2001

2001

WOMEN IN WORLD HISTORY

A Biographical Encyclopedia

WOMEN IN WORLD HISTORY

A Biographical Encyclopedia

VOLUME
10
Maa-Mei

Anne Commire, Editor
Deborah Klezmer, Associate Editor

YORKIN PUBLICATIONS

GALE GROUP

Detroit
New York
San Francisco
London
Boston
Woodbridge, CT

Yorkin Publications

Anne Commire, *Editor*
Deborah Klezmer, *Associate Editor*
Barbara Morgan, *Assistant Editor*

Eileen O'Pasek, Gail Schermer, Patricia Coombs, James Fox,
Catherine Cappelli, Karen Rikkers, *Editorial Assistants*
Karen Walker, *Assistant for Genealogical Charts*

Special acknowledgment is due to Peg Yorkin who made this project possible.

Thanks also to Karin and John Haag, Bob Schermer, and to
the Gale Group staff, in particular Dedria Bryfonski, Linda Hubbard, John Schmittroth, Cynthia Baldwin,
Tracey Rowens, Randy Bassett, Christine O'Bryan, Rebecca Parks, and especially Sharon Malinowski.

The Gale Group

Sharon Malinowski, *Senior Editor*
Rebecca Parks, *Editor*
Laura Brandau, *Assistant Editor*
Linda S. Hubbard, *Managing Editor*

Margaret A. Chamberlain, *Permissions Specialist*
Mary K. Grimes, *Image Cataloger*

Mary Beth Trimper, *Production Director*
Evi Seoud, *Assistant Production Manager*

Cynthia Baldwin, *Product Design Manager*
Tracey Rowens, *Cover and Page Designer*
Michael Logusz, *Graphic Artist*

Barbara Yarrow, *Graphic Services Manager*
Randy Bassett, *Image Database Supervisor*
Dan Newell, *Imaging Specialist*
Christine O'Bryan, *Graphics Desktop Publisher*
Dan Bono, *Technical Support*

Library of Congress Catalog Card Number 99-24692
A CIP record is available from the British Library

ISBN 0-7876-4069-7
Printed in the United States of America.

Library of Congress Cataloging-in-Publication Data

Women in world history : a biographical encyclopedia / Anne Commire, editor, Deborah Klezmer, associate editor.
p. cm.
Includes bibliographical references and index.
ISBN 0-7876-3736-X (set). — ISBN 0-7876-4069-7 (v. 10). —
ISBN 0-7876-4070-0 (v. 11) — ISBN 0-7876-4071-9 (v. 12) — ISBN 0-7876-4072-7 (v. 13) — ISBN 0-7876-4073-5 (v. 14)
1. Women—History Encyclopedias.2. Women—Biography Encyclopedias.
I. Commire, Anne. II. Klezmer, Deborah.
HQ1115.W6 1999   99-24692
920.72'03—DC21

10 9 8 7 6 5 4 3 2 1

Mac and Mc.

Names beginning with the prefix Mac and Mc are listed in alphabetical order.

Maacah (fl. 1000 BCE)

Canaanite princess. Name variations: Maachah. Flourished around 1000 BCE; daughter of Talmai, the king of Geshur (a nation northeast of the Sea of Galilee); one of the wives of David, Israelite king (r. 1010–970 BCE); children: son, Absalom; daughter, Tamar.

The daughter of the King of Geshur and one of the wives of David, Maacah had at least one daughter, *Tamar, and three sons, the last of whom was Absalom. All her children were born during David's early reign over Judah at Hebron. David had many other wives, including *Michal (who was Saul's daughter and David's first wife), *Ahinoam of Jezreel, *Abigail, *Abishag of Shunem, *Bathsheba (widow of Uriah and mother of Solomon), Abital and Elah.

Maacah (fl. 931 BCE)

Biblical woman. Name variations: Maachah; Michaiah. Daughter of Abishalom; third wife of Rehoboam, king of Judah (r. 931–913 BCE); children—four sons: Abijah; Attai; Ziza; and Shelomith.

Characterized as a strong-willed woman, Maacah was the third and favorite wife of Rehoboam, king of Judah. They had four sons, the eldest of whom, Abijah, succeeded his father as king. Maacah retained her position as queen-mother for many years, until her grandson Asa had her removed.

There is conflicting information in the Bible surrounding the names Maacah and Michaiah. In 2 Chr. 13:2, Michaiah is identified as the mother of Abijah and the daughter of Uriel of Gibeah, but in 1 Kings 15:2, Abijah's mother is said to be Maachah, the daughter of Abishalom. "The explanation is that Maachah is just a variation of the name Michaiah, and that Abishalom is probably the same as Absalom, the son of David," writes M.G. Easton. "It is probable that 'Uriel of Gibeah' married Tamar, the daughter of Absalom (2 Sam. 14:27), and by her had Maachah. The word 'daughter' in 1 Kings 15:2 will thus, as it frequently elsewhere does, mean grand-daughter."

Maachah (fl. 1575 BCE)

Biblical woman. Flourished around 1575 BCE; concubine of Caleb, one of 12 men sent out by Moses to assess the Promised Land.

Maansdatter, Katherine (1550–1612)

Mistress, then wife, of King Eric of Sweden. Born on November 6, 1550; died on September 13, 1612; married Eric XIV (1533–1577), king of Sweden (r. 1560–1568, deposed in 1568), on July 4, 1568; children: Henry; Sigrid (b. 1566, who married Henry Tott and Niels Natt); Gustav (b. 1568); Henry (b. 1570); Arnold (b. 1572).

Maar, Dora (1907–1997)

French artist, mistress of and model for Picasso, whose countenance adorns the walls of museums and pages of art books throughout the world. Born Theodora Markovitch on November 22, 1907, in Tours, France; died on July 16, 1997; buried in Clamart, a small town south of Paris; only child of a Yugoslavian father (an architect) and a French mother; studied painting in Paris at the École d'Art Décoratif, Académie de Passy, Académie Julien, and with André Lhote.

Subject of numerous of Picasso's portraits, including Bust of a Seated Woman, *which sold at auction for $3 million in 1995.*

Dora Maar was born in 1907 near Paris but grew up in a contentious household in Argentina, where her father worked as an architect in

Buenos Aires. "My father is the only architect who failed to make a fortune in Buenos Aires," Maar told James Lord. "All he got was a decoration from the Emperor Franz-Joseph for having designed the Austro-Hungarian legation." There was constant strife between parents, and between mother and child.

Before turning 20, Maar reappeared in Paris. Beautiful, bright and sexually progressive, she lived the life of a bohemian, hanging out with artists and writers in the cafes of Montparnasse, taking up with the married Parisian writer Georges Bataille. She studied painting but, self-critical and unsure, then took up surrealist photography; her first exhibition was held at the Galerie de Beaune in Paris in 1937. When Maar met Pablo Picasso in the spring of 1936, he was past 60, separated from his wife *Olga Khoklova, and had a mistress, Marie-Thérèse Walter. During their ten-year affair, Picasso drew and painted scores of portraits of Dora and her dark eyes, including *Dora in a striped blouse*; *Dora with cigarette holder*; *portrait of Dora, 1937*; and *portrait of Dora, 1944*.

Maar was now well into her 30s, and the conflicts with her mother continued. "There were times when I even wished my mother would die. We had such appalling disputes. And no faith to save her, no will, nothing to make her ruthless. Unlike me. Without ever knowing what she wanted from life, she knew she hadn't received it. . . . And yet it was awful when she did die." It was after the Germans had invaded France in World War II. "One night we were talking on the telephone, arguing terribly, and then suddenly she stopped talking. It was during the Occupation, and after the curfew. When I went around the next morning, I found her dead on the floor with the telephone in her hand."

At war's end, Picasso abandoned Maar for *Françoise Gilot, a woman 40 years younger than himself. (Gilot would be superseded by model *Jacqueline Roque, who eventually became his wife.) Maar, who had been deeply involved with the painter, suffered a nervous breakdown, becoming hysterical in a movie theater. Removed by police, she was taken to Sainte Anne, a psychiatric hospital, and given electroshock. Soon, a friend of Picasso's managed to get her into a private clinic. With the help of analysis, a smattering of Buddhism, and a return to her Catholic roots, Maar took charge of her life. "Dora excelled in conversation," wrote Lord, "possessed a very well organized mentality, and could marshal ideas with tactical exper-

tise. It was religion, its nature and necessity, that most engaged her conviction and passion."

For the rest of her days, she lived alone, a legendary recluse, working at her own painting, sometimes in her flat in Paris, sometimes in a large empty house Picasso had purchased for her long ago in Ménerbes, Vaucluse. So successful was Maar in withdrawing from society, people in the art world were generally amazed when periodically they learned she was still alive. She died, age 89, in 1997. "Look at that tree," she once said to Lord during a drive in the countryside. "To you it is just a tree, commonplace as can be. If Picasso painted it, it would become an object of veneration. To a person who has faith, it is a miracle in itself."

SOURCES:
Lord, James. *Picasso and Dora*. NY: Farrar, Straus, 1993.

RELATED MEDIA:
Julianne Moore portrayed Dora Maar in *Surviving Picasso*, a Merchant-Ivory film based on *Françoise Gilot's memoir, starring Anthony Hopkins, screenplay by *Ruth Prawer Jhabvala (1996).

Maass, Clara (1876–1901)

American nurse and victim of yellow fever immunity experiments. Born in East Orange, New Jersey, on June 28, 1876; died in Las Animas, Cuba, on August 24, 1901; interred in East Orange, New Jersey; oldest of nine children of B. Maass (father) and H.A. Maass (mother); graduated from the Newark German Hospital Training School for Nurses, 1895.

Awards: Newark German Hospital Training School for Nurses was renamed in her memory; inducted into the Hall of Fame of the American Nurses' Association; U.S. post office issued a memorial stamp.

Served in the Spanish-American War (1898); volunteered for yellow fever immunity experiments conducted by the U.S. Yellow Fever Commission, Cuba (1901).

Clara Maass was born in East Orange, New Jersey, in 1876, the oldest of nine children of a German immigrant mill worker. At age 15, she was forced to quit school to earn money for her family. While training at the Newark German Hospital Training School for Nurses, she sent half her wages home each month; after graduating in 1895, she was made head nurse of the school.

Starting in April 1898 during the Spanish-American War, Maass served as a contract nurse for the U.S. Medical Department in army camps in Florida, Georgia, and Cuba. In 1900, she volunteered once more and was sent to the Philippines, where she came down with severe joint pain, diagnosed as dengue fever, and nearly died. Sent home, she recovered and was then stationed in Havana.

Maass was in perpetual danger while serving as a nurse. Many of the soldiers she had been treating had been felled not by bullets but by the deadly yellow fever. The disease had killed over 1,500 soldiers, far more than those killed in battle, and 20,000 American soldiers had come down with the malady, which is marked by high fever, vomiting, and liver complications that cause the skin to turn yellow. In 1901, while at Las Animas Hospital in Havana, Maass volunteered for yellow fever experiments being conducted in Cuba by Major Walter Reed for the U.S. government. At the time a dispute raged among clinicians as to whether the illness was transmitted by poor sanitary conditions or mosquitoes. Under an experiment directed by Major William C. Gorgas and Dr. John Guitéras, Maass was one of about 20 volunteers who agreed to expose themselves to mosquito bites. It was believed that under controlled conditions and immediate hospital care, infected patients would recover. Maass wrote her mother: "Do not worry, Mother, if you hear that I have yellow fever. Now is a good time of the year to catch it if one has to. Most of the cases are mild, and then I should be an immune and not be afraid of the disease anymore."

On August 4, she was bitten by an infected *Stegomyia* mosquito and soon developed a case of yellow fever, but doctors decided the case was too mild; it would not make her immune. On August 14, they recommended she be bitten once more. From the second exposure, Maass suffered excruciating pain and died ten days later. She was only 25, the only woman and the only American to die during the yellow fever experiments of 1900–1901. (Dr. Jesse W. Lazear had died in September 1900 but in an uncontrolled experiment which was not under the auspices of Walter Reed.) Clara Maass did not die in vain, however, for the dispute over the transmission of yellow fever was resolved, and a treatment eventually discovered. At the time of her death, *The New York Times* noted: "No soldier in the late war placed his life in peril for better reasons than those which prompted this faithful nurse to risk hers."

In 1952, the Newark German Hospital Training School for Nurses, which had become Lutheran Memorial, was renamed the Clara Maass Memorial Hospital. She was inducted into the Hall of Fame of the American Nurses' Association, and the U.S. Postal Service issued a stamp of her in 1976, after a pastor from East Orange led an impassioned campaign. "Here we have a martyr," he said, "and no one has ever heard of her."

U.S. postage stamp issued in 1976 in honor of Clara Maass.

SOURCES:

Forbes, Malcolm, with Jeff Bloch. *Women Who Made a Difference.* NY: Simon and Schuster, 1990.

McHenry, Robert, ed. *Famous American Women.* NY: Dover, 1980.

The New York Times. August 25, 1901, October 21, 1901.

SUGGESTED READING:

O'Neill, Lois Decker. *The Women's Book of World Records and Achievements.* Garden City, NY: Anchor Press, 1979.

Hugh A. Stewart, M.A.,
University of Guelph, Guelph, Ontario, Canada

Mabel of Bury St. Edmunds
(fl. 1230)

English professional embroiderer. Flourished in 1230 in London, England.

Mabel of Bury St. Edmunds was an English embroiderer who flourished around 1230. Her early life is obscure; she moved to London as an adult and her name is found frequently in the royal treasury records of King Henry III (r. 1216–1272). Apparently Mabel was one of the finest artisans of her trade, for she was given several important commissions by the king himself. It is not certain how old she was when her work became so highly recognized, but she was considered an artist and allowed to design as well as embroider veils, banners, and ecclesiastical clothing for Henry and his officers.

Mabel was well paid for her works, some of which took her a year or more to complete. Henry also approved reimbursement for any ornamentation or precious materials she wanted to use in the execution of a piece, such as spun gold thread and pearls, which she used quite liberally. King Henry remembered Mabel even after her retirement to Bury St. Edmunds, giving her gifts of cloth and a fur robe when he visited that town years after she had ceased to work for him.

SOURCES:

LaBarge, Margaret. *A Small Sound of the Trumpet: Women in Medieval Life.* Boston, MA: Beacon Press, 1986.

Laura York,
Riverside, California

Mabley, Jackie (1894–1975)

Popular American entertainer, who was the first black female comedian to gain widespread recognition. Name variations: Moms Mabley. Born Loretta Mary Aiken in 1894 (some sources cite 1897 or 1898) in Brevard, North Carolina; died of natural causes at age 81 in White Plains, New York, on May 23, 1975; one of several children of Jim Aiken (a businessman and volunteer firefighter); never married; children: five, including Christine, Yvonne, Bonnie, and Charles.

Left home at 14 and moved to Cleveland, Ohio; began entertainment career in Pittsburgh, Pennsylvania (c. 1910); changed name to Jackie Mabley soon after beginning performing career; performed on Chitlin' Circuit (c. 1910–23), developing act; debuted at Connie's Inn in New York (1923), where career took off; performed regularly at black venues from then on; by 1939 was a regular at the Apollo Theater in Harlem; performed in several Broadway shows, including Fast and Furious *and* Swinging the Dream; *was a regular on radio show "Swingtime at the Savoy"; was discovered by white audiences (1960s), began recording comedy records, including* Moms Mabley—The Funniest Woman in the World, Now Hear This, Moms Mabley at the U.N., *and more than 20 others; made television debut (1967) on all-black comedy special "A Time For Laughter" (ABC); appeared on several television variety shows, including* "The Ed Sullivan Show," "The Flip Wilson Show," *and* "The Smothers Brothers Comedy Hour"; *appeared at Copacabana and Carnegie Hall in New York City and at the Kennedy Center in Washington, D.C.; starred in film* Amazing Grace *(1974). Member of NAACP; was guest at White House Conference on Civil Rights (1966).*

Jackie Mabley spent most of her life in show business, becoming the first African-American female comedian to achieve widespread recognition and popularity. She spent half a century performing in nightclubs on the black vaudeville circuit, constantly refining her act. Her stand-up persona was described in *Notable Black American Women* as "a cantankerous, spicy, raucous old lady with [a] shabby wardrobe and [a] broad, toothless smile." As **Elsie Arrington Williams** observed, Mabley had "a remarkably durable career that stretched from minstrel shows to the Harlem Renaissance to movies to record albums to television."

Fellow performers soon discovered Mabley's deep compassion and generosity and gave her the nickname "Moms." The name stuck, becoming a natural addition to her already established act. Williams noted that "salty, . . . wisecracking Jackie Mabley was called 'Moms' for so many years that it was easy to believe that she was ancient when she started out in show business." In fact, however, Mabley was remarkably young when she embarked on her performing career—barely a teenager.

Born Loretta Mary Aiken in 1894 in Brevard, North Carolina, Mabley was one of several children of Jim Aiken and his wife (name unknown). Aiken owned several businesses, including a grocery store in Brevard. A volunteer firefighter as well, he died in a fire truck explosion when Mabley was young, and her mother soon married a difficult man with whom Mabley did not get along. She was raped twice as a child, once when she was 11 and again two years later; each attack produced a child. Finally heeding her grandmother's advice that any future lay somewhere down the road, Mabley left her children in the care of two women and left home at age 14. She went to Cleveland, living for a time with a minister and his family. A rooming house next door catered to vaudevillians, and she became friends with a performer named **Bonnie Belle Drew** who was taken with her beauty and encouraged her to get into show business. Still calling herself Loretta Aiken, she lied about her age, claiming to be 16, and accompanied Drew to Pittsburgh, where she joined a minstrel show

Opposite page
Jackie
Mabley

and began performing on the Theater Owners Booking Association Circuit. At this time, she met a Canadian performer named Jack Mabley, to whom she became engaged. Although the marriage never took place, Loretta Aiken took his name; from then on, she was known as Jackie Mabley. Her ex-fiancé took a lot from her, she said, so the least she could do was take his name.

Jackie Mabley was performing on the Chitlin' Circuit, a network of black-owned venues around the country that welcomed African-American vaudevillians. Earning $12 a week, she sang, danced, acted in skits, and did comedy bits. The act for which she is remembered, a wise, sassy old lady with a funny hat and a baggy dress and stockings, began to evolve in the 1920s. According to *Notable Black American Women*, "Her trademarks became her bulging eyes, rubbery face, gravelly voice, and later, her toothless grin." Addressing her audience as "children," Mabley fashioned herself after her own wise grandmother. During these years, Mabley performed with such black vaudeville greats as Bill "Bojangles" Robinson, Dusty "Open the Door, Richard" Fletcher, Pigmeat Markham, and Cootie Williams. She also met *Pearl Bailey and took credit for convincing Bailey to tap her own comedic talents.

In the early 1920s, Mabley was "discovered" by the dance team Butterbeans and Susie, who took her to New York. Her debut, at Connie's Inn in 1923, was a hit, and her career finally took off. She appeared at big venues such as the Savoy Ballroom, the Cotton Club in Harlem, and Club Harlem in Atlantic City, New Jersey, often sharing billing with luminaries such as Duke Ellington, Louis Armstrong, Cab Calloway, and Count Basie.

Toward the end of the decade Mabley began to get bit parts in films, and appeared in *Boarding House Blues* (also known as *Jazz Heaven*) in 1929, and in the film version of Eugene O'Neill's *The Emperor Jones*, starring Paul Robeson, in 1933. By 1939, she was a regular at the Apollo Theater in Harlem. She would eventually appear at the Apollo more times than any other performer in the history of that institution. Mabley also appeared in Broadway shows such as *Blackbirds* and *Swinging the Dream*. She teamed up with Harlem Renaissance writer *Zora Neale Hurston* in 1931, writing and performing in *Fast and Furious: A Colored Revue in 37 Scenes*. Mabley was also a regular on the radio show "Swingtime at the Savoy" and continued her stand-up performances throughout the 1940s and 1950s.

The 1960s brought Mabley more widespread fame, as white audiences finally discovered this wise and folksy comedian. She also began recording comedy albums. Her first album, *Moms Mabley—The Funniest Woman in the World,* sold more than a million copies for Chess Records. Switching to Mercury Records in 1966, she recorded *Now Hear This, Moms Mabley at the U.N.,* and *Moms Mabley at the Geneva Conference.* All told, she would record more than 25 comedy albums.

Mabley made her first television appearance on "A Time for Laughter," a 1967 comedy special featuring an entirely black cast. After the special's success, Mabley was a frequent guest on various television shows, including "The Smothers Brothers Comedy Hour," "The Mike Douglas Show," and "The Flip Wilson Show." Although she appeared once on "The Ed Sullivan Show," she turned down a repeat offer, because Sullivan would not give her at least four minutes on the air. Television exposure widened Mabley's popularity even further, and she was much in demand, appearing at the Copacabana in New York and the Kennedy Center in Washington, D.C. At age 80, Mabley had a starring role in the 1974 film *Amazing Grace.*

Jackie "Moms" Mabley died of natural causes on May 23, 1975, in White Plains, New York. She was 81. In 1986, Mabley was honored with a play by *Alice Childress entitled *Moms, A Praise for a Black Comedienne.*

SOURCES:

Estell, Kenneth, ed. *The African-American Almanac.* 6th ed. Detroit, MI: Gale Research, 1994.

Smith, Jessie Carney, ed. *Notable Black American Women.* Detroit, MI: Gale Research, 1992.

Williams, Elsie Arrington. *Black Women in America: An Historical Encyclopedia.* Vol. II. Edited by Darlene Clark Hine. Brooklyn, NY: Carlson, 1993.

Ellen Dennis French,
freelance writer in biography, Murrieta, California

Mabley, Moms (1894–1975).

See Mabley, Jackie.

Mac and Mc.

Names beginning with the prefix Mac and Mc are listed in alphabetical order.

MacAdams, Roberta (1881–1959).

See Price, Roberta Catherine MacAdams.

Macardle, Dorothy (1889–1958)

Irish historian, novelist, and drama critic. Born Dorothy Margaret Macardle in Dundalk, County Louth, Ireland, on March 7, 1889; died in Drogheda, *County Louth, Ireland, on December 23, 1958; daughter of Sir Thomas Callan Macardle, KBE, DL, and Minnie Lucy (Ross) Macardle; attended Alexandra College, Dublin; University College, Dublin, B.A. with First Class Honors in English Language and Literature, 1911.*

Selected writings: (plays) Atonement *(1918),* Ann Kavanagh *(1922); (fiction)* Earthbound *(1924),* The Old Man *(1925),* Uneasy Freehold *(1944),* Fantastic Summer *(1946),* Dark Enchantment *(1953),* The Uninvited; *(history)* Tragedies of Kerry *(1924),* The Irish Republic *(1937); (nonfiction)* Children of Europe *(1949),* Shakespeare Man and Boy *(1961).*

Born in 1889, Dorothy Macardle was a member of a well-known brewing family in Dundalk, County Louth, Ireland. In later life, she referred to her family's pro-British and unionist sympathies, which conflicted with her own republicanism. She had a distinguished academic career at Alexandra College, where she also participated in the philanthropic activities of the Alexandra Guild. After graduating from University College, Dublin, with a first class degree in English (she also spoke fluent French), Macardle returned to Alexandra to teach and maintained a close connection with it for the rest of her life. The college even kept her teaching position open when she was imprisoned for her republican activities.

Before 1916, Macardle was active in Sinn Fein and the Gaelic League. She supported the 1916 Rising, even though two of her brothers were fighting with British forces at the time. Between 1919 and 1921, during the Irish war of independence, she worked as a publicist for Sinn Fein and for a time lived in the same house as *Maud Gonne and *Charlotte Despard. When the Anglo-Irish Treaty was signed in December 1921, Macardle sided with the republicans in rejecting its terms as inadequate. She worked for republican publicity but was arrested at the end of 1922 after civil war had broken out. In a talk years later at Alexandra, she recalled how she had longed for something to write with while incarcerated, even the stub of a pencil. Instead, she received a parcel of cosmetics which she considered a prime example of lack of imagination on the part of the well-meaning sender. She was released from prison in 1923 and, in 1924, published *Tragedies of Kerry.* One of her most famous books, it is a short account of the civil war in Kerry which had seen some of the worst atrocities of the war. She wrote of the "ominous wall of silence" which surrounded events in Kerry in 1922–23, events which her own book did much to uncover. It has never gone out of print, with the most recent edition being published in 1991.

Macardle resumed her teaching and literary career. She wrote several plays, one of which, *Dark Waters,* was performed at the Gate Theater in 1932 and showed the influence of Maurice Maeterlinck, whose work she studied and admired. She also published volumes of short stories. When Eamon de Valera, the republican leader, founded a new political party, Fianna Fail, in 1926, she was elected to the first executive. When de Valera started his own newspaper, the *Irish Press,* in 1931, Macardle became the drama critic and a regular feature writer. In 1932, when de Valera was president of the League of Nations Council, she went to Geneva as a special correspondent to cover the event. She was also a frequent broadcaster on Irish radio.

In the late 1920s, de Valera had asked her to write a history of the turbulent revolutionary years between 1916 and 1923, a task which was to take nearly ten years and which took valuable time away from her own literary work. The result was *The Irish Republic* (1937), a massive, scrupulously researched chronicle which for several decades was the standard reference work on the period. In her foreword, Macardle allowed a glimpse of some of the tensions, and admiration, in her relationship with de Valera. The book was, she made clear, "an account of the Irish Republican struggle from the viewpoint of an Irish Republican." She thanked de Valera doubly, not only because he had read the manuscript and written the preface for the book but also because "when he disagreed with my expressed or implied opinions he resisted the temptation to exert all his formidable powers of persuasion to make me alter them."

Although Macardle admired and respected de Valera, she was not uncritical of him. In 1935, she was vice-chair of the committee set up by the National Council of Women to examine legislation being introduced by the de Valera government which was considered discriminatory towards women. In 1937, just as *The Irish Republic* was published, she was expressing her opposition to the clauses of his new constitution relating to women.

Macardle continued to write fiction; two of her novels, *Uneasy Freehold* and *The Uninvited,* were made into successful films. During World War II, she worked for refugee causes and at the end of the war traveled to Czechoslovakia, Poland, Greece, Yugoslavia, Norway, Denmark, Holland, Belgium, Luxemburg, France and Austria where she gathered reports on what had happened during the Nazi occupation. The results of these investigations were published in a moving book, *Children of Europe* (1949), about the plight of Europe's children during and after the war. "The tale of what children endured in country after country," she wrote, "is a repetitive one burdened with a bitter reiteration, a monotony of terror and distress." She was most aware of the mental trauma which hurt children's "faith in life." She was particularly concerned with the plight of Germany's children, as was her close friend Dr. *Kathleen Lynn.

When she returned to Ireland in the late 1940s, Macardle became vice-president of the Irish Association for Civil Liberties. She was not a pacifist, unlike many of her friends, and had refused to join the Women's International League for Peace and Freedom because "you can't put peace before freedom. You've got to have freedom first." She also took a keen interest in youth movements. Dorothy Macardle died in December 1958; her funeral was attended by an Old IRA guard of honor. "I have never met anyone more intellectually honest," wrote de Valera in the *Irish Press*. "She had a horror of hypocrisy or pretence in any form. She worked incessantly. Of her indeed could it be truly said she was 'a lover of labour and truth.'"

SOURCES:
Irish Press. December 24–27, 1958.
Irish Times. December 24–29, 1958.
The Times. December 24, 1958.
Ward, Margaret. *Unmanageable Revolutionaries: Women and Irish Nationalism.* Brandon, 1983.

RELATED MEDIA:
The Uninvited (98 min. film), starring *Ruth Hussey, Ray Milland, and *Gail Russell, screenplay by *Dodie Smith and Frank Partos, 1944.

Deirdre McMahon,
Lecturer in History, Mary Immaculate College,
University of Limerick, Limerick, Ireland

Macarthur, Elizabeth (1767–1850)

*English diarist and letter writer who pioneered the Australian wool industry. Name variations: Elizabeth Veale Macarthur. Born Elizabeth Veale in 1767 (some sources cite 1768 or 1769), in Devon, England; died in Australia in 1850; daughter of Richard Veale (a farmer) and Grace (Hatherley) Veale; married John Macarthur (a Scottish soldier), in 1788, in England; children: nine, one of whom died in infancy; grandmother of *Elizabeth Macarthur-Onslow (1840–1911).*

Following marriage (1788), accompanied husband to Botany Bay in New South Wales, Australia; husband amassed a fortune and established Elizabeth Farm at Camden Park (1793), founded initial colonial wool trade and was first to establish sheep farming in

New South Wales, participated in rebellion against colonial governor (1808) and was forced to leave Australia for eight years (1809–17), during which time she ran wool business in correspondence with husband, was responsible for increasing flocks and expanding sales to English market, establishing New South Wales as a noted wool-producing region, and founding Australian wool industry overall; retired as manager of Elizabeth Farm (1817) upon husband's return; following husband's death (1834), again managed wool operation with sons.

Elizabeth Macarthur, the woman who founded the wool industry in Australia, was born Elizabeth Veale in Devon, England, in 1767. The daughter of Richard Veale, a wealthy farmer, and **Grace Hatherley Veale**, she was raised by her grandfather after her father died and her mother married again. Letters she wrote during her adult life indicate that she received a good education. Biographers have speculated that this instruction may have been received in part from the Reverend John Kingdon, who was the father of a close friend. She married John Macarthur, a Scottish soldier, in 1788, the same year that Britain founded the penal colony of New South Wales in Australia. John Macarthur was promoted the next year from ensign to lieutenant in the New South Wales Corps, the purpose of which was to maintain order in the convict settlement of Sydney Cove. The young family, which now included an infant son, sailed for Australia on a convict ship, arriving in mid-1790.

Elizabeth Macarthur was the first educated, non-convict woman in the new colony, and as such, she would dominate Sydney Cove social circles for the next two decades. Upon their arrival, living conditions were primitive and bleak even for those who were not prisoners, but the situation gradually improved as other colonists arrived. The family's prospects improved when John was made paymaster of his regiment, and he soon began to breed sheep. Receiving land grants in 1793 and expanding herd stock, John Macarthur built Elizabeth Farm at Camden Park. According to **Jennifer Uglow**, Elizabeth Farm was "the first great Australian estate, complete with elegant mansion and gardens," and for some while the Macarthurs were the biggest private landowners in New South Wales. John Macarthur was also involved in the lucrative liquor trade. By 1808, Macarthur had given birth to nine children (one of whom did not survive infancy); her sons were sent to England to complete their educations, while her daughters remained at home.

John Macarthur was involved in the 1808 Rum Rebellion against Governor William Bligh who had arrived in the colony in 1806. Bligh, captain of the HMS *Bounty* who had been set adrift after the infamous mutiny, was attempting to curb the powers enjoyed by the officers of the New South Wales Corps. In 1809, as a result of his role in the uprising, John was forced to leave Australia and spent the next eight years in England. During this time, Elizabeth Macarthur ran the farm and the wool business with her daughters while in correspondence with her husband. Shrewd and hard working, she traveled throughout the Australian colonies, increased the flocks, and expanded wool sales to Britain, thus becoming a primary force behind the establishment of New South Wales as a viable center of wool production.

Her husband returned to Australia with several of their sons in 1817, at which time Macarthur retired from active management of the estate. The steady deterioration of John's mental health was a great source of sadness for Macarthur until his death in 1834. At that point, she again assumed management of the estate, with assistance from her sons. Elizabeth Macarthur died in Australia in 1850. Her diaries and letters, detailing passage on a convict ship and life in a penal colony, are considered valuable historical documents; collected as *Journals and Letters 1789–1798*, they were published in 1984.

SOURCES:

Blain, Virginia, Patricia Clements, and Isobel Grundy. *The Feminist Companion to Literature in English: Women Writers from the Middle Ages to the Present.* New Haven, CT: Yale University Press, 1990.

Todd, Janet, ed. *A Dictionary of British and American Women Writers 1660–1800.* Rowman and Allanheld, 1985.

Uglow, Jennifer, ed. and comp. *The International Dictionary of Women's Biography.* NY: Continuum, 1989.

Ellen Dennis French,
freelance writer in biography, Murrieta, California

Macarthur, Mary Reid (1880–1921)

Scottish trade unionist. Name variations: Mary Reid Anderson; Mary Reid MacArthur. Born Mary Reid Macarthur in Glasgow, Scotland, in 1880; died of cancer in 1921; daughter of a Conservative Glasgow draper; attended Glasgow Girls' High School, followed by a year of study in Germany, 1896; married Will C. Anderson, in 1911; children: two, one of whom died at birth.

Was a member of the Shop Assistants' Union (1901); served as president of the Scottish National District of the Union (1902); was a secretary,

Women's Trade Union League (1903–21); was a dele-gate, International Congress of Women (1904 and 1908); was founder and first president, National Federation of Working Women (1906); was a member, National Council of the Independent Labour Party (1909–12); was a member, Central Committee of Women's Training and Employment (1914–18); was a Labour candidate for Parliament (1918). Publications: several articles.

In 1896, when Mary Reid Macarthur returned from a year of study abroad, she was at loose ends. Only 16 and not quite sure what career she should pursue, she decided to help out in her father's shop, working as his bookkeeper. Macarthur also freelanced for a local newspaper and, while covering the speech of an organizer for the Shop Assistants' Union, became interested in trade unionism. Despite being the "boss's daughter," Macarthur soon joined the Shop Assistants' Union and convinced the rest of her father's employees to do the same.

Shortly after that, she became president of her local and in 1902, at age 22, became president of the national council for her union. At that year's conference, Macarthur met *Margaret Bondfield, an English trade unionist and organizer for the Women's Trade Union League (WTUL). Encouraged by Bondfield, who even offered to share her London apartment, Macarthur left Scotland in 1903. She became secretary for the WTUL, a post she would hold the rest of her life. Before leaving home, however, Macarthur also met the man she would eventually marry, Will C. Anderson. Anderson, chair of the Glasgow Shop Assistants' Union and a Socialist, would go on to be a Labour Party official as well as president of the International Labour Organization (ILO). Anderson was able to convert Macarthur to Socialism but not until 1911 did she agree to marry him, saying that her work had to come first.

Working conditions in London seemed even worse than in her native Scotland, and Macarthur sought to change that soon after her arrival. While the conditions of labor for women and children in sweatshops and factories were horrific, she was just as troubled by women engaged in outwork. In the journal *Woman Worker*, which she established and served as editor of from 1907 to 1909, Macarthur wrote that "the plight of the sweated factory worker is as bad as her sister who toils in the home." When a minimum wage became law for English women workers in 1909, Macarthur was one of those who saw to it that the law covered women em-ployed in factories as well as those who worked out of their home. For Macarthur, the Trade Boards Act of 1909 was compromised enough in that it only covered women and not all workers, male and female, as initially proposed.

Despite her willingness to advocate protective labor legislation, Macarthur's first priority was trade unionism. The organization of women was especially critical. "Women are badly paid and badly treated because they are not organized," wrote Macarthur. "They are not organized because they are badly paid and badly treated." She sought to end this vicious circle and helped organize women chain-makers and hosiery knitters, lace makers and garment workers. From its beginnings, the British WTUL sought to organize women workers into unions already established by men. However, in some cases, unions did not exist for the trades in which women worked or, in other cases, certain male-dominated unions did not allow women to join. In response, the WTUL formed the National Federation of Women Workers (NFWW) in 1906. Open to all women working in those industries where unions did not exist or were not open to them, the NFWW had as its first president Mary Reid Macarthur.

During World War I, Macarthur, a pacifist, served on the Central Committee of Women's Training and Employment, ensuring that the women who flooded into the English munitions plants were treated fairly and earned a decent wage. Working in high government circles, she became nationally known and even became acquainted with Queen *Mary of Teck. During the war, the woman suffrage movement gained momentum in Great Britain. While she supported the right of women to vote, Macarthur sought to emphasize the economic needs of women, needs that could be met through trade unionism. Nonetheless, she saw the efficacy in establishing an alliance between working women and the British Labour Party. In 1906, Macarthur and three other WTUL activists joined in the formation of the Women's Labour League which sought to give women a voice within the party.

In 1918, a franchise bill was passed in Great Britain, giving women over the age of 30 the vote. At the same time, property requirements for voters were lifted, and the vote was extended to all men over 21. Given the high loss of life during the war, had women over 21 been given the vote, they would have been a majority of British voters. Not until 1928 was the voting age for women lowered to 21. However, in 1918, the 38-year-old Macarthur, who was old enough to vote and campaign for office, ran as the first woman Labour candidate for Parliament. Hampered in part by her acknowledged pacifism, Macarthur's campaign was further hurt by the fact that election officials insisted that she run under her married name, Mary Anderson, and not the name by which she was well known, Mary Reid Macarthur. In any case, she lost her bid for political office.

An even more devastating loss was the death of her husband and friend, Will Anderson, during the great influenza pandemic of 1918–19. Macarthur died two years later, in 1921, of cancer. Her loss was keenly felt by the WTUL. Unlike her predecessors, *Emma Paterson* and *Emily Dilke*, Macarthur had come to the WTUL with solid labor credentials, both in terms of her union work and her Socialist politics. Historians of the period credit her with revitalizing the WTUL, vastly increasing its membership and its clout. In part, this was due to her vital personality. One contemporary remarked that Macarthur "acted as if something great was always going to happen and she made an atmosphere in which it usually did."

SOURCES:
Hart, Vivien. *Bound by Our Constitution: Women, Workers, and the Minimum Wage.* Princeton, NJ: Princeton University Press, 1994.
Jacoby, Robin Miller. *The British and American Women's Trade Union Leagues, 1890–1925: A Case Study of Feminism and Class.* Brooklyn, NY: Carlson, 1994.
Soldon, Norbert C. *Women in British Trade Unions, 1874–1976.* London: Gill and Macmillan, 1978.

Kathleen Banks Nutter,
Manuscripts Processor at the Sophia Smith Collection, Smith College, Northampton, Massachusetts

Macarthur-Onslow, Elizabeth

(1840–1911)

*Australian property owner and businesswoman. Born on May 8, 1840, at Camden Park, Menangle, New South Wales; died on August 2, 1911, while visiting England; only child of James Macarthur and Emily (Stone) Macarthur; granddaughter of Australian wool industry pioneers *Elizabeth Macarthur (1767–1850)* and John Macarthur; married Arthur Alexander Walton Onslow (a navy captain), on January 31, 1867 (died 1882); children: six sons and two daughters (one son and one daughter died in infancy).*

The only child of James Macarthur, scion of an Australian family that had amassed a fortune in the sheep industry, and **Emily Stone Macarthur**, Elizabeth Macarthur-Onslow was born on May 8, 1840, at the family estate of Camden Park in New South Wales. She was educated at home and as a young adult spent four years on a European "Grand Tour" with her parents. In January 1867, she married Arthur Onslow, a captain in the navy. With her father's death later that year, she inherited a share in Camden Park as well as valuable real estate elsewhere in the state. Her husband died in 1882, and at the end of that decade she lived abroad for several years with her surviving six children while studying recent improvements in the dairy industry. Around 1890, the deaths of two childless uncles brought the whole of the Macarthur property into her possession.

Macarthur-Onslow (she legally adopted this name in 1892) returned to Australia and established profitable dairies and a central creamery at Camden Park. The dairies were set up in a semi-cooperative style, with workers and their families provided with housing, equipment, and 60 head of cattle each. The resulting milk, cream and butter were heavily promoted as "hygienic" due to the use of steam processing. Macarthur-Onslow also planted mulberry trees at the estate to use in breeding silkworms for raw silk, and was a member of the Women's Cooperative Silk-Growing and Industrial Association and the Victorian Silk Culture Association. A local philanthropist, she contributed to the Agricultural Society, Camden's School of the Arts, and Macarthur Park, and was a member of the women's branch of the Society for the Prevention of Cruelty to Animals. Possessed of sharp business acumen, she converted the family estate into a corporation in 1899, naming her children as shareholders and thus consolidating the fortune.

SOURCES:
Radi, Heather, ed. *200 Australian Women: A Redress Anthology.* NSW, Australia: Women's Redress Press, 1988.

Macaulay, Catharine (1731–1791)

Controversial British historian, political radical, and champion of women's education who was an ardent supporter of America in 18th-century England. Name variations: Catherine or Catharine Macaulay-Graham; Catherine Graham Macaulay; Catherine Sawbridge Macaulay. Born Catharine Sawbridge on April 2, 1731, at Olantigh (pronounced: Ollantee), the family estate near Wye, Kent, England; died in Binfield, Berkshire, on June 22, 1791, of a long, unidentified illness; daughter of John Sawbridge (a wealthy country gentleman) and Elizabeth Wanley Sawbridge (an heiress); largely self-educated; married Dr. George Macaulay, in June 1760 (died 1766); married William

Catharine
Macaulay

Graham, in 1778; children: (first marriage) one daughter, Catharine Sophia Macaulay, born sometime between 1760 and 1766.

Moved to London following marriage (1760); published first volume of History of England (1763); seven additional volumes followed intermittently until 1783; moved to Bath (1774); spent one year in America, including ten days at Mount Vernon with the Washingtons (1784–85); published Letters on Education (1790).

Selected publications: History of England from the Accession of James I to that of the Brunswick Line (8 vols., 1763–83); Loose Remarks . . . with a Short Sketch of a Democratical Form of Government (1769); Observations on a Pamphlet, Entitled, Thoughts on the Cause of the Present Discontents (1770); An Address to the People of England, Ireland and Scotland, on the Important Crisis of Affairs (1775); Letters on Education with Observations on Religious and Metaphysical Subjects (1790); Observations on the Reflections of the Right Hon. Edmund Burke on the Revolution in France (1791).

Few could have imagined that the sickly girl from rural Kent who spent much of her time reading ancient history in her father's library would grow up to become one of the most famous women in England in the 1770s—second only to the queen, *Charlotte of Mecklenburg-Strelitz.

Catharine Macaulay was born Catharine Sawbridge in 1731, one of four children of **Elizabeth Wanley Sawbridge**, an heiress, and John Sawbridge, a wealthy country gentleman. When Catharine was only two years old, her mother died, and her grieving father stayed mainly in London, leaving Catharine, her sister and brothers at Olantigh, the family estate near Wye, Kent. There, they were cared for by a governess whom Catharine later described as "ignorant and ill-qualified." In time, the two boys would go off to boarding school while the daughters stayed home with the governess.

*L*et it be remembered that everything new is alarming to the ignorant and prejudiced.

—Catharine Macaulay

According to Macaulay's first biographer, **Mary Hays**, Catharine did not care for dolls and doll houses, preferring books and news periodicals. At age 20, she came across a book of ancient history and from that time on was enthralled with the subject. Descriptions of the Greek and Roman republics proved as intriguing to her as the tales of tyranny and human cruelty proved distressing. These accounts led her to study the relationships among government, public morality, human happiness, and roots of evil.

Although nothing more is known of her early years, her fascination with ancient history and philosophy surfaced again when she attended a party in nearby Canterbury. *Elizabeth Carter*, a contemporary intellectual and avid correspondent, wrote to a friend in 1757:

> Did I tell you . . . of a very fine lady who . . . is a very sensible and agreeable woman and much more deeply learned than beseems a fine lady; but between the Spartan laws, the Roman politics, the philosophy of Epicurus, and the wit of St. Evremond, she seems to have formed a most extraordinary system. To be sure I should have been mighty cautious of holding any such conversation in such a place with a professed philosopher or scholar, but as it was with a fine fashionable well-dressed lady, whose train was longer than anybody's train, I had no manner of scruple.

It is generally assumed that she was referring to the 26-year-old Catharine Sawbridge.

Living in pastoral Kent, about 70 miles from London, Catharine and her brother John followed events of the capital and of the outside world. They shared their father's anti-aristocratic views and suspicion of autocratic government. Raised in the Age of Enlightenment (Age of Reason), the Sawbridges were influenced by such political and social philosophers as Locke, Montesquieu, and, later, Rousseau. These revolutionary writers challenged the power of despotic kings and abusive aristocrats, asserting that the common people should have certain natural, fundamental rights and liberties.

In 1760, at the age of 29 (a relatively advanced marital age for the time), Catharine married the widower Dr. George Macaulay, a Scottish physician practicing in London. Nothing is reported concerning the circumstances of their meeting or marriage. She may well have deferred marriage as long as possible, knowing that for the bride loss of legal and financial rights were the consequences. A married woman at that time could own no wealth or property, had no legal rights, could legally be beaten by her husband, and stood a good chance of dying in childbirth. Above all, society decreed that she was not to read, write or discuss serious subjects such as politics, history, or world affairs. Those who dared defy this code risked social rejection. Moreover, among the well-to-do, marriage arrangements were usually based on money, not mutual attraction. A wealthy father could, with a suitable dowry, "buy" a husband for his daughter with money and property to which she had no claim after the marriage. But George Macaulay was a rare man, who admired and encouraged his wife's intellectual interests. In a London seething with political debates, he introduced her to his circle of liberal friends, who cared deeply about human rights, liberty, and democracy. Indeed, she was soon accepted as a worthy colleague by these men.

The Macaulays lived on fashionable St. James's Place, a few blocks from St. James's Palace where George III had just taken up residence as king. As the monarch became increasingly determined to be a strong king, control Parliament, and crush dissent in the American colonies, the Macaulays and their friends protested in alarm. Long years of war with France, the beginnings of the Industrial Revolution, limited parliamentary representation, and a mentally unstable king all contributed to a London aboil with controversy. Within this environment of political ferment, Catharine Macaulay found her milieu.

With a loving husband, considerable wealth, and a houseful of servants, she easily could have enjoyed a life of leisure. As an intellectual, she might have joined the "Bluestockings," brilliant, well-read women who produced and discussed literature; but the Bluestockings chose to avoid discussions of political events, an intolerable limitation for Macaulay. She preferred talking with political dissenters such as her husband's friend Thomas Hollis, a wealthy radical who promoted liberty, espoused the American cause in the 1760s and early 1770s, and encouraged pro-American writers. He would help launch Macaulay upon her career as a historian by furnishing research materials and arranging for the publication of her first volumes, copies of which he would then send to Harvard College.

By 1763, Macaulay had produced the first volume of her controversial *History of England from the Accession of James I to that of the Brunswick Line.* This bombshell elicited reactions from admiration to ridicule, anger, and disbelief. According to the thinking of the time, women were not capable of understanding or writing history. Women could write novels, poetry and letters—but not history. Some even asserted that a man had actually written the *History.* As Macaulay later reflected, "when we compliment the appearance of a more than ordinary energy in the female mind, we call it masculine."

Ridicule for overstepping the gender boundaries was combined with wrath over the bias of the book. Among the author's stated purposes in writing an account of the 17th-century monarchy and the brief republic was to demonstrate the abuses of despotic power. To do so, she attacked the kings, praised Parliament and the Commonwealth (1649–1653), but blamed Oliver Cromwell's tyranny for the downfall of the short-lived republic.

On the other hand, her political kindred applauded her anti-monarchical views and her audacity. Above all, American colonists, who by 1765 were protesting what they perceived to be England's unfair tax policies, cheered Macaulay who became their new champion. In 1770, after the publication of two more volumes of her *History,* John Adams wrote to her: "I have formed the highest opinion of [Catharine Macaulay] as one of the brightest ornaments not only of her sex but of her Age and Country." Additional volumes of the *History,* eight in all, would appear intermittently until 1783.

Meanwhile, in 1766, her husband had died leaving her with one daughter, Catharine Sophia. After a period of deep mourning, Macaulay resumed her historical writing. Strongly involved in a number of political controversies, she wrote a letter to the city of Boston to apologize on behalf of the English people for the Boston Massacre, and she joined with others to urge parliamentary reforms in England. At that time, the high costs of running for office, long terms, and tight restrictions on voting eligibility meant that Parliament represented only the interests of the wealthy. Dedicated to making England a democracy, these reformers pressed for parliamentary changes which they hoped would weaken the power of the king and the wealthy landholders. They believed that broadening the electorate and shortening the terms of office of parliamentary members would help to create a more representative and democratic legislature. These reforms, however, would not come about until the 19th century.

Macaulay supported the cause of the fiery politician and journalist John Wilkes. By defying Parliament and the king, Wilkes became identified both in England and America with the cause of liberty. Macaulay contributed financially to his legal defense. During the decade of the 1770s, she also corresponded with a number of American leaders such as John Adams and James Otis, a leader of opposition to British rule.

When not engaged in writing her *History,* Macaulay wrote pamphlets, one of which attacked certain views of Edmund Burke, the renowned parliamentary leader. Burke complained later in a letter to a friend that "the Amazon" was "the greatest champion" of the reformers and that "no heroine in Billingsgate can go beyond the patriotick [sic] scolding of our Republican Virago. You see I have been afraid to answer her."

Macaulay moved to a new London home which became a gathering place for reformers, American sympathizers, and visiting Americans. Their hostess, with the aid of her liveried servants, is said to have presided over these weekly salons with the "air of a princess." A frequent visitor was Macaulay's brother, John Sawbridge, a member of Parliament and strong defender of American liberties. During the same period, Macaulay continued to be vilified and ridiculed by those opposed to her political philosophies, her assertiveness, and her "unwomanly" pursuits. Contemporary newspapers and magazines frequently ran cartoons lampooning her hairstyle, her cosmetics and her views. The famous Dr. Samuel Johnson spared no opportunity to jeer. Johnson, composer of the first English dictionary and prominent conversationalist, was a dedicated monarchist and arch-conservative. It is reported that he once teasingly reminded her: "You are to recall, Madam, that there is a monarchy in Heaven." To which she replied: "If I thought so, Sir, I should never wish to go there." Most of Johnson's attacks on her, however, were not so lighthearted.

In another of her pamphlets, written in 1775 on the eve of the American Revolution, Macaulay called upon the British public to petition Parliament for leniency in its colonial policies. She reasoned that English liberty, too, was at stake, for if Parliament and King George failed to recognize American grievances, the government would be emboldened to do likewise in the mother country. "Rouse my countrymen," she urged, "otherwise you . . . will be left to the bare possession of your foggy islands and under the imperious sway of a domestic despot."

The virulence of her opponents and the passion for her causes evidently took their toll. Her intermittent poor health had led her in 1774 to forsake the ferment of London for the curative waters of Bath. For the next four years, she enjoyed the social life of the spa's "smart set" while seeking relief from her unnamed physical ailments. Her correspondence with friends refers frequently to recurrent fever and bilious attacks of many months' duration. In Bath, she at last found help from a Dr. James Graham whose unorthodox treatments earned him the epithet "quack doctor." Macaulay, however, claimed that Graham saved her life.

About two years after Macaulay's arrival in Bath, an elderly admirer, the Reverend Thomas Wilson, invited her and her daughter to live in his house. Sharing her political views, he evidently felt that, as his protégée, the famous and colorful woman would bring distinction to his home as well as to his church in London. He even commissioned a larger-than-life-size statue of her and had it placed within the chancel of his church. The presence of a statue of a controversial, antigovernment radical in a place of worship was not popular among the congregation, however, and they demanded and won its removal.

By 1777, Macaulay was again ill, evidently beyond Graham's help, for she and his sister traveled to France in search of improved health. On the way to southern France, they stopped in Paris where Macaulay's fame as a lover of liberty had preceded her arrival. She was lionized by those opposed to the autocratic French monarchy; her History had helped inspire some who would become leaders of the French Revolution 12 years hence.

While in Paris, she also met Benjamin Franklin who was seeking assistance from the French monarchy for the new American republic, which was fighting for its life. Before leaving, she wrote a letter to Franklin apologizing for not having entertained him herself. Doing so, she states, would have subjected her to imprisonment for consorting with the enemy, and, because of her weak constitution, she probably could not survive life in prison. Although she would willingly give her life for American freedom, she added, she did not believe that a purely social meeting would contribute to the cause. Life in Paris seems to have agreed with her, for, instead of proceeding south, she returned to Bath.

Within a year, Macaulay, a leader of Bath society, would defy social convention and fall from grace, committing what was then considered a grievous sin. At age 47, she abandoned the Reverend Wilson's home and eloped with Dr. Graham's 21-year-old brother, William, an unemployed former ship surgeon's mate from Scotland, who was of lower social status than she. Scandalized, Bath society ostracized them. The 75-year-old Reverend Wilson was reportedly "consumed by rage and hatred."

From that time on, she and William lived quietly out of the public eye, moving frequently while she produced the last three volumes of her History. The marriage, according to observers, was apparently a happy one and lasted 14 years, until her death.

By 1784, the American Revolution was over, and, at last, Macaulay could travel with her husband to the United States to see firsthand the new republic she had so strenuously supported. It was the embodiment of the political philosophies she had been promoting for over 20 years. Also, she would meet face-to-face the colonial leaders with whom she had been corresponding for many years. She was especially eager to meet *Mercy Otis Warren of Massachusetts, with whom she had corresponded for the past ten years. As the sister of James Otis, signer of the Declaration of Independence, and wife of General James Warren, Mercy Otis Warren was directly acquainted with most aspects of the Revolution and its prelude. Like Macaulay, Warren was a writer, thinker, and activist who was devoted to liberty, republicanism, and the American cause. During Macaulay's one-year sojourn in America, these two women cemented their friendship and undoubtedly discussed Macaulay's plans to write a history of the American Revolution.

To this end, George and *Martha Washington entertained Catharine and William at Mount Vernon for ten days. Here, Washington allowed the historian to read his journals and records of the war. Macaulay, however, never wrote the history. Poor health was a factor, but she may also have realized from many conversations with Mercy Warren that the American woman was the logical candidate for the project. In a letter to Warren in 1787, Macaulay announced that she must decline the task. Perhaps, this was the green light Warren had been awaiting. Her *History of the Rise, Progress, and Termination of the American Revolution* appeared in 1805.

Three years after leaving America, Catharine and William were living in the small town of Binfield, Berkshire, west of London, for, as Macaulay told Warren, she was "quite tired of the absurdities of the capital." In their continuing correspondence, the two friends exchanged family news as well as other news and views. Macaulay happily announced the marriage of her daughter, Catharine Sophia, and, later, the birth of her first grandchild.

Though nearing the end of her life, Macaulay had yet to write the book which would in later years prove more significant than her voluminous *History of England*. In 1790, she published *Letters on Education With Observations on Religious and Metaphysical Subjects*. This single volume of "letters" to a fictitious friend sums up her philosophies on a myriad of topics ranging from human nature to the institutionalized church and Christianity, good government, cruelty to animals, penology, the problem of pain and evil, relations between the sexes, intellectual abilities of women, and the education of children. The last two subjects were of special concern to the author for, at this time, the education of girls was confined largely to domestic skills (and that at the hands of family retainers, not formal institutions). Some boarding schools for girls existed but served only the wealthy. Most women of learning such as herself and the "Bluestockings" were self-taught. Considering Macaulay's own educational history, these *Letters on Education* are of special interest. Most of the expressed views reflect the "new thinking" of the Age of Enlightenment and advocate replacing the old, restrictive ways with liberal and more humanitarian attitudes. "[A]ll those vices and imperfections which have been generally regarded as inseparable from the female character," she wrote, "do not . . . proceed from sexual causes, but are entirely the effects of situation and education."

> Confine not the education of your daughters to what is regarded as ornamental nor deny the graces to your sons. . . . Let your children be brought up together. . . .

The happiness and perfection of the two sexes are so reciprocally dependent on one another that, till both are reformed, there is no expecting excellence in either.

The *Letters* was not Macaulay's final publication, as even seclusion in Binfield and her last illness could not suppress her concern with current events. Only a few months before her death, she wrote a tract defending the French revolutionists in response to Edmund Burke's attack on the events of 1789–90 which toppled the Old Regime of France. Macaulay expressed her "exultation" over the new regime with its Declaration of the Rights of Man and King Louis XVI's acceptance of the new constitution. She did not live to see the Reign of Terror and the execution of Louis and Queen *Marie Antoinette. She did, however, live to see two nations, America and France, throw off the yoke of monarchical oppression.

Macaulay did not enjoy the realization of the reforms in England which she had advocated. Parliamentary changes and the broadening of the electorate awaited the next century, as did the granting of certain legal and educational rights to women. Nevertheless, Macaulay inspired later generations to continue working for human rights. Both *Mary Wollstonecraft, author of *A Vindication of the Rights of Woman*, and *Susan B. Anthony, renowned American suffragist, have acknowledged their debt to her.

After a long and painful illness, Catharine Macaulay died in Binfield on June 22, 1791. She was buried in the Binfield church where a plaque bearing her portrait was placed by her husband.

SOURCES:

Beckwith, Mildred. "Catharine Macaulay: Eighteenth-Century Rebel." Ph.D. dissertation, Ohio State University, 1953.

Hays, Mary. *Female Biography: or Memoirs of Illustrious and Celebrated Women of All Ages and Countries*. 6 vols. London: Printed for Richard Phillips, 1803.

Macaulay, Catharine. *Letters on Education with Observations on Religious and Metaphysical Subjects*. London: C. Dilly, 1790 (reprinted NY: Garland Press, 1974).

SUGGESTED READING:

Donnelly, Lucy Martin. "The Celebrated Mrs. Macaulay," in *William and Mary Quarterly*. Vol. VI. April 1949, pp. 173–205.

Hill, Bridget. *The Republican Virago: The Life and Times of Catharine Macaulay, Historian*. Oxford: Oxford University Press, 1992.

Emily Gilbert Gleason,
freelance writer in history, Sylvania, Ohio

Macaulay, Rose (1881–1958)

British novelist, poet, historian, journalist, literary critic, anthologist, travel writer, and broadcaster who was known for her caustic wit, satirical comedy, and, in late life, for her religious quest. Name variations: Emilie Macaulay; Dame Rose Macaulay. Born Emilie Rose Macaulay on August 1, 1881, in Rugby, England; died on October 30, 1958, in London of coronary thrombosis; one of seven children of Grace Mary (Conybeare) Macaulay and George Campbell Macaulay (a literary critic, translator, and academic); educated by parents at home, Varazze, Italy, 1887–94, except for six months at an Italian convent school in 1892; Oxford High School for Girls, 1894–99; Somerville College, Oxford University, 1900–03.

Awards: Femina-Vie Heureuse Prize for Dangerous Ages *(1921); Honorary Litt.D from Cambridge University (1958); James Tait Black Memorial Prize for best novel in 1956 for* The Towers of Trebizond; *Dame Commander of the British Empire (1958).*

Returned to parental home, Aberystwyth, Wales, to begin career as novelist; with parents in Cambridge (1906–22), overlapping with London literary life from 1911 onward; formed liaison with Gerald O'Donovan (1917–42); central to London literary world (1922–58); published 23 novels of social satire and moral quest, a critical biography of Milton, five books of criticism, four books of history and travel, two volumes of poetry, an anthology, plus numerous uncollected book reviews, essays and newspaper articles (1906–56); frequent BBC radio performer (1934–54).

Selected writings: (novels) Abbots Verney *(1906),* The Furnace *(1907),* The Secret River *(1909),* The Valley Captives *(1911),* Views and Vagabonds *(1912),* The Lee Shore *(1912),* The Making of a Bigot *(1914),* Non-Combatants and Others *(1916),* What Not: A Prophetic Comedy *(1918),* Potterism: a Tragi-farcical Tract *(1920),* Dangerous Ages *(1921),* Mystery at Geneva *(1922),* Told by an Idiot *(1923),* Orphan Island *(1924),* Crewe Train *(1926),* Keeping Up Appearances *(1928),* Staying with Relations *(1930),* They Were Defeated *(1932),* Going Abroad *(1934),* I Would Be Private *(1937),* And No Man's Wit *(1940),* The World My Wilderness *(1950),* The Towers of Trebizond *(1956); (poetry)* The Two Blind Countries *(1914),* Three Days *(1919); (essays and criticism)* A Casual Commentary *(1925),* Catchwords and Claptrap *(1926),* Some Religious Elements in English Literature *(1931),* Milton *(1934),* Personal Pleasures *(1935),* The Writings of E.M. Forster *(1938); (anthology)* The Minor Pleasures of Life *(1934); (history and travel)* Life Among the English *(1942),* They Went to Portugal *(1946),* Fabled Shore: from the Pyrenees to Portugal *(1949),* Pleasures of Ruins *(1953),* They Went to Portugal Too *(1990); (letters)* Letters to a Friend: 1950–1952 *(1961),* Last Letters to a Friend: 1952–1958 *(1962),* Letters to a Sister *(1964).*

In 1956, Rose Macaulay, British author and wit, published her last and most admired novel, *The Towers of Trebizond*, in which her androgynous narrator quests for spiritual perfection in an imperfect modern world of charlatans and fools. The narrator journeys from the ancient Turkish city of Trebizond, site of successive historical Hellenic, Byzantine, and Ottoman empires, to Jerusalem, nexus of continuing religious quarrel. The trek is empowered by a careening, insane, lovelorn white camel, and ends in the company of an ape who cannot make the decisions necessary to shift the gears of a car but can learn Anglican ritual: "When the congregation made the responses and joined the service, it joined too, softly chattering." The flawed, self-excusing narrator, unlike camel and ape, seeks spiritual absolution between poles of unrelinquished love with a married man and Christian morality: "the Church was meant to be a shrine of the decencies, of friendship, integrity, love, of the poetry of conduct, of flickering, guttering candles of conscience." The fictional narrator seeks but denies herself religious solace: "Still the towers of Trebizond, the fabled city, shimmer on the far horizon, gated and walled and held in luminous enchantment. It seems that for me, and however much I must stand outside them, this must for ever be." Macaulay's anguished, spiritually questing *Towers of Trebizond* was awarded the prestigious James Tait Black Memorial Prize for best novel in 1956. It departed from the caustic, comic novels that had brought Rose Macaulay her first fame in the 1920s.

Moreover, *The Towers of Trebizond*'s rendering of the narrator's clandestine heterosexual love affair contrasted sharply with Rose Macaulay's cultivated public persona. Tall, lean, and athletic, she was seen as "sexless though not unfeminine," this according to her friend *Rosamond Lehmann. *Storm Jameson found her "elegantly sexless." Observers commonly remarked upon her "sexless" and "ageless" presentation. Indeed, many of Macaulay's prior works had explored gender identities. Her own extremely discreet romantic liaison of 20 years' duration was not made public until a decade after her death and then only after the death of her lover's wife. However, her biographers concur in their understanding that, as Macaulay herself had asserted, *The Towers of Trebizond* was prompted by her "own story" about an adulterous affair in conflict with Anglican absolution. In 1930, she had alluded to her secret life in an epigraph she had written to introduce her novel *Staying With Relations*:

Shifting as mist, men's secret selves
Slip like water and drift like waves,

Flow shadow-wise, and peer like elves
Mocking and strange, from the deep caves.

Born on August 1, 1881, in Rugby, England, Emilie Rose Macaulay was the second child, one of four daughters and two sons, of **Grace Conybeare Macaulay** and George Campbell Macaulay. In his essay included in *Studies in Social History*, Noel Annan uses Rose Macaulay's pedigree as a hook that unravels the tangled line of intermarriages within the "intellectual aristocracy" of 19th-century England, a group of families characterized by liberal-minded, philanthropic intellectuals. Many in the Macaulay-Conybeare line were clerics. At the time she was born, her father was assistant headmaster at Rugby School. He left this post in 1887, sacrificing his professional career for the sake of his wife's health which was tubercular and deteriorating in the damp British climate. The Macaulays settled southeast of Genoa in the Italian fishing village of Varazze. Grace Macaulay's small inheritance allowed them to live abroad, if frugally; George Macaulay supplemented their income by translating classics and writing works of literary criticism. A gift of £1,000 from Grace's mother allowed them to purchase a villa with terraces that opened directly to the beach and sea, an idyllic playground for Rose and her siblings.

The five older children formed a cohort of "dolphin children." As home teachers, their parents encouraged questioning rather than rote learning: their father taught Latin, Italian, and mathematics, while their mother taught reading, writing, literature, and needlework. George gave benediction and read aloud to his family each evening; Grace ended the day with hymns, readings from *The Book of Common Prayer,* and fanciful stories about the Christian battle between good and evil. Afternoons were for outdoor play and private reading. Rose Macaulay lived her prepubescence "like a boy," boasting that she would have a naval career once she became a man. The six months she spent in 1892 at a convent school for girls seemed silly to her; learning was by memorization and behaviors rule-bound. Such restriction was in contrast with her free run of the shelves in her parents' library, where she read widely from Herodotus and Homer, Cervantes and Shakespeare, and 19th-century novelists and poets, including Swinburne, Tennyson, Browning, and Shelley. The Macaulay children were also encouraged to write their own verse. Looking back on her childhood, Rose Macaulay reminisced that "poetry flowed into life with surges of exquisite excitement."

In 1894, when Macaulay was 13, her family returned to England to live near Oxford. She and her sisters attended Oxford High School for Girls until she graduated in 1899. According to **Jane Emery**, one of Macaulay's biographers, the school's late Victorian education in which "moral rectitude was confused with appearance, etiquette, punctuality, and tidiness, . . . froze the Macaulay girls into social shyness." Although not an outstanding student, Rose did receive a Distinction in History which qualified her for admission to Oxford or Cambridge University. Constrained by family finances, she could not immediately attend university; money for advanced education was reserved for her brothers. A year later, however, her uncle Reginald Macaulay offered her money and secured a place for her as a resident student at Somerville College in Oxford, where she concentrated in modern history and bloomed into a talkative, debating young woman. Rose Macaulay graduated with an Aegrotat, a special ranking for students who would have scored at least a good second but were unable to sit because of illness. Women were allowed to sit for and be ranked on all Oxford University examinations, but it was not until 1920 that they could receive degrees.

At the worse, a house unkept cannot be so distressing as a life unlived.

—**Rose Macaulay**

In order to avoid controversy, Somerville College followed an official policy of not taking in the suffrage debate that raged at the turn of the century; Macaulay also avoided the suffrage campaign. Even after suffrage had been attained and she began to write for the feminist journal *Time and Tide* in the 1920s, she refused to write about women's issues, not wishing to be identified as "a writer for women."

As was expected of a young woman of her class, Rose Macaulay returned home to live with her parents who now resided in Aberystwyth, Wales, where her father had taken a position as professor of English language and literature at University College. Here, she began to write her first novel, *Abbots Vernay* (1906). In 1905, her father was appointed to a lectureship at Cambridge University where Macaulay continued to be a companion to both father and mother. Nevertheless, gradually by 1912 she was spending more and more time immersed in London literary life.

By 1912, she had already published several more novels: *The Furnace* (1907), *The Secret River* (1909), and *The Valley Captives* (1911), all of which asserted the values of conventional lifestyles and virtuous behavior. *Views and Vagabonds* (1912) lampooned Fabian socialism; for *The Lee Shore* (1912), she won a best-novel competition sponsored by the publisher Hodder and Stoughton. She was also writing parodies and poems for the *Westminster Gazette* in London, as was Rupert Brooke, a widely admired poet, who became her swimming and walking companion in a platonic friendship beginning in 1909. Macaulay never shared Brooke's agnosticism and Fabian socialism; instead she began to grope toward some sort of deeper religious faith to relieve the depression caused by the murder of her younger brother on the northwest frontier of India. By 1914, she was actively pursuing Anglican answers to murky ethical issues in consultation with an Anglican confessor in Westminster.

In London during 1910 and 1911, Rupert Brooke introduced Macaulay to his poet friends. Renting a flat of her own, she began to balance time between her parents' home and London. Her circle of friends gradually widened as did her reputation as a splendid conversationalist, gifted in repartee. Through ❧➤ **Naomi Royde-Smith**, the successful literary editor of the *Westminster Gazette* whom she met in 1912, Macaulay was further introduced into literary society and assimilated into the Bloomsbury group. Royde-Smith presented her to Walter de la Mare, Hugh Walpole, John Middleton Murry, and ***Katherine Mansfield**, among others. In the essay "Coming to London," Macaulay wrote: "[They] seemed to me, an innocent from the Cam, to be more sparklingly alive than any in my home world . . . . They were all gay and intelligent and young or youngish, and haloed to me with the glamour and sophistication of Londoners." She was especially enamored of Royde-Smith together with her lover Walter de la Mare: "He and she with her gay and ridiculous wit and her wide literary range and critical appreciation, fitted exactly together."

Macaulay's reaction to the initial months of the First World War was one of high adventure and intensified longing to do man's work. She produced another novel, *The Making of a Bigot* (1914), and a volume of poetry, *The Two Blind Countries* (1914). Rupert Brooke died in April 1915 of septicemia contracted in military service; her father then died three months later of a stroke. Macaulay would officially live with her mother until her mother's death in 1925. She began war work as a Voluntary Aid Detachment (VAD), scrubbing floors in a military convalescent hospital near her mother's home in Great Shelford near Cambridge. Subsequently, she was happier working as a land girl on a nearby Sta-

tion Farm. Once again living solely at home, she wrote *Non-Combatants and Others* (1916). In 1917, she took a position as a junior administrative clerk in the Exemptions Bureau of the Ministry of War in London, commuting from her mother's new domicile in Hedgerly near Beaconfield. Because of her knowledge of Italian culture and language, Macaulay was soon appointed to the Italian Section of the Department for Propaganda in Enemy Countries. Her novel *What Not: A Prophetic Comedy* (1918) ridiculed the type of bureaucracy she found in the Ministry of War. Her volume of poetry *Three Days* (1919) includes descriptions of war on the home front.

In the Department for Propaganda during the winter of 1918–19, Macaulay, age 38, met Gerald O'Donovan, age 46, married, an Irish Catholic ex-priest, a novelist (*Father Ralph*, 1913), and publisher's reader. They were in love by 1920, and as biographer Emery writes, "It was a year in which they moved toward a lifetime commitment to be both together and apart, in disregard of their moral convictions." Macaulay lapsed from the Anglican Church; by 1922, she no longer felt she could legitimately receive Holy Communion.

From the end of the First World War until 1922 when Macaulay again moved to her own London flat, she and Naomi Royde-Smith shared a house in Kensington where Macaulay stayed some nights each week. Many observers of the period comment on Royde-Smith's weekly parties, known as "Naomi's Thursdays." They were attended by between 50 and 60 people, mostly writers, publishers, and artists, a mixture of established figures and newcomers. Storm Jameson, then an aspiring novelist, described Royde-Smith as "a little formidable with the air of a younger more affable Queen ***Victoria**" and Macaulay as having a head covered with curls "like a Greek head in a museum" and a way of speaking "in arpeggios" and with "salty tongue." Nevertheless, in her autobiography written 20 years later, Jameson judged Naomi's salon to be "an urbane backwater." Macaulay and Royde-Smith had an emotionally charged falling out in 1922 over Royde-Smith's too public talk about Macaulay's relationship with Gerald O'Donovan. Royde-Smith went on to write novels, the most valued of which is *The Tortoiseshell Cat* (1925). In 1926, she married Ernest Milton, a well-known British actor.

With the popular success of Macaulay's tenth novel, *Potterism* (1920), she was able to live on the proceeds of her fiction. Her slang term "potterism" became a faddish '20s expres-

Royde-Smith, Naomi Gwladys (c. 1880–1964)

British journalist, novelist, anthologist, biographer, translator, and playwright. Name variations: Smith (Naomi Gwladys Royde); Mrs. Ernest Milton. Born Naomi Gwladys Smith in Llanwrst, Wales, around 1880 (some sources cite 1875 but birth date unknown); died on July 28, 1964, in a London hospital; eldest daughter of Ann Daisy (Williams) Smith and Michael Holroyd Smith; educated at Clapham High School, London, and at a private school in Geneva, Switzerland; married Ernest Milton (a British actor), in 1926.

Selected writings: (fiction) The Tortoiseshell Cat *(1925),* The Housemaid *(1926),* Skin-Deep *(1927),* In the Wood *(1928),* The Lover *(1928),* Summer Holiday *(1929),* The Island *(1930),* The Delicate Situation *(1931),* The Mother *(1931),* The Bridge *(1932); (short stories)* Madame Julia's Tale *(1932),* Incredible Tale *(1932),* David *(1933),* Jake *(1935),* All Star Cast *(1936),* For Us in the Dark *(1937),* Miss Bendix *(1938),* The Younger Venus *(1938),* The Altar-Piece *(1939),* Urchin Moor: A Tale *(1939),* Jane Fairfax *(1940),* The Unfaithful Wife *(1942),* Mildensee: A Romance *(1943),* Fire-Weed *(1944),* Love in Mildensee *(1948),* The Iniquity of Us All *(1949),* Rosy Trodd *(1950),* The New Rich *(1951),* She Always Caught the Post *(1953),* Melilot: A Tale *(1955); (plays)* A Balcony *(1926),* Mafro, Darling *(1929),* Mrs. Siddons *(1931),* Pilgrim from Paddington *(1933),* The Queen's Wigs *(1934),* Private Room *(1934); (miscellaneous)* The Double Heart: A Study of Julie de Lespinasse *(1931);* The Private Life of Mrs. Siddons *(1933),* Outside Information *(1941),* The Ox and the Ass at the Manger *(translation from French of J. Supervielle, 1945),* The State of Mind of Mrs. Sherwood: A Study *(1946),* The Idol and the Shrine *(biography and translation from French of journals of E. de Guérin, 1949).*

In the years before the First World War, Naomi Royde-Smith adopted the novelist *Rose Macaulay as her protégée, introducing her to her literary friends, including Walter de la Mare, Hugh Walpole, John Middleton Murry, and *Katherine Mansfield. Macaulay remembers that she was especially enamored of Royde-Smith and her lover Walter de la Mare, the poet: "He and she with her gay and ridiculous wit and her wide literary range and critical appreciation, fitted exactly together." As the successful literary editor of the *Westminster Gazette* and a dashing host of literary gatherings, Royde-Smith's patronage was considered enormously influential.

Royde-Smith was born in Llanwrst, Wales, the daughter of **Ann Daisy Williams Smith** and Michael Holroyd Smith. All biographical references omit her birth date. The Smith family moved to London where Royde-Smith attended Clapham High School and then a private school in Geneva, Switzerland. By 1906, she was responsible for the popular "Problems and Puzzles" page of the *Westminster Gazette*, characterized in 1964 as the "last literary evening paper that London has known." Between 1912 and 1922, she was the *Gazette*'s powerful literary editor. Many of the important writers of the '20s published their first contributions in her columns.

After the war, until 1922, observers of the period comment on "Naomi's Thursdays," Royde-Smith's weekly parties which were prominent events in postwar London. Her salons, given together with her house mate, Rose Macaulay, attracted a mixture of established and aspiring writers, publishers, and artists. *Storm Jameson described Royde-Smith as "a little formidable with the air of a younger more affable Queen *Victoria."

In 1926, Royde-Smith married the British actor Ernest Milton and began to write well-received novels which gently satirized class and gender, such as *The Tortoiseshell Cat* (1925) and *The Delicate Situation* (1931), a historical novel set in the Victorian 1840s. Her childhood is detailed in her novel *In the Wood*, published in America as *Children in the Wood*. Of *The Housemaid* (1926), the reviewer for *The New York Times* wrote: "Cutting as it does across a wide spectrum of contemporary British life, it holds an almost sociological interest." Nevertheless, by 1929 Royde-Smith's novels were considered romantic, whimsical, sentimental comedies. Of her long short story *The Lovers* (1929), the reviewer for *The Spectator* noted: "It is all an intangible web of music, golden light, regret, the transmission of dreamy suprasensual emotion." Royde-Smith also wrote a play about *Sarah Siddons and *A Study of *Julie de Lespinasse* (1933). Although her plays were performed in London, they were not as highly regarded as her fiction. None of Naomi Royde-Smith's novels have been reprinted. Even her 50 books in the British Library seem hidden, listed as they are under a name that she never used: Smith (Naomi Gwladys Royde).

Royde-Smith died in a London hospital on July 28, 1964. Lovat Dickson wrote in tribute that one could tell that Royde-Smith had been "beautiful and young and romantic and clever" because she was beautiful when old and still sharply clever, "keeping her mind in working condition, by writing her novels, plotting them with extreme care and ingenuity."

SOURCES:

Dickson, Lovat. "Miss Naomi Royde-Smith [obituary]," in *The Times* (London). July 30, 1964.

Emery, Jane. *Rose Macaulay*. London: John Murray, 1991.

Kunitz, Stanley, and Howard Haycroft, eds. *Twentieth Century Authors*. NY: H.W. Wilson, 1942.

Smith, Constance Babington. *Rose Macaulay*. London: Collins, 1972.

Jill Benton,
Professor of English and World Literature,
Pitzer College, Claremont, California

sion; it referred to second-rate sentimentalism, cheap short-cuts, mediocrity, muddle, cant, and self-interest. Attacking shoddy journalism, Macaulay dedicated *Potterism* "to the unsentimental precisions in thought, who have, on this confused, inaccurate, and emotional planet, no fit habitation." She was striking the satirical note that would characterize her famous novels of the 1920s, including *Dangerous Ages* (1921), which presented problems central to four generations of women and for which she was awarded the Femina-Vie Heureuse Prize. Others novels followed: *Mystery at Geneva* (1922), *Told by an Idiot* (1923), *Orphan Island* (1924), *Crewe Train* (1926), *Keeping Up Appearances* (1928), and *Staying With Relations* (1930). The critic William C. Frierson described these works in his essay "The Post War Novel, 1919–1929": "The tone of Rose Macaulay's work is sprightly and belies the author's pessimism. But pessimism gradually obtrudes as the reader discovers that the characters which are presented sympathetically acknowledge no values, no obligations, and the pressure of no lasting affection."

In 1925, soon after her mother's death, Rose Macaulay, age 44, established a permanent residence in London. During the mid- to late-1920s, Macaulay traveled often in Italy, France, and the Pyrenees with Gerald O'Donovan. She also joined her brother and sister for an automobile tour of the United States, motoring from Oregon southward to the Mexican border and then across the southwest to Florida. She was an intrepid driver, dangerous and nonchalant, writing in 1935: "I love driving my car. . . . All is bliss. We hum songs of triumph, as all charioteers have." Her friendships with Leonard and *Virginia Woolf deepened. In her diary, Virginia Woolf appraised Macaulay: "In some lights she has the beautiful eyes of all of us distinguished women writers; the refinement; the clearness of cut; the patience & humbleness. It is her voice and manner that makes me edgy." *Vita Sackville-West and Harold Nicholson were also intimates. Macaulay became a regular member of the Friday Hampstead Circle, meeting for games, charades, recitations and sing-alongs with *Ivy Compton-Burnett, Victor Gollancz, Max Beerbohm and sometimes James and *Nora Joyce. Her biographers assert that no dinner party in London was considered complete without Rose Macaulay's conversational sparkle and wit.

By the early 1930s, according to Emery, Rose Macaulay was worried lest her writing be too popular and not be considered intellectual, this despite the collection of essays, *A Casual Commentary* (1925), which had been aimed by her publisher at highbrow readers, and another selection of essays, *Catchwords and Claptrap* (1926) which was published by Leonard and Virginia Woolf's highbrow Hogarth Press. Macaulay began to limit her journalistic assignments to critical and social commentary. In 1931, she produced two works of literary criticism, *Some Religious Elements in English Literature* and *Milton*. Her novel of 1932, *They Were Defeated,* was unlike any she had written before; it was a historical novel about the poet Robert Herrick who lived in the 17th century. The few novels she produced in the comic vein were written half-heartedly, to please her publishers. She began to write a regular column, "Notes on the Margin," for *Time and Tide* and in 1936 wrote a weekly column, "Marginal Comments," for *The Spectator*. She was also making frequent appearances in BBC debates and broadcasts. She closed the decade with the first book-length criticism to be published about the works of E.M. Forster.

Macaulay entered politics in the mid-1930s in order to speak for peace. She never became a Marxist, nor did she abandon her Liberal Party affiliation, but she shared many of the younger generation's concern with justice and wrongful use of force; she became friends with younger literati such as Stephen Spender and Rosamond Lehmann. She was a member of the National Council for Civil Liberties headed by E.M. Forster; she collaborated with Daniel George Bunting, compiling a book for the International Peace Campaign on the subject of humanity's varying attitudes toward peace and war; she was a speaker for the Peace Pledge Union, resigning in 1938 after the Germans invaded Austria. When the Second World War broke out, Macaulay, age 59, was quick to find war work; she volunteered and was accepted as an ambulance driver in London, driving on night shifts during bombing raids so that she would have time to write during the day. Her apartment was completely burned out by a bomb in 1941, destroying her own valuable library as well as her father's. She grieved: "My lost books leave a gaping wound in my heart and mind."

In 1939, Gerald O'Donovan, Macaulay's love of over 20 years, was seriously injured in an automobile accident for which she was responsible. Macaulay suffered. Three years later, in 1942, O'Donovan died of cancer. Her guilt, remorse, and pledged love are poignantly described in a short story, "Miss Anstruther's Letters," which, according to her biographer **Constance Babington Smith**, she wrote in farewell to O'Donovan on his deathbed. The novel she produced eight years later, *The World*

My Wilderness (1950), reflected the sadness of these years. About this novel **Penelope Fitzgerald** writes: "However faulty the main characters may be, there is one striking fact about them; their mistakes are not the result of caring nothing about each other, but of caring too much."

Macaulay worked to forget her despair. She toured Portugal in 1943 gathering information for her tome on British and Portuguese history, 400 pages of which was published in *They Went to Portugal* (1946); the rest was published after her death in *They Went to Portugal Too* (1990). She was a well-known public figure, frequently participating in the BBC radio programs "Critics," "Brains Trust," "Book Reviews," and "Frankly Speaking." She also sat on the Council for the International Liberal Party. In 1946, she motored, alone, some 4,000 miles in Spain and Portugal in order to amass material for her well-received travel and history book, *Fabled Shore: From the Pyrenees to Portugal* (1949). She sought new friendships. Her relationship with the Classical scholar and historian Gilbert Murray blossomed in 1949. In 1950, she began correspondence with Father John Cowper Hamilton Johnson who had been her Anglican confessor between 1914 and 1916 in Westminster. He was now living in a religious community in Boston. Macaulay made her first confession in 30 years and received absolution in the Anglican Church. Her epistolary friendship with Father Johnson lasted for eight years until her death and is recorded in two volumes of collected letters.

Although Macaulay did not call herself a feminist, she lived her life insisting that women and men were equal. In her novel of 1920, *Potterism,* she asserted through one of her female avatars that "young women had to wrest what they wanted," and she had done exactly this in her lifetime, believing that all women could. In her last novel, *The Towers of Trebizond*, she created a feminist narrator who typically recognizes the shared qualities of women and men although she acknowledges that women are clearly disadvantaged:

> And it is a fact that women get called rude names more often than men, because it is not expected that they will hit the people who call them names so that they are called old trouts, old bags, cows, tramps, bitches, whores, and many other things, which no one dares to shout after men, though when they are not there men may safely be called sharks, swine, hogs, snakes, curs, and other animals.

Independent and class-bound, eccentric, libertarian, and anti-authoritarian, Rose Macaulay was, nevertheless, keenly aware of the human struggle between human desire and moral behavior located somewhere in Trebizond between the poles of camels and apes. She wrote to Father Johnson in 1951: "Human passions against eternal laws—that is the everlasting conflict." Her moralism based on her faith in Christian sensibilities and human rationality was the foundation of her satire.

On October 30, 1958, at age 77, Rose Macaulay, having chosen a life of "love with no ties," died quickly of a heart attack in her London apartment. She had recently returned from a Hellenic cruise to Trabzon on the Black Sea, the modern incarnation of Trebizond.

SOURCES:

Bensen, Alice. *Rose Macaulay*. NY: Twayne, 1969.

Emery, Jane. *Rose Macaulay: A Writer's Life*. London: John Murray, 1991.

Macaulay, Rose. "Miss Anstruther's Letters [short story]," in *London Calling*. Ed. by Storm Jameson. NY: Harper and Brothers, 1942 (reprinted in *Rose Macaulay* by Constance Babington Smith. London: Collins, 1972).

———. *Potterism*. NY: Boni and Liveright, 1920.

———. "Problems of a Woman's Life [essay]," in *A Casual Commentary*. NY: Boni and Liveright, 1926.

———. *The Towers of Trebizond*. NY: Farrar, Straus and Cudahy, 1956.

———. *The World My Wilderness*. London: Collins, 1950 (reprinted with an Introduction by Penelope Fitzgerald. London: Virago, 1992).

Smith, Contance Babington. *Rose Macaulay*. London: Collins, 1972.

SUGGESTED READING:

Annan, Noel. "The Intellectual Aristocracy," in *Studies in Social History*. Ed. by J.H. Plumb. London: Longmans, Green, 1955.

Crawford, Alice. *Paradise Pursued: The Novels of Rose Macaulay*. NJ: Fairleigh Dickinson University Press of the Associated University Presses, 1995.

Howatch, Susan. Introduction to *They Were Defeated* by Rose Macaulay. Oxford: Oxford University Press, 1981.

Passty, Jeanette N. *Eros and Androgyny: The Legacy of Rose Macaulay*. NJ: Fairleigh Dickinson University Press, 1988.

Spender, Dale. *Time and Tide Wait for No Man*. London: Pandora Press, 1984.

Wedgwood, Cicely Veronica. Introduction to *They Were Defeated* by Rose Macaulay. London: Collins, 1960.

COLLECTIONS:

Correspondence held in the Humanities Research Center at the University of Texas, Austin.

Correspondence with Gilbert Murray, 1934–57, held in Bodleian Library, Oxford University, England.

Family and personal papers, juvenilia, and correspondence held in the E.M. Macaulay Archive in the Wren Library of Trinity College, Cambridge University, England.

Recorded radio broadcasts held in the BBC Archive of Written Records at Reading, England, and in the BBC Archive of Recorded Sound in London.

Jill Benton,
Professor of English and World Literature,
Pitzer College, Claremont, California

Macbeth, Lady (fl. 1020–1054).

See Gruoch.

MacBride, Maud Gonne (1866–1953).

See Gonne, Maud.

MacDonald, Betty (1908–1958)

American writer whose life provided material for several humorous, bestselling autobiographical books.

Name variations: Anne Elizabeth Campbell Bard MacDonald; Anne Bard; Betty Bard MacDonald; Betty Heskett MacDonald. Born Anne Elizabeth Campbell Bard on March 26, 1908, in Boulder, Colorado; died on February 7, 1958, in Seattle, Washington; daughter of Darsie Campbell Bard (a mining engineer) and Elsie Tholimar (Sanderson) Bard; sister of Mary Bard (1904–1970); attended University of Washington in Seattle; married Robert Eugene Heskett, in 1927 (divorced); married Donald Chauncey MacDonald, on April 24, 1942; children: (first marriage) **Anne Elizabeth Heskett**; **Joan Sydney Heskett.**

Operated small chicken farm with first husband (1927–31); pursued business career (1931–43); began writing career (1943); published bestseller The Egg and I *(1945); published three other autobiographical works (1948–55); published several children's books (1947–57).*

Writings for adults: The Egg and I *(Lippincott, 1945);* The Plague and I *(Lippincott, 1948);* Anybody Can Do Anything *(Lippincott, 1950);* Onions in the Stew *(Lippincott, 1955);* Who Me? The Autobiography of Betty MacDonald *(contains parts of* The Egg and I, The Plague and I, Anybody Can Do Anything, *and* Onions in the Stew, *Lippincott, 1959).*

Writings for children: Mrs. Piggle-Wiggle *(Lippincott, 1947);* Mrs. Piggle-Wiggle's Magic *(Lippincott, 1949);* Nancy and Plum *(Lippincott, 1952);* Mrs. Piggle-Wiggle's Farm *(Lippincott, 1954);* Hello, Mrs. Piggle-Wiggle *(Lippincott, 1957).*

A popular writer in the 1940s and 1950s, Betty MacDonald turned the raw material from difficulties she faced into four humorous autobiographical books. She was born Anne Elizabeth Campbell Bard on March 26, 1908, in Boulder, Colorado, the daughter of Darsie Campbell Bard and **Elsie Sanderson Bard**. The family, which included five children, moved frequently to accommodate her father's job as a mining engineer. By the time Betty was nine, they had lived in mining camps in Colorado, Idaho, Montana, and Mexico. Around 1917, three years before her father's death, the family finally settled in Seattle, where

Betty would live until she was a young adult. The Bards believed their children should be well-rounded, versatile individuals able to meet life's challenges. Toward that end, Betty and her siblings' educations included lessons in piano, ballet and folk dancing, singing, and acting. They also learned French, cooking, and shooting, and, as part of a health program instituted by their father, rose at dawn to take cold baths and perform rigorous exercise routines.

Graduating from Roosevelt High School in Seattle at age 17, MacDonald entered the University of Washington to study art. She soon met and fell in love with Robert Eugene Heskett, an insurance salesman 13 years her senior. Dropping out of college, she married Heskett in 1927. On their honeymoon, Heskett confided that his life's dream was to operate a chicken ranch. Although MacDonald did not share this dream, she had been taught that it was a wife's duty to help ensure her husband's occupational happiness, and therefore agreed to invest their savings in a chicken farm. Located in Washington's Olympic Mountain region, the 40-acre homestead they bought was isolated and run-down, without electricity or running water. Wrote MacDonald:

> It was the little old deserted farm that people point at from car windows, saying "Look at that picturesque old place!" Then quickly drive by toward something not quite so picturesque but warmer and nearer to civilization. That first spring and summer I alternated between delirious happiness and black despair. . . . And then winter settled down and I realized that defeat, like morale, is a lot of little things.

There, she braved the next four years, giving birth to the couple's two daughters, attempting to cook on an explosive wood-burning stove, and struggling to keep chicks alive. Their nearest neighbors were the Kettles. Noted MacDonald:

> [Mrs. Kettle] began most of her sentences with Jeeeesus Keyrist and had a stock disposal of everything of which she did not approve, or any nicety of life which she did not possess. "Ah she's so high and mighty with her 'lectricity," Mrs. Kettle sneered, "She don't bother me none—I just told her to take her hold vacuum cleaner and stuff it." Only Mrs. Kettle described in exact detail how this feat was to be accomplished.

These years on the chicken ranch would later form the basis for MacDonald's first book, *The Egg and I.*

The Heskett marriage having foundered, the couple separated in 1931 (they later divorced), and MacDonald moved with her daughters into her mother's house in Seattle. Finding work during the Depression was difficult, and she had several jobs that lasted only a week or so. "[E]ven tips about jobs from friends were embarrassingly unreliable," she wrote. "I applied for a supposedly excellent secretarial job and was coldly informed, to my horror, that they weren't quite ready to interview new applicants as the former secretary had only just jumped out the window." The struggles of this period she would later detail in another autobiographical book, *Anyone Can Do Anything.* "I went to work in a credit bureau," wrote MacDonald. "One day when my boss was out of his office I sneaked over and looked up our family's credit. . . . From what I read it sounded as if the credit bureau not only wouldn't recommend us for credit, they wouldn't even let us pay cash."

Finally finding regular employment with the National Recovery Administration (NRA), MacDonald became the organization's first female labor adjuster in July 1931. Two and a half years later, she was hired by the procurement division of the U.S. Treasury Department. There she contracted tuberculosis, a contagious lung disease, from a co-worker and from September 1938 until June 1939 she was confined to Firland Sanitorium. She kept a journal during her stay, and the experience provided the raw material for what would be her second book, *The Plague and I.* MacDonald tried to adjust herself to the fact that she might be at Firland for the rest of her life. "At least I will go through menopause under medical supervision," she told herself. During her stay, she learned a stiff test of friendship from her wardmates: "Would she be pleasant to have tb with?"

Following her recovery from tuberculosis, MacDonald found work with another government agency, serving as supervisor of publicity for the National Youth Administration from 1939 to 1942. She subsequently worked for the U.S. Office of Emergency Management as a purchasing agent and then for the Western Construction Company. On April 24, 1942, she married second husband Donald Chauncey MacDonald. Their life together on rural Vashon Island ("a medium sized island . . . being approximately fifteen miles from shoulder to calf and five miles around the hips") in Puget Sound was detailed in *Onions in the Stew,* her fourth autobiography. She also lived in Carmel Valley, California.

Although she had previously written a few short stories, Betty MacDonald's writing career began in earnest in 1943, when her older sister ❧▶ Mary Bard—who would soon become a humorous autobiographical author herself—recognized her talent and made an appointment with a publisher looking for material about the Northwest. Then she persuaded MacDonald to keep the appointment. As Kathy D. Hadley wrote in *The Oxford Companion to Women's Writing in the United States,* "MacDonald hastily composed an outline about her life on a chicken farm, was fired . . . when her boss learned that she had called in sick to finish the outline, and thus began writing full-time." The result was *The Egg and I,* which was partially serialized in *The Atlantic Monthly* before appearing in book form in 1945. According to MacDonald, the book was "a sort of rebuttal to . . . I-love-life books by female good sports whose husbands had forced them to live in the country without lights or running water." *The Egg and I* was an instant bestseller. Published in late 1945, it had sold a million copies by August 1946. The story was adapted for the screen by Universal under the same title in 1947, starring *Claudette Colbert and Fred MacMurray. The Kettles, MacDonald's egg ranch neighbors, inspired the popular "Ma and Pa Kettle" film series starring *Marjorie Main and Percy Kilbride, which first appeared in 1949 and continued until 1957.

The Plague and I, which describes MacDonald's bout with tuberculosis and subsequent con-

❧▶ **Bard, Mary** (1904–1970)

American writer. Name variations: Mary Ten Eyck Bard; Mary TenEyck Bard; Mary TenEyck Bard Jensen. Born on November 21, 1904, in Butte, Montana; died in 1970; daughter of Darsie Campbell Bard (a mining engineer) and Elsie Tholimar (Sanderson) Bard; sister of Betty MacDonald (1908–1958); University of Washington, 1924–26; married Clyde Reynolds Jensen (a pathologist), in 1934; children: Mary, Sally, Heidi.

After a peripatetic childhood spent following her mining engineer father's career from state to state, Mary Bard married a doctor and wrote several books that detailed events in her personal life with a humorous slant. These included *The Doctor Wears Three Faces* (Lippincott, 1949), about the trials of a doctor's wife, *Forty Odd* (Lippincott, 1952), concerning life after 40, and *Just Be Yourself* (Lippincott, 1956). She also wrote several books directed at young girls, all published by Lippincott, including *Best Friends* (1955), *Best Friends in Summer* (1960), and *Best Friends at School* (1961). Her younger sister, the writer *Betty MacDonald, dedicated *The Egg and I* "to my sister Mary who has always believed that I can do anything she puts her mind to."

SOURCES:
Current Biography. NY: H.W. Wilson, 1956.

Betty MacDonald

(1949), *Nancy and Plum*, illustrated by **Hildegarde Hopkins** (1952), *Mrs. Piggle-Wiggle's Farm*, illustrated by Maurice Sendak (1954), and *Hello, Mrs. Piggle-Wiggle*, illustrated by Hilary Knight (1957). HarperCollins published three other "Mrs. Piggle-Wiggle" titles in the 1990s: *Mrs. Piggle-Wiggle Treasury* (1994), *Mrs. Piggle-Wiggle's Won't-Pick-Up-Toys Cure* (1997) and *Mrs. Piggle-Wiggle's Won't-Take-A-Bath Cure* (1997).

Betty MacDonald died of cancer in Seattle, Washington, on February 7, 1958, at the age of 49.

SOURCES:
Blain, Virginia, Patricia Clements, and Isobel Grundy. *The Feminist Companion to Literature in English*. New Haven, CT: Yale University Press, 1990.
Commire, Anne, ed. *Yesterday's Authors of Books for Children*. Detroit, MI: Gale Research, 1977.
Contemporary Authors. Vol. 136. Detroit, MI: Gale Research, 1998.
Current Biography. NY: H.W. Wilson, 1946.
MacDonald, Betty. *Anybody Can Do Anything*. Philadelphia, PA: Lippincott, 1950.
———. *The Egg and I*. Philadelphia, PA: Lippincott, 1945.
———. *Onions in the Stew*. Philadelphia, PA: Lippincott, 1955.
———. *The Plague and I*. Philadelphia, PA: Lippincott, 1948.
The Oxford Companion to Women's Writing in the United States. Edited by Cathy N. Davidson and Linda Wagner-Martin. NY: Oxford University Press, 1995.
Saturday Review. May 14, 1955.

RELATED MEDIA:
The Egg and I, starring Claudette Colbert and Fred MacMurray, was adapted for film by Universal, 1947.
Onions in the Stew was adapted for the stage by William Dalzell and **Anne Coulter Martins** for Dramatic Publishing, 1956.

Ellen Dennis French,
freelance writer in biography, Murrieta, California

finement, appeared in 1948, and was partially serialized in *Good Housekeeping* prior to publication by Lippincott in book form. In 1950, MacDonald published *Anybody Can Do Anything*, a testimonial to her sister Mary Bard's encouraging influence on her family as well as a wry depiction of her own Depression-era quest for employment. "As time went on I became more and more convinced that Mary was right and that anybody could do anything," wrote MacDonald, "but I had sense enough to realize that it was a hell of a lot harder for some people than for others." Her fourth autobiography, *Onions in the Stew*, was published in 1955. "Even if MacDonald never writes another book," claimed **Helen Beal Woodward** in *Saturday Review*, "she has earned the right to appear in any anthology of American humor." *Who Me?*, an abridgment of all four autobiographies, was published posthumously in 1959.

Betty MacDonald's first children's book appeared in 1947. Illustrated by Richard Bennett, *Mrs. Piggle-Wiggle* launched the series which featured the eponymous mother who proffers wise and witty advice for dealing with recalcitrant children. It was followed by *Mrs. Piggle-Wiggle's Magic*, illustrated by Kurt Wiese

MacDonald, Finula (fl. 1569–1592)

*Queen of Tirconnell (or Tir Chonaill). Name variations: (nickname) Inghean Dubh; Finula O'Donnell. Flourished between 1569 and 1592; daughter of James MacDonald of Isla and Agnes (Campbell) MacDonald; married Hugh O'Donnell, king of Tirconnell or Tir Chonaill, in 1569; children: Hugh Roe O'Donnell, known as Red Hugh (1572–1602, who married **Finula O'Neill**); Ruaidhrí O'Donnell (1575–1608); daughter Nuala O'Donnell (fl. 1608–1617); and at least two other sons.*

Finula MacDonald, wife of Hugh O'Donnell, king of Tirconnell, was determined that her son Hugh Roe O'Donnell, known as Red Hugh, succeed his father. At age 16, Red Hugh was taken hostage by Sir John Perrott and imprisoned in Dublin Castle where he spent the next four years until his escape in bitter winter weather to his parents' castle in Ballyshannon, County Donegal. Frostbite necessitated amputation of his two big toes. Meanwhile, his competitor for clan leadership, Hugh O'Gallagher, was gaining strength. Finula invited O'Gallagher to visit her house at Mongavlin and had him killed. In 1590, she also had another threat, Donnell O'-Donnell, killed at Doire Leathan, Tirconnell. Her influence and military strength contributed decisively to her son's succession as king of Tirconnell in 1592. Finula's daughter **Nuala O'-Donnell** was the subject of a poem, "Truagh liom Máire agas Mairghrég," by Fearghal Óg mac an Bhaird. Nuala lived in Rome in exile.

Macdonald, Flora (1722–1790)

Scottish heroine who ferried Bonnie Prince Charlie out of danger to the Isle of Skye after the failure of his rebellion in 1746. Born Fionnghal nighean Raonuill'ic Aonghais Oig, an Airidh Mhuillinn (Gaelic for "Flora, daughter of Ranald, son of Aungus, Younger of Milton"), in 1722; died in 1790; daughter of Ranald Macdonald of Milton, South Uist, and Marian Macdonald; married Allan Macdonald, in 1750; children: seven, two daughters (including Anne) and five sons (including Charles, Alexander, and James).

Took Prince Charles to the Hebrides and Skye by boat after Culloden (1746); imprisoned in London (1746–47); emigrated to North Carolina (1774); Battle of Moore's Creek Bridge (1776); reunited with Allan in New York (1778); spent winter in Nova Scotia followed by return to Scotland (1779).

In 1745, Prince Charles Edward Stuart, "Bonnie Prince Charlie," landed at Glenfinnan in the Scottish highlands and gathered volunteers for a rebellion against the Hanoverian King George II of Britain. Charles' Catholic grandfather, King James II, had been deposed in the Glorious Revolution of 1688–89 and Parliament had resolved to have no more Catholics on the throne. The "Protestant Succession" had a weaker dynastic claim to the throne than the Stuarts, however, and Charles, the "Young Pretender," hoped that the Scottish clans, especially those which had stuck to the Old Religion, would rise up and restore the Stuarts.

At first the adventure prospered as he conquered Scotland, gathered recruits and marched southward. But by the time he reached the English midland city of Derby, his clansmen were falling out among themselves and doubting their ability to overthrow the Hanoverians. Ironically, London was in panic. Had the rebels pressed on, they would probably have been able to seize it; but instead, demoralized, they turned and retreated to Scotland. By April 1746, the regime had recovered its composure and a pursuing British army under the Duke of Cumberland shattered the Scots' force at the Battle of Culloden Moor and routed the remnants. Charles and a handful of followers fled the battlefield and hid in the hills during the next few weeks. Only by getting off the Scottish mainland and returning to his exile court in France would he be safe. Flora Macdonald enabled him to escape.

She had been born 23 years earlier in the Hebridean island of South Uist, daughter of a prosperous farmer. He died when she was two, but her mother married another Macdonald, from the nearby island of Skye, who had earlier served in the king of France's army and was a legend for his strength and swordsmanship. Flora was raised under the protective gaze of Scottish nobility and probably lived all her early years in the islands, though one tale describes her spending three years at an Edinburgh seminary for young ladies. Her writing was poor but she was a fluent talker in English and Gaelic and a talented singer and storyteller.

Flora's family, who were not Catholics, played no role in the uprising; instead, her stepfather was made an officer in an anti-Jacobite militia company. But like many of the nominally anti-Jacobite highlanders, he was willing to help the fugitive prince escape detection in the summer of 1746 as the prince traveled incognito on the islands of Harris and Lewis. British soldiers and sailors searched for him in vain and even their threats of reprisals could not induce a betrayal. As their net gradually closed, however, the prince came to Ormiclade, home of the Clanranald family, where he met Flora Macdonald on June 20. At first, she refused to have anything to do with the fugitive but when she realized that her stepfather had planned the prince's escape her sense of duty moved her to action. According to historian Hugh Douglas, "The Prince's appeal to her honour won her over. As a Highland lady she could not refuse to assist a stranger in need." Flora was not political herself, but as Douglas adds, "in the Hebrides she was surrounded by relatives and kinsmen who either supported the Stuarts openly or at the very least had room in their hearts for them even if their heads held them back from rallying to the Prince's standard."

Flora
Macdonald

Macdonald recognized that the existence of a £30,000 reward on the prince's head would tempt everyone who knew about him to give the game away, so she decided to disguise him as a woman. From her stepfather, she obtained three passports for a voyage to Skye, one for herself, one for the prince's servant Niel MacEachainn, and one for "Betty Burke," an Irish seamstress who, she said, she was taking to her mother. Betty Burke was not happy with her new clothes. "The company being gone, the Prince, stript of his own cloaths was dressed by Miss Flora in his new attire," wrote MacEachainn, "but could not keep his

hands from adjusting his headdress, which he cursed a thousand times." With six sturdy sailors, they had to cross a stormy strait called The Minch, 40 miles wide, on the night of June 27, 1746, blown fast by favorable winds. Arriving the next morning, they ran into an anti-Stuart militia company which opened fire on them but were able to pull away from the shore and escape. When they came ashore again, this time in a deserted cove, Flora walked up to a close relative's house and calmly chatted there with a local militia colonel of the McLeod clan, who was opposed to the Pretender, while servants and family members spirited the fugitive to a safe hiding place. From there, Flora saw him first to her mother's house and then safely onto a boat bound for the island of Raasay, which stood between Skye and the mainland. It took several more journeys around the islands before the prince could finally get aboard a ship back to France, but his long journey with Flora Macdonald soon became the centerpiece of his legendary escape.

Well known in the islands, Macdonald was eventually identified by British soldiers, who had tortured several hostages into revealing information. She was arrested, held first on a ship, and then taken south to prison in the Tower of London. There, ironically, Londoners soon began to treat her not as a traitor or conspirator but as a romantic heroine. Even the king's son, Frederick, prince of Wales, came to visit her and was charmed by her good manners and dignified defense of her actions for which, she said, there had been no political motive. She was released into the custody of a sympathetic family but still confined to their house until her freedom came as part of the terms of a General Indemnity granted in 1747. The government's spies in France assured George II that there was no danger of any more rebellions and indeed Charles, despite constant plotting, deteriorated into alcoholism and was powerless to try again for the British throne. In 1748, the king of France evicted him too, and Charles spent the rest of his life wandering unwanted through Europe. Meanwhile, the British army was forcibly dismantling the Scottish clan system which had supported the Pretender, transforming the social and economic structure of Scotland in the process.

In 1750, age 29, Flora married Allan Macdonald, son of "Old Kingsburgh" of Skye. They lived together at his family farm, Flodigarry, where he experimented in new farming techniques, and they were still there in 1773 when Dr. Samuel Johnson and James Boswell, making their famous tour of Britain, went to stay with them for the night. Boswell described Allan Macdonald as "completely the figure of a gallant Highlander, exhibiting the graceful mien and manly looks which our popular Scotch song has justly attributed to that character." They broke with tradition by naming their oldest son Charles, in honor of the prince (whom Allan had not even supported) instead of naming him after his paternal grandfather. Six other children followed in the next fifteen years but the family's farming reforms did not go well. Poor prices, local resistance to innovations, and a certain lack of common sense on Allan's part led to successive years of failure, which ate up both

his own fortune and the money Flora had brought to the marriage as a dowry. In 1767, Allan lost his job as "tacksman" or land-agent for the clan chief and their fortunes continued to dwindle.

Many Scots had been emigrating to the American colonies in the face of hard times, and when Allan's father died in 1772 he and Flora decided to take the same course in the hope of making a fresh start. Just before they left in 1774, Flora wrote the family lawyer:

> There will soon be no remembrance of my family in this miserable island, the best of its inhabitance [sic] are already making ready to follow their friends to America, while they have anything to bring them and among the rest we are to go . . . as we cannot promise ourselves but poverty and oppression [if we stay in Scotland].

The Atlantic voyage in the fall of 1774 was stormy but the growing difficulties of their old life led the Macdonalds to look forward with hope to America.

This is not a simple Highland girl that legend has handed down but a clever, strong-willed young woman who commands attention.
—Hugh Douglas

When they arrived in Richmond County, North Carolina, near the present-day town of Fayetteville, they were greeted by the many Highland settlers in the district who knew of Flora's heroic deeds and had themselves, in some cases, been at Culloden. For Highlanders from the islands, especially the bare, windswept Hebrides and Skye, North Carolina presented a dramatic contrast, both in its high summer temperatures and its dense forest coverage, the like of which many of them had never previously seen. The Macdonalds bought a large plantation, "Killiegray," consisting of 70 acres of arable fields and a group of orchards, which they worked with their sons and eight indentured servants, but they had hardly begun their lives as farmers when the Revolutionary War began.

Whatever their earlier disputes with the Hanoverians, the Macdonalds now emerged as staunch opponents of the Revolution and defenders of King George III's government. The colony's governor, Josiah Martin, recognized Allan as a leading clansman from the moment of his arrival, and Allan reciprocated by swearing loyalty to the throne, just as he had done during the "Forty Five." He toured the colony with his two sons, both now old enough for

Flora Macdonald meets Bonnie Prince Charlie for the first time.

military service, trying to raise troops, and ignored a summons to join a highland regiment which was forming far to the north in Nova Scotia. Historian Hugh Douglas argues that Allan "was the key figure in the fight to save North Carolina for the King. Because of Flora's fame and his own enthusiasm for the Loyalist cause, it was natural that the Highlanders should look to [him] for leadership." He spent £300 of his own money equipping his soldiers, but even so they were a reluctant and poorly trained band.

According to a local tradition which is probably greatly embroidered, Flora rode a white pony and set up a royal standard on February 18, 1776, the day her husband's column set out, exhorting the recruits in Gaelic to fight for the king. Almost at once they were ambushed at the Battle of Moore's Creek, when they rashly tried to charge across a damaged bridge brandishing their Scottish broadswords in the face of withering cross fire. The battle "was over in minutes," writes Douglas, "a defeat almost as violent and swift as Culloden and

just as complete. Once again highland bravery and the broadsword had counted for nothing in the face of devastating musket fire."

Among those taken prisoner by the victorious patriots were Allan and sons Alexander and James. James managed to escape and return to his mother with the news that all three of them had at least survived the battle, but Allan and Alexander remained captives for a year and a half until they were ransomed during a general exchange of prisoners in New York. Flora endured two wretched years after the defeat and later told a chronicler:

> Mrs. Flora Macdonald, being all this time in misery and sickness at home, being informed that her husband and friends were all killed or taken, contracted a severe fever, and was deeply oppressed with straggling parties of plunderers from their army and night robbers, who more than once threatened her life wanting a confesion [sic] where her husband's money was. Her servants deserting her, and such as stayed grew so very insolent that they were of no service or help to her.

Flora spent time visiting other highland women whose men had been killed or captured, and on one such visit fell from a horse and broke her arm. There was no doctor in the colony to treat her, and it caused months of severe pain. She was finally able to leave North Carolina when a relative, Alexander MacLeod, sailed under a flag of truce to Wilmington in a small ship and picked her up with her daughter **Anne Macdonald**, a fellow colonist. They sailed to New York City, headquarters of the British forces, and were reunited with Allan.

Allan, however, had spent time since his release raising a new regiment of volunteers, whom he soon took to join the loyalist Highlanders in Nova Scotia. Flora followed him a few months later but had a rough sea voyage and a gruelling winter march. North Carolina's heat and the bitter winter of Canada were both taking a severe toll on her health and now, approaching 60, she became a near invalid. She remained high spirited in the face of adversity, however. Rather than spend a second winter in the icy garrison, she managed to get a place on a British ship heading back to England in the fall of 1779. It sighted a French man of war, and Flora, as she hurried the female passengers below decks, broke her other arm. In London, where the ship landed, she learned that her son Alexander had been lost at sea. This was the final straw which made her severely ill for the next six months. Old Jacobite friends remembered her from 33 years before and cared for her in this illness until she was well enough to return to the Scottish islands. At the end of the American wars, she was reunited with her husband Allan, and they lived together on Skye, surrounded by family and friends, until her death in 1790.

A lot of sentimental nonsense has been written about Macdonald, not least by Americans of Scottish descent trying to mimic the language of Robert Burns. In 1916, for example, a Canadian newspaper editor, James MacDonald penned these deathless lines:

> It was granted to Scotland that out of the gloom there should flash forth a deed so full of high patriotism that so long as the true sons of the Gael shall foregather, it will be remembered with glad hearts and high-lifted bonnets. Think you that this honor was granted to some great chief in the forefront of battle . . . ? Nay, it was but a bit sonsie lassie, her hair yet bound with the blue snood of maidenhood, who offered her all, even life itself, to save Scotland's "Bonnie Prince."

More sober historians like Hugh Douglas have in recent years sorted out the facts from the myth and shown that in the case of Flora Macdonald,

as with so many others, the truth is as strange, and more interesting, than the fiction. Although there are still many gaps in our knowledge of Flora Macdonald, we can now piece together the story of her life as a flesh and blood woman rather than a legendary Jacobite presence.

SOURCES:

Black, Jeremy. *Culloden and the '45*. Stroud, UK: Alan Sutton, 1990.

Douglas, Hugh. *Flora Macdonald: The Most Loyal Rebel*. Stroud, UK: Alan Sutton, 1993.

Macdonald, James A. *Flora Macdonald: A History*. Washington, DC: Scottish Society of America, 1916.

MacGregor, A., and W. Jolly. *The Life of Flora Macdonald*. Stirling, UK: Eneas Mackay, 1932.

SUGGESTED READING:

Carruth, J.A. *Flora Macdonald, the Highland Heroine*. Norwich, 1973.

Lenman, Bruce. *The Jacobite Risings in Britain*. London: 1980.

MacLean, Alasdair. *A Macdonald for the Prince*. Stornoway, 1982.

MacLean, J.P. *Flora Macdonald in America*. Morgantown, PA: 1984.

COLLECTIONS:

National Library of Scotland.
Scottish Record Office.

Patrick Allitt,
Professor of History, Emory University, Atlanta, Georgia

MacDonald, Frances (1874–1921)

English-born artist and designer. Born Frances Macdonald in England in 1874; died in 1921; sister of Margaret Mackintosh (1865–1933); studied at the Glasgow College of Art; married J.L. Herbert MacNair (a painter).

A member of the Glasgow group, Frances MacDonald painted portraits and figurative subjects. In 1894, she and her sister *Margaret Mackintosh** opened a studio and worked with stained glass, metal, embroidery, and illustration. Frances MacDonald's work was exhibited in Vienna in 1900 and at Turin in 1902. Following her marriage to artist Herbert MacNair in 1899, Frances moved to Liverpool, teaching arts and crafts there at the university. Her work was strongly influenced by her brother-in-law Charles Rennie Mackintosh. In fact, the sisters and their husbands worked so closely together that they were known as "The Four." In 1907, Frances returned to Glasgow where she taught various crafts.

MacDonald, Jeanette (1903–1965)

Broadway and Hollywood singer and actress. Name variations: Jeanette MacDonald Raymond; (nicknames) "Jessie," "Jimmie," "Jim-Jam," and "The Iron Butterfly." Born Jeanette Anna MacDonald in

Philadelphia, Pennsylvania, on June 18, 1903 (her burial crypt reads 1907, but as a young girl she enrolled in school by presenting birth records that stated 1903); died while preparing for open heart surgery on January 14, 1965, in Methodist Hospital, Houston, Texas; daughter of Daniel MacDonald (a building contractor) and Anna (Wright) MacDonald; sister of actress Marie Blake; attended Dunlap Grammar School and West Philadelphia School for Girls in Philadelphia, and Washington Irving High School and Julia Richman High School in New York City; only finished the 10th grade; married Gene Raymond (born Raymond Guion, an actor), on June 16, 1937; no children.

Appeared in "mini operas" at four years old (1907); toured summer resorts on East Coast with Al White's "Six Sunny Song Birds" (1914); joined sister Blossom in The Demi-Tasse Revue *in New York City (1919); quit school to appear in Broadway's* The Night Boat *(1920); after several small parts, played a lead in* A Fantastic Fricassee *and continued a secondary career in modeling (1922); received star billing in* Yes, Yes, Yvette *(1927); while appearing in the title role of Broadway's* Angela, *made a screen test at Paramount Studios in New York (1928–29); appeared as the female star in the movie* The Love Parade *(1929); after several films with Paramount and Fox, signed with Metro-Goldwyn-Mayer and made* Naughty Marietta, *first of eight films with Nelson Eddy (1935); as operetta began to lose favor with moviegoers, toured in concert (1939); debuted as Juliette in Gounod's opera,* Romeo et Juliette, *in Montreal (1943); made 29th and final film,* The Sun Comes Up *(1949); continued recording and personal appearances (through 1957); had an arterial transplant (1963).*

Selected filmography: The Love Parade *(1929);* The Vagabond King *(1930);* Monte Carlo *(1930);* The Lottery Bride *(1930);* Let's Go Native *(1930);* Oh, For a Man! *(1930);* Galas de la Paramount *(Spanish-language version of* Paramount on Parade, *1930);* Annabelle's Affairs *(1931);* Don't Bet on Women *(1931);* Love Me Tonight *(1932);* One Hour With You *(1932);* The Merry Widow *(1934);* The Cat and the Fiddle *(1934);* Naughty Marietta *(1935);* San Francisco *(1936);* Rose Marie *(1936);* Maytime *(1937);* The Firefly *(1937);* Sweethearts *(1938);* The Girl of the Golden West *(1938);* Broadway Serenade *(1939);* New Moon *(1940);* Bitter Sweet *(1940);* Smilin' Through *(1941);* I Married an Angel *(1942);* Cairo *(1942);* Follow the Boys *(1944);* Three Daring Daughters *(1948);* The Sun Comes Up *(1949).*

Louella Parsons.
See joint entry under Hopper, Hedda and Louella Parsons.

Hollywood critic ◄❦ **Louella Parsons** once said that Jeanette MacDonald was "Holly-wood's greatest show-woman," a person who gave the public what it demanded. By modern-day standards, her movies and manners are passé, part of an age when American tastes were uncomplicated and easy to please. But in her heyday, she not only registered box-office successes for a youthful film industry, she also helped promote the independence of female movie stars. She combined her abilities as an outstanding singer and superb comedic actress with good business sense. Her Hollywood nickname, "The Iron Butterfly," sums up her beauty, artistry, business acumen, and independence. In an age that endured sexual harassment with so-called "studio couch auditions," she kept unwanted advances in check, despite appearing in risqué comedies and musicals. Of Scottish, Irish, and English ancestry, MacDonald once said, "I've been told I have an Irish temper, I know I have Scottish thrift, and, like the English, I love a good show."

Jeanette MacDonald began life in 1903 in Philadelphia, the youngest daughter of a middle-class, Presbyterian family, whose father was a building contractor. All of the MacDonald offspring showed interest in entertainment and were encouraged by their parents. The oldest daughter, **Elsie MacDonald**, ran a dancing, singing, and acting school in her hometown for several years. Blossom, the second child, had a modest career on Broadway and became a character actress in movies and television using the name **Marie Blake**.

Jeanette began performing with a local music and dance school while only four years old and by six was appearing in mini opera with other child prodigies. She played in Philadelphia vaudeville houses and when eleven years old toured with the "Six Sunny Song Birds," making summer resort engagements along the East Coast.

When Jeanette was 16, her sister Blossom, a member of the chorus line of *The Demi-Tasse Revue* in New York City, got her a dancing part in the same production. At about this time, the family moved to New York, and Jeanette, whose job lasted only several weeks, enrolled in school. When a minor performer broke her leg while appearing out of town in Jerome Kern's *The Night Boat*, Jeanette, who had joined the troupe's chorus in Rochester, replaced her, never to pursue a formal education again. The play, which began at the Liberty on February 2, 1920, ran through 148 performances.

Briefly unemployed when *The Night Boat* closed, MacDonald began training her voice and took dancing lessons. She may also have begun

Jeanette
MacDonald

studying at the local Berlitz language school, for she ultimately mastered French and Spanish. After playing a small part in *Irene* in Chicago, she managed a larger role in *Tangerine,* a huge success that opened on Broadway in September 1921 and ran through 337 performances. When not en-

gaged as a performer, she sometimes modeled for New York furriers and lingerie merchants.

Her first important role was in *A Fantastic Fricassee* at the Greenwich Village Theater on September 11, 1922. After its moderately successful run, she appeared as the second female lead in *The Magic Ring*. Opening on October 1, 1923, it ran through 96 performances, a respectable figure for Broadway musicals and operettas in the Cinderella years of the 1920s. In it, MacDonald was billed as "the girl with golden red hair and sea-green eyes," who sang "eloquently."

Having played several times at the Liberty Theater, she returned there on December 28, 1925, in *Tip Toes*, a musical with songs written by George and Ira Gershwin. She was the lead ingenue, attracting the attention of the Broadway Shuberts, who signed her to a contract. The brothers, Sam, Lee, and J.J. ("Jake"), owned theaters in New York and elsewhere. With them, she starred in several so-so musicals, the first being *Bubbling Over*, a road success which lasted one week on the New York stage. Her next appearance was in *Yes, Yes, Yvette*, a musical which debuted in New York on November 3, 1927. It was by the same producer as *No, No, Nanette* (1925) and did well in Chicago but failed after 45 performances in New York. MacDonald played the title role, receiving what were generally good reviews.

I never realized how much movie stars mean to people. Not what you do or what you say, but just your presence, your being there. It makes you feel embarrassed and rather humble.

—Jeanette MacDonald

Sunny Days, based on a French farce, opened at the Imperial in February 1928 and was a better vehicle for her. She played Ginette, a young flower shop girl, who is the mistress of a banker. Although it lasted four months, the music was considered lackluster, with the presentation relying on comedy and dance for its success. One critic, however, wrote that Jeanette was "a charming blonde who sings and dances expertly and looks better in lingerie."

Her next two appearances, which would be her last on Broadway, were flops. *Angela*, which started in Philadelphia as "The Queen's Taste," moved to the Ambassador on December 23, 1928. How it managed 40 performances is baffling since it was described variously as having "stilted dialog," "tired dance routines," "abominable lighting," and "drab comedy."

Although entering her late 20s, MacDonald had never spent much time socially, devoting herself to her career. She did enjoying shopping and dining out but had established no serious relationships outside her family. During *Angela*,

she met New York stockbroker Robert Ritchie, who became a constant companion and finally her business manager. The extent to which their romance developed is pure conjecture, and they separated in 1935.

Also during that play, her performance impressed movie star Richard Dix, who arranged a screen test for her. Though he planned to have her appear in a movie with him, the Shuberts would not release her from her contract. Later, while appearing in *Boom, Boom* in Chicago, she was noticed by director Ernst Lubitsch, who asked to see her screen test and subsequently bought her contract from the Shuberts. Known for his "sophisticated sex comedies," Lubitsch cast her in *The Love Parade* (1929) with Maurice Chevalier. It is considered by some as "a milestone in the development of talking-film technique." As the haughty Queen Louise of mythical Sylvania, MacDonald was at her sauciest, wearing revealing negligees and appearing in bathtub or boudoir. The movie was what one author called a "sophisticated musical sex farce" even by modern standards.

Soon after, she cut her first recording with RCA Victor, singing selections from the film *The Love Parade*, the first of several films she made with Chevalier, a difficult man to work with under almost all circumstances. The strait-laced MacDonald found his "derriere pinch[ing]" distasteful. For his part, he could not understand why she did not like his off-color jokes. Still, they worked well together and made three more movies.

Fresh from her first success, she appeared in *The Vagabond King* (1930), an adaptation of Rudolf Friml's operetta, directed by Ludwig Berger. But Paramount's first talkie in full color was panned by the critics. She also sang in the all-star revue *Paramount on Parade*. Though cut from the American release, MacDonald remained in the Spanish version, *Galas de la Paramount* (1930), acting as an emcee and speaking and singing in Spanish. Lubitsch, impressed by her natural beauty and hardworking eagerness, cast her in *Monte Carlo* (1930). As in the earlier movies, she played aristocracy, a countess who falls in love with her hairdresser, only to discover happily that he is a count in disguise. One of her songs, "Beyond the Blue Horizon," became a hit.

Before movie musicals went temporarily out of style in the early '30s, she made *Let's Go Native* (1930) for Paramount and *The Lottery Bride* (1930) for United Artists. The former, a wild burlesque of shipwreck castaways with much singing and dancing, was fairly well accepted. The latter, despite songs by Friml, was not well received. She

From the movie Bittersweet, *starring Nelson Eddy and Jeanette MacDonald.*

was also put on loan to Fox studio where she made three comedies that featured her mostly in non-singing roles—*Oh, For a Man!* (1930), *Don't Bet on Women* (1931), and *Annabelle's Affairs* (1931).

In 1931, the French novelist Andre Ranson spread the rumor that MacDonald had been killed by a woman she had wronged in an illicit love affair. To correct these misimpressions, Mac-Donald made a smashingly successful singing tour of Europe. Lubitsch brought her back to America and paired her again with Chevalier in *One Hour With You* (1932). Because of previous commitments, Lubitsch named George Cukor to direct. But when the production was deep into filming, Lubitsch found himself free of his assignment and began to make frequent appearances on the set, offering suggestions. When the fed-up Cukor quit, Lubitsch took over. The movie, though not lucrative, received an Academy Award nomination for Best Picture, losing to that year's winner, *Grand Hotel.*

Chevalier also co-starred in her next picture, *Love Me Tonight* (1932), which featured songs by Richard Rodgers and Moss Hart, costumes by *Edith Head, and a deadpan, risqué turn by *Myrna Loy. It proved to be a money maker for Paramount but was to be MacDonald's last movie for them. Hollywood critic and playwright DeWitt Bodeen believed *Love Me Tonight* was not only the best film she and Chevalier made but considered it "one of the very best and brightest movie musicals ever made." It was also the first "integrated" musical, notes the *Motion Picture Guide,* with the score "seamlessly sewn into the story." Still, with all her success, MacDonald was unhappy with the way her career seemed to be heading in America. She toured Europe again, buying a villa in southern France. Louis B. Mayer, impressed by her talent and recent performance, followed her to the Continent and signed her to a contract at MGM, where she became one of the most beloved musical stars of all time.

Her first two productions for the company were *The Cat and the Fiddle* (1934), with the fading silent-film legend Ramon Novarro, and *The Merry Widow* (1934), her last picture with

Chevalier. Once again Lubitsch, now working for MGM, directed the pair in this operetta by Franz Lehar. One of her biographers, James Harvey, called it the best film of her career, writing that "her parodic talent, her gift for ardent nonsense, her ability to convey sexual longing in a direct, pure, unembarrassing way—all were qualities exactly and deeply suited to Lubitsch's comedy of dry astonishment." Editors of the *Motion Picture Guide* agree: "MacDonald more than held her own in the comedy department as she snapped off the lines with *Carole Lombard-like expertise." Despite her accomplishments, MacDonald had not yet achieved superstardom. But opportunity for it came with her next picture.

Mayer planned to star Allan Jones with her in *Naughty Marietta* (1935). But Jones, also a contract player for the Shuberts in New York, was unable to break his contract. So Mayer chose a bit player, Nelson Eddy, who had appeared in small parts in three movies. It was a stroke of genius. Ed Sullivan, in the New York *Daily News,* was soon writing that the team of MacDonald and Eddy were becoming the "sensation of the industry." *Naughty Marietta,* which received high praise, became one of the 100 top-grossing films in history. MacDonald would make seven more pictures with Eddy in the next six years: *Rose Marie* (1936), *Maytime* (1937), *The Girl of the Golden West* (1938), *Sweethearts* (1938), *New Moon* (1940), *Bitter Sweet* (1940), and *I Married an Angel* (1942).

Over the years, MacDonald's and Eddy's names became inseparable and rumors abounded of a secret love affair. Both were moralists and conservatives. Both loved opera. Both came from Philadelphia, Eddy having moved there from Rhode Island. And neither had finished high school. Their movies became steady money makers for MGM. "When they sang they lifted your soul from an abyss to the highest floating cloud in the sky," noted *Eleanor Powell. "They were the epitome of perfect blending and perfection."

In between her movies with Eddy, MacDonald made other films. By far the best was *San Francisco* (1936), which gave her a larger acting and smaller singing part opposite box-office greats Clark Gable and Spencer Tracy. She finally appeared with Allan Jones in *The Firefly* (1937), and then with Lew Ayers in *Broadway Serenade* (1939). During these years, she was associated with many of the great names of filmdom and American entertainment.

After parting with Ritchie, she began a romance with actor-singer Gene Raymond, whom she married in "Hollywood's wedding of the year" in 1937. The marriage lasted until her death. (**Sharon Rich** maintains in her 1995 book *Sweethearts* that Louis B. Mayer engineered the marriage, that Raymond was a closeted gay, and that MacDonald had an enduring affair with Eddy for 30 years. Biographer Edward Baron Turk claims that MacDonald and Eddy had little use for each other.) MacDonald's only movie with Raymond was *Smilin' Through* (1941)—a romantic drama that covered two centuries and allowed her to play a dual role: Moonyeen of the 19th century and Kathleen of the 20th. Her last picture with MGM was *Cairo* (1942), a spoof of espionage films. Although the idea of camp entertainment was yet to surface, she was well on her way to becoming a superb camp player.

With World War II underway, MacDonald became a regular on the USO circuit. As her movie career declined, she became increasingly interested in opera and began serious study, debuting with Ezio Pinza in *Romeo et Juliette* in Montreal in 1943. She also sang with Pinza in the Chicago Civic Opera Company's presentation of Gounod's *Faust* in 1944. Recital appearances and stock productions drew huge crowds. Although plans to pair her with Eddy in still another movie were considered, it never happened. They did appear together on Eddy's radio show, and songs from their movies were released by recording companies. She was featured in three more films: *Follow the Boys* (1944), *Three Daring Daughters* (1948), and *The Sun Comes Up* (1949). In the latter, she played with Lloyd Nolan, Claude Jarman, Jr., and one of Hollywood's famous movie dogs, Lassie.

Although she gave concerts and made radio and television appearances in the early 1950s, increasingly MacDonald spent more time at home being Jeanette MacDonald Raymond, a name she used in her everyday life. One of her last public appearances was at Louis B. Mayer's 1957 funeral where she sang, "Ah, Sweet Mystery of Life." Her own health deteriorated rapidly. She collapsed during a performance in Washington, D.C., and had an emergency appendectomy. In 1963, she entered Methodist Hospital in Houston to have an arterial transplant. Two years later at the same medical facility, while being prepared for open heart surgery on January 14, 1965, Jeanette MacDonald suffered a heart attack and died. *Newsweek* called her subsequent burial at Forest Lawn in Hollywood the "Funeral of the Year." Among the honorary pallbearers were two living former presidents of the United States and two justices of the U.S. Supreme Court. Senator Barry Goldwater, General Lauris Norstad, Nelson Eddy, and several movieland stars were the actual pallbearers. Hauntingly, recordings of her singing "Ave Maria" and "Ah, Sweet Mystery of Life" were played.

During much of her career, Jeanette Mac-Donald handled her own business arrangements with skill and determination. Soft and lovely while performing, she was a shrewd bargainer when dealing with show-business executives. She brought decency and decorum to a Hollywood in need of such leavening. Few entertainers have had as great an impact on their times as she, and though she belonged to a less complex, more pristine America, her songs and movies remain forever.

SOURCES:

Boardman, Gerald. *American Musical Theater: A Chronicle.* NY: Oxford University Press, 1978.

Bodeen, DeWitt. *More From Hollywood: The Careers of 15 Great American Stars.* NY: A.S. Barnes, 1977.

Castanga, Philip. *Films of Jeanette MacDonald and Nelson Eddy.* Foreword by Eleanor Powell. Secaucus, NJ: Citadel Press, 1978.

Ewen, David. *New Complete Book of the American Musical Theater.* NY: Holt, Rinehart and Winston, 1970.

Nash, Jay Robert, and Stanley Ralph Ross. *The Motion Picture Guide.* Chicago: Cinebooks, 1986.

Newsweek. Vol. 65, February 1, 1965, pp. 22–23.

Parish, James Robert. *The Jeanette MacDonald Story.* NY: Mason/Charter, 1976.

———, and Ronald L. Bowers. *The MGM Stock Company: The Golden Era.* New Rochelle, NY: Arlington House, 1973.

Sicherman, Barbara, and Carol Hurd Green. *Notable American Women: The Modern Period: A Biographical Dictionary.* Cambridge, MA: The Belknap Press of Harvard University, 1980.

Springer, John, and Jack Hamilton. *They Had Faces Then: Super Stars, Stars, and Starlets of the 1930s.* Secaucus, NJ: Citadel Press, 1974.

SUGGESTED READING:

Goodrich, Diane. *Farewell to Dreams.* Burbank, CA: MacDonald-Eddy Friendship Club, 1986.

Jeanette MacDonald's Favorite Operatic Airs and Concert Songs. NY: G. Schirmer, 1940.

Knowles, Eleanor. *The Films of Jeanette MacDonald and Nelson Eddy.* South Brunswick, NJ: A.S. Barnes, 1975.

Rhoades, Clara. *Lookin' in and Cookin' in with the Jeanette MacDonald Raymonds at Twin Gables.* Topeka, KS: Jeanette MacDonald International Fan Club, 1984.

Rich, Sharon. *Jeanette MacDonald: A Pictorial Treasury.* Los Angeles: Times Mirror Press, 1973.

———. *Sweethearts.* 1995.

Stern, Lee Edward. *Jeanette MacDonald: An Illustrated History of the Movies.* NY: Jove, 1977.

Turk, Edward Baron. *Hollywood Diva.* CA: University of California Press, 1999.

COLLECTIONS:

The Jeanette MacDonald Collection, Department of Special Collections, University of California at Los Angeles.

Oral History Interview with Jeanette MacDonald, June 1959, Popular Arts Project, Oral History Collection, Columbia University, New York.

Robert S. La Forte,
Professor of History,
University of North Texas, Denton, Texas

Macdonald, Lucy Maud (1874–1942).

See Montgomery, Lucy Maud.

Macdonald, Marcia (1865–1947).

See Hill, Grace Livingston.

MacDonald, Margaret (1865–1933).

See Mackintosh, Margaret.

MacDonald, Margaret

(c. 1907–1956)

English philosopher. Born in England around 1907, an abandoned child; had surgery at St. Thomas Hospital in London, to treat a heart condition, but died in recovery on January 7, 1956; fellow of Girton College, Cambridge University, 1932; granted Ph.D., Bedford College, by 1938.

Lecturer at St. Hilda's College, Oxford University, from 1938; editor of the academic philosophy journal Analysis.

Selected works: Notes from Ludwig Wittgenstein's lectures and discussions, published as The Blue and Yellow (or Brown) Books; Art and Imagination *(1953).*

Margaret MacDonald was always active in academic philosophy. Her early work was in the analytic tradition that was spreading across Britain and North America at the beginning of the 20th century. She edited the journal *Analysis* for several years.

MacDonald, with *Alice Ambrose, was responsible for the early transmission of Ludwig Wittgenstein's teachings at Cambridge University. At the time, she was a fellow at Girton College, and she and Ambrose secretly took notes of Wittgenstein's lectures and discussions. He had forbidden his students to record his talks in any form, but MacDonald and Ambrose hid the notebooks under their skirts. As the skirts were blue and yellow (or brown), the records became known as "The Blue and Yellow (or Brown) Books." Eventually Wittgenstein changed his mind and was happy to have the notes distributed and eventually published.

MacDonald's later work was more concerned with aesthetics, the philosophy of art, moving away from the questions about knowledge and language which concern the analytic tradition. While still interested in language, she was more interested in how language relates to art.

Catherine Hundleby, M.A. Philosophy,
University of Guelph, Guelph, Ontario, Canada

MacDowell, Marian (1857–1956)

American founder of the MacDowell Colony for artists and writers in Peterborough, New Hampshire. Name variations: Marian Griswold Nevins MacDowell; Marian Griswold MacDowell; Mrs. Edward MacDowell. Born Marian Griswold Nevins on November 22, 1857, in New York City; died in Los Angeles, California, on August 23, 1956; daughter of David Henry Nevins (a banker and broker) and Cornelia (Perkins) Nevins; briefly attended a school in New London, Connecticut, but was largely educated by her father; married Edward Alexander MacDowell (a composer and musician), on July 9, 1884 (died 1908); no children.

Awarded several honorary degrees; Pictorial Review's $5000 Achievement Award (1923); Henry Hadley Medal for outstanding service to music (1942); National Institute of Arts and Letters grant for distinguished service to the arts (1949).

The founder and tireless champion for nearly half a century of the MacDowell Colony, America's premier artists' colony, Marian Mac-Dowell was over 50 when she began the work for which she is honored. A country retreat where painters, writers, sculptors and musicians can work within the luxury of solitude and uninterrupted days in private studio cabins, the Mac-Dowell Colony is unparalleled in this country in its fostering of artistic creation. At the dawn of the 21st century, nearly 100 years after the colony's inception, Marian MacDowell's contribution to the world continues to thrive.

Born in New York City on November 22, 1857, MacDowell was descended through her father from Scottish ancestors who had immigrated to Connecticut in the 1720s and, through her mother, from English forebears who had arrived in 1636. The family was wealthy, and when Marian was three years old her father David Henry Nevins retired from banking and moved with his wife and five children to Shaw Farm in Waterford, Connecticut. In 1866, her mother **Cornelia Perkins Nevins** died. Already a solemn child, Marian readily shouldered the additional responsibility of helping to care for her two younger sisters. During this time, she also went to a school in New London which two of her aunts founded, but her attendance there was brief and her education was largely accomplished by her father, himself a self-educated man.

Becoming interested in the piano at age ten and showing musical promise, Marian took instruction from an aunt for four years and decided to pursue a career as a pianist. In 1880, she went to Germany intending to study piano under *Clara Schumann. Instead, she met Edward Alexander MacDowell, a musician and composer, and received musical instruction from him for two and a half years. Edward MacDowell would eventually gain distinction as the first internationally known American composer. Their relationship developed beyond that of teacher and student, and they were married in New York City on July 9, 1884.

Upon her marriage, Marian MacDowell sublimated her own musical aspirations and entered her husband's orbit. The couple returned to Germany and MacDowell became her husband's housekeeper, secretary, scribe, critic, booster and, during their four years in Germany, financial supporter, for they lived on an inheritance from her mother. In 1886, Mac-Dowell suffered what is variously reported as either a stillbirth or a miscarriage. Due to complications, she was unable to bear any more children. A series of depressions and illnesses followed that would linger and recur; some biographers have speculated that the origins of these can be found in MacDowell's sorrow and "frustration."

In 1888, the MacDowells moved to Boston, where they lived for eight years. Her supporting role continued, while Edward made a living teaching piano and giving recitals. He became the first professor of music at Columbia University in New York in 1896, and for the next two years also conducted the city's Mendelssohn Glee Club. After a clash with university officials which was well reported at the time, Edward MacDowell resigned his professorship in 1904, and soon thereafter began to suffer ill health. Afflicted by syphilis, he deteriorated rapidly. A fund-raising drive was begun for his benefit by the Mendelssohn Glee Club, but he died in 1908, before it was completed. On MacDowell's recommendation, the money (some $30,000) was contributed to the Edward MacDowell Memorial Association. This had been created in 1907, to establish an artists' colony at Hillcrest, the MacDowell summer estate in Peterborough, New Hampshire, where Edward had worked. It had been his wish that the peaceful setting be opened to other artists as well, and so Marian MacDowell had deeded title to the new association, while retaining lifetime rights. Thus was created the MacDowell Colony.

Although still locked in service to her husband's memory, MacDowell became zealous about the management and promotion of the Colony, pursuing both with vigor and skill. From 1910, she traveled throughout the United States—until she was past 80—giving recitals of her husband's compositions and explaining and publicizing the Colony's mission. With solicited donations and the proceeds of her lecture and recital tours, MacDowell was able to expand the Colony from 135 acres to more than 700, incorporating a farm to assist with provisions and building a library and additional studios and dormitories (although days are spent alone, down to box lunches deposited on studio doorsteps, participants sleep in group dormitories). Those who could not scrape together even the token cost of room and board were granted "scholarships." Artists who had been given the solitude to work there found success in their fields, thereby adding luster to the Colony's name, and ran the gamut from sculptor *Helen Farnsworth Mears, who attended in 1907, to artists such as *Amy Cheney Beach, Aaron Copland, *Elinor Wylie, *Willa Cather, James Baldwin, Thornton Wilder, Edward Arlington Robinson, Virgil Thomson, and DuBose Heyward. The Colony was a significant part of the artistic milieu in the United States by the 1930s.

Marian MacDowell was forced to retire from active management at the Colony in her late 80s. Her health was poor and her eyesight nearly gone. She spent the last ten years of her life in Los Angeles, living with **Nina Maud Richardson** (1885–1969), who had been her friend and assistant for more than three decades. Marian MacDowell died at Richardson's home at the age of 98, on August 23, 1956. She was buried beside her husband's grave near the MacDowell Colony.

SOURCES:

Bailey, Brooke. *The Remarkable Lives of 100 Women Artists*. Holbrook, MA: Bob Adams, 1994.

Rubinstein, Charlotte Streifer. *American Women Artists*. Boston, MA: G.K. Hall, 1982.

Sicherman, Barbara, and Carol Hurd Green. *Notable American Women: The Modern Period*. Cambridge, MA: The Belknap Press of Harvard University Press, 1980.

COLLECTIONS:

Some of Marian MacDowell's papers are held by the Schlesinger Library at Radcliffe College. Others are held at the Library of Congress; unpublished memoirs and extensive correspondence of Marian and Edward MacDowell are in the Music Division, and files of the MacDowell Colony are in the Manuscript Division.

Ellen Dennis French,
freelance writer in biography,
Murrieta, California

Macdowell, Susan Hannah (1851–1938).

See Eakins, Susan Hannah.

Macedonia, queen of.

See Thessalonike (c. 345–297 BCE).

See Statira III (fl. 324 BCE).

See Stratonice I for sidebar on Phila II (c. 300 BCE–?).

See Arsinoe II for sidebar on Nicaea (fl. 300 BCE).

Maceo, Mariana Grajales de (1808–1893).

See Grajales, Mariana.

MacEwen, Gwendolyn (1941–1987)

Canadian writer who published poetry, novels, short stories, radio plays, and children's fiction. Born Gwendolyn Margaret MacEwen on September 1, 1941, in Toronto, Ontario, Canada; died on November 30, 1987, in Toronto; daughter of Alick James MacEwen and Elsie Doris (Mitchell) MacEwen; married poet Milton Acorn (divorced); married Nikos Tsingos (a Greek singer), in 1971 (divorced 1978).

Awards: Canada Council Arts Scholarship (1964–65); CBC Prize (1965); Arts Bursary (1966–67); Governor-General's Award for Poetry (1970); Canada Council grants (1973, 1977, 1981); A.J.M. Smith Award (1973); DuMaurier Gold and Silver Awards (1983); Governor-General's Award for Poetry (1987).

Selected writings: (poetry) Selah (Aleph, 1961); (poetry) The Drunken Clock (Aleph, 1961); (poetry) The Rising Sun (Contact Press, 1963, published as The Rising Fire, 1964); Julian the Magician: A Novel (Corinth Books, 1963); (poetry) A Breakfast for Barbarians (Ryerson, 1966); (poetry) The Shadowmaker (Macmillan, 1969); King of Egypt, King of Dreams: A Novel (Macmillan, 1971); (short stories) Noman (Oberon, 1972); (poetry) The Armies of the Moon (Macmillan, 1972); Magic Animals: Selected Poems Old and New (Macmillan, 1974, published as Magic Animals: Selected Poetry of Gwendolyn MacEwen, Stoddart Publishing, 1984); (poetry) The Fire-Eaters (Oberon, 1976);

Gwendolyn MacEwen

(travel) Mermaids and Ikons: A Greek Summer *(Anansi, 1978)*; The Trojan Women: A Play *(Playwrights' Co-op, 1979)*; *(translator, with Nikos Tsingos)* Trojan Women: "The Trojan Women" by Euripides and "Helen and Orestes" by Ritsos *(Exile Editions, 1981)*; *(juvenile fiction)* The Chocolate Moose *(illustrated by Barry Zaid, NC Press, 1981)*; *(poetry)* The T.E. Lawrence Poems *(Mosaic, 1982)*; Earthlight: Selected Poetry of Gwendolyn MacEwen, 1963–1982 *(General Publishing, 1982)*; *(translator, juvenile fiction)* The Honey Drum: Seven Tales from Arab Lands *(Mosaic, 1983)*; Noman's Land: Stories *(Coach House Press, 1985)*; *(poetry)* Afterworlds *(McClelland & Stewart, 1987)*; *(juvenile fiction)* Dragon Sandwiches *(Black Moss Press, 1987)*; The Birds: A Modern Adaptation of Aristophanes' Comedy *(Exile, 1993)*; The Poetry of Gwendolyn MacEwen *(2 vols., edited by **Margaret Atwood** and Barry Callaghan, Exile, 1993, 1994)*.

Poet and author Gwendolyn MacEwen was born on September 1, 1941, in Toronto, Canada, the daughter of Alick James MacEwen and **Elsie Mitchell MacEwen**. She published her first poem at the age of 17 in *The Canadian Forum* and left school a year later to become a writer, because, as she said, "I didn't want to spend a whole lot of time having to learn what literature was all *about*. I simply wanted to make it myself." A prolific writer, MacEwen produced volumes of poetry, novels, children's fiction, a travel documentary, radio plays, and verse dramas. She was also a frequent contributor to literary journals, and her work has been included in many anthologies.

MacEwen helped edit the journal *Moment* from 1960 to 1962 with Al Purdy and poet Milton Acorn. She was briefly married to Acorn before the publication of her first two chapbooks of poetry in 1961, *Selah* and *The Drunken Clock*. Her reputation as a poet was established with *A Breakfast for Barbarians* (1966) and further enhanced with *The Shadow-maker* (1969), which won the 1970 Governor-General's Award for Poetry.

In 1971, MacEwen married Greek singer Nikos Tsingos and entered a phase in which her output was largely informed by mythology. During this time, she published a novel about Egyptian pharaoh Akhenaton, *King of Egypt, King of Dreams* (1971), the poetry collections *The Armies of the Moon* (1972), *Magic Animals* (1975), and *The Fire-Eaters* (1976), as well as the travel documentary *Mermaids and Ikons: A Greek Summer* (1978). With Tsingos, she also translated two long poems by Greek writer Yannis Ritsos, which appeared in her *Trojan Women* in 1981. *Twentieth-Century Poetry in English* noted that "the voice she developed during this period is haunted by doubts about the border between dream and reality."

During the 1980s, MacEwen served as a writer in residence at the University of Western Ontario (1984–85) and at the University of Toronto. That decade also saw the publication of what critics regard as the most complete synthesis of her canon, *The T.E. Lawrence Poems* (1982). Told in the first person, this sequence of poems in three parts recreates Lawrence's experiences from boyhood to death. Calling this work an "extraordinary feat of empathy," George Woodcock noted in *The Oxford Companion to Canadian Literature* that "the voice seems to be Lawrence's own."

In a statement included in *Contemporary Poets* (1985), MacEwen noted, "I write to communicate joy, mystery, passion . . . not the joy that naively exists without knowledge of pain, but that joy which arises out of and conquers pain. I want to construct a myth." Her poetry has been praised for its combination of surrealism and realistic imagery vividly rendered, and for a fluid, playful use of language. One critic called her poems "a balancing act between convictions and questions."

MacEwen's last work was a collection of poetry entitled *Afterworlds*, published in 1987. *Twentieth-Century Poetry in English* called this "a hauntingly poignant book" and suggested that several of the poems anticipated her death in November of that year. The work was posthumously awarded the 1987 Governor-General's Award for Poetry.

SOURCES:

Bartley, Jan. "Dedication: Gwendolyn MacEwen (1941–1987)," in *Canadian Woman Studies*. Summer 1988.

Blain, Virginia, Patricia Clements, and Isobel Grundy. *The Feminist Companion to Literature in English*. New Haven, CT: Yale University Press, 1990.

The Bloomsbury Guide to Women's Literature. Edited by Claire Buck. NY: Prentice Hall General Reference, 1992.

Contemporary Poets. 4th ed. Edited by James Vinson and D.L. Kirkpatrick. NY: St. Martin's Press, 1985.

Creative Canada: A Biographical Dictionary of Twentieth-Century Creative and Performing Artists, Vol. 1. Compiled by Reference Division, McPherson Library, University of Victoria, British Columbia. Toronto: University of Toronto Press, 1971.

Grace, Sherrill E. "Gwendolyn MacEwen," in *Dictionary of Literary Biography*, Vol. 53: *Canadian Writers Since 1960.* Detroit, MI: Gale Research, 1986.

The Oxford Companion to Canadian Literature. Edited by William Toye. Toronto: Oxford University Press, 1983.

The Oxford Companion to Twentieth-Century Poetry in English. Edited by Ian Hamilton. Oxford, England: Oxford University Press, 1994.

Ellen Dennis French,
freelance writer, Murrieta, California

MacFall, Frances E. (1854–1943)

British novelist. Name variations: Frances Elizabeth MacFall, McFall, or M'Fall; Frances Bellenden-Clarke; Frances Elizabeth Clarke; (pseudonym) Sarah Grand. Born Frances Elizabeth Bellenden-Clarke in Donaghadee, County Down, Northern Ireland, in 1854; died in Bath, Calne, Wiltshire, on May 12, 1943; fourth of five children of Edward John Bellenden-Clarke (a lieutenant in the Royal Navy) and Margaret Bell (Sherwood) Bellenden-Clarke; attended boarding school in England; married David MacFall (an army surgeon), in 1870 (separated); children: one son.

Principal works: Ideals (1888); A Domestic Experiment (1891); The Heavenly Twins (1893); The Beth Book (1898); Adnam's Orchard (1912); The Winged Victory (1916); Variety (1922).

Novelist Frances MacFall was born in Donaghadee, County Down, Northern Ireland, in 1854, the daughter of Edward Bellenden-Clarke, a lieutenant in the Royal Navy, and **Margaret Sherwood Bellenden-Clarke**. MacFall spent her formative years in Northern Ireland, then went to live with her mother's family in England after her father's death in 1861. Suffering an unhappy adolescence in two repressive boarding schools, she eloped at the age of 16 with an army surgeon 23 years her senior, who was also a widower with two children. For five years, the couple traveled to Hong Kong and the Far East and then returned to England. It was an unhappy union that produced one son, but eventually ended in separation. In 1888, MacFall completed her first novel *Ideals,* selecting a pseudonym, Sarah Grand, that reflected both her feminist pride and her liberated persona. With the profits from *Ideals,* MacFall permanently separated from her husband and took her son with her to London.

It was with her two feminist novels, *The Heavenly Twins* (1893) and *The Beth Book* (1898), that she established her reputation. The former, a rambling 700 pages, tells the life stories of three women, through which MacFall addresses a myriad of feminist issues, including the double standard and a woman's right to independence. The book was reprinted six times in the first year and went through 13 editions and several foreign translations before going out of print in 1923. *The Beth Book* (1898), a quasi-autobiographical novel, dealt with the frustration encountered by an intelligent woman seeking emancipation.

MacFall became extremely active in the suffrage campaign, joining the Women Writers' Suffrage League. After the death of her husband in 1898, she lived in Tunbridge Wells, where she became president of the local branch of the National Union of Women's Suffrage Societies. Her later works, including *Adnam's Orchard* (1912), *The Winged Victory* (1916), and *Variety* (1922), a collection of short stories, were said to be of little consequence. In 1920, she moved to Bath, where she was elected mayor for six separate terms. She died there at age 88. Her major work, *The Heavenly Twins,* reappeared in a 1993 edition, published by the University of Michigan Press.

SOURCES:

Postlethwaite, Diana. "Victims of Victorianism," in *The Women's Review of Books.* Vol. X, no. 10–11. July 1993.

Shattock, Joanne. *The Oxford Guide to British Women Writers.* Oxford: Oxford University Press, 1993.

Uglow, Jennifer, ed and comp. *The International Dictionary of Women's Biography.* NY: Continuum, 1989.

Barbara Morgan,
Melrose, Massachusetts

MacGill, Elsie (d. 1980)

Canadian aeronautical engineer and feminist. Name variations: Elizabeth MacGill; E.G. MacGill; (incorrectly) McGill. Born Elizabeth Gregory MacGill; died in 1980; daughter of Helen Gregory MacGill (1871–1947) and James H. MacGill; married in 1943 but continued to use her maiden name.

Awards: Gzowski Medal of the Engineering Institute of Canada (1941); Award for Meritorious Contribution to Engineering from the Society of Women Engineers (U.S. organization, 1953); awarded the Order of Canada (1971).

Elsie MacGill, the daughter of *Helen Gregory MacGill and James H. MacGill, became the first woman to graduate in electrical engineering from the University of Toronto (1927). She was also the first woman to graduate from the University of Michigan's master's program in aeronautical engineering (1929). In 1934, MacGill was hired by Fairchild Aircraft Limited in Montreal; she then worked as chief aeronautical engineer for the Canadian Car and Foundry Company, where she designed the Maple Leaf Trainer, possibly the first airplane designed by a woman. During World War II, Elsie MacGill was the engineer in charge of Canadian production of the Hawker Hurricane fighter plane at Fort

William, Ontario, with a staff of 4,500. Following the war, she started her own business as a consulting aeronautical engineer in Toronto, was a prominent member of the Toronto Business and Professional Women's Club, and campaigned on issues involving paid maternity leave, day care facilities, and liberalization of abortion laws. Elsie MacGill published a biography of her mother, *My Mother the Judge*, in 1955. She died in 1980.

COLLECTIONS:
Personal papers, dating from 1911, held in the Public Archives of Canada under #MG 31, K7.

MacGill, Helen Gregory
(1871–1947)

Canadian feminist, lawyer and first woman judge in British Columbia. Name variations: (incorrect) Helen McGill; Helen Gregory-Flesher. Born Helen Gregory into a socially prominent family in Hamilton, Ontario, Canada, in 1871; died in 1947; Trinity College, Toronto, B.A., 1888; married Dr. Lee Flesher (died 1901); married James H. MacGill, in 1902; children: (first marriage) two sons; (second marriage) one daughter, Elizabeth "Elsie" Gregory MacGill (d. 1980).

Helen Gregory MacGill

The daughter of an early suffragist, Helen MacGill was born in the industrial town of Hamilton in Ontario, Canada, in 1871. An outstanding student, she attended Trinity College in Toronto and was the only woman to graduate in the school's class of 1888. She then began working as a journalist, and traveled to Japan to write about social conditions in that country and cover the opening of the Japanese Diet. She would later also write an extensive series of articles about immigrant settlers in Manitoba for the Toronto *Globe*.

After returning to Canada, she married Lee Flesher, and with her mother the couple moved to California. While Flesher attended medical school, MacGill and her mother ran two newspapers, *The Searchlight* and *Society*. With Flesher and their two sons, MacGill then moved to Minnesota and became the editor of a daily newspaper in St. Paul. She remained in Minnesota after her husband died in 1901, and campaigned for women's rights and penal reform. In 1902, she married James H. MacGill, with whom she had a daughter *Elsie MacGill who would one day become the first qualified female aeronautical engineer in Canadian history. Soon after their marriage, the couple moved to Vancouver, British Columbia, where Helen established a legal practice and founded the Vancouver Women's Press Club and the University Women's Club.

The first woman judge in British Columbia, MacGill served on the British Columbia juvenile court from 1917 to 1929 and again from 1934 to 1945. She also served on the national level as a member of the Minimum Wage Board in 1918, and as chair of the Mother's Pension Board from 1920 to 1921. She helped found the Vancouver Women's Building, and remained active in welfare reform and women's rights issues throughout her life. Helen Gregory MacGill died in 1947, two years after she had retired from the bench.

SUGGESTED READING:
MacGill, E.G. *My Mother the Judge*. Reyerson, 1955.

> **Grant Eldridge**,
> freelance writer, Pontiac, Michigan

Macinghi, Alessandra (1406–1469).
See Strozzi, Alessandra.

MacInnes, Helen (1907–1985)
Scottish author known as the "Master Teller of Spy Stories." Name variations: Helen Clark; Helen Clark MacInnes; Helen Highet. Born Helen Clark MacInnes on October 7, 1907, in Glasgow, Scotland; died on September 30, 1985, in New York City; daughter of

Donald MacInnes and Jessica (McDiarmid) MacInnes; Glasgow University, M.A., 1928; diploma in librarianship, University College, London, 1931; married Gilbert Highet (a classical scholar), in 1932 (died 1978); children: one son.

Immigrated to United States (1937); wrote first novel (1941); became U.S. citizen (1951); published last book (1984).

Selected writings: Above Suspicion *(1941);* Assignment in Brittany *(1942);* While Still We Live *(published as* The Unconquerable *in UK, 1944);* Horizon *(1945);* Friends and Lovers *(1947);* Rest and Be Thankful *(1949);* I and My True Love *(1953);* Pray for a Brave Heart *(1955);* North from Rome *(1958);* Decision at Delphi *(1961);* The Venetian Affair *(1963);* The Double Image *(1966);* The Salzburg Connection *(1968);* Message from Màlaga *(1972);* The Snare of the Hunter *(1974);* Agent in Place *(1976); (play)* Home Is the Hunter *(1976);* Prelude to Terror *(1978);* The Hidden Target *(1980);* Cloak of Darkness *(1982);* Ride a Pale Horse *(1984).*

Helen MacInnes was the author of 21 spy novels that detail a world of international adventure not dissimilar to her own globe-trotting exploits. Her works of fiction are known for a wealth of site detail woven into intrigue-laden plots, and she did much of the research and legwork for the books herself.

MacInnes was born in Glasgow, Scotland, in 1907, and later attended that city's university until receiving her M.A. in 1928. For a time she worked as a cataloguer at a Glasgow University library, then went to London to earn a diploma in librarianship from University College. In 1932, she married Gilbert Highet, a scholar, and they honeymooned in Bavaria. Over the next few years, MacInnes worked with her husband on translations, which allowed them to save enough money to spend summers traveling across Europe. She received joint translator credit for two works from the original German: *Sexual Life in Ancient Rome,* by Otto Kiefer, and a biography of Friedrich Engels. With Highet, she lived in Oxford, and became active in the university town's Experimental Theater; she was also an avid tennis player and loved to attend the theater and concerts. They settled in New York City in 1937, when Highet took a post at Columbia University, but with the onset of World War II he was requested to join England's famed military intelligence service, as were many other scholars.

This request and the devastating events taking place in Europe led to the genesis of MacInnes' first novel. Keen on current events, she kept a journal chronicling world affairs from newspaper stories, and was often able to predict political outcomes correctly. Furthermore, she had kept a journal during her Bavarian honeymoon in 1932, while Adolf Hitler and the National Socialist Party had been rising to power (particularly in southern Germany); this journal provided the basis for a novel about the situation. An immediate bestseller upon its publication in 1941, *Above Suspicion* chronicles the adventures of a pleasant, scholarly couple from Oxford, England, who spend summers mountaineering. Wishing to visit Europe one more time, as war seems imminent, they are deemed "above suspicion" by the German government and are granted permission for another Alpine vacation in 1937. In actuality, however, they have been sent by their government to ferret out a secret agent working for Britain. In the course of the novel, the couple meet up with old friends from past visits who are sympathetic to the Nazi government, and meet new ones who are not. The book was made into a 1943 movie of the same title starring *Joan Crawford and Fred MacMurray.

Above Suspicion launched MacInnes' career as an espionage writer. Like many of her subse-

Helen MacInnes

quent works, the novel features villainous fascists or communists and an abundance of European intrigue. Though she became an American citizen in 1951, MacInnes traveled frequently to Europe with her husband after World War II, and her familiarity with both its cities and more rustic areas allowed for a surfeit of detail that delighted armchair-bound readers. Local customs and culture, cuisine and wines, and even street names were all faithful; in some cases MacInnes had her characters pass through actual restaurants or shops. Highet, with the benefit of his military intelligence work, helped to provide realistic procedures and dialogue for her professional spies. Her 1942 novel *Assignment in Brittany* was used by the Allies when training agents to assist the French Resistance because of its accuracy in showing the extreme difficulty of undercover work. After the 1944 publication of *While Still We Live,* Department of War officials in Washington, D.C., called MacInnes in for questioning, wishing to know how she came by so much abundant detail on the activities of the Polish resistance movement during the Nazi occupation.

In 1945's *Horizon,* MacInnes utilized her knowledge of mountain climbing to add excitement to the narrative, and *Rest and Be Thankful,* published in 1949, is set in Wyoming, where she had once spent time on a ranch. *I and My True Love* reflects the height of Cold War fears in 1953, and 1960's *Decision at Delphi* (for which she located and interviewed veterans for battle specifics) revisits World War II events in Italy and Greece. For *The Venetian Affair* (1963), MacInnes made certain that her characters' flights through Venice's maze of streets, some of them one-way, were accurate to the last. Some of her later works used the division of Europe into fenced-off communist and Western spheres in plots of political double-cross. MacInnes' protagonists were usually innocents drawn into the world of espionage who, during the course of the novel, came of age politically after being forced to act upon their personal beliefs and patriotic ideals. In many cases the protagonist was a young woman traveling abroad, and a romance with her American or British spy contact served as subplot. Said to have been influenced by the writings of George Orwell and *Rebecca West, MacInnes displayed throughout her career distrust for and horror of totalitarianism and all its trappings. She sometimes suffered criticism for the heavy hand with which she drew her Nazi or Soviet villains; in her books, democracy always emerges the rightful victor. Nonetheless, she earned the sobriquet of "Master Teller of Spy Stories," and her novels, which

sold over 23 million copies in America, have appeared in 22 languages.

MacInnes and Highet, who had one son together, lived the rest of their lives divided between New York City, Long Island's East Hampton, and their travels abroad. Gilbert Highet died in 1978. *Ride a Pale Horse,* published in 1984, was Helen MacInnes' last book, and she died after a stroke in New York City on September 30, 1985.

SOURCES:

Contemporary Authors. Vol. 117. Detroit, MI: Gale Research, 1986.

Macdonald, Gina. *Dictionary of Literary Biography,* Vol. 87: *British Mystery and Thriller Writers Since 1940.* Detroit, MI: Gale Research, 1989, pp. 284–294.

McHenry, Robert, ed. *Famous American Women.* NY: Dover, 1980.

Mote, Dave, ed. *Contemporary Popular Writers.* Detroit, MI: St. James Press, 1997.

Reilly, John M., ed. *Twentieth-Century Crime and Mystery Writers.* NY: St. Martin's Press, 1985.

COLLECTIONS:

Helen MacInnes' manuscripts are held at the Princeton University Library, Princeton, New Jersey.

Carol Brennan,
Grosse Pointe, Michigan

MacIver, Loren (1909–1998)

American artist. Born Loren Newman on February 2, 1909, in New York City; died on May 3, 1998, in New York City; daughter of Charles Augustus Paul Newman and Julia MacIver Newman; married Lloyd Frankenberg (a poet), in 1929 (died 1975).

A 20th-century artist acclaimed for her half-abstract landscapes, city views, and close-ups of inanimate objects, all rendered with a luminous use of color, Loren MacIver was born in New York City in 1909. Self-taught except for a single year of Saturday classes at the Art Students League in Manhattan when she was ten, MacIver (who as a young woman began using the maiden name her mother had retained after her marriage) painted throughout her youth but felt no special ambition to turn what she considered a hobby into a career. Others, however, recognized her considerable talent—particularly her husband, Lloyd Frankenberg, a poet whom she married in 1929. Their relationship was mutually stimulating, as her paintings often inspired his poetry and displayed many of the ideals he put into words. He began her professional career without her knowledge in 1935, when he showed *The Shack* to Alfred H. Barr, the director of the Museum of Modern Art (MoMA), who purchased it for the museum. (Barr also purchased another of her paintings for his private collection.)

From 1936 to 1939, MacIver achieved her first measure of fame while working on the New York Federal Arts Project. She had her first solo show in 1938, at **Marian Willard**'s East River Gallery; the catalogue contained an introduction by Alfred Steiglitz. A second show was held in 1940, at the Pierre Matisse Gallery, which would continue to represent her until it closed 50 years later.

MacIver has been called "one of the few genuinely independent artists" of the 1940s and early 1950s. Her themes were, for the most part, decidedly urban during this period. Among her best-known pieces were *Hopscotch* (1940), *Oil Slick* (1940), *The Violet Hour* (1943), *Pushcart* (1944), and *Taxi* (1951), although she also undertook such non-urban topics as *Tree* and *Puddle* (both 1945). A portrait series of clowns, including one of Jimmy Savo in 1944 and another of Emmett Kelly in 1947, is an example of her infrequent use of human subjects. The work created in those productive years afforded the means for MacIver and her husband to travel to England, France, Ireland, Scotland, and Italy in 1948. These locations provided new vistas for her talent, resulting in larger and more vivid paintings. *Cathedral* (1949), *Dublin and Environs* (1950), and *Venice* (1949)—the latter considered by some to be one of her best—were products of her trip to Europe.

MacIver counted among her friends such American poets as *Elizabeth Bishop, *Marianne Moore, and e.e. cummings, and with her husband spent many summers in Cape Cod, Massachusetts, local details of which were occasionally the subjects of her paintings. By 1960, she was experimenting with texture, using cloth, paper, and pastels. She continued to paint, expanding on her poetic, introspective style, most obviously in *Night Shadows* (1961). During the 1960s, MacIver and Frankenberg returned several times to Europe and also visited Istanbul, which was the inspiration for her 1965 paintings *Byzantium* and *Blue Mosque*. In 1966, she moved to Paris, a location she always favored, and was given a retrospective at the Musée d'Art Moderne de la Ville de Paris in 1968. She returned to the United States in 1970. Among the works inspired by her time in France were *Le Marché à Toulon*, *Patisserie*, and *First Snow*.

MacIver received numerous awards and grants for her work, including a Ford Foundation grant in 1960, a Mark Rothko Foundation grant in 1972, a Guggenheim Foundation fellowship in 1976, and a grant from the Pollock-Krasner Foundation in 1992. She was awarded first prize from the Corcoran Gallery of Art in 1957 and from the Art Institute of Chicago in 1961, exhibited at the Venice Biennale in 1962, and received a purchase prize from the Krannert Art Museum at the University of Illinois-Urbana in 1963. In addition to these prestigious accomplishments, MacIver was one of the few women at the time to be elected to the American Academy and Institute of Arts and Letters in New York City. She had several retrospectives across the country, including ones at the Whitney Museum of Art, the Phillips Collection in Washington, the Montclair Museum of Art in New Jersey, Newport Harbor Museum in Orange County, California, and the Addison Gallery of American Art in Andover, Massachusetts. Highly regarded in Europe as well, MacIver also had exhibitions at the Toulouse Museum of Fine Arts, the Musée des Beaux Arts in Lyons, and the Musée Ponchettes in Nice. Among the many museums which hold her work in permanent collections are the Metropolitan Museum of Art, the Whitney Museum of Art, the Museum of Modern Art, the Bibliothèque Nationale, the Detroit Institute of Art, the Corcoran Gallery of Art in Washington, D.C., the Brooklyn Museum, and the Los Angeles County Museum of Art in California.

Although she rarely spoke or wrote publicly about her art, a statement included in the catalog to a 1946 group exhibition may serve to illustrate how successful the artist was in achieving her aims. "My wish is to make something permanent out of the transitory," she wrote. Loren MacIver died at her home in Greenwich Village on May 3, 1998.

SOURCES:

Candee, Marjorie Dent, ed. *Current Biography*. NY: H.W. Wilson, 1953.
The New York Times. May 24, 1998, p. 36.

RELATED MEDIA:

Loren MacIver, film by **Maryette Charlton** (late 1960s).

Judith C. Reveal,
freelance writer, Greensboro, Maryland

Mack, Ruth (1897–1946).

See Gardiner, Muriel for sidebar on Ruth Mack Brunswick.

Mackay, Mary (1855–1924).

See Corelli, Marie.

MacKillop, Mary Helen (1842–1909)

Australian religious leader and founder of the Sisters of St. Joseph of the Sacred Heart. Name variations:

*Mother Mary of the Cross; Mary Helen McKillop.
Born Mary Helen MacKillop on January 15, 1842, in
Melbourne, Australia; died on August 8, 1909, in Sydney, Australia; daughter of Alexander MacKillop and
Flora (MacDonald) MacKillop; educated in Melbourne public schools.*

Born on January 15, 1842, in the Fitzroy
neighborhood of Melbourne, Australia, Mary
MacKillop was the eldest of eight children of
Alexander and **Flora MacKillop**, both of whom
had immigrated from Scotland. Looking back
on her early years, MacKillop wrote: "My life as
a child was one of sorrow, my home when I had
it a most unhappy one." Much of this unhappiness was probably linked to a lack of financial
security. For most of MacKillop's young life, her
family was forced to depend on relatives for
food and shelter; by some accounts, her father
had caused their impoverishment through his
charity to others. When she was 16, Mary became the principal provider for her large family,
working first as a governess, then as an assistant
at a stationery store, and later as a schoolteacher
in Portland, Victoria.

Alexander MacKillop was the principal
source of his daughter's education, particularly
in matters of the Roman Catholic church. Before
marriage, he had studied for the priesthood in
Rome, and he provided his daughter with a solid
foundation of knowledge about Catholicism,
which was not based on fear of the fierce God of
the Old Testament but was instead an embodiment of the love for all people felt by Jesus
Christ. In her teens, MacKillop began to feel
drawn to a religious life, although her family
commitments initially kept her from acting on
these feelings. In 1861, she met Father Julian
Tenison Woods of Penola, South Australia, who
encouraged her to seek a religious vocation. Five
years later, in 1866, she finally was able to accept his invitation to teach in the priest's school
in Penola. Woods had been directed by his bishop to provide a Catholic education for the children of his district, which covered more than
25,000 square kilometers (approximately
15,500 square miles). Father Woods believed
that such an education would be most effective if
the teachers were dedicated nuns willing to live
under the same conditions as the families of the
children they taught, and so he wanted to establish a new religious order, to be called the Sisters
of St. Joseph of the Sacred Heart. On March 19,
1866, MacKillop became the first sister of this
order of nuns, which was the first such established on Australian soil by Australians. The

school was called the Institute of the Sisters of
St. Joseph of the Sacred Heart. Before long,
other young women who felt called to a religious
vocation joined MacKillop in the school and in
the Sisters of St. Joseph (later affectionately
known as the "Little Joeys"). Their school was
open to all children in the district, and parents
who were financially unable to enroll their children received assistance.

The religious community of the Sisters of St.
Joseph was organized along egalitarian lines, and
the sisters (many of whom, like MacKillop, had
not been born into privilege) lived among the
people of the district in tents, shanties, and low-rent accommodations. All of this was a sharp departure from the accepted practice in orders that
had been imported from Europe, most of which
were made up of women sufficiently well-born to
afford a dowry to bring to the convent where
henceforth they would live, to a greater or lesser
degree, secluded from the world. The local bishop formally approved the new school and appointed Woods director of Catholic education,
transferring him to Adelaide. A short time later,
Father Woods called MacKillop to the city, and
in July 1867, the school was officially relocated
to Adelaide. In its new location in the capital city
of South Australia, enrollment at the Institute increased dramatically, and the Sisters of St. Joseph
soon extended their reach beyond the Institute to
other schools and charitable institutions. Some
conflicts arose between the sisters (and therefore
MacKillop) and Father Woods, who had little experience in working with nuns and apparently
tended to be overly demanding of inexperienced
members of the order.

Conflicts also arose between Father Woods
and other clergy who disapproved of the unorthodox manner in which the Institute was run, and
these eventually spread to MacKillop and her fellow nuns. A number of local priests called upon
the bishop to either impose strict rules on the operations of the Institute or to dissolve it. MacKillop stoutly resisted these calls for conformity and
encouraged her fellow nuns to do as their consciences dictated. Citing her insubordination, the
local bishop excommunicated MacKillop on September 21, 1871, and dismissed nearly half of the
127 nuns who taught at the Institute. Despite this
setback, MacKillop remained loyal to the Catholic
Church, and less than six months later the bishop
relented, revoking her excommunication and reinstating her as mother superior of the order. Soon
the Institute was flourishing again.

In 1873, with money she had begged,
MacKillop made a pilgrimage to the Vatican to

seek approval for the Institute. While approving the Institute in principle, Vatican officials decided that the school's rules needed to be rewritten; the centralized authority structure of the Institute was retained, but major changes were made regarding the order's observance of poverty. The end result of MacKillop's Vatican trip was a rift between her and Father Woods, who was angered that she had failed to resist these changes more vigorously.

MacKillop was elected superior general in 1875, under the new Vatican-imposed regulations. She traveled widely throughout Australia and New Zealand, setting up schools and charitable institutions. Through the years, she frequently came into conflict with bishops who disliked the lack of local power that resulted from the Institute's central government structure. Although intensely uncomfortable being at odds with bishops, she consistently resisted their calls for change, and this resistance led in 1883 to a temporary banishment from Adelaide and the loss of her position as superior general for several years.

Despite this, in July 1888, the Vatican, which had been closely observing the conduct of MacKillop and the other Sisters of St. Joseph, signaled its approval of their behavior with a formal ratification of the Institute. It ordered the Institute's Mother House relocated to Sydney. At the new Sydney headquarters, MacKillop established a center for the training of teachers, enabling the order to make further strides in Catholic education. Although her health was beginning to falter, MacKillop was reelected superior general in 1899, and she continued to work to advance both her order and the cause of Catholic education throughout the region until her death at the age of 67 in Sydney on August 8, 1909.

Mary MacKillop's leadership and advocacy of education made a significant contribution to changing the status quo in Australia and beyond, despite the fact that women were, and still are, routinely denied power both by the Roman Catholic Church and society as a whole. She devoted much of her life to those who had been discarded by most of society, including rural and urban poor children, street people, prostitutes, ex-convicts, and unmarried mothers. In her own words, MacKillop felt that all people, regardless of their background or the lives they led, deserved to be "given a go." The case for her beatification was presented in 1925 and formally introduced by the Vatican 50 years later. While visiting Sydney in 1995, Pope John Paul II declared her "Blessed," an important milepost on the road to the formal acknowledgement of Mary MacKillop as Australia's first saint.

SOURCES:
Radi, Heather, ed. *200 Australian Women: A Redress Anthology*. NSW, Australia: Women's Redress Press, 1988.

Don Amerman,
freelance writer, Saylorsburg, Pennsylvania

Mackin, Catherine (1939–1982)

American journalist who was the first woman to serve as a network television floor reporter at the national political conventions. Name variations: Cassie Mackin. Born Catherine Patricia Mackin in Baltimore, Maryland, on August 28, 1939; died in Towson, Maryland, on November 20, 1982; daughter of Francis Michael Mackin and Catherine Gillooly Mackin; attended public schools in Towson, Maryland; University of Maryland, B.A., 1960; selected as a Nieman fellow in 1967 and enrolled in Harvard University's "Great Lectures" program.

Born on August 28, 1939, in Baltimore, Maryland, Catherine Mackin, known as Cassie,

Catherine Mackin

was the third daughter of Francis Mackin and **Catherine Gillooly Mackin.** She was raised in suburban Towson, the town, she later observed, that "gave the world Spiro Agnew." Mackin graduated magna cum laude from the nearby University of Maryland in 1960 with a degree in journalism and moved quickly into a job at the Washington bureau of the Hearst family newspapers. Although she was interested in television work and had many opportunities to move into broadcasting, she felt that newspaper work was more rewarding.

Selected in 1967 as a Nieman fellow, Mackin enrolled in the "Great Lectures" program at Harvard University during the 1967–68 academic year. Her course of study at Harvard included lectures by a German-born professor named Henry Kissinger, who was at that time little known outside of Cambridge. After her studies at Harvard, Mackin returned briefly to Hearst's Washington bureau as an urban affairs correspondent. In 1969, she switched to television journalism by joining the staff of Washington's NBC affiliate, WRC-TV, where she spent two years as an investigative reporter and the anchorwoman of a local news broadcast. From 1971 to 1973, while remaining based in Washington, she took on the responsibilities of a general assignment reporter for the network.

Mackin won national recognition in 1972 when she became the first female television floor reporter at the national political conventions. She had moved up the ladder within NBC's news organization at a break-neck pace, a turn of events that she later attributed mostly to luck, although she said she thought her newspaper training had helped her make the most of that luck. Mackin attributed her quick metamorphosis from local newscaster to a floor reporter at the national conventions to the solid training she had received in reporting during her newspaper days. "I could honestly say that I had prepared for [the conventions] all my life," she explained. "It began at the supper table, where my family would talk about politics."

In 1973, Mackin was named a congressional correspondent for NBC, concentrating on the Senate. Although she faithfully reported their deliberations on a daily basis, Mackin never took senators or members of congress too seriously, and noted that the Capitol was "the only place where you'll never hear anyone say, 'I said that first.'" The years she spent in the political trenches were turbulent ones, beginning with the assassination of President John F. Kennedy and continuing on to the Watergate scandal and the subsequent resignation of another president, Richard Nixon. Throughout her career, Mackin, a member of the Women's National Press Club and the White House Correspondents Association, maintained a bipartisan outlook on the stories she covered. She was a master of professional detachment, able to handle emotional stories and tough deadlines with equal cool-headedness. Asked to single out what she considered her best stories, she responded: "I always hope my best stories are ahead of me."

While working in Washington, Mackin for several years made her home in a ninth-floor apartment at Watergate West, part of the apartment/office complex that figured prominently in the undoing of the Nixon presidency. Living at the Watergate was akin to living in a fishbowl since tourists visiting the nation's capital flocked to the complex to snap photos of its scandal-tinged nameplate. Mackin continued to work for NBC as a congressional correspondent until 1977, when she was hired by ABC as a Washington correspondent. Five years later, Catherine Mackin died of cancer at the age of 43 in Towson, Maryland.

SOURCES:
Buursma, Bruce. "Catherine Mackin: Reporting from Capitol Hill," in *Grand Rapids Press* (Grand Rapids, Michigan). January 19, 1975.
Newsweek. October 16, 1972, November 29, 1982.
Time. March 21, 1977, November 29, 1982.

Don Amerman,
freelance writer, Saylorsburg, Pennsylvania

Mackintosh, Elizabeth (1896–1952).

See Tey, Josephine.

Mackintosh, Margaret (1865–1933)

English-born artist. Name variations: Margaret MacDonald. Born Margaret MacDonald in Staffordshire, England, in 1865; died in 1933; sister of Frances MacDonald (1874–1921); studied at the Glasgow College of Art; married Charles Rennie Mackintosh (1868–1928, a Scottish architect, designer and watercolorist), in 1900.

Known for her watercolors, stained glass, and book illustration, Margaret Mackintosh worked closely with her sister *Frances MacDonald* from 1894 until Margaret's marriage to Charles Rennie Mackintosh in 1900. From then on, Margaret collaborated with her husband, an influential architect, designer, watercolorist, and exponent of Art Nouveau, on much of his work, especially in textile design. Margaret Mackintosh exhibited widely on the Continent and won the Diploma of Honor at the Turin International Exhibition in 1902. Following the Mackintoshes' move to London from Glasgow, Margaret's work as a painter supported them, as Charles' career tapered off in his later years.

Macklin, Madge (1893–1962)

American geneticist. Name variations: Madge Thurlow Macklin. Born Madge Thurlow on February 6, 1893, in Philadelphia, Pennsylvania; died on March 14, 1962, in Ontario, Canada; daughter of William Thurlow (an engineer) and Margaret (De Grofft) Thurlow; graduated from Goucher College, A.B., 1914; graduated from Johns Hopkins, M.D., 1919; married Charles Macklin (a physician), in 1918 (died 1959); children: Carol Macklin (b. 1919); Sylva Macklin (b. 1921); Margaret Macklin (b. 1927).

Selected writings: The Role of Inheritance in Disease (Baltimore: Williams & Wilkins, 1935).

Born Madge Thurlow in Philadelphia on February 6, 1893, Madge Macklin displayed a precise and logical mind early in life, studying calculus at the age of 12. Her understanding of mathematics would serve her well in her future endeavors in the field of genetics, where her methodical, meticulous approach to research uncovered the importance of the field in the study and treatment of disease.

When she was a child, Macklin and her family moved to Baltimore where she was educated in the public school system. Although her family later moved back to Philadelphia, she remained behind with a teacher to complete her high school education and later attended Goucher College. She graduated with an A.B. from Goucher in 1914 and went on to attend Johns Hopkins medical school on a fellowship, studying physiology. In 1918, Macklin entered the medical program and married Dr. Charles C. Macklin, an associate professor of anatomy, with whom she would have three daughters. She received her M.D. with honors from Johns Hopkins in 1919. Within two years, Macklin's husband received an appointment in histology and embryology at Western Ontario University and the family moved to London, Ontario, Canada.

Macklin's time at Western Ontario was pivotal to her professional growth, for it was there that she began her research in genetics. At a time when most universities discouraged husbands and wives from working together, Macklin assisted her husband with his histology classes. She

did not, however, secure anything more than a series of part-time positions for herself, and was not allowed to teach anything on her own except embryology to first-year students. Despite a career at the university that would span 23 years, she never received tenure and was consistently paid far less than her male colleagues (during the years of the Depression, she was paid nothing).

Although her hands were tied in the classroom, Macklin was a powerhouse in the laboratory. Through her research, which analyzed statistics culled from family histories and scientific studies, she demonstrated the value of genetics in diagnosis, therapy, prognosis, and prevention of disease. Using rigorously controlled data, she provided convincing evidence that both hereditary and environmental factors contribute to various kinds of cancer in human beings, such as stomach cancer and breast cancer. This evidence was a correlation of the data provided by *Maud Slye through her animal studies. As a result of her methodical research, Macklin became a staunch advocate of genetics studies at a time when only one medical school in either Canada or the United States had a compulsory course in genetics. While genetics was still in its infancy, she recognized the vital role this area of study would eventually play in the diagnosis and treatment of disease, and for years campaigned vigorously for the mandatory inclusion of genetics courses in medical schools. In large part due to her research and advocacy, over half the medical schools in America had such courses by 1953.

Macklin's intense belief in the importance of genetics was not without controversy. She became a vocal supporter of the eugenics movement, seeing it as a form of preventive medicine. Developed in the late 19th century, eugenics was intended to improve human intelligence and behavior through controlled breeding for "superior" characteristics, and was widely and seriously discussed throughout the early years of the 20th century. Macklin was a founder of the Canadian Eugenics Society in 1930 and continued her support of the movement for some years, although by that time its theories had fallen out of favor among many scientists. She suggested that doctors should be the ones to, in her own words, "determine who are physically and mentally qualified to be parents of the next generation." She further believed that people with certain mental deficiencies should be sterilized; among the more than 20 papers she published on eugenics was one titled "Genetical Aspects of Sterilization of the Mentally Unfit." It should be noted, however, that she was not alone in her views on this subject; even after the revelations of Nazi eugenic policies, some states in the U.S. had discreet sterilization programs up until the 1970s (*See Buck, Carrie*).

Whether because of her outspoken views, clashes with colleagues, or simple sexism, Macklin was never promoted beyond assistant professor at Western Ontario. Throughout her years there, she had been offered only yearly positions, despite the fact that she was a popular teacher. When the university did not renew her appointment in 1945, the National Research Council quickly offered her a position as an associate in cancer research at Ohio State University in Columbus. She accepted and was granted appointments in the zoology department and the medical school, lecturing in genetics and working with Dr. Lawrence Snyder, who also taught a course in human genetics. After over 20 years of accomplishment in the field, this was her first opportunity to teach genetics.

Macklin was recognized as a brilliant researcher and a superb teacher, with over 200 papers to her credit by 1961. Strong-willed and aggressive, especially with regard to her views on her subject, she made important contributions to the fledgling science of genetics. She received recognition throughout her life, including an honorary LL.D from Goucher College in 1938, the *Elizabeth Blackwell Medal of the American Medical Women's Association in 1957, and, in 1959, election to the presidency of the American Society for Human Genetics, which she retained for the rest of her life. Madge Macklin retired from Ohio State University that year and returned to Canada to look after her husband, who was ill. After his death later that year, she moved to Toronto to be close to her three daughters and their families. In 1962, Macklin suffered a coronary thrombosis and died at the age of 69.

SOURCES:

Bailey, Martha J. *American Women in Science*. Denver, CO: ABC-CLIO, 1994, p. 228.

Sicherman, Barbara, and Carol Hurd Green. *Notable American Women: The Modern Period: A Biographical Dictionary*. Cambridge, MA: The Belknap Press of Harvard University, 1980.

Siegel, Patricia Joan, and Kay Thomas Finley. *Women in the Scientific Search*. Metuchen, NJ: Scarecrow Press, 1985.

Soltan, Hubert C. "Madge Macklin—Pioneer in Medical Genetics," in *University of Western Ontario Medical Journal*. Vol. 38. October 1962, pp. 6–11.

Judith C. Reveal, freelance writer, Greensboro, Maryland

Mackworth, Margaret (1883–1958).

See Rhondda, Margaret.

Maclean, Letitia Elizabeth (1802–1838).

See Landon, Letitia Elizabeth.

Maclehose, Agnes (1759–1841)

Scottish woman who corresponded with Robert Burns under the name Clarinda. Name variations: Agnes M'Lehose; Clarinda. Born Agnes Craig in 1759; died in 1841; daughter of an Edinburgh surgeon; grandniece of Colin Maclaurin (1698–1746, a mathematician and natural philosopher); married James Maclehose (a Glasgow lawyer), in 1776 (separated 1780).

Two years after her separation from James Maclehose, a Glasgow lawyer, in 1780, Agnes Maclehose moved to Edinburgh where she met the poet Robert Burns at a party in 1787. Maclehose corresponded with Burns under the name Clarinda until 1794. Their correspondence was published in 1843.

MacLeod, Banda (1898–1919).

See Zelle, Margaretha for sidebar.

MacLeod, Juana-Luisa (1898–1919).

See Zelle, Margaretha for sidebar.

MacLeod, Margaretha (1876–1917).

See Zelle, Margaretha.

MacMahon, Aline (1899–1991)

American actress who was nominated for an Academy Award for her performance in Dragon Seed. *Born on May 3, 1899, in McKeesport, Pennsylvania; died on October 12, 1991, at her home in New York from pneumonia; graduated from Erasmus Hall and Barnard College; married Clarence S. Stein (an architect), in 1928 (died 1975).*

Selected theater: made Broadway debut in The Mirage *(1921); appeared in* Grand Street Follies *(Neighborhood Playhouse),* Artists and Models *(1925),* Beyond the Horizon *(1926),* Maya *(1928),* Winter Bound *(1929),* The Eve of St. Mark *(1942),* The Confidential Clerk *(1954),* A Day by the Sea *(1955); appeared as the Nurse in* Romeo and Juliet *(Stratford, Connecticut), the Countess in* All's Well That Ends Well *(Stratford, Connecticut, 1959), Volumnia in* Coriolanus *(Stratford, Connecticut, 1965).*

Selected filmography: Five Star Final *(1931);* The Heart of New York *(1932);* The Mouthpiece *(1932);* Life Begins *(1932);* One Way Passage *(1932);* Once in a Lifetime *(1932);* Gold Diggers of 1933 *(1933);* Heroes for Sale *(1933);* The World Changes *(1933);* Heat Lightning *(1934);* Side Streets *(1934);* Big-Hearted

From the movie
Dragon Seed,
starring Aline
MacMahon.

Herbert *(1934);* Babbitt *(1934);* While the Patient Slept *(1935);* I Live My Life *(1935);* Kind Lady *(1935);* Ah Wilderness! *(1935);* When You're in Love *(1937);* Back Door to Heaven *(1939);* Out of the Fog *(1941);* The Lady Is Willing *(1942);* Dragon Seed *(1944);* Guest in the House *(1944);* The Mighty McGurk *(1947);* The Search *(1948);* Roseanna McCoy *(1949);* The Flame and the Arrow *(1950);* The Eddie Cantor Story *(1953);* The Man From Laramie *(1955);* Cimarron *(1960);* The Young Doctors *(1961);* Diamond Head *(1963);* I Could Go on Singing *(UK, 1963);* All the Way Home *(1963).*

Once publicized as "the perfect screen secretary," Aline MacMahon made her mark in films as a character actress, often turning minor roles into small masterpieces. The actress came to Hollywood in 1931, via the New York stage, where she had already built a solid reputation.

The daughter of a stockbroker turned magazine editor, MacMahon was born in McKeesport, Pennsylvania, in 1899, and raised in New York City. She caught the acting bug at Barnard College. After graduating, she worked in stock and in 1921 landed her first Broadway role in *The Mirage*. She then did a stint with the Neighborhood Playhouse, which led to a contract with the Shuberts. Following a stellar performance of *Once in a Lifetime* in Los Angeles, she was tapped for the role as Edward G. Robinson's secretary in Warner Bros.' *Five Star Final* (1931), for which she won rave reviews. She then signed a contract with the studio, but only after they included a clause restricting her work to certain specific time periods so that she could live in New York with her husband, architect Clarence S. Stein. The couple had married in 1928.

Tall and a bit ungainly, with dark soulful eyes and a sad expression, MacMahon was usually cast in dramatic films, although she was equally adept at comedy, notably opposite Guy Kibbee (*Big-Hearted Herbert*). She also played opposite Kibbee in *Babbitt*, a film version of the Sinclair Lewis bestseller, and in *While the Patient Slept* (1935), a murder mystery. The actress received an Oscar nomination for Best Supporting Actress for her work in *Dragon Seed* (1944), in which she played Walter Huston's wife, but her best film role was as a volunteer officer looking after misplaced persons in *The Search* (1948), one of the top films of the 1940s. In *Sight and Sound* (1955), Albert Johnson recalled MacMahon's work in the film: "Here is Aline MacMahon as Mrs. Mallory, the careworn directress of this outpost of destitute youngsters," he wrote. "Her uniform somehow enhances a warm, matriarchal sympathy, and although she is a secondary figure, one is curious to know more about her. This is MacMahon's forte, to make everything she does stick in the memory."

Aline MacMahon made only a few screen appearance during the 1950s and 1960s, notably as **Judy Garland*'s dresser-companion in *I Could Go on Singing* (1963) and as Aunt Hannah in *All the Way Home* (1963), a role she also created on stage. Along with films, she continued to work in theater in New York, California, and Stratford, Connecticut, and was also seen on television.

SOURCES:
Katz, Ephraim. *The Film Encyclopedia*. NY: Harper-Collins, 1994.
Shipman, David. *The Great Movie Stars: The Golden Years*. Boston, MA: Little, Brown, 1995.

Barbara Morgan,
Melrose, Massachusetts

MacManus, Anna Johnston

(1866–1902)

Irish writer of poetry and short stories. Name variations: Mrs. Anna Johnston; Mrs. Seamus MacManus; *(pseudonym) Ethna Carbery. Born Anna Johnston in Ballymena, County Antrim, in 1866; died in 1902 (some sources cite 1911); married Séamus or Seumas MacManus (a poet).*

Selected writings: (poetry) The Four Winds of Eirinn *(1902); (short stories)* The Passionate Hearts *(1903); (short stories)* In the Celtic Past *(1904); (contributor)* We Sang for Ireland *(includes works of Séamus MacManus and Alice Milligan).*

Credited with influencing the early Sinn Fein movement, Anna MacManus wrote poetry that was first published in the journals *Nation* and *United Ireland*, then in a collection called *The Four Winds of Eirinn* (1902). In conjunction with a Belfast workingmen's club, MacManus and **Alice Milligan* founded the monthly newspaper *Northern Patriot*, and in 1896, following a dispute with the club, founded *Shan Van Vocht,* which MacManus edited until 1899. MacManus was also active in Inghinidhe na hÉireann, which offered free classes in music, dance, and drama, and purportedly motivated William Butler Yeats to start the Irish National Theater. The writer, who was married to poet Seumas MacManus, died in 1902 or 1911.

Macmillan, Chrystal (1871–1937)

Scottish feminist and pacifist. Born in Edinburgh, Scotland, in 1871; died in 1937; educated at St. Leonard's School, St. Andrews, and Edinburgh University; also studied in Berlin.

In 1908, on behalf of women Scottish graduates, Chrystal Macmillan became the first woman to address the House of Lords; she was arguing for their right to vote for parliamentary candidates to the Scottish Universities seat. A week later, the bill was defeated. She then joined the National Union of Suffrage Societies, serving as a leader with this group for a number of years until she resigned in opposition to proposals for protective legislation for women. In 1923, Macmillan founded the Open Door Council which espoused the elimination of legal restrictions on women. Six years later, she was named president of the Open Door International for the Economic Emancipation of the Woman Worker. As a pacifist, Macmillan was a major organizer for The Hague Congress in 1915 and secretary of the International Alliance of Women from 1913 to 1923. In 1935, she ran unsuccessfully as a Liberal candidate for the Edinburgh election.

MacMillan, Shannon.

See Soccer: Women's World Cup, 1999.

MacMonnies, Mary Fairchild
(1858–1946).

See Low, Mary Fairchild.

Macnamara, Jean (1899–1968)

Australian doctor and scientist who championed the use of an immune serum to treat pre-paralytic patients with polio and helped pave the way toward the development of the Salk vaccine with her discovery that more than one strain of the polio virus existed.
Name variations: Annie Jean Connor; Jean Connor. Born in Beechworth, Victoria, Australia, on April 1, 1899; died on October 13, 1968; daughter of John Macnamara (a court clerk) and Anne Fraser Macnamara; educated at Melbourne's Presbyterian Ladies' College; University of Melbourne, M.B.B.S., 1922, M.D., 1925; married Joseph Ivan Connor (a dermatologist), on November 19, 1934 (died 1955); children: two daughters.

The second daughter of John and **Anne Fraser Macnamara**, Jean Macnamara was born on April 1, 1899, in Beechworth, Victoria, Australia. In 1907, the Macnamara family moved to Melbourne, the capital of Victoria. There Jean attended the Presbyterian Ladies' College and later the University of Melbourne, from which she graduated with a medical degree in 1922. She began her medical practice as a resident medical officer at the Royal Melbourne and Royal Children's hospitals, graduating as a medical doctor in 1925. The following year, Macnamara was named clinical assistant to the outpatients' physician at Royal Children's Hospital and at the same time established a private practice specializing in the treatment of polio (poliomyelitis), a literally crippling disease that was running rampant not only in Australia but throughout the world. Also, beginning in 1925 and continuing until 1931, she served as a consultant and medical officer to the Poliomyelitis Committee of Victoria, an organization led by Dr. John Dale. Between 1930 and 1931, Macnamara also served as an honorary adviser on polio to three other states. For more than two decades, between 1928 and 1951, she held the post of honorary medical officer to the Yooralla Hospital School for Crippled Children.

In 1925, a polio epidemic swept through Australia, prompting Macnamara to conduct tests of immune serum in the treatment of pre-paralytic patients. (An infectious virus that struck particularly hard at children, polio often resulted in some form of paralysis or laming.) Confident that her treatment plan had merit, she published accounts of her experimental therapy in Australian and British medical journals between 1927 and 1935. An attempt to duplicate her treatment methods in New York produced discouraging results, which Macnamara blamed on flawed procedures. Discredited by the disappointing test results from the United States, the immune serum therapy program was largely abandoned by other medical practitioners, although Macnamara herself continued to use it privately. Working with fellow medical researcher Macfarlane Burnet, she discovered the existence of more than one strain of polio virus. This finding, which was reported in a 1931 issue of the *British Journal of Experimental Pathology*, was later credited with helping to lay the foundation for the development of the polio vaccine by American Jonas Salk in 1954 that virtually eliminated the disease from industrialized countries.

Macnamara traveled from Australia to the United Kingdom and the United States between 1931 and 1933 on a fellowship from the Rockefeller Foundation. During her overseas travels, she placed an order for Australia's first artificial respirator (polio sometimes attacked the muscles of the chest and throat, leaving the patient unable to breathe without the assistance of an "iron lung") and collected ideas for new splinting and rehabilitation techniques. The controversy over her immune serum therapy for the treatment of polio had caused a rift between Macnamara and her co-worker John Dale, so she determined to concentrate her future efforts on orthopedics. However, she did not totally abandon her interest in serum research, and worked part-time at Melbourne's Walter and Eliza Hall Institute on the polio immune serum and on psittacosis, another infectious virus.

On November 19, 1934, Macnamara married dermatologist Joseph Ivan Connor, with whom she would have two daughters. A year later Macnamara was named a Dame Commander of the Order of the British Empire (DBE). Shortly thereafter, she moved her Melbourne practice to larger quarters. A tireless worker, she often treated indigent patients free of charge and worked through the weekend when the need arose. When a new polio epidemic swept Australia in 1937 and 1938, she supervised patient care at both the Royal Children's and Fairfield Hospitals in Melbourne. So popular had she become among her patients, most of whom were children, that her clinics were almost always filled, despite the fact that patients faced lengthy waits to see her.

One of the methods Macnamara employed to try to get polio patients back on their feet was to splint the paralyzed limb until the damaged nerves had time to recover. After the nerves had recovered, she helped patients reeducate the muscles in the afflicted limb so that function could be restored. She spent much of her time trying to devise new splinting methods to help immobilize limbs that had been rendered useless by paralysis. To reach out to patients who had been paralyzed by polio, Macnamara set up a system of visiting physiotherapists, who went to patients in their homes to try to help them on the road to recovery. She established a clinic in the Melbourne suburb of Carlton that treated 30 children a day. To meet the needs of patients in outlying areas, she conducted country clinics. Macnamara also served on the Queensland Royal Commission on polio, which explored the innovative polio treatments pioneered by Sister *Elizabeth Kenny, a native of New South Wales in Australia. The Queensland commission supported the establishment at Brighton of an experimental treatment center utilizing the Kenny method. As an outgrowth of her work with polio patients, Macnamara eventually expanded her practice to include victims of cerebral palsy and lead poisoning, as well as healthy patients with poor posture. On her recommendation, the first Australian center for the treatment of spastic children opened at Royal Children's Hospital in Melbourne.

When she had learned in 1933 that researchers at Princeton University were experimenting with ways to combat the myxomatosis virus in rabbits, it occurred to Macnamara that perhaps the virus could be used as a weapon to combat Australia's enormous rabbit population, which posed a significant threat to agriculture. First it was necessary to make certain that the virus would pose no danger to domestic animals. She dispatched a sample of the virus to Melbourne for testing, but it was destroyed in transit. Macnamara called upon S.M. Bruce in London to help determine if the virus could be used safely without threatening other domestic animals, and such testing was carried out successfully in Cambridge. Between 1937 and 1944, Australia's Council for Scientific and Industrial Research conducted a series of field trials of the virus on rabbits, but the virus failed to spread. From Macnamara's point of view, it was clearly another case of a promising innovation being pushed aside after inadequate or flawed testing. She went public with her campaign to have testing of the virus revived, waging a war of words with other scientists in the Australian press and lobbying wool growers' organizations for a resumption of testing. In 1950, her efforts paid off, and testing of the virus was resumed in a location Macnamara felt was more favorable, although at first it produced no favorable results. A year or two later, the experiment triggered a widespread outbreak of disease among rabbits. During the 1952–53 wool season, the drop in the rabbit population caused by the virus was said to have increased wool revenues by millions of dollars. Growers showed their appreciation for Macnamara's efforts with a clock and a check.

Macnamara and her husband owned a farm, used mainly for weekend getaways, in the Romsey district, which she continued to visit after the death of her husband in 1955. Although she was not a full-time farmer, Macnamara campaigned against the indiscriminate use of pesticides in agriculture and even joined the Compost Society. In 1966, she was awarded an honorary LLD degree by the University of Melbourne. Right up until the time of her death on October 13, 1968, Jean Macnamara continued treating paralytic patients.

SOURCES:
Radi, Heather, ed. *200 Australian Women: A Redress Anthology.* NSW, Australia: Women's Redress Press, 1988.

Don Amerman,
freelance writer, Saylorsburg, Pennsylvania

Macomber, Mary Lizzie

(1861–1916)

American artist. Born in Fall River, Massachusetts, on August 21, 1861; died in Boston, Massachusetts, on February 4, 1916; studied drawing in Fall River with a local artist and later for a year at the school of the Boston Museum of Fine Arts.

A descendant of Pilgrims and Quakers, Mary Lizzie Macomber was born on August 21, 1861, in Fall River, Massachusetts. At age 19, she began taking instruction in painting from Robert S. Dunning, a major force in the Fall River school of still-life painting. For the next three years, Macomber spent much of her time executing paintings of flowers and fruit under Dunning's tutelage. She next studied at the school of the Boston Museum of Fine Arts, concentrating on painting figures, although ill health forced her to drop out after one year. Three years later, she studied briefly with Boston artist Frank Duveneck, after which she opened her own studio in Boston.

Among Macomber's earliest work in the Pre-Raphaelite style for which she is known were such paintings as *Love Awakening Memory* and *Love's Lament,* produced in 1891 and 1893, respectively. Characterized by an abundance of Madonnas, Mary Magdalenes, and Annunciations, Macomber's early paintings depicted these sacred images with "sweet, solemn sadness, illuminated by immortal faith" and "delicate coloring . . . with refined, spiritual conceptions," according to critics of the day. She exhibited over 20 paintings at the annual National Academy of Design shows between 1889 and 1902, and in 1897 won the Dodge Prize at the National Academy exhibition in New York for her *St. Catherine,* painted in 1896 and similar in style to the work of Sir Edward Burne-Jones. Her allegorical and symbolical panels, executed in a rarefied, decorative manner, were much admired.

The surge in Pre-Raphaelite painting during America's Gilded Age was fueled by some artists' disdain for the new industrial society. Painters of this school, two of the earliest proponents of which were Dante Gabriel Rossetti and John Everett Millais, harkened back to an earlier, less complicated era in an almost religious attempt to appeal to what they saw as a nobler spirit in man. Macomber and others of the Pre-Raphaelite school tried to emulate the style of some of the greatest artists of the Renaissance.

In 1903, a fire ripped through Macomber's studio in Boston, destroying much of her work. In the wake of this disaster she traveled to England, the Netherlands, and France to view firsthand the works of the great masters. When she returned to the United States her new work, which utilized broader brushwork and an innovative use of lighting, showed the influence of Rembrandt. Among the more memorable of her later paintings were *Night and Her Daughter* and *Memory Comforting Shadow.* Much of her later work was in portraiture. On February 4, 1916, Mary Macomber died in Boston. At her funeral in Boston's historic Old South Church, hundreds of artists and art lovers gathered to mourn her passing and to recognize the distinctive place she had created for herself in the world of American art.

SOURCES:

McHenry, Robert, ed. *Famous American Women.* NY: Dover, 1980.

Rubinstein, Charlotte Streifer. *American Women Artists.* Boston, MA: G.K. Hall, 1982.

Don Amerman,
freelance writer, Saylorsburg, Pennsylvania

Maconaqua (1773–1847).

See Slocum, Frances.

Maconchy, Elizabeth (1907—)

Irish-born composer of works for orchestra, chamber orchestra, opera and voice, whose unique style, combining the best in modern and classical techniques, has been a great influence on modern music both in Great Britain and internationally. Name variations: Dame Elizabeth Maconchy. Born Elizabeth Maconchy in Boxbourne, Hertfordshire, England, on March 19, 1907; attended the Royal College of Music in London, 1923–29; married William Lefanu, in 1930; children: two daughters, one of whom is the composer Nicola Lefanu (b. 1947).

Was a star pupil at the Royal College of Music (1923); won the Blumenthal and Sullivan scholarships, and the Octavia Traveling Scholarship (1929); by her mid-20s, major orchestras in England and Europe had performed her work; withdrew from the London musical scene to recover from tuberculosis (1932); lived in Essex, continuing to compose after birth of her daughters and throughout WWII; won the Edwin Evans Prize (1948); won the GEDOK International prize (1961); received the Radcliffe award (1969); became a Commander of the Order of the British Empire (CBE, 1977); became a Dame of the British Empire (DBE) for her contributions to music (1987); composed hundreds of works, increasingly performed and recorded.

Selected works—orchestral: "Concerto" (1928); "Christmas music" (1928); "Concertino" (1928); The Land Suite (1929); "Suite" (1930); "Dialogue" (1940); "Theme and Variations" (1942); "Variations on a well-known theme" (1942); "Concertino" (1945); "Symphony" (1948); "Concertino" (1951); "Nocturne" (1951); "Symphony for double string orchestra" (1952); Proud Thames (1953); "Sinfonietta" (1953); "Double concerto" (1957); "Serenata concertante" (1962); An Essex Overture (1966); Three Cloudscapes (1968); Two Dances from Puck Fair (1968); and half a dozen operas, many vocal and string quartet compositions.

With the dawning of the 20th century, when the musical world was dominated by the richly beautiful works of composers like Johannes Brahms, a rebellion arose among young British composers who referred to such music of the lyrical tradition as the "cowpat school." This rude but expressive term, referring to the many pastoral music works set in the green and cow-filled English countryside, gave vent to the musical aspect of the new century's struggle to find its own aesthetic. Composers like Schönberg, Webern, and Berg wrote atonal music that many found to be an assault on the ears just as Picasso, Dubuffett, and Pollack were assaulting the eyes in the visual arts. Lines were drawn between groups of artists who felt that modern was synonymous with ugly and those who believed that creative individuals must be freed from the past. As the 20th century progressed, one musician who managed to combine the best aspects of the older classical styles with the exciting elements of the new was Elizabeth Maconchy.

Of Irish ancestry, Maconchy was born in Boxbourne, Hertfortshire, on March 19, 1907, and lived in Britain until her family moved to Dublin shortly after World War I, when she was 12. Her father was mildly musical; her mother not at all. She had one sister who was tone deaf and another who was bored by music. There was no radio or phonograph in the family home, so her father's piano-playing was the only music she heard. But once she began piano lessons at age six, Elizabeth immediately began composing as well. She was 15 when she first heard a symphony orchestra in concert, when the Hallé Orchestra played in Dublin. Her father died of tuberculosis that same year, and the family returned to Britain. Elizabeth's obvious musicianship was by then well recognized, and at age 16 she entered the Royal College of Music in London. The girl who had heard only a single symphony concert, a performance of *Carmen*, and a piano recital by *Myra Hess was soon studying under Charles Wood and Ralph Vaughn Williams, two composers whose influence on 20th-century British music was profound.

> [Maconchy] is a born composer and has never been anything but a composer.
>
> —Frank Howes

The composer *Elisabeth Lutyens, a fellow student at the Royal College, described Maconchy in her autobiography as "the star pupil of those College days." During her years of study from 1923 to 1929, Maconchy won both the Blumenthal and Sullivan scholarships. She was denied the prestigious Mendelssohn Scholarship because, as Sir Hugh Allen explained, "if we give you the scholarship, you will only get married and never write another note." In 1929, she won the Octavia Traveling Scholarship, which gave her the opportunity to visit Vienna and Prague. She spent two months studying with Karl Jirák in Prague, and returned there in 1930 to attend the premiere of a piano concerto she had written. That same year, in a remarkable coup for a composer not yet in her mid-20s, another of Maconchy's works was produced at one of London's famous Promenade Concerts ("Proms"). *The*

Land, a suite of four numbers written for a large orchestra, depicted the seasons through the poetic vision of *Vita Sackville-West, and was highly praised for its imaginative and original style.

Because there were few places where the works of young composers could be performed, Maconchy, with Elizabeth Lutyens, **Anne Macnaghten**, and **Iris Lemare**, founded the Macnaghten-Lemare concerts, which strongly favored women composers. Held at the tiny Mercury Theater in London's Notting Hill Gate, these musical events also offered a means for up-and-coming composers to make contact with each other. In speaking of the series, which exists to this day, Maconchy commented, "It was probably the best thing that ever happened for young composers here, and it was the only thing that happened for a long time."

Maconchy married William Lefanu, with whom she would have two daughters (their second daughter, ✎➤ **Nicola Lefanu**, would later establish her own reputation as a composer), in 1930. Two years later, when she was 25, she contracted tuberculosis, the disease that had killed her father. The clear mountain air of Switzerland was considered the only cure for the disease in this era before antibiotics, but Maconchy moved to Kent instead, to breathe the fresh air in her own country. Although she had withdrawn from London's hectic music scene in her determination to restore her health, she continued to compose, and her husband encouraged her to combat this interruption to her career. Speaking of his support, she later said, "It certainly helped to be married to a man sympathetic to my work. For the 30 years we have lived in Essex, two thick walls divide his study from the room where I work at my piano composing. He maintains a keen interest in everything I write."

Beginning in 1933, Maconchy concentrated increasingly on the composition of string quartets, writing 13 of them within the next five decades and becoming the English composer most associated with the form. Although she continued to write larger orchestral works in the late 1930s and after, she considered the string quartet the perfect vehicle for dramatic musical expression, with the four instruments, like four characters, engaged in statement and comment. Maconchy said she that she composed to display the various abilities of the instruments, or "The clash of their ideas and the way in which they react upon each other." Early quartets featured a classic multimovement format, but with the passage of time her compositions in this form became more compact, often with only one continuous movement and very economical use of material.

Despite Maconchy's self-imposed distance from the London musical world, between 1932 and 1936 pieces of hers were featured at the Macnaghten-Lemare Concerts, helping to keep both her name and her music before the public. She was invited twice by Donald Tovey for performances of her work in Edinburgh, and Sir Henry Wood, founder of the Promenade Concerts, presented several of her works to London audiences. Maconchy's music was also played at the I.S.C.M. Festivals, held in Prague in 1935 and in Paris in 1937, and would be performed at various concerts in Warsaw in 1939. In 1938, she returned to London for a concert at the London Contemporary Music Center featuring her work along with that of Elisabeth Lutyens, Benjamin Britten, Lennox Berkeley, and Walter Leigh. Maconchy's photo appeared in the advance publicity for the concert, and she joined those who trooped off afterwards to a party given by Elisabeth Lutyens at her flat. Parties of the period were lively affairs, with drinks at the ready, where the musicians' conversation was likely to center on the difficulty faced by living artists who were trying to compete with "the towering dead and their nightingales and psalms" for the attention of concertgoers who rarely ventured into modern music.

Maconchy continued to compose after the birth of her first child in 1939 and the advent of World War II. One of the major influences on her unique style was the music of the modern Hungarian composer Bela Bartók, whose compositions, she found, set fire to her imagination. (His influence may have been due in part to her earlier visits to Central Europe.) Although she borrowed a great deal from him in matters of technique, Maconchy's work was to prove quite different from Bartok's. Some have found her style more Celtic than English, although without apparent reliance on Celtic folk music. Describing how she went about composing, Maconchy said:

> The form . . . must proceed from the nature of the musical ideas themselves—one cannot simply pour music into a ready-made mold. The composer must try to evolve a form that is the inevitable outcome of his own musical ideas and provides for their fullest expression.

Discussing the extreme economy of thematic material that characterizes her work, she said:

> To me music is a sort of impassioned argument, propelled by the force of its own inner logic, and by virtue of this logic each new idea will derive from the original premise

Lefanu, Nicola (b. 1947)

*English composer. Born in 1947; daughter of *Elizabeth Maconchy (b. 1907) and William Lefanu; studied at Oxford University and Royal College of Music; studied with Maxwell Davies at Dartington and in Siena.*

Following her studies with Maxwell Davies, Nicola Lefanu was appointed lecturer at King's College, London. Her compositions, including *Antiworld* (1972) and *Dawnpath* (1977), earned her many awards, as did her radiophonic operas, *The Story of Mary O'Neill* (completed in 1986, broadcast in 1989), and *Wind Among the Pines: Five Images of Norfolk* (1987).

and throw new light on the whole. The rigid self-discipline which the composer must impose on himself must always be directed to the fullest expression of the underlying emotion and never to its exclusion. This passionately intellectual and intellectually passionate musical discourse is what I seek to express in my music.

Although music is sexless, composition was for centuries divided according to whether it was "masculine" and "feminine." "Masculine" music demanded the best performers and large orchestras (almost all of which were comprised solely of male musicians), was performed on concert stages throughout the world, and could be innovative without being condemned. "Feminine" music was expected to be pleasant and pretty, like those who composed it, and performance of it was generally restricted to the home, which was where a great deal of music was performed before the advent of phonographs, radios, movies and television. As technology replaced musicians in the home in the early years of the 20th century, public and private performances were forced to merge. In the Western music world, women increasingly began insisting on filling the roles of performers and composers. Women first began to be taken seriously as composers at about the same time many were obtaining the right to vote.

Conscious of those "feminine" stereotypes about women composers, Maconchy clearly intended to avoid them. Her energetic music, with brazen tempos characterized by strong motor rhythms, has, perhaps not surprisingly, been described as "tough and masculine." She established thematic connections between movements, and sometimes based a whole work on a single idea. Austerity and severity prevailed, particularly in slow movements. Summing up her philosophy of composition, Maconchy said,

"Every note is an essential part of the whole structure—there is no place for 'effects without causes.'" She further noted:

> To crowd new and extraneous notes into existing harmonies may perhaps add a certain colour, but it does not represent any real development. On the other hand, the several threads of the music moving in melodic lines can coalesce vertically to create a new harmonic interest. A counterpoint of rhythm exists side by side with melodic counterpoint. By the free movement of several rhythms simultaneously we can hope for more rhythmic development than by any amount of experiment with monadic rhythms.

Fusing many traditions, her style seemed to move past the debate about classical tonal harmonies versus modern atonality.

Maconchy was accorded growing recognition after World War II. In 1947, her work was chosen for inclusion at the Copenhagen International Festival, and her fifth string quartet won the Edwin Evans Prize the following year. Her overture *Proud Thames* won the L.C.C. Prize in 1953, the Coronation Year of Queen *Elizabeth II. With each new composition, she remained concentrated on developing a single concept. Speaking of her intense focus, Maconchy said:

> Writing music, like all creative art, is the impassioned pursuit of an idea. . . . The great thing is for the composer to keep his head and allow nothing to distract him. The temptations to stop by the way and to be sidetracked by felicities of sound and colour are ever present, but in my view everything extraneous to the pursuit of this central idea must be rigorously excluded—scrapped.

Her music of this period is characterized by a preoccupation with short themes playing around a few notes, with the notes described by some as a "finger print." Intense movements, given a disturbing and sometimes vehement sense of pent-up energy and emotion by her strong sense of rhythm, are interspersed with movements of serenity. Some critics have said that while the music of Ralph Vaughn Williams and other members of the English School portrays the beauty of the Cotswolds, Maconchy's music portrays the "bare mountains, dark loughs, black bogs and turf stacks of Connemara, the country nearest her heart."

In the mid-1950s, Maconchy experienced a creative block and briefly stopped composing. When she returned to work it was in the operatic form, and between 1957 and 1967 she wrote three one-act operas, several choral pieces, and several pieces for children's voices. The latter works, including *Samson* and *The King of the*

Golden River, are dramatic without overstepping the bounds of children's musical abilities, and while simple and approachable also make full use of Maconchy's creative powers. In the 1970s, she became interested in the characteristics and foibles of particular instruments, exploring the freedom and expressive quality of a wide-ranging vocal line in *Ariadne* and the character of the solo cello in *Epyllion*. *The Leaden Echo and the Golden Echo,* written in 1978, continued her experimentation with vocal works, combining mixed chorus, alto flute, viola and harp. These successful vocal compositions marked both growth and expanded interest since the early years of her career, when she focused primarily on musical instruments (in 1938, Frank Howes had noted that Maconchy "shows no great partiality for vocal writing").

In 1989, Maconchy's "Music for Woodwind and Brass," written two decades before, was finally published. Scored for a classical orchestra without strings (paired woodwinds, four horns, three trumpets, three trombones, tuba, and timpani), the work was a true chamber piece, like so many of her best compositions. Critics particularly liked the piece for its use of numerous pianissimo passages without a single fortissimo passage, a rarity in wind music. She has received numerous awards, including a GEDOK International prize in 1961, a Radcliffe award in 1969, and membership in the Worshipful Company of Musicians in 1970. She was granted the title of Commander of the Order of the British Empire (CBE) in 1977. In 1987, Elizabeth Maconchy was named a Dame of the British Empire (DBE), the equivalent of a knighthood, for her contributions to music, in fitting tribute both to her own lasting compositions and to her important influence on 20th-century classical music.

SOURCES:
Britten, Benjamin. "England and the Folk-Art Problem," in *Modern Music*. Vol. 18, no. 2. January–February 1941, pp. 71–75.
"Contemporary Composers: Elizabeth Maconchy," in *Women and Music: A History*. Ed. by Karin Pendle. Bloomington, IN: Indiana University Press, 1991, pp. 178–179.
"Elizabeth Maconchy," in Le Page, Jane Weiner. *Women Composers, Conductors, and Musicians of the Twentieth Century: Selected Biographies.* Vol. III. Metuchen, NJ: Scarecrow Press, 1988.
Gruenberg, Louis. "Modern Youth at Prague, 1935," in *Modern Music*. Vol. 13, no. 1. November–December 1935, pp. 38–44.
Howes, Frank. "The Younger English Composers, III: Elizabeth Maconchy," in *The Monthly Musical Record*. Vol. 68, no. 798. July–August 1938, pp. 165–68.

J.V.R. "Recordings: Maconchy: String Quartets Nos. 1, 2, 3 and 4," in *Chicago Tribune*. Sunday, July 1, 1990, p. 22.

Lopatnikoff, Nicolai. "England's Young Composers," in *Modern Music*. Vol. 14, no. 4. May–June 1937, pp. 204–207.

Macnaghten, Anne. "Elizabeth Maconchy," in *The Musical Times*. Vol. 96, no. 1348. June 1955, pp. 298–302.

"Maconchy, Elizabeth," in *The New Grove Dictionary of Music and Musicians*. Vol. 11. Ed. by Stanley Sadie. London: Macmillan, 1980, pp. 448–449.

Matthew-Walker, Robert. "Maconchy, (Dame) Elizabeth," in *Contemporary Composers*. Ed. by Brian Morton and Pamela Collins. Chicago: St. James Press, 1992, pp. 599–602.

John Haag,
Associate Professor,
University of Georgia, Athens, Georgia

Macphail, Agnes (1890–1954)

First woman elected to Canada's federal Parliament, who was a tireless defender of the rights of women, farmers, prisoners and the disadvantaged through a political career spanning three decades. Name variations: originally "MacPhail," changed the spelling to "Macphail" in 1925. Born Agnes MacPhail in Proton Township, Grey County, southwestern Ontario, Canada, on March 24, 1890; died in Toronto on February 13, 1954; daughter of Henrietta Campbell MacPhail and Dougald MacPhail; never married; no children.

Like many Scottish emigrants in the mid-19th century, Agnes Macphail's ancestors came to central Canada with the dream of religious freedom and independent farm ownership. Choosing to settle in the Grey-Bruce area of southwestern Ontario, both the Campbells and the MacPhails were successful in acquiring their own farms. However, the soil in this area was poor, making farming and economic survival difficult. On March 24, 1890, Agnes Macphail (who changed the spelling to "Macphail" in 1925) was born in a small, dilapidated farm house, the first daughter of Dougald and **Henrietta MacPhail**. The MacPhails were hard working and determined to get ahead. In 1902, with the help of a small inheritance, they managed to buy a larger, better quality farm with a nicer house. Although the family never became wealthy, they did manage to acquire a degree of financial security by the time Agnes was in her late teens. Still, the impact of years of struggle remained with Macphail, making her sensitive to the plight of farmers throughout her life.

Sometime during these years, Agnes Macphail also became sensitive to the relative inequality of women in Canadian society. Farming was a difficult life for women, with its hard physical labor accompanying the demands of motherhood and housework. Whatever the source of Macphail's feminism, she revealed early on a determination to be independent and to live a life unconstrained by societal views of women's "place." As a student, she excelled and was gravely upset when her parents refused to allow her to attend high school. At the time, high schools were only available in the cities, thereby placing financial demands on rural families who would have to pay for room and board. As extended education was not considered necessary for girls, her parents initially refused to pay. After two years of their daughter's persistence, however, they finally relented and the 16-year-old was sent to the city of Owen Sound to live and study. "At last I was a real person starting out on my own," said Macphail.

Agnes continued to excel at school, both academically and athletically. She completed high school and then teachers college by 1910. For the next decade, teaching school became her vocation in rural areas around the province. During these years, Macphail also became involved with a growing farmers' movement. By the early 20th century, the farming community was declining in both numbers and prosperity. Discontented farmers had come to believe that the solution lay in cooperative action, education, and political reform. To achieve these goals, the United Farmers of Ontario (UFO) was formed in 1914. With her roots firmly planted in rural life and the farming community, Macphail joined the affiliated United Farm Women of Ontario (UFWO). Never content to be simply an auxiliary, she became an important figure in the work of organizing local chapters and publicizing the goals of the UFO. She also took up a position as a columnist for the *Farmers' Sun* (the newspaper of the UFO). Through these activities, Macphail quickly became a well-known and popular activist in rural Ontario.

By 1919, the rising tide of farmer discontent resulted in the UFO winning the election and forming the government in Ontario. Inspired by these results, the party decided to field candidates in the forthcoming federal election. Obviously a party based strictly in Ontario could not hope to secure a majority in the national Parliament. However, due to Ontario's large number of seats, the party could hope to affect the direction of federal policy by winning a significant number of seats. Convinced of the importance of the farmers' movement, Macphail decided to run as a candidate for the UFO. At the nomination meeting for Southeast Grey, she was the only female among 151 delegates. Yet through her forceful speaking ability and sensitivity to rural concerns, she managed to secure the nomination, an enormous victory for a woman in 1921 Ontario. Women in the province had only been allowed to vote since the end of World War I. The obstacle that Macphail faced was summed up by one farmer who was thrown by news of her victory: "What! Are there no men left in Southeast Grey?"

Having secured the nomination, Macphail confronted the much greater task of winning the election. Not only did she face barriers due to her gender, but she also represented a new party and faced an opponent who had held the riding for three terms. Throughout the election, Macphail concentrated solely on farm and labor issues, emphasizing farmer exploitation at the hands of the "big interests." Her message was clear: the only way for farmers to protect their interests was by electing farm representatives independent of the two mainstream parties. On the night of the election, she waited for the results at her family's home. History was made that night in Southeast Grey. They elected the first woman to the Parliament of Canada.

If there is any good point about me, it is that I am what I am, and I tell them what I think.

—Agnes Macphail

One might have expected that Macphail's public career would be dedicated to women's issues. There is no doubt that she experienced the frustrations of male prejudice. Press and opposition often resorted to derogatory, sexist remarks to undermine her parliamentary efforts. Still, Macphail generally emphasized social reform above women's rights, a position not uncommon among feminists of the time. The belief was that reforms such as labor legislation or old age pensions would ultimately lead to an improvement in women's position along with that of other disadvantaged members of society. Nonetheless, Macphail often stood as the sole champion of women's rights in a Parliament dominated by men. Throughout her career, she defended the right of women to work. She believed that women, like men, needed work to have fulfilling lives. Though Agnes recognized that domestic labor and childcare were "work," she felt that equal opportunity for employment should be available for those women not involved in these activities, by choice or life circumstances. Thus, Macphail was a firm supporter of "equal pay for equal work" laws and opposed female minimum wages as a hindrance to women in the fight for

jobs. Having fought so hard against the limitations imposed upon women, Macphail firmly believed that women needed and deserved greater freedom.

In particular, she believed that more women needed to be involved in the political process. This is not surprising considering her often solitary position within Canada's male-dominated Parliament. It was also the result of contemporary beliefs about the nature of men and women. Like other feminists, Macphail subscribed to what has become known as "maternal feminism." Influenced by prevailing beliefs that men and women were psychologically different, maternal feminists argued that women's greater morality, passivity, and nurturance were positive characteristics that should be present in public life to influence policy. Women, it was argued, would naturally oppose war and enact laws to support children and the family. Macphail said in 1925:

Whereas men naturally place business values, economic values, first, we women naturally place the emphasis on human values. So I wish to push human values to the forefront of politics. I believe this to be the fundamental effect of the political enfranchisement of women.

Still, for Macphail, the fight for women's rights was part of the larger fight for the rights and dignity of all disadvantaged people in society.

One of the most compelling examples of Macphail's commitment to human dignity was her fight for prisoners' rights; a fight which spanned her entire political career. Her battle for prison reform began in the 1920s but became a public issue only after the riots at Kingston penitentiary in 1932. Canada's prison population had been rising steadily, partly due to the imprisonment of political prisoners. A series of prison riots finally culminated in October 1932 with a sizable riot at Kingston. The incident became a national issue and a political embarrassment when it became known that shots had been fired into the cell of Communist Party leader Tim Buck (who ostensibly was not involved in the rioting). There was already some question as to whether Buck deserved to be incarcerated; to many, his only crime was his persistence in expressing his Communist beliefs. To end the riot, it was agreed that the rioters would be tried in criminal court rather than being punished by the warden. The subsequent trial brought to public attention the cruel and degrading conditions within Canada's prisons. The guards were untrained and administering corporal punishment according to personal likes and dislikes. Prisoners were not allowed to talk to one another and

Agnes
Macphail

were often locked in their cells for long periods. According to the press, one prisoner had apparently been in solitary confinement for 23 years. In the face of public outcry against this cruelty, Macphail placed a motion before the House that a public inquiry be held into prisons, their role and the sources of crime. Although the government did not immediately respond to her request, she became the leader of a movement to reform Canada's prisons.

From 1934 to 1936, Macphail maintained pressure on the government. She believed that the prison system should not just incarcerate

criminals but should reform them. Finally, in 1935, the government agreed to appoint a royal commission into prison conditions. The commission's report of 1938 proposed sweeping reforms, many of which had been previously advocated by Macphail. Although it took years for the reforms to be implemented, she was undoubtedly instrumental in their eventual success. For her efforts, she was admired greatly by the country's reformers and prisoners.

Macphail's concern for human rights and dignity went through a transformation during these years. Earlier, she had completely rejected socialism. This was common among farmers who firmly supported the principle of private property and, thus, felt threatened by socialism. Over the years, however, Macphail embraced a form of moderate socialism. While still committed to private property, she gradually came to believe that society needed greater government intervention in order to secure the dignity and rights of all people. She supported motions for better old-age pensions, government health insurance, and the nationalization of some critical industries such as insurance. While initially Macphail believed that less government would be better for all, the depression years led her to the conviction that government was necessary to force equalization within society, in order to ensure social justice.

Consequently, she was an instrumental figure in the creation of Canada's Social Democratic Party (which became the New Democratic Party). While believing that a greater role for government was necessary, she, like many reformers, believed that the two main parties would never institute reforms because of their alliance to big business. Thus, she was a delegate at the founding convention of the Cooperative Commonwealth Federation (CCF). A loose coalition of Canada's farmer, labor, and socialist groups, the new party accepted a platform based on socialist and reform principles. Macphail brought the UFO into affiliation with the new organization and tried to unify farmers and workers, believing that only through cooperation could they achieve their goals. In the federal Parliament, Macphail generally voted with the CCF members, although she was officially an independent (since the UFO had left federal politics).

Concern for social reform inevitably led to an interest in international affairs. Like many social democrats, Macphail believed that peace was necessary to ensure social justice. In Parliament, she spoke out frequently on foreign affairs and was an active member of the Women's International League. Eventually these activities led to her appointment in 1929 to the League of Nations as Canada's first woman delegate. At the League conferences, Macphail's stubborn determination and feminism surfaced. She refused to accept an appointment to the committee on women and children, which was an unimportant body reserved solely for women. Instead, she managed to secure a position as the first woman on the important and active disarmament committee. For her performance on this committee, she received widespread, international praise.

By the 1930s, Macphail's course had been set. Politics had become her chosen career, but it was not her only public activity. International peace, the farmers' movement, and social reform kept her involved in groups and activities outside of politics. For example, she was an active member in the campaign to create an effective cooperative system for farmers. Macphail also became a popular public speaker. When Parliament was not in session, she went on extensive speaking tours throughout Canada and the United States. This emphasis on a public career may have led to her decision to remain single, for it was extremely difficult to be both a wife and a career woman during the 1920s and 1930s. Even so, Macphail had several significant relationships during her life. As a young woman, she dated regularly, eventually becoming engaged to a young man named Robert Tucker. He enlisted and went overseas during World War I. Though he returned at war's end, the relationship was over. During the early 1930s, she became involved with a fellow MP, Robert Gardiner. In many ways, they held similar views. He was the leader of the Independent group in Parliament and president of the United Farmers of Alberta. However, around 1935, Macphail broke off the relationship.

After the initial election victory in 1921, Macphail won four successive victories, remaining the representative for Southeast Grey until 1940. During those years, she managed to remain responsive to her constituents' concerns in a time of crisis and change. The election of 1940 was different. Concentrating on farm issues, Macphail failed to realize that the primary concern of her constituents was the war. When the polls were counted, the result was a resounding defeat. She placed third behind her two contenders.

At first, she was devastated. Politics had become her life, and suddenly, at 50 years old, she had to find a new career and a new means of supporting herself. Although politics had provided a good income, Macphail had never been a saver, and she tended to give generously to charitable causes. As well, in 1940, there were no pensions for MPs. Eventually, she became involved in a number of pursuits, such as organizational work for the CCF and writing a farm column for the *Globe and Mail*. Politics was her first love, however, and when the opportunity arose to run for the CCF in the Ontario provincial election, Macphail accepted.

The 1943 election was an astounding victory for the CCF. The party won 34 seats, including Macphail's riding of York East. This victory made Macphail and another woman the first female MPPs (members of provincial parliament) in the Ontario legislature. Although the Conservative Party formed the government, it had only four more seats than the CCF, giving the CCF substantial influence. Generally, Macphail did not like provincial politics because it seemed unimportant compared to the national level. Her first session in the Ontario legislature did not allow her much time to adjust. Another election in 1945 resulted in a reversal for the CCF and defeat for Macphail. The defeat was brief, however, for she won back her seat in the 1948 election.

Once again, Macphail threw herself into reform causes. In particular, she focused on the concerns of the aged and of women workers. Annoyed by the slow pace of reform, she supported issues directed towards improving old-age pensions and "equal pay" for women workers. Ostensibly successful when the government introduced "equal pay" legislation in 1951, Macphail was disappointed and critical as she realized that the act, as written, would be completely ineffective. Her ability to reform Ontario was dwindling. Throughout the Western world, reform sentiment began to die in the face of the cold war. In the 1951 election, the CCF and Macphail were defeated once more.

Following this, Macphail decided to retire. A modest inheritance and an annuity allowed a small degree of comfort and entertainment. Retirement, however, did not mean inactivity. A vigorous social schedule and allegiance to various reform groups kept her involved and busy. In 1952, she accompanied friends on a trip to Scotland, the home of her ancestors. But Agnes Macphail's health deteriorated rapidly after her retirement, and she suffered a cerebral hemorrhage in 1952. A heart attack two years later resulted in hospitalization and eventual death on February 13, 1954, at the age of 63.

In 1955, a bust of Agnes Macphail was unveiled in her honor in the federal Parliament. Liberal MP Chubby Power, who had served with Macphail for many years, summed up her significance. Her importance, he said, did not stem only from the fact that she was the first female member of Parliament, or from her many other "firsts" as a woman. Rather, said Power, the "respect she won" and the "influence she played on Canada's national life" stemmed from "personal qualities of intelligence, courage, and unselfish industry."

SOURCES:

Crowley, Terry. *Agnes Macphail and the Politics of Equality.* James Lorimer, 1990.

Stewart, Margaret, and Doris French. *Ask No Quarter: A Biography of Agnes Macphail.* Longmans, Green, 1959.

SUGGESTED READING:

Pennington, Doris. *Agnes Macphail, Reformer: Canada's First Female M.P.* Simon & Pierre, 1989.

Catherine Briggs, Ph.D. candidate,
University of Waterloo, Waterloo, Ontario, Canada

Macpherson, Jeanie (c. 1884–1946)

American screenwriter, actress, and director. Born in Boston, Massachusetts, around 1884 (differing sources give birth date as early as 1878 and as late as 1897); died in 1946.

Filmography as actress: Mr. Jones at the Ball *(1908);* Mrs. Jones Entertains *(1909);* A Corner in Wheat *(1909);* Winning Back His Love *(1910);* Fisher Folks *(1911);* Enoch Arden *(1911);* The Outlaw Reforms *(1914);* The Merchant of Venice *(1914);* Rose of the Rancho *(1914);* The Ghost Breaker *(1914);* The Girl of the Golden West *(1915);* Carmen *(1915).*

Filmography as screenwriter: The Captive *(1915, also acted);* Chimmie Fadden Out West *(1915);* The Cheat *(1915);* The Golden Chance *(1916);* The Trail of the Lonesome Pine *(1916);* The Heart of Nora Flynn *(1916);* The Love Mask *(1916);* The Dream Girl *(1916);* Joan the Woman *(1916);* A Romance of the Redwoods *(1917);* The Little American *(1917);* The Woman God Forgot *(1917);* The Devil-Stone *(1917);* The Whispering Chorus *(1918);* Old Wives for New *(1918);* Till I Come Back to You *(1918);* Don't Change Your Husband *(1919);* For Better for Worse *(1919);* Male and Female *(1919);* Something to Think About *(1920);* Forbidden Fruit *(1921);* The Affairs of Anatol *(1921);* Saturday Night *(1922);* Manslaughter *(1922);* Adam's Rib *(1923);* The Ten Commandments *(1923);* Triumph *(1924);* The Golden Bed *(1925);* The Road to Yesterday *(1925);* Red Dice *(1926);* Young April *(1926);* The King of Kings *(1927);* The Godless Girl *(1929);* Dynamite *(1929);* Madam Satan *(1930);* Fra Diavolo *(1933);* The Plainsman *(research story material only, 1937);* The Buccaneer *(adaptation only, 1942);* Reap the Wild Wind *(co-adaptation only, 1942).*

A pioneer in the movie industry, Jeanie Macpherson was one of the first women to become a screenwriter and director. Born in Boston, Massachusetts, around 1884, she was initially a dancer and stage performer, then began acting in films in 1908, appealing directly to D.W. Griffith for her first role. She later became a lead actress for the newly formed Universal Studio, where she also directed and wrote many two-reelers. Around 1915, she began screen writing exclusively, eventually becoming a screenwriter for the legendary Cecil B. De Mille. Over the course of their 27-year relationship, she worked with De Mille on most of his silent films.

Their early collaboration on the classic *Joan of Arc story, *Joan the Woman* (1916), provides an good example of how the two merged their very different approaches. While De Mille provided the huge framework for the story, consisting of large-scale sets and hundreds of extras, Macpherson crafted a simple human drama characterizing Joan as a frightened young girl with whom the audience could easily identify. The small story played out against the huge backdrop became a winning combination. During the early 1920s, the team also produced a series of social dramas, including *Something to Think About*, *The Affairs of Anatol*, and *Adam's Rib*, based on their shared belief that although people have numerous weaknesses, they can learn from their mistakes and become stronger in the process.

In addition to her film career, Macpherson was also an aviator, and apparently the only woman to pilot a plane for the noted stunt flyer, Lieutenant Locklear.

SOURCES:
Acker, Ally. *Reel Women*. NY: Continuum, 1991.
Katz, Ephraim. *The Film Encyclopedia*. NY: Harper-Collins, 1994.

Barbara Morgan,
Melrose, Massachusetts

Macquarie, Elizabeth (1778–1835)

Scottish diarist who authored Diary of Journey from England to New South Wales 1809. *Born Elizabeth Campbell in 1778 in Airds, Scotland; died in 1835 in Scotland; daughter of John Campbell; married Lachlan Macquarie (1762–1824, governor of New South Wales in Australia [1809–1821]), before 1809.*

Born in 1778, Elizabeth Macquarie was raised and well educated in Scotland before becoming the second wife of Lachlan Macquarie sometime before 1809. A career military man who had served with the British army in Canada, America, Egypt, and India, Lachlan was in 1809 appointed governor of New South Wales in Australia. Elizabeth Macquarie accompanied her husband on the trip to his new posting and recorded the journey in a volume entitled *Diary of Journey from England to New South Wales 1809*. New South Wales had been established by Britain as a penal colony in 1788, and the appointment of the new governor was the result of what is known as the Rum Rebellion (fomented by officers posted to control the colony's convicts) against the previous governor. The Mac-

quaries were therefore entering into a delicate situation, and from the outset Elizabeth Macquarie proved a valuable partner to her husband.

She counseled him on ticklish matters of state and supported him vigorously in disputes he had with a variety of factions in New South Wales. Governor Macquarie was a strong proponent of the convicts, and his long term in office, generally acknowledged as one of the most successful in that nation's early history, saw the struggle between the "emancipists," freed or pardoned ex-convicts who remained in the colony, and the "exclusionists," who were generally wealthy settlers (or squatters) or officers seeking to stake their claims to potentially valuable land. Elizabeth Macquarie displayed particular concern for women convicts, and was interested in ensuring that all people, including the colony's Aboriginal inhabitants, were treated equitably by the state. Earlier training in architecture also enabled her to supply valuable advice to Francis Greenway, her husband's architect.

New South Wales was officially opened to immigration by free settlers in 1820. (Convict transportation would cease 20 years later.) Lachlan Macquarie's governorship came to an end in 1821, and the couple left the continent the following year. They returned to the Macquarie family estate at Jarvisfield, Scotland, where he died in 1824. Much of what is known of his final years has been gleaned from letters written by Elizabeth Macquarie to friends back in New South Wales. A biography, *Elizabeth Macquarie*, was published by **Lysbeth Cohen** in 1979, and *No Barrier*, a historical novel by *Eleanor Dark** published in 1953, features her as a character. Biographies of her husband, including *Macquarie's World* by *Marjorie Barnard** and *Lachlan Macquarie* by Malcolm Ellis, also include details of her life. A number of natural and man-made landmarks in and around Sydney, Australia, bear the names of either Elizabeth Macquarie or her husband, including a prominence overlooking Sydney Harbor that is called Mrs. Macquarie's Chair.

SOURCES:
The Oxford Encyclopedia of World History. Oxford and NY: Oxford University Press, 1998.
Wilde, William H., Joy Hooton, and Barry Andrews. *The Oxford Companion to Australian Literature*. Melbourne: Oxford, 1985.

Don Amerman,
freelance writer, Saylorsburg, Pennsylvania

Macrina (327–379)

Byzantine composer, singer, teacher, and saint who was the founder of a religious community for women in the Eastern Church. Name variations: Makrina.

Born in Caesarea (modern-day Kayseri), capital of Cappadocia, in 327 CE; died in 379; one of ten children of Basil (a distinguished lawyer and professor of rhetoric in Cappadocia) and Emmelia; sister of Peter, bishop of Sebaste, Basil the Great (329–379), bishop of Caesarea, whose authority extended over 11 provinces of Asia Minor, and Gregory of Nyssa (335–387), one of the fathers of the Eastern Church.

The family of Macrina played a leading role in Christianity. Her grandmother **Macrina the Elder**, who tended the chapel at Annesi, was influenced by Gregory the Illuminator, while her grandfather was a Christian of property. During the persecutions by Galerius and Maximianus, these same grandparents had to flee into the forests of Pontus, where they lived for seven years.

Macrina was born in Caesarea (modern-day Kayseri), the capital of Cappadocia, in 327, one of ten children of Basil, a distinguished lawyer and professor of rhetoric in Cappadocia, and **Emmelia**. Growing up in a household that has been described as "a nursery for bishops and saints," Macrina and her brothers were strong supporters of orthodox Christianity as delineated by the Nicene Creed. Along with Macrina, three of the brothers were later declared saints. At 12, when Macrina's chosen fiancé died, she renounced all future suitors.

Eventually, she became the deaconess of the church of St. Sophia in Byzantium. A woman of vivid imagination and what has been described as "terrifying" selflessness, she had enormous influence over her brothers, because positions of leadership in the early church were familiar to her. She accused a young Basil (the Great), newly offered the chair of rhetoric at the University of Caesarea, of being "puffed up beyond measure with the pride of oratory." That, along with the death of their younger brother Naucratius in a hunting accident, caused Basil to renounce his chair and turn to his sister, learning from her "the secret of renunciation and Christian virtue which had eluded him."

With Naucratius' death, Macrina's mother Emmelia was plunged into grief. While comforting her, Macrina also convinced her mother to treat the slave girls as equals, close the house, and move with her to the family estate at Annesi in the mountains of Pontus on the edge of the Iris River. There, Macrina founded a small community of religious women, taught the scriptures, and established a hospital. But renunciation was foremost—renunciation of wealth, rank, and all pleasures of the body. All thoughts must be of God. "It was the beginning of monasticism,"

writes Robert Payne in *The Fathers of the Eastern Church*, "and Macrina was its true founder. Women, not men, were the first monks."

Following her mother's death, Macrina raised and educated her younger brother Peter who became bishop of Sebaste. But Macrina owes her fame to another brother, Gregory of Nyssa. The opposite of Basil, who was a gifted ruler, Gregory was a soft, tender, joyful, compassionate man who leaned toward mysticism. As a child, he held no interest in the intense Christianity of his mother. Appointed by Basil to the bishopric of Nyssa, Gregory unwillingly administered to his diocese. But when Basil died in 379, Gregory felt the blow. A few months later, his beloved sister Macrina was dying at Annesi. Hastening to her, he was led into her cell, where he found her lying on the floor, with boards for a pillow, choking with asthma. He hardly recognized her. After leaving her side to take refreshment, Gregory returned to find that Macrina had regained some strength. Together, they spoke not of their youth but of the nature of death, the soul, and the Resurrection. Macrina urged her brother to play an expanded role in the spread of Christianity. Gregory explored this conversation at length in *Concerning the Soul and the Resurrection*. The chronicler of the family, Gregory wrote "enchantingly of divine things," notes Payne, and "just as enchantingly about the nature of man, which he was continually celebrating." Gregory spoke in poetic and reasoned terms, at times "putting the words into the mouth of his sister Macrina as she lay dying in a blaze of philosophy." In Gregory's treatise, Macrina appears sometimes under her own name, sometimes under the name "teacher." Writes Payne, "He was to say from her dying lips he learned more than anyone else ever taught him."

According to Gregory, the singing of songs never ceased night or day in the convent Macrina founded, and she wrote both the text and music of many songs performed there. Having learned the art of psalm singing from her mother, she wanted music to be a central part of her religious house.

SOURCES:

Cohen, Aaron I. *International Encyclopedia of Women Composers*. 2 vols. NY: Books & Music (USA), 1987.

Deen, Edith. *Great Women of the Christian Faith*. Harper, 1976.

Payne, Robert. *The Fathers of the Eastern Church*. Dorset, 1989.

Macruari, Amy (fl. 1300s)

Lady of the Isles. Flourished in the 1300s; daughter of Roderick Macruari; married John Macdonald, first

Lord of the Isles; children: John Macdonald; Godfrey Macdonald, lord of Uist; Ronald Macdonald.

Macurdy, Grace Harriet

(1866–1946)

American Greek scholar and teacher. Born Grace Harriet Macurdy on September 15, 1866, in Robbinston, Maine; died on October 23, 1946, in Poughkeepsie, New York; daughter and one of at least three children of Simon Angus Macurdy (a carpenter) and Rebecca Bradford (Thomson) Macurdy; attended high school in Watertown, Massachusetts; graduated from the Society for the Collegiate Instruction of Women (later Radcliffe College), in 1888; studied at the University of Berlin, 1899–1900; Columbia University, Ph.D., 1903.

A respected Greek scholar and a long-time professor at Vassar College, Grace Macurdy devoted her life to researching and teaching in her chosen field. The daughter of a carpenter, she was born in 1866 in Robbinston, Maine, and attended high school in Watertown, Massachusetts, where the family moved before she was ten. She graduated from the Society for the Collegiate Instruction of Women (later Radcliffe College) in 1888, and immediately began her teaching career at Cambridge School for Girls. Macurdy was appointed instructor of Greek at Vassar College in 1893, and remained there until her retirement in 1937.

During the early years of her career, Macurdy continued her own education, spending a year at the University of Berlin on a fellowship from the Woman's Education Association of Boston, and receiving her Ph.D. degree from Columbia University in 1903, after which she was promoted to associate professor. Her further advancement at Vassar was slowed by her frequent clashes with *Abby Leach, who was the chair of the classics department until her death in 1918. Macurdy became a full professor in 1916 and was appointed chair of the department in 1920, a post she held until her retirement. For ten years (1908–18), she also taught summer courses in Greek language and literature at Columbia University, before she began using her summers to travel abroad, carrying on research at the British Museum and in Greece, France, Italy, and Austria.

Macurdy's scholarly writings included extensive contributions to both American and British classical journals, and five books: *The Chronology of the Extant Plays of Euripides* (her doctoral dissertation, 1905), *Troy and Paconia* (1925), *Hellenistic Queens* (1932), *Vassal-Queens and Some Contemporary Women in the Roman Empire* (1937), and *The Quality of Mercy* (1940), a study of Greek literature written to commemorate Vassar's 75th anniversary. Much of Macurdy's written work reflects her deep interest in the achievements of women and in their battle through the ages for political and social equity. As might be expected, she was an ardent supporter of the suffrage movement of her own day.

Characterized as outspoken and a tad outrageous, Macurdy was hardly the stereotypical college professor. Dubbed "the Mad Queen" because of her wild hair and oversized hats, she was adored by her students who responded to her enthusiastic teaching methods by working particularly hard in her classes. Aside from her nemesis Abby Leach, Macurdy was also much loved by the entire Vassar community and beyond. When she retired, Vassar's president, Henry MacCracken, spoke of "her humor, her gaiety, and her eloquence," and her perpetual "spirit of youth."

Grace Macurdy continued to live at the college following her retirement, pursuing her research and occasionally lecturing, despite encroaching deafness. During World War II, she worked for Greek and British relief, and was awarded the British King's Medal in 1946. She died of cancer at the age of 80.

SOURCES:

James, Edward T., ed. *Notable American Women 1607–1950.* Cambridge, MA: The Belknap Press of Harvard University Press, 1971.

Barbara Morgan,
Melrose, Massachusetts

Macy, Anne Sullivan (1866–1936).

See Keller, Helen for sidebar.

Madame Mère (1750–1836).

See Bonaparte, Letizia.

Madame Royale.

See Jeanne of Nemours (d. 1724).
See Marie Thérèse Charlotte (1778–1851).

Madame Sans-Gêne (fl. 1764–after 1820).

See Lefebvre, Catherine.

Maddalena.

Variant of Magdalena.

Maddalena of Canossa

(1774–1833)

Saint. Name variations: Magdalena. Born in Verona in 1774; died in 1833.

Maddalena of Canossa founded the congregation of the Daughters of Charity, an order that taught the peasants and cared for the sick. As a young girl, she had caught the eye of Napoleon; her demeanor reminded him of an angel. Maddalena's feast day is April 10.

Maddern, Minnie (1865–1932).
See Fiske, Minnie Maddern.

Madelberte (fl. 7th c.)
Saint and abbess. Name variations: Madelberta. Flourished in the 7th century; daughter of St. Vincent Madelgaire and St. Wandru (d. 688); sister of Aldetrude, abbess of Maubeuge.

Madelberte, the daughter of St. *Wandru and St. Vincent Madelgaire, succeeded her sister Aldetrude as abbess of Maubeuge. The convent had been founded by her aunt Saint *Aldegund at the beginning of the 7th century. Madelberte's feast day is September 7.

Madeleine (1914–1944).
See Khan, Noor Inayat.

Madeleine (b. 1982)
*Duchess of Halsingland and Gastrikland. Name variations: Madeleine Bernadotte. Born on June 10, 1982; daughter of *Silvia Sommerlath (1943—) and Carl XVI Gustavus (b. 1946), king of Sweden (r. 1973—).*

Madeleine de la Tour d'Auvergne (1501–1519)
*Duchess of Urbino and mother of Catherine de Medici. Name variations: Madeleine de Medici; Madeleine of Auvergne; Madeline of Auvergne. Born in 1501; died of puerperal fever on April 28, 1519, three days after the birth of her only child; daughter of John de la Tour, count of Auvergne, and *Jane of Bourbon-Vendome (d. 1511); sister of *Anne de la Tour (c. 1496–1524); married Lorenzo de Medici, duke of Urbino, on June 13, 1518 (also died in 1519); children: *Catherine de Medici (1519–1589).*

Madeleine de Saint-Nectaire (fl. 1575)
French soldier. Name variations: Comtesse de Miremont; Countess of Miremont. Flourished around 1575.

The leader of a company of 60 Huguenot cavaliers, Madeleine de Saint-Nectaire distinguished herself during the French civil wars by defending her château at Miremont, in the Limousin, against Catholic invasion. One of her most celebrated battles occurred in 1575, when the governor of the province laid siege to her château, attacking with 15,000 soldiers on foot and 50 on horseback. Madeleine rode out with her small force and defeated the governor. Finding that the enemy had retreated into her own fortress, she rode to a neighboring town, rallied a band of supporters and rode back to vanquish the intruders. Madeleine's renown was such that her enemy Henry IV once quipped: "If I were not King, I would like to be Mlle. de Saint-Nectaire!"

Madeleine of Anhalt-Zerbst (1679–1740)
*Duchess of Saxe-Gotha-Altenburg. Name variations: Magdalena Augusta of Anhalt-Zerbst. Born Madeleine Augusta on October 13, 1679; died on October 11, 1740; daughter of Charles William (b. 1652), prince of Anhalt-Zerbst, and Sophie of Saxe-Weissenfels (b. 1654); married Frederick II, duke of Saxe-Gotha-Altenburg; children: Frederick III, duke of Saxe-Gotha (b. 1699); Wilhelm or William, duke of Saxe-Gotha (b. 1701); John August (b. 1704); *Augusta of Saxe-Gotha (1719–1772).*

Madeleine of Auvergne (1501–1519).
See Madeleine de la Tour d'Auvergne.

Madeleine of France (1443–1486)
*Queen of Hungary and Bohemia. Name variations: Madeleine de France; Magdalen. Born in 1443; died in 1486; daughter of Charles VII the Victorious (1403–1461), king of France (r. 1422–1461), and *Marie of Anjou (1404–1463); married Ladislas V (or VI) Posthumus (1440–1457), king of Hungary (r. 1444–1457) and Bohemia (r. 1452); married Gaston de Foix, vicomte de Castelbon and prince of Viane or Viana; children: (second marriage) Francis, king of Navarre; *Catherine de Foix (c. 1470–1517); possibly *Anne de Foix (fl. 1480–1500).*

Madeleine of France (1520–1537).
See Margaret Tudor for sidebar.

Madeleine Sophie Barat (1779–1865).
See Barat, Madeleine Sophie.

Madeleva, Sister Mary (1887–1964)

American religious educator, poet, and college administrator who was president of St. Mary's College, Notre Dame, for 26 years. Name variations: Sister Madeleva; Mary Evaline Wolff; Sister Madeleva Wolff. Born Mary Evaline Wolff on May 24, 1887, in Cumberland, Wisconsin; died on July 25, 1964, in Boston, Massachusetts; daughter of August Wolff (a harness maker) and Lucy (Arntz) Wolff; St. Mary's College, B.A., 1909, M.A., 1918; University of California at Berkeley, Ph.D., 1925; post-graduate study at Oxford University, 1933–34.

Was first woman religious to receive a doctorate from Berkeley; served as first dean and president of College of St. Mary-of-the-Wasatch in Salt Lake City, Utah (1925–33); was president of St. Mary's College, Notre Dame (1934–1961).

Selected writings: Knights Errant and Other Poems *(1923);* Chaucer's Nuns and Other Essays *(1925);* Penelope and Other Poems *(1927);* A Question of Lovers and Other Poems *(1935);* The Happy Christmas Wind *(1936);* Gates and Other Poems *(1938);* Four Girls *(1941);* Lost Language and Other Essays *(1951);* My First Seventy Years *(1959);* The Last Four Things *(1959);* Conversations with Cassandra *(1961).*

Born Mary Evaline Wolff in Cumberland, Wisconsin, in 1887, Sister Mary Madeleva had an early appreciation for education. Her mother had been a schoolteacher prior to her marriage and her father, a skilled harness maker, was also the mayor of Cumberland. Both parents encouraged her to continue her education through college. She enrolled in the University of Wisconsin at Madison with plans to specialize in mathematics. The young woman's plans were diverted, however, when she transferred to St. Mary's College at Notre Dame in Indiana in 1906. While there, she developed a friendship with Sister **Rita Heffernan** who encouraged her to write poetry and was instrumental in steering her towards a religious vocation. In 1908, she entered the novitiate of the Holy Cross Sisters who governed St. Mary's. At this time, she took the name Sister Mary Madeleva.

In 1909, Sister Mary Madeleva received her B.A. from St. Mary's and embarked on a lifelong quest to educate women. She continued her own education, receiving an M.A. in 1918. She was the principal of Sacred Heart Academy in Ogden, Utah, from 1919 to 1922, and then the principal of Holy Rosary Academy in Woodland, California, from 1922 to 1924. While at Holy Rosary, she studied at the University of California at Berkeley and, in 1925, became the first woman religious to receive a doctorate from Berkeley.

Sister Mary Madeleva served as college president of the College of St. Mary's-of-the-Wasatch in Salt Lake City from 1925 to 1933 and at Notre Dame's St. Mary's College from 1934 until 1961. While president at St. Mary's College, she saw enrollment and faculty size triple. Her desire to improve the educational opportunities for religious women was fulfilled when the graduate school of sacred theology—the first of its kind for women—was established in 1944. At a time when Catholic universities accepted only men for graduate study in theology, the new program at St. Mary's prepared women to teach religion in colleges. By 1969, when St. Mary's closed its program because other Catholic universities, including Notre Dame, began allowing women to study theology at the graduate level, 76 doctorates and over 300 master's degrees had been awarded.

Another important improvement in the education of women instigated by Sister Mary Madeleva came as a result of a panel she led at the 1949 National Catholic Education Association (NCEA). Papers presented at the panel led directly to a reformation of novitiate training programs in the 1950s, ensuring that female novices (who were often barely out of their teens) were not immediately charged with apostolic work but first could, like their male counterparts in Catholic seminaries, achieve a higher education.

Sister Mary Madeleva's unrelenting drive to provide opportunities for higher education to women religious caused her to suffer from chronic insomnia and exhaustion, and she frequently found solace from her health problems by writing poetry. In 1923, she published her first book, *Knights Errant and Other Poems.* Her short poems often dealt with religious themes drawn from her own experiences, in addition to the more general themes of beauty, love, and serenity. Over almost four decades, she published over 200 poems, essays, and autobiographies, collected in such books as *Chaucer's Nuns and Other Essays* (1925), *Penelope and Other Poems* (1927), *A Question of Lovers and Other Poems* (1935), *The Happy Christmas Wind* (1936), *Gates and Other Poems* (1938), *Selected Poems* (1939), *Four Girls* (1941), *Lost Language and Other Essays* (1951), *My First Seventy Years* (1959), *The Last Four Things* (1959), and *Conversations with Cassandra* (1961).

Sister Mary Madeleva served as vice president of the Indiana Conference on Higher Education and Indiana director of the National Confer-

Sister
Mary
Madeleva

ence of Christians and Jews, was a member of the Catholic Commission on Intellectual and Cultural Affairs, and was the president of the Catholic Poetry Society of America. Her awards included seven honorary degrees, the Siena Medal, the Cum Laude Poets' Corner Medal, and the Campion Award of the Catholic Book Club (1959).

Although she officially retired in 1961, Sister Mary Madeleva continued a rigorous schedule of speaking engagements, acted as a consultant to her successor at St. Mary's, and continued to write. Her bouts with insomnia and exhaustion did not lessen, and on July 25, 1964, she died of septicemia after undergoing surgery for a non-malignant condition. She was buried at St. Mary's at Notre Dame.

SOURCES:

Sicherman, Barbara, and Carol Hurd Green. *Notable American Women: The Modern Period: A Biographical Dictionary.* Cambridge, MA: The Belknap Press of Harvard University, 1980.

Judith C. Reveal,
freelance writer, Greensboro, Maryland

Madeline.

Variant of Madeleine.

Mademoiselle, La Grande (1627–1693).

See Montpensier, Anne Marie Louise d'Orleans, duchess de.

Madge.

Variant of Margaret.

Madgett, Naomi Long (1923—)

African-American poet, professor, publisher, and editor. Name variations: Naomi Witherspoon; Naomi Cornelia Long. Born Naomi Cornelia Long on July 5, 1923, in Norfolk, Virginia; daughter of Clarence Marcellus Long (a minister) and Maude (Hilton) Long (a teacher); Virginia State College, B.A., 1945; Wayne State University, M.Ed., 1956; International Institute for Advanced Studies, Ph.D., 1980; married Julian F. Witherspoon, in 1946 (divorced 1949); married William Harold Madgett, in 1954 (divorced 1960); married Leonard Patton Andrews, in 1972 (died 1996); children: (first marriage) Jill Witherspoon (b. 1947).

Naomi Long Madgett

Selected writings: Songs of a Phantom Nightingale *(1941);* One and the Many *(1956);* Star by Star *(1965);* Pink Ladies in the Afternoon: New Poems *(1972);* Exits and Entrances *(1978);* Octavia and Other Poems *(1988);* Remembrances of Spring: Collected Early Poems *(1993).*

The daughter of Clarence and **Maude Long**, Naomi Long Madgett was born on July 5, 1923, in Norfolk, Virginia, and experienced a lonely childhood in an intensely religious home. Her father's extensive library offered her refuge in such diverse literature as *Aesop's Fables* and Robert T. Kerlin's *Negro Poets and Their Poems*, and she found solace in the dissimilar works of Alfred, Lord Tennyson and Langston Hughes, two poets she credits for having a strong influence on her writing.

In addition to reading poetry, she also began writing it at an early age, expressing herself in verse. Madgett spent her childhood in East Orange, New Jersey, before moving with her family to St. Louis, Missouri, in 1937. She later identified the consequent transfer from an integrated high school to an all-black one as a positive turning point in her life. In an environment free from institutional racism, she began to recognize the achievements of African-Americans. In 1941, she published *Songs of a Phantom Nightingale*, a collection of poems she had written in high school. These poems reflect her lonely childhood and a growing awareness of her black heritage. Reviewers criticized her style for its youthful imitation of romantic poetry, but recognized her innovations with language and technique.

In 1945, Madgett earned a B.A. from Virginia State College and began graduate studies at New York University; however, she withdrew early in her studies to marry Julian F. Witherspoon in 1946. They moved to Detroit, where Madgett worked as a reporter and copyreader for an African-American weekly, *The Michigan Chronicle*. In 1947, she gave birth to their daughter Jill, and two years later she and Witherspoon divorced. She married her second husband, William Madgett, in 1954, and continued to use his last name after that marriage also ended in divorce. She began teaching in the Detroit school system in 1955 and earned a master's degree in education at Wayne State University in 1956. Madgett later earned a Ph.D. in 1980, from the International Institute for Advanced Studies (Greenwich University).

The long interval after her first publication ended in 1956, when Madgett published her second collection of poems, *One and the Many.*

Documenting her life to the mid-1950s, these poems covered a wide variety of feelings, from her sense of satisfaction as a mother to her sense of life passing and leaving her unfulfilled. The poems express feelings of entrapment as a homemaker, and the heartbreak of a failed love. In *One and the Many*, Madgett also began to deepen her expression of the African-American experience, although the nine poems dealing with this subject do not appear until the end of the book. One of her most important poems, "Refugee," appeared in this collection, and had been included by Langston Hughes and Arna Bontemps in their anthology *The Poetry of the Negro: 1746–1949* (1949).

Madgett's third collection of poems, *Star by Star* (1965), further explored the African-American experience. In it, the poet emphasized the beauty of the black race and the often crippling effects of the white-black relationship on black America. At this time Madgett was becoming increasingly concerned that black children were losing touch with many of their best literary representatives, such as Langston Hughes, and in the summer of 1965 she taught the first African-American literature course offered in the Detroit school system. She spent that school year at Oakland University as a Mott fellow and returned to Detroit to teach her African-American literature class as a regular part of the curriculum. Resigning from the public schools in 1968, Madgett accepted an assistant professorship at Eastern Michigan University, where she would remain until her retirement as professor emeritus in 1984.

Her fourth book of poems, *Pink Ladies in the Afternoon: New Poems*, was published in 1972. In the volume, she reflects upon her life in the 1960s and 1970s; her dual career, middle age, and the ongoing awareness of her heritage. Her love poems in this series express a quiet dignity. Madgett and her third husband, Leonard P. Andrews, also took over the Lotus Press in Detroit (which had published three of her collections) that year. The Lotus Press has since gone on to publish such writers as **Gayl Jones**, **Paulette White**, and Ray Fleming. *Exits and Entrances* (1978), her fifth collection, is presented in three sections: the first continues her autobiographical approach, the second her African-American themes, and the third contains her most recent poems to that time. A sixth collection of poetry, *Octavia and Other Poems* (1988), explores her deep family history, focusing on an aunt, **Octavia Cornelia Long**. The poems also extol the deep resolve of other family members and their efforts to make good lives for themselves and their families. In 1993, *Remembrances of Spring: Collected Early Poems* was published. In addition to her poetry collections, Madgett wrote *Deep Rivers* (a teachers' guide, 1974) and *A Student's Guide to Creative Writing* (1980), and edited *A Milestone Sampler: 15th Anniversary Anthology* (1988) and *Adam of Ifé: Black Women in Praise of Black Men* (1992).

Naomi Long Madgett has received many awards, including the **Esther R. Beer** Poetry Award from the National Writers Club for "Native" (1957); the **Josephine Nevins Keal** Development Fund Award (1979); the Robert Hayden Runagate Award and the Heritage House and Arts Achievement Award, both from Wayne State University (1985); the Creative Artist Award from the Michigan Council for the Arts (1987); the Creative Achievement Award from the College Language Association, for *Octavia and Other Poems* (1988); "In Her Lifetime" tribute from the Afrikan Poets Theater (1989); the Arts Foundation of Michigan literature award (1990); an honorary doctorate of literature from Siena Heights College (1991); the Award of Excellence from *Black Scholar* magazine (1992); the American Book Award and the Governor's Arts Award (both 1993); the Michigan State University American Arts Award (1994); and the George Kent award (1995). In 1993, the Hilton-Long Poetry Foundation began granting the annual Naomi Long Madgett Poetry Award in her honor.

SOURCES:

Contemporary Authors. Vol. 33–36. Revised. Detroit, MI: Gale Research.
Dictionary of Literary Biography. Vol. 76. Detroit, MI: Gale Research.

COLLECTIONS:

Special Collections Library at Fisk University, Nashville, Tennessee.

Judith C. Reveal,
freelance writer, Greensboro, Maryland

Madison, Cleo (1883–1964)

American silent-film actress and director. Born in 1883; died in Hollywood, California, in 1964.

One of the first women directors in the film industry; acted in and directed, or acted in only, at least 80 silent films, including Captain Kidd *(1913),* Shadows of Life *(1913),* Dolores D'Arada, Lady of Sorrow *(1914),* The Love Victorious *(1914),* Unjustly Accused *(1914),* The Trey O' Hearts *(1914),* Sealed Orders *(1914),* Alas and Alack *(1915),* A Woman's Debt *(1915),* Extravagance *(1915),* The Mystery Woman *(1915),* Her Bitter Cup *(1916),* The Severed Hand *(1916),* Priscilla's Prisoner *(1916),* Her Defiance *(1916),* A Soul Enslaved *(1916),* The Daring Chance

(1917), The Girl Who Lost *(1917),* The Romance of Tarzan *(1918),* The Great Radium Mystery *(1919),* The Price of Redemption *(1920),* The Lure of Youth *(1921),* The Dangerous Age *(1922),* Souls in Bondage *(1923),* The Roughneck *(1924),* Discontented Husbands *(1924).*

Born in 1883, Cleo Madison spent most of her life in show business, beginning as a vaudeville performer in her teens around the turn of the century. She made her vaudeville debut in the Midwest and spent a good deal of time performing in Bloomington, Illinois, not far from Peoria. The growing popularity of the "flickers," as motion pictures were known in the early years, lured Madison away from vaudeville and into the world of silent film. In 1913, at age 30, she began making films for Universal. A short time after her film debut, she became involved in serials, continuing stories told in short episodes, each of which ended with a cliffhanger that left the audience in doubt as to the survival of the hero or heroine, or of both. The reigning monarchs of the serial films at Universal were **Grace Cunard* and her partner, Francis Ford, brother of John Ford. In addition to her work in serials, Madison made a number of films with Lon

Cleo Madison

Chaney, who was later to become known the world over as "the man of a thousand faces."

In the early days of the silents, movies were generally made quickly, and so Madison had over a dozen films to her credit by the time she achieved stardom with a double role as twin sisters in the 1914 serial, *The Trey O' Hearts.* In the wake of the acclaim for her performance, the actress determined that her ultimate goal was to direct herself, therefore achieving near-total control of the productions in which she was involved. But Hollywood was not yet ready for a woman director, and she experienced rejection in her early attempts to gain that position.

Undaunted, Madison devised a relatively simple strategy. She would make life so miserable for directors that no one would be willing to work with her. Since Madison's temperament had already caused consternation for executives at Universal, she soon found herself in charge of her own production company. Before taking on the responsibility of writing, directing, and starring in a film, Madison first directed at least three films in which she did not appear. One of her earliest westerns was 1914's *Sealed Orders,* which was replete with roof-top chases and a fierce gun-fighting episode. She felt as comfortable directing a western as a romantic drama.

Madison, who felt women filmmakers were seriously needed, told *Moving Picture Weekly*:

> Every play in which women appear needs the feminine touch. **Lois Weber*'s productions are phenomenally successful, partly because her woman creations are true to the spirit of womanhood. I believe in doing most of the work before the camera is called into action. It should never be necessary, exception in the case of accident, to retake a scene.

Asked by reporters if she was intimidated by the responsibilities placed on a director, she replied: "Why should I be? I had seen men with less brains than I have getting away with it, and so I knew that I could direct if they'd give me the opportunity." Back in her vaudeville days in the Midwest, she had acted as the stage manager of the Cleo Madison Stock Company, which served as some preparation for the new duties she was assuming in Hollywood. She garnered the following backhanded compliment from an assistant cinematographer: "Cleo has taken up the methods of the best directors. . . . She's second to none. There isn't a director on the lot that's got the flow of language or can exhibit the temperament she can."

Her Bitter Cup, which Madison wrote, directed, and starred in, was one of the earliest films to take the women's suffrage movement as its theme. The film was released in 1916, as American women moved closer to winning their decades-long battle for the vote. A reviewer for *Photoplay*, in a breathless burst of benignancy, assessed the movie and Madison: "With the lovely but militant Cleo at their head, the suffragettes could capture the vote for their sex and smash down the opposition as easily as shooting fish in a bucket. She is so smart and businesslike that she makes most of the male population of Universal City look like debutantes when it comes right down to brass tacks and affairs."

Cleo Madison continued to direct herself in films until 1921, when a nervous breakdown forced her to take a hiatus. A year or two later, she returned to make a handful of films, the last of which was released in 1925, before fading from the scene altogether. She died in obscurity in 1964, but, through her work in silent films, left behind mute testimony that women could play a significant role behind the cameras in Hollywood. While still at the height of her fame in the early 1920s, she had remarked, "One of these days, men are going to get over the fool idea that women have no brains and quit getting insulted at the thought that a skirt-wearer can do their work quite as well as they can. And I don't believe that day is very far off."

SOURCES:

Acker, Ally. *Reel Women*. NY: Continuum, 1991.

Don Amerman,
freelance writer, Saylorsburg, Pennsylvania

Madison, Dolley Payne

(1768–1849)

American socialite who as first lady became a famous Washington hostess. Name variations: often spelled Dolly; Dorothea Payne Madison. Born Dolley Payne on May 20, 1768, in Guilford County, North Carolina; died in Washington, D.C., on July 12, 1849; daughter of John Payne (a planter and a businessman) and Mary (Coles) Payne; attended the Cedar Creek Meeting Society of Friends elementary school as a child; married John Todd, Jr., on January 7, 1790 (died, October 24, 1793); married James Madison (president of the United States, 1809–1817), on September 15, 1794 (died, June 28, 1836); children: (first marriage) John Payne Todd (b. February 29, 1792); William Temple Todd (1793–1793).

Payne family moved from North Carolina to Virginia (1769); moved to Philadelphia (1783); married John Todd, Jr. (January 7, 1790); son William Temple born (summer 1793) and died (autumn 1793); returned with husband James Madison to Virginia from Washington, D.C. (1797); moved to Washington, D.C. after James Madison became secretary of state (1801); became first lady when husband was inaugurated president (1809); rescued portrait of George Washington (August 24, 1814); returned to Virginia after James Madison's presidential term ended (1817); following husband's death, moved from Virginia to Washington, D.C. (1837); joined St. John's Church in Lafayette Square (1845); attended the laying of Washington Monument cornerstone (July 1848); attended President James K. Polk's farewell reception (February 7, 1849).

As the War of 1812 raged, Dolley Madison wrote to her sister at three o'clock in the afternoon, Wednesday, August 24, 1814, describing an event that would make her forever loved and admired. With the enemy closing in, prepared to torch the White House, and the sounds of battle within earshot, this courageous first lady steadfastly refused to flee until George Washington's portrait had been saved from destruction.

> Our kind friend, Mr. Carroll, has come to hasten my departure, and is in a very bad humour with me because I insist on waiting until the large picture of General Washington is secured, and it requires to be unscrewed from the wall. This process was found too tedious for these perilous moments; I have ordered the frame to be broken, and the canvas taken out; it is done,— and the precious portrait placed in the hands of two gentlemen from New York, for safe keeping.

Only then did she write, "And now, dear sister, I must leave this house, or the retreating army will make me a prisoner in it, by filling up the road I am directed to take. When I shall see or write you, or where I shall be tomorrow, I cannot tell!"

Although Dolley Payne Madison is remembered as a Virginian, she was born on May 20, 1768, in Guilford County, North Carolina. The following spring, she moved with her family to Little Bird Creek farm in Hanover County, Virginia. Six years later, her father purchased a more imposing plantation called Scotchtown where Dolley would live until her parents, John Payne and **Mary Coles Payne**, sold the property. Staunch Quakers, the Paynes both assumed leadership positions at the Cedar Creek Meeting of Friends. As conscientious Quakers, they believed that slavery was morally wrong; thus, when in 1782 Virginia legalized manumission, John and Mary Payne freed all their slaves. The following year, they moved to Philadelphia, Pennsylvania.

In Philadelphia, Dolley met and fell in love with a fellow Quaker, John Todd, Jr.; they married on January 7, 1790. In time, John Todd, five years older than Dolley, became a highly successful Philadelphia lawyer. On February 29, 1792, Dolley gave birth to a son, John Payne, named after Dolley's father, who passed away later that same year. In the summer of 1793, Dolley had a second son, William Temple, named in honor of one of her brothers.

About the time of William's birth, a yellow fever epidemic raged in Philadelphia. "The fever has assumed a most alarming appearance," wrote Dr. Benjamin Rush. "It not only mocks in most cases the power of medicine, but it has spread through several parts of the city remote from the spot where it originated." In the midst of the epidemic, John Todd, concerned that his wife and children be spared, moved his family out of the city to a place called Gray's Ferry, but John "like the honorable and good Quaker citizen that he was" felt compelled to return "to the plague-stricken city to do his duty." In Philadelphia, as John Todd battled the epidemic, he saw both of his parents die of the dreaded disease. When, on October 24, 1793, he returned to visit his own family, he was infected with yellow fever. As Dolley's mother Mary met him at the door, he gasped, "I feel the fever in my veins, but I must see her once more." A short time later, he died in his wife's arms. The plague would also claim Dolley's infant son, William Temple.

Following the death of her husband, Mary Cole Payne had taken in boarders, one of whom was Aaron Burr, who later became vice-president of the United States and in 1804 fatally wounded Alexander Hamilton in a duel at Weehawken, New Jersey. Dolley and Burr became good friends. Thus, when Dolley drew up a will following the death of her husband, she named Burr the sole guardian of her surviving son, now known as Payne Todd.

It was Aaron Burr who introduced Dolley to his friend James Madison, then serving as a congressman from Virginia in the U.S. House of Representatives. The courtship proceeded so smoothly that on September 15, 1794, Dolley and James Madison were wed at Harewood, the Virginia country estate where Dolley's sister **Lucy Payne Washington** and brother-in-law George S. Washington, the nephew of George Washington, lived. Dolley's marriage to a non-Quaker resulted in her expulsion from the Society of Friends. On December 12, 1794, the Society declared that she was no longer considered a member because "of her marriage with a person not in membership with us, before a hireling priest."

James Madison served in the House of Representatives until his term ended in March 1797. After the wedding, the Madisons therefore returned to the nation's capital, which at the time was Philadelphia. As the wife of a rather prominent public figure, Dolley quickly learned "the dress and ways of polite society" for she "was required to receive the great and small of the government and distinguished foreign visitors." Vice-president John Adams after one visit wrote to his wife ***Abigail Adams**, "Mrs. Madison is a fine woman, and her two sisters are equally so."

James Madison made his final public appearance as a member of the House at John Adams' presidential inauguration. It was also the last time that the Madisons saw George Washington. Katharine Anthony in her biography of Dolley Madison describes a crowd gazing "with awe" at Washington "clad as usual in black velvet." As he moved from Congress Hall to the door of the Hotel Indian Queen many followed him. After he entered the hotel, the crowd called for him whereupon the great man reappeared "for a second and last farewell."

After James retired from the House of Representatives, the Madisons lived for four years at Montpellier (also spelled Montpelier), a large country estate located approximately 30 miles from Monticello, Thomas Jefferson's Virginia home. Although Jefferson during those years served as vice-president, the Madisons frequently visited him at Monticello. When George Washington died in 1799, Jefferson accompanied the Madisons to Mount Vernon to console ***Martha Washington**. Because of the death of James Madison, Sr., shortly before Thomas Jefferson became president, the Madisons were unable to attend Jefferson's inauguration.

When Thomas Jefferson named James Madison secretary of state, the Madisons moved to Washington, D.C. (now the nation's capital), along with Dolley's nine-year-old son, Payne Todd, and **Anna Payne**, a niece. Jefferson was a widower, and so until the Madison family secured a home of their own, they lived with their old neighbor in the White House.

The arrival of Dolley Madison, the wife of the secretary of state and a friend of the president, had a decided effect on Washington society. One biographer avers that it "may be said truly that she took Washington." Wrote a prominent Philadelphia socialite, "I have become acquainted with and am highly pleased with her; she has

Dolley
Payne
Madison

good humour and sprightliness, united to the most affable and agreeable manners." After the Madisons moved from the White House to a home at 1333 F Street, "Dolley remained practically on call for the President's dinner parties whenever they included women guests," continued the socialite, who appreciated Dolley's vivacity: "Mrs. Madison was foe to dullness in every form, even when invested with the dignity which high ceremonial could bestow."

After Thomas Jefferson had served two terms, in 1809 he retired to his Monticello home. James Madison, Jefferson's only secretary of state, then assumed the presidency with Dolley as first lady. On the day of James' inauguration, one of Dolley's biographers asserts that "Dolley took the limelight away" from him for "she looked a queen." Not only did she seem radiant and regal in appearance but, said the Philadelphia socialite, "it would be absolutely impossible for any one to behave with more perfect propriety than she did." She further observed that Dolley's "unassuming dignity, sweetness and grace" seemed to "disarm envy itself, and conciliate even enemies."

As first lady, Dolley Madison exercised social leadership in ways that most of her predecessors had not. She genuinely enjoyed Washington social life. Her regular Wednesday receptions became known as "Mrs. Madison's levees," and she made certain that all guests were properly greeted. Said one of her guests, "We have not forgotten how admirably the air of authority was softened by the smile of gaiety, and it is pleasing to recall a certain expression that must have been created by the happiness of all dispositions,—a wish to please and a willingness to be pleased."

Washington Irving described how with eager anticipation he looked forward to meeting Dolley Madison when he visited the nation's capital. "I arrived at the Inn about dusk," said the famous author, "and understanding that Mrs. Madison was to have her levee or drawing-room that very evening, I swore by all my gods I should be there." He told of his emergence "from dirt and darkness into the blazing splendor of Mrs. Madison's drawing-room" where he "was most graciously received" by the first lady "who has a smile and a pleasant word for everybody."

One reason for her popularity was that she was an excellent conversationalist with wide-ranging interests. Wrote a contemporary, "We remarked on the ease with which she glided herself into the stream of conversation and accommodated herself to its endless variety. In the art of conversation she is said to be distinguished."

While Dolley was first lady, Congress authorized the expenditure of $6,000 to refurbish the White House. She played a significant role in the planning and execution of this venture. Her tastes were reportedly "graceful, beautiful and harmonious." Her fondness for yellow was reflected in the satin and damask utilized in creating an elegant drawing room. The drabness of the president's home disappeared with the addition of "gorgeous mirrors," "elaborate mantelpieces," and "handsome oil lamps of the period."

Dolley Madison deliberately avoided partisan politics or "public business" as she called it. This does not mean, however, that she was politically insignificant. In fact, one critic of James Madison believed that DeWitt Clinton would have been chosen president in 1812 if it had not been for the first lady, who was more popular than her husband. Dolley's hospitality extended to political foes as well as friends. As the War of 1812 became more unpopular and came to be called "Mr. Madison's War" in some parts of the country, Dolley's composure and élan countered some of the negative feelings that some citizens had towards the war and the president.

After Dolley rescued the portrait of George Washington during the War of 1812, the British invaders burned the White House as well as other public buildings before retreating. Because the chief executive's mansion required extensive restorative work, the Madisons spent one year living in the Octagon House and then from October 1815 in a home located where Pennsylvania Avenue and Nineteenth Street merge.

James Madison's presidential term ended in March 1817, whereupon the Madisons returned to Montpellier. Until her husband died in 1836, Dolley seldom ventured forth from her Virginia home, though she continued to be the amiable hostess she had always been. It mattered little, it seemed, how many guests came and how long they stayed. One of her great joys in retirement was her garden which was filled with a variety of flowers. During these years, too, she tenderly cared for her husband's mother **Nelly Conway Madison** who also lived at Montpellier. Nelly Madison lived to be 98.

James Madison outlived his mother by only seven years, dying on June 28, 1836. In the fall of 1837, Dolley moved to Washington, where she lived for the rest of her life with her niece Anna Payne. As always, her door was ever open to guests that came to visit. Some of the well-known personages that passed her way included John Quincy Adams, Henry Clay, Daniel Webster, and Mrs. Alexander Hamilton (*Elizabeth

Schuyler Hamilton). President Martin Van Buren, a widower, often invited Dolley to the White House. On one occasion, she was accompanied by "a vivacious southern girl" who so "bewitched" the son of the president that he wooed and won her as his bride. *Angelica Van Buren then served as the White House hostess much as Dolley had many years before. When John Tyler became president, his daughter-in-law, *Priscilla Cooper Tyler, had charge of many social affairs, because the president's wife *Letitia Tyler was a paralytic. The young Priscilla, somewhat intimidated by such responsibilities, sought out Dolley for advice which Dolley freely gave with no condescension.

In her last years, the former first lady was on the scene on some historic occasions. She was present, for example, when Samuel F. Morse demonstrated the electric telegraph. After the famous message "What hath God wrought" crackled over the wire from Baltimore to Washington, Morse turned to Dolley who was at his side for a return message. "Message from Mrs. Madison. She sends her love to Mrs. Wethered," was the response. (Mrs. Wethered was the wife of a member of the House living in Baltimore.) Along with President John Tyler and other important dignitaries, Madison was aboard the U.S.S. *Princeton* on February 28, 1844, when an accident occurred, killing the secretary of state, the secretary of the Navy, plus three others. On July 4, 1848, the cornerstone for the Washington Monument was laid, and Dolley was in attendance. She heard George Washington Parke Custis, the grandson of America's first president, give the address.

Dolley Madison's life, however, was not unclouded. Her only son John Payne Todd was a ne'er-do-well constantly in need of financial aid. She never disowned him, often doing what she could to help him escape difficulties that he usually brought on himself. Financial problems often plagued her during these years. Thus, for $30,000, she sold to the federal government James Madison's manuscripts of debates in the Congress under the Articles of Confederation, including those made during the 1787 constitutional convention. Later, for $25,000, she sold other James Madison papers to the government. She eventually was forced to sell Montpellier, the old Virginia estate, where she had lived with her husband for many years.

On March 4, 1849, President James K. Polk retired from the presidency; he scheduled one final reception for March 7. It proved to be not only the last of such social events during the Polk administration, but also the last time that Dolley Madison would be present for such an affair. Although now she was an old lady of more than 80 years, on this occasion she was reportedly sprightful as ever. In his diary, the president described the event and then concluded, "Towards the close of the evening I passed through the crowded rooms with the venerable Mrs. Madison on my arm. It was near 12 o'clock when the company retired."

Dolley Madison died four months later, on July 12, 1849. In the summer of 1845, she had formally joined the St. John's Church in Lafayette Square. In accepting her as a member, the rector, Smith Pyne, had written, "God bless you and keep you in His Holy Favor. Gladly will I enroll you in my list of candidates." On July 16, 1849, Dolley Madison's funeral service was conducted in this church by her longtime friend, Smith Pyne.

SOURCES:

Anthony, Katharine. *Dolly Madison: Her Life and Times.* Garden City, NY: Doubleday, 1949.

Clark, Allen C. *Life and Letters of Dolly Madison.* Washington, DC: W.F. Roberts, 1914.

Cutts, Lucia Beverly. *Memoirs and Letters of Dolly Madison, Wife of James Madison, President of the United States.* Edited by her grandniece (**Lucia B. Cutts**). Boston, MA: Houghton Mifflin, 1886.

Dean, Elizabeth Lippincott. *Dolly Madison: The Nation's Hostess.* Boston, MA: Lothrop, Lee, and Shepard, 1928.

Goodwin, Maud Wilder. *Dolly Madison.* NY: Scribner, 1896.

Moore, Virginia. *The Madisons.* NY: McGraw-Hill, 1979.

SUGGESTED READING:

Arnett, Ethel. *Mrs. James Madison: The Incomparable Dolley.* Greensboro, NC: Piedmont Press, 1972.

Barnard, Ella Kent. *Dorothy Payne, Quakeress: A Sidelight upon the Career of "Dolly" Madison.* Philadelphia: Ferris and Leach, 1909.

Robert Bolt,
Professor of History, Emeritus,
Calvin College, Grand Rapids, Michigan

Madison, Dorothea Payne (1768–1849).

See Madison, Dolley.

Madison, Helene (1913–1970)

American swimmer. Born on June 19, 1913, in Madison, Wisconsin; died of cancer on November 27, 1970; married and divorced three times; first husband Art Jarrett (a band leader); second husband Billy Rose (a theatrical producer).

Selected championships and honors: named Associated Press Female Athlete of the Year (1931); won an individual gold medal in the 100 meters, a gold medal in the 400 meters, a team gold medal in the 4x100m free-style relay, all at the Olympic Games in Los Ange-

Helene
Madison

les (1932); named to International Swimming Hall of Fame; named to U.S. Olympic Hall of Fame.

Called the queen of the waters, 6' free-styler Helene Madison was in a class by herself. In 1930, at age 17, she held 26 world free-style records in distances from 50 yards to one mile, and between 1930 and 1932, she won 14 world free-style championships at a variety of distances. At the 1932 Summer Olympics in Los Angeles, Madison won two individual gold medals, and a third gold as part of the world-record-setting relay team. An attractive, shapely blonde, the swimmer also had a brief career in show business, initially as a singer in her first husband's (Art Jarrett) band, and then as a star in the New York World's Fair Aquacade, produced by her second husband, Billy Rose (who also married swimmer *Eleanor Holm). In 1938, Madison ventured to Hollywood, playing Jane opposite Glenn Morris' Tarzan in *Tarzan's Revenge*. The actress was married and divorced three times. She died of cancer in 1970, at age 57.

Madonella (1666–1731).

See Astell, Mary.

Madonna.

See Mary the Virgin.

Madrid, duchess of.

See Margaret of Parma (1847–1893).

Maeder, Clara Fisher (1811–1898).

See Fisher, Clara.

Maehata, Hideko (1914—)

Japanese swimmer. Born in Japan on May 20, 1914.

At the Los Angeles Olympics in 1932, with a time of 3:06.4, Hideko Maehata won the silver medal in the 200-meter breaststroke; Australia's **Clare Dennis** finished first with a time of 3:06.3. In the same event at the Berlin Olympics in 1936, Maehata mounted the swimmers' platform with a prayer written on a piece of paper; she read it one last time, then ate the paper. She won the gold medal at a time of 3:03.6; 14-year-old **Martha Geneger** of Germany finished second, while 12-year-old **Inge Sorensen** of Denmark took the bronze. Maehata was the first Japanese woman to medal in Olympic swimming and one of the first swimmers to use the butterfly stroke, recovering her arms above the water rather than under, which was controversial at the time.

Maesa, Julia (c. 170–224 CE).

See Julia Maesa.

Mafalda.

Variant of Matilda.

Mafalda (c. 1197–1257)

*Portuguese princess. Born around 1197; died on May 1, 1257, in Arouca, Lisbon, Portugal; daughter of *Douce of Aragon (1160–1198) and Sancho I (1154–1211 or 1212), king of Portugal (r. 1185–1211 or 1212); married Enrique also known as Henry I (1184–1252), king of Castile (annulled in 1216).*

Mafalda of Hesse (1902–1944)

Italian-born princess, daughter of the king and queen of Italy, who died in a concentration camp during World War II, accused of poisoning Tsar Boris of Bulgaria. Name variations: Princess Mafalda of Savoy; landgravine of Hesse. Born Mafalda Maria Elizabeth, princess of Savoy, on November 19, 1902, in Rome, Italy; died on August 29, 1944, in Buchenwald concentration camp; daughter of Elena of Montenegro (1873–1952) and Victor Emmanuel III (1869–1947), king of Italy (r. 1900–1946); sister of Giovanna of Italy (1907–2000) and Maria of Savoy (b. 1914); married Philip (b. 1896), landgrave of Hesse, on September 23, 1925; children: Maurice Frederick (b. 1926), prince of Hesse; Henry William (b. 1927); Otto Adolf (b. 1937); Elizabeth Marguerite Elena (b. 1940), princess of Hesse (who married Friedrich Carl, count of Oppersdorf).

One of the countless dark stories that emerged from the Buchenwald concentration camp following World War II concerns Princess Mafalda of Hesse, the daughter of the king and queen of Italy, who was wounded in an American air raid on the camp on August 24, 1944, and died of her injuries a day later. Princess Mafalda was imprisoned by order of Adolf Hitler in 1943, after she and her husband Philip, landgrave of Hesse, were implicated in the mysterious death of Hitler ally Boris III, tsar of Bulgaria. Boris was married to Mafalda's sister *Giovanna of Italy (1907–2000). Many of the facts surrounding Mafalda's death were not revealed until after the war, and to this day her involvement in any plot to murder Boris has never been proven.

Mafalda Maria Elizabeth, the second of the five children of Victor Emmanuel III, king of Italy, and *Elena of Montenegro, was born in 1902, a year after

Mafalda of Hesse

her sister *Yolanda Margherita of Italy, and two years before her brother Umberto (Umberto II), the heir to the throne. Two more girls, Giovanna and *Maria of Savoy (b. 1914), completed the family. The king and queen, noted for their unpretentious lifestyle, brought the royal children up in a modest villa in the countryside outside of Rome. (It was said that Elena, who was raised in a small Balkan village, even did some of her own cooking and cleaning.) Mafalda grew up to be an accomplished young woman, who spoke four foreign languages, as well as her native Italian, played four musical instruments, and was an avid sportswoman. In 1923, she and her younger sister Giovanna were simultaneously stricken with typhoid fever and nearly died from the illness. Following her lengthy recovery, Mafalda remained in frail health and suffered life-threatening bouts of influenza in 1925, 1936, and again in 1939.

As a young woman, Mafalda was linked romantically with the prince of Wales and Crown Prince Leopold of Belgium (Leopold III), but in June 1925 she became engaged to Prince Philip of Hesse, whom she met at a garden party on the grounds of a Roman villa. The son of Prince Frederick Charles of Hesse and Princess **Margaret Beatrice**, and the nephew of exiled Kaiser Wilhelm II, Philip was an architect and engineer by training and served as a lieutenant in the German army during World War I. His engagement to Mafalda marked the first betrothal between the former opposing royal families since the war. In order to marry the Catholic princess, Philip, a Protestant, renounced all rights to his succession, and agreed that any children of the union would be raised Catholic. The couple married at an elaborate medieval ceremony held at the royal castle in Racconigi on September 23, 1925. On the eve of the wedding, while the royal guests dined in splendor within the confines of the castle, the royal family hosted a slightly more modest banquet for the villagers of Racconigi at a local hostelry, and even made a surprise appearance at the event. After the nuptials, the newly-weds honeymooned on the Italian Riviera, and in Germany, then returned to Rome, where they settled in a villa designed by Prince Philip. In 1933, when Philip was appointed governor of the province of Hessen-Nassau by Chancellor Hitler, they moved to Cassel, Germany. In the meantime, the couple began a family which eventually grew to include four children, three sons and a daughter, **Elizabeth Marguerite Elena** (b. 1940).

During the war, Philip rose to the honorary rank of general in Hitler's Brown Shirts and served as a go-between for Hitler, Benito Mussolini, and Heinrich Himmler, although according to *The Goebbels Diaries*, Philip was never trusted because of his Italian connections. Indeed, Hitler had nothing but disdain for the House of Savoy, once referring to Mafalda as "the trickiest bitch in the Italian royal house." In August 1943, when Tsar Boris of Bulgaria was struck by a disease of "mysterious suddenness" and died a short time later, Hitler made note of the fact that the illness coincided with a visit from Mafalda to her sister Giovanna. David Irving, in his book *Hitler's War*, asserts that Hitler's physician, Professor Hans Eppinger, who assisted on the case, strongly suspected that Boris had been poisoned. "The King's Italian wife Giovanna would not permit an autopsy, but Eppinger noticed that the royal corpse's lower extremities had turned black—a phenomenon he had seen only once before, after the Greek prime minister Ioannis Metaxas, had been poisoned in January 1941." Hitler also learned from other sources that around the time of Boris' death, Prince Philip had dictated groups of ciphers to Mafalda over the telephone. Armed with only this circumstantial evidence, Hitler had the princess arrested that summer and jailed along with her servant. He then invited Philip to be his guest at headquarters, telling his guards not to let the prince out again.

At Buchenwald, which was primarily a concentration camp for men, Princess Mafalda was confined to a special compound for dignitaries, which also housed approximately 54 other prominent personalities whom the SS wanted to separate from the rest of the prisoners. They had a special guard for the building which was surrounded by a ten-foot stockade. Others in residence there were the former Social Democratic Reichstag deputy Rudolph Breitscheid and Jehovah's Witness **Maria Ruhnar**. When the building was destroyed in the American raid, Mafalda survived the bombing but emerged with a badly wounded arm, which was amputated by the prison doctor. The operation, carried out in one of the recently established camp brothels, was botched. The princess suffered from excessive bleeding and an infection set in; she died the following day. After her naked body was dumped into the crematory, the prisoner in charge, Father Joseph Thyl, dug it out of the heap, covered it, and arranged for a speedy cremation. He also cut off a lock of her hair which would be smuggled out of the camp and sent to her Hessian relatives.

Prince Philip endured a two-year imprisonment in Darmstadt, Germany, existing for some time in a crowded coal bin dubbed "Camp Despair" by its inmates. He was later a witness at the Dachau trial of Flossenburg concentration camp guards, and in December 1947 he received a suspended two-year prison sentence from a German denazification court. The court also confiscated a third of the prince's property, estimated at $68,600.

Mafalda of Hesse was not forgotten by her nation. To commemorate the 50th anniversary of the end of World War II, the Italian government issued a stamp on which the image of the princess is superimposed against a barbed-wire fence.

SOURCES:
"Asserts Mafalda Will Wed Shortly," in *The New York Times.* June 20, 1925, p. 13.
"Blum, Schuschnigg and Niemoeller Found With 130 Others in Italy," in *The New York Times.* May 8, 1945, p. 12.
"Gala Day in Italy for Royal Wedding," in *The New York Times.* September 23, 1925, pp. 1–2.
"German Prince Says Jail Toughened Him," in *The New York Times.* February 8, 1947, p. 43.
Goebbels, Joseph. *The Goebbels Diaries, 1942–1943.* Edited, translated and with an introduction by Louis P. Lochner. Garden City, NY: Doubleday, 1948.
Hackett, David A., ed. *The Buchenwald Report.* Boulder, CO: Westview Press, 1995.
Irving, David. *Hitler's War.* NY: Avon Books, 1990.
"Italian Princess Future Belgian Queen," in *The New York Times.* February 12, 1923, p. 3.
"Italian Princess Ill," in *The New York Times.* December 20, 1936, p. 31.
"Italian Princess is Ill," in *The New York Times.* January 11, 1939, p. 10.
"Italian Princesses are Critically Ill," in *The New York Times.* September 18, 1923, p. 3.
"Italian Princesses Are Now Better," in *The New York Times.* September 17, 1923, p. 4.
"The Italian Royal Wedding," in *The Times* [London]. September 24, 1925, p. 14.
"Italian Sovereigns at London State Ball," in *The New York Times.* May 29, 1924, p. 19.
Judd, Denis. *Eclipse of Kings.* NY: Stein and Day, 1974.
Katz, Robert. *The Fall of the House of Savoy.* NY: Macmillan, 1971.
Kogon, Eugen. *The Theory and Practice of Hell.* Translated by Heinz Norden. NY: Octagon Books, 1979.
"Mafalda and Philip Wed in Royal Pomp; Gay Crowds Cheer," in *The New York Times.* September 24, 1925, pp. 1, 4.
"Mafalda's Romance Delights Italians," in *The New York Times.* September 19, 1925, p. 4.
"Philip of Hesse Freed," in *The New York Times.* December 18, 1947, p. 17.
"Prince and Princess Modern in Training," in *The New York Times.* September 21, 1925, p. 2.
"Princess Dead in Prison," in *The New York Times.* April 20, 1945, p. 5.
"Princess Mafalda to be Wed in Old Palace of Racconigi," in *The New York Times.* Sec. VIII. September 20, 1925, p. 8.
"Wales is an Escort to Italian Princess," in *The New York Times.* September 25, 1925, p. 25.

Barbara Morgan,
Melrose, Massachusetts

Mafalda of Portugal (c. 1149–1173).

See Matilda of Portugal.

Mafalda of Savoy (c. 1125–1157).

See Matilda of Maurienne.

Mafalda of Savoy (1902–1944).

See Mafalda of Hesse.

Magafan, Ethel and Jenne

American painters and muralists who were well known during the 1930s and 1940s.

Magafan, Ethel (1916–1993). Born in Chicago, Illinois, on October 10, 1916; died in 1993; daughter of Petros Magafan, also seen as Peter J. Magafan, and Julia (Bronick) Magafan; twin sister of artist Jenne Magafan; studied in the public schools in Colorado Springs, Colorado, and at the Colorado Springs Fine Arts Center; married Bruce Currie (an artist), on June 30, 1946; children: one daughter, Jenne Magafan Currie.

Awards: Tiffany Foundation award (1950s); Fulbright fellowship (1950s); Childe Hassam Purchase award from the Academy of Arts and Letters (1970); Altman prize from the National Academy of Design; the Hallgarten Award; Edwin Austin Abbey Mural Award (1980).

Magafan, Jenne (1916–1952). Born in Chicago, Illinois, on October 10, 1916; died in Woodstock, New York, in 1952; daughter of Petros Magafan, also seen as Peter J. Magafan, and Julia (Bronick) Magafan; twin sister of artist Ethel Magafan; studied in the public schools in Colorado Springs, Colorado, and at the Colorado Springs Fine Arts Center; married Edward Chavez (an artist).

Awards: Tiffany Foundation award (1950s); Fulbright fellowship (1950s).

Born in Chicago, Illinois, on October 10, 1916, twin sisters Jenne Magafan and Ethel Magafan were the daughters of Petros Magafan, who had emigrated from Greece in 1912, and **Julia Bronick Magafan.** Petros soon moved his family from Chicago to Colorado Springs, Colorado, the mountains of which reminded him of Greece. The Magafan sisters grew up with their father's love of mountainous terrain.

Both sisters showed a remarkable talent for art, which was encouraged by their teachers in public school, and they decided to pursue careers in painting while still quite young. Jenne won the Carter Memorial Art Scholarship, carrying a stipend of $90, which she shared with Ethel. The two began their formal art studies at the Colorado Springs Fine Arts Center, where they were taught by Frank Mechau, Boardman Robinson, and Peppino Mangravite. After two months of study, when their scholarship money was gone, Mechau was so impressed by their talent that he hired them to work as assistants on some of his mural projects. This early training helped prepare the sisters to enter juried competitions sponsored by the Treasury Department's Section of Fine Arts (one of the federal projects created during the Great Depression). In one such competition in 1937, Ethel won her first commission to create a mural, *Wheat Threshing,* for the post office in Auburn, Nebraska. Later that year, her design for the mural *The Lawrence Massacre,* intended for a post office in Fort Scott, Kansas, was rejected because the subject matter was too disturbing. The same official who rejected the mural nonetheless praised its design.

Jenne's first major commission was the mural *Western Town,* which depicts a typical town in the West during frontier days. Inhabited largely by tough-looking cowboy types, the mural was executed for the post office in Helper,

Ethel Magafan

Utah. It shows a blacksmith contemplating his handiwork, a woman entering the town's general store-*cum*-post office, two hard-bitten horsemen entering town on their mounts, and a saloon in the distance. The artist's signature appears on a scrap of discarded paper that lies on the street of the town. The influence of such early Renaissance masters as Massacio and Giotto is evident in the murals of both sisters.

The twins exhibited a number of their easel-size paintings together at least seven times and jointly produced the large-scale mural, *Mountains and Snow,* for the boardroom of the Social Security Building (later known as the Health, Education, and Welfare Building) in Washington, D.C.

During a visit to Los Angeles in pursuit of an assignment, the Magafans met artists **Doris Lee** and Arnold Blanch, who spoke so enthusiastically about the artists' colony at Woodstock, New York, that the sisters soon moved their base of operations to this village on the Hudson River. Soon thereafter each met and married a fellow artist. Jenne married Edward Chavez and

Ethel wed Bruce Currie. While the relationship between the two sisters and their spouses remained extremely close, the twins were now working in separate studios for the first time, which eventually led to the development of distinct styles. In a review of their joint exhibition at New York's Ganso Gallery in 1950, a writer for *Art News* observed: "Ethel is the more rugged painter, interested primarily in horses. . . . Jenne, whose style is similar but more sensitive, more often makes people the center of interest."

When both sisters received Tiffany Foundation awards and Fulbright fellowships for study abroad in the early 1950s, Ethel used hers to visit Greece, the homeland of their father, while Jenne studied in Italy. Both returned to their homes in Woodstock in 1952. Only a few days after her return, Jenne suffered a massive cerebral hemorrhage and died at the age of 36. Although, in time, Ethel continued with her career, producing murals into her late 60s, she later described her sister's death as "a tragedy from which I have never fully recovered." She named her only daughter **Jenne Magafan Currie**. Ethel died in 1993.

Murals by Ethel Magafan can be found in the U.S. Senate Chamber, the Recorder of Deeds Building in Washington, D.C., and in post offices at Wynne, Arkansas; Mudill, Oklahoma; and Denver, Colorado.

SOURCES:
Bailey, Brooke. *The Remarkable Lives of 100 Women Artists.* Holbrook, MA: Bob Adams, 1994.
Rubinstein, Charlotte Streifer. *American Women Artists.* Boston, MA: G.K. Hall, 1982.

Don Amerman,
freelance writer, Saylorsburg, Pennsylvania

Magafan, Jenne (1916–1952).
See joint entry under *Magafan, Ethel and Jenne.*

Ma-gcig Lab-sgron (c. 1055–c. 1149)
Eminent Tibetan Buddhist master who codified the Gcod ("cutting") practice. Name variations: Magcig Labsgron. Born in Labphyi, Tibet, possibly in 1055; died in 1149; taught by Skyo-ston Bsod-nams Bla-ma and Grwa-pa Mngon-shes; children: (with an Indian Tantric yogin) five; her son or grandson, Thod-smyon Bsam-grub, was an accomplished mediator.

The most eminent female Buddhist master in Tibetan history, Ma-gcig Lab-sgron professed that she gave up all regard for personal appearance and social convention to become a Gcod practitioner. Nevertheless, when she ran off with an Indian Tantric yogin, she was vilified as "the

nun who had repudiated her vows." It is believed that she lived in Kong-po for many years, and gave birth to five children before leaving her family to study with the famed Indian teacher of the Zhi-byed tradition, Pha Dam-pa Sangs-rgyas. She then retired to Mt. Zangs-ri Mkhar-dmar, living in retreat for the rest of her life.

Ma-gcig Lab-sgron also wrote a treatise on the Gcod meditational practice, which is comprised of indigenous pre-Buddhist ideas and the Prajnaparamita and Mahamudra doctrines she studied with Pha Dam-pa. In the treatise, she described setting up a tent in a haunted area, contemplating emptiness, and offering up (in visualization) her flesh and bones to the demons, whereby she attained transcendence and power. Ma-gcig Lab-sgron had many disciples, including her son or grandson, whom she purportedly cured of epilepsy. Tibetans still practice Gcod and Ma-gcig Lab-sgron remains a source of inspiration for new liturgies and lineages.

Magdalen.
Variant of Madeleine.

Magdalen (fl. early 1st c.).
See *Mary Magdalene.*

Magdalena (1532–1590)
German princess. Born in Innsbruck on August 14, 1532; died in Hall, Tyrol, on December 10, 1590; daughter of *Anna of Bohemia and Hungary (1503–1547) and Ferdinand I, Holy Roman Emperor (r. 1556–1564); possibly married the duke of Neuburg.

Magdalena (fl. late 1500s)
Countess Palatine. Flourished in the late 1500s; daughter of *Mary (1531–1581) and William V, duke of Cleves (r. 1539–1592); sister of *Maria Eleanora (1550–1608), duchess of Prussia; married John I, Count Palatine of Zweibrucken; children: John II, Count Palatine of Zweibrucken.

Magdalena Augusta of Anhalt-Zerbst (1679–1740).
See *Madeleine of Anhalt-Zerbst.*

Magdalena Sybilla (1587–1659)
Electress of Saxony. Name variations: Magdalene Sibylle of Brandenberg; Magdelene Sibylle Hohenzollern. Born on January 9, 1587 (some sources cite De-

cember 31, 1586); died on February 22 (some sources cite February 12), 1659; daughter of *Maria Eleanora (1550–1608) and Albert Frederick (b. 1553), duke of Prussia; sister of *Anna of Prussia (1576–1625); married John George I (1585–1656), elector of Saxony, on July 29, 1607; children: *Marie Elizabeth of Saxony (1610–1684); John George II, elector of Saxony (b. 1613); August, duke of Saxe-Weissenfels (b. 1614); *Magdalena Sybilla (1617–1668).

Magdalena Sybilla (1617–1668)

*Danish royal. Name variations: Magdalene Sibylle of Saxony. Born on December 23, 1617; died on January 6, 1668; daughter of *Magdalena Sybilla (1587–1659) and John George I (1585–1656), elector of Saxony; married Christian Oldenburg (1603–1647, son of Christian IV, king of Denmark), on October 5, 1634.*

Magdalena Sybilla of Holstein-Gottorp (1631–1719)

*Duchess of Mecklenburg-Gustrow. Name variations: Magdalene Sibylle of Holstein-Gottorp. Born on November 24, 1631; died on April 22, 1719; daughter of *Marie Elizabeth of Saxony (1610–1684) and Frederick III, duke of Holstein-Gottorp; married Gustav Adolf, duke of Mecklenburg-Gustrow, on December 28, 1654; children: *Marie of Mecklenburg-Gustrow (1659–1701); *Louise of Mecklenburg-Gustrow (1667–1721).*

Magdalene (fl. early 1st c.).

See Mary Magdalene.

Magdalene of Brandenburg (1582–1616)

*Landgravine of Hesse-Darmstadt. Born on January 7, 1582; died on May 4, 1616; daughter of *Elizabeth of Anhalt (1563–1607) and John George (1525–1598), elector of Brandenburg (r. 1571–1598); married Louis V, landgrave of Hesse-Darmstadt, on June 5, 1598; children: *Anne-Eleanor of Hesse-Darmstadt (1601–1659); George II (b. 1605), landgrave of Hesse-Darmstadt.*

Magdalene of Oldenburg (1585–1657)

Princess of Anhalt-Zerbst. Name variations: Magdalene von Oldenburg. Born on October 6, 1585; died on April 14, 1657; daughter of John XVI (b. 1540), count of Oldenburg, and *Elizabeth von Schwarzburg (b. 1541); married Rudolf, prince of Anhalt-Zerbst, on August 31, 1612; children: John (b. 1621), prince of Anhalt-Zerbst.*

Magdalene of Saxony (1507–1534)

*Princess of Saxony. Born on March 7, 1507; died on January 28, 1534; daughter of *Barbara of Poland (1478–1534) and George the Bearded (b. 1471), duke of Saxony; married Joachim II Hector (1505–1571), elector of Brandenburg (r. 1535–1571), on November 6, 1524; children: John George (1525–1598), elector of Brandenburg (r. 1571–1598).*

Magdalen women.

See Mary Magdalene for sidebar.

Magdelaine de France (1520–1537).

See Margaret Tudor for sidebar on Madeleine of France.

Magdelene.

Variant of Magdalena or Magdalene.

Magee, Martha Maria (d. 1846)

Irish philanthropist. Born Martha Maria Stewart in Lurgan, County Armagh, Northern Ireland; died in 1846; married William Magee, a Presbyterian minister, in 1780 (died 1800).

Born into the Stewart family in the town of Lurgan in County Armagh, Northern Ireland, Martha Maria Stewart married Presbyterian minister William Magee in 1780. Twenty years later, her husband died; she then inherited what was then considered a fortune upon the deaths of her brothers. When Magee died in 1846, she bequeathed a sum of £20,000 sterling to be used for the construction and endowment of a college to educate and train Irish Presbyterian ministers. That institution, named Magee College in her honor, opened in Londonderry in 1865. It is now part of the University of Ulster.

Don Amerman,
freelance writer, Saylorsburg, Pennsylvania

Maggie.

Variant of Margaret.

Magill, Helen White (1853–1944).

See White, Helen Magill.

Magnani, Anna (1908–1973)

Italian actress who won an Academy Award for her performance in the screen adaptation of Tennessee Williams' The Rose Tattoo. *Born on March 7, 1908, in Rome, Italy; died on September 26, 1973, in Rome; daughter of Marina Magnani, from Romagna; father unknown, except that he was from Calabria; married Goffredo Alessandrini (a director), in 1935 (annulled 1950); children: (with actor Massimo Serato) son, Luca Alessandrini (b. 1942).*

Studied at Rome's Academy of Dramatic Art while earning her living as a nightclub singer; began appearing in plays and variety shows (mid-1920s); made her first film appearance (1927), though she did not receive recognition as a film actress until 1941, in Vittorio De Sica's Teresa Venerdi; *became international star with appearance in Roberto Rossellini's* Roma, città aperta *(Open City) and given the American Board of Review's Best Foreign Actress award (1945); won an Oscar for her performance in the screen adaptation of Tennessee Williams'* The Rose Tattoo *(1955); continued to work steadily in film and television until her death.*

Filmography: Scampolo *(1927);* La Cieca di Sorrento *(1934);* Tempo Massimo *(1934);* Cavalleria *(1936);* Trenta Secondi d'Amore *(1936);* Tarakanova *(1938);* Una Lampada alla Finestra *(1940);* Finalmente Soli *(1941);* La Fuggitiva *(1941);* Teresa Venerdi *(1941);* La Fortuna viene dal Cielo *(1942);* La Vita è Bella *(1943);* L'Avventura di Annabella *(1943);* Campo dè Fiori *(1943);* L'Ultima Carrozzella *(1943);* T'amero sempre *(1943);* Il Fiore sotto gli Occhi *(1944);* Roma, città aperta *(1945);* Abbasso la Miseria *(1945);* Un Uomo ritorna *(1946);* Davanti a lui tremava tutta Roma *(1946);* Il Bandito *(1946);* Abbasso la Ricchezza *(1946);* Lo Sconosciuto di San Marino *(1947);* Quartetto Pazzo *(1947);* L'Onorevole Angelina *(1947);* Assunta Spina *(1947);* L'Amore *(1948);* Molti Sogni per le Strade *(1948);* Vulcano *(1950);* Bellissima *(1951);* Camicie rosse *(1952);* La Carrozza d'Oro *(1953);* Siamo Donne *(1953);* The Rose Tattoo *(1955);* Suor Letizia *(1956);* Wild Is the Wind *(1957);* Nella Città l'Inferno *(1958);* The Fugitive Kind *(1960);* Risate di Gioia *(1960);* Mamma Roma *(1962);* Le Magot de Joséfa *(1963);* Volles Herz und leere Taschen *(1964);* Made in Italy *(1965);* The Secret of Santa Vittoria *(1969);* Correva l'Anno di Grazia 1879 *(1972);* Fellini's Roma *(1972).*

On a bright autumn morning in 1973, crowds thronged the narrow streets of Rome hoping to catch a glimpse of the funeral cortège carrying its sad burden to a final resting place. The outpouring of tears and grief was of a de-

gree normally reserved for popes or lofty public officials, but the mourning on this occasion was for Italy's beloved "Nannarella," Anna Magnani, the actress whom director William Dieterle called "the last of the great, shameless emotionalists." Dieterle was referring not only to Magnani's acting, but to the passionate personality that was its genesis.

Even Magnani's birth and childhood evoked a great deal of dramatic speculation and innuendo during her lifetime. For years, she fought rumors that she was not really Italian, but had been born in Alexandria, Egypt, to an Italian mother and an Egyptian father. Magnani could never produce a birth certificate, having been born out of wedlock, but she claimed throughout her life that she had been born in Rome on March 7, 1908, in the Porta Pia section. Her mother was **Marina Magnani**, from Romagna; Anna knew nothing of her father, except that he was from Calabria. The story about her Egyptian birth may have arisen after Marina escaped the scandal of being an 18-year-old unwed mother by leaving her daughter in the care of her own mother and emigrating to Egypt, where she later married.

One of Magnani's earliest memories was the sobriquet which was given to her, *la figlia della colpa* (the daughter of sin). Her grandmother, she said, refused to talk about Marina, and Anna's most treasured possession was an album of photographs of her mother. "Mamma was beautiful," she once said, "with brown hair and eyes the color of steel. I was never allowed to speak of my dreams and fantasies about her, to hear her voice or feel the warmth of her affection." Magnani imagined Marina living like a princess in Egypt and was surprised when the two were briefly reunited in Rome in 1917 that her mother wasn't wearing the silks and brocades she had given her in dreams. Equally surprising was the little girl Marina brought with her, a daughter born after her marriage to a German living in Alexandria. The child, with her striking blonde hair and blue eyes, became an object of intense jealousy after Marina had gone back to Egypt, for Magnani felt the little girl was stealing the caresses and hugs that were meant for her.

Magnani also spent a good deal of her very public life denying stories of a wild, undisciplined life as a child of the streets. "How many times do I have to explain that I wasn't a waif or a stray," she complained in exasperation to journalist **Oriana Fallaci** in 1967, "that I went through high school, that I learned the piano for eight years, that I went to the conservatory of

Santa Cecilia?" It is true that Magnani received a standard public school education and studied music at Santa Cecilia with an eye toward becoming a concert pianist. Her grandmother, she said, had always sung to her as a child; and Anna remembered her delight in accompanying her grandmother on the old piano at home. Sometime in the early 1920s, with her grandmother in failing health, Magnani enrolled at Rome's Academy of Dramatic Art, earning her tuition and a living by singing bawdy songs in less-than-elegant nightspots around Rome. During this period, she appeared in her first play, taking the role of a maid in *La Nemica e Scampolo* for 25 lira a day. The play was later filmed, marking her first motion-picture appearance. In 1926, her grandmother died and Magnani, now without a family of any kind, took to the road for the next six years with a traveling repertory company, living out of a trunk and sleeping on the train that carried the troupe from one sleepy country village to the next. During this period, she met a young comic actor learning his trade named Vittorio De Sica, who was struck by Anna's laugh, which he later described as "loud, overwhelming, and tragic." She left the company after a tour of Argentina in 1932, returning to the nightclub circuit and gaining a reputation for herself as the Italian *Edith Piaf. One night, a handsome young film director, Goffredo Alessandrini, introduced himself. Alessandrini came from a wealthy Roman family, had attended Cambridge University, and had just returned from Hollywood, where he had been studying American film production techniques. He would be one of the first Italian filmmakers to adopt the new sound technology from America and was involved in the design of Rome's legendary studio complex, Cinecittà, built as part of Benito Mussolini's plan to boost Italian film production. But Alessandrini's interest in Magnani, at least initially, had little to do with film work. Soon after their meeting, Anna had become his mistress.

𝒲omen like me can submit only to men capable of dominating them, and I have never found anyone capable of dominating me.

—Anna Magnani

The Italian film industry during the late 1920s and early 1930s was at a low ebb, after an initially prosperous two decades during the silent era. Overwhelmed by an influx of more imaginative and better made American films, Italian studios did little more than release static versions of stage plays, such as Magnani's first film in 1927, *Scampolo*, which was merely a filmed replica of the stage presentation. With the rise of Mussolini's Fascists during the 1920s, Italian studios came under increasing pressure to produce not only more native product, but product that was in keeping with Mussolini's political authoritarianism. By the 1930s, Italian cinema consisted mainly of either propagandizing social dramas reflecting the Fascist party line or innocuous, sentimental comedies or dramas set against a glamorous, high society background which had little to do with the actual lives of most Italians. Moviegoers jokingly referred to these films as *telefoni bianchi,* or "white telephone."

It was this sort of superficial cinema in which Magnani labored after becoming Goffredo Alessandrini's lover and, in 1935, his wife. Alessandrini did not consider her suitable for the screen, though he cast her in a secondary role in his *Cavalleria* in 1936. It was true that Magnani was no match for the elegant, Hollywood-inspired actresses of the *telefoni bianchi*. She was short, somewhat plump, with a mass of unkempt dark hair and large, dark, pleading eyes. Fallaci once wrote that Magnani had "that look of a wounded bird that doesn't know where to beat its wings." Anna took small roles in a series of forgettable pictures, usually as maids or peasant women, but spent most of her time trying to hold together a marriage that was in trouble almost as soon as the ring was on her finger. "When I married [Alessandrini]," she once said, "I was only a young girl. And as long as I was his wife, his infidelities gave me more horns than a basketful of snails. I did nothing but weep and moan." Alessandrini was considerably older than Magnani, and friends noted that he treated her like a child rather than a wife, while Magnani may have seen him as more of a father figure than a husband. Such was not the case, however, when she met a young actor on the set of one of her films, in 1940. Her passionate affair with Massimo Serato, nine years her junior, resulted in a son, Luca, born in 1942.

By the time of Luca's birth, Magnani and Alessandrini had separated, but Alessandrini agreed to help support the boy and even gave Luca his family name, the same agreement they had reached some years earlier when a child was born to one of Alessandrini's mistresses. Despite the separation, the marriage would not be formally dissolved by annulment until 1950, but Magnani, always frank in her low opinion of most men, would speak kindly of Alessandrini in years to come. "Whenever I see him I feel a great tenderness," she said more than 20 years after their separation. "[He is] the only man, of all I've known, for whom I have ungrudging re-

Anna
Magnani

spect and of whom I am really fond." Even two years after the annulment was formalized, she appeared in Alessandrini's *Camicie Rosse*. Her passion for Massimo Serato quickly cooled, and by 1944, the two lovers had gone their separate ways. "Great passions don't exist," Magnani later observed. "They're liars' fantasies." For the rest of her life, Anna's only passion would be for Luca, who was diagnosed with polio during an epidemic which swept Rome in 1944 and whose care and education would become her life's work.

During her years with Alessandrini, Magnani worked several times with her old friend Vittorio De Sica. By the late 1930s, De Sica had turned from acting to directing, and in 1941 cast Magnani in what he grandly called "her first true film," *Teresa Venerdi* (*Theresa Friday*). Although hers was not the leading role in the film, Magnani's work drew the attention of another young director who had collaborated on several of Alessandrini's films. Anna probably first met Roberto Rossellini while visiting the set of one of her husband's pictures, *Luciano Serra, Pilota*, in the late 1930s, although their affair did not begin until several years later, in the midst of World War II. Like Alessandrini, Rossellini was the scion of a wealthy, aristocratic Roman family and frankly admitted that he had been drawn to the film world as a way to meet beautiful women. But he developed into one of Italy's most creative directors of the so-called neo-realist school, and La Magnani became his muse. They seemed drawn to each other, Rossellini having recently separated from his wife **Marcella de Marquis**, and Magnani despondent over the end of her own marriage. Anna said she was fascinated by "this forceful, secure, courageous man."

In later years, each would accuse the other of starting the affair. "It was Rossellini who wouldn't leave me alone, who wouldn't let me move a step," Magnani claimed, "not I who ran after him. Let Rossellini say what he likes. If I had shared that great passion, I would have been able to keep it alive, be sure of that." But even Magnani would readily admit that it was Rossellini who was responsible for her meteoric rise to international stardom. "I've worked better with Rossellini than with any other director," she said. "Whenever he was setting up a sequence, it was always the sequence I'd have shot if I'd been in his shoes."

Their first collaboration has often been called the opening salvo of Italian neo-realism. *Roma, città aperta* (*Open City*), shot in 1945, was a brutal, gritty depiction of war-ravaged Italy, the complete antithesis of "white telephone" films. Even the title was a sardonic comment on the state of affairs when Rome was declared an "open city" after the fall of Mussolini in 1943. The Nazi regime took control in the interim and kept the city in a grip of terror until its liberation by the Allies two years later. Rossellini began shooting the picture during the last days of the Nazi occupation, with his cast and crew continually dodging German military police determined to shut the film down. He was forced to shoot his scenes on the scraps and loose ends of film which were all that could be found in a looted and ruined city. *Roma, città aperta* told the story of a Nazi manhunt for a Communist leader of the Italian resistance movement, and painted a bitter portrait of Romans betraying their fellow compatriots and switching loyalties as the moment demanded. Few could forget Magnani's wrenching portrayal of Pina, whose attempts to keep her brother out of German hands ends in disaster. The scene in which a distraught Pina, chasing the truck carrying her brother away to be tortured, is shot dead and falls to the rubble-strewn pavement remains a potent symbol of Italy's suffering during the war.

Magnani had not been Rossellini's first choice for the role, for she was not regarded, even by her peers in the business, as a serious actress. After discovering that his first choice was under contract for another film, Rossellini found himself in an argument with Magnani, who demanded equal pay with the film's leading male actor before accepting the part. It very nearly went to yet a third actress before she relented, and she later laughed that a few hundred lira almost cost her the most important film of her career. It made her an international star, as well as publicizing her affair with Rossellini, with whom she toured Europe and the United States to promote the film. In America, the National Board of Review named Magnani the Best Foreign Actress of 1946, marking the beginning of her reign as Italy's best-known screen presence in theaters around the world.

Two years later, she was again directed by Rossellini in a pair of films that were released together as *L'Amore*. The first was *La Voce Umana* (*The Human Voice*), a 35-minute adaptation of the Jean Cocteau play in which Magnani was the only character—a woman talking to her lover on the telephone. The film, shot in long takes with Cocteau's abstract dialogue, was a *tour de force* for Magnani. Rossellini trusted her instincts so well that some sequences were shot with Anna's back to the camera, her voice and gestures powerful enough to carry the scene. Rossellini included a dedication to Magnani's talent in the film's opening credits, and said the phenomenon he wanted to explore in the picture "was called Anna Magnani." The second part of *L'Amore* was *Il Miracolo* (*The Miracle*), based on a village tale remembered by a young Federico Fellini, who was working for Rossellini as a writer at the time. Magnani plays a simpleminded peasant who believes a stranger she meets in the forest (played by Fellini) is Saint Joseph. Yielding to the stranger's advances, she later becomes pregnant and is rejected by her village as a sinner and outcast, much as Magnani's own mother had been in real life. Her character is thus condemned to giving birth to her child alone, but chooses to do so in the village church, where she clings to the bell rope for support during her labor and announces her "miracle" with peals of God's music. Under pressure from the Roman Catholic Church, the film was banned as blasphemous in the United States, where only *La Voce Umana* was released.

The next ten years contained Magnani's best work for directors that included, besides Rossellini and De Sica, Luchino Visconti (*Bellissima*) and France's Jean Renoir (*La Carrozza Doro*), who called her "the greatest actress I have ever worked with. She is the complete animal—an animal created for the stage and screen." Her career peaked in 1955, when she won an Academy Award for Best Actress for her performance as Serafina in the film adaptation of Tennessee Williams' *The Rose Tatoo,* playing opposite Burt Lancaster. "Miss Magnani sweeps most everything before her," *The New York Times*' reviewer wrote: "She overwhelms all objectivity with the rush of her subjective force." It was the first of two film versions of Williams' plays in which she appeared, the second—Sidney Lumet's 1959 *Orpheus Descending*—faring less well.

Although she was nominated a second time for Best Actress for 1957's *Wild Is the Wind*, Magnani's career had begun to decline as Italy left behind its postwar traumas and began to produce more sophisticated material for the world market, starring glamorous young actresses like *Gina Lollobrigida** and *Sophia Loren*. Magnani, with her plainer looks and passionate acting, seemed out of step with the new style. "I'm bored stiff with these everlasting parts as hysterical, loud, working-class women," she complained in 1963, perhaps thinking of the previous year's *Mamma Roma*, in which she had played just such a character and which had been the latest in a string of box-office failures. "The day has gone when I deluded myself that making movies was art. Movies today are made up of . . . intellectuals who always make out that they're teaching something," she said, pointing out that a film's first duty was to amuse its audience—a surprising statement from the woman who owed her success to films like *Roma, città aperta*. "Everyone blames la Magnani for the failure of her movies," she went on. "Everyone forgets I'm not a drama-school type actress, that my work comes off only when I'm free to do what I want, like a writer when he writes or a painter when he paints."

While Magnani's self-professed freedom had been an asset ten years earlier, the new Italy began

to look on her as a bitter, vulgar, ill-mannered holdover from a painful past—"a woman who lives on foul language and beans," as Fallaci described the prevailing view. Magnani's very public affair with Roberto Rossellini had ended in 1949, when Rossellini became infatuated with *Ingrid Bergman*. The two remained close friends for the rest of Magnani's life, but there were no more of the grand passions of which she was so suspicious. Fellini, who some said had been a rival for her affections in the old days, wrote in his memoirs of her bawdy behavior at parties and industry gatherings and told of a dance Magnani would perform only for close friends, in which she mimicked a man with an erection by stuffing stockings under her dress. "She talked about sex often, and in a vulgar way," he said, "but because it suited her persona, it didn't seem startling that she had a man's sense of humor." Indeed, when Magnani sought Fallaci's opinion of her notorious behavior, Fallaci replied, "I think you're a great man, Signora Magnani."

Despite her opinions of the current state of the cinema, Magnani continued to work frequently during the 1960s, her most commercial film during the period being Stanley Kramer's *The Secret of Santa Vittoria* in 1969. She devoted most of her off-screen time to Luca, her only source of consistent affection, who continued to suffer from the paralysis brought on by his childhood polio. Her personal habits included never rising much before noon and, late at night, wandering the streets of Rome feeding the stray cats of which she was so fond. "She was their best friend," Fellini said. "When she died, all the stray cats of Rome mourned for her." Anna Magnani died of pancreatic cancer on September 26, 1973, and was buried in Roberto Rossellini's family mausoleum.

It was Fellini, as it turned out, who acted opposite her in her last film, his own *Roma*, in 1972. Ill and tired, Magnani took only a small, cameo role, but, as was her habit, asked Fellini who would play opposite her. Having not yet cast the male role, Fellini spontaneously said that *he* would play it, and thus found himself in front of his own cameras one soft Rome night, following Anna Magnani up a flight of stairs to her apartment door. "May I ask you a question?" he asks her. Her reply, her last words spoken on film, is simply, "Ciao, go to sleep." Then she quietly closes the door.

SOURCES:

Bondanella, Peter. *The Films of Roberto Rossellini*. NY: Cambridge University Press, 1993.

Brunette, Peter. *Roberto Rossellini*. NY: Oxford University Press, 1987.

Chandler, Charlotte. *I, Fellini*. NY: Random House, 1995.

Fallaci, Oriana. "Tragic Mother," in *The Egotists: Sixteen Surprising Interviews*. Chicago, IL: H. Regnery, 1968.

Governi, Giancarlo. *Il Romanzo di Anna Magnani*. Milan: Bompiani, 1981.

Katz, Ephraim. *The Film Encyclopedia*. 2nd ed. NY: HarperCollins, 1994.

Norman Powers,
writer-producer, Chelsea Lane Productions, New York

Magnes, Frances (1919—)

American violinist who played with major orchestras throughout the world. Born Frances Shapiro in Cleveland, Ohio, on April 27, 1919.

Frances Magnes began lessons at age six with her grandfather, Herman Rosen. Musicians were the norm in Magnes' family; one of her ancestors had been a musician at the court of Nicholas II, tsar of Russia. Magnes was 14 when she made her debut with the Cleveland Orchestra under Artur Rodzinski. She became a member of the Busch Chamber Players, touring America with that group in 1945–46. She won great critical acclaim and went on to tour England, France, Israel, Canada, South America, and Europe. Magnes made recordings with Ernö Dohnányi and the New York Philharmonic Orchestra. Because of her interest in modern music, Magnes was the first to perform and record Stefan Wolpe's Violin Sonata (1949) and Tibor Serly's Sonata (1950); both works were also dedicated to her. In the 1960s, she increasingly appeared with the Westchester Symphony Orchestra where she was concertmaster. She taught as well.

John Haag,
Athens, Georgia

Magnus (d. 1676)

Sunksquaw of the Narragansett tribe. Name variations: Matantuck; Quaiapan; Old Queen. Born in the area now known as Rhode Island, during the middle 1600s; died in 1676, near Warwick, Rhode Island; married Mriksah.

Magnus was one of the women warriors often misidentified as "Queen" by British colonists. A member of the powerful Narragansetts, Magnus led her tribe into battle during King Philip's (Metacom's) War, 1675–76. When the Narragansetts were defeated by Major Talbot's troops, Magnus was taken prisoner. Though other women and children were sold to West Indian slavers, Magnus was executed as a warrior with 90 of her tribe.

SOURCES:

Allen, Paula Gunn. *The Sacred Hoop: Recovering the Feminine in American Indian Traditions*. Boston, MA: Beacon, 1986.

Dockstader, Frederick J. *Great North American Indians: Profiles in Life and Leadership*. NY: Van Nostrand Reinhold, 1977.

Deborah Jones,
Studio City, California

Magoffin, Susan Shelby (1827–c. 1855)

American diarist, best known for her journal Down the Santa Fe Trail and Into Mexico. *Born Susan Shelby in Arcadia, Kentucky, on July 30, 1827; died in Barrett's Station, Missouri, about 1855; married Samuel Magoffin, in 1845; children: two daughters.*

Was the first white woman to travel the Santa Fe Trail; kept a written record of that journey; Down the Santa Fe Trail and Into Mexico: The Diary of Susan Shelby Magoffin, 1846–1847 *published (1926).*

Born into a prosperous and prominent Kentucky family on July 30, 1827, in Arcadia, Kentucky, Susan Shelby Magoffin was the granddaughter of the first governor of Kentucky and was raised on an expansive estate. In 1845, she married neighbor Samuel Magoffin, who was 26 years her elder. For several years prior to their marriage, Samuel had been transporting goods between Independence, Missouri, and Mexico with his brother James. Despite her protected and pampered childhood, Susan chose to accompany her husband on his next trip to Mexico and, in 1847, became the first white woman to travel the Santa Fe Trail. She chronicled the daunting journey on the trail, which had first been traveled in 1821, and which linked Independence, Missouri, and Santa Fe (at that time still part of Mexico), in her diary. Published as a book in 1926, the diary remains a valuable source of insight into the rigors of life on the trail.

One of the early entries in Magoffin's journal reflects the protected environment in which she had grown up and her horror at hearing the profanity of mule drivers who were putting together the wagon train in which she would travel: "It is disagreeable to hear so much swearing; the animals are unruly 'tis true and worries the patience of their drivers, but I scarcely think they need be so profane." Later, while the caravan stopped at Pawnee Rock, a landmark on the Santa Fe Trail that served as something of a trail register, Magoffin wrote: "I cut my name among the many hundreds inscribed on the rock and many of whom I knew." Unlike some travelers, her party did not come under attack by hostile tribes, but the journey had its moments of tragedy; pregnant at the start of the trip, she gave birth to a stillborn son en route after catching yellow fever.

In later entries, Magoffin described her surprise at the informal nature of dress of most women in what is now New Mexico. Seeing a woman in Santa Fe hike her skirt to cross a stream was a revelation to Magoffin, since similar behavior back home would have been scandalous. The openness and independence of local women were equally surprising to her. Her diary contrasts the differences between the women she met in Santa Fe and American women: married American women, she noted, had few legal rights, and whatever property they brought into the marriage or later earned belonged to their husbands. Women in New Mexico, in keeping with the customs of early Spanish colonists, were not considered chattel of men and retained their maiden names, property, and wages after marriage.

The Magoffins eventually settled in Barrett's Station, Missouri, and had two daughters. The exact date of Susan Magoffin's death is unknown, but she passed away suddenly at the age of 28.

SOURCES:
Edgerly, Lois Stiles. *Give Her This Day.* Gardiner, ME: Tilbury House, 1990.

Don Amerman, freelance writer, Saylorsburg, Pennsylvania

Magogo ka Dinizulu, Constance (1900–1984)

South African composer, singer, ugubhu player, and princess whose songs were connected with Zulu life and history. Born in Nongoma, South Africa, in 1900; died in Durban on November 21, 1984; daughter of Chief Dinizulu Ka Cetshwayo; married Chief Mathole Shenge Buthelezi; children: son, Chief Mangosutho Buthelezi, was chief minister of KwaZulu.

Princess Magogo Ka Dinizulu learned the Zulu musical repertoire from her mother and grandmothers, memorizing songs that date back to the 18th century. She learned to play the *ugubhu*, a musical bow, the *umakhweyana* bow, and the European autoharp. When Magogo Ka Dinizulu married, she became the primary wife of Chief Mathole. The couple moved to Kwa Phindagene, living in the hills above Mahlabathini. Their son, Chief Mangosutho Buthelezi, would become a powerful figure in South African politics like his parents. Princess Ma-

gogo continued to sing and compose songs of a court and ceremonial nature after her marriage, and also sang traditional songs. Her singing was recorded by Hugh Tracey in 1939; other experts followed suit in the 1950s. Recognized as an authority, she was frequently consulted on her knowledge of Zulu music and served as musical consultant for the film *Zulu*. Articles on her composing and singing career appeared in South African and European journals. Through her singing and composing, Princess Magogo helped to keep Zulu traditional culture alive.

John Haag, Athens, Georgia

Magri, Lavinia Warren (1841–1919).
See Warren, Lavinia.

Maguire, Mairead (b. 1944).
See joint entry under Williams, Betty and Corrigan, Mairead.

Mahalde.
Variant of Matilda or Maud.

Mahalath.
See Bashemath.

Mahapajapati (fl. 570 BCE)
Indian nun who was aunt and foster mother to Prince Siddhartha Gautama, also known as the Buddha. Name variations: Mahaprajapati; Mahaprajapati Gautami; Gautami Mahapajapati. Flourished around 570 BCE in Nepal, near the Indian border; younger sister of Maya; married Suddhodana or Suddhodanaa (who was also married to her sister Maya); aunt and foster mother to Prince Siddhartha Gautama or Gautami, also known as the Buddha (c. 563–483 BCE).

During the 45 years between the Buddha's enlightenment and his death, he traveled and preached in central India, staying primarily in Magadha and Kausala. He won many converts to the religion and established a community of monks, nuns and laity to live and teach his message. Mahapajapati, Buddha's aunt and foster mother (his own mother *Maya had died seven days after his birth), expressed her desire to become a nun. At first the Buddha refused her request but later reluctantly agreed after Ananda, his beloved disciple, interceded. To govern the relations between monks and nuns and to prevent sexual activity, the Buddha established stringent restrictions concerning the interactions between them. In addition to the already existing rules (*Vinaya*) for the community of monks, eight weighty rules were added that made the nuns subordinate to the order of monks. Despite such restrictions, many able nuns were active during the lifetime of the Buddha. Considering the very limited options for women at the time, the community of Buddhist nuns afforded some women the opportunity to exercise a considerable amount of control over their lives.

Maharani or Maharanee of Gondwana.

See Durgawati (d. 1564).

Maharani or Maharanee of Gurrah.

See Durgawati (d. 1564).

Maharani or Maharanee of Jaipur.

See Gayatri Devi (b. 1919).

Maharani or Maharanee of Jhansi.

See Lakshmibai (c. 1835–1858).

Mahault.

Variant of Matilda or Maud.

Mahaut.

Variant of Matilda, Maud, and Mahout.

Mahaut (c. 1270–1329)

Countess of Artois who was influential in the politics and culture of the French court in the early 14th century. Name variations: Matilda of Artois; Mahout or Mahaut Capet; Mahaut of Artois; Mahaut of Burgundy; Mahaut of Flanders. Pronunciation: Mah-o. Born around 1270 in Artois; died in Paris on November 27, 1329, of a sudden illness; daughter of Robert II, count of Artois, and Amicie de Courtenay (d. 1275), both high ranking members of the French nobility; married Othon also known as Otto IV, count palatine of Burgundy, in 1285; children: Jeanne I of Burgundy (c. 1291–1330, queen of France); Blanche of Burgundy (1296–1326, queen of France); Robert (born c. 1299); Jean (born c. 1300, died in infancy).

At her father's death, inherited the county of Artois (1302); became regent for her son as count of Burgundy when her husband died (1303); her eldest daughter Jeanne I of Burgundy married Philip, the second son of King Philip of France (1306 or 1307); the following year, her daughter Blanche of Burgundy married Charles, another son of the French king (1307); her daughters were involved in a scandal of adultery at the French court for which Blanche was imprisoned and Jeanne was acquitted (1314); her son Robert died, leaving Mahaut as sole heir to the county of Artois (September 1317); was cleared by her son-in-law, King Philip V of France, of charges of sorcery and treason (October 1317); Philip V upheld her claims to the county of Artois against counter-claims brought by her nephew, Robert (1318).

Mahaut, countess of Artois, was among the most important women in France during the early 14th century. Her achievements illustrate how a woman of intelligence and determination was able to utilize her social standing to be an active participant in the politics and culture of French courtly society.

Mahaut's accomplishments were founded in her position in the French nobility which resulted from her parentage, her marriage, and her daughters' marriages and allied her closely to the inner circles of the French court. She was born around 1270 to Robert II, count of Artois, and *Amicie de Courtenay. The county of Artois was one of the important apanages of the French crown. In the mid-13th century, King Louis IX instituted the apanage system to endow his brothers with territories and thus ally important provinces to the French royal house. Mahaut's grandfather, Robert I, was Louis IX's brother and the first count of Artois. Her father, the second count, was Louis IX's nephew. Mahaut, therefore, was the great-niece of Saint Louis, one of the most famous and revered of the medieval French kings.

Mahaut's mother Amicie de Courtenay died in 1275, when Mahaut was about five years old, and her father then married ❧➤ **Agnes of Bourbon**. Relations between Mahaut and her stepmother must have been cordial, judging by the care Mahaut later took to provide a tomb monument for Agnes. However, the absence of consistent maternal influence may be one reason why some of Mahaut's formative years were spent at the French court. She developed a close friendship with *Marie of Brabant, the young second wife of the reigning French monarch, Philip III (1270–1285). Her friendship with Queen Marie influenced the development of Mahaut's keen interest in the arts, and the two remained friends until Marie's death in 1321.

In 1285, Mahaut married Otto IV, count palatine of Burgundy, who at about 45 years of age was considerably older than his first wife. The marriage probably was arranged to draw the important territory of Burgundy, located on the border between France and the Holy Roman Empire, into closer alliance with France. For the next 18 years, until Otto's death in 1303, Mahaut was primarily occupied with her duties as wife and mother. Between around 1290 and

1300, she had four children; Jean, the youngest, died in infancy, but she raised two daughters, *Jeanne I of Burgundy and ✧➤ Blanche of Burgundy, and a son, Robert.

As a young woman in her 20s, Mahaut assumed responsibilities not only for the care of her children, but also for some of the administration of her husband's feudal territory of Burgundy, because Count Otto was frequently absent on military campaigns. Although he was a valiant knight, he was less capable in managing his feudal resources. His accumulation of debts from his military exploits led him to place the county of Burgundy and the education of his children in the hands of Philip IV, king of France, in return for Philip's payment of Otto's debts and provision of income for his family. These arrangements reinforced the close ties among Mahaut, her children, and the French royal family.

Mahaut's situation began to change in 1302 when her father, Count Robert II of Artois, was killed fighting with French forces in campaigns against Flanders, and she inherited the county of Artois. Her husband was killed in battle the following year. Mahaut, now a widow in her early 30s, assumed sole responsibility for raising three young children and added the administration of a second significant feudal territory, Burgundy, to her duties in Artois.

Though young widows at the time tended to remarry, Mahaut remained single and took charge of her own affairs; initially, her children were her primary concern. In 1306 and 1307, both of her daughters married sons of the French king, further strengthening Mahaut's ties to the French royal house. First her eldest, Jeanne I of Burgundy, became the wife of Philip (the future Philip V the Tall, king of France), count of Poitiers, the second son of King Philip IV the Fair in 1306. This marriage fulfilled an agreement made in 1291 between Otto of Burgundy and Philip the Fair by which Jeanne was promised to one of Philip the Fair's sons. The following year, Mahaut's second daughter Blanche of Burgundy married Charles, count of La Marche (the future Charles IV, king of France), the third son of the French king and Mahaut's godson. This second couple appeared to be well matched. Blanche was reportedly very beautiful, and her husband Charles was so handsome that he was also called "the Fair" like his father.

Mahaut's only surviving son Robert, who showed great promise, was brought up in Paris and also traveled through his future lands of Burgundy and Artois. Mahaut made certain that he received the education befitting a future

✧➤ **Agnes of Bourbon** (d. 1287)
*Countess of Artois. Died on September 7, 1287; daughter of Archimbaud or Archambaud VII, ruler of Bourbon, and **Alix of Burgundy** (1146–1192); became second wife of Robert II (1250–1302), count of Artois (r. 1250–1302), in 1277; stepmother of *Mahaut (c. 1270–1329).*

✧➤ **Blanche of Burgundy** (1296–1326)
*Princess of Burgundy. Name variations: Blanche Capet. Born in 1296; died in 1326; daughter of Otto IV, count of Burgundy, and *Mahaut (c. 1270–1329); sister of *Jeanne I of Burgundy (c. 1291–1330); married Charles IV the Fair (c. 1294–1328), king of France (r. 1322–1328), in 1307 (annulled, September 1322). Charles IV was also married to *Mary of Luxemburg (1305–1323) and *Joan of Evreux (d. 1370).*

knight and peer of the realm; he learned his letters as well as the knightly pursuits of combat and hunting. He also enjoyed musical entertainment and an early form of tennis. (Around 1314–15, Robert would be with the French forces campaigning in Flanders, though he would not see combat. In 1317, he would assist at the coronation of his brother-in-law Philip V of France.)

While Mahaut was arranging her daughters' marriages and supervising her son's education, she also continued to administer her feudal holdings in Artois and Burgundy. With the assistance of a trusted advisor, Thierry d'Hireçon, she managed these affairs well. She negotiated disputes between the nobility and the bourgeois in various towns of Artois, and also defended her claims to Artois against the counterclaims of her nephew Robert. He first raised these claims in 1307; two years later, Philip the Fair reached a judgment upholding Mahaut's inheritance of the county of Artois. This decision primarily reflected Philip's personal interest in keeping Artois close to the French crown through the alliances established by the recent marriages of Mahaut's daughters to the king's own sons.

From 1314, Mahaut experienced several years of personal turmoil, beginning when both of her daughters were involved in an infamous scandal at the French court. King Philip the Fair arrested Blanche as well as her sister-in-law *Margaret of Burgundy (1290–1315) for adultery with two knights at the court, Gautier and Philippe d'Aunay. Jeanne was also placed under house arrest at Dourdan for having known of the affair without exposing it. Found innocent, she was reunited with her husband Philip and reigned as queen when he became king of France in 1317. Blanche, however, was not so fortunate. She was initially imprisoned in the famous fortress Château-Gaillard, and while she maintained her innocence, her marriage to the future Charles IV of France was eventually annulled. She is reported to have retired to the abbey of Maubuisson, where she died in 1326. Although it is usually said that Mahaut had no contact with her after the scandal, documents indicate that Mahaut did continue to provide for her disgraced daughter, and that Blanche may have been forcibly retired not to Maubuisson but to the château of Gavray in Normandy.

$\mathcal{S}$he stands before us, not the ideal creation of a mediaeval romancer, but a real woman, with her virtues and failings, her joys and sorrows, . . . a woman trying to grapple with difficulties forced upon her by her position, and by an age when intrigue and cunning were as freely resorted to, and as deftly handled, as the sword and the lance.

—Alice Kemp-Welch

By 1315, Mahaut's nephew Robert had capitalized on the difficulties created for Mahaut by the scandal involving her daughters by renewing his attempt to claim the county of Artois. He provoked rebellion in the county against Mahaut, her advisors, and governmental officials. He also caused Mahaut to be accused of poisoning King Louis X (died June 1315) and his infant son Jean I (died November 1316), and of using sorcery to produce a love potion to effect the reconciliation of Mahaut's daughter Jeanne and her husband, now King Philip V. According to the accusation, these "crimes" were designed to make Jeanne queen of France. While Mahaut was countering these accusations, she was deeply grieved when her only surviving son and heir Robert died suddenly in Paris in September 1317. He was about 18 years of age and shortly was to have been knighted.

Gradually, Mahaut's life became more settled. In October 1317, a judgment proclaimed Mahaut's innocence of the accusations brought by her nephew. With her son-in-law and daughter, Philip and Jeanne, as king and queen of France, Mahaut's influence at court became stronger. Her claim to Artois was confirmed by a judgment of Parlement in 1318, and the county was restored to her when the rebels in Artois finally submitted in March 1319.

The final decade of Mahaut's life allowed her to enjoy more fully the benefits of her position as countess of Artois, peer of the realm, and close relative by birth and marriage to the French royal family. First, she reestablished her authority in Artois. Making a triumphal reentry into her territories in 1319, she reclaimed her residences and repaired and restored the damage done by the rebellion, especially to her favorite château at Hesdin.

Mahaut traveled extensively throughout her life. She spent considerable time at her principal residence (*hôtel*) in Paris, located by the city wall close to the north road. She had several residences in Artois and was also frequently in Burgundy both during her marriage to Count Otto of Burgundy and as regent after his death; the familial line through her daughter Jeanne eventually assumed the inheritance of the county of Burgundy. Mahaut usually traveled in a carriage, accompanied by an extensive household, and her baggage often included such comforts as a bed or couch, tapestries, books, and silver basins.

An intelligent, cultured woman, Mahaut patronized the arts, music, and letters, and extensive documents preserve records of her expenditures for these luxuries. She was an important patron of books, many of which were richly illuminated, and provided liturgical service books for chapels connected with her residences as well as for churches and abbeys to which she made donations. Her personal library included works of devotion such as books of hours, as well as copies of chronicles of the French kings, various works of romance literature, French translations of religious and philosophical treatises, and an early copy of the travels of Marco Polo. Most likely, she was literate at least in French, because she made provisions for traveling cases for the books and reading lecterns for her residences.

Mahaut was also associated with many types of artistic production. She engaged important sculptors, such as Jean Pepin of Huy, to provide tomb monuments for members of her family. Her own tomb effigy of dark Tournai marble, originally at the abbey of Maubuisson, is now located at Saint-Denis near Paris. Her residences were sumptuously furnished with tapestries, metalwork objects, paintings, and stained-glass windows, and she gave equal attention to personal appearance, providing herself, family members, and friends with beautiful, luxurious garments. She also entertained lavishly at her many residences. Food was ample; musicians sang and played instruments. Her château at Hesdin was famed for its trick water fountains.

With all this, Mahaut never neglected the administration of her feudal holdings, and accounts were presented for her inspection three times a year. She was an important figure at the Parisian court. As one of two women to hold the title of peer of France, she was present at the coronations of her son-in-law Philip V (1317), where she held the crown over his head, of her godson Charles IV (1322), and of Philip VI of Valois (1328). In addition to these visible ceremonial roles, her successful negotiation through numerous legal entanglements suggests that she was adept at political maneuvering. Although a number of important French lawyers assisted her in these cases, she was clearly capable of directing her own defense.

Medicine was another one of her interests, and physicians were in attendance to care for her and members of her family. The most notable of these was Thomas le Myésier, a native of Arras in Artois, who was her personal physician for about 25 years. In Paris, le Myésier was also an intellectual disciple of Ramon Lull, a Spanish philosopher, and wrote several compilations of Lull's philosophical ideas. Mahaut's patronage was a key factor in enabling le Myésier to disseminate Lull's doctrines in Parisian intellectual circles.

As was expected in an age of faith, Mahaut was a pious and charitable woman. She founded hospitals in Artois and Burgundy as well as the hospital at Hesdin, which opened in 1323. She seems to have held St. James in particular veneration, for she sent the devout on pilgrimages to the shrine of St. James at Compostela in Spain with special prayers for her son's recovery from a serious illness in 1304 and on behalf of his soul after his death in 1317. She and her daughter Queen Jeanne made frequent donations to the confraternity of St. Jacques-aux-Pèlerins in Paris, where they helped to lay the cornerstone for its church and hospital in 1319. Its sculptured porch, now destroyed, depicted Mahaut, her daughter Jeanne, and her four granddaughters, including *Jeanne II of Burgundy (1308–1347), *Margaret of Artois, and Isabelle Capet.

Mahaut was a particular patron of the abbey of Maubuisson, founded by *Blanche of Castile (1188–1252), queen of France and mother of Louis IX, and often retired there for prayer and meditation. Several members of her family, including her father Count Robert II and probably her daughter Blanche, were buried there. Appropriately, Mahaut spent time at this abbey just before her death, sleeping there on November 23, 1329, after dining with the French king Philip VI at Poissy. She returned to her residence at Paris but became seriously ill and died on November 27. Her final resting place was at Maubuisson, where she was buried near her father.

Mahaut's life represents in microcosm the activities and interests of a French noblewoman during the late Middle Ages. She was adept at protecting and managing her feudal territories, especially Artois. She also understood, negotiated, and withstood the vicissitudes of political intrigue at the French court. Her patronage demonstrates that she both appreciated and promoted the literary, philosophical, and artistic culture that made France, particularly Paris, the leading exponent of Gothic style. As a woman, she was constantly forced to defend her legal rights to her feudal possessions, and she staunchly rose to the challenge. Her life provides a dramatic illustration of the way an intelligent, capable woman could capitalize on the advantages bestowed upon her by noble birth.

SOURCES:

Baron, Françoise. "La gisante en pierre de Tournai de la cathédrale de Saint-Denis," in *Bulletin monumental.* Vol. 128, 1970, pp. 211–28.

Butler, Pierce. *Women of Mediaeval France.* Philadelphia, PA: George Barrie and Sons, 1907.

Dehaisnes, Chretien. *Historie de l'art dans la Flandre, l'Artois et le Hainaut avant le XVe siècle.* Lille: L. Quarre, 1886.

Hillgarth, J.N. *Ramon Lull and Lullism in Fourteenth Century France.* Oxford: Oxford University Press, 1971.

Kemp-Welch, Alice. *Of Six Mediaeval Women.* London: Macmillan, 1913.

Labarge, Margaret Wade. *A Small Sound of the Trumpet: Women in Medieval Life.* Boston, MA: Beacon Press, 1986.

Lord, Carla. *French Patronage of Art in the Fourteenth Century: An Annotated Bibliography.* Boston: G.K. Hall, 1985.

Richard, Jules-Marie. *Une petite-nièce de Saint Louis: Mahaut, comtesse d'Artois et de Bourgogne.* Paris: H. Champion, 1887.

SUGGESTED READING:

Hallam, Elizabeth M. *Capetian France, 987–1328.* London: Longman, 1980.

Strayer, Joseph R. *The Reign of Philip the Fair.* Princeton: Princeton University Press, 1980.

COLLECTIONS:

A large collection of documents (about 12,000 items) pertaining to Mahaut's administration of Artois is preserved in the Archives départmentales du Pas-de-Calais in Arras. Some of these documents are printed or summarized in the following works:

Dehaisnes, Chretien. *Documents et extraits divers concernant l'histoire de l'art dans la Flandre, l'Artois, et le Hainaut avant le XVe siècle* Lille: L. Danel, 1886.

Richard, Jules Marie. *Inventaire sommaire des archives départmentales antérieures à 1790, Pas-de Calais, Archives civiles.* 2 vols. Series A. 1877–1878.

Karen Gould,
independent scholar and expert on
medieval art history, Austin, Texas

Mahaut I (r. 1215–1242)

Ruler of Bourbon. Name variations: Dame Mahaut. Reigned from 1215 to 1242; heir of Archimbaud or Archambaud V, ruler of Bourbon (r. 1116–1171); married Gautier de Vienne, ruler of Bourbon (r. 1171–1215); married Gui II de Dampierre, in 1242; children: (second marriage) two daughters, Mahaut II de Dampierre (1234–1266) and Agnes de Dampierre (1237–1288).

Mahaut I was the heir of Archambaud V, who ruled Bourbon from 1116 to 1171, but it was her first husband Gautier de Vienne who succeeded to the throne upon Archambaud's death. After Gautier's death in 1215, Mahaut I ruled for 27 years, until her marriage in 1242 to Gui II de Dampierre, with whom she had two daughters, *Mahaut II de Dampierre and *Agnes de Dampierre. Following her marriage, Mahaut I was succeeded to the throne by Archambaud VI; his successor was Archambaud VII, followed by Mahaut II.

Mahaut II de Dampierre

(1234–1266)

*Countess of Tonnerre who ruled Bourbon (1249–1262) and Nevers (1257–1266). Name variations: Baroness Mahaut; countess of Tonnere; Mahaut II de Bourbon. Born in 1234; died in 1266 (some sources cite 1262); daughter of Mahaut I (r. 1215–1242) and her second husband Gui II de Dampierre; sister of Agnes de Dampierre; married Eudes de Bourgogne or Eudes (1230–1266), count of Nevers, in 1248; children: Yolande of Burgundy (1248–1280); *Marguerite de Bourgogne (1250–1308); Alix of Burgundy (1251–1290, who married John I, count d'Auxerre and Tonnerre).*

Mahaut II de Dampierre succeeded to the throne of Bourbon upon the death of Baron Archambaud VII, who died in 1249. She also succeeded her grandmother, Countess *Mahaut de Courtenay, who ruled Nevers from 1182 to 1257. In 1262, Mahaut II was replaced by her sister *Agnes de Dampierre as ruler of Bourbon, although she remained ruler of Nevers until her death in 1266, after which the throne went to her daughter *Yolande of Burgundy.

Mahaut de Boulogne (c. 1103–1152).

See Matilda of Boulogne.

Mahaut de Chatillon (d. 1358)

*Countess of Valois. Name variations: Mahaut of Chatillon; Mahaut de Chatillon-Saint-Pol; Matilda de Chatillon or Châtillon; Matilda of Chatillon. Died on October 3, 1358; possibly daughter of Gaucher de Chatillon, lord of Crevecoeur, count of Porcien, constable of France since 1302; possibly daughter of Guido III, count of St. Pol; became third wife of Charles I (1270–1325), count of Valois (son of Philip III the Bold, king of France), in June 1308; children: *Isabelle of Savoy (d. 1383); *Blanche of Valois (c. 1316–?). Charles' first wife was *Margaret of Anjou (c. 1272–1299); his second was *Catherine de Courtenay (d. 1307).*

Mahaut de Courtenay (d. 1257)

*Countess, ruler of Nevers (1192–1257). Reigned from 1192 to 1257; died in 1257; daughter of Pierre de Courtenay and Countess *Agnes de Nevers (r. 1181–1192); married Count Hervé de Donzy, in 1199 (died 1226); married Guy de Forez; succeeded in 1257 by her granddaughter *Mahaut II de Dampierre.*

Mahaut de Dammartin or Dammaratin (d. 1258).

See Matilda de Dammartin.

Mahaut Louvain (1224–1288).

See Maude of Brabant.

Mahaut of Artois (c. 1270–1329).

See Mahaut.

Mahaut of Burgundy (d. 1202)

Countess of Auvergne. Name variations: Mahaut de Bourgogne; Matilda of Burgundy. Died on July 22, 1202; daughter of Eudes II (1118–1162), duke of Burgundy (r. 1143–1162), and Marie of Blois (1128–1190); married Robert IV, count of Auvergne.

Mahaut of Burgundy (c. 1270–1329).

See Mahaut.

Mahaut of Flanders (c. 1270–1329).

See Mahaut.

Mahbuba (fl. 9th c.)

Arabian poet who was the only historical female singer mentioned in The Thousand and One Nights. Born in al-Basra (now Iraq); flourished 840s–860s.

Mahbuba, whose name means *Beloved*, became the property of a man of al-Taif who taught her poetry and how to play the lute and sing. When Mutawakki (r. 847–861) ascended the throne as caliph, Mahbuba was given to him as a gift. Infatuated with her beauty and talent, the caliph kept her at his side constantly. But Mutawakki was murdered in 861, and Mahbuba as well as all the other female singers in his court became the property of Wasif al-Turki who had initiated the caliph's assassination. When Mahbuba continued to mourn the slain caliph, Wasif al-Turki had her thrown in prison. A Turkish captain prevented her death, and Mahbuba was freed on the condition that she leave. She went to Baghdad where she disappeared into the mists of history. Stories of her faithfulness survived, however, and Mahbuba is the only historical female singer to appear in *The Thousand and One Nights*, Arabic literature's most famous collection of stories.

John Haag,
Athens, Georgia

Mahdiyya, Munira al- (c. 1895–1965).

See Egyptian Singers and Entrepreneurs.

Mahlah

Biblical woman. The eldest of the five daughters of Zelophehad, of the Manasseh tribe.

When Mahlah's father Zelophehad died without male heirs, Mahlah and her four sisters (**Noah, Hoglah, *Milcah,** and **Tirzah**) requested permission from Moses to inherit their father's property. Moses granted their request, with the stipulation that the sisters marry within their father's tribe. Afterwards, Moses' judgment concerning the inheritance became general law.

Mahler, Alma (1879–1964)

Cultivated and talented beauty from turn-of-the-century Vienna who, through her romantic involvements, provided both stimulus and emotional shelter to several of the leading figures in the European world of the arts. Name variations: Alma Mahler-Gropius; Alma Mahler-Werfel. Pronunciation: MAH-ler, VER-fel. Born Alma Marie Schindler on August 31, 1879, in Vienna, Austria; died in New York City on December 11, 1964, probably from complications of diabetes; daughter of (Emil) Jakob Schindler (a noted Viennese painter) and Anna Bergen (or von Bergen) Schindler (a former singer who was the daughter of a brewery owner); tutored at home; married Gustav Mahler, on March 9, 1902 (died 1911); married Walter Gropius, on August 18, 1915 (divorced 1920); married Franz Werfel, on July 6, 1929 (died 1945); children: (first marriage) Maria Mahler (1902–1907); Anna Mahler, known as Gucki (b. 1904); (second marriage) Manon Gropius (1916–1935); (with Franz Werfel) Martin (1918–1920).

Death of her father (1892); Carl Moll became her stepfather (1897); met Gustav Klimt (1898); met Gustav Mahler (1901); death of her oldest daughter (1907); with Gustav, made first trip to U.S. (1907); began love affair with Walter Gropius (1910); began love affair with Oscar Kokoschka (1912); Kokoschka painted Die Windsbraut (1914); began love affair with Franz Werfel (1917); went into exile from Austria with Werfel (1938); settled in U.S. (1941); became an American citizen (1946).

Although Alma Mahler had her own set of gifts as a composer, she possessed, as Walter Sorell has put it, "a sort of spell-binding intensity and the effortless ability to fascinate gifted—literally extraordinary—personalities." Thus, she is most prominent for her role as the companion—married and otherwise—of some of the most talented men on the European cultural scene from the close of the 19th through the first half of the 20th century.

The product of an artistic background marked by early family tragedy—her father, a noted landscape painter, died when she was only 13—Alma early departed from the model of the socially and sexually restrained young Viennese woman. She became a consort to genius in the persons of Gustav Mahler, Oscar Kokoschka, Walter Gropius, Franz Werfel, and a number of others. In her autobiography, written in the closing decades of her life, she wrote of realizing "my childhood dream of filling my garden with geniuses." Werfel, her third husband, described her as "one of the very few sorceresses of our time."

Alma Mahler was a product of the vibrant but troubled atmosphere of fin-de-siècle Vienna. One of the great centers of European culture, the city both produced and revered achievements in music, literature, and painting. Its educated elite and much of the rest of the population treated with deadly seriousness such questions as who would win the post of conducting Vienna's leading orchestras. But within this rich cultural world, a variety of ethnic and religious tensions existed. Central among them was anti-Semitism. Sometimes practiced in an illogical fashion—Vienna's anti-Semitic mayor Karl Lueger had Jewish friends—it nonetheless was a pervasive element in the mental world of much of the population. Alma exemplified both her native's city reverence for art and its murky bigotry.

She was born Alma Schindler in Vienna on August 31, 1879, the daughter of the successful painter Jakob Schindler and Anna Schindler, who had sung opera professionally under her maiden name of **Anna Bergen** (some authorities give it as Anna von Bergen). After years of struggle Jakob had become a favorite landscape painter for some of Vienna's wealthiest families, and Alma spent her earliest years in a castle estate he had purchased with his substantial earnings. She was educated at home by her parents and by private tutors.

Thirteen-year-old Alma's life was harshly disrupted in the summer of 1892 when Jakob died suddenly of an intestinal ailment during a family vacation on the German island of Sylt in the North Sea. Her mother soon remarried; her new husband was Carl Moll, one of Schindler's former assistants.

Within a few years, Alma entered the world of Viennese high society. Strikingly attractive and endowed with a gift for witty repartee, the young woman found that her family background gave her ready access to the luminaries of the artistic world. Her intense interest in intellectual affairs—she became an avid reader of philosophers ranging from Plato to Friedrich Nietzsche—removed her from the level of most of her girlish contemporaries.

Serious musical interests also made Alma different from most of the other Viennese girls of her generation. Recognizing her daughter's musical gifts, Anna sent Alma to study counterpoint with Josef Labor, a noted Vienna organist. With evident talent, she composed serious music and pursued a career in the musical world. In later years, she noted: "I have had a wonderful life for which I sacrificed my becoming the first great woman composer." Whatever her musical gifts, her beauty and social skills attracted men early on. Even as a teenager, she had a close, almost amorous, relationship with Max Burckhart, a prominent jurist, friend of her late father, and luminary in the world of the theater. At age 19, she became romantically involved with Gustav Klimt, then a rising painter almost two decades older than she. Her mother and stepfather stood effectively between the two of them, but, as an amorous interest, Klimt was soon followed by the composer Alexander von Zemlinsky, her latest music teacher.

Thus, it was as a stunning young woman, already the object of attention from several notables in the art world, that she met the distinguished conductor and budding composer Gustav Mahler in November 1901. Like her previous flames, Gustav was substantially older than Alma, 20 years in fact. Following a series of successful engagements in a number of major cities like Leipzig and Hamburg, he had arrived in Vienna in 1897, to become director of the renowned Vienna Imperial Opera, and he thus stood at the peak of the European musical world.

Within a matter of weeks after their first encounter, Gustav began to discuss marriage with Alma. He had made a strong impression on her. "I must say I liked him enormously," she recorded in her diary, but she also noted the dangerous energy he seemed to project. "He paced the room like a wild animal. He's pure oxygen. You get burnt if you go too near." A fanatically devoted musician and a bundle of personal quirks, Gustav accompanied his courtship of Alma with a long letter insisting that she give up her work as a composer. She was to devote herself entirely to her role as his wife, comforter, and supporter. In order to be happy together, Gustav insisted, she must be "my wife, not my colleague."

Alma had already written nine musical pieces based on poems by leading German authors like Heinrich Heine. Nonetheless, faced with the prospect of becoming Gustav's wife, she agreed, perhaps reluctantly, to put her own career aside. (In the final year of his life, Gustav would finally take her music seriously. He insisted for example that the songs she had written before their marriage had great musical merit. She must go back to her work, he urged, and her musical writings to date had to be published.)

Gustav apparently lacked confidence in his sexual ability, and Alma decided to reassure him on that score in January 1902. She was pregnant well before the wedding which took place on March 9, 1902. It was followed by a honeymoon in Russia, where Gustav was scheduled to conduct concerts in St. Petersburg. Their first child Maria was born in November 1902, and a second daughter, **Anna Mahler** (called Gucki), followed in 1904.

The marriage was a troubled one due largely to the way Gustav devoted himself totally to his career. Although in their early years together Alma could express some contentment, writing, "I am filled to the brim with my mission of smoothing the path of his genius," she soon complained of her limited role as wife, mother, and personal companion. Some authors suggest she began to find solace in excessive drinking. Nonetheless, biographers of Gustav Mahler like

Alma
Mahler

Edward Seckerson and Michael Kennedy give her substantial credit for the spectacular development of his creativity in the years following the marriage. Still primarily known as a conductor at the time of their wedding, in the years after it he produced five completed symphonies along with his unfinished tenth symphony and his *Song of the Earth* to establish himself as one of the great composers of the 20th century. In Seckerson's words, Alma "became his motivation and his anchor."

The tragic loss of Maria, their firstborn daughter, to diphtheria in 1907 was accompanied by bad news about Gustav. Doctors discov-

ered that his frantic lifestyle had weakened his heart and placed his life in danger. Earlier that same year, they received another jolt when Gustav was impelled to resign his position as director of the Vienna Opera. He had been a controversial figure from his arrival, partly because of his Jewish background, partly because of his insistence on a high level of behavior from both his performers and his audiences. Singers who did not measure up to his standards were dismissed regardless of their previous tenure in the opera company. Gustav also revised older classical scores to reflect the new instruments now available, much to the dismay of traditionalists in his audiences. In a deeply resented policy, he refused to have latecomers admitted to performances when he conducted. A decline in box-office receipts gave his many enemies their opportunity to oust him. Following his resignation in March 1907, the Mahlers escaped the envenomed atmosphere in Vienna with a series of American tours.

A serious blow to the stability of the Mahlers' marriage was Alma's set of involvements with other men. Sometimes this took a relatively innocent form, such as her infatuation with a talented young pianist, Ossip Gabrilowitsch, whom Gustav himself brought home as a guest. More threatening to the marriage was her intimate relationship with Walter Gropius. A rising young architect, Gropius met Alma in the summer of 1910 at a spa where she had gone to recover from exhaustion. At first only her dancing partner, he fell in love with her, a fact that became known to Gustav when Gropius inadvertently addressed to Gustav a letter he had written to Alma. The composer consulted Sigmund Freud, whom he reached through the good offices of one of Alma's cousins, a neurologist, for advice on handling this personal crisis. Unbeknownst to him, however, Alma's relations with Gropius went on secretly and became physical.

Any possibility of a new stage in the Mahlers' marriage was cut short in any case by Gustav's declining health. During a tour of the United States in the winter of 1910–11, he became seriously ill with a heart ailment compounded by a streptococcal infection. Alma threw her formidable energies into caring for her husband, and the two of them returned to Europe in the spring of 1911. Gustav never recovered his health, and he died in Vienna on May 18, at the age of 51. After ten years of marriage to this musical genius, Alma was now an attractive widow of 31.

Gustav's death left Alma financially secure. In 1912, she met the spectacularly talented young Viennese painter Oscar Kokoschka, who had been commissioned to paint the portrait of her stepfather, Carl Moll. The day following their introduction, at a lunch at Moll's home, Kokoschka sent Alma a letter asking her to become his wife. They soon became lovers, and their tempestuous love affair lasted for three years as he repeatedly urged her to consent to marriage and she resisted. According to biographer **Susanne Keegan**, Alma was partly motivated by a practical reason: "to give up all her hard-earned comforts and live a life of spartan aestheticism as the wife of a struggling young artist . . . was asking too much."

A glorious product of their troubled time together was Kokoschka's brilliant 1914 painting *Die Windsbraut* (*The Tempest* or *The Bride of the Wind*). The work shows the two of them on a shattered boat atop a stormy sea. Painted at Alma's instigation—she had suggested that she would consent to marry him if he produced a masterpiece—in fact it came as their relationship was nearing its end. That same year, Alma faced a crisis in her affair with Kokoschka when she discovered she was pregnant. Her abortion in 1914—she may have had one a year earlier as well—was a decisive step in separating her life from his.

Like all Europeans, the young widow found her personal world shaken by the calamity of World War I. Kokoschka enlisted shortly after war broke out and was seriously wounded on the eastern front. When Alma tried to resume contact with Gropius, whose growing reputation as an architect had reminded her of their time together, she found that he too had fought on the Russian front and had returned to Berlin following a nervous breakdown. Their renewed relationship led, on August 18, 1915, to Alma's second marriage. Kokoschka now faded from her life, giving up any hope of winning Alma over.

Alma Mahler-Gropius, as she was now named, gave birth to a daughter **Manon Gropius** in October 1916. In the fall of 1917, after Gropius had gone back to the front, she met the writer Franz Werfel. Werfel had also served in the war against Russia and, thanks to an influential patron of the artistic world, Count Harry Kessler, had been reassigned to a safe job in the Army Press Section at Vienna. By the end of 1917, she and Werfel were deep in a romantic liaison. Despite the fact that she was still Gropius' wife, in August 1918 she and Werfel had a child together, a boy named Martin who died only a year and a half after his birth.

Alma ended her marriage to Gropius formally in 1920. Their relationship had disintegrated partly from physical separation, partly from the gap between her musical interests and his immersion in another part of the cultural world. Walter Gropius went on to become one of the century's most eminent architects in the period after World War I.

The talented young poet and novelist Franz Werfel was the last and also the greatest love of Alma's life. Although they married only in July 1929, they were romantic companions by the closing days of World War I. The two were widely separated by age, with Werfel 11 years younger than Alma. One of the oddities of their attachment—and of Alma's personality in general—was the stream of anti-Semitic rhetoric that she produced. She had twice married men of Jewish background—although Gustav Mahler had converted to Catholicism in 1897 in order to promote his chances of becoming director of the Imperial Opera in Vienna—but she remained a ceaseless source of crude and often cruel remarks about the Jews. Alma and her new love were equally separated by politics. Werfel took an enthusiastic part in the revolution in Austria that helped bring down the old Habsburg dynasty in the closing days of the war. As a result, he was for a time wanted by the police. Alma's political interests were minimal, but her natural conservatism and love for the old order put her at odds with him.

Men of substance and talent continued to be drawn to Alma despite her tie with Werfel. A particularly tangled relationship developed between her and the young Catholic priest Johannes Hollnsteiner, an Austrian professor of theology, in the 1930s. (Werfel apparently decided to tolerate this intense friendship.) Meanwhile, her life was struck by personal tragedy: Manon, her daughter with Gropius, died of poliomyelitis in the spring of 1935, the third child Alma lost.

Hitler's annexation of Austria in 1938 forced Alma and Franz to become exiles, first in Switzerland and England, and finally in France. The outbreak of World War II and, in the spring of 1940, the Nazi invasion of France, made Werfel a likely victim of Hitler's anti-Semitism. Franz and Alma were fortunate in being able to leave Europe via Spain and Portugal, even though they went through dreadful months in southern France before being able to make their escape. They were particularly lucky, as others were not, in finding a sympathetic official manning Spain's border with France who was willing to let them cross over and proceed to Barcelona. They were greeted by friends upon their arrival in the United States in November 1940; it was in the comfort and security of that country that they spent the rest of the war years.

Alma Mahler never learned to speak any language fluently other than her native German. Thus, she and her husband were inclined to spend their time in America largely within the confines of the large German emigré colony in Los Angeles. Clustered in Hollywood and the coastal suburb of Pacific Palisades, it was a remarkably distinguished group of refugees from Nazi Germany, including Thomas Mann, Max Reinhardt, and Erich Maria Remarque.

Alma's influence on Werfel has been blamed by many critics for the shift in his career that moved him away from his immense promise as a poet to become the widely published and highly prosperous author of such novels as *The Forty Days of Musa Dagh* in 1933 and *The Song of Bernadette* in 1941. It can be argued, however, that life experiences turned Werfel in this direction. For example, *The Forty Days of Musa Dagh*, describing the resistance of an Armenian community to persecution by the Turks during World War I, did not only reflect the couple's trip to the Middle East in 1931; it was also Werfel's response to the rise of Nazism in Germany in the first years of the 1930s. *The Song of Bernadette*, recounting the story of a 19th-century French girl, *Bernadette of Lourdes, who sees visions of *Mary the Virgin, was inspired by the couple's harrowing stay in southern France as they tried to elude capture by the Germans in 1940. Werfel's novel *The Song of Bernadette* brought him literary acclaim and the book's substantial financial success was augmented by the subsequent movie adaptation, starring *Jennifer Jones.

Werfel suffered a series of heart attacks dating back to the couple's stay in southern France in the summer of 1940. His condition worsened after 1943, and he died of heart failure on August 25, 1945. In the aftermath of her last husband's death, Alma began work on her autobiography. She became an American citizen in 1946 and in 1952 moved to New York, where she spent the remainder of her life. She traveled extensively in Europe and completed her autobiography, which was published in English in 1958 under the title *And the Bridge is Love*. It appeared in German the following year. She also served as a living link with Gustav Mahler, since leading conductors made her the guest of honor at concerts where her first husband's music was performed. For many observers, Alma remained a beautiful woman into her 80s. She died in New York on December 11, 1964, probably from complications of diabetes.

Aged 85 at her death, Alma Schindler Mahler Gropius Werfel had outlived most of the men for whom she had been a companion and perhaps an essential stimulus. As Sorell put it, "She played the driving motor for the genius of other people. . . . Her lot was to be needed by men about to unfold their own genius." Her fellow Viennese, the critic Friedrich Torberg, seconded that view: "She was a catalyst of incredible intensity."

SOURCES:

Giroud, Françoise. Translated by R. M. Stock. *Alma Mahler or the Art of Being Loved*. Oxford: Oxford University Press, 1991.

Keegan, Susanne. *The Bride of the Wind: The Life and Times of Alma Mahler-Werfel*. London: Secker and Warburg, 1991, Penguin, 1992.

Kennedy, Michael. *Mahler.* London: J.M. Dent, 1990.

Monson, Karen. *Alma Mahler: Muse to Genius: From Fin-de-Siècle Vienna to Hollywood's Heyday.* Boston, MA: Houghton Mifflin, 1983.

Seckerson, Edward. *Mahler: His Life and Times.* NY: Hippocrene Books, 1982.

Sorell, Walter. *Three Women: Lives of Sex and Genius.* Indianapolis, IN: Bobbs-Merrill, 1975.

SUGGESTED READING:

Isaacs, Reginald. *Gropius: An Illustrated Biography of the Creator of the Bauhaus.* Boston, MA: Little, Brown, 1991.

Joll, James. "Tales from the Vienna Woods," in *The New York Review of Books.* October 8, 1992.

Mahler, Alma. *And the Bridge is Love.* NY: Harcourt, Brace, 1958.

———. *Gustav Mahler: Memories and Letters.* Edited by Donald Mitchell. Translated by Basil Creighton. NY: Viking, 1969.

Mahler-Werfel, Alma. *The Diaries: 1898–1902.* Edited by Antony Beaumont and Susanne Rode-Breymann. Translated by Antony Beaumont. Ithaca, NY: Cornell University, 1998.

Steiman, Lionel B. *Franz Werfel: The Faith of an Exile: From Prague to Beverly Hills.* Waterloo, Ontario: Wilfrid Laurier University Press, 1985.

Wagener, Hans. *Understanding Franz Werfel.* Columbia, SC: University of South Carolina Press, 1993.

Weidinger, Alfred. *Kokoschka and Alma Mahler.* Translated by Fiona Elliott. Munich: Prestel, 1996.

Neil M. Heyman,
Professor of History, San Diego State University,
San Diego, California

Mahler, Maria (1895–1942).

See Leichter, Käthe.

Mary Eliza Mahoney

Mahoney, Mary Eliza

(1845–1926)

African-American nurse who was the first black woman in America to graduate with a nursing degree. Name variations: Mary Elizabeth Mahoney. Born Mary Elizabeth Mahoney on April 15 (some sources cite April 16 and others May 7), 1845, in Dorchester, Massachusetts; died on January 4, 1926; daughter of Charles Mahoney and Mary Jane (Steward) Mahoney; New England Hospital for Women and Children, R.N., 1879; never married; no children.

Born in 1845 in Dorchester, Massachusetts, Mary Eliza Mahoney was the eldest of three children of Charles Mahoney and **Mary Jane Mahoney**. As a black woman coming of age in Civil War-era America, her career options were severely restricted, but she was determined to pursue nursing from the time she was a teenager. At age 18, she began working at the New England Hospital for Women and Children as a cook and scrubber and, 15 years later, at age 33, was finally accepted as a student nurse. Considered progressive for its time, the hospital was proud of its treatment of both white and black patients, and the charter of its affiliated School of Nursing contained a provision allowing the admittance of one black student and one Jewish student per class. Mahoney was one of 42 students accepted into the intense 16-month course in 1878, and she was one of only four students to graduate. On August 1, 1879, Mary Mahoney became the first black woman in America to earn a nursing degree.

Staff positions at hospitals were difficult to obtain, particularly for African-Americans, and like most newly graduated nurses Mahoney registered with the Nurses Directory as a private duty nurse. Her references specifically listed her as "colored," but her reputation for calm, quiet efficiency often overcame racial barriers. She fostered trust and performed her job skillfully, and cared for patients not only in Massachusetts but in North Carolina, Washington, D.C., and New Jersey. Mahoney also secured membership in the Nurses Association Alumnae of the United States and Canada, which later became the American Nurses Association (ANA).

Recognizing the difficulties faced by black women in the nursing field, Mahoney supported the efforts of *Martha Minerva Franklin, who founded the National Association of Colored Graduate Nurses (NACGN) in 1908, and delivered the welcoming address at the association's first annual convention in 1909. In 1911, Mahoney was awarded lifetime membership in NACGN and became the group's national chaplain, with duties that included conducting the opening prayers at meetings as well as the induction and instruction of new officers. That year she moved to New York and became supervisor of the Howard Orphan Asylum for Black Children in Kings Park, Long Island, where she remained until her retirement in 1922.

During her career of 43 years, Mahoney received numerous honors; several local affiliates of the NACGN were named after her, and the NACGN established an award in her name in

1936. The first recipient of the annual Mary Mahoney Medal, presented to an African-American nurse who has contributed significantly to the profession, was *Adah B. Thoms. The American Nurses Association continued this award after the NACGN dissolved in 1951. The Mary Mahoney Health Care Center, a comprehensive health care facility, is located in the Dimock Community Health Center (previously the New England Hospital for Women and Children), and, in 1976, Mahoney was named to nursing's Hall of Fame.

Mary Mahoney supported the efforts of the suffragist movement, believing that equality was essential for all women. In 1921, while in her mid-70s, she was among the first women in New York City to register to vote. A dignified woman not quite five feet tall, Mahoney was a devout Baptist who attended the People's Baptist Church in Roxbury, Massachusetts, and, although described as private, had many friends within Boston's black medical community. In 1923, she developed metastatic breast cancer. Mahoney died on January 4, 1926, and was buried in Woodlawn Cemetery in Everett, Massachusetts, where her grave is a place of pilgrimage for members of the American Nurses Association and the nursing sorority Chi Eta Phi.

SOURCES:

Sicherman, Barbara, and Carol Hurd Green. *Notable American Women: The Modern Period: A Biographical Dictionary.* Cambridge, MA: The Belknap Press of Harvard University, 1980.

Smith, Jessie Carney, ed. *Notable Black American Women.* Detroit, MI: Gale Research, 1992.

Williams, Elsie Arrington. *Black Women in America: An Historical Encyclopedia.* Vol. II. Edited by Darlene Clark Hine. Brooklyn, NY: Carlson, 1993.

Judith C. Reveal,
freelance writer, Greensboro, Maryland

Mahony, Bertha (1882–1869).

See Miller, Bertha Mahony.

Mahony, Marion (1871–1961)

American architect, the first woman licensed to practice architecture in Illinois, who contributed to Frank Lloyd Wright's "Prairie School" of architecture. Name variations: Marion Mahony Griffin; Marion Lucy Griffin. Born Marion Lucy Mahony on February 14, 1871, in Chicago, Illinois; died on August 10, 1961, in Chicago; daughter of Jeremiah Mahony (a schoolteacher and journalist) and Clara (Perkins) Mahony (a principal); Massachusetts Institute of Technology, degree in architecture, 1894; married Walter Burley Griffin (an architect), in 1911 (died 1937); no children.

Born on February 14, 1871, and raised in Chicago, Marion Lucy Mahony was the first daughter of Jeremiah Mahony, an Irish immigrant who worked variously as a journalist, teacher, and school principal, and **Clara Perkins Mahony**, a former teacher from a long-established New England family. Her father died when she was 11, and her mother went to work as a school principal while raising Marion and her four siblings. After graduating from Chicago public schools, Mahony received financial assistance from prominent Chicago citizen **Mary Wilmarth** in 1890, which enabled her to attend the Massachusetts Institute of Technology's architecture course. She was only the second woman to receive a degree from the program when she graduated in 1894.

Mahony then worked briefly with her cousin, Dwight Perkins, in his Chicago architectural studio. She became the first woman licensed to practice architecture in Illinois in 1896, and began working with Frank Lloyd Wright in his Oak Park studio. Wright became famous for developing the precedent-setting "Prairie School" of architecture, so named because its use of sleek, low lines and jutting horizontal eaves resembled the flat prairie landscape. Initially paid $15 per week, Mahony did not complain when her salary was soon lowered to $10 per week, and made fundamental contributions to the designs produced in the Oak Park studio. Although she designed some of the interior objects included in Wright's housing designs, such as furniture and mosaic fireplaces, historians of architecture tend to agree that one of her greatest skills, during her time with Wright and later, was as a delineator (or artist) of architectural plans. These include landscape murals showing carefully drawn trees with detailed foliage—works which are clearly marked by her style. Her most important contribution to Wright's work is considered to be the drawings of his designs that she executed for the *Ausgeführte Bauten und Entwurfe von Frank Lloyd Wright* (also called the Wasmuth Portfolio), published in 1910, which brought Wright his first significant international recognition.

In 1909, when Wright made a sudden decision to depart for Europe, he asked Mahony to take over the direction of the studio. Her considerable accomplishments notwithstanding, Mahony preferred all her life to defer to the men she worked with (indeed, she seems to have been quite vehement in proclaiming her own inferiority of talent compared to theirs), and she refused his request, proposing her colleague at the studio, H.V. von Holst, instead. Von Holst agreed only on the condition that Mahony remain as the designer for the studio, which at the time of Wright's departure had a number of unfinished commissions. During Wright's absence, Mahony designed the David Amberg House in Grand Rapids, Michigan (1909–1911, the sole credit for which von Holst claimed in writing has been disproved); the Adolph Mueller House in Decatur, Illinois (1910); and a designed but unexecuted house for Henry Ford. Upon his return, Wright falsely accused her of stealing his clients. This caused a permanent rift between them, and she promptly left the studio.

In 1911, Mahony married Walter Burley Griffin, a colleague from the Oak Park studio. While she continued to be active professionally, she claimed she could never be as great an architect as Griffin, although most historians agree that the beauty of her drawings and the perfection of her delineation enhanced his work. Their professional partnership seems to have been a complete one in practice if not in name, and her work was a major factor in his winning a commission to design Canberra, the new capital city of Australia, in 1912. They moved to Australia in 1914, and for the next two decades lived and worked in Sydney and Melbourne. During this time, Mahony adopted her husband's interest in horticulture, which led to her design of Castlecrag, a self-contained community on the banks of Sydney Harbor. Through this admiration for natural beauty, she developed a belief in anthroposophy, a "mystical philosophy" derived from the theosophy of Madame *Helena Blavatsky.

In October 1935, Griffin moved his practice to Lucknow, India, where Mahony joined him eight months later. He died in 1937. Mahony remained to complete his projects, and later returned to Chicago where she established her own practice and remained active for another 20 years. Chair of the Campaign for World Government and a member of the World Fellowship Society, she was commissioned by **Lola Maverick Lloyd** (a co-founder of the Women's International League for Peace and Freedom) to design the World Fellowship Center in Conway, New Hampshire, in 1942. In 1943, she received a commission to design the town of Hill Crystals near Bolene, Texas. Neither project came to fruition, but her designs for the projects remained true to her appreciation for nature and the environment. Before her death in Chicago on August 10, 1961, Mahony also wrote her memoirs. Still unpublished, *Magic of America* is both autobiographical and philosophical in nature; biographical material about her husband is also included in the manuscript, which is retained in the Burnham Library of the Art Institute of Chicago and at the New York Historical Society.

A number of important details in Frank Lloyd Wright's designs, although traditionally assumed to be his, are now understood to have come from various co-workers, including Mahony, and the difficult task of assigning credit has not been finished. Many believe that Mahony did not receive full credit for her later work because of her staunch defense of her husband and her stated beliefs that he was the true genius. Yet her designs that survive reflect a high order of professional skills, and her architectural drawings, replete with detailed landscape renderings, are proof of a skilled perfectionist.

SOURCES:

Bailey, Brooke. *The Remarkable Lives of 100 Women Artists.* Holbrook, MA: Bob Adams, 1994.

Johnson, Donald Leslie, and Donald Langmead. *Makers of 20th Century Modern Architecture.* Westport, CT: Greenwood Press, 1997.

Sicherman, Barbara, and Carol Hurd Green. *Notable American Women: The Modern Period: A Biographical Dictionary.* Cambridge, MA: The Belknap Press of Harvard University, 1980.

Torre, Susan, ed. *Women in American Architecture: A Historic and Contemporary Perspective.* Whitney Library of Design, 1977.

Judith C. Reveal,
freelance writer, Greensboro, Maryland

Mahzolini, Anna (1716–1774).

See Manzolini, Anna Morandi.

Maia (fl. c. 100 BCE).

See Iaia.

Maid of Antioch (c. 255–c. 275).

See Margaret of Antioch.

Maid of Norway (c. 1283–1290).

See Margaret, Maid of Norway.

Maid of Orleans (c. 1412–1431).

See Joan of Arc.

Maid of Saragossa or Zaragoza (1788–1857).

See Agostina.

Maid of the Mill (1864–1934).

See Jermy, Louie.

Maiden Queen, the (1533–1603).

See Elizabeth I.

Maier, Ulrike (d. 1994)

Austrian skier. Died in January 1994; married; children: at least one.

Three weeks before the Winter Olympics in Lillehammer in 1994, major contender Ulrike Maier of Austria was killed during a downhill race in Garmisch-Partenkirchen. She had won two World championships, one in 1989 while pregnant and one in 1991, and had been fifth overall in the 1992–93 World Cup.

Mailing Soong (b. 1898).

See Song Meiling.

Maillart, Ella (1903–1997)

Swiss-French writer, perhaps one of the last great 20th-century travelers to explore Asia before the onslaught of modern tourism, whose many travel narratives introduced Western readers to new, challenging perspectives on previously unexplored cultures. Name variations: Ella K. Maillart; Kini. Pronunciation: MY-ar. Born Ella Katherine Maillart in 1903 in Geneva, Switzerland; died at age 94 in her mountain chalet in Chandolin, Switzerland, on March 27, 1997; daughter of middle-class parents, her father was a fur-trader; never married; no children; spent the winter months in Geneva, summer months in the Alpine village of Chandolin.

Learned to sail on Lake Geneva as a child; left high school at 17 (1920); began university preparatory curriculum but did not finish; captained and organized first Swiss women's field hockey team; represented Switzerland in single-handed yacht competition in Paris Olympics (1924), the only woman among 17 entrants; sailed to Crete with an all-woman crew (1925); traveled to Berlin and later Moscow (1930) to study filmmaking; became a four-year member of international Swiss ski team, trekking to then-Soviet Caucuses, then-Soviet Central Asia, Peking, Tibet, Afghanistan, and India in 1930s, 1940s. Author, journalist, photographer.

Selected writings—in English: Turkestan Solo: One Woman's Expedition from the Tien Shan to the Kizil Kum *(Des Montes Celestes aux Sables Rouges, 1938),* Forbidden Journey: From Peking to Kashmir *(Oasis Interdites, 1937),* Gypsy Afloat *(1942),* Cruises and Caravans *(1942),* The Cruel Way *(1947),* Ti-Puss *(1951),* Land of the Sherpas *(1955).*

At once intrepid and introspective, Ella Maillart chronicles her life and adventures through the pages of her varied travelogues. There is perhaps no better way to trace the experiences of a career that spans nearly eight decades than to sift through the photographs, reflections, and observations that compose Maillart's narratives. Through her texts, the author, photographer, and journalist exposes the reader to far-off people and places. She consistently brings women's lives—both her own and those she meets in her travels—to the forefront. Maillart's prose not only qualifies her as one of the premier travel writers of the 20th century, but has also helped to move the genre of women's travel writing into well-deserved critical focus.

Ella Maillart's multiple expeditions and wanderings may indeed represent an effort to compensate for an early childhood plagued by illnesses. Until she was ten, Maillart lived vicariously through the characters in the books she read. Older brother Albert's discarded Jules Verne books may have paved the way for later reverie and excitement, but a true turning point came when Ella was ten: that summer her father

Ella Maillart

rented a small house on Lake Geneva, and so began her love of sailing. Landlocked Switzerland may seem like an odd place to begin one's nautical career, but in the small village of Creux, Ella and her lifelong friend **Hermine de Saussure** learned much about boats and life on the water. Better known as Kini and Miette, the two piloted their first sloops on the lake. After learning much from brothers and friends, they managed to acquire a series of sail boats christened *Poodle, Gypsy,* and finally *Perlette.* They undertook the sail from the southern coast of France to Corsica in 1923, a journey that earned them local celebrity status. Following their trip, the two young women encountered Alain Gerbault, who was about to attempt and successfully complete the first solo crossing of the Atlantic. Indeed, this brief encounter was not to be forgotten, and Gerbault would become a strong supporter of Maillart in her future travels. A year later, Maillart became the sole representative of Switzerland in the single-yacht regatta at the Paris Olympics. In 1925, Kini and Miette joined two other women and set sail for Crete. This initial contact with the people in Crete, people whose lives were radically different than those they left behind in Western Europe, inspired Maillart to continue her travels.

The details of Maillart's sailing exploits in the mid- and late-1920s are compiled in *Gypsy Afloat.* Maillart found herself in England teaching at a girls' school and desperately wanted work more to her liking: she managed to apprentice herself as a sailor on the ship the *Volunteer,* impressing both captain and crew. She used this apprenticeship as preparation to fulfill a dream shared by Miette and herself: they planned to sail to Polynesia. Miette procured a boat for the journey, the *Atalante,* and, after nearly two years of planning, their project was finalized. Much to Maillart's chagrin, their hopes were dashed when Miette fell ill and could not make the journey. Two months later, Maillart lost her sailing partner: Miette did not succumb to illness, but to marriage.

The loss of her partner ultimately prompted Maillart to abandon her illustrious sailing career, but she could not shake the yearning to travel. As **Françoise Blaser** notes in an interview with Ella Maillart, the young Kini had no intention of pursuing a more conventional career path. When her father suggested that she accept a job as a bilingual secretary at the United Nations, Ella answered that she would rather die. Neither marriage nor an office position, more typical paths for young women in the 1920s and 1930s, appealed to her. Instead, she turned her

sights east, first to Berlin where she occasionally worked on the English versions of the first sound movies, and then on to Moscow, a short 12 years after the Bolshevik Revolution.

In Moscow, Maillart announced her plans to learn more about Russian cinema, which was evoking much foreign interest. In truth, she was more intrigued by Russian youth and their activities. In the fall of 1930, Ella was invited to join a group of 12 young people in a voyage to the Caucuses. The group trekked through the mountains and on to the Black Sea at Batoum, where Maillart remained for a time. There she worked on perfecting her Russian before returning home to Switzerland. Upon her return, she was accused of having trafficked with the Bolsheviks, accusations that hurt both her and, especially, her father. As Maillart notes in *Cruises and Caravans:*

> It was bitter to find out that people would not believe I was independent. My ailing father was upset to see that, even after the papers had published my reply, some of his friends were still cutting him. This incident affected me mainly because of him and it taught me a lesson: never to write or lecture on subjects related to political questions that do not interest me.

In fact, this learned abstention from political rhetoric would come to characterize all of Maillart's future narratives.

Maillart's adventures in the Caucuses found their way into print as the subject of her first book, *Parmi la jeunesse russe* or *Among the Russian Youth,* published in French. This initial attempt at writing did not belie a deep love for literary composition; on the contrary, Maillart needed the money that a book would earn her. In Paris, she was again encouraged by Alain Gerbault, who introduced her to the publisher of his latest book. Ella, in turn, had her book published, and the money she received for her effort bought the essentials for her next voyage. As she notes in *Cruises and Caravans:* "It was more money than I had ever seen before, and with the cheapness of third-class travel in Russia, it could take me a long way east of Moscow." The pattern for her future was thus set: she wrote to continue her travels, and her travels prompted her to write. In the spring of 1932, Maillart declared her next destinations to be what were then Soviet Turkestan and Khazakstan, both at the outer periphery of the Soviet empire.

Turkestan Solo documents Maillart's fantastic voyage from Moscow to the Celestial mountains that divide Russia, China, and Afghanistan. One of the first Westerners to observe the influence of Soviet authority on Turkestan and Khazakstan, Maillart in her travelogue delved into the complexities and repeated difficulties of daily life for travelers and indigenous people alike. The intricacies of Soviet rail travel, the complex process of obtaining horses, and the perils of high mountain trekking are interwoven with tales of the still nomadic Khirgiz and the essentials of their family life. Maillart identified with the nomadic lifestyle of the Khirgiz as she had once so closely identified with sailors: "All ports and none are home to them, and all arrivings only a new setting forth." While Maillart completed the first half of her journey in the company of four Russian companions, she proceeded alone to Uzbekistan and the Turkestan cities of Samarakand, Bukhara, and Khiva. She crossed the red desert, the Kizil Kum, on a camel, and astonished the president of the tourist society of Tourtkol, where she was proudly deemed the first tourist. When the office secretary does not understand the meaning of the word tourist, the reader understands that Maillart has indeed crossed into a land full of the unknown. She proved herself to be one of the last true travelers in a world that would soon belong to tourists.

Upon her return, the photographs, articles and book about Turkestan brought Ella Maillart much merited attention and allowed her to fund yet another expedition. With the backing of a French daily, the *Petit Parisien*, Maillart planned a daring journey across China. She traveled by sea to Shanghai and Manchukuo, and by rail on to Peking. Maillart bided her time writing about the Japanese presence in Manchuria while preparing to arrive at her true goal: she intended to meet up with the tracks of her previous journey at the foot of the Celestial Mountains. In January 1935, she met with bad news: the province of Sinkiang, north of Tibet and en route to her destination, was inaccessible due to civil war. She thus rerouted her itinerary through Tibet, with the hope of later deviating north. At this point, Ella encountered Peter Fleming, English traveler and journalist for *The Times* in London, and husband of actress *Celia Johnson. Their voyage together became the subject of two books: Maillart's *Forbidden Journey* and Fleming's *News from Tartary*. Maillart's initial reaction to Fleming's accompanying her was hardly welcoming. Consider her remarks in *Cruises and Caravans*: "I was not very enthusiastic about our association, because I am sure that a weak girl travelling alone through a difficult country has a better chance of success than anybody else. . . . But this journey might be so long and monotonous that it was wiser to be together—also in case it should land us in jail." Maillart and

Fleming went on to present two very different takes on their common journey: Fleming's narrative focuses on the many miles undertaken and the number of wild game shot. He often reminisces about England and the bounty that awaits him upon his return. Maillart, on the other hand, appreciates the primitive lifestyle that they and their guides must lead. She describes the details of each oasis and the long stretches in between, and her only regret is that the journey must someday end. In August 1935, the unlikely team reached their goal of Kachgar on the Russian border before they turned south towards India. Maillart recorded her thoughts about her flight home in *Cruises and Caravans*: "Though this miraculous flying made me air-sick, I was thinking; returning home I was different than the person who had left. I was no longer Swiss, or European. I belonged now to the whole world, and it seemed now that I could nevermore feel fully at home in Geneva."

This desire to find her place as a citizen of the world and to learn to know herself characterized Maillart's final two travel narratives and marked yet another chapter in her life. *The Cruel Way* tells the story of Maillart's 1939 crossing of Iran and Afghanistan with her friend Christina, a pseudonym Maillart gave to the Swiss-German author ✍➤ **Annemarie Schwarzenbach**. The two embarked on this journey in Schwarzenbach's Ford: Ella jumped at the chance to cross the roads of Iran and Afghanistan in a private vehicle and, at the same time, hoped to liberate Schwarzen-

---

✍➤ **Schwarzenbach, Annemarie** (1908–1942)

Swiss-German author. Born in Zurich, Switzerland, in 1908; died in 1942; daughter of a wealthy industrialist.

Though Annemarie Schwarzenbach wrote many novels, travelogues, and stories, few have been published. She often appears, however, in the memoirs and biographies of many literati of the early and mid-20th century: Klaus and *Erika Mann, Roger Martin du Gard, André Malraux, and *Carson McCullers. *Ella Maillart, with whom she traveled through Iran and Afghanistan in 1939, refers to Schwarzenbach as "Christina" in *The Cruel Way* (1947), Maillart's story of their journey. Annemarie Schwarzenbach's *Eine Frau allein* (*A Woman Alone*) was published in 1989.

SUGGESTED READING:
Fleischmann, Uta, ed. *"Wir werden es schon zuwege bringen, das Leben": Annemarie Schwarzenbach an Erika und Klaus Mann. Briefe 1930–1942*. Pfaffenweiler: Centaurus-Verlagsgesellschaft, 1993.

COLLECTIONS:
Klaus und Erika Mann-Archiv/ Städtische Bibliothek, Munich.

bach from her addiction to morphine. The two looked to flee a Europe where war had already erupted in search of both interior and exterior tranquility. Maillart's account of their trip attests to the many people and varied cultures that the two observed, but the author could not help but dwell on her companion's drug addiction and her incessant relapses: "I worried about Christina. She was feverish, smoked more than ever and, though she suffered from a bad digestion, would not observe her diet when we dined out. My affection for her was far from sufficient to tell me how to help her. Rather, I thought that I was exasperating her, that I should leave her in peace." These lines signaled Ella's spiritual abandonment of Schwarzenbach: she knew not what to say and she had become tired of focusing so much energy on her companion. Ultimately, Maillart admitted failure, for Schwarzenbach remained drug addicted, and after a six-month journey the two separated. Schwarzenbach returned to Europe to do what she could to fight the fascists. Maillart refused to return to war, and, shortly before 1940, took up residence in southern India.

Ti-Puss recounts the five years that Maillart spent in India with Hindu sages, eager to know herself, to learn the inner wisdom that the sages offer. The book tells the story of Ella's inner and outer journeys, and the role that her attachment to her cat plays in her understanding of love of self and love of other. Ti-Puss, the elusive but charming cat adopted by Maillart, helps the author to understand the inner self of which the sages speak. Indeed, Ti-Puss represents at once independence and unconditional love to Maillart, thus embodying what she sought and what eluded her in Europe. Traveling from India to Tibet, the beloved Ti-Puss was separated from Maillart. This loss marked the end of her voyage to India: shortly thereafter, she returned alone to Switzerland in 1945 to look after her ailing mother.

Despite the sadness associated with the loss of her cat, Maillart called *Ti-Puss* the only book she enjoyed writing. Serge Guertchakoff notes Ella Maillart's words in his 1993 interview with her: "But the only work that I really wanted to write is the one about my cat in India, Ti-Puss. As far as that goes, I hate writing, I never learned to do it. I am not good at grammar." Despite her readily admitted distaste for the art of composition, her publications, in fact, always allowed Maillart to live independently and to fulfill her dreams. An ethnographer and traveler at heart, she wrote mainly out of necessity. Yet her writings brought her travels to life for her readers, and provided a wonderful vantage point from which to consider her reflections and adventures.

In 1946, not long after her return from India, Maillart purchased a small plot of land and had a chalet built in Chandolin, high in the Swiss Alps. After that, she curtailed her travels somewhat, and generally spent six months of the year at her isolated mountain paradise and the other six months in Geneva. Chandolin offered Maillart the majesty and solitude that inspired her, recalling the spirituality that she sought in all of her Asian voyages. She revisited Asia often, traveling with small groups of tourists in Nepal, China, Tibet, and other countries. As she noted in the epilogue to the French version of *Cruises and Caravans*, she no longer needed to travel to quench her desires: "I do not expect anything from the outside. I have patience. I possess my bearings to follow the path that leads to the immutable center, to the One without a second, that which is the first and last word of life."

The indomitable Ella Maillart continued to give conferences and interviews until she died, at age 94. Equally fluent in French and English, she spoke of the many people she had known during her travels: indeed, although she lived alone, she was constantly in good company. The celebrated *grande dame* of Swiss travelers continued her reign almost to the very end of the 20th century.

SOURCES:
Blaser, Françoise. "Rester, partir: il faut choisir" (To Stay, To Go: One Must Choose), in *Journal de Genève*. July 10, 1994, p. 17.
Guertchakoff, Serge. "Une grande dame vagabonde: Ella Maillart" (A Great Lady Vagabond: Ella Maillart), in *Revue du Vieux Genève*. 1993, pp. 72–86.
Maillart, Ella K. *Croisières et caravanes* (Cruises and Caravans). Paris: Ed. du Seuil, 1951.
———. *The Cruel Way*. London: Heinemann, 1947.
———. *Cruises and Caravans*. London: J.M. Dent & Sons, 1942.
———. *Turkestan Solo: One Woman's Expedition from the Tien Shan to the Kizil Kum*. Translated by John Rodker. London: Heinemann, 1938.

SUGGESTED READING:
Russell, Mary. *The Blessings of a Good Thick Skirt: Women Travellers and their World*. London: Collins, 1986.

Sara Steinert Borella,
Assistant Professor of French, Pacific University,
Forest Grove, Oregon, who had the pleasure of meeting and
speaking with Ella Maillart in January 1995

Maillé, Jeanne-Marie de (1331–1414).

See Women Prophets & Visionaries in France at the End of the Middle Ages.

Mailly, Louise Julie de Mailly-Nesle, Comtesse de (1710–1751).

See Pompadour, Jeanne-Antoinette for sidebar.

Mailly-Nesle, Marie Anne de (1717–1744).

See Pompadour, Jeanne-Antoinette for sidebar on the duchesse de Châteauroux.

Main, Marjorie (1890–1975)

American actress, best remembered for her work in the "Ma and Pa Kettle" film series. Born Mary Tomlinson on February 24, 1890, in Acton, Indiana; died in Los Angeles, California, on April 10, 1975; daughter of Reverend Samuel Tomlinson and Mary (McGaughey) Tomlinson; attended public schools in Elkhart, Indiana; attended Knickerbocker Hall and Franklin College, both in Indiana, and Hamilton College, Lexington, Kentucky; graduated in 1909 from a school of expression; studied dramatics in Chicago and New York; married Stanley L. Krebs (a psychologist), on November 2, 1921 (died 1934); no children.

Selected theater: Cheating Cheaters *(1916);* Yes or No *(1917);* The Wicked Age *(1927);* Burlesque *(1927);* Salvation *(1928); appeared as Mrs. Martin in* Dead End *(1935), Lucy in* The Women *(1936).*

Selected filmography: A House Divided *(1931);* Hot Saturday *(1932);* Crime Without Passion *(1934);* Dead End *(1937);* Stella Dallas *(1937);* Boys of the Streets *(1938);* King of the Newsboys *(1938);* Test Pilot *(1938);* Too Hot to Handle *(1938);* Three Comrades *(1938);* They Shall Have Music *(1939);* Angels Wash Their Faces *(1939);* The Women *(1939);* Another Thin Man *(1939);* I Take This Woman *(1940);* Dark Command *(1940);* Susan and God *(1940);* The Trial of Mary Dugan *(1941);* A Woman's Face *(1941);* Barnacle Bill *(1941);* The Shepherd of the Hills *(1941);* Honky Tonk *(1941);* The Bugle Sounds *(1942);* We Were Dancing *(1942);* Jackass Mail *(1942);* Tish *(1942);* Tennessee Johnson *(1942);* Heaven Can Wait *(1943);* Johnny Come Lately *(1943);* Rationing *(1944);* Gentle Annie *(1944);* Meet Me in St. Louis *(1944);* Murder He Says *(1945);* The Harvey Girls *(1946);* Bad Bascomb *(1946);* Undercurrent *(1946);* The Egg and I *(1947);* The Wistful Widow of Wagon Gap *(1947);* Big Jack *(1949);* Ma and Pa Kettle *(1949, and eight other films in the series through 1957);* Summer Stock *(1950);* Mrs. O'Malley and Mr. Malone *(1950);* The Law and the Lady *(1951);* It's a Big Country *(1952);* The Belle of New York *(1952);* The Long Long Trailer *(1954);* Rose Marie *(1954);* Friendly Persuasion *(1956);* The Kettles on Old MacDonald's Farm *(1957).*

A veteran of the Broadway stage and some 80 movies, including the extremely popular "Ma and Pa Kettle" series (nine films about an eccentric farm couple which were made between 1949 and 1957), Marjorie Main was one of the finest character actresses of her time. "Realism is the hallmark of the acting style of this character player," observed a critic in the New York *Herald Tribune.* "The rasping voice and swaggering stride she affects in so many of her screen characterizations are traits she observed in a number of aggressive Western farm women during her childhood."

Born Mary Tomlinson in 1890, the daughter of a minister, Main did indeed grow up in the heart of Indiana farm country, and used to entertain visitors with her impressions of those around her. While reciting in a school elocution contest, her voice "slipped up a couple of gears," as she put it, and the reaction was so satisfactory that she later adopted it for her comedy roles. After graduating from an elocution school and attending several colleges, Main taught dramatics at Bourbon College (Paris, Kentucky) for a year before joining a Shakespearean repertory company. While playing the Chautauqua circuit, she met psychologist and lecturer Dr. Stanley Krebs, whom she married in 1921. It was Krebs who came up with her stage name, which was said to have been inspired by the Sinclair Lewis novel *Main Street.*

Krebs was supportive of Main's career, and she subsequently toured on the Orpheum circuit and with a stock company out of Fargo, North Dakota. Around 1915, she played New York's Palace Theater, appearing in a comedy skit called "The Family Ford," starring W.C. Fields. In 1916, she made her Broadway debut in *Cheating Cheaters,* followed by *Yes or No* the following year. Main played small roles in *The Wicked Age* (1927), as *Mae West*'s mother, and *Burlesque* (1927), with *Barbara Stanwyck*, and then took several years off to be with her husband, who was having difficulty arranging his work around her schedule.

Following Krebs' death in 1934, Main returned to the stage in the breakthrough role of Mrs. Martin, the mother of a gangster, in *Dead End* (1935), which ran for a year on Broadway. "Remarkably played," said Percy Hammond, the reviewer for the New York *Herald Tribune.* Critic Kelcey Allen concurred: "In two minutes she galvanized the audience with the sharpness of her delineation of a mother who accords a killer unusual treatment," he wrote. Main next signed on for *Clare Boothe Luce*'s drama, *The Women* (1936), stealing the show with her brief appearance as a Reno hotel maid. The actress reprised both her roles in *Dead End* and in *The Women* for the film versions of the plays.

Marjorie Main

From 1937, Main devoted herself to movies, finding her niche in a series of comedies during the 1940s, many of them with Wallace Beery. Her role as the frazzled farm wife with 13 children and a lazy husband, in the film adaptation of *Betty MacDonald's *The Egg and I* (1947), earned Main an Academy Award nomination and spawned the nine spin-off films of the "Ma and Pa Kettle" series, in which she co-starred with the peppery Percy Kilbride. These low-budget films were never endorsed by the critics, but were extremely popular with the public. Main called Ma Kettle her favorite role, "good for a lot of laughs," she told *The Saturday Evening Post*, "and I would rather make people laugh than anything else." The last of the series was *The Kettles on Old MacDonald's Farm* (1957), after which Main retired.

In private life, Main was known as a charming, soft-spoken woman, who retained much of the conservatism she learned as the child of a minister. Known as one of the most unpretentious stars in Hollywood, she always did her own cooking and housework, claiming that it was good for her mental and physical health. After leaving films, the actress divided her time between homes in Los Angeles and Palm Springs until her death in 1975.

SOURCES:

Katz, Ephraim. *The Film Encyclopedia*. NY: Harper-Collins, 1994.

Lamparski, Richard. *Whatever Became of . . . ?* 2nd Series. NY: Crown, 1968.

Rothe, Anna, ed. *Current Biography 1951*. NY: H.W. Wilson, 1951.

Barbara Morgan,
Melrose, Massachusetts

Main, Mrs. (1861–1934).

See Le Blond, Elizabeth.

Maine, countess of.

See Rothild (c. 871–c. 928).
See Matilda of Château-du-Loir.
See Ermentrude (d. 1126).
See Jeanne of Lorraine (1458–1480).

Maintenon, Françoise d'Aubigné, Marquise de (1635–1719)

French noblewoman who was the second wife of Louis XIV and established an influential school for girls. Name variations: Madame or Mlle Maintenon. Born on November 27, 1635, in Niort Prison, Poitou, France; died on April 15, 1719, at St. Cyr; interred at St. Cyr; daughter of Constant d'Aubigné and Jeanne de Cardilhac; married poet Paul Scarron (d. 1660), in 1652; married Louis XIV (1638–1715), king of France (r. 1643–1715), on June 12, 1683 or 1684; no children.

Born Catholic but educated by Protestant aunt until age seven; moved with family to French West Indies (1645); returned to France (1647); returned to Catholicism; became nurse and governess of Louis XIV's illegitimate children (1667); made a marquise (1675); appointed lady-in-waiting to the Dauphine (1679); became Louis' mistress (1680); was secretly married to the king (1683); set up school for girls at St. Cyr (1686); retired to St. Cyr after death of Louis (1715).

Publications: Françoise d'Aubigné, marquise de Maintenon, Lettres.

It is doubtful that anyone in the 17th century could have predicted that a girl who was born in extraordinary and somewhat shameful surroundings would become the wife of the most powerful king in Europe. Indeed, the birth of Françoise d'Aubigné on November 27, 1635, was far from auspicious. Her father Constant d'Aubigné was a member of the lower aristocracy who had gambled away the majority of his inherited income. More seriously, in 1627 he was arrested for treason and imprisoned at Niort, in Poitou. While in prison, however, his charms soon won over the governor's daughter, **Jeanne de Cardilhac**, and they were married shortly thereafter. All of their children, two sons and one daughter, were born within the prison walls. Fortunately, shortly after she was born Françoise was removed to live with her aunt, **Louise-Arthémise d'Aubigné**.

Although she was born into the Catholic faith, for the first seven years of her life Françoise was brought up in a Protestant household. Her aunt was a Calvinist, or Huguenot, and had inherited a strong sense of religious piety from Françoise's grandfather, Agrippa d'Aubigné. While not much is known of Françoise's early childhood years, she remarked later in life that this was one of the happiest periods of her life. When her father was released from prison in 1642, Françoise was reunited with her family.

For the next three years, she lived with her family in Paris. In 1645, however, at age ten, Françoise left France when her father was promised a government post in the French West Indies. Unfortunately, the position was already filled when the d'Aubigné family arrived in Martinique, and Constant, in contrast to his name, returned alone to France. Françoise was now left in a foreign land where she lived for two years with her mother and two elder brothers. It appears that this experience did not have a great impact upon the young girl as she rarely referred to it in later life. What is known is that she was a very pretty and intelligent child who had an aptitude for learning but was unusually reserved for her age.

When the family returned to France in 1647, Françoise's mother was unable to care for her, and, consequently, the 12-year-old was given into the care of another aunt, **Madame de Neuillant**. Unlike Louise-Arthémise, however, Mme de Neuillant was a strict Catholic, and Françoise was immediately sent to an Ursuline convent where she was to be educated and in- doctrinated into the Catholic faith. Although Françoise did not initially like the convent, she gradually came to accept it and would remain a strong and pious Catholic for the rest of her life.

For much of her early life, Françoise was sheltered from political events in France. When Louis XIII died in 1643, he was succeeded by a boy who was not yet five years old. Fortunately, the government was in the capable hands of the late king's widow, *Anne of Austria, who ruled France for nine years until her son, Louis XIV, was old enough to govern independently. Once he turned 13, which was the age of legal majori- ty in France, Louis XIV began ruling in his own name, and he quickly brought an end to the civil war, known as the Fronde, which had racked France for five years.

> *I*n Madame de Maintenon the king found a woman who was always modest, always mistress of herself, always reasonable, and who in addition to such rare qualities was also witty and a good conversationalist.
>
> —Madame de Caylus

Many of these events remained far removed from Françoise's life while she lived behind con- vent walls. The situation changed, however, in 1651 when she was removed from the nunnery and sent to live with her aunt in Paris. The house she lived in was next door to one of France's most famous lyric poets, Paul Scarron. Although he was originally intended for the priesthood, Scarron's life in holy orders was abandoned abruptly at the age of 26, when he developed a mysterious and incurable disease, which was probably acute rheumatoid arthritis. While his fi- nancial situation was precarious, his charm, wit, and literary skills soon brought him attention from the royal court. After the death of Louis XIII, Scarron received a pension from Anne of Austria and from that point on held nightly ban- quets and entertainments in his apartments.

In 1651, 16-year-old Françoise d'Aubigné met 42-year-old Paul Scarron; they took an in- stant liking to one another. This was partly based upon mutual feelings of sympathy since both of them were lonely people who felt unloved and unwanted. Within months after their first meet- ing, Scarron proposed marriage. Françoise ac- cepted, and they were married on April 4, 1652. The eight years of her marriage to Scarron were happy ones. Their house was visited daily by witty and intelligent aristocratic women and men who attended her husband's literary salon. Scar- ron was at the height of his popularity, and his wife was blossoming into a beautiful young woman. Françoise, however, maintained her re- served manner and said later: "I was not interest- ed in being rich, I was a hundred degrees above self-interest, but I wanted to be respected."

Her desire not to be rich was realized when Scarron died on October 6, 1660. He had left no will, and, after paying off his debts, Françoise had little to live on. Fortunately, her husband's reputation enabled her to continue to receive the royal pension from Anne of Austria. Shortly after Scarron's death, Françoise moved into a convent, where she lived a quiet, though far from isolated, life. Devoted to her women friends, she was a popular guest at their salons, where she counseled and advised them on vari- ous household matters. She had no desire to re- marry, and her continued aspiration was to be liked and esteemed. For the next eight years, Françoise lived content. Her life changed forev- er, however, when she was called upon to look after King Louis XIV's illegitimate children.

Louis XIV had married *Maria Teresa of Spain, the daughter of Philip IV, king of Spain, in 1660. Like most royal marriages, however, it was based upon neither mutual love nor attraction but was instead the final component of a peace treaty with Spain. Consequently, Louis did not take his marriage vows seriously and continued to have a series of sexual liaisons with other women. One woman, *Madame de Montespan, managed to keep the king's interest and remained his mistress for 13 years. After the birth of Montespan's first child in 1669, Françoise d'Aubigné, the widow Scarron, was appointed to act as nurse and gov- erness for the royal children. Madame de Mon- tespan eventually gave birth to seven illegitimate children, all of whom were cared for with great love and affection by Françoise.

This appointment brought Françoise her first opportunity to meet the king of France. Tall, handsome and intense, Louis XIV took his office seriously. Believing that he was God's divine rep- resentative on earth, Louis left no aspect of his government alone and followed a strict daily work routine. Having experienced civil warfare and upheaval during the early years of his reign, he was determined to unite the country and en- sure that no further opportunities for rebellion would arise. As a result, Louis created an admin- istrative apparatus which included not only an elaborate system of spies but also the largest army in Europe. At the palace of Versailles, a rit- ualized court life was established in order to keep

Françoise
d'Aubigné,
Marquise
de
Maintenon

the nobility close by where they could be observed. More important, attendance at court kept them far away from their provincial lands where secret plots could be hatched. Finally, the king engaged in a series of foreign wars in an attempt to expand the borders of France.

All of these policies were not readily apparent to Françoise when the king, who was a devoted father, visited his children. This situation changed in 1674 when Louis had the royal children moved to the palace of St. Germain. Not only did the king begin to pay more attention to his children's governess, but Françoise was now exposed to court life. To someone so reserved and pious, the ritual, luxury, extravagance and intrigue of Louis XIV's court was not only shocking but difficult to live with. According to some historians, when Françoise attempted to leave her post and retire quietly to a convent, she was persuaded to stay at St. Germain not only by her confessor but, more significantly, by several high-ranking members of the Catholic Church. Noticing that Louis was becoming increasingly interested in the 39-year-old widow, they encouraged her to continue living at court in the hopes that she would have a positive moral influence on the king. For whatever reasons, Françoise decided to remain at court, and, after she received a pension and the marquisate of Maintenon from the king, she was forever after known as Madame de Maintenon.

For the next several years, Madame de Maintenon's life at court revolved around teaching and caring for the king's children. Although she had been friends with Madame de Montespan, now that they were in closer proximity to one another, the differences of opinion they held regarding the upbringing of Louis' children surfaced. They openly disagreed and fought, often to the point of tears. Madame de Montespan was under additional pressure due to the church's remonstrances to the king that he give her up. The Montespan-Louis XIV relationship showed signs of stress from 1674 although it did not end until 1680. Rumors circulating at the time placed the blame for Louis' coolness towards his mistress on his new-found affection for Madame de Maintenon. There is no evidence to suggest that Françoise was the king's mistress before 1680, but it became clear that he was attracted to her.

Of Madame de Maintenon's feelings towards the king, even less is known. Although she left over 4,000 surviving letters, only two of them were from Louis XIV; she destroyed the rest he wrote to her. Even though it is well-known that she began corresponding with the king in 1674, the contents of those letters will never be known.

By 1680, the king's infatuation with Madame de Montespan came to an end. Now wholly devoted to Madame de Maintenon, he spent at least two hours every afternoon in her presence, and when he appointed her as lady-in-waiting to his son's wife, the Dauphine (*Maria Anna of Bavaria), Françoise's position was secured. She was now no longer responsible for the king's illegitimate children but held a more pres-

tigious and important role at court. Sometime after this appointment, she finally became Louis' mistress. Under her influence, the king's behavior changed. He began to pay more attention to his estranged wife, whom he had ignored for the past 20 years. More significantly, he never took another mistress and remained faithful to Madame de Maintenon for the next 35 years.

When Queen Maria Teresa died of blood poisoning in July 1683, Louis proposed marriage to Françoise shortly after. In most instances, a widowed king normally chose another royal princess for his second wife. Louis, however, was so deeply in love with Madame de Maintenon that he refused to consider any other possibilities. His respect for her was evident in the fact that he married her, rather than keeping her on as his mistress, as he had done with so many other women. To solve the problem of their difference in rank, they made a morganatic marriage. This allowed a man of superior rank to take a woman of inferior birth as his lawful wife, because neither she nor her children could inherit his rank or possessions. Since Françoise was 48 years old and past childbearing age, the problem that additional heirs to the throne would have created was avoided. Similarly, this kind of marriage was more acceptable to the church and nobility of France.

The date when Françoise, Marquise de Maintenon, married King Louis XIV of France is not known. It was probably around October 1683. What is known is that while the marriage was kept a secret for as long as possible, and she was never crowned queen of France, Françoise's life as the wife of the most powerful man in Europe was a happy one. Life at court continued to be busy. After taking care of governmental affairs in the morning, Louis usually went out hunting for several hours each day. In the evenings, there was always some form of entertainment. Françoise's positive influence on the king was observed by the court, and she was soon accepted by most of his family as well as his legitimate children.

At the beginning of their marriage, Louis did not often consult Françoise on military or governmental matters. This included one of the most influential decisions he made in his reign. In 1685, in an attempt to establish religious unity, Louis revoked the Edict of Nantes. This legislation, which had been passed over 85 years before by King Henry IV, gave the Protestant minority in France freedom of conscience and worship in designated provinces and towns. Louis' Revocation not only initiated a massive emigration of thousands of talented and wealthy middle-class French Huguenots to Protestant countries in Western Europe, but launched a series of violent confrontations between French Catholics and Protestants. While Huguenot pamphlet writers blamed Madame de Maintenon for the Revocation, there is no historical proof that she made that fateful decision. She certainly did not condone violence, although she did agree with Louis' desire for religious unity.

Françoise's main concern even before she married the king was to improve the education of girls. From 1680, she formulated plans to set up a school for girls from impoverished aristocratic families, and, when Louis gave her a large pension in 1685, she drew up building plans. In July 1686, the Maison Royale de Saint Louis at St. Cyr was completed. It housed approximately 300 staff and students and was intended to act as a counterweight to the decadence and degeneracy of life at Versailles. Madame de Maintenon believed that the role of education was to make women more virtuous and, hence, the curriculum emphasized modesty, frugality, and domesticity. Girls at St. Cyr were taught reading, writing, arithmetic, needlework, sewing and moral and religious theater. In 1689, Racine, the famous French dramatist, wrote a play for the school entitled *Esther* that was performed in front of the king. As well as engendering religious piety, an additional goal of the school was to provide a new identity for aristocratic women. Instead of living their lives as idle social butterflies, women, Madame de Maintenon argued, should learn to be virtuous wives, devoted mothers, and knowledgeable homemakers. The school at St. Cyr was admired and became the model for similar institutions throughout Europe.

Françoise provided daily and personal input into the school, and it was there that she escaped from the endless string of petitioners, visitors, and courtiers who continually plagued her at court. Life at Versailles was becoming increasingly difficult for her, though she looked upon her days there as a mission from God. She knew that Louis would be lost without her presence and realized that he could only truly relax and be himself while he was in her company. By 1696, Louis' reliance on his reserved and pious wife was becoming more evident. He began to hold conferences with his ministers in her rooms and was increasingly relying on her advice in governmental matters.

In 1700, when Louis was faced with an important decision, it was Madame de Maintenon who cast the deciding vote. In that year, the king

of Spain died childless, having named Louis' grandson Philippe as his successor. Knowing that accepting the throne of Spain would lead to certain war, Louis, nonetheless, sent his grandson off to Spain to become Philip V. This decision, which launched the War of the Spanish Succession, was made against the advice of his ministers but with the assent of his wife. It brought not only 13 years of war, but severe economic hardship to France. By the end of Louis' reign, the French government was close to bankruptcy as a result of almost continual warfare and Louis' elaborate building schemes.

While she had counseled the king to accept the Spanish throne for his grandson, Madame de Maintenon hated the resulting war. "How cruel is war," she said to a friend, "and the mutual persecution of one another by these princes one has to witness, with the destruction of so many lives! I am extremely unhappy and can only see the horror of it." In addition to the devastation that war brought to the country, the king faced a series of personal tragedies within the royal family. In a short number of years, Louis' brother, son, and grandson died. Fortunately, in 1710 another grandson, the future Louis XV, was born, thus ensuring the succession. The king, while overwhelmed by sorrow, maintained his kingly dignity in public. It was only in his private moments with Françoise that he gave vent to his true feelings.

The war with Spain was finally concluded in 1713 and from that point on Louis' strength began to falter. By August 1715, he was seriously ill. Madame de Maintenon remained at his side both day and night, and it was during his last days that she burned all of the letters that he had written to her except two. On September 1, 1715, the man to whom she had devoted her life for 35 years was dead. Françoise was nearly 80 years old when she became a widow for the second time. After his death, she noted to a friend that "although my sorrow is very great, I feel calm and peaceful. I shall often weep for him but they will be tears of affection, for in my heart I feel great joy that he died like a true Christian."

After Louis' death, Madame de Maintenon retired to the school at St. Cyr. Although she was rich, she gave most of her money and clothes away to charity. Her rooms at St. Cyr were the only reminders of the opulence she had once been surrounded with. They were elaborately furnished and contained several portraits, both small and large, of Louis XIV. Françoise's life at St. Cyr was relatively quiet aside from periodic visits, including one from Peter the Great of Russia in 1717. Knowing that her remaining time on earth was limited, Françoise drew up her will early in 1719. On April 15, at age 84, Madame de Maintenon died peacefully in her sleep. Her death was ignored by most of the royal family, and she was buried, by request, at St. Cyr.

SOURCES:
Barnard, H.C. *Madame de Maintenon and Saint-Cyr.* London: Black, 1934.
Cruttwell, M. *Madame de Maintenon.* NY: E.P. Dutton, 1930.
Haldane, Charlotte. *Madame de Maintenon: Uncrowned Queen of France.* London: Constable, 1970.

SUGGESTED READING:
Erlanger, Philippe. *Louis XIV.* NY: Praeger, 1970.
Wolf, John B. *Louis XIV.* NY: W.W. Norton, 1968.

RELATED MEDIA
Affairs in Versailles (165 min.), film starring *Claudette Colbert, *Edith Piaf, Mary Margiut, directed by Sacha Guitry, 1954.

Margaret McIntyre,
Instructor in Women's History,
Trent University, Peterborough, Ontario, Canada

Mairet, Ethel (1872–1952)

English weaver. Born in 1872; died in 1952; married Philip Mairet (second husband).

Inspired by a visit to Ceylon (1903–06), Ethel Mairet began studying with Charles Robert Ashbee and the Guild of Handcrafts. By 1911, she was weaving in Devon, before establishing Gospels, her Ditchling-based workshop in Sussex. Gospels became a worldwide hub for weavers.

Maitland, Agnes Catherine (1850–1906)

English educator. Born in 1850; died in 1906.

As the principal of Somerville College, Oxford, from 1889 to 1906, Agnes Catherine Maitland was responsible for increasing enrollment, developing a tutorial system, and the construction of a college library. She was also the author of the highly popular *Rudiments of Cookery,* as well as novels.

Maitland, Elizabeth (1626–1698).

See Murray, Elizabeth.

Majerová, Marie (1882–1967)

Czech novelist whose 1935 novel Siréna *(The Factory Siren) is generally regarded as a classic. Name variations: Marie Majerova; Marie Stivinová; Marie Tusarová; (pseudonym) Marie Bartosova or Bar-* tosová. *Born Marie Bartosová in Úvaly, Austria (now Czech Republic), on February 1, 1882; died in Prague on January 16, 1967.*

For a half century, the prolific writer Marie Majerová wrote novels and short stories which reflected her belief in the necessity of creating a society based on socialist ideals. Born into a working-class family, she grew up in the grimy industrial town of Kladno near Prague and was working as a domestic servant in Budapest by age 16. The poverty and exploitation of proletarian life that she experienced made her determined to rise above her station through education and literature. Majerová's first poem, "Pisen" (A Song), appeared in the *Worker's Calendar* (1901), voicing the bitter frustrations of many working-class mothers:

> I hide all the poisons and anger in my bosom
> and in the corner, in secret, I keep vengeance.

During the next several years, she lived in Paris, Vienna, and Prague, completing her education and becoming active in both the feminist and Social Democratic movements. Her first novel, the largely autobiographical *Panenství* (Virginity, 1907), looks at the middle-class institution of marriage as part of the capitalist process of commodification: as a commodity, a woman's virginity enhances her capital value in a social system where the yardstick of worth is money.

While living in Vienna, Majerová moved in circles close to the Austrian Social Democratic Party and participated in the 1905 general strike that closed all the Habsburg monarchy's coal mines. Influenced by the Czech poet Stanislav Kostka Neumann and the circle of intellectuals gathered around the journal *Nový kult* (New Cult), she was at first attracted to the doctrines of social anarchism. These ideals are clearly reflected in her first collection of short stories, *Povídky z pekla* (Stories from Hell), published in 1907. A sojourn to Paris, however, during which she met leading writers of the day, including Romain Rolland, prompted a significant change in her thinking on political and social matters. Having found anarchist ideals to be inadequate, she joined the Czech Social Democratic Party in 1908. Published in 1914, her second novel, *Námestí Republiky* (Place de la République), reflected the new direction. The sufferings of World War I made Majerová more radical in her beliefs. In 1920, she published her third novel, *Nejkrásnejsí svet* (The Most Beautiful of Worlds), in which the bourgeois heroine abandons her familiar environment for the brave new world of Marxist revolutionary commitment. Convinced that capitalism had not only been the root cause of the war, but that it would bring on even greater suffering for humanity, Majerová became a founding member of the Czechoslovak Communist Party in 1921. In the same year, she published a collection of short stories entitled *Mučeny* (The Women Martyrs). These studies of bourgeois women made a point of the way in which women of the middle classes found themselves to be deluded by their own romantic ideals as well as by society's double standard of sexual morality.

The troubled decade of the 1930s proved to be the most artistically productive period of Majerová's writing career. Published in the depths of the Great Depression, her 1932 novel *Přehrada* (The Dam) was influenced by literary Futurism and Surrealism. The work presented a detailed blueprint for a revolutionary Marxist seizure of power in a crisis-ridden Czechoslovakia. Set three decades in the future, the plot indicts corrupt capitalists and their political lackeys for building a dam out of inferior concrete and thus endangering the lives of many thousands of innocent people. After members of the revolutionary underground spread rumors warning that the dam will soon collapse and bring catastrophic flooding to Prague's inhabitants, they arm the city's workers and seize power in a successful coup. Despite, or perhaps because of, the novel's incendiary message, it was both a critical and commercial success. The individuals most embarrassed by the book's popularity may have been a number of Marxist literary commentators, who criticized Majerová for misrepresenting the Czech Communist movement as a subversive element that would stoop to using rumors to foment a proletarian insurrection.

In 1935, Majerová published the work which is generally considered her masterpiece. *Siréna* (The Factory Siren) is a sweeping epic that traces three generations in the lives of the Hudecs, a Czech working-class family. Beginning in the 1850s and ending circa 1918, the novel is set in the industrial and mining center of Kladno that she knew so well from her early years. *Siréna* combines historical documentation with a novelistic form to create a detailed picture of the difficulties of proletarian life and the decades awakening of the family's political and class consciousness. A linchpin of the novel is the powerful personality of Mrs. Hudcovka, whose village origins provide the cultural energies essential for her to fill the roles of mother, wife, and daughter-in-law of the workers and revolutionaries who appear in the novel. Written mostly in a naturalistic style, the novel also includes lyrical elements, possibly reflecting the newly emerging Soviet literary ideal of Socialist Realism. One of the most striking features of *Siréna* is Majerová's use of regional dialects to create rich, convincing portraits of the workers. Her description of the 1905 strike, which she had witnessed as a young woman, resembles an eyewitness account and has been viewed by some critics as the novel's artistic high point.

Although even some Marxist reviewers of *Siréna* were not completely won over by all of its stylistic experimentation, which they regarded as "bourgeois" in its narrative technique as well as sometimes pedantic, the book was a success with the reading public. After the Communists seized power in Czechoslovakia in 1948, the work became required reading in the nation's schools, was extolled by the Marxist literary establishment, and was used as a standard text in the indoctrination of Communist Party cadres. By 1965, the novel had become an unchallenged classic. In that year, the 23rd edition of *Siréna* had a printing of 17,000 copies. The book was well known in the eastern bloc and particularly popular in the Soviet Union thanks to a Russian-language translation. It was also made into a film that was shown in Czechoslovakia and throughout the bloc.

Majerová again presented a portrait of proletarian life in her 1938 novella *Havířská balada* (Ballad of a Miner). Despite some critics who regarded its style as artificial and bombastic, it too became a classic work in the postwar years, when the goal of the Marxist government in Prague was the creation of a new and distinctly proletarian culture for the entire Czechoslovak Republic. During the Nazi occupation of Czechoslovakia, which lasted from March 1939 through May 1945, Majerová withdrew into the inner exile that most Czech intellectuals chose as a form of spiritual resistance to foreign rule. After the country's liberation, she was hailed as one of the nation's artistic giants and in 1947 was awarded the title of National Artist of Czechoslovakia. Majerová became well known throughout the Communist bloc, with translations of her major works appearing in Russian-, German-, and even Chinese-language editions. She was convinced that *Siréna,* as it was first published, had not been sufficiently inspired by the spirit of Socialist Realism and so in 1947 revised the work to fall into line with this new aesthetic imperative. Most critics feel that the second version is much inferior artistically to the original of 1935. During these years, Majerová also wrote a new version of her 1914 novel *Place de la République*, omitting the character of the Russian anarchist Nasta who among other things strangled her cat in the original before departing for New Zealand, the book's socialist Utopia.

The creation of a Communist state in 1948 brought Majerová's works to center stage, and she became the Grand Old Lady of Czech proletarian literature. In her last collection of short stories, *Cesta blesku* (The Path of Lightning), published in 1954, all of the characters zealously follow the party line to help create an ideal socialist society.

Between 1952 and 1961, Majerová's collected works appeared in print as a set of 19 volumes. When she died in Prague on January 16, 1967, she was eulogized as a major personality of modern Czech literature. The collapse of Communism in Czechoslovakia during 1989, however, has dealt a major blow to her reputation. Some critics, including Peter Hruby, simply dismiss her as a "third-rate writer" who was decreed without debate to be "a national socialist classic" by the Czech Communist Party and regime. Others argue that despite her obvious flaws and deficiencies as a writer, Majerová remains an author of considerable significance. Regardless of such major differences in critical assessments, her impact on Czechoslovakia in the mid-20th century remains unmistakable.

SOURCES:

Brusák, Karel. "Majerová, Marie," in Robert B. Pynsent and S.I. Kanikova, eds., *Reader's Encyclopedia of Eastern European Literature*. NY: HarperCollins, 1993, pp. 245–246.

Hruby, Peter. *Daydreams and Nightmares: Czech Communist and Ex-Communist Literature, 1917–1987*. NY: Columbia University Press, 1990.

Majerová, Marie. *Ballad of a Miner*. Translated by Roberta Finlayson Samsour. Prague: Artia, 1960.

———. *Den po revoluci: co jsem videla v SSSR*. Prague: Nakladem Komunistickeho knihkupectvi a nakl., 1925.

———. *The Siren: A Novel*. Translated by Iris Urwin. Prague: Artia, 1953.

Mihailovich, Vasa D. *Modern Slavic Literatures*. 2 vols. NY: Frederick Ungar, 1972–76.

Novák, Arne. *Czech Literature*. Edited by William E. Harkins. Translated by Peter Kussi. Ann Arbor: Michigan Slavic Publications, 1976.

Souckova, Milada. *A Literary Satellite*. Chicago: University of Chicago Press, 1970.

John Haag,
Associate Professor of History,
University of Georgia, Athens, Georgia

Makare (c. 1515–1468 BCE).

See Hatshepsut.

Makarova, Natalia (1940—)

Russian ballerina. Born in Leningrad (now St. Petersburg), Russia, in 1940; studied ballet at Leningrad's *Vaganova School, 1953–59; married Edward Karkar (a businessman), in 1976; children: son Andre Michael (b. 1978).*

Born in Leningrad (now St. Petersburg), Russia, in 1940, Natalia Makarova entered the famed Vaganova School of Ballet when she was 13 years old. She was enrolled in a special accelerated instruction program that compressed the school's normal nine-year curriculum into six years. Graduating in 1959, she immediately joined the Kirov Ballet, headquartered in Leningrad, and rose quickly to the rank of ballerina. Only two years later, Makarova created a sensation when she danced in *Giselle* in the Kirov's first appearance at London's Covent Garden. Following her triumph in London, she joined the Kirov in touring throughout the United States. While with the company, Makarova danced in such classic Russian ballets as *Aurora* and as Odette/Odile in *Swan Lake*. In 1965, competing at the Second International Ballet Competition at Varna, Bulgaria, she was awarded the Gold Medal.

On September 4, 1970, while performing with the Kirov in London, Makarova defected, requesting political asylum in the United Kingdom. By the end of 1970, she had signed with New York's American Ballet Theater (ABT), making her debut in *Giselle* in December of that year. Described as possessing great classical style with a "mysterious haunting stage presence," Makarova danced a number of roles in the company's extensive repertoire during her years at the ABT, and worked with such noted choreographers as George Balanchine, Jerome Robbins, Glen Tetley, and Antony Tudor. Less than two years after her debut with the ABT, Makarova began what was to be a lengthy and mutually beneficial relationship with the Royal Ballet of London. Among the ballets in her repertoire with the Royal Ballet were *Swan Lake, Giselle, The Sleeping Beauty, Les Sylphides, Manon, Song of the Earth, Concerto, Cinderella, A Month in the Country, Voluntaries, Dances at a Gathering, Serenade, Elite Syncopations, Rituals,* *Ninette de Valois'* *Checkmate,* and *Bronislava Nijinska's* *Les Biches*. Her last performance with the Royal Ballet came in 1989, when she danced in choreographer Kenneth Macmillan's modern version of *Romeo and Juliet*. Through the years, Makarova appeared as a guest dancer with the leading ballet companies of the world, including Roland Petit's Ballets de Marseille, the Paris Opera Ballet, National Ballet of Canada, Stuttgart Ballet, Royal Danish Ballet, London Festival Ballet, and Bejart's Ballet of the 20th Century.

In addition to her work as a ballerina, Makarova staged the "Kingdom of the Shades" from *La Bayadere* for the ABT in 1974. Six years later, in 1980, she staged a full-length production of *La Bayadere*, making the ABT the first company in the West to present this work. For this production, Makarova choreographed a reconstruction of the ballet's final act, which had not been staged anywhere since 1919.

Less than a year before her retirement from dance in 1989, Makarova had a joyful reunion with the Kirov when she danced an excerpt from *Swan Lake* during a Kirov appearance in London. Just about five months later, on February 1, 1989, she performed once again on the Kirov's home stage, becoming the first artistic exile from Russia to be invited to perform back in her homeland. The return to Leningrad was captured on film and later shown as part of the British Broadcasting Company (BBC) documentary, *Makarova Returns*.

In 1976, Natalia Makarova had married businessman Edward Karkar, with whom she had a son Andre Michael in February 1978. Outside of ballet, she became involved in a number of television productions while in the United Kingdom, including the widely praised "Ballerina" series, produced for the BBC in 1987; Channel 4's "In a Class of Her Own"; "Assoluta" for the BBC; and a special called "Natasha." On the stage, Makarova had earlier made her Broadway debut in a musical comedy when she appeared in a revival of George Abbott's *On Your Toes*, for which she received the Tony Award for the Best Actress in a Musical. She recreated her role in *On Your Toes* in London in 1984, winning the Laurence Olivier Award. In 1991, after her retirement from ballet, Makarova made her straight acting debut in a production of *Tovarich* at England's Chichester Festival. She performed in *Two for the Seesaw* in St. Petersburg and Moscow the following year. In 1994, as part of the BBC's acclaimed "Great Railway Journeys" series, she wrote and presented a segment on the train journey from St. Petersburg to Tashkent.

SUGGESTED READING:
Marakova, Natalia. *A Dance Autobiography*, 1979.

Don Amerman,
freelance writer, Saylorsburg, Pennsylvania

Makarova, Tamara (1907–1997)

Russian actress and teacher. Born on August 13, 1907, in St. Petersburg, Russia; died in January 1997; graduated from the Leningrad Theatrical Institute, 1930; married Sergei Gerasimov (a film director, died 1985).

While a student at the Leningrad Theatrical Institute, Tamara Makarova began her film career which was closely aligned with that of her husband, film director Sergei Gerasimov. She starred in *Seven Brave Men, Big Earth, The Young Guards*, and *To Love a Man*. She began teaching, eventually becoming a professor at the State Institute of Cinematographers in 1958.

Makeba, Miriam (1932—)

South African Xosa singer and activist, one of Africa's greatest vocalists, who lived in exile for 30 years, before being welcomed back to her homeland in the post-apartheid era. Name variations: (nickname) Mama Africa; (African name) Zenzile Makeba Qgwashu Nguvama Yiketheli Nxgowa Bantana Balomzi Xa Ufun Ubajabulisa Ubaphekeli, Mbiza Yotshwala Sithi Xa Saku Qgiba Ukutja Sithathe Izitsha Sizi Khabe Singama Lawu Singama Qgwashu Singama Nqamla Nqgithi (every child takes the first name of all male ancestors, which is then often followed with a descriptive word or two, telling about the character of the person, "making a true African name somewhat of a story," says Makeba). Born on March 4, 1932, in Prospect, South Africa; daughter of a teacher and a domestic worker; attended Kimerton Training Institute in Pretoria, South Africa; married James Kubay; married singer Sonny Pillay (divorced); married Hugh Masekela (a trumpeter and bandleader), in 1964 (divorced 1968); married Stokely Carmichael (a Black Panther activist), in 1968 (divorced); married Bageot Bah (an airline executive, divorced); children: (first marriage) daughter Bongi (died at age 35).

Was a domestic worker in Johannesburg, South Africa; toured South Africa, Rhodesia (now Zimbabwe) and the Belgian Congo (now Republic of Congo) with the Black Mountain Brothers (1954–57); came to U.S. (1959); put African music on the international map (1960s); was UN delegate from Guinea, West Africa; won the Dag Hammarskjold Peace Prize for her work against apartheid (1986); appeared with Paul Simon on his Graceland tour (1987); released CD Homeland for Putumayo records (2000).

Life as an entertainer in South Africa during the era of apartheid was difficult. Black entertainers were often prohibited from traveling and from entertaining in white clubs. Always suspect, they were punished at the first hint of dissension. Despite these overwhelming odds, a great many talented musicians and performers emerged in South Africa. Among the first to gain international recognition was Miriam Makeba.

In the mid-1950s, she joined the Black Mountain Brothers, a leading touring group in the 1950s and 1960s. The group appeared in variety shows and on radio broadcasts and made several recordings. Gaining increasing recognition as a vocalist, Makeba was recruited as a star attraction in *African Jazz and Variety*. She went on to perform in other shows which toured Africa. Despite the fact that she was one of South Africa's most successful performers, Makeba received only a few dollars for each recording session, since there were no provisions for royalties.

In 1959, Makeba starred in the semi-documentary *Come Back Africa*, which was about the system of apartheid. When she went to the film's premiere at the Venice Film Festival in 1959, she decided not to return, which was fortunate because the film caused such an uproar that the South African government invalidated her passport, making a return impossible. While performing with the Black Mountain Brothers, Makeba had met Hugh Masekela, a trumpeter and bandleader. He, too, was anxious to leave South Africa, as it was very difficult for bands to make a living. The Sharpeville massacres in 1960 extended the Group Areas Act, banning black musicians from the inner city, and they could no longer appear on government-controlled radio or travel. With the help of Trevor Huddlestone and Harry Belafonte, Makeba and Masekela obtained permission to enter the United States. They would marry in 1964.

In America, Makeba's career prospered along with Masekela's. Belafonte secured her a guest spot on the "Steve Allen Show" in 1959 as well as an engagement at the Village Vanguard, the prestigious Manhattan jazz club. Within a few months, she had become a nationally feted performer. In May 1963, she performed at a birthday celebration for President John F. Kennedy (the same night that *Marilyn Monroe sang "Happy Birthday"), and her 1965 collaboration with Belafonte earned a Grammy. Makeba continued to speak out against apartheid; in 1963, all her recordings were banned from South Africa. "When I came [to the U.S.], I wasn't even aware that people would think I was a politician or I was talking or singing politics," she said. "To me, I was just telling the truth about where I come from."

In 1968, Makeba divorced Masekela and married Stokely Carmichael, the Black Panther activist. This second marriage greatly damaged her recording career, as the entertainment industry was reluctant to be involved with "radical performers." "My marriage to Stokely Carmichael didn't change my life," she told Leigh Behrens in a *Chicago Tribune* interview, "it just made my career disappear." To find work, she and Carmichael moved to Guinea in West Africa where Makeba continued to perform on the international circuit. She did not stop speaking out against apartheid, and served as the Guinean delegate to the United Nations. In 1986, Miriam Makeba won the Dag Hammarskjold Peace Prize for her work. The following year, she was a guest artist on Paul Simon's Graceland tour. When apartheid was abolished and Nelson Mandela became president of South Africa, Miriam Makeba returned to her country after 30 years in exile; she was determined to be on hand to celebrate the new freedom. In 2000, Makeba released a new CD, *Homeland*. Wrote Christopher Farley: "You can hear her homeland in her voice. As she lags behind a beat, drawing out emotion, one feels the weight of apartheid bearing down. Caught up in one of her forceful, husky glissandos, it's hard not to imagine soaring above the lush expanse of the African veld." She began a worldwide tour that year, and was scheduled to act in November 2000 as master of ceremonies in South Africa's first major benefit concert, "One Billion Against

Miriam Makeba

AIDS." In an interview in New York City during the tour, after noting that she still needed to perform for financial reasons, Makeba said: "I feel very lucky that at my age I can still get up on that stage and hold my own. I've always been singing, and I will die singing."

SOURCES:

Behrens, Leigh. *Chicago Tribune*. March 20, 1988.

Farley, Christopher. "Voice from the Veld," in *Time*. May 1, 2000.

"Makeba, Miriam," in *The Guinness Encyclopedia of Popular Music*. Edited by Colin Larkin. London: Guinness Publishing, 1990.

The New York Times. June 18, 2000, p. AR28.

SUGGESTED READING:

Makeba, Miriam, with James Hall. *Makeba: My Story*. New American Library, 1987.

John Haag,
Athens, Georgia

Makeda (fl. 10th c. BCE).

See Sheba, Queen of.

Makemson, Maud Worcester

(1891–1977)

American astronomy professor and author noted for her work in archaeoastronomy and astrodynamics. Name variations: Maud W. Makemson. Born Maud Worcester on September 16, 1891, in Center Harbor, New Hampshire; died on December 25, 1977, in Weatherford, Texas; daughter of Ira Eugene Worcester and Fannie Malvina Davisson Worcester; attended Girls Latin School of Boston, 1908; attended Radcliffe, 1908–09; University of California, A.B., astronomy, 1925, A.M., astronomy, 1927, Ph.D., astronomy, 1930; married Thomas Emmet Makemson, on August 7, 1912 (divorced, July 1919); children: Lavon, Donald, Harris.

Awards: Morrison Fellow, Lick Observatory (1930); Guggenheim fellow (1941–42); Fulbright professor, Japan (1953–54).

Was newspaper reporter in Arizona (1917–21); was assistant professor of mathematics, Rollins College (1931–32); was assistant professor of astronomy, chair of astronomy department, director of observatory, Vassar College (1932–57); was research astronomer and lecturer, University of California, Los Angeles (1959–64); was consultant, Consolidated Lockheed-California (1961–63), General Dynamics, Ft. Worth (1965).

Selected writings: The Morning Star Rises *(1941);* The Astronomical Tables of the Maya *(1943);* The Book of the Jaguar Priest *(1951); (with Robert M.L. Baker, Jr.)* An Introduction to Astrodynamics *(1961).*

During her 86 years, Maud Worcester Makemson made the successful transition from housewife to astronomy professor to NASA consultant. Born Maud Worcester on September 16, 1891, in Center Harbor, New Hampshire, to Ira Eugene Worcester and **Fannie Davisson Worcester**, Maud discovered the beauty of the night sky at age eight, after receiving her first pair of eyeglasses. However, as a student at the Girls Latin School of Boston, she concentrated on the classics, a trend she continued during her term at Radcliffe College, in 1909–10. She taught for a year at a one-room school in Connecticut before moving with her family to Pasadena, California, where she married Thomas Emmet Makemson. Between 1913 and 1917, the couple had a daughter Lavon and sons Donald and Harris while farming in Southern California and Arizona. To help ends meet, Makemson became a reporter for the *Bisbee Review* in 1917 and later for the *Arizona Gazette*, while her husband joined the Marine Corps. The couple divorced in 1919.

Maud's life changed in 1921 when she witnessed a rare auroral display in Arizona and began studying astronomy, first on her own, and later as a student at the University of California where she received her A.B. in 1925, A.M. in 1927, and Ph.D. in 1930. After teaching math at Rollins College in 1931–32, she joined the faculty of Vassar College as assistant professor of astronomy; she later became chair of the astronomy department and director of the Observatory.

Makemson became interested in archaeoastronomy and received grants and fellowships to research Polynesian astronomy and celestial navigation and Mayan astronomy and calendar systems, resulting in numerous articles and her books *The Morning Star Rises* (1941) and *The Book of the Jaguar Priest* (1951). "Mayan astronomy offers a fascinating field for research to anyone who combines an interest in archaeology with a love for astronomy and who has the time and patience to learn to work with strange-looking hieroglyphs," she wrote.

Retired in 1957, she moved to California, where she became a research astronomer and lecturer from 1959 to 1964 and consultant at Consolidated Lockheed-California from 1961 to 1963. She also co-authored *An Introduction to Astrodynamics*. Makemson launched the final phase of her career in 1965, when she moved to Texas and became a NASA consultant at the Applied Research Laboratories of General Dynamics in Fort Worth. There she devised a method for astronauts to navigate on the moon without using radio or radar. Maud Makemson died on Christmas 1977, in Weatherford, Texas.

SOURCES:

Bailey, Martha J. *American Women in Science*. NY: ABC-CLIO, 1994.

Block, Maxine, ed. *Current Biography*. NY: H.W. Wilson, 1941.

Cattel, Jacques, ed. *American Men of Science*, Vol. 1. Lancaster, PA: Science Press, 1955.

"Maud Worcester Makemson," in Vassar College press release, January 4, 1978.

SUGGESTED READING:

Makemson, Maud W. "The Maya Calendar," in *Publications of the Astronomical Society of the Pacific*. Vol. LIX, 1947, pp. 17–26.

———. "South Sea Sailors Steer by the Stars," in *The Sky*. Vol. III. January 1939, pp. 3–21.

Kristine Larsen,
Associate Professor of Astronomy and Physics,
Central Connecticut State University, New Britain, Connecticut

Makepeace, Joan.

See Joan (1210–1238).
See Joan of the Tower (1321–1362).

Makin, Bathsua (1608–1675).

See Behn, Aphra for sidebar.

Makrina (327–379).

See Macrina.

Maksimovic, Desanka (1898–1993)

Serbian writer, regarded as the doyenne of Serbian poets, who glorified forgiveness and compassion in her 1964 volume Trazim pomilovanje (I Seek Clemency), *the work which brought her national fame. Name variations: Maksimović. Born in Rabrovica near Valjevo, Serbia, on May 16, 1898; died in Belgrade on February 12, 1993; daughter of Mihailo Maksimovic (a schoolteacher) and Draginja Petrovic Maksimovic; had seven brothers and sisters; educated at the University of Belgrade and the Sorbonne; married Sergej Nikiforovic Slastikov.*

Desanka Maksimovic, a poet who became so popular with her readers in Serbia that almost all of them would refer to her only by her first name, had a writing career that spanned seven decades. During that time, she wrote verse, short stories and novels. When she was well into her 60s, Maksimovic created what is generally regarded as her best work, the 1964 collection *Trazim pomilovanje* (published in English as *I Seek Clemency* but also seen as "I Seek Mercy" or "I Plead for Mercy"), about the need for a moral renaissance. The book swept Serbia like a storm. While continuing to assimilate elements of South Slavic cultural heritage, her latter works express a heightened compassion for an unforgiving century's victims of war and violent intolerance.

Maksimovic was born in 1898 in the village of Rabrovica near Valjevo, but she would spend much of her childhood in the small town of Brankovina to which her father, a schoolteacher, was transferred when she was only two months old. Situated in the heart of Serbia, and home to little modern industry, Brankovina was steeped in Serbian cultural traditions. Maksimovic absorbed this heritage from the town, her parents, and also from her maternal grandfather, Svetozar Petrovic, a Serbian Orthodox priest who like her father owned a large library of which he was immensely proud. Although she and her family left the town to move to Valjevo when she was ten, Maksimovic would never forget the happy years she had experienced as a child in Brankovina where she had roamed in the nearby meadows and woods. For the rest of her long life, she would often return there both physically and through her poetry; the memories of the nature and people of a town that had changed little over the centuries served as a constant inspiration.

World War I, which devastated Serbia, dealt a hard blow to Maksimovic's large family: while serving in the Serbian Army, her father contracted typhoid fever and died. The family was emotionally and financially devastated by this loss, and for a time Maksimovic dropped out of school. In addition to helping run the household, she also learned French on her own by repeatedly reading the works of Hippolyte Taine and several novels she found in her father's library. In 1919, she finally was able to complete her high-school education. Maksimovic then moved to the Serbian capital of Belgrade, where she began her studies at the university, taking courses in art history and comparative literature. By this time, she had been writing verse for a number of years. She gave some of these works to one of her former teachers, who in turn gave them to Velimir Massuka, chief editor of one of Serbia's leading cultural journals, *Misao* (Thought). Not expecting much of literary value from the pen of a young woman from the provinces, Massuka was astonished by the quality and originality of Maksimovic's verse. Decades later, Massuka would note in an interview that as he read the poems, which were essentially of a confessional nature, he detected "a new content [which] was different from anything I knew; her verse had a completely different never before used cadence; there was music in it, it had an internal metric harmony but without a strict metric rhythm. . . . There was something elusive, soft, feminine, and sparkling in that verse created with confidence and only seemingly shy and anxious." All of the poems Maksimovic had brought with her when she moved to Belgrade appeared in print in issues of *Misao* (1920 and 1921). She received what was to be the first of many literary awards when readers of the journal, taking part in a contest, voted her poem "Strepnja" (Anxiety) to be the best. Her reputation in Serbian literary circles grew during the next few years when Belgrade's most respected and influential literary journal, *Srpski knjizevni glasnik* (Serbian Literary Herald), began to print her poems, and several of her works appeared in book form in an anthology of Yugoslav lyric poetry.

In 1924, she published her first collection of poems, simply entitled *Pesme* (Poems). The reviews were positive, with the Croatian critic Antun Barac maintaining that her poems "are the best ever written in our language by a woman and are, undoubtedly, among the best created in our country in the last several years." Maksimovic graduated from the University of Belgrade the same year (1924) and was granted a fellowship from the French government for a year's study at the Sorbonne in Paris. On her return to Belgrade in 1925, she received a Saint Sava medal from the government for her literary achievements and was appointed professor at the city's elite First High School for Girls. Except for the almost four years of German occupation during World War II, she would serve at this institution until her retirement from teaching in 1953. During the next years, Maksimovic was a highly respected teacher and remained a well-known author. But in a Yugoslav literary scene which in the 1920s was at least as turbulent as the political landscape of that multinational state, she was not without critics.

First called the Kingdom of the Serbs, Croats and Slovenes, the nation was named Yugoslavia in 1929, but this move did not bring stability to a nation whose very survival was often threatened by deep-seated ethnic hatreds and resentments. Although less violent than the political turmoil that raged in the cafés and public forums of Belgrade, Sarajevo, and Zagreb, the theoretical controversies that convulsed the Yugoslav literary firmament in these years was also highly emotional in nature. The younger generation in literature, who were generally referred to as advocates of the New Modernism, were determined to make a clean break with all existing literary traditions. Their goal was to create a new literature—utilizing innovative, unconstrained forms—which would explain the modern era's contradictions and explore all facets of the human subconscious. Politically en-

gaged (many were sympathetic to Communism and a Soviet Union that appeared to foster artistic innovations), many of the New Modernists were also drawn to several other "isms" by the 1930s, including Surrealism and Expressionism, as well as the more obscure, short-lived artistic movements known as "zenithism" and "hypnoism." Maksimovic, however, remained loyal to more traditional literary forms and traditions, and during these years she became the subject of bitter polemical articles which attacked her for a lack of interest in revolutionary literary forms or political goals. She stood her ground in a dignified manner, holding steadfast to her own artistic path, and would later note: "I would not have had as many friends as I have now if I had not been able to forget the biting jokes or critical remarks about my poetry or myself."

Throughout the 1930s—when Yugoslavia's always precarious economic situation deteriorated to an alarming degree and its unstable political landscape became bloodstained with the assassination of King Alexander I (October 1934)—Maksimovic concentrated her energies on verse. She also drew on the support of a large number of colleagues and friends, many of them prominent poets, novelists, artists, and actors, who regularly

Yugoslavian postage stamp honoring Desanka Maksimovic issued in 1996.

gathered in the home of Smilja Djakovic, publisher of *Misao*. In 1933, Maksimovic married a Russian-born writer, Sergej Slastikov. Their union would be happy, and although they remained childless Maksimovic and her husband enjoyed the company of young people and children, often entertaining their friends' children at their home. They collaborated on a number of projects, including the translation of many classic Russian authors' works, such as those of folktales and literature, into Serbo-Croatian.

The German army began the occupation of Yugoslavia in April 1941. When she was involuntarily retired from her teaching post by the puppet Serbian regime set up by the Germans, Maksimovic and her husband were quickly reduced to a state of poverty. To survive, she gave private lessons, made dolls to sell at the marketplace, and sewed children's clothes. These she exchanged for morsels of food in Brankovina and nearby villages where the peasants were still able to create a surplus from the soil. Maksimovic walked from Belgrade to nearby Mount Avala to find scraps of wood to heat her apartment in the bitterly cold Balkan winter; often, she returned with enough sticks and twigs to heat her home at least some degrees above freezing. In secret, she wrote defiantly patriotic poetry, but the only works she would be able to publish during these years were several children's books.

Published after the war's end, the 1946 collection *Pesnik i zavicaj* (The Poet and His Native Land) contains Maksimovic's wartime poetry. These patriotic poems give voice to pride about her nation's resistance against the German and Italian armies of occupation. Works like "Ustanici" (The Rebels) and "Srbija je velika bajka" (Serbia is a Deep Secret) celebrate the heroism of ordinary people, many of whom were slaughtered by the occupation forces. The best known of this collection remains "Krvava bajka" (A Legend of Blood), a poetic requiem for the scores of schoolboys in the town of Kragujevac who were massacred in 1941 by the Germans. Despite the brutal subject matter, Maksimovic chose to present the stories of war in a lyrical, gentle tone, their purpose being to reflect on, and commemorate, the patriotism that had motivated individuals to choose resistance over collaboration with the enemy.

In 1958, Maksimovic was the recipient of many awards from a grateful Yugoslavia which was now led by a relatively benign dictator, Marshal Josip Broz Tito. (Tito was a veteran Communist revolutionary and the wartime leader of the partisan movement, who in 1948 had embarked on a course that was free of the dictates of the Soviet Union while at the same time continuing to search for a more realistic way to achieve socialism.) Although she was a traditionalist and certainly not a Marxist, Maksimovic had gained the respect of both the political and literary leadership of postwar Yugoslavia. By the time she celebrated her 60th birthday in 1958, many felt that her major literary achievements were behind her and that the time had come to honor her for significant lifetime achievements. The most important of several awards she received that year was her nomination as a corresponding member of the Serbian Academy of Sciences and Arts. Early in the following year, she was elected to that prestigious body.

In 1964, on the 40th anniversary of the publication of her first verse collection, Maksimovic published the book that would make her a major figure on the national stage of Yugoslavia. In a volume of reflective poetry entitled *Trazim pomilovanje* (I Seek Clemency: Lyrical Discussions with Tsar Dushan's Code of Law) were a number of poems dealing with the 14th-century Serbian tsar Dushan the Powerful, who reigned during the last epoch of Serb national freedom before the Ottoman Turks destroyed their nation in battle. Presenting Tsar Dushan, who displays compassion, as the embodiment of justice and wisdom, Maksimovic glorified forgiveness and compassion for all human beings, "the same as we are or different from us." The groups for whom Maksimovic seeks Tsar Dushan's mercy include the lowliest serfs, both female and male; heretics and monks; soldiers who gave their lives in the nation's many wars; people who have, or have been stripped by fate of, power; and a vast tableaux of saints, sinners, fools, and others replete with human failings.

Almost immediately after its publication, *Trazim pomilovanje* was embraced by the nation. Its veiled critiques of the Tito regime—which became increasingly riddled with corruption and arbitrariness as Tito aged—made it a book to read, ponder over, and savor. A bestseller, it went through three large print runs in less than a year's time. Serbia's leading actors, actresses, and even choral groups put on shows in which the words Maksimovic had put in Tsar Dushan's mouth were presented to sold-out audiences in theaters throughout the Serbian Federated Republic of Yugoslavia. Now a veritable national superstar, Maksimovic became the recipient of many more honors over the next several years. In 1965, she was elected into a small elite group with full membership in the Serbian

Academy of Sciences and Arts. By this time, her verse had become known throughout Serbia, appearing in countless anthologies as well as in reprints and new editions of her major works. Internationally, too, she had become well known. Translations of her works appeared in Russian (translated by, among others, *Anna Akhmatova and *Elisaveta Bagryana) and other Slavic languages, as well as in English, French, German, Hungarian/Magyar, Norwegian, Portuguese, and Spanish. In 1967, the high respect in which she was held in the Slavic world was formalized by a special Medal of Honor awarded her by the USSR Supreme Soviet.

In 1970, Maksimovic's husband died. In a collection she published in Belgrade (1973), she gave thanks to him for "embracing, even in death, our soil." After this loss, she wrote poetry which dealt with the issue of human mortality, and her verse reflected a serene, philosophical view of the inevitability of death as a basic fact of life. Death was related to the eternal processes of nature:

> We are earth.
> Every particle and thread of us
> the earth will soak up slowly,
> we are going to quench the thirst of the roots of
>   oaks. . .

In 1975, Maksimovic received a Special Vuk Award for Lifetime Achievement, only the second artist so honored (the first was Ivo Andric, a Serb novelist who in 1961 became Yugoslavia's first and sole recipient of the Nobel Prize for Literature). The next year, Maksimovic provided impressive evidence that she remained a creative force in Serbian letters by publishing *Letopis Perunovih potomaka* (A Chronicle of Perun's Descendants). Organized into two cycles of poetry, this 1976 verse collection is set in the 10th century and describes a war and religious conflict of that far-off age of Balkan history. The martial aspect of the book shows how the Croats and Serbs—rivals, even enemies, throughout most of their history because of their different religious allegiances (Croats are Roman Catholic, Serbs Orthodox)—were at one time allies in a struggle against Bulgarian invaders. The poet addresses religion by looking at the crucial period when the Croats began to turn to the Latin world of Rome, and the Serbs began to identify with Byzantium, and eventually with Moscow. Combining elements of medieval South Slav history, Maksimovic's poems mix reality with myth to create a universally valid portrait of human error, suffering, and lost opportunities for prosperity and unity. In light of the disintegration of Yugoslavia that began in the late 1980s and culminated in the bloodbath that devastated the region in the final decade of the 20th century, Maksimovic's poems can now be read as prophetic warnings.

In the 1970s and 1980s, Maksimovic enjoyed some of the fruits of fame and traveled widely. In addition to visiting many European nations, including the Soviet Union and the United Kingdom, she accepted invitations from academic and literary hosts in Australia, Canada, the United States, and the People's Republic of China. In 1980, during a visit to America, she was warmly received by the North American Society for Serbian Studies. On at least two occasions, after having visited Norway and Switzerland, Maksimovic wrote volumes that reflected her experiences while in other lands (a book of verse, *Poems from Norway* [1976], and a travel book, *Snimci iz Svajcarske* [Snapshots from Switzerland, 1978]).

In 1988, at age 90, she delighted readers by publishing a new collection of poems, *Pamtiću sve* (I Shall Remember Everything). Although the national mood was often gloomy and Yugoslavia was *in extremis*, for a few days the literary world forgot these woes to honor her. By this time, Maksimovic's many friends and admirers noted that not only was she a Serbian national treasure, but also that for many decades she had served as an important link to the rest of world. A sensitive translator, Maksimovic had produced versions of works by major world writers which would remain among the best known in Serbia, including her translations of writings by Chekhov, Dostoyevsky, and Pushkin, as well as modern writers like Anna Akhmatova and non-Slavic classic writers such as Balzac. Her works for children and young readers also remain an important part of her legacy; these books were meant not only to entertain but also to develop in the next generation those ethical values that Maksimovic always cherished, namely ideals of love and respect for all individuals and nations. By the time she died in Belgrade on February 11, 1993, the Balkans were aflame with the spirit of war and vengeful hatred against which Maksimovic had so often, and eloquently, warned. On May 7, 1996, Yugoslavia (the name retained by Serbia-Montenegro) issued a commemorative postage stamp in her honor.

SOURCES:

Delavan, Joanne. "Desanka Maksimovic," in *Review* [Belgrade]. Vol. 1–2, 1985, pp. 33–34.

"Desanka Maksimovic—Six Poems, Translated by Celia Hawkesworth and Marie Schulte," in *Scottish Slavonic Review*. No. 12–13. Spring–Autumn, 1989, pp. 142–153.

Egeric, Miroslav. "Verses of Love and Nature," in *Relations* [Belgrade]. Vol. 1, 1985, pp. 45–48.

Holton, Milne, and Vasa D. Mihailovich, eds. *Serbian Poetry from the Beginnings to the Present.* New Haven, CT: Yale Center for International Area Studies, 1988.

Lukic, Sveta. *Contemporary Yugoslav Literature: A Sociopolitical Approach.* Edited by Gertrude Joch Robinson. Translated by Pola Triandis. Urbana, IL: University of Illinois Press, 1972.

Maksimovic, Desanka. *Greetings from the Old Country: A Collection of Poems Old and New.* Edited by Milan Surducki. Toronto: Yugo-Slavica Publishers, 1976.

———. *I Seek Clemency.* Translated by Celia Hawkesworth, with examples from Dushan's Law Code. Belgrade: Association of Serbian Writers, 1988 (Offprint from *Serbian Literary Quarterly.* No. 2. Summer 1988, pp. 5–38).

———. *Poems from Norway.* Translated by Robert De Bray. Belgrade: Idea, 1984.

———. *The Shaggy Little Dog.* Pictures by Jozef Wilkon. Winchester, MA, and Mönchaltorf, Switzerland: Faber and Faber/Nord-Sud, 1983.

Mihailovich, Vasa D., ed. *Contemporary Yugoslav Poetry.* Iowa City: University of Iowa Press, 1977.

———, ed. *Cuj, reci cu ti svoju tajnu: Pesnicka antologija udruzenja knjizevnih stvaralaca "Desanka Maksimovic," Toronto.* Belgrade and Toronto: Serbian National Academy/Center for Emigrants from Serbia, 1998.

Schulte, Marie. "Images of Women in the Works of Desanka Maksimovic." M.A. thesis, Corpus Christi College, Oxford University, 1991.

Sljivic-Simsic, Biljana. "The Collective Hero-Victim in Desanka Maksimovic's *Letopis Perunovih potomaka* (1976)," in *Southeastern Europe.* Vol. 9, no. 1–2, 1982, pp. 70–83.

———. "Desanka Maksimovic (May 16, 1898–February 11, 1993)," in Vasa D. Mihailovich, ed., *South Slavic Writers Before World War II. Dictionary of Literary Biography,* Vol. 147. Detroit, MI: Gale Research, 1995, pp. 127–133.

———. "Flowers Have Been My Friends: An Interview with Desanka Maksimovic," in *Serbian Studies.* Vol. 1, no. 2, 1981, pp. 85–92.

John Haag,
Associate Professor of History,
University of Georgia, Athens, Georgia

Malaika, Nazik al- (1923–1992)

Iraqi poet and critic. Name variations: Nazik al-Mala'ika. Born in 1923; died in 1992; graduated from Higher Teachers' College, in Baghdad, Iraq.

Born into a family of poets in Iraq in 1923, Nazik al-Malaika became one of her country's leading poets and critics. In addition, she taught Arabic literature at the University of Mosul in Iraq and at the University of Kuwait. By 1978, al-Malaika had published seven volumes of poetry and three volumes of poetic criticism. Her poetry encompasses a variety of subjects, from world disasters to the cultured Arab's reaction to change. In one poem, written in 1958, she celebrates Jamila, an Algerian woman who fought with the Algerian Liberation Movement and was imprisoned and tortured by the French (*See entries on Bouhired, Djamila and Boupacha, Djamila*). Her poem "Cholera" (1947), written during the cholera epidemic in Egypt, broke with the classical verse forms and initiated the New Movement in Arabic poetry. In her 1962 critical work *Issues of Contemporary Arabic Poetry*, al-Malaika discusses the need for the new versification for Arabic, for which she also attempted to formulate some new rules. Many of al-Malaika's feminist writings are included in a social criticism entitled *Fragmentation in Arab Society* (1974).

Malak Hifni Nassif (1886–1918).

See Egyptian Feminism.

Malaspina, Ricciarda

Princess of Massa. Name variations: Ricciarda Cybo. Married Lorenzo Cybo or Cibo.

Malatesta (fl. 1504–1505)

Lyons courtesan. Flourished between 1504 and 1505.

Between 1504 and 1505, writes the Italian bishop Bandello of Agen, "there dwelt at Lyons a courtesan named Malatesta who went to her midnight assignations armed with sword and rotella, which she knew how to use in a bold and dexterous fashion." She is not to be confused with *Francesca da Rimini* (d. 1285?) who was infamously killed by her husband Gianciotto Malatesta in a "crime of honor."

Malatesta, Anna

*Noblewoman of Mantua. First wife of Rodolfo Gonzaga (1451–1495). Rodolfo was killed at Fornovo in 1495; his second wife was *Caterina Pico* (d. 1501).*

Malatesta, Battista da Montefeltro (1383–1450)

Italian scholar. Name variations: Battista da Montefeltro. Born Battista da Montefeltro in 1383; died in 1450; daughter of Antonio, count of Urbino; married Galeazzo Malatesta; children: one daughter. Became Sister of the Franciscan Order of Saint Claire.

Works: oration to the Holy Roman Emperor Sigismund I (Zygmunt I).

Battista da Montefeltro Malatesta was born in 1383, the daughter of Antonio, count of Urbino, and married Galeazzo Malatesta; her marriage was extremely unhappy. After Galeazzo was assassinated as a despot, however, she retained an intellectual friendship with his father. She taught philosophy and received much admiration from the professors. Leonardo Bruni dedicated his *De Studiis et Litteris* to her. Malatesta had one daughter, and then a granddaughter, **Constanza Varano**, who also became known for her scholarship.

Catherine Hundleby, M.A. Philosophy,
University of Guelph

Malatesta, Elisabetta.

See Montefeltro, Elisabetta.

Malatesta, Francesca (d. 1285?).

See Francesca da Rimini.

Malatesta, Ginevra (1414–1440).

See Este, Ginevra d'.

Malatesta, Margherita (d. 1399).

See Gonzaga, Margherita.

Malatesta, Michelina (1300–1356).

See Michelina of Pesaro.

Malatesta, Paola (1393–1453).

See Gonzaga, Paola.

Malatesta, Parisina.

See Este, Parisina d'.

Malatesta, Polissena.

See Sforza, Polissena.

Malavesse.

See Catherine David in entry titled French "Witches."

Malcolm, Sarah (c. 1710–1733)

Irish-born murderer who was executed for the infamous "Temple Murder" in London in 1733. Born in Ireland around 1710 (some sources cite 1711); executed in London, England, on March 7, 1733.

Born in Ireland around 1710, Sarah Malcolm came to London to work as a launderer in the household of **Lydia Dunscomb**, an elderly widow. For reasons unknown, Malcolm is believed to have gone berserk on the night of February 5, 1733. During her rampage, she is said to have sneaked into the bedroom of her mistress and strangled her to death. Reportedly a strongly built woman, Malcolm then strangled 60-year-old **Elizabeth Harrison**, another servant in the household, after which she slit the throat of still another servant, 17-year-old **Ann Price**. The murders of her fellow servants were apparently committed to prevent them from accusing her of her initial crime. Malcolm then tore apart the house looking for anything of value she could steal. She was apprehended in the street not far from the Dunscomb home only a short time after the murders, still carrying the items she had stolen.

Despite the damning evidence against her, Malcolm adamantly insisted that she was innocent. Because the Dunscomb home was located in Tanfield Court, in the Inner Temple of London, the crime came to be known as the "Temple Murder." Malcolm's vehement protestations of innocence swayed no one, and she was quickly convicted of the triple murder and sentenced to death by hanging.

On March 7, 1733, the day of her execution, Malcolm showed little or no expression as she was brought down Fleet Street to the place of execution, a gallows located between Fetter Lane and Mitre Court. As was the custom, the place of execution was intentionally located not far from the scene of the crime. Executions often served as a form of public entertainment during that time, and it was not unusual for enormous crowds of men, women and children to gather to enjoy the show. Among those on hand for Malcolm's execution was the noted English painter and engraver William Hogarth, who had earlier drawn a portrait of the condemned after a visit to her cell. He later commented that Malcolm had seemed to him "capable of any wickedness." Her cheeks heavily rouged for her last public appearance, Sarah Malcolm offered no reaction to the cries of the hundreds of spectators who had gathered to witness her death by hanging, which was then duly carried out.

SOURCES:

Concise Dictionary of National Biography. Oxford: Oxford University Press, 1992.

Nash, Jay Robert. *Look for the Woman.* NY: M. Evans, 1981.

Don Amerman,
freelance writer, Saylorsburg, Pennsylvania

Malgherita.

Italian variant of Margaret.

Malgorzata (fl. 1290s)

Queen of Poland. Flourished in the 1290s; daughter of Albert, duke of Brandenburg; fourth wife of Przemysl II (1257–1296), king of Poland (r. 1290–1296).

Malibran, Maria (1808–1836)

French-born Spanish soprano who was one of the world's first international superstars. Name variations: María Malibran; Maria Garcia or García. Born María Felicità García on March 24, 1808, in Paris, France; died on September 23, 1836, in Manchester, England; eldest daughter of Manuel del Popolo Vicente García also known as Manuel Garcia (1775–1832, the tenor); mother's name unknown; sister of Pauline Viardot (1821–1910, a mezzo-soprano); studied with her father; married François Eugène Malibran (a merchant), in 1826 (separated 1827, annulled 1836); married Charles de Bériot, in 1836; children: (with de Bériot) one son Charles Wilfred de Bériot (b. 1830) and a daughter (b. 1832) who died at birth.

First appeared on stage at age five in Naples in Paër's Agnese *(1813); made London debut as Rosina in Rossini's* Il barbiere di Siviglia *(Barber of Seville, 1825); made Paris debut in* Semiramide *(1828); appeared at Teatro alla Scala debut as Bellini's* Norma *(1834).*

Maria Malibran was the sensation of Europe and America during the 1820s and early 1830s. Liszt and *George Sand were profoundly influenced by her. In the words of one of her contemporaries, "She set the world on fire." Mass hysteria existed long before the advent of the rock star, as Malibran's career proves. Wherever she sang, crowds flocked to the theater. Drawings of her were sold by the penny press; fans fainted in her presence. She once entered a theater bearing one name, only to leave and discover it had been renamed in her honor. On her arrival in Venice, traffic was stopped for hours. After her La Scala debut, crowds unhitched the horses from her carriage and pulled it through the streets.

Maria Malibran was born in 1808 in Paris, where her father had arrived only two months before. Along with her younger sister, mezzo-soprano *Pauline Viardot, Malibran grew up on stage; their father Manuel Garcia was a famous singer, composer, conductor, and teacher. At age three, Maria was taken to Italy; at age five, she played the child's part in Paër's *Agnese* at the Fiorentini in Naples. She was so precocious that, within days of the opening, she began to sing the part of Agnese in the duet in the second act, and was applauded by the audience. Whenever an opera plot called for a child, Maria often sang the role.

Two years later, she studied *solfeggi* with Panseron at Naples. Hérold instructed her on the piano. In 1816, the family went back to Paris, then on to London in 1817. By then, Malibran spoke fluent Spanish, Italian, and French,

and she picked up a "tolerable" command of English in the two years spent in London. She would also learn German. While in England, she made such rapid progress on the piano that she was able to play J.S. Bach's clavier-works by the time she returned to Paris in 1819.

Although Malibran's voice seemed unpromising at first, her father was determined to make her a great singer, no matter the cost. At age 15, she began to study with him and with *Giuditta Pasta, his onstage partner. Pasta extended the young girl's upper and lower registers, giving her voice a dramatic range uncommon in many vocalists. Maria's childhood was unhappy, as Garcia was a brutal parent with a violent temper determined to make money from his daughter. Maria later remarked that she learned to "sing through her tears." In 1824, he allowed her to appear before a musical club which he had established. She was a great sensation and her future success was predicted.

Two months later, Garcia returned to London where he was engaged as a principal tenor. On June 7, 1825, when Maria was 17, there was a casting crisis at the King's Theater in London for the part of Rosina in *Il Barbiere di Seviglia*. Lord Mount-Edgecumbe writes: "The great favorite Pasta arrived for a limited number of nights. About the same time Ronzi fell ill, and totally lost her voice, so that she was obliged to throw up her engagement and return to Italy. *Madame Vestris having seceded, and [Marie] Caradori-Allan being unable for some time to perform, it became necessary to engage a young singer, the daughter of the tenor Garcia, who had sung for several seasons. She was as yet a mere girl, and had never appeared on any public stage; but from the first moment of her appearance she showed evident talents for it both as singer and actress. Her extreme youth, her prettiness, her pleasing voice, and sprightly easy action . . . gained her general favor." Garcia had offered his daughter's services for an absurdly high fee which was accepted, and she was engaged for the remainder of the season (about six weeks) at £500.

"But she was too highly extolled," continues Lord Mount-Edgecumbe, "and injudiciously put forward as a prima donna, when she was only a very promising debutante, who in time, by study and practice, would in all probability, under the tuition of her father, a good musician, but (to my ears at least) a most disagreeable singer, rise to eminence in her profession. But in the following year she went with her whole family (all of whom, old and young, are singers *tant bons que mauvais)* to establish an Italian opera in America." In November 1825, Garcia assembled a troupe consisting mainly of family members and took the first Italian opera to the United States. Malibran quickly became America's first prima donna, appearing in *Otello, Romeo, Don Giovanni, Tancredi, Cenerentola,* and in two operas written by her father, *L'amante astuto* and *La Figlia dell' aria.* This sojourn also allowed her to perfect her art before audiences less critical than those in Europe. During this time, on March 25, 1826, she married Eugène Malibran, a seemingly wealthy French merchant three times her age, despite her father's objection to the union. The marriage, though unhappy, allowed her to escape from her father's merciless authority.

Malibran initially retired from the stage after her marriage, but in 1827 her husband suffered great business reverses. While he faced bankruptcy, she returned to Paris on her own in September 1827, so that she might earn more money. In Paris, Malibran contacted **Countess Merlin** whose salon ensured her entrance into the musical world. The composer Rossini helped her as well. Maria appeared as Semiramide at the Académie Royale de Musique in January 1828. Her success was immediate and enormous, and for the next eight years she followed one triumph with another. When *****Henriette Sontag** retired from the stage in early 1830, Malibran had no rivals. She continued to sing in London, Naples, and Paris, earning unprecedented fees.

Since no recordings exist from this period, only contemporary descriptions document Malibran's voice, which was not exactly beautiful, but was considered unique. In the middle range, it was unfocused and hollow, but its range was a remarkable three octaves. When she sang in the middle range, Malibran could use either her sweet soprano register or her rich contralto. Malibran embellished passages as she sang, using arpeggios and trills which astonished her audiences, and often leapt two or three octaves to avoid the weakness of her middle register.

Maria Malibran was also a consummate actress, a quality which was somewhat rare for the period. Traditionally, opera performers used stock gestures to depict stock emotions, while Malibran, on the other hand, brought emotional realism to her roles, whether dramatic or comedic. In this respect, she owed Giuditta Pasta a great deal, as she was Malibran's only rival and had been her teacher. Malibran had an almost manic-depressive temperament, and varied her roles according to her acute mood swings. Although this technique might have produced poor results for many others, audiences flocked to see how Malibran would reinterpret roles. Noted a critic, "Few among her contemporaries could go home and sit in cool judgment upon one who, while she was before them, carried them as she pleased to the extremities of grave or gay."

Malibran lived her life at an extremely fast pace. Sometimes she performed two operas back-to-back and then rushed off to salons to perform for even more money. In 1829, she fell in love with Charles de Bériot, a violinist, and determined to divorce her first husband. Initially, she asked the Marquis de Lafayette to push a divorce law through the French Parliament; when this effort proved impossible, she asked her lawyers to annul her first marriage so that she could marry Charles. (It would be annulled by the Courts of Paris in 1836, and she would marry Charles on March 26, 1836) In the meantime, she gave birth to their son, Charles Wilfred, in 1830. Because he was born before her second marriage, Malibran suffered a great deal; society was unforgiving of such trespasses at the time. The couple built a handsome villa in a suburb of Brussels in 1831, to which they returned between engagements. In November 1832, Malibran gave birth to a daughter, but the infant did not survive.

Maria Malibran

In April 1836, while in London, Malibran was thrown from a horse and dragged some distance along the road, receiving serious head injuries from which she never fully recovered, although she continued to perform. Malibran returned to Brussels and gave two concerts at Aix-la-Chapelle with de Bériot. That September, she was to appear at the Manchester Festival in England. As described in the 1880 edition of George Grove's *Dictionary of Music and Musicians*: "She arrived, with her husband, after a rapid journey from Paris, on Sunday, September 11, 1836. On the following evening she sang in no less than 14 pieces. On Tuesday, though weak and ill, she insisted on singing both morning and evening. On Wednesday, the 14th, her state was still more critical, but she contrived to sing the last sacred music in which she ever took part, 'Sing Ye to the Lord,' with thrilling effect; but that same evening her last notes in public were heard, in the Duet, with Caradori Allan, 'Vanne se alberghi in petto,' from *Andronico*. This was received with immense enthusiasm, the last movement was encored, and Malibran actually accomplished the task repeating it. It was her last effort. While the concert-room still rang with applause, she was fainting in the arms of her friends; and, a few moments later, she was conveyed to her hotel. Here she died, after nine days of nervous fever, in the prostration which naturally followed upon the serious injuries her brain had received from the accident." Malibran died on Friday, September 23, 1836, and was buried in the south aisle of the collegiate church in Manchester. Her remains were re-interred in the cemetery of Lacken in Brussels soon after. She was only 28. News of her death swept the Continent, and the public mourned her passing. Wrote Alfred Bunn, the impresario: "The powerful and conflicting elements in her composition were gifts indeed, but of a very fatal nature—the mind was far too great for the body, and it did not require any wonderful gift of prophecy to foresee that, in their contention, the triumph would be short, however brilliant and decisive."

SOURCES:

Bushnell, H. *Maria Malibran: A Biography of a Singer.* University Park, 1979.

Gattey, C. *Queens of Song.* London, 1979.

Grove, George, ed. *Dictionary of Music and Musicians.* Vol. II. London: Macmillan, 1889.

Uglow, Jennifer, ed. *International Dictionary of Women's Biography.* NY: Continuum, 1985.

Warrack, John, and Ewan West. *Oxford Dictionary of Opera.* Oxford University Press, 1992.

SUGGESTED READING:

Fitzlyon, A. *Maria Malabran.* London, 1987.

Pougin, A. *Marie Malibran: histoire d'une cantatrice.* 1911.

John Haag,
Associate Professor of History,
University of Georgia, Athens, Georgia

Malinche (c. 1500–1531)

Indian translator, interlocutor, and mistress of Hernán Cortés, who aided immeasurably in forwarding the Spanish conquest of the Aztec Empire. Name variations: La Malinche; Doña Marina; Malintzin; Marina Malintzin; Mallinalli Tenepal; Martina; Marina de Jaramillo; Mariana. Born in the village of Painala in southeastern Mexico, probably around 1500; died near Orizaba in 1531; parents' names not recorded; married Juan de Jaramillo, in 1523, after four years of a semiofficial liaison with Hernán Cortés; children: (with Cortés) Martín (b. 1520).

Sold into slavery by her family and taken southward to the Maya-speaking Tabasco region (1512); together with 19 other Indian women, given as a gift to the Spanish conquerors of Tabasco (1519); began a personal and political relation with Cortés, acting as his translator and confidant with all of the Indian groups (1519); gave birth to Cortés' child Martín and uncovered a major anti-Spanish plot at Cholula (1520); the fall of the Aztec capital Tenochtitlán (August 1521) brought a change in her status—from translator and diplomat to a minor member of a rather large entourage of women surrounding Cortés; before departing for an expedition to Honduras, Cortés commanded her to marry Juan Jaramillo, an old though not very reputable associate of the captain (1523); caught in an unhappy marriage, she retired into obscurity, finally dying near Orizaba (1531).

The 20 Indian women could not have been more frightened. They had just been turned over by the Tabascan *caciques* to the barbarians from across the waters, the bearded men who wore armor all of metal, who rode immense stags, and who spoke a language totally unlike their own Maya or Nahuatl. Indeed, were they men at all? They had attacked the Tabascan warriors in the manner of mad coyotes, vicious and unyielding. And now, as part of the price of peace, the women found themselves delivered into the hands of the monsters, who took them aboard a massive war canoe and proceeded northward along the coast. Huddled together in a corner of the deck, the women prepared themselves for death. But for one of their number, this encounter with the Spaniards—for such they were—was the most fortuitous thing that could have happened. She set out immediately to know more about them, examining everything on board the ship, and trying, willy-nilly, to convey all sorts of questions, large and small.

The young Indian woman's name was Malintzin, which means "a twist on the thigh," but she has entered history by the European name she took upon her baptism, Doña Marina, or Malinche (the Spanish corruption of her Indian name). She was a Totonac Indian from the central coastal region of Mexico. As a small child, she had been given to merchants who had sold her to the people of the south. Consequently, she knew not only her native Nahuatl but the Maya language as well. The Tabascans had regarded her as being little better than a slave, and not an especially good one at that. They were happy to hand her over to the monsters. The "monsters" themselves soon saw in her the key to their victory over the Aztecs.

The conquest of Mexico had already begun in the minds of the Spaniards several years before. They had come to the New World in the 1490s looking for gold and adventure. They found a great deal of the latter but very little of the former. Instead, the West Indies offered the Spaniards only a large, docile population of Arawak Indians, whom they proceeded to enslave and to push en masse to an early death, all in an obsessive search for nonexistent gold. Among the many newcomers to the New World on this same quest was one Hernán Cortés, a native of Extremadura and, outwardly, little different from the rest. In fact, Cortés was no dreamer. He was a practical man, a born leader with little of the fatalism and superstition so common among other European immigrants to the West Indies. The Indians, for example, he regarded less as savages than as men—with weaknesses and interests, to be sure, but men just the same. If he could understand these weaknesses and interests then he could transform their world into his. It was precisely this sense of self-assurance, coupled with practicality, that earned him the command position on an expedition sent in 1519 from Cuba to the Mexican coast, an area that was known to be vast and potentially wealthy.

Cortés' meeting with Malinche was in the best sense historic. His fleet had skirted the same route opposite the Yucatán peninsula taken by earlier reconnaissance vessels. He had made landfall near Cozumel to take on water, and on several occasions engaged in battle with the Mayas. He rescued a Spanish castaway, Jeronimo de Aguilar, who proved quite useful, since he had learned to speak the Maya language well. But Cortés came to realize that this would not help for much longer, since his ships were entering the realm of the Aztecs, where only the Nahuatl language was understood. As Cortés pondered this problem, into his line of vision came Malinche, so engaging, so full of curiosity, so different from the other Indian women received from the Tabascans. Here was the solution for his difficulty, for she understood both languages. Malinche would turn Nahuatl into Maya for Aguilar, and he in turn would translate into Spanish for Cortés.

Had this been the sum of her historical role, then Malinche would today be regarded as only a clever translator. But she had ambitions of her own. First of all, as a Totonac, she was part of a major Indian group that had long been oppressed by the powerful Aztecs of Tenochtitlán; now she saw in Cortés the possible liberator of her people. Second, as a woman of humble background, she could not normally expect to rise especially high within her own society; but Cortés in effect offered her a different fate—and she quickly seized her opportunity. As rapidly as she could, she learned the Castilian language, thus making Aguilar's function in the Spanish party superfluous and her function all the more critical. She also began to cultivate a personal relation with Cortés. As time went on, their continual conversations together, his strong liking for women, the daily revelations of her unexpected qualities—all of these fed their relationship. Within a short time, Malinche became Cortés' shadow, his inseparable companion.

The Aztec codices invariably depict her near the camp chair of the conqueror, decked in her loose tunic, spouting from her mouth a cluster of coruscating hieroglyphics.

—Fernando Benítez

The Spanish fleet made landfall on the central coast on Holy Thursday 1519. Realizing that the local Indians would report his arrival to the Aztec emperor Moctezuma, Cortés had his troops stage a mock battle to impress them. He then instructed the local chief to send a message to the emperor to tell him that the Spaniards had a disease that could only be cured by gold. Advised by Malinche that the Indians thought him the lost god Quetzalcoatl, Cortés did nothing to correct their error. Soon all Tenochtitlán, some 200 miles inland, was abuzz with tales of the new deities.

Moctezuma sent the gold that Cortés had requested. He also asked the Spaniards to leave his realm with all dispatch. Rather than accept this dismissal, which, after all, had been prompted by fear, Cortés audaciously announced his intention to visit the Aztec capital. He would not think, so he told the emperor's emissaries, of missing the opportunity of greeting the great lord in person after having crossed the waters with that object in mind. Moreover, he said, he bore a message from his king that could be delivered only to Moctezuma himself. To demonstrate still further his unalterable determination, he gave orders to scuttle his ships. This convinced Spaniard and Indian alike that Cortés took literally the royal mandate of *plus ultra*—ever forward.

There was, of course, much bluff and much calculation in all this. Cortés' greatest victories were always diplomatic, and he made every effort to prepare his hand with great care before ever having to ungird his sword. In this, Malinche's help was crucial. She explained to him many aspects of the Indian character, when an Indian might be expected to exaggerate or lie, and when an Indian might tell the truth. Above all, she stressed that Moctezuma and the Aztecs were fanatically attached to their religion, which bore little resemblance to the Christianity she had grown to understand. Where the Europeans worshipped a man crucified, the Aztecs worshipped the execution itself—seeing in blood spilled for their gods the necessary ingredient for their own continued survival in the world. Since war prisoners were required for ceremonies of sacrifice, the Aztecs could not be expected to make meaningful peace on any long-term basis with the Spaniards; nonetheless, unlike the Europeans, they could ill afford to undertake the annihilation of the invaders, since there would then be no guarantee of prisoners. Cortés remembered this detail and in it he saw the possible key to victory.

Malinche's relations with Cortés had by now taken on the appearance, if not the legal status, of a marriage. She had originally been assigned as slave to a little-known Spaniard called Puertocarrero. When Cortés realized her true value, the other man slipped into the background. He was sent back to Madrid to deliver the captain's letters to the king (although the monarch evidently never read these missives, they were delivered and today constitute one of our chief sources on the conquest of Mexico). It is not known whether Malinche's intimate relations with Cortés began before Puertocarrero's departure. In any case, however, she soon found herself pregnant with their son.

Even today, the Sierra Madre Oriental presents a breathtaking aspect, with its greenery slowly giving way to windswept peaks. In the time of Malinche, the mountain chain was dangerous as well, since it provided refuge for those savage Indian groups that the Aztecs had never managed to subdue. The Tlaxcalans, in particu-

lar, were much feared throughout the region, but Malinche stressed that they might make useful allies for Cortés against Moctezuma. She had already set up a network of informants and spies that stretched all the way to Tenochtitlán, and her information was usually regarded as sound. On this occasion, however, her informants failed her. As the expeditionary force crossed into Tlaxcalan territory, the Indians launched a ferocious assault. In the ensuing battle, several Spaniards were killed as well as two horses. The Indians had viewed the Spanish horses as being almost certainly immortal. The word now spread that the beasts could be killed, and Cortés lost a great psychological advantage.

Malinche's poor information before the battle was more than offset by her diplomacy and good sense in its aftermath. She helped initiate negotiations with the defeated Tlaxcalans, after which they became steadfast allies of Cortés. But her loyalty to the Spaniards on this and many other occasions was beginning to cost her among her own people. More and more the name Malinche took on the sense of traitor. The Totonacs as well as the Aztecs now stood in awe of her power, of her influence with the bearded gods.

Nowhere was this influence more critical than at the Aztec community of Cholula. Cholula stood at the principal crossroads leading to Tenochtitlán, and it was there that Moctezuma directed the Spaniards to await his delegation. Cortés and his men had by this time gained some idea of the enormity of the land around them, the number of potential enemies in their midst, and how very far away they were from home. They therefore welcomed the chance to go to a safe town like Cholula for a rest to plan their next moves.

But Malinche and the Tlaxcalans, who had joined their armies to the European cause, suspected a trap. The lords of Cholula, at first reluctant to meet with Cortés, eventually appeared, pleading friendship and offering tribute. The inhabitants of the town turned out *en masse* to shower food and flowers on the strangers—but their leaders had other instructions. Moctezuma had apparently determined to test at Cholula the belief of his militant generals that the Spaniards were simply men of flesh and blood and could be killed like anyone else. The emperor sent 30,000 troops to ambush the Spaniards as soon as the Cholulans arranged an ambush.

Malinche's spy network, however, reached into the confines of Cholula as well as the other towns in the valley of Mexico. She uncovered the conspiracy and immediately informed

Cortés, who ordered a preemptive attack within the city limits. He executed all the Cholulan nobles and mercilessly slaughtered their minions. Before the night had passed, the Spaniards had killed 6,000 people and had burnt every important building in the town.

Moctezuma was forced to disavow any connection with the plot. Amazed that Cortés had discovered the trap, and that his reaction had been so very bloody, Moctezuma felt confirmed in his earlier judgment: the Spaniards *were* gods. He invited them to enter his capital, this time unopposed.

Over the next year, Cortés quelled a rebellion in his own ranks, disposed of Moctezuma, and made war on his successors. Aided by cannons, horses, his Tlaxcalan allies, and the Aztec penchant for fighting a limited over an unlimited war, the Spanish captain went from victory to victory. Malinche did not share directly in these victories. In fact, she was far removed from the fighting. She had given birth to their son Martín and stayed in seclusion with him. Her diplomatic skills were little needed by the Spaniards at that point, and Cortés was busy with other things. When Tenochtitlán fell in August 1521, the relation between the Spanish conquistador and his Indian lover clarified itself. Cortés was no longer a simple adventurer; now he was a royal administrator, all-powerful within his realm, and immensely wealthy. He could choose what he wanted and when, and he did. In his Coyoacan residence, he established Malinche, their son, ❧➤ **Tecuichpo** (daughter of the dead Moctezuma), two other Indian women, and three Spanish women, one of whom was Cortés' legitimate wife, **Catalina Xuarez**, who had arrived unexpectedly from Cuba.

The new situation sealed Malinche's fate. When final victory was achieved, far from enjoying its fruits she instead became part of Cortés' coterie of women. On the arrival of his legitimate wife, Malinche came to be considered an intruder, someone to be rid of.

History records one final episode concerning her fate. Cortés had no intention of leaving Malinche without any reward whatsoever. Having ended their personal relations, the captain gave her some rich lands and commanded her to marry one of his allies among the conquistadores, Juan Jaramillo. The latter was a drunkard, chosen more for his political connections than for any attention or love he might show Malinche. After the wedding ceremony, Cortés himself left immediately for Honduras, hoping to repeat the successes he had enjoyed in Mexi-

co. This expedition proved an utter failure, and Cortés was lucky to escape with his life.

Malinche, for her part, evidently hated her marriage of convenience. Jaramillo happily took her lands while at the same time denigrating her as a dirty Indian. Nor did she find any solace in her son, for Cortés had already taken Martín from her and given the boy to one of his cousins. As the essayist Fernando Benítez noted:

> Had there been in the heart of Cortés a vestige of love, he would not have snatched away the child, nor would he have sold Malinche to a man of the moral fiber of Jaramillo, but he would rather have been content to keep her to herself and see that she had all the protection necessary.

But Cortés was still looking at the horizon, still looking for further Tenochtitláns to conquer. This fatal wanderlust made him blind to his earlier associates, Malinche among them. She languished for a time on her estates in Orizaba and then died, probably of a European disease, in 1531. Jaramillo remarried within six months.

Nationalist historiography in Mexico vilifies the memory of Malinche. She was, it is alleged, an arch-traitor to her own people, having in effect sold them into bondage to the Spaniards, thus setting the pattern for a long history of exploitation that lasted until the 1910 Revolution. "Malinche" has taken on the worst sort of pejorative connotation in contemporary Mexico. But is this fair to the historical figure? She thought that by allying herself to Cortés she might liberate her people, not enslave them. And she worked hard toward that end. That Cortés should appear to her as a glimmering comet is no more a surprise than it is that she failed to see the long darkness that followed him. Finally, what the nationalists have missed is that by giving

❧➤ **Tecuichpo** (d. 1551)
Daughter of Moctezuma II, emperor of the Aztecs. Name variations: Tecuichpoch; Miahuaxochitl; (baptismal name) Isabel; Doña Isabel. Daughter of Moctezuma II (c. 1480–1520), Aztec emperor (r. 1502–1520); mother unknown; married Alonso de Grado; married Pedro Gallego; married Juan Cano de Suavedra, in 1531; some sources claim also married Cuauhtemoc, last emperor of the Aztecs; children: (with Hernán Cortés) daughter Leonor Cortés Motecuhzoma, also known as Marina.

SOURCES:
Gillespie, Susan D. *The Aztec Kings: The Construction of Rulership in Mexica History.* Tucson, AZ: The University of Arizona Press, 1989.

birth to Martín, in whose veins pumped both European and Indian blood, Malinche helped lay the foundations for modern Mexican society. She is as much mother of Mexico as she is the malignant spirit that haunts the country to this day.

SOURCES:

Benítez, Fernando. *In the Footsteps of Cortés.* NY: Pantheon, 1952.

Chaison, Joanne Danaher. "Mysterious Malinche: A Case of Mistaken Identity," in *The Americas.* Vol. 32. April 1976, pp. 514–523.

Krueger, Hilde. *Malinche or Farewell to Myths.* NY: Storm Publishers, 1948.

SUGGESTED READING:

Cortés, Hernán. *Letters from Mexico.* NY: Orion, 1971.

Díaz del Castillo, Bernal. *The True History of the Conquest of New Spain, 1517–1521.* NY: Farrar, Straus, and Giroux, 1966.

Meyer, Michael C., and William L. Sherman. *The Course of Mexican History.* NY: Oxford, 1991.

Thomas Whigham,
Professor of Latin American History,
University of Georgia, Athens, Georgia

Malintzen, Marina (c. 1500–1531).

See Malinche.

Mallinger, Mathilde (1847–1920)

Croatian soprano. Born in Zagreb on February 17, 1847; died in Berlin, Germany, on April 19, 1920; studied in Prague with Gordigiani and Vogl, in Vienna with Loewy.

Mathilde Mallinger made her debut in Munich as Norma in 1866; she remained there until 1868, singing Elsa, Elisabeth, and the first Eva. Mallinger appeared in Berlin from 1869 until her retirement in 1882. After that, she taught singing in Prague, where one of her students was *Lotte Lehmann. A great rivalry between Mallinger and *Pauline Lucca resulted in their both appearing in *Figaro* in 1872.

Mallon, Mary (1867–1938)

American of Irish descent who contributed to the spread of typhoid, earning the name Typhoid Mary. Name variations: Typhoid Mary; Mrs. Brown; Marie Breshof. Born, she said, in America in 1867; died on North Brother Island on November 11, 1938. Mallon would leave no record of her past, nor would she allow her photograph to be taken, though one or two exist.

As the first known symptom-free carrier of the typhoid bacilli, Mary Mallon was a nine-year nightmare for those employed at New York City's Department of Health.

When six members of the household of Charles Henry Warren of Oyster Bay, Long Island, were struck with typhoid in August 1906, investigators for the Department of Health, led by sanitary engineer George A. Soper, were sent out to the house. In that year alone, the infectious disease had claimed 23,000 American lives. After eliminating the usual culprits—water supply, drainage, cesspools, indoor and outdoor plumbing—Soper began to look for a human carrier, making him the first in the United States to test a new theory being advanced in Germany by bacteriologist Robert Koch. For years, it had been known that victims of typhoid fever were contagious while they were ill and sometimes during recovery, but Koch maintained that a carrier, someone who had never even experienced the fever, could spread the disease through their feces as they continually bred the bacilli inside their bodies.

Soper discovered that one of the cooks was missing from the Warren house, a cook the family had newly retained through a New York employment agency at the beginning of August. She was a pretty good cook though not particularly clean, remarked Mrs. Warren, and she had left abruptly, without giving notice, three weeks after the outbreak of typhoid. Her name was Mary Mallon.

Aided by eyewitness descriptions, Soper set out to find a tall, buxom, 40-year-old Irish-American woman with blue eyes and blonde hair, who was described as firm of mouth and jaw. After months of research, through interviewing, gathering clues, and following leads, he pieced together her employment history over the previous ten years. His discoveries were alarming. In 1897, Mary Mallon began work for a family in Mamaroneck, New York; three years later, a houseguest came down with typhoid ten days after he arrived. In 1901–02, she was employed by a Manhattan family; one month after her arrival, their laundress was hospitalized with typhoid. In June 1902, she was employed at the summer home of J. Coleman Drayton in Dark Harbor, Maine; a few weeks later, six members of the household fell ill with typhoid. Before she left, Mallon stayed to help nurse them. In June 1904, she was employed at the summer estate of Henry Gilsey in Sands Point, Long Island; another laundress and three more servants took sick with typhoid.

Soper also learned that, within a few days of leaving the Warren family, Mallon had taken a job in Tuxedo, New York. After another laundress in that household took sick with typhoid, Mary Mallon had again moved on, but no one knew her whereabouts. Soper was convinced that his dilemma would be solved if he could find her. He planned to tell Mallon of her contagion, persuade her to volunteer for specimen tests of blood, urine, and feces to make certain she was a carrier, and educate her to minimize the risk. With the proper precautions, there was no reason for her to be deprived of a normal life.

In March 1907, while investigating another case of typhoid in a brownstone on Park Avenue, Soper was conducted to the kitchen and introduced to a cook named Mary Mallon. The meeting did not go as he might have hoped; when he told her he suspected she was a carrier, she lurched at him with a carving fork. Soper fled the house.

Soper learned that Mallon often spent the night with a man who lived in a rooming house on Third Avenue. With another doctor on hand, he stationed himself in the hallway and waited. When Mallon arrived, they tried reasoning with her, promising they would not harm her and begging only for her help with specimens. Furious, Mallon said they made no sense, that she never had typhoid, that typhoid was everywhere and why blame it on her, a woman who had only nursed its victims. Once again, as curses whirled around his head, Soper was driven away.

Stymied, he appealed to the health commissioner. On March 18, 1907, Dr. *S. Josephine Baker was sent to implore Mallon to come in for tests voluntarily, but Mallon would not be cajoled. When Baker returned the following morning on the orders of her superior Dr. Walter Bensel, she was accompanied by an ambulance and three policemen. Baker had been instructed to get the specimens, period. If Mallon resisted, she was to be forcibly taken to the Willard Parker Hospital for Contagious Disease at the foot of East 16th Street.

Instructing the ambulance to remain at the corner, Baker positioned two of the policemen and, accompanied by the third, approached the house. Mallon opened the door narrowly, lunged with a kitchen fork, then ran to the rear of the house and disappeared. After a five-hour search, Baker finally found Mallon in the outside closet-shed of an adjoining house; trash cans had been stacked in front of its door by conspiring servant friends. "I made another effort to talk to her sensibly," said Baker, "and asked her again to let me have the specimens, but it was no use. By that time she was convinced that the law was wantonly persecuting her, when she had done nothing wrong. She knew she had never had typhoid fever; she was

maniacal in her integrity. There was nothing I could do but take her with us. . . . I literally sat on her all the way to the hospital; it was like being in a cage with an angry lion."

Analysis of specimens proved that Mallon was a carrier. Soper, evidently a compassionate man, visited and tried to reason with her. It was not her fault that she carried the disease, he told her, but when she went to the toilet, germs got on her hands, and because she did not wash her hands, the germs got on the food. If she had washed her hands there might not have been any trouble. He told her that the bacteria was probably propagating in her gall bladder and asked if she'd be willing to have it removed. He tried to help her understand how many people had suffered and died. He told her that if she cooperated with him, he would help her get out of the hospital. She listened angrily, then walked into the bathroom and slammed the door.

After a few weeks, Mallon was moved and detained at Riverside Hospital on North Brother Island, a secluded 13-acre island in the East River. While tests were continued for eight months, her body kept manufacturing the deadly bacilli. Now aware of symptomless carriers, the Health Department rounded up hundreds of suspects who dealt with food or worked with the milk supply, but when the suspects promised to avoid any job that involved food preparation, they were released. Mary Mallon, however, by now notorious and dubbed Typhoid Mary by the New York tabloids, adamantly refused to make that promise; it was said she loved to cook. Despite two legal actions to free her, she remained in the hospital cut off from contact with others for three years. During this time, she was allowed to work as a laundress and to have a dog.

By February 1910, Mallon had been worn down. She finally acquiesced, promising to abandon employment as a cook. She also agreed to report to the Health Department every three months. The hospital released her, whereupon she promptly disappeared. The facts suggest that at first she did attempt to give up her chosen occupation. Now known as Mrs. Brown or Marie Breshof, Mallon tried running a boarding house which went bust; she then tried taking in ironing, but made far less than she had as a cook. Avoiding employment agencies and private homes, she began cooking in hotels, a Broadway restaurant, and a sanatorium in New Jersey. Though typhoid was reported in each, Mallon was yet to be connected.

Four years later, in 1915, when an outbreak of typhoid at the Sloane Hospital for Women infected 25 and killed two, Soper was called in. Shown a sample of the handwriting of a cook who had been hired three months before and had left without notice after the outbreak, Soper knew he had found his Mary. On March 27, she was brought once again to North Brother Island. Though a sympathetic staff tried to engage her, Mallon wanted none of it. She was withdrawn and sullen, responding to kind gestures with anger. Slowly, over the years, the nurses and doctors broke through her outer shell. Given a job in the laboratories of the hospital, she became a knowledgeable aide, poring over textbooks brought in to her. For $60 a month, she prepared slides and kept records. In 1923, the city gave her a home of her own on the island, a one-room cottage with a plot of grass and two elms, where she sewed, took walks, and read Dickens. On nice days, she would sometimes entertain friends from the hospital on her porch.

Less than ten years later, on Christmas 1932, Mallon was paralyzed by a stroke and forced to live the rest of her days on a hospital ward, a helpless invalid. When she died in 1938, there were 349 known chronic typhoid carriers in the city; all had cooperated, and none had been quarantined. As for Mary Mallon, at least 53 cases and three deaths could be directly attributed to her; she also may have been responsible for starting an epidemic in Ithaca, New York, in 1903. But the actual number of those affected by her cooking will never be known.

SOURCES:

Sufrin, Mark. "The Case of the Disappearing Cook," in *American Heritage*. August 1970, pp. 37–43.

SUGGESTED READING:

Leavitt, Judith Walzer. *Typhoid Mary: Captive to the Public's Health*. Beacon, 1996.

Mallory, Molla (1892–1959)

Norwegian tennis player who won eight U.S. singles tennis championships, more than any other woman in history. Name variations: Anna Margrethe Bjurstedt; Molla Bjurstedt; Mrs. Franklin Mallory. Born Molla Bjurstedt in 1892 in Norway; died in 1959 in Norway; married Franklin Mallory (a stockbroker), in 1919 (died 1934).

Born Anna Margrethe Bjurstedt in Norway in 1892, Molla Mallory was an athletic child who took up tennis at an early age. Competing throughout Europe, she won the Norwegian National championship eight times. By the time she visited the United States in 1914, she was already known as the first lady of Norwegian tennis. Mallory found herself smitten with America and

decided to settle in New York City. Five years later, she married stockbroker Franklin Mallory.

What she lacked in some areas of her game, Mallory made up for with her sheer determination to win, a powerful forehand, and excellent mobility. Among the holes in her game were her serve, which was surprisingly weak, a backhand that was used almost exclusively defensively, and an unwillingness to play close to the net unless forced to by a drop-shot. Of course, all these weaknesses quickly fall by the wayside, considering the formidable record of wins that Mallory posted both in Europe and in the United States. In her initial bid for the U.S. National tennis championship in 1915, Mallory defeated *Hazel Wightman. A sports writer of the day described Mallory as "a panther stalking her prey."

Molla Mallory was one of the first female tennis players to hit the ball hard; her powerful returns influenced women players to concentrate on passing shots rather than on returning volleys. Known for her fast-paced backcourt style of playing (*Billie Jean King called her "a thunderous backcourt player"), she was the essence of the fighting spirit. "I find that the girls generally do not hit the ball as hard as they should," said Mallory. "I believe in always hitting the ball with all my might, but there seems to be a disposition to 'just get it over' in many girls whom I have played. I do not call this tennis." She took a somewhat less stringent approach to training; she smoked and particularly enjoyed a night out dancing, even if one of those nights happened to be the eve of a big match. Athletically built and sporting a perpetual tan, she was described by fans and rivals alike as the "fighting Norsewoman."

Mallory was a major factor in women's tennis for 15 years and won the singles championship in 1915, 1916, 1917, 1918, 1920, 1921, 1922, and 1926. Every year between 1915 and 1929, she made it at least as far as the quarterfinals. Playing with *Eleanora Sears, she won the doubles championship in 1916 and 1917. In mixed doubles, she shared the championship with Ian Wright in 1917, and again in 1922 and 1923, with Bill Tilden. All of Mallory's major titles were won in the United States, although she did compete in several international tennis competitions. She also played for the United States five times in the Wightman Cup and came in second in the World Hard Court championship of 1921.

Mallory's court mien was described by a former president of the U.S. Lawn Tennis Association, Bob Kelleher: "She walked around in a manner that said you'd better look out or she'd deck you. She was an indomitable scrambler and runner. She was a fighter." The high point of her tennis career occurred at the 1921 Nationals in Forest Hills, New York. Mallory faced undefeated French champion and media celebrity *Suzanne Lenglen in the first round. A sellout crowd of 8,000 filled the stands at the West Side Tennis Club. Lenglen had been ill with a recurrence of chronic asthma before leaving France, but newspapers reported (as they reported almost anything about her) that she looked healthy and confident on the day of her match with Mallory. From the outset, however, she played tentatively, while Mallory attacked with a vengeance. Already trailing, Lenglen began to cough. Mallory won the first set decisively, 6-2. Lenglen served in the first game of the second set and soon fell behind, love-30. She then double-faulted, something that happened no more than ten times in her entire career. She eventually approached the umpire's chair to say she was too ill to go on. As she was helped off the court, weeping, many in the crowd expressed their disapproval by hissing. The match ended in a victory by default for Mallory, although amidst the enormous publicity which ensued most commentators opined that Mallory almost certainly would have won had the match continued. The victory made Mallory the only woman to beat the French champion from the time Lenglen first won at Wimbledon in 1919 until 1926. (In 1922, Lenglen defeated Mallory in straight sets at Wimbledon.)

Mallory, who had lived a life of luxury while married to her successful stockbroker husband, fell on harder times when he died in 1934, and worked for the government to make ends meet. She also sold all but one of her hundreds of trophies. In 1958, she was inducted into the International Tennis Hall of Fame at Newport, Rhode Island. She died the following year while on a visit to her native Norway.

Tennis champion *Helen Hull Jacobs dedicated her 1944 book *Gallery of Champions* (which chronicled the accomplishments of such women tennis stars as Mallory, Lenglen, *Alice Marble, *Louise Brough, and *Pauline Betz) to Mallory with these words: "To Molla Mallory, whose domination of American women's tennis was less important than the legacy she left to those who came after her. Her great driving game was the beginning of an era of hard-hitters among women players. . . . [H]er courage and sportsmanship and, above all, her will to win were a contribution of unforgettable value."

SOURCES:
Hollander, Phyllis. *100 Greatest Women in Sports.* NY: Grosset & Dunlap, 1976.

King, Billie Jean, with Cynthia Starr. *We Have Come a Long Way: The Story of Women's Tennis.* NY: Mc-Graw-Hill, 1988.

Don Amerman, freelance writer, Saylorsburg, Pennsylvania

Molla Mallory

Mallowan, Agatha Maria (1890–1976).

See Christie, Agatha.

Malmfrid of Russia (fl. 1100s)

Queen of Denmark. Flourished in the early 1100s; married Erik Emune, king of Denmark (r. 1134–1137).

Malone, Annie Turnbo
(1869–1957)

African-American entrepreneur and pioneer in black beauty culture. Name variations: Annie Turnbo; Annie Turnbo-Malone. Born Annie Minerva Turbo in Metropolis, Illinois, on August 9, 1869; died of a stroke on May 10, 1957; tenth of eleven children of Robert Turnbo and Isabella (Cook) Turnbo; married a man named Pope in 1903; married Aaron Malone, in 1914 (divorced 1927); no children.

An orphan who grew up penniless, Annie Turnbo Malone learned the cosmetics business with the help of her older sister while living in Peoria. By 1900, Malone had developed several hair-care products for African-American women: straighteners, growers, tetter reliefs, and hair oils. In 1902, she moved from Illinois to St. Louis, where she began to sell her products, enlisting other women to help. During the 1904 World's Fair in St. Louis, which brought an influx of tourists, she opened her first shop to showcase her wares. Within two years, her business was incorporated under the name Poro (West African for "physical and spiritual fulfillment"). By 1917, Poro was a million dollar complex called Poro College, encompassing a beauty school, barbershops, a manufacturing plant, a theater, a bakery, an auditorium, and hospitality facilities, becoming the social center for blacks in St. Louis. Poro had an in-house staff of 175 by 1926 and claimed 75,000 at-home agents around the world.

Annie and her husband Aaron Malone were generous to their employees and to charities, making major contributions to schools, including Howard University, and women's projects, especially the YWCA. They endured a bitter and much-publicized divorce in 1927, which split black leaders into his-and-her camps. Annie negotiated a settlement and bought Aaron out of his share of the business for $200,000. Unfortunately, she had purchased a business with a heavy tax debt and future lawsuits, three years before the onset of the Great Depression. By 1951, Poro was in receivership, and Annie Turnbo Malone died in Chicago six years later.

Malone, Dorothy (1925—)

American actress who won an Academy Award for Best Supporting Actress for her performance in **Written on the Wind.** *Born Dorothy Eloise Maloney on January 30, 1925, in Chicago, Illinois; attended Southern Methodist University; married actor Jacques Bergerac (divorced); two subsequent marriages.*

Filmography: Gildersleeve on Broadway *(1943);* The Falcon and the Co-Eds *(1943);* Higher and High-

Dorothy Malone

er *(1943)*; Show Business *(1944)*; Seven Days Ashore *(1944)*; Youth Runs Wild *(1944)*; One Mysterious Night *(1944)*; Too Young to Know *(1945)*; Janie Gets Married *(1946)*; The Big Sleep *(1946)*; Night and Day *(1946)*; To the Victor *(1948)*; Two Guys from Texas *(1948)*; One Sunday Afternoon *(1948)*; Flaxy Martin *(1949)*; South of St. Louis *(1949)*; Colorado Territory *(1949)*; The Nevadan *(1950)*; Convicted *(1950)*; Mrs. O'Malley and Mr. Malone *(1950)*; The Killer That Stalked New York *(1950)*; Saddle Legion *(1951)*; The Bushwackers *(1951)*; Torpedo Alley *(1953)*; Scared Stiff *(1953)*; Law and Order *(1953)*; Jack Slade *(1953)*; Loophole *(1954)*; The Lone Gun *(1954)*; Pushover *(1954)*; Young at Heart *(1954)*; Security Risk *(1954)*; The Fast and the Furious *(1954)*; Private Hell 36 *(1954)*; Five Guns West *(1955)*; Battle Cry *(1955)*; Tall Man Riding *(1955)*; Sincerely Yours *(1955)*; Artists and Models *(1955)*; At Gunpoint *(1955)*; Pillars of the Sky *(1956)*; Tension at Table Rock *(1956)*; Written on the Wind *(1956)*; Quantez *(1957)*; Man of a Thousand Faces *(1957)*; Tip on a Dead Jockey *(1957)*; The Tarnished Angels *(1958)*; Too Much Too Soon *(1958)*; Warlock *(1959)*; The Last Voyage *(1960)*; The Last Sunset *(1961)*; Beach Party *(1963)*; Fate Is the Hunter *(1964)*; Femmine insaziabili *(It./Monaco, 1969)*; The Man Who Would Not Die *(Target in the Sun, 1975)*; The November Plan *(1976)*; Golden Rendezvous *(1977)*; Good Luck, Miss Wyckoff *(1979)*; Winter Kills *(1979)*; The Day Time Ended *(Sp., 1980)*; The Being *(1983)*; Basic Instinct *(1992)*.

The daughter of a telephone company auditor, actress Dorothy Malone was discovered by a talent agent while performing in a college play at Southern Methodist University. Signed by RKO, she played several small roles under her real name of Dorothy Maloney before moving to Warner Bros. in 1945 and changing her name to Dorothy Malone. Then a wholesome girl-next-door type, Malone played standard leading lady roles for the next decade, developing into a fine dramatic actress along the way. In 1956, she won an Academy Award for Best Supporting Actress for her role as a frustrated nymphomaniac in *Written on the Wind*, a portrayal that changed her screen image considerably. Following the award, however, she suffered a dry spell. "Instead of getting better, my parts just got worse," she said of her later career. Malone had a long run (1964–69) on the hit television series "Peyton Place," based on the novel by *Grace Metalious, and a small but meaty role in *Basic Instinct* (1992). The actress has been married three times; her first husband was the actor Jacques Bergerac.

Malraux, Clara (c. 1897–1982)

French novelist, critic, and translator. Name variations: Clara Malraux-Goldschmidt. Born Clara Goldschmidt around 1897; died on December 15, 1982, in Paris, France; first wife of Andre Malraux (b. 1901, a writer and politician).

Clara Malraux published travelogues of journeys with her husband, writer Andre Malraux. She also wrote six volumes of her memoirs, including *When We Were Twenty, The End of the Beginning*, and *The Sound of Footsteps*, and translated *Virginia Woolf's *A Room of One's Own* into French. Her novel, *Portrait de Grisélidis* (1945), combines fiction with autobiography to portray a woman's struggle for equality.

Maltby, Margaret E. (1860–1944)

American physicist and educator. Name variations: Minnie Maltby; Margaret Eliza Maltby. Born Minnie Maltby on December 10, 1860, in Bristolville, Ohio; died on May 3, 1944, in New York City; daughter of Edmund Maltby and Lydia Jane (Brockway) Maltby; Oberlin College, B.A., 1882, M.A., 1891; attended Art Students League, 1882–83; Massachusetts Institute of Technology, B.S., 1891; University of Göttingen, Germany, Ph.D., 1895; never married; children: Philip Randolph Meyer (adopted 1902).

Born on December 10, 1860, on the family farm in Bristolville, Ohio, Margaret Maltby was originally christened "Minnie" by her two older sisters. At her earliest opportunity, she legally changed her name to Margaret Eliza. Although she initially selected art as a career, and did, in fact, graduate from Oberlin College with a B.A. in 1882 and spend a year studying at the Art Students League in New York City, a growing interest in chemistry and physics led her to enroll at the Massachusetts Institute of Technology (MIT) in 1887. While at MIT, Maltby developed her teaching skills as a physics instructor at nearby Wellesley College (1889–93). She graduated from MIT with a bachelor's of science degree in 1891, and stayed on to do postgraduate work. In 1893, she took a hiatus from teaching to attend the University of Göttingen in Germany on a traveling scholarship and, in 1895, became the first American woman to receive a Ph.D. from the university. The subject of her dissertation was the measurement of high electrolytic resistances. A second scholarship from the Association of Collegiate Alumnae allowed her to stay in Germany for postdoctoral work.

Maltby returned briefly to the United States, during which time she headed the physics department at Wellesley College and then taught physics and mathematics at Lake Erie College in Ohio. In 1898, she joined Friedrich Kohlrausch, her mentor and the president of the Physikalish-Technische Reichsanstalt in Charlottenburg, Germany, as his research assistant. She remained in Germany until 1899, when she once again returned to America to work in theoretical physics at Clark University with A.G. Webster.

In 1900, Maltby began a long association with Barnard College, first serving as an instructor in chemistry until transferring to the physics department in 1903. She served as adjunct professor until 1913, and from 1913 until her retirement in 1931 as assistant professor and chair of the department. (She was never appointed to a full professorship.) Her reputation in the highly male-dominated field of physics was secure; in 1906, she was listed in the first edition of *American Men and Women of Science* as one of the 1,000 most important scientists in the country. Her name remained on the list throughout the next six editions of the publication, although in the course of her tenure at Barnard, Maltby became so involved with her teaching and administrative duties that she found little time for research. As a teacher, she was thorough and hard working, and insisted that her students exhibit the same characteristics; she was happy to provide individual assistance if necessary.

Maltby was a strong advocate for securing opportunities for capable women in graduate and postdoctoral programs. From 1912 to 1929, she served on the fellowship committee of the American Association of University Women (AAUW), chairing the organization from 1913 to 1924; in 1926, the AAUW established the Margaret E. Maltby Fellowship. In 1929, she published *A History of the Fellowships Awarded by the American Association of University Women, 1888–1929*. Maltby received considerable recognition and participated in numerous organizations, including the American Association for the Advancement of Science. She was elected a fellow of the American Physical Society, and in 1960 her photograph was included in the *American Journal of Physics* where she was one of eight physicists profiled, and the only woman.

Although she never married, Maltby had adopted Philip Randolph Meyer, the orphaned son of a close friend, in 1902. Throughout her life, she enjoyed music, frequently attending the opera and symphony, and prior to her retirement conducted the first known course in the physics of music. Margaret Maltby died on May 3, 1944, at the age of 83.

SOURCES:

Ogilvie, Marilyn Bailey. *Women in Science*. Boston, MA: Cambridge Press, 1993.

Sicherman, Barbara, and Carol Hurd Green. *Notable American Women: The Modern Period: A Biographical Dictionary*. Cambridge, MA: The Belknap Press of Harvard University, 1980.

Judith C. Reveal,
freelance writer, Greensboro, Maryland

Malthace (fl. 40 BCE)

*Samaritan who was briefly queen of Judea. Flourished around 40 BCE; third of ten wives of Herod the Great (73–4 BCE), king of Judea; children: Herod Archelaus II (d. before 18 CE), ethnarch of Judea; Herod Antipas (d. after 40 CE), tetrarch of Galilee who married *Herodias.*

Mama Cass (1941–1974).

See Elliot, Cass.

Mamaea, Julia (c. 190–235).

See Julia Mamaea.

Mama-Ocllo (fl. around 12th c.)

Co-founder and queen of the Incan Empire. Name variations: Mama Ocllo; Mama Oello Huaco; Mana-Ocllo; Mana Ocllo; Mama-baco; Coya (queen). Probably born around the 12th century; died in Cuzco, in what is now Peru; according to Incan mythology, she was the daughter of the Sun, whose wife was his sister the Moon; possibly three sisters (names unknown) and four brothers, one of whom was Manco Capac (co-founder and first ruler of the Incan empire); married Manco Capac; children: daughter Mama Cora (later queen of the Inca Empire); son Sinche Roca (later ruler of the Inca Empire).

According to its own mythology, the great Incan Empire, which flourished in Peru for some 400 years before the arrival of Francisco Pizarro and his Spanish conquistadors, was founded by two Children of the Sun, Mama-Ocllo and her brother Manco Capac. Together they selected the site for the holy city of Cuzco; Manco Capac caused its stone fortifications to be built, and as coya, or queen, Mama-Ocllo taught the women of her people the arts of spinning and weaving. To ensure the purity of their royal line, brother and sister married and, with the births of their children **Mama Cora** and Sinche Roca, began the Incan ruling dynasty. (Like the Egyptian pharaohs, who also practiced intermarriage to keep their bloodline pure, Incan rulers strictly enforced the taboo of incest among their subjects.) Father Bernabe Cobo, the Spanish chronicler whose *Historia del Nuevo mundo* is an important source of information on Incan culture, visited Cuzco in the early 17th century and referred to a fountain belonging, or dedicated, to Mama-Ocllo in which "very great and ordinary sacrifices" were still made to her; he states that she "was the most venerated woman there was" among the Incas.

Although Manco Capac is the first historically verifiable Incan ruler, there is debate as to exactly when he and his sister-wife lived. While the empire is generally thought to have been founded some 400 years before the Spanish Conquest, experts point out that after Manco Capac's reign there were only 13 rulers up until the time of the Conquest, which would seem to suggest an interval of some 200, not 400, years. Some older sources offer dates of as far as 500 or 550 years before the Conquest, though with little supporting evidence. Adding confusion to these various claims is the fact that there are ruins in and around Cuzco and nearby Lake Titicaca that have been dated to a far earlier era.

After death, the bodies of Incan royalty were mummified and placed in the temple of the Sun in Cuzco, where they were worshipped. These mummies were hidden after Cuzco fell to the Spaniards in 1533. In 1559, the corregidor (head of the municipal government) in Cuzco, Juan Polo de Ondegardo, discovered the mummies of four rulers and three coyas, including Mama-Ocllo. Garcilaso de la Vega Inca, the famous contemporary chronicler who was himself a member of the Incan nobility on his mother's side, saw these mummies the following year, and in the words of W.H. Prescott described them thus: "They were dressed in their regal robes, with no insignia but the *llautu* [woolen headband] on their heads. They were in a sitting posture, and, to use his own expression, 'perfect as life, without so much as a hair or an eyebrow wanting.'" Prescott continues: "As they were carried through the streets, decently shrouded with a mantle, the Indians threw themselves on their knees, in sign of reverence, with many tears and groans, and were still more touched as they beheld some of the Spaniards themselves doffing their caps, in token of respect to departed royalty. The bodies were subsequently removed to Lima; and Father Acosta, who saw them there some twenty years later, speaks of them as still in perfect preservation."

SOURCES AND SUGGESTED READING:

Cobo, Father Bernabe. *Inca Religion and Customs.* Trans. and ed. by Roland Hamilton. Austin, TX: University of Texas Press, 1990.

Griffin, Lynne, and Kelly McCann. *The Book of Women: 300 Notable Women History Passed By.* Holbrook, MA: Bob Adams, 1992.

Hemming, John. *The Conquest of the Incas.* San Diego, CA: Harcourt Brace Jovanovich, 1970.

Prescott, William H. *History of the Conquest of Peru,* 1847.

Mamas and the Papas, The.

See Elliot, Cass or Phillips, Michelle.

Mamlok, Ursula (1928—)

German-born American composer. Born in Berlin, Germany, on February 1, 1928; only child of Dorothy Lewis and John Lewis; married Dwight Mamlok, in 1949.

Escaped from Nazi Germany to Ecuador (1939); based on her compositions, received a full scholarship at the Mannes School of Music where she studied with George Szell; studied with Roger Sessions for a year; received a scholarship to study at the Manhattan School of Music; Mamlok's String Quartet (written 1962) gained her considerable attention; composed Sonar Trajectory (1966), an electronic composition which was not performed until 1984; continued her work with the help of many commissions as well as grants from the National Endowment for the Arts and the CUNY Faculty Research Foundation, and a Martha Baird Rockefeller Recording Grant.

Over half a dozen recordings attest to the success of Ursula Mamlok's compositions, which encompass orchestral, chamber, and piano solo works. When her *Variations for Solo Flute* premiered at Carnegie Hall in 1961, one reviewer called it a "landmark of difficult 20th-century pieces." This assessment proved erroneous, as many people have since performed this work. Some of Mamlok's compositions include an odd assortment of instruments; for example, her *Variations and Interludes* was written for xylophone, timpani, snare drum, temple blocks, triangle, glockenspiel, tom-tom, suspended cowbells, vibraphone, marimba, chime bongos, and suspended cymbals. The piece requires over 60 percussion instruments, and melody does not intrude. In 1981, the American Academy and Institute of Arts and Letters granted Mamlok its annual award, citing her for creating "an elegantly crafted, eloquently expressive body of chamber music, which, while making no effort to be timely, is as distinctively of its own time as it is distinguished by its persuasive claims to musical permanence." Mamlok has also composed extensively for children, believing it was important for them to have interesting music to play.

John Haag,
Athens, Georgia

Mammaea, Julia (c. 190–235).

See Julia Mamaea.

Mana Ocllo.

See Mama-Ocllo.

Mana-Zucca (1887–1981)

American pianist, operatic singer, and composer of over 1,100 compositions. Name variations: Mana Zucca. Born Gizella Augusta Zuckerman in New York, New York, on December 25, 1887; died in Miami Beach, Florida, on March 8, 1981; daughter of Samuel Shepard Zuckerman and Janet (Denow) Zuckerman; educated in Europe; married Irwin M. Cassel, on September 22, 1921; children: Marwin Shepard Cassel.

After studying piano with Alexander Lambert, Mana-Zucca made her debut at the age of seven with the New York Philharmonic Orchestra in Carnegie Hall. At 13, she embarked on a European tour which lasted for four years. In Berlin, she studied piano with Leopold Godowsky and the renowned composer Feruccio Busoni. In London, she studied composition with Hermann Spielter, and in Paris she studied singing with Von Zur Muehlen. In 1916, she changed her name, dropping her first name and rearranging the syllables in her surname. She premiered her Piano Concerto in 1919; she was always interested in the concerto form, and her Violin Concerto received its first performance in December 1955.

Mana-Zucca composed two operas and a ballet score. From the start of her career she was able to juggle her careers effectively, getting fine reviews as a concert pianist while at the same time moving into light opera. Thus she was able to appear as lead soprano in Lehar's *Count of Luxembourg* in 1914. Mana-Zucca had become seriously interested in composing at age 16. During her long career, she wrote over 1,100 published pieces; many of these were lyrical songs to her own texts. Some of her orchestral works were light in spirit, reflected in such titles as *Frolic for Strings* and *Bickerings*. One of her most ambitious works was *My Musical Calendar*, a collection of 366 piano pieces (one for each day of the year, with an extra item to prepare the performer for leap years). She also wrote memoirs and accounts of her European travels.

John Haag,
Athens, Georgia

Manahan, Anna Anderson (1902–1984).

See Anderson, Anna.

Mance, Jeanne (1606–1673)

One of the early colonizers of Canada, inspired by religious devotion and the desire to serve God, who is credited as the founder of the Hôtel Dieu hospital and the co-founder of Montreal. Pronunciation: Jan Monce. Name variations: Jeanne de Mance. Born Jeanne Mance in late 1606 (she was baptized on November 12, 1606) in the town of Langres, France; died in Montreal, Canada on June 18, 1673; daughter of Charles Mance (a lawyer) and Catherine Émonnot Mance; never married; no children.

Worked as a nurse attending to victims of war and plague (1635–36); immigrated to New France (1641); Montreal founded (1642); secured funds to stave off Iroquois attack (1651); journeyed to France, returned with nursing sisters to Montreal (1658); was present at the founding of the Church of Notre Dame (1673).

The early exploration and settlement of North America has traditionally been viewed as the work of men. Along the St. Lawrence River, however, in the small settlements of the 17th century which were to form the backbone of New France, women played a significant role in early colonial life. One of these women was Jeanne Mance, who was born in France and spent the first half of her life in relative obscurity. However, by the age of 33, she had decided that the best way for her to serve God was to go to the New World to aid in the process of settlement and in the spread of Christianity to the natives. Mance played a critical role in the fortunes of the new colonies. As one of the founders of the City of Montreal, she was instrumental in the colony's survival, advising the governor and securing financial aid. She was also given sole responsibility for establishing a hospital and worked tirelessly over the years overseeing its construction and administration, while providing nursing care to the colonists. As well, she arranged for the establishment of an order of nursing sisters at the hospital, thereby ensuring its independence and survival after her death. As a testament to her success, the hospital, the Hôtel Dieu, still exists in Montreal.

Jeanne Mance was born in late 1606 (she was baptized on November 12, 1606) in Langres, a town in the province of Champagne, France. She was the second of twelve or thirteen children born to Charles Mance and **Catherine Émonnot Mance**. The family may have been minor nobility, although there is no doubt they were middle class by the standards of the time. Charles Mance was a king's proctor, a legal position of relative importance in the king's bureaucracy.

The details of Mance's early life are sketchy. According to memories recorded later, she decided at the age of six or seven to devote her life to God. Although this may seem young (and is perhaps an exaggeration), it is important to understand both that this was a period of increased religious fervor in France and that the nature of faith in the 17th century was different from that of today. Religion was all-pervasive in the lives of believers, affecting their daily actions and thoughts. It was also more mystical in nature, particularly for Roman Catholics (the dominant religion of the French). Tales of miracles and encounters with saints or other representatives of God were common and must be understood as a feature of this period. Whatever the age at which she made the decision, there is no doubt that at an early stage in her life Mance had decided to serve God. However, she did not wish to become a nun, because that required withdrawal into the cloister. Instead, Mance seems to have believed that her "calling" lay in helping others. Thus, her early years were spent caring for the sick and injured.

Mance's commitment to nursing was forged during the years 1635–36. The region where she lived was invaded by the Lorrains in 1635. As often happened, battle was followed by the pillaging and destruction of homes and property and by the widescale massacre of the local population. By 1636, sickness and plague were the natural consequence, adding to the devastation of the region. Throughout this period, Mance acted as a nurse, caring for wounded soldiers on the battlefield and for the plague-stricken population.

Up to this point, Mance was unsure as to what her life course would be. In 1640, while attending Lenten services, she had the opportunity to converse with a canon of the Cathedral at Langres. Eventually, their conversation switched to the topic of missionary activity in "New France." (By 1640, France had a number of small colonies situated along the St. Lawrence in what is present-day Quebec.) Mance was impressed and inspired by the efforts of the Church to Christianize and "civilize" the native population. Among the faithful existed a genuine belief that it was God's will and in the best interests of the natives that they be converted and dissuaded from "pagan" ways. Mance was particularly impressed by the contributions of women in New France. In the French colonies, unlike in those of Britain, women played a prominent role in early

settlement and missionary activity. Convents existed, offering women an alternative to marriage and motherhood. Many of the orders were dedicated to social services such as teaching and nursing, thereby effectively offering Catholic women the opportunity to play a role in society. In New France, two orders of nuns were already involved in establishing hospitals and schools.

Following this conversation, Mance began to consider the possibility of going to New France. But this was not a decision made easily, and as it was extremely dangerous, her family was completely opposed. New France was an unsettled wilderness with a harsh climate, lacking even the most rudimentary comforts of civilization and faced with the threat of attack from the native population. The distance was formidable. The ocean voyage was also dangerous, took a minimum of six weeks, and could only be taken during the summer months, meaning there was no communication with the colonies for most of the year. Effectively, this meant that she would be completely cut off from her friends and country. As well, Mance was frail in constitution, making her susceptible to illness. And, of course, she was a woman. Because she did not belong to a religious order, it was questionable

Jeanne Mance

what she would do in New France and through what means she would even get there.

Nonetheless, Mance persisted. The canon was supportive and encouraged her to go to Paris and consult with Father Charles Lalemant, the Jesuit priest in charge of Canadian missionary activities. Mance hid her intentions from her family, claiming that she was going to Paris to visit cousins. While in Paris throughout the summer of 1640, her plans solidified; she met Father Lalemant twice, and was encouraged by him to attempt the journey. Still, serious obstacles stood in her way. However, word began to spread throughout élite Paris society about Mance's religious devotion and her desire to go to the colonies. Eventually, she was introduced to **Angelique Faure**, the widow of Claude de Bullion (the superintendent of finance for the French government), a very wealthy woman who was actively involved in supporting numerous charities. After four visits, Madame de Bullion was so impressed by Mance that she asked her to go to New France with the purpose of establishing a hospital there for the benefit of the colony. Though she would finance the hospital and support Mance, the widow requested that her name be kept secret.

*M*ontreal owes a great debt to [Jeanne Mance].

—Sophy L. Elliott

In the spring of 1641, Mance arrived at the port of La Rochelle ready to embark for the New World. In a church there, she met Jérôme de La Dauversière, the founder of an association called the Company of Montreal. Comprised of 45 devout men and women, the Company had been formed with the purpose of founding a colony in the New World to be named Ville Marie de Montréal (present-day Montreal, Canada). It was to be a religious colony, dedicated to the Holy Family, and some colonists, supplies, and the chosen governor of the new colony, Paul de Chomedey de Maisonneuve, were already assembled to leave. Believing that the small group of settlers needed a woman to be responsible for the administration of supplies and care of the sick, Dauversière asked her to join the Company. Thus, Jeanne Mance came to be a member of the Company of Montreal and was given a concrete destination in the New World where she could establish a hospital.

Before embarking, Mance suggested to Dauversière that the Company of Montreal extend its membership in order to have a larger base of financial support from which to ensure the colony's survival. She asked him to write and send to her several copies of an outline of the Company's plan. Once she received the outline, she distributed it, with a personal invitation from herself, to the many prominent and charitable people with whom she had become acquainted. Through this means, Mance was able to secure several new members for the Company who were willing to donate money.

The group set sail on two ships in the early spring of 1641, and Jeanne Mance arrived at the colony of Quebec (modern-day Quebec City) at the beginning of August. It was soon decided that it was too late in the season to attempt founding a settlement before the winter set in, and the group therefore decided to winter at Quebec. Over the next nine months, they encountered opposition from the governor and residents of Quebec. Some feared a new settlement would compete with them for furs from the natives, while others believed it would be better for all if the new arrivals stayed in Quebec and helped to develop that colony. Nonetheless, on May 17, 1642, Mance and her group arrived on the Island of Montreal to found a new colony. Consequently, Jeanne Mance and Paul de Maisonneuve are credited with being the founders of Montreal.

Once the colony was established, it still faced serious obstacles to its survival. Beyond the rigors of founding a settlement in the midst of wilderness was the ever-present threat of attack from the Iroquois Nations. In the early days of European intervention in Canada, Jacques Cartier and Samuel de Champlain, in their desire to secure a steady supply of furs from the native population, had forged an alliance with the Huron, who were at war with the Iroquois. From that time on, the Iroquois regarded the French as their enemies. Montreal, situated furthest inland in the midst of Iroquois territory, faced the greatest threat of all the colonies. Consequently, the homes and fields of the colonists were built around a stone fortress in which guns, ammunition, food, and clothing were stored. In the event of attack, all could retreat into the fort. The first winter passed peaceably, giving the settlers much-needed time to clear land, construct their fort, and build homes. Mance received word at this time that a large sum of money had been sent by Madame de Bullion for the construction of the hospital at Montreal. Feeling secure, Mance argued that the funds could be better used by the Jesuits in their missionary work among the Huron. But Madame de Bullion insisted a hospital was to be built, and construction was begun immediately, with a permanent structure completed by 1645. This insistence was fortunate, as Mance soon found herself using the nursing skills she had developed on the battlefield in France to care for colonists injured in sporadic attacks by the Iroquois.

In 1649, warfare between the Iroquois and Huron came to an end with the virtual extermination of the latter group. The Iroquois immediately turned the full force of their efforts towards the French. By 1651, the situation in Montreal was critical. Sustained attack had forced the colonists to retreat into their fort, and their numbers had become seriously depleted. In the summer of 1651, one of the Montreal colonists, Dollier de Casson, wrote: "There is not a month in this summer when our book of the dead has not been stained in red letters by the hands of the Iroquois." It was obvious this state of siege could not go on for long; supplies would soon run out, and the colonists were not able to attend to the business of subsistence, such as caring for crops. But they did not have the money to purchase the necessary arms, munitions, and manpower. At this time, the French government, preoccupied with problems at home and unconvinced that the colonies had anything to contribute, was unwilling to supply the materials, men, and military strength needed to set the colonies on a firm footing. Wrote Mance:

> Every person was discouraged; I felt what a loss it would be to religion and what a disgrace for the State if we had to lose the colony after all we had done; I therefore urged M. de Maisonneuve to go to France for help.

It was hoped that, with the financial support of the Company of Montreal, Governor de Maisonneuve would be able to secure arms and soldiers, although all realized that the Company might not have the resources. At this point Mance developed a plan to save the colony. She explained to Maisonneuve that some of the money given to her by Madame de Bullion (a significant sum) still existed and could be used for the purposes of defense. Given her benefactor's determination that the money be used only for the hospital, Mance instructed the governor to explain to Madame that the hospital's survival was dependent upon the continued existence of a colony which required the protection of a company of soldiers. Thus, indirectly the money was to be used for the hospital. In return for the money, Mance demanded that the hospital be given 100 acres of cleared land to aid in its future support. Maisonneuve agreed to the proposal, although he had to approach Madame delicately given her continued desire to remain anonymous.

Maisonneuve then set sail for France, leaving the colony to wait through another winter for word of his return. Desperate for news, Mance headed to Quebec once the spring arrived in 1653. On arrival, she was relieved to hear that Maisonneuve was on his way back with a contingent of soldiers. The wait was tense: just two days after Mance had passed through Three Rivers on her way to Quebec that colony was attacked by the Iroquois. In Quebec, all realized that if Three Rivers were to fall, both Quebec and Montreal would be next. Finally, after delays due to bad weather, Maisonneuve arrived in Quebec on September 22, 1653, accompanied by soldiers as well as some new colonists and supplies. The presence of the soldiers frightened the Iroquois, causing them to end their aggression. Mance had saved the colony from extinction. Renewed and newly inspired, the colonists resumed the process of building their settlement.

A few years later, on January 28, 1657, while heading to the hospital to attend a patient, Mance fell on the ice, fracturing her arm and dislocating the wrist. While the fracture was repaired by a doctor, the dislocation was not initially noticed. Within six months, she could no longer use her right arm and hand. Unable to attend to her patients and in great pain, she left for France on October 14, 1658, accompanied by *Marguerite Bourgeoys, in the hope that a French physician could help. She also had to attend to some matters regarding the hospital. The original plan of Dauversière (and of Mance and her benefactor) was that a new order, the Hospitallers of Saint-Joseph of La Flèche, would go to Montreal once the hospital was founded to manage and operate it. Mance was concerned that this plan would not be fulfilled because of increasing pressure, particularly from the bishop of Montreal and the Jesuit Superior, that control of the hospital be given to the Hospitallers of Quebec. With two nuns from Quebec filling in while she was away, Mance knew that she had to secure the arrival of the Hospitallers of La Flèche or lose control of the hospital to the Quebec order. Her trip was successful. Through meetings with Madame de Bullion, she received additional funds to pay for the transportation and establishment of three nuns from La Flèche at Montreal. With this act, the establishment of a hospital in Montreal was finally complete. For years, Mance had overseen the building of the hospital from a small wooden room to a large, well-fortified structure. She had administered it and cared for the sick. As well, she had ensured the hospital's physical survival by securing the soldiers and its financial survival through the acquisition of the 100 acres of land and substantial funds from her benefactor. Now, she had ensured that the hospital would remain independent by establishing the Hospitallers of La Flèche to operate it in the years to come. The hospital Mance founded is now the Hôtel Dieu in Montreal.

While in France in 1658, Mance sought from various doctors, but did not receive, a cure for her injured arm and hand. Apparently on February 2, 1659, she went to the Chapel of Saint-Sulpice to pray at the tomb of M. Olier, one of the original members of the Company of Montreal. While there, she touched an urn containing the heart of Olier, which was kept as a relic, and according to the records a miracle occurred. Whether that is the case or not, there is no doubt that when Mance returned to Montreal in November 1659, she had regained the complete use of her hand.

If she stopped to pause in 1660, Jeanne Mance probably felt some satisfaction. Although she still lived in a state of hardship and poverty, the colony of Montreal was finally established on a firm footing as was the hospital to which she had dedicated half her life. With the arrival of the nursing sisters, Mance was able to work less, leaving the nuns to care for the sick while she concerned herself strictly with administration. The colony was still threatened by native attack, particularly during the years 1660–66. However, after 1663, the government of France began to take a more direct role in administering and protecting the colonies, and therefore the colonists did not have to secure and finance their own defense. The French government sent the Carignan-Salieres regiment to bring an end to war with the Iroquois. By 1667, fighting had virtually stopped, leaving the colonies safe once again to pursue settlement. The population of Montreal (and of the other colonies) was increasing steadily, partly due to government sponsorship of new immigrants. Through the presence of increasing numbers, including soldiers and adventurers, the religious nature of the colony was receding. This was probably disturbing to Mance who, with the other early members, had hoped to create a religious colony. Still, to this founder of Montreal, it must have been comforting to realize by 1672 that the colony was going to survive.

Mance's last official act in Montreal was in the spring of 1673, when she was one of five prominent people who laid a foundation stone for the Parish Church of Notre Dame. The fact that she was honored along with the four most prominent government officials in the colony (the governor general, the governor of Montreal, the intendant, and the superior of the seminary) shows the prominence and esteem with which she was regarded. By this time, Jeanne Mance was 66 years old. Considering how frail she was as a young woman, her health had been remarkably good during her years in Montreal, and she had lived a long life by the standards of the 17th century. Jeanne Mance died on the evening of June 18, 1673, not long after attending the foundation ceremony.

SOURCES:
Elliott, Sophy L. *The Women Pioneers of North America.* Gardenvale, Quebec: Garden City Press, 1941.
Foran, J.K. *Jeanne Mance: Her Life.* Montreal, Quebec: Herald Press, 1931.
Pepper, Mary Sifton. *Maids and Matrons of New France.* Boston, MA: Little, Brown, 1901.

SUGGESTED READING:
D'Allaire, Micheline. "Jeanne Mance à Montreal en 1642," in *Forces.* 1973, pp. 38–46.
Daveluy, Marie-Claire. *Jeanne Mance.* Montreal, Quebec: Fides, 1962.

Catherine Briggs, Ph.D. candidate,
University of Waterloo, Waterloo, Ontario, Canada

Mancini, Hortense (1646–1699)

Duchess of Mazarin. Name variations: Duchesse de Mazarin. Born in Rome in 1646 (some sources cite 1640); died in Chelsea, England, in 1699; fourth daughter of Laurent also seen as Lorenzo Mancini and a mother (maiden name Mazarini or Mazarino) who was the sister of Cardinal Jules Mazarin (chief minister to the young Louis XIV); sister of Olympia (c. 1639–1708), Marie Mancini (1640–1715), Marie-Anne Mancini (1649–1714), Laure Mancini (1635–1657); cousin of Anne-Marie Martinozzi (1637–1672) and Laura Martinozzi; married Marquis de La Meilleraye and Mayenne, who was elevated by the cardinal to the duke of Mazarin.

A Roman family, the Mancinis were introduced to the French court by Cardinal Jules Mazarin; they were the daughters of one of his four sisters and had come to live with him in Paris. There were five Mancini sisters, called the "Mazarinettes," who were married off to some of the oldest and noblest families in France and Italy, including *Laure Mancini who married Louis de Vendôme, duke of Mercoeur; *Olympia Mancini who married Eugene Maurice de Savoie-Carignan and was the mother of Prince Eugene of Savoy and the mistress of Louis XIV; *Marie Mancini who was in love with Louis XIV but married the Prince of Colonna; *Marie-Anne Mancini who married Godfrey Maurice de la Tour, duke of Bouillon; and Hortense. Mazarin had another sister **Laura Margaret Mazarini** who married Girolamo Martinozzi, adding their children *Anne-Marie Martinozzi**, who married the prince de Conti, and *Laura Martinozzi**, who married Alphonse d'Este, to his flock of nieces.

One of the most beautiful and flamboyant women in Europe, Hortense walked out on her miserable marriage to the duke of Mazarin. A religious fanatic, the duke had forced her to perform severe penances for her sins—real or imagined. He had also squandered her sizeable dowry. But Louis XIV refused to acknowledge Hortense's petitions to return the property she had brought to the marriage. After a brief dalliance with the duke of Savoy and an order by a French court to return to her husband and submit to his authority, Hortense fled to England in late 1675, accompanied by her pet parrot and her black page, Mustapha. Before long, she became the mistress of Charles II of England, following a considerable line of mistresses that included **Marguerite Carteret**, *Lucy Walter**, ☙➤ **Elizabeth Killigrew**, ☙➤ **Catherine Pegge**, ☙➤ **Moll Davies**, Lady **Elizabeth Byron**, *Frances Stuart**, *Louise de Kéroüalle** (duchess of Portsmouth), *Barbara Villiers**, countess of Castlemain, and *Nell Gwynn**. As a compulsive gambler and sexual free spirit, Hortense's term with the king was short. "Each sex provides its lovers for Hortense," commented an idle courtier. Her over-familiarity with a daughter of Charles, as well as her conspicuous flirtation in 1677 with the prince of Monaco, ended her reign as royal mistress. Her memoirs were probably written by the abbé de Saint-Réal from materials supplied by her. (*For more information see Gwynn, Nell.*)

SUGGESTED READING:
Les Nieces de Mazarin. Paris, 1856.

Mancini, Laura (1823–1869)

Italian poet. Born Laura Beatrice Oliva in Naples in 1823; died in Florence, Italy, on July 17, 1869; married Pasquale Stanislaus Mancini (b. 1817, an Italian diplomat and jurist).

An Italian poet, Laura Mancini was born in Naples in 1823 and is best-known for her patriotic poems.

Mancini, Laure (1635–1657)

*Duchess of Mercoeur. Name variations: Laura Mancini; Duchesse de Mercoeur. Born in Rome in 1635 (some sources cite 1636); died in Paris, France, on February 8, 1657; first daughter of Laurent also seen as Lorenzo Mancini and a mother (maiden name Mazarini or Mazarino) who was the sister of Cardinal Jules Mazarin (chief minister to the young Louis XIV); sister of *Olympia Mancini (c. 1639–1708), *Marie Mancini (1640–1715), *Hortense Mancini (1646–1699), and *Marie-Anne Mancini (1649–1714); cousin of *Anne-Marie Martinozzi (1637–1672) and *Laura Martinozzi; married Louis de Vendôme, duc de Mercoeur (grandson of Henry IV and *Gabrielle d'Estrees), in 1651; children: Louis Joseph, duc de Vendome (1654–1712, a well-known French soldier who conquered Barcelona and fought his cousin Prince Eugene of Savoy, son of Olympia Mancini, in the War of the Spanish Succession).*

Mancini, Marie (1640–1715)

*Princess of Colonna. Name variations: Marie de Mancini. Born in 1640 (some sources cite 1639); died in 1715 (some sources cite 1714); third daughter of Laurent also seen as Lorenzo Mancini and a mother (maiden name Mazarini or Mazarino) who was the sister of Cardinal Jules Mazarin (1602–1661, chief minister to the young Louis XIV); sister of *Olympia Mancini (c. 1639–1708), *Laure Mancini (1635–1657), *Hortense Mancini (1646–1699), *Marie-Anne Mancini (1649–1714); cousin of *Anne-Marie Martinozzi (1637–1672) and *Laura Martinozzi; married the prince of Colonna, connétable de Naples (High Constable of Naples), in 1661.*

As a frequent visitor to the Mazarin house, Louis XIV fell deeply in love with Marie Mancini. But her uncle Cardinal Jules Mazarin was determined that Louis choose a Spanish bride to ensure an alliance with Spain. (In 1660, Louis married *Maria Teresa of Spain.) Mazarin sent Marie away and pushed his niece *Olympia Mancini into the arms of Louis; he also made sure that Marie was apprised of this. Deeply hurt, the 21-year-old Marie married the prince of Colonna on the rebound in 1661, but she soon left him and returned to France where she was shut up in a convent by Louis XIV. She lived in Spain for most of her life, then returned to France where she died in obscurity in 1714 or 1715. Her *Mémoires de Madame la Connétable de Colonna* was published in 1678.

Mancini, Marie-Anne (1649–1714)

Duchess de Bouillon. Born in 1649; died in 1714; fifth daughter of Laurent also seen as Lorenzo Mancini and the sister (maiden name Mazarini or Mazarino) of Cardinal Jules Mazarin (chief minister to the young

☙➤
Elizabeth Killigrew, Catherine Pegge, and Moll Davies. *See Gwynn, Nell for sidebar.*

Marie Mancini (right), possibly flanked by Olympia or Hortense.

Louis XIV); sister of *Olympia Mancini (c. 1639–1708), *Marie Mancini (1640–1715), *Hortense Mancini (1646–1699), *Laure Mancini (1635–1657); cousin of *Anne-Marie Martinozzi (1637–1672) and *Laura Martinozzi; married Godfrey Maurice de la Tour, duke of Bouillon (a gallant soldier), in 1662.

Marie-Anne Mancini was renowned for her literary salon and patronage of La Fontaine, but she was accused of being involved with ❧ Catherine Deshayes (La Voisin) in the *cause célèbre* of the day, the "Affair of the Poisons," and was banished from France in 1680. Her innocence was later proven.

Deshayes, Catherine. See entry titled French "Witches."

Mancini, Olympia (c. 1639–1708)

*Princess of Savoy-Carignan, countess of Soissons, and mistress of Louis XIV. Name variations: Olympe or Olympie; comtesse de Soissons; countess of Soissons. Born around 1639; died in Brussels in 1708; second daughter of Laurent also seen as Lorenzo Mancini and the sister (maiden name Mazarini or Mazarino) of Cardinal Jules Mazarin (chief minister to the young Louis XIV); sister of *Marie-Anne Mancini (1649–1714), *Marie Mancini (1640–1715), *Hortense Mancini (1646–1699), *Laure Mancini (1635–1657); cousin of *Anne-Marie Martinozzi (1637–1672) and *Laura Martinozzi; married Eugene Maurice de Savoie-Carignan, prince of Savoy-Carignan, in 1657 (died 1673);*

children: Louis (who served in the army of Baden); Prince Eugene of Savoy (1663–1736).

Olympia Mancini was the wife of Eugene Maurice de Savoie-Carignan, and the mother of Prince Eugene of Savoy, a general who led the armies of Austria in victories over the French and the Turks, establishing Habsburg control over Northern Italy, Hungary, Serbia, and Transylvania, and ending the Turkish threat to Central Europe. Prince Eugene's origins and childhood were shadowed by the intrigues of Versailles, where Cardinal Jules Mazarin entertained hopes of engineering a romance between his niece Olympia and the future French king, Louis XIV. Though they had only a youthful affection for each other, Olympia and Louis were together for a time, prompting rumors that Louis was actually Eugene's father. Olympia was also embroiled, along with her sister *Marie-Anne Mancini, in the "Affair of the Poisons." Accused of poisoning her husband and *Marie Louise d'Orleans, queen of Spain, Olympia fled France to the Netherlands and eventually died in poverty in Brussels.

Mandel, Maria (1912–c. 1947)

Austrian SS Head Supervisor of the women's concentration camp at Auschwitz II (Birkenau) and convicted war criminal. Born in Münzkirchen, Upper Austria, on January 10, 1912; sentenced to death on December 22, 1947; did not attend high school.

Nazi Germany's genocidal war against those it defined as biologically "unworthy" (*lebensunwertes Leben*) was carried out by individuals, one of whom was Maria Mandel. Born in 1912 in Münzkirchen, Upper Austria, Mandel became an active member of the Austrian Nazi movement while it was banned as a subversive political party and, after the annexation of Austria by the German Reich in March 1938, became a member of the SS, the elite branch of the Nazi Party. A beautiful blonde, she quickly found suitable employment as a concentration camp guard.

Konzentrationslager [KZ] Lichtenburg, a concentration camp near Prettin in Kreis Torgau, Germany, had been established in 1933, during the first months of the Nazi dictatorship. Many of Lichtenburg's male inmates were tortured and beaten to death by the camp's SS guards. In August 1937, the male inmates were transferred to Buchenwald concentration camp, and in March 1938 Lichtenburg reopened as a women's camp. The savagery of the SS guards continued: many women were beaten to death, and two who had failed in an escape attempt were torn to pieces by dogs by order of the camp's commandant. On October 15, 1938, Maria Mandel began working as a supervisor at Lichtenburg. Seven months later, on May 15, 1939, the camp was disbanded and its inmates transferred to the newly established Ravensbrück camp. Mandel began working as a supervisor at Ravensbrück on the first day it opened.

Located near Berlin north of Fürstenburg an der Havel, Ravensbrück was exclusively a facility for women. Although it initially held only the inmates who had been transferred from KZ Lichtenburg, by the end of 1939 this number had grown significantly, with approximately 2,000 women incarcerated. As Nazi conquests added more land to the German Reich and as the domestic regime of terror intensified, the number of prisoners in Ravensbrück grew dramatically; by the end of 1942, there were 10,800 women behind the barbed wire fence.

From virtually the start of her tenure at Ravensbrück, Maria Mandel gained a reputation as one of the cruelest of the female SS guards there. Reichsführer-SS Heinrich Himmler visited Ravensbrück in 1940, at which time he authorized the details of punishment by flogging; Mandel, working in Ravensbrück's infamous Bunker, was thereafter involved in meting out this brutal punishment. Flogging could be "as few as" 10 to 25 lashes, but more serious cases merited 50 or 75 lashes, which were administered in installments of 25 because the full amount almost certainly would have brought about death. Mandel derived pleasure from flogging countless women, inflicting pain that seemed unbearable after the first four or five lashes. Many of her prisoners had to be ruthlessly revived in order for their punishment to continue, and after the flogging the beaten parts of their bodies became blue as ink. The swollen areas where Mandel's whip had cut deeply into flesh took many months to heal, and many of those women who survived Ravensbrück were scarred and crippled for the remainder of their lives.

On October 8, 1942, Mandel was appointed female Oberaufseherin (Head Supervisor) of the Auschwitz II (Birkenau) concentration camp near Cracow, Generalgouvernement (German-occupied Poland). Auschwitz I was the main camp and Auschwitz III was a series of satellite camps at industrial enterprises. Mandel replaced **Johanna Langefeld** (1900–1974), a veteran concentration camp guard who had begun her SS career in the first years of the Third Reich in the Moringen camp, the first created exclusively for women prisoners. From 1941 to April 1942, Langefeld had served as Head Supervisor in Ravensbrück, and from April until October 1942 was SS Oberaufseherin, and unofficial Camp Commander, of the women's camp at Auschwitz-Birkenau. Following a bitter quarrel with male Camp Commandant Rudolf Höss, Langefeld was removed from her post and imprisoned. Mandel, who had by now strongly impressed Höss and several other of her male SS superiors with her intelligence, "merit" and "conviction to the cause," was summoned to Auschwitz from Ravensbrück to take Langefeld's place.

Energetic and enthusiastic, Maria Mandel quickly asserted full executive authority in Auschwitz, spreading new terror among the prisoners of the women's camp. Before long, Mandel became known to the prisoners as "the beast." Not only did she participate in the infliction of savage punishments and torture on prisoners, she also became feared for her presence at the "selections," where she decided which prisoners would continue to live and which would die within the hour. Of the women she "selected," those who were not taken to the gas chambers had to submit to painful, crippling and often fatal medical experiments carried out by such SS "scientific investigators" as the infamous Dr. Josef Mengele. Some of the women chosen by Mandel became guinea pigs in experiments carried out on behalf of the I.G. Farben chemical trust. In one letter, a representative of I.G. Farben acknowledged that they had "received the order of 150 women. Despite their emaciated condition, they were found satisfactory. We shall keep you posted on developments concerning the experiment." In due course, another letter reported, "The tests were made. All subjects died. We shall contact you shortly on the subject of a new load."

As well as her official title of Oberaufseherin, Mandel held the unofficial post of Camp Commander in the Auschwitz-Birkenau women's camp until August 25, 1943, when SS Second Lieutenant Franz Hössler took over. While this constituted a slight loss of status for Mandel, her actual power of life or death over her prisoners remained virtually the same. In November 1943, Hössler was named Protective Custody Commander for the women's camp, and Mandel was made responsible for the deployment of female prisoners' labor within the entire facility. Throughout these redefinitions of bureaucratic authority, Mandel remained a zealous functionary of the death camp Auschwitz II.

At the same time, however, she exhibited a passionate love of music. In April 1943, Mandel decreed the creation of an orchestra for the enhancement of life in Auschwitz II. Instead of cleaning latrines or hauling rocks, a "privileged" group of women were made to perform as members of an ad hoc orchestra consisting of a few violins, a cello, accordions, guitars, and mandolins. The orchestra was conducted in an authoritarian fashion by the famous Viennese violinist *Alma Rosé and included such professional musicians as *Fania Fenelon. They played stirring marches while women newly arrived at the camp, dazed and exhausted from days of travel without food, water or sanitary facilities, were selected to live or die by Maria Mandel and other officials. On Sundays, the women musicians had to perform privately for an SS audience who looked forward to hearing operetta tunes, popular hits, and opera arias to help them relax after their arduous week's work. Mandel, who was proud of "her" orchestra, was one of the SS officials in mourning at Alma Rosé's bizarre funeral in April 1944.

In November 1944, with liberation of Auschwitz by the rapidly advancing Soviet Army only weeks in the future, Maria Mandel was replaced by **Elisabeth Volkenrath** as superintendent of the Auschwitz II women's camp. The various Auschwitz camps were liberated by Soviet forces in mid-January 1945, but most of the prisoners had already died. Of the many thousands who had been evacuated from the camp on forced marches by the Germans just prior to the liberation, many more perished. Mandel was

captured in the spring of 1945. Along with 35 men and 4 other women who had also been members of the Auschwitz death factories during World War II, she was placed on trial on charges amounting to the mass murder of more than 3,500,000 women, men, and children during World War II. The trial, held under the authority of the Polish Supreme National Tribunal, began at Cracow in November 1947. The massive and meticulously assembled documentation of their crimes filled 67 volumes of 200 pages each and testified to a systematic policy of genocide and extermination of Jews, Slavs, and others deemed politically, ideologically or morally unacceptable to the SS and the rulers of the Third Reich.

In one chilling session of the Cracow trial, **Janina Kowalczyk**, a prominent Polish pediatrician, testified that scores of women had been sterilized by X-rays and their ovaries removed for further examination in Berlin before they were sent to their deaths in the gas chambers and crematoria of Auschwitz. In order to save the cost of Zyklon-B poison gas crystals, the Auschwitz staff sometimes decided not to gas infants during the winter but simply left them in unheated rooms, where they soon froze to death. During the winter months, Kowalczyk testified, thousands of women had been forced to stand at attention in their bare feet in snow and freezing rain until they collapsed from exhaustion and hypothermia. They were then ordered to run to their barracks; those who were unable to do so were then selected by Maria Mandel and others for *Sonderbehandlung* (special treatment) in the gas chambers. Accused in court by Kowalczyk of having ordered these and similar "treatments" of prisoners, Mandel, her face pale and her body shaking with fear, responded in a voice that was barely audible, "I have always cared for the prisoners' well-being."

After Kowalczyk's chilling testimony, another witness told the tribunal of orgies at Mandel's richly furnished villa near Auschwitz. These parties were particularly uninhibited after "good" executions, when Mandel had whipped the selected women before sending them to their deaths. Maria Mandel sat with bent head after the conclusion of this testimony and kept silent. On December 22, 1947, the Cracow tribunal sentenced 23 of the Auschwitz staff members to death, including Maria Mandel. By this time, less than three years after the liberation of the infamous camps, most of the world had lost interest, and the trial received scant mention in the Western media. (Incredibly, only one Western reporter, France's Michel Gordey, was present at the trial.) It would take several more decades and another generation to begin to address the events in which Maria Mandel took such an enthusiastic part, the events of the Holocaust, a word that in 1947 did not even exist in the way it is now used.

SOURCES:

Adelsberger, Lucie. *Auschwitz: A Doctor's Story.* Translated by Susan Ray. Boston, MA: Northeastern University Press, 1995.

"Auschwitz Criminals to Die," in *Jewish Chronicle* [London]. No. 4106. January 2, 1948, p. 1.

Czech, Danuta. *Auschwitz Chronicle 1939–1945.* NY: Henry Holt, 1990.

Gordey, Michel. "Echoes from Auschwitz," in *New Republic.* Vol. 117, no. 25. December 22, 1947, pp. 14–15.

Hájková, Dagmar. "Middle Ages Nazi Style," in Vera Laska, ed., *Women in the Resistance and in the Holocaust: The Voices of Eyewitnesses.* Westport, CT: Greenwood Press, 1983, pp. 208–214.

Knapp, Gabriele. *Das Frauenorchester in Auschwitz: Musikalische Zwangsarbeit und ihre Bewältigung.* Hamburg: von Bockel Verlag, 1996.

Lasker-Wallfisch, Anita. *Inherit the Truth, 1939–1945: The Documented Experiences of a Survivor of Auschwitz and Belsen.* London: Giles de la Mare, 1996.

Newman, Richard, and Karen Kirtley. *Alma Rosé: Vienna to Auschwitz.* Portland, OR: Amadeus Press, 2000.

Philipp, Grit, and Monika Schnell. *Kalendarium der Ereignisse im Frauen-Konzentrationslager Ravensbrück 1939–1945.* Berlin: Metropol Verlag, 1999.

Segev, Tom. *Soldiers of Evil: The Commandants of the Nazi Concentration Camps.* Translated by Haim Watzman. NY: McGraw-Hill, 1987.

Shelley, Lore, ed. *Auschwitz—The Nazi Civilization: Twenty-Three Women's Accounts.* Lanham, MD: University Press of America, 1992.

Strzelecka, Irena. "Women," in Yisrael Gutman and Michael Berenbaum, eds. *Anatomy of the Auschwitz Death Camp.* Bloomington and Washington, DC: Indiana University Press/U.S. Holocaust Memorial Museum, 1994, pp. 393–411.

"23 Germans Sentenced to Death," in *The Times* [London]. December 23, 1947, p. 4.

"War Crimes—Subject: Women," in *Time.* Vol. 50, no. 21. November 24, 1947, p. 33.

RELATED MEDIA:

Playing for Time (148 min.), television drama, adapted by Arthur Miller, starring **Vanessa Redgrave**, **Melanie Mayron**, and **Jane Alexander** (1980), directed by Daniel Mann.

John Haag,
Associate Professor of History,
University of Georgia, Athens, Georgia

Mandelstam, Nadezhda

(1899–1980)

Russian memoirist. Name variations: Nadezhda Mandelshtam or Mandel'shtam; Nadezhda Yakovlevna; Nadezhda Yakolevna Mandelstam; Nadezheda. Born Nadezhda Khazina on October 31, 1899, in Saratov, Russia; died on December 29, 1980, in Moscow, USSR; daughter of Yakov Khazin (a physician) and a physician mother (name unknown); married Osip Mandelstam (b. 1891, the poet), in 1921, 1922, or 1924 (died in a Siberian labor camp in 1938).

Was responsible for the preservation of husband Osip Mandelstam's poetry; wrote the memoirs Hope Against Hope *and* Hope Abandoned, *chronicling the years of terror following Joseph Stalin's rise to power in the 1920s.*

Nadezhda Mandelstam was born Nadezhda Khazina on October 31, 1899, in Saratov, Russia, and enjoyed a privileged childhood as the daughter of well-educated Jewish parents, both of whom were physicians. She learned several languages, including German, French, and English, from a series of governesses, and traveled Western Europe with her parents. When she was older, she attended school in Kiev and studied art there under the cubist-futurist painter *Alexandra Exter.

The story of Nadezhda Mandelstam's life is intimately bound up with that of her husband Osip Mandelstam, one of 20th-century Russia's greatest poets. Osip was associated with an intellectual group of writers called the Acmeists whose writings were radical, allusive, and hostile to the new Communist government that had come into power after the overthrow of the tsar and the revolution in 1917. Among his peers and close friends were *Anna Akhmatova, Boris Pasternak, and Nikolai Gumilyov. Nadezhda met him in Kiev in 1919, and, after a separation while he traveled to the Crimea, they married "informally," keeping their wedding a secret. (Sources report the date of the marriage variously as 1921, 1922, or 1924.) In June 1921, they migrated to the Caucasus as refugees.

Their married life began roughly at the same time as the establishment, in 1922, of the Union of Soviet Socialist Republics (USSR) under V.I. Lenin and, after his death two years later, under Joseph Stalin. The Mandelstams' opposition to Stalin's government became the focus of their life's work and their ultimate undoing. Initially, it merely made employment almost impossible to find for Osip, and in the late 1920s Nadezhda Mandelstam worked as a translator of English novels. Osip's poetry of the 1920s and early 1930s established him as one of Russia's foremost poets of the 20th century, but it also made him an enemy of the state. At a private party late in 1933, he recited a poem to a group of friends which criticized Stalin, the "Kremlin mountaineer," as a murderer and peasant slayer; although the poem had not been written down, an informant in the group passed along news of the treasonous words to authorities, and Osip was arrested on May 30, 1934. A two-week interrogation resulted in his exile to the Urals and then to Voronezh, Russia—a rather fortunate sentence considering that it was only through the intervention of Nikolai Bukharin, a friend and member of the Central Committee of the Soviet Communist Party, that he escaped execution.

Nadezhda followed Osip into the harsh life of exile. The Mandelstams were forbidden to work or to publish and had to rely upon the generosity of those friends brave enough to associate with them for food, clothing, and lodging. Although a period of deprivation and fear for the couple, this was also one of the most creative times for the poet, who produced the "Voronezh Notebooks" while in exile.

In May 1937, they were allowed to return to Moscow, but lived as "convicted persons," continually under surveillance by the government. Stalin's bloody purges, the "Great Terror," had begun. Writers who did not write in the service of the state faced arrest and execution, but Osip resisted pressure to reject his outspoken political views. Fearing her husband would again face arrest, Nadezhda began to memorize his poetry and entrusted copies of his writings to close friends to smuggle out of the country. With the assistance of what has been called her "Homeric memory," Nadezhda was responsible for the preservation of his poems (including variants) at a time when the Communist government destroyed any evidence of ideas that ran contrary to those of the state.

Her worst fears were realized when, on May 1, 1938, Osip was again arrested and sent for five years' punishment to a Siberian labor camp. Although she was not allowed to accompany him, she worked a night job in a nearby factory so she could stand all day in line at the prison to deliver packets of food for him. Some months later, one of her food packets was returned marked "addressee dead." Nadezhda was never officially notified by the authorities of Osip's death; it was confirmed, in 1940, by a certificate issued by the Moscow Register Office to his brother Alexander. December 23, 1938, was listed as the official date of death. Relegated to the far provinces, Nadezhda Mandelstam worked as a teacher in Kalinin until 1941, when she and her mother were allowed to move to Tashkent. She taught English at the University of Central Asia (1943–46) and at the Teachers' Training College in Ulyanovsh

(1946–53). Until 1955, she was assigned a teaching position in Chita, eastern Siberia. In 1956, while head of the English department at the Chuvash Teachers' Training College in Cheboksary, she earned the degree *kandidat nauk* (equivalent to a Ph.D.) in English philology.

Mandelstam's devotion to her husband and his poetry did not end. She worked vigorously for the rehabilitation of Osip's reputation after Stalin's death in 1953. In 1960, she returned to Moscow, obtained a small apartment and was granted a widow's pension from the Writers' Union. She succeeded in getting some of his poems published in Soviet journals during the 1960s. Although the Soviet authorities were reluctant to popularize Russia's dissident son, his work was heralded abroad; a two-volume collection of his poetry was published in the United States. In 1973, his poetry was finally published in the Soviet Union, although he was not fully cleared of the charges which had led to his death.

Nadezhda Mandelstam earned her significant literary reputation with two memoirs, *Vospominaniya* (translated as *Hope Against Hope*) and *Vtoraya kniga* (translated as *Hope Abandoned*), both completed in 1970. (Nadezhda translates into English as "hope.") Smuggled out of the Soviet Union, the first volume was published in Russian and English in the United States in 1970, and the second was published in English in 1974. Ostensibly concerning her life with Osip, about which a great amount of detail is included, the books chronicle an entire generation of Russian literary figures who were silenced and destroyed by the Communist regime, as well as what Mandelstam described as "my battle with the forces of destruction, with everything that conspired to sweep me away, together with the poor scraps of paper I managed to keep." Her eyewitness accounts provide a rare glimpse of the decades of terror following the rise of Communism, and critics hailed the memoirs for a masterful portrayal of the writers of the period. Many also faulted *Hope Abandoned* for its relentless criticism of the Russian intelligentsia, a group which she blamed for allowing Stalin's excesses to occur, while admiring it for the portrayals of the author's friends and personal life. *Hope Against Hope* was not published in the Soviet Union until 1988.

In her later years, Mandelstam's small apartment in Moscow attracted foreign visitors and young Russians familiar with her husband's work, making her humble dwelling a literary salon in which she continued to champion his poetry. She was described as a small person, "steel-hard" and "vinegary," who was happy to compare all poets unfavorably to her husband, save for T.S. Eliot. Nadezhda Mandelstam died of a heart ailment on December 29, 1980, in Moscow. A line in *Hope Against Hope* may serve as an encapsulation of her life, and her struggles: "Silence is the real crime against humanity."

SOURCES:

Contemporary Authors. Vol. 110 and Vol. 102. Detroit, MI: Gale Research.

London Observer. May 23, 1971.

Magill, Frank N. *Cyclopedia of World Authors.* 3rd rev. ed. Englewood Cliffs, NJ: Salem Press, 1997.

New York Review of Books. February 7, 1974.

The New York Times. March 18, 1970, January 15, 1974, December 30, 1980.

Publishers Weekly. January 30, 1981.

SUGGESTED READING:

Holmgren, Beth. *Women's Works in Stalin's Time: On Lidiia Chukovskaia & Nadezhda Mandelstam.* Indiana University Press, 1993.

Mandelstam, Nadezhda. *Hope Abandoned.* Translated by Max Hayward. Atheneum, 1974.

———. *Hope Against Hope.* Translated by Max Hayward. Atheneum, 1970.

Judith C. Reveal,
freelance writer, Greensboro, Maryland

Mangano, Silvana (1930–1989)

Italian film actress. Born on April 21, 1930, in Rome, Italy; died in 1989; one of four children of a Sicilian railroad worker and an Englishwoman; married Dino De Laurentiis (a film producer), in 1949 (separated 1983); children: one son Frederico De Laurentiis, a film producer (died 1981), and three daughters, one of whom, Raffaella De Laurentiis, is also a film producer.

Selected films: Elisir d'Amore *(This Wine of Love, 1946);* Il Delitto di Giovanni Episcopo *(Flesh Will Surrender, 1947);* Gli Uomini sono Nemici *(1948);* Black Magic *(Cagliostro, 1949);* Riso Amaro *(Bitter Rice, 1949);* Il Lupo della Sila *(Lure of the Sila, 1949);* Il Brigante Musolino *(1950);* Anna *(1951);* Mambo *(1954);* L'Oro di Napoli *(Gold of Naples, 1954);* Ulisse *(Ulysses, 1954);* Uomini e Lupi *(1956);* La Diga sul Pacifico *(This Angry Age also known as The Sea Wall, 1958);* La Tempesta *(Tempest, 1958);* La Grande Guerra *(The Great War, 1959);* Jovanka e l'Altri *(Five Branded Women, 1960);* Crimen *(. . . And Suddenly It's Murder, 1960);* Il Guidizio Universale *(1961);* Barabba *(Barabbas, 1961);* Una Vita difficile *(A Difficult Life, 1961);* Il Processo di Verona *(1962);* La Mia Signora *(1964);* Il Disco Volante *(1965);* Io Io Io . . . e gli altri *(1966);* Scusi lei e' favorevole o contrario? *(1967);* Le Streghe *(The Witches, 1967);* Edipo Re *(Oedipus Rex, 1967);* Capriccio al'Italiana *(1968);* Teorema *(1968);* Scipione detto anche l'Africano

(1971); Morte a Venezia *(Death in Venice, 1971);* Il Decameron *(The Decameron, 1971);* Lo Scopone scientifico *(The Scientific Cardplayer, 1972);* D'Amore si muore *(1972);* Ludwig *(Ludwig II, 1972);* Gruppo di Famiglia in un interno *(Conversation Piece, 1975);* Dune *(U.S., 1984);* Oci Ciornie *(1987).*

Born in Rome in 1930 of Sicilian-English parentage, Silvana Mangano was trained as a dancer and entered films as a teenager after winning the title of Miss Rome. Her postwar roles were unremarkable, but she rocketed to fame in 1949, as the voluptuous lead in Giuseppe De Santis' socio-erotic film *Riso Amaro* (*Bitter Rice*), about the exploitation of women hired to work in the rice fields during the short growing season. (The color poster advertising this film about exploitation pictured the actress in a skimpy red top, hands on her hips, and eyes closed seductively.) Shortly after the film came out, Mangano married its producer Dino De Laurentiis and continued to play leading roles in films, although she was soon overshadowed by newcomers *Gina Lollobrigida and *Sophia Loren. Mangano retired from films for a few years following the death of her son Frederico in a plane crash in 1981, and was separated from

𝒮ilvana
𝑀angano

De Laurentiis two years later. She died from a heart attack following surgery for lung cancer in 1989. One of her three daughters, **Raffaella De Laurentiis**, is also a film producer.

Manikarnika (c. 1835–1858).
See Lakshmibai.

Mankiller, Wilma (1945—)

Native American activist and tribal leader who was the first woman elected as principal chief of the Cherokee Nation. Name variations: Wilma Pearl Mankiller. Born on November 18, 1945, in Tahlequah, Oklahoma; daughter of Charlie Mankiller and Irene Mankiller; attended Skyline Junior College in San Bruno, California, and San Francisco State College; Union for Experimenting Colleges and Universities, B.A., 1977; graduate studies at the University of Arkansas, 1979; married Hector Hugo Olaya de Bardi, in 1962 (divorced 1974); married Charlie Soap, around 1987; children: (first marriage) Felicia (b. 1964); Gina (b. 1966).

Wilma Mankiller was born at the Hastings Indian Hospital in Tahlequah, Oklahoma, on November 18, 1945. Her hometown was the last stop on the infamous Trail of Tears walked by the Cherokee during the forced removal from their southern homelands in 1838. Her father Charlie Mankiller was a full-blooded Cherokee, and her mother **Irene Mankiller** was of Dutch-Irish heritage; Wilma was the sixth of their eleven children. For her first decade, she lived a poor but comfortable life at Mankiller Flats, the 160-acre property which had been handed down from her grandfather. However, back-to-back droughts decimated the family farm, and when Wilma was ten the Mankillers accepted a government relocation offer and moved to San Francisco in the hopes of improving their economic status.

San Francisco drastically changed Wilma Mankiller's perspective on her Native American heritage. Although she experienced racism as a minority in the public schools, she also met Native Americans who inspired her to think of her goals in life as part of the greater Native community. She attended San Francisco State College during the tumultuous protest years of the late 1960s and early 1970s, and became involved with a group of Native Americans who set about reclaiming Alcatraz Island in 1969, asserting ownership based on an old treaty guaranteeing the reversion of unused government land to the tribe. Further involving herself in community ac-

tivism, she spent five years establishing a defense fund for the Pit River tribe's battle to reclaim ancestral lands from the Pacific Gas and Electric Company.

In 1962, at age 17, Mankiller had married Hector Hugo Olaya de Bardi, an Ecuadoran immigrant with whom she would have two daughters. He had expected a traditional marriage, and protested her growing involvement in political movements as well as her desire to improve her education. Mankiller's refusal to stop her activities contributed to their divorce in 1974.

As a single parent raising two children on hardly any income, Mankiller moved her family back to Mankiller Flats in 1976. She was hired by the Cherokee Nation and served as community development director from 1977 to 1983, during which time she also completed her undergraduate studies and enrolled in graduate courses at the University of Arkansas. The tribe then appointed her principal organizer of a grant-funded revitalization project. In 1983, the principal chief of the Cherokee Nation, Ross Swimmer, asked her to join him as his deputy chief in the upcoming elections. Mankiller overcame initial opposition from male members of the tribe and won the position.

In 1985, Swimmer left to head the Bureau of Indian Affairs in Washington, D.C., and Mankiller took over as principal chief to complete Swimmer's term. As such, she became the first woman ever to head a Native American nation. With the encouragement of her new husband Charlie Soap, Mankiller ran for this leadership position in the 1987 election. Having proven herself over the previous two years as a capable leader, she easily won, despite the annoyance of some men. In America's early days, "historians referred to our tribal government as a petticoat government because of the strong role of women in the tribe," said Mankiller. "Then we adopted a lot of ugly things that were part of the non-Indian world and one of those things was sexism. . . . So in 1687 women enjoyed a prominent role, but in 1987 we found people questioning whether women should be in leadership positions anywhere in the tribe." As elected chief, she assessed the primary problems of her nation as high unemployment, poor education and poor health care, and set out to address those issues. Mankiller represented a nation of over 70,000 people, with more than 45,000 acres of land and a yearly budget of over $75 million. During her tenure, the tribe's worldwide membership increased to 156,000, and she added three health centers and nine chil-

Wilma
Mankiller

dren's programs. She retired in 1994, to give others an opportunity to lead the nation.

Mankiller's personal life was marked by tragedy. In 1960, a brother died of burns sustained in a job-related accident. Her father died in 1971, of a kidney disease which would later afflict Wilma and require her to receive a kidney transplant from her brother Donald in 1990. In the mid-1970s, Mankiller was also seriously injured in an automobile accident that killed her best friend, and shortly thereafter was diagnosed with myasthenia gravis, a muscle disease. Throughout her personal struggles, she maintained a positive outlook on life, preferring to be instrumental in working toward change rather than to complain about disadvantages.

Wilma Mankiller co-authored her autobiography, *Mankiller: A Chief and Her People*, in 1984; she has also contributed fiction to magazines and authored the foreword to *Selu: Seeking the Corn-Mother's Wisdom* by **Marilou Awiakta**, published in 1993. Among the awards Mankiller has received are the Donna Nigh First Lady Award from the Oklahoma Commission for the Status of Women (1985), the American Leadership Award from Harvard University (1986), the John W. Gardner Leadership Award (1988), and an honorary degree from Yale University (1990). She was inducted into the Oklahoma Women's Hall of Fame in 1986, and, in 1994, was inducted into the Oklahoma Hall of Fame and the Women's Hall of Fame at Seneca Falls.

SOURCES:

Contemporary Authors. Vol. 146. Detroit, MI: Gale Research.

Contemporary Newsmakers 1986. Detroit, MI: Gale Research.

Magill, Frank N. *Cyclopedia of World Authors.* 3rd rev. ed. Englewood Cliffs, NJ: Salem Press, 1997.

McFadden, Margaret, ed. *Women's Issues.* Vol. II. Englewood Cliffs, NJ: Salem Press, 1997.

"Wilma Mankiller," in *Encyclopedia of World Biography.* Detroit, MI: Gale Research.

SUGGESTED READING:

Mankiller, Wilma, with Michael Wallis. *Mankiller: A Chief and Her People.* NY: St. Martin's Press, 1984.

Judith C. Reveal, freelance writer, Greensboro, Maryland

Mankin, Helen Douglas

(1894–1956)

U.S. congressional representative, state assemblywoman, and lawyer who was the first woman elected to Congress from Georgia. Name variations: Helen Douglas. Born on September 11, 1894, in Atlanta, Georgia; died on July 25, 1956; daughter of Hamilton Douglas (a lawyer, teacher, and founder of the Atlanta Law School) and Corinne (Williams) Douglas (a teacher and lawyer); Rockford College, A.B., 1917; Atlanta Law School, L.LB., 1920; married Guy Mark Mankin (an engineer), in 1927; children: (stepson) Guy, Jr.

Helen Douglas Mankin was born the third of five children, including four daughters, in Atlanta, Georgia, on September 11, 1894. Her parents had received law degrees from the University of Michigan; unable to practice because the Geor-

gia bar had not yet begun to admit women, her mother **Corinne Douglas** worked as a teacher and organized the first department of commercial studies for girls in the Atlanta high schools, and her father, Hamilton Douglas, president of the Board of Education, founded the Atlanta Law School, where he also served as dean. They maintained an intellectual household, entertaining such visitors as ***Jane Addams**, Charles W. Eliot, president of Harvard University, and William Howard Taft, future president of the United States. Helen attended public schools and was the only girl to play on the local baseball team.

Mankin graduated with a bachelor's degree from Rockford College in Illinois (her mother's and grandmother's alma mater) in 1917. She joined the American Women's Hospital Unit during World War I and drove an ambulance in France for 13 months. Returning to America, she entered Atlanta Law School and earned her LL.B. in 1920. That year both she and her mother, then over 60, were admitted to the Georgia bar and entered the family firm. At a time when women were still not accepted in traditionally male roles, particularly in the South, Mankin felt awkward and out of place. Searching for new adventures, she and her sister **Jean Douglas** set off on a whirlwind tour of America, covering over 13,000 miles by automobile in 1922. At the completion of their trip, they set off for Europe with their mother. Following an extensive automobile trip, they returned to America, and in 1924 Mankin opened her own law firm.

As a fairly new lawyer and a woman, she did not attract wealthy corporate clients. Most of her clients were poor African-Americans, with whom she quickly established good relationships. She supplemented her income by giving lectures at Atlanta Law School, and developed an interest in politics. In 1927, while working as the women's manager of I.N. Ragsdale's mayoral campaign, she met and married Guy Mark Mankin, a widower with a young son. Guy Mankin was a mechanical engineer and his work took them to a variety of locations, including Cuba, Brazil, Argentina, New York, and Chicago.

The family returned to Atlanta after several years, and by 1933 Mankin had resumed her law career. She lobbied without success for ratification of a child-labor amendment to the state constitution and her frustration led her to decide she would have more influence as a politician. In September 1936, Mankin was elected state representative. A Democrat, and only the fifth woman to sit in the Georgia legislature, she served from 1937 to 1946, being re-elected four times. Considered outspoken, independent and sometimes abrasive, Mankin championed causes such as education and child welfare. She worked for progressive legislation in such matters as improved salaries for teachers, better state policing, permanent registration laws, the separation of juvenile inmates from adult inmates in state prisons, and a state department of labor.

Mankin was an ardent supporter of Governor Ellis Arnall's liberal policies, including his repeal of the poll tax. In 1946, Arnall called a special election to fill the seat of Congressman Robert Ramspeck, who had resigned, and Mankin decided to leave the state legislature to seek the office. At a time when African-Americans were suing to end Georgia's white primary, she was the only candidate to actively pursue their vote. African-American voter registration doubled for the election, and Mankin won the seat. Facing derision from such locally important politicians as ex-governor and gubernatorial candidate Eugene Talmadge (who called her "the Belle of Ashby Street," an African-American neighborhood, and publicly mocked "the spectacle of Atlanta Negroes sending a Congresswoman to Washington"), she refused to disavow her black supporters. She also drew support from the Congress of Industrial Organizations (CIO), women's groups, church groups, and various progressive organizations. Mankin was considered a radical, and was one of the few Southerners to support Truman's veto of the Case anti-strike bill. Despite her labor support, she went on record voting for the Hobbs bill, which was directed against the CIO's Teamsters Union.

Mankin completed Ramspeck's term in Congress and filed to run again in the 1946 primaries. She won the popular vote against her closest opponent, Judge James C. Davis, but Davis claimed victory under an obscure county-unit system. The system awarded unit votes to the candidate receiving a plurality of its popular vote, and total units rather than majority were used to determine a winner. Although the system had not been used in recent times, it was revived to nullify African-American votes. Davis had received eight county-unit votes to Mankin's six. Mankin challenged the results and the State Democratic Executive Committee placed both names on the ballot. However, her political enemy Eugene Talmadge had won the gubernatorial election, and he removed her name. Mankin countered with a write-in challenge and, despite the involvement of white supremacists working for Davis, received an impressive

19,527 votes against Davis' 31,444. The racial disturbances drew national, and critical, attention, for which she was blamed by the local establishment. She challenged Davis again in 1948, was castigated again for stirring up trouble, and lost. In 1949, Mankin sued in *South* v. *Peters* to end the county-unit system. The Supreme Court did not rule in her favor, citing states' rights, and the system remained in effect until it was struck down in 1962.

Helen Mankin did not run for office again. She continued in private practice and also visited Israel and took up Zionist causes. In 1956, she was involved in an automobile accident in Georgia and died of her injuries on July 25.

Helen Douglas Mankin

SOURCES:

Current Biography. NY: H.W. Wilson, 1946.

Office of the Historian. *Women in Congress, 1917–1990.* Commission on the Bicentenary of the U.S. House of Representatives, 1991.

Sicherman, Barbara, and Carol Hurd Green. *Notable American Women: The Modern Period: A Biographical Dictionary.* Cambridge, MA: The Belknap Press of Harvard University, 1980.

SUGGESTED READING:

Spritzer, Lorraine N. *The Belle of Ashby Street: Helen Douglas Mankin and Georgia Politics.* Athens, GA: University of Georgia Press, 1982.

Judith C. Reveal,
freelance writer, Greensboro, Maryland

Manley, Delarivier (1663–1724).

See Manley, Mary de la Rivière.

Manley, Dorothy (b. 1927).

See Blankers-Koen, Fanny for sidebar.

Manley, Effa (1900–1981)

American co-owner of the Newark Eagles Negro League baseball team and civil-rights activist. Born Effa Brooks on March 27, 1900, in Philadelphia, Pennsylvania; died in Los Angeles, California, on April 16, 1981; daughter of Bertha Ford Brooks (a seamstress) and claimed to be daughter of John Marcus Bishop (a wealthy Philadelphia financier); married and divorced a man named Bush, sometime between 1916 and 1932; married Abraham L. Manley, on June 15, 1933 (died 1952); married Charles Alexander, in mid-1950s (divorced); no children.

*Effa
Manley*

When the subject arises of African-Americans playing baseball in the Negro Leagues of the 1920s, 1930s, and 1940s, most Americans who know anything about it quickly recall such luminaries as Leroy "Satchel" Paige, Josh Gibson, James "Cool Papa" Bell, and Jackie Robinson. Some others more familiar with the history remember a second tier of stars, Oscar Charleston, Rube Foster, Judy Johnson, Martin Dihigo, Buck Leonard, Buck O'Neil, Max Manning, Turkey Stearnes, Hilton Smith, and Monte Irvin, to name a few. But rarely does the name Effa Manley come up, even though, as co-owner of the powerful Newark Eagles black baseball club, she exerted a major influence on the game during the 1930s and 1940s.

The circumstances surrounding Manley's genesis are somewhat cloudy. At the time of her birth in Philadelphia on March 27, 1900, her mother **Bertha Ford Brooks**, a white seamstress, was married to Benjamin Brooks, an African-American. Manley always claimed that her father had been John Marcus Bishop, a wealthy white financier for whom her mother worked, and she was thus an illegitimate child. Benjamin Brooks certainly thought so at the time: he sued Bishop for alienation of Bertha's affections and garnered a $10,000 settlement. Technically then, if these facts were exact, Effa was born Caucasian. On her marriage certificate in 1933, however, she listed Brooks as her father and declared herself as "colored." Perhaps she did so because she had adopted black culture as her own so thoroughly.

Effa grew up mainly in an African-American culture, as her mother had six other children sired by black fathers. "I was always this little blond, hazel-eyed, white girl, always with Negro children," she remembered. She played and mixed with African-American children and even when she became aware of the prejudice directed at blacks, she chose to remain in that culture. Manley's complexion, which was olive toned, allowed her to mix fairly easily with blacks. But she also used her light skin to work jobs in New York City usually denied to people of color, and she stayed in posh hotels that allowed blacks in only as employees. Indeed, she sometimes played it both ways, trapping people into believing she was white and then asserting her "colored" status.

Sometime after graduating from William Penn High School in 1916, Effa departed Philadelphia for New York, and also was married for a short time to a man named Bush whom she met at an Atlantic City resort. During the 1932 World Series, however, Effa met Abraham L. Manley, a "numbers" gambling kingpin who had recently moved into Harlem from the Philadelphia area. Abe, an African-American originally from North Carolina, had migrated northward and latched onto his profession sometime in the early 1920s. He was an avid baseball fan, particularly of Philadelphia's Hilldale squad. Effa was more of a fan of Babe Ruth than of baseball in general, but she was a fan, so when they met in New York, where both lived by 1932, there was at least one reason for mutual attraction. Before meeting Abe, she had been "interested in the thing that interests most women, I suppose, clothes. I spent quite a few years in the millinery business making hats, [and] had taken a little additional training in designing," Effa later recalled. Their courtship progressed throughout the rest of the year. Abe purchased a five-carat ring for her at Tiffany's in 1933, and on June 15 of that year, they married.

The marriage allowed Effa full entry into African-American high society of the day. She was able to outrun the cloudy circumstances of her birth. "I was a bastard and 75 years ago that was a terrible thing," she said. "I was not accepted into the better circles of Negro society until I met Abe." The couple hobnobbed with such performers as Eubie Blake and such sports celebrities as boxer Joe Louis. Manley could have luxuriated in her good fortune and lived a quasi-sybaritic life, but she felt a certain amount of noblesse oblige toward the downtrodden of her adopted race and used her position to work for the betterment of black people. In 1935, for example, in the midst of the worst economic depression the country had ever known, merchants in Harlem were declining to hire African-American clerks. Scandalized by such racial insensitivity, Manley, along with a Methodist Episcopal minister, John Johnson, organized the Citizens' League for Fair Play. Carrying signs that read "Don't shop where you can't work," the League picketed shops along 125th Street. The boycott worked. Six weeks later, the store owners had a change of heart. Manley's actions were not as momentous as would be those of *Rosa Parks 20 years later in Montgomery, Alabama, but the tactics were the same. Within a year, perhaps as many as 300 black salespeople owed their new jobs in Harlem to the League's stand. Manley was also an officer of the Edgecombe Sanitarium Renaissance Committee (to save that Harlem medical institution) and the Children's Camp Committee of New York. She believed that African-Americans had great untapped potential. The black race "does not know its own strength," said Manley in 1936, "and when it begins to realize what really fine things the race is capable of doing it will show rapid progress."

But it was as co-owner of a franchise in Negro League baseball that Effa Manley gained renown. During the 1920s, thanks largely to the efforts of Rube Foster of Chicago, a Negro National League had offered some semblance of order to African-American players and fans whose previous fare of black baseball were barnstorming teams and tours. But in 1931, the Negro National League, minus Foster's leadership and losing fans because of the Depression, threw in the towel. Barnstorming resurfaced, but an organized league was sorely missing. Then in 1933, black "numbers" kings, such as Gus Greenlee of Pittsburgh and Abe Manley of Newark, put together a second Negro National League. Baseball historians generally credit Greenlee with this resurgence, because he built a black-owned stadium and talked the other "numbers" men into joining his venture. Effa Manley remembered the genesis differently. She admitted that Greenlee was important in 1933, but that he ran the league in "a permissive, self-defeating, and entirely unorthodox manner." According to Manley, it was not until her husband Abe reorganized the league in 1935 that it took on an air of professionalism. Greenlee would remain as president and Abe would be the treasurer and run a team in Brooklyn.

Abe [Manley] stayed mostly in the background. . . . Effa ruled the roost.

—**Max Manning**

The Manleys kept up their end of the bargain by setting up a franchise, the Brooklyn Eagles, which would play in Ebbets Field under a lease arrangement with the Brooklyn Dodgers. As co-owner, Effa swung into action, handling the business matters of the club, while Abe tended to recruitment. "I was surprised even myself with my rapid progress in absorbing the lesson so vital to the successful operation of a modern day baseball organization," she modestly marveled. She bought the team's equipment, scheduled their road trips and hotel accommodations, kept track of the corporation's payroll, and worked up the publicity for the game. Effa was justifiably proud of her accomplishments: "[I] succeeded in setting up a system of public relations that eventually made the Newark Eagles one of the most talked-about teams in the country." For the opening game, she got New York Mayor Fiorello La Guardia to throw out the first ball and numerous dignitaries to attend. But the opener was a disappointment. Only 2,000 or so fans showed up, and the Homestead Grays bombed the Eagles 21–7. Effa was furious. As first baseman George Giles recalled, "Mrs. Manley left. When she was displeased, the world came to an end. . . . Mrs. Manley didn't like a loser." Later that first season, she appointed Giles manager. But the team had a losing season, and despite coverage in the African-American newspapers, the Manleys decided to move the franchise to a more profitable location. Abe could continue to bankroll a club with his "numbers" money, but even that was not limitless, and competition with the Brooklyn Dodgers, even as a second-division club, was severe.

The Manleys decided on Newark and bought the Newark Dodgers, a black semi-pro team. Along with the purchase came the contract of Ray Dandridge, a young third baseman who would go on to have a Hall of Fame career. In 1936, the club officially became the Newark Eagles and set up a lease agreement with Ruppert Stadium, a New York Yankees property. Controversy immediately arose over control of bookings of exhibition games, because Abe did not want those games to cut into the Negro National League season. The agents retaliated by leaving the Eagles off the schedule for the profitable Sunday and holiday games in the major cities. Effa supported Abe publicly, blaming the booking agents for the Eagles' unprofitability and even later making a "fiery speech" against booking agent percentage cuts. But privately she disagreed with Abe, because she saw accurately that the exhibition games were often more lucrative than the regular Negro League games.

The Newark Eagles were never the most famous Negro League baseball team during their time—certainly the Kansas City Monarchs or Homestead Grays or Pittsburgh Crawfords held that honor—but the Manleys put together a rather respectable team. By 1937, the roster included the "Million Dollar" infield of Dandridge, "Mule" Suttles, Willie Wells, and Dick Seay, as well as the great pitcher Leon Day. Eventually, Abe recruited Larry Doby and Monte Irvin (albeit under other names to protect their amateur status). The Manleys also came close to landing the legendary Satchel Paige in 1938 and 1939, but he opted to pitch in Mexico and for his own traveling All-Stars team instead. Rumor had it that Satchel had asked Effa to be his girlfriend, but she had demurred. With or without Paige, the team was very popular in Newark. According to pitcher Max Manning, another important later addition, "The Eagles were to [black] Newark what the Dodgers were to Brooklyn." In 1941, the Manleys felt comfortable enough with the city to move from Harlem. Before World War II, the Eagles usually trailed the powerhouse Homestead Grays, but in 1946 the team won the league pennant and Negro League World Series with exciting victories over the Kansas City Monarchs.

As co-owner of the Eagles, Manley used the baseball games to promote civil-rights causes. The 1930s were witnessing an increase in lynching as whites unleashed their economic frustrations and racist anxieties against blacks. During this time, Effa was treasurer of the New Jersey chapter of the National Association for the Advancement of Colored People (NAACP). Determined to do something to raise consciousness and help deter lynching, she organized a "Stop Lynching" day at Newark's Ruppert Stadium. Wearing "Stop Lynching" sashes, the ushers went up and down the aisles collecting money for the benefit. Donn Rogosin, a historian of black baseball, later called it "probably the most remarkable special day in Negro baseball history." Manley also focused on spreading the proud message of baseball to kids, allowing the Knothole Gang free admission and sponsoring a youth team, the Newark Cubs.

World War II brought out her patriotism as well as a special pride in the 54 Negro Leaguers who volunteered to fight. Once she invited the entire 372nd regiment, an elite African-American unit of possibly as many as 2,500 men, to attend an Eagles game as her guests. She made sure that the soldiers at Fort Dix had entertainment, paying for a bus to transport performers there. Manley helped out with the NAACP's Crusade for Liberty, and at one point pinned a campaign button on Newark's deputy mayor. She also helped the federal government, as a member of the gas-rationing committee that decided on special exemptions for hardship cases. There is no indication that these were ploys to increase game attendance, but more likely examples of her sincere patriotism.

Effa did not play second fiddle to Abe in their business dealings with the Eagles or the Negro National League. Abe was nominally the league treasurer, but Effa seems to have handled the transactions. She had had no formal training in business administration, and women executives in any American business were scarce. But once in the co-owner position, her natural talents rose to the fore. The other owners may have chafed at this, but they did respect her financial abilities and strength. As Grays owner Cumberland Posey said, "Negro baseball owners can take a few tips from the lady member of the league when it comes to advertising." For example, she probably stopped the players from a threatened boycott of an East-West All-Star game by declaring flatly that no Newark Eagle was going to strike. Still the owners groused about taking any advice from a woman, despite her marriage to one of their peers. Dan Burley, sports editor for the Amsterdam, New York, *Star-News* noted, "Effa Manley has long been a sore spot in the N.N.L. setup . . . the rough and tumble gentlemen comprising its inner sanctum have complained often and loudly that 'baseball ain't no place for no woman.'" Similarly, a few of the Eagles staff may have resented her moves with the team as meddling. Certainly two of the managers, Willie Wells and Biz Mackey, thought she was too controlling of them. One story had it that Wells took a beaning one day, hit on the head by a pitch while he was trying to figure out a sign from Effa in the stands.

In many ways, however, the Manleys looked out for the well-being of their squad. Some players remembered them as tightwads, but Effa always claimed that she went a long way to promote the careers of her athletes. As early as 1935, she was instrumental in securing wintertime employment for some of her players on a ball team in Puerto Rico. The team won the winter league championship, and helped to open Latin America for more Negro Leaguers. She remembered it as "one of my most pleasant experiences in baseball," and the players appreciated the chance to earn sometimes double what the Manleys were able to pay. If a player, such as first baseman George Giles, needed some publicity, Effa made sure the press was attentive. If other players needed some financial assistance, as Monte Irvin did for a down payment on a house and Lenny Pearson did for financing a tavern, the Manleys pitched in. Occasionally, the aid would turn comical or backfire, as when Effa instructed the manager to put in Terris McDuffie, her favorite pitcher, so the crowd could see how good-looking he was. But more often than not, her heart and head were in the right place.

Many of the Newark Eagles understood that Manley's kindhearted qualities only went so far and that she was a hard-headed disciplinarian. Occasionally, she would chew out a player for sloppy attire or slackness. Pitcher James Walker reminisced, "She would call you in and tell you how to dress, what to do, who to associate with. When you had your problems, if they were personal, you went to Mrs. Manley, and she was very understanding, as long as you toed the line." She was a tough negotiator with the early contracts, and occasionally intercepted and held onto mail from female fans so the players would stay relatively intent on the games. As Max Manning remembered, "Abe mostly stayed in the background. . . . Effa ruled the roost." Some players tried to hide from her, if they thought she had a grudge against them. Johnny Davis, an outfielder and pitcher, recalled keeping to the back of the room in team meetings to stay out of her disfavor. But Davis also reckoned that her sternness added a needed measure of pride and fear that gave backbone to the club. "When I first started playing baseball, you needed drugs to stay awake!" he recalled. "But we never thought about drugs or anything. We were Mrs. Manley's boys."

Although the Eagles won the championship in 1946, the major changes in Negro League and Major League baseball already underway would undercut their glory. In 1945, Branch Rickey, the general manager of the Brooklyn Dodgers, had signed Jackie Robinson, a shortstop for the Monarchs, to a minor league contract. In 1946, Robinson played brilliantly for the Montreal Royals, and Rickey began signing other Negro Leaguers. At first, Effa cheered these developments as evidence of racial progress. Indeed, she was a member of the Citizens Committee to Get Negroes into the Big Leagues, and around 1943 had urged some sort of plan to make the Negro Leagues a farm system for the white majors. But as Rickey's aggressive posture mounted, she reached a different opinion. She complained about his recruiting tactics and privately claimed that he had "raped" the Negro Leagues.

Manley did manage to secure compensation for trading Larry Doby in 1947. When Bill Veeck, the aggressive owner of the Cleveland Indians, approached her about getting Doby, he offered $10,000. Manley, who had already indicated that she would not stand in Doby's way, chastised Veeck, "Mr. Veeck, you know if Larry Doby were white and a free agent, you'd give him $10,000 to sign with you merely as a bonus." Veeck, who had for several years been in favor of blacks breaking into the majors, agreed to pay the Manleys another $5,000 if Doby stayed with the Indians' organization past 30 days. Of course, Doby did that and more, helping the Indians to a World Series championship in 1948 and eventually hitting 253 home runs and driving in nearly 1,000 runs in a 13-year career with Cleveland and the Chicago White Sox. Effa claimed that the compensation paid by Veeck established a precedent; after that, Major League owners usually paid about $5,000 per player when they recruited a Negro Leaguer.

Receiving an occasional fee for a recruited player, however, was not enough to keep the Eagles franchise profitable. Like several other Negro League teams, the Newark club was feeling the financial pinch of losing black fans. In 1947, the Eagles suffered a loss of $22,000. By 1948, the Manleys had probably lost a total of $100,000. They sold the franchise for $15,000 to a consortium headed by Dr. W.H. Young, an African-American dentist in Memphis, who agreed to own the contracts of the players. This maneuver immediately created an incident in which Effa again displayed her tenacity and business acumen. Hearing that the Manleys had sold the club, Rickey approached star outfielder Monte Irvin about signing a contract with the Dodgers' St. Paul farm team. Manley intervened, and Rickey suspended the deal. Then the African-American press blasted her for ruining Irvin's chances with the majors. Effa turned around and eventually secured a deal for him with the New York Giants. The Giants paid her $5,000, which Manley considered minuscule for such a talented player as Monte, who went on to the Hall of Fame after contributing mightily to two Giant pennants and a World Series championship. Grumbling, Effa took the money, paid the attorney, and purchased a mink cape with her share. She kept the cape as a memento of the deal, but always thought Horace Stoneham, the Giants' owner, had gotten the far better deal.

In 1948, Manley squared off with none other than Jackie Robinson over the quality of Negro League baseball. Robinson had become legendary overnight in 1947 as the first African-American player to play in the Major Leagues in the 20th century (although undoubtedly some light-skinned blacks or Latinos "passed" as white and played before Robinson broke the color barrier). Many African-Americans and whites revered him for his perseverance. But in a 1948 article in *Ebony*, titled "What's Wrong with Negro Baseball?," Robinson attacked the Negro Leagues and their owners. Low salaries, lousy umpiring, and the shady business dealings of some of the owners hurt the leagues, he maintained. He also accused the owners of ignoring the welfare of their players by not providing them with better traveling and living conditions. Whether Robinson was speaking his own mind or voicing what some white executives such as Branch Rickey and owners in the Major Leagues believed is unclear, but Effa found his remarks unfair and damaging.

In an article in the August 1948 *Our World,* she took on Robinson's assertions. Negro League ballplayers made a handsome wage, she declared, pointing out that the $100 per week they earned on average was over twice as much as the typical American worker was making. She did not address the umpiring and business connections directly, but she reminded Robinson, who should have known very well, that Jim Crow segregation laws accounted for the substandard hotels and buses that marked Negro League life. "Until Congress makes statutory changes about race prejudice in hotels, I'm afraid there's very little that we can do to better such accommodation," she wrote. Then she went beyond Robinson's gripes and lambasted the Major Leagues for raiding players with no compensation to the Negro Leagues. African-American fans who cheered the black players in the Major Leagues were being naive, in her opinion. "Gullible Negro fans who think white owners take on colored players through any altruistic pangs of democracy had better quit kidding themselves," she warned. "There's a potential of two million Negro fans to draw from." The losers would be the Negro League teams, who had become, in the eyes of the sports press, black and white, "the step-child of American sport." The other Negro League owners appreciated her efforts, although they themselves remained relatively silent. Some writers from the African-American press responded forcefully. John Johnson, of the *Kansas City Call,* chided her for standing in the way of what he called progress and urged black fans to see baseball as colorblind. He also suggested that Effa was exercising her pet grievances against Branch Rickey and the black press in general. But as Effa stepped away from baseball, her departure drew some laments. Black newspaper columnist Wendell Smith forgave her occasional use of tears to get her way at meetings and declared, "The boys in the press box are gonna' miss her—tears and all!"

For the Negro Leagues, Manley's comments were accurate and sadly prophetic. The Newark Eagles collapsed in 1948. The Negro National League crumbled that same year. The Negro American League lost six teams and lurched along, with only four teams by 1953, all the way to its ultimate demise in 1960. Players who were not good enough for, or too old to make, the majors and those who were competent enough but were the victims of glacial progress on the integration front, found themselves with no baseball career or shrinking opportunities. Younger players both good and great such as Henry Aaron, Ernie Banks, and Willie Mays were able to latch on with the Major Leagues, but for the generation preceding them, the death knell of the Negro Leagues was disastrous. Effa Manley, by then no longer in an ownership position and unable to help the players, could only watch the slow fade.

In 1952, Abe Manley died. Effa moved back to Philadelphia to be near her family in 1955, but soon moved to Los Angeles, hoping to bring them along. Still only in her 50s, she married a musician named Charles Alexander, an old boyfriend, although the marriage lasted only a year. For the most part, she stayed away from baseball, still maintaining a grudge against the Dodgers, who under Rickey had helped demolish her Newark team. Several show-business friends from the East had moved to California and Effa socialized with them, easing her later years. Her health had deteriorated by 1980, and she moved into a rest home operated by former Negro League catcher Quincy Trouppe. In the spring of 1981 she contracted colon cancer and peritonitis, and died of a heart attack on April 16.

In her later years, however, Manley made many spirited efforts to remind people of the glory of the Negro Leagues. In 1976, with sportswriter Leon Hartwick, she co-authored a book, *Negro Baseball . . . Before Integration,* to try to set the record straight. She also granted several interviews to oral historians and graduate students. Although she disliked the Dodgers (who had long since abandoned Brooklyn for Los Angeles), she kept pressuring the team's management to recognize Negro Leaguers at the games. She peppered *The Sporting News* and the National Baseball Hall of Fame with letters advocating enshrinement of many Negro Leaguers. Even after the Hall of Fame admitted 11 Negro League players, she pressed for more, or at least for a significant exhibit noting the accomplishments of those not honored individually. The Hall did not act on her recommendation until four years after her death.

In 1985, the Hall of Fame in Cooperstown, New York, unveiled a new exhibit on Negro League baseball. The display prominently featured Effa Manley. But three years later, when the Hall of Fame developed an exhibit on women in baseball, the curators neglected to place Manley in the case, supposedly because it would duplicate her previous recognition. Never mind that plenty of male players, owners, and managers had appeared in more than one exhibit in the Hall. Although in the 1990s there was a resurgence of popular and historical interest in women and baseball due to the 1992 movie *A League of Their Own,* that renewed attention by and large ignored African-American women and baseball, particularly the contributions of Effa Manley. The full-scale biography of Manley by James Overmyer, published in 1993, might go a long way toward reversing this neglect by baseball historians. But Manley's life encompassed more than her baseball endeavors: she occupied a unique place as an African-American entrepreneur and a cultural and political activist.

SOURCES:

Berlage, Gai Ingham. "Effa Manley, A Major Force in Negro Baseball in the 1930s and 1940s," in *NINE: A Journal of Baseball History and Social Policy Perspectives.* Spring 1993, pp. 163–184.

Dixon, Phil, with Patrick J. Hannigan. *The Negro Baseball Leagues, a Photographic History.* Mattituck, NY: Amereon House, 1992.

Manley, Effa. "Negro Baseball Isn't Dead! But It Is Pretty Sick," in *Our World.* August 1948, pp. 27–29.

———, and Leon Hardwick. *Negro Baseball . . . Before Integration.* Chicago, IL: Adam Press, 1976.

Overmyer, James. *Effa Manley and the Newark Eagles.* Metuchen, NJ: The Scarecrow Press, 1993.

Rogosin, William Donn. *Invisible Men: Life in the Negro Baseball Leagues.* NY: Atheneum, 1987.

RELATED MEDIA:

Only the Ball Was White (video). Chicago: WTTW/Chicago, 1992.

Thomas L. Altherr,
Professor of History and American Studies at
Metropolitan State College of Denver, Denver, Colorado

Manley, Mary de la Rivière

(1663–1724)

English author and playwright. Name variations: Delarivier Manley; Mary de la Riviere Manley; Dela Manley; Mrs. Manley Delarivière. Born in 1663 in England; died in 1724 in England; daughter of Sir Roger Manley (a high-ranking British officer and writer); married cousin John Manley (dissolved because he was already married); lived with *Barbara Villiers, duchess of Cleveland (c. 1641–1709).

Selected writings: Letters (1696); Secret Memoirs and Manners of Several Persons of Quality of Both Sexes From the New Atalantis, an Island in the Mediterranean (1709); Memoirs of Europe . . . Written by Eginardus (1710); Court Intrigues (1711); The History of Rivella (also called The Adventures of Rivella, 1714); The Power of Love (1720).

Mary de la Rivière Manley was born in 1663, the daughter of Sir Roger Manley, a high-ranking officer in the British military and writer. According to a semi-autobiographical account of her life, she was drawn into an illegal marriage with her cousin, John Manley, who at the time of the ceremony was still married to another woman. He soon added insult to injury by taking control of her inheritance and deserting her. In another account, Manley identified herself as "a ruined woman" in the wake of her disastrous marriage to her cousin; she does indeed seem to have had a scandalous reputation among her contemporaries. She later wrote with considerable compassion about other such "ruined women," a group with which she clearly identified.

After John Manley left her, Mary Manley began to pursue her writing career in earnest, turning out plays, satiric prose, short stories, letters, and political articles (she was sympathetic to the Tory cause). She broke new ground in a number of literary areas, and is said to have been the first Englishwoman to work as a political journalist, the first to author a bestseller, and the first to be arrested because of something she had written. Her most famous work, *Secret Memoirs and Manners of Several Persons of Quality of Both Sexes From the New Atalantis, an Island in the Mediterranean,* published in 1709, was a satiric diatribe against the opposition Whig Party and other persons of importance, intended to expose personal scandals. Although the characters bore fictitious names, Manley helpfully appended a key to their real identities. Both she and her publishers were briefly arrested in the uproar over *Secret Memoirs.*

A collection of individual stories, *Secret Memoirs* is linked together by the framework of a tale of a goddess named Astrea, who returns to earth and visits an island in the Mediterranean called Atalantis. While on Atalantis, Astrea encounters Virtue and her mother, Intelligence, and the three share stories of what they have seen on their travels. Although the element of scandal (or slander) has faded, the stories retain a certain interest for modern-day readers for their revealing accounts of women's lives at the time. "Corinna" tells of a young woman who adamantly refuses to wed, and how circumstances conspire to punish her, while "The Cabal" offers a somewhat peculiar description of a circle of lesbians.

Encouraged by the success of her contemporary, the great playwright *Aphra Behn, Manley wrote several plays, including *The Lost Lover,* unsuccessfully staged in 1696, *The Royal Mischief,* also written in 1696, and *Lucius,* presented in Drury Lane in 1717. In 1710, she published *Memoirs of Europe . . . Written by Eginardus,* followed in 1711 by *Court Intrigues.* Although she had been attacked by Jonathan Swift in an issue of the *Tatler,* she later succeeded him as the editor of the *Examiner,* a popular Tory publication, and he assisted her on the job. In an entry in his *Journal to Stella,* Swift commented that "she has very generous principles, for one of her sort." Her memoir-novel *The History of Rivella,* thought by many to be largely autobiographical, opens with this description of the title character: "There are so many things

Praise- and yet Blame-worthy in Rivella's Conduct, that as her Friend I know not how with a good Grace, to repeat."

Mary de la Rivière Manley lived for a time with Barbara Villiers, duchess of Cleveland, and was said to have been the mistress of several men, including Alderman Barber. She died in 1724. A facsimile edition of her novels was published in 1971.

SOURCES:

Drabble, Margaret, ed. *The Oxford Companion to English Literature.* 5th ed. Oxford, NY: Oxford University Press, 1985.

Goreau, Angeline. *The Whole Duty of a Woman: Female Writers in Seventeenth Century England.* NY: Dial, 1985.

Goulianos, Joan, ed. *by a Woman writt: Literature from Six Centuries by and about Women.* Baltimore, MD: Penguin, 1974.

Don Amerman,
freelance writer, Saylorsburg, Pennsylvania

Mann, Carol (1941—)

American golfer. Born Carol Ann Mann in Buffalo, New York, on February 3, 1941.

Won the Vare Trophy (1968) with an average score of 72.04, a record which remained for a decade; won the Western Junior championship (1958); won the Women's Western (1964); won the USGA Open (1965); won ten tournaments (1968); won eight tournaments (1969); won the Lawson's Open, the Border Classic, the George Washington Classic, and the Dallas Civitan (1975); carded 200 strokes for 54 holes in LPGA competition at the Canongate Country Club in Palmetto, Georgia (1978), to win the Lady Carling.

One of golf's most successful and consistent players, Carol Mann was known on the golf course for her dependable putting and controlled driving. In 1958, she won both the Western Junior and the Chicago Junior. Two years later, she won the Trans-Mississippi and the Chicago Women's Amateur. That same year, 1960, Mann turned pro. Five years later in 1965, she won the U.S. Women's Open; she would take 35 more LPGA tournaments in her career, but never another major. Her best year was in 1968, when she won the Vare trophy and ten titles; her average score was 72.04, a record which remained unbroken for ten years. In 1982, Mann was elected to the Women's Sports Hall of Fame. In the early 1980s, she became an NBC commentator for televised coverage of both men's and women's tours; she also served on the President's Council for Physical Fitness, the LPGA executive board, and the board of the

Women's Sports Foundation. For two years (1974–75), Mann was president of the LPGA, at a time when the association pursued increased purses and status.

Karin Loewen Haag,
Athens, Georgia

Mann, Erika (1905–1969)

*German writer, journalist, and actress who was a life-long critic of political tyranny and champion of human freedom. Born Erika Julia Hedwig Mann in Munich, Germany, on November 9, 1905; died in Zurich, Switzerland, on August 27, 1969; daughter of Thomas Mann (1875–1955, the novelist) and Katia or Katja (Pringsheim) Mann; sister of **Elisabeth Mann** and **Monika Mann**, Angelus Gottfried (known as Golo) Mann, Klaus Mann, and Michael Mann; married Gustaf Gründgens, in 1926 (divorced 1929); married W.H. Auden (1907–1973, the poet), in 1935.*

Using biting satire to attack Nazism, Erika Mann was a thorn in the side of the Third Reich with her cabaret *Die Pfeffermühle* (The Peppermill) which toured Europe from 1933 through 1936. After coming to the United States in 1936, she was determined to alert Americans to the growing threat of fascism by lecturing and publishing several books. But in the postwar years, she found the Cold War hysteria which dominated American public life increasingly difficult to deal with, and in 1951 moved to Switzerland. There, she served as literary assistant to her famous father, Thomas Mann, during the last years of his life.

She was born on November 9, 1905, the first child and oldest daughter of Thomas and **Katia Mann**. Like all six children of the Nobel Prize-winning German novelist, Erika grew up in the shadow of her renowned father. She was particularly close to her brother Klaus (1906–1949), who would also embark on a literary career. Between 1906 and 1918, the growing Mann family spent their summers in near-idyllic surroundings at a spacious home in Bad Tölz, Upper Bavaria. Although they enjoyed many more privileges than most Germans, Erika and her siblings nevertheless could not help but be affected by the turmoil that assailed their country from the start of World War I in 1914. Imperial Germany's sudden and unexpected capitulation in November 1918, which was accompanied by the abdication and flight of Kaiser Wilhelm II, signaled the onset of a period characterized by a frenzy of artistic creativity. The Weimar Republic which succeeded the monarchical regime was often weak and unpopular with the German people, representing in their minds not a new democracy but chaos, starvation and moral anarchy. In these years, Erika Mann grew to maturity. Although she loved to read and had already begun to write, she was drawn most to the stage. In the early 1920s, she and her brother Klaus, with their mutual friend Richard ("Ricki") Hallgarten, formed an amateur theatrical group in Munich.

With their parents concerned about the negative environment of postwar Munich, Erika and Klaus were sent away in April 1922 to attend the Bergschule Hochwaldhausen in the Röhn mountains near the city of Fulda. The atmosphere there was oppressive, and after several months brother and sister left the school. Erika's formal schooling had effectively been ended, and she moved to Berlin to study acting with Max Reinhardt. Klaus also moved to Berlin and devoted himself to writing. Together they joined **Pamela Wedekind** and the talented actor Gustaf Gründgens to form a theater ensemble. On October 20, 1925, Erika Mann, Gründgens and Wedekind

Erika Mann

appeared on stage in Hamburg for the successful premiere performance of Klaus Mann's first play, *Anja und Esther*.

Over the next several years, Erika concentrated on building a reputation for herself as an actress. She appeared in a number of plays, including her brother's second play, *Revue zu Vieren* (Four in a Revue), which premiered to less favorable reviews in Leipzig on April 21, 1927. In her private life, she married Gustaf Gründgens in 1926, but the marriage was highly unconventional from the start and was probably never consummated since both partners were more attracted to members of their own sex. Mann and Gründgens became increasingly estranged not only personally but politically, with Gründgens moving largely in Communist circles at the time (in the Third Reich, his career was to thrive as a result of his having made peace with Nazism).

Closer than ever to her brother, in October 1927 Erika posed jokingly with Klaus before reporters as "the literary Mann twins," and they embarked on a trip around the globe. In the United States, they lectured at Columbia, Harvard, and Princeton universities. They also met such American literary luminaries as H.L. Mencken and Upton Sinclair, while enjoying reunions with old European friends, including Max Reinhardt and Hollywood celebrities such as *Greta Garbo, Emil Jannings, and Ernst Lubitsch. Continuing on their leisurely way, they visited the Hawaiian Islands, Japan, Korea, and the Soviet Union. Upon their return to Germany in July 1928, Erika and Klaus coauthored a travel book, *Rundherum* (Round About), which was published in the fateful year of 1929. Few of her friends were surprised when Erika obtained a divorce from Gründgens that year. In October, the New York Stock Exchange collapsed, marking the onset of a devastating worldwide economic depression.

By the time Mann and her brother published a second travel account, *Das Buch von der Riviera* (The Riviera Book), in 1931, the situation in Germany and the world in general had taken a dramatic turn for the worse. While Mann continued to act, making appearances in such films as *Christa Winsloe's *Mädchen in Uniform*, she also wrote and organized songs and skits for a cabaret revue. Her *Pfeffermühle* (Peppermill) cabaret opened in Munich on January 1, 1933, at the "Bonbonniere" next to the world-famous Hofbräuhaus, and it was an immediate hit with local audiences. In the years immediately after World War I, Munich had been the birthplace of National Socialism, and Hitler praised the city as "die Hauptstadt der Bewe-

gung" (the capital of the movement). Although Nazi brownshirts were to be seen everywhere in Munich, a significant number of the city's inhabitants remained anti-Nazi; many of them, however, were becoming demoralized. In songs and sketches performed by Erika Mann, **Therese Giehse**, Lotte Goslar, **Sybille Schloss**, and Magnus Henning, the Nazis were brilliantly satirized and demolished, while the morale of Munich's anti-Nazis was considerably improved. Writing in her 1939 book *Escape to Life* about her last days in pre-Nazi Germany, Mann noted:

> Our attack was masked; we told fairy stories and fables, but anyone listening knew what we meant. It was a boisterous festival. The devil-may-care mood of dying carnival could not entirely account for a gaiety so complete and so hectic. The farewell we were celebrating with such grim gaiety was not farewell to carnival, but to life in a free Germany, the farewell to all that had been dear to us. We did not know it then, but we must have had our forebodings.

The success of the *Pfeffermühle* would prove brief. Hitler was appointed chancellor of the German Reich on January 30, 1933, the result of a backroom deal by conservatives who naively believed they could manipulate the Nazi Führer into doing their bidding. Within weeks, the Nazis had established a blood-drenched dictatorship, using a bogus "Communist revolutionary plot" as a pretext for tearing up civil liberties. The last, short phase of German cultural freedom ended on February 27, 1933. The Reichstag building went up in flames, the fire likely having been set by the Nazis to provide an excuse for their seizure of power. In Munich, the Nazi dictatorship clamped down quickly on all signs of opposition, including the *Pfeffermühle*, which was banned. In the Munich suburbs, the Dachau concentration camp was in operation by the end of March 1933, and many hundreds of anti-Nazis found themselves prisoners of Nazi sadists.

Erika and Klaus fled Germany in mid-March 1933, having been for some time among the most hated anti-Nazis in Munich. As far back as early 1932, the Nazi newspaper *Völkischer Beobachter* had predicted a "war of liquidation" directed against the entire Mann family; Erika was targeted because she had advocated peace and disarmament at a women's rally. Realizing her life was at risk, she headed for Switzerland. Here, quickly assembling a brilliant cast of anti-Nazi exiles, Mann revived her *Pfeffermühle* as an exile ensemble, the first such free German group to appear after the creation of the Nazi dictatorship. Soon after its premiere performance on October 1, 1933, the cabaret was drawing capacity audiences in Zurich. The *Pfeffermühle* quickly became recognized as the most political of all the exile cabarets which appeared in the nations bordering Nazi Germany that had given refuge to individuals fleeing the Third Reich. But Mann's group was careful to avoid needlessly provoking the governments of nations increasingly fearful of the Reich's growing power. Nazi Germany was never explicitly named in any of the songs or sketches, although all of these were clearly intended as parables commenting on the contemporary situation in the Nazi dictatorship. Despite this precaution, it was universally obvious that the *Pfeffermühle* was an effective anti-Nazi statement as well as a good evening's entertainment. The German ambassador to Switzerland quickly lodged a formal complaint concerning its "provocative" nature. Soon, various Swiss pro-Nazi groups demonstrated against the cabaret, gas canisters were released during performances, and numerous death threats were made against Erika Mann and Therese Giehse. The actors in the *Pfeffermühle*, however, refused to be cowed and continued to delight audiences, which included German tourists vacationing in Switzerland.

Meanwhile, Erika Mann made a secret trip back to Germany to rescue the manuscript of her father's novel *Joseph and His Brothers*, which he had left behind upon fleeing the country to escape the Nazis. Erika was able to enter the family's house, which was under constant surveillance, disguised in a peasant costume. She spent several hours in total darkness inside her former home before stealing out again, carrying the precious manuscript under her arm. She drove off in the direction of the German-Swiss border with the manuscript under the seat of her car in a toolbox.

In 1935—caving in to pressure from both Nazi Germany and local Nazis, and uncertain of being able to guarantee performances free of violence—the Zurich cantonal government banned further *Pfeffermühle* appearances. Unfazed, Mann and her troupe took their show on tours of other Swiss cantons, as well as to Austria, Belgium, Czechoslovakia, Luxemburg, and the Netherlands. While the possibility of violence by Nazis and their sympathizers against Erika Mann and other members of her ensemble was always real, none of the group let this danger inhibit the enthusiasm of their performances. But Nazi pressure eroded the ensemble's ability to survive financially, as when the municipality of the Swiss town of Davos bowed in the spring of 1935 to local fascist groups, withdrawing their permit to perform.

The last public performances of the *Pfeffermühle* took place in Luxemburg on May 7–9, 1936. A private performance of the cabaret was given at Schloss Leopoldskron near Salzburg, and present among the elite audience on what must have been a bittersweet occasion were Max Reinhardt and ***Marlene Dietrich**. Although the *Pfeffermühle* had performed without incident before appreciative Dutch audiences in 1934 and 1935, in October 1936 Dutch Nazis, who were joined by local entertainers fearful of economic competition, were able to create a storm of controversy that was reported in newspapers and even became part of parliamentary debates. Under pressure, the Dutch authorities withdrew the group's performance permit. When the end came, the *Pfeffermühle* had presented 1,043 performances.

Mann, who had been a resident of Czechoslovakia since 1933, and her brother Klaus returned to the United States in the fall of 1936. She now believed that Nazi Germany could no longer be stopped by European nations alone. She knew that sooner or later the United States would have to enter the struggle against Hitler's regime, and she wanted to alert as many Americans as possible to the danger. Much had changed since their previous visit: Germany had become an aggressive dictatorship, the world had plunged into the worst economic depression in history, and far too many people remained complacent about the threat posed by Hitler and his followers to Western civilization. Over a period of four months, Erika and Klaus traveled from coast to coast, warning the American public of the need to prepare for a confrontation with a Nazi Germany which increased in power with each passing day. The siblings were encouraged by the fact that both of their parents had left Switzerland for the United States and that, after several years of public silence on political issues, Thomas Mann had finally made a definitive break with the Nazi regime, speaking out against it both forcefully and eloquently. Thomas Mann's breach with the Nazis was philosophical, but there was also a more personal factor involved. His wife Katia was Jewish, and thus his entire family was now regarded as being "non-Aryan" under the legal definitions of the 1935 Nuremberg Laws.

Although Erika would return to Europe after the end of her lecture tour, she may well have already decided by early 1937 to make the United States her future home. In January of that year, the cabaret phase of her life drew to a close when her English-language version of the *Pfeffermühle* in New York drew little public support. The show closed after a run of only a few weeks, and henceforth Mann would now fight Hitlerism through books, articles, and lectures. With her return to the U.S. in September 1937, she again hit the grueling lecture circuit. She became a successful lecturer almost immediately and would in fact be one of the best-known lecturers on the national circuit for the next decade or more.

In 1935, Mann married the British poet W.H. Auden in a marriage of convenience that gave her citizenship of a nation which could provide her with more security than her temporary Czechoslovak home. Since both Auden and Mann were homosexuals, the issues of a conventional marriage never arose; their union would endure until Mann's death in 1969. Erika's emotional life was strongly linked to her brother Klaus, a writer of considerable talent who like his sister lived with the burden of being a child of Thomas Mann, an author seen by many critics and readers as an Olympian figure comparable to Goethe. Fully in agreement on politics, Erika and Klaus continued the collaboration they had begun in the late 1920s. They spoke not only for themselves but also as representatives of the entire Mann family (one of Klaus' most successful lectures was entitled "A Family against a Dictatorship"). Sister and brother traveled to Spain, and in June and July 1938 they reported on the civil war then raging there in a series of articles that appeared in the leading newspaper of German emigrés in France, the *Pariser Tageszeitung*.

By the fall of 1938, Mann and her brother had settled permanently in the United States. They collaborated on a book entitled *Escape to Life* (1939), a collection of sketches depicting refugees from Nazi tyranny who, like themselves, were determined to continue the struggle against Hitler and make lasting contributions to their new homeland. The individuals portrayed in this volume included Albert Einstein, Max Reinhardt, and the musicians Adolf Busch and Rudolf Serkin. Klaus Mann also published a novel that year, *Der Vulkan: Roman unter Emigranten* (The Volcano: A Novel among Emigrants), in which he presented a panoramic view of the lives led by anti-Nazi German emigrés during the years 1933–38. His central female character, Marion von Kammer, is unambiguously modeled after Erika. Arguably the most inspiring personality presented in the book, Marion reveals great strength of character as well as the ability to adjust herself to new and difficult environments, both physical and psychological.

The year 1939 also brought British, Dutch, and Swedish editions of a work Erika had published in 1938 as part of her campaign to warn the American public of the evils of Nazism. Entitled *School for Barbarians: Education under the Nazis,* this short volume provided one of the first documentations of the massive perversions introduced by the Nazi regime into the German educational system. Any semblance of free inquiry had been abolished by the educational dictatorship set up in 1933. The goal of the system was now to crush the individual consciences of youths so as to transform them into automatons ready to serve the amoral military machine which the Reich had so quickly become. Mann provided her readers with both quotations from documents and anecdotes to illustrate the deformation of traditional culture carried out by the Nazis. Meant as a warning, *School for Barbarians* unfortunately turned out to be an objective documentation of the collapse of civilization in a nation once proud of its unparalleled cultural achievements.

Mann published another book documenting the threat of Nazism, *The Lights Go Down*, in 1940. Based on documentation which she included in an appendix, this volume presents what is claimed to be a typical Bavarian town. In ten stories of life in the Third Reich, the book chronicles the ways in which some of its citizens, which include a doctor, priest, small businessman, lawyer, farmer, and innkeeper, all try— mostly with little success—to halt the corrosive effects of Nazism in both their public and personal lives. Although some reviewers were positive in their evaluations, others were less than enthusiastic. The reviewer for *Commonweal* called Mann "altogether unequal to the great task of portraying the death of freedom in Germany," and a reviewer in *The Nation* wondered if "her oversimplified approach to the problem of Nazism is not ultimately dangerous to the very cause she serves."

Published in January 1940, *The Other Germany* proved to be the final book she would write in collaboration with Klaus. In it, Mann asked for sympathy on the part of Americans for the "civilized Germany" which she was convinced still existed despite seven years of the Nazi dictatorship. Reviews were mixed. While a review in *The New York Times* commented that the Manns had "evidently forgotten that a book is not a lecture hall," a reviewer for *The New Yorker* was impressed by the book's "brilliant exploratory operation on the German psyche," and called it, "almost painfully fair-minded."

After the publication of *The Other Germany,* Mann chose to direct her time and energy to journalism. In 1940, she was in London reporting on the Blitz. Over the next several years, she would report the war from the battlefields of North Africa, France, and eventually Germany itself. Her articles appeared in a wide variety of newspapers and periodicals, including London's *Evening Standard*, the *Toronto Star Weekly*, the *New York Herald Tribune*, the *Chicago Daily News*, *Vogue*, and New York City's *Aufbau*, a weekly newspaper published by German-Jewish refugees. Although Mann characterized herself during these years as "a militant liberal with a social conscience," her journalism betrays no rigid ideological position. Most of her reportage was in fact highly personal rather than theoretical in nature. By the end of the war, her fiercely independent spirit had served to alienate and antagonize both left and right sides of the political spectrum. Conservatives often regarded her as a dupe of the Communists, while those identified with the socialist left were increasingly annoyed by her hard-line attitude toward the treatment that should be meted out to defeated Germany. Convinced that the great majority of Germans, young and old, had become morally polluted by 12 years of Nazi rule, Mann believed that only a systematic reeducation program led by the victorious Allies (with but few exceptions, American, British and Allied teachers should staff German schools and universities) could restore Germany to the community of civilized nations. These and similar opinions made Mann a highly controversial and unpopular person in German emigré circles during and immediately after the war.

By 1945, Mann felt the emotional strain and psychological stress her years of exile had caused. The onset of the Cold War prompted her increased disillusionment with the foreign policy of her adopted homeland: American willingness, indeed eagerness, to embrace former Nazi and fascist enemies as new allies in the struggle against Communism appalled the woman who had volunteered during the war to assist the FBI in its battle against Nazis, as it did her brother Klaus, their father Thomas and uncle Heinrich. The year 1949 was a tragic one for the entire Mann family. No longer able to envision a way out of his despair, in May Klaus committed suicide in Cannes, France, by taking an overdose of sleeping pills. Thomas Mann's decision to visit both East and West Germany to commemorate the bicentennial of the birth of Goethe was interpreted by the American media as a sign of his—and his family's—"softness" on Communism. By 1950, Erika Mann shared many of the feelings that her brother suffered just before his suicide, namely those of being estranged from both one's native and adopted countries. In the newly created West Ger-

man Federal Republic, writers and intellectuals who had prospered under the Nazi regime once again enjoyed public favor and professional success, while exiled intellectuals like the entire Mann family found themselves to be distinctly *personae non gratae*, reviled and unwelcome.

From Erika's perspective, it was a tragedy of modern times that both of her homelands, Germany and the United States, had become distorted societies because of their paranoid fear of Communism, a phenomenon that was often much too broadly defined. With "multiple deracination" having taken a considerable toll of her energies, she uprooted herself from a country she had once loved and accompanied her aging father to Switzerland. There, she helped him to organize his vast personal archives and assisted in the preparation of his literary legacy for posterity. She would later note in a 1965 interview, "As of 1950 I was . . . finished, exhausted. . . . To begin over for a fourth time, with the probability that this too would soon be terminated, was a choice that I simply couldn't make, and that is the sad truth."

After her father's death in 1955, Mann wrote a book about his final years which received excellent reviews from most quarters. She also edited a collection of his letters which continues to be of value to both scholars and general readers. Erika Mann lived long enough to witness the onset of a new and intellectually more self-critical spirit in what had been a morally complacent West Germany. With the end of the chancellorship of Konrad Adenauer in 1963, a new generation began to enter the country's public life. The suicide of her ex-husband Gustaf Gründgens in October 1963 raised once again the issue of his—and many others'—collaboration with the Nazi regime, a human failing which had been brilliantly probed decades earlier in Klaus Mann's novel *Mephisto*, the protagonist of which is a thinly disguised Gründgens. Erika Mann did not live to see the vibrant and morally engaged West Germany that emerged in the early 1970s. She died, still an exile, in Zurich, Switzerland, on August 27, 1969.

SOURCES:

Der deutsche PEN-Club im Exil 1933–1948: Eine Ausstellung der Deutschen Bibliothek Frankfurt am Main. Frankfurt am Main: Buchhändler-Vereinigung GmbH, 1980.

Frisch, Shelley. "'Alien Homeland': Erika Mann and the Adenauer Era," in *The Germanic Review*. Vol. 63, no. 4. Fall 1988, pp. 172–182.

———. "'Die Pfeffermühle': Political Dimensions of a Literary Cabaret," in Alexander Stephan, ed., *Exil-Literatur und Künste nach 1933*. Bonn: Bouvier Verlag, 1990, pp. 141–153.

Hildebrandt, Irma. *Die Frauenzimmer kommen: 16 Zürcher Portraits.* 2nd rev. ed. Munich: Eugen Diederichs Verlag, 1997.

Jelavich, Peter. *Berlin Cabaret.* Cambridge, MA: Harvard University Press, 1996.

Keiser-Hayne, Helga. *Erika Mann und ihr politisches Kabarett die "Pfeffermühle," 1933–1937: Texte, Bilder, Hintergründe.* Rev. ed. Reinbek bei Hamburg: Rowohlt Verlag, 1995.

Kieser, Rolf. "Die Legende von der Pfeffermühle," in Helmut F. Pfanner, ed., *Der Zweite Weltkrieg und die Exilanten: Eine literarische Antwort/World War II and the Allies: A Literary Response.* Bonn: Bouvier Verlag, 1991, pp. 23–36.

Kolbe, Jürgen, and Karl Heinz Bittel. *Heller Zauber: Thomas Mann in München 1894–1933.* 2nd ed. Berlin: Wolf Jobst Siedler Verlag GmbH, 1987.

Lenschen-Ramos, Claudia. "'Aus der Fremde die Heimat beschreiben': Erika Mann und Vicki Baum im amerikanischen Exil," in Ernest W. W. Hess-Luttich, Christoph Siegrist and Stefan Bodo Wurffel, eds., *Fremdverstehen in Sprache, Literatur und Medien.* Frankfurt am Main: Peter Lang Verlag, 1996, pp. 209–223.

Lühe, Irmela von der. *Erika Mann: Eine Biographie.* Rev. ed. Frankfurt am Main: Fischer-Taschenbuch Verlag, 1997.

———. "Erika Mann (1905–1969)," in John M. Spalek, Konrad Feilchenfeldt and Sandra H. Hawrylchak, eds., *Deutschsprachige Exilliteratur seit 1933, Band 4: Bibliographien–Schriftsteller, Publizisten und Literaturwissenschaftler in den USA.* 2 vols., Bern: K.G. Saur Verlag, 1994, Vol. 2, pp. 1191–1199.

Mann, Erika. *Briefe und Antworten.* Edited by Anna Zanco Prestel. 2 vols. Munich: Deutscher Taschenbuch Verlag, 1988.

———. "Don't Make the Same Mistakes," in Stephen Vincent Benet *et al.*, *Zero Hour: A Summons to the Free.* NY: Farrar & Rinehart, 1940, pp. 11–76.

———. *The Lights Go Down.* Translated by Maurice Samuel. NY: Farrar & Rinehart, 1940.

———. *Mein Vater, der Zauberer.* Edited by Irmela von der Lühe and Uwe Naumann. Reinbek bei Hamburg: Rowohlt Verlag, 1996.

———. *School for Barbarians: Education under the Nazis.* NY: Modern Age Books, 1938.

———. "Who Has the Youth Has the Future," in *Proceedings of the 46th Annual Meeting of the National Congress of Parents and Teachers.* Washington, DC: National Congress of Parents and Teachers, 1942, pp. 56–64.

——— and Klaus Mann. *Das Buch von der Riviera.* Leipzig: Connewitzer Verlag, 1997.

——— and Klaus Mann. *Escape to Life.* Boston, MA: Houghton Mifflin, 1939.

——— and Klaus Mann. *The Other Germany.* Translated by Heinz Norden. NY: Modern Age Books, 1940.

——— and Klaus Mann. *Rundherum: Abenteuer einer Weltreise. Nachwort von Uwe Naumann.* Reinbek bei Hamburg: Rowohlt Taschenbuch Verlag, 1999.

Mann, Klaus. *Der Vulkan: Roman unter Emigraten.* Amsterdam: Querido Verlag, 1939.

Porterfield, Allen W. "Thomas Mann's Son and Daughter Write About the German Exiles," in *New York Sun.* April 20, 1939, p. 11.

Prater, Donald. *Thomas Mann: A Life.* NY: Oxford University Press, 1995.

Stephan, Alexander. "Die Akte Erika Mann: '. . . a liaison which might be of possible value'," in *Neue Deutsche Literatur: Zeitschrift für deutschsprachige Literatur und Kritik.* Vol. 41, no. 487. July 1993, pp. 124–142.

———. *Im Visier des FBI: Deutsche Exilschriftsteller in den Akten amerikanischer Geheimdienste.* Stuttgart: Metzler Verlag, 1995.

———. "Überwacht und ausgebürgert: Klaus Mann und Erika Mann in den Akten des Dritten Reiches," in *German Life and Letters.* Vol. 551, no. 2. April 1998, pp. 185–203.

Wysling, Hans. ". . . eine fast tötliche Bereitschaft," in *Schweizer Monatshefte.* Vol. 63, no. 7–8, 1983, pp. 615–631.

——— and Yvonne Schmidlin, eds. *Thomas Mann: Ein Leben in Bildern.* Zurich: Artemis & Winkler Verlag, 1994.

COLLECTIONS:

Erika Mann Archives, Handschriftenabteilung der Stadtbibliothek München, Munich, Germany.

RELATED MEDIA:

"I Bear the Scars of Our Time: Erika Mann, A Portrait" (video), Bonn: Inter Nationes, 1984.

John Haag,
Associate Professor of History,
University of Georgia, Athens, Georgia

Mann, Harriet (1831–1918).

See Miller, Olive Thorne.

Mann, Mary Peabody (1806–1887)

*American educator. Born Mary Tyler Peabody in Cambridgeport, Massachusetts, on November 16, 1806; died on February 11, 1887; daughter of Nathaniel and Elizabeth Palmer Peabody (1778–1853); sister of *Sophia Peabody Hawthorne (1809–1871) and Elizabeth Palmer Peabody (1804–1894); aunt of *Rose Hawthorne Lathrop (1851–1926); married Horace Mann, in 1843 (died 1859); children: Horace Mann, Jr. (b. 1844); George Combe Mann (b. 1845); Benjamin Pickman Mann (b. 1848).*

One of the notable Peabody sisters, Mary Peabody replaced her sister *Elizabeth Palmer Peabody** in a teaching position in Maine, then joined Elizabeth to open a dame school in Boston the following year. While there, Mary met Horace Mann and began to assist him with his educational research. The two were married in 1843. After the marriage, wrote **Louise Hall Tharp** in *The Peabody Sisters of Salem,* Mary came into her own. "Elizabeth had always assumed leadership; life had been made easy for Sophia, the youngest, the prettiest—the gifted daughter. Mary had been the forgotten middle sister to whom everyone turned for help or sympathy and then promptly forgot." The Manns moved to Antioch College in Ohio, when Horace Mann was appointed the school's president in 1853. Following his death, Mary rejoined her sister Elizabeth in Boston and helped promote the new kindergarten movement in 1859. Having dabbled with poetry throughout much of her life, Mary wrote her first novel at age 80.

SOURCES:
Edgerly, Lois Stiles, *Give Her This Day.* Gardiner, ME: Tilbury House, 1990.
Tharp, Louise Hall. *The Peabody Sisters of Salem.* Boston, MA: Little, Brown, 1950.

Mann, Shelley (1937—)

American swimmer. Born in Virginia on October 15, 1937.

Shelley Mann was born in Virginia in 1937; six years later, she was crippled by polio. Doctors prescribed swimming as therapy to regain strength in her arms and legs, and, at 12, she began to train for competition at the Walter Reed Swim Club in Washington, D.C. By 14, she was the U.S. national champion. Mann would be the first woman to win the gold medal in the 100-meter butterfly in Olympic swimming with a time of 1:11.0. When the inaugural event was held in Melbourne, Australia, in 1956, the Americans swept the field: Mann first, **Nancy Ramey** second, and **Mary Sears** third. The world record holder, **Aartje Voorbij**, had not competed because of the Dutch boycott of the Games. Mann also went home with a silver medal in the 4x100-meter freestyle relay. She held records in backstroke, freestyle, individual medley, and butterfly, and was inducted into the Swimming and Diving Hall of Fame in 1966.

Manner, Eeva-Liisa (1921–1995)

Finnish poet, playwright, novelist, and translator who was a leading figure in the modernist movement that changed the literary landscape of Finland in the 1950s. Name variations: (pseudonym) Anna September. Born in Helsinki, Finland, on December 5, 1921; died in Helsinki in January 1995; daughter of Leo Johannes Manner and Elsi Irene Kukkonen Manner; never married.

Born in the early years of Finland's independence from Russia, Eeva-Liisa Manner grew up in a middle-class family with a father who worked as an editor. Her formal education ended with junior high school. During the traumatic wartime years of 1940 through 1944—when Finland, an ally of Nazi Germany, twice went to war with the Soviet Union—she worked for an insurance company. Manner then worked for a publishing firm (1944–46) before turning to writing and translating to support herself. A precocious author, she had begun publishing collections of poems and short stories in 1944; by 1951, she had released three such volumes, all to respectful but fairly subdued critical responses. Of these books, the 1949 *Kuin tuuli tai pilvi* (Like the Wind or the Cloud) provided the most clues to the writer's potential talent. Shy and retiring, the unmarried Manner was often in fragile health and shunned publicity, choosing to live not in intrigue-ridden Helsinki, the political and cultural center of Finland, but in the nation's second city, the much more serene Tampere.

In 1956, with the publication of her verse collection *Tämä matka* (This Journey), Manner's writings finally received wide recognition in Finland. Emphasizing a rejection of strict form, as well as an elaborately structured, freely associative Imagism, the poems in this book were declarations of independence from traditionalism in Finnish poetry. Her bold modernist assertions brought free verse and new metaphors to a national poetic tradition that was ready for revitalizing. With this book, Manner literally changed the course of Finnish literary evolution. By 1964, *Tämä matka* had appeared in five editions, several of which contained modifications by the author. By the early 1960s, the influence of the poems was clearly evident in much of the verse being written by the younger generation of Finnish poets.

Like many European intellectuals of her generation, Manner rejected the school of thought based on reason and science which had dominated Western culture since the 17th century. In addition to regarding this system as having led to all manner of catastrophe—social, political, and moral—in the modern era, Manner also believed that sterile intellectualism had demystified the universe by stripping it of all magical and metaphysical meaning. In *Tämä matka*, she pokes fun at two of the founding fathers of modern thought, Descartes and Spinoza. Her Descartes declares that "philosophy is loneliness and loneliness is cold, and a dead body, which copulates with reason"; and Spinoza the apostate Jew offers to God his lenses, equated with philosophy, only to discover that they all give wrong refractions, and concludes: "I am agreeable now/ when I bring pain, solitude,/ without/ the written ignorance." Manner did not, however, entirely reject the tools provided by reason, asserting in her 1957 essay "Moderni runo" (Modern Poetry) that for a reader to truly grasp new forms of poetry "requires that the reader's . . . reason participate in the movement of the poem."

In her poem "Strontium," from the 1960 collection *Orfiset laulut* (Orphic Songs), she spoke for the millions who had become convinced that the nuclear age was not the start of a new Utopia but rather the creation of the distinct possibility of a global annihilation: "strange smokes are rising / invisible ashes are raining / bartering death. / For they, the Skilled Ones, / are almost destroying the whole world / although it is half dream."

Manner regarded the poet's mission as a unique one of acquiring and transmitting a wisdom that transcended knowledge. She was influenced by the more mystical of the ancient Greek philosophers, by Chinese mystical traditions, particularly Taoism, and by aspects of non-rational approaches to ultimate truth including astrology. Also inspired by music, Manner modeled many of her poems on musical forms and attempted to discover the polyphonic structures that organize the universe. Among those composers whom she found to most affect her creativity were Bach, Haydn, Mozart, and Webern. On more than one occasion, Manner stated her belief that the music of Bach had provided the key to the clarity and logic of modern poetic expression.

Manner's rejection of Christianity was indicated in many of her works. Making little or no distinction between the belief systems originating in the Old and New Testaments, she saw Christianity's vast body of ideas as inevitably responsible for legislating an intolerantly puritanical world which was incapable of seeing beauty in the earth's natural energies. In a well-known poem on childhood, she speaks of the grandmother who, when displeased that an organ-grinder had created a pretty tune in the courtyard, would take out her psalm book and start singing a harsh and "broken song." In her 1951 novel *Tyttö taivaan laiturilla* (The Girl on the Pier of Heaven), she defined all religions as being cold and hostile systems of human intellect, part of the "logical disorder" that she saw as continually at war with the infinitely more preferable system of "magical order." The latter, thought Manner, had the potential to empower us with the ability to better understand, and function within, our universe.

Called "the quiet Cassandra of Finnish poetry" by Philip Binham, Manner could not escape the conclusion that humanity was essentially a destructive force in the world. Contemporary events were alluded to in some of her works, including the 1968 Soviet bloc invasion of Czechoslovakia as well as the presence of grinding poverty and social injustice in Spain, where she lived for part of each year. But her most intense and concentrated writing in the final decades of her life can be found in her verse, which continued to examine the human need to seek an answer as to whether or not our existence had a meaning.

In addition to writing poetry which is becoming increasingly known worldwide through translations, Manner was a novelist, playwright, and translator of distinction. Her 1972 novel *Varokaa, voittajat* (Beware, Victors) has been described as "a significant analysis of violence." Set in an unspecified southern nation, it begins with a political assassination and depicts a world of oppression where the menacing presence of the poor is juxtaposed with obscene displays of wealth by the rich. Although they are not likely to attract mass audiences, Manner's plays are also distinguished. Her 1959 verse drama *Eros ja Psykhe* (Eros and Psyche) is a blend of lyrical and dream elements, while her 1965 play *Uuden vuoden yö* (New Year's Eve) is a spiky drama that bears a considerable resemblance to *Who's Afraid of Virginia Woolf?*, although Manner did not know of Albee's work at the time she wrote it. In both *Toukokuun lumi* (Snow in May, 1966) and *Poltettu oranssi* (Burnt-Out Ocher, 1968), Manner created poetic dramas that explored the psychological essences of very young women. Manner also provided the Finnish reading public with a large number of highly praised translations from the works of foreign authors including Shakespeare, Ben Jonson, Hermann Hesse, Georg Büchner, Edward Albee and Patrick White, as well as the works of several contemporary Japanese and Spanish authors.

As a sensitive writer who struggled not only with the perennial problems of her craft but also with the burden of being human in an age of cruelty and destruction, Manner had a largely pessimistic outlook. In the long philosophical poem that ends her 1968 book *Fahrenheit 121*, she speaks of a world "made as it is of fog and rust," expressing a despair which can also be found in her play *Burnt-Out Ocher*. Yet, in some of her later works, Manner gave indications that her pessimism was not an all-enveloping despair. In *Kamala kissa* (A Horrible Cat, 1976) and *Kauhukakara ja Superkissa* (Little Terror and Supercat, 1982), she found whimsical humor in a mirror world where cats play the roles of people (as did the equally austere T.S. Eliot from whose famous collection *Old Possum's Book of Practical Cats* Manner got the idea for some of her cat poems). These two books make a collection of international cat portraits and political satires, as well as of metaphysical and mystical cat aphorisms. One of the most memorable characters is the cat painter "Salve Dali," a wonderful portrait of the exuberant Spanish painter. In 1980, a wide selection of her poems from the years 1956 through 1977 appeared in print and was hailed by critics. Manner was the recipient of numerous Finnish literary awards, including the Michael Agricola Prize and the Alexis Kivi Prize. Universally respected by Finns, she died in Helsinki in January 1995.

SOURCES:

Ahokas, Jaako A. "Eeva-Liisa Manner: Dropping from Reality into Life," in *Books Abroad*. Vol. 47, no. 1. Winter 1973, pp. 60–65.

———. "Manner, Eeva-Liisa," in Virpi Zuck, *et al.*, eds. *Dictionary of Scandinavian Literature*. CT: Greenwood Press, 1990, pp. 400–402.

Binham, Philip. "Protest and After in the Finnish Theater," in *World Literature Today*. Vol. 54, no. 1. Winter 1980, pp. 58–61.

Bosley, Keith, ed. and trans. *Skating on the Sea: Poetry from Finland*. Newcastle upon Tyne: Bloodaxe Books, 1997.

Branch, Michael. "Manner, Eeva-Liisa," in Robert B. Pynsent and S.I. Kanikova, eds., *Reader's Encyclopedia of Eastern European Literature*. NY: HarperCollins, 1993, p. 249.

Dauenhauer, Richard, and Philip Binham, eds. *Snow in May: An Anthology of Finnish Writing 1945–1972*. Rutherford, NJ: Fairleigh Dickinson University Press, 1978.

Laitinen, Kai, ed. *Modern Nordic Plays: Finland*. NY: Twayne Publishers, 1973.

Lomas, Herbert, ed. *Contemporary Finnish Poetry*. Newcastle upon Tyne: Bloodaxe Books, 1991.

Manner, Eeva-Liisa. *Die Welt ist eine Dichtung meiner Sinne*. Translated by Ingrid Schellbach-Kopra and Stefan Moster. Eisingen: H. Heiderhoff, 1996.

———. *Selected Poems*. Translated by Herbert Lomas. Guildford, Surrey: Making Waves, 1997.

Niemi, Irmeli. "Finland: Women in the Limelight," in *The UNESCO Courier*. Vol. 36, no. 4. April 1983, pp. 36–37.

———. "Modern Women Playwrights in Finland," in *World Literature Today*. Vol. 54, no. 1. Winter 1980, pp. 54–58.

Partnow, Eaine T., and Lesley Anne Hyatt. *The Female Dramatist: Profiles of Women Playwrights from the Middle Ages to Contemporary Times*. NY: Facts on File, 1998.

Tuohimaa, Sinikka. "The Poetry of Eeva-Liisa Manner: Unveiling Reflections of Life," in *World Literature Today*. Vol. 61, no. 1. Winter 1987, pp. 37–40.

John Haag,
Associate Professor of History,
University of Georgia, Athens, Georgia

Manners, Lady Diana (1892–1986).

See Bagnold, Enid for sidebar on Cooper, Diana Duff.

Mannes, Clara Damrosch
(1869–1948)

American pianist and educator who co-founded the Mannes College of Music. Born on December 12, 1869, in Breslau, Prussia (now Wroclaw, Poland); died on March 16, 1948, in New York City; daughter of Leopold Damrosch (a musician and musical conductor) and Helene (von Heimburg) Damrosch; sister of Walter Damrosch (1862–1950) and Frank Damrosch (1859–1937), both musical directors; attended private schools in New York City, to which her family moved in 1871; began study of piano at the age of six; continued her musical studies in Dresden, Germany, during 1888 and 1889; married David Mannes (a violinist), in June 1898 (died 1959); children: Leopold Mannes; Maria von Heimburg Mannes (1904–1990), known as *Marya Mannes.

Best known as co-founder with her husband of New York's David Mannes Music School (now the Mannes College of Music), where she served as co-director until her death in 1948.

Clara Damrosch was born in Breslau, Prussia, on December 12, 1869. Two years later, her family moved to New York City, where her father Leopold Damrosch, a musician, played a key role in promoting music appreciation in the New York area. While attending private schools in New York, Clara began taking piano lessons at the age of six. From 1888 to 1889, she returned to Europe where she continued her musical studies in Dresden, Germany. Upon her return to New York, she began giving private music lessons. In addition to her continued work on the piano, she sang occasionally with the New York Oratorio Society, which had been founded by her father. While singing for the Society, she met violinist David Mannes, a member of the New York Symphony Orchestra, which also had been founded by her father.

David and Clara became engaged in 1897, while both were pursuing their music studies in Germany, and married in June 1898. For the first years of their marriage, the two musicians had separate careers. In 1901, however, they began performing together in public as a violin and piano sonata duo. Two years later, after studying with Eugene Ysaÿe in Belgium, the couple performed a series of sonata recitals that received both critical and popular acclaim. In addition to their concert schedule, they taught music at the Music School Settlement at East Third Street on the Lower East Side of Manhattan. David Mannes served as director. He was

Marya
Mannes

also concertmaster of the New York Symphony Orchestra, which was conducted by Walter Damrosch, Clara's brother. Clara and David's concert appearances took the couple all over the United States and to the United Kingdom in 1913. Clara also made occasional appearances as an accompanist to such popular artists as Pablo Casals and the Kneisel Quartet. The Manneses continued their joint concert appearances around the country until 1917, introducing both classic and contemporary sonata literature to many corners of the country previously unfamiliar with it.

As their careers in professional music matured, the Manneses began to feel the need to create a school of music to shape the musical growth of others. In the fall of 1916, they founded the David Mannes Music School on East 70th Street in Manhattan, which soon outgrew its original facility. In 1919, three contiguous brownstone apartment houses on East 74th were acquired and converted into new quarters for the school. The college moved to its present location on West 85th Street in 1984. Granted a provisional charter from the University of the State of New York in 1933, in 1934 it was incorporated as a tax-exempt, nonprofit institution, administered by a board of trustees with Clara and David as co-directors. It is now a division of the New School.

After the end of her concert career, Clara devoted most of her time and energy to her responsibilities as co-director of the music school. Both she and her husband were decorated in 1926 by the French government for their contributions to music education. Together, they edited with Louis Untermeyer a collection of songs for children entitled *New Songs for New Voices*. Clara Mannes died in New York City on March 16, 1948, age 78.

SOURCES:
McHenry, Robert, ed. *Famous American Women.* NY: Dover, 1980.

Don Amerman,
freelance writer, Saylorsburg, Pennsylvania

Mannes, Marya (1904–1990)

American writer and social commentator. Name variations: Marya Mannes Blow; (pseudonym) Sec. Born Maria von Heimburg Mannes on November 14, 1904, in New York City; died on September 13, 1990, in San Francisco, California; daughter of David Mannes (a violinist and co-founder of the Mannes College of Music) and Clara Damrosch Mannes (1869–1948, a pianist and co-founder of the Mannes College of Music); married Jo Mielziner (a theatrical designer), in 1926 (divorced 1931); married Richard Blow (an artist), in 1937 (divorced 1943); married Christopher Clarkson, in 1948 (divorced 1966); children: (second marriage) David Jeremy Blow.

Selected writings: (novel) Message from a Stranger (1948); (essays) More in Anger (1958); (poetry) Subverse (1959); (essays) The New York I Know (1961); But Will It Sell? (1964); (novel) They (1968); (autobiography) Out of My Time (1971); Last Rights (1974).

Marya Mannes achieved renown in the 1940s and 1950s as a writer on a variety of political and cultural matters, but may be best remembered for her incisive portrait of the postwar American psyche. She was born in New York City in 1904, to parents who were both accomplished musicians. *Clara Damrosch Mannes was a pianist, and David Mannes was a violinist; they frequently performed together, and, in 1916, would found the Mannes College of Music. Marya Mannes studied Latin, French, and drama at Miss Veltin's School for Girls and accompanied her parents on their trips to Europe. She spent a year abroad at the age of 18 and upon returning to New York began to audition for the stage, before realizing that she was probably too tall (nearly six feet) to achieve success.

She began writing reviews and articles in the 1920s that appeared in *Theater Arts, International Studio,* and *Harper's,* and was married to the Broadway scenic designer Jo Mielziner from 1926 to 1931. In 1933, she was hired as features editor at *Vogue* magazine, a job she quit a few years later when she moved to Florence, Italy, to live with her second husband, artist Richard Blow. During World War II, Mannes worked for the U.S. government in the Office of Strategic Service, the forerunner of the Central Intelligence Agency, and also wrote a series of articles about Spain and Portugal, both of which had supposedly neutral status in the conflict but exhibited clear pro-Fascist sympathies. The articles were published in *The New Yorker*, which also sent her to Jerusalem in 1946, to cover the flood of Jewish refugees from the Holocaust.

Mannes then returned to America and the women's magazine field, and was associated with *Glamour* for several years. Her first book, *Message from a Stranger*, was published in 1948. The novel centers around a poet who, after dying, gets a chance to return to earth and learn what her friends really thought of her. In 1952, she began to write pieces for *The Reporter* under the pen name "Sec." The word is French for "dry," and the erudite Mannes may have thought it an appropriate byline for her articles. Many of these evolved into her 1958 collection of essays, *More in Anger*. She once stated that she wrote to "communicate clearly and honestly what I see and what I believe about the world I live in"; the book's views on modern life in America, and her not-always-complimentary takes on American culture and mores, attracted no small amount of indignant attention.

Mannes won the George Polk Memorial Award for magazine criticism in 1958 and the following year published a collection of satirical poetry. *Subverse* was described as "alarmingly funny" by one critic, who went on to note that "[a] gay and diverting subject is introduced . . . and starts on its merry way and in the second stanza the reader is hit in the stomach." In addition to writing, Mannes worked as a television and radio commentator throughout the 1960s and 1970s, beginning with a stint as host of the television program "I Speak for Myself" in 1959. She freelanced after 1963 and wrote columns for both *McCall's* and *The New York Times*. Her autobiography, *Out of My Time*, appeared in 1971. After suffering a series of strokes, Marya Mannes died in San Francisco on September 13, 1990.

SOURCES:

Contemporary Authors, Vol. 132. Detroit, MI: Gale Research, 1991.

Current Biography. NY: H.W. Wilson, 1959.

Foremost Women in Communications. New York, NY: Foremost Americans Publishing, 1970.

McHenry, Robert, ed. *Famous American Women.* NY: Dover, 1980.

———. *Liberty's Women.* Springfield, MA: G.&C. Merriam, 1980.

Carol Brennan,
Grosse Pointe, Michigan

Mannin, Ethel (1900–1984)

British author and political activist whose many novels, travel books, and works of autobiography were enthusiastically awaited by a loyal readership for more than half a century. Born Ethel Edith Mannin in Clapham, London, England, on October 11, 1900; died in Devon, England, on December 5, 1984; daughter of Robert Mannin and Edith Gray Mannin; married J.A. Porteous, in 1919; married Reginald Reynolds, in 1938; children: (first marriage) daughter, Jean Porteous.

A largely self-educated woman and lifelong political maverick, Ethel Mannin was a pacifist, an anarchist, and an ardent supporter of the Palestinian cause. She published her first novel in 1922 and went on to publish 94 additional books, including numerous novels as well as travel reports that in many instances also served as political tracts. Her 1941 novel *Red Rose* was one of the first works of fiction about *Emma Goldman and is still considered one of the most interesting.

Born in a London suburb in 1900, Mannin was the daughter of a Post Office employee and grew up in the confining working-class world of Edwardian England. In her 1952 book *This Was a Man*, a work about her father which Mannin considered to be her finest book, she recalled the circumstances of her childhood: "even though other girls' fathers might be 'better off' and go to something called 'business,' whereas my own father merely went to 'work', we were really much superior as a family because of our rows of books." Ethel did not do well at school and regarded herself as physically ugly, deficiencies for which she compensated by becoming a proficient writer. "When I was writing I became someone," she wrote in *Privileged Spectator* (1939). "I was transformed, power was in me, the power of words . . . always this preoccupation with the written word, since I was seven years old."

Both of Ethel's parents opposed her ambitions of becoming a writer, believing that this was a guarantee of poverty. Instead, they hoped she might find employment with the Civil Service or security as a clerk in the Post Office. At age 14, she ended her formal education. Her parents breathed a guarded sigh of relief when, after taking some commercial courses, she found her first job as a stenographer in the Charles

Higham advertising agency. Mannin's work there soon shifted from stenography to assisting in the production of several trade publications. Before long, Charles Higham spotted her journalistic talents, and, although Mannin was only 17, he put her in charge of producing *The Pelican*, a theatrical newspaper he had recently acquired. In 1919, Mannin married J.A. Porteous and had a daughter named Jean.

In 1922, Mannin published her first novel, *Martha*, which neither she nor the reading public found particularly satisfactory. With her third novel, however, Mannin found her own voice as a writer. Entitled *Sounding Brass* (1924), this work is a biting satire of the advertising world and its values (or lack of them). Both a commercial and critical success, *Sounding Brass* was reviewed in the *Saturday Review*, with L.P. Hartley comparing it favorably with Aldous Huxley's novel *Antic Hay*, while across the Atlantic American reviewers made complimentary comparisons of Mannin's prose to that of Sinclair Lewis. Over the next decades, Mannin would write and publish at a furious pace, producing 30 novels by 1952. The goal she set for herself early in her career of writing two books a year, one fiction and one nonfiction, was rarely missed.

Motherhood brought forth an interest in various facets of education and child-rearing, subjects about which she developed strong opinions and dealt with in several books. Her politics and views on schooling were progressive, and the ideas of A.S. Neill, the radical advocate of child-centered education, are reflected in her books *Commonsense and the Child* (1931) and *Commonsense and the Adolescent* (1937). Mannin had equally unambiguous opinions on the great social and political controversies of the day. All of her books are in one way or another manifestations of her sympathy for the underdog, particularly the working classes. The various crises of the 1930s only served to heighten her sense of social justice. During these years, she joined the Independent Labour Party, which advocated taking a strong position against the growing threat of Fascism abroad and a more militant position in favor of domestic social change.

In 1930, Mannin published her first work of nonfiction, *Confessions and Impressions*, which reveals a desire to relate to the famous women and men of the period; some critics have detected in the book a basic insecurity in the author's personality, likely rooted in her working-class childhood and upbringing. Mannin traveled to the Soviet Union in 1936, a visit she recorded in *South to Samarkand*, and the sharply critical observations of the Stalinist regime included in the work made her very unpopular in British Marxist and pro-USSR circles. Her first marriage having ended, in 1938 she married the Quaker pacifist writer Reginald Reynolds. He resigned from the Independent Labour Party (1939) over the issue of British policies toward the Arab population of British-occupied Palestine, and she soon followed suit. During the next decades, Mannin would become deeply involved with issues relating to the rights of the Palestinian Arabs, eventually emerging as one of the most vocal and eloquent defenders of Palestinians at a time when most British intellectuals championed the Zionist-led cause of the Jewish population of Palestine.

During the Spanish Civil War of 1936–1939, Mannin helped American anarchist veteran Emma Goldman organize meetings in London to create public support for Spain's anarcho-syndicalist factions as well as to make possible meaningful British military assistance to the beleaguered Spanish Republic. She would draw an essentially sympathetic portrait of Goldman in her 1941 novel *Red Rose* (her second husband Reginald, however, was less impressed by Goldman's personality, finding her to be aggressive, dictatorial, and downright ungracious in temperament). The novel, which centered on the triangular relationship between Goldman, her lover Alexander Berkman, and Berkman's inamorata **Emmy Eckstein**, remains an important source on Goldman's life and personality. *Red Rose* has been described as the earliest attempt to reproduce and "complete" Goldman's own autobiographical opus, *Living My Life*. By the end of the decade, Mannin had undergone a political metamorphosis, moving away from Leftism, toward pacifism, philosophical anarchism, and defense of the rights of women and other disenfranchised groups in society. Publication of her *Privileged Spectator* in 1939 was evidence that her perspective had matured. Ending what she called "the bitter, dangerous 1930s" with a better understanding of politics, society and literature, Mannin had far more respect for her working-class friends and acquaintances, whom she saw as "good comrades of the class struggle," than for the "suede-shoed communists with Oxford accents and about as much knowledge of working class life and problems as they have of the word 'Left.'"

Although she continued to write novels until the final years of her long life, from the late 1930s more of Mannin's energy went into various nonfiction projects. In her 1938 volume *Women and the Revolution*, she made a vigorous case for full equality for women, at the same presenting a powerful attack on the entrenched prejudices and social inertia of the existing capitalist society.

In the mid-1940s, Mannin had a brief but intense attraction to the theology and rituals of the Roman Catholic Church. Eventually, she would decide to remain an atheist, but the depth of her exploration at this time was attested to by her 1948 novel *Late Have I Loved Thee*. With a title taken from the *Confessions* of St. Augustine, this realistic account of the saint's search for the divine force in the universe seems to parallel Mannin's own spiritual quest as she entered middle age. In the years after 1945, Mannin traveled around the globe for material for new books. She first spent time in Ireland, which made possible the writing of *Connemara Journal* (1947). A stay in war-ravaged occupied Germany resulted in *German Journey* (1948), while a number of other books were based on visits to Brittany, Egypt, Iraq, Japan, Jordan, Morocco, and Sweden. Although her trips were usually brief, Mannin's sharp powers of observation often resulted in considerable insights in her travel books. Some of these insights also found their way into her fiction, as was the case in her 1956 novel *The Living Lotus*. Set in rural upper Burma (now Myanmar), the book has been described as a realistic work with not only entertainment value but also information about the Burmese.

During the last two decades of her writing career, Mannin's time was consumed by her involvement in the cause of the Palestinian people. Believing that the Arab cause was essentially a just one, she felt that as such it deserved to be properly presented to the Western public. Her 1963 novel *The Road to Beersheba* was expressly written as an "answer" to *Exodus*, the immensely popular novel by Leon Uris. Mannin's 1966 novel *The Night and Its Homing*, a work about the Palestinian resistance movement, continued her advocacy of what was often a lonely and unpopular cause outside of the Arab world. Both of these books were translated into Arabic, and her work was praised in the media of several Arab nations. Mannin established friendships with Palestinians and other Arabs, and she believed that her writings on behalf of their national cause could contribute to a better understanding between the Arab world and the West. This commitment is perhaps most discernible in her 1963 volume *A Lance for the Arabs: A Middle East Journey*.

As an artist involved in contemporary controversies, Mannin sometimes walked a fine line between reality, fiction, and the "smoke and mirrors" of politics. This was particularly true in her relationship with General Abdel Karim Qassim, the Iraqi leader who had invited her to visit his country but who fell victim to an assassination plot in 1963. Mannin's 1969 novel *The Midnight Street* deals graphically with Qassim's bloody demise. Mannin had once noted that she could not help but be a part of her own books: "We are [shaped] by what we have experienced."

Mannin continued to live in her beloved home of Oak Cottage, Wimbledon, after the 1958 death of her husband. At the end of her writing career, when she was in her 70s, she moved to Teignmouth in Devon to be near her daughter Jean. In 1976, Mannin published her last novel, *The Late Miss Guthrie*. The next year, she published her final book, a fifth and last volume of autobiography, *Sunset over Dartmoor: A Final Chapter of Autobiography* (1977). In this work, she addressed her many loyal readers as old friends and demonstrated the charm that had kept them faithful to her even when in some instances her opinions were by no means palatable to every reader. She died of the infirmities of old age in Devon on December 5, 1984.

SOURCES:

"Ethel Mannin," in Margot Levy, ed. *The Annual Obituary 1984*. Chicago, IL: St. James Press, 1985, pp. 643–645.

Frankel, Oz. "Whatever Happened to 'Red Emma'? Emma Goldman, from Alien Rebel to American Icon," in *The Journal of American History*. Vol. 83, no. 3. December 1996, pp. 903–942.

Hartley, Jenny. *Hearts Undefeated: Women's Writing of the Second World War*. London: Virago, 1995.

Huxter, Robert. *Reg and Ethel: Reginald Reynolds (1905–1958), His Life and Work and His Marriage to Ethel Mannin (1900–1984)*. York, England: Sessions Book Trust, 1992.

Mannin, Ethel. *Confessions and Impressions*. Rev. ed. London: Penguin Books, 1936.

———. *The Living Lotus*. NY: Putnam, 1956.

———. *Young in the Twenties*. London: Hutchinson, 1971.

O'Rourke, Rebecca. "Were There No Women? British Working Class Writing in the Inter-War Period," in *Literature and History*. Vol. 14, no. 1. Spring 1988, pp. 48–63.

Silverstein, Josef. "Burma Through the Prism of Western Novels," in *Journal of Southeast Asian Studies*. Vol. 16, no. 1. March 1985, pp. 129–140.

John Haag,
Associate Professor of History,
University of Georgia, Athens, Georgia

Manning, Anne (1807–1879)

English novelist. Born in London, England, on February 17, 1807; died in Tunbridge Wells, England, on September 14, 1879; daughter of William Oke Manning (an insurance broker for Lloyd's) and Joan Whatmore (Gibson) Manning (daughter of the principal surveyor *of the London Docks and a distant cousin of Charles and *Mary Lamb); educated at home; never married.*

Selected writings: A Sister's Gift *(1826);* The Village Belle *(1838);* The Maiden and Married Life of Mary Powell *(1849);* Cherry and Violet *(1853);* The Household of Sir Thomas More *(1860);* Family Pictures *(1861).*

Born on February 17, 1807, in London, Anne Manning was the daughter of **Joan Gibson Manning** and William Oke Manning, an insurance broker, and the granddaughter of a Unitarian minister. Educated at home by her mother, who was an exceptionally well-read woman for the time, Manning was introduced to history, science, and languages. As a young girl, she showed a talent for painting, winning a gold medal from the Royal Academy for a copy she made of a painting by Murillo. Passing on the education that had been lavished upon her by her mother, she in turn taught her younger brothers and sisters. It was for her younger siblings that Manning wrote her first book, *A Sister's Gift*, published in 1826. This was followed by *The Village Belle* in 1838, and 11 years later by *The Maiden and Married Life of Mary Powell*, which went through a number of editions and is the novel for which she is probably best known. Her later books, several of which are set in the 16th century, include *Cherry and Violet* (1853), *The Household of Sir Thomas More* (1860), and *Family Pictures* (1861). She was also an occasional contributor to *Sharpe's Magazine*.

Never married, Manning lived a retired life within her family circle, moving from London to Mickleham with her parents and later, after their deaths, to Reigate Hill. She died at the age of 72 on September 14, 1879, while living in the Tunbridge Wells home of a sister.

Don Amerman,
freelance writer, Saylorsburg, Pennsylvania

Manning, Maria (c. 1821–1849)

English murderer who was the inspiration for a character in Charles Dickens' Bleak House. *Name variations: Marie Manning; Maria de Roux; Marie deRoux; Maria Manning DeRoux. Born Maria de Roux in 1821 (some sources cite 1825), in Lausanne, Switzerland; died by hanging on November 13, 1849, in London, England; married Frederick George Manning, in 1847.*

Maria Manning, a murderer whose much-publicized crime, conviction, and public execution enthralled Victorian England, was born Maria de Roux in Switzerland in 1821, of Swiss and French parentage. A domestic servant who had immigrated to England, she obtained a plum post as the personal maid to **Lady Blantyre**, who was a close friend of Queen *Victoria. Disliking or tiring of that line of work, however, and with few other options in that day and age, she appears to have decided to marry.

Maria was being courted by an Irish customhouse officer, Patrick O'Connor, whom she believed to be financially successful and a good prospect for a husband (unaware that he had bribed his way into the lucrative job), when she met a railway guard, Frederick George Manning. He, too, pursued her hand in marriage. Having to choose between the two suitors, she decided against O'Connor because of his penchant for alcohol; Frederick Manning's claim that he would inherit a large sum of money when his mother died may have also played a part in her decision. The Mannings were married in Piccadilly in 1847. As a wedding present Frederick gave Maria his newly written will, in which he bequeathed to her all of his property, including the future inheritance. They became tavern-keepers at the White Hart Inn in Taunton, but were forced to sell the business when Frederick mismanaged the finances. At this point, Maria apparently renewed contact with O'Connor, looking to escape from her decidedly unprosperous union—especially after learning that her mother-in-law was non-existent, and that there was no inheritance. She would later say that O'Connor urged her to take up lodgings at Minever Place in London with the promise that he would become a boarder to help defray the costs. He did not, and the Mannings took a medical student named Massey as a boarder. O'Connor was a frequent visitor, however, and it has been widely presumed that he and Maria Manning were conducting an affair. This was apparently unsuspected by her husband, who had also begun to exhibit a fondness for alcohol.

Maria had learned that O'Connor held valuable stock in foreign railroads. The medical student later said that at about this time Fred Manning began to ask him questions about chloroform and laudanum, both toxic substances. One day, the Mannings asked Massey to move out of the Minever Place quarters, saying that Maria's mother was arriving for a visit and they needed the room. Massey later told Scotland Yard detectives that a crowbar was being delivered to the house as he was leaving; he also remembered the delivery of a large quantity of lime (a drying agent, which therefore can be used to hasten the decomposition of dead matter) a few days before. That night, Mr. and Mrs.

Manning sent a note to O'Connor inviting him to dinner. No doubt to their chagrin, he brought a friend along. They invited him again the following night, August 9, 1849, and specifically requested that he come alone. Friends passed him walking on London Bridge on his way there. Neighbors on Minever Place also saw him that night, smoking a cigar and chatting with Maria Manning outside her kitchen door.

Maria allegedly took O'Connor to a lower kitchen to show him a basin where he might wash his hands before dinner, and fired a gun at his head. Going back upstairs, she announced the deed to her husband, and crowed that she would never be caught. He disagreed. Frederick Manning went into the lower kitchen and found O'Connor still alive, so he bludgeoned him with a chisel. The Mannings buried the dead man in the lower kitchen with a covering of lime, although not before Maria Manning removed O'-Connor's keys from his body. They then dined on the goose dinner she had prepared. The next day Maria was admitted into O'Connor's rooms by his landlady, and with the assistance of his keys stole from a trunk two gold watches, two gold chains, currency, and stock certificates worth several thousand pounds. Dismayed that she had not uncovered more assets, she returned the following day and was again admitted by the landlady, but found nothing more of value. Maria next persuaded her husband to pretend to be O'Connor in order to sell the stocks. As O'-Connor, he nervously sold less than £200 worth, and told her he would not do so again.

On August 12, some friends of the missing O'Connor came to Minever Place inquiring about him. Maria informed them that he had dined with them on the 8th of August, with a friend, and she had not seen him since. They told her that he had been seen crossing London Bridge the following night, and had mentioned that he was on his way to her house. She pleaded ignorance and feigned concern for his whereabouts, but panicked when, after they left, Frederick Manning voiced his suspicion that the "friends" were actually Scotland Yard detectives. Manning sent her husband out of the house on a spurious excuse, gathered up what she had stolen, and fled. When Frederick Manning returned to find her gone, he too fled. Not long after their departure, a servant at O'Connor's rooming house identified Maria as the woman who had entered the premises twice after his disappearance, and the Minever Place home was searched. Detectives found the body under the kitchen-floor stones.

With the intention of fleeing to America, Maria went first to Scotland and was easily apprehended not long after she tried to sell O'Connor's stocks at an Edinburgh broker's office. Shortly thereafter, Frederick Manning was taken into custody on Jersey, one of the Channel Islands. The London newspapers of 1849 seized upon the sensational nature of the case, and Maria was made into a salacious, French-accented femme fatale. Both of the accused claimed the other was the guilty party. After a two-day trial and 45 minutes of deliberation, the jury found wife and husband guilty, and they were sentenced to death by hanging. Manning clamorously protested the verdict, shouting at the judge, and later wrote numerous letters pleading for help, including to her former employer and to Queen Victoria. The queen actually did take the time to review the transcripts of the trial, only the second (and last) time in her long reign that she would do so; satisfied that the verdict was correct, she did not interfere. One correspondence Maria did not maintain was with her husband, who wrote to her often. She sent his letters back unopened, save for once, at the eleventh hour, when she wrote begging him to "confess" and prove her innocence.

The joint hanging of Maria and Frederick Manning was set for November 13. Prime viewing spots of the scheduled execution, to be held on the roof of London's Horsemonger Lane Gaol, were sold for good sums. Spectators began gathering at the spot days beforehand. The crowd was estimated to have been one of the largest—between 30,000 and 50,000—ever assembled for a public hanging in England. Hundreds were hospitalized after being trampled in the throng, and one woman died. In a letter to the London *Times,* novelist Charles Dickens described the crowd as consisting of "thieves, low prostitutes, ruffians and vagabonds of every kind," but other newspapers gleefully noted that no small number of the aristocratic, wealthy, or just plain respectable had watched from higher vantage points, with opera glasses. Dickens himself, against his better judgment, watched the executions from a nearby roof (which had been rented for the occasion). For her execution, Maria Manning wore a black dress made of satin, the most fashionable fabric of the time; sales of satin dropped sharply afterward because of the publicized association with the event. Watched by the enormous crowd, Maria and Frederick Manning together ascended the gallows set up on the roof of the jail and were hanged.

Three years later, newspaper serialization of Dickens' novel *Bleak House* began. One character was a French maid named Hortense, whose demeanor and actions instantly recalled Maria Manning to most readers. Yet Dickens, like other prominent writers and reformers of the day, had been regretful of his participation as a spectator in the hanging, and a movement to ban public executions gained strength. Executions were brought indoors, excluding the public, in 1868. By 1869, effigies of Maria Manning and her husband occupied a prominent spot in the popular Chamber of Horrors in Madame *Marie Tussaud's wax museum.

SOURCES:

Gatrell, V.A.C. *The Hanging Tree: Execution and the English People 1770–1868.* Oxford: Oxford University Press, 1994.

Nash, Jay Robert. *Look for the Woman.* NY: M. Evans, 1981.

Carol Brennan,
Grosse Pointe, Michigan

Manning, Marie (c. 1873–1945)

First American newspaper advice columnist, and one of the most popular, who was known as Beatrice Fairfax. Name variations: (pseudonym) Beatrice Fairfax. Born on January 22, c. 1873 (all sources are estimates, and include 1875 and 1878), in Washington, D.C.; died in Washington, D.C., on November 28, 1945; daughter of Michael Charles Manning (a War Department employee) and Elizabeth (Barrett) Manning; married Herman Eduard Gasch, in 1905; children: Oliver Gasch; Manning Gasch.

Selected writings: (novel) Lord Allingham, Bankrupt (1902); (novel) Judith of the Plains (1903); (advice) Personal Reply (1943); (autobiography) Ladies Now and Then (1944).

Journalist Marie Manning wrote the first newspaper advice column, a feature that was revolutionary at its inception in the 1890s for her forthright recommendations on pressing social issues. She was born in Washington, D.C., to English parents; the exact year of her birth is not known, because she kept it secret until her death, although her son has dated it in 1873. When she was six years old, her mother died, and thereafter she was raised by her father, a onetime employee of the U.S. War Department. She received schooling in London and New York City (she was disciplined at one school for reading tabloid papers during the meditation hour) and attended finishing school in Washington around 1890. Young women of her social station sometimes went off to college, but it was rare for one to work actively to establish herself in a career outside the home. Manning, however, was an avid newspaper reader, and harbored a secret ambition to become a journalist.

Her father died when she was 20, and she came under the guardianship of a family friend. At a Washington dinner party, she sat next to Arthur Brisbane, an editor at the *New York World.* She confessed her love of the media, and he helped her obtain a job at his paper writing filler, after she won a battle with her conservative guardian for permission to do so. Manning moved to New York City, where her job paid by the inch and only if the work actually made it into print. Intrepid and well connected, she managed to obtain an exclusive interview with President Grover Cleveland, and was then hired full-time by the paper. She moved to the *New York Evening Journal* in 1897, along with most of her colleagues at the *World,* and went to work for William Randolph Hearst, considered the founder of tabloid journalism. His papers featured true-crime stories and appealed to popular sentiments. At the *Evening Journal,* Manning wrote features for the "women's page," primarily concerning household and beauty tips. The section of the editorial room where she and two female colleagues sat was referred to by newspaper staff as the "Hen Coop."

The newspaper had been receiving an increasing amount of letters of a personal nature from readers, detailing various emotional hardships and requesting assistance. Manning suggested the creation of a separate column to respond to the letters, and received the approval of Brisbane, now her editor, to answer them in print under a pseudonym. Her first "Letters from the Lovelorn" column appeared on July 20, 1898, under the pen name "Beatrice Fairfax," and was an instant success. Readers were intrigued by the frank discussions of personal problems, discussions which, during the 1890s, were still subject to censure; the growth of urban populations due to the Industrial Revolution, and the resulting loss of community that people suffered, brought a host of social ills and little forum for remedy or even sympathy. Manning provided advice to women struggling to remain—or at least appear—virtuous in an era of great social change, and in time the paper would receive nearly 1,400 letters a day. "Beatrice Fairfax" became known for dispensing matter-of-fact advice regarding courtship and problems in love, with far less obligatory sentiment than was the norm; typical of her response was "Dry your eyes, roll up your sleeves, and dig for a practical solution, battle for it; if the law will help, invoke the law . . . pick up the

Marie
Manning
(c. 1873–1945)

pieces and keep on going." The paper's circulation, in her own words, "zoomed like an ascending airplane." Imitators soon sprang up at other newspapers, but her main competitor was the pseudonymous Dorothy Dix (*Elizabeth Meriwether Gilmer).

In addition to the column, Manning continued to write news articles for the paper under her real name ("Beatrice Fairfax" was a combination of Dante's *Beatrice [Portinari] and the county in Virginia where Manning's family had a farm), and also wrote fiction published in *Harper's*, some of it inspired by problems posed in letters to her column. She published two novels, *Lord Allingham, Bankrupt* (1902) and *Judith of the Plains* (1903). In 1905, she married real estate mogul Herman Gasch and retired from the newspaper, although she continued to turn in the occasional freelance piece at Brisbane's request. For most of the next two decades, Manning concentrated on raising her two sons, writing short stories that were published in such magazines as *Harper's, Ladies' Home Journal,* and *Collier's,* and championing women's rights. A longtime suffragist and founding member of the Women's National Press Club, she lectured, lobbied politicians, and marched in parades (later expressing regret that she had not had the courage to be jailed with other marching suffragists), and also worked for child-labor laws.

Like so many others, Manning was financially impoverished by the stock-market crash of 1929. She went back to work a year later on the "Beatrice Fairfax" column, which was still an enormously popular feature in the *New York Evening Journal* and had been ghostwritten by other female journalists since her departure. It had also been syndicated to 200 American newspapers, thanks to Hearst's King Features. She confronted an entirely new set of queries after a quarter-century hiatus. More married people were writing for advice, and men sent far more letters than they had at the turn of the century. Manning continued writing the column until her death 15 years later, and also wrote features for the International News Service. During World War II, she began to receive a record number of letters from military personnel and their families, and authored a book of advice for them titled *Personal Reply* (1943). An autobiography of sorts, *Ladies Now and Then,* appeared in 1944; it was only then that Marie Manning publicly revealed her identity as Beatrice Fairfax. She died of coronary thrombosis in Washington, D.C., on November 28, 1945.

SOURCES:

Current Biography. NY: H.W. Wilson, 1944.

Downs, Robert B., and Jane B. Downs, eds. *Journalists of the United States.* Jefferson, NC: McFarland, 1991.

McHenry, Robert, ed. *Famous American Women.* NY: Dover, 1980.

McKerns, Joseph P., ed. *Biographical Dictionary of American Journalism.* CT: Greenwood Press, 1989.

Read, Phyllis J., and Bernard L. Witlieb, eds. *The Book of Women's Firsts.* NY: Random House, 1992.

Sicherman, Barbara, and Carol Hurd Green. *Notable American Women: The Modern Period: A Biographical Dictionary.* Cambridge, MA: The Belknap Press of Harvard University, 1980.

Carol Brennan,
Grosse Pointe, Michigan

Manning, Olivia (1908–1980)

English novelist whose best-known works are two trilogies dealing with the Second World War. Name variations: Jacob Morrow. Born Olivia Manning on March 2, 1908, in Portsmouth, England; died of a stroke suffered in Ryde, Isle of Wight, on July 23, 1980; elder child of Lieutenant-Commander Oliver Manning, R.N. (retired) and Olivia (Morrow) Manning; attended Portsmouth Grammar School and Portsmouth Technical College; married Reginald (Reggie) Donald Smith, in 1939.

Moved to London (1926), where she became friends with Stevie Smith; had first novel published (1937); spent war years in Bucharest, Athens, Cairo and Jerusalem (1939–46); had first book of short stories published (1948); had first book of the Balkan trilogy published (1960); made a Commander of the British Empire (1976).

Selected writings: The Wind Changes (1937); Growing Up (1948); Balkan Trilogy: The Great Fortune (1960), The Spoilt City (1962), and Friends and Heroes (1965); The Play Room (1969); Levant Trilogy: The Danger Tree (1977), The Battle Lost and Won (1978), and The Sum of Things (1980).

Although she was always admired by other writers, Olivia Manning's books were slow to gain popularity with the general reading public, a state of affairs which depressed her. However, following the success of her *Balkan Trilogy,* she was published in paperback during the 1970s, and in 1976 she had further proof of her growing acclaim when she was awarded a CBE. In 1987, seven years after her death, the *Balkan Trilogy* was successfully serialized on television as "The Fortunes of War." Nevertheless very little has been written about her and no full-scale biography of her has yet been published.

Manning's father had been an officer in the Royal Navy. He had served during the days of sail and must have had a wealth of stories about distant times and places to tell his young children. It has been suggested that these stories may have fostered Olivia's historical interest. Olivia's mother Olivia Morrow Manning was Lieutenant-Commander Manning's second wife, and he had already retired by the time children were born. The Mannings, themselves called Oliver and Olivia, chose to call their two children Oliver and Olivia likewise. Olivia was the firstborn and it is thought that Mrs. Manning made no attempt to hide her preference for her son, and that Olivia never came to terms with being demoted from a favored only child to a daughter in secondary position to her brother.

Mrs. Manning was part American and part Irish. Olivia claimed that she herself felt like a "displaced person" and **Janet Todd** believes that her mixed background intensified her sense of belonging nowhere. Mrs. Manning came from Ulster but it was in Dublin that Olivia spent part of her childhood. By the time she was old enough to attend secondary school, she was in Portsmouth, a pupil in Portsmouth Grammar School and later at Portsmouth Technical College where she studied art.

A retired naval officer's pension was far from munificent, and the family was constantly short of money. It may have been the need to supplement her meager pocket money which encouraged Olivia, while still at school, to write some stories which she later described as "lurid serials." She used the pseudonym of Jacob Morrow, the surname being her mother's maiden name. Manning was paid £12 apiece for these stories, and a few years later, while still finding it hard to make ends meet, she sold their copyright for a small sum.

It was certainly a shortage of money within the family which caused Olivia to leave Portsmouth Technical College before she had completed her course, in order to start work. That she moved to London to do so probably had much to do with the fact that relations at home, particularly with her mother, were often strained. Once in London, she worked as a typist in the office of a city department store during the day and spent her evenings writing. Manning also made use of her artistic talents by painting reproduction furniture to supplement her income. She lived in Chelsea, where she rented a bed-sitter in Oakley Street, only a short walk away from the Chelsea Embankment and the Albert Suspension Bridge spanning the River Thames. At some time in the early 1930s, she met the poet and novelist *Stevie Smith. The two became friends, and Olivia often spent weekends with Stevie and her aunt at their home in Palmer's Green.

According to Stevie Smith's biographers, Jack Barbera and William McBrien, the friendship was "spiky." Early in the 1930s, Manning had a love affair with Hamish Miles who was Smith's editor at the publishing house of Jonathan Cape. When the affair foundered, Manning blamed Smith. However, it seems that Manning's friendships rarely ran smoothly; a mutual friend, **Kay Dick**, said, "Olivia's animosities were legendary and a bit of a joke among her friends." Despite the quarrel, it was on Smith's recommendation that Jonathan Cape accepted Manning's first novel after it had al-

ready been rejected by several other publishers. *The Wind Changes*, published in 1937, concerns Ireland's political troubles, especially during the settlement of 1921 which culminated in the signing of a treaty between Ireland and the rest of Great Britain and ultimately the formation of the Irish Free State. For her novel, Manning drew upon her knowledge of Ireland in general and of Dublin in particular.

In 1939, Manning married a British Council lecturer, Reginald Donald Smith. Stevie was a bridesmaid. When Olivia and Reggie went to Bucharest, where Reggie was already working, Stevie was put in charge of removing Olivia's books to her own home at Palmer's Green. At the outbreak of the Second World War, Manning and her husband found themselves marooned in Europe. Moving only just ahead of the hostilities each time, they escaped from Bucharest to Athens, from Athens to Cairo, and finally from Cairo to Jerusalem. In Cairo, Manning worked as a press officer in the U.S. Embassy and on her move to Jerusalem became press assistant at the

Olivia
Manning

Public Information Office there. During the war, Oliver was killed in action. Olivia was greatly distressed for, despite her mother's partiality, the brother and sister had been close.

Not surprisingly, Manning had no new novels published during this time, although in 1942 Stevie tried to get John Hayward to print one of Olivia's short stories. Manning and her husband did not return to England until after the end of hostilities in 1946. By 1947, Stevie was sending some of Olivia's poems to Kay Dick in the hope of getting them printed in the Windmill series. Olivia herself was preparing for publication her account of Sir Henry Morton Stanley's rescue of the Emir Pasha, titled *The Remarkable Expedition*. The year 1948 saw the publication of a collection of short stories, *Growing Up*, and 1949 that of her next novel, *Artist among the Missing*. From then on until her death in 1980, she brought out a book approximately every two years.

We have here [two trilogies,] an extraordinary body of work that should earn her a permanent place among the authors of that very considerable literature arising out of the Second World War.

—Harry J. Mooney, Jr.

During the 1950s, Olivia's relations with Stevie fluctuated and seem to have relied to some extent on the tone of Stevie's review of Olivia's latest book. Manning was always extremely sensitive to criticism and, like many writers, tended to remember the negative things said about her work while disregarding the positive. Stevie's reviews in the early 1950s were in the main appreciative and there is evidence that the pair were on amicable terms in 1953, for Stevie was invited to a party at Manning's home on July 23rd. But by 1955 the friendship had gone at least temporarily sour following Stevie's less favorable review in the *Observer* of Manning's newest book, *The Doves of Venus*. Olivia was offended by Stevie's criticism. Stevie in turn was less than pleased with one of the characters—Nancy Claypole—rumored to be based on her.

As well as being a novelist and short-story writer, Olivia Manning worked as a freelance literary critic and as a book reviewer. She contributed articles to many newspapers, journals, and magazines, including the *Sunday Times*, the *Observer*, the *Spectator*, the *New Statesman, Horizon, Vogue,* and *Punch*. In 1956, her sketches for *Punch* were collected into a book entitled *My Husband Cartwright*, which is said to throw light upon her relationship with her own husband, Reggie, who outlived her by only

four years. (In the late 1970s, a contribution she made to the *Sunday Times* "First Love" series dealt with her affair with Hamish Miles.)

In one sense all fiction can be claimed to be autobiographical, as a writer can only create out of her own actual or imagined experience, but much of Olivia Manning's work is more overtly autobiographical than that of many other writers. She herself said, "My subject is simply life as I have experienced it, and I am happiest when writing of things I know." Her story of adolescence, *The Play Room,* has been called an autobiographical novel and many of the situations contained therein were grounded in her own experience. Also autobiographical in nature are her two trilogies in which her two main protagonists, Guy and Harriet Pringle, traverse the same parts of the world at the same point in history as did Olivia and her husband. It would, however, be foolhardy to claim that the Pringles are reproductions of the couple. Harry J. Mooney, Jr. said of her writing, "She impresses me as a writer whose experience as historical witness compels her to creativity."

Barbera and O'Brien refer to Olivia's interest in the psychic and her desire that there should be some form of existence after death. They quote her admission to her friend, **Frances King,** "I have an absolute loathing of death, I really love life . . . and I do want to . . . believe that, even if it were far worse than any existence here on earth, there was the promise of an existence elsewhere." Some time after Stevie Smith's death in 1971, Olivia Manning was writing her memoirs. Evidently when a few pages which referred to Stevie went missing, Olivia blamed Stevie herself for removing them.

Manning had had an affection for the Isle of Wight since childhood, and while holidaying there in July 1980 she suffered a stroke and died. The final part of her *Levant Trilogy, The Sum of Things,* was published posthumously later the same year.

SOURCES:

Barbera, Jack, and William McBrien. *Stevie: A Biography of Stevie Smith.* London: Heinemann, 1985.

Mooney, Harry J., Jr. "Olivia Manning: Witness to History" in *Twentieth Century Women Novelists.* Edited by Thomas F. Staley. London: Macmillan, 1982.

Shattock, Joanne, ed. *The Oxford Guide to British Women Writers.* Oxford: Oxford University Press, 1993.

Todd, Janet, ed. *Dictionary of British Women Writers.* London: Routledge, 1991.

RELATED MEDIA:

"Fortunes of War" (VHS, 6 hrs.), starring Kenneth Branagh, **Emma Thompson,** Ronald Pickup, and Rupert Graves, a BBC production, 1987.

Barbara Evans,
Research Associate in Women's Studies at Nene College,
Northampton, England

Manny, Anne (b. 1355)

Countess of Pembroke. Name variations: Anne Hastings. Born around 1355; daughter of Walter Manny, 1st baron Manny (d. 1372), and *Margaret (c. 1320–1400), duchess of Norfolk; married John Hastings, 2nd earl of Pembroke (1347–1375); children: John Hastings, 3rd earl of Pembroke (1372–1389).

Manoliu, Lia (1932–1998)

Rumanian track-and-field athlete. Born on April 25, 1932, in Rumania; died on January 9, 1998, in Bucharest, Rumania; graduated from college in Bucharest with a degree in electrical engineering.

> *Participated as a discus thrower in six Olympic Games (1952–72), winning a bronze medal in Rome (1960) and Tokyo (1964) and a gold medal in Mexico City (1968); was the oldest woman in Olympic history to win a gold medal in a track-and-field event.*

Born in Rumania in 1932, the future Olympic athlete Lia Manoliu was raised in a family that placed a high value on intellectual pursuits. Her father was a professor of philosophy and instilled in his daughter a lifelong love of reading. She received a superior education, acquiring fluency in English, French, German, and Russian. She later graduated from college in Bucharest with a degree in electrical engineering. Early in her career, she studied the effects of light and noise on factory workers.

From 1952 through 1972, Manoliu competed for Rumania in six Olympic Games, more than any other woman track-and-field athlete. She made it to the finals as a discus thrower in all her Olympic appearances. In 1952, she placed sixth, and in 1956 reached a ninth-place finish. In 1960, she grabbed her first bronze medal in Olympic competition, a feat she repeated in 1964. In the 1968 Olympic Games at Mexico City, Manoliu was considered by sports commentators one of three favorites in the discus competition, along with East Germany's **Christine Speilberg** and West Germany's **Liesel Westermann**. (Competing in Brazil the previous year, Westermann had become the first woman to throw the discus more than 200 feet, heaving it 201 feet, or 61.26 meters.) At the Mexico City Games, Manoliu was suffering from a sore elbow, so she decided to give her first throw everything she had, hoping it would be good enough to take the day. Her first toss went 191'2", putting her in the lead after the first round. Although she performed poorly after that, the arrival of a sudden downpour so badly degraded the playing surface and the performance of her competitors that her first throw held up to give her first place and the gold medal. At 36 years of age, Manoliu became the oldest woman in Olympic history to win a gold medal in a track-and-field event. She competed again in the 1972 Games in Munich and finished in ninth place.

In 1990, Manoliu was named president of the Rumanian Olympic Committee, becoming only the third woman worldwide to head a national Olympic committee. Britain's Princess ***Anne** and Liechtenstein's Princess **Nora** had previously held such posts in their respective countries.

In Bucharest on December 31, 1997, Lia Manoliu went into a coma during surgery for a brain tumor. She never regained consciousness. On January 9, 1998, she suffered a massive heart attack and died.

Don Amerman,
freelance writer, Saylorsburg, Pennsylvania

Manos, Aspasia (1896–1972)

*Queen of the Hellenes. Born on September 4, 1896, in Athens, Greece; died on August 7, 1972, in Venice, Italy; daughter of Colonel Petros Manos and **Maria Argyropoulos**; married Alexander I, king of the Hellenes, on November 4, 1919; children: *Alexandra (1921–1993), queen of Yugoslavia.*

Mansberger, Margarita Nelken (1896–1968).

> *See Nelken, Margarita.*

Mansenée, Desle la (c. 1502–1529)

French victim of the Inquisition who was convicted of murder, heresy, and renunciation of the Catholic faith. Name variations: Desle la Mansenee. Born around 1502; executed on December 18, 1529, in Anjeux, France; married.

What has been called "the witch-craze" in Europe, which resulted in thousands of grisly deaths, mostly of women, from the mid-13th century through the 18th century, is aptly illustrated by the last months of Desle la Mansenée. Her trial also offers evidence of the continuing involvement of the Inquisition in witch trials.

In early 1529, France's inquisitor-general traveled to the village of Anjeux to collect villagers' reports of possible witches. There he heard rumors that a local woman named Desle la Mansenée was involved in communication with the devil and other acts of sorcery. Although many accused of such crimes against the faith were elderly women without protectors, usually widowed and poor, Mansenée was young, married, and, by all accounts, attractive. However, even the most unlikely candidates could, and did, fall victim to rumor, and nothing more substantial than such rumors was necessary to launch the prosecution of a suspected witch. All of the claims against Mansenée were unsubstantiated; some of the prosecution's witnesses could offer nothing more than testimony that they had heard rumors of her alliance with the devil.

Despite the weakness of the prosecution's case against her, Mansenée was questioned repeatedly, beginning in March 1529. She adamantly insisted that she was innocent of all such charges throughout these interrogations. The prosecution could not produce any real evidence of her guilt, and the trial itself uncovered nothing of significance. Therefore the prosecution ordered that Mansenée be subjected to squassation, a method of torture that was a mainstay of the Inquisition. There were five degrees to the torture, the first being the threat of it, and the second being taken to the place set aside for torture. The third degree (from which comes the phrase "put to the third degree") involved stripping the prisoner and tying her arms tightly behind her back, and the fourth consisted of raising her some five or six feet off the floor on a pulley through which was strung the rope tying the arms. Sheer body weight alone would be grievously painful, but heavy weights were also attached to the feet. If this was not enough to produce a confession from the prisoner, the final, fifth degree was employed, in which the torturer released the rope, plunging the prisoner down a few feet, and then pulled it taut again. The extreme strain produced by the weights attached to the prisoner's feet caused agonizing pain, and often dislocated arms and legs. This fifth degree could be repeated as often as the torturer cared to do so. Under the torture of squassation, Desle la Mansenée, by April 8, 1529, was willing to confess to anything, including a disclosure that the devil had promised to make her rich if she would reject Jesus Christ. She also claimed that the devil had empowered her to alter the weather and to poison cattle, and that in addition to worshiping the devil, she had had sexual relations with him. This was, of course, all the prosecution needed. Mansenée was convicted, however, not of witchcraft but of murder, heresy, and renunciation of the Catholic faith.

On December 18, 1529, she was hanged at Anjeux, and her body burned.

Don Amerman,
freelance writer, Saylorsburg, Pennsylvania

Mansfield, Arabella (1846–1911)

First woman admitted to the bar in the United States.
Name variations: Arabella A. Mansfield; Arabella Aurelia Babb Mansfield; Arabella Babb Mansfield. Born Belle Aurelia Babb on May 23, 1846, near Sperry Station, Iowa; died on August 2, 1911, in Aurora, Illinois; daughter of Miles Babb (a farmer) and Mary (Moyer) Babb (a farmer); earned undergraduate degree from Iowa Wesleyan University, 1866, M.A., 1870, LL.B., 1872; married John Melvin Mansfield (a professor of natural history), on June 23, 1868 (died 1894); no children.

Arabella Mansfield was born on her family's farm near Sperry Station, Iowa, on May 23, 1846. Christened Belle Aurelia Babb, she changed her name to Aurelia as a teenager and later became known as Arabella. Her father was a farmer who left the Midwest during the California Gold Rush of 1850. He was the superintendent of a mine there when a cave-in killed him and left Mansfield's mother, **Mary Babb**, a widow in Iowa with two young children. When the children were in their teens, Babb moved the family to Mount Pleasant, Iowa, where there was a high school. The school's principal, Samuel L. Howe, was a well-known abolitionist and proponent of women's suffrage, and these views probably made an impression on the young Mansfield. Deciding to attend college, she enrolled in Iowa Wesleyan University, also located in Mount Pleasant. After she graduated in 1866, she taught for a time at Simpson College in Indianola.

In June 1868, Mansfield returned to Mount Pleasant and married a professor of natural history named John Melvin Mansfield, and began teaching English and history at Iowa Wesleyan. She had been privately studying the law with her brother for some time, and her new husband joined her studies. (Attendance at law school had not yet become common practice for would-be lawyers.) They applied for the bar two years after their marriage. A liberal judge who was in charge of the district court at the time decided that the state law which indicated that the bar was open to "any white male person" did not necessarily exclude Mansfield, and appointed two examiners similarly progressive in their views. In the summer of 1869, Mansfield passed the exams with high marks and was admitted to the Iowa bar, becoming the first woman lawyer in America. The landmark event attracted little public notice aside from a few mocking newspaper editorials and positive mention in *Revolution*, a periodical published by women's suffrage movement leaders *Susan B. Anthony and *Elizabeth Cady Stanton.

Mansfield, who continued to teach, never practiced as a lawyer. She became involved in the suffrage cause in the 1870s and was one of the founders of the Iowa Woman Suffrage Society. For a time, she traveled through Europe with her husband and studied law in Paris at the Sorbonne. In 1879, both she and her husband were hired by Indiana Asbury University, in Greencastle, Indiana, but he suffered a nervous breakdown not long afterward, and Mansfield spent two years caring for him full-time. His condition deteriorated to the point where he had to be institutionalized, and after that Mansfield returned to her job at Indiana Asbury University, by then renamed DePauw University. She was active in many facets of campus life, and became dean of the school of art in 1893 and dean of the school of music a year later; she held the dual posts until her death. Known for her eye-catching millinery, Mansfield lived in the women's dormitory and gave popular Sunday lectures on a variety of topics. She learned she had cancer while traveling in Japan in 1909, but continued to work until several months before her death on August 2, 1911.

SOURCES:

McHenry, Robert, ed. *Famous American Women.* NY: Dover, 1980.

Read, Phyllis J., and Bernard L. Witlieb, eds. *The Book of Women's Firsts.* NY: Random House, 1992.

Sicherman, Barbara, and Carol Hurd Green. *Notable American Women: The Modern Period: A Biographical Dictionary.* Cambridge, MA: The Belknap Press of Harvard University, 1980.

Carol Brennan,
Grosse Pointe, Michigan

Mansfield, Jayne (1933–1967)

American actress who was one of Hollywood's leading sex symbols during the late 1950s and early 1960s. Born Vera Jayne Palmer in Bryn Mawr, Pennsylvania, on April 19, 1933; died near New Orleans, Louisiana, on June 29, 1967; daughter of Herbert Palmer (an attorney) and Vera Palmer; attended Parkland High School in Dallas, Texas, the University of Texas, the University of California at Los Angeles, and Southern Methodist University in Dallas; married Paul Mansfield, on May 6, 1950 (divorced 1956); married Mickey Hargitay (a bodybuilder), on January 13, 1958 (di-

vorced 1964); married Matt Cimber (a film producer and director), in 1964 (separated 1966); children: (first marriage) Jayne Marie Mansfield (b. 1950); (second marriage) Miklos Hargitay (b. 1958), Zoltan Hargitay (b. 1960), and **Mariska Hargitay** *(b. 1964); (third marriage): Anthony Richard Cimber (b. 1965).*

Selected films: The Female Jungle *(1954);* Pete Kelly's Blues *(1955);* Illegal *(1955);* The Burglar *(1956);* The Girl Can't Help It *(1957);* Will Success Spoil Rock Hunter? *(1957);* Kiss Them for Me *(1957);* The Sheriff of Fractured Jaw *(1958);* Too Hot to Handle *(1960);* The Loves of Hercules *(1960);* The George Raft Story *(1961);* Panic Button *(1962);* A Guide for the Married Man *(1967).*

Born Vera Jayne Palmer in the exclusive Philadelphia suburb of Bryn Mawr, Pennsylvania, on April 19, 1933, Jayne Mansfield was the only child of **Vera Palmer** and Herbert Palmer, a successful attorney. She spent her early years in the small town of Phillipsburg in northwestern New Jersey, where her father was the law partner of Robert Meyner, later governor of the Garden State. When she was only three, her father suffered a massive heart attack and died. Three years later, Vera Palmer married Harry Peers, a successful mechanical engineer, and the family moved to Dallas, Texas. From all reports, Mansfield had an idyllic childhood, pampered by doting parents who encouraged her precocity. At an early age, she discovered movie fan magazines and resolved that she would star in motion pictures—preferably like *Shirley Temple (Black), who had long been one of her favorites. Vera encouraged her daughter's aspirations.

While attending Parkland High School in Dallas, Mansfield boasted a B-average. Then a brunette, she physically matured early and, by age 17, was amply endowed. On May 6, 1950, though she seldom dated, a pregnant Jayne married 20-year-old Paul Mansfield. That November, Jayne and her newborn daughter Jayne Marie joined Paul in Austin, where he was attending the University of Texas. Although Mansfield took a couple of classes, she spent most of her time working to support the family, employed as a receptionist at a dance school and as a door-to-door saleswoman. Because the Mansfields had no money for a babysitter, Jayne took her infant daughter with her to class and to work.

In 1951, Mansfield took the first serious steps toward her goal. Leaving her daughter with Vera, she enrolled at the University of California at Los Angeles. While there, she reached the finals of the Miss Southern California

Pageant but dropped out when her husband expressed disapproval. In 1952, Paul was inducted into the U.S. Army and stationed at Camp Gordon, near Augusta, Georgia, where Jayne joined him. In a local beauty competition, she was named Miss Photoflash of 1952, only the first of many beauty titles she would eventually collect. She also picked up some acting experience at Camp Gordon, appearing in local productions of *Anything Goes* and *Ten Nights in a Ballroom*. After her husband was sent to Korea, Mansfield returned to Dallas where she attended classes at Southern Methodist University, earned money by modeling, and entered more beauty contests. She then came under the wing of Baruch Lumet, the father of film director Sidney Lumet. Founder and director of the Dallas Institute of Performing Arts, the elder Lumet saw some promise in Mansfield and agreed to give her free acting lessons. While studying under Lumet, she acted in a few local television productions and won a small part in a local presentation of *Death of a Salesman*, a role that brought her to

Jayne Mansfield

the attention of a Paramount executive, Milton Lewis. When Paul came back from Korea in 1954, he made good on an earlier promise to move to California so that Jayne could pursue a career in motion pictures.

Soon after their arrival in Southern California, Mansfield signed with an agent, Robert Schwartz, but work was not forthcoming. Paul found Jayne's quest for stardom more than he could tolerate and asked her to give up her career and return with him to Dallas. When she refused, he sued for divorce and sought custody of their daughter, citing a couple of Jayne's provocative pin-up posters; the court granted the divorce but turned down his custody petition.

Mansfield landed a part on television by camping out in the office of the casting agent for three consecutive days. It has been written, though perhaps apocryphally, that while still waiting to see the agent she scribbled "36–22–34" on a card and had it delivered to the show's producer. Supposedly, she was hired the same day. Although she then added a handful of small acting roles to her resume, her career was not successfully launched until early 1955. By that time, an appearance in Hugh Hefner's fledgling *Playboy* had increased her profile in Hollywood considerably. Howard Hughes ordered his executives at RKO Studios to sign Mansfield, which set off a bidding war with Warner Bros. In the end, she signed a six-month contract with Warner's for a mere $250 a week. Her first film was *Illegal*, and she also appeared in the television series "Casablanca." Unhappy with her roles at Warner's, Mansfield prevailed upon studio executives to allow her to appear in an independent film project, *The Burglar*, for which she was paid $5,000. While filming, she received word that the studio had terminated her contract.

Shortly after, Mansfield was signed to do George Axelrod's Broadway show *Will Success Spoil Rock Hunter?* Although reviews for the play were lukewarm at best, critics raved about her performance. Mansfield was suddenly a hot ticket in New York, leading to guest appearances on a number of television game shows, including "What's My Line" and "Down You Go," as well as a couple of 90-minute specials. While making a guest appearance on a *Mae West show, she met Mickey Hargitay, Mr. Universe 1955, who was one of the musclemen in West's entourage: Mansfield claimed it was love at first sight. Offered an attractive contract by 20th Century-Fox, which had also bought the rights to *Rock Hunter*, Mansfield left Broadway after more than 450 performances and headed back to Hollywood. *The Girl*

Can't Help It, her first film for Fox, was a box-office smash, rated among the top 20 films of that year. She next re-created her Broadway role in Fox's film version of *Rock Hunter.* Although it did not equal the success of *The Girl Can't Help It,* the film did well enough and eventually became something of a cult favorite.

Against the wishes of Fox, Mansfield married Hargitay on January 13, 1958. After their honeymoon, the newlyweds starred together in a nightclub act at the Tropicana in Las Vegas for six weeks. Before long, Mansfield and Hargitay welcomed the arrival of their first child, a son they named Miklos. About a year later, while they were both working on the film *The Loves of Hercules,* Mansfield became pregnant with their second son, Zoltan.

Mansfield's career peaked soon thereafter. In the wake of America's sexual revolution, her brand of sex appeal went out of style, and her inability to shape her image to the emerging sexual maturity resulted in parody; rather than copy for the Hollywood trade magazines, her life became fodder for the tabloids. Fox used her less and less and loaned her out to other studios for B (or lesser) movies. Even the offers from outside studios were becoming less frequent, leading Mansfield to appear more often on the nightclub circuit in Las Vegas, sometimes with Hargitay in tow. As her professional fortunes plummeted, so did her personal life, and reports of an imminent divorce from Hargitay ran rampant. In July 1963, Fox announced that it would not renew her contract. In January of the following year, she gave birth to daughter Mariska but soon made good on her threats to divorce Hargitay. Not long after, Mansfield married producer-director Matt Cimber, a match even she soon recognized as ill-considered. Pregnant and unhappy, Mansfield remained the trouper, acting in stage shows that she and her husband produced. They needed the income, but the shows were poorly received, and Mansfield, who had poured in her own money to cover production expenses, ended up further behind financially.

Anxious to terminate her marriage to Cimber, Mansfield separated from him and hired attorney Sam Brody to provide counsel. Shortly thereafter, she landed a role in *A Guide for the Married Man,* her first major film since 1961. Although still heavily burdened with debt, she managed to move back into her Hollywood mansion. To pay the bills, however, she found it necessary to stay on the road, playing engagements throughout the country. On the evening of June 28, 1967, after an appearance at a Biloxi, Missis-

sippi, nightclub, Mansfield, Brody, and three of her children piled into a car to be driven to New Orleans, where Mansfield was to appear on a talk show the next day. Early on the morning of June 29, 1967, the car in which they were riding ran into the back of a mosquito-control truck. The three children escaped serious injury, but Mansfield and Brody died gruesomely. It was a tabloid ending to a life lived largely in the tabloids.

SOURCES:

Agan, Patrick. *The Decline and Fall of the Love Goddesses.* CA: Pinnacle Books, 1979.

Katz, Ephraim. *The Film Encyclopedia.* NY: Harper-Collins, 1994.

Don Amerman,
freelance writer, Saylorsburg, Pennsylvania

Mansfield, Katherine (1888–1923)

New Zealand-born writer of short stories, poems, sketches, and reviews, who was also known for her letters, journals, and translations. Name variations: Kathleen Beauchamp; Kathleen Beauchamp Bowden; Kathleen Murry; Catherine, Katharina, Kathie Schonfeld; (nicknames) Kass, Kassie, Katie; (pseudonyms) Katherine Mansfield, K.M. Pronunciation: MANSfield. Born Kathleen Mansfield Beauchamp on October 15, 1888, in Wellington, New Zealand; died on January 9, 1923, in Fontainebleu, France; third of five children of Harold Beauchamp (a prosperous self-made banker) and Annie Burnell (Dyer) Beauchamp; attended Karori state school, Wellington Girls' High School, Miss Swainson's private school in Wellington, and Queen's College in London, England; married George C. Bowden, on March 2, 1909 (divorced, April 29, 1918); married John Middleton Murry, on May 3, 1918; no children.

Spent childhood in Wellington except for five years on the outskirts at Karori; attended state schools in Wellington (1895–99) and private school (1899–1903); attended Queen's College in Harley Street, London (1903–06); returned to Wellington and published several pieces in the Native Companion; *returned to London (1908) to pursue a career in music or writing; renewed friendship with Ida Baker; married George Bowden (1909), and left him the same day; pregnant by another man, went to Bavaria and suffered a miscarriage; returned to London (1910); began writing as Katherine Mansfield in periodicals; published her first book of stories,* In a German Pension *(1911); met John Middleton Murry (1912) and began relationship that continued until her death; diagnosed as tubercular (1918); divorced from George Bowden (April) and married Murry (May 1918); published* Prelude; *subsequently moved to Italy, France, and Switzerland, at times accompanied or visited by Murry, in search of a healthful climate; had a very productive period of writing (1920–22); began radium treatments (1922) and entered Gurdjieff Institute in Fontainebleu, France (October 1923), where she died.*

Major writings: In a German Pension *(1911);* Prelude *(1918);* Bliss and Other Stories *(1921);* The Garden Party and Other Stories *(1922);* The Dove's Nest and Other Stories *(1923);* Journal of Katherine Mansfield *("Definitive Edition," ed. by J.M. Murry, 1954).*

Caught in several cross-currents of change that marked the transition from the Victorian period to the modern era, the life of Katherine Mansfield reflects the many conflicts felt by colonial subjects, women, and writers during the first decades of the 20th century. Born in Wellington, New Zealand, on October 15, 1888, into an upwardly mobile family committed to achieving economic and social rank that would place their children on an equal footing with those of well-established middle-class families in England, Kathleen Mansfield Beauchamp was raised to assume a place in a world in which elegantly dressed women, as suitable ornaments of their husbands' success, ordered their households through directives to servants, pursued genteel leisure activities, supervised the arrangements of their gardens and conservatories, and participated in a social life marked by civic celebrations, teas, golf, tennis, and garden parties. The fierceness of her rebellion against this expected pattern brought her fame as a writer who helped to shape emerging themes and methods in modern fiction, as well as notoriety as a woman who casually dispensed with notions of traditional female roles and sexual behavior.

Kathleen's parents, born in Australia, carried their visions of mid-Victorian English culture with them to New Zealand, just as their own parents had carried fond images of "home" from England to Australia. Harold and **Annie Beauchamp** were among the fortunate colonials who found a better life in a place where their willingness to take risks gave them the fresh start that would lead to middle-class security, respectability, and eventually, prosperity and knighthood for Harold. The elements of rebellion, risk-taking, and willingness to recreate themselves that inspired her ancestors were the family characteristics that surfaced, much to her parents' consternation, in Kathleen, the third of their five children. **Vera, Charlotte** (Chaddie), and Kathleen (Kass), born respectively in 1885, 1887, and 1888, formed a close group, followed by a daughter who died in infancy in 1891, a

fifth daughter, **Jeanne**, born in 1892, and finally, the much desired son, Leslie, in 1894.

In 1893, the family moved from Wellington to Karori, on the outskirts of town, where Harold believed his children would enjoy the benefits of a country childhood. Here, Kass and her older sisters attended the village school, where her writing ability was first recognized when she won a prize in a school competition. She later attended Wellington Girls' High School and began to publish her work in the school newspaper. Following the family's return to Wellington and her father's appointment as a director of the Bank of New Zealand, Vera, Chaddie, and Kathleen were sent to Miss Swainson's private school, where Kathleen took the initiative to start a school magazine.

Kathleen was early identified in both family and school life as rebellious, less eager to please than her sisters, detached from the family and from classmates with whom she did not feel a special bond, and inclined to dramatize her difference through stories she fabricated about herself. Throughout her life, those who met her remarked on her reserve and the impression she often gave of wearing a mask or playing a role. She was not especially close to her mother, who often left the children in the care of their maternal grandmother while she traveled with her husband. Kass probably felt closest to and most loved by this grandmother, **Margaret Mansfield Dyer**, who lived with the family.

She cultivated special relationships with a chosen few she labeled "my people," and her early friendships prefigure relationships she had with women and men later in her life. She developed a close friendship with **Marion Ruddick**, with whom she was "sworn chums," and had an adolescent crush on **Maata Mahupuku**, the exotically beautiful descendent of Maori chieftains and heiress to a fortune. At 13, Kathleen thought she was in love with Arnold Trowell, a gifted young cellist of 15, who was largely indifferent to her ardent admiration. Arnold and his twin brother Garnet, a violinist, were anticipating going to Europe to develop their musical talents. Inspired by Arnold's promise of an exciting future, Kass persuaded her father that she should have cello lessons and practiced diligently. Thereafter her music vied with her writing as a means through which she could achieve distinction and so transcend the provincial life she already found commonplace.

In January 1903, when Kathleen was 14, she and her two older sisters, along with her parents and Aunt Belle, sailed for England; Harold

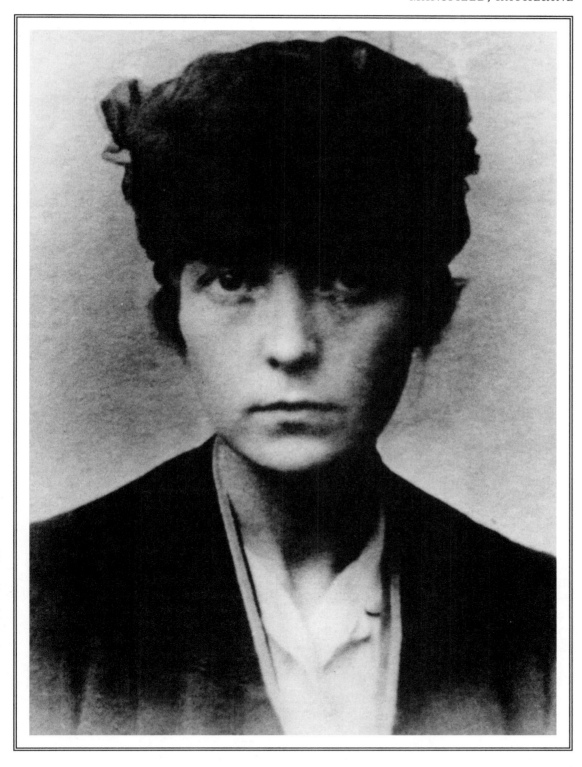

Katherine
Mansfield

Beauchamp had booked the entire passenger section for the family's exclusive use. The girls were to be left in London, with Belle as chaperon, to attend Queen's College in Harley Street, founded in 1848 as the first institution for higher education of women in England. Here Kathleen delighted in the larger world she had wished for. On the first day at school, she met **Ida Constance Baker**, another "Colonial," raised in Burma, with whom she would have a close and complex relationship for the rest of her life. At Queen's, Kathleen did not distinguish herself as a student, but learned German, practiced her cello, began writing in a notebook, the precursor of the journals she kept throughout her life, and wrote regularly for the college magazine, eventually becoming its editor in 1905. She discovered Oscar Wilde and the Decadents and was entranced by *The Portrait of Dorian Gray*. Taken with Wilde's insistence on the absolute freedom of the gifted individual, especially the artist, she began writing Wildean epigrams of her own. While at Queen's, she kept Arnold Trowell's photograph on her dresser and wrote to him in Frankfurt, where he and Garnet were studying music.

I feel always trembling on the brink of poetry. The almond tree, the birds, the little wood where you are, the flowers you do not see, the open window out of which I lean and dream. . . . But especially I want to write a kind of long elegy to you . . . perhaps not in poetry. Nor perhaps in prose. Almost entirely in a kind of *special prose*.

—Katherine Mansfield, *Journal*, January 22, 1916

Kathleen apparently visited the Trowell twins in Frankfurt in the fall of 1903. She also made a summer trip to Germany in 1904. Then for Easter in 1906, Aunt Belle took her three nieces to Brussels where the Trowells were now studying. Kass was attracted to the bohemian life of musicians and artists she saw on the Continent. When Harold and Annie Beauchamp arrived in England in April to take their daughters home in the fall, Kass found the prospect of returning to Wellington dismal. When the Trowells also came to London in April to give recitals for which Arnold won high praise, she became intensely emotional about the future of her relationship with him. She began the unfinished autobiographical piece "Juliet," in which she wrote, "If I do go back all will be over. It is stagnation, desolation that stares me in the face."

As the time to leave England approached, she spoke of taking a flat and staying in London; when her parents refused to entertain this notion, she resolved to make herself so objectionable that they would be glad to send her back to England. On the voyage back to New Zealand, just turned 18, she annoyed her father by flirting outrageously with a member of the English cricket team on the ship. Harold Beauchamp told his daughter he would not tolerate her "fooling around in dark corners with fellows"; he had serious misgivings about his wisdom in

sending his daughters "home" to finish their education and resolved to keep his two youngest children in New Zealand.

Back in Wellington, Kathleen continued to rebel against what she regarded as the conventional and materialistic values of her parents and the dullness of colonial social life. Resolved to pursue her desire to achieve independence as an artist and sexual freedom as a "new woman," she renewed her intimate friendship with Maata Mahupuku, toward whom she had always felt a strong sexual attraction, and developed a passionate relationship with **Edie Bendall**, nine years older than herself, who had recently returned from art school in Sydney. Kass and Edie planned to write and illustrate a book about children and spent time together in the holiday cottage Harold had built for the family at Day's Bay. In her journal, which had already become an important outlet for her intimate feelings, Kathleen recorded both the sexual yearning and comfort she felt in Edie's presence: "I feel more powerfully all those so-termed sexual impulses with her than I have with any man." At the same time, she was certain that she would one day marry Arnold and share the artist's life with him. An invaluable experience of her time at home, and one which gave her a new perspective on New Zealand, was the month-long camping trip she took with a small party to the Maori-speaking Urewara country in the volcanic central region of the North Island, where she saw for the first time scenes of untamed beauty of her native land and experienced the harsh living conditions of many settlers and indigenous people living in these remote areas.

During her 18 months in New Zealand before persuading her father to provide the allowance that would enable her to live in London until she could make her own way either through her music or her writing, the young woman who was to become Katherine Mansfield was shaped by the unresolved conflicts that would haunt her short life and provide many themes for her fiction. Throughout her life she needed—and hated to need—the support and ministrations of a woman who would give her unconditional love. At the same time she needed—and repeatedly denigrated or fled from—the safety net of heterosexual marriage to maintain what she seemed to recognize as her precarious hold on a world of security and respectability. Out of such conflicts she was to create satirical stories like "Marriage a la Mode" and "The Man Without a Temperament" about superficially sophisticated characters acting out roles with nervous gaiety that masks the frightening emptiness of their social and marital relationships. In time, she also came to understand her intense loneliness and her love-hate relationship with her family—especially her father—and with her homeland as a source of deep and poignant memories she would draw upon again and again in her best stories: those about childhood experiences ("Prelude," "The Garden Party," and "A Doll's House"); about moments of intense awareness of connection to the external world ("The Wind Blows," "At the Bay," "Bliss"); and about lonely and isolated characters whose lives of imaginative fantasy offer fragile and temporary protection from the cruelty of an indifferent world ("The Tiredness of Rosabel" and "Miss Brill").

The practice of daily writing during this period in New Zealand—in journals, diaries, notebooks, and letters—made her aware of the power of language to produce finely wrought, consciously crafted prose that recreates and reveals experience with the economy and intensity of poetry. When several of her pieces were accepted by the Melbourne *Native Companion* under the pen name of K. Mansfield, she was able to convince her father that she might have a future as a writer, if not as a cellist.

Kathleen left for England in July 1908, hopeful of finding the longed-for freedom and the range of "experience" that she believed would fuel her creative production. The next four years were in fact a traumatic and brutal initiation into the bohemian life of the early part of the century. This period of her life—about which there is a great deal of speculation and surmise among her biographers because she destroyed almost all of her diaries of 1909–12, and about which people who knew her at this time provided often conflicting recollections after her death—is characterized by a reckless pursuit of personal freedom, confusion about her sexual identity, and deep emotional hurt masked by assumed sophisticated indifference to failed personal relationships. The single truth that one can extract from the web of deliberate and unintentional lies and the protective half-truths that have accumulated about this period, and from the fragmentary evidence upon which her story has been variously reconstructed, is that Kathleen, in her frantic pursuit of a life of intense and varied experience, followed a path that led, by a series of tragic mistakes and misfortunes, to a future marked by increasingly debilitating illnesses, emotional and financial dependency on others, and frustration of her two deepest desires: for a permanent home and family, and for the sustained stamina to realize her talent as a writer.

Met when her ship docked at the end August 1908 by Ida Baker, who had idolized her when they were both at Queen's, Kass spent a few days with Ida's family before taking up residence at Beauchamp Lodge, a hostel for single music students with few rules for its residents. The Trowell family was living in London at the time, and although Kass was telling friends that she was secretly engaged to Arnold, he seems to have regarded her as no more than a family friend. During her frequent visits to the Trowell home, where she was treated as a member of the family, she very soon transferred her affections to Arnold's twin brother Garnet, a violinist in a traveling opera company who was more receptive to her overtures and, while he was on tour, her passionate letters.

Throughout the fall, she led a chameleon-like existence, assuming different roles according to the company she kept. She made ends meet between the days when she could pick up her monthly allowance through the Bank of New Zealand by entertaining for pay at fashionable parties with her gifts for recitation, singing, and music. For her birthday, Garnet Trowell evidently sent her a ring, which she proudly showed his family and her Aunt Belle, who was now married and living in England. At the same time, she told a friend that she feared she was pregnant as a result of an incident that had occurred on her journey to England when she went ashore with a male passenger and was drugged. Neither this melodramatic story nor the pregnancy has been verified. She went off to Paris to attend a wedding and wrote Garnet cheerfully about the sights she had seen. During the fall, she wrote "The Education of Audrey," which was probably published in London before it was reprinted in the Wellington *Evening Post*, and possibly the first version of a story that showed the promise of her mature writing, "The Tiredness of Rosabel." Toward the end of November, she may have joined Garnet on his tour and taken a small part in the opera chorus; upon Garnet's return to London, she lived with the Trowells for part of December as a paying guest.

Early in January, there was a serious falling out with Mr. and Mrs. Trowell—perhaps because of her affair with Garnet—and Kass left their home, never to return. Terribly hurt, confused, and now quite possibly pregnant, although it is not clear that Garnet or his parents were aware of this, she returned to Beauchamp Lodge. She first turned to Ida Baker for consolation, and then in early February accepted a marriage proposal from George Bowden, a tenor singer 11 years her senior whom she had recently met. They were married on March 2, 1909. On the evening of the wedding when, according to Bowden, "she lay on the bed [of their hotel suite] like a log" and he suggested that she "go and ring up Ida Baker," Kass left and returned to Beauchamp Lodge, where she announced casually the next morning at the breakfast table that she was married, a condition that made her ineligible to live there any longer. She shortly joined Garnet, who was on tour in Glasgow, and went with him to Liverpool before returning to London. It is unclear whether or not he knew about her marriage. On their return to London, Kass went to stay with Ida and her father. She never saw Garnet again, but wrote to him from Germany later in the year.

Annie Beauchamp, having learned of her daughter's marriage through the bank clerk who dispensed her allowance, sailed for England in early April. By this time, Kass was certainly pregnant. When Garnet, whose parents may have seen her marriage notice to Bowden posted in the papers on March 17, did not respond to her letters, Kass, having settled with Ida's help in a cheap flat, began to take Veronal to get to sleep. On a sudden whim, she went briefly to Brussels, traveling as Mrs. K. Bendall, thus beginning a pattern of abrupt moves and assumed identities to escape painful situations. Her mother arrived in England at the end of May. It is unclear whether or not she knew of Kass' pregnancy, but she promptly arranged interviews with Mr. Bowden and Ida's father, Dr. Baker. Apparently aware of her daughter's attraction to women, Annie hoped to "cure" what George Bowden referred to ten years later as Kathleen's "sexual imbalance" by separation: she took Kathleen to Germany and advised Dr. Baker to send Ida away on a trip. Once Kathleen was installed in an expensive hotel at a Bavarian spa at Bad Worishofen, where a Catholic priest advocated a regimen of ice cold showers, baths, barefoot walks, and a vegetarian diet as "nature therapy," Annie Beauchamp returned to Wellington and promptly cut Kathleen out of her will.

Left alone in Worishofen, Kass, under the name of Kathe Bowden, moved from the hotel to a small pension, which was to provide the setting and title of her first book of stories, *In a German Pension* (1911). In late June or early July, after lifting her trunk to the top of a cupboard, she had a miscarriage. The loss of her baby left her desolate, and she wrote Ida of her longing for a child to love. Ida, ever eager to fulfill Kathleen's slightest wish, promptly arranged for a poor shopkeeper's son, recovering from pleurisy and in need of a change and some sunshine, to be sent to spend several weeks with her.

In Worishofen, Kathleen met a Polish writer named Floryan Sobienowski, and her brief affair with him was to haunt the remainder of her professional and personal life. During their time together, they had apparently read and discussed Chekhov's short stories, and Kathleen's first published work after her return to England late in 1909, "The Child-Who-Was-Tired," was a "free adaptation" of Chekhov's story "Sleepy-head," printed without acknowledgment of Chekhov as a source or influence. This may have been the basis of later otherwise inexplicable favors and payments she agreed to grant Sobienowski. Equally important is the fact that through Sobienowski she probably contracted gonorrhea, undiagnosed for years—as was often the case with women at this time—while it destroyed her health and undermined her immune system, making her vulnerable to tuberculosis, the cause of her death in 1923.

Returning to London in 1909 with the help of Ida Baker, Kass appealed to George Bowden for assistance, lived in his flat, and through him met A.R. Orage, editor of the *New Age,* an innovative publication devoted to new perspectives in politics, literature, and art. This meeting marked the start of her professional career in England. Orage printed "The Child-Who-Was-Tired" in February and "Germans at Meat" in March. Her association with Orage and the *New Age* introduced her to the milieu of emerging modernist writers and artists in London, among whom she was to become known personally as well as professionally as Katherine Mansfield. Her new career was interrupted in the spring—as it would be often from now on—by a bout of illness, first an operation for "peritonitis," and then an infection, which she called rheumatic fever, but which was apparently an effect of the undiagnosed venereal infection which would recur frequently and which she thereafter called her "rheumatiz." Ida Baker, whom she had begun to refer to in her journals and letters as L.M. (for Leslie Moore), took her to the seashore to recover her health. In 1910, Katherine published several more of her Bavarian stories in the *New Age.*

At the beginning of 1911, she took a three-room flat in Clovelly Mansions, where she lived until September 1912, the longest period of residence at one address during her adult life. In 1911, she and her brother Leslie, who was visiting England with his mother and sisters for the coronation of George V, reestablished the close, loving relationship they had shared in childhood. She continued to publish in the *New Age,* and her first book of stories, *In a German Pen-*

sion, was published in December. She seemed to have emerged from a period of almost surreal existence and multiple personalities as a beautiful and fashionable young woman with a promising literary career; she was, however, about to enter the semi-invalid condition in which she would spend the rest of her life.

The next phase of her life began at the end of 1911 when she met John Middleton Murry, a 22-year-old scholarship student at Oxford and editor of *Rhythm*. By April 1912, Murry, at Katherine's invitation, moved into her flat first as her lodger and soon as her lover. As their relationship developed, she became assistant editor of *Rhythm*. In the fall, their first attempt to establish a home in the country and, Katherine hoped, begin a family failed after two months when the financial difficulties of *Rhythm* and the unwelcome appearance of Sobienowski, who moved in with them, made a return to London advisable. After spending Christmas in Paris with friends, the couple now known as the Murrys returned to London and, in March, again took a cottage in the country, keeping their one-room London flat as an office for *Rhythm*, which was reorganized in May 1913 as *The Blue Review*, but failed after three issues. For the remaining ten years of her life, Murry's need to make London the center of his career as a journalist and Katherine's need to escape London for the sake of her health determined the itinerant life they led despite frequent resolves to settle into a permanent home.

From 1913 to 1923, Katherine's life and career would be shaped by several new literary friendships, as well as by her continuing complicated relationships with Murry and Ida Baker. These new friendships led to connections with the coteries of unconventional writers, artists, and intellectuals who congregated in Bloomsbury and at Garsington, the fashionable country estate where Lady *Ottoline Morrell collected and entertained celebrities of the time.

In June 1913, D.H. Lawrence, who had by then published *The White Peacock* and *The Trespasser*, and had been in touch with *Rhythm* while in Italy about having his stories published, returned to England with *Frieda Weekley (Lawrence) after their dramatic lovers' flight of the previous spring and called at the journal's office. He took to Murry and Katherine immediately, and because of his similar situation with Frieda, identified with their inability to marry while Katherine was still married to Bowden, who went to America in 1914 without following up on preliminary steps he had made to get a di-

vorce. The two couples became close friends, and Murry and Katherine shared in the celebration of the Lawrences' wedding in July 1914, when Frieda gave Katherine her old wedding ring, which Katherine wore until her death.

Following the bankruptcy of the *Blue Review*, the Murrys stayed for a while in Paris and then in several flats in London, where they could live cheaply on Katherine's allowance while Murry worked on a novel and Katherine, who was not doing much writing, attempted to get work as an film extra. Meanwhile, Ida had gone to live with her father in Rhodesia. Following the outbreak of war in August, Katherine and Murry went for a brief holiday to Cornwall and then stayed with the Lawrences in Buckinghamshire before moving into Rose Tree Cottage, about three miles from the Lawrences.

Early in 1915, Katherine became discontented with Murry, returned to London, and planned to leave him to join Francis Carco, a friend Murry had introduced her to in Paris the previous year. She was detained by illness and by her brother Leslie's arrival in England to join a regiment and go to war. With money given her by Leslie, she went to Paris in February and managed to get into the war zone for a four-day affair with Carco. Within a week, she returned to England and reconciled with Murry, but in the next two months left him again twice to live in Carco's Paris flat to write, returning within weeks of each separation. In June, she and Murry moved together to a house in St. John's Wood after Murry was hired as a reviewer for the *Times Literary Supplement*. There, Leslie visited them for several weeks, and he and Katherine reminisced fondly about their childhood before he left for France on September 22. On October 7, Leslie was killed when a grenade blew up in his hand. Katherine was so devastated by the news and ill with the onset of winter that Murry took her to Bandol in the south of France in mid-November, hoping that there she would ease her grief and recover her health. She resolved to get well and pay tribute to her brother's memory by writing about their childhood in New Zealand. Murry left her there to return to England to spend Christmas at Garsington, to which he had been invited through Lawrence. At the new year, Murry returned to Bandol to write a book on Dostoevsky while Katherine rewrote "The Aloe," a story about her family and childhood, cast in a new mood of unsentimental reminiscence and written in a crisp, detached style. As it had for many of her fellow modernists, the war transformed Katherine's view of life and art.

In April 1916, the Murrys joined the Lawrences at Higher Tregerthen in Cornwall, possibly as a preliminary attempt to establish the utopian community of like-minded, free individuals Lawrence had been talking about for several years. By June, the violent arguments between Lawrence and Frieda and Lawrence's insistent urging of Murry to join him in a "blood-brother" relationship so distressed Katherine and Murry that they left to take a cottage some distance away, after which their relationship with the Lawrences cooled. Once more discontent, Katherine left Murry, but after spending a weekend at Garsington with Lady Ottoline and her guests, including Lytton Strachey and *Dora Carrington, returned to him. Through their new Garsington friends, Murry got a job as a translator with the War Office as an alternative to military service, which provided a regular salary for the first time in his life.

In September, Murry and Katherine moved into J.M. Keynes' house in Bloomsbury, which they shared with Dorothy Brett and Carrington. They soon became entangled in the unconventional relationships and gossip that characterized Bloomsbury and Garsington at the time. They developed friendships with Clive Bell, T.S. Eliot, and Bertrand Russell; Lytton Strachey arranged a meeting between Katherine and *Virginia Woolf, which took place the next year, after Katherine and Murry had moved to separate studio flats. Ida, back from Rhodesia, came to live with Katherine. Virginia and Leonard Woolf, who had just established the Hogarth Press, asked Katherine for a story they could publish, and she began reworking "The Aloe" as "Prelude," but became ill before she could finish typing it.

In December, a doctor, fearful that Katherine's persistent cough and chronic pleurisy indicated tuberculosis, advised her to go abroad, and in January 1918, Katherine left alone for Bandol. Ida, disturbed to hear of Katherine's poor health, joined her in February. On February 19, Katherine had her first lung hemorrhage. As her illness became worse, she and Ida tried to return to England by way of Paris, but were not permitted to leave Paris while it was under bombardment. On their return in April, Murry said that Katherine was barely recognizable. On April 29, her divorce from George Bowen became final, and on May 3, she and Murry were married. She spent two months in Cornwall in the hope of regaining her health, where Murry joined her after a while. When they returned to London in the summer, "Prelude" had been issued by the Hogarth Press, and in August, "Bliss" was published in the *English Review*. The Murrys moved to their own house in Hampstead, where Ida joined them as housekeeper, after Katherine, advised by specialists to enter a sanitorium, chose to undergo treatment at home under the care of a doctor who for the first time identified her "rheumatism" as a symptom of the gonorrheal infection she had contracted in 1911.

After Murry became editor of the *Athenaeum* in 1919, Katherine began reviewing novels for the journal and helped S.S. Koteliansky with his translation of Chekhov's letters. Too weak to go out much herself, Katherine was frequently visited by Virginia Woolf, who wrote in her *Journal* after Katherine's death "I was jealous of her writing—the only writing I have ever been jealous of. . . . Probably we had something in common which I shall never find in anyone else." In the fall, Lawrence visited and renewed their friendship. T.S. and Vivienne Eliot also visited her at Hampstead.

For the remaining years of her life, Katherine alternated between two beliefs: that she was on the brink of death, and that she would make a miraculous recovery, renewed in body and spirit, to live happily with Murry and the children they would have. Beginning in 1919, she spent long periods abroad seeking healthful climates in France, Italy, and Switzerland, usually accompanied by Ida and sometimes by Murry. She returned from time to time to their home at Hampstead. She continued to write reviews of novels for the *Athenaeum* as long as she was able to, and she wrote and published some of her best and most enduring stories during bursts of creative energy in 1920 ("The Daughters of the Late Colonel," "Miss Brill," "The Life of Ma Parker," and "The Lady's Maid") and 1921 ("At the Bay," "The Doll's House," "Her First Ball," "The Garden Party"). Two collections, *Bliss and Other Stories* (1921) and *The Garden Party and Other Stories* (1922), established her reputation as a major practitioner of the modern short story.

As her health continued to deteriorate, she sought desperate remedies, first in a series of radiation treatments she took in Paris in 1922, and finally through George Ivanovich Gurdjieff's Institute for the Harmonious Development of Man, organized as a commune in Fountainbleu, France, on the site of an old Carmelite monastery. There Gurdjieff preached that integrated mental, physical, and spiritual health could be achieved through exercise, diet, meditation, physical labor, music, dance, and painting. After a final visit to England, during which she saw her father and other members of her family, Katherine went to live at the Institute in Fountainbleu on October 16, 1922, and participated in the harsh regimen prescribed for her by Gurdjieff. In early January, she asked Murry to visit her there; he arrived on January 9 and spent the afternoon with her. As he walked her to her room that evening, she suffered a massive hemorrhage and died. She was buried in the communal cemetery in Avon, outside Fountainbleu.

As her widower and literary executor, John Middleton Murry became the guardian of Katherine Mansfield's reputation—personal and literary—a role many would say he performed with a mixture of shameless sentimentality and crass self-interest. At the time of her death, she was the author of some 88 stories and fragments and had published three books of collected stories, two in the last two years of her life. Although she earned a modest income in those years from the publication of individual stories in magazines and journals, she remained financially dependent on the allowance from her father throughout her life. After her death, Murry edited 11 books of her writings, including letters and various versions of her notebooks and journals. Jeffrey Meyers counts some 40 books, articles, poems, introductions, and letters to the press Murry wrote between 1923 and 1959 which contributed to the myths—indeed almost the cults—that grew around the idealized memory of Katherine Mansfield that Murry perpetuated. As manuscripts of letters, notebooks, journals, and unpublished works have become accessible in recent years, a much more complex portrait of Katherine Mansfield as woman and writer has begun to emerge. Continuing analysis of these new materials will undoubtedly lead to a fuller understanding of her life and a critical revaluation of her part in shaping the direction of modern fiction.

SOURCES:

Alpers, Antony. *The Life of Katherine Mansfield.* NY: Viking, 1980.

Meyers, Jeffrey. *Katherine Mansfield: A Biography.* NY: New Directions, 1978.

Tomalin, Claire. *Katherine Mansfield: A Secret Life.* London: Viking, 1987.

SUGGESTED READING:

The Collected Letters of Katherine Mansfield. Ed. by Vincent O'Sullivan and Margaret Scott. 4 vols. Oxford: Clarendon, 1993–96.

The Journal of Katherine Mansfield. Definitive Edition. Ed. by J. Middleton Murry. London: Constable, 1954.

The Katherine Mansfield Notebooks. Ed. by Margaret Scott. 2 vols. Canterbury, N.Z.: Lincoln University Press, 1997.

The Letters of Katherine Mansfield. Ed. by J. Middleton Murry. 2 vols. London: Constable, 1928.

Stories by Katherine Mansfield. NY: Knopf, 1930.

Patricia B. Heaman,
Professor of English, Wilkes
University, Wilkes-Barre, Pennsylvania

Manton, Sidnie (1902–1979)

English zoologist. Born Sidnie Milana Manton in 1902 in England; died in 1979; educated at the Froebel Educational Institute School and St. Paul's Girls' School in Hammersmith; Girton College, Cambridge, Ph.D., 1928, Sc.D., 1934; married Dr. John Philip Harding, in 1937; children: one daughter and one son.

Sidnie Milana Manton was born in 1902 in England. She attended Froebel Educational Institute School and St. Paul's Girls' School in Hammersmith, and Girton College in Cambridge. In 1928, after earning her Ph.D. in zoology at Girton, Manton visited Tasmania and participated in an exploration of the Great Barrier Reef, making advanced studies in arthropods. From 1935 to 1942, she served as director of studies in natural science at Girton. Remaining at her alma mater, she held the positions of staff fellow from 1942 to 1945 and research fellow from 1945 to 1948. In 1948, Manton was elected a fellow of the Royal Society. The following year, she was appointed as a reader (instructor) in zoology at King's College in London, where she remained until 1960. She was also associated with the British Museum Natural History section as an honorary worker. Her husband, Dr. John Philip Harding, whom she had married in 1937, became the Keeper of Zoology for the British Museum. The couple had two children, a daughter and a son.

Manton's research, much of which focused on evolution, added significantly to the knowledge of invertebrates, about which little had been studied previously, and she became eminent in the fields of arthropod embryology and functional morphology. Awards granted to Sidnie Manton included the Linnaean Gold Medal (1963) and the Frink Medal of the Zoological Society (1977). She also was named an honorary fellow of Queen Mary College in London. In 1930 she published her first work (coauthored by J.T. Saunders), *A Manual of Practical Vertebrate Morphology*; the fourth edition was released in 1969. She also wrote *Colourpoint, Himalayan and Longhair Cats.* The first edition was published in 1971, and the second edition in 1979. Her most comprehensive work appeared in 1977 as *The Arthropods: Habits, Functional Morphology and Evolution.*

Kari Bethel,
freelance writer, Columbia, Missouri

Mantua, duchess of.

See Gonzaga, Margherita (1510–1566).

See Catherine of Habsburg (1533–1572).
See Eleonora of Austria (1534–1594).
See Medici, Eleonora de (1567–1611).
See Medici, Caterina de (1593–1629).
See Gonzaga, Isabella (fl. 1600s).
See Margaret of Savoy (fl. 1609–1612).

Mantua, marchioness of.

See joint entry on Este, Beatrice and Isabella d' for Isabella d'Este (1474–1539).

Mantua, marquesa of.

See Gonzaga, Paola (1393–1453).
See Barbara of Brandenburg (1422–1481).
See Margaret of Bavaria (1445–1479).
See joint entry on Este, Beatrice and Isabella d' for Isabella d'Este (1474–1539).

Manuela (1847–1933).

See Uzès, Anne, Duchesse d'.

Manus, Rosa and Mia Boissevain

Dutch feminists who organized a major 1913 exhibition on the status of women, and who were advocates of women's suffrage, women's rights and the worldwide peace movement, as well as active in aiding war refugees.

Mia Boissevain (1878–1959). Name variations: Maria. Pronunciation: Bwha-se-VAY. Born Maria Boissevain on April 8, 1878, in Amsterdam, the Netherlands; died on March 8, 1959, in London, England; daughter of Jan Boissevain (director of a shipping company) and Petronella Brugmans; attended secondary girls' school; granted master's degree in biology at the University of Amsterdam, and Ph.D., University of Zurich, Switzerland, 1903; never married; children: two (adopted).

Was active in the International Woman Suffrage Alliance from 1908; organized an exhibition on the position of women, entitled "Woman 1813–1913"; was a member of the women's committee (and the general committee) to help mobilize families during World War I.

Selected writings: Beiträge zur Anatomie und Histologie von Dentalium (dissertation, Jena, 1903); The Women's Movement in the Netherlands (Leiden, 1915); Een Amsterdamsche familie (Diepenveen, 1967).

Rosa Manus (1881–1942). Name variations: Rosette. Pronunciation: MA-nus. Born Rosette Suzanne Manus on August 20, 1881, in Amsterdam, the Netherlands; died in 1942 at Ravensbrück concentration camp in Germany; daughter of Henry Philip Manus (a merchant in tobacco) and Soete Vita Israel; attended secondary girls' school and boarding school in Switzerland; never married.

Was active in the International Woman Suffrage Alliance from 1908 (known as the International Alliance of Women since 1926); organized an exhibition on the position of women, entitled "Woman 1813–1913"; was a member of the women's committee to help mobilized families during World War I; served as secretary of the Dutch Association for Woman Suffrage; vice-president of the International Woman Suffrage Alliance (1923); served as secretary of the Peace Committee of the International Alliance of Women (1926); was a member of the Women's Disarmament Committee of International Organizations; served as secretary of the International Peace Congress of the Rassemblement Universel pour la Paix (RUP) in Brussels (1936); was active in helping Jewish refugees (1933–42); co-founded the International Archive of the Women's Movement (IAV) in Amsterdam, the Netherlands (1935).

In 1913, the Netherlands had been a monarchy for a hundred years, since its liberation as the former Dutch Republic after being occupied by the French from 1806 to 1813. In celebration of a century of peaceful royal rule, a number of exhibitions were mounted in that year, including "De Vrouw, 1813–1913" ("Woman, 1813–1913") which was organized by two of the country's most influential feminists, Mia Boissevain and Rosa Manus. Opened by the reigning Queen *Wilhelmina in May 1913, its presentation of the changing status of women drew widespread attention in the Netherlands and from visitors from around the world.

Born in 1878, Mia Boissevain was a native of Amsterdam, the capital of the Netherlands. Both her parents were from distinguished Amsterdam families: her mother was Petronella Brugmans, the granddaughter of C.F. van Maanen, who served in the Cabinet of King William I for 30 years as minister of justice, and her father Jan Boissevain was a descendant of French Huguenots who fled France in the 1680s, after the revocation of the Edict of Nantes. The Boissevain family had become prosperous merchants and shipowners in the Netherlands, and in 1870, Jan had started one of the country's first steamship companies.

In contrast to her mother's education at home by a French governess, Mia joined other upper-class girls of her generation in attending school, advancing from primary school to the secondary "Golden School," a nickname for the place where the daughters of Amsterdam's

wealthiest citizens were educated. There she learned Dutch grammar and modern languages—English, French and German—as well as mathematics and handicrafts, and took little notice of a schoolmate, Rosa Manus, who was three years younger.

Mia did not like homework and looked forward to having school behind her, but she reached graduation without being sure what to do with her life. For a while she joined her eldest sister, **Elisabeth Boissevain**, a social worker for a private organization, Liefdadigheid naar Vermogen, on trips through the slums of Amsterdam. In the poorest neighborhoods of the city, she witnessed families living in stuffy single-room apartments, where wet laundry hung from the ceiling and stoves were used in dangerously close quarters, but the work brought her little satisfaction. Mia did not find poor people helped much by such charity, and viewed the efforts as a drop in the ocean.

Persuaded to take a botany course by her other sister, **Anna Boissevain**, who studied medicine, Mia began attending the lectures of professor Hugo de Vries. At the end of the 19th century, a growing number of women in Europe were attending college, but when the 17-year-old Mia first entered De Vries' lecture room, she caused a stir in the all-male class. Some of the young men made room for her in the front row, where women students were expected to sit, and Mia soon liked the course so much that she became a student of zoology at the University of Amsterdam in 1896. Within five years, she obtained her master's degree and then spent a year of study in Zurich, Switzerland, where she obtained her Ph.D. in 1903, with a dissertation entitled *Beiträge zur Anatomie und Histologie von Dentalium*. Back in the Netherlands, she was hired as a curator at Artis Magistra Natura, a museum of the Amsterdam Zoo. After the deaths of her parents in 1904 and 1905, her inheritance gave her an adequate income for the rest of her life, and she shared a household with her brother in the village of Bilthoven, near the city of Utrecht.

I have often wondered, what would have happened to the exhibition if Rosa Manus had not offered all her time and strength.

—Mia Boissevain

In the 1890s, much research was under way on the brain weight of humans and animals, and it was generally held that women's brains were of lesser weight (and therefore less intelligent) than men's, an assumption that Boissevain disputed, to many heated discussions with her colleagues at the laboratory. During her student days, although Mia Boissevain did not feel discrimination against her as a woman, she was conscious of undertaking an enterprise that was new for women. In her memoirs, she described the unease she felt when she met one of her colleagues from the laboratory at a ball or some other evening social occasion.

In Switzerland, Boissevain had also been drawn into discussions with female scientists interested in the feminist movement. Back in the Netherlands and wanting to know more about the position of women in her own society, she sought out Dr. *Aletta Jacobs, the first female student in the Netherlands and the country's most famous feminist, with an international reputation. Dr. Jacobs was kind and open to discussion, and gave Boissevain leaflets dealing with the legal position of women in the Netherlands; when preparations began for a congress on women's suffrage to be held in Amsterdam in 1908, Jacobs turned to Boissevain for help.

The congress was an initiative of the International Woman Suffrage Alliance, led by the American feminist *Carrie Chapman Catt. During the meeting Boissevain became acquainted with well-known Dutch feminists **Johanna Naber** and **Wilhelmina Drucker** as well as many militant English suffragists who were to be imprisoned over the next few years for their cause. Boissevain later remembered discussions between the militant and the moderate feminists as often heated, but always under the control of Catt. Around this time, Catt also "discovered" Rosa Manus.

Born in Amsterdam in 1881, Rosa Manus, the daughter of a tobacco merchant, was raised in another well-to-do family. She spent her childhood on one of the canals in the center of the city, the Kloveniersburgwal, where she was born at number 92 (Mia was born at number 74); later, her family moved to the neighboring small town of Baarn. Three years younger than Mia, Rosa had attended the same primary and "Golden" secondary schools, then followed another practice common to upper-class girls by spending a few years at a foreign "finishing" school, in Switzerland. (Two of Mia's sisters had attended such a school in France, where heat was lacking and the food was bad, which may be the reason that she, as the youngest, never enjoyed the finishing school experience.)

Like Boissevain, Rosa Manus never had to earn a living; as an unmarried woman of the bourgeoisie, she lived in the home of her parents, where she helped her mother to run the house and took part in many social and philanthropical activities. An inheritance from her grandmother gave Manus income of her own, which she wanted to use to open a shop. She had even rented a place when her father intervened, forbidding her to go into business because he believed it improper behavior for a girl of her class. Deeply disappointed, Rosa plunged back into philanthropic work, distributing soup to the poor, and was soon managing several soup kitchens.

In 1908, Manus took part in the International Woman Suffrage Alliance in Amsterdam,

as one of the performers of a wooden shoe dance. The story goes that Carrie Chapman Catt was so impressed by Rosa's display of passion and will power in the dance that she asked her to join the alliance's organizing committee. Soon Rosa and Mia were setting up an information desk for foreign visitors.

Three years apart in age, Rosa and Mia had not been friends at school, but at this third congress of the alliance they began a friendship that was to last the rest of their lives. According to Boissevain's later memory, it was during this meeting, when the issue of women's suffrage was raised, that she realized she had always been a feminist. At ages 30 and 27 respectively, Mia and Rosa belonged to their country's second generation of feminists; after the congress, they continued to be dedicated to the cause of women's suffrage. Together they founded a Committee of Propaganda, which was officially installed by Aletta Jacobs, and organized many evenings of debate. Sometimes no one showed up, but at other times there were so many people that the police would be summoned for crowd control.

Manus became secretary of the Dutch Association for Women's Suffrage and accompanied Jacobs in this capacity as Dutch representative to the next congress of the alliance, held in London in 1909. In 1910, she became special organizer of the alliance, traveling to the city to handle the advance planning for the next congress; later she was vice-president of the organization, but primarily she worked in the background.

In 1912, it was Boissevain's idea to organize an exhibition on the changing status of women over the period of 1813 to 1913. She and Manus coordinated the work of establishing 24 divisions, each with a separate theme. The preparation time was only eight months, a short period in which to launch such a huge project, and they did not receive the collaboration of some women's organizations. But in May 1913, "De Vrouw, 1813–1913" opened on time and won a request from Queen Wilhelmina for a guided tour, proudly given to her by Boissevain.

Separate pavilions housed portions of the exhibition organized around themes, such as The

Rosa Manus (right) with Carrie Chapman Catt during their world trip for the International Women's Alliance.

Woman in her Home, Education, Childrearing, Women's Rights, and Women's Work. Women's Work drew particular attention, with its display of women in home industries, where the pay was low and the conditions often humiliating. The display about the former Dutch colonies of the Dutch East and West Indies, with its replica of an Indonesian house, was outstanding; it also included a provisional Indonesian restaurant, which brought in considerable money. A large hall was devoted to the issue of women's suffrage, but when Carrie Chapman Catt arrived to make her passionate plea for the women's right to vote, it was not large enough for the crowd that had turned out, and an even larger hall had to be found for her lecture.

A year after the exhibition, when Europe was suddenly thrust into the First World War, Boissevain and Manus found their attention shifted to the issues of refugees and other war related problems. On August 1, 1914, Germany declared war on Russia; that same night, Rosa phoned Mia, who was then staying in the country with her youngest brother, and described a women's committee being formed in Amsterdam to help the wives of men mobilized for military service; in that period of uncertainty, it was feared that the men's families could not provide for themselves, and there was the question as well of who would take over the men's work. Meeting in an orphanage of the Walloon church, the committee was soon working in close cooperation with the city councilor of poor relief, collecting money, providing food and organizing courses in first aid. Later the committee became part of the General Aid Committee (*Algemeen Steuncomité*), of which Boissevain became a member.

In the fall of 1914, after the city of Antwerp, capital of neighboring Belgium, was captured by the Germans, thousands of Belgians fled across the border into the Netherlands. The Dutch government, located in The Hague, decided to accommodate as many as possible of the refugees, who at the time were forced to live and sleep in the open air. When the village of Bilthoven, where Boissevain lived, admitted 100 refugees, she went from house to house, collecting linens and mattresses, and asking people to lodge the Belgians. Boissevain herself accommodated seven refugees, four of whom—a mother with three children—remained with her throughout the winter of 1914–15.

After the war ended in 1918, Boissevain adopted two children and became less politically active, but traveled extensively in Europe. Boissevain and Manus saw each other less often after 1920, but in a letter to **Lucy E. Anthony** dated

November 15, 1926, Manus wrote, "We do not see each other often, but when we are together, we are very close friends again, and enjoy each other's company." In 1929, the two women went on holiday together, and from the city of Wiesbaden in Germany they wrote to Johanna Naber that the holiday "brought back memories from the good old days."

Manus continued to work for Carrie Chapman Catt. In 1922, she accompanied Catt on her women's suffrage campaign, making an excursion through South America. During this time, Manus was also drawn to the peace movement. In 1926, she became secretary of the Peace Committee of the International Alliance of Women, and she played an important role in organizing the big Disarmament Congress of the League of Nations held in 1932. As secretary of the Women's Disarmament Committee of International Organizations, she helped to collect eight million signatures from women all over the world in favor of peace. She was also active in organizing the International Peace Congress held in Brussels in 1936, a controversial undertaking because the organizers were accused of creating communist propaganda.

In the years after the First World War, women in many countries obtained the vote, and while many gender issues remained unchanged, the struggle for women's rights became less urgent. Like a number of feminists, Manus turned to other issues, such as disarmament and peace. Many members of the International Alliance of Women feared the dangers of Italian Fascism and German Nazism, and were witnessing the rise of anti-Semitism in Europe; some of the members of the alliance itself were not free of anti-Semitic feelings. At an alliance congress held in Copenhagen, Denmark, in 1939, a representative from Egypt stopped speaking to Manus after discovering she was Jewish.

After the death of her father in 1931, Rosa and her mother had moved back to Amsterdam, where she sensed the situation of Jews across Europe becoming more alarming. After Hitler came to power in Germany, she organized aid for German refugees as she had done earlier for the Belgians, and she became one of the founders of the General Women's Committee for Refugees (Neutraal Vrouwencomité voor Vluchtelingen). With family members living in Germany, she became well aware of what was happening to Jews under the Nazis. Her work, meanwhile, was hindered by the Dutch government, which was pursuing a restricted policy of admitting only a limited number of German refugees, while many more crossed the border illegally.

Frightened by this time, Rosa began to anticipate what would happen when the Nazis came to power in the Netherlands. Early in 1940, shortly before the outbreak of the Second World War, she collected her letters and personal documents and brought them to the International Archive of the Women's Movement (IAV) in Amsterdam, which she had co-founded in 1935.

In 1941, in a birthday greeting dated August 6 and sent for Manus' birthday on the 20th, which she probably never received, Carrie Chapman Catt wrote, "You certainly will become just as old as me, so you still have twenty-two years to go." A few days later, Manus was arrested in Amsterdam by the Gestapo, brought to a prison in Scheveningen, and afterwards transported to Ravensbrück, the women's concentration camp in Germany. In May 1942, her family received news that she had died there as a result of a kidney disease from which she had never previously suffered. Eyewitnesses later claimed that she was being transported to Auschwitz when she was shot, as a result of "maladjusted" behavior.

Mia Boissevain lived until 1959, and died during a trip to London.

SOURCES:

Boissevain, Mia. *Een Amsterdamsche familie.* Diepenveen: unpublished typescript, 1967.

Bosch, Mineke, and Annemarie Kloosterman. *Lieve Dr. Jacobs. Brieven uit de Wereldbond voor Vrouwenkiesrecht, 1902–1942.* Amsterdam: Feministische Uitgeverij Sara, 1985.

Hagemeijer, Pauline. "In de schaduw: Miss Manus." Carla Wijers et al, eds. *Tussen aanpassing en verzet. Vrouwen voor het voetlicht 1929–1969.* Culemborg: Uitgeverij Lemma, 1989, pp. 33–48.

Posthumus-van der Goot, W.H., and A. de Waal, eds. *Van moeder op dochter.* Utrecht: Bruna, 1968 (or. 1948).

COLLECTIONS:

Archive of the exhibition on the changing position of women entitled Woman, 1813–1913 is located in the Municipal Archive of Amsterdam, the Netherlands.

Correspondence and documents of Rosa Manus are located in the International Information Center and Archive of the Women's Movement (IIAV) in Amsterdam, the Netherlands.

Personal documents of Mia Boissevain and her family are located in the archive of the Boissevain family in the Municipal Archive of Amsterdam, The Netherlands.

Monique Stavenuiter, Ph.D.,
University of Groningen, and researcher at the
University of Nijenrode, the Netherlands

Manzini, Gianna (1896–1974)

Italian novelist and journalist. Name variations: wrote about fashion under the names "Vanessa" and "Pamela." Born on March 24, 1896, in Pistoia, Tuscany, Italy; died in Rome, Italy, on August 31, 1974; daughter of Giuseppe Manzini (a watch repairer); degree in modern literature from the University of Florence; married Bruno Fallaci (a journalist), in 1929 (divorced).

Published first novel (1928); moved to Rome (c. 1936); won prestigious literary award, Premio Viareggio, for autobiographical novel (1956); won Naples Prize (1965).

Selected writings: Tempo innamorato *(The Time of Love, 1928);* Incontro col faco *(Meeting with a Falcon, 1929);* Casa di riposo *(Rest Home, 1934);* Rive remote *(Far Shores, 1940);* Forte come un leone *(Strong as a Lion, 1944);* Lettera all'editore *(Letter to the Publisher, 1945);* Caro Prigione *(My Dear Prison, 1951);* Il valtzer del diavolo *(The Devil's Waltz, 1953);* La Sparviera *(The Sparrow-Hawk, 1956);* Allegro con disperazione *(Allegro with Despair, 1965);* Ritratto in piedi *(Standing Portrait, 1971);* Sulla soglia *(On the Threshold, 1973).*

Gianna Manzini was an Italian novelist of imposing intellectual capacity whose works have never been translated into English. Her writings reflect the heady erudition of modern Italian literature, especially of the interwar period, and Manzini has been praised as one of the premier practitioners of a style known as *prosa d'arte* (artistic prose), a form that combined the lyrical beauty of poetry with a narrative, sometimes surreal, structure.

Manzini was born into an impoverished Tuscan family in 1896, the only child of a middle-class mother and a father who had given up wealth to become a committed anarchist. As such, he rejected the idea of property ownership, and worked for most of his life as a watch repairer. When Manzini was a child, her mother left her husband, taking Gianna with her; her father later spent time in exile and eventually died in a political prison in 1925, after Mussolini's Fascist government had risen to power.

After graduating from the University of Florence with a degree in modern literature, Manzini began writing for the journals *Solaria* and *Letteratura* in Florence. She also wrote for a newspaper, *La Nazione*; all of these publications featured an intellectual style of writing common to Italian journalism of the time. Her first novel, *Tempo innamorato* (The Time of Love), was published to critical acclaim in 1928. She then concentrated on writing short stories and saw success with the positive reception garnered by such collections as *Incontro col faco* (Meeting with a Falcon, 1929) and *Casa di riposo* (Rest Home, 1934). Like many of her contemporaries, she was a great admirer of writers such as Marcel Proust, *Katherine Mansfield, and William Faulkner. Her stream-of-consciousness style and feminist tendencies earned her comparisons to James Joyce and *Virginia Woolf. The latter's influence on her early work was so strong that in a later essay Manzini commented: "For me, the courage to endure has a name: Virginia Woolf. In reading her, I learned to collect my soul and keep it in front of me as mine workers do with their lamp."

In 1933, Manzini moved from Tuscany to Rome. She believed that surroundings greatly affected one's disposition and output, and this belief imbued her work with what one critic has called "a sense of complete correspondence between characters and environment." After nearly two decades of short stories, she saw publication of her second novel, *Lettera all'editore* (Letter to the Publisher, 1945). Manzini won acclaim for this dual narrative tale of a novel-within-a-novel, in which a woman writer creates a tale of a disintegrating marriage in her fiction while the dramas in her own life are recounted through a series of letters to her editor. After World War II, Manzini became director of *Prosa*, a review that promoted contemporary fiction from around the world. She continued to write fiction as well, including *Caro Prigione* (My Dear Prison, 1951) and *Il valtzer del diavolo* (The Devil's Waltz, 1953), both collections of short stories. The title story of the latter recounts the tale of a woman plagued by the presence of a cockroach, which helps her realize how eager she is to please others around her.

The novel *La Sparviera* (The Sparrow-Hawk, 1956) was highly autobiographical in nature, and is considered by some critics to be perhaps her finest work. In it, a young boy is afflicted with a bronchial condition that stays with him into adulthood—the title is synonymous with "bird of prey," the name he has given his ailment—and through dialogues with a mysterious female he comes to understand that the infirmity is perhaps of his own creation. (Manzini herself suffered from a bronchial condition that had begun around the time of her father's death.) She was awarded the prestigious Italian literary award, the Premio Viareggio, for *La Sparviera* (that year's award also went to writer Carlo Levi).

Described as an elegant, regal woman with a memorable sense of style, Manzini for many years wrote about fashion under the names "Vanessa" and "Pamela" for the literary journal *La fiera letteraria*, of which she also served as fashion editor. After moving to Rome, she maintained a nearly four-decades long relationship with the critic Enrico Falqui. Manzini continued to write fiction until well into her 70s, enjoying a long relationship with the Milan publishing house of Mondadori and the respect of a small but reverent audience for books that were both highly praised and described as "elite" and "difficult." *Allegro con disperazione* (Allegro with Despair, 1965) details a troubled marriage in which the husband works as a female impersonator and the wife is a victim of a childhood rape; one day their child sees his father dressed as a woman, which introduces a raft of problems to the already troubled family. For this novel, Manzini received another distinguished literary honor, the Naples Prize. In *Ritratto in piedi* (Standing Portrait, 1971), she wrote about her father's life and her own emotional ties to him even after his death, and in her last book, *Sulla soglia* (On the Threshold, 1973), she reminisced about her mother. Gianna Manzini died in Rome on August 31, 1974.

SOURCES:

Bondanella, Peter, and Julia Conaway Bondanella, eds. *Dictionary of Italian Literature*. Westport, CT: Greenwood Press, 1996.

Miceli-Jeffries, Giovanna. "Gianna Manzini," in *Dictionary of Literary Biography*, Vol. 177: *Italian Novelists Since World War II*. Edited by Augustus Pallotta. Detroit, MI: Gale Research, 1997, pp. 171–179.

Robinson, Lillian S., comp. and ed. *Modern Women Writers*. NY: Continuum, 1996.

Wilson, Katharina M., ed. *An Encyclopedia of Continental Women Writers*. NY: Garland, 1991.

Carol Brennan,
Grosse Pointe, Michigan

Manzolini, Anna Morandi

(1716–1774)

Italian anatomist. Name variations: Anne Manzolini; Anna Morandi; Anna Mahzolini or Mohzolini. Born Anna Morandi in Bologna, Italy, in 1716; died in Bologna in 1774; married Giovanni Manzolini (a professor of anatomy), in 1736; children: six.

Anna Morandi was born in Bologna, Italy, in 1716. When she was 20 years old, she married anatomist Giovanni Manzolini, a professor at the University of Bologna. The university was one of the leading European centers for the study of anatomy, and her husband was an expert in making anatomically correct wax models from corpses, for use in the instruction of anatomy. (The various Christian churches had outlawed the dissection of human bodies, even for scientific purposes, during the Middle Ages, but some scientific study of the inside of the human body had begun with the growth of that intellectual curiosity that shortly would bring about the Enlightenment. Procuring corpses for dissection was difficult, however, and skillful anatomists were prized.) Her husband often worked at home, and Manzolini despised the presence of the dead bodies he brought into their small house. Nonetheless, when it became apparent that he was slowly dying of tuberculosis, she herself started creating wax models from corpses to support the family. She began studying anatomy at the same time, in order to perfect her modeling work, and also gave birth to six children over the course of five years.

When her husband became too ill to fulfill his lecturing duties at the university, Manzolini received permission from the school to step into his place. Because of her comprehensive knowledge of anatomy and her effective teaching style, she was appointed lecturer of anatomy in her own name upon her husband's death in 1760. The university also bestowed the title of *modellatrice* upon her. In 1766, she was elected to a professorship. Word of her work spread across the continent, and at the invitation of Empress *Catherine II the Great she subsequently lectured in Russia, where she was made a member of the Russian Royal Scientific Society, and in Britain, where she was made a member of the Royal Society. She remained a professor at the University of Bologna until her death at age 58 in 1774.

Although her career started from necessity, Anna Manzolini proved to be a skilled dissector, modeler, and teacher. Her precise observation and reproduction of the human body resulted in her discovery of the correct termination of the oblique muscle of the eye. Considered a vast improvement over those created by ☜➤ **Allessandra Giliani** some 400 years before, her models were on display throughout Europe and were purchased by such influential people as Joseph II, emperor of Austria. After her death, her bust was placed in the Pantheon in Rome and in the museum of the University of Bologna.

Kari Bethel,
freelance writer, Columbia, Missouri

Mao, Madame (1914–1991).

See Jiang Qing.

Mar, countess of.

See Helen (fl. 1275).
See Bruce, Christian (d. 1356).
See Marr, Margaret (d. after 1384).

Mar, Frances, Countess of
(1690–1761)

Sister of the well-known woman of letters Lady Mary Wortley Montagu, who married a Scottish Jacobite,

followed him into exile, and fell victim to severe depression which incapacitated her for much of her life. Name variations: Lady Mar. Born Frances Pierrepont in 1690; died in 1761; second daughter of Evelyn Pierrepont, earl of Kingston, and Lady Mary Pierrepont (daughter of William Fielding, earl of Denbigh); married John Erskine, 6th or 11th earl of Mar, on July 20, 1713 (died 1732); children: daughter Frances Erskine (b. 1715).

Frances Pierrepont was the younger sister of Mary Wortley Montagu, born only one year after her more famous sister, and they seem to have been very close. Their mother died in 1692, having given birth to four children in three and a half years. We first glimpse the adult Frances in 1711, scolding her sister for having illicit meetings with Edward Wortley against their father's instructions. Mary had to elope in 1712 to marry her less wealthy suitor; Frances married the following year. This time there was no difference in social rank; Frances' husband was John Erskine,

𝒜nna 𝓜orandi 𝓜anzolini

◂➤
Giliani, Allessandra.
See Trotula for sidebar.

earl of Mar. However, the 37-year-old widower was a supporter of the Tory cause, a fervent Scottish Jacobite, while Frances' family was staunchly Whig. Lady Mary was particularly displeased with the alliance, as she intensely disliked Lord Mar and was convinced of an unhappy outcome.

By 1715, the year that her daughter **Frances Erskine** was born, Lady Mar was living with her husband close to Whitehall Palace in London; like Mary and Wortley, the couple was attempting to win favor at the court of the new king, George I of Hanover. It was soon evident that Lord Mar could not expect to receive a position, and in August he left London to lead a Scottish rebellion; the Jacobite rebels were attempting to replace the Hanoverian ruler with James Stuart, the "Old Pretender." Despite her husband's defection, Frances continued to live in Whitehall and move in court circles. Her husband asserted that she had known nothing of his plans and her family was so supportive of the new regime that no action was taken against her. Frances was even able to stay in contact with Mar after his rebellion was defeated, and he fled to France; Lady Mary, returning from Turkey, met her favorite sister in Paris in 1718.

Frances had been given permission by the king to join her husband at the Pretender's court in Italy. There she found life difficult; some of the Jacobites suspected her of being sent by the king and her father of being a spy. Losing confidence in the Pretender's cause, Mar resigned his post and the couple settled in Paris, living on Frances' inheritance. She visited England occasionally but clearly felt the strain of her exile, and she was showing signs of mental instability by 1727.

Mary kept up a devoted and lively correspondence with her sister throughout the years of her exile, constantly attempting to revive her spirits, particularly following the deaths of their father and younger sister in 1726 and 1727. But despite her sister's resilient good cheer and advice ("galloping all day and a moderate glass of champagne at night in good company"), Frances became more and more withdrawn. In November 1727, she wrote to Mary in terms that are clearly indicative of severe depression:

> I fear a time will come when I shall neither write nor see anybody. . . . [M]y solitude comes from causes that you are too happy to have experienced, and gives me no other inclination but to doze upon a couch, or exclaim against my fortune, and wish . . . forgetfulness could steal upon me, to soften and assuage the pain of thinking.

In March 1728, Lady Mar returned to England in a state of mental breakdown and a battle for custody of her began between Lady Mary and Lord Mar's brother, Lord Grange. Grange had purchased his exiled brother's confiscated estates and was paying a substantial rent to Lady Mar. Lord Grange, who was rumored to have already locked up his own wife, attempted to carry off Frances and her daughter to Scotland, but the party was intercepted by Lady Mary with an officer and a judicial warrant, ordering Lady Mar to be returned to London.

In July 1728, a lunacy inquisition found Lady Mar to be of unsound mind; the investigators were unable to discover a reason for her insanity, unless "by the visitation of God." The Chancery Court awarded custody to her sister. Mary received an allowance from the estate for her support, and Frances seems to have been comfortably cared for (despite the poet Pope's accusation that the avaricious Mary had starved her sister) in her own residence in London. Frances appears to have made a temporary recovery in 1731 when Lord Grange, in a renewed effort to free her from her sister's influence, visited her. He found her judgment and memory sound, despite her moodiness and depression. However, she was soon in decline once again, and he observed that the "fancies which now perplext her brain were, like the clouds, fleeting, inconstant, and sometimes in monstrous shapes." Frances remained in Mary's care while her daughter joined the ailing Lord Mar in France. Mar died in exile in 1732.

As soon as Lady Mar's daughter, Frances Erskine, came of age in 1736 she concentrated her efforts on winning custody of her mother. She had always aligned herself with her father's side of the family, and she was to marry her cousin James Erskine, Lord Grange's son, several years later. Mary was doubtless reluctant to surrender her sister but, as she had fallen passionately in love with a handsome young Italian, she was now free to follow her heart, without the duty of caring for Lady Mar.

While Mary Wortley Montagu was about to embark upon the most notorious period of her life, Frances, Lady Mar, then faded from the spotlight of history. We can only assume that she spent her remaining years in her daughter's care, probably in Scotland. She died at the age of 71 in 1761.

SOURCES AND SUGGESTIONS FOR FURTHER READING:

Dictionary of National Biography, s.v., Erskine, John, 6th or 11th Earl of Mar. London: Smith Elder, 1894.

Halsband, Robert. *The Life of Lady Mary Wortley Montagu*. London: Oxford University Press, 1961.

Montagu, Lady Mary Wortley. *The Selected Letters of Lady Mary Wortley Montagu*. London: Longman, 1970.

(Dr.) Kathleen Garay,
Acting Director, Women's Studies Program,
McMaster University, Hamilton, Canada

Mara, Gertrud (1749–1833)

German soprano who was one of the first opera singers to become internationally famous. Name variations: Gertrude Elizabeth Mara; Gertrud Elisabeth Mara; Madame Mara. Born Gertrud Elisabeth Schmeling in Cassel, Germany, on February 23, 1749; died in Revel or Reval (present-day Tallinn), Russia, on January 20, 1833; studied violin; studied with Paradisi in London and Hiller at Leipzig; married Johann Mara (a cellist), in 1773 (divorced 1799).

Gertrud Mara was born Gertrud Elisabeth Schmeling in Cassel, Germany, in 1749. She made a successful debut in Dresden around 1767 and was selected by Frederick II the Great, king of Prussia, to become a court singer in Berlin, much to the consternation of Mozart who deplored her singing and her arrogance. In 1773, against the king's wishes, Gertrud married Johann Mara, a dissolute cellist, who treated her badly. Frederick had granted approval of the marriage only if Mara promised to stay at Berlin for life. After much friction, she left the court in 1778 and toured the Continent, enjoying a celebrated rivalry with *Luiza Todi.

In 1784, Mara journeyed to London, where she sang to equally enthusiastic audiences, notably at the Haymarket, and chiefly music by Handel. Though she was connected with the opera in London until 1791, singing in Nasolini's *Andromaca* and Cleopatra in Handel's *Giulio Cesare*, she was better suited for concerts and oratorios because of her small stature and poor acting. Her voice, however, has been described as one of great beauty and virtuosity with a range of G to E.

Having divorced Johann, Mara left London in 1802 with a flautist, Florio, with whom she successfully toured Paris, Vienna, and the German cities. Separating from Florio in 1893, she moved to Moscow and was living there in September 1812 when Napoleon's troops set fire to the city. Mara then settled in Reval (present-day Tallinn) and supported herself by teaching, eventually returning to London to sing in 1816.

Mara, La (1837–1927).

See Lipsius, Marie.

Maracci, Carmelita (b. 1911)

Spanish-trained American dancer. Born in Montevideo, Uruguay, in 1911; studied ballet and Spanish dance in California; taught dance in Los Angeles.

Brought to America as a child, Carmelita Maracci wove Spanish techniques into her style of dance with fine castanet and heel work. She made her professional debut in California in 1930. Appearing with her own group, she choreographed solos: *Viva Tu Madre, Nightingale and the Maiden, Etude, Cantine, Fandanguillo, Gavotta Vivace*; trios: *Another Fire Dance, Sonate, Portrait in the Raw España, Flamenco*; group dances: *Narrative of the Bull Ring* and *Suite*; as well as the ballet *Circo de España* for the Ballet Theater in 1951. Wrote *Agnes de Mille: "She is a true original, a satirist, a composer in the grand line, one of the great American choreographers." Poor health, however, often kept Maracci off the stage.

SOURCES:
de Mille, Agnes. *Book of the Dance*. Golden Press, 1961.

Marared (fl. 1173)

*Princess of Gwynedd. Flourished around 1173; daughter of Madog ap Maredudd, king of Powys, and *Susan of Powys (daughter of the king of Gwynedd and Angharad); married Iorwerth Drwyndwn, prince of Gwynedd; children: Llywelyn II the Great (1173–1240), Ruler of All Wales.*

Marble, Alice (1913–1990)

Four-time U.S. tennis champion who is generally credited with being the first woman to adopt the aggressive court strategy previously practiced only by male players. Born on September 13, 1913, in Beckwith, California; died on December 13, 1990, in Los Angeles, California; daughter of Jessie (Wood) Marble and Harry Marble; married Joseph Crowley, in 1942 (died 1944).

Began playing tennis in her teens and advanced to professional-level play under the coaching of Eleanor Tennant, whose movie-star clients introduced her to the major Hollywood stars of the day and made her a national celebrity; after collapsing on the court during a European tour, being diagnosed with tuberculosis, and hearing she would never play again, won the U.S. singles championship at Forest Hills (1936), Wimbledon (1939), and all major U.S. titles in both singles and doubles play by the outbreak of World War II; during war, was recruited by the U.S. government to spy on Nazi activities, using her position teaching tennis clinics in Europe as a cover, and was instrumental in discovering where the Third Reich had hidden much of its stolen wealth.

Alice Marble burst into tears the first time she saw a tennis racquet. "My life was over, and my brother was the cruelest man on earth," she later said of the day her brother Dan proudly unveiled the instrument that would bring her world fame. She was 13 at the time and convinced that her future lay in baseball, a game she had fallen in love with some years earlier and at which she was accomplished enough to be allowed to toss balls with the major league San Francisco Seals during practice games. Such was the unconventional fame of the little girl with the whiplash arm that the city's newspapers fondly dubbed her "The Queen of Swat," in a joking reference to Babe Ruth, but it was precisely that unconventionality that would catapult Marble to world attention on the tennis court.

You can't keep hanging around the ballpark . . . and acting like a boy.

—Dan Marble to his younger sister Alice, 1926

Before discovering baseball, Alice had adopted her mother's ambition to be a singer. **Jessie Wood** had had to give up that goal after marrying Harry Marble and moving to his farm in the Sierras of northeastern California, where she had five children. Alice, born on September 13, 1913, was the fourth. After the birth of their fifth child, the Marbles decided to seek a more financially secure future for their brood by moving to San Francisco in 1919, where Harry found a steady job. But injuries suffered in a car accident led to Harry's premature death from pneumonia in 1920, leaving his family to fend for themselves in genteel poverty. Jessie took a job as a cleaning woman, while her brother, a brakeman on San Francisco's famed cable cars, moved in to help. It was "Uncle Woody" who first taught Alice and her brothers to play baseball and who took them to Recreation Park to watch the San Francisco Seals play. Marble's devotion to the game became so passionate that she could be found in the bleachers tossing a ball with one of her brothers hours before the start of a game, as the Seals warmed up on the field below. When one of the team's players was astounded to find that the boy with the blond, close-cropped hair and the power arm was actually a girl, Alice eagerly took her seat in the dugout as the team's unofficial bat boy and mascot, becoming an overnight celebrity.

But as Marble approached young womanhood, her older brother Dan decided the tomboy image was unsuitable for a young lady and, saving up his money from the job he had left school to take, bought the hated tennis racquet. Under protest, Alice sought out a school friend who

was the only girl she knew who played tennis and, at 13, stepped onto a tennis court for the first time in her life. "In spite of myself, I was captivated," Marble wrote many years later. "I loved the sound of the ball striking my racquet, and wanted very badly to be able to control where it went when I hit it. Before the week was out, I was hooked." Marble found that her baseball years had served her well, for she had a powerful serve on the court right and quickly found her strength in a straightforward serve and volley game.

In no time at all, Marble was a regular at the Saturday tournaments at Golden Gate Park, which soon eclipsed the ball park as her favorite environment. By the time she was in her first year of high school, she was a regular fixture on the Golden Gate courts during weekdays, too, playing after school until the light began to fade. But on one such afternoon, as she was walking home through the Park, Marble was attacked and raped. The trauma took years to heal, as she struggled with the guilt and self-hatred that are the deepest wounds suffered by rape survivors. It would be ten years before Marble could endure a physical relationship with a man; but in later years, she credited her fight back to self-respect as a major influence on her game. "It made me tough," she said, "and made me turn all the more to tennis to counteract my low self-esteem. I didn't care much about winning, just the good feeling that came from playing the game well."

The tennis world of the West Coast began to notice that Marble was playing very well, indeed. Even as she struggled with the aftershock of being raped, Alice became the champion of Golden Gate Park's Girls' Tennis Club, her brother Dan acting as her trainer and seeing to it that she was on the court every day; and it was Dan who scrimped together $45 to buy her a junior membership at the California Tennis Club of San Francisco. The carefully tended courts of the Tennis Club were a far cry from the dirt courts of Golden Gate Park, but the social gulf between Marble's decidedly modest background and the rarified heights of San Francisco's elite was too wide to bridge. The haughty membership of the Tennis Club considered their sport of choice strictly for the leisured wealthy, free of the commercial stain of other mass-interest sports and certainly not to be seriously considered by the likes of an Alice Marble. Alice learned as much as she could from watching, but she played no tennis at the Club and soon gave up her membership to return to Golden Gate Park, where her game steadily improved.

The first recognition of her remarkable talent came in 1930, when she was invited by the Northern California Tennis Association to represent it in upcoming tournaments for the Northwest and Canadian championships, a two-and-a-half-month tour that paid $75 toward expenses. Marble was broken-hearted to learn that the state of her family's finances made the trip impossible, even with the expense money—until a mysterious envelope arrived in the mail with three $20 bills inside. There was no note. Marble never knew who donated the money, but it was enough to send her on her first tournament in a new level of competition. But now there was a new obstacle to overcome. Arriving in Canada at the start of the tour, Marble was faced for the first time with clay courts made slippery by three days of rain that delayed play and forced competitors to play extra matches to make up the lost time. The blisters that formed on her heels became so painful and infected that a doctor advised her to go home, but Marble simply cut away the heels of her shoes and went back for more. By the end of the tournament, she had captured her first championship outside of California.

The next year, Marble captured California's Junior championship and won a spot on her state's team that was to compete for the national Juniors Title in New York. This time, she found herself playing for the first time on the grass courts that were standard in the East. The differences in the ball's spin and bounce flummoxed her, leading to a near shut-out in singles play in the early matches of the tour and an equally humiliating defeat in doubles play with her fellow Californian, **Bonnie Miller**, as her partner. A comeback in the Philadelphia competition for the national Junior Title seemed within reach when Marble battled her way to the final singles match against **Ruby Bishop**, whom she had often defeated in California. But Bishop's coach had trained her on grass courts, and Alice won only five games in two sets before once again going down in defeat. Her anger and bitterness at losing the title almost cost her a doubles title, until Marble realized halfway through her matches partnering Bonnie Miller that her ungracious attitude was affecting somebody else's game, too. "We handed our opponents the first set before I realized that I was taking my anger out on Bonnie instead of on the other team," Marble later said, recalling how she and Miller went on to win the national doubles title that afternoon in Philadelphia. Alice's other realization was that she needed a trainer who could teach her to play on a grass court as well as Ruby Bishop did. With characteristic de-

termination, Alice settled for nothing less than Bishop's coach, ❧➤ **Eleanor Tennant**.

By the time Marble began working with "Teach" Tennant a year later, she had become the top-seeded woman in California tennis and had advanced to seventh in the national rankings, a record impressive enough that it was Tennant, in fact, who approached Alice. Born in San Francisco to British parents but based in southern California for many years, Tennant taught at her own school in La Jolla and at the Beverly Hills Hotel in Los Angeles, where movie stars and industry tycoons came to her for lessons. "She was witty and charming," Marble later wrote of the woman who would control her life for the next 15 years, "her strong voice with its slight British accent conveying an easy confidence. Everything I wanted was suddenly within my reach. With a coach like Teach, there was no telling what I could do." Realizing the Marble family's situation, so different from the status of her more exalted clients, Tennant had already arranged for Alice to work part-time at a sporting-goods store near her home by the time she approached Alice. Before long, Marble had moved to La Jolla and into the house shared by Tennant and a sister. Tennant came to rule not only Alice's tennis career, but every aspect of her life off the court, from the clothes she wore to the style of her conversation. "I wasn't allowed to cook or drive or make decisions," Marble later recalled. "She convinced me I was good at nothing *but* tennis, and I focused entirely on my sport, just as she intended." (Tennant would have a similar relationship with *****Maureen Connolly**.)

At first, it seemed as if Marble's dream come true was turning into a nightmare. Tennant, and Tennant's own coach, Harold White, forced a complete makeover of Alice's game. She was required to adopt the "Eastern," handshake-like grip on her racquet and learn to control her shots with the subtlety required on a grass court. Alice resisted mightily in the beginning. "My situation was worse than that of a beginner," Marble later said, "because I had to unlearn the skills I had come to depend on." Her frustration was evident in the initial rounds of unsuccessful tournament play after Tennant became her coach. But by July 1933, when Alice won the California women's singles title, the new style began to pay off. The win qualified her to travel East again, where Marble set her sights on the Wightman Cup matches, a tournament in which the top-seeded women players from the United States and from Britain faced off across the net. To win a place on the American team, however, Marble would have to prevail in pre-tournament play at the prestigious Maidstone Club in East Hampton, Long Is-

◆❧
Tennant, Eleanor. *See Connolly, Maureen for sidebar.*

land, a bastion of aristocratic tennis that did not look kindly on upstart young women from lower-class backgrounds. To her shock, Alice discovered that she had been scheduled to play in both singles and doubles matches, in nearly continuous competition over three days under a blazing August sun. The tournament chair, Julian Myrick, was unmoved by her complaints, or by an angry telephone call from Tennant, who had remained behind in California. "My dear," he sniffed to Alice, "you have to prove your worth by making a good showing here. Then *perhaps* you'll qualify for the Wightman Cup team." Marble knew only too well that Myrick also chaired the Wightman Cup selection committee.

The first two days went well for her. By the third day, however, as she faced semifinals play in both singles and doubles matches, Marble could feel the strain on her legs and back and in the dull headache that refused to go away as she walked onto the court for the doubles semifinal, partnering the reigning tennis diva of the aristocracy, then known as Helen Wills Moody (*Helen Newington Wills). Informing Marble that she didn't wish to strain her back, Wills forced Alice to play the more aggressive game, reaching for high shots and running after challenging volleys. She and Wills won the match in three hours of play, by the end of which the temperature had reached 104 degrees. As Marble staggered off the court to change for her upcoming singles final, Julian Myrick continued to turn a deaf ear to worried fellow tournament officials who urged him to remove Marble from further play. An exhausted Alice lost both the singles final and, to Helen Wills' displeasure, the doubles final, but the crowd recognized the astounding feat of endurance they had just witnessed and gave her a standing ovation as she walked off the court after playing 4 matches in 11 sets and 108 games over nine hours of play.

That night, Marble collapsed and was diagnosed with sunstroke and anemia. "TENNIS ASSOCIATION FORCES ALICE MARBLE TO PLAY 108 GAMES!" screamed the next day's newspapers, forcing an uncomfortable Julian Myrick to explain himself. Several days later, Marble learned that Myrick had not objected to her selection for the Wightman Cup team, but the punishment he had inflicted on her proved too much. Barred by her doctor from singles play at the Wightman tournament, Alice played badly in doubles matches and failed to make it into the semifinals. Still weak and dizzy from her ordeal, Marble also lost in quarterfinals play for the national women's title at Forest Hills. When she returned to California after the tour, she was quickly put under a doctor's care at her family's home in San Francisco. She took comfort from the fact that, despite her losses, she had advanced from seventh to third in the national rankings.

When she returned to La Jolla late in 1933, Marble's career took a new twist: she and Teach Tennant were invited to give tennis lessons at San Simeon, the extravagantly luxurious castle built by newspaper tycoon William Randolph Hearst. Hearst and his mistress, the actress *Marion Davies, were enchanted with Tennant's young pupil; and in Alice's time at San Simeon, others of Hearst's set—from George Bernard Shaw to *Jean Harlow to Charlie Chaplin—shared their hosts' opinion. She gave lessons and played doubles with many of them, earning a bear hug from Hearst himself, who told her she was the best partner he'd ever had. Hearst and Davies became two of Marble's biggest fans, once sending her a telegram that read: "To Alice, who will be champion whenever she wants to be." Also among Marble's admirers was actress *Carole Lombard, who would become a close friend and financial supporter.

Alice's third-place ranking brought an invitation from the U.S. Lawn Tennis Association in the spring of 1934 to join the Wightman Cup team again. This time, however, the tournament would be played at Wimbledon in England, the first time Marble would be playing in Europe; even more exciting, the USLTA had arranged for a series of matches to be played in Paris before the team traveled to Wimbledon. The previous year's experience at East Hampton was still painfully fresh, but Marble had no intention of putting herself at risk this time. "I promise, no marathons," Alice told Teach Tennant, who would remain behind in California. "I won't do anything stupid." Marble reported she felt a little tired when her ship docked in France. By the time of her first exhibition game in Paris, the rest of the team grew worried as Alice seemed to be struggling her way through a match she eventually lost, gasping for breath. The team doctor was called in. She was slightly anemic, he reported, but still able to play. The next day, Alice collapsed during her first match and woke up in a hospital bed. She would have to be sent home, the doctors said. She had tuberculosis and would never be able to play tennis again. "I was beaten, and my life was over," Marble remembered thinking. "Tennis was my life. I had never thought beyond it."

What lay beyond were long, dreary, idle days reclining in bed at her family's home in San Francisco, followed by nearly a year and a half

Alice Marble (right) with Kay Stammers before their Wimbledon match (1939).

at a sanatorium for tubercular patients in the California desert that Teach Tennant had located for her. Some consolation was to be found in a letter written to her by Carole Lombard, who had herself survived an automobile crash and returned to her acting career after being told she would never appear on film again. "I had nothing to lose by fighting, so I began to fight," Lombard wrote. "I made my career come true, just as you can—if you'll fight!" Marble took the advice to heart, working out an exercise regimen with Teach Tennant that was put into place as soon as Alice returned to La Jolla in 1936. She began by walking a block away from the house and back for a week; then another block was added. By the time her damaged lungs could withstand a three-mile walk, swimming was added and, in time, slow games of tennis with Tennant. A new doctor was consulted, who ventured the opinion that it was pleurisy, not tuberculosis, that had felled her and agreed that Marble could eventually return to the tennis court. Alice took his prediction to heart and, a year later, won her first tournament in nearly two years by defeating the woman who had succeeded her as the third-ranked player in the country. Although it was only a private tournament held at Palm Springs' Racquet Club, Marble knew she was back in the game.

But it was a different game Alice brought to the court when she appeared at the 1936 state championship tournament in Berkeley to defeat her opponent for the state title in just half an hour. One sports reporter characterized her as "the girl who played the same game as the fellas," for Teach Tennant had added power and aggression to her prize student's game. Rather than playing the base line and waiting for the ball to come to her, as was then the norm in women's tennis, Marble played close to the net and met the ball before it ever touched the ground, drilling it back at her opponent to cause maximum effort for the return. With her first title in three years behind her, Alice and Teach Tennant headed East by car for the U.S. National championship tournament in Forest Hills. It was during a stop in Ohio that Marble met former women's champion **Mary Brown**, a friend of Tennant's. "Brownie" would, in the end, have more influence over her life than even Teach Tennant. "You can do anything you want, if you care enough," Brownie told Alice, who proceeded to prove the truth of that statement by defeating four-time U.S. champion *Helen Hull Jacobs 4–6, 6–3, 6–2 at Forest Hills on September 12, 1936, becoming the new U.S. champion and a national celebrity. It would be the first of four National championships she won between 1936 and 1940, not only in singles matches but in doubles and mixed doubles play. (Marble nearly quit playing in 1937 after the death of her mother from cancer, and did not compete at the national level that year.) Her fortunes improved dramatically overseas as well, with titles at Wimbledon in 1939 (for singles, doubles and mixed doubles). By the outbreak of World War II, Marble had been named Woman Athlete of the Year and was co-chairing a national physical fitness program for the Office of Civilian De-

fense. "Now that Alice has regained her health, nothing can stand in her way," a proud Teach Tennant told reporters in 1939. "She is the best woman player in the world today."

There was more waiting in store for Marble. In 1938, when she was 26, Alice fell in love and embarked on a tempestuous affair with a man whom she would never identify by his real name. She called him Hans Steinmetz in her autobiography, and claimed he was a wealthy Swiss banker who introduced himself while she was in France for a series of exhibition matches. "Hans was handsome—not movie-star handsome, but striking, with an angular face that softened quickly and often into a smile," she wrote of the slim, attractive man who offered his compliments in a hotel lobby in Le Tocquet, on the Normandy coast, where Alice and Tennant were staying. Such was Hans' charm that, for the first time after having been raped over ten years before, Alice allowed a man to make love to her—on their first night together, and on a nearby beach where Hans had escorted her on a midnight walk. "At that moment, we were the only life on the planet, perhaps in the whole universe, and the stars were singing," she later said. The affair became public knowledge soon enough and was quickly ended by Teach Tennant, who mistrusted Hans' motives and feared that Alice's concentration on her game would be lost. It was the first rift between the two women in their ten years together, and one that would widen in coming years.

The outbreak of war in Europe, and America's entry into the conflict in 1941, put a stop to international competition. In addition to her duties for the Civil Defense Department, Marble played a series of exhibition games at military bases around the country and conducted tennis clinics with Tennant. The already weakening bond between teacher and student, however, was dealt another blow when Marble met an Army captain named Joseph Crowley and married him in 1942. The two met at the Stage Door Canteen in New York, a military club which Alice occasionally visited as part of her Civil Defense duties. Crowley worked for Army intelligence, but would reveal no details, telling Alice only that he would frequently be away in Europe while the war was on. He did, indeed, disappear for three months after their first meeting, but the two were secretly married in a quiet ceremony aboard a Navy ship docked on the Hudson River in New York in 1942. The Army insisted that the marriage remain secret as long as Crowley worked as an intelligence agent, but it wasn't long before Teach Tennant heard the news. "I suppose she thought I would come to my senses," Marble later wrote, "or something would happen to break us up. She didn't dislike [Crowley], just his intrusion on her grand plan for my life."

But Crowley's war work demanded longer and longer absences in Europe, during which Marble was unable to speak to him, even if she had been able to find the time during her touring schedule with Tennant, who was horrified to learn that Alice had become pregnant after Crowley's latest visit to the States. "You have obligations, a career," Tennant insisted. But tragedy struck when Marble was involved in a car accident and lost her baby. Then, on Christmas Eve, 1944, a telegram arrived informing her that her husband had been killed in action, his plane shot down over Germany. "There was nothing left for me but pain, and I couldn't face that," Marble recounted in later years. "I had been forced to be strong all my life, and I was tired of it. I didn't want to be strong anymore." She was rescued from a suicide attempt by Tennant and Brownie, who kept watch over her during the long weeks of her ensuing depression. Finally she was able to leave her apartment in New York for short walks, and the cure was completed when a telegram and flowers arrived from Clark Gable, who had been equally devastated by the death in a plane crash of his wife Carole Lombard that same year. "If I can do it, so can you," he wrote.

Shortly after her recovery, Marble's life entered a brand new chapter when she was approached by an Army intelligence officer (she gave him the name "Colonel Linden" in her memoirs) with a startling proposal. He asked her to become a spy to assist in her country's attempts to locate the whereabouts of the art treasures and other booty the Nazis had hidden somewhere in Europe to finance their faltering war effort. The cover was to be a series of tennis clinics that would be set up for her in neutral Switzerland. The Army was sure that her presence in Geneva would attract the man thought to be handling the transfer of art and money—none other than Marble's former lover "Hans." "If I could do what they wanted," Alice said, "it could hurt the bastards who shot Joe's plane out of the sky." The day after her meeting with Linden, Marble agreed. She was to tell no one, not even Tennant or Brownie, who believed she was taking afternoon classes at New York University when Alice was actually in a warehouse in Brooklyn being trained as a spy.

She had been in Geneva for only three days when Hans phoned her. What ensued could have come from a Hitchcock suspense film—the evening dinner at Hans' palatial mansion, the creep down to his wine cellar in his absence, the discovery of a hidden list of Nazi officials and the whereabouts of the art they had stolen which Marble committed to film using the tiny camera supplied to her, and a midnight car chase down a mountain road. Her pursuer was not Hans, but one of the Army's recruiters from New York who, as was now apparent, was a double agent. Shots were fired, the double agent was killed by other spies who had followed Marble in case help was needed, and Alice found herself in a hospital with a gunshot wound. But the information she gathered was used after the war at the Nuremburg Trials in 1945–46 and brought several Nazi war criminals to justice.

Safely back in New York by late 1945, Marble's next crisis involved her deteriorating relations with Teach Tennant, who was becoming increasingly abusive and dictatorial. "I was no longer a willing, malleable Eliza Doolittle," Alice later wrote. "Too much had happened. It was time for her to leave me and find another champion." The break finally came at the end of 1945, when Tennant moved out of the New York apartment the two had shared and went back to California. They would not speak again for nearly six years.

By 1950, with her national celebrity and reputation assured, Marble turned from professional play to coaching and lecturing. She spoke out strongly against the decision to bar African-American player *Althea Gibson from U.S. National championship games. Alice's public protest carried enough weight to make Gibson the first African-American woman admitted to the championship tour, after which she became the first black woman to win the U.S. National championship title and the first to win at Wimbledon. The vagaries of her health that had plagued Marble all her life returned during the 1950s; her lungs were now so severely scarred that one had to be removed, forcing her formal retirement from professional tennis and a return to California, where she and Eleanor Tennant made up their differences and embarked on joint coaching of promising young players. Among these players were *Billie Jean King, *Darlene Hard and Carole Caldwell. Marble was inducted into the Tennis Hall of Fame in 1964, and into the International Sportsman's Hall of Fame in 1967.

During her last years, Marble delighted in watching the new breed of players who took the "masculine" style of play she had introduced years earlier to new heights. She was especially impressed with *Martina Navratilova. "Not only is she stronger than I ever was," she wrote, "she's fitter. In my time, training didn't exist in any real sense. I thought I was doing great to run a little to build up my wind." She expressed outright fear at the thought of facing *Steffi Graf's serve and admired the grace and calm of *Chris Evert, whose father she had taught. ("I grew up on you!," Chris once told her.) But as the years went on, Marble's health continued its downward slide. She survived five operations for colon cancer between 1981 and 1989, but finally succumbed to pneumonia on December 12, 1990. She was 77.

"When you've lived as long as I have," she wrote in the autobiography she completed just before her death, "the sheer joy of having played the game comes to matter more than the victories, the records, the memories." But thanks to the strength and determination that ruled her life, Alice Marble left an abundant supply of just those items as her gift to the game she loved.

SOURCES:

Davidson, Sue. *Changing the Game: The Stories of Tennis Champs Alice Marble and Althea Gibson*. Seattle, WA: Seal Press, 1997.

Marble, Alice, with Dale Leatherman. *Courting Danger*. NY: St. Martin's Press, 1991.

Norman Powers, writer-producer, Chelsea Lane Productions, New York

Marbury, Elisabeth (1856–1933).

See de Wolfe, Elsie for sidebar.

Marcella of Rome (c. 325–410)

Roman founder of the first religious community for women in the Western church. Name variations: Marcella. Born between 325 and 335; died in 410 or 411; daughter of Albina; married briefly.

Born into the highest reaches of Rome's Senatorial aristocracy, Marcella of Rome could boast several consuls as ancestors. Her father died when she was very young and had little impact on her life. Marcella's mother was **Albina**, who seems to have avidly supported the decisions which molded her daughter's life. Married as befit one of her class, Marcella lost her husband after only seven months of marriage. Thereafter a much older ex-consul named Cerealis wooed the beautiful Marcella, reportedly seeking more a "daughter" to whom he could leave his estate than a true wife. Marcella declined Cerealis' offer of marriage, with the terse comment that if she wished to marry she would seek "a husband, not an inheritance." The religiously inclined Marcella then

embraced widowhood and a life of Christian asceticism, abandoning the material pleasures so ingrained in the Roman elite.

With her mother and a good friend, **Principia**, Marcella retired to her house on Rome's Aventine Hill. There the three came to live by a rule adapted from the monastic foundations of the East, knowledge of which circulated in Rome largely thanks to the efforts of Athanasius, bishop of Alexandria. This prelate had published a widely popular *Life of Antony* (an Egyptian who was one of the earliest hermit monks) and had visited Rome in 340 after the Arian Christians of Alexandria had temporarily driven him from his See. His reports on the developing monastic movement intrigued Roman society and stimulated a desire to learn more about the rules which regulated the lives thus being led.

As time passed, Marcella's fame grew among the women of Rome, and many were driven to join her in a life of seclusion, albeit a seclusion lived out in the midst of one of the greatest cities of the world. Thus developed what was probably the first organized community in the West consisting of Christian women living according to a religious rule. This community, led and endowed by Marcella, devoted itself to an existence of charitable works, prayer, and the study of Christian scripture.

When the famous Jerome visited Rome between 382 and 385, he met Marcella and undertook the religious instruction of her community. Marcella's community was not alone in seeking out Jerome, but his work with Marcella seems to have begun his cultivation of Rome's wealthy Christian women whose financial resources he helped channel into the development of the Church and whose behind-the-scene influence helped stamp out the last vestiges of Rome's pagan tradition. Marcella took the opportunity to pose a number of philological and exegetical questions about Christian scripture which had bothered her community. Marcella was not only the founder of her community, she was also its leading intellectual; her acumen impressed Jerome, as did her willingness to stand up to his arguments when she found them to be wanting. Of particular interest to Marcella was the contemporary dispute over the orthodoxy of Origenism, or that approach to the Bible which encouraged the use of certain pagan philosophical principles to interpret the text. Since Jerome was among the most vocal critics of Origen's methodology by the 380s, and since he once called Marcella "the glory of the women of Rome," it is virtually certain that she was also inclined to reject Origen's theology. Jerome came to know Marcella very well, both through personal contact and through a regular exchange of written correspondence. After he returned to Palestine without her (other Roman matrons followed him to the East), he offered the opinion that Rome would not suffer because Marcella was more than competent to take care of any difficulties within Rome's Christian community.

After Jerome's departure from Rome, Marcella continued with the well-established routine of her life until 410. In that year Rome was sacked by the Visigoths, whose king, Alaric, sought out Marcella as a probable possessor of hidden wealth. However, by that time Marcella's estate had been disbursed through the funding of charitable works, thus frustrating Alaric's lust for plunder from that source. Nevertheless, not convinced that Marcella was poor, Alaric had her subjected to torture in order to discover where she had "hidden" the fortune that no longer existed. Even though Marcella bore great physical abuse nobly, she died of her wounds in either 410 or early 411.

William Greenwalt,
Associate Professor of Classical History,
Santa Clara University, Santa Clara, California

Marcella the Elder (fl. 25 BCE)

Roman noblewoman. Born between 54 and 40 BCE; flourished around 25 BCE; daughter of *Octavia (c. 69–11 BCE) and G. Marcellus (Roman consul); niece of Gaius Julius Caesar Octavianus also known as Octavian or Augustus, Roman emperor; was first wife of Marcus Agrippa (Augustus demanded that Agrippa divorce Marcella to marry Augustus' daughter *Julia [39 BCE–40 CE]).

Marcella the Younger (fl. 20 BCE)

Roman noblewoman. Born between 54 and 40 BCE; flourished around 20 BCE; daughter of *Octavia (c. 69–11 BCE) and G. Marcellus (Roman consul); niece of Gaius Julius Caesar Octavianus also known as Octavian or Augustus, Roman emperor.

Marcellina (fl. 4th c.)

Saint. Flourished during the 4th century; daughter of the praetorian prefect of the Gauls; sister of Satyrus and Saint Ambrose. Her feast day is July 17.

Upon the death of her father, the praetorian prefect of the Gauls, Marcellina is believed to have returned to Rome with her mother and her two brothers, one of whom, Ambrose, would become a well-known saint. In 335, on the feast of the Epiphany, Marcellina received the virgin's veil in the Church of St. Peter, at which time Pope Liberius counseled her to serve Christ courageously. The pope cited the story of the Alexandrian page who, not wanting to disrupt a pagan ceremony, allowed the wax, dripping from the candle he held, to burn his hand to the bone rather than shake it off and cause a disruption. Marcellina's brother Ambrose was extremely supportive of her religious life, leaving her the income from all his lands so as to distance her from worldly affairs, and encouraging her monastic virtues in the treatise *De Virginibus* (c. 376), which he addressed to her. Marcellina remained close to Ambrose, corresponding with him frequently and relying on him to counsel her through difficult periods. She led an exemplary cloistered life, outliving both of her brothers.

Marcet, Jane (1769–1858)

First English-language author of scientific texts for women. Name variations: Jane Haldimand or Jane Haldimond; Jane Haldimand Marcet or Jane Haldimond Marcet. Born in 1769, in London, England; died in London in 1858; daughter of Anthony Francis Haldimand (a merchant) and Jane Haldimand; married Alexander John Gaspard Marcet (a physician), in 1799 (died 1822); three children.

Selected writings: Conversations on Chemistry: Intended More Specifically for the Female Sex *(1805);* Conversations on Political Economy *(1816);* Conversations on Natural Philosophy *(1819);* Conversations on Vegetable Physiology *(1829);* Bertha's Visit to Her Uncle in England *(1830);* John Hopkins's Notions on Political Economy *(1833);* Rich and Poor *(1851).*

Though it may seem remarkable that scientific texts were once geared exclusively to the gender of the reader, it is perhaps equally remarkable that the mere possibility, and even the safety, of this kind of education being permitted to women was a matter of heated debate in the Western world during the period of intellectual and social progress that was the Enlightenment. One woman who contributed much practical assistance to the cause of genuine education for women (as opposed to what was considered necessary for cultivating female charms) was Jane Marcet.

Born Jane Haldimand in London in 1769, Marcet was one of 12 children, the only surviving daughter, of Swiss parents **Jane Haldimand** and Anthony Francis Haldimand. Her father was a merchant who later founded a bank, and the family lived in comfortable circumstances. After her mother died when Jane was 15, she effectively became the female head of their household and looked after her younger siblings. Marcet was typical of the young women of her era who had little access to the solid, rigorous education her brother received. However, she was probably tutored privately, like other young women of her class, and it is assumed that she may have gleaned access to more challenging scientific disciplines through her brother's course of study. She most likely also heard conversation on economics between her banker father and her brother, who later became a director of the Bank of England.

At age 30, she married Alexander Marcet, a physician with a successful practice who derived far more satisfaction from his experiments in chemistry. This was a relatively new field of study in the early 19th century, and Alexander wrote papers on the subject and was eventually elected a fellow of the Royal Society. When Marcet received an inheritance upon the death of her father, her husband was able to spend less time as a physician and devote himself to his experiments. The Marcets were part of a social circle that included many prominent and learned members of English society, among them *Harriet Martineau, *Mary Fairfax Somerville, Thomas Malthus, Jöns Jakob Berzelius, and Auguste de la Rive, and both these friends and her husband encouraged Marcet to write a "beginner's" text on chemistry. This came about in part as a result of her attendance at the popular Royal Institution lectures by noted scientist Sir Humphry Davy. The celebrated Davy was considered a dashing figure, and Marcet was one of many women attracted to his lectures. Yet she found that her lack of formal education, and a resultant unease with more abstract ideas, kept her from properly appreciating Davy's scientific concepts until a post-lecture follow-up with a friend made a great difference in her understanding of chemistry.

Marcet's 1805 book, *Conversations on Chemistry: Intended More Specifically for the Female Sex*, was meant to remedy this gap. Like many of her subsequent books, it was centered around a dialogue between a woman teacher and two young female students. This Socratic method had been espoused by *Mary Wollstonecraft in her *A Vindication of the Rights of Woman* (1792) as ideally suited for a variety of subjects in the education of women. Marcet was no doubt influenced by Wollstonecraft, who argued vigorously for parity in education between the sexes.

Published anonymously, as was common at the time, *On Chemistry* was an instant success. It went through more than a dozen editions in both England and the United States (where it sold over 160,000 copies by 1853) and was frequently revised to incorporate the latest discoveries in chemistry. Somewhat ironically, its most famous reader was Michael Faraday, who as a young teen had little formal education but loved science and came across *On Chemistry* while working as a bookbinder. Considered one of the pioneers of electromagnetic induction, he later constructed the first dynamo, and throughout his life cited Marcet's book as a great influence.

Marcet wrote numerous other books intended for young women, and some for young people in general, a number of which followed the same successful formula as her first. Among these is *Conversations on Political Economy* (1816), which made her the first female scholar linked with this field. Still in its infancy at the time, economics was not yet fully considered a true academic discipline; it also drew disdain from many in the upper classes who preferred not even to think of such lower-class occupations as trades, much less assign them integral importance within the world at large. Nonetheless, in large part because of the success of Marcet's book, by 1822 the Irish writer *Maria Edgeworth commented in a letter that "fine ladies now require that their daughters' governesses should teach political economy." Other books in this vein were *Conversations on Natural Philosophy* (1819) and *Conversations on Vegetable Physiology* (1829), both of which went through numerous editions. Two more works in the field of economics ventured from the formula of the dialogue between the teacher and her female students, but nonetheless presented concepts in an accessible manner. *John Hopkins's Notions on Political Economy* (1833), meant to explain economics for people with little higher education, is a collection of anecdotes centered around the simple laborer of the title and a fairy. Each tale provides a different lesson in contemporary economic theory, although some of those theories were later debunked. Possessed of an inquisitive mind, Hopkins has a large family to feed, but earns little money. In one story, he loses his job after the fairy listens to his complaints about the luxuries of the rich, which class she then abolishes; in another tale, he asks her to double his wages, which does not make life any easier, as he had hoped, but instead catapults both his world and the larger one into fantastic turmoil. Marcet's obvious leanings were further reflected in one of her last books, *Rich and Poor*

(1851), which explains why each class is dependent upon the other (upper-class Victorians were rarely lamenting when they employed the phrase "the poor are always with us"). Enormously influential in popularizing science and in gaining respectability for women's studying of science, Jane Marcet died in London in 1858.

SOURCE:

Blain, Virginia, Patricia Clements, and Isobel Grundy, eds. *The Feminist Companion to Literature in English.* New Haven, CT: Yale University Press, 1990.

Millar, David, Ian Millar, John Millar, and Margaret Millar. *The Cambridge Dictionary of Scientists.* Cambridge: Cambridge University Press, 1996.

Ogilvie, Marilyn Bailey. *Women in Science: Antiquity through the Nineteenth Century.* Cambridge, MA: MIT Press, 1986.

Thomson, Dorothy Lampen. *Adam Smith's Daughters.* New York, NY: Exposition Press, 1973.

Zilboorg, Caroline, and Susan B. Gall, eds. *Women's Firsts.* Detroit, MI: Gale, 1997.

Carol Brennan,
Grosse Pointe, Michigan

March, countess of.

See Dunbar, Agnes (c. 1312–1369).
See Montacute, Philippa (fl. 1352).
See Mortimer, Philippa (1355–1382).
See Holland, Alianor (c. 1373–1405).
See Mortimer, Catherine (fl. 1402).
See Stafford, Anne (d. 1432).

March, Mrs. Frederic (1901–1988).

See Eldridge, Florence.

Marchant, Bessie (1862–1941)

Prolific British author of adventure tales for children.
Name variations: Elizabeth Comfort; Bessie Marchant Comfort; (pseudonym) John Comfort. Born on December 12, 1862, in Petham, Kent, England; died in Charlbury, Oxfordshire, England, on November 10, 1941; daughter of William Marchant (a farmer) and Jane (Goucher) Marchant; married Jabez Ambrose Comfort (a minister), on December 28, 1889 (died 1915); children: Constance (1891).

Selected writings: The Old House by the Water *(1894);* Yuppie *(1898);* Cicely Frome, The Captain's Daughter *(1900);* A Heroine of the Sea *(1903);* Athabasca Bill *(1906);* Juliette, The Mail Carrier *(1907);* A Countess from Canada *(1910);* A Girl of the Northland *(1912);* A Girl Munitions Worker *(1916);* A Dangerous Mission *(1918);* The Fortunes of Prue *(1923);* To Save Her School *(1925);* Millicent Gwent, Schoolgirl *(1926);* How Nell Scored *(1929);* Jane Fills the Breach *(1932);* Erica's Ranch *(1934);* Nancy Afloat *(1936);* Waifs of Woolamoo *(1938).*

Bessie Marchant wrote juvenile adventure fiction that was remarkable for the daring and cleverness of her young heroines. In her nearly 150 published titles, she also introduced readers to far-away locales and exotic escapades, a fact made perhaps even more remarkable because Marchant probably never ventured far from the English countryside where she spent her 78 years. Born in the Kent town of Petham in 1862, Marchant was educated primarily at home, although she may have attended a National School for a time. She had a brother and a sister, and she also attended school with the former in Canterbury so that she could become a teacher. Her family suffered from financial hardships, in part because of their Baptist religion. At one point Marchant's father was forced to give up his rented farm, the source of his livelihood, because of his beliefs. Some of these events Marchant would later use in her 1898 novel *Yuppie.*

As a young woman, Marchant taught at a Baptist school in London, and married a Baptist minister, Jabez Ambrose Comfort, when she was

$\mathcal{B}$essie
$\mathcal{M}$archant

27. Comfort was 28 years her senior, and with him she had one daughter, Constance, who was born in 1891. She had apparently been writing for some years before her marriage but, perhaps in need of extra income, began writing more seriously when her daughter was a toddler. Her first books were set in the Kent of her youth, and featured the usual moral messages imparted to young readers in all works of fiction during the Victorian era, among which was that honesty and hard work bring their own rewards. Soon, though, Marchant recognized a niche in the children's market that was relatively unfulfilled for the female reader: in this era of the vaunted British Empire, most children heard tales of, and from, relatives or neighbors sent off to exotic lands as military personnel, missionaries, or civil servants. She began writing adventure stories, featuring the usual intrepid English girl who found herself in a scrape in some far-off setting such as Borneo or Brazil.

Literary historians theorize that Marchant never ventured far from her home in Charlbury, Oxfordshire, where she lived in a place called Gothic House from 1904 onward. Instead she read voraciously, and also conducted research at Oxford University's famed Bodleian Library. Some details about life abroad were culled from *National Geographic* magazine, and she also corresponded with fans of her books from around the world who provided her with true-life accounts of poisonous snakes and blinding snowstorms. Marchant's books also reflected the changing geopolitical realities of her time. In *A Girl Munitions Worker* (1916), the heroine is employed in a factory during World War I, and *A Dangerous Mission* (1918) takes place during the Russian Revolution.

Marchant wrote for young women in Victorian and post-Victorian England who, despite their taste for adventure fiction, were expected to devote their future lives to their husband and children. Few women traveled independently or found themselves in such fantastical situations as her heroines did, and characters like "Di the Dauntless" and "Marta the Mainstay" were reunited in the end with the more settled goals of marriage and motherhood. Typically, one of her girl adventurers receives this compliment: "But you can do so many things no boy or man can ever manage, housekeeping and all that sort of work." Yet Marchant was also conscious of the hardships faced by women at the time who did not have the necessary protection of a male family member; in some instances, her fiction depicted young women at risk simply because of the absence of legal remedies or lack of control over their economic status. *A Girl of the Northland* (1912) is one example: the heroine's father is gone, and though the family owns valuable land with copper stores in it, they cannot profit from the resource because of his absence and so are forced to live in poverty.

Marchant wrote some books under the pseudonym John Comfort, and was sometimes compared with another juvenile adventure-fiction writer, G.A. Henty, whose stories were loved by boys of the era. Although her books were quite popular, she earned little money and considered herself successful if three or four publishing houses each accepted one of her books per year. Bessie Marchant remained a devout Baptist all of her life, and would sing a doxology, or hymn of praise, when she completed a novel. She died at the age of 79 in 1941.

SOURCES:
Blain, Virginia, Patricia Clements, and Isobel Grundy. *The Feminist Companion to Literature in English.* New Haven, CT: Yale University Press, 1990.

Brinkley-Willsher, Valerie. *Twentieth-Century Children's Writers.* 4th ed. Edited by Laura Standley Berger. Detroit, MI: St. James Press, 1995.

Hettinga, Donald R. "Bessie Marchant," in *Dictionary of Literary Biography, Vol. 160: British Children's Writers, 1914–1960.* Detroit, MI: Gale Research, 1996, pp. 166–169.

Major, Alan. "Bessie Marchant," in *This England.* Winter 1991, pp. 30–33.

Carol Brennan,
Grosse Pointe, Michigan

Marchant, Catherine (1906–1998).

See Cookson, Catherine.

Marchesi, Blanche (1863–1940)

French-born soprano. Name variations: Baroness A. Caccamisi. Born in Paris, France, in 1863; died in 1940; daughter of Marchese della Rajata Castone, a political refugee who adopted the nom de théâtre *Salvatore Marchesi (1822–1908, an Italian baritone and composer) and Mathilde Marchesi (1826–1913); educated in Vienna, Frankfort, and Paris; married Baron Caccamisi.*

Blanche Marchesi, the daughter of *Mathilde Marchesi, was born in 1863 and made her first professional appearance in Berlin in 1895 as a concert singer. She then toured extensively in England and Europe; sang in operas at Covent Garden, Prague, Brussels, and elsewhere; appeared before Queen *Victoria (from whom she received two decorations) and Queen *Alexandra of Denmark, as well as the courts of

Brussels and Germany; and was painted by Sargent, Shannon, and other well-known artists. Settling into a cottage she had built in Buckinghamshire, she had the largest private academy of singing in London; her pupils sang throughout the world.

Marchesi, Mathilde (1821–1913)

German mezzo-soprano and celebrated voice teacher whose students included Nellie Melba, Mary Garden and Emma Calvé. Name variations: Mathilde de Castrone Marchesi. Born Mathilde Graumann at Frankfort-Am-Main, Germany, on March 26 (also seen as March 20 and 24), 1826 (some sources cite 1821, but 1826 seems more probable); died in London, England, on November 17, 1913; studied in Vienna and Paris and was highly educated; married the Marchese della Rajata Castone, a political refugee who adopted the nom de théâtre Salvatore Marchesi (1822–1908, an Italian baritone and composer), in 1852; children: daughter *Blanche Marchesi (1863–1940), who was also a concert and opera singer.

Mathilde Marchesi was born Mathilde Graumann at Frankfort-Am-Main, Germany, in 1826, into a family of some distinction; one of her relatives was Baron Haussmann, the famous prefect under Napoleon III. Mathilde, who was persuaded to take up music as a profession by Mendelssohn, studied in Paris under Manuel Garcia, the father of *Pauline Viardot and *Maria Malibran. She also took lessons in acting from Joseph-Isidore Samson, the teacher of *Rachel, and had the opportunity to hear all the major singers of her age—Fanny Persiani, *Giulia Grisi, *Marietta Alboni, and Caroline Duprez. Mathilde's early aptitude for teaching was so apparent that when Garcia was temporarily incapacitated as the result of an accident, Marchesi took over the private lessons for every one of his students.

She first appeared as a mezzo-soprano concert singer in London in 1849 and then on the Continent. Though it was said her voice was pleasing, it was also said that it was not remarkable. As Mlle Graumann, she sang successfully in Germany, Belgium, Holland, Switzerland, France, and the United Kingdom.

In 1852, Mathilde met and married the Marchese della Rajata Castone, an Italian political refugee in London who was also a well-known baritone and composer; he adopted the nom de théâtre Salvatore Marchesi. Soon after, Mathilde became a teacher of singing, first as

professor at the Vienna Conservatory (1854–61 and 1868–78), then Paris (1861–64) and Cologne (1865–68). One of her early pupils was *Ilma di Murska. Eventually settling in Paris, Mathilde established École Marchesi around 1881, maintaining a salon that would become one of the most important circles of musical life in the city until 1908.

Marchesi, whose method stressed vocal longevity, published several books on vocalism, but is chiefly celebrated for the great opera singers who studied with her. Among her pupils were her daughter Blanche, *Etelka Gerster, *Mary Garden, *Nellie Melba, *Emma Eames, *Emma Calvé, *Sibyl Sanderson, *Selma Kurz, and *Frances Alda. In her lifetime, Marchesi was awarded the Golden Cross of Merit with the Crown from the emperor of Austria, and gold medals for Arts and Sciences from the royals of Italy, England, Saxony, Prussia, and Russia.

SUGGESTED READING:

Marchesi, Mathilde. *Marchesi and Music: Passages from the Life of a Famous Singing Teacher.* New York and London: Harper & Brothers, 1898.

Marcia (fl. c. 100 BCE).

See Iaia.

Marcia (fl. 100 BCE)

Roman noblewoman. Flourished around 100 BCE; daughter of Q. Marcius Rex; married Gaius Julius Caesar; children: Gaius Julius Caesar Maior (praetor in 85 BCE, who married *Aurelia); *Julia (d. 68 BCE, who married Gaius Marius); Sextus Julius Caesar (consul in 91 BCE); grandmother of Roman emperor Julius Caesar (101–44 BCE).

Marcia (fl. 177–192 CE)

Imperial concubine. Flourished in the late 2nd century, between 177 and 192 CE.

After the banishment of Empress *Bruttia Crispina in 177, Marcia became the mistress of Marcus Aurelius Commodus, the Roman emperor. Marcia, who is said to have been a Christian, became influential after the death of Commodus' longtime friend and chamberlain Cleander in 189. Three years later, in 192, she played a leading role, with Eclectus and Aemilius Laetus, in the plot to murder Commodus. On New Year's Eve, they tried to poison him to no avail. They then convinced an athlete named Narcissus to strangle him.

Marcia (fl. 1357).

See Marzia.

Marciana (fl. 98–117 CE).

See Ulpia Marciana.

Marcos, Imelda (1929—)

Philippine politician and first lady from 1965 through 1986 who ruled with her husband and amassed a fortune through corruption and the skimming of public funds. Born Imelda Romualdez on July 2, 1929, in Tacloban, Leyte Province, the Philippines; first of six children of Vicente Orestes Romualdez and Remedios Trinidad Romualdez; married Ferdinand Edralin Marcos (b. 1917, president of the Philippines, 1965–1986), on May 1, 1954 (died, September 28, 1989); children: Marie Imelda ("Imee") Marcos; Ferdinand Marcos, Jr.; Maria Victoria Irene Marcos.

Became first lady of the Philippines (December 30, 1965); legalized as head of state in event of death or illness by Presidential Decree 731 (June 7, 1975); was virtual ruler of the Philippines (after 1979) because of her husband's failing health; played the U.S. against the USSR to gain increasing aid; her conspicuous consumption in the 1980s became legendary; with husband, tried to fight off the Aquinos and their followers (1983–86); forced into exile (1986); returned to Philippines (1991).

Although her name is associated with the thousands of shoes found in her wardrobe, Imelda Marcos was much more than a fashion plate. During her husband's 20 years in office as president of the Philippines, Imelda Marcos was at the center of power, exercising dictatorial powers on her own authority.

𝓜rs. Marcos is ambitious and ruthless. Born a poor cousin of landed aristocracy, she has a thirst for wealth, power, and public acclaim.

—CIA report, 1975

Imelda Romualdez was born on July 2, 1929, in Tacloban, Leyte Province, the Philippines, the oldest of six children born to Vicente Orestes Romualdez and **Remedios Trinidad Romualdez**. Her father's family was a major political force in both provincial and national politics—one uncle had been a Supreme Court justice while another was elected mayor of Manila. Vicente Romualdez lagged behind other family members in personal accomplishments, with a rather lackluster record as a lawyer and law school professor. Indeed, he was probably best known for other forms of productivity—there were five children from his first marriage, and six from the second. Imelda's childhood was insecure. Her parents' marriage was filled with countless quarrels, separations, and reconciliations. In 1937, when Imelda was only eight, her mother died.

The Romualdez family was not well off, and Imelda grew up in genteel poverty. She was ashamed to invite the nuns from her Benedictine school into the house. Known as "Meldy," the attractive teenager was a good student and quite popular with her classmates. She loved to dance the rumba, watch *Ingrid Bergman** movies, and go to parties. In high school, she was crowned the "Rose of Tolosa." A talented singer, she often performed at weddings. Even at this stage of her life, Marcos possessed considerable political skills and ambition, demonstrated when she was elected student-body president. At home, she had long been exposed to political gossip and arguments because her father often entertained politicians from Manila.

Too confined by the small-town atmosphere of Tolosa, Imelda Romualdez moved to Manila in 1952, living with Daniel Romualdez, a cousin who was an influential politician. Family connections gave the young Imelda access to the highest strata of the city's political and business elites, although her earliest jobs were modest ones. She sang and played for potential purchasers of pianos in a music store and then worked as a clerk in the Central Bank. Among Imelda's more serious suitors was a dashing bachelor three years her junior. Scion of a wealthy and powerful family, he would meet Marcos at the music store at the end of the day, then take her to Luneta Park to watch breathtaking tropical sunsets over Manila Bay. The young man was Benigno Aquino, Jr., whose wealthy father served as both a Cabinet minister and senator. Some of their friends expected them to get married, but he broke off the relationship. The reason he gave in later years was that, at 5'6", Imelda was too tall.

Imelda soon met an ambitious older man in Manila's social swirl who took a liking to her. Ferdinand Marcos had been born on September 11, 1917, in Sarrat, Ilocos Norte, where his wealthy landowning family was deeply involved in politics, virtually controlling Ilocos Norte. The oldest of four children, Ferdinand was raised in a family atmosphere where his father, a strict disciplinarian, preached a doctrine of stoic self-reliance and a determination to win at all costs. From his mother, Ferdinand learned a respect for books and learning. As a youth, he became physically tough and excelled at shooting, tracking wild animals, and jungle survival skills. In 1939, he was tried for the 1935 murder of one of his father's political rivals. Arguing his own case as a newly minted lawyer, in 1940 Ferdinand won an acquittal. During the Japanese occupation of World War II, he claimed to be a leader of the resistance movement. Obviously impressed, Imelda accepted Ferdinand's engagement ring 11 days after they met and their marriage took place on May 1, 1954. Theirs was no doubt a love match, but the union also repre-

sented a synergistic fusion of two powerful political families, one dominating Ilocos Norte and the other Leyte.

A successful criminal defense lawyer and congressman when he married Imelda Romualdez in 1954, Ferdinand Marcos aimed much higher. When he first ran for Congress in 1949 on the Liberal Party ticket, he promised the district he represented there would be "an Ilocano President in twenty years." After three terms in the House of Representatives, he ran for Senate in 1959, winning his seat with the largest

Imelda Marcos

plurality ever obtained in a Philippine election. In the meantime, Imelda devoted herself to being a good political wife. **Marie Imelda ("Imee") Marcos,** the first of three children arrived. She would be followed by Ferdinand Marcos, Jr., and **Maria Victoria Irene Marcos.** From the outset, Imelda was highly ambitious for her husband. She often accompanied him on campaign trips where the couple dazzled voters by singing duets on the platform.

From 1954 to 1961, Ferdinand Marcos served as vice-chair of the Liberal Party. President Diosdado Macapagal agreed that he would retire after the first term to make way for the younger man. When he subsequently refused to do this, Ferdinand quit the Liberal camp and joined the Nationalist Party. Determined to win the Nationalist nomination for her husband, Imelda jumped into the fray, frequently entertaining badly needed allies in expensive nightclubs as well as on a barge in Manila harbor. In addition to charming conversation, 1,500 convention delegates often found envelopes generously stuffed with pesos next to their dinner plates. Several years later, Imelda proudly told William Bundy, American assistant secretary of state for East Asian Affairs, how she and her husband outmaneuvered their political rivals: "You've got to control the site; you've got to have your people everywhere. We had the bellhops; we had the waiters; we had the elevator boys; we had the desk clerks; we had everybody talking up [Ferdinand]: 'It's going to be Marcos.'" No detail escaped her eye, she told Bundy. She won over all the hotel's telephone operators at the political convention, ensuring that her husband's opposition never received their phone calls.

Imelda Marcos continued to lobby once her husband secured the Nationalist nomination for the presidency. Ferdinand, who needed a strong vice-presidential running mate, picked Fernando Lopez, a man of influence, status and wealth. However, Lopez and his powerful family did not want him to be number two, and they would not budge. Then Imelda met with Lopez in his suite at the Manila Hotel. It is said that she dropped on one knee, cried, and pleaded with him. He accepted the vice-presidential spot on the ticket.

When the campaign began, Imelda was a tireless adviser. Some political commentators argued she was worth at least a million votes to the Marcos-Lopez ticket. Imelda Marcos focused on women, whose votes might very well tip the election either way. She recruited thousands of women for the campaign, persuading large numbers from the social elite, debutantes and ma-

trons, to drive cars, organize receptions, and answer telephones on her husband's behalf. Their "uniforms" were blue dresses, so that in later years when Imelda went on shopping sprees in New York, Rome, or Tokyo as first lady, her retinue was known as the Blue Ladies.

Imelda Marcos' energetic campaigning paid off, and her husband's ticket amassed a plurality of 650,000 votes out of 8 million cast. It was an expensive campaign, with each candidate spending more than $8 million in a land where 60% of the population lived in poverty. An agrarian revolutionary movement known as the Huks (Hukbalahap) had come close to seizing power in the early 1950s, but it was crushed with massive U.S. assistance because of the strategic importance of two military bases in the Philippines: Clark Field and Subic Bay. The Philippines were considered crucial during the Cold War, and many in Washington felt festering domestic problems and poverty must be subordinated to geopolitical priorities. The Philippine oligarchy took advantage of this situation by labeling all attempts at change as "Communist inspired." This was a pattern the Marcoses could never break.

Ferdinand Marcos was inaugurated president of the Philippines on December 30, 1965. Although he spoke of social reform, the reality was dramatically different. He made attempts to curb crime, corruption and smuggling, but little had been accomplished. He sent troops to Vietnam, reversing earlier criticism of the conflict. Meanwhile, social inequalities got worse and a rural revolutionary movement, the New People's Army, began to grow while the middle class was more and more disgusted with corruption and economic injustice. Despite the fact that little was accomplished, the Marcoses were determined to have a second term. The 1969 election was marked by a great deal of corruption and vote buying, costing the Marcoses a staggering $50 million. In 1969, Ferdinand became the first (and only) Philippine president to secure a second term. Constitutionally, this would be his last term, since presidents were limited to two terms of office.

Life was changing in the Philippines. The nation's wealth continued to be in the hands of less than 5% of the population. Radicalized young men and women in the universities were particularly alienated, but growing sectors of the middle class now regarded the Marcos administration as part of the problem rather than a solution to national malaise. In January 1970, serious riots broke out after the State of the Nation address. The first couple was jeered by a mob of 20,000 and pelted with rocks, bottles, and a *papier-mâché* crocodile. In August 1971, a grenade attack on an opposition political rally left ten dead. President Marcos blamed Communists for the atrocity, used the attack to proclaim a state of emergency, and suspended the right of habeas corpus.

The November 1971 election was a strong rebuke of the Marcos administration. Of the eight contested Senate seats, six were won by the opposition Liberals—a stunning loss of face for Ferdinand and Imelda. Up to that time, Ferdinand had believed that he could choose his successor—either Imelda Marcos or his defense minister Juan Ponce Enrile. But the rapidly changing popular mood had radically altered the equation. The nationwide discontent crystallized around the candidacy of Benigno Aquino, Jr., leader of the Liberal Party and erstwhile suitor of Imelda Marcos. Born in 1932 to a wealthy landowning family, he was a journalist in the Korean War while still in his teens. At 22, he became the youngest mayor of his hometown and, at 28, was elected the youngest governor of Tarlac Province. Few were surprised when at age 34 he became the youngest senator in the history of the Philippines. Benigno described himself as "a radical rich guy" while managing his father-in-law's 18,000-acre sugar estate because he gave away plots of inherited land to field and factory workers. In the presidential elections scheduled for 1973, Benigno was regarded as the likely successor to the now increasingly unpopular Marcos regime. Without documentation of any kind, Ferdinand accused Benigno Aquino of aiding the Communists with weapons, asserting that he had been linked to revolutionary elements since 1965. Aquino vehemently denied the accusations and challenged the regime to file specific charges and try him in a court of law.

Ferdinand suspended the Constitution and declared martial law on September 23, 1972. He also imprisoned Benigno Aquino and thousands of opposition members. The pretext for the declaration was an "assassination attempt" against Defense Secretary Juan Ponce Enrile—an attack which later was revealed to have been faked. Until this time Imelda Marcos had played the traditional role of first lady, hanging in the background. Now she emerged as "co-president," eventually becoming the virtual dictator of the Philippines. Her role was widely recognized, and in December 1972 she narrowly survived an assassination attempt when a man armed with a foot-long bolo knife lunged at her. The injuries to her right arm and hand required 75 stitches. Imelda immediately received a telephone call from President Richard M. Nixon, who dispatched a noted Stanford hand surgeon to Mani-

la. The Marcoses had long been on the best possible terms with Nixon, secretly funneling contributions of more than $1 million to both his 1968 and 1972 campaigns.

With the establishment of dictatorship, Imelda Marcos became increasingly visible. Soon after the attempt on her life, she was in the United States wearing a gold necklace as a sling for her injured arm. She was a prominent guest at the January 1973 inauguration of Nixon. From this point forward, she began to pursue her own foreign policy. Although she wooed the United States, Imelda Marcos frequently courted other countries as well. The first woman to receive an official state welcome in Saudi Arabia, she also visited Nepal and Papua-New Guinea. Imelda was as warmly received by the military dictator of Bolivia as she was by the Marxist revolutionary Fidel Castro. As friendly with the left as with the right, she visited the People's Republic of China in September 1974. Royally received by her Marxist hosts, she spoke graciously of Mao Zedong's wife *Jiang Qing, describing her as "soft-spoken, very feminine" and "open-minded." Diplomatic relations between the two countries were established in 1975.

Imelda Marcos had learned the rules of an intriguing political game in which small countries like the Philippines pitted the U.S. against the U.S.S.R. Her object was to enhance her own status while pressuring the United States to increase its foreign aid. Her trips were also used to mute criticism of human rights abuses by the Marcos dictatorship. Although Communists and leftists were ruthlessly suppressed in her country, this did not stop Imelda Marcos from praising the Soviet Union for bringing "fullness to the lives of man" in the fall of 1977. American money inevitably followed after such pronouncements to keep this important ally happy.

Imelda Marcos' position in the regime was legalized on June 7, 1975, by Presidential Decree 731, which stipulated that, in the event of Ferdinand's death or incapacity, executive power would be exercised by a commission chaired by "Mrs. Imelda R. Marcos." Next, Metro Manila was created by merging the commercial metropolis of Manila with what had been until then the official national capital, Quezon City. In November 1975, Ferdinand named Imelda governor of Metro Manila, kicking out the mayor who had been democratically elected in 1971. This coup gave her control of over 6 million people, thousands of jobs, and hundreds of millions of dollars, many of which went into Imelda's pocket. In December 1975, *Cosmopolitan* magazine declared Imelda Marcos one of the richest women in the world, possibly even "the richest woman in the world, *bar none.*" This was certainly an extraordinary accomplishment in view of the fact that her husband's salary was only $5,700 a year. A 1975 Top Secret report from the CIA characterized her as "The Steel Butterfly," going on to describe her in these terms: "Mrs. Marcos is ambitious and ruthless. Born a poor cousin of landed aristocracy, she has a thirst for wealth, power and public acclaim. . . . Although she has little formal education, she is cunning." Imelda put the "squeeze" on corporations and wealthy individuals for "donations" to her private coffers. In 1978, her husband appointed her head of a new, ill-defined government agency called the Ministry of Human Settlements which provided further situations for skimming large amounts of public funds. Imelda Marcos also became chair or director of the National Electrification Commission, the National Food Authority, the National Housing Corporation, the National Home Mortgage Corporation, National Pollution Control Commission, and Rural Waterworks Development Corporation. Over the years, she had access to many hundreds of millions of dollars of American aid money. The Marcos marriage was described in the same CIA report as being essentially a business and political partnership. In this arrangement, Ferdinand was head of government while she was head of state. It was, in effect, a conjugal dictatorship.

In 1979, CIA station chief Herbert Natzke asserted that the Marcoses had accumulated at least $1 billion through various corrupt actions. Some of this money was spent on events like the Marcoses' silver wedding anniversary in 1979 when the couple renewed their wedding vows, with Cardinal Jaime Sin officiating, before a group of royalty specially flown in from Europe. Imelda wore a white veil while she fondled a two-foot long rosary, each bead a diamond, that some estimated to have cost at least $1 million. Music for the occasion was provided by the Manila Symphony Orchestra, and there was dancing until dawn. The opulent event was not shown on television, nor was it even reported in the state-controlled press. By now, even the Marcoses suspected that their conspicuous consumption might not meet with the approval of the average Philippine worker whose annual income was perhaps $500 a year. The transfer of billions of dollars from business to conspicuous consumption was a very heavy burden for a small country.

The Marcoses continued to profit enormously from Ferdinand's presidency, and Imelda's shopping sprees became legendary. On one day alone during a 1977 visit to New York, she spent $193,320 on antiques. A week later, she and her entourage stormed several of the most elegant jewelry stores. In one day, she spent a total of $2,181,000; her purchases included a Bulgari platinum and emerald bracelet costing $1,150,000. On another New York shopping spree, from May to July 1983, she spent almost $4.5 million. The more Imelda spent, the more the Marcos regime was criticized. Now, there were tough questions by human-rights activists who wanted to know why political leaders like Benigno Aquino had been imprisoned. The climate had changed at the White House also, and she felt snubbed when she was unable to secure even a brief meeting with President Jimmy Carter. "I have been to Peking. I have been to Moscow. I have been to Libya," she said. "Nobody ever treated me so rudely." When she returned to the Philippines, Ferdinand announced a suspension of negotiations about the military bases. Anti-American stories appeared in the controlled press, and vehement anti-base rallies were held by the government-sponsored youth organization Kabataang Barangay. The Marcoses made no secret of their involvement in these demonstrations. Daughter Imee Marcos was often seen chanting "Yankee, go home!" with the crowds.

Despite the increasingly corrupt and repressive nature of the Marcos dictatorship, successive U.S. administrations supported it. Fear of losing military bases deemed vital to American military security in the Pacific was an important factor. With the fall of the shah of Iran in 1979 and the Sandinista victory in Nicaragua, many observers were anxiously waiting for the Philippines to be next. The Carter administration distanced itself somewhat from the Marcoses, but there was no significant pressure to change. The Reagan presidency was, in contrast, friendly to the point of intimacy. One of the more dramatic signs of support from the new administration in Washington came from Vice President George Bush, who attended the Marcos inauguration in July 1981 and toasted the Philippine dictator by proclaiming, "We love your adherence to democratic processes, and we will not leave you in isolation." Ronald and *Nancy Reagan had known the Marcoses since the 1960s, and the two women had developed a strong friendship. Reagan's viscerally anti-Communist perspective on world affairs made it possible for him to ignore any flaws in the strong-willed couple who dominated the political and economic life of the strategic Pacific island chain.

The state visit of the Marcoses to Washington in September 1982 was a triumphal tour. The entire visit, which cost the Philippine government between $5 and $20 million, was orchestrated down to the last detail by Imelda's brother Benjamin ("Kokoy") Romualdez, who had been appointed ambassador to the United States three months before. Cultivated by Manila public relations executives and treated to numerous luncheons at exclusive restaurants, the Washington press corps proved to be, with few exceptions, remarkably friendly and uncritical. The Marcos party arrived, along with several hundred hangers-on, in two 747s. There were few protesters and nearly 1,000 Filipinos were on hand to cheer Ferdinand and Imelda. Lured by Kokoy Romualdez with promises of free food, lodging and entertainment, the crowd waved miniature flags and wore T-shirts proclaiming "I am a Filipino." *New York Times* reporter **Lynn Rosellini** noted with amazement that the arrival, which "easily could have been scripted by Cecil B. De Mille" was without any doubt "one of the most carefully orchestrated events of its kind Washington has ever seen." The show was meant to convince an increasingly disillusioned Philippine public that Washington truly loved the Marcoses. The Reagan administration, always fine-tuned to the world of television and show business, scheduled the White House opening ceremony for 10:00 AM Washington time, which allowed live transmission via satellite for prime time viewing at 10:00 PM in Manila. The staged welcome included crowds of Filipinos on the mall carrying banners inscribed "Long Live Marcos and Reagan." The 21-gun salute, and the fife and drum corps in colonial uniforms playing "Yankee Doodle," added color to the event as Nancy Reagan kissed her friend Imelda Marcos on the cheek. The festivities that filled the next few days were breath-taking. The entourage, probably the largest contingent ever to arrive in Washington for a state visit, sponsored some of the most opulent events within memory in the American capital. A reception hosted by the Marcoses at the Corcoran Art Gallery brought out 2,000 of Washington's elite. Diverted by a groaning buffet and folk dancers flown in from the Philippines, they paid court to Imelda, the "first lady of extravaganza." When her husband arrived late for this stellar event, Imelda grabbed a microphone and sang "Feelings."

Imelda Marcos had directly exercised political power since December 1975 when her husband fired Alejandro Melchor, his executive secretary, and gave her the job. According to a classified report of the Defense Intelligence Agency, she functioned as head of the Philippine government increasingly after 1979. Her power was vastly enhanced in early August 1983 when her husband had a kidney transplant. Ferdinand suffered from the operation as well as from lupus erythematosus, a chronic disorder of the immune system. Imelda became the de facto ruler of the country, and crisis followed. On August 21, 1983, Benigno Aquino, Jr., the most determined and popular of the Marcos dynasty's foes, returned to the Philippines from exile in the United States. He was assassinated immediately after stepping off his plane. Although the government accused others of the act, it was well known that Imelda had warned Benigno not to return home if he valued his life. It was also known that General Luther Custodio, head of airport security on the day of the assassination, was "owned" by Imelda Marcos "lock, stock and barrel."

The next three years were tumultuous. Imelda Marcos wielded ever greater power, but opposition continued to grow. Largely fraudulent elections in 1984 only served to further anger the anti-Marcos forces, who now began to crystallize around Benigno's widow, *Corazon Aquino. In late 1985, the Marcos regime, finally feeling significant pressure from the United States, called for a "snap election" to take place in February 1986. Corazon Aquino agreed to run for president after 1.2 million people petitioned her to do so. The election, held on February 7, 1986, was marked by fraud and bloodshed, and the Marcos regime almost managed to rig the vote successfully. But the end of the Marcos dictatorship became inevitable when two of the leading generals defected on February 22. The Catholic Church also withdrew support from the Marcoses and millions of ordinary Filipinos took to the streets in a display of "people power" to voice their outrage at the regime. Defiant to the last, Imelda and Ferdinand tried to ignore the inevitable collapse of their power by going through a bizarre "inauguration" at noon on February 25, a few hours after Corazon Aquino and her followers had held their own makeshift ceremony.

Intense pressure from Washington now forced the Marcoses to leave the nation they had looted for two decades. They left Malacanang Palace at 9:05 PM that same day and several hours later were flown out of Manila on a U.S. Air Force plane. Accompanied by an 86-member entourage, Imelda and Ferdinand brought along 22 boxes of currency and an astonishing 278 crates of jewelry, artworks, gold and real-estate deeds. After arriving at the island of Guam for a quick stopover, Imelda spent $12,000 at the U.S. military commissary. From their permanent place of exile in Hawaii, the Marcoses quickly began to denounce the new Aquino government, keeping in touch with pro-Marcos activists in the United States and the Philippines. In view of Ferdinand's declining health, most of these political maneuvers must be ascribed to a remarkably unrepentant Imelda.

Back in the Philippines, the full extent of the Marcos depredations of the public treasury began to be documented. When Malacanang Palace was opened, the public gawked at Imelda's boudoir with its two queen-sized beds on an elevated platform and a grand piano. Besides her solid-gold washbasin, there were 2,700 pairs of size-eight shoes, five shelves of Gucci handbags, and 105 clothes racks designed to carry 80 outfits each. The first couple's bedroom intercoms were marked "King's Room" and "Queen's Room."

The remarkable career of Imelda Marcos did not end in exile. She did not fade away when her husband died in Hawaii on September 28, 1989. She continued to lobby President Corazon Aquino to allow her husband's body returned to the Philippines for burial. Soon she faced charges in the United States of embezzlement and bank fraud totaling $268 million. Arriving at the U.S. federal building, she confidently held her head high, appearing distinctly glamorous in her sheer, low-cut turquoise *terno*, the Philippine national costume. She pled not guilty. In 1989, she was found guilty by a U.S. federal jury of liability in a 1981 murder of two anti-Marcos exiles in Seattle. She and her late husband were declared guilty of conspiracy in the murders, and the estate was ordered to pay $15 million to the survivors of the victims. In July 1990, Marcos was acquitted by a New York jury of charges of racketeering, fraud, and obstruction of justice.

After having lived in exile for nearly six years, Imelda Marcos returned to the Philippines on November 4, 1991, defiantly prepared to face criminal charges of graft and tax fraud. Despite the well-documented evils of the Marcos regime, she retained sufficient political talent to tap into old memories, stir up new discontents, and create a significant mass following. Since President Aquino had already announced her decision not to run for reelection, Imelda announced her own candidacy for the highest office in the land. In the election, held on May 11, 1992, she achieved a respectable fourth place, out of the seven candidates who ran, with 10.3% of the popular vote. In November 1996, she was elected to Congress, representing her home province of Leyte. By any criterion a remarkable human being, Imelda Marcos left a permanent mark on her nation's history. One can only speculate how different that history might have been had her energy, intelligence, and charm been harnessed to selfless goals.

SOURCES:

Baker, Richard. "The Ten Richest Women in the World," in *Cosmopolitan*. Vol. 179, no. 6. December 1975, pp. 160–165+.

Barber, Stephen. "First Lady in Distress," in *Far Eastern Economic Review*. Vol. 101, no. 32. August 11, 1978, pp. 22–24.

Bonner, Raymond. *Waltzing with a Dictator: The Marcoses and the Making of American Policy*. NY: Vintage Books, 1988.

Ellison, Katherine W. *Imelda: Steel Butterfly of the Philippines*. NY: McGraw-Hill, 1988.

Elson, John. "Mercenary Monsters from Manila," in *Time*. Vol. 132, no. 20. November 14, 1988, pp. 91, 93.

Francia, Beatriz Romualdez. *Imelda and the Clans: A Story of the Philippines*. Metro Manila: Solar, 1988.

Howard, Richard. "Manila Clipper," in *Yale Review*. Vol. 76, no. 2. Winter 1987, pp. 198–202.

———. "My Dinner with Imelda," in *Harper's*. Vol. 275, no. 1649. October 1987, pp. 29–30, 32.

Lamar, Jacob V. "From Ally to Pariah," in *Time*. Vol. 132, no. 20. November 14, 1988, p. 24.

The Marcos Revolution: A Progress Report on the New Society of the Philippines. Manila: National Media Production Center, 1980.

Mijares, Primitivo. *The Conjugal Dictatorship of Ferdinand and Imelda Marcos I*. San Francisco, CA: Union Square, 1976.

Pace, Eric. "Autocrat With a Regal Manner, Marcos Ruled for 2 Decades," in *The New York Times Biographical Service*. September 1989, pp. 946–949.

Pedrosa, Carmen Navarro. *Imelda Marcos*. NY: St. Martin's Press, 1987.

Polotan, Kerima. *Imelda Romualdez Marcos*. Cleveland, OH: World, 1969.

Romulo, Beth Day. *Inside the Palace: The Rise and Fall of Ferdinand and Imelda Marcos*. NY: Putnam, 1987.

Seagrave, Sterling. *The Marcos Dynasty*. NY: Harper & Row, 1988.

Spence, Hartzell. *Marcos of the Philippines: A Biography*. NY: World, 1969.

Steinberg, David Joel. *The Philippines: A Singular and a Plural Place*. Boulder, CO: Westview Press, 1982.

Wolmuth, Roger. "The Imelda Marcos Shopping Guide: A Cache 'n' Carry Way to Spend the Fortunes of a Nation," in *People Weekly*. Vol. 25, no. 14. April 7, 1986, pp. 139–141.

Zich, Arthur. "The Marcos Era," in *Wilson Quarterly*. Vol. 10, no. 3. Summer 1986, pp. 116–131.

John Haag,
Associate Professor,
University of Georgia, Athens, Georgia

Marcus, Adele (1905–1995)

American pianist and teacher of some of the 20th century's finest pianists. Born in Kansas City, Mis-

souri, in 1905; died in New York City on May 3, 1995; won the Naumburg Award in 1929; taught at Juilliard.

Adele Marcus studied with Josef Lhévinne in New York and with Artur Schnabel in Berlin. In 1929, she won the coveted Naumburg Award. Although she performed often in public, she was best known for her years of work at the Juilliard School, which she joined in 1954. A superb teacher, her distinguished students included Byron Janis, Agustin Anievas, Tedd Joselson, Santiago Rodriguez, Stephen Hough, Horacio Gutierrez, and many others. In 1980, she established a summer piano festival in Norway.

John Haag,
Athens, Georgia

Marcus, Ruth Barcan (1921—)

American philosopher. Born Ruth Barcan in New York City, on August 2, 1921; daughter of Samuel Barcan and Rose (Post) Barcan; New York University, B.A., magna cum laude, 1941; Yale University, M.A., 1942, Ph.D., 1946; married Jules Marcus; children: James Spencer Marcus; Peter Webb Marcus; Katherine Hollister Marcus; Elizabeth Post Marcus.

Was research assistant at Institute for Human Relations (1945–46); was visiting professor at Northwestern University (1950–53, 1959); served as assistant and then associate professor, Roosevelt University, Chicago (1956–59, 1960–63); was professor of philosophy, University of Illinois, Chicago (1964–70); was head of the Department of Philosophy, University of Illinois, Chicago (1964–68); was professor of philosophy, Northwestern University (1970–73); was Reuben Post Halleck Professor of Philosophy, Yale University (1973—), living in New Haven, Connecticut.

Selected works: "A Functional Calculus of First Order Based on Strict Implication" in Journal of Symbolic Logic *(vol. 11, 1946); "The Deduction Theorem in a Functional Calculus of First Order Based On Strict Implication" in* Journal of Symbolic Logic *(vol. 12, 1947); "Elimination of Contextually Defined Predicates in a Modal System" in* Journal of Symbolic Logic *(vol. 15, 1950); "Strict Implication, Deductibility and the Deduction Theorem" in* Journal of Symbolic Logic *(vol. 18, 1953); "Modalities and Intensional Languages" in* Syntheses *(vol. 27, 1962); "Essentialism in Modal Logic" in* Nous *(vol. 1, 1967); (ed.)* The Logical Enterprise *(1975).*

Ruth Barcan Marcus was born in New York City in 1921 and graduated magna cum laude from New York University in 1941. She earned her M.A. and Ph.D. at Yale University. Marcus was one of the few women who began to make forays into academic philosophy in the 20th century. Prior to this, women's opportunities for careers in that branch of academia had been limited, because they were largely restricted from even receiving an education within it. Marcus has had a very successful career as a professor at several prestigious American universities. She has published many articles in philosophy journals, particularly regarding symbolic logic in the subject of modal logic (systems that order the relationship between possibility and necessity) and how quantity can be accommodated in such systems, and also on the relationship between things being equal and their being identical.

Catherine Hundleby, M.A. Philosophy,
University of Guelph, Guelph, Ontario, Canada

Marek, Martha Lowenstein (1904–1938)

Austrian murderer. Born Martha Lowenstein in Vienna, Austria, in 1904; died by beheading in Vienna on December 6, 1938; educated at finishing schools in France and England; married Emil Marek, in 1924 (died 1932); children: one daughter and one son.

Born in Vienna in 1904, Martha Lowenstein Marek grew up in poverty. Orphaned at an early age, she came into the care of a poor Viennese family. In 1919, she began working in a dress shop, where her youthful beauty caught the attention of Moritz Fritsch, a wealthy 74-year-old department-store owner. In the early 1920s, Martha became a ward of Fritsch, who soon made his young charge his lover. He also sent her to expensive finishing schools in France and England, where she was surrounded by wealth and opulence.

When she finished school, Martha returned to live with Fritsch and began a secret affair with a young engineer, Emil Marek. Upon Fritsch's death, Martha inherited his entire estate. In 1924, the two young lovers married and lived lavishly upon the inheritance money; the funds were soon exhausted and the couple was forced to sell Fritsch's impressive mansion. They then devised a bizarre scheme to obtain money. Marek took out an insurance policy on her husband which covered accidents for £10,000. The Mareks then carried out a staged accident which called for Emil to actually lop off his own leg, supposedly while chopping wood. The plan went awry when he failed to fully sever his leg, although he inflicted injuries serious enough finally to result in hospitalization and amputation.

Their attempt to collect the insurance money went equally awry. Insurance agents were suspicious, and their misgivings were confirmed when doctors noted the presence of three separate cuts and decided that the accident had been deliberate. The Mareks were charged with attempted fraud. In a last attempt to save herself and her husband, Martha tried to bribe a nurse to say that her husband's doctor had himself been bribed by insurance agents to make the multiple cuts on Emil's leg. Ultimately, the fraud charges were dismissed, but the Mareks were convicted of bribery and served four months in prison. (They did eventually receive £3,000 from the insurance company, which barely covered the court costs.)

Released from prison, the Mareks moved to Algiers for a time, where they had two children and met with no financial success. Upon their return to Vienna, they were so impoverished that Martha was forced to sell vegetables on the street. Desperate for money, she turned to murder. In July 1932, Emil had difficulty swallowing and suffered numb limbs before dying of what was presumed to be tuberculosis. Just weeks later, their seven-year-old daughter died. Both deaths put insurance money in Martha Marek's pocket. Her next source of funds was a wealthy, aging aunt, **Susanne Lowenstein**. Marek moved in with her to care for her and, within months, Lowenstein was suffering symptoms akin to those of Emil. Lowenstein too soon died, and Martha inherited her aunt's small fortune, which she immediately spent.

Again desperate for money, Marek opened the Lowenstein house to two boarders, a man named Neumann and an elderly woman named Kittenberger. Soon after, Kittenberger was dead and Martha was the beneficiary of a small insurance policy, worth only $300. As this was not nearly enough to maintain her extravagant lifestyle, Marek devised another insurance fraud scheme whereby she had expensive paintings that still hung in her deceased aunt's house removed and hidden in a warehouse. The follow-

Martha Lowenstein Marek on trial.

ing morning she reported them stolen to the police and entered a claim with the company that had insured the paintings.

This proved to be Martha Marek's last deception, for Ignatz Peters, the detective assigned to investigate her claim, had also investigated the mishandled leg amputation years earlier. Instantly suspicious, Peters searched warehouses across Vienna until he uncovered the paintings. Marek was arrested and once again charged with insurance fraud. When Kittenberger's son learned of the arrest, he acted on his own suspicions and approached police with his belief that Marek had killed his mother.

As a result, Kittenberger's body was ordered exhumed, along with the bodies of Marek's deceased husband, daughter, and aunt. The police discovered that each body contained thallium, a rare and poisonous chemical compound. Peters then sought out Marek's son, and found him in a poor district of Vienna, suffering from the effects of thallium poisoning; he recovered after being hospitalized. Not surprisingly, Marek had recently taken out an insurance policy on her son.

Martha Marek maintained her innocence to the end of her trial, which was held in 1938. The prosecution, however, sealed its case by proving that she had been a steady customer of a Viennese chemist who sold thallium to her. Martha Marek received the death penalty, which had been reintroduced to Austria by the controlling Nazi Party, and was beheaded by a single blow of the executioner's axe on December 6, 1938.

SOURCES:
Nash, Jay Robert. *Look for the Woman*. M. Evans, 1981.

Kari Bethel,
freelance writer, Columbia, Missouri

Mareri, Filippa (c. 1190–1236)

Saint and Franciscan nun—belonging to the family of the Counts Mareri, feudatories of Cicolano—who was the founder of the nunnery of St. Peter of Molito. Name variations: Philippa Mareria. Born around 1190, in the Rieti valley, along the valley of the Salto River that marked the border between the territory of St. Peter and the Kingdom of Naples; died on February 16, 1236; daughter of Imperatrice Mareri and Filippo Mareri, prince of Cicolano.

Franciscan nun Filippa Mareri lived out her days against the backdrop of early 13th-century Italy, during which time Francis of Assisi began preaching a new path for the spiritual life, caring for the sick, giving away worldly goods, and depending on God for sustenance. His monastic order, founded in 1209, embraced the principals of poverty, chastity, and obedience. Although Filippa's choice of a religious life preceded the arrival of Francis in Rieti and Cicolano, where she lived, she later embraced his message, as did his disciple *Clare of Assisi who founded the Pauperes Dominae (Poor Ladies of San Damiano).

An article in the *Officium beatae Philippae* recounts that even before Filippa's birth, around 1190, her mother **Imperatrice Mareri** foresaw the extraordinary personality of the child she was going to bring into the world. While still very young, Filippa revealed a strong religious sensitivity, preferring prayer and acts of charity to childhood games. As she approached marriageable age, she obstinately refused to honor a contractual union arranged by her father and brother, even though it would have helped to strengthen her family's political alliances. She further defied her family's wishes by cutting her long hair (an act referred to as the "deed of tonsure") and turning her room into a sacred space, meant for isolation and prayer. According to legend, when her brother Tommaso tried to stop her from taking alms to the poor of the village, she left her home (an ancestral castle) and took refuge in a consecrated cave, a place of pilgrimage.

Eventually the Mareri family came to honor Filippa's religious aspirations, giving her an estate and administrative power in St. Peter de Molito's church, which she accepted gratefully. With a devoted group of followers, she took up the hermetic, reclusive life advocated by Francis of Assisi. Thus, St. Peter de Molito was transformed into a nunnery, becoming the first Franciscan settlement in the territory of Naples. Assuming the role of *mater et domina*, Filippa distinguished herself in proselytizing and charity. Unlike Clare's Poor Ladies of San Damiano, whose purpose was solely to contemplate God and lead holy lives, Filippa's nunnery became a landmark for the inhabitants of the Salto Valley, exercising a positive influence in the spiritual and civic life in Cicolano, and becoming a source of political and economic power.

Filippa lived a relatively short life, dying around the age of 46 on the night of February 16, 1236. The inhabitants of the Salto Valley claimed they were foretold of the event by a heavenly voice announcing: "*Mortua este sancta Filippa.*" Filippa Mareri became the first Franciscan nun to be proclaimed a saint.

SOURCES:
Cerafogli, E. *La baronessa santa Filippa Mareri*. Città del Vaticano, 1979.

Chiappini, A. *S. Filippa Mareri e il suo monastero di Borgo S. Pietro de Molito nel Cicolano*. Biography, liturgy, documents. Perugia, 1922.

Officium beatae Philippae Virginis de Ciculo Ordini Sancti Francisci.

Pasztor, E. "Filippa Mareri e Chiara d'Assisi, modelli della spiritualità femminile francescana," in *L'Italia francescana*. Vol. 63, 1988.

Tozzi, Ileana. "Filippa Mareri, francescana feudataria," in *Deputazione di Storia Patria negli Abruzzi* (Cultural meetings of the fellows). Extract before the publication of the gazette, *L'Aquila*, 1994.

SUGGESTED READING:

Santa Filippa Mareri e il monastero di Borgo S. Pietro nella storia del Cicolano, Records of the meeting of study in Borgo S. Pietro, October 24–26, 1986, Borgo S. Pietro, 1989.

Ileana Tozzi, D. Litt., and member of Società Italiana delle Storiche and Deputazione di Storia Patria, Rieti, Italy

Maretskaya, Vera (1906–1978)

Soviet actress. Born in Moscow, Russia, on July 1, 1906; died in 1978.

Selected filmography: The Tailor from Torzhok *(1925);* Simple Hearts *(1928);* A Living Corpse *(1929);* The Black Hut *(1933);* Love and Hate *(1935);* The Generation of Conquerors *(1936);* Member of the Government *(1939);* The Artomonoy Affair *(1940);* The Wedding *(also called* Marriage, *1944);* Village Teacher *(1947);* Mother *(1955);* My Little Field *(1956);* Mother and Daughter *(1962);* An Easy Life *(1964).*

Born in Moscow in 1906, Vera Maretskaya studied acting at that city's Bakhtangova Studio. Her initial stage appearance came in 1924, followed one year later by her first silent-film role in *The Tailor from Torzhok*. She achieved a measure of fame as an actress with the help of the Soviet propaganda machine, primarily undertaking stock comedic characters such as domestic servants and the naive villager just arrived in the big city. In the early 1930s, she played a series of frivolous women.

Maretskaya evolved her acting style to match the changing currents in Soviet films. When sound was introduced, Soviet directors began taking on more serious matters. A common theme of many films became the rise of the lowly woman into some type of liberation. Maretskaya achieved stardom as the liberated woman in the films *The Generation of Conquerors* (1936) and *Member of the Government* (1939). In *The Generation of Conquerors*, she portrayed a domestic servant transformed into a revolutionary heroine. In *Member of the Government*, she played a poor peasant who successfully learns to run a collective farm; as the story progresses, she denounces an enemy of the state (a common thread in all Soviet films of this era), struggles to maintain her relationship with her husband, and ultimately enters the Supreme Soviet. Maretskaya also starred in the talking version of Maxim Gorky's *Mother*, winning the title role over *Vera Baranovskaya, another popular actress who had played the part in the silent-film version.

Vera Maretskaya was admired for her ability to bring her characters to life; the maturity and depth of her performances distinguished her from those actresses of her time known primarily for their beauty. Her last film, *An Easy Life*, was released in 1964. She died in 1978.

Kari Bethel, freelance writer, Columbia, Missouri

Marfa.

Russian form of Marta or Martha.

Margaret.

Variant of Marguerite.

Margaret (fl. 1000s)

Queen of Scots. Flourished in the 1000s; married Donalbane or Donelbane also known as Donald III (c. 1033–1099), king of the Scots (r. 1093–1098); children: Bethoc (who married Hadria of Tynedale).

Margaret (d. 1209)

*Queen of Norway. Name variations: Margaret Ericsdottir. Died in 1209; daughter of Erik or St. Eric IX, king of Sweden (r. 1156–1160), and *Kristina; married Sverre (c. 1152–1202), king of Norway (r. 1177–1202), in 1185; children: Christine Sverresdottir (d. 1213, who married Philip, king of Bagler); Erling.*

Margaret (d. 1228)

*Countess of Huntingdon. Name variations: Margaret Dunkeld. Died in 1228; daughter of *Maude of Chester (1171–1233) and David Dunkeld, 1st earl of Huntingdon; married Alan, lord of Galloway, in 1209; children: *Christian (d. 1246, who married William de Forz); *Devorgilla (d. 1290, who married John Balliol).*

Margaret (d. 1270)

Queen of Norway. Name variations: Margaret Skulisdottir. Died in 1270; daughter of Jarl Skule; married Haakon IV the Elder (1204–1263), king of Norway (r. 1217–1263), on May 25, 1225; children: Haakon the

Younger (b. 1232), king of Norway (co-r. 1232–1257); Magnus VI the Law-mender (1238–1280), king of Norway (r. 1263–1280); *Christine of Norway* (1234–1262, who married Felipe of Castile, archbishop of Seville); Olav (b. 1227). Haakon IV was first married to *Kanga.

Margaret (d. 1275)

Countess of Bar. Died on November 23, 1275; daughter of Henry II, count of Bar, and *Philippa de Dreux (d. 1240); married Henry V the Blond, count of Luxemburg (r. 1226–1281); children: Henry VI (1240–1288), count of Luxemburg (r. 1281–1288); Walram of Luxemburg; *Philippine of Luxemburg (d. 1311).

Margaret (1240–1275), queen of Scots.

See Eleanor of Provence for sidebar.

Margaret (1275–1318)

Duchess of Brabant. Name variations: Margaret Plantagenet. Born on September 11, 1275, at Windsor Castle, in Windsor, Berkshire, England; died in 1318 in Brussels, Belgium; interred at the Collegiate Church of St. Gudule, Brussels; daughter of Edward I Longshanks (b. 1239), king of England (r. 1272–1307), and *Eleanor of Castile (1241–1290); married John II (1275–1312), duke of Brabant (r. 1294–1312), on July 9, 1290, in Westminster Abbey; children: John III (b. 1300), duke of Brabant (r. 1312–1355).

Margaret (c. 1320–1400)

Duchess of Norfolk. Name variations: Countess of Norfolk; Margaret Plantagenet; Margaret Segrave; Margaret Manny. Born around 1320; died on March 24, 1400; daughter of Thomas of Brotherton, earl of Norfolk, and *Alice Hayles; married John Segrave, 3rd baron Segrave, in 1327; married Walter Manny, 1st baron Manny, around 1354; children: (first marriage) *Anne Segrave; *Elizabeth Segrave (d. 1399); (second marriage) *Anne Manny.

Margaret (1346–1361)

English princess. Name variations: Margaret Plantagenet; Margaret Hastings. Born on July 20, 1346, in Windsor, Berkshire, England; died at age 15 after October 1, 1361; buried at Abingdon Abbey, Oxfordshire, England; daughter of *Philippa of Hainault (1314–1369) and Edward III (1312–1377), king of England (r. 1327–1377); married John Hastings

(1347–1375), 2nd earl of Pembroke, in 1359, in Reading, Berkshire, England.

Margaret (1395–1447)

Duchess of Bavaria. Name variations: Margarethe. Born on June 26, 1395, in Vienna; died on December 24, 1447, in Burghausen; daughter of *Johanna of Bavaria (c. 1373–1410) and Albrecht also known as Albert IV (1377–1404), duke of Austria (r. 1395–1404); sister of Albert V (1397–1439), duke of Austria (r. 1404–1439), king of Hungary (r. 1437); king of Bohemia (r. 1438) and Holy Roman emperor as Albert II (r. 1438–1439).

Margaret (1473–1541), Countess of Salisbury.

See Pole, Margaret.

Margaret (d. 1993)

Duchess of Argyll. Name variations: Margaret Whigham; Margaret Sweeney also seen as Sweeny. Died in August 1993; daughter of George Hay Whigham (a Scottish textile millionaire); married Charles Sweeney (American stockbroker and golfer), in 1933; married Ian Douglas Campbell (1903–1973), 11th duke of Argyll, on March 22, 1951 (divorced 1963); children: (first marriage) Frances Helen Sweeney (who married David Manners, duke of Rutland).

In her early years, Margaret Whigham was a well-known debutante, famed for her beauty, whose every coming and going was chronicled on England's society pages. Following her 1933 marriage to Charles Sweeney, an American stockbroker and golfer, Cole Porter immortalized her in his song "You're the Top" with the lines: "You're Mussolini, / You're Mrs. Sweeney, / You're Camembert." Eventually, Margaret divorced Mr. Sweeney and in 1951 married Ian Douglas Campbell, 11th duke of Argyll, who would have a total of four wives (**Janet Aitken, Louise Clews, *Matilda**, and Margaret). Eight years later, the duke sued for divorce, accusing Margaret of "multiple adultery." Her fame turned into notoriety, and the Argylls were officially divorced in 1963. Margaret's lifestyle changed completely. In February 1990, she was evicted from the Grosvenor House hotel for nonpayment of rent.

Margaret (b. 1949)

Rumanian princess in exile. Name variations: Margaret Hohenzollern. Born on March 26, 1949, in Lausanne, Switzerland; daughter of Michael, king of Rumania (r. 1927–1930 and 1940–1947) and *Anne of Bourbon-Parma (b. 1923).

Margaret's father, King Michael of Rumania, was deposed two years before she was born.

Margaret, Lady (1443–1509).

See Beaufort, Margaret.

Margaret, Maid of Norway
(c. 1283–1290)

Child-queen of Scotland. Name variations: Margaret of Norway; Margaret Ericsdottir. Born before April 1283 in Tönsberg, Norway; died at age eight on September 26, 1290, en route to Kirkwall, Orkney, Scotland; buried in Bergen, Norway; daughter of Margaret of Norway (1261–1283) and Eirik the Priest-Hater also known as Eric II Magnusson (1268–1299), king of Norway (r. 1280–1299); granddaughter of Alexander III, king of Scotland (r. 1249–1286).

At age three, in 1286, Margaret, known as the Maid of Norway, succeeded her grandfather Alexander III, king of Scotland. She was the only child of Alexander's daughter, *Margaret of Norway, who had married Eric II, king of Norway. In 1289, the young Margaret was affianced to Prince Edward (the future Edward II, king of England), but she mysteriously died at sea en route to the Orkneys from Bergen, Norway, by way of the North Sea. Her death left Scotland without a monarch, prompting a bitter conflict, the first Interregnum, between the families of Bruce and Balliol for the throne.

Margaret, Saint.

See Margaret of Antioch (c. 255–c. 275).
See Margaret, St. (c. 1046–1093).
See Margaret of Hungary (1242–1270).
See Margaret of Cortona (1247–1297).

Margaret, St. (c. 1046–1093)

Saint and Saxon princess who, after her marriage to Malcolm III of Scotland, conducted a revival of church discipline and reform, performed spiritual and charitable exercises, and left an influential legacy of equally pious sons and daughters. Name variations: Saint Margaret; Margaret Atheling; Margaret of Scotland. Born sometime in 1046 in Hungary; died in Scotland in Edinburgh Castle on November 16, 1093; buried in Dunfermline, Fife, Scotland; daughter of Ed-

ward the Exile also known as Edward the Atheling (1016–1057, son of Edmund II Ironside) and Agatha of Hungary (c. 1025–?); well educated; married Malcolm III Canmore or Caennmor, king of Scots (r. 1057–1093), around 1070; children: Edward (d. 1093); Edmund, king of Scots (r. 1094–1097); Edgar, king of Scots (r. 1098–1107); Ethelred, abbot of Dunkeld; Alexander I (1077–1124), king of Scots (r. 1107–1124); David I (b. around 1084), king of Scots (r. 1124–1153); Matilda of Scotland (1080–1118); Mary of Atholl (d. 1116, mother of *Matilda of Boulogne [c. 1103–1152]).

With family, returned to England (1057); spent nine years at the court of Edward the Confessor; escaped to Scotland after the Conquest of England (1067); held several conferences of clerics (1070–93), canonized by Pope Innocent IV (September 16, 1249).

Women in early medieval Europe were enjoined to be chaste, passive, and self-effacing. Circumstances, however, often led many women to act in ways which belied this popular image. This was particularly true of early medieval queens. Many monarchs in 11th-century Europe were engaged in the slow process of rejuvenating and consolidating their kingdoms after the Barbaric—and later the Viking—invasions of the 5th and 9th centuries. A queen's role in the royal household was especially significant since the household was, at that time, the center of government. Thus, many early medieval queens worked hand-in-hand with their husbands in the governance of their kingdoms, and both monarchs together exercised considerable power and influence. St. Margaret of Scotland was one such queen.

Born in Hungary sometime in 1046, she grew up at the royal court of Stephen I, king of Hungary, and was the eldest daughter of the exiled Edward the Atheling, son of King Edmund II Ironside, and ❧➤ Agatha of Hungary, a kinswoman of *Gisela of Bavaria, queen of Hungary. When they were infants, Margaret's father and his brother Edmund had been banished from England by the Danish King Canute the Great to Sweden and thence to Hungary. Margaret's father grew up in a very pious court, as Hungary had been newly converted to Christianity just prior to King Stephen's reign. Like her father, therefore, Margaret lived her early years surrounded by strong Christian influences and devout monarchs who served as important role models.

In 1057, Margaret, her brother Edgar the Atheling, sister ❧➤ Christina, and her mother and father returned to England at the behest of her great-uncle, Edward III the Confessor. Almost immediately after they landed in England, however, Margaret's father died suddenly. For the next nine years, Margaret lived at the equally pious court of the Confessor. Here, she lived a strict and religious life with her sister Christina, with much of their time being spent in meditation and prayer. Like all royal princesses, Margaret was well educated, and it was said that she could read Latin and speak French. Not much is known of her physical appearance except that she was tall and had blue eyes and fair hair.

These happy, tranquil years were shattered when Edward the Confessor died on January 5, 1066, and Harold II Godwineson of Essex was elected king of England. Nine months later, on October 14, 1066, Harold was defeated and killed at the Battle of Hastings by the Norman duke William I the Conqueror who was ordained king of England on Christmas Day in Westminster Abbey. Realizing that the conquest was permanent, Margaret and her family became concerned for their safety since her brother, Edgar the Atheling, was a direct heir to the English throne through the old Saxon line, and therefore represented a considerable threat to William the Conqueror.

Accordingly, in the summer of 1067, the 21-year-old Margaret, her siblings and her mother, set off to return to Hungary. They never reached their destination. Rough and stormy weather blew their ship north to Scotland and into the Firth of Forth where they dropped anchor in a bay since known as St. Margaret's Hope. Scotland was governed at this time by Malcolm III Canmore (Gaelic for Great Head or Chief), who was described by a contemporary, St. Ailred of Rievaulx, as "a king, very humble in heart, bold in spirit, exceeding strong in bodily strength, daring, though not rash and endowed with many other good qualities." Like Margaret, Malcolm had spent a great part of his early life in England at the court of Edward the Confessor, where he took refuge when his father Duncan was overthrown by Macbeth, the powerful lord of Moray. After 14 years of exile, Malcolm returned to Scotland in 1054, accompanied by Earl Siward of Northumbria, to claim back the throne of Scotland from Macbeth. Achieving his goal four years later when Macbeth was killed in battle, Malcolm was finally crowned king of Scotland on April 25, 1058. Nine years later, his kingdom was eagerly sought out by Saxon refugees escaping from the Norman court of William the Conqueror.

When he met the young Saxon princess, Malcolm, whose first wife *Ingebiorge died around this time, was immediately smitten.

Margaret, however, was not as keen as her ardent suitor and, indeed, expressed a strong desire to take the veil and retreat into a convent. Malcolm persisted and, after much coaxing, the 24-year-old Margaret was married to the 40-year-old king of Scots in 1070 at Dunfermline by Fothad, the Celtic bishop of St. Andrews.

Fortunately, much more is known about Margaret's life after she arrived in Scotland thanks to an account written 20 years after her death by her confessor and confidant, Turgot, prior of Durham and later the bishop of St. Andrews. Turgot's biography portrays a determined, strong, and pious woman who, although stern, had a great devotion to performing spiritual and charitable exercises as well as a keen interest in reforming the Church in Scotland.

When Margaret first arrived in Scotland there were no formal, organized monastic orders. Thus, she set about establishing religious orders based on the rule of St. Benedict. In 1070, she invited three Benedictine monks sent from Canterbury by Archbishop Lanfranc to found a priory at Dunfermline. This was the beginning of a wave of monastic foundations in Scotland which would be continued enthusiastically after her death by her sons. Margaret did not neglect the indigenous Celtic orders

Agatha of Hungary (c. 1025–?)
*Saxon noblewoman. Born around 1025; died after 1067 in Scotland; some sources erroneously claim that she was the daughter of Stephen I, king of Hungary, and *Gisela of Bavaria (d. 1033); other sources claim that she was the daughter of *St. Cunigunde and Henry II, Holy Roman emperor; more than likely she was the daughter of Bruno, bishop of Augsburg (brother of Henry II, Holy Roman emperor); married Edward the Exile also known as Edward the Atheling (son of King Edmund II), before 1045; children: Edgar the Atheling (b. around 1050); St. *Margaret (c. 1046–1093); *Christina (fl. 1086).*

Christina (fl. 1086)
*English nun of Romsey. Born in Hungary around 1055; died before 1102; daughter of *Agatha of Hungary and Edward the Exile also known as Edward the Atheling (son of King Edmund II); sister of St. *Margaret (c. 1046–1093); brought to England in 1057.*

By 1086, Christina was a nun at Romsey Abbey in Hampshire. There, she brought up her niece *Matilda of Scotland (1080–1118) and was opposed to Matilda's marriage to Henry I in 1100.

and was benefactor of at least two Culdee communities at Loch Leven and Abernethy. She was also responsible for rebuilding the monasteries at Iona and St. Andrews. Nonetheless, Margaret was concerned that the Church in Scotland was indifferent to, and unaware of, the revivalist movement of the Roman Catholic Church on the Continent. Throughout most of her life, therefore, she strove to bring the Celtic Church into closer conformity with the Church of Rome.

She was poorer than any of her paupers. . . . When she went out of doors, either on foot or on horseback, crowds of poor people, orphans and widows flocked to her, as they would have done to a most loving mother, and none of them left her without being comforted.

—Bishop Turgot

Matilda of Scotland. See *Matilda, Empress for sidebar.*

To this end, she held many church councils, one of which, described by Turgot in some detail, reformed various malpractices. Malcolm, Turgot noted, "took part as an assessor and chief actor, being fully prepared both to say and do whatever she might direct in the matter at issue." The king also acted as her interpreter, as the queen did not know how to speak Gaelic. The reforms she initiated were concerned with points of observance, rather than with any radical change to the organization and administration of the church. Thus, they included establishing uniform methods for dating and observing Lent, prohibitions on marriage with a stepmother or with a brother's widow, having the unconfessed participate in communion at Easter (despite their feelings of unworthiness), strict observance of Sunday as a day of rest, and a prohibition on the celebration of Mass according to "a barbarous rite" (this probably meant refraining from the use of Gaelic). Margaret's enthusiasm left an important legacy in Scotland. Historian Geofrrey Barrow has concluded that:

> in introducing . . . a wholly new kind of religious life north of the Forth, above all in inspiring in her sons and her husband's successors a zeal and devotion towards the forms of religious life and ecclesiastical observance familiar in Norman England and on the Continent, Queen Margaret was knowingly and deliberately instigating changes which for both Church and Nation were of fundamental, far-reaching significance.

Turgot's observations of the queen's daily life are indicative of her piety and devotion to good works. She built shelters for pilgrims and established the Queen's Ferry which took them across the Firth of Forth to the holy shrine at St. Andrews. Much of her day was spent in prayer, and she periodically withdrew to a secret cave where she worshiped in private. The rest of the time she devoted to alleviating the hardship of those less fortunate than herself. Hence, she maintained 24 poor people throughout the year in food and shelter, ministered daily to orphans during the seasons of Lent and Advent, and fed 300 indigent persons, serving them personally, while she herself fasted. At court, she established a school of church work where noblewomen embroidered altar cloths and vestments. It was, in Turgot's words, "a workshop of sacred art."

Margaret was also an intellectually keen woman and thus had a strong interest in reading. Malcolm often adorned her books with gold and gems, and, though he could not read, noted Turgot, he would "turn over and examine books which she used either for her devotions or her study; and whenever he heard her express liking for a particular book, he also would look at it with special interest, kissing it, and often taking it into his hands." Margaret's love of books was also passed on to her six sons and two daughters, **Matilda of Scotland** (1080–1118) and *Mary of Atholl** (d. 1116). Although she loved her children dearly and was a devoted mother, Margaret was a product of her time; hence, she ordered the children's nurse "to curb the children, to scold them, and to whip them whenever they were naughty." According to Turgot, "her children surpassed in good behavior many who were their elders [and] they were always affectionate and peaceable among themselves."

Secular life in Scotland was also touched by this devout queen's inspiration. By birth and inclination she looked toward England and the Continent, while her influence contributed to a more outward-looking, less isolated Scotland. It has been noted that none of her eight children were given Scottish names. Under her guidance, Scottish government was refined, as it became more ceremonial and dignified. Like many Continental kings, Malcolm now had a permanent coterie of nobles who accompanied him whenever he walked or rode abroad. Margaret introduced colorful, fine quality fabrics and elegant fashions, new foods and dishes, as well as a custom of saying grace after meals which has been known since as St. Margaret's Blessing. These Continental and Norman practices would be continued by three of her sons when they succeeded to the throne of Scotland, and closer ties with the English royal house would be established when Margaret's daughter Matilda of Scotland married William the Conqueror's son Henry I.

Although Margaret was canonized 156 years after her death, no miracles were ascribed to her during her life. Her biographer Turgot wrote: "I leave it to others to admire the tokens of miracles which they see elsewhere, I admire much more the works of mercy which I perceived in Margaret; for signs are common to the good and the bad, whereas works of piety and true charity belong to the good only." Nonetheless, Turgot recorded one miraculous event which occurred during Margaret's lifetime. It concerned a Book of Gospels which had been adorned with gold and precious stones. One day the person responsible for carrying it accidently let it fall into the middle of a stream where it lay at the bottom for several days. When it was finally discovered, the book was retrieved entirely undamaged from the water; it was believed to have been preserved by God out of His love for the saintly queen.

Margaret's last years were punctuated by a growing illness and a concern for Malcolm who was invading England regularly in the hopes of regaining territory which he had captured earlier in his reign. Her illness stemmed from excessive fasting; she had also suffered from stomach pains throughout most of her life. Six months before she died, she was unable to ride on horseback or rise from her bed. In November 1093, Malcolm launched his last invasion of England despite warnings from Margaret who had a premonition that this campaign would end disastrously. On the day when her husband and her eldest son were slain at Alnwick, she said: "Perhaps on this very day such a heavy calamity may befall the realm of Scotland as has not been for many ages past." Four days after this disaster, her son Edgar arrived at her sickbed and, unwilling to tell her the news of the deaths of her husband and son, was finally pressed into revealing the truth. Grief-stricken, Margaret died on November 16, 1093.

Scotland's new king was Malcolm's brother, Donalbane, who was head of a faction which reacted against the English influences that Margaret had introduced. As some feared that an outrage might be committed on her corpse, Margaret's body was smuggled out of Edinburgh Castle under cover of a heavy fog which had descended on the burgh that day. Her body was carried down the steep face of the Castle Rock and across the Queen's Ferry to Dunfermline where she was laid to rest in the Church of the Holy Trinity which she had built many years before.

One hundred and fifty-three years later, in July 1246, her great-grandson, Alexander II, petitioned Pope Innocent IV to have Margaret included in the Catalogue of Saints. Enquiries into her life and works were made, including her "miracles" (The Book of the Gospels and the fog which enabled her body to be taken from Edinburgh Castle) and, finally, on September 16, 1249, Margaret was formally canonized. Her bones were placed in a silver casket adorned with precious stones and jewels under the high altar at Dunfermline where they remained until the Reformation. St. Margaret's oratory in Edinburgh Castle still stands today where it serves as a lasting symbol of this devout and influential queen.

SOURCES:

Barnett, T. Ratcliffe. *Margaret of Scotland: Queen and Saint*. Edinburgh: Oliver and Boyd, 1926.
Barrow, G.W.S. *The Kingdom of the Scots*. London: Edward Arnold, 1973.
Menzies, Lucy. *St. Margaret, Queen of Scotland*. London: J.M. Dent, 1925.
Turgot, Bishop of St. Andrews. *Life of St. Margaret, Queen of Scotland*. Edinburgh: William Paterson, 1884.

SUGGESTED READING:

Burleigh, J.H.S. *A Church History of Scotland*. London: Oxford University Press, 1960.
Dickinson, W.C. *Scotland from the earliest times to 1603*. London: Thomas Nelson, 1961.
Donaldson, Gordon. *Scotland: Church and Nation Through Sixteen Centuries*. Edinburgh: Scottish Academic Press, 1972.

Margaret McIntyre,
Instructor of Women's History at Trent University,
Peterborough, Ontario, Canada

St. Margaret

Margaret I of Denmark

(1353–1412)

Queen of Denmark and one of Scandinavia's greatest monarchs, who unified Denmark, Norway, and Sweden by the Union of Kalmar. Name variations: (Danish) Margrete, Margrethe I, Margareta; Margaret of Denmark, Margaret Valdemarsdatter or Valdemarsdottir; Margaret Waldemarsdatter or Waldemarsdottir; "Semiramis of the North." Reigned as queen of Denmark, 1387–1397, queen of Norway, 1388–1405, and regent of Sweden, 1389–1412. Born in 1353; died on board her royal ship anchored in Flensburg's harbor on October 28, 1412; second daughter of Valdemar IV also known as Waldemar IV Atterdag, king of Denmark (r. 1340–1375), and Queen Helvig of Denmark (sister of Waldemar III, duke of Schleswig); sister of Ingeborg (1347–1370); married Haakon VI (1338–1380), king of Norway (r. 1355–1380), king of Sweden (r. 1362–1364), in 1363; children: Olaf or Oluf (born at the royal castle of Oslo in 1370), king of Denmark (r. 1376–1387), king of Norway (r. 1380–1387).

At the death of her father Waldemar IV (1375), persuaded the council of the realm to elect son Olaf as king of Denmark and appoint herself guardian; when Olaf inherited kingdom of Norway at the death of her Norwegian husband Haakon VI (1380), became guardian for that country as well; at Olaf's sudden death (1387), was declared "Denmark's proxy and guardian"; Norwegians made her regent for life and even the Swedes allied themselves with her to rid themselves of their German-born king; to ensure royal succession in all three countries, adopted six-year-old grandson of her sister, Erik of Pomerania, who was crowned king in each of the Scandinavian kingdoms (1397), while she remained regent; summoned the Union of Kalmar which unified the three Nordic countries, Denmark, Norway and Sweden (1397); maintained rulership till her death (1412).

In the 11th century, the kingdoms of Scandinavia were a relatively new feature of medieval Europe. During the earliest phase of Viking attacks on Europe, the area was characterized by disunity; bands of Vikings from various Scandinavian areas looted Western Europe for personal or regional gain. But from the late 9th through the 11th centuries, the Scandinavian rulers had consolidated the area; by 1100 three distinct kingdoms—Norway, Sweden and Denmark—had been created. By this time, there were significant regional differences in language and in rules of royal succession which ensured the separate development of the kingdoms. Of these

northern realms, only Iceland existed without a king; by the mid-13th century, however, the king of Norway claimed jurisdiction there. Notwithstanding the 11th-century achievements of King Canute the Great of Norway, Denmark and England, the Scandinavian kingdoms remained separate realms with separate monarchs until the 14th century. The individual who succeeded in uniting the three was a woman—Margaret Waldemarsdatter, later Margaret I of Denmark.

This Danish princess, second daughter of Waldemar IV Atterdag, king of Denmark, and Queen *Helvig of Denmark, spent only the first ten years of her life at her father's court on the island of Sealand. In her 11th year (1363), she was married to the Norwegian king, Haakon VI, and shortly thereafter was sent to the castle of Akershus near Oslo to become acquainted with the country of which she was to be queen. Because she was considered too young to consummate her marriage, she was given into the tutelage of a Swedish noblewoman, ✒➤ Merete Ulfsdatter, who brought her up with her own daughter, Ingegerd. Merete Ulfsdatter was a displaced royalist. With her husband, she had sided with the Swedish king, Magnus Eriksson (Haakon's father), when a faction of Swedish nobles had dethroned him and invited a German duke, Albert II of Mecklenburg, to take his place. Those same nobles would later ally themselves with Margaret to send Albert back to Mecklenburg and thus return the kingdom to the old Scandinavian line. From the very first, then, this Danish princess who married a Norwegian king at whose court she was reared by a woman of Sweden's bluest blood seemed destined by birth as well as circumstance to become the unifier of the three countries and earn the postscript among Danes of "greatest statesman in Danish history." The Swedes were less generous.

Sources of information regarding Margaret's early years in Norway are scarce, but the birth of her only child, Olaf (V), is recorded to have taken place in 1370. Margaret was then 17 years old. That she and her husband lived together in good understanding is suggested by a letter from Margaret to Haakon written during one of his frequent journeys about Norway to raise an army to liberate his father from the hold of the Swedish nobles. She lets him know that she and her household are on the point of starvation, and she urges her husband to write a German merchant with assurances that he will cover any loans extended to the queen in his absence for the purpose of buying food. She requests a copy of the letter as well as the king's permission to be granted cash from the treasurer of the realm in the event of ships entering the harbor with goods she needs to buy. At 18, she not only demonstrates her ability to manage the royal household but shows her knowledge of affairs of state and her participation in the solution of problems. She reports the receipt of a letter of apology from a certain jeweler who had failed to heed a royal summons, and she asks the king's indulgence on the jeweler's behalf. Finally, she seeks her husband's approbation for having mortgaged some royal possessions to obtain a pardon for an alleged criminal. This demonstrated ability to assess a situation and make choices in accordance with inborn intelligence and ingenuity, careful upbringing, and a sense of fairness would become her hallmark as she advanced from queen of one country to ruler of three.

In 1375, at age 22, Margaret was summoned to Denmark at the death of her father, King Waldemar IV. No successor to the Danish throne had been chosen even though Waldemar's son, the acknowledged heir, had died several years earlier. The first in line at this time was the son of Waldemar's eldest daughter, *Ingeborg, who before her death in 1370 had been married to Henry, duke of Mecklenburg. As the younger daughter, Margaret had the lesser claim for her son, but she appeared with Olaf by the hand immediately after learning of her father's death and persuaded the state council to proclaim the five-year-old Olaf king of Denmark with his mother as guardian. That began 37 years of rule during which she would gather the three Scandinavian countries under her dominion, one by one.

When Margaret's husband King Haakon of Norway died in 1380, ten-year-old Olaf inherited his father's kingdom and, again, his mother became his appointed guardian. She and Olaf subsequently traveled to Norway where Olaf was crowned king in Oslo. With two crowns in place, Margaret was ready to challenge the power of the Hanseatic League which not only dominated trade in the Baltic, but which also held extensive land holdings in all three Scandinavian countries. These had been obtained by purchases or leases from the succession of weak or profligate kings who had preceded Margaret's father, Waldemar IV. She targeted the most lucrative first, the possessions in southwest Sweden (Scania) with their castle strongholds which guarded the entry to the Baltic. Her father had been forced to mortgage them for 15 years, but the year of repossession,

---

Merete Ulfsdatter (fl. 1320–1370)

Swedish noblewoman. Name variations: *Marta Ulfsdottir.* Born around 1320; daughter of St. *Bridget of Sweden (1303–1373) and Ulf Gudmarsson (d. 1342), prince of Nericia; sister of Saint *Catherine of Sweden (c. 1330–1381); children: Ingegerd, who became an abbess at Vadstena.

1385, was approaching. The merchants, however, refused to release either property or castles, so Margaret had Olaf dispatch a letter expressing his royal wrath at being thwarted in his princely claims and threatening severe repercussions. Her own letter to the Hanseatic merchants subsequently promised her aid in smoothing matters over if they yielded to her son's demands. Simultaneously, pirates attacked the Hanseatic vessels in the Baltic with unaccustomed vigor. When their League complained to Margaret, reminding her that it was the duty of the Danish king to keep the sea safe for trade, she agreed but professed her inability to do anything without her Scanian castles. Realizing they had been outwitted and unwilling to go to war to keep their estates, the Hanseatic merchants yielded them up. Margaret had had her way, and once again the Danish monarch, now in possession and control of both sides of the Sound which connects the North Sea and the Baltic, could demand and receive the tariff from ships entering that inland sea. The incident shows Margaret as her father's daughter, intelligent and shrewd; for his violence, however, she had substituted flexibility, and experience had taught her patience to bide her time.

This extraordinary patience and willingness to negotiate were trump cards as well in the realization of her dream to build a Baltic empire. To be successful at that, Margaret had to include Sweden in her Dano-Norwegian sphere of influence. Again, time and circumstance were on her side, and she took advantage of the proffered opportunity. She learned that the same nobles who had grown weary of Magnus Eriksson, Olaf's grandfather, and ousted him, had grown equally disenchanted with Albert of Mecklenburg, the German whom they themselves had invited to rule. He and his fellow Germans, they complained, sat like eagles on the mountain tops tyrannizing the country. With her accustomed sense of timing, Margaret therefore had had her son proclaimed heir of Sweden as the last descendant of the Swedish royal line simultaneously with her regaining possession of the Scanian

---

provinces. The positive results of that proclamation measure the degree of dissatisfaction experienced by the Swedish nobles: they preferred to ally themselves with the daughter of King Waldemar, their one-time enemy in the battle for control of the Baltic, than to be ruled by their invited king. Another fortuitous circumstance which served to strengthen Margaret's position was the death of Sweden's greatest and richest landholder, Bo Jonsson. Void of heirs, he had left his estates in the hands of a group of nobles who as executors of his will were to further the politics of Swedish nobility and prevent his property and manors from reverting to the crown. The Swedes were concerned, however, that the wealthiest estate in the country and the power connected with it would be claimed by Albert of Mecklenburg, and that they would be powerless to prevent it. They therefore offered the estate to Margaret, or rather to Olaf, in the hope that he would return it to Swedish aristocracy. The gesture signalled the first step towards the deposition of Albert of Mecklenburg. It was now up to Margaret and Olaf to demand the castles from those who were managing them.

Margaret saw the Swedish crown within her reach when Olaf died suddenly in the year 1387. She grieved as a mother for the loss of her only child, but she acted quickly and decisively. She had the Danish council of state proclaim her "Mistress of our realm, Master of our house, and guardian." In Norway, she was declared "Regent for life," and, in Sweden, she continued her negotiations with the disenchanted nobles, avoiding war against Albert of Mecklenburg until no other option was possible. At that point, in 1389, she met Albert's forces in the battle of Falkoebing in Southern Sweden and defeated them. "Praise be to God who gave an unexpected victory into the hands of a woman," wrote a contemporary chronicler. Albert of Mecklenburg was captured by the Danes and kept in prison until he was ready to cede all claims to Sweden, including the city of Stockholm where the Germans had wielded their greatest influence. Subsequently, all of Albert's estates and holdings as well as those he had bequeathed to German officials reverted to the crown; possessions lost in the war were restored to the nobles, and all castles and fortifications erected during Albert's reign were demolished. Peaceful rule, order, and unity were the pillars of Margaret's empire.

Yet she was in a precarious position as ruler of all three countries but queen only of Norway. She was firm in her conviction, however, that a country could not be ruled well without a royal monarch. She therefore adopted her sister's six-

year-old grandson, Bugislav of Pomerania, whom she diplomatically renamed Erik (VII of Denmark) in memory of the Swedish national saint and numerous Scandinavian kings, and once again she toured the three kingdoms with a youth to have him proclaimed king of all.

Half a century after her father had started reconstituting the Danish kingdom which previous kings had parcelled out in mortgages and leases or downright sold to German dukes, Margaret had finished what he began: she had not only reconstituted Denmark, she had unified the three Scandinavian kingdoms. The event which celebrated and ratified that union is the now-famous Convention of Kalmar summoned by Margaret in 1397. Here were gathered nobles from all three kingdoms, and Erik VII was crowned king of the Scandinavian countries. The coronation document praises Margaret for her work which has yielded such glorious rewards. It reads, "God grant her heaven for her great deeds and her presence among us," and in it her subjects thank her for leading the Nordic countries out of the difficulties that had arisen with the infighting of nobles and their relationship to the king. Sixty-seven nobles attached their seals to the document. The charter which sealed the union was, however, signed by only a minority. Despite the brilliant conceptualizing of a Nordic union unlike any before or since, fear of dominant Danish rule prevented the consensus necessary to ensure its survival. It was nonetheless in effect for 126 years, until 1523, when Sweden broke away. The union between Denmark and Norway remained undisrupted until 1814 when England forced it asunder. By then Denmark and Norway had been united for 434 years.

The Kalmar Union was intended to ensure peace among the three countries. Together, they would elect one king, and each country would respect the independence of the others. They were equals, and no one country was to dominate another. For the time being, Erik was king of all three countries—with Margaret as ruler. In the future, one king was to be elected for all. If one country were forced into battle, all three were to consider it a declaration of war.

With the Scandinavian union in place, Margaret could turn her attention to a problem she had ignored in her efforts to tie Sweden to the Scandinavian alliance: the dukedom of Schleswig. In a seemingly brilliant move, she had made peace in 1386, shortly before Olaf's death, with the Holstein dukes who were clamoring for possession of Schleswig. She had offered that southernmost Danish province as a fiefdom to a

Holsteiner who would then consider the Danish king his lord. Historians have criticized Margaret for sacrificing Schleswig, but throughout her reign she remained constant in her decision to fight one battle at a time. With the Swedes in her corner, she could address the problem of dominion in southern Denmark. Her opportunity for intervention came in 1404 when the Holstein duke who had been installed in Schleswig with the rights and privileges of a Danish duke died, leaving a widow, with one daughter and three young sons, in urgent need of money. Fearful of the Holstein dukes who were eager to relieve her of the guardianship of Schleswig, the widowed duchess **Elizabeth of Brunswick** allied herself with Margaret. Elizabeth found Margaret willing to come to her rescue by paying cash for either mortgages or estates in Schleswig, in the manner practiced so successfully by Germans in other times. Thus, when Margaret acquired the city of Flensburg as a mortgage, young King Erik moved in and openly undermined the rule of the Holsteiners. They grew nervous at the vision of a separation between Holstein and Schleswig and consequently revolted in 1409. Erik took up the gauntlet and readied for war against the rebels. With her characteristic reliance on peaceful resolutions, Margaret nonetheless managed to intervene and secure an armistice for five years. She entered Flensburg on October 24, 1412, to receive the citizens' oath of fealty on Erik's behalf. That journey of reconciliation cost her her life. She caught the plague which during those weeks was ravaging the city and died on October 28 on board her royal ship anchored in Flensburg's harbor. She was 59 years old.

Her body was brought to Soro where she was to be interred with her father, grandfather, and son; but her chancellor, the bishop of Roskilde, wanted her close by and insisted she be brought to Roskilde Cathedral.

Approximately ten years later, King Eric erected a sepulchral monument for his famous foster mother. On the lid is a figure of alabaster, a young, gothic queen with an elaborate hairdo, a linen headpiece topped by a crown, a low-cut gown, and bells fastened to her belt with chains. Historians concede they know nothing about how Margaret looked. No paintings or drawings or even descriptions of her exist. They see in the alabaster woman an idealized figure, possibly even a rendering of *Mary the Virgin, whose resemblance Margaret herself might want to emulate after a long life's devotion to the heavenly queen.

Margaret had been especially tied to the cloister of Vadstena, housed in the castle which

her father-in-law, King Magnus Eriksson, had deeded to St. *Bridget of Sweden to house her order of Brigettines (Birgittines). Bridget, the mother of Merete Ulfsdatter, was famous throughout Europe for her visions and healing powers, and after her death in 1373 Margaret had been instrumental in her sanctification. A devout Catholic, Margaret had repeatedly returned to Vadstena where her childhood playmate, Ingegerd, the grandchild of Bridget, was an abbess. There she had been generous with her gifts as was also her custom *vis-a-vis* the church in general. She donated substantial holdings in exchange for daily masses for her soul and those of her parents.

The 18th-century Danish historian Ludvig Holberg, who was a wise and prudent observer of humanity, lauds Margaret as one of the great rulers of history. She managed, he writes, "through victories and through sagacity and statesmanship to unite three contentious kingdoms and become one of the mightiest if not the mightiest ruler of her time." Others consider her an enigma and wonder what she was really like, this strong woman, who after the death of her husband never remarried yet managed—with the help of her friends but with unfailing self-reliance—to bend the wills of Scandinavian nobles to her ends.

SOURCES:

Danstrup, John, and Hal Koch, eds. *Danmarks Historie.* Copenhagen: Politikens Forlag, 1977.

Holboll, C. Th. *Dronning Margrete.* Copenhagen: Arne Frost Hansens Forlag, 1968.

Jacobsen, Helge Seidelin Jacobsen. *An Outline History of Denmark.* Copenhagen: Host & Son, 1986.

Lauring, Palle. *A History of the Kingdom of Denmark.* Copenhagen: Host & Son, 1960.

Linton, Michael. *Drottning Margareta.* Aarhus: Aarhus Stiftsbogtrykkerie, 1971.

Olsen, Olaf. *Gyldendal og Politikens Danmarkshistorie.* Copenhagen: Nordisk Forlag, 1989.

Stangerup, Henrik, ed. *Holbergs Helte- og Heltindehistorier.* Copenhagen: Lindhart og Ringhof, 1990.

Inga Wiehl,
a native of Denmark, teaches English at
Yakima Valley Community College, Yakima, Washington

Margaret II of Denmark (b. 1940).
See Margrethe II.

Margaret Atheling (c. 1046–1093).
See Margaret, St.

Margaret Balliol (c. 1255–?).
See Balliol, Margaret.

Margaret Balliol (fl. 1300s).
See Balliol, Margaret.

Margaret Beatrice (1872–1954)

*Landgravine of Hesse-Cassel. Name variations: Margaret Hohenzollern. Born Margaret Beatrice Feodore or Feodora on April 22, 1872, in Potsdam, Brandenburg, Germany; died on January 22, 1954, in Kronberg; daughter of *Victoria Adelaide (1840–1901) and Frederick III (1831–1888), emperor of Germany (r. 1888), king of Prussia (r. 1888); married Frederick Charles, landgrave of Hesse-Cassel, on January 25, 1893; children: Frederick Victor (b. 1893); Maximilian (b. 1894); Philip (b. 1896), landgrave of Hesse; Wolfgang (b. 1896); Richard (b. 1901); Christopher of Hesse-Cassel (1901–1943).*

Margaret Beaufort (1443–1509).
See Beaufort, Margaret.

Margaret Bernadotte (1934—)

*Swedish royal. Name variations: Margaret Ambler; Margaretha. Born Margaret Desiree Victoria on October 31, 1934, at Haga Castle, Stockholm, Sweden; daughter of Gustavus Adolphus (1906–1947), duke of Westerbotten, and *Sybilla of Saxe-Coburg-Gotha (1908–1972); sister of Carl XVI Gustavus, king of Sweden; married John Kenneth Ambler, on June 30, 1964; children: Sybilla Louise Ambler (b. 1965); Charles Edward Ambler (b. 1966); James Patrick Ambler (b. 1969).*

Margaret Bruce (c. 1286–?).
See Bruce, Margaret.

Margaret Bruce (1296–1316).
See Bruce, Margaret.

Margaret Bruce (d. 1346).
See Bruce, Margaret.

Margaret Burgo (d. 1303).
See Margaret de Burgh.

Margaret Capet (1158–1198).
See Margaret of France.

Margaret Capet (d. 1271)

*French princess. Name variations: Margaret of Brabant; Marguerite. Died at an early age in 1271; daughter of *Margaret of Provence (1221–1295) and Louis IX, king of France (r. 1226–1270); sister of Philip III the Bold (1245–1285), king of France (r. 1270–1285); married John I (c. 1252–1294), duke of Brabant, around 1270. Two years after Margaret Capet's death, John I married *Margaret of Flanders (d. 1285).*

Margaret Capet (1290–1315).
See Margaret of Burgundy.

Margaret Capet (d. 1382).
See Margaret of Artois.

Margaret Christofsdottir
(c. 1305–1340)

Danish princess. Born around 1305; died in 1340; daughter of *Euphemia of Pomerania (d. 1330) and Christopher II (1276–1332), king of Denmark (r. 1319–26, 1330–32); became first wife of Louis V the Brandenburger (1316–1361), duke of Bavaria (r. 1347–1361), in December 1324. Louis' second wife was *Margaret Maultasch (1318–1369).

Margaret Clementine (1870–1955)

Princess of Thurn and Taxis. Name variations: Margarethe; Margaret Clementine of Habsburg-Lotharingen. Born on July 6, 1870; died in 1955; daughter of *Clotilde of Saxe-Coburg-Gotha (1846–1927) and Archduke Josef Karl Ludwig also known as Joseph Charles Louis (1833–1905); married Albert Maria, 8th prince of Thurn and Taxis; children: Franz Joseph (b. 1893), 9th prince of Thurn and Taxis; Charles Augustus (b. 1898), prince of Thurn and Taxis.

Margaret de Burgh (c. 1193–1259)

Scottish princess and duchess of Kent. Name variations: Princess Margaret; Margaret Dunkeld. Born around 1193; died in 1259; interred at Church of the Black Friars, London; daughter of William I the Lion, king of Scots (r. 1165–1214), and *Ermengarde of Beaumont (d. 1234); married Hubert de Burgh, 1st earl of Kent, on June 19, 1221; children: Magota de Burgh (died young); *Margaret de Burgh (c. 1226–1243).

Margaret de Burgh (c. 1226–1243)

English noblewoman. Born around 1226; died in 1243 (some sources cite November 1237); daughter of Hubert de Burgh, 1st earl of Kent, and *Margaret de Burgh (c. 1193–1259); married Richard de Clare, 6th earl of Hertford and 2nd earl of Gloucester, in 1232 (divorced). She was married to ten-year-old Richard de Clare, then count of Gloucester, when she was six. She died at age 17.

Margaret de Burgh (d. 1303)

Countess of Ulster. Name variations: Margaret Burgo. Died in 1303; daughter of John de Burgh; married Richard de Burgh the Red (c. 1259–1326), 2nd earl of Ulster (r. 1271–1326) and 4th earl of Connaught, before February 27, 1280; children: *Elizabeth de Burgh (d. 1327, queen of Scots); *Matilda de Burgh (d. 1315, who married Gilbert de Clare, earl of Gloucester); John, earl of Ulster; Sir Edmund de Burgh; Lady Joan de Burgh (who married Thomas FitzGerald, 2nd earl of Kildare, and John Darcy, Lord Darcy of Naith); Katherine de Burgh (d. 1331, who married Maurice Fitzgerald, 1st earl of Desmond); Aveline de Burgh (who married John de Birmingham); Alianore de Burgh (who married Thomas, Lord Multon).

Margaret de Chatillon (d. 1404).
See Marie of Guise.

Margaret de Clare (fl. 1280–1322).
See Siege Warfare and Women for sidebar.

Margaret de Foix (d. 1258)

Queen of Navarre. Name variations: Marguerite de Foix; Margaret of Foix; Margaret of Bourbon. Died on April 13, 1258; daughter of Archibald also known as Archimbaud or Archambaud VIII of Bourbon; became third wife of Teobaldo or Theobald I (1201–1253), king of Navarre (r. 1234–1253, also known as Theobald IV of Champagne), in 1232; children: Theobald II (1237–1270), king of Navarre (r. 1253–1270); Enrique or Henry I (c. 1240–1274), king of Navarre (r. 1270–1274). Theobald I was also married to Gertrude of Metz and *Agnes of Beaujeu.

Margaret de Foix (fl. 1456–1477).
See Marguerite de Foix.

Margaret del Balzo

Countess of St. Pol. Married Peter of Luxemburg, count of St. Pol; children: Louis St. Pol, count of St. Pol; *Jacquetta of Luxemburg (c. 1416–1472).

Margaret de Mâle.
See Margaret of Brabant (1323–1368).
See Margaret of Flanders (1350–1405).

Margaret de Rohan (1397–1428)

Viscountess de Rohan. Name variations: Margaret de Dreux. Born in 1397; died in 1428; daughter of John IV de Montfort, 5th duke of Brittany (r. 1364–1399) and *Joanna of Navarre (c. 1370–1437); married Alan de Rohan, viscount de Rohan.

Margaret de Rohan (fl. 1449)

Countess of Angoulême and grandmother of Francis I, king of France. Name variations: Marguerite de Rohan. Flourished around 1449; married John Valois (1404–1467), count of Angoulême, in 1449; children: Charles Valois (1459–1496), count of Angoulême.

Margaret Dunkeld (1261–1283).

See Margaret of Norway.

Margaret Habsburg (1480–1530).

See Margaret of Austria.

Margaret Habsburg (c. 1577–1611).

See Anne of Austria (1601–1666) for sidebar on Margaret of Austria.

Margaret le Brun (d. 1283)

French noblewoman. Died in 1283; daughter of *Isabella of Angoulême (1186–1246), queen of England, and Hugh X, count of Lusignan; married Raymond VII, count of Toulouse (divorced 1245); married Aymer, viscount of Thouars; married Geoffrey, seigneur de Chateaubriand; children: (first marriage) *Joan of Toulouse (d. 1271).

Margaret Louvain (1323–1368).

See Margaret of Brabant.

Margaret-Mary of Hungary (c. 1177–?)

Eastern Roman empress. Born around 1177; death date unknown; daughter of *Anne of Chatillon-Antioche (c. 1155–1185) and Bela III, king of Hungary (r. 1173–1196); sister of Emeric I, king of Hungary (r. 1196–1204), and Andrew II (1175–1235), king of Hungary (r. 1205–1235); married the widowed Isaac II Angelus, Eastern Roman emperor (r. 1185–95 and 1203–04); married Boniface of Montferrat; children: (first marriage) Alexius IV Angelus (d. 1204), emperor of Byzantium (r. 1203–1204); *Irene Angela of Byzantium (d. 1208, who married Philip of Swabia); (second marriage) Demetrius of Thessalonica.

Margaret Maultasch (1318–1369)

German ruler of Tyrol and Carinthia who was known and respected for her intelligence and political skills. Name variations: Margarete, countess of Tirol or Tyrol and duchess of Carinthia; Margaret of Carinthia; Margaretha Maultasch or Maultasche; Margarete von Karnten or Kärnten. Born in 1318 somewhere in Germany; died in Vienna in 1369; daughter of Henry of Carinthia, king of Bohemia (r. 1306–1310) and duke of Tyrol, and Anna of Bohemia; granddaughter of Meinhard II; married Johann also known as John of Bohemia or John Henry of Luxemburg, margrave of Moravia (brother of Charles IV, Holy Roman emperor), in 1330 (marriage annulled 1342); married Ludwig also known Louis V (1316–1361), duke of Bavaria and margrave of Brandenburg (r. 1347–1361), in 1342; children (second marriage) Meinhard, margrave of Brandenburg and duke of Bavaria (r. 1361–1363).

Became countess of Tyrol and duchess of Carinthia after her father's death and governed those territories (1335–1369); received annulment of first marriage on grounds of sorcery and married Louis of Bavaria (1342); ceded Tyrol to Rudolf of Habsburg after death of her son (1363); retired to Vienna (1363) and died there (1369).

Although the incidence of witch trials was fewer in the late medieval period than during the 16th and 17th centuries, accusations of sorcery were often used to get rid of an enemy or to relieve oneself of an intolerable situation. In 1342, Margaret Maultasch, countess of Tyrol and duchess of Carinthia, used the charge of witchcraft as the means of extricating herself from her first marriage. Since her marriage to John Henry of Luxemburg had never been consummated, it was easy for the judges to believe that he had been made impotent due to some sort of bewitchment; consequently, they granted her an annulment. Shortly thereafter, she married Louis V, duke of Bavaria and margrave of Brandenburg. Margaret Maultasch was a strong woman who knew what she wanted and often made sure that her desires were fulfilled. As a woman ruling in 14th century Europe, however, she was a convenient target for contemporaries who admired and yet feared her skills as a politician. Margaret's appearance, which was not within the preferred standards of beauty, resulted, ironically, in accusations of sorcery being leveled against her. Nevertheless, she ruled her territories effectively despite the complicated politics of medieval Germany.

Germany, as a united, independent country with a single ruler, did not exist in the Middle Ages. Instead, it was a conglomerate of several territories each governed by an independent ruler. Since the reign of Charlemagne, however, the German territories had been congregated into a loose confederation ostensibly ruled by the Holy Roman emperor. Thus, the Holy

Roman Empire consisted of a number of large kingdoms and duchies including at various times Bohemia, Hungary, Poland, Austria, and Bavaria as well as over 1,600 autonomous principalities, free towns and sovereign bishoprics. Each emperor was elected by a selected number of German magnates and was then crowned by the pope. Because the monarchy was elective, the emperors had little control over the greatest lords. In addition, the necessity of obtaining and, more important, sustaining the magnates' political support, particularly for military campaigns in Italy, led the emperors to grant the lords greater rights and autonomous powers within their own territories. Similarly, since it was the goal of every great aristocratic family to extend its own territory, family politics became the primary means by which the leading aristocratic families competed for political dominance in the empire.

In the 14th century, there were three aristocratic families who rose to prominence. The Luxemburg family succeeded in expanding their territorial base so that by mid-century it included Luxemburg, Brabant, Lusatia, Silesia, Moravia, Meisen, and Brandenburg. Their enemies, the Wittelsbachs, had acquired Holland, Hainault and Frisia through various marriage alliances. Finally, the Habsburgs, who were allies of the Luxemburgs, had acquired Austria and Carinthia, and by the end of the 14th century Tyrol and Carinthia. Margaret Maultasch's fortunes were intricately tied to the political maneuverings of each of these families.

Born in 1318, the daughter of *Anna of Bohemia and Henry of Carinthia, duke of Tyrol and Carinthia, Margaret grew up in Tyrol. Like most aristocratic girls, she received a good education which included the usual array of "feminine" accomplishments such as dancing, drawing and singing. Unlike her counterparts, however, Margaret also studied theology and took a keen interest in politics and diplomacy. She spoke and wrote fluently in Latin and German and was, by all accounts, an intelligent and sharp pupil. Her father Henry, on the other hand, was a friendly, if ineffective, ruler. In 1307, several years before Margaret's birth, he was elected king of Bohemia through a claim on the female side. However, he was not a successful ruler, and plans soon formed to oust him from the monarchy. In 1310, the Holy Roman emperor Henry VII of Luxemburg drove Margaret's father out by force. Henry of Carinthia was quickly replaced with the emperor's son and heir, John I of Luxemburg, who sealed the position by marrying *Elizabeth of Bohemia

(1292–1339), one of the last remaining members of the ancient Bohemian royal dynasty. For the next 36 years, John of Luxemburg ruled Bohemia primarily in absentia. Although he was king, John regarded his kingdom as little more than a source of revenue for what he felt were more important concerns. From 1314, when his Wittelsbach rival Louis (IV) of Bavaria became Holy Roman emperor, John of Luxemburg spent much of his time acquiring additional territory and doing whatever mischief he could to thwart any ambitions that Louis IV may have had of consolidating or expanding the empire.

One of John's policies was to isolate the emperor from potential allies and, as a result, he sought a marriage alliance with the man he had deposed 15 years before. In 1330, John of Luxemburg's youngest son, John Henry, was betrothed to Margaret Maultasch, daughter of Duke Henry of Carinthia. The significance of this alliance was not lost on Emperor Louis IV of Bavaria. Through this marriage, John of Luxemburg now had control of Carinthia, Carniola,

Margaret
Maultasch

and Tyrol in addition to Bohemia, Moravia, Silesia, and Poland. Louis IV, therefore, made a secret treaty with the Habsburg family whereby he promised to give them Carinthia upon Henry of Carinthia's death if they would help to secure Tyrol for the Wittelsbachs. In essence, Margaret's inheritance of her father's lands was being bargained away without her knowledge.

Despite these secret dealings, which were kept even from her father, the marriage of 12-year-old Margaret and 10-year-old John Henry took place with great pomp and ceremony in September 1330 and concluded with several days of feasting and tournaments. Unfortunately, the newlyweds did not much like one another. Margaret was serious, intelligent and interested in books and politics. Her young husband, on the other hand, was more interested in hunting and physical combat than in the intricacies of court intrigue. Consequently, their marriage began on a sour note which did not improve as the years progressed.

[Margaret Maultasch] was clever, was not importunate, and neither gave nor asked for sentimentality.

—Lion Feuchtwanger

In 1335, Margaret's father died and, at age 17, she became duchess of Carinthia and countess of Tyrol. According to the secret treaty between Emperor Louis IV of Bavaria and Albert II of Habsburg, duke of Austria, however, her lands were to be taken away from her and divided between the two men. Shortly after her father's death, Carinthia and Carniola were occupied by Habsburg troops without much resistance. Having lost these lands, Margaret was determined not to give up Tyrol so easily. Over the course of the year, Louis' attempts to get possession of Tyrol by force failed as the Tyrolese magnates rallied around their rightful ruler and defended Margaret's right to her inherited lands. Once she had secured possession of her lands, Margaret threw herself into administrative work, and she quickly gained a reputation in Western European courts for her intelligence and diplomacy.

Although Louis IV of Bavaria's schemes to take Tyrol away from Margaret angered her, the state of her marriage proved to be a more serious problem. John Henry was neither a willing nor an able partner, particularly in areas of governance. More seriously, Margaret had not conceived an heir, and some historians have argued that this was because the marriage had never been consummated. In addition, her father-in-law, John of Luxemburg, stationed his eldest son, Charles (IV) Luxemburg, in Tyrol to assist Margaret. Unfortunately, Charles' heavy-handed policies only served to alienate the majority of the Tyrolese magnates. In 1342, therefore, a plot was hatched to oust John Henry and bring in Louis V of Brandenburg, the emperor's son, who would then marry Margaret. The plan succeeded. Margaret's marriage to John Henry was quickly annulled based on grounds of impotence from bewitchment, and, although Margaret and Louis V were within the prohibited degrees of consanguinity, they did not wait for the pope's dispensation to marry.

It is from this point on that Margaret received the nickname Maultasch which roughly translates as "sack-mouth" or "pocket-mouth." It is not known why she received this moniker at this particular time, although she had never been considered a great beauty.

Despite the circumstances surrounding their marriage, Margaret's second husband was more compatible and able than her first. They had common interests, and Louis V was willing to assist her in governing Tyrol. More important, a year after their marriage Margaret gave birth to a boy, Meinhard, who became the heir to her lands and titles. Although her marriage was a success, the policies of her new father-in-law, Emperor Louis IV of Bavaria, were slowly eradicating the support he had previously enjoyed. By 1346, the majority of the magnates who were responsible for electing the Holy Roman emperors were dissatisfied with Louis' lust for territory. In addition, in April 1346 he was excommunicated by the pope, who called on the electors to choose a new emperor. The new candidate was none other than Charles, the eldest son of Louis' old enemy, John of Luxemburg. His election as Emperor Charles IV was quickly proclaimed in 1346.

As the new Holy Roman emperor, Charles IV sought to reclaim some of the Luxemburg territories that had been previously lost as well as to retaliate against any members of the Wittelsbach family. As a result, one of his first campaigns was an attempt to conquer Tyrol. Thus, Margaret was forced to defend her lands once more from the encroachments of a land-hungry emperor. Although her husband was away from Tyrol during the emperor's military campaign, Margaret's small but loyal army defended her territory well, and Charles IV was forced to retreat. When Louis IV of Bavaria died in October 1347, Charles gave up all claim to Tyrol, leaving Margaret in secure possession.

For the next 20 years, Margaret ruled alongside her husband. She initiated several reform policies which strengthened the central government and encouraged commercial trade in towns. When the plague broke out in 1348, Margaret was able to retain control over the populace to a greater extent than many of her contemporaries. In addition, she tried, albeit unsuccessfully, to protect the Jews living in Tyrol from persecution. Margaret was one of the most efficient and well-respected rulers of her day.

In 1361, her husband Louis V died. Two years later, she received another devastating blow when her son and heir, Meinhard, also died. Although there is no historical evidence, some of her contemporaries believed that she had poisoned both her husband and son. In that respect, Margaret was like many medieval women who, when placed in positions of power and authority, were often accused of unlawful and suspect behavior such as murder or adultery. Long-held beliefs about women's subordination were obstacles that every woman had to face, and Margaret Maultasch was no exception.

After the death of her son, Margaret became depressed and lost interest in governing. She pledged her lands to the Habsburg family and at age 45 left her homeland for Vienna, where she lived out her remaining years. Although her surroundings were not as grand as they had been in Tyrol, Margaret received a pension from Duke Rudolf IV of Austria which enabled her to live comfortably. In 1369, she died peacefully in Vienna.

SOURCES:
Maurice, Charles Edmund. *Bohemia: From the Earliest Times to the Fall of National Independence in 1620.* London: Unwin, 1896.

Stubbs, William. *Germany in the Later Middle Ages, 1200–1500.* NY: Howard Fertig, 1969.

Tanner, J.R., *et al. The Cambridge Medieval History.* Vol. VII. Chapters IV–VI. Cambridge: Cambridge University Press, 1958.

RELATED SOURCES:
Feuchtwanger, Lion. *The Ugly Duchess.* Viking Press, 1928.

Margaret McIntyre,
Instructor of Women's History at Trent University, Peterborough, Ontario, Canada

Margaret of Alsace (c. 1135–1194)

*Countess of Hainault and ruler of Flanders. Name variations: Margareta of Alsace; Marguerite. Born around 1135; died on November 15, 1194; daughter of Sybilla of Anjou (1112–1165) and Theodore of Alsace (also known as Didrik, Dietrich, or Thierry), count of Flanders (r. 1128–1157); sister of Philip of Alsace, count of Flanders (r. 1157–1191); married Baudouin also known as Baldwin V, count of Hainault (Baldwin VIII of Flanders); children: *Isabella of*

*Hainault (1170–1190); Baudouin also known as Baldwin IX (1171–1205), count of Flanders and Hainault (r. 1195–1205), also crowned Baldwin I, emperor of Constantinople; *Yolande of Courtenay (d. 1219), empress of Constantinople; Philip of Namur.*

Margaret of Alsace was born around 1135, the daughter of *Sybilla of Anjou** and Theodore of Alsace. Margaret succeeded her brother Philip of Alsace as ruler of Flanders when he died in 1191. She died in 1194.

Margaret of Angoulême
(1492–1549)

Queen of Navarre who was a poet, patron of reformers and humanists, and author of The Heptaméron.

Name variations: Margaret of Angouleme; Margaret of France; Margaret or Marguerite of Navarre; Marguerite d'Navarre; Marguerite de Navarre; Marguerite d'Angoulême or Marguerite of Angouleme; Margaret of Orleans; Margaret of Valois; duchess of Alençon or Alencon; duchess of Berry. Pronunciation: ON-gyou-lame. Born in the castle of Angoulême on April 11, 1492; died in the castle of Odos-in-Bigorre, near Tarbes, on December 21, 1549; buried in the cathedral of Lescar; daughter of Charles de Valois-Orléans (1460–1496), count of Angoulême, and Louise of Savoy (1476–1531); sister of Francis I, king of France (r. 1515–1547); married Charles, duke of Alençon, on October 9, 1509, at Blois; married Henry II (1517–1555), king of Navarre, on January 24, 1527, at St. Germain-sur-Laye; children: (second marriage) Jeanne d'Albret (1528–1572), later queen of Navarre; son Jean (died on Christmas Day 1530, aged five months); twins (b. 1542, died within hours).

Selected writings: Correspondance (ed. by P. Jourda, Paris, 1930); The Heptaméron (ed. by M. François, Paris, 1950); Les Poésies Dernières (Paris, 1896); Les Marguerites de la Marguerite des Princesses (2 vols., Lyons, 1547); Lettre et Nouvelles (pub. by F. Génin, Société de l'Histoire de France (2 vols., Paris, 1841–42).

Margaret of Angoulême, of Valois, of France, queen of Navarre (r. 1527–1549), duchess of Alençon and Berry, was highly respected as a person, poet, and patron of the Renaissance in France. She was praised for both her beauty and her intelligence, showing unusual brilliance in theology and language skills. Together with her brother Francis I, the king of France, and her mother *Louise of Savoy**, the noted regent of France, they formed the renowned *trinité*, which ruled over the French court in the early 16th century. Margaret supported and shared her mother's lifelong devotion to Francis as the king of France, often at the cost of her own happiness and health. Always obedient to the demands of Francis and Louise, she acted as her mother's deputy, traveling many miles, serving as mediator and messenger, most notably in Spain during Francis' captivity in 1525. It was Margaret of Angoulême who was called upon to care for Francis' motherless children after his wife *Claude de France died in 1524, and to nurse Louise during her last illness in 1531. Margaret was destined never to find true happiness in human relationships. Her mother and her brother shamelessly exploited her devotion. Both her marriages proved to be loveless; Charles, duke of Alençon, was a weak, mean-spirited man, and Henry II, king of Navarre, some years her junior, soon tired of her. Her only son Jean died as an infant and her relationship with her daughter *Jeanne d'Albret was a strained and difficult one. Margaret's unhappiness forced her to seek fulfillment in religion, and, through her correspondence over many years with Guillaume Briçonnet, she sought solace in matters spiritual. She became a friend and supporter of those who saw the need for reform in the church, defending them and protecting them during periods of persecution. She was loved by them for her integrity, sympathy, and understanding. She was a prolific writer, both of letters, personal and official, and of poetry; all of these have been preserved in the French national archives. Apart from her correspondence with Briçonnet, Margaret also wrote to her brother, to Montmorency, the constable of France, to the pope, and to other leading figures, such as Erasmus and *Margaret of Austria (1480–1530). It was said that she wrote continuously during long, tedious journeys by litter. Her poetry has lived on and is as popular today as it was in the 16th century. The work for which she is most remembered is *The Heptaméron,* which she wrote to amuse Francis I during his last illness. After his death in 1547, she, the sole survivor of the *trinité,* retired to Navarre and a semi-reclusive life. By the time of her death in 1549, she had become partially reconciled with her husband and her daughter.

One of the most brilliant and attractive women of the whole sixteenth century.

—S. Harrison Thomson

In a century of outstanding women, Margaret of Angoulême holds her own both as a patron of the arts and sciences and as a defender and protector of reformers and humanists. It was Margaret who inspired and encouraged Francis I to form the Collège de France, and it was her support and participation that ensured the survival of the Renaissance in France. Her name was linked with the Cercle de Meaux, and she counted its members—Clément Marot, Bonaventure des Periers, Étienne Dolet and William Farel—among her friends, together with other learned minds, such as François Rabelais. She accepted the views of Briçonnet and Lefèvre d'Étaples, although she never left the Catholic Church. Her courts in Navarre attracted scholars and artists and became a refuge for the persecuted. She was the first of a feminine dynasty of evangelical reformers, followed by her daughter, the Calvinist Jeanne d'Albret, and then by her granddaughter, the Huguenot *Catherine of Bourbon (c. 1555–1604). Much admired by her contemporaries, Margaret still retains a hold over the imagination and affection of the French people.

Margaret of Angoulême was born on April 11, 1492, the first child and only daughter of Charles of Orleans, count of Angoulême (r. 1460–1496), and Louise of Savoy (1476–1531). Her birth was recorded in her mother's journal thus:

> My daughter Margaret was born in the year 1492, the eleventh day of April, at two o'-clock in the morning, that is to say, the tenth day, fourteen hours and ten minutes counting after the fashion of the astrologers.

Her father was a direct descendant of Charles V, king of France (r. 1364–1380), and in position to claim the French crown should Charles VIII die and Louis (XII), his heir, fail to produce male offspring. His marriage with Louise of Savoy, many years his junior, had been arranged by *Anne of Beaujeu (c. 1460–1522), daughter of Louis XI, king of France (r. 1461–1483), when Louise was two years old as a means of preventing Charles VIII's proposed marriage with *Mary of Burgundy (1457–1482), an alliance which would have seriously threatened the power of the French crown. But Charles of Orleans was not politically ambitious; he was content with his own small court at Cognac, preferring books and women to the intrigues of the French royal court. He gathered around him artists and musicians and collected a library of rare books and manuscripts. As his wife, Louise, herself no mean scholar, participated in these activities and in turn passed on a love of learning and the arts to her daughter and her son. Margaret's brother Francis, destined to be Francis I, king of France (r. 1515–1547), had been born in September 1494.

Charles of Orleans died on January 1, 1496, when Margaret and Francis were still infants, leaving them in the care of their young mother. From Francis' birth Louise had been obsessed by him and his destiny as she believed it to be, and she instilled in her daughter the same sense of devotion and dedication. For the rest of her life, Margaret, like her mother, would put Francis and his needs before everything else. It would cost her dear in terms of her own personal relationships, but she never begrudged him or complained at the demands made on her by him or by Louise, acting in Francis' name. Rather, Margaret submitted to his will and served him well as official hostess, mediator, and personal messenger whenever the need arose. For his part, he accepted her devotion without question, returning her love by showering her with honors and, when necessary, protecting her from those who would have called her heretic. She was usually at his side, and foreign ambassadors and those currying favor sought her help.

In adult life, *nôtre trinité,* as Francis, Louise, and Margaret liked to call it, ruled the French royal court. Their mutual understanding conferred upon them an impregnability and independence that enabled them to function as one, with the single-minded purpose of preserving the ideal of the absolute monarch. They complemented each other perfectly; Francis was allowed to indulge his appetites for hunting, eating, drinking, and women, while Louise took on the practical roles of domestic adviser, diplomat, and foreign ambassador. Margaret, who was compassionate and caring, took on the roles of nurse and companion to Francis' wife Claude and their children, and it was she who provided the spiritual element necessary for a complete whole. Her two preoccupations in life, that of her brother and her religion, are illustrated by her adoption of a sunflower as her device, indicating that she knew she lived in the brilliance of her brother, and by her motto *non in feriora secutus* ("I have not followed lesser [or earthly] things").

As Francis moved nearer to the throne so Margaret and her mother moved with him, leaving Cognac in 1498 when Charles VIII died and making their home at Amboise under the protection of the new king, Louis XII. Louise oversaw every aspect of her daughter's education which, as Louise was a firm believer in sexual equality, Margaret shared with her brother. She shared not only his tutors and lessons but also his companions. There were five of them, and they were to play important roles in the lives of both Margaret and Francis: Gaston de Foix, whom Mar-

garet loved and who was killed at the battle of Novara in 1513; Guillaume de Bonnivet, a philanderer who was killed at Pavia in 1525; Philippe Brion, who became admiral of France; Anne de Montmorency, who became constable of France and with whom Margaret corresponded regularly for many years; and Charles de Bourbon, also constable of France, but a traitor who betrayed his king.

Margaret of Angoulême proved to be a willing pupil and soon surpassed in learning both her mother and her brother. In 1502, Maréchal de Gié described her as *"très belle et bitn sage de son âge"* and Brantôme, the famous commentator on life at court, described her as "a princess of enlarged mind being very able both as to her natural and acquired endowments." Scholars taught her Latin, philosophy and divinity, Hebrew, German, Spanish, and Italian. She loved to read Petrarch, Dante, and Boccaccio. She never lost her thirst for knowledge and love of learning, and even at 40 years of age was taking lessons in Greek. In 1498, Louis XII approved

Margaret of Angoulême (1492–1549)

the appointment of ◄ Louise de Montmorency, Madame de Châtillon, as governess to Margaret, who was now the sister of the heir to the French throne. The wife of a former royal chamberlain, Mme de Châtillon was described by Brantôme as "a wise and virtuous dame of unblemished virtue and descent." She proved to be a good friend to the young princess, encouraging her to read the scriptures and remaining in her household after Margaret's marriage in 1509 to Charles, duke of Alençon, though now in the position of maid-of-honor. But Madame de Châtillon had been much influenced by Lutheranism and indeed brought up her three sons, the Coligny brothers, who in the 1550s became leaders in the Calvinist movement, as Protestants. She left Margaret's employ in 1520, when she feared that her Lutheran sympathies were in danger of compromising Margaret's position at court.

The important question of Margaret's marriage had been of concern for many years. She had been named as a possible bride for Arthur, prince of Wales, the prince of Wales, as well as his brother Prince Henry (later Henry VIII) and Charles of Austria (later Charles V, Holy Roman emperor). Louise of Savoy certainly favored such a match for her daughter and was not happy with Louis XII's choice of a mere duke. However, Louis saw the marriage of Margaret with Charles, duke of Alençon, as a means of settling a long and tedious lawsuit concerning the county of Armagnac. This rich county had reverted to the crown due to a lack of male heirs, but Charles still held a hereditary claim. By marrying him to Margaret, who would receive the county, plus 60,000 crowns, as her dowry, the hardheaded Louis was able to retain possession of the county and its revenues. Alençon could be considered a worthy husband since he was a direct descendant of Charles, brother to Philip the Fair, king of France (r. 1285–1314), but he was far from being a suitable mate for the intelligent, quick-witted, liberally educated Margaret. He

was a dull, melancholic man with a mean, bad-tempered disposition. The marriage took place at Blois on October 9, 1509, and the ceremony was performed by the Cardinal of Nantes. Four days of festivities followed.

The marriage, loveless and childless, was never more than a simple business arrangement. Their incompatibility was not helped by Margaret's frequent visits to court at the demand of her brother and Alençon's all-consuming interest in his estate. In her disappointment and loneliness, Margaret turned to religion for consolation, encouraged by her pious mother-in-law, *Margaret of Lorraine (1463–1521). After Madame de Châtillon left, Margaret looked beyond her immediate circle for help and guidance. She found it in the bishop of Meaux, Guillaume Briçonnet, and they began a correspondence which lasted for three years. A total of some 123 letters, 59 of them from Margaret, are housed in the Bibliothèque Nationale. The letters are very nearly unintelligible, written in an elaborate style with involved figures of speech. Margaret herself struggled to understand Briçonnet and in her letters frequently begs him to write more simply. It has been suggested that Briçonnet's letters were deliberately obtuse in order to confuse his enemies who might obtain access to them.

Briçonnet hoped that in return for the guidance he gave to Francis' sister he might gain the king's support for reform. He was a cautious man, as evidenced by his letters, and always endeavored to steer clear of outright controversy. He was not a Lutheran; he sought, as many others did, a spiritual reform and a revival of piety that could be achieved within the existing framework of the church. Meaux, a town near Paris noted for priests and weavers, attracted the scholarly, pious, and wise minds of the day, including Lefèvre d'Étaples, Clément Marot, and William Farel. The group became known as the Cercle de Meaux, and they rapidly acquired a reputation for preaching and teaching the gospels; but, at the same time, they incurred the enmity of the orthodox theologians of the Sorbonne. Traditionally, noblewomen patronized such men, offering them shelter and protection in exchange for learning and scribal duties within the household. Margaret herself took Michel d'Arande and Gérard Roussel, both from Meaux, into her household. D'Arande preached as he traveled around the country with her, and Roussel was her almoner. Years later in 1531 and 1533 when Roussel was accused of heresy, Margaret's support saved him. In 1555, he was appointed to the bishopric of Oloron in Béarn and was responsible for the spread of reform

---

◄ Louise de Montmorency (fl. 1498–1525)

French governess of Margaret of Angoulême. Name variations: Madame de Chatillon or Châtillon. Flourished from 1498 to 1525; married a former royal chamberlain; married Gaspard I de Coligny, Maréchal de Châtillon (c. 1440–1522, marshal of France); children—three sons, known as the Coligny brothers: Odet de Coligny (1517–1571); François de Coligny (1521–1569); Gaspard II de Coligny (1519–1572, an admiral and leader of the Huguenots and father of *Louise de Coligny).

there. In her support of the reformers, Margaret was following the pattern already set, but her position as the king's sister drew more publicity to the reformers and their practices.

Margaret's own position on the matter of religious reform is none too clear. On her death bed she asserted that she had supported the reformers not because she shared their beliefs, but merely out of compassion. Her conduct certainly lent credibility to this. She sympathized with, aided and protected but never openly supported the cause for reform since that would have exiled her from her brother's court, and she loved Francis too deeply to risk losing his love for her. Nevertheless, the reformers themselves believed that there was no one in France more evangelical than Margaret of Angoulême. In her personal belief, she inclined towards the mystical piety which is expressed so profoundly and eloquently in her poetry, but in some of her less spiritual writings she was not above ridiculing priests and friars and pouring scorn on superstitious practices. She had turned to religion when the love she so much desired and needed was denied her. She was not worldly at heart and did not recognize, as Francis and Louise did, the dangers the reform posed to the security of the crown.

It was Francis' support that saved her from persecution as a heretic. In 1531, her poem "Miroir d l'âme pechers" (translated by *Elizabeth I of England in 1548 as "A Godly Meditation of the Soul") was condemned by the Sorbonne as a heretical work; instead of extolling the virtues of saints and purgatory, it stressed the saving blood of Christ, an emphasis seen by those theologians as proof of her Protestant sympathies. In 1533, they added it to the list of banned literary works. Francis was furious. Such an act against a member of his family and therefore against himself could not be tolerated. He ordered an inquiry. The theologians were forced to retract and revoke the censure. But soon after, in October of the same year, Margaret faced another attack, this time from the students of the Collège de Navarre, who staged a morality play in which Margaret was portrayed as a witch and accused of consorting with the Devil. Francis ordered the arrest of all concerned with the production. They were thrown into prison and threatened with the galleys for life. They were released with only a warning after Margaret herself had pleaded with Francis for mercy for them; even so, feeling against Margaret grew daily. She continued to defend the reformers, and then, when it seemed that at last there was hope of a breakthrough for them, there came the episode known now as the Affaire des Placards.

On October 18, 1534, Paris woke to find that every church and public building bore posters attacking the Mass, the prayers for the dead, and transubstantiation. The reformers were blamed, although there was no proof, and the author of the posters was never discovered. Swelled by the discovery of similar posters in five large provincial French towns, a wave of hysteria swept France, so strong it threatened the security of the king himself. Margaret, who had retired to Nérac, was ordered to return and answer the charges. She defended herself successfully but had lost forever the chance to win Francis over to reform.

Instead, on January 21, 1535, there was a national display of atonement. Francis, bareheaded, dressed in black and carrying a lighted candle, led a procession of all prelates, members of court and the universities, in a very public act of penance. Trials and mass burnings followed. It was the end for the reformers and reformation in France. From this time until her death in 1549, Margaret no longer interceded with Francis on their behalf. Her hope had been for changes effected within the existing religion, and she was not interested in the extremes now offered by Calvinism, finding them alien and distasteful. For the future, she would confine her spiritual activities to private prayer, meditation, and writing. The Affaire des Placards had clarified an ideological situation but had driven Margaret away.

But all that was in the future; in the early 1520s it was the wars in Italy that most occupied the minds of Margaret and her mother. In February 1525, the Habsburg-Valois rivalry, personified by the Spanish Charles V, the Holy Roman emperor, and Francis I, the French king, reached a climax at the battle of Pavia. Francis was captured by the Spanish and taken first to Barcelona and then to Tarrigona as prisoner of Charles V. His mother Louise of Savoy, now the regent, set about the joint tasks of preserving the status quo in France and securing the release of her son. Both she and Margaret were alarmed by the reports that reached them of the serious decline of Francis' health. At the same time, on a more personal level, Margaret's marriage to Alençon had reached its nadir with his disgrace at the battle of Pavia.

Although Alençon had fought alongside his king before, notably at Marignano where he had acquitted himself well, as a soldier and a leader he was regarded as unreliable. Despite this, Francis had given him on this occasion the important command of the vanguard, and it was his failure to carry out his command successfully and support the king during the battle that led to the king's capture, a heinous enough crime which was compounded by his running away from the battlefield. As he made his way home to Margaret, now with her mother's court at Lyons, taunts of *fuyard* (deserter) followed him, and derogatory rhymes were composed about him. He arrived back at the end of March, desperately ill with pneumonia and shame. Feeling only contempt for him, Margaret nevertheless was moved to pity and nursed him until his death on April 11, 1525. She even sent, at Alençon's urgent request, a letter to Francis pleading for a pardon for him, though detailed study of the letter reveals little warmth in her references to her husband.

As well as nursing her husband, Margaret also had the care of Francis' six young children, now motherless after the death of Queen Claude in July 1524. In the autumn of the same year, the children caught measles and were very ill, especially the Princess *Charlotte. Her death in October 1524, at the age of eight years, caused Margaret to write a memorial for her in the form of a poem with the lengthy title of *A dialogue in the form of a nocturnal vision between the right honourable and excellent Princess, my Lady Marguerite of France, only sister of our Sire the King, by the grace of God Queen of Navarre and Duchess of Alençon and Berry, and the Holy Soul of the deceased Madame Charlotte of France, eldest daughter of the said Sire and niece of the said Lady and Queen.* It was published in 1533, after Margaret's second marriage, and became one of the literary monuments of France.

After Charlotte's death, Margaret, now a 33-year-old widow and still childless after 16 years of marriage, was about to reach the pinnacle of her success as the king's most faithful subject and ambassador. As concern for the king deepened with no sign of any agreement on the terms for his release, it was decided that Margaret should go to Spain offering her proven nursing skills to the benefit of Francis and her reputed diplomatic skills to the aid of those already working in Madrid for the king's release.

This was no mean undertaking. Margaret was setting out on a four-month journey which was hazardous, strenuous, and made all the more grueling by the weather, for a series of delays had meant her setting off in the heat of the summer. Leaving Lyons in August 1525, she had arrived at Aigues-Mortes, her port of departure, after traveling down the river Rhône by barge, accompanied by her mother, only to be delayed

for a further two weeks awaiting a safe-conduct from the emperor. When Charles V's permission for her to travel finally arrived, it stipulated first that Margaret would be regarded as a personal ambassador only and not as part of the embassy already discussing the terms for the French king's release, and second that she was limited to a stay of three months. It was September when she arrived at Palamos, in Catalonia, only to learn that her brother had been moved to Madrid, adding many miles to her journey. She arrived at his bedside on September 22. Francis was very ill with a high fever, and his life was so despaired of that Charles himself had arrived in Madrid concerned that he might lose this most valuable of prisoners. Francis did not recognize her. She remained at his side praying for several days. Suddenly the abscess in his head, the cause of the fever, burst, and he regained consciousness and began to recover. Francis declared that Margaret had saved his life. This was to be the sole achievement of her epic journey, for she failed even to soften the terms of the treaty or to bring a solution any closer. Dressed in mourning for the dead Alençon, without jewels of any kind, in black robes covered by a white veil that fell from her head to the ground, she was an impressive figure, her dignity and grace capturing the sympathy of the Spanish people but not of their king. As the talks dragged on, the expiry date of her safe-conduct drew closer, and Margaret learned of Charles' plan to arrest her if she stayed longer than the permitted three months. She made a dash for the border traveling 12 hours a day, on horseback for speed, and reached Narbonne on Christmas Day. The Madrid treaty was finally agreed in the New Year, and Francis left captivity on February 21, 1526, arriving on March 16 at the border where he was exchanged for his two young sons, who now became the hostages.

Back in France, Margaret was praised for her efforts to save the king. Francis made her duchess of Armagnac in her own right. She now directed her energies to securing the release of her nephews, whose condition in prison worsened as efforts were slowly made to raise the money for their ransom. Margaret's affection for her brother's children was such that she gave all she had in money and pawned her jewelry. The boys were eventually returned in 1530 after four years as prisoners.

In 1529, Margaret accompanied her mother to Cambrai to offer support in Louise's negotiations with Margaret of Austria that brought about the "Ladies Peace" and a break in the wars between France and Spain. In 1531, Louise of Savoy died, nursed faithfully to the end by her daughter. The *trinité* was broken. From that time, Margaret and Francis drifted apart.

The battle of Pavia had made reputations as well as destroyed them. One who had benefited was Henry II d'Albret, king of Navarre (r. 1517–1555). Captured with Francis and imprisoned in the castle of Pavia, he escaped in December 1525 dressed as a page, made his way to Lyons and offered his services to the regent. Margaret and Henry d'Albret were mutually attracted. He saw a beautiful, accomplished woman, pale and dignified in her mourning and acclaimed by the people of France for saving the king's life, and she believed she had found her savior, her knight in shining armor. He appeared to have every quality that Alençon had lacked, including courage, determination, and intelligence; he was a cultivated man, a patron of the arts and sympathetic to the reformers. Although he was 11 years her junior, they shared this interest in religious reform and a mutual hatred for Charles V. He admired her skills as a diplomat and recognized her potential as his queen. After withdrawing his initial objection, Francis approved the match, and the marriage was celebrated on January 24, 1527, at St. Germain-sur-Laye. The festivities and tournaments lasted for eight days.

Henry d'Albret, vicomte de Béarn, king of Navarre, was born in 1502, the son of John III, and 🌣▶ **Catherine de Foix**, king and queen of Navarre. Navarre, the domain of the counts of Foix, sovereign lords of Béarn or "kings" of Navarre, lay between the Basque country and the central Pyrenées. Henry d'Albret's early life was spent on the Spanish side of the Pyrenées, but in 1512 Ferdinand II of Aragon had conquered these southern parts, so that only the northern part remained for the lords of Béarn. Henry d'Albret had fled with his mother to France. After her death in 1517, he had assumed the title of king and from that time was filled with an all-consuming desire to win back the rest of his land. The area continued to be a minor cause of friction between Spain and France, exploited to its utmost by Charles V but regarded as unimportant compared with other problems by Francis I. The 1526 Treaty of Madrid, through which Francis had obtained his release from captivity, contained proposals for the surrender of Navarre to Spain, but, since Francis had little intention of keeping the treaty, Henry d'Albret had every reason to hope that his marriage to the king's sister would lend weight to his cause. Margaret supported Henry in his claims, and Francis' continued refusal to discuss the matter was a great disappointment to her.

At first all went well with the marriage. "I have found my pearl and placed it in my heart," Henry d'Albret is reported to have said. With financial support from Francis, they were able to set up their court at Nérac and at Pau. Margaret presided over the court in much the same way as she had over the French court. She continued to administer to her duchies of Alençon and Armagnac, and took pains to learn the Basque language and to get to know her new subjects. She devoted her time to her charities, her letter writing, and to planning gardens, which provided employment for the poor. She and Henry d'Albret together worked to the benefit of the little mountain kingdom, improving agricultural methods and commerce and introducing new skills such as cloth weaving. They made political, financial, and legal reforms. Through her influence and efforts, Nérac became both a center for culture, attracting poets, writers and physicians, and a safe haven for those persecuted for their support of religious reforms. John Calvin, d'Arande, Lefèvre, and Marot were among those who sought sanctuary; none were denied. But any pleasure she could have derived from her modest achievements in Navarre was diminished by her failure to give birth to the much longed-for son and heir and by Francis' continued indifference to their claims in Navarre.

On January 7, 1528, their daughter and only living child was born at Fontainebleau. Neither Henry d'Albret nor Francis attended the birth of Jeanne d'Albret, who was destined to become queen of Navarre in her own right and to go much further in her support of religious reform than ever her mother did. Margaret's subsequent children died as infants. Her son Jean died aged five months on Christmas Day 1530, a grievous loss, and twin children born in 1542 lived only a few hours. Made impatient by the lack of response from the French king, Henry d'Albret took matters into his own hands and

🌣▶ **Catherine de Foix** (c. 1470–1517)
Queen of Navarre. Name variations: Catalinda de Albret; Catherine of Navarre; Katherine. Reigned as queen of Navarre from 1483 to 1517. Born around 1470; died in 1517; daughter of *Madeleine of France (1443–1486) and Gaston de Foix, vicomte de Castelbon and prince of Viane; married Jean also known as John III (d. 1512), duc d'Albret, king of Navarre, around 1502; children: Henry II d'Albret (1503–1555), vicomte de Béarn, king of Navarre (r. 1517–1555, who married *Margaret of Angoulême [1492–1549]).

entered into secret negotiations with Charles V through the spy Descurra. By 1537, he was heavily involved in plans to marry Jeanne d'Albret to Charles V's son, Philip (II), the future king of Spain.

Gradually the marriage that had begun so well fell apart, and Margaret found herself alone again. For a time, she had been useful as a go-between for both her husband and her brother, but now Henry d'Albret began to spend more and more hours away from her, and Francis demanded her presence at the French court less and less. Her daughter Jeanne d'Albret was a stranger living with her governess in a castle in Alençon. Once again in need of solace, Margaret turned to study and to poetry and sought answers in her religion. Her best literary work was produced from these years to her death in 1549.

Margaret's relationship with her daughter was always an unusual one. At birth, Jeanne d'Albret was placed in the care of Madame **Aimée de la Fayette** at the castle of Alençon. When Jeanne was two, Francis, who was determined to maintain strict control of his niece, ordered her to be moved nearer to him and to be housed in the castle of Plessis-les-Tours in Touraine. Jeanne d'Albret had exchanged one gloomy castle for another. Despite the oppressive nature of her early years, or perhaps because of it, she grew into a wilful, determined young woman at odds with both her parents and her uncle. Margaret was neither a heartless nor thoughtless mother, but the demands of her public life in both France and Navarre meant long absences, and she was never able to contradict Francis' will even in the matter of her own daughter's welfare. However, when Jeanne d'Albret fell dangerously ill in 1537, Margaret set out immediately to be with her and remained with her until Jeanne was completely recovered.

Unlike her mother, Jeanne d'Albret felt no obligation towards the French king and saw no reason to bend her will to his. Her marriage to Guillaume de la March, the duke of Cleves, proved how far she was prepared to go in opposing him. Francis saw the marriage both as a means of preventing her father Henry d'Albret from making a successful alliance for her with Charles V's son, and of annexing the lands and support of the Cleves—almost a repeat of the marriage Louis XII had arranged for Margaret with Alençon. Jeanne d'Albret defied everyone and every order and was set firmly against the marriage. Lectures on her duty, royal commands, and physical chastisements, ordered, uncharacteristically, by her mother, deterred her

none. She wrote two declarations witnessed by members of her household, which still exist, setting forth her case and her objections to the match and stating that it was only through coercion that she finally agreed. On her wedding day, June 15, 1541, she had to be carried up the aisle. Whether, as was said, this was because her robes were too heavy for a 12-year-old or because she refused to walk is not known. What is known is that Francis used the episode to humiliate Anne de Montmorency, the constable of France. By ordering him to carry the bride, when as constable it was his right to carry the Sword of State, Francis effectively degraded Montmorency and demanded his resignation. Three years later, Francis ordered the annulment of the Cleves marriage when the duke of Cleves turned his back on France and gave his support to Spain. Jeanne d'Albret later fell in love with and married Anthony de Bourbon, duke of Vendôme (r. 1518–1562) on October 20, 1548. She always kept an expensive household in Paris and lived very extravagantly, all at her mother's expense. Jeanne d'Albret never had any affection for her mother but always defended her memory and was proud of her literary achievements. When, after Margaret's death, doubt was voiced about the true authorship of *The Heptaméron*, Jeanne had it republished with a preface dedicated to herself to mark it forever as Margaret's work.

The Heptaméron, the work for which Margaret of Angoulême is best known, was written between 1538 and 1542, probably during 1541, to amuse Francis during his last illness. It is based on Boccaccio's *Decameron*, which she is known to have delighted in reading with her brother. It is said that when he looked to her for amusement to ease the discomfort of his pain she remembered Boccaccio and devised a similar volume, planning to write ten stories but only completing seven. The stories, told by a group of men and women travelers delayed by flooded roads on their return from the Cauteret Baths in the Pyrenees, are semi-autobiographical, and the characters are supposedly based on persons well known to Francis and herself. Scholars have written extensively about them and their real life counterparts. A mixture of spirituality and broad, bawdy humor, the tales illustrate the triumphs of virtue, honor and quick-wittedness over the evils of vice and hypocrisy. The satirical element, with licentious and grasping monks and clergy, is possibly drawn from Margaret's own experiences at court. It was said that she read Francis only the spicy passages, keeping the endings, when sensual love was raised to a higher plane, to herself. The volume was originally published in 1558, nine years after her death, and republished in 1559.

Concerning her other works, *Les Marguerites de Marguerite des Princesses,* published in 1547, is a mixture of poems and farces written in an elaborate artificial style. Her best verse is in *Les Poésies Dernières,* which includes *Les Prisons,* a pilgrimage of love from its first glow to its disillusionment, and *Le Navire,* an expression of her desolation at the death of her brother.

Francis' health declined from 1540 to his death in 1547. Margaret saw him last in January 1546. Although appointments were made to see him during the last year of his life, they were never kept. Margaret took refuge in a monastery at Tosson in Poitou, her health fluctuating according to the news of her brother's state of health. His death devastated her, and she spent 40 days in solitude during which she wrote *Chanson faicte par la Royne de Navarre, ung Mois après la Mort du Roy.* Her attire, according to a contemporary manuscript, was "a black velvet robe cut away slightly under the arms; a black jacket with a sable lined collar fastened down with brooches in the front; a mob cap low over her head; her blouse slightly ruffled about the neck."

The remainder of her life was spent mainly in Navarre. Her nephew Henry II, king of France (r. 1547–1559), continued to pay her a pension, but she no longer had any political significance. In September 1548, she witnessed Henry II's triumphal entry into Lyons as king, and in October she attended Jeanne d'Albret's marriage to Anthony de Bourbon at Moulins, after which she returned to Béarn and Pau. Henry d'Albret became more attentive, and they traveled together seeking a cure for her ills, to no avail. For a short period, she returned to Tosson and lived in a *logis* (dwelling) specially constructed for her. In 1549, she moved to Odos-en-Bigorre, near Tarbes, in the hope that the waters there would be beneficial. She died there alone on December 21, 1549, aged 57 years, following an attack of pleurisy or apoplexy. Henry d'Albret, having been summoned, arrived just hours too late. Jeanne and Anthony de Bourbon attended her funeral on February 10, 1550. She was buried in the cathedral of Lescar, the last resting place of the house of Navarre. The funeral oration was delivered by the poet Charles Saint-Marthe, who said that she "showed in her eyes, her countenance, her deportment, her speech, and, indeed, in all her actions that the spirit of God had been vouchsafed to her." There was no representation by the French court, but her own subjects turned out in full to follow the

solemn procession, and throughout the civilized world poets and people of learning poured out their grief in epitaphs and eulogies.

Henry d'Albret's health gradually deteriorated, and he died some five years later on May 24, 1555, at the castle of Hagetmau, leaving their daughter Jeanne d'Albret, now aged 27, as queen in her own right; her son became Henry IV, king of France (r. 1589–1610).

Margaret of Angoulême was a gentle and compassionate woman ever heedful of the needs of others. Her brother said of her: "She is the only woman I ever knew who has every virtue and every grace without one admixture of vice and yet, she is never tiresome or stupid, as good people are apt to be." (She must never be confused with the notorious *Margaret of Valois, queen of Navarre [1553–1615], who is sometimes also referred to as Margaret of Angoulême.) Margaret occupied an influential position in the intellectual movements of the day as well as a unique place at the court of France earned by hard work and at considerable personal sacrifice. Her humility and Christian idealism prevented her from expressing her true feelings when she was deserted by those she had looked to for love, and instead she retreated into melancholy and meditation. Her genuine and technically accomplished poetry remains as a testimony to the depth of her convictions and her spirituality.

SOURCES:

Knecht, R.J. *Francis I.* Cambridge University Press, 1982.
Putnam, Samuel P. *Marguerite of Navarre.* London, 1936.
Robinson, A. Mary E. *Margaret of Angoulême, Queen of Navarre,* 1886.
Roelker, Nancy Lyman. *Queen of Navarre, Jeanne d'Albret (1538–1572).* Cambridge, MA: Harvard University Press, 1986.
Williams, H. Noel. *The Pearl of Princesses: The Life of Marguerite d'Angoulême, Queen of Navarre,* 1916.

SUGGESTED READING:

*Fawcett, Millicent Garrett. *Five Famous French Women.* London, 1905.
Jourda, Pierre. *Marguerite d'Angoulême, Duchesse d'Alençon, Reine de Navarre (1492–1549).* 2 vols. Paris, 1903.
Roelker, Nancy L. "The Appeal of Calvinism to French Noblewomen in the Sixteenth Century" in *Journal of Interdisciplinary History.* Vol. 2, 1972, pp. 391–418.

COLLECTIONS:

Margaret of Angoulême's letters are in the Bibliothèque Nationale.

PORTRAITS:

The Bibliothèque Nationale has several drawings and portraits of Margaret of Angoulême; as well as a medallion dated c. 1509.

Margaret E. Lynch, M.A.,
Teaching Fellow in the Department of History at Lancaster University,
Lancaster, United Kingdom, and an independent scholar

Margaret of Angoulême (1553–1615).

See Margaret of Valois.

Margaret of Anjou (c. 1272–1299)

*Countess of Valois. Name variations: Margaret of Valois; Marguerite of Anjou-Sicily. Born around 1272; died on December 31, 1299; daughter of *Marie of Hungary (d. 1323) and Charles II (1254–1309), duke of Anjou (r. 1285–1290), king of Naples and Anjou (r. 1285–1309); sister of *Blanche of Naples (d. 1310), Robert the Good, king of Naples (r. 1309–1343), and *Lenore of Sicily (1289–1341); married Charles of Valois also known as Charles I (1270–1325), count of Valois (son of Philip III the Bold, king of France), on August 16, 1290; children: Philip VI of Valois (1293–1350), king of France (r. 1328–1350); *Jeanne of Valois (c. 1294–1342, mother of *Philippa of Hainault). Charles of Valois' second wife was Catherine de Courtenay (d. 1307); their daughter, also called *Jeanne of Valois (b. 1304), married Robert III of Artois. Charles' third wife was *Mahaut de Chatillon (d. 1358).*

Margaret of Anjou (1429–1482)

Queen of England who was a principal player in the Wars of the Roses. Name variations: Margaret d'Anjou; Marguerite d'Anjou. Born on March 23, 1429 (some sources cite 1430), at Château Keure in Lorraine (France); died on August 25, 1482, at Château de Dampierre in Anjou (France); daughter of René I the Good, duke of Anjou and titular king of Sicily, Hungary, and Naples, and Isabelle of Lorraine (1410–1453); sister of Yolande of Vaudemont (1428–1483); married Henry VI, king of England (r. 1422–1461, 1470–1471), on April 22, 1445, in Titchfield, England; children: Edward, prince of Wales (October 13, 1453–1471).

Crowned queen of England (May 1445); founded Queen's College at Cambridge University (1448); led Lancastrian party against Yorkists in civil war (1456–71); fled to Scotland after Yorkist seizure of throne (1461); met final defeat in Battle of Tewkesbury (1471); returned to Anjou (1476).

Margaret of Anjou is one of the most well known of English queens, primarily due to her long involvement as a principal figure in the Wars of the Roses, the English civil war which lasted through most of the 15th century. She was the leader of the party of Lancaster, and fought for many years, though in the end unsuccessfully, to restore to her husband and her son their right to rule England.

Margaret was the fourth child born to René I the Good, duke of Anjou, and *Isabelle of Lorraine. René had inherited from his father a claim to many crowns, including Hungary, Sicily, Naples, and Jerusalem. In reality, however, he possessed only the duchies of Anjou, from his father, and Lorraine and Provence, which were his wife's dowry. His many claims had led René to engage in constant warfare with his French feudal neighbors and foreign powers; when he was taken prisoner by the powerful duke of Burgundy, Isabelle took over the struggle. Because of the dangers inherent in warfare, in 1434 Isabelle sent her young daughters, Margaret and *Yolande of Vaudemont, to be raised by her mother-in-law, *Yolande of Aragon, who was acting regent of Sicily but resided at Saumur in Anjou. Yolande's court was a sophisticated cultural and artistic center, and there Margaret remained until 1442. She was highly educated in both academics and the accomplishments necessary to noblewomen, such as dancing, playing music, and embroidery. Yet, endowed as she was with a keen intelligence, she was also a student of politics and intrigue, skills she learned by the example of her grandmother and mother. Thus Margaret's emergence in later years as a political leader can be traced back to her upbringing by two women actively involved in the political and military events of their time. In 1442, Margaret of Anjou returned to her parents' home after her father was released from prison.

The years of Margaret's youth saw the winding down of the skirmishes between France and England collectively known as the Hundred Years' War. In 1444, King Henry VI of England offered to marry a daughter of the French nobility as part of a peace treaty between the countries. By this time, Duke René, having had enough of battles, had proven himself disinclined to further warfare and to any further claims to kingship. Margaret was unmarried and unbetrothed, despite the fact that she was already 15 years old, past the age when most women of her rank were married. Many negotiations for her marriage had taken place before 1444 but with no success, due to the constant feuding and shifting loyalties of the feudal houses. The king of France, Charles VII, felt it safe to offer the duke's daughter Margaret of Anjou to the English king, since he did not fear that René would try to use the alliance with England for his personal aggrandizement as more self-interested nobles would. Thus a treaty for a two-year truce was sealed by a marriage contract between Margaret and the king of England.

Margaret's own feelings toward this change in her fortunes can easily be guessed. Not only

The wedding of Margaret of Anjou and Henry VI.

was she French, raised to think of England as the traditional enemy of France, but her own grandmother and uncle, Duke Louis III, had been forced to defend Anjou some years earlier when Henry VI's army invaded the duchy. Thus she had no reason to think of King Henry as anything but an enemy. The king himself was somewhat disappointed that his bride-to-be would come to England with no tangible dowry—René being too impoverished by years of warfare to provide any—but Henry and his ministers believed the political benefits of this French-English marriage outweighed the financial loss.

Margaret of Anjou sailed to England in April 1445, having already been married to Henry VI by proxy. The actual ceremony was held April 22 at the Abbey of St. Mary in Titchfield. On May 30, Margaret was crowned queen of England in another elaborate ritual. She found the English people initially very receptive to their new French queen, for they saw her as the instrument of a new, lasting peace between England and France. However, the popularity enjoyed by the beautiful young queen was not to last. Margaret immediately involved herself in the political debate over the terms of peace with

France, promoting the surrender of English-held territories in France, to which the English people, despite their longing for peace, were unwilling to agree.

Margaret of Anjou is described as being impetuous and extravagant, freely spending the crown's money for her own entertainment. She loved hunting, costly clothing, dancing, and other amusements, but her husband did not. Henry VI was a solemn and pious man who strongly disapproved of the sorts of entertainments Margaret loved. Yet despite the differences in their characters and in their ages—he was eight years her senior—and the traditional enmity between their countries, the couple seem to have grown quite intimate and been happy together.

Margaret continued to earn the distrust of her subjects when she became a companion and friend of ◄❦ Alice Chaucer and her husband William de la Pole, duke of Suffolk. The duke was strongly in favor of peace with France at any cost and subsequently became regarded as a traitor to England. Margaret was his most ardent supporter, leading to accusations of treason against her as well as other stories, including that she was Isabelle's illegitimate daughter and that she was having an affair with Suffolk. After several years, Margaret began speaking openly against Richard, the powerful duke of York, Suffolk's enemy, whom she accused of wanting to depose her husband so that he could rule. Yet again she chose a political position contrary to the will of the English people. They supported York and believed that he could help England end the hardships it suffered, including high taxes, low international prestige, and a corrupt government bureaucracy. There was truth in her accusations of York's wish for the crown, however, for in 1450, York used his royal lineage to claim the right to succeed Henry, as the king and queen were still childless after four years of marriage and thus had no heir. York's popular support made his claim a serious threat to Margaret and Henry, for even if Henry accepted York as his heir, York might depose Henry before his death. Instead of York, Margaret supported Ed-

mund Beaufort, duke of Somerset, another leading noble who claimed the right to succeed Henry VI but one whom she trusted far more. For a time between 1450 and 1453, Margaret's influence led Parliament to support Somerset as Henry's heir-apparent.

But Margaret was fated to suffer from the vagaries of the English political scene and from her husband's weakening mental condition. In August 1453, Henry VI suffered a mental breakdown. Panicked, Margaret and her advisors tried to keep his condition a secret, but the truth became public when, three months later, Margaret gave birth to a son. Although the birth of an heir under earlier conditions would have been a blessing and likely eliminated the duke of York's threat to the throne, with Henry incapacitated York remained as much a threat as ever. When Parliament became aware of Henry's collapse, it appointed Duke Richard of York as "protector and defender of the realm" until the infant Prince Edward came of age. Margaret tried to win parliamentary support for a regency she would head, but her sex combined with her French heritage prevented Parliament from agreeing. What began then was a power struggle between York and the queen for control of the government. The queen is described at this time as passionate, single-minded, and unwilling to compromise. She took on many of the duties reserved for advisors and other functionaries and tried to prevent York from exercising his authority. In 1455, she recalled the exiled Somerset to England; the duke of York, recognizing that Margaret was now in a position of strength, withdrew to the north of England to mobilize his forces. Conflict between those supporting the rights of King Henry and Queen Margaret, called the Lancastrians, and those supporting the claims of Richard of York, called the Yorkists, began to divide the kingdom as each side recruited troops for the inevitable fight ahead.

The first armed conflict between the two groups occurred in May 1455, when a Lancastrian army was soundly defeated at the Battle of St. Albans. Queen Margaret was acknowledged by all as the de facto leader of the Lancastrians due to her high rank and close connection to King Henry VI and Prince Edward, both of whom were, of course, unable to lead for themselves. After St. Albans, Margaret, never dispirited, wrote to her allies in France to urge them to attack England, thereby hoping to show York's weakness as the realm's protector. She displayed early on one of the political blind spots which would appear during her struggles over the next 16 years: she would always consider herself

❦► **Chaucer, Alice** (fl. 1400s)

Duchess of Suffolk. Flourished in the 1400s; daughter of Thomas Chaucer of Ewelme (son of Geoffrey Chaucer, the writer) and Maud Burghersh; married Thomas Montacute, 4th earl of Salisbury; married William de la Pole, duke of Suffolk; children: (second marriage) John de la Pole, 1st duke of Suffolk.

French and would ignore the opinions of the English people when it came to seeking foreign aid for her cause. Thus she failed time and again to give due respect to one of the most important factors in civil warfare, the will of the people.

In late 1455, Henry recovered from his illness only to suffer another breakdown a short time later, a pattern which would continue for the rest of his life. During his recovery in 1455 and the long period of sanity he experienced in 1456, it became clear that Henry VI, who had always been a man of peace, wanted compromise and conciliation rather than civil war. To this end, he retained York as his chief minister over Margaret's protests. The queen, whose popularity had been waning steadily for many years, continued to lose support at the court and among the English by her steadfast refusal to compromise over the sharing of power and her insistence on being informed of and involved in every detail of the administration. Her reputation suffered further when, in 1457, King Charles VII of France answered her requests for French intervention by sending his ships to raid the English coast.

Despite peace negotiations in 1458, Yorkists and Lancastrians continued to prepare for war throughout that year and the year following, seizing treasure, recruiting troops, and seeking foreign support for their causes. At all times both sides claimed to represent good government and to be acting as loyal supporters of the crown. In November 1459, Margaret and Henry advanced on the town of Ludlow, where York's forces were waiting. The Lancastrian army was larger than York had expected and he ordered a retreat; he himself fled to Ireland while other Yorkists fled to Calais, the English-controlled port town on the French coast. Margaret rejoiced in the victory but knew that this was not the end of the Yorkist threat, and she and Henry continued to prepare for war. To this end, they began a program of heavy taxation and forced loans from the nobility and the towns of England which increased the discontent of their subjects and decreased their popularity.

The two armies met again in July 1460 at Northampton; the Yorkists were victorious this time, taking King Henry VI prisoner and slaying many of his staunchest supporters on the field. Upon hearing of Henry's defeat, Margaret fled to the northern counties which were loyal to Henry. She realized how important it was for her to remain at large with her son; if she and Edward were taken prisoner as well, York would be allowed to reign unchallenged. She sought military and financial aid from Scotland's Queen *Mary of Guelders (1433–1463) and France's King Charles VII; both monarchs wished to support the winning side but, being uncertain of which side this would be, only made vague promises of support with little tangible evidence.

Meanwhile, Parliament, faced with Richard of York's new claim to be the rightful king, agreed to a compromise by which York would succeed King Henry VI. But a few months later, in December 1460, another battle at Wakefield ended with the death of Duke Richard of York and a surprising victory for the Lancastrian cause. In a vengeful act not uncommon for her time, Margaret ordered the duke's corpse beheaded along with those of several other Yorkist leaders, and had the heads mounted on pikes outside the city of York. The Yorkist cause had lost its leader but not its core of supporters, however, and Margaret was still far from claiming a final victory. In February 1461, another victory led to the return of King Henry to his wife. Nonetheless, Margaret continued to prepare to defend the rights of her husband and child unwisely, seeking aid from foreign leaders by offering English territory in exchange for assistance and thus further antagonizing her subjects.

> *tiger's heart wrapped in a woman's hide!*
> —William Shakespeare, *Henry VI*

In March 1461, the duke of York's son and heir, Edward of March, proclaimed himself King Edward IV. Edward, a young man with his father's determination but far more military skill, was to prove a more formidable enemy than his father had been. Margaret realized how much popular support she had lost when the English readily accepted Edward IV as their new rightful king. On March 29, the Yorkist and still-strong Lancastrian armies met again on the battlefield at Towton. It was a decisive victory for Edward IV. Pursued by the usurper king's forces, Margaret fled to Scotland with Henry and her son. Demonstrating her indomitable spirit, she began once again to seek help from foreign lands.

The battles fought on the field during this phase of the Wars of the Roses were mirrored in the diplomatic maneuvers in which both Yorkist and Lancastrian leaders engaged to either win the support of foreign allies or negate the alliances secured by the opposing party. Margaret constantly sought the aid of France, Scotland, and Burgundy, and also appealed for help from the king of Aragon. As before, no foreign power supported her cause with any enthusiasm; all could see that it would take more than a few discontented Lancastrians to bring down the strong, popular Edward IV. Yet none would provide wholehearted support to Edward, either, fearing that at some point the Lancastrian cause could gain the upper hand and Henry VI be restored to the throne. Margaret of Anjou hoped to exploit the constant tension between the French and English monarchs to her own advantage, by forming a French-Lancastrian alliance united against Edward. For a time the French king, now Louis XI, Charles VII's son, supported Margaret and her cause in an effort to keep England too busy with its civil war to act against France.

In 1462, Margaret sailed to France at Louis XI's invitation, where she and Louis signed a secret agreement of French aid for the Lancastrian struggle. She did receive some aid, but Louis backed out of the pact fearing a Yorkist-Burgundian alliance united against France. A failed invasion of England in late 1462 by the Lancastrians forced Margaret, Henry, and their army to flee once again to Scotland for refuge. Yet again, she refused to give up hope, and in August she went to Burgundy to entreat Duke Philip of Burgundy, leaving Henry in Scotland. As time would prove, this was their final parting.

Margaret's efforts to win a substantive promise of aid from Duke Philip were fruitless. With no strong allies—Scotland wanted peace with England, while France and Burgundy were too concerned with their own affairs to be counted upon—Margaret retired for the time being to her father's estates to rest and plan her next move. She and her small band of loyal followers lived in relative poverty, mostly surviving off loans from Duke René. A brief partnership in the spring of 1464 with the duke of Somerset, the exiled former Yorkist, led to an abortive invasion of England headed by Somerset; he and many Lancastrians were executed on King Edward's orders after their defeat in battle. Henry VI, however, who had accompanied Somerset, escaped and remained a fugitive for over a year, until in July 1465 he was captured and imprisoned in the Tower of London.

Between 1464 and 1465, Margaret remained in exile with her son in France, always considering her next move and waiting for news from England of her husband's whereabouts. After learning that he had been captured, she was forced to waste another year in exile, for the Lancastrians did not have the strength to challenge King Edward IV without foreign aid, especially without Henry around which to rally support. In 1467, King Louis XI of France had Margaret and her small court brought to his castle at Chartres, thus giving Margaret hope for a French alliance, even though at this time he was also negotiating peace terms with King Edward. A treaty between Burgundy and England in 1468 ended French-English negotiations and led Louis to decide to aid the Lancastrians. To this end, he mediated an agreement between Margaret and Richard Neville, earl of Warwick—once King Edward's chief supporter but now estranged from him—to invade England. Margaret reluctantly agreed to accept Warwick's help, despite the fact that he had been a primary player in her husband's downfall, and even agreed to allow her son to marry Warwick's daughter, Lady Anne Neville (*Anne of Warwick), to seal their alliance.

In September 1470, a surprisingly effective invasion was launched by the exiled queen and led by the earl of Warwick, although Margaret did not dare risk her son's safety or her own by leaving France. Because Edward was ill prepared to resist, Warwick won an easy victory, forcing Edward to seek refuge in the Netherlands. Henry VI, weak, sickly, and mentally unstable, was freed from the Tower of London and nominally restored to the throne, after eight years as either a prisoner or an exile; Lancastrian loyalists replaced Yorkists in the administration of the kingdom.

After establishing himself in control, Warwick wrote to insist that Margaret return to England with her son to take possession of the government. However, at this point Margaret made a crucial mistake—she refused to bring the prince to England, fearing capture by the ships of Edward IV's ally, the duke of Burgundy. Yet it is likely that had she and the prince landed in England soon after Warwick's victory they could have rallied support among the war-weary English for the reign of the young prince. However, it was not until after the exiled King Edward had returned with an army to England in March 1471 that Margaret decided she needed to get to England quickly.

As it turned out, she was too late to salvage the victory which Warwick had gained for her. The English had become disillusioned with Warwick's governing and welcomed the return of Edward IV eagerly. On April 13, Margaret and Prince Edward landed in England, the same day that Edward IV's forces demolished Warwick's army and killed Warwick at the Battle of Barnet, again capturing Henry VI. Following a brief bout of depression, Margaret recovered her fighting spirit and, after recruiting new troops, spent the rest of April at the head of her forces, alternately pursuing and being pursued by Edward's army.

On May 4, 1471, both armies met for the final time at the Battle of Tewkesbury. For the first time, Margaret allowed her son Edward, now a young man of 17 and untried in warfare, to lead their army into combat. Each side was confident of victory, and each army was large and heavily armed with archers and mounted soldiers. The battle was engaged while Margaret waited anxiously some miles away. At first the forces were evenly matched, but a surprise attack by a hidden troop of Yorkists tilted the battle in the Yorkists' favor. The Lancastrians retreated, but the victorious Yorkists pursued them, managing to capture or kill every Lancastrian leader (the captured were later executed). Among the dead on the field was Prince Edward himself. When she heard the tragic news, Margaret, heartbroken, fled to the north, but she was captured and brought a prisoner to London on May 21.

The death of Prince Edward shattered Margaret's determination; preserving his right to inherit the throne by restoring Henry VI had been the only purpose of her many years of intrigue, warfare, and political machinations. She no longer had any reason to continue to fight, and her captor recognized this. King Edward shrewdly realized that this woman, who had been his and his father's constant enemy for 17 years, no longer posed a threat to him and was no longer a player on the political stage of Western Europe. Because of this, he refused to exact any vengeance on her. She was to remain a captive, but she was treated with dignity and respect. Edward did not, however, extend this clemency to her husband, still held in the Tower of London. On May 21, the same day Margaret was imprisoned in the Tower, Henry was secretly murdered on Edward's orders, to prevent any future rebellions in Henry's name by discontented English subjects. Although the official word was that he had died of natural causes, many suspected that the peaceful, simple-minded king had been put to death, and sympathy for his tragic life led some to consider him saintly.

At the end of 1471, Margaret of Anjou was put in the custody of her old friend Alice Chaucer, duchess of Suffolk. She remained with the duchess until 1475, when an unexpected treaty between King Louis XI of France and Edward IV included a stipulation that Louis would ransom Margaret for 50,000 crowns, an enormous sum. In return, Margaret agreed to renounce any holdings she had in England to Edward; after she returned to France in 1476, she agreed to pay Louis back by renouncing all her rights of inheritance to her father's territories and estates—even though their value was far higher than the total amount Louis XI had given her over the years for her support and for her ransom. Thus Margaret gained her freedom, but at the cost of giving up all her worldly possessions. Louis did, however, grant her a small pension to support herself.

She remained at her elderly father's court until his death in 1480; dispossessed, she retired to Château de Dampierre, the home of René's personal servant, in the same region of Anjou in which she had grown up. She remained in the quiet château until her death at age 53, on August 25, 1482. Margaret of Anjou was buried, at her own request, at the Cathedral of St. Maurice at Angers, where her mother and father were also buried.

SOURCES:

Bagley, J.J. *Margaret of Anjou, Queen of England*. London: Herbert Jenkins, 1948.

Crawford, Anne. "Margaret of Anjou" in *Europa Biographical Dictionary of British Women*. London: Europa Publications, 1983.

SUGGESTED READING:

Abbott, Jacob. *History of Margaret of Anjou, Queen of Henry VI of England*. NY: Harper and Brothers, 1861.

Ross, Charles Derek. *Wars of the Roses: A Concise History*. London: Thames and Hudson, 1976.

Strickland, Agnes. "Margaret of Anjou" in *Lives of the Queens of England*. Philadelphia: Lea and Blanchard, 1850.

RELATED MEDIA:

Dame *Peggy Ashcroft played Margaret of Anjou in the trilogy *The Wars of the Roses* which opened in Stratford, England, in 1963, and was reprised in London, 1963–64.

The Plantagenets, three of Shakespeare's plays performed together (earlier presented as *The Wars of the Roses*), starring **Penny Downie** as Margaret of Anjou and Ralph Fiennes as Henry VI, opened at the RSC in Stratford, England, in October 1988.

William Shakespeare's *Henry VI*.

Laura York,
freelance writer in medieval history
and women's history, Riverside, California

Margaret of Anjou (1553–1615).

See Margaret of Valois.

Margaret of Antioch (c. 255–c. 275)

Saint. Name variations: Marina of Antioch; Margarete or Margaret the Dragon Slayer; Maid of Antioch. Born at Antioch in Pisidia around 255 CE; beheaded around 275 at Antioch; daughter of Aedisius or Aedesius (a high-ranking pagan priest). Her feast day is July 20.

The legend of St. Margaret of Antioch, who is called St. Marina by the Greeks, came west with the crusades and survives in various interpretations. The daughter of a high-ranking pagan priest named Aedesius, Margaret was converted to Christianity by her childhood nurse and devoted her life to God at an early age. Her father, outraged by her conversion, drove her from the house, and she became a shepherd in the countryside. One day she captured the attention of the prefect Olybrius, who immediately wished to make her his bride, or, if she were a slave rather than a free woman, his concubine. He sent his servant to fetch her from the field for questioning. Upon meeting Olybrius, Margaret told him her name, and that she was of noble birth and a Christian, to which he responded that it was unworthy of her to "adore a crucified God." Whatever she said in reply made Olybrius so angry that he had her imprisoned. The next day when she was brought before an audience, she again infuriated the prefect with her statements of faith, and he retaliated by having her tortured. She was then returned to prison, where she performed a series of miracles, not the least of which was subduing a dragon which tried to devour her. (In a second version of the legend, she was swallowed by the dragon, whose body was then torn in two by her Christian faith, so that she emerged unscathed. In yet a third interpretation, she was additionally confronted by Satan whom she wrestled to the ground.) Unfortunately, neither the miracles nor her prayers could save her and she was beheaded.

In the Henry VII Chapel at Westminster Abbey, St. Margaret of Antioch is depicted holding a cross and standing on the dragon, illustrating the power of Christianity over evil. In other images, she is shown wearing a string of pearls and holding daisies in her lap. It is also said that St. Margaret, along with St. *Catherine of Alexandria, appeared to *Joan of Arc, telling her to go to war for France.

Barbara Morgan,
Melrose, Massachusetts

Margaret of Antioch-Lusignan
(fl. 1283–1291)

*Regent of Tyre. Flourished between 1283 and 1291; daughter of Henry of Antioch and *Isabella of Cyprus (fl. 1230s); sister of Hugh III, king of Cyprus (r. 1267–1284), king of Jerusalem (r. 1268–1284); married John of Montfort, lord of Tyre.*

Margaret of Artois (d. 1382)

Countess of Artois. Name variations: Marguerite of Artois; Margaret Capet; Joan. Reigned as countess of Artois from 1361 to 1382. Died in 1382; daughter of Philip V the Tall (c. 1294–1322), king of France (1316–1322), and Jeanne I of Burgundy (c. 1291–1330); married Louis I (d. 1346), count of Flanders (r. 1322–1346); children: Louis II de Male (1330–1384), count of Flanders and Artois (r. 1346–1384).

Margaret of Artois was the daughter of Philip V the Tall, king of France, and *Jeanne I of Burgundy. As countess of Artois, Margaret reigned from 1361 to 1382. After her death, the county of Artois merged with that of Flanders, which had belonged to her husband Louis.

Margaret of Attenduli (1375–?)

Italian military leader. Name variations: Margherita Sforza; Margaret of Attendolo; Margaret Attenduli. Born in 1375 in Italy; date of death unknown; daughter of Romagna peasants; sister of Muzio Attenduli or Attendolo (c. 1369–1424), the founder of Italy's famous Sforza family.

An aggressive politician and military leader, Margaret of Attenduli was an Italian noblewoman and sister of Muzio Attenduli, founder of the powerful Sforza family and later constable under *Joanna II of Naples. Muzio was also leader of the condottieri for Pope Martin V. Margaret of Attenduli was brought up in great wealth and was quite well educated, learning, among other skills, the art of warfare. She played an important role in her family's political games. Once, for example, an Italian prince kidnapped Margaret's brother and demanded a large ransom. Margaret was left in defense of Tricarico while her brother was imprisoned in Naples. When the enemy demanded the surrender of Tricarico, she met them dressed in armor with sword in hand, and took the envoys hostage. She was thus able to obtain her brother's release. Little else is known about Margaret of Attenduli's life.

Laura York,
Riverside, California

Margaret of Austria (fl. 1200s)

German queen. Flourished in the 1200s; married Henry VII (d. 1242), king of Germany (r. 1219–1235); children: Frederick and Henry.

Margaret of Austria (1480–1530)

Duchess of Savoy who governed the Low Countries for most of the period between 1506 and 1530. Name variations: Marguérite; Marguerite d'Autriche; Margaret Hapsburg; Duchess of Savoy and regent of the Netherlands. Born in Brussels, Belgium, on January 11, 1480; died in Malines on November 30 or December 1, 1530; daughter of Maximilian I, Holy Roman emperor (r. 1493–1519) and king of Germany, and Mary of Burgundy (1457–1482); sister of Philip I the Fair (also called the Handsome [1478–1506], husband of Juana La Loca); stepdaughter of *Bianca Maria Sforza (1472–1510) of Milan; engaged to future Charles VIII of France, in 1482; married Infante Juan also known as John of Spain (1478–1497), Spanish crown prince and son of Ferdinand and Isabella I, on April 3, 1497 (he died a few months later on October 4); married Philibert II, duke of Savoy (1497–1504), in 1501; children: none.

Margaret's maternal grandfather, Charles the Bold, duke of Burgundy, died (1477); Margaret's mother, Mary of Burgundy, died (1482); Treaty of Arras, subjecting duchy of Burgundy to French crown (1482); Louis XI died (1483); accession of Maximilian as Holy Roman emperor (1493); marriage of Philip to Juana La Loca of Castile and Margaret to John of Spain (1496); Charles VIII died (1498); Charles V born (1500); Isabella I of Castile died (1504); Philip the Fair died (1506); Margaret was appointed regent of the Netherlands (1507–15, 1519–30) and guardian of her nephew Charles, later Charles V (1507); Catherine of Aragon and Henry VIII married (1509); Ferdinand of Aragon died (1516); Charles became king of Spain (1517); Lutheran Reformation began (1517); Charles elected Holy Roman emperor (1519); Comunero Revolt broke out in Castile against Charles V (1520–21); Charles V and Martin Luther confrontation at Diet of Worms (1521); battle of Pavia and Francis I captured (1525); Charles V married Isabella of Portugal (1526); Henry VIII attempted to annul marriage to Catherine of Aragon (1526); Charles V's army sacked Rome (1527); Philip II born (1527); Margaret and Louise of Savoy negotiated the treaty of Cambrai, known as the "Ladies Peace" (1529) between France and the Netherlands; Mary of Hungary appointed regent of the Netherlands (1531).

Margaret of Austria was born on January 11, 1480, in Brussels, the second child of *Mary of Burgundy and Archduke Maximilian I, the future Holy Roman emperor. Margaret's brother, Philip the Fair, was two years older. In 1482,

their mother died from a riding accident. The tragedy touched off a dynastic crisis for Maximilian. As an Austrian, he had claim to Burgundy only through his wife, the daughter of Charles the Bold. With her dead, the Burgundian leaders refused to recognize Maximilian's authority. They pledged their loyalty to Philip, as long as he remained in the Low Countries to be raised as a Burgundian. This tension between dynastic ambition and nationalist sentiment foreshadowed one of the challenges of Margaret's public life.

To counterbalance Maximilian's influence, the Netherlandish provinces could always appeal to France for assistance. Thus, French intervention in the Low Countries menaced Maximilian's own authority and Philip's Burgundian inheritance. To forestall such trouble, in early 1483 Maximilian negotiated with Louis XI three-year-old Margaret's marriage to the Dauphin Charles, crown prince of France. Terms of the betrothal required Margaret to live in France, where the French could raise and educate her. During the summer of 1483, Margaret made her official entrance into Paris, and shortly thereafter in Amboise the three-year-old girl married her twelve-year-old prince. When Louis XI died two months later, Charles became King Charles VIII and Margaret was queen of France. She spent a happy childhood at Amboise. *Anne of Beaujeu (1461–1522), Charles' older sister and regent of France, acted as Margaret's guardian, and she developed the young girl's intellect and aesthetic sensibilities. The child's happiness lasted until 1491, when Charles decided to annul their unconsummated marriage and wed *Anne of Brittany (1477–1514).

Bitter about the snub, Margaret finally returned to the Low Countries and her father Maximilian in 1493. For the rest of her life, she remained culturally French but did not forgive what Charles and the Valois dynasty had done to her. Writes historian Henri Pirenne: "She had preserved tastes and a spirit totally French. She was not at all the enemy of France but of the house of France."

In late 1493, Maximilian became Holy Roman emperor, and he shortly arranged another marriage for Margaret to serve his political aims. His negotiations with Ferdinand of Aragon and *Isabella I of Castile produced a double wedding between the Spanish and Habsburg royal families. These marriages joined Spanish and German forces to curb French intervention in the Low Countries and Italy. On November 5, 1495, by proxy, Margaret married John of Spain, heir to the kingdoms of Castile and Aragon. Arriving in Spain in early 1497, she pleased the Spaniards with her intelligence and beauty: "a lovely girl, tall and fair, with masses of waving golden haire, a brilliant complexion, soft brown eyes, and a rather long narrow face, with the full under-lip so peculiar to the house of Austria." Meanwhile, her brother Philip wed *Juana La Loca (1479–1555), another of Ferdinand and Isabella's children. But fate snatched the Spanish crown from Margaret's head just as it had stolen the French throne from her. She was pregnant when John suddenly died of a fever on October 4, 1497. The grieving widow suffered another blow when she delivered a stillborn child. With neither husband nor heir, Margaret served no great geo-political purpose in Spain. Ferdinand and Isabella treated her kindly and reluctantly bid her farewell when she departed for the Low Countries in September 1499 at Maximilian's insistence.

By her talents, ability, and rare aptitude for business, [Margaret of Austria] eclipsed more powerful rulers, and soon became the pivot of political life in Europe.

—Eleanor E. Tremayne

Back in Flanders, she attended the baptism of her nephew, the future Charles V, on March 7, 1500. Meanwhile, Margaret's father negotiated another marriage for her, this time with Duke Philibert II of Savoy. Handsome and virile, the duke was Margaret's age. Wed on December 2, 1501, she began the happiest period of her life. Devoted to the hunt and his wife, Philibert showed little interest in governing his domains. Margaret willingly managed his affairs from their residence in the castle of Pont d'Ain at Bourg. Her bliss did not last. Philibert took ill and died of pleurisy on September 10, 1504. Margaret cut off her long blonde hair and donned widow's clothing. For a while, she considered taking religious vows.

But despair did not drive her from the world. She endowed the construction of a monastery at Brou, together with an elaborate tomb for Philibert and herself. Adept at word games, she created a new device for herself, displayed prominently on the tomb: *FORTUNE. INFORTUNE. FORT. UNE.* According to a biographer, **Eleanor Tremayne**, the motto means "Fortune strongly persecutes a woman." Other interpretations have also been suggested. But as biographer Ghislaine de Boom notes regarding Philibert's death: "It could be that, had he lived, his amiable frivolity would have ended by boring his wife's noble in-

telligence; but his premature death consecrated him" as the widow's "prince charming."

Margaret of Austria remained in Savoy for two years following her husband's death. Meanwhile, Queen Isabella of Castile died in late 1504, raising Margaret's brother Philip and his wife Juana La Loca to the throne. They eventually went to Spain to claim the Castilian crown. Their son Charles (V) stayed behind, for the Burgundians refused to accept him as their ruler unless he were raised in the Low Countries. Without Margaret's consent, her brother Philip and father Maximilian negotiated her marriage to Henry VII, king of England. She refused to cooperate, determined to avoid further marital sorrow. Then, on September 25, 1506, Philip died. This plunged the House of Burgundy into a new crisis. Charles was alone in the Low Countries, and his mother, Queen Juana La Loca, could not return to raise him: the Castilians would not allow her to abandon the kingdom and furthermore she was mentally unstable.

With Charles too young to govern, the provinces of the Low Countries voted to make Maximilian their regent. Preoccupied with his affairs in Germany, Maximilian urged Margaret to return to the Low Countries and care for Charles. She arrived in early 1507. Maximilian appointed her Charles' *mambour* or governess-tutor and empowered her to exercise the regency. Margaret, of course, was no political neophyte. Her education under Anne of Beaujeu had prepared her for civic life, and her marriages had placed her on the public stage. In Savoy, Philibert's disinterest in the affairs of state had given Margaret political opportunities that she gladly seized. Of those years in Italy, Ghislaine de Boom wrote: "For the first time, Margaret was revealed as an able and energetic woman, even imperious." Now, at age 27, her true public career began, and Margaret remained a chief player in European politics for the rest of her life.

As regent of the Low Countries, she shared the stage with some of the great figures of European history: Ferdinand of Aragon, Charles V, Henry VIII, Francis I, Erasmus, Martin Luther, Pope Julius II, Suleiman the Magnificent, and the Emperor Maximilian. When he visited the Low Countries in 1509, her father officially invested her with full, independent authority. Each of her acts was to carry the same weight "as though we ourselves did it." Her task was not easy. The Low Countries lacked any centralized political institutions. Furthermore, writes Pirenne, "she was and always remained a foreigner," having been raised at the French court.

Margaret knew neither Flemish nor German, and her principal advisers were Italians who had followed her north. Thus, she was less concerned about the interests of the Low Countries than how she could use their resources to her family's benefit. Margaret's chief responsibilities were to maintain political stability and economic prosperity in the Netherlandish provinces, while caring for Charles and then providing funds for his international gambits once he became emperor in 1519.

At Malines, she purchased the palace of Jean Laurin, lord of Watervliet, and installed herself there. She treated her nephew Charles with maternal love and lavished great care on his education, as her ambitions for the Habsburg dynasty depended on him. Almost immediately, she confronted the hostility of Guillaume de Croy, lord of Chièvres, who had been Charles' tutor and a dominant political figure at court. Chièvres retained the boy's trust, but his pro-French leanings brought him into conflict with Margaret's support for Maximilian. Furthermore, Maximilian was at war with the French, yet Louis XII was feudal sovereign of some Netherlandish provinces. As duke of Burgundy, for example, Charles was a vassal of the French king. To preserve the Low Countries for Charles, Margaret persuaded Maximilian to make peace with Louis. She then journeyed to Cambrai in November 1508, where "she revealed herself as the most able diplomat of her time," according to Pirenne. The treaty forming the League of Cambrai, signed on December 10, 1508, largely removed the French threat to the Low Countries and made it easier for Margaret to deal with an internal rebellion led by Charles of Egmont, duke of Guelders.

Margaret and the Low Countries were enmeshed in Charles' and Maximilian's political entanglements and Habsburg dynastic objectives. Where possible, she tried to keep the Low Countries at peace. In 1513, she persuaded her father to join a papal alliance with Spain and England against France, although she maintained the Low Countries in neutrality. To curb Chièvres' pro-French influence over Charles, Margaret created a council containing representatives of Maximilian, Ferdinand, and Henry VIII. The traditional animosity between France and England made it nearly impossible to align the Low Countries with either of their Western neighbors without antagonizing the other.

Jealous of Margaret's power, Chièvres and some nobles, working through the provincial Estates, pressed Maximilian to declare Charles of

age to rule. The Estates paid Maximilian to resign as regent and installed Charles, who was not yet 15 years old, on January 5, 1515. Negotiated secretly behind Margaret's back, her dethronement was a public humiliation. In his aunt's place, Charles established a council of regency. Margaret served on the council but had no vote in its deliberations. She was angry and hurt, and Maximilian shortly saw his mistake. Chièvres completely dominated Charles and urged upon him policies that conflicted with Habsburg interests. On March 24, 1515, Chièvres persuaded Charles to sign a treaty with France that recognized Francis I's sovereignty over Burgundy and gave little in return. Margaret's ministers, such as Mercurino de Gattinara, found themselves thrust aside and even persecuted.

The death of Charles' two grandfathers, Ferdinand and Maximilian, enabled Margaret to regain her powers. Ferdinand of Aragon died on January 23, 1516, opening the way to Charles' Spanish inheritance. His mother Juana's insanity allowed him to claim the crowns of both Castile and Aragon. To make an effective claim, however, he had to go to Spain. Maneuvering adroitly behind the scenes, Margaret paved the way for Charles to become king. After much hesitation

Margaret of Austria (1480–1530)

and delay, he departed in September 1517 for Spain, taking Chièvres and other Flemish and Walloon advisers with him.

Charles soon recognized his need for Margaret and her ministers. In June 1518, he appointed Gattinara grand chancellor, and he helped arrange Margaret's return as regent of the Low Countries. On June 24, 1518, from Zaragoza, Charles restored his aunt's powers. Given her father's poor health, Margaret and Charles began to negotiate the latter's election as emperor even before Maximilian's death on January 12, 1519. The papacy and French strongly opposed Charles. Margaret, thinking first of the dynasty, then suggested supporting instead Charles' younger brother Ferdinand I (b. 1502). But Charles refused to withdraw and eventually prevailed on June 28, 1519.

When Charles arrived as emperor in the Netherlands, he retracted the council of regency's power and proclaimed Margaret "regent of the Low Countries . . . in consideration of the great, inestimable and praiseworthy services that our said lady and aunt has done us." On a subsequent visit to the Low Countries in mid-1520, he renewed her authority and made her governor-general. Again, she loyally served the dynastic ambitions of her family. Ignoring the Netherlandish nobility except for Antoine de Lalaing, lord of Hoogstraeten, she formed a privy council of non-aristocratic outsiders to help her rule. "She governed them well," writes Pirenne, "for she was intelligent and hardworking, but she governed them without sympathy."

The Low Countries occupied a crucial position between France, England, and the Empire and represented the northern most bulwark of Charles and Spain's power. Serving her nephew's policies, Margaret of Austria gathered money, troops, and supplies to support Charles' wars, especially against Francis I and the German Protestants. In 1521, Habsburg forces seized the bishopric and city-state of Tournai and added it to Margaret's jurisdiction. In following years, the Habsburgs consolidated their hold over Friesland, Utrecht, and Overijssel.

Margaret also cooperated in the emperor's campaign to eliminate Protestantism. In late 1521 and 1522, Charles created a secular inquisition, headed by François van der Hulst, to ferret out heretics. In Brussels on July 1, 1523, the inquisitorial fires claimed their first Protestant victims, two former Augustinians from Antwerp. More moderate than her nephew, Margaret feared that intense persecution of Protestants would only strengthen them. Ignor-

ing her opposition, Clement VII also appointed an inquisitor-general in 1525. Repression of heresy in the Low Countries grew with the publication in 1529 of Charles V's "Placard." Despite the efforts of the emperor, his aunt, and the inquisitors, local officials were often lax in persecuting the heretics. Their negligence sometimes reflected sympathy for Protestantism and other times a desire to assert autonomy against the centralizing efforts of the Habsburgs.

Meanwhile, Margaret's court at Malines helped to introduce the energy and aesthetic values of the Italian Renaissance to Northern Europe. A poet herself, she collected books and paintings and patronized writers and artists. Visiting Malines in 1521, Albrecht Dürer wondered at her many "precious things and precious library." Among them was Jan van Eyck's *Arnolfini Wedding*. She continued to finance construction of the church and tomb at Brou.

Margaret of Austria's last diplomatic achievement was the Peace of Cambrai, sometimes called the Ladies Peace (1529). Journeying to Cambrai, she met *Louise of Savoy, Philibert's sister and the mother of Francis I. They arranged an end to a war that Francis could no longer sustain. The pact favored the dynastic interests of Charles; besides withdrawing French forces from Italy, Francis renounced his claims to Flanders, Artois and Tournai, which were part of Charles' patrimony. This diplomatic triumph placed Margaret at the peak of her glory throughout Europe. She was busy negotiating a double marriage between the children of Charles and Francis when she died.

According to a legend about Margaret's death, she stepped on a shard of glass, and the resulting wound became gangrenous. In reality, however, her health had declined since 1527, and an abscessed leg had tormented her during the negotiations in Cambrai. On November 20, 1530, a high fever caused by her infected leg forced Margaret to bed, and neither piety nor medicine made any headway against the spreading gangrene. She died shortly after midnight on December 1. Margaret had previously provided an endowment for the completion of the magnificent tomb at Brou, and her will, amended shortly before her death, left her remaining possessions to Charles V. She also urged her nephew to protect the sovereignty of the Low Countries against the centralizing tendency of his imperial administrators. Upon completion of her tomb, Margaret's body was transferred to Brou in 1532 and buried next to Philibert's remains.

An able diplomat, patron of the Renaissance, and effective ruler, Margaret of Austria was a central political figure of the early 16th century. Although unfortunate in her private life, she compensated by caring for her brother Philip's children. Margaret also helped Charles V overcome his uncertain steps at the outset of his reign and became an invaluable asset to his rule. The emperor had both personal and political motives to mourn her passing. He bemoaned "the loss that we have made and principally I who held her as a mother and for the lack she does me in the government of the countries where she was in charge."

SOURCES:

Boom, Ghislaine de. *Marguerite d'Austriche*. Brussels: La Renaissance du Livre, 1946.

Evans, Mark. *The Sforza Hours*. London: The British Library, 1992.

Halkin, Léon-E. *La Réforme en Belgique sous Charles-Quint*. Brussels: La Renaissance du Livre, 1957.

Hare, Christopher [Mrs. Marian Andrews]. *The High and Puissant Princess Marguerite of Austria: Princess Dowager of Spain, Duchess Dowager of Savoy, Regent of the Netherlands*. NY: Scribner, 1907.

Pirenne, Henri. *Histoire de Belgique des origines a nos jours*. 4 vols. Brussels: La Renaissance du Livre, 1948.

Rady, Martyn. *The Emperor Charles V*. Seminar Studies in History. NY: Longman, 1988.

Tremayne, Eleanor E. *The First Governess of the Netherlands: Margaret of Austria*. NY: Putnam, 1908.

SUGGESTED READING:

Altmeyer, Jean Jacques. *Marguerite d'Autriche, sa vie, sa politique et sa cour*. Liège: Jeunehomme frères, 1840.

Correspondance de l'empereur Maximilien Ier et de Marguerite d'Autriche: sa fille gouvernante des Pas-Bas, de 1507 à 1519. 2 vols. Paris: J. Renouard et Cie, 1839.

Correspondance de Marguerite d'Autriche et de ses ambassadeurs à la cour de France concernant l'exécution du traité de Cambrai, 1529–1530. Ed. by Ghislaine de Boom. Bruxelles: M. Lamertin, 1935.

Correspondance de Marguerite d'Autriche, gouvernante des Pays-Bas, avec ses amis sur les affaires des Pays-Bas de 1506–1528. 2 vols. Leiden: S. et J. Luchtmans, 1845–1847.

Headley, John M. *The Emperor and His Chancellor: a Study of the Imperial Chancellery under Gattinara*. NY: Cambridge University Press, 1983.

Kendall W. Brown,
Professor of History, Brigham Young University, Provo, Utah

Margaret of Austria (1522–1586).

See Margaret of Parma.

Margaret of Austria (c. 1577–1611).

See Anne of Austria (1601–1666) for sidebar.

Margaret of Babenberg (fl. 1252)

Queen of Bohemia and duchess of Austria. Flourished around 1252; daughter of Leopold VII, one of several claimants to the title of duke of Austria (r. 1250–1253); first wife of Otakar or Ottokar II (b. 1230?), king of Bohemia (r. 1253–1278), duke of Austria and Styria (r. 1252–1276).

Margaret of Baden (d. 1457)

*German noblewoman. Died on October 24, 1457; daughter of James I of Baden, margrave of Baden; became first wife of Albert Achilles (1414–1486) also known as Albert III (1414–1486), elector of Brandenburg (r. 1470–1486), in 1446; children: John Cicero (1455–1499), elector of Brandenburg (r. 1486–1499). Albert's second wife was *Anne of Saxony (1437–1512).*

Margaret of Baden (1932—)

*Grand duchess of Baden. Name variations: Margarita Alice Scholastica, grand duchess von Baden. Born Margaret Alice Thyra Victoria Mary Louise Scholastica on July 14, 1932, in Salem, Baden, Germany; daughter of Berthold (b. 1906), margrave of Baden, and *Theodora Oldenburg (1906–1969, sister of Prince Philip of England); married Tomislav Karadjordjevic (1928–2000) also known as Prince Tomislav (brother of Peter II, king of Yugoslavia), on June 5, 1957 (divorced 1981); children: Nicholas (b. 1958); Catherine Karadjordjevic (b. 1959).*

Margaret of Bavaria (fl. 1390–1410)

*Duchess of Lorraine. Flourished between 1390 and 1410; married Charles II, duke of Lorraine; children: *Isabelle of Lorraine (1410–1453), queen of Naples.*

Margaret of Bavaria (d. 1424)

*Duchess of Burgundy. Died in 1424 (some sources cite 1426); daughter of Albert I, duke of Bavaria (r. 1353–1404); married John the Fearless (1371–1419), duke of Burgundy (r. 1404–1419), on April 12, 1385; children: Philip III the Good (1396–1467), duke of Burgundy (r. 1419–1467); *Margaret of Burgundy (d. 1441); *Mary of Burgundy (c. 1400–1463, who married Adolf I of Cleves); Joan (d. around 1413); Isabella of Burgundy (d. 1412, who married Oliver, count of Penthièvre); Catherine (who married Louis, duke of Guise); *Anne Valois (c. 1405–1432, who married John, duke of Bedford); *Agnes of Burgundy (d. 1476, who married Charles I, duke of Bourbon).*

Margaret of Bavaria (1445–1479)

*Marquesa of Mantua. Name variations: Margherita of Bavaria; Margherita Gonzaga. Born in 1445; died in 1479; married Frederigo also known as Federico Gonzaga (1441–1484), 3rd marquis of Mantua (r. 1478–1484); children: *Chiara Gonzaga (1465–1505); Francesco Gonzaga (1466–1519), 4th marquis of Mantua (r. 1484–1519, who married *Isabelle d'Este); Sigismondo (1469–1525, a cardinal); *Elisabetta Montefeltro (1471–1526); *Maddalena Sforza (1472–1490); Giovanni (1474–1523, who married Laura di Giovanni Bentivoglio).*

Margaret of Blois (d. 1404).

See Marie of Guise.

Margaret of Bohemia (d. 1212).

See Dagmar of Bohemia.

Margaret of Bourbon (d. 1258).

See Margaret de Foix.

Margaret of Bourbon (d. 1483)

*Duchess of Savoy. Name variations: Marguerite de Bourbon. Born Margaret de Beaujeu; died in 1483; sister of Pierre de Beaujeu, who was married to *Anne of Beaujeu (1460/61–1522); married Philip II, count of Bresse, later duke of Savoy; children: *Louise of Savoy (1476–1531); Philibert II (1478–1504, who married *Margaret of Austria [1480–1530]); Charles II the Good of Savoy, duke of Savoy; Philippe, marquis of Saluzzo; René, count of Villare and Tende.*

Margaret of Brabant (d. 1311)

*Holy Roman empress. Name variations: Marguerite of Brabant. Died in 1311; married Henry of Luxemburg also known as Henry VII (c. 1274–1313), Holy Roman emperor (r. 1308–1313), in 1292; children: *Mary of Luxemburg (1305–1323, who married Charles IV, king of France); John Limburg (1296–1346), count of Luxemburg and king of Bohemia (r. 1310–1346).*

Margaret of Brabant (1323–1368)

*Countess of Flanders. Name variations: Margaret Louvain; Margaret de Mâle; Margaret of Male or Mâle. Born in 1323; died in 1368; daughter of John III (1300–1355), duke of Brabant (r. 1312–1355), and *Marie of Evreux (d. 1335); sister of *Joanna of Brabant (1322–1406) and *Marie of Guelders (1325–1399); married Louis II de Male (1330–1384), count of Flanders and Artois (r. 1346–1384); children:*

Margaret of Flanders (1350–1405, who married Philip the Bold, duke of Burgundy).

Margaret of Brandenburg (c. 1450–1489)

*Duchess of Pomerania. Name variations: Margaret von Brandenburg. Born around 1450; died in 1489; daughter of *Catherine of Saxony (1421–1476) and Frederick II (1413–1471), elector of Brandenburg (r. 1440–1470, abdicated); married Bogislav X also known as Boleslav X (b. 1454), duke of Pomerania, on September 20, 1477.*

Margaret of Burgundy (1290–1315)

*Queen of Navarre and France. Name variations: Margaret Capet; (Fr.) Marguerite of Bourgogne. Born in 1290; died on August 14, 1315, in Château Gaillard, France; daughter of Robert II (b. 1248), duke of Burgundy, and *Agnes Capet (1260–1327, daughter of Louis IX of France); sister of *Jeanne of Burgundy (1293–1348, first wife of Philip VI of France); married Louis X the Headstrong (1289–1316), king of France (r. 1314–1316), on September 23, 1305 (annulled before August 1315); children: *Joan II of Navarre (1309–1349)*

Margaret of Burgundy, queen of Navarre and France, was married for ten years to Louis X, king of France. She was convicted of adultery, imprisoned, then smothered to death on August 14, 1315. Louis married *Clemence of Hungary (1293–1328) that same month.

Margaret of Burgundy (d. 1441)

*Duchess of Guienne. Died in 1441; daughter of *Margaret of Bavaria (d. 1424) and John the Fearless (1371–1419), duke of Burgundy (r. 1404–1419); married Louis (d. 1415), duke of Guienne; married Arthur III of Brittany (1393–1458), count of Richmond, duke of Brittany (r. 1457–1458).*

Margaret of Burgundy (c. 1376–1441)

*Countess of Hainault and Holland. Name variations: Margaret Valois; Margaret of Ostrevent, countess of Ostrevent. Born around 1376; died in 1441; daughter of Philip the Bold (1342–1404), duke of Burgundy (r. 1363–1404), and *Margaret of Flanders (1350–1405); sister of John the Fearless, duke of Burgundy (r. 1404–1419); married Count William VI (d. 1417),* count of Hainault and Holland (r. 1404–1417), on April 12, 1385; children: *Jacqueline of Hainault (1401–1436).

Margaret of Burgundy (1446–1503).

See Margaret of York.

Margaret of Carinthia (1318–1369).

See Margaret Maultasch.

Margaret of Cleves (fl. early 1400s)

Duchess of Bavaria. Flourished in the early 1400s; married William II, duke of Bavaria (r. 1397–1435); children: Adolph, duke of Bavaria (r. 1435–1441).

Margaret of Connaught

(1882–1920)

*Swedish royal and granddaughter of Queen Victoria. Name variations: Margaret Saxe-Coburg; Margaret of Sweden; Crown Princess Margaret of Sweden; Margaret Victoria of Sweden. Born on January 15, 1882, in Bagshot Park, Surrey, England; died on May 1, 1920, in Stockholm, Sweden; daughter of Arthur Saxe-Coburg, duke of Connaught (son of Queen *Victoria of England), and *Louise Margaret of Prussia (1860–1917); married Gustavus VI Adolphus (1882–1973), king of Sweden (r. 1950–1973), on June 15, 1905, at St. George's Chapel, Windsor Castle, England; children: Gustav Adolphus, duke of Westerbotten (1906–1947); Sigvard (1907—); *Ingrid of Sweden (b. 1910, who married Frederick IX, king of Denmark); Bertil (b. 1912), duke of Halland; Charles John, duke of Dalecarlia (b. 1916).*

Following the death of Margaret of Connaught in 1920, Gustavus VI Adolphus married *Louise Mountbatten.

Margaret of Constantinople

(1202–1280).

See Margaret of Flanders.

Margaret of Corigliano

Neapolitan noblewoman. Married Louis of Durazzo; children: Charles III, king of Naples (r. 1382–1386), king of Hungary as Charles II (r. 1385–1386).

Margaret of Cortona (1247–1297)

Saint and Franciscan nun. Name variations: "The Magdalene of Cortona." Born in Alviano (Laviano), near Chiusi, in Tuscany, in 1247; died in Cortona, in Tuscany, on February 22, 1297; children: (with the lord of Montepulciano) one son.

Believed to have been driven from her home at an early age by her stepmother, the young and beautiful Margaret of Cortona became the mistress of the lord of Montepulciano, with whom she lived for nine years, and with whom she had a son. When her lover was subsequently assassinated by robbers, Margaret was overcome by shock and contrition, and returned to her father's house hoping to find solace within the family fold. When she was turned away yet again, she took refuge in a neighboring vineyard where "a tempting demon" urged her to return to her wayward life. Margaret resisted, praying that God would come into her life to replace all that she had lost. It was then that she supposedly received the divine intervention that led her to the Franciscan convent in Cortona where, barefoot, with a rope around her neck, she begged to be admitted as a penitent into the order. Her reputation was such, however, that the brotherhood refused to admit her without a sign of her sincere repentance. Over the next three years, she lived an exemplary life of humility, charity, and purity, and was permitted to take the habit of the Third Order of St. Francis in 1272. It is related that one day as she prayed before the image of Christ, he bowed his head in compassion and forgiveness, and from that time on, she was regarded as "the Magdalene of Cortona." Margaret lived in divine grace until her death in 1297, after which she was buried in the Church of the Lowly Penitent, adjoining the convent. In a few extant pictures of the saint, who is little known outside of Tuscany, she is often depicted with a small dog, usually a spaniel, at her feet. The animal represents the pet dog which purportedly helped her locate the body of her slain lover. Her feast day is February 22.

Barbara Morgan,
Melrose, Massachusetts

Margaret of Denmark.

See Estrith (fl. 1017–1032).
See Margaret I of Denmark (1353–1412).

Margaret of Denmark (1456–1486)

*Queen of Scotland. Born on June 23, 1456; died on July 14, 1486, in Stirling, Scotland; buried in Cambuskenneth Abbey, Stirling; daughter of Christian I (1426–1481), king of Denmark, Norway, and Sweden (r. 1448–1481), and *Dorothea of Brandenburg*

(1430–1495); married James III (1451–1488), king of Scotland (r. 1460–1488), on July 13, 1469; children: James IV (1473–1513), king of Scotland (r. 1488–1513); James Stewart (1476–1504), archbishop of St. Andrews; Alexander Stewart, earl of Mar and Garioch; John Stewart (1479–1503), earl of Mar and Garioch.

Margaret of Flanders (1202–1280)

Countess of Flanders. Name variations: Black Meg; Margaret of Constantinople; Marguerite of Flanders; Marguerite de Flandre. Born in 1202 in Flanders; died in 1280 in Flanders; daughter of Baudouin also known as Baldwin IX, count of Flanders (and emperor of Constantinople as Baldwin I), and Marie of Champagne (d. 1203); sister of Johanna of Flanders (c. 1200–1244); married Bourchard d'Avesnes of Hainault, in 1212 (annulled around 1215); married William de Dampierre, around 1223 (died before 1245); children: (first marriage) two sons; (second marriage) three sons, including Guy de Dampierre, later count of Flanders, and two daughters (names unknown).

Countess Margaret of Flanders was a religious founder and a great contributor to the commercial growth of the 13th century. Her mother was *Marie of Champagne; her father was Baldwin IX, count of Flanders, who rose to fame after his victories in the Fourth Crusade in 1204 when he helped effect the capture of Byzantium and was made emperor. Unfortunately, Baldwin's glory was short-lived, for he died a young man a few months later. On his death he had only two surviving children, both daughters. Margaret's older sister, *Johanna of Flanders, inherited the county. Ruling Flanders was a difficult challenge in that time, for although Flanders was small it had several emerging capitalist regions and was territorially significant, and the French monarch wanted to annex it to his own kingdom.

Margaret married a French noble, Bourchard d'Avesnes, around 1212; they had two sons but their marriage was annulled several years later, ostensibly because Bourchard had been a deacon and thus could never legally marry; in reality, the annulment was probably the work of King Philip II of France, who wanted to increase his influence in Flanders by having Margaret marry one of his own loyal barons. Thus Margaret next married William of Dampierre, around 1223; eventually she had five children with William, three sons and two daughters. Johanna of Flanders was likewise pressured by her powerful neighbor into making marriage alliances beneficial to the French, although she wanted to keep Flanders independent.

Johanna had no surviving children or husband when she died in 1245; the county then passed to Margaret, who was in her 50s. By this time, Margaret of Flanders had also been widowed. Upon her succession as countess, a war broke out between her d'Avesnes sons and her Dampierre sons over which son was her legal heir. The d'Avesnes children were older, but if their mother's marriage to Bourchard was invalid, they were illegitimate and could not legally inherit. Battles ensued, with Flemish and French nobles lending support to one side or the other as seemed reasonable and politically expedient. The mother of these warriors did everything in her power to bring peace to the situation, but it was a difficult legal question, and Margaret's efforts to negotiate without seeming to support one cause over the other put her in an awkward position, especially as she personally favored the rights of her Dampierre children. A compromise was reached after ten years of fighting only with the aid of King Louis IX.

With peace restored, Margaret turned her attention toward the welfare of the towns and people under her rule. She became a respected founder of religious establishments, favoring the Dominicans, for whom she established a house at Ypres and one at Douai. Throughout her life, she gave generously to the support of Dominican nuns and monks as well as to other houses and various charitable causes. She knew the great Dominican leader St. Thomas Aquinas, and corresponded with him on questions of moral rule as it related to commerce and finance, including the sins of usury and simony.

In addition, Margaret became interested in promoting the trade of her region. She started projects to improve the canal system of Flanders and shipping times, and had currency struck that was easily exchanged with German and English coins, for she wanted to increase Flemish trade with merchants of those areas. She also passed legislation which granted special benefits and incentives for merchants of Spain and Poitou to trade in Flanders, helping to bring more commerce and money into her capital trading city of Bruges.

Around 1278, Margaret, now in her late 70s, retired from her active life, and allowed her son Guy de Dampierre to take over as count of Flanders. She died two years later.

SOURCES:

LaBarge, Margaret. *A Small Sound of the Trumpet: Women in Medieval Life.* Boston: Beacon Press, 1986.

Laura York,
Riverside, California

Margaret of Flanders (d. 1285)

Duchess of Brabant. Name variations: Margaret of Brabant. Died in 1285; daughter of Guy of Flanders (probably Guy de Dampierre, later count of Flanders, son of *Margaret of Flanders [1202–1280]); became second wife of John I (c. 1252–1294), duke of Brabant, in 1273; children: a son who died. John I's first wife was *Margaret Capet (d. 1271).

Margaret of Flanders (1350–1405)

Countess of Flanders, duchess of Burgundy, and countess of Artois and Nevers. Name variations: Margaret de Mâle; Margaret of Male or Mâle; Margaret II, countess of Flanders; (Fr.) Marguerite de Flandre. Reigned as countess of Flanders (r. 1384–1405); countess of Artois and Nevers. Born in 1350; died on March 16, 1405, in Arras; daughter of Margaret of Brabant (1323–1368) and Louis II de Male, count of Flanders and Artois (r. 1346–1384); married Philippe de Rouvre, count of Artois, on March 21, 1356 or 1357; married Philip the Bold (1342–1404), duke of Burgundy (r. 1363–1404), in 1369; children: John the Fearless (1371–1419), duke of Burgundy (r. 1404–1419); Antoine also known as Anthony, duke of Brabant (d. 1415); Philip (d. 1415), count of Nevers; *Margaret of Burgundy (c. 1376–1441); *Catherine of Burgundy (1378–1425); *Mary of Burgundy (d. 1428).

Margaret of Flanders was the only child of Louis II, count of Flanders, and ***Margaret of Brabant**. In 1369, she married Philip the Bold who was duke of Burgundy and brother of Charles V, king of France. When Louis II died in 1384, Margaret inherited Flanders and Artois, and the cities of Antwerp and Malines. Through marriages, alliances, and skillful negotiation, Margaret and Philip, and three successive dukes of Burgundy—John the Fearless, Philip the Good, and Charles the Bold—would manage to enlarge the dominion to include most of the Netherlands and much of the outlying area. The Burgundians became powerful rivals to the sovereigns of France.

Margaret of Foix.

> *See Margaret de Foix (d. 1258).*
> *See Marguerite de Foix (fl. 1456–1477).*

Margaret of France (1158–1198)

Queen of Hungary. Name variations: Margaret Capet. Born in 1158; died in 1198 in Acre (Akko), now Israel; daughter of *Constance of Castile (d. 1160) and

Louis VII (c. 1121–1180), king of France (r. 1137–1180); married six-year-old Henry Plantagenet (1155–1183), known as the Young King (son of Henry II and *Eleanor of Aquitaine), count of Anjou and duke of Normandy, on November 2, 1160; became second wife of Bela III (1148–1196), king of Hungary (r. 1173–1196), in 1185 or 1186; children: (first marriage) William (stillborn).

Margaret of France (c. 1282–1318)

Queen-consort of England. Name variations: Marguerite of France; Margaret of Westminster. Born around 1282 (some sources cite 1279) in Paris, France; died on February 14, 1318 (some sources cite 1317); buried at Christ Church, Newgate, London; interred at Grey Friars Church, Newgate, London; daughter of Philip III the Bold (1245–1285), king of France (r. 1270–1285), and *Marie of Brabant (c. 1260–1321); half-sister of Philip IV, king of France (r. 1285–1314) and Blanche of France (c. 1266–1305); aunt of Isabella of France (1296–1358); became second wife of Edward I Longshanks, king of England (r. 1272–1307), on September 10, 1299 (also seen as 1298); children: Thomas (b. 1300), earl of Norfolk; Edmund of Woodstock (1307–1330), earl of Kent; Margaret (b. 1306, died young); Eleanor (1306–1311); (stepson) Edward II, king of England (r. 1307–1327).

Within a year of the death of his beloved queen ***Eleanor of Castile** (1241–1290), Edward I Longshanks, king of England, began negotiations for a second wife. Initially, he had his eye on the beautiful ***Blanche of France**, daughter of Philip III, king of France, but Philip did not wish to sacrifice his eldest daughter to an aging king who already had an heir (Edward II), so at the peace of Montreuil in 1299 he delivered up her younger half-sister Margaret of France instead. She was 16.

Margaret's introduction to England and to married life was bleak indeed. As war still raged in Scotland, there was no time or money for a proper coronation, so following a hasty wedding ceremony at Canterbury on September 9, 1299, Edward returned to his military command. Margaret was left quarantined in the Tower of London to prevent her from contracting smallpox which had been brought to London by the Crusaders, and there she remained until Edward sent for him to join his campaign. Margaret was never given an official coronation, though she was acknowledged as his queen.

From this inauspicious royal debut, Margaret became a much admired and beloved

Margaret of France (c. 1282–1318)

queen and had four children: two sons, Thomas and Edmund of Woodstock, and two daughters, Margaret and Eleanor (both died young). When Margaret did accompany her husband on campaigns, she was known to intercede with him frequently to save lives and forgive debts. It was recorded that on one occasion she pleaded for the life of the goldsmith who had made the crown for Robert I Bruce, king of Scotland. Captured and threatened with death, he was spared "solely at the intercession of our dearest consort, Margaret, Queen of England."

Before his death in 1307, Edward made it known that he wanted his son Edward II to marry *Isabella of France (daughter of Margaret's half-brother Philip IV and his late wife *Joan I of Navarre); thus, in 1308, the 26-year-old Margaret traveled with her stepson to Boulogne to witness his wedding on January 25. Margaret would exercise great influence over her niece Isabella, who was only 13 when she married Edward.

Margaret then retired to Marlborough Castle in Wiltshire, and spent the next ten years of her life doing charitable work and offering patronage to historians and architects. She was instrumental in the building of London's Grey Friars Church where she was buried following her death in 1318, age 36.

Margaret of France (1492–1549).

See Margaret of Angoulême.

Margaret of France (1523–1574).

See Margaret of Savoy.

Margaret of France (1553–1615).

See Margaret of Valois.

Margaret of Geneva

(fl. late 1100s–early 1200s)

*Countess of Savoy and poet. Born in the late 1100s; married Thomas I, count of Savoy (a troubadour); children: Amadeus IV (b. 1197), count of Savoy; Thomas (b. 1199), count of Flanders; *Beatrice of Savoy (d. 1268); Peter II (b. 1203), count of Savoy; Philip (b. 1207); Boniface, archbishop of Canterbury; and three others.*

Margaret of Germany (1237–1270)

*Landgravine of Thuringia and ancestor of house of Saxe-Coburg-Gotha. Born in February 1237; died on August 8, 1270; daughter of Frederick II, Holy Roman emperor (r. 1215–1250), and *Isabella of England (1214–1241, Holy Roman empress and daughter of King John of England); married Albert, landgrave of Thuringia; children: Frederick, margrave of Meissen and Thuringia.*

Margaret of Hainault (d. 1342)

*Countess of Artois. Name variations: Margarete of Hainault; Margaret of Hainaut. Died on October 18, 1342; daughter of John II, count of Hainault and Holland, and *Philippine of Luxemburg (d. 1311); became third wife of Robert II, count of Artois, in 1298.*

Margaret of Holland

(d. 1356)

*Countess of Hainault and Holland. Died in 1356; daughter of William III the Good, count of Holland and Hainault, and *Jeanne of Valois (c. 1294–1342, sister of Philip VI, king of France); sister of *Philippa of Hainault (1314–1369) and *Joan of Hainault (c. 1310–?); became second wife of Louis III, duke of Bavaria (r. 1294–1347), king of the Romans (r. 1314–1328), also known as Ludwig IV of Bavaria or Louis IV, Holy Roman emperor (r. 1314–1347); children: Louis the Roman, also known as Louis the Younger (1330–1365), elector of Brandenburg (r. 1350–1365); William V, duke of Bavaria (r. 1347–1358), count of Holland (r. 1354–1358), count of Hainault (r. 1356–1358); Albert I, count of Holland (r. 1353–1404); Otto V (1341–1379), elector of Brandenburg (r. 1365–1373). Louis IV's first wife was *Beatrice of Silesia.*

Margaret of Hungary

(1242–1270)

*Dominican nun, saint, and mystic. Name variations: Saint Margaret of Hungary. Born in 1242 in Dalmatia; died on January 18, 1270, in what is now Budapest, Hungary; daughter of Béla IV (b. 1206), king of Hungary (r. 1235–1270), and Queen *Maria Lascaris (fl. 1234–1242); never married; no children.*

Margaret of Hungary, born in Dalmatia in 1242, dedicated her existence to God at an early age, and, although she was the daughter of a king, lived a life of extreme asceticism and humility. Born while her parents were fleeing the Mongol invasion of Hungary, Margaret was promised to the church as an infant. At age three, she was given to the care of a community of Dominican nuns at Veszprém, and she made her formal religious vows at age 12. Margaret resisted pressure to return to the secular life, moving to another Dominican nunnery established by her parents on an island in the Danube. The island, now part of the city of Budapest, is called Margaret Island after her. She was determined to receive no special favors because of her royal birth and resolutely subjected herself to the most menial and squalid tasks as an expression of her devotion to God. Margaret's health was so weakened by her extreme asceticism, in particular her frequent fasts and refusal to sleep, that she died at the age of 28. Her feast day is January 26.

Dr. K.E. Garay,
McMaster University, Hamilton, Canada

Margaret of Huntingdon

(c. 1140–1201)

Duchess of Brittany and countess of Hereford. Born around 1140; died in 1201; interred at Sawtrey Abbey, Huntingdonshire; daughter of *Adelicia de Warrenne (d. 1178) and Henry Dunkeld, 1st earl of Huntingdon; sister of Malcolm IV and William I the Lion, both kings of Scotland, David Dunkeld, 1st earl of Huntingdon, and *Ada Dunkeld (c. 1145–1206); married Conan IV, duke of Brittany, in 1160; married Humphrey de Bohun, constable of England, in 1175; children: (first marriage) *Constance of Brittany (1161–1201); (second marriage) Henry de Bohun, 5th earl of Hereford (r. 1200–1220); Maud de Bohun (who married Henry de Oilly).

Margaret of Kent (1327–before 1352)

English royal. Name variations: Margaret Plantagenet; Margaret d'Albret. Born in 1327; died before 1352; daughter of Edmund of Woodstock (1307–1330), 1st earl of Kent, and *Margaret Wake of Liddell (c. 1299–1349); sister of *Joan of Kent (1328–1385); married Amanco d'Albret (also known as Amaneus d'Albret).

Margaret of Lancaster (1443–1509).

See Beaufort, Margaret.

Margaret of Limburg (d. 1172)

Duchess of Lower Lorraine. Died in 1172; married Godfrey III of Brabant, duke of Brabant and Lower Lorraine (r. 1142–1190), in 1155 (died 1190). Godfrey's second marriage was to Imagina von Loon (d. 1214/20).

Joanna of Sicily.
See Berengaria of Navarre for sidebar.

Margaret of Lorraine (1463–1521)

Duchess of Alençon. Name variations: Blessed Margaret of Lorraine, duchess of Alencon; Marguerite de Lorraine. Born in 1463; died on November 1, 1521; daughter of *Yolande of Vaudemont (1428–1483) and Ferrey de Vaudemont also known as Frederick, count of Vaudemont; married René (d. 1492), duke of Alençon, on May 14, 1488; children: Charles, duke of Alençon (who married *Margaret of Angoulême [1492–1549]); Françoise d'Alencon (who married Charles, duke of Vendome, and Francis II, duc de Longueville); Anne d'Alencon (who married William VII, marquis of Montferrat).

The pious Margaret of Lorraine married René, duke of Alençon, who was 23 years her senior. Widowed at 29, she continued to fulfill her duties as duchess of Alençon until her son came of age. She then became a Poor Clare at the convent of Argentan. Her feast day is November 2.

Margaret of Lorraine.

See Marguerite of Lorraine (c. 1561–?).
See Marguerite of Lorraine (fl. 1632).

Margaret of Mâle.

See Margaret of Brabant (1323–1368).
See Margaret of Flanders (1350–1405).

Margaret of Naples (fl. late 1300s)

Queen of Naples. Flourished in the late 1300s; daughter of *Marie of Naples and Charles of Durazzo; married Charles III of Durazzo (1345–1386), king of Naples (r. 1382–1386), also ruled Hungary as Charles II (r. 1385–1386); children: Ladislas I, king of Naples (r. 1386–1414); *Joanna II of Naples (1374–1435).

Margaret of Navarre (fl. 1154–1172)

Queen of Sicily and regent of Naples and Sicily. Name variations: Margherita. Queen of Sicily, 1154–1166; regent, 1166–1172; death date unknown; daughter of Garcia IV, king of Navarre (r. 1134–1150), and Marguerite de l'Aigle (d. 1141); married William I the Bad (1120–1166), king of Naples and Sicily (r. 1154–1166), in 1150; children: William II the Good (1153–1189), king of Naples and Sicily (r. 1166–1189, who married ⬅Joanna of Sicily); Henry.

The daughter of Garcia IV, king of Navarre, and *Marguerite de l'Aigle, Margaret of Navarre married William, prince of Capua, son of Roger II, ruler of the Norman kingdom of Sicily. By the time Roger II died in 1154, William's older brothers were also dead, and he inherited the throne as William I, making Margaret the queen-consort. Margaret was one of the few queens of Norman Sicily who seems to have played a significant political role in the kingdom. In part this was because her husband's inertia gave opportunity to her ambition. He preferred the luxury and comfort of isolation in the palace and hesitated to make decisions. She drove him, for example, to take revenge on the assassins of his chief minister, Maion de Bari. Her husband's indecisiveness contributed to his nickname "William the Bad."

When he died in 1166, Margaret faced the challenge of governing as regent until her 13-year-old son William II was old enough to take the throne. She struggled to impose order on a nearly chaotic situation, with the European barons conspiring to undermine the monarchy's power and Sicily's myriad ethnic and religious groups (the island was a jumble of peoples from North Africa, the Near East, and Mediterranean Europe) contending with each other. Her status as "the Spaniard" made her an outsider. At first she ruled through the eunuch Peter the Saracen, distrusting the ambitions of most of the courtiers. Margaret wrote to France, requesting that her cousin Stephen of Le Perche come and help her defend the realm. Meanwhile, many of the nobles exiled by her husband returned to Sicily. In 1167, when Stephen of Le Perche arrived with a detachment of French knights, she made him one of her chief ministers and secured for him the archbishopric of Palermo. The appointment provoked more envy among the nobility, and intrigues and conspiracies beset Margaret and the government. One of the chief conspirators was her own brother Henry, count of Montescaglioso.

With the kingdom beset by conspiracies, riots, and assassinations, Margaret of Navarre's rule was precarious. An insurrection in 1168 forced Stephen of Le Perche into exile (he went off to the Holy Land, which apparently had been his original reason for visiting the Mediterranean). The arch-conspirator and cleric, Englishman Walter Offamilio (Gualtiero Ophamil), emerged from the rebellion as the effective power behind the monarchy. Having driven Stephen from Sicily, Walter had himself elected archbishop of Palermo. Margaret tried unsuccessfully to persuade the pope to block Walter's installation, and Offamilio effectively became head of the state council. The regency ended in 1172, when William II the Good reached the age to take the throne, diminishing Margaret's role. Along with his supporters, Offamilio, who had been one of William's tutors, continued to wield political power.

SOURCES:

Chalandon, Ferdinand. *Histoire de la domination normande en Italie et en Sicile.* 2 vols. NY: Burt Franklin, 1960.

Smith, Dennis Mack. *Medieval Sicily, 800–1713.* NY: Viking Press, 1969.

Kendall W. Brown,
Professor of History, Brigham Young University, Provo, Utah

Margaret of Navarre (1492–1549).

See Margaret of Angoulême.

Margaret of Navarre (1553–1615).

See Margaret of Valois.

Margaret of Norway (1261–1283)

*Queen of Norway. Name variations: Margaret Dunkeld; Margaret of Scotland. Born on February 28, 1261, in Windsor Castle, Windsor, Berkshire, England; died on April 9, 1283, in Tönsberg, Norway; buried in Bergen, Norway; daughter of Alexander III (b. 1241), king of Scotland (r. 1249–1286), and *Margaret, queen of Scots (1240–1275); married Eirik the Priest-Hater also known as Eric II Magnusson (1268–1299), king of Norway (r. 1280–1299), on August 31, 1281; children: Margaret, Maid of Norway (c. 1283–1290).*

Daughter of the king of Scotland, Margaret of Norway was married to Eric II, king of Norway, in 1281. She died two years later while giving birth to *Margaret, Maid of Norway.* King Eric's second wife was *Isabel Bruce (c. 1278–1358), sister of Robert I the Bruce, king of Scotland.

Margaret of Norway (c. 1283–1290).

See Margaret, Maid of Norway.

Margaret of Orleans (d. 1466).

See Marguerite of Orleans.

Margaret of Orleans (1492–1549).

See Margaret of Angoulême.

Margaret of Ostrevent (c. 1376–1441).

See Margaret of Burgundy.

Margaret of Parma (1522–1586)

*Duchess of Parma, and illegitimate daughter of Charles V, who ruled the Netherlands as regent for eight years. Name variations: Margaret of Austria; Margaret or Margherita de Medici; (Italian) Margherita de Parma; (German) Margarete von Österreich; (Spanish) Marguerite of Spain. Born sometime in 1522 in the Netherlands; died in 1586 in Italy; illegitimate daughter of Charles V (1500–1558), Holy Roman emperor (also known as Charles I, king of Spain) and Johanna van der Gheenst; half-sister of Philip II, king of Spain, and *Joanna of Austria (1535–1573); married Alexander also known as Alessandro de Medici, in 1534 (died 1535); married Ottavio Farnese, duke of Parma, in 1540; children: (second marriage) Alessandro Farnese (also known as Alexander).*

Educated in the Netherlands by two female regents; lived in Italy after first marriage; appointed regent of the Netherlands by Philip II (1559); abdicated as regent (1567); returned to Netherlands for short regency (1580); died in Italy (1586).

Sixteenth-century Europe was an era characterized by female rule. During this century, an unprecedented number of women held the reins of government in several countries. While some were queens by blood, others ruled as regents for their infant sons or daughters. Still others were appointed by the reigning monarch to oversee the governance of recently annexed territory. The Netherlands (then comprised of Belgium and Holland), which had been under the rule of Habsburg kings since 1477, was governed by a succession of women. During one of the most important and tortuous events in its history, the Netherlands was ably governed by Margaret of Parma.

Margaret of Parma was born somewhere in the Netherlands in 1522. Although she was the illegitimate daughter of Holy Roman Emperor Charles V and noblewoman **Johanna van der Gheenst**, Margaret remained a favorite of her father's for many years. Very little is known about her early childhood, although it is established that she was given an excellent education fit for a legitimate princess. More significantly, she was exposed to two strong and influential female role models. From an early age, Margaret was sent to live at the royal court in Brussels where she saw firsthand the capabilities of a powerful female ruler. Until the age of eight, Margaret was brought up by her great-aunt *Margaret of Austria (1480–1530), regent of the Netherlands since 1507. When Margaret of Austria died in 1530, the government of the Netherlands was given to another woman, *Mary of Hungary (1505–1558). Thus, young Margaret grew up surrounded by capable, strong and independent women whose exercise of political power was not considered unusual.

As a daughter of the emperor, however, Margaret was a useful pawn in the marriage market. Consequently, her childhood was cut short when she was betrothed and unhappily married, at age 12, to 27-year-old Alessandro de Medici, grand duke of Tuscany. The marriage was short lived, as her husband died violently a year later. Margaret did not remain single for long, however, and was betrothed once again in 1540, this time to a younger man. At age 18, Margaret married 12-year-old Ottavio Farnese, duke of Parma. Probably as a result of their age differences, initially Margaret was not fond of her second husband. As a result, he left Italy in 1541 to go on a military campaign with Charles V. While in battle, Ottavio was injured and returned to Rome. From this point on it appears that Margaret developed more affectionate feelings for her husband. In 1545, her only child, Alessandro Farnese, was born. Little is known about Margaret's activities over the following 14 years when she lived in Italy. Her peaceful life was interrupted when she was appointed regent of the Netherlands in 1559.

The Netherlands was far from being a united country in the 16th century. It consisted of 17 provinces, each with its own semi-autonomous government made up of members from the clergy, the nobility, and towns. These provincial States had the power to raise troops and collect taxes, while every three years a meeting of delegates from each province met at the States-General. The watery landscape of the Netherlands, which consisted of bogs, rivers, marshes and lakes, made communication difficult. Nevertheless, the government of the Habsburgs, situated in Brussels, attempted to impose obedience and unity. Three years before Mary of Hungary's death in 1558, the government of the Netherlands was given to Charles V's son and heir, Philip (II).

Governing the Netherlands was becoming increasingly complicated due to religious dissent and financial difficulties. By the mid-16th century, a religious split between north and south was evident. The southern provinces tended to remain Catholic while their northern counterparts began to adhere to the reforming Protestant doctrines and, in particular, to Calvinism. Charles V's military campaigns, which included several wars, resulted in escalating taxation. Taxpaying Netherlanders were becoming ever more hostile towards the financial policies of the Habsburg government which, they felt, was requiring them to subsidize Spain. When Charles V died in 1558, Philip became king of Spain and left the Netherlands the following year. The government was taken over by 37-year-old Margaret of Parma.

Although she had lived in Italy since 1535, Margaret was popular in the Netherlands. Having been born and educated there, the people felt that she was one of their own, rather than a foreigner. Frugal in her habits, intelligent and good natured, the new regent was well liked. She was an excellent equestrian, which ensured her acceptance among members of the nobility. Margaret of Parma was also a devout, although not rigid, Roman Catholic. Her childhood confessor was Ignatius Loyola, father of the Jesuits, who instilled in her a strong sense of duty and responsibility. This was apparent in her annual practice of washing the feet of poor men, serving them food and sending them on their way with presents. Most significantly, the fact that their new regent was a woman was not troublesome to Netherlanders, as they were used to being governed by women. Margaret's problems

stemmed from the fact that Philip II intended her to act merely as his puppet. All executive power was retained by him, and she was ordered to write to him daily about everything of importance and not make any decisions without him. While these conditions were restrictive enough, Philip II's notorious tendency to agonize over every decision and, hence, cause unnecessary delays, severely undercut Margaret's ability to govern as effectively as possible.

Nevertheless, when Margaret of Parma arrived in the Netherlands in 1559 she set up her court and permanent residence in Brussels. As regent, she was advised by three councils: State, Finance, and Privy. Although many important members of the nobility sat on these councils, the most influential government minister was Antoine Perrenot, Cardinal Granvelle. Unfortunately, because he was a favorite of the king's, and had an arrogant personality as well, Granvelle was also very unpopular. In addition, Philip II's policies in the Netherlands caused increasing resentment which eventually turned into outright political rebellion. As Philip's attempts to impose these unpopular policies became more insistent, the resentment also took on religious tones. It was Margaret of Parma's misfortune to have been appointed governor and regent during these troublesome times.

When Philip II returned to Spain in 1559, he left behind 3,000 Spanish troops in the Netherlands ostensibly for protection against military action from the French. The people of the Netherlands did not view the presence of these troops in that light, however. They felt that the troops remained behind to enforce obedience. More seriously, they feared for their independence; they believed that the Netherlands would soon be reduced to the status of a Spanish colony. The issue became political when the States of the provinces refused to release any money to the central government until the Spanish troops left the country. Although Philip acceded to this request in 1561, his concession was merely a cloak for the introduction of an even more unpopular religious policy.

She did not want . . . in talents and possessed a particular turn for business.

—Friedrich Schiller

Religious problems in the Netherlands that Margaret of Parma was forced to deal with had their antecedents in the reign of her father, Charles V. Once it became apparent that the religious revolution sparked by Martin Luther was spreading, Charles V made a determined effort to stamp out heresy throughout his empire. A papal inquisition was established in 1522 and expanded in 1546, when inquisitors were given the right to question, arrest, and commit to trial anyone they suspected of being a heretic. In all of their efforts, the inquisitors were to be assisted by local magistrates and judges. In addition, anti-heresy legislation, known as placards, was introduced which included, among other things, a prohibition on reading certain books. More significantly, breaches of the placards were treated as treason and forfeiture of property was to be enforced. This not only threatened traditional inheritance customs but encroached upon the legal responsibilities of local authorities, who insisted that they had the right to try people accused of criminal acts within their boundaries. Although Protestantism had not made any serious inroads during the reign of Charles V, by the 1560s a few small, but vocal, groups of Calvinists had surfaced. When Philip II reintroduced all of his father's anti-heresy policies in 1559 as well as a new plan to reorganize the bishoprics, the stage was set for popular disturbance.

Anxiety over the new bishoprics scheme grew, and complaints that it had been developed in secret became prevalent. When Philip requested troops from the Netherlands to help the French monarchy suppress French Calvinists, Margaret hesitated. She was seriously worried that there might be a rebellion if troops from the Netherlands were sent to put down Protestants. When she called a meeting of the most important and influential nobles, they agreed to send money instead of troops. Hard on the heels of this victory, plans among the most influential nobles to oust Granvelle from the government proceeded. They chose their timing carefully, as Philip II was preoccupied with financial problems in Spain. In March 1563, the prince of Orange and the counts of Egmont and Horne sent an ultimatum to Philip indicating that they would resign unless Granvelle was dismissed. Philip refused, whereupon the three lords stopped attending council meetings. At the same time, the States of Brabant refused to grant any taxes to the government until Granvelle was dismissed.

Margaret soon realized that her government would be paralyzed unless she could persuade Philip to accede to the nobles' demands. She also had additional reasons for not supporting Granvelle. He had provided little help when she attempted to arrange an advantageous marriage for her son Alessandro, and she knew that he wrote private letters to Philip II which criticized her. Finally, Margaret realized that many people regarded her as a Granvelle supporter and that if she continued to back him, her popularity would wane. Consequently, she wrote a long letter to the king asking him to remove Granvelle. Her efforts succeeded, and Granvelle left the Netherlands in March 1564. From that point on, the nobles returned to sit on the Council of State to work closely with Margaret of Parma.

However, Margaret's efforts to govern successfully were thwarted by Philip II's intransigence over enforcing the heresy laws. In 1565, he sent several letters to the regent informing her that there was to be no compromise in this area and that none of the heresy laws were to be changed. Margaret's policy was to follow public opinion, which was lenient towards heretics as long as they did not disturb the peace. Margaret was, therefore, much more conciliatory than Philip wanted her to be. She did not, for example, arrest suspected heretics on the accusation of one person; instead, she wanted firmer evidence. Her attempts to be conciliatory fell on deaf ears. Philip was determined to stamp out heresy in the Netherlands and expected his representative to follow his orders.

Matters came to a head in December 1565 when several nobles formed a solemn league to secure the abolition of the inquisition and the moderation of the heresy laws. They drew up a document, called the Compromise, which set out the nobles' demands. By early 1566, several nobles had resigned from the government Councils and informed Margaret that they would not carry out the king's commands. On April 5, a group of 300 armed nobles presented a "Request" to Margaret which demanded suspension of the heresy laws and a new legal settlement of religious problems in consultation with the States-General. This event seriously compromised her authority, primarily because no one had been able, or willing, to prevent this group from submitting their demands to the regent—at gunpoint. The following day, Margaret agreed to instruct all magistrates and judges to be more lenient towards heretics. Thus, although she did not refuse their demands outright, she remained somewhat vague on the future of the heresy laws. Some dissidents, however, interpreted this as a sign that religious freedom was to be proclaimed, and several religious exiles returned to the Netherlands where they began to preach openly.

By August 1566, public preaching led to iconoclastic riots in several small towns. Although the groups were not large, they were well organized and met with little resistance from the local population. Margaret of Parma, however, saw these riots as proof that concessions to Protestants would only lead to disorder and the collapse of public authority. The only solution she felt was to take military action. When the nobles refused her request for troops, she reluctantly conceded to their requests for freedom of public Protestant worship in those areas where it was already taking place. This Accord did not, however, prevent militant Calvinists from continuing to pillage and destroy Catholic churches. These iconoclastic riots began to erode public sympathy for Protestants in the Netherlands and when Margaret sent garrisons to several towns in November, she had a majority of public support behind her.

In early 1567, the most prominent nobles threw their support behind the regent, and the rebellion began to collapse. By the end of May, the revolt was over, and open Calvinist worship was at an end. Margaret informed Philip that Spanish troops were not necessary and that order had been restored. Unfortunately, Philip had already sent Fernando Alvarz de Toledo, duke of Alva, to the Netherlands at the head of a large Spanish force. Although Alva was only to act as captain-general, Margaret soon realized that he had ambitions to be regent. When he arrived in August, Alva refused to comply with her request not to billet his troops in those towns that had remained loyal to the government during the rebellion. Alva was determined to establish a "new order" in the Netherlands which would not tolerate any dissent from Philip II's policies. Recognizing that her pleas for tolerance would fall on deaf ears, Margaret of Parma resigned as regent of the Netherlands and left Brussels in December 1567.

Margaret returned to Italy, where she settled down to a more peaceful life. Little is known about how she spent the following 13 years. When her son Alessandro was appointed regent of the Netherlands in 1578, the country was just as unsettled as it had been during his mother's regency. Demands from the nobles to rescind Parma's regency led Philip II to call upon the resources of Margaret once again. Thus, Alessandro remained in the Netherlands as military commander, while in 1580 his mother, at age 58, was once again appointed to govern. Although she set up her court at Namur, mother and son refused to cooperate with the nobles and the administration of the government soon ground to a halt. Realizing that this situation was getting them nowhere, the nobles agreed to have Alessandro return as regent. Margaret was no longer needed and returned to Italy in November 1581.

The last years of Margaret of Parma's life are obscure. All that is known is that she died, at age 64, in Italy.

SOURCES:

Hopkins, Lisa. *Women Who Would Be Kings: Female Rulers of the Sixteenth Century.* London: Vision Press, 1991.

Motley, John L. *The Rise of the Dutch Republic: A History.* NY: Thomas Y. Crowell, 1901.

Parker, Geoffrey. *The Dutch Revolt.* Harmondsworth: Penguin, 1979.

Tracy, James. *Holland under Habsburg Rule, 1506–1566.* Berkeley, CA: University of California Press, 1990.

Margaret McIntyre,
Instructor of Women's History at Trent University,
Peterborough, Ontario, Canada

Margaret of Parma (b. 1612)

Duchess of Parma. Name variations: Margherita of Parma; Margherita de Medici; Margaret de Medici; Margaret Farnese. Born in 1612; daughter of Cosimo II de Medici (1590–1620), grand duke of Tuscany (r. 1609–1620), and *Maria Magdalena of Austria (1589–1631); married Odoardo or Edward Farnese, duke of Parma (1612–1646, r. 1622–1646), in 1628.

In 1628, 17-year-old Margaret de Medici was married to Edward Farnese, the duke of Parma, to strengthen ties between the house of Tuscany and Parma, as well as Tuscany's position in Italy. Two generations later, when the throne of Tuscany became vacant, Margaret's descendants became the rightful heirs.

Margaret of Parma (1847–1893)

*Duchess of Madrid. Born on January 1, 1847; died on January 29, 1893; daughter of *Louise of Bourbon-Berry (1819–1864) and Charles III, duke of Parma; married Charles, duke of Madrid, on February 4, 1867; children: *Blanche of Bourbon (1868–1949); Elvira of Bourbon (1871–1929); Beatrix of Bourbon (b. 1874, who married Fabrizio, prince Massimo); Alicia of Bourbon (b. 1876, who married Friedrich, prince of Schönburg-Waldenburg, and Lino del Prete).*

Margaret of Pomerania (d. 1282)

Queen of Denmark. Name variations: Margaret of Pommerania. Died in December 1282; daughter of Sambor, duke of Pomerania; married Christopher I (1219–1259), king of Denmark (r. 1252–1259), in 1248; children: Eric V (or VII) Clipping (b. around 1249), king of Denmark (r. 1259–1286); Valdemar also known as Waldemar; Niels; Matilda Christofsdottir (died around 1300, who married Albert III, margrave of Brandenburg); Margaret Christofsdottir (died around 1306, who married John II, count of Holstein).

Margaret of Pomerania married Christopher I, king of Denmark, in 1248. Following his death in 1259, Margaret was regent for her son Eric V during his minority.

Margaret of Provence (1221–1295)

*Queen of France. Name variations: Marguerite de Provence; Marguerite of Provence. Born in Provence in 1221 (some sources cite 1219); died in 1295 in France; daughter of Raymond Berengar IV (some sources cite V), count of Provence, and Beatrice of Savoy (d. 1268); sister of *Eleanor of Provence (c. 1222–1291), *Sancha of Provence (c. 1225–1261), and Beatrice of Provence (d. 1267, who married Charles of Anjou, brother of Louis IX); married Louis IX, also known as Saint Louis (1214–1270), king of France (r. 1226–1270), in May 1234; children: eleven, including Philip III the Bold (b. 1245), king of France (r. 1270–1285); John, count of Nevers; Robert (1256–1317), count of Clermont; *Isabella Capet (who married Theobald of Navarre); *Margaret Capet (d. 1271, who married John of Brabant); *Agnes Capet (1260–1327); *Blanche of France (1253–1321, who married Ferdinand of Castile).*

Margaret of Provence was the oldest daughter of Raymond Berengar of Provence and *Beatrice of Savoy. At 14, she was betrothed and married to the king of France, Louis IX (Saint Louis). Louis and Margaret were deeply devoted to one another despite the political reasons that brought them together, and had 11 children. When Louis left Paris to lead the Seventh Crusade around 1244, Margaret accompanied him at his request; his mother, the indomitable *Blanche of Castile (1188–1252), remained as regent of France. This crusade (like all except the first) was a disaster, and the army returned home several years later.

Blanche of Castile was extremely jealous of Margaret of Provence, who was reportedly both beautiful and highly educated, and Blanche did her best to keep the couple apart. Chroniclers even wrote of the king and queen having to sneak through the castle in Paris at night to meet one another like lovers, because they feared Blanche's reaction if caught. When Blanche died in 1252, Margaret and Louis were free to act as they pleased. Margaret tried to take over Blanche's position as Louis' primary advisor, but she did not have the experience or the political shrewdness required, and Louis would not entrust her with important matters as he had his mother.

She accompanied her husband on the Eighth Crusade in 1270, where Louis died in battle at Tunis. Mourning him deeply, Margaret returned to France a widow and saw her son crowned king as Philip III. She then retired to her estates, where she died at age 60.

SOURCES:

Anderson, Bonnie S., and Judith P. Zinsser. *A History of Their Own.* Vol. I. NY: Harper & Row, 1988.

Gies, Frances, and Joseph Gies. *Women in the Middle Ages.* NY: Harper and Row, 1978.

Laura York,
Riverside, California

Margaret of Savoy (d. 1483)

*Countess of St. Paul. Name variations: Marguerite de Savoie. Died on March 9, 1483; daughter of *Anne of Lusignan and Louis I, duke of Savoy (r. 1440–1465); married Peter also known as Pierre II, count of St. Paul (r. 1476–1482); children: *Marie of Luxemburg (d. 1546).*

Margaret of Savoy (1523–1574)

Duchess of Savoy. Name variations: Margaret of France; Marguerite de France or Marguerite de Savoie; Marguerite of Berry, duchess of Berry. Reigned from 1550 to 1574. Born in 1523; daughter of Francis I, king of France (r. 1515–1547), and *Claude de France (1499–1524); sister of Henry II, king of France (r. 1547–1559); sister-in-law of *Catherine de Medici; married Emmanuel Philibert (1528–1580), 10th duke of Savoy (r. 1553–1580), in June 1559; children: Charles Emmanuel I (1562–1630), duke of Savoy (r. 1580–1630).

Called the Minerva, or the Pallas, of France, Margaret of Savoy wrote verses and was a patron of the young school of poets led by Pierre de Ronsard. Cherished by her brother, Henry II, king of France, Margaret was offered the Piedmont as her dowry in marriage to the duke of Savoy. "All that we had conquered and held in Piedmont was given back in one hour," wrote Saint-Beuve, "the greater part of France and Piedmont murmured and said it was too much." Even so, he wrote, she was so beloved in France and "in the lands and countries of her husband that when she died tears flowed from the eyes of all, both great and small."

Margaret of Savoy (fl. 1609–1612)

Duchess of Mantua. Name variations: Margherita of Savoy. Flourished between 1609 and 1612; daughter of *Catherine of Spain (1567–1597) and Charles Emmanuel I the Great, duke of Savoy (r. 1580–1630); sister of Victor Amadeus I (1587–1637), duke of Savoy (r. 1630–1637); married Francis also known as Francesco Gonzaga (1586–1612), 5th duke of Mantua (r. 1612); children: *Maria Gonzaga (1609–1660, who married Carlo, count of Rethel); Louis also known as Ludovico (1611–1612); Maria Margherita Gonzaga (b. 1612).

Margaret of Savoy (1851–1926)

Queen of Italy. Name variations: Margherita of Savoy; Margherita de Savoia. Born in 1851; died in 1926; daughter of *Elizabeth of Saxony (1830–1912) and Ferdinand of Savoy (1822–1855), duke of Genoa; married her cousin Humbert I or Umberto I (1844–1900, son of *Marie Adelaide of Austria and Victor Emmanuel II), king of Italy (r. 1878–1900); children: Victor Emmanuel III (1869–1947), king of Italy (r. 1900–1946, abdicated).

A proud and beautiful woman, Margaret of Savoy entered into a dynastic and loveless marriage with her cousin Umberto I who ascended the throne as the second king of Italy in 1878. Though a fervent nationalist who was also religious to the point of bigotry, Margaret could still charm republicans and inaugurated a new era at the Court Ball in 1875 when she attempted to reconcile Roman society by dancing the first quadrille with the leftist minister Baron Giovanni Nicotera. Later she would grumble that leaders of the Left were inexpert dancers. Considered a "queen to her fingertips," Margaret of Savoy would live long enough to back Benito Mussolini in his rise to power. Her husband had been assassinated at Monza by an anarchist in 1900.

Margaret of Saxony (c. 1416–1486)

Duchess and electress of Saxony. Name variations: Margarethe. Born in 1416 or 1417 in Wiener Neustadt; died on February 12, 1486, in Altenburg; daughter of *Cimburca of Masovia (c. 1396–1429) and Ernest (d. 1424, son of Leopold III of Austria); married Frederick II the Gentle (1412–1464), duke and elector of Saxony; children: *Anne of Saxony (1437–1512); Ernest of Saxony (b. 1441), elector of Saxony; Albert the Bold (b. 1443), duke of Saxony.

Margaret of Saxony (1449–1501)

Electress of Brandenburg. Born in 1449; died on July 13, 1501; daughter of William III the Brave of Saxony (b. 1425), duke of Luxemburg, and *Anne of Austria (1432–1462); married John Cicero (1455–1499), elector of Brandenburg (r. 1486–1499), on August 25, 1476; children: Joachim I Nestor (1484–1535), elector of Brandenburg (r. 1499–1535); *Anna of Brandenburg (1487–1514); *Ursula of Brandenburg (1488–1510).

Margaret of Saxony (1469–1528)

Duchess of Brunswick. Name variations: Margaret of Saxony Wettin. Born on August 4, 1469; died on December 7, 1528; daughter of Ernest of Saxony (b. 1441), elector of Saxony; sister of *Christina of Saxony (1461–1521), queen of Norway and queen of Denmark; married Henry (1466–1532), duke of Brunswick (r. 1471–1532), on February 27, 1487; children: Otto III of Luneburg; Ernest the Pious (b. 1497), duke of Luneburg; Francis, duke of Brunswick.

Margaret of Saxony (1840–1858)

Princess of Saxony. Born on May 24, 1840; died on September 15, 1858; daughter of *Amalia of Bavaria

(1801–1877) and Johann also known as John (1801–1873), king of Saxony (r. 1854–1873); became first wife of Karl Ludwig also known as Charles Louis (1833–1896), archduke of Austria, on November 4, 1856. Charles Louis' second wife was *Maria Annunziata (1843–1871); his third was *Maria Theresa of Portugal.

Margaret of Scotland (c. 1046–1093).
See Margaret, St.

Margaret of Scotland (1261–1283).
See Margaret of Norway.

Margaret of Scotland (1424–1445)

Scottish poet. Name variations: Margaret Stuart or Stewart; Marguerite d'Écosse. Born in Scotland on December 25, 1424; died in Chalons, Champagne, France, on August 16, 1445; eldest daughter of James I, king of Scotland (r. 1406–1437), and Joan Beaufort (c. 1410–1445); married Louis XI (1423–1483), king of France (r. 1461–1483), on June 24, 1436; no children.

In 1436, at age 13, Louis XI (then the dauphin) married the charming Scottish princess and poet Margaret of Scotland, daughter of James I, king of Scotland, and *Joan Beaufort. It is said that her marriage to Louis was so wretched that when she died at age 22, her parting words were: "Oh! fie on life! Speak to me no more of it." Louis later married *Charlotte of Savoy (c. 1442–1515), who became the mother of *Anne of Beaujeu (c. 1460–1522).

Margaret of Spain (1651–1673).
See Margaret Theresa of Spain.

Margaret of Sweden (1882–1920).
See Margaret of Connaught.

Margaret of Thouars (r. 1365–1377).
See Marguerite de Thouars.

Margaret of Turenne

Countess of Angoulême. Married Aimar IV, count of Limoges; married Guillaume also known as William IV Taillefer, count of Angoulême (r. 1140–1178); children: (second marriage) Vulgrin III Taillefer, count of Angoulême (1178–1181); William; Ademar.

Margaret of Valois (c. 1272–1299).
See Margaret of Anjou.

Margaret of Valois (1492–1549).
See Margaret of Angoulême.

Margaret of Valois (1553–1615)

French princess and queen of Navarre who was the sister of three French kings and the first wife of Henry of Navarre, the future King Henry IV. Name variations: Marguerite of Valois or Marguerite de Valois; Marguerite d'Angoulême; Margaret of Angoulême or Angouleme; Margaret or Marguerite of Anjou; Margaret of France; Margaret of Navarre; Queen Margot. Born on May 14, 1553, at St. Germain-en-Laye; died of pneumonia on March 27, 1615, in Paris; third daughter of Henry II, king of France (r. 1547–1559), and Catherine de Medici (1519–1589); sister of Francis II (r. 1559–1560), Charles IX (r. 1560–1574), Henry III (r. 1574–1589), all kings of France, and *Elizabeth of Valois (1545–1568), queen of Spain; married Henry of Navarre (future Henry IV, king of France, r. 1589–1610), on August 18, 1572 (divorced, December 1599); no children.

Educated at French royal court; at age 19, became queen of Navarre (1572); marriage sparked St. Bartholomew's Day Massacre; estranged from Henry for most of her marriage; forced into 19-year exile by her brother, King Henry III; returned to Paris (1605).

Publications: Memoires et lettres de Marguerite de Valois (n.d.).

On August 18, 1572, thousands gathered outside Notre Dame Cathedral in Paris to witness the marriage of the beautiful, young, and Catholic Margaret of Valois to the plain, Protestant Henry of Navarre (the future King Henry IV). Henry of Navarre was dressed in pale yellow satin embroidered with pearls and precious stones while his 19-year-old bride stood next to him dressed in a purple velvet gown embroidered with fleurs-de-lys and a cape of spotted ermine. Her head was covered by a wide, blue, jewel-encrusted mantle with four yards of train. The marriage was not a love match but rather an affair of state with the hoped-for intention of ending more than ten years of religious civil wars in France. Margaret was a reluctant bride and, according to legend, when she did not respond to the marriage question, her brother King Charles IX pushed her crown so that her head nodded "yes." Festivities continued over the next three days, and, although the marriage was intended to reconcile French Protestants (Huguenots) and Catholics, it precipitated one of the worst and bloodiest massacres in French history. Thus began the ill-fated career of Margaret of Valois, also known as Queen Margot.

Margaret of Valois was born on May 14, 1553, at the Palace of St. Germain-en-Laye. She was the third daughter of King Henry II of France and his Florentine wife, *Catherine de Medici. Margaret grew up in a large family with eight siblings. After the death of her father in July 1559, three of her brothers successively held the French throne. Margaret spent most of her early childhood away from court and grew up in the royal palaces of St. Germain and Amboise. Throughout her childhood and for most of her adult life, France was plagued by religious and political strife.

Dynastic politics ensured that the Valois kings of France, by pushing territorial claims in Italy, remained in conflict with the Spanish Habsburgs throughout most of the 16th century. More significantly, after the death of Henry II the succession of boy kings led to a resurgence of Protestantism in France and eight civil wars. More than half of the French nobility supported Protestantism and both sides were under the leadership of powerful noble houses. The Catholics were led by the influential Guise family who held important positions in the French government. The Huguenots were guided by several princes of the blood, the most important of whom, the Bourbons, came from the small kingdom of Navarre in southwestern France. Both sides were able to mobilize private armies and both sought aid from other European Protestant and Catholic countries. When Catherine de Medici became regent for her young sons, her policy was to maintain the authority of the monarchy as queen mother and to try for some kind of reconciliation with the Huguenots. Although she wanted to steer a middle course, her attempts at toleration and peace settlements were ignored by both sides.

While Margaret was sheltered from much of the turmoil during her early childhood, in March 1564, at age 12, she accompanied her mother and two brothers, King Charles IX and Henry, duke of Anjou (the future Henry III), on a two-year journey through France. It was hoped that by traveling through the kingdom, peace and religious harmony would be restored. Included in the royal family's train was young Henry of Navarre. Intelligent, bold and determined, Henry of Navarre was already exhibiting strong leadership qualities as well as an unfortunate tendency to gamble and spend money. Henry of Navarre had been raised in the Protestant faith by his mother *Jeanne d'Albret and

was next in line to the French throne if Charles IX and his two brothers died without male heirs. Henry of Navarre's leadership abilities were soon put to the test when he became leader of the Huguenot forces in 1569.

In that same year, Margaret's brother Henry of Anjou was appointed lieutenant-general and head of the Catholic army. Wishing to remain in his mother's good graces while he was away from court, Anjou asked Margaret to be his special agent with Catherine de Medici. Writing several years later in her *Memoires*, Margaret saw this as a turning point in her life. She noted: "I had been brought up in such awe of the Queen, my mother, that not only did I not dare to speak to her, but if she merely looked at me I trembled with fear of having done something to displease her." Her brother's confidence in her pleased Margaret, and she wrote that "it seemed to me that I had suddenly become something more than I was until then."

Following her brother's instructions, Margaret ensured that she was the first person in Catherine's presence in the morning and the last in her presence at day's end. For the next several months, she spent two or three hours daily talking with her mother during which time she never failed to mention Anjou's name. Suddenly, however, Margaret lost her mother's trust. Although it was never proven, Anjou accused Margaret of being in love with the duke of Guise and wanting to marry him. This conflicted with the queen's own plans for the marriage of her daughter. Margaret denied the accusation but noted in her *Memoirs*, "I would remember for the rest of my life the injury my brother had done me." According to the Spanish ambassador, when Charles IX heard the accusation of Margaret's affair with Guise he summoned her to his bedchamber and beat her severely. Both Charles and Catherine had different plans for Margaret's marriage.

Fearing that peace in France would never be achieved, Catherine de Medici began negotiations in 1570 for a peace treaty with the Huguenots. The treaty would be sealed by a marriage alliance between the Valois and Bourbon royal houses. Two years later, a formal contract for the marriage of Margaret of Valois and Henry of Navarre was signed in April 1572. Although the marriage was intended to engender dynastic stabilization as well as religious peace, it was able to do neither. First, Henry of Navarre's mother Jeanne d'Albret, who was opposed to the marriage, died suddenly two months before the wedding, in June 1572. While it is certain that she died of natural causes, the Huguenots spread a rumor that Catherine de Medici had poisoned her. Second, and more seriously, the marriage precipitated one of the worst massacres in French history.

Though the days following the wedding were spent celebrating, there were other, more sinister, forces at hand. At a secret meeting of the royal council, it was decided that Gaspard de Coligny, who was one of the most important and influential Huguenot leaders, had become too dangerous. Not only did Coligny exercise considerable influence over Charles IX (through witchcraft, some claimed), but he was urging the king to wage war against Spain. Fearing that all plans for peace would be jeopardized, the council decided that Coligny must be killed. On August 22, just four days after the wedding of Margaret and Henry of Navarre, Coligny was shot by an assassin hired by the ultra-Catholic Guise faction. Unfortunately for them, he was only wounded. It was then that a fateful decision was made. Not only was Coligny to be killed but other Huguenot nobles as well. Considering that over 1,500 of them were in Paris to celebrate the wedding, it was believed that a perfect opportunity had presented itself for their permanent extermination.

> [Margaret of Valois] was the greatest princess of her time, daughter, sister, and wife of great kings, yet despite these advantages she became the plaything of Fate, was despised by those who should have been her subjects, and saw another in the place she herself should have filled.
>
> —Cardinal Richelieu

On the morning of August 24, St. Bartholomew's Day, armed men broke into the houses of Coligny and other Protestant nobles and murdered them. Before these murders had ended, the Catholic populace of Paris began to riot; they murdered and mutilated, then degraded the corpses of anyone they suspected of being a Protestant. The victims numbered over 2,000. As news of the massacre spread, similar riots broke out in other French towns. Thus, the marriage that was supposed to engender peace merely crystallized existing hostilities.

After the St. Bartholomew's Day Massacre there was no longer any distance between the crown and the Catholic leaders. More significantly, the Huguenots could no longer claim that they were only fighting against the king's evil advisors. Consequently, several Huguenot writers began to publish political tracts in which they provided justification for armed rebellion against the king. In essence, both sides became increasingly rigid and less willing to compromise. Catherine de Medici's attempt to steer a middle ground had failed.

Margaret knew nothing of the plans for the assassination of Coligny or the massacre but, as she noted in her *Memoires*: "All the harm that ever came to me in life came through marriage. Do not let anyone say that marriages are made in heaven; the gods would not commit so great an injustice." Her husband was imprisoned for a short time in the Louvre and, fearing for his life, converted to Catholicism. For the next several years, Margaret, her husband and her youngest brother, Francis, duke of Alençon (not to be confused with her other brother King Francis II who had died in 1560), were kept at court under house arrest. Although they had access to the king and the court, they were not allowed to leave the grounds except under heavy guard. In addition, it became apparent that Margaret's marriage was not a happy one. Neither she nor Henry were sexually attracted to one another nor did they have many mutual interests. Margaret was a very intelligent, vivacious and well-educated princess. She could read and write poetry, was fluent in Latin, and studied Biblical and classical literature as well as philosophy. She also loved living at court and, in particular, dancing and entertaining. Henry of Navarre, on the other hand, was more interested in military tactics, hunting and fighting rather than learning the accoutrements of a successful courtier. Within a year after their marriage, both Margaret and Henry had taken lovers and rarely spoke to one another.

Their situation changed when Charles IX died on May 30, 1574, and was succeeded by his brother Anjou, now Henry III. Unfortunately for Margaret, the enmity between herself and her brother was not alleviated by his succession to the throne. He remained deeply suspicious and kept a close watch on her. Two years later, Henry of Navarre finally escaped from court, in February 1576, following the duke of Alençon who had escaped the previous September. The king accused Margaret of plotting and aiding their escapes and promptly ordered her confined to her bedroom. Here she remained for the next several months. While under confinement, Margaret spent much of her time reading. More significantly, she engaged in a secret correspondence with her husband. Although they both knew that their marriage was one in name only, they also realized that the alliance remained mutually beneficial. Margaret was queen of Navarre and second lady in France while Henry

Margaret
of Valois
(1553–1615)

of Navarre had access to the intrigues at court through his wife.

In May 1576, Margaret was released from her confinement. Her main concern now was forwarding the career of Alençon who had am-

bitions to lead a French army into Flanders. The majority of Catholics who lived in the southern Netherlands were unwilling to follow a Calvinist leader in the rebellion against Philip II of Spain. As a result they turned to France for help. While Henry III was not a friend of the Spanish king, he was not willing to engage in a full-scale war with Spain while civil war continued to rage in France. Nevertheless, Margaret wanted to help her younger brother realize his ambitions, and in July 1577 she journeyed to Flanders on the pretence of visiting a spa and recovering her health. In reality, she spent most of her time there trying to convince the Flemish nobles to invite Alençon to lead them.

After passing six weeks in the southern Netherlands, during which time she was royally and lavishly entertained, Margaret returned to France. Although the Flemish nobles were more than willing to accept Alençon's help, Henry III, who was insanely jealous of anyone who outshone him, kept the duke at court ostensibly as an important and necessary member of the royal council. Margaret, having accomplished her mission, decided that it was time to reconcile with her husband whom she had not seen for two years. Her purpose was to reinstate good relations between Navarre and the king. After his escape from court in 1576, Henry of Navarre had instantly revoked his conversion to Catholicism and become the leader of the Huguenots once more. The sixth war of religion had just ended when Margaret returned from Flanders, and she was bent on keeping the peace. As she noted in a letter to a friend, "I am determined to do everything in my power for the king in whatever will not be prejudicial to the greatness and maintenance of my husband; for I would prefer death to war."

On October 12, 1578, Margaret made her formal entrance into the kingdom of Navarre. For the next four years, she remained in her husband's kingdom, primarily at the royal court in Nerac where she felt most at home. It was neither as austere nor as Protestant as the other towns in Navarre, and Henry of Navarre embellished the royal palace with new tapestries and furniture as well as glassware and mirrors. He also lavished gifts upon his wife, including several expensive gowns and jewelry.

Margaret of Valois was now 25 years old and was one of the most accomplished and beautiful women in France. Her court was filled with poets, musicians, and philosophers whom the young queen of Navarre dazzled and charmed. She was pleased with her surroundings and noted that "our court was so brilliant that we had no cause to regret our absence from the court of France." In addition, she was also becoming increasingly proud of her husband. As the civil wars continued, Henry of Navarre was often absent on various military campaigns.

After one particularly brilliant victory in 1580, her pride was evident: "My husband showed himself not only a prince of renown but a resourceful and daring captain."

Despite the happy marital relations, rifts began to appear when Henry of Navarre fell in love with one of Margaret's ladies-in-waiting. Furthermore, Margaret was becoming increasingly upset that she was unable to become pregnant. Thus, in 1582 when her mother invited her to return to Paris, Margaret accepted. During this time, she fell in love with Jacques de Harlay, marquess of Chanvallon, who, although married, assured Margaret that he loved her.

Once Margaret moved into her own house in Paris, she and Chanvallon were able to visit one another more frequently. Unfortunately, this only aroused the ire of the king and the queen mother. By August 1583, Henry III ordered Margaret to leave Paris. The reasons for this remain cloudy, but it is generally concluded that her affair with Chanvallon had become too public. In addition, she continued to support her younger brother's ambitions in the Netherlands, against the wishes of the king. In any event, Margaret received no support from her husband who was involved in a new love affair of his own.

Relations with Navarre went from bad to worse when Francis, duke of Alençon, died on June 10, 1584. With no Valois heirs left, Henry of Navarre was next in line to the French throne. Ultimately, Alençon's death initiated the last of the religious civil wars, popularly known as the "War of Three Henrys," between Henry of Guise, the head of the Catholic party, Henry of Navarre the Huguenot leader, and the king, Henry III. By March 1585, Margaret left Paris for the Catholic city of Agen, believing that she had to protect it from her husband's forces. Unfortunately, Margaret was not an effective leader, and she soon became unpopular with the townsfolk. In an effort to fortify the city, she raised taxes, and the situation reached a climax when she refused to allow the townspeople to leave the city when plague broke out. Chaos and rebellion were the result, and Margaret narrowly escaped. She spent the winter of 1586 at Carlat but was eventually captured by the king's soldiers and taken to the mountain fortress of Usson.

This signaled the end of Margaret of Valois' exploits; she spent the next 19 years of her life imprisoned in the Castle of Usson. While war continued to rage on in France, Margaret whiled away her time peacefully, reading and establishing her own court. As always, poets, philosophers and musicians flocked to the court of the beautiful queen of Navarre and, although she was not allowed to leave Usson, she was never isolated or alone. She devoted much of her time to writing her memoirs and entertaining guests.

While Margaret lived peacefully, events in France changed the political situation substantially. Catherine de Medici died in January 1589 and eight months later, in August 1589, her last surviving son, King Henry III, was assassinated. Margaret's husband Henry of Navarre became king of France as Henry IV, and the civil wars finally came to an end. Realizing that his religion would remain a problem, Henry of Navarre again converted to Catholicism in 1593. From this point on, he also sent messages to Margaret requesting an annulment. Aware their marriage was over and that she would never be able to provide him with an heir, Margaret agreed. Her conditions were primarily financial. She asked for an annual allowance and full payment of her debts. Finally, in December 1599, Margaret and Henry of Navarre were granted an annulment on the grounds that their marriage had been coerced. She was allowed to retain her title as queen of Navarre, to which was added that of duchess of Valois. Ironically, from this point on Margaret's relations with Henry of Navarre were warm and friendly.

In 1605, Margaret returned to Paris. She remained on good terms with Henry IV and was particularly fond of his second wife, *Marie de Medici. When Marie gave birth to Henry IV's son and heir, the future Louis XIII, Margaret grew very close to the dauphin and eventually named him as her heir. In Paris, Margaret once again bought a house in which she established her own court. Although she had gained weight, wore too much makeup, and dressed in outdated fashions, she was no political embarrassment to Henry IV. She had promised him her undivided loyalty and kept her word.

When Henry IV was assassinated in 1610, Margaret became even closer to Marie de Medici, who acted as regent for the ten-year-old king. In 1614, Margaret caught a chill from which she never recovered. Her health steadily deteriorated and on March 27, 1615, at age 61, Margaret of Valois died of pneumonia.

SOURCES:

Haldane, Charlotte. *Queen of Hearts: Marguerite of Valois ("La Reine Margot") 1553–1615.* London: Constable, 1968.

Mariejol, Jean. *Daughter of the Medicis: The Romantic Story of Marguerite de Valois.* London: Harper and Brothers, 1930.

SUGGESTED READING:

Dumas, Alexander. *La Reine Margot* (novel).

Heritier, Jean. *Catherine de Medici.* NY: St. Martin's Press, 1963.

Mahoney, Irene. *Royal Cousin: The Life of Henri IV of France.* NY: Doubleday, 1970.

Waldman, Milton, *Biography of a Family: Catherine de Medici and her Children.* Boston, MA: Houghton Mifflin, 1936.

RELATED MEDIA:

Intolerance (123 min. silent film), starring *Lillian Gish, *Mae Marsh, Georgia Pearce, Douglas Fairbanks, directed by D.W. Griffith, 1916.

La Reine Margot (film), starring *Jeanne Moreau, directed by Jean Dreville, 1954.

Queen Margot (162 min. film), starring Isabelle Adjani and Daniel Auteuil, directed by Patrice Chereau, 1994.

Margaret McIntyre,
Instructor of Women's History at Trent University, Peterborough, Ontario, Canada

Margaret of Vendôme

*Duchess of Nevers. Name variations: Margaret of Vendome. Married Francis II, duke of Nevers (d. 1595); children: Jacques, duke of Nevers (r. 1562–1563); *Henrietta of Cleves, duchess of Nevers (r. 1564–1601); and two other daughters.*

Margaret of Westminster (c. 1282–1318).

See Margaret of France.

Margaret of York (1446–1503)

*Duchess of Burgundy and religious patron. Name variations: Margaret Plantagenet; Margaret of Burgundy; Margeret. Born into the House of York on May 3, 1446, at Fotheringhay Castle in Yorkshire, England; died on November 28, 1503, in Malines, Flanders; interred at the Church of the Cordeliers, Malines; daughter of Richard Neville (b. 1411), duke of York, and Cecily Neville (1415–1495); sister of Edward IV (1442–1483), king of England (r. 1461–1470, 1471–1483), George (d. 1478), duke of Clarence, Richard III (1452–1485), king of England (r. 1483–1485), Edmund (d. 1460), earl of Rutland, Edward (d. 1471), prince of Wales, *Elizabeth de la Pole (1444–1503, wife of John de la Pole, duke of Suffolk); became third wife of Charles the Bold (1433–1477), duke of Burgundy (r. 1467–1477), on July 3, 1468; no children.*

Margaret of York was the daughter of Richard Neville, duke of York, and *Cecily Neville; two of her brothers, Edward IV and Richard III, held the throne as the Yorkist monarchs. Her family arranged a marriage for her as a means of securing French support for the ongoing Wars of the Roses between the Yorkists (whose symbol was the white rose) and the Lancastrians (who used the red rose). Thus, in her early teens Margaret moved to France to wed Charles the Bold, duke of Burgundy. Margaret had been well educated in England, and possessed both a deep piety and a great love of learning. She is primarily remembered as a patron of the church, especially the Order of Poor Clares. She gave generously of her substantial wealth to support and establish religious institutions.

In addition, Margaret was an avid book collector. In her possession was a famous manuscript on the life of the religious reformer *Colette (1381–1447). The book was richly illuminated and cost a huge sum of money; on her deathbed, however, Margaret left it not to her family but to the Poor Clares of Ghent, asking them to pray for her soul in return. Duchess Margaret outlived her husband by 26 years, in which time she gained a reputation as a devout and holy woman; she was greatly mourned on her death at age 57.

SOURCES:
LaBarge, Margaret. *A Small Sound of the Trumpet: Women in Medieval Life.* Boston: Beacon Press, 1986.

SUGGESTED READING:
Weightman, Christine. *Margaret of York, Duchess of Burgundy 1446–1503.* NY: St. Martins Press, 1989.

Laura York,
Riverside, California

Margaret of Ypres (fl. 1322)

Surgeon of Paris. Flourished in 1322 in Paris.

Margaret of Ypres, a well-known Paris surgeon, built a successful practice using her empirical knowledge and common-sense methods. In 1322, she was caught in the ban on unlicensed physicians issued by the faculty of the University of Paris. Rather than being meant to ensure good medicine for Parisians, this restriction was principally designed to eliminate competition for university-trained doctors. Although it affected some male practitioners who were unable to afford formal schooling, the ban primarily affected women, who by definition were prohibited from such scholarship. Margaret was arrested for practicing without a degree but was not held in custody long. It is unknown whether she continued working after this period or not.

SOURCES:
Klapisch-Zuber, Christiane, ed. *A History of Women in the West, vol. II: Silences of the Middle Ages.* Cambridge: Belknap/Harvard, 1992.
Uitz, Erika. *The Legend of Good Women: The Liberation of Women in Medieval Cities.* Wakefield, RI: Moyer Bell, 1988.

Laura York,
Riverside, California

Margaret Rose (1930—)

English royal princess. Name variations: Princess Margaret Rose; Margaret Windsor; Margaret Armstrong-Jones; countess of Snowdon. Born on August 21, 1930, in Glamis Castle, Tayside, her mother's ancestral home in Scotland; second daughter of Albert Frederick Arthur George, 13th duke of York, later known as George VI, king of England (r. 1936–1952), and Elizabeth Bowes-Lyon (b. 1900); sister of Elizabeth II, queen of England (r. 1952—); educated privately by governesses and at a small school at Windsor Castle; married Anthony Armstrong-Jones, earl of Snowdon (a photographer), on May 6, 1960 (divorced 1978); children: David Armstrong-Jones (b. November 3, 1961), Viscount Linley; Sarah Armstrong-Jones (b. May 1, 1964).

Four years younger than her sister Queen *Elizabeth II, Princess Margaret Rose grew from a doll-like child into a beautiful, charming woman. "Margaret was also spoiled," wrote **Unity Hall**, "because her parents were aware that all her life she must play second fiddle to her older, more serious sister." Like Elizabeth, Margaret was educated privately at home and at the Royal School at Windsor Castle. She was described by her longtime governess, **Marion Crawford**, as possessing an intellect and curiosity that allowed her to keep pace with her sister's more advanced studies. From age three, Margaret also displayed a talent for acting and a musical ear that gave her almost perfect pitch.

At 21, she fell deeply in love with her father's equerry, Group Captain Peter Townsend, a divorced man with whom marriage was out of the question for a member of the royal family. The romantic misadventure played out in the international press, and by the time Margaret gave up Townsend she had evoked heart-felt sympathy from royal watchers throughout the world. In 1960, after years of continued intensive media coverage of her romances, she married the photographer Anthony Armstrong-Jones, who was later given the title earl of Snowdon. They had two children, David, Viscount Linley, and *Sarah Armstrong-Jones, before the marriage ended in a bitter divorce in 1978, the first in the royal family since Henry VIII legally parted from *Anne of Cleves.

For some time after the divorce, Margaret remained the subject of speculation about her romances. In 1987, concern shifted to her health when the Palace confirmed that she had undergone surgery. However, in 1995, looking quite robust, she joined the queen mother, *Elizabeth

Princess
Margaret
Rose

Bowes-Lyon, and her sister Elizabeth on the balcony of Buckingham Palace to celebrate the 50th anniversary of the end of World War II.

SOURCES:

Edwards, Anne. *Royal Sisters.* NY: William Morrow, 1990.

Hall, Unity. *The Private Lives of Britain's Royal Women.* Chicago, IL: Contemporary Books, 1990.

Sakol, Jeannie, and Caroline Latham. *The Royals.* NY: Congdon and Weed, 1987.

Barbara Morgan,
Melrose, Massachusetts

Margaret Saxe-Coburg (1882–1920).

See Margaret of Connaught.

Margaret Sophie (1870–1902)

Duchess of Wurttemberg. Name variations: Margarethe Sophie. Born on May 13, 1870, in Artstettn, Lower Austria; died on August 24, 1902, in Gmunden, Lower Austria; daughter of *Maria Annunziata (1843–1871) and Karl Ludwig also known as Charles Louis (1833–1896), archduke of Austria; sister of Franz Ferdinand (who was assassinated in 1914).

Margaret the Dragon Slayer

(c. 255–c. 275).

See Margaret of Antioch.

Margaret Theresa of Spain

(1651–1673)

Holy Roman empress. Name variations: Margaret of Spain; Maria Teresa or Maria Theresa of Spain; Margarita Teresa de España; Margareta Teresa; Infanta Margarita; Empress of Germany. Born on July 12, 1651; died on March 12, 1673; daughter of Philip IV (1605–1665), king of Spain (r. 1621–1665), and Maria Anna of Austria (c. 1634–1696); sister of Charles II, king of Spain (r. 1665–1700); half-sister of Maria Teresa of Spain (1638–1683); became first wife of Leopold I (1640–1705), Holy Roman emperor (r. 1658–1705), on December 12, 1666; children: Maria Antonia (1669–1692); Ferdinand Wenzel (1667–1668); John Leopold (1670–1670).

The daughter of Philip IV, king of Spain, and his second wife *Maria Anna of Austria, Margaret Theresa of Spain was born in 1651. Diego Velásquez painted several portraits of her as a child. Betrothed in 1663, she wed Holy Roman emperor Leopold I in December 1666, in a lavish ceremony; the marriage was arranged to strengthen political and dynastic ties between the Spanish and Austrian Habsburgs.

Both Margaret Theresa and Leopold were grandchildren of Philip III of Spain. As the reigning Spanish ruler, Philip IV had no surviving male offspring until the birth of Charles II in 1661. Because of this, Leopold was initially interested in marrying one of the Spanish princesses as a means of securing the Spanish throne for himself. These plans would fail, although the Austrian Habsburgs tried to claim the Spanish crown with the death of Charles II, who had no direct heirs, in 1700.

Leopold insisted that Philip IV recognize Margaret Theresa's right to the Spanish succession over that of her older half-sister, *Maria Teresa of Spain, the wife of Louis XIV of France. Margaret Theresa gave birth to a son, Ferdinand Wenzel, in September 1667, but he died a few months later. A daughter, *Marie Antonia, was born in January 1669. Her third child, John Leopold, died shortly after his birth in 1670. Three years later, Margaret Theresa died. Leopold than married *Claudia Felicitas, who would have no children, followed by *Eleanor of Pfalz-Neuburg, who would have five: Joseph I (1678–1711), Holy Roman emperor (r. 1705–1711); *Maria Elisabeth (1680–1741, stadholder of the Netherlands); Charles VI (1685–1740), Holy Roman emperor (r. 1711–1740); *Maria Antonia of Austria (1683–1754, who married John V, king of Portugal); and *Maria Magdalena (1689–1743).

SOURCES:

Spielman, John P. *Leopold I of Austria*. London: Thames and Hudson, 1977.

Kendall W. Brown,
Professor of History,
Brigham Young University, Provo, Utah

Margaret Theresa of Spain

Margaret Tudor (1489–1541)

Queen of Scotland who, while living in constant fear for her life and the lives of her children, strived within the complicated diplomatic and power struggles of Renaissance Europe to keep peace between Scotland and England and her son's throne secure. Born on November 28, 29, or 30, 1489, at the Palace of Westminster, England; died of "palsy" (probably a stroke) at Methven Castle, Perthshire, Scotland, on October 18, 1541; buried in the Carthusian Abbey of St. John, Perth, Scotland; eldest daughter of Henry VII, king of England (r. 1485–1509) and Elizabeth of York (1465–1503); sister of Henry VIII, king of England (r. 1509–1547) and Mary Tudor (1496–1533); grandmother of Mary Stuart, Queen of Scots (1542–1587); great-grandmother of James VI, king of Scotland (r. 1567–1625), who was king of England as James I (r. 1603–1625); married James IV (1473–1513), king of Scotland (r. 1488–1513), by proxy at Richmond Castle, Surrey, England, on January 25, 1502, and in person at Holyrood Abbey, Edinburgh, Scotland, on August 8, 1503; married Archibald Douglas, 6th earl of Angus, on August 6, 1514, at Kinnoul Church near Perth (divorced 1525); married Henry Stewart, 1st Lord Methven, on March 3, 1528; children (first marriage) six, of whom only two, James V (1512–1542), king of Scotland (r. 1513–1542) and Alexander (1514–1515), duke of Ross, lived for more than one year; (second marriage) Margaret Douglas (1515–1578), afterwards countess of Lennox.

Crowned queen of Scotland (August 8, 1503); on James IV's death on Flodden Field (1513), became regent of Scotland and guardian of the baby James V; after a secret marriage to earl of Angus, was forced (1515) to give up both the regency and the young king to John Stewart, duke of Albany (1515); escaped to England and gave birth to her daughter at Harbottle Castle in Northumberland (1515); held with little respect by either side, used and betrayed as it suited their best interests, she nevertheless continued to fight to keep her son's throne secure, changing sides as seemed expedient; after lengthy, frustrating negotiations, divorced Angus (August 1525) and married Henry Stewart and with him became James V's chief adviser; tried unsuccessfully to divorce Henry Stewart; became alienated from her son as he sank into a depression following the deaths of his sons and heirs; interceded with Henry VIII for her daughter, Margaret Douglas (1536), after her ill-advised marriage with Lord Thomas Howard; died alone and unmourned at age 52; had the unique distinction of being a double great-grandmother to the first ruler of a united England and Scotland, since her granddaughter Mary Stuart, Queen of Scots, married Lord Darnley, son of Lady Lennox (neé Margaret Douglas); Mary Stuart and Lord Darnley's son was James VI of Scotland and I of England.

Margaret Tudor was a disagreeable woman, a forceful personality, a Tudor without the charm and beauty of her sister, *Mary Tudor (1496–1533), ex-queen of France, or the wisdom and shrewdness of her niece, *Elizabeth I. She had been the child-wife of a superstitious monarch who modeled himself on the medieval rulers and kept the offspring of his earlier sexual relationships at court. She suffered great pain and discomfort during her numerous pregnancies and experienced the death in infancy of all but two of her children. The death of James IV on Flodden Field turned her into an embittered woman whose only aim was to secure the future of her son as James V of Scotland. Her decision to marry a Douglas and thereby forfeit the regency and guardianship of the baby king and deepen the gulf between the pro-French and pro-English factions at court, can be seen as ignorant, impetuous or simply the result of a fatal attraction. The marriage was certainly unfortunate and ill-considered and did neither herself nor her husband any good and resulted in separation from her dearly loved sons and a constant threat to her life and that of her son. Her attempts to extricate herself by divorce received no support from her brother, Henry VIII, who traded on her loyalty to England and himself, using her without mercy as a spy and just as callously betraying her when it suited his purposes. Her marriage to Henry Stewart was as impetuous as her second and bought her only more unhappiness. As life threw one disaster after another at her, she continued to struggle on beyond exhaustion, never admitting defeat or despair, seeking refuge in indifference. This indifference caused unsympathetic outsiders to see her as capricious, hysterical, selfish, and temperamental. She was labeled an evil woman, her loyalty to Scotland always in doubt. It is indeed remarkable that she retained her sanity. But she was popular with the people, had great determination and courage, and was, above all, a survivor.

Margaret Tudor was born in November 1489, the second child and eldest daughter of King Henry VII of England and *Elizabeth of York. She was the first princess in the new royal house of Tudor. Her father, the victor of Bosworth Field, had married Elizabeth, daughter of King Edward IV, in 1486, uniting the houses of Lancaster and York and putting an end to the Wars of the Roses. Margaret was thus born at a time when England was confidently looking outward towards the Continent and seeking to take a leading role in European politics. Her education reflected the new ideas and optimism of an English court where learning and the arts were highly valued.

Margaret's early years were spent at the Palace of Shene, Richmond, Surrey. Her governess was **Lady Guildford**, who was herself under the guidance of ****Margaret Beaufort** (1443–1509), Margaret's paternal grandmother, for whom she was named. From her birth, all instructions for her day-to-day care, her servants, clothes and studies were by order of Margaret Beaufort. This formidable woman was famous for her learning and scholarship and would have ensured that Margaret enjoyed the same educational benefits as her brothers, ensuring that she was perhaps better educated than most princesses of her day. She had the advantage of sharing her brothers' tutors who were well-versed in the new thinking. Erasmus, the greatest of all humanists, was reported to have visited the royal schoolroom in the company of Sir Thomas More when Margaret was aged about ten years. But by all accounts Margaret failed to make the most of these opportunities and has the reputation of having been an indifferent student. She learned to read and to write, though by her own admission, the latter was with "an evil hand." Her spelling, as with most of her contemporaries, was erratic. It is presumed that she learned French which would have been essential at the Scottish court with its traditional connections with the court of France. Like all Tudors, Margaret was very fond of music and enjoyed playing the lute and clavichord and dancing, at which she excelled. In short, she was given an education designed to equip her for her expected adult role.

At the same time, however, she grew up believing that the Tudors were superior beings who could do no wrong. Such an attitude served her ill when she became queen of Scotland and gave the Scots cause to doubt her loyalty to them. Her indulgent father spoiled her, and she developed a passion for clothes that never left her. She was very acquisitive, keeping more richly embroidered gowns than she could reasonably expect to wear simply for the pleasure of looking at them. She could always be appeased by such a gift.

Negotiations for her marriage began when she was about six years old. Her father favored an alliance with Scotland that would allow him to play a greater role in Europe, knowing that the northern border between England and Scotland was secure. The matter became more urgent in

1496 when James IV entertained Perkin Warbeck, imposter and pretender to the English throne, at his court and gave him a Scottish noblewoman, Lady **Catherine Gordon**, as a bride. Henry VII reacted quickly to this new threat to English security by sending Richard Fox, bishop of Durham, to Scotland with instructions to suggest a marriage alliance between Margaret and James IV. The proposal was received favorably. Margaret was, until her brothers married, the third in line to the throne. The prospect of Margaret's husband taking over England, however, did not appeal to the English. Henry VII swept their objections aside, declaring that in such an event Scotland would be absorbed by the more dominant England, in much the same way as Normandy had been drawn into England in the 12th century.

Papal dispensation for the marriage, which was necessary because Margaret and James had a common great-great-grandfather, was received in July 1500. The marriage settlement was agreed only after Henry had ensured that his daughter's future would be secure. She would receive dower lands sufficient to give her an income of £2,000 a year, and she would have plenty of servants, including at least 24 who were English. The signing of the treaty and the proxy marriage, with Patrick, earl of Bothwell, standing for James IV, took place at Richmond Palace on January 25, 1502.

Margaret's elder brother and heir to the English throne, Arthur, died in April 1502, moving her a step nearer the throne. The Scots, not unnaturally, pressed for her early departure for Scotland. Thus, in June 1503, at the age of 13 years, she left for Edinburgh where she would be married in person to James, a man twice her age. The splendor and pageantry of this journey has been described in great detail by John Young, Somerset herald, who was among the courtiers who accompanied the princess. Henry VII spared no expense in equipping his daughter for the trip and accompanied her as far as his mother's home in Northampton. For the remainder of the journey, she was in the care of Thomas Howard (d. 1524) and *****Agnes Tylney**, the earl and countess of Surrey. From the herald's account, it is clear that Margaret acquitted herself well not only during the rituals and formalities of her progress but also through the rigors and deprivations she must have experienced on such a trip.

Thirty-four days after they had left London, Margaret and her party crossed the border into Scotland. The new queen had her first sight of her bridegroom at the castle of the earl of Morton in Dalkeith. James IV (1473–1513), then 30 years old, had led the uprising against his father James III, who died in battle against his son's army. James IV had succeeded to the Scottish throne in 1488 at the age of 15 years. He aspired to the ideals of a medieval monarchy with its courtly graces, chivalrous behavior, and love of music, art and poetry; he had an intelligent and inquiring mind; but he was also vain, melancholic, superstitious, and pious to an extreme. The latter characteristics arose from the personal guilt he felt over the manner of his father's death. Since that day, he had worn an iron belt around his waist, which he never removed, adding a new link each year, as a self-imposed penance. He went on pilgrimages, visiting shrines in Scotland, and each year disappeared into retreat during Lent. His greatest unfulfilled ambition was to go on crusade. He had had several sexual relationships and provided for his illegitimate children, keeping them with him whenever possible. A popular and able king, noted for his kindness and the care and interest he took in his people, he was known to have traveled in disguise in order to discover for himself the needs of the poor and unfortunate.

A portrait of Margaret Tudor painted at this time shows her somberly posed against a conventional background, a plump white-skinned girl with red-gold hair tucked into a jewelled French hood; she has a round face, bovine eyes and a subdued almost sullen expression, which belies her wilful nature. A letter written to her father after her arrival in Scotland expresses her overwhelming unhappiness and homesickness. Although considerate and generous, James was twice her age, the Scottish dialect would have confused her, and Scotland did not appear at first sight to offer the same comforts as England. James lavished gifts on her and provided entertainments to amuse her. At her request, his children were removed from court, but she was too young and spoiled to fully appreciate his efforts to please her.

The marriage was apparently popular and applauded at court. William Dunbar (c. 1460–c. 1520), chief poet at the court of King James IV and Queen Margaret, wrote a poem to celebrate the occasion entitled *The Thistle and the Rose,* which he dedicated to the bride. (This is the earliest record of the use of the thistle as the national emblem of Scotland.) In the poem, he describes the young queen thus:

Nor hold no other flower in such dainty,
As the fresh Rose of colour red and white
For if thou dost, hurt is thine honesty
Considering that no flower is so perfite,
So full of virtue, pleasance and delight,

So full of blissful angelic beauty,
Imperial birth, honour, and dignity.

During the ten years of their marriage, Margaret and James had six children. All except one died before their second birthday, and after each birth Margaret was so ill that her life was despaired of. The one survivor was James, duke of Rothesay, born at Linlithgow Palace, Fife, in April 1512. He was their fourth child and would succeed to the throne as James V. Margaret's sixth child, Alexander, duke of Ross (1514–1515), was born after James IV's death at Flodden Field. Too many pregnancies, following in too quick a succession, together with the cold, draughty, unsanitary conditions prevailing in 16th-century Scottish castles were probably responsible for the high infant mortality. This does, however, provide further evidence of Margaret's stamina and will to survive. Time and again she followed James on pilgrimage to the more remote holy shrines in Scotland in their quest for a living, healthy child.

She managed to endure hardship and disaster, sustained by the fierce Tudor spirit that refused to admit defeat.

—Patricia H. Buchanan

James' marriage to Margaret was part of the "Treaty of Perpetual Peace" signed in 1502 with Henry VII. As long as England and France were at peace, James could reconcile the terms of this treaty with the traditional "auld alliance" between Scotland and France. But when England formally entered the Holy League with Spain and the pope in 1511 against France, James felt obliged to renew the alliance with France, and when England invaded France in 1513, he rallied his country, raised a huge army, and crossed the border into England and to Flodden Field. Margaret's quite desperate efforts to dissuade him were in vain. She appealed to his superstitious nature, by describing her dreams and even orchestrating visions, and to his conscience, by drawing his attention to her pregnancy and the delicate health of their only child. His death on the battlefield left her a bitter and angry woman. She was 24 years old, pregnant, and her 17-month-old son was the new king of Scotland. The golden days of her life were over. For the remainder of it, she was a woman alone fighting to survive.

She continued her regular correspondence with her brother Henry VIII, believing him to have her best interests at heart; he was her only link with happier, more comfortable times. Henry saw in her a useful ally and spy in the Scottish camp and encouraged her to write. Unfortunately, unbeknown to Margaret and sometimes to Henry as well, the letters were frequently intercepted, altered or delayed as best suited the bearers and/or the recipient.

James' will granted her the regency and guardianship of the new king. This unprecedented move, contravening established Scottish custom, upset a court already devastated by the loss of life at Flodden Field. Every noble family in Scotland had lost its head, its heir or both. The remaining younger sons were inexperienced and untried, intent only on revenge and asserting their new authority. It was now that Margaret had need of those very characteristics she lacked. Without the virtues of patience, wisdom, and political awareness, already held in suspicion because of her birth and relationship to the English king, she floundered and lost control. To be fair, it would have needed someone of extraordinary ability to have succeeded in this situation. The court was still divided between those who supported England and those who supported France. Despite Flodden Field, there were still those in the pay of England, just as there were those who received pensions from France. The French supporters demanded that Margaret be replaced as regent by John Stewart, 2nd duke of Albany, who was the king's nearest adult male kinsman and as such had this traditional right.

John Stewart was the son of James III's exiled brother, Alexander Stewart, 1st duke of Albany. At the time of James V's accession, he was 34 years old. John Stewart was to all intents and purposes French, having been brought up there by his French mother *Anne de la Tour** (d. 1512). He was married to a French heiress also named *Anne de la Tour** (c. 1496–1524) and had risen high in the service of the French crown, holding the post of lord high admiral. Although childless, he was rich and happy and had no desire to leave France and assert his claim to the Scottish crown. The duke of Albany was as much a victim of circumstances as Margaret and was used by both Henry VIII and Francis I, king of France, to satisfy their personal aspirations.

Margaret's hasty, secret marriage to Archibald Douglas, 6th earl of Angus, entered into for whatever reason, not only deepened the gulf between the factions but jeopardized her right to the regency and guardianship of the king. It was only a matter of time before her sons were removed from her, and she was daily proceeding in fear of her life and theirs. More than one historian has intimated that the marriage was made under duress. The secrecy surrounding it and the fact that it was conducted on Douglas land by a kinsman of the Douglases lend weight to their claims.

If she had looked for protection and support from the Douglases, she was disappointed. Angus' behavior throughout their marriage was ambiguous. How much of Margaret's actions were motivated directly or indirectly by him is debatable at this distance. She was continually on the move, never knowing whom she could trust, frequently making, what seem now, rash, impetuous decisions which only served to increase the precariousness of her situation. On his part, the "young witless fool," as his uncle Gavin Douglas described Angus, gradually developed into a cunning and ruthless man, whose actions caused Margaret to fear and distrust him. As she realized that she could, in fact, trust no one, she became, in **Hester Chapman**'s words, a "predatory, violent and menacing figure."

The duke of Albany's arrival in Scotland in 1515 saw Scottish internal politics enter a new phase. Almost immediately, there was a battle of wills between Margaret and Albany over the custody of the young king. When her sons James and Alexander, the baby duke of Ross, were taken into the custody of Albany, Margaret, heavily pregnant once more, escaped to England. In the relative safety of Harbottle Castle in Northumberland, she gave birth to her daughter, *Margaret Douglas. After regaining her health, Margaret Tudor continued on south to her brother Henry VIII's court in London. Angus remained in Scotland, always promising to join her but never doing so. Instead, he helped himself to her rents and revenues and comforted himself with a new mistress. Leading the pro-English faction, he continued to keep the English court informed regarding Scottish affairs. Henry's spymasters knew much more about Angus' movements and whereabouts than Margaret did.

Margaret's stay in London was a happy one. For once, she had the luxury of female company whom she could love and trust. She spent many hours with her younger sister, Mary Tudor, and her sister-in-law, *Catherine of Aragon, but the visit came to an end when the news reached them that Albany had left Scotland for France. Margaret returned to Scotland hoping to regain the regency and possession of her remaining son James. Alexander, duke of Ross, had died in 1515. It was not to be. She was not even allowed to visit James. Angus' behavior was now public knowledge; Margaret ceased to be part of his faction, remaining neutral for a short time, and, in 1519, applied to the pope for a divorce. Her action was immediately condemned by her brother, who had his own reasons for wanting the marriage kept intact.

Albany returned in 1521 and Margaret turned to him for help, finding him an unexpected ally in her desire to divorce Angus. They were seen together so much that rumors of a sexual liaison circulated and were reported to Henry VIII. There is little evidence to substantiate the rumors.

Angus took custody of their daughter Margaret Douglas, who was forced to travel about with him, before eventually finding a home at the English court as companion to *Mary (I), daughter of Henry VIII and Catherine of Aragon. Margaret and Angus never lived together again and, even though she was granted her divorce in 1525 by Pope Clement VII, Angus never acknowledged the divorce or recognized her third marriage. He himself did not remarry until after Margaret Tudor's death.

When Albany went back to France in 1524 never, as it turned out, to set foot in Scotland again, Margaret turned to James Hamilton, 1st earl of Arran, the sworn enemy of Angus and the Douglases. With the support of Arran and Henry Stewart, her treasurer and lord chancellor, she finally got possession of her son James, now 13 years old. It was agreed that he should be in the custody of the leading nobles in rotation. But when it was Angus' turn, he refused to release James, and for three years Margaret and her supporters sought to free the young king. This was finally achieved in 1528 and James, now in his 16th year, was deemed of an age to assume the trappings of government. Margaret and Henry Stewart were his chief advisers.

Margaret's infatuation with the young Henry Stewart had already been noted. It had been reported to Cardinal Wolsey, and thence to Henry VIII, that Margaret had "a young man about her who kept all seals and orders everything." Henry Stewart was a likeable young man who was attracted to older women. He was 32 years old; she was 38. He had none of the brashness or open defiance of Angus, and he supported rather than dominated her, but their marriage in 1527 was no happier than her earlier ones. It cost her her political influence, and she soon grew tired of him and began to despise him. Eventually, she sought to divorce him, for he, like Angus, had misappropriated her revenues and taken a mistress.

James V appeared to consent to the marriage. He created Henry Stewart the first lord Methven and bestowed on the couple the lands of Methven in Perthshire. Henry was also made Master of Ordnance. Despite the gradual breakup of the marriage, Stewart retained the favor of the king while Margaret withdrew more and more from the court, spending her time at Methven.

During the last years of her life, her relationship with her son remained good, and she was on equally good terms with her daughters-in-law. In 1536, James V married ◄⊰ **Madeleine of France**, elder daughter of Francis I and ***Claude de France**. Madeleine died of consumption within six months of her arrival in Scotland. His second marriage, in 1538, was to ***Mary of Guise**, widow of the duc de Longueville. When the two infant sons of this marriage died within days of each other, it was to Margaret that the young couple turned for comfort. James' subsequent decline into melancholy following this tragedy alienated him from everyone, including his mother.

In 1536, Margaret Tudor interceded with Henry VIII on behalf of her daughter, Margaret Douglas, after her hasty and ill-judged marriage with Thomas Howard (d. 1536), son of Thomas Howard and his first wife ***Elizabeth Tylney** and uncle to ***Anne Boleyn**. The penalty for marriage without the king's consent, and to a kinsman of the disgraced queen, sent Margaret Douglas and Thomas Howard to the Tower. Margaret Tudor's intervention saved her daughter's life; Thomas Howard was executed. However, Margaret Douglas was still in danger, because she was, after all, a Tudor and could have a claim on the English throne. To safeguard against this, Henry VIII had her declared illegitimate on the grounds that her mother's marriage to Angus had been annulled. Young Margaret Douglas' second marriage in 1544 to Matthew Stewart, earl of Lennox, was more favorably received. It was their son, Henry, Lord Darnley, who would marry ***Mary Stuart, Queen of Scots**, James V's only surviving child.

⊰► Madeleine of France (1520–1537)

*French princess. Name variations: Madeleine Valois; Madeleine de France; Magdelaine de France. Born on August 10, 1520, in St. Germain-en-Laye, near Paris, France; died at age 17 at Holyrood, Edinburgh, Scotland, on July 7, 1537; interred at Holyrood; elder daughter of Francis I, king of France (r. 1515–1547), and *Claude de France (1499–1524); married James V (1512–1542), king of Scots (r. 1513–1542), on January 1, 1537, at Notre Dame, Paris, France.*

Margaret Tudor died alone except for her servants at Methven on October 18, 1541. Her sudden illness had not been deemed fatal. A message sent to her son arrived too late for him to attend her. She left all her goods to her daughter, but James ignored her wishes, taking what little there was for himself. He organized an elaborate funeral for his mother who was interred in the Carthusian Abbey of St. John, Perth, where many members of the royal family of Scotland were buried. The tomb was later desecrated by Calvinist soldiers. A slab of blue stone now marks the place where it once was.

Historians have tended to overlook Margaret Tudor, her life overshadowed by the dominance and brilliance of the reign of Henry VIII and played out against the confusion of Scottish internal politics during the minority of James V. But during her lifetime, Margaret Tudor could not easily be disregarded. Because of Henry VIII's inability to produce an heir, she was for a long time in the line of succession to the throne of England. This gave her an importance that no one could ignore. Married as part of a peace treaty, she was penalized for her efforts to keep the peace between England and Scotland. She was a victim of the ambitions of ruthless men. She never succeeded in forming a trusting relationship with them and was constantly betrayed by them. Her rents and revenues were withheld or misappropriated, leaving her almost destitute and dependent on others. She never had full knowledge of the facts or was wise to the full politics of any situation. Frequently, information of great importance was withheld from her with malice and intent. She was also a victim of her own impetuosity and belief that as a Tudor she could do no wrong. But she never lost the common touch and remained popular with the people. It was in her character to fight against misfortune, and she did just that, showing great courage and stamina in the will to survive.

In 1603, with the accession of her great-grandson, James VI of Scotland, as James I of England, the crowns of England and Scotland were finally united.

SOURCES:

Buchanan, Patricia H. *Margaret Tudor, Queen of Scots.* Edinburgh: Scottish Academic Press, 1985.

Chapman, Hester W. *The Sisters of Henry VIII.* London: Jonathan Cape, 1969.

Mackie, R.L. *King James IV of Scotland.* Edinburgh: Oliver & Boyd, 1958.

SUGGESTED READING:

Bingham, Caroline. *James V, King of Scotland, 1512–1542.* London, 1971.

Ellis, H. *Original Letters Illustrative of English History, Vol. I.* 1824.

Leland, J. *de Rebus Britannicus Collectanea.* Vols. IV and V. Edited by Thomas Hearne, London, 1774.

P.R.O. Letters and State Papers of Henry VIII. London, H.M.S.O., 1830–52.

Strickland, Agnes. *Lives of Queens of Scotland and Princesses of England.* Vol. I. 2nd ed. London, 1853.

Wood, Mary A.E. *Letters of Royal and Illustrious Ladies of Great Britain from the beginning of 12th c. to close of reign of Queen Mary.* 3 Vols. London, 1846.

PORTRAITS:

Margaret Tudor. Anon. (National Portrait Gallery, London, England).

Margaret Tudor with the Earl of Angus by Anon (private collection of the Marquess of Bute and Rothesay; now in National Scottish Portrait Gallery). The man Angus is pointing to has been identified by some as Albany but is more probably Henry Stewart.

Margaret Tudor, Queen of Scots by Daniel Mytens (private collection of H.M. Queen Elizabeth II).

Queen Margaret praying to Saint Margaret from the *Book of Hours* given to Margaret by her father, Henry VII (private collection of the Duke of Northumberland at Alnwick Castle, Northumberland, England).

Margaret E. Lynch, M.A.,
Teaching Fellow in the Department of History at Lancaster University, Lancaster, United Kingdom, and an independent scholar

Margaret Valdemarsdatter or Valdemarsdottir (1353–1412).

See Margaret I of Denmark.

Margaret Valois (c. 1376–1441).

See Margaret of Burgundy.

Margaret Wake of Liddell
(c. 1299–1349)

Duchess of Kent. Name variations: Baroness Wake of Lydell. Born Margaret Wake around 1299; died on September 29, 1349; daughter of John Wake, 1st baron Wake of Liddell; married Edmund of Woodstock (1307–1330), 1st earl of Kent (son of Edward I Longshanks, king of England), in 1325; children: *Margaret of Kent (1327–before 1352); Edmund (c. 1327–1331 or 1333), 2nd earl of Kent; *Joan of Kent (1328–1385); John (1330–1352), 3rd earl of Kent.

Margaret Waldemarsdatter or Waldemarsdottir (1353–1412).

See Margaret I of Denmark.

Margareta.

Variant of Margaret.

Margareta Leijonhufvud
(1514–1551)

Queen of Sweden. Name variations: Lejonhufvud. Born on January 1, 1514; died on August 26, 1551; became second wife of Gustavus I Adolphus Vasa (1496–1560), king of Sweden (r. 1523–1560), in 1536; children: John III (1537–1592), king of Sweden (r. 1568–1592, who married *Catherine Jagello, sister of Sigismund II, king of Poland); Katharina (1539–1610, who married Edward, count of East Friesland); Cecilie (1540–1627, who married Christopher, margrave of Baden); Magnus, duke of East Gotland (b. 1542); Karl (b. 1544); Anna Marie (1545–1610, who married George John of Veldenz); Sten (b. 1546); Sophie (1547–1611, who married Magnus, duke of Saxe-Luneburg); Elizabeth (1549–1597, who married Christopher of Mecklenburg); Charles IX (1550–1611), king of Sweden (r. 1604–1611). Gustavus I's first wife was *Katarina of Saxe-Lüneburg; his third was *Katarina Stenbock.

Margarete.

Variant of Margaret.

Margarete of Prussia (1872–1954).

See Margaret Beatrice.

Margarete of Styria (c. 1577–1611).

See Anne of Austria (1601–1666) for sidebar on Margaret of Austria.

Margarete von Karnten (1318–1369).

See Margaret Maultasch.

Margaretha.

Variant of Margaret.

Margaretha of Sweden (1899–1977)

Swedish royal. Name variations: Margaretha Bernadotte. Born Margaretha Sophie Louise on June 25, 1899; died in 1977; daughter of *Ingeborg of Denmark (1878–1958) and Charles of Sweden; sister of *Martha of Sweden (1901–1954, who married the future Olav V, king of Norway) and *Astrid of Sweden (1905–1935); married Axel Christian George Oldenburg, on May 22, 1919; children: George (b. 1920); Flemming (b. 1922).

Margarethe.

Variant of Margaret.

Margarethe (1370–c. 1400)

Margravine of Moravia. Born around 1370; died after 1400; daughter of *Virida Visconti (1350–1414) and Leopold of Habsburg also known as Leopold III (1351–1386), archduke of Austria, Styria, and Carniola, co-emperor of Austria (r. 1365–1379).

Margarethe of Västergötland
(fl. 1100)

Danish royal. Name variations: Margaret of Vaster-gotland. Flourished around 1100; first wife of Niels, king of Denmark (r. 1104–1134). The Danish king's second wife was *Ulfhild.

Margarets, The Three.

See Margaret of Angoulême (1492–1549); Margaret of Savoy (1523–1574); and Margaret of Valois (1553–1615).

Margarita.

Variant of Margaret and Marguerite.

Margarita Maria (b. 1939)

Spanish crown princess. Born on March 6, 1939, in Anglo-American Hospital, Rome, Italy; daughter of *Maria de las Mercedes (1910–2000) and John or Juan (1913–1993), count of Barcelona; sister of Juan Carlos I (1938—), king of Spain (r. 1975—); married Carlos Zurita y Delgado, on October 12, 1972; children: Alfonso Juan (b. 1973); Maria Sofia Zurita y de Borbón (b. 1975).

Marge (1905–1993).

See Buell, Marjorie Henderson.

Margeret.

Variant of Margaret.

Margherita.

Italian variant of Margaret.

Margherita of Italy (1851–1926).

See Margaret of Savoy.

Margherita of Parma (b. 1612).

See Margaret of Parma.

Margherita of Savoy (1851–1926).

See Margaret of Savoy.

Margherita of Taranto (fl. 1300s).

See Balliol, Margaret.

Margherita Paleologo (1510–1566).

See Gonzaga, Margherita.

Margo (1918–1985)

Mexican-American actress who starred in the film version of **Winterset.** *Born Marie Marguerita Guadalupe Teresa Estela Bolado Castilla y O'Donnell in Mexico City, Mexico, on May 10, 1918; died from a brain tumor on July 17, 1985, at her home in Pacific Palisades, California; married Francis Lederer (an actor), in 1937 (divorced 1940); married Eddie Albert (an actor), on December 6, 1945; children: (second marriage) Edward Albert (later an actor) and one adopted daughter.*

Selected films: Crime Without Passion *(1934);* Rumba *(1935);* The Robin Hood of Eldorado *(1936);* Winterset *(1936);* Lost Horizon *(1937);* A Miracle on Main Street *(1940);* Gangway for Tomorrow *(1943);* Behind the Rising Sun *(1943);* The Leopard Man *(1943);* The Falcon in Mexico *(1944);* Viva Zapata *(1952);* I'll Cry Tomorrow *(1955);* From Hell to Texas *(1958);* Who's Got the Action? *(1962).*

Mexican-American actress Margo was born in Mexico City, Mexico, on May 10, 1918, as Marie Marguerita Guadalupe Teresa Estela Bolado Castilla y O'Donnell. She was groomed for stardom from an early age, being coached as a dancer by ***Rita Hayworth**'s father, Eduardo Cansino, and was dancing professionally when she was nine years old. When her aunt married the then little-known bandleader Xavier Cugat, Margo joined him, dancing with his band. At the age of 12, she moved to New York when invited to perform with Cugat at the Waldorf Astoria. Cugat quickly gained popular-

Margo

ity in the United States as the "Rhumba King," and Margo, dancing the rhumba that became the craze of the time, soon attracted the attention of filmmakers.

In 1934, Charles MacArthur and Ben Hecht chose Margo to star in the film *Crime Without Passion*. After receiving excellent reviews for her performance, she tried the stage, starring on Broadway in *Winterset* in 1935. Although critics praised her, RKO Radio Pictures required her to do a screen test before she was chosen for the same role in the film version of *Winterset* (1936), now considered to be one of her best roles. In 1937, she was chosen over Rita Hayworth by director Frank Capra for one of the leads in *Lost Horizon*, a part that required her to portray her character from adolescence to old age.

Margo appeared in numerous films and on stage during her career as an actress. Other film roles included *Miracle on Main Street* (1940), *The Leopard Man* (1943), *Viva Zapata* (1952), *I'll Cry Tomorrow* (1955), and *Who's Got the Action?* (1962). Along with *Winterset*, her credentials on Broadway included *Masque of Kings* (1937) and *A Bell for Adano* (1944).

In 1937, Margo married actor Francis Lederer, from whom she was divorced in 1940. She became an American citizen in 1942, and on December 6, 1945, she married actor Eddie Albert (later of the television show "Green Acres"). After the birth of their son Edward Albert in 1951, Margo devoted more time to her family, which grew to include an adopted daughter, and less to her career, although she performed in nightclub revues with her husband during the 1950s. She also taught acting classes for a number of years. Making her home in Pacific Palisades, California, she became deeply involved with the Chicano Cultural Center, Plaza de la Raza, in Los Angeles, and was a member of the Board of the National Council of the National Endowment of the Arts (NEA). Margo died in 1985.

Kari Bethel,
freelance writer, Columbia, Missouri

Margot.
Variant of Margaret or Marguerite.

Margot (1553–1615).
See Margaret of Valois.

Margrete.
Danish variant of Margaret.

Margrethe I of Denmark (1353–1412).
See Margaret I of Denmark.

Margrethe II (1940—)

Queen of the constitutional monarchy of Denmark who has reigned since 1972. Name variations: Margaret II or Margrete II; Daisy. Born Margrethe Alexandrine Thorhildur Ingrid on April 16, 1940, in Copenhagen, Denmark; daughter of Frederick IX, king of Denmark (r. 1947–1972), and Queen Ingrid of Sweden (b. 1910); sister of Princess *Benedikte (b. 1944) and Princess *Anne-Marie Oldenburg (b. 1946), ex-queen of Greece; graduated from Danish and English primary and secondary schools, attended the Universities of Copenhagen and Aarhus, Cambridge University, and the Sorbonne; married Count Henri or Henrik of Laborde De Montpezat, in 1967; children: two sons, Crown Prince Frederik (b. 1968) and Prince Joachim (b. 1969). The royal family of Denmark has permanent residences at Amalienborg in Copenhagen and Fredensborg in Northern Sealand.

Princess Margrethe was born on April 16, 1940, exactly one week after Hitler's troops occupied Denmark, the daughter of Frederick IX, king of Denmark, and Queen *Ingrid of Sweden. The affection and hopefulness with which the Danish people greeted Margrethe's arrival laid the base for the popularity she has enjoyed throughout her reign. The constitutional revision of June 5, 1953, which instituted women's rights of succession, was approved by referendum and thus made Margrethe the first Danish queen to be elected by the population.

Possibly the 13-year-old Margrethe's realization that she would not be "married out of the country," as her mother had been and her sisters were likely to be, reinforced her efforts towards obtaining a well-grounded education. Arguably, she is among the best-educated monarchs of Europe. She graduated from Danish and English primary and secondary schools, attended the Universities of Copenhagen and Aarhus, Cambridge University, and the Sorbonne. She also served in the Danish Women's Flying Corps and the Women's Auxiliary Air Force (WAAF) in England. Her avocations are archeology and art. She has done extensive field work, and her artistic talents have been well demonstrated in, among other works, her illustrations for *Lord of the Rings* and the costumes and scenery she designed for a TV production of Hans Christian Andersen's "The Shepherdess and the Chimney Sweep."

Queen Margrethe works closely with her government and has numerous social and diplomatic engagements in Denmark as well as abroad. On New Year's Eve, she invites the entire population into her home at Amalienborg via her

*M*argrethe II

televised speech. It has become a much-anticipat-
ed event because although she gets a draft from
members of Parliament, the final version and its
execution are entirely her own. She scolds and
encourages in tune with the times, but her comments are informed by the vision her intelligence,

courage, and sense of humor have consistently
granted her. Consequently, she is a respected,
honored, and deeply cherished monarch.

SOURCES:

Hansen, Thorkild. *Samtale med Dronning Margrethe.*
Copenhagen: Forum, 1979.

MacHaffe, Ingeborg S., and Margaret A. Nielsen. *Of Danish Ways*. Minneapolis: Dillon Press, 1979.

Taylor-White, Doreen, ed. *Denmark*. APA Publications. Singapore: Hofer Press, 1991.

Wolden-Ratinge, Anne. *Dronning i Danmark*. Copenhagen: Gyldendal, 1989.

Inga Wiehl,
a native of Denmark, teaches English at Yakima Valley Community College, Yakima, Washington

Margriet Francisca (b. 1943)

*Dutch princess. Name variations: Margaret. Born on January 19, 1943; daughter of *Juliana (b. 1909), queen of the Netherlands (r. 1948–1980), and Prince Bernard of Lippe-Biesterfeld; sister of Queen *Beatrix of the Netherlands (b. 1938) and *Irene Emma (b. 1939); married Pieter von Vollenhoven, in 1967.*

Marguerite.

Variant of Margaret.

Marguerite (r. 1218–1230)

*Countess of Blois. Reigned from 1218 to 1230; eldest daughter of Thibaut or Theobald V, count of Blois and Chartres (r. 1152–1218), and possibly *Alice, countess of Blois (1150–c. 1197); married Gauthier d'Avesnes.*

Following her father's death in 1218, Marguerite ruled Blois with her third husband, Gauthier d'Avesnes. She died in 1230 and was succeeded by *Marie de Chatillon.

Marguerite d'Angoulême.

See Margaret of Angoulême (1492–1549).

Marguerite d'Autriche (1480–1530).

See Margaret of Austria.

Marguerite de Bourgogne (1250–1308)

*Queen of Naples and Sicily and countess of Tonnerre. Name variations: Margaret of Burgundy, countess of Tonnere. Born in 1250; died on September 4, 1308, in Tonnerre; daughter of *Mahaut II de Dampierre (1234–1266) and Eudes (1230–1266), count of Nevers; married Charles I of Anjou, king of Naples (r. 1268–1285) and Sicily (r. 1266–1282), on November 18, 1268. Charles I's first wife was *Beatrice of Provence (d. 1267).*

Marguerite de Brabant (c. 1192–?)

*Countess of Guelders. Name variations: Margaretha. Born around 1192; daughter of Henry I (1165–1235), duke of Brabant, and *Maude of Alsace (1163–c. 1210); married Gerhard III of Gelre or Geldeland, ruler of the Netherlands (d. 1229); children: Otto II, called Otto the Lame (b. around 1220).*

On the death of Gerhard III, ruler of the Netherlands, Marguerite de Brabant's son Otto II the Lame became ruler. Marguerite was his guardian from 1229 until 1234 when he came of age.

Marguerite de Bressieux (d. 1450)

French noble and warrior. Died in 1450 in France.

Marguerite de Bressieux was a French noblewoman who took a bloody revenge on her enemies. She and several other noblewomen living in her father's castle were raped by the soldiers of Louis de Chalons when they invaded the castle. Marguerite and the other victims clad themselves in black and covered their faces, then joined the battle against Louis. The women proved to be excellent fighters and pitiless foes in exacting their revenge on Louis' men; supposedly, they even revealed their faces to their attackers as they killed them. Their leader Marguerite was mortally wounded in the battle and died soon after; she was celebrated for her bravery.

Laura York,
Riverside, California

Marguerite d'Écosse (1424–1445).

See Margaret of Scotland.

Marguerite de Duyn (d. 1310).

See Oignt, Marguerite d'.

Marguerite de Flandre (1350–1405).

See Margaret of Flanders.

Marguerite de Foix (d. 1258).

See Margaret de Foix.

Marguerite de Foix (fl. 1456–1477)

*Duchess of Brittany. Name variations: Margaret of Foix; Marguerite of Foix; Margaret de Dreux; Margaret of Dreux. Flourished between 1456 and 1477; daughter of Francis I (b. 1414), duke of Brittany, and *Isabel Stewart (d. 1494); married François or Francis II, duke of Brittany (r. 1458–1488); children: *Anne of Brittany (c. 1477–1514); and possibly one other daughter.*

Marguerite de l'Aigle (d. 1141)

Queen of Navarre. Died on May 25, 1141; daughter of Gilbert de l'Aigle and Julienne du Perche; married Garcia IV the Restorer, king of Navarre (r. 1134–1150); children: Sancho VI (d. 1194), king of Navarre (r. 1150–1194); *Blanche of Navarre (d. 1158, who married Sancho III, king of Castile); *Margaret of Navarre (fl. 1154–1172). Garcia's second wife was *Urraca of Castile (d. 1179).

Marguerite de Navarre (1492–1549).

See Margaret of Angoulême.

Marguerite de Provence (1221–1295).

See Margaret of Provence.

Marguerite de Savoie (1523–1574).

Margaret of Savoy.

Marguerite de Thouars

(r. 1365–1377)

Joint ruler of Dreux. Name variations: Margaret of Thouars. Reigned from 1365 to 1377; daughter of Simon de Thouars, ruler of Dreux (r. 1355–1365); sister of Peronelle de Thouars.

Marguerite de Thouars was a co-parcener of Dreux with her brother Peronelle de Thouars. They sold the fief in 1377–78 to Charles VI, king of France. Charles then conferred it on the house of Albret.

Marguerite Louise of Orleans

(c. 1645–1721)

Grand duchess of Tuscany. Name variations: Marguerite Louise de Medici. Born around 1645; died in Paris, France, in September 1721; daughter of Gaston d'Orleans (1608–1660), duke of Orléans (brother of Louis XIII), and *Marguerite of Lorraine (fl. 1632); first cousin of Louis XIV, king of France; stepsister of *Anne Marie Louise d'Orléans, Duchesse de Montpensier (1627–1693); married Cosimo III de Medici (1642–1723), grand duke of Tuscany (r. 1670–1723), in April 1661; children: Ferdinand (1663–1713); *Anna Maria Luisa de Medici (1667–1743, who married John William of the Palatinate); Giovan or Gian Gastone (1671–1737).

Marguerite Louise of Orleans, niece of Louis XIII, was brought up to be the future queen of France as wife of Louis XIV. She was considered beautiful and clever, a brilliant conversationalist with a biting wit. As the young charge of governess Madame du Deffant, she rode, hunted, and had great spirit. Her future husband Cosimo III de Medici would be her exact opposite.

When the plans for her marriage to Louis XIV fell through, Marguerite Louise was unfazed, for she was in love with Prince Charles of Lorraine. Her mother, the widowed **Marguerite of Lorraine**, was sympathetic with her daughter's wish and equally opposed to a marriage to Cosimo. But Louis XIV, under the urging of Cardinal Jules Mazarin, offered the young Marguerite Louise two options: Cosimo or the convent. Marguerite Louise married Cosimo by proxy in the Louvre chapel in April 1661.

Homesick and with a broken heart, Marguerite Louise began to hate all things Italian. She balked at learning the language and begged the French king to let her enter a convent rather than remain in Tuscany, but to no avail. At one point, she refused to eat; she also went through a period of silence. When she finally began to speak, she showered invective on all within reach. Madame du Deffant was sent to reason with her; it had no effect. Finally, Marguerite Louise withdrew to the Medici villa at Poggio a Caiano and sent a message to Cosimo that if he dared to follow she would hurl a missal at his head. Then amazingly she returned to the Tuscan court, admitted that she had been wrong, and calm was restored.

Eventually, the couple's relationship became tempestuous again, and Cosimo sent Marguerite Louise to the family palace at Pisa where she remained a virtual prisoner, kept from communicating with anyone outside the palace. "Finding her circumstances becoming thus ever more intolerable, and that she could get no help from her relatives in France," writes G.F. Young, "she evolved the idea of escape from the contemptible Cosimo by joining a party of gipsies, with whom she was discovered one night settling all the arrangements from a window of the palace at Pisa; whereupon that mode of escape was made impossible." By that time, Marguerite Louise had had a son; she soon added a daughter **Anna Maria Luisa de Medici**; another son arrived in 1671.

On the death of his father Ferdinand II in 1670, Cosimo took his position as grand duke of Tuscany, but he was strongly influenced by the church and his mother **Vittoria de Medici**. Concerned with this turn of events, the bright Marguerite Louise demanded a share in governing, but Cosimo refused. Marguerite returned to Poggio a Caiano once more, saying, "You make the unhappiness of my life, and I make the unhappiness of yours." She demanded a separation, and finally, reluctantly, he agreed. Thus, after 13 years in Tuscany, Marguerite Louise of Orleans returned to France and settled at the convent of Montmartre, near Paris. She became a popular member of the French court, and her ridicule of things Tuscan amused Louis XIV.

At the dawn of the 20th century, two silver coins in the Archaeological Museum were "discovered to be hollow," writes Young, "and to be in reality boxes; and in one of these was a miniature of Prince Charles of Lorraine in his youth, believed to have been concealed in this manner by Marguerite Louise so that she might wear it without detection."

SOURCES:
Young, Col. G.F. *The Medici.* NY: Modern Library, 1930.

Marguerite of Bourgogne (1290–1315).
See Margaret of Burgundy.

Marguerite of Flanders.
See Margaret of Flanders (1202–1280).
See Margaret of Flanders (1350–1405).

Marguerite of Foix (fl. 1456–1477).
See Marguerite de Foix.

Marguerite of France (c. 1282–1318).
See Margaret of France.

Marguerite of Hainault.
See Women Prophets & Visionaries in France at the End of the Middle Ages for Marguerite Porete.

Marguerite of Lorraine (c. 1561–?)
Duchess of Joyeuse and sister of the queen of France. Name variations: Margaret of Lorraine; Margaret of Vaudemont-Lorraine; Madame de Joyeuse. Born around 1561; daughter of Nicolas of Lorraine, count of Vaudemont, and **Marguerite d'Egmont**; sister of ***Louise of Lorraine** (1554–1601), queen of France, and Philippe-Emmanuel, duc de Mercoeur; married Anne, duc de Joyeuse (governor of Normandy), in 1581; married M. de Luxembourg.

Marguerite of Lorraine (fl. 1632)
Duchess of Orléans. Name variations: Margaret of Lorraine. Flourished in 1632; sister of Charles IV, duke of Lorraine (r. 1624–1675, sometimes referred to as Charles III); became second wife of Gaston d'Orléans (1608–1660), duke of Orléans (brother of Louis XIII, king of France), in January 1632; children: ***Marguerite Louise of Orleans** (c. 1645–1721);

***Françoise d'Orleans** (fl. 1650); stepmother of ***Anne Marie Louise d'Orléans, Duchesse de Montpensier** (1627–1693). Gaston's first wife was ***Marie de Bourbon** (1606–1627).

Marguerite of Navarre (1492–1549).
See Margaret of Angoulême.

Marguerite of Orleans (d. 1466)
Countess of Étampes. Name variations: Margaret of Orleans or Margaret of Orléans; Marguerite de Orléans; countess of Etampes or Estampes or d'Etampes. Died in 1466; daughter of ***Valentina Visconti** (1366–1408) and Louis (1372–1407), duke of Orléans; married Richard of Brittany also known as Richard Montfort, count of Etampes or d'Etampes (d. 1438); sister-in-law of ***Joanna of Navarre** (c. 1370–1437); children: Francis II, duke of Brittany (r. 1458–1488); ***Catherine of Brittany** (1428–c. 1476).

Marguerite Porete.
See Women Prophets & Visionaries in France at the End of the Middle Ages.

Marguerites, Les Trois.
See Margaret of Angoulême (1492–1549); Margaret of Savoy (1523–1574); and Margaret of Valois (1553–1615).

Maria.
Variant of Marie and Mary.

Maria (fl. 700s)
Byzantine empress. Flourished in the 700s; married Leo III the Iconoclast, Byzantine emperor (r. 717–741); children: Constantine V Kopronymus, Byzantine emperor (r. 741–775); **Anna** (who married Artabasdus).

Maria (fl. 995–1025)
Dogaressa of Venice. Name variations: Maria Arpad; Maria of Hungary. Flourished between 995 and 1025; daughter of Geza (d. 997), prince of Hungary (r. 970–997), and ***Sarolta** (fl. 900s); sister of ***Judith of Hungary** and King Stephen I of Hungary (d. 1038); married Otto Orseolo, doge of Venice; children: Peter (d. 1046), king of Hungary (r. 1038–1041, 1041–1046).

Maria (fl. 1200s)
Byzantine princess. Name variations: Maria Lascaris. Flourished in the 1200s; daughter of ***Helen Asen of

Bulgaria and Theodore II Lascaris, emperor of Nicaea (r. 1254–1258); married Nicephorus I of Epirus (d. 1296). Nicephorus was also married to *Anna Paleologina-Cantacuzene.

Maria, Dowager Countess of Waldegrave (1736–1807).

See Walpole, Maria.

Maria I of Braganza (1734–1816)

First queen to rule Portugal, from 1777 to 1792, who ended the despotic regime of the Marquis of Pombal, her father's chief minister, and reigned during a period of relative peace and prosperity before succumbing to mental illness in 1792. Name variations: María I Braganza; María I of Braganza; María Francisca. Born María Francisca Isabel Josefa Antonia Gertrudes Rita Joana on December 17, 1734, in Lisbon, Portugal; died in Rio de Janeiro, Brazil, on March 20, 1816; interred at the Basilica of Estrela, Lisbon; daughter of José I also known as Joseph I Emanuel (1714–1777), king of Portugal (r. 1750–1777), and Maria Ana Victoria (1718–1781); married her uncle, Pedro or Peter III (1717–1786), king of Portugal (r. 1777–1786), on June 6, 1760; children: José or Joseph (August 21, 1761–1788), prince of Beira; John de Paula (1763–1763); João or John VI (b. May 13, 1767), king of Portugal (r. 1816–1826); Mariana Victoria (1768–1788); Maria Clementina (1774–1776); Maria Isabel (1776–1777). Heir and successor: John VI (João VI).

Reign of John V began (1706); Peter III born (1717); death of John V and accession of Joseph I Emanuel (1750); Portuguese Jesuits expelled (1759); death of Joseph I Emanuel and ascension of Maria I to Portuguese throne (February 24, 1777); death of Pombal (1782); death of Maria I's husband, Peter (1786); death of crown prince Joseph (1788); death of Maria's daughter Mariana Victoria (1788); onset of the French Revolution (1789); Maria I's mental illness forces Prince John to become regent (1792); execution of Louis XVI by French revolutionaries (1793); Maria I declared incurably insane and John elevated to Prince-Regent (July 15, 1799); French invasion of Portugal (1807); flight of Portuguese royal family and court to Brazil (1807–08); death of Maria I in Brazil (1816); return of John to Portugal (1821).

Born on December 17, 1734, the infant princess received the name of María Francisca Isabel Josefa Antonia Gertrudes Rita Joana from her parents, Joseph I Emanuel and ✧▶ **Maria**

Ana Victoria. Joseph Emanuel was crown prince of Portugal, and as he had no sons, the baby became princess of Beira, second in line to the throne occupied by her grandfather, John V (João V). At the time, nothing predicted the political tumult which would color the years before Maria came to the throne nor the mental illness which overshadowed the end of her life. Nor would it have been possible to surmise, as historian Stanley Payne later concluded, that after Maria became queen in 1777, she "presided over the happiest and most prosperous period the Bragança dynasty had seen since the palmy early years of [John] V."

Contemporary observers described her as a bright, perhaps even precocious child, although somewhat reserved and pensive. She began speaking at 17 months and was soon reciting poems and catechisms. At four, Maria could read both Portuguese and Spanish. She also demonstrated excellent penmanship and a fine memory, described as "prompt in receiving, tenacious in conserving." The princess acquired an excellent education in matters deemed appropriate to royalty, and she enjoyed art, music, and the opera so fashionable in Lisbon at the time. She also showed a strong religious piety and was devoted to charitable works.

When Maria was 16, her grandfather John V died on July 31, 1750. This elevated her father to the throne, but he had little aptitude or training for rule, as historian Harold Livermore notes: Joseph Emanuel "had not been allowed to take any part in public affairs. Nor had he shown much interest in them. His benevolent and rather superficial nature did not admit of intense exertions. His main interests were riding, shooting, cards, the theater and music: these, with frequent devotions and religious holidays, easily filled an otherwise vacant existence." King Joseph I Emanuel immediately named as his chief minister Sebastião José de Carvalho e Melo, the future marquis of Pombal. Within a short time, the minister had taken the reins of power from the relieved monarch. For the rest of Joseph Emanuel's reign, Pombal, with the king's acquiescence, governed as a virtual dictator.

Meanwhile, Maria was a young woman, and it was time for her to marry. As she was the probable heir to the throne, it seemed best that she marry a countryman. John V had intended to wed Maria to his son Peter (III). Maria was receptive to the idea, but as Peter was her uncle, John V had to secure a dispensation from the papacy. Although Rome agreed to bless the union, John V died before it could be celebrated. To

Maria's frustration, neither Joseph Emanuel nor Pombal wanted her marriage to take place. The king was not fond of his brother Peter, and the minister feared that if Peter were prince-consort, he would become the leader of aristocratic and clerical opposition to Pombal's ministry. Maria's father considered marrying her to a Portuguese aristocrat, and the English proposed George II's son, the duke of Cumberland. In 1760, Madrid formally requested her hand for the son of Charles III, Don Luis. By then, however, Pombal and Joseph Emanuel had less to fear from her marriage to Peter, whom Maria preferred anyway. Pombal had broken the power of the Portuguese aristocracy, making it unlikely that Peter would constitute any threat to the ministry. Thus, on June 6, 1760, Maria married her uncle, 17 years her senior.

The bride was tall and thin but physically robust, with a delicate, pale face that was pleasing, if not beautiful. She and Peter enjoyed an affectionate life together. Their first child Joseph was born on August 21, 1761. Another son, John (VI), arrived on May 13, 1767, and on December 15, 1768, a daughter, ❧▶ Mariana Victoria, named for Maria's mother. The family settled at Queluz, outside Lisbon, where Peter expanded and lavishly decorated the palace. Maria and her husband entertained sumptuously but generally avoided politics to preclude conflict with Pombal. On occasion, however, Maria voiced dismay with or opposition to Pombal's actions.

The marquis stood at the apogee of his power in 1775, but Maria was shortly to take her place at center stage. Pombal had exiled the Jesuits in 1759, imprisoned or executed defiant nobles, strengthened Portuguese industry and commerce, and enriched himself and his family. But Joseph Emanuel's health was poor, and he took seriously ill in 1776. Fearful that as monarchs Maria and Peter would strip him of his power, Pombal maneuvered to have the king put aside Maria's claim to the throne. According to some accounts, the king dutifully acceded to Pombal's suggestion that Salic law (restricting the succession to men) be instituted in Portugal. This would allow them to make Maria's son Joseph the heir. Pombal had cannily tried to influence the boy's loyalty by manipulating his education. Despite these maneuvers, Queen Maria Ana Victoria and Maria learned of the scheme and persuaded Joseph Emanuel to reverse himself. When the king died on February 24, 1777, Maria became queen.

Sensing Pombal's impending fall, many Portuguese greeted her with "great and general con-tentment." Tired of "the most ferocious despotism ever exercised in Portugal," the populace anticipated a reaction against Pombal's policies. Among nobles and clergy ran a desire for revenge against the marquis. Joseph Emanuel's will counseled Maria to rule with "gentleness, peace and justice, promoting the happiness" of the people. She began by allowing political exiles to return and pardoning state prisoners. From Pombal's prisons emerged 800 inmates. Some had endured 20 years of incarceration; many others had died without their families ever receiving notice. A foreign diplomat described the emergence of the prisoners as a "resurrection of the dead." On March 1, Pombal asked Maria's permission to retire to his estate. She gave her approval on March 4 and provided an armed escort to protect the fallen minister from his vengeful enemies.

Strife over Pombal's policies colored Maria I's early reign. Pombal had led the public to believe that royal finances were in good order, but Maria I and her ministers discovered the treasury bereft of funds. The government had failed to pay salaries and pensions for many years, and Pombal had spent little on the army or navy since 1764. To save money, she quickly stopped work on some of Pombal's grandiose public pro-

❧▶ **Maria Ana Victoria** (1718–1781)
*Queen and regent of Portugal. Name variations: Mariana Victoria or Vitória; María Ana Victoria of Spain; Marianna Victoria; Maria Anna of Spain; Marie-Anne Bourbon; Marie Anne of Spain. Regent of Portugal (1776–1777). Born on January 31, 1718, in Madrid; died on January 15, 1781, at Ajuda Palace, Lisbon; interred at Sao Francisco de Paula, Lisbon; daughter of *Elizabeth Farnese (1692–1766) and Philip V, king of Spain (r. 1700–1724, 1725–1746); sister of Ferdinand VI and Louis I, kings of Spain; married José Manuel also known as Joseph I Emanuel, king of Portugal (r. 1750–1777), on January 19, 1729; children: *Maria I of Braganza (1734–1816); Maria Ana Francisca (1736–1813); Maria Francisca Dorotea (1739–1771); daughter (1741–1741, stillborn); daughter (1742–1742, stillborn); Maria Francisca Benedicta (1746–1829, who married José Francisco Xavier, prince of Beira).*

❧▶ **Mariana Victoria** (1768–1788)
*Portuguese princess. Born Mariana Ana Victoria on December 15, 1768; died of smallpox in 1788, shortly after giving birth; daughter of *Maria I of Braganza (1734–1816) and Pedro or Peter III (1717–1786), king of Portugal (r. 1777–1786); married Gabriel Antonio Francisco of Spain.*

jects and cut back on spending for royal entertainments. Her economy meant laying off workers, which fomented some discontent. But an economic recovery soon ensued, and the country was relatively prosperous for most of her reign.

Maria I found it impossible to escape altogether the outcry against Pombal. Her official acclamation by the cortes (parliament) and people on May 13, 1777, was accompanied by loud attacks against the marquis. On the one hand, the people greeted the new queen with tremendous enthusiasm: "This was for her the sweetest moment of her life; some threw themselves on their knees, others kissed the hem of her robe; she was touched almost to tears." On the other hand, many also demanded Pombal's head. The queen tried to ignore the rancor. But Pombal and his enemies engaged in polemical broadsides, upsetting the public satisfaction at Maria's coronation.

The royal couple infused an element of humanity and moderation into the new reign. [Maria I] had had little education or preparation to fit her for the affairs of state. But she had application and some common sense, and took pains to try to understand the papers submitted to her and to give sensible replies.

—David Francis

She found it extremely stressful to deal with the controversy, as evidenced by her handling of the Távora affair. Pombal had arrested and executed the duke of Aveiro, the count of Atouguia, and some of their family members for an attempted assassination of Joseph Emanuel on September 3, 1758. During interrogation, the accused had implicated the marquis of Távora. Released from prison by Maria I, the surviving members of the Távora and Aveiro families petitioned for redress, asking that the crown review the evidence used against them and that it restore their confiscated properties. In August 1780, Maria finally agreed to reopen the inquiry. The investigation unfolded slowly, the judges perhaps waiting to know the queen's will. But she was apparently torn between a desire to see justice served and fear for her father's reputation (he had approved the punishments). The case weighed more and more on her mind until she became very distressed. One morning, she demanded that the judges be called into session and that they render a verdict that day. After meeting all night, they declared the Aveiros guilty, but exonerated the other accused aristocrats. Pressed by her confessor, she finally ordered the return of the Atouguia estate, which

was in Pombal's possession. But her psychological agitation was evident: after signing the decree, she crossed out her signature "exclaiming that she was condemned to very Hell." Her actions censured Pombal and indirectly her father.

Soon thereafter, circumstances forced her to render a verdict on Pombal himself. On August 16, 1781, she declared him "culpable and deserving of exemplary punishment." But Maria I decided to treat him mercifully in view of his age, illnesses, and his request for pardon. The decision reflected her own propensity to show clemency, her ambivalence about her father's behavior as king, and her aversion to the controversies of power politics. She found the latter particularly agonizing. Throughout her reign, Maria I seemed able to deal with such debates only through the strong support of her husband, her mother Maria Ana Victoria, and other close advisors.

Yet her reign, even in its early years, was not a mere reaction against Pombal's absolutists policies. Martinho de Melo e Castro, minister of the navy and overseas dominions in her first cabinet, had served with Pombal. She refused to allow the Jesuits, whom Pombal had exiled, to return to Portugal, despite her own religious scruples and her husband's pro-Jesuit stance. In part, she wanted to respect the memory of her father, who had approved Pombal's actions, but Maria I was determined to steer a moderate course. Poorly prepared to govern because of Pombal's determination to set her aside in favor of Joseph, she wisely consulted with her husband and her mother, Maria Ana Victoria.

According to Maria I's foremost biographer, Caetano Beirão, "three great preoccupations dominated her thought: to repair the offenses to God, moralize political life and exercise a government both gentle and progressive." One of her priorities was to re-establish good relations with the papacy, which had suffered under Pombal's anticlericalism. She restored the papal nuncio's privileges and guided a far-reaching reform of Portuguese monastic houses. In fulfillment of a vow made prior to the birth of her eldest son, Maria I also built a large church dedicated to the cult of the Sacred Heart of Jesus.

In terms of economic life, her government was less interventionist than Pombal's regime had been. Maria I disbanded several of the state trading companies established by the marquis, including the Grão-Pará and Maranhão Company in 1778 and the Pernambuco and Paraíba Company in 1780. She also limited the concessions made by the crown to the Port-Wine Company, reduced subsidies to the Portuguese silk industry, and turned other industries over to private entrepreneurs. To provide the nation with better infrastructure, Maria I fostered road- and canal-building.

She steered a moderate political course. While she rehabilitated many of Pombal's aristocratic enemies, she did not restore full power to the nobility. The prosperous mercantile class that had emerged during her father's reign continued to prosper and served as a counterweight to aristocratic pretensions. In 1790, she undercut feudal rights by abolishing seignorial courts and bringing administration of justice under the auspices of the crown.

In the arena of foreign affairs, Maria I and her ministers sought greater independence from Great Britain, Portugal's traditional ally, and a rapprochement with Spain. Her mother, Maria Ana Victoria, herself a Spanish princess, worked to establish better relations between Portugal and Maria's uncle, Charles III of Spain. The result was a treaty between the two nations, signed in 1778. Meanwhile, the revolt of the British colonies in North America threatened to draw Portugal into a general European conflict. France and Spain supported the Americans, whereas Great Britain pressed Maria I to stand with the British. She was determined, however, to avoid the conflict and steered a neutral course to the extent the British permitted her. In July 1782, Maria I agreed to a joint proclamation with the Russian tsar, in which the neutral nations asserted their right to trade as they deemed fit. Several years later, a British diplomat wrote of Maria I's policy: "During the fatal contest betwixt England and its colonies, the wise neutrality she persevered in maintaining was of the most vital benefit to her dominions, and hitherto, the native commerce of Portugal has attained under her mild auspices an unprecedented degree of prosperity." She cemented her ties with Spain through marriages. Her daughter, Mariana Victoria, was betrothed to a Spanish prince, and her son John married *Carlota Joaquina, daughter of the future Charles IV of Spain. A Spanish-Portuguese expedition against Muslim pirates in Algiers proved unsuccessful.

Maria I's reign was the height of the Portuguese Enlightenment. At the outset, she transformed the University of Coimbra library into a public institution and ordered that the faculty be drawn from all disciplines rather than only from theology. In 1778, Maria I ordered a review of Portuguese laws, which had not been codified for two centuries. At the instigation of the duke of Lafões, in 1779 she created the Royal Academy of Sciences, which proved crucial in promoting Enlightenment science and technology in Portugal. In the same year, Maria I issued a decree reforming public instruction in the ex-Jesuit schools, and in 1790 she created 18 schools for girls in Lisbon. Equally influential and very practical was her support of General Intendant of the Police Diogo Inácio de Pina Manique, who worked to improve public safety and cleanliness in Lisbon. This was a major challenge, given the damage caused by the great earthquake of 1750. Always fond of almsgiving and other acts of charity, she founded a house for abandoned children (Lisbon's Royal House of Charity) in 1782. It provided food, training in crafts, and education.

Despite these achievements, the queen's life was becoming unsettled. Death took a heavy toll on family and close advisors, leaving her with a sense of isolation and overwhelming burden. Her mother died in 1781, followed two years later by her confessor, Frei Inácio de São Caetano. Her husband Petro, the king-consort, expired on November 25, 1786, from a stroke. Thus Maria I's three closest confidants and advisors were now dead. But even greater tragedy struck her. On September 11, 1788, her son and heir, Joseph, died of smallpox, reportedly after the queen had refused to let doctors vaccinate him. Less than two months later, her daughter Mariana Victoria succumbed in Spain to the same disease shortly after giving birth. The child died a few days later, as did Don Gabriel, Mariana Victoria's husband.

Distraught over such disaster, Maria I struggled on, only to confront the French Revolution, which cost the head of more than one monarch. As news from France became more alarming and the British and Spanish sought Portuguese support in dealing with the revolutionaries, the burden of rule pressed more heavily upon her. By late October 1791, she was obviously suffering from acute depression and nightmares. A morbid fear of eternal damnation obsessed her. Liberals criticized her new confessor, José Maria de Melo, bishop of the Algarve, for his propensity to speak of the punishments of Hell. He perhaps heightened her sensitivity but certainly did not cause her mental illness. In January of the following year, her obsessions left her incapacitated. John, her only surviving child, reluctantly agreed to rule for her during the duration of her illness. Meanwhile, the government acquired the services of Francis Willis, a British doctor who had won fame for his treatment of George III's insanity. Willis went to Portugal and voiced optimism regarding the queen's condition, despite finding her possessed of a morbid fear that she was eternally damned. However, his attempts to sedate her met opposition from clerics and ministers who advocated religious consolation for the infirm queen. His suggestion that sea voyages might prove beneficial also came to naught, and Willis returned to England in frustration.

Maria I thus slipped into a state of deep melancholy. In 1799, the government determined that her illness was incurable, and John officially became prince-regent. When French armies invaded Portugal in 1807 and the court fled to refuge in Brazil, John took his mother along. During the Atlantic crossing, her condition reportedly showed some temporary improvement, perhaps justifying Dr. Willis' earlier diagnosis and treatment. Inadvertently the first European monarch to visit the Americas, Maria I died in Rio de Janeiro on March 20, 1816, whereupon the prince-regent became John VI.

SOURCES:

Beirão, Caetano. *D. María I, 1777–1792; subsídios para a revisão da história do seu reinado.* 3rd ed. Lisbon: Empresa Nacional de Publicidade, 1944.

Ferrás Gramoza, José Pedro. *Successos de Portugal; memórias históricas políticas e civís.* Lisbon: Typographia do Diário da Manhã, 1882.

Francis, David. *Portugal 1715–1808: Joanine, Pombaline and Rococo Portugal as Seen by British Diplomats and Traders.* London: Tamesis Books Limited, 1985.

Livermore, Harold. *A New History of Portugal.* Cambridge: Cambridge University Press, 1969.

Payne, Stanley. *Spain and Portugal.* 2 vols. Madison: University of Wisconsin Press, 1973.

SUGGESTED READING:

Domingues, Mário. *D. María I e a sua época.* Lisbon: Romano Torres, 1972.

Kendall W. Brown,
Professor of History,
Brigham Young University, Provo, Utah

Maria II da Gloria (1819–1853)

Queen of Portugal who ruled as a symbol of constitutional monarchy during an era of intense strife between Portuguese conservatives and liberals. Name variations: María II da Glória. Born on April 4, 1819, in Rio de Janeiro, Brazil; died in Lisbon on November 15, 1853; reigned 1826–1828 and 1834–1853; eldest child of Peter IV, king of Portugal (r. 1826), also known as Pedro I, emperor of Brazil (r. 1822–1831), and the Archduchess Leopoldina of Austria (1797–1826); named Maria da Gloria and given the title of princess of Grão-Pará; married Prince August of Leuchtenburg also known as Auguste Beauharnais (1810–1835), on January 28, 1835 (died two months later); married Ferdinand of Saxe-Coburg-Gotha (1816–1885), also known as Ferdinand II of Portugal,

*duke of Saxony, on April 9, 1836; children: Pedro de Alcântara (1837–1861), later known as Pedro V or Peter V, king of Portugal (r. 1853–1861); Luís Filipe (1838–1889), later known as Luís I or Louis I, king of Portugal (r. 1861–1889); João or John (1842–1861), duke of Beja; *Maria Anna of Portugal (1843–1884); *Antonia of Portugal (1845–1913); Fernando or Ferdinand (1846–1861), duke of Coimbra; Augusto or August (1847–1889); plus Maria (1840–1840), Leopoldo (1849–1849), Maria (1851–1851), and Eugénio (1853–1853), who died at birth.*

Royal family arrived in Rio de Janeiro, seeking refuge from the Napoleonic invasion of Portugal (March 1808); John VI (João VI) returned to Portugal (1821); Maria's father declared Brazilian independence and began to rule as Emperor Pedro I; death of Maria's mother Leopoldina (1826); death of John VI in Portugal; Pedro I's promulgation of Constitutional Charter for Portugal (1828); Portugal's acclamation of Maria II (1828); Maria sent to Europe (1828); Maria returned to Brazil (1829); Pedro I abdicated as Brazilian emperor (1831); Maria returned to France (1831); Maria arrived in Lisbon (1833); Maria II declared of age to rule (1834); death of Pedro (1834); September Revolution (1836); Belemzada (1836); Maria awarded Rose of Gold by Vatican (1842); Maria de Fonte revolt (1845); beginning of "Regeneration" (1851).

For a queen who ruled 19 years until her premature death at age 34, Maria II da Gloria of Portugal faced a life of insecurity and political turmoil from her earliest years. The first European monarch native to the New World, Maria da Gloria was born on April 4, 1819 in Rio de Janeiro, Brazil. Her father Pedro (I) had fled to South America along with the royal court when Napoleon's armies invaded Portugal in 1807. From Brazil, Maria's grandfather, John VI (João VI), ruled the Portuguese empire as prince-regent for his mentally ill mother, ***Maria I of Braganza,*** until her death in 1816. He then assumed the crown himself. By then, the Portuguese had freed themselves of the French and insisted that their monarch return to Europe. John VI did not depart Brazil until 1821, however, and then left his son Pedro to rule Brazil. The latter declared Brazil independent of Portugal in 1822 and began to reign as Emperor Pedro I.

Three-year-old Maria da Gloria was heir to her father's throne because her younger brother John (João) Carlos, born in 1821, had died in infancy. A blonde, vivacious child, Maria spent her early years on the beautiful São Cristóvão estate outside Rio. Life at court was "lax and voluptuous," according to one of her biographers. Nowhere was this more evident than in her domestic arrangements. Maria's father took a Brazilian mistress, **Domitila de Castro**, who lived at the palace. For a while it must have seemed to Maria that she had two mothers, *****Leopoldina of Austria** and Domitila. But the empress died in 1826, somewhat resolving the confusion at home but leaving Maria motherless.

Meanwhile, the emperor tried to secure his daughter's claim to both the Brazilian and Portuguese crowns. In 1822, he proposed that his brother Michael (I) come back to Brazil and wed Maria. When John VI died in 1826 and Pedro was acclaimed king of Portugal, he developed a complicated strategy to secure both kingdoms for his family. Realizing that he personally could not rule both, he offered to abdicate as king of Portugal in favor of Maria. His plan was to have Michael marry her and then rule as regent until Maria, 15 years his junior, was old enough to govern. They would then reign together. Anxious to gain power, Michael agreed. To complicate the matter, however, Pedro considered himself a liberal, and one of the conditions of his abdication was that the Portuguese swear fealty to the liberal Constitutional Charter which he gave them in 1828. On March 3, 1828, Pedro abdicated, whereupon the European powers recognized the young girl as Portugal's new monarch, Maria II.

To prepare her for her future marriage and reign, Pedro then sent Maria to Vienna, where she was to be educated by her mother's family. Arriving at Gibraltar, the girl and her advisers found that Pedro's plan was in disarray. With Leopoldina dead and Pedro advocating a constitutional monarchy in Portugal, the Habsburg absolutists had no interest in supporting Maria. Instead, they backed Michael, who had become the champion of absolutism in Portugal, against the liberal regime imposed from Brazil. Under the Duke of Wellington's conservative leadership, the British permitted Michael's acclamation as king in June 1828. While the Austrians and British were willing to allow the marriage to proceed, they urged Michael to ignore Pedro's Charter. In the meantime, 9-year-old Maria went to Britain, little realizing that she had come to symbolize such abstractions as liberty and civil equality for Portuguese liberals. Their sympathy for her misfortune also made her the legitimate queen for many Portuguese. In London, she became the center of her nation's liberal émigrés. Back in Brazil, Pedro considered his brother Michael a traitor.

Presented to the steely Wellington, who earlier had fought in Portugal against the Napoleonic invaders, Maria reportedly said, "I hope that your influence will defend my rights as decisively as your sword defended those of my grandfather." Her appeal was to little avail, despite the liberals' assurances that she would soon be going to Portugal. Instead, her father called her back to Brazil. She accompanied *****Amelia of Leuchtenburg**, who was en route to Brazil to become Pedro's new bride. They arrived in Rio de Janeiro in October 1829, and Pedro set up a court-in-exile for his daughter. With the British supporting Michael, Maria II's prospects were faint, and Portuguese liberalism seemed doomed.

> *The* queen, many times denigrated and calumniated by the political passions of her contemporaries, . . . appears today as a rare and very lively personality—bold, decisive, loyal and strong.
>
> —Ester de Lemos

Adding to the confusion of Maria's situation was her father's forced abdication as emperor of Brazil on April 7, 1831. Leaving Brazil to Maria's young brother Pedro (II), the father sailed with his daughter for France. He claimed to act as her "tutor and natural defender." Their arrival and warm reception by Louis Philippe, the Citizen King, whose July Monarchy had come to power the previous year, breathed new life into Portuguese liberalism. Maria II became close friends with his daughter *****Clementine of Orleans**, and their subsequent correspondence helps illuminate the remainder of Maria's life. On January 25, 1832, Maria's father, dressed in a general's uniform, knelt before her and swore fealty to her as queen. This increased respect for him among Maria's supporters, some of whom had feared that Pedro might try to seize her crown.

While 13-year-old Maria continued her education in Paris, Pedro and the liberals, from a base at Terceira in the Azores, captured Oporto on July 9, 1832. But much of Portugal remained indifferent to or opposed to Maria, Pedro and the liberals. Victories at the cape of St. Vincent and in the Algarve allowed Pedro and his army to enter Lisbon on July 24, 1833. Maria then went to Portugal, arriving in Lisbon harbor on September 21, 1833, aboard the British steamer *Soho*. Her father acted as regent. The war dragged on until the following May, when Michael was finally defeated and forced into permanent exile. Earlier that year, Pedro had reinstituted his Constitutional Charter. With their victory, the liberals began purging conservatives from the army, church and civil bureaucracy. On September 18, the national cortes (parliament) declared Maria II da Gloria of age to rule, and she presided over her first council of ministers that day. On September 24, Pedro died of tuberculosis. He left her a nation devastated by intermittent warfare since 1807 and a government in financial crisis.

To strengthen her monarchy and in accordance with her father's wish, Maria II gave permission to negotiate her marriage with August of Leuchtenburg. From birth, Pedro had taught her to expect no voice in the choice of her husband. Maria and August, brother of Maria's stepmother Amelia, were married in Lisbon on January 28, 1835, but the bridegroom died suddenly on March 28. This led to unfounded rumors that the duke of Palmela, president of the queen's council, had poisoned August in order to wed his own son to Maria II. Popular riots provoked Palmela's dismissal and reflected growing political and ideological factionalism regarding Portugal's future. Only two weeks after her husband's death, each house of Parliament requested that she quickly remarry to stabilize the government. Still in mourning for her father and her husband, she lamented: "To hear the same proposal twice in the same day is too much for my anguished heart!" Politicians openly debated what to do about the succession should she die without an heir.

Ever mindful of her duty, Maria II authorized negotiations with the French royal family for a new husband. Those failed due to British opposition to a marital alliance between France and Portugal. Maria's stepmother Amelia also resisted such a union, hoping her son Pedro might inherit the throne. Relations between the two women became more and more difficult. In the end, Maria married 19-year-old Prince Ferdinand of Saxe-Coburg-Gotha on April 9, 1836. Their first child, Pedro de Alcântara, was born the following year and eliminated controversy over the succession. Ferdinand and Maria soon developed a genuine love for each other, giving the queen an emotional anchor in her otherwise storm-tossed life. This happened even though they had "political attitudes almost diametrically opposed: what was in her pride, tenacity, violence—was in him good nature and condescending indifference," writes Maria II's biographer, Ester de Lemos.

Between 1836 and 1853, Maria had 11 pregnancies, and 7 of her children survived infancy. She lavished great care on their education and demanded proper behavior of them. Once, while walking with one of her small children in the park, another child came up to the prince and enthusiastically embraced him. Taken aback, the prince recoiled and rebuked the little boy. Maria immediately grabbed the prince by the arm and forced him to embrace and ask pardon of the commoner. Even her political enemies credited the quality of her family life. The opposition paper *Espectro* admitted in 1847: "There is no queen more virtuous as wife and mother. Her house can serve as example to all those of Europe."

In the public sphere, however, Maria II faced repeated controversy and crisis. Loyal to her father's Charter, she represented a politically moderate position. Pedro's Charter did not recognize popular sovereignty and gave the crown an absolute veto over the legislature. Parliament consisted of two houses: the crown appointed members of the aristocracy to the Senate for life, while the Charter allowed elections for seats in the Chamber of Deputies. In supporting the Charter, Maria faced opposition from both the right and the left. Despite Michael's defeat, absolutism appealed to many Portuguese, either from ideological revulsion against the French Revolution or from tradition. This conservative element posed a significant threat to Maria's government during the early years of her reign, although its importance waned. Meanwhile, her monarchy found itself beleaguered by growing pressure from the left. Debating clubs, Masonic lodges, and much of the press called for greater freedom. They wanted a one-house legislature, with all deputies elected. They insisted on either a return to the more liberal constitution of 1822 or a new document which recognized popular sovereignty. They demanded that the monarch have only a suspensive, rather than an absolute, veto over the legislature.

By mid-1836, the moderates had failed to solve Portugal's economic and financial problems, and discontent was running high. Radicals from Oporto called for a return to the constitution of 1822. Dissident liberals in Lisbon rallied to their cause. This provoked the September Revolution. Troops from the National Guard sided with the radicals, and demonstrations disrupted Lisbon. Ferdinand urged Maria to take shelter on a British naval vessel in the harbor. Maria refused, persuaded that such action might provoke the protestors to demand the abolition of the monarchy. Growing popular pressure forced a tearful Maria to take an oath to the constitution of 1822. With tension still high in November, Maria and the royal family sought refuge in Belém, from whence she reinstated the Charter, to enormous popular indignation.

The so-called *Belemzada* was essentially an attempted coup d'état by the monarchy. Its failure discredited the moderates and threw the nation into the hands of the radicals or Septembrists. Rather than resurrecting the old constitution, they called a constituent cortes to write a new one and began to purge the Chartists (supporters of Pedro's Charter) from the government. In 1837, a failed coup by the moderates, the Revolt of the Marshals, further discredited the Chartists. Nonetheless, Maria II managed to rise above the turmoil. While sympathetic to the Charter, she was not ideologically committed to it. She seemed more devoted to the cause of peace and stability, even if it meant working with the radicals. The anarchy in the streets was a greater enemy to her than the radicals.

In 1838, on her 19th birthday, she gave her approval to the new constitution, which was acceptable to both Septembrists and Chartists. It provided for an elected rather than appointed upper house but otherwise retained many of the Charter's provisions. Maria II thereupon became a staunch defender of the new constitution, refusing to support recalcitrant Chartists. She remarked: "I do not intend to change the institutions which I have sworn [to uphold]." Several years of relative political peace ensued. Many liberals gave up their anti-clericalism, which allowed Maria and the government to establish better relations with the Vatican. In 1842, the pontiff awarded her the prestigious Rose of Gold and agreed to be godfather to her baby John (João).

That year also brought to power a ministry dominated by António Bernardino da Costa Cabral, who reinstituted the Charter. His authoritarian methods provoked revolts, especially in the countryside. Such rebellions were in part a reaction against Costa Cabral's centralizing and modernizing tendencies, and they pitted rural against urban Portugal. The most famous revolt was that of *Maria de Fonte, which led the queen to dismiss Costa Cabral in May 1845. More political turmoil ensued, and the Septembrists resurfaced. Unwilling to turn the government over to them, Maria da Gloria and her political advisers sought support within the military to impose a new ministry against the will of Parliament. This "ambush" of October 6, 1846, was probably Maria's most serious mistake as monarch. It polarized the nation and touched off a bloody civil war.

Peace was restored through the intervention of the British and Spanish in support of Maria. The foreign intervention, plus her willingness to back a non-factional transitional ministry, enabled her to overcome the crisis. Only in 1851 did Portugal reach a political compromise regarding the nature of its government and the transferral of political power, the centrist "Regeneration."

Meanwhile, the political turmoil made it nearly impossible for Maria II and her ministers to address the nation's social and economic problems. "What I want is to do all the good I can," she wrote. Maria was sincerely interested in creating asylums and nurseries for foundlings and in reforming primary education. She also had the energy to rule. But the unrest made governance difficult, and her commitment to constitutional rule subjected her to the factionalism which ravaged the country.

By the time the Regeneration began, Maria was only 32. Her recent pregnancies had become more difficult, and friends cautioned her about the risks. But ever the devoted mother, she responded, "If I die, I die at my post." She perished during childbirth on November 15, 1853, at the age of 34. Reports asserted that during her funeral procession, a white dove landed on her coffin and remained there as it was carried to St. Vincent for burial. The woman who symbolized Portugal's transition from absolutism to constitutional monarchy and who knew so little tranquility during her lifetime was finally at peace.

SOURCES:

Almeida, Fortunato de. *História de Portugal*. 6 vols. Coimbra: Fortunato de Almeida, 1957, vol. 6.

Lemos, Ester de. *D. Maria II (A Rainha e a Mulher) no Centenário da Sua Morte*. Lisbon: Fundação da Casa de Bragança, 1954.

Livermore, H.V. *A New History of Portugal*. Cambridge: Cambridge University Press, 1966.

Macaulay, Neill. *Dom Pedro: The Struggle for Liberty in Brazil and Portugal, 1798–1834*. Durham, NC: Duke University Press, 1986.

SUGGESTED READING:

Bastos, Francisco Antonio Martíns. *Memorias para a História de El-Rey Fidelíssimo o Senhor Dom Pedro V e de Seus Augustos Irmãos*. Lisbon: Typographia Universal, 1863.

Fonseca Benevides, Francisco da. *Rainhas de Portugal; Estudos Históricos com Muitos Documentos*. 2 vols. Lisbon: Typographia Castro Irmão, 1878–1879.

Kendall W. Brown,
Professor of History,
Brigham Young University, Provo, Utah

Maria Alexandrovna (1824–1880).

See Marie of Hesse-Darmstadt.

Maria Amalia (1724–1730)

*Austrian princess. Born in 1724; died in 1730; younger sister of *Maria Theresa of Austria (1717–1780); daughter of Charles VI (1685–1740),*

*Holy Roman emperor (r. 1711–1740), and *Elizabeth Christina of Brunswick-Wolfenbuttel.*

Maria Amalia (1746–1804)

*Duchess of Parma. Name variations: Amelia; Maria Amalie. Born on February 26, 1746, in Vienna; died on June 18, 1804, in Prague; daughter of *Maria Theresa of Austria (1717–1780) and Francis I, Holy Roman emperor (r. 1745–1765); niece of *Maria Amalia (1724–1730); sister of *Maria Carolina (1752–1814), Joseph II, emperor of Austria and Holy Roman emperor (r. 1765–1790), *Maria Christina (1742–1798), *Elizabeth of Austria (1743–1808), Leopold II, Holy Roman emperor (r. 1790–1792), and *Marie Antoinette (1755–1793), queen of France; married Ferdinand I (1751–1802), duke of Parma (r. 1765–1802), on July 19, 1769; children: *Caroline of Parma (1770–1804); Louis I (1773–1803), duke of Parma (r. 1801–1803); Marie Antoinette (1774–1841, an Ursuline abbess); Charlotte of Parma (1777–1813); Philipp of Parma (1783–1786); Louise (1787–1789).*

Maria Amalia (1782–1866)

*Queen of France. Name variations: Amélie; Maria Amélie or Marie Amélie, or Marie-Amelia of Bourbon; Maria Amalia of Naples; Marie Amélie of Sicily; Marie Amelie de Bourbon. Born in Caserta on April 26, 1782; died on March 24, 1866, in Esher, Surrey, England; daughter of Ferdinand I, king of the Two Sicilies (r. 1816–1825), also known as Ferdinand IV, king of Naples and Sicily (r. 1759–1806, 1815–1825), and Maria Carolina (1752–1814); married Louis Philippe I (1773–1850), king of France (r. 1830–1848), on November 25, 1809; children: Ferdinand (1810–1842); *Louise d'Orleans (1812–1850); *Marie d'Orleans (1813–1839, who married Alexander, duke of Württemberg); Louis, duke of Nemours (1814–1896); Fransisca (1816–1818); *Clementine of Orleans (1817–1907, who married Augustus, prince of Coburg); Francis, prince of Joinville (1818–1900); Charles (1820–1828);*

Maria Amalia (1782–1866)

Henry, duke of Aumale (1822–1897); Antoine, duke of Montpensier (1824–1900).

Maria Amalia was the daughter of Ferdinand IV, king of Naples, and *Maria Carolina. She married Louis Philippe, duke of Orléans, who was elected king of France in 1830. When Louis Philippe was deposed in 1848, she retired with him to England.

Maria Amalia of Saxony (1724–1760)

*Queen of Spain. Name variations: Marie-Amelia Saski. Born on November 24, 1724; died on September 27, 1760; daughter of Frederick Augustus II (1696–1763), elector of Saxony (r. 1733–1763), also known as Augustus III, king of Poland (r. 1733–1763), and *Marie Josepha (1699–1757); married Carlos III also known as Charles III (1716–1788), king of Spain (r. 1759–1788), also known as Charles IV, king of Naples and Sicily (r. 1735–1759), on June 19, 1738; children: Marie Elizabeth (1740–1742); Marie Josepha (1742–1742); Marie Elizabeth (1743–1749); Marie Josepha (1744–1801); *Maria Louisa of Spain (1745–1792, who married Leopold II, emperor of Austria); Philipp Anton (b. 1747); Charles IV (1748–1819), king of Spain (r. 1788–1808); Marie Therese (1749–1750); Ferdinand IV (1751–1825), king of Naples and Sicily (r. 1759–1806, 1815–1825), later known as Ferdinand I, king of the Two Sicilies (r. 1816–1825); Gabriel (b. 1752); Marie Anna (1754–1755); Anton (b. 1755); Franz Xaver (b. 1757).*

Maria Ana of Austria (1683–1754).
See Maria Antonia of Austria.

Maria Ana Victoria (1718–1781).
See Maria I Braganza for sidebar.

Maria Anna (1718–1744)

*Austrian princess. Born in 1718; died in 1744; younger sister of *Maria Theresa of Austria (1717–1780); daughter of Charles VI (1685–1740), Holy Roman emperor (r. 1711–1740), and *Elizabeth Christina of Brunswick-Wolfenbuttel.*

Maria Anna of Austria (c. 1634–1696)

Queen and regent of Spain. Name variations: Maria of Austria; Marie-Anne of Austria; Mariana de Austria;

Mariana of Austria; Mariana Teresea of Austria. Born on December 24, 1634 or 1635; died on May 16, 1696; daughter of Ferdinand III, king of Hungary and Bohemia, Holy Roman emperor (r. 1637–1657), and Maria Anna of Spain (1606–1646); became second wife of Philip IV (1605–1665), king of Spain (r. 1621–1665), on November 8, 1649; children: Margaret Theresa of Spain (1651–1673); Charles II the Bewitched (1661–1700), king of Spain (r. 1665–1700).

The daughter of Ferdinand III of Austria and *Maria Anna of Spain, Maria Anna of Austria was born around 1634. She was originally betrothed to Baltasar Carlos, crown prince of Spain, but when he died, his father, Philip IV, decided to marry her. Even though Maria Anna was Philip's niece, they wed in 1649, whereupon she left Austria to join the old king in Spain. She had a daughter, *Margaret Theresa of Spain, in 1651, who was eventually wed to Leopold III of Austria. Several other children were either stillborn or did not survive infancy. In 1661, Charles II, the long-desired male heir, was born. Frequent intermarriage between the Spanish and Austrian Habsburgs was probably responsible for the boy's genetic problems. Mentally retarded and physically deformed, Charles II, known as Charles the Bewitched, became king as a four-year-old when Philip died in 1665.

Philip IV named Maria Anna regent until the boy was old enough to rule. Maria Anna depended heavily upon the counsel of Fernando Valenzuela and especially of her confessor, the German Jesuit Johann Eberhard Nithard. This caused resentment among Spanish courtiers. She gave up the regency in 1675, when Charles II turned 14. Philip IV left her an annual pension of 300,000 ducats. She tried to remain in Madrid, close to the court and power, but John of Austria, Philip's illegitimate son who enjoyed great influence over his half-brother, forced her to move to Toledo. Maria Anna remained there until 1679, when John died, and then returned to Madrid. Charles II married *Marie Louise d'Orleans (1662–1689) that year, and his mother lived in her daughter-in-law's apartments. Maria Anna's influence did not wane with Marie Louise's death in 1689. She chose a new wife for her son, her choice falling on *Maria Anna of Neuberg (1667–1740). Charles proved unable to sire a child with either of his wives, and his mother understood the dynastic crisis that loomed should he die without a direct heir. Death claimed her on May 16, 1696, and Charles the Bewitched four years later, whereupon the Spanish crown passed to Philip V and the Bourbon dynasty.

SOURCES:

Kamen, Henry. *Spain in the Later Seventeenth Century, 1665–1700.* NY: Longman, 1980.

Kendall W. Brown,
Professor of History,
Brigham Young University, Provo, Utah

Maria
Anna of
Austria
(c. 1634–1696)

Maria Anna of Bavaria
(1574–1616)

*Queen of Bohemia and Hungary. Name variations: Mary; Mary Anne of Bavaria; Marie-Anne of Bavaria. Born on December 12, 1574, in Munich; died on March 8, 1616, in Graz; became first wife of Ferdinand II, king of Bohemia and Hungary (r. 1578–1637), Holy Roman emperor (r. 1619–1637), on April 23, 1600; children: *Maria Anna of Bavaria (1610–1665, who married Maximilian, elector of Bavaria); Ferdinand III (1608–1657), king of Bohemia and Hungary, and Holy Roman emperor (r. 1637–1657); *Cecilia Renata of Austria (1611–1644). Ferdinand II's second wife was *Eleonora I Gonzaga (1598–1655).*

Maria Anna of Bavaria

(1610–1665)

*Electress of Bavaria. Born on January 13, 1610, in Graz; died on September 25, 1665, in Munich; daughter of *Maria Anna of Bavaria (1574–1616) and Ferdinand II, king of Bohemia and Hungary (r. 1578–1637), Holy Roman emperor (r. 1619–1637); sister of Ferdinand III (1608–1657), king of Bohemia and Hungary, and Holy Roman emperor (r. 1637–1657); married Maximilian, elector of Bavaria (r. 1623–1651); children: Ferdinand Maria (1636–1679), elector of Bavaria.*

Maria Anna of Bavaria

(1660–1690)

Dauphine of France. Name variations: Marie Christine, dauphine or dauphiness of France; Marie-Anne; Mary Anne Christine of Bavaria; Marie-Anne Christine-Victoire of Bavaria. Born Marie Anne Christine Victoire de Baviere on November 17, 1660; died on April 20, 1690, in France; married Louis (1661–1711), le Grand Dauphin (son of Louis XIV, king of France), on March 17, 1680; children: Louis (1682–1712), duke of Burgundy; Philip V (1683–1746), king of Spain (r. 1700–1724, 1724–1746); Charles (1685–1714), duke of Berry.

Maria Anna of Neuberg

(1667–1740)

*Queen of Spain and wife of Charles II. Name variations: Maria Anna of Bavaria-Neuberg. Born in Dusseldorf on October 28, 1667; died on July 16, 1740; daughter of Philip Wilhelm or Philip William, Elector Palatine of the Rhine, and Elizabeth Amalia of Hesse (1635–1709); sister of *Maria Sophia of Neuberg (1666–1699); second wife of Charles II the Bewitched (1661–1700), king of Spain (r. 1665–1700), on May 4, 1690; no children.*

Born in Dusseldorf on October 28, 1667, Maria Anna of Neuberg was the daughter of Philip William, Elector Palatine of the Rhine, and *Elizabeth Amalia of Hesse. With the death of King Charles II of Spain's first wife, *Marie Louise d'Orleans, the king's Habsburg mother *Maria Anna of Austria arranged his marriage with Maria Anna of Neuberg to strengthen Austria's influence at the Spanish court against France and Louis XIV. Maria Anna wed Charles by proxy on May 4, 1690, and then journeyed to Spain.

The king's first wife had borne no children, and Spaniards waited to see if the new queen would produce an heir. It soon became obvious, however, that Charles II would leave no children, a consequence of his own genetic deficiencies. Thus, Maria Anna's hopes of perpetuating Habsburg claims to the Spanish throne were frustrated. She exercised great influence over her mentally deficient husband but lacked any significant group of political supporters. Indeed when Spaniards understood she would have no children, Maria Anna's initial popularity faded, and courtiers criticized her haughtiness.

When Charles II's health declined, and France and Austria began intriguing to pick his successor, Maria Anna did everything possible to swing the decision in the Habsburgs' favor. Charles died on November 1, 1700, and the succession passed to Philip of Anjou, grandson of Louis XIV. Maria Anna remained in Spain and supported the Austrian cause during the War of the Spanish Succession (1701–1713). On July 16, 1740, she died in exile in Bayonne. She was the heroine of Victor Hugo's *Ruy Blas*.

SOURCES:
Adalbert, Prince of Bavaria. *Das Ende der Habsburger en Spanien*. Munich: F. Bruckmann, 1929.

Kendall W. Brown,
Professor of History,
Brigham Young University, Provo, Utah

Maria Anna of Portugal

(1843–1884)

*Portuguese princess. Name variations: Maria Ana or Maria Anna of Saxe-Coburg-Gotha. Born on July 21, 1843, in Lisbon, Portugal; died on February 5, 1884, in Dresden; daughter of *Maria II da Gloria (1819–1853) and Ferdinand of Saxe-Coburg-Gotha; married George (1832–1904), king of Saxony (r. 1902–1904), on May 11, 1859; children: Frederick Augustus III (1865–1932), king of Saxony (r. 1904–1918, abdicated in 1918); *Maria Josepha of Saxony (1867–1944); John George; Maximilian.*

Maria Anna of Savoy (1803–1884)

*Empress of Austria. Name variations: Marianna of Savoy. Born Maria Anna Caroline Pié on September 19, 1803, in Turin; died on May 4, 1884, in Vienna; daughter of *Maria Teresa of Austria (1773–1832) and Victor Emmanuel I (1759–1824), king of Sardinia (r. 1802–1821, abdicated); married Ferdinand I the Good (1793–1875), emperor of Austria (r. 1835–1848), on September 5, 1823; children: Louise (1821–1823); Charles III (1823–1854), duke of Parma (r. 1849–1854).*

Maria Anna of Saxony (1795–1865)

Grand duchess of Tuscany. Born on May 27, 1795; died on January 3, 1865, at Brandeis Castle in Bohemia; second wife of Ferdinand III (1769–1824), grand duke of Tuscany (r. 1790–1802 and 1814–1824). Ferdinand's first wife was *Louisa Amelia (1773–1802).

Maria Anna of Saxony (1799–1832)

Grand duchess of Tuscany. Name variations: Marie Anna of Saxony. Born on November 15, 1799, in Dresden, Germany; died on March 24, 1832, in Pisa; first wife of Leopold II (1797–1870), grand duke of Tuscany (r. 1824–1859), on November 16, 1817; children: (second marriage) three daughters, including *Augusta of Tuscany (1825–1864, who married Luitpold of Bavaria).

Maria Anna of Spain (1606–1646)

Holy Roman empress and queen of Bohemia. Name variations: Maria of Austria; Maria of Hungary; Infanta Maria. Born on August 18, 1606, in Madrid, Spain; died on May 13, 1646, in Linz; daughter of *Margaret of Austria (c. 1577–1611) and Philip III (1578–1621), king of Spain (r. 1598–1621); sister of *Anne of Austria (1601–1666) and Philip IV (1605–1665), king of Spain (r. 1621–1665); became first wife of Ferdinand III (1608–1657), king of Bohemia (r. 1627–1646), king of Hungary (r. 1625), Holy Roman emperor (r. 1637–1657), on February 20, 1631; children: Ferdinand (1633–1654); *Maria Anna of Austria (c. 1634–1696, who became the second wife of Philip IV, king of Spain); Leopold I, Holy Roman emperor (r. 1658–1705). Ferdinand's second wife was *Maria Leopoldine (1632–1649); his third was *Eleonora II Gonzaga (1628–1686).

Maria Annunziata (1843–1871)

Princess of Sicily and archduchess of Austria. Name variations: Annunciata of Sicily; Maria Annuziata of Bourbon and the Two Sicilies; María Annunciata of Bourbon-Naples; Maria Annunziata of Naples. Born on March 24, 1843, in Naples; died on May 4, 1871, in Vienna; daughter of *Theresa of Austria (1816–1867) and Ferdinand II, king of the Two Sicilies (r. 1830–1859); became second wife of Karl Ludwig also known as Charles Louis (1833–1896), archduke of Austria, on October 21, 1862 (drank from the river Jordan while on a pilgrimage and died from an intestinal infection); children: Francis Ferdinand also known as Franz Ferdinand (1863–1914),

archduke of Austria (assassinated with wife *Sophie Chotek at Sarajevo in 1914); Otto (1865–1906, who married *Maria Josepha of Saxony); Ferdinand Karl (1868–1915, who became known as Ferdinand Burg when he renounced his title in 1911); *Margaret Sophie (1870–1902). Charles Louis was also married to *Margaret of Saxony (1840–1858) and *Maria Theresa of Portugal (1855–1944).

Maria Annunziata (1876–1961)

Austrian royal. Name variations: Miana. Born on July 31, 1876, in Reichenau an der Rax; died on April 8, 1961, in Vaduz; daughter of *Maria Theresa of Portugal (1855–1944) and Karl Ludwig also known as Charles Louis (1833–1896), archduke of Austria.

Maria Antonia (1669–1692)

Electress of Bavaria. Name variations: Maria Antonieta or Antoinette. Born in 1669; died in 1692; daughter of Leopold I, Holy Roman emperor (r. 1658–1705), and *Margaret Theresa of Spain (1651–1673); married Maximilian II Emmanuel (1662–1726), elector of Bavaria (r. 1679–1726), in 1685; children: Joseph Ferdinand, electoral prince of Bavaria (d. 1699). Following Maria Antonia's death in 1692, Maximilian married *Cunigunde Sobieska, the mother of Charles VII, Holy Roman emperor.

Maria Antonia of Austria (1683–1754)

Queen of Portugal and archduchess of Austria. Name variations: Marie-Anne of Austria; Maria Ana. Born Maria Antonia Josefa in Linz, Austria, on September 7, 1683; died on August 14, 1754; daughter of Leopold I, Holy Roman emperor (r. 1658–1705), and his third wife, Eleanor of Pfalz-Neuburg (1655–1720); married Joao or John V (1689–1750), king of Portugal (r. 1706–1750), in 1708; children: Pedro (1712–1714); Maria Barbara of Braganza (1711–1758, who married Ferdinand VI, king of Spain); José or Joseph I (1714–1777), king of Portugal (r. 1750–1777); Carlos (1716–1736); Pedro or Peter III (d. 1786), king of Portugal (r. 1777–1786); Alexander (1723–1728).

Birth of John V (1689); War of the Spanish Succession (1701–14); construction of palace complex at Mafra began (1717).

Born in Linz, Austria, on September 7, 1683, Maria Antonia of Austria was the daughter of the Habsburg ruler Leopold I and his third wife, *Eleanor of Pfalz-Neuburg. To strengthen an alliance with Portugal during the War of the Spanish Succession, Maria Antonia married John V, king of Portugal, on July 9, 1708, by proxy in Vienna. A fleet of 11 ships carried her to her new homeland.

Despite her own virtues, Maria Antonia's marriage was unhappy because of her husband's infidelities. To the royal couple's consternation, their first years of marriage bore no children. Maria Antonia eventually gave birth to *Maria Barbara of Braganza in 1711, in celebration of which John V built the great basilica of Mafra. Two of her sons also survived to adulthood: Joseph I and Peter III, both of whom ruled.

On two occasions Maria Antonia governed as regent. The first occurred in 1716, when the king secluded himself at Vila Viçosa suffering from depression. In 1742, John became very ill. Maria Antonia intermittently governed as regent until his death, despite the fact that her son, Joseph, was already an adult. Perhaps her chief political action, however, was to help launch the governmental career of Sebastião José de Carvalho e Melo, the future marquis of Pombal. Upon John V's death in 1750, Maria Antonia recommended Joseph appoint Carvalho e Melo as minister, recognizing her son's disinterest in politics and frivolous personality. Joseph complied immediately, and by 1756 the future marquis had become chief minister. He governed as virtual dictator of Portugal from 1756 to 1777.

Maria Antonia died in Belem Palace on August 14, 1754. She was buried in the São João Nepomuceno convent for Discalced Carmelites that she had founded. Her reign was a period of prosperity, largely due to the Brazilian gold-and-diamond boom.

SOURCES:

Fonseca Benevides, Francisco da. *Rainhas de Portugal; estudos históricos com muitos documentos.* 2 vols. Lisbon: Typographia Castro Irmão, 1878–79.

Livermore, H.V. *A New History of Portugal.* Cambridge: Cambridge University Press, 1966.

Kendall W. Brown,
Professor of History,
Brigham Young University, Provo, Utah

Maria Antonia of Austria

(1724–1780)

Princess of Bavaria, electress of Saxony, and German composer, pianist, harpsichordist, poet, singer, composer, and patron of the arts. Name variations: Maria Antonia Walpurgis; (pseudonym) ETPA (Ermelinda Talea Pastorella Arcada). Born in Munich, Germany, on July 18, 1724; died in Dresden on April 23, 1780; daughter of Karl Albert also known as Charles VII Albert (1697–1745), elector of Bavaria (r. 1726–1745), later known as Charles VII, Holy Roman emperor (r. 1742–1745); sister of Maximilian III Joseph, elector of Bavaria (r. 1745–1777); married Friedrich Christian also known as Frederick Christian (1722–1763), elector of Saxony (r. 1763), on June 20, 1747; children: Frederick Augustus III (1750–1827), elector of Saxony (r. 1763–1806), also known as Frederick Augustus I the Just, king of Saxony (r. 1806–1827); Anthony Clement I (1755–1836), king of Saxony (r. 1827–1836); Maximilian (b. 1759), duke of Saxony (who married *Caroline of Parma).

Princess Maria Antonia of Austria showed many talents at an early age. Giovanni Ferrandini, director of the electorate's chamber music group, taught her piano. After her marriage to Frederick Christian, elector of Saxony, in 1747, she studied composition and singing with Nicola Porpora and Johan Adolf Hasse. A writer and poet, she composed her own music and libretto for operas in which she sang, while some of her works were set to music by Graun, Ferrandini, Hasse, Risteri, and Nauman. Maria Antonia was also a painter, rendering her own self-portrait, and a patron of the arts. As a result of her support, Gluck produced his *Orpheus and Euridice* in Munich. This innovative work marked the beginning of a reform in the operatic world.

John Haag,
Athens, Georgia

Maria Antonia of Naples (1784–1806).

See Maria Carolina for sidebar.

Maria Antonia of Portugal

(1862–1959)

*Duchess of Bourbon-Parma. Born on November 28, 1862, in Bronnbach; died on May 14, 1959, in Luxemburg; daughter of *Adelheid (1831–1909) and Miguel also known as Michael I (1802–1866), king of Portugal (r. 1828–1834); married Robert, duke of Bourbon-Parma, on October 15, 1884; children: Adelaide of Parma (b. 1885, a nun); Sixtus (b. 1886); Franz Xaver (b. 1889); Francisca Josephe (b. 1890, a nun); *Zita of Parma (1892–1989); Felix (b. 1893), prince consort; René Charles (b. 1894), prince of Bourbon-Parma; Maria Antonia of Parma (b. 1895); Isabella of Parma (b. 1898); Ludwig (b. 1899); Maria Antonia of Parma (b. 1895); Isabella of Parma (b. 1898); Ludwig (b. 1899); Henriette of Parma (b. 1903); Gaëtan (b. 1905).*

Maria Antonia of Sicily
(1814–1898)

*Grand duchess of Tuscany. Name variations: Antonietta of Bourbon-Two Sicilies; Maria Antonia of Bourbon-Two Sicilies. Born on December 19, 1814, in Palermo; died on November 17, 1898, in Orth, near Gmunden; daughter of *Marie Isabella of Spain (1789–1848) and Francis I, king of the Two Sicilies (r. 1825–1830); married Leopold II (1797–1870), grand duke of Tuscany (r. 1824–1859), on June 7, 1833; children: ten, including *Maria Isabella (1834–1901, who married Francesco, count of Trapani); Ferdinand IV (1835–1908), grand duke of Tuscany; Charles Salvator (1839–1892, who married *Maria Immaculata of Sicily); *Maria Ludovica (1845–1917, who married Charles of Isenburg-Birstein); Louis Salvator (1847–1915); John Nepomucen (1852–1891, who renounced rights in 1889 and took the name Johann Orth); and four others who died young. Leopold's first wife was *Maria Anna of Saxony (1799–1832).*

Maria Antonia of Spain
(1729–1785)

*Duchess of Savoy. Name variations: Marie Antoinette of Spain; Mary of Spain; (Spanish) Maria Antonieta Fernanda; (Italian) Maria Antonia Ferdinanda. Born Marie Antoineta Fernanda on November 17, 1729; died on September 19, 1785; daughter of *Elizabeth Farnese (1692–1766) and Philip V, king of Spain (r. 1700–1724, 1725–1746); married Victor Amadeus III (1726–1796), duke of Savoy (r. 1773–1796), on May 31, 1750; children: 12, including Charles Emmanuel IV (1751–1819), duke of Savoy (r. 1796–1802); Joseph Benedict; *Marie Josephine of Savoy (d. 1810, who married Louis XVIII, king of France); *Maria Charlotte of Sardinia (c. 1761–c. 1786); *Maria Teresa of Savoy (1756–1805, who married Charles X, king of France); Victor Emmanuel I (1759–1824), king of Sardinia (r. 1802–1821); Charles Felix, duke of Genoa (r. 1821–1831).*

Maria Antonia Walpurgis (1724–1780).

See Maria Antonia of Austria.

Maria Augusta of Thurn and Taxis (1706–1756)

Duchess of Wurttemberg. Born on August 11, 1706; died on February 1, 1756; daughter of Anselm Franz, prince of Thurn and Taxis; married Charles I Alexander (1684–1737), duke of Wurttemberg (r.

1733–1737), on May 1, 1727; children: Charles Eugene (1728–1793), duke of Wurttemberg (r. 1737–1793); Louis Eugene (1731–1795), duke of Wurttemberg (r. 1793–1795); Frederick II Eugene (1732–1797), duke of Wurttemberg (r. 1795–1797).

Maria Barbara of Braganza
(1711–1758)

Queen of Spain and wife of Ferdinand VI who ruled during his illnesses. *Name variations: Marie-Barbara of Portugal; Barbara of Braganza or Barbara de Bragança; Maria Barbara, Marie-Barbara, or Mary Barbara; Marie Magdalena Barbara; Maria Magdalena Josepha de Bragança. Born in Lisbon on December 4, 1711; died on August 27, 1758, in Aranjuez; daughter of Joao V also known as John V, king of Portugal (r. 1706–1750), and Maria Antonia of Austria (1683–1754); sister of Joseph I (1714–1777), king of Portugal (r. 1750–1777), and Peter III (d. 1786), king of Portugal (r. 1777–1786); married Fernando or Ferdinand VI el Sabio (1713–1759), king of Spain (r. 1746–1759), on January 20, 1729; children: none.*

War of the Spanish Succession (1701–1714); birth of Ferdinand VI (1713); Treaty of Utrecht guarantees Philip V's claim to the Spanish throne (1715); abdication of Philip V in favor of Luis I (1724); death of Luis I (1724); death of Philip V (1746); death of Ferdinand VI (1759).

The daughter of John V of Portugal and *Maria Antonia of Austria, Maria Barbara of Braganza was born in Lisbon on December 4, 1711. She became a tool of dynastic diplomacy in 1725 when her father betrothed her to Ferdinand (VI), a son of the Spanish monarch Philip V. To strengthen the alliance further, the royal houses also agreed to the marriage of Maria Barbara's brother, Joseph (I), to Ferdinand's sister, ❧ Maria Ana Victoria (1718–1781). Given the youth of the parties involved, however, the marriages did not occur until January 1729, in a gala celebration. The rites took place in a wooden palace built solely for the occasion across the Caya River, on the Spanish-Portuguese border between Elvas and Badajoz. In another fit of extravagance, Maria Barbara's father built the Vendas Novas palace solely to host the Portuguese wedding guests for a night en route to the ceremony and another night on their return to Lisbon.

Spaniards rejoiced at the marriage, despite their initial perceptions of Maria Barbara. In 1725, Ferdinand had become heir to the Spanish

❧
Maria Ana Victoria (1718–1781). See Maria I of Braganza for sidebar.

throne when his elder brother Luis died of small-pox. Furthermore, their father's second wife, *Elizabeth Farnese (1692–1766), was imperious and widely unpopular, dominating her husband and Spanish policy. Many Spaniards looked to Ferdinand as a counterweight to his stepmother's influence, and his marriage to Maria Barbara seemed to convert him into an adult rival. On the other hand, Spaniards found the Portuguese bride homely and lamented that Ferdinand had to make such a sacrifice for the monarchy.

Nonetheless, Ferdinand and Maria Barbara fell deeply in love, and within a short time he became very reliant upon her. By nature, Ferdinand was docile, melancholic and irresolute. Although timid, Maria Barbara had received a good education, spoke several languages, and adored sacred music, which she also composed. She was especially remembered as the patron of the Italian opera star Farinelli (Carlos Broschi), who performed often at court. Love of music and the arts heightened the bond between Maria Barbara and her husband.

Perhaps three worries troubled Maria Barbara more than any others. First, she and Ferdinand had no children. Second, without children she could not prevent the Spanish throne from passing to Charles III, the son of Elizabeth Farnese, whom Maria Barbara resented. Third, Portuguese by birth, Maria Barbara inherited that nation's pro-British sentiments, which were contrary to the traditional French leanings of the Spanish Bourbons.

On July 9, 1746, Philip V died, thereby elevating Ferdinand VI and Maria Barbara to the Spanish throne. Farnese defied protocol by remaining at court, until Maria Barbara insisted that Ferdinand order her to depart. To Maria Barbara's chagrin, however, he allowed Farnese to occupy La Granja Palace at San Ildefonso. Despite palace intrigues between pro-French and pro-British factions attempting to influence royal policies, Ferdinand and Maria Barbara ruled over a period of relative prosperity and tranquility. Ferdinand was, according to historian William Coxe, a "prince of inferior capacity but upright intentions and pacific disposition." He lacked the energy or will to govern, and thus it remained for Maria Barbara and royal ministers such as the Marquis of Ensenada and José de Carvajal to manage the government.

Prior to 1746, Maria Barbara had largely avoided politics, in part fearing Farnese's wrath. Ascended to power and wedded to a weakling, she overcame her personal timidity. Writes John Lynch, "although she had power over her hus-band and an eye for Portuguese interests, she did not use her position to distort Spanish policy. She strongly supported the diplomacy of neutrality and joined her husband on the path of peace." Maria Barbara's ties to the Portuguese crown proved valuable to the negotiation of the Treaty of Limits (1750), which adjusted the boundaries between the Iberian nations' South American colonies. When the pro-French Marquis of Ensenada fell from power, she stepped in to prevent the complete triumph of the British faction.

Queen Maria Barbara died on August 27, 1758, and was buried in the chapel of Las Salesas convent, which she had founded in 1750. Her will confirmed rumors of her notorious avarice. She left a huge fortune, acquired since her arrival in Spain, to her brother, and Spaniards were outraged that it would be transferred out of the country. Her death left Ferdinand VI deeply depressed and unable to live without his beloved companion. He isolated himself in the royal palace at Villaviciosa and refused to govern. Ferdinand died on August 10, 1759, less than a year after his wife.

SOURCES:

Coxe, William. *Memoirs of the Kings of Spain of the House of Bourbon, from the Accession of Philip V, to the Death of Charles III, 1700 to 1788.* 5 vols. London: Longman, Hurst, Rees, Orme, and Brown, 1815.

Danvila, Alfonso. *Fernando VI y dona Bárbara de Braganza (1713–1748).* Madrid: J. Rates Martín, 1905.

Lancastre-Laboreiro e Souza de Villalobos, Anna de. *Infantas lusitanas reinas de España e infantas españpas reinas de Portugal.* Cáceres: Imprenta Moderna, 1931.

Lynch, John. *Bourbon Spain, 1700–1808.* Cambridge, MA: Basil Blackwell, 1989.

Kendall W. Brown,
Professor of History,
Brigham Young University, Provo, Utah

Maria Beatrice of Modena

(1750–1829)

*Duchess of Massa and Carrara. Name variations: Archduchess Beatrice of Modena; Maria Beatrice d'Este; Beatrix of Modena-Este; Maria Riccarda; Maria Beatrix Riccarda of Este; Mary Beatrice of Modena. Born on April 6 or 7, 1750, in Modena; died on November 14, 1829, in Vienna; daughter of Hercules also known as Ercole III d'Este (1727–1803), duke of Modena; married Archduke Ferdinand (1754–1806, governor general of Lombardy in Milano and son of *Maria Theresa of Austria [1717–1780]), on October 15, 1771; children: *Maria Teresa of Austria (1773–1832, who married Victor Emmanuel I, king of Sardinia); Josepha (1775–1777); *Maria Leopoldina (1776–1848, who married*

Charles Theodore of Bavaria); Francis IV (1779–1846), duke of Modena (r. 1814–1846); Ferdinand (1781–1850); Maximilian Joseph (1782–1863); Maria Antonia (1784–1786); Charles (1785–1809); *Maria Ludovica of Modena (1787–1816, who married Francis I, emperor of Austria).

Maria Beatrice of Modena

(1824–1906)

Spanish royal. Name variations: Beatriz of Austria Este; Marie Beatrix of Modena. Born on February 13, 1824, in Modena; died on March 18, 1906, in Gorz; daughter of Franz or Francis IV (1779–1846), duke of Modena (r. 1814–1846) and *Maria Beatrice of Sardinia (1792–1840); married the infante Juan de Borbon also known as John of Bourbon or John of Molina (1822–1887), on February 6, 1847; children: Charles (b. 1848), duke of Madrid; Alphonse Carlos (b. 1849), duke of San Jaime.

Maria Beatrice of Sardinia

(1792–1840)

Duchess of Modena. Name variations: Beatrix of Modena-Este; Maria Beatrice of Modena; Maria Beatrix of Savoy. Born Maria Beatrice Victoire Josephine on December 6, 1792; died on September 15, 1840; daughter of *Maria Teresa of Austria (1773–1832) and Victor Emmanuel I (1759–1824), king of Sardinia (r. 1802–1821, abdicated); married Franz or Francis IV (1779–1846), duke of Modena (r. 1814–1846), on June 20, 1812; children: *Therese of Bourbon (1817–1886); Francis V (1819–1875), duke of Modena (r. 1846–1859, who married *Adelgunde of Bavaria); Ferdinand (1821–1849, who married *Elizabeth [1831–1903], daughter of Archduke Joseph); *Maria Beatrice of Modena (1824–1906, who married the infante Juan de Borbon).

Maria Cantacuzene (fl. 1300s)

Byzantine princess. Flourished in the 1300s; daughter of *Irene Asen and John VI Cantacuzene, emperor of Nicaea (r. 1347–1354); married Nicephorus II of Epirus.

Maria Carolina (1752–1814)

Queen-consort of Ferdinand I, king of Naples and Sicily, who exercised the real power behind the throne. Name variations: Maria of Austria; Marie Caroline; Mary Carolina or Mary Caroline; Maria Karolina. Born on August 13, 1752, in Vienna, Austria; died on September 7 or 8, 1814, in Vienna, Austria; 13th of 16 children of Empress Maria Theresa of Austria (1717–1780, queen of Hungary, Bohemia and the Netherlands, archduchess of Austria) and Francis I, Holy Roman emperor (r. 1745–1765), also known as Francis Stephen of Lorraine, grand duke of Tuscany; sister of Marie Antoinette (1755–1793); married Ferdinand IV (1751–1825), king of Naples (r. 1759–1806, 1815–1825), later known as Ferdinand I, king of the Two Sicilies (r. 1816–1825), on May 13, 1768; children: Maria Teresa of Naples (1772–1807); Louisa Amelia (1773–1802), grand duchess of Tuscany; Anna (1775–1780); Carlo or Charles (1776–1778); Gennaro (d. 1789); Carlo or Charles (d. 1789); Leopold; Carlo Alberto or Charles Albert (d. 1798); Francis I (1777–1830), king of the Two Sicilies (r. 1825–1830); Maria Amalia (1782–1866), later queen of France (r. 1830–1848); Christine of Bourbon (1779–1849); Maria Antonia of Naples (1784–1806); and six others who did not survive to adulthood.

Crowned queen of Naples and Sicily on her marriage to Ferdinand I (1768); dominated her passive, uneducated husband; within a few years of marriage, was ruling the country in Ferdinand's name; first 20 years of her joint reign were extremely successful and marked by several efforts to reform and modernize Naples; last 20 years were clouded by the results of the French Revolution, including the execution of her sister Marie Antoinette, the temporary occupation of Naples by Jacobin forces, and finally the annexation of Naples as part of the Napoleonic empire; died at the very end of the Napoleonic wars, just before Naples was restored to her husband by the Congress of Vienna.

Maria Carolina was born in 1752, the 13th of 16 children of Empress *Maria Theresa of Austria and Francis Stephen, duke of Lorraine (Holy Roman Emperor Francis I). Trained from infancy to become part of Europe's ruling aristocracy, all of Maria Theresa's children were carefully tutored in the arts of music, drawing, history, geography, and Latin. Maria Theresa zealously oversaw not only her children's education, but also their religious training (she was a devoted Catholic who attended masses every morning and evening), their recreation, their behavior, and their dress. She was instantly suspicious of any tendency to idleness or carelessness in her children, determined that they would grow up to become wise, thoughtful, diligent, and intensely religious rulers.

Maria Theresa was determined to secure for her children diplomatically advantageous marriages. She had decided early on that one of her daughters would marry the king of Naples, Ferdinand I. Because he was too young to be a good match for her older daughters, Maria Theresa decided that her daughter **Johanna**, then only 12 years old, would be betrothed to Ferdinand. When Johanna died of smallpox in December 1762, Maria Theresa still refused to give up the idea of the Naples match, so she simply substituted her daughter **Josepha**, who was one year younger. Josepha objected to the match, but Maria Theresa put her under the care of a governess with the intention of sending her to Naples when she reached the age of 16. To the **Countess von Lerchenfeld**, whom she had chosen to educate Josepha for her future role, she admitted, "My mother's heart is very uneasy. I look upon poor Josepha as a sacrifice to politics. If only she fulfills her duty to God and her husband and attends to the welfare of her soul, I shall be content even if she is not happy." When the time arrived for Josepha to set off to Italy in 1767, Maria Theresa insisted that she visit the family vault at the Capuchin church in Vienna to pay respects to her father, the Emperor Francis, who had died two years previously. Josepha was horrified, and begged to be spared from such a gloomy and melancholy task, but Maria Theresa was obstinate. Josepha burst into tears and shuddered throughout the visit to the vault, in which not only her father but her sister-in-law *Maria Josepha of Bavaria, who had died of smallpox four months earlier, lay. Within hours of returning to the palace, Josepha began to complain of illness, and she soon showed signs of having contracted smallpox herself. On October 15, 1767, the day on which she was to have begun her journey to Italy, Josepha died.

Undaunted in her determination to elevate one of her daughters to the throne of Naples, Maria Theresa wrote to Charles III of Spain, Ferdinand I's father, who had given up the throne of Naples in order to inherit the throne of Spain from his brother when Ferdinand was but a child. She proposed that Charles choose between two of her daughters: *Maria Amalia, who was five years older than Ferdinand, and Maria Carolina, who was but eighteen months younger than Josepha. Ferdinand begged his father not to saddle him with a wife five years older than himself, and the betrothal, therefore, fell upon Maria Carolina. Maria Carolina cried and entreated her mother not to force her into this match; in light of her sisters' deaths, she proclaimed the Neapolitan match must be cursed. But Maria Theresa would not be moved. Maria Carolina was placed under the tutelage of Josepha's teacher, the Countess von Lerchenfeld,

who was given all of nine months to prepare the 15-year-old to become a queen. Maria Theresa had confidence that Maria Carolina could succeed in her future role. Maria Carolina resembled her mother remarkably in physical appearance, and her mother considered Maria Carolina, like herself, to be a born ruler.

As Maria Carolina was preparing for her journey to Italy, her mother gave her specific advice on how to prosper in her new role. Even if Maria Carolina could not bring herself to love her new husband, Maria Theresa warned, she should be careful to make Ferdinand think that she was enchanted by him, so that she could eventually bend him to her will, since Ferdinand was not considered competent to rule on his own. After a proxy marriage on April 17, 1768, Maria Carolina set out on the long journey to Italy. When she arrived, she described her new husband as "very ugly," and complained that "he thinks he is handsome and clever, and he is neither one nor the other." She was dreadfully homesick when first left on her own in a foreign land, depressed and unhappy, but remembering the advice of her mother, she promised Frau von Lerchenfeld in a letter that she was doing all in her power to hide her feelings from Ferdinand: "I don't love him except from duty," she admitted, "but I do all I can to make him think I have a passion for him." At first she was frustrated by Ferdinand's obstinacy in his old habits—on the morning of their wedding he arose early to go out shooting—but gradually Maria Carolina was able to inspire his interest, his respect, and finally his utter devotion. Never interested in the grueling work of administration, Ferdinand eventually entrusted all major decisions to Maria Carolina: "My wife," he bragged in later years, "knows everything."

Maria Carolina's rise in her husband's esteem and confidence earned her her first political enemy in Naples. Bernardo Tanucci had been appointed as regent for young Ferdinand I in 1759 by Charles III. As regent, Tanucci exercised ruling authority in Naples and Sicily, subject only to the oversight of Charles, to whom he sent frequent reports. Tanucci sorely neglected Ferdinand's education and training for leadership during his youth in favor of outdoor activities, in part because of Charles' fear that a contemplative life would catapult Ferdinand into the hereditary insanity which had been exhibited by Charles' brothers as well as by his oldest son. Tanucci had taken Charles' prescription a bit too far, and as a result Ferdinand was well known to be one of the most profoundly ignorant sovereigns in Europe. Maria Carolina's arrival and her

growing political power were a threat to Tanucci's position as the power behind the throne.

Even as Maria Theresa's children dispersed throughout Europe—her daughter Maria Amalia married the duke of Parma in 1769, and

*Marie Antoinette married the dauphin of France, later Louis XVI, in 1770—she continued to maintain contact with them by sending correspondence three times a week. Maria Carolina was the most attentive of all of the younger daughters to their mother's advice, and Maria

Theresa gave her detailed instructions for influencing Ferdinand and governing his kingdom, which Maria Carolina followed to the best of her abilities. As part of the marriage contract, Maria Theresa had wisely insisted upon a clause giving Maria Carolina the right to sit and vote in the State Council as soon as she had borne an heir for the kingdom. Although for the first few years Maria Carolina and Ferdinand had no children, a matter of some consternation for both of them, their first child, daughter *Maria Teresa of Naples, was born in 1772, followed in quick succession by another daughter, *Louisa Amelia, and finally a son, Carlo, in 1776 (he would die in 1778). In all, Maria Carolina gave birth to 18 children between 1772 and 1794. As was common during the 18th century, a number did not live to adulthood.

Of all my daughters, she is the one who resembles me the most.

—Maria Theresa of Austria

The 18th century was the great age of the Enlightenment, and Maria Carolina could not fail to be affected by the spirit of reform that was sweeping through Europe. Her own brother, Joseph II, was deeply moved by reforming zeal, and was already laying the groundwork in the Holy Roman Empire for the abolition of serfdom, the reduction of the influence of the Roman Catholic Church over secular policy, and the spread of education. Soon after her arrival in Naples, Maria Carolina had been drawn to the intellectual circles where professors, philosophers and civil servants reveled in the same utopian dreams of government based on reason. From the beginning of their reign, Ferdinand and Maria Carolina showed great concern for the plight of the poor, and their projects of public charity brought them great popularity among the *lazzaroni*, or common people.

During the eight years of his personal reign, Tanucci had followed an anti-clerical policy, even banishing the Jesuit order from Naples and confiscating their land, but he was not, in the Enlightenment sense, an avid reformer. He did nothing to ease the feudal burdens on the common people, and jealously guarded the rights and privileges of the landed aristocracy. He had no interest in building schools, hospitals, or orphanages. In comparison with England, France, and even Maria Carolina's native Austria, Naples was hopelessly feudal and backward. Maria Carolina's great chance to change the direction of public policy came with the birth of her first son, the prince royal, in 1776. When she formally requested the privilege of sitting on the Council which had been promised as part of her marriage agreement, Tanucci insisted to Ferdinand that she must be blocked. Ferdinand, more in love with his wife than ever now that she had given him an heir, refused to break his promise to her, and Tanucci's fate was sealed. By 1777, he had been driven from the Council, and he retired to the country, where he died six years later. Maria Carolina, now 25, quickly rose to become the practical head of state.

Under Ferdinand and Maria Carolina's rule, Naples and Sicily broke off their previous connection with the Bourbons, severing relations with Spain and even giving preference to England over France. Maria Carolina dreamed of creating a large navy, and to that end in 1779 she appointed Sir John Acton, a French-born adventurer and son of an English Jacobite, to lead the admiralty. Acton would rise in Maria Carolina's favor, in part due to her father-in-law Charles III's objections to him, to the extent that he would become her political favorite and minister of war. Acton's rapid ascent in the Neapolitan government gave rise to rumors that he was Maria Carolina's lover. These whisperings Maria Carolina vehemently denied, and though Ferdinand teased her about Acton on more than one occasion, the relationship between husband and wife did not seem adversely affected by Acton's position. Under Acton's leadership, the Neapolitan navy became the envy of all Italy, a force able to contend with the major powers of Europe and to discourage threatening exhibitions by Spain.

The 20 years following Maria Carolina's marriage were undoubtedly the most successful and carefree of her life. Ferdinand was willing to continue his outdoor pursuits with his old abandon while Maria Carolina took on the day-to-day burden of governing the nation. Like Maria Carolina, Ferdinand was concerned with the plight of the poor in Naples, and he supported Maria Carolina's efforts to reform some of the most oppressive feudal laws that worked against the interests of the poor. While open handed with government projects designed to relieve the physical hardship of the common classes, Maria Carolina had no interest in giving the populace greater political rights. Contrary to many of the revolutionary ideas in vogue during the Enlightenment, Maria Carolina considered the people largely unable to govern themselves, and, trained from birth to be a ruler, she viewed the relationship between ruler and subject as similar to that of a parent and children. Although the Habsburgs were very "enlightened" about certain social issues, politically they were all confirmed absolutists. Maria Carolina was no exception.

The outbreak of the French Revolution in 1789 shook Maria Carolina's ideals of enlightenment to their very foundations. Within a year of the storming of the Bastille, aristocratic families began fleeing from France in droves, many to settle in the various provinces of Italy until the revolutionary fervor had subsided. With growing horror, Maria Carolina began to see the violent potential of many of the seemingly innocent reform doctrines which she had encouraged and sheltered within her own country. Desperately, she tried to convince her younger sister Marie Antoinette to escape from France with her children, but King Louis XVI, naively convinced of the goodwill of his subjects, vacillated until it was too late, and after an abortive escape attempt in 1792, the entire French royal family was imprisoned. In January 1793, Louis XVI was convicted of treason and sent to the guillotine. Marie Antoinette fell to the same fate the following year.

The barbaric execution of her beloved sister changed Maria Carolina forever. Her zest for reform gave way to a grim determination to survive. Wrote one historian: "Her chief endeavours were to protect herself, her kingdom, and those dear to her from the horrors which threatened them, and, so far as she could, to avenge the sufferings of her friends and punish the wretches who had inflicted them." The queen quickly terminated the protection and support of reformers and intellectuals in Naples. The tendency towards secular education and away from the direct authority of the church, which had begun under Charles III, was halted, and Maria Carolina allowed Neapolitan bishops wide latitude. Government leaders denounced the French Revolution at every turn, and Maria Carolina offered succor to the increasing number of émigrés fleeing from revolutionary France, many of whom were granted pensions.

Terrified that the intellectual movements which she had previously tolerated and even encouraged in Naples were destined to create a similar revolution in her own country, Maria Carolina clamped down on universities, the church, and municipal governments, putting conservative royalists in positions of power and stifling political reformers. She established a circle of spies, who reported to her personally, to root out revolutionaries in coffee houses and salons. She developed a close friendship with *Emma Hamilton, the wife of the English ambassador Sir William Hamilton. Through Emma, she forwarded secret correspondence to the English government to aid them in opposing the French forces, which had withstood the opposition of the Austrians, Prussians and English and were poised for expansion—Maria Carolina realized that the divided kingdoms of Italy would be an all-too-tempting target for Republican France.

By the late 1790s, Maria Carolina was tracking with growing interest the rising star of the French general Napoleon Bonaparte. Alarmed by Napoleon's battlefield successes and his bold strategies, she began to offer information and aid to the English admiral Horatio Nelson against Napoleon. In fact, it was the surreptitious offer of the port of Syracuse to Nelson to use for refurbishing and supplying his ships that enabled him to destroy the French fleet at Aboukir Bay, leaving Napoleon's troops stranded in Egypt, in 1798.

The interminable struggle that Maria Carolina and Ferdinand carried on with revolutionary France drained the royal coffers. Rising taxes and repressive political measures whittled away at Maria Carolina's popularity. Murmuring by her own people, combined with French propaganda which accused her of public and personal immorality, gradually changed the public view of the monarchy from one of benevolent absolutism to one of repression and despotism. The widespread rejoicing of Nelson's victory on the Nile was short lived. By the end of 1798, French troops had broken through the Neapolitan defenses and were advancing on the capital. Terrified by the outbreak of rioting in the streets, especially in light of the recent example of Louis XVI and Marie Antoinette, who had hesitated to leave Paris until it was too late, Ferdinand and Maria Carolina fled Naples in December 1798 to take refuge in Palermo. In the perilous journey to Sicily, the youngest prince, Carlo Alberto, only seven, died of seasickness. Naples became a bloody battleground between the pro-French Jacobin forces and the loyal but savage *lazzaroni*. To ensure that the Neapolitan navy would not be captured by the advancing French, the ships which had been Maria Carolina's great pride were set on fire. Within two weeks, the French army occupied Naples, rechristening it "The Parthenopian Republic."

The humiliating defeat of the Neapolitan army put a strain on Maria Carolina's relationship with Ferdinand, shaking his faith in his wife's leadership. He announced, after 30 years of neglect, his intention to take over the reins of government and win back Naples at any cost.

With the help of the English navy and a fervent anti-Jacobin uprising in the countryside, the French were expelled from Naples in June 1799. After the triumphal reentry of the royal court into Naples in 1799, a purge of the Jacobin rebels who had cooperated with the French invaders began which did much to discredit Maria Carolina among later historians. Although Maria Carolina was criticized widely, especially by French republicans, for her cruelty in punishing the traitors, she authorized pardons for many condemned traitors.

In order to escape the continuing upheaval of Naples, Maria Carolina determined in 1800 to travel to Austria with her younger children, to visit the court of her son-in-law (also her nephew) Francis I of Austria (Holy Roman emperor Francis II), who was married to her daughter Maria Teresa of Naples. After a treacherous journey which took them dangerously close to enemy lines, the royal family was finally reunited with their cousins in Vienna, where they stayed for almost two years. Maria Carolina bided her time renewing her acquaintance with her only living sister, *Elizabeth of Austria, and taking care of the many nieces and nephews of the Viennese court. When the Peace of Luneville was signed with Napoleon in 1801, the entire family breathed a sigh of relief, for even though the peace was bought at the cost of losing many of the Habsburg dominions, war had bankrupted and exhausted all of Europe. Much revived in spirits, Maria Carolina and her children finally bid farewell to Austria and traveled towards home in 1802.

Maria Carolina was coldly received by the Neapolitans, who tended to blame her for all the misfortunes suffered under the Jacobin invasion. Ferdinand, on the other hand, was still wildly popular: the people tended to credit him with all the good done during his reign and blame Maria Carolina for all their misfortune. Soon after her return to Naples, Maria Carolina suffered another round of misfortune in the deaths, within weeks of each other, of one of her grandsons, her beloved daughter-in-law *Maria Clementina of Austria (wife of Francis, now the prince royal), and her second daughter, Louisa Amelia, grand duchess of Tuscany.

Peace with Napoleon was not destined to last; Napoleon wanted peace only long enough to build up his forces for renewed invasions in Europe. In 1805, Vienna fell to Napoleon's troops, and in the following year Naples suffered the same fate. Maria Carolina, who believed that the royal family's flight in 1798 might have been too precipitous, declared her intention of staying on and fighting to the end, but Ferdinand insisted on sending the family back to Sicily. In February 1806, the royal family entered Palermo much lower in spirits and fortunes. In a storm which blew up during the crossing, the ships containing the family's furniture and much of its supplies were lost. Almost constant warfare had drained the royal treasury, and the royal court was neither as glamorous nor as popular in Sicily as it had been before. Soon after their landing, Maria Carolina received word that her daughter ❧▸ Maria Antonia of Naples, who had been married to the Prince of Asturias (the future Ferdinand VII) in Spain in 1802, had died under mysterious circumstances rumored to be poison. In the following year, 1807, Maria Carolina's eldest daughter, the Empress Maria Teresa of Naples, died in childbirth.

Napoleon sent his brother Joseph Bonaparte to rule Naples while he turned his attention towards the conquest of Spain. It pained Maria Carolina to hear tales of her own courtiers pledging their loyalty to a man she considered a worthless upstart. Using all of her diplomatic connections and skill, she begged the English government to send her military aid. The English agreed to defend Sicily from a French attack, primarily because of their own diplomatic interests, but they refused to help her recapture Naples. The final humiliation for Maria Carolina was to hear that Joseph Bonaparte had been recognized as the lawful sovereign in Naples by the Austrians, who had sent an ambassador to his court.

Ferdinand's response to the royal family's declining fortune was to retreat to his hunting lodge and his mistress, *Lucia Migliaccio, sanguinely accepting the current situation with the calm assurance that, one day, Naples would be returned to him. Maria Carolina, once again put in charge of the daily affairs of government, railed against her enemies to everyone who would listen, and spent countless sums subsidizing plots and counterplots in Naples against the pretender to the throne. Joseph Bonaparte was sent to rule Spain in 1808, but the throne of Naples was then given to Napoleon's sister *Carolina Bonaparte and her husband Joachim Murat.

Two bright spots for Maria Carolina were the marriages of two of her daughters. In 1807, ❧▸ Christine of Bourbon was married to Charles Felix, duke of Genoa, whose suit for Christine's hand had previously been denied due to his lack of fortune. The subsequent rise in Charles Felix's position due to the death of his brother, and the fall of the Neapolitan royal family's status, made this love match more tolerable. In 1808, Maria Carolina's last unmarried daughter, Maria Amalia, was married to Louis Philippe, duke of Orléans. Although Maria Carolina would not live to see it, Maria Amalia would become queen of France when Louis Philippe was crowned in 1830.

By 1810, Napoleon Bonaparte as emperor of France was the undisputed master of Europe. As such, he was free to pursue his most fervent dream—to provide legitimacy to his seizure of power by marrying into Europe's nobility and producing an heir to his throne. In return for the restoration of his kingdom, king of Austria Francis I offered his daughter *Marie Louise of Austria (1791–1847) as a fit sacrifice. On hearing of the engagement of her granddaughter to the man she considered an unregenerate beast, Maria Carolina wrote a series of disparaging letters to her son-in-law, telling him that in her mind he was "dead, lost, dishonored, and soiled." Francis' nonchalant reply was "Better one princess should go to the devil, than the whole monarchy." To her friends she exclaimed, "That's it! That's what is missing in my fortune—to become the devil's grandmother!" As for the stunned Marie Louise, she wrote to Maria Carolina that it all seemed like a dream; all her life she had been told by her family that Napoleon was a usurper, a monster, the anti-Christ. He had driven her family from Vienna twice. How, then, could she be expected to become the wife of the archenemy?

Napoleon was thrilled with the prospect of becoming part of the House of Habsburg. Snobbishness, Maria Carolina later observed, had always been his greatest weakness. He wrote to her soon after the marriage, "Is your Majesty's mind, so distinguished among women, so unable to divest itself of the prejudices of your sex that you must treat affairs of state as if they were affairs of the heart?" The acquisition of this new and unwanted grandson actually worked to Maria Carolina's advantage. In answer to the pleading of his new wife, Napoleon ordered Murat not to invade the island of Sicily, although burdensome taxation and Maria Carolina's absolutist policies were making the position of the ruling family there increasingly tenuous.

Consumed with rage at the unfair treatment of her family, Maria Carolina refused to compromise with her Sicilian nobles on even the smallest points, and continued to oppress the people with taxes to finance her exorbitant but fruitless schemes to retake Naples. She drove the Sicilians to the point of rebellion, precipitating a takeover of the government by the English troops which had been stationed on the island. A governor sent from England to maintain order on Sicily, Lord William Bentinck, set up a parliamentary system on the English model and implemented a constitution placing limitations on the monarchy. When Maria Carolina hinted that she would rather throw over the island to Napoleon and Murat than submit to the illegal interference of the English, Bentinck insisted that Ferdinand send Maria Carolina into retirement in Austria. Unable to resist the force of English arms, Ferdinand was obliged to sign the order for her departure in June 1813.

Reduced in status from a powerful queen to a wandering exile, Maria Carolina returned to the land of her birth, accompanied only by her youngest surviving son Leopold, who had remained fiercely loyal to his mother. Although she was filled with rancor against Bentinck and the English, she also admitted that she had not always acted wisely: "For a long time," she later admitted, "I have believed that I knew how to govern, and I have only found out my mistake when it was too late. In order to rule men wisely one should study and understand them; this I did not do." Francis I provided her with a castle for her household, and she busied herself with caring for her grandchildren and watched while, in the wake of the disastrous Russian campaign, Napoleon was

᭦➤ **Maria Antonia of Naples** (1784–1806)
*Neapolitan princess. Name variations: Antonia of Sicily; Antoinette; Princess of Asturias. Born in 1784; died under mysterious circumstances in 1806; daughter of *Maria Carolina (1752–1814), queen of Naples and the Two Sicilies, and Ferdinand IV (1751–1825), king of Naples (r. 1759–1806, 1815–1825), later known as Ferdinand I, king of the Two Sicilies (r. 1816–1825); sister of *Maria Amalia (1782–1866, who married Louis Philippe, king of France); became first wife of Ferdinand, prince of Asturias (the future Ferdinand VII, king of Spain, r. 1813–1833), in 1802; no surviving children.*

᭦➤ **Christine of Bourbon** (1779–1849)
*Duchess of Genoa. Name variations: Cristina; Maria Christina of Bourbon. Born on January 17, 1779; died on March 12, 1849; daughter of *Maria Carolina (1752–1814), queen of the Two Sicilies, and Ferdinand IV (1751–1825), king of Naples (r. 1759–1806, 1815–1825), later known as Ferdinand I, king of the Two Sicilies (r. 1816–1825); married Charles Felix (Carlos Felice) of Sardinia, duke of Genoa (r. 1821–1831) and king of Sardinia, on April 6, 1807.*

finally defeated by the allies in 1814. Napoleon was forcibly granted the throne of the tiny island of Elba, but Marie Louise, together with her infant son, returned to her father's court in Vienna. Maria Carolina expressed open disapproval that Marie Louise had not followed Napoleon to Elba, had not "tied her bed-curtains together and let herself down from her window to join him." After all, Maria Carolina admonished her granddaughter, "when one is married it is for life." Napoleon II, Maria Carolina's only great-grandchild, was the object of Maria Carolina's untiring caresses and indulgences.

The defeat of France opened the way to a restoration of the Habsburgs to all of their wealth and position in Europe. But Maria Carolina would never see this come to pass. On the night of September 7, 1814, she retired to bed with no apparent symptoms of ill health, but the following morning her ladies-in-waiting found her dead in her bed, apparently having suffered a seizure in the night. Soon after her death, Ferdinand married his mistress, Lucia Migliaccio, and it was they, together with Maria Carolina's sons, who entered Naples victoriously to reclaim the Neapolitan throne.

SOURCES:
Acton, Harold. *The Bourbons of Naples: 1734–1825.* London: Methuen, 1963.
Bearne, Catherine Mary Charlton. *A Sister of Marie Antoinette: The Life-Story of Maria Carolina, Queen of Naples.* NY: E.P. Dutton, 1907.
Bonnefons, Andre. *Une ennemie de la revolution et de Napoleon; Marie-Caroline, reine des Deux-Seciles, 1748–1814.* Paris, 1905.
Croce, Benedetto. *History of the Kingdom of Naples.* Chicago: University of Chicago Press, 1970.
Fraser, Flora. *Emma, Lady Hamilton.* NY: Alfred A. Knopf, 1987.
Jeaffreson, John Cordy. *The Queen of Naples and Lord Nelson.* 2 vols. London: Hurst and Blackett, 1889.
Tamussino, Ursula. *Des Teufels Grossmutter: Eine Biographie der Königin Maria Carolina von Neapel-Sizilien.* Vienna: Deuticke, 1991. English translation by Myron E. Schirer.

SUGGESTED READING:
Connelly, Owen. *Napoleon's Satellite Kingdoms.* NY: Free Press, 1965.
Steegmuller, Francis. *A Woman, A Man, and Two Kingdoms: The Story of Madame d'Épinay and the Abbé Galiani.* NY: Alfred A. Knopf, 1991.

Kimberly Estep Spangler,
Associate Professor of History and Chair, Division of Religion and Humanities, Friends University, Wichita, Kansas

Maria Charlotte of Sardinia
(c. 1761–c. 1786)

Princess of Savoy. Name variations: possibly Caroline. Born around 1761; died around 1786; daughter of *Maria Antonia of Spain (1729–1785) and Victor Amadeus III, duke of Savoy (r. 1773–1796); married Anthony I Clement of Saxony (1755–1836), king of Saxony (r. 1827–1836), on October 24, 1781. Anthony Clement married his second wife, *Theresa (1767–1827), in 1787.*

Maria Christina (1742–1798)

*Archduchess and governor-general of Austrian Netherlands. Name variations: Maria Cristina; Marie Christine, stattholder or stadholder of the Netherlands; (nickname) Mimi. Born on May 13, 1742, in Vienna; died on June 24, 1798, in Vienna; daughter of Maria Theresa of Austria (1717–1780) and Francis I, Holy Roman emperor (r. 1745–1765); sister of *Marie Antoinette (1755–1793), *Maria Carolina (1752–1814), and Joseph II, Holy Roman emperor (r. 1765–1790); married Albert, duke of Saxony-Teschen.*

Maria Christina was one of 16 children of Empress *Maria Theresa of Austria*, and the empress' favorite daughter. Quick-minded and pretty, Maria Christina was governor-general of the Austrian Netherlands (present-day Belgium), during her brother Joseph II's reign as Holy Roman emperor.

Maria Christina (1947—)

*Dutch princess. Name variations: Maria-Christina; Maria Christina of Marijke. Born on February 18, 1947; daughter of *Juliana (b. 1909), queen of the Netherlands (r. 1948–1980), and Prince Bernard of Lippe-Biesterfeld; sister of Queen *Beatrix of the Netherlands (b. 1938) and *Irene Emma (b. 1939); married Jorge Guillermo (a Cuban-born New York teacher of deprived children), in 1975.*

Maria Christina I of Naples
(1806–1878).

See Isabella II for sidebar on Maria Cristina I.

Maria Christina of Austria
(1858–1929)

*Queen and regent of Spain. Name variations: Maria Cristina of Habsburg Lorraine; Marie-Christine of Austria. Born in Moravia on July 21, 1858; died on February 9, 1929; daughter of Charles Ferdinand (1818–1874), archduke of Austria, and Archduchess Elizabeth; became second wife of Alfonso or Alphonso XII (1857–1885), king of Spain (r. 1875–1885), on November 29, 1879; children: *Maria de las Mer-*

cedes (1880–1904); *Maria Teresa (1882–1912, who married Ferdinand of Bavaria); Alfonso also known as Alphonso XIII (1886–1941), king of Spain (r. 1886–1931).

Maria Christina of Austria was born on July 21, 1858, in Moravia, the daughter of Archduke Charles Ferdinand and Archduchess *Elizabeth. Studious and broadly educated, Maria became engaged in November 1879 to Alphonso XII, king of Spain, whose first wife *Maria de las Mercedes (1860–1878) had died after five months of marriage. Alphonso sought to remarry immediately, concerned with stabilizing the monarchy, which had been restored in December 1875 when the First Republic collapsed. Maria Christina went forthwith to Spain, and they wed on November 29, 1879. She had two daughters—*Maria de las Mercedes (1880–1904) and *Maria Teresa (1882–1912)—and was again pregnant when Alphonso XII died on November 25, 1885. The posthumous child was born on May 17 and proved to be a boy, the future Alphonso XIII.

The young widow faced daunting challenges. She governed as regent for 17 years, presiding over Spain's fragile constitutional monarchy until her son was old enough to rule. Maria Christina worked as an impartial arbiter between the conservatives, headed by Antonio Cánovas del Castillo, and the liberals, led by Práxedes Mateo Sagasta. She rotated the government between the two parties, and local political bosses rigged the votes to provide the desired electoral results. This produced a superficial stability.

By the time she ended the regency and turned over power to Alphonso XIII in 1902, however, Spain was beginning to fragment. The liberal and conservatives parties were disintegrating, the military sought extra-parliamentary means of controlling the nation, and Spain had lost its last overseas colonies during the Spanish-American War of 1898. Whereas Maria Christina had governed with decorum and impartiality, Alphonso XIII conspired with the military and acquiesced in General Miguel Primo de Rivera's dictatorship from 1923 to 1930. Maria Christina died on February 9, 1929. Within two years, her son abdicated, giving way to the Spanish Second Republic. The Spanish Civil War soon followed.

SOURCES:

Cortés Cavanillas, Julián. María Cristina de Austria: madre de Alfonso XIII. Madrid: Ediciones Aspas, 1944.
Herr, Richard. An Historical Essay on Modern Spain. Berkeley: University of California Press, 1971.

Romanones, Alvaro Figueroa y Torres, conde de. Doña María Cristina de Habsburgo Lorena. Madrid, Espasa-Calpe, 1933.

Kendall W. Brown,
Professor of History,
Brigham Young University, Provo, Utah

Maria Christina of Bourbon
(1779–1849).

See Maria Carolina for sidebar on Christine of Bourbon.

Maria Christina of Marijke (b. 1947).

See Maria Christina.

Maria Christina of Saxony
(1779–1851)

Duchess of Savoy-Carignan. Name variations: Marie of Saxony. Born in 1779; died in 1851; married Charles Emmanuel (1770–1800), duke of Savoy-Carignan (r. 1780–1800); children: Charles Albert, king of Sardinia (r. 1831–1849).

Maria Clementina of Austria
(1777–1801)

Florentine princess. Name variations: Clementina of Austria; Marie Klementine. Born on April 4, 1777, in Florence; died on November 15, 1801, in Naples; daughter of Leopold II (1747–1792), count of Tuscany, ruler of Florence (r. 1765–1790), Holy Roman emperor (r. 1790–1792), and *Maria Louisa of Spain (1745–1792); married Francis I, later king of the Two Sicilies (r. 1825–1830); children: *Caroline of Naples (1798–1870, who married the duke of Berri); Ferdinand (b. 1800). Francis I's second wife was *Marie Isabella of Spain (1789–1848).

Maria Comnena (fl. 1090s)

Byzantine princess. Flourished around 1090; daughter of *Irene Ducas (c. 1066–1133) and Alexius I Comnenus, Byzantine emperor (r. 1081–1118); sister of *Anna Comnena (1083–1153/55).

Maria Comnena (fl. 1100s)

Queen of Jerusalem. Name variations: Mary Comnena. Flourished in the 1100s; second wife of Amalric I (1136–1174), king of Jerusalem (r. 1162–1174); married Balian II of Ramla; children: (first marriage) *Isabella I of Jerusalem (d. 1205); (second marriage) Helvis (who married Reginald of Sidon, lord of Sidon); Margaret (who married Hugh of Tiberias and

*Walter of Caesarea). Amalric's first wife was **Agnes of Courtenay** (1136–1186).*

Maria Cristina (1911–1996)

*Spanish princess. Name variations: Infanta. Born on December 12, 1911, at Royal Palace, Madrid, Spain; died on December 23, 1996, at Villa Giralda, Madrid; daughter of **Ena** (1887–1969) and Alphonso XIII (1886–1941), king of Spain (r. 1886–1931); married Enrico Eugenio, 1st count of Marone, on June 10, 1940; children: **Victoria Marone** (b. 1941, who married José Carlos Alvarez de Toledo y Gross, 8th count of Villapeterna); **Giovanna Marone** (b. 1943, who married Jaime Galobart y Satrústegui and Luis Angel Sanchez Merlo y Ruiz); **Maria Teresa Marone** (b. 1945, who married José Ruiz de Arana y Montalvo, 5th marques of Brenes); **Anna Sandra Marone** (b. 1948, who married Gian Carol Stavro Santarosa).*

Maria Cristina I of Naples (1806–1878).

See Isabella II for sidebar on Maria Cristina I.

Maria Cristina of Habsburg Lorraine (1858–1929).

See Maria Christina of Austria.

Maria Cristina of Sicily (1877–1947)

*Archduchess of Austria. Name variations: Maria Cristina of Bourbon-Sicily. Born on April 10, 1877; died on October 4, 1947, in St. Gilgen; daughter of **Antonia von Trapani** (b. 1851) and Alphonse of Sicily (1841–1934), count of Caserta; married Peter Ferdinand (1874–1948), archduke or grand duke of Austria, on November 8, 1900; children: Gottfried also known as Godfrey (1902–1984, who married **Dorothea of Bavaria**); **Helene** (1903–1924); George (1905–1952, who married **Marie Valerie of Waldburg-Zeil**); **Rosa** (1906–1983).*

Maria da Fonte (fl. 1846).

See Maria de Fonte.

Maria da Gloria (1819–1853).

See Maria II da Gloria.

Maria da Gloria (1946—)

*Princess of Orleans-Braganza. Born on December 13, 1946, in Petropolis, Brazil; daughter of Peter Gonzaga (Prince Peter of Orleans and Braganza) and **Maria de la Esperanza** (b. 1914); married Alexander Karad-*jordjevic *(son of Peter II, king of Yugoslavia), on July 1, 1972 (divorced 1985); married Ignacio Medina y Fernandez, 21st duke of Segorbe, on October 24, 1985; children: (first marriage) Peter (b. 1980); twins Philip and Alexander (b. 1982).*

Maria dal Pozzo

*Duchess of Aosta. First wife of Amadeo also known as Amadeus of Savoy, duke of Aosta, king of Spain (r. 1871–1873); children: Emmanuel (who married **Helen of Bourbon**); Victor; Louis. Amadeus' second wife was **Marie Laetitia** (1866–1890).*

Maria de Fonte (fl. 1846)

Portuguese dissenter. Name variations: Maria da Fonte Arcada; Maria of Fonte.

In 1846, the liberal Portuguese government tried to carry out a series of reforms, among which were a new tax and a law forbidding, on sanitary grounds, the burial of bodies within churches. In the conservative Minho district of northern Portugal, where opposition to the government was already strong, a number of peasant women violently opposed the new burial ordinance. They held precious the belief that their beloved family members could await the end of time buried in the sacred precincts of the churches. The worst riot erupted in the parish of Fonte Arcada, where a woman by the name of Maria allegedly took a leading role. With her at their head, a mob of women forced a local priest to bury **Custódia Teresa** inside the chapel at Simães. These protests took on Maria's nickname, Maria de Fonte Arcada, shortened to Maria de Fonte. Soon other conservatives exploited the confusion, and even moderates and liberals who disliked the Portuguese dictator António Bernardino da Costa Cabral joined in. A long and bloody civil struggle culminated in his dismissal.

Kendall W. Brown,
Professor of History,
Brigham Young University, Provo, Utah

Maria Déia or Maria Déia de Nenem (c. 1908–1938).

See Bonita, Maria.

Maria dei Conti d'Aquino (fl. 1300s)

Princess. Name variations: called Fiammetta in the writings of Boccaccio. Illegitimate daughter of Robert the Good, duke of Anjou, king of Naples (r. 1309–1343).

Said to be an illegitimate daughter of Robert the Good, king of Naples, Princess Maria dei Conti d'Aquino was beloved by Boccaccio and portrayed by him under the name Fiammetta.

Maria de la Esperanza (1914—)

*Princess of the Two Sicilies. Born on June 14, 1914; daughter of *Louise of Orleans (1882–1952) and Carlos, prince of Bourbon-Sicily, also known as Charles (1870–1949), prince of the Two Sicilies; sister of *Maria de las Mercedes (1910–2000); married Pedro de Alcantra, prince of Grao Para, also known as Peter Gonzaga (Prince Peter of Orleans and Braganza); children: *Maria da Gloria (1946—).*

Maria de la Paz (1862–1946).

See Isabella II for sidebar.

Maria de las Mercedes (1860–1878)

*Queen of Spain. Born in 1860; died in 1878; daughter of Antoine, duke of Montpensier (1824–1900), and *Luisa Fernanda (1832–1897); became first wife of Alfonso also known as Alphonso XII (1857–1885), king of Spain (r. 1875–1885), in 1878. Alphonso married his second wife, *Maria Christina of Austria (1858–1929), in 1879.*

Maria de las Mercedes (1880–1904)

*Queen infanta of Spain. Name variations: Maria Mercedes. Born on September 11, 1880; died on October 17, 1904; daughter of Maria Christina of Austria (1858–1929) and Alphonso XII (1857–1885), king of Spain (r. 1875–1885); sister of Alphonso XIII (1886–1941), king of Spain (r. 1886–1931); married Carlos, prince of Bourbon-Sicily, also known as Charles or Charles of Bourbon (1870–1949), conti de Caserta, prince of the Two Sicilies, on February 14, 1901; children: Alphonse of Bourbon-Sicily (b. 1901); Ferdinand (b. 1903); Isabella of Bourbon-Sicily (b. 1904, who married John, count Zamoyski). Charles of Bourbon's second wife was *Louise of Orleans (1882–1952).*

Maria de las Mercedes was queen of Spain for one year (1885–1886). When her father Alphonso XII died without a male heir on November 25, 1885, the five-year-old Maria was named queen. But her mother *Maria Christina

of Austria gave birth to a boy on May 17, 1886. Named Alphonso XIII, he succeeded his sister on the day of his birth.

Maria de las Mercedes (1910–2000)

*Countess of Barcelona and mother of Juan Carlos I. Name variations: Mercedes of the Two Sicilies; Maria Mercedes; Maria-Mercedes; Maria Mercedes of Bourbon; María de Borbón; princess of Bourbon-Sicily. Born Maria de la Mercedes Christine Januaria Isabel Louise Caroline Victoria on December 23, 1910, in Madrid, Spain; died on January 2, 2000, in her residence on the Canary Island of Lanzarote; daughter of Carlos, prince of Bourbon-Sicily, also known as Charles of Bourbon (1870–1949), prince of the Two Sicilies, and *Louise of Orleans (1882–1952); married John or Juan (1913–1993), also known as Juan de Borbón y Battenberg, count of Barcelona, on October 12, 1935; children: *Maria del Pilar (b. 1936); Juan Carlos I (b. 1938), king of Spain (r. 1975—); *Margarita Maria (b. 1939); Alfonso or Alphonso (1940–1956, who died in a shooting accident).*

Maria del Pilar (b. 1936)

*Duchess of Badajoz and sister of the king of Spain. Name variations: Maria de Pilar Bourbon; Maria de Bourbon or Maria of Bourbon. Born on July 30, 1936, in Cannes, France; daughter of *Maria de las Mercedes (1910–2000) and John or Juan (1913–1993), count of Barcelona; sister of Juan Carlos I (b. 1938), king of Spain (r. 1975—); married Louis de la Torre Gómez-Acebo, duke of Estrada; children: Fatima Simoneta Gomez-Acebo (b. 1968); Juan (b. 1969); Bruno (b. 1971); Beltran (b. 1973); Fernando (b. 1974).*

Maria de Molina (d. 1321)

*Queen-regent of Castile and Leon. Name variations: Maria of Molina; Mary of Molina. Born between 1260 and 1270 in Spain; died on July 1, 1321, in Castile; daughter of Alphonse de Castilla de Molina and Mayor Alfonsa de Meneses; married cousin Sancho IV the Fierce (1258–1295), king of Castile and Leon (r. 1284–1296), in July 1281 or 1282; children: *Isabel de Limoges (1283–1328); Ferdinand IV, king of Castile and Leon (r. 1296–1312, who married Constance of Portugal); Alfonso (1286–1291); Enrique (1288–1299); Pedro (1290–1319), regent of Castile; Felipe or Philip (1292–1327); ❧ Beatrice of Castile and Leon (1293–1359, who married Alphonso IV of Portugal).*

See sidebar on the following page

> ### ❧ Beatrice of Castile and Leon (1293–1359)
>
> *Queen of Portugal. Name variations: Beatriz. Born in Toro, Spain, in 1293; died on October 25, 1359, in Lisbon, Portugal; daughter of *Maria de Molina (d. 1321) and Sancho IV, king of Castile (r. 1284–1296); married Alphonso IV, king of Portugal (r. 1325–1357), on September 12, 1309; children: *Maria of Portugal (1313–1357, who married Alphonso XI of Castile); Alfonso or Alphonso (1315–1315); Diniz or Denis (1317–1318); Pedro also known as Peter I (1320–1367), king of Portugal (r. 1357–1367); Isabel (1324–1326); Joao (1326–1327); *Eleanor of Portugal (1328–1348, who married Peter or Pedro IV of Aragon).*

Maria de Molina, queen and regent of Castile, was born between 1260 and 1270, the daughter of Alphonse de Castilla de Molina and **Mayor Alfonsa de Meneses**. Of noble birth, Maria married Sancho of Castile (later Sancho IV) and was the mother of Ferdinand IV. When Sancho died, Maria retained her authority as regent of the kingdom in her young son's name. She proved to be a successful regent, a difficult accomplishment given the great number of would-be usurpers of the Castilian throne that she was forced to war against. Maria de Molina's strong central government and her own strength and determination kept Castile intact until Ferdinand came of age. Maria was both an effective, astute ruler and a popular one. Her son Ferdinand did not share her talent for rule, and quickly lost control of his court, nobility, and subjects. When the situation became desperate upon Ferdinand's death in 1312, Maria was called upon by the people of Castile to restore order and to act again as regent, this time for her infant grandson Alphonso XI.

SOURCES:
Echols, Anne, and Marty Williams. *An Annotated Index of Medieval Women.* NY: Markus Wiener, 1992.
Salmonson, Jessica. *The Encyclopedia of Amazons.* NY: Doubleday, 1991.

> **Laura York,**
> Riverside, California

Maria de Portugal (1521–1577)

Infanta of Portugal. Name variations: Maria of Portugal. Born on June 8, 1521, in Lisbon; died on October 10, 1577, in Lisbon; daughter of Manuel I the Fortunate (1469–1521), king of Portugal (r. 1495–1521), and Eleanor of Portugal (1498–1558); half-sister of João also known as John III, king of Portugal; never married; no children.

Maria de Portugal was born on June 8, 1521, in Lisbon, the daughter of Portuguese ruler Manuel I and his third wife, *Eleanor of Portugal, who was the sister of Emperor Charles V. Maria's father died when she was only a few months old, and soon thereafter, in 1523, Charles insisted that Eleanor marry Francis I. Eleanor went to France to live, forced by the Portuguese to leave Maria behind.

Maria de Portugal received an outstanding education at the Portuguese court and proved herself intellectually precocious. She mastered Latin, played the harp and organ, and discussed literature, mathematics, astronomy, and philosophy with celebrated intellectuals. Some scholars have speculated, without offering conclusive evidence, that she inspired some parts of Luis de Camões' *Os Lusiadas*, the great classic of Portuguese literature.

She inherited her mother's Portuguese properties, and John III bestowed other riches upon her. Meanwhile, her mother Eleanor of Portugal attempted to arrange a marriage for her with a Frenchman, including the dauphin, as a means of ending their separation. On other occasions, negotiators proposed her marriage to the Austrian Habsburg Maximilian, Ferdinand of Guise, and Philip II of Spain, following the death of his wife *Mary Tudor. John III frustrated all the negotiations, however, because of his reluctance to lose control of Maria's tremendously rich dowry. As a result, she never married.

Maria and her mother met on the Spanish-Portuguese border at Badajoz in 1558, but she returned to spend the rest of her days in her royal palaces in Portugal. Known for her charitable donations to religious houses and hospitals, Maria died in Lisbon on October 10, 1577. Twenty years later, her remains were moved to the convent of Our Lady of Light, which she had established during her life.

SOURCES:
Vasconcelos, Carolina Michaëlis de. *A Infanta D. Maria de Portugal (1521–1577) e as Suas Damas.* 2nd ed. Lisbon: Biblioteca Nacional, 1994.

> **Kendall W. Brown,**
> Professor of History,
> Brigham Young University, Provo, Utah

Maria de Sancto Paulo (1304–1377).

See Marie de St. Pol.

Maria de Ventadour (b. 1165)

Literary patron and poet of France. Name variations: Marie de Ventadorn. Born 1165 in Turenne; died after 1221 in Ventadour; daughter of Raimon II of Turenne and Helis de Castelnau; married Ebles V, viscount of Ventadour, around 1183 (separated 1221); children: two sons.

A patron of the Provençal troubadours, Maria de Ventadour also composed poetry herself. She was the daughter of Raimon II of Turenne and **Helis de Castelnau**. She was about 18 years old when she married Viscount Ebles V of Ventadour, himself the descendent of a literary family. Maria supported several important male troubadours at her court, among them Gui d'Ussel.

During this time, Maria turned her own hand to composing the highly stylized love poems favored by the troubadours. Only one of her works has been preserved; it is a verse dialogue (*tenson*) between herself and Gui d'Ussel, in which they discuss whether a suitor should have as much authority over his lady as she has over him; Maria maintains that it is the lady who should be served by her lover as a superior, not as an equal. In 1221, Maria's husband took vows to become a Cistercian monk, leaving his wife and their two sons. No records of her life after this time exist.

Laura York,
Riverside, California

Maria Dorothea of Austria
(1867–1932)

Duchess of Orléans. Born on June 14, 1867; died on April 6, 1932; daughter of *Clotilde of Saxe-Coburg-Gotha (1846–1927) and Archduke Josef Karl Ludwig also known as Joseph Charles Louis (1833–1905); married Louis Philippe (1869–1926), duke of Orléans, on November 5, 1896.

Maria Ducas (fl. 1070–1081).

See Anna Dalassena for sidebar on Maria of Alania.

Maria Eleanora (1550–1608)

Duchess of Prussia. Name variations: Marie Eleonore of Jülich-Cleves; Marie Eleonore von Julich-Kleve. Born on June 15, 1550; died on May 23, 1608; daughter of *Mary (1531–1581) and William V, duke of Cleves (r. 1539–1592); married Albert Frederick (b. 1553), duke of Prussia, on October 14, 1573; children: *Anna of Prussia (1576–1625, who married John Sigismund, elector of Brandenburg); Marie Hohenzollern (1579–1649); Albert Frederick (b. 1580); Sophie Hohenzollern (1582–1610); Eleonore Hohenzollern (1583–1607); Wilhelm Friedrich (b. 1585);

*Magdalena Sybilla (1586–1659, who married John George, elector of Saxony).

Maria Eleonora of Brandenburg
(1599–1655).

See Christina of Sweden for sidebar.

Maria Elisabeth (1680–1741)

Stadholder of the Netherlands. Born on December 13, 1680, in Linz; died on August 26, 1741, in Mariemont Castle near Morlanwelz, Hennegau; daughter of *Eleanor of Pfalz-Neuburg (1655–1720) and Leopold I of Bohemia (1640–1705), Holy Roman emperor (r. 1658–1705).

Maria Francisca of Sulzbach

Bavarian noblewoman. Married Frederick Michael (died 1767); children: Maximilian I Joseph, elector of Bavaria (r. 1799–1805), king of Bavaria (r. 1805–1825).

Maria Gabriele of Bavaria
(1878–1912)

Bavarian princess. Born on October 9, 1878; died on October 24, 1912; daughter of *Maria Josepha of Portugal (1857–1943) and Charles Theodore also known as Karl Theodor "Gackl" (1839–1909), duke in Bavaria [sic]; became first wife of Rupprecht also known as Rupert, crown prince of Bavaria, on August 10, 1900; children: Luitpold (b. 1901); Irmingard (1902–1903); Albert (b. 1905), duke of Bavaria; Rudolf (b. 1909).

Maria Henrietta of Austria
(1836–1902)

Queen of the Belgians. Name variations: Marie Hendrika; Marie Henriette or Marie-Henriette. Born on August 23, 1836, in Ofen; died on September 19, 1902, in Spa, Belgium; daughter of archduke Joseph of Austria (1776–1847) and *Maria of Wurttemberg (1797–1855); married Leopold II, king of the Belgians, on August 22, 1853; children: *Stephanie of Belgium (1864–1945); Leopold (d. 1869); *Louise of Belgium (1858–1924, who married Philip of Saxe-Coburg-Gotha); *Clementine of Belgium (1872–1955).

Maria Immaculata (1878–1968)

Duchess of Wurttemberg. Name variations: Maria Immakulata. Born in 1878; died in 1968; daughter of Charles Salvator of Tuscany (1839–1892) and *Maria Immaculata of Sicily (1844–1899).

Maria Immaculata of Sicily
(1844–1899)

Archduchess. Name variations: Maria Immakulata. Born on April 14, 1844, in Caserta; died on February 18, 1899, in Vienna; daughter of *Theresa of Austria (1816–1867) and Ferdinand II, king of the Two Sicilies (r. 1830–1859); married archduke Karl Salvator also spelled Charles Salvator of Tuscany (1839–1892); children: seven, including Leopold Salvator (1863–1931, who married *Blanche of Bourbon) and *Maria Immaculata (1878–1968).

Maria Innocentia, Sister (1909–1946).
See Hummel, Berta.

Maria Isabel Francisca (1851–1931).
See Isabella II for sidebar.

Maria Isabel of Portugal (1797–1818).
See Carlota Joaquina for sidebar.

Maria Isabella (1834–1901)

Countess of Trapani. Name variations: Isabella; Maria Isabella of Tuscany. Born on May 21, 1834, in Florence, Italy; died on July 14 or 16, 1901, in Burgenstock; daughter of Leopold II (1797–1870), grand duke of Tuscany (r. 1824–1859) and *Maria Antonia of Sicily (1814–1898); married Francesco also known as Francis of Sicily (1827–1892), count of Trapani, on April 10, 1850.

Maria Isabella (1848–1919)

Countess of Paris. Name variations: Isabella d'Orleans; Isabella of Orleans. Born on September 21, 1848; died on April 23, 1919; daughter of Antoine (1824–1900), duke of Montpensier, and *Luisa Fernanda (1832–1897); married Louis Philippe (1838–1894), count of Paris, on April 30, 1864; children: *Marie-Amelie of Orleans (1865–1951, who married King Charles I of Portugal); Helene (b. 1871, who married Emanuel Philibert, duke of Aosta); Karl (b. 1875); *Isabella of Orleans (b. 1878); Jacob (b. 1880); *Louise of Orleans (1882–1952, who married Charles of Bourbon, prince of the Two Sicilies); Louis Philippe (1869–1926, who married *Maria Dorothea of Austria); Ferdinand, duke of Montpensier (d. 1924).

Maria Josepha of Austria (1699–1757).
See Marie Josepha.

Maria Josepha of Bavaria
(1739–1767)

Empress of Austria. Name variations: Josepha of Bavaria. Born on March 20, 1739, in Munich; died of smallpox on May 28, 1767, in Vienna; became the unhappy second wife of Joseph II (1741–1790), emperor of Austria (r. 1765–1790) and Holy Roman emperor (r. 1765–1790).

Maria Josepha of Portugal
(1857–1943)

Princess of Portugal. Name variations: Marie-José Bragança von Wittelsbach; Infanta of Portugal. Born on March 19, 1857; died on March 11, 1943; daughter of *Adelheid (1831–1909) and Miguel also known as Michael I (1802–1866), king of Portugal (r. 1828–1834); married Karl Theodor "Gackl" (1839–1909), on April 29, 1874; children: *Elizabeth of Bavaria (1876–1965); *Maria Gabriele of Bavaria (1878–1912).

Maria Josepha of Saxony
(1803–1829)

Queen of Spain. Name variations: Mary Josepha. Born on December 6, 1803; died on May 17, 1829; daughter of *Caroline of Parma (1770–1804) and Maximilian of Saxony, duke of Saxony (r. 1830–1838); became third wife of Ferdinand VII, king of Spain (r. 1813–1833), on October 20, 1819; no children. Ferdinand VII's first wife was *Maria Antonia of Naples (1784–1806); his second was *Maria Isabel of Portugal (1797–1818); his fourth was *Maria Cristina I of Naples (1806–1878).

Maria Josepha of Saxony
(1867–1944)

Archduchess of Austria. Name variations: Marie Josepha of Saxony. Born on May 31, 1867, in Dresden; died on May 28, 1944, at Wildenwart Castle, Upper Bavaria; daughter of *Maria Anna of Portugal (1843–1884) and George (1832–1904), king of Saxony (r. 1902–1904); married Otto (1865–1906, son of Charles Louis and *Maria Annunziata), archduke of Austria, on October 2, 1886; children: Karl also known as Charles I (1887–1922), emperor of Austria (r. 1916–1918, who married *Zita of Parma); Maximilian (1895–1952, who married Frances of Hohenlohe).

Maria Juliana of Brunswick (1729–1796).
See Carolina Matilda for sidebar.

Maria-Kyratza Asen
(fl. late 1300s)

Empress of Nicaea. Flourished in the late 1300s; daughter of Ivan Alexander; married Andronicus IV Paleologus, emperor of Nicaea (r. 1376–1379); children: John VII Paleologus (d. 1408), emperor of Nicaea (r. 1390).

Maria-Kyratza Asen was married to the Byzantine emperor Andronicus IV Paleologus. When he tried to overthrow his father John V, Andronicus was blinded and thrown into prison along with Maria-Kyratza and their infant son. It was said that Maria rubbed salve into his eyes and restored his sight.

Maria Lascaris (fl. 1200s).
See Maria.

Maria Lascaris (fl. 1234–1242)

*Queen of Hungary. Name variations: Mary Lascaris; Laskaris. Flourished between 1234 and 1242; daughter of Theodore I Lascaris, emperor of Nicaea (r. 1204–1222) and probably *Anna Angelina (daughter of Alexius III, Byzantine emperor); married Bela IV, king of Hungary (r. 1235–1270); children: *Cunegunde (1234–1292); Stephen V, king of Hungary (b. 1239, r. 1270–1272); *Margaret of Hungary (1242–1270). Bela IV's second wife was Saint *Salome of Hungary (1201–c. 1270).*

Maria Lesczinska (1703–1768).
See Marie Leczinska.

Maria Leopoldina
(1776–1848)

*Electress of the Palatine. Name variations: Maria Leopoldine; Leopoldine. Born on December 10, 1776, in Milan; died on June 23, 1848, in Wasserburg; daughter of *Maria Beatrice of Modena (1750–1829) and Archduke Ferdinand (1754–1806, son of *Maria Theresa of Austria [1717–1780]); sister of Francis IV, duke of Modena (r. 1814–1846); married Charles IV Theodore of Bavaria, elector of the Palatine, on February 15, 1795; married Ludwig, count of Arco, on November 14, 1804.*

Maria Leopoldina of Austria
(1797–1826).
See Leopoldina of Austria.

Maria Leopoldine (1632–1649)

*Queen of Bohemia and Holy Roman empress. Name variations: Maria Leopoldina. Born on April 6, 1632, in Innsbruck; died on July 7, 1649, in Vienna; daughter of *Claudia de Medici (1604–1648) and Leopold V (1586–1632), archduke of Austrian Tyrol or Tirol; second wife of Ferdinand III (1608–1657), king of Bohemia (r. 1627–1646), king of Hungary (r. 1625), Holy Roman emperor (r. 1637–1657). Ferdinand III's first wife was *Maria Anna of Spain (1606–1646), the mother of three of his children. His third was *Eleonora II Gonzaga (1628–1686).*

Maria Leopoldine (1776–1848).
See Maria Leopoldina.

Maria Louisa of Savoy (1688–1714).
See Marie Louise of Savoy.

Maria Louisa of Spain (1745–1792)

*Holy Roman empress, empress of Austria, and grandduchess of Tuscany. Name variations: Marie-Louise Bourbon; Maria Ludovica; infanta Maria Ludovica of Bourbon-Spain. Born on November 24, 1745, in Naples; died on May 15, 1792, in Vienna; daughter of Charles III, king of Spain (r. 1759–1788), also known as Charles IV, king of Naples and Sicily (r. 1735–1759), and *Maria Amalia of Saxony (1724–1760, daughter of Augustus III of Poland); married Leopold II (1747–1792), count of Tuscany, ruler of Florence (r. 1765–1790), Holy Roman emperor (r. 1790–1792); children: Ferdinand III (1769–1824), grand duke of Tuscany; Alexander Leopold (1772–1795); *Theresa (1767–1827); Francis II (1768–1835), last Holy Roman emperor (r. 1792–1806), also known as Francis I, emperor of Austria (r. 1804–1835); Maria Anna (1770–1809); *Maria Clementina of Austria (1777–1801); Maria Amalia (1780–1798); John (1782–1859), vicar-general; Joseph (1776–1847), archduke Palatine of Hungary; Anthony Victor (1779–1835); Rainer (1783–1853), viceroy of Lombardy; Louis (1784–1864); Rudolf (1788–1831), cardinal-archbishop of Olmutz.*

Maria Ludovica (1798–1857)

*Tuscan noblewoman. Name variations: Marie Louise or Marie Luise. Born on August 30, 1798, in Florence, Italy; died on June 15, 1857, in Florence; daughter of Ferdinand III, grand duke of Tuscany (r. 1790–1802 and 1814–1824) and *Louisa Amelia (1773–1802); sister of Leopold II, grand duke of Tuscany (r. 1824–1859).*

Maria Ludovica (1845–1917)

*Tuscan noblewoman. Name variations: Maria Luisa. Born on October 31, 1845, in Florence, Italy; died on August 27, 1917, in Hanau; daughter of Leopold II, grand duke of Tuscany (1797–1870, r. 1824–1859) and *Maria Antonia of Sicily (1814–1898); married Charles of Isenburg-Birstein.*

Maria Ludovica of Modena
(1787–1816)

*Empress of Austria. Name variations: Maria Ludovica Beatrix. Born on December 14, 1787, in Monza; died on April 7, 1816, in Verona; daughter of Archduke Ferdinand (1754–1806, son of *Maria Theresa of Austria [1717–1780]) and *Maria Beatrice of Modena (1750–1829); became third wife of Franz or Francis II, Holy Roman emperor (r. 1792–1806), also known as Francis I, emperor of Austria (r. 1804–1835), on January 6, 1808.*

Maria Luisa of Etruria (1782–1824)

*Queen of Etruria (Tuscany). Name variations: Luisa, Regent of Etruria, Duchess of Lucca; Marie Louise and María Luisa of Spain. Born in Madrid, Spain, on July 6, 1782; died on March 13, 1824; daughter of Charles IV, king of Spain (r. 1788–1808), and *Maria Luisa Teresa of Parma (1751–1819); sister of *Carlota Joaquina (1775–1830) and Ferdinand VII, king of Spain (r. 1813–1833); married Louis de Bourbon also known as Louis I (1773–1803), duke of Parma (r. 1801–1803), on August 25, 1795; children: Charles Louis (1799–1803), duke of Parma; *Louise of Parma (1802–1857).*

The kingdom of Etruria (located in present-day Tuscany) was created in the Treaty of Lunéville and bestowed to Louis de Bourbon in 1801. Upon the death of her husband in 1803, Maria Luisa became regent of the province for her son Charles Louis. In 1807, Maria Luisa lost her kingdom, failed an 1811 attempt to flee to England, and was imprisoned in a Roman cloister until 1814. After the fall of Napoleon in 1815, she was granted the province of Lucca by the Congress of Vienna. She ruled as the duchess of Lucca until her death in 1824.

Maria Luisa Teresa of Parma
(1751–1819)

*Queen of Spain, wife of Charles IV, and mother of Ferdinand VII, whose support of an alliance with Napoleon helped weaken the Spanish monarchy. Name variations: María or Maria Louisa Teresa of Parma; Marie-Louise of Parma; Maria Luisa of Parma; Maria Luisa of Spain; Marie Louise Therese; Luisa Maria Teresa. Born on December 9, 1751; died on January 2, 1819; daughter of Philip de Bourbon (1720–1765, duke of Parma and son of *Elizabeth Farnese), and Louise Elizabeth (1727–1759, daughter of Louis XV of France); married Charles IV (1748–1819), king of Spain (r. 1788–1808), on September 4, 1765; children: *Carlota Joaquina (1775–1830); Maria Luisa of Etruria (1782–1824); Ferdinand VII (1784–1833), king of Spain (r. 1813–1833); Charles or Carlos Maria Isidro or Don Carlos (1788–1855); Francisco de Paula (1748–1865), duke of Cadiz; Maria Amalia (1779–1798, who married Anton Pascal de Bourbon); *Marie Isabella of Spain (1789–1848).*

The daughter of Philip, duke of Parma, and *Louise Elizabeth, Maria Luisa Teresa of Parma was born on December 9, 1751. As a young woman, she received a good education from tutors such as Condillac, but was too frivolous and impetuous to fully profit from it. Although her portraits by Goya, made in middle age, picture her as a heavy, homely woman, she was a pretty, charming youth. Engaged at 13 to her cousin Charles (IV), crown prince of Spain, she married him in 1765. In Spain, she fretted at the austere court of Charles III, who suspected her frivolous nature and kept her under watch. She gave birth to a son, Ferdinand (VII), in 1784, and 23 other pregnancies followed, but only seven children survived to adulthood.

In 1788, her husband succeeded to the throne as Charles IV. His good intentions did not overcome his indecision and lack of energy, and Maria Luisa had room to maneuver. She secured the advancement of her favorite, an obscure guard named Manuel de Godoy, who by 1791 sported the Grand Cross of Charles III and according to rumor shared the queen's bed. When the French revolutionaries beheaded Charles IV's cousin, Louis XVI, in early 1793, war fever gripped Spain. Godoy's influence over the monarchs grew, to popular dismay.

Maria Luisa supported Spain's alliance with Napoleon, which eventually had disastrous consequences for the monarchy. To secure a domain for her daughter *Maria Luisa of Etruria as queen of Etruria in Tuscany, Spain agreed to the Second Treaty of San Ildefonso (1800) and returned Louisiana to France. Meanwhile enemies of Maria Luisa and Godoy played on Ferdinand's jealousy of the favorite, and by 1804 Ferdinand

Maria Luisa Teresa of Parma

had joined conspiracies to eliminate his mother's protege. When Charles and Maria Luisa refused to dismiss Godoy, Ferdinand began to plot again his father. In 1807, crisis enveloped the monarchy. Both Spanish factions appealed to Napoleon for support. He resolved the imbroglio by forcing the abdication (May 1808) of both Charles IV and Ferdinand VII in favor of his own brother Joseph Bonaparte.

Charles IV and Maria Luisa went to exile in France, never to return to Spain. They lived in comfort and eventually moved to Rome. Maria Luisa died there on January 2, 1819. Lacking wisdom in politics and circumspection in her private life, she helped weaken the Spanish monarchy, which could not withstand the tempest unleashed by the French Revolution and Napoleon.

SOURCES:

Hilt, Douglas. *The Troubled Trinity: Godoy and the Spanish Monarchs*. Tuscaloosa: University of Alabama Press, 1987.

Lynch, John. *Bourbon Spain, 1700–1808*. Cambridge, MA: Basil Blackwell, 1989.

Kendall W. Brown,
Professor of History,
Brigham Young University, Provo, Utah

Maria Maddalena de' Pazzi (1566–1607).

See Mary Magdalen of Pazzi.

Maria Magdalena (1689–1743)

*Bohemian princess. Born on March 26, 1689, in Vienna; died on May 1, 1743, in Vienna; daughter of *Eleanor of Pfalz-Neuburg (1655–1720) and Leopold I of Bohemia (1640–1705), Holy Roman emperor (r. 1658–1705).*

Maria Magdalena of Austria
(1589–1631)

*Grand duchess of Tuscany. Name variations: Maria Maddalena; Maria Maddalena of Austria; Maria Maddalena de Medici; Marie-Madelaine. Born on October 7, 1589, in Graz; died on November 1, 1631, in Passau; daughter of Mary of Bavaria (1551–1608), duchess of Styria, and Charles (1540–1590), archduke of Styria; sister of Ferdinand II, king of Bohemia and Hungary (r. 1578–1637), Holy Roman emperor (r. 1619–1637), *Margaret of Austria (c. 1577–1611), *Anna of Styria (1573–1598), and *Constance of Styria (1588–1631); married Cosimo II de Medici (1590–1620), grand duke of Tuscany (r. 1609–1620), on October 19, 1608; children: Ferdinand II (1610–1670), grand duke of Tuscany (r. 1620–1670); *Maria Cristina de Medici (1610–1632, twin sister of Ferdinand II); Giovanni Carlo, cardinal (1611–1663); *Margaret of Parma (b. 1612, who married Edward Farnese, duke of Parma); Mattia or Mattias (1613–1667); Francesco (d. 1634); *Anna de Medici (b. 1616, who married Ferdinand of Austrian Tyrol); Leopoldo (1617–1675), cardinal.*

A German princess of imperial descent, Maria Magdalena of Austria was the daughter of Archduke Charles of Austria and Styria and *Mary of Bavaria. Maria Magdalena was exceptionally well educated and showed considerable interest in contemporary art and the intellectual movement known as humanism. These cultural interests served Maria well in her marriage to the powerful leader of the Italian province of Tuscany, Grand Duke Cosimo II de Medici, since the Medici were renowned for their artistic patronage. Like virtually all marriages between aristocrats in early modern Europe, the union was politically motivated as an attempt to create a diplomatic alliance between the Austrian monarchy and the Medicis. Maria and Cosimo were married in 1608, when Maria was about 19 years old; her new husband was also 19.

Despite being a foreigner, the young grand duchess fit in fairly well in the culturally refined, ostentatious Medici court in Florence, and seems to have gotten along well with her husband; Cosimo had a palace built for Maria, called the Poggio Imperiale in honor of Maria's imperial family. Maria Magdalena of Austria matched the disposition of her husband: tolerant, agreeable, and friendly. The attractive couple became a popular subject of portrait painter Susterman. The results hang in the Corsini Gallery in Florence.

Maria and Cosimo had eight surviving children in their twelve years of marriage, four sons and four daughters. But in 1620 Cosimo died suddenly, at age 31. Maria's eldest son, Ferdinand, succeeded his father as Grand Duke Ferdinand II, but since he was only ten years old he could not rule. Cosimo's will had provided for the rule of the duchy during the young duke's minority. He had named his mother, *Christine of Lorraine, and Maria Magdalena to serve as joint regents for Ferdinand. However, it was understood that Christine would carry the burden of administration while Maria spent her energy on raising her eight children. The two women worked amicably together, sharing similar tastes for art and luxurious living and between them spending much of the large treasury Cosimo had built up. Maria did not live to see her son take over the reins of government, however. In November 1631, she went on a combined personal and diplomatic mission to see her brother, Holy Roman Emperor Ferdinand II. En route Maria fell ill and died suddenly at Passau. Her body was carried back to Tuscany and buried at San Lorenzo. Grand Duchess Maria Magdalena of Austria was 42 years old.

SOURCES:
Micheletti, Emma. *The Medici of Florence.* Florence: Scala, 1980.
Young, George F. *The Medici.* 2nd ed. NY: E.P. Dutton, 1911.

Laura York,
Riverside, California

Maria Maliuta (d. 1605).
See Maria Skuratova.

Maria Mercedes (1910–2000).
See Maria de las Mercedes.

Maria Nagaia (d. 1612)

Empress of Russia. Name variations: Maria Nagoy; Martha. Died on July 20, 1612; daughter of Theodor Nagaia (a minor landowner); became the seventh wife of Ivan IV the Terrible (1530–1584), tsar of Russia (r.

1533–1584), in September 1580; children: Demetrius also known as Dmitri (b. 1583, killed in 1591). Ivan IV had previously married Anastasia Romanova (d. 1560) in February 1547; Maria of Circassia (d. 1369) in August 1561; *Marta Sobakin (d. 1571) in October 1571; Anna Koltoskaia (d. 1626) in April 1572 (divorced 1574); *Anna Vassiltschikov around 1574 (divorced in 1576); and Vassilissa Malentieva around 1576 (divorced 1577).

The marriage of Maria Nagaia to Russian tsar Ivan IV in September 1581 was one of the most ill-fated unions in history. The bridegroom had already been married six times and was at the end of his "reign of terror," which had left the country in ruins. It was with the death of his first wife *Anastasia Romanova, in 1560, that Ivan began to run "along the broad highway that leads to Hell," as one chronicler put it. Certain that Anastasia had been killed in a plot by the boyars, whom he was convinced also had murdered his mother *Elena Glinski and his uncles, he now feared for his sons and heirs Ivan and Theodore (I).

Ivan IV's paranoia only increased with the death of his second wife *Maria of Circassia, at which time he began executing his advisors and destroying whole cities, believing that the citizens therein were part of an enormous plot against him. By the time Maria Nagaia entered the picture, the third of Ivan's wives had died, and he had made three more hasty marriages, all of which ended in divorce. (Canon law only recognized three of Ivan's marriages.) His wedding with Maria Nagaia was a double ceremony at which Ivan's son Theodore (I) married *Irene Godunova, the sister of Boris Godunov.

Ivan apparently turned a blind eye to his wife, and to the increasing military threat from Poland. However, when his son, Ivan Ivanovich, demanded to take over the imperial troops, Ivan grew enraged and struck the young man with the royal scepter, mortally wounding him. When Ivan Ivanovich died several days later, Ivan IV realized the enormity of his actions and sank into a deep despair from which he never recovered. Even Maria Nagaia's gift of another son, Dmitri, in 1582, did not revive him. Ivan seemed only to await death, which claimed him on March 18, 1584, during a game of chess with an aide. His son Theodore succeeded as him as tsar, although Ivan IV, knowing his son's shortcomings, had appointed a Regency Council headed by Boris Godunov and Nikita Romanovich Yuriev, the two men also serving as joint guardians to Theodore. Upon Nikita Yuriev's

death later in 1584, Boris Godunov became the most powerful man in Russia.

Meanwhile, when word of Ivan's death reached Maria Nagaia's family, they planned a coup to place her son Dmitri on the throne. The Regency Council, however, learned of the plot and arrested the entire family, exiling them to Uglich where they were permitted a small court overseen by council-appointed administrators. But the Nagaia family was not out of the picture for long. In May 1591, young Dmitri, an epileptic, was killed while playing the game tychka (similar to mumbletypeg), during which he collapsed and fell onto a knife which lodged in his throat. Dmitri's uncle Mikhail, believing the boy's death was the result of a plot executed by agents of Boris Godunov, immediately had the government agents hunted down and murdered. Later, when a church council determined that the death was "an act of God," Mikhail was charged with the murder of government officials and exiled, while Maria Nagaia was forced to a nunnery, where she took the name Martha.

Over the course of the next seven years, a series of events brought Boris Godunov into full power. Crowned tsar on September 1, 1598, he reigned over a two-year period of peace and prosperity. In the midst of this tranquil period, however, a rumor surfaced that Maria Nagaia's son Dmitri had not died and was being hidden by the Romanovs. Rumors of Dmitri's escape persisted over several years and in early summer of 1603, a servant claiming to be Dmitri turned up in Poland and quickly advanced to a position of considerable power.

When Godunov learned of this, he had Maria Nagaia—now Martha—brought to Moscow for questioning. When she refused to declare whether her son was dead or alive, the Russian Church declared that "Dmitri" was in fact the defrocked monk Grishka Otrepev, and had him excommunicated. Still, the man known as Dmitri invaded Russia in 1604, and Godunov, now ill following a stroke in the spring of 1603, was powerless against him as he continued to draw peasants, landowners, and Cossacks into his ranks. Following Godunov's death on April 13, 1605, and the succession to the throne of his son Theodore II, "Dmitri" managed to win over the Russian imperial generals. On June 2, it was announced that the 1591 report was indeed a lie and Dmitri had not died. Tsar Theodore I was murdered a week later, and "Dmitri" entered Moscow, where on July 18 he was reunited with his mother.

But there was yet another surprising turn of events. Within a year, Maria Nagaia recanted, stating that her son Dmitri had indeed been killed on Boris Godunov's orders. Upon her pronouncement, the man claiming to be Dmitri was murdered, and the body of the real Dmitri was brought to Moscow for canonization. Maria Nagaia died in 1612, taking whatever she knew about her son's death to her grave.

SOURCES:

Fletcher, Giles. *Of the Russe Commonwealthe*. Edited by Richard Pipes. Cambridge, MA: Harvard University Press. 1966.

Graham, Stephen. *Boris Godunof*. New Haven, CT: Yale University Press, 1933.

Grey, Ian. *Boris Godunov. The Tragic Tsar*. NY: Scribner, 1973.

Margeret, Jacques. *The Russian Empire and Grand Duchy of Muscovy*. Edited and translated by C.S.L. Dunning. PA: University of Pittsburgh Press, 1983.

Massa, Isaac. *A Short History of the Muscovite Wars*. Edited and translated by G.E. Orchard. Toronto, Canada: University of Toronto Press, 1982.

Platonov, S.F. *Boris Godunov*. Translated by L.R. Pyles. Academic International Press, 1973.

Skrynnikov, R.G. *Boris Godunov*. Translated by H.F. Graham. Academic International Press, 1982.

Maria Nikolaevna (1819–1876)

Duchess of Leuchtenburg. Name variations: Nicholia-va; Maria Romanov; duchess of Leuchtenberg. Born on August 6, 1819; died on February 21, 1876; eldest daughter of Nicholas I (1796–1855), tsar of Russia (1825–1855), and *Charlotte of Prussia (1798–1860); sister of Alexander II, tsar of Russia, *Olga of Russia (1822–1892), and *Alexandra Nikolaevna (1825–1844); married Maximilian de Beauharnais also known as Maximilian (1817–1852), duke of Leuchtenburg, on July 14, 1839; married Gregory Alexandrovna, count Stroganov, on November 16, 1856; children: (first marriage) George (b. 1852), count of Leuchtenburg.

Maria of Alania (fl. 1070–1081).

See Anna Dalassena for sidebar.

Maria of Alexandria (fl. 1st, 2nd, or 3rd c.).

See Mary the Jewess.

Maria of Amnia (fl. 782).

See Irene of Athens for sidebar.

Maria of Anjou (1371–1395).

See Maria of Hungary.

Maria of Aragon (fl. 1311)

Sicilian princess. Flourished in 1311; daughter of *Blanche of Naples (d. 1310) and James II or Jaime, king of Sicily and Aragon (r. 1291–1327); married Peter, regent of Castile, in December 1311; children:

Blanche of Castile (c. 1320–1375).

Maria of Aragon (1403–1445)

Queen of Castile and Leon. Name variations: María; Mary Trastamara. Born in 1403; died on February 18, 1445, in Villacastin; daughter of Ferdinand I, king of Aragon (r. 1412–1416), and *Eleanor of Albuquerque (1374–1435); became first wife of Juan II also known as John II (1404–1454), king of Castile and Leon (r. 1406–1454), on August 4, 1420; children: Catalina of the Asturias (1422–1424); Leonor of the Asturias (1423–1425); Enrique also known as Henry IV (1425–1474), king of Castile and Leon (r. 1454–1474, who married *Blanche of Navarre and *Joanna of Portugal); Maria of Castile (1429–1430). John II's second wife was *Isabel of Portugal) (1428–1496, mother of *Isabella I).

Maria of Aragon (fl. 1440)

Marquesa of Ferrara. Name variations: Maria d'Este. Flourished around 1440; married Leonello (1407–1450), 13th marquis of Ferrara. Leonello's first wife was *Margherita Gonzaga (1418–1439).

Maria of Armenia (fl. 1300)

Byzantine empress. Name variations: Xene. Flourished in the early 1300s; married Michael IX Paleologus (d. 1320), Byzantine emperor, co-emperor of Nicaea (r. 1295–1320); children: Andronicus III, emperor of Nicaea (r. 1328–1341); Manuel; *Theodora Paleologina (who married Theodore Svetoslav and Michael Shishman); Anna (who married Thomas of Epirus and Nicholas Orsini).

Maria of Austria (1505–1558).

See Mary of Hungary.

Maria of Austria (1584–1649)

Austrian royal. Born on June 16, 1584, in Innsbruck; died on March 2, 1649, in Innsbruck; daughter of *Anna Caterina Gonzaga (1566–1621) and Ferdinand II, archduke of Austria; sister of *Anna Gonzaga (1585–1618).

Maria of Austria (1752–1814).

See Maria Carolina.

Maria of Bavaria (1805–1877)

*Queen of Saxony. Born in 1805; died in 1877; daughter of Maximilian I Joseph, elector of Bavaria (r. 1799–1805), king of Bavaria (r. 1805–1825), and *Caroline of Baden (1776–1841); twin sister of *Sophie of Bavaria (1805–1872); sister of *Elizabeth of Bavaria (1801–1873, who married Frederick William IV of Prussia); second wife of Frederick Augustus II (1797–1854), king of Saxony (r. 1836–1854). Frederick Augustus' first wife was *Caroline of Austria (1801–1832).*

Maria of Bavaria (1841–1925).

See Maria Sophia Amalia.

Maria of Bavaria (b. 1872)

*Duchess of Calabria. Name variations: Marie of Bavaria. Born on July 6, 1872; daughter of *Maria Teresa of Este (1849–1919) and Louis also known as Ludwig III (1845–1921), king of Bavaria (r. 1913–1918); married Ferdinand Pio (1869–1934), duke of Calabria, on May 31, 1897; children: Maria Antoinette (b. 1898); Maria Cristina (b. 1899); Roger (1901–1914); Barbara (1902–1927, who married Franz Xaver of Stolberg-Wernigerode); Lucia (b. 1908); Urraca (b. 1913).*

Maria of Byzantium

Queen of Hungary. Married Stephen IV, king of Hungary (r. 1162–1163).

Maria of Castile (1401–1458)

Queen of Aragon, Naples, and Sicily, a talented monarch and an able administrator, who ruled Aragon successfully for a quarter of a century. Name variations: María of Castile; Mary Trastamara; infanta of Castile. Born on November 14, 1401, in Segovia; died on September 7, 1458 (some sources cite 1457), in Valencia; daughter of Catherine of Lancaster (1372–1418) and Enrique also known as Henry III (1379–1406), king of Castile (r. 1390–1406); married Alfonso or Alphonso V the Magnanimous (1396–1458), king of Aragon (r. 1416–1458), king of Sicily as Alphonso I (r. 1443–1458), in Valencia, Aragon, on June 12 or 13, 1415; children: none. Ferdinand or Ferrante I of Naples (b. 1423, r. 1458–1494) was Alphonso V's illegitimate son.

Her marriage contract negotiated between Castile and Aragon (1408); death of King Ferdinand I of Aragon (April 2, 1416); was viceroy of Aragon (1421–24); negotiated truce between the armies of Aragon and Castile (July 1, 1429); was viceroy of Aragon (1434–58); postponed permanent reunion with Alphonso due to illness (1437); urged neutrality in conflict between Navarre and Castile (July 1444); peace treaty with Castile signed (May 16, 1454); death of Alphonso V (June 27, 1458).

The daughter of *Catherine of Lancaster and Henry III of Castile, Maria of Castile was born in 1401. In 1415, she wed her cousin Alphonso V, the future king of Aragon, in a ceremony presided over by Pope Benedict XIII. Alphonso ascended to the throne of Aragon in 1416. During a three-year absence from 1421 to 1424, Alphonso appointed his wife viceroy of Aragon. In 1429, Queen Maria negotiated a truce between the forces of Aragon and Castile. When Alphonso became king of Naples in 1434, Maria of Castile was again appointed his viceroy. With Alphonso in Naples, the two were never to see each other again.

Maria of Castile proved herself both on the battlefield and in the council chamber. She was a deft negotiator, and initiated policies which benefited the common people of Aragon and fostered economic growth. A generous patron of the arts, Maria of Castile also favored monastic reform.

Maria died on September 4, 1458, a few months after her husband. She had been a successful medieval monarch in every respect, save one. Plagued by ill health throughout her life, Maria of Castile failed to provide an heir. A period of political instability followed.

SOURCES:
Bisson, T.N. *The Medieval Crown of Aragon: A Short History.* Oxford: Clarendon Press, 1986.
Ryder, Alan. *Alfonso the Magnanimous: King of Aragon, Naples and Sicily.* Oxford: Clarendon Press, 1990.

SUGGESTED READING:
Miron, E.L. *The Queens of Aragon: Their Lives and Times.* Port Washington, NY: Hippocrene, 1970.

Hugh A. Stewart, M.A.,
Guelph, Ontario, Canada

Maria of Castile (1482–1517).

See Isabella I for sidebar.

Maria of Circassia (d. 1569)

*Russian empress. Name variations: Maria Tscherkaski. Died on September 1, 1569; daughter of Temrink Tscherkaski; became second wife of Ivan IV the Terrible (1530–1584), tsar of Russia (r. 1533–1584), in August 1561; children: Vassilli (1563–1563). Ivan IV also married *Anastasia Romanova (d. 1560) in Feb-*

ruary 1547; *Marta Sobakin (d. 1571) in October 1571; Anna Koltoskaia (d. 1626) in April 1572 (divorced 1574); *Anna Vassiltschikov around 1574 (divorced in 1576); *Maria Nagaia (d. 1612); and Vassilissa Malentieva around 1576 (divorced 1577).

Maria of Cordova (d. 851).

See joint entry on Flora and Maria of Cordova.

Maria of Habsburg (1528–1603).

See Elisabeth of Habsburg (1554–1592) for sidebar on Marie of Austria.

Maria of Hungary (fl. 995–1025).

See Maria.

Maria of Hungary (1371–1395)

Queen of Hungary and Bohemia. Name variations: Maria of Anjou; Mary of Anjou. Born in 1371 in Hungary (some sources cite 1370); died on May 17, 1395, in Hungary (some sources cite 1392); daughter of Louis I the Great, king of Hungary (r. 1342–1382), king of Poland (r. 1370–1382), and Elizabeth of Bosnia (c. 1345–1387); sister of Jadwiga (1374–1399), queen of Poland (r. 1384–1399); became first wife of Sigismund I (1368–1437), margrave of Brandenburg, king of Bohemia (r. 1419–1437), duke of Luxemburg (1419–1437), king of Hungary (r. 1387–1437), and Holy Roman emperor (r. 1410–1437), in October 1385.

⚜▶
Elizabeth of Bosnia. *See Jadwiga for sidebar.*

Maria of Hungary was born in 1371, the daughter of King Louis I the Great of Poland and Hungary, and Queen ⚜ **Elizabeth of Bosnia.** Louis conquered the kingdom of Naples for his young relative, Charles of Durazzo, but reserved his major holdings for his two daughters, Maria and **Jadwiga.* When Louis died in 1382, Jadwiga became queen of Poland, while Maria inherited Hungary at age 17. She married the German noble Sigismund (I), margrave of Brandenburg, who soon became king of Germany and Bohemia (he later was crowned Holy Roman emperor). This put Maria and Sigismund in control of most of Central and Eastern Europe, from the French border across almost to the Black Sea.

The emperor and empress ruled well together; both were ambitious and politically astute, making important alliances and preserving their empire for 12 years. Their powerful positions also led them into numerous wars and engagements; at one time, Maria was captured by enemy forces within Hungary and imprisoned. Sigismund had to pay a huge ransom and make large land con-

cessions to her captors in order to gain her release. Empress Maria of Hungary died suddenly after a fall from her horse at the young age of 29; her unborn child died with her. She was greatly mourned by her husband and subjects.

SOURCES:
Anderson, Bonnie S., and Judith P. Zinsser. *A History of Their Own.* Vol. I. NY: Harper & Row, 1988.
Opfell, Olga. *Queens, Empresses, Grand Duchesses, and Regents.* Jefferson, NC: McFarland, 1989.

Laura York,
Riverside, California

Maria of Hungary (1606–1646).

See Maria Anna of Spain.

Maria of Julich-Berg (fl. 1515)

Duchess of Cleves. Name variations: Marie of Julich; Mary of Jülich-Berg-Ravensburg. Flourished around 1515; daughter of William III (or IV), duke of Juliers, and *Sybilla of Brandenburg; married John III, duke of Cleves (r. 1521–1539); children: *Sybilla of Cleves (1514–1554); *Anne of Cleves (1515–1557, who married Henry VIII, king of England); William IV (or V), duke of Cleves (r. 1539–1592); *Amelia of Cleves (1517–1586).

Maria of Kiev (d. 1087)

Queen of Poland. Name variations: Dobronega Maria. Born before 1015; died in 1087; daughter of Vladimir I, grand prince of Kiev (r. 980–1015) and one of his nine wives; sister of Yaroslav I the Wise, grand prince of Kiev (r. 1019–1054); married Kazimir or Casimir I the Restorer (1015–1058), king of Poland (r. 1038–1058), in 1043; children: Boleslaw II Szczodry also known as Boleslaus II the Bold, king of Poland (r. 1058–1079); Wladyslaw I or Ladislas Herman (1043–1102), king of Poland (r. 1079–1102); Swietoslawa (who married Vratislav, king of Bohemia); Mieszko.

Maria of Kiev (d. 1146)

Princess of Kiev. Died in 1146; daughter of *Gyseth (fl. 1070) and Vladimir II Monomakh or Monomach (1053–1125), grand prince of Kiev (r. 1113–1125); married Leo Diogenes of Byzantium (d. 1116).

Maria of Kiev (d. 1179).

See Marie of Kiev.

Maria of Macedonia (d. around 864)

*Macedonian wife of Basil I. Born in Macedonia; died around 864; first wife of Basil I the Macedonian, Byzantine emperor (r. 867–886); children: Constantine (crowned as co-emperor on January 6, 869, but died young in 879). Basil's second wife was *Eudocia Ingerina.*

Maria of Mecklenburg-Schwerin (1854–1920)

*Grand duchess. Name variations: Grand duchess Vladimir; Mary of Mecklenburg-Schwerin. Born Mary or Maria Alexandra Elizabeth Eleanor on May 14, 1854; died on September 6, 1920; daughter of Frederick Francis II, grand duke of Mecklenburg-Schwerin; married Vladimir Alexandrovitch (son of Alexander II, tsar of Russia, and *Marie of Hesse-Darmstadt), on August 16, 1874; children: Cyril Vladimorovitch (1876–1938); Boris (1877–1943); Andrew (1879–1956); *Helena of Russia (1882–1957).*

Maria of Molina (d. 1321).

See Maria de Molina.

Maria of Montpellier (1181–1213)

Queen of Aragon who devoted her short life to protecting her inheritance, the town of Montpellier, from greedy husbands and rebellious city nobles, to preserve it for her son who became James I, king of Aragon. Name variations: Marie of Montpellier or Montpelier; Mary of Montpellier or Montpelier. Born in 1181 (some sources cite 1182); died in 1213 (some sources cite 1219); daughter of Guillaume or Guillem or William VIII, lord of Montpellier, and Eudocia of Byzantium (niece of the Byzantine emperor Manuel I Comnenus); married Barral, viscount of Marseilles, in 1192 (died 1192); married Bernard IV, count of Comminges, in 1197 (Maria was repudiated and sent home in 1201); married Pedro or Peter II, king of Aragon (r. 1196–1213), in 1204; children: daughter Sancia; Jaime or James I the Great of Catalonia (1208–1276), king of Aragon (r. 1213–1276); two other daughters (names unknown).

Maria of Montpellier was the daughter of William VIII, lord of Montpellier, and *Eudocia of Byzantium, niece of the Byzantine emperor Manuel I Comnenus (r. 1143–1180). Born in 1181, Maria lost her birthright at the age of six when her father repudiated her mother in order to marry Agnes of Castile. Agnes quickly satis-

fied William's need for heirs, bearing a son who became William IX and seven more children for backup.

Maria's prospects as the daughter of a repudiated mother were poor. Although Eudocia was the niece of the emperor of Constantinople, she did not command any clout. Eudocia consented to sending Maria away from Constantinople at the tender age of 11 (1192), and, following her daughter's departure, Eudocia disappeared from history. Maria was supposed to marry King Alphonso II of Aragon, but when it turned out that Alphonso had married somebody else, she had to settle for Barral, viscount of Marseilles. This cut her off from succession to Montpellier. However, the viscount was old and ill, and he died before the year was out.

Next, in 1197, Maria was married to Bernard IV, count of Comminges, as his second wife (or third—sources differ). In return for her dowry, Maria was forced to renounce all claims to her paternal inheritance. After bearing two daughters, she was repudiated by her husband and sent home in 1201.

In 1202, her father died, naming William IX as heir. But in 1204, the city of Montpellier expressed itself: the ruling elite rebelled and expelled its new ruler. Either because they expected Maria to be a weak ruler or because they welcomed her soon-to-be new husband, the city of Montpellier declared itself loyal to Maria.

On June 15, 1204, Maria was married to Peter II, king of Aragon, known in his day as Pere II or En Pere II. He was the most powerful political figure in the region, and he no doubt had had his eye on Montpellier for some time. After swearing his marital oath of fidelity in the presence of the local bishop and agreeing to honor the city's custom, Peter promptly mortgaged the castle of Lattes, which was the port of Montpellier. In the next year (1205), he mortgaged the city itself. By September 1205, he persuaded Maria to surrender all her rights to Montpellier, which radically altered the terms of the marriage contract. Although in October Maria gave birth to a daughter (christened **Sancia**), Peter immediately betrothed her to the newly born son of Raymond of Toulouse. Not only did he do this without her mother's consent, but he bequeathed the city of Montpellier as the little girl's dowry. The next year (1206), Peter initiated divorce proceedings against Maria. In two years, then, Maria had again lost her seignorial rights to Montpellier along with her new daughter's future and her own third husband.

In sum, by the time she was 25, Maria of Montpellier was widowed, divorced, and separated from three husbands, respectively. At this point, she launched her campaign to fight back. She resorted to two time-honored strategies available to victimized women: 1) pregnancy and 2) litigation, the particular remedy available to Biblically certified "women and orphans" in Medieval Christianity.

> *I*, Maria, Queen of Aragon and Lady of Montpellier, ill in body but of healthy mind, not wishing to die intestate, make my testament in which I institute James, the son of the King of Aragon and myself, as my heir in all my goods both real and personal.
>
> —**Codicil of Maria's will dictated before her death**

In 1208, at the advanced age of 27, Maria gave birth to James (I). According to the romantic version of the story, Maria had lured Peter to bed in the middle of the night by pretending to be his currently favored mistress, and a few weeks later triumphantly announced that she was pregnant. James offered a more discreet account written decades later in his *Book of Deeds*:

> Now I will relate in what wise I was begotten, and how my birth was. Firstly, in what manner I was begotten. Our father would not see our mother, and it chanced that once the King, our father, was in Lattes, and the Queen, our mother, in Miravals. A nobleman named En Guillen Dalcala came to the King and besought him till he made him go to Miravals where the Queen, my mother, was. And that night both were together it was the will of our Lord, that I should be begotten. And when the Queen, my mother, perceived that she was with child, she and my father went to Montpellier. . . . When they took me back to my mother's house . . . she made twelve candles all of one weight and one size, and had them lighted all together, and gave each of them the name of an Apostle, and vowed to our Lord that I should be christened by the name of that which lasted the longest. And so it happened that the candle that went by the name of Saint James lasted a good three fingers' breadth more than all the others. And owing that circumstance and to the grace of God, I was christened "En Jaume."

When James was duly born, all Montpellier cheered for their sovereign-to-be, and Maria seemed to have cemented her hold on Montpellier. But she had not cemented her hold on Peter. From 1210 to 1213, he continued to press for the divorce from Maria and the subsequent acquisition of Montpellier. And he did not play by the rules.

Against the backdrop of the bloody Albigensian crusade (in which Innocent III, the most medieval pope, enlisted Philip II Augustus, the most powerful medieval king of France, to pit northern Frenchmen against the alleged heretics of southern France), Peter betrothed Maria's only son to a daughter of Simon IV de Montfort, the leader of northern crusaders who were hammering at the border of his southern kingdom. Seizing the infant heir from his mother, Peter sent him more or less as a hostage to live in the Montfort household.

Next, backed by a papal decree in 1212, Peter tried to take Montpellier, intending to give it back to Maria's half-brother William IX. At this point, Maria's popularity in Montpellier evidently saved her possession. The city fathers refused to accede peacefully to the transfer, and the whole town arose in insurrection. Unfortunately, this provoked mobs who destroyed the castle, filled the moat, and pillaged goods belonging to Catalan merchants. All this was to no avail, for Maria still lost her city. By the beginning of 1213, then, her fortunes were at their lowest ebb. She had lost her son, and she had lost Montpellier.

She resorted next to the legal system, moving to Rome to litigate at the highest court. The issue on which the case hinged was consanguinity. Peter's lawyers argued that even though Peter and Maria did not have a common ancestry within the prohibited range of kinship, their marriage was nullified by two other facts: 1) he had fornicated with one of Maria's kinswomen and was thereby rendered ineligible to marry Maria; and 2) Maria had committed adultery by marrying him because she had never divorced Bernard IV, count of Comminges, even though he had cast her out. Maria's lawyers were countering the second point by denying the validity of her earlier marriage on the grounds of consanguinity when they discovered that this errant count had sandwiched in another marriage without a divorce. This made him even more ineligible to marry her. As for the first point about fornicating with Maria's kinswoman, even male chauvinist medieval Christians drew the line at this kind of legal argument to excuse male philandering. It is interesting to note that neither parent considered custody of the child to be legally pertinent. Consanguinity, not custody, was the issue.

Luckily for Maria, there was at the same time an even more notorious case taking place. King Philip II of France had married and rejected **Ingeborg* (c. 1176–1237/38), princess of Denmark, and he had compounded his repudiation by refusing to return her. After years of litigation, Ingeborg's appeal finally reached the pope, and the pope was about to vindicate her.

So it was that on January 19, 1213, that Pope Innocent III decided in favor of Maria of Montpellier. The politically most powerful pope in history decreed that Peter's attempt to divorce Maria was invalid. He ruled as follows:

> Having diligently heard and subtly examined all those things which the parties prudently and faithfully presented to the judges delegate and to us, since it appears to us evident that the Count Comminges is related to you in the third and fourth degree, and the Count had earlier married the noble woman Beatrice before the Church, and it is not proved that they had been separated by ecclesiastical judgment, and since nothing legitimate has been proved against you on the matter of kinship. . . . [Be it enjoined upon him, King Peter] to take the Queen back with kindness into the fullness of His grace and treat with marital affection; especially since you have had a son by her, and she is a God-fearing woman possessed of many virtues.

Moreover, on April 8, in a second decree, the pope ordered the archbishop of Narbonne to compel the rulers of Montpellier to return the seignorial rights and revenues to their rightful lord, Maria of Montpellier:

> Those goods [which were mortgaged by her husband the illustrious King of Aragon, although the law does not assent to the mortgaging of dowry property, . . . plus] money which has been collected for so long from these revenues . . . ought to be paid back to her. . . . We, who owe the debt of justice to all persons, wish to stand with her in her rights. We therefore order you by apostolic writing that you summon the parties and hear what they have to propose, and decide what is just, without appeal, and enforce your decision by ecclesiastical penalties. You should force the men of Montpellier by ecclesiastical censure, and without right of appeal to pay the Queen her expenses in this matter.

The papal documents presume that the pope did indeed have jurisdiction over secular holdings. More significantly, however, the decrees of Pope Innocent III revealed that women were not powerless. While not in a commanding position legally, their legal status did not reflect their low theological estate. At the very least, women were not pawns in male power struggles. Rather, they had rights of their own. To be sure, these rights had to be articulated in court by male lawyers; but then, so did the rights of kings, princes, nobles, merchants, etc., have to be defended in court by male lawyers. For latter-day despisers of the Middle Ages who subscribe to the liberal theory of historical progress, it is ironic that Maria of Montpellier, as queen of Aragon in the early 13th century, fared better than her descendant, ❧➤ **Catherine of Aragon**, Henry VIII's queen of England, who three centuries later became history's most famous spurned queen.

On April 20, 1213, Maria dictated her last will and testament and died soon afterwards. In July of the same year, her husband Peter died on the battlefield of Muret fighting against Simon de Montfort, the guardian of their son. James, aged five, inherited his parents' possessions: Peter's kingdom and Maria's city.

Maria of Montpellier had been politically orphaned at 6; married at 11 to be widowed at 12; married at 16 to be repudiated at 20; married again to the most powerful king at 23 to be separated at 25. At 27, she was the mother of three daughters and of a son who became the most powerful king in the history of the region. Finally, vindicated at 32 by the most powerful medieval pope, she died only four months later. At each marital repudiation, she had her children and her possessions stripped from her. Obviously, Maria of Montpellier's struggle over her city, her inherited and acquired properties, and her three husbands raise many questions about women's rights and power in the 12th century which cast shadows down to the present day. She was a miracle worker for her age. Reported her son James the Conqueror, "Many sick to this day are cured by drinking in water, or in wine, the dust scraped from her tombstone."

SOURCES:

There are no biographies of Maria of Montpellier in English. There is one in Spanish by Rafael Dalmau i Ferreres entitled "Maria de Montpellier," Barcelona, 1962. It is in the series *Episodis de la Historia*, edited by Rafael Dalmau, *Bonavista* 26, Barcelona, Spain.

Cheyette, Frederic I. *Resource Book for the Teaching of Medieval Civilization.* Amherst, MA: Five Colleges, 1984, pp. 113–140.

James I. *Book of Deeds.* Translated by John Forster from *Libre dels fevts,* or *Llibre dels Feits del rei en Jacme.* London, 1883.

SUGGESTED READING:

Duby, Georges. *Medieval Marriage: Two Models from Twelfth Century France.* Translated by E. Forster. London, 1978.

David Stevenson,
former Associate Professor of History at the
University of Nebraska at Kearney, Nebraska

Catherine of Aragon. See Six Wives of Henry VIII.

Maria of Navarre (fl. 1340)

Queen of Aragon. Flourished around 1340; first wife of Pedro IV also known as Peter IV the Ceremonious

(b. 1319), king of Aragon (r. 1336–1387). Peter IV's second wife was *Eleanor of Portugal (1328–1348); his third was *Eleanor of Sicily (d. 1375).

Maria of Portugal (1313–1357).

See Guzman, Leonora de for sidebar.

Maria of Portugal (1538–1577)

Duchess of Parma. Name variations: Maria Farnese. Born on December 8, 1538, in Lisbon; died on July 18, 1577, in Parma; daughter of *Isabella of Braganza (c. 1512–1576) and Duarte (1515–1540), duke of Guimaraes; married Alexander also known as Allesandro Farnese, duke of Parma, in November 1565; children: Ranuccio I (1569–1622), duke of Parma (r. 1592–1622).

Maria of Prussia (1825–1889)

Queen of Bavaria. Name variations: Marie of Prussia. Born Marie Hedwig on October 15, 1825, in Berlin; died at the castle of Hohenschwangau on May 18, 1889; daughter of *Mary of Hesse-Homburg (1785–1846) and William (son of Frederick William II, king of Prussia, and *Frederica of Hesse); niece of Frederick William III of Prussia; married her cousin Maximilian II (1811–1864), king of Bavaria (r. 1848–1864), on October 12, 1842; children: Ludwig II (1845–1886), the mad king of Bavaria (r. 1864–1886); Otto (1848–1886), king of Bavaria (r. 1886–1913).

Maria of Savoy (fl. 1400s)

Duchess of Milan. Flourished in the early 1400s; married Filippo Maria Visconti (1392–1447), duke of Milan (r. 1402–1447). Filippo had an illegitimate daughter, *Bianca Maria Visconti (1423–1470), with Agnes del Maino.

Maria of Savoy (1914—)

Italian princess. Name variations: Marie of Savoy; Maria di Savvia. Born in 1914; daughter of *Elena of Montenegro (1873–1952) and Victor Emmanuel III (1869–1947), king of Italy (r. 1900–1946, abdicated); sister of *Mafalda of Hesse.

Maria of Sicily (d. 1402)

Queen of Sicily. Name variations: Mary of Sicily. Reigned from 1377 to 1402 (some sources cite 1401); died in 1402; daughter of Frederick III the Simple, king of Sicily (r. 1355–1377) and *Constance of Aragon (c. 1350–?); married Martin I the Younger, king of Sicily (r.

1390–1409); children: one son (d. 1402).

Following the death of her father Frederick III the Simple, king of Sicily, in 1377, Maria of Sicily came to the throne in name only. In 1390, she was abducted from her castle and taken to Barcelona to marry her cousin, the son of Martin I the Humane, king of Aragon. In 1392, her husband became Martin I the Younger, king of Sicily. Maria of Sicily died the same year as her only son, in 1402. Two years later, Martin I married *Blanche of Navarre.

Maria of the Palatinate.

See Anna Maria of the Palatinate.

Maria of Trebizond (d. 1439)

Byzantine empress. Name variations: Maria Komnene or Comneni of Trebizond. Died in 1439; third wife of John VIII Paleologus (1391–1448), emperor of Nicaea and Byzantine emperor in exile (r. 1425–1448).

Little is known of Maria of Trebizond, the third wife of John VIII Paleologus. John had previously been married briefly to *Anna of Moscow, who died of the plague, and to his Italian cousin, *Sophie of Montferrat, whom he had divorced. Apparently Maria was the most beloved of his wives, and following her death, he lost much of his zest for living.

Maria's death occurred while John was at the ecumenical Council of Florence, at which he had sought official reunion of the Greek Orthodox and Italian Catholic churches in order to win military support from Western Europe. In Florence, where the Council had moved when rumors of plague surfaced in Ferrara, a decree of union was signed, but when John returned to Constantinople, he found widespread opposition to the "unionizers." Now shattered by the death of his wife, John lacked the strength or desire to implement the union, and although he remained committed to the work of the Council, he did not force the union upon his subjects. Since Maria had not produced an heir, John was succeeded by his brother Constantine XI when he died in 1448.

Barbara Morgan,
Melrose, Massachusetts

Maria of Tver (c. 1440–1467)

Grand Princess of Moscow. Born in 1440 or 1442, in Tver, a town northwest of Moscow; died on April 22, 1467; daughter of Prince Boris of Tver and Anastasia of Mojaisk (d. 1451); betrothed to Ivan III when she was six; married Ivan III (1440–1505), tsar of Russia (r. 1462–1505), on June 2, 1452; children: Ivan the Younger (1456–1490), prince of Moscow (r. 1471–1490, who married *Helene of Moldavia).

The daughter of Prince Boris of Tver and **Anastasia of Mojaisk**, Maria of Tver was betrothed to Ivan III in 1446, when both were six years old. Ivan's father, Basil II, grand duke of Moscow, was trying to consolidate his position. Little is known of the subsequent years, except that Maria of Tver married Ivan in 1452 and had a son in 1458, and Ivan fought a campaign against the Dnieper Tatars in the same year. He succeeded to the Grand Ducal throne in 1462, aged 22, after his father's death from gangrene. Moscow at that time had not established the principle of primogeniture, by which the oldest son inherited all his father's duchy. Although Ivan received the lion's share, Basil was careful in his will to share almost half of his lands and wealth among his four other sons. Ivan honored the will, but for most of his reign he had to face the anger of his resentful brothers without yielding to them any more than was necessary.

Maria died in 1467. Although she had been forced on Ivan solely for political reasons, her death caused him genuine regret. He was only 27 at the time, and she had borne him only one son. Like all monarchs of the era, he had to think at once of securing the succession by remarrying, lest he outlive this son and expose the state to a fratricidal succession war. Ivan employed a handful of Italian military and architectural advisors and through one of them he learned that the pope, Paul II, was guardian of a princess who might become his new bride. She was *Sophia of Byzantium, a huge woman whose uncle had been the last Byzantine emperor, Constantine XI, when that ancient Empire fell to the Turks in 1452.

Maria of Waldeck (1857–1882)

*Princess of Waldeck and Pyrmont. Name variations: Marie of Waldeck and Pyrmont. Born on May 23, 1857; died on April 30, 1882; daughter of George II Victor, prince of Waldeck and Pyrmont, and *Helen of Nassau (1831–1888); became first wife of William II (1848–1921), king of Wurttemberg (r. 1891–1918, abdicated), on February 15, 1877; children: *Pauline of Wurttemberg (1877–1965, who married Frederick, prince of Wied); Ulrich (b. 1880). William II married*

his second wife, Princess **Charlotte of Schaumburg-Lippe** (1864–1946), on April 8, 1886.

Maria of Wurttemberg (1797–1855)

*Archduchess of Austria. Name variations: Maria Dorothea. Born on November 1, 1797; died on March 30, 1855; daughter of *Henrietta of Nassau-Weilburg (1780–1857) and Ludwig Frederick Alexander, duke of Wurttemberg; married Joseph, archduke of Austria, on August 24, 1819; children: Elizabeth (1820–1820); Archduchess *Elizabeth (1831–1903); Alexander (b. 1825); Joseph (b. 1833); *Maria Henrietta of Austria (1836–1902).*

Maria Padilla (1335–1365).

See Marie de Padilla.

Maria Paleologina (fl. 1278–1279)

Tsarina of Bulgaria. Name variations: Maria Palaeologina. Flourished around 1278 and 1279; daughter of Eulogia Paleologina; niece of Michael VIII Paleologus, emperor of Byzantium (r. 1261–1282); became second wife of Constantine Tich, tsar of Bulgaria (r. 1257–1277), around 1271; married Ivajlo, tsar of Bulgaria (r. 1278–1279), around 1277.

Following the death of his first wife *Irene Lascaris, Tsar Constantine Tich of Bulgaria married Maria Paleologina, daughter of *Eulogia Paleologina and niece of Michael VIII Paleologus, emperor of Byzantium. Tensions between Bulgaria and Byzantium seemed to ease, until Michael refused to surrender the seaports of Anchialus and Mesembria, the promised dowry, and war broke out in 1272. When the Bulgarians invaded Byzantium, however, they were turned back by the Tartars, allies of Michael.

When Michael demanded that the Byzantine church unite with Rome, a storm swept the nation and beyond. Eulogia, Michael's favorite sister, opposed the union, and teamed up with her daughter Maria, now the tsarina of Bulgaria, turning the Bulgarian court, writes George Ostrogorsky, "into a nest of anti-imperial intrigue." When Constantine Tich was murdered in 1277, Maria married Ivajlo who was proclaimed tsar in 1278. In 1279, he was deposed, and the Byzantines placed Ivan Asen III on the throne of Bulgaria.

SOURCES:
Ostrogorsky, George. *History of the Byzantine State.* New Brunswick, NJ: Rutgers University Press, 1969.

Maria Pia (1847–1911)

Queen of Portugal and daughter of Victor Emmanuel II of Italy. Name variations: Marie-Pia; Maria Pia of Italy; Maria Pia de Savoie. Born in Turin on October 16, 1847; died on July 5, 1911, in Stupinigi, Italy, from heart disease; daughter of Victor Emmanuel II, king of Italy (r. 1849–1878), and Marie Adelaide of Austria (1822–1855); married Luis or Louis I (1838–1889), king of Portugal (r. 1861–1889), on September 27, 1862 (some sources cite October 6); children: Carlos or Charles I (1863–1908), king of Portugal (r. 1889–1908); Afonso also known as Alfonso Henrique (1865–1920), duke of Oporto.

Birth of Louis (1838); proclamation of the Kingdom of Italy by Victor Emmanuel II (1861); abolition of slavery in Portuguese colonies (1868); death of Louis (1889); assassination of Charles (1908); proclamation of Portuguese republic (1910).

Maria Pia

(1847–1911)

The daughter of Victor Emmanuel II of Sardinia and *Marie Adelaide of Austria, Maria Pia was born in Turin on October 16, 1847. Her mother died when Maria Pia was seven, and the girl's childhood was beset with the wars between Sardinia and the Austrian empire, as Victor Emmanuel fought to expel foreign powers and unify the Italian states. Maria Pia was 14 when emissaries of the Portuguese king approached Victor Emmanuel to negotiate a marriage between her and Louis I. Her father approved, and Maria Pia was married by proxy to Louis on September 27, 1862, in Turin. She departed immediately for Portugal, arriving there on October 5.

Louis I had acceded to the Portuguese throne the year before, and the royal couple ruled over a period of rising liberalism and political chaos. Portugal's declining economic fortunes weakened the government, as did political factionalism. Maria Pia rarely intervened in government affairs, preferring to devote her energies to charitable works. The queen did press for the abolition of slavery in the Portuguese colonies, which occurred in 1868.

Although Louis ruled as a constitutional monarch, Portuguese liberalism and republicanism agitated his reign. The political opposition accused Maria Pia of extravagant expenditures and considered her politically too conservative. On the other hand, she enjoyed popularity in pro-monarchy circles. She heroically rescued her two sons when they were caught by an undertow at Cascaes in 1873. When widespread flooding destroyed homes and fields in 1876, she successfully organized relief campaigns to raise funds. Even the political opposition approved, and the people called Maria Pia the "Angel of Charity."

Her husband died in 1889, succeeded by their son Charles I. Maria Pia remained in Portugal as the dowager queen, but her final years were filled with tragedy. Her brother Umberto I, king of Italy, was assassinated in 1900. Eight years later, political extremists in Portugal killed her son Charles and her grandson. When the republican revolution of 1910 exiled her from Portugal, she took refuge with her sister-in-law *Margaret of Savoy, the dowager queen of Italy. The tragedies, however, left her clinically depressed, a condition complicated by arteriosclerosis. She died on July 5, 1911, in Stupinigi from heart disease.

SOURCES:

A Morte da Rainha Maria Pia. Rio de Janeiro: Jornal do Commercio, 1911.

Mowlam, Kay. *A Rainha D. Maria Pia: Iconografia.* Portugal: Palacio Nacional da Ajuda, 1987.

Kendall W. Brown,
Professor of History, Brigham Young University, Provo, Utah

Maria Skuratova (d. 1605)

Tsarina of Russia. Name variations: Maria Maliuta; Mary of Malyuta; Maria Godunov, Godunova or Godunovna; Maria Gudunov; Maria Skurateva. Born Maria Maliuta-Skuratova; killed in 1605; daughter of Grigorii Maliuta-Skuratov or Skuratev (leader of Ivan IV's terror squad); married Boris Godunov (1552–1605), tsar of Russia (r. 1598–1605), in 1570; children: (daughter) *Xenia Godunova (1582–1622); Fyodor or Fedor Borisovich also known as Theodore II (1589–1605), tsar of Russia (r. 1605).

Maria Sobieska (1702–1735).

See Sobieski, Clementina.

Maria Sophia Amalia (1841–1925)

Duchess in Bavaria and last queen of the Two Sicilies. Name variations: Maria of Bavaria. Born on October 4, 1841; died on January 19, 1925; daughter of Maximilian Joseph, duke of Bavaria, and *Ludovica (1808–1892); sister of *Elizabeth of Bavaria (1837–1898), empress of Austria and Hungary; married Francesco II also known as Francis II (1836–1894), king of the Two Sicilies (r. 1859–1861), on February 3, 1859; children: Marie Christine (1869–1870).

Maria Sophia Amalia was briefly queen of the Two Sicilies from 1859 until 1861. Then Italy was united under Victor Emmanuel II of Sardinia.

Maria Sophia of Neuberg (1666–1699)

Queen of Portugal. Name variations: Marie-Sophia; Maria Sophia of Palatinate. Born on August 6, 1666, in Neuberg; died on August 4, 1699, in Lisbon, Portugal; daughter of Philip Wilhelm or Philip William, elector Palatine of the Rhine (r. 1667–1706), and *Elizabeth Amalia of Hesse (1635–1709); sister of *Maria Anna of Neuberg (1667–1740); became second wife of Pedro or Peter II, king of Portugal (r. 1667–1706), on August 11, 1687; children: John of Portugal (1668–1688); John V (1689–1750), king of Portugal (r. 1706–1750); Francisco (b. 1691); Antonio Francisco (b. 1695); Teresa (1696–1704); Manuel (b. 1697); Francisca Josefa of Portugal (1699–1736).

Maria Telles (d. 1379).

See Leonora Telles for sidebar.

Maria Teresa (1882–1912)

Spanish princess. Born in 1882; died in 1912; daughter of *Maria Christina of Austria (1858–1929) and Alfonso or Alphonso XII (1857–1885), king of Spain (r. 1875–1885); married Ferdinand of Bavaria (1884–1958), in 1906.

Maria Teresa of Austria (1773–1832)

Queen of Sardinia. Name variations: Maria-Theresa. Born on November 1, 1773; died on March 29, 1832; daughter of *Maria Beatrice of Modena (1750–1829) and Archduke Ferdinand of Austria (1754–1806, son of *Maria Theresa of Austria [1717–1780]); married Victor Emmanuel I (1759–1824), king of Sardinia (r. 1802–1821, abdicated), on April 25, 1789; children: *Maria Beatrice of Sardinia (1792–1840, who married Francis IV, duke of Modena); *Theresa of Savoy (1803–1879, who married Charles, duke of Parma); *Maria Anna of Savoy (1803–1884, who married Ferdinand I, emperor of Austria); *Christina of Sardinia (1812–1836, who married Ferdinand II of Naples).

Maria Teresa of Este (1849–1919)

Queen of Bavaria. Name variations: Maria Theresa; Maria Theresa of Modena. Born on July 2, 1849, in Brunn; died on February 3, 1919, in Schloss, Wildenwart; interred at Dom Church, Munich, Germany; daughter of Ferdinand (1821–1849), archduke of Austria-Este (r. 1835–1848), and Archduchess *Elizabeth (1831–1903); married Louis III also known as Ludwig III (1845–1921), king of Bavaria (r. 1913–1918), on February 20, 1868; children: eleven, including Rupert (1869–1955), and *Maria of Bavaria (b. 1872).

Maria Teresa of Naples (1772–1807)

Holy Roman empress. Name variations: Marie-Thérèse of Bourbon-Naples; Maria Teresa of the Two Sicilies; Maria Theresa of Naples; empress of Austria. Born on June 6, 1772, in Naples; died in childbirth on April 13, 1807, in Vienna; daughter of *Maria Carolina (1752–1814) and Ferdinand I, king of the Two Sicilies (r. 1816–1825), king of Naples and Sicily as Ferdinand IV (r. 1759–1806, 1815–1825); became second wife of Francis I (1768–1835) emperor of Austria (r. 1804–1835), also known as Francis II, Holy Roman emperor (r. 1792–1806), on September 19, 1790; children: *Marie Louise of Austria (1791–1847, who be-

came second wife of Napoleon I Bonaparte); Ferdinand I the Good (1793–1875), emperor of Austria (r. 1835–1848); Caroline (1794–1795); Caroline (1795–1799); *Leopoldina of Austria (1797–1826, who married Pedro I of Brazil); *Clementine of Austria (1798–1881); Joseph (b. 1799); *Caroline of Austria (1801–1832, who married Frederick Augustus II of Saxony); Francis Charles (1802–1878, who married *Sophie of Bavaria); Mari Anna (1804–1858); Johann (b. 1805); Amalie (1807–1807). Holy Roman emperor Francis II had four wives: *Elizabeth of Wurttemberg (1767–1790), Maria Teresa of Naples, *Maria Ludovica of Modena (1787–1816), and *Caroline Augusta of Bavaria (1792–1873).

Maria Teresa of Savoy (1756–1805)

Queen of France. Name variations: Marie Thérèse; Maria Theresa of Sardinia; Clotilde of Savoy. Born in 1756; died in 1805; daughter of *Maria Antonia of Spain (1729–1785) and Victor Amadeus III (1726–1796), duke of Savoy (r. 1773–1796); married Charles X (1757–1830), king of France (r. 1824–1830, abdicated); children: Louis XIX (1775–1844), duke of Angoulême; Charles Ferdinand (1778–1820), duke of Berry.

Maria Teresa of Spain (1638–1683)

Queen of France. Name variations: Marie Theresa or Thérèse; Marie Therese of Austria; Marie-Thérèse of Spain; Maria Theresa; Maria Teresa; Marie-Theresa; Infanta of Spain. Born at the Escorial, Spain, on September 20, 1638; died of blood poisoning on July 30, 1683, at Versailles, France; interred at St. Denis; daughter of Philip IV (1605–1665), king of Spain (r. 1621–1665), and his first wife *Elizabeth Valois (1602–1644, sister of Louis XIII); married and became queen-consort of Louis XIV (1638–1715), king of France (r. 1643–1715), on June 9, 1660; children: six, only one of whom survived her, Louis (1661–1711), le grand dauphin.

The year before the royal marriage between Louis XIV, king of France, and Maria Teresa of Spain in 1659, the 21-year-old Maria signed the Treaty of the Pyrenees, renouncing any claim to Spanish succession. The queen fell in love with her husband on their wedding night and remained so, but she was neglected by Louis for his many mistresses, including *Louise de la Vallière, the ☙ Duchesse de Fontanges, and *Olympia Mancini, Comtesse de Soissons. On Maria Teresa's death, the king was known to have said to his mistress, the *Marquise de Maintenon, "This is the only time she has ever given me any trouble." He then married Mlle Maintenon.

Maria Teresa of Spain (1651–1673).

See Margaret Theresa of Spain.

Maria Teresa of the Two Sicilies (1772–1807).

See Maria Teresa of Naples.

Maria Teresa of Tuscany (1801–1855).

See Maria Theresa of Tuscany.

Maria the Jewess.

See Mary the Jewess.

Maria Theresa of Austria

(1717–1780)

Habsburg monarch who ascended a throne threatened on all sides, repulsed most of her adversaries, and instituted a series of social and administrative reforms largely credited with ensuring the survival of the Habsburg empire through the 19th century. Name variations: Maria Theresia (German spelling). Pronunciation: tay-RAY-zee-ah. Born on May 13, 1717, in Vienna, Austria; died on November 29, 1780, in Vienna; daughter of Charles VI, Holy Roman emperor (r. 1711–1740), and Elizabeth Christina of Brunswick-Wolfenbuttel (1691–1750); educated at home by Jesuit tutors; married Francis Stephen, duke of Lorraine, later Holy Roman emperor (r. 1745–1765) as Francis I; children: 16, of whom six died before the age of 17, including Johanna (d. 1762) and Josepha (d. 1767); those surviving to adulthood include: Joseph II (1741–1790) emperor of Austria (r. 1765–1790), who succeeded his mother and became Holy Roman emperor; Leopold II (1747–1792), grand duke of Tuscany, Holy Roman emperor (r. 1790–1792); Maximilian Francis (who became elector of Cologne); Maria Carolina (1752–1814, who married into the Bourbon family and became queen of Naples and the Two Sicilies); Maria Amalia (1746–1804, who married the duke of Parma); Marie Antoinette (1755–1793, who married Louis XVI and became queen of France); Elizabeth of Austria (1743–1808, who became abbess in Innsbruck); Ferdinand (1754–1806, who was governor general of Lombardy in Milano and married *Maria Beatrice of Modena); Maria Christina (1742–1798, who married Duke Albert of Saxony-Teschen and became duchess and governor-general of Austrian Netherlands); Maria Anna (who became abbess of Klagenfurt).

Succeeded to her father's hereditary domains (1740), which she was forced to defend against an overwhelming armed coalition in the Austrian Succession War (1740–48); led the anti-Prussian coalition during the Seven Years' War (1756–63); participated with Prussia and Russia in the First Polish Partition (1772); intervened to end the Bavarian Succession War (1778–79), promoted by her son, Holy Roman Emperor Joseph II; with aid of two highly capable ministers, Counts Haugwitz and Kaunitz, instituted far-reaching reforms in virtually every domain of public life, the most durable of which were the foundation of a progressive educational system and the modernization of the realm's administrative structure; therefore, considered an "enlightened despot" by some, but not all, scholars.

Tradition has it that a disarmingly pretty Austrian archduchess, barely 24 years of age and utterly unprepared to assume the reins of state in her ethnically diverse and geographically far-flung domains, appeared before the Hungarian Diet at Pressburg on September 11, 1741, to plead for military aid against a mighty European coalition, including France, Bavaria, Saxony and Spain, and led by "the monster"—as she called him—her arch-enemy, Frederick II the Great, king of Prussia. Her treasury was empty, her troops scattered and demoralized, and her richest province, Silesia, was in enemy hands. Choked with emotion, and cradling her whimpering infant son, Joseph (II), in her arms, she delivered a passionate address to the assembly, moving the hearts of the chivalrous Hungarian magnates, otherwise known for their intractable relations with Vienna. Rising to their feet in an outburst of sympathy, the Magyars pledged their "life and blood" to defend the young queen and mother. The striking scene has been memorialized in art and literature, and Austrian schoolchildren can recount the episode by heart. But, as with much high drama in history, the facts were embellished by later generations—her plea for help and the appearance with her baby were actually separate incidents—while an essential core of truth kept the myth alive.

On October 20, 1740, the Habsburg dynast and Holy Roman emperor Charles VI died, leaving to his daughter a grand array of crown domains and connected territories. These included the hereditary Habsburg lands (*Erblande*) of Upper and Lower Austria, Inner Austria (Styria, Carinthia, Carniola), Tyrol, Vorarlberg and Freiburg-im-Breisgau; also the Kingdom of Bohemia, Margravate of Moravia, Duchies of Upper and Lower Silesia, Kingdom of Hungary

◄❧
Duchesse de Fontanges. See *Montespan, Françoise* for sidebar.

Opposite page

𝓜aria 𝒥eresa of 𝒮pain

(1638–1683)

(with Croatia and Slavonia), Principality of Transylvania, Duchy of Milano (Lombardy), and the Austrian Netherlands (modern Belgium). Yet the structural nature of this impressive legacy implied significant difficulties for its administration. For one, the Habsburg lands included important geographically non-contiguous regions (Belgium, Lombardy), both hard to defend and coveted by rival powers. In addition, its ethnic and religious diversity made for a heterogeneous and hard-to-manage mass of subjects. Finally, traditions of limited self-rule, jealously guarded by regional and local estates, rendered it politically difficult to manage.

Charles VI also left behind a government in disarray. The Habsburg domains were being managed by a gerontocratic ministry; indeed, the average age of permanent members of the Privy Conference was 71. The state was in a severe fiscal crisis, total debt amounting to 103 million florins, with only 87,000 florins available on hand. Lastly, the realm was virtually defenseless, for only half the army was in any state resembling combat preparedness.

If the domestic outlook was bleak, Charles' foreign policy legacy hardly looked any better. Not having achieved his aims of succeeding to the Spanish throne—and thus re-uniting the empire of Charles V, during the Spanish Succession War (1701–14)—he had been defeated twice more in the course of six years, during the Polish Succession War (1733–38) and the Fourth Austro-Russian-Turkish War (1737–39). Both conflicts had entailed the painful loss of territory, in Italy (Naples and Sicily) and on his southeast flank (northern Serbia and parts of Walachia). Habsburg prestige—at its peak after the Turks had been stopped at the gates of Vienna in 1683 and humiliated in the Treaties of Carlowitz (1699) and Passarowitz (1718)—had plummeted to new depths.

Not surprisingly, looking back on the early days of her reign from the vantage point of 1756–57, Maria Theresa was to write: "No one, I believe, will disagree that it would be hard to find an example, in history, of a crowned head of state succeeding to the throne under more difficult circumstances than I." Not only were the circumstances of succession extremely difficult, but the young successor was singularly unprepared for the duties of a monarch.

Maria Theresa was born on May 13, 1717, in the Vienna Hofburg. Her older brother Leopold, the designated successor, had recently died, and the arrival of a girl was a disappointment to court and town alike. Unlike many other Habsburgers, she was through-and-through German, since her parents and grandparents were all ethnic Germans and Germanophones. Significantly, religion played an important role in both parents' lives, as it was to do in Maria Theresa's. Her mother ◄◈ **Elizabeth Christina of Brunswick-Wolfenbuttel** was born and raised in Brunswick in the Calvinist faith and had reluctantly agreed to convert to Catholicism upon marriage; some sources contend she remained a crypto-Protestant long after conversion. Charles VI was of a fairly simple and devout faith, stressing outward signs of belief, such as frequent local pilgrimages to shrines of the Virgin. He appears to have been an attentive father who saw his children, of whom he had four, almost daily. Unfortunately for Maria Theresa, however, she was not given the education befitting an heir to empire.

While material on her childhood is sparse, it is clear that Maria Theresa's training was characteristic of any princess at a typical 18th-century Catholic court. Jesuit tutors and a governess, Countess **Charlotte Fuchs**, oversaw her daily exercises. Language instruction figured prominently, and Maria Theresa became fluent in French. Her Latin was also excellent, her Italian fair, she had little Spanish, and her written German remained erratic throughout life. The scholar and court historiographer, Gottfried Wilhelm Spannagl, taught her mainly church and world history with a significantly anti-papal tendency. Mathematics lessons were administered by the famous astronomer and geometer Johann Jakob von Marinoni. Finishing touches were provided by the drawing, riding, and music masters. Indeed,

---

❧➤ **Elizabeth Christina of Brunswick-Wolfenbuttel**
(1691–1750)

*Holy Roman empress. Name variations: Elizabeth Christina of Brunswick-Wolfenbüttel; Elizabeth Christina of Brunswick; Elizabeth of Brunswick; Elizabeth Christine. Born Elizabeth Christine of Brunswick-Lünebrug-Wolfenbüttel, princess of the German house of Brunswick-Wolfenbüttel, on August 28, 1691, in Wolfenbüttel; died on December 21, 1750, in Vienna; daughter of Ludwig Rudolf also known as Louis Rudolph, duke of Brunswick-Wolfenbüttel; her younger sister *Charlotte of Brunswick-Wolfenbüttel (1694–1715) married Alexis, son of Peter the Great of Russia; married Charles VI (1685–1740), Holy Roman emperor (r. 1711–1740); children: Leopold (died in infancy in 1716); *Maria Theresa of Austria (1717–1780); *Maria Anna (1718–1744) and Maria Amalia (1724–1730).*

Maria Theresa of Austria

much stress was placed on music, and Maria Theresa became a good clavacin player and sang well, appearing in a court musical drama at age eight. Most sources point out the irony that Charles VI invested so much effort into securing his daughter's title politically, while leaving her completely untutored in the art of statecraft. Austrian historian Adam Wandruszka has speculated that Charles was perhaps hoping that his son-in-law, Francis Stephen (Francis I), would in fact take over the reins of state, leaving his daughter with the title alone.

Maria Theresa had three siblings. Leopold, Charles' only son, died in infancy (1716). Maria Theresa was born next, followed by two more daughters, *Maria Anna (1718–1744) and Maria Amalia (1724–1730).

While Charles VI long hoped to father a male heir, and made opulent offerings to churches and frequent pilgrimages to shrines of the Virgin in an effort to obtain divine help, his last years were plagued with the succession issue. This he attempted to solve with a unique document, issued early in his reign and indicating an almost uncanny foresight. The Pragmatic Sanction of April 19, 1713, proclaimed a complex female succession—in the absence of a male heir—beginning with the direct progeny of Charles VI; and it declared all Habsburg lands "indivisible and inseparable." Thus, it was both a legal attempt at securing the throne for his eldest daughter, and a constitutional charter proclaiming the territorial unity of the realm.

The problem with this highly innovative settlement was how to gain its acceptance with the Habsburg estates and the family of European monarchs. The former raised no significant obstacles, but the latter virtually had to be bribed for support. In the end, Russia, Prussia (Charles promised aid in the acquisition of the Duchy of Berg), and the Empire signed on by 1732; and France (he pledged help in its quest for the Duchy of Lorraine) joined in 1735. To sweeten the deal for the colonial powers—Spain, England, and Holland also gave their support by 1732—Charles had to dissolve the Ostende Trading Co., a promising enterprise founded in 1714. Bavaria held out until 1745. Yet the Pragmatic Sanction proved a worthless piece of paper, for an array of signatories descended upon Maria Theresa shortly after her succession, eager to exploit her weakness.

> *She is very ambitious and possesses talents in more than one area; herein I must do her justice.*
>
> —Frederick the Great

The assault was led by Frederick II, who had recently inherited a bursting treasury and modernized army from his father, Frederick William I. On December 16, 1740, Frederick kept his "rendez-vous with glory," as he put it, and invaded the rich province of Silesia, attaining his objective in a four-week campaign. The fat province was a rich prize: counting over a million souls, it included fine farmland, rich forests, mineral deposits, and a thriving weaving industry; it was easily the most productive of Habsburg lands. Able to justify his act outwardly through dubious legal claims, his real motives were clearly territorial expansion and a thirst for personal glory. Though he had offered Maria Theresa financial and military aid in exchange for the province, she had refused, since acceptance was tantamount to abrogation of the indivisibility provision of the Pragmatic Sanction. By July 1741, Saxony, Bavaria, France and Spain had formed a coalition with Prussia, intent on despoiling Austria territorially. According to their cynical pact, largely outlined in the Treaty of Nymphenburg, the allies were to support Bavaria's claim to the Austrian *Erblande* and Elector Charles Albert's bid for the imperial crown; France was to obtain Belgium, Spain to obtain Lombardy, and Saxony to obtain Moravia. Maria Theresa's main ally, Britain, provided meager subsidies, and virtually no troops, for these were needed overseas—and to protect the dynastic home of Hanover against possible French aggression.

At first, developments were nothing less than grim. The bulk of her troops was stationed on the geographical periphery of her lands, where they were of little use, and both her husband, Francis Stephen (Francis I), and his brother, Charles of Lorraine, proved incompetent military leaders. Scores of Bohemian and Upper Austrian nobles deserted the young archduchess and, by December 1741, Elector Charles Albert of Bavaria, leading the Franco-Bavarian-Saxon forces, had taken both Linz and Prague and crowned himself king of Bohemia; in 1742, he was elected Holy Roman Emperor Charles VII—the first non-Habsburg emperor since 1437. Yet after these initial setbacks, Maria Theresa was able to recoup all her territorial losses, except Silesia. While Frederick II had given her a breather by withdrawing from the conflict for a time, and the Hungarian estates finally came through with a contingent of 22,000 intrepid infantry and 14,000 hard-fighting horse, her personal courage and fortitude in adversity can hardly be overestimated in assessing the causes of her survival. Following various interim arrangements, an overall settlement was reached in the Treaty of Aix-la-Chapelle (October 18, 1748), in which Maria Theresa accepted the Prussian acquisition of Silesia, gave up Parma, Piacenza and Guastalla to the Spanish Infant Philip, but all the Powers finally recognized the Pragmatic Sanction. In fact, the treaty was considered little more than a ceasefire by contemporaries, and both Prussia and Habsburg began preparing for the next duel: Frederick, by consolidating his hold on Silesia; and Maria Theresa, by putting her army and administration in order.

The First Theresian Reforms issued directly from the realization that, in times of war, she had to overcome her dependence on unreliable foreign and wavering domestic support. Given the ethnic and political diversity of her land, Maria Theresa sought the cooperation of her subjects, rather than disciplining them by force—contrary to most other contemporary monarchs. Thus, both impetus and mode of implementation characterize the reforms as pragmatically oriented. The ultimate goal—were it to stand a chance against Frederician Prussia—was to regain Silesia, and to attain that goal the Habsburg state needed a thorough restructuring.

The centerpiece of the post-1748 reforms was the anti-feudal administrative transformations directed by Count Frederick William

Haugwitz, who is largely credited for bringing Habsburg government into modernity. Influenced by the Prussian model to such an extent that detractors accused him of the "Prussification" of Austria, Haugwitz centralized the political and financial administration of the German and Bohemian lands—the domains of prime economic and strategic importance—in Vienna, drastically reducing the powers of the regional estates in the process. Not surprisingly, German historian Heinz Duchhardt has aptly labeled the transformation "much more than just an administrative reform, but rather a fundamental constitutional and state reform." Haugwitz wanted an army of 200,000 men and annual revenues of 15 million florins (compared with 6 million in 1748). To that end, regional diets no longer administered the collection of revenue and military affairs; this was now done by the *gubernium,* a province-level agency directly answerable to the Directorium in Publicis et Cameralibus, or State Chancery, the new streamlined central governing council. On the local level *Kreise,* or districts, were headed by trained civil servants (*Kreishauptmann*). Far-off Belgium, Lombardy and the traditionally independent-minded Hungarian nobility were largely left with their special status, another indication of Maria Theresa's pragmatism and diplomacy.

In fiscal affairs, centralized and expanded collection of revenue met with much regional opposition—not all of which was successfully overcome—but nonetheless resulted in a dramatically increased income. Diets were made to vote taxes for ten years as against the previous one, guaranteeing the crown both greater disposable income and continuity of planning; and nobles and clergy were taxed for the first time. Commercial policy was classically mercantilist. The importation of luxury items as gilded coaches and brocade was banned, and luxury manufacturing in Vienna (e.g. porcelain) stimulated, as were mining and textile fabrication in Bohemia, Styria, and Carinthia. Domestic duties in the dynastic territories were lowered, while stiff tariff walls were erected on the outside. Finally, a monetary reform created a new silver coin— the famous Maria Theresa taler, soon to become the primary currency used in the Balkans and throughout the Near East. In the domain of law, Haugwitz established the Oberste Justizstelle, a judiciary agency independent of the rest of the administration, thus laying the cornerstone for a modern legal system.

To implement Haugwitz's comprehensive changes, an educational reform was essential, for an army of loyal and trained bureaucrats was necessary to staff the renovated ship of state. To meet this need, the Theresianum, a civil servant academy, was founded in 1746 and followed by the Oriental Academy, a diplomatic school for service in the Balkans, in 1754.

Military reforms included the creation of the General War Commissary as an independent ministry, the new *contributionale* tax, to be paid in cash and not in kind, the strategic redistribution of forces throughout the provinces, and the foundation of two academies in Vienna—the aristocratic Military Academy (1752) and the Engineering Academy (1754). With increased funding and improved training, Haugwitz was able to field a modernized army of 180,000 men by 1756. These, Maria Theresa was soon to need, in yet another struggle with Frederick II.

Meanwhile, the major players of the Austrian Succession War had had time to reflect on the relationship with their partners during that conflict. Maria Theresa was disappointed with Britain's paltry aid and constant pressure to make peace with Prussia in order to concentrate on France—Britain's primary rival. Given the success of her domestic reforms, it appeared Maria Theresa need no longer depend on the Court of St. James in times of distress. Count Wenzel Anton von Kaunitz, who directed foreign policy from 1753 on, strongly favored giving up the alliance with Britain and seeking an understanding with France, in the belief that the real strategic threat came not from that state in the traditional theaters of the Low Countries and northern Italy, but from Prussia and in Silesia. For its part, France realized that the days of Habsburg encirclement under Charles V were long gone, while the real menace came from Britain overseas. Britain, however, had signed the Westminster Convention with Prussia (1756), in which Prussia pledged to help defend Hanover against France. France considered this proof of its former ally's perfidy. Therefore France, after some wooing, embraced its inveterate foe, Austria, and contemporary observers marvelled at the new Bourbon-Habsburg rapprochement, writing of the grand *renversement des alliances,* or Diplomatic Revolution. Maria Theresa, characteristically overcoming her moral qualms in pragmatic state affairs, even sent Louis XV's mistress, *Madame de Pompadour,** costly presents out of gratitude for her behind-the-scenes role in forging the new Vienna-Versailles axis.

Frederick II kept a wary eye cocked on these developments, knowing that Maria Theresa's goal was the forging of a coalition to aid her in regaining Silesia. In fact, her ambitions were greater: both Frederick's general threat to the peace of the Empire, and the concomitant advance of Protestantism were to be checked. To this end, she agreed with France that Prussia was to be dismantled. Habsburg would regain Silesia, Sweden would acquire Stettin, and Saxony would get Magdeburg. A joint attack on Prussia, with Russian aid, was scheduled, but Frederick II got wind of the plan and launched a preemptive strike, attacking Saxony on August 29, 1756. With Prussia out in the open as the aggressor, an overwhelming alliance including Russia,

France, Austria, Saxony, Sweden and a number of German principalities, converged their forces on Prussia, whose sole ally was Britain, with its usual subsidies.

The first phase of the Seven Years' War was marked by Prussian successes. With his superior generalship, initiative, the strategic benefits of an inner line, and the initial disarray and problems of motivation of the anti-Prussian coalition—France's prime interests still lay in the colonial conflict with Britain—Frederick racked up a series of spectacular victories against overwhelming odds at Rossbach (November 5, 1757, against France and the Empire) and Leuthen (December 5, 1757, against Maria Theresa), earning his epithet "the Great." Soon Saxony was in his hands. But at Kunersdorf (August 13, 1759), Frederick's luck ran out, and his army was devastated by Habsburg and Russian forces. Yet the allies, still lacking strategic coordination, failed to deliver the *coup de grâce,* an error which Frederick termed the "miracle of the House of Brandenburg." Though the battle did usher in a succession of Prussian defeats, the conflict had become a war of attrition, resulting in the general exhaustion of all parties. On January 5, 1762, Empress *Elizabeth Petrovna of Russia died and was succeeded by the Prussophile Peter III, who changed sides and joined Frederick, but was soon murdered and succeeded by his wife, *Catherine II the Great. The new empress, for her part, chose to remain neutral, prompting Sweden to desert the anti-Prussian coalition, as well. France, meanwhile, had been expelled from Canada by the British and made a preliminary separate peace with that power, to be followed by the definitive Treaty of Paris (February 2, 1763). The grand coalition, forged by Maria Theresa to humble "the monster," had crumbled. Alone and exhausted, she made peace with Frederick in the Treaty of Hubertusburg (February 2, 1763), bitterly recognizing his acquisition of Silesia. She had lost the war, failing to attain any of her objectives.

The end of the Seven Years' War was a watershed in Maria Theresa's reign in more ways than one. As in 1748, the defeat of 1763 provoked a round of introspection and reform. This time, however, Kaunitz provided the ministerial leadership. Francis Stephen, Maria Theresa's husband and co-regent since 1740, had died in 1765 and was succeeded as co-regent—and Holy Roman emperor—by her eldest son, Joseph II (born 1741), who was to inject many reforms with a dose of Enlightenment thought. Joseph read such moderate Enlightenment authors as the political scientist Pufendorf or the historian Muratori, but also admired more radical thinkers his mother abhorred, even holding her arch-foe, Frederick II, in secret esteem. His own character differed markedly from that of his mother; while very intelligent and perceptive, he was also impatient, daring, and uncompromising to a fault. Given his more radical ideas about social reform, particularly in the area of religious policy, and his more aggressively expansionist foreign policy—both of which he shared with Kaunitz—he was bound to clash with his mother, the pragmatic and essentially peaceable "mother of her people," as she was often called. While Maria Theresa retained final authority, Joseph II was a highly active co-regent who attempted to assert his policies at every turn. Thus, their relationship was often strained.

The first concern in 1763 was fiscal reform, for state debt had doubled to 280 million florins since 1740. Cameralist ideas of thinkers like Justi and Sonnenfels convinced Maria Theresa that some social reform was necessary to boost revenue. (The economic theory of cameralism advocated a strong public administration of a centralized industrial economy.) This meant broadening the tax base and paying special attention to agriculture and the peasantry. Productivity was to be enhanced, and feudal burdens reduced. She therefore issued a number of decrees to limit or reduce the *robot* (forced labor the peasant owed his lord, in practice over 100 days per year in many regions of the realm), fix the customary feudal dues, prohibit noble land encroachment on peasant land, and provide for better enforcement of government regulations in these matters. Joseph's frequent fact-finding missions into the countryside, where he often traveled under the alias of "Count Falkenstein," contributed firsthand information, and anecdotes of his plowing a peasant's field were widely circulated. Outside the hereditary domains of Austria, the impact of these reforms was real but limited by aristocratic intransigence and the deep-rooted traditions of regional independence, particularly in Hungary. In her own lands, where she exercised greater control, Maria Theresa instituted the highly progressive Raab system (after Councillor Franz Anton von Raab): the *robot* was commuted to cash payments, and the *demesne*—or crown lands—were parcelled out to peasant small-holders. These small-holders became personally free, were given long or hereditary leases, and paid cash rents. The system was highly successful, soon generating 50% more output than before its initiation. Sadly, Maria Theresa's hopes that the nobility throughout her realm would emulate this enlightened approach to agrarian policy came to nought.

To increase revenue, Joseph proposed to abolish all tax exemptions, as well as the independent administrative status of Hungary, Lombardy, and Belgium. Such radical and unimplementable measures Maria Theresa characteristically refused to take. She did, however, assent to Kaunitz's further centralization and streamlining of administration and finance in the *Erblande*, which resulted in the revamping of agencies built up by Haugwitz during the first reform period. In addition, Kaunitz succeeded in imposing a general land tax on the nobility, though not in Hungary. Nonetheless, the totality of social, fiscal, and administrative reforms succeeded in increasing annual revenue from 35 million florins in 1763 to 50 million in 1780, and in 1775 Kaunitz balanced the budget for the first time in Habsburg history.

Educational reform after 1763—perhaps her most enduring attainment—was ambitious, despite Maria Theresa's initial disinterest. According to Charles Ingrao, her real motivation was religious, for in 1769 the bishop of Passau had informed her of the ignorance of his parishioners and that many were in fact crypto-Protestants. The reform was directed by the highly enlightened Studienhofkommission (Education Commission). Ironically, its key element was the secularization of schools. This measure, however, was not implemented until after 1773 with the abolition of the Jesuit Order, and despite Maria Theresa's religious qualms. Here, Kaunitz's and Joseph's influence are in evidence. Inspired largely by the Pietist model of Silesian Prussia, with its stress on education as a potent tool for social control, two General School Ordinances for the *Erblande* (1774) and Hungary (1777) standardized teacher training at mandatory Normal schools, as they did the curriculum. Structurally, the new school system distinguished the Trivialschule (compulsory elementary school), Hauptschule (middle school in the district capital, providing vocational training or preparation for high school), and the Gymnasium (elite high school with a university preparatory curriculum). Again, traditionalist attitudes hampered implementation: peasants grumbled that their children were kept away from the fields, while priests considered the whole scheme too secular. Still, it proved highly successful in increasing the sheer number of schools and students, for by 1780 Austria had surpassed the Prussian model in quantity and quality.

Joseph's imprint was also evident in this period's judicial reform. In 1766, Maria Theresa had created a commission designed to consolidate, but not humanize, existing codes, e.g. she was adamantly against the abolition of torture and the death penalty, despite the influence of Italian jurist Beccaria's book, *On Crimes and Punishments* (1764). Her code, the *Nemesis Theresiana* (1768), still allowed impalement, breaking on the wheel, and burning alive. Not until 1776 could Joseph, Kaunitz, and other enlightened advisers force her to abolish torture.

In religious matters, Maria Theresa's stance was a mix of progressivism, traditionalism, and pragmatism, reflecting her modern ideas on the separation of church and state, her deeply felt Catholic personal piety, and contemporary diplomatic realities. In 1765, she instructed her son Leopold (II), shortly before his departure to assume the reins of government in Tuscany: "Be a good son, devoted to the Holy Father in all matters of religion and dogma. But remain sovereign, and do not tolerate the least interference of the Roman curia in matters of state." Not surprisingly, she continued the general Habsburg policy, followed since the 1650s, to strengthen the control of state over church. This included the taxation of the clergy without papal consent, confiscation of Jesuit assets, suppression of monasteries, subjection of Church courts and property to state control, and the abolition of numerous religious holidays. True to her dogmatic nature, however, she was intolerant towards non-Catholics, unlike several other contemporary enlightened monarchs. Believing that the existence of multiple creeds within a realm caused disunity, she tended to infringe on the rights of Lutherans and Calvinists, and particularly of Jews. In one instance, she attempted to forcibly reconvert Moravian Protestants in 1777. Fortunately, Joseph II and Kaunitz were able to prevent the most egregiously intolerant policies. External pressures—this time from the Bourbon courts, with whom she had aligned herself against Frederick II, eventually marrying five of her children into that dynasty—helped push her towards the abolition of the Jesuit Order.

In foreign affairs after 1765, the overall situation was favorable for Habsburg security, though a wary eye towards the ascendant powers Prussia and Russia was always called for. With the Ottomans in decline, Prussia preoccupied with consolidating Silesia, and the French alliance precluding a threat to Belgium or Lombardy, Joseph II and Kaunitz could give policy a more aggressive thrust, albeit only with Maria Theresa's reluctant assent. While dependable allies were still a scarcity, she could now field over 300,000 troops, although their costliness suggested use only *in extremis*. Two events stand out during the last decade of her rule: the First Polish Partition and the Bavarian Succession War.

Although Maria Theresa did not share the cynical statecraft mentality of the day, she participated with Prussia's Frederick the Great and Russia's Catherine the Great in the first partition of Poland in 1772. Indeed, she had little choice. The alternatives, Poland as a Russian satellite or Poland partitioned between Russia and Prussia, would have considerably weakened the position of the Habsburgs. Much has been made of the cynicism of this agreement, and Peter Berglar eloquently denounced it as particularly disgusting because it was "powdered and perfumed, in the rococo fashion." Indeed, the Polish Diet itself was pressured into ratifying the partition on September 30, 1773. Maria Theresa has repeatedly been charged with hypocrisy, her first and most famous accuser being Frederick II himself—everywhere quoted as having said: "She cries, but she always takes." Family correspondence indicates a real moral dilemma on her part, and her acquiescence clearly represented the choice of reason of state over Christian ethics. The richest slice of the Polish cake, Galicia, with its three million inhabitants and its famous salt mines, was her prize.

The Bavarian Succession War (1778–79) can best be characterized as a bungled attempt by Kaunitz and Joseph to profit from Bavarian Elector Maximilian III's death without male issue (December 30, 1777), with subsequent damage control by Maria Theresa. Complex plans included demands for Bavarian territory, and at one point even a trade-off for all of Bavaria, in exchange for Belgium. Austrian troops entered Bavaria on January 16, 1779, but Joseph and Kaunitz not only failed to respect Prussia's justified demands for compensation, but also refused to give up all of Belgium to the Bavarian heir presumptive, Elector Palatine Charles Theodore. These blunders prompted Frederick II to intervene and invade Bohemia, invoking the protection of "German liberty." Blocked by Austrian troops, the war soon degenerated into a winter stand-off, highlighted by soldiers scrounging for potatoes in the frozen ground, earning it the German nickname, *der Kartoffelkrieg*. Maria Theresa, diplomatically isolated, weary of war, and loath to see her subjects suffering to no avail, secretly met with Frederick II and signed the Treaty of Teschen, ending the conflict on May 13, 1779. Her cool appraisal of the risks to her house, and willingness to sacrifice Habsburg prestige, had prevented a general assault on her domains.

The following winter, her conservatism and good sense would no longer be there to temper her son's more radical policies. She signed her last will on October 15, 1780, and died on November 29, in Vienna. Having suffered long from emphysema, Maria Theresa probably also had cardial bronchitis and hypertension, for she had grown quite obese during the last two decades of life. She bore her final illness with equanimity and dignity, working hard until the very end.

With her husband and close adviser, Francis Stephen, whom she dearly loved, Maria Theresa had 16 children, of which 6 died before the age of 17—mostly of smallpox. Of the children surviving to adulthood, Joseph II succeeded his mother and became Holy Roman emperor; Leopold II became grand duke of Tuscany, then succeeded his brother Joseph; Maximilian Francis became elector of Cologne; *Maria Carolina married into the Bourbon family of Naples; *Maria Amalia (1746–1804) married into the Bourbon house of Parma; *Marie Antoinette married Louis XVI of France; *Elizabeth of Austria became abbess in Innsbruck; Ferdinand was governor-general of Lombardy in Milano; *Maria Christina, Maria Theresa's favorite daughter, married Duke Albert of Saxony-Teschen; and Maria Anna became abbess of Klagenfurt. After the death of her husband, Maria Theresa always wore mourning.

SOURCES:

Anderson, M.S. *Europe in the Eighteenth Century*. 3rd ed. London: Longman, 1987.

Berglar, Peter. *Maria Theresia*. Hamburg: Rowohlt Taschenbuch Verlag, 1980.

Dickmann, Franz, Hrsg. *Geschichte in Quellen. Renaissance, Glaubenskämpfe, Absolutismus*. 2nd ed. München: Bayerischer Schulbuch-Verlag, 1976.

Duchhardt, Heinz. *Das Zeitalter des Absolutismus*. 2nd ed. München: R. Oldenbourg Verlag, 1992.

Ingrao, Charles. *The Habsburg Monarchy, 1618–1815*. Cambridge: Cambridge University Press, 1994.

Krieger, Leonard. *Kings and Philosophers, 1689–1789*. NY: W.W. Norton, 1970.

Mandrou, Robert. *Staatsräson und Vernunft*. Frankfurt/M: Verlag Ullstein GmbH, 1975.

Pick, Robert. *Empress Maria Theresa: The Earlier Years, 1717–1757*. NY: Harper and Row, 1966.

Taddey, Gerhard, Hrsg. *Lexikon der deutschen Geschichte*. 2nd ed. Stuttgart: Alfred Kröner Verlag, 1983.

Wandruszka, Adam. "Die Historiographie der theresianisch-josephinischen Reformzeit," in *Ungarn und Österreich unter Maria Theresia und Joseph II. Neue Aspekte im Verhältnis der beiden Länder. Texte des 2. österreichisch-ungarischen Historikertreffens Wien 1980*. Hrsg. Anna M. Drabek, Richard G. Plaschka and Adam Wandruszka. Wien: Verlag der österreichischen Akademie der Wissenschaften, 1982.

———. *Maria Theresia. Die grosse Kaiserin*. Göttingen: Muster-Schmidt Verlag, 1980.

Williams, E.N. *Penguin Dictionary of English and European History, 1485–1789.* Harmondsworth: Penguin, 1980.

Woloch, Isser. *Eighteenth-Century Europe. Tradition and Progress, 1715–1789.* NY: W.W. Norton, 1982.

SUGGESTED READING:

Arneth, Alfred von. *Geschichte Maria Theresias.* 10 vols. Wien: Braumüller, 1863–1879.

Beales, Derek. *Joseph II: In the Shadow of Maria Theresa, 1741–1780.* Cambridge: Cambridge University Press, 1987.

Crankshaw, Edward. *Maria Theresa.* NY: Atheneum, 1986.

Dickson, P.G.M. *Finance and Government under Maria Theresa, 1740–1780.* 2 vols. Oxford: Clarendon Press, 1987.

Drabek, Anna M. *et al.,* Hrsg. *Ungarn und Österreich unter Maria Theresia und Joseph II: neue Aspekte im Verhältnis der beiden Länder.* Wien: Verlag der österreichischen Akademie der Wissenschaft, 1982.

Duffy, Christopher. *The Army of Maria Theresa. The Armed Forces of Imperial Austria, 1740–1780.* North Pomfret, VT: David & Charles, 1977.

Fussenegger, Gertrud. *Maria Theresia.* Wien: Molden, 1980.

Gooch, George P. *Maria Theresa and Other Studies.* London: Longmans, 1952.

Guglia, Eugen. *Maria Theresia. Ihr Leben und ihre Regierung.* 2 vols. München-Berlin: R. Oldenbourg, 1917.

Koschatzky, Walter, Hrsg. *Maria Theresia und ihre Zeit: eine Darstellung d. Epoche v. 1740–1780.* Wien: Residenz-Verlag, 1979.

Kretschmayr, Heinrich. *Maria Theresia.* Gotha: Flamberg Verlag, 1925.

Kunisch, Johannes. *Das Mirakel des Hauses Brandenburg: Studien zum Verhältnis von Kabinettspolitik und Kriegsführung im Zeitalter des siebenjährigen Krieges.* München: Oldenbourg, 1978.

Kutschera, Rolf. *Maria Theresia und ihre Kaisersöhne: ein Beitrag zum Habsburgerjahr 1990.* Innsbruck: Wort und Welt, 1990.

Macartney, C.A. *Maria Theresa and the House of Austria.* London: English Universities Press, 1969.

Mraz, Gerda, Hrsg. *Maria Theresia als Königin von Ungarn.* Eisenstadt: Selbstverlag des Instituts für österreichische Kulturgeschichte, 1984.

Reinhold, Peter. *Maria Theresia.* Wiesbaden: Insel-Verlag, 1958.

Vallotton, Henry. *Marie-Thérèse impératrice.* Paris: Fayard, 1963.

COLLECTIONS:

Printed documents:

Arneth, Alfred von, and Auguste Geffroy, Hrsg. *Briefe der Kaiserin Maria Theresia an ihre Kinder und Freunde.* Vols. 1–4. Wien: Braumüller, 1881. facsimile reprint Osnabrück, 1978.

———. Hrsg. *Marie-Antoinette. Correspondence secrète entre Marie Thérèse et le Cte de Mercy-Argenteau. Avec les lettres de Marie-Thérèse et de Marie-Antoinette.* vols. 1–3. 2nd ed. Paris: Firmin-Didot frères, fils et cie., 1874.

———. Hrsg. *Maria Theresia und Joseph II. Ihre Korrespondenz sammt Briefen Josephs an seinen Bruder Leopold.* Vols. 1–3. Wien: C. Gerold's Sohn, 1867–68.

Christoph, Paul, Hrsg. *Maria Theresia und Marie-Antoinette. Ihr geheimer Briefwechsel.* Wien: Cesam-Verlag, 1952.

Jedlicka, Ludwig F., Hrsg. *Maria Theresia in ihren Briefen und Staatsschriften.* Wien: Bergland Verlag, 1955.

Kallbrunner, Josef, Hrsg. *Kaiserin Maria Theresias Politisches Testament.* Wien: Verlag für Geschichte und Politik, 1952.

Khevenhueller-Metsch, Johann. *Aus der Zeit Maria Theresias. Tagebuch 1742–1776 . . . u. Nachtr. von anderer Hand 1774–1780.* Hrsg. Rudolf Khevenhueller-Metsch. Wien-Leipzig T. 1–8. 1907–1925. New edition Maria Breunlich-Pawlik and Hans Wagner, Hrsg., Wien: A. Hozhausen, 1972.

Walter, Friedrich, Hrsg. *Maria Theresia. Briefe und Aktenstücke in Auswahl.* 2nd ed. Darmstadt: Wissenschaftliche Buchgesellschaft, 1982.

Manuscript Document Collections in Vienna Archives:

Allgemeines Verwaltungsarchiv.

Haus-, Hof- und Staatsarchiv.

Hofkammerarchiv.

Kriegsarchiv.

Österreichische Nationalbibliothek.

William L. Chew III,
Professor of History, Vesalius College, Vrije
Universiteit, Brussels, Belgium

Maria Theresa of Modena (1849–1919).

See Maria Teresa of Este.

Maria Theresa of Portugal
(1855–1944)

Archduchess of Austria. Name variations: Maria Teresa da Imaculda. Born on August 24, 1855, in Kleinheubach; died on February 12, 1944, in Vienna, Austria; daughter of Michael I (or Miguel), king of Portugal (r. 1828–1834) and *Adelheid (1831–1909); became third wife of Karl Ludwig also known as Charles Louis (1833–1896), archduke of Austria and governor of Tirol (r. 1855–1861), on July 23, 1873; children: Elisabeth Amalia (b. 1878, who married Aloys, prince of Liechtenstein); *Maria Annunziata (1876–1961).

Maria Theresa of Sardinia (1756–1805).

See Maria Teresa of Savoy.

Maria Theresa of Spain (1638–1683).

See Maria Teresa of Spain.

Maria Theresa of Spain (1651–1673).

See Margaret Theresa of Spain.

Maria Theresa of Spain
(1726–1746)

French dauphine and infanta of Spain. Name variations: Marie Therese de Bourbon; Mary Theresa;

*Marie Raphaëlle or Marie Raphaelle of Spain. Born Marie-Thérèse Raphaele de Bourbon on June 11, 1726; died four days after giving birth to a girl on July 22, 1746, at age 20; daughter of Philip V (b. 1683), king of Spain, and *Elizabeth Farnese (1692–1766); became first wife of Louis le dauphin (1729–1765, father of Louis XVI), on February 23, 1745; children: one girl (name unknown). Louis the Dauphin's second wife was *Marie Josephe of Saxony (1731–1767).*

Maria Theresa of Tuscany (1801–1855)

*Queen of Sardinia. Name variations: Maria Teresa of Austria; Archduchess Therese of Austria; Teresa of Tuscany; Theresa of Modena; queen of Savoy-Piedmont. Born on March 21, 1801, in Vienna, Austria; died on January 12, 1855; daughter of Ferdinand III, grand duke of Tuscany (r. 1790–1802 and 1814–1824) and *Louisa Amelia (1773–1802); sister of Leopold II, grand duke of Tuscany (r. 1824–1859); married Charles Albert (1798–1849), prince of Carignano and king of Sardinia (r. 1831–1849); children: Victor Emmanuel II, king of Italy (r. 1849–1878, who married *Marie Adelaide of Austria); Ferdinand (who married *Elizabeth of Saxony).*

Maria Theresa of Wurttemberg

Countess of Clermont. Name variations: Maria-Theresa of Württemberg. married Henri or Henry of Clermont (b. 1933), count of Clermont, in 1957; children: Francis Henri (b. 1961).

Mariamme.

Variant of Mariamne.

Mariamne (fl. 1st c.)

Saint and Biblical woman.

It is claimed that after Jesus' ascension, Mariamne, a pious widow, accompanied the apostle Philip to teach the gospel to the Scythians at Hieropolis, and that afterwards she carried the Gospel to Lycaonia and died there. Her feast day is on February 17.

Mariamne the Hasmonian (c. 60–c. 29 BCE).

See Berenice (c. 35 BCE–?) for sidebar.

Mariana.

Variant of Maria or Marie.

Mariana de Austria (c. 1634–1696).

See Maria Anna of Austria.

Mariana de Paredes (1618–1645)

Ecuadoran saint. Born in Quito, Ecuador, in 1618; died in Quito in 1645.

Mariana de Paredes longed to be a Dominican nun; instead, she lived the life of a contemplative in the house of her relatives. When an earthquake hit Quito in 1645, Mariana died after she "offered herself as a victim to divine justice for the deliverance of the city." The Republic of Ecuador conferred on her the title of "national heroine." Her feast day is May 26.

Mariana of Jesus (1565–1624)

Saint. Born in 1565; died in 1624.

Blessed Mariana of Jesus was the founder of the discalced (barefoot) nuns of Our Lady of Mercy in Spain. Her feast day is April 17.

Mariana Victoria (1768–1788).

See Maria I Braganza for sidebar.

Marianne of Molokai, Mother (1838–1918).

See Cope, Mother Marianne.

Marianne of the Netherlands (1810–1883)

*Princess of the Netherlands. Born on May 9, 1810; died on May 29, 1883; daughter of *Frederica Wilhelmina of Prussia (1774–1837) and William I (1772–1843), king of the Netherlands (r. 1813–1840, abdicated in 1840); married Albert (1809–1872), prince of Prussia, on September 14, 1830 (divorced 1849); children: Charlotte (1831–1855, who married Bernard II, duke of Saxe-Meiningen); Albert (b. 1837); Elizabeth (1840–1840); Alexandrine (1842–1906, who married William, duke of Mecklenburg-Schwerin). Prince Albert's second wife was Rosalie von Rauch (1820–1879), countess of Hohenau.*

Maric, Ljubica (1909—)

Serbian conductor and composer who fought as a partisan during WWII. Born in Kragujevac, Serbia, on March 18, 1909.

Ljubica Maric studied under J. Slavenski at the Music School in Belgrade from 1929 until the early 1930s. She then went to the Prague Conservatory where she studied with Josef Suk and Alois Haba. Nikolai Malko taught her conducting in Prague, and Hermann Scherchen instructed her in Strasbourg. World War II erupted shortly after Maric completed her musical studies; like many young people, she soon found herself fighting against the Nazis with the partisans. When the war ended, Maric began teaching and in 1957 came to the Music Academy of Belgrade.

John Haag,
Athens, Georgia

Maríc, Mileva (1875–1948).

See Einstein-Maríc, Mileva.

Marie.

French form of Maria and Mary.

Marie (1393–1438)

Prioress of Poissy. Name variations: Mary Valois; Marie de Bourbon; Mary de France or Mary of France. Born in 1393; died in 1438; daughter of Charles VI, king of France (r. 1380–1422), and *Isabeau of Bavaria (1371–1435); sister of *Catherine of Valois (1401–1437); *Isabella of Valois (1389–c. 1410, who married Richard II, king of England), and Charles VII, king of France (r. 1422–1461).

Marie (1876–1940)

Greek princess. Name variations: Mary Oldenburg. Born on March 3, 1876; died on December 13, 1940; daughter of George I, king of the Hellenes, and *Olga Constantinovna (1851–1926); married George Michaelovitch (grandson of Tsar Nicholas I of Russia); children: two.

Marie (1900–1961)

Queen of Yugoslavia. Name variations: Mignon; Maria or Mary Hohenzollern; Marie of Rumania. Born on January 9, 1900, at Schloss Friedestein, in Gotha, Thuringia, Germany; died on June 22, 1961, in London, England; daughter of Ferdinand I, king of Rumania (r. 1914–1927), and *Marie of Rumania (1875–1938); married Alexander I (1888–1934), king of Yugoslavia (r. 1921–1934), on June 8, 1922 (he was assassinated by a Croatian in Marseilles, France, on October 9, 1934); children: Peter II (1923–1970), king of Yugoslavia, who married *Alexandra Oldenburg; Prince Tomislav Karadjordjevic (1928–2000); Andrej Karadjordjevic (b. 1929).

Marie, abbess of Romsey (d. 1182).

See Marie of Boulogne.

Marie, empress (1824–1880).

See Marie of Hesse-Darmstadt.

Marie, grand duchess (1899–1918).

See Alexandra Feodorovna for sidebar.

Marie, grand duchess of Russia (1847–1928).

See Marie Feodorovna.

Marie, Jeanne (1809–1875).

See Héricourt, Jenny Poinsard d'.

Marie, princess of Orleans (1813–1839).

See Marie of Württemberg.

Marie-Adelaide d'Orleans (1698–1743).

See Louise-Adelaide.

Marie Adelaide of Austria (1822–1855)

Queen of Sardinia and Italy. Name variations: Adelaide of Austria; Maria Adelaide di Asburgo-Lorena. Born on June 3, 1822; died on January 20, 1855; daughter of Rainer, archduke of Austria, and Elizabeth of Savoy-Carignan; married Victor Emmanuel II, king of Italy (r. 1849–1878), on April 12, 1842; children: Carlo Alberto also known as Charles Albert; Oddone Eugenio; *Maria Pia (1847–1911, who married the king of Portugal); *Clotilde of Savoy (1843–1911); Amadeus (b. 1845), king of Spain (r. 1870–1873); Humbert I also known as Umberto I (1844–1900), king of Italy (r. 1878–1900, assassinated); Vittorio Emanuele also known as Victor Emmanuel (b. 1855).

Born in Milan on June 3, 1822, Marie Adelaide of Austria was the daughter of Archduke Rainer and *Elizabeth of Savoy-Carignan. She married her cousin Victor Emmanuel II, the duke of Savoy and later king of Italy, on April 12, 1842. Tall and attractive, Marie Adelaide won respect as a pious, charitable woman known for her kindliness to the poor and for raising her family in a simple, circumspect manner. She died on January 20, 1855, a few days after giving birth to her son Victor Emmanuel.

SOURCES:
Giovannini, Gemma. *Le donne di Casa Savoia: dalle origini della famiglia fino ai nostri giorni.* Milan: L.F. Cogliati, 1900.

Kendall W. Brown,
Professor of History,
Brigham Young University, Provo, Utah

Marie Adelaide of Luxemburg

(1894–1924).

See Charlotte, grand duchess of Luxemburg, for sidebar.

Marie Adelaide of Savoy

(1685–1712)

Duchess of Burgundy. Name variations: Marie Adélaïde; Marie-Adelaide of Savoy; Maria Adelaide, Duchesse de Bourgogne. Born on December 6, 1685; died on February 12, 1712; daughter of Anne-Marie d'Bourbon-Orleans (1669–1728) and Victor Amadeus II (1666–1732), duke of Savoy (r. 1675–1713), king of Sicily (r. 1713–1718) and Sardinia (r. 1718–1730); married Louis (1682–1712), duke of Burgundy (grandson of Louis XIV), on December 7, 1697; children: Louis Bourbon (1704–1705), duke of Brittany; Louis XV (1710–1774), king of France (r. 1715–1774).

Marie Adelaide of Savoy was born in 1685, the daughter of *Anne-Marie d'Bourbon-Orleans** and Victor Amadeus II, duke of Savoy, king of Sicily and Sardinia. In 1697, in a silver dress dotted with rubies and a 25-foot-long train, 12-year-old Marie Adelaide married Duke Louis of Burgundy, grandson of Louis XIV. She became one of King Louis XIV's favorites and was extremely popular at court.

SUGGESTED READING:

Elliott, Charles. *Princess of Versailles: The Life of Marie Adelaide of Savoy, 1993.*

Marie Alexandra of Baden

(1902–1944)

*German royal. Name variations: Zahringen. Born Mary Alexandra Thyra Victoria Louise Carol Hilda on August 1, 1902, in Salem, Baden, Germany; killed in an air raid, age 42, on January 29, 1944, in Frankfurt-am-Main, Germany; daughter of Maximilian, margrave of Baden, and *Marie-Louise Guelph (1879–1948); married Wolfgang of Hesse-Cassel, on September 17, 1924.*

Marie Alexandrovna (1853–1920)

Russian grand duchess and duchess of Edinburgh. Name variations: Maria or Mary Alexandrovna, Mary Romanov; Grand Duchess of Russia. Born on October 17, 1853, in St. Petersburg, Russia; died on October 24, 1920, in Zurich, Switzerland; daughter of Alexander II (1818–1881), tsar of Russia (r. 1855–1881), and

*Marie of Hesse-Darmstadt (1824–1880); sister of Alexander III, tsar of Russia (r. 1881–1894); married Alfred Saxe-Coburg (1844–1900), duke of Edinburgh, on January 23, 1874; children: Alfred Saxe-Coburg (b. 1874); *Marie of Rumania (1875–1938); *Victoria Melita of Saxe-Coburg (1876–1936); *Alexandra Saxe-Coburg (1878–1942); *Beatrice of Saxe-Coburg (1884–1966).*

Marie Amélie (1782–1866).

See Maria Amalia.

Marie-Amelie of Orleans

(1865–1951)

*Queen of Portugal. Name variations: Amalia of Paris; Amélia or Amélie; Amelia of Orleans. Born on September 28, 1865, in Twickenham, Middlesex, England; died on October 25, 1951, at Château de Bellevue, Le Chesnay, Versailles; daughter of Louis Philippe (1838–1894), count of Paris, and *Maria Is-*

Marie Adelaide of Savoy

abella (1848–1919); married Carlos also known as Charles I (1863–1908), king of Portugal (r. 1889–1908), on May 22, 1886; children: Luis Filepe also known as Louis Philippe (1887–1908), duke of Braganza; Maria Ana of Portugal (1887–1887); Manuel II (1889–1932), king of Portugal (r. 1908–1910).

Born in Great Britain in 1865, Marie-Amelie of Orleans was the daughter of the counts of Paris, exiled descendants of the French Bourbon family. In 1886, she married Charles I of Portugal. Queen Amelia, as she was best known in Portugal, founded the Carriage Museum in 1905 and dedicated much of her time to the campaign against tuberculosis. She was present when her husband and her son Louis Philippe were assassinated on February 1, 1908.

Amelia was the last Portuguese queen. Her second son, Manuel II, succeeded to the throne following the assassinations, and he did not marry until after he had been deposed in 1910 by a republican insurrection. Amelia accompanied her son into exile in England, although she later took up residence at Versailles. With the permission of the Portuguese government, she returned to visit Portugal in 1945. Her death occurred on October 25, 1951.

SOURCES:

Sá, Aires de. *Rainha D. Amélia*. Lisbon: Parceria A.M. Pereira, 1928.

Kendall W. Brown,
Professor of History,
Brigham Young University, Provo, Utah

Marie Angelique, Mere.

See Port Royal des Champs, Abbesses for Jacqueline Arnauld.

Marie-Anne de la Trémouille

(c. 1642–1722)

Princess of the Ursins and ambitious French aristocrat who headed the household of Queen Marie Louise of Savoy, wife of Philip V of Spain, and wielded great political influence during the War of the Spanish Succession. Name variations: Madame or Princess des Ursins; Marie Anne Ursins; Anne Marie de la Trémouille, Duchess of Bracciano; Marie-Anne de la Tremouille; Marie-Anne Orsini. Probably born 1642 (perhaps as early as 1635); died in Rome on December 5, 1722; eldest child of Louis de la Trémouille, marquis of Noirmoutier, and Julie Aubry; married Adrien-Blaise de Talleyrand, prince of Chalais, July 5, 1659 (died 1670); married Flavio deglio Orsini, duke of Bracciano, on February 17, 1675 (died, April 5, 1698); no known children. Appointed camarera mayor (1701); dismissed and exiled (December 1714).

Birth of Louis XIV (1638); accession of Louis XIV to throne (1643); Peace of the Pyrenees between France and Spain (1659); marriage of Louis XIV to Maria Teresa of Spain (1660); birth of Charles II of Spain (1661); accession of Charles II (1665); birth of Philip of Anjou (1683); death of Charles II (1700); coronation of Philip V (1701); marriage of Philip V and Marie Louise of Savoy (1701); start of the War of Spanish Succession (1701); Treaty of Utrecht (1713); death of Marie Louise (1714); marriage of Philip V and Elizabeth Farnese (1714); death of Louis XIV (1715).

Marie-Anne de la Trémouille spent her first half century as a minor aristocratic figure in France, Spain, and Rome. She then played a central role during the War of the Spanish Succession (1701–13), after which she submitted to a forced retirement in Italy during her remaining days. The date and place of her birth are unknown, except that she was born by 1642 (perhaps as early as 1635) in France, the eldest child of Louis de la Trémouille, marquis of Noirmoutier, and his bourgeois wife, **Julie Aubry.**

Marie-Amelie of Orleans

Marie-Anne's family enjoyed social prestige and her father held political office. On July 5, 1659, she married Adrien-Blaise de Talleyrand, prince of Chalais. Three years later, Adrien-Blaise participated in a duel, despite a law condemning to death those involved in such brawls. To save his life, he fled to Spain. Marie-Anne waited to go there until 1666, meanwhile gathering the financial resources to support them in exile. When she arrived in Madrid, another predicament faced her: Chalais had joined Spanish forces fighting the Portuguese, who had captured and imprisoned him. Her acumen and independence of spirit carried her through until he returned to Spain in 1668. She quickly became prominent at the Spanish court, gaining the friendship of the queen regent *Maria Anna of Austria (c. 1634–1696) and her chief minister, the Austrian Jesuit Johann Nithard.

In mid-1670, the couple moved to Venice, rented a modest house, and participated on the fringes of aristocratic life. Both soon came down with fever, and Chalais died. The French refused to help, out of fear of Louis XIV, but the Spanish community aided her. She retired briefly to a convent but soon emerged with her worldly ambitions intact. At Marie-Anne's urging, Nithard petitioned the Austrian emperor to recognize her as a princess of the empire. That failed, but in 1673 her fortunes rose. She charmed Cardinal d'Estrées, and he interceded with Louis XIV, who appointed her France's secret envoy to the papacy. With her Spanish connections, Louis XIV hoped she could influence the succession to the Spanish throne; Spain's king, Charles II, had no children and Europe's royal families were maneuvering to claim his crown. Marriage between the French and Spanish royal families gave Louis' grandson, Philip of Anjou (the future Philip V of Spain), a strong claim to succeed Charles.

A sizeable pension accompanied Marie-Anne's appointment, and she became a charming, energetic fixture of Roman society. In March 1675, she married Flavio deglio Orsini, duke of Bracciano, and received a personal letter of congratulations from Louis himself. Nonetheless, other than his titles, which included prince of the Austrian empire and grandee of Spain, the duke was a disappointment. He was bankrupt and lacked the intellect or energy to satisfy Marie-Anne's powerful ambitions. Unlike her marriage to Chalais, love had little role in her second union. During ensuing years, she often lived apart from Bracciano, and spent long periods in France.

Marie-Anne's contacts at Versailles served her well. She became friends with *Madame de Maintenon, whom Louis XIV had secretly married. This rapport was crucial because Maintenon helped persuade the king that Marie-Anne could be useful to French interests in Italy and Spain. Marie-Anne also made the acquaintance of the duke of St. Simon, and featured prominently in his gossipy chronicle of the later decades of the Louis XIV's reign. In 1697, she helped arrange the marriage of the duke of Burgundy (Louis' grandson and father of the future Louis XV) to *Marie Adelaide of Savoy. Meanwhile, her public life in Rome was "brilliant and pompous in spite of debts and poverty," and she constantly entertained diplomats, political leaders, and aristocrats who could help persuade Spaniards to support France. Having sold some of his titles to raise money, her husband began calling himself the prince of the Orsini. He died in April 1698. Modifying the name slightly, she took the title princess des Ursins.

The widow had no intention of fading into obscurity. Indeed, her greatest years lay ahead, though she was nearing 60. Charles II of Spain died in November 1700. As his heir, Charles named Philip of Anjou, the duke of Burgundy's younger brother. The French, the Spaniards, and the papacy agreed to Philip's accession, but Archduke Charles of Austria (the future Holy Roman emperor Charles VI) also tried to claim the throne. Louis XIV's numerous enemies sided with Charles, and the War of the Spanish Succession erupted. Trained from youth to be submissive and pious so he would not challenge his elder brother for the French crown, Philip was ill-suited to rule. Louis intended to establish the general policies for Philip's realm, but the new king, only 17 years old, had to make the daily decisions of government. Philip also needed a wife, and his grandfather chose for him *Marie Louise of Savoy.

This gave the Princess des Ursins an opening to the European stage. She requested of Louis permission to chaperon the bride to Spain. After all, she noted, her second marriage had given her the title of a Spanish grandee. From her years in Madrid, she could speak the language, and she still had many influential friends at the Spanish court. One was the powerful chief minister, Cardinal Portocarrero, who supported Ursins' petition. In April 1701, Louis approved it, to her great delight. Leaving Rome on August 27, she attended Marie Louise's marriage by proxy to Philip on September 11. They then departed for Spain, with a large retinue. The Spaniards refused to let the queen's Italian servants and courtiers cross the border, leaving Ursins as Marie Louise's chief confidante. On November

3, in Figueras, Philip met them and married Marie Louise amid general celebration.

Ursins' handling of an unexpected problem quickly showed Louis XIV her potential value in Spain. The morning of November 4, she met a sexually frustrated Philip, who reported that rather than consummating the marriage, his 13-year-old bride had harangued him about European politics. Victor Amadeus II, duke of Savoy, who soon joined the cause of Archduke Charles, had instructed his daughter Marie Louise to make anti-French demands of Philip. Ursins immediately informed Versailles about the state of affairs, and her counsel smoothed out the monarchs' marital discord. Philip's sensuality made it easy for the queen to manipulate him, however, especially as he was generally passive in other respects.

> *Madame des Ursins was born to mould and direct great public affairs and to have a high hand in the intrigues of state.*
>
> —Constance Hill

Louis XIV knew that Philip's strong-willed bride would dominate her husband. The great monarch also foresaw that as the young queen's chief confidante, Ursins could influence Philip's decisions. Thus, Louis instructed his grandson to name Ursins *camarera mayor* (head of the queen's household). Ursins' friends in Versailles, including Madame de Maintenon and Marie Adelaide, also supported the princess. Even before leaving Italy, Ursins had probably begun maneuvering to obtain the post. It positioned her to implement Louis XIV's policy for Spain and further her own ambitions. As *camarera mayor,* she occupied the bedroom next to the queen's and controlled access to Marie Louise's apartments. In processions, her coach followed directly after that of the monarchs and her servants wore the royal livery. She attended the queen constantly.

Her own intelligence, ambition, and energy meant that Ursins became more than a mere conduit for Louis XIV's policies. Philip soon left for Italy to lead Spanish forces there, appointing the queen to act as regent in his absence. Ursins, Cardinal Portocarrero, and the French ambassador, the Marquis de Louville, attempted to rule Spain. The two men preferred to remove Spaniards from the government and appoint the French to fill the more important positions. Ursins resisted this policy. She recognized that Philip and Marie Louise needed support from their subjects if they were to reign successfully. Ursins thus guided the monarchs to be more than simple tools of

France, at the same time recognizing that Philip could not protect his crown without military assistance from Louis XIV. She introduced French and Italian culture and fashions at court, to the dismay of some Spanish conservatives. Ursins also tried to curb the influence of the Inquisition, with little success. According to historian John Lynch, Ursins "came to monopolize power from 1702 to 1704, marginalizing the Spanish ministers, excluding the grandees, and alienating even the French ambassadors."

After Cardinal d'Estrées replaced Louville as French ambassador to Madrid, and both he and his nephew, the abbé d'Estrées, quarreled with Ursins, she secured the cardinal's dismissal and even dared intercept her enemies' correspondence. Louis tired of her independence and engineered her removal. He anticipated that Marie Louise would insist that Philip protect Ursins. Louis thus encouraged Philip to go with the army on its campaign against the Portuguese. Having separated the royal couple, Louis then ordered his grandson to dismiss the princess. Philip reluctantly did so in mid-1704, to Marie Louise's outrage. Louis ordered Ursins to return to Rome, but later that year her friends persuaded him to allow the princess to go to Versailles instead.

By then things in Spain were in such disarray that Louis XIV reconciled himself to restoring Ursins as *camarera mayor.* In January 1705, he received her at Versailles with great public favor and on January 13 announced his intention of sending her back to Madrid. Serving with her were ambassador Michel-Jean Amelot and financial expert Jean Orry. Their task was twofold: to win the war, and to centralize the power of the Spanish monarchy by curbing the independence of the grandees and clergy and by abolishing the *fueros* (privileges) of Aragon. Ursins reached Madrid on August 3, to the delight of Marie Louise. Writes Lynch, the princess "immediately recovered control of court patronage, throwing out her enemies and bringing in her own clients, and she reestablished her domination over the queen, to such an extent that even Philip was secretly jealous of her."

With the war going badly, Ursins' task was difficult. In late August 1705, the archduke's fleet besieged Barcelona, which fell on October 4. Philip's enemies soon penetrated the Spanish heartland and forced the monarchs to flee Madrid in June 1706. Harshly criticizing the great aristocrats who refused to defend their sovereigns but waited instead to learn which side would prevail, Ursins accompanied Marie

Louise on her desperate flight to Burgos in June and July. Throughout it all Ursins showed great fortitude, strengthening the will of the monarchs to continue the struggle. Her endurance was remarkable, given her age and poor eyesight (cataracts had rendered her nearly blind). Hungry for power themselves, the grandees resented Ursins. When she and the queen returned to Madrid in late 1706, Ursins reportedly engineered the dismissal of 300 ladies-in-waiting who had refused to accompany the queen to Burgos. She forced the Church to contribute heavily to Philip's cause and worked to strengthen the king's will. Biographer François Combes wrote: "If the King inspired respect and fear, it was through Madame des Ursins that he did so. She alone . . . kept him up to a high standard of principle and of action." Meanwhile, through Madame de Maintenon and her other correspondents at Versailles, she also besieged Louis XIV with requests for more soldiers and aid.

For a while the war turned in Philip's favor. Unable to hold Castile, the archduke's armies withdrew. The duke of Berwick arrived from France to command the Spanish-French forces, which dealt the enemy a crushing defeat at Almansa on April 25, 1707. On August 25 of that year, the queen gave birth to Louis (I), the crown prince, to general celebration in Castile. But Philip and Louis could not vanquish their enemies. The terrible winter of 1709–10 caused great suffering in France and made it hard for Louis to sustain the war. France was attacked on several fronts, and the archduke invaded Castile again in 1710. Ursins held firm in her support for Philip, despite flagging enthusiasm in Versailles. When Philip was ready to abdicate, she upbraided him: "How is this, sire? Are you a king? Are you a man? You, who value so lightly your sovereignty!" Her correspondence with Madame de Maintenon took on a chilly and sometimes sarcastic tone, for Louis' wife had become a pacifist, willing to accept peace on nearly any terms. Louis opened secret negotiations with the enemy and offered to sacrifice Philip and Spain.

Led by the duke of Vendôme, Spanish-French forces achieved victories at Villaviciosa and Saragossa (Zaragoza) in 1710, convincing the archduke's allies that he could not subdue Castile. Then, in April 1711, the Austrian ruler died, leaving the title to his brother, the archduke, who became Emperor Charles VI. The English and other allies had no interest in seeing Austria annex the Spanish empire. Divisions among the allies enabled Philip to make slow progress against Charles' forces in Catalonia. The Peace of Utrecht (1713) ended the European conflict, although

Barcelona held out against the Bourbon siege for another year. In the peace negotiations, Ursins had confidently requested that Louis obtain a small Dutch principality for her. She intended to trade it for territory in Touraine. Nothing came of her demands, however, which were considered presumptuous by the negotiators.

Ursins still continued to wield wide power over Philip and Marie Louise and thus over Spain. A serious illness in 1711 and her advancing age (she was now about 70) had not curbed Ursins' energy or her ambition. Nonetheless, an unforeseen crisis awaited. On February 14, 1714, the queen died of tuberculosis. Philip turned his children over to Ursins' care and talked of abdicating. Philip's melancholy and lethargy foreshadowed the mental illness that afflicted his later years. To forestall an abdication and to protect her own position, Ursins isolated Philip. Enemies of the princess spread rumors that she was trying to force Philip to marry her. More realistically, Ursins set about to find him another wife. Giulio Alberoni, envoy of the duke of Parma, shrewdly suggested *Elizabeth Farnese, the duke's niece. The girl, Alberoni assured Ursins, was "plump, healthy, and well bred, brought up in the petty court of her uncle Duke Francis, and accustomed to hear of nothing but needlework and embroidery." Thinking she would be able to dominate Farnese as she had Marie Louise, Ursins recommended the marriage to Philip and the negotiations were soon completed. Elizabeth Farnese married Philip by proxy on September 25, 1714, and then set out for Spain.

As it turned out, the new queen was not the submissive girl described by Alberoni. As *camarera mayor,* Ursins went out to the village of Jadraque to meet Elizabeth, while Philip awaited his bride nearby in Guadalajara. Alberoni had coached Farnese on how to deal with the princess. When they met on December 23, Elizabeth accused Ursins of disrespect and ordered the guards to arrest her. She further commanded them to escort the princess out of Spain without delay. Ursins had no time to gather possessions or make any arrangements. Guards placed her in a carriage with an attendant and hastily drove her to the French border. His new wife's presumption surprised Philip, but his anticipation of spending a pleasurable night in the wedding bed foreclosed any possibility that he would intercede on Ursins' behalf. He allowed her to be cast aside ignominiously although she had served his cause faithfully for more than a decade.

Ursins' fortunes improved a little in France. Louis XIV and Madame de Maintenon received her on March 27, 1715, and Louis doubled Ursins' pension to 40,000 livres. Royal finances made it doubtful, however, that she would ever receive much from Versailles. Influenced by Farnese, Philip refused to provide any assistance. Meanwhile, Ursins decided to return to Italy. She feared to stay in France, where her enemies could persecute her after the death of the aged Louis XIV. Philippe Bourbon-Orleans, 2nd duke of Orléans, one of the princess' most implacable foes, became regent when the great king died on September 1, 1715. Ursins, who had already left Paris, made her way to Genoa, where she resided for a while. In 1718, she moved to Rome. For many years, she had dreamed of returning to the Eternal City, "because there one sees only those one wishes and the climate is gentle and agreeable to a lazy woman who likes to be well lodged, to hear the best music that exists, and seeks also to pass the rest of her life in some tranquility." She died there on December 5, 1722.

Marie-Anne de la Trémouille, princess of Ursins, played a remarkable political role during the first decade and a half of the 18th century. Of her, historian Henry Kamen observes, "In Spain Madame des Ursins achieved an eminence perhaps greater than that of Madame de Maintenon in France. Louis XIV treated directly with her as though she were arbiter of the destinies of Spain, and ministers appointed in Madrid had invariably to pass under her scrutiny." Many resented her power, for her ambition and her gender, but her "extraordinary mental faculties and physical energy" made her formidable. Biographer **Maud Cruttwell** concludes, "Thanks to her clear brain, energy, and ability, Spain was twice saved—first from becoming a mere province under the domination of France and later from being partitioned out by Louis to half the European powers to save his own skin."

SOURCES:

Combes, François. *La Princesse des Ursins; essai sur sa vie et son caractére politique.* Paris: Didier et Cie, 1858.

Cruttwell, Maud. *The Princess des Ursins.* NY: E.P. Dutton, 1927.

Hill, Constance. *The Story of the Princess des Ursins in Spain (Camarera-Mayor).* NY: John Lane, 1906.

Kamen, Henry Arthur Francis. *The War of Succession in Spain, 1700–15.* Bloomington: Indiana University Press, 1969.

Lynch, John. *Bourbon Spain, 1700–1808.* Oxford: Basil Blackwell, 1989.

Ribardière, Diane. *La Princesse des Ursins: Dame de fer et de velours.* Paris: Librairie Académique Perrin, 1988.

The Secret Correspondence of Madame de Maintenon, with the Princess des Ursins; from the Original Manuscripts in the Possession of the Duke de Choiseul. 3 vols. London: G.B. Whittaker, 1827.

SUGGESTED READING:

Rosseeuw Saint-Hilaire, Eugene François Achille. *La Princesse des Ursins.* Paris: Furne, Jouvet, 1875.

Saint-René Taillandier, Madeleine. *La princesse des Ursins: une grande dame française à la cour d'Espagne sous Louis XIV.* Paris: Hachette, 1926.

Kendall W. Brown,
Professor of History,
Brigham Young University, Provo, Utah

Marie-Anne of Austria (1683–1754).

See Maria Antonia of Austria.

Marie-Anne of Braganza
(1861–1942)

*Princess of Portugal. Name variations: Maria Anna of Portugal. Born on July 13, 1861, in Bronnbach; died on July 31, 1942, in New York; daughter of *Adelheid (1831–1909) and Miguel also known as Michael I (1802–1866), king of Portugal (r. 1828–1834); married William IV (1852–1912), grand duke of Luxemburg (of the House of Nassau), on June 21, 1893; children: *Marie Adelaide of Luxemburg (1894–1924); Hilda (b. 1897, who later married Prince Adolf of Schwartzenberg); *Antoinette of Luxemburg (1899–1954, who married Crown Prince Rupprecht of Bavaria); Elisabeth (1901–1950, who married Prince Ludwig-Philipp of Thurn and Taxis); *Sophie of Nassau (1902–1941); and *Charlotte, Grand Duchess of Luxemburg (b. 1896).*

Marie Annunziata of Naples
(1843–1871).

See Maria Annunziata.

Marie Antoinette (1755–1793)

*Austrian-born queen of France whose misfortune was to be the wife of Louis XVI when that monarch was overthrown in the French Revolution of 1789, and whose poor judgment and provocative behavior led to her execution in the name of the Revolution. Name variations: Marie-Antoinette. Born in Vienna, Austria, on November 2, 1755; died by the guillotine in Paris, France, on October 16, 1793; daughter of Francis Stephen of Lorraine, grand duke of Tuscany, also known as Francis I, Holy Roman emperor (r. 1745–1765), and Maria Theresa of Austria (1717–1780), empress of the Habsburg domains; sister of *Maria Carolina (1752–1814), Joseph II, emperor of Austria and Holy Roman emperor (r. 1765–1790), *Maria Christina (1742–1798), *Elizabeth of Austria (1743–1808), Leopold II, Holy Roman emperor (r. 1790–1792), and *Maria Amalia (1746–1804); mar-*

ried Louis XVI, king of France (r. 1774–1792), in 1770; children: first daughter, Princess Marie Thérèse Charlotte (1778–1851), was exchanged by the Revolutionary government to the Court of Vienna and grew up to be the duchess of Angoulême; the first dauphin, Louis Joseph (1781–1789); the second dauphin, Louis Charles (b. 1785), imprisoned during the Revolution, was proclaimed "Louis XVII" by royalists, and apparently died in prison in 1795; Princess Sophie Beatrix (1786–1787).

Marie Antoinette was raised at the Schonbrunn palace and indifferently educated; betrothed to the dauphin of France, the future Louis XVI (1769) to reinforce the alliance between the House of Habsburg and the House of Bourbon; married the dauphin (1770); gave birth to four royal children (1778–86); engaged in court intrigues and flirtations until outbreak of French Revolution (1789); failed in attempted flight from France with the king (June 1791); arrested by revolutionaries (1792) and tried before Revolutionary Tribunal (October 14, 1793); guillotined in Paris (October 16, 1793). Marie Antoinette was the very symbol of a failed and hated monarchy in the most profoundly symbolic revolution of modern history, the sad fulfillment of all the prophecies of vanity.

Marie Antoinette, a queen forever associated with the French Revolution of 1789, was—along with her royal husband, Louis XVI—one of its two most prominent victims. Undoubtedly self-indulgent and proud, she nevertheless did not deserve the calumny heaped upon her by the revolutionaries of France. Indeed, the excessive nature of the accusations brought against her before the revolutionary tribunal suggest an obsession with the queen as a hated symbol as much as an individual guilty of treason.

It has been noted by biographers, particularly Stefan Zweig, whose writing was greatly influenced by the theories of psychoanalysis, that Marie Antoinette was in most ways an unremarkable person. Attractive with her blue eyes and blonde curls, despite her Habsburg features, she was, even so, no match for the great beauties of the court at Versailles. Only the most gallant would compare her with the influential mistress of Louis XV, ***Madame du Barry**, who dominated affairs in 1770 when Marie Antoinette arrived France to marry the heir to the throne. Nor did she possess more than ordinary intelligence and education. Lively and personable, she gave her heart to many, and her body, it would seem, to some. Yet her adultery has been attributed, in part, to her husband's incapacity to engage in normal sexual intercourse during their first six

years of marriage (he suffered a genital defect called phymosis, which was corrected when the king finally submitted to minor surgery). But Marie Antoinette was hardly the libertine of popular mythology. Events, rather than personality, would thrust her onto the pages of history.

If not a ***Valeria Messalina** or a ***Fredegund**, Marie Antoinette was a foreigner. Austrian born, she found herself at an early age in a strange court, at the center of intrigues and expectations, and the wife of an indifferent and inept prince. Far from the steady hand of her capable mother, Empress ***Maria Theresa of Austria**, and lacking good counsel or the wisdom to seek it, Marie Antoinette behaved poorly and became queen at a time when France was drifting toward financial ruin and political chaos. When she became the subject of court gossip and then the object of unbridled popular speculation, detractors of the monarchy fixed upon her as a root cause of political decline and royal extravagance. Failing to be French in a country awash in nationalism, Marie Antoinette became the symbol of foreign influ-

Marie Antoinette

ence for millions of French citizens, an emblem of financial irresponsibility, and the personification of moral corruption. It was as the most obvious representation of the Bourbon monarchy, the reputed "Austrian whore" who, it was claimed, had suggested that the hungry French eat cake, that Marie Antoinette mounted the scaffold and was decapitated by the "national razor" on October 16, 1793.

She was born in imperial splendor on November 2, 1755. Her father was the lackluster Francis I, but her mother was a conscientious and intelligent heir to the Habsburg name and empire. Preoccupied with heavy responsibilities, particularly in foreign affairs, Maria Theresa could spare but little time for her energetic daughter. While her mother struggled to maintain the empire through war and diplomacy, Marie Antoinette romped and indulged herself, failing to take any formal instruction seriously. Most official attention was directed to her royal brother, Joseph II, who would share imperial power with his mother after 1765.

Marie Antoinette's emergence from the historical obscurity of most royal princesses can be traced to the formation of a state alliance between France and Austria after the War of the Austrian Succession, which ended in 1748. Austria, having lost valuable territories to Prussia, needed a strong continental ally to protect it against additional piracy. Although France was the ancient enemy of the Habsburgs, the court at Vienna and the court at Versailles found they had common enemies. As blood was thicker than ink, discussions began early on to link the two dynasties together with a wedding ring. Yet it was not until 1766 that Louis XV of France, a singularly ineffective monarch who was controlled by his mistresses and his degeneracy, signaled that a marriage between the dauphin, or heir to the French throne, and the 11-year-old Marie Antoinette would be welcomed. Maria Theresa, fearful that her archenemy, Frederick I the Great of Prussia, would somehow unhinge the Franco-Austrian understanding, pressed for a rapid conclusion of the business. She was indifferent to reports that the dauphin would hardly be an appealing son-in-law. As for Marie Antoinette, she seems to have thought but little of the engagement, continuing in her amusements and failing to master even written German, much less French. Child that she was, she enjoyed the last years of her girlhood while the politicians argued interminably over the particulars of her coming marriage. It was three years before a final understanding was obtained. By then, Marie Antoinette was 14 years old.

On April 19, 1770, Marie Antoinette was married by proxy in Vienna to the dauphin of France, a man she had never seen. Shortly thereafter, a magnificent procession accompanied her to a wooden pavilion on an island in the Rhine near Strasbourg where she was handed over to French courtiers. In a specially constructed room, she was stripped of her Austrian garments and dressed in French clothing; from that moment Marie Antoinette became legally French. At Compiegne, she was met by Louis XV and his grandson, the dauphin. It could not have been a joyful moment for the girl. Her groom, besides being plain in appearance, was completely devoid of enthusiasm, a condition that was to prove enduring. Although not yet the corpulent man he would be in a few years, the dauphin already displayed a torpor that would increase with the passage of time.

On May 16, 1770, the actual wedding took place at Versailles. After extraordinary celebrations, Marie Antoinette and her husband were finally alone. Almost certainly she learned then of her husband's incapacity; it would not be long before almost everyone else at court and in foreign governments knew as well. Eight years were to elapse before the dauphiness would deliver a child.

In the early years, Marie Antoinette was relatively popular among the subjects of the Bourbon crown. Many hopes and ambitions rode upon her narrow shoulders, because the old king was widely detested. When the dauphin ascended the throne, it was thought, his young wife would have borne him many children. The dynasty would be reinvigorated, secure, and France would march forward along the road of enlightenment and progress. But no children were conceived. Meanwhile, Marie Antoinette found the French court stiff and cool, her husband distant and inept. Ignoring her mother's cautionary letters, the young woman drifted into intrigues at court, going so far as to insult the king's favorite, Madame du Barry, whom Marie Antoinette, as the ranking woman at Versailles, saw as undeserving of the influence she commanded. This marked the beginning of a road that would lead her into ever-deeper factionalism and spite.

The year 1774 was a critical one in the life of Marie Antoinette. Louis XV died and Louis XVI succeeded him with Marie Antoinette as his proud queen. In the same year, the queen met the comte de Fersen, a young Swede who was eventually to become her lover and, until the end of his life, her most devoted admirer and defender. And it was the year that Marie Antoinette first saw a particular diamond necklace that was to do her incalculable harm. Encountering the disapproval of the older, sedate elements at court, she appears to have retaliated by launching herself onto a treacherous sea of conspicuous hedonism.

The France that the new royal couple inherited was the focus of the Enlightenment, a progressive movement at once reformist, literary, and scientific. Yet it was not the serene realm dreamed of by the celebrated philosophers of the day. The nation had been defeated in war, was financially insecure, and was torn between the claims of the aristocracy, the royal courts, and the bureaucracy. France was also regarded as despotic by its great thinkers such as Voltaire, Diderot, and Rousseau and so became the object of intellectual disdain. Most of this was beyond Marie Antoinette's comprehension. Bored with the endless ceremony of Versailles, the queen discovered the entertaining world of Parisian society while the larger world of France discovered its new monarch well intended but ineffective. Many were sure that her mother, the Austrian queen, was to blame.

As Marie Antoinette lived only for amusement and paid scant attention to Louis, he, strangely enough, doted on her. He indulged her every whim, including expending two million livres on the Little Trianon, a miniature palace on the Versailles grounds. There, Marie Antoinette and her friends put on amateur plays, indulged in flirtations, and, when the mood struck them, pretended to be cowherds and milkmaids and simple folk. In these last years of the 1770s, Marie Antoinette's reputation declined not only because of her extravagance, but also because it was widely believed that she had taken a series of lovers and, therefore, betrayed her husband and sovereign. Even her friendships with women, such as the *Princess de Lamballe (1749–1792) and the *Comtesse de Polignac (1749–1793), were rumored to be indecent. To a considerable degree, these allegations stemmed from the Diamond Necklace Affair.

A cunning cardinal, Prince Louis de Rohan, sought the queen's favor for personal advancement. Duped by a dishonest young woman, Madame 🎵▶ Jeanne La Motte, and her friends, he was persuaded that the queen coveted a particular diamond necklace worth more than a million and half livres. By 1785, Rohan had bought the necklace and, in the night hours, met a young woman in the Versailles gardens, whom he assumed to be the queen, and gave her the necklace. The woman gave Rohan a note promising

to pay with Marie Antoinette's forged signature. Of course, it was all a swindle. Though Marie Antoinette was not involved in the proceedings, it was made to look as though she, rather than the imposter, had been responsible—that she had taken the necklace without paying for it. The affair became public, and the queen was insulted and outraged. The king had Rohan arrested and tried, but the justices exonerated him, probably because of their growing hatred of the queen. The populace sided with Rohan, seeing the queen as duplicitous and the king as a cuckold and a fool. From then on, no libel against the queen was too extravagant to believe. Pornography featuring the queen as a nymphomaniac and lesbian flourished and could be found in the Parisian streets and the halls of Versailles.

> *The handful of pale dust . . . was the last trace of that long-dead woman who in her day had been the goddess of grace and of taste, and subsequently the queen of many sorrows.*
>
> —Stefan Zweig, on the uncovering of Marie Antoinette's remains

Ironically, as the queen's reputation diminished in this period of her life, she and her husband finally accomplished the most important task of any royal couple. They conceived children. A simple operation in 1777 corrected the king's phymosis, and in December 1778 the queen gave birth to a girl, *Marie Thérèse Charlotte. A dauphin was born in 1781, only to die in 1789. But a second dauphin, Louis Charles, was born in 1785 and Princess Sophie Beatrix in 1786, only to die a year later. The children sobered the queen somewhat, and the delivery of male offspring restored a small measure of royal popularity. But the queen's basic personality was not altered, and the king remained benign but befuddled by events he could not control. Still searching for the great passion of her life, Marie Antoinette, long in love with the comte de Fersen, found her fulfillment with him in 1785. She was 30 years old.

Meanwhile, the ground was beginning to tremble beneath them. France's economy was in a long decline, and royal government suffered from costly and unsuccessful wars and inefficient financial management. The royal debt climbed yearly, and Marie Antoinette's extravagances helped not at all. The root of the problem was not so much national poverty but a hopelessly complex and antiquated system of administration and taxation. By the 1780s, the fear of royal bankruptcy haunted the middle classes, and, influ-

🎵▶

See sidebar on the following page

✤▶ La Motte, Jeanne de Valois, countess de
(1756–1791)

French adventurer. Name variations: Madame La Motte; Jeanne Lamotte; Jeanne de Valois, countess de la Motte; Countess de La Motte. Born Jeanne de Saint-Rémy de Valois in 1756; died in 1791; daughter of a poor farmer in Champagne; married Nicolas de La Motte (a soldier).

Jeanne de Saint-Rémy de Valois was born in 1756, the daughter of a poor farmer from Champagne who was one of the last of the Valois; he was a direct descendant of the French king, Henry II. After her father died and left her penniless, Jeanne de Valois was aided by a kindly marquise who had her background authenticated, and she was granted an annual pension of 800 livres by Louis XVI. She spent the next few years petitioning the court for more. *Madame Elisabeth convinced the king to double the amount.

Jeanne de Valois married Nicolas de La Motte, a soldier in the police militia, whom she referred to as a count, and together they set out to recoup the Valois estates. Since the legacy had already been put in the hands of the Orléans family, Jeanne had to recover the money some other way. Thus, she became involved in the Affair of the Diamond Necklace (L'Affaire du Collier), which took place during 1783–84.

Jeanne de Valois, now the Countess de La Motte, befriended the cardinal Louis de Rohan, who for eight years had been out of favor at court, most especially out of the queen's favor. La Motte persuaded him that she was an intimate friend of *Marie Antoinette and promised that she would use her influence to help the queen change her mind about him. In May 1874, she told Rohan that on his next visit to Versailles, the queen would show her change of heart by slightly inclining her head. Subsequently, while in the queen's presence, Rohan was sure he saw her do just that, not once, but several times. La Motte then hired a Palais Royal prostitute to impersonate Marie Antoinette. Wearing a flowing gown and a wide-brimmed hat with veil, the prostitute met with the cardinal in the park of Versailles at 11 o'clock on a moonless summer night; the cardinal kissed her hem, and she gave him a rose.

Meanwhile, the queen's jeweler had made an opulent diamond necklace expressly for Marie Antoinette but could not convince her to purchase it. The queen said she had a diamond necklace, wore it rarely, and did not need another. When King Louis offered to buy it for her, she again turned it down, saying that the money would be better spent on a ship for the French fleet.

Aware of the jeweler's frustration, La Motte confided to Rohan that the queen wished to buy a diamond necklace, on credit and without the king's knowledge, and wanted him to act as security. With the help of a duped Rohan and a forged document that stated the queen's acceptance of the terms of purchase—1,600,000 livres to be paid off in three monthly installments—La Motte convinced the jeweler to give her the necklace. She and her husband then broke up the necklace and sold the jewels.

In 1786, the plot was revealed, and Rohan and La Motte were arrested. Rohan was acquitted, but La Motte was branded and imprisoned. The following year, she escaped from jail and joined her husband in England. Countess de La Motte then wrote her memoirs before dying from a drunken fall from a three-story window. Though historians now know that Marie Antoinette was completely innocent in the Affair of the Necklace, at the time she was discredited by the incident, and it exacerbated the public's suspicions about her. Countess de La Motte's autobiography was published in 1793, two years after her death, and Alexander Dumas père later wrote the well-known historical novel, *Le Collier de la Reine* (1849–50), based on her scam.

---

enced by the Enlightenment, they demanded a modern, efficient, constitutional state. Inspired by the American Revolution, all classes of French society yearned for personal liberty and an end to the absolute model of the state, which, no doubt, allowed for many injustices and abuses. Louis tried to take matters in hand and appointed a series of reformist ministers such as Jacques Turgot and Jacques Necker. But serious change would alter France's ancient social structure and reduce the privileges of the aristocracy and the clergy. Resistance was certain, and the friends of the old order, including the king's younger brothers, the comte de Provence and the comte d'Artois, found their champion in the queen. Convinced that her associates would lose the generous allowances she had secured for them should the schemes of the reformers be implemented, Marie Antoinette became known as "Madame Veto" by influencing Louis to evade change and dismiss the reformers.

It is doubtful that Marie Antoinette guessed at the profound currents animating French society by the late 1780s. No more than the king could she have foreseen the consequences of the summoning of an Estates General to Versailles in 1789. Hard pressed by the mounting debt, stung by criticisms by the nobility, and worried

by popular disturbances caused by food shortages and high prices, the king decided to call elected deputies of the clergy, nobility, and commons to find a way out. Unwilling to settle for a limited agenda or half measures, however, the deputies of the Third Estate, or commons, demanded far-reaching changes, including a written constitution to limit the monarchy and define the rights of French "citizens." These demands were underscored by ominous popular violence in Paris, in other French cities, and in the countryside. Unwittingly, Louis, by issuing an invitation for limited reform to save the royal finances, had touched off an uncontrollable revolution.

The Revolution that began in 1789, commenced as an endeavor by nobles and progressive members of the middle-class to modernize France, was altered almost immediately by the explosion of popular violence directed toward the destruction of legal and economic inequality, and matured in the early 1790s into a determined crusade to create a democratic republic of virtue. In time, the Revolution displayed an in-

tolerance of dissent more bloody and grim than any tyranny of the Bourbon monarchy.

When the Estates General was transformed into a National Assembly in June 1789, drastic changes in French life came rapidly. Many nobles and some of the royal family fled the realm. But Louis and Marie Antoinette stayed on, trying to shore up what was left of the monarchy. Perhaps still unaware of the magnitude of events, the king and queen were surprised when a mob of women, angry over rising bread prices in Paris, marched on Versailles in October and demanded that the royal couple come to the city and "do something" to relieve their plight. Marie Antoinette barely escaped death at the hands of the women, for whom she was plainly a symbol of royal indulgence and corruption, but that was only the beginning of a long melancholy train of humiliations and endangerments.

Taken to the Tuileries in Paris, the king and queen and their children were, in effect, held hostage to the demands of both the National Assembly and the more radical city government.

Marie Antoinette imprisoned in the Temple.

Around them swirled innumerable intrigues and counterplots, but the tide was running strongly against them. Louis finally accepted the idea of a constitutional monarchy, but the queen was made of stronger stuff and urged him to resist. If necessary, the royal family should flee the country and find help at foreign courts to destroy the Revolution in its infancy. Louis procrastinated, but, outraged by revolutionary assaults on the Church, finally agreed to a scheme to escape Paris on June 20, 1791, under a plan developed by the comte de Fersen.

By an incredibly bad stroke of fortune, the royal couple, with Marie Antoinette disguised as a noblewoman and Louis as her manservant, were recognized and apprehended at Varennes, only a few miles from the French border. Returned to Paris, the king sullenly agreed to the newly drafted Constitution of 1791, which severely limited his powers.

The royal couple were now virtually prisoners, although Louis tried to play the role of constitutional monarch. For a time, little could be done. Then, in 1792, the revolutionary government went to war with Austria and Prussia, determined to liberate Europe from kings. When the war went badly, however, suspicion of treachery fell upon the king and queen and their moderate supporters. In August, a mob broke into the Tuileries, murdered the king's bodyguards, and demanded the overthrow of the king. The frightened Assembly concurred, and the royal family was imprisoned in a tower called the Temple.

Time was running out for Marie Antoinette and her husband. A terrible terror seized Paris in September, leading to a horrible massacre of royalist and noble prisoners in the thousands. Among the victims was Marie Antoinette's closest friend, the Princess de Lamballe, whose mutilated body was displayed to the appalled queen. In December, Louis was brought to trial for treason against the Revolution. Compromising documents were discovered in a secret safe that incriminated the king by showing his correspondence with counter-revolutionaries. No one doubted the queen's connivance. Separated from his family until the night before his execution, Louis exhibited quiet courage and dignity as he said his farewells to his family. For Marie Antoinette, it must have been painful to say goodbye to the father of her children. How far they had come together since she first saw him at Compiegne 23 years before. On the next day, January 21, 1793, the king was executed.

Marie Antoinette now awaited her own inevitable end. But, before then, she would be forced to drink the full bitter cup. The "Widow Capet," as she was called, was repeatedly insulted and humiliated, then, in July, separated from her remaining son. She never saw him again. Meanwhile, he was subjected to great pressures to bring evidence against his mother. Eventually, he was made to say that she, along with *Madame Elisabeth, her sister-in-law, had introduced him to masturbation. No crime was too extreme to charge against the "Austrian harpy." Before the Revolutionary Tribunal, the queen conducted herself with a resolution unknown to her earlier years. Rejecting the infamous charges of incest, she appealed beyond the court to the generations to come by asking any mother who might hear her words if such an act were imaginable.

The revolutionary painter Jacques Louis David sketched Marie Antoinette in the tumbrel on the way to the guillotine on October 16, 1793. She is depicted as a barren, haggard old woman with hands tied behind her back. Her hair had gone entirely white, but in the portrait, as in history, she showed no sign of fear. Moments later, her bleeding head was lifted to the crowd. Then it was placed between the legs of

The revolutionary painter Jacques Louis David sketched Marie Antoinette in the tumbrel on the way to the guillotine.

her corpse and carried away to be tossed in a common grave in the Madeleine cemetery. She was not yet 38 years old.

SOURCES:

Schama, Simon. *Citizens: A Chronicle of the French Revolution.* NY: Alfred A. Knopf, 1989.

Scott, Samuel F., and Rothaus, Barry, eds. *Historical Dictionary of the French Revolution 1789–1799.* CT: Greenwood Press, 1985.

Zweig, Stefan. *Marie Antoinette: The Portrait of an Average Woman.* NY: Viking Press, 1933 (reissued, Harmony Books, 1984).

SUGGESTED READING:

Erickson, Carolly. *To the Scaffold: The Life of Marie-Antoinette.* NY: Morrow, 1991.

Gershoy, Leo. *The French Revolution and Napoleon.* NY: Appleton-Century Crofts, 1964.

Haslip, Joan. *Marie Antoinette.* London: Weidenfeld & Nicolson, 1987.

Seward, Desmond. *Marie Antoinette.* London: Constable, 1981.

C. David Rice, Ph.D.,
chair and professor, Department of History, Central Missouri State University, Warrensburg, Missouri

Marie Antoinette of Spain (1729–1785).

See Maria Antonia of Spain.

Marie-Barbara of Portugal (1711–1758).

See Maria Barbara of Braganza.

Marie Caroline (1752–1814).

See Maria Carolina.

Marie Caroline Ferdinande Louise of Naples (1798–1870).

See Caroline of Naples.

Marie Casimir (1641–1716)

Queen of Poland. Name variations: Maria Casimira; Marie Casimere d'Arquien; Marie de la Grange d'Arquien; Marie Casimire de la Grange d'Arquien; Marysienka; Marie Kazimiere or Kazimierz; Marie Sobieski. Born in 1641 in Nevers, France; died on January 30, 1716, in Blois, France; daughter of Henri, marquis d'Arquien, and Françoise de la Chatre; married John Zamoyski (a Polish noble), in 1658 (died 1665); married Jan III also known as John III Sobieski (1624–1696), king of Poland (r. 1674–1696), in 1655; children: Constantine Sobieski; Alexander Sobieski; Teresa Sobieski also known as Cunigunde Sobieska; James Sobieski (who married Hedwig Wittelsbach); grandchildren: *Clementina Sobieski (1702–1735, who married James Francis Edward, the Old Pretender).

Marie Casimir, known as Marysienka, was born into the minor French nobility. Her mother served as governess to the princess *Louise Marie de Gonzague. When Louise Marie left France for Poland in 1645 to marry the Polish king, four-year-old Marie Casimir accompanied her as part of her entourage. Marie Casimir was thus raised in the Polish royal court at Warsaw, and became the queen's favorite maid of honor. In 1658, the queen arranged a marriage for 17-year-old Marie with John Zamoyski, a 31-year-old wealthy noble and a leader of the Polish army. Zamoyski was highly favored by the king and queen, who encouraged his marriage to the young French noblewoman as a means of showing their desire for friendship with the powerful French king, Louis XIV. The couple moved from the royal palace in Warsaw to Zamoyski's vast estates at Zamosc, but the marriage soon proved to be a failure. Zamoyski was an alcoholic, and was jealous and controlling of his young wife. Marie had three children, all of whom died shortly after birth.

To escape her domestic problems, Marie Casimir often returned for long periods to Warsaw, residing again in the queen's household. There she developed a friendship with John (III) Sobieski, a Polish noble who was quickly emerging as a great military leader. By the time he met and fell in love with Marie Casimir, Sobieski was already regarded as a national hero by the Polish people for protecting Poland from its Swedish, Russian, and Ottoman enemies. Over the course of several years the two developed a close relationship, primarily through an increasingly intimate correspondence.

When John Zamoyski died suddenly in 1665, Marie Casimir quickly agreed to marry Sobieski, who was by now commander in chief of the army. Queen Louise Marie made every effort to hasten the nuptials, because she saw a potential advantage in strengthening the ties between Poland and France through this union between the young French widow and Poland's military commander. Marie Casimir and John Sobieski were married in a secret ceremony only three weeks after Zamoyski's death; they were married again in a public ceremony two months later. The extreme haste of Marie Casimir's second wedding was a scandal at the royal court and brought her the disapproval of her own family, the Polish nobility, and the Polish people, criticism which would follow her throughout her life.

Despite the uproar, neither Marie Casimir nor John Sobieski regretted their marriage. They were in love and shared ambitions for Sobieski's political advancement. Marie Casimir did not hesitate to use her French relatives to try to help her husband's career by seeking support for his endeavors from the French king and nobility. As Sobieski was often away on campaigns, their marital life is preserved in the long letters he wrote Marie (most of her letters have not survived). These letters describe his battles, Marie's political intrigues at the court in Warsaw and abroad, as well as the intimate details of their relationship. It is clear from his letters that Sobieski trusted her political instinct, while depending on her to find support for him from France and to keep him current on events in the capital. Writes historian L.R. Lewitter:

> Her beauty and vivacity were to Sobieski and Poland, what Cleopatra's nose had been to Caesar and Rome. Though to explain the whole of Sobieski's conduct from now on in terms of the sublimation of his passion for Marysienka would be a piece of gross oversimplification, it cannot be denied that she was a major and sometimes dominant influence in his life.

With the reigning king John II Casimir aging and his power weakening, Marie and John Sobieski began planning for Sobieski's election as the next king of Poland. Hoping to win important financial and military aid from France, Marie Casimir made several extended journeys back to France in the late 1660s, where she successfully solicited support from Louis XIV. It was on one of these journeys that her first son, James, was born in Paris in 1668.

Despite her efforts and Sobieski's national status, however, in 1669 the Polish nobility elected another candidate, Michael II Wisniowiecki, as king. Even so, Marie Casimir and John Sobieski continued their campaign in Poland and abroad for Sobieski's advancement, and when the new king died in 1673, Sobieski was chosen king of Poland. Aid from the French in money and troops was important in determining the outcome of the election, for which Marie Casimir deserves some of the credit.

As with most foreign-born queens, Marie Casimir was never popular with her subjects, although her husband enjoyed great popularity. At the time, France and its powerful army were viewed with suspicion by Poles, and a French queen was easily suspected of disloyalty to her adopted country. Marie Casimir was criticized for extravagant spending and accused of wasting the national treasury, and her subjects feared she would influence the king to allow France to dominate Polish affairs, even that she would help Louis XIV take control of Poland. It is true that Marie Casimir made every effort to win Louis' favor, but not with the intention of giving him

power in Poland; instead, she wanted him to raise her family's status in France. She petitioned King Louis frequently, and often successfully, for grants of estates and titles for her parents and siblings.

The queen also figured frequently in Louis XIV's correspondence with his diplomats in Warsaw, as he encouraged them to keep themselves in her favor because of her political influence. Yet by 1683 the Polish-French alliance had foundered, as John III and Marie Casimir came to prefer an alliance with the Habsburg rulers of Austria—France's enemy—for Poland's protection against the Ottoman Empire and Russia. The French alliance was later revived, but Marie Casimir shrewdly negotiated the marriage of her eldest son James Sobieski with a Habsburg princess, *Hedwig Wittlesbach, to maintain Austria's friendship.

After 1692, John Sobieski's age and declining health forced him to withdraw from active military and governmental leadership. As his efforts to unite the Polish aristocracy and strengthen the monarchy had for the most part failed, there was increasing instability within the kingdom during his final years, although his military achievements had made it safe from foreign invasion. There was also growing discord within the Sobieski family, as the king's three sons each hoped to be the new elected ruler; in particular, Marie Casimir promoted her son Alexander against her eldest son James.

With the king incapacitated, the queen acted as unofficial regent of Poland from 1692 until his death in 1696. She reaffirmed relations with France and arranged for a treaty of aid from Louis XIV; with Louis' support she was gratified to see her father named a cardinal by the pope in 1695. Marie Casimir also negotiated the marriage of her only daughter, *Cunigunde Sobieska, with the elector of Bavaria. However, Marie was unable to achieve a lasting peace with the Ottoman Empire, though it had been much weakened by the Polish king's military victories.

King John III died in 1696, leaving a kingdom uncertain of its future and a family divided in its political ambitions. The election of the new king was violently contested. Marie Casimir initially hoped to arrange for the election of her favorite son, Alexander, as the next king; her oldest son James also wanted the throne, and the French king was backing a French candidate. Marie Casimir eventually came to question Alexander's chances, and alternately favored James and her son-in-law Maximilian II Emmanuel, elector of Bavaria. In June 1697, a fifth candidate was finally chosen by the Polish nobility.

Defeated in her attempts to promote the Sobieski dynasty, Marie Casimir moved to Rome with her son Alexander in 1698, leaving her sons James and Constantine in Poland. She was welcomed in Rome, honored as the widow of the celebrated warrior who had conquered the Turkish threat to European security. She participated actively in the court life of Rome's elite and was often at the Vatican, where she enjoyed the friendship of Pope Clement XI. After her father's death in 1707, Marie Casimir successfully petitioned Louis XIV for permission to return to France, although seven years were to pass before she actually left Rome. In 1714, she settled in the royal château at Blois, which had been lavishly redecorated and furnished at King Louis' expense to make it suitable for a widowed queen. In her final years at Blois, she was reconciled with her sons James and Constantine.

Marie Casimir died at Blois on January 30, 1716, at age 75. The French king ordered a state funeral to be held, but conflicts arose over where she should be buried. Finally, in December 1716 James Sobieski arranged for her body to be taken to Warsaw and interred near King John III, in accordance with her final wishes.

SOURCES:

Lewitter, L.R. "John Sobieski: Savior of Vienna," in *History Today*. March–April 1962.

Morton, J.B. *Sobieski, King of Poland*. London: Eyre and Spottiswoode, 1932.

Verneret, Hubert. *Marie de la Grange d'Arquien, 1641–1716*. Paris: Editions de l'Armançon, 1997.

SUGGESTED READING:

Dalerac, M. *Polish Manuscripts: or the Secret History of the Reign of John Sobieski, The III. of that Name, K. of Poland*. Printed for D. Rhodes, at the Star, near Fleet-Bridge, 1700.

Davies, Norman. *God's Playground: A History of Poland*. Columbia University Press, 1982.

Garlicki, Andrzej, ed. *Poczet krolow i ksiazat polskich*. Czytelnik, 1980.

Laskowski, O. *Sobieski: King of Poland*. Glasgow, 1944.

Mizwa, Stephen, ed. *Great Men and Women of Poland*. Macmillan, 1941.

Stoye, John. *The Siege of Vienna*. Holt, 1964.

Swiecicka, Maria, trans. *The Memoirs of Jan Chryzostom z Goslawic Pasek*. Kosciuszko Foundation, 1978.

Laura York,
freelance writer in medieval and women's history,
Riverside, California

Marie-Cecile Hohenzollern (1942—)

Prussian royal. Name variations: Marie-Cecile of Oldenburg. Born Mary Cecily Kira Victoria Louise on May 28, 1942; daughter of Louis Ferdinand, prince of Prussia, and *Kira of Russia (1909–1967); married Frederick Augustus of Oldenburg, December 3, 1965; children: three.

Marie Christine of Bavaria (1660–1690).

See Maria Anna of Bavaria.

Marie Clotilde (d. 1794)

Saint. Died in 1794; her feast day is October 23.

Caught in the upheaval of the French Revolution, Marie Clotilde, mother superior of an Ursuline convent at Valenciennes, became a political and religious martyr, as did the 32 sisters under her supervision. In August 1792, the Ursulines were ordered by municipal officials to vacate their convent, at which time they were also deprived of their teaching rights. By September 17 of that year, all but five of the sisters (left behind due to illness) were furnished with passports and taken to the Belgian city of Mons by carriage. They remained there until November of the following year when they returned to Valenciennes, now occupied by the Austrians. Permitted back into the convent, with their teaching rights restored, the order flourished for a short time, even taking in three dispossessed nuns—two Brigittines and a Poor Clare. However, when the French liberated Valenciennes in August 1794, the nuns were numbered among those suspected of sympathizing with the former regime and were imprisoned in their convent. While two-thirds escaped, 11 others, including Marie Clotilde and three who also became saints, **Marie Claire, Marie Anne,** and **Marie Rose,** were sentenced to die by hanging. They were executed in the marketplace in two groups, on October 17 and 23, 1794. All mounted the scaffold with the courage of the faithful, declaring that they were happy to have returned to Valenciennes "to teach the Catholic, apostolic, and Roman religion."

Barbara Morgan,
Melrose, Massachusetts

Marie Clotilde (1759–1802)

Queen of Sardinia. Name variations: *Clotilde or Clothilde; Clotilde de France or Clotilde of France; Marie-Clotilde. Born on September 23, 1759; died on March 7, 1802; daughter of *Marie Josèphe of Saxony (1731–1767) and Louis (1729–1765), dauphin of France; sister of Louis XVI, king of France (r. 1774–1792); married Charles Emmanuel IV, king of Sardinia (r. 1796–1802), on September 6, 1775.*

Marie d'Autriche (1505–1558).

See Mary of Hungary.

Marie d'Autriche (1528–1603).

See Elisabeth of Habsburg (1554–1592) for sidebar on Marie of Austria.

Marie de Bourbon (1393–1438), **prioress of Poissy.**

See Marie.

Marie de Bourbon (fl. 1350s)

French noblewoman and prioress of Poissy. Flourished in the 1350s at convent of Poissy, France; daughter of Isabelle of Savoy (d. 1383) and Pierre or Peter I (1311–1356), duke of Bourbon (r. 1342–1356); sister of Jeanne de Bourbon (1338–1378), queen of France; never married; no children.

Marie de Bourbon, the daughter of *Isabelle of Savoy and Peter I, duke of Bourbon, became a highly respected prioress. She was closely connected to the royal house of France through her sister *Jeanne de Bourbon who married Charles V, king of France (1337–1380). Marie seems to have been a younger daughter whom her parents did not need for a marriage alliance, for she was given to the Dominican convent of Poissy (near Paris) when she was only four years old. She took the vows of a nun at age 17 and remained at Poissy the rest of her life. Marie grew up extremely well educated among over 200 other noble daughters who had not married for one reason or another, for Poissy was at the time a fashionable convent. Admission was restricted to noble girls whose parents gained permission from the king for their daughter's entrance. The convent was atypical for this very reason, for most often convents were the shelter of poor women or women who felt a strong calling to a religious life. The noblewomen at Poissy also brought substantial wealth with them in the form of lands granted or cash "dowries."

Marie de Bourbon was elected prioress of Poissy in her early 30s, and distinguished herself in that position for 20 years. Although she was a pious administrator, she ran the house almost as if it were a rich noble's castle; the prioress entertained noble guests, maintained a large garden with a fountain and pond complete with white swans, and dined with her nuns on gold and silver plates. Among the nuns at Poissy under Marie's rule was the daughter (name unknown) of the renowned poet and author *Christine de Pizan. In a poem Christine composed after a visit to Poissy, she describes Marie as a gracious and awe-inspiring spiritual leader.

SOURCES:

Gies, Frances, and Joseph Gies. *Women in the Middle Ages.* NY: Harper and Row, 1978.

LaBarge, Margaret. *A Small Sound of the Trumpet: Women in Medieval Life.* Boston: Beacon Press, 1986.

Laura York,
Riverside, California

Marie de Bourbon (fl. 1440s)

*Duchess of Calabria. Flourished in the 1440s; daughter of *Agnes of Burgundy (d. 1476) and Charles I, duke of Bourbon (r. 1434–1456); married John II (1424–1470), duke of Calabria; children: Nicholas, duke of Anjou (1448–1473).*

Marie de Bourbon (1606–1627).

See Montpensier, Anne Marie Louise d'Orléans, Duchess de for sidebar.

Marie de Bourbon

*Princess of Carignan. Married Thomas Francis, prince of Carignan or Carignano (died 1656); children: Emmanuel Philibert (d. 1709); Eugene (d. 1673, who married *Olympia Mancini).*

Marie de Bourgogne.

Variant of Mary of Burgundy.

Marie de Brabant (c. 1530–c. 1600)

French poet. Born around 1530 in France; died around 1600 in France; daughter of John of Brabant (Jean de Brabant); married Claude de Tourotte.

A well-educated daughter of the nobility, Marie de Brabant married Claude de Tourotte, a French noble who seems to have encouraged his wife's intellectual pursuits. Marie showed a remarkable aptitude for learning and composing poetry, and by virtue of her class was allowed to nourish her talents. Somewhat of a moralist, she composed epistles against what she considered the lewd and scandalous behavior of French women of the lower classes. She also translated foreign works in verse into French, achieving a considerable reputation. In 1602, she published *A Declaration of the Spirit of the Faithful Soul* as well as her translation of the *Song of Songs.*

Laura York,
Riverside, California

Marie de Champagne (1145–1198)

*Countess of Champagne. Name variations: Marie, countess of Champagne; Marie of Champagne; Mary of Champagne; Mary Capet; Mary of France; possibly, Marie de France. Born in 1145; died in 1198; daughter of Eleanor of Aquitaine (1122–1204) and Louis VII, king of France (r. 1137–1180); sister of *Alice (1150–c. 1197), countess of Blois; married Henry I, count of Champagne, around 1164; children: Henry I, king of Jerusalem (Henry II of Champagne); Theobald III, count of Champagne; *Marie of Champagne (c. 1180–1203); *Scholastica of Champagne (d. 1219).*

*Eleanor of Aquitaine's daughter Marie, who became the countess of Champagne, was a literary patron in her own right, commissioning courtly romances from such poets as Chretien de Troyes. Chretien's works include "Lancelot, or The Knight of the Cart," and other Arthurian romances. Some think that the woman known only as *Marie de France, who wrote many popular *lais* (story-songs), was either Marie of Champagne or ❧➤ Emma de Gatinais, an illegitimate sister of Henry II and thus Eleanor of Aquitaine's sister-in-law.

Marie de Champagne (c. 1180–1203).

See Marie of Champagne.

Marie de Chatillon (r. 1230–1241)

Countess of Blois and Chartres. Reigned from 1230 to 1241; died in 1241; married Hugues de Chatillon, count of Saint-Pol; children: son Jean de Chatillon, count of Blois and Chartres (r. 1241–1279); granddaughter: Jeanne de Chatillon, countess of Blois and Chartres (r. 1279–1292).

Marie de Chatillon inherited Blois on the death of *Marguerite, countess of Blois, in 1230; she ruled until 1241. Her granddaughter *Jeanne de Chatillon would be ruler of Blois from 1279 to 1292.

Marie de Courtenay (fl. 1215)

Empress of Byzantium. Name variations: Marie or Mary of Courtenay; daughter of Yolande of Courtenay (d. 1219) and Pierre II also known as Peter II of Courtenay, emperor of Constantinople; third wife of Theodore I Lascaris, Byzantine emperor (r. 1204–1222); no children.

❧➤ **Emma de Gatinais** (fl. 1150–1170)
Princess of Gwynedd. Daughter of Geoffrey IV, count of Anjou; mother unknown; illegitimate half-sister of Henry II, king of England (r. 1154–1189); married David I, prince of Gwynedd, about 1174; children: two.

Marie de Courtenay, the third wife of Theodore I Lascaris, was a pawn in her husband's political career. Following the death of the first empress ❧➤ **Anna Angelina**, and his divorce from his second wife, *Philippa of Lesser Armenia, Theodore was eager to end hostilities with Constantinople, which at the time was ruled by empress *Yolande of Courtenay. He convinced Yolande to allow him to marry her young daughter Marie de Courtenay, believing, no doubt, that any male offspring from the union might heal the breach between the rival imperial lines. As it turned out, however, the couple had no children, and upon Theodore's death, the throne went to his daughter by Anna Angelina, *Irene Lascaris, who ruled with her husband John III Ducas Vatatzes.

SOURCES:
Head, Constance. *Imperial Byzantine Portraits.* New Rochelle, NY: Caratzas Brothers, 1982.

Marie de France (c. 1140–1200)

French writer who lived and worked in England and is most famous for her short tales dealing with romantic love and court life. Name variations: Marie of France. Specifics of Marie's life are not known with certainty. She was born around 1140 and died around 1200; she was French but lived in England in the late 12th century, at, or associated with, the court of Henry II and Eleanor of Aquitaine; she may have been an abbess; wrote fables, a religious tract, and courtly short stories (called lais*).*

Selected writings: Fables; Lais: "Bisclavret," "Chaitivel," "Chevrefoil," "Eliduc," "Equitan," "Guigemar," "Lanval," "Laüstic," "Le Fresne," "Les Deus Amanz," "Milun," "Yonec"; The Purgatory of Saint Patrick.

The exact identity of Marie de France is a mystery. We know from her writings that she was French; however, she spent her life in England. Marie's birth and death dates are not known, but we deduce that she wrote between approximately 1155 and 1199. She might have lived in the Angevin (Anglo-French) court of Henry II of Eng-

◀❧
Anna Angelina.
See Irene Lascaris for sidebar.

land to whom the *lais* were probably dedicated. Some theorize that Marie was ❧▶ **Emma de Gatinais**, the illegitimate daughter of Geoffrey of Anjou (which would make her a half-sister to Henry II), and that she later became abbess of Shaftesbury where early manuscript copies of her *lais* were found. Others have speculated that she was a nun at Reading, or ◀❧ **Isabel of Beaumont,** or one of the daughters of Stephen of Blois. Marie's contemporary, Denis Pyramus, referred to her simply as Dame Marie. Emil Winkler has suggested that Marie de France and *Marie de Champagne (daughter of *Eleanor of Aquitaine and Louis VII of France) were one and the same person. Much of the speculation as to Marie's identity is based on the tone of her works. Emanuel Mickel argues that the *lais* which are predominately worldly in style and theme, were written early, in a secular, courtly setting, and that the more pietistic *Purgatory of Saint Patrick* and *Fables* were written at a later point when Marie had retired to religious life. This hypothesis is questionable, however, because in the literary climate of the 12th century, profane, sacred, allegorical, satirical, and didactic works were produced alike in and out of monastic circles.

Whatever her exact identity, Marie was well educated, and, therefore, has been assumed to be high born. If, in fact, she was raised in the court of Henry II, Marie would have been acquainted with noted intelligentsia and literati of the period as Henry and his wife Eleanor were famed patrons of the literary arts. Marie knew Latin, French, English, Welsh, and the dialect of the Bretons. In the prologue to the *Fables*, the first *lai*, and *The Purgatory of Saint Patrick,* Marie indicates that she is intimate with, and jealously competitive within, contemporary literary circles. The prologue to the *Fables* states, "It may be that many clerks will take my labor on themselves. I don't want any of them to claim it."

Marie de France composed her works at a time when Western Europe was the scene of a confluence of cultural trends which had been developing for several centuries. Many factors favored an acceleration of societal change in what has been called the 12th-century Renaissance.

The demands of and opportunities for commerce, stimulated, in part, by the crusades, made city living a possibility for increasing numbers of people. Urban centers provided the environment in which cathedral schools and, by the end of the century, universities developed.

The monastic population also changed in the 12th century. The Cistercian order drew part of its membership from adult converts who had known the world—men and women who had married, parented children, been to war. This resulted in a changed intellectual and literary emphasis in some monasteries. A secular or courtly literary style was developed and romance themes and sources, originating in the lay world from which the converts had come, were allegorized. The ubiquitous love theme was also expanded in works such as those by Bernard of Clairvaux, where love is expressed in various ways—for instance, by the love of Christ for the Church.

The distinctiveness of the century lies in the manner in which various trends and views were reorganized, reevaluated and codified. Marie de France was in the forefront of this process of cultural introspection and redefinition. The particular element of 12th-century culture which Marie engaged was the subject of romantic love, which is the dominant theme in the most important of her works, the *Lais*.

Marie's position as an innovator in the genre of the courtly *lai* is generally agreed upon. The word *lai* comes from a Celtic root meaning song. The *lai* was originally a musical composition commemorating an important historical event. It is organized for maximum intensity and based around symbols which parallel the plot of the *lai* and give a hint to its meaning. It was Marie who first retold the Celtic stories in French and changed the form of the material into narrative, rhyming, octosyllabic couplets which de-emphasize the lyric content and are not intended to be sung. Marie's style is distinctive in its use of unifying motifs, deceptively simple language, repetition, and economy of expression.

Marie de France also influenced the literature of the period by her contribution to the vogue of retelling Celtic legends, the most famous of which are stories of King Arthur and his court. An important element of this Celtic literary tradition which Marie manipulates masterfully is the use of magic as a plot device. The *lai* called "Lanval," set in Arthur's court, is about a knight who attains the love of a fairy princess and the conflict he experiences in moving between the imperfect world of Camelot and the ideal sphere created by love. In "Guigemar," a

❧▶

Emma de Gatinais. *See Marie de Champagne for sidebar.*

❧▶ **Isabel of Beaumont** (fl. 1150)

English royal. Name variations: Isabel Beaumont; Isabel de Beaumont. Flourished around 1150; daughter of Waleran of Meulan also known as Waleran de Beaumont (1104–1166), earl of Worcester; married Maurice de Craon.

talking fawn reveals the hero's destiny, and a mysterious, un-manned, exotic ship transports him across the ocean to a strange land. At the end of this *lai*, quasi-magical knots reveal the lovers' identities to each other after a long separation. "Yonec" is about a clairvoyant knight from another world who can shape-shift into the form of a bird and, from afar, discern the wishes of his lady as soon as she expresses them. The protagonist periodically, and involuntarily, transmutes into a werewolf and, at one point, is unable to resume his human shape because his clothes are stolen. However, though Marie frequently relies on magic as a narrative device, her major interest is in the forms and varieties of human love, and her *lais* provides an extensive examination of the subject.

For Marie, love is more than just a passion, it is a process of discovery—of the self and of the world in which the self-aware person must live. Love is appraised by Marie based on the manner in which her characters manipulate the emotion. In most of the *lais,* the lovers are in conflict with a world which does not understand them, but the best love is one which is enduring enough to mold the public environment of the character so that the new individual, whom love has created, can exist comfortably within his or her society. In order for a character to maintain the integrity of love and to live in the world, he or she must generally be long suffering, loyal, charitable and ingenious. When characters are too indulgent, concupiscent or anti-social, the world ruins them. Love forms an individual who must, to be successful, recreate the world. A lover who ignores social roles in order to insulate private passions will probably be destroyed by them. At the other extreme, the happiness of a character who ignores private needs in deference to public demands will atrophy. He or she will actualize neither those needs, nor any possibilities for personal growth.

Love is not univocally defined by Marie nor is it morally evaluated in absolute terms, but there is an internal ethical system established in the *lais* by which the author's judgment of her characters is based more on motivation than it is on behavior. Marie (speaking through the *lais*) is clearly a champion of love, even when it is adulterous or premarital; however, she does not value all love relationships equally. For example, in "Equitan," the king and his mistress are ultimately boiled to death when they are caught in a trap set for the lady's husband. They are destroyed because they are guilty of *demesure* (lack of moderation) and flagrant, unjustified disloyalty. By contrast, the love relationship in "Laüstic" dissolves, leaving the couple lonely and un-

fulfilled, because the lovers are not willing enough to impose their will on external impediments, to exercise *engin* (ingenuity), in the service of love. The affair is quickly terminated when it is discovered by the lady's husband. In short, love will not prosper and grow when it is expressed either too rashly or too cautiously.

> *I* shall name myself so that it will be remembered; Marie is my name, I am of France.
>
> —Epilogue, *Fables*

Strength of will, persistence, and personal *engin* must be balanced with passive qualities, such as loyalty and patience, to test and transform love from an enslaving passion to a virtue. To Marie, love and the anguish it brings are natural, but each individual defines himself by the manner in which he responds to this passion. The lady in "Milun" waits 20 years for her valorous knight to return and acknowledge their love and the son who is a product of it. The protagonist of "Yonec" suffers a lifetime in a loveless marriage with an abusive husband before her sufferings are avenged by the son conceived with her hawk lover. The heroine in "Le Fresne" is finally able to marry the king, because through her selfless forbearance, her aristocratic identity is revealed. Relationships suffer when the participants are not able to endure hardship—sometimes humiliation—in the service of love. The young knight in "Les Deus Amanz" is willing to suffer physical asperity to win his lady, but ultimately fails in his task because he can not endure a more difficult trial—the loss of face in the presence of the townspeople. In short, in Marie's *lais*, love demands moral rectitude, forbearance, and restraint, but the rewards to those who endure are a fulfilling relationship and a self made wiser and more complete.

Whether or not Marie should be considered a proponent of courtly love is not clear. There has been a great deal of discussion over the last century about the concept of courtly love and courtly love literature. A particular mode of behavior which operates in medieval literature was identified and labeled *courtois* (courtly) by Gaston Paris in 1883. Since then, scholars have disagreed over whether representations of courtly love reflect an aristocratic code of conduct which was practiced in the courts of Europe or whether it was simply a short-lived literary convention produced for the amusement of a small, elite leisure class. Definitions of courtly love are frustrated by the fact that the precepts of the code vary among courtly authors. Even within the body of work of one writer, the "rules" of the game can be inconsistent. Generally speaking, courtly love is a highly stylized romance between an aristocratic man and woman who are not married to each other, although the woman is usually married to someone else. The man in a courtly love relationship must submit himself to his lady (*domina*) in complete obedience. His service to love parallels the service a feudal vassal owes his lord and is accompanied by a great deal of conventionalized flattery, cajoling, sophistic argumentation and secrecy. The appearance, social standing, and character traits of courtly lovers are also strictly standardized: the ladies are beautiful and wise, the knights are handsome and brave, both are sophisticated in the ways of the court and high-born, although the woman often has a higher social status than the man.

Romance literature and the courtly love *topos* provide a frame of reference for the *lais* of Marie de France; however, her work does not fit simply into either model. Marie often uses the romance motif of "the quest" (*aventure*) to test her characters, and some of the *lais* such as "Equitan," "Chaitivel," and "Laüstic" follow courtly formulas. Other *lais* show only superficial evidence of courtliness. So though Marie often uses courtly terminology and situations, she is not ultimately in sympathy with courtly love as a model of behavior. She frequently associates courtly conduct with characters who do not love "properly" or sincerely. Also, the marital status of her characters is not determinate of their ability to participate in a *fin'amor* (ideal love). For example, the couples in "Le Fresne," "Guigemar," "Milun," and "Eliduc" experience romantic love within their marriages. A few of the stories actually mock chivalric love ideals. In "Guigemar," Marie interjects a telling condemnation of courtly lovers "who have affairs everywhere they go/ then boast about their conquests/ that's not love but folly,/ evil and lechery."

Some historians consider Marie's religious sensibilities important as a clue to her identity: if she was a nun, as suggested by some evidence, why would she compose the *lais*, which are secular, even a-religious, in content and tone? It is difficult, however, to determine Marie's views from the *lais*, especially in regard to sexuality. In some stories, Marie places a Christian veneer on her borrowed material, which is, in many cases, pagan and so inherently non-Christian (in "Yonec" the lady insists that her bird lover take the Eucharist before she will accept him). Some characters specifically articulate that love and sex outside of marriage are wrong. Yet for the most part, violations of Catholic teachings regarding adultery and fornication do not cause a serious moral dilemma for any of Marie's characters. At certain points, Marie herself interrupts the story to make an authorial comment championing the extramarital affairs of her characters. She says of Guigemar and his mistress, "They lie down together and converse,/ kissing and embracing often./ I hope they also enjoy whatever else others do on such occasions."

In many ways, however, Marie's thinking on male-female relationships is compatible with 12th-century religious thought on the subject. Writes Georges Duby: "The Church too was fighting to give free reign to affection and showed the greatest indulgence for extramarital sexuality." Ecclesiastics, such as Peter Lombard, held that games of love were deployed as a lead-in to marriage. Hugh of St. Victor articulated the importance which the period placed on consent and affections by saying that marriage involved both wife and husband "in a unique and special way by the love they share" (*De amore sponsi ad sponsam*, PL 192.920). Bernard of Clairvaux deferred to St. Paul by insisting that the law of marriage required that neither party be captive to the other and that equality of lovers rests in conformity of will. The language of Marie and numerous churchmen indicates that there were many common expectations regarding love relationships. For example, in the *Lais*, taken as a whole, there is a sense of equality between the two lovers, once two people have loved there is a bond or commitment to continue the relationship (stronger in some *lais* than in others), and personal attraction and devotion are essential to a *fin'amor*. In short, Marie's views on romantic love are not, over all, at odds with religious thinking of the late 12th century.

"Eliduc" makes a religious statement different from the other 11 *lais*. In this story, Eliduc, although married and specifically pledged to marital fidelity, loves and successfully woos the young daughter of his overlord. The hero is torn between a sense of responsibility towards his wife and passion for his mistress Guilliadun. After a series of *aventures,* Eliduc's dilemma is solved when his wife agrees to retire to a convent leaving him free to remarry. Ultimately, however, both Eliduc and Guilliadun themselves enter monasteries. The protagonists in "Eliduc" reject the game of courtly love, and come to recognize that any love of another human being, even when ennobling and heartfelt, is ultimately inferior to Christian charity and pales before the value of a life dedicated to God.

Most historians who investigate the work of Marie de France deal with the question of the order of the *lais*. We do not have Marie's original manuscript. The earliest and most complete copy of the works was produced in the 13th century. The order of the tales found in most translations of the *Lais* is the same as that of the 13th-century manuscript which ends with the story of "Eliduc." The reason the sequence of the stories is important is that many scholars have tried to deduce Marie's meaning (and identity) based on her ordering. Robert Hanning, **Joan Ferrante**, and Emanuel Mickel see in the collection of *lais* a hierarchy of love from the carnal (human and less worthy) to the divine (love of God). If, in fact, "Eliduc" is the final story, one can ask whether this *lai* is a type of apology for the frivolous nature of the first 11 tales. Perhaps Marie was following a pattern discernible in some of her sources (Ovid's *Ars amatoria* and *Remedia amoris* and Andreas Capellanus' *De amore*) where a final statement of orthodoxy softens the flagrant "turpitude" of the first part of the work.

The other works of Marie de France are the *Fables* and *The Purgatory of Saint Patrick*. Marie's collection of 102 fables was very popular in the later Middle Ages. This is attested to by the fact that they survive in 23 manuscripts and were incorporated into the fable collections of many writers in the centuries after her death. Marie claims that her fables were adapted from Aesopic tales translated into English by King Alfred. An analysis of her work, however, suggests that the source of the fables was more likely a combination of Latin texts, which reveal Arabic influences, and a sprinkling of oral tradition. In many cases Marie tells a well-known story but gives it a unique twist. The fables are short, didactic episodes teaching moral lessons and involving, for the most part, personified animals with stereotypical characteristics: the lion is regal, the fox deceitful, the lamb meek. The morals of Marie's fables are often surprising. Fable 44, for example, is a story of a husband who finds his wife with another man. The woman uses an imaginative ploy to convince her husband that she is innocent. Her deception is successful, and, rather than faulting her, the epimythium of the story praises her ingenuity. The collection as a whole emphasizes the importance of personal and feudal loyalty, the immutability of social class (the Affectionate Ass who tries to imitate his master's pet dog is nearly beaten to death for his presumption), the necessity of compassion for the under-privileged, and a critique of political, legal, and familial institutions. As in the *Lais,* many of the fables deal with the challenges of the individual functioning in society.

The Purgatory is a poem based on a Latin work entitled *Tractatus de Purgatorio Sancti Patrici* by the English Cistercian Henry of Saltrey. It is a moralizing, mystical tale about a knight called Owen and his journey through Purgatory, the entrance of which was revealed to Ireland's Saint Patrick. Marie's poem differs from the Latin model in two important ways. Her characters use direct and vivid discourse, and Marie designed the work to speak to a lay audience: "I, Marie, have put/ the Book of Purgatory into French,/ as a record, so that it might be intelligible/ and suited to lay folk." In Marie's hands the story becomes an *aventure* undertaken by a knight who bravely passes every test put to him by the devils of the underworld. When Owen emerges from his *geste,* he rejects the temptation to join a religious order, rather he uses his experience in Purgatory to guide him to a more virtuous lay life. The concept of love so central to the *lais* motivates Owen to become a crusader "out of love/ and honor for God his Creator."

An important feature of Marie's work, which is perhaps appreciated more by modern readers than it was in the 12th century, is her portrayal of female characters. The women in the *lais* are active; they, just as much as the men, must endure hardship, explore their own interiority, and successfully surmount obstacles to love. Marie is as concerned with the development of the lady as with the knight. This is an unusual feature in romance literature where the female often plays a passive role as the vehicle for bringing about moral growth in the hero. The women in "Yonec" and "Guigemar" are not rescued from their towers; they escape. The heroine in "Yonec" is the real protagonist in the *lai.* She undertakes *aventures* in order to realize her individual needs in a hostile environment. Le Fresne is saved because she makes sound ethical choices. In "Les Deus Amanz," the tragic figure is the princess. She, although loyal, patient, and resourceful, is ultimately a casualty of the young knight's pride.

Marie de France had a marked influence on medieval literature. The genre of the narrative *lai* and her fable collection inspired the admiration of subsequent generations of writers and led to a number of English imitations. She developed a distinctive stylistic technique and was innovative in her use of Celtic plots and motifs woven together with Classical imagery. Finally, Marie, herself a woman struggling in a field dominated by men, created memorable female characters who relied on their intellectual, moral and physical faculties to create a world receptive to their interior needs.

SOURCES:

Clifford, Paula. *Marie de France: Lais*. London, 1982.

Duby, Georges. *Medieval Marriage: Two Models from Twelfth Century France*. Translated by Elborg Forster. Baltimore, 1978.

The Fables of Marie de France. Translated by Mary Lou Martin. Birmingham, Alabama, 1984.

The Lais of Marie de France. Translated by Robert Hanning and Joan Ferrante. Durham, 1982.

Marie de France. *Saint Patrick's Purgatory: A Poem*. Translated by Michael J. Curley. Binghamton, NY, 1993.

Mickel, Emanuel J. *Marie de France*. New York, 1974.

SUGGESTED READING:

Burgess, Glyn S. *Marie de France: An Analytical Bibliography: Supplement 1*. London, 1986.

Capellanus, Andreas. *The Art of Courtly Love*. Translated by John Jay Parry. New York, 1941.

Ferrante, Joan M. *Woman as Image in Medieval Literature*. New York, 1975.

Gold, Penny S. *The Lady and the Virgin: Image, Attitude and Experience in Twelfth-Century France*. Chicago, 1985.

COLLECTIONS:

Four redactions of the *Lais* are found in the British Library, London and the Bibliotheque Nationale, Paris. *The Purgatory* survives in a unique manuscript at the Bibliotheque Nationale, Paris. The oldest and most complete manuscript containing the *Fables* is held at the British Library, London.

Martha Rampton,
Assistant Professor of History,
Pacific University, Forest Grove, Oregon

Marie de France (d. 1335).

See Marie of Evreux.

Marie de Gonzaga (1611–1667).

See Louise Marie de Gonzague.

Marie de l'Incarnation (1566–1618).

See Acarie, Barbe.

Marie de l'Incarnation (1599–1672)

French educator and founder of the Ursuline Order in New France (Canada). Name variations: Marie de L'Incarnation; Mary of the Incarnation; Marie Guyard or Marie Guyart. Born Marie Guyard or Guyart on October 28, 1599, at Tours, France; died on April 30, 1672, in Quebec City, New France (Quebec, Canada); third child of Florent Guyart (a master baker) and Jeanne Michelet; educated at elementary religious school in Tours; married Claude Martin, in 1617; children: Claude (b. 1619).

Champlain founded Quebec City, the first French settlement in New France (1608); first members of the Jesuit Order arrived in New France (1625); war between French settlers and the Iroquois nation (1642–67); Roman Catholic Bishopric established in New France (1674).

Selected writings: Relation Autobiographique (1633); Lettres de Conscience (1625–34); Exclamations et Élévations (1625–38); Exposition du Cantique des Cantiques (1631–37); École Sainte: Explication des Mystères de la Foi (1633–35); Relation Autobiographique (1654); Mémoire Complémentaire (1656).

On the 24th of March 1620, Marie Guyart underwent a remarkable mystical experience in the middle of a busy street in Tours, France. As she later described the event, an irresistible force seemed to descend upon her, and she saw herself immersed in the blood of Christ. The eye of her spirit was miraculously opened and all her faults and imperfections were suddenly revealed with "a clearness more certain than any certitude." This revelation, the culmination of a series of events, convinced Guyart to abandon her secular life and enter holy orders. In turn, that decision eventually came to have a profound effect on the development of religious life and civil society in the colony of New France (modern-day Quebec, Canada).

Marie was born on October 28, 1599, in Tours, then one of the most important commercial centers in west-central France. Her father Florent came from a humble background but, thanks to hard work and his own skill, had risen to a prominent position in the local guild of master bakers. By contrast, Marie's mother Jeanne was descended from one of the leading noble families in the area—the Babou De La Bourdaisières—who for many years had held influential positions in both the church and government service. Despite the marked contrast in social origin (then an important consideration), Florent and Jeanne were devoted to each other and enjoyed a happy marriage.

Both parents were deeply religious and were determined to provide all their seven children with a sound education based on Christian principles. From an early age, therefore, Marie and her siblings attended one of the small religious schools in Tours. Nothing of detail is known about the subjects studied, though it may be safely assumed that she received a fundamental grounding in reading, writing, mathematics, and the Bible.

What is definitely known, however, is that, even at this early stage in her life, Marie enjoyed her own deep and committed religious faith. Later, she would recall how, as a youngster, she would spend hours telling "personal matters" to God and how often she would repeat the sermons that she had memorized from church. One of Marie's earliest recollections concerned what she believed was her first mystical experience.

God, she said, had come to her in a dream and had asked her if she wanted to be His. Her immediate answer was "yes!"

When Marie was 14, she asked her parents' permission to enter holy orders in order to be-come a nun. The Guyarts recognized the depth of their daughter's religious convictions but, probably for economic reasons, preferred that she marry. Shortly after, a marriage contract was formalized between Marie and a young silk worker, Claude Martin, who was also a native of Tours. Their marriage took place early in 1617, but it became clear almost immediately that the union was not a happy one. Marie had to cope with a mother-in-law who appears to have been extremely jealous of the intrusion in her son's life. This, coupled with a number of financial difficulties which eventually resulted in Claude's bankruptcy, set the final seal on their relationship. The only bright event of this period was the birth of a son, also named Claude, in April 1619.

Six months after Claude's birth, Marie's husband suddenly died. In these circumstances, the young 19-year-old widow had no option but to return to her father's house with her infant son. There she was strongly urged to remarry in order to secure her own personal and financial well-being. Although aware of this need, Marie was still strongly drawn to the religious life. As a result, she entered a period of seclusion in which she spent most of her time engrossed in the Bible or communing and conversing with God. It was in this frame of mind that Marie received her most powerful mystical revelation in the street in Tours in March 1620.

[S]he was eminently endowed with all the virtues, especially with the gift of such lofty prayer and with so perfect a union with God.

—Bishop Laval

Although Marie was now more determined than ever to follow a religious life, this was not immediately possible. Despite her late husband's lack of financial acumen, Marie herself had such a good head for commerce that one of her sisters, who was married to a moderately successful carrier, asked her to come and live with them and assist in running their business. Not long after, Marie assumed sole responsibility for an increasingly successful and profitable operation.

These earthly concerns did not distract Marie from her deep commitment to God, as witnessed by her adoption of a personal vow of poverty, chastity and obedience. Finally, in late 1625, Marie entered into holy orders. Her son Claude, then eight, was entrusted to the care of her sister and Marie formally joined the novitiate of the Ursuline order of nuns in Tours. In 1633, she took her final vows and adopted a new name—Marie de l'Incarnation—a name also taken by the Carmelite *Barbe Acarie a few years earlier.

Although Marie was soon appointed assistant mistress of novices and instructor of Christ-

ian doctrine in the convent, she was still not fully satisfied in her vocation. Convinced that God had another, more important task for her, she dreamed that she had been commanded to travel to a new land across the seas. At first, Marie was confused at what this command meant, but God soon made His purpose clear. As she later recounted, God told her: "It was Canada that I showed you; you must go there to build a house for Jesus and Mary."

This was indeed a daunting task. The original colony of New France (centered around modern-day Quebec City) was a small, remote community where, with the exception of a few hardy Jesuit missionaries, there was no organized religious presence. Fortunately, Marie was introduced to **Mme De Chauvigny de la Peltrie**, a noblewoman of Tours eager to support evangelization missions among the native children of New France. She provided sufficient financial support to permit Marie and two other Ursuline nuns (**Marie de Saint-Joseph** and **Cécile de Sainte-Croix**) to set sail on the May 4, 1639, for the colony. After a hazardous and dangerous journey (during which their ship was almost crushed by an iceberg), they reached Quebec a few months later.

The problems of running a new religious foundation in a young colony made many demands on Marie. In this situation, her previous business experience proved invaluable in dealing with the local French settlers. By 1642, she had raised enough funds to allow her and her sisters to build an impressive convent (although it was destroyed by fire three years later). Local merchants recognized her business sense and often came to her for advice in their own dealings. Similarly, local representatives of the French state (including the governor of the colony) came to consult her on political matters. In 1646, with the help of Jesuit brothers, Marie helped draw up the first constitution for the colony of New France. She also found time to become fluent in several native languages and eventually wrote the first French-Algonquin and French-Iroquois dictionaries as well as a catechism in Iroquois that was extensively used by Jesuit missionaries.

The principal purpose of Marie de l'Incarnation's mission, however, had always been educational. To this end, she began by establishing a small boarding school to instruct the daughters of the local French settlers in godliness and morality. Although this school gradually expanded in size over the years, Marie was also deeply interested in providing similar opportunities to native children. This latter task was complicated by the official French government policy of assimilation, whereby native customs and ways of life were to be subordinated to those of the French. Quickly recognizing how disruptive and disastrous such a policy was for the native population, Marie unsuccessfully attempted to resist its implementation.

Not all natives were willing to accept the situation. In particular, the Iroquois (with the active assistance and encouragement of the British) vigorously resisted French incursions on their territory and way of life. Throughout this period, they launched a series of punishing raids on the settlements in New France, burning farms and killing settlers. In 1660, the Iroquois besieged Marie's convent.

Her problems were not confined to native raids. In 1659, Bishop François De Laval, who had recently been appointed to take charge of religious affairs in the colony, paid his first episcopal visit to the Ursulines. During his stay, he announced that he intended to bring about a significant number of changes to the constitution that Marie and the Jesuit brothers had drawn up a few years previously. Marie, whose knowledge and insight into the political and economic reality of life in New France was second to none, strongly protested the bishop's proposed changes. Shortly after, she wrote to Laval on behalf of all local settlers stating that "the matter has been thoroughly considered and our mind is fully made up: we will not accept it, unless we are pushed to the limits of obedience." Marie's determination so impressed Laval that he relented and agreed to make only a smaller number of largely cosmetic changes to the constitution.

Throughout these years, Marie de l'Incarnation maintained an extensive correspondence with other members of the Ursuline order, Jesuits, entrepreneurs, government officials, and friends. It has been estimated that she wrote over 13,000 letters, a number that is prestigious by any gauge but especially when given the conditions and remoteness of her place of residence. Few of the original letters still exist but it is known from other sources that they covered a wide range of topics. Although primarily religious in orientation, they also frequently contained Marie's insights into the economic and political conditions as well as her observations on the natural environment of New France.

Perhaps Marie's most enduring legacy, however, was the series of religious tracts she wrote both before and after her arrival in the New World. These leaflets represent the most fundamental expression of the nature of her relationship with, and understanding of, God. Among the most significant of these can be counted her *Exclamations et Élévations* written between 1625 and 1638. Now largely lost, this work apparently consisted of a series of *epithalamia* or "lover's complaints" which Marie wrote, as she explained, to "dissipate the fervour of the spirit." They were intended to express her profound emotional attachment to God, that "infinitely adorable, ineffable, incomprehensible unity."

Similarly, the *École Sainte: Explication des Mystères de la Foi* (1633–35) subsequently came to be considered, by the distinguished Jesuit theologian Father Pierre Charlevoix, as one of the best and most important catechisms ever written in the French language. Finally, in 1654, Marie composed her *Relation Autobiographique,* an open and honest account of her life and the principal spiritual influences upon it. This work (not to be confused with a similarly titled book previously produced by Marie while in Tours in 1633) is profoundly mystical and its full religious significance has not, perhaps, been fully understood or appreciated even today.

The combination of hard work, harsh conditions, and the prolonged penances which she imposed on herself eventually took a toll on Marie's health. Her sight gradually failed, her appetite faded, and she could no longer kneel to pray. Not surprisingly, for so deeply religious a person, her faith became ever stronger as her predicaments grew with the passing years. Marie rejoiced in the thought that she would soon be with the Savior whom she had adored for so long.

Shortly before her death on April 30, 1672, Marie de l'Incarnation sent a last message to her son Claude. The latter had followed his mother into the church as a member of the Benedictine order of monks. In 1652, Claude was appointed superior of the abbey of Saint-Maur and in 1668 received further recognition by his elevation to the post of assistant to the superior-general of the order. Marie had never forgotten the boy she had left behind so many years before and wrote a friend to inform her son "that I am carrying him with me in my heart."

Immediately following her death, Marie became venerated and a number of personal objects that she had used throughout her life came to be considered as relics by many French settlers and members of the local native community. In the middle of the 18th century, this practice was brought to the attention of the pope, but further action to formally recognize Marie's status was delayed by the Treaty of Paris (which ceded the French territories in Canada to the British crown). It was not until 1867 that the then bishop of Quebec, Charles-François Baillargeon, initiated proceedings to officially recognize Marie as one of the venerated of the Church. Eventually, in 1911, the Papal See issued a decree which evidenced the "heroic virtues" of Marie de l'Incarnation.

SOURCES:

Beaumier, Jean-Louis. *Marie Guyart de L'Incarnation, Fondatrice des Ursulines au Canada, 1599–1672*. Trois-Rivières, 1959.

Chabot, Marie-Emmanuel. *Marie de L'Incarnation d'apres ses Lettres*. Ottawa, 1946.

Jetté, Fernand. *La Voie de la Sainteté d'apres Marie de L'Incarnation, Foundatrice des Ursulines de Quebec*. Ottawa, 1954.

Repplier, Agnes. *Mère Marie of the Ursulines: A Study in Adventure*. New York, 1931.

SUGGESTED READING:

Cuzin, Henry. *Glimpses of the Monastery: Scenes from the History of the Ursulines of Quebec during Two Hundred Years, 1639–1839, by a Member of the Community*. Quebec, 1897.

Dave Baxter,
Department of Philosophy,
Wilfrid Laurier University, Waterloo, Ontario, Canada

Marie de Medici or Medicis

(c. 1573–1642).

See Medici, Marie de.

Marie de Padilla (1335–1361)

Mistress of Peter the Cruel, king of Castile, and possibly his wife. Name variations: Maria Padilla; Marie Padilla. Born in 1335 (some sources cite 1333); died in July 1361 (some sources cite 1365), in Seville, Spain; daughter of Diego or Juan García de Padilla and Meria de Henestrona also seen as María González de Hinestrosa; secretly married Pedro el Cruel also known as Peter the Cruel (1334–1369), king of Castile and León (r. 1350–1369), in 1353; children: Constance of Castile (1354–1394, who married John of Gaunt); Isabel of Castile (1355–1392, who married Edmund of Langley, duke of York); Beatriz of Castile (1354–1369); Juan (1355–1405, who married Elvira de Eril); Alfonso (1359–1362). Peter also married Blanche of Bourbon (c. 1338–1361), in 1353.

Marie de Padilla was born in 1335, the daughter of Juan García de Padilla and **María González de Hinestrosa**. Perhaps in 1350 or 1351, she joined the household of the wife of John of Albuquerque, one of King Peter the Cruel of Castile's chief advisers. Marie's beauty caught the king's attention and she began a relationship with him that lasted until her death in July 1361. She lacked sufficient rank to marry the king, but her status as royal mistress brought her social and economic benefits.

These were controversial and tumultuous years in Castile. The Black Death struck Europe at mid-century, and constant warfare wracked the peninsula, both sectarian conflict between the Christian and Moorish kingdoms and civil strife between the monarchs and their restless nobility. Although Peter agreed to marry the French noblewoman *Blanche of Bourbon for political reasons, he had already fallen in love with Marie de Padilla. He married Blanche in June 1353 but immediately returned to Marie, leaving his unfortunate bride imprisoned in the royal fortress of Toledo. Marie secured from Peter rich properties, including the major port of Huelva on the Atlantic coast of Andalusia, plus other royal favors for her family. In turn, Marie had three daughters (*Constance of Castile, *Isabel of Castile, and Beatriz of Castile) and two sons (Juan and Alfonso). She showed little interest in becoming involved in the political disputes surrounding the court, although it was inevitable that Henry II of Trastamara, Peter's half-brother and bitter enemy, saw Marie and her sons as obstacles to his own power.

In 1361, Blanche died while still imprisoned, leading to speculation that Peter had ordered her death, perhaps to prepare the way for legitimating Marie and her children. His plans were frustrated, however, by Marie's death in Seville in July of that same year. Soon thereafter Peter publicly announced that he and Marie had secretly wed sometime prior to his marriage to Blanche of Bourbon and produced witnesses to support his claim. He persuaded the cortes (parliament) to legitimate Marie's children and recognize Alfonso as heir to the throne, although the boy's death shortly thereafter made that issue moot.

SOURCES:

Estow, Clara. *Pedro the Cruel of Castile, 1350–1369*. NY: E.J. Brill, 1995.

Sitges y Grifoll, Juan Bautista. *Las mujeres del rey Don Pedro I de Castilla*. Madrid: "Sucesores de Rivadeneyra," 1910.

Kendall W. Brown,
Professor of History, Brigham Young University, Provo, Utah

Marie de St. Pol (1304–1377)

Countess of Pembroke and religious founder. Name variations: Marie de St. Paul; Marie of St. Paul; Marie de Saint-Pol; Mary of St. Pol; Maria de Sancto Paulo. Born in 1304 in France; died in 1377 in Pembroke, England; daughter of Guy IV de Châtillon, count of St. Pol, and Mary of Brittany; married Aymer de Valence, earl of Pembroke, around 1320 (d. 1324); children: none.

Marie de St. Pol, a French noblewoman, was the daughter and heir of Count Guy de Chatillon of St. Pol and **Mary of Brittany**. In 1321, Marie married the powerful and wealthy English count, Aymer de Valence, earl of Pembroke, who was in his 50s at the time. He died only three years later; thus at age 20, Marie had already become a childless widow living in England with great estates both there and in France. It was expected that a young widow of such importance would remarry, but Marie refused to do so. The countess of Pembroke divided her time between castles in England and her house in Paris, trying to maintain a neutral political position between the two constantly warring nations.

She seems to have striven to achieve the medieval ideal of a wealthy noblewoman, for she gave generously to charity and used her resources and time to found both a religious establishment and a hall for the university at Cambridge. Marie de St. Pol was an important patron of the Franciscan order of nuns (called Poor Clares or Minoresses), although she was a somewhat demanding patron. She donated generously to a Franciscan convent at Waterbeach in England, but then requested that the convent be moved to Denny, one of her manors. A fight ensued, but Marie finally had her way; she was eventually buried at Denny. She also founded the still-extant Pembroke College at Cambridge in 1347 and endowed it to support 30 students; in the rules she made for the future use of the endowment, Marie specified that French scholars be given priority over English students.

Marie de St. Pol's forceful personality helped her achieve many of her personal goals. She utilized the prestige and power of her rank to influence her superiors; she constantly wrote to the kings of France and England and even to the pope, requesting special favors and privileges for the convent at Denny, for Pembroke College, and for herself, usually successfully. Yet she also seems to have had many close personal friends, particularly *Elizabeth de Clare (1295–1360), the wealthy widow of Clare who shared her interests and whom she often visited and entertained. On her death, Elizabeth left Marie two gold rings as a token of her affection. Marie de St. Pol was 73 when she died in 1377.

SOURCES:

LaBarge, Margaret. *A Small Sound of the Trumpet: Women in Medieval Life.* Boston, MA: Beacon Press, 1986.

Laura York,
Riverside, California

Marie d'Oignies (1177–1213).

See Mary of Oignies.

Marie d'Orleans (1813–1839)

Duchess of Wurttemberg and artist. *Name variations: Marie of Wurttemberg; Marie of Württemberg; Marie, Princess of Orléans; Marie of Orleans. Born in Palermo on April 12, 1813; died on January 2, 1839; daughter of Maria Amalia (1782–1866) and Louis Philippe I (1773–1850), king of France (r. 1830–1848); married Alexander (1804–1881), duke of Württemberg, on October 17, 1837.*

Marie d'Orleans was born in 1813, the daughter of *Maria Amalia and Louis Philippe I, duke of Orléans, who was proclaimed "citizen king" but overthrown in the Revolution of 1848. Marie was a talented painter and sculptor who is best known for her statue of *Joan of Arc at Versailles. She depicted the maiden warrior as having, for the first time, killed a man with her battle-axe. Writes **Clara Clement**: "Full of spirit and animation, Joan is moved with contending and powerful emotions; she believes that God has strengthened her arm, and will help her to deliver France, and this imparts a noble pride to her features; at the same time, the young maiden trembles and gazes upon blood and death with consternation."

Marie d'Orleans also modeled a dying Bayard, which was never executed in large size. An angel in white marble which she sculpted adorns the sarcophagus of her brother Charles in the chapel of Sablonville. She also made some designs for glass painting. In a chapel at Fontainebleau, there is a glass painting of Saint **Amalia**, the patron of her mother, made from her design. Marie d'Orleans was as beautiful in her life as in her art, writes Clement. When she proceeded to Württemberg, she was received with enthusiasm. But joy turned to misfortune: the castle was burned, then her health failed. She journeyed to Pisa in hopes of restoration, but it was not to be. There, a few days before her death, she asked for more light in her apartment and spent an hour drawing.

SOURCES:

Clement, Clara Erskine. *Painters, Sculptors, Architects, Engravers, and Their Works.* Hurd & Houghton, 1874.

Marie d'Savoy-Nemours (d. 1724).

See Jeanne of Nemours.

Marie Elizabeth of Saxony
(1610–1684)

*Duchess of Holstein-Gottorp. Born on November 22, 1610; died on June 24, 1684; daughter of *Magdalena Sybilla (1587–1659) and John George I (1585–1656), elector of Saxony; married Frederick III, duke of Holstein-Gottorp, on February 21, 1630; children: Sophie Auguste (b. 1630); *Magdalena Sybilla of Holstein Gottorp (1631–1719); Christian Albrecht, duke of Holstein-Gottorp (b. 1641); *Augusta Maria of Holstein-Gottorp (1649–1728, who married Frederick VII, margrave of Baden-Durlach).*

Marie Feodorovna (1759–1828).

See Sophia Dorothea of Wurttemberg.

Marie Feodorovna (1847–1928)

*Russian empress, known as the "Lady of Tears," who was related by birth or marriage to three European monarchies and survived the violent upheavals of the late 19th and early 20th centuries that claimed many in her family. Name variations: Princess Dagmar of Denmark; Maria Feodorovna or Fyodorovna or Fedorovna; Mary Feodorovna or Fyodorovna or Fedorovna; Mary Oldenburg; Minny; Maria. Born Marie Sophia Frederika Dagmar on November 26, 1847, at Gule Palace in Copenhagen, Denmark; died at Hvidore Villa near Copenhagen, Denmark, on October 13, 1928; second daughter of Prince Christian of Schleswig-Holstein-Sönderborg-Glücksburg, later Christian IX, king of Denmark (r. 1863–1906), and Louise of Hesse-Cassel (1817–1898); sister of Frederick VIII (1843–1912), king of Denmark (r. 1906–1912), Alexandra of Denmark (1844–1925), queen of England, *Thyra Oldenburg (1853–1933), and William of Denmark, who was elected king of the Hellenes as George I (r. 1863–1913); taught languages, dance, music, literature and physical education by her parents; married Alexander III (1845–1894), tsar of Russia (r. 1881–1894); children: Nicholas II (1868–1918), tsar of Russia (r. 1894–1917); Alexander (1869–1870); George (1871–1894, died of tuberculosis); Xenia Alexandrovna (1876–1960); Michael (1878–1918, who married *Natalia Sheremetskaia); Olga Alexandrovna (1882–1960).*

Married Grand Duke Alexander Alexandrovitch (1866); became empress of Russia at the coronation of Alexander III (1881); became dowager empress fol-

lowing Alexander III's death (1894); was a prisoner of the Bolshevik Revolution (1917–19); embarked for England after the World War I Armistice (1919); took permanent residence in Denmark (1919–28).

Marie Feodorovna, dressed in a sweeping robe of silver, had no idea at her coronation with her husband, Tsar Alexander III, that she would be known as the "Lady of Tears" in 20th-century Europe. Her life would witness the assassination of her brother, King George I of Greece, the premature death of her husband in 1894, the abdication of her son, Tsar Nicholas II, and the execution of many members of her family during the Bolshevik Revolution. But her own miraculous escape from Russia, and the dignity she maintained during her exile, won Marie Feodorovna the admiration and respect of the world.

Marie Sophia Frederika Dagmar was born on November 26, 1847, at Gule Palace, Copenhagen, Denmark. Known as Princess Dagmar until her marriage, she was the second daughter and fourth child of Prince Christian of Schleswig-Holstein-Sönderborg-Glücksburg and *Louise of Hesse-Cassel, daughter of *Charlotte Oldenburg and Landgrave William of Hesse-Cassel. Marie's parents lived in unpretentious surroundings in Copenhagen, but Louise's mother Charlotte, a sister of King Christian VIII (r. 1839–1848), was the natural heiress to the Danish throne after her childless cousin, King Frederick VII (r. 1848–1863). When a succession struggle became apparent, several European nations reached an agreement in 1852 known as the London Protocol which established the borders of Denmark and named Prince Christian and Princess Louise as heirs to the throne of Denmark. In 1863, Marie's father became king of Denmark as Christian IX (r. 1863–1906); her brother William became King George I of Greece the same year.

Marie spent her youthful years living in the Yellow Palace, a modest home provided by her maternal grandfather, on a street lined with similar houses near the harbor. She shared a room with her sister, *Alexandra of Denmark, who would later marry the British prince of Wales (future king Edward VII). Prince Christian, only a captain in the Danish Guards, had a small income which made it difficult for his growing family to make ends meet. The girls made their own clothes and knitted their own stockings. Education was expensive, so their mother taught them music and religion and their father looked after their physical education. They were taught foreign languages and learned English from their English nannies. Sometimes the girls would spend the summers at the 18th-century château of Bernstorff, ten miles from Copenhagen. Author Hans Christian Andersen was a family friend and visitor; Marie and her siblings knew him very well.

Little is known about the individual personalities or childhood experiences of Marie and her siblings. An oil portrait made when Princesses Alexandra and Marie were about ten and seven confirms that Alexandra was the more beautiful and Princess Marie the more lively of the two. In her early youth, Marie was both charming and pretty, with dark violet eyes and an elfin, sparkling face. It was her idea to dress alike, and she and Alexandra almost gave the appearance of twins. Marie was the only one of Christian's daughters to demonstrate any interest in books and literature. The girls, generally not very artistic or intellectual, were happy, boisterous children with good manners and natural senses of humor. In March 1863, Marie accompanied her family to London for Alexandra's marriage to the prince of Wales.

Shortly thereafter, Marie was herself betrothed to Tsarivitch Nicholas, heir to the Russian throne. Nicholas, however, died of pulmonary problems before their wedding, at the age of 22. His last wish from his deathbed was that Princess Marie marry his younger brother, Alexander. Both the Russian and Danish royal families accepted that arrangement, and the engagement and marriage dates were set. Just before the wedding ceremony, Marie converted to the Russian Orthodox Church and changed her name from Dagmar to Marie Feodorovna. She married Grand Duke Alexander Alexandrovitch, heir to the Russian throne, on November 9, 1866, at the Winter Palace in St. Petersburg. Among the wedding guests were her sister, Alexandra, and the prince of Wales.

Their marriage was a happy one. Alexander, never expecting to succeed to the throne, had received an education for the military profession. He would remain throughout his life a plain and blunt soldier with excellent qualities and character. His honesty was sterling and his demeanor unceremoniously straightforward. Alexander possessed incredible physical strength but was extremely tender and affectionate to his family. He spent hours of recreation with his children, and his matrimonial relationship to Marie was impeccable.

Quite unexpectedly, Alexander and Marie became the rulers of Russia. On March 1, 1881, Tsar Alexander II (r. 1855–1881) was assassinated by revolutionary terrorists on the very day he

Marie Feodorovna

had signed a decree approving a representative assembly. Badly wounded by a bomb, he died at the Winter Palace shortly after the attack. Alexander III (r. 1881–1894), as he was now called, and Marie Feodorovna were forced to take the strictest precautions for their safety because of the political radicalism in Russia. Instead of living in the Winter Palace or the palace of Tsarskoe Selo, they took up residence in the strongly guarded palace at Gatchina. During their rare stays in St. Petersburg in the summer months, they resided in the small, secure Anitchkoff Palace. The fear of terrorism strengthened a political reaction that saw Alexander III reject the constitutional reforms of his father. Konstantin Pobiedonostzeff, a fanatical defender of autocracy, presided over the reactionary policies of the new reign. Alexander III, as a result of his protective isolation from his public, was probably ignorant of many of the excesses committed by his zealous officials.

Their coronation did not take place until May 15, 1883. The emperor and empress were escorted by heralds arrayed in cuirasses, plumed hats, and gilded spurs. Appearing small beside her husband, Marie wore a sweeping robe of silver covered with jewels. Four court pages carried her long gold-and-ermine train. Although her coronation gown, robes and train were so heavy as to fatigue her, Marie maintained a radiant smile for everyone present. After a lengthy ceremony, the Metropolitan of St. Petersburg passed the crown to Alexander who placed it on his own head. The tsar then took the second crown and turned to Marie, kneeling in front of him, and placed it upon her head.

> [S]he saw the face of Europe transformed; saw dynasties flourish and fall . . . saw that country over which she had ruled as a joint sovereign descend into the very Valley of the Shadow.
>
> —Edmund A. Walsh

Marie and Alexander's marriage produced five children between 1868 and 1882. Nicholas, born on May 18, 1868, would eventually succeed his father as Emperor Nicholas II. George, born on May 9, 1871, entered the Russian navy and died of consumption at the age of 23. *Xenia Alexandrovna, born on April 6, 1876, married the Grand Duke Alexander Mikhailovitch in 1894. Michael was born on December 5, 1878, and served as the heir to the Russian throne from the time his brother ascended the throne until the birth of a son in 1904. *Olga Alexandrovna, born on June 13, 1882, married the duke of Oldenburg but their marriage was later dissolved. She then married to Major Nicholas Koulikovsky. The children were raised in a simple way in a warm family environment. Little effort was exerted to prepare them for their future roles as the imperial rulers of Russia. They were in a narrow sense well-educated by tutors. The royal family probably lost some touch with reality and the necessity of protocol and training in the seclusion and isolation at Gatchina. The children were often uneasy around their father, who, while loving and caring, was a taciturn and gruff man.

The Empress Marie found her happiness in the serenity of domestic life and family. She had little interest in politics beyond discussions with her husband. The only political influence known to have been exerted by Marie was over Russian policy toward Finland. She so strongly disliked Russian infringement upon the autonomy of their neighbor that Alexander III moderated policies toward Finland out of consideration for her feelings.

Apart from her family, she spent most of her time in philanthropic and educational work. She was generous in both effort and financial support for her projects, and became head of the Department of the Institution of the Empress Marie, which provided for special girls' schools. Marie, who had thrown herself into this project during the reign of Alexander II, completely changed the character of the department. It grew and expanded under her leadership into a network of not just schools but also hospitals, relief centers, and refuges. She improved the finances of the department by introducing the concept of voluntary contributions to supplement government subsidies. More than being head of this department, she took an emotional and personal role in trying to alleviate the suffering of thousands of unfortunate girls.

Marie Feodorovna was also the head of the Russian Red Cross. Her involvement helped to remedy several deficiencies while enlarging both its size and service. She had been trained as a nurse during the Russo-Turkish War of 1877–78, and her personal knowledge of Red Cross duties helped her during her stewardship at its head.

The private life of the royal couple was for the most part uneventful, although there was an unsuccessful attempt on Alexander's life on March 1, 1887, by university student radicals. Of the 15 men indicted in the assassination plot, five were ultimately given the death penalty. One of those executed was Alexander Ulianov, older brother of V.I. Lenin. In October 1888, the royal train was accidentally derailed near Kharkov as the tsar and his family were eating in the dining car. The badly damaged roof caved in, but Alexander, using his Herculean strength, lifted the ceiling on his shoulders while Marie and the children crawled uninjured from the car. Marie, forgetting her own plight, helped the doctors with other members of the court who had been injured in the crash.

In 1894, Alexander began to suffer from insomnia, headaches, and pain in his legs. The family traveled, on doctors' advice, to the royal hunting lodge near Spola, Poland, but his condition continued to worsen and was finally diagnosed as nephritis. It was decided that the warm weather in the Crimea would benefit the tsar, but after a brief period of improvement his health again began to deteriorate. Marie spent day and night beside her husband and, despite her deep grief, nursed him until his death on the afternoon of November 1, 1894, at age 49.

Following the traditional period of mourning, Marie Feodorovna returned to public life. She served as an advisor to Nicholas II (r. 1894–1917), who was conscientious but poorly prepared to govern his empire. In time, a bitterness developed between Marie and her daughter-in-law, *Alexandra Feodorovna (1872–1918), because Russian court protocol gave precedence to a dowager empress over the reigning empress. Marie, always splendidly dressed in jewels and fine clothes, made public appearances on the arm of her son, while Alexandra was escorted by one of the grand dukes. They even quarreled about sharing the imperial jewels. This unintended rivalry died away in 1895, however, when Marie took a long visit to her family in Denmark and Nicholas moved his family to the Peterhof Palace.

Marie lived in the Anitchkoff Palace after her return to Russia and devoted herself to her philanthropic work. A coldness always remained between the pragmatic Marie and the often unstable Alexandra. Marie openly expressed her dislike of the charlatans, fortune-tellers and mediums serving and advising her daughter-in-law. She found her most pleasant times to be her visits to the family in Copenhagen and to her sister, Queen Alexandra of Great Britain.

Marie, who was in England when World War I broke out, left immediately for Russia, but she was detained in Berlin on August 4, 1914, and given the choice of returning to England or traveling to Denmark. Refusing to appeal to the German government, she eventually reached Russia by traveling through Denmark, Sweden, and Finland.

During the war, Marie spent much of her time with the Russian Red Cross, which did exceptional work under her leadership and patronage. As the war progressed, the Russian public began to turn against the imperial family. Empress Alexandra's constant meddling and the people's concerns about the influence of her confidant and advisor, Gregory Rasputin, made Nicholas II appear weak. Marie, at the request of several influential people, attempted to warn her son of the unrest. Events moved rapidly in both the imperial family and the Russian nation. Rasputin was murdered in December 1916. Three months later, the March revolution forced Tsar Nicholas II to abdicate. Marie traveled to the General Headquarters at Mogilev to see her son. They spent three days together before he was taken prisoner on March 21, 1917. As the train took him away, a tearful Marie waved at her son and made the sign of the cross to him. They would never see each other again.

Marie joined other members of the royal family in the Crimean city of Sebastopol, where several loyal officers protected them from the chaos created by the revolution. Life was difficult and dangerous. Conditions improved during the German occupation of the Crimea, and the Germans offered her safe passage to Denmark through their territory. She refused and remained in the Crimea until British forces arrived after the Armistice ended the war. In April 1919, as the Russian Communist army advanced on the Crimea, Marie left Russian soil on the British battleship H.M.S. *Marlborough* for Great Britain. Nicholas II, Alexandra Feodorovna and their five children had been murdered by Bolshevik forces in July 1918.

Marie Feodorovna never acknowledged the execution of Nicholas II and his family at Ekaterinburg. She eventually left England and returned to her native Denmark, taking up residence in the Hvidore Villa which she and her sister Alexandra had earlier built for themselves. She constantly feuded over money with her nephew, King Christian X, and stubbornly refused to sell the jewels she had brought from Russia when the king suggested she could pay her own expenses. Her sister, Alexandra, sent her £1,000 annually toward the maintenance of the villa. In the end, King George V, Alexandra's son, generously established a yearly pension of £10,000 for Marie—"his dear Aunt Minnie."

Marie Feodorovna, dowager empress of Russia, died at the age of 81 at her residence on October 13, 1928. Her daughters, the Grand Duchesses Olga and Xenia, who had also escaped from Russia, were at her bedside. Services were held at the Russian Church in Copenhagen, and, despite her desire to be buried on Russian soil, she was laid to rest in her father's vault in Roskilde Cathedral.

SOURCES:

Alexander, Grand Duke of Russia. *Once a Grand Duke.* NY: Farrar and Rinehart, 1932.

Battiscombe, Georgina. *Queen Alexandra.* Boston, MA: Houghton Mifflin, 1969.

Lowe, Charles. *Alexander III of Russia.* Freeport, NY: Books for Libraries Press, 1895 (reprinted, 1972).

Marie, Grand Duchess of Russia. *Education of a Princess.* NY: Viking Press, 1931.

———. *A Princess in Exile.* NY: The Viking Press, 1932.

Tisdale, E.E.P. *Marie Feodorovna: Empress of Russia.* NY: The John Day, 1958.

SUGGESTED READING:

Massie, Robert K. *Nicholas and Alexandra.* NY: Atheneum, 1967.

Vorres, Ian. *The Last Grand Duchess: Her Imperial Highness Grand Duchess Olga Alexandrovna.* NY: Scribner, 1965.

COLLECTIONS:

Bing, Edward J. *The Secret Letters of the Last Tsar: The Confidential Correspondence Between Nicholas II and his Mother, Dowager Empress Marie Feodorovna. NY: Longmans, Green, 1938.*

Phillip E. Koerper,
Professor of History,
Jacksonville State University, Jacksonville, Alabama

Marie Feodorovna (1876–1936).

See Victoria Melita of Saxe-Coburg.

Marie Françoise of Savoy

(1646–1683)

Queen of Portugal. Name variations: Maria Francisca Luisa de Savoie; Maria Francisca Isabel of Savoy. Born Marie de Savoie-Nemours on June 21, 1646; died on December 27, 1683; daughter of Charles Amedeé of Savoy (who was killed in a celebrated duel with his brother-in-law, François de Vendome, duke of Beaufort) and Elizabeth de Bourbon; sister of *Jeanne of Nemours (d. 1724); married Afonso or Alphonso VI (1643–1683), king of Portugal (r. 1656–1667), on August 2, 1666 (annulled in 1668); married his brother Pedro or Peter II (1648–1706), king of Portugal (r. 1667–1706), on April 2, 1668; children: (second marriage) Isabel Luisa Josefa (1669–1690).

Marie-Ileana (1933–1959)

Granddaughter of Marie of Rumania. Name variations: Marie Ileana Habsburg. Born on December 18, 1933, in Modling, Austria; killed in a plane crash on January 11, 1959, in Rio de Janeiro, Brazil; daughter of Anthony, archduke of Austria, and *Ileana (b. 1909).

Marie Isabella of Spain

(1789–1848)

Queen of Sicily. Name variations: Maria Isabel. Born on July 6, 1789; died on September 13, 1848; daughter of *Maria Luisa Teresa of Parma (1751–1819) and Charles IV (1748–1819), king of Spain (r. 1788–1808); became second wife of Francis I, king of Sicily (r. 1825–1830), on October 6, 1802; married Franz de Balzo, on January 15, 1839; children: (first marriage) *Louisa Carlotta of Naples (1804–1844); *Maria Cristina I of Naples (1806–1878); Ferdinand II (1810–1859), king of the Two Sicilies (r. 1830–1859); *Maria Antonia of Sicily (1814–1898); Marie Amalie (1818–1857, who married Sebastian de Bourbon); *Caroline of Sicily (1820–1861); *Teresa Cristina of Bourbon (1822–1889, who married Pedro II of Brazil); Francesco, count of Trapani (1827–1892). Francis I's first wife was Maria Clementina of Austria (1777–1801).

Opposite page

Marie José of Belgium with Humbert II.

Marie José of Belgium (b. 1906)

Queen of Italy for 34 days. Name variations: Marie Jose of Belgium; Maria-José or Marie-Jose; countess of Sarre. Born on August 3, 1906; daughter of Albert I (1875–1934), king of the Belgians (r. 1909–1934), and Elizabeth of Bavaria (1876–1965); attended boarding school in Florence; married Humbert II also known as Umberto II (1904–1983), king of Italy (r. 1946, for 34 days), on January 8, 1930; children: Maria Pia (b. 1934); Victor Emmanuel (b. 1937); Maria Gabriella (b. 1940); Beatrice (b. 1943).

The intelligent and spirited daughter of Albert I, king of Belgium, and Queen *Elizabeth of Bavaria, Marie José married into the Italian House of Savoy in 1930, becoming the bride of Umberto II, the handsome and self-indulgent heir to the throne. Despite her husband's philandering and his alleged homosexuality, the princess gave birth to four children, the first two of whom were purportedly conceived after artificial insemination. An adoring mother, she also worked tirelessly during the war as inspector general of the Red Cross. While popular with her subjects, Marie José never won the respect and trust of her father-in-law, King Victor Emmanuel III (called "the little king" because of his short stature), who objected to her unconventional habits of smoking cheroots and traveling about incognito, and bristled at her reputation of being the only ruler in the House of Savoy.

By 1943, Marie José was estranged from both her husband and her father-in-law, and had set up a four-room "bachelor-girl" apartment in the royal residence, the Palazzo del Quirinale, in Rome. What no one knew at the time was that for three years, since 1940, Quirinale had been a center of the underground movement against Benito Mussolini (1883–1945), and that the princess was waging her own private war against the dictator whom she had dubbed "Provolone" (Big Cheese). In her apartment, Marie received emissaries from the political underground that was threading its way through Rome and even through Vatican City. Working closely with her friend and confidante Marchesa **Giuliana Benzoni**, also an avowed anti-Fascist, Marie José became an important factor in the overthrow of Mussolini. In her quest, the princess enlisted the trust and support some of Italy's most important political revolutionaries, including Ivanoe Bonomi, former premier of Italy, Alcide de Gasperi, a Christian Democrat who would later serve as his party's first premier, Professor Ferdinando Arena, physician to the House of Savoy, Dr.

Carlo Antoni, Marie José's tutor in constitutional law, and Guido Gonella, diplomatic correspondent of the official Vatican newspaper *L'Osservatore Romano*. Although she had no personal contact with the king, Marie José kept him informed of the escalating plots against Mussolini by feeding information to him through his trusted financial advisor Pietro, duke of Acquarone, who had a secret crush on her.

In 1942, the princess met secretly with Marshal Pietro Badoglio, who was part of the coup that forced the Fascist premier's resignation in 1943. Mussolini was imprisoned at that time, but was rescued within two months and set up a republican fascist government in German-occupied northern Italy. He was finally captured and killed by anti-fascist forces in 1945.

King Victor Emmanuel retired from public office in 1944, but exercised control of the crown through his son Prince Umberto. He abdicated to his son in 1946, but Umberto's reign ended after 34 days when the country voted to become a republic. With the end of the 1,000-year rule of the House of Savoy, Umberto retired to Portugal without Marie José, who went to live in Switzerland. She later wrote a book about the first duke of Savoy.

SOURCES:

Collier, Richard. *Duce!: A Biography of Benito Mussolini.* NY: The Viking Press, 1971.

Judd, Denis. *Eclipse of Kings: European Monarchies in the Twentieth Century.* NY: Stein and Day, 1974.

Barbara Morgan,
Melrose, Massachusetts

Marie Josepha (1699–1757)

*Queen of Poland. Name variations: Marie Josephine; Maria Josepha of Austria; Marie Josephe. Born on December 8, 1699; died on November 17, 1757; daughter of Joseph I (1678–1711), Holy Roman emperor (r. 1705–1711), and *Wilhelmina of Brunswick (1673–1742); married Frederick Augustus II (1696–1763), elector of Saxony (r. 1733–1763), also known as Augustus III, king of Poland (r. 1733–1763), on August 20, 1719; children: Frederick Christian (1722–1763), elector of Saxony (r. 1763); *Maria Amalia of Saxony (1724–1760, who married Charles III, king of Spain); *Marie Josephe of Saxony (1731–1767, who married Louis, the dauphin of France).*

Marie Josephe of Saxony
(1731–1767)

French royal. Name variations: Marie Josèphe; Marie or Maria Josepha of Saxony; Marie-Josephe de Saxe;

*Marie Josephine. Born on November 4, 1731; died on March 13, 1767; daughter of Frederick Augustus II (1696–1763), elector of Saxony (r. 1733–1763), also known as Augustus III, king of Poland (r. 1733–1763), and *Marie Josepha (1699–1757); became second wife of Louis the Dauphin of France (1729–1765), on February 9, 1747; children: duke of Burgundy (1751–1761); duke of Aquitaine (1753–1754); Louis XVI (1754–1793), king of France (r. 1774–1792); Louis XVIII (1755–1824), king of France (r. 1814–1824); Charles X (1757–1836), king of France (r. 1824–1830); *Marie Clotilde (1759–1802, who married Charles Emmanuel IV of Sardinia); *Madame Élisabeth (1764–1794). Louis the Dauphin's first wife was *Maria Theresa of Spain (1726–1746).*

Marie Josephine of Savoy (d. 1810)

*Countess of Provence. Name variations: Josephine Louise of Savoy; Marie Joséphine; Louise Benedicta; Maria Josepha Louisa; Joséphine. Died in 1810; daughter of *Maria Antonia of Spain (1729–1785) and Victor Amadeus III (1726–1796), duke of Savoy (r. 1773–1796); married Louis Stanislas Xavier, count of Provence, who later became Louis XVIII (1755–1824), king of France (r. 1814, 1815–1824), in 1771.*

Marie Leczinska

Marie Josephine of Savoy, the daughter of the duke of Savoy, married the future king of France, Louis XVIII, in 1771. She died in exile in England in 1810, before Louis took the throne, and was buried in Westminster Abbey with all the pomp befitting a queen.

Marie Laetitia (1866–1890)

*Duchess of Aosta. Born Marie Laetitia Eugenie on December 20, 1866; died on October 25, 1890; daughter of Prince Napoleon (Plon-Plon) and *Clotilde of Savoy (1843–1911); married Amadeo also known as Amadeus of Savoy (b. 1845), duke of Aosta, king of Spain (r. 1871–1873), on September 11, 1888; children: Umberto also known as Humbert or Humberto (b. 1889), count of Salemi. Amadeus' first wife was *Maria dal Pozzo.*

Marie Leczinska (1703–1768)

*Queen of France. Name variations: Marie, Maria, or Mary Leszczynska; Maria Lesczinska. Pronunciation: (French) Lek-ZON-skah. Born on June 23, 1703, in Breslau, Silesia, Poland; died on June 24, 1768, in Versailles, France; daughter of Stanislaw also known as Stanislaus I Leczinski or Leszczynski (d. 1766), duke of Lorraine (r. 1737–1766), king of Poland (r. 1704–1709); married Louis XV (1710–1774), king of France (r. 1715–1774), on September 5, 1725; children: ten, including (twin daughters) *Louise Elizabeth (1727–1759) and *Henriette (1727–1752); Louis le dauphin (1729–1765, father of Louis XVI); *Adelaide (1732–1800); *Victoire (1733–1799); *Sophie (1734–1782); *Louise Marie (1737–1787).*

Following his banishment from Poland in 1709, King Stanislaus I and his daughter Marie Leczinska settled in Alsace, destitute exiles. When she married Louis XV, she was a princess "who knew no cosmetics but water and snow," writes **Nancy Mitford**, "and who spent her time embroidering altar cloths." At first glance, Marie Leczinska was no one's idea of a queen of France. She won the right to marry Louis with the help of *Madame de Prie (who assumed that Marie would be extremely grateful and grant much favor) after spirited competition between 40 princesses and courtwide wagering on the winner. Marie came to the throne with neither beauty, possessions, nor connections, and she was seven years older than the 15-year-old Louis. But she was kind and dignified, and the king was besotted on first sight.

Later, however, Marie began to tire of always being "in bed, or pregnant, or brought to bed"; a pious woman, she excused herself from her husband's attentions on the feast days of major saints. Soon, she became interested in the minor saints. One saint too many caused an explosion on the part of Louis, who then turned to others, many others. Of Marie Leczinska's ten children, only six daughters and one son reached maturity.

SOURCES:

Mitford, Nancy. *Madame de Pompadour*. NY: Harper & Row, 1968.

Marie Leopoldina or Leopoldine (1797–1826).

See Leopoldina of Austria.

Marie Lesczinska (1703–1768).

See Marie Leczinska.

Marie Louise (1695–1719)

Duchess of Berry. Name variations: Mary Bourbon-Orleans; duchesse de Berri; Marie-Louise d'Orleans. Born on August 20, 1695; died on July 21, 1719; daughter of Philip Bourbon-Orléans (1674–1723), 2nd duke of Orléans (r. 1701–1723), and *Françoise-Marie de Bourbon (1677–1749); married Charles (1686–1714), duke of Berri or Berry, on July 6, 1710; married a von Rioms, in 1716.

Marie Louise (1872–1956)

Princess. Name variations: Marie Louise of Schleswig-Holstein. Born Franziska Josepha Louise Augusta Marie Christiana Helena on August 12, 1872, in Windsor, Berkshire, England; died on December 8, 1956, in London; daughter of Christian of Schleswig-Holstein-Sonderburg-Augustenburg and Helena (1846–1923, daughter of Queen Victoria); married Prince Aribert of Anhalt, on July 6, 1891 (marriage annulled, 1900).

Marie Louise was born in England in 1872, the daughter of Christian of Schleswig-Holstein-Sonderburg-Augustenburg and Princess *Helena, daughter of Queen *Victoria. After her marriage to Prince Aribert of Anhalt was annulled, Princess Marie Louise returned to England and devoted her life to charitable and artistic causes; she was heavily involved in the creation of Queen *Mary of Teck's Dolls' House. Her autobiography *My Memories of Six Reigns* was published in 1956.

Marie Louise (1879–1948)

Margravine of Baden. Name variations: Marie Louise Guelph. Born Mary Louise Victoria Caroline Amelia Alexandra Augusta Fredericka on October 11, 1879, in Gmunden, Austria; died on January 31, 1948, in Salem, Baden, Germany; daughter of Ernest Augustus, 3rd duke of Cumberland and Teviotdale, and *Thyra Oldenburg (1853–1933); granddaughter of George V, king of Hanover; married Maximilian, margrave of Baden, on July 10, 1900; children: *Marie-Alexandra of Baden (1902–1944); Berthold, margrave of Baden (1906–1963).

Marie Louise Albertine of Leiningen-Heidesheim (1729–1818)

Landgravine of Hesse-Darmstadt. Name variations: Princess George. Born in 1729; died in 1818; married imperial lieutenant field marshal Prince George William, landgrave of Hesse-Darmstadt (1722–1782); children: *Frederica of Hesse-Darmstadt (1752–1782); Charlotte of Hesse-Darmstadt (1755–1785).

Marie Louise d'Orleans (1662–1689)

Queen-consort of Spain as wife of Charles II. Name variations: Marie Louise of Orleans or Orléans; Marie-Louise Bourbon-Orleans; Maria Luisa de Orleans, Maria Luisa de Borbon. Born April 26 (some sources cite March 27), 1662; died on February 12, 1689; daughter of Henrietta Anne (1644–1670) and Philip also known as Philippe I (1640–1701), 1st duke of Orléans (r. 1660–1701); married Charles II (1661–1700), king of Spain (r. 1665–1700), on August 31, 1679 (some sources cite November 19); no children.

Born on April 26, 1662, Marie Louise d'Orleans was the daughter of Philip, 1st duke of Orléans, and *Henrietta Anne, daughter of the king and queen of England. Louis XIV was Marie's uncle. To strengthen peace between Spain and France, Louis XIV betrothed her to Charles II, the last Habsburg monarch of Spain. The marriage contract was signed on August 30, 1679, and Marie Louise wed Charles by proxy at Fountainbleau a day later.

In several ways, Marie Louise faced a difficult situation. Her husband, known as Charles the Bewitched, was mentally retarded and physically deformed. Nor did he prove capable of fathering an heir, to her disappointment. Meanwhile, Spain had fallen from its former glory, and the monarchy faced a prolonged financial retrenchment. Marie Louise comported herself with dignified piety, occasionally ruling for her husband, but governmental councils generally determined policy. Her death on February 12,

1689, at age 27, occasioned rumors that she had been poisoned, although little evidence substantiated the allegation. Marie Louise was buried in the royal pantheon at the Escorial.

SOURCES:

Bassene, Marthe. *La vie tragique d'une reine d'Espagne, Marie Louise de Bourbon-Orleans.* Paris: Calmann-Lévy, 1939.

Maura Gamazo, Gabriel, duke of Maura. *María Luisa de Orléans, reina de España: leyenda e historia.* Madrid: Saturnino Calleja, 1943.

SUGGESTED READING:

Harrison, Kathryn. *Poison* (fiction). NY: Random House, 1995.

Kendall W. Brown,
Professor of History,
Brigham Young University, Provo, Utah

Marie Louise d'Orleans (1695–1719).

See Marie Louise.

Marie Louise d'Orleans (1750–1822)

Duchess of Bourbon. Name variations: Princess de Bourbon; duchesse de Bourbon. Born Louise-Marie-Thérèse d'Orléans on July 9, 1750; died on January 13, 1822; daughter of *Louisa Henrietta de Conti (1726–1759) and Louis Philippe (1725–1785), 4th duke of Orléans (r. 1752–1785); married Louis-Joseph, duke of Bourbon (later Prince de Condé in 1818), on April 24, 1770 (divorced 1780).

Marie-Louise Gonzaga or Gonzague (1611–1667).

See Louise Marie de Gonzague.

Marie Louise of Austria

(1791–1847)

Empress and regent of France, duchess of Parma, who was Napoleon's second wife. Name variations: Maria Louisa or Maria Luisa; Marie-Louise; Marie-Louise of France; Marie-Louise Habsburg; Mary Louise of Austria. Archduchess of Austria (1814–1847). Born in Vienna, Austria, on December 12, 1791; died in Parma, Italy, on December 17, 1847; daughter of Francis II, Holy Roman emperor (r. 1792–1806), who was king of Austria as Francis I (r. 1804–1835), and Maria Teresa of Naples (1772–1807); sister of Ferdinand I, emperor of Austria (r. 1835–1848), and *Leopoldina of Austria (1797–1817); daughter-in-law of *Letizia Bonaparte (1750–1836); became second wife of Napoleon I, emperor of France (r. 1804–1815), in 1810; married Count Adam Adalbert von Neipperg, in 1821; married Count Charles de Bombelles, in 1834; children: (first marriage) Napoleon II (1811–1832), also known as the duc de Reichstadt, king of Rome; (second marriage) two.

Marie Louise of Austria was born in 1791, the daughter of Francis II, Holy Roman emperor, and ***Maria Teresa of Naples**. Marie Louise's marriage to Napoleon I Bonaparte was arranged for the purpose of producing an heir and in hopes of establishing a bond between his regime and the Habsburgs, one of Europe's oldest royal houses. However political the bond may have been, Napoleon, who had reluctantly divorced ***Josephine**, grew genuinely fond of Marie Louise, especially when she gave birth to an heir in 1811. When Napoleon abdicated in 1814 and went into exile on the island of Elba, Marie Louise returned home to her father and was granted sovereignty over Parma, Piacenza and Guastalla. She was a liberal ruler. After Napoleon's death, she married Count Adam von Neipperg in 1821 and had two children. Following Neipperg's demise in 1829 and an uprising in 1831, she was driven from Parma but was later

Marie
Louise of
Austria

WOMEN IN WORLD HISTORY

returned by the Austrians. Marie Louise married Count Charles de Bombelles in 1834, 13 years before she died of pleurisy at Parma.

SOURCES:

Decaux, Alain. *Napoleon's Mother.* London: The Cresset Press, 1962.

Seward, Desmond. *Napoleon's Family.* NY: Viking, 1986.

Stirling, Monica. *Madame Letizia: A Portrait of Napoleon's Mother.* NY: Harper & Brothers, 1961.

Marie Louise of Bulgaria (b. 1933)

Bulgarian princess. Born on January 13, 1933, in Sofia, Bulgaria; daughter of Boris III, king of Bulgaria, and *Giovanna of Italy (b. 1907); married Charles Vladimir Ernst, prince of Leiningen, on February 14, 1957 (divorced 1968); married Bronislav Chrobok, on November 16, 1969, in Toronto, Ontario, Canada; children: (first marriage) Boris of Leiningen (b. 1960); Hermann of Leiningen (b. 1963); (second marriage) Alexandra Nadpichida Hrobok; Pavel Alister Hrobok.

Marie Louise of France (1727–1759).

See Louise Elizabeth.

Marie-Louise of France (1791–1847).

See Marie Louise of Austria.

Marie Louise of Orleans (1662–1689).

See Marie Louise d'Orleans.

Marie Louise of Orleans (1695–1719).

See Marie Louise.

Marie Louise of Parma (1727–1759).

See Louise Elizabeth.

Marie Louise of Parma (1751–1819).

See Maria Luisa Teresa of Parma.

Marie Louise of Parma (1870–1899)

Queen of Bulgaria. Name variations: Maria Louisa of Parma; Mary of Parma. Born on January 17, 1870; died on February 1, 1899; daughter of Robert (b. 1848), duke of Bourbon-Parma, and *Pia of Sicily (1849–1882); married Ferdinand I (1861–1948), king of Bulgaria (r. 1887–1918, abdicated), on April 20, 1893; children: Boris III (1894–1943), king of Bulgaria (r. 1918–1943); Cyril (b. November 17, 1895); Eudoxia (b. January 17, 1898); *Nadejda of Bulgaria (b. 1899, who married Albert Eugene of Württemberg). Ferdinand's second wife was *Eleanora of Reuss.

Marie Louise of Savoy (1688–1714)

Queen of Spain. Name variations: Maria Louisa; María Luisa Gabriela; María Luisa Gabriel of Savoy; Louise Marie. Born María Luisa Gabriela in Savoy, Italy, on September 17, 1688 (some sources cite 1687); died on February 14, 1714; daughter of Anne-Marie d'Bourbon-Orleans (1669–1728) and Victor Amadeus II (1666–1732), duke of Savoy (r. 1675–1713), king of Sicily (r. 1713–1718) and Sardinia (r. 1718–1730); sister of *Marie Adelaide of Savoy (1685–1712), duchess of Burgundy (mother of Louis XV of France); became first wife of Philip V (1683–1746), king of Spain (r. 1700–1724, 1725–1746), on November 2, 1701; children: Luis or Louis I (August 25, 1707–August 1724), king of Spain (r. 1724–1724); Felipe (1712–1719); Ferdinand VI (b. September 23, 1713), king of Spain (r. 1746–1759).

The daughter of Victor Amadeus II of Savoy and ✥ Anne-Marie d'Bourbon-Orleans, Marie Louise of Savoy was born in Turin on September 17, 1688. Louis XIV arranged her marriage in 1701 to his grandson, Philip of Anjou (the future Philip V of Spain), whom the last Spanish Habsburg monarch, Charles II, had named as his heir to the throne of Spain. She was 13 at the time and chosen by Louis XIV in part because of Savoy's strategic location in France's struggle with Austria to control Italy. As Philip was not in line to succeed to the French throne, Louis had trained him to be docile and pious rather than kingly, and Marie Louise was able to exert considerable influence over him as a result.

Marie Louise of Savoy and Philip V married in November 1701 at Figueras in Catalonia. In an attempt to prevent Marie Louise from pulling Spain toward the interests of Savoy, Louis XIV refused to permit her to take her own ladies-in-waiting to her new home. Before proceeding to Madrid, Marie Louise passed through Zaragoza, where in her husband's name she swore to respect the traditional rights and privileges of Aragon. Accompanying the queen was *Marie-Anne de la Trémouille (c. 1642–1722), princess of the Ursins, whom Louis XIV had chosen as head of the queen's bedchamber, with the understanding that Ursins would champion French interests. She did, in fact, exert significant influence over the queen, and consequently over Philip V.

The War of the Spanish Succession overshadowed Marie Louise's reign as queen. In 1706, she acted as regent while Philip was away on military campaign and had to abandon Madrid when the enemy occupied it. The following year, she gave birth to a son and heir, Louis, on August 25, cementing popular support for the new dynasty. With the war still continuing, in 1711 Marie Louise fell ill with scrofula.

Anne-Marie d'Bourbon-Orleans. See Henrietta Anne for sidebar.

In a weakened condition she gave birth to another son, Ferdinand, in September 1713. Her health declined, and she died of tuberculosis on February 14, 1714, in Madrid. Marie Louise had four children, all sons, and two reigned as Louis I and Ferdinand VI. Her youth, energy, and kindliness made her more popular among Spaniards than Philip V's second wife, *Elizabeth Farnese.

SOURCES:

Bergamini, John D. *The Spanish Bourbons.* NY: Putnam, 1974.

Hill, Constance. *Story of the Princess des Ursins in Spain.* NY: R. H. Russell, 1899.

Lynch, John. *Bourbon Spain, 1700–1808.* Cambridge, MA: Basil Blackwell, 1989.

> **Kendall W. Brown,**
> Professor of History,
> Brigham Young University, Provo, Utah

Marie Louise of Schleswig-Holstein (1872–1956).

See Marie Louise.

Marie Magdalena Barbara (1711–1758).

See Maria Barbara of Braganza.

Marie Melita of Hohenlohe-Langenburg (1899–1967)

*Duchess of Schleswig-Holstein-Sonderburg-Glucksburg. Born on January 18, 1899, in Langenburg, Germany; died on November 8, 1967, in Munich, Bavaria, Germany; daughter of Ernest, 7th prince of Hohenlohe-Langenburg, and *Alexandra Saxe-Coburg (1878–1942); married Wilhelm Fredrich also known as Frederick, duke of Schleswig-Holstein-Sonderburg-Glucksburg, on February 15, 1916; children: Hans (1917–1944); William (1919–1926); Peter, duke of Schleswig-Holstein-Sonderburg-Glucksburg (b. 1922); Marie-Alexandra of Schleswig-Holstein-Sonderburg-Glucksburg (b. 1927).*

Marie of Anhalt (1898–1983)

*Princess of Prussia. Name variations: Marie Auguste von Anhalt. Born on June 10, 1898, at Schloss Ballenstedt; died on May 22, 1983, at Essen; daughter of Eduard Georg Wilhelm, duke of Anhalt, and **Marie of Saxe-Altenburg**, duchess of Saxony; married Joachim Francis Humbert, prince of Prussia, on March 11, 1916; married Johann Michael, baron von Löen or Loen, on September 27, 1926 (divorced 1935); children: (first marriage) Charles Francis Joseph (b. 1916), prince of Prussia.*

Marie of Anjou (1404–1463)

*Queen of France. Name variations: Marie d'Anjou; Mary of Anjou; Mary d'Anjou. Born in 1404 in Angers, France; died in 1463 at Amboise, France; daughter of Louis II (1377–1417), duke of Anjou and king of Sicily, and Yolande of Aragon (1379–1442); sister of King René I the Good, duke of Anjou and Lorraine (husband of *Isabelle of Lorraine); married Charles VII (1403–1461), king of France (r. 1422–1461), on December 18, 1422; children: 14, including Louis XI (1423–1483), king of France (r. 1461–1483); Jean (b. 1426); *Catherine de France (1428–1446, who married Charles the Bold); Jacques (b. 1432); *Jeanne of Bourbon (1434–1482, who married John II of Bourbon); *Yolande of France (1434–1478, who married Amadeus of Savoy); Marguerite (1437–1438); Marie (1437–1439); Charles of Berri (1446–1472); *Radegonde (b. 1445); *Madeleine of France (1443–1486, who married Ladislas Posthumus); and adopted daughter Louise de Laval.*

The life of the French queen Marie of Anjou is often overshadowed by the lives of three other women who had a profound influence over her husband, King Charles VII: her mother *Yolande of Aragon, *Joan of Arc, and Charles' mistress *Agnes Sorel. Born into the ducal family of Anjou, which also claimed the kingdoms of Sicily and Naples, Marie was the great-granddaughter of the French king John II on her father's side and the granddaughter of John I, king of Aragon, on her mother's.

In 1413, her parents and Queen *Isabeau of Bavaria (1371–1435) arranged a marriage between nine-year-old Marie and Isabeau's eldest son and Marie's cousin, the Dauphin Charles Valois. As was customary for a royal bride, Marie of Anjou soon moved to the royal palace in Paris along with her mother and a large entourage. Charles, about 14 years old in 1414, became attached to his intelligent, ambitious, and politically savvy future mother-in-law, who would exercise enormous sway over him personally and politically. Her influence apparently prevented Marie from developing a close relationship with her future husband; there is no evidence from his reign, or before, that he valued his wife's advice much.

In October 1422, one of the final years of the protracted war with England known as the Hundred Years' War, King Charles VI died, leaving a kingdom destroyed by war and mostly held by English forces. Marie's husband nominally succeeded to the throne, but the ongoing war prevented his coronation. In December 1422, Charles and 18-year-old Marie were finally wed. Over the 24 years of their marriage, Marie of Anjou had fourteen children, only six of whom survived to adulthood, including the future king Louis XI.

Charles was finally crowned king in 1429 at Rheims, after the remarkable young heroine Joan of Arc led the French army to victory against the English there. The queen was conspicuously absent from the coronation ceremony in 1429; the king felt that Rheims was too dangerous for her and her ladies. But the political and public role of the French queen was minor compared to that of the king anyway, and it was not believed that her coronation was significant in establishing royal authority. Marie was crowned in a rather small ceremony some months later in Paris.

After 1429, Charles VII began to rule in actuality, displaying military prowess combined with a deep piety and generosity but also a weak constitution. He was always susceptible to the manipulation of others, however, which led in 1433 to a conspiracy by Marie and Yolande of Aragon against one of his favorites, Georges de La Trémouille. They feared that Georges had gained too much influence over Charles' actions and convinced three nobles to attempt to assassinate him. The plot failed, but Georges was exiled when Charles realized that Georges was costing him his mother-in-law's goodwill.

Eventually the king and his well-chosen advisors succeeded in reconquering all of France's territory held by the English. Having no political role to play during these years, Marie of Anjou was occupied in presiding over the royal courts in Paris and the other royal residences across France, and performing other ceremonial functions. She also spent her time raising her many children. The queen was particularly involved in their education, unlike many queens who left child-rearing to servants and tutors. Marie also devoted herself to charitable works. Like Charles, she was intensely religious, and supported the church by establishing religious foundations. She did not regularly stay with the king, who spent much of his time on military campaign, but lived a rather quiet life with her children.

After the death of Yolande of Aragon in 1442, whatever sway Marie had held with her husband diminished. Charles then came under the influence of another woman, Agnes Sorel, a lady in the queen's entourage. The first royal mistress to hold an official title, *maitresse en titre*, she quickly became a sort of second queen,

Marie of Anjou (1404–1463)

and gave birth to three children acknowledged by Charles as his own. Agnes presided over many royal social functions and was referred to as *Dame de Beauté*, Lady of Beauty. After Agnes' death, probably by poison, in 1450, a series of less influential mistresses took her place.

Marie of Anjou was not with her husband when he died in July 1461. After her son succeeded as Louis XI, she retired to her estates at Amboise. There she died in 1462, at age 58.

SOURCES:

Pernoud, Regine and Marie-Veronique Clin. *Joan of Arc: Her Story*. NY: St. Martin's Press, 1998.
Vale, M.G. *Charles VII*. Berkeley, CA: University of California, 1974.

Laura York,
Riverside, California

Marie of Antioch (d. 1183)

Empress and regent of the Byzantine empire. Name variations: Mary of Antioch; Maria of Antioch. Born before 1149, possibly in the 1130s; died in 1183;

daughter of *Constance of Antioch (1128–1164) and Raymond I of Poitiers, prince of Antioch; sister of Bohemund III, prince of Antioch (r. 1163–1201); second wife of Manuel I Comnenus or Komnenos (c. 1120–1180), Byzantine emperor (r. 1143–1180); children: Alexius II Comnenus (c. 1168–1183), emperor of Byzantium (r. 1180–1183).

After the death of his first wife *Bertha-Irene of Sulzbach in 1161, Manuel I Comnenus married Marie of Antioch. Their son Alexius II Comnenus was born around 1168. When the king died in 1180, the frail Alexius acceded the throne at age 11, and his mother became regent. Marie of Antioch's pro-Western policies and indulgence of corrupt favorites made her unpopular. She was also Italian, and Italians were resented by the Byzantines. Opportunistic Italian merchants held a monopoly on trade. In 1182, Andronicus I Comnenus, a cousin of the imperial family, invaded Constantinople, ostensibly as a protector to the boy-king and foe to the Latins. Citizens took the opportunity for widespread revolt. In the "Latin Massacre," they slaughtered thousands, including the Italian merchants. Andronicus compelled the boy Alexius to sign a death warrant for his mother, then had himself crowned co-emperor. Two months later, Alexius was murdered. Then his ordered execution was carried out: Marie of Antioch was strangled to death in 1183.

Marie of Austria (1505–1558).
See Mary of Hungary.

Marie of Austria (1528–1603).
See Elisabeth of Habsburg (1554–1592) for sidebar.

Marie of Baden (1817–1888)

Duchess of Hamilton and princess of Zahringen. Born on October 11, 1817; died on October 17, 1888; daughter of *Stephanie de Beauharnais (1789–1860) and Charles Ludwig, grand duke of Baden; married William Alexander, 11th duke of Hamilton, on February 23, 1843; children: William Alexander (b. 1845), 12th duke of Hamilton; Charles George (b. 1847), earl of Selkirk; Mary Victoria (b. 1850), Lady Douglas-Hamilton.

Marie of Blois (d. 1404).
See Marie of Guise.

Marie of Boulogne (d. 1182)

Countess of Boulogne and abbess of Romsey. Name variations: Marie, Abbess of Romsey; Mary, countess of Boulogne; countess of Mortain; countess of Mortaigne. Born around 1136; died in 1182 (some sources cite 1181) in St. Austrebert, Montreuil, France; interred at St. Austrebert; daughter of Matilda of Boulogne (c. 1103–1152) and Stephen of Blois (c. 1096–1154), later king of England (r. 1135–1154); married Matthew I (Matthieu d'Alsace), count of Boulogne, around 1160 (annulled in 1169); children: daughter Ide d'Alsace (c. 1161–1216); *Maude of Alsace (1163–c. 1210).

Marie of Boulogne, the daughter of *Matilda of Boulogne and King Stephen of Blois of England, became prioress of Lillechurch, a nunnery founded for her by her parents. She was then the abbess of the celebrated Romsey before succeeding her brothers Eustace IV and William II (also known as Guillame II) as ruler of Boulogne in 1159. It is said that because of her rich inheritance she was abducted by Matthew I of Alsace, son of the earl of Flanders, and forced by her cousin King Henry II to marry her abductor, in order to secure an alliance. After nine years of marriage, her husband allowed her to return to the religious life in 1169. Her daughter *Ide d'Alsace succeeded her as countess of Boulogne in 1173 and ruled until 1216.

Marie of Brabant (c. 1260–1321)

Queen of France. Name variations: Mary Louvain; Mary of Brabant; Marie de Brabant. Born around 1260; died in 1321; daughter of Henry III (d. 1261), duke of Brabant, and *Adelaide of Burgundy (d. 1273); became second wife of Philip III the Bold (1245–1285), king of France (r. 1270–1285), in 1274; children: Louis of Evreux (d. 1319); *Margaret of France (c. 1282–1318, who married Edward I, king of England). Philip's first wife was *Isabella of Aragon (1243–1271).

Marie of Brabant (fl. 1250)

Countess Palatine. Flourished around 1250; first wife of Ludwig also known as Louis II the Stern (1229–1294), count Palatine (r. 1253–1294), duke of Bavaria (r. 1255–1294). Louis' second wife was *Anna of Silesia.

Marie of Brandenburg-Kulmbach (1519–1567)

Electress of the Palatinate and duchess of Simmern. Name variations: Marie von Brandenburg-Kulmbach.

Born on October 11, 1519; died on October 31, 1567; daughter of *Suzanne of Bavaria (1502–1543) and Casimir, margrave of Brandenburg; married Frederick III the Pious (1515–1576), duke of Simmern and elector of the Palatinate (r. 1559–1576), on October 21, 1537; children: Louis VI (b. 1539), elector of the Palatinate; *Elizabeth of Wittlesbach (1540–1594). Following Marie of Brandenburg-Kulmbach's death, Frederick III married Amalie von Neuanahr on April 25, 1569.

Marie of Brunswick (1729–1796).

See Carolina Matilda for sidebar on Maria Juliana of Brunswick.

Marie of Bulgaria (c. 1046–?)

Bulgarian princess. Name variations: Maria of Bulgaria. Born around 1046; death date unknown; possibly daughter of King Samuel of Bulgaria; possibly sister of *Catherine of Bulgaria; married Andronicus Ducas (general, known as the traitor of Manzikert); maternal grandmother of *Anna Comnena; children: two sons and three daughters, including *Irene Ducas (c. 1066–1133).

Marie of Champagne (1145–1198).

See Marie de Champagne.

Marie of Champagne (c. 1180–1203)

Countess of Flanders and Hainault. Name variations: Maria of Champagne; Mary of Champagne. Born around 1180; died during an epidemic while on crusade in 1203; daughter of *Marie de Champagne (1145–1198) and Henry I, count of Champagne; married Baudouin also known as Baldwin IX (1171–1206), count of Flanders and Hainault (crowned Baldwin I of Constantinople), in 1186; children: *Johanna of Flanders (c. 1200–1244), countess of Belgium; *Margaret of Flanders (1202–1280).

Marie of Cleves (1426–1486)

Duchess of Orléans. Name variations: Mary of Cleves; Marie de Clèves; Anne de Cleves; Anne of Cleves. Born in 1426; died in 1486 (some sources cite 1487); daughter of Adolph or Adolf IV, duke of Cleves; became third wife of Charles Valois (1391–1465), duke of Orléans, in 1441; children: Louis XII (1462–1515), king of France (r. 1498–1515); *Marie of Orleans (d. 1493, who married Jean de Foix, comte d'Etampes); Anne of Orleans

(d. 1491), abbess of Fontevrault. Charles' first wife was *Isabella of Valois (1389–c. 1410); his second was *Bonne of Armagnac (d. 1415).

Marie of Dreux (1391–1446)

Duchess of Alençon. Name variations: Mary of Dreux; Mary de Dreux; duchess of Alencon. Born in 1391; died in 1446; daughter of John IV de Montfort, 5th duke of Brittany (r. 1364–1399) and *Joanna of Navarre (c. 1370–1437); married John I, duke of Alençon.

Marie of Evreux (d. 1335)

Duchess of Brabant. Name variations: Marie de France or Marie of France; Mary of Evreux. Died in 1335; daughter of Louis, count of Evreux; married John III the Triumphant (1300–1355), duke of Brabant (r. 1312–1355), around July 19, 1311; children: *Margaret of Brabant (1323–1368); *Joanna of Brabant (1322–1406); *Marie of Guelders (1325–1399); John of Brabant (1327–1335); Henry of Brabant (d. 1349); Godfrey of Brabant (d. after February 1352). Her husband John III had many illegitimate children, including John Brant; William Brant; John van Veen; Joanna (who married Costin von Raenst); Jeanette (who married Godfrey van der Dilft); Marie van Veen (a nun in Brussels who died in 1394); Arnold van der Hulpen (who married Elisabeth Moedels); Henry van der Hulpen; Margareta van der Hulpen (who married Bernardus van der Spout and Walter de Melin); Barbe van Ophem (a nun who died in 1354); Nikolaus de Sweerthere; Nikolaus de Werthusen; Henry of Brussels; John van Linden; John van Overysche; Dionysius van Louvain; Katharina (who married Godefroy de Henri-Chapelle); another daughter who married Winand de Henri-Chapelle; another daughter who married Clerembaut de Hauterive.

Marie of France (c. 1140–1200).

See Marie de France.

Marie of France (1198–c. 1223)

Duchess of Brabant. Name variations: Maria de France. Born in 1198; died on August 15, 1223 or 1224; daughter of Philip II Augustus, king of France (r. 1180–1223), and *Agnes of Meran (d. 1201); married Philip of Namur (son of Margaret of Alsace and brother of Baldwin IX); became second wife of Henry I (1165–1235), duke of Brabant, on April 22, 1213; children: two daughters.

Marie of France (1344–1404)

*Countess of Bar. Born in 1344; died in 1404; daughter of *Bona of Bohemia (1315–1349) and John II the Good (1319–1364), king of France (r. 1350–1364); married Robert I, duke of Bar.*

Marie of Gascony (d. 1399).

See Marie Robine in Women Prophets & Visionaries in France at the End of the Middle Ages.

Marie of Guelders (1325–1399)

*Duchess of Guelders. Name variation: Countess of Gelderland. Born in 1325; died in 1399 (some sources cite 1398); daughter of John III (1300–1355), duke of Brabant (r. 1312–1355), and *Marie of Evreux (d. 1335); married Reginald also known as Renaud III (1333–1371), duke of Guelders, in 1347.*

Marie of Guise (d. 1404)

Countess of Guise. Name variations: Margaret of Blois; Margaret de Chatillon or Châtillon; Marie of Blois. Died in 1404; daughter of Charles de Chatillon, count of Blois; married Louis I (1339–1384), count of Provence, duke of Anjou, king of Naples, Sicily and Jerusalem (r. 1360–1384), in 1360; children: Louis II (1377–1417), duke of Anjou and king of Sicily; Charles, count de Roucy; Marie of Anjou (d. 1370).

Marie of Guise (1515–1560).

See Mary of Guise.

Marie of Hainault (fl. 1300)

Countess of Clermont. Name variations: Marie of Hainaut. Flourished around 1300; married Louis I the Grand (1270–1342), count of Clermont; children: Pierre or Peter I (1311–1356), duke of Bourbon; Jacques I or James I (1315–1361), comte de la Marche.

Marie of Hesse-Darmstadt (1824–1880)

*Empress of Russia and wife of Tsar Alexander II. Name variations: Mariia Aleksandrovna or Alexandrovna; Mary of Hesse-Darmstadt; Princess Wilhelmine (before 1841), Empress Marie; Empress Marie of Russia. Born Princess Maximilienne Wilhelmine Auguste Sophie Marie on July 27, 1824, in Hesse-Darmstadt; died of tuberculosis on May 22, 1880 (o.s.) in St. Petersburg; illegitimate daughter of Baron August Ludwig de Senarclans-Grancy (a minor state official) and Princess Wilhelmine of Baden (1788–1836); education uncertain; married Alexander II, tsar of Russia (r. 1855–1881), in 1841; children: Alexandra or Aleksandra (1842–1849); Nicholas (1843–1865); Alexander III (1845–1894), tsar of Russia (r. 1881–1894); Vladimir (b. 1847, who married *Maria of Mecklenburg-Schwerin); Aleksei (1850–1908, who married Alexandra Zhukovskaya); *Marie Alexandrovna (1853–1920); Sergei or Sergius (1857–1905, who married *Ella); Paul (1860–1919, who married *Alexandra Oldenburg [1870–1891]).*

Raised in German duchy of Hesse-Darmstadt (1824–40); lived in St. Petersburg as wife of Alexander II (1841–80); was empress of Russia (1855–80); was active in numerous charitable activities.

On September 8, 1840 (o.s.), Marie of Hesse-Darmstadt arrived in St. Petersburg in a great gold coach. Next to her sat her future mother-in-law, the Empress Alexandra Feodorovna (*Charlotte of Prussia). Behind them Tsar Nicholas I rode on horseback followed by Marie's handsome fiancé, the tsarevich Alexander Nikolaevich (Alexander II), at the head of a cavalry honor guard. All around them church bells rang and cannon boomed to welcome the future empress of Russia. Despite this warm reception, the 16-year-old girl from the small and isolated German duchy of Hesse-Darmstadt could not help but be awed and frightened by her new surroundings. She knew no Russian; she was a Lutheran in an Orthodox country; and she had no training for the responsibilities which confronted her. Much like her more famous predecessor, *Catherine II the Great, who also came from an obscure German principality to be empress of Russia, Marie turned out to be as bright as she was pretty. She soon became the helpmate as well as the wife of Alexander, a liberal and stabilizing influence on her weak-willed husband, the mother of eight of his children, and the benefactor of many Russian charities. Unfortunately, she also was the victim of court intrigue and of Alexander's philandering. She spent the last 15 years of her life in poor health and in undeserved humiliation.

Alexander first met Marie on March 13, 1839, when he was in the middle of a 16-month tour of Western European capitals in search of a suitable royal bride. Given the insignificance of Hesse-Darmstadt, a "remarkably dull and stagnant duchy," it is not surprising that Marie was not on the list of princesses to be interviewed. Moreover, her youth and family background seemed to disqualify her. Her mother, Princess

Marie
of Hesse-
Darmstadt

❧▸ **Wilhelmine of Baden,**
had left her husband Grand
Duke Ludwig II in 1809, 15 years
before Marie was born. Marie's real father was August Ludwig Senarclans-Grancy who
held a minor post as master of horse in Hesse-
Darmstadt. To avoid further scandal, the grand
duke generously accepted Marie as his own child
and raised her after her mother's death in 1836.
This family imbroglio was well known to the
courts of Europe even if not to Alexander and his
advisors. After attending an opera in their honor,
the Russian party returned to the duke's castle
where the tsarevich met Marie, who was serving
as her adoptive father's hostess. Despite her
youth—she was not yet 15—"she attracted me

enormously from the first
moment I saw her," Alexander informed his father. Though
he did not state the nature of his attraction, one of his biographers notes that "Marie
was beautiful but she was also alarmingly intelligent. She seemed to have been educated far
above her age." Alexander declared to one of his
advisors: "We don't have to go further. I have
made my choice."

In the face of considerable parental opposition, the tsarevich stuck to his "choice" even to
the point of threatening to renounce the throne
unless he had his way. A year later, they were engaged, and, in September 1840, Marie came to
St. Petersburg to face the problems of being the

❧▸

*See sidebar
on the
following page*

wife of the future tsar of Russia. Given the Russian name of Mariia Aleksandrovna, but known universally as Marie, she became an enthusiastic convert to Russian Orthodoxy; she learned to read the classics of Russian literature in the language in which they were written; and she worked to understand the problems of her new country. The royal couple were married in the chapel of the Winter Palace on April 16, 1841, with all the pomp and ceremony imperial Russia could muster. Their early married life was happy and fruitful. Marie had four children (one of whom died in infancy) during the first six years of their marriage. The young couple surrounded themselves with friends interested in music, poetry, and the arts. Marie and Alexander read together Turgenev's *Sportsman's Sketches* as it appeared serially, and they discussed the need for peasant reform which it revealed. The tsarevich also developed the habit of reading state papers with his wife in the evening and listening to her advice on liberal policies he might pursue on becoming tsar.

The Empress is a woman of sense and ability and is believed to have great influence with her husband when he is with her.

—Lord Granville

Conservative elements in the court, however, resented Marie's strong convictions and stabilizing influence on her often vacillating and perhaps less intelligent husband. Rumors were spread that she sought to "Germanize" Russia, and she was criticized for hiring English nannies to look after her children. As much as possible, she was isolated from influencing policy once Alexander ascended to the throne in 1855. The new tsar then chose the inopportune time of

Marie's seventh pregnancy in 1857 to have an affair with one of her ladies-in-waiting, *Alexandra Dolgorukaia, an affair which may have been encouraged by Marie's enemies at court. When reproached for his infidelity, Alexander angrily decided to spend more of his time hunting and less of it listening to his complaining wife. The death by meningitis of their eldest and favorite son Nicholas in 1865, followed soon after by the tsar's very public infatuation with *Ekaterina Dolgorukova, a woman 30 years his junior, effectively ended the royal marriage in all but name.

Marie devoted much of the last two decades of her life to charitable activities, serving as president of the Russian Red Cross and fostering better education for women. She also became interested in Pan-Slavism and promoted greater Russian support for their Slavic and Orthodox brethren in the Balkans. As her health as well as her marriage deteriorated, she spent more of her time in Germany visiting relatives and seeking medical treatment abroad. She also increasingly turned to mysticism and the Orthodox Church for inner salvation. As a result, she rarely engaged in court activities, which merely reinforced the popular perception that she was aloof and cold. The empress' final indignity came in 1878 when Alexander moved Ekaterina Dolgorukova into the Winter Palace. Sick in bed, Marie was forced to listen to the "other woman's" three illegitimate children playing immediately above her bedroom. When she sought the emotional support of her own children and her sisters-in-law in the face of Alexander's inconsiderate behavior, she caused even further division in an already unhappy royal family. Two years later, this intelligent and progressive woman died a lonely and lingering death from tuberculosis on May 22, 1880, at the age of 55.

SOURCES:

*Almedingen, E.M. *The Emperor Alexander II.* London: The Bodley Head, 1962.

Mosse, W.E. *Alexander II and the Modernization of Russia.* NY: Collier Books, 1962.

Tarsaïdzé, Alexandre. *Katia: Wife Before God.* NY: Macmillan, 1970.

R.C. Elwood,
Professor of History,
Carleton University, Ottawa, Canada

Marie of Hohenzollern-Sigmaringen (1845–1912)

Countess of Flanders. Born on November 17, 1845; died on November 26, 1912; daughter of Charles Anthony I of Hohenzollern-Sigmaringen (1811–1885), prince of Rumania, and *Josephine of Baden

(1813–1900); sister of Carol I, king of Rumania (r. 1881–1914); married Philip (1837–1905), count of Flanders, in 1867; children: Baudouin (1869–1891); twins *Henrietta of Belgium (1870–1948, who married Emmanuel of Orléans) and Josephine (1870–1871); *Josephine of Belgium (1872–1958, who married Charles Anthony II of Hohenzollern-Sigmaringen); Albert I (1875–1934), king of the Belgians (r. 1909–1934).

Marie of Hungary (d. 1323)

*Queen of Naples and Anjou. Name variations: Maria; Mary of Hungary. Born in Hungary; died on March 25, 1323; daughter of Stephen V, king of Hungary (r. 1270–1272) and *Elizabeth of Kumania (c. 1242–?); married Charles II the Lame (1254–1309), duke of Anjou (r. 1285–1290), king of Naples (r. 1285–1309), in 1270; children: Charles Martel of Hungary; *Blanche of Naples (d. 1310, who married James II of Aragon); Robert the Good, king of Naples (r. 1309–1343); Philip of Tarento (d. 1332); *Margaret of Anjou (c. 1272–1299); *Lenore of Sicily (1289–1341, who married Frederick II of Sicily); John of Gravina (who married Agnes of Perigord).*

Marie of Kiev.

See Maria of Kiev (d. 1087).
See Maria of Kiev (d. 1146).

Marie of Kiev (d. 1179)

*Grand princess of Kiev. Died in 1179; daughter of *Christina of Sweden (d. 1122) and Mstislav I (b. 1076), grand prince of Kiev (r. 1125–1132); sister of *Ingeborg of Russia, Izyaslav II also known as Yziaslav II, prince of Kiev (r. 1146–1154), and *Irene of Kiev; married Vsevolod II, grand prince of Kiev; children: Svyatoslav also known as Sviatoslav III, prince of Kiev; Jaroslav also known as Yaroslav (b. 1139), prince of Kiev.*

Marie of Leiningen (1907–1951).

See Marie of Russia.

Marie of Lusignan (d. 1260)

*Countess of Eu. Died on October 1, 1260, in Melle, Poitou; interred at Fourcarmont Abbey; daughter of *Yolande de Dreux (d. 1238) and Raoul III de Lusignan, count of Eu; married Alfons de Brienne, count of Eu, in 1249; children: John de Brienne, count of Eu.*

Marie of Luxemburg

*Duchess of Brittany. Name variations: Luxembourg. Daughter of Sebastian of Luxemburg, duke of Penthièvre; married Philippe-Emmanuel (1548–1602), duc de Mercoeur, brother of *Louise of Lorraine; children: at least a daughter.*

As her father's only heir, Marie of Luxemburg inherited the duchy of Brittany, which she and her husband governed.

Marie of Luxemburg (d. 1546)

*Countess of Vendome. Died on April 1, 1546; daughter of *Margaret of Savoy (d. 1483) and Peter also known as Pierre II, count of St. Paul (r. 1476–1482); married Jacques de Romont, in 1460; married François also known as Francis of Bourbon, count of Vendôme, on September 8, 1487; children: (second marriage) Charles (b. 1489), duke of Vendome; Francis (b. 1491), duke of St. Pol; *Antoinette of Bourbon (1494–1583).*

Marie of Mecklenburg (fl. 1380)

*Danish royal. Name variations: Marie von Mecklenburg. Flourished in 1380; daughter of *Ingeborg (1347–1370) and Henry, duke of Mecklenburg; married Vratislav or Vratislas of Pomerania (d. 1394); children: Erik VII of Pomerania (c. 1382–1459), king of Denmark, Norway, and Sweden (r. 1397–1438); *Catherine of Pomerania (d. 1426, who married Johan or John of Bavaria).*

Marie of Mecklenburg-Gustrow (1659–1701)

*Duchess of Mecklenburg-Strelitz. Name variations: Marie von Mecklenburg-Güstrow. Born on July 19, 1659; died on January 16, 1701; daughter of *Magdalena Sybilla (1617–1668) and Christian Oldenburg (1603–1647, son of Christian IV, king of Denmark); married Adolf Frederick II, duke of Mecklenburg-Strelitz, on September 24, 1684.*

Marie of Montferrat (d. 1212)

*Queen and regent of Jerusalem. Name variations: Maria or Mary of Montferrat; Marie de Montferrat; Maria La Marquise; Mary la Marquise of Jerusalem. Died in 1212; daughter of Conrad of Montferrat, king of Jerusalem (r. 1190–1192), and *Isabella I of Jerusalem (d. 1205); married John of Brienne also known as John I de Brienne, king of Jerusalem (r.*

1210–1225), emperor of Constantinople (r. 1228–1237), in 1210; children: Yolande of Brienne (1212–1228), queen of Jerusalem.

Marie of Montferrat was queen under a regency from 1205 to 1212. Her death deprived her husband John I de Brienne of any title to the throne, though he ruled as regent for their daughter *Yolande of Brienne until 1225. John de Brienne also married Agnes de Beaumont, daughter of Raoul IV de Beaumont, and *Berengaria of Castile (b. around 1199), the infanta of Castile and daughter of *Berengaria of Castile (1171–1246) and Alphonso IX of León.

Marie of Naples (fl. 1300s)

*Heir to the throne of Naples. Flourished from 1320s to 1350s; daughter of Charles of Calabria and *Marie of Valois; sister of *Joanna I of Naples (1326–1382); granddaughter of Robert the Good, king of Naples (r. 1309–1343); married Charles of Durazzo; married Philip II of Constantinople; children: (first marriage) *Margaret of Naples (who married Charles III of Durazzo, king of Naples, r. 1382–1386, who ruled Hungary as Charles II, r. 1385–1386).*

Marie of Nassau (1841–1910)

*Princess of Wied. Born on July 5, 1841; died on June 22, 1910; daughter of *Louise (1808–1870) and Frederick Orange-Nassau (son of William I of the Netherlands); married William (1845–1907), 5th prince of Wied, on July 18, 1871.*

Marie of Orleans (d. 1493)

*Countess of Étampes. Name variations: Marie de Orléans; countess of Etampes or Estampes or d'Etampes. Died in 1493; daughter of *Marie of Cleves (1426–1486) and Charles Valois (1391–1465), duke of Orléans; married Jean de Foix, comte d'Etampes.*

Marie of Orleans (1813–1839).

See Marie d'Orleans.

Marie of Rumania (1875–1938)

*Queen of Rumania and English princess who married the heir to the Rumanian throne and played an important role in the affairs of her adopted country during and immediately after World War I. Name variations: Marie of Romania; Marie of Roumania; Mary of Saxe-Coburg; Marie of Saxe-Coburg-Gotha; called Missy by her family. Born Marie Alexandra Victoria of Saxe-Coburg on October 29, 1875, at the family country home in Eastwell Park, Kent, England; died on July 18, 1938, at Castle Pelesch, Sinaia, Rumania, of an intestinal hemorrhage; daughter of Prince Alfred Saxe-Coburg, duke of Edinburgh (who was the son of Queen Victoria) and Grand Duchess Marie Alexandrovna (daughter of Tsar Alexander II of Russia); sister of *Alexandra Saxe-Coburg (1878–1942), ✥ Beatrice of Saxe-Coburg (1884–1966), duchess of Galliera, and Victoria Melita of Saxe-Coburg (1876–1936); educated by governesses and private tutors; married Ferdinand I of Hohenzollern-Sigmaringen (1865–1927), king of Rumania (r. 1914–1927), on January 10, 1893; children: Carol II (1893–1953), king of Rumania (r. 1930–1940); Elisabeth (1894–1956); Marie (1900–1961, also known as Mignon); Nicholas (1903–1978); Ileana (1909–1991); Mircea (1913–1916).*

Spent portion of early years in Malta (1885–89); moved with family to the Duchy of Coburg in Germany, where Prince Ferdinand of Hohenzollern-Sigmaringen became heir to the Rumanian throne (1889); attended coronation of Tsar Nicholas II of Russia (1896); while Ferdinand was ill with typhus, began first extramarital love affair (1897); began friendship with Waldorf and Pauline Astor (1902); during Rumanian peasant revolt, began longstanding love affair with Barbo Stirbey (1907); performed relief work when Rumania fought Second Balkan War against Bulgaria (1913); with outbreak of World War I, Rumania declared its neutrality; following German invasion, performed relief work when Rumania entered war (1916); continued relief work until Rumania left the war, German occupation began (1917); Prince Carol eloped and Rumania reentered the war against Germany (1918); conducted mission to Paris Peace Conference (1919); coronation (1922); toured U.S. (1926); widowed by death of Ferdinand (1927); Carol returned from exile to take the throne (1930); published her autobiography (1934).

Queen Marie of Rumania was one of the most colorful and influential monarchs of the early 20th century. Her physical beauty, her vast energies and talents, and her vibrant personality combined with her sense of style to set her apart from most members of Europe's royal houses. Moreover, in contrast to royalty in most other countries, Rumania's monarchs wielded crucial influence in political affairs. Marie's qualities of leadership came to the fore during World War I.

The country that became Marie's adopted homeland was one of the most turbulent nations in the troubled Balkan peninsula. Rumania was freed from Turkish domination to become an independent nation only in the middle of the 19th century. Shortly after independence, Rumania's political leaders called in a member of a reigning German family to become the country's monarch. Monarchy was still the normal form of government in Eastern Europe, and Prince Karl of Hohenzollern-Sigmaringen, who became King Carol I of Rumania, turned out to be a forceful and intelligent ruler. In 1889, he turned to his nephew Prince Ferdinand (I) of Hohenzollern-Sigmaringen to become crown prince and heir to the Rumanian throne.

The country, despite its vast agricultural and mineral wealth, faced numerous problems. Its relations with its neighbors were particularly difficult. The adjoining great power, Austria-Hungary, had a large number of Rumanians within its territory in the province of Transylvania. The desire of most Rumanians to obtain Transylvania meant strained relations with a country Rumania could not hope to challenge militarily. In its internal affairs, Rumanian stability was threatened by a large, impoverished peasantry presided over by a small, wealthy, and privileged native aristocracy. The periodic persecution of Rumania's Jewish minority made the country the target for bitter criticism from abroad, both from Western governments and from public opinion. The political system was notoriously corrupt, with leaders using public office to enrich themselves with impunity.

The future queen of Rumania was born into the most rarefied levels of European society. Her father Prince Alfred Saxe-Coburg was the second son of Britain's Queen *Victoria, the most eminent monarch of the 19th century. Her mother was *Marie Alexandrovna, daughter of Tsar Alexander II, the Russian emperor who reigned from 1855 to 1881 and the author of the reform movement that ended serfdom.

In the style of British royalty, the young princess was given a nickname, Missy, which her relatives in Britain used throughout her life. Her childhood included visits to her imposing grandmother Queen Victoria, as well as trips to see her mother's family, the ruling Romanov dynasty in Russia. She acquired vague memories of her maternal grandfather, Tsar Alexander II, and she was shocked in March 1881, at age seven, when her tearful mother told her the tsar had just been assassinated. A crucial friendship dating from childhood linked Marie to her younger sister, Princess *Victoria Melita of Saxe-Coburg, who was known as Ducky.

Marie's father had made his career in the Royal Navy, and thus her childhood included a

⁂▶ **Beatrice of Saxe-Coburg** (1884–1966)
*Duchess of Galliera. Born Beatrice Leopoldine Victoria on April 20, 1884, in Eastwell Park, Kent, England; died on July 13, 1966, in Sanlucar de Barrameda, Andalusia, Spain; daughter of Alfred Saxe-Coburg, duke of Edinburgh, and *Marie Alexandrovna (1853–1920); sister of *Marie of Rumania (1875–1928); married Alphonso Bourbon, 5th duke of Galliera, on July 15, 1909; children: Alvaro (b. 1910); Alonso (b. 1912); Ataulfo (b. 1913).*

long stay in Malta, starting in 1885 and lasting until 1889. An active and athletic young teenager, she spent much of her free time using her vast skills as an equestrian riding around the island. There, she had a first romance with her cousin, Prince George, who would take the British throne as King George V in 1910. At the close of their stay in Malta, Marie moved to a German environment. Her father, the heir to the duchy of Coburg, moved to that small region of southern Germany.

She loved being a queen. She gave herself to the Rumanians with exuberance and played her role with drama and humor.

—Hannah Pakula

In the custom of European royalty, Marie's mother sought a suitable spouse for the girl while she was still a teenager. Already strikingly beautiful with blonde hair, blue eyes, and an attractive figure, the exuberant young princess seemed destined for a brilliant marriage. Prince George of England, an old companion from her Malta days who had just become heir to the throne upon the death of his older brother, tried and failed to get Marie's parents to accept him as her future husband. Marie's Russian-born mother had found her life in England uncomfortable and wished her daughter to marry a German.

Marie's family now turned their efforts to securing Prince Ferdinand of Rumania, heir to the Rumanian throne, as Marie's husband. Ferdinand was a tall, painfully shy young man, totally dominated by the force of his uncle's personality. In 1892, King Carol had compelled Ferdinand to give up his hopes of marrying a young Rumanian noblewoman. Carol welcomed the diplomatic advantages of a marriage between Marie and Ferdinand: it meant closer ties for Rumania with both Britain and Russia.

Even during their courtship a cloud came into the relationship between the two young

Volume Ten   **403**

members of European royalty. Ferdinand gave his bride-to-be hints of both the country's primitive nature as well King Carol's dominant presence in family affairs. Despite her fiance's only middling good looks, Marie was enchanted with the prospects of marriage. In her memoirs, she described how "the love I read in Nando's eyes meant nothing to me but a promise of perfect happiness." In an emotional farewell meeting with her father, he told her how he had hoped for a different kind of happiness for her, and how he regretted her departure for such a distant country.

The marriage took place at Sigmaringen in 1893. As with many weddings involving European royalty, monarchs and their representatives gathered from throughout the Continent. Among the guests were Kaiser Wilhelm II of Germany and Prince Albert (I), the heir to the Belgian crown. Like her peers, Marie had been sheltered from any detailed knowledge of the physical side of marriage, and after the wedding she was shocked by her husband's passionate overtures.

A few weeks after the wedding, the young couple made their way to Rumania. Marie was surprised by the primitive appearance of the capital city, Bucharest, and the modest royal palace. Under Carol's orders, she was not permitted to have extensive contact with the Rumanian aristocracy, and she soon found herself isolated and lonely. In short order, she discovered she was pregnant. Her first child, Carol, was born in October 1893.

As Marie's biographer Terence Elsberry notes, King Carol "regarded his Crown Prince and Princess as necessary, but potentially dangerous" to his rule. Thus, he kept them both isolated and under close control. Marie was particularly disappointed to find that she could only travel abroad on infrequent occasions, even for family weddings. Her lively and spirited nature did not mix well with Ferdinand's quiet and shy personality. Marie also learned that Ferdinand was often unfaithful to her.

She had a rare moment of freedom in May 1896, when she attended the coronation of her cousin Tsar Nicholas II. In a memorable event in her life, she rode to victory in a horse race against a Russian cavalry officer. Upon her return to Rumania, she insisted on a new measure of personal freedom, epitomized by rides in the countryside. She also became the honorary commander of a distinguished Rumanian cavalry regiment.

In the summer of 1897, Ferdinand fell seriously ill with typhus. He was for a time feared to be dying. His recovery was a prolonged one, and

it left him physically weakened. While Ferdinand was convalescing, Marie of Rumania had her first extramarital relationship, a romance with an aristocratic young army lieutenant. Word of the liaison spread in Rumanian society, and Marie fled for a time to visit her family in Germany. She returned in November 1899 upon hearing that her eldest child, Prince Carol, was ill with typhoid. The boy recovered, and she and Ferdinand responded to the emergency with a personal reconciliation.

While visiting England in 1902, Marie began a lifelong friendship with Waldorf Astor and his sister **Pauline Astor**, the children of an American millionaire who had settled in England. The friendship with the young Astor developed into an intense, albeit platonic, love affair. The birth of a fourth child, Nicholas, her second son, in 1903 led to a wave of gossip in Rumania that the boy was Waldorf's son, although his physical resemblance to Prince Ferdinand, his legal father, was striking.

By the start of the new century, Marie of Rumania had developed into a confident as well as a physically attractive woman. She had shaken off much of the confining supervision of the early years of her marriage and widened her circle of friends. A symbol of her growing freedom was her extensive contact with the wealthy, often dissolute, members of the Rumanian aristocracy.

In 1907, her life took a new turn in several ways. The oppressed peasantry rose in revolt, and thousands marched on the capital city of Bucharest. Marie and her children left the city to guarantee their safety. In her refuge at the mountain resort of Sinaia, she began her longstanding romantic attachment to Barbo Stirbey, a Rumanian noble and a prominent leader in the country's economy. As a longtime student of Rumanian politics, he provided Marie with her first serious introduction to the nation's problems. Word of their personal tie spread through European aristocratic circles, and rumor had it that the last of her six children, *Ileana, born in 1909, and Mircea, born in 1913, were the offspring of their relationship.

When Rumania participated in the Second Balkan War in 1913, sending its army to invade Bulgaria, Marie of Rumania took on a public role for the first time. She visited the dismal and poorly equipped Rumanian military hospitals. Appalled by what she saw, she took the initiative in setting up an emergency center for treating soldiers with cholera. "Devoid of physical fear herself," writes **Hannah Pakula**, "the Crown Princess obtained permission from the King to

Marie of Rumania (seated).

personally administer one of the cholera camps." It was a preview of one of her roles in World War I.

That same year, Stirbey received an important royal appointment when Carol made him superintendent of the crown's estates. It was a significant sign of royal influence; it also meant Stirbey would have daily contact with Marie.

In July 1914, when World War I began, Marie's relatives in Germany and Russia were rulers on opposite sides of the battle lines. King Carol, now suffering from severe illness, tried to bring Rumania into the war on the side of Germany and Austria, the Central Powers. He found his efforts blocked: all the major political leaders called for neutrality, a position that in fact reflected sympathy for the side of Britain, France, and Russia. Rumanian public opinion was virulently hostile to Austria-Hungary, since that country held Transylvania with its large Rumanian population. Marie, with her close ties to both Britain and Russia, shared the sympathies of most Rumanians, but she was tormented by

the course of events. As she wrote a friend at the time, "One cannot know where or how we shall all be when this horrible nightmare is ended."

The death of King Carol less than two months after the start of the war placed Ferdinand and Marie on the throne as rulers of Rumania during this precarious era. The war came steadily closer to Rumania as Turkey entered the conflict on the side of Germany in late 1914, while Bulgaria did the same at the close of the following year. As monarch, Ferdinand remained the timid and indecisive figure he had always been. Personally inclined to favor Germany's side, he was swayed by those around him, notably the prime minister Ion Bratianu. Marie's influence too promoted sympathy for the Entente (Britain, France, and Russia). At Bratianu's request, she corresponded with King George V of Britain and Tsar Nicholas II of Russia, asking for future territorial concessions to Rumania, especially the acquisition of Transylvania. Notes Pakula, "Being everyone's relative warmed diplomatic waters."

In the spring and summer of 1916, the position of the Entente seemed increasingly favorable in Eastern Europe. The key event was the successful offensive by Russia's General Aleksei Brusilov against the Austro-Hungarian army. Pushed by Marie, Stirbey, and Bratianu, Ferdinand declared war on Austria-Hungary in late August. Germany immediately joined its ally against Rumania.

In short order, the military situation shifted. Brusilov's offensive stalled; the Rumanian offensive into Transylvania brought early successes but at the cost of stripping Rumania of its own defenses. By mid-September, powerful German armies were pouring into Rumania from the north and the south. Meanwhile, the German air force bombed Bucharest. In November, as German armies approached the nation's capital, personal tragedy struck Marie's family: her young son Mircea died of typhus. The Rumanian government and the royal family fled to Jassy, in the unoccupied area in the country's northeastern corner.

Marie of Rumania now became a heroine-queen, one of few effective leaders in her country. She directed the Rumanian Red Cross, worked long hours setting up relief efforts, and personally worked in the nation's bulging military hospitals. Dying soldiers held her photograph, and, when she visited the wounded, she was greeted with the cry of "Mamma Regina," the mother queen.

The new year brought worse news. The March 1917 Revolution in Russia, led by V.I. Lenin, toppled the Romanov monarchy and threatened to remove Rumania's large neighbor from the war. Marie's sister Victoria Melita, married to a Russian grand duke, seemed to be in great personal danger. A partially restored Rumanian army was able to hold defensive positions against an attack by the Central Powers at the battle of Marasesti in August 1917, but Russia's departure from the war threatened to isolate Rumania completely. In November, the Bolsheviks came to power in Russia and the threat became reality. Russia made peace with the Central Powers at Brest-Litovsk in March 1918; Rumania was forced to do the same.

The international public soon heard that Marie refused to accept the peace settlement. These difficult months brought both a new romantic interest and new personal difficulties into her life. She became the firm friend, and perhaps the lover, of Joe Boyle, a representative of the Canadian Red Cross, who heroically delivered supplies from Russia into Rumania. Meanwhile,

Lambrino, Jeanne. See Lupescu, Elena for sidebar.

her eldest son Carol, the heir to the throne, caused deep personal and political embarrassment. He abandoned his duties as an officer in the Rumanian army and eloped to marry a young society woman, **Jeanne Lambrino**, nicknamed Zizi. Marie fought successfully to have the marriage annulled and to permit Carol to retain his right to succeed his father someday as king.

In the closing days of the war, Austria-Hungary collapsed, a pro-Entente government took power in Rumania, and the country re-entered the war on November 9. Marie was overjoyed at the turn of events. At the close of the month, the royal couple, accompanied by their French military adviser, General Henri Berthelot, returned in triumph to Bucharest. They soon discovered that the Germans had looted and devastated much of the country. Russian troops in Rumania, undisciplined in the aftermath of revolution, had also used their stay in Marie's realm to pillage.

At the request of Bratianu, who was serving as Rumania's delegate at the Versailles Peace Conference, Marie came to France to aid her country's diplomatic efforts. Bratianu was pursuing a policy of gaining vast territories for Rumania, but he found the representatives of the major victorious powers unsympathetic. Marie of Rumania answered Bratianu's call with enthusiasm, and received a warm welcome in Paris. Supplied with information and talking points by Bratianu, the queen applied her charm. She held press conferences, lobbied leaders like Prime Minister Georges Clemenceau and President Woodrow Wilson, and visited military hospitals. Marie was also able to renew her longtime friendship with the Astor family. The Peace Conference ended with Rumanian success in gaining a vast amount of territory at the expense of the defeated powers. Due mainly to the strength of the Rumanian army and the power vacuum in Eastern Europe, her country's success was attributed by many, nonetheless, to Marie's personal efforts. Said Marie, "I had given my country a living face."

Marie of Rumania's life in the postwar period contained glamorous elements, many of them which she herself fostered. She continued to be famous for a flamboyant style of dressing, featuring wide hats, long gowns, fur wraps, capes, and turbans. She saw to it that her image was distributed throughout the world on millions of postcards. Rumania's queen even wrote a syndicated column for the newspapers of North America. In 1926, she toured the United States, beginning with a ticker-tape welcoming parade in New York. There, one newspaper greeted her as "the world's first ultra-modern queen." She visited with President Calvin Coolidge and General John Pershing, Sioux Indians, and the cadets at West Point. She was even fodder for the wit of *Dorothy Parker:

> Oh, life is a glorious cycle of song.
> A medley of extemporanea;
> And love is a thing that can never go wrong;
> And I am Marie of Roumania.

Despite Marie's long-standing success in the public eye, the trip soon became an embarrassment to the government back home due to her lavish style of travel, her occasional verbal indiscretions, and the unrelenting curiosity of the press. Word of her husband's illness encouraged her to cut the visit short.

These years were burdened by the disreputable behavior of her oldest son. Carol continued romantic attachments with unsuitable women and refused to fulfill his duties as an army officer. Although he married Princess ✣➤ **Helen of Greece** in February 1921 and their child Michael was born in late October, the marriage soon broke down. To Marie's consternation, he soon took up a scandalous relationship with a commoner from a Jewish family, *Elena Lupescu. In 1925, Carol left the country, renounced his rights to the throne, and set up housekeeping with his mistress in Paris.

On a happier note for Marie, she saw one daughter, *Marie, known as Mignon, married to Alexander (I), the crown prince of Yugoslavia, and another, *Elisabeth, married to George, the crown prince of Greece. A signal event in these postwar years was the formal coronation of Ferdinand and Marie on October 15, 1922, as monarchs of the newly expanded Rumania.

Marie's own troubled marriage was transformed into a more serene tie in the postwar years. She and Ferdinand each accepted the other's extramarital alliances. They found common ground in devotion to their children and their royal responsibilities. Marie's skilled hand in public ceremonies complemented the shy Ferdinand's behind-the-scene political influence.

Ferdinand died of cancer in July 1927. In the last months of the monarch's life, Marie moved frantically to get Carol to return to Rumania. Like many politically astute figures in the country, she knew that it would be dangerous to have Carol's child Michael take the throne under a regency. Rumania's neighbors like Hungary might seize on such an opportunity to retake territory they had lost to the Bucharest government after World War I. But Carol had little interest in returning to Rumania without Elena Lupescu. The death soon afterward of Ion Bratianu, the country's only powerful political leader, only heightened her anxiety.

Marie soon witnessed even more political difficulty. The onset of the Depression struck Rumania's farm-based economy with stark force. Marie was frozen out of the regency council and became frustrated by her lack of political influence. She busied herself with her relationship with Barbo Stirbey; she also wrote a number of romantic novels and started work on her memoirs.

Carol returned in a successful coup in June 1930. He flew to Bucharest and soon received majority support from the regency council. Marie received word of these events while in Germany. She was well acquainted with her son's personal failings, but she accepted his return. The country, in her view, needed the kind of leadership that would restore national unity. She herself hoped to play a role in the new political environment.

Events soon disappointed Marie. King Carol II exiled Barbo Stirbey, whom he had disliked for years. He scandalized Rumanian opinion when he brought his mistress, Elena Lupescu, back home from France. Marie found her own activities restricted, and the new monarch cut off a substantial part of her income. A solitary bright spot in Marie's life was the marriage of her daughter Ileana to an Austrian noble.

Meanwhile, the political scene in Rumania grew uglier. Opposition to the power of Elena Lupescu spurred the growth of a Fascist movement. Led by the attorney Corneliu Codreanu, it was first called the Legion of the Archangel Michael, then renamed the Iron Guard. In 1933, the movement claimed a prominent victim when a member assassinated Marie's friend, Prime Minister Jean Duca. The following year, Marie was shaken by another assassination: her son-in-law, King Alexander of Yugoslavia, was murdered by a Croatian in Marseilles. Marie's daughter Mignon was a widow at the age of 34.

In 1934, Marie published the first portion of her autobiography and received favorable reviews as well as a prestigious British literary prize the following year. She then marked her 60th birthday, still a strikingly attractive woman as a number of portraits painted by Sir Philip de László have recorded. The sadness in one of them reflects her grief at the death of her sister and oldest friend Victoria Melita. At Victoria's deathbed in 1936, Marie had a final reunion with all of her sisters.

✣➤
Helen of Greece. See *Lupescu, Elena for sidebar.*

Her final illness became evident in March 1937. Marie collapsed at her home in Rumania, and her doctors discovered she suffered from repeated bouts of internal bleeding, possibly due to liver disease. King Carol seemed indifferent to her suffering; it took an angry confrontation between him and his sister Mignon to make the monarch call in noted specialists. Marie was able to continue writing her memoirs, but suffered a relapse at the end of the year. Her last months were filled with political pain as King Carol abolished the existing constitution in 1938 and declared himself the country's dictator.

Marie died at Sinaia on July 18, 1938. Her last words to her son were a plea that he be "a just and strong monarch." She was buried at the royal tomb at Curtea de Arges. Following her own typically romantic request, her heart was cut out and placed in the chapel at Balcic, her private retreat on the Black Sea.

Marie of Rumania remains a complex and fascinating figure to students of her time. In an era when European royalty seemed a useless anachronism, her personality was striking, and she played a significant, at times heroic, role for her country both in World War I and at the Peace Conference.

SOURCES:

Blanch, Lesley. *Pavilions of the Heart: The Four Walls of Love*. NY: Putnam, 1974.

Elsberry, Terence. *Marie of Roumania: The Intimate Life of a Twentieth Century Queen*. NY: St. Martin's, 1972.

Pakula, Hannah. *The Last Romantic: A Biography of Queen Marie of Roumania*. NY: Simon and Schuster, 1984.

SUGGESTED READING:

Blanch, Lesley. *Under a Lilac-Bleeding Star*. NY: Atheneum, 1964.

Marie, Queen of Roumania. *The Story of My Life*. NY: Scribner, 1934.

Seton-Watson, Hugh. *Eastern Europe between the Wars, 1918–1941*. 3rd ed. Hamden, CT: Archon Books, 1962.

Stavrianos, Leften. *The Balkans since 1453*. NY: Holt, Rinehart and Winston, 1958.

Neil M. Heyman,
Professor of History,
San Diego State University, San Diego, California

Marie of Rumania (1900–1961).

See Marie.

Marie of Russia (1907–1951)

Princess of Leiningen. Name variations: Mary Cyrillovna; Marie of Leiningen. Born on February 2, 1907, in Coburg, Bavaria, Germany; died on October 27, 1951, in Madrid, Spain; daughter of Cyril Vladimirovitch (son of Tsar Alexander II of Russia) and *Victoria Melita of Saxe-Coburg (1876–1936); married Charles, 6th prince of Leiningen, on November 25, 1925; children: seven, including Emrich, 7th prince of Leiningen (b. 1926); Charles (b. 1928); *Kira of Leiningen (b. 1930); Margaret of Leiningen (b. 1932); Matilda of Leiningen (b. 1936); Frederick (b. 1938).

Marie of Salerno (fl. 1000s)

Countess of the Principate. Flourished around 1000s; married William, count of the Principate (d. 1080); children: Robert, count of the Principate (r. 1080–1099); Tancred (who fought under Roger I in Sicily and received lands of the country of Syracuse); Richard (who was with Bohemund in Antioch in 1096); Rainald (who was with Bohemund in Antioch in 1096).

Marie of Savoy-Nemours (d. 1724).

See Jeanne of Nemours.

Marie of Saxe-Coburg-Gotha (1875–1938).

See Marie of Rumania.

Marie of Saxe-Weimar-Eisenach (1808–1877)

Princess of Prussia. Born on February 3, 1808; died on January 18, 1877; daughter of *Marie Pavlovna (1786–1859) and Charles Frederick, duke of Saxe-Weimar; married Charles Hohenzollern, prince of Prussia, on May 26, 1827; children: Frederick Charles (b. 1828), prince of Prussia; Marie Louise Anne (1829–1901, who married Alexis William, landgrave of Hesse); Anne Frederica (1836–1918).

Marie of Swabia (c. 1201–1235)

German princess. Name variations: Marie de Swabia; Marie von Hohenstaufen. Born around 1201 in Constantinople; died in 1235; daughter of *Irene Angela of Byzantium (d. 1208) and Philip of Swabia (c. 1176–1208), Holy Roman emperor (r. 1198–1208); sister of *Beatrice of Swabia (1198–1235) and *Cunigunde of Hohenstaufen; became first wife of Henry II (1207–1248), duke of Brabant (r. 1235–1248), before August 22, 1215; children: *Maude of Brabant (1224–1288); Henry III (b. 1233), duke of Brabant (r. 1248–1261). Henry II's second wife was *Sophia of Thuringia (1224–1284).

Marie of Valois

Neapolitan noblewoman. Married Charles of Calabria (son of Robert the Good, king of Naples); children: *Joanna I of Naples (1326–1382) and *Marie of Naples.

Marie of Wurttemberg (1813–1839).

See Marie d'Orléans.

Marie Padilla (1335–1365).

See Marie de Padilla.

Marie Pavlovna (1786–1859)

Russian royal and duchess of Saxe-Weimar. Name variations: Mary Pavlovna; Princess Mary. Born on February 15, 1786; died on June 23, 1859; daughter of Paul I (1754–1801), tsar of Russia (r. 1796–1801), and *Sophia Dorothea of Wurttemberg (1759–1828); sister of *Anna Pavlovna (1795–1865) and *Helena Pavlovna (1784–1803); married Charles Frederick, duke of Saxe-Weimar, on August 3, 1804; children: *Marie of Saxe-Weimar-Eisenach (1808–1877); *Augusta of Saxe-Weimar (1811–1890, who married Wilhelm I, emperor of Germany); Charles Alexander (b. 1818).

Marie Pavlovna (1890–1958)

Duchess of Sodermanland. Name variations: Mary Pavlovna Romanov. Born Marie Pavlovna on April 6, 1890; died on December 13, 1958; daughter of Paul Alexandrovitch (son of Alexander II, tsar of Russia) and *Alexandra Oldenburg (1870–1891); married William Bernadotte, duke of Sodermanland (son of Gustavus V, king of Sweden, and *Victoria of Baden), on May 3, 1908 (divorced 1914); married Serge Michailovitch, count Putiatin, on September 6, 1917 (divorced 1924); children: (first marriage) Lennart Gustaf, count of Wisborg (b. 1909).

Marie Poveka (1887–1980).

See Martinez, Maria Montoya.

Marie Raphaelle of Spain (1726–1746).

See Maria Theresa of Spain.

Marie Sophie of Hesse-Cassel
(1767–1852)

Queen of Denmark. Name variations: Marie Sofie Frederikke of Hesse-Cassel. Born on October 28, 1767, in Hanau; died on March 21, 1852, in Amalienborg, Copenhagen, Denmark; daughter of *Louise of Denmark (1750–1831) and Charles of Hesse-Cassel,

regent of Schleswig-Holstein; sister of *Louise of Hesse-Cassel (1789–1867); married Frederick VI, king of Denmark (r. 1808–1839), on July 31, 1790; children: Christian (1791–1791); Marie Louise (1792–1793); Caroline (1793–1881, who married Frederick Ferdinand, prince Oldenburg); Louise (1795–1795); Christian (1797–1797); Louise Juliane (1802–1802); Frederica Maria (1805–1805); *Wilhelmine (1808–1891, who married Frederick VII, king of Denmark).

Marie Stuart (1542–1587).

See Mary Stuart.

Marie Thérèse Charlotte
(1778–1851)

Duchess of Angoulême, daughter of Louis XVI and Marie Antoinette, who survived her parents and lived most of her life in exile. Name variations: Marie Therese Charlotte; Marie-Thérèse-Charlotte; Madame Royale; Filia Dolorosa, the Modern Antigone; Comtesse de Marnes. Born at Versailles, France, on December 19, 1778; died of pneumonia on October 19, 1851, in Austria; daughter of Louis XVI (1754–1793), king of France (r. 1774–1792), and Marie Antoinette (1755–1793); educated at French court; married Louis Antoine de Bourbon (1775–1844), duke of Angoulême, in 1799.

Imprisoned with her family in the Temple (1792); mother and father guillotined (1793); released from prison (1795); married the duke of Angoulême (1799); lived in exile with her uncle Louis XVIII in various European countries (1799–1814); Louis XVIII restored to the French throne (1814–15); lived at French court; revolution in Paris and abdication of Charles X and the duke of Angoulême (1830); spent remaining years in exile.

On August 13, 1792, *Marie Antoinette and her husband Louis XVI and their two children were imprisoned in the Temple in Paris. The French Revolution, which had begun three years before, was reaching a crucial stage and the actions of the king, who had attempted to escape the country, were increasingly under suspicion. Fearing a Royalist counter-revolution, the National Assembly agreed that the royal family must be kept under close guard. These years of imprisonment were to have a profound effect upon the young princess Marie Thérèse Charlotte.

Born on December 19, 1778, Marie Thérèse Charlotte was the eldest daughter of Louis XVI and Marie Antoinette. As a child of royalty, she was given a thorough education. Her mother was particularly influential and ensured that Marie Thérèse learned not to neglect the feelings and opinions of others. Author Joseph Turquan concludes that Marie Antoinette inculcated in Marie Thérèse "respect for the virtues of others, gratitude for services rendered, love of humanity, compassion towards misfortune, moderation in luxury, charity, kindness and forbearance." Perhaps the young girl took this training too close to heart, as she was very serious as a child and was called "mousseline la sérieuse" ("Muslin the Serious") by her mother. Nevertheless, these qualities stood her in good stead when the fortunes of her family took a turn for the worse.

With the storming of the Bastille in July 1789, the French Revolution had begun. Although he attempted to maintain his authority, Louis XVI continued to make unwise and politically disastrous decisions, including an attempt to flee the country with his family in June 1791. When they were discovered at the French border, the royal family was escorted back to Paris under heavy guard. A year later, 14-year-old Marie Thérèse, her mother, father, brother and aunt were imprisoned in the Paris dungeon known as the Temple. She spent the next three years there with few comforts and little reliable news of the political situation. During her imprisonment, Marie Thérèse kept a personal journal detailing her experiences. These entries express the hopes, fears, and, ultimately, strength of a young woman living under extraordinary circumstances.

As the Revolution progressed, the fate of the king became increasingly precarious. When the National Convention abolished the institution of the monarchy in September 1792, Louis' fate was sealed. After a short trial in December, the king was found guilty of treason and was guillotined on January 12, 1793. This event affected the young princess deeply. For the rest of her life, she never failed to hold at least two days of prayer and memorial services every January 21 to commemorate the death of her father. Yet, although it was a heavy blow, his death did not signal the end of misfortunes for the royal family. Shortly after the king's execution, Marie Antoinette was removed from her daughter and imprisoned in a separate room where she was interrogated. Although Marie Thérèse attempted to obtain news of her mother's situation, the government refused to disclose any information to her. From that point on, she came to rely on her aunt *Madame Elisabeth (1764–1794) for maternal support. When Marie Antoinette was

executed in October 1793, Marie Thérèse was not told. Whenever she asked for news about her mother, her questions were avoided. She only learned of her mother's death one and half years after the event.

Life in prison was difficult for the young princess. Frequent searches were made of her room, sometimes three times a day and by officials who were often intoxicated. Marie Thérèse coped with her situation by relying increasingly on religion, and the majority of her reading material consisted of prayer books. In May 1794, her aunt Elisabeth was taken away and guillotined. Marie Thérèse was now left completely alone. When she received a visit from the duchess of Tourzel in 1795, she explained how she survived the isolation: "Without religion it would have been impossible. Religion was my only resource, and it procured for me the only consolations of which my heart could be susceptible." While her situation was difficult, her brother's was even worse. Louis Charles' quarters were filthy, he was left alone, and received few visits from his guards or anyone else for several days. Upon the death of his father, he became Louis XVII although this position held no sway with his jailers. Marie Thérèse stopped writing in her journal when she learned of her brother's death on June 9, 1795. She was now truly an orphan—without mother, father, brother or aunt.

As she was the last remaining member of the royal family who was still in prison, some people in the government felt that Marie Thérèse should be released. While this was being debated, the conditions of her imprisonment improved. She was now allowed to have a female companion, visitors, new dresses, paper and ink, and books. She was also allowed to have walks in the Temple gardens. It was obvious that public opinion was becoming more favorable towards her. At 17, Marie Thérèse was a slender young woman, with chestnut hair and fine features. Shortly before her release, a visitor to the Temple noted how she had changed: "When we left her at the Temple about the 10th of August, she was frail and delicate-looking. Now, after three years of misfortune, mental agony, and captivity, she is handsome, tall and strong, and bears on her countenance the imprint of that nobility of mind which is her distinguishing feature."

In November 1795, the volatile French government changed hands once more and steps were taken to release the young princess. It was decided that she would be liberated in exchange for several French prisoners who were being held in Austria. On the night before her 18th birthday,

Marie
Thérèse
Charlotte

Marie Thérèse Charlotte was finally released from the prison where she had spent the majority of her adolescence. Traveling incognito under the name "Sophie," she left Paris on the night of December 18, 1795. As she made her way towards the Austrian border, she was soon recognized by French citizens who treated her with much sympathy. She burst into tears when she crossed the border into Austria and exclaimed: "I quit France with regret for I shall never cease to regard it as my country." Thus, after all that she had gone through, Marie Thérèse Charlotte remained strong and warm hearted with little bitterness towards the country that had caused her such heartbreak.

Although she was no longer a prisoner, the Austrian government, which was still at war with France, was not very liberal with her. In essence, the government wanted to keep her as a hostage for political leverage. Marie Thérèse, however, wanted to join her uncle, now Louis XVIII, who was living in Verona. The Austrian emperor refused her request, and she was obliged to make an attempt to settle down to her new life in Vienna. She was granted some new freedoms, however. She was, for example, finally allowed to pray inside a church—something she had not done since her imprisonment. Marie Thérèse was also able to wear mourning clothing, thus honoring the deaths of her parents, aunt and brother. Although she aroused much sympathy in Austria, she continued to experience difficulties. The emperor took away most of the French servants who had traveled with her to Austria. He also tried to persuade her to marry an Austrian duke. Despite these and other slights, Marie Thérèse remained in Vienna for more than three years. In May 1799, she was finally allowed to join her uncle who was now living at Mittau in Russia.

*A*sk your selves, all ye who pause here, if your sorrows are equal unto mine.

—Inscription on tombstone of Marie Thérèse Charlotte

In Russia, Marie Thérèse was given a warm welcome by Tsar Paul I, son of *Catherine I the Great. She and her uncle, Louis XVIII, were allowed to live in one of the tsar's palaces and were also given a pension. It was at Mittau that Marie Thérèse met her future husband, Louis Antoine de Bourbon, duke of Angoulême. As the son of Louis XVI's younger brother, the count of Artois, Louis Antoine was Marie Thérèse's first cousin. Since her marriage to the duke had been the wish of her parents, 20-year-old Marie Thérèse held no objections to the match, and she married him six days after her arrival in Russia. Her husband, who was four years older than his bride, was short, frail and not very handsome. Whether or not she truly loved him never will be known. Her duty was to honor the wishes of her dead parents, and Marie Thérèse would have never contemplated going against their desires. By all accounts, wife and husband lived peacefully together whenever he was not away on frequent military campaigns.

As exiles, Marie Thérèse and her uncle depended upon the goodwill and support of their hosts. Unfortunately for them, Tsar Paul I was not very trustworthy. When Napoleon Bonaparte defeated the French Royalist forces in several battles, Paul decided to throw his support behind Napoleon and, consequently, gave orders for Louis XVIII and his court to leave Russia immediately. On January 22, 1801, Marie Thérèse and Louis XVIII left Russia incognito under the names Count of Lille and Marchioness of La Meilleraye. They finally found refuge in Warsaw, where they remained under the protection of the king of Prussia. In March, Louis Antoine rejoined his wife, and they attempted to settle down in their new surroundings.

The political situation in France became worse for the exiles when Napoleon was made First Consul for life in May 1802. By 1803, Napoleon asked Louis XVIII to give up any claim to the French throne, which Louis refused to do. When Napoleon proclaimed himself emperor of France in 1804, it appeared that any hopes for a restoration of Louis XVIII to the French crown were lost forever. The financial situation of Marie Thérèse and her uncle improved, however, after the assassination of Paul I. The new tsar of Russia, Alexander I, supported Louis XVIII and gave him much-needed subsidies. In 1805, they returned to Mittau. As always, however, the political sympathies of their hosts determined the fate of the exiles. When Russian troops suffered two major defeats at the hands of Napoleon's army, Tsar Alexander signed the Treaty of Tilsit on June 25, 1807. Although Louis XVIII was not banished outright, he soon left for England. Marie Thérèse joined him there one year later. From 1808, France was engaged in war with most of Europe. By 1810, however, after a series of military victories, Napoleon was master of continental Europe. With the placement of his relatives and friends on the thrones of Italy, Westphalia, Holland and Spain, it appeared that his power was complete.

For Louis XVIII and his niece, these victories meant six years of exile in England. Upon her arrival there in July 1808, Marie Thérèse was given shelter at the home of the marquis of Buckingham in Essex. Desiring a dwelling closer to London, she and her uncle moved to Hartwell in 1809. During her exile in England, Marie Thérèse lived a quiet, relatively peaceful life. She spent much of her time meditating, reading and praying. Each January, she continued to hold her own private memorial service to mark the death of her father. Louis XVIII set up a small court at Hartwell and made every attempt to maintain the semblance of a royal routine. Although Marie Thérèse supported him as best as she could, she was not very interested in the intricacies of court etiquette and ritual. Contact with the king and queen of England was infrequent; Marie Thérèse appeared at the royal court in London only once in 1811. From this point on, she was often referred to as Madame Royale, signifying her status as the only surviving child of Louis XVI.

The fortunes of the exiles took a positive turn when cracks in Napoleon's seeming invincibility began to appear by 1812. Despite the fact that his troops reached Moscow in September 1812, the Russian winter soon decimated what remained of the French army. At Leipzig, French troops were forced to retreat after the Battle of Nations in October 1813. From this point on, events leading to Napoleon's defeat followed rapidly. In January 1814, Louis Antoine, his father the count of Artois, and the duke of Berry left England and invaded France. By March, the French Royalist army, with assistance from British troops, entered Bordeaux, proclaimed the restoration of the Bourbon monarchy and named Louis XVIII king of France. On March 31, Paris was captured by the allied forces, and on April 6 Napoleon abdicated and was sent into exile on the island of Elba. On April 24, 1814, Marie Thérèse and Louis XVIII left England for France.

Twenty-one years after the deaths of her parents and nineteen years after her release from the Temple, Marie Thérèse had finally returned home. Her joy was short lived, however, as one year later Napoleon escaped from Elba and invaded France in an attempt to regain power. Fearing for their safety, the majority of the royal family, including her uncle, fled the country. Marie Thérèse, however, refused to leave France and remained in Bordeaux. Upon hearing of her stand against him, Napoleon was impressed. Despite her best efforts, however, the French troops were unwilling to fight for a king they had never seen, and Marie Thérèse was forced to flee. On June 15, 1815, Napoleon was defeated for the last time at the Battle of Waterloo and exiled to the island of Saint Helena. From this point on, the threat to the restoration of the French monarchy was gone. Marie Thérèse could return to her native land in security.

For the next 15 years, Marie Thérèse lived a quiet and reserved life in Paris. She set up her own court at the Tuileries, which was renowned for its simplicity and order. Under her influence, French court life in general improved and became better mannered. When her uncle died in 1824, Marie Thérèse's father-in-law, the count of Artois, became King Charles X. Her husband was now heir to the throne and, as such, was called the Dauphin. Unfortunately, the new king was not sympathetic to the form of constitutional monarchy that had been set up when Louis XVIII was restored to the throne. Following the ideals of his eldest brother, Louis XVI, Charles X attempted to re-establish pre-revolutionary kingship. When elections were held in 1830, a liberal majority was returned that was unfavorable towards Charles. These political tensions were coupled with a downturn in the French economy. Bad harvests caused near-famine conditions in many urban areas along with a huge rise in prices for grain and other commodities. On July 28, 1830, a protest by workers erupted into a full-fledged revolution. Three days later, Louis Philippe I, the former duke of Orléans, was set up as the new constitutional monarch. Charles

X and his son, Marie Thérèse's husband, both abdicated their rights to the French throne. Once again, she was forced to flee the country of her birth and live in exile.

In 1830, Marie Thérèse was 52 years old and her fortunes remained unsettled. She and her husband's family returned to England, where they were allowed to remain on the proviso that they renounced all outward symbols of royalty. Consequently, Marie Thérèse and Louis Antoine changed their names to the Comte and Comtesse de Marnes. They lived at Lulworth Castle in Dorset for one year and then moved to Edinburgh, where they spent two years at the palace of Holyrood. In 1833, Marie Thérèse and her husband moved to Prague where they set up a small household. On November 6, 1836, Charles X died. From this point on, the life of Marie Thérèse and her husband became simple and austere. She enjoyed reading novels and tending to her garden. When Louis Antoine died of complications from blood poisoning in 1844, Marie Thérèse settled in the small town of Frohsdorf, about 30 miles from Vienna.

The royal princess spent her remaining years in near seclusion. Content with her simple

Painting of Marie Thérèse Charlotte by Madame Vigée-Le Brun.

life, she had no desire to spend time at the Austrian court. In 1851, she caught a chill after taking a long walk. She died of pneumonia on October 19, 1851, at the age of 72.

SOURCES:

Powers, Elizabeth. *The Journal of Madame Royale.* NY: Walker, 1976.

Saint-Amand, Imbert de. *Famous Women of the French Court: The Duchess of Angoulême and the Two Restorations.* NY: Scribner, 1899.

———. *The Youth of the Duchess of Angoulême.* NY: Scribner, 1892.

Turquan, Joseph. *Madame Royale: The Last Dauphine.* London: T. Fisher Unwin, 1910.

SUGGESTED READING:

Desmond, Alice Curtis. *Marie Antoinette's Daughter.* NY: Dodd, Mead, 1967.

Margaret McIntyre,
Instructor of Women's History at
Trent University, Peterborough, Ontario, Canada

Marie-Thérèse de Soubiran
(1834–1889)

Founder of the Society of Mary Auxiliatrix. Born on May 16, 1834, at Castelnaudary (Aude), France; died on June 7, 1889, in Paris, France; beatified by Pius XII in 1946.

Born in 1834 into a family that included St. Elzéar de Sabran, the Franciscan tertiary, and Urban V, the sixth pope of Avignon, Marie-Thérèse de Soubiran also chose the religious life. At age 14, she took a vow of chastity, began to eat nothing but bread and water, and slept on a board. After spending some time in a convent in Ghent, Marie-Thérèse established her own congregation, which eventually came to be known as the Society of Mary Auxiliatrix. Receiving pontifical approbation in 1869, the order practiced perpetual adoration of the Blessed Sacrament.

During the war of 1870, Marie-Thérèse took refuge in London. In her absence, one of her nuns supplanted her, and upon her return she was disowned by her own institution. She had a great deal of difficulty finding a convent that would accept her, but in 1874 was finally received at Notre Dame de Charité in Paris. She remained there for 15 years, relegated to small duties which she performed with resignation. "Oh! richness of the present moment, thou art infinite, since thou containest my God!," she proclaimed. "Why not love you? Why not enclose myself wholly in you." Marie-Thérèse de Soubiran died there on June 7, 1889, and was beatified by Pope Pius XII in 1946.

SOURCES:

Englebert, Omer. *The Lives of the Saints.* Translated by Christopher and Anne Fremantle. London: Thames and Hudson, 1951.

Marie Therese of Austria (1638–1683).

See Maria Teresa of Spain.

Marie Therese of Bourbon

Princess of Hohenzollern. Married William (1864–1927), prince of Hohenzollern; children: *Augusta Victoria (1890–1966, who married Manuel II, king of Portugal).

Marie Therese of Spain (1638–1683).

See Maria Teresa of Spain.

Marie Valerie (1868–1924)

Archduchess of Austria. Name variations: Marie Valérie. Born in 1868; died in 1924; daughter of *Elizabeth of Bavaria (1837–1898) and Franz Josef also known as Francis Joseph, emperor of Austria (r. 1848–1916); married Francis (Franz) Salvator, archduke of Tuscany; children: Elisabeth Franziska, known as Ella Salvator (1892–1930); Franz Karl Salvator (1893–1918); Hubert Salvator (1894–1971); Hedwig Salvator (1896–1970); Theodor Salvator (1899–1978); Gertrud Salvator (1900–1962); Maria Salvator (1901–1936); Klemens Salvator (1904–1974); Mathilde Salvator (b. 1906).

Marie Vetsera (1871–1889).

See Vetsera, Marie.

Marietta (fl. 1430s)

Mistress of the king of Cyprus. Born in the Greek city of Patras; mistress of John II, the Lusignan king of Cyprus (r. 1432–1458); children: illegitimate son, James II the Bastard, king of Cyprus (b. in either 1440 or 1441); possibly mother of *Anne of Lusignan.

Marietta was the mistress of the king of Cyprus, John II. At some point, John's queen *Helen Paleologina literally bit off Marietta's nose. Henceforth, Marietta was commonly referred to as "Crop-nosed," and the rivalry between Helen's and Marietta's children, which had been bitter, grew rancid.

Mariia.

Variant of Maria.

Marillac, Louise de (1591–1660)

Saint who founded the Sisters of Charity in 1633. Name variations: Madame le Gras. Born in Paris, France, on August 15, 1591; died of gangrene on March 15, 1660; daughter of Louis de Marillac (counselor to Parliament) and his second wife Marguerite (le Camus) de Marillac; married Antoine le Gras, in 1613 (died 1626); children: one son. Her feast day is March 15.

The daughter of a counselor to the French Parliament, Louise de Marillac lost her mother at an early age, after which she assumed the management of the family household. A pious young girl, she vowed to become a nun, but she married instead in 1613. When her husband Antoine le Gras was stricken with an incurable disease nine years later, Marillac accepted his illness as divine punishment for having broken her earlier religious vow. After his death in 1626, she became a nun, keeping her son, her only child, with her.

Under the blessing and guidance of St. Vincent de Paul, Marillac founded the Sisters of Charity in 1633, with a group of five young country girls. The order first devoted itself to teaching catechism, but as it increased in membership, it broadened its purview, opening small schools and conducting retreats. Later, the order founded hospitals for the poor and mentally afflicted. The Congregation of Sisters of Charity was sanctioned by King Louis XIV in 1657, and by the pope in 1668, the same year that Marillac was elevated to superior-general. She died two years later and was mourned by her mentor St. Vincent. Ill himself and unable to visit her on her deathbed, he sent a message that "she should go on ahead and he would hope to see her soon in heaven."

SOURCES:

Englebert, Omer. *The Lives of the Saints.* Translated by Christopher and Anne Fremantle. London: Thames and Hudson, 1951.

Marina (c. 1500–1531).

See Malinche.

Marina of Antioch (c. 255–c. 275).

See Margaret of Antioch.

Marina of Greece (1906–1968)

Duchess of Kent. Name variations: Marina Oldenburg; Dame Marina. Born on December 13, 1906, in Athens, Greece; died on August 27, 1968, at Kensington Palace, London, England; daughter of Helena of Russia (1882–1957) and Prince Nicholas (Oldenburg) of Greece (uncle of England's Prince Philip); sister of *Olga Oldenburg (1903–1981) and *Elizabeth Oldenburg (1904–1955); married George Windsor (1902–1942), 1st duke of Kent, on November 29, 1934; children: Edward Windsor (b. 1935), 2nd duke of Kent; Princess *Alexandra of Kent (b. 1936); Prince Michael of Kent (b. 1942).*

The youngest of the three daughters of Prince Nicholas of Greece and ***Helena of Russia**, Marina of Greece married George, 1st duke of Kent, in 1934, and had three children before her husband's untimely death in a plane crash in 1942. Marina, who served during the war as commandant, and later chief commandant, of the Women's Royal Naval Service (WRNS), was also colonel-in-chief of the Queen's Own Royal West Kent Regiment and the Corps of Royal Electrical and Mechanical Engineers. Marina was a chancellor of Kent University and a patron of the National Association for Mental Health. She also served as president of the Royal National Lifeboat Institution and of the All England Lawn Tennis Club. She was named Grand Cross of the British Empire (GBE) in 1937 and Grand Cross of the Royal Victorian Order (GCVO), in 1948.

Mario, Queena (1896–1951)

American soprano and writer. Name variations: wrote under names Queen Tillotson and Florence Bryan. Born Queena Mario Tillotson on August 21, 1896, in Akron, Ohio; died in New York, on May 28, 1951; attended Ogonta (Pennsylvania) School, 1907–08; attended Plainfield (New Jersey) High School, 1908–10; daughter of James Tillotson and Rose (Carewe) Tillotson; married Wilfred Pelletier (a conductor at the Metropolitan Opera House), on November 23, 1925 (divorced 1936).

The daughter of a Civil War soldier turned Broadway playwright, Queena Mario was born on April 21, 1896, in Akron, Ohio, but later moved with her family to Plainfield, New Jersey. As the result of a family financial reversal, she gave up dreams of becoming an opera singer and went to work as a journalist, writing women's columns and features for several leading New York papers under the names Queen Tillotson and Florence Bryan. Her salary was such that in addition to helping out her family, she was able to indulge her desire to take voice lessons. In 1916, after studying with Oscar Saenger, she auditioned for the Metropolitan Opera, but was turned away. She continued her studies with *Marcella Sembrich, but a second audition in 1918 was also unsuccessful. Still determined to reach her goal, and with some additional intervention from Enrico Caruso, she prevailed upon Fortuno Gallo, the director of the San Carlo Opera to invite her to join the company. Caruso was reportedly so sure of Mario's gifts that he promised Gallo he would pay the singer's first-year salary out of his own pocket if she did not work out.

In September 1918, Mario made her debut with the San Carlo Opera in *Tales of Hoffmann*, for which she received excellent reviews. "Her voice has the advantage of youth and freshness," wrote one critic. "It is flexible, but it is also warm in quality." Mario remained with the San Carlo for two seasons, singing the roles of Violetta, Lucia, Gilda, and Juliet, then joined the Scotti Grand Opera Company for two seasons.

In 1922, Mario auditioned for the Metropolitan yet a third time. The singer was about to debut at Paris' Opéra-Comique when she received news of her acceptance by the Met; she was so excited that she immediately booked passage home, canceling her Paris engagement. Mario debuted with the Met on Thanksgiving Day that same year, singing the role of Micaëla in *Carmen*. She remained with the Metropolitan for the next 15 years, singing over 20 leading roles in Italian, French, and German operas, and committing to memory 25 additional roles. By one account, Mario learned each new role by first whistling it from beginning to end before making any attempt to sing it. The singer's private life also flourished at the Met. In 1925, she married Wilfred Pelletier, then the conductor at the opera house. (They would divorce in 1936.)

Although she received much acclaim for her interpretations of the roles of Inez, Aennchen, Ah-Yoe, and Sophie, Mario became best known for her performance of Gretel in the Humperdinck opera *Hansel and Gretel*. She sang the role in the first full performance to be broadcast on the radio from the stage of the Met (Christmas Day, 1931), and again at her farewell performance in 1938. During her years at the Met, Mario also made guest appearances with the San Francisco Opera (1923–24 and 1929–30), where she won particular acclaim as the Child in the premiere of Ravel's *L'Enfant et les Sortilèges* (1930). Following her retirement from the stage, Mario devoted her later years to teaching. Among her more notable students were *Rose Bampton and *Helen Jepson.

In addition to her operatic career, Mario wrote a successful murder mystery, *Murder in the Opera House*, which centers around a performance of *I Pagliacci* at the Met.

SOURCES:
Ewen, David, ed. *Living Musicians.* NY: H.W. Wilson, 1940.
Sadie, Stanley, ed. *The New Grove Dictionary of Opera.* Vol 3. London and NY: Macmillan Press, 1992.

Barbara Morgan,
Melrose, Massachusetts

Marion.

Variant of Mary and Miriam.

Marion, Frances (1888–1973)

American screenwriter who was the first female writer to win an Academy Award. Name variations: (pseudonym for westerns) Frank M. Clifton. Born Marion Benson Owens in San Francisco, California, on November 18, 1888; died on May 12, 1973, of an aneurysm; daughter of Len Douglas Owens (in advertising business) and Minnie Benson Hall Owens; married Wesley de Lappe, on October 23, 1906 (divorced 1911); married Robert Dickson Pike (an industrialist), on November 14, 1911 (divorced 1917); married Fred Thomson, on November 2, 1919 (died 1928); married George Hill, in January 1930 (divorced 1931); children: (third marriage) Fred Thomson, Jr. (b. December 8, 1926); (adopted) Richard Gordon Thomson (1927).

Won Academy Award for Screenwriting for her original story The Big House *(1930); won second Oscar for* The Champ; *served as vice president and only woman on the first board of directors of the Screen Writers Guild; wrote 325 scripts.*

Women were powerful in the early years of Hollywood; half of all copyrighted films between 1911 and 1925 were written by women. "With few taking moviemaking seriously as a business, the doors were wide open," writes **Cari Beauchamp**. By the time Frances Marion won a 1930 Academy Award for her original story *The Big House*, she was the highest-paid screenwriter in Hollywood. That evening, four of her films had nominees for Best Actress or Actor: Wallace Beery for *The Big House*, Lawrence Tibbett for *The Rogue Song*, *Norma Shearer for *Their Own Desire*, and *Greta Garbo for *Anna Christie*; the following year, *Marie Dressler would take Best Actress honors for appearing in another Marion screenplay, *Min and Bill*. By then, Frances Marion had written over 100 produced films, including *Rebecca of Sunnybrook Farm*, *Pollyanna*, *A Little Princess*, and a dozen others for *Mary Pickford. She had also penned *Stella Dallas, Poor Little Rich Girl, Dinner at Eight, Camille,* and *The Champ.* But that night in 1930, when she returned to her seat with Oscar in hand, Marion sized up the statuette: "I saw it as a perfect symbol of the picture business: a powerful athletic body clutching a gleaming sword, but with half of his head, the part which held his brains, completely sliced off."

Frances Marion was born Marion Benson Owens on November 18, 1888, in San Francisco, California, the middle child of Len and **Minnie Owens**; her sister Maude was two years older; her brother Len, Jr., two years younger. Len, Sr., was successful in advertising and owned a drug company, and the family was firmly ensconced in San Francisco society. Len loved the outdoors and organized a bicycle club; Minnie, whose parents were musicians, preferred life indoors, maintaining her household on O'Farrell Street as a hub for such artists as *Luisa Tetrazzini, *Nellie Melba, and Enrico Caruso. Minnie's uncle and aunt, George and **Jane Benson**, also lived with the family.

In the fall of 1898, when Marion was ten, her parents divorced; two years later, Len married **Isabel Preston**. Though Marion was generally a well-behaved child who had, in her own words, learned the "hypocrisies of social graces," a few months after her father's wedding she was caught at her classroom blackboard, drawing caricatures of her teachers, and was expelled from "all public schools."

With her days thus free, Marion became the channeler for the weekly spiritualist sessions held by Aunt Jane, and Uncle George, a retired seafarer, took his niece with him to his favorite haunts, the saloons of the Barbary Coast. She was then waylaid by polio for several months and turned to reading, as well as to writing in her secret diary. After her recovery, she was sent to the exclusive preparatory boarding school, St. Margaret's Hall in San Mateo, an Episcopalian enterprise that promised to raise girls to "noble womanhood." Summers, she traveled with her mother to such places as Alaska. Marion was in Mexico when she first saw the disparities between the wealth of the Church and the poverty of the poor. She began to loathe hypocrisy and was an early student of human behavior.

At St. Margaret's, Marion excelled in writing, and friends of the family, Jack London and *Ella Wheeler Wilcox, encouraged her to send her stories to magazines. "California's Latest," an ode to Luther Burbank, was printed in *Sunset* magazine in May 1905. Marion also took to art

at school, under the tutelage of Charles Chapel Judson. When he transferred to the Mark Hopkins Art Institute, 16-year-old Marion followed and once again lived at home in the rarified society of her mother, while at the same time taking advantage of San Francisco's bohemian community. She also fell in love with her art teacher, Wesley de Lappe, who had just been hired to draw for the *San Francisco Chronicle*. On April 18, 1906, while sitting together on a park bench, Marion and de Lappe heard a loud rumbling sound. The San Francisco earthquake leveled 250 city blocks and killed 1,000. Workers and socialites pitched in side-by-side to save the city. Though her parents' home was left standing, Marion claimed that the family "lost everything" in the quake; it was the end of the Mark Hopkins Art Institute and her father's drug company. With hopes of college in the East dashed, 18-year-old Marion wed 19-year-old de Lappe on October 23, 1906, and the cash-strapped couple lived with her family.

> *I* spent my life searching for a man to look up to without lying down.
>
> —**Frances Marion**

Marion continued to write but, at the urging of Jack London, took odd jobs to study human behavior. She pitted peaches at a cannery, operated a telephone switchboard, and then signed on as an assistant to well-known photographer Arnold Genthe, who not only did informal portraits of society's elite but took his camera to the streets of the city. Marion, who was 5'2", with chestnut hair and deep blue eyes, was considered a beauty, and Genthe, who was struck by her looks, used her as a model. She also learned layout and color photography and met many of the theatrical elite who sought out Genthe for portraits.

Economic stress hampered her marriage, however, and the de Lappes were divorced in 1910. Hungry for experience, Marion became a reporter for the *San Francisco Examiner,* but "her sympathy for victims," writes Beauchamp, "prevented her from writing flamboyantly enough for William Randolph Hearst's news desk, and she was transferred to the theater department." One of Marion's first interviews was with Marie Dressler, in town on a theatrical tour, and the two hit it off.

Marion then met Robert Dickson Pike, a member of the Bohemian Club and an up-and-comer in his father's steel firm. For Marion, Pike offered economic security and social respect; her father's approval, a rarity, was an added bonus.

Married in November 1911, the newlyweds moved to Los Angeles, where Robert opened a branch office for his father, and Marion was hired to paint posters for Oliver Morosco, owner of the Morosco theater. But unlike sophisticated San Francisco, Los Angeles was provincial, and Marion was soon appalled at the bias against Jews, actors, artists, and anyone in the burgeoning movie industry. Her conservative husband tended to side with the "conscientious citizens" who deplored the outcasts who worked in the "flickers." Since husband and wife were rarely together, however, the inevitable breakup was postponed. Marion was learning that she preferred work to the life of a society matron. When she bumped into Marie Dressler, who was in Los Angeles to film *Tillie's Punctured Romance* for Mack Sennett, the two picked up their conversation where they had left off.

Marion, who would mother a retinue of women friends, also became close to *Mabel Normand* as well as *Adela Rogers (St. John)*, an old friend from San Francisco who was now writing for the *Los Angeles Herald Examiner*. On first meeting Mary Pickford, Marion sensed the vulnerability of the young actress, writes Beauchamp, and "instantly developed a fiercely protective attitude toward Mary that was to be a hallmark of their friendship." The new confidants soon shared the truth about their failed marriages. Marion's second would end that year.

In the summer of 1914, 26-year-old Marion was hired by the director *Lois Weber* at Bosworth Studio to do a little of everything: write press releases, paint backdrops, learn to edit film, and, despite her protests, act. Though Marion Benson Owens was handed the new name of Frances Marion for the screen, she wanted to write, not act. Then Weber moved to Universal, and Marion joined the writing department at Balboa Studios. To her consternation, she found herself in front of the cameras once more. Marion was baffled; as far as she was concerned, she was a "tall, gawky girl" on screen, "a stranger who made a few grimaces and then dashed off." But when Pickford said "come act" at Famous Players, "we'll have fun together," Marion readily complied. Pickford had also agreed to let her friend dabble with scenarios. In short order, Frances Marion wrote *The Foundling* for Pickford, and Adolph Zukor bought the script for $125. "I ceased walking on this earth," wrote Marion. But just as the film shoot was wrapping up in New York, the negative burned in a studio fire. No prints had yet been made.

A devastated Marion, who had been counting on the film to establish her writing credentials, remained in New York, taking a small room at the Algonquin, and was soon working for William Brady at his World Studios in Fort Lee, New Jersey. She was earning $200 a week, an unheard-of salary for a scenarist, writing films for *Clara Kimball Young*, *Doris Kenyon*, and *Alice Brady*. She was also ghostwriting a syndicated column for S.S. McClure's "Daily Talks" for Mary Pickford, who then lived in New York.

Meanwhile, Pickford had reshot *The Foundling*, and it was released in 1916 to popular acclaim. Marion then wrote *Woman Against the Sea* for Fox for $5,000; by the time filming began, the woman against the sea was being played by William Farnum and was called *The Iron Man*, but Marion retained her $5,000. By March 1916, she was head of the scenario department at World and was casting films, directing scenes, and supervising screen tests for fresh faces. But Marion was overworked and exhausted. When her 30-year-old sister Maude put a .22 to her head and killed herself, Marion broke down and was hospitalized. It was Marie Dressler who nursed her back to health. After a month, Marion returned to her work at World, but she stopped writing the Pickford column and tried to slow down. She also added two more women friends, *Mary Roberts Rinehart* and *Anita Loos*, to her close-knit group.

When Pickford signed for *Poor Little Rich Girl*, to be filmed by Cecil B. De Mille in Fort Lee, she demanded that Frances Marion write the scenario. De Mille was adamant that he would choose the scriptwriter; soon De Mille was out and a new director, Maurice Tourneur, was in. But during the shoot, to Tourneur's annoyance, Pickford and Marion repeatedly added bits of comedy. The women were devastated when, at the private screening for executives, not one man laughed. So, with little advance publicity, *Poor Little Rich Girl* was shown at the Strand on Broadway. The audience roared. Pickford and Marion vowed that they would never again question their instincts because of the disapproval of the powers that be. The film was a major success, and Marion signed a contract with Famous Players-Lasky at $50,000 per year to write for Pickford. Their next project, *Rebecca of Sunnybrook Farm*, was another smash; they followed that with an adaptation of *Frances Hodgson Burnett*'s *The Little Princess*. By then, Marion had written 50 films and returned to Los Angeles to much favorable press. Movies had become respectable.

With Europe at war, Pickford talked her friend into writing *Johanna Enlists*. While securing the 143rd Field artillery unit to appear in the movie, Marion met Lieutenant Fred Thomson, the unit's chaplain and a world-class athlete. It was love at first sight; she had fallen, she said, for a Boy Scout. Fred sailed off to war, Pickford went on bond-selling tours, while Marion headed for France and the front as a correspondent for the Committee on Public Information. Her job was to film the work of Allied women—over 20,000 were serving overseas as army and navy nurses, entertainers, decoders, and interpreters for the Red Cross, Salvation Army, and YMCA. Marion was the first correspondent to cross the Rhine, days before the Armistice; the outcome was her 15-reel serial, *American Women in the War*.

Back home again, Frances Marion adapted four stories from *Lucy Maud Montgomery's "Anne of Green Gables" series into one scenario for *Mary Miles Minter. She then signed with William Randolph Hearst's studio in New York, Cosmopolitan, to write for *Marion Davies. Now proclaimed in studio ads as "the highest salaried photoplaywright in the industry," Frances Marion shared a house with Anita Loos on Long Island and wrote *The Cinema Murders*, leaving plenty of room to showcase Davies' comedic talents despite Hearst's tendency to cast her in costume epics which did nothing for her career. Marion, maid of honor when Loos married John Emerson in the summer of 1919, moved back to the Algonquin where she wrote the scenario for *A Regular Girl* for *Elsie Janis. Frances Marion was then loaned out to work once more with Pickford: they chose to do *Pollyanna* but soon found the storyline too simple for their tastes. "I hated writing it and Mary hated playing in it," said Marion. Nevertheless, the critics and the public were again enthralled.

On November 2, 1919, despite bitterly regretting her "two marital indiscretions," Marion married Fred Thomson because, she said, she "couldn't get him any other way." Spending time shepherding her friend Mary through divorce and marriage to Douglas Fairbanks, Marion then adapted *Fannie Hurst's *Humoresque* for Davies. To William Randolph Hearst's

Frances Marion (with Mary Pickford)

amazement, the film, which was set on New York's Lower East Side and concerned a Jewish mother's love for her son, was a huge success. Wrote the critic for the *New York Herald Tribune*: "It is doubtful if a better picturization has been placed on the screen in a decade." Frances Marion made her directorial debut with another Fannie Hurst short story, *Just Around the Corner.* When one of the actors failed to show up during production, Marion convinced her husband to replace him. Marion's film did well at the box office, and Fred Thomson would go on to appear in an adventure series 2-reeler and in westerns for Monogram; at one point, with his loyal mount Silver King, he was the highest-paid western star in films.

Frances Marion's next major venture was directing Thomson and Pickford in *The Love Light,* based on a true story Marion had stumbled on while in Europe. It concerned an Italian heroine, a lighthouse keeper's daughter, who pulled a German from the sea during World War I, fell in love, then betrayed him when she learned that he was sending signals to German allies from the lighthouse. But directing her best friend and her husband may not have been wise; working so closely put a damper on the Pickford-Marion friendship, and though they remained loyal, they did not work together again for over ten years. It was also Frances Marion's final film as solo-director. Having withstood a violent storm off the rocky coast of Carmel to film the shipwreck, almost losing her assistant director to the waves in the process, she was devastated when one reviewer commented, "Only a woman director would use such an obvious miniature in that phony storm."

Frances Marion's continual disagreement with William Randolph Hearst over the way to best showcase Davies wore thin, and she moved on as a freelancer. She wrote two movies for *Constance Talmadge, *The Primitive Lover* and *East Is West* for First National, and four for *Norma Talmadge: *Smilin' Through, The Eternal Flame, The Voice from the Minaret,* and *Within the Law.* She then wrote the second all-color movie, *Toll of the Sea,* for *Anna May Wong, and the epic 12-reeler *The Dramatic Life of Abraham Lincoln,* one of the few films of which she was truly proud. By 1924, Marion was back on Hearst's payroll with two more movies for Davies, both comedies. She also wrote a pair of films for Norma Talmadge and Ronald Colman for Samuel Goldwyn. To gain more control, Frances Marion turned to producing, resulting in *The Flaming Forties, Simon, the Jester,* and *Paris at Midnight.* She soon learned,

as she had with directing, that producing took too much of her time and energy.

With a great deal of money coming in, the Thomsons bought property in Beverly Hills, building a large estate with a waterfall. Marion began to work on Fred's successful westerns under the pseudonym Frank M. Clifton. In 1925, Goldwyn obtained the rights to *Stella Dallas,* a story of mother love and sacrifice; Marion tried, she said, to walk the "thin line between convincing sentimentality and lachrymose melodrama." Writes Beauchamp: "She mixed comedy scenes with drama in such a sophisticated way that her script was barely tampered with" in the *Barbara Stanwyck remake 12 years later. The original film, starring **Belle Bennett**, took in over $1 million, bringing Goldwyn his highest gross to date.

Irving Thalberg signed Frances Marion to write the scenario for *The Scarlet Letter* for *Lillian Gish. Her next, *The Winning of Barbara Worth,* cast with the then-unknown Gary Cooper, was another hit. Marion then adapted the Victor Hubert musical comedy *The Red Mill* for Marion Davies. Her *The Son of the Shiek* for Rudolph Valentino premiered in L.A. on July 9, 1926, five weeks before Valentino died.

After ten years of what was from all accounts a successful marriage, Marion gave birth to a son, Frederick Clifton Thomson, Jr., on December 8, 1926; the Thomsons adopted another boy the following year, and Marion decided it was time to settle down. Instead of jumping from one lot to another, she signed with Thalberg at MGM to write, help supervise, and edit her own productions. Her first assignment was *The Wind* with Lillian Gish, now considered one of the last great films of the silent era. Both women were adamant that the story they were doing would not have a typical Hollywood happy ending. Thalberg agreed to back them. Then *The Wind* was previewed, and Louis B. Mayer demanded they change the ending. Gish was "heartbroken" and left the studio. Marion, who admitted to Gish that she'd write a happy ending for *Romeo and Juliet* if told to, was also devastated; she told Gish that it would be the "last film to which she gave her heart as well as head."

From literary agent ◄❧ **Elisabeth Marbury** in New York, Marion learned that her old friend Marie Dressler was down on her luck and contemplating taking a job as housekeeper for a Long Island household, so Frances wrote an original story of battling female buddies, *The Callahans and the Murphys,* for Dressler and *Polly Moran. Though Thalberg was reluctant

Marbury, Elisabeth. See de Wolfe, Elsie for sidebar.

to use Dressler, he went along. Despite the backlash from the Catholic community over the obviously Irish Catholic characters, the film put Dressler's career back on track, and Marion wrote a sequel for Moran and Dressler, *Bringing Up Father*, based on the popular syndicated cartoon characters Maggie and Jiggs.

Her next venture was the script for Leo Tolstoy's *Anna Karenina* for Greta Garbo. After some discussion, Metro's honchos wanted to rename the movie *Heat,* but Marion pointed out that the marquee would read "Greta Garbo in Heat"; they settled on *Love.* They also asked Marion, to her continued chagrin, to change Tolstoy's ending: though Anna leaves for the train station, she turns up alive three years later. *Love* opened in November 1929; it was a huge hit.

Meanwhile, Fred was caught in a snare. His producer, Joseph P. Kennedy (father of the future American president), had him tethered to an impossible contract. When Kennedy signed Fred's major competitor Tom Mix, he priced Fred's movies out of the market, effectively killing his career. Following an operation for kidney stones on Christmas Day 1928, Fred Thomson died suddenly from tetanus. The 40-year-old Marion, who always remained convinced that the dealings with Kennedy led to her husband's death, was left with two children, ages two and one. Devastated, she sold off all her holdings, kept her books and clothes, moved into a furnished apartment with her sons, and continued to be, as one friend put it, "prodigal in her generosity" to others. Friends were fearful of complimenting her on anything she owned, because it would be wrapped and waiting at the door for them when they took their leave.

After writing two sound movies for Norma Shearer, *Their Own Desire* and *Let Us Be Gay,* Marion adapted Eugene O'Neill's *Anna Christie* for Garbo's first talking picture and successfully plugged for Marie Dressler to play the part of Marthy, a waterfront hangabout. With ads proclaiming GARBO TALKS, the movie broke box-office records. Then Marion began to date an old friend, director George Hill; intent on spurring prison reform, they worked together on the movie *The Big House.* Following a tour of San Quentin, Marion wrote the script and recommended Wallace Beery for casting. The movie, shot realistically, earned raves, but the Marion-Hill marriage that took place in January 1930 would last less than one year. George turned out to be a periodic drinker and a menacing drunk. Marion placed him in a house she owned as an investment in Venice, bought a

two-story house on Selma Avenue, just off Fairfax, added a Saint Bernard and a pair of baby lambs, and settled in.

Throughout her career, Frances Marion was an inveterate helper of friends. When screenwriter **Lorna Moon** was battling tuberculosis and low on funds, Marion borrowed a storyline from one of her novels, writes Beauchamp, concerning a "rough-and-tumble boardinghouse owner with a heart of gold and . . . her old curmudgeon sailor boyfriend cum straightman." Marion rewrote it to fit the talents of Wallace Beery and Marie Dressler and talked the studio into paying a delighted Lorna a then whopping $10,000 for the story. (Sadly, within weeks, Moon was dead.) *Min and Bill* was a smash hit and helped save MGM from financial disaster during the first stages of the Depression. Frances Marion won her second Oscar for her original story for *The Champ,* a tearjerker that starred Beery and little Jackie Cooper. Soon after, on March 18, 1932, Marion collapsed from overwork. While she lay in bed recovering, she learned of the plight of the financially strapped Lois Weber and agreed to work for Goldwyn on *Cynara* if she could hire Weber to assist in the adaptation.

David Selznick, now at MGM, hired Marion for the screenplay for *Dinner at Eight* which would star Dressler, Beery, *Jean Harlow, and John and Lionel Barrymore. But with the arrival of Franklin Roosevelt in the White House and the closing of the banks, Louis B. Mayer was claiming poverty and Marion took a paycut. Aware of Hollywood's metamorphosis into very big business, Marion felt it was time to protect the writer. In 1933, Frances Marion, Anita Loos, *Bess Meredyth, and a few others revived the moribund Screen Writers Guild, with Marion its first vice president. Within a year, the group went from a membership of 100 to nearly 750. Despite Thalberg's fury over Marion's seeming betrayal with the union, he hired her to adapt *Pearl S. Buck's *The Good Earth,* and, prodded by Marion, hired her ex-husband George Hill to direct. But in quick succession Marie Dressler died of cancer and George Hill, after quitting the picture in a drunken rage, committed suicide. Saying she needed a change of scene, Marion went back to San Francisco; on her return to L.A. with family and friends, the driver of their car lost control after a blowout and swerved into an oncoming car. A young boy in the other car was killed. Marion experienced internal injuries, a crushed shoulder, and a broken collarbone, and she was in a cast for months. While recovering at her father's home in Napa Valley, she wrote a series of short stories about the women of the valley, published under the title *Valley People;* she saw it as a "tribute to my suffering sex." Marion then wrote another novel, *Molly, Bless Her,* based on her good friend Marie Dressler. With an agreement with Thalberg in her pocket to write, direct, and produce for him, Marion left for a six-month vacation in London; she learned of Thalberg's death while she was there.

On her return, she was unhappy with the contract offered by MGM, and, though she tried to make it work, things were different without Thalberg. Sick of the studio power plays and disgusted over the way a friend was being used by Mayer, she broke her contract. Frances Marion, now 48, again became a freelancer. Her first project was her book *How to Write and Sell Films.* She also wrote a film advice column for *Cinema Progress,* a magazine published by the American Institute of Cinematography at the University of Southern California.

After a deal with Harry Cohn at Columbia did not pan out, Marion returned to MGM, but she spent most of her time there doctoring scripts written by others. Then Lois Weber died at age 56 with Frances at her bedside, and Marion felt the old Hollywood receding; many of her friends had died. Intent on a sea change, she left MGM and put her energy into sculpting; it was refreshing, she said to have "total control of the result."

Just after Pearl Harbor, young Fred graduated from high school and joined the navy. Marion, who needed money, returned to MGM in 1943 as "editorial assistant to Louis B Mayer." Her earnings had been reduced by two-thirds, and she had the feeling that the new generation of writers saw her as a "pre-Columbian artifact." The work she so loved had become a job. On October 23, 1946, by mutual agreement, she quit MGM for the last time. In April 1948, with her children grown, she moved to New York. That June, she published *Westward the Dream* and co-authored a play with Loos, *Red Lamp in My Window,* but Loos could not agree with the director over the third act and the project was quietly dropped. Marion returned to California for awhile on the death of her mother, then moved to Woodbridge, Connecticut, to be near her son and his family.

There she wrote her autobiography, *Off With Their Heads* (1972). "I hope my story shows one thing—how many women gave me real aid when I stood at the crossroads," she told DeWitt Bodeen. "Too many women go around these days saying women in important positions don't help their own sex, but that was never my experience. The list is endless, believe me." Added Beauchamp, "And of course, she didn't

mention all the women she in turn had helped." Frances Marion died on May 12, 1973, of an aneurysm. She was 84.

SOURCES:
Beauchamp, Cari. *Without Lying Down: Frances Marion and the Powerful Women of Early Hollywood.* NY: Scribner, 1997.

COLLECTIONS:
Papers in the cinema library at the University of Southern California.

Mariscotti, Hyacintha (d. 1640)

Saint. Died at Viterbo in 1640.

Hyacintha Mariscotti entered the religious life as a Franciscan nun at Viterbo against her wishes and for ten years remained indifferent to her surroundings. She was eventually converted and became a distinguished saint. Her feast day is January 30.

Marisol (1930—)

Venezuelan-American artist and portrait sculptor, noted for her use of multimedia assemblages and monumental scale. Name variations: Marisol Escobar. Pronunciation: Mah-ree-SOLE Acekoh-BARR. Born Marisol Escobar on May 22, 1930, in Paris, France; daughter of Gustavo Escobar (a wealthy real-estate broker) and Josefina Hernandez Escobar; attended Catholic and boarding schools until age 11, Westwood School for Girls in Los Angeles, Jepson School, École des Beaux-Arts in Paris, Art Students League in New York, Hans Hofmann's painting schools in New York and Provincetown, Massachusetts, New School for Social Research; never married; no children.

Established her reputation in the art world following a solo exhibition at the prestigious Stabler Gallery in 1962.

Selected works: The Family from the Dust Bowl, Babies, and The Generals (all from her 1962 exhibition); The Party (1965–66); LBJ Himself (1967); Lick My Bicycle Tire (1974); Pablo Picasso (1977); The Last Supper (1983).

One night at The Club, a Greenwich Village establishment that catered to local artists during the 1950s, a new face appeared. But it was a face covered with a mask, pure white and fashioned in Japanese style. Club members, who enjoyed a reputation for friendly harassment of young artists who appeared at their gatherings, demanded that the mask be removed to reveal the identity of the wearer. When the demands became sufficiently insistent, Marisol lifted the mask only to

Marisol,
masked, 1964.
*Photograph by
Hans Namuth.*

reveal a face made up in pure white, Japanese style. Granted, this was a stunt, but at another level it reveals much about Marisol. She has worn many masks in her life, masks that protect her privacy, the mask of silence as a defense against the dangers of the outside world, masks that disguise a search for self-identity which blurred appearance and reality. Her art is a form of revelation that transforms solitude into communion through the repeated recreations of herself.

Little is known about Marisol's early life, save what she has imparted to interviewers over the years. Her parents were wealthy Venezuelans who traveled frequently in Europe. Gustavo Escobar, her father, made a fortune in real estate. Marisol, a name that in Spanish means "sea and sun" (*Mar y sol*), was born in Paris in 1930. The family, which included a son also named Gustavo, returned to Caracas, Venezuela, in 1935 but traveled regularly to the United States. Enrolled in Catholic schools, Marisol remembers that she had a difficult time communicating with anyone her own age. As she told **Grace Glueck**: "I was always a little bit strange. In school they treated me like an oddball. I never wanted to talk at all." Following the death of her mother **Josefina Escobar**, in 1941, she decided never to talk again. "I didn't want to sound the way other people did," she told interviewer Jeff Goldberg. "I really didn't talk for years except for what was absolutely necessary in school and on the street." Indeed, Marisol would become famous for her mask of taciturnity.

While World War II raged in Europe, Marisol's family remained in Caracas. It was in 1946, at age 16, that Marisol decided to become a painter. She had always been interested in drawing and won a clutch of art prizes at every school she attended. Fairy stories and comic books provided early inspiration, and techniques were learned in the Catholic schools where "you spent months doing one drawing" of a saint. It was also at this time when Marisol became interested in embroidery.

Gustavo embraced his daughter's interest in art and in 1946 enrolled her in the fashionable Westwood School for Girls in Los Angeles, California. "He liked that I was an artist and he supported me. . . . I had an income through him." While pursuing a normal liberal arts curriculum during the day, Marisol in the evening took classes with the humanist painters Howard Warshaw and Rico Lebrun at the Jepson School. It is difficult to determine if they had an influence on the later development of her unique style, although art historian **Charlotte Streifer Rubinstein** noted that "some of their Goya-like influence might be subtly discerned under the humorous facade of her work."

Marisol traveled to Paris in 1949 to further her education as an artist at the École des Beaux-Arts but left after just one year. In her words: "It was like nothing. They wanted me to paint like [Pierre] Bonnard." Study with Yasuo Kuniyoshi at the Art Students League in New York in 1950 also proved unsatisfactory and was followed quickly by classes taken at Hans Hofmann's painting schools in New York and Provincetown, Massachusetts. This experience proved more enduring and lasted from 1951 to 1954. Although on one occasion she stated that Hofmann, an abstract expressionist, had taught her to paint like a Hofmann student, at another time she admitted that he was the only teacher from whom she had learned anything.

Hofmann may in fact have influenced Marisol's decision to turn to sculpture. **Nancy Grove** noted that although Hofmann taught painting, in 1948 he wrote an essay in which he stated that sculpture "deals with basic forms. The basic forms are: cubes, cones, spheres, and pyramids. Every subject has a characteristic basic form. These forms can be intensified by opposing them to other basic forms [push-pull]." Interestingly, an art critic in 1963 saw in Marisol's sculpture a variation of Hofmann's push and pull where "three dimensions sink into two" and "two grow into three."

While taking classes with Hofmann, Marisol also studied at the New School for Social Research but was unimpressed by the students. They "were really unaware. I didn't want to go to college because it was so dead. . . . Only a few people were protesting," she told **Cindy Nemser**, and they "were the beatniks. I used to hang around with them in the Village, and everyone thought they were a bunch of kooks." By her own admission, the main influences on her life, if not her art, during the early 1950s, were the streets and the bars. She was searching.

It was at this time that she turned to sculpture and was influenced by the work of William King, who shaped figures in wood, clay and other materials. King and some of his circle "bought some houses in Maine," Marisol told Nemser, "and they had early American furniture [and artifacts] in their homes. . . . That's why I got involved with [Early American Art]. I was looking at all the things that people didn't take seriously before, instead of getting influenced by the Hofmann painting. But I'm not really a folk artist." Marisol appreciated folk art, however. She told Grace Glueck that she began to work with sculpture in 1953 after viewing both an exhibition of pre-Columbian Mochica pottery from South America and a friend's collection of hand-carved and painted South American folk-art figures in boxes. Her experimentation with sculpture, Marisol said, "started as a kind of rebellion. Everything was so serious. . . . I started doing something funny so that I would become happier—and it worked."

As she gained confidence in her work, Marisol forged a new identity by dropping her family name, Escobar, in 1957. *Marisol* would stand alone. In that same year, the Leo Castelli Gallery in New York City featured a solo exhibition of her work, which won high praise from the critics. Some wrote of Marisol's search for identity or commented on how her work reflected primitive folk art that would not have been out of place on an archaeological dig in the South American jungles.

Abstract expressionism was new and controversial in 1950 and its artists were accorded a cold reception by mainline galleries and museums, such as the Metropolitan Museum of Art.

Undaunted, they organized their own showings and sponsored their own galleries. Marisol exhibited a sampling of her early sculpture at the Tanager Gallery, which was founded by King and other artists. Some of her pieces reflected fresh influences on her work. According to Grove, Robert Rauschenberg, who experimented with paintings that combined paint and "found" or appropriated objects, made an impression on Marisol. Jasper Johns, who incorporated plaster casts of parts of his body in his painting, was a direct source of inspiration. His 1955 work, *Target with Four Faces,* combined art, or appearance, with life, or reality.

Marisol, who was experimenting in the 1950s, was worried by the attention given to her works. She was still unsure of her direction and felt that such critical scrutiny was premature. She told Glueck: "I got scared . . . . I thought when you start getting publicity, you lose everything you have." To escape briefly and to gather her thoughts, she traveled to Rome. Upon her return to the United States in 1960, she entered the most productive period of her life. Many of her assemblages featured plaster-cast masks of her face or other body parts and the themes Marisol developed apparently reflected a degree of social commentary. Both the critics and Marisol herself reflect some ambivalence as to the content and meaning of her work.

When asked about the use of her own face in her work, Marisol's initial explanation was that she was "available" and free of charge. She later admitted to Glueck that her self-focus was in part a search for identity. "There comes a point where you start asking, 'Who am I?' I was trying to find out through my sculpture. That's why I made all those masks and each one of them is different." A few critics saw her self-focus as narcissism while others supposed that Marisol used herself to project an image of present-day society. If Marisol's Latin American heritage is considered in an interpretation of her work, a more profound image emerges. The Mexican author Octavio Paz in his classic *Labyrinth of Solitude* wrote:

> We are not afraid or ashamed of our bodies; we accept them as completely natural and we live physically with considerable gusto. It is the opposite of Puritanism. The body exists, and gives weight and shape to our existence. It causes us pain and gives us pleasure; it is not a suit of clothes we are in the habit of wearing, not something apart from us: we are our bodies. But we are frightened by other people's glances, because the body reveals rather than hides our private selves. Therefore our modesty is a defense.

Roberta Bernstein captured this dimension perfectly when she wrote that when Marisol did a self-portrait she felt "self-consciously that it is a part of herself and in using her own body parts she feels she is brought back to reality."

With regard to social commentary, Marisol again initially argued—perhaps as a form of self-defense—that she was primarily interested in shapes and colors, or, as she told Glueck: "an artist is an artist. I have no social intention. I think about the forms, not the meaning. People think too much about subject matter in art. But whatever they want to call me is okay—Pop or anything." Interpreters of her art found much social content. Nemser noted that Marisol in the 1960s created tableaux that mirrored the political and social attitudes of the period. Her work brought to life people from all classes, from *Family from the Dust Bowl* to the stereotyped women in *The Party* to Britain's *Royal Family.* Political leaders such as Lyndon Baines Johnson and Francisco Franco became the targets of "her deft political and social analysis." Critic **Katharine Kuh** commented in 1963 on "the pathos, irony and outrageous satire with which [Marisol] invests her sculpture. Whether she designs a single figure or a large group, she invariably ends up with a biting comment on human foibles. . . . No one has deflated human pomposity with greater insight."

Be that as it may, on occasion Marisol's work has been misinterpreted. "I'm surprised that . . . some people never understood what I was saying," she noted. "People don't think." By way of example, her sculpture *Baby Boy,* a giant infant holding an adult toy, has been cast as the power of a child to manipulate adults. Marisol said that, for her, the baby "meant America. This huge baby monster taking over. I even had the flag here—stripes." South Americans were more adept at seeing the messages that Marisol intended. Once she took a piece to South America "and they wouldn't show it. There they notice."

Marisol's niche in the history of art is equally unclear. Pop Art expert **Lucy Lippard** concluded that "Marisol has contributed enormously to the enrichment and scope of Pop imagery." Grove argued that even though Marisol's works were based on mass-media images of popular figures and utilized found objects, "her techniques have never been impersonal, and her work has elements of absurdity and irony that are unlike the deadpan literalness of hard-core New York Pop." Others, such as Rubinstein, place her in the "New Realism" school.

Even though her art was not "pop," she frequented the Pop Art scene. She played a glamorous role, seemed to be a fixture at jet-set parties in the company of Andy Warhol, and even starred in one of his underground films, *The Kiss*. Her work was featured on the cover of *Time* magazine. The themes in her assemblages—social role playing and isolation in a group—were played out in life. Marisol became known as the "Latin Garbo" and was famous for her long periods of silence in the midst of a party. Artist friend Conrad Marca-Relli observed that Marisol used her silence "like a shield. But she seems comfortable behind it." Silence, too, was a mask.

By the late 1960s, as life in the United States turned menacing and as her fame produced a growing alienation, she journeyed to Asia, South and Central America and the Caribbean. Impressed with the art of India, Nepal, Thailand and Cambodia, Marisol said that its magnificence surprised and shocked her. "I was influenced there." Scuba diving off Tahiti and in the Caribbean in combination with what she had seen in the Far East set her on a new course. She returned to New York in 1970 with the intent to do "something very pure . . . I wanted to do something very beautiful." The result was a school of large, beautifully carved, stained and varnished mahogany fish—almost all bearing a mask of her face.

It was also in the 1970s that Marisol's work turned sharply inward, and she focused on graphics, making prints, and "a series of disturbingly explicit and autobiographical erotic drawings" that, in the view of Bernstein, told of anger, pain and sexual frustration. Marisol also produced in the 1970s a whole series of masks that included not only the usual self-portraits but also archetypal females—goddesses, shamans, and fertility figures. Bernstein feels that this was an expression of the interconnectedness of nature and humanity and of the archaic with the contemporary.

Casts of her face were no longer used by Marisol after 1975 as she entered yet another phase of her career. The crisis of the late 1960s and 1970s, if, indeed, there had been a crisis, was past and she carved rough portraits of older artists whom she admired, including Picasso, *Georgia O'Keeffe, Willem de Kooning, *Louise Nevelson, choreographer *Martha Graham and writer William Burroughs. In 1983, she produced her version of da Vinci's *Last Supper*, which for her symbolized the decline and fall of Western culture and its loss of morality. "I inserted myself because I am watching it happen."

A number of critics have attempted to interpret Marisol from a feminist perspective. Two other female artists, *Elaine de Kooning and *Grace Hartigan, impressed Marisol. "Those women paved the way for me." Bernstein correctly observes that Marisol was never overtly "identified with feminist concerns." Her role has always been that of the "artist" and not the "woman." "However, because her works are self-portraits of an introspective, sensitive and independent woman, they present a powerful and insightful examination of female identity which lends itself to feminist analysis."

When art historian **Elsa Fine** asked her about problems she may have encountered as a woman artist, Marisol replied: "I always knew I would have [difficulties] whoever I was, because of the way I have always lived outside society. I never expected to be treated nicely by people and their customs I was rebelling against."

SOURCES:
Bernstein, Roberta. "Marisol's Self-Portraits: The Dream and the Dreamer," in *Arts Magazine*. Vol. 59. March 1985, pp. 86–89.
Glueck, Grace. "It's Not Pop. It's Not Op. It's Marisol," in *The New York Times Magazine*. March 7, 1965, pp. 34–35, 45–49.
Goldberg, Jeff. "Pop Artist Marisol—20 Years After Her First Fame—Recalls Her Life and Loves," in *People Weekly*. Vol. 3. March 24, 1975, pp. 40–43.
Grove, Nancy. *Magical Mixtures: Marisol Portrait Sculpture*. Washington, DC: Smithsonian Institution Press, 1991.
Nemser, Cindy. *Art Talk: Conversations with 12 Women Artists*. NY: Scribner, 1975.
Rubinstein, Charlotte Streifer. *American Women Artists: From Early Indian Times to the Present*. NY: Avon, 1982.

SUGGESTED READING:
Andersen, Wayne. *American Sculpture in Process, 1930–1970*. Boston, MA: New York Graphic Society, 1975.
Lippard, Lucy. *Pop Art*. NY: Praeger, 1966.

Paul B. Goodwin, Jr.,
Professor of History,
University of Connecticut, Storrs, Connecticut

Maritain, Raïssa (1883–1960)

Russian-born French writer, wife and collaborator of the philosopher Jacques Maritain, who played a key role with her husband in the revival of Catholic intellectual life and advocated for a modern rekindling of the thoughts of the medieval philosopher St. Thomas Aquinas. Name variations: *Raissa Maritain; Raïssa Oumancoff, Oumançoff, Oumansov, or Oumansoff.* Born Raïssa Oumansov in Rostov on the Don, Russia, on September 12, 1883; died in Paris, France, on November 4, 1960; daughter of Ilia Oumansoff and Issia Oumansoffa; sister of Véra Oumansoff (spelled Vera

Oumancoff in entry on *Gwen John; also seen as Oumançoff, d. 1959); married Jacques Maritain (1882–1973), on November 26, 1904.

In tsarist Russia during 1883, Raïssa Oumansoff was the first daughter born to a moderately successful Jewish tailor named Ilia Oumansoff. She lived in the river port of Rostov on the Don until age three, when her family moved to the Ukrainian port of Maripol. There, in a fiercely anti-Semitic Russian Empire, she met with an unusual opportunity for a Jewish girl of her day, namely the chance to study in a state school. In 1893, Raïssa, along with her mother **Issia Oumansoffa** and younger sister **Véra Oumansoff**, emigrated to Paris; Ilia had moved there some time before to find a refuge for his family from the hatred and pogroms of the tsar's realm. The highly intelligent Raïssa quickly mastered the French language, developed a familiarity with French cultural values and traditions, and became an ardent Francophile. In a family which prized educational achievement, she easily earned her baccalaureate degree and at age 17 began her studies at the Sorbonne.

A serious young woman, she embarked upon her higher education hoping to find nothing less than convincing answers to the question of why she and other mortals were alive, "a justification for existence." Convinced that the answer was to be found in the natural sciences, she endeavored to master them. It quickly became apparent to Raïssa, however, that for all of the facts that the modern scientific disciplines had assembled, deeper truths that might illuminate the purpose of life continued to elude the great minds of science. In 1900, she met a fellow student at the Sorbonne who was engaged in a similar quest. Equally obsessed in his search for truth, Jacques Maritain came from a distinguished Protestant family of liberal and secular views. Jacques, the son of a prosperous lawyer, was the grandson on his mother's side of Jules Favre, one of the founders of the French Third Republic (created in 1870). By the time he began studying at the Sorbonne, Jacques no longer found a convincing explanation of the meaning of life in the rationalism of his parents.

Raïssa and Jacques fell in love soon after they met, but their mutual affection did not solve the problem that plagued them. Science and reason no longer provided answers, and religious doctrines too brought no solace. For Raïssa, the Judaism of her parents was outmoded and irrelevant in regard to representing either a coherent religious or cultural tradition. For Jacques, liberal Protestantism failed to answer any of the big questions that plagued him. Living in a state of profound spiritual disarray, for a time the couple contemplated suicide, making a pact in the Jardin des Plantes to end their lives. They were prevented from carrying out this act by attending, and being inspired by, the public lectures of College de France professor Henri Bergson. A highly influential philosopher, Bergson was in the vanguard of the full-blown attack on scientific positivism that was well underway by the last decades of the 19th century. By pointing to a world in which higher metaphysical truths could in fact be discovered by humanity, his subtle and persuasive ideas gave hope to Raïssa and Jacques.

They married on November 26, 1904, and continued their search for a way out of a world they regarded as obsessed with material success and power. By the time of her marriage, it appears likely that Raïssa had already altered her plans of preparing herself for university degree examinations. Whereas Jacques continued to pursue a course of study leading to the agrégation degree (which he would be awarded in 1905), Raïssa would earn no university degree despite the strong encouragement of her parents, her obvious abilities as a student, and a love of learning that had been central to her nature since childhood. Her biographer Judith D. Suther has argued that already at this stage in her life, she had "[i]mperceptibly and without conscious design . . . cast herself into the traditional ancillary role that until very recently in Western culture has been taken for granted." In a world that Suther has described as being organized around "the encoded misogyny of patriarchal culture," Raïssa Maritain, though intellectually gifted, would remain largely hidden behind the spotlight on her husband.

Raïssa's fragile state of health also played an important role in her life. An illness in the summer of 1904, only months before she married Jacques, had compelled her to abandon all regular work, academic or otherwise, and began a regular pattern of illness and recovery that was to continue for the rest of her life. A number of her statements give credence to the notion that she almost enjoyed these illnesses. She commented on one occasion, "I am ill because illness is salutary for me," and, on another, "I feel the debility of recovery, not of illness." For her entire married life, Raïssa appears to have suffered from lethargy and a general sense of being unwell. In 1906, one of these unidentifiable illnesses left her semi-comatose and prompted a desperate Jacques to pray (for the first time in his adult life) for his wife's recovery. It was not his prayers but rather a medal of *Mary the Virgin placed around Raïssa's neck by Jeanne Bloy—the wife of their close friend, the pious and eccentric Catholic novelist and pamphleteer Léon Bloy (1846–1917)—that seems to have revived her. Soon after this incident, encouraged by their spiritual mentor Bloy, Raïssa and Jacques were secretly baptized, along with Raïssa's sister Véra, into the Roman Catholic faith on June 11, 1906, at Saint-Jean-l'Évangéliste in Montmartre. The eccentric Léon Bloy served as godfather to all three converts.

For the next two years after her conversion, Raïssa's vocation as a Catholic contemplative emerged as she spent her days in study and prayer. Her sister Véra, who moved in permanently with the couple starting in December 1906, made it possible for Raïssa to avoid virtually all contact with the outside world. Apparently without resentment, Véra took on most of the daily household chores. From this time until her death in 1959, Véra would be a member of a "small flock of three." Jacques, who took considerable time off from his own studies and prayers to attend to household tasks, also took on the psychological burden of consoling both sets of parents on the "loss" of their children to the demands of the Roman Catholic faith. In January 1907, Raïssa was seriously ill, possibly from amoebic enteritis, and received the last rites of the Catholic Church, ecstatically experiencing the sacrament as "a new baptism." She would describe the experience as having flooded her with "grace and peace" and bringing her "the joy of suffering." She soon had what she called a "sudden and undeniable" physical recovery. As a consequence of this event, she offered to God "the total gift of herself" and shortly after began attending daily Mass.

Over the next several years, Raïssa sought ways to deepen her religious devotion, and discussions on this issue took place between her, Jacques, and Véra. In time, the triumvirate discerned a clear path. On September 29, 1912, in the presence of the Dominican priest Humbert Clerissac, who now served as their charismatic spiritual father, the three took vows of celibacy, becoming oblates on that day at St. Paul's Abbey in Oosterhout. Several days later, Jacques and Raïssa offered their marriage to God as a pledge of their future celibate life together. These decisions, as well as Raïssa's recurring mysterious illnesses and mystical spirituality, confounded both the Oumansoff and Maritain families. The estrangement between Jacques and his mother Genevieve Favre (whose marriage to Jacques' fa-

ther had all but collapsed before her husband committed suicide) was only slowly—and never totally—bridged over the next years. Both Ilia and Issia Oumansoff, however, not only became reconciled to the decisions their daughters had made, but over time became converts themselves to Roman Catholicism.

In 1918, a substantial legacy to Jacques from a dead soldier, Pierre Villard, made it possible for the trio to attain a state close to financial independence. In 1923, Jacques purchased a house in Meudon, a suburb south of Paris, where he would write the many books that would eventually make his name known throughout the world, not only to Roman Catholics and other believing Christians but also to many of the non-religious intellectually engaged citizens of the 20th century.

At around the same time, first Raïssa and then Jacques discovered the vast body of work left behind by St. Thomas Aquinas (c. 1225–1274), the "Prince of Scholastic Philosophers" and "Doctor Angelicus" whose *Summa Theologica* was intended by its author to be the sum of all known learning. Both Maritains regarded the teachings of Aquinas not as part of a dead medieval world but rather as a living doctrine, the essence of which could be made viable once again for the contemporary world. Known as Thomism, these teachings formed a complex intellectual structure which proclaimed that faith and knowledge could be made totally compatible with one another by use of reason. Aquinas was the thinker who would become the central passion of the couple's lives. They were convinced that the 20th century could learn much from Thomism, a modernized version of which Jacques tirelessly spread to bring the modern age back to spirituality and moral truth. In her own, less philosophical and more personal, fashion, Raïssa also spread the same message.

Although Raïssa was usually ailing and self-absorbed, Jacques admired her and regarded her as both a poet and a mystic. Over the years, while he would describe her as a person who was "in the world but not of it," she wrote a number of books including four volumes of poetry, two volumes of memoirs (*We Have Been Friends Together* [1942], and *Adventures in Grace* [1945]), and the posthumously published *Notes on the Lord's Prayer* (1964) and *Raïssa's Journal* (1974). One of her books, *The Situation of Poetry* (1955), was co-authored with her husband. Unlike the many French Catholics who, attracted to Fascism and Nazism, were willing to grant Adolf Hitler the benefit of the doubt because he had been able to destroy Marxism and "restore order" in Germany, Jacques Maritain fully recognized the dangers of authoritarian racism. At least in part, this was based on his realization that a Nazified Europe would gravely endanger the two persons with whom he had shared virtually all of his adult life, Raïssa and Véra. Although both women had been devout Catholics since they were in their 20s, according to Nazi Germany's Nuremberg Laws they remained Jews.

The three arrived in the United States in late December 1939. During World War II, they lived in Manhattan's Greenwich Village, and Jacques was active in Free French politics while also lecturing and writing. In the evenings, the Maritains often gave parties at which philosophical ideas, frequently of a Thomist nature, flowed easily along with the ginger ale. In November 1944, Jacques was appointed France's ambassador to the Vatican, a post he held until 1948. At that point, he resumed his teaching at Princeton University, where the trio continued to live after he achieved emeritus status in 1952. The Maritains maintained their residence at 26 Linden Lane in Princeton, with Jacques, Raïssa, and Véra carrying on in their accustomed patterns for a number of years. Then in 1956, Véra's health began to decline dramatically. She died in December 1959 after enduring much pain and suffering. In a letter dated February 8, 1960, to **Anne Green** (a writer and sister of the writer Julien Green), Raïssa noted: "There was a special bond, a naive playfulness, a perpetual game between Véra and me. Although she was younger than I, in the game she was my little mother and I was her little child."

Raïssa was deeply shaken by her sister's death and the many months of suffering that preceded it. Robert Speaight, who had written of Raïssa as being frail but also in many ways ageless ("a queen in a fairy tale who had kept the secret of eternal youth"), now noted that within weeks of Véra's death she took on the appearance of "a little old lady with greying hair." It was decided that, to lift her spirits, Jacques and Raïssa would take a trip to France in the summer of 1960. Departing from New York on June 30, they arrived in Paris on July 7. They checked into the Hôtel de Bourgogne, where they had stayed on previous visits. As soon as the couple entered their room, Raïssa collapsed. A stroke was diagnosed, and, after a period of aphasia, her condition began to improve markedly. With therapy, Raïssa regained the ability to speak intelligibly. Brief visits from friends seemed to cheer her up, but in mid-September her condition deteriorated quickly, and she received the last rites of the Catholic Church. She was taken by ambulance to the apartment of close friends, Alexandre and **Antoinette Grunelius.** Throughout October and early November, no longer being able to eat, she became progressively weaker and died on November 4, 1960. After the funeral Mass, held at St. Clotilde in Paris, her body was taken to the village of Kolbsheim, where she was buried in the local cemetery. After living the last decades of her life in a foreign land which she never fully understood, in death Raïssa Maritain returned to the "terre aimée," the beloved soil of France.

After a brief return to the United States, Jacques was soon back in France. In March 1961, he began to live with Les Petits Freres de Jésus (the Little Brothers of Jesus), a Dominican community in Toulouse, on the banks of the Garonne river in southern France. During the extended sessions of the Second Vatican Council, which took place between October 1962 and December 1965, Jacques Maritain's ideas—and indirectly, those of Raïssa—were often cited during the deliberations. In October 1970, Jacques donned the habit of the Little Brothers of Jesus and in 1971 took his vows. He died in Toulouse on April 28, 1973, and on May 2 was buried at Kolbsheim next to his beloved Raïssa. The intellectual partnership they had shared created a body of ideas that helped to bring the Roman Catholic Church into the world of the 20th century.

SOURCES:

Barre, Jean-Luc. *Jacques et Raïssa Maritain: Les Mendiants du Ciel.* Paris: Stock, 1997.

Bloy, Léon. *Pilgrim of the Absolute.* Selected by Raïssa Maritain. Translated by John Coleman and Harry Lorin Binsse. NY: Pantheon Books, 1947.

Castori, Michael T. "Jacques Maritain and the Jews," in *America.* Vol. 168, no. 19. May 29, 1993, pp. 18–21.

Dunaway, John M. *Jacques Maritain.* Boston, MA: Twayne, 1978.

———, ed. *Exiles and Fugitives: The Letters of Jacques and Raïssa Maritain, Allen Tate, and *Caroline Gordon.* Baton Rouge, LA: Louisiana State University Press, 1992.

Gardet, Louis, and James V. Zeitz, S.J. "Poetry and Mystical Experience: Contribution of Jacques and Raïssa Maritain," in *Renascence: Essays on Values in Literature.* Vol. 34, no. 4, 1982, pp. 215–227.

Hudson, Deal W., and Matthew J. Mancini, eds. *Understanding Maritain: Philosopher and Friend.* Macon, GA: Mercer University Press, 1987.

Kernan, Julie. *Our Friend, Jacques Maritain: A Personal Memoir.* Garden City, NY: Doubleday, 1975.

Maritain, Jacques, and Raïssa Maritain. *Liturgy and Contemplation.* NY: P.J. Kenedy, 1960.

Maritain, Raïssa. *Patriarch Tree: Thirty Poems.* Translated by a Benedictine of Stanbrook. Worcester, England: Stanbrook Abbey Press, 1965.

————. *Raïssa's Journal presented by Jacques Maritain.* Albany, NY: Magi Books, 1974.

————. *We Have Been Friends Together and Adventures in Grace: Memoirs.* Translated by Julie Kernan. Garden City, NY: Image Books, 1961.

"The Maritains Honored," in *America.* Vol. 99, no. 10. June 7, 1958, pp. 306–307.

O'Brien, Astrid M. "Raïssa's Hasidic-Catholic Spirituality," in Robert Royal, ed., *Jacques Maritain and the Jews.* Mishawaka, IN: American Maritain Association-University of Notre Dame Press, 1994, pp. 168–178.

Schall, James V. *Jacques Maritain: The Philosopher in Society.* Oxford: Rowan & Littlefield, 1998.

Suther, Judith D. "Marc Chagall, by Raïssa Maritain: A Translation," in *The French-American Review.* Vol. 1, 1976, pp. 54–64.

————. *Raïssa Maritain: Pilgrim, Poet, Exile.* NY: Fordham University Press, 1990.

————. "Raïssa Maritain in America, 1940–1960," in *Research Studies.* Vol. 45, 1977, pp. 61–72.

————. "Thomas Merton Translates Raïssa Maritain," in *Renascence: Essays on Values in Literature.* Vol. 28, 1976, pp. 181–190.

————. "The Tree Motif in Raïssa Maritain's Poetry," in *Research Studies.* Vol. 44, 1976, pp. 165–174.

Whitman, Alden. "Jacques Maritain Dies at 90," in *The New York Times Biographical Edition.* April 1973, pp. 657–658.

John Haag,
Associate Professor of History,
University of Georgia, Athens, Georgia

Mariya.

Variant of Maria.

Marja.

Variant of Maria.

Marjorie.

Variant of Margery or Marjorie.

Marjorie of Carrick (c. 1254–1292)

Scottish royal and mother of Robert the Bruce, king of Scotland. Name variations: Marjory or Marjorie, Countess of Carrick. Born around 1254; died before October 27, 1292; daughter of Neil, 2nd earl of Carrick, and **Margaret Stewart***; married Adam, 3rd earl of Carrick, before October 4, 1266; married Robert Bruce, earl of Carrick, in 1271; children: Robert Bruce (1274–1329) also known as Robert the Bruce and Robert I, king of Scotland (r. 1306–1329); Edward Bruce (d. 1318), king of Ireland; Thomas Bruce (d. 1307);* *Isabel Bruce *(c. 1278–1358, who married Eric II, king of Norway); Alexander (d. 1307); Nigel (d. 1306);* *Mary Bruce *(fl. 1290–1316);* *Christian Bruce *(d. 1356, who married Gratney, 7th earl of Mar, and Christopher Seton and Andrew Moray of Bothwell);* *Matilda Bruce *(who married Hugh Ross, 4th*

earl of Ross); **Margaret Bruce** *(d. 1346, who married William de Carlyle).*

Marjory.

Variant of Margery or Marjorie.

Marjory (fl. 1200s)

Daughter of the king of Scots. Name variations: Marjorie; Marjory Dunkeld; Marjory Durward. Illegitimate daughter of Alexander II (1198–1249), king of Scotland (r. 1214–1249), and an unknown mistress; married Alan Durward.

Marjory (d. 1244)

Countess of Pembroke. Name variations: Marjory Dunkeld; Margaret; Marjory Marshall. Died on November 17, 1244; interred at Church of the Black Friars, London; daughter of William I the Lion, king of Scots (r. 1165–1214), and *Ermengarde of Beaumont *(d. 1234); married Gilbert Marshall, 4th earl of Pembroke, on August 1, 1235.*

Markandaya, Kamala (b. 1924).

See Taylor, Kamala Purnaiya.

Markey, H.K. (1913–2000).

See Lamarr, Hedy.

Markham, Beryl (1902–1986)

Famous adventurer and accomplished horse trainer and bush pilot who is most widely known for her record-breaking solo flight from east to west across the Atlantic in 1936 and her bestselling memoir West with the Night. *Born Beryl Clutterbuck on October 26, 1902, in Ashwell, Leicestershire; died on August 4, 1986; daughter of Charles Baldwin Clutterbuck (a British army officer and farmer) and Clara Agnes (Alexander) Clutterbuck; raised on a ranch in British East Africa; married Captain Alexander Laidlaw "Jock" Purves (a British army officer and farmer), on October 15, 1919 (divorced 1925); married Mansfield Markham (a wealthy aristocrat and landowner), on September 3, 1927 (divorced 1942); married Raoul Schumacher (a writer), on October 15, 1942 (divorced 1960); children: (second marriage) Gervase.*

Brought to Kenya to join her father (1905); mother left for England (1906); began career as horse trainer (1921); pursued career as pilot (1929); flew the Atlantic solo (1936) from England to Nova Scotia; moved to California (1938) where she worked as a consultant for the film industry as well as working on her memoir West with the Night *and short stories; returned to Kenya (1949) to resume her career as a horse trainer where she won the top trainer's award for five years, then the Kenya Derby for six years; moved to South Africa (1967) where she continued her career as a trainer but with limited success; returned to Kenya for the last time (1969), but her training career was far less successful; lived in semi-poverty until* West with the Night *was republished (1983) to great acclaim and popularity; royalties allowed her freedom from poverty; fell and broke hip, dying a few days later, at age 83, from pneumonia which set in after a long operation (1986).*

Publications: West with the Night *(1942, reissued 1983).*

One day in December 1932, Beryl Markham, who had been riding horses since she was four, was putting John Carberry's grey Somali mare through her paces. J.C., as he was known in Kenya, was impressed, and having a somewhat sadistic fondness for challenges, dared Beryl to ride the mare at full gallop and pick up a handkerchief he had just dropped on the ground. Markham took the horse around to get a running start. Urging her mount to top speed, she raced towards the spot and, leaning far over the horse's side like a Mongolian warrior, scooped up the handkerchief. She was just 30 and the feat was only one of many wild stunts she had pulled by that point. Within four years, it would pale in comparison to her greatest accomplishment, the first solo flight across the Atlantic from east to west.

Having been raised on a ranch in the Rift Valley of what was then British East Africa (modern-day Kenya), it is no wonder that Beryl Markham was unsatisfied with an ordinary life. Her father Charles Clutterbuck came to Africa in 1904 after being educated at the Royal Military College at Sandhurst and a brief career in the military. After establishing himself on Lord Delamere's farm in the fabled White Highlands of Kenya, he sent for his wife Clara and their two children: Beryl, age 2, and Richard, age 4. In two years, the young couple had separated, and **Clara Clutterbuck** returned to England with her son, leaving Beryl in Africa to be raised by her father and the African servants he employed.

As her father was preoccupied with running a ranch and training race horses, Beryl spent much of her formative years with Africans, hunting in the woods and learning their traditions. In Beryl Markham's authorized biography, **Mary Lovell** writes:

Beryl seemed to tread easily between the two cultures, taking from each what she needed. Had she remained in England with her mother and brother, her life would have been vastly different. . . . Had she been born African she would certainly never have been allowed to participate in the hunting pastimes which are purely the preserve of the male warrior.

Indeed, East Africa was a comparatively free and open society for European women in the early 20th century, allowing many to reach their full potential and explore lifestyles and careers that would have been closed to them in the more restrictive social milieu of Western Europe.

From an early age, Markham was out in the Mau forest hunting wild boar with her young African friend Kibii. Like her companion, she went barefoot everywhere and was indoctrinated into the many social customs held by the Kipsigi and Masai tribes. Markham's first language was Swahili. The Africans taught her how to endure pain, avoid emotion, and gave her a fatalistic outlook. Many of these qualities would help her in the challenges she encountered and hinder her in establishing permanent relationships.

> *S*he was absolutely wild and would try anything, no matter how dangerous it was.
>
> —Nigel N. Clutterbuck, cousin

Like the legends of a mythical figure, stories of Markham's early life abound, and it is unclear how many of them are based on fact. There is the well-documented account of how she was mauled by a neighbor's "tame" lion at the age of 11, but it is unclear whether she had harassed the lion or not. There are other stories, less well documented, of Beryl fighting off with a club a revengeful African boy who attacked her with a sword, even though her thigh was slashed open in the melee. There is the story of how, after being beaten by an unruly governess, Markham ran away from home during a four-day downpour and slept for two nights in a pig-hole wearing nothing but a pair of flimsy cotton pajamas. It is known that Markham went through several governesses, and it may also be true that she scared some of them away by placing dead vipers in their beds at night.

Markham never took well to authority. Sent off to school in Nairobi twice, she was expelled both times, and her formal schooling added up to only a few years. Shortly after Markham's mother left Africa, her father hired a housekeeper, **Ada Orchardson**, with whom he soon fell in love. They lived openly together as a couple, though they did not marry until years later. Markham took an instant dislike to Orchardson but was fond of her son, Arthur Orchardson, who was a few years younger than Beryl. Though her formal education was piecemeal and far from adequate, Markham did learn a skill from her father that would serve her well; how to train a race horse.

Though its European population was only 7,000, Kenya during this time was very much consumed with horse racing. Many Europeans, such as the Clutterbucks and the Delameres, were aristocrats from England who had either become disaffected with their mother country, fallen in love with Kenya's sweeping beauty, or been separated by fate from their fortunes and looked upon Kenya as a land of opportunity. These upper-class English women and men brought to this untamed country many of the diversions of the old world; cricket, polo, rugby, horse racing and especially hunting came to dominate many of their lives. These Europeans bought enormous tracts of land ranging from 500 to 10,000 acres, which were worked by hundreds and sometimes thousands of African laborers. This cheap labor enabled the European landowners to go to the races, or on safari, or to their all-white clubs, unhindered by the daily duties a farm entails.

Of course, many of these landowners went bankrupt. Africa was an unforgiving place with its drought, diseases and locusts. Markham's father, after having established himself on a large ranch on the edge of the Mau forest, lost it all in 1920 when the currency used in Kenya was revalued to the detriment of anyone in debt. He packed his bags and moved to Peru where he had accepted a position as horse trainer. Markham was only 18, and yet she had already been married for over a year.

Jock Purves came to East Africa during the Great War as one of the Madras Volunteers and later transferred to the King's African Rifles. He met Beryl sometime during the war, and they were married on October 15, 1919. Markham was only 16. Jock, who was twice her age, bought a 600-acre ranch in the Rift Valley of Kenya and settled down to a life as a farmer. Markham had other ideas. She took up where her father had left off by training race horses, several of which had been given to her by her father and others which were owned by her husband. She was the first woman in Kenya to be granted a trainer's license, and in 1922 one of her horses placed second in the East African Derby, the most prestigious race of the season.

During the 1920s, as a young, beautiful, active woman, Markham became more and more ensconced in the lively social milieu of Kenya. Her marriage with Jock fell on hard times as her circle of friends expanded and her success at racing increased. Jock was intensely jealous of the men Beryl associated with through her racing and even went so far as to physically assault and severely injure Lord Delamere, the "father" of British East Africa, because Jock suspected Beryl was having an affair with his son or his farm manager. Markham soon left Jock, and they were finally divorced sometime around 1925, though no records remain that can verify the exact date.

Once separated from her husband, Markham had to make a living on her own and did admirably well as a horse trainer, though she was never fiscally responsible and never managed to save anything. She moved around frequently during the years after she left Jock, living for periods with the Delameres and staying occasionally with Karen Blixen (*Isak Dinesen) and her lover Denys Finch Hatton at Mbogani, Blixen's coffee farm. In a letter home, Blixen described Markham as "one of the most beautiful girls I have seen, but she has had such bad luck," referring to her marriage to Jock. Some claim that Markham was in love with Denys Finch Hatton and that her close proximity to Karen Blixen was a ploy in order to be closer to him. Indeed, Errol Trzebinski, who wrote biographies of both Finch Hatton and Markham, believes that they were lovers during the first part of 1931, and that Markham was Finch Hatton's last love before he died in a plane crash in May of that year.

If Markham did fall in love with Finch Hatton on first sight, it was over eight years before her feelings were returned, and in the meantime she had remarried. Mansfield Markham was the son of Sir Arthur Markham, an extremely wealthy coal magnate. Sir Arthur had died when Mansfield was only 11, leaving him and his brother each about £2 million. Mansfield was as sophisticated and cultured as they came, with a particular fondness for all things Parisian. It was an odd match; a somewhat effete, refined aristocrat and a zesty beauty raised in a new African colony. They honeymooned first class in the capitals of Europe, Beryl's first trip. They were accompanied by Beryl's childhood friend Kibii, now called Ruta and her personal servant, who made quite a stir in Europe's finest hotels, sometimes being mistaken for Indian royalty. Upon their return to Kenya, Mansfield bought a huge and beautiful ranch in the Rift Valley and stocked it with some of the finest race horses available.

Beryl
Markham

Since Markham was always an extremely private person, her love affairs are poorly documented, except for one, which also happens to be her most famous. It occurred almost one year to the day of her marriage to Mansfield, when she was three months' pregnant. Prince Henry, 1st duke of Gloucester, along with his brother Edward, prince of Wales and duke of Windsor (the future Edward VIII), came to Kenya in 1928 to go on safari. Markham, being part of the inner social circle, was introduced to him, and Henry was instantly besotted. Their affair in Kenya continued in England when Markham traveled there in November, even though she was by that time nearly six months' pregnant. On February 25, 1929, Gervase Markham was born with a number of physical complications and was not expected to live. Shortly after the birth, Markham renewed her affair with Prince Henry, and in a few months this liaison caused a row with Mansfield Markham. Allegedly, Mansfield found out about the affair when he discovered letters to Beryl from Prince Henry in Beryl's hotel room. The couple were soon officially separated, and Gervase went off to live with Mansfield's mother **Gar O'Hea**, who raised the sickly child.

Not long after the breakup of her marriage and the birth of her son, Markham's career changed course as well. In October 1929, as she turned 27, she decided to pursue a life as a pilot. It was then the rage; Denys Finch Hatton, Prince Henry, and the prince of Wales had all learned to fly or owned their own airplanes. As with race horse training, Markham would quickly become established and successful at another occupation dominated by men. In 1931, she received her A license and passed the test for her B license in 1933, making her the first woman in Kenya to become a commercial pilot. "Beryl had instinctively found a way to avoid female destiny," wrote Trzebinski in *The Lives of Beryl Markham*:

> Kenya's space, its raw growth, was responsible for such latitude, offering a different dream (as it has for many other women), allowing Beryl to mature with relatively unfettered ambition in its abstraction of human endeavor; through necessity, pioneering has always dictated that the best person for the job gets it, regardless of sex.

And indeed Markham was possibly the best pilot to fly out of Kenya, certainly the boldest. Some likened her courage to that of a lion. In April 1932, with only 127 hours of flying time, she set off alone in a single-engine Avro Avian for England. She had been in such a hurry that there had been no time to service the plane. She set off for Lake Victoria, then over Uganda and down the Nile, refueling when necessary. Crossing the seemingly endless expanse of marsh and swamp known as the Sudd was a risky venture for any pilot, alone or otherwise. Her plane was forced down at Juba with engine trouble, and from then on hopped across the Sudd, landing at major trading centers for repairs. Near Cairo, she ran into a sand storm and had to make a quick landing. She continued along the coast of North Africa and finally crossed the Mediterranean over Malta and Sicily. The European portion of the trip was relatively safe in comparison.

The airplane made Markham's life immensely mobile. She flew several times between Kenya and Britain during the early 1930s. While in Kenya, she worked as a bush pilot, transporting people and supplies. She also worked for the safaris, delivering essentials and spotting elephant herds. All of these daring escapades eventually culminated in one flight that would top them all. In 1934, while having afternoon drinks with friends at the White Rhino in Nairobi, J.C. challenged Markham to fly across the Atlantic alone and against the wind, from east to west. "Think of all the black water," he said. "Think how cold it is, Beryl." With a taunt like that she could not back down.

Two years later, J.C. Carberry provided Markham with a single-engine Vega Gull. Beryl returned to England to prepare for the historic solo flight across the Atlantic from east to west. The plane's passenger and cargo space had been filled with fuel tanks, and the plane had been taken to Abingdon because its military runway was long enough to allow the fully loaded plane to take off. September was a terrible time to fly the Atlantic. The Royal Air Force (RAF) officers at Abingdon and the Air Ministry were against Markham making the attempt, arguing the foul weather and unusually strong headwinds at this time of year made a crossing foolhardy. Markham was unperturbed. On September 4, 1936, as the sun's light drained from a clouded sky, she took off alone, "west with the night."

Most of her 22-hour flight was at night, flying by instruments. Markham tried to stay close to shipping lanes in case she went down, though she knew that a crash-landing in the North Atlantic would mean her death. Halfway across, one of the fuel tanks went dry and the engine quit. Her plane began to descend quickly toward the ocean from its cruising altitude of 2,000 feet. By the time she found the fuel switch for the other tank and got the engine started again, her plane had dropped to only 50 feet above the waves. "Eventually land did show up," she said later. Having battled strong headwinds the entire way, her plane was much lower on fuel than she had planned. Not far from Sydney, Nova Scotia, she attempted a landing in a bog, which she thought was a field. The plane nose-dived, damaging it severely, but only slightly injuring Markham.

In another plane, she flew on to **New York** City, her intended destination, to the applause of thousands and a ticker-tape parade. She was now famous. But her fame brought her little satisfaction and little financial reward. Carberry took back the plane that could have made

Markham a fortune had she been allowed to tour with it. She traveled around the world looking for another opportunity to break a flying record but none revealed itself. Finally, she was wooed to Hollywood, only to be disappointed by an unsuccessful screen test. She remained in California and met Raoul Schumacher, a writer, who was to become her third husband.

The late 1930s and early 1940s are a poorly documented and highly controversial period of Markham's life. She traveled much and worked at various jobs, including consultant to the movie *Safari*, starring *Madeleine Carroll and Douglas Fairbanks, Jr. Sometime in 1940 or 1941, Markham's memoir *West with the Night* was written. Whether she wrote it herself or whether it was ghostwritten by Raoul Schumacher is not known. The book was published in 1942 to wide critical acclaim. Ernest Hemingway later called it a "bloody wonderful book." Because of the war and the rationing of everything including paper, the book was not as successful as it might have been at another time.

Markham went on to write a number of short stories, though these too are considered by a number of Markham's researchers to be the work of Raoul Schumacher. Schumacher was an American writer from Minnesota about whom little is known and who wrote mostly under pseudonyms. He was married to Markham until 1946, when they separated under unpleasant circumstances. Markham had little money at this point, living far beyond her means and relying on the generosity of friends and creditors to remain afloat. In 1950, she left the United States disillusioned and almost penniless to resume her life in Kenya as a horse trainer.

After a slow start, Markham eventually resumed her place in the racing elite of Kenya. The horses she trained won the Kenya Derby for six years, and she won the top trainer's award for five years. But after a strange disease, called "Beryl's blight," prevented any of the horses under her charge from racing, she moved, with a number of her finest horses, to South Africa, to try her luck there.

Markham continued training in South Africa for six years, from 1964 to 1970, but never again reached the prominence she had attained in Kenya; she moved back to Kenya after a brief stay in Zimbabwe. Life in Kenya had changed, however, and her resources were as low as they had ever been. Her house was broken into several times; once, when the burglars discovered that she was home, they beat her senseless. In 1980, during a coup attempt, she drove through a roadblock and was shot at, a bullet nicking her chin. In 1983, with Markham nearly destitute, a San Francisco restaurateur named George Gutekunst rediscovered her book and helped to convince publishers to reissue it. The book again met with wide critical acclaim, which this time was accompanied by brisk sales. It had soon sold 100,000 copies and to date has sold well over a million. This windfall did not alter Markham's life substantially, except to bring a legion of admirers, reporters, and moviemakers to the door of her humble bungalow.

In 1986, after 83 years of one harrowing event after another, Beryl Markham fell while leaning over to pet her dog and broke her femur. A long operation ensued and pneumonia set in during her recovery. A few days later, on August 4, 1986, she died. It had been a wild life, a life fuller than any other ten individuals combined. But Markham, though she had three husbands and countless lovers, had few enduring friendships. She ended her life essentially alone, having touched so many with her daring and her charm.

SOURCES:
Lovell, Mary S. *Straight On Till Morning: The Biography of Beryl Markham*. NY: St. Martin's Press, 1987.
Trzebinski, Errol. *The Lives of Beryl Markham*. NY: W.W. Norton, 1993.

SUGGESTED READING:
Markham, Beryl. *West with the Night*. San Francisco; North Point Press, 1983.

RELATED MEDIA:
"A World Without Walls" (VHS, 55 mins.), television documentary chronicling the life of Beryl Markham, George Gutekunst Productions, 1984.

Taylor Harper,
freelance writer, Amherst, Massachusetts

Markham, Mary (c. 1584–1659).
See Frith, Mary.

Markham, Violet Rosa (1872–1959)
English public servant. Born in Chesterfield, England, in 1872; died in 1959; daughter of a Chesterfield colliery owner; married James Carruthers (a lieutenant colonel), in 1915 (died 1936).

Born in 1872, Violet Rosa Markham was the daughter of a Chesterfield colliery owner and the granddaughter of Sir Joseph Paxton, the architect who designed London's Crystal Palace. As an adult, her house in London was often the meeting place of important members of the art, social service, and political communities. She joined the Liberal Party and, from 1914, served on the Central Committee on Women's Training and Employment, which she chaired for numerous years. She was also a member of the executive committee of the National Relief Fund. In 1915, Markham married Lieutenant Colonel James Carruthers, who died in 1936. From 1919 to 1946, she was a member of the Industrial Court, and in 1927 was elected mayor of Chesterfield. She joined the Assistance Board in 1934, serving as deputy chair from 1937 to 1946, was a member of the Appeals Tribunal on Internment from 1939 to 1945, and chaired the Investigation Committee on Welfare of Service Women in 1942. Markham was awarded honorary degrees from Sheffield University (1936) and Edinburgh University (1938), and recorded her life in her autobiography *Return Passage* (1953). She died in 1959.

Kari Bethel,
freelance writer, Columbia, Missouri

Markievicz, Constance (1868–1927)

Irish revolutionary who was both symbol and exemplar of the crucial role played by many active, though less visible, women in Irish nationalist politics between 1909 and 1922. Name variations: *Countess de Markiewicz; Constance Gore-Booth.* Pronunciation: *Mark-ee-vitz.* Born Constance Georgina Gore-Booth at Buckingham Gate, London, England, on February 4, 1868; died in Dublin, Ireland, on July 15, 1927, of peritonitis; daughter of Sir Henry Gore-Booth of Lissadell, Sligo, Ireland, and Georgina Mary Hill of Tickhill Castle, Yorkshire, England; sister of Eva Gore-Booth (1870–1926); educated privately and at Julien's of Paris, France, 1897–99; married Count Casimir Dunin-Markievicz, on September 29, 1900; children: Maeve Alys (b. November 14, 1901).

Founded Fianna na hEireann (1909); joined labor movement during Great Lockout in Dublin (1913); fought in Dublin during 1916 rebellion as member of Irish Citizen Army; sentenced to death but reprieved, and spent year in prison; elected to first Dail Eireann and appointed secretary for labour (1919); opposed Anglo-Irish Treaty of 1921 and played active part in civil war (1922–23).

In 1966, when the 50th anniversary of the 1916 Easter Rebellion was the occasion of flamboyant and sometimes xenophobic celebration in Ireland, Countess Constance Markievicz occupied a unique position in popular Irish history: she was, apparently, the only clearly identifiable woman who had been actively engaged in revolutionary pursuits. She was, it was implied rather than stated, the token exception amongst the smallish group of women participants in the Rising (as the rebellion became generally known) whose role was to clerk, cook, nurse, load weapons, and eventually bear white flags. Much emphasis was placed on her patrician and Anglo-Irish background, and her conversion to Irish nationalist principles was quietly referred to as a further sign of the legitimacy of those principles. She was truly the "Rebel Countess," each side of that description lending support to the other. Unsurprisingly, the reality was a touch more complicated.

The society into which Constance Gore-Booth was born in 1868 was already developing into the state of crisis at the height of which she would have her finest hour. But had it not been for her own individual qualities historians would certainly have regarded her more as a part of the Irish problem than a partial key to its solution. For Constance was one of the Anglo-Irish aristocracy, a socio-political group which has now all but disappeared but which between 1700 and 1920 was the ruling elite in Ireland. It was one of the less endearing characteristics of that elite to abandon their Irish estates and responsibilities for at least part of each year and repair to London for the social season. The Gore-Booths, it should be said, were not "absentees" in the true economically disastrous sense of the time; but Constance's mother **Georgina Hill Gore-Booth** was an English aristocrat, and Constance's birth in London was not quite the "mere accident" she herself liked to claim.

The Gore-Booths' Irish estate was "Lissadell" at Drumcliffe, Sligo, on Ireland's west coast. The family had first come to Ireland during the Reformation of the 16th century. By the time Constance arrived, however, her immediate forbears had begun to depart from the pattern of financial fecklessness, social unconcern, and political introversion which had long characterized Anglo-Irish rule. It was a process that Constance was to carry to its eventual self-destructive conclusion. During the Great Potato Famine of the 1840s, when most Anglo-Irish landowners wavered between genuine but helpless distress at the plight of their starving tenantry, and the dogmatic view that the forces of markets and nature should be allowed to take their course, the Gore-Booths continued to collect rents where possible, but returned much of it in the form of food to their tenants. When the rents were no longer forthcoming and the food finally ran out, the family went into debt to protect their tenantry. A generation later, in 1879–80, when conditions bordering on famine returned to the Irish countryside, the 12-year-old Constance joined her el-

Opposite page

Constance

Markievicz

ders in distributing food to the hungry and so acquired some of the organizing skills and much of the sense of social responsibility for which she would one day become renowned.

But for the most part Constance's upbringing was conventional for a girl of her time and class, and both she and her family were quite content that it should be so. Her educational agenda, which she shared with her younger sisters, *Eva Gore-Booth and Mabel Gore-Booth, consisted almost entirely of the acquisition of narrow social mannerisms and the polite skills of sketching and music. It was intended that she should be decorative rather than useful, and cultivated rather than intelligent. Only in middle age did she perceive the essential inadequacy of her early formal education, and only then also did she at last cross the boundary away from "Lady Bountiful"-type philanthropy and into a mental world where socialist and nationalist ideologies governed and informed her attitudes. In her youth much of her energy, drive and enthusiasm, which were later channeled into political objectives, found an outlet in horse-riding. As long as it was on a purely amateur (i.e. unpaid) basis, proficiency in handling horses was considered by upper-class Victorians—especially in the predominantly rural environment of Ireland—to be a perfectly respectable female accomplishment. It was a pursuit in which Constance excelled from an early age. When wintry weather kept them indoors at Lissadell, amateur theatricals occupied the girls.

Although known domestically and locally in Sligo as a young woman of spirit and determination, Constance showed little sign in her adolescent years that she was willing to press these personality traits beyond the ordinary boundaries laid down by respectable society. In due course, she was conducted by her governess on a "grand tour" of Italy, presented to Queen *Victoria in that lady's golden jubilee year of 1887, then made her formal entry into society and its well-structured marriage market. For some years, Constance seemed fully occupied by the glittering social whirl, and her progress was rendered only slightly unusual by her tardiness in acquiring a husband. Politically, she veered from her designedly "shocking" participation in 1891 in the procession through Sligo of the disgraced Home Ruler Charles Stewart Parnell, to occasional appearances at anti-Home Rule meetings in 1893. Her presidency of the Sligo Women's Suffrage Society (of which her sisters acted as secretary and treasurer) was short lived and her interest in the movement apparently superficial. The liberal outlook of Constance's parents,

which probably accounted for her continuing unmarried state, no doubt also underlay the fulfillment of her ambition to study art in Paris. A fellow student was Casimir Dunin-Markievicz, a Polish aristocrat and a widower with one son. Though he was six years younger than Constance, her parents raised no objection when the conventional courtship led to engagement and marriage in the summer and fall of 1900 (Constance's father Henry had, in fact, died in January). Their first and only child, **Maeve Alys Markievicz**, was born a year later.

Constance Markievicz's road to 1916 was a long one, and its stages are still not altogether clear. There was no dramatic moment of conversion or any indisputable evidence of a steady change in her personal ideology. The changes in Markievicz, such as they were, may have reflected simply the gradual, almost imperceptible, shifts in social and political attitudes which took place in the conservative society that was Edwardian Ireland. It was a time when the IRB (Irish Republican Brotherhood), that most long-surviving of Irish nationalist organizations, began to infiltrate and assume command of many of the country's sporting and cultural bodies.

Sacrifice, misunderstanding and scorn lay on the road she adopted, but she trod it unflinchingly.
—Eamon de Valera

The Markieviczs spent much of their abundant spare time acting and writing for the Dublin theater movement, which was then undergoing a revival that had strong Gaelic and cultural overtones. Her repeated performances in the role of "Ireland" as personified by a wronged maiden led her to enquire beneath the surface of the analogy, and inevitably she was brought into contact with active nationalist politicians. Because of her establishment credentials, however, she was treated with great suspicion, and even the female nationalist body of the time, Inghinidhe na hEireann (Daughters of Ireland, pronounced in-y-ee-an na hair-on), regarded her as a possible government spy.

Markievicz was forced to prove the sincerity of her attachment to the nationalist cause through a unilateral gesture, but one which was to have the most profound long-term significance. Fianna na hEireann (pronounced fee-an-a na hair-on), founded by Constance in 1909, took their format from the then-omnipresent boys' brigades and their name from a body of ancient Irish warriors. Unlike the IRB which worked by subterfuge and infiltration, Markievicz had founded an explicitly militaristic

body whose aim was the overthrow of the establishment. Many of the youths who filled its ranks would one day fight in the 1916 Rising and in the War of Independence of 1919–21. Its popularity became so obvious and its growth was so rapid that soon it was afforded the ultimate accolade: it was quietly taken over by the IRB. Constance believed that secret bodies like the IRB often proved to be fertile ground for the second-rate and the self-important, but she was helpless to prevent the development.

In any event, the boy-members of the Fianna needed time in which to grow up. Meanwhile Markievicz, now solidly integrated into the world of Irish underground nationalism, turned her attention to the developing labor movement. Several prominent nationalists known to Constance had become involved at one point or another with the labor unrest that had gradually threatened to paralyze Dublin during the course of 1913. Constance herself was catapulted from the periphery into the center of the unrest when she was savagely assaulted by the police in one of their most bloody and notorious efforts at crowd control. When a general lockout of the striking workers was introduced a few weeks later, she began to assist in a direct and, to her, very familiar manner. Of the several bodies which sprang up to feed and clothe the Dublin poor during the hungry locked-out winter of 1913–14, Constance Markievicz's was virtually unique in being apolitical and non-sectarian.

The strike eventually collapsed, a humiliating defeat for the workers, but by then it had been overtaken by events of far greater significance. To protect themselves against the attacks of the police and to preserve morale for as long as possible, the workers formed themselves into the Irish Citizen Army. It would eventually be an armed, uniformed, and well-drilled organization, and Markievicz was one of its first members.

At Westminster, home of the British Parliament in London, the Irish Parliamentary Party was about to crown a generation of effort with the attainment of Home Rule, a form of limited self-government for Ireland which kept it constitutionally still within the British Empire. The measure was resented by republican nationalists who desired a more total political separation of Britain and Ireland, but it was resented even more by the loyalists of Ulster in North-East Ireland who in 1913–14 armed themselves and prepared to resist Home Rule. In response to Ulster, southern Irish nationalists formed the Irish Volunteers in November 1913.

The drifting together of the socialist and nationalist armies was to be gradual, but Markievicz was by then involved in both movements. It was she who presided over the absorption of Inghinidhe na hEireann into the new Cumann na mBan (roughly, The Irish Women's Council, pronounced come-in na mon), the female wing of the Irish Volunteers. With the outbreak of the First World War, the British government postponed the implementation of the Home Rule measure. The resultant political vacuum was filled by the Irish Volunteers, now driven increasingly by the IRB, which laid plans for a military uprising, the goal of which would be an Irish republic independent of Britain. When the Volunteers secured rifles and ammunition in July 1914, Constance's Fianna boys were of particular service. Their "handbook" was quickly adopted for military training purposes by the adult Volunteers.

It was perhaps the measure of Markievicz's achievement as a woman in a male-dominated nationalist movement that, on the eve of the rebellion, she was confirmed in her role as a lieutenant in the Citizen Army rather than as a support-person of Cumann na mBan. Last-minute disagreement at the policy-making level led to confusion in the ranks and from the outset the 1916 rebellion was doomed to military failure. It was no fault of hers that Constance was posted to one of the most ludicrous and militarily suicidal positions. This was St. Stephen's Green, a park in central Dublin surrounded by high buildings. Due to shortage of troops, plans to seize the buildings were abandoned early and the Green itself was occupied instead, reducing the insurgents to the role of fish in a barrel. They eventually retreated to one of the nearby unoccupied buildings, and it was there, after a week of indifferent action, that she received orders to surrender. Many prominent leaders of the uprising were executed in the weeks that followed. Despite Markievicz's own account of her coolness and bravado in the face of the death sentence passed upon her, her defense counsel remembered her as having broken down and begged that her life be spared because she was a woman. It was a plea accepted by the military court which then commuted her sentence to penal servitude for life.

The executions of the 1916 leaders proved to be, from the British point of view, a grave error. During the year that Markievicz spent in prison, first in Dublin and then in Aylesbury, England, the political climate in Ireland changed drastically. The republican movement, once a minority pursuit (even if it was a somewhat large minori-

ty), became a national obsession. Ex-prisoners and relatives of the executed leaders succeeded in being elected to the British Parliament and by mid-1917 the bulk of the interned rebels had been released. As a prominent survivor of the rebellion, Markievicz's position in future nationalist endeavors was assured. In the election of December 1918, which saw the destruction of the old parliamentary party and its effective replacement by republican Sinn Fein (pronounced shin fane) representatives, Markievicz was elected with a large majority for a Dublin constituency.

By this time, however, she was again in an English prison, having been arrested for treasonable activities during the failed British attempt to introduce conscription to Ireland during the last critical spring of the First World War. She was not present, therefore, for the early meetings of Dail Eireann (pronounced doyle air-on), the parliamentary body into which Sinn Fein members had formed themselves by the simple expedient of refusing to take their seats at Westminster. On her release in April 1919, she was the only woman appointed to the Dail's "cabinet" or "government"; she was the first ever Irish secretary for labour. The British government, not surprisingly, refused to recognize the new Dail institutions. A shooting war involving the reconstituted Irish Volunteers (soon to be called the Irish Republican Army or IRA) began early in 1919 and the prospects for Markievicz's personal safety deteriorated rapidly. Along with her Cabinet colleagues and most of the Dail, she became a fugitive member of a fugitive administration. She spent two more periods in prison and was released only after hostilities ceased in July 1921.

The final years of Constance Markievicz's life were sad and unfulfilled. Her hopes (such as they may have been) of a ministerial career vanished when she became part of the opposition to the Anglo-Irish Treaty of 1921. The Treaty, which set up the Irish Free State, contained an oath of allegiance to the British monarch and other clauses which were objectionable to die-hard republicans such as Constance. A tour of America in the spring of 1922 helped to raise public awareness of the anti-Treaty position, but, by the time Markievicz returned in June, a civil war was about to erupt between the two factions.

She played an active part in the conflict, but the years of imprisonment and hardship had taken their toll; her spirit remained unbowed but her once-formidable energy and drive had begun to slacken. Because the anti-Treaty party, even in the wake of defeat in the civil war, refused to participate in the democratic processes of the

Free State's parliamentary system, Constance Markievicz was unavoidably excluded from the center of events. She remained loyal to the futile politics of extra-parliamentary opposition, but the unfamiliar lack of activity and her advancing years took their toll upon her health. She seemed much older than her 58 years when she collapsed at a political meeting in July 1927. An emergency appendectomy failed, and within a fortnight (two weeks) peritonitis had put an end to her brave, lifelong struggle.

SOURCES:

Van Voris, Jacqueline. *Constance de Markievicz: In the Cause of Ireland*. MA: University of Massachusetts Press, 1967.

SUGGESTED READING:

Haverty, Anne. *Constance Markievicz: Irish Revolutionary*. London: Pandora, 1988.

Marreco, Ann. *The Rebel Countess*. London: Weidenfeld and Nicolson, 1967.

COLLECTIONS:

Regrettably there is no single body (or even small bodies of any consequence) of Constance Markievicz's papers. However, a publication of some value, *Prison Letters of Countess Markievicz*, was edited by Esther Roper in 1934 (reprinted London: Virago, 1987).

Gerard O'Brien,
Senior Lecturer in History,
University of Ulster, Northern Ireland

Markova, Alicia (1910—)

Distinguished English-born ballerina who was one of the stars of the dance world from the 1930s to the early 1960s. Name variations: Lilian Alicia Marks; Dame Alicia Markova. Pronunciation: Mar-COVE-ah. Born Lilian Alicia Marks in Finsbury, North London, on December 1, 1910; daughter of Arthur Marks (a mining engineer) and Eileen Barry Marks; studied dance with Serafima Astafieva, 1921–25; never married; no children.

Met Anna Pavlova (1919); began career as dancer in pantomime show (1920); met Patrick Healey-Kay and received first offer to dance in a production by Diaghilev (1921); death of her father (1924); joined Diaghilev's Ballets Russes and danced first solo role in Le Rossignol (1925); death of Diaghilev (1929); joined Old Vic-Sadler's Wells ballet (1933); gave first performance of Giselle (1934); formed Markova-Dolin Ballet (1935); joined Ballet Russe de Monte Carlo and made debut in America (1938); joined Ballet Theatre (1941); had surgery for hernia (1943); appeared in Broadway show (1943–44); founded London Festival Ballet (1950); left London Festival Ballet (1952); received Order of the British Empire (OBE, 1953); gave final performance (1962); announced her retirement and named

Dame of the British Empire (DBE, 1963); served as ballet director, Metropolitan Opera (1963–69); taught at the University of Cincinnati (1970–74); presented television series on BBC (1981); was given gala birthday celebration at Sadler's Wells (1990).

Selected roles: title role in The Dying Swan; *title role in* The Firebird; *title role in* Giselle; *Juliet in* Romeo and Juliet; *the Nightingale in* Le Rossignol; *title role in* La Sylphide; *Odette-Odile in* Swan Lake; *Sugar-Plum Fairy in* The Nutcracker; *Swanhilda in* Coppélia.

Alicia Markova was one of the most eminent dancers of the 20th century. Taken into the world of Russian ballet by the distinguished impresario Sergei Diaghilev, she moved on to form her own ballet company in the 1930s. In 1950, along with her longtime partner and friend, Anton Dolin, she founded the London Festival Ballet and promoted interest in classical dance in Great Britain. In all, she stands as a pioneer in the formation of British ballet. Writes her English biographer Maurice Leonard: "Before her only foreigners had been ballerinas. No one thought we could do it."

During the first decades of the 20th century, the ballet world was dominated, in all its aspects, by Russians like Diaghilev. His Russian ballet had taken Paris, then the other major cities of Western Europe, by storm in the years before World War I. In the 1920s, cut off from Russia by the Bolshevik Revolution, his touring company still set the standard for the ballet world. Dancers of several nationalities were attracted to the company, and some were invited to join. With the death of Sergei Diaghilev in 1929, his Ballets Russes collapsed, and his dancers went their separate ways, sometimes bringing ballet to their own countries and setting up national companies. Alicia Markova, whose Russian name disguised her English background, was one of the most renowned products of the Diaghilev company.

The future ballet star was born Lilian Alicia Marks in the north London neighborhood of Finsbury Park. Her father Arthur Marks was a Jewish mining engineer whose family had originally come from Poland, and her mother **Eileen Marks** was an Irish-born Roman Catholic who converted to Judaism. Markova grew up in a loving, increasingly prosperous household, and her childhood was marked by the arrival of a housekeeper with a powerful personality. **Gladys Hogan**, whom everyone called "Guggy," became a crucial figure in Alicia's life and early career.

An initial turning point came when a doctor advised ballet lessons to deal with Alicia's flat feet. Her ballet teacher saw her extraordinary natural talent almost immediately, and, encouraged by her teacher, the young girl soon won a dance contest at a London theater. In 1919, Alicia met the greatest ballerina of the day, *Anna Pavlova. She had already seen Pavlova's performances, but this time she pushed her father to arrange an introduction. The visit to Pavlova's house led to a private lesson. Like Alicia's first ballet teacher, Pavlova saw the talent in the young girl and encouraged her to think of a professional career.

Within a year of her meeting with Pavlova, Alicia, still a young child, was launched as a professional dancer. On April 1, 1920, she gave her first paid performance, at a charity show for the Italian Red Cross. With special permission from the local government and with Hogan accompanying her in the role of governess, she began regular performances at a local music hall. The minimum age for someone undertaking such work was ten; Alicia had just celebrated that birthday. Presented as "The Child Pavlova," she was hailed by one critic as "a very accomplished ballerina in miniature."

Only at this point did Alicia begin her formal training in the classical tradition. She auditioned for the famous Princess *Serafima Astafieva in 1921, made her usual striking impression, and began her studies with Astafieva immediately. A fellow pupil was a young English dancer named Patrick Healey-Kay, who was to become her lifelong partner. When Sergei Diaghilev visited the school, he too was struck by the young girl's talent, and he planned on creating a special dance for her in the prologue of his production of *The Sleeping Beauty.* This was an extraordinary opportunity for such a young dancer, and Alicia was crushed when she was temporarily disabled by diphtheria. The disease not only destroyed her first chance to perform in one of Diaghilev's productions, it almost took her life.

By this time, Diaghilev was finding it difficult to maintain his company with Russian-born dancers. Patrick Healey-Kay had already joined his company; to give him a Russian facade, his name was soon changed to Anton Dolin. Three years later, at the start of 1925, Astafieva persuaded Diaghilev to allow Alicia, still only 14, to join the Ballets Russes. Legally she could not take a full-time position, but Diaghilev decided to ignore the law; for professional purposes, she was to be presented as 16 years of age. The previous year, Alicia's father had died after seeing the family's fortune dwindle due to bad investments. She entered upon a full-time dancing ca-

reer mainly because of the growing financial pressures on her family.

Both Alicia's family and Diaghilev recognized that the young prodigy needed to be supervised, and Hogan continued to travel with her in the role of governess. Meanwhile, Diaghilev appointed one of his established dancers, *Ninette de Valois, to look after the girl. De Valois took on the task reluctantly, expecting to encounter a spoiled brat. Instead, she found, "there was never a sweeter child. . . . Everything you told her to do she immediately did." Nonetheless, young Alicia found herself out of place and lonely in a group that contained no one close to her age.

Diaghilev took the young dancer under his wing, seeing to it that she had French lessons, changing her name to the Russian-sounding "Alicia Markova," and offering her steadily larger parts. She began a longstanding relationship with the young choreographer George Balanchine, and her debut in a solo part was in Balanchine's version of *Le Rossignol,* his first original production since his arrival in Western Europe from the Soviet Union. Meanwhile, under Hogan's supervision, Markova led a disciplined life of practice, rehearsal, and performances, all the while continuing to do her schoolwork. For four years, writes **Sarah Montague,** "her life was immensely exciting artistically and completely sheltered socially."

During those years from 1925 to 1929, the tiny young dancer, who weighed only 80 pounds, traveled throughout Europe with Diaghilev's company. Illness forced Hogan to give up her role as governess, and Eileen Marks stepped in to accompany her daughter. Meanwhile, Diaghilev took a direct role in promoting her career. Some of his decisions Alicia accepted only with reluctance. He insisted, for example, that she abandon her position as a soloist for an entire season; by dancing with the corps de ballet, she would thereby improve her technique. She would also free herself from later accusations that she had advanced too quickly because of favoritism. The impresario also restricted her social life, barring her, until she reached the age of 18, from joining the company at the various functions to which they were invited. The Diaghilev company stressed modern dance, and Markova's years with the group gave her a firm grounding in this branch of ballet.

In 1929, Alicia Markova's career seemed on the verge of a major advance. She danced publicly for the first time with Anton Dolin, and Diaghilev informed her that she was to be promoted to the rank of prima ballerina. She would alternate in roles already held by some of the most illustrious and established members of his troupe. She was also to receive a formal contract, symbolizing her arrival as a full-fledged professional. All of these expectations exploded for Markova on August 19. While taking a holiday in England, she learned of Diaghilev's sudden death.

In the next year and a half, Markova spent much of her time away from the world of dance. By the beginning of 1931, however, she began a new and decisive phase in her career: she became a leading figure in the new world of British ballet. She danced for the Camargo Society, an organization recently founded to promote the art of dance in Markova's native country. She also renewed her relationship with Ninette de Valois, who was now becoming a prominent ballet producer in Britain. At the Camargo Society and at the equally new Ballet Club, Markova found herself paid a pittance, dancing on cramped stages, and dealing more with up-and-coming British dancers than with the great Russian stars of the Diaghilev company. She covered the gaps in her finances by dancing in stage shows that took place in the intermissions at movie theaters in London's fashionable West End.

Alicia's art, through sheer concentration and focussing of impulse, became transfigured gradually to the beauty and cold endurance of the stars.

—Agnes de Mille

Markova became increasingly involved in the efforts of Ninette de Valois to promote British ballet. In March 1932, she began to dance important roles in the Sadler's Wells Company, an organization founded by de Valois that would eventually become the Royal Ballet. Later that year, Markova was a featured star in de Valois' troupe of dancers sent to perform in Copenhagen, the first time a company comprised entirely of British dancers went abroad to perform.

Markova's performances at Sadler's Wells drew huge audiences for the new, and still struggling, company, and she shifted from guest artist to full member in 1933, then broadened her work to appear in the musical *A Kiss in Spring*. The critics panned the overall production, but they praised the ballet interlude at the close of the evening that featured Markova. In June 1933, at the final performance put on by the Camargo Society, Markova appeared before Queen *Mary of Teck* and other members of the British royal family.

Ninette de Valois' dance company stressed the great Russian classics, and Markova now found herself steeped in this tradition. Thus, in 1934, she took on the title role in *Giselle,* a part with which her name would be associated for the remainder of her career. Markova had been attracted to the role since seeing one of her Russian mentors, *Olga Spessivtzeva*, perform it in the early 1930s. Partnered with Anton Dolin, Markova now danced it for the first of many times. She received lavish praise, one critic noting that "her ethereal grace attained a truly poignant beauty."

In 1935, Markova and Dolin left Sadler's Wells to form their own company; they had become increasingly convinced of their power to draw an audience based upon the success of a recent Sadler's Wells tour throughout Britain. Their departure from the company founded by Ninette de Valois was accompanied by harsh feelings and the threat of lawsuits. In the end, de Valois let them go, placing Robert Helpmann and the young *Margot Fonteyn* at the center of her future efforts. Fonteyn, another English dancer, had long since made Markova her model.

The Markova-Dolin Company, which would became Alicia Markova's artistic home for the next three years, gave its opening performance in Newcastle on November 11, 1935, then toured extensively. Shy as usual, Markova refused to make speeches from the stage after performances, leaving this task to Dolin. Combined with her Russian name, this gave many audiences the impression that she was a foreigner who could not speak English.

The tours were grueling. Wrote Markova in her memoirs in 1986: "My life was, literally, spent between my hotel room and the stage, and my dressing-rooms were my real home." Meanwhile, critical success followed, but it came at enormous cost. The company ran up huge deficits too great to be sustained even with the help of wealthy patrons. There was also a physical cost. Markova gave eight performances each week, and, in the fall of 1937, she suffered a serious foot injury.

By now, Markova was one of the leading ballerinas in the world, but she had confined her performances to Britain throughout the 1930s. The possibility of appearing before foreign audiences was something she had rejected repeatedly in order to build up the dance world in her own country. In 1937, she received an offer she decided to accept. Leonid Massine and the American impresario Sol Hurok were building an American ballet company. Markova signed with

Alicia
Markova

Hurok, and the Markova-Dolin Company ended its last tour at the close of 1937.

Before leaving for America, Massine's company performed in Europe, where Markova joined them in Monte Carlo, Paris, and London in the spring of 1938. Her early months with the new company were marred by a difficult relationship with her partner Serge Lifar. His efforts to overshadow her, notably as she danced her favorite role as *Giselle,* made their dancing styles incompatible. In London, where her interpretation was well known and popular, audiences booed Lifar. Markova had a triumphal American debut in *Giselle* in October 1938, but there was a poisonous atmosphere surrounding her performance due to hostility and jealousy towards her from other members of the troupe. She received a threatening note after one rehearsal, and a stage prop lily she was supposed to pick up during her performance was nailed to the stage. The most disturbing event occurred on the second night. Lifar slipped, sending her crashing to the floor. When the two of them were disentangled, Markova was found to have a bone fracture in her foot. Although she was dancing in agony, she finished the first act before passing out. Lifar soon left the company.

The American tour continued for six months, with the company visiting more than 100 cities before returning to Monte Carlo in May 1939. According to biographer Leonard, acts of sabotage continued throughout the tour. A costume she needed in the midst of a performance turned up mysteriously mutilated. On another occasion, a long needle was embedded in a costume she was wearing.

Soon after the outbreak of World War II in September 1939, Markova left for America. Though she would have preferred to remain in Britain to do war work, Sol Hurok had threatened legal action unless she honored her contract to appear once again in New York. Her stay abroad lasted for eight years. Together with *Alexandra Danilova, who accompanied her from Europe, and dancers whom Hurok and Massime recruited in America, Markova toured the U.S. and Latin America with the Ballet Russe de Monte Carlo, as the company was now called. In 1942, she set an attendance record for the Hollywood Bowl, attracting an audience of 35,000. In the changing and competitive world of ballet companies, Sol Hurok established a link with the newly created Ballet Theatre. In 1941, Markova followed him.

A new turn in Markova's career came in late 1943. Responding to a long series of invitations by producer Billy Rose, Markova agreed to appear in the Broadway show *The Seven Lively Arts.* From November 1943 to May 1944, she and Dolin danced in the show to music specially commissioned from composer Igor Stravinsky. Along with Dolin, she also appeared briefly in the Hollywood film *A Song for Miss Julie.* But the wartime years saw Markova struggling with a variety of illnesses. In 1943, for example, she had to undergo surgery for a hernia. In the aftermath of the operation, a doctor ordered her to take a prolonged period for recuperation, but he was mistaken when he warned her that she might never dance again.

In the postwar years, the English star continued to dominate the ballet world. She toured widely in both North and South America, even traveling to dance in the Philippines in 1947. This whirlwind of activity put enormous strain on her slender physique. Newspaper accounts of her career noted how she kept her strength with a routine diet of steaks and chocolate sundaes after her performances; she usually weighed less than 100 pounds.

In 1948, Markova returned to her native country after an absence of eight years. Dancing *Giselle* at Covent Garden with the Sadler's Wells troupe, she received a tumultuous reception from both the audience and the press. One critic wrote, "Markova gave us a Giselle whose quality has not been seen in London for ten years." She was also idolized by the younger generation of English dancers, most of whom were seeing her perform for the first time. Now based in Britain, Markova and Dolin formed their own small company in 1950. With the country gearing up for the Festival of Britain scheduled for the following year, she decided to call their troupe the Festival Ballet. That same year, she and Dolin made a brief, black-and-white film version of *Giselle* for American television.

Markova continued her frantic schedule of traveling, dancing on both sides of the Atlantic throughout the 1950s. Leaving the London Festival Ballet in 1952, she performed as a guest artist with numerous companies. In 1958, she fulfilled a longstanding desire to dance in Israel. As always, her most popular role was in *Giselle.* She once calculated that she had danced it with more than 15 different partners, and she found a new and frequent partner, the Danish dancer Erik Bruhn. In a different group of settings, she performed in variety shows at the London Palladium and on British television. In 1953, Markova received her first honor from the British government, the title of Commander of the Order of the British Empire (CBE).

At the start of 1963, Markova announced her retirement to a group of reporters who had come to interview her at Heathrow Airport as she prepared to leave for the United States. Now 52, she had recently undergone a series of illnesses, and, even though her physician told her she could continue with her career, she decided to end her work as a performer. "Things would have to be whittled away," she noted. "I didn't want that." In the aftermath of her retirement, she received from Queen *Elizabeth II an additional honor, the title of Dame of the British Empire (DBE).

Nonetheless, Markova's work continued in other forms. She served as ballet director for the Metropolitan Opera from 1963 to 1969. She was hailed, along with George Balanchine at the New York City Ballet, as one of the outstanding directors in the dance world. In 1970, still active in the dance world at the age of 60, Markova joined the faculty of the Conservatory of Music at the University of Cincinnati. She quickly became an active fan of the university's basketball team, but she kept some of the trappings of a star ballerina and arrived to teach her classes in a chauffeured limousine.

Markova remained at the university for four years, then returned to London in 1974, where she continued to be an influential and respected member of the dance world. In 1981, she was the star of her own BBC television series, "Markova Master Classes," and her birthdays were the occasions of celebrations in the artistic community. In 1985, the Royal Ballet marked her 75th with a special performance of *Giselle*. Sadler's Wells presented a gala performance five years later to mark her 80th. Even in what some would consider old age, Markova still struck acquaintances with her beauty and grace. A young journalist who interviewed her in 1994 noted that, compared to Markova, "I . . . have never felt less gainly in my life."

Markova has remained a shy person throughout her career. Many were struck by the way in which the ballerina, who so dominated a stage, preferred to sit by herself at a party. She never married. In her autobiography, she referred to proposals she had received, ranging from one from a leading Danish dancer to offers from a number of millionaires. She turned them all down. Her longstanding relationship with Anton Dolin led to rumors of romance, and Maurice Leonard claims her longtime partner proposed to her twice. Here again she declined. "I suppose I really am one of those people married to their careers," she said.

SOURCES:

Leonard, Maurice. *Markova: The Legend.* London: Hodder and Stoughton, 1995.

Markova, Dame Alicia, DBE. *Markova Remembers.* London: Hamish Hamilton, 1986.

Montague, Sarah. *The Ballerina: Famous Dancers and Rising Stars of Our Time.* NY: Universe Books, 1980.

SUGGESTED READING:

Au, Susan. *Ballet and Modern Dance.* London: Thames and Hudson, 1988.

Clarke, Mary, and Clement Crisp. *Ballerina: The Art of Women in Classical Ballet.* London: BBC Books, 1987.

Fisher, Hugh. *Alicia Markova.* 2nd ed. London: Adam and Charles Black, 1958.

Markova, Alicia. *Giselle and I.* NY: Vanguard Press, 1960.

Neil M. Heyman,
Professor of History, San Diego State University, San Diego, California

Markovic, Mirjana (1942—)

Serbian founder and president of the modern Marxist party Yugoslav United Left (YUL) and wife of Slobodan Milosevic, former president of the Yugoslav Federal Republic. Name variations: Mira; Dr. Mirjana Milosevic. Born on July 10, 1942, in the village of Brezane; daughter of Moma Markovic (a high-ranking Communist) and Vera Miletic; received an undergraduate degree from Belgrade University; University of Nis, Ph.D. in sociology; married Slobodan Milosevic (later president of Serbia and then of the Yugoslav Federal Republic), on March 14, 1965; children: daughter Marija Milosevic (b. 1965); son Marko Milosevic (b. 1976).

Characterized as a "Balkan Lady Macbeth," Mirjana Markovic, known as Mira, is the powerful wife of Slobodan Milosevic, former president of the self-declared Yugoslav Federal Republic who ruled for 13 years. Milosevic's atrocities in the name of ethnic cleansing have made him a pariah in the world's press and among the world's governments. Although he and four of his officials were indicted for war crimes in Kosovo in May 1999, he remained in tenuous rule for nearly another year and a half. Markovic is considered dangerous not only for her own declarations of vengeance, but because of the enormous influence she has with her husband.

Mira Markovic is the daughter of **Vera Miletic** and Moma Markovic, devoted members of the Communist Party who became partisan fighters following the German attack on Belgrade in 1941. While Moma went off to the mountains to organize partisan resistance, Vera joined the underground in Belgrade. Shortly after Markovic's birth in the village of Brezane in 1942, Vera sent her to live with her grandparents in Pozarevac, while she continued her underground activities. In 1943, Vera was captured by the Gestapo, at which time it is believed that she revealed the names of key Communist officials to her torturers. Even Moma Markovic condemns his lover as a traitor, stating in his memoir, *War and Revolution*, that she and a fellow prisoner "revealed everything about the work of the party in a detailed report they wrote for the police. Both were executed in 1944." According to Dusko Doder and **Louise Branson**, in *Milosevic: Portrait of a Tyrant*, it is likely that Vera was not executed by her Gestapo torturers, but by the Communists who captured Belgrade in 1944 and gained access to the police reports. (All the documents concerning the case mysteriously disappeared when Slobodan Milosevic came into power.) After the war, Markovic remained with her grandparents and was visited only occasionally by her father who married and began another family. She blamed her stepmother for her father's rejection. "If I had been in her place, I would have behaved differently," she later wrote.

As a girl, Markovic idolized her mother's memory and harbored great bitterness over her death. She was in high school when she met Slobodan Milosevic, a lonely outsider with an equally unfortunate childhood (both his parents had committed suicide). The two quickly became inseparable. "We nicknamed them Romeo and Juliet," recalled an old school friend, "because from about the age of sixteen they were never apart. She always dressed like a middle-aged woman." Markovic went on to graduate from Belgrade University and earn a Ph.D. in Sociology from the University of Nis. She became a university professor, although in her official biography and articles she has written, she claimed that literature was her real love, and she would have liked to have been a writer. She also bemoans her husband's study of the law, having urged him to take up the more "romantic" subject of architecture. Markovic was pregnant with her daughter Marija when she married Milosevic in 1965. The couple later had a son Marko, born in 1976.

During the early years of their marriage, as her husband was serving in the Belgrade city government, Markovic taught Marxist sociology at Belgrade University and raised her children. With her husband's rise to power in the 1980s, she served as his main adviser, though she remained in the background and was seldom seen at political events. She also carefully guarded her husband's privacy, frequently changing their home phone number and giving out the correct number only to a select group of top officials. Markovic began to emerge into the limelight in 1990, the year after her husband was elected president of Serbia, founding the Yugoslav United Left (YUL). An alliance of some 20 Communist groups aligned with her husband's Socialist Party of Serbia, the organization would become a kind of Mafia, doling out favors to high-ranking businessmen.

In 1993, when the deepening Bosnian crisis threatened Milosevic's standing, Markovic began writing a column in the fashionable biweekly magazine *Duga*, using it to both humanize and defend her husband. Calling him a loving family man "who had never been a nationalist," she also described his adversaries as "lunatics who instead of being in an asylum are sitting in their so-called political parties and who, instead of taking medicine, are making pronouncements." Doder and Branson suggest that Markovic's column added significantly to her sense of power. "She began commenting on Serbia's political life and personalities, weaving in bizarre details about her own habits or observations." She told readers, for example, that she never let her husband see her brushing her hair, and in one column, she waxed lyrical about the season: "The winter is so beautiful, with white trees, bluish mist and the pale light of distant lonely stars." Since Markovic's column was often an indicator of what her husband was thinking, Serbs dubbed it "The Horoscope," especially since she seemed to consult the heavens regularly. "I say often," she wrote, "with a mixture of sadness and irony, that things that some governments or some ministries cannot resolve, may be resolved by the stars."

But, as Doder and Branson point out, Markovic was also in the position to make her own predictions come true. Following a trip to China with fellow Belgrade University professor Slobodan Unkovic, she remarked to a group of journalists that "Unkovic would make a terrific ambassador to Beijing." Not long afterwards, he was indeed appointed to the post. On the other hand, a disparaging word in her column about a Serbian official resulted more than once in a dismissal. Markovic's friends, as well as her husband's closest political cronies, never knew when she would turn on them and begin to negotiate their downfall. "It's like fire," says one political victim. "If you are too close you'll burn. She's a great consumer of people. She wants maximum obedience. She's good at provoking people, and then assesses and judges later, in private with [Milosevic]. You can say everything to him and he'll support it and praise it, but already the next morning everything is different. It will be the way he agreed with Mira in the night."

Markovic might well have orchestrated the purge of her husband's innermost circle following the pull-out of troops in Kosovo in October 1998. Amid a popular revolt, Milosevic resigned his presidency on October 6, 2000, conceding his electoral defeat by the people's choice Vojislav Kostunica.

SOURCES:

Chua-Eoan, Howard. "Slobo, Mira and Their Wild Brood," in *Time*. December 16, 1996, p. 42.

Doder, Dusko, and Louise Branson. *Milosevic: Portrait of a Tyrant*. NY: The Free Press, 1999.

Erlanger, Steven. "Slobodan Milosevic's Wife May Influence Outcome of War," in *The Day* [New London, CT]. May 31, 1999.

Perlez, Jane. "Milosevic Purges his Entire Cabinet," in *The Day* [New London, CT]. November 29, 1998.

Barbara Morgan,
Melrose, Massachusetts

Marks, Hertha (1854–1923).

See Ayrton, Hertha Marks.

Marks, Josephine (1874–1922).

See Peabody, Josephine Preston.

Marks, Nora (1863–1942).

See Atkinson, Eleanor.

Markus, Fanny (1811–1889).

See Lewald, Fanny.

Marlborough, duchess of.

See Churchill, Sarah Jennings (1660–1744).

See Churchill, Sarah Jennings for sidebar on Henrietta Churchill (1681–1733).

See Churchill, Jennie Jerome for sidebar on Fanny Churchill (d. 1899).

See Vanderbilt, Consuelo (1877–1964).

Marlitt, Eugenie (1825–1887)

German novelist. Name variations: Eugenie John; E. Marlitt. Born in Arnstadt, Thuringia, on December 5, 1825; died in Arnstadt on June 22, 1887; her father was a portrait painter.

At age 17, Eugenie Marlitt was sent by her foster mother, the princess of Schwarzburg-Sondershausen, to Vienna to study vocal music. After appearing in concert in Leipzig, Linz, and Graz, she became deaf and was obliged to give up a contemplated music career. Subsequently, she lived for 11 years at the court of the princess, but ultimately took up residence in her hometown of Arnstadt, in Thuringia. Beginning with *Die zwölf Apostel* (The Twelve Apostles), which was published in 1865, all her stories first appeared in the journal *Die Gartenlaube*. Other works include *Goldelse* (Gold Else), *Blaubart* (Blue Beard), *Das Geheimniss der alten Mamsell* (The Old Mamsell's Secret), all written in 1868, *Thüringer Erzählungen* (Thuringian Tales, 1869), *Reichsgräfin Gisela* (Countess Gisela, 1879), *Heideprinzesschen* (The Moorland Princess, 1872), *Die zweite Frau* (The Second Wife, 1874), *Im Haus des Kommerzienrats* (In the House of the Counselor, 1877), and *Im Schillingshof* (1879).

Marlowe, Julia (1866–1950)

English-born actress who was one of the most popular Shakespearean actresses on the American stage of her day. Name variations: earliest stage name, Fanny Brough; performed as Julia Marlowe from 1887; also known as Mrs. Robert Taber (1894–1900), then Mrs. Edward H. Sothern (from 1911); Julia Marlowe Sothern. Born Sarah Frances Frost (family changed name to Sarah Frances Brough) on August 17, 1866, at the village of Upton Caldbeck, near Keswick, Cumberlandshire, England; died in New York City on November 12, 1950; daughter of farmers; attended Kansas and Cincinnati, Ohio, public schools; married Robert Taber (an actor), in 1894 (divorced 1900); married E.H. Sothern (1859–1933, an actor), on August 17, 1911 (died October 28, 1933).

Brought to U.S. as a child of four (1870); made first stage appearance in a children's performance of Gilbert and Sullivan's light opera H.M.S. Pinafore, *in Vincennes, Ohio, under the name Fanny Brough (1878); appeared in* Rip Van Winkle, Macbeth, Romeo and Juliet, Richard III, The Chimes of Normandy, The Hunchback, Pygmalion and Galatea *(in repertory, 1878–84); made New York debut in* Ingomar *(1887); made subsequent appearances* inter alia *in* Twelfth Night, *and* As You Like It *(1887),* The Rivals *(1896),* Countess Valeska *(1898),* Barbara Frietchie *(1899),* When Knighthood Was in Flower *(1901),* The Hunchback *and* Romeo and Juliet *(1904),* The Sunken Bell *and* Gloria *(1907); subsequently appeared in repertory in* Romeo and Juliet, The Taming of the Shrew, Hamlet, Twelfth Night, Macbeth, The Merchant of Venice, Jeanne d'Arc, John the Baptist, *and in revivals of* The Sunken Bell, When Knighthood Was in Flower, *etc.; retired from the stage (1924).*

Born Sarah Frances Frost on August 17, 1866, at Upton Caldbeck, near Keswick, Cumberlandshire, in the north of England, Julia Marlowe came from a family of farmers of pure English descent. By sheer coincidence, she was born in the same village as *Adelaide Neilson, who also went to America and became a famous actress. Marlowe's father was forced to flee England after having assaulted a neighbor with a horsewhip. When Marlowe was four, she crossed the ocean with her mother, brother, and sister to join him in America. The family settled first in Kansas, where Marlowe began her schooling, and then moved to Cincinnati, Ohio, where for some reason the Frosts changed their surname to Brough, and where Marlowe attended the local public schools. No one in her family had ever been on the stage, and there was no sign that acting was to become her life's work until she was 12 years old. When she did appear on the stage, she first went by the name of Fanny Brough.

Julia Marlowe's career began fortuitously in 1879. A theatrical manager in Cincinnati, Colonel Robert E.J. Miles, undertook to stage the popular comic opera, Gilbert and Sullivan's *H.M.S. Pinafore,* in Vincennes, Ohio, using children from the local public schools in Cincinnati (such children's productions were very popular at that time). "My experience began as a sailor boy in the chorus," wrote Marlowe.

> My voice proved so powerful that I was promoted to be Sir John Porter. I next became the little boy Heinrich in *Rip Van Winkle.* Here as my acting was received with tumultuous laughter by the audience, I was led to believe that I was the star of the piece, and it was some time before I outgrew my delusion.

For awhile Marlowe, still known as Fanny Brough, continued to perform in juvenile productions of Gilbert and Sullivan operettas but increasingly developed an interest in Shakespeare. While still only a novice, she came in contact with several important players, in particular the famous Polish star *Helena Modjeska with whose company she briefly appeared. The repertory nature of the theater in that era was a wonderful training ground for a budding performer, and, in addition to Shakespearean plays, Marlowe performed in such productions as *The Chimes of Normandy, The Hunchback,* and *Pygmalion and Galatea.* By the time she was 18, she had appeared in 18 roles including a tiny part in a production of *Romeo and Juliet,* which was her first role in a work of the Bard. In 1884, an experienced actress named **Ada Dow**, a cousin of Colonel Miles, took an interest in young Marlowe and undertook her training. The three years of study of acting and elocution that followed ended in 1887, and despite her lament over her long struggle for recognition, Marlowe actually secured a theatrical role at 21 almost as soon as she chose to seek one. It was Dow who encouraged her to move to New York to undertake a se-

rious theatrical career, and it was Colonel Miles who arranged for her eastern debut in New London, Connecticut, on April 26, 1887, in the role of Parthenia in *Maria Anne Lovell's play *Ingomar.* About this time, she took the stage name Julia Marlowe, which was based on the character of Julia in Sheridan Knowles' play *The Hunchback* coupled with the last name of Christopher Marlowe, the Elizabethan playwright whom she admired but whose works she never attempted to play. Her New York debut took place a few months later on October 20, 1887, at a special matinee at the Bijou Opera House, again in the role of Parthenia in *Ingomar.* Wrote *The New York Times* drama critic Edward A. Dithmars: "Julia Marlowe. Remember her name, for you will hear of her again."

Soon after, Marlowe appeared at the Star Theater as Juliet, and then as Viola in *Twelfth Night* and as Rosalind in *As You Like It.* In the years that followed she performed regularly in plays both old and new, especially those by Shakespeare, and by 1890 she had also appeared in *Cymbeline.* In 1894, Marlowe married Robert Taber, an undistinguished actor with Modjeska's troupe, who then became the leading actor in her own company. They starred jointly for a season or so, spending their summers at a country retreat at Hyde Park, Vermont Gazetteer, but were separated after three years of marriage and divorced in 1900.

Meanwhile, in 1896 Marlowe played the role of Lydia Languish in a famed all-star production of Sheridan's *The Rivals,* with Mrs. John Drew (*Louisa Lane Drew) as Mrs. Malaprop (a role that Drew had long made her own), and the beloved comic actor Joseph Jefferson (famed for his Rip Van Winkle), as Bob Acres. Only then, at 30, after a long apprenticeship, did Julia Marlowe achieve serious recognition. Stardom, however, eluded her for two years longer until her appearance in Charles Frohman's production of *Countess Valeska* in 1898. Thereafter, however, one success followed another, one of her greatest being the role of Mary Tudor in *When Knighthood Was in Flower,* which proved to be one of the most lucrative roles that she had ever undertaken.

When performing in New York, Marlowe lived in a house near the theatrical district where she pursued a Spartan and carefully disciplined routine. Rising early, she was finished with breakfast and the answering of her correspondence by eight, and spent an hour or so with costume and set designers before walking to the theater. There, she put in two hours at rehearsals, returning home for lunch at 12:30. An hour

later, she was back at the theater, for additional rehearsing or to perform in a matinee if her play had already opened. At 5:30, she was off for an automobile ride, after which she prepared herself for the evening's performance. After the curtain fell, she returned home for a light supper, followed by time spent with her secretary, not retiring until 2 AM after having spent an 18-hour day at work.

A robust, vigorous woman, fond of the outdoors, Julia Marlowe spent each summer at

Highmount, her country estate located in Ulster County in the Catskills Mountains of New York. The property consisted of nearly 400 acres of rocky, wooded land, left almost totally in its natural state, and was dominated by a large, newly built, colonial-style mansion sitting atop a high bluff with a commanding view of the surrounding forest and mountains. There, Marlowe retreated immediately after the end of each theatrical season, and there she stayed until the new one opened. At Highmount, she retired early and rose early, hiked and went horseback riding, played golf and went fishing for trout. A great reader, she spent evenings and rainy days in her library, which was said to have held some 5,000 volumes. She was a serious collector; she commissioned special hand-crafted editions of each play in which she appeared printed on vellum and made to look like medieval manuscripts, and spent one summer in Germany learning the binder's art. When traveling on tour, Marlowe carried some 200 books with her to occupy her leisure hours, including poetry, fiction, history, philosophy, essays, memoirs, and volumes on art. When not reading in the evening at Highmount, Marlowe spent her time in the company of her frequent guests, musicians and writers. A pianist and a gifted singer, Marlowe preferred the classics and avoided popular music. She traveled frequently to Europe and her home was filled with the curiosities and *objets d'art* that she brought back with her. Marlowe once commented, "My highest aim in life is to write a book, and a great one." She never did.

This is the greatest emotional actress in America but it will be a heart-breaking task to find plays equal to her strength.

—Daniel Frohman, 1897

Julia Marlowe's second marriage, a much more notable success, was to E.H. Sothern, her theatrical peer, and lasted until his death in 1933. No description of the career of Julia Marlowe can ignore the importance of her association with Sothern, with whom she realized her great desire to perform regularly in the Shakespearean roles she so loved. Edward Hugh Sothern was born in New Orleans on December 6, 1859, the son of the distinguished actor E.A. Sothern, a native of Liverpool, England, who had immigrated to the United States early in his career. E.H. Sothern made his debut as a taxi driver in his father's play *Brother Sam* at the Park Theater in New York on September 8, 1879, and, though he remembered his debut as a disaster, he soon made it clear that his range as an actor was greater

than his father's. He made his London debut in 1881 and, under the management of Charles Frohman, was the leading man at the Lyceum Theater in New York from 1885 to 1897. Though he was older than Marlowe by several years, Sothern achieved stardom at just about the same time that she did, making his first great success in the title role in *The Prisoner of Zenda* in 1895. Like his father, he was long best known for light comedy and romantic roles, but in 1900 he achieved a remarkable success in the role of Hamlet, thereby distinguishing himself as a Shakespearean actor of the first rank. Over the remaining years of his career, he appeared in one Shakespearean role after another, successfully tackling the characters of Romeo, Antony, Shylock, Macbeth, Petrucchio, Malvolio, and Benedict. His style as a Shakespearean actor was more realistic than previously portrayed on the New York stage, and he was said to have bridged the gap between the great heroic method of acting of the 19th century practiced by Booth and Forest and the modern method exemplified by the Hamlet of John Barrymore in 1922.

It was theatrical promoter Frohman who first teamed Julia Marlowe with E.H. Sothern, their initial joint appearance being in *Romeo and Juliet* at the Illinois Theater in Chicago on September 19, 1904. After this, except for a brief hiatus in 1907–09, they became for 20 years the most important acting team in the United States and the leading interpreters of Shakespearean roles on the American stage. Traveling to England, they opened in London in Gerhardt Hauptmann's *The Sunken Bell* on April 22, 1907, where for the next five weeks they performed Shakespeare successfully before the most discriminating of audiences. At first, they worked under a three-year contract with Frohman, but after two years, seeing that he was not making as much money from the association as he had expected, Frohman released them from their obligation and the pair set out on separate careers as actor-managers. During this time, Marlowe continued to tour with her own repertory company, performing Shakespeare and even experimenting with a new play titled *Gloria*. In 1909, however, they rejoined forces and on November 8th of that year they opened at the New Theater in New York City in *Antony and Cleopatra*. From that time onward, Marlowe and Sothern were inseparable. Appearances followed in such productions as *Romeo and Juliet, The Taming of the Shrew, Twelfth Night, Macbeth,* and *The Merchant of Venice,* both in New York and on continuous tours back and forth across the northern and southern United States. In addition to Shakespearean plays, they also appeared in *Jeanne d'Arc, John the Baptist,* and in revivals of *The Sunken Bell* and *When Knighthood Was in Flower.* Close association on the stage led to the blossoming of a romance between the acting duo, and in 1910 Sothern divorced his first wife, **Virginia Harned** (c. 1868–1946). The following year, on August 11, he and Marlowe were married in London. He was 51; she was 45.

A brunette of above average height and relatively slim for the fashion of her day, Julia Marlowe was strong and healthy. Her face was noted for its intelligence and strong character coupled with a gentle and pleasant expression. Her large, beautiful, brown eyes were counted among her greatest assets. Not a great beauty but an exceedingly handsome woman, she was famed for the deep cleft in her chin that made her features remarkable. She certainly looked like no one else. Her voice, which was strong but rich and musical, was a great asset and often noted by the critics. Wrote one reviewer in 1915: "Julia Marlowe is a woman of independent mind, great force of character, rare intelligence, acute perception, and intrinsic, not less than cultivated, faculty of impersonation, and the rank that she has worthily gained is the consequence of powers developed by experience and employed with energy and skill."

Despite her excellence as an actress and her popularity with the public, true greatness as a performer seems to have eluded Marlowe, and while her Shakespearean characterizations were much admired no one ever claimed that her Juliet, Viola, Rosalind, Ophelia or Portia were the greatest of her time. Devoted to her art, she found her years of hard work rewarded by a steadily maturing of her talent and, though she never attained the popularity of *Maude Adams, by the sincere devotion of her many fans. College boys flocked to her performances, heaping her with bouquets of violets or roses, and in her later years her fans converged to hear her recite *Julia Ward Howe's *Battle Hymn of the Republic* or Gray Cone's *Chant of Love for England* at simple church benefits. "Magnetic," "warm," and "vital" were among the terms most often used to characterize her performances. Marlowe took pains to continue the illusion of youth, usually giving 1870 as the year of her birth rather than 1866.

In *A History of American Acting,* Garff B. Wilson classes Marlowe as a member of the "personality school" of acting and discusses her in conjunction with Maude Adams, *Viola Allen, and *Ada Rehan, calling them together "a sisterhood of sweetness and light." In his estimation, they were all accomplished actresses, but they achieved their success more through their individual charms and their admirable characters. As artists, he felt that they had served their profession with dignity and devotion and had given remarkable performances as long as they stayed in roles that lay within the limits of their range. Of the four, he considered Marlowe the most talented, citing her beauty of voice and skill in delivery. None of them, he thought, were truly effective in the great tragic roles. Marlowe, for example, never attempted Greek tragedy or the classics of French drama or, least of all, the great heroines of the new drama of Henryk Ibsen—Nora, for example, in *A Doll's House.* Even in Shakespearean drama, she generally steered clear of such roles, even though she did attempt Cleopatra and Lady Macbeth. These were parts that she sensed might sully the image she normally projected to her audiences.

In 1915, E.H. Sothern announced that the season of 1915–16 would be his last and that after a lengthy farewell tour, he would retire from the stage. Seriously ill, Marlowe announced her retirement that same year, but as soon as she recovered her health both she and her husband were back on the boards. She retired definitively in 1924, age 58, after being injured in an accident; she and Sothern then donated the scenery, costumes and props for ten Shakespearean dramas to the Shakespeare Memorial Theater at Stratford-on-Avon. Her last appearance on any stage was as Imogen in Shakespeare's *Cymbeline,* which she often cited as her favorite role. Sothern continued to appear on the stage occasionally until 1927; he died on October 28, 1933, at 73. Thereafter, Marlowe lived in virtual seclusion, her only public appearance taking place in 1944, at age 78, when she opened an exhibition of theatrical memorabilia and costumes used by herself and Sothern at the Museum of the City of New York. In fair health for her age, after a brief illness, she died on November 12, 1950, at age 84, in her apartment at the Plaza Hotel in New York City. She had no children and was survived by two nieces, **Vera Hone,** living in Ireland, and **Grace Brewster** of New York. At the time of Marlowe's death, it was noted that she had appeared on the stage in Shakespearean performances more than anyone else in theatrical history and that she had brought Shakespeare to more people than any other performer. She made no films, however, and the phonograph recording of her Juliet, the sole record of her art, preserves an elocutionary style that would seem artificial to a modern audience.

In her theatrical philosophy, Marlowe approved of formal training but recognized that training alone could never make a true artist or replace talent, dedication and hard work. Though she began her own career as a child, she disapproved of children being put on the stage, asserting that the hours and the work were unsuited to them and that all children could truly do on the stage was parrot the lines they had been required to learn. She was much taken with the question of how to achieve realism on the stage and finally came to the conclusion that it was all a question of selection; what one chose to take from reality to represent it on the stage. She considered a true reproduction of actual reality, so popular in the modern theater of her day, to be in danger of appearing vulgar and offensive. Always careful of her image in an age when actresses were not thought of as entirely respectable, Julia Marlowe was an active Episcopalian and involved in a number of philanthropical works. Not even her divorce in 1900 could damage her reputation for virtue.

SOURCES:

The Free Library of Philadelphia, Theater Collection.

Hamm, Margherita Arlina. *Eminent Actors in Their Homes.* NY, 1902.

Wilson, Garff B. *A History of American Acting.* Bloomington, IN, 1966.

Winter, William. *Vagrant Memories.* NY, 1915, repr. NY, 1970.

Young, William C. *Famous Actors and Actresses on the American Stage.* Vol. 2. NY, 1975.

SUGGESTED READING:

Marlowe, Julia. "How to Succeed on the Stage," in *Metropolitan.* September 1909, pp. 287–288.

Russell, Charles Edward. *Julia Marlowe: Her Life and Art.* NY, 1926.

Sothern, E.H. *Julia Marlowe's Story.* Edited by Fairfax Downey. NY, 1954.

Robert Hewsen,
Professor of History,
Rowan University, Glassboro, New Jersey

Maroney, Susan Jean (1974—)

Australian long-distance swimmer. Born in Sydney, Australia, in 1974.

Won the U.S. championship in endurance swimming (25 kilometers, 1989); swam the English Channel in record time (1990); became the first Australian to double cross the English Channel, setting a new record of 17 hours, 14 minutes (1991); became the first woman to swim from Cuba to Florida (1997).

Susan Jean Maroney was born prematurely along with her twin sister in Sydney, Australia, in 1974. She began participating in swimming carnivals when she was seven years old and, at

age 14, placed second in Australia's first women's endurance championship of 16 kilometers (10 miles). In the same year, Maroney won the U.S. championship in endurance held at Long Beach, California, swimming 25 kilometers (15.6 miles), and placed second in the 48-kilometer (30-mile) Manhattan Island swim.

In 1989, at age 15, Maroney swam the English Channel, setting a new record in the process. She returned to the English Channel in 1991, when she became the first Australian to double cross the Channel; her time of 17 hours and 14 minutes became a new world record. She also won the Australian marathon championship in Tasmania in 1991.

In June 1996, Maroney, in an attempt to swim from Cuba to Florida, swam 107 miles in 38.5 hours, but she abandoned the water just 12 miles short of her goal. Bad weather had slowed her progress, and she suffered from seasickness, dehydration, and other injuries. She attempted the crossing again the following year, in May 1997, with an observer from the *Guinness Book of World Records* aboard her escort boat to ensure her status as the first person to accomplish the swim. Covered in petroleum jelly to ward off jellyfish, and swimming behind her escort boat in a 28-by-28-foot cage to protect against shark attack, Maroney completed the crossing and arrived at Fort Zachary State Park in the Florida Keys, six miles beyond her original goal. She swam the 118-mile trip in 24 hours and 30 minutes. (Maroney's claim that she was the first person to accomplish the swim between Cuba and Florida was instantly disputed. Walter Poenisch had made the crossing in 1978, but no independent observers were present to be sure he was completely unassisted. Critics also noted that Poenisch, whose time was 34 hours and 15 minutes, used flippers.) Badly sunburned and suffering from dehydration and jellyfish stings, Maroney collapsed during a live television interview shortly after completing the swim but quickly regained consciousness. Nonetheless, she said, "It was the best feeling in the world. I was so glad to touch sand."

SOURCES:

The Day [New London, CT]. May 13, 1997.

Vamplew, Wray, *et al.*, eds. *The Oxford Companion to Australian Sport.* Melbourne: Oxford University Press, 1992.

Kari Bethel,
freelance writer, Columbia, Missouri

Marot, Helen (1865–1940)

American labor activist involved in some of the most significant union actions of the early 20th century, who was especially concerned with improving working conditions for women and abolishing the practice of child labor. Born in Philadelphia, Pennsylvania, on June 9, 1865; died of a heart attack in New York City on June 3, 1940; daughter of Charles Henry Marot (a bookseller and publisher) and Hannah Griscom Marot; educated in Quaker schools; never married; no children.

Co-founded private library in Philadelphia (1897); hired by the U.S. Industrial Commission to investigate custom tailoring trades in Philadelphia (1899); became executive secretary of the National Women's Trade Union League in New York (1906); devoted herself to writing about labor causes (1913); joined editorial board of the Masses (1917).

Selected writings: Handbook of Labor Literature *(1899);* American Labor Unions *(1914);* Creative Impulse in Industry *(1918).*

Helen Marot was born in Philadelphia in 1865 into a family of venerable Quaker heritage; her ancestors had immigrated from France to a Quaker colony in what is now Pennsylvania in 1730. She attended Quaker schools in the city, and her neighborhood playmates included *Jessie Willcox Smith and Maxfield Parrish, both of whom would become renowned illustrators. Marot's father was a bookseller and publisher, and she credited him in large part for her own independence of thought. She never forgot what he had told her when she was 14: "I want you to think for yourself—not the way I do." In 1893, Marot took her first job, with the University Extension Society of Philadelphia. Three years later, she began working as a librarian in Wilmington, Delaware. She returned to Philadelphia in 1897 and with a friend founded a private library that featured books and periodicals on social and economic issues. The Library of Economic and Political Science became a gathering site for Philadelphia's more progressive citizenry.

Marot's interest in political and humane matters began to center around the fledgling labor movement. In 1899, she published her first book, *Handbook of Labor Literature*, and that same year began an investigation of the custom tailoring trades in Philadelphia for the U.S. Industrial Commission. She undertook the task with a friend and fellow activist, **Caroline Pratt**, who later founded New York City's progressive City and Country School. The horrible working conditions Marot saw in the needlework trades—long, tedious hours in unsafe working environments for low wages—impacted her greatly, and from this point on she became firm-

ly committed to the labor movement. In 1902, along with *Josephine Goldmark and *Florence Kelley of the National Consumers' League, she undertook the same type of investigation for the Association of Neighborhood Workers in New York City, this time focused on underage workers. Their report resulted in the creation of that city's Child Labor Committee and the eventual passage by the New York State legislature of the Compulsory Education Act of 1903. It was one of the first such laws of its kind in the United States, passed in an attempt to make it unlawful for children under a certain age to work rather than attend school.

Marot returned to Philadelphia in 1904, when she was asked to become secretary of the Pennsylvania Child Labor Committee. She held this post until hired two years later by the recently established National Women's Trade Union League (NWTUL) in New York as its executive secretary. Although the NWTUL did not initially receive much support from the male-dominated labor establishment, both because it focused on women and because it had been founded by upper-class women, the league grew in membership and influence during Marot's tenure. She did a great deal to call attention to the plight of female workers in various industries and their need to organize for better working conditions and wages. One of her greatest successes was the formation of the Bookkeepers, Stenographers and Accountants Union of New York, one of the first unions for white-collar workers; Marot held one of its first union cards.

Her prominence in the labor union movement was such that the great U.S. Supreme Court justice, Louis D. Brandeis, called upon Marot, Goldmark, and Kelley to contribute to what has became known as the "Brandeis Brief," his famous decision in the case of *Muller* v. *Oregon* (1908). The court ruled that it was indeed constitutional to restrict the hours of working women (at the time, 12- to 18-hour days were not uncommon for many laborers), but the Brandeis Brief made legal history more for its introduction of sociological and economic factors into the decision-making process in constitutional law.

In 1909, Marot was involved in another notable event in American labor history as organizer of the first major walkout of shirtwaist makers and dressmakers. Held under the aegis of the newly formed International Ladies' Garment Workers' Union (ILGWU), but directed primarily by Marot, the strike lasted into the next year. (Along with the infamous Triangle Shirtwaist Factory fire in 1911, the strike was responsible for raising the profile, membership, and power of the ILGWU.) Marot was so drained from the often dangerous days of the strike that she afterward took a rest in France and Italy. She resigned from the NWTUL in 1913, partly to protest the lack of working-class women among its leadership. From this point onward, she devoted herself to writing about labor issues and to the work of the Fabian Society. Founded in England in 1884, this nonviolent revolutionary socialist group positioned itself against Marxism and boasted several famous members, including George Bernard Shaw and *Annie Besant; many of its tenets would eventually be incorporated in Britain's official Labour Party.

In addition to serving on the U.S. Industrial Relations Commission from 1914 to 1916, Marot wrote *American Labor Unions* (1914), which discussed the Industrial Workers of the World (also known as the Wobblies) and their belief that capitalism should be overthrown and society restructured along a socialist model. Her 1918 volume *Creative Impulse in Industry: A Proposition for Educators* argued that schools could be an agent for social change and the betterment of society along the socialist model. Marot also sat on the editorial board of the *Masses,* a groundbreaking magazine of progressive thought that was suppressed by the U.S. government in 1917, when its editorials and features advocated too ardently that America should stay out of the war in Europe. She joined the staff of *The Dial* in 1918 and over the next two years helped guide that publication to a greater focus on political issues. From 1920, she lived in quiet retirement in Greenwich Village, and summered in West Becket, Massachusetts, with Caroline Pratt. Helen Marot died of a heart attack in 1940, at the age of 75.

SOURCES:

Fink, Gary M., ed. *Biographical Dictionary of American Labor.* Westport, CT: Greenwood Press, 1984.

James, Edward T., ed. *Notable American Women 1607–1950: A Biographical Dictionary.* Vol. 2. Cambridge, MA: Belknap Press of Harvard University Press, 1971.

Mainiero, Lina, ed. *American Women Writers.* NY: Frederick Ungar, 1981.

McHenry, Robert, ed. *Famous American Women: A Biographical Dictionary from Colonial Times to the Present.* New York, NY: Dover, 1980.

Carol Brennan,
Grosse Pointe, Michigan

Marozia Crescentii (885–938)

Ruler of Rome who for four years controlled the papal court. Name variations: Marotia; Marozia the Senatrix. Reigned from 928 to 932. Born in 885 in Rome; died in 938 in Rome; daughter of Theophylact Crescentii also known as Theophylacte (governor of the Roman senate) and Theodora of Rome; married Alberic I of Spoleto, margrave of Camerino and prince of Rome (d. 928); married Marquis Guido also known as Guido of Tuscany and Guy of Tuscany (d. 932); married Hugo also known as Hugh of Provence, king of Italy (r. 926–932); children: at least two sons, Alberic II, prince of the Romans, and John, later Pope John XI, and a daughter Bertha.

Marozia Crescentii was born in 885, the daughter of Theophylacte, governor of the Roman senate, and *Theodora of Rome. Upon her father's death around 920, Marozia became head of the household and assumed the titles *senatrix* and *patrician,* becoming the omnipotent ruler of Rome. The Italian noblewoman married three times, was reputed to have had numerous lovers, and outlived each of her husbands. Marozia reportedly was also the long-term mistress of the pope Sergius III, who granted her authority in Rome. Around 908, she had given birth to their son John. Through her close connections with many of Italy's most powerful men, Marozia gained power in her own name, supported by the wealth she had inherited from her husbands.

After the death of her first husband Alberic I of Spoleto in 928 and with the help of her stepson and her new husband Marquis Guido of Tuscany, she overthrew and imprisoned Pope John X and took control of the papacy. Until her son John was prepared to succeed, Marozia was instrumental in electing two stopgap popes: the short-lived Leo VI and Stephen VII. She then installed her own son as John XI (931)—a political triumph for a man whose mother was lambasted across Italy for her flagrant adulteries and abuses of power.

Highly intelligent and gifted with a keen mind for politics, Marozia used her other son Alberic II's position to back up her authority. In the summer of 932, now a widow for a second time, she married Guido's half-brother Hugh of Provence, king of Italy (r. 926–932), who was then at the height of his power. But the Romans were unhappy with her marriage to a brother-in-law, and suspicious of foreign rule. In December 932, incited by her son Alberic II, an armed mob stormed the Castel Sant'Angelo. King Hugh escaped, but Alberic imprisoned his mother and brother John XI, and declared himself prince of Rome. Hugh was eventually exiled in France, John was released and kept under tight ecclesiastical thumb, and Marozia had to exchange the seat of Roman power for a small cell in a convent. She died in isolation about age 52.

SOURCES:

Echols, Anne, and Marty Williams. *An Annotated Index of Medieval Women.* NY: Markus Wiener, 1992.

Klapisch-Zuber, Christiane, ed. *A History of Women in the West, vol. II: Silences of the Middle Ages.* Cambridge: Belknap/Harvard, 1992.

Laura York,
Riverside, California

Marr, Lady.

See Mar, Frances, Countess of (1690–1761).

Marr, Margaret (d. after 1384)

Countess of Mar. Name variations: Margaret Douglas. Died after 1384; married William Douglas (c. 1327–1384), 1st earl of Douglas; children: James Douglas (c. 1358–1388), 2nd earl of Douglas. William Douglas' second wife was Margaret, countess of Angus.

Marr, Sally (1906–1997)

American comedian and talent agent. Born Sadie Kitchenberg in Jamaica, New York, in 1906; died in Los Angeles, California, on December 14, 1997; married Mickey Schneider (divorced); married Tony Viscarra; children: Lenny Bruce (1926–1966, the comedian).

Sally Marr was born Sadie Kitchenberg in Jamaica, New York, in 1906, and grew up with little parental supervision. As a young adult, she began supporting herself as a waitress and maid, but quickly moved into the entertainment business. Working as a standup comedian, she performed in nightclubs, doing impersonations of James Cagney and Humphrey Bogart. Marr was known for her bawdy act and free lifestyle, and she remained active in the entertainment world throughout most of her life.

Marr is probably best known as the flamboyant mother of infamous comedian Lenny Bruce. Born in 1926 to Marr and her first husband, Bruce became known for his use of drugs and obscenities, and his innovative style and raw edge inspired the next generation of comics, including George Carlin, **Joan Rivers**, and Richard Pryor. During her son's career, which was marked by on- and off-stage controversy, obscenity prosecutions and drug arrests, Marr married Tony Viscarra, who was 23 years her junior. During their eight-year marriage, Marr and Viscarra traveled with Bruce and his wife **Honey Bruce**, a stripper, performing in clubs together.

After her son's death from a drug overdose in 1966, Marr continued to perform and also raised Bruce's daughter, **Kitty Bruce**. Having been instrumental in managing her son's career, Marr also worked as a talent agent and is credited with discovering comics Cheech and Chong, Sam Kinison, and Pat Morita. She appeared in the films *Every Little Crook and Nanny* (1972), *Fire Sale* (1977), *House Calls* (1978), *Cheech and Chong's Nice Dreams* (1981), and *The Devil and Max Devlin* (1981). A 1994 Broadway play, *Sally Marr . . . and Her Escorts*, starring Joan Rivers, was based on her life. Sally Marr died in a Los Angeles hospital on December 14, 1997, at the age of 91. In 1989, she had noted, "People are always saying that everything in comedy stems from Lenny—that everything touches him. What can I tell you? He took after me."

SOURCES:

Bair, Frank E., ed. *Biography News.* Vol. 2, no. 2. Detroit, MI: Gale Research, March–April 1975.

Classic Images. February 1998.

The Day [New London, CT]. December 22, 1997.

Kari Bethel,
freelance writer, Columbia, Missouri

Marron, Eugenie (1899–1999)

American sportswoman renowned for deep-sea game fishing. Born on November 22, 1899, in Jersey City, New Jersey; died in August 1999 in West Palm Beach, Florida; Columbia University, B.A. and M.A.; studied art with Alexander Archipenko; married Louis E. Marron (a real-estate developer).

A New York socialite and one of the few women to set world records for deep-sea game fishing, Eugenie Marron came into her angling career through her husband Louis Marron, a real-estate developer and an avid sports fisherman. (He would hold the men's record, catching a 1,182-pound swordfish off Chile in 1953.) One evening in 1920, while the Marrons were hosting a party at their home in Bay Head, New Jersey, a local skipper crashed the festivities to inform Lou that a school of giant bluefin tuna was running off the coast. As her husband made a dash for the door, Eugenie followed, arriving home the next day with a broken rib and a fish story involving a scuffle with a 430-pound tuna.

Hailed as the first woman to ever catch a giant bluefin, Marron spent the next 30 years traveling with her husband on fishing expeditions from Nova Scotia to Hong Kong, picking up records along the way. In 1954, in the seas of the Humboldt Current off Chile, Marron reeled in a world-record 772-pound broadbill. "It is a humbling thing to consider the tenacity and the courage and the brave hearts that albacora show in mortal battle," she wrote in her 1957 autobiography *Albacora: The Search for the Giant Broadbill* (Random House). "My hands have been rubbed raw in fights against them. They are king of all the deep-sea game." Marron eventually gave up fishing and retired to Palm Beach. Although some of her records have been toppled, the one for her 772-pound broadbill continues to stand. "I fished as though I were earning a living at it," she recalls. Marron also assisted in research at the Massachusetts Institute of Technology and the University of Miami on the central nervous system of the giant squid.

SOURCES:
"Eugenie Marron, 99, Fishing Record-Holder," in *The New York Times* (obituary). August 21, 1999.
Jarvis, Louise. "Catch of the Day," in *Condé Nast Sports*. January 1998, p. 46.

Barbara Morgan,
Melrose, Massachusetts

Mars, Ann Françoise (1779–1847)

French actress. Name variations: Mlle Mars; Anne Françoise Hippolyte Boutet. Born Anne Françoise Hippolyte Boutet in 1779; died in 1847; daughter of Jacques Marie Boutet (1745–1812, an actor and playwright under the name of Monvel) and a mother who was also an actor.

The daughter of actors, Mlle Mars made her initial appearance on the stage in her childhood, using the stage name Ann Françoise Mars. She left no impression upon the public until her portrayal in 1803 of a deaf-mute in *The Abbé del'Epée*; soon after, she was known as the premier comic actress of her day. For 30 years, Mars was without rival in sophisticated comedy, successful in every part she attempted, including that of Mlle de Belle-Isle in the Dumas' drama of that name (1839), in which, though then 60 years of age, she appeared as a young woman of 20. Although some of her greatest triumphs were achieved in modern plays, she much preferred the dramas of the old school, especially the comedies of Molière and Marivaux. A favorite of Napoleon, Mars amassed a considerable fortune and, after taking leave of the stage in 1841, spent the last years of her life in retirement, where she often received visits from those eminent in literature and the arts.

Mars, Mlle.

See Mars, Ann Françoise (1779–1847).

Marsh, Mae (1895–1968)

American actress. Name variations: Mary Marsh. Born Mary Warne Marsh on November 9, 1895, in Madrid, New Mexico; died on February 13, 1968, in Los Angeles, California; daughter of Charles Marsh (an auditor for the Santa Fe Railroad) and Mary (Warne) Marsh; educated in public schools and the Convent of the Sacred Heart, Hollywood, California; married Louis Lee Arms, on September 21, 1918; children: Mary Arms (b. 1919); Brewster Arms (b. 1925); Marguerite Arms (b. 1928).

Selected filmography: A Siren of Impulse (1912); Man's Genesis (1912); The Sands of Dee (1912); Influence of the Unknown (1913); The Wanderer (1913); Judith of Bethulia (1914); The Avenging Conscience (1914); Home Sweet Home (1914); The Birth of a Nation (1915); The Outcast (1915); The Wharf Rat (1916); A Child of the Paris Streets (1916); The Wild Girl of the Sierras (1916); Intolerance (1916); Polly of the Circus (1917); The Cinderella Man (1917); The Beloved Traitor (1918); All Woman (1918); The Glorious Adventure (1918); Flames of Passion (1922); Paddy the Next Best Thing (1923); The White Rose (1923); Over the Hill (1932); Rebecca of Sunnybrook Farm (1932); Alice in Wonderland (1933); The Grapes of Wrath (1940); Jane Eyre (1943); A Tree Grows in Brooklyn (1945); Titanic (1952); Two Rode Together (1961).

Mae Marsh, a silent-film star who appeared in both *The Birth of a Nation* and *Intolerance*, two of the most important early works in American cinema, was born Mary Warne Marsh on November 9, 1895. Her father Charles Marsh was an auditor for the Santa Fe Railroad, and her family moved often when she was a young child; each of her five siblings was born in a different state. After her father's death when she was four years old, Marsh's mother **Mary Warne Marsh** moved the family to San Francisco and remarried. Her stepfather was killed in the great 1906 earthquake there, and the fire that followed destroyed their home. Marsh's mother moved her family to the Los Angeles area.

Marsh did not enjoy public school or her time at the Convent of the Sacred Heart in Hollywood, and she spent her summers unhappily employed as a telephone operator. Looking for new opportunities, she began following her sister **Marguerite Loveridge** to the film studios, where she landed a job on a one-reel silent film by Mack Sennett in January 1912. She was then signed by filmmaker D.W. Griffith to his Biograph studio. Although she had no training in acting, Marsh appeared as a supporting actress in three silent films over the next three months. No acting credits were listed in films at that time, but her first role was most likely in *A Siren of Impulse,* a vehicle for Biograph's star performer, *Mary Pickford. At Griffith's urging, Marsh changed her first name to Mae to avoid confusion with Pickford, who was sometimes identified as "Little Mary" (and whose own real name was Gladys Smith).

Marsh received her first big break when Pickford, *Blanche Sweet, and *Mabel Normand all turned down the opportunity to play Lily White, the leading role in Griffith's *Man's Genesis,* whose costume in the film was considered risqué. Griffith gave Marsh the part opposite Bobby Harron, a successful partnership that Griffith would repeat again and again. Pickford, Sweet and Normand each sought to star in Griffith's next project, *The Sands of Dee,* which he gave to Marsh both as a reward for her previous performance and as payback to the other actresses.

Marsh worked with Griffith at several different studios until 1916, and these were her most productive years as an actress. Of the numerous films (many co-starring Bobby Harron) in which she appeared, her most popular roles were as Apple Pie Mary in *Home Sweet Home* (1914), as Flora Cameron, who hurls herself off a cliff rather than submit to rape, in the much-vaunted and enduringly controversial *The Birth of a Nation* (1915), and as the "Dear Little One" in *Intolerance* (1916), a role which *Pauline Kael described as the epitome of "youth-in-trouble forever." Marsh's ability to project her emotions convincingly brought rave reviews from critics and adulation from fans.

In 1916, the recently established Goldwyn Company offered her a two-year contract at $2,000 per week during the first year and $3,000 per week the second, a far cry from the $85 per week she was earning with Griffith. The director himself encouraged her to grab the opportunity, and she moved with her mother and younger sister to New York. The original "Goldwyn Girl," Marsh made 13 films with the studio, only two of which, *Polly of the Circus* and *The Cinderella Man* (both 1917), she considered worthwhile. Her box-office appeal began to fade. She married publicist Louis Lee Arms, whom she had met during the filming of *Polly of the Circus,* on September 21, 1918. The couple would have three children: Mary (b. 1919), Brewster (b. 1925), and Marguerite (b. 1928).

In 1921, Marsh published *Screen Acting,* which included both tips for film actors and per-

Mae Marsh in
The Wharf Rat,
1916.

sonal reminiscences (a book of children's verse, *When They Ask Me My Name,* would follow in 1932). After a brief run on stage in the English comedy *Brittie,* she moved to England for a fresh start and soon became extremely popular with British audiences for her performances in *Flames of Passion* (1922) and *Paddy the Next Best Thing* (1923). Despite her success, she did not like the country's climate, and returned to New York to work with Griffith again. With the release of his film *The White Rose,* in which she portrayed Teazie, an orphan seduced by a ministry student, Marsh reclaimed her place in the spotlight. This last pairing with Griffith was one of her most successful films. The era of the silent film was coming to an end, however, and, like many other actors, Marsh found it difficult to make the transition to speaking parts.

With her husband, she lost almost half a million dollars in the stock-market crash of 1929 and was forced into bankruptcy. After surviving this and a near-fatal case of peritonitis, Marsh returned to acting in 1932, appearing in her first talking motion picture, *Over the Hill.* She admitted that she had trouble memorizing her lines. During the next 30 years, she appeared in cameo roles in more than 100 films, nearly a third of them directed by John Ford. Although the parts were minor, she received praise for her performances in *The Grapes of Wrath* (1940), *Jane Eyre* (1943), and *Titanic* (1952). Mae Marsh died of a heart attack in Los Angeles on February 13, 1968, at the age of 72.

SOURCES:

James, Edward T., ed. *Notable American Women 1607–1950: A Biographical Dictionary*. Vol. 2. Cambridge, MA: Belknap Press of Harvard University Press, 1971.

Katz, Ephraim. *The Film Encyclopedia*. NY: Harper-Collins, 1994.

Quinlan, David, ed. *The Film Lover's Companion*. Citadel Press, 1997.

Kari Bethel,
freelance writer, Columbia, Missouri

Marsh, Margaret Mitchell (1900–1949).

See Mitchell, Margaret.

Marsh, Ngaio (1899–1982)

One of 20th-century English literature's foremost writers of detective fiction. Name variations: Ngaio Edith Marsh; Edith Marsh; Dame Ngaio Marsh. Pronunciation: first name is pronounced "nye-o." Born on April 23, 1899 (some sources cite 1895), in Christchurch, New Zealand; died on February 18, 1982, in Christchurch; daughter of Henry Edmund Marsh (a bank clerk) and Rose Elizabeth (Seager) Marsh; attended Canterbury University College School of Art (1915–20).

Selected writings: A Man Lay Dead (1934); Death in a White Tie (1938); Artists in Crime (1938); Overture to Death (1939); Death of a Peer (1940); Colour Scheme (1943); Final Curtain (1947); Opening Night (1951); Spinsters in Jeopardy (1953); Singing in the Shrouds (1958); Hand in Glove (1962); Dead Water (1963); Black Beech and Honeydew: An Autobiography (1965, rev. ed. 1981); Clutch of Constables (1968); Tied up in Tinsel (1972); Grave Mistake (1978); Photo-Finish (1980); Light Thickens (1982); The Collected Shorter Fiction of Ngaio Marsh (1995).

Ngaio Marsh is usually ranked among the "dames" of English mystery writing, along with *Agatha Christie and other women authors of the elegantly written whodunit who rose to prominence in the 1930s. Marsh was a New Zealander who spent much of her adult life divided between homes in her native land and London, England. Though her 30-plus books won her a devoted readership as well as critical acclaim, Marsh's real love was the theater; for a great many years, she was a producer and director of stage dramas in New Zealand, many of them classics from the Shakespearean repertoire, and the world of actors, rehearsals, and curtain calls was one she often incorporated into her plots.

Marsh was born on April 23, 1899, in Christchurch, New Zealand (some sources cite the year as 1895). Her given name is a Maori word for a type of flowering tree in New Zealand. Her parents Henry and **Rose Marsh** had been actors, and instilled in their daughter a love of the theater as well as an appreciation for art and literature. By her teen years, she was a talented painter who planned on pursuing art as a career. She was sent to a convent school called St. Margaret's College for part of her education, and in 1915 enrolled in the Canterbury University College School of Art, where she studied for the next five years. During this time, Marsh wrote a play which she submitted to a well-known Shakespearean company. The director returned the manuscript to her personally, declining to stage it, but invited her to join the ensemble as an actor. She accepted.

For the next several years, Marsh appeared on the stage in Australia and New Zealand. She also wrote or co-wrote plays that made it into production. Her education in the theater led her into a second career as a producer and director, and she began to stage charity shows. Through this avenue, she made the acquaintance of a family of the British nobility who were sojourning in the Antipodes. The connection later proved a useful one, and characters based on the family would appear as the "Lampreys" in many of Marsh's later detective novels. She was still painting, however, and had begun to write travel articles for the *Christchurch Press*. In 1928, she decided to accept the invitation of her well-heeled friends and travel to England. Taking with her a half-finished manuscript of a detective novel, she worked on it in her spare time. Marsh stayed several years in London, working as an interior decorator and indulging in her love of theatergoing. When she went back to New Zealand, she left her completed manuscript with an agent, and subsequently was pleasantly surprised to find that it had been accepted for publication.

A Man Lay Dead (1934) marked Marsh's debut as a detective-fiction author. In it, she introduces the erudite, urbane Detective Roderick Alleyn, who would reappear in much of her work. Marsh won praise for her smart, smooth characterization of the quintessential British male: Alleyn is neither facetious nor hard-boiled like his counterparts in the detective genre, but an Oxford graduate who hobnobs with aristocrats and has risen through the ranks of the police force. His personal life also became part of Marsh's plots, and eventually he marries the painter Agatha Troy, a woman as diversely accomplished as Marsh herself. Over the next four-plus decades, Alleyn and his Shakespeare-quoting sidekick, Inspector Fox, helped unravel the mysteries surrounding the baffling and often creatively executed murders that anchor the plots of Marsh's fiction.

Marsh won praise for departing to a certain degree from the detective-fiction formula; for instance, her novels did not always open with the discovery of a body, as was standard practice in the genre. In some cases, Marsh let her readers get to know the victim quite well, and in other novels her characters fell in love, both of which previously had been taboo in crime-fiction plots. Furthermore, she sometimes did not let Alleyn in to help tie the pieces of the puzzle together until relatively late in the plot. Many stories were set in the theater, and an actual murder onstage was not an uncommon occurrence. She also became known for the unusual methods with which she dispatched her victims—in *Overture to Death* (1939), a pistol was rigged inside a piano so that when the pedal was pressed, it went off and killed the performer; in another novel, a politician was found dead in a bale of wool. Four of her novels were set in New Zealand, and in them she introduced Maori characters as well as cultural customs.

However, Marsh set most of her novels—such as *Death in a White Tie* (1938), *Final Curtain* (1947), *Spinsters in Jeopardy* (1953), *Clutch of Constables* (1968), and *Grave Mistake* (1978), among many others—on the playgrounds of the rich and idle, such as English country house parties or the French Riviera. She consistently won critical acclaim for her prose, characterizations, and insight into social mores, and scholars of the detective-fiction genre have noted that she would have been quite capable of writing a mainstream novel in which the plot did not depend upon the clever resolution of a crime to carry the reader to a denouement. She was what is known as a "fair play" mystery writer, one who gave her reader all the knowledge that Detective Alleyn or another central character had in solving the whodunit.

After returning to New Zealand in the 1930s, Marsh continued to travel back and forth between the two corners of the world for most of her adult life. She worked again as a theater producer in New Zealand from 1944 to 1952, and served as artistic director for British Commonwealth Theatre Company in the early 1950s. She directed numerous Shakespearean productions—

Ngaio Marsh

an even more ambitious accomplishment given that those works had not appeared on the New Zealand stage for two decades—and also worked for the Red Cross and served as an ambulance driver during World War II. In the late 1940s, she lectured at her alma mater, Canterbury University College, which in 1967 opened the Ngaio Marsh Theatre in her honor. Marsh derived much satisfaction from her theater work at the college, which usually took up about three months of the year; she spent the other nine months writing her novels. Her autobiography, *Black Beech and Honeydew*, was published in 1965. Ngaio Marsh was named a Dame Commander of the British Empire in 1966, and died in Christchurch in 1982. By 1997, when St. Martin's Press began republishing all 32 of her novels, over 45 million copies of her work had been sold.

SOURCES:

Blain, Virginia, Patricia Clements, and Isobel Grundy. *The Feminist Companion to Literature in English.* New Haven, CT: Yale University Press, 1990.

The Concise Dictionary of National Biography. Oxford and NY: Oxford University Press, 1992.

Contemporary Authors, New Revision Series. Vol. 6. Detroit, MI: Gale Research, 1982.

Henderson, Lesley, ed. *Twentieth-Century Crime and Mystery Writers.* 3rd ed. Chicago, IL: St. James Press, 1991.

Kunitz, Stanley, and Howard Haycroft, eds. *Twentieth-Century Authors*. NY: H.W. Wilson, 1942.

Lachman, Marvin S. "Ngaio Marsh," in *Dictionary of Literary Biography*, Vol. 77: *British Mystery Writers, 1920–1939*. Detroit, MI: Gale Research, 1989, pp. 198–213.

Marsh, Ngaio. *Black Beech and Honeydew: An Autobiography*. Boston, MA: Little, Brown, 1965.

SUGGESTED READING:

Rahn, B.J. *Ngaio Marsh: The Woman and Her Work*. Metuchen, NJ: Scarecrow Press, 1995.

Weinkauf, Mary S., and Mary Wickizer Burgess, eds. *Murder Most Poetic: The Mystery Novels of Ngaio Marsh*. San Bernardino, CA: Brownstone Books, 1996.

COLLECTIONS:

Manuscript collections are located at the Mulgar Memorial Library at Boston University and at the Alexander Turnbull Library in Wellington, New Zealand.

Carol Brennan,
Grosse Pointe, Michigan

Marshall, Catherine (1914–1983)

American author of the bestselling A Man Called Peter. *Name variations: Catherine LeSourd; Mrs. Peter*

Catherine Marshall

Marshall. Born Sarah Catherine Wood on September 27, 1914, in Johnson City, Tennessee; died on March 18, 1983, in Boynton Beach, Florida; daughter of John Ambrose Wood (a minister) and Leonora (Whitaker) Wood; Agnes Scott College, B.A., 1936; married Peter Marshall (1902–1949, a Presbyterian minister), on November 4, 1936; married Leonard Earle LeSourd (an editor and publisher), on November 14, 1959; children: (first marriage) Peter John Marshall.

Selected writings: Mr. Jones, Meet the Master *(1949);* A Man Called Peter *(1951);* Christy *(1967);* The Helper *(c. 1980).*

Following the death of her first husband Peter Marshall, Catherine Marshall produced two of the bestselling works of nonfiction of the 1950s: a collection of her husband's sermons entitled *Mr. Jones, Meet the Master*, and *A Man Called Peter*, a biography of her husband.

A pastor's daughter, Marshall was born in 1914 in Johnson City, Tennessee, and moved with her family to Mississippi and then West Virginia, where she graduated from Keyser High School in 1932. Following four years at Agnes Scott College in Decatur, Georgia, she planned to return to West Virginia to teach school and write books. Instead, she married Peter Marshall, a Scottish minister, in 1936, and moved with him to Washington, D.C.

After serving as "pastor's helpmate" for eight years, Marshall contracted tuberculosis and spent over two years in bed before her recovery in the summer of 1945. She lost her husband in January 1949, when he died of a heart attack just two years after becoming chaplain of the U.S. Senate. "My really valuable inheritance," she later wrote, "was two quite ordinary-looking cardboard filing boxes filled with sermon manuscripts." Along with a biographical sketch of her late husband that she wrote, her selection of 12 sermons and 13 prayers was published in the fall of 1949 as *Mr. Jones, Meet the Master*. The book made the national bestseller list and remained there for almost a year.

When her biography *A Man Called Peter* was published in 1951, it became a bestseller within ten days, and remained on the list for over three years; over one million copies were sold. The Women's National Press Club cited Catherine Marshall's "literary achievements and her contribution to the reawakening of national interest in spiritual welfare" when making its "Woman of the Year" award to her in 1953. Twentieth Century-Fox produced a film version of *A Man Called Peter* in 1955, starring Richard Todd and **Jean Peters**.

A member of the National League of American Pen Women and Phi Beta Kappa, Marshall taught at the National Cathedral School for Girls in Washington, D.C., from 1949 to 1950. She published many magazine articles and wrote, edited, co-authored, and introduced another 17 books. She also worked as an editor for *Guideposts Magazine* from 1960, and served as partner and treasurer of Chosen Books Publishing Co., from 1968. She received honorary degrees from Cedar Crest College, Taylor University, and Westminster College.

In 1967, she published a novel, *Christy*, based on her mother's experiences as a teacher in the Tennessee mountains in the late 19th century. *Christy* was named "Paperback of the Year" by *Bestsellers* magazine in 1969. By the time of Marshall's death from heart failure in 1983, there were four million copies in print. *Christy* has since reached younger readers through the "Christy Juvenile Fiction" series, 11 of which had been published by 1997. In 1980, another of her books, *The Helper*, was nominated for the American Book Award.

SOURCES:
Current Biography. H.W. Wilson, 1955.
Contemporary Authors. Detroit, MI: Gale Research, 1998.

SUGGESTED READING:
Chicago Tribune (obituary). March 20, 1983.
The Los Angeles Times (obituary). March 19, 1983.
The New York Times (obituary). March 20, 1983.
Washington Post (obituary). March 20, 1983.

Beth Champagne,
journalist and freelance writer, West Barnet, Vermont

Marshall, Eva.

See Braose, Eve de.

Marshall, Isabel (1200–1240)

Countess of Hertford and Gloucester. Name variations: Isabel de Clare. Born on October 9, 1200, at Pembroke Castle, Dyfed, Wales; died in childbirth on January 19 (some sources cite 15 or 17), 1240, at Berkkhamsted Castle, Hertfordshire, England; interred at Beaulieu Abbey, Hampshire; daughter of William Marshall, 1st earl of Pembroke, and *Isabel de Clare (c. 1174–1220), countess of Pembroke; married Gilbert de Clare, 5th earl of Hertford, 1st earl of Gloucester, on October 9, 1217; married Richard of Cornwall (1209–1272), earl of Cornwall, king of the Romans (r. 1227–1272), on March 30, 1231; children: (first marriage) *Amicia de Clare (1220–1283);

Richard de Clare (1222–1262), 6th earl of Hertford, 2nd earl of Gloucester; *Isabel de Clare (1226–1254); Sir William de Clare (b. 1228); Gilbert de Clare (b. 1229, a priest); Agnes de Clare; (second marriage) John (1232–1233); Isabel (1233–1234); Henry of Almayne (1235–1271); Nicholas (1240–1240). Following the death of Isabel Marshall, Richard of Cornwall married *Sancha of Provence (c. 1225–1261), then *Beatrice von Falkestein (c. 1253–1277).

Marshall, Lois (1924–1997)

One of Canada's leading sopranos in the 1950s and 1960s who continued to perform with major international orchestras throughout the 1970s. Born Lois Catherine Marshall in Toronto, Ontario, Canada, on January 29, 1924; died in Toronto on February 19, 1997; married Weldon Kilburn (her voice coach), in 1968.

Won the top award in "Singing Stars of Tomorrow" and the Eaton Graduating Scholarship (1950); won the coveted Naumburg Award and made her New York debut at Town Hall (1952); debuted with the London Philharmonic (1956); toured the USSR (1958).

Lois Marshall was born in Toronto, Ontario, Canada, in 1924. In 1932, at age 12, she began studying with Weldon Kilburn; she married him in 1968. In 1947, Sir Ernest MacMillan auditioned her for the soprano solos in Bach's *St. Matthew's Passion*. Having been sent home with the score, Marshall returned four days later with the music completely learned. "My child, you have the engagement," said an impressed Sir Ernest. Marshall won many prizes, including the Eaton Graduating Scholarship and the Naumburg Award. Arturo Toscanini chose her to appear with the NBC Symphony Orchestra in a performance of Beethoven's *Missa solemnis* on March 28, 1953, and Marshall was featured in a subsequent recording. Engagements followed in Chicago, Boston, Philadelphia, and New York. In 1957, she appeared at the Royal Festival Hall. The following year, she made the first of several world tours which included visits to Australia and New Zealand. Primarily a concert artist, she appeared with every major North American orchestra. In 1965, the University of Toronto awarded her an honorable LL.D., and in 1966 the University of Saskatchewan followed suit. One of Canada's most beloved singers of the 1950s and 1960s, Marshall made many recordings which document her artistry.

John Haag,
Athens, Georgia

Marshall, Maud (d. 1248)

*Countess of Warrenne and Surrey. Name variations: Maud de Warrenne; Maud Marshal. Died on April 4, 1248; daughter of *Isabel de Clare (c. 1174–1220) and William Marshall (b. 1146), 4th earl of Pembroke; sister of *Sybilla Marshall; married Hugh Bigod, 3rd earl of Norfolk (r. c. 1200–1225) and earl marshal of England; married William de Warrenne, 6th earl of Warrenne and Surrey (r. 1202–1240), before October 13, 1225; children: (first marriage) Roger Bigod (c. 1212–1270), 4th earl of Norfolk; Hugh Bigod, Justiciar of England; Isabel de Bigod (who married Gilbert de Lacy and John FitzGeoffrey, justiciar of Ireland); Sir Ralph Bigod; William Bigod; (second marriage) John de Warrenne (b. 1231), 7th earl of Warrenne and Surrey; *Isabel de Warrenne (d. 1282).*

Marshall, Mrs. Peter (1914–1983).

See Marshall, Catherine.

Marshall, Sybilla (fl. 1230)

*Countess of Derby. Name variations: Sibyl Marshal. Flourished around 1200; daughter of *Isabel de Clare (c. 1174–1220) and William Marshall (b. 1146), 4th earl of Pembroke; sister of *Maud Marshall (d. 1248); married William de Ferrers, 6th earl of Derby; children: Agnes de Ferrers (d. 1240, who married William de Vesci); Isabel de Ferrers (d. 1260); Maud de Ferrers (d. 1299); Sibyl de Ferrers; Jean de Ferrers (d. 1267); Agatha de Ferrers (d. 1306).*

Marta.

Italian form of Martha.

Martel, Adeloga (fl. 775)

*Frankish abbess and founder of religious communities for women. Flourished around 775 in France; daughter of Charles Martel (c. 690–741), mayor of Austrasia and Neustria (r. 714–741), and possibly *Sunnichild (d. 741); granddaughter of *Alphaida (c. 654–c. 714); never married; no children.*

Adeloga Martel was a Frankish princess, the daughter of the famous ruler Charles Martel, who reunited the Franks after the end of the Roman empire, and possibly *Sunnichild. Adeloga showed an inclination towards holy work even as a girl, and was allowed to enter a convent rather than be used as a marriage pawn in a political alliance. She was soon elected abbess, and throughout her life was renowned for her learning and deep devotion to serving God through charitable works. Adeloga used her influence and wealth as the daughter of the Frankish leader to found numerous churches and communities for women. These communities became places where women of all classes could live in seclusion, studying holy writings and producing manuscripts.

SOURCES:
Dunbar, Agnes. *Dictionary of Saintly Women, vol. I.* London: G. Bell and Sons, 1904.

Laura York,
Riverside, California

Martel, Gisela (d. 919).

See Gisela Martel.

Martel, Judith (c. 844–?)

*Countess of Flanders. Name variations: Princess Judith. Born around 844; death date unknown; daughter of Charles I the Bald, king of France (r. 840–877), also known as Charles II, Holy Roman emperor (r. 875–877), and *Ermentrude (d. 869); became second wife of Ethelwulf, king of Wessex and the English (r. 839–858), on October 1, 856; then married Ethelwulf's son Ethelbald (c. 834–860), king of Wessex and the English (r. 855–860), in 858 or 860 (annulled); married Baldwin I (d. 879), count of Flanders (r. 862–878), in 863; children: (third marriage) Charles of Flanders; Baldwin II (d. 918), count of Flanders (r. 878–918); Ralph (b. 865), count and abbott of Cambrai; Gunhilda of Flanders; (stepchildren) Alfred the Great, king of the English (r. 871–899).*

Contrary to tradition, the 13-year-old Judith Martel was crowned queen-consort when she married Ethelwulf, king of the English, at Verberie-sur-Oise, France, on October 1, 856. Since this made her Ethelwulf's equal, the deed was not well received by the Saxons across the Channel and would cause problems some years later. At the time of the marriage, Ethelwulf had already had an illegitimate child (an Oxford don) and five children with his first wife, *Osburga (d. 855), including Alfred the Great, king of the English.

Following Ethelwulf's death in 858, Judith married her stepson Ethelbald, king of Wessex and the English, but the marriage was annulled. She was then abducted by and married to Baldwin I, known as Ironhand, whom one historian called a "Flemish thug."

Martel, Matilda (943–c. 982).

See Matilda Martel.

Martel de Janville, Comtesse de (1850–1932)

French novelist. Name variations: Comtesse de Mirabeau; (pseudonym) Gyp. Born Sybille Gabrielle Marie Antoinette de Riquetti de Mirabeau at the Château de Koëtsal, Morbihan, in Brittany, around 1850; died in Neuilly in 1932; descendant of Gabriel-Honoré Riqueti, Count Mirabeau (1749–1791).

A French writer, known to millions under her pseudonym Gyp, Sybille Gabrielle, countess de Martel de Janville, wrote for *La Vie Parisienne* and *La Revue des Deux Mondes*. She created several well-known characters (notably Paulette, Loulou, and le petit Bob) who appeared in her sketches and gave titles to several of her humorous novels. Among the latter are *Autour de mariage* (1883, dramatized in the same year with M. Crémieux), *Ce que femme veut!* (1883), *Sans voiles* (1885), *Autour du divorce* (1886), *Bob au salon*, with illustrations by "Bob" (1888–90), *C'est nous qui sont l'histoire* (1890), *Passionette* (1891), and *Mariage de Chiffon* (1894). On Martel de Janville's death, *Janet Flanner wrote: "No popular French writer ever covered so much time or took so little trouble about it, since she wrote as easily as she remembered. She was a trenchant conversationalist, no prude, despised the tepid mind, hated fakes, fatuousness, and, on the whole, the Third Republic, under which she died." In her writings, Martel de Janville skewered Dreyfus.

SOURCES:
Flanner, Janet. *Paris Was Yesterday.* NY: Viking, 1972.

Martelli, Camilla (fl. 1570s)

*Grand duchess of Tuscany. Name variations: Camilla de Medici. Flourished in the 1570s; mistress, then wife, of Cosimo I de Medici, grand duke of Tuscany (1519–1574), around 1571; children: Giovanni de Medici (d. 1621); *Virginia d'Este (who married Cesare d'Este, duke of Modena). Cosimo's first wife was *Eleonora de Medici (1522–1562).*

Martha and Mary of Bethany (fl. early 1st c. CE).

See Mary Magdalene for sidebar.

Martha and the Vandellas.

See Reeves, Martha (b. 1941).

Martha de Freitas (1958—)

Norwegian royal. Born on April 5, 1958, in Rio de Janeiro, Brazil; daughter of Jose Marie Gomes de Freitas and Maria Bernadette Aragao Carvalho; married Haakon Lorentzen (grandson of Olav V of Norway), on April 14, 1982; children: one.

Martha of Denmark (c. 1272–1341)

*Queen of Sweden. Name variations: Margaret of Denmark; Margaret Eriksson. Born around 1272; died on March 2, 1341; daughter of Eric V, king of Denmark (r. 1259–1286) and *Agnes of Brandenburg (d. 1304); sister of Eric VI Menved (1274–1319), king of Denmark (r. 1286–1319), and Christopher II (1276–1332), king of Denmark (r. 1319–1326 and 1330–1332); married Birger also spelled Berger (d. 1321), king of Sweden (r. 1290–1318, deposed 1318), on November 25, 1298; sister-in-law of *Ingeborg (c. 1300–1360); children: Magnus Bergersson (b. 1300); Eric Bergersson; Agnes Bergersdottir; Katherina Bergersdottir.*

Martha of Sweden (1901–1954)

*Crown princess of Norway. Name variations: Crown Princess Martha or Märtha; Martha Bernadotte. Born Martha Sophia Louise Dagmar Thyra on March 28, 1901, in Stockholm, Sweden; died on April 5, 1954, in Oslo, Norway; daughter of Charles of Sweden (1861–1951) and *Ingeborg of Denmark (1878–1958); sister of *Astrid of Sweden (1905–1935, queen of the Belgians); married Olav V, king of Norway (r. 1957–1991, and son of Haakon VII), on March 21, 1929; children: *Ragnhild Oldenburg (b. 1930); *Astrid Oldenburg (b. 1932); Harold or Harald V, king of Norway (b. 1937, r. 1991—).*

Crown Princess Martha of Sweden died three years before her husband was crowned Olav V, king of Norway, in 1957.

Martha the Nun (1560–1631)

Founder of the Romanovs. Name variations: Marta the Nun; Xenia Chestov or Shestov; Martha Romanov. Born in 1560; died on January 27, 1631; daughter of Ivan Shestov; married Fedor also known as Theodore the Metropolitan (1558–1663), also known as the Monk Philaret or Theodore Romanov; children: Mikhail also known as Michael III (1596–1645), tsar of Russia (r. 1613–1645). Martha could claim descent from Rurik, the 7th century founder of the Russian monarchy.

Martha the Nun married Theodore Romanov, son of Tsar Ivan IV's friend Nikita Romanov; Theodore was driven to cloisters under the name Monk Philaret by Boris Godunov. Martha and Theodore spent most of their adult years sheltered in monasteries. When Martha's son Michael (III) became a candidate for tsar of Russia, Martha extrapolated a promise from the notification committee that his reign would be supported by all Russia. A new dynasty was founded—the Romanovs.

Marthe or Marthon.

French form of Martha.

Martia.

Variant of Marcia.

Martia (fl. c. 100 BCE).

See Iaia.

Martin, Agnes (1912—)

American artist. Born Agnes Bernice Martin on March 22, 1912, in Macklin (also seen as Maklin), Saskatchewan, Canada; daughter of Malcolm Ian Martin and Margaret (Kinnon) Martin; immigrated to United States, 1932, naturalized citizen, 1940; attended Western Washington College, 1932; attended Columbia University, 1941–42, 1951–52; University of New Mexico, B.F.A., 1954.

Had first solo exhibition in New York (1958); inducted into American Academy and Institute of Arts and Letters (1989); held major retrospective exhibitions in Europe (1991) and the United States (1992). Wrote The Perfection Underlying Life *and* The Untroubled Mind.

Selected works: White Study *(1958);* Little Sister *(1962);* Orange Grove *(1965);* Morning *(1965);* Desert *(1966).*

Agnes Martin, born in Macklin, Saskatchewan, in 1912, came to live in the United States in 1932. She became a U.S. citizen in 1940 and earned a B.A. (1941) and M.F.A. (1954) at Columbia University in New York City. In 1947, she headed west to paint and teach in New Mexico, working intermittently at the University of New Mexico into the 1950s; she also worked in New York, teaching children in Harlem, in the early 1950s. Returning to live full time in New York in 1957, Martin settled into an artists' community in Coenties Slip in lower Manhattan. There, over the next ten years, she developed the "grid" style for which she became famous.

Originally portraying human figures and landscapes, Martin's paintings moved into Surrealism and were influenced by Abstract Expressionism in the 1950s. In the 1960s, she began to create a new style, veering towards geometric minimalism, later recognized as "minimal" or "boundless field" art. The change came after Martin joined her Coenties Slip neighbors, Ellsworth Kelly and Ad Reinhardt, in a revolt against Abstract Expressionism and what she saw as egotistical romanticism. "I would like my work," she noted, "to be recognized as being in the classic tradition"; she also stressed the spiritual significance of her paintings, which were composed of vertical and horizontal lines with extremely subtle variations. The artist has said that looking at her boundless field paintings is like looking at a waterfall, or at the sea.

Starting with paintings like *White Study* (1958), in which two rectangles are situated on the canvas, Martin moved on to paint rectangles filled with grids, always with borders around them. Eventually, a single rectangle filled the entire canvas, and after 1964 most of her paintings consisted of canvas or paper entirely covered by a grid, as in *Little Sister* (1962), *Orange Grove* (1965) and *Desert* (1966). Naturalistic details and color disappeared, and the grids, frequently pencil on acrylic, were usually monochromatic (for example, *Play*, *Hill* and *Adventure* of 1966 and 1967). According to **Charlotte Streifer Rubinstein**, Martin produced her most minimal, pure paintings in 1966 and 1967. Critic Lawrence Alloway has assigned her a historic role in the development of modern art. In her poetry and lectures, Martin implied that her paintings might contain Christian and Buddhist symbolism, and referred to the need to defeat pride in order to achieve humility. "When pride is lost," she wrote, "we feel a moment of perfection."

Agnes Martin had solo exhibitions annually between 1958 and 1967, and also exhibited in dozens of prestigious group shows in the United States and Europe. Although she left New York in 1967 to return to New Mexico, and for six years gave up painting for writing, she continued to be a presiding figure in the New York art scene. She also produced a film, *Gabriel*, in 1976. Martin received the Alexej von Jawlensky Prize from the city of Wiesbaden, Germany, in 1991 and the Oskar Kokoschka Prize from the Austrian government in 1992. Her works are in the collections of museums throughout the United States and Europe, including the Guggenheim, the Museum of Modern Art, and the Whitney Museum of American Art, all in New York City; the Tate Gallery in London, England;

the Stedelijk Museum, Amsterdam, Netherlands; and the Musée national d'art moderne in Paris, France. In addition, her work is displayed in the Australian National Gallery, Canberra, and the Art Gallery of Ontario in Toronto, Canada.

Agnes Martin, who moved from Galisteo, New Mexico, to Taos, New Mexico, in 1992, continued to exhibit in individual and group shows, both nationally and internationally, through the late 1990s. She was a featured artist at the 1995 Whitney Biennial. Pace Wildenstein, the gallery that has represented her since 1975, presented an exhibition of Martin's work in 1997, just before her 85th birthday.

SOURCES:

Harrap's Illustrated Dictionary of Art and Artists. Harrap's Reference, 1990.

Rubinstein, Charlotte Streifer. American Women Artists. Boston, MA: G.K. Hall, 1982.

SUGGESTED READING:

Haskell, Barbara. Agnes Martin. With essays by Anna Chave and Rosalind Krauss and writings by Agnes Martin. NY: Whitney Museum of Art, 1992.

Morris, Linda. Studio, 1973–74.

Ratcliff, Carter. Art News, 1973.

Beth Champagne,
journalist and freelance writer,
West Barnet, Vermont

Martin, Ann (1757–1830).

See Taylor, Ann Martin.

Martin, Anne Henrietta
(1875–1951)

American pacifist and suffragist. Name variations: (pseudonym) Anne O'Hara. Born in Empire City, Nevada, on September 30, 1875; died in Carmel, California, on April 15, 1951; attended Whitaker's School for Girls in Reno; University of Nevada (Reno), A.B., 1894; Stanford University (Palo Alto), B.A., 1896, M.A. in history, 1897.

Anne Martin was the first woman to run for the U.S. Senate in 1918 and 1920, polling 20% of the vote in the state of Nevada. In 1897, she founded the University of Nevada history department and was its head until 1903. An inveterate traveler, Martin became interested in the suffragist movement while in England about 1910. Returning home, she was elected president of the state suffragists and successfully led the movement for Nevada women to win the vote (1914). Following her run for the Senate, she moved to Carmel, California, and became active in the Women's International League for Peace; she was opposed to America's involve-

ment in World War II, just as she had been to its involvement in World War I.

SUGGESTED READING:

James, Edward T., ed. *Notable American Women 1607–1950: A Biographical Dictionary*. Vol. 2. Cambridge, MA: Belknap Press of Harvard University Press, 1971.

McHenry, Robert, ed. *Famous American Women: A Biographical Dictionary from Colonial Times to the Present*. New York, NY: Dover, 1980.

Martin, Mrs. Bell (1815–1850).

See Martin, Mary Letitia.

Martin, Joan (1899–1962).

See Adler, Polly.

Martin, Lady (1817–1898).

See Faucit, Helena Saville.

Martin, Lillien Jane (1851–1943)

American psychologist. Born Lillie Jane Martin on July 7, 1851, in Olean, New York; died on March 26, 1943, in San Francisco, California; oldest of four children of Russell Martin (a merchant) and Lydia Hawes Martin (a college matron); Vassar College, B.A., 1880; University of Göttingen, Germany, Ph.D., 1898; never married; no children.

Lillien Martin, who was born on July 7, 1851, may well have been the first four-year-old to enter the first grade at Olean Academy in her hometown of Olean, New York, and her involvement with academia continued uninterrupted until she was forced into mandatory retirement at age 65. She then proceeded to distinguish herself in another professional career, and continued consulting, writing, and publishing until her death at age 92.

Although a precocious child, young Lillie Jane (she later changed her name to Lillien) preferred riding her pony to reading; as she grew older, she fell in love with geometry and trigonometry, and solved arithmetic problems for fun. After an introduction to surveying instruments when she was 15, she independently mapped a small field. In 1867, at 16, she began studying psychology, physics, and chemistry, the subjects on which her life's work would be based. That year, she also graduated from Olean Academy and began teaching to earn money for college. Her family had lost much of the money that her father had left, which had once made their lives comfortable, but her mother was determined that her daughter should have a college education. In 1876, after nine years of teaching and saving, Martin sought admission to Cornell University in Ithaca, New York. Although female students were not expressly forbidden, that was apparently only because the authorities had not expected any to apply, and she was not welcomed. Martin therefore took the entrance examination at Vassar College, a women's college in Poughkeepsie, New York, where her high scores won her a full scholarship. Upon her graduation in 1880, she accepted a position at Indianapolis High School, teaching botany, physics, and chemistry.

In 1889, after addressing a teachers' convention in San Francisco, California, Martin was offered three positions in the area and accepted the post of vice-principal and science department head at Girls' High School in San Francisco. Five years later, with the encouragement of her close friend, **Fidelia Jewett**, she resigned in order to fulfill her desire to study psychology. She went to the University of Göttingen in Germany and, somewhat to the consternation of university officials, became the first woman to enroll in the science department. In 1898, at age 47, she received a Ph.D., and the following year accepted an assistant professorship at Stanford University. As a member of the international scientific community, Martin continued researching and writing, publishing four technical volumes on psychology in German between 1899 and 1914, and spent alternate summers in Germany. She was named a full professor in 1911, and in 1913, in honor of the discoveries she had made in psychology, became the first American to be awarded an honorary Ph.D. from Germany's University of Bonn. In 1915, she was appointed head of the psychology department at Stanford, becoming the first woman to head an academic department at that university. One year later, she turned 65 and in accordance with faculty rules was forced to retire.

After several frustrated months of unwanted relaxation, Martin rebelled against her sense of loss and discouragement by teaching herself touch typing and devising exercises to strengthen her hands, her gait, and her speech. A professor emerita, she began preparing for a new career, and from 1917 to 1920 served as president of the California Society for Mental Hygiene. In 1920, she founded the nation's first guidance clinics for preschoolers, at the Polyclinic and Mt. Zion hospitals in San Francisco. Martin ran the clinics while also working as a consulting psychologist in private practice until 1929, using regular and frequent rest periods to enable her to remain as productive as she had been in younger years.

In 1929, in response to a comment from her colleague **Clair deGruchy** that the grandmother of one of the children at a clinic was causing the child's problems, Martin opened the Old Age Center in San Francisco. Believed to be the first old-age counseling center in the United States, it provided rehabilitative physical and mental exercises which restored over 800 elderly men and women to effective functioning. She also bought and ran a farm in California to provide work and purpose for older men who otherwise would have eked out their days in a county home for the indigent. The project succeeded both as rehabilitation and as a profitable business. During World War II, the shortage of younger workers led her to open a second Old Age Center in New York City. Martin was deeply pragmatic. "Age is an accident," she said, "and nothing to pride oneself on. The important thing is to adapt oneself to the requirements of each successive age-class, and to function in each as an active participant in life, a fully adjusted human being."

Lillien Martin traveled around the world with her companion Fidelia Jewett in 1925, and in 1927 traveled alone to Soviet Russia. In 1929, at age 78, she earned a driver's license, and three years later, by herself, made a cross-country automobile trip. An excellent manager of her money, she had lost nothing in the stock-market crash of 1929. A lifelong feminist with a strong political bent—she had once led a suffragist parade in London with *Anna Howard Shaw*— Martin had served as a delegate from California to the first national convention of Theodore Roosevelt's Progressive Party, but was won over by Woodrow Wilson (himself a progressive) and switched her affiliation to the Democrats. She strongly supported Franklin Delano Roosevelt's New Deal policies. From 1917, she authored or co-authored a number of psychology monographs and books, including *Salvaging Old Age* (1930) and *Sweeping the Cobwebs* (1933).

In 1939, at 87, Lillien Martin traveled with Clair deGruchy to South America, journeying by boat up the Amazon River. When told by physicians that the strain of sightseeing flights at high altitudes would be too much for her heart, she responded "that would be a fine way to die"— and flew. After her return to San Francisco, she served as educational counselor of the Democratic Women's Forum and worked regularly as a consulting psychologist until the week before her death of bronchopneumonia at age 92.

SOURCES:

Bailey, Brooke. *The Remarkable Lives of 100 Women Healers and Scientists.* Holbrook, MA: Bob Adams, 1994.
Current Biography, 1942. H.W. Wilson, 1942, pp. 575–577.

James, Edward T., ed. *Notable American Women 1607–1950: A Biographical Dictionary.* Vol. 2. Cambridge, MA: Belknap Press of Harvard University Press, 1971.

McHenry, Robert, ed. *Famous American Women: A Biographical Dictionary from Colonial Times to the Present.* New York, NY: Dover, 1980.

Ogilvie, Marilyn Bailey. *Women in Science: Antiquity through the Nineteenth Century.* Cambridge, MA: The MIT Press, 1986.

Read, Phyllis J., and Bernard L. Witlieb. *The Book of Women's Firsts.* New York, NY: Random House, 1992.

Zilboorg, Caroline, ed., and Susan B. Gall, managing ed. *Women's Firsts.* Detroit, MI: Gale Research, 1997.

SUGGESTED READING:

deFord, Miriam Allen. *Psychologist Unretired: The Life Pattern of Lillien J. Martin.* Stanford, CA: Stanford University Press, 1948.

Fenton, Norman. *Psychological Review.* July 1943.

Merrill, Maud A. *American Journal of Psychology.* November 1943.

National Cyclopedia of American Biography. Vol. XVI, p. 153.

The New York Times (obituary). March 28, 1943.

Readers' Guide to Periodical Literature. 1939–40.

Ruess, Christopher. *American Sociological Review.* June 1943.

Sicherman, Barbara, and Carol Hurd Green, eds. *Notable American Women: The Modern Period. A Biographical Dictionary.* Cambridge, MA: The Belknap Press of Harvard University Press, 1980.

Titchener, E.B. "Professor Martin and the Perky Experiments," in *American Journal of Psychology.* January 1913.

COLLECTIONS:

Kaiser, Mrs. William Martin, and/or other family members have documents and clippings.

Vassar College, Poughkeepsie, New York, has records in registrar's office and a clipping file in alumnae office.

Beth Champagne,
journalist and freelance writer, West Barnet, Vermont

Martin, Lynn (1939—)

U.S. Republican congressional representative and secretary of labor. Born Judith Lynn Morley on December 26, 1939, in Evanston, Illinois; daughter of Lawrence Morley and Helen (Hall) Morley; University of Illinois, Urbana, Illinois, B.A., 1960; married John Martin (an engineer), in 1960 (divorced 1978); married Harry Leinenweber (a U.S. district court judge), in 1987; children: (first marriage) Julia Martin; Caroline Martin.

Was a teacher; served as member, Winnebago County Board (1972–76); was a member, Illinois House of Representatives (1977–79), and Illinois Senate (1979–80); was a delegate to the Illinois State Republican Convention (1980); elected as Republican to the 97th and to the four succeeding Congresses (1981–91); stood but was not elected to U.S. Senate (1990); was secretary of labor (1991–93); professor at J. Kellogg Graduate School of Management at Northwestern University (1993—); fellow at Harvard University's Kennedy School of Government.

Born in Evanston, Illinois, on December 26, 1939, to Lawrence Morley and **Helen Hall Morley**, Lynn Morley Martin attended William Taft High School in Chicago, graduating in 1957 with honors. After receiving a B.A. from the University of Illinois in 1960, she worked as a high school teacher, teaching English and economics, and married engineering student John Martin. They had two daughters. Lynn Martin was elected in 1972 to the Winnebago County Board and four years later she gained a seat in the Illinois House of Representatives, moving to the state senate in 1979.

In 1980, U.S. congressional representative John Anderson decided to run for president, creating an opening for the House seat in Illinois' 16th District. Martin beat four Republicans in the primary and then won the general election. She would soon gain the reputation of being unbeatable, winning the next four elections by comfortable margins.

Lynn Martin

Entering Congress, Martin was appointed to the influential Budget Committee where she served for three Congresses. An outspoken, skilled and confident politician, she was to establish herself as a Republican Party leader. Martin was regularly a floor manager for the Republican Party in the House chamber. In 1984 and 1986, she won election as vice chair of the Republican Conference in the House, the first time a woman had held a position in the congressional Republican Party's hierarchy. In 1984, she also helped then Vice President George Bush prepare for his debate with *Geraldine Ferraro; he selected Martin to deliver the vice presidential nomination speech in Dallas that year.

In the Budget Committee negotiations of 1986, Martin was leader of her party's delegation, largely responsible for the acceptance of a Republican-sponsored reconciliation bill. She also served on the Committee on House Administration in the 97th and 98th Congresses, the Committee on Public Works and Transportation in the 98th Congress, and the Committee on Armed Services in the 99th and 100th Congresses. In the 101 Congress, she was given a widely sought seat on the Committee on Rules.

Lynn Martin was known as a fiscal conservative but a social moderate, a supporter of abortion rights and the Equal Rights Amendment. In 1989, she was named Republican Woman of the Year and decided to run for the U.S. Senate from Illinois rather than seek reelection to the House of Representatives. Unsuccessful in this bid, she was appointed secretary of labor in the Cabinet of President George Bush, replacing **Elizabeth Dole**. When he announced her nomination, Bush referred to Martin as a "cherished friend," even though she had voted against him several times during her career in Congress, including on a critical labor issue. As secretary of labor, she pushed for greater representation of women and minorities in corporate America.

Martin was divorced from her first husband in 1978 and married U.S. district court judge Harry Leinenweber in 1987. After serving as secretary of labor from 1991 until 1993, Martin took up a teaching position at the J.J. Kellogg Graduate School of Management at Northwestern University's business school, teaching public policy. She has also been a fellow at Harvard University's Kennedy School of Government and consulted for the international accounting firm Deloitte & Touche.

Paula Morris, D.Phil.,
Brooklyn, New York

Martin, Maria (1796–1863)

One of the best nature artists of the 19th century who created flower and plant backgrounds for many of Audubon's bird paintings, including some of the most popular prints from Birds of America. *Name variations: Maria (Martin) Bachman. Born on July 3, 1796, in Charleston, South Carolina; died on December 27, 1863, in Columbia, South Carolina; daughter of John Nicholas Martin (a Lutheran minister) and Rebecca Murray Martin (a widow, maiden name unknown); married her widowed brother-in-law, John Bachman (a Lutheran minister and naturalist), in 1848; no children.*

Maria Martin was born in 1796, in Charleston, South Carolina. In 1827, as an unmarried adult, she went to live in, and assist with, the household of her older sister **Harriet Bachman**. Harriet, who was married to John Bachman, a minister and ardent naturalist, had 14 children and was often ill; Maria handled most of the tasks involved in running the house and caring for the children. Whether she had ever received any formal education is unknown, but she was by all accounts extremely intelligent and well read, with particular interests in literature, art, and natural history.

Maria met ornithologist and painter John James Audubon during his 1831 visit to Charleston. By 1833, he had taught her to paint birds, and she was supplying backgrounds for his watercolors of American birds. Audubon generally painted his birds on blank canvases, leaving the backgrounds to be painted in later, either by himself or by an assistant, and Martin occasionally worked directly on his canvases. Her drawings are notable for their combination of scientific accuracy and artistic judgment, as well as for their seamless blending of bird with background. "Miss Martin, with her superior talents, assists us greatly in the way of drawing. . . . [T]he insects she has drawn are, perhaps, the best I've seen," wrote Audubon.

Martin was the sole woman among his three principal assistants. She created the backgrounds for many of the prints in his *Birds of America* (the "Elephant Folio," engraved and printed in England), and also supplied paintings for the American editions of the prints issued by Audubon's sons. In addition, she contributed drawings of Carolina reptiles to John Edward Holbrook, who used them in his five-volume work *North American Herpetology* (1836–1842).

Two years after the death of her sister in 1846, Martin married her brother-in-law John Bachman. She assisted him in his collaboration with the Audubons, furnishing studies providing the color and form of various details for *Viviparous Quadrupeds of North America* (1846–54). According to family tradition, Martin also contributed paintings of occasional plants. Audubon named a subspecies of hairy woodpecker, *Picus martinae* (also called the Maria's woodpecker), after her, and they remained friends until his death in 1851.

By the start of the Civil War in 1861, Maria Martin was caring for four motherless grandnieces. She also plunged into war work, and her health declined. After Charleston was shelled, she fled with her grandnieces to Columbia, where she died in 1863 and was buried in the graveyard of Ebenezer Church.

SOURCES:

James, Edward T., ed. *Notable American Women, 1607–1950.* Vol. II. Cambridge, MA: Belknap Press of Harvard University Press, 1971, pp. 505–506.

Kass-Simon, G., Patricia Farnes, and Deborah Nash, eds. *Women of Science, Righting the Record.* Bloomington and Indianapolis, IN: Indiana University Press, 1990.

McHenry, Robert, ed. *Famous American Women, A Biographical Dictionary from Colonial Times to the Present.* NY: Dover, 1980.

SUGGESTED READING:

Audubon, John James. *Ornithological Biography.* 5 vols., 1831–39.

Bachman, C.L. *John Bachman.* 1888.

Coffin, Annie Roulhac. *Art Quarterly.* Autumn 1960.

———. *New York Historical Society Quarterly.* January 1965.

Corning, Howard, ed. *Letters of John James Audubon, 1826–1840.* 1930.

Herrick, Francis H. *Audubon the Naturalist.* 2 vols. 1917.

COLLECTIONS:

Charleston Museum, Charleston, S.C., has family papers, including original sketches, watercolors, etc. by Maria Martin, in the possession of her nine great-grandnieces in Charleston.

Beth Champagne,
journalist and freelance writer, West Barnet, Vermont

Martin, Mary (1907–1969)

British painter and sculptor. Born Mary Balmford in 1907, in Kent, England; died in 1969; educated at the Goldsmiths School of Art and the Royal College of Art in London; married Kenneth Martin (an artist), in 1930; two children.

Mary Martin received artistic training in London at the Goldsmiths School of Art and the Royal College of Art, where she specialized in painting. In 1930, she married fellow artist Kenneth Martin; their son, Paul Martin, would also become a professional artist. Abandoning repre-

sentational art in the late 1940s, Martin started painting geometrical shapes, simply arranged, and along with her husband and artists Anthony Hill and Victor Pasmore created what became known as the post-war Constructivist movement. A growing interest in abstraction led her to relief sculpting, with which she would be associated for the remainder of her career. Her first construction, *Columbarium,* appeared in 1951. Although influenced by Pasmore and Ben Nicholson and American sculptor Charles Biederman, Martin's art, called by one critic an "orderly presentation of repeated modular designs," was unlike anything else being produced at the time. Often working with bronze, her favorite material, she used simple shapes, varying color, mirrored surfaces, and folded forms to create illusion and complexity in her work.

Mary Martin began collaborating with architects in 1956, and eventually received commissions on numerous architectural structures, including fountains and large wall constructions; by the early 1960s, several of her designs had been published. She spent her last years teaching art, and died in 1969. A retrospective of her work was mounted by the Tate Gallery in London in 1984.

SOURCES:

Harrap's Illustrated Dictionary of Art and Artists. Harrap's Reference, 1990.

Heller, Nancy G. *Women Artists: An Illustrated History.* New York and London: Abbeville Press, 1987.

Kari Bethel,
freelance writer, Columbia, Missouri

Martin, Mary (1913–1990)

Tony-Award winning actress, singer, dancer, and leading lady of the American musical comedy stage, best known for her portrayal of Peter Pan on stage and television. Born Mary Virginia Martin on December 1, 1913, in Weatherford, Texas; died of cancer in California on November 4, 1990; daughter of Preston Martin and Juanita (Presley) Martin; had one older sister, Geraldine Martin; married Benjamin Hagman, in 1930 (divorced around 1936); married Richard Halliday (a story editor at Paramount), in 1940; children: (first marriage) one son, actor Larry Hagman (b. 1931); (second marriage) one daughter, Heller Halliday (b. 1941).

Taught dancing in her hometown before entering show business in Los Angeles as a nightclub singer; first appeared on Broadway (1938); created the roles of Nellie Forbush in Rodgers and Hammerstein's South Pacific *(1949), Peter Pan in Jerome Robbins' musical production of* Peter Pan *(1954), and Maria von Trapp in* The Sound of Music *(1959).*

Selected filmography: Rage of Paris *(1938);* The Great Victor Herbert *(1939);* Rhythm on the River *(1940);* Love Thy Neighbor *(1940);* New York Town *(1941);* Kiss the Boys Goodbye *(1941);* Birth of the Blues *(1941);* Star Spangled Rhythm *(1942);* True to Life *(1943);* Happy Go Lucky *(1943);* Night and Day *(1946);* Main Street to Broadway *(1953).*

Stage: appeared in Leave It to Me, One Touch of Venus, Lute Song, Pacific 1860 *(U.K.),* Annie Get Your Gun *(tour),* South Pacific, Kind Sir, Skin of Our Teeth, Jenny, Peter Pan, The Sound of Music, I Do!, I Do!, Legends.

On any school day during the early 1920s, the residents of Weatherford, Texas, would be treated to the spectacle of a slim young girl cartwheeling downhill from Weatherford's only school to a trim farmhouse two blocks away. Everyone in town, numbering a few thousand, knew it was the daughter of Preston and **Juanita Martin** who gave them this acrobatic display, and that Mary Virginia Martin was a musical child, indeed.

"From the time I was born," Mary Martin would say many years later, "I could *hear* notes and reproduce them," and it was true that she had been exposed to music from the day of her birth, on December 1, 1913. Her mother was a music teacher and taught her daughter early on to play the violin. Even before she entered first grade, Martin was singing with the Weatherford band on Saturday nights in the town square, being especially remembered for her renditions of "Moonlight and Roses" and "When the Red, Red Robin Comes Bob-Bob-Bobbin' Along." From her father, a lawyer, she learned a certain dramatic style, for Preston Martin was known for his stirring elocution at the town's courthouse and would attract a good turnout when he was arguing a case. Then, too, there was the Weatherford movie house, whose owner, a client of her father, gave her passes to all the films that came to town. Before long, Mary had added imitations of ***Ruby Keeler**, Bing Crosby, and other movie stars to her repertoire and won prizes for them at local affairs.

After spending a childhood in relative freedom on a very large farm in a very small town, Martin was sent off to a girls' finishing school in Nashville, Tennessee, when she was 14. Cut off from the open fields and blue skies of home and, even worse, from her childhood sweetheart, Ben Hagman, Mary spent a miserable two years broken only by short visits from her mother and the occasional vacation trip back home. She finally persuaded her mother to bring Ben to visit her in

Nashville, and it was then that Juanita learned of Mary's determination to marry Ben, a plan hatched in a flurry of surreptitious letters between the two young people. Juanita gave in after several days of pleading and, barely a month before her 17th birthday, on November 3, 1930, Mary became Mrs. Benjamin Hagman. The plan had the added benefit of getting her expelled from school. She returned to Weatherford, where she and Ben lived with her parents. A son, whom they named Lawrence, was born in September of the following year.

Marriage, however, failed to meet the rosy expectations of a 17-year-old farm girl. After Ben left for law school, Mary grew restless and hit upon a plan to open a dancing school in the hayloft of her uncle's barn. Thirty pupils enrolled, enough to convince Martin that some formal training could bring her even more business. Once again, after several days of Mary's pleading, Juanita agreed to look after the baby and Preston agreed to finance a semester at a school in Hollywood, California, that Mary had read about—The Fanchon and Marco School of the Dance. After she returned home with new routines and techniques, Martin's school flourished. She was able to open a branch in a town some 20 miles from Weatherford and soon had enough students to form a troupe, The Martinettes, which toured Prince County. Excited by the prospects of an even larger school with classrooms throughout Texas, Martin returned to Hollywood for more training, this time with her mother and four-year-old Larry, and before long was assigned as a singer to the Fanchon and Marco School's troupe, The Fanchonettes. The school was just then forming a road show that would appear in Los Angeles and San Francisco, and Martin found herself riding the bus north to her first paying job in show business, at $75 a week, including costume. The school neglected to mention that she would be singing from the wings while the rest of the troupe danced on stage, the costume only being necessary for curtain calls. Still, it was enough to attract her to the world of show business and make-believe.

It was Broadway entrepreneur Billy Rose who inadvertently propelled her into the business for good. On her return to Texas, Martin learned that Rose was bringing a touring musical revue to Fort Worth and would be holding casting sessions for chorus girls and incidental dancers to back up his major stars. Mary hustled her Martinettes on a bus to Fort Worth and after their audition, with Martin as lead singer and dancer, a telegram arrived inviting her to Rose's hotel room. The good news: the Martinettes

Mary
Martin
(1913–1990)

were hired. The bad news: Mary Martin was not. Apprised of her son and husband, Rose told Martin: "My advice to you is to tend to them. Tend to the family, the diapers. Stay out of show business." The depth of her heartbreak told Martin that she wanted the exact opposite. She talked with her parents and then with Ben, who amicably agreed to a divorce in a year's time. In 1935, Martin left Weatherford for good, moving permanently to Hollywood and leaving five-year-old Larry in her mother's care until she could find an agent and work.

At first, it seemed as if she had made the right decision. She did, indeed, find an agent who got her a non-paying job on a national radio show and sent her out on a round of auditions that got her introductions to some of the leading names in musical comedy of the day, if not actual jobs. Among those she met were Jerome Kern and Oscar Hammerstein II, with whom she would form a particularly close relationship that would prove important a decade later. Nonetheless, those first two years in Hollywood were financially disastrous. Even her agent began calling her "Audition Mary." After a bleak two years, Martin finally found a paying job at the Cinegrille in Hollywood's Roosevelt Hotel, where she sang nightly for $40 a week and began a career on the nightclub circuit that provided a measure of financial security. With a day job as a dancing coach at Universal, she was earning enough by 1937 to allow Larry and her mother to join her in California. When young fans would ask her many years later how the big break in show business happens, she would remember these early times in Hollywood and reply, "Work and work and work. Be ready for when the break comes."

Martin's break came because of a song a rehearsal pianist at Universal had taught her, an Italian love ballad called "Il Bacio" (The Kiss). The pianist suggested she spice the tune up by doing it in swingtime, and Martin developed the number for a talent audition to be held at The Trocadero, a Los Angeles night spot. She began the song traditionally, almost operatically, but gradually turned it into a swing tune worthy of Benny Goodman. The audience, including an admiring Jack Benny, gave her a standing ovation. Within ten minutes, Benny had introduced her to producer Lawrence Schwab, who offered her the lead in a Broadway musical he was preparing, along with the train fare to Broadway and hotel accommodations. Martin felt that those ten minutes had made the last two years worth it.

Just as she was boarding the train for New York, however, the bad news arrived. A telegram from Schwab told her that the financing for his show had fallen through and the project had been scrapped. But he urged her to come to New York anyway, and after the celebrations and goodbyes to her friends in California, Mary was reluctant to tell anyone what had happened. She kept her silence even when she stopped in Weatherford to leave Larry with her mother, and was welcomed as the local girl who had made it to Broadway. She arrived in New York in 1937 as she had arrived in Los Angeles in 1935—with no work and no prospects. But Schwab did not let her down. He paid her expenses while sending her out on auditions until, in 1938, she was cast in Cole Porter's new musical, *Leave It to Me*, which he had written as a vehicle for the legendary *Sophie Tucker. Martin played the enterprising mistress of a succession of admiring young men unaware of her particular attachment to a much-older benefactor. She was given the number that would make her the talk of Broadway, "My Heart Belongs to Daddy," a sly song with such typically Porter-esque lyrics as, "If I invite/ a boy some night/ To dine on my fine finnan haddie."

Martin later claimed that she was naive enough at the time to entirely miss the double entendres peppered throughout the song, but it was precisely her innocence that sold the song and made her a star, even though the crowded theater marquee only had room for "M. Martin." She became known as "The Daddy Girl," not to mention gaining a reputation from a carefully choreographed striptease in the third act that left her on stage in nothing but a pink silk chemise—her "Teddy Bare," soon copied in lingerie shops all over New York. "Texas Girl Hits New York with a Storm!" wrote Walter Winchell the day after the show opened. *Life* featured her in a major article, and a film contract from Paramount started her on a string of movie musicals lasting into the 1950s.

While working at Paramount, Martin fell in love with a young story editor named Richard Halliday and married him in 1940, in a civil ceremony in Los Angeles. A daughter **Heller Halliday** was born in 1941; "heller," Mary explained, was a Texas term for a rambunctious young hellian. Halliday would be her constant companion for the next 30 years, although the success of her next show tested the relationship.

In *One Touch of Venus*, Martin played a goddess whose statue comes to life in the New York City of the 1940s. The show's credentials were impeccable. Kurt Weill had written the score, *Agnes de Mille** was choreographer, and Elia Kazan, who would later make his mark in such films as *On the Waterfront*, was directing. The musical opened in October 1943, played to full houses during its run, and then went on the road. Halliday still had his editing work at Paramount, and the two missed each other terribly. While the show was playing Chicago, the couple realized one career was going to have to be sacrificed if the marriage were to survive. The decision was, as Mary put it, that "Richard would edit *me*," by becoming her manager. It was to prove a fortuitous choice.

In late 1948, while Martin was touring as *Annie Oakley in *Annie Get Your Gun,* Halliday mentioned he had gotten a call from director Josh Logan about a new musical Logan and producer Leland Hayward were mounting, a show about an army nurse who falls in love with a French plantation owner on a Pacific island during World War II. It didn't sound promising to Mary, and she told Richard as much. But Logan called back with the news that her old friend from the "Audition Mary" days in Los Angeles, Oscar Hammerstein, was insisting on her for the part. Despite her initial skepticism, Martin would later say that *South Pacific* was the greatest thing that ever happened to her.

James Michener's book *Tales of the South Pacific,* on which the musical was based, stressed an ill-fated romance between an American navy lieutenant and a Polynesian woman. But Rodgers and Hammerstein thought this was too much like rewriting *Madame Butterfly* and decided to concentrate instead on the book's second, and more successful, romance between army nurse Nellie Forbush and the plantation owner, to be played by Italian baritone Ezio Pinza. The cast approached the New York opening nervously—not because of problems in tryouts but, rather, the opposite. The show had been such a smash in New Haven and Boston that it consistently ran 45 minutes long because of repeated demands for encores.

There were, however, mishaps. During Nellie's number "I'm in Love with a Wonderful Guy," for example, Martin had to cross from stage left to stage right, and a bit of stage business was needed to get her there. It was Mary's suggestion, much to Logan's surprise, that she cartwheel across the stage. It was, after all, a much shorter distance than those two blocks back in Weatherford, Texas, and she assured Logan she could cartwheel and sing at the same time, demonstrating on the spot—"I'm in love" (cartwheel) "I'm in love" (cartwheel) "I'm in love" (cartwheel) "with a WONDERFUL GUY!" It worked perfectly in rehearsal, but disaster struck at the show's first tryout performance in New Haven because no one had considered the difference between rehearsal lighting and the full lights of a performance. Mary, blinded by the glare, became disoriented and cartwheeled off the stage and into the orchestra pit, knocking herself, the conductor, and the piano player unconscious. Although everyone recovered, Martin had to wear a heavy body bandage under her costume for the rest of the New Haven run.

The show came to New York with a $500,000 advance sale, a record for the time. It opened in April 1949, ran for two years to packed houses and nearly universal critical acclaim, won Martin a Tony Award, and brought to the American musical comedy stage some of its most beloved show tunes, including "I'm Gonna Wash That Man Right Out of My Hair," for which Martin washed her hair on stage eight times a week for three years (counting the year's tour after Broadway).

When the tour of *South Pacific* closed, Mary and Richard took a cruise to South America to recharge and were invited by friends to recuperate at a ranch in Brazil. This was the beginning of the Hallidays' infatuation with that country, and would lead to their purchase, in the mid-1950s, of their own Brazilian retreat, Nozza Fazenda, to which they would return whenever time allowed. Their South American sojourns were frequent during the 1950s, as Mary appeared in several shows that were unsuccessful and closed quickly, among them 1953's *Kind Sir,* with Charles Boyer ("When they review the clothes, you know something's wrong with the show," Mary noted), and a musical version of Thornton Wilder's *Skin of Our Teeth* in 1955.

All my life, when things seemed at lowest ebb, something good was waiting.

—Mary Martin

By then, Martin was preparing for the role she considered "perhaps the most important thing . . . I have ever done in the theater." Another friend from the "Audition Mary" days who had become the director of the San Francisco and Los Angeles Light Opera Company offered her the lead in a musical version of J.M. Barrie's 1905 classic, *Peter Pan.* The show had not been remounted since its premiere 50 years previous with *Maude Adams and had never been done as a musical. The production, which had a score by Jule Styne, Adolph Green, and *Betty Comden, *Carolyn Leigh, and Mark Charlap, would be directed by Jerome Robbins, with British actor Cyril Ritchard cast as the venomous Captain Hook.

The show was a challenge for Martin, not only because she would be playing a boy of indeterminate age, but because Peter had to fly. Peter Foy, who had been rigging flying acts for circuses in Europe with great success, was brought from England. Martin told him she wanted Peter to fly "all over the place," and used her training from the Fanchon and Marco days to choreograph the aerial ballet that carries Peter, Wendy, and the boys to

Never-Never Land—a technical nightmare for Foy that required the intricate coordination of five actors suspended on wires 20 feet or more over the stage. Yet another problem was singing while "flying," since voices tended to get lost in the flies overhead rather than being projected straight out to the audience. *Peter Pan* thus became the first musical to make use of specially designed wireless microphones concealed on the body.

The role was the most physically challenging Martin, now 42, had ever undertaken, but when she let out with her first "crow" in "I Gotta Crow" at the show's opening performance in San Francisco, she knew it was worth it. "Oh!," she would remember, "what joyous bedlam followed!," as everyone in the audience—and not only the children—crowed back, clapped their hands to revive Tinkerbelle, shouted warnings to Peter as Captain Hook closed in for the kidnapping, and stared in wonder as Peter soared overhead. Jerome Robbins complained that the tumult was preventing him from accurately assessing the show's rhythm and blocking, but Martin knew the "joyous bedlam" was precisely what *Peter Pan* was all about.

Given the technical hurdles, it is remarkable that there were so few accidents during the show's run. During one performance in Los Angeles, the wire attached to Martin's body harness slipped off its pully, dropping her 30 feet and then snatching her back up again. The whiplash injured her back, and she had to take painkillers in order to perform. Later, when she inadvertently assumed the wrong spot just before flying, there was a mid-air collision between Mary and the actress playing Wendy, **Kathy Nolan**. But Martin's enthusiasm was unflagging. "I think that after all that money and faith and anticipation," she said, "a few shots and a little pain are far less important than the performance." *Peter Pan* opened on Broadway in late 1954, toured the country the following year, was adapted for a live television broadcast, and remains a landmark memory for many a baby-boomer.

Martin called her next stage success a "triumph of audience over critics." *The Sound of Music* was too sticky-sweet for most critical tastes, but Mary loved the role of *Maria von Trapp* so much that she was a major investor in the show and spent three years preparing for it. She was proved right, appearing as Maria throughout the show's run from 1959 on Broadway until its close on tour in 1962.

Martin hadn't long to wait for her next hit show, *I Do! I Do!*, which had been adapted by Harvey Schmidt and Tom Jones from Jan de

Hartog's *The Four Poster.* (Schmidt and Jones would later collaborate on *The Fantasticks*.) De Hartog's play followed a married couple from their wedding night through the next 50 years—a considerable acting exercise for Martin, her co-star Robert Preston, and their director, Gower Champion. It was a tribute to their skills that the show ran for more than a year after it opened in 1966—a remarkable run for a two-character musical. But on tour with the show, Martin suffered from colds, flu, and a persistent pain near her abdomen. Growing weaker and weaker as the tour neared its end, she was finally hospitalized and found to be in need of a hysterectomy. She and Halliday flew to Brazil after the operation for much needed rest.

Although Martin toured Southeast Asia in *Hello, Dolly!*, which she brought to Korea, Vietnam, and Japan during the Vietnamese war, the hectic pace of the past 20 years began to slow, with longer and longer periods spent at Nozza Fazenda. One morning in 1973, Halliday was found collapsed on the floor of his bathroom. He had suffered an intestinal blockage during the night, with such pain that he had been unable to call anyone for help. Rushed to Brasilia, he survived an operation but developed pneumonia and died. The Hallidays had been married for 33 years.

Devastated, Martin sold the ranch and moved back to California. It took her three more years before she could write: "I was always so busy living that I didn't have much time to think about [life itself]. We *can* learn, I am sure, until the day we die and I, for one, am looking forward to each new day, each new thought." Now she was able to take pleasure in the successful career of her son, Larry Hagman, soon to become notorious as "J.R." on "Dallas"; and she accepted the occasional television appearance or film cameo. But with the exception of an unsuccessful show called *Legends*, which she toured with *Carol Channing*, there were to be no more stages graced with her presence.

Mary Martin died of cancer on November 4, 1990, at her home in Rancho Mirage, California. She was 77 and had spent nearly 50 of those years bringing a special dignity and glamour to American musical comedy. She considered the stage her home where, like Peter Pan in Never-Never Land, she was free to live her dreams. "Neverland," she once said, "is the way I would like real life to be: timeless, free, mischievous, filled with gaiety, tenderness, and magic."

SOURCES:

Atkinson, Brooks. *Broadway.* NY: Macmillan, 1970.

Martin, Mary. *My Heart Belongs*. NY: William Morrow, 1976.

Skouras, Thana. *The Tale of South Pacific*. NY: Lehman Books, 1958.

Norman Powers,
writer-producer, Chelsea Lane Productions,
New York, New York

Martin, Mary Letitia (1815–1850)

Irish novelist. Name variations: Mrs. Bell Martin; Princess of Connemara. Born Harriet Mary Letitia Martin at Ballinahinch Castle, County Galway, Ireland, on August 25, 1815; died in childbirth in New York on November 7, 1850; only child of Thomas Barnewall Martin (an MP); granddaughter of "Humanity Dick" Martin; married Arthur Gonne Bell, in 1847.

An Irish novelist, known as Mrs. Bell Martin and the Princess of Connemara, Mary Letitia Martin was born in 1815 at Ballinahinch Castle, County Galway, and, on the death of her father in 1847, inherited a sizeable estate, mortgaged to the Land Life Assurance Company for £200,000. During the Irish famine of 1846–47, the Martin family had spent large sums on food and clothing for their tenant laborers. In 1847, Mary married Arthur Gonne Bell of Brookside, County Mayo, who brought no money into the marriage and assumed the surname of Martin by royal license. When Mary could not meet the mortgage payments on the property, the matter was taken up by the Encumbered Estates Court, and Mary Letitia Martin was left penniless. The couple moved to Belgium where she turned to writing for monetary support; she then sailed to New York in 1850, hoping to better her fortune. Martin died there in childbirth on November 7, 1850. Her chief works are *St. Etienne, a Tale of the Vendean War* (1845) and *Julia Howard: A Romance*, published the year of her death.

Martin, Mary Steichen (1904–1998).

See Calderone, Mary Steichen.

Martin, Mother Mary (1892–1975)

Irish founder of the Medical Missionaries of Mary. Name variations: Mary Martin. Born in 1892, in Glenageary, County Dublin, Ireland; died on January 27, 1975, in the hospital she had founded in Drogheda, County Louth, Ireland; father was a timber merchant; educated at Sacred Heart Convent, Leeson Street, Dublin, and Holy Child College, Harrogate, Yorkshire, England; never married; no children.

Mother Mary Martin advocated untiringly for permission from the Roman Catholic Church to allow women's religious orders to perform medical work. Once this permission was granted by Pope Pius XI in 1936, she would found a religious order, the Medical Missionaries of Mary, that has since opened hospitals in Spain, Italy, the United States, and throughout Africa.

While serving as a VAD (Voluntary Aid Detachment) nurse during World War I in England, France, and Malta, Martin had determined to dedicate her life to medical service. In 1921, having trained as a midwife, she went to Nigeria at the request of Bishop Shanahan, a missionary in Africa. There she conceived the idea of founding a religious order for women that would establish clinics and hospitals to serve Africans. In 1923, she returned to Ireland on the bishop's advice, but left the new congregation to which he had directed her after two years. Although in ill health, Martin continued to advocate that women in holy orders should be permitted to perform maternity and medical work. Encouraged by the Papal Nuncio to Ireland, she sought permission for this from the Vatican throughout the next ten years, and in 1936 succeeded in winning papal authorization for her plan. In April 1938, while seriously ill in a hospital in southern Nigeria, Martin was professed as a nun.

On medical advice, she returned home to Ireland, where she opened a house for students at Booterstown, County Dublin, a novitiate at Collon, County Louth, and, in response to local requests, a maternity hospital in Drogheda in December 1939. When she opened the International Missionary Training Hospital in Drogheda in 1957, Cardinal Richard Cushing, archbishop of Boston, Massachusetts, became a patron. Through his assistance, a hostel for extern sisters and students was opened two years later.

Martin was awarded the *Florence Nightingale Medal from the International Red Cross in 1963. In 1966, she was the first woman to be made a freeman of Drogheda and was also the first woman to be inducted into the honorary fellowship of the Royal College of Surgeons, Ireland (RCSI), which cited "her singular achievements in the field of medical missions." Mother Mary Martin died on January 27, 1975, in the hospital in Drogheda that she had founded.

Beth Champagne,
journalist and freelance writer, West Barnet, Vermont

Martin, Sara (1884–1955)

African-American blues singer. Name variations: Sarah Dunn Martin; Margaret Johnson; Sally Roberts.

Born on June 18, 1884, in Louisville, Kentucky; died of a stroke on May 24, 1955, in Louisville; daughter of William Dunn and Katie (Pope) Dunn; married William Myers (marriage ended); married Hayes Withers; children: (first marriage) one son.

Selected discography: Sugar Blues/ Achin' Heart Blues (1922, OK 8041); Graveyard Dream Blues (1923, OK 8099); Yes, Sir, That's My Baby (1925, OK 8262); Death Sting Me Blues/ Mistreatin' Man Blues (1928, QRS 7042); Mean Tight Mama (1928, QRS 7043).

Stage performances and recordings by 1920s vaudeville blues queen Sara Martin played a central role in popularizing the emerging American art form of the blues, and one of her first records, "Sugar Blues," recorded in 1922, has since become a classic.

A contemporary of *Bessie Smith and *Ma Rainey, Martin was born in 1884 in Louisville, Kentucky, and as a teenager started performing in vaudeville there. Around 1915, she took her act north to Chicago, and within five years had made it to the entertainment circuit in New York City. She was sought after as much for her dramatic performances and her versatility as for her

Sara
Martin

voice, which was reportedly unexceptional and sometimes abrasive in tone. When Martin began singing in New York City clubs and cabarets, she attracted the notice of Clarence Williams (1898–1965), an African-American composer who was also the most frequently recorded jazz pianist in the 1920s. As a music publisher and promoter who founded a New York publishing house and opened several music stores, he recorded more African-American jazz musicians than anyone else at the time, frequently for the Okeh label, and through him Martin became one of the first female blues singers to be recorded.

Her first recordings with Okeh Records in 1922 included "Uncle Sam Blues" and "A Green Gal Can't Catch On," and "Sugar Blues" and its flip side, "Achin' Heart Blues." In the same year, she also recorded on the Columbia label with her own group, the Brown Skin Syncopators. In 1923, she recorded again on the Okeh label with *Eva Taylor, Shelton Brooks, and Fats Waller; when Louisville guitarist Sylvester Weaver came to New York, Martin recorded with him, and so sponsored the first American recordings by a country bluesman. She also toured with Waller (1922–23) and with the W.C. Handy Band (1923) on the Theatre Owners Booking Association (TOBA) circuit, the main circuit for black entertainers, performing among other places in Nashville, New Orleans, Atlantic City, Washington, D.C., and Chicago.

Sara Martin appeared in many 1920s revues, theatrical shows, and musicals, singing everything from traditional 12-bar and 16-bar blues to vaudeville comedy songs and even foxtrots which she delivered in the style of *Sophie Tucker. She wore lavish gowns onstage, and frequently appeared in two or three different outfits in one show. At one point, she performed with her husband, William Myers, on banjo, and their three-year-old son onstage. She sang on radio in 1924 and 1927, and appeared in the 1927 film *Hello Bill*. In 1928, she toured Jamaica, Cuba, and Puerto Rico with the *Get Happy Follies Revue*, and the following year appeared with *Mamie Smith in *The Sun-Tan Frolics* at the Lincoln Theater in New York City. During 1930, Martin again toured East Coast theaters, and performed also in Cleveland, Ohio clubs.

Shortly after that, Martin left blues and vaudeville behind and began singing gospel music with Thomas Dorsey, who had also recently switched from the blues. They toured Chicago-area churches in 1932. (She had earlier recorded gospel music with Sylvester Weaver, Arizona Dranes, and, in 1927, her future husband, Hayes Withers.) As a gospel singer, however, she never achieved the renown she had won on the vaudeville and blues club circuits. During the last decade of her life, having retired from performing, Sara Martin owned and managed a private nursing home in Louisville. She died of a stroke on May 24, 1955, and was buried at the Louisville Cemetery.

SOURCES:

Cohn, Lawrence, *et al. Nothing But the Blues: The Music and the Musicians.* NY: Abbeville Press, 1993.

Kernfeld, Barry, ed. *The New Grove Dictionary of Jazz.* NY: St. Martin's Press, 1994.

Smith, Jessie Carney, ed. *Notable Black American Women.* Detroit, MI: Gale Research, 1992.

SUGGESTED READING:

Harris, Sheldon. *Blues Who's Who: A Biographical Dictionary of Blues Singers.* New Rochelle, NY: Arlington House, 1979.

Harrison, Daphne Duval. *Black Pearls: Blues Queens of the 1920s.* New Brunswick, NJ: Rutgers University Press, 1988.

Kellner, Bruce, ed. *The Harlem Renaissance: A Historical Dictionary for the Era.* NY: Methuen, 1987.

"Sara in New York," in *Chicago Defender.* April 23, 1927.

"Sara Martin," in *Living Blues.* Number 52, 1982, p. 23.

COLLECTIONS:

Materials on Sara Martin are located in the James Weldon Johnson Memorial Collection, Beinecke Rare Book and Manuscript Library, Yale University.

Materials on Martin from around 1924 are located in the Music Division, vertical files, New York Public Library, Lincoln Center.

Beth Champagne,
journalist and freelance writer, West Barnet, Vermont

Martin, Steffi.

See Walter-Martin, Steffi.

Martin, Mrs. Theodore (1817–1898).

See Faucit, Helena Saville.

Martin, Violet Florence (1862–1915).

See joint entry under Somerville and Ross.

Martín Gaite, Carmen (1925—)

Spanish novelist and historian. Name variations: Carmen Martin Gaite. Born in Salamanca, Spain, on December 8, 1925; graduated from the University of Salamanca in 1948; married Rafael Sánchez Ferlosio (a writer), in 1953 (divorced 1987); children: two.

Carmen Martín Gaite was born in the university city of Salamanca, Spain, on December 8, 1925. Her progressive bourgeois parents provided private tutors for her early schooling. The Spanish Civil War (1936–39) and the subsequent consolidation of Francisco Franco's dictatorship overshadowed her youth, especially as her family's sympathies lay with the defeated Republic. Martín Gaite graduated from the University of Salamanca in 1948 and then went to Madrid, where she began work on a doctorate in history and philology. There, however, she fell in with a group of young writers interested in social criticism.

Turning to short stories and novels, Martín Gaite began to establish a reputation as one of Spain's foremost writers with the publication of the short novel *El balneario (The Spa)* in 1954. It won the important Gijón Prize, in part for innovatively combining fantastic and realistic elements. Her novel *Entre visillos (Behind the Curtains,* 1958) won the Nadal Prize, Spain's most prestigious literary award. Other novels include *Ritmo lento* (1962), *Retahílas* (1974), *Fragmentos de interior* (1976), and *El cuarto de atrás* (1978). The last received Spain's National Literature Prize in 1979 and is her most widely acclaimed work.

Meanwhile, Martín Gaite also returned to her study of history. She completed her dissertation and published it in 1969 as *El proceso de Macanaz: Historia de un empapelamiento.* She also researched and wrote *Usos amorosos del siglo XVIII en España* (1972), which examines customs of love in 18th-century Spain.

Martín Gaite's technical innovations, her sensitive rendering of women and their concerns, and her portrayal of contemporary Spanish society earned her wide recognition as one of late 20th-century Spain's foremost literary figures. In 1987, she was the first Spanish woman to become an honorary member of the Modern Language Association.

SOURCES:

Brown, Joan L. "Carmen Martín Gaite: Reaffirming the Pact between Reader and Writer," in *Women Writers of Contemporary Spain: Exiles in the Homeland.* Edited by Joan L. Brown. Newark, NJ: University of Delaware Press, 1991, pp. 72–92.

Kendall W. Brown,
Professor of History, Brigham Young University, Provo, Utah

Martina (fl. 600s)

Byzantine empress. Flourished during the 600s; second wife of Herakleos also known as Heraclius I of Carthage, Byzantine emperor (r. 610–641); children: ten, including Heraklonas also known as Heraclonas II, Byzantine emperor (r. 641).

The Byzantine Empire that Heraclius I of Carthage inherited in 610 was sadly reduced from its former glory and still being decimated by enemies. These included Slavs, Avars, Lombards, and the Persians, who soon captured Palestine and Syria and removed the True Cross from Jerusalem. Although moody and subject to phobias, Heraclius rallied his armies, retook much of the land that had been lost, and restored the holy relic to Jerusalem. Martina, his second wife, traveled with him on his campaigns, and gave birth to some of their ten children at far-flung military outposts. The royal couple appear to have been devoted to each other; they were also related by blood, for Martina was Heraclius' niece, and many Byzantines believed the marriage to be incestuous. This does not seem to have harmed the emperor's high standing with his subjects, but it made Martina widely scorned and unpopular.

By the early 630s, Heraclius had vanquished his foes, and the empire seemed set for prosperity. Then the warriors of the new religion of Islam swept into Byzantium. Jerusalem fell to their onslaught in 637, and by the end of the decade Islamic forces had conquered the Byzantine provinces of Palestine and Syria, and Heraclius was suffering from a crisis of nerves that rendered him virtually unable to rule. Martina remained by his side throughout. Heraclius' designated successor was Heraclonas-Constantine, his son with his first wife *Fabia-Eudocia, but Martina's influence over her husband was such that before his death in 641 she was able to secure a joint kingship for their 15-year-old son Heraclonas II. Heraclius agreed to this arrangement in part due to the poor health of Heraclonas-Constantine, and, indeed, the new co-emperor died, probably of tuberculosis, after just three months on the throne. Martina's enemies in the imperial court spread rumors that she had poisoned him so her son Heraclonas II could rule as sole emperor. Despite the fact that Heraclonas II promptly raised his nephew Constantine III to the status of co-emperor, those same enemies took Martina and her son into custody a few months later. Martina's tongue was cut out, Heraclonas' nose was mutilated, and they were banished to the island of Rhodes. Nothing further is known of Martina's fate.

SOURCES:

Head, Constance. *Imperial Byzantine Portraits*. New Rochelle, NY: Caratzas Brothers, 1982.

Grant Eldridge,
freelance editor, Pontiac, Michigan

Martindale, Hilda (1875–1952)

British civil servant. Born in London, England, in 1875; died in 1952; daughter of William Martindale (a merchant) and Louisa (Edwards) Martindale (1839–1914, a suffragist and educational advocate); sister of Louisa Martindale (a well-known obstetrician and gynecologist); educated in Germany, Brighton High School, and the Royal Holloway College and Bedford College in London.

Hilda Martindale was born in London, England, in 1875, the second of two daughters of **Louisa Martindale**, a noted advocate of women's suffrage and an outspoken supporter of the Liberal Party, and William Martindale, who died when she was a child. After attending primary school in Germany, Martindale returned to England when her mother and sister, also named Louisa, moved to Brighton in 1885. She attended the Brighton High School for Girls before leaving to study hygiene and sanitary sciences at the Royal Holloway College and Bedford College in London.

Following her graduation from college, Hilda Martindale went on a world tour with her mother and sister to study state programs for the care of indigent children. (Her sister would later become a well-known obstetrician and gynecologist.) Upon her return to England, Hilda secured a position in the civil service as a factory inspector under the supervision of **Adelaide Anderson**. Martindale's work as an inspector led her in 1903 to write an influential report on lead poisoning suffered by workers in brick factories, and to become a supporter of ◄⧖ **Gertrude Tuckwell**'s efforts to eradicate lead in household and occupational environments. Hilda went on to conduct an examination of working conditions in Ireland in 1905.

Martindale rose steadily through the ranks of the civil service, obtaining the posts of senior lady inspector in 1908, superintending inspector in 1921, and deputy chief inspector in 1925. She was especially noted for her work in integrating women into formerly male-dominated areas of industrial employment, which was of crucial importance during World War I. Notwithstanding her conviction that separate treatment violated the principle of equal opportunity, she was in 1933 named director of women establishments in the Treasury Department; this made her one of the first women to secure a position in the highest ranks of the civil service. Martindale served as a member of the Whitley Council Committee on the Women's Question and became an advocate of equal pay for women and an opponent of mandatory retirement for women who married while employed. She was awarded the Order of the Commander of the British Empire in 1935. Hilda Martindale retired in 1937 to pursue a writing career and published several books, including *Women Servants of the State,*

◆▶
Tuckwell, Gertrude. See Bondfield, Margaret for sidebar.

1870–1938 (1938), *One Generation to Another* (1944), which was about her family, and *Some Victorian Portraits* (1948). She died in 1952.

SOURCES:

The Concise Dictionary of National Biography. Oxford and NY: Oxford University Press, 1992.

Uglow, Jennifer S., ed. *The International Dictionary of Women's Biography.* NY: Continuum Press, 1989.

Grant Eldridge,
freelance writer, Pontiac, Michigan

Martineau, Harriet (1802–1876)

English author of fiction, reviews, travel writings, and religious, philosophical, and sociological essays, who was an advocate for women's rights, education, the abolition of slavery, and other liberal and radical causes of the 19th century. Pronunciation: MAR-tin-O. Born Harriet Martineau on June 12, 1802, in Norwich, England; died at Ambleside, in the Lake District, on June 27, 1876; daughter of Thomas Martineau (a textile manufacturer) and Elizabeth (Rankin) Martineau; educated at home before being sent to Reverend Isaac Perry's school from 1813 to 1815; continued education at home under private teachers; never married; no children.

Grew up in Norwich in middle-class family of Unitarian faith; led an unhappy childhood beset by fears, illnesses, and the onset of deafness at age 12; sent from home at age 15 to relatives in Bristol for 15 months, and came under the influence of philosophical traditions of Locke, Hartley, and Priestley; published her first writings in the Unitarian journal, the Monthly Repository *(1822–23); following her father's death and an engagement that ended with the death of her fiancé, contributed to household support first through needlework and eventually by her writing (1826); gained fame by popularizing principles of political economy through a series of didactic narratives (1832–34); traveled extensively in America (1834–36); became a strong advocate of abolitionism and women's rights; established her reputation as a social analyst through writings on her American travels; suffered a period of invalidism (1839–44), from which she announced her cure through mesmerism; settled in the Lake District (1845) where she continued to write, lectured to the working classes, and established a model farm and low-income housing; traveled to the Near East (1846–47); published* Household Education *and her most important historical work,* The History of the Thirty Years' Peace 1816–1846 *(1849); declared her break with religious faith (1851); following a recurrence of illness (1855) from which she did not expect to recover, wrote her Autobiography; continued writing to support herself until incapacitated by illness (1866).*

Major writings: Illustrations of Political Economy *(25 vols., 1832–34);* Poor Laws and Paupers Illustrated *(10 vols., 1833–34);* Illustrations of Taxation *(5 vols., 1834);* Society in America *(1837);* Retrospect of Western Travel *(1838);* Deerbrook, a novel *(1839);* Eastern Life, Past and Present *(1848);* Household Education *(1849);* The History of the Thirty Years' Peace 1816–1846 *(1849);* Letters on Man's Nature and Development *(1851); a popular translation and abridgment of Comte's* Positive Philosophy *(1853); and a posthumously published* Autobiography *(1877).*

Many prominent figures of 19th-century England can be described as both typical and eccentric. Certainly Harriet Martineau's life reflects typical patterns of development of individuals who rose to distinction during a century that saw an unprecedented transformation in the material conditions of English life and serious challenges to the intellectual, political, and religious traditions of the English people. Like Charles Dickens, she learned firsthand the precarious nature of traditional middle-class social and economic stability and responded by forging a new professionalism based on ambition and talent rather than inherited position. Like George Eliot (*Mary Anne Evans), Martineau underwent a spiritual conversion from an ardent religious faith to a hopeful secular belief in human progress. The far-reaching social and economic changes of the century put her in the position of *Mary Wollstonecraft and *Charlotte Brontë, educated middle-class women who had to support themselves or accept a life of dependence, and who resolutely took as their tool the pen rather than the traditional needle. Martineau was among the pioneering women of her time who extended their sphere to the public space of authorship and the popular press from the private space of the nursery and schoolroom that had previously marked the limits of respectable female employment.

While the social and intellectual patterns of her life have much in common with those of her contemporaries, her distinctiveness, indeed her eccentricity, emerges from a character marked by fierce independence, strong opinions, and fearless self-assertion. Martineau's unwavering belief in democratic principles and egalitarianism led to her association with unpopular causes ranging from abolitionism to women's right to obtain a divorce; her receptiveness to unconventional ideas and experiences allowed her to proclaim a cure from invalidism through mesmerism and to enjoy a good cigar; her independence and principles motivated her to build a home of her own, she wrote in her *Autobiography,* where she could enjoy her life as "probably the happiest single woman in England" and to turn down pensions offered by the government three times because she feared they would compromise her reputation for intellectual and political autonomy.

Believing as she did from early adulthood in the inevitable operation of the law of causality, Martineau looked back at her life when she wrote her *Autobiography* in 1855 to trace how her family background, childhood experiences, and physical and mental health shaped her character and opinions. As the third daughter and the sixth of eight children of Thomas and **Elizabeth Martineau,** she was born in 1802 into a family well able to provide for the material needs of their children. Her father, a descendant of French Huguenots who settled in the cathedral city of Norwich in the 17th century, was a cloth manufacturer and wine importer in Norwich, a largely Nonconformist and economically prosperous manufacturing town and cultural center. As a member of the intellectual community that included such literary figures as William Taylor, *Anna Letitia Barbauld,** and *Amelia Opie,** he provided for the education of his large family of sons and daughters equally during their early childhood. From 1813 to 1815, he sent Harriet and her sister **Rachael Martineau** to Reverend Isaac Perry's school, where girls were taught the same curriculum as boys: Latin, French, composition, and arithmetic. When the school closed, Harriet continued lessons in Latin, French, and music at home. The Martineau daughters thus received a deeper education than girls in most middle-class families of the time. Thomas Martineau passed the values he espoused as a Unitarian, a political radical, and a manufacturer on to his children, and Harriet's understanding and advocacy of *laissez-faire* capitalism owe much to his views and example. Elizabeth Martineau, like most middle-class women of the 19th century, was responsible for domestic arrangements and supervision of the children. She was a stern disciplinarian who seems to have regarded motherhood as a moral duty rather than an intimate relationship. Harriet especially among her children was frustrated by the inability to establish a warm and trusting relationship with her mother.

Harriet was described as difficult and delicate from infancy. Her *Autobiography* shows that she retained vivid memories of an unhappy childhood, which she summarized bleakly: "My life began with winter. . . . I have had no spring."

She records memories of fears that haunted her, the yearning for love she desperately needed and missed, and the pain she suffered physically and mentally from poor health and perceived emotional neglect. It seems clear that her physical and mental symptoms reinforced and intensified one another. She suffered from digestive problems and nervous fears through much of her early childhood. She was easily upset by the rough play and bullying of her older siblings. Choosing solitude to avoid conflict, she became an astute observer and avid reader, completing *Paradise Lost* by the time she was eight and having memorized it shortly after. When she was 12, the first signs of deafness added to her sense of isolation and intensified her tendency to be withdrawn and sullen. She claimed to have no sense of smell or taste. By the time she was 16, deafness made personal relationships and social situations difficult. Her closest family relationships were with her younger brother, James, on whom she lavished her frustrated affection, and **Ellen Martineau,** the baby of the family, toward whom she consciously assumed the role of surrogate mother. The lack of love she felt during her childhood accounts to a great extent for the independence she assumed throughout her adult years and also for her sympathetic insight into the feelings of children, invalids, the disadvantaged, and the disabled.

A turning point in Harriet's life came at the age of 15 when she was sent away from home to relatives in Bristol in the hope that a change of scene would improve her health and disposition. In her aunt, she found for the first time a warm and affectionate adult in whom she could confide, and in her cousins she found companionship within her peer group she had not experienced at home. Her aunt kept a school for girls, and the intellectual discussions of the school and the household stimulated her active mind. She was taught by Lane Carpenter, a Unitarian minister whose influence intensified the religious fervor she had turned to earlier as a substitute for family affection. Through Carpenter, she became acquainted with the philosophical ideas of Locke on the importance of sensation and experience, and of Hartley on the principles of association and causation. As a result, she became attracted to the branch of Unitarian thought associated with Joseph Priestley, who had achieved, through Hartley's doctrine of "philosophical necessity," an optimistic reconciliation between the scientific, materialist thought of the Enlightenment and faith in a divine creator as a first cause. Harriet readily adopted Hartleyan necessarianism as a governing principle for

Harriet
Martineau

much of her later thought on politics, morals, and education.

Upon her return home in 1819, Harriet's family found her much improved in mind and temper. She studied the Bible systematically and continued reading philosophy. Over the next few years, the ideas that were to inform Martineau's mature opinions—the concept of necessity and an optimistic faith in individual and social perfectibility—guided her intellectual development. Encouraged by her brother James, she submitted an article she had written on "Female Writers and Practical Divinity" to the *Monthly Repository*, a Unitarian journal. Her first literary production was published pseudonymously in 1822, to be followed in 1823 by "On Female Education." Thus her literary debut announced one of the persistent themes in the writing she produced over a 54-year career: the position of women in society.

During the decade when Martineau was developing her literary talent, she confronted several crises in her family and personal life. She began writing when her brother James suggested it as a distraction from the loneliness she felt when he left home to attend college in 1821. The death of her oldest brother Thomas of consumption in 1824 was a devastating blow to the family, especially her father, whose manufacturing business was in a serious decline, partly as a result of competition from the power looms gaining wide use in the Yorkshire textile industry and partly because of the general economic depression of 1825–26. Her father died of an incurable liver ailment in 1826, after he had been forced to reduce the inheritances he had set aside for his daughters to save his business. When the firm he left behind finally went bankrupt in 1829, the family was nearly penniless; two of the daughters, Rachael and Ellen, found positions as governesses, and Harriet, limited in her choices even more than most women of her time by her deafness, realized that she would have to make her way in the world through her needle or her pen.

It seems that marriage had been ruled out of the question by her experience of 1826, when she became engaged to John Hugh Worthington, a fellow seminarian introduced to her in 1823 by her brother James. In what appears to be the closest approximation to a romantic relationship in her life, Harriet was strangely ambivalent toward her fiancé. When Worthington suffered a mental and physical breakdown and lapsed into insanity in December 1826, Martineau reacted at first with shock, then broke off the engagement and distanced herself abruptly, refusing to visit him and shutting him out from her thoughts. When he died a few months later, she seemed more relieved than grieved.

The prospect of a single, independent life as a writer was attractive to her, and although beset by grief, disappointment, and precarious health between 1826 and 1829, she was encouraged by her success in earning small sums for the religious works, novellas, stories, and tracts she wrote. With the final collapse of her father's business in 1829, the need to earn a reliable in-come became urgent. Her literary ambition was thwarted, however, by her mother's reluctance to allow her to move to London where she hoped to find markets for her work. After a three-month stay with relatives in London in 1829, during which she made her first acquaintance with a literary community and first used the trademark ear trumpet that made social relationships much easier, her mother called her home to Norwich, where Harriet continued to produce the fancy needlework that was her chief source of income and did what writing she could at night. By appearing tractable to her mother's wishes, she extracted a promise that she might spend three months of each year in London to cultivate literary relationships and pursue a career as a writer.

Liberated from middle-class conventionality by her circumstances following her father's economic failure and death, yet dedicated to the ideals of competitive individualism and a belief in the benevolent workings of capitalism that he had represented for her, Martineau discovered her special gifts and her appeal as a writer in the intellectual and political ferment that led to the passage of the Reform Bill of 1832. The confluence of personal, national, and international events that transformed her from a provincial but ambitious young woman of unconventional religious and political views to a celebrated, controversial, cosmopolitan speaker for radical causes must have reinforced her necessarian beliefs. Surely, Martineau and the decade of the tumultuous '30s were made for one another.

The transformation began when Martineau won in all three categories of a contest sponsored by the Unitarian Association in 1830 to argue the superiority of Unitarianism to Catholicism, Mohamedanism, and Judaism. She used her prize money to visit her brother James in Dublin in 1831. With his encouragement, she conceived the plan of writing a series of narratives to illustrate the principles of "political economy," a term with a great deal of currency as a slogan but with little meaning to the general public at the time. Martineau was convinced that she could make the theories on political economy of the "philosophical radicals" comprehensible to moderately educated artisan and middle-class readers through narratives. After rejections from several publishers, she persuaded Charles Fox to publish the series, agreeing to his condition that she raise a subscription to guarantee a market for the project. The series began in February 1832 and was an immediate popular success. Readers awaited the publication of the monthly tales as eagerly as the installments of serialized novels. Martineau produced the tales rapidly, writing a story a month for 25 numbers, the last appearing in February 1834. Each tale illustrated specific principles associated with the radical reform movement of the time, particularly Bentham's greatest happiness principle, Smith's *laissez-faire* doctrine, Malthus' theory on population, and Ricardo's anti-Corn Law rationale. Martineau's chief source for her series was James Mill's *Elements of Political Economy,* a primer intended for students of the subject. Through this project, she discovered her strength as a writer, that of translating contemporary political, social, and economic theoretical concepts and texts into forms and language suitable for a growing mass audience. The market for what **Dierdre David** has called such "textual services" as Martineau provided is attested to by the institution of the Society for the Diffusion of Useful Knowledge, which provided informative publications at reasonable prices to educate the public on the many contemporary issues during this era of rapid cultural change. The extent of the public's need for information in accessible language and form is suggested by the fact that the first number in Martineau's series sold the entire first edition of 1,500 copies in ten days, and that by 1834, the series was selling 10,000 copies monthly. By contrast, John Stuart Mill's *Principles of Political Economy,* published for a more sophisticated audience in 1848, sold 3,000 copies in four years. Although Mill wrote to Thomas Carlyle in April of 1833 that Martineau "reduces the *laissez-faire* system to absurdity," by November of the same year, he also wrote to Carlyle that Harriet Martineau and the "political economy tales" that made her famous were "surely a sign of this country and Time."

Harriet Martineau had become a celebrity. She settled in London with her mother and aunt, where she dined out almost every night and was visited daily by journalists, novelists, and political figures. Her views on capital and labor, which she saw as bound by an "identity of interests"; her opposition to governmental regulation of wages and working conditions; her support of mechanization of industry as a sign of progress; her advocacy of birth control, emigration, and colonization as means of balancing population and resources; and her support of free trade and the repeal of the Corn Laws put her in the mainstream of the Benthamite Radicals and Whig Reformers. Although she repeatedly denied affiliation with the Whigs and held firmly to her radical credentials, she was courted by the Whig Cabinet and press, praised by Lord Brougham as "a deaf girl from Norwich" who was doing

more good for the country than any man and recruited by him as a publicist for Poor Law reform. He supplied her with private government reports, and she responded by writing a series of tales, *Poor Laws and Paupers,* for the Society for the Diffusion of Useful Knowledge. Her career as a writer was firmly established and sufficiently compensated to permit her to refuse a civil-list pension. She wisely invested her earnings in a deferred annuity that would pay her £100 a year beginning in 1850.

> *I* believe myself possessed of no uncommon talents, and of not an atom of genius; but as various circumstances have led me to think more accurately and read more extensively than some women, I believe that I may so write on subjects of universal concern as to inform some minds and stir up others.
>
> —**Harriet Martineau**

Martineau was exhausted by the pace and volume of her literary production and the demands of her social life; her health once again suffered. When a voyage to America was suggested for rest, she was excited by the prospect of viewing the American experiment in democracy at firsthand and quickly arranged to sail in August of 1834 on an extended holiday that was to take her on a demanding two-year itinerary that included virtually all of the existing 24 states. On her voyage to New York, she wrote *How to Observe: Morals and Manners,* a handbook that outlined a primitive sociological methodology that would permit a traveler to "read" the correlation between social theory and practice much as her tales had illustrated the connection between the theory and practice of political economy. This handbook, and the two other volumes that resulted from her American travels, earned her the title of the "first woman sociologist."

Her fame having preceded her, Martineau had dinner at the White House with President Andrew Jackson, stayed with James Madison, attended debates of the Senate and House of Representatives, and visited the homes of the socially and intellectually prominent from New England to New Orleans. Although her opposition to slavery was well known from her writings, she refrained from judgment and assumed the role of an objective observer as she traveled south from New York, observing the social scene and enjoying the generous hospitality provided through the Carolinas, Georgia, and west to Louisiana before sailing up the Mississippi to Tennessee, Kentucky, and Ohio. She found anti-abolitionist feeling at its height in the southern and middle states during the time of her visit. William Lloyd Garrison and his abolitionist colleagues were regarded as dangerous extremists whose radical methods opposed a policy of gradual emancipation and colonization supported by moderates, including many people in the northern states. In Massachusetts, she was asked to attend an abolitionist meeting, which presented a threat of physical danger because such meetings had been mobbed in the past. Although she had not agreed entirely with Garrison's call for immediate emancipation and integration of slaves and free blacks into the full privileges of American citizenship, when she was asked to speak at the meeting, she spoke unequivocally in favor of abolition. Following her endorsement of the abolitionist cause, she found her welcome in many quarters less enthusiastic, and during the remaining months of her travels, she was sometimes forced to cancel plans because of apprehension about her personal safety. She maintained her connection with abolitionist leaders and her fervor for the cause throughout her lifetime.

Martineau kept a detailed journal of her travels, observations, and conversations, and on her return to England had several offers from publishers for books on her impressions of America. She wrote *Society in America* (1837), in which she declared her purpose was "to compare the existing state of society in America with the principles on which it was professedly founded." On the basis of her analysis, she announced that America had indeed been founded on admirable egalitarian principles and in many ways exemplified and validated the theories of political economy; nonetheless, she found that America's democratic ideals could not be realized while slavery persisted and while women were denied equal rights and representation under the law. In her chapter on "The Political Non-Existence of Women," she took issue with the idea prevalent in both England and America that women's interests were fairly represented through a system of surrogate representation by males. She criticized the limitations of women's education and deplored their limited opportunities to earn an independent living. She wrote about marriage as an institution that, like slavery, was based primarily on economics. As a proponent of divorce and as an outspoken advocate of women's political and economic rights, Martineau was ahead of the mainstream of public opinion in both England and American by several decades. A second book to come from her American journey, *Retrospect of Western Travel* (1838), is a less analytical, more personal account of her travels that still holds interest as a vivid and detailed contemporary depiction of American life and society in the 1830s.

On her return to England, she continued to write for various periodicals, was offered but did not accept the editorship of a proposed sociological journal, wrote three volumes for *The Guide to Service*, manuals commissioned by the Poor Law authorities to train girls for domestic service, completed a three-volume novel, *Deerbrook*, attended Queen *Victoria's coronation, and traveled to the north of England and Scotland. In the spring of 1839, she left England for an extended continental tour, but became so seriously ill in Venice shortly after her departure that her brother James and her future brother-in-law were sent to bring her back to England, where she was immediately placed under the care of another brother-in-law, Thomas Greenhow, who practiced medicine in Newcastle.

Greenhow diagnosed an enlarged and prolapsed uterus, and suspected an inoperable uterine tumor as the source of her pain. He prescribed leeches, bed rest, and opiates for discomfort. After staying six months with her sister and brother-in-law in Newcastle, she took lodgings in nearby Tynemouth, on the North Sea. There she lived as an invalid for the next five years in a two-room apartment where she could observe, from her bed or couch, the activities of the outside world through a telescope given her by a friend. During her illness, she continued to write, completing a novel based on the life of Toussaint L'Overture, *The Hour and the Man*, four children's stories for the Playfellow series, and *Life in the Sickroom*, a book that describes the psychological effects of physical illness. She and *Elizabeth Barrett (**Browning**) maintained a correspondence from their respective sickbeds, and she welcomed visits from friends when she was not in pain.

In 1844, her symptoms began to abate, probably as a result of a shift in the position of the tumor so that it no longer pressed on her abdominal organs. At about the same time, she was introduced by friends to a visiting mesmerist, Spencer Hall, and experienced a sense of health and well being after her first treatment. She continued the mesmeric treatments and gained enough strength in a few months to give up opiates; she ventured out of doors for the first time in five years. By December of 1844, she was walking 15 miles a day. Having been convinced that she was dying for the last five years, she was now equally convinced that her cure was a result of mesmerism, and with characteristic haste and conviction, she published "Letters on Mesmerism" in the *Athenaeum*, linking mesmerism, an almost respectable alternative medical treatment of the time, with clairvoyance, which was much more generally suspect. Her advocacy in this case stretched the credulity of many of her friends, and she was the subject of sharp criticism from medical authorities and her family, including her brother James, with whose religious views she increasingly disagreed. Her association with Henry Atkinson, who promoted a self-styled "scientific" philosophy based largely on phrenology and mesmerism, further alienated her from James, who had become a prominent voice in theological writing of the time.

Following her recovery, she energetically set about reestablishing her active life by building a home in the Lake District, near Ambleside, where she spent the rest of her life. There she wrote according to a regular schedule, received visits from such luminaries as Charlotte Brontë and George Eliot, exchanged neighborly visits with William and *Dorothy Wordsworth and the Arnolds, gave lectures on social improvement, and established a small model farm to demonstrate that agricultural workers could gain self-sufficiency through industry, careful planning, and thrift. She joined friends for a trip to Egypt, Palestine, and Syria in 1847, an experience that apparently confirmed her conversion to a secular philosophical perspective. Her travel book on the journey, *Eastern Life, Past and Present* (1848), was a great success. In 1849, she wrote *Household Education* and researched and wrote a social history of England during the first half of the 19th century, *A History of the Thirty Years' Peace*, an astute analysis of the changes wrought through the influence of the philosophical radicals and informed by the meliorist view of social progress that became the basis of her secular faith. She shocked many of her friends and readers by declaring her religious apostasy publicly in *Letters on the Laws of Man's Social Nature and Development* in 1851, letters largely written by Atkinson, with commentary by Martineau. The book, widely attacked for its atheism, caused her final break with her brother James, who wrote a devastating review for the *Prospective Review.* They never again met or spoke to one another.

Acting as "governess to the nation," the role that Martineau had fashioned for herself over the past 20 years, she undertook a translation and condensation of Comte's *Positive Philosophy* to make accessible to the public Comte's view of social development as an inevitable reflection of the progression of human thought from a religious to a metaphysical to a scientific

Harriet Martineau

understanding of the world. Although she disagreed with much of Comte's thought as authoritarian and anti-egalitarian, she was in sympathy with his general meliorist tendencies.

As signs of deteriorating health in 1854 led her to believe that time was short, she set about writing her *Autobiography*, in effect an *apologia* to offer an "account of my conscious transition from the Xn faith to my present philosophy." The *Autobiography* remains her most important work for modern readers. In the great tradition of such 19th-century autobiographical writing as Wordsworth's *The Prelude*, John Stuart Mill's *Autobiography*, and Cardinal Newman's *Apologia Pro Vita Sua*, its appeal lies in the account it provides of the individual mind struggling with the imperatives of faith, knowledge, and self-discovery, the essential experience of humanity coming to terms with modernity. In this work, Martineau looks forward to a future in which "men will have risen to a capacity for higher work than saving themselves,—to that of 'working out' the welfare of their race, not in 'fear and trembling,' but with serene hope and joyful assurance."

Martineau's indomitable spirit and resilience again triumphed, and she was to live for

22 more years. Though debilitated and often in pain, she continued to write until 1866, contributing articles as a regular leader writer for the *Daily News* from 1852. She pursued her mission as governess to the nation in her journalism, writing on the Crimean War, the American Civil War, the Indian Mutiny, and continuing her advocacy for a more democratic world in her pieces on education, women's issues, abolitionism, and the condition of the working class. She roused herself from virtual retirement to work with *Florence Nightingale and *Josephine Butler for the repeal of the Contagious Diseases Acts of 1866 and 1869, deploring the double standard that permitted the forcible medical examination for venereal disease of any woman in a military town but did not require the soldiers themselves to be examined. Finally too ill to write, she lingered under the palliative effects of opiates until her death at Ambleside on June 27, 1876. The many tributes of those who wrote memoirs for the third volume of her *Autobiography* testify that she was indeed "a sign of this country and Time."

SOURCES:

David, Dierdre. *Intellectual Women and Victorian Patriarchy: Harriet Martineau, Elizabeth Barrett Browning, George Eliot.* Ithaca, NY: Cornell University Press, 1987.

Harriet Martineau's Autobiography. 2 vols. London: Virago Press, 1983.

Pichanick, Valerie Kossew. *Harriet Martineau: The Woman and Her Work, 1802–76.* Ann Arbor, MI: University of Michigan Press, 1980.

Rossi, Alice S., ed. *The Feminist Papers: From Adams to deBeauvoir.* NY: Columbia University Press, 1973.

Thomas, Gillian. *Harriet Martineau.* Boston, MA: Twayne, 1985.

Webb, R.K. *Harriet Martineau: A Radical Victorian.* NY: Columbia University Press, 1960.

Wheatley, Vera. *The Life and Work of Harriet Martineau.* Fair Lawn, NJ: Essential Books, 1957.

Patricia B. Heaman, Ph.D.,
Professor of English, Wilkes University,
Wilkes-Barre, Pennsylvania

Martinelli, Elsa (1932—)

Italian actress. Born in Grosseto, Italy, in 1932; married; children: Cristiana Mancinelli (an actress).

Selected filmography: The Indian Fighter *(US, 1955);* La Risaia *(Rice Girl, 1956);* Donatella *(1956);* Four Girls in Town *(US, 1957);* Manuela *(Stowaway Girl, UK, 1957);* I Battellieri del Volga *(Prisoner of the Volga, 1958);* Gosta Azzura *(1959);* Ciao Ciao Bambina *(1959);* La Notte Brava *(1959);* Un Amore a Roma *(1960);* Et Mourir de Plaisir *(Blood and Roses, Fr.-It., 1960);* Hatari *(US, 1962);* The Pigeon That Took Rome *(US, 1962);* Le Procès *(The Trial, Fr.-It.-Ger.,* 1962); Rampage *(US, 1963);* The V.I.P.s *(UK, 1963);* De L'Amour *(Fr.-It., 1965);* La Fabuleuse Aventure de Marco Polo *(Marco the Magnificent, Fr.-It.-Ger., 1967);* La Decima Vittima *(The Tenth Victim, 1965);* Maroc 7 *(UK, 1966);* Sept fois Femme *(Woman Times Seven, Fr.-It.-US, 1967);* Le plus Vieux Métier du Monde *(The Oldest Profession, Fr.-It.-Ger., 1967);* Candy *(US-Fr.-It., 1969);* El Millón de Madigan *(Madigan's Millions, Sp.-It., 1969);* Maldonne *(Fr.-It., 1969);* L'Amica *(1969);* Les Chemins de Kathmandou *(Fr.-It., 1969);* La Part de Lion *(Fr., 1971);* Una sull'altra *(One on Top of the Other, 1971);* L'Araucana Massacro degli Dei *(1972);* Il Garofano Rosso *(1976);* Sono un Fenomeno paranormale *(1986);* Pygmalion 88 *(1988);* Once Upon a Crime *(1991).*

The daughter of a minor government employee, Elsa Martinelli was a barmaid and a model before being discovered by Kirk Douglas, who launched her film career by securing her a role in his movie *The Indian Fighter* (1955). The actress, slim, with cat-like qualities, graced Italian and international films throughout the 1960s, although her early unsophisticated roles were said to have far surpassed the cosmopolitan roles of her later career. Martinelli's daughter **Cristiana Mancinelli** is also a screen actress.

Martinez, Maria (1886–1951).

See Cadilla de Martínez, Maria.

Martinez, Maria Montoya (1887–1980)

Tewa potter, known primarily for developing matte black-on-black ware, who was the key figure in the 20th-century revival of Pueblo pottery. Name variations: Marie. Signed work: Poh've'ka, Marie, Marie & Julian (1923–1922); Marie & Santana (1943–1956); Marie Poveka (Pond Lily); and Maria/Popovi (1956–1971). Born Poh've'ka or Pond Lily (Tewa) or Maria Antonita Montoya (Spanish) in the Tewa Pueblo P'owo'ge, or Place Where the Waters Meet (in Spanish: San Ildefonso, New Mexico) on April 5, 1887; died on July 21, 1980, in Santa Fe, New Mexico; daughter of Reyecita Pena and Tomas Montoya; attended St. Catharine's Indian School (Santa Fe, New Mexico); married Julian Martinez, in 1904 (died 1943); children: Adam Martinez (who married Santana Roybal Martinez); Juan Diego Martinez; Popovi Da Martinez; Felip Martinez; and a daughter and son who died in infancy.

Survived epidemic that decimated Pueblo population (c. 1890); participated with husband Julian in

"Anthropology Exhibit" at St. Louis World's Fair (1904); with Julian, joined archaeological excavation of the Pajarito Plateau at Tyuonyi and Frijoles Canyons under Dr. Edgar L. Hewett (1908); began reproduction of ancient Frijoles pottery, originally polychrome; employed at the Museum of New Mexico (1909–10); experimented with black-on-black ware (1910–12); developed black ware; exhibited at San Diego World's Fair (1912–15); discovered matte-on-black ware method (1919–21); developed pottery-making as full-time industry (1921–22); exhibited at Chicago World's Fair (1934); demonstrated pottery-making at San Francisco World's Fair with Julian (1939); Julian died (1943); worked with Santana Martinez (1943–1956); worked with son, Popovi Da (1956–1971); Popovi Da died (1971).

Awards and shows: Bronze Medal, Chicago World's Fair and Indian Fire Council's Bronze Medal for Indian Achievement (1934); University of Colorado Bronze Medal (1953); American Institute of Architects Craftsmanship Medal and France's Palmes Academie Award (1954); Rockford College-*Jane Addams Award for Distinguished Service (1959); the "Three-Generation Show," sponsored by the Center for the Arts of Indian American, featuring Maria, son Popovi Da, and grandson Tony Da (1967); American Ceramic Society Presidential Citation (1968); Minnesota Museum of Art "Symbol of Man" Award; honorary Ph.D. in Fine Arts from New Mexico State University at Las Cruces; NEA grant for pottery workshop, Idyllwild, California (1973); New Mexico Arts Commission Governor's Award for Outstanding Service to the Arts (1974); National Council on Education for Ceramic Arts Award (1976); honorary Ph.D., Columbia College, Chicago (1977); "Maria: The Legend, The Legacy," retrospective exhibition presented by Wheelwright Museum, New Mexico (June 1980).

Twenty-five miles northwest of Santa Fe, New Mexico, where the Rio Grande snakes through high desert covered by pinyon pines, sits the Tewa Pueblo named P'owo'ge ("Place Where the Waters Meet"). Situated on the river bank between the Jemez Mountains on the west and the snow-capped Sangre De Cristos on the east, the Pueblo has been inhabited since 1300 CE and was renamed San Ildefonso by Spanish invaders in 1617. The once-thriving Tewa community of 3,000 tumbled into a 200-year spiritual and physical decline reaching rock bottom at the end of the 19th century when an influenza epidemic reduced the population to 80. Among the survivors was young Maria Montoya. Her mother

Reyecita Montoya is said to have taken the child's resilience to be a sure sign that she would withstand great hardship in years to come. Indeed, Maria, who grew up to become one of her Pueblo's greatest potters, overcame personal tragedy many times in her long life.

As with most native endeavors, pottery-making is an ancient blending of the practical with artistic and spiritual expression. The designs and techniques of Pueblo pottery date back centuries and employ materials natural to the region: clay from the four sacred mountains, vegetal pigments (*guaco*) for color, and the sharp bristles of the yucca plant for brushes. Unlike European potters, North American natives never used the potter's wheel, preferring to coil rather than throw and to bake the pots in a hot fire of sheep dung rather than in a man-made kiln.

Maria's first attempts at making pottery began when she was a girl. She would later tell author **Susan Peterson**: "I watched my Aunt, Nicolasa . . . she didn't teach. Nobody teaches pottery. I was about ten or twelve." She also had the advantage of watching **Martina Montoya** (no relation) who was, and still is, considered one of the finest Tewa potters of all time. Despite these artists, however, the early 20th century saw a serious shortage in quality pottery coming out of the Pueblos, a circumstance which could be attributed to the overall economic and cultural depression experienced throughout all of the Pueblos in the southwest. So in decline was the Pueblo culture that many experts feared the Pueblos were on the verge of dying out altogether.

Myriad factors fueled this deterioration. Like many children from Indian nations, Maria and her sisters were sent away from the Pueblos to Indian schools, where speaking their native language (Tewa) was forbidden, and even Spanish was considered a language secondary to the preferred English. Traditional religious practices were frowned upon by priests who continued the centuries-old practice of their predecessors of attempting to convert the natives. For the Tewas, relinquishing their spiritual identity was impossible because of the intertwining of Tewa ceremonial life with daily living, with the cycles of planting and harvest, and with the cycles of birth and death. These ideas are sustained throughout the culture, and particularly in the art work. From the beginning, Maria's work reflected the close ties to family, as well as to Pueblo and ceremonial life, of a Tewa Indian.

In 1904, the 17-year-old Maria married Julian Martinez, who was from her village. A saddlemaker by trade, Julian agreed to learn farming, the Montoya family business. Maria's father Tomas was to teach his new son-in-law everything he knew, so that Julian could be a steady provider. But Maria's and Julian's lives were soon to take another turn. In an understatement about what some consider to be one of the most covertly racist events in the 20th century, she later told curator Richard Spivey: "When I was married in 1904, I went to the St. Louis Fair and there I made little pots." Maria's narration said more about her generous and forgiving nature than it did about the event.

I just learned [pottery] for myself. I learned it with . . . my whole heart.

—Maria Martinez

Deciding that the citizens of the United States needed to be exposed to "primitive" cultures, the architects of the St. Louis World's Fair set about creating an "Anthropological Exhibit." To that end, they sent for native peoples from across the United States and the world, inviting them to participate in what amounted to living dioramas: little scenes depicting "primitives" in their natural habitats. The visitors to the fair, largely descendants of white European settlers, viewed dioramas that featured cultures and peoples as diverse as African Pygmies, Fiji islanders, and Native Americans. Even the great Apache warrior and mystic Geronimo was featured as an attraction. Maria and Julian were viewed depicting scenes in the life of the Pueblo Indians. Maria, fluent in three languages including English, was curious and startled by the rude comments made by whites about the indigenous peoples, whom they assumed could not understand them. Though Maria may have been quietly offended by the paternalistic remarks, her experience and spirituality provided a means by which to maintain an interest in, and liking for, people of all races and backgrounds.

Later that year, the couple returned to San Ildefonso. Julian set about the task of learning his adopted occupation; unfortunately, he did not particularly enjoy farming, making it all the more difficult for him because at the time no one was making a good living. Maria gave birth to their first son almost immediately and to a daughter the following year.

In 1907, the couple suffered their first tragic loss when their infant girl died of a sudden illness. Maria was consumed with grief, and the child's death may have been a watershed event for Julian, who developed a drinking problem. For many native people, the hardships of economic oppression seemed unending. Though al-

cohol was forbidden in Indian territory, saloon owners made a habit of strategically placing their bars just off Indian land. No matter how much he fought it, Julian suffered bouts of chronic alcoholism for the rest of his life.

In 1908, Dr. Edgar L. Hewett, professor of archaeology and director of the Museum of New Mexico in Santa Fe, began archaeological excavations of the ancient Tewa Pueblos at Tyuonyi and Frijoles Canyons. Native men were offered work as diggers and, though it meant his leaving the Pueblo for an extended period, Maria urged Julian to take the job, hoping that the isolation of the digs would help curb his appetite for alcohol.

Hewett and his colleagues were successful at unearthing ancient polychrome ware, examples of the characteristic black-on-red or black-on-cream pottery. But they also found fragments of pottery not previously discovered in the Southwest. These shards were jet and charcoal black in color, and some were polished. Unable to find a piece intact, the archaeologists wanted a native woman to recreate the unusual style of pottery. Maria Martinez, who at the time signed her polychrome pots with her given name Poh've'ka, made the thinnest, roundest pots in the least amount of time. She was thrilled when asked to attempt the recreations.

For the next year, Maria and Julian began to experiment with different methods of firing the clay to achieve the black ware. At the same time, she continued to make polychrome pieces that Julian painted with traditional Tewa symbols, in particular the *avanyu* or plumed serpent. Though it was unusual for a Tewa man to participate in any phase of pottery-making, Julian and Maria's collaboration was not only a perfect artistic match but it was also probably critical to keeping their marriage intact, as they were able to augment their income with sales of their work. This period—from 1907 until Julian's death in 1943—is considered the first phase of Maria's long career. She told Spivey in 1979: "Julian helped me. He helped me with everything. . . . And when Dr. Hewett came . . . there's where we started making money, and we were very happy."

Edgar Hewett was excited by the success of Maria's reproductions. He and a colleague, Dr. Kenneth Chapman, encouraged the couple to continue their experiments which they were convinced would spark a renaissance in Tewa pottery. So positive were Hewett and Chapman in this prediction that by 1911 Maria, Julian, and several other potters had been hired to demonstrate their craft at the Museum in Santa Fe and to sell directly to the public. By 1914, when the Museum sent

Maria
Montoya
Martinez

a group of potters, including Maria and Julian, to the San Diego World's Fair to demonstrate this work, a full-scale revival was on the rise. Though they were accomplished at rendering beautiful pieces of traditional pottery, and their efforts were critical in improving the artistic integrity of the native ware, Maria and Julian had not yet made their own artistic mark. That was soon to come.

Around 1919, the couple reached a turning point in their lives and work. The more Maria worked with black ware, the less Julian was needed in their collaboration, and it seemed that

whenever Julian was at creative loose ends, he found his way into a saloon. Fortunately, the couple decided to experiment with the black ware. With a red clay slip, Julian painted a design on one of Maria's black pots after she had polished it but before it was fired. Neither of them knew what would result. To their great surprise, when the pot was pulled from the fire a new kind of pottery had been created—matte black (where Julian had painted) on polished black.

The black-on-black pottery became an instant success both artistically and commercially.

The first black-on-black pots were finished in matte with a polished design. The couple continued to perfect the new style, and eventually the technique was reversed, producing the Martinez family signature style seen today: a polished design within a matte band on a highly polished, silvery black vessel. In addition to being the innovators of the matte black-on-black ware, the Martinezes were the only Tewas who worked with black fired clay. The potters of the Santa Clara Pueblo have been working for decades in black ware and are most known for the "bear claw" pottery, its design fired into the clay.

While the family grew to include two more sons, Juan Diego and Popovi Da, and their pottery-making flourished, Maria and Julian's accomplishments were not well accepted by the rest of the Pueblo, who viewed the success of the group as more important than the achievement of any individual. Sensitive to the Pueblo's attitudes, Maria willingly shared what had been a secret technique, and her generosity single-handedly turned around the economic conditions of the village. Also helpful was a road which opened San Ildefonso to tourists from Santa Fe in 1924. Maria's pots were already well known, and now her neighbors' wares were sought after as well.

Maria and Julian worked on improving their techniques while teaching and displaying the black-on-black ware nationwide. By 1931, when the rest of the country was in the midst of a depression, Maria's income was over $5,000. She hired a Spanish maid to take over the household chores and to help with the three youngest boys (the last son, Felip, was born during this time), which allowed her to work at her craft full time. Martinez's life, however, was not without challenges. She lost another child, a son, in infancy and was given the care of her baby sister **Clara Montoya** when their mother Reyecita died in childbirth.

Julian's bouts with alcohol increased with time. Even as his drinking became progressively worse, the couple traveled extensively throughout the 1930s and 1940s, demonstrating their skills and accepting various awards and citations. Their reputation as master artisans was becoming known nationwide. Meanwhile, with alcoholism not yet recognized as a disease, Julian went untreated. In 1943, he disappeared for several days before he was found dead in the mountains near the Pueblo where he was born.

His death marked both an ending and a beginning for Maria. She mourned the man with whom she had lived most of her life. But she could not let the grief destroy her when she had her children, and by now grandchildren, to consider.

Her eldest son Adam had married **Santana Roybal (Martinez)**, a woman from a respected family of Pueblo artisans. Julian had instructed Santana in his painting techniques, and Maria now began a collaboration with Santana. Their work together, which lasted seven years, continued the Maria-Julian tradition.

In 1956, Maria Martinez began the third phase of her artistic career when she began working with her son Popovi Da. Like his father, "Po" was a painter by nature and used his skill to decorate his mother's pots; he had also inherited his father's spirit of experimentation. By this time, Martinez's technical excellence had reached its zenith, and together they developed a new line of pottery: sienna ware and black-on-sienna ware. Po added his trademark signature when he invented a polished gun-metal finish. This period, one of Martinez's most creative, came to an abrupt and tragic end with Po's untimely death. Before his passing in 1971 at the age of 50, he was Martinez's last living child. Juan Diego and her youngest son Felip had died in 1966. Martinez, now 84, had survived her husband and most of her children.

After Popovi's death, Martinez retired as a practicing artist, though she continued to teach. In 1973, a National Endowment for the Arts grant allowed her to hold a pottery workshop at Idyllwild, California, in the mountains above Los Angeles, where she passed on her techniques to a new generation of potters.

After decades of national and international recognition, Martinez was honored by her home state of New Mexico with a retrospective exhibition at the Wheelwright Museum. Opening June 15, 1980, it was to be the last tribute during her lifetime. She died just over a month later, on July 21, 1980. Her work can be found in many private collections and museums including the Museum of New Mexico in Santa Fe. Martinez's legacy continues in the work of her grandchildren and great-grandchildren, as well as that of the hundreds of other potters she inspired.

SOURCES:

Marriott, Alice. *Maria: The Potter of San Illdefonso.* Norman, OK: University of Oklahoma Press, 1948.

McGreevey, Susan Brown. *Maria: The Legend, The Legacy.* Santa Fe, NM: Sunstone Press, 1982.

Peterson, Susan. *The Living Tradition of Maria Martinez.* San Francisco: Kodansha International, 1977.

Spivey, Richard L. *Maria.* Northland Publishing, 1979.

Trimble, Stephen. *Talking With Clay.* Santa Fe, NM: American Research Press, 1987.

Deborah Jones,
freelance writer, Studio City, California

Martinez, Marianne (1744–1812)

Austrian composer, patron, pianist, harpsichordist, singer, and teacher who composed around 200 works. Name variations: Marianne von Martinez. Born Anna Caterina Martines in Vienna, Austria, on May 4, 1744; died in Vienna on December 13, 1812; father was Spanish in origin and master of ceremonies to the Papal Nuncio; friend and associate of Haydn and Mozart.

Marianne Martinez was born in Vienna in 1744 and grew up in one of the world's most important musical circles. On the first floor of the house in which she lived, the Dowager **Princess Esterhazy** resided, while Esterhazy's son, the prince, was the patron of Joseph Haydn who lived in the attic. As well, Pietro Metastasio, the court poet and opera librettist, lived with Marianne's family. Although Haydn was the poorest among the occupants in the large house, he soon became part of the active life which unfolded there. Haydn taught Marianne harpsichord and accompanied her to singing lessons; she also showed talent for composition. The young girl studied with Porpora, Bonno and Hasse.

By the 1760s, Martinez was writing large church works. She would compose around 200 pieces, including four symphonic masses, six motets, and three litanies for choir and orchestra. One of her masses, probably her third, was performed at the court chapel in 1761; it was a large work with more than 150 pages of score. But when Joseph II came to the throne, he reinstated an old rule against women "speaking" in church, that is "singing" in church. This meant two things: women composers like Martinez could no longer hear their works played in churches, and male castratii were substituted for women. (The practice of castrating young boys to ensure that their soprano voices would not change at puberty became popular in church choirs in the mid-14th century; by the 17th century, the vogue had spread to opera, and thousands of young boys, at their parents' request, were being castrated per year in Europe.) This did not, however, stop Martinez from composing, and her fame continued to spread. She was admitted to the Philharmonic Academy of Bologna in 1773.

Martinez also became acquainted with the young Amadeus Mozart in Vienna. Many believe that he modeled his 1768 Mass, K. 139, on one of her works. He also probably wrote his Piano Concerto in D major, K. 175, for her. Throughout her life, Marianne Martinez was very close to Pietro Metastasio, the bachelor who lived with her family. He encouraged her composing and wrote the libretti for two of her oratorios. When Metastasio died, he left his considerable fortune to the Martinez siblings. Their home was already a center for musical evenings which everyone in Vienna wanted to attend, and even visitors from foreign capitals had heard of them. In 1796, Martinez opened a singing school in her home and trained many professional singers. Throughout her life she remained close to Joseph Haydn.

Marianne Martinez was active as a composer, performer, and teacher during Vienna's golden age and her contributions to the city's cultural life were significant. Although most of her music was forgotten in the next century, it has been revived in recent years, and her considerable creative ability has again been recognized. Martinez's reputation, as well as those of many women like her, suffered in the 19th century when it became fashionable to criticize feminine creativity and label it as inferior. She has, however, been restored to the important status which she once occupied in Vienna's golden age and again her compositions are played.

SOURCES:

Cohen, Aaron I. *International Encyclopedia of Women Composers.* 2 vols. NY: Books & Music (USA), 1987.

Sadie, Stanley, ed. *New Grove Dictionary of Music and Musicians.* 20 vols. NY: Macmillan, 1980.

John Haag,
Athens, Georgia

Martino, Angel (1967—)

American swimmer and winner of several Olympic gold medals. Name variations: Angel Meyers. Born on April 27, 1967; attended Furman University, in 1980s; married Mike Martino (a swimmer).

Won first place in the national NCAA Division II swim meets (1986); became first American woman to swim 100-meter freestyle in under 55 seconds (1988); won a bronze medal for the 50-meter freestyle, and a gold medal for the 400-meter freestyle relay in Summer Olympic Games, Barcelona, Spain (1992); set world record for the 100-meter backstroke (1993); won gold medals for 400-meter freestyle relay and 400-meter relay, and bronze medals for 100-meter freestyle and 100-meter butterfly, all in Summer Olympic Games, Atlanta, Georgia (1996).

Competitive swimmer Angel Martino was the oldest female athlete on the U.S. Swim Team assembled for the 1996 Summer Olympic Games in Atlanta, Georgia. A gold-medal winner in the previous Olympics in Barcelona, Martino was encouraged by the cheering crowds of her home state in the Atlanta Games, and her victory capped a decade of both personal triumph and career setback. Martino was born Angel Meyers in 1967. Both her parents were avid swimmers who, when they moved to the small town of Americus, Georgia, were dismayed to find there was no public pool—so they founded one themselves. Martino thus spent much of her youth in the water, swimming competitively, encouraged by her family. At one point in high school, her cheerleading coach complained about the time she devoted to the pool; Martino toyed with the idea of giving up swimming, but her parents convinced her to give up cheerleading instead.

Unable to win a college scholarship despite her talents, Martino attended South Carolina's Furman University, where in 1986 she set national records in the National Collegiate Athletic Association (NCAA) Division II swim meets. At Furman, she also began dating another swimmer, Mike Martino, and the two started training for the 1988 Olympics together (they would later marry). At the peak of her powers in 1988, Martino became the first American woman to swim the 100-meter freestyle in under 55 seconds. Just two weeks before the start of the Summer Olympics in Seoul, South Korea, Martino was disqualified from competing because her blood had tested positive for a banned substance. Although she contended that she had not used performance-enhancing drugs, and that the contraceptive pills she was taking had probably caused the positive reading, her appeal was denied. Martino became skeptical about drug tests: "Because of what happened to me, I'm not going to automatically assume that someone is guilty."

Martino decided to restore her reputation simply by continuing to compete and excel. She resumed training, and again qualified for the U.S. Women's Swim Team for the 1992 Summer Games. In Barcelona, she won a bronze medal for the 50-meter freestyle, and a gold medal for the 400-meter freestyle relay. The following year, she set a world record for the 100-meter backstroke in the Short Course World championships, and in 1995 took first place in the 100-meter freestyle at the Pan American Games.

Martino's greatest restoration of her reputation came with her performance in the 1996 Summer Olympic Games in Atlanta. At an age when most competitive swimmers have retired, Martino qualified for a spot on the U.S. team, becoming its senior member. She won gold medals for 400-meter freestyle relay and 400-meter relay, and bronze medals for 100-meter freestyle and 100-meter butterfly at the Olympics, and a few days later attended a parade in her honor in her hometown of Americus.

SOURCES:
Johnson, Anne Janette. *Great Women in Sports*. Detroit, MI: Visible Ink Press, 1998.
People Weekly. August 19, 1996, p. 43.

Carol Brennan,
Grosse Pointe, Michigan

Martinozzi, Anne-Marie

(1637–1672)

*Niece of Cardinal Jules Mazarin. Born in 1637; died in 1672; daughter of Hieronymus Martinozzi also seen as Girolamo Martinozzi and Laura Margaret Mazarini (who was the sister of Cardinal Jules Mazarin, chief minister to the young Louis XIV); sister of *Laura Martinozzi; cousin of *Laure Mancini (1635–1657), *Olympia Mancini (c. 1639–1708), *Marie Mancini (1640–1715), *Hortense Mancini (1646–1699), and *Marie-Anne Mancini (1649–1714); married the prince de Conti (brother of Louis II de Bourbon, the Great Condé), in 1654.*

Anne-Marie Martinozzi, sister-in-law of *Anne Geneviève, duchesse de Longueville, became a Jansenist and devoted herself to piety.

Martinozzi, Laura (fl. 1658)

*Duchess of Modena. Name variations: Laura d'Este. Flourished around 1658; daughter of Hieronymus Martinozzi also seen as Girolamo Martinozzi and Laura Margaret Mazarini (who was the sister of Cardinal Jules Mazarin, chief minister to the young Louis XIV); sister of *Anne-Marie Martinozzi (1637–1672); cousin of *Laure Mancini (1635–1657), *Olympia Mancini (c. 1639–1708), *Marie Mancini (1640–1715), *Hortense Mancini (1646–1699), and *Marie-Anne Mancini (1649–1714); married Alphonse d'Este (heir of the duke of Modena), in 1656; children: Mary of Modena (1658–1718), queen of England; Francis II, duke of Modena.*

Laura Martinozzi was regent of Modena for 12 years following the death of her husband Alphonse d'Este. Her daughter *Mary of Modena married James II, king of England.

Martinson, Helga Maria (1890–1964).

See Martinson, Moa.

Martinson, Moa (1890–1964)

Swedish proletarian-feminist, political activist, syndicalist sympathizer and experimental modernist writer whose literary reputation has been overshadowed by her husband's fame as a poet. Name variations: Helga Svartz. Pronunciation: MO-wah MARtin-son. Born Helga Maria Svartz on November 2, 1890, in Vårdnäs, a suburb of Norrköping, Sweden; died in Södertälje, Sweden, on August 5, 1964; daughter of Kristina Svartz (an unmarried textile-factory worker); father unknown; attended six years of public school and one semester at Fogelstad Women Citizens College; married Karl L. Johansson (after publication of marriage banns in 1911), in April 1922 (committed suicide, 1928); married Harry Martinson, on October 3, 1929 (divorced 1940); children: (first marriage) Olle (b. 1910); Tore (b. 1911); Erik (b. 1913); Manfred (b. 1914); Knut (b. 1916).

First seven years spent in slum foster homes; quit school (1903); became syndicalist union organizer (1921); resumed education at college level (1924); received first literary recognition in exchange of letters published in Swedish newspaper Arbetaren *(1922); saw publication of first novel* Women and Appletrees *(1933); traveled to Soviet Union (1934); won Sweden's De Nois Prize for Literature (1944); published poetry, essays and novels (1933–59).*

Novels: Kvinnor och appelträd *(1933, Eng. tr.* Women and Appletrees, *1985);* Sallys söner *(Sally's Sons, 1934);* Rågvakt *(Rye Watch, 1935);* Mor gifter sig *(1936, Eng. tr.* My Mother Gets Married, *1988);* Drottning Grågyllen *(Queen Grågyllen, 1937);* Kyrkbröllop *(1938, Eng. tr.* Church Wedding*);* Kungens rosor *(The King's Roses, 1939);* Vägen under sjärnorna *(The Journey Under the Stars, 1940);* Brandliljor *(Firelilies, 1941);* Den osynlige älskaren *(The Invisible Lover, 1943);* Livets fest *(Life's Celebration, 1949);* Du är den enda *(You Are the Only, 1952);* Kvinnorna på Kummelsjö *(The Women at Kummelsjö, 1955);* Klockor vid Sidenvägen *(Bells at Sidenvägen, 1957);* Hemligheten *(The Secret, 1959).*

Short story and essay collections: Armén och horisonten *(The Army and the Horizon, 1942);* Bakom svenskvallen *(Behind the Swedish Field, 1944);* Kärlek mellan krigen *(Love Between Wars, 1947);* Jag möter en diktare *(I Meet a Poet, 1950).*

Poetry collection: Motsols *(Counter-clockwise, 1937).*

The writing career of Moa Martinson was launched in October 1922, at age 32, when she sent a letter to the Swedish newspaper *Arbetaren* (The Worker) in response to an article by *Elise Ottesen-Jensen. Martinson's letter challenged Ottesen-Jensen for the patriarchal tone she had used in writing about women. *Arbetaren's* publication spurred a lengthy written debate between the two on the *Kvinnosidan* (Women's Page), which had previously been reserved for writings on homemaking and childcare. Martinson's references were to August Strindberg, Rudyard Kipling, and Emile Zola, and she wrote about "men's subjects" such as philosophy, religion, and history. The style and content of her letters served to prove her high level of scholarly achievement, despite her lack of even a high school diploma. Two years later, in 1924, when women in Sweden earned 55% of what men earned, Martinson dared to suggest in the column she was then writing for *Arbetaren* that women receive equal pay for equal work; the newspaper's editors began to censor the Women's Page. It was 11 years and hundreds of articles and short stories after her first provocative article had appeared in print before the publication of Martinson's first book, *Women and Appletrees*. By then, the prolific Swedish proletarian-feminist author was 43 years old.

Moa Martinson was born Helga Maria Svartz in 1890, to an unmarried and impoverished factory worker in an industrial suburb of Norrköping, Sweden. Tradition has it that her father was a soldier who refused to marry beneath his station and died the year the girl was born. Since her mother could not support her, the child spent her first seven years living in slum foster homes, until her mother finally married. She then had to vie with an alcoholic and abusive stepfather for her mother's attention. During the next two years, the family moved seven times in the hope of bettering their lives through new jobs or new surroundings. Known in childhood as Helga, Martinson attended nine different schools before she quit at age 13; her report card at the time described her work as "excellent."

Childhood taught Martinson survival skills. She knew how to knit, sew, clip rags to weave rugs, and could carry water great distances from a well. Her mother had worked as a scrubwoman in homes as well as at factory jobs. Birth control was illegal in Sweden between 1910 and 1938, and in Martinson's youth, her mother gave birth at least three times. The infant girls, born to a malnourished mother, all died within their first year. These years of poverty and hardship made lasting impressions on the young girl and became the powerful subject matter chronicled in an autobiographical trilogy that takes its protagonist from age six to seventeen. The first volume, *My Mother Gets Married* (1936), is regarded as Martinson's "classic" work and describes the adventures of a six-year-old girl named Mia. The life of Mia exactly parallels Martinson's as she moves through different environments and situations, making new friends only to leave them and mourn the loss. The account also includes humorous tales about classroom happenings, schoolmistresses and masters, skipping school and exciting adventures the child has with Gypsy (Roma) children.

The second book of the trilogy, *Church Wedding* (1938), continues with Mia at ages eight through fourteen, and describes her first job as a nanny. The central event in this book is the planning of the wedding of Mia's Aunt Charlotte, a strong and stylish woman who has remained single long past the usual age, and consequently has enough money saved for a church wedding, which were generally restricted to the wealthy in turn-of-the-century Sweden. For Mia, the aunt's wedding is a major status symbol, and the book concludes with the girl's refusal to marry a boy who has emigrated to America, even though he has offered to pay for her trip there. Since economic conditions like those Martinson experienced caused 25% of Sweden's population to emigrate between 1850 and 1900, the girl's choice was one faced by many in her country.

In *The King's Roses* (1939), the trilogy's final book, Mia works in a city restaurant as a bread-slicer. Aged 16 during the summer of 1906, she works 15 hours a day, shares a sleeping room with 11 other women and misses her mother terribly. In the kitchen, she finally puts a stop to harassment by her male co-workers by repeatedly striking back physically at one of the offenders. These three volumes illuminate Mia's progression from vulnerable waif to an assured, if still struggling, young woman.

At age 17, Martinson was determined never to marry. Her aim was to work, become rich and help her mother, and her highest hope was to write poetry. But at 19 she became pregnant, just as her mother had. In 1911, banns were read in church for her and Karl Johansson, proclaiming their intentions to marry, but the marriage did not actually occur until 1922, probably for economic reasons. Johansson was not rich but had a house and farm called Johannedal, which his father had built during the 1860s. Like Martinson's stepfather, he was also an abusive alcoholic. By 1916, the couple had five children, all boys. Unemployment in the country was high, and Johansson rarely had work. In 1922, the economic stress may have lifted temporarily when the couple finally married. In 1925, their two youngest sons, Olle and Tore, ages eight and nine, drowned in a creek near the house. Three years later, Johansson committed suicide, leaving Martinson a widow with three children at age 38.

Before the death of Johansson, Martinson had become a supporter of syndicalism, a revolutionary doctrine somewhat akin to socialism which advocated that workers seize control of the economy and the government by direct means, as in a general strike. In 1921, she walked 30 kilometers from their farm to the harbor town of Nynashamn, Sweden, in order to attend her first union meeting. She became an active organizer and outspoken supporter of the labor movement in industrial cities as well as on farms. She also became a prominent advocate of feminist issues of the day, including equal wages and birth control.

After the loss of her two children, Martinson wrote her first short story during 1924–25, but found no publisher for the work. Encouraged by a friend, the writer *Elin Wägner, she attended the spring semester at Fogelstad Women Citizens College and began to improve her writing skills. While still in school, she began the novel *Women and Appletrees*, which would be published in 1933. This work intertwines the lives of women from many generations and focuses on a friendship between two characters, Sally and Ellen. In 1934, it was followed by *Sally's Sons*.

The semester at college served to strengthen Martinson's ideas about women, their capacity for greatness, and the unfair manner in which they were treated. It was at this time that she renamed herself Moa, after a character in an early 20th-century novel *Jökeln* (The Glacier) by Johannes V. Jensen. The meaning of the new name was "the mother of all humankind," seen as a developer of her own skills, the inventor of agriculture, and an herb-gathering healer.

In 1928, Martinson's first story, *Pigmamma* (Maidservant-Mother), reached print in serial form in the socialist newspaper *Brand* (Fire). She also became a writer for the feminist paper *Tidevarvet* (The Turning of Time). Because of her lack of basic education, her work sometimes required extensive editing, but the newspapers liked her ideas. She wrote about the common, unknown people, discussing the work of women, the importance of educating children, unemployment, child abuse, and other issues of general concern among the proletariat. In her 1956 foreword to *My Mother Gets Married*, Martinson asked:

Did my mother's life, my own, and millions of other anonymous lives in our country need to be so hard in spite of peace, in spite of hard work, and the eager, unceasing search for work that hardly paid for daily bread? With good reason I ask this question for my mother's sake, my own, and in the name of two-thirds of the people of Sweden.

In the year she went back school, Moa met a well-known seafarer-turned-poet named Harry Martinson. Fifteen years younger than herself, Harry was poor, unemployed, and sick with pneumonia at the time. Some scholars believe that she saved his life and provided the nourishment for his creative work. They married in 1929 and would divorce in 1940. In 1949, Harry would be elected to the Swedish Academy, and he would receive the Nobel Prize for Literature in 1974. In contrast, Moa Martinson's achievements have historically been undermined by critics who saw her merely as Harry Martinson's wife "who also wrote." Although there are critics who argue that their styles are so different that it is pointless to compare their books, those comparisons have been made, and most often to

her detriment. Ill-informed literary critics have argued that he taught her to write and played a large role in her work, despite the number of articles and short stories, she had published, and the novel she had begun, prior to their meeting.

By the 1930s, however, Martinson was recognized for her place in the community of literary Swedish women that included Elin Wägner, *Selma Lagerlöf, and *Karin Boye. She was already well known as a political figure and the author of short stories, poetry and historical essays when the autobiographical fiction that would become her most famous work began to reach print in Sweden. Perhaps because of the harshness of her early years, she was not easily intimidated by negative criticism, even when one critic called her work "food for the dump."

Toward the end of the 1930s, Martinson began to write historical novels. In *Drottning Grågyllen* (Queen Grågyllen), published in 1937, she wrote about the effects of World War I on Europe. A three-volume historical epic describing farm life in the area of Östergötland,

Sweden, included *Vägen under sjärnorna* (Journey Under the Stars) in 1940, *Brandliljor* (Firelilies) in 1941, and *Livets fest* (Life's Celebration) in 1949.

In her novels, Martinson often depicts brave, thrifty, and hardworking women and responsible young girls, while her male characters are usually careless and unable to hold steady jobs; they are absent fathers who spend the family rent money on alcohol and violate marital fidelity, all descriptions of life as Martinson knew it. In *Women and Appletrees,* Sally gives birth alone at home, just as Martinson had done with her youngest son.

Paradoxically enough, I am mostly indignant not because I was denied the possibility to get a university education, but because I landed right in the same anonymous hell as my mother. Maybe it was even harder for me, for I was fully conscious that it was hell.

—Moa Martinson

Martinson's poetry broke new ground in addressing subjects then rarely addressed in European literature. In a poetry collection called *Motsols* (Counter-clockwise, 1937) is a poem called "Världens väverskor" (The World's Weavers), about peace and justice, framed in the world of women textile workers, weavers and spinners.

In her political speeches, writing and appearances on radio shows, Martinson took the side of the weak and unfairly treated. Known simply as "Moa," she was revered for her honesty and humility and became a figure widely adored by the Swedish populace. In 1944, she received the Samfundet De Nois literary prize; more recently, she has been depicted on Swedish postage stamps. Nonetheless, Moa Martinson's work is not widely known outside Scandinavia, and thus far only two of her books have been translated into English. She has been compared to the American author and activist *Agnes Smedley (1890–1950), and there are indeed strong parallels in their life stories and writing careers. When Martinson read Smedley's *Daughter of Earth* (1929), she is said to have felt a sisterhood with the American author.

In later life, Martinson wrote four books about a woman named Betty, which are also argued to be depictions of herself: *Den osynlige älskaren* (The Invisible Lover, 1943), *Du är den enda* (You are the Only, 1952), *Klockor vid Sidenvägen* (Bells at Sidenvägen, 1957), and her final book, *Hemligheten* (The Secret, 1959). Scholarship on the works of Moa Martinson

began in earnest only in the last decades of the 20th century. **Ebba Witt-Brattström**'s 1988 doctoral dissertation on Martinson as a representative of Swedish women authors of the 1930s continues to sell as a popular Swedish paperback. The future holds further exploration of both Martinson and her community of "forgotten" Swedish women writers.

SOURCES:
Dahlström, Britt, ed. *Litteraturhandboken* (Literature Handbook). Stockholm: Forum Press, 1984.
Witt-Brattström, Ebba. *Moa Martinson: Skrift och drift i trettiotalet* (Moa Martinson: Life and Letters in the 1930s). Denmark: Nörhaven A/S, 1989.
Wright, Rochelle. "The Martinsons and Literary History," in *Scandinavian Studies*. Vol. 64, 1992, pp. 263–269.

SUGGESTED READING:
Martinson, Moa. *My Mother Gets Married.* Translated and with an afterword by Margaret S. Lacy. Old Westbury, NY: The Feminist Press, 1988.
———. *Women and Appletrees.* Translated and with an afterword by Margaret S. Lacy. Old Westbury, NY: The Feminist Press, 1985.

COLLECTIONS:
Correspondence, manuscripts, papers and memorabilia located at Martinson's home, Johannedal, in Ösmo, Sweden, now a museum.

RELATED MEDIA:
"Moa: Filmen om Moa Martinson" (Moa: The Film about Moa Martinson), starring **Gunilla Nyroos**, directed by Anders Wahlgren, Filmstallet A/B et al, 1986 (in Swedish).

Mara M. Johns,
translator of Moa Martinson's *Kyrkbröllop* (*Church Wedding*)
and a freelance writer in San Diego, California

Martius, Hedwig (1888–1966).
See Conrad-Martius, Hedwig.

Martyn, Edith How- (1875–1954).
See How-Martyn, Edith.

Marucha (1944–1991)
Cuban photographer, cartoonist, and graphic designer. Born Maria Eugenia Haya in 1944, in Havana, Cuba; died in Havana in 1991; studied at the Instituto Cubano de Arte e Industria Cinematográfica (1962–63), the Biblioteca Nacional de José Marti (1964–65), and with painter Raúl Martínez (1965–66); attended Havana University (1972–78); married Mario García Joya (director of photography at the Instituto Cubano de Arte e Industria Cinematografía); children: Mayitín and María.

Born Maria Eugenia Haya in Havana, Cuba, in 1944, Marucha was involved in photography, film, and the graphic arts throughout her adult life. She studied the history of photography under Mario Rodríguez Alemán at the Instituto Cubano de Arte e Industria Cinematográfica from 1962 to 1963, also acting as the institute's cartoonist and animator from 1962 to 1964. From 1965 to 1966, she studied photographic theory with **Adelaida de Juan** at the Biblioteca Nacional de José Marti. Marucha became a photographer for the Chamber of Congress in Havana in 1970, a position she would hold for eight years, and served as a researcher and script supervisor for filmmaker Tomás Gutierrez Alea in 1975 and 1978. Marucha also studied philology at Havana University from 1972 to 1978. The breadth and quality of her art was recognized by her selection as a member of the Unión Nacional de Escritores y Artistes Cubanos.

Marucha's work took first prize from the union's National Salon as well as the Salon of the University of Havana in 1978, and she organized an exhibition on the history of Cuban photography which was presented in Mexico in 1979. She also played a key role in organizing the Coloquio de Fotografía Latinoamericana in Havana in 1984.

SOURCES:
Rosenblum, Naomi. *A History of Women Photographers.* Paris and London: Abbeville Press, 1994.

Grant Eldridge,
freelance writer, Pontiac, Michigan

Marvelettes (fl. 1960s)

American popular music group of the early 1960s whose songs "Don't Mess With Bill," "Please Mr. Postman," and "Beachwood 4–5789" reached the top of the charts. Part of the Motown sound of the early 1960s; originally comprised of Wanda Rogers, Katherine Schaffner, and Gladys Horton (later replaced by Ann Bogan).

During the late 1950s, while **Wanda Rogers, Katherine Schaffner** and **Gladys Horton** were in high school in Detroit, Michigan, they often sang harmonies at parties. Spotted at a talent show, the friends were brought to the attention of Berry Gordy's Motown recording studio and the Marvelettes were born. With Rogers singing lead vocal and Schaffner and Horton (who was later replaced by **Ann Bogan**) on backup vocals, the Marvelettes' first album, *Please Mr. Postman*, was released in November 1961. It was a great success, with the title song reaching #1 the following year. The group's sound influenced the most important popular musicians of

the day, and "Please Mr. Postman" was covered by the Beatles on their second album.

The Marvelettes produced an astonishing three albums in 1963, with *Live on Stage* released in June and *Marvelettes Sing* and *Playboy* released in November. These albums proved less successful than their first release, however, and the group's popularity fell off markedly. Motown waited three years to release their next album, *Marvelettes' Greatest Hits*. The group returned to the studio in 1967 to produce *The Marvelettes*, but the record did not prove a success. Their last recording, *Sophisticated Soul*, was released in 1968. Despite the group's brief career, the Marvelettes' songs have remained part of the American popular music scene, and their work can still be heard regularly on radio stations dedicated to music of the 1960s.

Grant Eldridge,
freelance writer, Pontiac, Michigan

Marx, Eleanor (1855–1898).

See Marx-Aveling, Eleanor.

Marx, Jenny von Westphalen (1814–1881)

Prussian of aristocratic lineage who married her childhood playmate, Karl Marx, and became his lifelong companion in the struggle for socialism. Name variations: Jenny von Westphalen. Born Johanna Bertha Julie Jenny von Westphalen on February 12, 1814, in the small north German town of Salzwedel; died in London on December 2, 1881; daughter of Johann Ludwig von Westphalen (a Prussian civil servant) and Caroline Heubel von Westphalen; education uncertain, but perhaps attended a private Catholic school in Trier; married Karl Marx (1818–1883, philosopher, economist and sociologist who wrote The Communist Manifesto), *on June 19, 1843; children: Jenny Marx (1844–1883); Laura Marx (1845–1911); Edgar Marx (1846–1855); Heinrich Marx (1849–1850); Franziska Marx (1851–1852); Eleanor Marx-Aveling (1855–1898), and an unnamed last child who died shortly after birth on July 6, 1857.*

Family moved to Trier (1816); confirmed as a Protestant (1828); broke off engagement to Lt. von Pannewitz (1831); secretly engaged to Karl Marx (1836); married to Karl and moved to Paris (1843); "Letter from a German Lady" published (1844); expelled from Paris, moved to Brussels (1845); became Brussels secretary of Communist correspondence committees (1848); arrested by Belgian police, returned to Paris (March 1848); moved to Cologne and became secretary of German Workers Party (summer 1848); took up residence in London (1849); finished copying Capital *(1867).*

Socialism did not come automatically to Jenny von Westphalen Marx, who left behind an aristocratic heritage when she joined her husband Karl Marx in a lifelong commitment to the emancipation of the working class and the abolition of capitalism. But she threw her whole being into that struggle, giving to the socialist cause her unremunerated services as financial manager, organizational secretary, scribe and critic.

One of her daughters, *Eleanor Marx-Aveling, wrote in her reminiscences that without the aid of Jenny Marx her father, the founder of modern communism, would never have accomplished what he did. In addition to raising their six surviving children, Jenny Marx was his constant companion, advisor and assistant. She was, in short, the unsung orchestrator at the center of one of the key command posts of the 19th-century European revolutionary movement: the Marx home, which served as a meeting place and headquarters, not simply a household.

The world belongs to the fearless.

—Jenny Marx

Jenny von Westphalen was born in 1814 in a small town in northern Germany to Johann Ludwig von Westphalen, a 44-year-old civil servant whose grandfather had been ennobled in 1763 in recognition of his services in the Seven Years' War. Baron von Westphalen was father to four children by his first marriage to the daughter of a large landowning aristocrat, but she died suddenly in 1807. Several years later, he married a middle-class woman, **Caroline Heubel**, who became mother to those four children and gave birth to three others, including Jenny.

In 1816, the Prussian government transferred Baron von Westphalen, who was fluent in French, to Trier, a city in the Rhineland close to the French border. The baron was more influenced by the times than by his lineage. As first councillor in the government of Trier, he was reluctant to enforce reactionary measures passed down from Berlin, because he had been inspired by the Enlightenment and the ideals of the French Revolution. "We live in fateful times," he wrote to a friend, "a time in which two contradictory principles are at war: that of the divine right of kings and the new one which proclaims that all power belongs to the people."

Because Jenny was born more than a decade after the last of her father's children by his first marriage, and because her little sister Laura (b. 1817) died at age five, Jenny's only contemporary sibling was her younger brother Edgar (b. 1819). Jenny was highly literate, but not much is known of her formal education. She was confirmed in the Protestant faith in 1828, but may nevertheless have attended a Catholic school, since the only private schools in Trier were Catholic. The family home was a center of spirited social life, with poetry readings and dinner parties for visiting dignitaries.

Sometime around 1817, First Councillor von Westphalen met Heinrich Marx, a 35-year-old lawyer descended from a rabbinical family, who had just undergone a Christian baptism. The conversion had been forced upon Heinrich by a Prussian decree excluding Jews from public office, including law practice. Rather than convert to Catholicism, the predominant faith in Trier, Heinrich Marx chose Protestantism, which he identified with intellectual freedom. Heinrich and Ludwig found they had much in common as middle-aged Protestants deeply involved in Trier's civic and legal deliberations.

Soon the two jurists' children, too, grew close. **Sophie Marx**, two years younger than Jenny von Westphalen, became her best friend. Jenny first met Karl, who was born in 1818, when she was five years old and he was a one-year-old baby. Karl quickly showed exceptional creativity and became dominant in the circle of children. When Karl was eight and Jenny was twelve, wrote Marx-Aveling, "He was a terrible tyrant; he forced them all—Jenny, her brother Edgar and Sophie—to push him in a cart fast down the Markusberg, and what was even worse, he insisted that they eat the pie he had baked with his dirty hands from even dirtier dough. They submitted to it because, as their reward, Karl told them marvelous stories."

The road to marriage was not without ruts. When Jenny was 17, she was beautiful, elegant and caught up in the midst of Trier's social whirl. A young Prussian lieutenant, Karl von Pannewitz, asked Jenny's hand in marriage, and she accepted. But Jenny soon found herself at odds with her fiancé over his belief in the duty of the soldier to blind obedience regardless of his own sentiments—even when ordered to shoot into a protest of the poor. After several months, Jenny broke off her engagement, and the lieutenant's regiment left Trier soon afterward.

Karl Marx was still only 13, but already he gave evidence of a keen mind. Baron von Westphalen became the mentor of the adolescent boy, taking him on long walks, reciting and analyzing passages from Homer, Dante, Shakespeare and Goethe. Along with Jenny and her brother Edgar von Westphalen (who was a year older than Karl, a friend of his at Friedrich Wilhelm Gymnasium, and later a dedicated Communist), the baron and the young Karl discussed the fate of European politics. It was, indeed, through Ludwig von Westphalen that Karl was first exposed to socialism, when, without much luck, the baron tried to induce him to read the French utopian socialist Saint-Simon. Years later, Karl would acknowledge his intellectual debt by dedicating his Ph.D. dissertation to the baron.

In October 1835, Karl left for Bonn to study law. While he was home on vacation in August 1836, intent on transferring to the University of Berlin the following term, he proposed to the 22-year-old Jenny, and she accepted. Karl had begun to read deeply in critical philosophy. He had also returned with a bushy beard which, combined with his dark skin, led her to nickname him her "darling wild boar." When he left for Berlin, only his sister and father knew of the young couple's feelings for each other. "I have talked with Jenny and wish I could calm her," his father wrote to him. "She does not know how her parents will accept the news. And what her relatives and the rest of the world will say. . . . The sacrifice she is making to you is inestimable. Woe to you if you should ever forget it. You must now show that you are a man who deserves the respect of the world."

From Berlin, Karl sent Jenny flowery letters and, for Christmas in 1836, three books of romantic poetry he had written and dedicated to her. "Love is Jenny," ended one poem, "Jenny is love's name." Ferdinand von Westphalen, Jenny's older half-brother who had climbed past his father in the Prussian civil service and would one day serve as minister of the interior, learned from the Berlin police that Karl was keeping the company of radicals and atheists. He urged his father to force Jenny to break off the engagement. But Baron von Westphalen was fond of Karl. He believed Jenny could make up her own mind, and he held out hope that Karl might yet settle down.

Karl Marx, however, was on a decidedly unconventional path. In April 1841, he at last finished his dissertation on Greek philosophy and took his doctorate from the University of Jena, an institution he had never attended. The times were not propitious for scholars with Karl's dissident politics, so he accepted the offer of an acquaintance, Moses Hess, to join the staff of the liberal newspaper *Rheinische Zeitung*. Jenny,

Jenny von Westphalen Marx

28, still in Trier and as yet unmarried, was not thrilled. "Oh, my dear, dear darling," she wrote to him, "now you even start meddling in politics. That is the most daredevil undertaking. Remember, Karlchen, that you have a sweetheart at home who hopes and cries and is entirely dependent on your fate. Tell me, Karlchen, that I shall soon be yours completely."

In March 1842, Baron von Westphalen died, leaving his son Ferdinand as titular head of the family. Jenny's mother forbade Ferdinand from preventing her marriage to Karl, but as a journalist Karl was still receiving an income insufficient to support a wife. His career, moreover, was quickly engulfed in controversy. His first published article, on May 5, 1842, argued for free speech and press. Soon he was decrying restrictions on peasants' rights to gather wood. But in October 1842, he was made editor-in-chief of the *Rheinische Zeitung*, which improved his income, and that Christmas he and Jenny decided that they would marry the following June. Early in 1843, however, the Prussian ministers in charge of censorship decided to move against the *Rheinische Zeitung.* On March 17, Karl resigned his post. He hoped that his dissociation would save the paper, but the gesture did not satisfy the censor and the *Rheinische Zeitung* was suppressed shortly afterward.

Outraged, Karl decided to leave Germany and publish a paper in Paris with his friend Arnold Ruge. But before leaving he intended to marry Jenny, to whom he had been engaged for more than seven years. He wrote to Ruge that he was in love "with heart and soul" and that Jenny had "fought the hardest fights for me, fights that have undermined her health, partly against her pietistic-aristocratic relatives to whom the Lord in Heaven and Lord in Washington are equal objects of veneration, partly against my own family where some priests and other enemies of mine have installed themselves." On June 19, 1843, the marriage took place at last. By October, the newlyweds were on their way to join Ruge in Paris.

Paris, a large metropolis that was home to a substantial German exile community, awed Jenny. She quickly became friends with **Emma Herwegh** (1817–1904), who oversaw a literary salon and was married to the poet George Herwegh. She also participated in the animated conversations that took place among political exiles such as Heinrich Heine and Michael Bakunin in the Marxes' rented house. The first issue of the *Deutsch-Französische Jahrbücher,* as the Marx-Ruge paper was called, appeared in February 1844. It turned out to be the only issue. The paper was banned in Prussia and confiscated at the border. Furthermore, Ruge became horrified by Karl Marx's nascent alliance with the proletariat against private property and reneged on Karl's pay, leading Jenny to call Ruge an "ass."

In May 1844, Jenny gave birth to her first child, **Jenny Marx**—nicknamed "Jennychen" so as to distinguish mother from daughter. The baby suffered severe stomach pains, and in June, Jenny returned to Trier with her "mortally sick child" to visit her mother. In August 1844, she wrote a letter to her husband, who had stayed in Paris, with news about an assassination attempt on King Frederick William IV. The plot was not carried out by a radical, she wrote, but by a disgruntled ex-mayor who had been snubbed for a civil-service job. Karl saw that her analysis was published in *Vorwärts,* a German paper in Paris, under the title "Letter of a German Lady."

When Jenny returned to Paris in the autumn, she discovered that Karl had begun what would prove to be a lifelong friendship with Friedrich Engels, the radical son of a German manufacturer who owned cotton mills in Barmen and Manchester. But in February 1845, Karl was expelled from France at the request of Prussia's King Frederick William IV. Jenny, pregnant with her second child, was left to retire their debts to the landlord and sell the furniture. Sick and bitterly cold, she followed after her husband to Belgium, where the family found a small house in one of Brussels' working-class neighborhoods.

In Brussels, Engels and the Marxes spent many evenings discussing issues of the day in cafés with exiled Poles, Russians and Germans. In July 1845, while Karl Marx and Friedrich Engels left on a trip to Manchester and London to meet with Chartists (members of a British movement for social and electoral reform) and carry out research, Jenny again spent six weeks in Trier with her mother. She wrote Karl that Germany seemed nice in comparison to the "pettiest and meanest conditions" that she had experienced in "magnificent France and Belgium." But life in Brussels was not entirely bleak, for within two years it became the birthplace of their second daughter, &▶ **Laura Marx**, and first son, Edgar.

In Belgium, the Marxes were joined by **Helena Demuth**, known within the family by the nickname "Lenchen." Demuth had been a von Westphalen family servant ever since her childhood and was sent to Jenny by her mother when she learned of the difficult conditions they faced in Brussels. Six years younger than Jenny, Demuth took care of the cleaning, cooking, baking and washing in the Marx household for nearly 40 years. Since Demuth took on most of the housework, Jenny was able to spend hours copying letters and manuscripts from Karl's illegible handwriting for publication.

In Belgium, Jenny took part in the discussions between her husband and Engels which led to the *German Ideology,* and she acted as the Brussels secretary for the Communist correspondence committees which they set up after their return from England. Jenny and Karl were very poor and often sick, but they welcomed in the new year of 1848 at a New Year's Eve celebration of the German Workers' Union. A report in the *Deutsche Brüsseler Zeitung* noted, "The banquet was followed by music and then by a dramatic performance, where Madame Dr. Marx showed a brilliant talent for recitation. It is very impressive to watch exceptionally gifted ladies trying to improve the intellectual faculties of the proletariat."

The year 1848 proved momentous. The year before, Karl had agreed to join the League of the Just, a German exile group centered in

London, so long as it would agree to change its name to the Communist League. He and Engels began to work on the group's declaration, the now-renowned *Communist Manifesto,* which Jenny copied—putting the finishing touches on it in late January 1848.

The year was also a time when the aspirations of exiled revolutionaries became material. In late February, news reached Brussels of revolution in France. Karl began to make preparations to return to live under the new government, but he was caught up in the wave of reaction which swept France's neighbors. On March 4, he was arrested by the police on charges that he gave money to exiled German workers for the purchase of weapons. In autobiographical notes which she wrote in 1865 but never published, Jenny recalled that after the police took Karl away:

> I hurried after him in terrible anxiety and went to influential men to find out what the matter was. I rushed from house to house in the dark. Suddenly I was seized by a guard, arrested and thrown into a dark prison. It was where beggars without a home, vagabonds and wretched fallen women were detained. I was thrust into a dark cell. As I entered, sobbing, an unhappy companion in misery offered to share her place with me: it was a hard plank bed. I lay down on it. When morning broke . . . I was taken to the interrogating magistrate. After a two hours' questioning, during which they got little out of me, I was led to a carriage by gendarmes and towards evening I got back to my three poor little children.

Arrest and imprisonment were not the only indignity that Jenny Marx was forced to endure. Once again her husband was expelled from a European nation, this time at the instigation of Leopold I, king of the Belgians. As a result of the political shift in France, however, Paris was willing to accept Karl Marx again. Jenny and the children returned to the city they had left three years earlier.

In Paris, where barricades still remained in the streets, the family stayed in a hotel. Karl Marx and Engels quickly formed the German Workers Party, which advocated a "red Republic" as well as political freedom in Germany. Jenny Marx served as the party's secretary. The revolutionary feeling which captivated Europe in 1848 seemed to revive radical prospects in Germany, and Karl traveled to Cologne to see about launching a new paper. When the *Neue Rheinische Zeitung* was launched three months later in June 1848, Jenny and the children joined him in Cologne.

For nearly a year, the paper and the party kept both Marxes extremely busy, but as the fer-

Marx, Laura (1845–1911)

Daughter of Karl and Jenny Marx. Name variations: Laura Lafargue. Born Jenny Laura Marx (all of the Marx daughters carried the name "Jenny") in 1845; committed suicide in 1911 (her husband died by his own hand that same year); daughter of *Jenny von Westphalen Marx (1814–1881) and Karl Marx (1818–1883, philosopher, economist and sociologist who wrote* The Communist Manifesto*); sister of Jenny Marx (1844–1883) and *Eleanor Marx-Aveling (1855–1898); married Paul Lafargue (1842–1911); children: three, all died as infants.*

vor of 1848 began to wane, reaction again took hold. In May 1849, Karl Marx was expelled from Germany. Having been hounded out of three countries on the Continent, the Marxes decided to travel across the Channel to London, then a magnet for revolutionary exiles from across Europe, where they would stay for the rest of their lives.

The Marxes spent their first seven years in England in severe deprivation, with death around every corner. They rented a two-room attic on Dean Street that sometimes had to house eight people—Jenny, Karl, Helena, a nurse and four children. But the mood was more of loss than overcrowdedness.

In November 1849, Jenny gave birth to her fourth child, Heinrich ("Foxchen"), who suffered cramps and died in infancy. In March 1851, Jenny gave birth to Franziska, a girl, who died a year later of bronchitis. The family was so poor that it had to borrow money to pay for Franziska's burial. On January 16, 1855, Jenny gave birth to a sixth child, Eleanor ("Tussy"), who would outlive her parents. But a few months later, the Marxes' young son Edgar, who had struggled for a year with abdominal ailments, died at age seven. The loss of their son was particularly devastating to the Marxes. Jenny wrote that death had snatched from her "the best loved being I had in the world, my dear, only Edgar. It is a pain that never heals, never becomes a scar— because neither wound nor scar will heal." In 1856, Jenny's mother, then 80 and partially paralyzed, died when Jenny returned to Trier on a visit. Yet that was not her last lament of the decade. She also lost her seventh and last child, a girl born on July 6, 1857, who died before she could be given a name. Jenny, overtaken by melancholy, never recovered completely.

Despite the omnipresence of death, along with cold, illness and malnourishment (sometimes they had to live for a week or more on potatoes alone), the Marx family in the 1850s did manage to find some pleasures. They took picnics on their Sunday excursions to the open, half-wild grounds of Hampstead Heath. Karl also loved children, and he would let his daughters Jenny, Laura and Eleanor romp on his back, even as he worked at his desk. When he began to serve as a European correspondent for the *New York Herald Tribune,* moreover, the regular source of income led to some improvement in the family's conditions.

Jenny copied every *Herald Tribune* article and all of Karl Marx's pamphlets, but, for her, such labor was far from drudgery. "The memory of the days I spent in his study copying his scrawly articles," she recalled in 1865, "is among the happiest of my life." Karl's intellectual virtuosity, as manifested in such epochal works as the *Communist Manifesto* and *Capital,* was unexcelled by any radical of his day, including his famous friend and collaborator, Engels.

In the middle of the 1860s, a small family inheritance enabled the Marx family to move out of the desolate apartment where they had spent seven depressing years and to occupy a modest house. Even though Engels assisted the family with regular gifts, the Marxes barely made a living, however.

The damage to Jenny's spirit from the loss of her children and repeated political setbacks, including the defeat of the Paris Commune in 1871, led the pace of her participation in the socialist movement to slacken. She did, however, continue to assist in such projects as the defense of Communists put on trial in Cologne in 1852 and in the coordination of the International Working Men's Association.

Some of her responsibilities were shouldered by her young daughters. "Today little Jenny is copying the article in my place," she wrote mirthfully to Engels on December 24, 1859. "I believe my daughters will soon put me out of business, and I shall then come on the register of those 'entitled to assistance.' A pity that there's no prospect of getting a pension after my long years of secretarial duties." Yet it was Jenny Marx who copied the entirety of Karl Marx's magnum opus, *Capital,* finishing the manuscript in 1867.

Jenny Marx had a reputation for elegance and wit that seems to have been unaffected by her own trials. Paul Lafargue recalled that she "entertained working people in their working clothes in her house and at her table with the same politeness and consideration as if they had been dukes or princes." But she dispensed with elaborate custom, especially when it came to herself. In an 1867 letter to her comrade Ludwig Kugelmann, she asked, "Why do you address me so formally, even using the term 'gracious,' for me, who am such an old campaigner, such a hoary head in the movement, such an honest fellow-traveler and fellow-tramp?"

Eleanor Marx-Aveling later said that her parents' love derived from their humor as much as from their dedication to the workers' cause. She recalled many occasions when she saw them "laugh till tears ran down their checks, and even those inclined to be shocked at such awful levity could not choose but laugh with them."

Jenny Marx lived to see each of her eldest daughters marry a French socialist, soon thereafter making her a grandmother. In April 1868, Laura married Paul Lafargue (1842–1911), with whom she had three children who died as infants. But in October 1872, Jennychen married Charles Longuet (1839–1903), with whom she had six children, four of whom lived long into the 20th century. Most of Jenny Marx's final years, however, were spent in bed with liver cancer, nursed by her youngest daughter Eleanor and her faithful housekeeper Helena Demuth. When she died at the age of 67 on December 2, 1881, her last words were, "Karl, my strength is gone." With her passing, his strength also left. The untimely death of their daughter Jennychen in 1883 was the final blow. Within a month, Karl Marx succumbed to the many maladies that had long afflicted him.

Jenny and Karl Marx were buried together, along with their servant Helena Demuth and one of their grandsons, in London's Highgate Cemetery. At her graveside, Friedrich Engels delivered the eulogy for Jenny Marx:

> What such a woman with such clear and critical intellect, with such political tact, with such passionate surges of character, with such capacity for self-sacrifice, has done in the revolutionary movement, that has not been pushed forward into publicity, that is not registered in the columns of the periodical press. That is only known to those who lived near her. But that I know, we shall often miss her bold and prudent counsels, bold without brag, prudent without sacrifice of honor.

SOURCES:

Marx, Jenny. "Short Sketch of an Eventful Life," in *Marx and Engels Through the Eyes of Their Contemporaries.* Moscow: Progress Publishers, 1972.

Marx, Karl, and Friedrich Engels. *Collected Works.* 50 vols. NY: International, 1975. Appendices to the volumes of correspondence include many letters by Jenny Marx.

Peters, H.F. *Red Jenny: A Life with Karl Marx*. London: Allen and Unwin, 1986.

SUGGESTED READING:

Blumenberg, Werner. *Karl Marx*. London: New Left Books, 1972.

McClellan, David. *Karl Marx: His Life and Thought*. NY: Harper and Row, 1973.

Christopher Phelps,
Editorial Director at *Monthly Review Press* in New York City

Marx-Aveling, Eleanor (1855–1898)

Youngest daughter of Karl Marx, who worked much of her adult life to fulfill the vision of her father and to create a labor party in England. Pronunciation: Marks. Born Jenny Julia Eleanor Marx (all of the Marx daughters carried the name "Jenny") on January 16, 1855, in London, England; committed suicide at age 42, on March 31, 1898, in London; daughter of Karl Marx (1818–1883), the founder of Marxism, and Jenny von Westphalen Marx (1814–1881); sister of Jenny Marx (1844–1883) and Laura Marx (1845–1911); tutored by her father and by Friedrich Engels; took courses at the South Hampstead College for Ladies; not legally married, but maintained long-term household and "free marriage" with the socialist and freethinker Edward Aveling.

Questioned by French authorities during visit to France (1870); accepted teaching job at Brighton (1873); engaged to Hippolyte Prosper Olivier Lissagaray (1882); joined W.M. Hyndman's Democratic Federation and seceded from the organization a short time later (1884); toured the U.S. with Edward Aveling (1886–87); helped organize May Day demonstration for an eight-hour working day (1890); helped found the Independent Labour Party and was elected to the party's first executive committee (1893); rejoined the Democratic Federation (1895); was made financially independent from provision in Engels' will (1895).

Selected works: The Factory Hell *(1885); (with Edward Aveling)* The Woman Question *(1886); (translation) Hippolyte Prosper Olivier Lissagaray's* History of the Commune of 1871 *(1886); (translation) Gustav Flaubert's* Madame Bovary *(1886); (translation) Georgi Plekhanov's* Anarchism and Socialism *(1887); (translation) Henrik Ibsen's* An Enemy of Society *(1888);* The Working Class Movement in England: A Brief Historical Sketch *(1896); (edited) Karl Marx's* Value, Price, and Profit *(1898).*

Although Eleanor Marx-Aveling was born into a famous family, she was unaware that there was anything unusual about her childhood. Her mother ***Jenny von Westphalen Marx**, who was born into a German noble family, was married to the most famous socialist and one of the most famous writers of the 19th century, Karl Marx. While Marx-Aveling was growing to adulthood, her father was producing his epochal book *Capital*. Despite his future fame, Karl Marx's work was made possible only by the sacrifices of a family who lived on the economic edge, moving from place to place as events and finances dictated.

The Marxes had left their native Germany in 1849, during a period of monarchical reaction following the failed revolutions of 1848. They settled in England where, penniless and without many friends, they were evicted from lodgings in Chelsea and were forced to settle into a two-room apartment in the Soho section of London. In this crowded flat lived Karl and Jenny, their daughters **Jenny** and ✥➤ **Laura Marx**; their son, Edgar; a devoted housekeeper, **Helena Demuth**, affectionately known as Lenchen; and, after she was born, Eleanor.

Although Karl Marx was paid for work as a European reporter for the *New York Herald Tribune*, money was especially short during the economic downturn of the late 1850s. Karl's income as a newspaper correspondent was further reduced in 1861, when the New York newspaper decided to give less emphasis to its European coverage and more attention to the American Civil War. The next year, Karl stopped writing for the newspaper entirely.

The family was forced to borrow from friends and relatives constantly, and Jenny Marx, who frequently had to visit pawn shops to sell family silver and other valuables, developed physical symptoms from the emotional strain; at one point, she went partially deaf. During the harsh winter of 1858, only monetary gifts from Karl Marx's collaborator Friedrich Engels—who had returned to the hated cotton business of his father—kept the family afloat.

By the time Eleanor was born, the family had already lost a son, Heinrich (1849–1850), and a daughter, Franziska (1851–1852). The only surviving son, Edgar (1846–1855), was already showing symptoms of a disease, generally thought to have been a form of tuberculosis, which would take his life at age eight, some three months after Eleanor was born. Even Marx-Aveling was sickly—so sick that the family feared she might die until a doctor advised putting her on a special diet until she was five. When Eleanor subsequently developed whooping cough, she was given so much attention by

✥➤ *Marx, Laura.* See *Marx, Jenny von Westphalen* for sidebar.

the family, she later recalled, that "the whole family was my bond slaves."

Marx-Aveling seemed unaware that she had been born into near poverty, partly because by the time she was 21 months old, the family could afford to move to larger quarters. It was one of several moves to more "appropriate" lodgings as the older daughters approached marriageable age. Eleanor was keenly aware, however, that she was the only member of the Marx family born in England, and thus the only member of the family who was a British subject. While her older sisters maintained ties with friends on the European Continent, her friendships, and career, were centered in England.

Wilhelm Liebknecht, a fellow socialist and family friend, described the very young Marx-Aveling as "a merry little thing, round as a ball," who was also "restless . . . wanting to know everything." Although her father joked to associates that she was a sexual mistake, both Karl and the rest of the family, after the loss of two children, lavished affection on Eleanor. Her two sisters were so much older that she was raised almost as an only child, and a special bond developed between father and daughter.

Among the three daughters of Karl Marx, Eleanor alone grew into a fighter dedicated to a cause, a brave, ingenious, never tiring champion of Socialism.

—Chushichi Tsuzuki

Karl, who called Eleanor "Tussy," read to her and her sisters from Homer, the German Niebelungen stories, the *Arabian Knights*, and Miguel de Cervantes' *Don Quixote*. He carried her on his shoulders around their home and arranged flowers in her hair as he read stories to her. The entire family also admired Shakespeare's plays, sometimes performing improvised scenes as a group. By the time she was four, Eleanor could memorize passages from Shakespeare; her favorite was a soliloquy of Richard III. When she was six, her father presented her with her first novel as a birthday present. Karl took her to a Catholic church to listen to music, but he also described Christianity in "historical materialist" terms, as the story of an impoverished carpenter who was killed by the rich.

Like the rest of the family, Marx-Aveling called him by his nickname "Moor" (a name which referred to his dark complexion). She considered her father a friend, and wrote in a letter, "I am getting on very well with chess. I nearly always win, and when I do papa is *so* cross." The

bond between the two was so close that Karl Marx once said, "Tussy is me."

Eleanor seemed to flourish under her father's tutelage and from lessons at South Hampstead College for Ladies, which her sisters also attended. By age 14, she spoke German, although she could not write the language particularly well. She could also speak French. She began to develop an interest in politics, showing particular concern for the cause of the North in the American Civil War. She even wrote some letters of advice to Abraham Lincoln, which were apparently never mailed.

Engels served as a tutor as well. Before she visited Ireland in 1869, Eleanor stopped for a time in Manchester, where Engels had her read from the German writer Johann Wolfgang von Goethe, including some Serbian folksongs translated by Goethe.

A trip with her sister Jenny to the European Continent in 1870, in order to visit their sister Laura and her husband Paul Lafargue, became a lesson in politics. A supporter of the Paris Commune, Lafargue traveled with Laura into southern France after the Commune failed. Eventually, they sought safety in northern Spain. Eleanor and Jenny visited them there but were detained by French police, who suspected them of helping Communards, when they crossed the border back into France. Despite Eleanor's insistence ("You have no right to come near a British subject"), she and her sister were questioned by French government agents. The French agent who questioned Eleanor deceived her, claiming that Jenny had signed an admission of guilt. Proclaiming that the French police had told her the "most dreadful lies," Eleanor concluded that her father was correct to condemn European governments as he did.

As she reached adulthood, Marx-Aveling, while embracing her father's political outlook, began to assert how own independence. In 1873, she accepted a teaching position in a boarding school for ladies in Brighton. She was encouraged by her mother, who wrote her that work was one of the few things that could help with the "sorrow and cares of present-day society." Her parents were distressed, however, that Eleanor arranged for her own lodgings and declined to stay with family friends in Brighton.

When her father hosted a party for exiled Communards at their family home, Eleanor met Hippolyte Prosper Olivier Lissagaray. Drawn to the flamboyant Frenchman, she soon announced to her parents that she was engaged to Lissagaray;

Eleanor Marx-Aveling

Karl was furious. Not only was Lissagaray much older—34—but his dashing image and his reputation as a lover made him unsuitable as a husband. His other daughters were involved with Frenchmen, declared Karl, that was enough.

He forbade Eleanor to see Lissagaray, a decision that left her nervous and withdrawn, with little appetite. Karl twice traveled with her to a spa in Bohemia in search of a cure. Finally, he relented, declaring that Eleanor was allowed to see Lissagaray but that he might not, under any circumstances, call at the Marx house. The "en-

gagement" continued. When Lissagaray published a *History of the Commune of 1871*, and Eleanor insisted that she wanted to translate it into English, Karl gave her advice on particular sections.

By 1877, Marx-Aveling was working in the British Museum on a variety of projects for organizations such as the Chaucer and the Shakespeare societies. While there, she met George Bernard Shaw, who encouraged her to join the New Shakespeare Society. Shaw reported that he was impressed by her "verve and wonderful voice" and considered her "unusually vivacious." She began to appear in productions of plays at the Dilettante Theater. Shaw commented on the rift between Eleanor and her father, observing that Karl treated his daughter with an "indulgent affection" of the kind that one gives to a "willful child." Eleanor felt guilty when her mother died in 1881, saying that her mother had thought her to be cold and unfeeling. Eleanor became a nurse to her father as he experienced increasing bouts of poor health, although Karl told her: "I would not for anything in the world imagine that a child should sacrifice herself . . . as a nurse for an old man." Father and daughter struck a deal. Eleanor would agree to stop seeing Lissagaray—the engagement would be "at an end"—and Karl would help Eleanor finance acting lessons.

When her sister Jenny died in early 1883, and her father followed a short time later, Eleanor's interest in the theater became, for a time, the central part of her life. Her stage work brought her in contact with Edward Aveling, a socialist and freethinker who was unpopular in many British political and literary circles. Shaw described Edward as not being a handsome man, saying that although his voice had "beauty of tone," in looks he had "every aesthetic disadvantage." More damaging, Shaw added, was the widespread belief that Edward had character flaws so serious that "he would have been . . . interesting in a zoological museum as a reptile but [was] impossible as a man."

Many English socialists refused to attend political gatherings if Edward Aveling was present. When American anarchists were convicted of the deaths of police in the Chicago Square Haymarket riots of 1888, Edward collected money to send a telegram of protest to the U.S. president. The telegram was never sent; it was generally believed that he had simply pocketed the money. Yet Eleanor's relationship with Edward developed rapidly. As early as 1884, she was writing that she and Edward were "fond of each other" and intended to live together, or to "set up" with each other, in her words. She reported that she felt more independent and "purposeful" when she was with him, and that they had been married "without benefit of authorities." Edward already had a legal wife but told Eleanor he could not win his freedom from her.

The arrangement placed her in an awkward position, as she gradually came to realize. While couples might cause no waves in Victorian society as long as their relationship was discreet, flaunting such a relationship was frowned upon.

Marx-Aveling even told the headmistress of the school where she was teaching about the arrangement, knowing she would be fired, but believing that it was the correct thing for a modern woman to do.

Eleanor did all she could to help Edward establish himself as a playwright, urging influential friends to read his plays. In 1886, she participated, with Edward, in a group reading from Ibsen's *A Doll's House*. Among the other participants was Shaw. When Edward's play *By the Sea* was performed in 1887, she played the heroine, but to very tepid reviews; one critic said that her lines "were prettily spoken" but questioned her acting ability, while another complained that she was almost inaudible. Her involvement in the literary world did bring a commission from George Moore, which she eagerly sought, to translate into English Gustav Flaubert's *Madame Bovary*. She came to identify with the heroine of the novel, writing: "This strong woman feels that there must be some place in the world, there must be something to do—and she dreams." Her version remained the only English translation for a number of years, and its success resulted in her translation of Ibsen's play *An Enemy of Society* (later entitled *An Enemy of the People*).

In 1886, the German socialist Wilhelm Liebknecht organized a speaking tour of the United States to raise money for the German Social Democratic Party, then the major Marxist party in Germany. At the time, the party was under legal restrictions engineered by the German chancellor Otto von Bismarck. Liebknecht invited Eleanor and Edward to participate in the tour, which was being paid for by its U.S. sponsor, the Socialist Labor Party.

When Edward submitted a list of expenses at the end of their tour, a New York newspaper reported that the bills were so extravagant that some Socialist Labor Party leaders in the United States had come to regard Edward as a "swindler." It was reported that he had billed the party for some $1,300, including a two-day wine bill and a $42 charge for a hotel (an exorbitant amount at the time), $100 for theater tickets, as well as bills for corsages, cigars, and cigarettes. Edward replied to much of the charges—he had, he pointed out, had to pay the expenses of Liebknecht and his daughter during their visit to Boston—but the "swindler" charge was widely disseminated in English political and literary circles.

One reason that Eleanor was attracted to Edward appears to have been that he was a potential ally in promoting labor activism. When she visited London's East End, she had been appalled at the sights of children looking for bread, children she described as "like skeletons." She hoped that Edward might help her create a range of socialist or labor organizations in England that would prepare the way for the acceptance of her father's ideas. Comforted by her father's memory, she took flowers to her parents' graves every spring. She continued to visit in the home of her father's collaborator and benefactor, Engels, who was working to prepare further volumes of *Capital*. In fact, Engels was an emphatic defender of Edward Aveling.

Eleanor and Edward worked together in preparing for a Second International, and when they organized a May Day celebration in London in 1889, they were as shocked as many reporters by the sizeable crowd. They also founded the Legal Eight Hour and International Labor League. They worked in several unions and participated in efforts to create labor candidates for seats in Parliament, although they were largely unsuccessful in convincing labor unions to cooperate. As part of this effort, they cooperated, for a time, with the Democratic Federation of the prominent English Marxist H.M. Hyndman. They contributed regular articles on the working-class movement to the *Workingmen's Times* and tried, largely unsuccessfully, to convert the radical workingmen's clubs to the cause of Marxism.

Together, they also authored a book on the rights of women, *The Woman Question*. Marx-Aveling believed that women would forever be assigned the most menial jobs for the lowest pay and that since women felt the full effects of inequality between the sexes, they must fight for equality. When she spoke in 1891 at a demonstration for the eight-hour work day, she said that her "great object" was to create women's labor unions "as strong as men's."

The year 1887 proved to be particularly trying. Marx-Aveling participated in a demonstration in Trafalgar Square and once again experienced the dark side of political authority. When the demonstration was broken up by police on horseback and foot, Eleanor reported, "I have never seen anything like the brutality of the police. My cloak and hat were torn to shreds; I have had a blow across my arm from the policeman's baton, and a blow on the head knocked me down."

During the year 1887, Edward also became more distant. He was often away on trips, and Eleanor acknowledged that she often felt "very lonely." As well, the couple was short of money. "We have money troubles enough to worry an ordinary man or woman into the grave," she wrote. After an apparent suicide attempt from an opium overdose, she reportedly had to be fed strong coffee and walked repeatedly around her room by friends.

As Edward was less and less at home, Eleanor began to build her own career as a labor organizer. She was elected to the executive board of the gasworkers union. She kept records and accounting books for the union, and it was reported that she had taught the head of the union to read and write. She helped organize a strike by the union in 1889. Increasingly, she proved to be an adept public speaker. When a self-proclaimed "radical" interrupted one of her speeches to complain that she did not know what Karl Marx meant by "social democracy," Eleanor replied, "Heaven save Karl Marx from his friends."

Marx-Aveling found a special joy in speaking to unassimilated Jewish workers in the East End of London. She apparently became the only member of her immediate family to feel an identity and empathy with them. While Karl Marx, whose Jewish father had been forced to convert for political reasons, had seemed to believe that emancipation from bourgeois society meant separation from Judaism, Eleanor told friends, "My happiest moments are when I am in the east end among the Jewish work people."

In 1893, Eleanor had to battle, without help from Edward, to retain some control over the disposition of her father's papers. After Karl Marx's death, his papers had been given to Friedrich Engels, to help in preparing additional volumes of *Capital*. Engels had promised Eleanor and her sister Laura that the Marx papers would be returned to them, and Eleanor planned to use some of the papers to write a biography of her father. However, among Engels' close friends were two leading continental Marxists, the Austrian couple, Karl and *Luise Kautsky. When Karl Kautsky left Luise for another woman, Luise stayed behind and became part of the Engels household. Apparently at the urging of some leaders of the German Marxist Social Democratic Party, such as August Bebel, Luise Kautsky appeared to begin maneuvering to secure control of both the Marx and Engels papers for the German party.

Eleanor became suspicious when Luise warned her that Helena Demuth—the former housekeeper for the Marx family who now worked for Engels—might take the papers. Luise asked Eleanor to sign a document giving control of the papers to her. Eleanor also learned that Luise was making malevolent comments about her—reportedly telling Engels that "no society" could tolerate a "friendship" between a man and a woman such as Eleanor and Edward's. There were also reports that Luise was telling Engels that the Marx papers were "rightfully" his, and that the Marx daughters were trying to steal his "legacy." (It was about this time that Demuth claimed that her son had been fathered by Karl Marx; Eleanor believed that Luise Kautsky was somehow behind the timing of the allegation.)

Alarmed, Eleanor sent a letter to Engels expressing her outrage. "I should be blind indeed if I had not seen the efforts to set you against us," she wrote. Her pleas had some effect on Engels, who assured her that her father's papers would be returned to her family. But when Engels died in 1895, only a portion of the Marx papers were willed to Marx-Aveling. His will did, however, make a sizable monetary bequest to Eleanor. The bequest made Marx-Aveling financially secure for the first time in her life. Eleanor and Edward used the money to remodel their home, which they called "The Den." (Edward's wife had died in 1892.)

When Eleanor confronted Edward in 1897 with the rumor that he was having an affair with a woman named **Eva Frye**, he took everything in the house that could be sold and walked out, leaving no forwarding address. Eventually he returned to plead that he needed money to "free" himself from Frye. Eleanor gave him part of her bequest from Engels, and he promised that from now on their love would be "pure." When Edward needed a serious operation because of complications from an abscess in his side, she rented a room near the hospital so that she could be near him during his recovery. In June 1897, Edward Aveling married Eva Frye while Eleanor was attending a congress of a miners' union. He listed his own name on the marriage certificate as "Alec Nelson" and the name of his father as "Thomas William Nelson." Eleanor learned of the marriage from an anonymous letter sent to her on March 31, 1898. In a stormy scene with Edward, she threatened suicide.

Despite testimony at an inquest after her death, it is still unclear how he reacted. Some friends of Eleanor's believed that Edward must have promised to commit suicide with her. The maid, who was sent to a nearby drug store, testified that she was given a note asking the druggist for chloroform and prussic acid "for a dog." Although the maid said that Eleanor gave her the note, she also said that Eleanor and Edward's handwriting were similar enough that she was not certain who had written the note.

When the maid returned to "The Den," she brought from the druggist a book that purchasers of poison were required to sign. She gave the book to Eleanor, who took it into a nearby room, where Edward was present. When Eleanor returned the book to the maid, the signature in the book read "E.M. Aveling." A short time later, Edward left the house. Eleanor then took a bath, dressed herself in white, and went to bed. She left a note to Edward which said, "Dear, it will soon be all over now. My last word to you is the same that I have said during these long sad years—love." The maid later found her barely alive, but she was dead by the time a physician arrived. She was 42 years old.

At the subsequent inquest, Edward testified that Eleanor had threatened to commit suicide "several times." The coroner's jury returned a verdict of "suicide" in the midst of "temporary insanity." Yet Eleanor's friends continued, for a long time, to hold Edward responsible for her death, either directly or indirectly.

Her body was cremated, and Eleanor Marx-Aveling's ashes found no permanent resting place for many years. Her urn was kept initially in the offices of the Social Democratic Federation, later the headquarters of the British Communist Party. When the party offices were raided by police in 1921, the police kept the urn for a time. It was later housed in the Karl Marx Memorial Library in Clerkenwell Green. In 1956, it was given a final resting place in Highgate Cemetery, next to the graves of her mother and father.

SOURCES:
Florence, Ronald. *Marx's Daughters*. NY: The Dial Press, 1975.
Knapp, Yvonne. *Eleanor Marx*. Volume I: *Family Life (1855–1887)* and Volume II: *The Crowded Years (1884–1898)*. London: Lawrence and Wishart, 1972 and 1976.
Tsuzuki, Chushichi. *The Life of Eleanor Marx: 1855–1898: A Socialist Tragedy*. Oxford: Clarendon Press, 1967.

SUGGESTED READING:
Dutt, R.P. *The Internationale*. London: Lawrence and Wishard, 1969.
Hastings, Michael. *Tussy is Me: A Novel of Fact*. NY: Delacorte Press, 1977.
Hulse, James W. *Revolutionists in London*. Oxford: Clarendon Press, 1970.
Pelling, Henry. *The Origins of the Labour Party, 1880–1900*. Oxford: Clarendon Press, 1965.

COLLECTIONS:
After Eleanor Marx-Aveling's death, her papers, and the papers of her father and Engels, were divided between the International Institute of Social History in Amsterdam, the Netherlands (which obtained the archives of the German Social Democratic Party when party leaders were driven into exile in the 1930s); the Institute of Marxism-Leninism in

Moscow; and the archives of the Bottigelli family, in Paris, France. Materials regarding Marx-Aveling are also contained in the British Library of Political and Economic Science; the British Museum's Additional Manuscripts division; and the Ohara Institute for Social Research at Hosei University in Tokyo. The Dean street house in London in which the Marxes lived is still standing and bears a commemorative plaque to Karl Marx.

Niles R. Holt,
Professor of History,
Illinois State University, Normal, Illinois

Marx, Laura (1845–1911).
See Marx, Jenny von Westphalen for sidebar.

Mary.
Variant of Maria.

Mary (1278–1332)
Princess and nun of Amesbury. Name variations: Mary Plantagenet. Born on March 11, 1278, in Windsor, Berkshire, England; died in 1332 in Amesbury, Wiltshire, England; daughter of Edward I Longshanks, king of England (r. 1272–1307), and Eleanor of Castile (1241–1290).

Because Edward I Longshanks, king of England, and *Eleanor of Castile had 16 children, the Catholic Church pressured Eleanor to offer one of her daughters to God. Eleanor did not welcome the Church's suggestion but reluctantly capitulated. In August 1285, seven-year-old Princess Mary entered a nunnery at Amesbury where her fraternal grandmother, the dowager-queen *Eleanor of Provence (c. 1222–1291), acted as her guardian. Mary's life was far from secluded; she traveled and was often at court. After her death in 1332, Nicholas Trevet, a Dominican friar, composed an Anglo-Norman chronicle for her which became a principal source for Chaucer's *Man of Law's Tale.*

Mary (1531–1581)
*Duchess of Julich-Cleves-Berg. Name variations: Maria. Born on May 15, 1531, in Prague; died on December 11, 1581, at Hambach Castle; daughter of *Anna of Bohemia and Hungary (1503–1547) and Ferdinand I, Holy Roman emperor (r. 1558–1564); married William V of Cleves, duke of Juliers (r. 1539–1592); children: *Maria Eleanora (who married Albert Frederick, duke of Prussia); John William, duke of Cleves (r. 1592–1609); Anna (who married Philip Louis, count Palatine of Neuberg); *Magdalena (who married John I, count Palatine of Zweibrucken).*

Mary (1776–1857)
*Duchess of Gloucester. Name variations: Mary Guelph; Mary Hanover; Princess Mary. Born on April 25, 1776, at St. James's Palace, London, England; died on April 30, 1857; buried at St. George's Chapel, Windsor, England; fourth daughter of George III, king of England, and *Charlotte of Mecklenburg-Strelitz; married William, 2nd duke of Gloucester and Edinburgh, on July 22, 1816.*

Mary (1897–1965)
*Princess Royal of England and countess of Harewood. Name variations: Mary Lascelles. Born Victoria Alexandria Alice Mary on April 25, 1897, in York Cottage, Sandringham, Norfolk, England; died on March 28, 1965, in Harewood House, Leeds, West Yorkshire, England; daughter of George V, king of England (r. 1910–1936), and *Mary of Teck (1867–1953); married Henry Lascelles (1882–1947), 6th earl of Harewood, on February 28, 1922; children: George Lascelles, 7th earl of Harewood (b. 1923); Gerald Lascelles (b. 1924).*

Mary (b. 1964)
*Rumanian princess. Name variations: Mary Hohenzollern. Born on July 13, 1964, in Copenhagen, Denmark; daughter of Michael I (b. 1921), king of Rumania (r. 1927–1930, 1940–1947), and *Anne of Bourbon-Parma (b. 1923).*

Mary, Countess of Boulogne (d. 1182).
See Marie of Boulogne.

Mary, Countess of Falconberg or Fauconberg (1636–1712).
See Cromwell, Mary.

Mary, Duchess of Brittany (1344–1362).
See Philippa of Hainault for sidebar.

Mary, Queen (1867–1953).
See Mary of Teck.

Mary, Queen of Scots (1542–1587).
See Mary Stuart.

Mary, Saint (20 BCE–40 CE).
See Mary the Virgin.

Mary I (1516–1558)
Queen of England, 1553–1558, who restored Roman Catholicism as the established religion of England and was popularly known as Bloody Mary. Name

variations: Bloody Mary; Mary Tudor; Mary the Catholic. Born Mary Tudor at Greenwich Palace, near London, England, on February 18, 1516; died at St. James's Palace in London, on November 17, 1558; buried in Westminster Abbey, London; daughter of Henry VIII, king of England (r. 1509–1547), and the Spanish princess Catherine of Aragon (1485–1536, youngest child of Ferdinand of Aragon and *Isabella I [1451–1504]); ascended throne, July 1553; married Philip II, king of Spain (r. 1556–1598), and king of Portugal as Philip I (r. 1580–1598), on July 25, 1554; no children.

❦▶
Catherine of Aragon. *See Six Wives of Henry VIII.*

The birth of a healthy girl to King Henry VIII and ❦ **Catherine of Aragon** on February 18, 1516, was greeted in England with more than usual joy. Since 1510, the queen had tried and repeatedly failed to produce a viable child, yet it now seemed that the Tudor dynasty might after all be able to secure domestic peace and its own future by producing a direct heir to the throne. Mary's sex prompted some worry because there existed no historical precedent for a queen regnant and, more generally, the prospect of female rulership conflicted with established ideas about male precedence. But Henry interpreted his daughter's birth as a harbinger of more fruitful times, hoping that "by God's grace the sons will follow." They did not. As a result, Mary passed from childhood into adolescence under a darkening cloud as her father became increasingly desperate to beget a legitimate male heir to the throne. The disfavor, isolation, and even danger into which Mary was plunged during these formative years left indelible scars on her physical and mental constitution from which she never recovered and which limited her effectiveness once she succeeded to the throne as a prematurely middle-aged woman of 37.

In contrast to her later adversities, Mary's early years appear to have been happy ones. More than most royal children, she enjoyed a great deal of contact with her parents, who indulged her by arranging special Christmas entertainments for their daughter, much to her delight. As the heir apparent, Mary was proudly shown off at court to wide acclaim. A foreign delegation to England in 1520 remarked favorably upon Mary's "most goodly countenance" and "her skill in playing on the virginals, her tender age considered." In addition to music, the young princess studied, under her mother's careful direction, the fashionable new humanistic curriculum. Catherine of Aragon was herself a highly educated woman who greatly admired Erasmus and patronized a number of scholars,

among them the famous Juan Luis Vives who in 1523 wrote a treatise on the education of women, *De institutione Christianae feminae*, specifically for Mary. It was also Catherine who selected Mary's first tutor, Thomas Linacre, who wrote a Latin grammar for Mary's use in which, perhaps wistfully, he praised her love of learning. The truth is that Mary, though exposed to a fine education including the classics as well as modern authors like Erasmus and Thomas More, proved to be an indifferent pupil. She learned Latin and French but failed to acquire more than a smattering of Greek and Italian, and strangely never learned to speak or write Spanish, her mother's native tongue. She seems not to have had much taste for theology either, preferring to direct her religious energies into an emotionally fervent but unintellectualized piety. She reportedly studied astronomy, geography, and mathematics, but tellingly spent most of her time in needlework. Even as an adult, her privy purse expenses reveal much alms-giving but no patronage of scholarship or the arts save music.

Mary's marriage became the subject of diplomatic negotiation while she was still an infant since, as the heir apparent, her hand was a diplomatic prize that betokened political alliance and ultimately promised dynastic union. In 1518, she was betrothed to the dauphin, but when relations with France soured the following year Henry began to broker a marriage with Catherine's nephew, the Holy Roman Emperor Charles V, who was 16 years Mary's senior. Terms for the marriage were settled in 1522, but Mary's tender age precluded their enactment for another eight years, a length of time that rendered the agreement nugatory. Upon Charles' marriage to ***Isabella of Portugal** (1503–1539) in 1526, Henry VIII explored the possibility of marrying his daughter to the dissipated king of France, Francis I, a man older than himself. There were also rumors of a Scottish match, but like all of these marital prospects nothing resulted.

In any case, by the mid-1520s, Henry's increasing anxiety about the lack of a male heir had begun to affect Mary's political position and her marriageability. In 1525, she moved to Ludlow Castle and began nominally to exercise her rights and powers as princess of Wales, although she was not formally invested with that title. Such a move was entirely in keeping with the training of a royal heir, but Mary's absence from court also enabled Henry to showcase his bastard son, Henry Fitzroy, two years younger than Mary, whom Henry created duke of Richmond and even considered making heir to the throne. Catherine bitterly resented these indignities, but the fact that she was now 40 and past her child-bearing years seriously reduced her political clout. Although Mary's separation from her beloved mother was difficult, she at least was spared the pain of watching her mother's estrangement from Henry as he evolved a plan to annul his marriage to Catherine so that he could remarry. By the summer of 1528, Mary must have become aware of her mother's disgrace, which Catherine bore with an uncompromising stoicism that Mary would later emulate during her own times of trial. Henry sought to diffuse the unpopularity of his plans for divorce, which were widely seen as unfairly injuring his daughter's interests, by securing a papal dispensation for Mary to wed her half-brother, Henry Fitzroy. But the pope agreed to do so only if Henry ceased with his efforts to divorce Catherine, and the matter was dropped.

While Henry's game of brinkmanship with the pope proceeded, Mary remained fiercely loyal to Catherine, whose cause was also championed by Chapuys, the imperial ambassador, upon whom both she and Mary increasingly relied for support and advice. Mary and her mother remained in political limbo until 1531 when Henry finally ordered Catherine to retire from court and forbade Mary access to her. Then in 1533, with *Anne Boleyn pregnant, Henry took matters into his own hands, abjured the pope's authority, and obtained an annulment from his own archbishop. The legal consequences of Henry's schism with Rome now struck Mary with full force. The succession was reordered and, although she refused to acknowledge it, she was now designated illegitimate and styled "the Lady Mary, the king's daughter." Mary's household was broken up, the number of her servants reduced, and in December she was ordered to enter the household of Anne Boleyn's infant daughter, Elizabeth (later *Elizabeth I), at Hatfield, an establishment headed by Anne Boleyn's aunt, Lady Shelton, who was instructed to beat Mary if she disregarded her father's commands. Nevertheless, in defiance of the law, Mary continued to profess her fidelity to Rome, the validity of her mother's marriage, and to assert her title as heir apparent. But her father's threats, her virtual imprisonment by Anne Boleyn, her worst enemy, and her constant fear of assassination took their toll on her nerves. Under all this stress, Mary developed nervous illnesses and a susceptibility to hysteria from which she would never fully recover.

Mary's fortunes improved somewhat in 1536 after Anne Boleyn's execution and, ironically enough, her own mother's death. With her enmity with Anne Boleyn at an end and the issue

of Henry's divorce mooted, Mary finally reconciled with her father by publicly submitting to his supremacy over the English Church despite her private reservations. She maintained good relations with the new queen, ☙▶ Jane Seymour, and, with the birth of Edward (future king Edward VI) in October 1537, she was relieved of having to assert her position as heir apparent. Although Mary maintained a combative relationship with ☙▶ Catherine Howard, her father's fifth wife, the arrival in 1543 of Henry's sixth queen, the learned and accommodating ☙▶ Catherine Parr, ushered in a period of comparative stability for her. Despite their confessional disagreements and slight difference in ages, Catherine Parr supplied the maternal figure Mary craved. In 1544, Mary was restored officially to the royal succession directly behind Edward, but the other great matter of her life—her marriage—remained unsettled, the sterile outcome of Henry's constantly shifting diplomatic alliances. As Mary herself lamented, "while my father lives I shall be only the Lady Mary, the most unhappy lady in Christendom."

Mary I

◀☙
**Jane Seymour,
Catherine
Howard, and
Catherine Parr.**
*See Six Wives of
Henry VIII.*

Upon Henry VIII's death in January 1547, Mary, now 31 years old, acquired a greater measure of freedom. By her father's will, she inherited a number of estates which gave her an independent income and the practical ability to call upon men-at-arms from among her tenants. She was thus a magnate in her own right and once again the heir apparent, this time not of a domineering father but of a boy-king 20 years her junior. So when, under the direction of the Lord Protector, Edward Seymour, duke of Somerset, Edward's regime embarked upon a course of radical religious reform, Mary frankly registered her disapproval and defiantly held public masses in contravention of the first Act of Uniformity (1549). Given the widening confessional divide separating the ultra-Catholic Mary from the advanced Protestant regime taking shape under Edward, it is no surprise that further plans for Mary's marriage came to nought. The Privy Council sought to temper her Catholicism by marrying her to a Protestant prince, while Mary determined not to marry anyone without the Emperor Charles V's approval. Relations between Mary and the Council became still worse once Somerset was overthrown by John Dudley (later duke of Northumberland) who pursued a still more radical policy of religious reform. In March 1551, Mary provided a visible focus for conservative religious dissent by ostentatiously riding to court with a retinue of 130 gentlemen and women, each holding a rosary. A scolding before the Council by the king himself, who insisted that she cease her evil ways and conform to established religious practice, only made Mary more unyielding and even roused the imperial ambassador to threaten war if Mary continued to be harassed. In the end, Mary continued to hear mass but was forced to do so privately, though she derived satisfaction from the fact that her private worship was public knowledge. For the insecure Edwardian regime, Mary was a nettle too irritating to ignore but too dangerous to grasp.

In 1553, Edward's always frail health further deteriorated and on July 6 he died of tuberculosis, aged 17. Before his death, Northumberland had made a last-minute attempt to forestall Mary's accession by proclaiming his own daughter-in-law, Lady *Jane Grey, as queen. He had hoped to seize Mary by luring her to London, ostensibly to visit her ailing brother, but Mary learned that her brother in fact lay dying and instead rode to her Manor of Kenninghall in Norfolk, a fortress situated in the midst of sympathetic Catholic gentry. In one of her greatest acts of courage, Mary proclaimed her own accession and commanded the obedience of the Privy Council and of the towns and counties of the realm. The tide of public opinion responded to her call and support for Northumberland's regime rapidly melted away. When London proclaimed for Mary on the 19th, Northumberland was forced to surrender himself, and Mary marched triumphantly to the capital. Mary had Northumberland executed but otherwise displayed exemplary mercy to his co-conspirators.

When she ascended the throne, Mary was 37 years old. She was a slight woman with auburn hair, plain but pleasant features, a deep voice, and a myopic squint. She loved expensive jewelry and extravagant dress, though she lacked the theatrical demeanor that her father and younger sister used to such effect. She also possessed an iron resolve, forged in the adversity of her youth, that referred to the principle of a matter rather than to its pragmatic effects. This unshakable resolve and her essential impracticality hampered the effectiveness of Mary's three great aims: the restoration of England to the Roman Catholic fold, the accomplishment of her long-delayed marriage, and the production of an heir who could ensure the continuation of England's Catholic regime.

Immediately after her accession, Mary announced her intention to marry and began to choose her own husband—an extremely rare freedom for any female of royal birth. Although some of her councilors advocated English candidates, Mary sought the advice, as she had so often done before, of Charles V, who suggested his son, Prince Philip (II) of Spain. Despite the fact that Philip personally lacked much ardor, several factors made him the ideal choice for Mary: he was of royal birth, an experienced diplomat, Catholic, and Spanish. In October 1553, she agreed to the proposal of marriage scarcely having consulted her own Privy Councilors. The final agreement worked out in December conferred upon Philip the title of king but severely limited his political powers in England. Any child would be bound to rule by England's laws and, if the marriage proved fruitless, Philip and his heirs would have no further claim to the throne. Despite these advantageous terms, the Spanish match hit a xenophobic nerve in the public, raising fears that Protestantism would be endangered and English interests subordinated to the Spanish Habsburgs. In January 1554, hostility to the marriage erupted into open rebellion in Kent under the leadership of Sir Thomas Wyatt—a challenge which, after some hesitation and blundering on the part of the government, Mary bravely faced down.

Philip finally arrived in early July, and the two were married on the 23rd at Winchester. If Mary expected conjugal affection from Philip, she was to be sorely disappointed. Despite his initial efforts to charm his new queen and her court, his personal lack of interest in Mary, the chilliness of his reception by the English, and his limited access to political power soon led him to lose interest in England and to plan for his departure. He remained in England through May 1555, long enough to observe the grim progress of his wife's hysterical pregnancy, which embarrassingly dissolved as the spring advanced. With Philip gone, Mary's hopes for progeny were put on hold as she redoubled her efforts to stamp out the Protestant heresy.

The first steps on the way to the Catholic restoration were taken shortly after Mary's accession, but it was not at first clear in what manner she intended to accomplish this task or how far she intended to go. Assuming that the committed Protestants comprised a small but vocal minority, Mary initially attempted to remove the most prominent of them, including Thomas Cranmer, Nicholas Ridley, and Hugh Latimer, who were imprisoned. Protestant printers were shut down and Protestant refugees from the Continent expelled. Married clergy were deprived of their livings, although many were reinstated once they relinquished their wives. Mary's first Parliament repealed all ecclesiastical legislation passed during Edward VI's reign and implicitly affirmed the traditional Catholic doctrine of the Eucharist. With the arrival of Reginald Pole, the papal legate, on November 24, 1554, the stage was set to overturn the Henrician reformation as well, except for the sensitive issue of the return of former Church lands. Parliament repealed all ecclesiastical legislation passed after 1529, in return for which Pole granted absolution to the kingdom and welcomed "the return of the lost sheep" back to Rome. With the schism legally healed, Pole started to clean up the administrative and financial disorder of the English Church, as well as to suppress obstinate Protestants, thus ushering in the most notorious chapter of Mary's reign. Mary has earned the epithet "Bloody" for the nearly 300 Protestant martyrs who were convicted of heresy and burned between February 1555 and November 1557. Although by European standards of the time the toll was not great, the burnings gave the Marian regime a reputation for cruelty and ultimately proved counterproductive since the persecution only stiffened Protestant opposition.

After an absence of nearly two years, Philip returned to England in March 1557, seeking English financial and naval support for a war with France. Despite their misgivings, Mary and

her Privy Councilors were finally forced to yield and join in Spain's war effort. In July, Mary saw Philip for the last time as he left England for battle in the Low Countries. Although some of the operations the English forces undertook against the French and Scottish could be deemed successes, the Anglo-French war of 1557–59 is known chiefly for the devastating loss, in January 1558, of Calais—the last proud remnant of England's medieval European empire.

The hopelessness of Mary's vision of a world sans heresy, sans doubt, and sans discord was evidenced by the sterility of her means: her fruitless marriage to Philip of Spain, the use of fire to purge her church of error, and her dependence on ecclesiastics who were even more out of touch with reality than she was.

—Lacey Baldwin Smith

The spring of 1559 found Mary temporarily in better physical health but once again under the delusion that she was pregnant, a conclusion made more understandable given the periodic amenorrhoea from which she suffered. But, in the succeeding months, she suffered from a succession of fevers and continually moved from residence to residence in search of better air. By autumn, her condition worsened, and, in November, Mary took to her deathbed at St. James's Palace. In her last days, she is said to have lamented, "when I am dead and opened you shall find Calais lying upon my heart." She died on the morning of November 17, fittingly while bowing before the Host during mass.

SOURCES:
Loades, D.M. *Mary Tudor: A Life.* Oxford: Basil Black-well, 1989.
———. *The Reign of Mary Tudor.* NY: St. Martin's Press, 1979.
Tittler, Robert. *The Reign of Mary I.* London and NY: Longman, 1991.

SUGGESTED READING:
Erickson, Carolly. *Bloody Mary.* Garden City, NY: Doubleday, 1978.
Prescott, H.F.M. *A Spanish Tudor.* NY: AM Press, 1970.
Ridley, Jasper. *Mary Tudor.* London: Weidenfeld and Nicolson, 1973.

Geoffrey Clark,
Assistant Professor of History,
Emory University, Atlanta, Georgia

Mary II (1662–1694)

English princess who took over the throne from her father and ruled successfully as queen of England.

Name variations: Mary Stewart or Stuart. Reigned 1689–1694; born on April 30, 1662, at St. James's Palace, London, England; died of smallpox on December 28, 1694, at Kensington Palace, London; interred at Westminster Abbey; daughter of James, duke of York, later James II, king of England (r. 1685–1688), and Anne Hyde (1638–1671); sister of Anne (1665–1714), queen of England (r. 1702–1707), queen of Scotland (r. 1702–1707), queen of Britain (r. 1702–1714); educated under Protestant guidelines, apart from parents; married William III, prince of Orange (r. 1672–1702), later William III, king of England (r. 1689–1702), on November 4, 1677; children: three who died stillborn.

Spent twelve years in Holland at Dutch royal court (1677–89); became queen of England after father was deposed by English Parliament (1688); acted as regent for William on four separate occasions (1690–94).

On a cold, windswept morning in March 1694, a large and lengthy procession of mourners gathered at Whitehall Palace. As the snow began to fall, they followed an open purple-draped chariot drawn by six horses onto the street. Over 500 members of Parliament as well as various city and court officials walked behind the hearse that carried the body of their much-beloved queen, Mary II. Upon reaching Westminster Abbey, where the funeral ode by Henry Purcell filled the hall, Mary Stuart was finally laid to rest.

Although she died queen of England, Mary Stuart's birth at St. James's Palace on April 30, 1662, was neither auspicious nor welcome. Her parents, James, duke of York (the future King James II of England), and *Anne Hyde, had been married for over two years, and Anne Hyde had not yet produced the long-hoped-for male heir. The princess, who was named after her paternal aunt, *Mary of Orange, and her great-great-grandmother, *Mary Stuart, queen of Scots, soon became her father's favorite. More significantly, Mary became second in line to the English throne when her only surviving brother died in 1671. Anne Hyde died that same year, just one month short of her daughter Mary's ninth birthday.

Mary's life was complicated by the politics surrounding the English crown. In 1660, her uncle, Charles II (1660–1685), was restored to the English throne, which the Stuarts had lost in the English Civil War (1642–49). Because Charles and his queen *Catherine of Braganza were unable to provide an heir, Mary's father, as duke of York, was next in line for the throne. But

James had converted to Catholicism, and Charles II feared his influence over his daughters. Thus, Charles made sure that Mary and her only surviving sister *Anne (1665–1714) were declared wards of the state. They were given a separate lodging at Richmond Palace where they were raised by a Protestant governess, Lady *Frances Villiers, and two Anglican chaplains. For the rest of her life, Mary remained a constant and devoted member of the Church of England.

Mary's early education consisted of accomplishments that were typical for a royal princess; she was tutored in dancing, singing, drawing, and needlework. Unfortunately, the academic component of her education was not as comprehensive. She did not learn Latin, Greek, or history, and her spelling and arithmetic remained rudimentary. She was, however, given a strong grounding in French and religious instruction. In appearance, the princess was tall and slender. Her oval-shaped face, with clear complexion and almond-shaped eyes, was surrounded by dark curls. Fond of the latest fashions, she carried herself gracefully, with a majestic air.

Mary's childhood companions at Richmond were the daughters of Charles II's officers, including **Frances Apsley**, with whom Mary developed an intense and intimate friendship. When Mary's father married his second wife, 15-year-old *Mary of Modena, in 1673, she, too, became a close companion. Like all royal princesses, however, Mary was not allowed to remain a child for long, and plans were soon being made for her marriage. The choice of her husband was guided by politics rather than emotion and rested on William III of Orange, the son of Mary's aunt (Mary of Orange) and Prince William II of Orange.

Prince William III was Hereditary Stadholder and military leader of the Dutch United Provinces and spent most of his early life maintaining Dutch independence against the encroachments of the French king, Louis XIV. While William's English uncle, Charles II, had attempted to remain on friendly terms with the French king by engaging in a trade war with Holland, by 1674 it became apparent that Charles' pro-French policy was neither popular nor financially advantageous. Overtures to William were made and in February 1674, England and Holland signed the Peace of Westminster. Although a marriage alliance was suggested at this time, it was not finalized until three years later.

Historical opinions about William's character differ, but he is generally considered to have been reserved, somewhat humorless, and very formal. In appearance, he was a stark contrast to his tall, pretty, 15-year-old fiancée. Four inches shorter than Mary, and 12 years older, William of Orange was asthmatic, thin, with a beak-like nose and poor posture. Although he was next in line to the English throne after James, duke of York, and his children, William's interest in a matrimonial alliance with England was based upon English military and naval support rather than any personal ambitions for the English throne. The marriage served political and diplomatic purposes while assisting William in his continued attempts to prevent French dominance in Holland. When Mary was told of the marriage, she wept for two days before accepting her father's decision. Nevertheless, the marriage was solemnized on November 4, 1677. Fifteen days later, Mary and William left for Holland. For the next 12 years, Mary lived a quiet and reserved life in Holland.

Although initially homesick for England, Mary quickly grew to love her new home and was rewarded with love from the Dutch people. Over the years, she gradually came to cherish her husband, although the early years of her marriage were not happy. Mary suffered from frequent bouts of illness as well as an inability to conceive. More seriously, within three years of their marriage William was having an affair with one of Mary's former childhood companions and ladies-in-waiting, *Elizabeth Villiers. Confronted, William refused to give up his mistress, but he did make considerable efforts to keep the affair as secret as possible.

It is generally considered that Mary "grew up" in Holland. She became more religiously devout and broadened her education to include more diverse areas such as mathematics, science, and architecture. She also settled into a daily routine of walking, reading, painting, and needlework. Her usual residence was the "House in the Wood" near The Hague, although she and William drafted plans for a new palace at Het Loo. Mary had a fondness for flowers, and she soon began to amass a growing collection of rare plants and botanical catalogues. She also began a collection of Dutch china.

In 1679, James, Mary of Modena, and Princess Anne visited Mary at The Hague. While the visit was a pleasant one, her family had come in the wake of political crisis in England. In 1678, a plot to assassinate Charles II and place James on the English throne was discovered. Although James had played no part in the affair, anti-Catholic sentiment in England was rife. This visit to his Protestant daughter and son-in-law was intended to diffuse the tension.

Over the next several years, concerted, but ultimately unsuccessful, attempts were made to exclude James from the line of succession. Consequently, when Charles II died in February 1685, James ascended to the throne peacefully. While the early years of his reign caused little controversy, James II soon began alienating much of the political community not only for his increasing favoritism towards Catholics, but for his tendencies to practice arbitrary rule.

In addition, James began to apply pressure upon Mary in two of the most important areas of her life. In 1687, James began a correspondence with his daughter in which he urged her to divorce William, convert to Catholicism, and marry a Catholic prince. This was the first of the divided loyalties that Mary was forced to negotiate. As an obedient daughter, she was upset not only by her father's attempts to convert her, but also by his attempts to test her loyalty as a wife. Rejecting her father's proposals, Mary remained steadfast in her adherence to both her husband and her religion. Mary's unwavering loyalty to Protestantism had also been apparent three years earlier in 1685 when Louis XIV revoked the Edict of Nantes, the official toleration of French Protestants. When exiled French Huguenots arrived in Holland, she set up schools for them and continued to support them in whatever ways she could.

There was a union of their thoughts, as well as of their persons and a concurring in the same designs, as well as in the same interests. He was to conquer enemies, and she was to gain friends. She prepared and suggested what he executed.

—**Bishop Gilbert Burnet**

The political situation in England worsened, and in 1688 matters came to a head. On June 10, Mary of Modena gave birth to a boy to whom popular reaction was decidedly cool. A rumor circulated soon after the birth that the baby had been smuggled into the lying-in chamber in a warming pan, and, although there was no historical truth to the story, the birth precipitated a political crisis. A male heir would now take precedence over Mary and her sister, and, fearing that there would be an endless succession of Catholic kings, a group of parliamentarians sent a letter of invitation to William on June 30 urging him to come to England. Mary's support for her husband's expedition was based upon her belief that the baby was, indeed, a replacement. Similarly, although William insisted that he did not want to usurp the throne but rather protect England's laws, liberties, and religion, both Mary and William believed that James II was guilty of a fraud that represented the continuation of a Catholic succession.

Mary's participation in what became known as the "Glorious Revolution" led to contrasting imagery of her both during, and after, the Revolution. The Whigs, those parliamentarians who supported the Revolution, used propaganda that portrayed Mary as the good dutiful wife. The supporters of James II, who later came to be known as Jacobites, characterized Mary as the betraying daughter who broke the fifth commandment by dishonoring her father. William fared no better in Jacobite propaganda. He was portrayed as a cruel, negligent husband who used his wife to obtain power. In her own memoirs, however, Mary characterized herself as a reluctant queen, and she continued to feel guilt about the fate and safety of her father for the rest of her life. Nevertheless, Mary did not act alone.

In November 1688, when William landed in England with a force of 15,000 men, James II's fate was sealed. The king fled to France where he hoped to receive financial and military support from Louis XIV. However, when Parliament met in February 1689, it was declared that since James II had left the country, he had by implication abdicated and the throne was therefore vacant. The birth of his heir was conveniently ignored. While it was acknowledged that Mary's claim to the crown was the stronger, she refused to accept the throne unless her husband shared the royal title with her. It has been argued that William purposely delayed her arrival in England until his own position became stronger. Yet, Mary admitted publicly that she never wanted to rule alone. Similarly, she did not believe that women should govern independently.

The conflicting feelings that Mary felt about taking the throne from her father were apparent when she finally arrived in England on February 12, 1689. While happy to see her husband and her sister, she claimed that after this meeting, she was "guilty of a great sin. I let myself go on too much and the devil immediately took his advantage; the world filled my mind, and left but little room for good thoughts." The following day, Mary and William accepted the crown which they would share jointly, with administrative power vested in William. Over the next several years, several pieces of legislation were passed in order to legitimize the Revolution and set down in law the relationship between crown and country.

Mary remained reluctant to take on the reins of government. She noted that "my

Mary II

heart is not made for a kingdom and my inclination leads me to a retired life, so that I have need of the resignation and self denial in the world, to bear with such a condition as I am now in." Similarly, she was unused to the noisy and, for her, more decadent life at the English court. Consequently, in the early years of her reign as queen of England, Mary was not very involved in governmental affairs. William, on the other hand, had to tread carefully as he was not immediately accepted by the English people.

In addition, the early years of their reign were not peaceful. Rebellions erupted in Scotland and Ireland, and from April 1689 England was once again at war with France. When it became apparent that William would have to leave England in order to lead an army against France, Mary's reluctance to govern was overlooked. In June 1690, Parliament passed the Regency Act which allowed Mary to rule both in her name and William's when he was away. From 1690 to 1694, Mary reigned alone on four separate occasions. Although she gave up her power whenever William returned, it is generally concluded that she handled these periods of regency with political skill and strength. During this period, England continued to have problems with war, naval mismanagement, and frequent threats of invasion and counter-revolution. Mary, however, rose to the challenge and won over not only many members of Parliament, but the hearts of the English people as well. Her own self-confidence increased, and many people came to admire and respect her.

When William returned from his campaigns, Mary happily gave up governing and took to redecorating several royal palaces, which included planning and cultivating the royal gardens. She continued to collect and promote Dutch porcelain. Her love of clothing and jewelry did not abate over the years, and, whenever possible, she gave fancy dress balls where her grace and beauty charmed the royal guests. Mary's activities as queen of England were not confined to the ballroom. She championed various social, religious, and moral reforms. Since she was not only devout but rigorously educated in Protestant doctrine, William gave her control over appointments to ecclesiastical offices.

While Mary's relations with the government and the English populace were improving, her relationship with her sister Anne was steadily deteriorating. In 1692, matters came to a head when William refused to give command of the English forces in Flanders to John Churchill, duke of Marlborough. Fearing a coup, he also banished Marlborough from court. Since Princess Anne was not only Marlborough's patron but the best friend of his wife, *Sarah Jennings Churchill, she took the duke's dismissal as a personal slight. In addition, Anne was engaging in secret correspondence with her exiled father. Refusing to give up her friend, Anne left the court. Mary deeply regretted this alienation from her sister, but her loyalty to William overrode all other familial commitments.

When William returned from his last campaign in November 1694, the queen fell ill. It soon became apparent that she was suffering from a particularly virulent attack of smallpox. Realizing that her death was imminent, Mary became very calm and began to inventory her jewels and debts. William, on the other hand, became increasingly distraught. When her illness took a turn for the worse, he set up a bed in her sickroom where he sat by her side day and night. Her condition steadily deteriorated and on December 28, 1694, Mary II, queen of England, died at the age of 32. Upon her death, MPs cried openly, the people of England were grief-stricken, and William was in a state of shock and depression.

Although Mary had wanted a simple funeral, this last wish was not granted. Shortly after her death, her body was embalmed and lay in state for over eight weeks. On March 5, she was finally laid to rest in Henry VII's chapel in Westminster Abbey.

SOURCES:

Chapman, Hester. *Mary II, Queen of England.* London: Jonathan Cape, 1953.

Hamilton, Elizabeth. *William's Mary: A Biography of Mary II.* London: Hamish Hamilton, 1972.

van der Zee, Henri, and Barbara van der Zee. *William and Mary.* London: Macmillan, 1973.

SUGGESTED READING:

Maccubbin, R.P., and M. Hamilton-Phillips. *The Age of William III and Mary II: Power, Politics and Patronage, 1688–1702.* Williamsburg: College of William and Mary, 1989.

Margaret McIntyre,
Instructor in Women's History,
Trent University, Peterborough, Ontario, Canada

Mary Adelaide (1833–1897)

*Duchess of Teck. Name variations: Mary Adelaide Guelph; Fat Mary. Born Mary Adelaide Wilhelmina Elizabeth on November 27, 1833, in Hanover, Lower Saxony, Germany; died on October 27, 1897, at White Lodge, Richmond Park, Surrey, England; daughter of Adolphus Guelph, 1st duke of Cambridge, and *Augusta of Hesse-Cassel (1797–1889); married Francis, 1st duke of Teck, on June 12, 1866; children: *Mary of Teck (1867–1953); Adolphus, 1st marquess of Cambridge (1868–1927); Francis of Teck (1870–1910); Alexander of Teck, earl of Athlone (1874–1957).*

Mary Alexandrovna (1853–1920).

See Marie Alexandrovna.

Mary and Martha of Bethany

(fl. early 1st c. CE).

See Mary Magdalene for sidebar.

Mary Avis (1527–1545).

See Mary of Portugal.

Mary Barbara (1711–1758).
See Maria Barbara of Braganza.

Mary Bosomworth (c. 1690–c. 1763).
See Musgrove, Mary.

Mary Caroline (1752–1814).
See Maria Carolina.

Mary de Bohun (1369–1394)

*First wife of Henry IV. Name variations: Mary Bohun; Mary of Bohun. Born in 1369; died in childbirth on July 4, 1394, at Peterborough Castle, Cambridgeshire, England; buried at Leicester; daughter of Humphrey de Bohun, earl of Hereford, and *Joan Fitzalan (d. 1419); sister of *Eleanor Bohun (1366–1399, who married Thomas of Woodstock); married Henry Bolingbroke, later Henry IV, king of England (r. 1399–1413); children: Henry (1387–1422) also known as Prince Hal, later Henry V, king of England (r. 1413–1422); Thomas, duke of Clarence (1388–1421); John, duke of Bedford (1389–1425); Humphrey, duke of Gloucester (1390–1447); *Blanche (c. 1392–1409, who married Louis, duke of Bavaria); *Philippa (1394–1430, who married Eric VII, king of Denmark).*

Mary de Bohun, daughter and co-heir of Humphrey de Bohun, earl of Hereford and Essex, married Henry Bolingbroke, but died a few years before he became king of England as Henry IV. Henry then married *Joanna of Navarre (c. 1370–1437).

Mary de Coucy (c. 1220–c. 1260)

Queen of Scots. Name variations: Marie de Coucy; Mary de Couci; Mary di Coucy; Mary of Coucy. Born around 1220; died around 1260; interred at Newbottle, Scotland; daughter of Enguerrand de Coucy, 3rd baron de Coucy, and Mary de Montmirel-en-Brie; became second wife of Alexander II (1198–1249), king of Scots (r. 1214–1249), on May 15, 1239; married Jean de Brienne, before June 6, 1257; children: (first marriage) Alexander III (1241–1286), king of Scots (r. 1249–1286); (second marriage) Blanche of Brienne (who married William II de Fiennes). Alexander II's first wife was Joan (1210–1238).

Mary de Coucy (fl. 1370)

*English royal. Flourished around 1370; daughter of Enguerrand VII, lord of Coucy and earl of Bedford, and *Isabella (1332–1382, daughter of *Philippa of Hainault and King Edward III).*

Mary de Medicis (c. 1573–1642).
See Medici, Marie de.

Mary de Monthermer
(1298–after 1371)

*Duchess of Fife. Born in 1298; died after 1371; daughter of *Joan of Acre (1272–1307) and Ralph Monthermer, earl of Gloucester and Hertford; married Duncan Fife (1285–1353), 10th earl of Fife (r. 1288–1353), in November 1307; children: *Isabel of Fife (c. 1332–1389).*

Mary de Padilla (1335–1361).
See Marie de Padilla.

Mary Elizabeth, Mother (1784–1882).
See Lange, Elizabeth Clovis.

Mary-Elizabeth of Padua
(1782–1808)

*Duchess of Brunswick. Name variations: Mary Elizabeth of Padua Zähringen. Born on September 7, 1782; died on April 20, 1808; daughter of *Amalie of Hesse-Darmstadt (1754–1832) and Charles Louis of Padua (b. 1755), prince of Padua and Baden; married Major-General Frederick William (1771–1815), duke of Brunswick (r. 1806–1815), on November 1, 1802; children: Charles Frederick (b. 1804); William Maximilian (b. 1806), duke of Brunswick.*

Mary Feodorovna (1847–1928).
See Marie Feodorovna.

Mary Habsburg (1528–1603).
See Elizabeth of Habsburg (1554–1592) for sidebar on Marie of Austria.

Mary Henrietta (1631–1660).
See Mary of Orange.

Mary Henriques (1313–1357).
See Guzman, Leonora de for sidebar on Maria of Portugal.

Mary Katharine, Mother (1858–1955).
See Drexel, Mary Katharine.

Mary Louvain (c. 1260–1321).
See Marie of Brabant.

Mary Magdalen of Pazzi

(1566–1607)

Saint. Name variations: Maria Maddalena de' Pazzi. Born Catherine in 1566; died in 1607; daughter of Florentine nobles.

When she was 12, Mary Magdalen of Pazzi made a vow to refrain from marriage. At 18, she entered the Carmelite Monastery of Santa Maria degli Angeli, changing her name from Catherine to Mary Magdalen and taking as her motto "To suffer or die." She then endured corporal and spiritual sufferings which she had asked of God. She was beatified by Pope Urban VIII in 1626 and canonized by Alexander VIII in 1670. Her feast day is May 29, and a church in Florence bears her name.

Mary Magdalene (fl. early 1st c. CE)

Disciple of Jesus, ranked with the apostles because of her role at the resurrection, who, for much of Western history, has been thought to be a repentant prostitute. Name variations: Mariam; Mariamne or Mariamme, Mariham; Maria or Maryam; Maria Magdalene; the Magdalene; the Magdalen; Mary of Magdala or Magdalo.

Based on the four Gospels of the New Testament, Mary Magdalene was born in the late 1st century BCE in Magdala on the lake of Galilee. After being cured of "seven devils" by Jesus, she became a disciple, was with Jesus at the crucifixion, and came to anoint his dead body on Easter morning. Mary Magdalene was the first to discover the empty tomb and to see the risen Christ. Because she announced the resurrection to the other disciples, she is called "apostle to the apostles." By the 6th century, in the West the Magdalene was conflated with Mary of Bethany and with the repentant sinner in Luke 7 (assumed to be a prostitute), who, on encountering and anointing Jesus, reformed and devoted herself to his ministry. She is a Christian model of penitence and the contemplative life. According to legend, she ended her days as a solitary hermit in France about 50 CE. Mary Magdalene is symbolized by a scarlet cloak, loose red or golden hair, an ointment jar (alabastron), or a book.

Mary Magdalene is an enigma. Not only have multiple and conflicting mythologies about her life after the crucifixion flourished, but it is not completely clear from the Bible who this woman was. The foundational texts for the life of Mary are the New Testament and the apocryphal gospels, written in the first few centuries after

Jesus' death. However, from the 1st century, the identity of Mary was controversial. The references to the Magdalene in the Bible are scanty and confusing. There are perhaps seven different Marys mentioned in the Gospels, and at one point or another in Christian history most of those seven have been thought to be Mary Magdalene. Only recently has consensus been reached on which passages refer to the woman who has come to be known as the repentant sinner.

It is in the story of the passion and resurrection of Jesus that all but one of the explicit references to Mary Magdalene (in some versions of the Bible called Mary of Magdala), by name, occur (Mt. 27:55–28:11; Mk 15:40–16:11; Lk 23:49–24:11; Jn 19:25–20:18). She was among the women watching from afar as Jesus was nailed to the cross. This group "had followed Jesus from Galilee and waited on him." Mary Magdalene sat at the tomb after Joseph of Arimathaea laid Jesus' broken body into it, and on the third day after burial she and others returned to the grave. Matthew claims the Magdalene and "the other Mary" were there to look at the tomb (28.1), but the other Evangelists specify that Mary Magdalene came to carry out the traditional Jewish burial custom of anointing with oil the body of the recently deceased. John's Gospel differs slightly from the other three in that he places Mary Magdalene with *Mary the Virgin at the foot of the cross and has her coming alone to anoint Christ on the Sunday of the resurrection. On that Easter morning, a violent quake shook the earth, and angels, which Matthew says descended from heaven, spoke to the women, announcing that Jesus had risen and that they should announce the good news to his disciples. Matthew says the women, overjoyed, hurried to accomplish their mission, urged on by the resurrected Christ who appeared to them in the way, bidding "Be not afraid" (Mt 28:2–10). According to Luke, the women fulfilled their task, but the disciples did not believe their miraculous story. In Mark, the women were terrified and spoke to no one, and it was only after Jesus appeared to Mary Magdalene that she alone among the women carried the joyous news to the mourning disciples who did not believe her (Mk 16:1–11). In John's Gospel, as Mary Magdalene wept at the empty tomb, her savior spoke to her, asking, "Why are you weeping?" She, thinking Jesus was the gardener, replied, "They have taken my Lord away, and I do not know where they have laid him." However, at that point she turned and, recognizing Jesus, cried out, "'Rabbuni!' (which is Hebrew for 'My Master')." The ecstatic Mary Magdalene moved to embrace her Lord, at which he uttered the famous phrase, *"Noli me tangere"* (do not touch me) because he was at that point in a transformed state and not to be worshipped in the flesh (Jn 20:10–17). In Mark 16:9, where Mary Magdalene meets the risen Christ, we get the first (because Mark's was the first Gospel written) indication that Mary Magdalene was a repentant sinner, in a passage that some scholars believe to be a 2nd-century addition to the text. He describes her as the woman "from whom [Jesus] had formerly cast out seven devils." Luke, who undoubtedly knew Mark's Gospel, incorporates in his text the motif of the Magdalene's seven devils. He attests that the Mary "from whom seven devils had come out" traveled with Jesus and his chosen 12 apostles from village to village "proclaiming the good news of the kingdom of God" (Lk 8:1–2).

In addition to these references which name Mary Magdalene specifically, there are six other passages which, over the centuries, various exegetes have claimed allude to her. She has been identified as the unnamed woman who entered the house in Bethany of Simon the Leper in which Jesus was dining and liberally anointed Jesus' head with her costly oil of nard (Mt 26:6–13; Mk 14:3–9). The disciples were indignant that money which could have been given to the poor had been spent on this extravagance. Jesus calmed his followers by instructing them that the action foreshadows his anointing for burial, and went on to say that "what she has done will be told as her memorial" (Mk 14:8–9). It is understandable why later thinkers conflated this unnamed woman of Bethany with Mary Magdalene whom the Gospel texts say went to Jesus' tomb to anoint the dead body of her Lord, for that story of Mary Magdalene's attempt to anoint him did indeed become her "memorial." The act of anointing also connects Mary Magdalene to another nameless woman of a town called Nain. Jesus was dining with one of the Pharisees when a woman "who was living an immoral life" entered with a flask of oil of myrrh. She fell to Jesus' feet, "wetted them with her tears and wiped them with her hair, kissing them and anointing them with the myrrh" at which Jesus said, "Your faith has saved you, go in peace" (Lk 7:36–50). This is a critical passage to the legend of Mary Magdalene as it evolved in later centuries; the sin of this "immoral" woman was assumed to be prostitution, partially based on the fact that her hair was loose, not bound and concealed beneath a cloth as was proper for respectable women.

A third incident involving a Mary, which has also been attributed to Mary Magdalene, oc-

curred in Bethany where "a woman named Martha made [Jesus] welcome in her home. As ❧▶ **Martha of Bethany** was busy preparing the meal, her sister ❧▶ **Mary of Bethany** sat at their guest's feet listening attentively to his words. When Martha reproached her sister, Jesus assured Martha that Mary had "chosen the better way." In other words, while Martha was busy with worldly things, Mary was attending to things of the spirit (Lk 10:38–42). In addition, Martha and Mary of Bethany were the sisters of Lazarus whom Jesus resurrected, and the story of Lazarus in the Gospel of John (Jn 11–12) includes a version of the aforementioned story from Matthew and Mark. In this version, Mary of Bethany, in gratitude for the resurrection of her brother, anoints Jesus' feet with ointment

❧▶ **Martha and Mary of Bethany** (fl. early 1st c. CE)
Biblical women of the New Testament. Name variations: Sisters of Bethany; some think Mary of Bethany and *Mary Magdalene are one and the same. Flourished in the early 1st century CE; sisters of Lazarus.

The sisters of Lazarus, Martha and Mary of Bethany were also followers of Jesus, and he frequently used their home in Bethany as a retreat. Little is known about the sisters except that they were quite different in temperament. Martha, presumably the eldest, was constantly busying herself with the details of keeping an ordered home. Mary was more contemplative and spiritual. When Jesus visited, Martha endeavored to feed him and make him comfortable, while Mary sat at his feet and opened her heart to his teachings. Jesus frequently reminded Martha that she must not allow her daily chores to interfere with her inner spirituality. Once when Martha complained that Mary was not helping her, Jesus gently rebuked her. "You are worried and troubled about many things," he said. "But one thing is needed, and Mary has chosen that good part, which will not be taken away from her."

It is said in the Gospel of John (Jn 11–12) that when Lazarus died, the sisters went into a deep grief. When Jesus arrived following Lazarus' death, they admonished him for not coming sooner. "Lord, if You had been here my brother would not have died," Mary cried. Jesus was impatient at their disbelief, but he also wept. He then brought the four-day-dead Lazarus back to life, after which Mary expressed her gratitude by anointing Jesus' feet, using "a pound of very costly oil of spikenard," and wiping them with her hair. A variant of this story, concerning an unnamed woman who anoints Jesus' head at Simon the Leper's house, is told in Mt 26:6–13 and in Mk 14:3–9. Mary of Bethany was for centuries identified by Western church fathers as being Mary Magdalene, which has caused much confusion for scholars.

and wipes them with her hair, which has reinforced Mary of Bethany's identification with Mary Magdalene. In the Middle Ages, the Mary of Bethany (presumed to be that repentant ex-prostitute Mary Magdalene) who sat at the feet of Jesus was held up as a model of the contemplative or monastic life.

Some medieval thinkers grafted the story of the Samaritan woman onto the life of Mary Magdalene. While Christ and his followers were traveling in Judea, they met a Samaritan woman at the well, and Jesus correctly intuited that she was living in sin with a man who was not her husband. The Samaritan woman, amazed by this clairvoyance, converted and brought many of her townspeople over to Christ and thus became the first apostle to the gentiles. Presumably, the factor that for the medieval thinkers linked this incident with the Magdalene was the renunciation of sinful sexuality, which more and more became the hallmark of Mary Magdalene's persona (Jn 4:8–30). Finally, Mary Magdalene has been assumed by some writers to have been the woman whom the Pharisees caught in the act of adultery and whom Jesus saved from death by stoning when he suggested, "Let anyone among you who is without sin be the first to throw a stone at her" (Jn 8:3–11). The woman in these verses is not called Mary, nor does she share attributes with the woman from Magdala who first witnessed the risen Christ.

The absorption of all of the above six passages into the persona of the Mary Magdalene who followed and administered to Christ hinges on Mark's statement, repeated by Luke, that Christ cast seven devils from her. It was mere assumption that those unspecified devils were demons of lust, a deduction facilitated by the association in the classical world of the feminine and the corporeal. Also, Mary Magdalene is designated in the Gospels by her place of origin, Magdala, and not associated with a husband, father, or any other male. She was an independent female and therefore her respectability was suspect. Further, Magdala had a notorious reputation in the 1st century for the licentious behavior of its inhabitants. The Jews used the word "magdala" to denote a person with plaited hair, which was in use among prostitutes of the time. However, whether validated by the Biblical texts or not, as Christianity spread, with it spread a fluid mythology of Mary Magdalene, the penitent fallen woman who was beloved of Christ.

Discussions about which of the Biblical passages refer to Mary Magdalene date to the earliest centuries of Christianity. The fathers of the early Greek church (c. 300–400) generally distinguished Mary Magdalene, the sinner from Nain of Luke 7, and Mary of Bethany (the sister of Martha and Lazarus) as three separate people, but in the Western tradition the three have been treated as one person, based largely on a determination made by Pope Gregory the Great (d. 604). The unnamed sinner in Luke 7:37, who washed Jesus' feet with her tears and dried them with her hair, came to be viewed as the same woman who anointed his head just before the passion and who first saw the risen Christ. This composite Mary's feast day is celebrated on July 22. Although in the Western church Gregory the Great's position held firm, intellectuals in both the East and the West continued to struggle with the identity of Mary and to further interpret the Scriptures. At one point, Cyril of Jerusalem (d. 386) identified *Mary of Cleophas, the sister of Mary the Virgin, as the Magdalene, and in a later treatise he held that Mary the Virgin herself was one and the same as Mary Magdalene (whom he claimed was virgin and aged at the time of Christ's death). This appears to be a confusion of the three women who stood at the foot of the cross when Jesus was killed. The Western church father Ambrose (d. 397) suggested that there may have been several Mary Magdalenes, citing the discrepancies in Scripture: according to John 20:15, Mary did not recognize Jesus, whereas in Matthew 28:9, she did.

In the same time period that the four orthodox Gospels of the New Testament were written, other gospels appeared which, although never sanctioned by inclusion in the Bible as we know it, carried authority and wide currency in the late antique world. The apocryphal *Infancy of Jesus Christ* claims that the alabaster box in which Mary Magdalene kept her ointment was the same box in which Jesus' foreskin had been preserved since his circumcision. Another apocryphal text, *The Gospel of Nicodemus,* formulates a narrative in which Mary Magdalene travels to Rome after Jesus' death to publicly accuse Pontius Pilate before Tiberius, the Roman emperor. Two of the most significant of the apocryphal texts for the life of Mary Magdalene, both of which were discovered in Egypt in the mid-18th century, are *The Gospel of Mary* and *Pistis Sophia* (Faith Wisdom). In *The Gospel of Mary,* written in the 2nd century, Mary Magdalene consoles the disciples who are confused and disheartened by Christ's absence after his ascension into heaven by reassuring them that the spirit of Jesus is still among them. She alone was privileged to hear additional salvific words of Jesus at the end of his life because the Savior loved her more than any other woman. Mary tells of a mystic encounter she had in which she experienced the soul's sojourn through the spheres. This angers Andrew and Peter; they refuse to believe her, and Peter persuades the others that, had Christ had further revelations about the cosmos, he would have unveiled those secrets to them instead of to a woman. He demands of the other disciples, "Did Christ prefer her to us?" Levi answers that question in the affirmative, saying to Peter, "If the Savior made her worthy, who are you to reject her. [The Savior] loved her more than us." *Pistis Sophia* explains the existence of a goddess of wisdom, spouse of the Lord, who, like the Magdalene, experiences a fall from grace because of her attraction to material things, undergoes repentance, and regains elevation to a position of power and glory. In this text, there is also an antagonism between Mary and Peter because Peter accuses her of monopolizing theological conversations. Mary complains to Jesus that she is afraid of Peter because "he hates our sex." But Jesus exonerates Mary Magdalene before all his followers, declaring that it is she who will receive "the light" because her "heart strains toward the Kingdom of the Heavens more than all [her] brothers." The repeated focus on the conflict between Peter and Mary is certainly informed by the misogyny characteristic of the Roman world in the early centuries CE (the pagan Celsus [fl. 180] discounted the resurrection because it was based on the "reports of hysterical women"), but it also relates to a larger question as to where authority would lie within the emerging church.

The Gnostic Gospels are texts written in the first few centuries by groups of Christians who had a very different interpretation of Jesus' message than that represented in the New Testament, particularly evident in their position that the flesh and the whole of the created, material world is corrupt and evil and only the spirit is worthy. Those holding what we know as the orthodox position opposed and eventually condemned Gnostic religious views. Several proscribed Gnostic texts were hidden around 400 CE in Egypt and discovered only in 1945. One of the striking differences between the Christian Gnostic Gospels and Matthew, Mark, Luke, and John is the role of women in the cosmic design and in prominent leadership positions within the fledgling church. Mary Magdalene is an important figure in many Gnostic texts, yet she is not featured as a repentant prostitute, but rather as a woman who has a special and loving relationship with Jesus. *Gnosis* refers to a special or mystical knowledge, and Mary Magdalene is portrayed as most able to comprehend Christ's

Mary Magdalene

message and meaning in a way that the other disciples cannot, because she intuits through a lens of mystic and spiritual love. She is "the woman who knew the All" and "inheritor of the Light," the principle decipherer of *gnosis* for the other disciples. She is Christ's "partner" or "consort," and in the *Gospel of Philip* the sexual connotation of this image is developed: "the companion of the Savior is Mary Magdalene . . . he used to kiss her often on her mouth." In this text, Jesus and the Magdalene are lovers, but *Philip* is principally interested in the metaphorical dimension of human love, which symbolizes the union of Christ and the church. Some Gnostic writings, however, do focus on a physical relationship between Mary Magdalene and Jesus. A document called *Great Questions of Mary* has Jesus revealing to the Magdalene obscene, orgiastic ceremonies which must be performed before salvation can be achieved.

In the late antique and medieval periods, characters in the Old Testament were often viewed as "types"—a sort of parallel or precursor—of or for characters in the New Testament. ***Miriam the Prophet**, the sister of Moses, was often viewed as a type of Mary Magdalene inasmuch as they both appear as penitents; Miriam was cursed with leprosy and banished for seven days for questioning her brother's behavior (Nm 12). In a slightly different way, Hippolytus of Rome (d. around 235) saw the figure of Mary Magdalene as the Bride from the *Song of Songs* who seeks her Bridegroom at the tomb (3:1–4): an allegory of the love between Jesus and his church in which Mary is the church. He develops another important typological association between Mary Magdalene and *Eve. A mirror image of the first Eve who forfeited her right to eternal life in one garden (Eden), Mary Magdalene becomes the New Eve and counters that mistake by finding the new life, the risen Christ in the Easter garden.

Out of a prostitute, Christ made an apostle.

—Pierre de Celle

The most fertile period of speculation about Mary Magdalene was during the Middle Ages (accelerating in the 9th and 10th centuries, at its height in the 12th century), when legends of her life after the crucifixion proliferated. These legends were pieced together out of clues from the Gospels, bits of narrative borrowed from the lives of other saints, and the imaginations of medieval hagiographers. As one anonymous 14th-century biographer said in describing Mary's life, "I do not trouble myself about this [chronology] . . . it delights me to tell of the Magdalene and of what she did . . . according to my fancy." The persona of Mary Magdalene, the most beautiful of all women, lends itself to embellishment better than that of most saints because of the extremes which characterized her life; she knew wickedness and sanctity, grief and ecstasy. Tales of Mary's later life exist in virtually all vernaculars and locales in which Christianity has taken hold. She was much discussed by ecclesiastics in both the Eastern and Western churches. She was the subject of Latin hymns from the early church through the poetry of Francesco Petrarch (d. 1374), who was especially devoted to the Magdalene; he called her the "sweet friend of God." Mary was a favorite topic for Jacobus de Voragine in his compendium of saints' lives called the *Golden Legend* (1276). Both medieval France and England produced numerous sermons, poems, songs, and plays about the Magdalene, one of which was falsely attributed to Geoffrey Chaucer (d. 1400). Mary Magdalene naturally appears in virtually all literature, drama, and scholarly discourse on the events surrounding Easter.

For Modestus, patriarch of Jerusalem (fl. 630), Mary Magdalene died a virgin and a martyr in Ephesus. Isidore of Seville (d. 636) calls her "star of the sea" from an interpretation of the etymology of her name. Based on the Hebrew word for tower (*migdal*), Mary was often characterized as a tower well fortified by faith; writers saw Mary, the tower, as a metaphor for the church. It was widely accepted in the Middle Ages, and is recorded in the *Golden Legend,* that the Magdalene was married to St. John the Evangelist and that it was their nuptials being celebrated at Cana when Jesus turned water into wine (Jn 2.1–10). The association may derive from the scene in John 19:25–27 where Mary Magdalene and John are together at the foot of the cross with Mary the Virgin. A 14th-century Italian biography of Mary Magdalene says that after the wedding feast Jesus took John away with him, "wishing that he should remain pure." It was at this point, according to legend, that Mary Magdalene, in her resentment and despair, turned to a life of sin: "She became a common prostitute and of her free will founded a brothel of sin . . . for seven devils entered into her at once, and continually plagued her with foul desires" (Honorius of Autun, *De Sancta Maria Magadlena*). Clearly, Honorius is embellishing from Mark's reference to Mary's seven devils (Mk 16.9). Those seven devils were often interpreted as the seven deadly sins which, in Jean Michel's *Mystère de la Passion* (1486), are personified as actual characters who discourse with Mary. Another legend tells of two Mary Magdalenes, one of whom went to France while the other sailed to Spain with St. James. (The story of Mary's travels to France finds an airing in a current work entitled *Holy Blood, Holy Grail* in which Mary Magdalene makes her way to Marseilles carrying in her womb the "Holy Grail" which is the child of Jesus. Mary's descendants marry into the house of the Frankish kings, and thus the blood of Christ enters the veins of several European royal dynasties.)

In the high and late Middle Ages, a genre of writing called romance literature developed around chivalric themes and tales of courtly love into which the story of Mary Magdalene and her beloved Jesus fits nicely. In many texts Mary and Jesus are fashioned into courtly lovers; yet, consistent with the strictures of courtly love, that affection is not played out on the physical level, and often the passion shared by the two is largely allegorical of the soul's yearning for the divine. For instance, a 10th-century *vita* (life) of Mary Magdalene says that when Jesus died she "grieved with the grief of a forsaken lover." A 12th-century treatise mistakenly attributed to Rhabanus Maurus (d. 856) says of Mary, "the fire of love raged . . . into a burnt offering, in an insatiable desire for her Redeemer. . . Mary suffered as lovers are accustomed to suffer." The late medieval *Digby Mysteries* puts these words in Mary's mouth: "Show my best love that I was here!/ Tell him, as he may prove,/ that I am deadly sick/ And all is for his love." In Michel's *Mystère*, Mary is a coquette adorned with finery, a mistress of seduction, young, rich, exceedingly beautiful with the form, coloring, and proportions of the ideal heroine of the romance genre. Her suitors are aristocratic knights decked out with falcons on their wrists, gaily whistling lyric ballads of love. Thomas Robinson, in his *Life and Death of Mary Magdalene* (c. 1621), calls Jesus himself a "heavenly paramour." Despite the fact that most authors portrayed the reformed Mary Magdalene as pious and earnest, the Mary of the English Towneley Plays was not able to abandon her flippant flirtatiousness, and that is why women were not allowed at the last supper: "It was because of Mary, because [Peter] saw her smiling."

According to the most popular medieval legend of Mary Magdalene (which incorporates elements of the story of Mary of Bethany and of the unnamed woman of Nain), evident in England as early as the 8th century, but not gaining wide currency until the 12th century, Mary Magdalene was the daughter of noble parents who were descendants of kings. She, along with her sister, Martha, and brother, Lazarus, inherited Magdala, Bethany, and property in the city of Jerusalem. Mary, despite her advantages of wealth and breeding, became a common sinner until her conversion in the house of the Pharisee, where she performed the famous penitential act of washing and anointing Jesus' feet. After Christ's ascension into heaven, Mary lived on in Jerusalem for 14 years, at which time a great persecution against Christians ensued. "Unbelievers" put Mary along with several other people into a rudderless, oarless boat "for to be drowned." There is great variety in different traditions about who set out with Mary. Usually Martha, Lazarus, and Maximin, one of the 72 disciples (Lk 10.1), are among the party. The hapless group eventually arrived safely in Marseilles, France, where they found shelter under the portico of a pagan temple. Mary Magdalene preached the gospel to those coming to make sacrifices to "false gods"; she was even able to convert the king and queen of the land (after appearing in their dreams for three successive nights) by promising them that if they were faithful they would bear a son. The queen became pregnant, and the now-devout royal cou-

ple, seeking to deepen their understanding of Christianity, set out for Rome to visit St. Peter. On the journey a storm arose, and during the turmoil the queen delivered a son but died from complications, leaving the rest of the party with no choice but to leave the bodies of the mother and son on a forsaken, rocky island. The king went on to Rome, saw Peter, traveled to the Holy Land, and on his return to France insisted on stopping at the island to pay respects to his dead wife and son. Miraculously, the child was still alive, having taken nourishment from the milk-filled breast of his mother's corpse. She was also brought back to life by the intercession of Mary Magdalene, and the happy family returned to France and assisted in the conversion of the land to Christianity.

Mary Magdalene, her work as "apostless" now completed, "desirous of sovereign contemplation," and in remembrance of her former sin hoping to forever more avoid the sight of a male face, sought out a deserted cave called Ste. Baume in which there was "neither water, nor herb, nor tree" (some traditions place the cave in Arabia) and lived the last 30 years of her life there. At this point in the legend, the details of Mary's life are largely borrowed from the biographies of another saint who shares her name, *Mary of Egypt, who lived five centuries after the Magdalene. Both women were sinners and both ended their lives in repentant solitude. Mary of Egypt became a prostitute at the age of 12. At one point in her life, she made her way to Jerusalem, and, when her entry into a church was barred by an invisible force, she was struck with a horrible recognition of her sins. She repented and, with only three loaves of bread, retired to the desert where she lived in penitence for 47 years. In the version of this story tailored to the life of the Magdalene, Mary was provided nourishment by being lifted into the heavenly choirs at each of the seven canonical hours and fed on celestial food. A further detail of Mary's hermetic seclusion, which may have been borrowed from the life of a Roman martyr, *St. Agnes (d. possibly c. 304), is that when the Magdalene's clothes finally disintegrated from age, her golden hair grew long enough to cover her nakedness. When the hour of her death approached, Mary appeared in the nearby church where St. Maximin, with whom she had fled to France so many years before, was priest, received the Blessed Sacrament from him, and the Lord and his angels lifted her soul into heaven. She was buried at St. Maximin's church, and countless sick, blind, demon-possessed, and repentant sinners were miraculously cured at her tomb.

Because of the importance and attraction of Mary Magdalene, it is not surprising that controversy continued to follow her long after her death. In medieval Europe, her memory was kept fresh by a disagreement as to the location of her remains. From about 449, the Eastern Church claimed that after the resurrection Mary Magdalene moved to Ephesus with John the Divine and Mary the Virgin to preach the gospel, and that her body was buried first in Ephesus in the cave of the Seven Sleepers and then moved to Constantinople in the 9th century. In the West, by the end of the 13th century five different churches claimed to have her corpse; in addition, 60 other bits and pieces of her body, or objects she owned, were held in various locations as precious relics. Among them are a lock of the hair with which she wiped Jesus' feet, a portion of her forehead touched by the resurrected Christ, some of the spice she used in anointing Jesus, and the rock upon which she sat when Christ appeared to her in the garden. (This list also illustrates the Western assumption that Mary Magdalene was the unnamed woman in the Gospel stories previously cited.) The two churches whose claims to have Mary Magdalene's remains were most credited are St. Maximin and Vézelay. According to one tradition, Mary was interred at the church of St. Maximin in Provence—buried there by Maximin himself. A later tradition has it that her body was never in Ephesus or Provence at all but that the saint was laid to rest in Jerusalem and her bones carried to Ste. Marie-Madeleine in Vézelay, Burgundy, in 1042 by a monk called Badilon on his return from the Holy Land. Yet another camp said that Badilon transported the bones from Provence to Vézelay, and another version has it that in 745 Gerard, count of Burgundy, removed the body from Provence to Vézelay for safekeeping from Arab attack. When questioned about the validity of their claim, the monks of Vézelay assured the skeptical that the Magdalene herself had appeared standing outside her tomb saying, "It is me, whom many people believe to be here." They provided further "proof" in 1267 when they invited the French king, St. Louis IX, to witness the exhumation of Mary Magdalene's corpse (which, when exposed, was fragrant and adorned with copious tresses of yellow hair) and its reburial in a larger, more elaborate reliquary. To commemorate the occasion, the arm, jaw, and three teeth of the saint were distributed amongst the crowd, and the king himself kept a considerable portion of the body. This event did not deter the monks of St. Maximin from declaring in 1279 that they also had found the body of Mary Magdalene in the crypt of their monastery church. The saint's head was put in a golden reliquary shaped like a head, on which a royal crown was perched. Despite the wide disparity among the various versions of the Magdalene's resting place, droves of medieval pilgrims visited her remains in Ephesus, Provence, and Vézelay, which in the mid-11th century became the most popular pilgrimage center in France. During the 16th-century wars of religion, the remains of Mary Magdalene at Vézelay were burned along with the church. The cave at Ste. Baume (Holy Balm) in Provence, where Mary Magdalene was reputed to have lived the last 30 years of her life in solitary penitence, also became a center of pilgrimage after a Count William identified it in 935. The spot became especially popular in the 13th century, and in 1254 received as a pilgrim St. Louis IX. Although the site fell into neglect in the early modern period and was ravished during the French Revolution, in 1822 (before 40,000 people), the cult of Mary Magdalene at Ste. Baume was reinstated.

Because of Mary Magdalene's complex and disparate identifications, she lends herself to veneration by virtually every class of Christians and became the patron saint for several trades and institutions. Because she mistook Jesus for a gardener, she is the patron saint of gardeners. Her role as myrrhophore (one who carries myrrh) makes her a logical patron for apothecaries. As symbol of the contemplative life, she is a natural patron for monastic orders and mystics. As a penitent sinner, she became the patron, even the symbol, of the reformed prostitute. The 14th and 15th centuries saw the flourishing of the Order of the Penitents of St. Mary Magdalene, approved by Pope Gregory IX in 1227 and called "White Ladies" because of the white robes they wore. The group set up houses in towns and cities all over Europe to provide refuge for those prostitutes wishing to renounce their lives of sin and become brides of Christ. Not all of those seeking refuge in the order were destined for a religious vocation; the houses also acted as temporary havens for prostitutes who were making the transition to a new life. In 1324 at Naples, the Order of Magdalene, a community of reformed prostitutes cum nuns, was established. By papal decree, all the revenue of public prostitutes dying intestate went to the new order. By the 17th century, in England, repentant prostitutes were known as "magdalens" or ❧➤ "Magdalen women"; 18th-century reformatories for women were called "Magdalen-houses"; and in 19th-century Victorian England, Magdalenism became a synonym for prostitution.

Some who sought a patron in Mary Magdalene identified with her role as the consummate contemplative—the woman of Bethany who listened at Jesus' feet while her sister Martha fussed with dinner, the woman who spent the last 30 years of her life in a cave at St. Baume fasting and praying—rather than as a sinner. The Magdalene was a special friend of and model to both the Italian mystic *Catherine of Sienna (1347–1380) and the English *Margery Kempe (c. 1378–after 1478), whose most notable characteristic was her uncontrolled weeping. *Margaret of Cortona (1247–1297) was tortured by anxiety because she was not a virgin and therefore excluded from the highest celestial reward. But she found solace in her identity with Mary Magdalene who, though she had lived a carnal life, was elevated to the rank of virgin in heaven. In a mystical vision, Margaret of Cortona was assured that "there is none above Magdalene in the choir of virgins." Mary Magdalene appeared wearing a robe of silver and a crown of precious jewels which Christ told Margaret that Mary had earned in the "desert cave." Margaret of Cortona's biographer described her as "a second Magdalene."

Not all the discussions of Mary Magdalene have been adoring of her. Especially beginning in the 13th century, many medieval writers stressed her sinful nature, focusing on her role as the fallen woman and her identification as the common prostitute portrayed in Luke, who was saved by God's grace, not her own merits. Mary Magdalene was especially suspect because of her great beauty and rich, flowing, fair hair, which a Middle Low German poem claims was dyed. She was a metaphor for *luxuria* and *vanitas* and became a focal point for much misogynistic discourse which described the woman as a weak, carnal, insatiable temptress. The *Carmina Burana* has Mary Magdalene singing the words, "In worldly joy I shall end my life. . . I shall take care of my body and with different colors I shall adorn it." In a work produced in 1430, Mary Magdalene boasts of her "proud little breasts" and announces that she is "available to all." Michel's *Mystère* has Mary Magdalene (the woman of Nain) seeking out Christ at the home of the pharisee because she heard that Jesus was blond and beautiful, and she lusted after him. Some thinkers went so far as to deny that it was the Magdalene to whom the risen Christ first appeared, claiming the distinction for Mary the Virgin because of their objections to the notion that a fallen woman would be so honored. *Christine de Pizan (c. 1363–c. 1431) defends her sex by reference to Mary Magdalene: "If women's language is so blameworthy and of such small authority. . . our Lord Jesus Christ would never have deigned to wish that so wor-

thy a mystery as His most gracious resurrection be first announced by a woman." She scoffed at some preachers who claimed that Christ told Mary Magdalene to announce his resurrection because he knew that, women being gossips, the news of his return would thus spread all the more quickly.

Mary Magdalene became an extremely useful saint for the Catholic Church during the Counter-Reformation of the 16th and 17th centuries. The reform Council of Trent (1560s) put special stress on the humanity and affective attraction of the Christian message. The prevailing image of the Magdalene was of the faithful penitent in her French grotto, granted salvation as a gift of Christ. Given to extremes of emotion, a depth of feeling, and an unwavering love for the Savior, Mary Magdalene became the embodiment of the Counter-Reformation spirit. Not un-

---

✤ Magdalen women (c. 1820s–early 1970s)
Irish "fallen women" who were confined in convents, where they worked as unpaid launderers.

In Western society, the stigma attached to a woman who became pregnant while unmarried was until the last decades of the 20th century enormous and often irreparable. Magdalen women, so called in reference to *Mary Magdalene, the repentant prostitute who was the beloved follower of Jesus, were "fallen women" in Ireland who were confined to convents because of their transgressions. Beginning around the 1820s and continuing into the early 1970s, thousands of these women worked without pay in convent laundries until their deaths, when they were buried in unmarked graves on convent grounds. Magdalen women included not only unmarried women but sometimes also their daughters (some of whom left the convents upon attaining their majority), orphans, and ex-prostitutes. Families sometimes placed unconventional women there as well. This practice was revealed to the world at large in 1993, when the destruction of 133 graves of Magdalen women by a Dublin convent provoked a national scandal. (The land was intended for a real-estate development.) Grown daughters of Magdalen women, including some who had grown up working in convent laundries, came forward to talk of their experiences and attempt to locate, usually without success, their mothers or their mothers' graves. Although diocese authorities refused to comment, a Dublin nun, Sister **Meta Reid**, noted: "Society didn't want these women. Their families didn't want them. Yes, we were unjust, but we were unwittingly facilitating a system that was unjust." A monument to Magdalen women may be erected in Dublin.

SOURCES:
The Day [New London, CT]. October 25, 1993, p. A2.

---

predictably, she was a focus of criticism by Martin Luther (d. 1546), Ulrich Zwingli (d. 1531), and other reformers who demanded that her cult be abolished (however, this does not represent the only reaction to Mary Magdalene by Protestant denominations). The most significant furor of the period over the Magdalene came, however, not from the Protestant camp but from a leading French humanist, Jacques Lefèvre d'Etaples, who asked that the three women subsumed under the identity of Mary Magdalene be differentiated. He claimed that Mary of Bethany, the sinner in Luke, and the Mary who found the empty tomb were three different women. In 1521, Lefèvre d'Etaples was accused of heresy by the Faculty of Theology at Paris University, and his works were placed on the index of forbidden books; he recanted.

Artistic treatments of Mary Magdalene through the ages have been as abundant and diverse as her appearances in literature, and the way the Magdalene is portrayed (and the particular stories or legends stressed) mirrors in a predictable way the values and interests of the period in which the artwork was produced. The earliest representation of Mary Magdalene comes from a house at Dura-Europos in Syria and portrays that aspect of her biography which was most important in the first several centuries: as one of the myrrhophores who discovered the empty tomb. Through the medieval period, the images of the saint expanded beyond her role at the tomb, and she is portrayed in her many guises in multitudinous variations. But she appears most frequently as the penitent sinner—weeping, anointing, and adoring her Savior. Counter-Reformation art also stresses the penitential aspect of Mary Magdalene, but focuses not on the sinner in Luke, but on Mary's later life as a hermit in the cave of Ste. Baume where she is no longer beautiful but gaunt and thin from fasting, clothed only by her long flowing hair, her garments having long since rotted away. Some late medieval German art actually casts Mary Magdalene in the role of the mythical, animalistic "wild man" who inhabits remote unpeopled regions. She is shown with a covering fur, rather than hair. The representation of Mary Magdalene in scenes of Jesus' death are often designed to contrast her with the Mother of God. Mary the Virgin is generally restrained in her remorse because of her understanding of Christ's mission, whereas the Magdalene rushes like a maenad to weep at the feet of Jesus; she lets loose her sorrow in a flood of tears, a face distorted by grief, and gestures of despair. (The English word "maudlin" is derived from Mary Magdalene.)

In 15th-century Germany, however, began an artistic innovation in the representation of the saintly hermit that became a trend, then a fad. The naked penitent is not so much covered by her long hair as framed by it. Her curls swirl around her voluptuous form, revealing and describing her body which is no longer emaciated but comely and titillating. Artists of the Renaissance became less and less interested in the theological aspects of the Magdalene in her grotto and more intrigued by the aesthetic possibilities of the scene. From the 15th to the 18th centuries, despite censure by some church leaders who urged decorum, Mary Magdalene became a coquette, a Venus figure; her now fully revealed nakedness was (somewhat disingenuously) allegorized as unashamed divine love. Antonio Correggio painted her nude, lying on her stomach, absorbed in a book upon which rest the nipples of her sensuous breasts (1522). In reference to Titian's similar portrayals of the same scene (1560s), a contemporary commented, "The flowing mane makes a golden necklace around the naked alabaster [breasts]." Other famous Renaissance and Baroque representations of Mary Magdalene which fall into the same class are those by Domenico Tintoretto, Annibale Carracci, Correggio, and *Artemisia Gentileschi.

By the late 17th century, it was common for wealthy aristocratic women to have their portraits painted in the guise of various historical or mythological characters. One of the favorite "dress-up" characters was Mary Magdalene, except that she was often chosen because this particular subject allowed the high-class women an opportunity to undress. The Magdalene was not selected here for her virtues or vices, but because there was a long and generally respectable tradition of portraying her partially naked in her bucolic grotto. In France, it was particularly fashionable to be painted à la Madeleine, and several of the Sun King's (Louis XIV) mistresses were represented in this way. Representations of Mary Magdalene from the 19th and 20th centuries parallel the period's inclination to question the fanciful legends that have for centuries been spinning off of the basic Bible narrative. People seeking the "historical Jesus" were attracted to scenes of the Gospel characters in very human terms. The special love between Mary Magdalene and Jesus, which has been a subject from a very early period, was explored through the strongest visual images. For example, one Belgian artist portrayed Mary Magdalene masturbating below a cross to which is nailed a haloed penis. Auguste Rodin (d. 1914) represented Mary Magdalene and Jesus as very mortal, very physical lovers, and some artistic treatments show her pregnant, carrying Jesus' child. This representation is not unprecedented; some medieval art portrays Mary Magdalene in the late stages of pregnancy, but the image is allegorical: the womb is fruitful with spiritual gifts. The representation also creates correspondences between Mary Magdalene and the Virgin Mother of God.

Mary Magdalene has not been neglected in music. She was the subject of hymns in the medieval period, and in the early modern era, musical pieces commemorated Mary Magdalene in what was then the most popular conception of her: the penitent in her grotto. Some of the most famous works are by Andrea Gabrieli (d. 1586), Claudio Monteverdi (1617), and Lorenzo Giustiniani (d. 1620). In *Marie-Magdeleine* (1873), one of Jules Massenet's operas about women of questionable virtue, the artist envisions Mary Magdalene as a sultry oriental courtesan (1873).

In the 19th and 20th centuries, the conception of the Magdalene has reverted to a 1st-century view in some respects. She is first and foremost the faithful friend and assistant of Jesus, who stayed by her Lord at the end and was the first to see him resurrected. The Catholic Church has come into line with the traditional Eastern position that Mary of Bethany, the sinner in Luke, and Mary Magdalene were three separate women. Also, the stories about Mary Magdalene's later life in France, questioned as early as 1641 by Jean de Lyon, a scholar from the Sorbonne, and again by Louis Duchesne in 1894, have been discredited. One result of the 19th-century effort to find the "historical Jesus" has been a denigration of Mary Magdalene because of the layer after layer of myth attached to her. The scholar David Friedrich Strauss, who rejected the historicity of much of the Bible story, mocked the Gospel account of resurrection which had been founded upon "the ravings of a demented and lovelorn woman . . . she having been formerly a demoniac" (1836). Ernest Renan (d. 1892) was not flattering Mary Magdalene when he claimed that the "glory" of the resurrection belongs to her.

Strangely, however, at the same time that theologians and scholars are establishing that much of the traditional lore about Mary Magdalene is fictitious, novels, movies, and artistic images of her in her traditional guise as the repentant sinner continue to proliferate. In the 19th century, her name was firmly entrenched in the popular imagination with two issues that were no longer related to religion: the "Great Social Evil" of prostitution and the inequitable position of women in a society which often forced them to lead secret lives because of societal constraints on their options. Mary Magdalene was the acknowledged model for several beautiful fictional heroines who were forced by society's strictures to enter a life of sin; famous among them is *Madeleine Férat* (1868) by Emile Zola. Another way in which the Magdalene manifested herself in the 19th century was in association with the Western orientalist fascination with the East which arose as European imperialism brought more and more Westerners to the East. Mary Magdalene fit nicely into romantic conceptions of an exotic oriental beauty trapped by her own sexuality—which was thought to be so much a feature of the Eastern personality.

Martin Scorsese's 1988 film interpretation of the novel *The Last Temptation of Christ* by Nikos Kazantzakis, and the public reaction to it, demonstrate that Mary Magdalene is still an important emblem for our era. The *Last Temptation* further demonstrates that, despite virtual unanimity on the position that the sinner in Luke and Mary Magdalene were not the same person, Mary as a metaphor for human sexuality and its conflicted relationship with the spiritual or divine is still very necessary. Scorsese's film follows a fairly traditional composite of the Gospel story in which Mary Magdalene is the repentant prostitute who, once redeemed, joins Jesus' following. The portion of the film that resulted in cinemas being bombed, boycotted, and vandalized comes at the end as Jesus hangs dying on the cross. His last temptation is an opportunity to end his tortures, give up his mission, and live the life of an ordinary man. In a dream sequence, he chooses that option, marries, fathers a child by Mary Magdalene, and, when she dies, lives and procreates with Mary and Martha of Bethany. Although the film raised a storm of protest, its treatment of many themes, including Mary Magdalene, is very traditional. Mary Magdalene is first a sinner, then reformed—the special friend of Jesus. As is typical in Western culture, that which most tempts men to veer from the divine is represented by the feminine. Two other motion pictures of the late 1980s, Denys Arcand's *Jesus of Montreal* (1989) and Krzysztof Kieslowski's *A Short Film about Love* (1988), explore similar themes with similar treatments of Mary Magdalene. In Tim Rice and Andrew Lloyd Webber's opera *Jesus Christ Superstar* (1970), Mary Magdalene is the sinner, but is treated as an essentially positive force. The work stresses the scene in the home of Simon the Leper where the unnamed woman (in this case presumed to be Mary Magdalene) anoints the exhausted Jesus to the chagrin of Judas and the other disciples who think the money spent on the oil could better go to the poor and that Jesus compromises himself by associating with "women of her kind." A very intense Jesus assures the men that only Mary has understood his mission. The poor, he sings, will always be among us. But Mary intuits that he, the Savior, will be on earth only a short time and should be adored here and now. In a later scene, Mary Magdalene again reveals her deeper understanding of the uniqueness of Jesus when she ponders how to love this man who is clearly not "just one more."

Mary Magdalene has been firmly instated to her role as first apostle and participant in Christ's ministry. There is a growing tendency to see her as the leader of the group of women who provided the material means of support for the traveling preachers and who were full and equal participants in the movement. Even the negative stigma of the seven devils has been reinterpreted. The *New Catholic Encyclopedia* states that the seven devils is a reference to a "chronic nervous disorder, rather than a sinful state." One important difference between the positive view of the Magdalene in the late 20th century and affirmations of her in earlier Gnostic gospels is that for the Gnostics Mary was a valued apostle and leader of the new Christian community, but only because she has become like a man. She says to the other disciples, "He has prepared us and made us into men." In the *Gospel of Thomas*, Jesus assures Peter that it is proper that Mary, a woman, be part of the inner circle, for "every woman who will make herself male will enter the Kingdom of Heaven." The association between women and the profane, material world was so strong that despite Jesus' insistence that there be "neither male nor female" (Gal 3.28), placing a woman at the center of the Christian narrative of redemption caused discomfort and needed justification. Current scholarship has restored the Magdalene to her position as a respectable member of Jesus' inner circle whose gender was not of particular importance. She was a devoted and constant member of Jesus' radical revolution.

SOURCES:
Bruckberger, Raymond-Leopold. *Mary Magdalene*. Translated by H.L. Binsse. NY: Pantheon, 1953.

Garth, Helen Meredith. *Saint Mary Magdalene in Mediaeval Literature*. The Johns Hopkins University Studies in Historical and Political Science, series 67, no. 3. Baltimore, 1950.

Grant, Robert M., ed. *Gnosticism: A Sourcebook of Heretical Writings from the Early Christian Period*. NY: Harper & Bros., 1961.

Haskins, Susan. *Mary Magdalen: Myth and Metaphor*. NY: Harcourt Brace, 1993.

Pagels, Elaine. *The Gnostic Gospels*. NY: Random House, 1979.

Rushing, Sandra M. *The Magdalene Legacy: Exploring the Wounded Icon of Sexuality*. Westport, CT: Bergin & Garvey, 1994.

SUGGESTED READING:
Saxer, Victor. *Le Culte de Marie Madeleine en Occident des origines à la fin du moyen âge*. Auxerre-Paris, 1959.

Martha Rampton,
Assistant Professor of History,
Pacific University, Forest Grove, Oregon

Mary of Agreda (1602–1665).

See Agreda, Sor María de.

Mary of Alania (fl. 1070–1081).

See Anna Dalassena for sidebar on Maria of Alania.

Mary of Anjou (1371–1395).

See Maria of Hungary.

Mary of Anjou (1404–1463).

See Marie of Anjou.

Mary of Antioch (d. 1277)

*Princess of Antioch. Died in 1277; daughter of *Melisande* and Bohemund IV, prince of Antioch.*

When Mary of Antioch died in 1277, she left her claims to Charles of Anjou, king of Sicily.

Mary of Atholl (d. 1116)

*Countess of Boulogne. Name variations: Mary Dunkeld. Died on May 31, 1116; buried at Bermondsey Abbey, London, England; daughter of Malcolm III, king of Scots (r. 1057–1093), and Saint *Margaret* (c. 1046–1093); married Eustace III, count of Boulogne (brother of Baldwin I, king of Jerusalem), in 1102; children: two, including *Matilda of Boulogne* (c. 1103–1152).*

Mary of Baden (1834–1899)

*Princess of Leiningen. Born on November 20, 1834; died on November 21, 1899; daughter of Leopold, grand duke of Baden, and *Sophia of Sweden* (1801–1865); married Ernest, 4th prince of Leiningen, on September 11, 1858; children: two, including Emich, 5th prince of Leiningen (1866–1939).*

Mary of Battenberg (1852–1923)

*Aunt of Earl Mountbatten of Burma. Born on July 18, 1852; died in 1923; daughter of Alexander of Hesse-Darmstadt and *Julie von Hauke* (1825–1895); aunt of Lord Louis Mountbatten, Earl Mountbatten of Burma.*

Mary of Bavaria (1551–1608)

Duchess of Styria and Austria. Name variations: Maria of Bavaria. Born on March 21, 1551; died on April 29, 1608; daughter of Anna of Brunswick (1528–1590) and Albert V (d. 1579), duke of Bavaria; married Karl also known as Charles of Styria (1540–1590), archduke of Styria; children: Katharina Renea, known as Renata (1576–1595); *Margaret of Austria (c. 1577–1611, who married Philip III, king of Spain); Ferdinand II (1578–1637), king of Bohemia and Hungary (r. 1578–1637), Holy Roman emperor (r. 1619–1637); Leopold V, archduke of Austrian Tirol (d. 1632, who married *Claudia de Medici); Maximilian Ernst (1583–1616); *Maria Magdalena of Austria (1589–1631, who married Cosimo II, duke of Tuscany); *Anna of Styria (1573–1598, who married Sigismund III of Poland); Gregoria Maximiliane (1581–1597); Eleonore (1582–1620); *Constance of Styria (1588–1631, who married Sigismund III, king of Poland).

Mary of Bethany (fl. early 1st c. CE).

See Mary Magdalene for sidebar on Martha and Mary of Bethany.

Mary of Brabant (c. 1191–c. 1260)

Countess of Brabant and Holy Roman empress. Name variations: Marie of Brabant; Marie de Brabant. Born around 1191; died after March 9, 1260; daughter of Henry I (1165–1235), duke of Brabant, and *Maude of Alsace (1163–c. 1210); became second wife of Otto IV of Brunswick (c. 1183–1218), earl of York, count of Ponthieu, duke of Bavaria, and Holy Roman emperor (c. 1198–1214), in 1213 or 1214 (Otto was deposed in 1215); children: none.

Mary of Brabant was the second wife of Otto IV, Holy Roman emperor; he had previously been married to *Beatrice of Swabia (1198–1235). Otto was deposed in 1215 and died in 1218, and Mary of Brabant did not remarry. When Countess *Matilda de Dammartin died in 1258, Mary ruled Brabant briefly for that year. Eventually, the fief of Boulogne was passed on to Robert VI, count of Auvergne.

Mary of Burgundy (c. 1400–1463)

Duchess of Cleves. Born around 1400; died in 1463; daughter of *Margaret of Bavaria (d. 1424) and John the Fearless (1371–1419), duke of Burgundy (r. 1404–1419); sister of *Anne Valois (c. 1405–1432), duchess of Bedford, *Agnes of Burgundy (d. 1476), Philip the Good, duke of Burgundy (r. 1419–1467), and Margaret of Burgundy (d. 1441); married Adolphus also known as Adolf I, duke of Cleves; children: John I, duke of Cleves (r. 1448–1481).

Mary of Burgundy (d. 1428)

Duchess of Savoy. Died in 1428; daughter of *Margaret of Flanders (1350–1405) and Philip the Bold (1342–1404), duke of Burgundy (r. 1363–1404); married Amadeus VIII, duke of Savoy; children: Louis I, duke of Savoy.

Mary of Burgundy (1457–1482)

Duchess of Burgundy, countess of Flanders, and archduchess of Austria, who fought to save her land from France and preserved what was to become the modern country of Belgium. Name variations: Marie of Burgundy; Marie de Bourgogne; Maria van Bourgund; Duchess of Burgundy and Luxemburg; Queen of the Low Countries; (sometimes incorrectly known as Margaret of Burgundy because she has historically been confused with Margaret of York). Born in Brussels on February 13, 1457; died on March 27, 1482, at the Prinsenhof in Ghent; daughter of Charles the Bold, the last Valois duke of Burgundy (r. 1467–1477), and his second wife, Isabelle of Bourbon (d. 1465); became first wife of Maximilian I of the Habsburgs (1459–1519), archduke of Austria, and Holy Roman emperor (r. 1493–1519), in 1477 (by proxy on April 22, and in person on August 18); children: Philip the Handsome also known as Philip I the Fair (1478–1506, who married *Juana La Loca); Margaret of Austria (1480–1530, duchess of Savoy, regent of the Netherlands); Frederic (b. September 1481 and lived only a few months). Maximilian I, who had many illegitimate children, also married *Bianca Maria Sforza (1472–1510).

Inaugurated duchess of Burgundy and countess of Flanders (February 16, 1477); became archduchess of Austria upon marriage to Maximilian; had she lived, she would have become empress of Austria.

In Mary of Burgundy's day, Burgundy encompassed the area surrounding Dijon, Flanders, Picardy, and Brabant. It bordered France, Austria, and the English territories in the northeast part of continental Europe. The future of Burgundy was of utmost importance in the ongoing struggle for power between England and France, as well as in the many smaller conflicts throughout central and northern Europe. Mary's father, who was to be remembered as Charles the Bold, was the count of Charolois. Her grandfather, known as Philip the Good, reigned as the duke of Burgundy. Mary's mother was ◄⚜ **Isabelle of Bourbon**, the second wife of Charles. His first wife ◄⚜ **Catherine de France** had died young, with no children; Mary of Burgundy was therefore the sole heir to a large and rich territory.

Since Charles had no male heirs, potential marriages with Mary of Burgundy were plotted almost from the day of her birth on February 13, 1457. Her entrance into the world was celebrated in a grand style, and her baptism at the cathedral of Coudenberg was considered "the greatest magnificence ever seen for a girl." This elegance may have been due to the political position of the child, or it simply may have been expected of the stylish House of Burgundy. Whatever the reason, the festivities lasted an entire day, and Louis of France, later to rule as King Louis XI, was appointed as Mary's godfather. Mary's grandmother, *Isabella of Portugal (1397–1471), filled the role of godmother. Gifts were brought by representatives from across Europe, including some from a number of cities which were in rebellion against Duke Philip the Good at the time.

Mary of Burgundy spent most of her childhood at the ducal castle of Ten Waele at Ghent. She enjoyed an affectionate relationship with her father, even though he was almost constantly away from her. Especially after 1465, when

Charles became the duke of Burgundy, he was personally involved in controlling and governing the cities of his territory. He also developed a flair for conquering new cities, and military operations kept him occupied for months at a time. Isabelle of Bourbon died when Mary was eight years old, and the girl was raised primarily by **Lady Hallewijn**, the wife of the duke's chief steward. Lady Hallewijn was a constant companion and loyal attendant to Mary throughout her life. Several cousins and other children from noble families lived with the heiress as playmates during her childhood. Mary's great-aunt (possibly *Agnes of Burgundy) was responsible for arranging the series of governesses that educated the young lady. Not much is known about Mary's education, but it is clear that she could speak French, Flemish, and English. She enjoyed reading fables and Roman histories, and may have had some training in political philosophy. Her later actions as reigning duchess suggest that she was prepared early in life to govern.

Much more is known about how Mary of Burgundy was entertained and occupied as a child. Exotic animals were brought to her as pets from around the world. She had several dogs, parrots, monkeys, and a giraffe. Mary developed a keen interest in hunting, riding, and other outdoor sports, as well as in gardening. She cared for her falcons as if they were children; later in life, her husband would express surprise at Mary's insistence on keeping the birds of prey in the bedroom, even within a few days of their wedding. Mary's personal seal was a picture of herself on horseback with a falcon on her wrist. She had a complete court of attendants from her infancy, including a dwarf named **Madame de Beauregard**. In all ways, Mary was treated as royalty.

Within a few years of her mother's death, Mary of Burgundy developed the most important relationship of her short life. Upon his ascension to the ducal throne, Charles married for the third time; his new wife was ***Margaret of York**, the sister of Edward IV, the king of England. This alliance was significant for Burgundy because it connected the duchy to the English crown and frustrated the French. Though they were cousins and had previously enjoyed good relations, Charles and Louis of France had become foes in a contest for land acquisition. It was hoped that Margaret of York would have influence with her brother should Burgundy ever require English help. This marriage meant even more for young Mary, however, for she gained in Margaret of York a lifelong friend and mother figure. The two were almost inseparable; indeed, their lives became so intertwined that modern

⚜► **Isabelle of Bourbon** (d. 1465)

*Countess of Charolois. Name variations: Isabel or Isabella of Bourbon. Died in 1465 or 1466; daughter of *Agnes of Burgundy (d. 1476) and Charles I, duke of Bourbon (r. 1434–1456); second wife of Charles the Bold (1433–1477), duke of Burgundy (r. 1467–1477); children: *Mary of Burgundy (1457–1482, who married Maximilian I, Holy Roman emperor). Charles the Bold's first wife was *Catherine de France (1428–1446); his third wife was *Margaret of York (1446–1503).*

⚜► **Catherine de France** (1428–1446)

*French princess. Name variations: Catherine Valois; Catherine de Valois. Born in 1428; died in 1446; daughter of Charles VII (1403–1461), king of France (r. 1422–1461), and *Marie of Anjou (1404–1463); sister of Louis XI, king of France (r. 1461–1483); first wife of Charles the Bold (1433–1477), count of Charolois, later duke of Burgundy (r. 1467–1477); no children.*

Mary of Burgundy (top right) with Maximilian I and their grandchildren.

scholars sometimes confuse the two and the role that each played during the next ten years.

Beginning in 1468, Mary accompanied Margaret of York on her visits throughout Burgundy. Since the duke could not be everywhere at once, it was important for ducal representatives to make appearances in each of the major cities. The two women listened to petitions and assured the people that the duke would not ignore his territories. Charles was a strict ruler, and the women were especially needed to pacify dissatisfied factions and build loyalty. They were often successful in this respect, so much so that Margaret of York usually had little trouble collecting money and men for Charles when he needed them on the battlefield. The exposure of the heiress to so many of her subjects also served to encourage love and loyalty for her, something she would sorely need in the coming years.

Mary of Burgundy was still a child for the first several years of traveling, and Margaret of York took responsibility for the girl's education. They learned from each other; Mary learned to speak fluent English from her stepmother, and

Margaret of York learned French and Dutch from Mary. Together, they were quite a diplomatic team. Mary and Margaret of York were both pious women, and they made it a point to stop at many shrines while touring the country. They also went on a number of pilgrimages together. They shared a special devotion to the cult of *St. Colette, a reformer of convents in Burgundy and France. Together, they served as patrons of the Ghent guild of *St. Anne. The two were welcomed and celebrated everywhere they went. The city of Mons so impressed Mary with its splendid reception in 1471 that she decided to stay there a year without Margaret of York. Thus, by the age of 14, she was already prepared to stand independently as the ducal resident.

Her death was a great loss to her subjects; for she was a person of great honor, affability, and generosity to all people, and she was more beloved and respected by her subjects than her husband, as being natural sovereign of their country.

—Philip of Commines

At all times, negotiations for Mary of Burgundy's eventual marriage was taking place. Charles was a shrewd man, and he knew that offering Mary's hand could get him immediate support from any quarter. He shamelessly courted several alliances, possibly without the intention of honoring any of them. Starting when Mary was only a child, her father promised her to a long line of suitors, including Ferdinand of Aragon, Nicholas of Lorraine, George, duke of Clarence (brother of Margaret of York), Duke Francis II of Brittany, the dauphin Charles (the future Charles VIII), Charles of Berry, Philibert of Savoy, Nicholas of Anjou, and Maximilian (I), the Habsburg archduke and heir to the Austrian empire. Mary seemed to be unusually well informed of these negotiations, and on more than one occasion Charles had his daughter personally write to her suitor and pledge herself to the man, enclosing a ring or some other symbolic gift.

After 1473, Mary of Burgundy spent most of her time in residence at Ghent. That city had a reputation for uprisings, and the duke had taken most of the privileges away from its citizenry. He had most recently dismissed all of their magistrates and enforced the election of an entire new council. At the same time, the city had financed a good deal of the latest military expeditions. Mary's presence served to quiet the resentful citizens and reassure them that the duke's debt would be repaid. In this respect, she was some-

thing of a hostage; as long as she was in their care, the people of Ghent knew the duke could not ignore them. Back in 1467, shortly after Charles had become duke of Burgundy, the Gantois, as the citizens were called, had risen against him. Mary, aged ten at the time, had been staying at Ghent. Charles chose to give in to their demands rather than use force to put down the rebellion, which might have put his daughter at risk. These tactics had worked so well that the Gantois were determined to keep Mary again in residence there for as long as possible.

In late 1475, Charles came to a final agreement on Mary's marital future. He had negotiated with Frederick III, Holy Roman emperor and emperor of Austria, for the marriage of Mary to his son Maximilian; the match was designed to bring stability to the warring German cities and to outmaneuver France once and for all. This time, however, Charles' ambition proved too much. He brought his daughter with him to Treves, where he intended to persuade Frederick to bestow upon him the title "King of the Romans" in return for Mary's promised betrothal. His dream was to create a kingdom out of Burgundy called Lotharingia. Frederick refused to comply and left early one morning without a word to Charles. There was nothing for Mary to do except return to Ghent and await her father's next decision.

In January 1477, once again trying to expand his territories, Charles was involved in a war against the free cities of the Rhine valley and, despite a string of losses, decided to press on. Against advice, he laid siege to the city of Nancy, which was defended by a Swiss army. On January 5, his army was destroyed, and Charles' stripped and mutilated body was not recovered for a couple of days. This tragedy was the beginning of the most trying year of Mary of Burgundy's life. Without giving her a day to grieve, the citizens of Ghent approached the new duchess and demanded the reinstatement of their privileges. It was said at the time that the people of a country always adore the child of their prince while she is young, but hate her as soon as she becomes the governor. Mary's situation was no exception. While she dealt with formal petitions in her chambers, people in the streets rose up, setting fire to the prison and the hall of justice. They gathered up the magistrates who had been chosen under Charles' authority and executed them in the square. This uprising was put down by the ducal army that resided in the city, but Mary had to vow to make amends to the city and find a peaceful solution.

Mary of Burgundy summoned the Estates General, a body of citizens and councilors, to meet at Ghent in February 1477. Margaret of York, who had since taken on the title of duchess dowager, acted as Mary's top advisor. They wrote up a draft of the Great Privilege, a new charter for the city which included Mary's promise to submit any marriage proposals made to her for the people's approval. In return for peace, Mary promised not to make a move without the help and advice of her many advisors. Unfortunately, the Gantois were more concerned with their privileges than with the safety of their land. Burgundy was in a delicate position; Louis XI of France was eager for any excuse to take possession of Burgundian territory, and his armies and ambassadors had already started out for the nearest cities. Some of those municipalities readily gave their loyalty to France, and Louis was prepared to use force against any that were hesitant. Despite Margaret of York's pleas to her brother for help, the king of England was reluctant to offer assistance until he saw how far Louis could get. If enough of the territory fell without a struggle, and Mary proved incapable of keeping the land intact, Edward IV was willing to split the territory evenly with France.

Louis XI justified his invasion of Burgundy by pointing out the lack of a male heir; French law did not recognize a woman's right to inherit land, and thus he considered the land to be leaderless. Ironically, Flanders and other central European lands had often passed down through female hands, and those territories did not welcome France's intrusion. Most of these were not French-speaking territories, and they feared a great loss of cultural independence if France took over. Louis had many tricks at his disposal, however. He even wrote to Mary to promise his protection, calling upon his duty as her godfather to watch out for her and her land, which he more than likely hoped to claim as his own. He offered to marry the duchess to his son, the dauphin Charles, who was at the time a sickly seven-year-old. Mary of Burgundy was 19 and ready to bear children if she were matched with an adult husband. Louis knew that she and his son would probably never have children, leaving all of Burgundy in his possession.

In March, Louis sent as ambassador to Ghent a man named Oliver le Mauvais, a former barber and surgeon who had bought his noble status. There, Mauvais was supposed to rally the people of the city to France's side and to meet in private with Mary to persuade her to accept the marriage proposal. The citizens and councilors of Ghent were so insulted at the lowliness of the ambassador sent to meet with their sovereign, and at his insistence on speaking privately with the young woman, that they threatened to throw Mauvais into the river. He left without accomplishing his mission. During that same month, Mary of Burgundy wrote to Louis XI on the advice of Margaret of York and her other top advisors, the lords Ravenstein, Humbercourt, and Hugonet. In the letter, co-signed by her advisors, Mary humbly addressed the king of France as her godfather and suggested that she would consider his offer. Some modern scholars claim that this letter never really existed; since Louis would use it later to hurt her, some believe he forged the letter to turn her subjects against her. However, many contemporary French chroniclers accept the letter as authentic. France was a very real threat to Burgundy; Mary's letter may have been an acknowledgment of France's power or a device to buy some time.

Ghent and several other major cities sent ambassadors to France to meet with Louis XI and negotiate a peace treaty. They were sure of their own authority, as Mary had promised it to them in the Great Privilege. Louis convinced them that Mary was actually negotiating behind their backs, and showed them the letter as proof. He claimed that he had been instructed to ignore the ambassadors of the city and deal only with her top advisors. He also claimed that the duchess had agreed to marry his son against the wishes of her subjects. Even if the letter was real, however, Louis was considered by contemporaries to be devious for his use of it. He knew it would cause turmoil, and he cared little for the unwritten code of honor between nobles that would have prevented him from sharing a private correspondence with others. This ploy worked; the enraged ambassadors returned to Ghent and confronted Mary with the letter. They accused her advisors of conspiring with the king of France against the people of Burgundy, but chose to assume that Mary was personally innocent of the arrangements. Humbercourt and Hugonet, two of her advisors, were from French nobility, and may have actually wanted to see Mary wedded to French royalty. Thus, the citizens formally convicted these two men of treason and sentenced them to death. Mary's other advisors, Margaret of York and Lord Ravenstein, were exiled from the city. Mary of Burgundy was confined to the castle Ten Waele and deprived of visitors and correspondence.

Mary tried every political tool at her disposal to free the men from custody; when those failed, she attempted an emotional appeal. During Easter week of 1477, on the appointed day of execution for Humbercourt and Hugonet, Mary of Burgundy appeared in the public square, alone and on foot, and entered the crowd. She was disheveled, her head covered by a simple kerchief, and with tears in her eyes she begged the people of the city not to kill her friends. Many were moved by the sight of their princess, and a fight broke out between those who wanted to free the prisoners and those who wanted them killed. In the chaos that followed, the executioners performed their duty, and called for attention only after the men lay dead. Mary collapsed and was carried back to the castle. She spent the next few days making sure that the families of the executed advisors were safe and cared for financially.

Throughout the first year of Mary of Burgundy's reign, she was bombarded with the marital demands of "pretendants," men who insisted that they had been promised her hand in marriage by her father Charles before his death. Some of them, in fact, may have received such assurances. Nevertheless, Mary had to be wary of the stream of suitors who hoped to win her hand and her riches. She was well aware of Louis' intention to marry her to his son and claim Burgundy for himself. However, accepting a partner who was not powerful enough to fight France would also be tantamount to surrender. The only practical solution was to marry Maximilian of Austria. Fortunately for her, he was the only suitor who was able to produce a letter of promise from Mary, as well as one of her jewels sent to seal the pledge. Thus, Mary of Burgundy proceeded to finalize the marriage arrangements herself, despite a clause in the Great Privilege that gave the right of arrangement to the people of Burgundy. There was no time to lose in council meetings, and as reigning duchess Mary had no need of a dowry or lengthy marriage contract. The wedding was performed by proxy on April 22, 1477, and Maximilian began his journey from Cologne to Ghent, where the actual ceremony would be repeated in person on August 18.

Mary of Burgundy appeased the people of Ghent by promising that Maximilian would not inherit her land in the event of her death. The citizens of the Burgundian cities were afraid of having a foreign ruler. As things stood, however, the Flemish cities were pleased with her choice, because an Austrian duke was more likely to respect their culture and language than was the French king. Maximilian was celebrated and welcomed on his journey to Ghent, and when his money ran out only halfway to his destination, ambassadors financed the rest of the trip. Louis XI is said to have tried to delay the procession to Ghent—he persisted in believing he could force Mary to accept his son. Nevertheless, Maximilian arrived safely in the city, and the wedding was celebrated without further problems.

Mary and Maximilian seem to have had an ideal marriage. They were both young, attractive, and known for their intelligence and courage. While they could not, at first, speak each other's native languages, they taught each other and communicated well. They both enjoyed riding and hunting. Maximilian wrote to a friend that he found his wife beautiful, and he confided that they did not have separate bedrooms—something almost unheard of among the nobility of the day. Unfortunately, Maximilian was soon caught up in the fight with France over territory. With the power of Austria now behind Burgundy, England had no problem committing to support the tiny collection of states against the French king. Maximilian was absent for long periods, and he missed the birth and baptism of his first born child when on June 22, 1478, Mary gave birth to the boy who would someday reign as Philip I the Fair. A year and a half later, on January 10, 1480, Mary had her second child, *Margaret of Austria, who would eventually be betrothed to the same son of King Louis XI who had been offered to Mary.

A stern ruler, Maximilian was becoming hated and feared in some Burgundian cities. The people's love for Mary grew, however, as she became a patron of the arts and continued to hear petitions from citizens. Mary's subjects were overjoyed with the births so soon after her marriage, and they followed the growth of the ruling family with interest. In Brussels, on September 2, 1481, while Maximilian was again absent, Mary had a third child, another son whom she named Frederic. Sadly, Frederic died only a few months later. In the meantime, Mary had changed her will secretly so that Maximilian would get all of her territory, as well as guardianship of the children, should she die before him. This would be contested hotly after her death by the people of Ghent and the Estates General.

After the wedding, Mary and Maximilian had moved their primary residence to the castle Prinsenhof. In March 1482, Mary was there with her children when Maximilian came to stay for several weeks; they were enjoying one of their famous hunts together. Somehow, though she was an accomplished rider, Mary was thrown from her horse. Her injuries did not at first seem serious enough to warrant fetching a doctor, but during the next few days she developed a serious fever and asked for the last rites to be performed. Mary of Burgundy died on March 27, 1482, with her husband and children nearby. She was 25 years old. Some believe she was pregnant with her fourth child at the time of her death. Maximilian grieved publicly for her, and did not remarry for many years. Mary was buried at the church of Our Lady of Bruges. In 1502, she was reinterred beneath a magnificent monument created by the sculptor Pierre de Beckere. Her remains were moved once more in the turmoil after the French Revolution; in 1806, she and her father were moved to a simple tomb in the chapel of Lanchals.

SOURCES:

De Berente, M. *Histoire des ducs de Bourgogne de la maison Valois, 1364–1477*. Vol. 11–12. Paris: Le Normant, 1937.

Hommel, Luc. *Marie de Bourgogne; ou, le Grand Heritage*. Brussels: Les Ouevres, Ad. Goemaere, 1945.

Scoble, Andrew R., ed. *The memoirs of Philip de Commines, Lord of Argenton*. 2 vols. London: Henry G. Bohn, 1855.

Vaughn, Richard. *Charles the Bold: The Last Valois Duke of Burgundy*. NY: Longman Group, 1973.

Weightman, Christine. *Margeret of York, Duchess of Burgundy 1446–1503*. NY: St. Martins Press, 1989.

SUGGESTED READING:

James, G.P.R. *Mary of Burgundy; or, the Revolt of Ghent*. London: George Routledge, 1903.

Nancy L. Locklin, Ph.D. candidate,
Emory University, Atlanta, Georgia

Mary of Buttermere (d. 1837).

See Robinson, Mary.

Mary of Cleophas

*Saint and Biblical woman. Name variations: Mary Cleophas; Mary, the wife of Clopas. Sister or close relative of *Mary the Virgin; children: possibly James of Jerusalem and Joseph (called the brothers of Jesus in Mark 6.3).*

Mary of Cleophas followed Jesus to Calvary, was present at his burial, and saw him after he had risen. Her feast day is April 9.

Mary of Cleves (1426–1486).

See Marie of Cleves.

Mary of Coucy (c. 1220–c. 1260).

See Mary de Coucy.

Mary of Egypt (d. 430)

Saint and Christian ascetic. Name variations: Mary the Egyptian. Born in Egypt; died in 430, in the desert of Palestine, near the river Jordan.

Mary of Egypt was a half-mythical African saint whose history is founded on that of a female hermit who lived and died in a desert near the river Jordan in Palestine. According to legend, Mary was born in Egypt and left her home at age 12, embarking on a dissolute life in Alexandria which far exceeded the reputed deeds of *Mary Magdalene, with whom she is frequently confused. They are sometimes united in paintings as joint figures of female penitence. At age 29, Mary of Egypt accompanied a group of Libyans who were going to Jerusalem to witness the Exaltations of the Cross. Arriving in the Holy City, Mary of Egypt sought to join the crowd going into the temple, but found herself rooted to the ground, unable to cross the threshold. A light appeared, telling her that her sinful ways prevented her from entering, followed by a vision of *Mary the Virgin. Mary of Egypt prayed for veneration, vowing to follow the path she was shown. "Cross Jordan," she was told, "and you will find peace." After confessing her sins and receiving Communion, Mary of Egypt crossed the Jordan as instructed, taking with her three loaves of bread. She remained in the desert for the next 47 years, eating only roots and herbs and communing with God. A year before her death, Mary of Egypt was visited in the desert by St. Zosimus to whom she related the story of her life. As he was leaving, she requested that he return to her on Holy Thursday of the following year to bring her the Eucharist. The monk kept his promise but found that Mary had since died. As he began to dig a grave in which to bury her, a lion appeared and with his paw assisted the monk in preparing the grave.

The earliest depictions of Mary of Egypt are thought to be in a series on the wall of the chapel of the Bargello, in Florence, and there is a celebrated painting of her by Tintoretto at the Scuola de San Rocco in Venice. Her story is also depicted in one of the painted windows of the cathedral of Chartres. According to *Anna Brownell Jameson in her *Legends of the Monastic Orders* (1872), Mary of Egypt was also a popular saint in France, particularly with the Parisians, until she was eclipsed by the increasing popularity of Mary Magdalene. Her feast day is April 2.

Barbara Morgan,
Melrose, Massachusetts

Mary of Egypt (fl. 629).

See A'ishah bint Abi Bakr for sidebar on Maryam the Egyptian.

Mary of France (c. 1140–1200).

See Marie de France.

Mary of France (1496–1533).

See Mary Tudor.

Mary of Guelders (d. 1405)

*Duchess of Juliers. Name variations: Mary of Gueldres. Died in 1405; daughter of *Sophia of Malines (d. 1329) and Renaud, also known as Rainald or Reginald II the Black Haired (d. 1343), duke of Guelders (also known as count of Gelderland), count of Zutphen; married William VI (d. 1393), duke of Juliers.*

Mary of Guelders (1433–1463)

*Queen of Scotland. Name variations: Mary of Gelders; Mary of Gueldres; Mary of Gelderland; Marie von Geldern. Born on July 3, 1433, in Holyrood Abbey, Edinburgh, Scotland (some sources cite Guelders, the Netherlands); died on December 1, 1463, in Scotland; interred in Holy Trinity Church, Edinburgh; daughter of Arnold, duke of Guelders, and *Catherine of Cleves (1417–1479); married James II (1430–1460), king of Scotland (r. 1437–1460), on July 3, 1449; children: James III (1451–1488), king of Scotland (r. 1460–1488); *Margaret Stewart (fl. 1460–1520); Alexander (c. 1454–1485), 1st duke of Albany; David, earl of Moray (died in infancy); David (c. 1454–1456); John (c. 1456–1479), earl of Mar and Garioch; *Mary Stewart (c. 1451–1488).*

A Dutch noblewoman, Mary of Guelders became queen of Scotland upon her marriage to King James II. Over time, she became a great supporter and patriot of her adopted country, playing an important role in Scotland's continuous wars against English rule. Even after James died in 1460, Mary of Guelders maintained the Scottish campaigns against the British as regent of Scotland for her young son, now James III. The queen was a capable strategist and leader, heading the siege of several northern English towns and conquering the town of Berwick. She was a prominent political force in Scotland throughout her regency and even beyond, and was rewarded by the Scots' loyalty to her rule. In 1462, she founded the Church of the Holy Trinity in Edinburgh. She died young, the following year, at the age of 30.

Laura York,
Riverside, California

Mary of Guise (1515–1560)

French-born queen of Scotland who fought to retain the throne for her daughter, Mary Stuart, against Scottish nobles and Protestant reformers. Name variations: Mary of Lorraine; Mary of Guise-Lorraine; Marie of Guise; (Fr.) Mary de Guise, duchess of Longueville. Pronunciation: Geez or Geese. Born on November 20 (some sources cite 22), 1515, in Castle Bar-le-Duc, Lorraine, in northern France; died in Edinburgh Castle, Scotland, on June 10 or 11, 1560; buried in Rheims, Champagne, France; daughter of Claude I, duke of Guise, and Antoinette of Bourbon (1494–1583); married Louis II d'Orleans, duke of Longueville, on August 4, 1534; married James V (1512–1542), king of Scotland (r. 1513–1542), on May 9, 1538; children: (first marriage) François III also known as Francis III (b. October 30, 1535), duke of Longueville; Louis (b. August 4, 1537); (second marriage) James Stewart (b. May 22, 1540), 5th duke of Rothesay; Arthur Stewart (b. April 24, 1541), duke of Albany (also referred to in some sources as Robert); Mary Stuart (1542–1587), Queen of Scots.

Educated at Pont-au-Mousson convent; presented at court of Francis I of France (1531); crowned queen of Scots (February 22, 1540); widowed and assumed title queen dowager (December 14, 1542); appointed head of advisory council to Scottish governor (1544); made diplomatic visit to France (1550); appointed regent of Scotland (April 12, 1554).

In May 1538, the coastline of Scotland loomed large before Mary of Guise as she peered from the deck of a ship crossing the North Sea. She was traveling to meet her new husband, James V, king of Scotland. Behind her lay France and everything the 22-year-old widow had known and loved, including her young son; ahead was an alien country of people whose ways she did not know and a language she did not speak. Even her husband, married to her by proxy, was a stranger. Though they had only exchanged a few letters, the newlyweds would now face the challenge of being Scotland's king and queen.

Mary of Guise was born on November 20, 1515, in Bar-le-Duc castle in northern France, the oldest child of Claude, duke of Guise and ✤▶ **Antoinette of Bourbon**. It was an exciting time in the country of her birth. The cultural flowering known historically as the Renaissance had spread from Italy to northern Europe and taken hold in France, with all its artistic and literary splendor. A new king had ascended the throne that same year. Francis I was a patron of the arts and literature, and his court was to grow into a center for French thinkers and writers. The nobility of the country, including Mary's parents, were to be deeply influenced by his example.

Mary grew up in various of her father's castles but lived primarily at Joinville, left behind by her grandmother, *Philippa of Guelders, who had retired to the convent of Pont-au-Mousson on the northern French coast. During her earliest years, Mary was most strongly influenced by her mother, whose only child she was until the birth of a son when Mary was four. Three more sons, as well as five more daughters whose names are unknown, would follow in a span of some seventeen years, and from her mother Mary learned to care for her brothers and sisters, and all she would need to know about running a noble household.

Sometime near the beginning of her teens, Mary was sent to the convent of her grandmother to be educated. One effect of the Renaissance was to encourage many noble families to view the education of their daughters in reading, writing, and reasoning to be as important as the education of their sons. If a woman were to raise wise and thoughtful children capable of ruling, it was believed, she herself would need moral and philosophical education. Mary probably became well grounded in Christian philosophy while at Pont-au-Mousson.

In 1529, Mary was close to her 14th birthday when her uncle and aunt—Anthony, duke of Lorraine, and ❧▶ Renée of Montpensier—arrived at the convent to take her with them to their court at Nancy. It was a common practice among the nobility for children to be sent to the households of friends or family where they could learn etiquette and strengthen friendships between households. At Nancy, Mary spent the next year learning the finer points of courtly manners while her elders looked toward establishing her in a good marriage.

In March 1531, soon after she turned 15, Mary of Guise was presented by her uncle at the court of Francis I, where she spent the better part of the next three years serving as a waiting-woman to Queen *Eleanor of Portugal (1498–1558). During this time, a suitable husband was found in Louis, duke of Longueville, whose lands lay just to the north of the Guise lands. It is likely that Mary and Louis had known each other since childhood, and their marriage solidified friendly relations between the two families.

Mary and Louis married on August 4, 1534, in the chapel of the Louvre Palace. Much of the royal court was in attendance, and the celebration following the ceremony lasted two weeks. The couple took up residence at Louis' ancestral home of Châteaudun, where Mary began the life for which she had been raised. She became a strong patron of the tenants on her husband's land, seeing to both their grievances and their needs. On October 30, 1535, one month shy of her 20th birthday, her first son Francis was born. By December 1536, she was pregnant again. Whatever sense of contentment she may have felt was soon shattered by the death of her husband Louis on June 9, 1537, in Rouen. Her second son Louis was born two months later on August 4, 1537, but the infant died four months later. Determined to avoid remarriage, Mary of Guise set about caring for the Longueville lands until her son Francis was old enough to oversee them.

But the king of France had other ideas. In the winter of 1536, James V of Scotland had visited the court of Francis I in search of a wife, whom he found in ❧▶ Madeleine of France (1520–1537), one of Francis' and *Claude de France's daughters. The couple had been married on January 1, 1537, in an elaborate ceremony attended by many of the nobility, including Mary and her husband. Madeleine was not a physically strong woman, however, and the weather in Scotland apparently contributed to her death only a few months after the wedding, leaving James in search of another French noblewoman to marry. While he was eager to continue his alliance with Scotland, Francis I did not want to lose any more daughters to the Scottish climate. Pondering other acceptable candidates, the king remembered the recently widowed duchess of Longueville, whose rank and wealth made her the perfect choice. The only obstacle was Mary's vow not to marry again.

▲❧
Madeleine of France. See Margaret Tudor for sidebar.

❧▶ **Antoinette of Bourbon** (1494–1583)
*Duchess of Guise and Lorraine. Born on December 25, 1494 (some sources cite 1493); died on January 22, 1583; daughter of *Marie of Luxemburg (d. 1546) and François also known as Francis of Bourbon, count of Vendôme; married Claude I (1496–1550), duke of Guise-Lorraine, on June 9, 1513 (some sources cite 1510); children: *Mary of Guise (1515–1560); Francis, 2nd duke of Guise (1519–1563); Charles (b. 1524), cardinal of Lorraine; Claude (1526–1573), marquis of Mayenne and duke of Aumâle; Louis (d. 1578), 1st cardinal of Guise; René (1536–1566), marquis of Elbeuf; and five other daughters (names unknown).*

❧▶ **Renée of Montpensier** (fl. 1500s)
Duchess of Lorraine. Name variations: Renee of Montpensier. Flourished in the early 1500s; married Antoine or Anthony, duke of Lorraine (r. 1508–1544); children: Francis I, duke of Lorraine (r. 1544–1545).

James V had met Mary briefly in 1536, during his earlier visit to France. Now he set out to win her over by appealing to her sense of duty and purpose. According to **Rosalind Marshall**, "He was not simply offering her a ceremonial role in life but asking for her advice and assistance. She was to be his partner in a difficult endeavour."

The endeavor, which was indeed difficult, was to unite Scotland and France against England and its threats to the Catholic Church, which Henry VIII, king of England, had broken with in 1534. Only for reasons so broad and deep would Mary consider remarriage at this point, and she finally agreed to the arrangement. On May 9, 1538, she was married by proxy to James at Châteaudun; Robert, Lord Maxwell, who stood in place of James, then escorted the new queen to Scotland.

Leaving France, Mary also left behind Francis, her two-year-old son, in the care of her mother Antoinette. As heir to his father's lands, it was important that the infant duke of Longueville remain close to his possessions. Mary's ship landed with her entourage close to the city of St. Andrews, where she was met by James. Two days after Trinity Sunday, 1538, their marriage was confirmed at the Cathedral of St. Andrews.

*S*he took hold of her courage, constancy, and resolution during the consolations and desolations, the prosperities and adversities of this mortal life.

—Hilarion de Coste

For the next two years, Mary's time was mostly spent acquainting herself with her new country. In contrast to the custom in France, the new queen discovered that the Scottish nobility did not hold their king in high regard; while they recognized him as king, many of the nobles were closely related to James and remembered when his family had been in their position; some hoped eventually to usurp his crown for themselves or their sons. Slowly, Mary learned which nobles could be counted on to support James and which sought his downfall.

A primary duty of hers, meanwhile, was to provide Scotland with an heir, and more than one if possible. The issue was so important that she was six months' pregnant with the king's first child before she was crowned queen of Scots on February 22, 1540. On May 22, Mary of Guise gave birth to a healthy son baptized a week later as James, duke of Rothesay and prince of Scotland. This time, unlike with her son Francis, the raising of her child was not left to her. Almost from his first week of life, as the next in line to the throne, the young James had his own household, separate from the court.

On April 24, 1541, Mary gave birth to another son, Arthur. But while Scotland celebrated the news of the birth of a second prince, the infant James fell seriously ill, and the newborn Arthur also appeared frail. Only a week after his birth, Arthur died a few hours after the death of his older brother. The king and queen were both devastated.

James V never truly recovered from the loss of the infants. For months after the deaths, his relationship with Mary of Guise was strained; when they were reconciled, it was to join in facing foreign troubles. To the south, Henry VIII was threatening to invade Scotland if James would not join him in alliance. But James perceived Henry's overtures as a menace to Scotland, and saw no other recourse but to fight to keep his country independent. James set off for war, leaving Mary, pregnant for a third time, in the capital of Edinburgh. In November 1542, the Scots suffered an overwhelming defeat at the battle of Solway Moss, and James was crushed by the setback. In his weakened state, he contracted a fever, living only long enough to hear of the birth of a daughter, *****Mary Stuart**, on December 8. He died on December 14.

Mary of Guise, widowed a second time at age 27, was now dowager queen of Scotland. With her week-old daughter as queen, Mary of Guise was thrust to the center of a political and religious struggle to control the regency of her child. Soon two men were vying openly to be named regent. David Beaton, cardinal-archbishop of St. Andrews and formerly a close advisor to the dead king, had strongly supported the French alliance and was uncompromising in his belief of the Catholic Church's supremacy in Scotland. In contrast, James Hamilton, 2nd earl of Arran, second in line to the Scottish throne after the infant queen, was a man suspected of Protestant leanings. Mary of Guise, having spent most of her four years in Scotland sorting out the political intrigues of the court or sequestered in pregnancy, lacked enough support among the Scottish barons to declare herself regent. She decided to back Beaton, since they agreed on Scotland's ties with France and on the preeminence of the Catholic Church.

Throughout 1543, Arran and Beaton each connived to gain the upper hand. Because Beaton wanted links with France, Arran looked for support in England, negotiating a peace treaty

Mary of
Guise

and an agreement for Mary Stuart to marry England's Prince Edward (the future Edward VI) when she reached the age of ten; one demand of the marriage agreement was that the young queen be educated in England. None of this sat well with the Scottish nobles, however, and Arran eventually had to acquiesce to Beaton. Finally, in 1544, a council was formed, with Mary of Guise at its head, to oversee Beaton as regent.

Meanwhile, the rebuff by the Scots left Henry VIII eager to suppress the barons to the north. From 1543 to 1548, Henry first tried to intimidate them into an English alliance, then declared war. Scottish Protestants turned their support to him, in hopes of displacing the Catholic Church in Scotland, while the French aided the main Scottish force with soldiers and money.

For the first four years, it was a traditional war, fought in hopes of an overwhelming defeat that would lead to the loser's capitulation. But after 1547, English tactics changed: instead of engaging in battle after battle, the English fortified the lands they had taken and prepared to outlast the Scottish forces, waiting for them to make the next move. When the move came, it was under the influence of the dowager queen, who organized French troops at siege sites and gave a stirring speech before her armies in preparation for what was to be one of the final battles of the war. A final countermove from the English, with their Scottish support, forced her to remove herself and her daughter to the heavily fortified castle of Stirling. From there, through her contacts at the French court, Mary of Guise managed to arrange a treaty with France that secured the marriage of her daughter to Francis, the dauphin of France (later Francis II), son of King Henry II, who had succeeded his father Francis I in 1547. In July 1548, her daughter sailed for France, leaving the English outmaneuvered, not on the battlefield but through diplomacy.

In 1550, in celebration of this political success and to demonstrate to the Scots what an alliance with France meant, Mary of Guise invited several Scottish nobles to join her on a yearlong diplomatic visit to France. When the city of Rouen held pageants in honor of the victories of the Scottish and French troops, the visitors were suitably impressed. In Paris, King Henry II held lavish entertainments at the royal court, while Mary of Guise had time to be with her relatives, whom she had not seen in more than ten years, and especially with her two surviving children, Francis and Mary Stuart. It was to be the last time she would see the son of her first marriage; he would die in October 1551.

On her return from France, Mary of Guise's political position was strengthened to the degree that she was officially declared regent of Scotland by the Scottish Parliament on April 12, 1554. After the assassination of Cardinal Beaton in 1546, Arran had assumed the regency, and, in compensation for relinquishing it, he was awarded the French duchy of Châtelherault by Henry II. Mary of Guise, meanwhile, moved to shore up her own domestic and foreign policies, seeing her regency as a chance to bring stability and prosperity to Scotland.

But a miscalculation of the strength of religious interests was soon to help precipitate her downfall. A Catholic herself, she did not understand the hold that the Protestant reformation by then had on Scotland. Refusing to persecute Protestants, she believed that many of their conversions were political, and that the converts would eventually return to the Catholic Church. It was a view that left her ill-prepared to deal with the most strident of Scottish Protestant reformers, John Knox, who declaimed against Mary of Guise's regency as an abomination to Scotland both religiously and politically. Preaching for her overthrow and the establishment of a national Protestant Church in Scotland, he won a growing number of converts.

Mary of Guise also failed to understand the depth of the Scottish fear of foreign domination. In setting up her government, she drew many of her new state officials directly from France, without realizing the insult this was to the Scottish nobility. Appreciative as they were of French wealth and power, they did not want Scotland to be annexed to France. When they discovered that the 1558 marriage treaty between Mary Stuart and the dauphin included a clause granting the throne of Scotland to the dauphin in the event of Mary Stuart's death, they grew incensed, viewing Mary of Guise as a puppet of the French king.

By 1559, Mary of Guise was engaged in one battle after another against the forces seeking to depose her. The Protestants, led by John Knox, were requesting aid from England, which was willingly given, since Mary Stuart, through her marriage to the dauphin, now made claims to thrones of England and Ireland as well as of Scotland and France. At age 45, Mary of Guise was most likely suffering from acute heart disease when she became extremely ill while trying to lead the struggle against the English from Edinburgh. Taking to her bed, she continued to issue orders for her troops, but she succumbed, on June 11, 1560, to her exhausted and debilitated heart.

SOURCES:
Brown, P. Hume. *History of Scotland.* 2 vols. NY: Octagon Books, 1971.
Coste, Hilarion de. *Les elogies et les vies des reynes, des princesses, et des dames illustres . . . .* 2 vols. Paris: S. Cramoisy, 1647.
Jensen, De Lamar. *Reformation Europe: Age of Reform and Revolution.* Lexington, MA: D.C. Heath, 1992.
Lynch, Michael. *Scotland: A New History.* London: Century, 1991.
Marshall, Rosalind K. *Mary of Guise.* London: William Collins Sons, 1977.

RELATED MEDIA:
Elizabeth (film), starring **Cate Blanchett** as *Elizabeth I and **Fanny Ardant** as Mary of Guise, Polygram, 1999.

Elisa A. Litvin,
historian and freelance writer,
Farmington Hills, Michigan

Mary of Habsburg (1528–1603).

See Elizabeth of Habsburg (1554–1592) for sidebar on Marie of Austria.

Mary of Hanover (1849–1904)

Hanoverian princess. Born Mary Ernestine Josephine Adolphine Henrietta Theresa Elizabeth Alexandrina on December 2, 1849, in Hanover, Lower Saxony, Germany; died on June 4, 1904, in Gmunden, Austria; daughter of George V (b. 1819), king of Hanover, and *Mary of Saxe-Altenburg (1818–1907).

Mary of Hesse-Cassel (1723–1772)

English princess royal. Name variations: Mary, Princess of Hesse; Mary Guelph; Mary Hanover. Born on February 22 (some sources cite March 5), 1723, at Leicester House, St. Martin's, London, England; died in Hanau on January 14, 1772; daughter of George II (1683–1760), king of Great Britain and Ireland (r. 1727–1760) and Caroline of Ansbach (1683–1737); married Frederick II, landgrave of Hesse-Cassel or Kassel, on June 28, 1740; children: William (b. 1741); William IX, elector of Hesse (b. 1743); Charles of Hesse-Cassel (1744–1836); Frederick III (1747–1837), landgrave of Hesse-Cassel.

Mary of Hesse-Cassel was born in 1723, the daughter of George II, king of England, and *Caroline of Ansbach. She married Frederick II, landgrave of Hesse-Cassel, in 1740. When her husband became a Catholic in 1754, Mary separated from him and lived with her children at Hanau.

Mary of Hesse-Cassel (1796–1880)

Grand duchess of Mecklenburg-Strelitz. Born on January 21, 1796; died on December 30, 1880; daughter of Frederick III, landgrave of Hesse-Cassel, and *Caroline of Nassau-Usingen; married George, grand duke of Mecklenburg-Strelitz, on August 12, 1817; children: four, including Frederick (1819–1904), grand duke of Mecklenburg-Strelitz.

Mary of Hesse-Homburg
(1785–1846)

Princess of Prussia. Born on October 13, 1785; died on April 14, 1846; daughter of Frederick Louis, landgrave of Hesse-Homburg, and *Caroline of Hesse-Darmstadt (1746–1821); cousin of Louis II, grand duke of Hesse-Darmstadt; married William (1783–1851, son of Frederick William II, king of Prussia, and *Frederica of Hesse), prince of Prussia, on January 12, 1804; children: Frederica (1805–1806); Frederick (b. 1811); Adalbert (b. 1811), admiral in the Prussian navy; *Elizabeth Hohenzollern (1815–1885); Waldemar (b. 1817), Prussian major general; *Maria of Prussia (1825–1889, who married Maximilian II, king of Bavaria).

Mary of Hungary (1371–1395).
See Maria of Hungary.

Mary of Hungary (1505–1558)

Queen of Hungary and regent of the Netherlands. Name variations: Marie of Austria or Marie d'Autriche; Maria of Hungary; Maria of Castile; Mary Habsburg or Hapsburg. Born in 1505 in the Netherlands; died in 1558 in the Netherlands; daughter of Philip of Burgundy also known as Philip I the Fair, king of Castile and Léon (r. 1506), and Juana La Loca (1479–1555) of Aragon, queen of Castile; sister of Ferdinand I and Charles V, both Holy Roman emperors, and *Catherine (1507–1578), *Eleanor of Portugal (1498–1558), and *Elisabeth of Habsburg (1501–1526); married Lajos also known as Louis II (1506–1526), king of Hungary (r. 1516–1526), around 1520; no children.

Mary of Hungary served as regent of the Netherlands for 27 years. She was born in 1505 into the royal families of Spain and Austria, the daughter of Philip I the Fair, heir to Austria and the Netherlands, and *Juana La Loca, titular queen of Castile. Her father died in 1506; her

Mary of
Hungary
(1505–1558)

mother, who had always suffered from mental illness, became completely insane after Philip's death and had to be kept in isolation. Mary and her siblings, now effectively orphaned, were reared by their aunt, *Margaret of Austria, who had just taken over the government of the Netherlands for Mary's brother Charles (later Holy Roman Emperor Charles V).

At age seven, Mary of Hungary was betrothed to Prince Louis (II) Jagellon, heir to the throne of Hungary. When she was about 15, she left the Netherlands for Hungary, where she and Louis were married. The marriage did not last long; in 1526, Louis was killed in battle during an invasion of Hungary by Turkish forces. Since Mary had borne no children during her marriage, she thus lost her position as princess of Hungary. She soon returned to her native land, where she took up residence once again at the court of the regent, Margaret of Austria. Although Mary of Hungary's brother Charles V was now an adult and had been named Holy Roman emperor, Margaret of Austria had remained regent for him, because the vast empire he now controlled made it impossible for him to personally govern each region.

Mary of Hungary, who refused to remarry, remained a rather quiet figure at the court until Margaret of Austria's death in 1530. Charles V, needing a new regent who was familiar with the Netherlands and could be trusted to act as he wished, turned to his younger sister, and thus Mary of Hungary was named regent in 1531. She proved to be an astute choice, for she was a wise, thoughtful ruler, interested in promoting the welfare of her subjects. She left Charles V free to concern himself with the rest of his empire, and she enjoyed great popularity among her people.

In 1549, she acted as tutor to Charles' son and heir, Philip (II), who stayed at her court for two years to learn about the people and institutions of the Netherlands. Philip was impressed with Mary of Hungary's deft handling of domestic affairs; so much so that upon his accession as emperor in 1555, he asked Mary to continue as regent in his name. She agreed and governed successfully for another three years, until her death at age 53.

SOURCES:
Hopkins, Lisa. *Women Who Would Be Kings: Female Rulers of the Sixteenth Century.* NY: St. Martin's Press, 1991.

SUGGESTED READING:
Hale, John. *The Civilization of Europe in the Renaissance.* NY: Macmillan, 1993.

Laura York,
Riverside, California

Mary of Jerusalem

Biblical woman. A wealthy and influential woman of Jerusalem and the mother of John, also called Mark, possibly one of the writers of the four gospels (Acts 12:12).

A resident of Jerusalem, Mary of Jerusalem was the mother of John whose other name was Mark, thought by the 2nd-century Christian writer Papias to be one of the writers of the four gospels. In the Bible, no mention is made of Mark's father. Mary of Jerusalem was apparently of some wealth and influence, as her large and well-staffed house became a meeting place for the early Christians of Jerusalem, and it was there that the disciples gathered following the release of the Apostle Peter who had been imprisoned by Herod Antipas. When Peter was miraculously liberated, an angel accompanied him to Mary of Jerusalem's house, where he was met at the door by the servant **Rhoda**, and inside found "many gathered together praying."

Mary of Lorraine (1515–1560).
See Mary of Guise.

Mary of Luxemburg (1305–1323)

Queen of France. Name variations: Marie of Luxemburg. Born in 1305; died of puerperal fever around 1323 near Bourges, France; eldest daughter of *Margaret of Brabant (d. 1311) and Henry VII, Holy Roman emperor (r. 1308–1313); became second wife of Charles IV the Fair (1294–1328), king of France (r. 1322–1328), on September 21, 1322.

Mary of Magdala (fl. early 1st c. CE).
See Mary Magdalene.

Mary of Mecklenburg-Schwerin (1854–1920).
See Maria of Mecklenburg-Schwerin.

Mary of Modena (1658–1718)

Queen of England. Name variations: Mary Beatrice; Mary Beatrice d'Este; Mary Beatrice Eleanora d'Este. Born Mary Beatrice Eleanor on October 5 (some sources cite September 25), 1658, at the Ducal Palace, Modena, Italy; died of cancer on May 7 or 8, 1718, at Château St. Germain-en-Laye, near Paris, France; interred at the Abbey of Visitation of St. Mary, Chaillot, France; daughter of Alphonso IV or Alfonso IV, duke of Modena, and *Laura Martinozzi; became second *wife of James (1633–1701), duke of York, later James II, king of England (r. 1685–1688, deposed), on November 21, 1673; children: Catherine (1675–1675); James Francis Edward Stuart (1688–1766), duke of Cornwall, known as the Old Pretender; Isabel (1676–1681); Elizabeth (1678–1678); Charlotte (1682–1682); ❧ Louise (1692–1712); six others died at birth or in infancy of smallpox.*

Two years after the death of his first wife *Anne Hyde in 1671, James, duke of York (later James II), was betrothed to a 15-year-old Italian Catholic, Mary from the duchy of Modena. Mary was said to be beautiful and well educated, though she had never heard of England, and when told that her betrothed was 40 years old, "burst into tears and said she would sooner be a nun," writes **Norah Lofts** in *Queens of England*.

The marriage caused an uproar in Parliament. Most of the country was resigned to James' eventual succession, convinced that he would soon be followed by his Anglican daughters, *Anne (1665–1714) and *Mary (II, 1662–1694), the children of Anne Hyde. The possibility of a new Catholic heir set off a wave of anti-Catholic hysteria. By 1678, rumors of a fiendish "Popish Plot" warned that English Catholics, under orders from the pope, were planning to murder Charles II and replace him with James. The scandal was perpetuated by a roguish liar, Titus Oates, who testified in Parliament about leaders of the plot. Charles himself was skeptical about its existence, but before Oates was finally discredited, several prominent Catholics were sent to their deaths.

In the aftermath of the Plot, a political movement aimed at excluding James from the throne arose, under the direction of a group of men who were derisively referred to as *Whigs*, a name given to Scottish outlaws. They in turn called their opponents *Tories*, or Irish rebels. The party labels lasted beyond the unsuccessful Exclusion Crisis, and bickering between the two political parties blighted later reigns.

James, who became king in 1685, was highly unpopular, and his brief reign was predominantly concerned with furthering the cause of Catholicism. Though three children died in infancy during the first 15 years of their marriage and many assumed that Mary of Modena's childbearing years were over, the royal line seemed secure. Protestants of England looked forward to the ascendancy of Mary II and her Protestant husband William III of Orange on the death of King James II.

When Mary of Modena gave birth to a boy, James Francis Edward Stuart, in June 1688, he

was destined to be known throughout his years as the Old Pretender. Enemies of the royal family invented and popularized the story that the queen had only pretended to be pregnant that the boy was smuggled into the royal bed in a warming pan by Jesuits. In reality, it would have been all but impossible for Mary of Modena to have pulled off such a ruse, as the birth was almost a public event, attended by members of the royal family as well as by important figures of state. It did not matter that *Catherine of Braganza was in attendance and swore of the child's validity. Stepdaughter Anne, who had been

Mary of Modena

brought up in the Church of England, bore some of the blame, as she wrote in a letter, "I can't help but think Mansell's wife's great belly is a little suspicious."

The panic wrought by the birth of James Edward, the new prince of Wales, prompted many prominent Anglicans to begin negotiating with William of Orange to install Mary II on the throne. Now, with the possibility of a continued Catholic monarchy, Mary II and her husband William arrived on the coast of England to claim the throne by force. Mary of Modena and her baby son preceded her husband James II on his flight to France.

SOURCES:
Lofts, Norah. *Queens of England.* Garden City, NY: Doubleday, 1977.

SUGGESTED READING:
Fraser, Antonia. *Royal Charles: Charles II and the Restoration.* NY: Alfred A. Knopf, 1979.

Mary of Molina (d. 1321).
See Maria de Molina.

Mary of Montpelier (1181–1213).
See Maria of Montpellier.

Mary of Munster (d. 570).
See Ita of Ireland.

Mary of Nazareth (20 BCE–40 CE).
See Mary the Virgin.

Mary of Oignies (1177–1213)

Belgian holy woman. Name variations: Marie d'Oignies; Blessed Mary d'Oignies. Born in 1177 in Nivelles (Brabant), Belgium; died in 1213 in Belgium; married.

The Belgian holy woman Mary of Oignies' early life is obscure, but it is clear that she was an exceptionally pious child. Though married at age 14, she felt so strongly that she had a religious vocation that she persuaded her husband they should abstain from sexual intimacy. Her husband agreed, and the two began to devote their time to working with patients at a leper colony. Mary then began to live as a Beguine, part of an informal order of women who dedicated themselves to public service.

Mary of Oignies' faith led her to mystical visions, which she revealed and interpreted to people while traveling and preaching on the streets of Belgian cities. Her faith included an emphasis on Christ's humanity which was a growing trend in northern Europe at the time. In her sermons,

Mary, who attracted a considerable number of followers, emphasized what she felt were the most important characteristics of Christ: chastity, poverty, converting heretics, and educating others. Mary's piety and activism earned her the attention of the famous reformer and preacher Jacques de Vitry. Mary of Oignies traveled with him for some time and helped him write his sermons.

Around 1207, she separated permanently from her husband and joined the St. Nicholas convent at Oignies. There, her reputation as a holy woman increased, and miracles were attributed to her. She remained at Oignies for six years and was revered after her death as a popular saint, though she was never canonized. Her feast day is June 23.

SOURCES:
Anderson, Bonnie S., and Judith P. Zinsser. *A History of Their Own.* Vol. I. NY: Harper & Row, 1988.
LaBarge, Margaret. *A Small Sound of the Trumpet: Women in Medieval Life.* Boston: Beacon Press, 1986.

Laura York,
Riverside, California

Mary of Orange (1631–1660)

Princess of Orange and princess royal. Name variations: Mary Stuart; Mary Henrietta. Named princess royal around 1642. Born on November 4, 1631, at St. James's Palace, in London, England; died of smallpox on December 24, 1660, at Whitehall, London; interred at Westminster Abbey, London; daughter of *Henrietta Maria (1609–1669) and Charles I (1600–1649), king of England (r. 1625–1649); married William II (1625–1650), prince of Orange (r. 1647–1650), on May 2, 1648; children: William III (1650–1702), prince of Orange (r. 1672–1702), king of England (r. 1689–1702).

Mary of Portugal (1527–1545)

Portuguese princess. Name variations: Maria of Portugal; Mary Avis. Born on October 15, 1527, in Coimbra; died four days after giving birth on July 12, 1545, in Valladolid, Castile and Leon, Spain; daughter of João III or John III the Pious, king of Portugal (r. 1521–1557), and Catherine (1507–1578, daughter of Philip I of Spain); married Philip II (1527–1598), king of Spain (r. 1556–1598), and king of Portugal as Philip I (r. 1580–1598), on November 12, 1543; children: Charles (1545–1568).

Mary of Portugal was born in 1527, the daughter of John III the Pious, king of Portugal (r. 1521–1557), and ***Catherine**, the daughter of

Philip I, king of Spain. She married Philip II, the future king of Spain, in 1543. Mary of Portugal died four days after giving birth to her son Charles (Don Carlos) in 1545; he was born epileptic, as well as lame, with one leg shorter than the other.

Mary of St. Pol (1304–1377).

See Marie de St. Pol.

Mary of Saxe-Altenburg

(1818–1907)

Queen of Hanover. Name variations: Marie-Alexandrina. Born Alexandrina Mary Wilhelmina Katherine Charlotte Theresa Henrietta Louise Pauline Elizabeth Fredericka Georgina on April 14, 1818, in Hildburghausen, Germany; died on January 9, 1907, in Gmunden, Austria; daughter of Joseph, duke of Saxe-Altenburg, and *Amelia of Wurttemberg (1799–1848); sister of *Alexandra of Saxe-Altenburg (1838–1911); married George V, king of Hanover, on February 18, 1843; children: Ernest Augustus, 3rd duke of Cumberland and Teviotdale (1845–1923); *Fredericka of Hanover (1848–1926); *Mary of Hanover (1849–1904).

Mary of Saxe-Coburg (1875–1938).

See Marie of Rumania.

Mary of Teck (1867–1953)

Beloved queen of early 20th-century England and grandmother of Elizabeth II. Name variations: Queen Mary; May of Teck; Victoria Mary of Teck; duchess of York; princess of Wales. Born Victoria Mary Augusta Louise Olga Pauline Claudine Agnes on May 26, 1867, in Kensington Palace, London, England; died on March 24, 1953, at Marlborough House, London; daughter of Francis, duke of Teck, and Mary Adelaide (1833–1897); betrothed to Albert Saxe-Coburg, duke of Clarence and Avondale (son of Edward VII and *Alexandra of Denmark), in 1891; married George, duke of York, later George V, king of England (r. 1910–1936), on July 6, 1893; children: Edward VIII (1894–1972), duke of Windsor; Albert, later George VI (1895–1952), king of England (r. 1936–1952); Mary (1897–1965), princess royal; Henry Windsor (1900–1974), 1st duke of Gloucester; George (1902–1942), 1st duke of Kent; John Windsor (1905–1919).

Betrothed to duke of Clarence, the future king of England (1891); duke of Clarence died (1892); married duke of York and became duchess of York (1893);

first child born (1894); became princess of Wales (1901); crowned queen of England (1911); became queen mother and saw son abdicate throne (1936).

Queen Mary of Teck, who was the wife of King George V, the reigning English monarch from 1910 to 1936, was an extremely popular royal figure in her day, and serves as a historical link of sorts between the rigidly protocol-bound age of Queen *Victoria and the modern, *Diana-dominated House of Windsor. Hand-picked by the imperious queen, who ruled for over six decades, as a bride for Victoria's grandson, Mary lived to see her own granddaughter, the princess and future queen *Elizabeth (II), give birth to a new heir to the throne, Prince Charles. She has been called "one of the most regal and dignified, even formidable, figures ever to grace the throne." Her devotion to duty, loyalty to the monarchy, and genuine courtesy to, and interest in, her subjects were legendary, and survived the crises of two world wars, unexpected deaths in the family, and an unprecedented abdication.

Mary of Teck—called "May" because of the month of her birth—was born in Kensington Palace in 1867, in the same bedroom in which Queen Victoria had been born. She was the daughter of Prince Francis, a member of the Austrian royal house who was also the duke of Teck, and an English princess, *Mary Adelaide, who was the cousin of Queen Victoria and the granddaughter of King George III. Mary was quite shy as a child, and undoubtedly suffered because of her parents' lifestyle: they were impoverished royals who often lived far beyond their means and depended on Queen Victoria for support. They maintained close ties with the German royal house, and Mary of Teck spent holidays with her German cousins. She was not formally educated beyond what was thought necessary for a young woman of the upper crust to be taught by her governesses (which in her case included European history, the French and German languages, and needlepoint, all of which she mastered), but she possessed a large measure of intelligence and an excellent memory, and added greatly to her own education through reading and general curiosity. In 1883, her parents were sent by the queen to Italy, where at the time one could live very cheaply, because she was tired of paying their debts. Mary of Teck liked Italy a great deal, and did not mind living simply. When the family spent a year in Florence, she used the opportunity to gain a wealth of knowledge about art and art history by visiting its museums and churches full of Renaissance treasures; she would remain a lover and collector of art throughout her life.

Such an intellectual capacity made Mary of Teck somewhat suspect in royal circles, but she was nevertheless a popular young woman in society after she was formally presented at court in the mid-1880s. Her parents, naturally, were very interested in engineering a good match for her, but had little dowry to provide. Not until Mary was 24 did a marriage proposal come about, urged by none other than Victoria. The queen thought the sensible Mary would be a suitable bride for her undisciplined, playboy grandson Albert, duke of Clarence, who was known as "Prince Eddy." He was also second in line to the throne, behind his father. Mary accepted the proposal, the match was announced in December 1891, and a date was set. While the engaged couple was staying with his family at their royal castle at Sandringham the following month, Eddy caught a cold. The cold developed into influenza, and he became delirious; Mary helped to nurse him before he died. A year later, she accepted the marriage proposal of his brother George, the duke of York, who was the new heir to the throne.

They were married on July 6, 1893, in St. James's Palace Chapel, and Mary of Teck became the duchess of York. The marriage was by most reports happy, and the couple remained devoted to one another for the four-plus decades of their union. Over the next 12 years they had six children: Edward (called David), the heir to the throne, who was born in 1894; Albert, born in 1895, who would later be king of England as George VI; Princess *Mary, born in 1897; Henry, the first duke of Gloucester, born in 1900; George, the first duke of Kent, born in 1902; and John, born in 1905, who was epileptic and died of an attack at the age of 13. Like other royals and members of the upper class in that era, Mary and her husband left the upbringing of their children to the staff, and she was said to have remained distant from them throughout their lives. After the nanny in charge of their first few children had a severe nervous breakdown, it was rumored that the woman had been mentally unstable for some time.

The death of Queen Victoria in 1901, which brought Mary's husband one step closer to the throne, caused significant changes in their lives. The couple became the prince and princess of Wales and were sent by George's father, now King Edward VII, on major tours of the vast British empire to acquaint them with their future subjects. Mary's well-known robust health and energy served her well. She visited Australia with her husband for the first session of the former colony's Parliament in 1901 and made an arduous tour of India between 1905 and 1906.

King Edward VII died in May 1910, and George V was crowned in June 1911. Mary of Teck was now known as Queen Mary. The clouds of war were already gathering, however, and the outbreak of World War I in 1914 was made particularly difficult for the British royal house because of their close personal links with the royal house of the enemy, Germany. (George V and Kaiser Wilhelm II were first cousins.) Mary renounced her ties to her German relatives and devoted herself to the war effort at home. She launched the Queen's Work for Women Fund and Queen Mary's Needlework Guild, which sewed clothes for the poor, and worked extensively with the Red Cross. Like their subjects, the royal family ate rationed food and grew their own potatoes; King George locked up his wine cellar. They considered turning Buckingham Palace into a hospital, but this was vetoed by the government. Queen Mary also visited hospitals full of the war-wounded. She became a beloved public figure because of her unflinching attention to these self-imposed war duties. Personal sorrow came in July 1918, only four months before the end of the war, when the Bolsheviks murdered Nicholas II, former tsar of Russia, and his wife *Alexandra Feodorovna and their children; Nicholas was a first cousin and close friend of George V who had attended his wedding to Mary. At the war's end, George V changed the name of their royal house from the very German Saxe-Coburg-Gotha to Windsor, which it remains.

After the war, Mary of Teck supported the newly formed trade unions, met with the Indian nationalist leader Mohandas Gandhi, and maintained cordial relations with the first Labour government in Britain. She also lent her voice to help working women's causes, including the establishment of convalescent rest homes for them. In addition, the queen was known for her more domestic skills, and loved to sew. She created carpets based on antique designs, collected art, and, unlike her parents, was known to be a savvy household manager. Her husband was said to be dependent on her and her energies, particularly as he grew increasingly infirm with age.

The royal couple celebrated their Silver Jubilee in 1935, which was a great event in England in the midst of a world depression. Queen Mary, now 68 and a grandmother several times over, was cheered by massive crowds that assembled to pay homage to her and the king. He

passed away in January 1936, and their son David was crowned King Edward VIII later that year. Despite a deferential silence on the part of British newspapers and censorship of all mention of it in imported American newspapers, there were already rumors that the new king was involved with an American divorcée. This was a wholly unacceptable mate for a king of England, not least because he was the hereditary head of the Church of England, which frowned upon remarriage after divorce. Queen Mary, now the queen mother, intervened, and attempted to dissuade her son from the romance. No compromise could be reached, however, and amidst a worldwide frenzy of publicity King Edward VIII abdicated late in 1936 to marry *Wallis Warfield. Although Mary received her son (now the duke of Windsor) when he returned to England after World War II, she never met his wife.

The abdication was a devastating blow to the house of Windsor. Mary's second son Albert and his wife *Elizabeth Bowes-Lyon were crowned as King George VI and Queen Elizabeth, a change in status they had neither expected nor wanted, and to lend them the benefit of her popularity Mary appeared with them in public frequently during the difficult first years of their reign. (Once they got over their shock, the monarchs, particularly the new queen, proved to be immensely popular with their subjects.) Mary took an active role in the lives of her grandchildren, the princesses Elizabeth and *Margaret Rose, and spent a great deal of time with them. During World War II, Mary retired to Badminton, where she engaged in salvage work along with her servants and gave lifts to pedestrians on the country roads when fuel rations were drastic. Her youngest surviving son, George, duke of Kent, was killed in a Royal Air Force plane crash in 1942. After the war, she resumed her schedule of public engagements and kept them up until just before her death. She witnessed the wedding of Princess Elizabeth to Philip, made duke of Edinburgh, in 1947, and was thrilled with the birth of her great-grandson Prince Charles in 1949. Upon the death of her son the king in February 1952, Mary of Teck was one of the first to kiss the hand of the new queen, Elizabeth II, as "her old Grannie and subject." She died in March 1953, only a few months shy of Elizabeth's coronation, and was buried next to her husband in St. George's Chapel at Windsor Castle.

SOURCES:
The Concise Dictionary of National Biography. Oxford and NY: Oxford University Press, 1992.
Lofts, Norah. *Queens of England.* Garden City, NY: Doubleday, 1977, pp. 174–180.
"Queen Mary," in *British History Illustrated.* October–November 1978, pp. 28–37.
Softly, Barbara. *The Queens of England.* NY: Bell Publishing, 1976.

SUGGESTED READING:
Pope-Hennessy, James. *Queen Mary 1867–1953.* NY: Alfred A. Knopf, 1960.

Carol Brennan,
Grosse Pointe, Michigan

Mary of the Cross, Mother (1842–1909).
See MacKillop, Mary Helen.

Mary of the Incarnation.
See Acarie, Barbe (1566–1618).
See Marie de l'Incarnation (1599–1672).

Mary of Wurttemberg (1799–1860)
*Duchess of Saxe-Coburg-Gotha. Name variations: Marie of Wurttemberg; Mary von Württemberg. Born on September 17, 1799, in Coburg, Bavaria, Germany; died on September 24, 1860, in Gotha, Thuringia, Germany; daughter of Alexander, duke of Wurttemberg, and *Antoinette Saxe-Coburg (1779–1824); cousin of Queen *Victoria; became second wife of Ernest I (1784–1844), duke of Saxe-Coburg-Gotha, on December 23, 1832. Ernest I's first wife was *Louise of Saxe-Gotha-Altenburg (1800–1831).*

Mary Plantagenet (1278–1332).
See Mary.

Mary Plantagenet (1467–1482)
*English princess. Born in August 1467 in Windsor, Berkshire, England; died on May 23, 1482, in Greenwich, London; buried in St. George's Chapel, Windsor; daughter of Edward IV (1442–1483), king of England (r. 1461–1470, 1471–1483), and *Elizabeth Woodville (1437–1492).*

Mary Romanov (1853–1920).
See Marie Alexandrovna.

Mary Stewart.
See Stewart, Mary (c. 1451–c. 1488).
See Stewart, Mary (d. 1458).
See Mary Stuart (1542–1587).
See Mary II (1662–1694).

Mary Stewart (d. 1465), countess of Buchan.
See Joan Beaufort (c. 1410–1445) for sidebar.

Mary Stuart (1542–1587)
Queen of Scots, from six days after her birth until forced to flee the country in 1567, who lived in the turbulent period of the Counter-reformation and became caught up in scandals which ended her reign and resulted in her execution by Elizabeth I. Name variations: Mary, Queen of Scots; Mary Stewart; dauphine of France. Born on December 8, 1542, at Linlithgow, Lothian, Scotland; beheaded by order of Elizabeth I for treason at Fotheringhay Castle,

Northamptonshire, England, on February 8, 1587; daughter of James V, king of Scotland (r. 1513–1542), and Mary of Guise (1515–1560); married Francis, dauphin of France, later Francis II, king of France (r. 1559–1560), on April 24, 1558; married Henry Stuart, duke of Albany, Lord Darnley, on July 29, 1565; married James Hepburn, 4th earl of Bothwell, on May 15, 1567; children: (second marriage) James (1566–1625), king of Scotland as James VI (r. 1567–1625) and king of England as James I (r. 1603–1625).

Proclaimed queen of Scotland six days after her birth, with the death of her father James V; at age five, was betrothed to the dauphin of France, Francis, and sent to France to be brought up in the French court; was queen of France during the brief reign of her husband as Francis II (1559–60); following death of Francis, went back to Scotland to claim birthright; married Henry Stuart, Lord Darnley (1565); son James born (1566); under bizarre circumstances, husband Darnley strangled (February 1567); within months of murder, married the earl of Bothwell, who was widely believed to have been the perpetrator; these actions provoked a widespread rebellion, which led to her abdication from the Scottish throne (1567) in favor of her son and her flight to England; remained in England for almost 20 years, becoming the focus of many Catholic plots against the life of Queen Elizabeth I; though her degree of participation in plots is still debated by historians, Elizabeth eventually became convinced of Mary's duplicity and ordered her trial and execution for treason (1587).

Mary Stuart, queen of Scots, was born on December 8, 1542, under conditions that were less than auspicious and into circumstances which seemed hopeless. Scotland had been under constant pressure for centuries from its more wealthy and powerful neighbor to the south, England. The challenge from England had increased dramatically with the accession of the powerful Tudor dynasty in the 16th century. In addition, the era of the Protestant Reformation was spreading unrest throughout Europe, and although Scotland was still Catholic at the time of Mary's birth, rumblings of the approaching Protestant storm could already be heard.

Six days after her birth, Mary's father James V, who had sunk into illness and depression following the humiliating defeat of Scottish troops at the hands of the English at Solway Moss, "yielded the spirit" at Falkland. To compound all of the other threats to the stability of Scotland, now the crown passed to a six-day-old infant. The succession of a child heir was consid-ered calamitous in the 16th century; the succession of a female infant threatened imminent dis-aster. John Knox, who would later lead the Protestant Reformation in Scotland, noted that "all men lamented that the realm was left with-out a male to succeed."

No sooner had James V been laid to rest than a hotly contested struggle emerged over control of the regency for the young princess. Mary's mother *Mary of Guise was quickly pushed aside because of suspicion about her powerful French relatives. David Beaton, cardi-nal-archbishop of St. Andrews, vied unsuccess-fully for control of the regency, which was even-tually won by James Hamilton, second earl of Arran, who had the advantage of being the new queen's closest adult male relative, since he was the grandson of James III's sister *Mary Stewart (c. 1451–c. 1488). Arran, a lukewarm Protes-tant, was appointed Governor of the Realm and "tutor" of the young queen. He arranged a tem-porary halt in hostilities between Scotland and England by negotiating the Treaty of Greenwich with King Henry VIII of England. The treaty sealed the peace between the two countries by betrothing the infant Mary to Henry's son Prince Edward (future Edward VI). Henry hoped that the political union of the two kingdoms could be accomplished naturally through the children of Mary and Edward. In preparation for the even-tual inclusion of the Scottish Catholic Church under the Anglican cloak, Henry VIII suggested that Arran authorize the importation of English versions of the Bible, which he hoped would kin-dle the Protestant flame in Scotland. The influ-ence of Protestantism would continue to grow and reach a fever pitch by the time Mary Stuart grew to adulthood.

The appearance in Scotland of a rival claimant to the throne put a swift end to Arran's pro-English policy. Matthew Stuart, 4th earl of Lennox, was also descended from the Scottish royal house, but through the female line. Lennox arrived in Scotland in 1543 and immediately of-fered himself as a suitor to Mary of Guise. Arran, whose tie to the Scottish throne was through the male line but was besmirched by illegitimacy, found it convenient to ally with Cardinal Beaton and apply for restoration into the Catholic Church in an attempt to strengthen his claim. Arran repudiated the Treaty of Greenwich (which had not been ratified by Henry VIII either) in 1543, and in response Henry ordered two inva-sions of Scotland, in 1544 and 1545, which did massive destruction to buildings, farms, livestock, and population in southern Scotland. Blame for this "Rough Wooing" at the hands of Henry fell squarely on the shoulders of Arran, whose authority gradually began to trickle into the hands of Cardinal Beaton and Mary of Guise.

The assassination of Cardinal Beaton in May 1546 and the subsequent occupation of St. Andrews Castle by the murderers exacerbated the tension with England. Although Arran conducted a half-hearted siege of the castle, it was a French expeditionary force called in by Mary of Guise that freed the castle. After the death of Henry VIII in January 1547, retaliation by the English for the French intervention fell to Edward Seymour, duke of Somerset, who was head of the regency for the new king Edward VI. Somerset ordered an invasion of Scotland in September 1547, where the English troops routed the Scots at Pinkie. The English army then built several garrisons in Scotland, which Somerset intended to use to assist in the spread of Protestantism.

Mary of Guise took advantage of Arran's misfortune to engineer an alliance with France which she hoped would preserve her daughter's inheritance. She pressured Arran to approve a treaty offering Mary Stuart as a bride for the dauphin Francis (later Francis II), eldest son of Henry II and *Catherine de Medici. In July 1548, the five-year-old queen was spirited off to France, where she was brought up in the French court. Mary of Guise's influence in Scotland grew steadily, and in 1554 she was appointed regent of Scotland. The regency of Mary of Guise allowed for the reestablishment of Scotland's ties with France, but undermined her position in the eyes of the Scottish nobility. The potential of domination by France was no more popular with the Scottish peers than the prospect of domination by England had been ten years earlier. Many of Scotland's leading aristocratic families regarded Mary's pro-French policies as prejudicial to their own interests.

On April 24, 1558, Mary Stuart was married to the dauphin Francis. From this point in her life, her circumstances began to change with alarming speed. The Scots nobles, angry that Francis had been granted the "Crown Matrimonial," which would make him king of Scotland if Mary should predecease him, began to throw their support to the "Lords of the Congregation." These Protestant nobles and clerics, directed by the Calvinist minister John Knox, began the process of transforming Scotland from a Catholic country into a Protestant, Calvinist one. Calvinism spread rapidly through the Scottish nobility in the 1550s, who saw the new doctrine as both a lever to use against Mary of Guise's government and a means for purging the

Catholic Church hierarchy in Scotland of some of its most obnoxious abuses, including the collecting of multiple appointments and high fees by the upper clergy as well as ignorance and illiteracy among the lower. Despite Mary of Guise's repeated attempts to put it down, a Reformation rebellion effectively transformed Scotland into a Protestant country by 1559.

On July 6, 1559, the king of France, Henry II, was accidentally killed during a tournament when a sliver from an opponent's lance pierced his eye. The dauphin immediately succeeded his father, and Mary Stuart found herself queen of France at the tender age of 16. Meanwhile, Scottish rebels appealed for help to the new Protestant monarch of England, *Elizabeth I, who sent troops to assist in the removal of Mary of Guise from the regency. The Treaty of Berwick was signed between the Scottish rebels and Elizabeth in February 1560, promising mutual aid in the case of an invasion by France. Mary of Guise, forced out of the capital, fled to Leith and sent to France for assistance, but before it arrived she died on June 11, 1560. In July, Elizabeth I and Francis II signed the Treaty of Edinburgh, which stipulated the removal of both English and French troops from Scotland, recognized Elizabeth I as the legal ruler of England, and forbade Francis and Mary from displaying the English arms. Following this settlement, the Scottish "Reformation Parliament" formally adopted the Calvinist Confession of Faith as the new state religion and prohibited celebration of the Catholic mass in Scotland.

By the end of 1560, yet another change in Mary Stuart's circumstances took place, when Francis II died on December 5. Mary's status in France plummeted—a future as queen dowager of France offered little chance for grandeur or political power. The only useful position she still held in life was that of queen of Scotland. She decided to return to her native land, which she had not seen since she was five years old.

At 18 years of age, Mary Stuart was considered by her contemporaries to be an extraordinarily beautiful and well-educated Renaissance woman. Her face was oval and her features finely drawn. Her smooth skin was fair, her eyes hazel, and her hair was dark auburn brown. She was described as tall and graceful, and was noted for her accomplishments in dancing and riding. She spoke Latin, French, and Italian, in addition to her native Scots. In religion, she was a Catholic, but not a fanatical one.

When Mary Stuart announced her intentions to return to her native land, conservative Catholic nobles urged her to enter the country with a

Catholic army and overturn the Protestant revolution. Mary refused, in hopes that she could adopt a *politique* position between the two religions and thus conciliate both factions. Furthermore, she hoped that religious moderation would prompt Elizabeth I of England to recognize her as her heir. Elizabeth had no husband or children, so Mary was Elizabeth's closest kin and, in the eyes of many Catholics throughout Europe, Mary was the legitimate heir to the English throne. The pressures of their political and religious differences created a chilly diplomatic climate between the two cousins. Mary Stuart had never ratified the Treaty of Edinburgh, hoping to preserve her interest in the English throne. When Mary returned to Scotland in 1561, Elizabeth retaliated by refusing to grant Mary safe conduct through England. Elizabeth even sent a convoy of ships to intercept Mary's entourage, but a persistent sea mist allowed Mary to evade capture.

When Mary Stuart landed safely at Leith on August 19, 1561, John Knox commented upon the gloom that enveloped her arrival: "The very face of heaven, the time of her arrival, did manifestly speak what comfort was brought into this country with her, to wit, sorrow, dolour, darkness, and all impiety." Despite the strong opposition among Protestant lords to the homecoming of their Catholic monarch, Mary's arrival provoked surprisingly little resistance. With the exception of a violent outburst occasioned by the celebration of Mary's private mass in the Chapel Royal of Holyrood House and a minor outbreak led by the earl of Huntly which ended with his defeat in October 1762, Mary's subjects seemed largely tractable to her assumption of personal rule. Mary Stuart helped to ease tensions by firmly maintaining a neutral stance on religion. Although she insisted upon the right to continue her own Catholic mass in her household, she repeatedly issued proclamations which upheld the prosecution of Catholic priests for saying mass anywhere outside the confines of her court. She even attempted to smooth out her relations with Elizabeth I, by offering to ratify the Treaty of Edinburgh in return for formal recognition as Elizabeth's heir. Elizabeth refused to commit to the succession, but still insisted upon ratification of the Treaty of Edinburgh. Mary proposed a personal meeting between the two monarchs in September 1562 to hammer out a compromise. Although Elizabeth agreed, she later changed her mind, and the two cousins never met face to face.

&▶ **Erskine, Margaret** (fl. 1530s)
Mistress of James V. Flourished in the 1530s; daughter of John, 4th or 12th lord Erskine; mistress of James V (1512–1542), king of Scotland (r. 1513–1542); children: (with James V) James Stuart also seen as James Stewart, earl of Moray (1531–1570, legitimated in 1551); Robert Stuart also seen as Robert Stewart, earl of Orkney (c. 1533–1591, became the abbott of Holyrood House).

The character Lady Sensuality in David Lyndsay's *Satire of the Three Estates* was based on Margaret Erskine.

Mary's next course of action was to search for a husband, in the hopes that producing an heir would make her a more attractive candidate for the English throne. Serious negotiations with several foreign suitors, including the kings of Sweden and Denmark, the sons of the Holy Roman emperor Charles V, and the son of the Spanish king Philip II, provoked fear among the Scottish nobles that a foreign match would necessarily lead to foreign domination. Mary toyed with the idea of marrying a suitor of Elizabeth's choosing, but when Elizabeth suggested that Mary wed her own long-standing favorite, Lord Robert Dudley, earl of Leicester, then made it clear that she would not make any declarations about the succession until her own marriage or public announcement of her intention not to marry, Mary decided to give up the possibility of working out an official agreement with Elizabeth. Instead, Mary hastily concluded negotiations to marry her cousin, Henry Stuart, Lord Darnley. As a grandson of *****Margaret Tudor** (1489–1541), Darnley's greatest recommendation was his own strong claim to the English succession. Mary seemed charmed by her cousin at their first meeting, and she described him as "the lustiest and best proportioned long man that she had seen." Tall and thin, with blond hair and a boyish face, Darnley was well versed in the important courtly accomplishments of singing, dancing, and playing the lute.

Mary and Darnley were married on July 29, 1565, and Darnley was granted the titles king of Scots and duke of Albany, although Mary wisely chose not to vest her new husband with the Crown Matrimonial. The marriage was not universally popular, and provoked a rebellion led by Mary's own half-brother (the illegitimate son of James V and ◄⅜ **Margaret Erskine**), the earl of Moray. The queen of Scots put down the rebellion easily, riding at the head of her own army which drove the rebels across the border into England.

As attractive as Darnley had appeared on paper, unfortunately he failed to live up to Mary's expectations. Hopelessly spoiled and self-absorbed, Darnley quickly exhibited the darker side of his character by indulging himself in sexual escapades and alcoholic binges. By the end of 1565, Mary's relationship with Darnley grew distant, and she began to spend an increasing amount of time with other favorites and advisors, most notably an Italian musician named David Riccio. Mary appointed Riccio as her secretary for French correspondence, and Riccio began to exert an increasingly potent, though unofficial, influence on the queen's political policies.

Mary Stuart was calm and serene as attendants prepared for her beheading.

Riccio's appearance provided a perfect opportunity for a group of disaffected Scottish nobles to gain the ear of the new king. Playing on Darnley's natural jealousy and suspicion, the conspirators intimated that Riccio was the queen's lover and a secret agent of the pope.

Mary had become pregnant within a few months of her marriage to Darnley, and the conspirators succeeded in convincing Darnley that the child could be Riccio's. They were so successful in enraging the young king that they convinced him to take part in a plot to do away with his rival.

On March 9, 1566, the conspirators surprised Mary, Riccio, and the **Countess of Argyll** at supper: Darnley threw his arms around Mary to prevent her intervention while the conspirators dragged Riccio out of the room as he piteously clung to the queen's skirts screaming, "Justizia! Justizia, Madame! Save ma vie! Save ma vie!" Riccio was stabbed to death outside in the hall.

Although Darnley later repented of his role in the incident, Mary Stuart never forgave him. Even the birth of their son James, on June 19, 1566, did not prevent Mary from referring to Darnley in contemptuous terms. When Mary displayed the baby publicly to her husband, she was said to have announced: "My Lord, God has given you and me a son, begotten by none but you. Here I protest to God as I shall answer to him at the great day of Judgment, that this is your son and no other man's son. I am desirous that all here, with ladies and others bear witness. For he is so much your own son, that I fear it will be the worse for him hereafter." With the birth of an heir, the queen no longer saw much reason to uphold a sham marriage, and she began to hint to her closest advisors that Darnley's presence was no longer required, looking for an "outgait" from her unsatisfactory marriage. Darnley's response was to stay away from court as much as possible.

Burn the whore! Burn the murderess of her husband!

—Citizenry of Edinburgh, June 1567

By the fall of 1566, Mary had adopted another favorite as her primary councillor, James Hepburn, earl of Bothwell. Bothwell's contemporaries described him as conceited, ambitious, and ruthless, but Mary undoubtedly found him to be a perfect antidote to her weak and flaccid husband. It was later alleged that, early in 1567, Bothwell approached the conspirators who had murdered Riccio, whom Mary had conveniently pardoned a few days earlier, and asked for their assistance in getting rid of Darnley. Although the murderers refused to stain their hands with another murder, by the following month, on the night of February 9, Darnley, who had been suffering with syphilis and recuperating at the royal residence at Kirk o' Field, was murdered. The house at Kirk o' Field was blown up, but curiously, Darnley and his manservant were found outside the house in the garden, strangled to death but unhurt by the explosion.

Although the crime was never solved, public opinion in Edinburgh pinned the blame solidly on Bothwell. To this day, historians are divided in their judgments about what Mary Stuart's role in the murders was. It is evident, however, that Mary did not intend to allow Bothwell to be tried for the crime. As she refused to prosecute, Bothwell was eventually brought to trial by Darnley's father the earl of Lennox, but on April 12 Bothwell was acquitted for lack of evidence. Mary blatantly refused to heed advice from Elizabeth I and her former mother-in-law Catherine de Medici of France, who both urged her to move swiftly to exact justice for the crime. As a result, rumors of Mary's complicity in the plot spread through Europe like wildfire.

Then Mary committed what many Scots considered to be the final outrage—three months after the murder of Darnley, Mary married Bothwell on May 15, according to the rites of the Protestant Church. Before the marriage, Bothwell had staged an abduction scene, and had spirited the queen off to Dunbar Castle. Mary later claimed to have been abducted, raped, and forced into the marriage with Bothwell. Her new husband certainly brought her little happiness. Within days of the wedding, Mary began to express regrets at her hasty actions. In the weeks that followed, she seemed listless and depressed, and often threatened suicide.

It was only a matter of a few weeks before the nobles of Scotland moved to put an end to what they considered an intolerable arrangement. Bothwell had many enemies, and he had never cultivated a network of alliances which could be relied upon to come to his aid. Noble families with close ties to the throne were infuriated that Bothwell would seize the power behind the throne in such a brutal and illegal manner. By the middle of June, the earl of Morton had collected an army to fight the queen and Bothwell, under the banner of the murdered Darnley and his infant son James. The two armies met at Carberry Hill, where ambassadors approached the queen offering to restore her to her throne if she would abandon Bothwell. When the queen steadfastly refused, her own troops began deserting her. Bothwell was allowed to escape, and Mary never saw him again. Eventually, he was imprisoned in Denmark and died in captivity in 1578.

Mary was left alone, with no choice but to surrender to Morton's troops and be led as a prisoner into Edinburgh. Her arrival was met by an angry mob, who shouted cries of "Burn the whore! Burn the murderess of her husband!" Partly in an effort to protect her from the mob, her captors imprisoned her in an island fortress on Lochleven. Soon after, during the latter part of July, Mary miscarried twins, and it became apparent to contemporary observers that her pregnancy was so advanced that it must have dated from before her marriage to Bothwell in May; this fact may provide a more believable explanation for the bizarre circumstances of her recent marriage than the one she had offered. On July 24, Mary was compelled to sign a document of abdication, turning over the crown to her 13-month-old son James. Control of James' regency was given to Mary's half-brother, the earl of Moray.

On May 2, 1568, Mary escaped from Lochleven Castle, convinced that the sympathy of her people would allow her to repudiate her abdication. Although she succeeded in raising a force of some 5,000 men, her army was defeated by Moray on May 13. Mary fled after the defeat, determined to avoid imprisonment. She asked her cousin Elizabeth for sanctuary in England, having been encouraged by Elizabeth's sympathetic letters to her during her imprisonment. Elizabeth granted permission, but once Mary arrived in England she found herself a virtual hostage, confined to house arrest. To Elizabeth, Mary was still dangerous, still an obvious magnet for the ambitious Catholics who viewed Elizabeth as illegitimate and hoped to use Mary to reunite England with the Catholic Church.

Upon Mary's arrival in England, Elizabeth sent a trusted advisor to meet with Mary to discuss the circumstances of Mary's sanctuary in England. Elizabeth insisted that Mary make no effort to solicit French aid while in England, and that Mary wait in northern England until she could be thoroughly acquitted of the charges of her complicity in Darnley's murder. Disappointed that she was not allowed to approach Elizabeth immediately, Mary agreed to stay confined to Carlisle Castle for the duration of the investigation.

The earl of Moray traveled to the hearing, intent upon protecting his position as head of the regency and preventing Mary from returning to Scotland. He brought with him a small, gilded casket which contained a collection of letters which Moray claimed would decisively incriminate Mary in Darnley's death. The letters, none of which were complete and many of which were translations from French into Scots, were purported to be love letters between Mary and Bothwell written before the murder of Darnley. Since the copies which were retained in England were translations and not in Mary's handwriting, it is difficult for modern scholars to determine whether they were genuine or forged. Although the contents of the letters include several protestations of love for Bothwell, none of them prove that Mary was involved in a plot to murder Darnley. Queen Elizabeth was given copies of the letters, and claimed to see nothing in them which could prove that her cousin was guilty of murder.

Although the Casket Letters undoubtedly had an impact upon the English nobles whom Elizabeth had chosen to conduct the investigation into Darnley's murder, the investigators were not convinced of Mary Stuart's guilt. Unable to prove guilt or innocence, they took the highly irregular step of ruling that both sides of the case were "not proven." As a result, Mary was neither convicted nor completely cleared. Moray returned to Scotland (and the originals of the Casket Letters soon disappeared), and Mary returned to captivity, this time in a more secure house at Tutbury in Staffordshire. Tutbury was a medieval castle surrounded by damp marshes, and it had a noticeable effect on Mary's declining health and spirits. Her strident objections and the intervention of her "jailers," George and *Elizabeth Talbot, count and countess of Shrewsbury, led to her removal to Sheffield Castle later in 1569.

Mary Stuart's position in England remained vague. She was not a convicted criminal, and, as the crowned head of another sovereign state, she could not be considered a subject of the queen of England. Elizabeth was able to secure Mary's tacit consent to this continued imprisonment by dangling before her the carrot of possible aid in the future. Mary had good reason to hope that her cause could best be served by biding her time. Even during the course of the "trial," the possibility of an English marriage for Mary was in the air—and Mary nurtured that possibility by agreeing to divorce Bothwell and by participating in Anglican Church services. Mary's forces were still fighting Moray's adherents in Scotland, and for the next three years Moray's position as regent remained in question. Mary's imprisonment in England was not terribly restrictive: at English expense, Mary Stuart's household of 30 to 40 persons was provided for; Mary was given all the respect of a sovereign queen, including the right to use her royal cloth of state; and she secretly maintained correspondence with Catholic friends and supporters in England and on the Continent, using the income she still received as queen dowager of France.

Limitations on outdoor exercise and her declining health led Mary to take up new hobbies during her imprisonment. She became an expert embroiderer, and sent samples of her needle-work to friends throughout England, and even to Elizabeth, whom Mary was convinced could be won over if only she were allowed but two hours alone with the English queen. The other hobby in which Mary increasingly indulged was the more dangerous one of plotting and intrigue. Since Mary was not a citizen of England, and therefore Elizabeth had no legal basis for imprisoning her, Mary considered it within the bounds of accepted diplomacy to do all in her power to regain her birthright in Scotland. Her somewhat amateurish attempts at escape gave the Shrewsburys no end of grief, but all were inevitably foiled by Elizabeth's agents before they could be carried out. Although Mary considered herself perfectly within her sovereign rights, her brother-in-law, King Charles IX of France, noted with disturbing prescience: "Ah, the poor fool will never cease until she lose her head. In faith, they will put her to death. I see it is her own fault and folly, I see no remedy for it."

The first conspiracy which was linked to Mary was a plot by a group of northern English earls who wanted to do away with Elizabeth and bring back the Roman Catholic Church to England. Their plan was to convince Mary to marry Thomas Howard, duke of Norfolk, the highest peer in the realm and a Catholic, after which they would launch a rebellion to put Mary and Norfolk on the English throne. When Elizabeth caught wind of the plot, she called Norfolk to court and threw him into the Tower. The conspirators were also called to Westminster but chose to rebel instead. Before they could rescue Mary, Elizabeth ordered her removal to Coventry. When English troops arrived in Yorkshire, the rebels surrendered without a fight. Many of the leaders escaped into Scotland, and 500 of their humbler followers were executed for treason.

Elizabeth still continued to negotiate for a compromise settlement in Scotland that would rid her of responsibility for Mary and neutralize French influence in Scotland. When the earl of Moray was assassinated in January 1570, Elizabeth tried to convince the Scottish earls to accept a limited restoration of Mary coupled with a regency for young King James VI led by Darnley's father, the earl of Lennox. While these negotiations were underway, however, Elizabeth's feelings toward her cousin were hardened by two new developments: the publication of a papal bull excommunicating Elizabeth, and Mary's involvement in a more serious international plot led by a Florentine banker named Ridolfi. The Ridolfi plot centered around an uprising of English Catholics, which was intended to coincide with an invasion by the Spanish army. Norfolk, recently released from the Tower, played a role in the plot although he had been made to swear to have nothing further to do with the queen of Scots as a condition of his release. The Spanish government refused to act until the uprising of English Catholics had begun, and before an uprising could be coordinated, correspondence was seized and the plot discovered.

Norfolk was tried for treason and executed in June 1572. Elizabeth broke off negotiations for Mary Stuart's restoration in Scotland and published the incriminating evidence from Mary's trial, which she had been withholding from public scrutiny on condition of Mary's good behavior. The public reaction to the release of the documents, which included three of the infamous Casket Letters, was immediate. In May 1572, the English Parliament passed a bill excluding Mary and her heirs from the English succession and calling for Mary's execution, as one who had "heaped up together all the sins of the licentious sons of David, adulteries, murders, conspiracies, treasons and blasphemies against God." Elizabeth refused to give her assent to these bills and to others passed by Parliament declaring it treason to support Mary's claim to the English crown and providing for Mary's trial and execution if she were involved in any new insurrections. Elizabeth toyed with the idea of sending Mary back to Scotland to face justice by the Scottish earls after 1573, when the last Marian stronghold, Edinburgh Castle, was conquered by English artillery, ending the civil war in Scotland, but in the end Elizabeth's safest course seemed to be one that would keep Mary firmly under English surveillance.

The remainder of the 1570s were a relatively quiet time for Mary Stuart. No real opportunities for intrigue presented themselves; Mary contented herself with working at her embroidery, and she was allowed to visit the baths at Buxton for the good of her health. But, by 1580, Mary was again chafing against the yoke of her confinement. She hoped to gain the influence of her son, who had reached his 12th birthday in 1578, at which time he was allowed to begin taking an active role in governance. Mary offered to help him throw off the influence of his regents, now led by the earl of Morton, by proposing an "Association" whereby she would be allowed to rule jointly with James. James wrote polite letters in answer to his mother's proposal without committing himself either for or against the scheme. Elizabeth even considered the option, but in the end James abandoned the idea of an Alliance when his growing autonomy made cooperation unnecessary. In May 1585, James negotiated a treaty with Elizabeth without referring to the claims of his mother. Mary, who had always hoped that James' "natural" filial affection would make him one of her staunch defenders, was devastated by her son's abandonment of her cause. Mary retaliated to this slight by changing her will to name Philip II of Spain as her heir. In the meantime, Mary kept alive her negotiations with Spain, even proposing that Philip send an invasion force through which he could conquer England and rule with the queen of Scots at his side.

Unfortunately, Mary Stuart had chosen an inopportune time to renew her intrigues. In 1580, a papal pronouncement against Elizabeth declared that anyone who encompassed her assassination "with the pious intention of doing God's service, not only does not sin but gains merit." Elizabeth took such a threat seriously, especially after William of Orange, the leader of the Protestant Netherlanders, was successfully assassinated in 1584, following a similar declaration. A steady stream of Jesuits from Spain were entering England during the 1580s, and some were plainly implicated in plots against Elizabeth. Through the underground circuit of English Roman Catholics, most of these had some connection to Mary. The growing Puritan presence in Parliament made that body increasingly determined to snuff out what they considered to be the focus of all Jesuit intrigues, the queen of Scots.

Elizabeth again had Mary moved back to Tutbury. The Shrewsburys were released from their duties, and Mary was eventually put into the hands of a new jailer, the staunchly Puritan Sir Amias Paulet. Paulet was completely immune to Mary's charms, and he succeeded in stopping her secret pipeline of correspondence, so that she was cut off from her allies for over a year. When a Roman Catholic agent, Gilbert Gifford, was sent to try to reopen communication with Mary, he was captured upon landing and persuaded to turn double agent. Mary was moved again, to Chartley, where Gifford assisted in the establishment of a pipeline of correspondence utilizing waterproof packets slipped into casks of beer for the household. Mary was completely unaware of the trap, and threw herself into a flurry of correspondence. All of her "secret" letters were intercepted, copied and forwarded by Elizabeth's agents.

Within months of baiting the trap, Elizabeth's agents caught Mary engaging in correspondence with a group of starry-eyed young conspirators, led by a 25-year-old English lord,

Anthony Babington. The Babington plotters proposed to assassinate Elizabeth as a prelude for a foreign invasion. Babington wrote to Mary, sketching out the parameters of the plot, and Mary replied enthusiastically, concentrating on the means they proposed to effect her rescue and saying nothing about the proposed assassination of Elizabeth. When Mary sent this letter through the pipeline, Elizabeth's officials reacted by seizing Mary's papers and arresting the Babington conspirators, all of whom were convicted of treason. Babington and two other ringleaders were hung, drawn and quartered: "They were all cut down [from the gallows], their privities were cut off, bowelled alive and seeing, and quartered." Seven other Babington conspirators went to the scaffold on the following day, but at Elizabeth's order for mercy they were not cut down until they were dead.

At their trials, the Babington conspirators had all implicated Mary Stuart in their scheme, and although the original letter from Mary to Babington had been destroyed soon after its receipt, Babington had vouched for the authenticity of the copy held by Elizabeth's agents. Resolved to Parliament's demand that Mary Stuart be put on trial for her part in the conspiracy, Elizabeth had her cousin moved to the castle of Fotheringhay in Northamptonshire. A group of dignitaries was dispatched from London to try Mary for treason. Convinced that she would not survive this second trial, Mary claimed, "as Queen and Sovereign, I am aware of no fault or offense for which I have to render account to anyone here below"; nevertheless, she believed that she was to die as a martyr for her Roman Catholic faith. Just prior to the opening of the trial, Mary Stuart received a letter from Elizabeth accusing, "You have planned in divers ways and manners to take my life and to ruin my kingdom by the shedding of blood. I never proceeded so harshly against you; on the contrary, I have maintained you and preserved your life with the same care which I use for myself." She commanded Mary to answer to the English peers for the charges, and ended the epistle with the coy assurance, "But answer fully, and you may receive greater favour from us."

Mary Stuart's trial began on October 15, in the great hall of Fotheringhay. Entering the hall at nine o'clock, she was dismayed to see many of the lords dressed in riding clothes and boots—obviously they did not expect a lengthy hearing. As was the custom for all treason trials in the 16th century, Mary was given no counsel for her defense and had no access to her papers at the trial. She defended herself bravely before the 36 peers, privy counsellors, and judges, claiming her rights to be outside of English law as a sovereign queen. When those objections were laid aside, she pled her own illness and physical weakness, and while she admitted being privy to plots for her release, she claimed no knowledge of any plots against Elizabeth's life. After two days of testimony, the council prorogued and ten days later reconvened in Westminster and pronounced Mary guilty.

Within days of the verdict, Parliament passed a bill petitioning for Mary Stuart's execution, but Elizabeth hesitated. For the next three months, Elizabeth waited, perhaps fearful of the international repercussions of killing an anointed queen, and perhaps a little sympathetic to the cousin whom she had never met face to face. Finally, on February 1, 1587, the death warrant was signed—Elizabeth's secretary having conveniently placed it in a pile of other state papers requiring her signature. Even after the warrant was signed, Elizabeth hinted to Paulet that his assistance in Mary's "accidental" demise would be rewarded, but he refused. When Elizabeth continued to hesitate, her secretary, William Davison, took the signed warrant to the Privy Council, which sent it out on its own authority to be administered. On receiving word that the warrant had been sent, Elizabeth went on a rampage of tears and recriminations and ordered Davison to prison (temporarily), but her theatrics did not convince contemporaries that the warrant had been sent by mistake.

Mary Stuart was finally beheaded on February 8, 1587. A platform had been erected in the great hall of Fotheringhay. Mary was not informed of her impending execution until the evening of February 7. She spent the night calmly distributing gifts to her loyal servants and praying. On the morning of February 8, Mary walked to the scaffold calmly and serenely. Some 300 spectators filled the hall. Mary heard the commission for her execution read aloud without flinching, and when she was offered the services of the Protestant dean of Peterborough, she answered, "I am settled in the ancient Catholic Roman religion, and mind to spend my blood in defense of it." When the dean began to pray out loud anyway, Mary turned away from him and prayed in English for the preservation of the true Church, for her son James, and for Elizabeth, calling for God to spare England from his wrath. She ended by calling on Jesus to receive her and forgive her for her sins.

Mary Stuart was then stripped of her ornaments and outer garments, and a cloth was wrapped around her eyes. She knelt on the cushion in front of the block and carefully positioned her head. Stretching out her hands and legs, she cried out: "Into your hands, O Lord, I commend my spirit," three or four times. The first blow of the executioner's axe missed her neck and lodged into the back of her head. At this, Mary reportedly whispered, "Sweet Jesus." The second blow severed the neck almost completely; the last sinew was then sawed apart. The executioner lifted the head for the crowd, crying "God Save the Queen!"—but before he had shown it around, the auburn wig parted from the skull and Mary's head dropped to the ground; to the surprise of the audience, Mary's own sparse hair was very short and completely gray. Another surprise was in store when Mary's little pet terrier crept out from under her skirts where he had been hidden and settled himself between the body and the severed head, refusing to be moved. He subsequently refused to eat and pined away after his mistress.

Mary's executioners were careful to burn or scour everything which was stained with her blood, fearful of creating future religious relics. Her remains were embalmed that afternoon and placed in a heavy lead coffin, but they were not buried until July, and then were moved in the middle of the night. James VI did not break off relations with Elizabeth after his mother's execution. He was ultimately rewarded by being made heir to the English throne when Elizabeth died in 1603.

SOURCES:
Bingham, Caroline. *The Stewart Kingdom of Scotland: 1371–1603.* NY: Barnes and Noble, 1974.
Cowan, Ian B. *The Enigma of Mary Stuart.* Gollancz, 1971.
Donaldson, Gordon. *Mary Queen of Scots.* London: English Universities Press, 1974.
Fraser, Antonia. *Mary Queen of Scots.* NY: Dell, 1969.
Phillips, James. *Images of a Queen.* Los Angeles: University of California Press, 1964.
Zweig, Stefan. *Mary Queen of Scotland and the Isles.* NY: Viking Press, 1935.

Kimberly Estep Spangler,
Associate Professor of History and chair of the Division of Religion and Humanities, Friends University, Wichita, Kansas

Mary Stuart (1631–1660).
See Mary of Orange.

Mary Stuart (1662–1694).
See Mary II.

Mary the Catholic (1516–1558).
See Mary I.

Mary the Egyptian (d. 430).
See Mary of Egypt.

Mary the Jewess.

See also Miriam the Prophet.

Mary the Jewess (fl. 1st, 2nd or 3rd c.)

Hebrew alchemist. Name variations: Maria the Jewess; Miriam the Jewess; Maria Prophetissa; Maria of Alexandria; Miriam the Prophet; Miriam the Prophetess. Born in Alexandria, Egypt, in the 1st, 2nd, or 3rd century CE.

A shadowy historical figure, Mary the Jewess is often identified as *Miriam the Prophet, the sister of Moses.. Miriam the Prophet is a Biblical woman who is known by some of the same alternative names as Mary the Jewess. By other accounts, this is an erroneous association, and the seeming incongruity between the time periods when each one lived implies that they are different women. Yet details are muddled in the haze of myth and history, so many sources treat them as the same person. Some attribute the link to the concept of alchemy as a gift from God to his prophets, or to the Hebrews alone. Others ascribe it to the ancient alchemists' tendency to appropriate historical names for themselves as a way to gain prestige. Nonetheless, Mary the Jewess left behind enough fragments of her writings to establish for herself a revered place in scientific antiquity.

Ancient alchemy, "the art" linked with science, was an amalgamation of "the mystical, the rational, and the practical." The time and place in which Mary lived, the churning, heterogeneous society of Alexandria in the first few centuries after Christ, was the perfect environment for a female Jewish alchemist. Along with *Cleopatra (fl. 1st c. BCE), the physician and author, Mary the Jewess is considered one of the founders of alchemy, and in a 17th-century text is listed as one of the 12 sages of alchemy. Zosimus, in the 3rd century, states that she was the first alchemist to compose the "first material," copper burned with sulfur, necessary for the preparation of gold.

In simplest terms, alchemy sought to achieve the transmutation of base materials into precious materials; the ultimate goal was the creation of the Philosopher's Stone, which alchemists believed could both transform matter into gold and silver and bestow immortality. One of the central tenets of alchemy was the fusing of elements with their opposites, in particular those elements which "adepts" or skilled practitioners designated as "male" and "female." Although these terms were meant metaphorically (as was much in alchemy), the equal respect accorded to both male and female elements had the practical result of allowing male alchemists very little reason to shut women out of the art. Although the degree of acceptance fluctuated, throughout the centuries women alchemists frequently practiced both alongside men, who were often, but not always, their husbands or other family members, and independently, as did Mary the Jewess.

Mary believed that God had given the secret to alchemy exclusively to the Hebrews. She taught that all matter is one, and that successful creation of gold results when parts are combined, saying, "one becomes two, two becomes three, and by means of the third the fourth achieves unity; thus two are but one." Her writings also draw an analogy in this principle between metals and humankind. Although her philosophies and theories were influential, her most important legacies to science were her inventions or improvements of the physical apparatus of chemistry. She left the oldest description of the three-armed still, or *tribikos*, and invented the *kerotakis*, a sealed container in which metal shavings were exposed to vapors. Her most famous contribution is the water bath or double boiler, a twofold vessel in which contents of the inner part are heated by hot water in the outer part. Her affiliation with this device lingers in both the French name for it, *bain Marie*, and the German name, *Marienbad*.

SOURCES:

Doberer, Kurt K. *The Goldmakers*. London, 1948.

Kass-Simon, G., and Patricia Farnes, eds. *Women of Science: Righting the Record*. Bloomington, IN: Indiana University Press, 1990.

Ogilvie, Marilyn B. *Women in Science: Antiquity through the Nineteenth Century*. London: Cambridge Press, 1993.

Jacquie Maurice,
Calgary, Alberta, Canada

Mary the Virgin (20 BCE–40 CE)

Mother of Jesus of Nazareth and the most important Christian saint who is thought by some to be the most perfect of women as well as held to be an intercessor between God and mortals and dispenser of all graces. Name variations: Maria; Miriam; Mary of Nazareth; the Virgin Mary. Born approximately 20 BCE in Roman Palestine; died about 40 CE; daughter of Anne and Joachim; married Joseph (a carpenter of Nazareth); children: Jesus of Nazareth (c. 6 BCE/4 CE–c. 27/37 CE). James of Jerusalem and Joseph (called the brothers of Jesus in Mark 6.3), might be the sons of Joseph from a previous marriage, while some contend they were actually sons of another Mary, possibly Mary of Cleophas, the sister of the Virgin.

Scriptural narrative

Mary the Virgin, the mother of Jesus, is relatively inactive in the New Testament narrative. She is present in few Biblical scenes, and some of those appearances are cameos. Her centrality in Western religious and cultural history, however, significantly outstrips her role in the Gospel stories. Mary has taken on tremendous importance in Christian culture. She is among the pivotal personages in salvation history and is clearly the most famous Christian female figure.

From the Gospels we learn that Mary, a young Jewish woman, lived in Nazareth, a town in Galilee. She was betrothed to a carpenter named Joseph who was descended from the famous David, king of ancient Israel. Before the wedding took place, however, the young virgin was visited by an angel of the Lord. The Angel Gabriel told her not to fear, she was highly favored because she had been chosen among all women to bear the son of the Most High whom she should name Immanuel (Jesus). Mary questioned Gabriel saying, "How can this be? . . . I am still a virgin." The angel assured Mary that the presence of God would overshadow her, and she would conceive a son (Matthew 1.18; Luke 1.26–38). Mary became pregnant by the Holy Spirit. "Being a man of principle," Joseph wished to have the marriage contract annulled, but the angel appeared to him in a dream and counseled him that Mary had not been untrue and that her child would be a savior to his people (Matthew 1.19–21).

Soon after this event (called the Annunciation), Mary visited her elder kinswoman, *Elizabeth. Gabriel had announced to Mary that Elizabeth was not barren, as thought, but was also with child. When Mary and Elizabeth met, Elizabeth's child (John the Baptist) leapt in the womb with joy at the proximity of the Virgin and the baby she was carrying, and Elizabeth, recognizing the significance of her young cousin's pregnancy, addressed her as "mother of my Lord" (Luke 1.39–45). Mary then commenced her most extensive speaking part in the Gospels: the Magnificat, which is a traditional hymn celebrating God's goodness. The Magnificat invokes several Old Testament allusions to God's salvific plan which had come to fruition in Mary (Luke 1.46–55).

When the time of delivery was near, Mary and Joseph were obliged to travel to Bethlehem (the ancestral city of the house of David, Joseph's forebear) in order to register for the census. Bethlehem was crowded with travelers, and the couple, unable to find a place in the inn, slept in the stable. There, in fulfillment of a prophecy in Isaiah 7.14, the Virgin was delivered of a child. She wrapped him in swaddling clothes and used a manger for his crib. Shepherds from the nearby fields were told of the birth by an angel and came to honor the infant king. After eight days, the child was circumcised and named Jesus, according to Gabriel's instructions to Mary. By Mosaic law, the first-born son was to be dedicated to God, but an offering of turtle-doves or pigeons customarily acted as proxy for the child. When Mary and Joseph went to the temple to make their offering, they met the devout Simeon who recognized the sanctity of the boy but prophesied he would suffer a rejection that would "pierce [Mary's] heart" (Luke 2.1–35).

Matthew alone of the Evangelists tells the story of the Adoration of the Magi, the Massacre of the Innocents, and the Flight into Egypt. According to Matthew, Persian priests (called magi) saw a spectacular star rise on the night Jesus was born and knew it signified that a great king had come into the world. After a journey of two years, the three magi reached Judea. They asked the local ruler, Herod, where they could find the young king whose birth the star had announced to the world. Herod's aid was not needed after all, for the same star which had drawn them to Judea rose in front of the three wise men and led them to the home of Jesus where they paid homage to the boy and left gifts of gold, frankincense, and myrrh. Desperate to eliminate anybody who had the potential to challenge his dignity and position, Herod, in a jealous and paranoid rage, ordered that all boys in Bethlehem of two years of age or younger be killed. Mary and Joseph were alerted to this danger in a dream; the warning angel told them to take the child into Egypt for his safety (Matthew 2.1–18).

After a short time, the Holy Family returned from Egypt (Joseph having been advised in a dream that Herod was dead) to Nazareth, and the child grew in strength and wisdom (Matthew 2.19–23). When Jesus was 12, Joseph took Mary and Jesus to Jerusalem for the Passover festival. At the conclusion of the holiday, Mary and Joseph set out with a large party of their relatives for home, but Jesus stayed behind in Jerusalem. When the anxious parents realized that their son was missing, they returned to the city in search of him and, to Mary's astonishment, found Jesus in the temple expounding on the law for an audience of priests and teachers (Luke 2.40–52).

Madonna and Child with Angels.

Mary's next appearance in the Bible narrative is recorded only in the Gospel of John. She was with her son at a wedding in Cana and indicated to him there was a shortage of wine. Jesus mildly rebuked his mother with the enigmatic statement, "Woman, what have I to do with thee? Mine hour is not yet come." All the same, Mary instructed the stewards, "Whatsoever he saith unto you, do it," and Jesus changed water in several nearby jars to wine for the enjoyment of the wedding guests. This incident marked the beginning of Jesus' public ministry as a teacher and prophet, capable of miracles (John 2.1–11). Mary is next mentioned in connection with an incident which is a continuing source of bewilderment for Bible scholars. She was among the group of Jesus' kin who came from Nazareth to Capernaum to bring him home or at least to persuade him to cease preaching, because the family thought Jesus was mad (Matthew 12.46–50; Mark 3.31–35; Luke 8.19–21).

The Gospels differ in their telling of Mary's participation in the final passion (suffering) of Jesus. Matthew, Mark, and Luke indicate that the only supporters present at the crucifixion were a few men and women, watching from a distance, who had followed Jesus from Galilee. If Mary was among this group, the first three Evangelists do not mention her by name (Matthew 27.55–56; Mark 15.40–41; Luke 23.49). John's Gospel, on the other hand, puts Mary at the foot of the cross when Jesus was killed. He reports that Jesus delivered Mary into the care of John, his most beloved disciple, and asked his mother to consider John the Beloved her son (John 19.25–27). Mary's final appearance in the Bible is recorded in the Acts of the Apostles; she was present with the disciples at Pentecost when the Holy Spirit descended on the gathered apostles, marking the establishment of the church (Acts 1.14).

Biblical scholarship on Mary

Such then is the story of Mary as told in the New Testament, drawn from a composite of references to her, many of which were supposedly recited by Mary to the Evangelists years after the events. Outside the Gospels, there are few early sources which shed light on this figure who became so central in the Christian tradition. There is no mention of Mary in Q (a reconstructed collection of Jesus' sayings used by Matthew and Luke) or in Paul's letters (c. 50–60 CE). The paucity of scriptural attention and the near silence of other sources have challenged scholars and invited manifold speculation as to the character of Mary, her role in the early church, and her relationship with Jesus. One of the first questions scholarship asks of the infancy narratives, in which Mary is so prominent, is how historically accurate are they? The answers to that question vary tremendously, as might be expected when dealing with material which has been studied for 19 centuries by people from varying cultures with myriad agendas. Generally speaking, however, the consensus is that Jesus was a historical person and the basic outline of the Gospel account is true to the events it describes. Yet, even as there is virtual agreement on the veracity of the central nar-

rative, most would concede that some of the details of Jesus' life, many of them involving his mother, are embroidered or fabricated.

Matthew is particularly inclined to interpret the life of Jesus as a fulfillment of Old Testament prophecies so as to establish continuity between the Old and New Testaments. Matthew hopes to demonstrate that through Jesus, the Messiah, God continues his beneficent presence in Israel for the salvation of his chosen people and the rest of creation. The virgin birth of Jesus fulfills a prophecy from Isaiah 7.14 that "a virgin will conceive and bear a son." Nathan prophesied that the Messiah would be of the house of David; Mary's marriage to Joseph makes Jesus legally the scion of the Davidic line (2 Samuel 7.12–13). Isaiah foretold that the Messiah would come out of Bethlehem, and Matthew is the only Evangelist who indicates that Mary and Joseph were from Bethlehem. Only Matthew tells of Herod's massacre of the children, which satisfies a prophecy in Jeremiah (31.15), and the fact that the Holy Family settled in Nazareth after its sojourn in Egypt satisfies two predictions: "He shall be called a Nazarene" and "I called my son out of Egypt" (Isaiah 11.1; Hosea 11.1). In short, one of the two accounts of Mary's early motherhood is substantially informed (possibly transformed) by concerns outside the narrative itself.

During Jesus' life, and for some time thereafter, considerable confusion existed as to his paternity. The Gospels pursue two lines of argument. On the one hand, Jesus is the Son of God; on the other, he is descended from David through Joseph. In addition, there was a pertinacious tradition among Jews and pagan Romans that Jesus was the son of a soldier from Gaul named Tiberius Julius Abdes Panthera, who was serving in Palestine near the time of Jesus' birth. The name Jesus ben (son of) Panthera is used in the Talmud in connection with the story of Rabbi Eleazar ben Dama who suffered from a snake bite; Jacob of Sama sought to heal him in the name of Jesus ben Panthera. In the 3rd century, Origen responded to charges commonly directed against Christians, in this case by a Roman named Celsus, that Jesus had fabricated his miraculous birth, and that in fact he was the offspring of a poor country woman who was turned out by her fiancé when her adultery was discovered. According to this accusation, Mary "was wandering about in a disgraceful way [when] she secretly gave birth to Jesus . . . by a certain soldier named Panthera" (*Contra Celsum* 1.28, 32). Eusebius, a 4th-century bishop of Caesarea, also referred to the "slanderous" accusation that Jesus was "born of Panthera" (*Ecl. Proph.* 3.10). Christians defended Jesus by asserting that Panthera was the surname of Joseph's father, Jacob, and in the 8th century an archbishop of Crete suggested that Panthera was an ancestor of Mary. Another possibility is that Panthera is a corruption of *parthenos* (virgin or young girl), and may have been a term used to slur Mary and cheapen her son's origins.

The relationship between Mary and Jesus as represented in the Gospels is puzzling at several points. On various occasions, Jesus makes what could be read as disparaging comments about family in general and about his family in particular. In Luke and Matthew, he claims that one who hopes to be his disciple must hate his father and mother, wife and children, brothers and sisters (Luke 14.26; Matthew 10.37–38 omits wife and siblings). Jesus periodically predicts that, as a result of his mission, families will be split: father against son, daughter against mother (Matthew 10.21, 10.34–37; Luke 12.51–53). In Luke (11.27–28), a devotee of Jesus calls from the crowd, "Happy the womb that carried you and the breast that suckled you." Jesus lets pass the opportunity to praise his mother and responds instead that the most blessed are those who hear God's word and keep it. The three synoptic Gospels (Matthew, Mark, and Luke) relate an incident between Mary and her son which has perplexed scholars seeking to understand their relationship. When Jesus is preaching in Capernaum, his mother and brothers arrive to take charge of him. Unable to reach him due to the crowds, they send a message to Jesus instructing him to come out, to which he responds, "Who is my mother? Who are my brothers?" Pointing to his disciples, he continues, "Whoever does the will of God is my brother, my sister, my mother" (Matthew 12.46–50; Mark 3.31–5; Luke 8.19–21).

Mary's attitude towards her son is not clear. She is among the family members who seek to restrain the peripatetic preacher. Does she think him mad or possessed of the demon Beelzebub as the doctors of the law surmise earlier in the scene (as recorded by Mark)? It is difficult to say, because the description of the episode is laconic. Jesus' reaction to the presence of his family at Capernaum has been explained allegorically: he sought to pose a contrast between his natural and eschatological families. His remark could be read as an assertion that kinship bonds are less meaningful than affinity with the larger human family united by its devotion to God. Another interpretation has it that Jesus was disappointed by the skepticism of his fellow Nazarenes, including his family, as revealed in

Pietá *by Michelangelo.*

his lament, "A prophet will always be honored except in his home and among his kinsmen and family" (Mark 6.4). Alternatively, the comments derogating his family may have been later insertions meant to discredit Jesus' siblings by the Evangelists who were, in the last part of the 1st century when the Gospels were written, trying to wrest leadership of the young Christian community from the control of Jesus' brother James.

The strange incidents at Cana, and at the cross where Jesus addresses his mother with the pejorative term "woman," are difficult to understand unless placed against their Old Testament background. Some scholars have suggested that the term "woman" connects the wedding at Cana to a scripture in Isaiah (26.17) in which a metaphorical pregnant woman yearns for the kingdom of God but is unable to bring it about. In the same manner, at Cana Mary must wait on Jesus for the birth of the new Israel—the church. Jesus' use of "woman" to refer to his mother as she stands at the foot of the cross connects the scene at Cana with the crucifixion when Jesus, in his death and resurrection, finally makes the deliverance or delivery of Israel possible.

Through the Christian centuries, exegetes have plumbed the Scriptures for allusions to Mary. In Revelations, John writes of a woman in labor—"robed with the sun," the moon at her feet, and twelve stars for a crown. She gives birth to a male child who is delivered to God after evading a terrestrial dragon. Through her successful delivery this woman comes to personify the old and the new: the people of Israel and the Christian church. By the 4th century, this passage was thought to refer to Mary the Virgin (Ap 12.1–5).

*W*hat is holier than she? Neither Prophets nor Apostles . . . neither seraphim nor cherubim . . . nor any created being, visible or invisible.

—John Chrysostom

In the Old Testament, Israel is often personified as a woman: sometimes a virgin (Jeremiah 31.4), a faithless bride (Jeremiah 2; Ezekiel 16), a mother (Hosea 2.4–5; Isaiah 66.7), a daughter (Zephaniah 3.14–20; Isaiah 37.22), or a woman in labor (Jeremiah 6.24, 13.21; Isaiah 26.17). Since Mary was seen as mother to the new Israel, prophecies about the attributes of Israel in the Old Testament readily attached themselves to her. Gabriel's greeting to Mary at the Annunciation, "Hail, the Lord is with you," was thought to echo Old Testament prophecies in which the "daughter of Sion" is told to rejoice at her special status in the eyes of God (Joel 1.21–27; Zechariah 9.9). The phrase "the Lord is with you" was said to mirror passages which express the idea that God is about to inaugurate a new era (Genesis 26.24, 28.15, 46.4; Exodus 3.12; Judges 6.12, 6.16). When God chastises the serpent in the Garden, he allies Mary to the cosmic struggle against evil with the words, "I will put enmity between you and the woman" (Genesis 3.15). In the Annunciation when Gabriel explains to Mary that the spirit of God will "overshadow" her, he employs the same term used to describe the presence of God descending on the ark of the covenant (Exodus 40.35). Thus, Mary with the child in her womb is the ark of the new covenant. The ark was brought to Jerusalem in David's time and, in the same way, Mary, on learning of her pregnancy, goes to Jerusalem to visit Elizabeth. Another common allusion to Mary from Genesis 3.15 refers to a woman who "will bruise the serpent's head." *Eve was defeated by the serpent, but the new Eve, Mary, subdues it. In short, Mary who entered Christian history as a simple peasant from Nazareth became the embodiment of the church in its glory and humanity redeemed. She is a model to other Christians because she allowed the Word to permeate her body and soul.

Marian Apocrypha

If the New Testament is sparing in its treatment of Mary, the gnostic documents from Nag Hammadi and the apocrypha she generated in subsequent centuries are not. "Apocrypha" is a reference to religious writings which did not become part of the Biblical canon, were not officially sanctioned by church authorities, and were in many cases condemned. Such was the case with the Gospel of James (now referred to as the *Protoevangelium*). The oldest manuscript of this work was produced in the early 4th century and was reputed to have been copied from the original by James of Jerusalem, the brother of Jesus. It achieved immediate popularity and formed the basis of two later tracts on the birth, childhood, and domestic life of Mary (*The Gospel of the Nativity of Mary* and *The Book of the Infancy of Mary and Christ the Savior*). All three works continued to circulate despite the opprobrium of Pope Gelasius (d. 496). The *Protoevangelium* was the source of several medieval legends and iconographic representations of Mary. From this work, we learn for the first time of Mary's conception and birth, the notion that she was without sin from birth, her stay in the temple from her third to twelfth year, and her preternatural powers. This apocryphal account indicates that Joseph was an elderly widower at the time of his marriage to Mary, thus explaining the Biblical references to Jesus' siblings which presented a problem for the author of the work, who held that Mary had remained a virgin throughout her life and did not bear any children except Jesus.

The revision of the *Protoevangelium*, called *The Book of the Infancy of Mary and Christ the Savior* (part of which is also referred to as pseudo-Matthew), has a propensity for the miraculous (even the ridiculous). It dates from the 7th or 8th century and concentrates on Mary's time in the temple. *The Gospel of the Nativity of Mary*, written in the 9th century, uses material similar to the pseudo-Matthew but eliminates the shocking or unintelligible sections. Both works were well known in the High Middle Ages (c. 1100–1250) and were the source for art, literature, and dramatic narrative cycles concerning Mary the Virgin.

The Virgin Birth: Virgo concepit, virgo peperit, virgo permansit (*She conceived while virgin, gave birth while virgin, and she remained virgin*)

Among the multitude of virtues and miracles attributed to Mary over the centuries, the

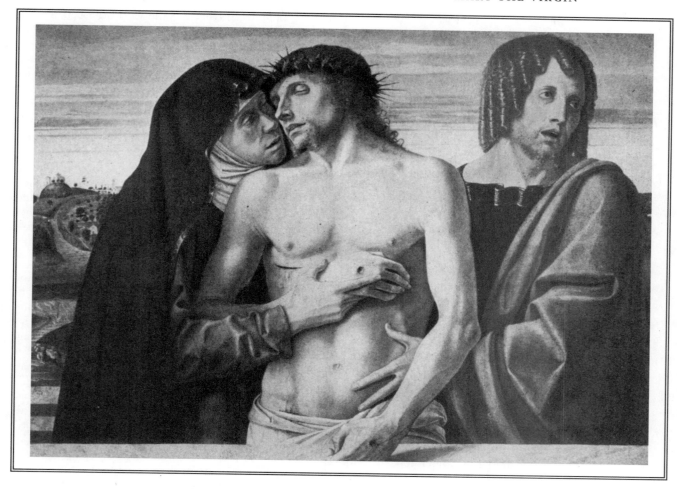

The Dead Christ, with Madonna and St. John.

earliest was her virginity during the conception and delivery of Jesus. In the primitive church, Mary's virginity was less important for what it said about her than for the implications it had on the nature of Jesus and the purity of his birth.

The notion of Mary's virginity did not, however, achieve wide currency in the lifetime of Jesus. Neither Mark, Paul, nor John refer to it. Matthew and Luke introduce the virgin birth principally for two reasons. First, particularly Matthew holds that the virgin birth fulfills a prophecy of Isaiah which he understood to state that a virgin would bear a child called Immanuel, which means God is with us (7.14). The word Matthew took from the Septuagint (Greek Old Testament) to mean virgin (*parthenos*) can also be interpreted as "young girl" without any connotation of virginity. Scholars do not agree on what meaning was originally intended in Isaiah, but in Matthew's view Isaiah foretold the birth of the Messiah from a virgin, and, in the Gospel of Matthew, Jesus is that Messiah and Mary is that virgin. Second, for Matthew and Luke the virgin birth

demonstrates Jesus' preeminent and unique authority over other itinerant preachers-healers. For them, the virginity of Mary is one of the critical signs that Jesus is not just another prophet, but the Christ.

In the Gospels, Jesus is referred to variously as the son of Mary, son of Joseph the carpenter, son of David, Son of Man, Son of God, and Son of the Most High. Even today Biblical commentators have not reached consensus on the implications of these various appellations. Mark's use of the term "son of Mary" is, according to some scholars, tantamount to calling Jesus a bastard. The usual form would have been to refer to a man as the son of his father. John and Paul argue that Jesus had no father other than God or the Holy Spirit. In other words, they understand the unique paternity of Jesus, but that does not necessarily imply that they recognize the conception and birth as virginal.

Although the idea of Mary's virginity was initially promoted because of its relevance to an understanding of Jesus, by the 3rd century celibacy was idealized as a virtue in itself, and Mary was elevated as the virgin *par excellence*. Not only was she held to be virginal in the conception and delivery of Jesus, but she was thought to have remained celibate throughout her life. This interpretation, promoted by many of the Church Fathers (particularly authoritative theologians writing from c. 150 to 600), is at odds with the Biblical account in which the siblings of Jesus are often mentioned. Also, Matthew (1.25) reports that Joseph "had no intercourse with [Mary] until her son was born," implying that the couple may have had conjugal relations after the birth of Jesus. Jerome, an early and indefatigable champion of female monasticism, was instrumental in articulating and actively advocating the perpetual virginity of Mary. In 383, he wrote a tract in which he argues that the marriage of Joseph and Mary was never consummated and the siblings of Jesus mentioned in the Gospels were actually his cousins. He claims the confusion is due to a misunderstanding created when the New Testament was translated from Aramaic to Greek. He also asserts that James and Joseph, called the brothers of Jesus in Mark 6.3, were actually sons of another Mary, the sister of the Virgin, possibly *Mary of Cleophas. Jerome's labored efforts to demonstrate that Jesus had no siblings demonstrates how important the perpetual virginity of Mary was to him. By about 400, the position of Jerome (and other Church Fathers such as Origen and Gregory of Nyssa) on the mother of Jesus became orthodox: Mary was held to be virgin *ante partum, in partu*, and *post partum* (before, during, and after the birth of Jesus).

Mary's role in Christological debates

The 4th and 5th centuries were characterized by serious, divisive debates over the nature of Jesus (Christology) in which disagreement about the corporeal relationship between Mary and Jesus played a role. John the Evangelist always refers to Mary the Virgin as "mother of Jesus"—never simply "Mary." When Paul speaks of God's son as "born of a woman" (Galatians 4.4), he introduces a theme which became increasingly important in Christian theology (fully worked out by the 12th century in a tract by Anselm of Canterbury called *Why God Became Man* [*Cur Deus Homo*]). By their disobedience in the Garden of Eden, Adam and Eve precipitated the fall of humanity. Because human beings committed the sin, only a human could atone for it. However, due to the enormity of the offense, it had to be rectified by a mortal of superior dignity, a dignity possible only to God. So Jesus, the man/God, redeemed the world through the humanity he received from the woman, Mary. This, contend some writers, is why many of the apostles refer to her as "woman." Mary the specific individual from Nazareth is not theologically significant; but her humanness is.

Once it was established that Jesus' humanity was real, questions arose over how a man, born of woman, could also be God. Proponents of Arianism, a wide-spread heresy (c. 300–600), claimed that the Son (Jesus) was not the same as, or co-eternal to, the Father (God). The Council of Nicaea (325) rejected the Arian position and affirmed the doctrine that Jesus and the Father are *homoousios* (of the same divine substance): in effect, Jesus is God—which makes Mary the mother of God.

Christological debates continued into the 5th century. Nestorius, patriarch of Constantinople in 428, was distressed over the increasing popularity of the cult of Mary the Virgin and rejected the notion that a created human being could be mother to deity. He argued that Jesus was not the *Logos* (word) incarnate but a man in close association with the *Logos*: more human than divine. On these grounds, he denied Mary the appellation *Theotokos* (bearer of God), although he was willing to concede her the title *Christotokos* (bearer of Christ). According to Nestorius, Mary was simply the mother of a human infant. A church council, convened at Ephesus in 431, denounced Nestorius and upheld the absolute unity of Jesus' humanity and divinity. Cyril of Alexandria responded to Nestorius by saying, "If the Incarnation was a phantom, salvation is a phantom too" (*Cat. Lect.* 4.9). A subsequent council at Chalcedon in 451 confirmed Mary's honorific, *Theotokos*, a term which spread quickly in the Eastern and Western churches. After Chalcedon, Mary's stature in salvation history continued to grow.

Development of Marian Theology (Mariology)

Mary's importance to the early church rested entirely on the fact that she was the mother of Jesus, or as Elizabeth said, "mother of my Lord" (Luke 1.43). She was honored strictly for providing Christ his humanity and for being graced by God (for no obvious merit of her own) as vessel for the Incarnation. Other than the anomaly of the virgin birth, Mary received little attention in the 1st century of the Christian era.

Beginning in the 2nd century, aspects of Mary as an individual and of her role in salvation history began to attract interest, and a theology of the Virgin herself (Mariology) took root. In seeking to clarify the relationship between Jesus' human and divine natures, thinkers such as Ignatius of Antioch, Irenaeus of Lyon, and Justin Martyr were led to consider the part played by the mother of Jesus. Irenaeus articulated a precept that became a permanent aspect of Mariology when he characterized Mary as a type of anti-Eve: through one woman, death entered the world; through another, humankind was redeemed and death overcome. Justin Martyr emphasized Mary's role in the redemption of mankind. Just as sin entered the world through Eve who came from Adam's side, redemption was made possible through the second Eve who, in a sense, experienced rebirth from the side wound Jesus received on the cross, for Mary only fully understood her mission as she watched her son die. The notion of Mary as anti-Eve continued to evolve; by the 9th century, Mary was occasionally referred to as *Redemptrix* or *co-Redemptrix* and by the 15th century as Queen of Heaven. These titles were recognized by Pope Pius XII in 1954 who reaffirmed that Mary was the "new Eve," *co-Redemptrix* with Jesus, the "new Adam" (*Mystici corporis*).

While the doctrine of the virgin birth, incipient in the Gospels, was expounded by the Church Fathers primarily because of information it provided about the nature of Jesus, there was also some interest in it for the light it shed on the person of Mary. Because she conceived without concupiscence, she was free of the "stain" of sexual desire. This notion of Mary's innocence gained wide popularity to the point that in the early centuries of the church she was viewed by many to be uniquely free of sin among mortals. The doctrine of Mary's sinlessness was officially confirmed by the Catholic Council of Trent in the 16th century.

Beginning in the 2nd century, a teaching circulated that Mary was free, not only of actual earthly transgression, but even of original sin, meaning she was unable to sin. Throughout the Middle Ages, many thinkers, even ardent devotees of the Virgin such as Augustine (d. 430), Bernard of Clairvaux (d. 1153), and Bonaventure (d. 1274), while conceding that Mary possessed a greater degree of sanctity than even the angels, doubted that any human being other than Jesus eluded the stain of original sin inflicted on humankind by the offense of Adam and Eve in the Garden. The tenet gradually gained acceptance until it was officially approved as Catholic dogma in 1854 by Pope Pius IX (*Ineffabilis Deus*). Pius explained that Mary was predestined to be the mother of God and was "adorned with an abundance of heavenly gifts"

even before her conception. That she was blessed with a supremacy of holiness is clear, he claimed, in Gabriel's greeting to her at the Annunciation: "Hail Mary, full of grace" (Luke 1.28). This teaching came to be known as the Immaculate Conception of Mary.

Within the Mariological tradition, the Virgin's life broadly parallels that of Jesus as she participates in the redemptive mission of her son. This is the case particularly in reference to three events: (a) the Incarnation, (b) the Cross, and (c) the Resurrection. (a) The Incarnation: Mary's cooperation in the birth of Christ was implicit at the Annunciation when she responded to the Angel Gabriel, "Behold the handmaid of the Lord; be it unto me according to thy words" (Luke. 1.38). The full implication of her participation in the Incarnation was "ratified" at the crucifixion when Mary became mother to all humanity. In 1943, Pope Pius XII fleshed out centuries of discussion on the subject when he asserted that Mary, in her response to Gabriel, not only accepted God's proposal that she bear the Christ, but also gave consent for the whole of the human race to a spiritual marriage between the Son of God and human nature.

(b) The Cross: God did not afford Mary the privilege of suffering martyrdom because she participated empathetically in the passion of her son. Her presence at the foot of the cross constituted her integration with Christ in the act of redemption. On this point Pope Benedict XV wrote, "To such an extent did [Mary] suffer and almost die with her suffering and dying son . . . that we may rightly say that she redeemed the human race together with Christ" (*Acts ApS* 10 [1918] 182). When Jesus said, "Woman, behold thy son," in reference to John, and to John, "Behold thy mother" (John 19.26–27), Mary's spiritual motherhood of all humankind was affirmed. She experienced no pain in the delivery of the baby Jesus, but at Calvary, where she became the mother of sinful humanity, her pain was tremendous, fulfilling Simeon's prophecy that because of Jesus, Mary's soul would be pierced (Luke 2.35).

At the cross, Mary's motherhood was extended beyond the simple maternity of Jesus to encompass all human beings. Origen, in the 3rd century, alluded to Mary's spiritual motherhood of the church (meaning redeemed humankind). Bernard of Clairvaux enlarged the metaphor when he wrote, "God is the Father of all created things, and Mary is the mother of all recreated things." The theology was further elaborated by Pope Sixtus IV in the 15th century and by a series of popes in the 20th century. "Bearing Jesus in her womb, Mary bore there also all those whose life was included in that of the Savior. . . . We ought to consider ourselves as having come forth from the womb of the Virgin" (Pope Pius X, *Ad diem illum*).

Mary's participation in the redemption of humankind earned her the title *Redemptrix,* and her position in the spiritual hierarchy between other mortals and Christ has resulted in the designation *Mediatrix*. The term was introduced in the 8th century, extended in the 12th century, generally accepted by the 17th century, and embraced by the papacy in the 19th and 20th centuries. *Mediatrix* is a reference to Mary's role as mediator between Christ and humanity which she was afforded because of her divine motherhood and plenitude of grace. According to the precept of the *Mediatrix,* all favors, blessings, and gifts of the Holy Spirit granted by God to human beings are brought about by Mary's intervention and dispensed by her. The Franciscan Bernardino of Siena (d. 1444) said, "[Mary] has received a certain jurisdiction over all graces. . . . They are administered through her hands to whom she pleases, when she pleases, as she pleases and as much as she pleases."

(c) The Resurrection: In the 4th century an apocryphal work called *Transitus Mariae* appeared which provides (in addition to tales of Mary's miracles) the earliest suggestion that Mary did not die in the normal fashion, but fell asleep (referred to as her Dormition or *Koimesis*) and was assumed into Heaven, body and soul, in a manner similar to Jesus; hence, she was resurrected before the general resurrection of the faithful. Although belief in the Assumption of the Virgin was condemned by Pope Gelasius, the legend gained credence in the Middle Ages and was formally approved by Pope Pius XII in 1950.

Mary has also been cast as a type (the completion of an Old Testament foreshadowing) of the church, and, although her ecclesial significance was noted in the patristic period, it was not a major theme then or in the Middle Ages. In Lucan theology, Mary is the ark carrying the new covenant. For Pope Leo I (d. 461), Mary and the church share the distinction of producing offspring in the purity of faith. As Mary is the virginal mother of Jesus, the church is the virginal (faithful and undefiled) mother of humans to whom it offers eternal life. As the church is the Mystical Body of Christ, the mother of Christ is also the mother of the church. Because Mary is the mother of Christ, the head of the church, she is mother of the whole body, the members. In

1964, Pope Paul VI formally proclaimed Mary *Mater Ecclesiae* (Mother of the Church).

The above presentation of Marian theology is based largely on the Catholic view of the mother of Jesus because it is in the Roman Catholic tradition that Mariology is most developed. The understanding of Mary varies in other Christian religions. Although she is highly extolled in Greek Orthodox doctrine and popular piety, the Orthodox Church does not recognize the Immaculate Conception of Mary and balks at the notion of her Assumption. During the Reformation, Luther, Calvin, and other Protestant leaders reacted adversely to what they considered abuses in devotions to Mary and forbade calling on her for assistance in prayer. Luther affirmed Mary's Immaculate Conception and bodily Assumption and retained some Marian feasts, but Luther and Calvin both expressed misgivings about titles such as Mother of God. They tended to see Mary as the virgin mother of the Gospels and a symbol of the believing church. Mary is also honored in Islam and extolled in the Quran (see *suras* 3, 4, 19, 21, and 66).

Marian feasts and the cult of the Virgin

Both popular and liturgical devotion to the Virgin began first in the East. The earliest liturgical commemoration of Mary occurred in a 5th-century feast (celebratory day of remembrance) called "remembrance of Mary" held on January 1. By the late 7th century, the four major Marian feasts developed in the East had been introduced to the West. They are the Annunciation (March 25), The Dormition and Assumption (August 15), the Nativity of the Blessed Virgin Mary (September 18), and the Purification at the Temple, a rite of cleansing that Mary underwent after the birth of Jesus (February 2). Three other feasts were in place by the end of the 15th century. The Presentation (of Mary) in the Temple is celebrated on November 21, the Feast of the Immaculate Conception is held on December 8 or 9, and the Visitation (of Mary to Elizabeth) takes place on July 2. In addition to these major feasts, several other Marian commemorations were developed and promoted, especially in tandem with the Counter-Reformation and often in response to local or special interests.

Devotion to Mary the Virgin grew gradually over the centuries. In Late Antiquity, she was honored as the mother of God. As early as the 4th century, churches were dedicated to her, she was praised and petitioned in private and public prayers and was the subject of popular devotion. Leaden seals have been found from the period with the inscription "servant of Mary." The Virgin came to be venerated by some sects even more than her human nature warranted or orthodoxy allowed. The embellishment of the historical person of Mary was influenced by myths of mother goddesses from pagan religions, in particular the figure of Isis nursing her child Horus, who is portrayed iconographically in a manner similar to the Christian Madonna with Child. In the 4th century, a small group of women called Collyridians from the Eastern Empire formed a cult of the Virgin (considered heretical); part of their ritual included offering cakes (*kollyrides*) to Mary, the virgin goddess.

Ambrose of Milan (d. 397) reminded Christians that the Incarnation was the work of the Holy Spirit and he admonished, "Let no one divert his adoration to the Virgin Mary; Mary was the temple of God, not the God of the temple" (*De Spiritu Sancto* 3.11.79–80). Participants at the second Council of Nicaea (787) felt it necessary to clarify the appropriate approach to Mary. They re-established that *latria* (worship) is due to God alone, *dulia* (veneration) is fitting for the saints, but Mary, more holy than all the other saints, is owed *hyperdulia* (more than reverence). Mary, although full of grace, was not equal to Jesus who had a plenitude of grace at birth; Mary's grace developed through her life experiences.

By the Carolingian period, four feasts of the Virgin were celebrated in the West (six in the East) and Charlemagne's councilor, Alcuin (d. 804), promoted Saturday as Mary's day. In the 12th century, the cult of the Virgin truly came into its own. Since Mary was thought to have been assumed into Heaven, there were no bodily remains, but her robe, belt, and breast milk became coveted relics. Along with a developed Mariology, a growing humanistic emphasis on Jesus the man stimulated interest, both popular and learned, in the Holy Family and focused attention on even the mundane, quotidian details of Mary's earthly existence. This devotion is evidenced by the dedication of numerous cathedrals to "Our Lady" (*Notre Dame*), increased concentration on Mary in art and literature (both sacred and profane), and the special adoration given her by major religious leaders in the High Middle Ages, such as Bernard of Clairvaux, Dominic (d. 1221), Francis of Assisi (d. 1226), Thomas Aquinas (d. 1274), and Duns Scotus (d. 1308).

Protestant reformers, although honoring Mary, questioned the validity of the cult of the Virgin and denied the ability of saints generally to intercede with Christ on behalf of humans. By contrast, among Catholics adoration of Mary blossomed in the 16th, 17th, and 18th centuries, especially as the Catholic Council of Trent (1545–1563) defended the cult, and devotions such as the rosary and scapular increased in popularity. While some individuals consecrated themselves to the "holy slavery of Mary," others took vows to defend to the death the doctrine of the Immaculate Conception. John Eudes preached the Immaculate Heart of Mary, and in 1750 Alphonsus de Liguori defended Marian devotion in the widely read *Glories of Mary*.

In the 19th and 20th centuries, several missionary orders were founded in Mary's name, as were lay organizations or sodalities which professed special friendship with Mary. Great national and international congresses and pilgrimages mark Marian devotion in our era. Several sightings of Mary have taken place around the world, including Lourdes (1858) and LaSalette (1846), France; Knock, Ireland (1879); and Fatima, Portugal (1917). Various Christian churches recognize some of these visitations as legitimate, some they reject. Twentieth-century popes have set the pattern for Catholic Marian devotion in this century by officially affirming many aspects of Mariology developed in pervious periods. Pius XII consecrated the world to the Immaculate Heart of Mary (1942) and inaugurated a new feast of the Queenship of Mary celebrated on May 31. The most recent trend in papal discourse on Mary is moderation. Since mid-century, popes such as John XXIII, and Paul VI have urged that veneration of the Virgin be realigned with "the most traditional Marian devotion."

Mary in art

Marian themes have varied over the centuries in response to theological and cultural developments. The earliest representation of Mary (found in the 2nd-century Roman catacomb of *Priscilla) is a fresco of a simple peasant woman holding her child. This motif of the Madonna and Child has persisted in Christian art for centuries, although the interpretation of it varies depending on cultural milieu. Images of the Madonna became more regal, for instance, in the 5th century in line with Mary's theological designation as mother of God and the general recognition of the Virgin as the beneficent Queen of Heaven. She is enthroned with the Christ child, surrounded by ministering angels, draped with costly oriental fabrics, and red slippers adorn her feet. Reflecting other aspects of Mariology as they were articulated, Mary is often iconographically assimilated to the Church (*Ecclesia*), or depicted as the Woman of the Apocalypse.

Most Marian themes are common to both the Eastern and Western artistic traditions, but there are differences in emphasis. Early and medieval Byzantine artists often portrayed Mary, seated or standing, holding the baby Jesus while he is in the act of blessing. We also have representations of the Virgin praying, standing at the foot of the cross, and, though less frequently, nursing Jesus or being kissed by the child. Icons (sacred pictures) of the Virgin were thought to be spiritually potent and were used to effect miracles, protect their owners, and even win battles. In 626, the emperor Heraclius placed an icon of the Virgin on the gates of Constantinople as a reminder that the city was under divine protection even when the sovereign was away. The Byzantine icon known as the *Mother of God of Vladimir* was often carried into battle by medieval Russian warriors.

Western artists borrowed heavily from Byzantine themes, but also developed distinctive iconographic motifs. The *Maria Regina*, a representation of Mary crowned as queen, evolved in the 6th century in Italy and was very popular throughout the Romanesque and Gothic eras (c. 1100–1250). Just as temporal monarchies were increasingly influential in Western medieval culture, the Virgin and her son were depicted in artistic images as enthroned in the heavenly kingdom. A common element of the *Maria Regina* theme is the Coronation of Mary by Christ the King. Kings, both terrestrial and eternal, were idealized as the final, often harsh, adjudicators of the law, but queens, including Mary, played the role of intercessor, softening the monarch's heart by gentle persuasion and arguments on the side of mercy.

The major source for the Marian pictorial tradition in both the East and the West was the apocryphal *Protoevangelium* and its revisions. From these works, numerous episodes of the life of Mary's parents were developed: The Marriage of *Anne and Joachim, the Annunciation to Anne that she would bear the Virgin Mary, and the Conception of Mary (which is symbolized in art by a kiss between Anne and Joachim outside the gates of Jerusalem). The most frequently rendered scene from Mary's childhood is her nativity. Anne and Joachim were thought to be rich, so the birth of Mary is portrayed as a splendid affair, involving servants, midwives, gift bearers, and the ceremonial bathing or cradling of the Virgin. In later compositions, the Nativity of Mary includes a representation of the presentation of the infant Mary to her mother, Anne.

Pictorial elaborations of mundane or quotidian events of Mary's life were of great interest, especially in the High Middle Ages which witnessed a trend towards sentimentalizing the Holy Family. Popular scenes include Mary's First Steps, Caresses, and the Blessing by the Priest. The theme of Anne teaching Mary to read became widespread in Western art beginning with the 14th century. Several groupings, including some or all members of the family (Anne, Mary, Jesus and Joseph), were produced during the High Middle Ages. The Presentation at the Temple (and associated activities) was a common artistic theme in Byzantine Marian art because of the importance of the liturgical feast commemorating the event. For similar reasons, Western visual accounts capture scenes of Mary's life in the temple, with a concentration on her weaving and miracles. Mary's stay in the temple was terminated by her marriage to Joseph, and the couple's nuptials are commonly recorded in Byzantine works of art.

The New Testament was the primary source for pictorial representations of Mary from her pregnancy to the crucifixion of Jesus. Although particular episodes from the Gospels are emphasized, embellished, and often conflated, every appearance of Mary in the Biblical text has found a place in the Christian artistic tradition, from the Annunciation (in which Mary is usually pictured weaving purple wool, praying, or reading), to the Crucifixion, Entombment, and Ascension of Jesus.

Apocryphal literature takes up the narrative of Mary's later years where the New Testament leaves off and is again the source of visual renderings of Marian themes. A 4th-century work incorrectly attributed to pseudo-Melito, bishop of Sardis (2nd century), formed the textual basis for the Dormition and funeral of Mary, especially in Byzantine iconography. Gabriel, or sometimes Christ, appears to the aged Virgin to inform her of her impending death and assumption. Holding a palm branch, she bids farewell to the apostles who surround her bed or (in 12th-century depictions) hover over the scene on clouds. Angels wait in the background to take the Virgin to Heaven, and Christ is present holding the soul of his mother. Sometimes Athanios, a legendary Jew whose hands were cut off for touching the funeral bier, is present. In Byzantine renderings of the Assumption of the Virgin, Mary is represented as an infant in swaddling clothes. In the West, it is usually the adult Mary who is pictured, flanked by angels, often surrounded by a mandorla. Some Renaissance artworks include Mary throwing her belt to Doubting Thomas in order to assuage his skepticism as she ascends to her glorious reward.

The Pieta (Mary with the dead Christ in her lap) first appeared at the beginning of the 14th century in German convents. Perhaps the most famous rendition of this theme is the *Pieta* by Michelangelo (d. 1564) now in the Vatican. Unlike the Lamentation in which Mary cries out in anguish at the sight of her lifeless child, the Pieta captures the mother's serene acceptance of Christ's sacrifice. In Michelangelo's vision, Mary, although mother of the adult Jesus, is a young woman frozen in her timeless perfection—a flawless image of the graceful, compassionate mother of a tortured humanity.

Mary in literature

Much of the most beautiful medieval poetry was inspired by Mary the Virgin, whether for private devotions or public liturgy (standardized church services). As in theology and art, Mary entered Christian literature gradually and references to her mirror Mariological developments. The earliest extant literary references to Mary can be found in the 2nd century, when the phrase "born of the Holy Spirit and the Virgin Mary" was attached to some baptismal creeds. Mary's name also appears in prayers for remembrance, patronage, intercession, and the ritual of the Eucharist. Fourth-century manuscripts preserve prayers such as *Sub tuum praesidium confugimus* (*We fly to thy Patronage*) that petition or praise Mary directly and were designed for private worship. In the 4th century, mention of Mary also increased in public liturgical prayers. For example, the mid-4th century liturgy of St. Basil includes the expression "remembering in the first place the Blessed Virgin Mary, Mother of God, and all the saints." By the 5th and 6th centuries, inclusion of the Virgin Mother was customary in a variety of standardized forms. For instance, the Greek hymn *Akathistos* contains an elaborate epithet for Mary, and Western liturgical antiphons like *Alma redemptoris mater* (*Sweet Mother of the Redeemer*) commemorate the Virgin.

As Marian feasts developed, liturgies were written for them, first in the East and then in the West. In the early 7th century, references to Mary became common in liturgies produced for other saints. The famous prayer *Ave Maria*, first written for private or individual worship, was quickly integrated into formal observances. The early form of this poem (likely a Syriac ritual attributable to Severus, patriarch of Antioch) incorporates the sense of Gabriel's greeting to Mary at the Annunciation (Luke 1.28 and 1.42), praising her and the fruit of her womb. The 8th-century writer John of Damascus was particularly devoted to the Virgin whom he extolled as "all holy."

Mary figures prominently in literature produced in Anglo-Saxon England beginning in the 7th century. Praises to her appear regularly in poetic form in works by such luminaries as Aldhelm (b. 640), Bede (d. 735), and Alcuin. Bede gives us evidence of Marian references in monastic offices (prescribed formulas for monastic services) when he speaks of a monk who sang "all the hours of St. Mary." A century later across the Channel, Carolingian clerics were producing masses in honor of Mary. The Office of the Blessed Virgin Mary was developed by Benedict of Aniane (d. 821), and there is widespread evidence that an Office of the Blessed Virgin Mary (which includes lessons, responses, psalms and hymns) was used throughout Europe in the 10th century.

The 11th and 12th centuries saw the flowering of Marian veneration in the West. The *Ave Maria* became a separate devotional formula commonly repeated several times in the context of private worship. Sermons, prayers, liturgical offices, and masses (especially for Saturday) proliferated. In this period, use of the votive Office of the Blessed Virgin Mary expanded, particularly promoted by Peter Damian (d. 1072). Geoffroy de Vigeois reports that at the Council of Clermont (1095) where Pope Urban II preached the First Crusade, the pontiff urged clerics to recite the Office of the Blessed Virgin Mary to assure the success of the Holy War. The Office, which had initially been designed for a monastic setting, was abridged into the Little Office of the Blessed Virgin Mary and became popular with the laity. It includes the *Ave Maria* along with other Marian hymns and poems (*Salve Regina, Ave Maris Stella, Gaude Maria Virgo*) and the recitation of five psalms, the first letters of which make up the word MARIA. By the end of the 12th century, churchmen recommended the *Ave Maria* to the laity and urged children to learn it by heart. Stories of Mary are common in popular literature, especially tales of her miracles, and she is a favorite in the homilies of Bernard of Clairvaux. An example of a typical tale about the Virgin which reflects high medieval Marian piety is *Our Lady's Tumbler*, a story about a lowly acrobat who had nothing to offer St. Mary but his craft. He tumbled for the Virgin who was pleased with his gift and appeared to him in her glory, as "the sweet and courteous Queen." Taking a white napkin, she gently fanned the face of the exhausted tumbler.

In the Late Middle Ages (c. 1250–1450), tributes to the Virgin flourished in scores of hymns and carols, with special devotion shown by Franciscans. A number of older Latin hymns were translated into English, many of which focus on appeals for intercession and aid at the hour of death. In the mid-13th century, the wealthy commonly owned prayer books or Books of Hours (so called because they contain texts to be recited and sung at each of the eight periods or hours of the liturgical day). These books frequently incorporate the Little Office of the Blessed Virgin Mary. There is great variety in the composition of the Marian material in the Books of Hours as they were produced on demand for individual patrons. *Margaret of Hungary (1242–1270) is said on certain days to have recited no fewer than a thousand *Ave Marias*.

Medieval writers, such as Bernard of Clairvaux, Bonaventure, Anthony of Padua (fl. 1224), and Pope Boniface VIII (d. 1303), proliferated the honorary titles, virtues and Old Testament antetypal allusions to Mary. She became at the pens of these poets and theologians the "Spouse of Christ," "throne of Solomon," "Ladder of Heaven," "rising sun," "Tower of David," "lily of the valley" (the lily is one of Mary's artistic symbols), "*Sarah," "*Deborah," "*Esther," "*Judith," a "Rose without Thorns," and a "garden enclosed." Her virginity is likened to the "burning bush," the "fleece of Gideon," and "the rod out of the root of Jesse."

In the 14th and 15th centuries, Books of Hours were so popular that artistic representations of the Annunciation often portrayed Mary in the act of reading one. They were also used in the home to teach children to read. Bernardino of Siena, a devotee of Mary the Virgin, added the phrase *ora pro nobis peccatoribus* (pray for us sinners) to the *Ave Maria* and wrote several sermons taking Mary as his theme. Mary appears as intercessor in Dante's *Paradiso*, Chaucer's Second Nun's prologue, and the works of John Wycliffe, who thought it "impossible that we should obtain the reward of Heaven without the help of Mary." A 15th-century cycle of 40 dramatic pieces on the *Miracles of Our Lady* was based on canonical narratives and Marian apocrypha.

Although Mary continued to play a prominent role in liturgical literature in the 16th and 17th centuries (for instance a 1568 *breviarium* reformed by Pope Pius V contained the complete form of the *Ave Maria*), she declined as a theme in secular literature. She figures in John Donne's sonnets and Robert Southwell's poems, but is scarcely mentioned by William Shakespeare. This change is due largely to the Protestant attitude towards the Virgin Mother. England's *Elizabeth I, "the Virgin Queen," often substitutes for Mary in literary compositions. In *Paradise Lost* and *Paradise Regained*, John Milton treats Mary as "blessed among woman" but does not credit her with a redemptive function in salvation history.

The modern literary treatment of Mary, unmoored from religious dogma, is eclectic. The liberalizing of anti-Catholic legislation and attitudes in several Protestant countries in the modern era unleashed a wave of new Marian poetry, much of which was produced and appreciated by Protestants as well as Catholics, especially in England among those associated with the Oxford Movement. Romantic literature tended to make of Mary a goddess. William Wordsworth describes her by use of pagan imagery as "pure sea foam, the moon, Venus, Aurora and Diana." In some Romantic literature, she becomes a goddess of fertility and love. The Victorian poet Robert Bridges begins his poem to the Blessed Virgin with "Goddess, azure-minded and aureoled,/ That standing barefoot upon the moon." The Catholic poet Gerard Manley Hopkins provides evidence that devotion to the Virgin has not weakened in the modern era in his poem entitled "The Blessed Virgin Compared to the Air We Breathe."

The persona of Mary the Virgin, a young woman from 1st-century Nazareth, has accreted to itself a host of literary, artistic, doctrinal, and social symbols. Although she was the first convert to Christianity (Luke 1.38), possibly a disciple of Jesus (John 2.12), and present at the establishment of the church (Acts 1.14), her active role in the New Testament is obscured, for in the cultural history of Europe and the Christian history of the world she is far more precious as the female counterpart to Jesus. Periodic efforts through the Christian period to establish her as a model for all women have not been successful because Mary, both virgin and mother, can never be a model for real women; rather, she is a Christian embodiment of the idealized, cosmic feminine.

SOURCES:

Brown, R.E., and K.P. Donfried, *et al.*, *Mary in the New Testament*. Philadelphia, PA: Fortress Press, 1978.

Dalton, Ormonde M. *Byzantine Art and Archeology*. NY: Dover, 1911, repr. 1961.

Dictionary of Biblical Tradition in English Literature. Grand Rapids, MI: William B. Eerdman, 1992.

Dictionary of the Middle Ages. NY: Scribner, 1984.

Encyclopedia of Religion. NY: Macmillan, 1987.

Graef, Hilda. *Mary: A History of Doctrine and Devotion*. NY: 1963–1965.

Grant, Michael. *Jesus*. NY: Scribner, 1977.

New Catholic Encyclopedia. NY: McGraw Hill, 1967.

Oberman, H. *The Harvest of Medieval Theology*. Cambridge, MA: Harvard University Press, 1967.

Smith, Morton. *Jesus the Magician*. San Francisco, CA: Harper and Row, 1978.

Warner, Maria. *Alone of Her Sex: The Myth and the Cult of the Virgin Mary*. NY: Knopf, 1976.

SUGGESTED READING:

Articles on most aspects of Mary can be found in the periodical entitled *Marian Studies*.

Clayton, Mary. *The Cult of the Virgin Mary in Anglo-Saxon England*. Cambridge: Cambridge University Press, 1990.

Cunneen, Sally. *In Search of Mary*. NY: Ballantine, 1996.

Graber, André. *Christian Iconography: A Study of its Origins*. Princeton, NJ: Princeton University Press, 1967.

Harthan, John. *The Book of Hours*. NY: Crowell, 1977.

Kitzinger, Ernst. *The Art of Byzantium and the Medieval West*. Bloomington, IN: Indiana University Press, 1976.

Pelikan, Jaroslav. *Eternal Feminines: Three Theological Allegories in Dante's Paradiso*. New Brunswick, NJ: Rutgers University Press, 1990.

———. *Mary Through the Centuries: Her Place in the History of Culture*. New Haven, CT: Yale University Press, 1996.

Schaberg, Jane. *The Illegitimacy of Jesus: A Feminist Theological Interpretation of the Infancy Narratives*. NY: Crossroads Publishers, 1990.

Witherington, Ben, III. *Women in the Ministry of Jesus*. Cambridge: Cambridge University Press, 1984.

RELATED MEDIA:

Mary of Nazareth (docu-drama, 115 min.), Questar Video, 1996.

Martha Rampton,
Assistant Professor of History,
Pacific University, Forest Grove, Oregon

Mary Trastamara (1403–1445).

See Maria of Aragon.

Mary Trastamara (1401–1458).

See Maria of Castile.

Mary Trastamara (1482–1517).

See Isabella I for sidebar on Maria of Castile.

Mary Tudor (1496–1533)

Queen of France and sister of Tudor king Henry VIII.
Name variations: Mary of France; Duchess of Suffolk. Born Mary Tudor on March 18, 1496, in Richmond-upon-Thames, Surrey, England; died on June 26, 1533, in Westhorpe, Suffolk; buried at Bury St. Edmunds, Suffolk; daughter of Henry VII, king of England (r. 1485–1509), and Elizabeth of York (1466–1503); sister of Henry VIII, king of England (r. 1509–1547); married Louis XII (1462–1515), king of France (r. 1498–1515), on October 9, 1514 (died January 1515); married Charles Brandon (1484–1545), 1st duke of Suffolk (r. 1514–1545), on May 13, 1515; children: Henry Brandon (1516–1534), earl of Lincoln; Frances Brandon (1517–1559, mother of Lady Jane Grey); Eleanor Brandon (c. 1520–1547). Charles Brandon was also married to *Anne Browne (d. 1511), *Margaret Neville (b. 1466), and *Catharine Bertie (1519–1580).

Married king of France (1514); widowed (1515); married the duke of Suffolk (1515); journeyed to Calais, France, with her brother, Henry VIII, for Field of the Cloth of Gold meeting (1520).

Mary Tudor, sometimes called Mary of France, was the daughter of King Henry VII of England. Her father created the Tudor dynasty when he married *Elizabeth of York and united the Houses of York and Lancaster. Mary's brother would become the notorious Henry VIII, who sundered the Roman Catholic Church's influence from England as a result of his penchant for new wives. That same Henry's daughter—Mary Tudor's niece—would also come to be known as Mary Tudor or *Mary I, and fared somewhat better than her namesake as the first woman to take the English throne by hereditary right.

Mary Tudor's father brokered marriages for his children that continued the legacy of his own union to Elizabeth of York and its political ramifications. At the age of 12, Mary was betrothed

Mary Tudor (1496–1533), with Charles Brandon, Duke of Suffolk.

to the prince of Castile, Charles (V), who would become Holy Roman emperor in 1519. The engagement was broken, however, by 1514, and she was married that same year to Louis XII of France of the Valois dynasty. He died on New Year's Day the following year, and Mary then wed in secret Charles Brandon, duke of Suffolk, on May 13, 1515. This union, however, raised the ire of her brother, now king of England, and from France the couple sent large sums of money to Henry VIII to appease him.

In 1520, Mary Tudor joined her brother and Francis I of France near Calais in a place referred to as the Field of the Cloth of Gold for a lavish ceremonial alliance between the two longtime enemy nations. Little good came of it, and Henry VIII eventually allied with Mary's former fiancé, now Holy Roman Emperor Charles V. Mary reportedly disliked *Anne Boleyn, her brother's second wife; Henry VIII's determination to marry Boleyn and conceive a male heir eventually led England to a schism with Rome and to Henry being declared head of the Church of England, superior to the pope.

Mary Tudor died on June 26, 1533, in Westhorpe, Suffolk. With Charles Brandon, she had had one son, Henry Brandon, and two daughters, ◄ Eleanor Brandon and ◄ Frances Brandon; Frances would be the mother of *Lady Jane Grey. In a power struggle between Mary I and anti-Catholic forces, 17-year-old Lady Jane Grey sat on the English throne for nine days in 1553 before meeting her death by beheading.

Carol Brennan,
Grosse Pointe, Michigan

Brandon, Frances. See Grey, Lady Jane for sidebar.

Mary Tudor (1516–1558).

See Mary I.

Mary Tudor (1673–1726)

*Countess of Derwentwater. Born in 1673; died in 1726; illegitimate daughter of *Moll Davies and Charles II (1630–1685), king of England (r.*

◄ Brandon, Eleanor (c. 1520–1547)

*Duchess of Cumberland. Born around 1520; died on November 1547 at Brougham Castle, Cumbria, England; buried at Skipton, North Yorkshire, England; daughter of Charles Brandon (1484–1545), 1st duke of Suffolk, and *Mary Tudor (1496–1533); married Henry Clifford, 2nd earl of Cumberland, in June 1527; children: Margaret Clifford.*

1661–1685); married Edward Radclyffe, 2nd earl of Derwentwater (1655–1705); married Henry Graham of Levens (d. 1707); married James Rooke.

Maryam of Egypt (fl. 629).

See A'ishah bint Abi Bakr for sidebar on Wives of Muhammad.

Marzia (fl. 1357)

Italian noblewoman and military leader. Name variations: Marcia. Flourished in 1357 in Italy; married Francesco Ordelaffi, lord of Forli; children: son and daughter.

Marzia boldly defended the town of Cesena during her husband's war against the papacy. An Italian noble of the Ubaldini family, Marzia married Francesco Ordelaffi, lord of Forli, and became one of his most trusted allies in his struggle against papal rule. He stationed her in Cesena in 1357, with orders not to surrender the town under any circumstances. She was accompanied by her young son and daughter, and by Sgariglino, a counselor of the Ordelaffis.

Marzia and her troops, about 400 in number, held the town against the papal soldiers' attacks for several months, despite the siege laid on the town. She was single minded in her desire to not let the town fall under any circumstances, and to punish any supporters who turned against her. When she discovered that Sgariglino had secretly been plotting against her, she had him arrested and beheaded. Marzia refused to surrender but eventually the starving townspeople of Cesena pressured her into negotiating with the enemy; the papal forces were able to take Cesena, and imprisoned its brave defender and her children. Nothing is known of Marzia after her capture.

SOURCES:
Starling, Elizabeth. *Noble Deeds of Women.* Boston: Phillips, 1857.

Laura York,
Riverside, California

Marzouk, Zahia (1906–1988)

One of Egypt's first trained social workers, the first Egyptian woman to study in the United States, and founder of her nation's first family planning association. Born in 1906; died in 1988; had two sisters; studied in London; studied in America at the Harvard Graduate School of Education, 1933–35; married.

Explosive population growth has long been characteristic of Egypt, the population of which is squeezed onto approximately 5% of the country's total land. Between 1922, when the land was granted (theoretical) independence from Great Britain, and 1999, population grew to 62 million from 13.5 million, and some projections have estimated a population of 105 million by the year 2025. In 1999, up to 35% of Egyptian households were believed to be living below the poverty line, and in Upper Egypt, 40% of the children were stunted because of severe malnutrition. For many decades, Zahia Marzouk sounded a cry to reduce the nation's high birth rate through family planning. To do so, she fought entrenched cultural attitudes which resisted a woman's participation in her chosen field of social work, but she succeeded in establishing a number of organizations to aid in the plight of her nation.

Zahia Marzouk was born in 1906 and lost her father when she was only three. Her illiterate mother, a woman of courage and tenacity, somehow found ways to educate all three of her daughters. After they completed their basic education, Marzouk's sisters decided they wanted to get married. Responding with "Not me; I want to study more," Marzouk was already resentful of the restrictions placed on women by Egyptian culture at that time. In 1923—the same year that *Huda Shaarawi created a sensation by publicly discarding her veil at the Cairo Railway Station upon her return to Egypt from the International Feminist Conference in Rome—16-year-old Marzouk also refused to continue wearing a veil. Although this action deeply upset her family, she would not back down.

Marzouk's extended family showed little understanding for her intention to prepare herself for a teaching career, arguing that she did not need the money. Though he said little, her paternal uncle provided her with encouragement by clearly not objecting when she spoke out. At this important juncture, his tacit backing was of great psychological importance. When Marzouk, already starting her teaching career, was chosen to further her studies in London, his support continued.

Upon her return to Egypt in 1931, Marzouk received an appointment to a teachers' college where she taught psychology to classes of advanced students. Two years later, in 1933, she became the first Egyptian woman chosen to study in the United States. At the Harvard Graduate School of Education, she focused on medical social work, psychology, and children with problems. Upon completion of her courses,

Marzouk did field work in Missouri and the mountains of Kentucky, becoming familiar with the lives of neglected Americans, Native Americans, and the rural poor. Returning home in 1935, she began to realize how little social work was being done in her homeland. In 1935 and 1936, she opened Egypt's first schools of social work in Alexandria and in Cairo, innovations that led in 1938 to the creation of Egypt's Ministry of Social Affairs. During this time, she worked as a psychiatric social worker at the Ministry of Education. She was the only woman there, and her presence created a considerable stir, but Marzouk held her ground and was permitted to stay at her post.

In 1937, she created a small, unofficial organization that was meant to discuss demographic issues. The nation's population explosion could only get worse, and threatened to bar the majority of Egyptians from ever achieving even a moderate level of economic security and well-being. By the end of 1937, Marzouk's energy, charm, and formidable lobbying skills had succeeded in convening a formal conference on population issues. Prestige came from the fact that the conference enjoyed the sponsorship of the Egyptian Medical Association. Muslim conservatives disapproved of her presence at the conference, and when she began her lecture she was pummeled with tomatoes and eggs. Nonetheless, when she had finished reading her paper, the ensuing applause signaled a slight shift in attitude.

During this busy time, Marzouk also founded an institution for disabled children in need of physiotherapy. In addition to seeking professional assistance for this and other projects, she also became a skilled fund raiser. Most important, she was constantly spreading word of the need to reduce Egypt's high birth rate through family planning. By the 1950s, her decades of work had resulted in the creation of several family welfare institutions, including the Happy Childhood Association, the Institute for Training and Research in Family Planning, and the Regional Federation of Social Services. Marzouk was also responsible for founding the Alexandria Family Planning Association, the first association of its kind in Egypt. Even in relatively liberal Alexandria, there was considerable skepticism and even hostility to the idea of family planning and birth control. But with Marzouk at its head, the organization flourished and was able to provide information to thousands of women who wanted to limit the size of their families and space their children's births.

Dressed in Western garb, usually trousers and a bright blouse, Marzouk was a familiar sight in clinics and social work centers for many decades. She was also a skilled administrator, painter, and sculptor. When she died in 1988, Egypt's medical and social welfare community mourned one of the nation's first trained social workers. Her legacy continued, however, with the generations of Egyptian women to whom Zahia Marzouk served as mentor.

SOURCES:
"Egypt: Life at the Bottom," in *The Economist*. Vol. 350, no. 8111. March 20, 1999, Survey Egypt supplement, pp. 10–11.

Huston, Perdita. *Motherhood by Choice: Pioneers in Women's Health and Family Planning.* NY: Feminist Press, 1992.

"Zahia Marzouk 1906–1988," in *People Weekly* [London]. Vol. 19, no. 1, 1992, p. 22.

John Haag,
Associate Professor of History,
University of Georgia, Athens, Georgia

Masabnik, Badi'a.

See Egyptian Singers and Entrepreneurs.

Masako Hojo (1157–1225).

See Hōjo Masako.

Masaryk, Alice Garrigue

(1879–1966)

Eminent Czech sociologist and social activist who was the daughter of Czech nationalist Thomas Masaryk. Name variations: Alice Garrigue Masaryková. Born in Vienna, Austria, on May 3, 1879; died in Chicago, Illinois, on November 29, 1966; eldest child of Thomas Garrigue Masaryk (1850–1937) and Charlotte Garrigue Masaryk (1850–1923); had brothers Herbert and Jan Masaryk (1886–1948, a diplomat and Czech foreign minister), and sister Olga Garrigue Masaryk; Charles University (Prague), doctoral degree in philosophy, 1903; never married.

The major events and accomplishments of Alice Garrigue Masaryk's long life would be profoundly linked to Czechoslovakia and the United States, the homelands of her parents, Thomas Masaryk (1850–1937) and *Charlotte Garrigue Masaryk (1850–1923). Her father was the son of impoverished Slovak serfs; through native intelligence and tenacity, he earned a doctorate in philosophy, became a professor of philosophy as well as a noted sociologist, and after decades of political struggle would emerge as the first president of the Czechoslovak Republic. Thomas met Charlotte Garrigue during 1876 in Leipzig, Germany, where she, a child of a large and financially comfortable American family,

had gone to study music. Despite the immense differences in their backgrounds, Thomas and Charlotte married in the United States in March 1878. They were living in Vienna when Alice, the first of their five children, was born in 1879. Alice was named for the heroine of *The Martyr of Tilbury*, a novel so obscure that when she wanted to read the book as an adult it proved impossible to track down. In 1882, the family moved to Prague, where Thomas had received a professorship at the newly founded Charles University (where the language of instruction was Czech rather than German). Growing up in a multilingual and multicultural home, Alice and her siblings achieved fluency in Czech, German, and English.

Alice began her formal education in 1886, dividing her time between classes at the St. Egidus School and private lessons at home in music, French, and Russian. She then enrolled in the Prague municipal middle school and in 1891 began her studies at "Minerva," the city's recently founded women's Gymnasium. Initially a pre-medical student, Alice decided after one year of this curriculum that she did not wish to become a physician and signed up instead for philosophy courses at her father's institution, Charles University. Now determined to earn a doctoral degree in philosophy, she completed her course work in Prague, attending lectures as well at the University of Berlin during the academic year 1901–1902. Soon she had a dissertation subject, the English Magna Carta of 1215, and made several research trips to London to gather data for her project. Masaryk was awarded her doctorate in philosophy by Charles University in June 1903.

In February 1904, she made her first trip to the United States. Most of the next year was spent in Chicago, where she worked in residence at the University of Chicago Social Settlement (UCSS). Masaryk became acquainted with a number of leading social reformers of the day, including ***Jane Addams** and UCSS director ***Mary McDowell**. In Chicago, she witnessed firsthand the harsh working and living conditions of a largely laissez-faire system that exploited the cheap labor of European immigrants in the city's stockyards and sweatshops. Soon after her arrival in the city, the tensions there exploded when the stockyard workers went out on strike and veritable social chaos ensued. Masaryk gained important insights into the emerging social-reform movement when she became acquainted with a fellow UCSS resident, the novelist Upton Sinclair, who at the time was gathering material for his novel *The Jungle*.

Returning to Prague in 1905, Masaryk accepted a teaching position at the Girls' Lycee in Ceské Budejovice. She remained there until moving on to a similar position at a newly founded lycee in Prague during 1910. The next year, she played a leading role along with the Czech Student Union in creating a Sociological Section at Prague's Charles University. The most important aspect of this innovation was a lecture series through which leading Czech intellectuals and social reformers informed both students and interested members of the public on the social pathologies of the contemporary urban-industrial world. Topics covered in the series included many of the unsolved dilemmas of the day, such as the substandard housing of the working class, broken families and neglected children, nutritional deficiencies, crime, alcoholism, and venereal diseases. While recognizing the presence of these social ills, Masaryk rejected Marxist revolution as a solution, looking instead to the use of reason, good will, and the tools of sociological analysis to achieve major improvements while remaining within the parameters of the existing social order.

When World War I broke out in August 1914, Alice's father Thomas Masaryk—by now one of the leading voices of the Czech nationalist movement—escaped with his younger daughter **Olga Garrigue Masaryk**, first to Italy and then to Switzerland. After his "declaration of war" on behalf of a Czech nation that thus far existed only in theory, his entire family began to feel the growing anger of Vienna's Habsburg regime. Thomas was sentenced to death in absentia for his treasonous actions, and his wife Charlotte, whose health was fragile at best, was harassed by the authorities. Accused of having engaged in illegal Czech nationalist activities, Alice, along with **Hana Benesova**, the wife of her father's close associate Eduard Benes, was interrogated for two weeks in Prague, and then moved to a prison in Vienna.

Alice was incarcerated there for eight months, and a massive pressure campaign from abroad was undertaken to secure her release. Her father wrote to many influential Americans about his daughter's plight, including a letter to UCSS director Mary McDowell in April 1916. Despite her declining health, Charlotte provided her daughter with moral support by writing to her several times a week. A petition signed by 40,000 Americans from all walks of life went to the Austrian authorities. In addition to Mary McDowell, Jane Addams, *Florence Kelley and *Lillian Wald were among the prominent individuals involved in the petition drive. A significant factor in

Masaryk's release from prison would be the involvement of *Julia Lathrop, chief of the Children's Bureau in the Department of Labor, who was at the time the highest-ranking woman serving in the U.S. federal government. Lathrop petitioned the U.S. State Department to intervene with high officials in Vienna on Masaryk's behalf. The pressure was effective, and Masaryk gained her freedom on July 3, 1916.

Although they no longer kept her behind bars, the Viennese authorities, with good reason, continued to regard Masaryk as a sympathizer of her father's nationalist movement and banned her from teaching for the duration of the war. Masaryk instead gave private tutorials at her home, emphasizing the importance of applied sociology as a tool for Czech national survival and renewal.

In the fall of 1918, the Habsburg state and armed forces disintegrated, and on October 28 the Czechoslovak Republic was proclaimed. Two months after the Republic was founded in Prague, Thomas Masaryk took office as president. By this time, the physical and psychological stresses of the war had taken their toll on the health of Alice's mother Charlotte, and from the very start, Alice substituted for her mother as first lady. Acting as her father's official host on state occasions, she drew on her considerable poise and culture to ease the ceremonial aspects of his presidential role, making less burdensome both the official and private aspects of his busy life. She retained this role after her mother's death in May 1923 and until her father's retirement in 1935.

Alice Masaryk was appointed president of the Czechoslovak Red Cross in February 1919, a post in which she would remain for fully two decades, until the German invasion of the crippled post-Munich Czechoslovak Republic in March 1939. During her first years as head of the Red Cross, she was responsible for the care of wounded and ill war veterans, as well as of civilian victims of the war. Having declared itself independent of the Austro-Hungarian state, the new republic faced the challenge of creating a working public-health and welfare system. Masaryk's experience as a social worker and reformer was of great value during this period. She was also astute enough to realize that Czechs and Slovaks alone would not be able to solve the many problems of their new nation. Consequently, soon after taking charge of the national Red Cross organization, she requested Mary McDowell of UCSS to send an American task force to assist local social welfare professionals in carrying out a survey of the existing educational, health, recreational, and welfare systems. This survey was completed within a year's time, and its published results would be regarded for many decades by professionals in the field as a model undertaking.

During the decade of the 1920s, Alice Masaryk was one of the best-known women in the world in the fields of sociology and social welfare. She was honored in 1928 by being chosen to preside over the First International Conference of Social Work, held in Paris. On this occasion, she reminded the assembled delegates that the responsibilities of national social welfare organizations were at least as important in an era of peace and stability as they had been in a time of war and chaos. She also pointed out the need for integrating both the organization and delivery systems of the world's varied public-health systems. In 1930, Masaryk received an additional honor when she became a member of the Executive Committee of the International Red Cross.

With her father's retirement in 1935 and his death in September 1937, Masaryk's roles changed considerably. No longer first lady of Czechoslovakia, she left her residence in the Presidential Palace in Prague and concentrated her energies on her Red Cross work. When this ended with the German invasion of March 1939, she fled to the United States.

Invited to stay at the UCSS in Chicago, Masaryk was asked to speak before various groups about the deteriorating situation in Europe. She also received an honorary doctorate from the University of Pittsburgh. Determined to do her utmost for the cause of Czechoslovak freedom, she began a lecture tour of the United States in September 1939. It soon became clear, however, that the stresses of recent years had undermined her emotional stability, and she was forced to cancel the tour in January 1940. With Masaryk mentally traumatized and suffering from depression, it was decided that she should be institutionalized, and she was moved to the Mitchell Sanatorium in July 1940. In November 1941, she was moved to a facility in White Plains, New York, where one of her frequent visitors was her brother Jan Masaryk, now an official of the Czechoslovak Government-in-Exile.

After the liberation of Czechoslovakia in May 1945, Masaryk was released from the hospital and returned to Prague. Although the city was physically intact, much had changed in the six years she had been absent. Aged and psycho-logically vulnerable, she found it difficult to create a stable life for herself. By the end of 1947, domestic and foreign Communist pressure was bringing the postwar Czechoslovak experiment in democracy to an end. In February 1948, the Communists seized power in a coup d'état, and several weeks later, on March 10, Jan Masaryk died under mysterious circumstances, having apparently committed suicide by hurling himself from the bathroom window of his apartment to the pavement below. Shattered by her brother's death, and with Czechoslovakia now in the grip of a Communist dictatorship, Alice Masaryk once again became an emigré, finding asylum for a last time in the United States.

Despite her poor health, Masaryk refused to retire after settling in the United States. She made frequent broadcasts to the people of Czechoslovakia via Radio Free Europe, reminding them from 1950 to 1954 that one day their democratic system would be restored. She began writing her memoirs in 1954 and in 1960 established the Masaryk Publications Trust, its purpose being the eventual publication in English of the most important writings of her father and other members of the Masaryk family. Her health failing, she spent several years in Florida and died in Chicago on November 29, 1966. A true daughter of both the New World and the Old World, Alice Garrigue Masaryk had been a humanitarian in the 19th-century mold. Her concept of sociology was that of the social organizer who believed that pragmatic solutions, rather than abstract ideologies, offered the best hope for human progress.

SOURCES:

Deegan, Mary Jo. "Transcending a Patriarchal Past: Teaching the History of Women in Sociology," in *Teaching Sociology*. Vol. 16, no. 2. April 1988, pp. 141–150.

———. "Women in Sociology: 1890–1930," in *Journal of the History of Sociology*. Vol. 1, 1978, pp. 11–34.

Keith, Bruce. "Alice Masaryk (1879–1966)" in Mary Jo Deegan, ed., *Women in Sociology: A Bio-Bibliographical Sourcebook*. NY: Greenwood Press, 1991, pp. 298–305.

Kovtun, George J. *Masaryk & America: Testimony of a Relationship*. Washington, DC: Library of Congress, 1988.

———, ed. *The Spirit of Thomas Garrigue Masaryk (1850–1937): An Anthology*. NY: St. Martin's Press-Masaryk Publications Trust, 1990.

Masaryk, Alice. "The Bond Between Us," in *Official Proceedings of the 66th Annual Meeting, National Conference of Social Work*. NY: Columbia University Press, 1939, pp. 69–74.

———. "From an Austrian Prison," *The Atlantic Monthly*. Vol. 126, no. 5. November 1920, pp. 577–587.

———. "A Message from Alice Masaryk," in *The Survey*. Vol. 46. June 1921, p. 333.

———. "The Prison House," in *The Atlantic Monthly*. Vol. 126, no. 6. December 1920, pp. 770–779.

Masaryk, Alice Garrigue. *Music in Spillville*. Translated by Esther Jerabek. St. Paul, MN: Minnesota Historical Society, 1969.

Masaryková, Alice Garrigue. *Detství a mladí: vzpomínky a myslenky*. 2nd ed. Prague: Ústav T.G. Masaryka, 1994.

Mitchell, Ruth Crawford. "Alice Masarykova," in *The Survey*. Vol. 63. March 1930, pp. 633–635.

———, comp. *Alice Garrigue Masaryk 1879–1966: Her Life as Recorded in Her Own Words and by Her Friends*. Pittsburgh, PA: University Center for International Studies, University of Pittsburgh, 1980.

Zeman, Zbynek. *The Masaryks: The Making of Czechoslovakia*. London: I.B. Tauris, 1990.

John Haag,
Associate Professor of History,
University of Georgia, Athens, Georgia

Masaryk, Charlotte Garrigue

(1850–1923)

American-born wife of Thomas Masaryk, who played an active role in Czech public life during the decades before 1914, encouraging women to fully utilize their talents and engage in political activity. Name variations: Charlotta Garrigue Masaryková; "Charlie" Garrigue. Born in Brooklyn, New York, on November 20, 1850; died at her country house at Lány, near Prague, on May 13, 1923; daughter of Rudolph Garrigue and Charlotte Lydia (Whiting) Garrigue; had ten siblings; married Thomas Garrigue Masaryk; children: daughters, Alice Garrigue Masaryk (1879–1966), Eleanora (died shortly after her birth in 1889), and Olga Garrigue Masaryk; sons Herbert Garrigue Masaryk and Jan Masaryk (1886–1948, a diplomat and Czech foreign minister).

A native of Brooklyn, New York, who at the age of four moved with her family to the Bronx, Charlotte Garrigue was called "Charlie" by her ten siblings. The large family was a happy one, headed by Rudolph Garrigue, who was descended from a Huguenot family and grew up in Denmark and Germany before immigrating to the United States, where he quickly became successful as the owner of a Brooklyn bookstore. After his shop burned, Rudolph founded the Germania Fire Insurance Company, also a successful enterprise, and the family lived in considerable comfort. Believing that no distinctions should be drawn between his sons and daughters, Rudolph wanted their intellectual and moral development to be as free as possible, and this independence included the right to choose their own religious denominations. These extremely liberal views were shared by his wife, **Charlotte Whiting Garrigue**, an intellectually adventurous individual who was strongly influenced by unorthodox Transcendentalist ideas and ideals.

The Garrigues' daughter Charlotte was drawn to the arts, particularly music, at an early age. After the family's relocation to a large house in the Bronx, much of her time was spent practicing the piano. Determined to become a famous virtuoso like *Clara Schumann, at 17 she traveled to Leipzig, Germany, to study. In Leipzig, she lived with the Goering family, for whom her father had worked in the book trade decades earlier. Her dreams of a musical career as a pianist had to be abandoned after three years of intensive practice resulted in permanent damage to her hands. Back in the United States, Charlotte began to resign herself to a life of giving piano lessons and studying mathematics. Via the post, she maintained contact with the Goerings, her substitute family in Germany, who in some of their letters described an interesting young man who was boarding with them. The son of Slovak serfs, Thomas Masaryk was a student of the new social science of sociology, and he supported himself by giving lessons to other students. The independent-minded Thomas was fiercely determined to be a success.

Obviously intrigued, Charlotte returned to Leipzig in 1876. She and Thomas proved mutually attracted to one another, as well as intellectually and spiritually compatible, and they spent much time together reading and studying. Thomas was impressed by Charlotte's love of mathematics and her strong religious impulses, which while hardly orthodox did include a firm belief in immortality. As a social scientist, he was also drawn to her search for precise knowledge through experience, observation, and disciplined analysis. Among the books they discussed was John Stuart Mill's classic *Subjection of Women*, a work Thomas Masaryk would later translate into Czech, turning it into a key text of the women's movement in the Czech provinces of the Habsburg Empire.

While visiting some German friends just prior to her return to the United States, Charlotte received a letter from Thomas proposing marriage; she immediately agreed. Soon after her return home, however, she was seriously harmed in a carriage accident. Charlotte's family wrote Thomas, urging him to come to America as quickly as possible due to the severity of her injuries. By the time he arrived in the Bronx, she had made a remarkable recovery, and they were married according to the traditions of Charlotte's chosen faith, Unitarianism, on the Ides of March (March 15, 1878) in the Garrigue family's double living room. In a move indicative of his progressive attitudes, Thomas replaced his patriotic middle name Vlastimil, with his wife's maiden name of Garrigue. Henceforth, he would be known as Thomas Garrigue Masaryk, and in time all of their children would have Garrigue as their middle names. Charlotte's father was taken aback when his son-in-law—noting that it would be difficult if not impossible to support Charlotte in decent circumstances on the meager salary from his new teaching post in Vienna—asked him for financial assistance. Somewhat reluctantly, Rudolph agreed to send a subsidy to Vienna, money which proved particularly needed as the Masaryk family grew rapidly. In all, five children would be born in the next few years, although one daughter, Eleanora, would die soon after her birth in 1889. In 1882, Charlotte joined her husband in Prague, where he had been appointed professor at the newly created Czech-language Charles University.

During her first years as a wife and mother, Charlotte Masaryk worked hard to master the difficult Czech language. In time, she became highly proficient in this venerable Slavic tongue, although she would never completely be at home with the intricacies of feminine verb endings. An enthusiastic mother, she enjoyed the time spent with her children, taking them to open-air swimming baths in the summer and to skating rinks in the winter. Years later, her daughter *Alice Garrigue Masaryk would recall her mother walking up and down alongside the skating rink, dressed in a black costume complete with a hat covered with ostrich feathers. She read to them from a great variety of books including Czech, German, and Russian fairy tales; the nursery rhymes of *Kate Greenaway; the Czech classic *The Grandmother* by **Bozena Nemcová**; and works by Dickens and other classic writers of the day. Additional forms of home entertainment included occasional musicales by the Masaryk parents, in which Charlotte played the piano, accompanying Thomas who played the violin.

Charlotte described their summer holidays, which were eagerly anticipated by the entire family, as "fairy tales come true." For a number of years, they went to Klobouky, the home of Thomas' parents' in Moravia, and in later years to a farm in the hills of Slovakia on the river Turec, at a village called Bystricka near Turcansky Sväty Martin. At Klobouky, Charlotte got to know and cherish her husband's peasant parents, while improving her mastery of the Czech language. At Bystricka, where the family lived in a white farmhouse, the girls liked their work in the flax and hemp fields, singing folk songs while carefully picking the plants by hand, and their brother Jan Masaryk enjoyed drilling the local Slovak fire brigade in the nearby village and working as a ploughman in the fields.

These idyllic summers were balanced by the rest of the year in Prague, where studies and Thomas' academic and political activities left their mark on the entire family. Once she had mastered the Czech language and felt at ease in Czech culture, Charlotte Masaryk became increasingly engaged in the most important Czech issues and controversies of the day. Since music remained her first love, she became both an expert and ardent advocate of the rapidly emerging national school of Czech musicians, with particular enthusiasm for the compositions of Bedrich Smetana and Antonin Dvorak. The Czech musical world was appreciative of her support, and an edition of Smetana's works was dedicated to her as "the true friend of [his] genius."

But not all of Charlotte Garrigue Masaryk's experiences in her adopted homeland would be pleasant ones. On more than one occasion, her husband's intellectual integrity resulted in difficult situations for the entire family. In 1886, he refused to accept as genuine a collection of ancient Czech manuscripts, which placed him at odds with fellow Czech nationalists. Thomas regarded upholding the truth on a matter of scholarship as being more crucial for the retention of his people's moral integrity than any propaganda victories based on deception. If the documents in question were forgeries, he argued in print and in public debate, this should be acknowledged even if it resulted in a temporary weakening of the Czech national struggle against Austrian domination. Thomas stood almost alone in public on the "manuscript question"; few of his academic colleagues supported him on this issue, and many shunned him. At times, he considered abandoning his teaching post and emigrating to the United States. Charlotte remained convinced that her husband was right in his position and supported him through this difficult period. The stress of the situation was almost more than she could bear—she had suffered a temporary nervous breakdown after the birth of their first child Alice—but while frayed, her nerves did not shatter.

Although in time the bitter memories of the manuscript controversy faded, a new crisis was to put the family's moral resolve even more to the test. In 1899, Thomas, again very much in the minority, spoke out to defend the innocence of Leopold Hilsner, a Jew who had been found guilty of murdering a young girl for purposes of ritual sacrifice. Condemning the case against Hilsner as a terrible miscarriage of justice that echoed the medieval anti-Semitic accusations of ritual murder, Thomas not only defended the accused, but also launched vigorous attacks against the Czech press. He denounced the press for its prejudicial partisanship in this case, which was reminiscent of the anti-Semitism it had displayed several years before when reporting on the Dreyfus affair that had torn apart France. Fearlessly, Thomas also criticized those professional elements among the Czech nation, particularly its doctors and lawyers, who either shared these savage prejudices or remained silent in the face of a grave miscarriage of justice.

Due to Thomas' spirited defense of Hilsner, almost overnight the Masaryks faced a "wave of hatred." Thomas became, in the words of his close friend and ally Jan Herben, "the most isolated man among the Czech public." He was accused of splitting the national cause, of loving the Jewish nation more than the Czech nation, and even of having taken money as bribes from unspecified Jewish sources. Once again, Charlotte provided the strength for him to continue his struggle and persuaded him not to emigrate. Thomas suffered through personal abuse on the street, difficulty in getting published, and countless threatening letters. On one occasion, anti-Semitic students assembled outside the Masaryk home in Prague's historical Malá Strana district, where Charlotte displayed her own gritty courage by successfully persuading them to disperse. Described as a helper and collaborator in all of Thomas' work, Charlotte was willing to make sacrifices: their simple, even stark, flat could boast of few modern conveniences, and in order to provide for the family's necessities she sold all of her jewelry and other luxuries.

Although she often remained behind the scenes in her husband's career, Charlotte Masaryk was an active participant in Czech political life in her own right. She was an enthusiastic advocate of women's rights, presenting her ideas publicly both in meetings and in print. While she maintained a critical stance toward certain aspects of Marxist ideology, in 1905 she nevertheless joined the Social Democratic Party—rather than her husband's Realist Party—because of its ongoing and militant support of the rights of workers, as well as its unequivocally feminist platform. In 1906, she joined street demonstrations of working men and women demanding free and equal suffrage along with the secret ballot. Charlotte saw to it that her older daughter Alice (who would later become an internationally renowned sociologist) was among

the first generation of Prague girls to go on to receive a university education, and she often reminded her husband of the necessity of including Czech women in all aspects of the ongoing national revival. Not surprisingly, Thomas would make an important part of his political credo the idea that the "modern Czech woman signifies for our small nation a doubling of our strength."

World War I would be the last great test of resolve for the Masaryk family. By 1914, the children were grown and settling into marriages and careers. With the start of hostilities in August of that year, Thomas, accompanied by his daughter **Olga Garrigue Masaryk**, escaped the Austrian police by fleeing first to Italy and then to Switzerland. In July 1915, he declared war on the Habsburg Empire in the name of a yet-to-be-born Czech nation, working thereafter to gain full recognition from the Allies for the Czechoslovak National Council. As a result, Thomas was declared a traitor and sentenced to death in absentia. Back in Prague, Charlotte, depressed, lonely and suffering from heart disease, was now under round-the-clock surveillance by Austrian authorities. Her daughter Alice was interrogated for two weeks in Prague and then imprisoned for eight months in a Viennese prison.

Charlotte Garrigue Masaryk (center) with her daughter Alice and son Jan.

Charlotte purposely did not know where her husband's writings might be secreted in their flat, nor did she accept news about his activities abroad, fearing that to do so would endanger those who might bring her such information. Her health was undermined by many personal blows, including her son Herbert's death from typhus while working in a refugee camp in Austrian Galicia and the plight of her younger son Jan, who was captured while attempting to flee abroad and drafted into the Imperial and Royal Austrian Army as punishment.

In late October 1918, the Czech and Slovak nations began the process of dissolving their centuries-old ties to the Habsburg Empire. The independence of the new Czechoslovak Republic, founded in Prague on October 28, 1918, was achieved without bloodshed. On December 21, Thomas Masaryk arrived in Prague to become president of the new nation. He would be elected president of Czechoslovakia in 1920, 1927, and 1934. Thomas retired in 1935 due to extreme age and died, deeply revered, in September 1937. But after 1918, Charlotte could no longer enjoy her husband's triumphs. Her health had been shattered both physically and psychologically during four years of war. She would spend the next years in seclusion, at times under treatment for her troubled emotions, until her death at the presidential summer home at Lány, near Prague, on May 13, 1923.

In his final years, when he looked back on a life rich in achievements and struggles, Thomas Garrigue Masaryk gave credit to his wife for the role she played in his career. On women's issues, he declared, "I am only a peddler of my wife's opinions," admitting that she had in fact been the actual author of one of his major statements in favor of full equality for Czech women, *Polygamy and Monogyny.* "Without her," he also noted, "I wouldn't have had a clear sense of . . . my political task." The Czech poet **Oldra Sedlmayer** summed up the nation's indebtedness to Charlotte Garrigue Masaryk by asserting, "Neither golden letters nor marble monuments can express the moral contribution, the price in human suffering which that daughter of free America paid in the life and work of our president."

SOURCES:

Belohlavek, Bedrich. *Charlotte G. Masaryk and the Czechoslovak Nation.* London: Czechoslovak Red Cross, 1941.

Garver, Bruce. "Masaryk and Czech Politics, 1906–1914," in Stanley B. Winters, ed., *T.G. Masaryk (1850–1937)*, Volume 1: *Thinker and Politician.* London: Macmillan & School of Slavonic and East European Studies, University of London, 1990, pp. 225–257.

Garver, Bruce M. *The Young Czech Party 1874–1901 and the Emergence of a Multi-Party System.* New Haven, CT: Yale University Press, 1978.

Hoogenboom, Olive. *The First Unitarian Church of Brooklyn, One Hundred Fifty Years: A History.* Brooklyn, NY: First Unitarian Church, 1987.

———. "Masaryk, Charlotte Garrigue," in John A. Garraty and Mark C. Carnes, eds., *American National Biography.* Vol. 14 of 24 Vols. New York and Oxford: Oxford University Press, 1999, pp. 633–635.

Karla G. Masaryková, prva ceska unitarka. Prague: Dr. N.F. Capek, 1923.

Kovtun, George J. *Masaryk and America: Testimony of a Relationship.* Washington, DC: Library of Congress, 1988.

———, ed. *The Spirit of Thomas Garrigue Masaryk (1850–1937): An Anthology.* NY: St. Martin's Press-Masaryk Publications Trust, 1990.

Ludwig, Emil. *Defender of Democracy.* NY: Arno Press and The New York Times, 1971.

McKinney, Donald W. *A Tribute to Charlotte Garrigue Masaryk.* Brooklyn Heights, NY: First Unitarian Church, 1973.

"Mme. Masaryk's Death," in *The Times* [London]. May 14, 1923, p. 7.

Masaryk, Thomas Garrigue. *President Masaryk Tells His Story, Recounted by Karel Capek.* London: George Allen & Unwin, 1934.

Neudorfl, Marie L. "Masaryk and the Women's Question," in Stanley B. Winters, ed., *T.G. Masaryk (1850–1937)*, Volume 1: *Thinker and Politician.* London: Macmillan & School of Slavonic and East European Studies, University of London, 1990, pp. 258–282.

Polák, Stanislav. *Charlotta Garrigue Masarykova.* Prague: Mláda Fronta, 1992.

Skilling, H. Gordon. *T.G. Masaryk: Against the Current, 1882–1914.* University Park, PA: Pennsylvania State University Press, 1994.

Veger, Mila. *Czechoslovakia's American First Lady.* Translated by Brackett Lewis. NY: Masaryk Institute, 1939.

Zeman, Zbynek. *The Masaryks: The Making of Czechoslovakia.* London: I.B. Tauris, 1990.

John Haag,
Associate Professor of History,
University of Georgia, Athens, Georgia

Masham, Abigail (1670–1734).

See Queen Anne for sidebar.

Masham, Damaris (1658–1708)

English scholar. Name variations: Lady Masham; Damaris Cudworth; Philoclea. Born Damaris Cudworth in England on January 18, 1658; died on April 20, 1708; buried in Bath Abbey; daughter of Ralph Cudworth (1617–1688, a philosopher); educated at home; studied under her father and John Locke; married Sir Francis Masham, 3rd baronet, of Oates, Essex, in 1685; children: Francis Cudworth Masham (b. 1686).

Selected works: wrote over 40 letters to the philosopher John Locke; corresponded with the philosopher Gottfried Wilhelm Leibniz; A Discourse Concerning the Love of God (1690); Occasional Thoughts in Reference to a Virtuous or Christian Life (1705); an essay on Locke for the Great Historical Dictionary; a biography of Locke in La Bibliotheque Universelle (1704).

Damaris Masham was born in 1658 and brought up around Cambridge University. Her father Ralph Cudworth, a philosopher at Cambridge who specialized in Plato, had a hand in teaching her; otherwise little is known about her education, though she became very well known for her intellect. She learned French, but not Latin which was usually included in men's education of the day.

In 1682, at about the age of 23, Damaris met the philosopher John Locke (probably through their mutual friend, Edward Clarke). Their early correspondence was romantic, and they addressed each other as Philander and Philoclea. They would remain good friends and intellectual companions after the romance faded, corresponding regularly on personal matters mostly, but also on philosophy, while Locke was away in Holland. In 1685, she married Sir Francis Masham, a landowner who already had eight children from a previous marriage. Together they had a son, Francis Cudworth Masham.

Early on, Masham had befriended John Norris, another Cambridge Platonist and a follower of the philosophy of Nicholas de Malebranche. She corresponded with Norris for several years. As time wore on and her views began to differ from his, he became her intellectual adversary. She also corresponded, almost exclusively on the topic of philosophy, with Gottfried Wilhelm Leibniz. She had sent him a copy of her father's book, *The True Intellectual System of the Universe,* and his letter in response sparked a dialogue between them. In later years, Leibniz would offer his sympathy on the death of Locke, and they would continue to write for a brief period, discussing Leibniz' and Locke's and her father's writings.

Masham's two philosophical treatises, which became very popular and went into second editions, were first published anonymously. As anonymous publication was usual for Locke, and he influenced her, the writings were at first attributed to him. Even when her authorship was made public, some still doubted it; for instance, *Catherine Trotter Cockburn was forced to defend Masham's authorship.

The first work, *A Discourse Concerning the Love of God,* published in 1690, is Masham's philosophical examination of the correspondence between her adversary John Norris and *Mary Astell, which they had published as *Letters Concerning the Love of God.* Also that year, Norris had published a treatise on love directed at Masham: *Reflections upon the Conduct of Human Life with reference to the Study of Learning and Knowledge, in a letter to an excellent Lady, the Lady Masham.* His writing shows that he believed her to have become blind; she had not, although her eyes did grow weak with age. *A Discourse Concerning the Love of God* is also directed also at this work, as well as at Astell's solo writing. Masham uses a Lockean theory of knowledge to argue that love of God is derived from sensory experience, disputing Norris' view that God can be the only source of any causation of love. Masham may have contributed at an earlier date to Norris' half of the correspondence, but by this time she was a confirmed Lockean, holding views directly in opposition to Norris'.

In *Occasional Thoughts in Reference to a Virtuous or Christian Life,* published in 1705, Masham argues that rationality should be the basis of moral conduct, and also that on this basis, women should be equally educated with men. She was concerned that lack of education made women unable to perform well their duties as wives and mothers. She argued that an educated woman would be more reasonable and a better educator of her children than one who lacked schooling.

Although Masham's views as represented in *Occasional Thoughts* are somewhat like Mary Astell's, they are written in response to Astell (in her 1705 work *The Christian Religion*), with an empiricist, rather than an idealist, background. Masham was greatly encouraged by Astell's representation of women as maligned in *A Serious Proposal to the Ladies* (published in 1694), but her own arguments for the equal education of women were based on pragmatism instead of Astell's ideals. As an idealist, Astell considered our experience of the world to be fundamentally dependent on our minds. Masham, following Locke, was an empiricist, believing that what we know depends on our concrete experience; therefore she focused more on practical matters.

When Locke returned from Holland in 1688, he and Masham were able to meet frequently, and so no longer corresponded. In 1691, Locke finally gave in to her requests that he stay (as a paying guest) with her family at

Oates, their country estate in Essex, bringing with him his 5000-volume library. Intellectual visitors to the estate during this time included Isaac Newton and Francis Mercury van Helmont. Locke helped educate her son, and remained on the estate until his death in 1704. Damaris Masham died four years later, in 1708.

SOURCES:

Atherton, Margaret. *Women Philosophers of the Early Modern Period.* Indianapolis, IN: Hackett, 1994.

Ballard, George. *Memoirs of Several Ladies of Great Britain, Who Have Been Celebrated for Their Writings or Skill in the Learned Languages, Arts and Sciences.* Detroit, MI: Wayne State University Press, 1985.

Kersey, Ethel M. *Women Philosophers: a Bio-critical Source Book.* NY: Greenwood Press, 1989.

Perry, Ruth. *The Celebrated Mary Astell, an Early English Feminist.* Chicago, IL: University of Chicago Press, 1986.

Stenton, Doris Mary. *The English Woman in History.* NY: Macmillan, 1957.

Waithe, Mary Ellen, ed. *A History of Women Philosophers.* Boston: Martinus Nijhoff Publications, 1987–1995.

Catherine Hundleby, M.A. Philosophy, University of Guelph

Mashin, Draga (1867–1903).

See Draga.

Masina, Giulietta (1920–1994)

Award-winning Italian actress who earned international recognition for her portrayal of Gelsomina in La Strada. *Born Giulia Anna Masina on February 22, 1920, in San Giorgio di Piano, Italy; died of lung cancer on March 23, 1994, in Rome; youngest of four children of Gaetano Masina (erstwhile first violinist with Milan's Teatro Scala); grew up under the tutelage of her aunt Giulia Pasqualin; married Federico Fellini (a director), in 1943; children: one son (b. 1945, died in infancy).*

First appeared as an actress while at university in Rome, performing with the school's drama society and attracting professional attention with her performance in a radio play written by Federico Fellini (1942); married Fellini (1943); won Best Supporting Actress award at the Venice Film Festival for her work in Without Pity *(1948), and Best Actress for her performance in Fellini's* The Nights of Cabiria *at the Cannes Film Festival (1956); became an icon of Italian television and cinema (1970s), although her only recognition outside her own country was mainly due to her work with Fellini.*

Films: Paisà/Paisan *(The Countryfolk, 1946);* Senza Pietà *(Without Pity, 1948);* Luci del Varietà *(Variety Lights, 1951);* Persiane chiuse *(1951);* Europa 51 *(1952);* Lo Sceicco Bianco *(The White Sheik, 1952);* Donne proibite *(1953);* La Strada *(The Street, 1954);* Il Bidone *(The Swindle, 1955);* Le Notti di Cabiria *(The Nights of Cabiria, 1956);* Fortunella *(1958);* Nella Città l'Inferno *(1958);* La Grande Vie *(1960);* Landru *(1972);* Giulietta degli Spiriti *(Juliet of the Spirits, 1965);* Non Stuzzicate la Zanzara *(1967);* The Madwoman of Chaillot *(1969);* Frau Holle *(1985);* Ginger e Fred *(Ginger and Fred, 1986);* Aujourd'hui Peut-Etre *(1991).*

It was an odd couple that met for lunch one spring day in 1943, amid the rubble of war-ravaged Rome—a pert, blonde, northern Italian girl, urban and sophisticated, and a dark, swarthy young man from the provinces of coastal Italy. Giulietta Masina wondered if she would end up paying for the meal when she first caught sight of her frightfully thin dining companion, wearing a wrinkled black hat and trousers too short for his bandy legs. Despite his insistence that she order lavishly, she prudently limited herself to a bowl of minestrone while he proceeded to consume courses of ham, roast meats, and ravioli. The surprisingly thick wad of money which he produced at the end of the meal put her concerns to rest, although more serious apprehensions lay in store during the years of her upcoming, if as yet unexpected, marriage to Federico Fellini—a marriage plagued not only by the normal pressures of conjugal living but by the conflicting creative impulses of two artists intensely devoted to their craft. The two would live and work together for 50 years, making it impossible to consider Giulietta's life and career without Fellini. "I feel I am in his shadow," she once lamented, "but I don't mind it, because it is a wonderful shadow."

Masina had come to Rome for an education in the classics and in music, little dreaming that she would become one of postwar Italy's most famous actresses and the wife of its most flamboyant film director. The oldest of four children, she had been born into a middle-class family on February 22, 1920, in the small village of San Giorgio di Piano, near Bologna. Her father Gaetano taught music in local public schools after having spent 30 years as first violinist with Milan's Teatro Scala, acquainting his daughter with the arts from an early age. Additional cultural exposure had come from time spent in Rome as a young girl with her aunt **Giulia Pasqualin**, who frequented the theater and concert halls and who was acquainted with some of the most famous Italian performers and artists of the day. Masina recalled being taken backstage one theatrical evening to meet the author of that night's play, Luigi Pirandello; and she was fascinated with the witty conversation and theatrical gossip of the actors and actresses who came to tea at her aunt's home on Via Lutezia.

Although Masina might have been a talented musician like her father, it was the University of Rome's experimental student theater that held her attention when she arrived there for her studies shortly after the outbreak of World War II. She first appeared on stage in a university program of three one-act plays, attracting attention by portraying a middle-aged woman in the first play, a girl of 14 in the second, and a young prostitute in the third. Although Masina refused several subsequent offers of professional theater work, out of respect for her family's wishes, she began to accept small roles in radio plays and was eventually cast as a newlywed in the radio comedy series "Cico e Pallina," written by a young writer fresh from Rimini named Federico Fellini. Still, the two never met until Fellini was approached with the idea of turning the series into a film and decided it was time to meet the young actress who had been playing his Pallina. "He telephoned me one day," Masina once remembered, "and he said 'My name is Fellini and I am fed up with life, but before I die I would like to see what my heroine looks like.' I thought he might be joking, but I couldn't risk a corpse on my conscience."

Their fateful lunch was in June 1943. By the end of that month, Fellini was introducing her as his fiancée, and on October 30, 1943, the two were married in Masina's aunt's apartment by a priest who conveniently lived next door. It was not a particularly auspicious time to wed, given that Mussolini's government had just collapsed, the Allies had begun their push from Sicily to wrest the country from the Germans, Allied bombs were falling on Rome daily, and Fellini had become a hunted man after escaping a conscription attempt by the German army. Nevertheless, Fellini insisted that he and his new wife go to the theater that evening, where his actor friend Alberto Sordi stopped the show to announce the marriage and call for a round of applause for the couple. The parents of both young marrieds, cut off by blockades and bombs from Rome, never learned of the marriage until well after the fact.

The couple's first two years together, during the turmoil of the Allied victory, were marked by tragedy, beginning with a miscarriage in 1944 when a pregnant Masina fell down a flight of steps and, the following year, the death of a two-

week-old son on April 1, 1945. Even worse, Masina had suffered an infection after her second pregnancy which left her unable to bear more children. She never spoke publicly about her pain, but she often peppered her conversation with maternal images, once describing the process of preparing for a role as making the character "my own chubby little darling." Fellini, when asked about the couple's lack of children, would only reply, "My films are my children."

He was my first and only love.
—**Giulietta Masina, speaking of Federico Fellini**

Masina's first film role came a year after the death of her son, in a picture her husband had written for Roberto Rossellini, *Paisà/Paisan* (*The Countryfolk*). She appeared in one of the film's six "chapters" detailing the advance of American troops northward through Italy from the points of view of the peasants they encounter. It was a small role and attracted little attention, but at least it meant she could travel with her husband from location to location during the shoot. For the next two years, while Fellini worked as a writer and assistant director for Rossellini, Masina did not appear again on screen, but she continued to accompany Fellini on location, even cooking for cast and crew at times. With Fellini occupied with learning his trade, Masina was forced to keep her distance—a characteristic of the marriage that would intensify as the years passed.

Masina's first significant film role was as the prostitute Marcella in 1948's *Senza Pietà* (*Without Pity*), Alberto Lattuada's gritty depiction of life in a small coastal town at the end of World War II. It was a role added by Fellini to the original script when Lattuada hired him as a collaborator. Marcella dreams of marrying an American GI and returning with him to the United States, only to have her hopes crushed in the conflicts arising from black-market trading in American arms supplies. Masina's poignant performance, generally considered one of the finest in any Italian film of the immediate postwar period, earned her a Silver Ribbon for Best Supporting Actress, equivalent to an Oscar, at the Venice Film Festival.

Although the award established Masina as a formidable dramatic actress, a reputation she consolidated in the next year's *Luci del Varietà* (*Variety Lights*), it was in the first film entirely directed by Fellini, 1952's *Lo Sceicco Bianco* (*The White Sheik*), that she displayed the comedic talent that would endear her to Italian audiences. For his first solo directing effort,

Fellini cast her in a small part at the end of the film in which, he later said, "she revealed herself capable of being a tragicomic mime in the tradition of Chaplin [and] Keaton." Two years later, he gave her the role which brought her international recognition—as Gelsomina in 1954's *La Strada* (*The Street*).

The film told the story of a small band of traveling street performers, with Masina playing opposite two American actors, Anthony Quinn as the strongman Zampano and Richard Basehart as Il Matto. Masina claimed many years later that she had introduced both men to Fellini (there were rumors at the time that she and Basehart were lovers) after they had fled a rigid Hollywood studio system to seek their fortunes as leading men in European cinema. The production was a challenge for all involved, since neither Masina nor Fellini spoke English, Quinn and Basehart spoke no Italian, and Fellini was required to shout and act out his direction during each take, in which the actors traded dialogue that none of them could understand (the entire dialogue track was recreated on a dubbing stage afterward). Gelsomina, a mime who becomes Zampano's ill-fated lover, had little dialogue, forcing Masina to convey the character through carefully considered movement and gesture which Fellini trusted her to work out for herself. His only direction to her, she later remembered, was to keep her mouth closed when she smiled. Gelsomina became an extremely popular character in Italy. A Gelsomina Club was established in Naples, and Masina received bags filled with letters from Italian women who knew exactly what Gelsomina had felt near the end of the film when Zampano leaves her. *La Strada* was Fellini's first film to be released in America, bringing both director and actress an adoring new audience and an Academy Award as Best Foreign Film.

Their next collaboration, however, was not as successful. *Il Bidone* (*The Swindle*, 1955), in which Masina again played opposite Richard Basehart in addition to Broderick Crawford, was one of Fellini's rare attempts at realism and was not well received by audiences in Italy or the United States, where it was not released until 1964 in a shorter version. Masina admitted years later that she had talked Fellini into making the picture against his wishes, and close friends of the couple said the film's poor reception generated a good deal of resentment toward her on Fellini's part. An encounter during the filming of *Il Bidone* led to further professional tensions, even though it would ultimately produce a Best Actress award for Masina at the 1956 Cannes Film Festival. One night during the shooting, Fellini spent consider-able effort and energy calming the ruffled nerves of a Rome prostitute into whose neighborhood the cast and crew had intruded and who complained of losing business from the disturbance. The result was the character of Maria Cecciara, nicknamed Cabiria, whose sordid life and ultimate redemption is explored in *La Notti de Cabiria* (*The Nights of Cabiria*). Relations between husband and wife on the set of *La Notti de Cabiria* were far from cordial, marked with very public arguments, because Fellini sensed that "Gelsomina's fallen sister," as he called Cabiria, was the most important role of his wife's career to date. As the conjugal waters calmed and the praise began building, Masina indirectly complimented Fellini for his creation. "She resembles me very much," she said of Cabiria. "[She is] naive, aggressive and finally very strong."

Despite the acclaim, Masina's career languished for the next decade. Deciding that her marriage to Fellini was more important than a career as his starring actress, she refused his offer to appear in *La Notte* (*The Night*), a role Fellini eventually gave to *Jeanne Moreau. She also declined the leading role played by **Daniella Rocca** opposite Marcello Mastroianni in what would become one of the most successful Italian films of the early 1960s, *Divorzio all'italiana* (*Divorce Italian Style*). As if to refute charges that she could work with no one but her husband, she appeared in several undistinguished productions (one of which, *Fortunella*, Fellini co-wrote) but was absent from the films which marked the crest of her husband's career, such as *8½*, *La Dolce Vita*. and *Boccaccio '70*. She often visited Fellini on the sets of his various pictures and was once likened by a Fellini associate to a political candidate's wife, "dutifully stumping. Her small face was almost hidden behind huge sunglasses. She took a chair and continued to smile at no one in particular." It wasn't until the spring of 1965 that the two again worked together, Fellini having created another role which even Giulietta admitted was the most challenging of her career, and one which even bore her name.

Giulietta degli spiriti (*Juliet of the Spirits*) was written expressly for her. "Giulietta is the soul of my film," Fellini said at the time, but even he was not prepared for the difficulty that lay ahead. From the start, she and Fellini differed violently over the interpretation of Fellini's middle-aged housewife who is driven into a world of hallucinatory fantasy by her husband's infidelities. The character was closely modeled on Masina herself, Fellini having exploited her well-known superstitious fears and imagined her thoughts and reactions to his own rumored af-

Giulietta
Masina

fairs with other women. Perhaps unprepared for the nearly autobiographical accuracy with which Fellini wanted her to play the part, Masina resisted her husband strenuously, even before production began. She refused to attend a séance, telling Fellini that although she believed in the spirit world, she feared what might come of communicating with it; and during filming, she resisted Fellini's angry insistence that she play herself, not a character. "Those who have seen *La Strada* or *La Notti di Cabiria* know her as a poignant clown, a comedienne who can wrench the heart," Fellini recalled many years later. "But that engaging creature had to go. And all along I knew what I was losing." For her part, Masina told an interviewer after filming had ended that she remained convinced that Fellini had been mistaken. "I feel that this film doesn't permit me to arrive at the . . . high tide . . . of this character," she said. "But that's the way Federico wanted it." In later years, Fellini admitted that Masina may have been right, for the film was poorly received in both Europe and the United States. Audiences and critics alike complained that *Giulietta degli spiriti* was all style and little substance. It would be Masina's last work with her husband for some 20 years.

As time wore on, the emotional distance between Masina and Fellini became more pronounced, noticeable even to casual acquaintances. Their apartment on Via Margutta, which had begun as a small one-bedroom flat and had grown as other apartments were added to it, included two sitting rooms and two bedrooms—because, as Fellini took pains to explain, Masina refused to give up her smoking habit and his health suffered from the fumes. Dinner guests at the Fellinis' seaside home, which had been modeled on the designs for the fictional villa in *Juliet of the Spirits*, would often see little of Masina once the meal was over and she retired to her private quarters. (The home later had to be sold to pay back taxes.) Masina accepted few film roles, taking up charity work, notably for UNICEF, and writing gardening and homemaking columns for *La Stampa* while Fellini created trademark works like *Satyricon, The Clowns,* and *Roma.* "The word marriage is not appropriate in our case," Masina told an interviewer in the early 1970s. "It would be better to speak of . . . two people who stay together by free choice." But the marriage was important enough for her to come to Fellini's defense after a much-discussed episode in which Fellini was seen enjoying an intimate dinner with the actress/model **Capucine**, marked by much kissing and petting. Masina told a press conference that rumors of his many affairs were greatly exaggerated. "He is an Italian man," she said, "and they have to talk about their sexual exploits in order to have the respect of other Italian men. I suppose the truth lies somewhere in between what he tells the world and what he tells me." A French journalist was perhaps more perceptive than most in evaluating the relationship, noting during an interview with Fellini, in which the director pompously discussed his films, that Giulietta "smiles, always impassive, next to her big adolescent, full of tempest."

Despite their marital tensions, Fellini continued to show great respect for Masina's talent as an actress. During the time she was in France playing opposite ***Katharine Hepburn** in Bryan Forbes' film of *The Madwoman of Chaillot,* Fellini appeared on the set each day and sat silently, observantly, through every one of her takes. Later, when Masina had become a household name in Italy thanks to two television series in which she starred, Fellini delightedly told her of the conversation he'd overheard between two women while crossing Rome's Piazza del Popolo. "Look," one of the women had exclaimed, "there goes Giulietta Masina's husband!"

In 1986, Masina agreed for the first time since 1965 to appear in one of her husband's films, *Ginger e Fred* (*Ginger and Fred*), in which she and Marcello Mastroianni play an ageing couple, known in younger years as imitators of ***Ginger Rogers** and Fred Astaire, who are reunited 40 years later on a bizarre television chat show, "Ed Ecco a Voi!" (This One's For You!). Masina claimed the film had been her inspiration, based on an idea she had once had for a television series. Whatever its source, Masina and Fellini once again found themselves at odds over interpretation. To Fellini, the film was a means to satirize the banal state of Italian television and society in general; to Giulietta, it was a poignant story of two old lovers reunited for the last time and, she hoped, a way to revive her film career. The arguments between the two were as violent as they had been 20 years before, with Masina insisting that she be lit differently, costumed differently, made up differently, and Fellini sinking into an increasingly foul mood. "She was ever the actress, never the writer," as he put it. Also as before, the film opened to a lukewarm reception, although Masina's performance was regarded with affection by some reviewers. "She infuses this role with a touching mixture of pride, regret, and a wry kind of humor born of the resignation of middle age," wrote film critic Ralph Novak, while *Time*'s Richard Schickel called her work "observant, original and infinitely appealing." The real Ginger Rogers disagreed, however, charging that Masina's imitation of her was offensive and suing Fellini for $8 million. (The suit was later dropped after Rogers admitted she had never actually seen the film but had been merely acting on the advice of lawyers.) Except for a French film released in 1991, *Ginger e Fred* was Masina's last screen appearance.

In the late 1980s, Masina was diagnosed with lung cancer and underwent a painful series of radiation treatments to halt the disease. At the same time, Fellini's health began to fail and his pace slowed. He released only two films in the seven years between *Ginger e Fred* and his death in November 1993. Near the end of his funeral service, Giulietta was seen to raise her arm and wave a final goodbye. "*Ciao, amore,*" she whispered. Five months later, on March 23, 1994, Giulietta Masina died in a Rome hospital.

Despite the tumult and the confusion of the personal and the professional that marked her years with Fellini, Giulietta Masina managed to develop a successful career while maintaining the love and respect of one of the world's most famous and difficult film directors. During her last illness, Giulietta often fondly recalled her courtship with the thin, poorly dressed young writer she met that June day in a Rome restaurant. "Maybe deep down, I already knew intuitively that he was going to be my hero," she remembered. For his part, Fellini regarded her as his heroine and his muse. "I don't know what would have become of me," he admitted not long before his death, "if I had not found Giulietta."

SOURCES:

Alpert, Hollis. *Fellini: A Life.* NY: The Marlowe Company, 1988.

Baxter, John. *Fellini.* London: Fourth Estate, 1993.

Chandler, Charlotte. *I, Fellini.* NY: Random House, 1995.

Katz, Ephraim. *The Film Encyclopedia.* 2nd ed. NY: HarperCollins, 1994.

Kezich, Tullio. *Giulietta Masina.* Bologna: Cappelli, 1991.

Novak, Ralph. "*Ginger and Fred* (movie review)," in *People Weekly.* Vol. 25. April 14, 1986.

Schickel, Richard. "*Ginger and Fred* (movie review)," in *Time.* Vol. 127. March 31, 1986.

Norman Powers,
writer-producer, Chelsea Lane Productions, New York

Mašiotene, Ona (1883–1949)

Lithuanian feminist and nationalist. Name variations: Ona Masiotene. Born Ona Brazauskaité in Slavenae, Lithuania, in 1883; died in 1949; attended the Advanced School of Moscow.

Born in what was then the Russian province of Slavenae, Lithuania, in 1883, Ona Mašiotene showed an early interest in science, and attended the Advanced School of Moscow. While in Russia, she developed an interest in the feminist movements of Western Europe and, upon her return to Vilnius in 1905, founded the Alliance of Lithuanian Women. She subsequently represented the Alliance at the Russian Women's National Congress. In addition to holding a position as a high school teacher in Vilnius from 1911 to 1914, Mašiotene remained active in the women's move-

ment until the outbreak of World War I in August 1914. She then moved to Moscow and became involved in nationalist movements there. In 1917, she founded the Lithuanian Women's Freedom Association, which campaigned for the independence of Lithuania.

Following the Treaty of Brest-Litovsk in 1918, by which Lithuania and the other Baltic provinces gained their independence, and the end of World War I the same year, Mašiotene returned to Vilnius. There she ran a girls' school and organized adult education classes. She founded and became president of the Council of Lithuanian Women in 1929, and wrote a history of the role of Lithuanian women in politics and nationalist movements, *Moteru politnis ir valstybiniai tautiskas darbas*, the last volume of which was published in 1937. Ona Mašiotene died in 1949, by which time Lithuania had again lost its independence and become a constituent republic of the Soviet Union.

SOURCES:

Uglow, Jennifer S., ed. *The International Dictionary of Women's Biography.* NY: Continuum Press, 1989.

Grant Eldridge,
freelance writer, Pontiac, Michigan

Mason, Alice Trumbull
(1904–1971)

Important American abstract painter of the mid-20th century who has begun to receive recognition only since her death. Name variations: Alice Trumbull; Alice Mason. Born in 1904 in Litchfield, Connecticut; died in 1971 in New York, New York; attended the National Academy of Design (1924–28); studied with Arshile Gorky at the Grand Central Art Galleries; studied at the Atelier 17 (1944–47); married Warwood Mason (a ship's captain), in 1928 (one source cites 1930); children: one son (died 1958); Emily Mason Kahn (an artist).

Selected paintings: Free White Spacing *(1934);* L'Hasard *(1948);* Magnetic Field *(1951);* Memorial *(1958–59);* Magnitude of Memory *(1962);* Urban White *(1969).*

During her lifetime, Alice Trumbull Mason never achieved the critical recognition she was due, but since her death art historians have identified her as an important figure in the movement to introduce European-centered abstract art into the canon of serious American painting. Born in Connecticut in 1904, Mason came from an old New England family whose origins dated back to the Revolutionary War era; among her father's ancestors were a governor of Connecticut and the painter John Trumbull. Her father was trained as a lawyer but never practiced law, and the family, devout Christian Scientists, enjoyed a life of leisure and often visited Europe. They also gathered in the evenings to play word games and charades and to recite poetry, making for an erudite environment that would later inform Mason's art.

She became interested in art as a career while on a trip to Italy in 1922, and began studying at the British Academy in Rome. After successfully pleading with her family to return to America so she could attend art school in New York, from 1924 to 1928 Mason took courses at the National Academy of Design in New York City. She then studied under Arshile Gorky at the Grand Central Art Galleries in New York, and through his influence became intently interested in abstract art. She began painting in earnest in 1928 after a trip through Greece and Italy, where she saw the links between the flat color fields of modern European abstract art and the formal structures of classical Byzantine art.

Mason married a ship's captain, Warwood Mason, probably around 1928, and did not paint for a period of five years after the birth of their two children; instead, she wrote poetry, some of which was published, and lived almost as a single mother because her husband was often away at sea. She took up painting again in the early 1930s, and in 1936 became a founding member of the American Abstract Artists group. This alliance of painters worked passionately to change opinion about non-representational art, which was viewed with skepticism by the art establishment and outright ridicule by the general public in some cases. At one point, Mason and the group picketed the Museum of Modern Art. She held a number of executive positions within the organization, including president, and remained an active member until 1963. She also belonged to the Federation of Modern Painters and Sculptors, and to the 14 Painters/Printmakers group.

Mason was meticulous about her craft as well as her art, and ground and mixed her own paints. She was influenced by Dutch artist Piet Mondrian, whom she had met, although she always employed a subtler palette of colors. As **Brooke Bailey** notes, Mason's "paintings are carefully laid out to keep their harmony no matter which side of the frame points up." Mason herself described her work as "architectural abstraction," and once commented that her art was "a building and not a destroying. It is making color, density, dark and light, rhythm and balance work together without depending on references and associations." She also studied soft-ground etching from 1944 to 1947 with Stanley Hayter at the Atelier 17, and created woodcuts and etchings.

The efforts of the American Abstract Artists bore fruit, for Mason and her fellow abstract artists did indeed begin to gain acceptance by the early 1940s. She held her first solo show in 1942, at the Museum of Living Art. Despite several more solo shows, Mason did not achieve the status of her male colleagues. She grew increasingly reclusive and never recovered from the death of her son at sea in 1958; *Memorial* (1958–59) was her homage to him. Alice Trumbull Mason died in 1971. Two years later, the first retrospective of her work was held at the Whitney Museum of American Art. Other retrospectives have followed, and her paintings have since been included in every major exhibition of the American Abstract Artists. Mason's work is in the permanent collections of the Whitney Museum of American Art, the Museum of Modern Art in New York City, the Guggenheim Museum, the Metropolitan Museum of Art, the Philadelphia Museum of Art, the Hirshhorn Museum, the Brooklyn Museum, and the Walker Art Center, among many others.

SOURCES:

Bailey, Brooke. *The Remarkable Lives of 100 Women Artists.* Holbrook, MA: Bob Adams, 1994.

Harris, Ann Sutherland, and Linda Nochlin. *Women Artists: 1550–1950.* Los Angeles County Museum of Art. NY: Alfred A. Knopf, 1976.

Rubinstein, Charlotte Streifer. *American Women Artists from Early Indian Times to the Present.* Avon, 1982.

SUGGESTED READING:

Mason, Alice Trumbull. *Alice Trumbull Mason: Etchings and Woodcuts.* Introduction by Una E. Johnson. NY: Taplinger, 1985.

COLLECTIONS:

Papers of Alice Mason Trumbull are held at the Archives of American Art, New York City, New York.

Carol Brennan,
Grosse Pointe, Michigan

Mason, Biddy (1818–1891)

American woman, born into slavery, who became a successful businesswoman and philanthropist. Name variations: Bridget Mason. Born on August 15, 1818, in Georgia or Mississippi; died on January 15, 1891, in Los Angeles, California; children: Ellen Mason Owens; Ann Mason; Harriet Mason.

Biddy Mason's remarkable life serves as a paradigm for the unchronicled lives of millions of women who endured hardship, overcame legal obstacles, and prospered through their own good sense. Mason was born into slavery in 1818, probably in Georgia or Mississippi; it is known for certain only that she was named Bridget upon her birth, and that she was the property of Robert and **Rebecca Crosby Smith**, Mississippi plantation owners. She gained a great deal of knowledge about midwifery and the folk arts from other slave women and healers, and became a well-regarded midwife. At age 20, she became a mother herself with the first of three daughters. The rape of female slaves by their male owners was not an uncommon occurrence in the antebellum South, and it is thought that Robert Smith may have been the father of Mason's daughters.

Robert Smith converted to the Mormon faith in 1847 and decided to move to the Utah Territory. With his extended family and their large retinue—90 in all—Mason traveled the 2,000 miles from Mississippi on foot. Slaves did not travel in the wagons, and one of her jobs was to keep track of the animals. With no choice but to accompany her owner, Mason perhaps believed her lot might improve in the new American West, but found that the Mormons who had settled the Utah Territory were greatly prejudiced against blacks. In 1851, Robert Smith moved the entourage to a more liberal Mormon enclave in San Bernardino, California; he was apparently unaware that the state's 1849 constitution prohibited slavery. This prohibition did not, however, automatically grant freedom to newly arrived slaves, whose legal status was murky. Some time later, unwilling to take the chance that he might be forced to give up his "property," Smith began making plans to relocate the entourage to Texas, where slavery was still legal.

Mason's teenage daughter Ellen and a friend of hers, the daughter of another of Smith's slaves named Hannah, had begun dating two free black men, Charles Owens and Manuel Pepper. Mason told the men of her desire to live as a free person outside the brutal constraints of slavery. Pepper and Owens, the son of an esteemed business owner in Los Angeles' African-American community, enlisted the aid of sheriffs to serve Smith with a writ of habeas corpus on behalf of Mason. Because an 1850 state law prohibited blacks, mulattos, and Native Americans from testifying in court against whites (both in civil and in criminal cases), Mason was not permitted to speak on her own behalf when the case came to court. However, the judge met with her privately and listened to her story. When Robert Smith failed to appear in court on January 21, 1856, the judge not only granted Mason's petition for manumission but freed the other members of her family as well.

Biddy Mason

Now free citizens, Mason and her family accepted the Owens family's invitation to take up residence with them in Los Angeles (Ellen Mason and Charles Owens would later marry). Mason quickly gained renown as an excellent midwife, assisting at hundreds of births of African-Americans, whites and Native Americans of all social classes. After just ten years of freedom, she had managed to save enough money to buy her own home on Spring Street in the city, making her one of the first African-American women to own property in Los Angeles. She deemed it her "homestead," and instructed her children that it should never pass from their hands. She accrued further savings to purchase more land, and in 1884 had a commercial property built in the downtown section of the city. The income from this and other shrewd investments gave Mason a fund from which to indulge her philanthropic bent. She became well known in Los Angeles for her relief aid to people of all colors who had encountered hardship, and visited the city jails frequently. With Charles Owens, in 1872 she hosted a meeting at her home of what became the founding congregation of the First African Methodist Episcopal Church of Los Angeles.

Biddy Mason died in Los Angeles in January 1891 and was buried in Evergreen Cemetery, in an unmarked grave. In 1988, her memory was honored with a proper gravestone bestowed in a ceremony involving Los Angeles mayor Tom Bradley and several thousand members of the city's First A.M.E. Church. A community center in Los Angeles, the Broadway Spring Center, features an 81-foot long mural that depicts Mason's lifetime of achievement, and her homestead has been preserved as a historical site.

SOURCES:

Igus, Toyomi, ed. *Book of Black Heroes, Volume Two: Great Women in the Struggle.* Just Us Books, 1991.

Smith, Jessie Carney, ed. *Notable Black American Women.* Detroit, MI: Gale Research, 1992.

Carol Brennan,
Grosse Pointe, Michigan

Mason, Lucy Randolph

(1882–1959)

American labor activist and social reformer who served as the highly effective "roving ambassador" for the CIO in the South for 16 years. Born Lucy Randolph Mason at "Clarens" on Seminary Hill near Alexandria, Virginia, on July 26, 1882; died in Atlanta, Georgia, on May 6, 1959; daughter of Landon Randolph Mason (1841–1923, an Episcopal minister) and Lucy (Ambler) Mason (1848–1918); sister of **Anna Mason**, *Ida Mason, John Mason, Landon Mason, and Randolph Mason; never married.*

Lucy Randolph Mason was a direct descendent of some of the oldest and most respected families of the South. Ralph McGill, editor of the Atlanta *Constitution*, was hardly exaggerating when he wrote of her ancestry—which entitled her to membership in both the Daughters of the American Revolution and the United Daughters of the Confederacy—that "When it came to ancestors she made all the others seem parvenus." On both parents' sides, she was related to George Mason, author of the Virginia Bill of Rights and a friend of George Washington and Thomas Jefferson. (In 1775, George Mason had urged his fellow revolutionary leaders to start their new nation in a spirit of justice by abolishing slavery, arguing prophetically, "Providence punishes national sins by national calamities.") On her mother's side, she was also related to John Marshall (first chief justice of the U.S. Supreme Court), and on her father's side to Robert E. Lee (her father's second cousin).

Her parents, whom she described as "deeply good, sincerely spiritual and most humanly kind," strove to transform their Christian beliefs into practical reality. Lucy's father Landon Randolph Mason was an Episcopal minister who had served with Mosby's Raiders in the Civil War; his social theology prompted him to such acts as carrying a sack of coal through deep snow to an impoverished widow who was not even a member of his congregation. Lucy's mother **Lucy Ambler Mason** was, if anything, more emphatic in her views of how the gospel should be lived in daily life. Years later, she would be described by her daughter as "a born social worker, without benefit of study for that profession. In addition to helping countless individuals, she frequently turned her attention to remedying evil institutions."

Shocked by the conditions of prisons, and convinced that reforms could achieved, Lucy's mother was a near-constant visitor at the state penitentiary in Richmond. She often appeared before the Virginia legislature to plead for prison reform and kept the issue alive through newspaper articles and pamphlets. The Mason home eventually became an unofficial halfway house for recently released convicts who, as her daughter would recall later, needed a helping hand to get back on their feet after being released from prison: "Nearly all of these men kept up with Mother afterwards and became good citizens—and mostly good Christians."

While rich in traditions and compassion for the less fortunate, the Mason family was relatively poor in financial resources. Neither Lucy nor her sister **Ida Mason** were able to complete high school. Lucy dreamed of becoming a foreign missionary, but lack of funds kept her in Richmond. With initiative likely prompted by necessity, she bought a shorthand manual and with a rented typewriter taught herself stenography, so that she could work at home. Around the same time, she taught Sunday School classes in a mission church located in one of Richmond's working-class areas. She also organized industrial clubs for her pupils, who were mostly working girls from the nearby tobacco factories. Industrial capitalism had not brought prosperity to the great majority of the city's wage earners, either black or white, and the harsh, squalid nature of their existences ignited a reform movement.

While working as a stenographer at a law firm in Richmond, Mason remained active in church-related and other local educational efforts. Increasingly drawn to the feminist movement, she was convinced that women could only achieve the social reforms they believed in if they possessed the ballot. In *The Divine Discontent*, a pamphlet published in 1912 by the Equal Suffrage League of Virginia, she noted that the women's suffrage movement was an expression of discontent rather than of "mere dissatisfaction or disquiet." "Divine discontent" she argued, "has been responsible for every reformation accomplished in the history of our race. It has furnished the incentive for progress and development. It has led to the purifying of religion, politics and all social institutions."

In 1914, Mason became the industrial secretary of Richmond's Young Women's Christian Association (YWCA), thus becoming the first woman to be appointed to such a position in any Southern state. She used her new post to educate working women and carry on lobbying activities for legislation that would bring about major reforms of women's working conditions, including an eight-hour day and restriction of night work. No doubt taking advantage of her family's prestige, Mason became involved in activities that were by no means totally endorsed by the Richmond establishment, such as organizing support for an all-female strike at a local company. Increasingly convinced that only collective bargaining and unionization would bring about significant social changes for female wage earners in the South, she became an active member of the Union Label League, which urged consumers to purchase only union-made products. Mason's work soon brought her to the attention of Samuel Gompers, head of the American Federation of Labor (AFL). In 1917, he named her the Virginia chair of the Committee on Women in Industry of the wartime National Advisory Committee on Labor.

With her mother's sudden death in 1918, Mason resigned from her YWCA position in order to take care of her father, who was in declining health. For the next five years, supported by her brother John, she carried out volunteer work as president of the Richmond Equal Suffrage League and of its successor organization, the Richmond League of Women Voters. Now that women had won the right to vote, noted Mason in her speeches and articles, they had a special role to play in the ongoing reform of the social order, most of all by advocating the passage of legislation that would bring about a significant "humanizing of the industrial processes." In 1923, after her father's death, she returned to her career at the Richmond YWCA, serving as the general secretary of that organization from then until 1932.

In 1931, Mason's various activities in Virginia brought her to the attention of *Florence

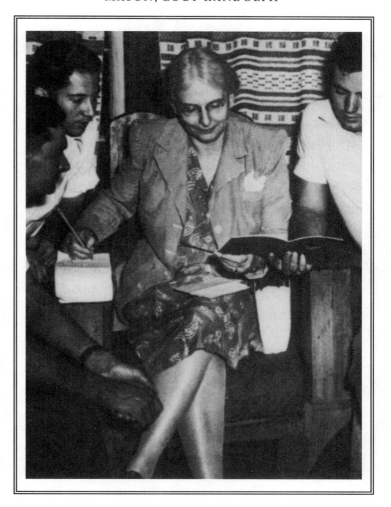

Kelley of the National Consumers' League (NCL), a major national labor-reform organization. For two months of that year, Mason worked on behalf of the NCL as director of the fledgling Southern Council on Women and Children in Industry. During this period, she helped publicize a progressive agenda of labor legislation and also wrote a pamphlet entitled *Standards for Workers in Southern Industry* that would prove to be of considerable influence over the next decade.

In September 1932, she moved to New York City to succeed Florence Kelley as NCL general secretary. Although the cause of labor, particularly in the South, was profoundly demoralized, better times were on the horizon; the start of Franklin D. Roosevelt's New Deal (March 1933) signaled a more sympathetic Federal role in regard to labor in the South.

Over the next four years, Mason spent countless hours promoting labor and social-welfare legislation aimed at improving working and

Lucy Randolph Mason

living conditions in the South, described by the National Emergency Council as "the Nation's Number One economic problem." During the first several years of the New Deal, working conditions and wages in the South improved little if at all. Although optimistic about the future, she had no illusions about the difficulties of organizing labor in the region. Mason was more than aware of the immense economic, racial, and social problems which remained endemic in the states of the former Confederacy, and at times she was bitterly disappointed. On one occasion, she wrote to a friend: "Virginia killed every social and labor bill except a mutilated amendment to the child labor law." Workers and their families faced violence if they attempted to organize into unions; state militia were called out to crush workers; and in one state, Georgia, Governor Talmadge imprisoned many strikers in compounds that soon became known as "concentration camps."

In 1937, Mason began working for the Congress of Industrial Organizations (CIO), a militant union based on industry-wide, rather than craft, organization of labor. While testifying before a congressional committee in support of a national Fair Labor Standards bill, she met John L. Lewis, the legendary leader of the coal miners, who was now CIO president. Lewis offered Mason the job of public-relations officer—in effect, a kind of "roving ambassador"—of the CIO in the Southern states. During her first months on the job, she began to realize the immensity of the task before her. Mason's initial visits to the South during this period quickly made it clear to her that labor had few if any friends among the politicians, press, police, or general public. "When I came South I had no idea of the frequency of attacks on people peacefully pursuing legitimate purposes," she wrote President Roosevelt (August 12, 1937). "I am appalled at the disregard of the most common civil rights and the dangers of bodily harm to which organizers often are exposed."

Although she remained proud of her Southern origins, Mason was disappointed by "a conspiracy of silence" from the region's press on matters of anti-worker violence and intimidation. In one despairing moment, she described the South as "Fascist," a place in which "the domination of the Negro had made it easier to repeat the pattern for organized labor."

During Mason's first months in her new position, she received helpful advice from local labor veterans, including Steve Nance. Having served as president of the Georgia AFL, Nance was now di-

rector of a unionization drive in the South by the Textile Workers Organizing Committee (TWOC). He quickly became Mason's trusted colleague and mentor, giving her confidence but also cautioning her that the "only possible way" to achieve lasting results in the region was by relying on "infinite patience and diplomacy." Mason took his advice to heart, using it to temper her sometimes impetuous desire to fell injustice—economic, racial, or social—with one dramatic blow. But Nance died soon after, at age 41 (April 1938), largely as the result of overwork.

For 16 years, Mason worked as public-relations officer for the CIO, striving to change Southern attitudes toward labor unions and working-class militancy. Her base of operations during these years was a small but comfortable apartment on Myrtle Street in northeast Atlanta, which served as her home, office and archive. Despite the South's skepticism, if not violent hostility, toward the ideals she stood for, she refused to be discouraged. Drawing from her earlier experience with the YWCA and NCL, she spoke before college and university classrooms, church groups, social worker conventions, and civic clubs. She pointed out that labor unions were not "un-American" conspiracies, but that they represented a progressive way to bring about positive social change. When CIO organizers and members suffered violence at the hands of employers or local police and other officials, Mason was on hand to intervene, bringing these violations of civil and human rights to the attention of the national media. On more than one occasion, Mason slipped into the White House to present labor's side in a conflict to her personal friend *Eleanor Roosevelt, whom Mason regarded as "the first lady of the world."

Playing a significant role in the slow but steady growth of Southern liberalism, Mason was for many years an active member of the key organizations that made possible the South's transformation from within by natives committed to the ideals of economic, racial and social justice. She was involved in the work of such organizations as the Southern Policy Committee, the Southern Conference for Human Welfare, and the Southern Regional Council, as well as the Highlander Folk School and the Southern Summer School for Women Workers. On more than one occasion, she used her illustrious lineage to awe a fellow Southerner who seethed with hostility to unionism. Labor organizer Miles Horton, noting her ancestry, remarked:

> You can't get more kosher than that in Virginia, but she kind of had an interest in working people that most people of that

kind of background don't have. . . . Boy, she was a power. We would all yell for Lucy anytime that we needed help and she would come into the toughest situation and was great. She played a tremendous role, a tremendous role.

There are literally hundreds of "Miss Lucy stories" recalling Mason's courage in the face of physical danger. On one occasion, she trailed a gang of thugs around a Georgia mill town because of her concern for the physical safety of a union official, reasoning that "the mob would think twice about attacking him if an old lady was there as a witness."

Lucy Mason retired from her CIO post in 1953 and died in Atlanta, Georgia, on May 6, 1959. In her obituary, Ralph McGill described Mason as a woman small in stature, prematurely grayhaired, who wore gold-rimmed glasses and blushed easily. She was a "very kind sweet lady, characterized, too, by all the graces of the old Virginia of plantations and the gentry." Above all, Lucy Randolph Mason impressed those who met her as being "a born lady." She advanced the cause of justice in the South, a region steeped in history, talent, and tragedy. While Mason was an experienced advocate with considerable political skills, a good deal of her prestige was derived from her character—the idealism, integrity, and courage she displayed throughout her life.

SOURCES:

Brinson, Betsy. "'Helping Others to Help Themselves': Social Advocacy and Wage-Earning Women in Richmond, Virginia, 1910–1932." Ph.D. dissertation, Union Graduate School, 1984.

Dunbar, Anthony P. *Against the Grain: Southern Radicals and Prophets 1929–1959.* Charlottesville: University Press of Virginia, 1981.

Egerton, John. "The Pre-*Brown* South," in *Virginia Quarterly Review.* Vol. 70, no. 4. Autumn 1994, pp. 603–622.

Frederickson, Mary. "'I Know Which Side I'm On': Southern Women in the Labor Movement in the Twentieth Century," in Ruth Milkman, ed., *Women, Work and Protest: A Century of U.S. Women's Labor History.* Boston, MA: Routledge & Kegan Paul, 1985, pp. 156–180.

Glen, John M. *Highlander: No Ordinary School, 1932–1962.* Lexington, KY: University Press of Kentucky, 1988.

Griffith, Barbara S. *The Crisis of American Labor: Operation Dixie and the Defeat of the CIO.* Philadelphia, PA: Temple University Press, 1988.

Krueger, Thomas A. *And Promises to Keep: The Southern Conference for Human Welfare.* Nashville, TN: Vanderbilt University Press, 1967.

Mason, Lucy Randolph. "The CIO and the Negro in the South," *Journal of Negro Education,* Vol. 14, Fall, 1945, pp. 552–561.

———. *The Divine Discontent.* Richmond: Equal Suffrage League of Virginia, 1912.

———. "I Turned to Social Action Right at Home," in Liston Pope, ed., *Labor's Relation to Church and Community: A Series of Addresses.* New York and London: Institute for Religious and Social Studies/Harper & Brothers, 1947, pp. 145–155.

———. *To Win These Rights: A Personal Story of the CIO in the South.* Foreword by Eleanor Roosevelt. NY: Harper & Brothers, 1952.

"Miss Lucy R. Mason, 77, Ex-CIO Official, Dies," in *Atlanta Constitution.* May 7, 1959, p. 21.

Reed, Linda. *Simple Decency and Common Sense: The Southern Conference Movement, 1938–1963.* Bloomington, IN: Indiana University Press, 1991.

Salmond, John A. *Miss Lucy of the CIO: The Life and Times of Lucy Randolph Mason, 1882–1959.* Athens: University of Georgia Press, 1988.

Scott, Anne Firor. *The Southern Lady: From Pedestal to Politics.* Chicago: University of Chicago Press, 1970.

Sternsher, Bernard, and Judith Sealander. *Women of Valor: The Struggle Against the Great Depression As Told in Their Own Life Stories.* Chicago: Ivan R. Dee, 1990.

Storrs, Landon. "Civilizing Capitalism: The National Consumers' League and the Politics of Fair Labor Standards in the New Deal Era." Ph.D. dissertation, University of Wisconsin-Madison, 1994.

Storrs, Landon R.Y. "Mason, Lucy Randolph," in John A. Garraty and Mark C. Carnes, eds., *American National Biography.* Vol. 14 of 24 Vols. Oxford: Oxford University Press, 1999, pp. 657–658.

COLLECTIONS:

Lucy Randolph Mason Papers, Perkins Library, Duke University, Durham, North Carolina.

John Haag,
Associate Professor of History,
University of Georgia, Athens, Georgia

Masriyya, Na'ima al-.

See Egyptian Singers and Entrepreneurs.

Massee, May (1881–1966)

American editor and children's literature specialist who was instrumental in establishing high critical standards for children's books. Born on May 1, 1881, in Chicago, Illinois; died on December 24, 1966, at her home in New York City; daughter of Francis Spink Massee and Charlotte Maria (Bull) Massee; attended Milwaukee public schools and two years at state normal school in Milwaukee; enrolled at Wisconsin Library School in Madison; attended Armour Institute in Chicago for two years; never married; no children.

During the beginning decades of the 20th century, interest in children's books developed rapidly. May Massee, who had briefly taught elementary school before becoming a children's librarian, had both the experience and the imagination to effect significant improvements in American publishing for children.

Massee graduated from public high school in Milwaukee at 16, then spent two years at the state normal school and one year teaching elementary school. After a winter spent working with a librarian in White Water, Wisconsin, she enrolled at the Wisconsin Library School, and later spent two years at the Armour Institute in Chicago as an assistant librarian. Originally interested in organizing libraries in western Illinois, Massee changed her plans after she met **Theresa West Elmendorf**, the first woman president of the American Library Association. Elmendorf encouraged her to join the public library staff at Buffalo, New York, as a librarian in the children's room. Massee stayed there for five years, loving every moment of it and developing a keen interest in children's literature.

In 1913, she accepted an offer from *The Booklist*, a publication of the American Library Association, to become its editor, and during her tenure saw the reputations of both her editing skills and the magazine itself grow. In 1919, **Louise Seaman (Bechtel)** at Macmillan established the first children's book publishing department in America. Three years later, Doubleday, Page publishers decided to follow suit, and sought out Massee. Believing that "pioneering is more fun than anything else," she moved to New York City and created the country's second children's book publishing department. She remained there until 1933, when she founded the Viking Press' children's book department, where she served as editor and director for 27 years.

Massee was willing to take risks, publishing some of the first children's books with minority protagonists who were portrayed in a non-derogatory light—books she regarded as "most truly American"—as well as stories set in foreign countries. In a 1950 interview, she commented that she wanted to provide books "that would bring the joy of living of all the world's children to our children." That year, she translated and published German author Eric Kästner's *Emil and the Detectives*, now a perennial favorite, the success of which led other American publishers to seek out children's books by foreign authors. Massee also encouraged authors to try something new; in 1939, she had published one of the earliest books dealing with the growth of a baby from conception to birth, **Marie Hall Ets'** *The Story of a Baby*. Massee worked hard to rid the field of "juvenile books," instead calling them junior books.

Massee was interested in illustration and design, and endorsed such new methods as offset lithography. In 1923, at Doubleday, she published the *ABC Book* by Charles B. Falls, a groundbreaking example of color printing in picture books. Her passion for illustration led her to seek out and publish the work of artists including **Elizabeth MacKinstry**, Boris Artzybasheff, Ludwig Bemelmans, and James Daugherty. Massee was the first woman member of the American Institute of Graphic Arts and in 1959 became the first woman to be awarded the Institute's gold medal, "for production of beautiful books."

May Massee edited ten children's books that won Newbery Medals, the American Library Association's coveted annual award for the "most distinguished contribution to American literature for children." She also edited four other books that were honored by the association with the Caldecott Medal, for the "most distinguished American picture book for children," and in 1950 was the recipient of the *Constance Skinner Medal for "achievement in the realm of books." Her office at Viking, decorated by her friend, the architect Eric Gugler, displayed a medallion of Taurus the Bull, Massee's astrological sign, which she treasured as a symbol of the creative life; around the top of the walls, her motto was carved in Latin: "Nothing too much, not even moderation." Noted for being an extremely kind and generous woman whose passion was her work, Massee continued as an advisory editor at Viking after her retirement in 1960 until she died of a stroke at home in New York City on Christmas Eve 1966.

In 1972, Massee was honored by the establishment of a collection in her name at the library of the Kansas State Teachers College at Emporia (later Emporia State University); her office was transported intact to the library.

SOURCES:

Read, Phyllis J., and Witlieb, Bernard L. *The Book of Women's Firsts*. NY: Random House, 1992.

Sicherman, Barbara, and Carol Hurd Green, eds. *Notable American Women: The Modern Period. A Biographical Dictionary*. Cambridge, MA: The Belknap Press of Harvard University Press, 1980.

Who's Who of American Women, 3rd ed. Chicago, Illinois: A.N. Marquis, 1964.

SUGGESTED READING:

Gottlieb, Robin. *Publishing Children's Books in America, 1919–1976, An Annotated Bibliography*, 1978.

The May Massee Collection: Creative Publishing for Children, pamphlet published in conjunction with opening of Massee Memorial Collection, contains two articles: "May Massee: Who Was She?" by *Elizabeth Gray Vining*, and "The May Massee Collection: What Is It?" by Annis Duff, along with a photo of Massee.

COLLECTIONS:

Books published under Massee's direction, examples of illustration and of iconographic films, reminiscences of Massee, correspondence, articles and transcripts of speeches, and interviews, are at Emporia State University, Emporia, Kansas.

Nine taped interviews, "The Reminiscences of May Massee (1964–66)," are in the Oral History Collection at Columbia University, New York City.

Jo Anne Meginnes,
freelance writer, Brookfield, Vermont

Massevitch, Alla G. (1918—)

Soviet astrophysicist, university professor, and vice-president of the USSR's Academy of Science, who organized and administered a network of stations that tracked movements of Soviet Sputniks. Born Alla Genrikohovna Massevitch on October 9, 1918, in Tbilisi, capital of the Georgian Republic (now Georgia); eldest daughter and one of three children of Genrikh Massevitch (a lawyer) and Natalie (Zhgenty) Massevitch (a nurse); graduated from the University of Moscow with a degree in physics, 1940; candidate's degree (the equivalent of a Ph.D.) from the Sternberg State Astronomy Institute in Moscow, 1946; married Joseph Friedlander (a metallurgical engineer), in 1941; children: one daughter, Natalie Friedlander.

Pursuing an interest in science that began at 13, Alla Massevitch entered the University of Moscow in 1937, intent on a career in space science and astronomy. After she earned her degree in 1941, her postgraduate studies were interrupted by the war and her marriage to a young engineer nine days after their meeting in an air raid shelter. She left the university and joined her husband in Kuibyshev (now Samara, Russia), where she worked with him at the Institute of Physics and taught astronomy at the Kuibyshev teachers' college. In 1943, when the military threat to Moscow ended, she returned to the capital and continued her studies at the Sternberg State Astronomy Institute. After completing the equivalent of a Ph.D. in 1946, she remained at Sternberg to pursue her research into the structure and internal energy sources of giant red stars, and to begin one of the first nonstatic approaches to the evolution of the sun. In 1946, she became a lecturer in astrophysics at the University of Moscow and in 1952 was named vice president of the Astronomical Council of the Academy of Sciences.

In 1957, the Astronomical Council was assigned the task of tracking space vehicles. With no precedent to guide her, Massevitch trained the leaders for a network of 70 tracking stations throughout the USSR and had them in place by October 4, 1957, when *Sputnik I* was launched. Her ongoing duties also included investigating new tracking methods and publishing the vast amount of data collected by the tracking stations. Known for her charming personality and inexhaustible energy, she also became a spokeswoman for Soviet science abroad, making trips to almost every European country and the United States. A strong advocate of international cooperation, she served as chair of the tracking group of the International Committee on Space Research and in 1962 became vice president of the IAU's Commission N44 on extraterrestrial astronomy. Massevitch was elected a foreign member of Britain's Royal Astronomical Society in 1963. In her own country, she was vice president of the Institute for Soviet-American Relations. During her career, she authored two books on stellar evolution and published over 60 papers, mainly in the *Astronomical Journal of the U.S.S.R.*

In an article for *This Week* (September 2, 1962), Massevitch spoke to Eric Bergaust about Russia's seemingly enlightened attitude about women in space, especially when compared to that of the United States. "In a sense," she said, "women represent one of Russia's secret resources as far as the space program is concerned. . . . I think women can do better jobs than men in many areas of the space field." On June 16, 1963, *Valentina Tereshkova became the first woman in history to be launched into orbit around the earth.

SOURCES:
Current Biography. NY: H.W. Wilson, 1964.

Barbara Morgan,
Melrose, Massachusetts

Massey, Ilona (1910–1974)

Hungarian-born American actress. Name variations: Ilona Hajmassy. Born in Budapest, Hungary, on June 16, 1910 (some sources cite 1912); died in Bethesda, Maryland, on August 20, 1974; married Alan Curtis (an actor), in 1941 (divorced 1942); married Charles Walker (a jeweler); married Donald S. Dawson (an air force general); married one other time; became a U.S. citizen in 1946.

Selected filmography: Knox aus die lustigen Vagabonden *(1935);* Der Himmel auf Erden *(1935);* Rosalie *(1937);* Balalaika *(1939);* International Lady *(1941);* New Wine *(1941);* Invisible Agent *(1942);* Frankenstein Meets the Wolf Man *(1943);* Holiday in Mexico *(1946);* The Gentleman Misbehaves *(1946);* Northwest Outpost *(1947);* The Plunderers *(1948);* Love Happy *(1950);* Jet Over the Atlantic *(1959).*

A native of Budapest, Ilona Massey began her career in the music halls of Vienna under her real name, Ilona Hajmassy, probably in the early 1930s. She made two films in Austria, *Knox aus* *die lustigen Vagabonden* and *Der Himmel auf Erden,* both released in 1935, and was discovered by an overseas scout employed by the American film studio Metro-Goldwyn-Mayer. She signed a contract and was brought to Hollywood, where she changed her surname to Massey. During this era, MGM was enjoying box-office success with the Nelson Eddy-*Jeanette MacDonald musicals, but the saccharine on-screen romance of the famous couple was rumored to be equaled by a real-life hostility towards one another, and MGM executives liked to keep a "back-up" star ready in case things disintegrated on the studio lot. In possession of an excellent singing voice and a credible presence in outlandish period costumes, Massey for a time waited in the wings as that back-up star before teaming up with Eddy in the 1937 picture *Rosalie.* They also made *Balalaika,* released in 1939, but neither film achieved commercial success, in part because of the public's shock at seeing Eddy crooning love songs to an interloper; some had thought that Eddy and MacDonald were actually married in real life.

Ilona Massey

Massey starred in some of the international espionage tales that were a staple of the World War II years, including *International Lady* (1941) and *Invisible Agent* (1942). In 1943, she made a Frankenstein movie, *Frankenstein Meets the Wolf Man,* with Bela Lugosi and Lon Chaney, Jr., and also appeared on Broadway opposite Arthur Treacher and Milton Berle in *Ziegfeld Follies.* Massey teamed once more with Nelson Eddy in *Northwest Outpost* (1947), and made a 1950 film with the Marx Brothers, *Love Happy.*

After the war, Massey obtained entry visas for some of her family members, and because of what she learned from them and other emigrés became intensely involved in anti-Communist political circles in Southern California. She even testified before a U.S. House Committee on Eastern Europe about the treatment of Hungarians by Soviet forces in the wake of World War II, when the Communist power was an occupying force there. She picketed Soviet premier Nikita Khrushchev on his 1959 visit to the U.S., and had her picture in the newspapers at one demonstration next to a sign proclaiming him "The Butcher of Bucharest."

Massey was married four times, the fourth to an American military officer, General Donald Dawson. After making her last film, *Jet Over the Atlantic,* in 1959, she retired to the Maryland area with her husband and remained active in the Hungarian expatriate community. She died in 1974.

SOURCES:

Katz, Ephraim. *The Film Encyclopedia.* New York, NY: HarperPerennial, 1994.

Lamparski, Richard. *Whatever Became of . . . ?* 2nd series. New York, NY: Crown, 1968.

Carol Brennan,
Grosse Pointe, Michigan

Massimi, Petronilla Paolini

(1663–1726)

Early 18th-century Italian poet and writer, an admired member of the Arcadian Academy, whose work is noted for its sharp defense of women and anticipation of gender theory. Name variations: *Fidalma Partenide (as member of the Arcadia Academy). Pronunciation: Pet-ro-KNEE-la Pay-o-LEE-nee Mah-SEE-mee; Fee-DAHL-ma Pahr-tuh-NEE-dee. Born Petronilla Paolini in Tagliacozzo, Abruzzo, in 1663; died in 1726; daughter of the Baron Francesco Paolini (owner of Marsica) and Silvia Argoli (a noblewoman); married, at age ten, the Marquis Francesco Massimi; after the death of one of her sons, entered the Convent of the Holy Spirit, and began the writing that led to her acceptance into the Arcadian Academy.*

Selected works: Non disdire alla Donna gli esercizi letterari e cavallereschi *(no date);* Oratorio per la morte del Redentore *(Vienna, 1697);* La corona poetica rinterzata in lode di Clemente XI *(Rome, 1701);* Canzoni epitalamiche *(Siena, 1704);* Le Muse in gala *(Perugia, 1704);* I giuochi olimpici *(Rome, 1705);* "Note sul Simposio di Platone," *in* Prose delgi Arcadi *(Tome III).*

A decade after the death of Petronilla Paolini Massimi, Monsignor Pietrantonio Corsignani set down a few details of her sad life in a biographical note tinged with affection and regret, relating much of what is known about the noblewoman who was:

> the only survivor of her father, and rich of means, married in Rome the Marquis Francesco Massimi, Roman patrician, then Lord of St. Angel Castle, and relative of the Pope Clemente X, in the time when she was being educated in the Convent of the Holy Spirit. She was a lady of great knowledge and deep sufferance; with which she bore many passions and restlessnesses of soul; and she had indeed a very high spirit and intellect; so that she spoke of Literature, Philosophy, and other Sciences with so much frankness and solid learning, that she excited admiration in any man of letters who listened to her. She was held in great esteem by the virtuous men and, among the members of the Arcadian Academy, she had a high position under the name of Fidalma Partenide: she was a famous poet and composed Italian verses of good savour.

In the lifetime of this "lady of great knowledge and deep sufferance," Monsignor Corsignani was her most discerning literary critic, and at her death he was author of the epigraph inscribed on her grave at the church of the Teresian nuns at St. Egidio, in Trastevere. A second contemporary, G.M. Crescimbini, has provided a few other biographical details, so that we know the young Petronilla was orphaned, while still a small child, by the murder of her father, Baron Francesco Paolini, in an ambush. His wife was a noblewoman, **Silvia Argoli**, who fled with their daughter to Rome, where the two took refuge at the court of Pope Clement X. The murder of the baron remained unpunished, however, and under the little girl made "rich of means" by her father's death became a pawn in the political alliances of the papal court. She received an excellent education during the time she spent at the boarding school of the Convent of the Holy Spirit, but at the age of ten Petronilla was removed from the convent and married to a nephew of Clement, Francesco Massimi, a rough, callous soldier with the title of marquis.

Confined to what she called the "closed horror" of her husband's St. Angel Castle, she endured her marriage to a taciturn and possessive man who aroused in her no feelings except a dutiful respect for the sacrament binding them together, and perhaps a pity for his meanness, which she bore with patience and detachment. The number of children she had is not known, but it was the death of one of her sons that effectively ended the marriage. She was then allowed to return to the Convent of the Holy Spirit, where she wrote the works for which she is known.

Lyrical, lucid, and at times pitilessly analytical, the poetry of Petronilla Paolini Massimi was written according to the strict rules of classicism that prevailed in the Arcadian poetry of the time, with its roots in the works of the Latins and Greeks. Her style left no room for the kind of sorrowful self-indulgence that might be expected in one who had endured her life. The pain of past experience never led to passivity, but to reaffirmations of strength, and to vigorously high ethics. For this attitude of ripening boldness and will, she was dubbed the "leopardian Arcadian" by Thovez. The steadiness and strength of Massimi are implicitly affirmed in the name she was given at birth, Petronilla, meaning "little stone." The name with which she presented herself before the Arcadian Academy, Fidalma Partenide, carries a more subtle yet eloquent metaphor of her poetical work, with its expression of purity of feeling, faith to moral principles, and indomitable will.

In one extended lyric, addressed to a friend, Massimi encourages him to face the difficulties of a bleak existence by reviewing the circumstance of her own life—the childhood marked by her father's murder, the greed of relatives and isolation endured by her and her mother, the girlhood denied her by the forced marriage—all tinged with incomprehension and coercion, and the feel of a long, dark confinement. Even the haven of the cloister in maturity is seen as merely a truce: she is far from her sons, whom she sees as stolen away from her custody by the dry partiality of the law and their father's despotical will, and mourning, with a sense of guilt, the death of one son, until the poet comes finally to desire her own death—to invoke it, even, in order to recover that nearness to the lost son, at least in heaven. But as the work continues, the poet flees indignantly from the temptation to commit suicide, finding an inner coherence in the divine commandment not to kill and in that categorical imperative which represents, for her, an exquisite human ethic. When the laws of men fail in their support of her, she takes comfort in the divine justice of *Mary the Virgin, the "high queen" of heaven, who lightens her sorrow through mercy.

Abstracting and extrapolating on the vicissitudes of her highly privileged but unhappy experience, Massimi arrived at a more general, even universal, description of the feminine condition. To modern-day feminist scholars, her works are remarkable for their conscious expression of a gender-oriented point of view; a pattern of thought that is neither neuter, nor oriented toward ratification by the unequivocally male culture of her time, but containing original reflections and feelings of what she has experienced, analyzed, lived and suffered on her own. The originality of her work lies in Massimi's setting herself as a critical conscience, a feminine voice speaking on behalf of her gender about suffering that otherwise went unexpressed.

The symbolic universe of the work is drawn from the literary tradition of Greco-Latin mythology. Although elements are traceable to classics from Ovid and Virgil to Dante and Petrarch, her message is nonetheless an expression of a feminine culture, a creative synthesis of experience oriented and determined by her own sex. Some of the striking originality of her work lies in the attributes of character she allots women.

In the case of her own mother, who seems to have been a woman dominated by the male world, their relationship is outlined in a few quick traits; she is hardly mentioned except for a gleam of piety and nostalgia suggesting denied affections. In contrast to this is the strength of the poet's declared bond with Mary, mother of Jesus and, in the Christian tradition, the redeemer of the feminine gender from Eve's guilt.

Piety itself, as represented by the poet's Mary, ripens beyond the conventions of her day: emerging out of the standard mildness, servitude and passivity in the poetical text are the stronger and more dynamic feelings of indignation, insistence on justice, and untamable pride. In the poems, even piety becomes "blazing," mindful of the Dantesque "upright zeal," giving the measure of a faith strengthened by a striving for justice through vindication of one's rights. Even the convent is not typically characterized for the isolation it offers from the world, but for the chance it offers to restore dignity, and to recover the pattern of life holding qualities of sacredness, dignity, and mutual respect.

Corsignani, who is a precise and reliable biographer on most grounds, misunderstands his subject when it comes to the convent. "God is then wise about new virtuous progresses," he writes in his account of the marquise's return there; "with the narrowness of the place she began to detach her heart from the womanly cares; and with learned application she devoted herself to overcome the heavy pains with the help of the letters." While granting that this noblewoman has good reasons for neglecting the accepted duties of her sex, he wants her isolation in the nunnery to be a beneficial retreat but implies that a devotion to intellectual pursuits is otherwise inadmissible, even inconceivable, for a woman. Massimi, on the contrary, declares, "Do not deny the Lady literary exercises," and explicitly and irrefutably views the convent as her place for restoring the intellectual and moral dignity of women, for seeking the dimension of life marked by respect, affection, and mutual care that had been shared by generations of cloistered women.

For the poet, the cloistered room offers the opportunity for real, practiced and deeply lived experience, in contrast to the secular world of relationships with men and the power they express and represent. The desirability of this setting may be seen partly in the fact that, as a woman of title and means, she could have left the convent for an independent life after her husband's death, but chose to remain within its walls. Massimi's work never demonstrates a biased hostility against men, however. On the contrary, it shows a serenity, and a suspension of judgment, couched in the lost and forever regretted affections toward her father and dead son, allowing her to imagine the best of all possible worlds existing in the celestial spheres, if not here on earth.

In Massimi's second Petrarchan canzone, or pastoral lyric, beginning "When from the dark urns," such themes are deepened. In search of the reasons which stir her woman's soul, she becomes more subtle and acute in her introspective analysis. The bitter vicissitudes of her life keep her deprived of rest, and in the silence of the night she returns to "sorrowful thought" and ponders the misery of her condition. Painful as the experience is, her spirit rises, indomitable, "with virtue armed" and tears kept back, still aimed at the arduous task of turning the weariness of living into lyric. The poem is her instrument of analysis, denouncement and condemnation.

In terms that are almost plain, she points at the "high cause" of her woes and proclaims her strategy. Stirred by the furor of the poet, Massimi will avenge the wrongs suffered by her gender. To poetry she commits the redemption from the misery not only of herself but of the entire "unwarlike sex, "with virtue and the firmness of her soul as her weapon and shield. She invokes Pallas, goddess of wisdom, as her protector, while sacralizing the classical daughter of Jupiter as Christian; the Pallas she describes in quick and effective traits is not borne from the forehead of a heathen god, but conceived in the mind of God. A queen of chastity and of high intellectual virtue, she blends the features of the Olympian deity with the Christian Mary the Virgin.

This bridging interpretation of the poetical traditions of Pallas Athena (as renewed and strengthened by the Arcadian Academy) and the Madonna (more clearly invoked in Massimi's first Petrarchan canzone) is informed by the "soul and divine light" which illuminates the way for the poet. It is the light that allows the poet, as protagonist, to go on praising the sorrow that tests her and deprives her of the delights of love and the charms of society, and it is the light that enables the attainment of her moral aim which is, as she states in a declaration reminiscent of the Roman poet Horace, the poetical fame that will be an everlasting affirmation of women's strength of soul. In a passage pronouncing her act of faith, experience becomes the purifying fire which will allow her cathartic release:

Yes, yes, on this stone
thou grind the weapons and thousands
sparks of glory will burst,
and awaken the fire, where I wish
I could die, phoenix, and overcome oblivion.

SOURCES:

Corsignani, P. *De viris illustribus Marsorum.* Rome, 1712.

Crescimbeni, G.M. *Vite degli Arcadi illustri scritte da diversi autori.* Rome, 1708.

Croce, B. Fidalma. "Partenide ossia la Marchesa Petronilla Paolini Massimi," in *La Letteratura italiana del Settecento.* Bari: La terza, 1949.

SUGGESTED READING:

Corsignani, P. *About the Marsican Royal Palace or topographic-historic memories of various colonies of the Marsi and Valeria.* 2 vols. Naples, 1738.

Tozzi, Ileana. *Petronilla Paolini Massimi, una donna in Arcadia.* Pescara: Nova Italica, 1981.

COLLECTIONS:

Prose degli Arcadi.

Rime degli Arcadi. Vols. I, III, VII, IX.

Ileana Tozzi, D. Litt.,
secondary school teacher in Rieti, Italy, and member of Società
Italiana delle Storiche and Deputazione di Storia Patria

Mastenbroek, Rie (1919—)

Dutch swimmer. Name variations: Ria Mastenbroek or Mastenbroeck. Born Hendrika W. Mastenbroek in Rotterdam, the Netherlands, on February 26, 1919.

Won three gold medals in the Berlin Olympics, the 100-meter freestyle at 1:05.9, the 400-meter freestyle at 5:26.4, and the 4x100-meter freestyle relay, as well as a silver in the 100-meter backstroke (1936); inducted into the International Swimming Hall of Fame (1968).

Hendrika "Rie" Mastenbroek burst onto the international swimming scene at the 1936 Berlin Olympics. Until 1934, the year she won the European championship, she had competed only in regional contests. At the Berlin Olympics, the Dutch women swimmers were a powerhouse, winning four gold medals. (The U.S. team had lost the talent of *Eleanor Holm, who had won the 100 meters in 1932, when she was dismissed from the team for disciplinary reasons.) Mastenbroek won two of these gold medals individually in the 100- and 400-meter freestyle (beating out *Ragnhild Hveger), and a third as a member of the 4x100-meter freestyle relay team where her finishing sprint gave the Dutch the gold over Germany; her teammates

Rie Mastenbroek

Ouden, Willemijntje den. See Fraser, Dawn for sidebar.

were **Johanna Selbach**, **Catherina Wagner**, and **Willemijntje den Ouden**. Mastenbroek was only three-tenths of a second from winning a gold in the 100-meter backstroke, but in this event first place went to her teammate, **Dina Senff**. Mastenbroek held nine world records, six in backstroke and three in freestyle.

Karin Loewen Haag,
Athens, Georgia

Masters, Sybilla (d. 1720).

See Inventors.

Masters, Virginia (b. 1925).

See Johnson, Virginia E.

Mata Hari (1876–1971).

See Zelle, Margaretha.

Matantuck (d. 1676).

See Magnus.

Matayer, Odette (1912–1995).

See Sansom, Odette.

Matchless Orinda, the (1631–1664).

See Philips, Katharine.

Mateld or Matelda.

Variant of Matilda.

Materna, Amalie (1844–1918)

Austrian soprano. Born on July 19, 1844 (one source cites July 10, 1845), in St. Georgen, Austria; died on January 18, 1918, in Vienna, Austria; married K. Friedrich (an actor).

Amalie Materna was born in St. Georgen, in the Austrian province of Styria, on July 19, 1844. The daughter of a schoolmaster, Materna made her professional debut in a performance of Suppé's *Light Cavalry* in Graz, Austria, in 1864. Her star rose steadily, and by 1869 she was named prima donna of the Austrian court opera in Vienna, a title she would hold until 1896.

Materna was an early admirer of the work of German composer Richard Wagner. Wagner in turn declared her the only woman capable of singing Brünnhilde in his epic *The Ring of the Niebelung,* and selected her to perform the part in the opera's first complete performance in Bayreuth in 1876. Materna also performed the part of Kundry in the debut of Wagner's 1882 opera, *Parsifal.* She toured the United States in 1884–85, during which time she made her debut at New York's Metropolitan Opera, and again in 1894. After her retirement in 1900, Amalie Ma-

terna taught singing in Vienna, where she died on January 18, 1918.

Grant Eldridge,
freelance writer, Pontiac, Michigan

Mather, Margrethe (c. 1885–1952)

American photographer. Born around 1885, in or near Salt Lake City, Utah; died in 1952, in Glendale, California.

Margrethe Mather, who was born around 1885, lived in an orphanage until she was adopted by a mathematics professor and his common-law wife. She was unhappy with them, and as a teenager ran away to San Francisco, where for a time she earned a living through prostitution. Around 1911, Mather began an affair with a wealthy woman identified as "Beau" who guided her cultural education. Exactly when she began to study photography is not known, but it was probably sometime before 1912, when she met noted photographer Edward Weston. They established an "essentially platonic" working and personal relationship that would last for nearly two decades, sharing a highly respected studio in Glendale, near Los Angeles. Producing portraits and other images as well as working with interior decorators, Mather was included in several photography exhibits in the late 1910s and early 1920s, and eventually took over the Glendale Studio.

Her photographs, which often featured isolated parts of the human body, exhibited a sense of artistry which is believed to have influenced Weston's work both during and after their collaboration. She was published in *Camera Craft, Pictorial Photography in America,* and *American Photography* magazines, and with her friend William Justema organized a 1931 exhibit, "Patterns by Photography," at San Francisco's M.H. de Young Memorial Museum. Despite her popularity and critical success, by the early 1930s Mather all but abandoned photography. Although she continued to take occasional photographic portraits of her friends, she spent most of the last two decades of her life working in retail stores. She died of multiple sclerosis in 1952.

SOURCES:

Rosenblum, Naomi. *A History of Women Photographers.* New York and London: Abbeville Press, 1994.
———. *A World History of Photography.* Paris and London: Abbeville Press, 1984.

Grant Eldridge,
freelance writer, Pontiac, Michigan

Mather, Winifred Holt (1870–1945).

See Holt, Winifred.

Mathers, Helen (1853–1920)

English novelist. Name variations: Helen Buckingham Mathers; Helen Reeves; Mrs. Henry Reeves; (pseudonym) David Lyall. Born at Crewkerne, Somerset, England, on August 26, 1853; died in London, England, on March 11, 1920; daughter of Thomas Mathers (a country gentleman) and Maria Buckingham Mathers; educated at Chantry School; married Henry Albert Reeves (an orthopedic surgeon), in 1876 (died 1914); children: one son, Phil.

Selected writings: Comin' Thro' the Rye (1875); Cherry Ripe! (1877); Land o' the Leal (1878); As He Comes up the Stair (1878); My Lady Greensleeves (1879); Jock o' Hazeldean (1884); Murder or Manslaughter (1885); The Fashion of this World (1886).

Born in Somerset, England, in 1853, Helen Mathers was raised at her parents' country home, where she and her 11 siblings had much vigorous physical activity to complement their strict schedule of home schooling. Her father was a tyrant over his children, and according to Mathers treated his daughters as "his white slaves." Of the character based on her father in her novel *Comin' Thro' the Rye*, she noted: "If he had his way he would keep all his daughters withering forever on their virgin stalks, and when they were miserable, peaky old maids turn round upon them, and twit them with their incapacity to get a man to marry . . . them." Mathers decided by the age of eight that she wanted to be a novelist, and often read her stories and poems to her family. She spent hours in her room writing on pieces of paper; when she had a large collection of pieces, she sorted them out and fashioned them into a narrative sequence, a practice she would follow well into her adult life. At 13, she went away to the Chantry School, where her ability landed her in a class with students who were much older. She worked so hard at her studies that she had a physical breakdown, causing partial deafness which was to last her entire life.

When she was 16, Mathers sent a poem to Dante Gabriel Rossetti, who encouraged her to keep writing. Her first story was published in 1872 in the illustrated monthly magazine *Belgravia* (later edited by *Mary Elizabeth Braddon, whose novels were popular with the same audience as Mathers' own). Her autobiographical first novel, *Comin' Thro' the Rye*, was published three years later. Mathers had written the book secretly, and after it was published anonymously she lived in fear that someone would tell her father how she had portrayed him; the novel describes a house similar to the one she had grown up in, a dominating and sadistic father, a kind and exhausted mother, and the passage from adolescence to maturity within this household of Nell, one of twelve children. A great success, *Comin' Thro' the Rye* sold over 35,000 copies, a huge number in those days, and was translated into many languages, including Sanskrit.

In 1876, Mathers married Henry Albert Reeves, later a prominent orthopedic surgeon, with whom she had one son. Although she was considered a "sensation" novelist in the style of *Rhoda Broughton, meaning that her work often broached topics that polite society considered risqué, *British Authors of the Nineteenth Century* opines bluntly: "Her life was completely uneventful." Mathers continued to write popular novels until nearly the end of her life, and died in London on March 11, 1920.

SOURCES:
Black, Helen C. *Notable Women Authors of the Day.* Freeport, NY: Books for Libraries Press.

Kunitz, Stanley J., ed. *British Authors of the Nineteenth Century.* NY: H.W. Wilson, 1936.

Shattock, Joanne. *The Oxford Guide to British Women Writers.* Oxford and NY: Oxford University Press, 1993.

Patrick Moore,
Associate Professor of English,
University of Arkansas at Little Rock, Little Rock, Arkansas

Mathews, Ann Teresa (1732–1800)

Co-founder of the first Roman Catholic women's religious order in the United States. Name variations: Sister Bernardina Teresa Xavier of St. Joseph; Mother Bernardina. Born Ann Teresa Mathews in 1732, in Charles County, Maryland; died on June 12, 1800, in Port Tobacco, Maryland; daughter of Joseph Mathews (a farmer) and Susannah (Craycroft) Mathews; never married; no children.

Ann Teresa Mathews was better known as Mother Bernardina, head of the first Roman Catholic religious order for women in the United States. Mathews was born in Charles County, Maryland, in 1732, into a devout Catholic family that was left in hardship after the death of her father two years later. Although the state originally had been founded as a haven for Catholics, prior to the American Revolution there were many strictures placed upon its Catholic citizens; public worship was banned, as were seminaries, convents, and other training institutions. At the age of 22, Mathews decided that she had a religious calling, and so journeyed to Hoogstraeten, Belgium, in order to enter a convent. She joined the English order of the Discalced (Barefoot) Carmelites, a contemplative order that neither taught nor tended to the sick, as most religious orders for women did. She took her vows in November 1755, becoming Bernardina Teresa Xavier of St. Joseph.

Mathews was elected prioress of her order in 1774. After the end of the American Revolution in 1783 and the lifting of restrictions on Catholic worship in Maryland, she began to consider founding an order in the new United States. (There was an Ursuline convent in New Orleans, but the city would remain under French rule until 1803.) Planning, the raising of money, and securing the legal rights for her goal took a number of years. In April 1790, Mathews sailed for America with **Frances Dickinson** (Sister Clare Joseph), two of her nieces who had joined the Discalced Carmelites, and Father Charles Neale, a priest who was a distant relative. Both he and her brother Ignatius, a Jesuit priest, had encouraged Mathews in her plan. In July 1790, Mathews and Dickinson founded the first convent in the United States at Chandler's Cove, Maryland. They moved not long afterward to land provided by a supportive Catholic landowner, and established the Port Tobacco convent on October 15, 1790. Mathews was its first prioress, and within a decade it was home to 14 other sisters. The bishop of their diocese was interested in having them teach, and received a papal dispensation in 1793 that would have permitted them to do so, but Mathews and the other nuns argued successfully to maintain their contemplative routine. They did, however, raise their own sheep and spin the wool for use in sewing their habits. Mathews died of cancer in 1800, and was later interred in Bonnie Brae Cemetery in the city of Baltimore, where the Carmelite order had relocated in 1831.

SOURCES:

James, Edward T., ed. *Notable American Women 1607–1950: A Biographical Dictionary.* Vol. 2. Cambridge, MA: Belknap Press of Harvard University Press, 1971.

McHenry, Robert, ed. *Famous American Women: A Biographical Dictionary from Colonial Times to the Present.* New York, NY: Dover, 1980.

Read, Phyllis J., and Bernard L. Witlieb. *The Book of Women's Firsts.* NY: Random House, 1992.

Carol Brennan,
Grosse Pointe, Michigan

Mathews, Lucia Elizabeth (1797–1856).

See Vestris, Lucia.

Mathews, Vera Laughton

(1888–1959)

British military officer who served as director of the British Women's Royal Naval Service (WRNS) during

World War II. Name variations: Vera Laughton. Born Vera Elvira Sibyl Maria Laughton in London, England, on September 25, 1888; died in London on September 25, 1959; daughter of Sir John Knox Laughton and Maria Josefa di Alberti Laughton; attended the Convent of St. Andrew at Streatham and was also educated in Tournai, Belgium; attended King's College, London; married Gordon Dewar Mathews, in 1924; children: one daughter; two sons.

Served in WRNS (1917–19) and was recalled as its director on the eve of World War II; created a Commander of the British Empire (CBE, 1942); created a Dame of the British Empire (DBE, 1945); retired from WRNS (1946).

Vera Laughton Mathews, the future director of the British Women's Royal Naval Service (WRNS), was born in 1888, the daughter of Sir John Knox Laughton, R.N., a highly respected naval historian, and **Maria di Alberti Laughton**, who was from Cadiz, Spain. Vera received an excellent education, first at the Convent of St. Andrew at Streatham, then in Tournai, Belgium, and finally at King's College, London. In 1917, determined to make a contribution to the war effort, she volunteered for service on the same day that the WRNS was created. Selected for the first officers' training course, she was placed in charge of a training depot at London's Crystal Palace, "H.M.S. Victory VI." Here her leadership talents came to the fore, and within six months Mathews had reached the rank of lieutenant commander and was in charge of a unit of 250 women. After the war, she was awarded an MBE for her achievements.

With victory, the WRNS was demobilized in 1919. Retaining close ties to her wartime colleagues and friends, Mathews was instrumental in forming an Old Comrades Association and served as editor of the organization's journal, *The Wren*, for many years. She also worked as a journalist, writing primarily for *The Ladies' Field* and *Time and Tide*. In her free time, Vera was active in the Girl Guide movement and helped to organize the London section of its newly formed Sea Ranger branch. After her 1924 marriage to the engineer Gordon Dewar Mathews, with whom she had two sons and a daughter, she lived for a number of years in Japan. While there, she remained active in the Girl Guide movement, serving as the organization's international commissioner for Japan. Following her return to London, Mathews served for almost a decade as Girl Guide division commissioner for one of the city's poorest areas.

Deciding that war was imminent, in early 1939 the British Admiralty made plans to revive a women's auxiliary service within the Royal Navy. In February of that year, Mathews was appointed director of the skeleton organization that would soon be the WRNS. By the time war with Germany was declared on September 3, 1939, considerable progress had already been made to create the new organization. Displaying immense confidence in the WRNS, Mathews declared: "Whatever the Navy demands of the Wrens shall be fulfilled." With few exceptions, this pledge would be kept, thanks to her efforts, abilities, and insistence that, both for and by the WRNS, only the best was good enough.

Mathews gained the affection of WRNS officers and enlisted women alike, at least in part because her remarkable memory enabled her to recognize every one of her officers at sight. Good judgment helped her more often than not to pick the best people for the jobs at hand, and she charmed the great majority of her officers into performing above and beyond the required limits of their responsibilities. A large woman physically, Mathews had a deep musical voice and cheerful laugh which reflected an essentially kindly, generous nature. Such traits allowed her to win over virtual strangers. She also relied on human psychology, once commenting, "It's difficult to recruit stewards to clean rooms, but put them in dungarees to swab a deck, call them 'Maintenance' and there's a queue."

In 1942, when the outcome of the world conflict was by no means certain, Mathews was honored by being appointed CBE, a Commander of the British Empire. For her work in connection with staff training for MARVA (the Free Dutch equivalent of the WRNS), she would receive the Cross of Orange Nassau from the Dutch Government-in-Exile. Mathews was unique among the directors of Britain's three women's services during World War II because she remained in her post from the very start to the end of the conflict. In 1945, she was created a Dame of the British Empire. In November 1946, having received the welcome news that the WRNS would continue as a permanent service, Dame Vera retired from her post. Over 100,000 women had served under her leadership as Wrens during the war.

After her retirement, Mathews continued to be active in various organizations, including the Gas Council, the Domestic Coal Consumers' Council (which she chaired), and the South Eastern Gas Board. Particularly concerned about the deterioration of the urban environment, she served for a number of years as president of the Smoke Abatement Society. Dame Vera Mathews died in London on her 71st birthday, September 25, 1959. Her life and accomplishments have been memorialized in an alcove in the north aisle of Westminster Cathedral in which St. Christopher is seen holding a boat with a wren perched on an anchor. A portrait of Mathews is displayed at London's Imperial War Museum, and a copy of the portrait also hangs in a place of honor at the WRNS establishment at Burghfield, Reading.

SOURCES:
"Dame Vera Laughton Mathews, D.B.E.," in *The Times* [London]. September 28, 1959.

Hartley, Jenny, ed. *Hearts Undefeated: Women's Writing of the Second World War.* London: Virago Press, 1995.

Mathews, Vera Laughton. *Blue Tapestry.* London: Hollis & Carter, 1948.

Palmer, J.M. "Mathews, Dame Vera (Elvira Sibyl Maria) Laughton (1888–1959)," in E.T. Williams and Helen M. Palmer, eds., *The Dictionary of National Biography, 1951–1960.* Oxford: Oxford University Press, 1971, pp. 716–717.

John Haag,
Associate Professor of History,
University of Georgia, Athens, Georgia

Mathieu, Simone (1908–1980)

French tennis champion. Born Simone Passemard in 1908; died in 1980; married name was Mathieu.

Won the French junior championship (1926); won French mixed doubles with Damien Mitic (1927) and Yvon Petra (1938); won Wimbledon doubles with *Elizabeth Ryan (1933, 1934) and with Billie Yorke of England (1937); won the French doubles championship with Elizabeth Ryan (1933, 1934), with Billie Yorke (1936, 1938), and with Jadwiga Jedrejowska of Poland (1939); runner-up for the French singles title (1929, 1932, 1933, 1935, 1936, 1937); runner-up in the U.S. doubles with Jedrejowska (1938).

One of the few married women to win the French junior title at age 18, Simone Mathieu inherited the French tennis crown from *Suzanne Lenglen, and was France's stellar player before World War II. In women's doubles, she was a six-time French champion. In women's singles, she was a five-time runner-up, including three losses to *Hilde Sperling, before finally taking the French singles title at age 30 in 1938 (she would win again in 1939). Known as a baseliner with a formidable temper, Mathieu also made the semifinals at Wimbledon six times. She once whacked a ball so hard in frustration that she nearly hit Queen *Mary of Teck in the Royal Box. Mathieu would later use her energy and rebelliousness working with the French Resistance during World War II, creating a women's auxiliary group.

Mathilda.

Variant of Matilda.

Mathilda (1925–1997)

Duchess of Argyll. Name variations: Mathilda Campbell; Mathilda Heller; Mathilda Mortimer. Born Mathilda Costner Mortimer in Geneva, Switzerland, on August 20, 1925; died in Paris, France, on June 6, 1997; daughter of Stanley Mortimer of Litchfield, Connecticut; married Clemens Heller (divorced 1961); married Ian Douglas Campbell (1903–1973), 11th duke of Argyll, on June 15, 1963 (died 1973).

Of American parentage but raised in France by her grandparents, Mathilda Mortimer wed the 11th duke of Argyll in 1963, following his notorious split with wife number three, *Margaret (d. 1993). The couple gave lavish parties at Inveraray Castle, their home in the Scottish county of Argyllshire.

Mathilde.

Variant of Matilda.

Mathilde (1820–1904)

*Princess of Westphalia. Name variations: Mathilde Bonaparte. Born Mathilde Laetitia Wilhelmine Bonaparte on May 27, 1820; died in 1904; daughter of Jerome Bonaparte (1784–1860), king of Westphalia (youngest brother of Napoleon), and *Catherine of Wurttemberg (1783–1835); sister of Prince Napoleon (Plon-Plon) and niece of Napoleon I, emperor of France; married Count Demidoff, a Russian count (separated 1845).*

Princess Mathilde was extremely influential during the Second Empire because of her close friendship with her cousin Napoleon III. (She was one of the many who opposed his marriage to Empress *Eugénie.) Mathilde held a salon at her country house in Saint-Gratien as well as in Paris which was frequented by writers and artists, including Flaubert, Gautier, Edmond de Goncourt, and Sainte-Beuve.

Mathilde de Mayenne

Duchess of Burgundy. Died after 1162; married Hugh II (b. 1085), duke of Burgundy (r. 1102–1143), around 1115; children: Clemence of Burgundy (b. 1117, who married Henri III de Donzy); Eudes II (b. 1118), duke of Burgundy; Gauthier, archbishop of Be- sancon (b. 1120); Hugh (b. 1121); Robert (b. 1122), bishop of Autun; Henri (b. 1124), bishop of Autun; Raymond (b. 1125); *Aigeline of Burgundy (d. 1163, who married Hugo I, count of Vaudemont); *Sibylle of Burgundy (1126–1150); Ducissa of Burgundy (b. 1128, who married Raymond de Grancey); Mathilde of Burgundy (b. 1130, who married William VII, lord of Montpellier); Aremburge of Burgundy (b. 1132), became a nun.*

Mathilde of Bavaria (1843–1925)

*Countess of Trani. Born on September 30, 1843; died on June 18, 1925; daughter of *Ludovica (1808–1892) and Maximilian Joseph (1808–1888), duke of Bavaria; married Louis of Sicily (1838–1886), count of Trani, on June 5, 1861; children: Maria Theresia (1867–1909, who married William, prince of Hohenzollern).*

Mathildis.

Variant of Matilda.

Mathis, June (1892–1927)

American actress, screenwriter, and scenarist. Born in Leadville, Colorado, in 1892; died in 1927 in Hollywood, California.

Selected filmography: The Legion of Death *(1918);* An Eye for an Eye *(1918);* To Hell with the Kaiser *(1918);* The Divorcee *(1919);* Satan Junior *(1919);* Polly with a Past *(1920);* Hearts Are Trumps *(1920);* The Willow Tree *(1920);* The Four Horsemen of the Apocalypse *(1921);* The Idle Rich *(1921);* The Conquering Power *(1921);* Camille *(1921);* The Sheik *(1921);* Hate *(1922);* Blood and Sand *(1922);* Turn to the Right *(1922);* Kisses *(1922);* Salome *(1922);* The Young Rajah *(1922);* The Spanish Dancer *(1923); (re-edited and rewrote)* Greed *(1923);* In the Palace of the King *(1923);* Three Wise Fools *(1923);* Sally *(1925);* We Moderns *(1925);* The Desert Flower *(1925);* Ben-Hur *(1926);* Irene *(1926);* The Greater Glory *(1926);* The Masked Woman *(1927);* The Magic Flame *(1927).*

June Mathis was born in Leadville, Colorado, in 1892. Following the death of her father in the mid-1910s, she played in vaudeville shows and appeared as an actress to support her family. Although she was a success on stage, she yearned to become a writer, and despite a total lack of experience began writing short stories which soon attracted the attention of studio owner Samuel Goldwyn. In 1918, Mathis was hired as a scenarist (someone who adapted theatrical and literary works for depiction in silent movies) at Goldwyn's Metro studios. The following year, she became head of the script department and began lobbying to adapt Vicente Blasco Ibáñez's 1916 novel *The Four Horsemen of the Apocalypse* for the screen. Many major Hollywood studios had considered filming this novel, which concerned the effects of World War I, but all had decided that it would be impossible. Mathis persisted in her efforts, however, and Metro bought the rights to the novel for $20,000 and began production. She also insisted that the picture star Rudolph Valentino, then an unknown actor, whom she had seen in only one film. Released in 1921, the film proved a resounding success, turning Valentino into a celebrity and securing Mathis a position among the top scenarists of the era.

Despite her professional success at Metro, Mathis came into conflict with management and in 1921 transferred to the Famous Players Studio (later Paramount). While at Famous Players, she adapted *The Sheik*, starring Valentino, and wrote the script for *Blood and Sand* (1922), the bullfight scenes of which were edited by ***Dorothy Arzner** and the movie that turned Valentino into a coast-to-coast sensation. Within a year, Mathis moved once again, this time to head the story division of the Goldwyn Studio. Shortly after, Metro and Goldwyn merged to form Metro-Goldwyn-Mayer; despite her past difficulties with Metro, Mathis played a critical role in the merger.

One of her first projects at the new studio was collaborating with the legendary ***Alla Nazimova** to create the screen version of *Salome*, which was released in 1922. (They had earlier worked together on *Camille*, based on the story of ***Alphonsine Plessis**, and other projects.) Mathis was then assigned to rewrite, re-edit, and reduce director Eric von Stroheim's epic film *Greed* from 24 reels to 10, a task which was completed in 1923. By 1925, Mathis had become so indispensable to Metro-Goldwyn-Mayer that Samuel Goldwyn insured her life for $1,000,000, and she was assigned to write the script and scenarios for the studio's new epic, *Ben-Hur*. Her adaptation of the novel proved so successful that the film is universally viewed as a classic of the silent screen. Mathis went on to write scripts and scenes for four more movies before her unexpected death in 1927. Although her career was brief, June Mathis occupies a leading role in American film history through her work on some of the most highly regarded films of the silent era.

SOURCES:

Acker, Ally. *Reel Women: Pioneers of the Cinema 1896 to the Present.* NY: Continuum, 1991.

Francke, Lizzie. *Script Girls: Women Screenwriters in Hollywood.* London: BFI Publishing, 1994.

Katz, Ephraim. *The Film Encyclopedia.* NY: Harper-Perennial, 1994.

Grant Eldridge,
freelance writer, Pontiac, Michigan

Matidia I (d. 119 CE)

Roman noblewoman. Died in 119 CE; daughter of *Ulpia Marciana and C. Salonius Matidius Patruinus; niece of Trajan, the Roman emperor; married L. Vibius Sabinus; children: Sabina (88–136 CE); *Matidia II.

Mother of the Empress ***Sabina**, Matidia I was present at the death of Trajan in 117 CE. When she died and was deified in 119 CE, Hadrian delivered her funeral oration.

Matidia II (fl. 110 CE)

Roman noblewoman. Flourished around 110 CE; daughter of *Matidia I (d. 119 CE) and L. Vibius Sabinus; sister of *Sabina (88–136 CE).

Matikainen, Marjo (c. 1966—)

Finnish Nordic skier. Born around 1966.

Marjo Matikainen collapsed at the finish line after winning the Olympic gold medal in the 5k Nordic skiing event at Calgary in 1988 with a time of 15:04.0. **Tamara Tikhonova** of Russia placed second; **Vida Vencienè** of Lithuania placed third. The following year, Matikainen retired from competitive skiing to study engineering. She was 23.

Matilda.

Variant of Mathilda, Mathilde, or Maud.

Matilda (fl. 680s)

Queen of Austrasia. Born an Anglo-Saxon princess and flourished in the 680s; married Saint Dagobert II, Merovingian king of Austrasia (r. 674–678); children: Saints *Adela (d. 735) and *Irmina (d. 716?); Clothaire or Lothair IV (c. 682–719), king of Neustria (r. 716–719).

Matilda (fl. 1100s)

Duchess of Brittany. Flourished in the 1100s; illegitimate daughter of Henry I (1068–1135), king of England (r. 1100–1135), and *Sybilla Corbett; sister of

*Sybilla, queen of Scots (d. 1122); married Conan III, duke of Brittany; children: Hoel Fergaunt, count of Nantes (d. 1158); *Bertha of Brittany (d. 1163).

Matilda (1046–1115).

See Matilda of Tuscany.

Matilda (d. 1252)

Countess of Winchester. Died in 1252; third wife of Roger de Quincy.

Matilda, countess of Winchester, was a patron of the arts. Matthew Paris, the chronicler and artist of St. Albans, was responsible for an illustrated psalter or Book of Hours for her.

Matilda (1813–1862)

Grand duchess of Hesse-Darmstadt. Born on August 30, 1813; died on May 25, 1862; daughter of Louis I Augustus also known as Ludwig I (1786–1868), king of Bavaria (r. 1825–1848, abdicated), and *Theresa of Saxony (1792–1854); married Louis III (1806–1877), grand duke of Hesse-Darmstadt, on December 26, 1833.

Christina (fl. 1086). See Margaret, St. for sidebar.

Matilda, Empress (1102–1167)

Daughter and heir of King Henry I of England, who waged a 15-year civil war to establish her right to rule the kingdom of England and the duchy of Normandy. Name variations: Aaliz, Aethelic, or Adela; Lady of England; Empress Maud, Mathilda or Matilda of England; Matilda Augustus of England; Mold. Born Matilda Alice on February 7, 1102, in Winchester, Hampshire, England; died at Rouen, duchy of Normandy, France, on September 10, 1167; daughter of Henry I (1068–1135), king of England (r. 1100–1135), and Queen Matilda of Scotland (1080–1118); married Henry V (1081–1125), Holy Roman emperor (r. 1106–1125), on January 7, 1114 (d. 1125); married Count Geoffrey of Anjou, on June 17, 1128; children: (second marriage) Henry II, king of England (r. 1154–1189, who married Eleanor of Aquitaine); Geoffrey de Gatinais (Geoffrey IV of Anjou), count of Nantes (r. 1134–1157); William de Gatinais, count of Poitou (r. 1136–1164).

Betrothed to Henry V, Holy Roman emperor (1109); widowed (1126); recognized as her father's heir (1126); allied with the house of Anjou through marriage to Geoffrey Plantagenet (1128); barons swore fealty to her a second time as her father's heir (1131); gave birth to future King Henry II of England (1133); fealty sworn to her a third time after birth of second son (1134); began struggle to secure holdings in Normandy after death of her father (1135); failed in appeal to Second Lateran Council to recognize her right to the English throne (1139); waged war against Stephen of Blois for English throne (1139–54); returned to Normandy, where she frequently acted as regent for her son (1148).

The exalted ancestry of the daughter born to King Henry I of England and Queen ✥▶ **Matilda of Scotland** assured that she would play a commanding role in the history of her time. Henry was the third son of William the Conqueror, who led the Normans in their takeover of England in 1066, while Matilda of Scotland was the daughter of King Malcolm III of Scotland and descended on her mother's side from Edmund Ironside, making their union a consolidation of the conquering dynasty with the Anglo-Saxon ruling house. In the political climate of the time that made heritage an important consideration in Henry's selection of a mate, it had also been virtually inevitable that the validity of the marriage would be questioned, since Matilda of Scotland had lived for a time at Romsey abbey, with her aunt ✥ **Christina.** The marriage had not received the blessing of Archbishop Anselm of Canterbury until a church council met, in 1100, to accept the word of Matilda of Scotland that she had never taken religious vows.

On February 7, 1102, the marriage produced a daughter, Matilda; the following year, her brother William was born and declared heir to the throne. Nothing is known of Matilda's early life or education, except that her mother was said to have kept a pious and learned court. In another political alliance through marriage, Matilda was betrothed, at age seven, to Holy Roman Emperor Henry V, who was then about 23. In February 1110, Matilda left England in an entourage destined for the court in Germany of her husband-to-be. According to one chronicler, the emperor sent her escort home at once in order to keep them from profiting from the position of their mistress, but it is more likely that he wanted to separate the child from English influences so that she would be quicker to learn the language and customs of her new homeland. On July 25, 1110, the young Matilda was crowned queen of the Romans at Mainz, then left in the care of Archbishop Bruno of Trier while her husband proceeded to Rome for his imperial coronation. In January 1114, before she turned 12, Matilda was formally married to Henry V.

From the time of her arrival in Germany, Matilda was firmly linked with her husband in the governing of his far-flung empire. Her name appears frequently in the records as both intercessor and co-sponsor of royal grants; she traveled with Henry to Italy to claim the lands he inherited from Countess *Matilda of Tuscany, and in 1117 she was crowned in St. Peter's Basilica by the Archbishop of Braga. When the emperor returned to Germany to deal with a rebellion, he left Matilda as regent of his newly acquired Italian lands, where she governed and often presided independently over courts of law. In 1119, she rejoined her husband in Lotharingia, and remained there as regent when Henry left to deal with another rebellion in Saxony.

On May 23, 1125, after entrusting the imperial insignia to his young wife on his deathbed, Emperor Henry V died of stomach cancer. If the empress had had a son, she might have remained in Germany as regent for the child, but as a childless widow at age 23, she lacked the power base to hold the throne. The insignia was turned over to the archbishop of Mainz for him to conduct the imperial election, and she returned to England in September 1126. Her departure was apparently regretted by the Germans, and chroniclers in later years reported that princes from Lorraine and Lombardy came to England to ask Matilda to be their sovereign.

In England, Matilda found her father's realm in the midst of a deepening succession crisis. Her brothers William and Richard had perished in a shipwreck in December 1120, leaving Henry I without an obvious heir and under pressure from his barons to recognize William Clito, the son of Robert II Curthose, his older brother and bitter enemy, to succeed him. At his Christmas court in 1126, King Henry instead took the unprecedented step of naming Matilda as his heir, and required that all his barons swear a solemn oath in support of his daughter's succession to the rule of the two great regions under his domain, the kingdom of England and the duchy of Normandy. According to contemporary chronicles, there was no immediate protest, and there even seems to have been a quarrel between Matilda's illegitimate half-brother Robert of Gloucester and her cousin Stephen of Blois, the son of William the Conqueror's daughter *Adela of Blois (1062–1137) and Stephen Henry, count of Blois, over who would be first to swear allegiance to the newly declared heir.

In May 1127, King Henry betrothed Matilda to Geoffrey Plantagenet, the son of Count Fulk of Anjou. The move was probably met with consternation by the Anglo-Norman barons, since the Angevins had always been ene-

> ⚜ **Matilda of Scotland** (1080–1118)
>
> *Queen of England. Name variations: Matilda Dunkeld; Mahalde; Edith Matilda of England, Maud; Good Queen Molde. Born Edith Matilda in 1080; died in Westminster, London, England, on May 1, 1118; buried in Westminster Abbey; daughter of Malcolm III, king of the Scots (r. 1057–1093), and *St. Margaret (c. 1046–1093); became first queen of Henry I (1068–1135), king of England (r. 1100–1135), on November 11, 1100 (his second wife was *Adelicia of Louvain, 1103–1151); children: Euphemia (b. 1101, died in infancy); Empress *Matilda (1102–1167); William Atheling (1103–1120), duke of Normandy; Richard (d. 1120).*

mies of the dukes of Normandy. For Henry, the issue at stake was more to secure his borders against a traditional enemy than to provide an acceptable future ruler; he may have hoped that his second wife, *Adelicia of Louvain, would produce a male heir. At the time of Matilda's marriage on June 17, 1128, Geoffrey was a youth of 16, ten years her junior, and neither found the match compatible. The following summer, Matilda returned to her father in Normandy, where she remained for two years. In September 1131, the barons swore fealty to her a second time as Henry's heir before she returned to her husband in Anjou.

In March 1133, Matilda gave birth to the couple's first son, the future Henry II of England. A second son, Geoffrey, was born the following spring, and Matilda was seriously ill after this birth. When she recovered, the barons swore a third oath in support of her right to the royal succession. Then a quarrel with Henry I ensued, after Matilda and Geoffrey demanded that the castles on the border between Normandy and Anjou be put under their rule. On December 1, 1135, the king suddenly died, still estranged from his daughter.

The couple moved quickly to secure their inheritance in Normandy. Matilda immediately went to take possession of the border castles that had been part of her dowry, at Exmes, Domfront, and Argentan, where the castles surrendered to her. Geoffrey was on his way to join her when he was forced to turn back because of a rebellion in Anjou. In September 1136, the Angevins besieged the castle at Le Sap, and Geoffrey was wounded. Matilda brought additional forces to his rescue, but the expedition eventually had to turn back, because of Geoffrey's wound and an outbreak of dysentery among the troops.

While Matilda and Geoffrey concentrated on securing their continental inheritance, Matilda's cousin Stephen of Blois rushed to take possession of the English throne. According to the contemporary document *Gesta Stephani,* Stephen of Blois was the ruler preferred by the English barons, who considered him the only one strong enough to put down the disorders that gripped the country after the death of King Henry. The archbishop of Canterbury, William of Corbeil, was at first unwilling to crown Stephen of Blois because of the oaths he and others had sworn to Matilda. Stephen of Blois and his supporters persuaded the prelate that the oath had been taken under duress, and that, on his deathbed, the king had repented exacting the oath. Stephen of Blois' coronation took place on December 22, 1135.

Never have I read of another woman so luckily rescued from so many mortal foes and from the threat of dangers so great.

—Gesta Stephani

In the first years of his reign, Stephen of Blois struggled to consolidate his power against rebellions in the West Country and Wales, as well as an invasion from the north by King David I of Scotland. By 1137, he had secured his English possessions enough to mount a military campaign against Matilda and Geoffrey in Normandy. His son Eustace did homage to King Louis VI of France for his support of their invasion of the duchy, but Stephen then abandoned the campaign in order to return to England to quell rebellious barons.

It may have been Stephen of Blois' ineffectual leadership that caused Robert of Gloucester to ally himself with Matilda after the failed invasion; certainly the alliance was an important one for the Angevins, giving them possession of two strategic castles on the mainland, at Bayeux and Caen. In 1139, Matilda also appealed to the Second Lateran Council for recognition of her right to the English throne. In the document known as *Historia Pontificalis,* John of Salisbury argued the points of King Stephen of Blois' case: Matilda was illegitimate because her mother had been a nun at Romsey abbey; the oath sworn in her support had been exacted under duress; the oath had been conditional and enforceable only in the event that Henry chose no other heir, and Henry had actually changed his mind and named Stephen of Blois on his deathbed. Matilda's representative was Bishop Ulger of Angers, who declared the charge of illegitimacy ridiculous since the marriage of her parents had been blessed by the saintly Archbishop Anselm of Canterbury; he also pointed out that Hugh Bigod, the man who had testified that Henry had made Stephen of Blois his heir, had not in fact been present at Henry's death. Settlement of the case was up to the pope, who declined to render a definite decision but demonstrated his preference by continuing to receive letters and gifts from Stephen of Blois and to recognize him as king.

In June 1139, King Stephen of Blois made a serious mistake by arresting three bishops, Roger of Salisbury, Alexander of Lincoln and Nigel of Ely, and forcing them to relinquish their castles. The powerful English Church, including even Stephen of Blois' own brother Henry, bishop of Winchester, was deeply alienated by the move. Matilda seized the opportunity to travel with Robert of Gloucester to England, where she was received by her stepmother, Adelicia of Louvain, at Arundel Castle. When Stephen of Blois laid siege to the castle, Adelicia persuaded him to grant Matilda safe passage to join Gloucester in Bristol.

The next two years were spent in a war comprised mainly of sieges, during which many English barons repeatedly switched their allegiance from one side to the other as self-interest dictated. In December 1140, Ranulf of Chester and William of Roumare sent their wives on a friendly visit to the wife of the castellan (governor) of Lincoln castle. At the end of the visit, Ranulf and William arrived with a small force to escort the women home, then suddenly produced weapons and subdued the castle guards. Stephen of Blois rushed to the scene, followed by Matilda and her forces, who routed the king's army and took him prisoner on February 2, 1141.

On March 3, Matilda was ceremoniously received at Winchester Cathedral by its bishop, Henry, the brother of and only remaining leader in Stephen of Blois' government, and the most powerful figure in the English Church. A church council under his leadership soon agreed to accept Matilda as queen, and she set off with her followers for London. Scholars disagree about what Matilda intended to happen there—most believe she meant to be crowned queen herself, but some think she planned to rule as regent for her son. Surviving charters describe her granting rewards and honors to her followers in documents in which she is referred to as "Lady of the English," a title she might have used either as regent or as an intermediate designation prior to her coronation. In any case, the ceremonies planned for London never occurred, because a violent uprising on June 24, 1141, forced Matilda to flee to Oxford. Sources are vague about

the causes of the rebellion, accusing the empress of haughtiness and excessive pride, of demanding money from the Londoners and of failing to follow the advice of her chief subjects, but it was probably instigated by Stephen of Blois' wife, *Matilda of Boulogne, who was popular with the Londoners and had kept her husband's cause alive since his imprisonment. On the eve of the rebellion, Matilda of Boulogne appeared just outside London with William of Ypres, the commander of Stephen of Blois' Flemish mercenaries, and a large body of troops, in a show of force that apparently inspired the expulsion of the former empress from London.

Faced with this setback, Henry of Winchester began to waver in his support of Empress Matilda. After she refused to grant possession of Stephen of Blois' ancestral lands to Stephen's son Eustace, the bishop left her court for Winchester, and in early August Matilda laid siege to Winchester. Stephen of Blois' forces, commanded by his queen and William of Ypres, laid siege to the besiegers; Matilda escaped, but Gloucester, her military commander and chief advisor, was cap-

tured. Faced with this disastrous loss, Matilda agreed to exchange the imprisoned King Stephen of Blois for her loyal half-brother, and the political situation was back to what it had been before the battle of Lincoln.

The exchange of prisoners took place on November 3, 1141, and Matilda's political fortunes subsequently went into decline. In December 1142, she was forced to escape from Oxford and walk through snow to Abingdon while camouflaged in a white cloak; according to *The Anglo-Saxon Chronicle,* she had been lowered from the castle tower by ropes. For six years she remained headquartered at the great castle at Devizes, controlled by Robert of Gloucester, in the heart of the West Country around Bristol. The domain allowed her some power to reward loyal followers and entice a few barons disenchanted with Stephen of Blois, but generally the two sides had reached a stalemate. In June 1148, Bishop Jocelyn of Salisbury obtained a papal mandate returning the castle at Devizes to him, on the grounds that it had been unlawfully taken from his predecessor in 1139, forcing Matilda to leave.

Returning to Normandy, Matilda settled at Rouen, which was under the strong control of her husband Geoffrey and their son Henry. After her success at Lincoln, Geoffrey had stepped up attacks on the barons with holdings in Normandy, many of whom had assumed Stephen of Blois' rule to be ended and tried to safeguard their possessions on that side of the Channel by surrendering to the count of Anjou. Since his capture of Rouen in January 1144, Geoffrey had been using the title duke of Normandy, and in 1151, a few months before his sudden death, Geoffrey turned rule of the duchy over to his son Henry.

The new duke spent two years subduing rebels against his claims to Normandy and Anjou. In 1153, he invaded England, where Stephen of Blois had apparently lost the will to fight following the recent death of his son Eustace. Stephen of Blois agreed to the Treaty of Winchester, which allowed him to remain king for his lifetime but named Matilda's son Henry as his heir. In 1154, Stephen of Blois died, and King Henry II succeeded peacefully to the English throne.

During the early years of her son's reign, Matilda lived in Normandy, usually at Rouen, where she interested herself in the affairs of the city and contributed money for the construction of a stone bridge called the "Pont Mathilde," which survived until the 16th century. She was a great patron of religious foundations in Normandy, particularly of the abbey of Bec, and when Henry's duties took him elsewhere she acted as regent in Normandy and heard court cases. Her influence was vital to his success in governing his vast empire, which encompassed England, Normandy, and Anjou. When King Louis VII of France, angered by Henry's marriage to *Eleanor of Aquitaine, stood ready to invade Normandy at the first sign of unrest within its borders, Matilda helped to maintain the region's stability.

Henry II often relied upon his mother's wisdom, but he ignored her advice in one crucial matter. Matilda warned against his appointment of his friend the chancellor Thomas Becket as archbishop of Canterbury. In the early stages of their struggle, both Henry and Becket sought Matilda's support, each asking her to help negotiate with the other. Matilda stood up for her son, although she preferred the guidance of unwritten custom to Henry's attempts to delimit the rights and responsibilities of the Church in the Constitutions of Clarendon. She died on September 10, 1167, and thus did not witness the tragic outcome of the struggle between the king and his stubborn archbishop in 1170.

Although the rule of England by a woman in her own name had to wait for her descendant *Elizabeth I four centuries later, Empress Matilda was no stranger to the exercise of power. As wife of Henry V, she often acted independently at a very young age, administering parts of the Holy Roman Empire on his behalf, and her failed quest for the English crown allowed her son's peaceful ascent to the throne. Two lines from the inscription on her tomb, in the abbey church at Bec, fittingly sum up her long and dramatic career:

> Great by birth, greater by marriage, greatest in her offspring,
> Here lies the daughter, wife and mother of Henry.

SOURCES:

The Anglo-Saxon Chronicle. Edited and translated by G. N. Garmonsway. London: J.M. Dent, 1986, p. 267.

Chibnall, Marjorie. *The Empress Matilda: Queen Consort, Queen Mother and Lady of the English.* Oxford: Basil Blackwell, 1991.

Gesta Stephani. Edited and translated by Kenneth R. Potter. Oxford: Clarendon Press, 1976, pp. 2–6, 144.

John of Salisbury. *Historia Pontificalis.* Edited and translated by Marjorie Chibnall. Oxford: Clarendon Press, 1986, pp. 83–85.

SUGGESTED READING:

Davis, R.H.C. *King Stephen, 1135–1154.* 3rd ed. London: Longman, 1990.

Leyser, Karl J. "The Anglo-Norman Succession 1120–1125," in *Anglo-Norman Studies.* Vol. 13, 1990, pp. 225–241.

Jean A. Truax, Ph.D. in medieval history, University of Houston, Houston, Texas

Matilda, Empress (c. 1103–1152).

See Matilda of Boulogne.

Matilda, Saint (c. 892–968).

See Matilda of Saxony.

Matilda I (c. 1031–1083).

See Matilda of Flanders.

Matilda Augustus of England (1102–1167).

See Matilda, Empress.

Matilda Bruce (c. 1285–c. 1326).

See Bruce, Matilda.

Matilda Bruce (d. 1353).

See Bruce, Matilda.

Matilda de Blois (d. 1120)

Countess of Chester. Name variations: Maud of Blois; Matilda of Blois. Born around 1100; drowned, along with her husband and sister Lucy de Blois, *in the wreck of the* White Ship *on November 25, 1120, in Barfleur, Normandy, France; daughter of Stephen*

Henry of Blois, count of Blois, and *Adela of Blois (1062–c. 1137); sister of Stephen of Blois (c. 1096–1154), later king of England (r. 1135–1154); married Richard d'Avranches (1094–1120), 2nd earl of Chester, in 1115.

Matilda de Burgh (d. 1315)

Countess of Hertford and Gloucester. Name variations: Matilda de Clare. Died in 1315 (some sources cite 1320); interred at Tewkesbury Abbey, Gloucester; daughter of Richard de Burgh the Red (c. 1259–1326), 2nd earl of Ulster (r. 1271–1326) and 4th earl of Connaught, and *Margaret de Burgh (d. 1303); married Gilbert de Clare, 8th earl of Hertford, 4th earl of Gloucester, on September 29, 1308, at Waltham Abbey, Essex; associated with John de Birmingham; children: John de Clare (b. 1312).

Matilda de Chatillon (d. 1358).

See Mahaut de Chatillon.

Matilda de Dammartin (d. 1258)

Countess of Dammartin, countess of Boulogne, and wife of Alphonso III, king of Portugal. Name variations: Mahaut de Dammartin or Dammaratin; Mahault; Matilda of Dammartin or Dammaratin; Matilde. Died in 1258 (some sources cite 1257); daughter of Ide d'Alsace (c. 1161–1216), countess of Boulogne, and Reinaldo, count of Dammartin; married Philippe Hurpel, count of Clermont, in 1216; married Alphonso III, future king of Portugal (r. 1248–1279), around 1238; children: (first marriage) Jeanne de Clermont; (second marriage) Robert (b. 1239, died in infancy).

Born in the early 13th century, Matilda de Dammartin was the only child of Reinaldo, count of Dammartin, and *Ide d'Alsace. In 1216, Matilda married Philippe Hurpel, count of Clermont, who died in 1234. Perhaps in 1238, she married again, this time to a Portuguese prince, the future Alphonso III, who was residing at the court of Louis VIII. Alphonso hoped to make his fortune in France. He also apparently envied and feared his brother Sancho II, who was then ruling Portugal. Matilda's marriage to Alphonso served his interests, as she was a wealthy heiress (the richest in France, according to some estimates).

When Portuguese nobles overthrew Sancho, Alphonso returned home to claim the throne, leaving Matilda in France. This led to a perma-

nent separation between the couple, which Matilda apparently did not protest. When Alphonso tried to wed *Beatrice of Castile and Leon (1242–1303) in 1253, however, Matilda sought redress from Pope Alexander IV, who excommunicated Alphonso. The marriage of Alphonso and Beatrice was celebrated in 1259, soon after Matilda's death in 1258.

SOURCES:

O Grande Livro dos Portugueses. Lisbon: Círculo de Leitores, 1991.

Oliveira, Américo Lopes de, and Mário Gonçalves Viana. Dicionário Mundial de Mulheres Notáveis. Porto: Lello & Irmão, 1967.

Kendall W. Brown,
Professor of History,
Brigham Young University, Provo, Utah

Matilda Martel (943–c. 982)

Queen of Burgundy. Born in 943; died around 982; daughter of *Gerberga of Saxony (c. 910–969) and Louis IV, king of France (r. 936–954); married Conrad the Pacific, king of Burgundy (r. 937–993); children: *Bertha of Burgundy (964–1024); Rudolf III (b. 970), king of Burgundy.

Matilda of Anjou (1107–1154)

Duchess of Normandy. Name variations: Isabel de Gatinais; sometimes referred to as Alice. Born in 1107; died in 1154 in Fontevraud, Anjou, France; daughter of Fulk V, count of Anjou and king of Jerusalem, and Ermentrude, countess of Maine (d. 1126); married William the Atheling, duke of Normandy, in June 1119 (d. 1120).

Matilda of Anjou was born in 1107, the daughter of Fulk V, count of Anjou and king of Jerusalem, and *Ermentrude, countess of Maine. She married William the Atheling, duke of Normandy, in June 1119; he died the following year. At the time of her death in 1154, Matilda of Anjou was the abbess of Fontevraud.

Matilda of Artois (c. 1270–1329).

See Mahaut.

Matilda of Bavaria (fl. 1300s)

Bavarian princess. Flourished in the 1300s; daughter of *Beatrice of Silesia and Louis III, duke of Bavaria (r. 1294–1347), also known as Ludwig IV of Bavaria and Louis IV, Holy Roman emperor (r. 1314–1347); sister of Louis V (1315–1361), margrave of Brandenburg (r. 1347–1361, who married *Margaret Maultasch) and Stephen II, duke of Bavaria (r. 1363–1375).

Matilda of Boulogne (c. 1103–1152)

*Queen of England and countess of Boulogne. Name variations: Mahaut de Boulogne; Empress Maud; Empress Matilda. Born around 1103 in Boulogne (France); died on May 3, 1152 (some sources cite 1151), at Heningham Castle (also seen as Hedingham Castle), Kent, England; buried at Faversham Abbey, Kent; daughter of Eustace III, count of Boulogne, and Mary of Atholl, princess of Scotland (d. 1116); niece of *Matilda of Scotland (1080–1118); cousin of Empress Matilda (1102–1167); married Stephen of Blois (c. 1096–1154), later king of England (r. 1135–1154), around 1120; children: Baldwin (c. 1126–1135); Eustace IV (c. 1130–1153), count of Boulogne; William (1134–1159), earl of Warrenne and Surrey (who married *Isabel de Warrenne [c. 1137–1203]); Matilda (c. 1133–c. 1135); *Marie of Boulogne (d. 1182).*

Matilda of Boulogne played an important role in the English civil war fought between her husband and Empress *Matilda of England. She was born in Boulogne, the daughter of Count Eustace III of Boulogne and *Mary of Atholl. When she was about 17, Matilda of Boulogne married Stephen of Blois. Upon the death of England's King Henry I, Stephen of Blois claimed the throne of England as a descendant of William the Conqueror; this began a long and bloody war against Empress Matilda who had inherited the throne as King Henry's heir and daughter.

As his wife, Matilda of Boulogne became Stephen of Blois' most significant ally, for she was intelligent, daring, loyal, and ultimately committed to becoming the undisputed queen of England. She planned battle strategies and even led troops. A skilled politician and negotiator, she mediated an alliance with Scotland, but was willing to resort to kidnapping and blackmail when negotiations failed. When Stephen of Blois was taken prisoner by Empress Matilda's allies, Matilda of Boulogne captured Robert of Gloucester and agreed to free him when Stephen of Blois was released. In 1148, with her constant support, the somewhat ineffectual Stephen of Blois secured the throne for himself, which he held until 1154. Matilda of Boulogne preceded her husband in death in 1152, at age 49.

SOURCES:

Williams, Marty, and Anne Echols. *Between Pit and Pedestal: Women in the Middle Ages.* Princeton, NJ: Markus Wiener, 1994.

Laura York,
Riverside, California

Matilda of Boulogne (1163–c. 1210).

See Maude of Alsace.

Matilda of Brandenburg (d. 1261)

*Duchess of Brunswick-Luneburg. Died on June 10, 1261; daughter of Albert II, duke of Brandenburg (r. 1205–1220); married Otto I Puer also known as Otto the Child (1204–1252), duke of Brunswick-Luneburg (r. 1235–1252), in 1228; children: Albert I (b. 1236), duke of Brunswick; John, duke of Brunswick-Luneburg; *Helene of Brunswick-Luneburg (d. 1273).*

Matilda of Canossa (1046–1115).

See Matilda of Tuscany.

Matilda of Château-du-Loir

*Countess of Maine. Married Elias I, count of Maine; children: *Ermentrude, countess of Maine (d. 1126).*

Matilda of Chester (1171–1233).

See Maude of Chester.

Matilda of England (c. 1031–1083).

See Matilda of Flanders.

Matilda of England (1102–1167).

See Matilda, Empress.

Matilda of England (1156–1189)

Duchess of Bavaria and Saxony. Name variations: Matilda, duchess of Saxony. Born in Windsor Castle, Windsor, Berkshire, England, in June 1156; died in Brunswick, Germany, on June 28, 1189 (one source cites 1198); buried in Brunswick Cathedral, Lower Saxony, Germany; daughter of Eleanor of Aquitaine (1122–1202) and Henry II, king of England (r. 1154–1189); married Henry XII also known as Henry V the Lion (1129–1195), duke of Saxony and Bavaria (r. 1156–1195), on February 1, 1168; children: Henry Welf, count palatine of the Rhine; Otto IV of Brunswick (c. 1175–1218), earl of York, count of Ponthieu, duke of Bavaria, and Holy Roman emperor (r. 1198–1214); William of Winchester (1184–1213), duke of Brunswick-Luneburg.

Matilda of England was born in 1156, the daughter of *Eleanor of Aquitaine and Henry II, king of England. She married Henry V the Lion, duke of Saxony and Bavaria, in 1168. In 1180, when her husband refused to submit to forfeiture of his lands to the emperor Frederick I Barbarossa, the town of Brunswick in Lower Saxony was besieged. Matilda appealed to the emperor's chivalry and the siege was ended, after which Matilda and Henry V sought refuge in

England. In 1181, Henry V the Lion submitted to the forfeiture, returning to Brunswick in 1185. He was again exiled in 1189, the year Matilda of England died.

Matilda of Essen (949–1011)

*Abbess of Essen. Born in 949; died in 1011; daughter of *Ida of Swabia (d. 986) and Liudolf also known as Ludolf (980–957), duke of Swabia (r. 948–957).*

Matilda of Flanders (c. 1031–1083)

*Queen of England, of noble birth and closely related to the kings of France, who married William, duke of Normandy, later king of England, was the mother of two future kings, and played a significant part in the political affairs of the period, especially in Normandy. Name variations: Matilda or Matilda I; Matilda of England. Born in Flanders around 1031; died in Normandy on November 3, 1083; daughter of Baldwin of Lisle also called Baldwin V le Debonnaire (c. 1012–1067), count of Flanders (r. 1035–1067), and his second wife Adela Capet (c. 1010–1097, daughter of Robert II and sister of Henry I, kings of France); sister of *Judith of Flanders (1032–1094) and Baldwin VI, count of Flanders; married William of Normandy (c. 1027–1087), later William I the Conqueror, duke of Normandy (r. 1035–1087), king of England (r. 1066–1087), in 1051 or 1053; children: Robert III also seen as Robert II Curthose (c. 1054–1134), duke of Normandy (r. 1087–1106); Richard (c. 1055–d. between 1069 and 1075), duke of Bernay; Cecilia (c. 1059–1126), abbess of Holy Trinity in Caen; Adeliza (d. 1066?); William II (c. 1060–1100), king of England; Constance (c. 1066–1090); Adela of Blois (c. 1062–1137, countess of Blois and Chartres, who married Stephen Henry, count of Blois); Agatha (betrothed to Harald or Harold II, king of the English, but died unmarried); Henry I (1068–1135), king of England (r. 1100–1135); and perhaps a Matilda (mentioned in Domesday Book, but nothing further is known).*

Born into the powerful ruling family of Flanders, was closely related, through her mother, to the ruling house of France; despite opposition of papacy, married William, duke of Normandy (1051 or 1053) and spent much of the rest of her life in the duchy; assisted William in administering the area and acted as his regent when he was absent; following William's conquest of England (1066), became queen of England and was crowned (1068); was a powerful, wealthy woman who was generous in her endowment of the church; had nine or ten children, including two future kings; was approximately 52 years old when she died (1083).

Matilda of Flanders bursts upon the historical record in 1049 as a beautiful young woman of perhaps 17 (we do not know the exact date of her birth). A determined young upstart, William (later William I the Conqueror), the illegitimate son of the duke of Normandy, had come to Flanders seeking a suitable bride. Few young women could have been considered more suitable than Matilda. Her uncle, Henry (I), was the reigning French king. Her mother ✒➤ **Adela Capet** was a member of the Capetian family, the ruling house of France. (In 998, Pope Gregory V had excommunicated Robert II the Pious, king of France, and voided his second marriage to his cousin ✒➤ **Bertha of Burgundy** because they were too closely related. Robert then married *Constance of Arles, and she gave birth to four children, including Adela Capet.) Count Baldwin V, Matilda's father, was the wealthy and influential ruler of Flanders, an area covering what is now western Belgium and part of northern France.

Since Roman times, Flanders had developed an international reputation as a producer of the

---

✒➤ **Adela Capet** (c. 1010–1079)

*Countess of Flanders. Name variations: Adela of France. Born around 1010; died on January 8, 1079, at Messinesmonastre, France; daughter of Robert II the Pious (972–1031, son of Hugh Capet) sometimes known as Robert I, king of France (r. 996–1031) and *Constance of Arles (c. 980–1032); sister of Henry I (1008–1060), king of France (r. 1031–1060), and Robert, duke of Burgundy (r. 1031–1076); married Richard III, 5th duke of Normandy, in January 1026 or 1027; became second wife of Baldwin V (c. 1012–1067), count of Flanders (r. 1035–1067), in 1028; children: (second marriage) possibly Baldwin VI, count of Flanders (d. 1070); *Matilda of Flanders (c. 1031–1083); *Judith of Flanders (1032–1094).*

Following the death of her second husband Baldwin V, count of Flanders, Adela Capet entered the convent.

✒➤ **Bertha of Burgundy** (964–1024)

*Queen of France. Born around 964; died in 1024; daughter of *Matilda Martel (943–c. 982) and Conrad, king of Burgundy (r. 937–993); became second wife of her cousin Robert II the Pious (972–1031, son of Hugh Capet) sometimes known as Robert I, king of France (r. 996–1031), in 996 (marriage annulled in 998); children: Almaric Montfort.*

Pope Gregory V voided the marriage of Bertha of Burgundy and Robert II, king of France, in 998, because they were too closely related. Robert then married his third wife *Constance of Arles (c. 980–1032).

finest woolen cloth, and from the late 10th century, under strong rulers and stable government, the region grew from strength to strength. Its favorable coastal location was ideal for trade with the Scandinavian countries of the north, and the Rhine River provided a vital link with the markets of France and Germany. It is, therefore, hardly surprising that the young man who sought to marry Matilda had no easy time in winning her.

First, there was the problem of the suitor himself: although William, at age 21, had already acquired a reputation for bravery and military skill and was the son of the duke of Normandy, that duchy had only been established in the 10th century to placate the Viking invaders. Normandy lacked both the illustrious history and the wealth of neighboring Flanders, and, to further diminish his eligibility, William's illegitimate birth made his claim to the duchy seem tenuous at best. In 1049, no one could be sure that he would manage to defeat the powerful opponents who were plotting to overthrow him, and no one could have foreseen the illustrious future which awaited him.

Sprung from a royal stem; child of a Flemish duke; her mother was Adela, daughter of a king of France, . . . married to William, most illustrious king.

—Epitaph on Matilda's tomb at Caen

Evidence suggests that Count Baldwin's response to the marriage proposal was less than enthusiastic, and a Norman chronicle (dismissed by one historian as an "idle legend") tells of Matilda's own reaction: she is said to have declared that she would never marry a bastard. William rode secretly to Bruges, so the chronicle recounts, caught her as she was coming out of church, and beat and kicked her. Matilda then took to her bed and told her father that she would marry no one but the duke. Another, and perhaps equally unreliable Norman chronicler provides a different reason for Matilda's reluctance to marry William: according to this account, she had already fallen in love with an Anglo-Saxon thane (a soldier of a king) who had come to Bruges on a diplomatic mission. Rejected by the young man, Matilda allegedly took vengeance upon him when she became queen of England.

Winning over the opposition of Matilda and her father, however it was accomplished, was to prove less difficult for William than gaining the approval of the pope. The papal council held at Rheims in 1049 refused to allow the match on the grounds of consanguinity (a fairly common impediment to politically significant medieval marriages), which meant that the parties were related in some way. Historians have not been able to discover the precise grounds of this alleged relationship; the most likely theory is that the difficulty arose because of a marriage contract between William's uncle, Richard III, duke of Normandy, and Matilda's mother Adela. Other speculative accounts have the two connected through a common great-grandmother, or have Matilda previously married, but none of these stories bear scrutiny. The fact that the marriage of Richard and Adela had never actually taken place did nothing to diminish the force of papal opposition to the match between Matilda and William, duke of Normandy.

William, however, refused to be swayed, and the marriage eventually took place at Eu, on his duchy's northeastern frontier, perhaps as early as 1051 but more likely in 1053, with Matilda subsequently being received in Rouen, William's Norman capital, with much rejoicing. The rejoicing may well have been short-lived, however, as the duchy was subsequently placed under a papal interdict, to punish William for his disobedience, and it may not have been until 1059, when Pope Nicholas II granted a dispensation, that the services of the church were fully restored to William and his subjects.

Matilda of Flanders was made to share in the requirement to make amends for the disobedient marriage: as a physical expression of her contrition, she financed, from her own revenues, the building of the Abbey of the Holy Trinity (La Trinité) at Caen, a magnificent convent for nuns, while William established the Abbey of St. Stephen (St-Etienne) in the same city. Building of the two abbeys as well as a castle commenced in the late 1050s, raising Caen to the status of the second city in Normandy, after the capital, Rouen.

Given what we know of the customs of the time and of the character of Duke William, it would seem wiser to ascribe his determined pursuit of Matilda to politics rather than passion. She was wealthy and well connected and his alliance with Flanders served William well, in Normandy and, later, in England. Yet Matilda of Flanders was well educated, cultured and, according to contemporary descriptions, beautiful, her tiny form a striking contrast to William's imposing size. If the marriage did not start out as a love match, it seems to have developed into one; unlike most of his ancestors and contemporaries, William seems to have been loyal to his wife, a facet of his character considered remarkable by those who observed it, and, though not without some disagreements, William and Matilda remained close for their 30 years together.

Matilda seems to have quickly come to share her husband's role as ruler of Normandy and with it his ambitions for England. Contemporary Norman sources are in agreement that King Edward III the Confessor of England, lacking an heir and grateful to the Normans for their support of his cause when his political survival was in doubt, promised the English throne to William sometime in 1051. Harold II Godwineson's visit to Normandy in 1064 or 1065 is seen, to these same Norman chroniclers, as a mission to confirm this promise and to swear his own oath of loyalty. Given Harold's ambitions to secure the throne for himself, such motivation seems unlikely, although it is probable that William cleverly exploited the visit to serve his own ends. Nor was William alone in his machinations; one account presents Matilda as spending many hours in conversation with Harold Godwineson during his time at the Norman court and alleges that she persuaded him to promise to marry one of her daughters—perhaps an attempt to develop an alternate strategy, should William's master plan fail to materialize.

It soon became clear to William what his master plan must be. Immediately following King Edward's death on January 5, 1066, Harold Godwineson announced that the king had promised him the throne with his dying breath. Then, Harold took advantage of popular support and had himself crowned. If he were to make good his claim, William had no choice but to invade England. It is obvious that he was not unprepared; Matilda was named as regent in Normandy, to be assisted, in the duke's absence, by a council of advisors. As he rallied his supporters before departure, Matilda presented her husband with a ship called the *Mora* to serve as his flagship. It is shown in the Bayeux Tapestry as a square-rigged Viking ship with a cruciform banner at the masthead. Matilda had placed on board the golden image of a boy, holding an ivory horn to his lips, his right hand pointing towards England.

The dedication of Matilda of Flanders' abbey of the Holy Trinity at Caen on June 18 represented a symbolic culmination of the invasion preparations. At what must have been a most magnificent and memorable ceremony, attended by almost all of the major religious and secular figures in Norman society, William and Matilda gave their eldest daughter ❧➤ Cecilia, then about seven years of age, to be a child oblate at the abbey.

William's fleet finally set sail for England on the night of September 27, 1066. In one of the most famous battles in history, fought at Hastings on October 14, he defeated Harold Godwineson's forces and, on Christmas Day 1066, William of Normandy, now William the Conqueror, was crowned king of England. Meanwhile, Matilda of Flanders successfully ruled in Normandy, ending her regency only with the return of her husband in March 1067 and resuming it once again upon his departure in December. The second regency was established in conjunction with their eldest son Robert, the first of their many children, who had been born shortly after their marriage and was now entering his teens.

Early in 1068, William sent a high-ranking delegation of Normans to escort his wife to their new kingdom. She "quickly obeyed her husband's commands with a willing mind and crossed the sea with a great attendance of knights and noble women." On Whit Sunday, May 11, 1068, she was crowned at Westminster by the archbishop of York, with William sharing in the ceremony to make it all the more splendid. One historian has suggested that this formal ceremony of coronation in the newly conquered land made Matilda the first real queen of England.

Matilda of Flanders was still in England when she gave birth to her fourth son, Henry (later Henry I), but soon after his birth she returned to Normandy, and she seems to have been greatly involved in Norman affairs for the rest of her life. The couple's eldest son Robert II, nicknamed "Curthose" because of his short legs, was to succeed his father in the duchy, but for many years Matilda, acting first as regent for her husband and then as Robert's guardian, had her name placed on charters alongside that of her son. Often, Matilda's name or seal appeared alone. She was certainly directing Normandy's

❧➤ **Cecilia** (c. 1059–1126)

*Abbess of the Holy Trinity at Caen. Name variations: Cecily. Born around 1059 (some sources cite 1055) in Normandy, France; died on July 30, 1126 (some sources cite 1127), in Holy Trinity Abbey, Caen, Normandy, France; buried in Holy Trinity Abbey, Caen; daughter of *Matilda of Flanders (c. 1031–1083) and William I the Conqueror (c. 1027–1087), duke of Normandy (r. 1035–1087), king of England (r. 1066–1087); sister of *Adela of Blois (1062–c. 1137). Elected abbess of the Holy Trinity Abbey at Caen in 1112.*

administration during William's absences of 1066–67, 1067–68 and 1071. Although William had returned to Normandy in 1070, Matilda's name still appears, alongside that of Robert, on important documents of that year. We find her joining her son in a petition to the learned Bishop Lanfranc, inviting him to leave Normandy and accept England's highest ecclesiastical office, that of archbishop of Canterbury. Later the same year, Matilda's orders sent a force from Normandy to Flanders to uphold the claims of her brother and nephew against the claims of Robert the Frisian. The chroniclers tell us that she was much disturbed by the death of her brother Baldwin VI and deeply concerned about the warfare in her native land.

There is no doubt that Matilda of Flanders was an affectionate mother to her numerous children, although there is some doubt about the children themselves; many historians have engaged in the somewhat unrewarding effort to ascertain their precise number and their names. As the eminent 19th-century historian Edward Freeman has observed, "about the number and order of the sons of William and Matilda there is no doubt. They were Robert, Richard, William and Henry. . . . But about the daughters, their number, names, and order, the statements are most contradictory." There seem to have been five or perhaps six daughters: Cecilia who became an abbess, ◄§ **Constance** who married Alan of Brittany, ◄§ **Adeliza**, *Adela of Blois** who married Stephen Henry, count of Blois, ◄§ **Agatha**, who was perhaps betrothed to Harold Godwineson but died unmarried, and possibly a Matilda.

It was the eldest of the children, Robert II, who caused what was perhaps the most significant rift between Matilda and her husband. One contemporary observer depicts him as an unstable, ungrateful young man, too easily influenced by his friends and unable to handle money. Father and son quarreled seriously late in 1077 or early in 1078. Since 1072, William had been spending increasingly lengthy periods with Matilda in Normandy, no doubt curtailing some of Robert's independence; indeed one chronicler records the son's claim that he was being treated like a hired soldier.

Having failed in an attempt to capture the castle at Rouen, Robert left Normandy with a group of other young malcontents and began to make raids across its borders from inside France. During the course of a battle in January 1079, both King William and his third son, William II, were wounded; accounts suggest that Robert himself attacked his father. Following the battle, Robert took refuge with his mother's relatives in Flanders.

Matilda of Flanders found herself emotionally torn by the dispute: as a loyal and devoted wife, she could not abandon her husband, and yet her maternal ties to her firstborn were too strong to sever. While Robert was in Flanders, she sent him large quantities of gold and silver without her husband's knowledge. Such largesse not only indicates the depth of her affection, but reveals the extent to which, after almost 30 years of marriage, she had been able to maintain independent control of her own considerable fortune. The chronicler Orderic Vitalis reports that William discovered what she was doing and reproached her; Matilda excused herself on the grounds of her great love for her son. Nor did the matter end there: William gave orders that the messenger who had carried the treasure be blinded, but, alerted by friends of the queen, the man escaped to a monastery where the abbot, at Matilda's request, granted him refuge. Undaunted, she seems to have continued to send aid to Robert even after William's discovery.

It was probably also during the turbulent year of 1079 that Matilda sent gifts to a famous hermit in Germany, with the request that he pray for her husband and Robert and predict what would become of them. The hermit, if he were able to foresee the future accurately, would have told Matilda that after vigorous efforts on the part of many mediators, including Pope Gregory VII, father and son finally sealed a peace at Easter (April 12) 1080.

As she grew older and her health declined, Matilda of Flanders seems to have turned increasingly to religion. We do not know the nature of her illness, but it is likely that her many pregnancies took their toll, particularly if she was as small of stature (about 4'3") as the bones found in her tomb at Caen suggest. On the death of her kinsman, the holy hermit Simon de Valois, count of Amiens, in 1082, she sent gifts to adorn his tomb. While continuing her generosity to her foundation at Caen, Matilda also founded the abbey of St. Mary de Pré at Rouen, and she sent gifts to the abbey of Le Bec and to many other churches.

To the English Church, the queen was less generous; one account has her ordering the abbey of Abingdon to send her some precious ornaments with which she intended to enrich a Norman house, and, when the items offered were not all she expected, demanding more. However, she did use her negotiating skills on several occasions to resolve quarrels among the disputatious ecclesiastical community in England; she persuaded the bishop of Exeter to return a church to the bishop of Wells, and assisted the bishop of Durham in making changes to his administration.

Matilda and William spent Easter 1083 at Fécamp, and by July they were at Caen. It was at Caen that Matilda died on November 3, 1083, and she was buried, with great ceremonial, in her own abbey church. A scurrilous story, reported by only one chronicler, alleges that William had taken a mistress who had been killed on Matilda's orders and, in his fury, William had beaten his wife to death. However, the chronicler, William of Malmesbury, also says that he knows the tale to be nonsense and records that the only "slight dispute" which had arisen between them had been over Matilda's support for their rebellious son. William seems to have been genuinely distraught at his loss of Matilda; Malmesbury has him "weeping most profusely for many days" and reports that, from the time of her death, "he refrained from every gratification" until his own death four years later. The grieving husband had an elaborate monument of gold and precious stones, which has since been destroyed, built over her tomb, but the tomb itself can be seen still, with its proud epitaph proclaiming Matilda's noble connections: "Sprung from a royal stem; child of a Flemish duke; her mother was Adela, daughter of a king of France, sister of Henry, Robert's royal son, married to William, most illustrious king."

Perhaps with something of a prescient eye, Matilda left her substantial English land holdings to her youngest son, Henry. After King William's death, Robert lost Normandy and was imprisoned by his brothers, Richard was killed in a hunting accident, and William II (called William Rufus because of his red hair) succeeded to the throne of England but was also killed while hunting. Only Henry, who succeeded his brother as Henry I in 1100, demonstrated the legacy of his parentage. No match for his father on the battlefield, for he was never more than an adequate military leader, Henry proved to be a vigorous and astute ruler in both England and Normandy. Such refined political skills may be attributed as much to the legacy of his mother as of his father.

Matilda of Flanders, like so many medieval women, especially medieval queens, is all but eclipsed by the shadow of her husband. This familiar situation is exacerbated in Matilda's case because her husband seems to have been, to both his contemporaries and to later historians, larger than life. When contemporary chroniclers, intent on focusing on the deeds of William, pause to consider her at all, they recount a conventional list of her virtues: beauty, learning, prudence, piety, charity, obedience, and fruitfulness, or they manufacture unlikely and completely unsupported tales of jealousy and vengeance, reflecting the popular misogyny of their times.

Even modern historians give little attention to the woman who, for 30 years, shared the life of one of history's most famous men. Perhaps the wisest course in rediscovering Matilda is to consider what we know of her life: a woman of her noble birth, education, and political experience must have been an invaluable asset to William as he struggled, during the first decade of their marriage, to create in Normandy something resembling the ordered and peaceful government of Flanders. Nor could he have been an easy partner; even by the standards of the day, William was said to be a stern, stubborn and sometimes brutal man. As her husband's attention increasingly turned towards England, Matilda was closely involved, first in planning a marriage alliance and then in supporting the invasion, and even providing William with his flagship. Despite her frequent pregnancies, Matilda was actively engaged in governing Normandy during the duke's many lengthy absences, especially after he became king of England in 1066. It is surely significant that, in an age where powerful women were rare, and hence the subjects of close scrutiny, none of the chroniclers has anything negative to report about Matilda as an administrator. Her magnificent coronation in 1068 is a clear testimony not only to William's high regard for her, but also to her political importance.

An astute and independent administrator of her own considerable fortune, she was also, as we have seen, a generous patron of the Church and a skilled negotiator on its behalf. She may also have been involved in the creation of the magnificent Bayeux Tapestry, for while most historians no longer see this giant piece of pictorial embroidery as the work of Matilda's own hand, it fits well with what we know of her character that she would have wished to immortalize her husband's great triumph in such a striking and permanent fashion.

Throughout much of her life Matilda of Flanders was, no doubt, responsible for supervising the intellectual, moral, and political education of her children, and she seems to have been deeply attached to them, as the quarrel with her husband over their son Robert indicates. This proud and powerful woman placed a high value on the importance of family ties, and not only as far as her sons were concerned. She chose for two of her daughters the names Adela and Constance, the first her mother's name, and the second the name of her grandmother.

SOURCES AND SUGGESTED READING:

The Anglo-Saxon Chronicle: A Revised Translation. Edited by D. Whitelock, D.C. Douglas, and S.I. Tucker. London: Eyre and Spottiswode, 1961.

Bates, David. William the Conqueror. London: George Philip, 1989.

The Ecclesiastical History of Oderic Vitalis. Edited and translated by Margery Chibnall, 6 vols. Oxford: Clarendon Press, 1969–1980.

Freeman, Edward A. The History of the Norman Conquest of England. Oxford: Clarendon Press, 1875.

Lofts, Norah. Queens of Britain. London: Hodder and Stoughton, 1977.

Malmesbury, William of. Chronicle of the Kings of England. Edited by J.A. Giles. London: Bell & Daldy, 1866.

"Matilda," in Dictionary of National Biography. Volume XXXVII. London: Smith Elder, 1894.

(Dr.) Kathleen Garay,
Acting Director of Women's Studies Program,
McMaster University, Hamilton, Canada

Matilda of Germany (d. before 1044)

Queen of France. Died before 1044; first wife of Henry I, king of France (r. 1031–1060); children: Hugh the Great (b. 1057), count of Vermandois. Henry's second wife was *Anne of Kiev (1024–1066).

Matilda of Guelders (d. 1380)

Princess of Guelders. Name variations: Matilda of Gueldres. Died in 1380; daughter of *Sophia of Malines (d. 1329) and Renaud, also known as Rainald or Reginald II the Black Haired (d. 1343), duke of Guelders (also known as count of Gelderland), count of Zutphen; stepdaughter of *Eleanor of Woodstock (1318–1355); married Godfrey, count of Hennenburg; married John, duke of Cleves; married John, count of Chatillon.

Matilda of Habsburg (1251–1304)

Duchess of Bavaria and countess Palatine. Name variations: Mathilda or Mathilde of Hapsburg. Born in 1251; died on December 22, 1304, in Munich; daughter of Rudolf I (1218–1291), king of Germany (r. 1273), Holy Roman emperor (r. 1273–1291), and *Anna of Hohenberg (c. 1230–1281); sister of Albert I (b. 1250), Holy Roman emperor (r. 1298–1308 but not crowned); sister of *Catherine of Habsburg (c. 1254–1282) and *Clementia of Habsburg (d. 1293); third wife of Louis II the Stern (1229–1294), count Palatine (r. 1253–1294), duke of Bavaria (r. 1255–1294); children: Ludwig, also known as Louis IV (1287–1347), Holy Roman emperor (r. 1314–1347); Rudolf or Rudolph I (b. 1274), duke of Bavaria (1294–1317), Elector Palatine (r. 1294–1319).

Matilda of Leiningen (b. 1936)

German royal. Name variations: Matilda Bauscher. Born on January 2, 1936, in Wurzburg, Bavaria, Germany; daughter of *Marie of Russia (1907–1951) and Charles, 6th prince of Leiningen; married Charles Bauscher, on November 25, 1961; children: Ulf (b. 1963); Berthold (b. 1965); John (b. 1971).

Matilda of Maurienne (c. 1125–1157)

Queen of Portugal. Name variations: Mafalda of Savoy; Matilda of Savoy. Born around 1125; died on November 4, 1157, in Coimbra, Portugal; daughter of Amadeus III of Maurienne and Savoy and *Matilde of Vienne (d. after 1145); married Alfonso or Alphonso Henriques also known as Alphonso I, count of Portugal (r. 1112–1139), king of Portugal (r. 1139–1185); children: Henrique (b. 1147, died young); *Urraca of Portugal (c. 1151–1188); Sancha (c. 1153–c. 1160); Sancho I (1154–1211 or 1212), king of Portugal (r. 1185–1211 or 1212); Joao or John (b. around 1156, died young); *Teresa of Portugal (1157–1218, who married Philip of Flanders); *Matilda of Portugal (c.

1149–1173, who married Alphonso II, king of Aragon).

Matilda of Narbonne (d. after 1348)

Castilian royal. Name variations: Mafalda de Narbonne. Died after 1348; daughter of **Sibylle de Foix** and Aimery IV, vicomte of Narbonne; married Alphonso de la Cerda (c. 1270–1327), Infant of Castile, after 1294; children: Luis de la Cerda, prince of Canary Islands; **Margarita de la Cerda** (c. 1300–1330, who married Felipe of Castile, sn de Cabrera); **Ines de la Cerda** (c. 1302–1362, who married Fernando Rodriquez de Villalobos); Juan Alfonso; **Maria de la Cerda** (b. 1306, who married Alfonso Melendez de Guzman); Alfonso de la Cerda.

Matilda of Nassau (fl. 1285–1310)

Countess Palatine. Flourished between 1285 and 1310; married Rudolf or Rudolph I of Bavaria, count Palatine (r. 1294–1319) and duke of Upper Bavaria; children: Adolph the Simple (1300–1327), count Palatine (r. 1319–1327); Rudolph II (1306–1353), count Palatine (r. 1327–1353); Rupert I (1309–1390), count Palatine (r. 1353–1390).

Matilda of Northumberland
(c. 1074–1131)

Queen of Scotland. Born around 1074; died in 1131; buried at Scone, Perth, Tayside, Scotland; daughter of ***Judith of Normandy** (c. 1054–after 1086) and Waltheof II, earl of Huntingdon and Northampton; married Simon, earl of Northampton, around 1090; married David I the Saint (c. 1084–1153), king of Scotland (r. 1124–1153), in 1113 or 1114; children: (first marriage) Simon (b. after 1103), earl of Huntington; St. Waldef (b. around 1100), abbot of Melrose; **Matilda of Northampton** (d. 1140, who married Robert FitzRichard); (second marriage) Malcolm (b. around 1114); Henry (c. 1115–1152), 1st earl of Huntingdon (r. 1136–1152); Claricia; Hodierna (died young).

Matilda of Portugal (c. 1149–1173)

Queen of Aragon. Name variations: Mafalda of Portugal; Mathilde de Bourgogne. Born around 1149; died in 1173; daughter of Alphonso Henriques also known as Alphonso I, count of Portugal (r. 1112–1139), king of Portugal (r. 1139–1185), and Matilda of Maurienne (c. 1125–1157); sister of ***Teresa of Portugal** (1157–1218), ***Urraca of Portugal** (c. 1151–1188), and Sancho I, king of Portugal (r.

1185–1211); became first wife of Alphonso II (1152–1196), king of Aragon (r. 1162–1196), count of Barcelona (r. 1162–1196), and count of Provence as Alphonso I (r. 1166–1196), in 1160.

Matilda of Portugal was born around 1149, the daughter of Alphonso I, king of Portugal, and *Matilda of Maurienne. At age 11, in 1160, she married Alphonso II, king of Aragon, but she died 13 years later, age 24. Following her death, Alphonso married *Sancha of Castile and Leon (d. 1208).

Matilda of Quedlinburg (c. 953–999).
See Adelaide of Burgundy (931–999) for sidebar.

Matilda of Ringelheim (c. 892–968).
See Matilda of Saxony.

Matilda of Savoy (c. 1125–1157).
See Matilda of Maurienne.

Matilda of Saxony (c. 892–968)

Holy Roman empress, queen of Germany, and saint. Name variations: Maud; Matilda of Germany; Matilda of Ringelheim; St. Matilda. Born around 892 (some sources cite 895) in Saxony; died on March (some sources cite May) 14, 968, in Quedlinburg, Germany; daughter of Dietrich, count of Ringelheim, and **Reinhild of Denmark**; became second wife of Henry I the Fowler (c. 876–936), king of Germany, Holy Roman emperor (r. 919–936), in 909; children: Otto I the Great (912–973), king of Germany (r. 936–973), Holy Roman emperor (r. 962–973); Henry I the Quarrelsome (918–955), duke of Bavaria (r. 947–955, who married ***Judith of Bavaria**); Bruno (925–965), archbishop of Cologne; ***Gerberga of Saxony** (c. 910–969); ***Hedwig** (c. 915–965, who married Hugh the Great). Henry I the Fowler was first married to Hatheburg.

The life of Saxon princess and saint Matilda has survived in two biographies by monks writing shortly after her death. She was educated at the convent of Erfurt, and although this experience made her a deeply pious woman, she was not destined for a cloistered life. In 909, her parents arranged a marriage for her with Henry the Fowler, the heir of the duke of Saxony. Henry, who had repudiated his first wife ***Hatheburg**, was 17 years older than his 17-year-old bride, who brought to the marriage extensive dowry lands in Saxony and Lotharingia.

In 912, Henry succeeded to the duchy of Saxony and Matilda gave birth to the first of five surviving children, a son who would become Holy

Roman emperor Otto I the Great. Like many medieval noblewomen, Matilda of Saxony spent little time with her husband, who after being elected to the German throne in 919 spent most of his time at war. The court Matilda established as queen was the opposite of Henry's military life; pious, quiet and intellectual, it was more like a convent than a seat of royal power. In 929, Henry promised Matilda numerous fortresses and towns for her dower inheritance to provide her income after his death. Over the next several years, Matilda converted three of the five towns into religious communities, including Quedlinburg and Nordhausen, later renowned as centers of learning.

In 936, Henry the Fowler died, beginning a period of civil conflict led by his sons in a struggle over the succession. Among the German nobles, Otto was the preferred choice to become the next king, but Matilda favored her younger son Henry I the Quarrelsome. After Otto's election, Henry raised an army in an unsuccessful attempt to take the throne. With Matilda's intercession, Otto pardoned Henry, but her support for Henry had cost her Otto's trust. Although he allowed her to remain at his court for several years, Otto accused her of wasting royal income with her generous charity to the poor, and had spies watch her movements. Henry reconciled with Otto and joined him in the persecution of their mother, refusing to allow her to keep the income generated by her dower lands.

Matilda eventually turned over her dower inheritance to her sons and settled on her estates in Saxony. After a decade of retirement, she reconciled with her sons and returned to court, taking up her charitable works once more and even acting as regent for Otto during his absences from court. Henry's second rebellion against Otto caused Matilda great suffering before his death in 955, which she is said to have foretold. After 965, Matilda retired again from public life, dividing her time between her religious houses, where she lived as a nun. She died at the convent of Quedlinburg in March 968, about age 76. Her granddaughter ◄❊ **Matilda of Quedlinburg**, abbess of Quedlinburg, inherited most of her establishments. For her devotion and charity to the poor, Queen Matilda of Saxony was canonized shortly after her death.

SOURCES:

Leyser, K.J. *Rule and Conflict in Early Medieval Society: Ottonian Saxony.* Bloomington, IN: Indiana University Press, 1979.

Thurston, Herbert, and Donald Attwater, eds. *Butler's Lives of the Saints.* Vol. I. London: Burns & Oates, 1956.

Laura York,
Riverside, California

❧►
Matilda of Quedlinburg.
See Adelaide of Burgundy (931–999) for sidebar.

Matilda of Saxony (978–1025)

Countess Palatine. Born in 978 in Saxony, Germany; died on November 4, 1025; daughter of *Theophano of Byzantium (c. 955–991) and Otto II (955–983), Holy Roman emperor (r. 983–983) and king of Germany (r. 973–983); married Ezzo of Palatine, count Palatine, around 992; children: *Richesa of Lorraine (d. 1067), queen of Poland; possibly nine others.

Matilda of Scotland (1080–1118).

See Empress Matilda (1102–1167) for sidebar.

Matilda of Tuscany (1046–1115)

Powerful ruler of extensive lands in Tuscany and Lombardy-Emilia (Italy), who was the most loyal and courageous supporter of the papal cause during the lengthy dispute between the popes and the German emperors known as the Investiture Conflict. Name variations: Matilda of Canossa; Matelda, Mathilda, or Mathildis. Born in 1046, somewhere in northern Italy (month, day, and place unknown); died on July 15 or 24, 1115, at the monastery of Polirone in northern Italy; daughter of Boniface II, margrave of Canossa and Tuscany, and Beatrice of Lorraine (c. 1020–1076); married Godfrey III the Hunchback (her stepbrother), in 1069 (died 1076); married Welf V of Bavaria (c. 1073–1120), in 1089 (separated by 1097); children: (first marriage) probably one child who died in infancy (birthdate unknown).

Born into a powerful Italian family during a time of political turmoil (relations between the German emperors and the Papacy were heading towards a crisis, and the rulers of states within the empire were forced to choose between the two warring sides); inherited sizeable and wealthy territories and soon showed her preference for the papal cause; devoted her life to the support, moral, financial and military, of the popes and earned the title "handmaiden of St. Peter"; had two brief and unhappy marriages; had no children who survived beyond infancy.

Countess Matilda of Tuscany was one of the few women of the Middle Ages to have had a prominent role in the political affairs of church and state. Medieval chroniclers traditionally ignored the women of their time, or made token references to them either as stereotypically good (saintly virgins or devoted mothers) or quintessentially evil (harlots or heretics). Matilda, however, is transmitted to us, through the letters of such dominant figures of the age as Pope Gregory VII and St. Anselm, as well as through the verses of her personal chaplain, as an individual: a woman of considerable resources, forceful convictions, and the courage to devote her life to a cause.

Matilda was of noble birth and was to inherit a large and wealthy domain. Her father, Boniface II, held sizeable estates in northern Italy, with the seat of his power located at Canossa, a virtually impregnable fortress in the Apennine mountains. Her mother, ✥➤ **Beatrice of Lorraine**, Boniface's second wife, was the daughter of the duke of Upper Lorraine and a niece of Emperor Conrad II. The marriage of Matilda's parents marked the high point of good relations between the house of Canossa and the emperors and, in 1028, Boniface added Tuscany to his Apennine-Alpine dominions as a reward from Conrad II for his support and as an incentive to continue it. After Conrad's death in 1039, however, the pattern of alliances began to change and, following the death of her husband in 1052, Matilda's mother embarked upon a course which was to shape and define her daughter's life.

It is impossible to fully understand Matilda without some grasp of the turbulent political circumstances in which the six-year-old found herself following her father's death. The first German emperor, Charlemagne, had managed to acquire his vast territories through a variety of stratagems: inheritance, alliances and, most productive of all, conquest. In the year 800, the title of Roman emperor, moribund in the West since the fall of Rome more than three centuries earlier, was revived and bestowed upon Charlemagne by the pope, in recognition of his preeminent political position and in gratitude for his support. The tripartite division of Charlemagne's territories among his warring grandsons in 843 had assigned the rights to the imperial crown to the ruler of the Italian lands, but during the 10th century the German kings acquired the title, and henceforth it became an elective office, awarded following the decision of the designated German electors and ratified by papal coronation.

Lacking the security of the hereditary principle, which was to gradually establish itself in such neighboring countries as England, France, and Hungary, the German emperors were forced to court the support of their powerful vassals,

---

✥➤ **Beatrice of Lorraine** (c. 1020–1076)

Marchioness and regent of Tuscany. Name variations: Beatrice of Tuscany; Beatrice of Canossa. Born in Upper Lorraine around 1020; died in 1076 in Tuscany, Italy; daughter of Frederick, duke of Upper Lorraine; niece of Conrad II; became second wife of Count Boniface II of Canossa, Marquess of Tuscany, around 1040 (died 1052); married Godfrey the Bearded, duke of Upper Lorraine, in 1054 (died 1069); children: three from first marriage, including Matilda of Tuscany.

Beatrice was born into the ruling family of Lorraine around 1020. In 1040, she married Count Boniface II of Canossa, the marquess of Tuscany (in northwestern Italy) and had three children, including a daughter *Matilda of Tuscany; the other two died in infancy. At this time, central European politics were dictated by the armed struggles between the Holy Roman emperor Henry III and Pope Gregory VII, who were vying for ultimate power across Germany and Italy. Beatrice and Boniface supported Pope Gregory's authority over Henry III; Tuscany's strategic location and wealth made them important allies for Gregory and detested enemies of Henry. Boniface was assassinated in 1052, probably on Henry's orders and certainly with his approval. Beatrice's only surviving child, Matilda, inherited her father's titles and estates at age six. Beatrice became regent of Tuscany for her small daughter, ruling by herself for two years. In 1054, she married the duke of Upper Lorraine, Godfrey the Bearded. Like her first husband, Godfrey was a supporter of the papacy.

The year after their marriage, Godfrey managed to escape Tuscany when the Holy Roman emperor had Matilda and Beatrice arrested and taken captive to Germany. Beatrice remained a prisoner in Germany for about a year, until Godfrey and Henry reached a settlement, and Henry allowed the mother and daughter to return home. Beatrice took up the reins of government again in Matilda's name, arranging a marriage for Matilda with Godfrey's son, Godfrey III the Hunchback. Even after she reached adulthood, Matilda seemed content to let Beatrice and Beatrice's husband continue administering her lands, and after her marriage in 1069 she moved to Lorraine. However, later that year Godfrey the Bearded died, and Matilda left Lorraine to return to Tuscany. Beatrice and Matilda co-ruled for the remaining six years of Beatrice's life. Matilda continued her parents' policy of staunch support for the papacy throughout her own eventful reign.

Laura York,
Northampton, Massachusetts

---

and they also had to avoid alienating the papacy. Emperor Henry III, who succeeded Conrad, seems genuinely to have attempted to assist the papacy through a difficult period and to have encouraged spiritual reform. Once awakened, however, the reforming impetus proved difficult to control, indeed it might be argued that a major confrontation between church and state was becoming inevitable. The Canossan territories, strategically located between Germany and Rome, could not remain untouched by the conflict, and Matilda was to find herself a leading player in the drama.

According to her chaplain and biographer Donizone di Canossa, Matilda's upbringing was strongly influenced by her mother Beatrice: "From early childhood she educated in a beautiful manner her daughter Matilda, who had an elevated and temperate mind." Matilda was taught French and German as well as Italian and we are told that she wrote Latin like the clerks. She shared her mother's love of learning and, from her youth, encouraged and funded the building of monasteries to assist in the spread of literacy and the transmission of written culture. Also from her childhood, Matilda seems to have been devout and pious; her favorite form of signature reads "Matilda, by the grace of God if she is anything."

Matilda, Countess of Tuscany . . . inherited vast domains in northern Italy . . . acting as the 'faithful handmaid of St. Peter,'—a hand-maid with a sharp sword in her hand and an army at her back.

—Antonia Fraser

On her father's death, the emperor Henry III attempted to transfer Boniface's Tuscan territories, held in feudal tenure, to a male heir, leaving Matilda (whose brothers—we are not sure whether she had one or two—predeceased their father) to inherit the Canossa lands. The law regarding the right of women to inherit lands varied widely throughout medieval Europe, and it was sometimes possible for females to succeed, even to feudal tenure, as long as they designated a man to perform the required military duties. Cases were often decided, not on the prevailing legal principles, but upon political circumstances and the support that female claimants were able to muster. Given her somewhat vulnerable situation, it is hardly surprising that Matilda's mother, Beatrice, should have remarried within two years to her cousin, Duke Godfrey of Upper Lorraine, a vigorous opponent of Emperor Henry III. The evidence suggests that Matilda's mother had now decided to give her support to the anti-

imperial forces, forces which were soon to be headed by a series of reform-minded popes.

The death of Henry III in 1056 provided a temporary respite in the political turmoil which defined Matilda's life. The future Henry IV was then a child of six and could not yet be the threat to Italian affairs that his father had been. With a regency established in Germany, Godfrey and Beatrice were left free to administer Matilda's lands until she came of age. In 1059, as a young girl of 13, Matilda had her first opportunity to observe the explosive conjunction of secular and papal politics when she and her parents attended the Council of Sutri, one of many assemblies held to determine which of rival claimants should be accepted as the true pope. The Sutri meeting was precipitated by the death of Godfrey's brother, who had headed the Church as Pope Stephen IX. At Sutri, the family was successful once again in having its candidate selected as Pope Nicholas II. However, Nicholas' death in 1061 caused yet another outbreak of factionalism. Matilda's family supported the candidacy of Alexander II, but an anti-pope assumed the title of Honorius II, setting off armed conflicts which were to rage on for years.

According to a somewhat romantic, and probably sometimes exaggerated, 17th-century account of Matilda's life, she first appeared on the battlefield in 1061. The Italian author, Vedriani, vividly describes Matilda, accompanied by her mother, leading her troops against the supporters of the evil anti-pope:

Now there appeared in Lombardy at the head of her numerous squadrons the young maid Matilda, armed like a warrior, and with such bravery, that she made known to the world that courage and valour in mankind is not indeed a matter of sex, but of heart and spirit.

We will probably never know for certain whether Matilda actually donned armor and "seized the spear of Pallas" as Vedriani would have us believe. Contemporary accounts, extolling her bravery and dedication to the papal cause, describe her leading her troops against the enemies of religion, but that may well mean only that she ordered them into battle. Given the generally negative reaction which *Joan of Arc was to provoke, some 300 years later, by wearing armor and riding into battle, it seems unlikely that Matilda, almost universally praised for her virtue and decorum, would have transgressed against the accepted convention that war was a "manly" pursuit. However, it is probably safe to assume that her role as director of the Canossan armies increased after the death of her stepfather, Godfrey of Lorraine, in 1069.

STIRPE·OPIBVS·FORMA·GESTIS
ET·NOMINE·QVONDAM
INCLYTA·MATILDIS·HIC·IACET
ASTRA·TENENS

Matilda of
Tuscany

During 1069, or perhaps earlier, Matilda, now 23 years old, had married her stepfather's son by an earlier marriage, a young man known as Godfrey III the Hunchback. While there is evidence to suggest that she might have preferred to dedicate her life completely to Christ, espousing perpetual virginity, Rangerius, the biographer of Matilda's spiritual advisor Anselm of Lucca, records that "her mother's exhortations prevented her from committing herself to the deep religious desire for a chastity which was, in her case, no longer permissible in view of the obligations she had assumed."

Not surprisingly, if Rangerius is to be believed, the marriage was not a happy one, and although it produced at least one child, none of Matilda's offspring survived infancy. As Matilda's devotion to the papal cause grew ever stronger, so her marriage seems to have diminished in importance. Apart from the couple's apparent lack of personal compatibility, Godfrey spent most of his time and military resources fighting in Lorraine, while Matilda's efforts focused on Italy, and she was displeased when her husband's forces failed to support her initiatives there. According to **Antonia Fraser**, the marriage "ended technically with Godfrey the Hunchback's death in 1076 but before that politics, far more than physical disinclination, had driven the couple apart."

Matilda's mother Beatrice, to whom she had always been close, also died in 1076, leaving Matilda to depend even more upon two men, Pope Gregory VII and Bishop Anselm of Lucca. Both served as advisors and confidants in matters political as well as spiritual; indeed, given the temper of the times, it was almost impossible to separate one sphere from the other. Perhaps Anselm's role was primarily that of Matilda's spiritual advisor, but the relationship between Matilda and Gregory was far more complex and interdependent, as the famous "incident at Canossa" of 1077 was to dramatically demonstrate.

Before his consecration as Pope Gregory VII in 1073, Hildebrand the monk had clearly aligned himself with the reformist cause in Rome, indeed he appears to have been the source of many of the reform initiatives of his predecessor, Alexander II. While he shared the monastic vision of what Abbot Hugh of Cluny called "the boundlessly rich and happy realm of heaven," he was not content with the monastic ideal of renunciation and flight from the world. Rather, the new pope applied all of his considerable talent and energy to the task of enforcing the claims of the successors of St. Peter, the popes, over the secular authorities, the kings and, in particular, the emperor. Throughout his life, Gregory held unflinchingly to one fundamental conviction:

> We must fight with the sword of the Holy Spirit, which is the word of God, to the death if need be, in the defence of righteousness (*iustitia*) against the enemies of God until they are converted.

In this fight Gregory was to rely heavily upon the faithful "daughter of Peter," Matilda.

The most important element of Gregory's reform program was to ensure the independence of the Church from outside interference; the practice of lay investiture, by which was meant the handing over of the symbols of office to bishops by secular officials, was formally prohibited in February 1075. Although the prohibition had serious implications for all the rulers of Christendom, since all of them tended to treat their bishops as members of their own staff, to be appointed, moved and even dismissed at will, the implications for the now adult Emperor Henry IV of Germany were the most serious of all. Not only was the assistance—less friendly observers might call it interference—of the German emperors in papal matters a long-established practice, but the German government, perhaps the most well developed in Western Europe during this period, could not function adequately without the bishops whom Henry and his predecessors had carefully selected and installed.

A vituperative war of words broke out between the emperor and the pope, during the course of which, on Christmas Eve 1075, the pope was assaulted in Rome and narrowly escaped being taken to Germany as a prisoner. At the Council of Worms in January 1076, Henry IV renounced his obedience to "Hildebrand, not Pope but false monk." In February, the pope responded with the most powerful weapon in his arsenal—excommunication.

Not only did the sentence of excommunication have spiritual consequences for Henry—if he died he could not be buried in consecrated ground and his soul would be damned forever—but there were also serious practical effects. If the ruler failed to do penance and have his sentence lifted within a period of 12 months, his subjects were absolved from their obedience to him and he forfeited his office. This threat of deposition was particularly serious in view of the elective nature of the imperial title; if Henry IV failed to reinstate himself into the pope's good graces, those entitled to elect the emperor could simply choose someone else to replace him. Given the constant struggles for power in Germany, and their resentment of Henry's growing power, there was little doubt that the princes would grasp their opportunity. Matilda of Tuscany and her stronghold at Canossa were to occupy a central place in the dramatic confrontation which was to follow.

There are few episodes in the history of the entire Middle Ages which have reached us with the completeness and vividness of the incident at Canossa, and for the intimate details of the affair we have to thank, not the chroniclers of the papal or the imperial courts, but a long (almost 3,000

lines) biographical poem, the *Vita Mathildis,* written while Matilda was still alive by her chaplain, Donizone. It is from him we learn of the proud and prosperous state of Canossa in 1077. But it was not the castle's grandeur or prosperity which Gregory was to come seeking; he was in need of the fortress' strength.

In December 1076, the pope, accompanied by a guard of Matilda's troops, was already on his way to Germany to preside at a meeting of the German Diet, called to discuss the mechanisms whereby, if certain conditions were not met, Henry IV might be deposed. Unwilling to be placed in such a potentially dangerous position, the emperor, with his wife *Bertha of Savoy by his side, determined to head the pope off and seek a resolution. With Germany now out of reach, Gregory headed for the safety of Canossa, Matilda's great, almost impregnable, fortress in the center of her dominions.

Henry IV was wise enough to realize that violence would not serve his interests on this occasion; halting a respectful distance from Canossa,

he begged for the intervention of Matilda and Abbot Hugh of Cluny, a saintly reformer who was also in the castle. Both Hugh and Henry agreed that Matilda had the best chance of softening the heart of the pope, and Henry implored his kinswoman to intercede. A charming illumination in Donizone's manuscript, still preserved today in the Vatican Library, shows Henry as a supplicant, sitting at the feet of a much larger Abbot Hugh, with both men gazing confidently at Matilda of Tuscany, who sits enthroned, surrounded by an elegant Romanesque canopy. The manuscript illuminator, the priestly poet, and especially the beleaguered emperor, were well aware of the potency of Matilda's influence.

But Pope Gregory was not a man to surrender his hard-won position of power easily. At first, he appeared to resist the attempts of all those who counselled moderation and forgiveness, even the pleas of the "faithful handmaiden of Christ," Matilda. Instead of granting absolution and lifting the sentence of excommunication, Gregory sent Henry IV prevaricating messages about the forthcoming Diet. According to

Henry IV stood barefoot in the snow, for three days, outside the castle at Canossa.

Donizone's eyewitness account, Henry, one of the most powerful secular rulers in Christendom, was forced to employ desperate measures. He donned the sackcloth shift of a penitent and stood, with bare head and bare feet, in the deep alpine snow. There, during three days spent in prayer and fasting, he knocked repeatedly at the castle gates, seeking Gregory's forgiveness. According to Gregory's own account of the incident, reported later to the German princes:

> [Henry] ceased not with many tears to beseech the apostolic help and comfort until all who were present, or who had heard the story, were so moved by pity and compassion that they pleaded his cause with prayers and tears. All marvelled at our unwonted severity, and some even cried out that we were showing, not the seriousness of apostolic authority, but rather the cruelty of a savage tyrant.

While Gregory the pope, with an eye to his political advantage, might have continued to resist Henry's pleas, Gregory the priest could not refuse a penitent, and he finally granted Henry absolution. The pope's fears proved only too well-founded; once Henry IV had averted deposition, he immediately resumed his opposition to papal policies and had soon arranged for the installation of an anti-pope in Rome, driving Gregory into exile at Salerno. The German princes, who had been preparing to select a new emperor, went ahead despite the lifting of the sentence of excommunication, for they had lost all faith in Pope Gregory and many of them rallied behind the rival king. The Diet at Augsberg never took place, and civil war ravaged the empire for the next three years.

Yet despite the weakness of the papal position, Matilda's faith never wavered, indeed she continued, "like a shining light," to actively support the papal side, putting, as Donizone tells us, "her weapons, her revenues, her servants and her property" at the disposal of the righteous cause. By 1080, she had agreed that, at her death, her lands should pass to the papacy, and she remained Gregory's one reliable source of support until he died, still in exile at Salerno, in 1085. Stalwartly refusing to recognize the anti-pope, despite mounting pressure from Henry, Matilda formed another firm alliance with Urban II who became pope in 1088. In 1089, she enraged the emperor still further by marrying Welf V of Bavaria, thus bringing this important region into the camp of papal supporters.

The marriage of the 43-year-old Matilda and the 17-year-old Welf has been variously interpreted by historians. **Shulamith Shahar** cites it as one of the isolated examples of medieval noblewomen "acting independently, evading the constraints of the law and overruling the customs of their society to select their own mates" and suggests that she made the selection "out of personal choice" as well as political considerations. Fraser, on the other hand, writes of Matilda's "personal reluctance" and concludes that this second marriage "was not only arranged by the Pope, but arranged for the benefit of his cause." What we know of Matilda's personality would suggest that, on this point, Fraser's version is closer to the truth. In any event, the marriage lasted only six unhappy years; by 1097, the couple had separated, and Welf had made his peace with the emperor.

The years which followed saw some significant deaths: Urban II in 1099, the anti-pope Clement III in 1100 and, in 1106, the death of Matilda's old enemy Emperor Henry IV. Matilda's relations with Henry V were better, partly because of Henry's somewhat more conciliatory attitude towards the question of church reform. While she continued to defend her own territories, she no longer went in person or sent aid to the papal supporters in other parts of Italy. In 1111, Matilda was formally reconciled with the emperor, and she appears to have revoked her earlier decision to give her lands to the papacy.

Now in her 60s, Matilda of Tuscany gradually came to accept the virtual independence of many of the cities within her domain; she spent less time waging war, devoting herself instead to visiting the monasteries which she had endowed, particularly St. Benedetto di Polirone, a reformed Benedictine house, founded by her grandfather. A magnificent manuscript, the so-called Matildine Gospels, presented to the monks of Polirone by Matilda, testifies to her love of learning and to her generosity. It was at Polirone in July 1115 that Matilda died, in her 70th year. Given the spiritual devotion with which she lived her life, there can be no doubt that she kept in mind the advice which St. Anselm of Canterbury had once given her:

> This counsel I presume to give you that if you feel the danger of death to be imminent, give yourself wholly up to God before you depart from this life; and for this purpose always keep a veil prepared secretly beside you.

Matilda of Tuscany was buried at Polirone. His great *Vita* unfinished and unpresented, Donizone lamented his patron's demise: "Now that thou art dead, oh great Matilda, the honour and dignity of Italy will decline." Certainly, Italy was not soon to see another woman of Matilda's determination and devotion. Profoundly revered by both popes and poets, she probably provided the model for Dante's Matilda, the beautiful young girl who appeared as guardian of the Earthly Paradise. In 1634, it was Pope Urban VIII who made arrangements for her body to be transferred to St. Peter's in Rome, the center of papal power. There her remains lie today, encased in an imposing tomb designed by Bernini. The famous Renaissance sculptor depicted the Countess Matilda larger than life size, young and beautiful, yet strong and determined. She carries the keys of St. Peter in her left hand and cradles the papal mitre protectively in her left arm, while with her right hand she grasps a staff. In death, as she had in life, Matilda of Tuscany stands ready to confront all who might wish to assail these sacred symbols of papal authority.

SOURCES:

Donizone di Canossa. *Vita Mathildis, Celeberrimae Principis Italiae.* Edited by Luigi Simeoni. Bologna, 1968.

Duff, Nora. *Matilda of Tuscany: La Gran Donna D'Italia.* London, 1909.

Fraser, Antonia. *Boadicea's Chariot: The Warrior Queens.* London, 1988.

Shahar, Shulamith. *The Fourth Estate: A History of Women in the Middle Ages.* London, 1983.

Strayer, Joseph R., ed. *Dictionary of the Middle Ages.* Vol. 8. 1982–1989.

(Dr.) Kathleen Garay,
Assistant Professor of History and Women's Studies,
McMaster University, Hamilton, Canada

Matilde.

Variant of Matilda.

Matilde of Vienne (d. after 1145)

Countess of Savoy. Died after 1145; married Amadeus III, count of Savoy (r. 1103–1148), around 1120; children: *Matilda of Maurienne (c. 1125–1157); Humbert III, count of Savoy (b. 1136).

Matoaka (c. 1596–1617).

See Pocahontas.

Matoko, Hani (1873–1957).

See Hani Motoko.

Matsukata, Haru (c. 1915–1998).

See Reischauer, Haru.

Matsuoka Moto (1873–1957).

See Hani Motoko.

Matthews, Burnita S. (1894–1988)

American jurist. Born Burnita Shelton in Burnell, Mississippi, on December 28, 1894; died in Washington, D.C., on April 25, 1988; daughter of Burnell

Shelton and Laura Drew (Barlow) Shelton; National University Law School, LL.B., 1919, LL.M., 1920, LL.D., 1950; married Percy Ashley Matthews, on April 28, 1917.

Born in rural Burnell, Mississippi, in 1894, Burnita S. Matthews proved an adept student of law, and received LL.B. and LL.M. degrees from the National University Law School (now a part of George Washington University) in 1920. Following her graduation, Matthews sought employment in the legal department of the Veterans Administration, but was told that the agency did not hire women. She then founded her own legal practice in Washington, D.C., although she was denied membership in the local law association due to her gender.

American women received the right to vote in 1920, and Matthews subsequently became a lawyer for the National Women's Party. In this position, she played a leading role in expanding the legal rights of women. In 1949, she was appointed by President Harry S. Truman to the Federal District Court for the District of Columbia, thus becoming the first woman in America to serve as a federal district judge. Among her cases was the bribery prosecution against new Teamsters Union president Jimmy Hoffa in 1957. Matthews became a senior judge (meaning one who is semi-retired, with a reduced caseload) in 1968, but remained an active jurist until her death in Washington, D.C., on April 25, 1988.

Grant Eldridge,
freelance writer, Pontiac, Michigan

Matthews, Jessie (1907–1981)

British actress and dancer. Born Jessie Margaret Matthews on March 11, 1907, in the Soho district of London, England; died of cancer on August 20, 1981; daughter of George Matthews (who ran a market stall) and Jane Matthews; educated at Pulteney Street School for Girls; married Henry Lytton, Jr. (an actor), in 1926 (divorced 1931); married Sonnie Hale (an actor), on January 24, 1931 (divorced 1944); married a third time; children: (second marriage) one adopted daughter.

Selected filmography: The Beloved Vagabond *(1923);* This England *(1923);* Straws in the Wind *(1924);* Out of the Blue *(1931);* There Goes the Bride *(1932);* The Midshipmaid *(Midshipmaid Gob, 1932);* Friday the Thirteenth *(1933);* Waltzes from Vienna *(1933);* The Good Companions *(1933);* Evergreen *(1934);* First a Girl *(1935);* It's Love Again *(1936);* Gangway *(1937);* Secrets of the Stars *(1937);* Sailing Along *(1938);* Climbing High *(1938); (as director)* Victory Wedding *(1944)*; Candles at Nine *(1944)*; Tom Thumb *(1958)*; The Hound of the Baskervilles *(1977)*.

Jessie Matthews was born in the working-class neighborhood of Soho in London, England, on March 11, 1907. Her father ran a stall in the local market, and her family, which ultimately included 16 children, was extremely poor. After seeing the silent-film serial *The Perils of Pauline,* Jessie became determined to become a professional actress. She began training in classical ballet in 1917 and had her first theatrical role in Seymour Hicks' production of *Bluebell in Fairyland* in London in 1919. Matthews was offered a role in *Charlot's Revue of 1924* and subsequently became the understudy to ***Gertrude Lawrence,** the revue's star. She was also in *Charlot's Revue of 1925* and secured the starring role in *Charlot's Revue of 1926.* Later the same year, Matthews married her co-star, Henry Lytton, Jr.

Known as the "Dancing Divinity," Matthews was famous in both England and America throughout the late 1920s and the 1930s. She made a number of light films in Britain and starred in such productions as *Earl Carroll's Vanities,* with which she toured the

Jessie Matthews

United States in 1927, *One Dam Thing After Another,* and Cole Porter's *Wake Up and Dream,* which introduced his song "Let's Do It." Perhaps her most memorable role was in Rodgers and Hart's *Ever Green* in 1930; she also starred in the 1935 movie version *Evergreen.* Matthews' on-stage fame did not negate the turmoil of her personal life. She entered into a long-running feud with fellow actress ***Evelyn Laye,** and eventually divorced Lytton to marry Laye's former husband, Sonnie Hale, in 1931.

Among the movies Matthews made was Alfred Hitchcock's 1933 *Waltzes from Vienna,* but her first love remained the stage. Her last starring role was in *Wild Rose,* which opened in London in 1942. During the play's production, Hale ran off with their daughter's nanny, and Matthews suffered a nervous breakdown. Her career never fully recovered. In 1944, she directed a 20-minute war propaganda piece, *Victory Wedding.* She continued to appear on stage sporadically in a series of nondescript productions throughout the 1950s, and had a role on the radio soap opera "Mrs. Dale's Diary" from 1961 to 1966. Matthews attempted several stage comebacks during the 1960s and 1970s, but these were also unsuccessful. She received the Order of the British Empire (OBE) in 1970, and in 1974 published an autobiography (co-written with **Muriel Burgess**), *Over My Shoulder.* Her last stage appearance was in the role of the Duchess of Berwick in *Lady Windermere's Fan,* which toured the United States in 1978. Jessie Matthews died of cancer on August 20, 1981.

SOURCES:

Katz, Ephraim. *The Film Encyclopedia.* NY: Harper-Perennial, 1994.

Lamparski, Richard. *Whatever Became of . . . ?* 2nd series. NY: Crown Publishers, 1968.

Morley, Sheridan. *The Great Stage Stars.* Australia: Angus & Robertson, 1986.

Grant Eldridge,
freelance writer, Pontiac, Michigan

Matthews, Mrs. Charles (1797–1856).

See Vestris, Lucia.

Matthews, Margaret (1935—)

African-American track-and-field champion. Born Margaret Rejean Matthews in Griffin, Georgia, on August 5, 1935; grew up in Atlanta and graduated from David T. Howard High School, the only member of her family to graduate from high school; married Jesse Wilburn (a Tennessee State football running back).

Was the first American woman to broad-jump 20 feet (1958); won the AAU broad jump title (1957,

1958, 1959); won an Olympic bronze medal in the 4x100-meter relay (1956).

Margaret Matthews belonged to a select group of American track-and-field champions who began their careers at Atlanta's David T. Howard High School under **Marian Armstrong-Perkins** and continued as Tennessee Tigerbelles under Ed Temple. This small circle, who won national and international championships at Howard High and Tennessee State, included **Mary McNabb**, *****Mildred McDaniel**, **Anna Lois Smith**, and *****Edith McGuire**. But if Matthews was a member of an elite squad as an athlete, her life outside school was one of poverty. She grew up on Butler Street, one of the poorest, roughest neighborhoods in Atlanta. The $26 per week her mother earned working in a laundry was the family's main income, as her infirm father worked only periodically. Neither of her parents had gone beyond third grade and no one in her family had graduated from high school. For Matthews, track and field was a way out. "I saw in athletics a chance to be something," she said. "I saw Mary McNabb and Mildred McDaniel win medals, and I felt if they could, I could."

Matthews did not attend Tennessee State University directly from high school. Instead, she went to Bethune-Cookman College in Florida, then left for Chicago to run for the CYO. Finally, she enrolled at Tennessee State where she roomed with her emotional opposite *****Mae Faggs**. While Faggs was mature and maternal, Matthews was immature, shrill, and determined to beat her teammates to prove herself. This was a tall order; the Tennessee Tigerbelles represented some of the world's best female athletes. Because she vacillated between overconfidence and self-doubt, Matthews' performances were erratic; she would win some meets, while at others she would not even place among the top runners. Competition with individuals seemed more important than winning an event. "The only time Margaret would jump was when I would jump," observed *****Willye B. White**. "She was determined to beat me." For Matthews, track was comparable to the mean streets of Atlanta—a place where one fought to survive.

In 1956, Matthews was considered America's best chance for a medal in the broad jump, as she set a new American record of 19'9¼" in the Olympic trials, beating Willye White by 6". In Melbourne, however, Matthews found the Olympics overwhelming and jumped a full 3' less than her record jump in the Olympic trials, though she did redeem herself by winning a

bronze medal on the U.S. 400-meter relay team. In 1957, Matthews won the broad jump title in the national outdoor AAU meet. At the AAU meet on July 6, 1958, she became the first woman to jump over 20' with a record 20'1". Matthews was pleased; she had topped Willye White. She was also delighted to beat another arch-rival *****Barbara Jones** in the 100-meter run. As well, Matthews anchored a victory for the Tigerbelles in the 4x100-meter relay.

During the Cold War, athletic events became battles; teams sought to prove the superiority of the system under which they trained. All this was lost on Matthews. "At that time I had not learned what it meant to win for the United States, or my school, or my hometown." Before participating in her first international event with the Soviet Union in Moscow, Matthews slacked off training and was scratched from the 100-meter run. She placed fourth in the broad jump, behind two Russians and Anna Lois Smith. Being beaten by Smith was particularly galling. Things got worse on the European tour when Willye White had a leap of 20'2½" inches in Warsaw, a new American record. Although Matthews did not particularly care if Eastern bloc teams won, White's victory spurred her on. In a dual meet with Hungary in Budapest, she made a record-breaking jump of 20'3½" and won gold medals in relay and sprints as well. In her final year at Tennessee State, Matthews successfully defended her broad jump title and was AAU All-American, but she placed second to **Vera Krepkina** in a meet between the U.S. and USSR. In the Pan American meet held in Chicago in 1959, Anna Lois Smith beat Matthews in the broad jump.

After college graduation, Matthews married Jesse Wilburn and moved to Memphis, where she became a teacher in the Klondike Elementary School and he became a coach at Melrose High School. "Even now," she said, "I want to be the best teacher here."

SOURCES:

Davis, Michael D. *Black American Women in Olympic Track and Field.* Jefferson, NC: McFarland, 1992.

Page, James A. *Black Olympian Medalists.* Englewood, CO: Libraries Unlimited, 1991.

Karin Loewen Haag,
Athens, Georgia

Matthews, Mary (c. 1690–c. 1763).

See Musgrove, Mary.

Matthews, Victoria (1954—)

Bishop of Edmonton who was the Anglican Church of Canada's first woman diocesan bishop. Born in

Toronto, Canada, in 1954; educated at Trinity College, University of Toronto, B.A., 1976, Th.M, 1987; Yale University Divinity School, M. Div. (Divinity), 1979.

Victoria Matthews was born in 1954 in Toronto, Canada, and spent most of her ministry in that city as well. After completing her studies at the University of Toronto and Yale University, she began her career as an assistant curate at the Church of St. Andrew in Scarborough, Ontario, Canada, in 1979, and served there until 1983. She then served as an incumbent at the parishes of Georgina, York-Simcoe, from 1983 to 1987, and at All Souls, Lansing, York-Scarborough, from 1987 to 1994. She also served as regional dean at the Deanery of York Mills, Ontario, from 1989 to 1994, as suffragan (assistant) bishop of the Diocese of Toronto in 1994. In 1997, at age 43, she was named bishop of Edmonton, Diocese of Edmonton, where she currently remains.

At the time of her seating as bishop of Edmonton, she was one of 6 women among the Anglican Church's 525 diocesan bishops and the Anglican Church of Canada's first woman diocesan bishop. (The first woman bishop chosen in the Anglican Communion was *Barbara Harris, a suffragan bishop in the United States. The first woman diocesan bishop was *Penelope Jamieson, elected in New Zealand.) When chosen diocesan bishop, Matthews, who was elected at a special synod meeting on the fifth ballot, said she was surprised with the decision. Election delegates maintained that gender was not an issue. Even so, Matthews has said that she would be gratified to see more women bishops in Canada, and that "I welcome the day when gender is no longer a concern in the church."

Jo Anne Meginnes,
freelance writer, Brookfield, Vermont

Matthews, Victoria Earle

(1861–1907)

African-American author and journalist. Name variations: (pseudonym) Victoria Earle. Born Victoria Earle Smith in Fort Valley, Georgia, on May 27, 1861; died of tuberculosis in New York City on March 10, 1907; interred at Maple Grove Cemetery, Kew Gardens, Long Island; one of nine children of Caroline Smith, a slave; according to family oral history, her birth father was her mother's slaveowner; attended Grammar School 48 in New York City; married William Matthews (a carriage driver), in 1876; children: one son, Lamartine.

The light-skinned Victoria Matthews wrote stories of her childhood for the *Waverly* magazine, the *New York Weekly* and the *Family Story Paper.* She told of her mother, **Caroline Smith,** who had escaped from her slave-owning master during the Civil War, only to return and find her daughters Victoria and Anna living in his home. According to family oral history, he was their birth father, and Caroline had to sue for custody. Moving to Virginia for four years, she then took her children to New York around 1873.

Victoria Matthews, who had been a fervent reader while growing up, freelanced for various newspapers in Brooklyn and Manhattan, including *The New York Times,* the *New York Herald Tribune,* and the *Brooklyn Eagle.* She then became a full-time journalist for the *New York Age.* Matthews was the organizer behind the fund-raising testimonial for *Ida Wells-Barnett and her anti-lynching crusade. Founder and first president of the Woman's Loyal Union, Matthews was also instrumental in forming women's clubs in New York City and Boston and was on the executive board of the National Federation of Afro-American Women.

Victoria Matthews

Matthison, Edith (1875–1955)

English actress. Born Edith Wynne Matthison in Birmingham, England, on November 23, 1875; died on September 23, 1955; daughter of Henry Matthison and Kate (Wynne) Matthison; married Charles Rann Kennedy (a playwright).

Edith Matthison, who first trod the boards in illustrator *Edith Holden*'s backyard, made her legitimate stage debut at Blackpool in December 1896 in *The School Girl*. A Shakespearean actress and leading lady for Sir Henry Irving and Herbert Beerbohm Tree, she first came to the public's attention when, at short notice, she played the part of Violet Oglander in *The Lackey's Carnival* at the Duke of York's Theater in September 1900. Her performance in *Everyman* in 1902 led to her New York debut in the same play. Matthison remained for two years in America, appearing as Viola in *Twelfth Night* and Kate Hardcastle in *She Stoops to Conquer*. On her return to England, she was engaged by Irving to tour with him as Portia to his Shylock in *Merchant of Venice* which then opened at the Drury Lane in May 1905. Matthison often played both sides of the Atlantic, appearing in *King Henry VIII* and *Merry Wives of Windsor* with Beerbohm Tree in New York in 1916. Back in London in 1926, she appeared as *Francesca da Rimini* in *The Salutation*; on her return to America in 1930, she was a great success when she appeared as Hamlet. She married Charles Rann Kennedy and also performed in many of his plays.

Mattingly, Marie (1878–1943).

See Meloney, Marie Mattingly.

Mattocks, Isabella (1746–1826)

English actress. Name variations: Isabella Hallam; Mrs. George Mattocks. Born Isabella Hallam in 1746; died in Kensington, England, on June 25, 1826; daughter of Lewis Hallam (d. 1756, a comedian) and Mrs. Lewis Hallam (an actress, first name unknown, who died in 1774); married George Mattocks who became a theater manager in Liverpool.

At four and a half, Isabella Hallam, the daughter of comedian Lewis Hallam and actress **Mrs. Lewis Hallam**, played children's parts at Covent Garden. When her family journeyed to America to seek their acting fortune, she remained in England with relatives. Isabella married George Mattocks in 1765, and was chief support of Covent Garden until her retirement in 1808. A comedian and singer, she was noted for her portrayals of chambermaids and old women.

Matute, Ana Maria (1926—)

Important Spanish novelist of the post-Civil War era. Name variations: Ana María Matute Ausejo. Born in Barcelona, Spain, in 1926; married Ramón Eugenio de Goicoechea, in 1954 (divorced 1963); children: Juan Pablo (b. 1956).

Ana Maria Matute was born in 1926 in Barcelona, where she spent her childhood beset by poor health. She studied first at a school run by nuns and then received an unhappy secondary education at a French-run institution. Although Matute did not attend university, she early showed literary genius. As a teenager, in 1943 she completed *Pequeño teatro*, which was later revised and published in 1954. Her first novel to appear in print was *Los Abel* (1948), exploring the conflict between Cain and Abel to understand Spain following the Civil War. It was a finalist for the Nadal Prize. In 1952, she married Ramón Eugenio de Goicoechea, and they had a son, Juan Pablo, two years later. Matute and Goicoechea were divorced in 1963.

Matute wrote prolifically, publishing novels, short stories, and children's books. She set many of her works in the countryside of Castile and explored themes related to the Civil War, of which she later remarked: "Even today, those of us who then were only ten years old, we haven't been able to forget it." Her novels won Spain's most prestigious literary awards, including the Nadal Prize and the Cervantes National Literature Prize. Matute's trilogy, *Los Mercaderes*, received great acclaim both at home and abroad, as did *Olvidado Rey Gudu* (1974).

Matute also taught at U.S. universities, including Indiana University and the University of Oklahoma. She donated her manuscripts and other papers to Boston University, which created a special library collection for them in her name.

SOURCES:
Díaz, Janet Winecoff. *Ana María Matute*. NY: Twayne Publishers, 1971.
Jones, Margaret. E.W. *The Literary World of Ana Maria Matute*. 1970.
Roma, Rosa. *Ana María Matute*. Madrid: E.P.E.S.A., 1971.

Kendall W. Brown,
Professor of History,
Brigham Young University, Provo, Utah

Matzenauer, Margaret (1881–1963)

Hungarian contralto, soprano and mezzo-soprano. Name variations: Margarete. Born on June 1, 1881, in Temeszvar, Hungary; died on May 19, 1963, in Van Nuys, California; studied in Graz with Januschowsky;

studied in Berlin with Mielke and Franz Emerich, and in Munich with Ernst Preuses; married three times.

Debuted in Strasbourg (1901); was a member of the Munich Court Opera (1904–11); made Metropolitan Opera debut (1911), appearing for 19 seasons until 1930; made Covent Garden debut (1914); retired and became a teacher (after 1938).

Possessed of a stupendous contralto voice, Margaret Matzenauer was born in Temeszvar, Hungary, in 1881, and she made her opera debut as Puck in Weber's *Oberon* at the Strasbourg Stadttheater in 1901. For seven years, from 1904 to 1911, she was featured in Wagnerian soprano roles with the Hofoper in Munich. She was then invited to participate in the Bayreuth Festival.

On November 13, 1911, Matzenauer opened the season at the New York Metropolitan Opera as Amneris in *Aïda*, with Toscanini conducting. Wrote one New York critic: "It is possible to praise not only the natural beauty of her voice, but the care and the intelligence evidenced in her singing." Matzenauer would be featured at the Metropolitan for the next 18 years, during which she successfully portrayed Leonore, the three Brünhildes, Kundry, Isolde, Donna Elvira, Selika, Orfeo, Carmen, and Delilah.

Matzenauer sang roles for mezzo-soprano or soprano as well. Although unsurpassed in the mezzo range, she was not content with limiting herself and in the process compromised her voice. By the time she was 40, the glory of her lower voice had been dulled by hard usage. Although she was accepted in Wagnerian roles, critics were less forgiving when she performed Mozart. But she was successful on the concert as well as the opera stage, and despite her attempts to succeed at all roles and the subsequent strain on her vocal cords, Matzenauer was a popular singer.

She was also an accomplished pianist who learned new and difficult music very quickly. After leaving the Met in 1930, Matzenauer moved to Los Angeles and devoted herself more and more to teaching.

John Haag,
Athens, Georgia

Margaret Matzenauer

Maubeuge, abbess of.
See Aldegund (c. 630–684).
See Madelberte (fl. 7th c.).

Maud.
Variant of Matilda, Mathilda, Maude, Mold.

Maud (1869–1938)
*Queen of Norway. Name variations: Maud Saxe-Coburg. Born Maud Charlotte Mary Victoria on November 26, 1869, in London, England; died on November 20, 1938, in London; daughter of Edward VII, king of England (r. 1901–1910), and *Alexandra of Denmark (1844–1925); married Haakon VII, king of Norway (r. 1905–1957), on July 22, 1896; children: Olav V (1903–1991), king of Norway (r. 1957–1991). Queen Maud Land in Antarctica was named in her honor.*

Maud, Empress (1102–1167).
See Matilda, Empress.

Maud, Empress (c. 1103–1152).
See Matilda of Boulogne.

Maud Carinthia (c. 1105–1160).
See Adele of Champagne for sidebar.

Maud Chaworth (1282–c. 1322).
See Chaworth, Maud.

Maud de Bohun.

See Bohun, Maud (fl. 1240s).
See Bohun, Maud (fl. 1275).

Maud de Braose.

See Braose, Maud de (d. 1211).
See Mortimer, Maud (c. 1229–1301).

Maud de Kevilioc (1171–1233).

See Maude of Chester.

Maud de St. Walerie (d. 1211).

See Braose, Maud de.

Maud of Lusignan (d. 1241)

*Countess of Hereford and Essex. Name variations: Maud d'Eu; Maud de Lusignan. Died on August 14, 1241; interred at Llanthony Priory, Gloucester; some sources say she was the daughter of *Isabella of Angouleme (1186–1246) and Hugh X, count of Lusignan; others say she was the daughter of Ralph de Lusignan and Alice d'Eu (d. 1246), countess of Eu; married Humphrey Bohun (1200–1275), 2nd earl of Hereford, 1st earl of Essex (some sources cite 6th earl of Hereford and Essex [r. 1220–1275]), and constable of England; children: *Maud Bohun (fl. 1240s); Humphrey Bohun (d. 1265, who married *Eleanor de Braose). Humphrey Bohun was also married to Maud of Avenbury (d. 1273).*

Maud of Mandeville (d. 1236)

Countess of Essex. Name variations: Maud de Mandeville or Mandville; countess of Hereford. Acceded as countess of Essex on January 8, 1226; died on August 27, 1236; daughter of Geoffrey, 4th earl of Essex (r. 1199–1213), and Beatrice de Say (d. before 1197); married Humphrey Bohun, 1st earl of Hereford (some sources cite 5th earl of Hereford); married Roger de Daunteseye (divorced 1233); children: (first marriage) Henry; Humphrey Bohun (1200–1275), 2nd earl of Hereford, 1st earl of Essex (some sources cite 6th earl of Hereford and Essex [r. 1220–1275]).

Maud of Normandy (d. 1017)

*Countess of Blois, Champagne and Chartres. Name variations: Matilda. Died in 1017; daughter of Richard I the Fearless (d. 996), duke of Normandy (r. 942–996), and *Gunnor of Denmark (d. 1031); married Eudes also spelled Odo I, count of Blois, Champagne, and Chartres (r. 978–995); children: Theobald II also known as Thibaut II, count of Blois, Champagne, and Chartres (r. 995–1004).*

Maud of Norway (1869–1938).

See Maud, queen of Norway.

Maud Plantagenet (c. 1310–c. 1377)

*Countess of Ulster. Born around 1310; died around 1377 in Campsey Abbey, Suffolk, England; daughter of Henry, 3rd earl of Lancaster, and *Maud Chaworth (1282–c. 1322); married William de Burgh, 3rd earl of Ulster, around 1330; married Ralph de Ufford; children: (first marriage) *Elizabeth de Burgh (1332–1363); (second marriage) *Maud de Vere. Maud Plantagenet became a nun at Campsey Abbey around 1348.*

Maud Plantagenet (1335–1362)

*Countess of Hainault and Holland. Name variations: Matilda; Maud Stafford. Born on April 4, 1335 (some sources cite 1339); died on April 10, 1362, in England; daughter of Henry (b. 1306), 1st duke of Lancaster, and *Isabel Beaumont (d. 1368); sister of *Blanche of Castile (1341–1369); married Ralph Stafford, Lord Stafford, on November 1, 1344; married William V, duke of Bavaria (r. 1347–1358), count of Holland (r. 1354–1358), count of Hainault (r. 1356–1358), in 1352.*

Maude of Alsace (1163–c. 1210)

*Duchess of Brabant. Name variations: Matilda of Boulogne. Born in 1163 at Pas-de-Calais, France; died around 1210 or 1211; daughter of Matthew I (Matthieu d'Alsace), count of Boulogne, and *Marie of Boulogne (d. 1182); married Henry I (1165–1235), duke of Brabant, in 1179; children: Godfrey de Brabant (b. 1186); Marle de Brabant (b. 1188); *Mary of Brabant (c. 1191–c. 1260); *Marguerite de Brabant, countess of Guelders (c. 1192–?); Alix de Brabant also known as Adelaide of Brabant (b. 1194); Mathilde de Brabant (b. 1200, who married Floris IV, count of Holland); Henry II (1207–1248), duke of Brabant. Following the death of Maude of Alsace, Henry I married *Marie of France in 1213.*

Maude of Brabant (1224–1288)

*Countess of Artois. Name variations: Mahaut Louvain; Matilde de Brabant. Born in 1224; died on September 29, 1288; daughter of Henry II, duke of Brabant, and *Marie of Swabia (c. 1201–1235); sister of Henry III (1233–1261), duke of Brabant; married Robert I the Good (1216–1250), count of Artois (r. 1237–1250), on June 14, 1237; married Guion de*

Chastillon, count of St. Pol; children: (first marriage) Robert II (1250–1302), count of Artois; *Blanche of Artois (c. 1247–1302, who married Henry I, king of Navarre, and Edmund the Crouchback, 1st earl of Lancaster); (second marriage) Beatrice of Chastillon (d. 1304, who married John de Brienne, count of Eu).

Maude of Chester (1171–1233)

Countess of Huntingdon. Name variations: Maud de Kevilioc or de Keveliock; Maud Dunkeld; Matilda of Chester. Born in 1171; died on January 6, 1233; daughter of Hugh de Kevilioc, 3rd earl of Chester (some sources cite 6th earl of Chester), and *Bertrada of Evreux; married David (c. 1144–1219), earl of Huntingdon (r. 1185–1219), on August 26, 1190; children: seven, including *Margaret (d. 1228, who married Alan of Galloway); *Isabella (1206–1251, who married Robert Bruce); *Ada Dunkeld (c. 1195–after 1241); Robert (died young); Henry (died young); John of Chester (c. 1207–1237), earl of Chester (r. 1232–1237).

Mauermayer, Gisela (b. 1913)

German discus thrower who won a gold medal in the 1936 Olympics. Born on November 24, 1913.

Gisela Mauermayer, a six-foot tall discus thrower, captured a gold medal at the 1936 Olympics, held in Berlin. Three weeks before the games, Mauermayer heaved the discus 158'6" to set a world record that remained unbroken for 12 years. Even her winning Olympic distance was slightly under her record, at 156'3". The Berlin games also netted a silver medal for **Jadwiga Wajs** of Poland, who threw a distance of 151'8", while Mauermayer's teammate **Paula Mollenhauer** took the bronze medal with a much less impressive distance of 130'7". Mauermayer went on to became a schoolteacher and a high-ranking member of the Nazi women's organization. Following the war, she lost her job because of her Nazi affiliation. She returned to school, receiving a doctoral degree in the Zoological Institute of Munich University, where she specialized in the study of ants. Later, she became a librarian.

Maultasch, Margaret (1318–1369).

See Margaret Maultasch.

Maunder, Annie Russell
(1868–1947)

Irish astronomer. Born in 1868 in County Tyrone, Ireland; died in 1947; daughter of W.A. Russell (an An-

glican vicar); attended Victoria College in Belfast; graduated from Girton College in Cambridge, 1889; married Edward Maunder (an astronomer), in 1895.

The daughter of an Anglican vicar, Annie Russell Maunder was born in County Tyrone, Ireland, in 1868. She received her primary education at home before attending Victoria College in Belfast. Continuing her studies at Girton College in Cambridge, she received the school's highest honor granted to a woman when she was named Senior Optime in the Mathematical Tripos in 1889. She then secured a position at the Royal Observatory at Greenwich, measuring and examining photographs of sunspots, which was one of the subjects that most interested her. Along with two other women, and despite her growing prominence as an astronomer, Maunder was denied admission to the Royal Astronomical Society in 1892. During her tenure at Greenwich, she met noted astronomer Edward Maunder, the head of the solar photography department at Greenwich who was also the founder of the British Astronomical Society, an organization which welcomed participation by women. The two struck up both a personal and a professional relationship, and she became the first editor of the *Journal of the British Astronomical Society* in 1894. She and Edward were married the following year.

Although Maunder's contributions to astronomy did not include any new theories, her work on sunspots and her photographic survey of the Milky Way galaxy secured her a place in the history of science. She also made field trips to Norway and India to study and document eclipses. With her husband, she published *The Heavens and Their Story*, a history of astronomy, in 1908. Maunder was otherwise not active as a scientist between 1898 and 1915, but she returned to her position at the Royal Observatory from 1915 to 1920, and resumed the editorship of the *Journal of the British Astronomical Society* from 1917 to 1930. She died in 1947.

SOURCES:
Ogilvie, Marilyn Bailey. *Women in Science: Antiquity through the Nineteenth Century.* Cambridge, MA: MIT Press, 1986.

Grant Eldridge,
freelance writer, Pontiac, Michigan

Maupin, d'Aubigny (c. 1670–1707)

Flamboyant French singer, renowned bisexual, and sword duelist, who was the first mezzo-soprano in French opera to play leading roles. Name variations: Julie d'Aubigny Maupin; Julie, Chévalier de Maupin;

Mlle de Maupin; Mlle d'Aubigny; Aubigny Maupin. Pronunciation: JHU-lee DOH-BEEN-YEE mo-PEH. Born Julie d'Aubigny in Paris around 1670 (some sources cite 1673); died in November 1707, probably in a suburb of Paris, perhaps in Provence; burial place unknown; daughter of Gaston, Sieur d'Aubigny; mother's name unknown; educated by private tutors; married Jean Maupin, around 1687; no children.

Was mistress of the Comte d'Armagnac (c. 1685–87); moved to Marseille, where she sang at the Academy of Music (c. 1687–89); condemned by the Parlement of Aix for taking a lover from a convent (c. 1689); made her way to Paris, fighting and singing (c. 1689–90); debuted at the Paris Opera (1690); fled to Brussels, where she became the mistress of the elector of Bavaria (1696–98); was possibly in Spain (c. 1698); starred at the Paris Opera (1698–1705); husband returned (c. 1701); had liaison with the Marquise de Florensac (1703–05); left the stage and took up religious pursuits (1705–07).

Debuts at the Paris Opera: Pallas in Cadmus et Hermione *(composer Lully, librettist Quinault, 1690); A (female) Magician in* Didon *(Desmarets, Mme. de Xaintonge, 1693); Cérès in* Les Saisons *(Collasse, ballet by Abbé Pic, 1695); Minerve in* Thésée *(Lully, Quinault, 1698); Cidippe in* Thétys et Pelée *(Collasse, Fontenelle, 1699); Cérès in* Proserpine *(Lully, Quinault, 1699); The High Priestess of the Sun in* Marthésie, Reine des Amazones *(Destouches, La Motte, 1699); Venus and Campaspe in* Triomphe des Arts *(La Barre, ballet by La Motte, 1700); A Singing Shepherdess and The (female) Musician in* Le Carnaval *(Lully, a masquerade revival, 1700); The Dawn and Nérine, confidante of Circé, in* Canente *(Collasse, La Motte, 1700); The Priestess of the Sun and A Priestess of Flora in* Hésione *(Campra, Danchet, 1700); The Nymph of the Seine and Thétys in* Aréthuse *(Campra, ballet by Danchet, 1701); France, Ismène, A (female) Magician, and Thétys,* Scylla *(Gatti, Duché, 1701); Clymène, mother of Phaéton, in* Phaéton *(Lully, Quinault, 1702); A Grace and Céphise in* Omphale *(Destouches, La Motte, 1702); Scylla in* Arcis et Galathée *(Lully, Campistron, 1702); Médée in* Médus, Roi de Mèdes *(Bouvard, Lagrange-Chancel, 1702); Polymnie, Iris, and Valfrina in* Fragments de Lully *(Campra, ballet by Danchet, 1702); Clorinde, lover of Tancrède, in* Tancrède *(Campra, Danchet, 1702); Pénélope in* Ulysse et Pénélope *(Rebel, Guichard, 1703); Cassiope, Queen of Ethiopia, in* Persée *(Lully, Quinault, 1703); title role in* Armide *(Lully, Quinault, 1703); Venus and a Distressed Woman in* Psyché *(Lully, Corneille de l'Isle, 1703); Madness in* Le Carnival et la Folie *(Destouch-*

es, ballet by La Motte, 1704); Junon in Isis *(Lully, Quinault, 1704); Diane in* Iphigénie et Tauride *(Desmarets, Duché, 1704); Felicity, Thétys, and A Nymph of Calypso in* Télémaque *(Campra, Danchet, 1704); Mélanie, Princess of Iceland, in* Alcine *(Campra, Danchet, 1705); Isabelle, lover of Octave, in* La Vénitienne *(La Barre, ballet by La Motte, 1705).*

D'Aubigny Maupin experienced enough adventure to fill a life far longer than the 37 years allotted her. In her day, she was notable for her powerful, warm mezzo-soprano voice and notorious for her duels and her male and female lovers. Yet little documentary evidence about her exists apart from notices of Paris Opera productions and a handful of letters and judicial documents. Even her first name is unknown save for a single letter addressing her as "Julie." Dates and places of her birth and death are disputed, and her mother's name is lost. Numerous anecdotes and passing mention in memoirs and diaries of her contemporaries comprise the bulk of what has survived. Nevertheless, a reasonably accurate account of her turbulent life can be pieced together.

Maupin was probably born in 1670 in, or near, Paris. Her father, Gaston, Sieur d'Aubigny, was secretary to Louis de Lorraine, Comte d'Armagnac, a prominent figure at the court of Louis XIV (r. 1643–1715). Armagnac was governor of Artois (mostly a title, not a job) and as grand equerry of France (responsible for the king's horses and stables) a holder of one of "the seven offices" of the Crown. Gaston himself was of the petty nobility at best and not related to the lords of Aubigny (Berry). He was a dashing sort, a swordsman and womanizer. Nothing is known about Maupin's mother; she may well have died soon after her birth.

Julie (assuming that was her name) was raised by her father in a male environment. He had her educated by the tutors of the king's pages, who taught her grammar, literature, writing, drawing, dancing, and such, leaving her better educated than most women of her time and class. He also insisted she learn to fence, probably to protect herself in a turbulent society where personal violence and dueling (albeit illegal) was endemic. (It is estimated that the wealthy quarters of Paris housed well over 10,000 professional duelists.) Fencing was not a common skill among women but was far from unknown, especially in Latin countries in the 16th and 17th centuries. Julie had favorable physical attributes: a lithe, agile body, strong limbs, wrists of steel, and swift reflexes. She probably started to fence at about age 12 and possibly was taught by masters Jean and François Rousseau and André Vernesson de Liancourt. Most uncommon about her as a duelist, however, was that apparently she fought only men, and on an equal footing.

At about age 15, she became Armagnac's mistress. An agreeable, handsome man, he had watched her grow up and became her guardian when her father died. Gaston may have died after the start of the affair, which he possibly promoted but in any case was powerless to prevent, as Armagnac well knew. Julie was exceptionally attractive. She had large blue eyes, an aquiline nose, a pretty mouth, excellent white teeth, very white skin, and a luxuriant crown of chestnut hair with shades of blonde. Of "medium" height (by modern standards probably not over 5'3"), she was slender, small-breasted, and lithe. No less striking was her personality, which has been described as brave, fiery, generous, ardent, impetuous, and seductive. The affair lasted maybe two years, after which Armagnac found her a husband, either because he was tiring under her pace or because they wanted a respectable cover. A mild young man from Saint-Germain-en-Laye filled the bill, one Jean Maupin.

I am made for perils, as well as for tenderness.

—d'Aubigny Maupin, in a letter, 1703

Estimates of how long this ill-matched pair stayed together range from a day to a year. Whatever the case, Armagnac or Julie (or both) wangled him a post in the tax service (Cour des Aides) in Toulouse. Julie stayed behind in Paris; whether with Armagnac's approval is in dispute.

His lax supervision and her independent spirit left her largely on her own. While haunting the stables and fencing halls, Maupin fell passionately in love with an aspiring masterswordsman, Henri(?) de Séranne (variant spellings abound). After a time, they took the road to Marseille, where he claimed to have property. One version of the story says Armagnac persuaded M. de La Reynie, the Paris chief of police, to pressure Séranne to leave, then became furious when Julie went too. Others say Séranne had fallen afoul of La Reynie because he had killed a man in a duel behind the church of the Carmelites or because he and some other gallants had had a run-in with a patrol.

This journey to Marseille, and her experiences once there, proved to be the turning point in Maupin's life. In Marseille, she discovered her future vocation and her bisexuality. Whether she had cross-dressed before is uncertain, but on the journey she did so. For the rest of her life, she cross-dressed frequently, having no trouble passing as a boyish cavalier due to her figure and her ease in a masculine environment. It should be noted, however, that female cross-dressing has a long history in the West; it made traveling much easier and opened otherwise forbidden pathways through a male-dominated society.

Once in Marseille (if not on the way), Séranne confessed he had no property there. Maupin forgave him. To survive, they gave fencing exhibitions in taverns, advertising her as a woman despite her attire. According to a famous anecdote, when a heckler called out that she really was a man, she settled the question by tearing open her shirt. To keep going, they added singing to their show since both had fine voices.

Maupin's singing success inspired her to dream of a career in opera. The Marseille Academy of Music, with theaters in Marseille and Montpellier, had been founded in 1685 by Pierre Gaultier, a friend of Jean-Baptiste Lully (1632–1687), the premier opera composer in France. Maupin auditioned for Gaultier and passed. Like the large majority of singers of her time, she could not read music; her prodigious memory helped her overcome this impediment, while her untutored but beautiful mezzo-soprano voice (then called *bas-dessus*—see below) was well received. She also revealed a gift for acting. Admission to the Academy was not overly difficult—Séranne was hired, too—but this step up was momentous.

Performing as "Mlle d'Aubigny," she won quick success in a variety of roles—only to throw it all away in a truly incredible escapade. Because of her cross-dressing, Maupin had drawn the attentions of young women who initially thought she was a man, and she became infatuated with a beautiful young girl, **Cécilia Bortigali**(?). She besieged Bortigali (or possibly the reverse) to the point that the girl's parents, fearing a scandal, packed her off to a convent in Avignon. Maupin straightaway abandoned Séranne and the Opera. Posing as a young woman seeking to become a nun, she located Bortigali's convent in Avignon and was soon admitted as a novice. The two, reunited, then plotted an escape. Maupin surreptitiously disinterred the body of a young nun who had recently died, hauled it to Bortigali's cell, laid it on the cot, and then set it afire, thus hoping to lead the nuns to think Cécilia had perished. During the ensuing confusion, the two fled over the walls of the convent and rode out of town.

The truth quickly emerged. The Parlement (high court) of Aix condemned "the sieur d'Aubigny" (in absentia) to the stake for sacrilege and an armload of other grave offenses. Why was Maupin portrayed as a male in the sentence? It seems implausible that the court did not know her true sex. More likely, the male identity was a tactful device to spare Bortigali's family the further embarrassment of revealing it was a lesbian affair.

Within three months, Maupin cooled on Bortigali, who crept back home after Maupin had a fling with a musketeer. Making her way north by degrees, probably intending to go to Paris when it appeared safe, Maupin again sang in taverns. While at the Écu-Neuf in Villeperdue, near Tours, she became embroiled with a drunken young cavalier whom she challenged and fought along with his two companions. (Probably she fought them in succession, although some versions say she took them on as a group.) Maupin ran the cavalier clear through the shoulder, pinning him and thus ending the duel. Within a day, he learned to his astonishment that his adversary was a woman, while she learned he was a grandee, Louis-Joseph d'Albert de Luynes (b. 1670), son of the Duc de Luynes and his wife *Anne de Rohan-Montbazon. Versions differ as to which one sought a meeting during Albert's recovery at the inn. She ended by nursing him back to health, and they became lovers. Once recovered, he received orders to join the army in Germany. They bade a tearful farewell, vowing to meet again. Both were to go on to many other lovers, but theirs was a special relationship, passionately renewed now and then until her death.

Again on the move, at Poitiers Maupin met a 50ish actor-musician named Maréchal, who recognized her talent and insisted that she make the Paris Opera her goal. A stern, competent teacher, he gave her much-needed acting and singing lessons until she left because of his alcoholism. Eventually, at Róuen, she met a young bass-baritone, Gabriel-Vincent Thévenard (1669–1741), a baker's son from Orléans who was also touring the provinces on the way to the Opera. The two became lovers and finally reached Paris. Still concerned about the warrant against her, Maupin boldly approached her old lover Armagnac. He readily succumbed to her familiar charms and put the case to Louis XIV, pleading that she was remorseful and had worked hard to become a singer at the Opera. The king, apparently amused by her gall and daring, annulled the warrant.

Thévenard won a place in the chorus immediately, but Maupin needed help and used Théve-nard, Armagnac, and possibly Albert to secure an audition, for which she needed to contact Jean-Nicolas de Francine (1662–1735), successor (from 1688) to his late father-in-law, Lully, as Superintendent of the King's Music. Through Thévenard, she learned that a boy soprano (later a composer), François Bouvard (c. 1683–1760), was close to Francine, so she auditioned for Bouvard. He then mentioned her to Francine, who needed a female warrior to play Pallas Athena in a revival of Lully and Quinault's *Cadmus et Hermione* (1673). This opera, writes Peter Pierson, was the first of Lully's series of *tragédies lyriques,* "brilliantly orchestrated and precisely sung operas that set the main direction of French operatic style for the following two hundred years." Lully welded the music to the texts; hence, acting assumed real importance—which aided Maupin's career. The plots, based on Roman myths and chivalric romances, emphasized themes of love and glory, again suiting Maupin well. Also, Lully's arias, note **Ellen Clayton**, are "simple, smooth, and easily learned," which helped since Maupin depended on her memory.

D'Aubigny Maupin won the role and admission to the Académie Royale de Musique, known as the "Paris Opera," which performed on Tuesdays, Thursdays, Fridays, and Sundays at the theater in the Palais-Royal, the residence of the king's brother Philip (1640–1701), duke of Orléans (known as "Monsieur"). Singing there was a challenge. Audiences behaved in ways later times would think outrageous: conversing, moving about, heckling, and even loudly singing along with the artists. She made her debut in December 1690 under the name "Mlle Maupin" and won immediate acclaim. Before she left the Opera temporarily in 1695, she also sang in two other roles that are known by name, originating both. Probably there were additional roles, the records of which have disappeared. Maupin could play both comic and serious roles and also dance. Often her parts were transposed to suit her lower register, sometimes (it has been said) an octave below the original soprano line.

Maupin early won respect in the company when she stood up against one Dumesnil/Dumény (d. 1702). He was a highly popular, golden-voiced tenor but a coarse, cowardly lout who made himself odious as an intimidating seducer who took souvenir ribbons from his conquests. During a rehearsal for *Cadmus et Hermione*, he tried his wiles on Maupin. She indignantly rebuffed him, and he called her a foul name. Bystanders prevented a duel then and there, but that evening she waited for him, dressed as a man, at the Place des Victoires. Accosting him, she demanded satisfaction for his behavior. Thinking she was a man, he begged for mercy, but she thrashed him soundly with a cane and took his watch and snuffbox. The next day, he regaled the company with a tale about being beaten and robbed by three men despite his valiant defense. When Maupin stepped forward, called him a liar, and produced the watch and snuffbox, he slunk off, trailed by mocking laughter. Thereafter, he treated her with fawning deference, while she basked in the gratitude of her colleagues.

Maupin led a tempestuous offstage existence. After Lully's death, Louis XIV, answering complaints, issued a code of conduct for the company. It had little effect. The *grande seigneurs* continued to raid the Opera and the Comédie for mistresses, and Maupin was accommodating. Albert also turned up once more; the couple passed several blissful months in 1695 before he was recalled for the siege of Namur. Maupin sought female lovers as well; some, like the beautiful **Fanchon Moreau** (1668–after 1743), were members of the company. (A questionable story claims that Maupin tried to commit suicide after Moreau repulsed her.) Following Albert's departure, she seems to have become especially willful, and in February 1696 she crossed the line too openly.

Dressed as a man, she crashed the duke of Orléans' annual pre-Lenten ball at the Palais-Royal and made persistent, obviously unwanted advances to a lovely young marquise. Three men, the marquise's suitors, warned Maupin to back off. She challenged them, and the four retired to a park on the Seine near the Louvre. Aided only by moonlight, she fought each in turn, seriously wounding all three. (Some accounts assert she killed them.) Returning to the ball, she told the duke that three men needed assistance and disclosed her identity. She also archly informed the distraught marquise of the fate of her champions. The court buzzed for a week. Louis disliked violations of the dueling law, but he again seems to have found Maupin amusing and evaded the issue by informing her that the law was silent on female duelers. Relieved, but concerned lest he change his mind, she left for Brussels to let the dust settle.

The Spanish Netherlands (as Belgium was called) was currently governed by the duke-elector of Bavaria, Maximilian II Emmanuel (1662–1726), a music lover, legendary Lothario, and widower of *Maria Antonia who had died in 1692. His Théâtre de la Cour housed a distinguished company, most of it French, for he was a devotée of Lully's operas. In 1694, Louis XIV, in a diplomatic offensive, had lent him musicians and dancers. Hence, Maupin joined the Théâtre, won acclaim, and soon became Maximilian's latest trophy.

The affair lasted for many months, much longer than was usual for either of them, before Maximilian, probably tiring of Maupin's brand of non-stop *ardeurs*, turned to **Mlle Merville**, a ballet dancer. Desperate, Maupin, while playing *Dido's suicide in Johan Wolfgang Franck's *Énée* (Aeneas), actually stabbed herself. This sensational display embarrassed the elector, who continued with Merville. But when Merville deceived him with the Comte de Dohna, Maximilian returned to Maupin. In time, he wandered again, neglecting her in favor of a beautiful blonde Fleming, **Mlle Popuel**, a quiet, gentle sort. To reward Popuel for bearing him a son, he married her off to the Comte d'Arco and continued with her in a *ménage à trois*. Deciding at last to end his relations with Maupin, he sent Arco around with a dismissal sweetened by 40,000 livres; she threw the money at him (some say at his groin). After lingering a while hoping for a reconciliation, she accepted a 2,000-livre pension from the ever-generous elector and left the country.

Most accounts say she went off to Spain, where the Affair of the Radishes occurred. After trying in vain to land a singing position, it is said, and needing money to return to Paris, she became a maid to a demanding harridan, **Countess Marino**, wife of a royal minister. Having saved enough, Maupin took her revenge. When she dressed Marino's hair for a ball, she pinned some small, fresh radishes to the back of her head. At the ball, Marino wondered why people were snickering. A kind soul finally told her the truth, and Marino flew home in a towering rage, but Maupin had long since taken the road north. No evidence supports this oft-repeated tale, which contains gross improbabilities. If she did go to Spain—again, nothing concrete supports this assertion—it may have been, as another version has it, with a woman lover after the elector had ditched her. All that is certain is that in November 1698 she was back at the Paris Opera, playing Minerve in Lully's *Thésée*. The following seven years marked the peak of her fame as a singer.

During this time, Maupin appeared in 20 operas, 4 opera-ballets and 2 gala concerts. She played 41 roles, originating 25 of them. She also sang at parties, spectacles, and entertainments for the king and high nobility, often at Versailles or Fontainebleau, appearing, for example, in Destouche's *Omphale* at the Grand Trianon on February 23, 1702. In his famous journal, the

Marquis de Dangeau noted that they had "heard la Maupin, who has the most beautiful voice in the world." She also sang chamber music that year accompanied by François Couperin (1668–1733).

After the retirement of **Marthe Rochois** (c. 1658–1728) in 1698, Maupin inherited her position as a diva. Her specialty was heroic, armed females in helmet and cuirasse. She was now at the top, a celebrity invited to the king's hunts. Fellow singers admired her self-possession and stage presence, her ability, for example, to dispense with such props as sticks, fans or handkerchiefs to occupy nervous hands. Her decisive bearing, cavalier manner, and unusually strong voice, however, made her less suitable in soprano roles, which as a rule emphasized the qualities of an ingénue—artlessness, simplicity, gentleness, naïveté. Among her most acclaimed performances were as Cérès in Lully's *Proserpine* (1699), Venus in La Barre's ballet *Triomphe des Arts* (1700), The Priestess of the Sun and A Priestess of Flora in Campra's *Hésione* (1700), Armide in Lully's *Armide* (1703) and Junon in his *Isis* (1704), Diana in Desmarets' *Iphigénie en Tauride* (1704), Isabelle in La Barre's ballet *La Véntienne* (1705, her last role), and above all as Médée in Bouvard's *Médus* (1702) and Clorinde in Campra's *Tancrède* (1702). In *Médus*, she stepped in for **Mlle Desmatins** (d. 1708?), something Rochois admitted she never would have done given the demands of the role. As for Clorinde, André Campra (1660–1744) and Antoine Danchet (1671–1748), who admired Maupin greatly, wrote this role containing great dramatic range specifically for her. *Tancrède*, it is believed, was the first French opera in which the principal female was not a soprano.

How to categorize Maupin's voice has posed problems, because terminology has changed over time. Clorinde is often described as a contralto role. Yet the "contralto" voice was virtually unknown in France before 1800. Maupin's voice was called a *bas-dessus* (low treble), a term used in France from the 17th to the early 19th century; its closest modern equivalent would be mezzo-soprano. Because pitch was about a tone lower than now, however, that range would significantly overlap with a modern contralto. In Clorinde's case, the part has more of a mezzo range than that of a true contralto. Writes James R. Anthony in *New Grove Dictionary of Opera*: "This suggests that voice quality, not vocal range, must have been at issue, and Maupin in fact later wanted to sing the role a tone lower." Hence the catchall term "soprano" in cast lists at that time does not of itself indicate the precise kind of voice thought suitable for a particular role. In France,

to give the leading female role to a *bas-dessus* voice was unheard-of before Campra's *Tancrède*. Maupin, thus, mostly sang secondary leads or supporting roles during her career.

Given her prominence, she drew criticism, too, notably in the form of *chansons* popular with the public. Her private life fed her notoriety—inordinately so, as it always had. Contrary to all expectations, at some point, most likely by 1701, her husband returned, and they lived together (amicably, it was said) until his death a few years later. Everything suggests his return was conditioned upon his ignoring her sexual escapades. From her perspective, possibly, having a husband around only proved the adage that "stolen fruit tastes sweeter."

One affair was with Frédéric-Jules de La Tour, Chevalier de Bouillon, younger brother of the Prince de Turenne. Like her a bisexual, he had been keeping company with Maupin's colleague and former lover Thévenard. The result—assuming the events are connected—was a confrontation in which Thévenard publicly insulted her one day. He immediately realized his mistake, being no duelist, so he lived in his dressing room for three weeks while she waited every night outside the theater. On stage, they continued to play opposite each other, even as lovers. When Francine and the company finally persuaded him to apologize, Thévenard wrote a graceful letter touched with humor—the one addressed to "Julie." She relented on condition he apologize before the company, which he did.

On another occasion, she fought the Baron de Servan, a pretentious fool from Périgord who was forever bragging about his swordsmanship and female conquests. Boasting to a group of men in the Opera foyer, he sullied the name of a young dancer, **Mlle Pérignon**, whose sterling reputation caused them to protest the calumny. Maupin, sitting nearby, dressed as a man and identifying herself to Servan as the "Chevalier de Raincy," was the only one present to call him out. They met the next day, and Maupin ran him through the arm. Servan, humiliated when he learned her identity, stole back to his hometown of Périgord, while Maupin basked in the bravos of the company.

An incident on September 6, 1700, illustrates how dangerous it could be to cross Maupin. Arriving famished about 9 PM at her magnificent apartment on the rue Traversière-Saint-Honoré after a performance, she descended to the kitchen and demanded a meal. Her landlord, the Sieur de Langlois, refused, saying meals were not part of her lease. She thereupon pulled a hunk of mutton off a spit taken from the oven and flung it at him, hitting the door through which he was beating a retreat. The cook, a woman, brandished the spit, so Maupin struck her with a huge door key and, with her "sister" (doubtless a current partner) and three lackeys, floored her with kicks and punches. A justice of the peace (*commissaire*) presently arrived and ended the brawl. Witnesses gave depositions the next day, but for some reason the case was filed away.

Maupin's belligerency erupted again in connection with Albert and the duchess of Luxemburg. He had continued his relations with Maupin whenever he was on leave, but he became Luxemburg's lover, too. Albert was imprisoned for two years for a duel with Luxemburg's former lovers, but after his release (December 29, 1702) he resumed his double affair. In a fit of cold rage one day, Maupin stole up beside Luxemburg while she was at prayer at Saint-Roch and murmured that if she did not break off with Albert she would blow her brains out with her pistol. The incident caused a stir for several days.

Maupin cooled off, but Albert continued to see Luxemburg. After he returned to the army, Maupin sent him a touching poem (probably ghost-written by Danchet), and he replied in kind. But when he arrived again on leave, he took up with the Prince de Condé's mistress, **Mme de Mussy**. Maupin now turned to what proved to be her last love.

Saint-Simon's memoirs describe **Marie-Thérèse-Louise de Sanneterre de Lestrange**, Marquise de Florensac (1671–1705), as "perhaps the most beautiful woman in France . . . the gentlest, the most simple in her beauty." She also was rich and promiscuous. Louis XIV exiled her to a convent for a time because of an affair with the dauphin. After her return in 1701, she continued her affairs, including one with the duke of Orléans. In 1703, she began a liaison with Maupin. Since Florensac had not been known as bisexual, her attraction to Maupin seems puzzling. The liaison remained astonishingly discreet; no mention appears in surviving *chansons*, which retailed every tidbit *du jour*.

On July 2, 1705, Florensac died after only a two-day illness, reportedly puerperal fever. Maupin, who had opened on May 26 in La Barre's *La Vénitienne*, was devastated. She immediately forsook the stage, never to return.

In her agony, religion became her stay. She contemplated entering an order, but the decision proved exceedingly difficult. She turned to Al-

bert, the only person still linking her to the world. In his return letter, he chose to assume she indeed was leaving society, and only insisted on how much it pained him. If in her heart of hearts she wanted him to dissuade her, he disappointed her. What became of her is largely a mystery. It appears she continued in prayer and repentance, but probably was still bracing herself to become a nun when she died, reportedly in November 1707. That she founded a chapel and hospice or moved to Provence, as some versions assert, seems unlikely. Her principal biographer speculates that she lived in a quiet Paris suburb. Where and how she died and was buried are unknown. In December, a long *chanson* about all the Opera stars and their doings omitted any mention of her.

Maupin did not disappear altogether from the public's consciousness. Théophile Gautier entitled his first novel *Mademoiselle de Maupin* (1835); and Balzac, in *Béatrix* (1839), has a female author disguise her name as "Camille Maupin." Gautier's cross-dressing heroine bears little resemblance to the historical figure; he uses a few attributes and names—Maupin in disguise is "Théodore de Sérannes"—but that is all. He and other Romantics used androgyny to challenge traditional social codes, especially in regard to sexual roles, so allusions to the historical Maupin served them well.

Cameron Rogers calls Maupin "one of the most baffling figures in history." Would even a Dumas or Maupassant have invented a sword-wielding, bisexual, transvestite opera star? Contemporaries shook their heads in amazement, admiring her talent and verve while making no pretense of understanding this woman who mocked all conventional norms.

For an all-too-brief time she was one of the most celebrated of opera singers, the first mezzo-soprano in French operas to play leading roles. At the same time, she was a crack swordswoman, the most famous female duelist on record. And not least of all, she was a renowned bisexual and transvestite with seemingly boundless sexual appetites yet, even so, capable of serious, sincere love. Like all people, but more sharply than most, she reflected her times, in her case the latter years of Louis XIV's reign, when courtly society, defying ***Mme de Maintenon** and the king's strictures, "cultivated vice with a refined dilettantism." Beautiful and brave, with a devil-may-care swagger absent affectation, d'Aubigny Maupin strode down the perilous streets of 17th-century Paris—in all her virtues and vices, truly one of a kind.

SOURCES:

Beaumont, Édouard de. *The Sword and Womankind: Being an Informative History of Indiscreet Revelations.* Adapted from the French version, *L'Épée et les femmes* (1882). NY: Panurge Press, 1929.

Clayton, Ellen Creathorne. *Queens of Song.* Freeport, NY: Books for Libraries Press, 1972. Repr. of 1865 ed.

Companion to Baroque Music. Julie Sadie, ed. NY: Schirmer Books, 1990.

Cook, Ellen Piel. *Psychological Androgyny.* NY: Pergamon Press, 1985.

Dautheville, Anne-France. *Julie, Chévalier de Maupin.* Paris: Jean-Claude Lattès, 1995. Informed but romanticized.

Donington, Robert. *The Rise of Opera.* NY: Scribner, 1981.

Gilbert, Oscar Paul. *Women in Men's Guise.* Trans. by J. Lewis May. London: John Lane, 1932.

Letainturier-Fradin, G.-J.-A.-P. *La Maupin: sa vie, ses duels, ses aventures.* Paris: Ernest Flammarion, 1904 (the most reliable single work).

Music and Society: The Late Baroque Era, from the 1680s to 1740. George J. Buelow, ed. Englewood Cliffs, NJ: Prentice Hall, 1993.

New Grove Dictionary of Music and Musicians. Stanley Sadie, ed. NY: Macmillan, 1980.

New Grove Dictionary of Opera. Stanley Sadie, ed. NY: Macmillan, 1992.

Pierson, Peter. "Music in the Reign of Louis XIV," in *The Reign of Louis XIV: Essays in Celebration of Andrew Lossky.* Paul Sonnino, ed. Atlantic Highlands, NJ: Humanities Press International, 1990.

Rogers, Cameron. *Gallant Ladies.* NY: Harcourt, Brace, 1928.

Smith, Albert B. *Ideal and Reality in the Fictional Narratives of Théophile Gautier.* Gainesville, FL: University of Florida Press, 1969.

SUGGESTED READING:

Barker, Nancy Nichols. *Brother to the Sun King: Philippe, Duke of Orleans.* Baltimore, MD: The Johns Hopkins Press, 1989.

Campardon, Émile. *L'Académie Royale de Musique au 18e siècle.* Paris: Berger-Levrault, 1884.

Fétis, François-Joseph. *Biographie universelle des musiciennes.* 2nd ed. 8 vols. Brussels: Culture et Civilisation, 1972. Orig. pub. 1873–75.

Lajarte, Théodore de, ed. *Bibliothèque musicale du Théâtre de l'Opéra.* Paris: Librairie des Bibliophiles, 1876.

Lewis, W.H. *The Sunset of the Splendid Century: The Life and Times of Louis Auguste de Bourbon, Duc de Maine, 1670–1736.* NY: William Sloane Associates, 1955.

Wolf, John B. *Louis XIV.* NY: W.W. Norton, 1968.

Ziegler, Gilette. *At the Court of Versailles: Eye-Witness Reports from the Reign of Louis XIV.* Translated by Simon Watson Taylor. NY: E.P. Dutton, 1966.

David S. Newhall,
Pottinger Distinguished Professor of History Emeritus,
Centre College, Danville, Kentucky

Maurizio, Anna (1900–1993)

Polish-born Swiss apiculturist who was one of the world's leading experts on honey bees for half a century. Born in Poland of Swiss parents in 1900; died at Liebefeld, near Bern, Switzerland, on July 24, 1993; never married.

In a scientific career that spanned more than 50 years, Anna Maurizio established a reputation as one of the world's leading apiculturists. Her knowledge of bees was immense, and many of her scientific papers were pioneering studies of various aspects of the life cycle of bees and the factors that influence their ability to produce honey.

Maurizio was born in 1900 in Poland, where her father was a professor of botany. In childhood, she developed an interest in science which never abated. The subject of her doctoral dissertation was mycology, the study of fungi, and she became interested in bees as a result of one of her first research projects, a study of fungi that were potentially pathogenic to honey bees. In 1928, she began working at the Bee Section of the Swiss Federal Research Institute for Milk Husbandry, located at Liebefeld near Bern.

From 1930 well into the 1980s, Maurizio published the results of her meticulous and innovative research. Among her most important discoveries were the differences between northern and southern bees, and her quantitative pollen analyses of honeys were of great consequence. She made significant contributions to an understanding of the considerable variability of the nutritive value of pollens taken from different plants (a variability that exists in part because each pollen contains different amounts of protein). Her classification of this nutritive value remains useful to both scholars and beekeepers. Her paper on the composition, collection, utilization, and identification of pollen, first published in 1954 in the journal *Bee World*, remains a classic.

In the 1950s and 1960s, Maurizio published some of her most important research, which contributed to a better understanding of the following areas: the functions of different glands in the digestive process of bees; the processes of honey production by honey bees; pollen morphology; nectar and honeydew honeys; the factors influencing bee pollination; and the toxicity of various substances to bees.

Despite the passage of time and the publication of much additional research, her papers continue to be cited as basic sources by scholars in the field. Maurizio published a large number of scientific papers and several books for which she served as author or co-author. Her most successful was *Das Trachtpflanzenbuch*, a popular explanation of nectar and pollen which has gone through several editions since it was first published in Germany in 1969 (most recently appearing in print in 1994). In 1975, she published a new and completely revised edition of *Der Honig: Herkunft, Gewinnung, Eigenschaften und Untersuchung des Honigs* (Honey: Origins, Extraction, Properties, and Investigation of Honey), a classic reference book originally written by Enoch Zander and Albert Koch. In the final decades of her life, Maurizio was universally recognized in the bee world as the most respected member of the International Bee Research Association.

SOURCES:

"Anna Maurizio—Liebefeld Scientist," in *American Bee Journal*. Vol. 91, no. 1. January 1951, pp. 24–25.

Crane, Eva. "Dr. Anna Maurizio: An Appreciation from IBRA," in *Bee World*. Vol. 75, no. 2, 1994, pp. 98–99.

Dietz, Professor Alfred. Personal Communication.

Hodges, Dorothy. *The Pollen Loads of the Honeybee; A Guide to their Identification by Colour and Form*. London: Bee Research Institute, 1974.

Maurizio, Anna. "How Bees Make Honey," in Eva Crane, ed., *Honey: A Comprehensive Survey*. London: Heinemann, 1975, pp. 77–105.

———— and Friedgard Schaper. *Das Trachtpflanzenbuch: Nektar und Pollen—die wichtigsten Nahrungsquellen der Honigbiene*. Munich: Ehrenwirth, 1994.

Winston, Mark L. *The Biology of the Honey Bee*. Cambridge, MA: Harvard University Press, 1991.

John Haag,
Associate Professor of History,
University of Georgia, Athens, Georgia

Maury, Antonia (1866–1952)

American astronomer noted for her contributions to stellar spectral classification and the study of spectroscopic binaries. Pronunciation: MAW-ree. Born Antonia Caetana de Paiva Pereira Maury on March 21, 1866, in Cold Spring, New York; died on January 8, 1952, in Dobbs Ferry, New York; daughter of Mytton Maury (an Episcopal minister) and Virginia (Draper) Maury; sister of Carlotta Maury (1874–1938); Vassar College, B.S., astronomy, 1887; never married; no children.

Awards: Annie J. Cannon Prize, American Astronomical Society (1943).

Served intermittently as an assistant, Harvard College Observatory (1888–96, 1918–35); was a science teacher, Gilman School, Cambridge, Massachusetts (1891–94); worked as teacher and lecturer (1896–1918); was custodian, Draper Park Observatory Museum (1935–38).

Selected publications: "Spectra of Bright Stars," in Annals of the Harvard College Observatory *(1897); "The Spectral Changes of Beta Lyrae," in* Annals of the Harvard College Observatory *(1933).*

The important role of women observers at the Harvard College Observatory from 1880 to 1930 has been the subject of numerous articles. The name Antonia Maury figures prominently in all such discussions, despite her intermittent relationship with the observatory.

Maury was born on March 21, 1866, in Cold Spring, New York, to Reverend Mytton Maury and **Virginia Draper Maury**. She and her sister *Carlotta Maury (a well-known woman paleontologist) inherited a love of science from their grandfather Dr. John Draper and uncle Dr. Henry Draper, prominent physicians and pioneering amateur astrophotographers. Maury studied astronomy at Vassar College under ***Maria Mitchell**, America's first woman astronomer, and graduated in 1887 with honors in astronomy, physics, and math. In 1888, Reverend Maury secured Antonia employment as an observer at Harvard, a post she held intermittently until 1935.

Antonia Maury became a central figure in the Henry Draper Catalogue project (funded by her aunt in honor of her husband Henry Draper) as a classifier of stellar spectra. Maury was assigned stars in the northern portion of the sky, while famed astronomer ***Annie Jump Cannon** was assigned the southern half. During her work, Maury discovered that the traditional classification scheme of assigning letters of the alphabet to classes of differing spectral line strengths was inadequate to explain the complexity of the structure being seen. Maury introduced an additional "second dimension" to her classification method, a letter which described the appearance of the spectral lines: "a" for wide and well-defined, "b" for hazy but relatively wide and of same intensity as "a", and "c" for spectra with lines due to hydrogen and helium appearing narrow and sharply defined. Class "ac" represented stars with mixed characteristics.

Maury left Harvard for a teaching job and travel in 1891, suffering from burnout. Documented conflicts with director Edward C. Pickering were a factor as well. According to noted astronomer *E. Dorrit Hoffleit (who knew Maury in her later years):

> She was one of the most original thinkers of all the women Pickering employed; but instead of encouraging her attempts at interpreting observations, he was only irritated by her independence and departure from assigned and expected routine.

Maury returned to Harvard in 1893 and her catalogue of spectra, in which she described her "c-characteristic," was published in 1897. Pickering did not believe in the validity of Maury's system, and instead Annie Cannon's system (which did not discuss the appearance of the spectral lines) was accepted as the official method at Harvard, and later worldwide. However, Maury did have her champions. Noted astronomer Ejnar Hertzsprung explained in a 1905 paper that the stars which Maury had classified as "c" were in fact not ordinary stars but red giants. "In my opinion," he wrote, "the separation of Antonia C. Maury of the c- and ac-stars is the most important advancement in stellar classification since the trials of Vogel and Secchi." Hertzsprung wrote to Pickering questioning why Maury's work was not utilized in all Harvard catalogues. This work by Hertzspung, as well as work by Henry Norris Russell, form the basis of our understanding of stellar evolution. Maury had meanwhile left Harvard again in 1896 for teaching jobs and lecturing, and did not return to Harvard in earnest until after Pickering's death in 1919, when she turned her attention to spectroscopic binaries and enigmatic binary Beta Lyrae. Ironically, for this work she was appointed Pickering fellow for 1919–20. After retiring, she spent three years as custodian of her uncle's observatory museum in Hastings-on-Hudson, New York, where she lived until her death. Antonia Maury was awarded the Annie J. Cannon Prize of the American Astronomical Society in 1943 and has a lunar crater named in her honor.

SOURCES:

Hoffleit, Dorrit. "Antonia Maury," in *Sky and Telescope*. Vol. XI, no. 5. March 1952, p. 106.

——. *Maria Mitchell's Famous Students; and Comets Over Nantucket*. Cambridge, MA: AAVSO, 1983.

——. *Women in the History of Variable Star Astronomy*. Cambridge, MA: AAVSO, 1993.

Jones, Bessie Zaban, and Lyle Gifford Boyd. *The Harvard College Observatory*. Cambridge, MA: Belknap Press, 1971.

SUGGESTED READING:

Bailey, Solon. *The History and Work of Harvard Observatory, 1839 to 1927*. NY: McGraw-Hill, 1931.

Hoffleit, Dorrit. "The Discovery and Exploitation of Spectroscopic Parallaxes," in *Popular Astronomy*. Vol. LVIII, 1950, pp. 428–438, 483–501.

——. "The Evolution of the Henry Draper Memorial," in *Vistas in Astronomy*. Vol. XXXIV, 1991, pp. 107–162.

Kristine Larsen,
Associate Professor of Astronomy and Physics,
Central Connecticut State University, New Britain, Connecticut

Maury, Carlotta (1874–1938)

American paleontologist. Born Carlotta Joaquina Maury in Hastings-on-Hudson, New York, in 1874; died in Yonkers, New York, in 1938; daughter of Mytton Maury (an Episcopal minister) and Virginia (Draper) Maury; sister of noted astronomer Antonia Maury (1866–1952); graduated from Radcliffe College, 1894; Cornell University, Ph.D., 1902.

Carlotta Maury was born in Hastings-on-Hudson, New York, in 1874, the daughter of Mytton Maury, an Episcopal minister, and **Virginia Draper Maury**. She shared an interest in science with her elder sister *** Antonia Maury**, who later became a noted astronomer, but also retained a fondness for philosophy and the Episcopal Church. Maury developed an abiding interest in paleontology at an early age. She received her post-secondary education at Radcliffe College, graduating in 1894, and taught high school in New York City from 1900 to 1901 while continuing her studies at Cornell University. In 1902, she received a Ph.D. from Cornell, and published *A Comparison of the Oligocene of Western Europe and the Southern United States* later the same year. Maury worked as an assistant in the department of paleontology at Columbia University from 1904 to 1906. She then served as a paleontologist with the Louisiana Geological Survey from 1907 to 1909, and returned to Columbia as a lecturer in paleontology from 1909 to 1912.

Carlotta Maury undertook her first field study in 1910, when she accompanied Arthur Clifford Veatch's geological expedition to Venezuela. She was also retained that year by the Royal Dutch Shell Petroleum Company as a consulting paleontologist and stratigrapher, a post she would continue to hold on a part-time basis until her death. From 1912 to 1915, she served as professor of geology and zoology at Huguenot College, University of the Cape of Good Hope, in South Africa. Her position in the field of paleontology was recognized when she was named the official paleontologist to Brazil in 1914, which post she retained for the rest of her life. Maury published a number of papers and reports on her specialties of fossil faunas and Antillean, Venezuelan, and Brazilian stratigraphy, and organized a geological expedition to the Dominican Republic in 1916. A fellow of the Geological Society of America, a member of the American Geographical Society and of the American Association for the Advancement of Science, and a corresponding member of the Brazilian Academy of Sciences, she remained active in the field of paleontology until her death in Yonkers, New York, in 1938.

SOURCES:

Ogilvie, Marilyn Bailey. *Women in Science: Antiquity through the Nineteenth Century*. Cambridge, MA: MIT Press, 1986.

Grant Eldridge,
freelance writer, Pontiac, Michigan

Mauteby, Margaret (1423–1484).

See Paston, Margaret.

Mavia (c. 350–c. 430 CE)

Queen of the Saracens. Name variations: Mania; Mawia; Mawia, Queen of Syria. Born around 350 CE on the southern or southwestern coast of Arabia; died around 430 CE; daughter of a Saracen chief; probably married a Roman military commander named Victor; children: possibly Mavia.

Mavia was probably the only offspring of a Saracen (Arab) chief whose territory abutted the land which the Romans called Arabia Felix (Arabia the Fortunate). This land lay along the southern and southwestern coast of the Arabia, and was so called because, unlike the arid interior of the peninsula, it produced the plants from which many highly sought-after spices came. Thus in relative terms it was wealthy and drew traders from many lands, both east and west. As such, Arabia Felix was a fairly cosmopolitan region in the 4th century CE. Although Mavia's clan seems to have been Asian in origin, Saracen tribes also inhabited that part of modern Egypt which touches the Red Sea. Given the geopolitical realities of the time, the lands occupied by the Saracens were very strategic since they drove a wedge between the great empires of the Romans to the west and northwest and the Persians to the east and northeast.

When Mavia was born around 350, the Saracens were a nomadic people, having no fixed homes or cities and only loosely defined home ranges (constantly under the press of other tribes). However, they did possess domesticated horses and camels to transport them about, and they used these assets to live according to their wits and military prowess. When the times afforded the opportunity, the Saracens raided sedentary populations and pillaged their accumulated stores. When such times did not exist and potential victims knew the security to be had from credible political authority, the Saracens survived off hunted game and the milk of their transport animals. Such an open life produced egalitarianism within the tribal groups, with women knowing freedoms not afforded to tillers of the soil, and men as well as women being more or less only as important as they were adept in accumulating wealth either through hunting or looting. Such neighbors could be difficult for established powers such as the Romans and the Persians, and in the paraphrased words of one Roman writer, the Saracens made "bad allies and even worse enemies."

During the 360s and 370s, the Roman Empire faced a series of problems which cumulatively produced a crisis. In the geographical proximity of Mavia's experience, the Romans had long been bitter enemies of the Persian Empire which stretched eastward from their common boundary of the Euphrates River. This enmity had led the Roman emperor Julian (363) to invade the Persian realm, but even when the major contestants were not fighting each other directly, they sparred indirectly by manipulating the inhabitants of their joint frontier to fight on their behalf. That is, both the Romans and the Persians exploited the local Arabian peoples to fight for their respective strategic interests. Since neither empire had the capacity to close their borders, and, since, even if either could, neither wanted to do so entirely because of the lucrative trade which passed from one empire into the other, both maintained their stakes through dispersed guerrilla activity. The fighting which resulted was sporadic but destructive, with each side attempting to intimidate the other's rural populations and induce those populations to lose faith in their government's ability to defend them.

For a long time, this system had generally favored the (usually) more powerful Romans. However, in 378 a powerful Visigothic army had defeated a major Roman army under Emperor Valens near the European city of Adrianople (in northwestern Turkey). This disaster shook the Roman world, for not only did Valens die amidst the slaughter, so too did 40,000 of his best troops, leaving the defense of the Eastern Empire in serious doubt. The ramifications of this calamity were many, but as far as Mavia, now the leader of her people, was concerned, it caused the Romans to approach her with the prospect of a formal alliance with potentially rich financial rewards. In 378, she apparently was elevated to the status of "phylarch" (nomadic chieftain whose status was recognized by Rome and whose loyalty was purchased through gifts [financial bribes]). Mavia was so honored because of the strategic nature of the territory over which her people ranged, and because the Romans desperately needed allies to help provide for the defense of Constantinople, lest the Eastern capital fall before the advancing Visigoths.

Mavia lived up to her end of the bargain, providing troops which helped to repel the Goths from the walls of Constantinople. In fact, the contribution of Mavia's troops was especially noteworthy, attracting the notice of Roman authors. For example, the historian Ammianus Marcellinus reports that a Saracen (probably under Mavia's command) made a huge impression on the Visigoths when, in the midst of a defensive sally, he heroically cut down a Gothic opponent and then drank the blood of his victim as the battle raged around him. In part put off by the barbarity of this act, the Goths fell back and Constantinople was saved.

However important Mavia's help was in the salvation of Constantinople, at the time the Romans were beset by too many obligations to deal fairly with each one. In Mavia's case, it became evident that the Romans would not live up to their promises even after Mavia's people had acted in good faith. As a result, Mavia led a revolt against the Romans (378) to extract from Rome's Eastern provinces the promised reward for services rendered. This was the first such large-scale attack upon Roman territory by a Roman phylarch of Arabian extraction, and the devastation left in Mavia's wake spread throughout the Roman East, including deep inroads into Palestine and Egypt. The destruction wrought upon the countryside was widespread, but Mavia did not have the engineering wherewithal to besiege Roman cities. Regardless, a solution to the "difference of opinion" over "wages" seems to have been hammered out rapidly, with Mavia apparently returning rather quickly to the Roman fold. Evidence for this exists in the fact that Mavia seems to have married a Roman military commander named Victor. This connection raised her status above that of the average phylarch, but it almost certainly came at a price: that is, in order to contract the marriage Mavia probably was forced to convert to Christianity, with the result that her tribe would have followed suit. Evidence that Mavia converted exists from about 425, when a Christian church in Syria was dedicated by a "Mavia," almost certainly either the phylarch herself or her daughter. It is not known when Mavia died, but 425 is probably close to the mark.

William Greenwalt,
Associate Professor of Classical History,
Santa Clara University, Santa Clara, California

Mavrogenous, Manto (d. 1848)
Greek freedom fighter. Died in 1848.

Manto Mavrogenous was living in the city of Trieste, which was then part of the Austro-Hungarian Empire, when the Greeks rose in revolt against the Ottoman Empire in 1821. She immediately moved to the Aegean island of Mykonos,

where she used her own personal wealth to raise and maintain an army of guerilla fighters and outfit two warships for the Greek cause. Mavrogenous retained personal command of the forces she equipped and successfully led them in battle on a number of occasions. She also proved an adept fund raiser and advocate of Greek independence, and her letters to friends in England and France brought in money and volunteers to aid the Greeks. (The war appealed to many liberal Europeans; among those who joined was George Gordon, Lord Byron, who went to Missolonghi to fight but instead died of a fever.) Mavrogenous was celebrated in poems and stories during the war, and portraits painted by her contemporaries still survive. In recognition of her services, the Greek revolutionary leadership awarded her the rank of lieutenant general.

After the Ottomans recognized Greek independence with the Treaty of Constantinople in 1832, Mavrogenous' lack of political influence forced her to the sidelines. She lived in obscurity on a small pension usually granted to war widows until her death in 1848.

SOURCES:
Griffin, Lynne, and Kelly McCann. *The Book of Women: 300 Notable Women History Passed By.* Holbrook, MA: Bob Adams, 1992.
Uglow, Jennifer S., ed. and comp. *The International Dictionary of Women's Biography.* NY: Continuum, 1989.

Grant Eldridge,
freelance writer, Pontiac, Michigan

Mavrokordatou, Alexandra
(1605–1684)

Greek intellectual. Born in Constantinople in 1605; died in prison in 1684; married and divorced twice; children: at least one son.

Alexandra Mavrokordatou was born in Constantinople, the capital of the Ottoman Empire (now Istanbul, Turkey), in 1605, and later moved to Greece, which had been under Ottoman control since the 14th century. She married twice while a young woman; one of these marriages produced a son, but both ended in divorce, leaving Mavrokordatou free to pursue her interests. Following a period of study of classical history, literature, and philosophy, Mavrokordatou founded Greece's first literary salon, which met in her own house. Her reputation was such that the new salon attracted both Greek and international intellectuals, and eventually produced many notable Greek politicians and artists. Mavrokordatou ran afoul of Turkish authorities late in her life when her son, a Turkish diplomat, was accused of aiding the forces of Austria-Hungary during the Turkish siege of Vienna in 1683. She was sent to prison for her role in the affair, where she died in 1684.

SOURCES:

Uglow, Jennifer S., ed. and comp. *The International Dictionary of Women's Biography.* NY: Continuum, 1989.

Grant Eldridge,
freelance writer, Pontiac, Michigan

Mawia (c. 350–c. 430 CE).

See Mavia.

Maxtone Graham, Joyce

(1901–1953)

British author. Name variations: (incorrectly) Joyce Maxtone-Graham; (pseudonym) Jan Struther. Born Joyce Anstruther on June 6, 1901; died on July 20, 1953, in New York City; daughter of Dame Eva Anstruther (a writer); married Anthony Maxtone Graham, in 1923 (divorced); married Adolf Kurt Placzek, in 1948; children: (first marriage) James Anstruther Maxtone Graham (b. 1924, a writer); **Janet Maxtone Graham**; Robert Maxtone Graham.

Joyce Maxtone Graham was born into a literary family on June 6, 1901. Her mother, Dame **Eva Anstruther**, was an author but was best known for her service to the British Empire during World War I as director of the Camps Library, which made available millions of books to military personnel overseas. Joyce received her primary education in London, England, and obtained her first writing job as a contributor to the court page of the London *Times,* using the pseudonym Jan Struther to differentiate herself from her mother. In 1923, she married Anthony Maxtone Graham, with whom she had two sons and a daughter. Maxtone Graham published her first book, *Betsinda Dances and Other Poems,* in 1931, and soon had a devoted following. Her most notable work was *Mrs. Miniver,* a semi-autobiographical series of sketches on family life during wartime that was a tremendous commercial success upon its release in 1939. In 1942, the book was made into a popular film, starring **Greer Garson* and Walter Pidgeon, that won six Academy Awards, including Best Actress for Garson (a sequel, *The Miniver Story,* was released in 1950).

During World War II, Maxtone Graham continued the tradition of service begun by her mother, lecturing throughout the United States on behalf of the British War Relief. She also published *The Glass Blower* in 1940 and edited *Women of Britain* in 1941. Her husband served in the war as

a member of the Scots Guards, and was taken prisoner by the Germans in Libya in 1942. After the war ended, she remained in the United States, becoming a member of the library staff at Columbia University and divorcing her husband. She published *Pocketful of Pebbles* in 1946 and married Adolf Kurt Placzek, a colleague at the library, in 1948. Joyce Maxtone Graham was working on a semi-autobiographical novel at the time of her death on July 20, 1953.

SOURCES:

Kunitz, Stanley J., ed. *Twentieth Century Authors.* NY: H.W. Wilson, 1942, and First Supplement, 1955.

RELATED MEDIA:

Mrs. Miniver (134 min. film), starring Greer Garson, Walter Pidgeon, **May Whitty*, and **Teresa Wright*, directed by William Wyler, released in 1942.

The Miniver Story (104 min. film), starring Greer Garson, Walter Pidgeon, John Hodiak, and **Cathy O'Donnell**, released in 1950.

Grant Eldridge,
freelance writer, Pontiac, Michigan

Maxwell, Caroline Elizabeth Sarah, Lady Stirling (1808–1877).

See Norton, Caroline.

Maxwell, Constantia (1886–1962)

Irish historian. Born Constantia Elizabeth Maxwell in Dublin, Ireland, on August 24, 1886; died at Pembury, Kent, England, on February 6, 1962; daughter of Patrick W. Maxwell and Elizabeth (Suckling) Maxwell; educated at St. Leonard's School, St. Andrew's, Scotland, Trinity College, Dublin and Bedford College, University of London.

Was a lecturer in history (1909–39), professor of economic history (1939–45), and Lecky Professor of modern history (1945–51) at Trinity College, University of Dublin; was a member of the Irish Academy of Letters.

Selected publications: Irish History from Contemporary Sources (Allen & Unwin, 1923); Dublin under the Georges (1936, new ed., Faber, 1956); Country and Town in Ireland under the Georges (1940, new ed., Tempest, 1959); A History of Trinity College, Dublin (University Press, 1946); The Stranger in Ireland, from the reign of Elizabeth to the Great Famine (Cape, 1954).

Constantia Maxwell was born in 1886 in Dublin, Ireland, where her Scottish father P.W. Maxwell had gone in the early 1880s when he was appointed an ophthalmic surgeon at the Royal Victoria Eye and Ear Hospital. Her sister, **Euphan Maxwell**, followed their father into ophthalmology and became the first woman ophthalmic surgeon in Ireland. In 1916, following the death of their brother in action, Euphan returned from war service with the Royal Army Medical Corps and succeeded her father at the Eye and Ear Hospital. Constantia went to school in Scotland but returned to Dublin for her university education at Trinity College. She entered Trinity in 1904, the first year it accepted women, and was soon marked out as one of the most brilliant of the distinguished women who took advantage of the change of regulations. She graduated in 1908, having won the gold medal and a senior moderatorship, and went on to postgraduate study at Bedford College in London. Maxwell was one of that first generation of Irish women historians, among them *Mary Hayden, **Maud Clarke** and **Síle Ní Chinnéide**, who were remarkably successful in obtaining university posts. Their successors were not as fortunate.

In 1909, Maxwell became the first woman member of the academic staff when she was appointed lecturer in modern history. In 1939, she was given a personal chair in economic history and in 1945 was appointed to the prestigious Lecky chair in modern history, the first woman to hold a full-time chair in Trinity. Despite these achievements, the position of Maxwell and other women academics at Trinity was difficult. They did not receive equal pay; they were excluded from the fellowship until 1968; they were not admitted to the staff Common Room until 1958 and they were not allowed to dine on High Table until 1966. For many years, they also were subject to the six o'clock rule whereby women had to leave the College precincts by 6 PM. Maxwell had retired by the time most of these changes were implemented. But, as the College historians D.A. Webb and R.B. McDowell have noted, Maxwell had "strongly conservative instincts and disliked upsetting the existing order."

Maxwell retained close connections with London and Cambridge. **Mary O'Dowd** claims that in many ways her historical writings are more clearly understood within an English historiographical context than an Irish one. As with other women historians of her generation, Maxwell wrote with a strong pedagogic purpose, for she was trying to provide for Irish history the kind of guides for students and teachers that the Historical Association in Britain was producing for British history. Her first book, *A Short History of Ireland* (1914), was for schools. *Irish History from Contemporary Sources* (1923) broke new ground in providing an accessible source book of documents for students. Equally important was her interest in economic history at a time when it was virtually ignored in Irish history syllabi. One her students, R.B. McDowell, later a distinguished historian, recalled that she had given him Marx's *Das Kapital* to read.

In 1936, Maxwell published *Dublin under the Georges* which was followed four years later by *Country and Town in Ireland under the Georges*. These studies of Ireland in the 18th and early 19th centuries were considered her best work. In 1946, she wrote a history of Trinity College which concluded with the college's tercentenary celebrations in 1892, a reflection of her lack of sympathy with the political changes which had occurred in Ireland after independence in 1922. Webb and McDowell wrote that for Maxwell her abiding city lay not in the new Irish Free State but rather in England or in pre-independence Ireland. She lived with her sister at the family home in Dublin and after her retirement in 1951 moved to Cranbrook, Kent, just south of London. She published one more book, *The Stranger in Ireland* (1954), and supervised new editions of *Dublin under the Georges* and *Country and Town in Ireland under the Georges*. Constantia Maxwell died in Kent in February 1962. An obituary in *Trinity* described her as "a deeply learned and cultivated woman of much sympathy and understanding, and much modesty and even humility for all her accomplishment and knowledge[;] her shrewd judgments on her subject and on her university [were] tinged always, it seemed, by an amused and ironic detachment which extended itself to all human affairs."

SOURCES:

Hogan, Robert, ed. *Dictionary of Irish Literature*. Rev. and expanded ed. Westport, CT: Greenwood Press, 1996.

Irish Times (obituary). February 8, 1962.

McDowell, R.B., and D.A. Webb. *Trinity College, Dublin 1592–1952: An Academic History*. Cambridge: Cambridge University Press, 1982.

O'Dowd, Mary. "From Morgan to MacCurtain: Women Historians in Ireland from the 1790s to the 1990s" in Maryann Gialanella Valiulis and Mary O'Dowd, eds., *Women and Irish History: Essays in honour of Margaret MacCurtain*. Dublin: Wolfhound Press, 1997.

Trinity (obituary). Vol. 14, Dublin: 1962.

Deirdre McMahon,
Lecturer in History, Mary Immaculate College,
University of Limerick, Limerick, Ireland

Maxwell, Elsa (1883–1963)

Renowned American hostess of the international society set who became a popular writer and radio host. Born on May 24, 1883, in Keokuk, Iowa; died on November 1, 1963, in New York City; daughter of James David Maxwell and Laura (Wyman) Maxwell; never married; no children.

An enormously popular personality in the decades before the middle of the 20th century, Elsa Maxwell was usually referred to as a professional party giver, though she termed her carefully engineered soirées veritable "works of art." According to her own life history, Maxwell was supposedly born in an opera box in Keokuk, Iowa, in 1883. She moved to California as a child, where she attended a private school for girls in San Francisco. Her first ambition was to be a musician, for it was apparent early on that she could play nearly any instrument by ear, although she never took lessons or pursued that goal seriously. One of her first jobs was playing the piano to accompany silent films. In 1905, she joined a traveling Shakespeare troupe as an assistant, visiting South Africa and other locales, and found she had a lucrative talent for song writing; she would eventually publish some 80 songs. Maxwell appeared in vaudeville, and later landed in Europe, where she fell in with a "smart" crowd. In the years before World War I, Maxwell was esteemed as a hostess by high-living American expatriates and wealthy Europeans, first in Venice and later on the French Riviera. It was said that she single-handedly changed many of the stuffy social customs that characterized formal entertaining during this era, most notably by forgoing the "dinner at eight" rule and serving her guests at ten, which was initially regarded as a near-heresy. In Venice, she organized a golf course, was the force behind an international motor-boat race, and ran a nightclub on a barge in the city's Grand Canal. Maxwell is credited with helping to make the French Riviera a desirable vacation spot during the 1920s, and in 1926 was invited by Monaco's royals to work her magic on that city; there, her name was associated with the success of a beach club and restaurants.

Elsa Maxwell returned to the United States in the 1930s. While living in New York City, she organized the revue *Who's Who* and wrote two books for serial publication: *I Live by My Wits*, which appeared in *Harper's Bazaar* in 1936, and *The Life of *Barbara Hutton*, published in *Cosmopolitan* in 1938. She then moved to Hollywood, where her daring ideas about entertaining found a ready audience—she once put a live (albeit tethered) baby duckling on every woman's plate at a dinner party. Maxwell lived at *Constance Bennett*'s house. In the late 1930s and early 1940s, she made a number of short films, including *Elsa Maxwell's Hotel for Women, Elsa Maxwell's Public Deb Number One,* and *The Lady and the Lug.* In 1942, she started a radio program, "Elsa Maxwell's Party Line," in which she chronicled the comings and goings of the rich and famous. She also began to earn money by sharing her hostessing secrets with the masses. Among her break-the-ice schemes for parties were the game of scavenger hunt, about which she noted that "it is inadvisable to include objects which can be procured only by violating the law," and a real-life version of what would later become the board game "Clue," complete with a play-acting dead body. Maxwell also wrote a nationally syndicated gossip column, appeared in the wartime revue *Stage Door Canteen*, and gave lectures. Her autobiography, *R.S.V.P.*, was published in 1954, followed in 1957 by *How to Do It: The Lively Art of Entertaining.* She was a frequent guest on Jack Paar's "The Tonight Show" before her death in 1963.

SOURCES:

Current Biography. NY: H.W. Wilson, 1943, 1964.

McHenry, Robert, ed. *Famous American Women.* NY: Dover, 1980.

Carol Brennan,
Grosse Pointe, Michigan

Maxwell, Kate.

See Watson, Ellen for sidebar.

Maxwell, Mary (fl. 1715)

*Countess of Traquair. Name variations: Lady Traquair; Lady Traquir; Mary Stuart. Flourished around 1715; daughter of Robert Maxwell, 4th earl of Nithsdale, and Lady Lucy Douglas; sister-in-law of *Winifred Maxwell (1672–1749); married Charles Stuart, 4th earl of Traquir or Traquair; children: Charles Stuart, 5th earl of Traquair; John Stuart, Lucy Stuart; Anne Stuart; Mary Stuart; Catherine Stuart (who married William Maxwell, 6th earl of Nithsdale).*

Maxwell, Mary Elizabeth (1835–1915).

See Braddon, Mary Elizabeth.

Maxwell, Mary Sutherland (1910–2000).

See Rabbani, Ruhiyyih.

Maxwell, Vera (1901–1995)

American fashion designer. Name variations: Huppe. Born on April 22, 1901; died in Rincon, Puerto Rico, in January 15, 1995.

A popular American designer of sportswear known as the American *Coco Chanel*, Vera Maxwell designed women's clothes for endurance and comfort as well as chic. She created the prototype of the jumpsuit for Rosie the Riveter during World War II, as well as a zipperless, buttonless dress, known as the "Speed Suit," that could be donned in seconds. Her "Weekend Wardrobe," consisting of two jackets, two skirts, and a pair of slacks, was said to have been inspired by the dapper tweeds of Albert Einstein, during a 1935 visit. Her clients included *Lillian Gish, *Martha Graham, *Pat Nixon and *Rosalynn Carter.

Maxwell, Winifred (1672–1749)

*Countess of Nithsdale. Name variations: Winifred Herbert; Lady Winifred Nithsdale. Born Winifred Herbert in 1672; died in 1749; daughter of William Herbert (1617–1696), 1st marquis of Powis or Powys, 3rd baron Powis or Powys, and *Elizabeth Somerset; married William Maxwell (1676–1744), 5th earl of Nithsdale, in 1699; children: William Maxwell, 6th earl of Nithsdale; Anne Maxwell.*

The name Winifred Maxwell might have been lost to history had it not been for her daring rescue of her husband William Maxwell from the Tower of London, where he was imprisoned while awaiting execution for his participation in the Jacobite rebellion of 1715. The Jacobites supported James Francis Edward, the Old Pretender, in his claim to the British throne after the death of Queen *Anne. Winifred not only hatched the elaborate scheme to save her husband, but assumed a major role in its execution, risking her life to do so. Her efforts, however, were not rewarded to any great extent. William Maxwell, never noted for his intelligence (Ian Fellows-Gordon referred to him as "one of the stupidest men in Scottish history"), made little of his second chance at life, and although Winifred certainly contributed her share to the family coffers, the couple suffered many years of poverty.

Winifred Maxwell was the beautiful and intelligent daughter of English lord William Herbert, 1st marquis of Powis, and Lady *Elizabeth Somerset, and an ancestor of the duke of Norfolk. She married Scotsman William Maxwell, 5th earl of Nithsdale, in 1699, and lived an uneventful life until 1715, when William became involved in the first of the two Jacobite uprisings. Captured at the Battle of Preston, William was tried with six of his compatriots, all of whom were convicted of treason and sentenced to die. The prisoners were housed in the formidable Tower of London to await execution.

News of her husband's plight reached Winifred at the family home in Scotland on De-

cember 8, and she immediately set off for London on horseback, taking along her devoted Welsh maid, Cecilia Evans. The journey, over a month in duration, was made almost entirely on horseback, and was frequently slowed by excessive cold and snow. "I must confess that such a journey I believe was scarce ever made, considering the weather, by a woman," Winifred wrote to her sister-in-law *Mary Maxwell, countess of Traquair, on Christmas Day, without making reference to the holiday. "However, if I meet my dear lord well, and am so happy as to be able to serve him, I shall think all my trouble well repaid." The two women arrived in London sometime in January, but Winifred was so weak and ill that she could do nothing until February.

After filing a petition for mercy with King George I to spare her husband's life, Winifred and Cecilia took rooms in Drury Lane. Winifred had already made several trips to the Tower to visit William, who was imprisoned in a small cell with a single window overlooking Water Lane approximately 60 feet below. At first, she had been denied permission to visit her husband, but she both charmed and paid off the guards, who eventually befriended her and gave her free access to William's room during daylight hours. This, of course, was all part of her plan, which was already taking shape. The day before the escape, Winifred would tell the guards that the petition for mercy had been granted and that the prisoners were free. She would also give them money to drink to the king, hoping that their celebration would occupy the greater portion of the next 36 hours. On the following afternoon, she would visit the Tower again, disguise her husband as a woman visitor, and walk him past the guards, down the staircase, and out of the Tower to a waiting stagecoach.

In execution, however, the plan was not quite so concise. In fact, when it was later related in a letter to her sister-in-law Mary Maxwell, Winifred used a thousand words to describe the intricacies of what seemed more an elaborate bedroom farce than a deadly serious rescue operation. After setting things in motion with her lie to the guards, and enlisting the help of her maid Cecilia as well as of her landlady, Mrs. Mills, and another boarder, Miss Hilton, Winifred arrived at the Tower late the following afternoon. While Cecilia stayed outside, Winifred took each of the other two women separately into her husband's room with her, where each relinquished the garments they had piled on themselves to aid in William's disguise. She dismissed the women with a loud and urgent order to go out and get "my woman" (Cecilia, of course). Winifred then quickly transformed her

Winifred Maxwell rescuing her husband from the Tower of London.

husband, using white paint to cover his growth of beard and tying false ringlets into his hair. Then, bulking him up with the contraband petticoats and wrapping him in a riding cloak, she opened the door and escorted him through the corridor and down the stairs, all the while keeping up a barrage of chatter as a distraction. Once outside, she handed him off to Cecilia, the maid, and hurriedly made her way back to his room. "When I got into my lord's chamber, I spoke to him as it were, and I answered as if he had, and imitated his voice as near as I could and walked up and down the room," she later related. When she felt she had made it clear that William was still in residence, she left, telling the guards that her husband was at prayers and should not be disturbed. She then made her way back to Drury Lane, where her husband was safely hidden in the attic.

With some further aid, William was seen safely to Dover and then to France, while Winifred, now pregnant, made an arduous journey back to Scotland to retrieve family papers and to sell whatever she could of the household items to raise money. On her way to France to join her husband, she suffered a miscarriage and almost died "in a cabin in the boat in which were seven other persons sleeping," as Cecilia related in a letter home. Upon reuniting with William in Lille, in September 1716, Winifred found little sympathy, merely a stack of unpaid bills. It was only through the help of her sister-in-law Lady Traquair that the Maxwells were able to keep afloat.

By 1718, Winifred and William were living in James Francis Edward's Court-in-Exile in Rome, where they received a modest allowance from the Old Pretender, who had since married the somewhat unstable Princess *Clementina Sobieski from Poland. Winifred later became governess to their offspring, Bonnie Prince Charlie, the Young Pretender, and Prince Henry, which greatly enhanced the family income as well as bringing stability into the lives of her young charges. Winifred also had two children of her own, Anne Maxwell and William Maxwell. While little is known of Anne, William the Younger, who was 12 when his father escaped the Tower, eventually returned to Scotland and took over the family estate. William the Elder died in 1744, and Winifred lived on in exile until her death in 1749. The story of her courageous rescue was handed down from generation to generation and was immortalized by the Scottish author John Buchan (1875–1940).

SOURCES:

Fellows-Gordon, Ian. *Famous Scottish Lives.* Watford: Odhams, 1967.

Barbara Morgan,
Melrose, Massachusetts

May.

Variant of Mary.

May of Teck (1867–1953).

See Mary of Teck.

May, Catherine Dean (1914—)

American politician and six-term Republican member of the U.S. House of Representatives. Name variations:

*Catherine Dean Bedell. Born Catherine Dean Barnes on May 18, 1914, in Yakima, Washington; daughter of Charles Henry Barnes and Pauline (Van Loon) Barnes (both real estate brokers); graduated from Yakima Valley Junior College, 1934; University of Washington, Seattle, B.A., 1936, M.Edn., 1937; studied speech at the University of Southern California, 1939; married John O. May, in January 1943 (divorced); married Donald W. Bedell, on November 14, 1970; children: (first marriage) James C. May; **Melinda E. May.***

Catherine Dean May was born Catherine Dean Barnes on May 18, 1914, in Yakima, Washington. She graduated from Yakima Valley Junior College in 1934 and received a B.A. from the University of Washington in 1936 and a five-year degree in education in 1937. She then taught English at Chehalis, Washington, from 1937 to 1940, and studied speech at the University of Southern California in 1939.

May launched a new career in 1940, serving first as a radio special-events broadcaster and

Catherine Dean May

writer in Yakima, and later as the director of the radio departments of an advertising agency and an insurance company in Seattle. She married John O. May in January 1943. The following year, Catherine May moved up to a national audience when she became a writer and assistant commentator for the National Broadcasting Company (NBC) in New York City, but she returned to Yakima in 1946. She served as the women's editor for a local radio station from 1948 to 1957, and also held the positions of office manager and medical secretary for the Yakima Medical Center.

May ran successfully as a Republican candidate for the Washington state legislature in 1952, in which position she served until 1958. That year, she won the seat vacated by Otis H. Holmes, an eight-term member of the U.S. House of Representatives from the fourth district of Washington; she was the first woman from Washington state elected to the House. As a member of the House, May served on the Committee on the District of Columbia, the Committee on Atomic Energy, and the Committee on Agriculture, where she quickly gained a reputation as an advocate of the protection and improvement of farm incomes. Although a member of the Republican Party, she remained true to her personal beliefs, and voted against the party majority on numerous occasions. May worked tirelessly to benefit the domestic sugar beet industry, which was important to her district, and in 1967 co-sponsored joint resolutions to create a U.S. World Food Study and Coordinating Commission and a Select Committee on Standards and Conduct. In 1970, she sponsored a proposal to provide free food stamps to families with incomes of less than $30 per month. May was defeated in her attempt to secure a seventh term in Congress in 1970, and withdrew briefly from public life. She married Donald Bedell later the same year.

Catherine May was appointed to the U.S. International Trade Commission by President Richard Nixon in 1971, and served in that capacity until 1981. The following year, she was named a Special Consultant to the president on the 50 States Project by Ronald Reagan. May is now president of Bedell Associates in Palm Desert, California.

SOURCES:
Office of the Historian. *Women in Congress, 1917–1990.* Commission on the Bicentenary of the U.S. House of Representatives, 1991.

SUGGESTED READING:
Moritz, Charles, ed. *Current Biography.* NY: H.W. Wilson, 1960.

Grant Eldridge,
freelance writer, Pontiac, Michigan

May, Geraldine (1895–1997)

One of the first female officers in the American military. Born Geraldine Pratt on April 21, 1895, in Albany, New York; died on November 2, 1997, in Menlo Park, California; daughter of Louis W. Pratt and Geraldine (Schuyler) Pratt; University of California at Berkeley, B.A., 1920; member of first graduating class of Women's Army Auxiliary Corps, 1942; married Albert May (a contractor), in 1928 (died 1945).

Commissioned a second lieutenant in the Women's Army Auxiliary Corps (1942); made captain (April 1943); made major (November 1943); made lieutenant colonel (May 1945); became director, Women's Army Corps (January 1947); retired (1951).

Geraldine May was born in 1895 in upstate New York, where her father Louis W. Pratt was an attorney from a prominent family best remembered for its involvement in the creation of the state's university system; her mother **Geraldine Schuyler Pratt** was descended from Dutch immigrants who had been among New York's first leading families. Called "Jerry" as a child, May moved with her family to Tacoma, Washington, and demonstrated a talent for athletics at an early age. After attending boarding school in Bryn Mawr, Pennsylvania, she enrolled in the University of California at Berkeley, where she served as coxswain of the women's rowing crew and president of the women's athletic association. Upon her graduation in 1920 with a degree in social economics, May became a social worker in San Francisco before moving to Sacramento to take a job with the city's department of recreation. For several years in the 1920s, she was an executive officer of the Camp Fire Girls in Sacramento, and in her paid position trained leaders and managed its camp. Geraldine quit working in 1928 when she married Albert May, a contractor, and for several years was a homemaker in Tulsa, Oklahoma.

May's life changed dramatically when the United States entered World War II at the end of 1941. Back in California with her husband, she enlisted in July 1942 in the Women's Army Auxiliary Corps (WAAC, which the following year became the Women's Army Corps or WAC), and was selected for its first women officers' training course in Des Moines, Iowa. After completing the course, she was assigned recruiting duties as a second lieutenant, which entailed a great deal of travel. With the creation of the Army Air Corps (the forerunner of the U.S. Air Force) and its auxiliary women's branch, May was transferred to the latter and became the WAC staff director for its Air Transport Command. In this capacity, she oversaw 6,000 female personnel on 41 different bases around the world, including places as disparate as the U.S., Labrador, North Africa, and the Hawaiian Islands. Again, the job required extensive travel: she was required to visit each base a first time to make sure it was suitable for women, and afterwards to make periodic progress checks. She received a promotion to major by the end of 1943.

With the cessation of the war in 1945, May was made lieutenant colonel, and accepted a job with the General Staff in Washington, D.C. Named director of the Women's Army Corps in January 1947, May became first director of the Women's Air Force (WAF) with the passage of the Women's Armed Services Integration Act of 1948, which made the "auxiliary" women's branches of the service a legitimate part of the armed forces. (Women would still not be allowed to enter the military as full-fledged members until decades later.) With that promotion, she was also elevated to the rank of full colonel. For her wartime service, she was awarded the Legion of Merit and a Commendation of Merit. May retired as head of the WAF in June 1951, and was succeeded by Colonel **Mary Jo Shelly**. Geraldine May died on November 2, 1997, at the age of 102, and was buried with full military honors in Arlington National Cemetery.

SOURCES:

Current Biography. NY: H.W. Wilson, 1949.

McHenry, Robert, ed. *Famous American Women*. NY: Dover, 1980.

Read, Phyllis J., and Bernard L. Witlieb. *The Book of Women's Firsts*. NY: Random House, 1992.

Carol Brennan,
Grosse Pointe, Michigan

May, Gisela (1924—)

German singer and actress, celebrated as Germany's "First Lady of Political Song," who reigned as one of the unchallenged superstars of the German Democratic Republic for more than two decades. Born in Wetzlar, Germany, on May 31, 1924; daughter of Ferdinand May (1896–1977, a well-known playwright and author) and Käthe (Käte) Mettig May (1898–1969, a successful actress).

Began acting (1942) and became a permanent member of the ensembles of the Deutsches Theater (1951) and the Berliner Ensemble (1962), two of East Berlin's leading theaters; regarded for a generation as the foremost singing actress of the GDR, combined her singing career with that of a major dramatic actress; among her most famous roles was that of Mother Courage in Bertolt Brecht's play of the same name.

A veteran of the German stage for almost six decades, Gisela May began her career as an actress in Nazi Germany, survived the final days of World War II, was considered the foremost singing actress of the German Democratic Republic for a generation, and continued to perform after the unification of the two German states in 1990. Regarded by many critics as the greatest interpreter of songs set to the sardonic texts of Bertolt Brecht and Kurt Tucholsky, she was still performing in her mid-70s to enthusiastic audiences. She is known as a formidable interpreter of the repertory of pre-Nazi Berlin songs by Kurt Weill, Hanns Eisler, and other composers, and her use of words is comparable to the styling of *Lotte Lenya and artistic newcomer **Ute Lemper**. Thousands gave May a standing ovation at the end of a two-hour recital of songs by Weill at the Eighth Kurt Weill Festival in his hometown of Dessau, Germany, in February 2000, the year of his birth centenary.

May's repertory and life mirror the history of 20th-century Germany. She was born in 1924 to parents who were successful artists. Her father Ferdinand May was a well-known playwright and author; her mother **Käthe Mettig May** was a successful actress. Both parents detested Nazism. In 1930, when Gisela, her brother Ulrich, and her parents settled in Leipzig, her mother joined the German Communist Party (KPD), which she viewed as the last hope for a successful resistance against Hitler's brownshirts. When the Nazis came to power in 1933, the May family found itself at the mercy of the regime. Because of Käthe May's revolutionary Marxist sentiments, her family was stigmatized, and their apartment was searched on many occasions by brownshirted storm troopers, agents of the criminal police, and the dreaded Gestapo. When the Leipzig Schauspielhaus, a hitherto private theater, came under direct state control in May 1938, Käthe May was pressured into ending her acting career lest her family face additional risks. She helped supplement family income by setting up a women's-stocking business and returned to her early love of painting, selling a number of canvases.

As a child, Gisela May was soon attracted to the artistic and intellectual causes which energized her parents. She was gifted in literature, music, and theater, and was aware of the interrelationship between art and politics. From the earliest days of Hitler's dictatorship, Käthe May was an active member of an anti-Nazi resistance circle that included Bruno Apitz (who would later describe his years in a Nazi concentration camp in the novel *Naked Among Wolves*) and the composer and music pedagogue Alfred Schmidt-Sas, who was Gisela's piano teacher for a number of years. Schmidt-Sas was arrested and executed in 1943 for his anti-Nazi activities. In 1943, the May family received notification that Gisela's brother Ulrich had been declared missing in action; the official date given for his disappearance at the front was April 20, 1943, Adolf Hitler's 54th birthday. Decades later, sharp-eyed visitors to Gisela's Berlin apartment would note a small bust of "Uli" on one of her bookshelves.

Not yet 21 when Nazi Germany surrendered in the spring of 1945, May had experienced much in her short life. The savagery of Nazism, which resulted in incalculable loss of life as well as the physical and moral destruction of her country, was deeply impressed upon her, and she wanted to participate in Germany's cultural reconstruction. May already had considerable preparation for a career in the arts. She had completed a course in acting studies between 1940 and 1942 and appeared on stage during the war years, starting in 1943 at Dresden's Kömedienhaus Theater, then going on to the Municipal Theater in Görlitz and the Landesbühne Theater in Danzig. Now living in the Soviet Occupation Zone (SBZ) of Germany, May accepted an offer at the theater in Halle an der Saale. Here, she broadened her repertory by appearing in classic plays by Goethe, Schiller, and other representatives of the German humanist tradition, as well as in plays by modernists including Bertolt Brecht. During the next half-dozen years, she also appeared on stage in theaters in other cities of the SBZ, including Leipzig and Schwerin.

As she was increasingly acclaimed for both the power and subtlety of her performances, May's reputation flourished. In 1951, she became an ensemble member of the East Berlin's prestigious Deutsches Theater. While her career was on the rise, she relied on her mother's advice and support. Käthe May could often be seen sitting at the back of the theater during rehearsals, unobtrusively observing her celebrated daughter. For the next few years, May expanded her repertory, which consisted entirely of supporting roles.

A turning point came in 1957, when at short notice she agreed to stand in for an indisposed fellow actress in a matinee performance of songs by Bertolt Brecht. Although May had never sung on stage before, the performance—in which she shared the spotlight with the famous singer-actor Ernst Busch—was a great success.

Noted composer Hanns Eisler, who was in the audience, told May that she had a talent that had to be further developed. From then on, May would be as much a singer as she was an actress. In 1959, she made a wildly successful international debut as a performer of Brecht's songs at Milan's Piccolo Teatro. In the same year, she was awarded the Arts Prize of the German Democratic Republic (GDR). Her husky contralto, ideal in many ways for interpreting the bitter songs of Brecht and Weill, rekindled for many in the audience memories of *Marlene Dietrich.

In 1962, May joined the world-famous Berliner Ensemble. Founded by Brecht and continued by his widow *Helene Weigel, this troupe specialized in performing Brecht's plays, and over the years became a mecca for Brecht enthusiasts on both sides of the Iron Curtain. Weigel had been impressed by May's performances for years and played a key role in making her a permanent member of the Ensemble. May's career flourished there. She soon became one of the theater's leading attractions, starring in most of Brecht's important plays. Her performance in the role of Mrs. Peachum in the *Dreigroschenoper* (*Threepenny Opera*) provided perhaps the most successful combination of acting and singing. Her Mother Courage in Brecht's *Mutter Courage* (*Mother Courage*) received the highest possible praise from Therese Giehse, who had created the role: "[May] possesses an extraordinary musicality—and a genuinely beautiful voice. Once she has heard a song, she has mastered it. That is really quite unbelievable and truly a splendid thing."

Few dissenting voices were heard when one of May's most impressive achievements, her recording of Kurt Weill's *Die Sieben Todsünden* (*The Seven Deadly Sins*), earned her the coveted Grand Prix du Disque in 1967. Starting in the late 1960s, she began to perform not only in the GDR and eastern bloc, but also in a number of Western nations, where she taught workshops on chanson performance. Official GDR recognition of May's unique talents came when she was invited to begin lecturing at East Berlin's Academy of Music. She also began to appear in motion pictures and television. During her several visits to the United States, a small but growing number of fans snapped up tickets for her performances. In 1974, she performed in Manhattan as well as before a gathering of United Nations delegates.

May's experiences in Nazi Germany had convinced her that the only way to prevent a recurrence of the evil of fascism on German soil was to build a strong society. Loyal to the eastern half of Germany, the GDR, she became a dedicated member of the leading party, the Socialist Unity Party (SED), serving on various boards and committees of artists. In 1966, she became an executive board member of the Association of Performing Theater Artists, and 1972 she received an additional honor by being elected a full member of the GDR Academy of Arts. Among the many GDR prizes May was awarded were the National Prize, third class (1963), the National Prize, first class (1973), and the Fatherland Merit Order in Gold (1980).

In early 1989, on the eve of the collapse of the GDR, May took advantage of her special status by crossing daily to West Berlin to perform in cabaret at the Theater des Westens, where enthusiastic audiences greeted her nightly. Deeply in debt, the GDR regime encouraged such cultural exchanges not only for prestige but as a means to acquire needed hard currency. Gisela May did not play a significant role, as did such women as *Bärbel Bohley and *Steffie Spira, in the events that brought down the SED dictatorship in the last months of 1989. She did, however, continue her career, remaining immensely popular in her live performances.

Many of May's more than 20 classic recordings, particularly those she made in the 1960s, were remastered and reissued in the compact-disc format in the 1990s. Her recordings of chansons based on Brecht texts are regarded by many critics as the definitive interpretations of these works. In a 1985 interview, May noted: "You must be an actress to interpret the lyrics of Brecht. Singing the songs, I am all the time an actress. You must always keep in mind the social situations of the songs. Singing Marlene Dietrich songs is, of course, a very different experience. You have wonderful melodies and a feeling of nostalgia. I have great respect for her as a woman and as an actress who always had a deeply human touch." She also recorded prize-winning interpretations of chansons based on texts by Heine, Tucholsky, Mehring, Mühsam, Kästner, Hollaender and Wedekind, as well as by Jacques Brel and Pablo Neruda. Ironically, with their sharp criticisms of capitalist and middle-class society, these songs were highly popular among Western intellectuals starting in the 1960s. May's renditions of the songs of Hanns Eisler played an important role in making this brilliant but relatively neglected composer (because of his Marxist allegiances) better known outside the eastern bloc. While becoming an internationally renowned singer of German chansons, May remained active on stage as one of the best-known actresses of the

Berliner Ensemble. By the 1990s, most theatergoers felt that she had earned the unofficial title of the Ensemble's "First Lady."

Gisela May

SOURCES:

Clark, Andrew. "Sign of Glasnost at the Wall," in *Financial Times* [London]. February 18, 1989, p. XXV.

Cultural Life in the GDR: Review and Current Trends. Dresden: Panorama DDR, 1982.

"Gisela May beim 8. Kurt-Weill-Fest in Dessau gefeiert," in *Deutsche Presse-Agentur-Europadienst.* February 26, 2000.

"Gisela May—Die First Lady des politischen Liedes," in *Der Standard* [Vienna]. August 29, 1990.

Harten, J. "Eerste Dame van het Berliner Ensemble," in *Maatstaf.* Vol. 39, no. 5. May 1991, pp. 62–63.

Holden, Stephen. "Summerfare Festival in Purchase Offers Cabaret," in *The New York Times.* July 5, 1985, p. C3.

Jäger, Manfred. *Kultur und Politik in der DDR 1945–1990.* Cologne: Edition Deutschland Archiv im Verlag Wissenschaft und Politik Claus-Peter von Nottbeck, 1995.

Kranz, Dieter. *Gisela May, Schauspielerin und Diseuse: Bildbiographie.* Berlin: Henschelverlag, 1988.

May, Ferdinand. *Die bösen und die guten Dinge: ein Leben erzählt.* Berlin: Verlag Neues Leben, 1978.

May, Gisela. *Mit meinen Augen: Begegnungen und Impressionen.* 3rd rev. ed. Berlin: Buchverlag Der Morgen, 1982.

"May, Käthe," in Frithjof Trapp *et al.,* eds., *Handbuch des deutschsprachigen Exiltheaters 1933–1945,*

Band 2: *Biographisches Lexikon der Theaterkünstler*, Teil 2: L–Z, Munich: K.G. Saur, 1999, p. 649.

Otto, Hans-Gerald. "Gisela May—Schauspielerin, Sängerin und Diseuse," in *Musik und Gesellschaft*. Vol. 24, no. 5. May 1974, pp. 298–300.

Papst, M. "Ein Koffer spricht: Gisela May im Theater am Hechtplatz," in *Neue Zürcher Zeitung*. March 16, 1999, p. 46.

Rehahn, Rosemarie. "Gisela May," in Sabine Ehrhardt-Renken, ed., *Chanteusen: Stimmen der Grosstadt*. Mannheim: Bollmann Verlag GmbH, 1997, pp. 157–167.

Rockwell, John. "A Concert Will Evoke Berlin in Weimar Days," in *The New York Times*. September 27, 1974, p. 48.

———. "Gisela May Sings Brecht, Tucholsky With Exhilaration," in *The New York Times*. October 6, 1974, p. 63.

Schumacher, Ernst. *Berliner Kritiken: Ein Theater-Dezennium 1964–1974*. 2 vols. Berlin: Henschelverlag Kunst und Gesellschaft, 1975.

Theater der Zeit. Vol. 38, no. 11, 1983, pp. 6–10.

Wekwerth, Manfred. *Notate: Über die Arbeit des Berliner Ensembles 1956 bis 1966*. Frankfurt am Main: Suhrkamp Verlag, 1967.

Wildenhains, Bernhard. *Schauspieler sein . . . Die Erinnerungen Bernhard Wildenhains*. Edited by Ferdinand and Käte May. Berlin: Henschelverlag, 1958.

RELATED MEDIA:

"Brecht-Songs" (Berlin Classics CD 2165-2).

"Gisela May: Live" (EMI Electrola LP C 062-31 136).

"Gisela May: Reflections on the Theater of Brecht" (videocassette in Creative Arts Television Archive Collection, VAE 0390, Library of Congress, Washington, D.C.), Camera Three television program with Gisela May and Carl Weber, November 26, 1972.

"Hanns Eisler Dokumente: Musik und Gespräche von und mit Hanns Eisler" (Berlin Classics CD 0090582).

"Reflections on the Theater of Brecht" (videocassette), NY: Columbia Broadcasting System, 1972.

"Die sieben Todsünden" (Berlin Classics CD 2069-2).

"Songs aus Happy End, Das Berliner Requiem, Die Dreigroschenoper, Aufstieg und Fall der Stadt Mahagonny" (Capriccio CD 10 180).

John Haag,
Associate Professor of History,
University of Georgia, Athens, Georgia

Maya (d. around 563 BCE)

Indian princess. Died around 563 BCE at Lumbini (in modern-day Nepal); elder sister of *Mahapajapati; married Suddhodanaa or Suddhodana (a noble prince of the Gautama [Gotama] clan, belonging to the Sakyas tribe who lived on the border of India and Nepal); children: Prince Siddhartha Gautama, also known as the Buddha (c. 563–483 BCE).

The years 563 and 483 BCE are generally accepted as the least controversial, if not the most plausible dates, for the birth and death of the Buddha. The historical facts of his life are these: he was born around 563 BCE in what is now Nepal, near the Indian border. His full name was Siddhartha Gautama of the Sakyas clan. His father was a prince; his mother was a princess, and by the standards of the day his upbringing was luxurious.

Legend has it that in the middle of summer, under a full moon, Queen Maya fell asleep and dreamed that she was transported to the Himalayas, where her future son, in the guise of a white elephant, entered her womb through her side (thus suggesting a virgin birth). "In the instant that the future Buddha was conceived, the world had quivered and quaked," write David Leeming and Jake Page:

> light filled the world; the blind saw; the deaf heard; the crooked of body grew straight; the lame walked; those in chains went free; the fires of hell were banked; disease disappeared; the weather grew fair; rain fell; rivers stopped flowing; . . . flowers fell in showers from the sky; the world became a garland. All these things happened for a brief time when the Buddha was conceived, and angels with swords arrived to guard the future Buddha and his mother from harm.

Near the time her baby was due to be born, Maya decided to visit her family in the city of Devadaha, and set off in a chair of gold carried by courtiers. She stopped on the way to admire beautiful Lumbini Grove, and there gave birth to the Buddha, standing up and holding on to a Sal tree (shorea robusta), an image often used in Buddhist art. (The Buddha himself would later meditate under a tree.) He was born clean and unbloodied, without afterbirth, and from the sky two streams of pure water washed over the newborn and his mother. Maya died seven days later, because "a womb that has held a future Buddha is like a temple shrine; it cannot be used again for another purpose," and was reborn, it is written, as the goddess Mahadevaputta.

SOURCES:

Leeming, David, and Jake Page. *Goddess: Myths of the Female Divine*. Oxford: Oxford University Press, 1994.

Mayer, Constance (c. 1778–1821)

French painter of the First Republic era. Name variations: Marie Françoise Constance Mayer; Marie-F-Constance Mayer Lamartiniere. Born in 1775 or 1778, in Paris, France; committed suicide on May 27, 1821; daughter of a customs official; studied art privately in Paris.

Selected works: Portrait of a Father and Daughter *(1801);* The Sleep of Psyche *(1806);* The Torch of Venus *(1808);* The Dream of Happiness *(1819);* Portrait of Mlle. Tretzel *(exhibited in 1822)*; Young Girl with a Cat *(exhibited in 1822)*.

Born in Paris in the late 1770s, Constance Mayer lived and painted during a heady time in European history, executing the domestic scenes, allegories, and portraits that were popular in the years following the French Revolution and during the reign of Napoleon I. As the daughter of a customs officer, she probably witnessed much of the violence and social upheaval that came with the French Revolution of 1789 and the ensuing Reign of Terror. Her first painting teacher, J.B. Suvee, was imprisoned during the latter episode. She then studied art alongside her best friend, *Jeanne Philiberte Ledoux, at the studio of Jean-Baptiste Greuze, and began to achieve a small measure of recognition for her work. Mayer exhibited in the Salons beginning in 1796, and was then invited by the painter Pierre-Paul Prud'hon to work in his atelier. (Prud'hon would later work as a drawing instructor to Napoleon's empresses, *Josephine and *Marie Louise of Austria.) From 1802 onward, Mayer both assisted Prud'hon and executed her own paintings; her hand is evident in several of works signed by Prud'hon, including *Innocence Seduced by Love* and *The Dying Laborer*.

Mayer was evidently close to her father, a tie that is apparent in her *Portrait of a Father and Daughter* (exhibited in the Salon of 1801), in which he is showing her a bust of Raphael. Although her paintings belonged to the traditional genre that was expected in the Salons during this era, Mayer exhibited a distinctive talent for conveying animated personalities and lively scenes on her canvases. In some cases, her works depict idyllic families, most often mothers and children. Empress Josephine commissioned her to paint *The Sleep of Psyche*, exhibited at the 1806 Salon under the title *The Sleeping Venus with Cupid Caressed and Wakened by Zephyrs*, but the painting's reception was representative of one of the obstacles faced by women artists: it was first shown and sold under her name; then, under Prud'hon's name, it was sold again for a higher price.

In 1810, Mayer's father died, and she accepted Prud'hon's invitation to live next to him in a designated artists' quarter near the Sorbonne. Although he was married, they worked closely and ate meals together, and are described by **Ann Sutherland Harris** and **Linda Nochlin** as "shar[ing] a strong emotional and professional dependency." Constance Mayer continued to paint and exhibit, at times weathering criticism that her work too closely resembled that of her

mentor. Around 1818, she began to be plagued by bouts of melancholy and anxiety. Three years later, upon her return from a holiday with Prud'hon, they learned that they both were being evicted; Mayer may have had nowhere else to live. Prud'hon—who had five children whom Mayer sometimes cared for, a brood that was said to treat her derisively—had repeatedly stated his intentions to remain single if his wife were to die. Constance Mayer was found dead on May 27, 1821, having slashed her throat with his razor.

SOURCES:

Harris, Ann Sutherland, and Linda Nochlin. *Women Artists: 1550–1950*. NY: Alfred A. Knopf, 1976.
Heller, Nancy G. *Women Artists: An Illustrated History*. NY: Abbeville Press, 1987.

COLLECTIONS:

Mayer's paintings are held in private collections and in the collections of the Louvre in Paris, the Wallace Collection in London, the Baltimore Museum of Art, and the museums of Dijon and Nancy, France, among others.

Carol Brennan,
Grosse Pointe, Michigan

Mayer, Emilie (1821–1883)

German composer, sculptor, and co-director of the Berlin Opera, whose instrumental works were frequently performed in Germany and Central Europe. Born in Friedland, Mecklenburg, on May 14, 1821; died in Berlin on April 10, 1883.

Emilie Mayer studied under Carl Loewe when her musical talent became apparent and also began composing, writing dances and variations. She studied counterpoint under B.A. Marx and orchestration under Wieprecht after she went to Berlin for further study in 1847. Three years later, Mayer gave a concert of her own works which included a concert overture, a string quartet, a setting of Psalm 118 for chorus and orchestra, two symphonies and some piano solos. The concert was a great success, and not long afterwards Mayer received the gold medal of art from the queen of Prussia, *Elizabeth of Bavaria (1801–1873). Mayer's instrumental works were increasingly performed, and she was appointed co-director of the Berlin Opera as a result of her growing fame. Also a talented sculptor, Mayer received a gold medal for a vase from the queen of Prussia.

John Haag,
Athens, Georgia

Mayer, Helene (1910–1953)

World-class athlete and winner of Olympic, national and international medals in fencing, who struggled against Nazi racial oppression and continued to compete successfully despite intolerance. Name variations: Hèléne Mayer. Born Helene Mayer on December 20, 1910, in Offenbach, Germany; died on October 15, 1953, in Heidelberg, Germany; daughter of Ludwig Mayer (1876–1931, a prominent Jewish physician) and Ida (Becker) Mayer (1883–1958, a Lutheran); attended public schools in Offenbach; studied international law at the University of Frankfurt, the Sorbonne, and obtained a degree in that field from Scripps College in Claremont, California; married Erwin Falkner von Sonnenburg, in 1952.

Won German foil championship at age 14 (1925); won the gold medal in the Amsterdam Olympics at age 17 (1928); won World championships (1929 and 1931); expelled from the Offenbach Fencing Club for being half Jewish, excluding her from competition (1933); won silver medal at the Berlin Olympics (1936); won U.S. indoor championships (1934, 1935, 1937, 1938, 1939, 1941, 1942, 1946).

Born on December 20, 1910, in Offenbach, Germany, Helene Mayer was the product of a mixed marriage, a common occurrence in Germany's upper-middle class: her father Ludwig Mayer was a prominent Jewish physician, whereas her mother **Ida Becker Mayer** was Lutheran. Mayer enjoyed a conventional middle-class childhood in Offenbach. She was athletic and took ballet lessons, but by age nine she showed great interest in fencing and began taking lessons at the town's excellent fencing club. Her teacher was the famous "Cavaliere" Arturo Gazzera, under whose tutelage she made great progress. In 1925, at age 14, she won the German foil championship.

The skill and art of using a sword was not commonly acquired by women until the late 19th century, when it was often part of the finishing school curriculum. Fencing was one of the few sports in which women could compete at national and international levels. When Baron Pierre de Coubertin founded the modern Olympic Games which first took place in Athens in 1896, the games were created for gentlemen amateurs. (One woman, *Melpomene, did participate in the 1896 Olympics, albeit illicitly.) Coubertin vehemently opposed female participation on the basis that women had no role in the original games. Furthermore, he felt that strenuous sports activities destroyed feminine charm. The objection was overcome, however, in 1900, when golf and lawn tennis were introduced as female events, followed by tennis and archery in 1904. In 1908, skating and gymnastics ap-

peared, then swimming in 1912. Fencing was introduced in 1924 at the games held in Paris. The first female Olympic fencing champion was ❧▶ **Ellen Osiier**, a Dane, who won all 16 of her bouts, scoring 80 touches and receiving only 34. One of the U.S. entrants at these same games was **Adeline Gehrig**, sister of the great New York baseball player Lou Gehrig.

At age 17, Helene Mayer represented Germany at the 1928 games held in Amsterdam, sweeping through the tournament with surprising ease, winning 18 bouts and losing two to win the gold medal. From this point forward, she was the sovereign master of women's fencing, winning the European championship in 1929 in Naples and again in 1931 in Vienna (these were later declared to be World championships). Catapulted into national fame, she was known as "die blonde He." Her only setback took place in the 1932 Olympics in Los Angeles, when she was off form and was only able to achieve a fifth place. Despite this, she continued to compete.

An all-around athlete, Mayer enjoyed skiing, tennis, rowing, swimming, and hockey. She did not confine her fencing skill to female opponents; Mayer was a match for men as well. "As for any mental hazard men may feel at lunging toward a woman," said one admirer, "it soon disappears when they meet her skillful foil."

In addition to her athletic prowess, Mayer was academically ambitious and looked forward to a career in the diplomatic service. She took courses in international law at the University of Frankfurt in 1929 and studied at the Sorbonne in Paris in the winter of 1930–31. She left Germany in 1932 to study international law at Scripps College in Claremont, California. Fiercely independent, she paid for her education by working as a governess, teaching German, and coaching to earn spending money, tuition, room and board. She bought a Plymouth roadster, which she named "Asthma" because of its leaky radiator, and liked her American classmates' open-mindedness, remarking, "Nobody minds what religion or sect I belong to."

The Nazi seizure of power in the first months of 1933 did not initially affect Mayer personally; indeed, the striking 5'10" green-eyed blonde was portrayed as a national hero in Nazi propaganda until her half-Jewish origins were discovered. Then she was expelled from the Offenbach Fencing Club. The German Fencing Association announced at the same time that the action of the local club did not affect her membership in the German National Fencing Federation. Despite this "exceptional" treatment, Mayer chose to continue her studies in the United States.

Harsh Nazi treatment of German Jews upset many American athletic leaders. They were shocked by the removal of Dr. Theodor Lewald from his post as president of the German Olympic Committee because of his partly Jewish ancestry. On June 6, 1933, at a meeting of the International Olympic Committee, American delegates threatened to remove the games from Germany if discrimination did not cease. On the next day, Lewald, who had been given the post of "adviser" to the German Olympic Organizing Committee, announced that the government would observe all Olympic resolutions and that "on principle" Jews would not be excluded from the German teams.

Brigadier General Charles E. Sherrill, U.S. delegate to the International Olympic Committee, was not convinced of Germany's good faith and demanded that Helene Mayer be invited to join the German Olympic team as concrete proof of compliance. Under the Nazis, Jews were barred from practice and from the clubs whose members had access to the Olympic trials, which effectively kept them from participating in the trials to make the German team. American athletic leaders were aware of this ongoing discrimination. At a meeting of the U.S. Amateur Athletic Union on November 21, 1933, the delegates, with one exception, voted to boycott the 1936 Olympic Games scheduled to be held in Berlin unless Germany changed its treatment of Jewish athletes "in fact as well as theory." Quickly responding to the threat of exclusion, German Olympic officials announced that Helene Mayer would be allowed to participate in the games as a member of the German team. Then with a further fanfare of international publicity, the German Olympic Committee announced in June 1934 that 21 Jewish athletes had been nominated for their training camps. Hitler's Reichssportsführer Hans von Tschammer und Osten recognized the importance of public relations and explained German acquiescence saying, "You are probably astonished by the decision in Vienna, but we had to consider the foreign political situation." Meanwhile, at a closed meeting of officials, he declared his pleasure at the ongoing racial cleansing of German sporting clubs.

The American Olympic Committee dispatched its president, Avery Brundage, to make an on-the-spot investigation. Brundage was dazzled by the "order and prosperity" which many then felt characterized the Nazi regime. Inter-

Osiier, Ellen (1890–1962)

Danish fencer. Name variations: *Ellen Ottilia Osiier; Ellen Osiier-Thomsen. Born on August 13, 1890; died in September 1962; married Dr. Ivan Osiier (1888–1965, an Olympic fencer who won the gold medal in individual epee in Stockholm in 1912).*

In 1924, 33-year-old Ellen Osiier became the first female Olympic fencing champion, winning the gold medal for individual foil in Paris. Her husband Ivan Osiier competed as a fencer in the Olympics over a span of 40 years, holding the competitive longevity record.

views with Jewish leaders convinced Brundage all was well despite one critical journalist's observation that they were always accompanied by Nazi officials. On the basis of Brundage's recommendations, the American committee voted to participate in the 1936 Olympics. Later it was learned that although 21 Jewish athletes had been nominated for participation in training camps, none were actually invited to attend.

> [T]he tall, statuesque, green-eyed blonde was portrayed in Nazi propaganda as a national heroine, until her half Jewish origins were discovered.
>
> —Robert Wistrich

The true face of the regime was revealed once again in September 1935 when the Nuremberg laws were proclaimed, officially transforming German Jews into second-class citizens. At this point, General Sherrill decided to make the best of a bad situation. Returning from a trip to Germany, he condemned Americans advocating a boycott of the games and claimed he knew many American Jews who opposed such a boycott. The secretary of the American Olympic Committee, Frederick W. Rubien, seconded this position, asserting, "Germans are not discriminating against Jews in their Olympic tryouts. The Jews are eliminated because they are not good enough as athletes. Why are there not a dozen Jews in the world of Olympic caliber?"

Continuing American pressure did produce results on the German team. Rudi Ball, a star ice hockey player who had fled to France, returned to Germany and rejoined the team. Gretel Bergmann (*Margaret Bergmann Lambert), a world-class high jumper, was allowed to compete in the "advanced" Olympic tryouts although as a "Jewess" she was excluded from the German championships. Reassured by these concessions by the Nazis, a number of Jewish athletes from other countries agreed to participate in the games. The Polish, Czechoslovakian, and Hungarian teams all included Jewish athletes.

Americans continued to be concerned about the inclusion of Jewish athletes on the German Olympic team, fearing the Nazis would renege on their promises. Although Helene Mayer had been assured a place on the team in 1933, no further invitations had been extended, and she continued to live in the United States. In the summer of 1935, Sherrill hectored Nazi sporting officials to make good on their two-year-old promise to include Mayer. Reichssportsführer Hans von Tschammer und Osten reextended the invitation and attempted to defuse the racial issue by declaring Mayer to be "Aryan," an easy assertion to make about the tall Teutonic athlete. Meanwhile, Mayer had already stated publicly she would be pleased to represent Germany as she had done in two previous Olympiads. Furthermore, she was eager to visit her mother and two brothers, one of whom, Eugen Mayer, was also a star fencer.

Nevertheless, some athletes decided to boycott the games. The president of the Maccabi World Union, an international organization of Jewish sporting clubs, urged "all Jewish sportsmen, for their own self-respect, to refrain from competing in a country where they are discriminated against as a race and our Jewish brethren are treated with unexampled brutality." Among those declining to attend were **Judith Deutsch**, an Austrian swimmer of world-record caliber, Philippe de Rothschild and Jean Rheims, French bobsled champions, and Albert Wolff, the famous French fencer.

The 1936 Olympic Games provided Hitler's regime with an opportunity to advertise the benefits of Nazism. As early as January 1934, Propaganda Minister Joseph Goebbels had taken over control of Olympic publicity. No expense was spared to create a superb venue for the games. A new Olympic stadium with seating for 110,000 was built, as well as a village for the almost 4,000 athletes from 50 nations. Great attention was paid to creature comforts. American mattresses were provided for the American athletes, the Swiss and Austrians slept under feather comforters, while the Japanese slept on floor mats. A sauna was provided for the Finns. Recipes of favorite foods were researched, and North German Lloyd, the shipping line, supplied individualized cuisines for each nation in order to make the athletes feel at home. Afterward the Americans declared, "The best place to eat in Berlin was the Olympic Village."

This careful attention to the needs of male athletes, however, did not extend to women competitors. The women's dormitory was a utilitarian structure surrounded by a high wrought-iron fence. For some time, the rooms went unheated. Food was inadequate, and its quality far below what male athletes enjoyed. The men's needs were catered to by Captain Wolfgang Fuerstner, chief of the German army's athletic program and also a part Jew. The women, on the other hand, were strictly supervised by **Baroness von Wangenheim** who was indifferent to their complaints about poor housing and food.

Hitler's regime was determined to put its best foot forward during the games. Anti-Semitic propaganda was discouraged. The stormtroopers were reminded to be courteous to everyone, including Jews, during the months of July and August. Goebbels issued an order forbidding political meetings from August 1 to September 7 to ensure that no anti-Semitic incidents would occur.

As usual the Nazis' split personality emerged. One song popular among Nazi activists urged them to "have patience" stating, "When once Olympia is past, then boys, the spring cleaning comes at last." Blatant anti-Semitism had already surfaced during the Winter Games held at the two villages of Garmisch and Partenkirchen. Although the German goal was to present typical Bavarian *Gemütlichkeit*, the effort failed at times. Count Baillet-Latour, president of the International Olympic Committee, had toured the winter games facilities and come across signs at the toilet facilities stating, "Dogs and Jews are not allowed." Requesting an interview with Hitler, he informed the chancellor that the signs were "not in conformity with Olympic principles." Hitler replied, "Mr. President, when you are invited to a friend's home, you don't tell him how to run it." After a moment Baillet-Latour responded, "Excuse me, Mr. Chancellor, when the five-circled flag is raised over the stadium it is no longer Germany. It is Olympia and we are masters there." The signs were removed.

No other Olympic sport in 1936 was as cosmopolitan as fencing. Three hundred contestants from 31 nations joined Helene Mayer in competition. Two gymnasiums and an amphitheater in Berlin as well as some hard clay tennis courts near the main stadium were the site of the matches, and eliminations went on for two weeks. As a competitor in a demanding sport which requires great stamina, it was not unusual for a fencer to begin early in the morning and compete until late at night. This was

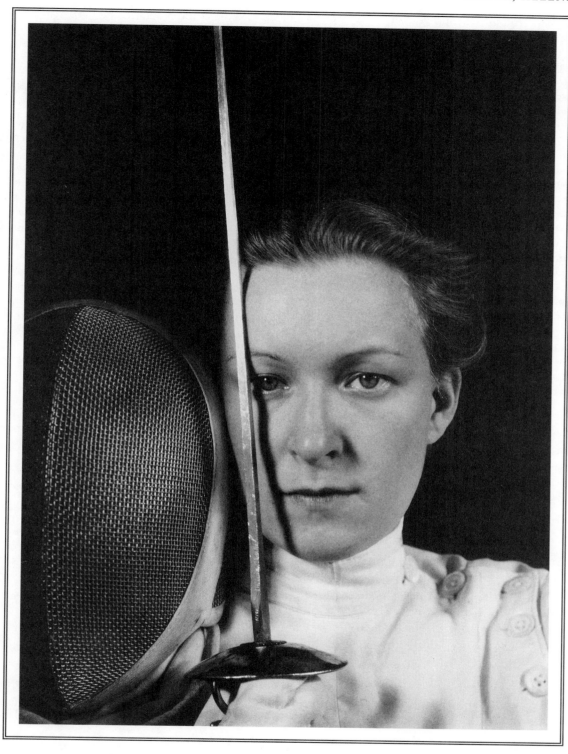

Helene Mayer.
Photo by
Imogen
Cunningham.

particularly true in 1936 when the long elimination trials shifted the balance toward youthful vigor. As well, for the first time the electrical touch apparatus had been adopted, which may have lessened the effect of dramatics and the confidence that comes with age.

In 1936, the only Olympic fencing competition for women was the individual foils. Elimination matches had narrowed the field to eight continental contestants, including three of the greatest fencers of the modern era. Helene Mayer was joined by ❧▶ **Ellen Preis**, the Austri-

See sidebar
on the
following page

❧▶

an who won the Olympic gold in Los Angeles in 1932, as well as ◄⚘ **Ilona Schacherer-Elek**, the 1934 and 1935 European champion from Hungary. According to reports, all three had never been in better form. Although fencing matches were often sparsely attended, theirs were sold out, and despite its size, the audience was hushed as the matches proceeded.

Helene Mayer was the star of two of the most hotly contested events. One match was with Schacherer-Elek who perceived Mayer's weakness and used a provocative air to make her nervous. At the end of three encounters, the Hungarian led 3:2, 4:4, and 5:4. In subsequent matches, however, Mayer improved her position and picked up more points than her rival. The two were tied before Mayer and Preis began their match, which has been described as the most dramatic fencing match of modern times. The Austrian, like her German opponent, was in deadly earnest. Tension was so high in the stadium that the crowd was absolutely silent. The two great athletes lunged at each other with uncanny skill, and the results for three matches were 2:2, 3:3 and 4:4—a draw. However, points

decided the victor and in the end Ilona Schacherer-Elek won the gold. Mayer had to be content with the silver while Ellen Preis took the bronze. All three champions were Jewish. Nonetheless, in the victory ceremony, Mayer held her profile high and offered a faultless "Heil Hitler!" salute.

After visiting her family, Helene Mayer returned to the United States. Her last great international victory came in Paris in 1937 when she won the World fencing championship, but she also won the U.S. indoor championship eight times (1934, 1935, 1937, 1938, 1939, 1941, 1942, 1946). Mayer earned her living teaching German at Mills College and later at the University of California, Berkeley. The war years brought her anguish, particularly as her family faced great danger. In 1952, she returned to Germany and married Erwin Falkner von Sonnenburg (1901–1980), an engineer. The following year, on October 15, 1953, Helene Mayer died of cancer in Heidelberg. She is still well known in Germany and was honored on an Olympic commemorative stamp issued by the Federal Republic of Germany in 1972.

SOURCES:

Arlott, John, ed. *The Oxford Companion to Sports and Games.* London: Oxford University Press, 1975.

Bernett, Hajo. *Der jüdische Sport im nationalsozialistischen Deutschland 1933–1938.* Schorndorf: Karl Hofmann, 1978.

Cuddon, J.A. *The International Dictionary of Sports and Games.* NY: Schocken Books, n.d.

Deutsche Sporthochschule Köln-Zentralbibliothek der Sportwissenschaften, press clippings on Helene Mayer, 1928–1953.

Güse, K.D., and Andreas Schirmer. *Faszination Fechten,* 1986.

Guttmann, Allen. *The Games Must Go On: Avery Brundage and the Olympic Movement.* NY: Columbia University Press, 1984.

Hart-Davis, Duff. *Hitler's Games: The 1936 Olympics.* NY: Harper & Row, 1986.

"Helene Mayer, 43, Fencing Star, Dies," in *The New York Times.* October 16, 1953, p. 27.

Hoberman, John M. *Sport and Political Ideology.* Austin: University of Texas Press, 1984.

Jonas, K.W. *Helene Mayer—Zur Erinnerung an den Olympischen Spiele in Berlin vor 50 Jahren,* 1988.

Kass, D.A. "The Issue of Racism at the 1936 Olympics," in *Journal of Sport History.* Vol. 3, no. 2. Summer 1976, pp. 223–235.

Kluge, V. *Olympische Spiele von 1886–1980,* 1981.

Kruger, Arnd. "The 1936 Olympic Games—Berlin," in Peter J. Graham and Horst Ueberhorst, eds., *The Modern Olympics.* West Point, NY: Leisure Press, 1976, pp. 172–186.

Lehnen, V.M. "Holokaust und Sport: Helene Mayer oder jüdische Sportler in Nazi-Deutschland," in *Olympische Jugend.* Vol. 3, 1979, pp. 4–5.

Levine, Peter. "'My Father and I, We Didn't Get Our Medals': Marty Glickman's American Jewish

⚘▶ **Preis, Ellen** (1912—)

Austrian-Jewish fencing champion. Name variations: Ellen Müller-Preis; Ellen Mueller or Muller-Preis. Born Ellen Preis in Berlin, Germany, on May 6, 1912.

A sports prodigy, Ellen Preis became an Austrian fencing champion in Damenflorett at the age of 12. She participated in five Olympics, winning a gold medal in individual foil in Los Angeles in 1932 (**Heather Guinness** of Great Britain won the silver, **Erna Bogen** of Hungary took the bronze). Preis also won a bronze medal in Berlin in 1936, and, as Ellen Müller-Preis, another bronze medal in London in 1948 (*Ilona Schacherer-Elek** of Hungary won the gold, **Karen Lachmann** of Denmark won the silver). Preis was still competing for World championships as late as 1959.

⚘▶ **Schacherer-Elek, Ilona** (1907–1988)

Hungarian-Jewish fencer. Name variations: Ilona Elek; Ilona Elek-Schacherer. Born Ilona Elek on May 17, 1907; died on July 24, 1988.

For 60 years, the Hungarians dominated fencing. Ilona Schacherer-Elek won her first Olympic gold medal in Berlin in 1936 in the individual foil events. She took her second gold in London in 1948, and then a silver in Helsinki in 1952. She was world champion in 1934, 1935, and again, an amazing 16 years later, in 1951.

Odyssey," in *American Jewish History*. Vol. 78, no. 3. March 1989, pp. 399–424.

Mandell, Richard D. *The Nazi Olympics*. NY: Macmillan, 1971.

Mayer, Paul Yogi. "Equality—Egality: Jews and Sport in Germany," in *Year Book XXV of the Leo Baeck Institute*. London: Secker & Warburg, 1980, pp. 221–241.

Meisl, Willy, and Felix Pinczower. "Sport," in Siegmund Kaznelson, ed., *Juden im Deutschen Kuturbereich: Ein Sammelwerk*. 3rd ed. Berlin: Jüdischer Verlag, n.d., pp. 926–936.

Mevert, F. *Olympische Spiele der Neuzeit*, 1983.

Mitchell, Sheila. "Women's Participation in the Olympic Games 1900–1926," in *Journal of Sport History*. Vol. 4, no. 1. Spring 1977, pp. 208–228.

Murray, Bill. "Berlin in 1936: Old and New Work on the Nazi Olympics," in *International Journal of the History of Sport*. Vol. 9, no. 1. April 1992, pp. 29–49.

"An Olympic 'Hymn of Hate,'" in *Jewish Chronicle* [London]. August 7, 1936, p. 14.

O'Neill, Lois Decker, ed. *The Women's Book of World Records and Achievements*. Garden City, N.Y.: Anchor Books, 1979.

Oppenheimer, John F., ed. *Lexikon des Judentums*. Bertelsmann Lexikon-Verlag, n.d.

Remley, Mary L. *Women in Sport: An Annotated Bibliography*. Boston: C.K. Hall, 1991.

Schirmer, Andreas. "Mayer, Helene, Fechterin," in *Neue Deutsche Biographie*. Vol. 16. Berlin: Duncker & Humblot, 1990, pp. 541–542.

Wallechinsky, David. *The Complete Book of the Olympics*. NY: Viking Press, 1984.

Wistrich, Robert. *Who's Who in Nazi Germany*. NY: Macmillan, 1982.

John Haag,
Associate Professor of History,
University of Georgia, Athens, Georgia

Mayer, Irene.

See Selznick, Irene Mayer.

Mayer, Maria Goeppert

(1906–1972)

German-American physicist who was the first woman to win the Nobel Prize for theoretical physics, awarded in 1963 for her explanation of the nuclear shell model theory. Name variations: Maria or Marie Goeppert-Mayer; Göppert, Geoppart, or Geoppert. Pronunciation: GER-pert MAY-er. Born Maria Gertrud Käte Göppert on June 28, 1906, in Kattowitz, Upper Silesia (now Katowice, Poland); died in San Diego, California, on February 20, 1972, of a pulmonary embolism; daughter of Friedrich Göppert (a pediatrician and professor of medicine at Georgia Augusta University in Göttingen, Germany) and Maria Wolff Göppert (a schoolteacher and musician); graduated Georgia Augusta University, Ph.D., 1930; married Joseph Edward Mayer, on January 18, 1930; children: Maria Anne Mayer (b. 1933); Peter Conrad Mayer (b. 1938).

Worked as "volunteer associate" at Johns Hopkins University (1931–39); was lecturer in chemistry at Columbia University (1939–45); was a research physicist for Substitute Alloy Materials Project (1942–45); was senior physicist for Institute for Nuclear Studies and Argonne National Laboratory at the University of Chicago (1945–59); published theory of nuclear shell model in Physical Review (1948); cowrote Statistical Mechanics in 1940 and Elementary Theory of Nuclear Shell Structure (1955); was the fifth woman elected to National Academy of Sciences (1956); named professor and given salary at the University of California at San Diego (1959–72); awarded Nobel Prize in Physics (1963).

Selected writings: (with Max Born) "Dynamische Gittertheorie der Kristalle," in Handbuch der Physik (Band 24, part 2, 1931, pp. 623–794); (with R.G. Sachs) "Calculations on a New Neutron-Proton Interaction Potential," in Physical Review (vol. 53, 1938, pp. 991–993); (with A.L. Sklar) "Calculations of the Lower Excited Levels of Benzene," in Journal of Chemical Physics (vol. 6, 1938, pp. 643–652); (with Joseph E. Mayer) Statistical Mechanics (NY: Wiley, 1940); "On Closed Shells in Nuclei," in Physical Review (vol. 74, 1948, pp. 235–239); "On Closed Shells in Nuclei, II," in Physical Review (vol. 75, 1949, pp. 1969–1970); (with Edward Teller) "On the Origin of the Elements," in Physical Review (vol. 76, 1949, pp. 1226–1231); "Nuclear Configurations in the Spin-Orbit Coupling Model. I. Empirical Evidence," in Physical Review (vol. 78, 1950, pp. 16–21); "Nuclear Configurations in the Spin-Orbit Coupling Model. II. Theoretical Considerations," in Physical Review (vol. 78, 1950, pp. 22–23); "The Structure of the Nucleus," in Scientific American (March 1951, pp. 22–26); (with J.H.D. Jensen) "Electromagnetic Effects Due to Spin-Orbit Coupling," in Physical Review (vol. 85, 1952, p. 1059); (with J.H.D. Jensen) Elementary Theory of Nuclear Shell Structure (NY: John Wiley & Sons, 1955); "The Shell Model," in Science (vol. 145, 1964, pp. 999–1006); "The Shell Model," in Les Prix Nobel en 1963 (Stockholm: The Nobel Foundation, 1964); (with J.H.D. Jensen) "The Shell Model. I. Shell Closure and jj Coupling," in Alpha-, Beta- and Gamma-Ray Spectroscopy (edited by Kai Siegbahn, Amsterdam: North Holland Publishing, 1965, p. 557).

Maria Gertrud Käte Göppert, whose family name was later Anglicized to Goeppert, was born on June 28, 1906, at Kattowitz in Upper Silesia, a German province now in Poland. The only child of a medical professor who was the sixth generation in his family of professors, she moved with her parents, Friedrich and **Maria Wolff Göppert**, to the medieval university town of Göttingen four years later. Mayer's father became director of a children's hospital as well as a professor, and established a day-care center for children of working mothers; her mother was a schoolteacher and a musician.

Maria was a thin, pale child who suffered painful headaches. Her father was a gentle man, who loved children and emphasized that they should be self-confident and adventurous and not limited by their parents' fears. He urged his daughter to be curious and a risk taker, taking her on fossil searches and crafting dark lenses for her to use in watching solar eclipses. After attempting various cures for his daughter's migraines, he finally told her that he was unable to mitigate the pain, and that she could either be an invalid or learn to ignore them; Mayer chose the latter.

Friedrich also counseled his daughter to "never become just a woman," a comment on the times that demanded women be solely housewives, interested only in their husbands and children. Mayer followed her father's advice, but her 40-year career, spanning original scientific research and teaching at four universities, and culminating in a Nobel Prize, was filled with numerous ironies.

From an early age, Maria's goal was to be educated at Georgia Augusta University, more commonly referred to as the University of Göttingen. "Ever since I was a very small child," she noted, "I knew that when I grew up I was expected to acquire some training or education which would enable me to earn a living so that I was not dependent on marriage." In Göttingen, she attended the Hohere Tochterschule, or public elementary school, where she was an excellent student, especially in mathematics and languages. At age 15, she matriculated in a private school, the Frauenstudium, which had been established by suffragists because the city had no advanced public schools for girls. Prepared by her teachers, Mayer successfully passed the series of written and oral examinations, known as the *abitur*, that admitted her to the University of Göttingen as a mathematics student in the spring of 1924.

In Germany, the interim separating World Wars I and II, known as the Weimar Republic, was a period of extraordinary artistic and scientific creativity. The development of quantum mechanics by physicists during the 1920s and 1930s is considered by many historians to be the greatest intellectual achievement of the 20th cen-

tury, and much of the ground-breaking research in the field was carried out at the University of Göttingen. The university was renowned for attracting superb scientific talent, particularly mathematicians and physicists, who brought the work there to its apex in the pre-Hitler years.

When Mayer began her course work, only ten percent of German university students were female, compared to at least one third of American college students during the same period. At Göttingen, a university rule allowed professors to refuse women admittance to their classes, few women professors were hired to teach, and most female students were there to become schoolteachers, a career that Mayer considered to be boring. The only woman in many of her classes, Mayer nonetheless thrived in the scholarly, male-dominated environment, and was often the best student in her courses. At a time when the methodology of quantum mechanics was fast maturing, she found mentors among the prominent scientists who were at work on discovering the atomic properties of matter. Max Born was the eminent atomic physicist who had initiated quantum mechanics research, and when Mayer was invited to join his seminar, her interest in physics blossomed. Born encouraged her to join in the pioneering effort of discovering the new physics methodology and served as her thesis advisor. "This was wonderful," as Mayer later recalled. "I liked the mathematics in it. . . . Mathematics began to seem too much like puzzle-solving. . . . Physics is puzzle-solving, too, but of puzzles created by nature, not by the mind of man. . . . Physics was the challenge."

Mayer was exceptionally strong in the mathematical concepts necessary to an understanding of quantum mechanics, and she found quantum mechanics, in contrast to her mathematics studies, "young and exciting." James Franck, who won a 1925 Nobel Prize for his theories of atomic structures, also taught her non-mathematical approaches to problem resolution. In a joint seminar taught by Born and Franck, students were expected to challenge the professors, who were often delivering new ideas about quantum mechanics within hours of their discoveries. In her advanced theory seminar, her classmates included Robert Oppenheimer, the future creator of the atomic bomb, who interrupted Born so much that Mayer circulated a student petition requesting that he be quiet. After eating with her mother at home, Maria would daily eat a second course with friends from her physics classes in order to debate the issues of quantum mechanics while they ate.

Following the unexpected death of her father in 1927, Mayer decided to pursue a doctorate as a tribute to him. In 1928, she won a German government fellowship to spend a term at Girton College at Cambridge University, in England, where she met Ernest Rutherford, winner of the 1908 Nobel Prize for his nuclear theory. Her father's death resulted in another significant event in 1929: her mother, like many Göttingen widows, began taking in university students as boarders. In January of that year, Joseph Edward Mayer, a postdoctoral fellow from California who had some to Göttingen to study with Franck, was inquiring at the Göppert home about renting a room when he met the elegant, blue-eyed blonde Maria.

Maria had had many suitors, none of whom had mattered to her. Joe Mayer changed her mind about matrimony. When they became engaged, she even considered ceasing her physics work, but he insisted that she finish her degree and become a professor. When she doubted that she could compile a scholarly thesis, he took her to visit physicist Paul Ehrenfest, a close friend of Albert Einstein, to inspire her, and he also offered to hire a maid to do the cooking and cleaning chores that Maria despised. Throughout their marriage, he was to encourage Maria in her intellectual pursuits.

On January 18, 1930, Maria Goeppert married Joe Mayer at Göttingen city hall. After a party in her mother's home, the couple honeymooned in Berlin. Maria retained her family name, linking it with Joe's surname. By March, she had completed her dissertation "Über Elementarakte mit zwei Quantensprüngen" ("On Elemental Processes with Two Quantum Jumps"), which was approved by her committee, consisting of Born, Franck, and future Nobel Laureate Adolf Windaus. Mayer's academic mentors enthusiastically promoted her scientific talents, and she contributed a section to a book on quantum mechanics written by Born.

As Nazi policies in Germany restricted academia, many European scientists began to emigrate to the U.S. in pursuit of intellectual freedom. Ambitious as she was, Mayer began to realize that administrators' attitudes toward female professors would limit her career in Germany, and in 1931 she and Joe sailed on the S.S. *Europa* to Baltimore, Maryland, where Joe took up a new position at the Johns Hopkins University. Known now as Maria Goeppert Mayer, she began to encounter a new round of professional obstacles, becoming what **Joan Dash** has labeled the "fringe benefit" faculty wife.

At the time, universities in the United States observed rules of anti-nepotism, entrenched since the 1920s and reinforced during the Depression, which were designed to prevent married women from depriving male heads of households from income-generating jobs. Their practical result was also to restrict many women scholars and scientists with good credentials from acquiring jobs or status equivalent to their male peers. At Johns Hopkins, where Mayer was denied access to an academic position, her desire to pursue scientific work allowed the university to take advantage of her skills by using her as a "voluntary associate" in physics, working without salary or tenure, until 1939.

Refusing to allow Joe to protest her treatment in any way that might damage his own professional standing, Maria remained publicly modest and quiet while privately exercising her intense competitive drive to solve physics problems. Working out of an attic office, she cared only about the opinions of her scientific peers, and believed that most of them accepted her ability, although she felt snubbed by some administrators and colleagues. "I sensed the resentment very early," she recalled later, "so I simply learned to be inconspicuous. I never asked for anything, and I never complained."

American physicists advocated experimental work in place of theoretical investigations, and Johns Hopkins was not a major focal point for quantum mechanics research. American scientists preferred to explore the wave theory of physics, and the theoretical work in particle mechanics was still the general provenance of German scientists. Basing her research approach on techniques she had learned in Germany, Mayer began to collaborate with her husband and with theorist Karl Herzfeld, who hired her to translate his German correspondence. In addition to teaching these men quantum theory, Maria began to apply quantum mechanics to chemical experiments such as the structure of organic compounds, and wrote several significant papers on molecular physics. With Enrico Fermi and Ehrenfest, whom she had first met in Europe, she also taught European quantum mechanics to American physicists at the University of Michigan summer school.

During her first years in America, Mayer was deeply homesick and spent her summers in Göttingen. Marrying Joe had caused her to lose her German citizenship, and as Hitler grew more dominant in German politics, travel in her homeland became more difficult. Mayer retained upper-class German beliefs reflecting her Prussian heritage, and during the early Nazi regime she hoped that traditional German values and culture would overcome the rapid political changes. Disturbed by the 1933 racial laws imposed by the Nazis that ousted Jewish professors, she became treasurer of a fund to help German refugees, including Franck, who came to Baltimore, and she began to shelter exiles in her home. She also began to encounter anti-German sentiment in America, which would increase during the Second World War.

Shortly after the birth of her daughter, **Maria Anne Mayer**, in 1933, Mayer became a naturalized citizen. She stayed home for a while with her new daughter, trying to balance her family, social life, and career, but admitted, "There is an emotional strain due to the conflicting allegiances, that to science and that to the children who, after all, need a mother." Nevertheless, Mayer later reminisced that her years at Johns Hopkins were her happiest. In addition to research, she taught and supervised the doctoral thesis of graduate student Robert G. Sachs, and wrote an article with him on nuclear physics. But problems continued to plague her professional advancement. Herzfeld demanded a salary for her, contending, "Her mind is really brilliant and penetrating," but the university administration refused to pay her.

In the late 1930s, Mayer's mother died, and she became pregnant with her second child, Peter Conrad Mayer, who was born in 1938. While she was pregnant, she and Joe had initiated work on a textbook in statistical mathematics. Then Joe was unexpectedly dismissed by Johns Hopkins. While his department head proffered various reasons for his termination, including the need to reduce expenses, Mayer believed that academic jealousy of her was to blame, despite her diligent attempts not to alienate colleagues.

From 1939 to 1946, Joseph Mayer became a lecturer at Columbia University. Maria applied for a position in the physics department at Columbia but was refused. The only person at Columbia to support her was Harold Urey, chair of the chemistry department and a Nobel Prize winner in 1934. Urey wangled her a small teaching position and an office, and bestowed the title of "lecturer in chemistry" on her, enhancing her stature for the title page of the Mayers' book, *Statistical Mechanics*, published in 1940. Describing molecular systems, this chemistry textbook was considered a classic in the field. Joe received primary credit for the work, with most physicists erroneously assuming Maria Mayer had only performed secretarial duties; nevertheless, Maria received a letter from the American Physical Society in 1940, addressed "Dear Sir," which named her a fellow.

With America's entry into World War II in 1941, the small supply of skilled physicists in the United States led to Mayer's first paying job. Fearing that the Germans would develop an atomic bomb first, the U.S. government was funding research in nuclear fission, code-named the Manhattan Project, for the purpose of developing atomic weaponry, particularly a bomb. At Columbia, Urey was director of a secret research group as part of the Manhattan Project, and assigned Mayer to the Substitute Alloy Materials (SAM) project for research. Initially reluctant to take the time away from her children, Mayer compromised by hiring nannies and agreeing to work half-time. During this period, she also taught a basic science course at Sarah Lawrence College, which earned her a part-time salary.

Now, for the first time in her career, Mayer began to find herself being treated in the same way as her male counterparts were. She did not encounter discrimination by the government because she was a woman, and she was allocated supervisory roles, directing researchers. "Suddenly I was taken seriously, considered a good scientist," she said. "It was the beginning of myself standing on my own two feet as a scientist, not leaning on Joe."

While Mayer worked in New York, investigating the possibility of separating uranium isotopes—atoms of the same element but differing in the number of neutrons in the nucleus—through photochemical reactions, Joe conducted work on classified weaponry at the Aberdeen Proving Grounds, in Maryland. Personal difficulties arose when Mayer discovered that nannies she had hired were abusive to her children, and her son was sickly and doing poorly in school, exacerbating her feelings of guilt for spending too much time on her work. A heavy drinker and chain smoker (known to puff on as many as four cigarettes at once), Mayer suffered declining health during the war, with pneumonia and a goiter, and underwent both thyroid and gallbladder surgery.

In May 1945, Mayer was assigned by Edward Teller, who would later design the hydrogen bomb, to the Columbia Opacity Project at Los Alamos, New Mexico, to analyze the possible behavior of uranium compounds at high temperatures and pressures in thermonuclear explosions. Sworn to secrecy, Mayer was uncomfortable in being unable to share her thoughts on her research with Joe. She also continued to express a love for her homeland, blaming the war on Adolf Hitler and attempting to reconcile her fears that her research might be turned against Germans. "We failed. We found nothing, and we were lucky," she observed later, "because we didn't contribute to the development of the bomb, and so we escaped the searing guilt felt to this day by those responsible for the bomb." After the war, Mayer made visits to both Germany and Hiroshima, which she found excruciatingly painful, and she sent clothes and money to relief organizations to help in the recovery of postwar Germany.

After the war ended in 1945, Mayer accepted a position at the recently established Institute for Nuclear Studies at the University of Chicago, which she would hold until 1959. Back in an atmosphere that resembled Göttingen, where colleagues were intellectually stimulating and encouraging, she observed, "This was the first place where I was not considered a nuisance but greeted with open arms by the administration." However, because of the university's nepotism rules, she received the title of full professor but, again, no salary. At Chicago, she taught physics-theory seminars, served on committees, hired faculty, advised graduate students, and established the standard of difficulty for graduate examinations.

Teller's Opacity Project continued at Chicago, and he hired Mayer as a part-time consultant at the Metallurgical Laboratory, where the initial work on nuclear chain reaction had occurred. Under the auspices of the Atomic Energy Commission, the Argonne National Laboratory replaced the Metallurgical Laboratory on July 1, 1946, and Mayer was hired as a senior physicist by her former student, Sachs, who was now director of Argonne.

Mayer's work centered on a basic physics problem: why certain atoms are stable or unstable. She pursued, as a part of this puzzle, the question of why some isotopes are more abundant than others, and Teller proposed that she catalogue the nuclear properties of the stable elements to determine the number of neutrons or protons in each. Eugene P. Wigner, a Göttingen friend, had labeled the quantification of nuclear particles "magic numbers." Mayer determined a series of "magic numbers" (2, 8, 20, 28, 50, 82, 126) wherein the nuclei with those numbers of neutrons or protons were unusually stable. She then began to devise a model for the nucleus of atomic particles, in which there were concentric shells of protons and neutrons, a structure similar to electrons orbiting around the nucleus. When she made an analogy of the particles orbiting in shells to the layers of an onion "with nothing in the center," physicist Wolfgang Pauli dubbed her "The Madonna of the Onion."

Because Mayer lacked experimental proof to verify her concept of the shell model, she hesitated to publish her findings until her husband, fearing that she would lose her original claim to her work, insisted she submit her paper. In 1948, her treatise appeared in the *Physical Review*. Meanwhile, as a result of a chance remark by Fermi suggesting that she consider spin-orbit coupling, she arrived at the analogy that was to give support to her theory. Comparing the nucleus to a room full of waltzers, she saw the particles as orbiting and spinning in different directions like dancers in a ballroom, some needing more energy depending on which way they re-

volved. This difference in energy requirement caused by spin-orbit coupling strengthened the shells' positions in the nucleus, resulting in the occurrence of the "magic numbers" in the most tightly bound shells.

Again, however, Mayer was reluctant to publish her findings, fearing most physicists would reject her theory. Urged by Fermi and her husband, she nonetheless submitted her research results to the *Physical Review* in late 1949, and soon became aware that three German scientists, Hans Jensen, Hans E. Suess, and Otto Haxel, had simultaneously and independently proposed a similar theory. Initially upset, Mayer soon realized that their publication confirmed her work and would aid in convincing skeptical researchers of its validity. Although the shell theory countered previous nuclear physics methodology, the conclusions arrived at in these diverse ways led to its rather quick acceptance by the scientific community, and it became an essential model for studies of nuclear behavior and structure.

After Jensen suggested that he and Mayer write a book, she traveled to Germany in 1950, where they began a collaboration on advanced interpretation of their model. Mayer, well organized and diligent, was slowed down by Jensen's procrastination, but in 1955 they published *Elementary Theory of Nuclear Shell Structure*, the bulk of which was written by Mayer. By this time, the nuclear shell model was gaining her the international renown she had long hoped for, along with various professional laurels. In 1951, she was inducted into the Heidelberg Academy of Science, and eminent physicist Niels Bohr invited her to the Institute of Copenhagen. Five years later, she was the fifth woman ever elected to the National Academy of Sciences in the United States.

In 1959, she officially achieved her long-sought goal as the seventh generation of college professors in her family. Harold Urey had transferred to the University of California at San Diego, where he offered her the position of professor with full salary and benefits. Chicago countered this offer with a full-time title and salary, but Mayer decided to move west. She was unpacking her voluminous library when she suffered a stroke that left her speech blurred and her left arm paralyzed; she had already suffered a loss of hearing in her left ear a few years earlier, which impeded her work. Now, although she attempted to continue her researching, she never fully recovered her health.

In 1963, Mayer became the first woman to win the Nobel Prize for theoretical physics when she was awarded the honor along with Jensen and

Wigner for their research on the structure of atomic nuclei. On December 12, 1963, she accepted her gold medal and diploma from Sweden's King Gustavus VI Adolfus in Stockholm, and in her Nobel lecture she described some of the difficulties of her struggle to gain acceptance for her ideas. Returning home, she was eager to continue her research, noting, "If you love science, all you really want is to keep on working. The Nobel Prize thrills you, but it changes nothing."

In San Diego, Mayer found the university environment invigorating, although she was limited by her health. With a pacemaker installed in her heart, she taught, did research, and refined the shell theory, writing several major articles in the 1960s. Her last publication was a review of the shell model with Jensen. She also became active politically, promoting civilian control of nuclear energy and protesting against the Vietnam War, and collected honorary doctorates in science from numerous colleges.

In December 1971, Maria Goeppert Mayer suffered heart failure and lapsed into a coma. On February 20, 1972, she died of a pulmonary embolism at her home in La Jolla, at age 65. She had overcome the obstacles of being a woman in the world of theoretical science and a German immigrant in the United States in the 1930s to rise to the top of her field, and she had avidly pursued the problems of physics until her death. She had also managed to balance a career, marriage, and family, raising a daughter, Maria Anne, who entered the field of astronomical research, and a son, Peter, who became the eighth generation of Goeppert professors, in the field of economics.

Mayer's papers were donated to the University of California at San Diego by her husband Joe, who had continually encouraged his wife to maintain her intellectual independence while forging a strong marriage and professional partnership. In the conglomeration of letters, scientific notes, manuscripts, menus, itineraries, and her daughter's report card that reside in those archives, is perhaps the best indication of what kind of woman Maria Goeppert Mayer ultimately defined herself to be.

SOURCES:
Dash, Joan. "Maria Goeppert Mayer," in *A Life of One's Own: Three Gifted Women and the Men They Married.* NY: Harper and Row, 1973, pp. 229–346, 368–369.
McGrayne, Sharon Bertsch. *Nobel Prize Women in Science: Their Lives, Struggles, and Momentous Discoveries.* Secaucus, NJ: Carol Publishing Group, 1993.
Opfell, Olga S. "Madonna of the Onion: Maria Goeppert-Mayer," in *The Lady Laureates: Women Who Have Won the Nobel Prize.* Metuchen, NJ: Scarecrow Press, 1986, pp. 224–238.

Rossiter, Margaret W. *Women Scientists in America: Struggles and Strategies to 1940.* Baltimore and London: The Johns Hopkins University Press, 1982.
Sachs, Robert G. "Maria Goeppert Mayer, June 28, 1906–February 20, 1972," in *Biographical Memoirs of the National Academy of Sciences.* Vol. 50. Washington, DC: National Academy of Sciences, 1979, pp. 310–328.

SUGGESTED READING:
Born, Max. *My Life: Recollections of a Nobel Laureate.* London: Taylor & Francis, 1978.
Cline, Barbara Lovett. *The Questioners: Physicists and the Quantum Theory.* NY: Thomas Y. Crowell, 1965.
Cropper, William H. *The Quantum Physicists.* NY: Oxford University Press, 1970.
Fermi, Laura. *Atoms in the Family.* Chicago: University of Chicago Press, 1954.
Fleming, Donald, and Bernard Bailyn, eds. *The Intellectual Migration: Europe and America, 1930–1960.* Cambridge, MA: Harvard University Press, Belknap Press, 1969.
Forman, Paul. "Environment and Practice of Atomic Physics in Weimar Germany," Ph.D. dissertation, University of California at Berkeley, 1967.
Gabor, Andrea. *Einstein's Wife: Work and Marriage in the Lives of Five Great Twentieth-Century Women.* Penguin, 1996.
Jungk, Robert. *Brighter Than a Thousand Suns.* NY: Harcourt, Brace, 1958.

COLLECTIONS:
Autobiography and 1962 interview located in Autobiographies Collection and Oral History Collection, American Institute of Physics, New York City.
Biographical file, including bibliography, membership activity, and photograph, located in Deceased Members Records, National Academy of Sciences-National Research Council Archives, Washington, D.C.
Correspondence, manuscripts, lecture notes, photographs, and memorabilia located in Maria Goeppert Mayer Papers, Mandeville Department of Special Collections, University of California at San Diego.
Interview with Mayer and 1964 memoir located in Nobel Laureates on Scientific Research Oral History Collection, Columbia University, New York City.
Interview with Mayer by Thomas S. Kuhn, February 1962, and interview with James Franck and Hertha Sponer by Thomas S. Kuhn and Maria Goeppert Mayer, July 1962, held in Archive for History of Quantum Physics, American Philosophical Society Library, Philadelphia, Pennsylvania.
Interview with Mayer, February 1962, Archive for the History of Quantum Physics, University of California at Berkeley.

Elizabeth D. Schafer, Ph.D.,
freelance writer in history of technology and science,
Loachapoka, Alabama

Mayfreda de Pirovano (d. 1300)

Italian heretic. Died in 1300 in Milan; never married; no children.

Mayfreda de Pirovano was a close friend and follower of the heretical sect leader *Guglielma of

Milan. When Guglielma declared herself the incarnation of God and began gathering supporters for her new religious movement, Mayfreda emerged as her most important supporter. Together the two women and their followers preached in and around Milan; Mayfreda believed that Guglielma was the hope of salvation for humanity, and wanted to establish a new church based on the spiritual superiority of women, with herself as pope. The cardinals, bishops, and priests would also be all female. She and Guglielma had attracted a substantial number of supporters by the time Guglielma died around 1282, probably burned at the stake by Milanese authorities. Mayfreda survived until around 1300, and it seems likely that she continued preaching for the eight years following Guglielma's death. Mayfreda was eventually arrested, condemned, and burned at the stake as a heretic.

Laura York, M.A. in history,
University of California, Riverside, California

Mayling Soong (b. 1898).

See Song Meiling.

Maynard, Frances (1861–1938).

See Greville, Frances Evelyn.

Maynor, Dorothy (1910–1996)

Acclaimed concert soprano and founder of the Harlem School for the Arts. Name variations: Dorothy Leigh Mainor; Dorothy L. Maynor; Dorothy Maynor-Rooks. Born on September 2 (some sources cite September 3), 1910, in Norfolk, Virginia; died on February 19, 1996, in West Chester, Pennsylvania; daughter of John Mainor (a minister) and Alice (Jeffries) Mainor; Hampton Institute, B.S., 1933; Westminster Choir College, B.Mus., 1935; married Shelby Albright Rooks (a Presbyterian minister), on June 27, 1942.

Became soloist with Westminster Choir (1935); moved to New York City (1935); made professional debut (1939); debuted at Carnegie Hall (1941); toured Europe (1949); retired from the stage (1963); founded Harlem School for the Arts (1964).

Dorothy Maynor

Called "one of the supreme communicative artists" of her time, Dorothy Maynor was a concert singer and an African-American at a time when discrimination—both official and implicit—was common in the world of American classical music. Although there were some venues to which she was denied entry because of her skin color, she won great acclaim for both her classical repertoire and her renderings of African-American spirituals, and after her retirement from performing founded the Harlem School for the Arts.

Dorothy Maynor was born in Norfolk, Virginia, in 1910. The daughter of a minister, she sang in her father's Methodist church choir and enjoyed accompanying him while he hunted and fished. At the age of 14, with plans to become a teacher, she enrolled in high school classes at the Hampton Institute, where she quickly distinguished herself as a member of the school's choir and toured Europe with it in 1929. The choir director saw her talent and encouraged her to switch to music education. After graduating with a B.S. in home economics in 1933, Maynor won a three-year scholarship for vocal training at the Westminster Choir College in Princeton, New Jersey, where she earned a bachelor of music degree. As a soloist with the school's choir, she acquired a number of supporters who were willing to serve as private benefactors. In 1935, she moved to New York City for further study under Wilfried Klamroth, and worked as a choir director in Brooklyn to make ends meet.

In 1939, Maynor's friends arranged for Serge Koussevitzky, founder of the Tanglewood Music Festival and conductor of the Boston Symphony Orchestra (BSO), to hear her sing at a picnic at Tanglewood. He was impressed (reportedly exclaiming "The whole world must hear her!"), and she received national press for her performance as well as a record contract to work with the BSO. Both helped to increase momentum for her professional debut in November of that year at New York City's Town Hall, and the debut itself inspired accolades. Maynor quickly became a well-regarded and critically acclaimed singer, and also recorded oratorio and opera for the Victor music label. She became the first African-American to perform in the concert hall of the Library of Congress when she was invited to sing at a special ceremony commemorating the 75th anniversary of the passage of the 13th Amendment, which outlawed slavery in the United States.

Maynor made her debut at Carnegie Hall in 1941, and in 1942 married Shelby Albright Rooks, a Presbyterian minister who would later serve for many years as pastor of New York City's St. James Presbyterian Church. During World War II, she often sang for armed forces on board military ships, and in these years also soloed with the Philadelphia Symphony, the New York Philharmonic Orchestra, the BSO, and the Chicago Symphony. In 1948 she performed at Harry Truman's presidential inauguration, and the following year toured Europe. In 1951, she was granted special permission by the Daughters of the American Revolution to perform at Constitution Hall (owned by the DAR) in Washington, D.C. The conservative group had in 1939 caused a national furor when they denied this permission to Maynor's contemporary and fellow African-American *Marian Anderson, and Maynor was the first African-American to perform there since that time. In the 1950s, she also toured in Australia, Europe, and Central and South America. Still, other singers of her caliber would have been offered a contract with a leading opera house—Maynor was known for agility in the German *lieder* repertoire—but she was not. Not until 1955 would a major opera company sign an African-American woman to a contract, when Anderson broke the color barrier by signing with the Metropolitan Opera.

Maynor retired from the concert stage in 1963. The following year, she founded the Harlem School for the Arts, which offered music, painting, drama, and dance instruction to children in Harlem, and of which she would serve as director until 1979. The school initially had but 20 students, and Maynor herself was the only staff member; she eventually built up a faculty roster that mined the graduate student bodies of the renowned Juilliard School and the Mannes School of Music (now the Mannes College of Music, co-founded by *Clara Damrosch Mannes) and taught 500 children. In 1977, Maynor led a fund-raising effort to construct a new facility that yielded $2 million.

The recipient of honorary degrees from Bennett College, Howard University, Duquesne University, Oberlin College, and Carnegie Mellon University, Dorothy Maynor was in 1975 invited to join the board of the Metropolitan Opera, becoming the first African-American so honored. She died of pneumonia in February 1996, at the age of 85.

SOURCES:

Current Biography. NY: H.W. Wilson, 1951.

The Day [New London, CT]. February 24, 1996.

Ewan, David, comp. and ed. *Living Musicians.* NY: H.W. Wilson, 1940.

People Weekly. March 11, 1996, p. 84.

Smith, Jessie Carney, ed. *Notable Black American Women.* Detroit, MI: Gale Research, 1992.

Carol Brennan,
Grosse Pointe, Michigan

Mayo, Virginia (1920—)

American actress. Born Virginia Jones on November 30, 1920, in St. Louis, Missouri; married Michael O'Shea (an actor), in 1947 (died 1973).

Selected films: Jack London *(1943);* Seven Days Ashore *(1944);* The Princess and the Pirate *(1944);* Wonder Man *(1945);* The Best Years of Our Lives *(1946);* The Kid From Brooklyn *(1946);* Out of the Blue *(1947);* The Secret Life of Walter Mitty *(1947);* A Song Is Born *(1948);* Smart Girls Don't Talk *(1948);* The Girl from Jones Beach *(1949);* Colorado Territory *(1949);* Always Leave Them Laughing *(1949);* The West Point Story *(1950);* The Flame and the Arrow *(1950);* Painting the Clouds With Sunshine *(1951);* Captain Horatio Hornblower *(US/UK, 1951);* King Richard and the Crusades *(US/UK, 1954);* The Silver Chalice *(1955);* The Proud Ones *(1956);* The Story of Mankind *(1957);* Young Fury *(1965);* Fort Utah *(1967);* Won Ton Ton, The Dog Who Saved Hollywood *(1976);* French Quarter *(1977);* Evil Spirits *(1991).*

$\mathcal{V}$irginia
$\mathcal{M}$ayo

Virginia Mayo, who was born Virginia Jones in 1920, began her entertainment career as a show girl before her dancing talent and voluptuous blonde beauty brought her to the attention of Hollywood movie producers. After a series of minor roles, during World War II she began starring in a number of films designed primarily for viewing by U.S. military personnel abroad, including *Stand for Action* in 1942 and *Salute to the Marines* in 1943, and was often cast as a foil opposite comedians such as Danny Kaye and Bob Hope. She was once described by the sultan of Morocco as "tangible proof for the existence of God." Her most critically acclaimed roles were in the Academy Award-winning classics *The Best Years of Our Lives* (1946) and *The Secret Life of Walter Mitty* (1947). Mayo continued to secure starring roles throughout the 1950s and 1960s, and appeared in films into the 1970s, including *Won Ton Ton, The Dog Who Saved Hollywood* (1976) and *French Quarter* (1977). She was married to the actor Michael O'Shea, who had starred in her first major picture, *Jack London* (1943), from 1947 until his death in 1973. Her last screen role was in *Evil Spirits* in 1991.

SOURCES:

Katz, Ephraim. *The Film Encyclopedia.* NY: Harper-Collins, 1994.

Quinlan, David, ed. *The Film Lover's Companion.* Carol Publishing Group, 1997.

Grant Eldridge,
freelance writer, Pontiac, Michigan

Mayreder, Rosa (1858–1938)

Austrian painter, writer, sociologist, feminist, and peace activist. Born Rosa Obermayer on November 30, 1858, in Vienna, Austria; died on January 19, 1938, in Vienna, Austria; daughter of Franz Obermayer (a restaurant owner) and Marie Obermayer; attended the Institute for Girls, and Sophie Paulus' School, both private girls' schools in Vienna; studied painting with Hugo Darnaut; married Karl Mayreder (an architect), in 1881 (died 1935).

At the age of 18, objecting to being a "stuffed doll," Rosa Mayreder abandoned her corset and refused to submit to any more constraints on body or mind. Now, along with *Marianne Hainisch, **Marie Lang**, and **Auguste Fickert**, she is remembered as one of the founders of the Austrian feminist movement.

Born in Vienna in 1858, Mayreder was the daughter of the well-to-do owner and landlord of Winter's, a famous Vienna beer hall. She received a private school education and took French and piano lessons, but was thwarted in her pursuit of a higher education. "While my sisters never doubted for a moment that the sons of the family enjoyed absolute precedence as regards to educational opportunities, I responded to this situation with a constantly growing feeling of indignation, which was further kindled by the behavior of my brothers," she recalled.

Mayreder, as it turned out, was not only intelligent, but had a gift for painting and writing. Encouraged by her fiancé, Karl Mayreder, whom she married in 1881, she studied painting with Hugo Darnaut and by 1891 was exhibiting her landscapes and flower paintings at the Vienna *Künstlerhaus*. She also became a member of the Club of Water-Color Painters, and for many years wrote art criticism for a Vienna newspaper under the male pseudonym Franz Arnold. While pursuing painting, she also published a collection of short stories in 1896, *Aus meiner Jugend* (*From my Youth*). In addition, she wrote the libretto for the comic opera *The Corregidor*, by Hugo Wolf, whom she had met and befriended in 1882.

In 1894, Mayreder became active in the feminist movement, which was just then gaining a foothold in Vienna. On February 20, 1897, as a representative of the General Austrian Women's Union, she appeared before a meeting of women at the Old City Hall, speaking out against compulsory registration and medical surveillance of prostitutes. She also helped author the "Petition to the Austrian Parliament against the Official Sanctioning of Houses of Prostitution," expressing her belief that such establishments encouraged the exploitation of women. In 1900, along with Auguste Fickert and Marie Lang, Mayreder edited the journal *Dokumente der Frauen* (*Documents of Women*). (Fickert would leave to found her own journal, *Frauenleben* [*Women's Life*], following a disagreement between the three women.) In 1903, Mayreder was elected vice president of Allgemeiner Österreichischer Frauenverein, one of Vienna's largest women's organization, of which she had been a co-founder with Auguste Fickert.

Rosa Mayreder also addressed feminism in her first novel *Idole, Geschichte einer Liebe* (*Idols, A Love Story*, 1899), in which she stressed that love can lead to idolizing. In 1905, she published a volume of essays in cultural philosophy, *Zur Kritik der Weiblichkeit* (*Contributions to a Critique of Womanhood*). "I consider the feminist movement to be one of those phenomena by which the present age differs favorably from all previous epochs of human history," she stated in the preface. For Mayreder, the unleashing of the creative forces within the feminist movement was as important as the struggle for women's rights. "Without the cooperation of Women as an equal partner," she wrote, "the community on which the ideal of higher humanity is based cannot be realized; and the contribution to civilization which women, in accord with their historical evolution, can offer is an indispensable complement to the achievements of men." A second volume of essays, *Geschlecht and Kultur* (*Gender and Culture*), was published around 1914.

In 1917, as the First World War raged, Mayreder addressed the Vienna Sociological Society, reading a paper entitled "The Typical Progress of Social Movement," in which she addressed ideological and political questions, and also the abuse of power. The paper may have been inspired by an incident the year before, when Mayreder was banned by the authorities from publishing a lecture entitled "Women and Internationalism."

Mayreder remained active throughout her life. In 1921, at the third congress of the International Women's League for Peace and Freedom, she was elected vice president of the Austrian branch (founded in 1915). As the years went on, she became a fervent pacifist and antimilitarist, and was instrumental in organizing an exhibition of antimilitarist toys and pacifist literature for children.

After 1912, Mayreder's personal life became quite difficult; her husband Karl began suffering psychotic episodes, resulting in intermittent outbursts of rage and obsessive behavior. Karl was treated by both Sigmund Freud and Alfred Adler, but did not improve. (In later years, Mayreder would be quite critical of Freud. "Indeed, the artistic interpreter in him by far surpasses the scientific observer," she wrote.) Upon Karl's death in 1935, Mayreder published a cycle of poems entitled *Ein Schicksal* (*A Fate*), celebrating their years of happiness before his illness.

Rosa Mayreder lived into her 80th year, dying on January 19, 1938, just two months before the Nazis destroyed Austria. In 1997, a new Austrian 500 schilling banknote bearing her likeness was issued in her honor.

Barbara Morgan,
Melrose, Massachusetts

Mayson, Isabella Mary (1836–1865).

See Beeton, Isabella Mary.

Maywood, Augusta (1825–1876)

First American ballet dancer to win international renown. Name variations: Augusta Williams. Born in 1825, probably in New York City; died in Lemberg,

Austrian Galicia (now Lvov, Poland), on November 3, 1876; daughter of Henry August Williams (an itinerant actor) and Martha Bally (a former actress); married Charles Mabille (a dancer), in 1840 (separated 1848); married Carlo Gardini (a physician, journalist, and impresario), in 1858 (separated 1864); children: (with Mabille) Cecile Augusta Mabille (b. 1842); (with Pasquale Borri) Paul Maywood (b. around 1847); one who died young (b. 1864).

Selected roles: The Mountain Sylph *(New York, 1838);* La Tarentule *(Paris, 1838);* Le Diable boîteux *(Paris);* Giselle *(Vienna);* Uncle Tom's Cabin; La Dame Aux Camélias; Faust *(Milan, 1848);* L'Araba *(Milan, 1853).*

Although she was the first American ballet dancer to achieve critical acceptance in Europe, where xenophobic cultural prejudices still ran high during the 19th century, and was for a number of years a darling of the ballet world, Augusta Maywood died in obscurity, after a life that was iconoclastic above all else. The daughter of two traveling English actors, she was born in 1825, probably in New York City. Her mother **Martha Bally** divorced her father and married another actor, Robert Maywood, who gave both Augusta and her sister his surname. Robert became the manager of the Chestnut Street Theater in Philadelphia, the city in which she grew up. Hoping to profit from their children, the Maywoods enrolled Augusta in ballet lessons, where she showed great promise early on. Her stage debut in 1837 launched a media sensation in the city. She was forced into a rivalry with another child prodigy, **Mary Ann Lee**, with whom she had studied. Both made their New York debuts the following year, and in the spring of 1838 Augusta and her mother sailed for Paris on one of the first steam-powered ocean liners.

In Paris, she began classes with ballet teachers affiliated with the Paris Opera, and easily won a small role there. She made her Paris debut in November 1839 in *Le Diable boîteux*, which starred *Fanny Elssler; Theophile Gautier wrote of her that "there is something brusque, unusual, fantastic . . . which sets her quite apart." After being cast in other Opera productions, Maywood was on her way to a promising career there when one day in 1840 she simply vanished. Her mother enlisted the help of her teachers, the Paris police, and even the newspapers to discover her whereabouts. They soon learned that Maywood had run off with another dancer from the Opera, Charles Mabille, who by dressing as a woman had gained entry to the Maywood apartment when both knew her mother would

Augusta
Maywood

be out; they had fled the apartment with Maywood hidden underneath his skirts. Although they had planned to marry in England, the underage Maywood had no passport and could not cross the border. Both were arrested. Mabille was jailed, but at the request of his father no charges were pressed, and the young couple accompanied Maywood's mother to Ireland, where they were married a short time later.

Maywood and her new husband lost their contracts with the Opera because of the scandal, and resigned themselves to dancing on the stages of lesser cities across Europe, including Lisbon and Marseilles. In 1842, Maywood had a daughter, **Cecile Augusta Mabille**, with Mabille, but she left them in 1845 and relocated to Vienna, where she began a successful engagement at the Kaerntnertor Theater. In 1847, however, she received a personal request from Empress *Maria Anna of Savoy to quit the stage, since it was apparent that the unwed ballerina was pregnant. (Her second child Paul Maywood, who was probably the result of a liaison with another dancer in the company, Pasquale Borri, was placed in a foster home after his birth.)

After briefly dancing in Budapest, Maywood went to Milan in 1848 and made her debut at La Scala, where she won enormous acclaim and steady engagements. Five years later, she was named La Scala's *prima donna assoluta*, the company's highest honor, for her interpretations of classic ballets such as *Giselle* and *La Gypsy*. After *Harriet Beecher Stowe's 1852 novel *Uncle Tom's Cabin* was first staged in the United States, Maywood quickly devised a ballet version; she also danced the role of Rita Gauthier (*Alphonsine Plessis) in the first Italian production of *La Dame aux Camélias*. She was the first woman to tour with her own company of dancers and technicians, which made performances run much more smoothly than was usual on tours, and booked many of her own touring performances. A legitimate star in Europe, she consistently avoided returning to the United States. Her stepfather sometimes fed items to American newspapers that printed the sad tale of how much money her parents had invested in her training, and how she had gone off to Europe to lead a dissolute life and left them poverty-stricken.

Divorce was technically illegal in France, and Maywood was still married to Mabille, who had quit the stage and taken over his father's popular Parisian amusement park and entertainment complex, the Bal Mabille. They were involved for a time in a bitter legal battle he instigated to ensure that he would not be held as the father of her son Paul Maywood (who otherwise might inherit his assets). After Mabille's death in 1858, Maywood retired from the stage and married Carlo Gardini, a doctor, literature professor, one-time American consul in Italy, and impresario. Now in her early 30s, she moved to Vienna with her new husband and founded a school of ballet there. The marriage fell apart, however, when in 1864 Maywood gave birth to a child whom Gardini knew was not his. The infant died on the same day that Gardini departed. For a time, Maywood lived near Lake Como in Italy,

and continued to teach at her school, achieving great success through the accomplishments of her pupils. Nonetheless, when during a visit to what is now the city of Lvov in Poland she contracted smallpox and died on November 3, 1876, the news attracted little mention in the European cities that only decades ago had feted her, and was not even reported in America.

SOURCES:

James, Edward T., ed. *Notable American Women, 1607–1950*. Cambridge, MA: The Belknap Press of Harvard University Press, 1971.

McHenry, Robert, ed. *Famous American Women*. NY: Dover, 1980.

Migel, Parmenia. *The Ballerinas from the Court of Louis XIV to Pavlova*. NY: Macmillan, 1972, pp.179–193.

Read, Phyllis J., and Bernard L. Witlieb. *The Book of Women's Firsts*. NY: Random House, 1992.

Carol Brennan,
Grosse Pointe, Michigan

Mayy Ziyada (1886–1941).
See Ziyada, Mayy.

Mazarin, duchess of (1646–1699).
See Mancini, Hortense.

Mazarin's nieces.
See Mancini, Laure (1635–1657); Martinozzi, Anne Marie (1637–1672); Mancini, Olympia (c. 1639–1708); Mancini, Marie (1640–1715); Mancini, Hortense (1646–1699); Mancini, Marie-Anne (1649–1714); Martinozzi, Laura.

Mazeppa (1835–1868).
See Menken, Adah Isaacs.

Mazzetti, Enrica von Handel (1871–1955).
See Handel-Mazzetti, Enrica von.

Mc and Mac.
Names beginning with the prefix Mac have been separated from Mc and are listed earlier in alphabetical order.

McAfee, Mildred Helen (1900–1994).
See Horton, Mildred McAfee.

McAliskey, Bernadette Devlin (1947—)
Irish socialist republican who was a prominent and well-remembered figure in the 1960s civil-rights campaign in Northern Ireland. Name variations: Bernadette Devlin; Bernadette Devlin-McAliskey. Pronunciations Mack-AL-is-KEE. Born Bernadette Josephine Devlin at Cookstown, County Tyrone, Northern Ireland, on April 23, 1947; daughter of John James Devlin and Elizabeth Bernadette Devlin, both of

Cookstown; educated at St. Patrick's Academy, Dungannon, County Tyrone, and at Queen's University, Belfast; married Michael McAliskey, on April 23, 1973; children: Roisin McAliskey (b. August 1971); Deirdre McAliskey (b. 1976); Fintan McAliskey (b. 1979).

Became a founder-member of the People's Democracy movement (1968); took part in the civil-rights march from Belfast to Derry (January 1969); elected to British House of Commons and sat for Mid-Ulster constituency (1969–74); unsuccessfully contested European election (1979) and Irish Republic's election (1982); narrowly survived assassination attempt (1981); campaigned against extradition from Irish Republic to Northern Ireland (1987–88); was opposed to the Downing Street Declaration of December 1993; continued to take an active part in socialist republican politics.

A relative silence surrounded Bernadette Devlin McAliskey in the last decade of the 20th century, but it was a silence which deepened her mystique and copperfastened her image as the popular champion of nationalist Derry during the ferment of 1969–70. One of the new university-educated generation of Roman Catholics, a woman from a poor background, a product of a people the quality of whose lives had been destroyed by barbaric discriminatory policies, Bernadette Devlin in her 22nd year became a living symbol both of Northern Ireland's most intractable political problems and of the need for and inevitability of change.

𝓘 am not a politician but a political thinker.

—Bernadette Devlin McAliskey

"Change" had never been part of any government's agenda in the society into which she was born at Cookstown, County Tyrone, on April 23, 1947. Northern Ireland itself had been the outcome of a refusal on the part of its Protestant and Presbyterian majority to acquiesce in a transfer of political power which would have placed them under a Roman Catholic-dominated government. The settlement which the Unionists negotiated in 1921 allowed them to remain part of the United Kingdom and to separate politically from the new Irish Free State which was set up and governed largely by nationalists. Fear of possible treachery from the large minority of Catholic nationalists who lived in the new Northern Ireland fused with a sectarian bitterness that already was centuries old, and successive governments operated a policy of covert and often open discrimination against Catholics in practically all areas of social and political life.

Bernadette's childhood was marked by an awareness of the muted ineffectual hostility of her Catholic community towards the Unionist regime. The history of the government's policy had been written clearly across her own family. Her father, born a decade before the Northern Irish State itself, had been one of the upwardly mobile Catholics of the period who by his own initiative had freed himself from an unpropitious background to become a skilled carpenter. The uncertainties of the Ulster economy, which had often forced John James Devlin to seek temporary employment in England, were exacerbated for the Devlins by an inexplicable (and still unexplained) official view that he was a "Political Suspect." This damning cachet on his insurance card (which had to be presented to every prospective employer) meant that Bernadette saw her much-loved father "only at Christmas and Easter and occasional weekends in between." Bernadette's mother **Elizabeth Devlin** came from a middle-class, almost affluent, background. Not surprisingly, her marriage to a carpenter whose father had been a streetsweeper was ill-received by her family, whose barbed attitude was to remain a feature of McAliskey's childhood memories.

Her father's experience of a segregated State and Ulster's segregated school system fused to form and define Bernadette's political outlook. The seeds of awareness were sown early, and childhood bedtime stories were laced with accounts of the oppressed Irish and their English oppressors: "In our family we developed an unconscious political consciousness from listening to the story of our country," she wrote. She was nine when the Irish Republican Army began an ill-organized and episodic guerilla campaign against the Ulster government. It lasted for six years, ending in failure, but provided for the young Bernadette a realistic backdrop to the songs, stories and lore of conflict.

But the schools were the principal battleground in the struggle for the hearts and minds of Ulster's youth. On the Catholic side of the divide, religion and Irish nationalism were skillfully combined and extolled, by the religious teaching orders in particular. By the time she came under the tutelage of **Mother Benignus**, vice-principal at St. Patrick's Academy in Dungannon, Bernadette and her peers already knew "what we were for and against." The school, like many others of a republican slant, survived almost independently in a postwar society where state-supported education had become the norm. To Mother Benignus, the government was English-based and therefore was The Enemy.

Despite recurring financial difficulties, an apparently lax disciplinary system, and a poor social cachet, the academy fostered a strong sense of identity and cultural values that bred a certain academic excellence. Sadly, Mother Benignus' religious, even more than her political, views, made her part of the on-going problem and no part of any solution: "She didn't hate Protestants," writes McAliskey, "but her view was that you couldn't very well put up with them."

But McAliskey was bright and able. She won coveted prizes for proficiency in the Irish language (which in most instances was not spoken at home and had to be learned) and was one of those who formed an unofficial senior pupils' common room in which "we analyzed the situation in Northern Ireland and discussed why most of us were going to leave it." Even at that age, the pupils were conscious that their future presented a stark choice: either they could leave Ulster and so leave the problem behind them, or become Catholic-trained teachers in Catholic schools and so help perpetuate it.

McAliskey chose not to leave Ulster. So, to examine the problem more thoroughly (and so also to avoid becoming an immediate obvious part of it), she became one of the first generation of Catholics to attend Queen's University in Belfast. Later she would recall that she had gone there "with some vague notion of being able, one day, to improve some aspect of life in Northern Ireland." In 1966, a period when students throughout the world saw themselves as a potential instrument of social and political change, student life at Queen's was repressed, intellectually timid, and socially unimaginative. McAliskey toured all the various student groups and societies with growing frustration. Even the Republican Club "didn't seem to have anything but an existence." Only the Folk Music Society which, significantly, articulated both black civil-rights concerns and Belfast's unemployment problem, displayed any promise of things to come.

It seems unsurprising, therefore, that Bernadette arrived at her first civil-rights march through reading about its imminence in a newspaper. Rising Catholic expectations in an improved economic climate which was not including them, a growing liberal and secular atmosphere, and the entry into office of Prime Minister Terence O'Neill, whose strategic (and slow) liberalizing policy barely concealed an odd political vacuity, all combined with several other factors to lead to the setting-up of the Civil Rights Association in April 1967. The British governing system, which has always emphasized the virtues of leading from

the top, has likewise always been wary of attempts to reverse the emphasis by those who would lead from below. The Ulster government had even greater reason to be wary of those "below," and reacted unwisely (though very much in character) when challenged by a civil-rights body which based its methods on those of black counterpart organizations in America. Certainly both black and white inhabitants of Alabama at that time would have recognized certain familiar aspects in the police attack on civil-rights demonstrators in Derry in October 1968, a fateful occasion to which McAliskey was an uninjured witness. For Bernadette, within the space of a few minutes, State repression ceased to be merely the manipulation of economic resources or the bureaucratic hostility of faceless civil servants; it was a physically violent, bloody reality, measured finally in the smug partisanship of Protestant hospital staff and in the "evil" delight on the faces of the attacking policemen. For her fellow students at Queen's also, the ill-fated march was a watershed: "People were talking and thinking about the society they

Bernadette Devlin McAliskey

were living in—not as an intellectual exercise, but realistically and emotionally as if it mattered."

Further determined, though less bloody, attempts by the police to obstruct civil-rights marches led to the formation of a body equally determined that the marches should proceed. The People's Democracy movement set its sights on an end to the gerrymandering system by which Northern Ireland maintained the essentially non-Catholic character of its establishment; repeal of the Special Powers legislation which enabled the police to protect the well-being of the establishment in as forceful a manner as they considered necessary; an end to discrimination in housing and employment; and, above all, the right to publicly pursue these objectives. More immediately, a four-day march across the province from Belfast to Derry was planned for the New Year 1969.

The march was successful in the short-term sense, in that it stirred the popular imagination; but in Ulster that stirring had more than one meaning. On the one hand, the small group of 20 or so students had swelled to many hundreds by the time it reached its destination. On the other hand, the loyalist community was sufficiently alarmed by this unprecedented display of Catholic solidarity that the march was attacked at several points, most memorably and most violently at Burntollet Bridge outside Derry. The incident was particularly notable for the passive acquiescence, and occasionally even the active participation, of the police. McAliskey was among the injured, though she managed to continue on to Derry.

Popular awareness of the People's Democracy was now at such a pitch that, when an election was called for February 1969, the movement attempted to take on the establishment within the confines of its own rules. McAliskey, who contested the South Derry constituency against a government minister, lost the election but took over a third of the votes. A month later, a by-election in Mid-Ulster (this time for the British House of Commons in Westminster rather than Northern Ireland's Parliament at Stormont) brought her victory against the widow of a Unionist MP (member of Parliament). Of the several voices in the British House of Commons which were raised in condemnation of the Stormont regime during those years, hers was the most rancorous, the most unrestrained, and the best remembered.

When the rising political tension of the previous several months finally erupted into unprecedented rioting and destruction in the summer of 1969, both Derry and McAliskey became high-profile features of the media coverage. In a sea of unknown persons manning the makeshift barricades, hers was the familiar face behind the megaphone, urging on the defenders of the Bogside against the police, "making sure that everybody had two petrol-bombs." The media continued its close pursuit as she conducted a tour of American cities which resulted in a largesse of £84,000 for the relief of those who had suffered in Ulster's summer of unrest. In November, she published an autobiography which became a classic document of the early "Troubles" era. She increased her majority in the general election of 1970, but little more than a week later she was jailed for her activities on the barricades the previous year. She returned to her post in October 1970, but while she had remained near the center of the storm, the very complexities of the tempest were causing the media focus to shift.

Her energy seemed unabated even by the birth of her daughter ❧▶ Roisin in August 1971, and she took a prominent role in publicizing and protesting against the abuses which accompanied the imposition of internment that same month. Possibly her last memorable appearances during this period were on Bloody Sunday when she addressed the crowd, some of whom became victims of the paratroopers' fire, and two days later, when, as parliamentary speaker for the public's outrage, she physically attacked the Home Secretary during a House of Commons debate. She married Michael McAliskey, a schoolteacher, in April 1973.

The clear anti-Unionist ticket of previous elections was wrecked in February 1974, when the Catholic-dominated center-left Social, Democratic and Labour Party fielded their own candidate, thus splitting the vote and allowing McAliskey's Mid-Ulster seat to be retaken by an extreme Unionist. Those close to her, however, were aware that her growing disillusionment with public life had contributed to the event. In the increasingly polarized state of Ulster politics during the 1970s, her republican socialism seemed too anodyne to the extremists, while her occasional endorsements of the Provisional IRA as fighters of British imperialism alienated the middle classes as well as some working-class Catholics who had experienced the complexities of life under the IRA's stewardship. On one hand, she dismissed the Peace Movement as "dishonest," but conversely she was unable to find an acceptable niche in the increasingly popular Sinn Fein movement. Ultimately, her attempt at contesting the European election of 1979 in order to publicize and defend republican prisoners who were seeking political status, was relatively a lone one. The republican movement refused to support her, and she lost heavily.

An end of a more decisive nature came very close in February 1981, when loyalist gunmen, incensed by her continuing loud support for republican prisoners, almost succeeded in murdering both McAliskey and her husband. Despite the severity of their injuries, the government used her six-month prison sentence of 1970 as an excuse to refuse her any financial compensation. Her efforts to return to "institutional" politics, however, continued to fail; in particular, her bid for a seat in the Irish Dail (parliament) of southern Ireland in 1982 when she attempted to unseat the Taoiseach (prime minister) Charles J. Haughey, came to nothing. She remained the unbowed champion of the republican cause in its broadest and most traditional sense. She spoke against the extradition of wanted republicans from the safety of southern Ireland to the custody of the Belfast authorities in 1987–88, and was one of those who helped to establish a group to preserve in the Irish Constitution the articles (2 and 3) which assert the southern Republic's territorial claim to Northern Ireland. Official confusion as to her precise status within republican circles was demonstrated in 1993 when the British Broadcasting Company was forced to revoke a decision to include her in a legal voice-ban which hampered both republican and loyalist broadcasts until the ceasefire of the following year. She was among the first in republican circles to reject the Downing Street Declaration.

It was, however, her statement at the funeral of the controversial Dominic McGlinchy that he was "the finest republican the struggle has ever produced," an assertion made perhaps with regard more to the distant than to the recent past, that drew her back into the headlines. The journalists rediscovered a woman who had gained nothing and had lost much through her life in socialist republicanism, but who believed in it more passionately than ever. While acutely aware of her "legend," she was dismissive of it as a mere media creation; historical realities for her transcended such chimera. Far from reading the only other account of her life (written in the mid-1970s), she has never read the published version of her own autobiography. When she was first elected to Westminster, she had insisted that she had not intended merely "to join your club." In retrospect, she still maintains that all her elections were fought "on a tactical basis" and "for a specific purpose." She was never a politician but rather "a political thinker." The long-ago refusal of Queen's University to allow

McAliskey, Roisin (1971—)

*Irish activist. Born in August 1971; daughter of *Bernadette Devlin McAliskey and Michael McAliskey.*

In 1997, ill and pregnant, Roisin McAliskey was jailed in connection with an Irish Republican Army mortar attack on a British army base in Osnabrueck, northwest Germany. There were no injuries. Protesters were convinced that she was being held in solitary confinement in Holloway Prison without bail in direct retaliation against her mother.

her the degree which she had largely earned still rankles. She feels no bitterness against her would-be assassins (one of whom has since been murdered), even though her husband, already made redundant through government economic cutbacks, has not worked since that fateful morning. She resents, however, the necessity to move from the countryside into a built-up urban area which was a consequence of the attack.

History may well remember Bernadette Devlin McAliskey as the one Ulster idealist for whom conformity and compromise were never real options. Even in 1996–97, when the shooting stopped, the unsullied clarity and essential historicity of her vision of the Irish conflict was a disturbing reminder to those who were tempted to accept less than that which they knew to be their due.

SOURCES

Devlin, Bernadette. *The Price of My Soul*. Andre Deutsch: London, 1969.

Target, G.W. *Bernadette: The Story of Bernadette Devlin*. London: Hodder and Stoughton, 1975.

SUGGESTED READING:

Bell, J. Bowyer. *The Irish Troubles: A Generation of Violence, 1967–1972*. Dublin: Gill and Macmillan, 1993.

Farrell, Michael. *Northern Ireland: The Orange State*. London: Pluto Press. 1976.

Gerard O'Brien,
Senior Lecturer in History,
University of Ulster, Northern Ireland

McAliskey, Roisin (b. 1971).

See McAliskey, Bernadette for sidebar.

McAuley, Catherine (1778–1841)

Irish nun who founded the Institute of Our Lady of Mercy (Sisters of Mercy). Name variations: (incorrectly) Catherine McCauley. Born in Ballymun, County Dublin, Ireland, in 1778 (some sources cite 1781); died in Dublin on November 11, 1841; second of three children of James McAuley and Elinor (Conway) McAuley; founded the Institute of Our Lady of Mercy (Sisters of Mercy), in December 1831.

Selected writings: The Correspondence of Catherine McAuley, 1827–41 *(Sisters of Mercy, 1989).*

Catherine McAuley's father James McAuley was part of the growing Catholic middle class in 18th-century Ireland. Having started out as a carpenter, he became by turns a builder, timber merchant and grazier, ending as a country gentleman on his estate at Stormanstown House in north Dublin. Her mother **Elinor Conway McAuley** was over 30 years younger than James when they married at the end of the 1770s. James McAuley died in 1783 when Catherine was still a small child. Elinor, who was fond of pleasure and fashion, gave up Stormanstown House and moved into central Dublin. She was also irked by the social and legal stigmatism that came with Catholicism, so she and two of her children converted to Protestantism and joined the Church of Ireland. Catherine remained Catholic.

These familial religious divisions persisted after her mother's death in 1798. McAuley went to live with her uncle Owen Conway and his daughter **Ann Conway**, who became her closest friend, while her brother and sister went to live with relatives of her mother, the Armstrongs, who were also Protestant. Ann Conway's confessor, Father Andrew Lube, became a trusted adviser of Catherine. When the Conways fell on hard times, McAuley joined her siblings at the Armstrongs', where she came under considerable pressure to change her religion. Although she refused, she always remained close to her brother and sister despite their religious differences. She was subsequently invited by the Callaghans, friends of the Armstrongs, to become a companion to Mrs. Callaghan, who lived in Coolock, north Dublin. McAuley soon became involved in helping the poor of the village and in organizing classes for the local children. After Mrs. Callaghan died in 1819 and her husband died three years later in 1822, McAuley inherited the Callaghan estate which was valued at almost $150,000.

Her inheritance gave her the opportunity to extend her involvement in charitable work. There were enormous social problems in Dublin, with poor housing, overcrowding, insanitary conditions and epidemics of typhus and cholera. Although she became acquainted with the Sisters of Charity and visited their convent at Stanhope Street in Dublin, McAuley was not at this point attracted to the religious life. Such a choice was still considered unusual, as the great expansion of Irish religious life was in the future. Her aim was to build a large house which would serve as a school for poor children and a shelter for homeless young women, and she wanted to invite other lay women to join her in this project. McAuley bought a site on Baggot Street, in the heart of fashionable south Dublin, to the considerable disapproval of some of the residents who did not welcome the new establishment. In 1827, she and her friend **Fanny Tighe** went to France to study the educational system there. Later that year, the first group of women moved into Baggot Street. Also in 1827 her sister **Mary McAuley** died, and following the death of Mary's husband two years later Catherine became responsible for their children. Consumption cut a swathe through the family and four of the children were to die before their aunt.

The Baggot Street foundation encountered increasing problems with the Catholic Church authorities, partly because of their lay status and partly because some church leaders feared her group would become a rival to the Sisters of Charity. These problems prompted McAuley to reassess the issue of canonical status, and in September 1830, as a preliminary to founding her own order of nuns, she entered the Presentation Convent at George's Hill in Dublin to serve her novitiate. She took her final vows in December 1831 and within days the new Institute of Our Lady of Mercy was established. The Sisters of Mercy soon proved their value when a cholera epidemic broke out in the spring of 1832 and they took charge of one of the temporary hospitals at the request of the Board of Health.

McAuley was a formidable administrator with a gift for developing administrative talent among her subordinates. She faced enormous problems in the early years of the Sisters of Mercy, including the myriad difficulties in establishing new foundations in Ireland and Britain, lack of money, poor health, and continuing problems with certain Catholic church leaders, but she overcame most of them by her determination, practicality and good humor. The new order spread rapidly, and in the last seven years of her life she founded 11 convents in Ireland and Britain. Her biographer, Roland Burke Savage, attributed the expansion of the order to the fact that McAuley gave complete local autonomy to the different foundations. She believed that the family spirit, which she regarded as an essential element of her order, could not be maintained under centralized control. In her view, the local superior was much better able to understand local problems and conditions. It was also the case that many novices preferred to enter local convents rather than go to some central novitiate far away from their homes. By 1841, the order had two foundations in England and had been invited to go to Newfoundland in Canada. But by late 1841, the family weakness, consumption, was beginning to affect McAuley's health. She kept up her reassuring manner while privately arranging her affairs. Few of her nuns realized how ill she was. Catherine McAuley died on November 11, 1841, and was buried in the Baggot Street cemetery.

SOURCES:

Bolster, Angela M. *Catherine McAuley 1778–1978: Bicentenary Souvenir Booklet*. Dublin: Irish Messenger Publications, 1978.

Savage, Roland Burke. *Catherine McAuley: The First Sister of Mercy*. Dublin: M.H. Gill, 1949.

Sullivan, Mary C. *Catherine McAuley and the Tradition of Mercy*. Dublin: Four Courts Press, 1995.

Deirdre McMahon,
Lecturer in History, Mary Immaculate College, University of Limerick, Limerick, Ireland

McAuley, Mary Ludwig Hays

(1754–1832).

See "Two Mollies."

McAuliffe, Christa (1948–1986).

See Astronauts: Women in Space.

McAvoy, May (1901–1984)

American star of the silent-film era. Name variations: Mae McAvoy. Born on September 18, 1901, in New York City; died after a heart attack on April 26, 1984, in Sherman Oaks, California; daughter of a livery-stable owner; married Maurice G. Cleary (a United Artists and Lockheed Aircraft executive), in 1929 (divorced); children: Patrick Cleary.

Selected filmography: Hate *(1917);* To Hell with the Kaiser *(1917);* Mrs. Wiggs of the Cabbage Patch *(1919);* The Truth About Husbands *(1920);* The Devil's Garden *(1920);* Sentimental Tommy *(1921);* A Private Scandal *(1921);* The Top of New York *(1922);* Her Reputation *(1923);* The Enchanted Cottage *(1924);* Three Women *(1924);* The Mad Whirl *(1925);* Lady Windermere's Fan *(1925);* Ben-Hur *(1926);* The Jazz Singer *(1927);* A Reno Divorce *(1927);* The Lion and the Mouse *(1928);* The Terror *(UK, 1928);* Two Girls on Broadway *(1940);* Luxury Liner *(1948);* Mystery Street *(1950);* Executive Suite *(1954);* Gun Glory *(1957).*

May McAvoy was born in New York City in 1901, into a well-off family of Scots-Irish ancestry who owned extensive livery stables on a stretch of Park Avenue where the Waldorf-Astoria Hotel would later be built. She dreamed of becoming an actress from an early age, although her mother would have preferred that she become a schoolteacher, and dropped out of high school around 1916. At the time, Hollywood had not fully supplanted New York City as the center of the motion-picture industry, and McAvoy began applying to casting agencies in Manhattan. Initially, she received modeling jobs instead, including an advertisement for Domino Sugar; her first real film role came as an ingenue in *Hate* (1917), which led to steady work in the Pathé studio's silent films. In 1919, she played one of the title character's many children in *Mrs. Wiggs of the Cabbage Patch*, the second film version of *Alice Hegan Rice*'s 1901 novel. McAvoy received good reviews for her work in the 1921 film *Sentimental Tommy* (adapted from a short story by J.M. Barrie), and, though the film was not a commercial success, won a contract with Paramount, which required her to move to the West Coast.

McAvoy made numerous films in Hollywood, becoming a well-known screen presence; the poet Carl Sandburg sang her praises when he was still a film critic for a Chicago daily. Famed director Cecil B. De Mille wanted to cast her in *Adam's Rib*, but when she learned her costume

May McAvoy

would be virtually nonexistent, she declined. Because of this Paramount stopped giving her leading roles, but she was savvy enough to buy out her contract with the studio and work as a free agent, immediately tripling her fee. Over the next few years, she appeared in such films as *The Enchanted Cottage* (1924), Ernst Lubitsch's *Lady Windermere's Fan* (1925), and opposite heartthrob Ramon Novarro in *Ben-Hur*, a film that cinema historians would later refer to as the last great epic of the silent period. There were reportedly numerous problems on the set during production of *Ben-Hur* because of an army of well-paid technicians and extras interested in extending the length of their employment. The movie went into cost overruns and was consistently thwarted by acts of sabotage; there were even threats of a plot to kidnap McAvoy. While she was talking one day to the writer F. Scott Fitzgerald, who was visiting the production, a nearby set erupted in flames.

In 1927, she signed a contract with Warner Bros., which cast her opposite Al Jolson in *The Jazz Singer*, the film that introduced spoken dialogue. McAvoy also appeared in the first British talkie, *The Terror* (1928), after which she dropped from sight. Many stars of silent films, whose fans never would have known of their regional accents or squeaky voices, found their careers unexpectedly terminated with the introduction of sound, and there were rumors that McAvoy had been dropped because she had a lisp. In fact, in 1929 she had married Maurice G. Cleary, an executive at United Artists who later worked for Lockheed Martin, and retired to Beverly Hills to devote her time to raising their son. (They would later divorce.) May McAvoy appeared on the Los Angeles stage occasionally, and returned to the screen as a contract player for MGM in the 1940s and 1950s. She died in 1984.

SOURCES:

Katz, Ephraim. *The Film Encyclopedia.* NY: Harper-Collins, 1994.

Lamparski, Richard. *Whatever Became of. . . ?* 3rd Series. NY: Crown Publishers, 1970.

Wagenknecht, Edward. *Stars of the Silents.* Metuchen, NJ: Scarecrow Press, 1987, pp. 64–75.

Carol Brennan,
Grosse Pointe, Michigan

McBride, Clara (1905–1992).

See Hale, Clara.

McBride, Mary Margaret

(1899–1976)

American journalist and writer who was one of the most popular radio hosts of the first half of the 20th century. Name variations: (early radio name) Martha Deane. Born on November 16, 1899, in Paris, Missouri; died in West Shokun, New York, on April 7, 1976; daughter of Thomas Walker McBride (a farmer) and Elizabeth (Craig) McBride; University of Missouri, B.A., 1919.

Selected writings: (with Paul Whiteman) Jazz (1926); (with Alexander Williams) Charm: A Book about It and Those Who Have It, For Those Who Want It (1927); (with Helen Josephy) Paris Is a Woman's Town (1929); (with Josephy) London Is a Man's Town (1930); The Story of Dwight Morrow (1930); (with Josephy) New York Is Everybody's Town (1931); (with Josephy) Beer and Skittles: A Friendly Modern Guide to Germany (1932); The Life Story of *Constance Bennett (1932); Here's Martha Deane (1936); Tune In for Elizabeth: Career Story of an Interviewer (1945); How Dear to My Heart (autobiography, 1940); A Long Way from Missouri (autobiography, 1959); Out of the Air (autobiography, 1960).

Awards and honors: Medal for outstanding journalism from the University of Missouri; medal from the Woman's National Exposition of Arts and Industries (1936); Haiti's National Order of Honor and Merit; special medal of honor from the city of Vienna; special recognition from the Virgin Islands; One World Award (1950).

Mary Margaret McBride, who was a fixture on American radio networks for two decades and whose personality-driven, nationally broadcast radio program was heard by an estimated six million listeners daily at the height of her career, was born in Paris, Missouri, in 1899, only two years before the birth of radio itself via Guglielmo Marconi's famous transatlantic wireless communication. She moved frequently as a child, partly as a result of her farmer father's restlessness. Encouraged by her book-loving grandfathers to pursue her dream of becoming a writer, McBride put herself through the University of Missouri by working on the school paper—including typesetting duties—and babysitting for faculty families, earning a journalism degree in 1919. For a time after graduation she worked in Washington, D.C., and was then offered a job as a reporter for the *Cleveland Press* through a college classmate, **Pauline Pfeiffer** (who would later marry Ernest Hemingway). McBride dreamed of moving to New York City, however, and obtained a publicity job with the Interchurch World Movement there around 1920. Living in Greenwich Village, she worked for a few years at the *New York Evening Mail*, where she was only the second female writer to be hired. She covered fires and tragic cases involving orphaned children and the indigent, common assignments for women reporters, but fought to get the hard-news assignments.

McBride left the *Mail* around 1924 to begin freelancing. She wrote articles for the *Saturday Evening Post, Good Housekeeping*, and other popular periodicals, and began to travel. After writing two books, *Jazz* with Paul Whiteman (1926) and *Charm: A Book about It and Those Who Have It, For Those Who Want It* with Alexander Williams (1927), McBride began

writing light-hearted travel guides with **Helen Josephy**. These included *Paris Is a Woman's Town, London Is a Man's Town, New York Is Everybody's Town*, and *Beer and Skittles: A Friendly Modern Guide to Germany*, all published between 1929 and 1932. McBride suffered financial hardship as a result of the Great Depression in the early 1930s (she was also supporting her parents back in Missouri by this point), and needed money when the magazine market shrank. In 1934, she went to an audition at a New York radio station, WOR, and to her surprise was offered the job as host of a newly

Mary Margaret McBride

created radio program aimed at women. She began as "Martha Deane," a grandmother who gave housekeeping hints and talked about her grandchildren, but after just a few weeks on the air misspoke while in the middle of an anecdote about a nonexistent grandchild; she then confessed that she was not even married. She told listeners to write to the station if they thought she should stay, and they did.

Over the next few years, McBride's show evolved from advice-giving and recipes to more sophisticated topics, especially when the CBS Radio Network hired her in 1937 and gave her a show under own name. She switched to NBC from 1941 until 1950, when she jumped to ABC. Extremely popular, McBride interviewed noted celebrities of the day, including Queen *Elizabeth II, *Eleanor Roosevelt, and President Harry S. Truman, broadcast from remote locations, and took her listeners on a great many adventures. Much of her show was ad-libbed, a risky practice in the days of live radio. Known as a convincing spokesperson for a range of products (she had a waiting list of sponsors), McBride was adamant about not endorsing goods that she had not personally tested, and so gave quite convincing testimonials.

Called "the First Lady of Radio," McBride was such a success that her anniversary broadcasts were attended by huge audiences: the 10th, held in Madison Square Garden, attracted 25,000, and the 15th had to be held in Yankee Stadium to accommodate a crowd of 40,000. She was once named one of the five most important women in America (along with Sister *Elizabeth Kenny, *Emily Post, *Dorothy Thompson, and Eleanor Roosevelt). McBride retired from a six-day-a-week schedule in 1954 after the death of her longtime confidant and business manager, **Stella Karn**. A friend since their days together at the Interchurch World Movement, Karn figures prominently in many of the adventures that McBride chronicled in one of her autobiographies, *A Long Way from Missouri* (1959). Mary Margaret McBride also wrote two other volumes of memoirs, *How Dear to My Heart* (1940) and *Out of the Air* (1960). She spent her remaining years in a renovated Hudson Valley barn, making the occasional radio or television appearance, and died in April 1976.

SOURCES:

Current Biography. NY: H.W. Wilson, 1941.

Lamparski, Richard. *Whatever Became of . . . ?* 3rd Series. NY: Crown Publishers, 1970.

McHenry, Robert, ed. *Famous American Women.* NY: Dover, 1980.

100 American Women Who Made a Difference. Vol. 1, no. 1. Cowles, 1995.

Carol Brennan,
Grosse Pointe, Michigan

McCambridge, Mercedes (1918—)

Stage, screen, and radio actress who won an Academy Award for her first film and was later the off-camera voice of the demon in The Exorcist. *Born Carlotta Mercedes Agnes McCambridge on March 17, 1918, in Joliet, Illinois; daughter of John Patrick McCambridge (a farmer) and Marie (Mahaffry) McCambridge; Mundelein College, B.A., 1937; married William Fifield (a writer), in 1939 (divorced 1946); married Fletcher Markle (a writer and director), in 1950 (divorced 1962); children: (first marriage) John Lawrence (died 1987).*

Selected filmography: All the King's Men *(1949);* Lightning Strikes Twice *(1951);* Inside Straight *(1951);* The Scarf *(1951);* Johnny Guitar *(1954);* Giant *(1956);* Suddenly, Last Summer *(1959);* Cimarron *(1960);* Angel Baby *(1961);* Crackshot *(1968);* 99 Women *(1969);* Sixteen *(1972);* Two for the Money *(1972);* The Girls of Huntington House *(1973); (voice only)* The Exorcist *(1973);* Thieves *(1977);* The Sacketts *(1979);* Amazing Stories: Book Two *(1987).*

Born in 1918 in Joliet, Illinois, actress Mercedes McCambridge grew up on the South Side of Chicago, where she attended St. Thomas Apostle High School. A talented student, she won a scholarship to Mundelein, a Catholic women's college in the city, and received solid dramatic training from nuns in the drama department there. By the time she graduated in 1937, she had already been signed to a five-year contract with NBC Radio.

In this pre-television era of the Great Depression, radio was perhaps the most pervasive form of entertainment in the United States, and Chicago was the center of much of radio production. McCambridge soon became an acclaimed actress in the medium, greatly in demand for her versatility even after she moved briefly to Hollywood and then, in 1942, to New York. Over the years, she appeared in numerous radio series, including "Inner Sanctum," "Abie's Irish Rose," "I Love a Mystery," "Bulldog Drummond," "Dick Tracy," and "The Thin Man." She was called "the world's greatest living radio actress" by no less an authority than Orson Welles, with whom she worked on the "Ford Theater" series. She starred in her own series on CBS radio, "Big Sister," in 1945.

Though McCambridge was considered an outstanding radio performer, she encountered a streak of bad luck during her first attempts on Broadway in the mid-1940s, with miscast roles and abysmal productions. In 1946, she divorced her husband, writer William Fifield, and the following year took her six-year-old son on a trip that included long sojourns in Italy and the West Indies. She later published an account of this year as *The Two of Us* (1960). After returning to the United States, McCambridge continued working in radio and in 1948 was cajoled by a friend into showing up at a cattle call at Columbia Pictures. Signed to a contract, she made her film debut in the 1949 drama *All the King's Men*, based on the Robert Penn Warren novel about a Huey Long-type politician. McCambridge won great reviews for her 17 minutes on screen, and, much to her surprise, was awarded the Academy Award for Best Supporting Actress in 1950. Roles in an array of other outstanding films followed, including *Johnny Guitar* (1954), a Western in which she battled *Joan Crawford, *Giant* (1956), a classic based on the *Edna Ferber novel that also starred *Elizabeth Taylor, Rock Hudson, and James Dean, and for which she received her second Academy Award nomination, and *Suddenly, Last Summer* (1959), an adaptation of the Tennessee Williams play with *Katharine Hepburn, Montgomery Clift, and Elizabeth Taylor (whose mother McCambridge played onscreen). Although she also appeared in the worthwhile *Angel Baby* (1961), her film career then began to stall, in part due to her battle with alcoholism. Among her later movies, which include *99 Women* (1969) and *Thieves* (1977), certainly the most well known is *The Exorcist* (1973), for which she provided the demonic voice that issues from the mouth of the possessed **Linda Blair**.

McCambridge had married her second husband, writer and director Fletcher Markle, in 1950, but her personal life was plagued by a series of tragic events that began around the time of their divorce in 1962. Her college-age son John was severely beaten by muggers late that year; in early 1963, her home was destroyed by fire, she broke a leg, and her son again suffered injuries, this time in an automobile crash. The news of the latter event drove McCambridge to a suicide attempt. In 1987, her son shot and killed his wife and two daughters before killing himself. McCambridge wrote a candid autobiography in 1981, *The Quality of Mercy*.

SOURCES:

Current Biography. NY: H.W. Wilson, 1964.

Katz, Ephraim. *The Film Encyclopedia.* NY: Harper-Collins, 1994.

McCambridge, Mercedes. *The Quality of Mercy: An Autobiography.* NY: The New York Times Books, 1981.

Carol Brennan,
Grosse Pointe, Michigan

Mercedes
McCambridge

McCardell, Claire (1905–1958)

One of the foremost American sportswear designers of the mid-20th century. Born on May 24, 1905, in Frederick, Maryland; died of cancer on March 22, 1958, in New York City; daughter of Adrian Leroy McCardell (a banker and politician) and Frances (Clingan) McCardell; degree from New York School of Fine and Applied Arts, 1928; married Irving Harris (an architect), in 1943; children: two stepchildren.

Moved to New York City (1925); traveled to Paris (1927); hired at Townley Frocks (1930); became chief designer (1931); created designs for Hattie Carnegie's Workshop Originals line (1938–40); returned to Townley Frocks (1940); received Coty Award from the American Fashion Critics Association (1944); became partner at Townley Frocks (1952).

Designer Claire McCardell helped push American fashion toward its own singular, individualistic style. Before the 1930s, when her designs first won acclaim, affluent American women could choose either clothing made by, and purchased from, Parisian couture houses or American-made items that were copies of the French designs. McCardell felt that her customers led a different lifestyle than did European women; they were more physically active and had far less time for the care and maintenance of impractical fabrics. Her designs, which made her a household name by the 1940s, were practical yet stylish and helped define what came to be called the "American Look." In her own words, her style embodied "America—it looks and feels like America. It's freedom, it's democracy, it's casualness, it's good health. Clothes can say all that."

Claire McCardell was born in Frederick, Maryland, in 1905, the first of Adrian and **Frances McCardell**'s four children. Her father was a bank president in Frederick, and would be elected to the state legislature as well as serve as an elder in the Evangelical and Reformed Church. Her mother hailed from Mississippi, and reportedly McCardell grew up in a home where a portrait of Confederate general Robert E. Lee was enshrined on a parlor wall. She developed an interest in dressmaking from an early age, and was sewing her own clothes by the time she graduated from Frederick's Girls High School in 1922. She then spent two years at Hood College in her hometown but, after dismal grades, was able to convince her father to fund an education in New York and Paris at the School of Fine and Applied Arts (later Parsons School of Design). McCardell soon became acquainted with the work of the best-known European couture houses, and like other fledgling designers of the era would purchase sample dresses after the Paris showings and take them apart to study how they were made. She was particularly intrigued by the work of *Madeleine Vionnet, renowned as the inventor of the bias cut.

After earning her degree in 1928, McCardell had a difficult time finding a job with a design house, and worked as a model, sketcher, and even lampshade painter in New York City. A designer named Robert Turk hired her in 1929, and when Townley Frocks hired him as its chief designer a year later, he brought McCardell with him. Turk died in 1932, and McCardell took over her mentor's duties at the company. She would remain with Townley until her death, with the exception of two years spent working for designer *Hattie Carnegie. In a major break with European-inspired fashion, McCardell created at Townley a line of "separates" that could be worn in various combinations for varying occasions. The concept did not initially win a huge following, but, several decades later, separates had become the backbone of most designers' ready-to-wear collections. Another famous design of McCardell's was her caftan, called the "Monastic," which was inspired in part by Moroccan garb.

World War II brought an enforced break with French fashion, creating a pocket of opportunity for American houses, while wartime shortages necessitated design innovations. McCardell created a denim "Popover" wraparound housedress for women whose domestic servants had moved on to better-paying factory work. Fuel rationing meant that college dormitories were chilly, and another McCardell innovation was a wool leotard to be worn under sweaters and skirts during the winter months. Throughout her career, a hallmark of McCardell's designs was her introduction of new or unusual fabrics. American cotton, for instance, had rarely been used for anything but golf togs or housedresses, but she employed it for a range of sportswear items. She also favored wool jersey for evening wear.

McCardell married architect Irving Harris in 1943 and enjoyed a close relationship with his two children. By the time Townley made her a partner in 1952, she was an American celebrity who had received most of the top awards in her field. She was an advisor to the Costume Institute at the Metropolitan Museum of Art, taught at Parsons, and was feted with a 1953 retrospective of her work by the Los Angeles art gallery Perls. McCardell wrote one book, *What Shall I Wear?*, published in 1956, and died of cancer two years later. Collections of her work can be found at the Design Laboratory of the Fashion Institute of Technology in New York City, the Costume Institute of the Metropolitan Museum of Art, and the Los Angeles County Museum. Twenty-five years' worth of her design sketches are held by Parsons School of Design.

SOURCES:

Pile, John. *Dictionary of 20th-Century Design.* NY: Facts on File, 1990.

Sicherman, Barbara, and Carol Hurd Green, eds. *Notable American Women: The Modern Period.* Cambridge, MA: The Belknap Press of Harvard University, 1980.

Carol Brennan,
Grosse Pointe, Michigan

McCarthy, Kathryn O'Loughlin
(1894–1952)

American politician and U.S. representative to the 73rd Congress. Born Kathryn Ellen O'Loughlin on April 24, 1894, near Hays, Kansas; died in Hays,

Kansas, on January 16, 1952; daughter of John O'Loughlin and Mary Ellen (McIntosh) O'Loughlin; Fort Hays State College (later Kansas State Teachers College), B.S. in Edn., 1917; University of Chicago Law School, J.D., 1920; married Daniel M. McCarthy (a Kansas state senator), on February 4, 1933.

Kathryn O'Loughlin McCarthy was born on April 24, 1894, near Hays, Kansas, where she attended rural primary and secondary schools. She continued her education at the Kansas State Teachers College and the University of Chicago Law School, from which she received her law degree. After a brief stint practicing law in Chicago, in 1928 she returned to Hays to open her own practice. She also became active in the state Democratic Party and in 1931 was elected to the Kansas State House of Representatives. She then defeated Republican incumbent Charles Sparks to gain election in 1932 to the U.S. House of Representatives from the Sixth District of Kansas. She married Kansas state senator Daniel McCarthy shortly before the start of her term in March 1933.

A supporter of New Deal policies, McCarthy was also a strong backer of the Agriculture Adjustment Act, for many of her constituents were farmers who had been devastated by the Depression. She was assigned to serve on the House Committee of Insular Affairs, an appointment she protested in favor of participation on the Committee on Agriculture which she considered more appropriate to a representative from rural Kansas. Although her protest was denied, she was transferred to the Committee on Education, in which role she sought increased federal funding for vocational schools.

McCarthy lost her bid for reelection to the House in 1934. She returned to her law practice in Hays, and later operated a car dealership. Remaining active in Democratic politics, she participated in national party conventions until her death in Hays on January 16, 1952.

SOURCES:
Office of the Historian. *Women in Congress, 1917–1990.* Commission on the Bicentenary of the U.S. House of Representatives, 1991.

Grant Eldridge,
freelance writer, Pontiac, Michigan

McCarthy, Lillah (1875–1960)

British actress. Name variations: Lady Lillah Keeble. Born in 1875; died in 1960; married Harley Granville-Barker (a playwright, director, translator, and writer), in 1906 (divorced 1918); married Sir Frederick Keeble, in 1920.

Lillah McCarthy was born in 1875, and showed an early inclination to be an actress. She studied elocution and voice production with Hermann Vezin and secured her first theatrical role in 1896. McCarthy worked with Wilson Barrett until 1904, when she was discovered by playwright George Bernard Shaw. Moving to the Court Theater, for the next two years she starred in Shaw's plays. Most of these were directed by Harley Granville-Barker, a former actor who was also a playwright, daring director, producer and writer. They were married in 1906.

McCarthy appeared in the title role of *Nan* and as Lady Sybil in J.M. Barrie's *What Every Woman Knows* in 1908, as Margaret Knox in *Fanny's First Play* in 1911, and as Lavinia in *Androcles and the Lion* in 1913. She also worked with her husband in his revolutionary series of Shakespearean productions at the Savoy Theater from 1912 to 1914. McCarthy divorced Granville-Barker in 1918, and married Sir Frederick Keeble in 1920, after which she left the

Kathryn O'Loughlin McCarthy

stage. She published an autobiography, *Myself as Friends*, in 1933. Lillah McCarthy died in 1960.

Grant Eldridge,
freelance writer, Pontiac, Michigan

McCarthy, Mary (1912–1989)

American literary critic, novelist, journalist of the anti-Communist left, and author of **The Group,** *who was one of the nation's most prominent intellectuals.*

Name variations: Mary McCarthy (1912–1933 and in her professional life throughout); Mary Johnsrud (1933–36); Mary Wilson (1937–45); Mary Broadwater (1948–60); Mary West (1961–89). Born Mary Therese McCarthy in Seattle, Washington, on June 21, 1912; died of lung cancer on October 25, 1989; daughter of Roy Winfield McCarthy and Therese (Preston) McCarthy; sister of Kevin McCarthy (an actor); Vassar College, A.B., 1933; married Harold Johnsrud, in 1933 (divorced 1936); married Edmund Wilson (a writer), in 1937 (divorced 1945); married Bowden Broadwater (a writer and deputy headmaster), in 1948 (divorced 1961); married James West (a Public Affairs officer), on April 15, 1961; children: (second marriage) one son, Reuel K. Wilson (b. 1938).

Selected writings: The Company She Keeps *(1942);* The Oasis *(1949);* The Groves of Academe *(1952);* A Charmed Life *(1955);* Memories of a Catholic Girlhood *(1957);* The Group *(1963);* Venice Observed *(1956);* The Stones of Florence *(1959);* Vietnam *(1967);* Hanoi *(1968);* Birds of America *(1971);* Medina *(1972);* The Seventeenth Parallel *(1974);* Cannibals and Missionaries *(1979);* How I Grew *(1987);* Intellectual Memoirs: NY: 1936–1938 *(1992).*

Mary McCarthy was a leading American novelist, critic, and travel writer of the 20th century whose sardonic social observations made her widely feared as well as much admired. In a long succession of novels, she scrutinized, and often debunked, intellectuals, people who live by ideas, revealing the vanity, greed and ambition which drove them as much, or more, than their high-mindedness. She made strong friends but also passionate enemies throughout her long life and incurred a libel suit in 1980 when she declared on the "Dick Cavett Show" that every word the playwright *Lillian Hellman* had ever written was "a lie, including 'and' and 'the.'" Four times married and famous for a long succession of stormy love affairs with literary figures, McCarthy was also a prominent figure in the anti-Communist left and a high-profile critic of America's role in Vietnam during the late 1960s.

Mary McCarthy was born in Seattle, Washington, in 1912. Her devoted parents were taken ill while traveling to Minnesota, in the severe influenza epidemic which swept America at the end of the First World War. They both died in the same week, leaving her an orphan at the age of six. With her siblings Preston, Sheridan, and Kevin McCarthy (who would become a well-known film and television actor), she went to live with a great-uncle and great-aunt in Minneapolis who brought her up strictly and inflexibly, depriving her of toys and playmates, beating her for disobedience, even taping her mouth shut each night to be sure she would breathe through her nose. Some of the most effective passages of McCarthy's *Memories of a Catholic Girlhood* (1957) describe, with Dickensian vividness, her bitter confrontations with them and show how she developed a combative streak in the face of persecution.

In 1923, at age 11, she went to live with a richer and much more benevolent grandfather back in Seattle who indulged her. Another wonderful passage of *Memories* explores her religious development as a Catholic. At the age of about 12, she realized that her grandfather, a Presbyterian, was destined for Hell, according to her Catholic teachers. She came to believe that his only hope was "invincible ignorance," the Catholic doctrine that no one can go to Hell if they have had no opportunity of learning the religious truth. She therefore ceased what had been her ostentatious devotions, but the grandfather, misinterpreting her motives, chided her for backsliding. She then relished the "martyrdom" of suffering despite doing the *right* thing. A little later, she made a bid for her teachers' and friends' attention at her elite Catholic school by alleging that she had lost her faith. As she tells it, what began as a social gambit suddenly turned into a reality, and she discovered that she was more convinced by the arguments *against* the existence of God than those for it. From then on, she had no religious life though, like many brilliant 20th-century intellectuals, she later substituted psychoanalysis and morbid self-scrutiny for the Christianity she had left behind.

Mary McCarthy was passionately devoted to a succession of female teachers and studied hard. She also grew up quickly, longing for the adventures of adulthood. She first had sex at the age of 14, with a man in his mid-20s, and later posed secretly for an artist who also slept with her. At the same time, she excelled in her West Coast schools before going to college back East, at Vassar, where she quickly gained a reputation among her fellow students as an intellectual *enfant terrible*. McCarthy mixed learning with acting, dating, and an enthusiastic social life. One of the rituals of college life for "fast" students at that time of Prohibition was buying and enjoying illegal alcohol, especially cocktails, which she enjoyed from the beginning. Always materialistic, McCarthy loved good clothes and the pleasures of wealth, and enjoyed social climbing, which never abated even when she was an active political leftist. She mentions in *How I Grew* that she disguised from her high-toned WASP friends the fact that one of her grandmothers was Jewish because of the social stigma it carried. Her most successful novel *The Group* (1963), a national bestseller which would make her name a household word, describes the fortunes of a circle of Vassar graduates in the New York of the 1930s, and depends heavily for characters and situations on her actual college friends. It is a sometimes affectionate, sometimes critical account of changing social mores, as these gifted young women go to work, experiment with sex and contraception, live in their own apartments, and try to apply the lessons of their elite education in a tough, Depression-afflicted city.

While still a college junior, McCarthy became engaged to Harold Johnsrud, an actor, theater director, and aspiring movie scriptwriter. Friends who knew him warned her that he was a womanizer, prone to heavy drinking and fits of depression. He even told her that a drunken car crash, from which he walked away, was really an attempted suicide. The idea that he was a suffering artist appealed to her Byronic side and encouraged her to marry him just after graduation, even though, during a college vacation, he had made her miserable with his bullying when they lived together for a few weeks. Their wedding day in 1933 was also her 21st birthday.

Though the couple lived in New York, Johnsrud was often away directing or acting in the following years. In his absence, McCarthy began writing regularly, soon establishing herself as a hard-hitting and controversial literary critic. Most of her early reviews were for the *New Republic* and the *Nation*. One set of articles for the *Nation*, a survey of contemporary book critics, was bitingly satirical about many big names of the era. *Time* magazine nicknamed the series, which gave the 22-year-old McCarthy an instant notoriety, the "Saint Valentine's massacre of reviewers and critics." Her husband's frequent absences also led her to befriend and then become the lover of John Porter, an unemployed writer, and she wrote to friends that although she had married Johnsrud she had never really loved him. She asked him for a divorce after three years of marriage and later fictionalized their

breakup in a short story, "Cruel and Barbarous Treatment." She soon discovered, however, that she was less enamored of Porter than she had imagined, and could not bring herself, after her Reno divorce, to marry him.

In the mid-1930s, McCarthy found regular work and a circle of new friends at the *Partisan Review*, a journal of the American left for which she became drama critic. *Partisan Review* was run mainly by secular Jewish intellectuals, the sons of recent immigrants, who were leftists but anti-Soviet and foes of Stalin. Many described themselves as Trotskyites and like Leon Trotsky himself (an occasional contributor from his Mexican exile) they were fascinated by the achievements of the great literary modernists (W.B. Yeats, T.S. Eliot, James Joyce, *Virginia Woolf) despite political differences. Eager to hack away at what she thought of as inflated reputations, McCarthy continued to take on famous authors; she described Graham Greene in one characteristic review of the period as an "ersatz great novelist." She also began a passionate love affair with the journal's editor, Philip Rahv.

Rahv was eager to get Edmund Wilson, America's premier literary critic, to add the luster of his name to *Partisan Review*. Wilson agreed and soon after his first contributions to the journal McCarthy met him and became his lover. For a while she tried to keep it secret but finally admitted to Rahv what was going on. Rahv was sufficiently impressed with Wilson's and McCarthy's talents that he continued to publish their work despite this mortifying jolt. McCarthy and Wilson married in 1937, when she was 25 and he was 42. Their marriage led to the birth of a son, Reuel Wilson, her only child, who was born on Christmas Day, 1938. Their union was also important for McCarthy's development as a writer. With Wilson's encouragement, she began to concentrate on writing fiction and published her first novel, *The Company She Keeps,* in 1942. It still glitters, is full of daring self-revelation about her indiscretions, and contains many portraits of friends, lovers, and employers. One section in particular, "The Man in the Brooks Brothers Suit," about the protagonist's getting drunk and having violent sex with a businessman while traveling across country by train, gave her the reputation of being a "racy" writer. The book elicited divided judgments from critics, many of whom were impressed by her sharp eye and candid style, but a few of whom were dismissive of the novel's subject and its jumpy narrative.

The years of her marriage to Wilson were, however, a period of emotional storm and stress.

Theirs is probably the most famous literary bad marriage of the 20th century, and it ended in acrimony and bitter mutual recriminations. In many later novels, notably *The Groves of Academe,* McCarthy drew thinly veiled fictional versions of Wilson, making him physically grotesque, violent, abusive, egotistical, and drunk. And she often claimed later that she had never loved him but saw him only as a bullying reincarnation of the cruel great-uncle who had raised her. Wilson must certainly have been a difficult man to live with—he *was* vain and given to drinking binges, and sometimes lectured her for hours on whatever literary subject currently preoccupied him— but as his biographer Jeffrey Meyers points out, for a while the two exchanged affectionate love letters and took great pleasure in each other. When she was pregnant, however, McCarthy suffered a nervous breakdown and was committed to a New York hospital. After the birth of Reuel, she continued to make regular visits to New York from their home in Provincetown, Massachusetts, on Cape Cod, partly to visit a Freudian psychoanalyst, partly to pursue more sexual affairs, including one with *Partisan Review*'s art critic Clement Greenberg. By her own admission, she was, at this and several other times of her life, very active sexually. She and Wilson had several trial separations and finally divorced in 1945, with her gaining custody of their son during school terms and he during vacations.

*M*cCarthy's beauty was accompanied by an uncommon intelligence . . . but there was truth in the fear that she had the goods on everybody, and was not above using what she knew.

—Carol Brightman

The year of her second divorce, McCarthy met and befriended Nicola Chiaromonte, an Italian exile intellectual also living in Massachusetts, who made a calm contrast to her stormy life with Wilson. Unlike most of her acquaintances up to that time, he was an enthusiast neither for any variety of Marxism, nor for psychoanalysis. He was suspicious of all abstract, intellectual master systems, and McCarthy, formerly an ardent leftist, learned to share this suspicion. She later told him that his influence, during the summer of 1945 when they were often together, had transformed her view of the world. Her skepticism of intellectual systems became clear in much of her subsequent fiction.

McCarthy next took a job teaching Russian and English literature at Bard College, in the Hudson Valley, where another *Partisan Review* writer, Fred Dupee, was head of the English department. She enjoyed teaching but found it difficult to write as well, and so resolved to give up the job which, in any event, was not sufficiently well-paid to finance her often-extravagant way of life. After her first trip to Europe in the summer of 1946, she returned to New York and married Bowden Broadwater, an aspiring writer who was eight years her junior and had been courting her for the previous year. He could not find regular work and suffered from prolonged writer's block, so for much of their 14 years of marriage he played the role of housekeeper and companion to Reuel while McCarthy got on with her writing. In the mid-1950s, he became a teacher at Reuel's school and later its deputy headmaster.

McCarthy's second novel, *The Oasis* (1949), described an intellectuals' commune in which her friends Philip Rahv and Dwight Macdonald were distinctly visible in the characters of Will Taub and Macdougall Macdermott. Her third, *The Groves of Academe* (1952), was based partly on her experiences as a teacher at Bard and a semester of teaching at Sarah Lawrence College in 1948. Written in the midst of the era of anti-Communist McCarthyism, about which she and her many leftist friends were dismayed, it nevertheless avoided the easy approach of contrasting good liberals with mendacious anti-Communists. McCarthy depicted liberal intellectuals as muddle-headed dupes, rather than staunch guardians of academic freedom and integrity. The novel's unscrupulous protagonist, Professor Henry Mulcahy, has been fired from one college because of allegations that he is a Communist. On the verge of being fired next from progressive Jocelyn College, in Pennsylvania, whose crusading President Hoar had sympathetically hired him, he reacts by claiming, falsely, that he *is* a Communist, because he anticipates that Hoar will then protect him in the name of standing up to McCarthyism. Sure enough, the disgusting Mulcahy gathers a committee of defenders, appealing to their interest in civil liberties, and keeps his job. In his place, the good-natured but naive Hoar is forced to resign. The novel showed that Mary McCarthy envisioned the paradoxical side of McCarthyism, and her humorous treatment of the whole issue indicates that she looked on it as anything but a reign of terror.

By the early and mid-1950s, now in her 40s, McCarthy was a well-established author who could command high fees for writing projects. On the strength of these fees, and taking advantage of rich friends with European houses, including the art connoisseur Bernard Berenson,

she spent more and more time there, which culminated in two fine books about Italy, *Venice Observed* and *The Stones of Florence*. The works were good for her career and checkbook but bad for her marriage. In 1956, she had a passionate affair with an English reviewer, John Davenport, only to discover, on her return to Europe, that he had boasted of his conquest to his friends, and was a liar and cheat. More significant was her meeting with James West, a Public Affairs officer at the American Embassy in Warsaw whom she met while lecturing in Eastern

Europe on behalf of the Congress for Cultural Freedom. West was 46, had three young children, and was married. He and McCarthy fell in love at once and resolved to break their ties and marry one another, which they did, despite great prolonged legal difficulties, in 1961. The service was held in Paris. They had hoped to return to Warsaw, but the Wests' divorce had caused a scandal there which the Polish Communist authorities were eager to exploit. Instead, after nine months in the United States, West got a job with the Organization for Economic Cooperation and Development (OECD) in Paris, where the newlyweds moved in 1962. Friends like Macdonald and Chiaromonte were amused to see McCarthy acting like a girl in love for the first time even though she was a 49-year-old with her fourth husband. She insisted that she had never really been in love before and that she was faithful to this husband, as she had not been to any of the others.

McCarthy had been working on *The Group,* based on the experiences of her Vassar friends, ever since the early 1950s and finally completed it in 1963. One long section was written in the Libyan mansion of one of her wealthy European friends. A vastly entertaining and witty book, it came out to almost universal critical acclaim and confirmed her popular standing as a leading American novelist. It also ensured that the busyness of the preceding years would continue, as she went on publicity tours and speaking engagements. It also prompted another literary critic, **Doris Grumbach,** to undertake a literary biography of McCarthy, following up on an article Grumbach had written about how few women became first-class novelists. McCarthy met Grumbach and tape-recorded several interviews with her. Indiscretions in the transcript of these conversations alarmed her, and the manuscript had to be modified to avoid libels, but it was duly published in 1967 as *The Company She Kept.* From then on, McCarthy was the subject of a steady stream of interviews, articles, studies, and biographies.

Mary McCarthy, like most American intellectuals of the late 1960s, deplored America's role in Vietnam and responded to an invitation from Robert Silvers, editor of the *New York Review of Books,* to visit Saigon, the capital of South Vietnam. Her articles described the depressing transformation of the city by the American military, and the apparent inability of South Vietnam to prevail in the war. They were followed by a sharp debate between McCarthy and *Diana Trilling, a former colleague in the Congress for Cultural Freedom, because Trilling re-

mained committed to the war on orthodox anti-Communist grounds. Next, in mid-1968, McCarthy took the more daring step of visiting the North Vietnamese enemy's capital, Hanoi. A succession of young leftists and idealists, notably the film star **Jane Fonda,** had visited Hanoi. McCarthy, who by then was in her mid-50s, added weight to the American antiwar movement by lending it the prestige of her reputation and was already a regular speaker on the antiwar and draft-resisters' circuit. Her visit to Hanoi was an embarrassment to her husband, an American State Department official, but he supported her work and agreed to her going. Even so, her books *Vietnam, Hanoi, The Seventeenth Parallel,* and *Medina* (about one of the My Lai massacre defendants) were far less successful than her fiction and won an audience only among other outspoken foes of the war, rather than the large, uncertain center of the American population which she had hoped to sway.

In the 1970s, McCarthy resumed the writing of fiction with two fine novels, *Birds of America* (1971) and *Cannibals and Missionaries* (1979), weaving, as before, episodes of her own life and those of her friends into imaginary dramatic settings. *Cannibals and Missionaries,* which describes the fate of a group of art collectors when their airliner is hijacked by Iranian terrorists, came out at the same time as the national trauma of the Iranian "hostage crisis." In the 1980s, as she entered her 70s, McCarthy took up the writing of memoirs, the first volume of which was *How I Grew.* She had always had the power to shock readers, as had been clear with "The Man in the Brooks Brothers Suit." She now did it again by describing her teenage sexual encounters, in graphic and unsparing detail, to the surprise of many of her friends, and followed up this first memoir by writing two more, one on her intellectual life and friends in the New York of the late 1930s, the other on her stormy relationship with Edmund Wilson. Mary McCarthy died of lung cancer in 1989 after a succession of illnesses, at the age of 77.

SOURCES:
Brightman, Carol. *Writing Dangerously: Mary McCarthy and Her World.* NY: Clarkson Potter, 1992.
Gelderman, Carol. *Mary McCarthy: A Life.* NY: St. Martin's Press, 1988.
Grumbach, Doris. *The Company She Kept.* NY: Coward-McCann, 1967.
McCarthy, Mary. *How I Grew.* NY: Harcourt, 1987.
———. *Intellectual Memoirs: New York: 1936–1938.* NY: Harcourt, 1992.
———. *Memories of a Catholic Girlhood.* NY: Harcourt, 1957.
Meyers, Jeffrey. *Edmund Wilson: A Biography.* Boston, MA: Houghton Mifflin, 1995.

SUGGESTED READING:

Brightman, Carol, ed. *Between Friends: The Correspondence between *Hannah Arendt and Mary McCarthy, 1949–1975*. NY: Harcourt, 1995.

Kiernan, Frances. *Seeing Mary Plain*. NY: W.W. Norton, 2000.

COLLECTIONS:

Mary McCarthy Papers, Vassar College Library; Edmund Wilson Papers, Yale University Library.

Patrick Allitt,
Professor of History, Emory University, Atlanta, Georgia

McCarthy, Maud (1858–1949)

Nurse and Matron-in-Chief of the British armed forces during World War I. Name variations: Dame Maud McCarthy; Emma Maud McCarthy. Born in 1858, in Sydney, Australia; died in 1949.

Maud McCarthy was born in Sydney, Australia, then a dominion of Great Britain, in 1858. She traveled to England to train in nursing at the London Hospital, and after completing her courses entered the nursing service of the British armed forces. McCarthy went to South Africa as an army nurse during the Boer War from 1899 to 1902, and upon the war's end entered Queen Alexandra's Imperial Military Nursing Service. She remained in that post until 1910, when she was named principal matron of the War Office. At the outbreak of World War I in August 1914, McCarthy was named Matron-in-Chief of the British armies in France. Her services to the British Empire were formally recognized in 1918, when she was created Dame Grand Cross of the Order of the British Empire (GBE) and allowed to use the title "Dame." After the British armies in continental Europe returned to Britain in 1919, Maud McCarthy headed the Territorial Nursing Service from 1920 to 1925. She died in 1949.

COLLECTIONS:

Letters and a small collection of papers of Maud McCarthy are held at the Queen Alexandra's Royal Army Nursing Corps Museum in Aldershot, Hampshire, England.

Grant Eldridge,
freelance writer, Pontiac, Michigan

McCartney, Linda (1941–1998)

American photographer, vegetarian cookbook author, entrepreneur, animal-rights activist and wife of Paul McCartney. Name variations: Linda Eastman. Born Linda Louise Eastman on September 24, 1941, in Scarsdale, New York; died of breast cancer in Tucson, Arizona, on April 17, 1998; daughter of Lee V. Eastman (an entertainment lawyer) and Louise (Linder) Eastman; graduated from Scarsdale High School,
1959; attended University of Arizona in Tucson; married Joseph Melville See (a geology student), around 1960 (divorced 1963); married Paul McCartney (British composer, musician, and member of the Beatles), on March 12, 1969; children: (first marriage) Heather See (a potter); (second marriage) **Mary McCartney** (a photographer); **Stella McCartney** (a fashion designer); James McCartney (a musician).

Discovered photography while a student at University of Arizona; moved to New York City with daughter (1965); began career as a photographer (1966), getting exclusive photos of the Rolling Stones rock band; specialized in photos of pop and rock bands, often at the beginning of their careers; photographed the Beatles in London (1967), and met Paul McCartney; continued to pursue career as a rock photographer, with work published in magazines around the world, while conducting an on-and-off romance with McCartney; moved to London to live with McCartney (1968); married McCartney (1969); sang harmonies on husband's solo albums post-Beatles (1970–71); became a vegetarian in early 1970s, campaigned for animal rights until her death; sang and played keyboards despite no musical training with husband's band Wings (1971–80), and with husband's unnamed band (1980–97); published first cookbook (1989); launched McVege line of frozen vegetarian products (1991); company had grown to sales of $50 million by 1998; first solo album, 20 years in the making, released posthumously; photographs appeared in two posthumous exhibits: in Liverpool, England, and as part of a traveling exhibit of Rolling Stone magazine covers (1998).

Selected writings: Linda's Pictures: A Collection of Photographs (Random House, 1976); Photographs (Simon & Schuster, 1982); Linda McCartney's Sun Prints (Salem House, 1989); Linda McCartney's Home Cooking (Arcade Pub., 1989); Linda McCartney's Sixties: Portrait of an Era (Bulfinch Press, 1992); Linda's Kitchen: Simple and Inspiring Recipes for Meatless Meals (Little, Brown, 1995); Roadworks (Bulfinch Press, 1996); Linda McCartney on Tour: 200 Meat-Free Dishes from Around the World (Little, Brown, 1998).

Album credits: (backing vocals) McCartney (Apple/Capitol, 1970); (with husband) Ram (Apple/Capitol, 1971), McCartney II (Columbia, 1980), Tug of War (Columbia, 1982), Pipes of Peace (Columbia, 1983), Give My Regards to Broad Street (Columbia, 1984), Press to Play (Capitol, 1986), All the Best (Capitol, 1987), Flowers in the Dirt (Capitol, 1989), Tripping the Live Fantastic (Capitol, 1990), Off the Ground (Capitol, 1993), Flaming Pie (1997); (with

Wings) Wildlife *(Apple/Capitol, 1971),* Red Rose Speedway *(Apple/Capitol, 1973),* Band on the Run *(Apple/Capitol, 1973),* Venus and Mars *(Capitol, 1975),* Wings at the Speed of Sound *(Capitol, 1976),* Wings Over America *(Capitol, 1976),* London Town *(Capitol, 1978),* Wings' Greatest *(Capitol, 1978),* Back to the Egg *(Columbia, 1979); (with husband, as Suzy and the Red Stripes) single "Seaside Woman" (1977), single "The White-Coated Man" (1994); (solo)* Wide Prairie *(1998).*

Films: Give My Regards to Broad Street *(1984);* Get Back *(1991).*

Linda McCartney, a non-technical photographer who could not be bothered much with shutter speeds and f-stops, nonetheless produced an impressive body of work, resulting in several published photography collections. As a nonviolent animal-rights activist and passionate proponent of vegetarianism, she also authored cookbooks and established a successful business featuring a line of frozen vegetarian products. As well, she was an indifferent vocalist and keyboard player who freely admitted her lack of talent, but her enduring celebrity resulted from her 29-year marriage to Paul McCartney of the Beatles, the seminal British rock band of the 1960s.

Born Linda Louise Eastman in 1941 in Scarsdale, New York, she was one of four children, and grew up in a wealthy and artistic environment. Her mother **Louise Linder Eastman** was an heiress, the daughter of the head of the Linder department store chain. Her father Lee V. Eastman, the son of Russian-Jewish immigrants named Epstein, was a self-made man who received a scholarship to Harvard University when he was 16, changed his last name to Eastman, and became a show-business lawyer. His friends and clients, who were frequent dinner guests, included Hopalong Cassidy, Fritz Kline, Hoagy Carmichael, and Willem de Kooning. One of them, composer Jack Lawrence, wrote the song "Linda" for Eastman's six-year-old daughter. A hit in 1947 for Buddy Clark, it was later recorded by both Perry Como and the duo Jan and Dean.

An animal lover even as a child, Linda recalled for *OK Magazine* that she "was forever filling the house with injured squirrels or birds that needed nursing." She was very close to her mother, who died in a plane crash when Linda was 18. Moving to Tucson, for a time she studied art history at the University of Arizona, where she was an unexceptional student. (She did not attend Sarah Lawrence College, as has often been written.) At 19, she married geology

student Joseph Melville See, with whom she had a daughter, **Heather See**, before the marriage ended in 1963.

Discovering photography through her friend **Hazel Archer**, Linda was struck by the idea that photography could be art. "Photography made me a different person," she told Barry Miles, "because it was something I loved doing and just nothing else mattered." Without formal training, she learned by trial and error. When a visiting Shakespearean actor performing in Tucson asked her to take a publicity still, it resulted in her first published photo, in the British actors' directory *Spotlight.*

Moving to New York City with her daughter in 1965, Linda found employment as a receptionist at *Town and Country* magazine. In that position, she was able to intercept a press pass for a Rolling Stones press conference in 1966. Because the reception was being held on a yacht, space was limited, and a decision had been made to bar all photographers. Wrote Miles, "Linda refused to take no for an answer, and the Stones . . . so enjoyed the ensuing argument that they . . . let her stay." As the only photographer present, she was in a unique position; the journalists begged for her photos to go with their copy, and valuable contacts were made. As a result, Linda quit her job to pursue photography full time. Australian rock critic **Lillian Roxon** began to use her work in her *Sydney Morning Herald* column. Linda also did publicity stills for the Blues Project, a rock band, and soon was making a decent living. Her photos of the British supergroup Cream were included in the first issue of *Rolling Stone* magazine, and she continued to photograph many of the practitioners of rock before it became an industry, including Bob Dylan, the Doors, *Janis Joplin, Simon and Garfunkel, Frank Zappa, and Jimi Hendrix. "There are few rock photographers with such a complete portfolio of sixties stars, in most cases taken at the very beginning of their career[s]," wrote Miles. "Linda always used natural light, never flash, which partially accounts for the intimate feeling of her portraits." Her collection would be published in 1992 as *Linda McCartney's Sixties: Portrait of an Era.*

In 1967, while photographing the Beatles in London, she met Paul McCartney; their romance was off-and-on for the next year. Although she was becoming well known in her field and her income was rising, by 1968 she had become disenchanted with the evolving big-business atmosphere of the music industry. That September, at Paul's invitation, the 25-year-old Linda moved to

London, where their relationship flourished. Heather was brought over to join them, and the couple married on March 12, 1969, at London's Marylebone Registry Office. The Beatles had released the *White Album* in 1968 and would release both *Yellow Submarine* and *Abbey Road* in 1969; their fame was enormous, and Paul was the last unattached member of the band. Huge crowds of weeping female fans jammed the sidewalks in front of the registry office, although the wedding was supposed to have been a secret. Linda paid dearly for marrying Paul. "They would get back home and there was graffiti—American Slut Go Home," said her friend Danny Fields. "She had to deal with the hatred of fans. That was a difficult time for her."

But when the Beatles disbanded in 1970, *Entertainment Weekly* observed that Linda "more easily sidestepped the 'she broke up the Beatles' accusations that dogged **Yoko Ono**. . . . Indeed, with her grace and affability, Linda came to be seen as the good Beatle wife." Paul persuaded her to sing harmony on his first two post-Beatles solo albums, *McCartney* (1970) and *Ram* (1971). Although she was untrained musically, he wanted her with him as a member of Wings, the band he formed in 1971. "Her unpolished vocals invited derision," noted *People*, and although she frequently thought of quitting, a stubborn dislike of being told what to do and the lure of being with her husband always held sway. She stayed in the band, and the couple toured and performed together for many years; eventually, the fans were won over. In addition to her contributions to Wings, Linda wrote a few songs of her own. Two of these, "Seaside Woman" (1977) and "The White-Coated Man" (co-written with **Carla Lane**, 1994) were recorded with her husband under the name Suzy and the Red Stripes. As well, Paul has long told interviewers that any love song he has written since 1968 has been written for his wife, including "The Lovely Linda" and "My Love."

In the early 1970s, the McCartneys sat down to a meal of lamb, only to observe lambs ambling about outside their window. In that moment, they became vegetarians and advocates for animal rights. Linda's activism led the McCartneys to campaign against veal crates in France, to write letters to governments protesting whale hunting, and to spend thousands of pounds to save animals from slaughterhouses or testing facilities. The animal-rights group People for the Ethical Treatment of Animals (PETA) awarded the McCartneys its Lifetime Achievement Award in 1996. The first of her vegetarian cookbooks, *Linda McCartney's Home Cooking*, was published in 1989. It was a bestseller in the United States and the biggest-selling cookbook ever in Great Britain. She also published *Linda's Kitchen* (1995) and had finished putting together *Linda McCartney on Tour* (1998), which featured 200 international vegetarian recipes, just before her death. In 1991, she introduced a successful line of frozen vegetarian foods called McVege; by 1998, sales had reached $50 million. Linda once noted that "vegetarianism isn't a business for me, it's a mission."

In 1995, Linda McCartney was diagnosed with breast cancer. With aggressive treatment, it was thought that she was beating the illness, but in March 1998 she received word that the disease had spread to her liver. She died the following month, while vacationing with her family in Tucson. (In an effort to deflect the attention of the press, an emissary for the family initially announced that she had died in Santa Barbara, California.) Her ashes were scattered at the family's estate in Sussex, England.

Following her death, several of her projects were brought to completion. Her last cookbook was published, and a photographic exhibit was mounted in Liverpool, England. An album, *Wide Prairie*, featuring 13 songs Linda had written over a 20-year period, was finished and released in 1998. Paul vowed to keep alive her crusade for animal rights, and two California performances of his *Standing Stone* Symphony were dedicated to her memory.

Mary Riddell, in recognition of Linda's stable 29-year marriage to a public icon, suggested in the *New Statesman* that despite her activism, talent and bravery, perhaps the most important aspect of Linda McCartney's legacy was her fulfillment of the role of wife and mother. (It has often been noted that in the course of their marriage the McCartneys never spent a night apart, except for Paul's short stint in jail for marijuana possession in 1980.) Calling the marriage "a bucolic vista of family togetherness and contented children," Riddell noted that Linda "exemplified the success of a mutually supporting, enduring relationship although McCartney herself noted that all marriages are difficult. She showed couple power was more exciting than power couples."

Linda McCartney's photographic work appeared on her husband's album covers for years, and has been shown all over the world, including exhibits at the International Center for Photography in New York City, the National Museum of Photography in Yorkshire, England, London's Victoria and Albert Museum, and the Royal Photographic Society in Bath, England. The first woman to shoot a *Rolling Stone* magazine cover (May 11, 1968), and the only woman both to have photographed (three) as well as appeared on *Rolling Stone* covers (twice, with her husband), she was represented in the touring commemorative show "30 Years of *Rolling Stone* covers," launched in May 1998. "I've had all sorts of labels stuck on me," she told *OK Magazine* in March 1998. "Now the new label is 'businesswoman.' Sure, I have this business. But what I am, what I am in myself, is a photographer."

SOURCES:

The Day [New London, CT]. April 20, 1998; April 22, 1998.

Entertainment Weekly. May 1, 1998.

Helander, Brock. *The Rock Who's Who,* 2nd ed. NY: Schirmer Books, 1996.

The International Who's Who 1998–99. 62nd ed. London: Europa Publications, 1998.

Kansas City Star [MO]. April 19, 1998.

Los Angeles Times. July 21, 1998.

Media Industry Newsletter. April 27, 1998.

Miles, Barry. *Paul McCartney: Many Years From Now.* NY: Henry Holt, 1997.

The New York Times. April 20, 1998; May 20, 2000.

OK Magazine. March 6, 1998.

People Weekly. May 4, 1998.

Press-Enterprise [Riverside, CA]. August 7, 1998; September 4, 1998; September 18, 1998.

Riddell, Mary. *New Statesman.* April 24, 1998.

SUGGESTED READING:

Fields, Danny. *Linda McCartney: A Portrait.* Renaissance, 2000.

RELATED MEDIA:

"The Linda McCartney Story" (television movie), starring **Elizabeth Mitchell** and Gary Bakewell, was first shown on CBS on May 21, 2000.

Ellen Dennis French, freelance writer in biography, Murrieta, California

McCauley, Catharine (1778–1841).

See McAuley, Catharine.

McCauley, Mary Ludwig Hays (1754–1832).

See "Two Mollies."

McClain, Katrina (1965—)

American basketball player. Born on September 19, 1965, in Atlanta, Georgia; daughter of Edward McClain (an A.M.E. minister and former Baltimore Colts running back) and Sara McClain; graduated from the University of Georgia.

Two-time All-America selection as a basketball player at the University of Georgia; named National Player of the Year and Southeast Conference Player of the Year (1987); member of the U.S. women's Olympic basketball teams (1992 and 1996).

The daughter of **Sara McClain** and former Baltimore Colts running back Edward McClain, Katrina McClain was born in Atlanta, Georgia, on September 19, 1965, and grew up with her five sisters and two brothers in Charleston, North Carolina. Katrina quickly showed an aptitude for playing basketball and, at 6'2", became a star player with the University of Georgia. While a collegian, McClain was twice named to the All-America team, and she was recognized as the National Player of the Year and the Southeast Conference Player of the Year in 1987. In her senior year, McClain averaged 24.9 points and 9.5 rebounds per game.

Katrina McClain graduated from college at a time when there was no professional women's basketball league in the United States. She therefore started her professional career overseas, playing for Kyodo Petroleum in Japan from 1988 to 1991. She continued to play for professional leagues in Italy and Spain until the fledgling American Basketball League started up in 1996. Although the Atlanta Glory team drafted her that year, she opted for a more lucrative deal with a Turkish team, Istanbul's Galatasary club. After her year-long stint overseas, she returned to Atlanta to become a cornerstone of the Glory team, shooting 52.5% from the floor and averaging more than 14 points and 8 rebounds per game.

McClain twice represented the United States in the Olympic Games, playing on the 1992 team, which captured the bronze medal, and on the 1996 gold medal-winning squad. She is the all-time U.S. women's Olympic scoring leader, with 258 points and an average of more than 8 rebounds per game.

Grant Eldridge, freelance writer, Pontiac, Michigan

McClements, Lyn (1951—)

Australian swimmer. Born in 1951, in Nedlands, Western Australia.

Lyn McClements was born in the small town of Nedlands, Western Australia, in 1951. She participated in competitive swimming from an early age, but began to focus on the butterfly stroke after coming under the tutelage of coach Kevin Duff in 1967. The following year, she captured the state senior titles in the 100- and 200-meter butterfly stroke, with times impressive enough to secure her a position on the 1968 Australian Olympic team. Although she did not win an individual medal at the Mexico City games, she swam the butterfly on the 4x100-meter medley team that captured the silver medal. Mc-

Clements was disqualified at the 1970 Australian championships, and subsequently retired from competition. After a long layoff, she returned to swimming to participate in senior events.

Grant Eldridge,
freelance writer, Pontiac, Michigan

McClendon, Rosalie "Rose"
(1884–1936).

See Women of the Harlem Renaissance.

McClintock, Barbara (1902–1992)

Outstanding researcher in the field of genetics who discovered the way genetic material moves and alters chromosomes, and therefore heredity, winning the Nobel Prize for her pioneering work. Pronunciation: Mc-CLIN-tock. *Born on June 16, 1902, in Hartford, Connecticut; died at the Huntington Hospital on Long Island, New York, on September 2, 1992; third of four children of Thomas Henry McClintock (a physician) and Sara (Handy) McClintock; graduated from Cornell University, B.S., 1923, M.A., 1925, Ph.D. in botany, 1927; never married; no children.*

Awards: honorary doctorates in science from the University of Rochester (1947), Western College (1949), Smith College (1958), University of Missouri (1968), Williams College (1972), Rockefeller University (1979), Harvard University (1979). Kimber Genetics Award, National Academy of Sciences (1967); National Medal of Science (1970); Rosenstiel Award from Brandeis University (1978); Albert Lasker Basic Medical Research Award (1981); Wolf Foundation Prize from Israel (1981); (shared with Susumu Tonegawa) Horwitz Prize, Columbia University (1982); MacArthur Laureate Award (annual lifetime award, $60,000 tax-free); Nobel Prize in Physiology or Medicine (1983).

Following the birth of her brother (1904), lived periodically with her father's aunt and uncle in Massachusetts; family moved to the Flatbush section of Brooklyn, New York (1908); graduated Erasmus Hall High School, Brooklyn (1918); worked in an employment agency; enrolled in Cornell University (1919), majoring in biology; studied graduate-level genetics while working on her bachelor's degree; began studies of plant genetics at Cornell which had an active research program in the Agriculture College; worked with maize (Indian corn); granted doctorate at age 25 (1927); began publishing research papers (1929); awarded fellowship by the National Research Council; divided time conducting research for two years at Cornell University, the University of Missouri, and the California Institute of Technology; received Guggen-

heim fellowship to work in Berlin at the Kaiser Wilhelm Institute (1933); returned to U.S. after witnessing rise of Nazism in Germany; worked in research at Cornell; became assistant professor at the University of Missouri (1936), teaching and conducting research; became vice-president of the Genetics Society of America (1939); began working at the Cold Spring Harbor Laboratory on Long Island, New York (1941); joined staff of the Carnegie Institution (1941–67); became president of the Genetics Society of America (1944); experimented with chromosomes in maize (1940s), making many original discoveries; presented findings (1951); trained Latin American cytologists in methods of conducting research of maize (1958–60); appointed Andrew White professor-at-large by Cornell University (1965); gained recognition for her discoveries (1970s); worked at Cold Spring Harbor Laboratory until the end of her life.

Selected writings: The Discovery and Characterization of Transposable Elements: The Collected Papers of Barbara McClintock *(NY: Garland Press, 1987); many journal articles and speeches.*

Barbara McClintock, who conducted research in genetics, made immensely important discoveries about the nature of genes and chromosomes years before other researchers. She found that genes can move around chromosomes to form new heredity patterns, a discovery that did not fit the prevailing thinking which pictured genes as fixed and stable segments of chromosomes. McClintock worked independently and intensely, and for a long time her work was not understood by her peers, though she was well respected in the field. She persisted throughout her life in her goal of conducting important research in a male-dominated field that discouraged women from attaining leadership roles. Recognition that Barbara McClintock was one of the geniuses in the history of genetics finally came when her theories of genetic transposition were confirmed.

Barbara McClintock's mother **Sara Handy McClintock** came from a distinguished Massachusetts family that could trace its ancestry to the *Mayflower*. When Sara wanted to marry Thomas Henry McClintock, there was a great deal of opposition, because Thomas, whose parents had immigrated to the United States from Great Britain, was perceived as a foreigner. As well, he had run off to sea in his teens and was now a medical student, incapable of supporting a family. Sara married Thomas in 1898, against her father's wishes and aware that he would not aid them financially. Instead, she used some of her own funds from an inheritance and, over the years, gave piano lessons to earn income. The McClintocks were an attractive, intelligent, and compatible couple who supported each other during difficult times, especially when their children were young and Thomas was starting his medical practice.

On June 16, 1902, Barbara McClintock was born in Hartford, Connecticut, the third daughter, following sisters **Marjorie** and **Mignon**, and a disappointment to her parents who had wanted a son. She was originally called Eleanor, but that delicate appellation did not suit the independent child, so her name was changed to Barbara. Though she loved her family, she felt she did not quite belong. After a son, Malcolm Rider McClintock (called Tom), was born in 1904, the strain of raising four young children proved too trying for Sara McClintock, so Barbara was sent to live on-and-off with her father's aunt and uncle in a small town in Massachusetts. (Sara herself had lived with an aunt and uncle in California after her mother died when she was a year old.) Barbara enjoyed Massachusetts and would often accompany her uncle, a fish vendor, when he made his rounds with horse and wagon. She learned about the natural and mechanical worlds, particularly after a truck replaced the horse. When she was old enough to attend school, she moved home permanently.

The thrill comes from being intensely absorbed in the material.

—Barbara McClintock

In 1908, the McClintocks moved to Flatbush, in Brooklyn, New York, which—unlike Hartford, an already developing city—had some untouched areas that allowed the children to explore nature. The McClintocks would have agreed with some modern-day theories on child-raising; for example, they believed that children should have freedom to do what they wanted and not be bound by rules. Thomas McClintock cautioned the children's teachers that they were not to be assigned homework, and when the youngsters wanted a day off from school, or disliked a teacher, they were allowed to stay home. Barbara enjoyed playing street games with her brother and his friends; her parents had bloomers made for her so that she could be as active as a boy, playing football and climbing trees (later she would wear slacks for her work in the corn fields). McClintock had boxing gloves and ice skates as well, yet she also enjoyed spending time alone reading and thinking. Her outdoor activities irritated a neighbor who advised Barbara to take up more feminine pastimes. Sara McClintock informed the woman that she was never to interfere with her daughter again.

The McClintock youngsters attended Erasmus Hall High School, where they were good students and where Barbara discovered her love of science. During her adolescence, she felt different from her peers. She was uninterested in boys or clothes but had a keen intellectual curiosity and an eagerness to learn. Although the McClintock sisters were extremely intelligent, Sara discouraged them from attending college, believing that higher education was a hindrance to marriage. Although Barbara wanted to attend Cornell, she settled for working as an interviewer at an employment agency and studying at the library.

Thomas McClintock had been away, serving in the military as a surgeon during the First World War. At war's end in 1918, he returned home and convinced his wife to allow their third-born daughter to travel to Cornell and register. The fact that the College of Agriculture did not charge tuition may have helped, because one of Sara's arguments had been the family's lack of money.

Barbara enjoyed an active social life in college: she was elected president of the women's freshman class and became friends with a group of young women, most of whom were Jewish. She learned some Yiddish, and rejected a sorority bid when she realized that her friends would not be included. Friendly and attractive, Barbara McClintock dated frequently but soon realized that close personal attachments and marriage were not what she had in mind. She was the first woman on campus to have her hair cut short in a "shingle," causing a stir, because women wore their hair long at that time. But life was changing for women. In the United States, after many years of struggle, women won the right to vote after Congress passed the 19th Amendment to the Constitution in 1920. In the '20s, many young women began cutting their hair (the "bobbed" look), wearing pants, and smoking cigarettes, as did Barbara McClintock.

As a college senior, she played a banjo in a jazz band, but quit when she realized that she could not spare the time. McClintock found that she loved to immerse herself in her work, and chose to focus on biology. At the time, many young women were attending college, often women's colleges. In the U.S., women comprised between 30 and 40% of all graduate students during the decade, and accounted for approximately 12% of the science and engineering Ph.D.s awarded, a proportion not seen again until the 1970s.

Barbara
McClintock

During the 1920s, researchers at Cornell's College of Agriculture were investigating plant genetics, using maize (Indian corn), an ideal plant to analyze because kernels come in a variety of colors, blue, brown, and red, indicating to the naked eye that changes occur from generation to generation. McClintock, who studied genetics as an undergraduate, wanted to continue to do so in graduate school, but she had to remain in the botany department because women could not matriculate in the plant-breeding department that taught genetics. Lester Sharp, a cytology professor, taught McClintock methods of studying cells. She had already mastered some of the techniques and in fact had discovered how to identify the chromosomes in maize while working for another cytologist who had been trying to solve this problem for quite some time.

McClintock proved to be brilliant both at the meticulous care needed to prepare slides of the various stages of cell division in maize and at the interpretation of what was going on. "When I look at a cell," she said, "I get down in that cell and look around. . . . You're not conscious of anything else. . . . You are so absorbed that even small things get big. . . . Nothing else matters. You're noticing more and more things that most people couldn't see because they didn't go intently over each part, slowly but with great intensity. . . . It's the intensity of your absorption. I'm sure painters have the same thing happen right along."

McClintock's responsibilities included planting, growing, tending, and pollinating the maize plants in a field. The plants required full days of hard work: tagging, watering, and watching. Pollination had to be carefully done to ensure that only certain pollen would fertilize a particular ear of corn. If there was too much rain, the plants could be washed out and would have to be replanted. "No two plants are exactly alike," said McClintock. "They're all different, and as a consequence, you have to know that difference. . . . I start with the seedling, and I don't want to leave it. I don't feel I really know the story if I don't watch the plant all the way along. So I know every plant in the field. I know them intimately, and I find it a great pleasure to know them."

Many brilliant young scientists were drawn to Cornell for their doctorates during that era because of the exciting work that was being done under the leadership of Rollins A. Emerson, the foremost maize geneticist of the day. In 1927, after attaining her doctorate, 25-year-old McClintock worked at Cornell as an instructor. Even before she finished her degree, she had become the leader of a group of doctoral students and graduates: Marcus Rhoades, George Beadle, Charles Burnham, Harold Perry, and H.W. Lee. They shared an enthusiasm for the subject, worked long hours at their research, and stimulated each other into advancing the boundaries of knowledge in the field. Said Rhoades, "I've known a lot of famous scientists. But the only one I thought really was a genius was McClintock."

In 1929, 20-year-old **Harriet Creighton** arrived at Cornell to undertake graduate studies, and McClintock became her mentor and friend. They worked together, designing experiments to prove that genetic material accompanies the exchange of chromosomal matter during cell division. When the well-known scientist Thomas Hunt Morgan asked them about their progress, he urged them to publish the information. Another scientist, working with fruit flies, was coming to the same conclusions, but the Cornell team published first, in 1931. McClintock would publish nine important journal articles about her work between 1929 and 1931, but her male colleagues were more assured of their future careers. A woman's options in science were limited: she could teach in a woman's college, accept an instructor's position in a university where she might be hired, or, if her husband were a scientist, assist him in his work. But she could not become a research scientist.

Rollins Emerson, who was the department chair, thought highly of McClintock's work, but the faculty refused to hire a woman to join them. Though McClintock was frustrated in her career, between 1931 and 1936 she had research fellowships at Cornell, the California Institute of Technology, and the University of Missouri. She criss-crossed the country in her Model-A Ford and was known as a daring driver.

Cornell had become home for McClintock, partly because of a friendship with Dr. **Esther Parker**, a physician who had treated McClintock when she was ill and had invited her to convalesce in her home, which was a temporary haven for many students. But McClintock realized, with regret, that she needed to move on, despite the support she had obtained for her research, be-

cause her position at Cornell was not permanent. In 1933, McClintock was awarded a Guggenheim fellowship to study in Berlin with Richard B. Goldschmidt, head of the Kaiser Wilhelm Institute. But the rise of Nazism and the persecution of Jews troubled her deeply, and she returned to the United States. "It was a very, very traumatic experience," she said. "I was just unprepared."

Lewis Stadler, at the University of Missouri, was raising maize from irradiated kernels because X-rays increased the speed of mutations (changes), and he asked McClintock to investigate the genetic changes in the mature plants. In doing so, she made some fundamental discoveries: that chromosomes are physically broken by X-rays and that they rejoin, sometimes in rings, sometimes breaking again. She called this the "breakage-fusion-bridge cycle." In 1936, when the University of Missouri offered McClintock a position as assistant professor, she accepted. Though she had excellent research privileges, she was not treated well and never felt a part of the faculty, despite the fact that her reputation as a geneticist continued to grow. Realizing that she would be fired if her mentor Stadler were no longer there, she left in 1941.

That summer, she joined her friend Marcus Rhoades at the Cold Spring Harbor Laboratory, a research facility on Long Island, New York. The Carnegie Institution of Washington at Cold Spring Harbor first hired McClintock for a year, and then permanently. She would work there for the rest of her life, living in a small apartment nearby but spending most of her time in her lab, corn field, or greenhouse. Always fond of mechanical things, McClintock took her microscopes apart, cleaned, and reassembled them. She took good care of her cars as well, changing her own tires until she was 80. While at Cold Spring Harbor, McClintock would receive some important recognition: she was listed in *American Men of Science*, became the first woman president of the Genetics Society of America, and was elected to the National Academy of Science. Only two other women had become members in 81 years.

During the 1940s, McClintock conducted the experiments that led to her discoveries of "jumping genes," the movement of genes from one place to another in the chromosomes, which thus change the expected patterns of heredity. These discoveries were in opposition to current theories of the time that held that genes were in fixed positions. Further, she found that chromosomes actually exchange genetic material, and that there are controlling factors signaling the genes to be active or passive. One of these factors was the Dissociation locus (Ds). Upon insertion next to the gene responsible for pigment production, the Ds caused that gene to stop functioning; that is, it acted as the equivalent of a mutation. Any subsequent movement of Ds to another location resulted in the restoration of the pigment-producing gene to its normal function. These discoveries were extremely important to the understanding of heredity in all living organisms.

McClintock presented her findings at Cold Spring Harbor in 1951, but the information was so new, dense, and contrary to the thinking at the time that her audience did not understand or accept her theories. She was vindicated, however, later in the 1950s, when molecular biologists, using powerful new tools (crystallographic techniques and X-ray diffraction patterns), found the basic double helix structure of DNA, which comprises genes. "Gene splicing" in the 1970s was possible because of scientists' further knowledge about genes and the technical tools that were developed: micromanipulators, enzymes, or other molecules, which accomplish the fine work of removing, cutting, and inserting the submicroscopic genes into cells.

One of the amazing facts about McClintock's work was that she used the techniques of "observation, documentation, and microscopic analysis" to uncover new data. Young scientists objected to such old-fashioned methods, but McClintock was a superb observer: she knew each corn plant intimately and understood more from her observations than other scientists. It was her amazing intellect and attunement to her work that facilitated her discoveries. McClintock was a voracious reader; she read everything from biology to biography to Tibetan Buddhism and felt that there were important roads to knowledge outside Western traditions.

From 1958 to 1960, McClintock trained cytologists from Latin America to collect and identify indigenous maize, because modern maize seeds were crowding out the native strains. She studied the geographical distribution of the corn and discovered that they formed a map of old patterns of human commerce and travel. Twice a year, for many years, she visited sites in South America where a great deal of research on maize was conducted. Always ready to learn, she prepared for her Latin American trips by mastering Spanish, which she augmented by watching Spanish television.

Many scientists who make landmark contributions to human knowledge are not honored for decades, often because their peers have not caught up to them. McClintock's recognition was characteristic: she received many honors and awards from science organizations in the 1970s and 1980s for work she had done in the 1940s, as well as the MacArthur "genius" award of $60,000 a year for life, and the Nobel Prize for Medicine or Physiology in 1983, which the scientific community by then expected her to receive.

The slight, 5'-tall McClintock was known to be forthright, energetic, and private. Her biographers **Evelyn Fox Keller** and **Sharon Bertsch McGrayne** present two very different views of their subject. Keller sees McClintock as a "brilliant recluse, a mystic," but McGrayne writes that McClintock's friends "stressed that McClintock was neither a recluse nor a mystic." She herself, upon receiving the Nobel Prize, simply noted, "It may seem unfair . . . to reward a person for having so much pleasure, over the years, asking the maize plant to solve specific problems and then watching its responses." Barbara McClintock, whose immense intelligence and curiosity about life were coupled with a wry sense of humor, lived a full life, working until the end, dying of old age in her 90th year.

SOURCES:

"Barbara McClintock," in *Current Biography*. NY: H.W. Wilson, 1984.

Hammond, Allen L. *A Passion to Know: 20 Profiles in Science*. NY: Scribner, 1984.

Keller, Evelyn Fox. *A Feeling for the Organism: The Life and Work of Barbara McClintock*. NY: W.H. Freeman, 1983.

McGrayne, Sharon Bertsch. *Nobel Prize Women in Science: Their Lives, Struggles, and Momentous Discoveries*. NY: Carol Publishing, 1993.

The New York Times (obituary). September 4, 1992, Section A, p. 1.

SUGGESTED READING:

Dash, Joan. *The Triumph of Discovery: Women Scientists Who Won the Nobel Prize*. Englewood Cliffs, NJ: Julian Messner, 1991.

Dr. Evelyn Bender,
librarian, Philadelphia, Pennsylvania, School District

McClung, Nellie L. (1873–1951)

Canadian suffragist, temperance activist, politician, writer, and public speaker who was a crucial force in the fight for women's political and legal rights. Born Nellie Letitia Mooney on October 20, 1873, in Grey County, Ontario; died on September 1, 1951, in her home outside Victoria, British Columbia; daughter of John Mooney and Letitia (McCurdy) Mooney; married R.W. (Wes) McClung; children: four sons and one daughter.

Selected writings: Sowing Seeds in Danny (1908); Purple Springs (1921, reprinted with a new introduc-

tion by *Randi R. Warne, University of Toronto Press, 1993*); Clearing in the West: My Own Story (*Thomas Allen & Son, 1935*); The Stream Runs Fast: My Own Story (*Thomas Allen & Son, 1945*).

Born on October 20, 1873, Nellie Letitia McClung was the sixth and last child of John and **Letitia Mooney**. John Mooney had arrived in Canada from Ireland at age 18 to escape the famine and hardship that plagued his homeland. In 1858, he married Letitia McCurdy, a recent immigrant from Scotland, and established a farm in Grey County, Ontario. From childhood, Nellie was influenced by the contrasting personalities of her parents. John Mooney, warm and affectionate with a lively sense of humor, enjoyed joking and playing with his young daughter. Letitia, however, perhaps due to her Scottish Presbyterian background, was much sterner. Deeply religious and hard-working, she frowned upon these playful antics. Despite a childhood preference for her father, McClung as an adult was the product of both parents. Active participation in politics, social reform, writing, and motherhood was accomplished through tireless energy and hard work. Yet in all these activities, Nellie was guided by values derived from religious conviction and a lively sense of humor, both of which colored her work and endeared her to people.

Farming in Grey County was a hard life. The last area of the province to be colonized for farming, its land was poor, making only bare subsistence possible. However, by the 1870s the Canadian west was finally beginning to open up to settlement. Glowing reports of plentiful and productive land began to filter into Ontario with the commencement of railway construction and government suppression of western native populations. By 1879, Letitia and her eldest son, Will, had decided the family would go west. Will went ahead, staking out a large plot of land for the family 80 miles southwest of Portage La Prairie (near present-day Wawanesa, Manitoba). A year later, the rest of the family followed. The first settlers in the area, the Mooneys were at the forefront of a migration that was to populate the Canadian west within 30 years.

For six-year-old Nellie, the move west and homesteading was an adventure, remembered fondly in later life. Within several years, a small community had sprung up around the family, bringing with it services such as schools and social interaction. Naturally, it also brought with it the propriety of eastern society. Reflecting back, McClung remembered being stung by the sexual inequality present even within a frontier society. Writing in 1935, she described a picnic planned for the summer of 1882:

> A committee was formed and a program of sports arranged. . . . I was hoping there would be a race for girls under ten, or that girls might enter with the boys. But the whole question of girls competing in races was frowned on. Skirts would fly upward and legs would show! And it was not nice for little girls, or big ones either, to show their legs. I wanted to know why, but I was hushed up. Still, I kept on practising and tried hard to keep my skirts down as I ran. . . . I could see my dress which was well below my knees, was an impediment, and when I took it off I could run more easily. I suggested that I would wear only my drawers. . . . My suggestion was not well received.

McClung's schooling was intermittent throughout her youth. When a school was finally established in 1883, she attended only sporadically due to responsibilities on the family farm. Still, by July 1889, she had passed the exams which allowed her attendance at the Normal school in Winnipeg for teacher training. At age 15, she headed for Manitoba's largest city.

At an early age, Nellie faced the choice between having a career or a family. In those days it was believed, and was in fact a reality for most women, that the demands of motherhood were too great to allow for work outside the home. Years later, McClung wrote about the dilemma she faced:

> I had thought I was strong like Queen Elizabeth who kept clear of sex complications, but now I could see I was wavering. I knew that I would like to have a baby of my own sometime. . . . [Yet] marriage to me had a terrible finality about it. It seemed like the end of all ambition, hope and aspiration.

After five months of training, McClung chose a career and moved to the small town of Hazel, Manitoba, to teach all eight grades in a small schoolhouse. At the time, she believed she had rejected the call of babies, marriage and love.

Events did not go exactly as planned, however. While living in Hazel, Nellie met and was deeply impressed by **Annie E. McClung**, wife of the local minister. It is reported that Nellie decided that Annie would make an excellent mother-in-law and took the liberty of seeking out and meeting the eldest McClung son, Wes, who worked in the local pharmacy. In the fall of 1892, Nellie secured a teaching job in the larger community of Manitou. By this time, the McClungs were also living in Manitou and invited Nellie to board with them. There, Nellie's relationship with Wes blossomed. Wes appreciated her lively sense of humor and intelligence and was receptive to ideas about women's rights. From the beginning, Nellie knew that he would not expect her to devote all of herself to him. On August 25, 1896, they were married.

The new couple decided to settle in Manitou, where Wes established himself as a pharmacist. Nellie immediately left teaching and devoted herself to the tasks of housework and childcare. With the three young children she had by 1901, there is no doubt that being a wife and mother had become a full-time responsibility. However, McClung's decision to embrace motherhood did not mean that she had rejected her desire to find fulfillment in a career. As the following years would prove, she would be one of the few women of the time to succeed in both of these areas.

McClung became actively involved in the Manitou branch of the Women's Christian Temperance Union (WCTU). Formed in Cleveland, Ohio, in 1874, the WCTU advocated total abstinence based on the belief that alcohol was the cause of many of the social and economic problems plaguing society. Its goal, in most cases, was enforced abstinence through legislated prohibition. By the standards of today, the women of the WCTU often seem backward or anti-feminist. Although they glorified motherhood as the natural state of women, they were progressive in that they also believed that women should be involved in public life (through the professions, politics, etc.). In their view, men and women were different but complementary, and it was necessary to have the attributes of both sexes represented in the public realm in order to ensure a stable and prosperous society. McClung subscribed wholeheartedly to these beliefs, which guided her involvement in the temperance movement and in other causes throughout her life.

During this period, she also began to write, encouraged in this as in her temperance activities by her mother-in-law, Annie McClung. Finding the time and energy was difficult as she noted in her journal: "With three small children and a house to run you can imagine the sort of frame of mind I'm in. In fact, the frame is all that is left of my mind." Still, encouragement came when several of her articles and stories were published in Methodist Sunday school publications. Finally, in 1908 her novel *Sowing Seeds in Danny* was published. The book was instantly successful, becoming bestseller of the year in Canada with over 100,000 copies sold. In the years to follow, McClung would publish an additional 15 books

and many articles, most attaining wide readership. For McClung, who had always wanted to be a writer, this success brought not only fulfillment but recognition and popularity among Canadians, a factor which was helpful in her later crusades for women's rights. It also brought a sizeable income, a rarity for women at this time and a help in paying for domestic care and other expenses.

Never retreat, never explain, never apologize. Get the thing done and let them howl.

—Nellie L. McClung

In 1911, Wes decided to work for a life insurance company, moving the family to Winnipeg (the capital of Manitoba). The move marked a change in Nellie's thoughts about social reform. Although she remained committed to temperance throughout her life, the reality of female inequality in Canadian society moved progressively more into focus for her. Unlike Manitou, Winnipeg provided the specter of poverty, disease and "immorality," with women and children the most visible victims. As well, city living provided extended social opportunities. Through organizations like the Canadian Women's Press Club, McClung was exposed to troubling issues. Of primary concern, as in the case of alcohol abuse which temperance was meant to negate, was women's vulnerability in a society which offered them no legal or political status and protection. Legally, a woman's husband could sell the family property or will it away without any provision for her care. Women did not even have rights to their own children. Thus, Nellie's concerns spread beyond temperance to social reform, landing eventually in the suffrage movement.

During the decade leading up to 1920, suffrage was the primary focus of McClung's public life. She had come to the conclusion that the only way to address female inequality was to secure the vote for women. Consequently, in 1912 she helped found the Political Equality League (PEL), one of several provincial associations dedicated to the cause of female suffrage. The League held public speeches, distributed leaflets and petitioned Parliament, all to no avail. Suffrage was not popular in early 20th-century Canada. However, the presence of women like Nellie McClung was beneficial to the suffrage movement, for she was not threatening to established concepts of femininity. She was, after all, an attractive woman with a husband and five children (two more children had been born between 1904 and 1911). As well, her popularity as a writer and public speaker, combined with a humorous and gentle nature, had the effect of disarming critics. This is not to say that Mc-Clung was not capable of biting satire and criticism, or that she did not suffer a great deal of abuse at the hands of critics. However, in her writing and speaking she employed a sense of humor that was not threatening and was greatly successful at publicizing suffrage ideas. This was exactly the tactic used when the League decided to stage a "mock parliament" in 1914.

The idea of a mock parliament was not new, having been used by other suffrage groups. However, the PEL developed a strategy to maximize its effectiveness. First, they went to the Manitoba legislature to request the vote be granted to women, fully expecting the premier, Sir Rodmond Roblin, to reject the request. Mc-Clung, who had been nominated as the group's speaker, presented an eloquent and compelling argument for female suffrage. Luckily for their plan, Roblin was not swayed and replied with fawning condescension, expressing his concern for womanhood should the weaker sex become involved in the dirty business of politics. The group had booked the Walker Theater, and in it, for the next three days, their mock parliament depicted a session of Parliament with heckling, bills, and the usual activity, except that all the members of the legislature were women, with Nellie McClung as premier. In the final scene, the "government" received a delegation of men requesting the right to vote. McClung's reply was a perfect reversal of Roblin's arguments. Accurately mimicking the premier's mannerisms and speaking techniques, she complimented the men on their appearance while expressing concern for the sanctity of the home if men were allowed to vote.

> It gives me great pleasure to receive you here tonight. I want to compliment the deputation for their courtesy—and candor—and gentlemanly appearance. . . . If all men were as intelligent as these representatives of the down-trodden sex seem to be, it might not do any harm to give them the vote. But all men are not as intelligent. . . . Politics unsettle men, and unsettled men lead to unsettled bills—which lead to broken furniture, broken vows—and divorce!

The event was a resounding success. Reported extensively in the Canadian press, it raised public awareness and sympathy for the suffrage cause.

The mock parliament has been deemed the turning point of the Canadian suffrage movement; female enfranchisement was now only a matter of time. Within months, the opposition

Liberal Party endorsed female suffrage and placed it in their platform. Growing popularity meant that it was now considered politically advantageous to support this issue. However, even after the Liberal victory in 1915, there was hesitation, forcing the suffrage organizations to apply pressure on the government. On January 27, 1916, Manitoba women became the first Canadian women with the right to vote. Within the next few years, the rest of the provinces (except Quebec) and the federal government followed suit.

By 1918, it would seem that McClung had much of which to be proud. Both suffrage and Prohibition had been passed in Manitoba and were steadily achieving success in the rest of Canada. Wes had been transferred to Edmonton, Alberta, in 1914, forcing Nellie to commute extensively between the two provinces during the campaign. Consequently, following the victory, she decided to settle down and devote herself to writing. By 1921, however, she was back in the public spotlight as a member of the Alberta legislature. Although elected as a Liberal, McClung remained true to her convictions, supporting or rejecting bills according to conscience rather than party affiliation. During the next five years, she supported legislation for old age pensions, mothers' allowances, factory regulation, minimum wages and birth control.

Despite all the victories of these years, by 1926, McClung must have been questioning the value of her success. In that year, she lost her seat in the election. A heated battle during the last four years had led to the repeal of Prohibition, despite her best efforts. Furthermore, there was no evidence that female enfranchisement had led to the great social and moral reform that many had envisioned. Generally, women tended to vote like men. Perhaps it was the recognition that enfranchisement alone would not lead to the liberation of women that led Mc-Clung to become involved in the now-famous "Persons Case."

The "Persons Case" was initiated by *Emily Murphy, a popular writer, political activist and magistrate. As a magistrate, Murphy was bothered by an 1876 British common law ruling which declared that "Women are persons in matters of pain and penalties, but are not persons in matters of rights and privileges." Still in effect, this ruling meant that women were not equal in Canadian society. In order to challenge it, Murphy seized on the issue of the Canadian Senate. According to the constitution, the Senate was to be filled by "qualified persons" appoint-

Nellie L. McClung

ed by the governor-general (the prime minister in practice). Thus Murphy, through various women's groups, started a campaign to force the government to appoint a woman to the Senate. Fed up with being ignored, a group of five women—McClung, Murphy, ***Irene Parlby**, ***Henrietta Muir Edwards**, and ***Louise McKinney**—decided in 1927 to petition the prime minister to decide if the word "persons" included women. Choosing to avoid the issue, the prime minister and his associates passed the matter along until it ended up before the Canadian

Supreme Court, which decided that women were not "persons" within the meaning of the Act. The "Famous Five" (as they later became known) decided to take their case to the Privy Council in London, England, which at that time was the final court of appeal for Canadians as well as the British. Finally, on October 18, 1929, the news came that the Privy Council had decided that women were "persons."

Prime Minister William Lyon Mackenzie King knew he would have to appoint a woman to the Senate. Emily Murphy was the most obvious choice, due to her involvement in the matter and experience as a magistrate; vengeful after so many years of Murphy's persistence, however, King refused to consider her. In 1930, he appointed the first woman, *Cairine Wilson, to sit in the Senate.

The importance of the "Persons Case" was found not so much in the presence of a woman in the Senate, but in its symbolic and legal value. The declaration that women were in fact "Persons" was a great step towards ensuring female equality in Canadian society. With the "Persons Case" and her participation in the suffrage movement, McClung had played an instrumental role in the two most important victories of the women's movement in early Canadian history.

As Canada entered the Depression and the Second World War, McClung again devoted her energies to writing. Two collections of short stories were published in 1930 and 1931, followed by two volumes of collected essays in 1936 and 1937. It was during this period that she also wrote her autobiography in two volumes entitled *Clearing in the West* (1935) and *The Stream Runs Fast* (1945). In 1935, the McClungs moved to their final home at Gordonhead, B.C. (near the capital of Victoria), where Wes retired.

Nellie, however, was not ready for retirement. Along with prolific writing, she remained active in public life. In 1936, she was the first woman appointed to the new Canadian Broadcasting Corporation's board of governors. The CBC had been created by the government to regulate radio wave use and licensing to ensure that all Canadians were served by the new medium of radio and to guarantee the presence of Canadian content. McClung, recognizing the potential influence of radio, and thus of the CBC, on Canadians, took her role very seriously. Two years later, she was appointed as a delegate to the League of Nations, the predecessor to the United Nations. Although McClung recognized the League's ineffectiveness in preventing interna-

tional conflict, she felt that it nonetheless played an important role through its efforts to ensure international standards in labor relations, social welfare and human rights. Thus, she was pleased by her appointment to the Fifth Committee which studied social legislation, refugees, narcotics, nutrition, housing and labor conditions.

Gradually, McClung was forced to slow down, as arthritis and heart problems took their toll. She and her husband spent more time together, becoming avid gardeners. In 1946, they celebrated their 50th wedding anniversary. "The day I married Wes I did the best day's work I have ever done," she said. In many ways, their marriage was a model for women contemplating a career. Popular conceptions held that suffragists did not make good wives or simply could not find someone to marry them. Yet for 50 years, McClung had successfully combined a public career with the demands of marriage, and she and Wes had remained happy together.

Five years later, illness had finally overtaken her, and she lay dying at home. Reportedly, during her last few days, there was a moment when she became quite still. As Wes bent over to check on her, she quickly opened her eyes. "Oh, I'm still here," she said. "I'll never believe I'm dead till I see it in the paper." On September 2, 1951, the papers reported that Nellie McClung had died the previous day at the age of 77.

SOURCES:

Benham, Mary Lile. *Nellie McClung.* Fitzhenry & Whiteside, 1984.

Hancock, Carol L. *No Small Legacy.* Wood Lake Books, 1986.

Savage, Candace. *Our Nell: a Scrapbook Biography of Nellie L. McClung.* Western Producer Prairie Books, 1979.

SUGGESTED READING:

Strong-Boag, Veronica. "Introduction," in *In Times Like These.* University of Toronto Press, 1972.

Catherine Briggs, Ph.D. candidate in history, University of Waterloo, Waterloo, Ontario, Canada

McCollum, Ruby (1915—)

American murderer. Born in Live Oak, Florida, in 1915; children: at least one daughter.

Ruby McCollum was born in Live Oak, Florida, in 1915. As an African-American woman in the South before the era of the civil-rights movement, she suffered discrimination throughout her life. Although the exact circumstances of their relationship are unknown, McCollum was alleged to have become the mistress of a local white politician, Dr. C. LeRoy Adams, and to have borne a child by him. McCollum was convicted of murdering Adams in 1952, and was saved from the death penalty only through the efforts of white attorney Frank Cannon, who took her case without pay. After spending two years in the state penitentiary, McCollum was transferred to a high-security mental hospital, from which she was eventually released into the custody of her daughter. She was the subject of William Bradford Huie's book, *Ruby McCollum: Woman in the Suwanee Jail.*

Grant Eldridge,
freelance writer, Pontiac, Michigan

McCord, Louisa S. (1810–1879)

American writer, plantation owner, and defender of slavery. Name variations: Louisa Susannah Cheves McCord; (pen name) L.S.M. Born Louisa Susannah Cheves on December 3, 1810, in Charleston, South Carolina; died on November 23, 1879, in Charleston; daughter of Langdon Cheves (a lawyer and politician) and Mary Elizabeth (Dulles) Cheves; educated privately and at Mr. Grimshaw's Academy; married David James McCord (a lawyer, journalist, and politician), on May 2, 1840; children: Langdon Cheves McCord (b. 1841); Hannah Cheves McCord (b. 1843); Louisa Rebecca Hayne Smythe (b. 1845); ten stepchildren.

Selected writings: translation of Frédéric Bastiat's Sophismes Economiques *(1848); articles published in* Southern Quarterly Review, DeBow's Review, Southern Literary Messenger *(1850s);* Caius Gracchus *(play, 1851).*

The fourth of fourteen children in an affluent family, Louisa S. McCord was born in 1810 in Charleston, South Carolina. Her grandfather had traded with the Native Americans in the area beginning in the 1760s, and her father Langdon Cheves was a self-taught lawyer and prominent Southern politician who once served as Speaker of the U.S. House of Representatives. When McCord was a child, President James Monroe appointed Langdon Cheves president of the Bank of the United States, and the family lived in Philadelphia for a time during his tenure. There, her Northern classmates at the private academies she attended taunted McCord about the slaves owned by her family, and thus at an early age she became a staunch defender of the South's "peculiar institution."

Although she was sent, along with her sisters, to Mr. Grimshaw's Academy and to a school run by a French couple, McCord longed for the more rigorous education given her brothers. After she was caught covertly listening to

their lessons, her father allowed her to study Latin and math alongside the boys. With her family she also spent time in Washington, D.C., before their move in 1829 back to Charleston, where she was overshadowed socially by her older sister **Sophia Cheves**. In 1830, at the age of 20, McCord took over Lang Syne, a cotton plantation near Columbia that had been bequeathed to her by an aunt. There she owned 200 slaves, and reportedly made their clothing herself; she also supervised a nursery for the children of field hands, and trained some slaves to run a rudimentary plantation hospital.

At the age of 29, Louisa wed a man 13 years her senior, David McCord, a lawyer in Columbia who also sat in the state legislature and edited a nullification newspaper. (Nullification was an antebellum Southern political doctrine, predecessor of the secession concept, that maintained that a state could declare "null and void" a federal law it deemed unconstitutional.) A widower, her husband also came with ten children and plantations of his own. Together they had two daughters and a son, and lived at Lang Syne. In 1848, at the behest of her husband, McCord put her French to use to translate an economic treatise that became an important part of the South's anti-tariff political platform. Her English-language version of *Sophismes Economiques* (Economic Sophism or Fallacy) by Frédéric Bastiat was published under the pen name "L.S.M.," and was well received; McCord was offered other assignments, and moved from translation to full-fledged writing. She was reportedly most proud of her five-act tragedy *Caius Gracchus*, written entirely in verse and published in 1851. Psychological parallels have been drawn between the author and Gaius (Caius) Gracchus' mother *Cornelia (c. 195–c. 115 BCE).

McCord's articles appeared in such political journals as the *Southern Quarterly Review*. With a conservative pen, she wrote about women's rights—arguing, for instance, that women should receive access to education, but remain out of the political sphere. Some biographers have speculated that she may have been familiar with such arguments from having used them earlier to convince herself to be satisfied with her own domestic-oriented lot in life. A spirited, energetic woman, both the daughter and wife of politicians, McCord may well have yearned for her own political career, aware that she was equal in intellect to the men in her family. Unlike some defenders of slavery who considered it a necessary evil, McCord, as she stated in 1853 while attacking *Harriet Beecher Stowe's novel *Uncle Tom's Cabin*, thought slavery "a God-like dispensation, a providential caring for the weak, and a refuge for the portionless."

When David McCord died in 1855, Louisa moved to Columbia and began to focus her energies on her son and his political aspirations. She funded and equipped a company which he commanded during the Civil War, but Langdon Cheves McCord, named in honor of her beloved father, died in 1862 during the Second Battle of Bull Run. Back in Columbia, McCord supervised a military hospital that would later be encompassed by the campus of the University of South Carolina, and exhibited bravery under duress when the city was torched by Union troops; this is mentioned in her friend *Mary Boykin Chesnut's war diary. The end of the war and the Emancipation Proclamation ruined her financially, and she moved to Cobourg, Ontario, for a time, to avoid having to pledge an oath of allegiance to the federal government. Eventually she conceded, however, in order to sell her remaining property. McCord lived the rest of her years in Charleston with her daughter, **Louisa Rebecca Smythe**, and was buried in that city's Magnolia Cemetery after her death in 1879.

Patty McCormack

SOURCES:
James, Edward T., *Notable American Women, 1607–1950*. Cambridge, MA: The Belknap Press of Harvard University Press, 1971.

Carol Brennan,
Grosse Pointe, Michigan

McCormack, Patty (1945—)

American actress. Born on August 21, 1945, in Brooklyn, New York.

A prototypical child star, Patty McCormack worked as a professional model at the age of four and appeared in the television series "Mama" for four years beginning at the age of seven. Her most notable role, however, was that of Rhoda Penmark in both the stage and screen versions of Maxwell Anderson's *The Bad Seed*. A little girl with pigtails, a flat stare, and an apparently inherent capacity for evil, Rhoda was quite a shock to 1950s America as she drowned a little boy at a picnic and burned to death a gardener. McCormack was barely ten during the play's 1954 run in New York. The movie version of *The Bad Seed*, which featured a new ending in which Rhoda was struck dead by lightning, was released in 1956 and has since gone on to become a cult classic. (*Nancy Kelly, who won a Tony award for her performance on Broadway as Rhoda's mother, also reprised that role in the film.) McCormack never again played a role as significant as that of Rhoda in *The Bad Seed*, although she was briefly the star of her own television show, "Peck's Bad Girl," in 1959, and had a fairly prolific career playing wild girls and troubled teens in films in the 1960s and 1970s. These included *The Explosive Generation* (1961), *The Mini-Skirt Mob* (1968), *The Young Runaways* (1968), and *Bug* (1975). McCormack also sang for various rock bands during that period, and later appeared on the television sitcom "The Ropers" (1979–80). Following a long absence, she returned to films in 1988 in *Saturday the 14th Strikes Back*, playing the role of a mother.

Grant Eldridge,
freelance writer, Pontiac, Michigan

McCormick, Anne O'Hare (1880–1954)

Foreign correspondent who was the world's most honored newspaperwoman of her day. Name variations: Anne O'Hare. Born Anne Elizabeth O'Hare on May 16, 1880, in Wakefield, Yorkshire, England; died in New York City on May 29, 1954; daughter of Thomas O'Hare (a life insurance employee) and Teresa Beatrice (Berry) O'Hare (a writer and poet); attend-

ed St. Mary of the Springs Academy; B.A., College of St. Mary of the Springs, Columbus, Ohio; married Francis J. McCormick (an engineer and importer), on September 14, 1910.

On staff at The New York Times (1922–35), on editorial board (1935–54).

Selected writings: Hammer and the Scythe: Communist Russia Enters the Second Decade (NY: Knopf, 1928); (edited by Marion Turner Sheehan) The World at Home: Selections from the Writings of Anne O'Hare McCormick (NY: Knopf, 1956); (edited by Sheehan) Vatican Journal, 1921–1954 (NY: Farrar, Straus, and Cudahy, 1957).

In 1921, a 42-year-old woman, 5'2", with reddish hair and blue eyes, sent a brief note to Carr V. Van Anda, managing editor of The New York Times. She noted that as the wife of an engineer and exporter, she traveled frequently overseas. Was it possible, she asked with some timidity, to send him some dispatches from abroad? She would gladly serve as a freelance contributor, not in competition with regular foreign correspondents. Van Anda's reply was brief: "Try it."

By the time Anne O'Hare McCormick died in 1954, she had won practically every major award in the field of journalism, including the Pulitzer Prize in 1937 for distinguished foreign correspondent. Equally important, in her role as Times writer and editor, she was one of the most influential opinion-makers in the American press.

Anne Elizabeth O'Hare was born on May 16, 1880, in Wakefield, Yorkshire, England, the daughter of Thomas O'Hare and **Beatrice Berry O'Hare**. The eldest of three children, she grew up in Columbus, Ohio, and graduated from the academy and college of the city's St. Mary of the Springs Academy. While she was still in high school, her father, a regional manager for Home Life Company of New York, deserted the family. To earn money, Anne's mother ran a dry-goods store and sold a book of her own poetry door-to-door.

After O'Hare's graduation from college, the family moved to Cleveland, where Anne served as an associate editor of the Catholic Universe Bulletin, a weekly. Her mother contributed poetry, wrote a column, and served as the women's page editor for the same journal. On September 14, 1910, O'Hare married Francis J. McCormick, eight years her senior, an engineer and importer whose work frequently took the couple to Europe. At first they lived in Dayton, where she wrote poetry for the Smart Set and Bookman; her work was included in the annual

Braithwaite's Anthology of Magazine Verse. She also began contributing feature articles on a freelance basis. Eventually, she was published in the Atlantic Monthly, Catholic World, Reader Magazine, and The New York Times Magazine.

In 1921, McCormick was hired by The New York Times as a stringer, but within a year she carried a roving commission as regular correspondent. At first, she wrote so much that Times editors nicknamed her "Verbose Annie," but she gradually streamlined her prose so that it needed virtually no further work. She initially made her reputation by covering the rise of fascism in Italy. Very early she made contacts with dictator Benito Mussolini. Although other journalists were dismissing Il Duce as just "an upstart Milanese newspaper editor," McCormick correctly insisted that his was "the master voice" to which Italy was responding.

McCormick's initial interview with Mussolini was revealing of her journalistic technique. When Il Duce asked her what interested her the most in Italy, she replied, The Law of Corporations, a thick legal volume that she had read in the original Italian. Upon discovering that she had actually mastered it, he took her hand and said, "My congratulations; you and I are the only ones who have!"

McCormick was not only a strong Italophile; she genuinely admired Mussolini the man. The Italian dictator, she said, was not intoxicated but rather mellowed by power. In describing Italian fascism, she wrote approvingly of its "elan" and "vitality." Only during World War II did she drop her admiration, and even then she claimed that the Allies should back the nation's monarchy and the military.

After 1925, McCormick wrote almost exclusively for the Times. Her book Hammer and the Scythe: Communist Russia Enters the Second Decade (1928) was a firsthand account of the Soviet experiment, based upon her Times articles. Avoiding polemics usual to the topic, she wrote, "Nothing in Russia is fixed enough to hang a judgment on." In addition to covering events overseas, she reported on occurrences in the United States, including national political conventions, life in the modern South, and the hardships inflicted by the Great Depression.

In 1935, Times publisher Arthur Hays Sulzberger appointed McCormick the first woman member of the editorial board, a position she held for the remainder of her life. Sulzberger urged her to be the "freedom editor: to stand up and shout whenever freedom is interfered with in any part of the world." From 1936 to 1954, she wrote three weekly columns, first called "In Europe," then "Affairs of Europe," then "Abroad," for the op-ed page, alternating with columns by *Times* Washington correspondent Arthur Krock. In addition, whenever she was not traveling, she wrote two unsigned editorials each week.

A strong believer in the League of Nations, McCormick wrote in 1935, "Nothing better or more stable can be established by more war but in the long view it is equally certain that there must be war—not all the sanctions in the world can stop it—unless there is a league not only to enforce but to create peace." But in June 1936, McCormick sensed "a world-wide storm" in the offing. She wrote:

> The face of the world has changed. You walk familiar streets and they are strange. People everywhere are like houses with the shutters down, withdrawn and waiting, as if life were held in suspense; or they are quarreling within their houses, because long-drawn-out uncertainty has rasped their nerves to the breaking point.

Anticipating the bitter isolationist-interventionist debate of 1939–41 in America, she continued: "In another four years we may face a division on principles as fundamental as the issues of the Civil War."

Anne McCormick was an extraordinary reporter primarily because she was an extraordinary human being.

—James Reston

In 1939, over a five-month period, Anne O'Hare McCormick studied conditions in 13 countries. During her trip, she witnessed both the birth and death of a republic within 24 hours. This took place on March 14, at the time of the second partition of Czechoslovakia. She saw Father Augustin Voloshyn, head of the autonomous Ruthanian government, proclaim the independence of Ruthania, renaming it Carpatho-Ukraine. From its capital city, Huszt, McCormick cabled hourly reports. However, independence lasted only one day, for the Germans then authorized Hungary to annex the nation.

The *Times* correspondent had other good beats, so many that her colleagues accused her of having an uncanny knack of being where the news was "breaking." "Crises were popping all over Europe at the time," replied McCormick, "so it isn't strange that I bumped into a few." Be that as it may, in 1939 she was in Rome when British Prime Minister Neville Chamberlain visited Mussolini and in the British Parliament when Chamberlain discarded his appeasement

policy. When Hitler invaded Poland on September 1, 1939, McCormick went immediately to Rumania, to capture the odyssey of Polish refugees pouring over the border.

McCormick's greatest influence came during the 1940s. Her writings at the time reflected her belief in an unchanging moral order and conveyed her sober optimism. Her enthusiasm for the League spilled over to the new United Nations. Recalling the disillusion in the U.S. at the end of World War I, she warned that the Americans would again withdraw from the global scene, "if there are shabby compromises in the peace and the ordinary citizen sees the principles he is fighting for scuttled to serve the ambitions of the great powers."

Her account of the Greek civil war was something of a classic. In 1949, at age 69, McCormick was scrambling up mountains with soldiers less than half her age. After an inspection of refugee and prison camps, she wrote:

> It is easy to say that the Greek war is an affair of daily raids in which armed bands . . . swoop down from the cracks and crevices of a mountain . . . to sack or burn villages and carry off able bodied men and girls to forced service in their armies. But the imagination cannot picture the desolation that this hit-and-run fighting leaves behind it. . . . Everywhere the atmosphere was heavy with suspense. In such fearful quiet must the early settlers in the West have waited for the descent of the Indians.

McCormick opposed the militancy of President Dwight D. Eisenhower's secretary of state John Foster Dulles. When Dulles announced his retaliation policy at a 1953 dinner of the Overseas Press Club, McCormick commented, "I've watched Dulles' performance at a number of international conferences, and in my opinion he's demonstrated a complete lack of sensitivity and understanding."

To McCormick, public opinion was most significant. Hence, in addition to interviewing leaders of a nation, she drove over the country, chatting with farmers, small shopkeepers, mechanics—people who could give her a cross-section of a nation's life. Her gift for catching small details was uncanny. In covering Berlin early in World War II, McCormick wrote, "Groping along the tunnel-like streets you almost never hear a voice. Other gropers are shadows and footsteps." A McCormick dispatch from liberated France described "the symbol and promise" of "the woman with a broom trying to clear away the debris that used to be her home." In her account of the Russian capture of Budapest, she noted the rows of empty food stores and cattle being driven down the street, thereby capturing the mood of an occupied city.

At the same time, McCormick could use dramatic metaphors, as when in 1940 she wrote, "Daily it becomes plainer that the struggle in Europe is the Apocalypse of the long drawn-out fight of man to control the machine." Upon watching the founding of the U.N. in San Francisco, she said she was at the place "where the desperation of the peoples of the world beats upon the Golden Gate. For if the forum does not take the place of the battlefield this war is lost and the next begins." An unidentified French diplomat once commented: "She is more than a journalist, she is a historian writing history."

Not surprisingly, McCormick won many awards. In addition to receiving the Pulitzer, she was elected to the National Institute of Arts and Sciences, was made 1939 Woman of the Year by the National Federation of Business and Professional Women's Clubs, and received 16 honorary degrees. Furthermore, in February 1942 she was named to the Advisory Committee on Post-War Foreign Policy, a 15-member blue-ribbon group that met secretly to engage in postwar planning. In 1946 and 1948, she was a delegate to United Nations Educational, Scientific, and Cultural Organization (UNESCO) meetings.

McCormick did not believe journalists should become media personalities. Indeed, she was so reticent about self-promotion that for years she even refused to fill out a questionnaire from *Who's Who in America*. (Her secretary eventually did.) McCormick claimed that fame would interfere with "the kind of impersonal and uncolored reporting . . . on which the maintenance of a free press and therefore a free society depend." While O'Hare was covering postwar Berlin and Frankfurt at age 68, press colleagues contrasted her quiet personality with the egocentric style of the two female stars of the *New York Herald Tribune*, *Dorothy Thompson and *Marguerite Higgins.

Over the years, McCormick's reporting took on a definite pattern. She and her husband would leave New York every fall, traveling throughout Europe until spring. They never established a permanent residence, preferring the amenities of the Carlyle or Gotham hotels in New York, the Ritz or Crillon in Paris, and Claridge's in London. Whenever she was in Europe, no matter what the local hour, she called in her column to the *Times* so that it arrived at 9:30 PM, New York time.

During her long career, McCormick interviewed most of the prominent political leaders of her day. Joseph Stalin gave her an unprecedented six hours. Adolf Hitler, not on speaking terms with the press, was willing to talk to her. She was a particular favorite of Franklin D. Roosevelt, who felt so relaxed in her company that he often broke his own ban on individual interviews to give her three hours at a stretch. Other leaders included Eisenhower, Winston Churchill, and Harry S. Truman as well as Eamon de Valera of Ireland, Leon Blum of France, Eleutherios Venizelos of Greece, Gustav Stresemann of Germany, and Engelbert Dollfuss and Kurt von Schuschnigg of Austria. While interviewing, she took no notes ("It makes people too cautious," she asserted), but rather relied on her superb memory. She sought no political statements since, she maintained, interviews were for revealing personality.

Two collections of her columns were published posthumously. *The World at Home* (1956), edited by **Marion Turner Sheehan**, in-

Anne
O'Hare
McCormick

cluded articles from 1925 to 1945 that centered on U.S. domestic life. In his introduction, *Times* editor James B. Reston stressed her "rare gift of sympathy for all sorts of people." Her *Vatican Journal, 1921–1954* (1957), also edited by Sheehan, contained a preface by author *Clare Boothe Luce, who called her "a rare combination of brilliance and goodness." Included in the anthology was material on the Lateran Treaty of 1929, conflict between church and state in Nazi Germany, the U.S. debate over President Truman's proposal to send a U.S. ambassador to the Vatican, and the position of the Roman Catholic Church in Spain.

Anne O'Hare McCormick died in New York City on May 29, 1954, at the age of 74; she was survived by her husband, who had suffered a stroke. In its tribute, the *Times* blackened the border of the "Abroad" column, and called her a "reporter in a rare sense. She understood politics and diplomacy but for her they were not the whole truth and no abstraction was ever the whole truth. The whole truth lay in people." It was an appropriate epitaph.

SOURCES:

Belford, Barbara. *Brilliant Bylines: A Biographical Anthology of Notable Newspaperwomen in America.* NY: Columbia University Press, 1986.

Edwards, Julia. *Women of the World: The Great Foreign Correspondents.* Boston, MA: Houghton Mifflin, 1988.

SUGGESTED READING:

Sheehan, Marion Turner, ed. *The World at Home: Selections from the Writings of Anne O'Hare McCormick.* Introduction by James Reston. NY: Knopf, 1956.

COLLECTIONS:

The papers of Anne O'Hare McCormick, which include correspondence, are at the manuscripts collection of the New York Public Library.

Justus D. Doenecke,
Professor of History, New College,
University of South Florida, Sarasota, Florida

McCormick, Edith Rockefeller

(1872–1932)

Chicago socialite and patron of the arts. Name variations: Edith Rockefeller; Mrs. Harold McCormick. Born Edith Rockefeller on August 31, 1872, in Cleveland, Ohio; died of liver cancer on August 25, 1932, in Chicago, Illinois; daughter of John Davison Rockefeller (1839–1937, founder of Standard Oil Trust in Ohio and philanthropist) and Laura Celestia (Spelman) Rockefeller (1839–1915); educated privately and briefly attended the Rye (New York) Female Seminary; married Harold Fowler McCormick (son of Nettie Fowler McCormick [1835–1923]), on November 26, 1895 *(divorced 1921); children: John Rockefeller McCormick (died young); Fowler McCormick;* **Muriel McCormick**; *Editha McCormick (died young);* **Mathilde McCormick**.

Moved to New York City (early 1880s); dominated Chicago society after 1895; helped found Chicago Opera Company (1910); moved to Switzerland to study with Carl Jung (1913); divorced husband and returned to Chicago (1921).

Edith Rockefeller McCormick was one of the most eccentric of America's art patrons in the early decades of the 20th century. Heiress to the Standard Oil fortune, for many years she ruled over Chicago society and gave lavishly to her city's cultural institutions. In later years, she became a student of Swiss psychoanalyst Carl Jung and even practiced psychology herself. Her biographers estimate that over a three-decade span McCormick probably gave away well over $10 million to various causes. She was born in 1872 in Cleveland, Ohio, the third of four children of John D. Rockefeller and *Laura Spelman Rockefeller. Her father had founded a New York oil refinery, and by 1870 established the Standard Oil Trust in Ohio, a consortium that controlled virtually all oil refining in the United States and became the Standard Oil Company in 1899; over his lifetime, he would give away an estimated $500 million to philanthropic causes, setting a precedent which his daughter and many other members of the family would follow.

By most accounts, McCormick was a gifted musician who balked at the constrictions of her parents' Baptist household, which by the early 1880s had left Cleveland far behind for the grander precincts of Manhattan. In 1895, she wed Harold Fowler McCormick of Chicago, the son of *Nettie Fowler McCormick and Cyrus McCormick, inventor of the reaper machine that revolutionized agriculture. Like the Rockefellers, the McCormicks were one of the country's emergent dynasties. Together, McCormick and her husband would have five children: John Rockefeller, Fowler, Muriel, Editha, and Mathilde (both John and Editha died young). McCormick became Chicago's premier hostess and most formidable grand dame, throwing opulent soirées at the McCormick mansion at 1000 Lake Shore Drive. She was known as much for the orthodoxy that guided her entertaining as for the headstrong nature of her personality.

McCormick used her fortune both lavishly and charitably. Among her many civic-minded contributions to Chicago was the funding of the payroll for the first juvenile probation officers in

Opposite page

ℰ**dith**

ℛ**ockefeller**

ℳ**cCormick**

the country, and the founding (with her husband) of the John Rockefeller McCormick Memorial Institute for Infectious Diseases, named in honor of their late son. Borrowing the concept of early education from European "kindergartens," McCormick founded a nursery school for girls located in her mother-in-law Nettie's ballroom; all instruction was in French. The McCormicks also gave generously to the Chicago Opera Company, and Edith McCormick's grand arrival there in a Rolls-Royce, trailing a vast ermine cape, assured a sellout crowd. She was also known for her spectacular jewelry, including a Cartier necklace featuring ten massive emeralds along a chain strung with over 1,600 diamonds and a pearl necklace worth $2 million. At her mansion, she hosted dinners for 200 guests with a footman stationed behind every second chair, but always adhered to a promise once made to her conservative father never to serve alcohol in her home; the sober guests ate from an enormous dinner service that had been given by Napoleon to his favorite sister *Pauline Bonaparte. Her home was filled with antiques and treasures in every room, including a library that held 15,000 rare books and a rug that was once a gift to Peter the Great from the shah of Persia. No servant was permitted to address her directly (in later years, even her three surviving children were required to make appointments to see her), and all communication between McCormick and her immense household staff was delivered by either her steward or her personal secretary.

McCormick's name became associated with scandal when she left her husband to study in Switzerland with Carl Jung in 1913 (the McCormicks would not formally divorce until 1921). She was already a devotee of the occult and astrology, and thought herself the reincarnation of **Ankhesenpoaten**, the bride of Tutankhamun. She also gave generously to Jung and his research aims, and helped promote his pioneering work. She continued to serve as a patron to the arts, and supported James Joyce for a time during his writing of the novel *Ulysses*. After 1921, she remained in Chicago, and built a lavish suburban estate called Villa Turicum in Lake Forest. She continued to give abundantly, establishing the Chicago Zoological Gardens in 1923 and funding a $17 million trust in her name to erect the works of two architects she had come to know in Zurich. One of them, Edwin Krenn, established himself in Chicago, and was her usual companion on the rounds of her still busy social whirl.

Edith McCormick lost a great deal of money in the stock-market crash of 1929 and

collapse of the real-estate market, and died in 1932 with a fortune estimated at only $10 million, one quarter of its original figure. She was buried in Chicago's Graceland Cemetery.

SOURCES:

Birmingham, Stephen. *The Grandes Dames.* NY: Simon & Schuster, 1982.

James, Edward T., ed. *Notable American Women, 1607–1950.* Cambridge, MA: The Belknap Press of Harvard University Press, 1971.

Carol Brennan,
Grosse Pointe, Michigan

McCormick, Mrs. Harold (1872–1932).

See McCormick, Edith Rockefeller.

McCormick, Katharine

(1875–1967)

American philanthropist and advocate for women's reproductive freedom. Name variations: Katharine Dexter McCormick. Born Katharine Dexter on August 27, 1875, in Dexter, Michigan; died on December 28, 1967, in Boston, Massachusetts; daughter of Wirt Dexter and Josephine (Moore) Dexter; Massachusetts Institute of Technology, B.S., 1904; married Stanley Robert McCormick (son of Nettie Fowler McCormick [1835–1923]), in September 1904 (died 1947); no children.

Inherited family fortune (1894); became active in national suffrage moment (1909); began funding research into an oral contraceptive for women (1952); because of her efforts, first wing of M.I.T. dormitory for women opened (1962).

Katharine McCormick, who for years gave generously of her fortune to scientists working to develop a reliable method of contraception for women, was born in 1875 in Dexter, Michigan, a town bearing her family name. Her father Wirt Dexter was a prominent Chicago attorney, while her former schoolteacher mother **Josephine Moore Dexter** was descended from an esteemed New England family; McCormick's maternal grandfather had led settlers from New England to Michigan. When Wirt Dexter died in 1889, and his only son died five years later, McCormick and her mother inherited a great deal of money.

Not yet 20, McCormick left the Midwest for Boston, where she and her mother lived in a Commonwealth Avenue mansion. Free to follow their own intellectual and personal convictions without the disapproval or legal domination of husbands, fathers, or brothers, both women turned their energies to the growing women's suffrage movement. McCormick desired a solid education, and was able to enroll at the rigorous Massachusetts Institute of Technology (MIT) after spending three years preparing for the school's admission exam. She earned her B.S. in biology in 1904 with a thesis on "Fatigue of the Cardiac Muscles in Reptilia."

That same year, she married Stanley McCormick at her mother's second home on Switzerland's Lake Geneva. An heir to the McCormick fortune, he was the son of *Nettie Fowler McCormick and Cyrus McCormick, inventor of the reaper machine that revolutionized agriculture, and a comptroller for the family business, International Harvester. Stanley soon began to display signs of mental illness and was declared legally incompetent by 1909. Katharine spent years working with psychiatrists and a host of other health professionals trying to ascertain the root of his affliction. Some doctors asserted that Stanley McCormick's apparent schizophrenia was due to unresolved problems with his family and to sexual guilt; when some tried to restrict her from visiting him, she launched a series of legal challenges from which she emerged victorious in 1930. McCormick also gave generously to medical research in the field of mental health during these years. She founded the Neuroendocrine Research Foundation at Harvard Medical School in 1927 and funded publication of the journal *Endocrinology*. Stanley McCormick's condition never improved, however, and he died in 1947 in the palatial Santa Barbara, California, home that had served as his asylum.

Katharine McCormick had also devoted her time and assets to other causes. In 1909, she began actively participating in the women's suffrage movement and spoke at Massachusetts' first outdoor demonstration by women for the right to vote. McCormick, along with *Mary Ware Dennett and several others, went on to organize 97 more open-air rallies for women's rights while also lobbying the state legislature. For years she worked with *Carrie Chapman Catt in the National American Woman Suffrage Association (NAWSA), and chaired its War Service Department during World War I. The social changes wrought by that international conflict eventually brought success to the movement, and American women won the right to cast ballots in federal elections in 1920.

But it was in the realm of reproductive freedom that Katharine McCormick's convictions and support resulted in direct progress. During

World War I, she became an ally of *Margaret Sanger, a prominent activist in the birth-control movement in the early decades of the 20th century, when even supplying information on contraceptive methods was illegal. McCormick supported Sanger's efforts financially, and was one of many travelers who smuggled European diaphragms into the United States to give American women access to them. For years McCormick funded research projects on contraception, and eventually came to know a biologist and hormone researcher named Gregory Pincus. In 1953 she solicited his help in developing a safe and effective contraceptive for women, and provided him and his research institute with funds to continue his experimental research with synthetic hormones. This research had been dismissed as unpromising by a pharmaceutical company, but McCormick thought otherwise because of her scientific background and knowledge of endocrinology. Enovid, the first oral contraceptive for women, came on the market seven years later and quite literally changed the world. Popularly known as the pill (as are its lower-dose successors), it is considered one of the most significant inventions of the 20th century.

At her alma mater, McCormick funded the construction of two dormitories for women. M.I.T. had long balked at rescinding its annual quota on female students, declaring that it did not have sufficient space to house them, but the construction of two Stanley McCormick Halls, in 1962 and 1968, effectively negated that argument. Before her death in 1967, McCormick also gave money in her husband's name to the art museum of Santa Barbara, and in her will left a $5 million bequest to the Planned Parenthood Foundation of America.

SOURCES:
Sicherman, Barbara, and Carol Hurd Green, eds. *Notable American Women: The Modern Period*. Cambridge, MA: The Belknap Press of Harvard University, 1980.

Carol Brennan,
Grosse Pointe, Michigan

McCormick, Katherine Medill

(d. 1932)

American socialite and leading stockholder in the Chicago *Tribune. Name variations: Kate Medill; Kate McCormick; Catherine Medill McCormick. Born Katherine Van Etta Medill; died in 1932; daughter of Joseph Medill (1823–1899, proprietor and editor of the* Chicago *Tribune); sister of* Elinor (Nellie) Medill Patterson *(d. 1933, mother of* *Eleanor Medill "Cissy" Patterson*); married Robert Sanderson Mc-*

Cormick *(1849–1919, an American diplomat and ambassador to Austria, Russia, and France); children:* Joseph Medill McCormick *(1877–1925, a journalist and politician who married* *Ruth Hanna McCormick*); Robert (Bertie) Rutherford McCormick *(1880–1955, editor of the* Chicago Tribune, *who married* Amie Irwin Adams).

McCormick, Kelly (1960—)

American diver. Name variations: Kelly McCormick Robertson. Born on February 13, 1960, in Anaheim, California; daughter and one of two children of Glenn McCormick (a diving coach) and Patricia (Keller) McCormick (b. 1930); married.

Won silver medal in the springboard event, Olympic Games, Los Angeles, California (1984); won bronze medal in the springboard event, Olympic Games, Seoul, South Korea (1988).

Kelly McCormick was born in Anaheim, California, in 1960, the daughter of diving coach Glenn McCormick and Olympic gold-medal diver *Patricia McCormick. "My mother showed me her medal when I was a little girl. I made a bet with her that someday I'd make an Olympic team and win," Kelly McCormick told *Sports Illustrated* in 1983, recalling that she started diving as a youngster because she wanted her own prizes. In a career that nearly paralleled her mother's, Kelly did win her own medals, a silver and a bronze, in consecutive Olympic Games (1984 and 1988). It was not quite the "double-double" win of the elder McCormick (two gold medals in each of two consecutive Games), but impressive nonetheless, particularly given the changes in the competition since the 1950s.

Kelly began training as a gymnast, but gave it up after eight years because she hated being cooped up inside. As a diver, she possessed the same grace and strength as her mother, although she was frequently criticized as inconsistent. In the 1984 Olympics in Los Angeles, facing intense scrutiny from the media, Kelly finished three points shy of a gold medal in the springboard event, winning the silver instead. Four years later, she took home a bronze medal in the same event. In addition to her Olympic wins, she won nine national titles, two Pan American gold medals, and a World Cup bronze medal. At the end of her career, McCormick admitted that comparisons to her mother had been hard on her, and she was glad it was over. After retiring from competition, she married and took up coaching in Washington state.

McCormick, Nettie Fowler

(1835–1923)

Chicago business leader and philanthropist who was a major donor to the Presbyterian Church. Born Nancy Maria Fowler on February 8, 1835, in Brownville, New York; died on July 5, 1923, in Lake Forest, Illinois; daughter of Melzar Fowler (a merchant) and Clarissa (Spicer) Fowler; married Cyrus McCormick (an inventor and industrialist), on January 26, 1858 (died 1884); children: Cyrus Hall McCormick II; Mary Virginia McCormick; Anita Eugenie Blaine McCormick; Harold Fowler McCormick (who married *Edith Rockefeller McCormick); Stanley Robert McCormick (who married *Katharine McCormick).

Nettie Fowler McCormick

When Nettie Fowler McCormick died at the age of 88 in 1923, she left behind letters and journals that lent great insight into what drove a lifelong philanthropy. Orphaned at an early age and an unexpected heir to one of the Midwest's greatest manufacturing fortunes through her marriage, McCormick had always felt somewhat alienated from those close to her, and came to believe that immense wealth made her especially accountable in the eyes of her God. Her papers reveal a woman dedicated to leading a diligent and sober life and to putting her fortune to altruistic use.

McCormick was born Nancy Maria Fowler in 1835, the daughter of devout New York State Methodists Melzar and **Clarissa Fowler**. Her father was a merchant who died unexpectedly when she was an infant; Clarissa Fowler then took over the family's dry-goods business, but died in 1842 and orphaned seven-year-old Nettie and her two brothers. With her brother Eldrige Merick Fowler, a future lumber baron of the Midwest, she was taken in by the family of their shipbuilder uncle and grew up in Clayton, New York.

As a young woman, McCormick was schooled at three seminaries, including Genesee Wesleyan Seminary in Lima, New York, and for a time taught school in Clayton. Her life changed with a visit to a cousin in Chicago, where she met Cyrus McCormick. Twenty-five years her senior, McCormick was a wealthy industrialist who had invented the reaper machine. It revolutionized agriculture, and the company Cyrus McCormick founded eventually became the farm-machinery giant International Harvester. Of similarly devout and sober personalities, the two were wed in 1858; they would have seven children, two of whom died in infancy and two of whom would suffer from severe mental illness as adults. For many years McCormick served as her husband's personal secretary, and was an integral part of many important business decisions. After the Chicago Fire of 1871 destroyed the famed McCormick Reaper plant, for instance, Cyrus McCormick considered abandoning the business altogether, but she convinced him to rebuild and even expand.

When she became a widow in 1884, McCormick inherited a vast fortune. By that point a long-time Presbyterian, she became one of the top American donors to the Presbyterian Church in the 19th century. She was a firm believer in education, and came to see her mission as one of providing educational opportunity around the globe. Although the McCormick Theological Seminary in Chicago was the recipient of much of her largesse, she contributed to over 40 different educational institutions. McCormick was also active in funding the World's Student Christian Federation (housed in the same castle where ***Bridget of Sweden** had founded her religious

order) and gave generously to religious conversion efforts by Protestant clerics around the globe. For over three decades, she served in various capacities on the Woman's Board of the Presbyterian Mission of the Northwest, including treasurer, vice-president, and honorary vice-president. Her Rush Street home was a center of Christian missionary movement meetings for many years; she even traveled to Egypt in 1896 to check on one of her schools. A Democrat, she also donated sums to political campaigns, including the presidential candidacies of Woodrow Wilson in 1912 and 1916.

Though she grew deaf in her 60s, McCormick was still active in company matters as late as a 1913 labor dispute. She moved out of her home at 135 Rush to her "House-in-the-Woods," as she named it, a retreat on Sheridan Road in suburban Lake Forest. There she died of pneumonia in 1923, and was buried in Graceland Cemetery in Chicago.

SOURCES:

Deen, Edith. *Great Women of the Christian Faith.* NY: Harper & Row, 1959.

James, Edward T., ed. *Notable American Women, 1607–1950.* Cambridge, MA: The Belknap Press of Harvard University Press, 1971.

Carol Brennan,
Grosse Pointe, Michigan

McCormick, Patricia (1930—)

American diver who was the only woman in Olympic diving history to achieve a "double-double," winning two gold medals in each of two consecutive Olympic Games. Born Patricia Keller in Seal Beach, California, on May 12, 1930; daughter of Robert Keller and Harriet Keller; married Glenn McCormick (a diving coach), in 1949; children: one son and one daughter, Kelly McCormick, also a diver.

Won gold medals in springboard and platform events, Olympic Games, Helsinki, Finland (1952); won gold medals in springboard and platform events, Olympic Games, Melbourne, Australia (1956); named Associated Press Athlete of the Year and Sullivan Award winner (1956); was inaugural inductee (with **Katherine Rawls**) *into the International Swimming Hall of Fame (1965); named to International Women's*

$\mathcal{P}$atricia
$\mathcal{M}$cCormick

Paula Myers
Pat McCormick
Juno Irwin

Sports Hall of Fame (1984); named to U.S. Olympic Hall of Fame (1985).

Growing up on the California coast, Patricia McCormick was lured into the waters off Seal Beach and Muscle Beach at an early age, and performed her first aerial acrobatics on her surfboard. As a teenager, she focused on diving, refining her technique at the Los Angeles Aquatics Club where she practiced six days a week, sometimes executing up to 100 dives a day. At age 14, she won her first title, and in 1951, at age 22, she became the first diver to win all five national championships. Difficult dives were especially appealing to McCormick, who frequently attempted maneuvers considered too risky for men. Her ambition came at a price; during one medical examination, a doctor discovered a scar on her scalp and several at the base of her spine, as well as a variety of impact welts, laceration, and chipped teeth. "I've seen worse casualty cases," he told her, "but only where a building caved in."

Although she had missed making the 1948 Olympic team by a mere two points, McCormick was ready for the 1952 games in Helsinki, having married her diving coach, Glenn McCormick, who helped her stick to her rigorous training routine. Despite considerable pressure (American women had captured the gold in the springboard event since it was introduced for women at the 1920 Antwerp Games), McCormick won both the springboard and platform events. "Helsinki was really fun," she said later. "It was like receiving your first kiss. You never know what to expect." She also recalled the thrill of standing on the top step of the podium to receive her medal. "I still get goose pimples when I think of the national anthem. I still get tears in my eyes when I think of it."

Extraordinary as it was, McCormick's Olympic triumph commanded little attention back in the United States. So little, in fact, that when she arrived home from Helsinki, her neighbor inquired as to whether she had been on vacation. Following the games, McCormick resisted offers to turn professional, setting her sights on the next Olympic competition. In the interim, she became pregnant with her first child but did not use her "delicate condition" as an excuse to slow down. She continued to train up until two days before the birth of her son, who arrived just five months ahead of the Olympic trials. McCormick was one of the first to prove that women could successfully train as athletes during pregnancy.

At the Melbourne Games, McCormick, at age 26, was the "old lady" of the team, making her performance in the competition all the more extraordinary. She won the springboard event easily, beating runner-up **Jeanne Stunyo** 142.36 to 125.89. The platform competition proved slightly more elusive. With only two dives remaining, she suddenly found herself in second place behind teammate **Paula Jean Myers**. McCormick recalled telling herself, "You can't go out now after so many years of hard work without a fight." Although her fifth dive went well, she was still in second place, increasing the pressure to make the sixth dive, a difficult full twisting one-and-one-half, as near perfect as possible. After executing the plunge of her life, McCormick could only wait and hope. When Myers' dive fell short, McCormick walked away with her second gold medal, and her "double-double."

After 1956, a banner year in which she also won the Associated Press Athlete of the Year award and the Sullivan Trophy, McCormick retired from competition. She later opened a diving camp, where one of her prize students, her daughter *Kelly McCormick, trained for her own career in diving. With a style described as "eerily similar" to her mother's, Kelly went on to win her own silver and bronze medals in consecutive Olympic Games.

SOURCES:

Grace and Glory. Washington, DC: MultiMedia Partners, 1996.

Greenspan, Bud. *100 Greatest Moments in Olympic History.* Los Angeles, CA: GPG, 1995.

Johnson, Anne Janette. *Great Women in Sports.* Detroit, MI: Visible Ink, 1998.

Markel, Robert, Susan Waggoner, and Marcella Smith, eds. *The Women's Sports Encyclopedia.* NY: Henry Holt, 1997.

Woolum, Janet. *Outstanding Women Athletes: Who They Are and How They Influenced Sports in America.* Phoenix, AZ: Oryx Press, 1992.

McCormick, Ruth Hanna

(1880–1944)

*American politician who worked for suffrage, was elected "congressman-at-large" from Illinois, was the first woman from a major party to be nominated for the Senate, and managed the first presidential campaign of Thomas E. Dewey. Name variations: Ruth Hanna McCormick Simms. Born Ruth Hanna on March 27, 1880, in Cleveland, Ohio; died in Billings Hospital, Chicago, Illinois, on December 31, 1944, of pancreatitis following a fall from a horse; daughter of Marcus Alonzo Hanna, known as Mark Hanna (a U.S. senator) and Augusta Rhodes Hanna; attended Miss *(Sarah) Porter's School, Farmington, Connecticut; married (Joseph) Medill McCormick (1877–1925, a* *journalist and politician), in 1903 (died 1925); married Albert Gallatin Simms, in 1932; children: (first marriage) Katrina "Triny" McCormick; Medill McCormick (d. 1938); **Ruth "Bazy" McCormick.***

Moved to Chicago (1903) with husband Medill McCormick; founded women's division of National Civic Federation and Women's City Club of Chicago; served as chair of women's committee of Progressive Party in Chicago (1912); led successful suffrage campaign in Illinois (1913); served as chair of Congressional Committee of National American Woman Suffrage Association (1914); served as chair of Republican National Party Women's Executive Committee (1918–19); was Republican National Committeewoman for Illinois (1924); was at-large Representative to U.S. Congress, Illinois (1928); was Republican nominee for U.S. Senate (1930); moved to Albuquerque, New Mexico, with husband Albert Simms (1932); founded Manzano School and Sandia School for Girls (1932) and the Albuquerque June Music Festival (1942); was co-manager of preconvention presidential campaign of Thomas E. Dewey (1940).

The cover of *Time* magazine on April 23, 1928, featured a woman in a cloche hat with a wide grin and flashing brown eyes. "She learned the law of the jungle," announced the caption beneath the picture. Ruth Hanna McCormick had just defeated seven men in the Republican primary for "congressman-at-large" for Illinois; in November, she became the first woman to win a state-wide election for national office, ahead of the runner-up by 90,000 votes. Two years later, she beat the incumbent senator, Charles S. Deneen, twice governor and undefeated in 38 years of public service, to become the first woman nominated for the U.S. Senate by a major party. She lost the general election in the Democratic landslide at the onset of the Depression in 1930, but came back ten years later to break new ground for women when Thomas E. Dewey appointed her to manage his campaign for the Republican presidential nomination.

Ruth Hanna McCormick learned the love and practice of politics from her father Mark Hanna, a businessman who was just beginning his career in politics when she was born in 1880. In 1896, the year she turned 16, Hanna managed the successful presidential campaign of his Ohio neighbor, William McKinley. Ruth also worked for the McKinley campaign, serving lemonade to voters who came to see McKinley speak on the front porch of his home in Canton, Ohio. After McKinley was elected president, Hanna himself was elected to the U.S. Senate.

Hanna liked to invite all kinds of people to his house, and always said he could learn more from talking to people than from reading books. His daughter Ruth was the same. She was not a good student, and, after graduation from boarding school, she worked as her father's personal secretary in Washington. The Hannas lived across Lafayette Park from the White House, and she was hostess at her father's famous breakfasts, attended by the important politicians of the day, including Presidents McKinley and Theodore Roosevelt. She always craved her father's approval, but, she said later, "In all my life I never had one word of praise from my father. If he accepted the work, it was satisfactory. Otherwise, it came back to me to do over."

Even her marriage in 1903 to Chicago *Tribune* heir apparent Joseph Medill McCormick was a political affair. Hanna was Roosevelt's only serious rival for the Republican presidential nomination in 1904, and the president invited himself to the wedding in order to get on a friendly footing with "Uncle Mark." But the wedding date conflicted with a planned presidential speaking tour. When Roosevelt suggested that Ruth postpone the nuptials, she told the press: "The wedding has been set for the tenth of June. I am sure if Mr. Roosevelt understands this, he will arrange to reach Cleveland by that time." The president changed his itinerary.

ℛeal political achievement asks for all you've got, including all the years of your life. Nowhere is that better illustrated than in the life of Ruth [Hanna McCormick].

—**Raymond Moley**

Ruth McCormick moved to Chicago with her husband, who eventually forsook the newspaper business for politics. The two were involved in many early progressive reform groups in the city, including the Northwestern Settlement House behind the stockyards that provided material for Upton Sinclair's exposure of the meatpacking industry, *The Jungle*. Tensions at the Chicago *Tribune*, where Medill's powerful mother *Katherine Medill McCormick* was a controlling stockholder, led to his nervous breakdown in 1909. Ruth McCormick persuaded him to spend some months in Europe consulting Carl Jung, but Medill probably suffered from manic depression, and analysis was ultimately of little help. They did decide that he would be better off out of the family business.

When Roosevelt lost the Republican presidential nomination in 1912 to his successor

William Howard Taft, the McCormicks joined his breakaway Progressive "Bull Moose" Party. Medill McCormick was the Western campaign manager, while Ruth McCormick headed a group of Chicago women. Roosevelt privately considered her the more astute politician, remarking of the couple, "My money's on the mare!"

The Progressive Party was the only one to endorse woman suffrage in 1912. Although Roosevelt lost the presidential election, Medill won a seat as a Progressive in the Illinois state legislature. With Medill working with fellow Progressives who held the balance of power inside the statehouse in Springfield, Ruth McCormick joined **Grace Wilbur Trout, Elizabeth Booth**, and **Antoinette Funk** to lobby legislators outside. Together they worked to successfully pass, in 1913, the first woman suffrage bill east of the Mississippi, granting women the right to vote in presidential and municipal elections.

The year 1913 was also a significant one for the national suffrage movement. *Alice Paul had persuaded the National American Woman Suffrage Association (NAWSA) to allow her to reopen the Congressional Committee in Washington, D.C., to lobby Congress for a constitutional amendment granting women everywhere the right to vote. Paul had learned the strategies of civil disobedience working with suffrage advocates in England, but her use of them in the United States was unpopular with the rank and file of the suffrage movement. Ruth McCormick was chosen to replace Paul as chair of the Congressional Committee in 1914, and Paul continued to work with the smaller Congressional Union. The Congressional Union (later the Woman's Party) used controversial tactics such as holding the incumbent Democrats responsible for the passage of a suffrage amendment, campaigning against them when it did not pass, and picketing the White House. McCormick kept NAWSA on a political course, organizing grassroots support in the states and publishing a "black list" of congressional representatives opposed to a suffrage amendment, without alienating the large conservative membership.

By 1918, it seemed clear that women would soon win the vote (the 19th Amendment was ratified in August 1920), and the Republican Party, eager to attract new voters, named McCormick chair of the National Women's Executive Committee. She urged the men on the Republican National Committee to hold fast to progressive principles, which would appeal to women voters. She soon found, however, that she had no real power, and resigned at the end of 1919.

Medill had been elected, as a Republican, to the U.S. House of Representatives in 1916, and to the U.S. Senate in 1918, where he was a member of the Foreign Relations committee. A significant number of Republicans in the Senate objected to the Treaty of Versailles which President Woodrow Wilson helped negotiate at the end of World War I. Led by Henry Cabot Lodge and William Borah, the "Irreconcilables" were particularly opposed to the idea of a League of Nations, believing that it could commit the United States to unwise foreign intervention without due consultation with the Senate. This was an issue upon which Ruth McCormick's own political career would be based. Once again, she worked on the outside, together with her friend *Alice Roosevelt Longworth, Theodore Roosevelt's daughter, to lobby members of the Senate.

At the 1920 Republican Convention, the party reorganized itself to include the newly enfranchised women. Eight of the 21 members of the Executive Committee were women, including Ruth McCormick, who represented the Central Division. She was wryly amused at the condescension of male colleagues who said the women would learn the political game in time: "I wonder, if they think at all, how they think we became enfranchised." She believed that women needed to be involved in political parties to effect the changes they wanted. The Woman's Party or the League of Women Voters (successor organization to NAWSA) was as dependent upon political parties as the suffrage groups had been, she argued. Because of this belief, and also to support her husband's re-election in 1924, she began to organize Republican Women's Clubs all over Illinois, with a membership by the late 1920s of over 200,000. At the Republican Convention in June, the women were given equal representation with the men, one from each state, and McCormick was elected Republican National Committeewoman for Illinois.

Despite her efforts, Medill was narrowly defeated in the primary election by Charles S. Deneen, who went on to win the general election in November. Medill's term was due to expire in March 1925. One week before that, overcome by depression, he took his life, probably with an overdose of barbiturates.

Ruth McCormick had little time to grieve in private. The year before, she had organized a Women's World's Fair in Chicago to showcase the achievements of women in the world of work. Its underlying purpose, however, was to raise money for the Republican Women's Clubs, which had not been reimbursed for campaign expenses by the national committee. The fair,

Ruth
Hanna
McCormick

which opened just six weeks after Medill's death, succeeded in raising more than $50,000, and continued, larger every year, through the 1920s.

Ruth McCormick had managed a dairy farm in Byron, Illinois, beginning in 1913, and in 1927

she bought a newspaper in Rockford which she published until her death. These activities were not enough. She needed to redefine her political career, which had been, like that of many politically minded women of the era—including *Molly Dewson, *Belle Moskowitz, *Eleanor

Roosevelt—tied to the career of a man. She was urged to run for governor, to replace the corrupt Len Small. One supporter assured her, "I think you are the man for the job." She felt, however, that the complicated alliances of Illinois politics would make it impossible for her to win.

Instead, she decided to run for a seat as "congressman-at-large." In the early 20th century, as population grew rapidly, some states, instead of redistricting, added "congressmen-at-large," representing the whole state. Illinois had two "at large" seats. Ruth McCormick, who was an unconventional candidate in many ways, refused to repeat the old platitudes about the sacrifice she was making. "In all candor and honesty I must say that nobody asked me to run," she announced. Some were frankly appalled at the idea: one downstate farmer wrote that he would sooner vote for one of his cows than to vote for a woman for such a responsible office. Most voters saw her as an appealing alternative to politics as usual; the primary that year was termed the "pineapple primary" because grenades were thrown at the homes of other prominent politicians. She led the field of seven candidates, ahead of the runner-up by almost 100,000 votes.

Ruth McCormick was more of a politician than a legislator. Her two years in Congress were less an occasion to make laws than an opportunity to campaign. Although she seems to have been very responsive to constituent requests, she never spoke on the floor of the House at all. Instead she was thinking about a new campaign. She suspected that the 1930 census would lead to redistricting and the elimination of her seat. Information that she would run for the U.S. Senate in 1930 was leaked to the press in May 1929. The news, reported *The New York Times,* fell like a "bombshell" among the politicians of Illinois, now uncertain whether to support McCormick or her rival Deneen. Even though a candidate for senator would represent the same constituency as a "congressman-at-large," there was more opposition to a woman senator. There were eight women in the 435-member House of Representatives; the first, *Jeannette Rankin, had been elected in 1916. The 96-member Senate was more of a men's club, arguably the most powerful in the world, and even Hiram Johnson, Theodore Roosevelt's Progressive running mate in 1912, was concerned that her victory would mean "a punch in the eye to the Senate. . . . [I]ts thorough breakdown and demoralization, in my opinion, will come with the admission of the other sex."

McCormick had expanded her power base among Republican women to include support from labor and the African-American community. **Irene McCoy Gaines** (1892–1964), a prominent organizer among black women in Chicago, criticized Deneen's record, and recommended a vote for McCormick for the Senate "because we have nobody there." McCormick chose to run against Deneen because he had voted in favor of the World Court, which she denounced as the "back door" to the League of Nations. She waged an extensive campaign, speaking in all 102 counties in Illinois, and mounting a huge grass-roots organization. She won by over 200,000 votes, a victory doubly sweet because she vanquished the man who had defeated her husband.

Her sense of triumph was short-lived, for she had to face another seasoned politician in the general election. James Hamilton Lewis had been the minority whip in the Senate during the Wilson administration, and had, coincidentally, been defeated by Medill McCormick in 1918. He supported the repeal of Prohibition, which was becoming increasingly unpopular because it had given rise to gangsters like Al Capone. Illinois was also beginning to feel the effects of the beginning of the Great Depression.

Another problem for Ruth McCormick was a Senate investigation into her campaign expenditures, which had amounted to over $250,000. Even though she showed that all of the money spent had been hers, and claimed that large expenditures were needed to offset an incumbent's advantages, it seemed extravagant to many in the face of hard times. Also, as a United Press syndicated column observed, there was unease at the thought of a woman with such economic power: "What be, if women were permitted to spend their money like that? Certainly there would be no political sanctuary for men if such carryings on were allowed." However, the backlash against the Republicans in the first election after the stock-market crash of 1929 was the most decisive factor. The 1930 returns gave the Democrats eight seats in the Senate and 51 in the House. Ruth McCormick went down in the landslide. She was never one to look back in regret. Her daughter **Katrina "Triny" McCormick** observed, "I saw her through many triumphs and defeats, and you could hardly tell the difference."

Also defeated was a fellow Republican congressional representative from New Mexico, Albert Simms. They were married the following year, and Ruth moved herself, her children, and her cattle out to Albuquerque to begin a new life. The 1930s were not a good time for Republicans, and although she remained modestly active, seconding the nomination of Alf Landon for president in 1936 and campaigning for him, she became involved in her new community. She founded a school for girls in 1932, the Manzano and Sandia Schools. She was active in the Little Theater, founded the Albuquerque June Music Festival in 1942, and used an annex to her house for art exhibits and lecture series. She seemed content, according to her younger daughter **Ruth "Bazy" McCormick**, to be a "semi-retired suburban woman."

In the summer of 1938, however, her middle child and only son, Medill, was killed mountain-climbing outside of Albuquerque at the age of 21. His body was not recovered for a week, and the search was an ordeal that tested her to the limit. The following autumn, Ruth broke her hip, and was bedridden in view of the mountain where her son had died. As she listened to the radio, she began to hear about a dynamic young man in New York, District Attorney Thomas E. Dewey. In the summer of 1939 she went to New York to meet him, and by fall, she was working as his campaign manager.

The year 1939 was an auspicious one for her to re-enter the political scene. The Republicans had made a comeback in the 1938 congressional elections, and Franklin Delano Roosevelt, if he ran, would be seeking an unprecedented third term. Dewey was more charismatic than other Republican contenders, but he was young—only 37—and inexperienced. He needed a seasoned political mentor like Ruth Hanna McCormick. The principal issue was American involvement in the growing European war; McCormick and Thomas Dewey represented the widespread antiwar sentiment of that time. Once again, she ran an extensive and meticulously organized campaign, touring all over the West at the age of 60. Dewey was leading in the primaries when, on June 10, Italy entered the war on the side of the Axis powers. Dewey's youth and inexperience told against him, and the convention turned to Wendell Willkie, who was older and had more international leanings. Willkie, however, was defeated in November by Roosevelt, whom the American public preferred during the time of crisis.

Ruth returned to the West to manage a cattle and sheep ranch she had bought in southern Colorado, but continued to advise Dewey about strategy for the 1944 election. At first Dewey seemed eager for her opinions, but gradually consulted her less and less. When a reporter called her to ask the cause of the break between them, she wrote him one last letter, announcing that she would campaign for him whether he

welcomed it or not: "I will always be active in party affairs. . . . It is my inheritance and my conviction of my participation as a citizen. It is my right and my pleasure."

Just before the election, her horse tripped when she was riding out to inspect her sheep, and she fractured her collarbone. McCormick was making a good recovery when, six weeks after the accident, she suddenly developed pancreatitis, from which she died on December 31, 1944.

At the time women entered electoral politics, Ruth Hanna McCormick was unusually well qualified to take advantage of the new opportunities, and her career illustrates the possibilities and limitations of women's expanding role. She was a leader in many fields: the suffrage movement, party politics, campaigns and elections. However, her colleague and friend **Helen Bennett** believed that her most important accomplishment was to draw large numbers of women into the partisan political process itself.

SOURCES:

Miller, Kristie. *Ruth Hanna McCormick: A Life in Politics 1880–1944.* Albuquerque, NM: University of New Mexico Press, 1992.

Moley, Raymond. *27 Masters of Politics in a Personal Perspective.* NY: Funk & Wagnalls, 1949.

Time. April 23, 1928.

SUGGESTED READING:

Chamberlin, Hope. *A Minority of Members: Women in the U.S. Congress.* NY: Praeger Publishers, 1973.

COLLECTIONS:

Hanna-McCormick Family Papers. Manuscript Division. Library of Congress, Washington D.C.

Kristie Miller,
journalist and author of *Ruth Hanna McCormick: A Life in Politics 1880–1944* (University of New Mexico Press, 1992),
and Ruth Hanna McCormick's granddaughter

McCorquodale, Barbara (1901–2000).

See Cartland, Barbara.

McCoubrey, Margaret (1880–1955)

Scottish suffragist, trade unionist and economist. Born in Eldersley, Scotland, in 1880; died in Carnlough, County Antrim, Northern Ireland, in 1955; attended Manchester University; married.

Margaret McCoubrey was born in 1880 in the small town of Eldersley, Scotland, near Glasgow. At age 12, she went to work in a men's outfitters shop, but also continued her education and in 1896 qualified as a junior shorthand typist. McCoubrey secured employment as the secretary to the managing director of the first private telephone service in Scotland in 1899, and also became a teacher at Skerries Business Training College. She was named deputy headmistress of the college in 1904.

McCoubrey married and moved to Belfast, Northern Ireland, in 1905. Five years later, she joined the suffragist movement, becoming a militant. She also developed an interest in trade unionism, and served as general secretary of the Cooperative Guild from 1910 to 1916. During World War I, she was active in the pacifist movement, and taught economics and history in the educational department of the Cooperative Guild.

Following the end of World War I, McCoubrey was elected Labour Party councillor for the Dock Ward of Belfast in 1920. During the 1920s, she spent a year studying economics at Manchester University and contributed scholarly pieces to economic and trade-union periodicals, including the *Co-op News* and the *Wheat Sheaf*. McCoubrey moved to Carnlough, County Antrim, in 1933, to run Drumalla House, a nonprofit retreat for members of the Belfast Girl's Club Union. She remained active in politics and the trade-union movement as an orator (her voice was powerful enough for her to disdain the use of a microphone) for the rest of her life, and died in Carnlough in 1955.

SOURCES:
Newmann, Kate, comp. *Dictionary of Ulster Biography*. The Institute of Irish Studies, the Queen's University of Belfast, 1993.

Grant Eldridge,
freelance writer, Pontiac, Michigan

McCoy, Elizabeth (1903–1978)

American bacteriologist. Born in Madison, Wisconsin, in 1903; died in Madison, Wisconsin, in 1978; daughter of Cassius McCoy (a farmer) and Esther (Williamson) McCoy (a nurse); received undergraduate degree and Ph.D. in bacteriology (1929) from the University of Wisconsin.

Elizabeth McCoy was born on her family's farm in Madison, Wisconsin, in 1903. Her mother, **Esther Williamson McCoy**, had considered attending medical school before deciding to study nursing and for six years put off marrying her fiancé Cassius McCoy so that she could continue to work as a nurse. Elizabeth McCoy inherited her mother's love of science, although as she was growing up she also demonstrated such an interest in farming that her father decided to groom her rather than her brother to take over the family spread. An apt student, McCoy completed an accelerated secondary education and then attended the University of Wisconsin to study general bacteriology. She was so dedicated to learning all she could in her field that she took graduate courses before completing her undergraduate degree. She received a doctorate in 1929 and was hired by the university as an assistant professor of bacteriology the following year.

Although female scientists were rare at the time, McCoy distinguished herself in bacteriology. She began to specialize within her field after joining the faculty at Wisconsin, and became an authority on the bacteria of lake ecosystems. She also studied butyl alcohol-producing bacteria, known as *clostridia*, and traveled to Puerto Rico to help the territorial government establish a butyl alcohol fermentation plant. (This work led her to develop a new culture of *clostridia*, which she patented.) McCoy's expertise in creating new strains of bacteria yielded many useful results, but the single most important was probably her creation of Strain X1612, a bacterium which made the production of penicillin for civilian use economically and scientifically feasible. She remained an active student, researcher, and teacher of bacteriology until her retirement in 1973, after which she concentrated on researching the development of bacteria to treat sewage. McCoy was still engaged in this research when she died in Madison in 1978, bequeathing her beloved family farm to the University of Wisconsin.

SOURCES:
Bailey, Brooke. *100 Women Healers and Scientists*. Holbrook, MA: Bob Adams, Inc., 1994.

Grant Eldridge,
freelance writer, Pontiac, Michigan

McCoy, Iola Fuller (1906–1997)

American writer. Name variations: Iola Fuller. Born on January 25, 1906 (or 1905), in Marcellus, Michigan; died on July 19, 1997, in Morgan, Ohio; daughter of Henry Fuller and Clara (Reynolds) Fuller; graduated from the University of Michigan, A.B., 1935, A.M., English, 1940, A.M.L.S., 1962; married first husband; married Raymond McCoy (an artist); children: (first marriage) Paul Goodspeed.

Born in Marcellus, Michigan, on January 25, 1906, Iola Fuller McCoy was the daughter of Henry Fuller and **Clara Reynolds Fuller**. Married twice, she had one son, Paul Goodspeed, from her first marriage. She received an A.B. in 1935 from the University of Michigan, and an M.A. in English in 1940. She later went on to study library science, receiving an A.M.L.S. degree in 1962. From 1964 to 1969, she was an associate professor of English at Ferris State College. During her career, she also helped to set up new school libraries.

Greatly influenced by her creative writing professor at the University of Michigan, Roy W. Cowden, McCoy started writing historical novels in the late 1930s. She valued accuracy in historical material in her work, and her stories often focused on characters who had to strive against great odds to attain their goals. She traveled extensively throughout Canada, Mexico, the United States, and Europe to gather research for her novels. A Phi Beta Kappa scholar, McCoy received the Avery Hopwood Award for Creative Writing in 1940 and the Michigan Distinguished Alumni Award in 1967. Her novels include *The Loon Feather* (1940), about the history of Mackinac Island in Michigan; *The Shining Trail* (1943), a portrait of the Native American chief Black Hawk; *The Gilded Torch* (1958), about La Salle's discovery of the mouth of the Mississippi River; and *All the Golden Gifts* (1966), which details life in the court of King Louis XIV.

SOURCES:

Commire, Anne. *Something About the Author.* Vol. 3. Detroit, MI: Gale Research, 1972.

Contemporary Authors. Vol. 13–16. Detroit, MI: Gale Research, 1975.

Michigan Authors. 2nd ed. Michigan Association for Media in Education, 1980.

Lolly Ockerstrom,
freelance writer, Washington, D.C.

McCoy, Memphis Minnie (1897–1973).

See Douglas, Lizzie.

McCracken, Elizabeth

(c. 1865–1944)

Irish suffragist. Name variations: (pseudonym) L.A.M. Priestly. Born around 1865; died in 1944.

Elizabeth McCracken's exact birth date is unknown, but she is believed to have been born around 1865. She spent her summers in Bangor, County Down, in what is today Northern Ireland, and gained renown as one of Ulster's leading advocates of women's suffrage. (Women over the age of 30 in Britain gained the right to vote in 1918, followed in 1928 by the right to vote for those under 30.) McCracken published numerous articles on women's suffrage under the pseudonym L.A.M. Priestly; her books include *The Feminine in Fiction.* Elizabeth McCracken died in 1944.

Grant Eldridge,
freelance writer, Pontiac, Michigan

McCracken, Esther Helen

(b. around 1902)

English playwright and actress. Born Esther Helen Armstrong in Newcastle-upon-Tyne, England, around 1902; married Angus McCracken (a lieutenant-colonel who would die in action in World War II in 1943); married Mungo Campbell.

Esther Helen McCracken acted with the Newcastle Repertory Company from 1924 to 1937. Her first play, *The Willing Spirit,* was produced in 1936; two years later, *Quiet Wedding* sealed McCracken's reputation as a first-rate playwright of domestic comedy. She also wrote *Quiet Weekend* (1941) and *No Medals* (1944).

McCracken, Mary Ann

(1770–1866)

Irish political feminist, radical, and philanthropist who was prominent in a range of charitable and reforming societies. Name variations: Mary McCracken. Born on July 8, 1770, in Belfast, County Antrim, Ireland; died in Belfast on July 26, 1866; sixth of seven children of John McCracken (a ship's captain and merchant) and Ann (Joy) McCracken; attended David Manson's Play School in Belfast; never married; children: none of her own, but cared for her brother Harry's illegitimate daughter Maria.

Soon after leaving school, started a small muslin manufacturing business with her sister, Margaret; shared her brother Henry's interest in radical politics and social justice; attended his trial on charges of involvement in the United Irishmen's rebellion of 1798, and accompanied him to his execution at the old Market House in Belfast (July 17, 1798); continued to assist former United Irishmen and their dependents, including Thomas Russell who was executed at Downpatrick (October 21, 1803); retired from business (about 1815); was a member of the ladies' committee of the Belfast Poorhouse (1814–16); was a member of the ladies' committee reconstituted (1827) and secretary (1832–51); was a member of the committee of the Ladies' Industrial School (1847–66); was a member of the Belfast Ladies' Clothing Society and of the Society for the Relief of the Destitute Sick; involved in the temperance and anti-slavery movements and in the campaign to outlaw the use of climbing boys as chimney sweeps.

On July 8, 1798, Mary Ann McCracken's 28th birthday, word was received at the family home in Rosemary Street, Belfast, that her much-loved brother, Harry, had been arrested. The news, though shocking, was not unexpected. As one of the leaders of the radical political society the United Irishmen, Henry Joy McCracken had been a fugitive since the defeat, a few weeks earlier, of the rising against British rule in Ireland. During that period, Mary Ann had spent two days searching for her brother in the mountains outside Belfast and, having found him, had supplied him with money and clothes and had tried to arrange his escape by ship to America. The scheme failed: Harry was taken prisoner on the eve of his departure and, having been held for a few days in Carrickfergus, where he was visited by McCracken and her father, was taken on the evening of July 16 to his home town of Belfast, where he was to stand trial. McCracken, in her correspondence and in later recollections, has left a vivid account of the traumatic events of those days, in which she herself was to play a central part.

On hearing of Harry's arrival in the city, she and her sister, **Margaret McCracken**, immediately set out to try to see him, and eventually succeeded in gaining access to the prison. Very early on the following morning, and in accordance with her brother's instructions, Mary Ann traveled to Lisburn to fetch a witness whom he wished to testify on his behalf, and, on her return to Belfast, hurried to the Exchange, where the trial had just begun. Having listened to the evidence against her brother, she herself appeared as a witness, drawing attention to some inconsistencies in the prosecution's evidence. However, the outcome was never really in doubt. Having refused to give information on his fellow rebels to the authorities, Harry was already resigned to conviction. As he admitted to his sister, though some of the prosecution witnesses had perjured themselves, "the truth would have answered the same purpose." Mary Ann, despite her exertions, "little expected that any efforts to save him would be successful; but I felt I had a duty to perform—to prevent misrepresentation, and to put it out of the power of his enemies to injure his character while living, or his memory when dead." Visiting him in his cell after the trial, she was in time to hear him informed of his imminent execution. She quickly regained her composure and self-possession in order to support Harry in these final hours. "I knew," she wrote,

> it was incumbent on me to avoid disturbing the last moments of my brother's life, and I endeavoured to contribute to render them worthy of his whole career. We conversed as calmly as we had ever done. . . . We had been brought up in a firm conviction of an all-wise and overruling Providence, and of the duty of entire resignation to the Divine Will. I remarked that his death was as much a dispensation of Providence as if it had happened in the common course of nature; to which he assented. . . . About 5 p.m. he was ordered to the place of execution, the old Market House, the ground of which had been given to the town by his great-grandfather. I took his arm, and we walked together to the place of execution, when I was told it was the General's orders I should leave him, which I peremptorily refused to do. Harry begged I would go. Clasping my hands around him—I did not weep till then—I said I could bear anything but leaving him. Three times he kissed me, and entreated I would go; and looking round to recognise some friend to put me in charge of, he beckoned to a Mr. Boyd, and said, 'He will take charge of you' . . . and, fearing any further refusal would disturb the last moments of my dearest brother, I suffered myself to be led away.

The strength, the religious faith, and the independence of mind which McCracken displayed during this period of crisis, and which were to characterize her entire career, were derived from a strong family tradition of self-reliance and of service to the community. In the rapidly growing Belfast of the late 18th century, the McCrackens and the Joys were noted not only for their enterprise, demonstrated by their involvement in the trade and industry upon which the city's fortunes were founded, but also for their sense of civic duty and moral responsibility. Francis Joy, Mary Ann's maternal grandfather, was a lawyer, a leading citizen of Belfast and the founder in 1737 of the *Belfast Newsletter*, the first newspaper to be printed in the city. Of Francis' sons, Henry was a notable entrepreneur, active in municipal politics, while Robert Joy was the founder of the Volunteer Company in Belfast, a movement established initially to protect Ireland from invasion in time of war, but which quickly became a mouthpiece for demands for the removal of legal disabilities on Catholics and Dissenters and for the establishment of an Irish Parliament for the Irish people. Both men were also active in the creation of the Belfast Charitable Society, founded in 1752 with the object of establishing a poorhouse and hospital in the city. Their sister **Ann Joy**, Mary Ann's mother, showed a comparable streak of independence when, before her marriage, she opened a milliner's shop and later, after her children had grown up, started a small muslin industry. Her husband John McCracken was, like the Joys, a Presbyterian. A sea captain and a merchant, he was a deeply religious and upright

*Mary Ann
McCracken
with her niece
Maria, c. 1801.*

man, and it was recount-
ed of him as proof of his integrity that at a time when smuggling was a commonplace and profitable
activity, he would not engage in it, nor allow his
sailors to do so on his behalf. He was also charitable, taking part with Robert Joy and others in
efforts to improve the conditions of French prisoners of war held at Belfast, and founding the
Marine Charitable Society as a fund to assist
sailors at times of need.

Mary Ann was born on July 8, 1770, the
second youngest of Ann and John McCracken's
six surviving children. She received what was for
a girl of the time an unusually full education.
Like her brothers, she attended a school which

had been founded in
Belfast a few years earlier by
David Manson, whose views on
the education of children were remarkably humane and progressive. Believing that "tuition should be made a labour of love to both the
pupil and the master," Manson urged his teachers to gain the affection and confidence of their
pupils, to "make them sensible of kindness and
friendly concerns for their welfare; and when
punishment becomes necessary . . . convince
them 'tis not their *persons* but their *faults* which
he dislikes." Manson was an enthusiastic exponent of co-education, and female pupils received
exactly the same education as their male counterparts. In McCracken's case, this early training

must have reinforced the sense of confidence and of responsibility which she was already imbibing at home, while also providing her with the practical skills necessary to achieving a degree of independence. Some time after leaving school, wishing to have some money of her own and following her mother's example, she proposed to her sister Margaret that they should go into business together. The two started a muslin manufacturing industry, which was initially a small scale operation employing workers in their own homes, but which by 1809 had moved into factory production. While Mary Ann paid tribute to the contribution of her sister, it was apparently she who was the moving spirit in the enterprise, and she, with her talent for figures, who was in charge of its financial affairs.

While the McCrackens were an affectionate and united family, Mary was particularly close to Margaret and to her older brother, Henry Joy, called Harry. Harry had been a clever, passionate and popular boy; as he grew older, his idealism showed itself in efforts to improve social conditions and in dissatisfaction with the political establishment. In 1791, he joined the United Irishmen, a new society, inspired by the example of the French Revolution, and dedicated to the achievement of complete legislative reform "founded on a communion of rights, and a union of power among Irishmen of every religious persuasion." The Society became increasingly radical, ultimately demanding a complete separation from Britain rather than merely reform, and was suppressed by the government in 1794. Mary Ann sympathized with her brother's republican and revolutionary views, and was herself deeply interested in the reforming ideology of contemporary writers such as William Godwin, Thomas Paine and *Mary Wollstonecraft. Indeed, drawing on her reading of Wollstonecraft, she went considerably further than her brother and his associates in her conception of the rights of man as also applying to members of her own sex. While the United Irishmen themselves gave no indication of any concern for the rights of women as citizens within the democratic and secular republic which they envisaged, Mary McCracken rejected any suggestion of women's inability to participate on equal terms within the social and political structure. As she argued, writing to her brother in 1797 when he was imprisoned in Dublin, "if we suppose woman was created for a companion for man, she must of course be his equal in understanding, as without equality of mind, there can be no friendship, and without friendship, there can be no happiness in society." Optimisti-

cally, she suggested that the creation of a democratic republican system would usher in a new era of egalitarianism in which women too would assume the obligations as well as the rights of citizenship. "Is it not almost time," she asked,

> for the clouds of error and prejudice to disperse and that the female part of the Creation as well as the male should throw off the fetters with which they have been so long mentally bound? . . . I do not hold out the motive of interest as an inducement for man to be just, as I think the reign of prejudice is nearly at an end, and that the truth and justice of our cause alone is sufficient to support it, as there can be no argument produced in favour of the slavery of women that has not been used in favour of general slavery. . . . I therefore hope that it is reserved for the Irish nation to strike out something new and to shew an example of candour, generosity, and justice superior to any that have gone before them.

The defeat of the United Irishmen's rising of 1798 put a sudden and decisive end to such hopes. In its aftermath, Henry Joy McCracken, who had acted as general of the rebel forces in the North, was executed, another brother, William McCracken, was imprisoned, and a third, Francis McCracken, also a member of the United movement, left the country temporarily for his own safety. One shred of comfort was provided for Mary Ann in the fact that Harry's friend and fellow radical, Thomas Russell, was currently in prison and could not be implicated in the rising. Writing to inform him of her brother's death, she expressed the hope "that the cause for which so many of our friends have fought and have died may yet be successful and that you may be preserved to enjoy the fruits of it." In fact, Russell was himself to be executed in 1803 for his involvement in Robert Emmet's abortive rising of that year. In the period before his arrest, he had been in hiding in Ulster, during which time Mary had supplied him with money, met him on at least one occasion and, when he was arrested, undertook to pay for his defense from the profits of her own business and from a collection among sympathetic friends.

There is little doubt that McCracken was in love with Russell, but there is also little reason to doubt her protestation that her actions on his behalf were a response to:

> a call to duty of such sacred importance that no person similarly situated could have resisted; for how was it possible to shrink back when told that human lives were at stake, which my exertions might be instrumental in saving. . . . Even had [Russell] not been of the number, I would have felt it my bounden

duty to go forward in the business, and, once having undertaken it, there was no question of drawing back from pecuniary risk.

Characteristically, McCracken sought comfort for her losses in practical action. Following Harry's death, she had taken on responsibility for the care of his illegitimate child, Maria, to whom she offered a home and a stable and loving environment. Now she also sent assistance to Russell's sister, **Margaret Russell**, and to other members of his family, and for the rest of her life was to act as an advisor and benefactor to many needy former insurgents and their dependents. Like many other former Belfast radicals following the defeat of the 1798 rising and the subsequent union of the Irish and British legislatures, she herself had turned from politics and, indeed, from the overt feminism of her youth to a more approved form of service. As an employer and through her family's involvement in various charitable undertakings, she had become aware of the condition of the workers and of the poorest classes in Belfast; in 1803, a letter probably written by her appeared in the *Belfast Newsletter,* in which factory proprietors were urged to regard themselves as fulfilling a parental role towards their workers and to do all in their power to prevent "emaciation, ignorance, and vice" in their establishments. When in 1815 she was forced by a serious decline in trade and by financial losses to give up her business, she sought new outlets for her energy, embarking in middle age on a second career as a philanthropist and social reformer.

As a child, she had often been taken by her mother to visit the Belfast Poorhouse, founded in 1771 by her uncle Robert Joy, and, in what must have been one of the first of her benevolent enterprises, she and her cousin Bab had collected funds and arranged for the making of new gowns for the girls resident there. By the beginning of the 19th century, the expansion of Belfast, growing rural unemployment, and the decline of the domestic linen industry had resulted in increased destitution, putting pressure on the poorhouse's resources. In 1814, in an effort to deal with the range of problems arising within the institution, the all-male governing body inaugurated a ladies' committee to oversee the welfare of women and children residents. Mary Ann McCracken, who had maintained her interest in the poorhouse and had from time to time offered suggestions to the governors on its conduct, was an obvious recruit, and from the beginning took a leading part in its business. Over the next two years, the committee put forward a number of recommendations for a more humane and efficient regime within the institution, press-

ing for the provision of an extra dormitory, for improvements in the girls' school, and for increased attention to cleanliness and the avoidance of infection. Although the committee apparently ceased to exist in 1816, McCracken continued to take an interest in the running of the poorhouse and in the condition of its inmates. When in 1827 a visit to Belfast by the prison reformer *Elizabeth Fry prompted the foundation of a new ladies' committee, McCracken was once more included, quickly becoming its dominant and most hard-working member. One of her major concerns, reflected in the work of the committee, was the provision of an education which would adequately equip the girls for their future lives: instruction in needlework, straw plaiting, and housework was introduced and, in an innovative move, an infant school was established for the younger children in the house. The ladies also supervised the running of the girls' school, sought employment for children leaving the home, enquired into their progress and treatment during their first months after departure, and made recommendations for improvements in the cleanliness of the living quarters and inmates and in the diet provided. From 1848, the ladies' committee began to be less active, as the functions of the poorhouse increasingly passed to the workhouse established under the recent Poor Law legislation. On some occasions, McCracken was the only member to attend its regular meeting, and in October 1851, when the committee ceased its operations, she made the final entry in its minute book. She was then 81 years old and had been secretary to the committee for the past 19 years.

> *I*s it not almost time for the clouds of error and prejudice to disperse and that the female part of the Creation as well as the male should throw off the fetters with which they have been so long mentally bound and, conscious of the dignity and importance of their nature, rise to the situation for which they were designed?
>
> —Mary Ann McCracken

The poorhouse was only one among a range of Mary McCracken's concerns during the half century of her "retirement." As she told a friend, "I have allowed my out-of-door avocations to increase so much, that I have less command of time now than when I was occupied with business. . . . I fear that undertaking too many things prevents me from doing anything as it ought to be; but somehow one gets entangled unawares, and cannot draw back, particularly if they [sic] think that they are usefully employed."

The numerous bodies to which she gave her assistance included the Belfast Ladies' Clothing Society and the Society for the Relief of the Destitute Sick, for both of which she was a collector. In 1847, at the height of the Great Famine in which up to a million people died, she was involved in a ladies' relief association and was instrumental in the establishment of an industrial school for poor girls, with which she continued to be associated for many years. In addition to a range of private and church-based charities, she also campaigned against the use of children as chimney sweeps and was an active and voluble opponent of the slave trade. Having seen the abolition of the trade in the British colonies, she continued to agitate against its survival in the United States, noting sadly in extreme old age that America, whose struggle for democracy and independence had inspired her brother and his associates in the 1790s, might now "more properly be styled the land of the tyrant and the slave," and that Belfast, "once so celebrated for its love of liberty is now so sunk in the love of filthy lucre that there are but sixteen or seventeen female anti-slavery advocates . . . and none to distribute papers to American emigrants but an old woman within seventeen days of eighty nine."

Mary McCracken never lost the passion for justice and the willingness to fight to achieve it which had marked her entire life. "She had naturally," her grand-niece, **Anna McCleery** noted, "a quick and hasty temper, though evidence of this was rarely seen; but even when at an advanced age, if a helpless person were wronged, or an animal cruelly treated, it was startling to see how her eye would flash, and to hear her indignant words." Increasing weakness, however, gradually forced her retirement from public activities, although, as one of the very few surviving witnesses, she continued to be an invaluable source of information on the republican movement of the 1790s and on the rising of 1798, contributing substantially, for instance, to Dr. R.R. Madden's monumental *Lives and Times of the United Irishmen* (published 1843–46).

On July 26, 1866, at the age of 96 and having outlived virtually all of her contemporaries, she died in the home which she had shared for many years with Maria, Harry's child and her own "only and affectionate daughter." Her death removed one of the doughtiest fighters for the rights of the poor of her own city, and tributes from the many causes to which she had given assistance celebrated the achievements of "a life so rich in all good works, and a spirit so full of love."

Disappointed in her early hopes of a radical reform in the political and social order, Mary Ann McCracken turned instead to one of the few public areas open to women in the 19th century and, while denied the rights of citizenship, demonstrated her ability to fulfil its obligations through her commitment to public service. It was a commitment based on religious convictions which she saw as the indispensable basis of public no less than of private virtue; in a letter to her long-time friend Dr. Madden, she declared the principles upon which her early radicalism and republicanism as well as the philanthropy of her later years were founded:

> Religion also should be called to aid the regeneration . . . of our political as well as our social and individual character. Its Divine precepts are simple and easily comprehended—to do to others as we would wish others to do to us; to do no evil that good may come of it; to love our neighbour as ourselves, and to be guided by the parable of the good Samaritan, to consider all who are within reach of our kindness as our neighbours, however they may differ from us in our religious belief; thus endeavouring to become in reality what we profess to be, true and sincere Christians; for then indeed would this world become a paradise of peace.

SOURCES:

Curtin, Nancy J. "Women and Eighteenth-Century Irish Republicanism," in *Women in Early Modern Ireland*. Edited by Margaret MacCurtain and Mary O'Dowd. Dublin: Wolfhound Press, 1991, pp. 13–146.

Gray, John. "Mary Ann McCracken: Belfast Revolutionary and Pioneer of Feminism" in *The Women of 1798*. Edited by Daire Keogh and Nicholas Furlong. Dublin: Four Courts Press, 1998.

McCleery, Anne. "Life of Mary Ann McCracken, sister of Henry Joy McCracken, by her grand-niece," in *Historical Notices of Old Belfast*. Belfast, 1896, pp. 175–197.

McNeill, Mary. *The Life and Times of Mary Ann McCracken, 1770–1866*. Dublin: Allen Figgis, 1960.

SUGGESTED READING:

Chart, D.A., ed. *The Drennan Letters*. Belfast: HMSO, 1931.

Dickson, David, Daire Keogh, and Kevin Whelan. *The United Irishmen: Republicanism, Radicalism and Rebellion*. Dublin: Lilliput Press, 1993.

COLLECTIONS:

Copies of correspondence of the McCracken family, Public Record Office, Belfast.

Joy Mss., Linenhall Library, Belfast.

Madden Papers, Trinity College, Dublin.

Rosemary Raughter,
freelance writer in women's history, Dublin, Ireland

McCrea, Jane (c. 1752–1777)

Young Hudson Valley woman murdered during the American Revolution. Born around 1752, near Bed-

minster (later Lamington), Somerset County, New Jersey; died of bullet wounds and scalping on July 27, 1777, near Fort Edward, New York; daughter of James McCrea (a Presbyterian minister) and Mary (Graham) McCrea.

For decades after her death in 1777, the name of Jane McCrea symbolized romantic martyrdom and the loss of innocent life as British, American colonial, and indigenous forces battled for hegemony on the North American continent during the American Revolution. It has been said that McCrea's ignoble murder and the furor that resulted from it fueled the support needed for American colonial forces to emerge victorious at Saratoga later that year, a turning point in the American War for Independence.

Jane McCrea was born around 1752 in what is now Somerset County, New Jersey, into a family of Scots-Irish descent. Her father was a Presbyterian minister, and her mother died when Jane was around a year old. James McCrea later remarried, and in total Jane would have six brothers and sisters and five younger half-siblings. After her father died when she was a teenager, she moved to the home of her brother John near the Hudson Valley town of Northumberland. John was a Princeton graduate, a lawyer in Albany, and a colonel in the American colonial army. The McCrea family was a divided one during this era of revolution: some of Jane's brothers served in the militia of the colonial "patriot" forces, while others were loyal to the British side.

Described as an attractive young woman, tall and with long blonde hair, McCrea had been courted for several years by David Jones, whom she had known in New Jersey. When the war intensified in 1776, Jones enlisted in the British army and came under the command of General John Burgoyne. With a military objective to sever the lower colonies from the rest of New England, Burgoyne and his forces attacked settlements and forts along the important Hudson River route that led from Lake Champlain to New York City. By the summer of 1777, many families were fleeing the area, and McCrea's brother urged her to go with him to Albany. But David Jones, now a colonel, had written to her that he would be in the area, and hoped to see her at nearby Fort Edward. There was some later speculation that they had planned to be married by the British chaplain the next day.

On July 27, 1777, while Jane McCrea was visiting a friend, **Sarah McNeil**, who was preparing to leave the area imminently, they were surprised by a party of Indians working on behalf of Burgoyne and the British. It remains unclear whether the women were taken prisoner as part of a military objective, or whether the Indians had been sent to escort McCrea to meet Jones. (Understandably, McCrea's sympathies probably lay with the English cause.) The exact reason for her death is also unclear; the Indians may have quarreled over whose prisoner she was, although they claimed that colonial soldiers pursuing them had accidentally killed her. What is known is that she was shot while on horseback and then scalped. Sarah McNeil arrived in British hands safely, but the Indians carried McCrea's distinctive scalp (reportedly she possessed very long tresses) and demanded the reward that the British allegedly were paying for colonial scalps. McCrea's body, which David Jones retrieved, was riddled with bullet wounds.

McCrea's remains were initially interred near Fort Edward at Moses Kill, and later moved to the Union Cemetery near Hudson Falls, New York. Jones deserted the British army and lived out the rest of his life in the Canadian wilderness. McCrea's death became a great sensation of the time, a classic tale of fateful tragedy befalling star-crossed lovers that took on even greater dimensions in a time of war. More significantly, her murder provoked intense sentiment against the British. The American side used the incident to stir sympathy for their cause and to portray the British as a dishonorable, loathsome bunch, and indeed the death of an attractive civilian swung many previously neutral colonists to the patriot side. Even a member of England's House of Commons publicly condemned his army's use of Native American allies in the war against the colonists. Burgoyne and his forces were defeated just three months later.

The tale of Jane McCrea was standard in many contemporary accounts of the American Revolution and later histories, and was the subject of an 1839 play called *The Bride of Fort Edward* by *Delia Salter Bacon. A Currier & Ives print even commemorated the horrific incident (and was quite popular). During the first half of the 19th century, devotees of her legend used to make pilgrimages to her grave on July 27, but over the decades this descended into a cult of sorts and her bones were stolen and the headstone chipped for souvenirs. By the time of the Civil War, Jane McCrea's death had faded from popular memory.

SOURCES:

Edgerton, Samuel Y., Jr. "The Murder of Jane McCrea," in *Early American Life*. June 1977, pp. 28–30.

James, Edward T., ed. *Notable American Women, 1607–1950*. Cambridge, MA: The Belknap Press of Harvard University Press, 1971.

McHenry, Robert, ed. *Famous American Women*. NY: Dover, 1980.

RELATED MEDIA:

A (factually inaccurate) painting by John Vanderlyn of *The Murder of Jane McCrea* is in the collection of the Wadsworth Athenaeum in Hartford, Connecticut.

Carol Brennan,
Grosse Pointe, Michigan

McCue, Lillian de la Torre Bueno (c. 1902–1993)

American writer of historical mysteries. Name variations: (pseudonym) Lillian de la Torre. Born Lillian de la Torre Bueno in New York City around 1902; died in Colorado Springs, Colorado, on September 13, 1993; graduated from New Rochelle College; earned master's degrees from Columbia and Harvard-Radcliffe; taught high school English; married George McCue (an English professor at Colorado College), in 1932 (died 1984).

As a child, Lillian de la Torre Bueno McCue became fascinated with detective stories shelved in her father's library and later could hardly recall a time when she was not "addicted." She did not, however, begin writing until her middle years, when she began to speculate about how Samuel Johnson might have approached mysteries of his era. Describing herself as a histo-detector, McCue used scholarly research to delve into old crimes and scandals, especially those in 18th-century Britain, and arrive at her own modern solutions. In related work, she also took real people and events and wove them into fictionalized plots. Her first book *Elizabeth Is Missing or Truth Triumphant* dismissed 12 theories on the famous 1753 disappearance of **Elizabeth Canning**, a maidservant near the Tower of London, and offered the author's own. McCue had combined, said *The New York Times*' reviewer, "the scholarly patience of a candidate for a Ph.D." with the "ingenuity of a Nero Wolfe." She followed with a similar book, *Villainy Detected* (1947). But her most popular fiction comprised a series of short stories about Samuel Johnson and James Boswell under the title *Dr. Sam: Johnson, Detector*. A founding member of the Colorado Springs Chorale and a former president of the Mystery Writers of America, McCue wrote for nearly 50 years and was working on a manuscript at the time of her death.

McCullers, Carson (1917–1967)

One of the most gifted and original writers to emerge from the American South in the 1940s, whose haunting novels and stories about loneliness and frustrated love have long appealed to readers, scholars, and critics throughout the world. Born Lula Carson Smith in Columbus, Georgia, on February 19, 1917; died at Nyack Hospital in Nyack, New York, following a massive cerebral hemorrhage, on September 29, 1967; oldest child of Lamar Smith (a watchmaker and jeweler) and Marguerite Waters Smith (a homemaker); sister of Margarita G. Smith (fiction editor for Mademoiselle); attended public schools in Columbus, graduating from Columbus High School in 1933; also studied piano for a dozen years; married James Reeves McCullers, on September 20, 1937 (divorced 1941, remarried February 1945); no children.

Attack of rheumatic fever marked the beginning of a long struggle against debilitating illness (1932); left for New York to study at the famed Juilliard School of Music but instead decided on a writing career (1934); took creative writing courses at Columbia University and New York University (1935–37); published first story, "Wunderkind," in Story (December 1936); after marriage, moved to Charlotte and then to Fayetteville, North Carolina; completed her first novel, The Heart Is a Lonely Hunter (1937–39), which was published by Houghton Mifflin (June 1940); lived on and off at a home in Brooklyn Heights, New York, rented with celebrities such as W.H. Auden and Gypsy Rose Lee, who became lifelong friends (1940–42); published second novel Reflections in a Golden Eye at Houghton Mifflin, and suffered a stroke that temporarily impaired her vision (February 1941); also suffered repeated bouts of influenza, pneumonia, and pleurisy both before and after the stroke; published novella The Ballad of the Sad Cafe (August 1943); her father died and her mother Marguerite and younger sister Rita moved to Nyack to share her home (1944); remarried (1945); published her fourth novel, The Member of the Wedding, to universal acclaim (1946); suffered a second stroke that left her paralyzed on the left side (1947); unable to write, attempted suicide (1948); persuaded by Tennessee Williams to dramatize her 1946 novel, which was a huge success on Broadway (1950–51) and which restored her self-confidence; however, the suicide of her husband (1953), the sudden death of her mother (1955), and the failure of her second play, The Square Root of Wonderful (1957), undermined her ability to write; helped and encouraged by a psychiatrist and friend, Dr. Mary Mercer, was able to finish her fifth and last novel, Clock Without Hands (end of 1960); during the remaining seven years of life, wrote some stories and poems for Harper's Bazaar and other fashion magazines, and Houghton Mifflin published* *her collection of children's verses,* Sweet as a Pickle, Clean as a Pig *(1964).*

With the exception of her second novel, Reflections in a Golden Eye, *which took her only two months to write, it took McCullers three to six years to complete each of her other works. As a result, she finished a total of only 5 novels over a period of 30 years. Several editions of her best fiction,* The Heart Is a Lonely Hunter, The Ballad of the Sad Cafe *and* The Member of the Wedding *remain in print. She also wrote a number of stories, essays and a few poems, most of which appeared in fashion magazines such as* Harper's Bazaar, Mademoiselle *and* Vogue *from the early 1940s through the mid-1960s.*

Carson McCullers, like most of the characters in her fiction, grew up in the deep South when segregation was in full force. Her father's jewelry and watchmaking business prospered during the postwar boom of the 1920s, and when Carson was a child the family moved from the downtown area to an upscale suburb of Columbus, Georgia, a mill town of some 30,000 inhabitants. As the family could well afford hired help, Carson and her younger siblings Lamar Smith, Jr. and **Margarita G. Smith,** known as Rita, became intimately acquainted with a succession of black housemaids who worked for the Smith family over the years. Some of McCullers' most memorable characters, such as the black maid Portia in *The Heart Is a Lonely Hunter* (1940) and the black housekeeper Berenice in *The Member of the Wedding* (1946), were drawn from life. In his 1940 review of her first novel, *The Heart Is a Lonely Hunter,* the eminent black writer Richard Wright praised McCullers' "astonishing humanity" that enabled "a white writer, for the first time in Southern fiction, to handle Negro characters with as much ease and justice as those of her own race."

From early childhood, Carson's parents, especially her mother **Marguerite Waters Smith,** were sure that their eldest child was a "wunderkind" or child prodigy. They noticed and nurtured her lively imagination, her passion for books, and her early interest in music. At the age of five, her parents bought her a piano and for the next twelve years, from approximately 1922 to 1934, Carson, inspired by two excellent teachers, practiced for at least four hours a day. Not surprisingly, music plays a prominent role in the lives of McCullers' most autobiographical adolescent characters, Frances in her first published story "Wunderkind" (1936), Mick Kelly in *The Heart Is a Lonely Hunter* (1941), and

Frankie Addams in McCullers' masterpiece, *The Member of the Wedding* (1946).

When McCullers was 13, she dropped her baptismal name Lula in favor of her middle name, Carson. Oliver Evans, McCullers' first biographer, pointed out "that the names Mick and Frankie, like Carson's own, are, though sexually ambiguous, more generally applicable to boys than to girls." And like Mick of *The Heart Is a Lonely Hunter* and Frankie of *The Member of the Wedding,* Carson was a tall, lanky tomboy who felt quite out of place in a region that viewed tall women (McCullers was 5'8½") as freaks, and androgyny as an abomination.

While Carson grew up in a warm, harmonious and supportive household, the world beyond her doorstep was hostile. She was often called a freak by children and adolescents, not only because of her height but because she was a voracious reader and a serious student of music, both rarities in small-town America. And to increase her estrangement from her contemporaries, at the age of 15 and in her senior year in high school, McCullers suffered a severe attack of rheumatic fever that kept her in bed for months. Misdiagnosed as "growing pains," the attack damaged her heart badly, although this was not known until much later. Ill health and finally invalidism were to plague McCullers for more than half of her relatively short life.

Although no one seems to have made the connection, it is possible that McCullers began to abandon the idea of a musical career because of the attack of rheumatic fever. However, she continued to study piano with her beloved teacher, **Mary Tucker,** the wife of an officer at nearby Fort Benning, until Colonel John Tucker was reassigned to a post in California in 1934. In retrospect, McCullers was wise to abandon the piano and devote herself to fiction, for the two strokes she suffered before the age of 30 left her with the use of only her right hand.

McCullers read every work of fiction in her family's library and at the local public library and began writing stories and plays before graduating from high school in 1933. Once again Lamar and Marguerite Smith fully supported their daughter, buying her a typewriter when it was clear that she was serious about writing. Carson was pleased enough with one story "Sucker" to show it to her parents; however, it was not published for another 30 years.

The decision to abandon music for writing was finally made for Carson after she left Columbus in 1934 to study music at Juilliard in New

York. Her parents sold a valuable heirloom ring to pay for Carson's tuition at Juilliard and her living expenses in New York, but the money was somehow lost in the subway. To support herself and to pursue her true calling—writing—Carson worked at odd jobs in the city while studying creative writing in evening classes at Columbia University and later New York University.

Carson returned to Georgia in June 1935, working briefly for the Columbus *Ledger*. That same summer, Edwin Peacock, a good friend who encouraged her writing, introduced Carson to another aspiring writer, James Reeves McCullers, a well-spoken, well-read and charming young man originally from Alabama, who left the Army in 1936 to pursue a writing career in New York. The following year, Carson and Reeves were married in Columbus, and the couple moved first to Charlotte and then to Fayetteville in North Carolina where Reeves found work with a credit company. They agreed to alternate at breadwinning, and that once Carson was an established writer (her first published story, "Wunderkind," had already appeared in *Story* in December 1936) she would support Reeves while he took a turn at writing.

Everything significant that has happened in my fiction has also happened to me—or it will happen eventually.

—Carson McCullers

The agreement never worked, and by the time Carson's first novel, *The Heart Is a Lonely Hunter*, catapulted her to fame in 1940 their marriage had unravelled. Reeves, it turned out, was not a gifted writer, which had a disastrous effect on his sense of self-worth. To make matters worse, both Carson and Reeves were bisexual, with Reeves the more passive of the two. Carson's pursuit of women completed the destruction of their first marriage. They reconciled after Reeves, who re-enlisted in the Army after Pearl Harbor, was thrice wounded in Europe, but their second marriage came to a tragic end when Reeves, severely alcoholic, took his own life in November 1953.

Domestic bliss and joyous sex are as rare in McCullers' fiction as they were in her own life. Most of her characters suffer spiritual loneliness, and are engaged in a frustrated search for communion with, and understanding by, their fellow human beings. The lover is seldom appreciated or even noticed by the loved one, and the loss of love often leads her characters to defeat, despair, and, in the case of the deaf-mute John Singer in *The Heart Is a Lonely Hunter*, to suicide. The themes of estrangement, frustrated love, and solitariness that inform Carson's novels, from *The Heart Is a Lonely Hunter* (1940) to *Clock Without Hands* (1961), and her passionate plea for racial and social justice, gained her millions of readers in the United States and abroad.

A celebrity by the age of 23, McCullers befriended and was befriended by many of the famous that she met at the Yaddo Artists' Colony in Saratoga Springs, New York, in the 1940s and at a house in Brooklyn Heights, New York, that Carson rented in the early 1940s with her mentor, George Davis, the fiction editor at *Harper's Bazaar*, the poet W.H. Auden, and the entertainer *Gypsy Rose Lee. The house at 7 Middagh Street, which the diarist *Anais Nin dubbed "February House" because some of its tenants were born under the sign of Pisces, was, from 1940 until the building was demolished in early 1945, the most extraordinary literary salon in the United States. Some of the leading writers, artists, and musicians of the war years either lived there for a time or visited its distinguished tenants.

In the mid-1940s, Carson also became a close friend of the dramatist Tennessee Williams, who convinced her to dramatize *The Member of the Wedding*. Because of Carson's paralyzing stroke in 1947, she was unable to finish the play for years, and it did not open until January 5, 1950. The play featured *Julie Harris as the motherless adolescent Frankie Addams, Brandon de Wilde as Frankie's young cousin John Henry, and the legendary *Ethel Waters as the compassionate and nurturing housekeeper Berenice. *Member of the Wedding* was a runaway success, and played 501 performances until it closed in mid-March 1951. It won both the New York Drama Critics' Circle Award and the Donaldson Award for Best Play of the 1950 season. Carson was also awarded a Gold Medal of the Theater Club as the Best Playwright of the year. Within two years, the play was made into a highly successful film starring the Broadway cast. Carson McCullers received many honors and awards from the 1940s through the early '60s, including two Guggenheim fellowships, but none of them pleased her more than those accorded *Member of the Wedding*.

By 1952 and at the age of 35, Carson McCullers was one of the most highly regarded and financially successful writers in the United States, but during the remaining 15 years of her life she suffered such devastating personal losses and so much physical pain that her writing faltered. First, her inability to grieve over her hus-

band Reeves' tragic death in 1953 was viewed as callousness by friends who had known them both. Two years later, her reaction to the sudden death of her mother, Marguerite Smith, with whom Carson and her younger sister Rita had shared a house in Nyack, New York, since the mid-1940s, brought renewed charges of callousness and irresponsibility. Marguerite Smith had devoted her life to her eldest daughter, nurturing her career and caring for Carson through one illness after another. Carson was not there when she was needed, and her sister Rita, still recovering from an appendectomy, had to make all the funeral arrangements with long-distance support from their brother, Lamar. Carson made matters worse when she insisted on claiming her third of their mother's estate despite the fact that she was much more affluent than her siblings.

Many of Carson's friends noticed that she was as contradictory as a child, and that under stress she could be callous, stingy, and morose while she was normally compassionate, generous, and animated. Constant physical pain and the growing fear of death may account for McCullers' otherwise inexplicable behavior at the passing of the two most important persons in her life.

From the movie The Member of the Wedding, *starring Julie Harris, Ethel Waters, and Brandon de Wilde.*

Ever-debilitating illness certainly accounts for McCullers' decline as a writer, especially after her play *The Square Root of Wonderful* (1957), which concerns a failed writer who commits suicide, was a flop. It opened on Broadway on October 30, 1957, and closed on December 7, after only 45 performances. In February 1958, Carson's close friends, fearing for her life (she had made one attempt at suicide in 1948),

brought her to the attention of Dr. **Mary Mercer,** an excellent psychiatrist who lived and practiced near Carson's home in Nyack. Everyone who has written about McCullers' last nine years agrees that Mary Mercer was an exemplary friend who not only saved her life but who, in Carson's estimation, saved her soul as well.

As a result of Mercer's help and guidance, Carson resumed writing a work she had begun years before, and when *Clock Without Hands*, a novel about a Southern pharmacist who is dying of leukemia, appeared in 1961, Carson dedicated it to Mercer. The critics treated McCullers' novel gently, but most agreed that it did not fulfill the promise of her earlier work. By the late 1990s, all of McCullers' novels of the 1940s and many of her stories were in print, but *Clock Without Hands* has been out of print for years.

McCullers' last years were brightened by the knowledge that another two of her novels, *Reflections in a Golden Eye* and *The Heart Is a Lonely Hunter*, were either filmed or were in production. She struck up an especially warm

friendship with the distinguished film director John Huston, and after he finished filming McCullers' gothic novel *Reflections in a Golden Eye* early in 1967, the bedridden but indomitable McCullers visited Huston at his home in Ireland. It was her last journey; on August 15, Carson McCullers suffered a massive cerebral hemorrhage and lay comatose in Nyack's hospital until her death on September 29, 1967.

At a memorial service at St. James Episcopal Church in Manhattan and at the burial service in Nyack's Oak Grove Cemetery, her sister Rita, her brother Lamar, and her ever faithful friend Mary Mercer greeted the countless celebrities from the literary, artistic and theatrical world including Carson's old friends W.H. Auden, Gypsy Rose Lee, Ethel Waters, Julie Harris, *Janet Flanner, and Truman Capote, who came to bid farewell to one of America's most original writers.

Over 30 years after her death, Carson McCullers' fame remains undiminished. The universal and timeless themes of alienation, isolation, and loneliness that inform her fiction were more relevant than ever as the 20th century drew to a close and the 21st century began.

SOURCES:

Carr, Virginia Spencer. *The Lonely Hunter: A Biography of Carson McCullers.* Garden City, NY: Doubleday, 1975.

Cook, Richard M., *Carson McCullers.* NY: Frederick Ungar, 1975.

Evans, Oliver. *The Ballad of Carson McCullers.* NY: Coward-McCann, 1965.

James, Judith Giblin. *Wunderkind: The Reputation of Carson McCullers, 1940–1990.* Columbia, SC: Camden House, 1995.

McDowell, Margaret B. *Carson McCullers.* Boston: G.K. Hall, Twayne Publishers, Twayne United States Authors Series, No. 354, 1980.

Smith, Margarita G., ed. *The Mortgaged Heart: Carson McCullers.* Boston, MA: Houghton Mifflin, 1971.

SUGGESTED READING:

Dews, Carlos, ed. *Illumination and Night Glare: The Unfinished Autobiography of Carson McCullers.* WI: University of Wisconsin, 1999.

McCullers, Carson. *The Ballad of the Sad Cafe and Other Stories.* Boston, MA: Houghton Mifflin, 1951.

———. *Clock Without Hands.* Boston, MA: Houghton Mifflin, 1961.

———. *The Heart Is a Lonely Hunter.* Boston, MA: Houghton Mifflin, 1940.

———. *The Member of the Wedding.* Boston, MA: Houghton Mifflin, 1946.

———. *Reflections in a Golden Eye.* Boston, MA: Houghton Mifflin, 1941.

Rich, Nancy B. *The Flowering Dream: The Historical Saga of Carson McCullers.* Chapel Hill, NC: Chapel Hill Press, 1999.

RELATED MEDIA:

The Ballad of the Sad Cafe, adapted by Edward Albee, starring *Colleen Dewhurst, Michael Dunn, directed by Alan Schneider, lighting by *Jean Rosenthal, opened on Broadway at the Martin Beck Theater on October 30, 1963, and ran for 123 performances.

The Heart Is a Lonely Hunter (124 min. film), starring Alan Arkin, **Sondra Locke, Cicely Tyson,** Warner Bros., 1968.

The Member of the Wedding (91 min. film), starring Julie Harris, Brandon de Wilde, Ethel Waters, produced by Stanley Kramer, directed by Fred Zinnemann, Columbia, 1952.

Reflections in a Golden Eye (109 min. film), starring *Elizabeth Taylor, Marlon Brando, Julie Harris, Brian Keith, produced by Ray Stark, directed by John Huston, Warner Bros., 1967.

Anna Macías,
Professor Emerita of History, Ohio
Wesleyan University, Delaware, Ohio

McCulloch, Catharine (1862–1945)

American lawyer and suffragist. Name variations: Catharine Waugh McCulloch; Catharine Gouger Waugh McCulloch. Born Catharine Gouger Waugh on June 4, 1862, in Ransomville, New York; died of cancer on April 20, 1945, in Evanston, Illinois; daughter of Abraham Miller Waugh and Susan (Gouger) Waugh; attended Union College of Law, 1885–86; Rockford Female Seminary, B.A., M.A., 1888; married Frank Hathorn McCulloch (a lawyer), on May 30, 1890; children: Hugh Waugh (b. 1891); Hathorn Waugh (b. 1899); Catharine Waugh (b. 1901); Frank Waugh (b. 1905).

Became partner of Chicago firm of McCulloch & McCulloch (c. 1890); admitted to the bar of the U.S. Supreme Court (1898); elected justice of the peace (1907); co-founded the Mississippi Valley Conference (1912); served as president of the Women's Bar Association of Illinois (1916–20); named senior counsellor of the Illinois Bar Association (1940).

Selected writings: Mr. Lex *(1899);* Bridget's Daughters *(1911);* A Manual of the Will Contests in Illinois *(1929).*

Catharine McCulloch practiced law in an era when many of the legal protections granted to free male citizens of the United States did not extend to women. Born in 1862 to parents of Irish and French Huguenot ancestry, she spent her first years on a farm in New York state. When she was five, the family moved to another farm in Illinois, where she attended public school in New Milford. Her father was well versed in the law, though not formally trained, and often helped his neighbors with land claims; from him, she developed a keen interest in the subject. She graduated from Rockford Female Seminary in 1882 and in 1885 entered Chicago's Union College of Law (forerunner of Northwestern University Law School). Though she was admitted to the Illinois bar, she found it difficult to practice in Chicago because of a bias against woman attorneys, and so returned to Rockford and established a practice there.

McCulloch also went back to school, and was granted bachelor's and master's degrees in 1888 from Rockford Seminary after producing a thesis on women's wages. In 1890, she married a former law-school classmate, Frank Hathorn McCulloch, who was supportive of all her endeavors, in a ceremony presided over by temperance activist and suffragist Reverend *Anna Howard Shaw. Catharine then joined her husband's firm (the name of which was changed to McCulloch and McCulloch) in Chicago, and had the first of their four children in 1891. She also became involved in women's suffrage. McCulloch served as legislative superintendent of the Illinois Equal Suffrage Association, and in that capacity wrote a suffrage bill that was not ratified by the state legislature for 20 years; it finally passed in 1913, giving Illinois women the right to vote in presidential elections some seven years before the 19th amendment made women's suffrage the law of the land. More quickly passed was a 1905 law she wrote which raised the age of consent for women from 14 to 16 years of age.

An accomplished attorney admitted to the bar of the U.S. Supreme Court in 1898, McCulloch was also a popular public speaker and interview subject for newspapers. Her forays into literature reflected her interest in women's rights: *Mr. Lex* (1899) dealt with the lack of legal status for married women and mothers, and helped to pass a 1901 Illinois law that granted women equal status as guardians of their children. She also wrote a suffragist play, *Bridget's Daughters,* in 1911. A year later, she co-founded the Mississippi Valley Conference, a coalition of suffrage leaders that became the locus of the suffrage movement in the Midwest and organized annual conventions for a number of years. From 1916 to 1920, she was the president of the Women's Bar Association of Illinois.

A longtime legal adviser to the Women's Christian Temperance Union (WCTU), McCulloch played an active role in a movement toward another constitutional amendment that became effective in 1920—the ban on the manufacture and sale of alcoholic beverages. After 1920, she served on committees of the newly formed League of Women Voters, was active in numerous Chicago organizations, and was twice elected justice of the peace for the Chicago suburb of

Evanston. With her husband, she wrote *A Manual of the Will Contests in Illinois,* published in 1929. In her later years, she and her husband traveled extensively, studying legal systems in other countries; their three sons became lawyers, and their daughter **Catharine Waugh** married one. Catharine McCulloch died of cancer in Evanston, at age 82, and was buried in Chicago's Graceland Cemetery.

SOURCES:
James, Edward T., ed. *Notable American Women, 1607–1950.* Cambridge, MA: The Belknap Press of Harvard University Press, 1971.

Carol Brennan,
Grosse Pointe, Michigan

McCullough, Myrtle Reed (1874–1911).
See Reed, Myrtle.

McCutcheon, Floretta (1888–1967)
American bowler who is considered one of the greatest woman bowlers of all time. Name variations: Mrs. Mac. Born Floretta Doty in Ottumwa, Iowa, on July 22, 1888; died in Pasadena, California, on February 2, 1967; married Robert J. McCutcheon; children: Barbara McCutcheon.

*Challenged Jimmy Smith, world champion bowler, to a three-game set and defeated him 704 to 697 (1927); with the exception of *Marion Ladewig, was perhaps the greatest woman bowler of all time.*

As a pivotal figure in the history of women's athletics, Floretta McCutcheon was an unprepossessing figure. In her prime, she was once described as "a quiet, studious, smiling, [prematurely] gray-haired little woman who might have just dropped her knitting." In the bowling alley, however, she was unbeatable.

Born in Iowa in 1888, Floretta McCutcheon moved with her parents to Denver, Colorado, when she was 13. After finishing public school in Denver, she married Robert J. McCutcheon, a bowling enthusiast. McCutcheon was also physically active, playing on a women's volleyball team at the local YWCA. Though her husband and friends encouraged her to bowl, McCutcheon begged off, claiming too many family and church obligations. As well, at the turn of the century, bowling was considered a masculine sport with a rather coarse reputation. In 1923, when her husband formed a new league, he added Floretta to the team without asking her. She was 35 when she bowled her first game.

"I often wonder why I didn't break my neck running the way I did," said McCutcheon, describing those early efforts. "I stood as far back as I could, ran to the foul line, swinging the 16-pound ball. My impression of the way to bowl was to throw as hard as possible." At the end of that first season, she dropped out for three years because of ill health. Returning to bowling in 1926, McCutcheon worked on controlling her delivery, which dramatically improved her score. By 1927, she had rolled her first perfect game and several three-game series of 700 or more. She began doing exhibitions and bowled three 800 three-game series with an average of more than 266 per game. That same year, she challenged world champion Jimmy Smith to a three-game set, beating him 704 to 697 to the delight of sports-page headline writers nationwide and Ripley's "Believe It or Not." "She is simply the greatest bowler I have ever seen," said Smith after the match. Suddenly Floretta McCutcheon found herself sharing the spotlight with the famous swimmer *Gertrude Ederle.

A year later, in 1928, the Brunswick Corporation employed McCutcheon as an instructor. With her daughter **Barbara McCutcheon** attending college, Floretta had decided the money would come in handy for tuition. Exhibition matches initially took precedence over bowling instruction, with McCutcheon bowling 788 games in 66 cities. Then someone had the idea of patterning bowling schools after the popular cooking schools of the era. In 1931, the first Mrs. McCutcheon School of Bowling was announced in the *Peoria Star.* When the *Chicago Herald Examiner* sponsored a similar school, over 3,500 women attended. Suddenly local bowling alleys and corporate entities like Brunswick saw the opportunity to double the number of participants in the sport by appealing to women.

From 1930 to 1938, McCutcheon set up schools and organized leagues; she was the only bowling instructor in the country who taught women specifically. Her classes varied widely, from high school girls to blind bowlers to female students at Vassar College and New York University. "Bowling is one of the few sports at which women and men can have such hilarious fun while participating as equals," noted McCutcheon. "Since bowling depends on rhythm and timing rather than on strength, women often make more rapid progress than men."

After ten years on the road, McCutcheon retired from touring, first moving to New York, then to Chicago, then to Pasadena. She continued to compete and averaged 201 for 8,067 games. In her 26 years as an instructor, McCutcheon taught almost 300,000 women how to

Floretta McCutcheon

bowl. In 1956, she was inducted into the Women's International Bowling Congress Hall of Fame and in 1973 into the Colorado Sports Hall of Fame. "Mrs. Mac," as everyone fondly called Floretta McCutcheon, probably did more for bowling in America than any other individual. She had 10 games of 300, nine more of 299, and, all told, 85 games of 279 or better. She once rolled an 832 three-game series.

SOURCES:

Hollander, Phyllis. *100 Greatest Women in Sports.* NY: Grosset & Dunlap, 1976.

Woolum, Janet. *Outstanding Women Athletes: Who They Are and How They Influenced Sports in America.* Phoenix, AZ: Oryx Press, 1992.

Karin L. Haag,
freelance writer, Athens, Georgia

McDaniel, Hattie (1895–1952)

First African-American actress to win an Academy Award. Born on June 10, 1895 (some sources cite 1898), in Wichita, Kansas; died on October 26, 1952, in Los Angeles, California; daughter of Henry Mc-

Daniel (a Baptist minister) and Susan (Holbert) Mc-Daniel; sister of Etta McDaniel (an actress); married James Lloyd Crawford (a real-estate agent), in 1941 (divorced); married Larry C. Williams (an interior decorator), in 1949 (divorced 1950); married once more and possibly once again.

Sang on Denver radio station (1915); made film debut (1931); won Academy Award (1940); cast in title role of "Beulah" for radio (1947).

Selected filmography: The Golden West (1931); Blonde Venus (1932); I'm No Angel (1933); Imitation of Life (1934); Judge Priest (1934); The Little Colonel (1935); Alice Adams (1935); Show Boat (1936); Nothing Sacred (1937); The Mad Miss Manton (1938); Gone With the Wind (1939); The Great Lie (1941); George Washington Slept Here (1942); Never Say Goodbye (1946); Song of the South (1946); Margie (1946); The Flame (1947); Mickey (1948); Family Honeymoon (1949).

The image of singer and actress Hattie Mc-Daniel as "Mammy," one of Gone With the Wind's most memorable background characters, is indelibly etched in the American pop-culture consciousness. Her portrayal of the slave house-maid in the Civil War epic won her an Academy Award, but for this and other roles McDaniel was accused of participating in the perpetuation of African-American stereotypes. "I'd rather play a maid than be a maid," she once said.

McDaniel was born in Kansas in 1895, the last of Henry and **Susan McDaniel**'s 13 children. Her father was a Baptist minister, a former slave who had fought in the Civil War, and a performer in minstrel shows. After the family moved to Denver, Colorado, McDaniel completed two years at East Denver High School and began a singing career while still in her teens. She sang on the radio, took top prizes in drama contests, and joined the traveling tent show run by her brother Otis after he convinced their parents of her talents and his responsibility. They played throughout the South, and by 1924 McDaniel had enough performing experience to join the Pantages Circuit of vaudeville shows.

Such work was far from steady, however, and McDaniel often supplemented her income with jobs as a cook. Stranded in Milwaukee once, she took a job as a ladies' room maid in a hotel; when the night's entertainment walked out, she sang "St. Louis Blues" and was hired for the floor show. After a successful run there, Mc-Daniel decided to try her luck in Hollywood. Although initially she found little work and had to take in laundry to make ends meet, persistence

paid off and she began appearing in a number of minor roles, beginning with The Golden West in 1931. Usually cast as a servant, one of the few roles in which Hollywood would then cast African-Americans, McDaniel tried to inject some personality into these generally invisible roles. Over the course of a decade, she perfected the character of the maid who, though loyal and respectful to her employers, is wiser and deeper than they are. Audiences of all colors loved to see snooty lead characters get their comeuppance, and McDaniel's comic timing was flawless.

The number of outstanding Hollywood films McDaniel appeared in during the 1930s includes I'm No Angel (1933) with *Mae West, Judge Priest (1934), in which she sang with Will Rogers, the screen version of Booth Tarkington's Alice Adams (1935) with *Katharine Hepburn, The Little Colonel (1935), one of the most popular of the *Shirley Temple (Black) vehicles, and Show Boat (1936), a film adaptation of the stage musical based on *Edna Ferber's novel that paired her with Paul Robeson. When she auditioned for the part of Mammy in the highly anticipated screen version of *Margaret Mitchell's novel Gone With the Wind, she was signed immediately to a contract. Her performance in the 1939 movie won her the Academy Award for Best Supporting Actress, marking the first time an African-American had been so honored, but in subsequent years the pejorative term "mammy" was employed by African-Americans angered by Hollywood's persistent portrayal of blacks almost exclusively as subservient domestic workers.

McDaniel's real-life persona was anything but meek, however. She initiated a lawsuit over a discriminatory real-estate policy in California and emerged victorious. Married several times, she was active in charity work in Hollywood, entertained military personnel during World War II, and continued to work in films and on radio during the decade. (Her brother Sam and sister **Etta McDaniel** also made a living in Hollywood for some years in minor roles.) But after the war, some African-American groups, including the NAACP, successfully petitioned Hollywood studios to stop portraying blacks as servants and slaves, and roles for McDaniel grew scarcer. She appeared on the "Amos 'n' Andy" radio program, and in 1947 was cast as the title character in the successful radio series "Beulah." With this part she became the first African-American to play a lead role in a program not geared specifically to the minority community. (The part had originated with a white actor, Marlin Hurt, on the "Fibber McGee and Molly" radio series.) "Beulah" moved to television a few years later

Hattie
McDaniel

and first starred *Ethel Waters. McDaniel replaced Waters in 1951 but was unable to continue. She had suffered a heart attack during the show's first season, and battled breast cancer for two years before dying of the disease on October 26, 1952. *Louise Beavers replaced McDaniel.

In her will, McDaniel had stipulated: "I desire a white casket and a white shroud; white gardenias in my hair and in my hands, together with a white gardenia blanket and a pillow of red roses. I also wish to be buried in the Hollywood Cemetery." But the Hollywood Cemetery was segregated; blacks were not allowed. Instead, McDaniel was buried at Angelus-Rosedale Memorial Park. In October 1999, 47 years later, new owners of the Hollywood Cemetery (renamed Hollywood Forever) installed a memorial there to honor Hattie McDaniel. The gray-and-pink granite monument was placed next to a lake and in view of the famous hillside "Hollywood" sign.

SOURCES:

Current Biography. NY: H.W. Wilson, 1940, 1952.

Igus, Toyomi. ed. *Book of Black Heroes, Volume 2: Great Women in the Struggle.* Just Us Books, 1991.

Katz, Ephraim. *The Film Encyclopedia.* NY: Harper-Collins, 1994.

Sicherman, Barbara, and Carol Hurd Green, eds. *Notable American Women: The Modern Period.* Cambridge, MA: The Belknap Press of Harvard University Press, 1980.

Carol Brennan,
Grosse Pointe, Michigan

McDaniel, Mildred (1933—)

African-American track and field star. Born Mildred Louise McDaniel in Atlanta, Georgia, on November 4, 1933.

Was AAU national high jump champion (1953, 1955, and 1956); won the high jump title in the Pan American Games (1955); won the Olympic gold medal in high jump in Melbourne Olympics (1956), setting a world record with a jump of 5'9¼", and also won the bronze in the 4x100-meter relay.

Mildred McDaniel did not consider herself an athlete when she was a student at David Howard High School in Atlanta, Georgia. She took gym because it was required, and would shoot baskets while waiting for class to start. But her gym teacher arrived early one day, and after watching her play, invited McDaniel to try out for the basketball team. Mildred refused, but her teacher was adamant: "Any girl who can shoot ten straight foul shots will get her sneakers tomorrow and will be a member of the team." McDaniel soon became a major player with teammates **Mary McNabb** and ***Margaret Matthews**, who would also become Olympic track-and-field champions.

Students at David Howard generally went out for track and field when the basketball season was over, but McDaniel was reluctant. When her coach advised her to watch the other athletes and decide if a particular track-and-field event interested her, McDaniel became intrigued with high jumping and tried out for that event. Soon she was high jumping, running the hurdles,

broad jumping, and had become a member of the relay team. When she graduated from high school, McDaniel received a scholarship to Tuskegee Institute, where she trained under Coach Cleveland Abbott and became the high-jump champion in the outdoor AAU meet in 1953. In 1955 and 1956, she was indoor and outdoor AAU champion in the high jump. Although she had a sore heel in the 1955 Pan American Games, she won the title in the high jump. McDaniel qualified for the 1956 Olympics with a jump of 5'4". At that time, her best jump was 5'6½".

In Melbourne, McDaniel was not considered a contender. "At the bottom of the news story it said, 'They might have a little trouble with Mildred McDaniel of the United States,' and that's the way I wanted it," she said. "If the girls know you can jump a certain height, they are always watching. So I was going to let them watch each other, and I was going to win the event. But my plan backfired on me because I was named first up to jump." Although several international competitors had jumped 5'8" in previous competitions, they failed to match their earlier records in Melbourne. At the end of the day, officials reckoned the competition was all but over as the time neared for McDaniel's final jump. As she came on the field, she heard one official say to another, "Well, we might as well pack up, she can't go any higher."

But McDaniel surprised the officials and delighted 100,000 spectators by asking that the bar be raised to 5'9¼"—an inch over the world record and two inches over her highest jump. She missed the first time, but on her second jump she flung herself over the pole, winning the gold with 5'9¼", and beating Great Britain's **Thelma Hopkins** and the Soviet Union's **Mariya Pisareva**, who tied for the silver with jumps of 5'5¼". She had also beaten the future world-record holder, ***Iolanda Balas** of Rumania. McDaniel's record remained unbroken for two years.

SOURCES:

Davis, Michael D. *Black American Women in Olympic Track and Field.* Jefferson, NC: McFarland, 1992.

Page, James A. *Black Olympian Medalists.* Englewood, CO: Libraries Unlimited, 1991.

Wallechinsky, David. *The Complete Book of the Olympics.* NY: Viking, 1988.

Karin Loewen Haag,
Athens, Georgia

McDonagh, Paulette (c. 1901–1978)

Australian filmmaker. Born in Sydney, Australia, around 1901; died on October 11, 1978, in Sydney;

one of seven children of Dr. J. McDonagh (a resident doctor for the J.C. Williams theater company); sister of Isobel McDonagh (c. 1899–1982) and Phyllis Mc-Donagh (c. 1900–1978).

Filmography: Those Who Love (1926); The Far Paradise (1928); The Cheaters (1930); Two Minutes' Silence (1933).

Paulette McDonagh, the first woman to write and direct silent films for the commercial cinema in Australia, was born around 1901 in Sydney and educated there. She was an avid moviegoer and was particularly intrigued with films exported from Hollywood. With no other option open to her, McDonagh taught herself to direct by viewing the same movie over and over. After a short stint at P.J. Ramster's acting school, McDonagh decided to make a movie. She wrote several drafts of her first script, Those Who Love, then hired her former teacher, P.J. Ramster, to direct it. When he proved unsatisfactory, McDonagh finished directing the project herself.

Produced in 1926, Those Who Love is a romantic melodrama, typical of the era, about a daughter who gets revenge on her dying mother's unfaithful paramour. The movie was shot in the McDonagh family home, and Paulette recruited her sister **Phyllis McDonagh** to serve as producer and her eldest sister **Isobel McDonagh** to star. Isobel, working under the stage name Marie Lorraine, had an established acting career, having appeared in Beaumont Studios' Joe (1924) and another film titled Painted Daughter (1925). Despite its melodramatic plot, the few extant scenes of Those Who Love clearly establish McDonagh as a talented director with a sense of realism rarely seen in silent movies, particularly those made by Australians.

In 1928, the McDonagh Sisters, as they were known, resumed their previous roles to make The Far Paradise, another melodrama similar in tone and story to Those Who Love. A box-office success, the movie established the threesome as popular and unique filmmakers, and emboldened them to take on more risky material. Naturalistic in style, their next film, The Cheaters, was a radical departure from melodrama. Fans of the McDonaghs were nonplussed by the story of a woman safecracker, and the premiere was a disaster. Even so, critics greeted the film with good reviews.

The McDonaghs' next film was also the last Paulette ever directed. Made in 1933, Two Minutes' Silence was a serious drama based on a play by Leslie Hayden. Decidedly antiwar in sentiment, it was a box-office disaster. Years later,

McDonagh told **Andree Wright**: "We were fools to have made Two Minutes' Silence. The whole world would have eaten out of our hands if we'd made another romantic film. Two Minutes' Silence was too true." Because of the film's failure, McDonagh was unable to raise money to direct a planned picture about the Royal Flying Doctors' Service. Though she directed a series of documentaries, including a film about the legendary Australian race horse Phar Lap, she was never able to direct a commercial feature again. Film historians have often wondered whether her career would have continued to flourish had she left Australia.

Not long after the release of Two Minutes' Silence, Isobel married Charles Stewart and moved to London, where she would die nearly 50 years later on April 14, 1982. Phyllis McDonagh had a long career as a journalist and respected film critic. In August 1978, the McDonaghs were presented with the prestigious Langford Award from the Australian Film Institute. Paulette McDonagh died in Sydney two months afterward on October 11, 1978. Her sister Phyllis died a few weeks later.

SOURCES:

Foster, Gwendolyn. Women Film Directors: An International Bio-Critical Dictionary. Westport, CT: Greenwood Press, 1995.

Kuhn, Annette, and Susannah Radstone, eds. Women's Companion to International Film. Berkeley and Los Angeles: University of California Press, 1990.

McFarlane, Brian. Australian Cinema. NY: Columbia University Press, 1988.

Tulloch, John. Legends on the Screen in Narrative Film in Australia 1919–1929. Sydney: Currency Press, 1981.

Wright, Andree. Brilliant Careers. Sydney: Pan Books, 1986.

Deborah Jones,
Studio City, California

McDonald, Golden (1910–1952).

See Brown, Margaret Wise.

McDowell, Anne E. (1826–1901)

American publisher. Born in Smyrna, Delaware, on June 23, 1826; died in Philadelphia, Pennsylvania, in 1901.

Anne E. McDowell was born in Smyrna, Delaware, on June 23, 1826, and early in life developed an interest in women's and labor rights. She founded the Philadelphia Woman's Advocate, a weekly newspaper, in 1855. The Advocate was unprecedented, not only in that it was written for and about women but also because all of its staff, including printers and typesetters, were women. The paper's stated goal was "the elevation of the female industrial class," which McDowell put into practice by paying her employees the same wages earned by men in similar jobs, and its stance reflected her advocacy of the rights of laborers.

Despite her best efforts, the *Woman's Advocate* went out of business in 1860. McDowell then became editor of the women's department of the Philadelphia *Sunday Despatch*. For a woman to occupy such a position of authority in the publishing industry was nearly unheard of at the time; she stayed for 11 years. In 1871, McDowell became the editor of the Philadelphia *Sunday Republic*. While she remained active in the publishing business, she also took an increasing interest in labor issues. In 1884, she created an organization to secure sickness and death benefits for employees of Wanamaker's department store, and also founded the McDowell Free Library for women employed by Wanamaker's. She died in Philadelphia, Pennsylvania, in 1901.

SOURCES:

Edgerly, Lois Stiles, ed. *Give Her This Day*. Gardiner, ME: Tilbury House, 1990.

Read, Phyllis J., and Bernard L. Witlieb. *The Book of Women's Firsts*. NY: Random House, 1992.

Grant Eldridge,
freelance writer, Pontiac, Michigan

McDowell, Katharine Bonner
(1849–1883).

See Bonner, Sherwood.

Mary Eliza McDowell

McDowell, Mary Eliza (1854–1936)

"Angel of the Stockyards" who helped to improve living conditions in Chicago's squalid meat-packing district. Born on November 30, 1854, in Cincinnati, Ohio; died after a stroke on October 14, 1936, in Chicago, Illinois; daughter of Malcolm McDowell and Jane Welch (Gordon) McDowell; attended Elizabeth Harrison's kindergarten training school in Chicago, late 1880s.

Moved to Chicago (c. 1866); was active in relief efforts after Chicago Fire of 1871; served as national organizer for Women's Christian Temperance Union (c. 1887); was first director of the University of Chicago Settlement House (1894); traveled to Europe to study sanitation plants (1911); appointed Commissioner of Public Welfare (1923); retired from Settlement House (1929).

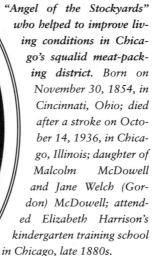

Reformer Mary Eliza McDowell, called the "Angel of the Stockyards," belonged to a breed of activists who at the turn of the 20th century fought big business and apathetic government to improve the lives of the poor, the desperate, and the immigrant, which often intersected. Born in Cincinnati, Ohio, in 1854, McDowell came from a family of strong abolitionists in the era of slavery. During the Civil War, her father Malcolm McDowell served as paymaster of the Tennessee army. After the war ended, they moved to Chicago, where he established a steel-rolling mill. As the eldest daughter, McDowell was responsible for many household duties and child-rearing tasks, since her mother **Jane Gordon McDowell** was often ill. She also grew close to her father, with whom she had converted from the Episcopal faith to the Methodist faith back in Ohio. Living on Chicago's northwest side, she became active in her parish, and helped in the relief efforts organized by her pastor after the Chicago Fire of 1871.

These activities inspired McDowell to work on behalf of the needy, and when her family moved to the suburb of Evanston she came to know the temperance activist *Frances Willard. She became active in the Women's Christian Temperance Union (WCTU), and served as a national organizer for the anti-alcohol group. She also developed an interest in early elementary education, and after attending *Elizabeth Harrison's teacher training college in Chicago, worked as a kindergarten teacher in New York City around 1890. Returning to Chicago, she worked with *Jane Addams' Hull House settlement on the South Side and established its kindergarten. Through these activities, she became interested in the conditions of the industrial working class, about which little was widely known in the days before extensive public transportation and automobiles (and, later, television) made the areas in which the urban poor lived accessible to middle-class viewing. At the urging of Addams, McDowell was invited to assume the directorship of a "settlement" house similar to Hull's that was created by the University of Chicago.

In the fall of 1894, McDowell took up residence near the University of Chicago Settlement

House, on what was then called Gross Avenue. "No social climber ever desired more earnestly to be accepted by the elite than I wished to be accepted by my neighbors," she later wrote. It was an abominable neighborhood, treeless and filthy, where the exploited immigrant workers of the giant meat-packing industries lived. Known as Packingtown, or Back-of-the-Yards, it was home to numerous German, Irish, and later Slavic immigrants and grew in infamy for its stench and miserable conditions. The ward was surrounded by open garbage dumps and decimated by political corruption, a situation later detailed but not overtly fictionalized in Upton Sinclair's 1906 novel *The Jungle*. Running through Packingtown was a branch of the Chicago River that was called Bubbly Creek because it was so toxic it literally fizzled. McDowell spent her days running the Settlement House and fighting city hall to improve the neighborhood. Her efforts eventually resulted in the first public bath, the first library, and the first park in the area, Davis Square. She also exposed political payoffs and battled illegal dumping. McDowell became so adamant about raising awareness about the open pits that ringed the district that she became known as the "Garbage Lady." In 1913, when the city created a City Waste Commission, she was appointed to it.

The University of Chicago Settlement House was a focal point of the Packingtown neighborhood and featured a gymnasium, social activities, day care, adult-education classes, and an Indiana summer camp for youth. McDowell's sympathies for the workers and the unsafe and precarious conditions under which they worked naturally made her sympathetic to the organized labor movement. She co-founded the National Women's Trade Union League in 1903 and served as president of its Chicago branch. During a heated 1904 Packingtown strike, she was the only well-known figure in the district to publicly side with the strikers. This pro-labor stance cost her some support for her Settlement House, but her wider efforts helped to bring about a federal investigation into the use of women and child labor in industry by 1907. She also campaigned to establish a Women's Bureau in the U.S. Department of Labor, which was created in 1920.

Mary McDowell's sympathies knew neither class nor race barriers. After the infamous race riots in Chicago in 1919, she established the Interracial Cooperative Committee, and was active in the National Association for the Advancement of Colored People (NAACP) as well as the Chicago Urban League. In 1923, a sympathetic new city government appointed her commissioner of public welfare, a post in which she served for four years. McDowell had traveled twice to Europe: once in 1911 to visit its sanitation treatment public-works projects, and later in the 1920s, when she received honors from the governments of Lithuania and Czechoslovakia for her service to immigrants from those countries who lived in Chicago and toiled in the meat-packing industry. A volume of her collected essays, *Mary McDowell and Municipal Housekeeping*, was published in 1929, the same year she retired from her Settlement House duties. McDowell died after a stroke in 1936 and was buried in Chicago's Rosehill Cemetery. Gross Avenue, the street on which she had lived for so many years, was renamed McDowell Avenue in her honor.

SOURCES:

Edgerly, Lois Stiles, ed. and comp. *Give Her This Day*. Gardiner, ME: Tilbury House, 1990.

James, Edward T., ed. *Notable American Women, 1607–1950*. Cambridge, MA: The Belknap Press of Harvard University Press, 1971.

McHenry, Robert, ed. *Famous American Women*. NY: Dover, 1980.

SUGGESTED READING:

Hill, Caroline, ed. *Mary McDowell and Municipal Housekeeping*, 1929.

Carol Brennan,
Grosse Pointe, Michigan

McElderry, Margaret K. (1912—)

American children's editor and publisher. Born in Pittsburgh, Pennsylvania, in 1912; graduated from Mt. Holyoke College, 1933.

Margaret K. McElderry was born in Pittsburgh, Pennsylvania, in 1912, and graduated from Mt. Holyoke College with a major in English and a minor in economics at the height of the Depression in 1933. Upon informing her career advisor that she wanted to go to New York City and "work with books," McElderry was told that she had absolutely nothing to offer the publishing industry. Nevertheless, she set off to pursue her dream. After one year at the Carnegie Library School in Pittsburgh, she obtained employment with the New York Public Library System as an assistant to *Anne Carroll Moore, the system's superintendent of children's works. For the next nine years, McElderry filled increasingly responsible positions in the children's works area of the system, and eventually assisted Moore in the preparation of the New York Public Library's prestigious annual list of best children's books.

McElderry left the library in 1943 to participate in the Allied war effort during World War

II, and served in the Office of War Intelligence in London, England, from 1944 to 1945. At the war's end, she returned to New York City, where she became the head of the children's department of the Harcourt Brace publishing house. The first separate department for children's literature in American publishing had been founded in 1919, and McElderry, along with *May Massee, ◄☙ Ursula Nordstrom, and Elizabeth Reilly, was largely responsible for shaping the field of modern children's literature. In 1952, works she had edited won both the Newbery Medal, given by the American Library Association to the year's most distinguished American children's book, and the Caldecott Medal, given by the association to the most distinguished American picture book; no other editor had won both awards in the same year before that, and no other would again until 1994. She edited *Mary Norton's classic *The Borrowers,* and was a champion of both picture books and stories by foreign authors at a time when few American publishers looked beyond their own shores.

After 25 years at Harcourt Brace, in 1972 McElderry, at age 60, was told by the publishing firm that "the wave of the future has passed you by" and unceremoniously forced into early retirement. Rather than taking up gardening, however, she moved to Atheneum (later Macmillan and currently, Simon and Schuster), where she became the first children's editor to receive her own imprint. In the year 2000, Margaret K. McElderry Books was still publishing some 25 titles per year. McElderry, who has an apartment in Greenwich Village and a summer cottage in Nantucket, is also a frequent speaker before publishing and library groups; many in her audiences were not even born when she began her career.

SOURCES:
The New York Times. November 17, 1997.

Grant Eldridge,
freelance writer, Pontiac, Michigan

McElroy, Mary Arthur (d. 1916).
See Arthur, Ellen Herndon for sidebar.

McFall, Frances E. (1854–1943).
See MacFall, Frances E.

McGee, Anita Newcomb
(1864–1940)

American physician and founder of the army nurse corps. Born Anita Newcomb on November 4, 1864, in Washington, D.C.; died on October 5, 1940; eldest of three daughters of Professor Simon Newcomb (an astronomer at the U.S. Naval Observatory) and Mary

Caroline (Hassler) Newcomb (daughter of Ferdinand Rudolph Hassler, founder and first superintendent of the U.S. Coast and Geodetic Survey); graduated from private school; traveled and studied for three years in England and Switzerland, took special courses at Newnham College, Cambridge, and the University of Geneva; studied medicine at Columbian (later George Washington University), M.D., 1892; took a postgraduate course in gynecology at Johns Hopkins University; married William J. McGee (an ethnologist), in 1888; children: daughter Klotho (b. 1889); son who died in infancy; son Eric (b. 1902).

Four years after her marriage in 1888, Anita McGee received the degree of M.D. from Columbia University. During the Spanish-American War in 1898–1900, she was acting assistant surgeon, the only woman officer in the U.S. Army, and established and had charge of the nurse corps division of the Surgeon-General's office, the Army Nurse Corps.

In 1904, McGee took a party of American nurses to Japan, and served successfully in the military hospitals there for six months, holding rank as supervisor of nurses in the Japanese army. After her death in 1940, Anita McGee was buried with full military honors in Arlington National Cemetery.

COLLECTIONS:
Anita Newcomb McGee Papers at the Library of Congress.

McGee, Molly (1896–1961).
See Jordan, Marian.

McGill, Helen (1871–1947).
See MacGill, Helen.

McGinley, Phyllis (1905–1978)

Pulitzer Prize-winning poet, author of children's books, and essayist. Born Phyllis McGinley on March 21, 1905, in Ontario, Oregon; died of a stroke on February 22, 1978, in New York City; daughter of Daniel McGinley (a land speculator) and Julia Kiesel McGinley; graduated from the University of Utah, 1927; married Charles L. Hayden, in 1937; children: Julia Elizabeth Hayden (b. 1939); Phyllis Louise "Patsy" Hayden (b. 1941).

Before marriage taught school and worked in publishing; published first book of poetry, On the Contrary *(1934); published first children's book,* The Horse Who Lived Upstairs *(1944); won Pulitzer Prize for* Times Three: Selected Verse from Three Decades

***Nordstrom, Ursula.** See Brown, Margaret Wise for sidebar.*

(1961); published essays, The Province of the Heart *(1959) and* Sixpence in Her Shoe *(1964). Honorary degrees from institutions including Dartmouth College (1961), Boston College (1962), Smith College (1964), St. John's University (1964).*

Phyllis McGinley was most recognized for her light verse describing suburban life in America from the 1930s to the 1960s. Her writing career, however, covered more than middle-class life in the New York suburbs, as McGinley was an observer of humanity whose interests included everything from the qualities of sainthood to myths and social criticism.

McGinley called herself "a pure third-generation immigrant." Her heritage was a mixture of Irish on her father's side and German on her mother's. She was born in 1905 in Ontario, Oregon, but her earliest memories were of the ranch in eastern Colorado where her family moved when she was three years old and remained until she was twelve. Her father's land investments were not successful and the family lived some miles from the nearest town, which McGinley remembered as resembling a scene from a television western, characterized by muddy streets, hitching posts, and bronco busting as a favorite pastime. The weather was harsh, with blizzards in winter and muddy roads in spring, and coyotes and antelope roamed the plains. She and her brother rode ponies to a one-room schoolhouse which was so isolated that sometimes they were the only pupils and other times they had no teacher. There was no public library within a reasonable distance, but McGinley, an eager reader, devoured the heavy history and law books in her father's collection. At the age of six, she composed her first poem; she would later date her determination to become a poet from that point.

When she was 12, her father died. With her mother and brother, Phyllis moved to Ogden, Utah, where her mother's family had settled when they immigrated from Germany, and where her mother had a sister, also widowed. The McGinleys moved in with their relatives in what Phyllis described as a sort of "communal home." This arrangement was apparently not to the young girl's liking, as she later contended that she did not have a "real" home until after she married. She attended Ogden High School and later the Sacred Heart Academy which she called a "decorous boarding school." McGinley did not find either high school intellectually stimulating.

Nor was college at the University of Utah, which had few entrance requirements, a challenge for her. McGinley remembered her fellow students as more interested in football games and dances than in education. If female students seemed too bright, they would become social outcasts. Thus, McGinley maintained, she managed to graduate as an English major without any familiarity with the great works of literature, discovering most of the important writers on her own after college.

Ironically, after her graduation in 1927, McGinley taught school for one year in Ogden, Utah. She then moved to New Rochelle, New York, where she would work as a high-school teacher until 1934. In 1928, she wrote a children's operetta, *The Toy Shop.* Meanwhile, she had begun writing both prose and poetry and submitting her work to magazines, teaching all day and writing into the night. Her early poetry was somber, but McGinley developed a lighter touch after being told by Kate White (***Katharine S. White**), an editor at *The New Yorker,* that all contemporary female poets "sang the same sad song." This less serious verse was, apparently, what publishers wanted. In 1934, McGinley resigned her teaching position, moved from the suburbs into Manhattan, and took a variety of jobs in publishing, as poetry editor of *Town and Country* and as a copywriter at an advertising agency. Her first book of poems, *On the Contrary,* was published that same year. *One More Manhattan* followed three years later, while *A Pocketful of Wry* was published in 1940.

Her first two collections of verse were written while the United States suffered through the Great Depression. Some of the poems refer to the effects of the economic disaster, and others address issues of social inequality. McGinley also developed the theme that too many people were preoccupied with foolishness and triviality—the doings of celebrities or some ephemeral fashion—while others starved or lived in the shadow of fascism. In her later collection, *Times Three,* she referred to the 1930s as "The Threadbare Years," an apparent pun on both the financial and spiritual poverty of the period. Irony was McGinley's weapon of choice to criticize hypocrisy.

Other poems written during the 1930s relate to her personal preferences: winter, hot baths, and an orderly universe. In many of these works, she seems to be speaking for normality, conventional man-woman relationships, and a comfortable world. Some of the later poems, no doubt, reflect changes in McGinley's personal life. In 1937, she married Charles L. Hayden, an executive with the Bell Telephone Company and an amateur jazz musician, and gave up her paid employment to focus on homemaking and her writing. A series of poems entitled *Husbands Are Difficult* appeared in 1940. Shortly after her marriage, McGinley and her husband moved from Manhattan to a large, old house in Larchmont, New York. Much of the poetry and essays written during the rest of her life would concentrate on the suburban milieu, and she has been described as "an *Erma Bombeck who rhymed."

McGinley's first child Julie was born in 1939, her second daughter Patsy in 1941. Her first children's book, *The Horse Who Lived Upstairs,* appeared three years later. An artist friend had brought over some drawings of horses, suggesting that McGinley might create a poem or story around them. She discovered a stable in Greenwich Village where horses lived on the second floor and wrote a story about a horse that lived in an apartment building and had a job pulling a vegetable wagon. Here, as in other later children's books, McGinley was determined to challenge her young audience with some unfamiliar words. She believed that children needed new ideas, new words, and new situations to help them grow both morally and intellectually.

Her next children's book, *The Plain Princess* (1945), was a fairy tale in which a "plain" princess who is vain and selfish learns the value of work and responsibility, and incidentally wins the love of the handsome prince. Again McGinley used a demanding vocabulary along with a moral lesson and a happy ending. *All Around the Town,* an alphabetical tour of New York City, was published in 1948, as was *A Name for Kitty,* a book for toddlers. McGinley continued to write for children throughout her career, believing that young readers and listeners needed well written and interesting stories that provided a positive and cheerful moral message.

During the 1940s, a decade dominated by World War II, McGinley also wrote poems about the war. *Stones from a Glass House* (1946) includes poetry that depicts the horrors of war, the fear, and the loneliness. She also wrote socially critical verse, as well as poems that conveyed her joy and contentment with suburban life. The latter type of verse resonated well in the postwar years, as Americans began to move past the conflict into the "baby boom" era, characterized by an idealization of home and family life.

Many of McGinley's poems of the 1950s echo those themes. As her daughters grew up, she wrote more of childhood and adolescence, themes she believed most poets did not address. In 1954, she published *The Love Letters of Phyllis McGinley,* which focused on the joys of sub-

urban living and was one of her most popular collections of verse. Because several readers wrote to the author asking her assistance in finding a home in the suburbs, a realtor is alleged to have hung her picture in his office—a tacit testimony to her approval of his listings. She also included a poem, "The Old Feminist," which assails the proponent of women's equality who "takes no pleasure in her Rights/ Who so enjoyed her Wrongs."

Through her work, McGinley wanted to narrow the distance between light and serious verse, using the light-verse form to deal with more somber subjects. For example, in "Ballade of Lost Objects," she juxtaposes misplacing small objects with the passage of time and the loss of her maturing daughters.

In 1954, McGinley was designated Columbia University's Phi Beta Kappa poet. For the occasion, she wrote "In Praise of Diversity," one of her best-known works. Though it does not refer specifically to politics, the poem, written against the anti-Communist hysteria of the McCarthy era, is clearly meant as a statement in favor of tolerating differences.

In addition to reading at Columbia, McGinley received a number of significant awards during the 1950s. *The Love Letters of Phyllis McGinley* was granted both the *Edna St. Vincent Millay Memorial Award and the Christopher Book Award. In 1955, she was elected to the National Institute of Arts and Letters. She also received recognition from several Catholic organizations, including the Catholic Writers Guild Award in 1955, and the St. *Catherine of Siena Medal in 1956. As well, Wheaton College and St. Mary's College at Notre Dame presented her with honorary degrees. McGinley's work clearly struck a responsive chord in the 1950s, as she achieved unusual popular acclaim for a poet.

Her children's books were also well received. *All Around the Town* (1949) and *The Most Wonderful Doll in the World* (1950), which describes a little girl who has difficulty telling her dreams from reality, were chosen as Caldecott Honor Books. Imagination is the theme in *The Make Believe Twins* (1953), about real twins who like to pretend to be other things. A number of characters from her earlier works reappeared in new juvenile works. Joey, the hero of *The Horse Who Lived Upstairs,* returned in *The Horse Who Had His Picture in the Paper* (1951), and the bus from *All Around the Town* was featured in *Blunderbus* (1951), in which the vehicle demonstrates a code of morality that includes kindness and consideration for others.

Phyllis McGinley

One of her most popular books, *The Year Without a Santa Claus* (1957), is written as poetry and tells of the year in which Santa decided to take a vacation on Christmas. The work would later be adapted as a stage musical. *Lucy McLockett* (1959) alternates poetry and prose, telling the story of a little girl who seemed to lose everything but recovers miraculously when her new tooth grows in. McGinley also wrote the lyrics for a musical review, *Small Wonder* (1948), and the narration for a 1951 film, *The Emperor's Nightingale.*

McGinley's audience expanded further in 1959 when she published a book of essays, *The Province of the Heart*. Her prose frequently developed themes expressed in her poetry, and this volume includes an expansive defense of the right of women to flourish and take pleasure in the role of homemaker. She staunchly supports the notion of a woman's place in the home, and argues that keeping house is a serious and important career, that children need full-time mothers, and that fathers should be heads of families. Although McGinley frequently cites her own experience as evidence for her conventional views, she does not come to terms with the contradiction implicit therein—that she herself was, throughout her life, a woman with a career outside the home.

In style, McGinley's essays are anecdotal, while her language resembles that of her poetry. In the later years of her career, she turned increasingly to prose, apparently because she could express her message in more detail and depth without the constraints imposed by poetic forms. She could also reach a wide audience through her articles in magazines such as *Saturday Review*, *Ladies' Home Journal*, and *Good Housekeeping*.

Ironically, when McGinley had virtually stopped writing new poetry she received the Pulitzer Prize in 1961 for *Times Three: Selected Verse from Three Decades* (1960). W.H. Auden wrote the introduction to the volume, in which he praised McGinley as the most feminine of women writers. The book included some 300 poems, many previously published in the 1930s and 1940s, as well as approximately 70 unpublished poems from the 1950s. Her receipt of the award marked the first time the Pulitzer Prize had ever been given to a writer of light verse. McGinley described her own accomplishment as "poetry of wit" and asserted that her only claim to genius was her painstaking approach, her determination to make her writing clear and accessible to "common people."

McGinley's last real book of poetry, *A Wreath of Christmas Legends*, appeared in 1967. It includes 15 poems, each based on a traditional Christmas fable. Her purpose in the collection was to present human reactions to a supernatural event, the birth of Christ, and to focus on the value of love.

Although she contended that middle age may have caused "the lyric impulse to fade," McGinley continued to write children's books and essays during the 1960s. Self-help books for young women, *Sugar and Spice: The ABC of Being a Girl* (1960) and *A Girl and Her Room* (1963), offered traditional advice. She also wrote a 1961 poem *Aren't Boys Awful* which was published as a companion piece to Ogden Nash's *Girls Are Silly*. *Mince Pie and Mistletoe* (1961), a collection of ethnic Christmas traditions, and *How Mrs. Santa Claus Saved Christmas* (1963) were seasonal works. Her final compilation of original children's poems, *Wonderful Time* (1966), centered on the theme of time. In 1968, McGinley edited an anthology of poems for young people called *Wonders and Surprises: A Collection of Poems*, including classic works by Shakespeare, *Emily Dickinson, Robert Frost, and others.

Sixpence in Her Shoe (1964) reiterates many of the themes discussed in *The Province of the Heart*. McGinley offers the collection of essays as a reward to housewives, just as an old English legend promised that the good housewife might be rewarded by finding a sixpence in her shoe. The essays are written in a chatty, first-person style, and although McGinley calls them autobiographical, they might better be described as memoirs. Again, McGinley describes her profession as housewife and argues that homemaking is women's natural and noblest calling. In one essay, "The Moonlight Adventure," which argues against work outside the home, McGinley maintains that although women have had the vote for many years, they "have made no impression at all on the nation or on the universe." They have accomplished no reforms, alleviated no problems, they have failed to abolish war or poverty. She wants such failures "hammered into feminist skulls," so women can be left alone to continue their one true career. Whereas McGinley's poetry and essays during the 1950s seemed to be in harmony with the conventional prevailing views of women, not long after *A Sixpence in Her Shoe* was published, a new generation of women found her views out of step.

McGinley issued her last book, *Saint Watching: A Personal View of Several Saints*, in 1971. She had earlier written poems which humorously described the eccentricities of some Christian saints. *Saint Watching* tells the life stories of several saints, focusing on their human qualities, such as wit, friendship, love of animals, and compassion. McGinley considers the cultural variables that may influence the definition of holiness. *Saint Watching* seems to be another of her efforts to emphasize models of goodness in her writings, as against an environment she perceived as too preoccupied with violence and evil.

After receiving the Pulitzer Prize in 1961, McGinley continued to be honored by many groups for her work. The Catholic Poetry Society of America gave her the Spirit Gold Medal in 1962, and the University of Notre Dame awarded her its Laetare Medal in 1964. That year, McGinley was also invited to read at the White House Arts Festival, where she read, with minor adaptations and updates, "In Praise of Diversity." Her children's collections were also recognized; *The New York Times* chose *Wonderful Time* as one of the Best Illustrated Books of the Year in 1966, and *Wonders and Surprises* became one of the Child Study Association's Children's Books of the Year in 1968.

In 1972, McGinley's husband Charles Hayden died. At her daughters' urging, McGinley sold her beloved house in Larchmont and moved into an apartment in New York City. She died of a stroke in Manhattan in 1978.

SOURCES:

Auden, W.H. "Foreword" to *Times Three: Selected Verse from Three Decades*. NY: Viking, 1960.

McGinley, Phyllis. *The Province of the Heart*. NY: Viking, 1959.

————. *Sixpence in Her Shoe*. NY: Macmillan, 1964.

"Moment with Phyllis McGinley," in *Newsweek*. September 26, 1960, p. 120.

"Phyllis McGinley," in *Contemporary Literary Criticism*. Vol. 14. Detroit, MI: Gale Research, 1980, pp. 364–369.

Wagner, Linda Welshimer. *Phyllis McGinley*. NY: Twayne, 1971.

Mary Welek Atwell,
Associate Professor of Criminal Justice,
Radford University, Radford, Virginia

McGrath, Peggy (d. 1996).

See Rockefeller, Margaret.

McGroarty, Sister Julia

(1827–1901)

American nun, educator, and founder of Trinity College. Born Susan McGroarty on February 13, 1827, in Donegal, Ireland; died on November 12, 1901, in Peabody, Massachusetts; daughter of Neil McGroarty and Catherine (Bonner) McGroarty; received teachers' training from the Sisters of Notre Dame de Namur; never married; no children.

Left Ireland (1831); death of father (1838); began preparations to enter women's religious order (1846); took vows as Sister Julia (1848); moved to Massachusetts (1854); became superior of Philadelphia convent school (1860); became provincial superior in Cincinnati (1887); founded college (1900).

Through her accomplishments as an administrator, Sister Julia McGroarty left behind an educational legacy that benefited generations of Catholic schoolchildren in America. She also battled great opposition to establish a college for women attached to the prestigious Catholic University of America in Washington, D.C. One of ten children, she was baptized Susan McGroarty after her 1827 birth on the family farm in Donegal, Ireland. With her family, she emigrated to the United States in 1831, settling for a time in Ohio before moving to Cincinnati when her father gave up farming for good. He died in 1838, which meant certain hardship for the large brood, but her mother's brother, who was a physician in Cincinnati, provided assistance.

As a child, McGroarty did poorly in school, but nevertheless was bright enough to memorize her lessons and books in order to fool teachers into believing she could read, a ruse that was only uncovered when she was ten. At 13, she was sent to a much stricter convent school, run by the Sisters of Notre Dame de Namur in Cincinnati. She surprised many when she decided to become a nun herself at the age of 18. Two years later, in 1848, she took her vows as Sister Julia and began teaching school. After a time, she was sent by the order to Roxbury, Massachusetts, to serve as mistress of boarders at the Academy of Notre Dame there. She spent six years at the school and in 1860 was transferred to the post of superior of the Notre Dame order's Philadelphia school, becoming the first American nun to hold that position.

At the time, anti-Catholic sentiment ran high in many cities, including Philadelphia, and McGroarty attempted to fight prejudice in her community by running a faultless, charitable organization. Her school educated girls from affluent families, but also held evening classes for immigrant families and had a school for African-American children. In 1885, she returned to Cincinnati when her mentor, Sister Superior **Louise van der Schrieck**, became ill and needed an assistant. McGroarty helped her in her administrative duties of supervising all Notre Dame de Namur houses east of the Rocky Mountains, and upon Sister Louise's death in 1887 succeeded her as provincial superior with responsibilities for overseeing all 26 houses. From 1892 to 1901, her duties also included overseeing all the houses in California.

Over the next decade, McGroarty worked to standardize the curriculum in all schools run by the Notre Dame sisters, and implemented an examination system; she also set up an orphanage and established 14 new schools. Yet McGroarty also saw that while the Catholic educational system in the United States did a fine job of educating young women, it often left them stranded at the threshold of a college education; there were many secular women's colleges across the country, but mixing with people of other religions was seen as a potentially corrupting situation by strict Catholics of the era. The Catholic University of America, founded in 1889, observed the strict gender separation found in Catholic schools and did not admit women (although it received applications from them every year). Backed by Catholic educators and even many male administrative clergy, McGroarty began working to establish a women's college near the Catholic University that would borrow some of its faculty. There was great opposition to the proposed Trinity College, however, for it was seen by some of the more traditionally minded Catholics as a liberal plot to corrupt Catholic values by imposing American customs upon its institutions.

McGroarty fought the indignant cries against "coeducation" with characteristic good grace, though she was even censured by the superior of her own order. The first class of Trinity College was matriculated in 1900. McGroarty never saw its graduation day, however. She died in November 1901, and was buried in the chapel of the Summit School, one of the institutions she had founded.

SOURCES:

James, Edward T., ed. *Notable American Women, 1607–1950.* Cambridge, MA: The Belknap Press of Harvard University Press, 1971.

McHenry, Robert, ed. *Famous American Women.* NY: Dover, 1980.

Carol Brennan,
Grosse Pointe, Michigan

McGrory, Mary (1918—)

Nationally syndicated American columnist who in 1975 became the first woman to receive the Pulitzer Prize for commentary. Name variations: sometimes signs work as "Mary McG"; also referred to as "Mother McGrory." Born on April 22, 1918, in Boston, Massachusetts; daughter of Edward Patrick McGrory (a postal worker) and Mary (Jacobs) McGrory; attended Girls Latin High School in Boston; Emmanuel College, B.A., 1939; never married; no children.

Worked in publishing (1939–42); joined Boston Herald *staff as a secretary (1942), and became book reviewer; served as regular book reviewer for* Washington Star *(1947–54); covered McCarthy hearings (1954), and assigned to national desk; started first regular column (1960); won Pulitzer Prize for commentary on*

Watergate scandal (1975); covered Three Mile Island story (1979); had column syndicated nationally (1985).

One of the most respected journalists in Washington, D.C., Mary McGrory earned a Pulitzer Prize in 1975 for a series of columns that captured the mood of the Watergate scandal during the Nixon administration. A columnist who is really a reporter and bases her stories on what she herself sees and hears, McGrory finds writing extremely difficult. Despite that fact, it is generally acknowledged that her articles covering the Army-McCarthy hearings, the Three Mile Island nuclear reactor accident (1979), and the Nixon-Watergate political operatives scandal are among the best ever written on those subjects.

Born in Boston, Massachusetts, on April 22, 1918, McGrory was the daughter of **Mary Jacobs McGrory** and Edward Patrick McGrory. She learned about words by listening to the lilt of Irish voices as they recounted endless stories, and through her father, who died when she was 21. Edward supported his family as a postal clerk, but was an avid reader in his off-duty hours and often quoted Shakespeare to his children. Mary McGrory went to a strict Catholic girls school in Boston for her high school education and then to Emmanuel College, also in Boston, graduating in 1939 with a B.A. degree in English. Upon completion of her education, she worked for Houghton Mifflin publishers, cropping pictures for $16.50 a week. In 1942, she joined the *Boston Herald* as a secretary to the book review editor. She fought to become a book reviewer there, eventually succeeding, and in her spare time also critiqued books for *The New York Times*. In 1947, she became a book reviewer for the *Washington* [D.C.] *Star* and continued there for seven years, which once prompted *Doris Fleeson, a *Daily News* columnist, to note that McGrory was "curled up on a bookshelf" all those years gathering strength to become a columnist.

McGrory spoke as well as she wrote, and in this way she impressed Newbold Noyes, the *Star*'s national editor in the 1950s, enough that in 1954 he asked her to cover the Army-McCarthy hearings. The first major congressional event to be shown on live television, the hearings riveted America and dealt a mortal blow to the previously unstoppable Senator Joseph McCarthy and his Communist witch hunt when defense lawyer Joseph Welch asked McCarthy, "Have you no decency, sir, at long last? Have you no decency?" McGrory, who saw McCarthy as an Irish bully, produced 32 stories on the hearings with what came to be her trademark incisive thumbnail descriptions, and "all of a sudden," she said, "people wanted to adopt me, marry me, poison me, run me out of town."

She moved to the national desk after the McCarthy hearings, an unheard-of promotion, and assumed a leadership position that gained her her "Mother McGrory" reputation. She was not always easy to work with, maintaining her gutsy and often controversial views, but these were counterbalanced with enormous grace and generosity, and she earned great respect from her co-workers. In 1960, she began her first regular column, heeding the advice of her colleague Walter Lippmann to "ignore" what she thought others wanted to read. "Write what you want, and don't fret if a paper doesn't run it." Later in her career, she would help younger, inexperienced journalists just as Lippmann had helped her. She won the George R. Polk Memorial Award in 1962 for her coverage of Nixon's "last press conference," after his defeat in the California gubernatorial race, at which he seemed to be having a nervous breakdown and told the assembled members of the press, "You won't have Nixon to kick around any more."

McGrory, who once described Nixon as "still stalk[ing] the light touch with all the grimness that the butterfly collectors bring to pursuit of a rare specimen," was delighted when, some 12 years after that press conference, her columns on the Watergate scandal garnered her a spot on White House counsel John Dean's list of enemies. They also won her the 1975 Pulitzer Prize for commentary, making her the first woman so honored. Her passionate columns against the Vietnam War also earned her both enemies and admirers, and ran defiantly contrary to the Star's pro-Vietnam editorial policy. In 1979, in the wake of the Three Mile Island nuclear reactor accident, she searched far and wide for the mother she had seen in a photograph fleeing from the scene while attempting to shield her infant from radiation with a blanket. After extensive investigation, McGrory finally located the woman, who was staying with a relative 75 miles away, and interviewed her by telephone, putting an individual human face on the story that panicked the nation.

Unlike other columnists who depended upon researchers to track down their information and staff members to do their legwork, McGrory gathered all the research for her columns herself. She considered this a disadvantage only when people would not return her phone calls or in situations (which she said were rare) like the fol-

lowing. While interviewing Mississippi senator John Stennis, she wrote, "[He] said to me, 'Well now, Little Lady, I don't think I'd want to comment on that, Miss Mary.' Then he went down the hall and said to [reporter] Roger Mudd, 'I'd like to tell you what we were talking about.'"

After the Star folded, she took a news position at the Washington Post. In 1985, her thrice-weekly column was syndicated through the Universal Press Syndicate, and had 160 subscribers, many of which were major American papers. Over the years, the number of subscribing papers grew, but, she pointed out, "It's hard to be a liberal columnist in a conservative world." Having volunteered for decades at the St. Ann's Infant Home, an orphanage in Washington, D.C., she was known for her annual Christmas party for the children there. With friends, she had an informal choral group that sang Irish songs, and she frequently traveled to Italy. She said she would like to die in the newsroom; in a 1980 interview, she called politics "the most entertaining thing possible. It involves high risk and ex-

Mary
McGrory

citement and suspense, human nature and comedy and tragedy. What more do you want?"

SOURCES:

Belford, Barbara. *Brilliant Bylines: A Biographical Anthology of Notable Newspaperwomen in America.* NY: Columbia University Press, 1986.

Read, Phyllis J., and Witlieb, Bernard L. *The Book of Women's Firsts.* NY: Random House, 1992.

Spencer, Duncan. "Mary McGrory: A Reporter at Her Primitive Best," in *Washington Star.* May 6, 1975.

Jo Anne Meginnes,
freelance writer, Brookfield, Vermont

McGuinness, Norah (1901–1980)

Irish artist who was a major proponent of the modern movement in Ireland. Born Norah Allison McGuinness in Derry, Northern Ireland, on November 7, 1901; died in Monkstown, Co. Dublin, on November 22, 1980; daughter of Joseph Allison McGuinness and Jessie McCleery McGuinness; educated at Victoria High School; Dublin Metropolitan School of Art; Chelsea Polytechnic; married Geoffrey Taylor also known as Geoffrey Phipps (a poet), in 1925 (marriage dissolved 1929, partially because of his affair with *Laura Riding).

Awards: Royal Dublin Society medal (1923); Tailteann Competition medal (1924); honorary doctorate, Trinity College, Dublin (1973).

Norah McGuinness was born in 1901 in Derry, Northern Ireland. Though her financially comfortable family was opposed to her ambition to be an artist, she was able to support herself when she won a three-year scholarship to the Dublin Metropolitan School of Art in 1921. There, she studied under Patrick Tuohy, Oswald Reeves, and Harry Clarke. Clarke influenced her career as an illustrator, which remained an important source of income throughout her life. In 1923–24, the *Dublin Magazine* published some of her illustrations. In 1925, just after she had gone to London to study at the Chelsea Polytechnic, she received a commission to illustrate a deluxe edition of Laurence Sterne's *A Sentimental Journey through France and Italy.*

McGuinness returned to Dublin frequently in the late 1920s to work at the Abbey Theater, designing the sets and costumes for W.B. Yeats' *Deirdre* and *The Only Jealousy of Emer* in 1926. She also conceived the garden scene for Oscar Wilde's *The Importance of Being Earnest.* For the opening of the Abbey's studio theater, the Peacock, in 1927 she designed the sets for Georg Born's *From Morn to Midnight.* Yeats, a great admirer of her work, asked her to illustrate his *Stories of Red Hanrahan and the Secret Rose* and

dedicated the introductory poem to her. In 1929, *Mainie Jellett advised McGuinness to go to Paris to study under André Lhote, who had taught Jellett and *Evie Hone a decade earlier. McGuinness worked with Lhote for nearly two years and was influenced by the work of Braque, Lurçat, Dufy and Vlaminck. She did not embrace Cubism completely and commented later that pure abstraction "would be an empty field for me."

In 1931, she returned to London to live, remaining there until 1937, though she continued to spend summers in Ireland at her cottage in Donegal. Landscapes became a favorite form in the 1930s, and in the opinion of S.B. Kennedy her landscapes were "a breath of fresh air to Irish painting at this time." She also illustrated for books and periodicals such as *The Bystander* and *Vogue.* There were exhibitions of her paintings in London, Paris and Dublin and she also continued to design for the stage, most notably for Denis Johnston's *A Bride for the Unicorn* at the Westminster Theater in London. In 1939, McGuinness had her first exhibition in New York, at the Reinhardt Gallery, and received commissions from *Harper's Bazaar* and to design window displays for Altman's department store.

After her return to Dublin, she was hired by Brown Thomas, one of Dublin's leading department stores, to do their window displays, and she did this regularly for the next 30 years. McGuinness had regular exhibitions of her paintings in Dublin and also became a considerable portrait artist, painting many of the leading cultural figures in Ireland. Her career took a major turn in 1943–44, when she became a founder member of the Irish Exhibition of Living Art and, after Mainie Jellett's death in 1944, president. McGuinness held this position until 1972, and as such became the speaker for the modern movement in Ireland and its champion against the forces of reaction symbolized by the Royal Hibernian Academy (RHA). She was also known for generous support of younger artists. The critic and art historian Brian Fallon described her as "a formidable personality and organizer in the Hone-Jellett and *Sarah Purser tradition, with an acute social sense and firm opinions about virtually everything. In short, another masterful woman in the Irish Protestant mould, and a useful person to lead the official opposition to [Sean] Keating and the RHA." McGuinness had known Jellett for some time but was closer to Evie Hone with whom she went on painting holidays in Ireland and abroad.

After the war McGuinness painted in Italy, and in 1947 had the first in a series of solo shows at the Leicester Galleries in London. She also continued to design for the stage in Dublin at the Abbey and at the Gaiety Theater. In 1950, she and Nano Reid were chosen to represent Ireland at the Venice Biennale, and her work was also included in the exhibition of Contemporary Irish Painting which toured North America during the same year. In 1957 she was elected an honorary member of the RHA and in 1959 the first exhibition of her work in her native Northern Ireland was held in Belfast. That same year, her painting *The Yellow Table* was one of five pictures by Irish artists selected to compete in the International Guggenheim Award.

A retrospective of McGuinness' work, including paintings, drawings, prints, theatrical designs and illustrations, was held at Trinity College in 1968 and was subsequently shown at the Crawford Gallery in Cork and at the Brooke Park Gallery in her native Derry. In 1973, she was awarded an honorary doctorate of literature from Trinity College, and the following year one of her works was featured on an Irish postage stamp. Norah McGuinness had a solo show at the Taylor Galleries in Dublin in 1979 and continued to work until shortly before her death in 1980.

SOURCES:

Fallon, Brian. *Irish Art 1830–1990*. Belfast: Appletree Press, 1994.

Kennedy, S.B. *Irish Art and Modernism 1880–1950*. Belfast & Dublin: Institute of Irish Studies and Hugh Lane Municipal Gallery of Modern Art, 1991.

Snoddy, Theo. *Dictionary of Irish Artists: 20th Century*. Dublin: Wolfhound Press, 1996.

Walker, Dorothy. *Modern Art in Ireland*. Dublin: Lilliput, 1997.

Deirdre McMahon,
Lecturer in History, Mary Immaculate College,
University of Limerick

McGuire, Dorothy (1918—)

American actress who was nominated for an Academy Award for her work in Gentleman's Agreement.
Born Dorothy Hackett McGuire on June 14, 1918, in Omaha, Nebraska; daughter of Thomas Johnson McGuire and Isabelle (Flaherty) McGuire; attended Pine Manor Junior College, c. 1936; married John Swope (a photographer), in 1943; children: one son; daughter Topo Swope.

Moved to New York City (c. 1937); won title role in first Broadway play (1940); made film debut (1943); nominated for Academy Award (1948).

Selected filmography: Claudia *(1943);* A Tree Grows in Brooklyn *(1944);* The Enchanted Cottage *(1945);* The Spiral Staircase *(1946);* Claudia and David *(1946);* Gentleman's Agreement *(1947);* Mother Didn't Tell Me *(1950);* Three Coins in the Fountain *(1954);* Trial *(1955);* Old Yeller *(1957);* The Remarkable Mr. Pennypacker *(1959);* The Dark at the Top of the Stairs *(1960);* Susan Slade *(1961);* Summer Magic *(1962);* The Greatest Story Ever Told *(1965); (voice only)* Jonathan Livingston Seagull *(1975).*

Born in Omaha, Nebraska, in 1918, Dorothy McGuire began acting as a child and appeared in a local theater production of *Cinderella* at age 12; her costar, a friend of the family, was Henry Fonda. McGuire's father died when she was a teenager, and as a result she was sent to a convent school in Indianapolis. Afterward, she went on to Pine Manor Junior College in Wellesley, Massachusetts, but departed in the late 1930s to try her luck in New York City. Aside from a job as understudy to *Martha Scott in *Our Town* (1938), she found little success in her audition rounds, and barely survived with summer stock work and touring companies. In 1940, her luck changed when she won the coveted title role in *Claudia*, *Rose Franken's stage adaptation of her popular stories. McGuire made her Broadway debut the following February to effusive critical praise, and was signed to a studio contract to reprise the role on the silver screen. The 1943 film version of *Claudia*, the story of a naive newlywed who breaks free of her attachment to her mother, marked her screen debut.

Dorothy McGuire went on to appear in a number of other critically acclaimed films, including *A Tree Grows in Brooklyn* (1944), based on the novel by *Betty Smith, *The Spiral Staircase* (1946), for which studio executive David O. Selznick gave her a convertible as a bonus, and the film version of *Laura Z. Hobson's novel *Gentleman's Agreement* (1947), a role that earned her an Academy Award nomination. During the 1950s, she was cast in *Three Coins in the Fountain* (1954), *Old Yeller* (1957), and *The Remarkable Mr. Pennypacker* (1959), among other films. Later credits included *The Dark at the Top of the Stairs* (1960), based on the Pulitzer Prize-winning play by William Inge, *The Greatest Story Ever Told* (1965), in which she portrayed *Mary the Virgin, and a voice role in *Jonathan Livingston Seagull* (1975).

McGuire was known for her determined attitude. She earned some enmity within the studio for refusing to be made up to look extremely ugly for her role as a homely woman who finds love with a disfigured man in *The Enchanted Cottage* (1945), although film critics generally agree that her choice was correct. She also turned down the lead in *Anna and the*

Dorothy McGuire

King of Siam (1946), the movie version of *Margaret Landon's book about *Anna Leonowens (*Irene Dunne took the part instead), and declined to be part of the studio publicity machine by being seen on the town with actors. In 1943, she married photographer John Swope, with whom she had two children, and made her home in Beverly Hills. Though she went back to Broadway in 1976 in a revival of Tennessee Williams' Night of the Iguana, McGuire confined her screen work after 1973 to television movies.

SOURCES:

Current Biography. NY: H.W. Wilson, 1941.

Katz, Ephraim. *The Film Encyclopedia.* NY: Harper-Collins, 1994.

Lamparski, Richard. *Whatever Became of . . . ?* 5th Series. NY: Crown, 1974.

Quinlan, David, ed. *The Film Lover's Companion.* Carol Publishing, 1997.

Carol Brennan,
Grosse Pointe, Michigan

McGuire, Edith (1944—)

African-American track star. Born Edith Marie McGuire in Atlanta, Georgia, on June 3, 1944.

Won an Olympic gold medal in the 200-meter run at 23.05, a silver in the 4x100-meter relay, and a silver in the 100-meter run at 11.62 (1964).

Several American schools produced outstanding women in track and field, among them Tuskegee Institute and Tennessee State University, both African-American institutions. One high school which fed these colleges with soon-to-be celebrated track-and-field-competitors was David T. Howard High School in Atlanta, Georgia. Howard High's coach, **Marian Armstrong-Perkins**, produced some of America's finest, including **Mary McNabb**, *****Mildred McDaniel**, *****Margaret Matthews**, **Anna Lois Smith**, and Edith McGuire. An honor student in high school, Edith was named best all-around student in her class. Because of her athletic and academic ability, no one was surprised when McGuire was awarded a scholarship to Tennessee State and given the opportunity to run with some of the world's finest women athletes as a member of the Tennessee Tigerbelles.

In 1961, as a freshman, McGuire qualified for the U.S. women's international team and was soon on her way to Europe. Armstrong-Perkins described McGuire's reaction:

> I think Edith was the most surprised person of us all when she made the team. When she realized what the trip entailed, being away from home for at least a month, she became very depressed. She began crying when she got to New York, and she cried all the way into Germany. She had a terrific homesickness and only realized that the trip was worthwhile when we got into Poland.

In the early 1960s, the Cold War was in full force. Western and Eastern athletes worked to prove that their ideological and economic systems were superior not only in the business world but also on the playing fields. When Edith McGuire arrived at Kiev's Central Stadium in the USSR, the competition between East and West that greeted the young American runner was fierce. *****Wilma Rudolph** and *****Wyomia Tyus**, two Tennessee Tigerbelles, had held the world record in the 100 meters until *****Irena Szewinska** and **Ewa Klobukowska**, two Poles, wrested the title from them in Prague, Czechoslovakia, three weeks before. The Americans were determined to win back their titles. In the 100 meters in Kiev, Wyomia Tyus finished first and Edith McGuire finished second, matching the new world record set by Szewinska and Klobukowska. In the 200 meters, McGuire finished first while Tyus finished second. In the 4x100-meter relay, McGuire, Tyus, *****Willye B. White**, and **Diana Wilson**, all from Tennessee, took first place. They left Kiev having established clear American dominance, and Edith McGuire had unquestionably contributed to the Americans' success. But the Tigerbelles had less success in Warsaw, where Irena Szewinska won the 100 and 200 meters as well as the long jump and Klobukowska helped win the 400-meter relay. (In 1967, Klobukowska would fail a sex-determination test and a *Times* story would report that she had "one chromosome too many.")

McGuire went on to a remarkable career at Tennessee State. In 1963, she won the 100 meters and the long jump at the AAU indoor and outdoor meets. She also led the 100 meters at the Pan American Games that year in Sao Paulo, Brazil, with a Pan Am record of 11.5 seconds. In 1964, McGuire established a world record in the 70-yard dash, an American record in the 100-meter run, an American record in the 200-meter run, and an American outdoor record in the 220-yard dash. That same year, she won the AAU 200-meter run. She qualified for the Olympic team at the 1964 Tokyo Games, where she finished ahead of Irena Szewinska and won a gold medal in the 200 meters with a time of 23.05, an Olympic record. She also won silver medals in the 4x100-meter relay, with a time of 43.92, and in the 100 meters, with a time of 11.62.

In 1965, McGuire defended her title in the 220-yard dash at the AAU and repeated this feat in 1966. During seven years of national and international competition, she held World, Olympic, Canadian, AAU American, and AAU champion records in the 200-meter run and the 220-yard dash. She won a place on six AAU All-American track-and-field teams. After graduating from Tennessee State University in 1966, McGuire became a schoolteacher in Detroit, where she specialized in working with underprivileged children.

SOURCES:

Davis, Michael D. *Black American Women in Olympic Track and Field*. Jefferson, NC: McFarland, 1992.

Page, James A. *Black Olympian Medalists*. Englewood, CO: Libraries Unlimited, 1991.

Wallechinsky, David. *The Complete Book of the Olympics*. NY: Viking, 1988.

Karin Loewen Haag,
Athens, Georgia

McGuire, Phyllis (1931—)

American pop singer. Born on February 14, 1931, in Middletown, Ohio; youngest sister of Christine McGuire (b. 1928) and Dorothy McGuire (b. 1930).

Won national talent show with sisters (1954); signed to record contract (1954); single "Sincerely" reached No. 1 (1955); released "Volare" (1957); had last top ten hit (1961).

Selected discography: Best of the McGuire Sisters; McGuire Sisters; Our Golden Favorites.

Phyllis McGuire was one-third of the McGuire Sisters, a wholesome singing act that sang in the close three-part harmony style prevalent in pop music just before the arrival of rock 'n' roll. With her older sisters **Christine** and **Dorothy McGuire**, Phyllis left her Middletown, Ohio, home and received her first big break when the group won a showdown on the popular "Arthur Godfrey Talent Hour" in 1954. They were signed to a contract with Coral Records and had a hit with their first single, "Goodnight, Sweetheart, Goodnight," released in June 1954. Later that year, they recorded "Sincerely," which reached No. 1 in 1955 and would remain their best-known hit. The song previously had been a bestseller for the rhythm and blues group the Moonglows; some thought the McGuire Sisters' version was decidedly more saccharine. They had several other top ten hits, with "Sugartime" reaching No. 1 in 1957. Singles such as "Give Me Love," "Volare," "Theme from Picnic," "Delilah," and "Tears on My Pillow" appeared on the three albums McGuire recorded with her sisters for Coral. By the time of their last top ten hit in 1961, the trio had already become successful performers on the Las Vegas nightclub circuit.

As a result of her popularity in the high-flying Nevada gambling mecca, in the 1960s McGuire met and became romantically linked with alleged organized crime figure Sam Giancana, who was later murdered. Their affair was the basis for the HBO cable channel's 1995 movie *Sugartime*, which McGuire publicly, and bitterly, denounced. Supposedly, transcripts of FBI wiretaps of conversations between McGuire

and Giancana were used in writing the script. McGuire was still performing both as a solo act and with her sisters in the 1990s.

SOURCES:

Amende, Coral. *Legends in Their Own Time*. NY: Prentice Hall, 1994.

Claghorn, Charles Eugene. *Biographical Dictionary of American Music*. West Nyack, NY: Parker Publishing, 1973.

Nite, Norm N. *Rock On: The Illustrated Encyclopedia of Rock 'n' Roll*, Vol. 1: *The Solid Gold Years*. NY: Thomas Y. Crowell, 1974.

The Penguin Encyclopedia of Popular Music. Edited by Donald Clarke. NY: Viking, 1989.

People Weekly. November 27, 1995, pp. 15–16.

TV Guide. November 25, 1995, p. 38.

RELATED MEDIA:

Sugartime (110-min. television movie), starring **Mary-Louise Parker** and John Turturro, shown on HBO in 1995.

Carol Brennan,
Grosse Pointe, Michigan

McIntosh, Caroline C. (1813–1881)

Second wife of Millard Fillmore. Name variations: Caroline Fillmore. Born Caroline Carmichael on October 21, 1813, in Morristown, New Jersey; died on August 11, 1881, in Buffalo, New York; daughter of Charles Carmichael (a New Jersey merchant) and Temperance (Blachley) Carmichael; married Ezekiel C. McIntosh (one of the builders of the Mohawk and Hudson Railroad); married Milliard Fillmore (former U.S. president), on February 10, 1858, in Albany, New York; no children.

Little is known about Caroline McIntosh. She attended a finishing school in New York and married Ezekiel C. McIntosh in Morristown, New Jersey. His date of death is unknown. In 1858, after a brief courtship, she married former president Millard Fillmore. A prenuptial agreement allowed Fillmore complete control, with no accountability, over her fortune from her first husband. It further stated that upon her death, he would receive her entire estate, while if he died first, she would receive only a third of his money. Millard Fillmore died first, in 1874. After his death, Caroline became senile, died seven years later, and was buried in Buffalo next to Fillmore, his first wife *Abigail Powers Fillmore*, and his daughter from that earlier marriage, **Mary Abigail Fillmore**.

McKane, Alice Woodby (1865–1948)

African-American physician and educator. Name variations: Alice Woodby-McKane. Born Alice Wood-

by in 1865 in Bridgewater, Pennsylvania; died on March 6, 1948; daughter of Charles Woodby and Elizabeth B. (Frazier) Woodby; attended public school in Bridgewater; Hampton Institute, 1883–86; Institute for Colored Youth in Pennsylvania, 1886–89; Women's Medical College of Pennsylvania, M.D., 1892; married Cornelius McKane (a physician), on February 2, 1893; children: Cornelius, Jr. (b. 1897), Alice Fanny (b. 1898), William Francis (b. 1902).

Selected works: contributed to a number of religious magazines and journals; The Fraternal Society Sick Book (1913), which dealt with art of healing; Clover Leaves (Boston, 1914), a book of poems.

After a childhood in which both her parents died before she was seven years old and she suffered blindness for three years, Alice Woodby McKane received a medical degree from the Women's Medical College of Pennsylvania in 1892. She then worked as resident physician and instructor in physiology and chemistry at the Haines Institute, founded by *Lucy Craft Laney, and privately taught a class on nursing. In 1893, she married another physician, Cornelius McKane, who would become an early civil-rights activist. The grandson of a Liberian king, he had been born in British Guiana (now Guyana), and together they founded the first training school for nurses in southeast Georgia in 1893. The school doubled as a free clinic for destitute people, although lack of funds and space forced the clinic to turn away about ten patients a week.

McKane and her husband then traveled to Monrovia, Liberia, where they helped to organize health facilities and she served as the Assistant United States Pension Medical Examiner for Civil War veterans who had moved to Liberia. She also co-organized and headed the department of women's diseases at Monrovia's first hospital, but was forced to return to Georgia after she contracted an African fever. Regaining her health in 1896, she and her husband established the McKane Hospital for Women and Children and Training School for Nurses in Savannah. Several white physicians who became interested in their project donated money and helped to treat the sick.

In search of better educational opportunities for their three children, the McKanes then moved to Boston, where they reestablished their medical practice in a matter of weeks. McKane concentrated on treating diseases affecting women, and also lectured weekly to nurses in training at the Plymouth (Massachusetts) Hospital. An active member of the National Associa-

tion for the Advancement of Colored People (NAACP) after its founding in 1910, she was also involved in the women's suffrage movement and wrote magazine articles and poetry. McKane published *The Fraternal Society Sick Book*, about healing, in 1913, and a book of poems, *Clover Leaves*, a year later. She died in 1948.

SOURCES:

Bailey, Brooke. *The Remarkable Lives of 100 Women Healers and Scientists.* Holbrook, MA: Bob Adams, 1994.

Smith, Jessie Carney, ed. *Notable Black American Women.* Detroit, MI: Gale Research, 1992.

SUGGESTED READING:

Davis, Marianna W., ed. *Contributions of Black Women to America, Vol. II.* Columbia, SC: Kenday Press, 1992.

COLLECTIONS:

Papers on Alice Woodby McKane are in the Black Women Physicians Project, Archives and Special collections on Women, Medical College of Pennsylvania. The archives of Hampton University also have materials on McKane.

Jo Anne Meginnes,
freelance writer, Brookfield, Vermont

McKay, Heather (1941—)

Australian squash champion. Born Heather Pamela Blundell on July 31, 1941, in Queanbeyan, New South Wales, Australia.

Won first Australian Amateur Squash championship title (1960); won first British Open title in the sport (1962); won the inaugural Women's World championship title (1976, 1979).

Heather McKay lost only two squash matches in twenty years, and is recognized as one of the leading players of the game (known in the United States as racquetball). Born in the town of Queanbeyan in New South Wales, Australia, in 1941, McKay was already a skilled field hockey player when she took up a squash racquet in order to improve her field hockey game. Though she would play on the Australian women's national field hockey team, she came to excel in squash and began making a name for herself in the sport in the late 1950s. In 1960, she won her first Australian Amateur championship title, and retained control of that title through 1973. She also won the British Open title for 16 seasons straight, from 1962 to 1977. She was named ABC Sportsman of the Year (now Sports Person of the Year) in 1967, and after winning the Women's World championship title in 1976 turned professional. She moved to Toronto, Canada, in the late 1970s and became a coach. In 1979, she won both the Women's World Open Squash championship as well as the

U.S. Amateur Women's Racquetball title. She also took the Professional Women's Racquetball titles in the United States in 1980, 1981, and 1984. Returning to Australia in 1985, she became a coach in Brisbane.

SOURCES:

Hemery, David. *The Pursuit of Sporting Excellence.* Champaign, IL: Human Kinetics Books, 1986.

Vamplew, Wray, *et al.*, eds. *The Oxford Companion to Australian Sport.* Melbourne: Oxford University Press, 1992.

Carol Brennan,
Grosse Pointe, Michigan

McKenna, Marthe (1893–1969)

Belgian spy and novelist. Born Marthe Cnockaert in Belgium in 1893; died in 1969; married Jock McKenna.

Marthe McKenna was born Marthe Cnockaert in Belgium in 1893, and became a qualified nurse. During World War I, when she was pressed into service in military hospitals set up by the occupying Germans, McKenna became a spy, gathering information from her patients and their superior officers and passing it to Allied forces. The information she provided was important enough to secure her mention in a dispatch from British Field Marshal Earl Haig, who praised her "gallant and distinguished services in the field." She was eventually caught and sentenced to death by a German military court, but the end of the war in 1918 came before the sentence could be carried out. Marthe married British soldier Jock McKenna after the war, and moved to Britain where she began writing spy fiction. Her most notable work was the autobiographical *I Was a Spy*, published in 1953 with a foreword by Winston Churchill. Marthe McKenna died in 1969.

Grant Eldridge,
freelance writer, Pontiac, Michigan

McKenna, Rollie (1918—)

American photographer who specialized in black-and-white architectural studies and portraits. Born in Houston, Texas, in 1918; daughter of Henry Thorne (an army pilot) and Bel (Bacon) Thorne; awarded undergraduate and graduate degrees from Vassar College; married Henry Dickson McKenna (an architect), on April 27, 1945 (divorced 1949); no children.

A classic late bloomer, Rollie McKenna was 30 years old before she picked up a camera and discovered her life's purpose. "Bought camera. Wanted one so badly, hope it's wise," she recorded in her journal following the purchase of a Pontiac 35mm during a visit to Paris in 1948. McKenna began her new found career photographing architecture, then moved into portraiture, becoming best known for her penetrating images of poets, artists, and musicians. The camera "gives me a sense of power," she wrote in *Rollie McKenna: A Life in Photography*, "not to use as a weapon, but to interpret the force and frailty of life as I see it. I love to take pictures; an act both aesthetic and kinesthetic. There is satisfaction in coordinating muscle and sensibility—as with sailing or executing a well-placed tennis stroke."

Rollie McKenna had an unusual childhood, which she later credited with preparing her for the unconventional life that followed. Born in 1918 in Houston, Texas, four days after the end of World War I, she was sent to live with her maternal grandparents Henry and **Mabel Marks Bacon** at the age of three, when her parents separated. The Bacons ran a hostelry in Pas Christina, Mississippi, which eventually evolved into a large resort, The-Inn-by-the-Sea. After an absence of several years, McKenna's mother **Bel Bacon Thorne**, now divorced from her husband, returned to the family and shortly thereafter married Roger Generelly, a tall, handsome man who subsequently became the assistant manager of the inn. Hotel life brought a variety of interesting people into McKenna's life, and provided her with a youthful playground like no other, complete with swimming pools and ponies. Life was idyllic until the stock-market crash in 1929, when the family lost everything. Boarding a 78-foot schooner loaned to them by a friend, they cruised up and down the Mississippi and Alabama coasts for months, finally taking refuge on Dauphin Island, Alabama, where they turned an abandoned Civil War fort into another hotel, The-Sea-Fort-Inn.

In the climate of the Depression, the inn barely turned a profit, and McKenna, her mother, and stepfather spent the early 1930s on the move, settling wherever Roger could find work: New Orleans, Paris (where they located briefly after a job offer in Majorca fell through), Rye Beach, St. Louis, and Manchester, New Hampshire. Meanwhile, Bel and Roger's marriage slowly unraveled and by 1935, when McKenna entered Gulf Park Junior College in Gulfport, Mississippi, they had divorced. In the college's coastal setting—reminiscent of The-Inn-by-the-Sea—she felt very much at home, and earned her tuition by teaching tennis and sailing. Upon finishing her second term at junior college, McKenna was rescued financially by her paternal grandfather, Victor Thorne, who made it possible for her to continue her education at Vassar College. Thorne, an architect with a passion for Renaissance painting, became increasingly important to McKenna during her college years, as did the various other Thorne relatives she came to know during that time. Her great-grandmother *Harriet V.S. Thorne had pursued photography as a hobby when the medium was still in its infancy, and had been one of the first members of the New York Camera Club when it was incorporated in 1888. Harriet had produced a treasure trove of negatives, which McKenna received from two of her cousins in the early 1960s but put aside until 1978. Upon graduating from Vassar, McKenna was given an additional gift of $5,000 from her grandfather Thorne which she used to purchase 14 acres of land and a ramshackle house in Millbrook, New York. It became her first real home and what she called "the beginning of long-sought security."

To support her new house, which she repaired and remodeled with the help of a Yale University architectural student, McKenna took some technical training and became a medical technician at the first Vassar College infirmary. Bored with the job after a year, she secured a position at *Time* magazine as a researcher in science and medicine, a position that led her to flirt briefly with the idea of becoming a doctor. With the outbreak of the war, however, McKenna left the magazine and retired to Millbrook, taking up the management of a victory garden and serving as an airplane spotter until 1942, when she joined the WAVES (Women Accepted for Voluntary Emergency Service). While posted in Washington, D.C., she met and married Henry Dickson McKenna, called Dickson, a Yale architectural school graduate who had just finished a stint as a photo interpreter on General Douglas MacArthur's staff.

Following the war, the newlyweds settled into a sunless apartment in New York City, where Dickson worked as a draftsman and McKenna was hired again by Time, Inc., this time as a researcher at *Life* magazine. She and Dickson eventually bought an old-law tenement in the German section of New York, which they remodeled. Meanwhile, they took advantage of New York's postwar cultural boom, and in the process became friendly with many of the artists and theater personalities of the time. The marriage floundered, however, and following an illness which necessitated an operation to remove her appendix, McKenna left her husband to recuperate at her house in Millbrook. She had just settled in when her grandfather Thorne died, leaving her devastated.

Rollie McKenna

Recuperating slowly from surgery and the loss of her grandfather, McKenna searched for direction in her life. Having received a generous inheritance from Thorne, she left *Life* and returned to Vassar to pursue a master's degree in art history. A three-month trip to Europe in late May 1948 clarified McKenna's path even further. After purchasing her first camera in Paris, she used it to record the rest of her trip, the Italian leg, in a rush of photographs. Returning to the United States, McKenna finished her degree, made plans to end her failing marriage, and set out to perfect her photography. While fulfilling a six-month residency in Florida in order to get a divorce (Florida being one of the few states at the time to allow partners to divorce on grounds of incompatibility), she obtained several new cameras and began to learn the rudiments of developing and printing. At the suggestion of her mentor at Vassar, Professor Richard Krautheimer, she charted a photographic project concentrating on the Renaissance architecture of Italy, and in August 1950 she boarded the French liner *Liberté* for the trip abroad.

By 1951, McKenna was committed to photography; a second trip abroad in the spring of that year increased her skill and confidence. She subsequently sold many of her architectural prints and slides to Vassar, and also assembled and circulated a traveling exhibition called *Three Renaissance Architects: Brunelleschi, Alberti and Palladio*, which was later purchased by the American Federation of Art for educational purposes. While continuing her architectural work, McKenna became interested in portraiture. Shooting in her usual black and white, she took as her mission to strip away the pretence and "prettification" of studio photography, and to create a more truthful image. One of her early projects, a series on poets for the Poetry Center in New York, was displayed at the center in November 1951, serving as her first solo exhibition. That same year, another exhibition of her portraits was held at Vassar. Through a friend, several of the pictures were purchased by the State Department to create an exhibition called *Young American Poets*, for distribution in Europe, the Middle East, and Japan. Around the same time, *Vogue* did a story on poets using several of her photographs, and *Harper's Bazaar* also bought and published several images. McKenna summed up the year as a banner one.

From 1951, portraits of literary personalities became a photographic obsession for McKenna, who subsequently produced some exquisite images of writers such as Robert Graves, Truman Capote, Sir Herbert Read, *Elizabeth Bishop, *Marianne Moore, Dame *Edith Sitwell, Robert Frost, T.S. Eliot, and Ezra Pound, among many others. Some of McKenna's most haunting images of this period are of the Welsh poet Dylan Thomas, whom she first met in January 1952, when he and his wife *Caitlin Thomas visited her in Millbrook. She subsequently photographed the poet and his family several times before his untimely death in November 1953. Shortly after, *Mademoiselle* magazine ran a story on him using McKenna's pictures. "It is sad and ironic that Dylan's fame would turn on so tragic an end, and that my career would be accelerated by it," McKenna wrote. As well, many of McKenna's photographs of Thomas appeared in Bill Read's *The Days of Dylan Thomas* (1964), a title also used for McKenna's prize-winning film about the poet, which she painstakingly created from her numerous still photographs. **Judith Crist** called the film "documentary creativity at its best," while Archer Winsten of the *New York Post* wrote: "It is a curiously touching memorial, at once objective and supported upon a foundation of poetic emotion."

In addition to her portraits of writers, McKenna produced numerous portraits of other creative artists, including painters, sculptors, actors, and musicians. "My challenge is to reach inside myself to catch the essence of a person—or what I feel is *an* essence," she said. To achieve this, she often took numerous exposures ("Pick a number from one to a hundred"). Overshooting, she explained, could help warm up a wary subject and guarded against darkroom mishaps. "However many exposures I make, it's important to me to give my subject a loose rein and myself all the awareness, openness and concentration I can muster," she added. "It's the result, not the method that counts, for when the actual shooting is over and done, another 'decisive moment' occurs—editing."

Just as McKenna was achieving recognition for her portraits, other opportunities began coming her way. Between 1954 and 1955, she accompanied the architectural historian Henry-Russell Hitchcock to Latin America, to photograph buildings for an exhibit at New York's Museum of Modern Art entitled "Latin American Architecture Since 1945" (1955). In 1956, she became a contract photographer for the U.S. Information Agency's new Russian-language publication *America Illustrated*, a nonpolitical journal circulated in what was then the Soviet Union. McKenna's assignments for the publication were extremely varied, ranging from photographing the United Nations during the Suez crisis to traveling to Florida to record the activities of retirees. She also photographed *Eleanor Roosevelt and created a picture story of *Helen Keller for the magazine. McKenna was so moved by Keller that at first she was unable to photograph. "When I did, I wondered if doing so might be taking advantage of her blindness," she wrote.

During the 1960s, McKenna divided her time between her house in New York City and a home by the sea in Stonington, Connecticut, where she eventually moved her business in 1965. In 1961, she had mounted a successful one-woman show at the Limelight Gallery in Greenwich Village, her first New York exhibit. Another well-received exhibit, "The Face of Poetry," opened at Princeton University and subsequently toured 20 other institutions. Many of the pictures in the exhibit also appeared in *The Modern Poets: An American-British Anthology* edited by John Malcolm Brinnin and Bill Read. (A second edition was published in 1970, with several new poets and updated photographs.) As McKenna's career flourished, so did her personal life. **Pat Willson**, who moved next door to

McKenna with her three children following her divorce in 1962, gave the photographer a family identity she had never before known. She helped Willson raise the children, sailed and traveled with her throughout the 1960s and 1970s, and nursed her through the lung cancer which claimed her life in 1981.

Soon after Willson's death, McKenna's own health began to deteriorate, the result of a heart condition similar to that which had killed her father in 1959. Despite a less strenuous work schedule, and winters spent in the mild climate of Key West, Florida, McKenna had to undergo open heart surgery to repair the problem. Calling her operation a gift, she recovered to resume her work and become involved with a new circle of writers and artists.

At the end of her book *Rollie McKenna: A Life in Photography*, McKenna includes a series of photographs called "Continuum," in which she displays—side-by-side—past and more recent portraits of W.H. Auden, Robert Lowell, *Elizabeth Hardwick, W.S. Merwin, *Anne Sexton, *Barbara Howes, and Leonard Bernstein, among others. "Photographing is my connection to the world," McKenna wrote at the beginning of the section. "As I grow older, I identify more and more with the people I have photographed over the years. Although many are gone, we remain attached, and through my pictures, I share them with the world."

SOURCES:
McKenna, Rollie. *Rollie McKenna: A Life in Photography*. NY: Alfred A. Knopf, 1991.

Barbara Morgan,
Melrose, Massachusetts

McKenna, Siobhan (1922–1986)

Irish actress, director, and translator who was celebrated for her interpretations of Shaw's St. Joan *and Pegeen Mike in Synge's* Playboy of the Western World. *Name variations: Siobhán McKenna; Siobhán Nic Cionnaith. Pronunciation: SHE-vawn. Born Siobhán McKenna on May 24, 1922, in Belfast, Northern Ireland; died on November 16, 1986, in Dublin, Ireland; daughter of Eoin McKenna (a university professor) and Margaret (O'Reilly) McKenna; educated at Dominican Convent, Taylors Hill, Galway, and St. Louis Convent, Monaghan; graduated with B.A. (1st class honors) in French, English and Irish, University College, Galway, 1943; married Denis O'Dea, in September 1946; children: son Donnacha O'Dea (b. August 30, 1948).*

Awards: London Evening Standard Best Actress (1954); Life Member, Abbey Theater (1966); Gold

Medal, Eire Society of Boston (1971); Hon. D.Litt, Trinity College, Dublin (1971); Hon. D.Litt, University College, Galway (1974); Member of Council of State (1975); Life Member, Royal Dublin Society (1983).

Joined Abbey Theater (1944); made film debut (1946); made London stage debut (1947); made American stage debut (1955).

Repertoire: Le Bourgeois Gentilhomme, Abbey (1944); The End House, Abbey (1944); (film) Hungry Hill (1946); The White Steed, London (1947); (film) Daughter of Darkness (1947); Mary Rose, her own Irish translation, Abbey (1948); Fading Mansions, London (1949); Heloïse, London (1948); Countess Cathleen, Abbey (1950); directed and acted in her own Irish translation of St. Joan, Galway and Dublin (1950); Playboy of the Western World, Edinburgh (1951); As You Like It, Coriolanus, Macbeth, Stratford-upon-Avon (1952); Purple Dust, English tour (1953); Playboy of the Western World, Arms and the Man, Dublin (1953); Love of Four Colonels, Anna Christie, St. Joan, Dublin (1953); St. Joan, London (1954); Chalk Garden, New York (1955); St. Joan, Cambridge, Mass., Philadelphia, New York; Hamlet, New York (1957); Twelfth Night, Stratford, Ontario (1957); Macbeth, Cambridge, Mass. (1957); The Rope Dancers, New York (1957); Playboy of the Western World, Dublin (1961); (film) King of Kings (1961); St. Joan of the Stockyards, Dublin and London (1961, 1964); (film) Playboy of the Western World (1962); directed Daughter from over the Water, Dublin (1964); (film) Of Human Bondage (1964); (film) Philadelphia Here I Come (1965); (film) Dr. Zhivago (1965); The Cavern, London (1965); Juno and the Paycock, Dublin (1966); directed Playboy of the Western World, New Haven, Connecticut (1967); Loves of Cass Maguire, Abbey (1967); Cherry Orchard, Abbey (1968); Here Are Ladies, one-woman show (1970–75); Fallen Angels, Dublin (1975); A Moon for the Misbegotten, Dublin (1976); The Plough and the Stars, Abbey and U.S. tour (1976); Sons of Oedipus, London (1977); directed Rising of the Moon, Cat and the Moon, Purgatory, Pot of Broth, Riders to the Sea, London (1978); Juno and the Paycock, Abbey (1979); directed Shadow of a Gunman, Vienna (1980); Britannicus, London (1981); directed The Midnight Court, Abbey (1984); Arsenic and Old Lace, Dublin (1985); Long Day's Journey into Night, Abbey (1985); Bailegangáire, Galway, London, and Dublin (1986).

After the Second World War, Siobhan McKenna achieved an international reputation as an actress both on stage and screen, but, unlike a previous generation of actors who had been trained at the Abbey Theater in Dublin, she retained close links with Irish drama and continued to work regularly in Ireland until her death. She was born in 1922 in Belfast, where her father Eoin McKenna was a mathematics teacher. Both her parents had a love of the Irish language, employed an Irish-speaking housekeeper, and brought up Siobhan and her sister speaking Irish. Her parents also loved the theater and from an early age Siobhan attended performances at the Opera House in Belfast. In 1927, the family moved to Galway when her father was appointed to a lectureship in mathematics at University College Galway (UCG). For Siobhan, the beautiful, wild countryside of the west of Ireland was "love at first sight . . . I think there must be something in the air of the West which is wild and untameable and soaring."

Shaw's definition of a miracle is something strange to those who witness it and simple to those who perform it.

—Siobhan McKenna

McKenna attended the Dominican Convent School at Taylors Hill, Galway, but after a diagnosis of primary tuberculosis had to spend nearly a year in bed during which she read extensively. She then went to St. Louis Convent School in County Monaghan which had a reputation for academic excellence and which taught in the Irish language. She won a scholarship to University College, Galway, where she studied Irish, French and English. In Galway, there was a semi-professional, Irish-speaking drama company called An Taibhdhearc (Thive-yark) which regularly used students from the university. McKenna was recommended to the director by her French professor, Liam O Briain. The director, Walter Macken, was impressed with McKenna and offered her a small salary, but her father, who did not want her distracted from her studies, refused to allow her to accept it. She continued to act with the company without a salary and appeared in Eugene O'Neill's *Emperor Jones* and in *Macbeth* and *Mary Rose* (which she translated herself). In 1943, she graduated from UCG with a first class honors degree and won a scholarship to University College, Dublin, to study for a master's degree in French.

Liam O Briain mentioned her to Ernest Blythe, the director of the Abbey Theater in Dublin, who asked her to audition. The Abbey had increased the number of plays performed in Irish, and there were opportunities for Irish-speaking actors like McKenna. Though Blythe

was unimpressed by her audition, he offered her a contract, and she gave up her postgraduate work, to her father's dismay. McKenna made her debut at the Abbey in April 1944 in Peadar Ó hAnnracháin's *Stiana*. The following month, she appeared in an Irish translation of Molière's *Le Bourgeois Gentilhomme*. Her first part in English was in Joseph Tomelty's *The End House*, in which she played a Belfast factory girl. The cast included the finest Abbey actors of the time, F.J. McCormick, Cyril Cusack, Denis O'Dea, **Eileen Crowe**, and *May Craig. Siobhan deeply admired McCormick whom she described, after his untimely death in 1947, as "one of the greatest actors in the world." She and McCormick played opposite each other in Shaw's *A Village Wooing*, and it was McCormick who advised her not to rush into a film career, and to get more experience at the Abbey, after she had film successes in *Hungry Hill* and *Daughter of Darkness*. In September 1946, McKenna married Denis O'Dea, to whom she had been secretly engaged for nearly two years. O'Dea, a handsome, long-established Abbey actor who had been in John Ford's film of Sean O'Casey's *The Plough and the Stars*, could have had a Hollywood career, but he was unambitious and preferred his familiar Dublin surroundings (he was a noted poker player). McKenna trusted his professional advice, but he was 19 years older than she and this led to forebodings from their respective families and friends. Although the marriage endured, there were strains because of the long absences. Their only child, son Donnacha, was born in 1948. From the 1950s, McKenna was the main breadwinner in the family while O'Dea looked after Donnacha.

Siobhan McKenna was anxious to extend her range beyond Irish repertory and appeared in two plays in London, Olivier's production of Jean Anouilh's *Fading Mansions* and James Forsyth's *Heloïse*. In 1950, McKenna's first company, An Taibhdhearc, was in severe financial difficulties, and she agreed to give some performances. In what seemed a daring venture, she was determined to stage Shaw's *St. Joan* in Irish. When Shaw was asked for permission, he replied that he had never seen any sense in the Irish language revival but would let them have the play without a fee. When the director fell ill, McKenna took over and made her directorial debut. The premiere at Christmas 1950 was enthusiastically received, and the play had a short season in Dublin. McKenna also played *St. Joan* in more illustrious productions, and it became one of her most famous roles, though her inspiration had a more intimate, domestic source, her mother **Margaret O'Reilly McKenna**, who had a

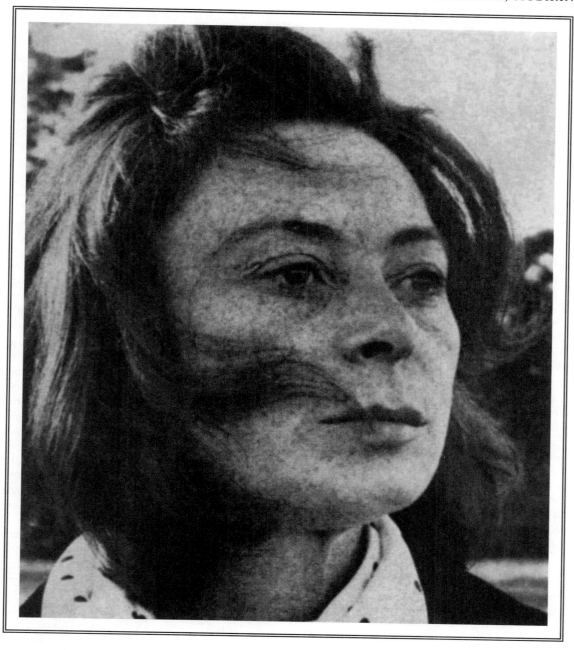

Siobhan
McKenna

strong, unquestioning faith. In an interview which she gave to Des Hickey and Gus Smith in 1970, McKenna said: "I am sure it has something to do with prayer, and prayer could be just wishing. My mother had this extraordinary faith and complete acceptance, which used to get on my father's nerves sometimes. . . . She was like Joan. You couldn't answer back because she had this remarkable common sense."

After seeing McKenna in *St. Joan,* the director *Shelah Richards* thought that Siobhan would be an ideal Pegeen Mike in a production

of John Millington Synge's *The Playboy of the Western World* which she was planning for the Edinburgh Festival in 1951. McKenna had played Synge only once before, a minor part in *The Playboy.* Richards, an ex-Abbey actress, felt that the Abbey's playing of their classic had become too stale and tradition-encrusted. In an extract from her unpublished memoirs quoted in Micheál Ó hAodha's *Siobhán,* Richards said that the play had lost its original fire and "had turned rather drearily into a sing-song recitation." Richards turned the actors away from this style, and McKenna gave, in Richards' opinion, "a consummate performance." This was also the view of the actor Carroll O'Connor, who played Michael James in the production. O'Connor noted particularly the way McKenna used her magnificent voice which was "capable of the most wonderful contrasts—of great emotional power, and soft, deep gentleness."

In 1952, McKenna played a nine-month season at the Shakespeare Memorial Theater in Stratford-upon-Avon, performing in *As You Like It, Coriolanus,* and *Macbeth.* In 1953, she toured England in Sam Wanamaker's production of O'Casey's *Purple Dust,* but to her disappointment it did not get a London production. She also had several arguments with O'Casey and on one occasion was furious when he criticized F.J. McCormick. O'Casey, she told her husband in a letter quoted by Ó hAodha, "contradicts himself all the time by saying things just for effect." Later that year, Cyril Cusack invited her to play Pegeen Mike to his Christy in a Dublin production of *Playboy* directed by Jack McGowran. In Cusack, McKenna would be playing opposite the foremost interpreter of the Playboy of his generation. As Ó hAodha observed, after her Edinburgh experience she "knew instinctively that she must hold the stage from the first to the last lines . . . she must be the Muse who sets the Playboy's imagination on fire." The production was a great success, and was later taken to Paris. The partnership between McKenna and Cusack was a memorable one but was not really established until the 1960s and 1970s when they both returned to the Abbey. It was also honed by a competitive edge, and neither was above upstaging the other.

Later in 1953, McKenna joined the MacLiammóir-Edwards company and gave her first performance in English of *St. Joan,* helped by a fine supporting cast. It received superb notices. McKenna spoke Joan's lines in a simple but direct Connemara (west of Ireland) accent which disconcerted more conservative members of the audience. McKenna recalled that when she first went to the Abbey everyone said she was "real P.Q. I didn't know what they were talking about. . . . I finally found out it meant 'Peasant Quality.' I felt really complimented." She was less amused when, asked to play the part in London, she was told to discard her "brogue." She refused. In an article on Shaw for the journal *Chrysalis* in 1956, McKenna said that the distinguished conductor Sir John Barbirolli advised her to approach the role musically, an approach she found congenial:

There is fine music in *St. Joan.* There is orchestration of voices. The trial scene actual-

ly roars. I picture the bullying Duc de Tremouille as a saxophone. I can see the Dauphin as a pathetic flute. There are fiddles, bugles and drums. There's an organ in the cathedral scene. Shaw knew his music—he was a music critic at one time—and his knowledge of the art makes itself felt in *St. Joan.*

McKenna won the London *Evening Standard* Best Actress award for her St. Joan. She wanted to take the play to New York, but a production of Anouilh's *Joan of Arc play *The Lark,* starring *Julie Harris, was in preparation there. Instead, McKenna's Broadway debut took place in a new play, *Enid Bagnold's *The Chalk Garden,* in which McKenna portrayed the enigmatic governess of a troubled girl who was the granddaughter of an autocratic old woman (played by *Gladys Cooper). McKenna found the stylized English manner of *The Chalk Garden* difficult and was convinced it would flop, but it was a success. Siobhan stayed on in New York after her run ended, determined to play St. Joan in America in 1956 which was Shaw's centenary. She finally got the chance in August of that year at the Cambridge Drama Festival in Massachusetts in a production directed by Albert Marre. Elliot Norton, the critic of the *Boston Globe,* called her the finest Joan of her generation: "There has never been and probably never will be a Joan of such vitality and intensity." The production went on to Philadelphia and reached New York in September 1956. In January 1957, McKenna played Hamlet in an experimental version of Shakespeare's play, but for audiences and critics it was rather too experimental at a time when cross-gender performances were still rarities. McKenna stayed in North America for another year, playing Viola in *Twelfth Night* at Stratford, Ontario, Lady Macbeth to Jason Robards' Macbeth at Harvard, and on Broadway in Morton Wisengrad's *The Rope Dancers.*

For the 1960 Dublin Theater Festival, McKenna returned to the role of Pegeen in *The Playboy of the Western World.* The production transferred to London, where her interpretation was regarded as definitive by even the most exacting critics. Plans were underway for a film of *The Playboy,* to be directed by Brian Desmond Hurst who had directed *Riders to the Sea* in the 1930s. Though enthusiastic, McKenna soon became aware of problems. The producers' priority was a cast which would be intelligible internationally, and not necessarily, as McKenna wanted, one experienced in Synge's verbal richness. McKenna's husband, who had considerable film experience, was not cast in any of the character parts, while the role of Christy went to a young Welsh actor, Gary Raymond. When the film appeared, the characters seemed dwarfed by the majestic Kerry landscapes, and, to compound this, Hurst was too stage-bound in his treatment of the actors. McKenna was also, by this time, too old for the part of Pegeen. Nevertheless, the film is valuable as recording the essence of an eminent interpretation.

In the 1960s, Siobhan McKenna began to concentrate on the great O'Casey plays. In 1966, she played Juno in *Juno and the Paycock* with Peter O'Toole and Jack McGowran. That same year, the new Abbey Theater was opened, replacing the old theater which had burned down in 1951. McKenna and her husband were two of the ten life members appointed to celebrate the new theater. In 1967, she appeared in the new theater in Brian Friel's *The Loves of Cass Maguire,* which Friel had written with her in mind. In this and as Ranevskaya in Chekhov's *Cherry Orchard,* also at the Abbey in 1968, she gave two of her finest performances.

For some years, the actor and director Micheál MacLiammóir, whose solo show on Oscar Wilde had been an international success, had been urging McKenna to think about her own one-woman show. McKenna was adamant that she did not want anything that smacked of stage-Irishy, and arranged a selection of dramatic vignettes featuring some of the most famous speeches by women in Irish drama and literature: Ginnie Gogan and Mrs. Tancred in *The Plough and the Stars,* Maurya in *Riders to the Sea, St. Joan,* Winnie from Beckett's *Happy Days,* Anna Livia Plurabelle from Joyce's *Finnegan's Wake,* and most memorably of all, Molly Bloom's soliloquy from *Ulysses.* The show, which McKenna called *Here Are Ladies,* opened in London in 1970 and was a triumph for her, especially the Molly Bloom sequence. She subsequently toured the show throughout America, Canada, and Australia. Ironically, it did not reach Dublin until 1975.

The outbreak of the Northern Ireland troubles stirred McKenna's deeply nationalist feelings; she never forgot her Belfast childhood. In 1974, she spoke out against the introduction of internment without trial in Northern Ireland and also protested the forcible feeding of republican women prisoners. She attracted criticism because of her outspoken views but was surprised and gratified when in 1975 her old friend Cearbhall Ó Dálaigh, now president of Ireland, appointed her to his advisory Council

of State, making her only the second woman to be named. In 1976, she played Bessie Burgess to Cyril Cusack's Fluther Good in the Abbey's 50th-anniversary production of *The Plough and the Stars.* The production then went on tour to the U.S. She and Cusack had lost none

of their competitive edge, and Cusack complained several times about the length of her death scene.

Despite her acting successes of the late 1960s and 1970s, McKenna increasingly preferred to direct and in 1978 had one of her biggest challenges when she was invited to London to direct five one-act Irish plays for the Greenwich Theater's Horniman season. The year was marred by the death of her husband in November, but McKenna continued to work. She appeared as Juno in the Abbey's 75th-anniversary production of *Juno and the Paycock* and directed O'Casey's *The Shadow of a Gunman* in 1980 for Vienna's English Theater. In 1982, she performed Molly Bloom's soliloquy for the last time at the Abbey for the Joyce centenary celebrations. In 1984, in what was to be her last work with the Abbey, she directed Brian Merriman's *Midnight Court* in Irish. Before her sudden death in November 1986, there was one last remarkable performance, as Mommo in Thomas Murphy's *Bailegangáire* (Town Without Laughter), which Murphy had written for McKenna. The play brought McKenna back to Galway to perform with the Druid Theater company. In an interview with the Dublin *Sunday Tribune* in December 1985, just after the play's premiere, Murphy explained the character of Mommo, a senile woman in her 80s recalling her past for her two granddaughters: "She has a compulsion to tell her story and yet a fear of it. As if distancing herself from the experience, she remembers it in the third person." Fintan O'Toole of the *Sunday Tribune* found McKenna's Mommo "foul, terrifying and insidious, as well as being somehow haunting and very moving." The praise was repeated when the play moved to London in 1986, but the part of Mommo was an exhausting one for McKenna. In November 1986, she was diagnosed with lung cancer and died from a heart attack following two operations; she was buried in Galway. In his funeral address, the playwright Brian Friel said that "in theater, a star was an actress who was unique in that she personified an idea a country has of itself at any particular time. . . . For people of my generation, Siobhan personified an idea of Ireland."

SOURCES:

Hickey, Des, and Gus Smith. *A Paler Shade of Green.* London: Leslie Frewen, 1972.

McKenna, Siobhán. "Belfast of My Nostalgia," in *Irish Press.* November 13, 1969.

———. "GBS: A Centenary Bouquet," in *Chrysalis.* Vol. 9, 1956.

———. Interview in *Sunday Tribune* (Dublin). November 23, 1986.

Ó Dulaing, Donncha, ed. "Siobhan McKenna," in *Voices of Ireland.* Dublin: O'Brien Press/RTE, 1984.

Ó hAodha, Micheál. *Siobhán: A Memoir of an Actress.* Dingle, County Kerry: Brandon Press, 1994.

SUGGESTED READING:

Hogan, Robert. *The Modern Irish Drama* (multivolume survey beginning in 1975). Atlantic Highlands, NJ: Humanities Press.

Ó hAodha, Micheál. *Theater in Ireland.* Oxford: Blackwell, 1974.

Deirdre McMahon,
Lecturer in History, Mary Immaculate College,
University of Limerick, Limerick, Ireland

McKenney, Ruth (1911–1972)

American author best known for her first book, **My Sister Eileen,** *which was subsequently made into a Broadway play, two movies, and a musical. Name variations: Ruth McKenney Bransten. Born on November 18, 1911, in Mishawaka, Indiana; died on July 25, 1972, in New York City; daughter of John Sidney McKenney and Marguerite (Flynn) McKenney (a schoolteacher); sister of Eileen McKenney West; graduated from Shaw High School in Cleveland, Ohio; attended Ohio State University; married Richard Bransten (an editor and historian who wrote under the pseudonym Bruce Minton), on August 12, 1937 (died 1955); children: Eileen Bransten; Thomas Bransten; (adopted her sister Eileen's child) Patrick West.*

Selected works: My Sister Eileen *(1938);* Industrial Valley *(1939);* The McKenneys Carry On *(1940);* Browder and Ford: For Peace, Jobs and Socialism *(1940);* Jake Home *(1943);* The Loud Red Patrick *(1947); (with Richard Bransten)* Here's England: An Informal Guide *(1950);* Love Story *(1950);* All About Eileen *(1952);* Far, Far From Home *(1954);* Mirage *(1956).*

Born in 1911 in Mishawaka, Indiana, to John Sidney McKenney and **Marguerite McKenney,** Ruth McKenney moved with her family to Cleveland, Ohio, when she was six. Her mother, a schoolteacher and Irish Nationalist, died two years later. As a child she was smart, rather unattractive, and not very popular. Her sister **Eileen McKenney (West)** was just the opposite, and Ruth idolized her. At age 14, McKenney apprenticed as a printer in Cleveland. A few years later, she entered Ohio State University, where she reported for the college newspaper and for the *Columbus Dispatch* before dropping out of school to travel through Europe with a friend. On her return to the United States, McKenney became a reporter for the *Akron Journal*, winning awards for feature articles. In 1933, she accepted an offer from a newspaper in Newark, New Jersey, and moved East with her sister, only to find that the newspaper was on strike. She soon signed on with the *New York Post* as a feature writer, and moved with Eileen to Greenwich Village.

After leaving the *Post* in 1936, she began writing stories for *The New Yorker* based on her childhood experiences in Ohio and her experiences in New York City. Many of these later evolved into the humorous *My Sister Eileen*, an immensely popular book published in 1938 which, despite the title, is somewhat more concerned with the author herself than with her sister. The book was a bestseller and eventually became the basis for two plays, a musical (*Wonderful Town*), two movies and a television series. Shortly before the premiere in January 1941 of the first of these adaptations, a Broadway play of the same title that would prove hugely successful, Eileen and her husband, the novelist Nathanael West (author of *Miss Lonelyhearts*), were killed in an automobile accident. McKenney, who in 1939 had married Richard Bransten, an editor and historian who wrote under the pseudonym Bruce Minton, adopted her orphaned infant nephew Patrick. (She would later name her daughter after her sister.)

During the time she had been writing for *The New Yorker,* McKenney had interrupted her work long enough to gather material about the Goodyear rubber strike in Akron, Ohio, that led to the formation of the CIO (originally the Committee on Industrial Organization, later the Congress of Industrial Organizations). She developed her research into the novel *Industrial Valley* (1939), which was generally hailed by critics and won an award at the 1939 Writer's Congress. It is now considered the strongest of her books and an important depiction of a crucial development in American labor history. McKenney was proudest of this book out of all her work, a few years later commenting "I am not a humorist. I only wrote the funny stories to make a living. . . ; I doubt if I shall ever write anything else funny, for the truth is, I have very little sense of humor, and suffer a good deal while writing what is supposed to be funny."

Although she did in fact go on to write other "funny" books, including *The Loud Red Patrick* (1947), about her grandfather, and *All About Eileen* (1952), McKenney preferred to consider herself a labor activist and sociologist. The writings closer to her heart, however, such as the short work *Browder and Ford: For Peace, Jobs and Socialism* (1940) and the novel *Jake Home* (1943), found little success with the public. In the early 1940s, McKenney and Bransten moved to Washington, D.C., and became mem-

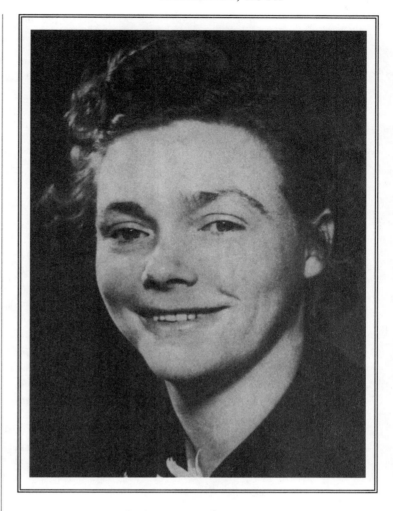

Ruth McKenney

bers of the Communist Party. For a while, McKenney wrote a column, "Strictly Personal," for the Communist weekly *New Masses,* but both McKenney and her spouse were ousted from the party in 1946 for deviating from party doctrine. They lived in various places during the war years, including Washington, D.C., Hollywood, Brussels (which she wrote about in 1954's *Far, Far From Home*), London, New York, and France. Her last book, *Mirage* (1956), set during the French Revolution and the Napoleonic era, received mixed reviews from critics. Ruth McKenney died in New York City from complications of diabetes and a heart ailment on July 25, 1972.

SOURCES:

American Women Writers. Edited by Lina Mainiero. NY: Frederick Ungar, 1981.
Contemporary Authors. Vol. 93–96. Detroit, MI: Gale Research.
Current Biography, 1942. NY: H.W. Wilson, 1943.
Current Biography, 1972. NY: H.W. Wilson, 1972.
Encyclopedia of American Humor. Edited by Steven H. Gale. NY: Garland, 1988.

Twentieth Century Authors. Edited by Stanley J. Kunitz and Howard Haycraft. NY: H.W. Wilson, 1942.

RELATED MEDIA:

My Sister Eileen (96 min. film), starring *Rosalind Russell, Brian Ahearn, **Janet Blair** and *June Havoc, directed by Alexander Hall, Columbia, 1942.

My Sister Eileen (108 min. musical film), starring **Betty Garrett**, *Janet Leigh, and Jack Lemmon, directed by Richard Quine, screenplay by Blake Edwards and Quine, Columbia, 1955.

Jo Anne Meginnes,
freelance writer, Brookfield, Vermont

McKillop, Mary Helen (1842–1909).

See MacKillop, Mary Helen.

McKinley, Ida Saxton (1847–1907)

American first lady of indomitable spirit who, though plagued by ill health most of her life, was a trusted advisor to her husband. Born on June 8, 1847, in Canton, Ohio; died on May 26, 1907, in Canton; eldest daughter of James Asbury Saxton (a banker) and Katherine (DeWalt) Saxton; married William McKinley (1843–1901, president of the United States, 1897–1901), on January 25, 1871, in Canton, Ohio; children: Katherine (b. 1871 and died before her fourth birthday); Ida (b. 1873 and died five months later).

Ida Saxton McKinley

At formal White House receptions, Ida McKinley received guests seated on a thronelike velvet chair, holding a large bouquet of flowers so she would not have to shake hands. Cabinet wives and relatives flanked her chair and were designated to assist the first lady. At state dinners, contrary to protocol, Ida was seated to the president's right so he could watch for what was then regarded as her "fainting spells," but were, in fact, epileptic seizures. If one occurred, he would calmly place his large white handkerchief over her face, wait for it to pass, and proceed as though nothing had happened. If guests were alarmed, they said nothing. Even the press was discreet. Only recently have the facts about Ida McKinley's illness been disclosed.

Ida Saxton was a cheerful, intelligent, and spoiled child. As the eldest of three children in one of the oldest and wealthiest families in Canton, Ohio, she attended the finest schools. At age 16, she was forced her to leave Brooke Hall Seminary in Media, Pennsylvania, because of "delicate health," foreshadowing the problems that would dominate her later life. After an eight-month grand tour of Europe, accompanied by her younger sister **Mary "Pina" Saxton**, Ida took her place in the fashionable young society of Canton, but found herself somewhat bored. Her father, in an unconventional gesture, employed and trained her as a clerk in his bank. She loved the work and earned a promotion to cashier.

When Major William McKinley, who had come to Canton to set up a law practice, met the vivacious, auburn-haired Ida, he thought she was the most beautiful girl he had ever seen, and the couple wed on January 25, 1871. Happiness was short-lived. Two daughters, Katherine and Ida, were born in 1871 and 1873. Ida lived only five months, and Katherine contracted typhoid fever and died before her fourth birthday. It was during the birth of her second child that Ida's mother died, and her extreme grief contributed to premature labor and complications. Ida contracted phlebitis in her legs and began to suffer a nervous disorder that was diagnosed as mild epilepsy coupled with recurring headaches and bouts of severe depression. She was devastated by the death of her children and, it is said, refused to part with their clothes and toys. With the loss of their family, the McKinleys found solace in each other.

William McKinley, as a congressional representative and then governor of Ohio, altered his life considerably so he could take care of Ida. She managed some charitable work but spent most of her time seated in a favorite childhood rocking chair, doing needlework. (It is said she crocheted thousands of pairs of slippers for relatives and various hospitals.) By the time William won the presidency in 1897, and the couple moved to the White House, Ida was a confirmed invalid. But she made a brave effort to manage as many of the demanding duties of first lady as possible.

Despite her frail health, and the need to walk assisted by a cane, Ida accompanied her husband on many of his travels, including his ill-fated trip to the Pan Am Exposition held in Buffalo in September 1901, soon after his second inauguration. When the president was shot by an assassin, his first thoughts were of Ida and how she would receive the news. To the surprise of many, she summoned the strength to remain at his bedside until he died eight days later. She also insisted on handling all of the burial arrangements. Ida McKinley lived for six years after his death, cared for by her sister Mary, and visited her husband's grave almost daily. Ida died on May 26, 1907, at the age of 60. She is buried with the president and her daughters in Westlawn Cemetery in Canton, Ohio.

SOURCES:

James, Edward T., ed. *Notable American Women, 1607–1950.* Cambridge, MA: Belknap Press of Harvard University Press, 1971, pp. 470–471.

Klapthor, Margaret Brown. *The First Ladies.* Washington, DC: The White House Historical Association, 1979.

Melick, Arden David. *Wives of the Presidents.* Maplewood, NJ: Hammond, 1977.

Paletta, LuAnn. *The World Almanac of First Ladies.* NY: World Almanac, 1990.

Willard, Frances E., and Mary A. Livermore, eds. *A Woman of the Century: Biographical Sketches of Leading American Women.* New York, Buffalo, Chicago: Charles Wells Moulton, 1893 (reprinted by Gale Research, Detroit, 1967), p. 183.

Barbara Morgan,
Melrose, Massachusetts

McKinney, Louise (1868–1931)

Canadian suffragist and legislator who was one of the first two women legislators in the British Empire. Name variations: often listed as one of the Alberta Five also known as the Famous Five; Mrs. James McKinney. Born Louise Crummy in Frankville, Ontario, Canada, on September 22, 1868 (one source cites 1863); died in Claresholm, Alberta, Canada, in 1931 (one source cites 1933); married James McKinney.

Louise McKinney was born in Frankville, Ontario, Canada, in 1868, and after attending normal school in Ottawa became a teacher. She subsequently moved to North Dakota, where she continued teaching, got married, and be-

came active in the Women's Christian Temperance Union (WCTU). In 1903, she moved with her husband to Claresholm, Northwest Territories (later Alberta), where she founded a local chapter of the WCTU. She became a member of the Non-Partisan League (NPL), a political party in favor of agrarian reform and the criminalization of the sale and consumption of alcohol, in 1916. That same year, Canadian women obtained the right to vote and the right to stand for election to office. McKinney won election to the Alberta Legislative Assembly as an NPL candidate the following year, and holds the distinction of being one of the first two women elected to a legislature in the British Empire. (The other is *Roberta MacAdams Price.) Although McKinney was defeated in her bid for reelection in 1921 and retired from politics, she remained an active orator and advocate of temperance and women's rights. She was also a dynamic member of the Imperial Order Daughters of the Empire and of the Methodist Church, and was the only woman to sign the Church's Basis of Union of the United Church of Canada in 1925.

Although the Canadian constitution granted "persons" the right to hold public office, a historical prohibition against women serving as senators in the national Parliament had effectively negated that right. McKinney, with *Emily Murphy, *Nellie McClung, *Henrietta Muir Edwards, and *Irene Parlby, challenged this prohibition in the 1920s with a court case now known as the "Persons Case." The Canadian Supreme Court upheld the prohibition in 1928, citing an 1876 British Common Law ruling that

Louise McKinney

"Women are persons in matters of pains and penalties, but are not persons in matters of rights and privileges." McKinney and the others, who became known as the Alberta Five or the Famous Five, appealed in 1929 to what was then Canada's highest court of appeal, the British Privy Council, and won a reversal of the Supreme Court's decision. The first woman in the Canadian Senate, *Cairine Wilson, was appointed in 1930.

Louise McKinney served as the acting president of the Canadian WCTU in 1931 and died in Claresholm, Alberta, that same year. Canada's annual Governor-General's Award is given to distinguished Canadian women in honor of the achievements of the Alberta Five.

SUGGESTED READING:

Cochrane, Jean. "Reformers in the House," in *Women in Canadian Politics*. Toronto: Fitzhenry and White-side, 1977.

Innis, Mary Quayle. *The Clear Spirit: Twenty Canadian Women and Their Times*. Toronto: Published for the Canadian Federation of University Women by the University of Toronto Press, 1973.

MacEwan, Grant. *Mighty Women: Stories of Western Canadian Pioneers*. Vancouver: Greystone, 1995, pp. 138–145.

Grant Eldridge,
freelance writer, Pontiac, Michigan

McKinney, Nina Mae

(c. 1912–1967)

African-American actress, singer, and dancer. Born on June 12, around 1912 (some sources give dates as early as 1909 or as late as 1914), in Lancaster, South Carolina; died in New York City on May 3, 1967; daughter of John McKinney (a postal worker) and Nina McKinney; married James Monroe, in 1940 (divorced 1941).

Raised by grandmother before moving to New York City to join parents (c. 1924); as a self-taught dancer and singer, auditioned and won a place in a black vaudeville revue and was discovered by Hollywood; appeared in MGM all-black musical Hallelujah, *but after landing only minor roles in little known films, toured Europe as a jazz singer for a year (1929–30); finding few film roles on return to U.S. (1930), returned to Europe (1935–38); toured U.S. as a singer (1940s), and appeared in last film (1949); subsequent career obscure.*

Filmography: Hallelujah *(1929);* Congo Road *(1930);* Safe in Hell *(1931);* Swan Boat *(1931);* Pie, Pie Blackbird *(1932);* Reckless *(1935);* Sanders of the River *(1935);* Gang Smashers *(1938);* St. Louis Gal *(1938);* Pocomania *(1939);* Straight to Heaven *(1939);* Devil's Daughter *(1939);* Together Again *(1944);* Night Train to Memphis *(1946);* Mantan Messes Up *(1946);* Dark Waters *(1947);* Danger Street *(1947);* Pinky *(1949).*

The box office at Harlem's Lafayette Theater was particularly busy the week of February 12, 1930, as eager crowds lined up to buy tickets for that week's show, *Snap Out of It*. The vaudeville revue featured a popular dancing and comedy team, Buck and Bubbles, but it was the show's lithe, sensuous female star who was selling out the house every night. Nina Mae McKinney was back in New York, and each night's audience gave a standing ovation to the Harlem woman that Hollywood had made a sensation.

McKinney's fame among both African-American and white audiences had come virtually overnight, when she was barely 16 and had been in New York for less than five years. She had been born on June 12, around 1912, in rural Lancaster, South Carolina, to John and Nina McKinney. There had been McKinneys in South Carolina since the antebellum days of the early 19th century, and McKinneys had been living and working on the same estate in Lancaster for as long as anyone could remember. John McKinney was employed by the postal service, traveling the muddy roads of Lancaster County, midway between Columbia, the state capital, some distance to the southeast and the North Carolina border to the northwest; but shortly after Nina Mae's birth, the McKinneys moved to New York, leaving their daughter in the care of John's mother. Little is known of Nina Mae's childhood years with her grandmother, who is described as an "old and trusted servant" of the family which owned the estate, but it is likely that at some time during this period one of the traveling vaudeville shows that toured the South set up a tent in the area. Such shows were virtually the only form of entertainment for America's rural Southern blacks in the first decades of the century, and served as springboards for the careers of such notable African-American entertainers of the day as *Bessie Smith, *Ma Rainey, and *Ethel Waters. It is tempting to think that Grandmother McKinney provided her granddaughter with her first exposure to show business, either at one of the traveling shows or at an all-black movie theater showing one of any number of films produced by a then-lively African-American motion-picture industry.

Since the earliest days of motion pictures, white producers and studios had been making films featuring white performers in blackface, little more than filmed minstrel shows for white audiences built around the prevailing stereotypes of the "American Negro." But as early as 1910, William Foster, a white educator, had produced a short film in Chicago with an all-black cast; and the Lincoln Film Company established in Los Angeles in 1916 was the first formed by blacks to produce films directed specifically at black audiences. Lincoln's *Realization of a Negro's Ambition*, released in 1916, was the first film with an all-black cast that attempted to portray the middle-class aspirations of African-Americans in a realistic manner. Its success was the catalyst for a number of black-owned film companies, such as Unique Films, Million Dollar Productions, and the longest-running of them all, Oscar Michaux's Film and Book Company, which not only produced films but operated a booking circuit of all-black theaters until the 1950s. There were eight such theaters in South Carolina during McKinney's childhood, most of them in Columbia.

By the time McKinney was sent to join her parents in 1924, the black film industry was in full swing, especially in New York, where many such films were produced. Nina was enrolled in P.S. 126 in lower Manhattan, where vaudeville shows and films were much more accessible than in South Carolina; and Harlem theaters like the Alhambra, the Apollo, the Franklin, and the Roosevelt, just a subway ride away, all included films in their weekly entertainment offerings. It was at such theaters, and by listening to records, that McKinney taught herself to sing and dance. By the time she was 16, just as she was graduating from high school, she won a place in the chorus line of Lew Leslie's *Blackbirds*, a long-running all-black Broadway revue modeled on Florenz Ziegfeld's *Follies*. By this time, white Hollywood had begun to realize that there was money to be made in so-called "race pictures," especially now that talking pictures had become technically feasible. In the audience at one night's *Blackbirds* performance was King Vidor, who had been hired by MGM to direct the film that would make McKinney a star, 1929's *Hallelujah*.

MGM was well aware that rival Twentieth Century-Fox was preparing to release *Hearts in Dixie*, starring the African-American actor Stepin Fetchit. Billed as the first "all-singing, all-dancing, all-Negro" musical film, it was set on an idyllic Southern plantation full of lazy, irresponsible, but nonetheless tuneful slaves serving benevolent white masters. *The New York Times'* critic Mordaunt Hall thought the film was "truthful in its reflection of the black men in those days down yonder in the cornfields," but

fellow critic Henry Dobbs, also white, pointedly disagreed. "It is obvious," he wrote, "that *Hearts in Dixie* director Paul Sloane has not yet emerged from that state of mind which conceives of the Negro film as leaning towards open-necked shirts, banana hats, and the melodic charms of 'Old Black Joe' and 'The Lonesome Road.' If *Hearts in Dixie* is a specimen of colored expression under the aegis of Hollywood, let us, next time, hand the whole process over to the Negroes themselves."

King Vidor believed that *Hallelujah* would answer some of Dobbs' criticisms, and would later claim that Nina Mae McKinney, more than any other cast member, carried the film and made it a success with black and white audiences alike. Vidor cast her as Chick, the film's seductive female lead who lures the son of a poor sharecropping family into temptation before he renounces her, becomes a preacher, eventually leads Chick to baptism and salvation, only to kill her out of jealousy of her new lover. Although McKinney was Vidor's second choice for

Nina
Mae
McKinney

the role, he professed himself well-satisfied with his decision and labeled her performance as "sensational." *Hallelujah* was a lavish production, featuring 40 musical numbers (including one by Irving Berlin) and a huge cast with some of the best African-American talent of the day—*Victoria Spivey, **Fannie Belle De Knight**, and William Fountaine among them.

Because of McKinney's light-skinned complexion, Chick is referred to in the film as "that cinnamon gal" and "high yeller," and Vidor's choice of his leading lady was a commercial one. White audiences would accept her as the screen's first black "love goddess," while they would only accept darker-skinned actresses—like *Hattie McDaniel, *Louise Beavers, and *Butterfly McQueen—in the roles of maids, housekeepers, or queens of the jungle. "Only light-skinned women," writes black cultural historian Gary Hull, "who represented a basically white style of beauty were shown as sexually desirable." McKinney certainly helped the image with the sinuous dance she performed in the film, the "Swanee Shuffle," and with her delivery of seductive musical numbers in a brassy voice, her hands planted enticingly on her hips.

Hollywood tells the world [that a black is] only . . . a trespasser in the world of make-believe.

—Film critic Earl Morris, 1948

"Miss McKinney is Lilith herself, a pure child of emotion," the New York *Amsterdam News* told its black readership, while Mordaunt Hall wrote, "Nina Mae McKinney . . . gives a clever performance as Chick," and went on to praise the film's revival meeting sequences with the characteristically blunt racism of the period. "In portraying the peculiarly typical religious hysteria of the darkies and their gullibility," he noted, "Mr. Vidor atones for any sloth in preceding scenes." When the film opened in London, the British weekly *Theater and Film Illustrated* called it "a song of the American Negro," asserting that "rarely has the spirit of the Negro people been so finely portrayed as in this picture." Though Vidor probably intended the film to accurately and sympathetically portray African-Americans, much of the black press vehemently pointed out that the film's characterizations were more racist imaginings of white Americans. "King Vidor's Filthy Hands Reeking With Prejudice," read one headline; and in the same review of the film which praised McKinney's performance, the *Amsterdam News*' Paul Holt wrote that *Hallelujah*, "while pretending to

be a fervent appeal for understanding, is really just an opportunity for white Americans to say, 'Yes, that's what they really are, barbaric, stupid, child-like, dangerous.'" The great black actor and humanitarian Paul Robeson complained that "the burlesquing of religious matters appeared sheer blasphemy."

Still, it was Nina Mae McKinney's singing, tap dancing, and shimmying that captured the imagination and brought full houses to the Lafayette and other theaters in which she appeared after the film's release. Fans wanted to see for themselves the woman who "made a preacher lay his Bible down," especially when it was reported that McKinney had become engaged and would soon marry. McKinney denied the reports and told the *Amsterdam News* that far from settling down, she had just signed a five-year contract with MGM and was thinking of embarking on a European tour. "From a carefree little miss," the *News* verbosely reported, "she has been forced to assume responsibilities of a prominence which bids fair to find her basking in the realities of undreamed monetary returns for her work that will from time to time furrow her little brow."

The truth was that there were no more starring roles for McKinney. Although MGM, in its enthusiasm following *Hallelujah*'s release, had indeed put her under contract, there were no parts to be found for her at a major studio catering to a mostly white market. After turning down the more typical maids or slaves which were the only roles available to black actors in the majority of films being made, McKinney decided that Europe might prove to be a more fertile ground for her talents. In 1930, she set sail for the Continent in the company of a pianist.

Her reputation preceded her, for *Hallelujah* had been even more successful abroad. She was billed as "the black Garbo," and when the *New York Post*'s music critic Richard Watts, Jr., happened to see her cabaret act in Athens, he wired back that she was one of the most beautiful women in the world. Over the next year, McKinney played to jazz-hungry audiences throughout Europe, at some of the Continent's most chic night spots, such as Chez Florence in Paris and the Trocadero in London, as well as clubs in Dublin, Berlin, and Budapest. While in London, she was introduced to Robeson, who was so taken with her that he insisted she star with him in his next film, United Artists' *Congo Road*, which was released in 1931, just as McKinney was returning to the United States. Back home, film roles for her seemed as sparse as ever, certainly in major studio films, but McKinney managed to find a few parts in the studios' "race pictures." She was directed by a young William Wellman in 1931's *Safe in Hell* for MGM, an escaped-convict film set in the Caribbean that, according to Mordaunt Hall, had little to recommend it except McKinney's performance as the barmaid Leonie, which he called "about the most entertaining item in the film." The 1935 musical comedy *Reckless,* also for MGM, was the only mainstream white film in which she made an appearance as herself, in a nightclub sequence. McKinney's voice, to which the film's star, *Carole Lombard, lip-synched her own musical numbers, went uncredited.

A string of nightclub appearances in New York, Chicago, and Los Angeles kept McKinney busy between films, but after completing work on *Reckless* she headed back to the steadier work offered in Europe. There, McKinney once again co-starred with Robeson in London Films' 1935 *Sanders of the River*, a jungle epic adapted from the "Mr. Commissioner Sanders" stories of Edgar Wallace. McKinney played Lilongo, the wife of Robeson's tribal chief Bosambo, both of whom nearly lose their lives for siding with their British colonial rulers in a tribal uprising before being rescued by Commissioner Sanders. Robeson had taken the role based on a script in which scenes that did not include him were later altered, giving the final picture a smug British colonial gloss at the expense of the "savage" natives. (Robeson stormed out of the screening and unsuccessfully tried to have the film's release blocked.) The film, in any event, was not well received, the *Times'* Andrè Sennwald noting that "the talented Nina Mae McKinney is likely to impress you more as a Harlem nightclub entertainer than a savage jungle beauty." During the next few years, McKinney was one of a number of American black performers who met with great success before European audiences, including *Josephine Baker, Ethel Waters, and Robeson. But by the late 1930s, a Europe in turmoil was heading for World War II. For the second time in less than ten years, McKinney came home.

While McKinney was again frustrated in her search for work in mainstream, white-produced films, she had much better luck in a resurgent black-film industry. After a slump in the face of competition from the bigger budgeted "race pictures" released by the major studios, Oscar Micheaux's company, as well as other black companies, began to prosper just before the war. By now, the balconies of formerly all-white theaters had been opened to African-Americans, vastly increasing the number of blacks looking

Nina Mae McKinney with Daniel Haynes in Hallelujah, *1929.*

for filmed entertainment; and many white theaters throughout the South instituted special "midnight shows" for black audiences, thus boosting the number of outlets for all-black films. Black-produced films at this time were usually low-budget replicas of prevailing genres popular with white audiences—gangster pictures, domestic dramas, even Westerns. Most were shot in less than a week for under $15,000, with little or no rehearsal time, and their production values seem laughable by today's standards. But their importance lies elsewhere than in cinematic quality, for these films were countering the self-image foisted on blacks by whites and reinforced by the performances of such actors as Stepin Fetchit. While *Gone With the Wind*'s only black characters were plantation servants, films like 1937's *Black Manhattan* and 1938's *God's Stepchildren* presented contemporary African-Americans in contemporary settings, with characterizations which mirrored those of the major studios' white product, good, bad, and everything in between. McKinney, like many other of her contemporaries, churned out a string of these black-produced films during the late 1930s and early 1940s—among them *Devil's Daughter*, a tale of two sisters competing for control of their dying father's Haitian estate; *Mantan Messes Up*, one of several "Mantan" comedies starring Mantan Moreland, who would gain fame with white audiences as the wide-eyed chauffeur-valet in Charlie Chan films; and two gangster pictures, *Gang Smashers* and *Gun Moll*, both set in Chicago. All were produced by black-owned production companies, directed by blacks, and released by black-operated distributors.

But the white-controlled film world remained a restricted one to McKinney, as it would to most black actors of her day, although Hattie McDaniel gained distinction as the first black actress to win an Academy Award for her performance in *Gone With the Wind*. What few roles McKinney could find in white films were small, and almost always as a maid, such as her appearance in United Artists' *Dark Waters* in 1947. In 1949, Elia Kazan cast her as the spiteful Rozelia in *Pinky*, in which white actress *Jeanne Crain won the lead role that might have seemed eminently suitable for the light-complexioned McKinney—that of a light-skinned black nurse who passes herself off as white to win the affections of a white doctor in a Southern town. Although the film was the most socially significant and controversial in which McKinney appeared, repeatedly selling out Broadway's Rivoli Theater during its New York run and attracting the suspicions of Joseph McCarthy's House Un-American Activities Committee as "communistic," Kazan never even mentions McKinney in his recollections of the film, dwelling instead on the only black with a major part in the picture, Ethel Waters, who played the role of the loyal Southern "mammy," Aunt Dicey, opposite *Ethel Barrymore's imperious white aristocrat, Miss Em. The strains of struggling for a livelihood after 20 years in the business were beginning to show on McKinney, with one critic noting the contrast between the "stocky, bleary-eyed harridan" Rozelia in 1949's *Pinky* and the "bright-eyed, carefree Chick" of 1929's *Hallelujah*. *Pinky* would prove to be McKinney's last film.

Throughout the war years, McKinney relied on her musical and theatrical talents to survive, touring the country with her own 13-piece band and appearing in traveling productions of *Good Neighbor* in 1941 and as Sadie Thompson in a Brooklyn stage adaptation of Somerset Maugham's *Rain* in 1951. Her private life remained out of the tabloids, although her brief marriage, in 1940, to jazz trumpeter Jimmy Monroe, was reported. The two were separated by 1941 and divorced shortly thereafter.

From 1950 on, McKinney virtually disappears from the show-business record. There is a brief mention of her in a 1953 article recounting her appearances at several Hollywood parties some years earlier in the company of a wealthy Indian maharajah, the article still referring to her, nearly 30 years on, as the "star of the movie *Hallelujah*." There is an elusive reference to a possible second marriage, in the early 1950s, but little else is known of McKinney's final years. She died in New York City on May 3, 1967. In a delayed tribute to her short, overlooked career, she was inducted into the Black Filmmakers' Hall of Fame in 1978.

Although Nina Mae McKinney never reached the heights of fame accorded to African-American actors of later generations—*Dorothy Dandridge, Sidney Poitier, Cicely Tyson, James Earl Jones, to name only a few—their careers would not have been possible without her. She was the first African-American actress to win wide acceptance and recognition among white audiences; and she was among the first of her contemporaries to legitimize African-American culture, first in Europe and, later, in films produced by and for black American audiences. Wrote Donald Bogle: "McKinney endured a fate that such talented black female stars as Dorothy Dandridge and Lonette McKee would later experience: after one dazzling performance . . . few, if any, important follow-up roles materialized. McKinney was left floundering. . . . [H]er full potential was left untapped."

SOURCES:

Annotated motion picture stills from the collection of the Prints and Photo Division, Schomburg Center for Research in Black Culture, New York Public Library.

Bogle, Donald. *Toms, Coons, Mulattoes, Mammies and Bucks*. NY: Viking Press, 1973.

"Darlings of Royalty," in *Ebony*. June 1953.

Holt, Paul. "The Truth About Hallelujah," in the *Amsterdam News*. February 12, 1930.

Kisch, John and Edward Mapp. *A Separate Cinema*. Introduction by Donald Bogle. NY: Farrar, Straus, 1992.

Lenwood, Davis. *A Paul Robeson Research Guide*. Westport, CT: Greenwood Press, 1982.

Mapp, Edward. *Directory of Blacks in the Performing Arts*. Metuchen, NJ: Scarecrow Press, 1990.

Noble, Peter. *The Negro in Films*. London: S. Robinson, 1948.

Null, Gary. *Black Hollywood: The Black Performer in Motion Pictures*. NY: Citadel Press, 1975.

Sampson, Henry T. *Blacks in Black and White*. Metuchen, NJ: Scarecrow Press, 1977.

Smith, Jessie Carney, ed. *Notable Black American Women*. Detroit, MI: Gale Research, 1992.

Springer, John, and Jack Hamilton. *They Had Faces Then: Superstars, Stars, and Starlets of the 1930s.* NY: Citadel Press, 1974.

Norman Powers,
writer-producer, Chelsea Lane Productions, New York

McKinney, Tamara (1962—)

American skier who won 18 World Cup races and competed in two Olympics. Born in Lexington, Kentucky, on October 16, 1962; one of seven children of Rigan McKinney (d. 1981, a veteran steeplechase rider) and Frances McKinney (d. 1988, a ski instructor); sister of Sheila McKinney and Steve McKinney (both skiers).

Won three races and took World Cup giant slalom title (1981); finished in top four in seven of twelve races entered (1982); was the first American to win the World Cup competition overall (1983); won the World Cup giant slalom (1983), and slalom (1984); won the national slalom championship (1984); won bronze medals in combined events at the World championships (1985, 1987); took first place in the World Cup races (1986); won the gold medal in women's combined event, World championship Alpine races (1989); also an accomplished equestrian.

Tamara McKinney's family had two passions—riding and skiing. In Kentucky, famous for its thoroughbreds, the desire to be a horsewoman was considered to be as natural as breathing. Skiing, on the other hand, was a more exotic sport in a state with a moderate climate. Nevertheless, Tamara was a child when she put on her first pair of skis, and she was only 15 when she raced in her first World Cup event in 1978. Physically petite, McKinney had tremendous speed but less control. In the 1980 Winter Olympics, she fell in both the slalom and giant slalom. McKinney had to work hard to develop the strength to control her speed on the slopes.

In 1982, skiing with a fractured hand, McKinney finished in the top four in seven of the twelve races she entered. Perseverance continued to pay off as in 1983 Tamara McKinney won the giant slalom and was the first American to win the World Cup championship overall. She had high hopes for the 1984 Winter Games in Sarajevo but was .43 seconds behind the bronze medalist, veteran **Perrine Pelen** of France, in the giant slalom. Her chances for a medal in the slalom were also ruined when her ski hooked a gate. McKinney was back in her best form in the 1984 World Cup winning the slalom title and finishing third overall. She was 1984 national champion as well.

Though a broken leg thwarted a medal at the Winter Olympics of 1988, she came back in 1989 to win a gold medal in the women's combined at the World championship Alpine races in Vail, Colorado, beating the favored *Vreni Schneider. McKinney retired in the early 1990s. Throughout her skiing career, Tamara McKinney continued her love of horseback-riding and when she was named 1983 Kentucky Sportswoman of the Year, it was as a skier and equestrian. Like American speed skater and cyclist *Sheila Young, Tamara McKinney excelled in two sports.

Karin Loewen Haag,
Athens, Georgia

McKolly, Mary (1754–1832).

See "Two Mollies."

McLachlan, Laurentia (1866–1953)

English abbess and scholar. Name variations: Dame Laurentia McLachlan. Born Margaret McLachlan on January 11, 1866, in Coatbridge, Lanarkshire, England; died on August 23, 1953, in Worcester, England; daughter of Henry McLachlan and Mary (McAleese) McLachlan; received education at Stanbrook Abbey under Benedictine clergy; never married; no children.

Laurentia McLachlan

Entered Benedictine order (1884); became subprioress (c. 1910); became abbess (1932).

Although Dame Laurentia McLachlan lived cloistered in a Roman Catholic abbey in England for nearly 70 years, she maintained lively friendships with renowned humanists, intellectuals, and writers. Born Margaret McLachlan in Lanarkshire in 1866, she was sent away to school in Edinburgh as a teen, and then on to Worcester's Stanbrook Abbey convent school. There she was taught by Benedictine nuns, members of a religious order dating back to early medieval England. When she finished school, McLachlan returned to her parents' home for six months, then entered the convent for good in September 1884. With her vows, one of which was never to leave the premises of the abbey, she took the name Laurentia, and to that added the title "Dame," as Benedictine sisters in England are called. She lived her life as did other sisters of the Abbey, spending six hours a day in prayer or singing the liturgy, two hours in manual labor, and the remainder in study or reading. McLachlan became a learned scholar of medieval liturgical texts. She also became a subprioress around 1910, and in 1932 was elected abbess by her community.

McLachlan engaged in several years-long correspondences with various intellectuals of her day, most notably the playwright George Bernard Shaw. A socialist and unabashed atheist, Shaw stopped occasionally at Stanbrook Abbey to visit McLachlan, as did her other correspondents. A breach in their friendship occurred in 1933 with the publication of his play *The Adventures of a Black Girl in Her Search for God*, which contained several scenes considered blasphemous, including the destruction of a crucifix. To mend the friendship, McLachlan sent him an announcement that commemorated her 50th anniversary as a Benedictine, which he mistook for a death announcement. Their correspondence continued until Shaw was well into his 90s. The abbess' trove of extant letters reveal a spirited woman adept at defending her faith from non-believers.

SOURCES:
Corrigan, D. Felicitas. *The Nun, the Infidel, and the Superman.* Chicago, IL: University of Chicago Press, 1985.

Carol Brennan,
Grosse Pointe, Michigan

McLaughlin-Gill, Frances (1919—)

American photographer and filmmaker. Born in New York City in 1919; twin sister of Kathryn Abbe; Pratt Institute, B.F.A., 1941; married Leslie Gill (a photographer and artist), in 1948 (died 1958); children: one daughter, Leslie Gill (b. 1957).

Frances McLaughlin-Gill was born in New York City in 1919, and began studying photography seriously at the age of 18. She graduated from the Pratt Institute in Brooklyn with a B.F.A. in art and design in 1941, and that year won *Vogue* magazine's Prix de Paris contest. From 1940 to 1942, she also studied painting at the New School for Social Research and at the Art Students League in New York City. She served as a member of the photography staff of the Condè Nast magazines from 1944 to 1954, photographing still lifes, portraits, celebrities, and fashion and travel shots for magazines including *Vogue, Glamour,* and *House and Garden.* In 1948, she married artist and photographer Leslie Gill. The couple had a daughter, Leslie, in 1957; McLaughlin-Gill was widowed the following year. She worked as an independent film producer and director from 1964 to 1973, shooting television commercials for major soap and cosmetics manufacturers. She also produced short films, and received a gold medal at the International Film and Television Festival in New York City in 1969 for the one-hour film *Cover Girl: New Face in Focus,* commissioned by the Cover Girl cosmetics company. In 1978, she retired from filmmaking and production to take a teaching post at the School for Visual Arts in New York City. With her twin sister *Kathryn Abbe, she published the book *Twins on Twins* in 1980. McLaughlin-Gill continued to produce photographs for magazines until 1985.

SOURCES:
Rosenblum, Naomi. *A History of Women Photographers.* NY: Abbeville Press Publishers, 1994.

Grant Eldridge,
freelance writer, Pontiac, Michigan

McLean, Alice (1886–1968)

Founding director of American Women's Volunteer Services during World War II. Name variations: Alice T. McLean; Alice Throckmorton McLean; Alice Tinker. Born on March 8, 1886, in New York City; died in Baltimore, Maryland, on October 25, 1968; daughter of James T. McLean and Sara (Throckmorton) McLean; married Edward Larocque Tinker (a lawyer and writer), around 1903 (divorced); children: James McLean; Edward T. McLean.

Founded American Women's Volunteer Services (1940); founded National Clothing Conservation Program to address wartime fabric shortages (1944).

During World War II, Alice McLean founded and ran a volunteer organization for American women, based on England's wartime civil-service corps, that carried out numerous activities aimed at helping military personnel and their families. Born in 1886 into a wealthy family of English-Scottish ancestry, McLean was raised in affluent surroundings in New York City, receiving her education at the exclusive Manhattan private schools Spence and Miss Chapin's, and spending time at a family estate in Delaware County, New York. Her mother **Sara Throckmorton McLean** was active in charity work. McLean eagerly accompanied her father James T. McLean on his business travels, including visits to mining camps in the American Southwest. The family were inveterate travelers, and as a youth McLean learned to speak four languages on her frequent travels in Europe, and even journeyed to the Middle East. She became an avid equestrian, and played polo as a teen. At age 17, she married Edward Larocque Tinker, a lawyer who later became a novelist; the couple had two sons before they divorced.

McLean, who reverted to the use of her family name after her divorce, maintained ties to her English heritage, and traveled to England every fall to take part in the traditional country hunt activities of the landed class. Through these visits, in the years just prior to World War II she became interested in the Women's Voluntary Services, an arm of the civil-defense organization that was preparing for what seemed to be a looming conflict with fascist powers on the European Continent. McLean believed that the United States would also become involved in the coming European war. Upon returning home in 1938, she engineered a poster campaign aimed at women to explain ways in which they could be prepared for war. In 1940, she officially founded the American Women's Volunteer Services (AWVS), and set up offices on East 62nd Street in New York City.

Initially, few women seemed interested, for although England and France had gone to war against Germany and Italy in September 1939, America was still determinedly isolationist and officially neutral, and it seemed hard to imagine that the war would reach American shores. Calls for women to sign on as air-raid wardens or evacuation clerks seemed almost alarmist, and military and civic authorities were of little help to McLean in her organizing efforts. Therefore, the AWVS instead offered classes in first aid, and by the time of Pearl Harbor and America's entry into the war in December 1941, it boasted a membership of over 18,000.

After the bombing of Pearl Harbor, when American men began being drafted in large numbers to the European and Pacific theaters of conflict, patriotic fervor swelled, and McLean's AWVS shifted into high gear. Membership increased dramatically, reaching 325,000 nationwide by the end of the war in 1945. McLean, whose two sons both served as military officers, once said that the business skills she learned from traveling with her father proved invaluable in running such a large and diverse organization. Her promotional talents were also legendary. She once held a barbecue for 250 people at her Delaware County farm, only to have 3,000 local residents appear as well. Her response was to send out a car with a loudspeaker to invite the entire Valley; she used the opportunity to publicize the AWVS and how the average citizen might help the war effort.

The AWVS offered an array of services spread out across its local chapters in 33 states. Childcare was one such important service, because many women were now working in factories converted over to military production while their husbands were serving in the armed forces overseas. The organization also ran canteens and transport operations, taught Braille to recently blinded veterans in San Francisco, sold war bonds and stamps (over a billion dollars' worth by war's end), took photographs of the children of military personnel and mailed them to their posts, sewed clothes, and ran a clothing conservation program. Perhaps more importantly, McLean directed an organization that was anything but elitist, and the AWVS brought together women from all walks of life. It was nondenominational and nondiscriminatory, open to all races at a time when even the U.S. military still had segregated units for African-Americans. In 1944, McLean was given an award for these efforts in promoting interracial harmony by *Mary McLeod Bethune, the African-American educator who was special advisor on minority affairs to President Franklin D. Roosevelt. After the war McLean continued to own and manage her stock farm and dairy in upstate New York; she died in Baltimore in 1968.

SOURCES:

Current Biography. NY: H.W. Wilson, 1945.

McHenry, Robert, ed. *Famous American Women.* NY: Dover, 1980.

Carol Brennan,
Grosse Pointe, Michigan

McLean, Evalyn Walsh

(1886–1947)

American socialite and owner of the Hope diamond.

Born on August 1, 1886, in Denver, Colorado; died

on April 26, 1947, in Washington, D.C.; daughter of Thomas F. Walsh (a carpenter and gold miner) and Carrie Bell (Reed) Walsh; married Edward Beale McLean, on July 22, 1908 (separated 1928); children: Vinson McLean (died young); John R. McLean; Edward Beale McLean; Evalyn Washington McLean Reynolds (died 1946).

Father found gold (1896); moved to Washington, D.C. (1898); moved to Paris (1904); bought Hope diamond (c. 1909); entered upper stratum of Washington society (1916); left husband (1927); became involved in Lindbergh kidnapping reward campaign (1932).

Selected writings: Father Struck It Rich (autobiography, 1936).

Evalyn Walsh McLean was a mining heiress and renowned Washington hostess best remembered for her extravagant soirées and profligate spending habits. She also owned the storied Hope diamond, a 44.52-carat jewel rumored to bring bad luck to its owners. McLean was born Evalyn Walsh in Denver, Colorado, in 1886, under anything but moneyed surroundings. Her father was an Irish immigrant and carpenter who bought and sold small abandoned mines in the West, hoping to strike it rich. He also spent

Evalyn Walsh McLean

time as a storekeeper and hotelier. At age ten, McLean's life was changed forever when her father did indeed find gold quartz near Ouray; she detailed this rags-to-riches tale in her 1936 autobiography *Father Struck It Rich*.

McLean initially had a hard time making the transition to wealth; a notorious tomboy, she had little formal schooling even after her family moved to Washington, D.C. They frequently sailed to Europe, and on one occasion there her parents put her in a convent to restrict her troublemaking. In 1904, she was allowed to move to Paris to study music, and was provided by her father's bankers with a $10,000 letter of credit. She used it to buy a sports car. Her parents worked diligently, though unsuccessfully, to prevent her marriage to Edward Beale McLean, with whom she had a tempestuous relationship. The scion of a newspaper family that owned both the *Cincinnati Enquirer* and the *Washington Post*, "Ned," as he was called, had spending habits as lavish as her own. In 1905, McLean was in an automobile accident in which her brother Vinson was killed. Her leg was seriously injured, then badly set, and as a result she underwent a dangerous operation that brought on an addiction to morphine for a time.

Evalyn and Ned eloped in 1908, after which both sets of parents reconciled themselves to the situation and gave the newlyweds generous cash gifts. They spent the money on an extravagant European honeymoon, during which Ned bought her a famed jewel called the Star of the East. They also viewed the Hope diamond at Cartier in Paris; after their return to the United States, McLean bought that huge stone as well, although she knew of its reputation as a bringer of bad luck. Raised a Catholic, she simply called a priest and had him bless the stone in a gesture to remove the alleged curse.

The McLeans lived in a summer home in Bar Harbor purchased for them by her father, who also gave them an allowance of $1,000 a month that never lasted the 30 days. Ned McLean drank and teetered on the edge of bankruptcy several times. McLean had her first child in 1909, a son she named after her late brother Vinson (the boy would die in a traffic accident at the age of nine); three more children followed. The McLeans' life was further stabilized when Ned gained control of his family's newspapers in 1916, after his father appeared to grow mentally unstable. Control of the *Post* placed the McLeans inside Washington's upper echelons of non-elected power-brokers, a position they relished. The family home was a rambling northwest D.C. estate called Friendship, where McLean kept a llama, and which reportedly had the highest private electric bill in the capital. They were known for throwing outstanding dinner parties that included both the city's old guard and new legislators; McLean loved to seat ideological or personal enemies next to each other at her tables. At one of her lavish soirées, a senator surveyed the ballroom and remarked, "This sort of thing is what brings on a revolution."

Ned McLean became friends with President Warren G. Harding, who often dined at their home, and in 1924 became involved in Harding's Teapot Dome scandal. Under oath, he lied to protect Albert B. Fall, secretary of the interior, then recanted his testimony. The debacle ended the McLeans' social prominence in Washington for a time. McLean left her husband several years later and raised their three children in a much stricter manner than her own upbringing. Like his father, Ned McLean grew unstable; in 1933, he entered a mental hospital, and died there in 1941.

During the depression years of the 1930s McLean, while maintaining her opulent lifestyle, became known for her extravagant acts of charity. She grew sympathetic to what was called the Bonus Army—the thousands of out-of-work men who converged on the nation's capital for aid during the only massive protest of the Great Depression—and convinced a restaurant owner to make them 1,000 sandwiches in the middle of the night. She also bought them cots, books, and cigarettes with her own funds before they were driven out of town. In 1932, McLean pawned the Hope diamond to raise $100,000 which she gave to a convicted felon who said he knew the whereabouts of the kidnapped baby of Charles and *Anne Morrow Lindbergh; the man promptly disappeared. (He was later sent to prison for the scam, and the diamond was returned to McLean.) Gradually such acts dissipated her fortune, and the *Post* was sold in 1933 to the Meyer family right around the time their daughter, *Katharine Graham, was in college; it is still in the Graham family.

McLean continued to entertain lavishly at her Georgetown home during the war years as well. Her daughter **Evalyn McLean Reynolds** married a senator, but died while still in her 20s. McLean herself died of pneumonia at the age of 60 on an April night in 1947. Her servants phoned U.S. Supreme Court Justice Frank Murphy, a family friend, upon her death, unsure of how the priceless jewel collection should be guarded. Murphy took the Hope diamond and

the rest of the jewels and rode around in a taxicab all night, finally putting them in a safety-deposit box after the banks opened in the morning. Two years later, the McLean jewels were sold to New York jeweler Harry Winston; in 1958, Winston donated the Hope diamond to the Smithsonian Institution in Washington, D.C., where it remains on display.

SOURCES:
Current Biography. NY: H.W. Wilson, 1943, 1947.

James, Edward T., ed. *Notable American Women, 1607–1950.* Cambridge, MA: The Belknap Press of Harvard University Press, 1971.

Kernan, Michael. "Around the Mall and Beyond," in *Smithsonian,* May 1995, p. 18.

McHenry, Robert, ed. *Famous American Women.* NY: Dover, 1980.

SUGGESTED READING:
McLean, Evalyn Walsh, with Boyden Sparks. *Father Struck It Rich,* 1936.

Carol Brennan,
Grosse Pointe, Michigan

McLean, Kathryn (1909–1966).

See Dunne, Irene for sidebar.

McLeod, Alice (b. 1937).

See Coltrane, Alice.

McMein, Neysa (1888–1949)

American commercial illustrator and portraitist.
Name variations: Marjory Edna McMein. Born Margary Edna McMein on January 24, 1888, in Quincy, Illinois; died on May 12, 1949, in New York City; daughter of Harry Moran McMein (a newspaper editor) and Isabelle Lee (Parker) McMein; attended School of the Art Institute of Chicago and the Art Students League; married John Gordon Baragwanath (an engineer and writer), on May 18, 1923; children: daughter Joan Gordon Baragwanath; stepson.

Sold first drawing (1914); sold first magazine cover (1915); rode in dirigible airship (1916); hired by McCall's (1923).

Perhaps the first female artist ever to be invited to the White House to execute a portrait of a sitting president, Neysa McMein was born in 1888 in Quincy, Illinois, where her father was a newspaper editor. After high school, she went to study at the School of the Art Institute of Chicago, supplementing the small allowance her parents sent her by playing the piano in movie theaters and the organ in church; she also worked as a sales assistant to a milliner and then as a hat designer. With a friend who had ambitions for the stage, McMein moved to New York City in

1913, around the age of 25. There a numerologist suggested the name "Neysa," which she used for the rest of her life. Thriving within the cultural scene in the city, she appeared as a stage extra in opera productions and took classes at the Art Students League. After working as a sketcher and clothing designer for Butterick, the patternmaker, in 1915 McMein sold her first magazine cover, to the *Saturday Evening Post.* From that point, her career as a commercial artist was well underway, in part because the women she drew looked as intelligent as they did attractive, which was a far cry from the doe-eyed, gamine-like females that were then standard magazine or advertisement fare.

McMein did magazine covers for the best-known publications of the era, including *Collier's* and the *Women's Home Companion.* Her pastel illustrations were on the covers of every issue of *McCall's* magazine between 1923 and 1937, for which she was paid $2,500 per cover, a small fortune in those days. She also continued to do commercial illustrations, and her work was used to sell a range of products, from Palmolive soap to Lucky Strike cigarettes to Betty Crocker baking mixes. She donated sketches to illustrate the annual "One Hundred Neediest Cases" Christmas giving campaign of *The New York Times.*

An avid athlete and adventurous traveler who once rode 100 miles on a camel through North Africa, McMein was considered a devastatingly attractive blonde. During World War I, she worked as a lecturer and entertainer for the YMCA in France, and in 1916 was invited by Count Ferdinand von Zeppelin to fly in his new invention, the dirigible airship; she and her friend **Beulah Livingstone,** who later handled publicity for McMein, were probably the first American women to take such a ride. (The experience went quickly out of fashion after the dirigible *Hindenburg* exploded in 1937.) She also wrote a screenplay, *Three Miles Out,* as well as songs, short stories, and magazine articles. In 1923, McMein married a mining engineer and writer of adventure stories, John Gordon Baragwanath, with whom she had what has been called an unconventional but happy marriage; the couple had one daughter.

About this time, as the use of color photographs for magazine covers started narrowing the market for her commercial work, McMein began to devote more time to oil portraiture. She painted portraits of two sitting presidents, Warren G. Harding (c. 1922) and Herbert Hoover (c. 1931), and of many other well-known figures of the day, including *Anne Morrow Lindbergh, *Beatrice Lillie, Charlie Chaplin, *Dorothy

Parker, *Edna St. Vincent Millay, and *Janet Flanner, but she never gained serious recognition as an artist, in part due to her work as a commercial illustrator. Many of the artists and entertainers she painted were personal friends; McMein was a vivid figure in New York's literary scene, and was a frequent diner at the "Vicious Circle" table at the Hotel Algonquin presided over by Parker and Alexander Woollcott. Her New York painting studio was a gathering place for these friends and others, including Irving Berlin and *Edna Ferber. During Prohibition, she made her own liquor in the bathtub there. Neysa McMein died in 1949, after suffering an embolism during surgery for cancer.

SOURCES:

Bailey, Brooke. *The Remarkable Lives of 100 Women Artists.* Holbrook, MA: Bob Adams, 1994.

Current Biography. NY: H.W. Wilson, 1941 and 1949.

James, Edward T., ed. *Notable American Women, 1607–1950.* Cambridge, MA: The Belknap Press of Harvard University Press, 1971.

Read, Phyllis J., and Bernard L. Witlieb. *The Book of Women's Firsts.* NY: Random House, 1992.

Rubinstein, Charlotte Streifer. *American Women Artists.* Boston, MA: G.K. Hall, 1982

SUGGESTED READING:

Gallagher, Brian. *Anything Goes: The Jazz Age Adventures of Neysa McMein and Her Extravagant Circle of Friends.* NY: Times Books, 1987.

Carol Brennan,
Grosse Pointe, Michigan

McMillan, Clara Gooding

(1894–1976)

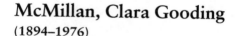

U.S. representative in the 76th Congress (November 7, 1939–January 3, 1941). Name variations: Clara Eloise McMillan. Born Clara Eloise Gooding on August 17, 1894, in Brunson, South Carolina; died on November 8, 1976, in Barnwell, South Carolina; daughter of William James Gooding and Mary Emily (Webb) Gooding; attended Savannah (GA) High School, Flora MacDonald College (Red Springs, NC), and Confederate Home College (Charleston, SC); married Thomas Sanders McMillan (1888–1939, a congressional representative), on December 16, 1916 (died September 29, 1939); children: Thomas Sanders; James Carroll; William Gooding; Edward Webb; Robert Hampton.

Chosen by House Democrats to finish late husband's Congressional term (1939); affiliated with National Youth Administration (1941); hired at Department of State (1946); retired from public service (1957).

In Clara McMillan's day, few women held public office of any sort, let alone a seat in Con-gress. There was a precedent, however, of widows of elected representatives winning special elections and serving out the remainder of their late husband's terms in office. Born in 1894 in South Carolina, Clara Gooding attended two South Carolina colleges, Confederate Home and Flora MacDonald, before marrying Thomas McMillan. When he died in the middle of a term as representative from the First District of South Carolina in 1939, the state's Democratic Party leadership backed her candidacy in a special election. She won the election in November 1939, and took her seat in the U.S. House of Representatives the following January. McMillan served a full year in Washington, D.C., during which she spoke in favor of a bill establishing America's first peacetime draft and sat on the Committee on Public Buildings and Grounds, the Committee on Patents, and the Committee on the Election of President, Vice President, and Representatives in Congress. She chose not to run for a second term, and after 1941 worked for the National Youth Administration and later in the Office of War Information. From 1946 to 1957, McMillan was an information liaison officer at the Department of State. She died in South Carolina in 1976.

*Clara
Gooding
McMillan*

*Opposite page
Neysa
McMein*

SOURCES:

Office of the Historian. *Women in Congress, 1917–1990.* Commission on the Bicentenary of the U.S. House of Representatives, 1991.

Who's Who in America, 1940–41. Chicago, IL: A.N. Marquis, 1941.

Carol Brennan,
Grosse Pointe, Michigan

McMillan, Margaret (1860–1931)

American-born English reformer. Born in New York in 1860; died in 1931; brought up in Inverness, Scotland; sister of Rachel McMillan (1859–1917).

A pioneer of nursery schools, Margaret McMillan campaigned tirelessly for medical inspection of schoolchildren and school clinics in the north of England. In 1902, she joined her sister **Rachel McMillan** in London. In 1908, the McMillan sisters opened their first school clinic, and their first open-air nursery in Deptford in 1914. Numerous nursery school openings followed. When Rachel died in 1917, Margaret carried on the work with the mystical belief that they were still working together; she dedicated the Rachel McMillan Training College for nursery teachers, also in Deptford, to her sister.

McMurry, Lillian Shedd

(c. 1922–1999)

American blues producer. Born Lillian Shedd in Purvis, Mississippi, around 1922; died of a heart attack in Jackson, Mississippi, on March 18, 1999; daughter of itinerant Southern musicians; studied law in Jackson, Mississippi; married Willard McMurry (a store manager), in 1945 (died 1996); children: daughter Vitrice McMurry.

Founded Trumpet Records (c. 1950); discovered and promoted numerous African-American blues musicians; inducted into Blues Hall of Fame (1998).

As a Southerner and a white woman in the 1950s, Lillian Shedd McMurry was an unlikely pioneer in the popularization of black music, but as a devotee of Southern black blues, she founded Trumpet Records around 1950 and produced the first recordings of two major Delta blues musicians, Sonny Boy Williamson and Elmore James, as well as recordings by such leading figures as Willie Love, Big Joe Williams, and Jerry McCain.

Although born around 1922 in Purvis, Mississippi, to a musical family who moved from town to town, in the first decades of her life McMurry was never exposed to the evocative, local blues music that became her passion. During the 1940s, she took a position as a state secretary in Jackson, Mississippi, and began taking law courses. In 1945 she married Willard McMurry, a manager of several furniture stores in Jackson. One day in 1949, while helping her husband clean out a building at 309 Farish Street, McMurry found a stack of old records. Upon listening to "All She Wants to Do Is Rock," a song by Wynonie (Mr. Blues) Harris, she was transfixed. She called it "the most unusual, sincere and solid sound" she had ever heard, and was entranced by the rhythm and freedom in the music.

McMurry opened a record department in her husband's furniture store, specializing in African-American music, particularly blues and gospel. The record department grew in popularity following her use of radio advertising, and soon became an independent store. Less than a year later, McMurry turned the store into a recording studio and began recording local gospel groups under the newly created Trumpet label. She then sought out Sonny Boy Williamson, a harmonica player who had performed for 20 years in the Delta without receiving a record contract. Williamson, whose real name was Alex "Rice" Miller, was an escaped convict, and thus was forced to hide his identity under an alias. He had chosen the name of another popular blues singer called Williamson, performed on radio station KFFA in Helena, Arkansas, and built up a devoted following in the area. (McMurry did not learn about Williamson's past until later.) With a tendency to curse and to carry both a gun and a knife, Williamson could be cantankerous when he drank too much, which was often, and tended to engage in fisticuffs which frequently landed him in jail. McMurry regularly paid his bail. According to legend, one day he was spouting expletives in the recording studio when McMurry instructed him to stop. When he refused, McMurry took his own pistol (which she had previously required him to check), pointed it at him, and marched him outside, telling him not to return. Two weeks later, Williamson reappeared to apologize, and McMurry allowed him back. When he died in 1965, she paid for his tombstone.

With McMurry's production skills, Williamson produced a number of blues classics, including "Eyesight to the Blind," "Nine Below Zero," "Mr. Down Child," "Mighty Long Time," and "Red Hot Kisses," written by McMurry. "Pontiac Blues" is Williamson's tribute to McMurry's car. Williamson's friend, slide guitarist Elmore James, also recorded a major hit, "Dust My Broom," on the Trumpet label. But the label went out of business in 1955, unable to compete with bigger record companies. McMurry, unlike many producers of her generation, nonetheless continued to ensure that her recording artists received residuals from Trumpet songs that were re-released throughout the years. She was inducted into the Blues Hall of Fame in 1998, and died of a heart attack in Jackson the following year, at the age of 77.

SOURCES:

The New York Times. March 29, 1999.

Lolly Ockerstrom,
freelance writer, Washington, D.C.

McNair, Denise (d. 1963).

See Davis, Angela for sidebar.

McNall, Belva (1830–1917).

See Lockwood, Belva Bennett.

McNamara, Julianne (1966—)

American gymnast. Born in Flushing, New York, on October 6, 1966.

Won the American Cup; won a bronze in the vault in World Cup (1982); shared a gold in the uneven bars in the Los Angeles Olympics (1984).

Five years after she began gymnastics, Julianne McNamara made the 1980 Olympic team. She performed well enough to make the last place berth, despite her relative lack of experience and a strained ligament. Unfortunately, her hopes of Olympic competition were dashed when the United States boycotted the 1980 Moscow Olympics after the Soviet Union invaded Afghanistan. McNamara continued to compete, however, and in the 1981 World championships she placed 7th in the all-around, the highest an American woman gymnast had ever placed until that time. That same year, she won two American Cup titles and a bronze in the vault in the 1982 World Cup. McNamara often competed with *****Mary Lou Retton**, the two scoring very close in points in match after match. Her best event was the uneven bars, and McNamara often used moves from the men's repertoire that were seldom attempted by other women gymnasts. In 1984, Julianne McNamara finally competed in the Olympics, where she shared a gold medal in the uneven bars with **Ma Yanhong** of China; Mary Lou Retton placed third.

SOURCES:

Markel, Robert, Nancy Brooks, and Susan Markel. *For the Record: Women in Sports*. NY: World Almanac Publications, 1985.

Karin Loewen Haag,
Athens, Georgia

McNamara, Maggie (1928–1978)

American actress. Born on June 18, 1928, in New York City; died of an overdose of pills in New York City on February 18, 1978; married director David Swift (divorced).

Maggie McNamara was born in New York City on June 18, 1928. A fashion model while still in her teens, she wanted to be an actress and studied drama and dance from 1948 to 1951, when she made her Broadway debut. She later replaced *****Barbara Bel Geddes** in the lead role in the play *The Moon is Blue*, a comedy that was considered quite racy for its time. She became a film star when she reprised the role in the 1953 movie version, directed by Otto Preminger, and was nominated for an Academy Award for Best Actress. Despite this promising start and starring roles in her next two films, *Three Coins in the Fountain* (1954) and *Prince of Players* (1955), lasting fame eluded her. McNamara returned to Broadway in *Step on a Crack* in 1962, but failed to secure any subsequent stage roles, and appeared on film for the fourth and last time in 1963's *The Cardinal*, in which she had only a supporting role. McNamara abandoned her acting career and began working as a typist, but suffered from mental illness and committed suicide by taking an overdose of sleeping pills in 1978.

Grant Eldridge,
freelance writer, Pontiac, Michigan

McNeil, Claudia (1917–1993)

African-American actress. Born in Baltimore, Maryland, on August 13, 1917; died in Englewood, New Jersey, on November 25, 1993.

Selected theater: Mamie in Simply Heavenly *(1957); Tituba in* The Crucible *(1958); Lena Younger in* A Raisin in the Sun *(1959); Sister Margaret in a London production of* The Amen Corner *(1965); the Jewish mother in* Something Different *(1967); Fatateeta in* Her First Roman *(1968).*

A nightclub singer before making her off-Broadway debut in Langston Hughes' *Simply Heavenly* (1957), Claudia McNeil is best known for her role as Lena Younger in *A Raisin in the Sun* (1959), the *****Lorraine Hansberry** drama about a struggling black family that won the Drama Critics' Circle Best Play award and ran on Broadway for three years. McNeil recreated her role for the film version of the play in 1961. The actress later portrayed Sister Margaret in a London production of James Baldwin's *The Amen Corner* (1965), for which she was voted Best Actress of the year by the

From the movie
Raisin in the
Sun, *starring*
Claudia McNeil
and Sidney
Poitier.

critics. McNeil appeared in a variety of film and television roles before returning to cabaret in 1978. She was hospitalized for surgery in 1982, after which she was confined to a New Jersey nursing home. She died in 1993, at age 76.

SOURCES:
Pace, Eric. "Claudia McNeill, 77 [*sic*], an Actress Best Known for 'Raisin in the Sun,'" in *The New York Times.* November 29, 1993, p. B11.
Willis, John. *Theater World: 1993–1994.* Volume 50. NY: Theater Book Publishers, 1996.

Barbara Morgan,
Melrose, Massachusetts

McNulty, Dorothy (b. 1908).

See Singleton, Penny.

McNulty, Mrs. William.

See Tait, Agnes.

McPartland, Marian (1920—)

English-born jazz pianist who organized her own trio, made numerous recordings, and hosted her own show

on public radio. Name variations: Marian Page. Born Margaret Marian Turner in Slough near Windsor, England, on March 20, 1920; daughter of Frank Turner (a civil engineer) and Janet (Payne) Turner (a pianist); attended Guildhall School of Music, London; married Jimmy McPartland, on February 4, 1945 (divorced then remarried two weeks before he died in 1991).

Composed "Twilight World" and "Ambience." Albums include: Ambience, Fine Romance, Now's the Time, Solo Concert at Haverford, Personal Choice, and In My Life.

Studied classical music at the Guildhall School of Music before moving into jazz; toured English vaudeville theaters as pianist with Billy Mayerl (1941); toured with Britain's ENSA in Europe (1943) and with USO camp shows in France (1944); came to U.S. (1946); formed group with husband, played with Billie Holiday; formed own trio (1951); toured U.S. nightclubs; played Hickory House in New York City (1952–60); performed with Benny Goodman (1963); founded Halcyon Records (1969); toured South America with Earl Hines and Teddy Wilson (1974); made numerous recordings; won Peabody Award for hosting her National Public Radio series "Piano Jazz" (1984); given lifetime achievement award from Down Beat (1994).

As a jazz artist, Marian McPartland had three strikes against her—she was English, white, and a woman. Jazz was created by black musicians, many of them male, and some of them unwilling to share the spotlight with an interloper. Once, a group of eminent black male musicians played an entire set with their backs turned to her. Over time, however, McPartland earned their respect, because she was an extremely fine musician. After many decades at the keyboard, she became a much-beloved figure, her musicianship winning over her critics.

Marian McPartland's background was atypical for a jazz musician. She was born in Slough (a name she disdains), near Windsor, England. "I like to say I was born near Windsor Castle, which is true," she said. "Members of my family actually had homes inside the castle grounds and I've been able to tour places in the castle the public never sees." She began to play the piano by ear at the age of three or four, picking out the Chopin waltzes she heard her mother playing on the piano. In kindergarten, she was already a performer, playing away at the keyboard while admirers gathered around. When she was in her late teens, a teacher convinced her parents that she should study music seriously. McPartland was accepted at London's Guildhall School of Music, one of the world's preeminent institutions. Here she studied theory, sight-singing, piano, violin, and composition, sometimes practicing eight hours a day. Her piano teacher, Orlando Morgan, disapproved of popular music, but McPartland listened to it anyway and played it whenever she had the chance; she always played by ear. McPartland knew little about jazz; when she picked out tunes from Duke Ellington, Art Tatum, or Teddy Wilson, she knew nothing about the performers or their music.

Before McPartland received her degree at Guildhall, she snuck off to play for Billy Mayerl, a popular pianist in the West End. When he hired her for a piano act, her parents were frantic. Her father, who wanted her to become a nurse, offered her £1,000 to turn him down, until he learned she would be paid £5 a week, then a small fortune. McPartland began traveling with Mayerl's four-piano group, performing throughout Great Britain in vaudeville theaters; it was a happy period for her. In 1943, during World War II, she volunteered for the Entertainments National Service Association (ENSA) and later switched to the USO, going to France with the first group after the Normandy invasion. She enjoyed the opportunity to meet and hear American performers like Fred Astaire, *Dinah Shore, James Cagney, and Edward G. Robinson. She was sitting in on a jam session in Belgium when Jimmy McPartland, the famed cornetist, walked in; he reacted like many musicians: "O, God, a woman player!," he groaned. "And she's going to sit in—I know she's going to be lousy." Wrote McPartland: "It so happens he was right. In those days I hadn't learned how to back up a jazz soloist. I didn't really keep steady time, or listen enough to the other players. I was so eager to prove myself that I just went barging in with lots of enthusiasm and not too much expertise." Soon they were entertaining troops on the front lines, and he began to appreciate her talent and her harmonic ideas. They were married in Aachen, Germany, on February 4, 1945. Shortly afterwards, she returned with him to Chicago, and then to New York.

Marian McPartland had entered the center of the jazz world at the right time. Her husband encouraged her to form her own group, so in 1951 the Marian McPartland Trio opened at the Embers Club. In February 1952, they opened at the Hickory House; she would play there off and on throughout the 1950s. "Having my own combo," said McPartland, "I was never in the position of waiting to be hired by some leader who might have harbored one prejudice or another. . . . Being a woman could be an asset. It was unusual enough for people to remember me, and club owners hire musicians who draw audiences; they don't care if the draw is a man or a woman."

Having started her own trio, in 1969 McPartland founded her own recording label, Halcyon, on which her work as well as that of other musicians was released; she also wrote songs including "Twilight World," and "There'll Be Other Times." Her radio career began on WBAI, New York's public radio station, with a two-hour jazz show, "A Delicate Balance." She has since hosted an hourly show, "Piano Jazz," for over 15 years on National Public Radio (NPR), conversing and improvising duets with top musicians, including Bobby Short, Stephen Sondheim, and **Susannah McCorkle**.

A legend in her own right, McPartland has been hailed by jazz critic Leonard Feather as "one of the great jazz pianists." When "she gets her left hand going," wrote jazz commentator Len Lyons, "she can make the piano seem to be strutting across the stage." But McPartland not only plays a good show, she talks it. Educating the public about jazz has been an ongoing mission, in jazz workshops and clinics at all levels, as well as on radio. She particularly enjoyed touring public schools to teach about jazz. Improvisation, she felt, is an important skill for children. When *Down Beat* singled McPartland out for its annual lifetime achievement award in 1994, they were recognizing in her work "her ongoing interest in subsequent generations of jazz musicians."

Marian McPartland is synonymous with piano jazz. Her soothing, upper-class voice conveys elegance and style as does her piano playing. Although jazz was born in the drums of Africa, the streets of New Orleans, Memphis, and Chicago, and in black churches throughout America, it is not a culturally narrow form. It invites diversity and creativity. Marian McPartland's career demonstrated the international nature of this musical form. She has recorded over 40 albums, the latest being a salute to composer *Mary Lou Williams. "If you go hear a Chopin recital," said McPartland, "you know what you're going to hear. But if you're going to hear a jazz group, you really don't know what you're going to hear. It's all very on the spur of the moment. It's such a creative thing."

SOURCES:

Carlson, Elliot. "Jazz with an English Accent," in *AARP Bulletin.* July–August 1994.

Gottlieb, Annie. "Marian McPartland—Everything a Jazz Musician is Not Supposed to Be." *Ms.* Vol. 6, no. 9. March 1978, pp. 24–30.

Parade Magazine. August 6, 1995.

SUGGESTED READING:

McPartland, Marian. *All in Good Time.* NY: Oxford University Press, 1987 (contains a portrait of Mary Lou Williams).

John Haag,
Associate Professor of History,
University of Georgia, Athens, Georgia

McPherson, Aimee Semple

(1890–1944)

Canadian evangelical preacher with melodramatic tastes, who enjoyed massive success in Los Angeles during the 1920s but damaged her reputation in a 1926 kidnapping hoax. Born Aimee Kennedy in Ingersoll, Ontario, Canada, on October 9, 1890; died in Oakland, California, on September 27, 1944; daughter of James Morgan Kennedy (an Ontario farmer) and Minnie (Pearce) Kennedy (a Salvation Army fund raiser); married Robert Semple, in 1908 (died in Hong Kong in 1910); married Harold Stewart McPherson, in 1912 (divorced 1918); married David Hutton, in 1930 (divorced 1935, on grounds of mental cruelty); children: (first marriage) daughter, Roberta Semple; (second marriage) son, Rolf.

Moved to Providence, Rhode Island (1912); migrated to California (1918); opened the Angelus Temple, Los Angeles (January 1, 1923); involved in disappearance and "kidnapping" scandal (1926).

Many American evangelists have been marred by scandal; the sensational disappearance of Aimee Semple McPherson in 1926 is one of the best-known examples. America's first woman evangelist to enjoy international renown, she claimed to have been kidnapped and tortured in the Mexican desert, but skeptical investigators maintained that she had been hiding out with a married lover in Carmel, California. Denying it to the end of her life, McPherson retained thousands of loyal disciples and her church of the Foursquare Gospel continued to grow.

She was born Aimee Kennedy in a small Ontario farm community in 1890. Her father James Morgan Kennedy was an ardent Methodist, her mother, **Minnie Pearce Kennedy**, a Salvationist. Growing up in an intensely religious rural environment, she longed for a career on the stage, and as a teenager rebelled against religion and took the side of the evolutionary modernists in the great debate on human origins. When she was 17, however, the preaching of a traveling revivalist, Robert Semple, precipitated a religious experience, and she was "born again." The revivalist proposed marriage to her soon there-

after, she accepted, and they laid plans to go as missionaries to China. "He was my theological seminary, my spiritual mentor, and my tender, patient, unfailing lover," she would write of him later. This was the era when confident missionaries spoke of "the evangelization of the world" and anticipated mass conversions among the "heathen" of China. Many of the American Protestant churches had mission boards to finance their evangelists overseas, but Robert Semple was an independent and decided to trust in God to provide the necessary funds. His spellbinding preaching brought him crowds wherever he went, and, from their contributions, he raised enough to pay for the voyage.

Aimee and her husband sailed first to Ireland, to visit his family, then to London, where they enjoyed the hospitality of millionaire evangelist Cecil Polhill. While there, she preached for the first time at a London revival, claiming that the Holy Spirit had possessed her when she felt powerless to speak alone. Wrote Aimee:

> Then the Lord took possession of my tongue even as he had on that memorable day when he had baptized me with Pentecostal fire, only this time it was in England. The words seemed to flow forth without conscious volition or self-will. It seemed as though I was caught away by the oratory of another.

Boarding a ship for China, the couple landed in the devastating heat of a South China summer. Robert Semple went out to preach the gospel in the heat of the day (with an interpreter at his side), but before their mission was well under way he developed dysentery and died, leaving the 20-year-old Aimee Semple a widow and mother of a newborn daughter **Roberta Semple**. Returning to America, she moved disconsolately from New York to Chicago and then back to Ontario, nursing her frail child.

Fearing for her daughter's life and in need of some stability, she accepted a marriage proposal from Harold McPherson, a young contemporary whom she had met in Chicago just after her return. But "before the marriage took place . . . I made one stipulation, telling Mr. McPherson that all my heart and soul were really in the work of the Lord, and that if at any time He called me back into active ministry, no matter where or when, I must obey God first of all." They had a son, Rolf, but Aimee Semple McPherson remained depressed and dissatisfied. Suffering what seems to have been a nervous breakdown, she finally decided she could live with her husband no longer but must answer her call to preach. Taking both her children, she set off without notice in the middle of the night and joined the revival circuit. The oratorical power she had shown in London returned—she again gave full credit to the Holy Spirit—and as her reputation spread, she began to receive invitations to hold revivals throughout the United States. Her willingness to hold a revival in the African-American community of Corona showed an unusual readiness, for that era, to cross the color line. Harold McPherson was so impressed with her speaking when he came to listen that he urged her to continue. They were not reunited, however, and divorced in 1918.

According to her autobiography, Aimee McPherson had been wondering what role women should play in evangelism from the time of her conversion.

> I found that *Deborah, a woman, led forth her gleaming armies beneath flaming banners under the sunshine of God's smile. The woman at the well preached the first salvation sermon and led an entire city to Christ . . . [and] a woman had delivered the first Easter message.

Coming out of a tradition where scriptural validation was all-important, she apparently had no further doubts about her right to play a role usually reserved for men, even though the evangelical Christians in many cities regarded her as a dangerous and slightly scandalous figure.

Aimee McPherson bought a moth-eaten revival marquee with some of her collection funds, founded an evangelical newspaper, the *Bridal Call*, in 1916, and was soon publishing it monthly. It specialized in sentimental religious tales and moral advice. She began ranging along the East Coast of the United States, moving to Florida each winter and back to New England and Canada for the summers. Her two children and her mother came along as well, and her successes enabled them all to prosper. Frequently sick, she claimed that pain left her the moment she began to preach, and became convinced that, through her, God had the power to heal. Even the severe burns she suffered after an explosion in a faulty carbide lighting system during a camp revival meeting in Florida healed themselves, she claimed, as she plucked up her courage and returned to the pulpit with singed hair and blackened skin burns. During the terrible influenza epidemic of 1918, she preached three times a day despite being desperately ill. When her daughter Roberta was on the brink of death, suddenly Jesus appeared before McPherson and promised that her child would live, adding that the family's future lay in California, in a bungalow, with a rose garden outside and a caged canary within.

Following Jesus' instructions she bought a new car, painted "Jesus is coming soon—get ready!" on its doors, and drove the family across the country. She got as far as Tulsa, Oklahoma, when she heard that the First World War had ended. Completing the westward journey, she quickly made a name for herself in Los Angeles and along the West Coast, preaching a cheery gospel of good health, family love, and wholesome simplicity, which appealed to her mainly lower-middle-class audience. Many of her followers were also middle-class migrants who, like McPherson, had traveled to the Golden Land of California from other parts of America. She once defined her mission as an essentially middle-class affair, adding that the poor should turn to the Salvation Army and that the rich could take care of themselves. The idea of naming her brand of revivalism the "Foursquare Gospel," first came to her during a revival in Oakland, California, in 1922, as a way of dodging the then-much-debated question of whether or not she lined up with Pentecostalism. The four sides of the square were Jesus the Savior, Jesus the Baptizer with the Holy Spirit, Jesus the Healer, and Jesus the Coming King. Within two years of her arrival in Los Angeles, volunteers from the

Aimee
Semple
McPherson

congregation had built and paid for the cottage she had foreseen. It was complete, right down to the canary, but would soon be upstaged by something grander still.

McPherson's chief rival in Los Angeles was Bob Shuler, a sour, irritable evangelist who preached a ferocious blend of hellfire and damnation and loved to denounce sinners by name from his pulpit. Though their styles were totally different, each soon enjoyed a huge following. McPherson at first held her meetings in the Philharmonic Auditorium, the largest meeting place in Los Angeles, but found that it was not big enough. With her Midas touch for money-raising, however, she collected enough to build the stupendous "Angelus Temple," then the largest religious building in American history, seating 5,300 worshippers, which was dedicated on New Year's Day of 1923. She and her mother (now her business manager) were joint owners of the building, and of the adjacent mansion to which they moved; they had no bank debts and no financial accountability to the congregation.

McPherson evolved a technique of costumed sermonizing linked to a theme. Dressed as a USC football player, she preached on carrying the ball for Christ. Entering the Temple on a motorcycle in a policeman's uniform, she placed sin under arrest and urged her audience not to speed to ruin.

—Kevin Starr

McPherson had a well-developed sense of the dramatic. She loved to dress up in different costumes to give added emphasis to her messages, collecting costumes on her frequent revival tours throughout the United States, Europe, and Australia. Her strawberry blonde hair became famous, and newspapers sometimes featured successive photographs showing how she gathered the loose tresses and arranged them into her elaborate performance coiffure. Other accessories were flowing white robes, glittering costume jewelry, and theatrical kleig lights, all of which added impact to her performances. A well-trained choir backed up the preaching, a brass band punctuated the prayers, and for those worshippers whose excitement led to ecstasy and "holy rolling" there was even a padded cell in the Angelus Temple where they could writhe without serious injury. Preaching services often culminated in faith healings, as McPherson implored the sick and the lame to rise from their beds of suffering. Dozens did just that, and one area of the Temple was given over to a display of the discarded crutches, wheelchairs, and stretchers of sufferers who claimed to have been healed through her intercession. The theatricality of her preaching certainly contributed to her success; so did her unerring eye for publicity. Historian Lately Thomas aptly summarized that "her tastes, sentimental, garish, heartily and healthily vulgar, matched those of the multitude."

Along with the Temple, she created a music conservatory, a Bible college (attended by 1,000 students) which was soon thriving, and radio station KFSG, only the third radio station to be licensed in Los Angeles. Evangelical preachers were some of the earliest Americans to understand the power of broadcasting to create and enlarge an audience. When inspectors closed the station down temporarily in 1925, for veering off its assigned frequency, she cabled Secretary of Commerce (later president) Herbert Hoover: "Please order your minions of Satan to leave my station alone. You cannot expect the Almighty to abide by your wavelength nonsense." She also pioneered in the use of telephones as an aid to evangelizing. Her assistants would set up tents in Los Angeles suburbs and welcome crowds to listen to her sermons over the air, then converts would call in word of their salvation (and contributions) by phone. In all these enterprises, some of them anticipating evangelical techniques of the 1970s and 1980s, McPherson showed a high measure of entrepreneurial skill.

On a sunny May 18, 1926, at the height of her fame, McPherson went to the beach near Los Angeles. After pitching a tent, she sent her secretary, and only companion, on an errand. But when her secretary returned, Aimee Semple McPherson had disappeared. It was assumed that she had drowned. The exact sequence of events in that spring and summer was never settled beyond dispute, but the conflicting stories are soon told. During a massive search for her body, one diver and one enthusiast from the Angelus Temple were themselves killed by drowning. But then, two days after thousands of mourners had attended a memorial service at the Temple to grieve her loss, she appeared once more, in the Mexican city of Agua Prieta. She told police and journalists that she had been walking toward the water that day when a distraught couple hailed her and asked for her help. Their child was sick in a nearby car. When they reached the car, McPherson was shoved in, thrown to the floor, anesthetized, and driven first to an unidentified house and later to a desert shack, where she had been tortured. She managed to escape, she added, by severing her bonds, climbing through a window, and staggering off

into the desert, walking 20 miles in the midsummer Mexican sun to Agua Prieta. She claimed that a ransom note demanding $500,000, delivered to her mother at the Temple during her absence, proved that her story was true.

The story did not convince investigators for long, and as more sleuths, amateur and professional, became involved, the gaps in her tale grew larger. Why did her dress show no sign of wear? Why wasn't she dehydrated? Why hadn't she even asked for a glass of water when she arrived out of the desert? Most of the evidence pointed towards another version of events. As she rested in bed in a Los Angeles hospital, there was a new development. Kenneth G. Ormiston, a married man who ran KFSG, had also been missing. He had spent several weeks traveling with a blonde companion who some said resembled McPherson. Authorities began to speculate that she had left her clothes on the beach to give the illusion of drowning, and then had gone with her lover, Ormiston, to a honeymoon cottage in Carmel. Neighbors reported seeing a mysterious

veiled woman on several occasions during the month in question, and a local shopkeeper had a grocery list written in her distinctive handwriting. According to this version of events, the ransom note was part of the hoax, arranged by McPherson and Ormiston to substantiate her kidnapping claim. The district attorney gathered evidence in preparation for a trial, on the charge that McPherson had conspired to produce false testimony. In his view, Minnie Kennedy, McPherson's mother, had known perfectly well that her daughter was still alive and had orchestrated the search efforts while knowing that there was no body to be found. After months of costly evidence-gathering, however, he decided against prosecuting, partly because of McPherson's immense popularity and partly because of his inability to get incontestable proof. This decision offered true believers in McPherson's story the reasonable doubt they had been looking for, despite the strength of the circumstantial evidence. Their jubilation knew no bounds. A crowd of 50,000 turned out to greet her at the station when she returned to Los Angeles. Thou-

Aimee
Semple
McPherson

sands more flocked to her sermons; they saw the allegations as a vicious affront to a virtuous woman who had already suffered enough. A triumphant cross-country preaching tour (with plenty of paid publicity flacks on board) fortified her rehabilitation.

McPherson insisted to the end of her life that Ormiston had been no more than a business associate. Ormiston, who stayed in Los Angeles as a radio station engineer and died in 1937, denied to the end that there had been an affair. Soon after the scandal, Ormiston's wife applied for a divorce on grounds of desertion but declined to name any "other woman" in the case. McPherson's spectacular career continued, even though among more skeptical Angelenos she had become a laughingstock. The Foursquare Gospel continued to grow, and by the Second World War had opened 400 churches in America and 200 more throughout the world, preaching the same message of "feel-good" religion. And as biographer Thomas noted, McPherson retained and exploited many of the advantages of notoriety: "During the decade 1927–1936, her name appeared on the front pages of the Los Angeles newspapers an average of three times a week."

When Sinclair Lewis, America's first Nobel-Prize winning novelist, wrote *Elmer Gantry* (1927), the tale of a fraudulent evangelical preacher, he included a thinly fictionalized version of McPherson in the character of Sister Sharon Falconer. In his portrayal of Falconer, Lewis blended disdain with a sort of grudging admiration for her organizational powers and her rhetorical dash. In several scenes, he showed her offstage entrepreneurial character, as she reminded her volunteers of the need to raise hard cash to keep the evangelical empire running. During the Great Depression of the 1930s, McPherson recovered some of her former esteem by playing a distinguished part in Los Angeles poor relief work. She set up a "commissary," offering food to thousands of the unemployed each day, along with an employment and housing bureau which aimed at helping the thousands of homeless people in Los Angeles.

Her personal life remained chaotic. In 1930, she was married for a third time, to David Hutton, a baritone from the Angelus Temple choir. Hutton began to play a role in the business side of the Temple, and before long the two of them were squabbling, often in public. The press had always relished the way she and her mother would fight over business matters; now they had a field day with the Huttons' not-so-secret con-

flicts. In 1934, the marriage reached a crisis, with him suing for divorce on grounds of mental cruelty and her countersuing on the grounds that his posing for publicity photographs with scantily clad dancing girls had damaged the Temple's reputation for moral probity. He won his suit; hers was thrown out.

During the Second World War, as during the First, Aimee Semple McPherson turned her oratorical powers to fund raising on behalf of war loan drives and was always an energetic patriot. But, in 1944, aged only 53, she had a series of heart attacks and died (some sources cite an overdose of sleeping pills).

Aimee Semple McPherson had been an unbending foe of Hollywood and of decadent night-life, a supporter of Prohibition during the 1920s, and an enemy of all criminals. She believed she had been kidnapped by racketeers whose business she had tried to interrupt, and the sincerity with which she described the whole episode in several books makes it difficult to see her as a cynical, knowing liar. The exact sequence of events in the summer of 1926 and many strange details of the case have still not been unravelled beyond all doubt, though most evidence does support the theory of a Carmel tryst. Kindly, affable, entertaining, self-indulgent, taking unashamed pleasure in wealth and luxury, and yet hard-working and in her own way devout, McPherson became an important precursor of one side of the postwar evangelical revival, in addition to being a pioneer for women preachers and evangelical broadcasters.

SOURCES:
Hadden, Jeffrey, and Charles E. Swann. *Prime Time Preachers: The Rising Power of Televangelism.* Reading, MA: Addison Wesley, 1981.
Lewis, Sinclair. *Elmer Gantry* (fiction). NY: Grosset and Dunlap, 1927.
McPherson, Aimee Semple. *The Story of My Life.* Waco, TX: Word Books, 1973.
Starr, Kevin. *Material Dreams: Southern California Through the 1920s.* NY: Oxford University Press, 1990.
Thomas, Lately. *Storming Heaven.* NY: William Morrow, 1970.
———. *The Vanishing Evangelist.* NY: Viking, 1959.

SUGGESTED READING:
Blumhofer, Edith. *Aimee Semple McPherson: Everybody's Sister.* Eerdmans, 1993.
Epstein, Daniel Mark. *Sister Aimee: The Life of Aimee Semple McPherson.* NY: Harcourt Brace, 1993.

Patrick Allitt,
Professor of History, Emory University, Atlanta, Georgia

McQueen, Butterfly (1911–1995).

See McQueen, Thelma.

McQueen, Thelma (1911–1995)

African-American actress best known for her role as Prissy in the movie Gone With the Wind. *Name variations: Thelma "Butterfly" McQueen. Born Thelma McQueen on January 8, 1911, in Tampa, Florida; died in Augusta, Georgia, on December 22, 1995, after suffering critical burns when a kerosene heater caught fire; her father was a stevedore and her mother was a domestic worker (names unknown); graduated New York City College, B.A. in Spanish, 1975; never married; no children.*

Made stage debut at New York City College (1935); made Broadway debut at Biltmore Theater in New York (1937); made movie debut as Prissy in Gone With the Wind *(1939); produced one-woman shows,* Butterfly McQueen and Friends *(1969) and* Prissy in Person *(1976); conferred Rosemary Award (1973); conferred Black Filmmakers Hall of Fame Award (1975); given Emmy Award for "The Seven Wishes of Joanna Peabody" (1979); wrote, produced, and starred in* Tribute to *Mary Bethune (1978); active in the 50th anniversary celebration of the release of* Gone With the Wind *(1989).*

Filmography: Gone With the Wind *(1939);* The Women *(1939);* Affectionately Yours *(1941);* Cabin in the Sky *(1943);* I Dood It *(1943);* Since You Went Away *(1944);* Flame of the Barbary Coast *(1945);* Mildred Pierce *(1945);* Duel in the Sun *(1946);* Killer Diller *(1947);* The Phynx *(1969);* Amazing Grace *(1974);* The Seven Wishes of Joanna Peabody *(1979);* Mosquito Coast *(1986).*

Known to many only for her role as Prissy in *Gone With the Wind*, Thelma "Butterfly" McQueen was an accomplished dancer and stage actress as well as a screen actress. Her humorous depictions of confused, somewhat hysterical maids raised the genre to an art form. Never one to succumb to stereotyping, however, McQueen courageously refused many demeaning roles, often to the detriment of her popularity with producers and film casters.

An only child, Thelma "Butterfly" McQueen was born in Tampa, Florida, on January 8, 1911. Her father was a stevedore on the Tampa docks. Her mother, who worked as a domestic, was born in the 1880s in Augusta, Georgia, in a neighborhood described to writer **Helen Smith** as a place where "whites and blacks lived side by side." In 1916, McQueen's father left the family, and a court decision awarded custody of Thelma to her mother. To provide financial support, Mrs. McQueen sought work in numerous locations from Florida to New Jersey, finally set-tling in Harlem. In the meantime, Thelma had begun to attend school in a Tampa church, but she was soon sent to Augusta, Georgia, while her mother looked for employment elsewhere. In Augusta, McQueen lived at St. Benedict's Convent and attended school there as well. Later, she moved in with an aunt and went to school at Walker Baptist Church. Mrs. McQueen sent for her daughter after she had secured a steady job in Harlem as a cook. When Thelma McQueen arrived in New York, she was enrolled in what was then Public School Number 9 on West 83rd Street. In 1924, her restless mother decided to move again, this time to Babylon, New York, where they remained long enough for McQueen to finish high school.

After graduation, McQueen entered a nursing program at the Lincoln Training School in the Bronx, completing her instruction several years later at Georgia Medical College in Augusta. In 1946, she began taking liberal arts courses in various subjects, including political science, Spanish, drama, dance, and music. McQueen attended City College of Los Angeles, the University of California at Los Angeles, Southern Illinois University, Queens College, and New York City College. In 1975, she would earn a bachelor of arts degree with a major in Spanish from New York City College.

McQueen's introduction to the theater occurred shortly after she had finished high school, when she became a dancer in **Venezuela Jones'** Negro Youth Group. Membership in a dramatic club and a Works Progress Administration (WPA) youth theater project provided McQueen with her first acting opportunities. She began to study dancing, music, and ballet with various instructors including *Janet Collins, *Katherine Dunham, Geoffrey Holder, Venezuela Jones, **Mabel Hunt** and *Adelaide Hall. In 1935, McQueen made her stage debut as part of the Butterfly Ballet in Jones' adaptation of *A Midsummer Night's Dream* performed at New York City College. "Butterfly" became her stage name during this production and remained with her thereafter.

McQueen made her Broadway debut on December 2, 1937, at the Biltmore Theater in New York in the George Abbott production *Brown Sugar*. The play was a murder melodrama set among the blacks of Harlem and acted by an all-black cast. McQueen played the part of Lucille, the first of her many maid roles. It was a minor part—she had only one spoken line. Nonetheless, her talents did not go unnoticed. *The New York Times* critic John Anderson wrote of "the extraordinary artistry of a high-stepping little dusky creature with a piping voice who describes herself as Butterfly McQueen."

> In "Brown Sugar" she is an over-genteel parlor maid in an apartment of iniquitous leanings. All she does is flutter at the door, announce the black thugs with a gesture of grandeur and say, "Step forward, please," as though she were joyfully admitting them through the pearly gates. But she does it like a whole encyclopedia of etiquette. Butterfly has something on the ball.

McQueen's favorable review for her role in *Brown Sugar* prompted Abbott to cast her in further productions, including *Brother Rat* and *What a Life*. Her role as Mary in *What a Life* was again a small one with only a few speaking lines. With her "piping" voice, she was credited with skillfully providing comic relief during the more solemn moments of the production. By now, she had become a regular in the informal Abbott Acting Company and part of what was critically described as an impeccable cast. When Abbott decided to take *What a Life* on the road, he selected McQueen to be a member of the touring company.

ℒawsy, Miss Scarlett, Ah don' know nuthin' 'bout birthin' babies.

—"Butterfly" McQueen as Prissy in *Gone With the Wind*

In the late 1930s, while still working for Abbott, McQueen auditioned for the part of Prissy in the film *Gone With the Wind*. At first, she was told that she was too fat, too dignified, and too old to play the part of a slave girl half her age. Later, producer David O. Selznick had other casting ideas. He preferred seasoned actors, choosing *Hattie McDaniel to play Scarlett O'Hara's Mammy and McQueen, by now a veteran of Broadway, to play Prissy. McQueen succeeded in winning the one role that, according to film writer Ronald Haver, author *Margaret Mitchell wished she herself could have played.

Susan Myrick, representing Mitchell on the set of *Gone With the Wind* and serving as technical advisor, noted in her journal her satisfaction with the choice of McQueen for the role of Prissy. Myrick's image of Prissy was that of a purveyor of subtle humor, and in her eyes, McQueen's Prissy remained loyal to the novel. She reported back to Mitchell in a letter that McQueen was "really good in the role though not so young nor pipe-stemmed-legged as I could wish." In her Macon, Georgia, newspaper column "Straight from Hollywood" Myrick wrote:

> I can hardly wait for the picture to be shown so you can laugh at the scenes where Prissy

does her stuff. Butterfly McQueen is a good actress. . . . Every time Prissy worked in a scene we had a grand time. I know you'll get laughs when you see her.

It was not until McQueen actually arrived in Hollywood that she took the time to reflect upon the role she was about to play. She had serious misgivings about the way Mitchell portrayed blacks in her novel. In particular, McQueen expressed a strong distaste for Mitchell's presentation of Prissy as inane and dull-witted. McQueen was stubbornly resistant to stereotyping, yet she played Prissy with remarkable conviction. Still, she was outspoken about certain aspects of her role: she refused to be filmed eating watermelon and spitting seeds, and she disapproved of the scene in which Scarlett slaps Prissy's face. In another scene, McQueen objected when the script called for Rhett Butler to refer to Prissy as a "simple-minded darky" when Mitchell's words were "simple-minded wench." A debate flared between Myrick and McQueen over the head attire to be worn by the female black servants; McQueen preferred colored bows while Myrick insisted on the more stereotyped "wrapped heads." With Mitchell's approval, Myrick won out in the end. Off the set, McQueen asserted her own brand of individualism as well, joining a delegation of blacks who threatened a protest if restroom segregation were not abolished. She spoke out when all the black actors in the cast were packed into one car, while the white stars were provided with several limousines.

Preparation for filming *Gone With the Wind* required numerous rehearsals and coaching sessions to perfect the Southern accents of the novel's characters. McDaniel and McQueen both spent hours learning Mitchell's black dialect. Years later, Myrick reminisced to reporter Ron Taylor that "the most paradoxical dialect problem was presented by Butterfly McQueen who found the Uncle Remus-style dialect required by the film all but impossible." McQueen later explained to *The New York Times* reporter John Wilson that she "was not allowed to speak in dialect as a child."

Filming of *Gone With the Wind* started in January 1939 under the direction of George Cukor. Almost immediately, Selznick's disapproval of Cukor's script interpolations became apparent—a disagreement that eventually led to Cukor's resignation. Even so, much of what Cukor filmed remained in the final version of the movie, including the famous birthing scene in which Prissy squeals, "Lawsy, Miss Scarlett, Ah don' know nuthin' 'bout birthin' babies." For her terrified and ill-timed confusion, the screenplay called for Prissy to be rebuked by a slap in

the face from Scarlett. Film historian Thomas Cripps recounted an incident that occurred during the first take, when *Vivien Leigh slapped too hard, causing McQueen to step out of character. The exasperated McQueen cried, "I can't do it, she's hurting me. . . . I'm no stunt man; I'm an actress." She insisted that Leigh apologize before shooting could continue. Cukor was a stickler for detail, and wanted Prissy to scream loudly when she was reprimanded by the irate Scarlett. McQueen later recalled to Chris McCarter, "I told them, if you really slap me, I won't scream, but if you pretend to slap me, I'll make the best scream you ever heard." Cukor acquiesced and in the second shooting of the scene Leigh did not actually slap McQueen; instead, a sound man clapped his hands off the set when Leigh swung her hand toward McQueen's face.

Myrick described Cukor's relationship with McQueen during the filming of *Gone With the Wind* in amicable terms. In her journal, Myrick wrote that Cukor became "so tickled at her sometimes he could scarcely direct, and when Butterfly sees George is amused she breaks down

and laughs." Cukor enjoyed exchanging quips with McQueen, though they were often laced with racial overtones. He borrowed lines from the novel, threatening to "sell Butterfly down the river if she didn't get the action just right," or to "use the Simon Legree whip on Prissy." In another scene, Cukor admonished, "Prissy, you better be careful how you try my patience. We had one Prissy here before you came, and I really did sell her South."

Despite the controversy and the love-hate relationship McQueen had with *Gone With the Wind,* she considered her part in the movie to be her best work. The role brought her instant international notoriety and financial security, albeit temporary. She later told film historian Malcolm Vance that the role of Prissy paid well: "I went through a full semester at UCLA on one day's pay."

Three weeks into production of *Gone With the Wind,* Cukor's resignation brought filming operations to a temporary standstill while a replacement was sought. Cukor, who immediately

From the movie Gone with the Wind, *starring Vivien Leigh and Butterfly McQueen.*

resurrected another dormant project, the film version of *Clare Booth Luce's play *The Women*, assigned McQueen the part of Lolla, a maid. Appearing in only one scene, she played opposite *Joan Crawford and **Virginia Grey**. McQueen's recollection of working for Cukor in this project was anything but pleasant. She related to Murray Summers that Cukor's sole purpose in giving her the bit part was to vent his frustrations:

> The hurt I felt in having Mr. Cukor scream at me for some mistake I made, I remember vividly and will take with me to my grave. In the employment of David Selznick, he could not have done such a thing.

After the filming of *Gone With the Wind*, McQueen returned to New York and to the stage. She appeared as Puck in the 1939 production *Swingin' the Dream*, a reinterpretation of *A Midsummer Night's Dream* which premiered on November 29 at the Center Theater and lasted only 13 performances. McQueen was singled out by critic Brooks Atkinson for her "piping-voiced Puck whose travesty is genuinely comic, her clowning as 'ladylike,' representing her peculiar artistry in finest fettle."

During the early 1940s, McQueen appeared in several more films, though never to the acclaim associated with *Gone With the Wind*. In 1941, she was again a maid, this time in *Affectionately Yours*. Playing opposite Hattie McDaniel, she uttered the infamous line, "Who dat say who dat when you say dat." Sometime later, according to film writer Donald Bogle, she remarked, "I never thought I would have to say a line like that. I had imagined that since I am an intelligent woman, I could play any kind of role." Ironically, her performance was considered by some critics to be the best of the film. As Bosley Crowther described it: "The only glints of brightness in the film are contributed by a hair-spring brownie called Butterfly McQueen, as a maid. Her frequent dissolves into tears upon the slightest provocation are ludicrous—and strangely prophetic."

Her next movie, *Cabin in the Sky*, released in 1943, was a monumental showcase for black musical talent. The all-star and entirely black cast included Louis Armstrong, *Ethel Waters, Oscar Polk, Duke Ellington and his orchestra, the Hall Johnson Choir, and **Ruby Dandridge**, the mother of *Dorothy Dandridge. The filming of *Cabin in the Sky* proved troublesome for McQueen, and owing to her thin-skinned nature, she found herself frequently at odds with various personalities in the cast. In particular, she felt beset upon by a sarcastic Eddie "Rochester" Anderson; *Lena Horne regarded her with contempt, and director Vincente Minnelli spoke

critically of her. Writes Chris McCarter, McDaniel advised McQueen to be more tolerant and patient: "You complain too much, you'll never come back to Hollywood."

During the next few years, McQueen appeared in more minor film roles: *I Dood It* (1943), *Mildred Pierce* (1945), *Flame of Barbary Coast* (1945), *Duel in the Sun* (1947) and *Killer Diller* (1948). The 1950s and 1960s were lean years for her. Film producers weren't offering many non-servant roles to black actors, so she returned to the stage. In 1951, she produced her own one-woman show in Carnegie Recital Hall (now Weill Recital Hall). She also played the part of Queen Elizabeth Victoria in the 1956 all-black production *The World's My Oyster*. It was not a critical success; reviewer Arthur Gelb called the plot "dreary," the musical numbers "bumbling," adding, "even . . . potentially funny and charming players such as Butterfly McQueen . . . are victimized by their material." The critics were not much more enthusiastic about a 1957 comedy, *School for Wives*. Reviewer Gelb noted, "Admittedly, the idea was an intriguing one, if just for the trick of putting Butterfly McQueen in the role of the addlepated Georgette. But McQueen, for all her fluttery personal charm, heaving bosom and silver fingernails, is a fish out of water." In the 1964 production *The Athenian Touch*, McQueen was Ora, a maid and cook. The play was reviewed by Lewis Funke as "an exercise in tedium. . . . Butterfly McQueen tries hard to make merry" but was trapped by the material.

In her next few theater appearances, McQueen fared somewhat better. The character Hattie was added to the off-Broadway musical *Curley McDimple*—a role written expressly for McQueen. She premiered the part on May 9, 1968. Her own musical revue, *Butterfly McQueen and Friends,* appeared off-Broadway, premiering August 4, 1969. That same year, she worked again with George Abbott, this time in *Three Men on a Horse*. She played the part of Dora Lee, an elevator operator, drawing favorable reviews. Clive Barnes wrote that he enjoyed "the itsy-little voice, fading over the far horizon of comprehension, that Butterfly McQueen contributed with elevation and style."

The 1970s were sparse as well, but the decade was marked by McQueen's return to film. She appeared in a cameo role in the critical flop *The Phynx* in 1970. In 1974, she was Clarine in *Amazing Grace*, which showcased the aging *Jackie "Moms" Mabley. "The people around [Mabley] never came up to her instep," wrote critic Vincent Canby. "Two black performers associated with an earlier movie age—Stepin Fetchit and Butterfly McQueen—turn up in cameo roles that are unrewarding, both to us and to them."

McQueen continued to find work in musical theater as well during the 1970s. She secured a part in a pre-Broadway production of *The Wiz* in 1975, and in 1976 she presented another one-woman show, *Prissy in Person*. In 1980, Mc-Queen was a member of the touring company of the musical *Showboat*. She returned to the limelight in the later 1980s as a guest of honor at celebrations commemorating the 50th anniversary of the publication of the novel *Gone With the Wind* and the premiere of the film. She appeared at numerous showings of the movie, signing autographs and squealing Prissy's "birthin' babies" line, much to the delight of her admirers.

In between stage and film commitments, McQueen, whose contribution to dramatic television had begun with a part in the 1957 Hallmark Hall of Fame movie "The Green Pastures," made numerous television appearances. She was a guest on several talk shows such as those hosted by Mike Wallace, **Virginia Graham** and Mike Douglas, and on the "Today Show." She had parts in the 1979 children's special "The Seven Wishes of Joanna Peabody," and the 1987 drama "Our World." She also took part in radio shows produced by *Dinah Shore, Jack Benny and Danny Kaye.

Even though her movie roles were temporarily lucrative, McQueen found it necessary to support herself with various odd jobs. She taught at Southern Illinois University, sold toys at Macy's, dispatched taxi cabs in the Bronx, operated a restaurant, and managed a theater group. Much of her savings from her early movie successes financed her one-woman shows and paid fees in two legal suits. In 1968, McQueen won a court decision awarding her damages for unauthorized use of her photographs for promotional purposes by Stone Mountain Park in Georgia. Twelve years later, McQueen filed a $300,000 suit against Greyhound Bus Lines and International Security of Virginia for injuries and damages sustained in a scuffle that erupted after a security guard at a Washington, D.C., bus station accused her of pickpocketing. During the altercation, Mc-Queen had been thrown against a metal bench, injuring her ribs. A court settlement in 1984 awarded her $60,000.

Throughout McQueen's career, community service also occupied much of her time. "Community work comes first. I don't like people to call me a star. I'm not a star. I'm a community worker," she insisted to reporter **Terri Smith**. In

her later years, she enjoyed teaching at neighborhood recreational centers, working with both the young and the elderly. A tireless supporter of animal rights, McQueen became a life member of the Anti-Vivisection Society in the 1940s. She was also active in urban cleanup and beautification projects and environmental protection.

McQueen the actress is best remembered for her high-pitched voice, ready smile, and large expressive eyes. Myrick once described her voice as "higher than soprano . . . about as high as the top note on Kreisler's violin." Author Bogle characterized her as a "surreal creature . . . with a perplexed stare. . . and a quivering tremor of a voice . . . almost otherworldly." McQueen never married, preferring the company of the residents of her Harlem neighborhood and her many cats. A selfless individual, she chose to work for racial equality rather than seek wealth or take advantage of fame. She once described her lifestyle to reporter Helen Smith as "square and straight-laced." McQueen apprised Murray Summers of her refreshingly simple philosophy: "Each of us is born perfect; we acquire habits of hate."

The many honors bestowed upon Thelma McQueen included the Rosemary Award in 1973, the Black Filmmakers Hall of Fame Award in 1975, and an Emmy Award for "The Seven Wishes of Joanna Peabody" in 1979. On December 22, 1995, McQueen died in Augusta, Georgia, after suffering critical burns when a kerosene heater caught fire. She was 84.

SOURCES:

Anderson, John. Review of *Brown Sugar,* in *New York Evening Journal.* December 3, 1937.

Atkinson, Brooks. "Swinging Shakespeare's 'Dream' with Benny Goodman, Louis Armstrong and Maxine Sullivan," in *The New York Times.* November 30, 1939.

Barnes, Clive. "All-star Cast Excels in Betting Tale," in *The New York Times.* October 17, 1969.

Bogle, Donald. *Toms, Coons, Mulattoes, Mammies, and Bucks.* Expanded ed. NY: Continuum, 1989.

Canby, Vincent. Review of *Amazing Grace,* in *The New York Times.* November 2, 1974.

Cripps, Thomas. *Slow Fade to Black.* NY: Oxford University Press, 1977.

Crowther, Bosley. "Offer Rejected," in *The New York Times.* May 24, 1941.

Funke, Lewis. Review of *The Athenian Touch,* in *The New York Times.* January 15, 1964.

Gelb, Arthur. Review of *School for Wives,* in *The New York Times.* June 20, 1975.

———. "*World's My Oyster* is Staged Downtown," in *The New York Times.* August 10, 1956.

Howard, Sidney. "*GWTW*": The Screenplay. Edited by Richard B. Harwell. NY: Macmillan, 1980.

McCarter, Chris. "Actress Had a Strong Love-Hate Relationship with 'Prissy' Role," in *Columbus* [GA] *Ledger-Enquirer.* November 5, 1989.

Mitchell, Margaret. *Gone With the Wind.* NY: Avon, 1973.

——. Letter to Susan Myrick, January 19, 1939. The Margaret Mitchell Marsh Collection, Hargrett Rare Books and Special Collections, University of Georgia Library.

Myrick, Susan. Letters to Margaret Mitchell, January 15, 1939 and February 12, 1939. The Margaret Mitchell Marsh Collection, Hargrett Rare Books and Special Collections, University of Georgia Library.

——. *White Columns in Hollywood: Reports from the "Gone With the Wind" Sets.* Edited by Richard Harwell. Macon, GA: Mercer University Press, 1982.

Smith, Helen C. "Butterfly: Still Flitting at 69," in *Atlanta Constitution.* February 19, 1980.

Smith, Terri K. "She Sounds Like Prissy and She Looks Like Prissy, But Butterfly McQueen Isn't 'Stupid and Backward'," in *Macon* [GA] *Telegraph and News.* April 2, 1984.

Summers, Murray. "Butterfly McQueen Was One of *The Women,* Too," in *Filmograph* 3. November 4, 1973, pp. 7–8.

Taylor, Ron. "Movie Memories Not Gone with Wind," in *Atlanta Journal.* March 25, 1976.

Vance, Malcolm. *Tara Revisited.* NY: Award Books, 1976.

Wilson, John S. "Butterfly McQueen Squeaks Along," in *The New York Times.* July 12, 1978.

SUGGESTED READING:

Bronner, Edwin. *The Encyclopedia of the American Theater, 1900–1975.* NY: A.S. Barnes, 1980.

Haver, Ronald. *David O. Selznick's "Gone With the Wind."* NY: Bonanza, 1986.

Karpf, Juanita. "McQueen, Thelma ('Butterfly')," in *African American Women.* Edited by Dorothy C. Salem. NY: Garland, 1993, pp. 343–344.

——. "Thelma 'Butterfly' McQueen," in *Notable Black American Women.* Edited by Jessie Carney Smith. Detroit, MI: Gale Research, 1992, pp. 710–715.

Knock, Thomas J. "McQueen, Butterfly," in *Black Women in America.* Edited by Darlene Clark Hine. Vol. 2. Brooklyn, NY: Carlson, 1993, pp. 777–779.

Lamparski, Richard. "Butterfly McQueen," in *Whatever Became of . . . ?* 2nd series. NY: Crown, 1968, pp. 96–97.

Leab, Daniel J. *From Sambo to Superspade.* Boston, MA: Houghton Mifflin, 1975.

Leiter, Samuel L. *The Encyclopedia of the New York Stage, 1930–1940.* Westport, CT: Greenwood, 1989.

Schomburg Library, ed. *The Kaiser Index to Black Resources, 1948–86.* Vol 3. Brooklyn, NY: Carlson, 1992, p. 311.

Williams, Michael W., ed. *The African American Encyclopedia.* Vol. 4. NY: Marshall Cavendish, 1993, pp. 1015–1016.

COLLECTIONS:

Clipping file located at Hargrett Rare Books and Special Collections, University of Georgia Library, Athens, Georgia.

Correspondence and papers of Margaret Mitchell located at The Margaret Mitchell Marsh Collection, Hargrett Rare Books and Special Collections, University of Georgia Library.

Juanita Karpf,
Assistant Professor of Music and Women's Studies,
University of Georgia, Athens, Georgia

McRae, Carmen (1920–1994)

Acclaimed African-American jazz artist. Born on April 8, 1920, in Brooklyn, New York; died after a stroke on November 10, 1994, in Beverly Hills, California; daughter of Oscar McRae and Evadne McRae; married Kenny Clarke (a drummer), in the 1940s (divorced 1947); married Ike Isaacs (divorced); no children.

Joined Benny Carter Orchestra (1944); recorded first album (1954); retired from performing (1990); named master of jazz by the National Endowment for the Arts (1993).

Selected recordings: Just a Little Lovin' *(1970);* I'm Coming Home *(1980).*

Carmen McRae was a contemporary of jazz vocalists *Sarah Vaughan and **Shirley Horn**, and equally lauded for the vocal stylings she delivered in her smoky, smart contralto. Born in 1920 in Brooklyn, New York, McRae was an only child who grew up in Harlem. She studied piano from an early age, and her parents hoped she would become a classical concert pianist. McRae had other plans, however, and at age 17 won a talent contest at the famed Apollo Theater that launched her career. She began singing in New York City nightclubs, and met *Billie Holiday,** for whom she wrote "Dream of Life." She would later record an album in tribute to that great singer, *Carmen McRae Sings 'Lover Man' and Other Billie Holiday Songs.*

For a time McRae worked as a secretary by day while singing at night. In 1944, she joined the Benny Carter Orchestra, and her piano skills later

Carmen McRae

got her a job as the intermission pianist at Minton's Playhouse in New York, considered the birthplace of bebop. McRae also sang with Count Basie during this year. She was signed to the Decca label in 1954 and recorded the first of what would eventually be close to two dozen albums on various labels, including *Bittersweet*, *Woman Talk*, *Just a Little Lovin'*, *The Great American Songbook*, *I'm Coming Home*, and *Carmen Sings Monk*. Also in 1954 she won *Down Beat* magazine's new singer award, and the following year tied with *Ella Fitzgerald for best female vocalist in a *Metronome* magazine poll.

McRae sang with her own trio from 1961 to 1969, and over the course of her career recorded duets with *Betty Carter, the hugely successful "Take Five" with Dave Brubeck, a tribute album to Sarah Vaughan, versions of "God Bless the Child," "I've Got you Under My Skin," and even Billy Joel's "New York State of Mind." She also appeared in several movies, including the film version of Jack Kerouac's *The Subterraneans* (1960), *Hotel* (1967), and *Monterey Jazz* (1968). In her later years, she lived in Los Angeles, where she appeared on the occasional television program or in a feature film. In 1990, McRae suffered respiratory failure during a performance at New York City's Blue Note, and never sang in public again. Early in 1994, she was named a "master of jazz" by the National Endowment for the Arts (NEA), which praised her "instinctive feeling for rhythm, her skillful vocal technique, her innovative scat singing, as well as her relaxed manner of presentation." Carmen McRae suffered a stroke in October 1994 and died a month later.

SOURCES:
Current Biography. January 1995.
The Day [New London, CT]. November 12, 1994.
Lees, Gene. *Jazz Lives: 100 Portraits in Jazz.* Firefly, 1992.
Smith, Jessie Carney, ed. *Notable Black American Women.* Detroit, MI: Gale Research, 1992.

Carol Brennan,
Grosse Pointe, Michigan

McTier, Martha (c. 1743–1837)

Irish letter writer. Born Martha Drennan in Ireland around 1743; died in 1837; sister of William Drennan (a member of the United Irishmen); married Samuel McTier (a politician).

Martha McTier was born around 1743 in what is now Northern Ireland. Her brother, William Drennan, was a member of the United Irishmen, an organization inspired by the French Revolution that hoped to separate Ireland from

Britain and institute a united, secular republic. Through her association with him, McTier met many of the leading Irish politicians and reformers of the day. Her political connections were further extended through her marriage to Samuel McTier, president of the First Belfast Society of United Irishmen. McTier maintained an extensive correspondence, and her political commentary has proven valuable to historians studying Irish and British politics in the turbulent period around the turn of the 19th century. She was also an avid gambler who held her own with men, writing, "I play as well as any of them, and when I lose too much, I will quit it."

SOURCES:
Newmann, Kate, comp. *Dictionary of Ulster Biography.* The Institute of Irish Studies, the Queen's University of Belfast, 1993.

Grant Eldridge,
freelance writer, Pontiac, Michigan

Mdluli, Labotsibeni (c. 1858–1925).

See Labotsibeni Gwamile LaMdluli.

Mead, Andrea (b. 1932).

See Lawrence, Andrea Mead.

Mead, Elizabeth Storrs (1832–1917)

American educator who was the first president of Mt. Holyoke College. Born Elizabeth Storrs Billings on May 21, 1832, in Conway, Massachusetts; died on March 25, 1917, in Coconut Grove, Florida; daughter of Charles Eugene Billings and Sally Williston (Storrs) Billings; attended Ipswich Female Seminary; married Hiram Mead (a minister and professor), on August 5, 1858 (died 1881); children: Alice Edwards Mead; George Herbert Mead.

Moved to New York (1837); ran a girls' school in Massachusetts (c. 1852); moved to Ohio (1869); named president of newly created Mt. Holyoke College (1890); retired (1901).

Elizabeth Storrs Mead was the first president of Mt. Holyoke College, one of New England's "Seven Sisters" string of women's colleges established in the 19th century to provide a solid liberal arts education for American women. She is credited with laying the foundation upon which much of Mt. Holyoke's modern reputation as a prestigious educational institution rests. Born in 1832 into an old New England family, Mead and her twin sister **Harriet Billings** were the last of 11 Billings children. Her father was a colonel who sat on the Massachusetts General Court, and her mother was related to key leaders of the New England Congregationalist faith. The family moved to Trenton, New York, in 1837, and then to Andover, Massachusetts. Elizabeth Mead was educated at the Ipswich Female Seminary and taught at Northampton High School for a year before becoming co-director, with her eldest sister **Jerusha Roberts**, of a school for girls in Andover. She left this line of work when she married Hiram Mead, a minister and professor, in 1858.

With her husband, Elizabeth Mead relocated to South Hadley, Massachusetts, where Hiram sat on the board of Mt. Holyoke Seminary. From there, they moved to Oberlin College in Ohio for several years, where Elizabeth taught part time. Widowed in 1881, she returned with her two children to Andover around 1883 and served as assistant principal of the Abbott Academy there. It was this combination of teaching and administrative experience which led to her selection as the first president of Mt. Holyoke Seminary and College. The school had been founded by *Mary Lyon as Mt. Holyoke Seminary in 1837, and was one of the first educational institutions in America open to women of all economic means. In 1890 it was chartered as a college, with authority to grant degrees, and renamed Mt. Holyoke Seminary and College. Mead was chosen that year as president of the institution as much for her background in education as for her sophistication and people skills. She quickly established herself as an ally of the college faculty—revoking the rule, for instance, that required teachers to share in housekeeping chores. She also raised salaries, revamped the students' social code to reflect greater trust in them, and created a music department and sports teams. In 1893, after receiving a solely collegiate charter, the school stopped offering its seminary course and became Mt. Holyoke College.

Mead and her plans for the school suffered a great setback when the main building of Mt. Holyoke was destroyed by fire in 1896, but she began a fund-raising campaign immediately and used the opportunity to create a better campus with smaller, "cottage-plan" dormitories. She also implemented other progressive actions that brought women's higher education on par with men's during this era, such as creating a gymnasium facility, a student government, the establishment of professor chairs at the college, and a variety of degree programs. During Mead's decade as president, Mt. Holyoke's student body increased from 272 to 600. She was succeeded by *Mary E. Woolley upon her retirement in 1901. Mead lived her remaining years in Oberlin; she died in Coconut Grove, Florida, in 1917.

SOURCES:
James, Edward T., ed. *Notable American Women, 1607–1950.* Cambridge, MA: The Belknap Press of Harvard University Press, 1971.
Woman: Her Position, Influence, and Achievement Throughout the Civilized World. Springfield, MA: King-Richardson Co., 1900.

Carol Brennan,
Grosse Pointe, Michigan

Mead, Kate Campbell (1867–1941).

See Hurd-Mead, Kate Campbell.

Mead, Lucia Ames (1856–1936)

American writer and lecturer who promoted reform causes, including women's suffrage and world peace.

Name variations: Lucy True Ames; Lucia Ames. Pronunciation: Meed. Born Lucy Jane Ames on May 5, 1856, in Boscawen, New Hampshire; died in Boston, Massachusetts, of injuries suffered in a fall, November 1, 1936; daughter of Nathan Plummer Ames (a farmer) and Elvira (Coffin) Ames; aunt of *Mary Ware Dennett (1872–1947); attended public and private schools in Illinois and Massachusetts, graduated from Salem Normal School; married Edwin Doak Mead (a writer and reformer), on September 29, 1898.

Mother died (1861), moved near Chicago; father died (1870), moved to Boston to live with brother Charles; began career as piano teacher (1875); offered courses for women on literature, history, and philosophy (1886); published novel, Memoirs of a Millionaire (1889); attended first peace conference, Lake Mohonk Conference on International Arbitration (1897); elected president of Massachusetts Woman Suffrage Association (1903–09); selected as peace committee chair, National American Woman Suffrage Association (1904) and National Council of Women (1905); wrote Patriotism and the New Internationalism (1906) and Swords and Ploughshares (1912); named national secretary, Woman's Peace Party (1915–18); named national secretary, U.S. branch of Women's International League for Peace and Freedom (1919–21); lectured for National Council for the Prevention of War (1922–33); wrote Law or War (1928).

In 1897, Lucia True Ames traveled from her home in Boston to the Catskill Mountains of New York, site of the third annual Lake Mohonk Conference on International Arbitration. The writer and reform activist had never attended a major peace conference before, but meeting organizers prevailed upon her to deliver an address. Ames' talk focused on the role that women, as mothers and teachers, could play in promoting peace. While instructing children, they should discuss the negative economic consequences of warfare, portray patriotism as not simply "pride in our country but . . . service to our country," and encourage toleration of all peoples and diverse beliefs. In addition, Ames urged peace advocates to start employing imaginative techniques, such as placing advertisements in street cars, to bring their message before a larger number of Americans of all classes.

This address by Lucia Ames, a talented writer and speaker who became a leader of the U.S. peace movement within a few years of her first visit to Lake Mohonk, foreshadowed her subsequent peace activism in two ways. First, she focused on the potential role of women within the movement. Second, she argued for a campaign of public education. Though she contributed to the cause in many ways during the next 40 years, her attempts to involve women's groups and individual women in the peace crusade, and her personal efforts to publicize antiwar sentiment among non-elites, render her among the most important American peace activists of the late 19th and early 20th centuries.

Born in Boscawen, New Hampshire, in 1856, Lucy Jane Ames was the second daughter and third child of **Elvira Coffin Ames** and Nathan Plummer Ames. Her father, a farmer, served as a colonel in the New Hampshire Militia during the Civil War. After the death of his wife in 1861, Nathan Ames moved his family near Chicago, where Lucy attended both public and private schools. In 1870, following her father's death, she returned East to live with her older brother Charles, a recent college graduate who worked for a publishing house. Together with their maternal uncle Charles Carleton Coffin, the well-known war correspondent, brother Charles provided an excellent informal education for his inquisitive sister which served to supplement her training at Salem High School in Massachusetts, from which she graduated. Lucy devoted tremendous energy to examining literature, history, theology, and philosophy, among other subjects, often setting rigid goals for completing her studies.

Shortly after moving to Massachusetts, Lucy changed her name to Lucia True Ames, undoubtedly in anticipation of becoming a published author. Beginning in the mid-1870s, she worked as a piano teacher, an occupation which allowed her to avoid the life of dependency most women of the era faced. She wrote some articles for newspapers and journals while in her 20s, and her first books—one a manual for Sunday School teachers and the other a reform novel—appeared in 1888 and 1889 (she ultimately wrote four others, including three on peace). Her earliest scholarly interests were primarily in theology and philosophy. A devout Congregationalist who later became a Unitarian, Lucia recognized that her "whole instinct [was] for religion . . . [and her] strongest, deepest feeling religious." This led to a thorough study of philosophy, and her studying with one of the nation's leading philosophers and educators, William Torrey Harris, who later served as U.S. Commissioner of Education. Ames attended the Concord Summer School of Philosophy, run by Harris after 1879, and arranged an annual "Saturday Club" of friends who met regularly to hear Harris' teachings. When Harris was away, Lucia Ames directed the sessions, a practice which ultimately evolved in 1886 into Ames offering her own classes to women on "Nineteenth-Century Thought."

By the early 1890s, Ames had authored a number of pamphlets and journal articles favoring a host of reform causes. She called for the creation of an educational system that would provide adequate training for recent immigrants, blacks, and other underprivileged Americans. She attacked municipal government corruption and irresponsibility, the greed of the large corporations, and "extravagant self-indulgence" among the wealthy. She also delivered lectures on these subjects, and others, to church congregations, literary societies, and women's clubs, earning a reputation in the Boston area as a fine public speaker.

In 1898, she married reformer Edwin Doak Mead, editor of the *New England Magazine*. Over the next few years, the commitment of the Meads to the peace movement gradually intensified, fueled initially by the couple's outrage over American involvement in the war with Spain. After the fighting with Spain ended, Lucia Mead joined the Anti-Imperialist League. She wrote and lectured in opposition to America's Philippine policy, and was among the first three women named as vice-presidents of the organization in 1904.

Lucia Mead also began attending international peace congresses in Europe. A 1901 trip to the Glasgow Universal Peace Congress brought her for the first time into direct contact with leading European pacifists, and provided the final push which caused the Meads to devote their lives to the movement. Between 1902 and the outbreak of World War I, Lucia Mead emerged as arguably the most prominent female peace activist in the nation. She served on the American Peace Society's board of directors, attended every Lake Mohonk Conference between 1902 and 1916, and traveled as a delegate to dozens of national and international peace congresses. Like most peace advocates of the period, she argued for the establishment of international peacekeeping mechanisms such as arbitration treaties, a world legislature, and a world court. But it was not her ideas on peace and war that rendered Lucia Mead an extraordinary peace activist. It was her actions. No American pacifist of the immediate pre-World War I movement came close to equalling Mead's efforts to recruit women into the crusade, or to publicize the goals of pacifists among the general population.

> The teacher who has the spirit of internationalism is alone fitted to lead today.
>
> —Lucia Ames Mead

After 1902, Mead spoke to thousands of audiences, about three out of four of which were women's groups or school assemblies. Her goal, as she often told her pacifist colleagues, was to awaken "the great body of hitherto silent women," to encourage them to learn about the dangers of war and the promise of international cooperation. Mead undertook a concerted effort to interest the major women's organizations in peace activism. By 1905, she chaired the peace committees of both the National American Woman Suffrage Association (NAWSA) and the National Council of Women (NCW). At each organization's annual convention, she urged prominent female activists in attendance to do more to promote peace. Mead, who served as president of the Massachusetts Woman Suffrage Association from 1903 to 1909, called on suffragists to closely link the fight for the ballot with the pacifist crusade. "Suffragists may work for the abolition of war," she observed, "not merely because it is a great evil, but because whenever militarism obtains, women's influence decreases." Chairing the peace committees also afforded her a small budget to distribute pamphlets to women, or, as she did in 1910, send copies of two of her pamphlets to every congressional representative.

Lucia Mead never achieved her goal of inaugurating a massive women's war against war, but her efforts were notable. The same can be said of her attempts to reach all non-elites, including men. During the first three decades of the 20th century, she became "the most successful newspaper letter writer in the United States," as pacifist Frederick J. Libby noted. She turned out scores of short articles and letters each year in hundreds of publications. She usually produced two pieces a week, then sent them off to varied publications, usually in different locales so that the same letter could appear in a number of newspapers and journals.

To supplement her literary efforts, Lucia Mead also undertook extensive annual lecture tours. As many contemporaries noted, she was a fine public speaker whose ability could shock audiences. *Jane Addams believed that "no one [of her day] in the United States has done more through that most valuable method of instruction, direct speech, to educate the public in the history of the peace movement, nor has any one been more successful in securing new adherents" to the cause. The Boston activist usually made a five- or six-week lecture tour in January and February, then embarked on another trip in the fall. All told, she would speak to a hundred or so audiences on "The End of International Dueling," "Women's Work for Peace," "The New Internationalism," and similar topics.

When World War I broke out in the summer of 1915, Lucia Mead helped found the Woman's Peace Party. Named national secretary of the group, she helped devise policy as a member of the executive board throughout the war, lectured under the auspices of the group, wrote its annual reports, and generally played a crucial leadership role within the first significant national women's peace organization in American history. Before the American war declaration in 1917, Mead's speeches and writings focused on minimizing armament and other military expenditures, and resisting attempts to begin compulsory military training for all young men. After April 1917, she shifted her focus to making sure conscription ended with the cessation of hostilities, defending conscientious objectors, minimizing intolerance of dissenters during war, calling for a just war settlement, and most important, supporting the idea of a postwar league of nations.

In April 1919, Lucia Mead joined a large American contingent who attended the international women's peace congress in Zurich, where the Women's International League for Peace and Freedom was born. During the 1920s, often speaking under the auspices of the National Council for Prevention of War, she brushed aside repeated attacks upon her by the American Legion, Daughters of the American Revolution, and other intolerant groups. She challenged her adversaries to radio debates to take advantage of this new propaganda opportunity. Lucia Mead, one of only a few American women who made the "short list" of great activists considered for the

Nobel Peace Prize, continued to write extensively on peace and other issues until the middle 1930s.

In late October 1936, while Mead waited to board a Boston subway, a crowd of schoolchildren knocked her from the platform by accident. The fall broke her hip, and "ill more from the shock than from the fracture," she died a few days later. Her passing deprived the peace movement of an important transitional figure whose career spanned the period from the Spanish-American War to the year of Germany's occupation of the Rhineland. Though her colleagues were slow to respond to the call for a campaign of education among non-elites and women, the peace movement finally moved in this direction during the 1920s.

SOURCES:

Craig, John M. *Lucia Ames Mead and the American Peace Movement.* Lewiston, NY: Edwin Mellen Press, 1990.

Patterson, David S. *Toward a Warless World: The Travail of the American Peace Movement, 1887–1914.* Bloomington, Indiana: Indiana University Press, 1976.

SUGGESTED READING:

Alonso, Harriet Hyman. *Peace as a Women's Issue: A History of the U.S. Movement for World Peace and Women's Rights.* Syracuse, NY: Syracuse University Press, 1993.

Crapol, Edward P., ed. *Women and American Foreign Policy: Lobbyists, Critics, and Insiders.* Wilmington, DE: Scholarly Resources, 1992.

COLLECTIONS:

Papers of Lucia Ames Mead, Swarthmore College Peace Collection, Swarthmore, Pennsylvania.

John M. Craig,
Professor of History, Slippery Rock University, Slippery Rock, Pennsylvania, author of *Lucia Ames Mead and the American Peace Movement* and numerous articles on activist American women

Mead, Margaret (1901–1978)

The most prominent anthropologist in the world.
Born Margaret Mead on December 16, 1901, in Philadelphia, Pennsylvania; died in New York City on November 15, 1978; daughter of Edward Sherwood Mead (an economist) and Emily Fogg Mead (a sociologist); attended DePauw University, 1919–20; Barnard College, 1920–23, A.B., 1923; M.A., Columbia, 1924; Ph.D., Columbia, 1929; married Luther Sheeleigh Cressman (an Episcopal priest; later sociologist, archeologist), on September 3, 1923 (divorced 1928); married Reo Franklin Fortune (an anthropologist), on October 8, 1928 (divorced 1935); married Gregory Bateson (an anthropologist), on March 13, 1936 (divorced 1950); children (third marriage): Mary Catherine Bateson (b. 1939, an anthropologist).

Appointed assistant curator of ethnology, American Museum of Natural History (1926), associate cu-

rator (1942), curator (1964), curator emeritus (1969); appointed adjunct professor of anthropology, Columbia (1954–78); named professor of anthropology and chair, division of social sciences, Fordham University (Lincoln Center campus, 1968–70); named visiting lecturer, department of psychiatry, school of medicine, University of Cincinnati (1957–58); was visiting lecturer, Menninger Foundation, Topeka, Kansas (1959).

Selected writings: Inquiry into the Question of Cultural Stability in Polynesia (Columbia University Contributions to Anthropology Series, 1928); Coming of Age in Samoa: A Psychological Study of Primitive Youth for Western Civilization (Morrow, 1928); Growing Up in New Guinea: A Comparative Study of Primitive Education (Morrow, 1930); Social Organization of Manu'a (Bernice P. Bishop Bulletin #76, Honolulu, 1930); The Changing Culture of an Indian Tribe (Columbia University Press, 1932); "Kinship in the Admiralty Islands," in Anthropological Papers of the American Museum of Natural History (New York, 1934); Sex and Temperament in Three Primitive Societies (Morrow, 1935); From the South Seas: Studies of Adolescence and Sex in Primitive Societies (Morrow, 1935); (editor) Cooperation and Competition among Primitive Peoples (McGraw-Hill, 1937); And Keep Your Powder Dry: An Anthropologist Looks at America (Morrow, 1942); (with Gregory Bateson) Balinese Character: A Photographic Analysis (Special Publications of the New York Academy of Sciences #2, 1942); Male and Female: A Study of the Sexes in the Changing World (Morrow, 1949); Soviet Attitudes Toward Authority: An Interdisciplinary Approach to Problems of Soviet Character (Rand Corporation & McGraw-Hill, 1951); (with Frances Cooke Macgregor) Growth and Culture: A Photographic Study of Balinese Childhood (Putnam, 1951); The School in American Culture (Harvard University Press, 1951); (editor) Cultural Patterns and Technical Change: A Manual Prepared by the World Federation for Mental Health (UNESCO, 1953); (editor, with Heinz von Foerster and Hans Lucas Teuber) Cybernetics: Circular Causal and Feedback Mechanisms in Biological and Social Systems (Josiah Macy, Jr. Foundation, 1953); (editor, with Nicolas Calas) Primitive Heritage: An Anthropological Anthology (Random House, 1953); (editor, with Rhoda Métraux) The Study of Culture at a Distance (University of Chicago Press, 1953); (editor, with Rhoda Métraux) Themes in French Culture: A Preface to a Study of the French Community (Stanford University Press, 1954); (editor, with Martha Wolfenstein) Childhood in Contemporary Cultures (University of Chicago Press, 1955); New Lives for Old: Cultural Transformation—Manus 1928–1953 (Morrow, 1956); (editor) An Anthropologist at Work:

Writings of Ruth Benedict *(Houghton Mifflin, 1959)*; People and Places *(World, 1959)*; *(editor, with Ruth L. Bunzel)* The Golden Age of American Anthropology *(Braziller, 1950)*; *(with Gregory Bateson)* Balinese Character: A Photographic Analysis *(New York Academy of Sciences, 1962)*; Continuities in Cultural Evolution *(Yale University Press, 1964)*; Anthropology, A Human Science: Selected Papers, 1939–1960 *(Van Nostrand, 1964)*; Anthropologists and What They Do *(Watts, 1965)*; *(with Ken Heyman)* Family *(Macmillan, 1965)*; *(editor, with Frances B. Kaplan)* American Women: The Report of the President's Commission on the Status of Women and Other Publications of the Commission *(Scribner, 1965)*; *(with Muriel Brown)* The Wagon and the Star: A Study of American Community Initiative *(Rand McNally, 1966)*; *(with Paul Byers)* The Small Conference: A Innovation in Communication *(Mouton, 1968)*; *(editor, with Theodosius Dobzhansky, Ethel Tobach, and Robert E. Light)* Science and the Concept of Race *(Columbia University Press, 1968)*; Culture and Commitment: A Study of the Generation Gap *(Natural History Press & Doubleday, 1970)*; *(with James Baldwin)* A Rap on Race *(Lippincott, 1971)*; *(editor, with J. Edward Carothers, Daniel D. MacCracken, and Roger L. Shinn)* To Love or to Perish: The Technological Crisis and the Churches *(Friendship Press, 1972)*; Blackberry Winter: My Earlier Years *(Morrow, 1972)*; Twentieth Century Faith: Hope and Survival *(Harper & Row, 1972)*; Ruth Benedict *(Columbia University Press, 1974)*; *(with Rhoda Métraux)* A Way of Seeing *(Morrow, 1974)*; World Enough: Rethinking the Future *(Little, Brown, 1975)*; Letters from the Field 1925–1975 *(Harper & Row, 1978)*; *(with Rhoda Métraux)* An Interview with Santa Claus *(Walker, 1978)*; *(with Rhoda Métraux)* Aspects of the Present *(Morrow, 1980)*.

On August 31, 1925, at the lush port of Pago Pago, Samoa, a somewhat fragile-looking woman, age 23, embarked from a steamer. She was just over five feet tall, weighed under 100 pounds, and had never been west of the Mississippi. As the U.S. Pacific fleet was in port, she saw battleships filling the harbor. "Airplanes scream overhead," she wrote home; "the band of some ship is constantly playing ragtime." Her baggage: a typewriter, a change of clothes, and a small metal strongbox to hold her papers and notes. Her occupation: anthropologist.

For six weeks, Margaret Mead lived in a ramshackle hotel that was the setting for W. Somerset Maugham's short story "Rain." As she began her research, the study of adolescence among the Polynesians, she was held suspect by other whites, experienced a hurricane, and contacted a case of pinkeye that afflicted her years afterwards. When a visiting chief from British Samoa sought her favors, she convinced him that she lacked his rank and was therefore unworthy of him. Yet Mead persevered, soon moving to the island of Ta'u, where—except for the family of a naval pharmacist—she was the only white person. She believed she was part of what she called a "giant rescue operation," the study of primitive cultures before they perished. Remaining there nine months, in some ways she lived the life of a Samoan woman, eating dried fish and helping care for their ailing children. In the process, she interviewed 68 Samoan females between the ages of 8 and 20, though most of her data came from 25 who trooped daily into the medical station office. During this time, she picked up elements of the language from a nurse.

Five years afterwards, the results of the young anthropologist's research were published. *Coming of Age in Samoa* (1928) by Margaret Mead was a bestseller, launching its author into worldwide fame. The book portrayed Samoa as a veritable Eden, due in large extent to the lack of sexual inhibitions among its youth. At the end of her first chapter, "A Day in Samoa," she wrote of young couples who would dance in the moonlight, then "detach themselves and wander away among the trees. Sometimes sleep will not descend upon the village until long past midnight; then at least there is only the mellow thunder of the reef and the whisper of lovers, as the village rests until dawn." Asserting that the Samoan maidens sought to acquire as many lovers as possible before settling down to family life, she found both sexes possessing no notion of "romantic love as it occurs in our civilization, inextirpably bound up with ideas of monogamy, exclusiveness, jealousy and undeviating fidelity."

Philosopher Bertrand Russell, sexologist Havelock Ellis, anthropologist Bronislaw Malinowski, and critic H.L. Mencken all praised her work. The public was enamored as well. Here was a society marked by overwhelming ease and casualness, in which conflict was minimal, family ties were loose, and guilt did not exist. Rather than the nuclear family, "a larger family community, in which there are several adult men and women, seems to insure the child against the development of the crippling attitudes which have been labeled Oedipus complexes, Electra complexes, and so on." In the words of Mead biographer **Jane Howard**, Mead had portrayed "a romantic paradise of a place where no one ever had acne or blushed from embarrassment or squirmed from frustration." If only, many readers extrapolated, Americans would abandon their notions of

Margaret
Mead

fidelity, competition, and the tight nuclear family in favor of the more casual Samoan life, problems caused by shame and neurosis would not exist. By the 1940s, people were quipping:

> Margaret Mead, Margaret Mead,
> Helps to Fill our country's need,
> Thinks our culture is much lower
> Than the one in Samoa.

From that point, Mead built upon her celebrity status until at last she became a national oracle, pronouncing on all topics from Soviet child-rearing to Anglican liturgy. In a lifetime of 77 years, she wrote close to 30 books, edited a dozen more, contributed hundreds of articles, helped lead major professional associations, and was one of the most sought-after lecturers in the nation. Always she conveyed a tone of boundless optimism. To Margaret Mead, all problems were solvable, all guilt a waste of time. Brilliant, naive, enchanting, obstreperous, demanding, forgiving, Margaret Mead encompassed a universe.

Mead was born on December 16, 1901, the eldest of five children, in Philadelphia. Her father Edward Sherwood Mead was a professor of economics at the Wharton School of the University of Pennsylvania and an expert on corporate finance. Her mother **Emily Fogg Mead** was a suffragist, reformer, and sociologist whose doctorate focused on Italian immigrant families. Yet Mead always found **Martha Ramsay Mead**, her maternal grandmother, the most decisive influence on her life. A former high school principal, Martha tutored Margaret through adolescence, once assigning her the task, at age eight, of observing the speech patterns of her younger sisters.

Mead's parents raised their children in various towns in New Jersey and Bucks County, Pennsylvania, from which her father commuted to work. As Edward was helping to establish extension branches of the university through the state, the family moved frequently. Hammonton, Holicong, Doylestown, Buckingham, Landsdowne—all were temporarily her home. By the time she was 11, Margaret had lived in 60 houses and eaten food prepared by 107 cooks. "In a sense," she said, "we were like a family of refugees, always at odds with and well in advance of the local customs." Little wonder Margaret grew up bright, precocious, restless, and, above all, impatient.

Graduating from Doylestown High School, in 1919 she enrolled in DePauw University, in Greencastle, Indiana. Here the precocious Mead, incredibly sophisticated in some ways and quite awkward in others, was a social outcast. After her freshman year, she transferred to Barnard College, from which she graduated in 1923. In the urban, highly sophisticated environment of New York City, Mead thrived. Already impressing her peers by her intelligence and maturity, she was remembered by a classmate as appearing "so much older than the rest of us." After Barnard, she attended Columbia University, from which she received her M.A. in psychology.

At Columbia, two anthropologists changed the course of Mead's life. First was Franz Boaz, who already possessed an international reputation and whose paternalism led students to call him "Papa Franz." Very much the iconoclast, Boaz stressed the autonomy of culture and language at a time when race was seen as the ultimate determinant. The so-called "savage," he said, was certainly not mentally inferior to the Westerner. The second influence, ***Ruth Benedict**, was Boaz's earliest disciple as well as his doctoral student and teaching assistant. Mead quickly absorbed Benedict's contagious enthusiasm over cultural relativity while becoming, as she later said, "the child Ruth never had."

In September 1923, Mead married Luther Sheeleigh Cressman, a graduate student in soci-

ology who had just received his divinity degree at New York's General Theological Seminary. The couple had been secretly engaged from the time she was 16. Within two years, however, they drifted apart. Mead had a brief affair with Edward Sapir, a noted anthropologist and linguist who implored her to divorce Cressman and marry him.

By 1925, Mead had obtained a National Research Council fellowship, received an appointment at the ***Bernice Pauahi Bishop** Museum in Honolulu, and traveled to Samoa. In seeking to prove Boaz's contention that adolescent behavior was more cultural than biological, she asked: "Are the disturbances which vex our adolescents due to the nature of adolescence itself or to civilization? Under different circumstances does adolescence present a different picture?" In part, Boaz recommended Polynesia to her because she would not need many languages, in part because a steamer arrived every three weeks.

Mead had left Cressman with the comforting words that she would never leave him—unless, that is, she found somebody else. The "somebody else" was Reo Franklin Fortune, a 24-year-old New Zealander heading for graduate studies at Cambridge. Mead and Fortune met on board the *Chitral* en route to Europe after Mead's stay in Samoa. A reunion of Margaret and husband Luther in Marseilles, with Reo then joining them in Paris, led to awkwardness all around, but Mead soon found solace in her work. Once back in New York, she became assistant curator of ethnology at the American Museum of Natural History, beginning an association that lasted until her death.

In October 1928, having divorced Cressman, Mead married Fortune in Auckland, New Zealand. The couple immediately went to the central island of the Great Admiralty archipelago, Manus, settling in a village called Peri. Here they sought to study the minds of primitive children. In some ways, life was a bit bizarre, with Mead becoming an arbiter in apparently age-old village feuds. "You write down every single transaction and we won't need to quarrel any more," the inhabitants told her. Mead and Fortune constructed a house with several exits so that mothers-in-law could depart as sons-in-law entered. During her stay, Mead fractured her foot and suffered from insomnia. The product of her research, *Growing Up in New Guinea: A Comparative Study of Primitive Education* (1930), caused less stir than the Samoa work but was well received. In this book, she argued that the gap between the "civilized" mind and the "primitive" one had been greatly exaggerated; human nature was essentially malleable.

Once fieldwork was accomplished, the couple settled in New York, where Mead found her book on Samoan adolescence catapulting her to fame. In the summer of 1930, they went to Nebraska, there to study the Omaha Indians, whom—to protect their identity—Mead called the "Antlers." Noting the degree to which Omaha culture had shrunk markedly from a richer past, Mead and Fortune felt devastated.

A year later, they were in New Guinea, where their carriers unceremoniously dropped them off at a village called Alitoa. Yet, being left stranded proved to be a blessing in disguise, for they found the inhabitants there ideal subjects of study. Certainly there was variety. Mead found one group, mountain people whom she and Fortune named the Arapesh, almost totally pacifist. By contrast, another tribe, the Mundugumor, was so violent that "small children of eleven and twelve had all taken part in cannibal feasts." People committed suicide by surrendering to neighbors who would eat their flesh. By the end of 1932, Mead's marriage was in trouble. She found Fortune "a crank"; Fortune reciprocated by referring to her as a "psychopathological case."

On Christmas Day 1932, Mead's life was again transformed. At a party at Ambunti, she met British ethnologist Gregory Bateson, of St. John's College, Cambridge, who was in New Guinea researching the Iatmul people of the Sepic River area. Soon Mead and Bateson were falling in love. For the rest of their time in the field, the trio constituted a *mélange à trois*. As Bateson later said, "All three of us together were pretty psychotic." Mead once reminisced, "It was the closest I've ever come to madness." Indeed, their relationship reminded Mead of the lake-dwelling Tchambuli, a group they were studying. At one point, life was physically precarious as well. While staying with the Washkuk tribe, the three anthropologists expected a raid from a hostile group. Fortune had to protect the trio by brandishing a revolver as all took turns sleeping on the floor.

When the New Guinea project ended, all three returned to their respective homelands—Bateson to Britain, Fortune to New Zealand, and Mead to Manhattan. In October 1933, *The New York Times* greeted Mead's return with the headline: NEW GUINEA SONGS ARE SOLD FOR A PIG. It continued, "Woman Explorer, Back, Says Old Times Bring High Prices Among the Aborigines—THEY KILL GIRL BABIES—But Spare Enough to Do All Their Work—

'Sweetest' of People, Even So." She was quoted as saying: "The women shave their heads and bear burdens, while the men decorate their long hair with peacock feathers and strut around like lords." Mead added to the exotic aura about her when her *Sex and Temperament in Three Primitive Societies* (1935) was published. She told of how the Mundugumor took "frank, sadistic enjoyment of other people's discomfiture" and of how their conversations on sex had the character of "playing ball with hand grenades." Soon Mead was teaching at Columbia's extension division and was frequently on the lecture circuit.

Her's was the most complex life imaginable.

—Jane Howard

In 1935, Mead divorced Fortune and, in March 1936, married Bateson. After the wedding in Singapore, the couple worked for two years in Bali. Here they pioneered in using photography as a research tool, taking some 28,000 stills in the process. While living on the Sepik River, they built a house without walls so that nothing around them would take place unobserved. Mead was less than enamored with their research subjects, at one time writing psychologist John Dollard:

> Not an ounce of free intelligence or free libido in the whole culture. The whole culture is arranged like a sling, and most of the time the people swing into it, their knees barely gripping, working alone, without either punch or kick. . . . Anything new or strange leads to total panic.

Without trances, she said, the Balinese would lead dreary lives. After further research with a New Guinea tribe, the Iatmul, the couple returned to New York City.

In December 1939, the 38-year-old Mead gave birth to **Mary Catherine Bateson**, her first and only child. Few births ever received so much attention. The event, writes Mead biographer Jane Howard, bore the air of a Nativity project. The delivery was delayed until a friend who was filming the event could rush to her car for flashbulbs. The prominent pediatrician Benjamin Spock was on hand, as he later put it, "to certify the baby's normalcy."

If Mead's life had been somewhat unsettled to this point, the war years were close to anarchy. World War II separated Mead and Bateson much of the time. "Cathy" was left with close friends in New York, who supplied the role of extended family. Mead's greatest wartime activity was with the National Research Council's Committee on Food Habits, a branch of the National Academy of Sciences' National Research Council. This work frequently took her to Washington. From this body evolved the Committee on Living Habits, the National and World Federations of Mental Health, and, after the war, the United Nations Economic, Social, and Cultural Organization (UNESCO).

In the summer of 1943, the Office of War Information sent Mead to England. Her task: to study the budding relationships between young British women and newly arrived American GIs. In 1944, Mead and Ruth Benedict launched the Institute for International Studies, financed by the Office of Naval Research. The aim of the body was nothing if not cosmic: to "develop a series of systematic undertakings of the great contemporary cultures so that the values of each may be orchestrated in a world built new," in short an examination of national character. How does national character, the task force asked, determine the behavior of enemies, allies, and the Americans themselves? The project involved some 120 social scientists, representing 16 nationalities and 14 disciplines.

In October 1950, Mead and Bateson divorced. Bateson later said of Mead:

> It was almost a principle of pure energy. I couldn't keep up, and she couldn't stop. She was like a tugboat. She could sit down and write three thousand words by eleven o'-clock in the morning, and spend the rest of the day working at the museum.

For decades, Mead held down posts at the Museum of Natural History while continuing to teach at Columbia and Fordham. From her tower office in the museum, she supervised 15 assistants. Frequently, she held visiting academic and consulting posts. When, in 1968, she taught a course at Yale, 600 students signed up, the largest enrollment in the university's history. Until the end of her life, she was a globetrotter par excellence. Never known for possessing a diminutive ego, she once responded to a Toronto clerk who told her a plane was full: "But I'm Margaret Mead!"

In 1953, Mead returned to Peri, there to see what changes the war had made. She was accompanied by budding anthropologists Theodore Schwartz and **Lenona Shargo**. "It is all rather like a family gathering," she said, "with cousins one hasn't seen for twenty-five years." Believing that the local Manus tribe had made a 4,000-year leap, she entitled her study *New Lives for Old* (1956).

All this time Mead remained a prolific writer, one who at times could produce a book in less than a month. *And Keep Your Powder Dry: An Anthropologist Looks at America* (1942) examined American character in light of seven "primitive" cultures she had studied. *Balinese Character: A Photographic Analysis* (1942), written with Bateson, was an ethnographic analysis of 700 thematically arranged photographs. *Male and Female: A Study of the Sexes in the Changing World* (1949) advanced her theory that sexual differences resulted from social conditioning, primarily maternal influence. *Culture and Commitment: A Study of the Generation Gap* (1970) examined how rapid cultural change influences the transferal of information from one generation to the next. One of Mead's most provocative works was her autobiographical *Blackberry Winter* (1972). Though offering much insight into her early years, it downplayed a number of sensitive matters, including her stormy marriages.

Not surprisingly Mead received many tributes, including some 28 honorary degrees. She was president of seven professional organizations, including the World Federation of Mental Health (1956–57), the American Anthropological Association (1960), and the American Association for the Advancement of Science (1975). Always seeing her mission as one to a wider community, she could give over a hundred speeches a year and frequently appeared on talk shows. From 1961 to 1978, she wrote a column for *Redbook* magazine with anthropologist **Rhoda Métraux**, with whom she long shared a Greenwich Village flat. As she grew older, she always carried a forked stick and wore a cape.

A devout Episcopalian, Mead served in 1967 on the denomination's Subcommittee for the Revision of the Book of Common Prayer. Already an admirer of the King James translation of the Bible, she sought to preserve as much of the old liturgy as possible. During a discussion of Noah's flood, a bishop commented, "Nobody believes *that* in this day and age." Mead snapped back, "Bishops may not but anthropologists do." She was particularly concerned to keep the renunciation of "Satan and all his works" in the baptismal rite.

Margaret Mead was always good for a quotation, even if many would find some of her positions outlandish. Just before World War II broke out, she thought that the conflict could be avoided if Franklin Roosevelt would "have a talk" with Hitler "in terms of building Europe." Once, during the Cold War, she told a friend she was glad to be an American for "I think we can do more harm than any other country on earth at the moment"; better to be within such a soci-

Margaret
Mead

ety than without. In an attempt to explain the Russian character, Mead and fellow anthropologist Geoffrey Gorer said, "We've got to pursue swaddling in every direction, including metaphors or any kind of figures of speech." Critics labeled the preoccupation "diaperology."

It seemed as if Margaret Mead had an opinion on everything. She called for trial marriage, a single world language, salaries for college students, and the legalization of drugs for addicts. In the 1970s, she argued that American colleges were 400 years out of date. When she endorsed decriminalization of marijuana, Governor Claude Kirk of Florida called her "a dirty old lady." Instead of the "isolated" nuclear family, she advocated "cluster" units, comprised of older married couples, singles, and teenagers from other households.

Some of Mead's comments concerning the relationship between the sexes could appear particularly outlandish. Americans were "appallingly poor lovers." Newlyweds should purchase divorce insurance. American men were losing their "sense of adventure" because with the advent of bottle-feeding, males could suckle babies just as well as females. An ideal society would consist of people who were homosexual in their youth, heterosexual in middle age, and homosexual again in later life. In 1969, she spoke on the evils of co-education to Radcliffe students: "Twenty-four hours a day with boys can be appalling—it's bad enough to have to eat breakfast every day with your husband."

On some matters, however, she appeared conservative. Abortion, she said, was "an incredibly brutal, lazy, cruel way of handling life," "an abominable method of birth control." People who turned children over to day-care centers were better off not having any. Calling women's liberation too anti-male, she said women "cannot build on the fantasy that [they] have been held down by a conspiracy." She favored a daily period of silent prayer in the public schools. In calling for a coed draft, she opposed giving women firearms; females "are too fierce," she remarked.

Biographer Jane Howard denies that anyone knew "the whole Mead." Obviously one of the most energetic public women of her time, she was also one of the most enigmatic. As Howard notes, "She was loving, scolding, ebullient, irksome, heroic, and at times vindictive. Like most great characters, she was inconsistent."

As the 1970s waned, Mead became physically thin and quite irritable. Fortunately for her she did not live to see the devastating attack on her Samoa research by Derek Freeman, a New Zealand-born professor at the Australian National University. She also did not have to confront accusations that she had reinforced colonialism and romanticized the Pacific Islands by portraying the inhabitants in terms of savagery, cannibalism, and wanton sexuality.

On November 15, 1978, in New York Hospital, Margaret Mead died of pancreatic cancer. *Time* magazine's obituary bore the headline: "grandmother to the global village." When she told the nurse she was dying, the nurse gently replied, "Yes. We all will, someday." "But," said Mead, "this is different."

SOURCES:

Bateson, Mary Catherine. *With a Daughter's Eye*. NY: Morrow, 1984.

Cassidy, Robert. *Margaret Mead: A Voice for the Century*. NY: Universe Books, 1982.

Howard, Jane. *Margaret Mead: A Life*. NY: Simon and Schuster, 1984.

Mead, Margaret. *Blackberry Winter: My Earlier Years*. NY: Morrow, 1972.

———. *Letters from the Field, 1925–1975*. NY: Harper and Row, 1977.

SUGGESTED READING:

Cressman, Luther S. *The Golden Journey: Memoirs of an Archeologist*. Salt Lake City: University of Utah Press, 1988.

Foerstel, Lenora, and Angela Gilliam. *Confronting the Margaret Mead Legacy: Scholarship, Empire, and the South Pacific*. Philadelphia: Temple University Press, 1992.

Freeman, Derek. *Margaret Mead and Samoa: The Making and Unmaking of an Anthropological Myth*. Cambridge, MA: Harvard University Press, 1983.

Sargeant, W. "Profiles: It's All Anthropology," in *The New Yorker*. Vol. 37. December 30, 1961, pp. 31–44.

COLLECTIONS:

The papers of Margaret Mead are contained in the Manuscripts Division, Library of Congress, Washington, D.C.

Justus D. Doenecke,
Professor of History, New College,
University of South Florida, Sarasota, Florida

Mead, Sylvia Earle (1935—)

American marine biologist. Name variations: Sylvia Earle. Born Sylvia Alice Earle in Gibbstown, New Jersey, on August 30, 1935; only daughter and one of three children of Lewis Reade (an electrical contractor) and Alice Freas (Richie) Mead (a nurse); graduated from Clearwater High School, Clearwater, Florida, in 1952; Florida State University, B.S., 1955; Duke University, M.A., 1956, Ph.D., 1966; married Giles W. Mead (an ichthyologist and museum curator and later director of the Los Angeles County Museum of Natural History), in 1967; children: daughter Gale Mead, two adopted children, and three stepchildren.

In the summer of 1970, Dr. Sylvia Earle Mead made history as the leader of the five-member team of women aquanauts participating in the Tektite project of underwater research in the Great Lameshur Bay of the Virgin Islands. At the time, the 35-year-old marine biologist was an associate in botany at the Los Angeles County Museum of Natural History, and held appointments at Harvard University, the University of California at Berkeley, and the University of Southern Florida. She also had 20 years of diving experience behind her and had conducted systematic and ecological studies of marine plants, and the interrelationship between marine animals and plants, in the Gulf of Mexico, the northwest Indian Ocean, and the southeast Pacific. Following the Tektite project, Mead participated in numerous other undersea operations, including one under the aegis of SCORE (Scientific Cooperative Operational Research Expedition), during which she successfully completed the longest and deepest lock-out dive ever done by a woman. Later, she surpassed her own record, surveying the ocean floor untethered at 2,500 feet. Today, Mead is still involved in research diving, and is considered one of the world's most respected aquanauts and marine scientists.

Sylvia Earle Mead, one of three children, was born in 1935 and grew up on a small farm near Camden, New Jersey, where her father was an electrical contractor and her mother worked as a nurse. She spent her early years exploring the woods near her house and learning to swim in what she described as a "rinky-dink backyard pool." The family spent many vacations at Ocean City, where she first fell in love with the sea, and she credits her parents with encouraging her natural curiosity. "I was turned loose with a watchful eye, but without the 'Great No' which dulls the curiosity of so many children," she recalls. "The 'Great No': that's the 'don't pick up frogs, don't go into the water, don't do this, don't do that.'" When Sylvia was 12, the family moved to Florida, where the waters of the Gulf of Mexico offered new opportunities for exploration. After graduating from Clearwater High School in 1952, Mead attended Florida State University, receiving a B.S. degree in biology in 1955. During her sophomore year, in the summer of 1953, she took an 8-week course in marine biology, which included her first instruction in scuba diving. "They almost had to haul me back to get me out of the water," she said.

From an early obsession with crabs, Mead's interest turned to photosynthesis and then to marine algae, which eventually became her focus. She earned both her M.A. and Ph.D. degrees from Duke University (in 1956 and 1966, respectively), combining her academic studies with various jobs in her field, including a stint as a fisheries biologist for the U.S. Fish and Wildlife Service in Beaufort, North Carolina, and one as an herbarium assistant at the University of Florida, where she also served as an instructor in botany. In 1964, she joined the long-term cooperative research project known as the International Indian Ocean Expedition, serving as a marine biologist—and the only woman—aboard

the National Science Foundation's research vessel *Anton Bruun*. She subsequently participated in four other *Anton Bruun* cruises.

In 1966, while working as resident director of the Cape Haze Marine Laboratory, Sylvia met Dr. Giles W. Mead, an ichthyologist and curator of fishes at the Harvard University Museum of Comparative Zoology. She later joined Giles as a research scholar at Radcliffe Institute, and the two married in 1967. Giles brought to the marriage three children from a previous marriage, so Mead now found herself with a ready-made family. (The couple later had one child of their own, and adopted two more.) Despite the additional responsibilities, Mead forged ahead with her career, diving for private research in collaboration with the New England and Steinhart Aquariums, and for the Smithsonian-Link Man-in-Sea Project in the Bahamas in 1968.

When Mead joined the Tektite project (which took its name from the glassy nodules, probably originating from meteorites, found on land and on ocean floors), it was in the second phase of its twofold mission to increase our knowledge of the sea and to investigate means of space exploration by studying the behavior of crews living and working in isolated and confined quarters for prolonged periods of time. Mead was accepted for the project on merit and headed the project's only all-female team. The other members were **Ann Hurley Hartline**, a graduate student at Scripps Institute of Oceanography; **Alina Szmant**, a marine biologist; Dr. **Renate Schlenz True**, a teacher at Tulane University; and **Margaret Ann Lucas**, an electrical engineer studying at the University of Delaware. Mead and her crew, like the all-male crews of the project, were subjected to a rigorous predive training period lasting two weeks. "Although a particular effort was made to treat male and female aquanauts alike, it soon became clear that we were receiving an unusual amount of protective interest," she wrote in an article about the project for *Redbook* magazine (April 1971), "well-intended but sometimes harassing. Mostly we joked about it." The underwater capsule in which the women lived and worked for two weeks was a combination laboratory-dormitory which was constantly monitored by closed-circuit television cameras. The only concession to privacy was a shower curtain.

On their second night in the capsule, shortly after midnight, the aquanauts were jarred awake by an earthquake. Although *The New York Times* reported that the women were "probably the human beings closest to the center of the quake," they treated the unexpected event routinely. After checking to see that the capsule was still intact, the women simply went back the sleep.

During the mission, the team spent as much time out of the habitat as possible, as much as six to ten hours a day. Their dives, confined to four hours in length, provided them a range of 1,500 feet from which to view the marine life. Mead informally reported some of her findings in *National Geographic* (August 1971). "My own studies had turned up 153 different species of marine plants, including 26 never before recorded in the Virgin Islands," she wrote. "In addition, I was able to make new observations on the day-night behavior of garden eels and basket stars. The study also added new details on the habits of 35 different species of plant eating fish and the breeding behavior of deepwater damselfish." Mead concluded that one of the greatest advantages of the habitat was "gaining the perspective of a resident." A more formal account of the mission, "Scientific Results of the Tektite Project," was published in 1972.

The Tektite project brought nationwide attention to Mead and her team, in the form of a ticker-tape parade, press conferences, awards ceremonies, and television appearances. "We were hailed as 'aquanettes,' 'aquabelles,' 'aquachicks,' 'aquababes,' 'aquanaughties,' and even 'aqua-nuts,'" said Mead. "I wonder what the reactions would have been if newspapers had hailed the men who landed on the moon as astronuts." In a more sedate acknowledgment of their accomplishment, the team was invited to a White House luncheon where Mead received a Conservation Service Award from the secretary of the interior. She also received the County of Los Angeles Commendation and the Los Angeles *Times* Woman of the Year Award.

In 1975, during the SCORE undersea operation in the Bahamas, Mead stayed for a week in *Hydro-Lab*, an undersea habitat at 60 feet, from which divers were shuttled in the submersible *Johnson-Sea-Link* to the face of a vertical coral wall at 250 feet. Here, in water that dropped off to 3,000 feet, the divers were able to examine the reef environment. "I felt like a hawk as I left the submarine and swam out freely along the face of this submerged cliff," she recalled, "knowing that more than 3,000 feet below was just empty, blue, deep, open water. It was like swimming into the sky on the side of a mountain. I wanted to spread my arms and take off." On this particular project, Mead discovered several new species and genera of algae, which would be named for her. Later explorations deeper and deeper into the ocean resulted in the discovery that photosynthe-

sis can occur where light intensity is extremely low, destroying the theory that plants could not survive below 300 feet.

In addition to several additional missions during the 1970s, Mead also began a collaboration with undersea photographer Al Giddings, with whom she investigated the battleship graveyard in the Caroline Islands of the South Pacific. In 1977, they began a series of expeditions tracking the great sperm whales from Hawaii to New Zealand, Australia, South Africa, Bermuda and Alaska, journeys that were recorded in a documentary film, *Gentle Giants of the Pacific* (1980).

In 1979, Mead had the ocean walk of her life when she explored the sea floor untethered at a depth lower than anyone before or since. Wearing a state-of-the-art pressurized one-atmosphere garment called a Jim suit, she was transported to a depth of 1,250 feet below the ocean's surface off the Hawaiian island of Oahu. Reaching the bottom, she detached from the vessel and investigated on her own for two hours. She described the extraordinary adventure in the book *Exploring the Deep Frontier* (1980).

During the 1980s, with engineer Graham Hawkes, Mead formed Deep Ocean Engineering and Deep Ocean Technologies, companies which design and build undersea vehicles that allow scientists to maneuver at much lower depths than ever thought possible. During the early 1990s, she took time away from her business ventures to serve as chief scientist of the National Oceanographic and Atmospheric Administration (NOAA), a post from which she monitored the health of the nation's waters.

Since 1998, Mead has been involved with the Sustainable Seas Expedition, a five-year project of underwater exploration focusing on the national marine sanctuaries of the United States. Conceived and led by Mead, the expeditions are a project of the National Geographic Society (of which she is explorer-in-residence), in cooperation with NOAA, as well as other government agencies, industries, and private institutions. The expeditions are chronicled daily on the Web by Mead's daughter **Gale Mead**, who is working on the mission and also serves as Expedition Log editor. Sylvia Earle Mead was inducted into the Women's Hall of Fame at Seneca Falls, New York, in the fall of 2000.

SOURCES:

Hauser, Hillary. *Women in Sports: Scuba Diving*. NY: Harvey House, 1976.

Moritz, Charles, ed. *Current Biography 1972*. NY: H.W. Wilson, 1972.

Barbara Morgan,
Melrose, Massachusetts

Meadows, Audrey (1922–1996)

American television actress best remembered for her role in "The Honeymooners." Name variations: Audrey Cotter; Audrey Six. Born on February 8, 1922, in Wuchang, China; died of lung cancer on February 3, 1996, in Los Angeles, California; daughter of Francis James Meadows Cotter (a missionary and minister) and Ida Taylor Cotter; younger sister of Jayne Meadows (b. 1920, an actress); married Randolph T. Rouse (a builder), on May 26, 1956 (divorced 1958); married Robert Six (an airline executive), on August 24, 1961 (died 1986); no children.

Moved to United States (c. 1927); made stage debut at Carnegie Hall (c. 1938); moved to New York City (c. 1940); won Emmy Award (1955); retired (1961); returned to show business (1986); named to Broadcasting Hall of Fame (1990).

Selected television appearances: "The Bob and Ray Show" (1951–52, 1953); "The Jackie Gleason Show" (1952–55); "The Honeymooners" (1955–57); "I've Got a Secret" (late 1950s); "Too Close for Comfort" (1985–90).

Audrey Meadows had a relatively brief career in television, but her portrayal of the tart-tongued young Alice Kramden in "The Honeymooners" opposite Jackie Gleason made her one of the more memorable characters in the annals of the medium. Meadows was born Audrey Cotter in 1922 in China, where her father served as an Episcopalian missionary. When she was five, the family—which included her older sister *Jayne Meadows—returned to the United States to live in Providence, Rhode Island. Meadows fell through a skylight as a child, and her self-consciousness about the resultant scars on one leg made her somewhat shy and reserved. She studied opera at Miss Hill's School in Great Barrington, Massachusetts, and made her stage debut at New York's Carnegie Hall when she was just 16. Her sister, also a gifted performer, convinced Meadows to abandon her plans to enter Smith College, and they moved to New York City instead.

Success on Broadway proved elusive, however, and for a time Meadows toured the Midwest as a coloratura soprano with light opera

Audrey Meadows (center) with co-stars Jackie Gleason, Art Carney, and Joyce Randolph in "The Honeymooners."

companies. She also sang in nightclubs and was a USO performer during World War II. In this line of duty, she was involved in three plane crashes, walking away uninjured from all of them, although she did catch malaria. Around this time, both she and her sister changed their stage name to Meadows, and Audrey soon found work in the new medium of television. In 1951, she began appearing as a comedy-sketch player on the "The Bob and Ray Show," alternating this with work on Broadway. The following year, Jackie Gleason hired her to play his on-screen wife in "The Honeymooners" sketches that were part of his hour-long show on the Du-Mont network. Gleason had rejected Meadows at her first audition, deeming her too glamorous to play the role of a working-class Brooklyn housewife, but changed his mind and hired her after Meadows sent him some test photos taken when she had just gotten out of bed one morning. She was cast as Alice Kramden, the strong-willed wife of Gleason's blustery, loudmouthed bus driver Ralph Kramden. Their on-screen quarrels hit a nerve with postwar audiences—Meadows was adept at scoring verbal victories that quickly deflated Ralph's rage—but it was the obvious affection in the marriage that made the couple so endearing. Meadows was lauded for her comic timing and ability to ad lib (especially important in light of the fact that Gleason preferred not to rehearse, even during the initial shows that were taped before a live audience), and won an Emmy in 1954 for her performances on "The Jackie Gleason Show." For many of the show's viewers, she came to represent the spirited American everywoman of her era.

"The Honeymooners" sketches were such a hit that they became an official half-hour show in 1955. Although the show as such lasted only one season, switching formats in 1956 and ending in 1957, it has since gone on to gain a hallowed place in American pop culture. Considered "landmarks of small-screen entertainment," the 39 episodes that were taped in the 1955–56 season have been rebroadcast almost continuously ever since, and remain a staple of late-night television. (Meadows was the only member of the cast, which included Gleason, **Joyce Randolph** as Trixie Norton, and Art Carney as Ed Norton, to insist on rights to residuals.) A fan club for the show, the Royal Association for the Longevity and Preservation of "The Honeymooners" (RALPH), was founded in 1982.

Audrey Meadows was married in 1956 to a Washington, D.C., builder, then divorced; she married Robert Six in 1961, and enjoyed 25 years of a decidedly un-Kramden-like life as wife

of the chair of Continental Airlines. She retired from television and film almost completely after her second marriage, and divided her time between a Southern California home and international travel. Widowed in 1986, Meadows returned to television on the ABC sitcom "Too Close for Comfort" and also appeared on "Uncle Buck." She was inducted into the Broadcasting Hall of Fame in 1990, and wrote a memoir, *Love, Alice: My Life as a Honeymooner,* in 1994. She died of lung cancer in 1996.

SOURCES:
Amende, Coral. *Legends in Their Own Time.* NY: Prentice Hall, 1994.
Current Biography. NY: H.W. Wilson, 1958.
The Day [New London, CT]. February 5, 1996.
People Weekly. February 19, 1996.
Publishers Weekly. September 19, 1994.
Ragan, David. *Who's Who in Hollywood.* NY: Facts on File, 1992.
Remember. December 1995.
Smith, Ronald L. *Who's Who in Comedy.* NY: Facts on File, 1992.
Time. February 19, 1996.
TV Guide. February 24, 1996.

SUGGESTED READING:
Meadows, Audrey, and Joe Daley. *Love, Alice: My Life as a Honeymooner.* NY: Crown, 1994.

Carol Brennan,
Grosse Pointe, Michigan

Meadows, Jayne (1920—)

Stage and screen personality of the 1950s. Name variations: Jane Cotter; changed stage name to Jayne Meadows (c. 1946). Born in 1920 in Wuchang, China; daughter of Francis James Meadows Cotter (a missionary and minister) and Ida Taylor Cotter; sister of Audrey Meadows (c. 1922–1996); married Milton Krims (divorced); married Steve Allen (an actor and comic), on July 31, 1954; children: (second marriage) William Christopher Allen.

Selected stage roles: Spring Again *(1942);* Another Love Story *(1943);* Kiss Them for Me *(1945).*

Selected film roles: Undercurrent *(1946);* Lady in the Lake *(1947);* Song of the Thin Man *(1947);* The Luck of the Irish *(1948);* Enchantment *(1949);* David and Bathsheba *(1951).*

Selected television appearances: I've Got a Secret *(c. 1952–58);* "The Drop of a Hat," Studio One *(May 7, 1956);* General Motors Motorama *(1956);* High Society *(1996).*

Born Jane Cotter in 1920 in China, where her father was a missionary, Jayne Meadows was a popular actress on stage, film, radio and television in the 1940s and 1950s. She is also known as the sister of *Audrey Meadows, who played Alice Kramden on "The Honeymooners," and as the wife of actor and comic Steve Allen. Meadows grew up in Rhode Island, Pennsylvania, Connecticut, and Massachusetts, after her family returned to the United States. She attended private schools, and exhibited a flair for the stage at a young age; by her early 20s, she and her sister were living in New York City and auditioning for roles on Broadway.

Meadows' first stage role came in January 1942, when she was cast in *Spring Again*. She also appeared in *Another Love Story* (1943) and *Kiss Them for Me* (1945) before deciding to change her last name from Cotter and try her luck in Hollywood. Her first screen role was in *Undercurrent* (1946); parts in *Lady in the Lake* and *Song of the Thin Man* (both 1947) and *The Luck of the Irish* (1948) followed, but it was with her role as a manipulative foster sister in the 1949 film *Enchantment* that she made a name for herself. Two years later, she won praise for her supporting role in the Biblical drama *David and Bathsheba*.

In 1952, Jayne Meadows began appearing regularly on television, and, with her husband Steve Allen, whom she wed in 1954, became one of the medium's first big names (Allen was the inaugural host of the first version of NBC's "The Tonight Show"). Meadows was a panelist on the popular quiz show "I've Got a Secret" from 1952 to 1958, and with Allen appeared on the television program "Danger" as well as in skits called "The Psychiatrist" on "The Tonight Show." She also acted in a number of playhouse series, among them "Studio One" and "General Motors Motorama." In the mid-1950s, she recorded several songs with her sister Audrey, including "Hot Potato Mambo" and "Dungaree Dan and Chino Sue."

SOURCES:

Current Biography. NY: H.W. Wilson, 1958.

Ragan, David. *Who's Who in Hollywood*. NY: Facts on File, 1992.

> **Carol Brennan,**
> Grosse Pointe, Michigan

Meagher, Mary T. (1964—)

American swimmer. Pronunciation: MAH-her. Name variations: Mary Meagher-Plant. Born in Louisville, Kentucky, on October 27, 1964; married.

Won three Olympic gold medals in the 100-meter butterfly, the 200-meter butterfly, and the 4x100-meter medley relay in Los Angeles (all 1984); won the Olympic bronze in the 200-meter butterfly and the silver in the 4x100 medley relay in Seoul, Korea (1988).

The tenth of eleven children, Mary T. Meagher was born in 1964 in Louisville, Kentucky, and began swimming at a young age. The career of a competitive swimmer is one of the briefest in athletics; few compete past the age of 20. Meagher's specialty was the butterfly, one of swimming's most difficult events. She set her first world record at the Pan American Games in 1979 in the 200-meter butterfly and set another world record not long after in the 100 meters. Meagher was certain she would do well in the upcoming 1980 Olympics, but the United States boycotted the games, which were held in Moscow, because of the Soviet Union's invasion of Afghanistan. Even so, her world records of 2:07.01 in the 200 meters and 59.26 in the 100 meters were not broken at the Moscow Olympics. Shortly after, she lowered her records to 2:06.37 and then to 2:05.96 in the 200 meters and to 57.93 in the 100 meters.

Despite her success, the self-effacing Meagher felt depressed after the 1980 boycott, and her performance suffered. She also added 15 pounds to her weight after she enrolled in college. As the 1984 Olympics approached, her resolve returned. She left school to get into condition, though she was not satisfied with her performance at the Olympic trials. Once in Los Angeles, Meagher, fighting off a stomach ailment and bronchitis, surprised herself by winning gold medals in both the 100-meter butterfly (with a time of 59.26) and the 200-meter butterfly (with the third fastest time ever of 2:06.90). With teammates **Theresa Andrews**, *****Tracy Caulkins**, and *****Nancy Hogshead**, Meagher won a third gold in the 4x100-meter medley relay. She swam the third leg and was the fastest women's "flyleg" ever, turning a half second deficit into a two-body-length lead. In the 1988 Olympics in Seoul, Meagher competed once more and walked away with the bronze medal in the 200-meter butterfly and a silver in the 4x100 medley relay. She was 24 years old.

SOURCES:

Markel, Robert, Nancy Brooks, and Susan Markel. *For the Record. Women in Sports*. NY: World Almanac Publications, 1985.

Wallechinsky, David. *The Complete Book of the Olympics*. NY: Viking, 1988.

> **Karin Loewen Haag,**
> Athens, Georgia

Means, Jacqueline (1936—)

First woman to be officially recognized as an ordained priest by the Episcopal Church in the United States. Name variations: Jacqueline Allene Means-Bratsch. Born Jacqueline Allene Ehringer in Peoria,

Illinois, on August 26, 1936; daughter of Theodore R. Ehringer and Minnett M. Ehringer; married Delton Means (divorced 1979); married David H. Bratsch; children: (first marriage) **Deborah Means**; *David Means; Delton Means; Patrick Means.*

Although women have been excluded in modern times from serving as priests in the Episcopal (or Anglican) Church, the tide began to change in the middle of the 20th century. In 1944 in war-torn China, Right Reverend R.O. Hall, the bishop of Hong Kong, ordained a Chinese woman deacon, Reverend **Li Tim Oi** (1907–1992). Li ministered in parts of mainland China and in the Portuguese colony of Macao while chaos, revolution, and war ravaged Asia. After the Second World War ended (1945), Bishop Hall brought the matter of ordaining women as priests before the meeting of Anglican bishops held at the Lambeth Conference (1948). His proposal—that women continue to be ordained on an experimental basis for 20 years—was denied by the assembled ecclesiastics, and the bishops petitioned Hall to ask Li Tim Oi to renounce her orders. She never did, however, and in fact continued her ministerial duties. In 1970, in Hong Kong, she was finally vindicated when the Anglican province of that British Crown Colony officially recognized that her ordination had always been valid. Seven years later, Jacqueline Means became the first woman to be "regularly" or "legally" ordained an Episcopal priest.

Born Jacqueline Ehringer in 1936 in the heartland city of Peoria, Illinois, during the Great Depression, she grew up under less than ideal circumstances. Both her father, a traveling salesman, and her mother became alcoholics. The family was often on the move, but her parents saw to it that she attended a Roman Catholic school in each town in which they settled. At age 16, Jacqueline dropped out of high school and married Delton Means. The couple settled in Indianapolis, where Delton found work as a truck driver. For some years, Jacqueline concentrated on raising their four children, and the Means family attended an Episcopal church.

Looking back on her early years, Jacqueline Means would recall in 1977: "I was the resident bitch, very dissatisfied with my life and a very unhappy person who channeled my energy in a negative direction." Life began to look brighter when she passed a high-school equivalency test and became a licensed practical nurse. Restless as ever, she sought other areas in which to direct her energies and in time turned to the field of religion, enrolling in courses at both Roman Catholic and Disciples of Christ seminaries in Indianapolis. Her new direction upset her husband, resulting in violent arguments between the couple. In 1974, Jacqueline Means was ordained a deacon in the Episcopal Church and was assigned to All Saints', an inner-city parish in a racially mixed neighborhood of Indianapolis.

By the late 1960s, when her religious odyssey was beginning, the issue of women's ordination in the Anglican-Episcopal Church was once again a contested subject within that religious community. In 1965, the controversial Bishop James Pike declared **Phyliss Edwards**, an Episcopal deaconess, to be a deacon. This changed Edwards' status, allowing her to be placed into Holy Orders. As the Reverend Phyliss Edwards, she was now a priest and Bishop Pike put her in charge of a parish. Soon the entire church took up the matter. In 1967, a study commission that had been appointed by the Episcopal House of Bishops reported that it could find no reason why women could not be ordained to all orders of ministry. The issue, however, was by no means resolved because of considerable opposition posed by both clergy and laity. At the 1973 General Convention, a resolution to ordain women was defeated by a narrow margin.

Frustrated after an inconclusive meeting with supportive bishops in November 1973, and with the public refusal of the bishop of New York to ordain five women bishops who presented themselves for ordination in December, some Episcopal women now decided that legalistic stalling could go on for many years. These women felt that the clear call to ordination need not, indeed could not, be delayed. On July 29, 1974, at the Church of the Advocate, a predominantly African-American parish in the heart of a black community in North Philadelphia, a decisive step was taken. On this day—the feast of Saints ◄☀ **Mary and Martha of Bethany**—three retired white bishops ordained eleven women deacons to the priesthood. Serving as master of ceremonies was the parish's African-American rector, the Reverend Paul Washington; the preacher was Dr. Charles V. Willie, the Episcopal Church's highest-ranking lay leader, and an African-American as well. Senior warden, and leading the procession carrying the cross, was the Church of the Advocate's lay leader, *****Barbara Harris**, who would go on to become the first woman bishop in the Anglican Communion. (At the 1989 ceremony that elevated Harris, the elderly Li Tim Oi celebrated the Eucharist.) Although the 1974 ordinations were ruled to be invalid several weeks later by an emergency meeting of bishops, the women so or-

❧▶
Mary and Martha of Bethany. See *Mary Magdalene for sidebar.*

dained began to function as priests. After much soul-searching and agitation within the Episcopal world, that church's General Convention of 1976 voted that women could be ordained to all orders of ministry, including the episcopate.

The first "regular" or "legal" ordinations of Episcopal women priests began in January 1977. Among this group, Jacqueline Means was the first. At her ordination at All Saints' Church in Indianapolis, Bishop Donald Davis asked the congregation, "If any of you know of any impediment or crime because of which we should not proceed, come forward now and make it known." Traditionally no more than a formality, on this occasion the question was responded to by a man who rose to condemn the proceedings as "heresy" and "sacrilege," at which point a dozen people, many of them in tears, marched out of the church (10 out of a parish membership of 150 would officially resign in protest). But 45 male priests, who joined in the service, clothed Jacqueline Means in a white chasuble, the outer vestment of her new office. A neighbor provided homemade wine for the service, and one of the parish's older women, **Sarah Mallory**, expressed her delight, noting: "Now I've seen God's man put together as he should be—male and female. Remember where it says in Genesis: 'He gave *them* dominion.'"

In the years after her ordination, Means was often an object of controversy within her church. Some felt she was "too aggressive," or even profane, as she was known to say "Oh Jesus" on occasion. On her first day as a priest, working as the institutional chaplain of her diocese, she cleaned her own house, then went out to call on the sick at a psychiatric hospital. She ended that day with a visit to a local women's prison, where she was greeted with hugs and kisses and a comment by one inmate, "Maybe I can make it too."

In 1979, Means raised some eyebrows when she divorced her truck-driver husband of 26 years and married David H. Bratsch, a Moravian minister, less than a year later. Although she received the support of her church's officials on this occasion, Jacqueline Means conceded, "I don't imagine they would have chosen to write that scenario for the first woman priest." By 1982, she had advanced to the position of associate pastor of St. John's Episcopal Church in Indianapolis. While pleased with her own situation, in which she was no longer treated merely as a novelty, she went on to assess both the present and future for women within the Episcopal Church from a realist's point of view: "The battle has not really been won, because so few women have their own churches."

SOURCES:

Constable, Anne. "'Father, Make Her a Priest,'" in *Time*. Vol. 109, no. 3. January 17, 1977, p. 41.

Donovan, Mary Sudman. *A Different Call: Women's Ministries in the Episcopal Church, 1850–1920*. Wilton, CT: Morehouse Barlow, 1986.

Heyward, Carter. *A Priest Forever*. NY: Harper and Row, 1976.

Hiatt, Suzanne Radley. "Women's Ordination in the Anglican Communion: Can This Church Be Saved?," in Catherine Wessinger, ed., *Religious Institutions and Women's Leadership: New Roles Inside the Mainstream*. Columbia: University of South Carolina Press, 1996, pp. 211–227.

Morgan, John H. *Women Priests: An Emerging Ministry in the Episcopal Church (1975–1985)*. Bristol, IN: Wyndham Hall Press, 1985.

Schneider, Carl J. and Dorothy Schneider. *In Their Own Right: The History of American Clergywomen*. NY: Crossroad Publishing, 1997.

Seligmann, Jean, Lea Donosky and Kim Foltz. "Women Pioneers Find Their Pulpits," in *Newsweek*. Vol. 99, no. 13. March 29, 1982, p. 16.

John Haag,
Associate Professor of History,
University of Georgia, Athens, Georgia

Meany, Helen (1904–1991)

American diver. Born on December 15, 1904; died on July 21, 1991.

Participated in the Olympics (1920, 1924, and 1928); won a gold medal in springboard diving at the Olympics in Amsterdam (1928); won 17 national AAU diving championships for the New York Women's Swimming Association; her career ended when she appeared in a water show unsanctioned by U.S. Olympic Committee.

Athletic competition used to be a more haphazard affair. When American diver Helen Meany participated in the 1920 Olympics, there was no Olympic Village, athletes stayed in hotels, the YMCA, or makeshift accommodations, and swimming and diving took place in a moat that encircled the city of Antwerp. Because the summer of 1920 was cold and rainy, the water temperature was only about 60°; one swimmer fainted as she entered the water, and the American water polo team refused to compete. A group of American swimmers then formed a team and, though they knew nothing about polo, played against a foreign team. They pulled competitors under water, stood on their shoulders, and generally clowned around. The referee could barely contain himself.

Although Meany did not medal in 1920, she returned for the 1924 games in Paris, where the American swim team performed exceptionally well. Following the diving competition, at which she again did not medal, some Parisian fans requested an exhibition. A platform was rigged up on a derrick next to the Seine, and two ladders were provided for Meany to climb. Though the platform was 40' higher than she had ever dived and the river unknown, Meany performed three dives to the delight of the crowd.

Helen Meany journeyed to Amsterdam for the 1928 Olympics. In those days, divers reported for the competition at 1 PM, but were not told when their turn might come. Though Meany spent five tense hours in anticipation, she won the gold medal in springboard diving, with **Georgia Coleman** and *Dorothy Poynton finishing second and third. Women's swimming and diving was dominated by the Americans, and no one was surprised by the sweep.

Although Helen Meany was the only American female diver to be invited to a three-day meet in Tokyo held in honor of *Princess Chichibu's wedding, her career as an amateur was terminated when she appeared in a Miami Beach watershow with Johnny Weissmuller, Pete Desjardins, and *Martha Norelius (two-time 400-meter freestyle gold-medal winner). During that time, Olympic athletes were required to maintain amateur status, and all events they entered had to be sanctioned by the Olympic Committee, as the watershow had not been. It would be decades before this policy changed. Helen Meany was later inducted into the Swimming and Diving Hall of Fame and the Citizens Savings Hall of Fame Athletic Museum.

SOURCES:

Carlson, Lewis H., and John J. Fogarty. *Tales of Gold.* Chicago and NY: Contemporary Press, 1987.

Soderberg, Paul, *et al.*, eds. *The Big Book of Halls of Fame in the United States and Canada Sports.* NY: R.R. Bowker, 1977.

Karin L. Haag,
freelance writer, Athens, Georgia

Mears, Helen Farnsworth

(1872–1916)

American sculptor. Born in Oshkosh, Wisconsin, on December 21, 1872; died in New York City on February 17, 1916; the youngest of three daughters of John Hall Mears (a dealer in farm implements) and Mary Elizabeth (Farnsworth) Mears (a poet, essayist, and playwright, who had published a book of poetry under the name Nellie Wildwood); attended Oshkosh public schools and Oshkosh State Normal School; briefly attended the Art Students League, New York City; apprentice to Augustus Saint-Gaudens; studied sculpture under Frederick MacMonnies in Paris; studied abroad with Alexander Charpentier and Denys Puech; never married; no children.

The youngest of three sisters, all of whom pursued artistic careers (**Mary Mears** as a writer and **Louise Mears** as a book illustrator), Helen Mears was apparently predisposed at a young age to become a sculptor. Although information about her is limited, anecdotal accounts have survived recounting her ability as a baby to bite her pieces of bread into the shapes of horses and dogs. When she grew a little older, she was said to have fashioned clay portraits of the neighbors, some of them embarrassingly accurate. Apparently, Mears' talent was recognized by her father, who saw to it that she received the proper training in anatomy and was outfitted with tools and a suitable place to work.

At age 20, Mears received her first commission: a statue of a woman and a winged eagle entitled *Genius of Wisconsin,* for the Wisconsin Building at the 1893 World's Columbian Exposition. Mears traveled to Chicago to work on the nine-foot marble piece, which was executed at a studio in the Art Institute, where she met and was encouraged by the sculptor Lorado Taft. The work was widely acclaimed and was later installed in the Wisconsin State Capital. With an additional fee of $500 that she won from the Woman's Club of Wisconsin, Mears traveled to New York City. After briefly studying at the Art Students League, she became an apprentice to Augustus Saint-Gaudens, working in his studio for several years. With his encouragement and with the help of a wealthy Milwaukee patron, **Alice Chapman,** Mears was able to spend a year studying abroad with sculptors Alexander Charpentier and Denys Puech.

Mears returned to New York in 1899 and set up a studio in Washington Square which she shared with her sister Mary. Although small in stature, Mears continued to tackle large-scale projects, including a full-length statue of *Frances E. Willard (1905) for Statuary Hall in the U.S. Capitol rotunda. Other commissions, smaller in scale, included portrait bas-reliefs of Saint-Gaudens (Peabody Institute, Baltimore) and Edward MacDowell (replica in the Metropolitan Museum of Art, New York), a bust of George Rogers Clark for the Milwaukee Public Library, and a bust of Dr. William T.G. Morton for the Smithsonian Institution. Although not viewed as an innovator, Mears was respected among her contemporaries for her energy, artistic integrity, and superb skills.

Mears' masterpiece was an ambitious, three-panel bas-relief *Fountain of Life,* which won medals in several competitions. The work, Grecian in mood, represented a change of direction for the sculptor and may have reflected her desire to vary and expand her form of expression. Another bas-relief, *Portrait of My Mother,* which won honorable mention at the San Francisco Panama-Pacific Exposition in 1915, appears to owe a compositional indebtedness to James Whistler.

Helen Mears died unexpectedly on February 17, 1916, at age 43, of pulmonary edema. Among a number of works left unfinished at her death was the portrait of a laborer, *The End of Day,* a piece that was never permanently cast. In 1927, the Wisconsin Federation of Women's Clubs honored the sculptor by establishing an art competition for schoolchildren in her memory.

SOURCES:

James, Edward T., ed. *Notable American Women 1607–1950.* Cambridge, MA: The Belknap Press of Harvard University Press, 1971.

McHenry, Robert, ed. *Famous American Women.* NY: Dover, 1983.

Barbara Morgan,
Melrose, Massachusetts

Mechthild.

Variant of Mechtild.

Mechtild of Driessen (d. 1160)

Saint. Died in 1160.

Mechtild of Driessen, a Bavarian Augustinian, was related to Frederick I Barbarossa (1123–1190), Holy Roman emperor and king of Germany. Mechtild died at the abbey of Driessen in 1160. Her feast day is July 6.

Mechtild of Hackeborne (1241–1298).

See Gertrude the Great for sidebar.

Mechtild of Holstein (d. 1288)

Queen of Denmark. Name variations: Mechtild von Holstein. Died in 1288; daughter of Adolf V, count of Holstein; married Abel (1218–1252), king of Denmark (r. 1250–1252, killed), on April 25, 1237; children: Erik, duke of Schleswig; Valdemar also known as Waldemar, duke of Schleswig; Sophie Abelsdottir (b. around 1240, who married Bernard, prince of Anhalt-Bernburg); Abel (b. 1252).

Mechtild of Magdeburg

(c. 1207–c. 1282)

German Christian mystic and Beguine whose writing describes the love affair between God and her soul.

Name variations: Mechtild von Magdeburg; Mechthild of Magdeburg; Mechthild von Magdeburg; Mechtilde de Magdebourg. Pronunciation: MECH-tild of MAG-de-berg. Born between 1207 and 1212 near Magdeburg in Lower Saxony (Germany); died in the convent at Helfta in 1282 (although some suggest her death might be as late as 1297).

Had religious experience (c. 1219); left home for Magdeburg (c. 1229 or 1230), where she led a semi-religious life as a Beguin; wrote the first six books of The Flowing Light of the Godhead *(1250–70); retired to the Cistercian convent at Helfta (1270), and wrote book seven of* The Flowing Light *before her death.*

Selected writings: The Flowing Light of the Godhead, *also referred to as* The Flowing Light of the Divinity.

In 1860, when Mechtild of Magdeburg's *The Flowing Light of the Godhead* was found in a dusty corner of a monastery, it was considered a major discovery. Here was a work by a 13th-century woman describing the life of a mystic. Not only was it the first Christian mystical text known to be written by a man or a woman in the vernacular (or language of the common people) rather than in Latin, it also contained one of the first descriptions of a type of Christian devotion known as the Sacred Heart. With this discovery, German literary historians and theologians declared Mechtild of Magdeburg one of the first and best examples of the German mystic movement.

Yet it is difficult to say anything with certainty about the woman who wrote this text. What we do know comes primarily from references she recorded in her book. She was probably born in the Lower Saxony area of Germany near Magdeburg, which was one of the emerging towns of that time. Her birth date (between 1207 and 1212) is deduced from dates given in the prologue to her book. It is generally agreed that she was born of well-to-do parents because of her knowledge of scripture and Christian tradition, suggesting she was educated in some manner, and because of her knowledge of courtly life and customs, suggesting she may have had firsthand experience of life at court.

Mechtild herself reveals little about her upbringing. She states that the status of one's birth is not of primary importance, declaring that "discipline and good habits render one noble and well-bred." While she notes that as a child she was "the best loved of her family," only once does she mention her parents, saying that she will pray for them and "all the souls in Purgatory." We also know that she had a brother, Baldwin, a well-educated monk of the Dominican order, who distinguished himself by making an entire copy of the Bible single-handedly. As to her own education, Mechtild confessed that she could not write in Latin and was "unlearned," but her book begins and ends with the declaration that she wrote it with her own hand—a very unusual accomplishment for a woman of the 13th century. We do not know if she received her education from a noble upbringing or later in life. Either way, her writing ability suggests that she possessed the discipline and good habits which rendered her noble and well-bred.

At age 12, Mechtild had what she considered the defining moment of her early life, this being her first religious experience during which she was reportedly greeted by the Holy Spirit. In the context of her day, such an experience was not unheard of, but it was unusual. Mechtild understood this event as a calling to a special religious life as a mystic, one who devotes herself to a life of union with God. Before this event, she "knew nothing of God save the usual Christian beliefs." She calls herself "one of the simplest people who was ever in the spiritual life." Afterwards, she was a changed person who "could no longer have given way to serious daily sins." For the next 31 years, she daily experienced "a loving greeting" from the Holy Spirit.

More and more, her life centered around these experiences with the Holy Spirit until, around age 22, she decided to leave home to live a religious life. She states that she "longed to be despised through no fault of her own," meaning that she wanted to live a life modeled on the life of Christ even if it meant persecution. Therefore, she chose not to enjoy the relative comfort of religious life provided inside convent walls, but to travel to Magdeburg and live the semi-religious life of a Beguine.

Beguines were a diverse group of women who lived a life of religious devotion and community service. Their lifestyle is called "semi-religious" because they did not take permanent vows of poverty, chastity, and obedience like nuns and monks did. Instead, they vowed chastity as long as they were Beguines, but they could leave the community and marry later in life. They were allowed to keep private property and worked in a number of trades to support themselves. They also engaged in a wide variety of work for the poor, sick and orphaned. Most important, they took no vow of obedience to any monastic rule, house, or superior, although they were often associated with a monastic order and received spiritual direction from the monks

there. Thus, Beguine life was less supervised than convent life, because supervision through a monastic order or parish priest was minimal.

Beguine life was also more vulnerable and dangerous than convent life. In the Middle Ages, women were subject to physical attack and poverty if not protected by a husband or religious order, but Beguines often lived in small groups in or near their place of service, usually in urban areas such as Magdeburg. They endured persecution, sometimes accused of heresy for their religious practices and ideas, other times accused of laziness or charged with illicit begging. At the heart of these criticisms was a concern for the protection of these women and disapproval of their independent lifestyle. In 1311, the Beguine movement was generally condemned at the Council of Vienne by Pope Clement V. It was endorsed by later popes, but eventually evolved into charitable institutions by the 15th century.

This life of independence and persecution fit Mechtild's needs. She wanted a way of life that would free her from earthly attachments, so that she could devote herself to love of God as well as challenge herself to walk in Christ's footsteps. Mechtild describes her life in Magdeburg as like "an exile in a foreign land." So dedicated was she to her goals that Mechtild ignored the one person she did know in Magdeburg upon her arrival for fear that friendship would keep her from "disdain of the world and the pure love of God."

For 40 years, Mechtild lived as a Beguine. During this time, she states: "God never left me. He brought me such sweetness of love, such heavenly knowledge, such inconceivable wonders, that I had little use for earthly things." However, these divine graces did not come easily. Mechtild confesses that she constantly struggled to overcome her angry and weak nature in an effort to foster love of God in her heart. Like many mystics of her time, she engaged in physical trials to increase her dedication. A Beguine, she writes, should foster humility, discipline, good habits, love and degradation. She notes that in addition to weeping, confessing, fasting, and constant worship she endured whippings and tremendous blows upon her body.

The result of this lifestyle was "many days of bodily illness," which Mechtild understood to be a test from God of her ability to trust the Lord to take care of her. When she revealed her thoughts to her confessor, he not only confirmed the authenticity of her experience but commanded her to write down all her experiences. Mechtild states, "Then he commanded me to do that for which I often weep for shame when my unworthiness stands clear before my eyes, namely, that I, a poor despised little woman, should write this book out of God's heart and mouth." Thus, Mechtild's writing was born. From the book's prologue, we know that the year was 1250.

For the next 20 years, Mechtild wrote down her thoughts on scraps of paper. Scholars agree that her writing was collected and arranged into six chapters (called books) by someone else, probably her spiritual director, who distributed them to the surrounding community. Mechtild never names her director but did refer to the reaction of Master Heinrich to her text. From this, it is deduced that her director was probably Heinrich of Halle, a member of the Dominican order, who is known to have translated her work into Latin near the time of her death.

Mechtild portrays herself as a reluctant writer urged on by God and her director to continue her work. She calls her director "my dear schoolmaster," who taught her, "simple and stupid as I am, to write this book." About the urging of God she states, "I cannot nor do I wish to write," unless feeling the power of the Holy Spirit. At other times, she complains of the inability to express herself, declaring that she is no expert in writing, and at one point saying, "German now fails me and I do not know Latin." It is difficult to interpret the meaning of these remarks because Mechtild is expressing a theme familiar to Christian writers: that God chooses the weak and poor. At one point, Mechtild wonders why God did not choose a priest rather than herself for this work, and she is told that God always seeks out the lowest and smallest so that "unlearned lips can teach the learned tongues of the Holy Spirit."

The contents of her writing, however, reveal anything but a poor and unlearned writer. Her work is a collection of diverse styles and themes. It consists of poems, love songs, allegories, visions, and moral reflections, gathered in no particular order. Most often quoted are the dialogues between God and her soul which are cast in the courtly language of a lord wooing a queen at court. Their courtship expresses the complexities of love with all its yearning and pain as well as closeness and joy. As to the latter, Mechtild writes, "Lord, now am I a naked soul and Thou a God most Glorious! Our two-fold intercourse is Love Eternal which can never die." **Elizabeth Petroff** observes that this combination of spiritual love expressed in courtly literary form is a reflection of the Beguine goal "to be in the world but not of it."

Another major theme of her work is criticism of corruption in the church. Mechtild calls cathedral clergy "goats" because of their impurity and urges them to confess and repent. She maligns the priesthood as a whole as the tarnished crown of the holy church because of their love of power. Even her own sisters, the Beguines, are criticized for their worldly ways, which she calls a "gruesome service" to Lucifer. In prophetic style, she not only criticizes but suggests characteristics of true servants of God, urging clergy to be good preachers, holy examples, and friendly counselors.

> *It* grieves me to the heart that I, a sinful woman, must so write . . . in these words which seem so insignificant compared to the eternal truth.
>
> —**Mechtild of Magdeburg**

Mechtild indicates that her writing was not well received by some. At one point, she refers to her critics as "my pharisee," a reference to those who criticized Jesus. Another time, she refers to being barred from taking communion, a punishment for those accused of heresy. Reflecting on the mounting criticism, she writes, "I was warned about this book and was told by many people that if there were no wish to preserve it, then flames could consume it." Given the context of the day—in which Beguines were always targets for criticism and those who veered too far from orthodox Christian beliefs were often branded as heretics—Mechtild could very well have suffered persecution. Despite criticism, she continues to be convinced of the validity of her work. She states that she is reassured by God that no one can burn the truth. "He who would take it from My [God's] hand must be stronger than I!"

Some have speculated that due to increased persecution and failing health Mechtild was forced to retire to the convent of Helfta around 1270. There, she met three other notable writers of the time, ❧➤ **Gertrude of Hackeborne**, ❧➤ **Mechtild of Hackeborne**, and *Gertrude the Great. Helfta was a good place for a writer such as Mechtild. Under the leadership of Gertrude of Hackeborne, it had become a hub of learning and writing for women and a center for book collecting, copying and illumination.

Mechtild spent her final days at Helfta. Soon after her arrival, she suffered a serious illness and became totally blind. She asked God if she should stop writing but was reassured that God would give her the strength to continue her work through the assistance of her sisters. Though

❧➤ *Gertrude of Hackeborne and Mechtild of Hackeborne.* See Gertrude the Great for sidebar.

poor, blind, and unable to write by herself, Mechtild rejoiced that she was cared for by the goodness of others who served as her eyes, hands and heart. With their help, she completed the seventh book of *The Flowing Light of the Godhead.*

A major theme of the last book is Mechtild's reflection on old age and death. Calling old age a time that is cold and without grace, she laments that she is powerless to maintain the level of spiritual existence she had enjoyed for so long, for she can no longer "bear the fiery love of God." In reflecting on her life, she paints a picture of life as a house of suffering furnished with a bed of restlessness, a chair of trouble, and a table called indignation dressed with a cloth of poverty on which sit bitterness of sins and willingness to work. Her drink is rare praise, she writes, because of the few good works to her credit.

But despite all this, Mechtild does not despair. Even her present state is not to be grieved. "And yet a good old age is worth waiting for a long time," she writes, "and may be entrusted to God alone." She looks forward to the last day when her suffering will end and she will be filled with gladness. Reflecting on death, she thanks God that she was called to be a Christian and came to "real Christian belief." She takes leave of her friends, who have been her help in need, and her enemies, who have not vanquished her. To those left behind, she leaves this advice, "Any truthful woman or good man should read this little book if after my death he wishes but cannot speak to me."

A number of women and men have read her work through the years. The original was collected and arranged by Heinrich of Halle in German soon after her death and translated into Latin by him so that the work would be available to a larger audience. Some have speculated that Dante was familiar with this translation and had Mechtild in mind when he wrote of Matelda in his work *Purgatorio*, but there is not much evidence to support this claim.

In 1344–45, Heinrich of Nordlingen made another German translation and sent it to friends with the note: "This book, in delightful and vigorous German, is the most moving lovepoem I have ever read in our tongue." It was the Nordlingen translation, bound with a few pages from a Christian group called Friends of God, along with essays and sermons by the German writer Meister Eckhart, that was found at Einsiedeln in 1860. A modern translation was made by Gall Morel in 1869, but it remained relatively unknown. *Evelyn Underhill introduced English readers to Mechtild in her classic text *Mysticism*.

For many years, the only English translation was that of **Lucy Menzies**. Today, those "truthful women and good men" who want to speak to Mechtild can read the work translated by **Christiane Galvani**.

SOURCES:

Howard, John. "The German Mystic Mechthild of Magdeburg," in *Medieval Women Writers*. Edited by Katharina M. Wilson. Athens: University of Georgia Press, 1984, pp. 153–163.

Mechthild von Magdeburg. *The Flowing Light of the Divinity.* Translated by Christiane Mesch Galvani. Edited with an Introduction by Susan Clark. NY: Garland, 1991.

Menzies, Lucy. *The Revelations of Mechthild of Magdeburg (1210–1297) or the Flowing Light of the Godhead.* London: Longmans, 1953.

Petroff, Elizabeth Alvilda, ed. *Medieval Women's Visionary Literature.* NY: Oxford University Press, 1986.

SUGGESTED READING:

Bynum, Caroline Walker. *Jesus as Mother: Studies in the Spirituality of the High Middle Ages.* Berkeley: University of California Press, 1982.

Labarge, Margaret Wade. *A Small Sound of the Trumpet: Women in Medieval Life.* Boston: Beacon Press, 1986.

Jane McAvoy,
Associate Professor of Theology at
Lexington Theological Seminary, Kentucky

Mechtilde.
Variant of Mechtild.

Meck, Nadezdha von (1831–1894).
See Von Meck, Nadezdha.

Mecklenburg, duchess of.
See Euphemia (1317–after 1336).
See Ursula of Brandenburg (1488–1510).
See Sophie of Holstein-Gottorp (1569–1634).
See Cecilia of Mecklenburg-Schwerin (1886–1954).
See Wilhelmina for sidebar on Juliana (b. 1909).

Mecklenburg-Gustrow, duchess of.
See Elizabeth of Denmark (1524–1586).
See Anna Sophia of Prussia (1527–1591).
See Magdalena Sybilla of Holstein-Gottorp (1631–1719).

Mecklenburg-Schwerin, duchess of.
See Anna of Brandenburg (1507–1567).
See Catherine of Mecklenburg-Schwerin (1692–1733).
See Louise of Saxe-Gotha (1756–1808).
See Caroline Louise of Saxe-Weimar (1786–1816).
See Alexandrina of Mecklenburg-Schwerin (1879–1952).

Mecklenburg-Schwerin, grand duchess of.

See Louise of Prussia for sidebar on Alexandrine of Prussia (1803–1892).

See Anastasia Romanova (1860–1922).

See Alexandra Guelph (1882–1963).

Mecklenburg-Strelitz, duchess of.

See Marie of Mecklenburg-Gustrow (1659–1701).

See Elizabeth of Saxe-Hildburghausen (1713–1761).

See Louise of Prussia for sidebar on Frederica of Hesse-Darmstadt (1752–1782).

See Augusta Guelph (1822–1916).

See Romanov, Catherine (1827–1894).

Mecklenburg-Strelitz, grand duchess of.

See Charlotte of Hesse-Darmstadt (1755–1785).

See Mary of Hesse-Cassel (1796–1880).

See Elizabeth of Anhalt-Dessau (1857–1933).

Medea (d. 1440)

Queen of Cyprus. Died in 1440; became the first wife of John II, the Lusignan king of Cyprus (r. 1432–1458), around 1440. John II's second wife was *Helen Paleologina (c. 1415–1458).

Meders, Mary (1643–1673).

See Moders, Mary.

Medforth-Mills, Helen (b. 1950).

See Helen, Princess.

Medhavi, Ramabai (1858–1922).

See Ramabai, Pandita.

Medici, Alfonsina de (d. 1520)

Florentine noblewoman. Name variations: Alfonsina Orsini. Born Alfonsina Orsini; died in 1520; married Pietro the Unfortunate also known as Pietro de Medici (1471–1503), ruler of Florence, on May 22, 1488; children: Lorenzo de Medici, duke of Urbino (1492–1519); *Clarice de Medici (1493–1528, who married Filippo Strozzi).

Alfonsina de Medici, a daughter of the powerful Orsini family, was known to be haughty and showed an "unconcealed contempt" for the Florentines. She was driven out of Florence with her equally unpopular husband, Pietro de Medici, two infant children, and the rest of the Medici clan, on November 9, 1494.

Medici, Anna de (1616–?)

Italian princess. Born in 1616; daughter of Cosimo II de Medici (1590–1620), grand duke of Tuscany (r. 1609–1620), and Maria Magdalena of Austria (1589–1631); sister of Ferdinand II (1610–1670), grand duke of Tuscany; married Ferdinand, archduke of Austrian Tyrol (son of *Claudia de Medici); children: one daughter, *Claudia Felicitas who married Leopold I, Holy Roman emperor (r. 1658–1705).

Anna de Medici was born in 1616, the daughter of Cosimo II de Medici, grand duke of Tuscany, and *Maria Magdalena of Austria. Following her marriage to her first cousin, Ferdinand, archduke of Austrian Tyrol, Anna de Medici and her husband spent more time in Florence than in their duchy in the Austrian Tyrol, preferring the Tuscan court.

Medici, Anna Maria de (d. 1741)

Grand duchess of Tuscany. Name variations: Anna Maria of Saxe-Lauenburg; Anne of Saxe-Lauenburg. Died in 1741; daughter of the duke of Saxe-Lauenburg; married Philip of Neuberg, count Palatine (died); married Giovan also known as Giovanni or Gian Gastone de Medici (1671–1737), grand duke of Tuscany (r. 1723–1737), in July 1697; no children.

Daughter of the duke of Saxe-Lauenburg and widow of the count Palatine, Anna Maria was "more like a Bohemian peasant than a princess," writes C.G. Young, when she married Gian Gastone de Medici in Dusseldorf. Gian Gastone had vigorously opposed the match, but his father Cosimo III had won out. Since Anna Maria much preferred living on her inherited property in Reichstadt, a small village isolated in the mountains of Bohemia, to living in Tuscany, Gian Gastone was forced to settle in the remote Bohemian village. To add to his misery, Anna Maria's interests tended toward horses, dogs, and field sports, while he was more inclined toward intellectual pursuits. He soon took to drink and within one year was fleeing to Paris to be with his mother *Marguerite Louise of Orleans. Though compelled to return by his father, Gian Gastone began to spend more time in Prague in intemperate pursuits than in his wife's tiny castle.

Cosimo, with his health failing and aware that his son would soon be heir, tried to convince Anna Maria to come to Tuscany, but she would have none of it. Cosimo finally allowed his son to return to Florence without her, and from then on, they lived apart. Instead, Gian Gastone's sister-in-law, *Violante Beatrice de Medici, served as his host at court.

Medici, Anna Maria Luisa de

(1667–1743)

Electress of the Palatinate and the last of the Medicis. Name variations: Anna Maria Luisa of the Palatinate; Anna Maria Ludovica. Born in 1667; died in 1743; daughter of Cosimo III de Medici (1642–1723), grand duke of Tuscany (r. 1670–1723), and Marguerite Louise of Orleans (c. 1645–1721); married John William of the Palatinate.

Ruler, benefactor, and the last member of the famous Medici family, Anna Maria Luisa de Medici is not a name that is well known in her native province of Tuscany. Yet among her other contributions to Florentine history, Anna Maria played a vital role in establishing Florence's modern status as an artistic and tourist center of Italy. Born into the wealthy reigning patrician family of Florence, Anna was the daughter of Grand Duke Cosimo III and his French duchess, *Marguerite Louise of Orleans. Anna was only seven when her mother, unhappy in her marriage to the grand duke, left Italy and her three children to retire to a French convent.

In 1691, at the rather late age of 24, Anna Maria married John William, Elector Palatine of the Rhine (one of the seven German nobles who had the hereditary privilege of electing the German emperors), and moved to John William's capital at Dusseldorf. The marriage was part of Cosimo's plan to improve diplomatic relations between Tuscany and the Holy Roman Empire, because Cosimo needed the support of the German emperor due to the increasing threats against the political independence of the Tuscan city-state by the armies of France and Spain. Before long, however, the emperor himself was sending Austrian armies to invade the state. After the death of Anna's eldest brother in 1713, which left only her brother Gian Gastone de Medici as heir, the Florentine Senate passed a decree that Anna Maria would succeed Gian Gastone to the ducal throne if she outlived him. Naming a daughter as a potential heir, especially to such a wealthy state, was rare in the 18th century; Cosimo's actions perhaps speak to his doubts about the continuation of the Medicis and his desire to keep Tuscany in their hands, since there were no other surviving children in the immediate family.

When Elector John William died in 1716, Anna Maria, who was childless and thus had no heirs to keep her in Dusseldorf, returned to the Florentine court. Unlike her status when she had left 25 years earlier as a political pawn, on her return the 50-year-old widow Anna Maria was a political figure of great importance, the potential ruler of a vast and prosperous state. After 1722, the elderly Cosimo III essentially gave up ruling directly and allowed Anna Maria, who seems to have been his favorite child, to act in his name. Her brother and Cosimo's heir, Gian Gastone, apparently showed little inclination to leadership and was content to let Anna Maria take over her father's administrative duties, including diplomatic negotiations. She was a competent administrator and became a popular ruler.

Yet on Cosimo's death in 1723, Gian Gastone took over the reins of government; Anna Maria was forced into semi-retirement, although she remained in the grand ducal palace in Florence. During Gian Gastone's reign, Spain and Austria continued to maneuver for control of Tuscany. Fighting one another over the conquest of Tuscany, each used Gian Gastone's lack of a male heir as a pretext for invading Tuscany. Both tried to force him to name their own princes as his heir instead of Anna Maria. Gian Gastone refused to agree to these demands, but with a weakened army and his own weak leadership, there was little he could do to protect his state from its enemies.

The question of who would control Tuscany—Spain, Austria, or Anna Maria—remained unresolved on Gian Gastone's death in 1737. Austria's superior army was triumphant, and Francis II of Austria was named grand duke of Tuscany, the first who was not a member of the Medici family. Francis, who remained in Vienna, installed an administrator in the grand ducal palace in Florence where Anna Maria lived. Anna Maria was allowed by Francis to remain in the palace as well, perhaps as a means of pacifying the Tuscan people for the conquest of their state by showing respect for their beloved former ruler. She was, however, completely removed from power, and lived in a separate section of the palace. Yet she was not inactive, despite her advanced age (she was 70 when Gian Gastone died), failing health, and her status as last surviving member of the conquered ruling house of the Medici.

In her last years, Anna Maria became renowned as a benefactor and art collector. Using her vast personal wealth—from family inheritances to which Francis II of Austria had no claim—she added substantially to the Medici family art collections, already the largest and most valuable private art collection in Europe. Her purchases of new works included paintings, sculptures, jewels, and books, as well as the funding of the completion of the long-planned Medici family mausoleum. She also spent copious sums on charity for the poor of Florence, which further endeared her to her former subjects.

It was one particular bequest made in her will, however, which should have assured Anna Maria's fame in Florentine memory. Without a relative to name as heir to the immensely valuable Medici treasures, and clearly conscious of the permanent loss of Medici control of Tuscany to foreign rule, Anna Maria decided to make a gift of the entire Medici collection of art to the city of Florence. This vast treasure included much of the modern collections in the Uffizi and Pitti galleries and the Medici library, as well as numerous other museums and galleries which still form the basis of Florence's artistic and cultural artifacts. Having promised this invaluable gift to her native city, the much-beloved Electress Anna Maria died at the grand ducal palace at age 76. She was buried in the newly finished Medici mausoleum.

The treasures she left to the city remain virtually intact in Florence, drawing vast numbers of visitors to the city, in large part due to Anna Maria's stipulation that the collections never be removed from Florence and that they always be available to the public.

SOURCES:
Micheletti, Emma. *The Medici of Florence.* Florence: Scala, 1980.
Young, George F. *The Medici.* 2nd ed. NY: E.P. Dutton, 1911.

Laura York, M.A. in history, University of California, Riverside, California

Medici, Bianca de (fl. late 1400s)

*Sister of Lorenzo the Magnificent. Name variations: Bianca dei Pazzi. Flourished in the late 1400s; daughter of Piero or Pietro de Medici (1416–1469, a preeminent figure in Florence) and *Lucrezia de Medici (1425–1482); sister of Lorenzo de Medici, the Magnificent (1449–1492), unofficial ruler of Florence; married Guglielmo dei Pazzi.*

Medici, Bianca de (1548–1587).

See Cappello, Bianca.

Medici, Camilla de (fl. 1570s).

See Martelli, Camilla.

Medici, Caterina de (c. 1462–1509).

See Sforza, Caterina.

Medici, Caterina de (1593–1629)

*Duchess of Mantua. Name variations: Catherine de Medici; Caterina Gonzaga. Born in 1593; died in Siena of smallpox in 1629; daughter of *Christine of Lorraine (c. 1571–1637) and Ferdinand I (1549–1609), grand duke of Tuscany (r. 1587–1609); sister of *Claudia de Medici (1604–1648); married Ferdinando also known as Ferdinand Gonzaga (1587–1626), 6th duke of Mantua, in 1617.*

Caterina de Medici, known for her piety, married Ferdinand Gonzaga, duke of Mantua, in 1617. When he died in 1626, the 33-year-old widow returned to Tuscany, where she was made governor of Siena. She died there of smallpox in 1629, at age 36.

Medici, Catherine de (c. 1462–1509).

See Sforza, Caterina.

Medici, Catherine de (1519–1589)

*Influential queen mother who tried to put an end to the French Wars of Religion, alternating between attempts at encouraging peaceful coexistence between Catholics and Protestants and attempts to eliminate the Protestant minority. Name variations: Catherine or Katherine de Médicis or Medicis; Catherine de' Médici or de' Medici; Caterina Maria Romola; Caterina de Medici or Caterina de Médicis. Pronunciation: (Italian) MEH-de-chee or MED-ee-chee; (French) MAY-dee-sees. Born in Florence, then an independent city-state in Italy, on April 13, 1519; died in Blois, Anjou, France, on January 5, 1589; daughter of Lorenzo de Medici (1492–1519), duke of Urbino (and grandson of Lorenzo the Magnificent) and French noblewoman Madeleine de la Tour d'Auvergne (1501–1519); trained by private tutors in skills requisite of a Renaissance lady: languages, writing, rhetoric, dancing, riding; married Henry, duke of Orléans, the future Henry II, king of France (r. 1547–1559), on October 28, 1533; children: Francis II (January 19, 1543–1560), king of France (r. 1559–1560); Elizabeth of Valois (1545–1568, queen of Spain); *Claude de France (1547–1575); Louis (February 3, 1549–1550); Charles IX (June 27, 1550–1574), king of France (r. 1560–1574); Henry III (September 20, 1551–1589), king of France (r. 1574–1589); Margaret of Valois (May 14, 1553–1615); Hercule, later confirmed as Francis (b. March 18, 1555, later pronounced duke of Anjou but died in 1584 before he had an opportunity to ascend the throne of France); twins Jeanne and Victoire (b. June 24, 1556, died at birth, almost costing their mother's life).*

Was a prisoner of the Florentine republic (1527–30); served as regent of France for the first time (1552); made regent for her son Charles IX (1560); called the Colloquy of Poissy (1561); issued edicts favoring the toleration of French Protestantism (1562 and 1563); start of the French Wars of Religion (1562); the St. Bartholomew's Day Massacre (1572); entered into peace negotiations with Henry of Bourbon, the Protestant king of Navarre (1578 and 1586).

The future Catherine de Medici, queen of France, was born on April 13, 1519. Three days later, she was baptized Caterina Maria Romola; by early May, she was an orphan. Her mother *Madeleine de La Tour d'Auvergne died of puerperal fever on April 28, and her father Lorenzo de Medici died within five days, more the victim of his life's dissipations than of grief. Still less than a year old, Catherine was taken to Rome to live under the guardianship of her great-uncle Pope Leo X, who, with tears in his eyes, was reported to have called her a "child of sorrow."

Though Catherine's father bore the impressive title of duke of Urbino, the Medici family's roots were mercantile rather than noble. Her great-grandfather was Lorenzo the Magnificent (1449–1492), head of Europe's most powerful banking firm and political power-broker in the Italian city-state of Florence. It was he who used the Catholic Church's reliance on Medici credit and financial support to have both a son and nephew made cardinals in the church hierarchy. Each would go on to be pope, and it was Catherine's great-uncle Leo X who had made her father duke of Urbino, an Italian city controlled by the papacy.

When Pope Leo X died in 1521, Catherine became the ward of Cardinal Giulio de Medici, who, in turn, became Pope Clement VII in 1523. Having little desire to supervise the girl's upbringing directly, Clement returned her and her illegitimate half-brother Alessandro (duke of Florence) to Florence in June 1525. There, they lived in the Medici mansion under the guardianship of the pope's representative, Cardinal Silvio Passerini. On April 26, 1527, a Florentine republican opposition to Medici dominance forced Cardinal Passerini and Alessandro to flee Florence. Young Catherine was not part of the escape, and she would be held hostage by the rebel republic until August 1530, when the Holy Roman emperor and king of Spain, Charles V, restored Medici rule on behalf of Pope Clement VII. Alessandro would return in triumph as the duke of Florence, having missed all the threats and dangers faced by Catherine.

In 1527, Catherine de Medici had been placed in one of Florence's convents by the republican government. When Clement VII and Charles V commenced the siege of the city-state in 1529, members of the city's leadership suggested that the little girl be placed in a brothel or raped by the common soldiers so that the pope would never then be able to use her to arrange an advantageous marriage for the Medici clan. Though it was finally determined that she was too valuable a hostage to be treated in such a fashion, these brutal suggestions demonstrate the extent to which male political actors viewed her as a mere pawn. This was even more apparent when the pope finally used her to attain a marriage alliance to the benefit of the Medici family.

On October 28, 1533, Catherine married the duke of Orléans (the future Henry II), second son of Francis I, the king of France, with Pope Clement VII officiating at the ceremony. Catherine was 14 years old, and her husband Henry was only 13 days older. In many ways, the union, like so many in past ages, was much more an alliance between two powers than a matter of romance. In fact, when Henry, the duke of Orléans, turned 17, the very same year that he became the heir to the French throne through the death of his elder brother, he also took as his lover the 37-year-old *Diane de Poitiers, who was to remain his mistress until his own death in 1559. In old age, Catherine would admit in a letter that she was only publicly polite to Diane in order to maintain royal dignity, "for never did woman who loved her husband succeed in loving his whore."

In an age when political stability was tied to the succession of legitimate monarchs, when governments were literally identified with individual kings, and when the term "Crown" was used interchangeably for both the monarch and the state, the chief responsibility of any princess or queen was the production of heirs. For nearly ten years, Catherine de Medici failed to produce an heir, though Henry had at least three illegitimate children by three different mothers, including ❧ Diane de France. Catherine, in her attempt to do her duty, submitted herself to the "cures" of her day: she wore magical amulets and drank elixirs of rabbit's blood and sheep's urine. Though some at court spread rumors that the king intended to find another wife for his heir, Catherine had an ally in Francis I, who admired her as an embodiment of the multifaceted talent he so revered in Italian Renaissance culture. As a young princess, she demonstrated skill with a pen and a crossbow. Fond of hunting, she was an accomplished rider who introduced a style of riding sidesaddle which, for the first time, allowed women to trot and gallop alongside men on the hunt.

Finally, on January 19, 1543, her father-in-law's patience was rewarded with the birth of a grandson who would bear his name and eventually become King Francis II of France. His birth was followed by that of nine other children, but Francis I only witnessed this one and that of Princess *Elizabeth of Valois. In March 1547, at 53, Francis I died, and 28-year-old Catherine became queen of France, as her husband ascended to the throne as King Henry II. They inherited a problem which had first reared its head on October 17, 1534, when a number of placards appeared in Paris denouncing the Catholic faith as idolatrous. Protestantism, an early 16th-century development, was making inroads in France, and much of Catherine's political career would be dedicated to issues surrounding religious strife.

In 1552, when Henry II went to war in an alliance which bound Catholic France to German Protestants rebelling against Charles V, Holy Roman emperor and king of Spain, he left the regency of France in the hands of his wife. Catherine took her position quite seriously, silencing Catholic sermons which denounced the king's alliance with Protestants against fellow Catholics. She also threw herself into her role as commissary general, providing the army with its supplies. However, with taxes already high, cannon and mercenary troops costly, and inflationary spirals dominating 16th-century economic life, the French Crown could not afford the war for long, and a truce was signed in February 1556. Animosities with the Habsburgs, the royal family of Spain and Austria, were such, however, that war soon broke out again in 1557. On April 3, 1559, yet another temporary peace was achieved when the Treaty of Câteau-Cambrésis was signed. In an attempt to make the treaty more than a temporary reprieve, Catherine's daughter Elizabeth of Valois was to be married to the new Habsburg king of Spain, Philip II, in June. As part of the celebrations, a joust was held on June 30. During the joust, Henry II was mortally wounded by accident. He lingered until July 10, 1559, when he died.

Francis II was the first of Catherine's incompetent sons to reign in France. He had no desire to govern, and he almost immediately handed over most fiscal, military, and diplomatic responsibilities to Francis, duke of Guise, and Charles, cardinal of Lorraine, the maternal uncles of his wife *Mary Stuart, queen of Scots (1542–1587). Above all else, this clearly identi-

fied the royal household with a very Catholic faction in the midst of growing tensions between French Catholics and Protestant followers of John Calvin, who had become the spiritual leader of an expanding Protestant movement centered in French-speaking Geneva, Switzerland. In France, Calvin's followers were called Huguenots, and they were a substantial minority, represented among nobles, merchants, artisans, and peasants alike. In addition to religious tensions, the French national public debt stood at 40 million livres in 1559, an enormous sum for the day. The Guise family responded to this by cutting royal pensions and other expenditures aimed at pacifying the nobility. This only exacerbated problems, creating enemies who turned to Protestantism as a rallying point for the anti-Guise opposition. When a plot involving the stockpiling of arms by French Protestant nobles was uncovered, the House of Guise responded by executing the Sieur de La Renaudie and many of his co-conspirators.

In the midst of all this, Catherine de Medici was quietly and efficiently maneuvering for influence herself. In March 1560, the post of chancellor to the king was vacant, and Catherine pro-

---

❧➨ **Diane de France** (1538–1619)

*French duchess of Montmorency and Angoulême. Name variations: Madame d'Angoulême; Diana of France or Diane of France. Born in Piedmont, Italy, in 1538; died on January 3, 1619; legitimized daughter of Henry II (1519–1559), king of France (r. 1547–1559), and *Filippa Duci; married Orazio Farnese, duke of Castro (son of the duke of Parma), in 1553; married François de Montmorency (d. 1579), governor of Ile-de-France, on May 3, 1559.*

Though fathered by Henry II out of wedlock, Diane de France was acknowledged by the king, legitimized in 1547, and fully accepted as a daughter of France. She was also accepted by her half-brothers and half-sisters. Known as a beauty and fine equestrian, Diane was given the duchy of Chastellerault, until she took over the title and estate of Angoulême. After her first husband Orazio Farnese, duke of Castro, was killed in battle at the siege of Hesdin, she married François de Montmorency, though he was betrothed to **Mademoiselle de Piennes**. Diane de France was close to her half-brother Henry III. When Henry was in danger and in need of financial assistance during his conflict with the duke of Guise, it was Diane who, at great risk, brought him 50,000 crowns which she had saved. She was also politically astute and influential at the court of her brother-in-law Henry IV, who married her half-sister *Margaret of Valois (1553–1615).

posed Michel de L'Hospital, a man who had been trained in law at the University of Padua in Italy, wrote poetry, and favored the development of a compromise where Catholics and Huguenots were concerned. The Guise household accepted Catherine's choice, for, aside from his reputation as a Renaissance scholar, he had dedicated a number of his poems to the House of Guise. Catherine now had a man who reflected her own politics as one of the king's senior advisors, but before any of this could bear fruit, the ever-sickly Francis II died on December 5, 1560. Catherine's second son, suddenly Charles IX of France, was only ten years old and in need of a regent to rule on his behalf. To the royal council, the young king's mother and guardian became the natural choice, and Catherine supplanted the Guise family and Mary Stuart, queen of Scots, as regent. The Italian republic of Venice quickly received word from its representative that "the Queen Mother is considered the one whose will is supreme in all matters."

Vive la France! That was what Catherine wanted to hear, and not Long Live the Pope! or Long Live Calvin!

—Jean Héritier

To counterbalance the disgruntled Guise faction, Catherine turned to the Huguenot nobility. Above all others, she targeted Antoine, duke of Bourbon and king of Navarre, a small subordinate protectorate of the French monarchy just north of the Pyrenees. Antoine was the closest male relative to King Charles IX, aside from his two brothers. Catherine readily told the royal council that he would thus occupy first place in the council, advising the queen regent and her son in all matters. She also noted that Antoine was, as Calvin himself noted, "entirely given to Venus," and she selected one of her most intelligent and beautiful maids of honor to become Antoine's lover and her spy, thereby initiating the practice of consistently employing her attendants in sexual adventures which provided her with influence and information. Once in possession of that information, she would try to neutralize dangerous factions by maintaining a balance of power. In fact, in a letter she told her inflexibly Catholic son-in-law, Philip II of Spain, that attempts at "cutting out the contagion" of Protestantism had only increased its spread. She said that it was her intention to eliminate Protestantism by means of persuasion rather than violence. She also wrote that she intended to call a general council to that effect.

In 1561, she held her council at the Dominican monastery of Poissy, near Paris. Though the pope disapproved and refused to recognize the meeting as an official church council, all five of France's cardinals attended the "Colloquy" of Poissy, and Calvin himself sent a Genevan delegation which included his protégé Theodore Beza. Catherine truly hoped for compromises, but these religious leaders spent their time preaching at each other from irreconcilable positions. In fact, Beza's opening remarks started with an attack on the Catholic mass. Catherine was able to ease over the initial tension which thereby resulted, but the colloquy only demonstrated the extent to which many Catholics and Calvinists viewed each other as heretical and morally reprehensible. Despite the lack of real unity at the colloquy, Catherine, on January 17, 1562, issued an edict which effectively allowed Huguenots to worship in peace "until such time as God will do us the grace to be able to reunite them in one fold." In short, as long as Huguenots were peaceful and loyal subjects of France, she was willing to leave their conversion to Catholicism in God's hands, effectively meaning that no political force would be used to bring about that conversion.

The noble House of Guise was furious. When the duke stopped in the small village of Vassy to hear mass on March 1, 1562, he first demanded that the local Huguenot population not hold its service, and then had his retainers slaughter 30 of the Protestants and wound another 130 when they threw stones in response to his demands. Throughout the rest of the country, Huguenots attacked Catholic churches and Catholics set upon Protestant congregations. Though Catherine and her chancellor Michel de L'Hospital attempted toleration, the age was not tolerant. By July 1562, the French Wars of Religion truly commenced.

The Huguenots actually aimed at seizing the king and controlling him through one of their leaders, the noble Prince of Condé, whom they wished to have appointed chief advisor to the Crown. Meanwhile, the House of Guise wished to extirpate all Protestantism. Catherine was caught in the middle of hostile forces, both international as well as domestic, for Catholic and Protestant powers abroad took an interest in the events in France. The Huguenots received 100,000 crowns and 6,000 men from *Elizabeth I's Protestant England, and Spain, in turn, favored the arch-Catholic cause.

In the midst of this chaos, Catherine de Medici proved that she was quite capable of taking to the battlefield to inspire troops and protect her son from capture by the Huguenots. Ca-

Catherine
de Medici

sualties mounted, and Antoine of Bourbon, king of Navarre, died in 1562, while Francis, duke of Guise, died early in 1563. Throughout all this, Catherine continued to issue edicts of toleration, even as she made war. In March 1563, for example, the Edict of Amboise called for French unity and allowed for Huguenot worship in towns held by Huguenot garrisons. Quite literally, religious conflict was too costly for France, and Catherine desired its end. In addition, to pay for the wars with rebellious Protestants, Catherine issued bonds, called *rentes*, which only increased the government's debt in a period of price inflation and bad harvests. While Henry II had issued rentes totalling 6.8 million livres, Charles IX and Catherine sold 25.9 million livres in bonds. New rentes were used to pay old debts as the wars consumed revenues as well as lives.

Increasingly, Catherine thought in terms of a bold stroke to eliminate the conflict. Though arch-Catholics, following the Guise cardinal of Lorraine, ignored edicts of toleration and fueled the flames of conflict, they naturally fought against rebellious Huguenots who had attempted to seize the person of the king. Most important, while the Huguenots numbered approximately 1 million, French Catholics numbered about 15 million, and more and more of them cried for Huguenot blood as the atrocities continued on both sides. Given the numbers and general sentiment, Catherine gravitated toward the Catholic side. In 1568, she dismissed the chancellor L'Hospital, who had increasingly come to be identified with a policy of toleration and coexistence. Then, as the year 1572 opened, Charles IX, now in his early 20s and no longer in need of an official regent, apparently intended to strike out on his own and initiate a policy which blatantly favored the Huguenot minority in their foreign policy aims. The Huguenot leaders of the day, including the supreme leader Admiral Gaspard de Coligny, even began to attend the king's court, and to convince Charles of the need for new alliances with England and Dutch Calvinists against Philip II's attempts to build Spanish hegemony (influence) in Europe. By August, Catherine was trying to regain influence with her son and thereby prevent heavily indebted France from going to war with Spain, then the most powerful country in Western Europe. This proved to be a precipitous time for Catherine to strike, since that very month, as part of an old policy of forming alliances with moderate Huguenot leaders, she had arranged for her daughter *Margaret of Valois to marry Henry of Bourbon (the future Henry IV), the new Huguenot king of Navarre.

The wedding of Henry and Margaret of Valois took place on August 18, 1572. Eight days earlier, on August 10, the Huguenot faction had been outvoted in the royal council by Catherine and her allies: war with Spain was avoided. Then, four days after the wedding, on August 22, an assassination attempt, most likely masterminded by Henry, the new duke of Guise, was made on the life of Coligny, the Huguenot aristocrat and leader. To the present day, it is not clear whether Catherine was part of the plot to eliminate Coligny, though it is quite clear that she opposed his growing influence over her son and that she planned to capitalize on the assassination attempt. On August 23, Catherine and her supporters deliberated with Charles IX, somehow convincing him that the Huguenots were not only threatening to take justice into their own hands where the duke of Guise was concerned, but that they also intended to overthrow Charles himself. Charles IX then sanctioned the slaughter of the Huguenot nobility. This was the St. Bartholomew's Day Massacre, August 24, 1572, and it cannot be doubted that Catherine played a major role in its implementation. Three thousand Huguenots, including the wounded Coligny, were killed in Paris alone, where they had assembled to celebrate the wedding of Margaret of Valois and Henry of Bourbon. Henry of Bourbon and some others were spared by converting to Catholicism, but throughout the rest of France some 10,000 Huguenots were slaughtered in the next few days. To the present day, many still see the massacre as a premeditated plot concocted by Catherine, Guise, Charles IX and a few others—the wedding celebration merely being a lure to draw the Huguenot leadership out into the open. Some historians, like J.E. Neale, have speculated that Catherine wished to see the Huguenot leadership decimated, but that the mass slaughter was more a function of hatreds and prejudices long festering in the mostly Catholic mobs of France. On August 25, the Crown even issued an edict calling for the massacre to stop, but the genie had been let out of the bottle. Huguenot tracts and pamphlets would often now place the blame for Protestant misfortunes on a manipulative Catherine, who was wildly accused of being the poisoner of numerous individuals who stood between her and power.

The Wars of Religion were renewed with a vengeance after the St. Bartholomew's Day Massacre. Then, in 1574, Charles IX died of consumption, leaving the kingdom to his brother Henry III, an unpredictable man given to the pursuit of male favorites. Catherine had reached the twilight of her political career. All her efforts turned to an attempt to maintain a balance of power regulated by the Crown.

In the autumn of 1578, at the height of the wars, Catherine decided to meet with her son-in-law, Henry of Bourbon, the king of Navarre. This was clearly a case of putting France's interests before the interests of family since Henry had abandoned Paris, his wife, and his Catholicism in 1576. Rather than his Protestantism and abandonment of her daughter, Catherine determined to focus on Henry of Bourbon's desire for

peace and order. At this time, Catherine was hated and distrusted by both Catholics and Protestants, but Henry of Navarre saw merit in her renewed call for compromise, agreeing to the opening of negotiations for peace in 1579. In February, Catherine and Henry came to terms at Nérac—terms which once again promised religious toleration and Huguenot loyalty—but Henry of Navarre did not control all Huguenot forces. In the north, the Huguenot noble Condé continued hostilities, and the dream of peace once again disintegrated.

By 1585, the Guise family's Catholic League had the upper hand in the religious struggle. In an attempt to save Henry III's crown, Catherine encouraged capitulation to the League in the Treaty of Nemours, which recognized a Guise successor to Henry III. Then, in 1586, in yet another attempt to restore balance, she again negotiated for peace with her son-in-law Henry of Navarre, but the Catholic League pressured Henry III to take the offensive against the Huguenots. This proved to be disastrous, as the royal army was defeated by Henry of Navarre in

October of 1587. Finally despairing over Guise power, Henry III independently ordered the assassination of Henry, duke of Guise, and his brother Louis, Cardinal of Guise. Other prominent Catholic League members were arrested, leading to an open revolt of the League in January of 1589.

That same month, on January 5, 1589, Catherine de Medici died. However, one of her last gambles finally bore fruition. In April of that year, Henry III drew up an alliance with Henry of Bourbon, the Huguenot king of Navarre. This alliance and the Guise assassinations eventually cost Henry III his life at the hands of a Catholic assassin, but it provided Henry of Bourbon with the legitimacy he needed to ascend to the throne of France that same year. As the most closely related male relative of the deceased king, he became Henry IV on the condition that he return to Catholicism, which he did, using his newfound power to eventually put an end to the Wars of Religion. Then, secure in his position, in 1598, he issued the Edict of Nantes, granting religious toleration to his former Huguenot

Artist's conception of Catherine de Medici on the morning after the St. Bartholomew's Day Massacre.

brethren—an edict which would remain in effect until 1685 and its revocation by the absolutist Louis XIV.

In her last years, Catherine found in Henry of Bourbon an unexpected ally who could understand her policy and goals. For Catherine, the task of government was not to promote eternal salvation, but to provide as much order and peace as possible on earth, even if that meant the use of deception and violence to defeat those who would kill others in order to promote their religions. In 16th-century Europe, when so many believed that there could only be "one true faith" in any well-ordered society, Catherine de Medici experimented with both religious pluralism and balance of power politics.

SOURCES:
Héritier, Jean. *Catherine de Medici*. Translated by Charlotte Haldane. NY: St. Martin's Press, 1963.
Kingdon, Robert M. *Myths about the St. Bartholomew's Day Massacres, 1572–1576*. Cambridge, MA: Harvard University Press, 1988.
Neale, J.E. *The Age of Catherine de Medici*. NY: Harper and Row, 1962.
Salmon, J.H.M. *Society in Crisis: France in the Sixteenth Century*. London: Methuen, 1979.
Strage, Mark. *Women of Power: The Life and Times of Catherine de' Medici*. NY: Harcourt Brace Jovanovich, 1976.
Van Dyke, Paul. *Catherine de Médicis*. 2 vols. NY: Scribner, 1924.

SUGGESTED READING:
Salmon, J.H.M., ed. *The French Wars of Religion: How Important Were Religious Factors?* Boston: D.C. Heath, 1967.

Abel A. Alves,
Associate Professor of History, Ball State University, Muncie, Indiana, and author of *Brutality and Benevolence: Human Ethology, Culture, and the Birth of Mexico* (Greenwood Press, 1996)

Medici, Christine de (c. 1571–1637).

See Christine of Lorraine.

Medici, Clarice de (c. 1453–1487)

Florentine noblewoman. Name variations: Clarice Orsini. Born around 1453; died in August 1487 (some sources cite 1488); came from a celebrated Roman noble family, the Orsinis; daughter of Jacopo also known as Giacomo Orsini of Monterotondo; married Lorenzo de Medici, the Magnificent (1449–1492, unofficial ruler of Florence), on June 4, 1469; children: (four daughters) *Lucrezia de Medici* (b. around 1480, who married Giacomo Salviati); *Maddalena de Medici* (d. 1519, who married Franceschetto Cybo); Luisa or Luigia (who died before age 12); *Contessina de Medici* (who married Piero Ridolfi); (three sons) Pietro (1471–1503, who was briefly mas-

ter of Florence upon his father's death and married Alfonsina Orsini de Medici), Giovanni (1475–1521, who became Pope Leo X, r. 1513–1521); Giuliano (1479–1516, who became duke of Nemours and married *Philiberta of Savoy*).

Born into the one of the great families of the Italian Renaissance, Clarice Orsini was the daughter of Jacopo Orsini of Monterotondo, a man whose family had made its fortune as mercenaries. Most of the Orsini men were soldiers, a profession which allowed them to amass huge territories around Rome and Naples. Clarice was not particularly well educated, which is perhaps not surprising given her family's military rather than aristocratic background. Yet she was chosen as a bride for one of the most cultured and intellectual men of Italy, Lorenzo the Magnificent of Florence, so called because of his immense political talents and generous patronage of the Florentine Renaissance. He was the eldest son of Piero de Medici, who was the undisputed ruler of Florence, despite its ostensibly republican form of government. Lorenzo would succeed to this unofficial but immensely powerful position on Piero's death in late 1469.

Earlier in that year, 16-year-old Clarice was betrothed to 20-year-old Lorenzo by his mother, *Lucrezia de Medici* (1425–1482). Lucrezia traveled to Rome to meet and evaluate Clarice as a potential daughter-in-law before the formal negotiations began. As a newer family, the Medicis sought a marriage alliance with the well-established Orsinis as a means of cementing their own status as one of Italy's leading houses. In letters to Lorenzo, Lucrezia described Clarice as tall and fair but not pretty, with red hair and a modest, shy disposition. The marriage negotiations were then completed, with the Orsinis providing a dowry of 6,000 florins in gold, dresses, and jewels. For her part, Clarice showed in her private letters that while she was resigned to the marriage, she considered it a step down socially for herself and her family. She and Lorenzo were married by proxy in February 1469 and a great tournament was held in Florence in celebration. Three more days of public celebration followed Clarice's arrival in Florence on June 4, 1469.

Their years of marriage seem to have followed 15th-century expectations for aristocrats: the couple got along adequately, but were not particularly loving. Lorenzo had overt affairs with various mistresses, and Clarice and Lorenzo did not share any interests that might have brought them closer. Their formally worded letters reveal little emotional attachment. They had ten children, three of whom died in infancy. Clarice was a devoted parent, as was Lorenzo; their letters show the sincere affection and love for their children that is missing in their correspondence with each other. In the mid-1480s, Clarice's health began to fail. She died in 1487, while about 34 years old. Lorenzo the Magnificent did not remarry, and died only five years later, in 1492.

SOURCES:

Ady, Cecilia M. *Lorenzo dei Medici and Renaissance Italy*. London: English Universities Press, 1955.

Micheletti, Emma. *The Medici of Florence*. Florence: Scala, 1980.

Young, George F. *The Medici*. 2nd ed. NY: E.P. Dutton, 1911.

Laura York, M.A. in history,
University of California, Riverside, California

Medici, Clarice de (1493–1528)

Florentine noblewoman. Name variations: Clarice Strozzi; Clarice de Medici degli Strozzi. Born Clarice di Pietro de' Medici in 1493; died on May 3, 1528; daughter of Pietro also known as Piero de Medici (1471–1503) and Alfonsina de Medici (d. 1520); married Philip Strozzi also known as Filippo Strozzi, in 1508; children—ten: three daughters and seven sons.

The Italian noblewoman Clarice de Medici has been the subject of high praise by her family's many historians and biographers. The granddaughter of the Florentine ruler Lorenzo the Magnificent de Medici, Clarice was born in the Medici Palace in Florence in 1493, daughter of *Alfonsina de Medici, of the powerful Orsini family, and Piero de Medici. At her birth, her family was at the height of its power; yet when she was only one year old, the Medici were overthrown and exiled from the province of Tuscany, and spent the next 18 years moving between the palaces of their supporters across Italy. In 1508, the 15-year-old Clarice was married to Filippo Strozzi, the young head of the powerful Strozzi family of Florence. In making an alliance with an exiled family, 19-year-old Filippo was betting that the Medici would rise again; and indeed he was right. The Medici returned to power in 1522, and the Strozzi were connected closely to the major family in Florentine and Italian politics. Clarice divided her time over the next 15 years between the Strozzi palace in Florence and the papal palaces of Rome, where first her uncle Giovanni was pope as Leo X (1513–1521), and then her distant relative Guilio served as pope as Clement VII (1523–1534). She had an excellent relationship with Leo X, who admired her as an intelligent and spirited woman; he is quoted as

saying that it would have been better for the Medici if she had only been born male so that she could lead the family. Altogether, Clarice gave birth to ten surviving children with Filippo.

But the peaceful times did not last in this era of almost constant warfare between the Italian states. In 1526, Filippo Strozzi was given by Pope Clement to his enemies, the Colonna, as a hostage to guarantee his good faith. When Clement instead attacked the Colonna, the Colonna planned to execute their hostage. But Clarice acted quickly, and, traveling to Rome from Florence, she negotiated Filippo's release from his captors. The next year, Clement, head of the Medici family, faced strong opposition to his corrupt and despotic rule from the Florentines. Despising Pope Clement and the other Medici who supported him, Clarice was not afraid to act for what she saw as the honor of the Medici name. Boldly, she instigated the expulsion of Clement's supporters from the Medici Palace, showing the people of Florence that the "true" Medici did not support Clement and his harsh rule. Although Clarice helped regain peace within the city, she could not solve the feuding among the Medici, and the fighting continued.

Clarice died the following year at the villa of Le Selve. She was only 35, and left behind seven sons and three daughters. Clarice de Medici was buried in a Strozzi chapel in Florence. In his will, Filippo Strozzi stipulated that a monument be erected in Clarice's memory.

SOURCES:

Young, George F. *The Medici*. 2nd ed. NY: E.P. Dutton, 1911.

Laura York, M.A. in history,
University of California, Riverside, California

Medici, Claudia de (1604–1648)

*Princess of Urbino and regent of Austrian Tyrol. Name variations: Claude de' Medici; Claudia of Tuscany; Claudia della Rovere; archduchess of Austrian Tyrol. Born on June 4, 1604, in Florence; died on December 25, 1648, in Innsbruck; daughter of Ferdinand I de Medici (1549–1609), grand duke of Tuscany (r. 1587–1609), and *Christine of Lorraine (c. 1571–1637); married Federigo della Rovere, hereditary prince of Urbino, in 1620; married Leopold V (1586–1632), archduke of Austrian Tyrol or Tirol, in 1625; children: (first marriage) Vittoria de Medici (d. 1694); (second marriage) two sons and two daughters, including Ferdinand Karl or Ferdinand Charles, archduke of Austrian Tyrol (b. 1626, who married his first cousin *Anna de Medici); Isabella Clara (1629–1685);*

Sigmund Franz (1630–1665), archduke of Austrian Tyrol; *Maria Leopoldine (1632–1649).

At age 16, the year of her brother Cosimo II's death in 1620, Claudia de Medici was married to Federigo della Rovere, hereditary prince of Urbino, a boy two years her junior. Federigo, the only son of the duke of Urbino, was said to have been immoderate and died of "his excesses" before he was 18. Claudia returned to Florence with her baby daughter, *Vittoria (de Medici), in her arms; Vittoria would be the sole heir of her grandfather, the aging duke of Urbino.

In 1625, leaving her daughter in the care of her sister *Maddalena de Medici, who was a nun at the convent of Crocetta, 21-year-old Claudia married Leopold V, archduke of Austrian Tyrol. Leopold was the brother of Claudia's sister-in-law *Maria Magdalena of Austria as well as the brother of Holy Roman emperor Ferdinand II. For the rest of her life, Claudia resided at Schloss Amras, a modest villa in comparison to her former Tuscan home, which overlooked Innsbruck. She had two sons and two daughters with her second husband, and when he died in 1632 she was made regent of Tyrol for her eldest son Ferdinand Karl. Claudia ruled as regent from 1632 to 1646, and ruled well. She "not only greatly improved the administration and resources of Tyrol," writes G.F. Young, "but also by her wisdom and watchful care over the defences of the country she saved it from being drawn into the Thirty Years' War in which all the rest of the German empire was involved." Hanging in the museum at Innsbruck is a portrait of Claudia de Medici presiding at a meeting at Landstag during the crisis. Another portrait by Sustermans which hangs in the Uffizi Gallery depicts her at age 30. Claudia de Medici died in 1648 after having relinquished the government of Tyrol to her son Ferdinand Karl in 1646.

SOURCES:
Young, Col. G.F. *The Medici.* NY: Modern Library, 1930.

Medici, Contessina de
(fl. 1400–1460)

Florentine noblewoman, one of the matriarchs of the Medici family. Name variations: Contessina de' Bardi. Born Contessina de Bardi (Contessina was her Christian name, not a title) in Florence; eldest daughter of Giovanni de Bardi (a partner in the Rome branch of the Bardi bank); married Cosimo de Medici the Elder (1389–1464), also known as Pater Patriae, ruler of Florence (r. 1434–1464); children: Piero de

Medici (1416–1469), ruler of Florence; Giovanni de Medici (1421–1463); Lorenzo.

Contessina de Bardi came from an old Florentine family. In the 14th century, the Bardi were rich bankers; by the 15th century, after England's King Edward III reneged on a loan, they had fallen on hard times. With Contessina's marriage to Cosimo the Elder, the Bardi palace, which still stands in Florence, came into the possession of the Medici family as part of her dowry.

"Contessina appears to have been a rather unimaginative, fussy, managing woman," writes Christopher Hibbert. "Fond of good food, fat, capable and cheerful, she was also domestic and unsociable. Far more scantily educated than her granddaughters were to be, she was, like many another Florentine wife, denied access to her husband's study. Cosimo was quite fond of her; but he was never in the least uxorious, and bore his long partings from her with equanimity, writing to her seldom." During one of these long partings, Cosimo had a son Carlo with a slave-woman named Maddalena. Carlo, who was brought up by Contessina with her sons Piero, Giovanni, and Lorenzo, became rector of Prato and Protonotary Apostolic. Donatello sculpted a bronze head of Contessina.

SOURCES:
Hibbert, Christopher. *The House of Medici: Its Rise and Fall.* NY: William Morrow, 1975.

Medici, Contessina de

Florentine noblewoman. Name variations: Contessina Ridolfi. One of four daughters of Lorenzo de Medici (1449–1492), the Magnificent, unofficial ruler of Florence, and *Clarice de Medici (c. 1453–1487); married Piero Ridolfi; children: Niccolo Ridolfi, cardinal.

Medici, Eleonora de (1522–1562)

Italian noblewoman and warrior, duchess of Florence. Name variations: Eleonora of Toledo; Eleonore of Toledo; Eleonora da Toledo. Born in 1522; died of malarial fever in 1562; daughter of Pedro de Toledo (a rich Spanish viceroy at Naples and marquis of Villafranca); became first wife of Cosimo I or Cosmos de Medici (1519–1574), grand duke of Tuscany (r. 1569–1574), in 1543; children: five sons, Francesco (1541–1587); Giovanni, cardinal (d. 1562); Garzia (d. 1562); Ferdinand I (1549–1609); Pietro (1554–1604); and three daughters, Maria (b. 1540, died at 17); Isabella de Medici (1542–1576); *Lucrezia de Medici (c. 1544–1561).

Eleonora de Medici was a noblewoman who married the Italian prince Cosimo I de Medici. Sixteenth-century Italy was a place of incessant civil warfare carried on by the lords of its powerful city-states, and Cosimo was no exception to the rule. He spent most of his career trying to defeat the House of Strozzi, hereditary enemies of the House of Medici. Eleonora was not a passive witness to Cosimo's warfare; instead, she was an active participant and seems to have been a bold warrior. She fought in pitched battles alongside her husband, and in some cases led troops herself. A chronicler of the time recorded an instance when Eleonora was riding with only a few soldiers and met Filippo Strozzi. A battle ensued, and in the end Eleonora took Strozzi captive. She later participated in the capture of the town of Siena in 1554.

Her daughters Maria and Lucrezia died young; Maria died of malaria at 17, and Lucrezia died at 16, one year after her marriage to Alfonso d'Este, duke of Ferrara. Her daughter *Isabella de Medici, who was married to Paolo Giordano Orsini and lived in the Medici Palace, was murdered by her husband. (*See also Accoramboni, Vittoria.*)

Eleonora de Medici died in 1562, following the death of her favorite son Garzia; Cosimo, who was with her to the end, never fully recovered from the loss, though he did go on to marry his young mistress, *Camilla Martelli. Together, they had two children: Giovanni (d. 1621) and *Virginia d'Este.

Laura York, M.A. in history,
University of California, Riverside, California

Medici, Eleonora de (1556–1576)

*Tuscan noblewoman. Name variations: Eleonore or Eleonora or Eleanora of Toledo; Eleonora di Toledo; Leonora. Born around 1556; murdered in 1576; niece of *Eleonora de Medici (1522–1562); married Pietro de Medici (1554–1604), in 1571; children: Cosimo.*

At age 15, in 1571, Eleonora de Medici arrived in Florence to marry her cousin Pietro de Medici. It was a ceremony that aroused pity in all who attended, for Pietro, a dissipated member of the Medicis, was not a prize catch. For the next few years, as her husband scandalized Florence with consecutive orgies and openly insulted her, the neglected Eleonora fell in love with Bernardino Antinori. When Bernardino was accosted by an angry rival in a narrow passage near the Strozzi Palace, he killed his assailant in self-defense and then gave himself up and was

confined as a prisoner in his family's palace until the matter could be looked into. A terrified Eleonora, who could no longer hide her love, drove round and round the Antinori palace, hoping to speak to her beloved through an open window. But Bernardino was exiled to Elba.

From Elba, he wrote to Eleonora, but the missive was intercepted and handed over to Francesco I de Medici, brother of Pietro and grand duke of Tuscany. Brought back to Florence, Bernardino was executed on June 20. On July 11, Eleonora was told to meet her husband Pietro at the villa of Cafaggiolo. Leaving her four-year-old son Cosimo, she drove the 15 miles from Florence and arrived at the villa that evening. Following supper, Pietro drew his sword and killed her, then claimed that she had died from heart disease. Eleonora's son died a few months later.

*Eleonora de Medici
(1522–1562)*

Medici, Eleonora de (1567–1611)

Duchess of Mantua. Name variations: Eleonora Gonzaga. Born Eleonora de Medici in 1567; died in 1611; daughter of Joanna of Austria (1546–1578) and Francis or Francesco I de Medici (1541–1587), grand duke of Tuscany (r. 1574–1587); sister of Marie de Medici *(c. 1573–1642); married Vincenzo I (1562–1612), 4th duke of Mantua (r. 1587–1612), in 1583; children: Francesco (1586–1612), 5th duke of Mantua (r. 1612–1612); Ferdinando also known as Ferdinand (1587–1626), 6th duke of Mantua (r. 1612–1626); *Margherita Gonzaga (1591–1632); Vincenzo II (1594–1627), 7th duke of Mantua (r. 1626–1627); Eleonora I Gonzaga (1598–1655).*

Eleonora de Medici was born into the ruling family of Florence, Italy, the oldest child of Francesco I de Medici, later Grand Duke Francesco I of Tuscany, and his first wife, ***Joanna of Austria**. She received an excellent education in the tradition of the Italian Renaissance aristocracy, which included the study of languages, ancient literature, music, and philosophy.

When Eleonora was about 15, her father entered into negotiations with Guglielmo Gonzaga, ruler of Mantua, to arrange a marriage between Eleonora and Guglielmo's son Vincenzo Gonzaga. The matter of 20-year-old Vincenzo's marital career was of scandalous interest in the courts of Europe, as Vincenzo was accused by many prominent Italian men of being impotent. Since impotency was seen as a sign of weakness in a man, and since fathering children was crucial to being a ruler, no family wanted to marry their daughter to a man suspected of impotency unless he could prove it to be false. Negotiations between the Medici and the Gonzaga were completed concerning Eleonora's dowry and other property issues, but the agreement could not be finalized until the Medici were convinced of Vincenzo's worthiness. This led to a series of "tests" designed to let Vincenzo prove himself a potential husband, as well as to scientific debates over the nature of impotence and much gossip at Vincenzo's expense across the courts of Europe. But at last the "tests," which involved witnesses (including women he had supposedly had affairs with) testifying to Vincenzo's sexual abilities, satisfied the Medici's suspicions. Eleonora left Florence for Mantua, and married Vincenzo in 1583.

Eleonora's thoughts about her husband and her marriage are revealed in some of the letters she wrote later to her sister ***Marie de Medici**, queen of France. She and Vincenzo appear to have been compatible, but it was not a love match. They shared many of the same interests—love of theater, appreciation for the visual arts, and the desire to create a splendid court which passed its days in luxury, expensive feasts, and lavish entertainment. They had six children, three daughters and three sons.

But Vincenzo, though a cultured and intellectual man, was also the product of his times, which valued violence as a sign of masculinity. He was frequently drunk, and more than once the courts of Europe learned of Vincenzo knifing some courtier, entertainer, or stranger in a fit of rage over a perceived insult. He also had a particularly antagonistic relationship with his father which Eleonora tried unsuccessfully to diffuse, even goading Vincenzo into a short-lived reconciliation with his father on his father's deathbed. All this was enough to make Eleonora's married life difficult, but Vincenzo was also, as were many aristocratic men of his time, notorious for his affairs with prostitutes and court women. As her letters to her sisters reveal, Eleonora sometimes railed against her situation, even advising Marie de Medici to avoid similar marital hardships by refusing to get married. Eleonora also suffered from ill health for most of her married life, illnesses compounded by her numerous pregnancies. Duchess Eleonora died early, at age 44, in 1611. Her husband survived her by less than a year. All three of her short-lived sons eventually succeeded their father to the throne of Mantua. The portrait of Eleonora de Medici by Pulzone, located in the Pitti Gallery, shows her to be of considerable beauty.

SOURCES:
Simon, Kate. *A Renaissance Tapestry: The Gonzaga of Mantua.* NY: Harper & Row, 1988.
Young, George F. *The Medici.* 2nd ed. NY: E.P. Dutton, 1911.

Laura York, M.A. in history,
University of California, Riverside, California

Medici, Eleonora de (1591–1617)

Tuscan noblewoman. Born in 1591; died, age 26, in December 1617; daughter of Christine of Lorraine (c. 1571–1637) and Ferdinand I de Medici (1549–1609), grand duke of Tuscany (r. 1587–1609); sister of Cosimo II de Medici (1590–1620), grand duke of Tuscany (r. 1609–1620).

Eleonora de Medici was born in Tuscany in 1591, the daughter of ***Christine of Lorraine** (c. 1571–1637) and Ferdinand I de Medici, grand duke of Tuscany. She was betrothed to Philip III, king of Spain, but he reneged on the agreement, and it is said that she died of a broken heart. Her portrait hangs in the Uffizi Gallery.

Medici, Eleonora de (fl. 1690)

Tuscan noblewoman. Name variations: Eleonora Gonzaga. Flourished around 1690; married Francesco

Maria de Medici (1660–1711, who was cardinal until 1709).

Medici, Ginevra de (fl. 1450–1460)

Florentine noblewoman. Name variations: Ginevra degli Alessandri. Born Ginevra degli Albizzi; married Giovanni de Medici (1421–1463); children: one son who died in 1461 at age nine.

Medici, Ginevra de

Tuscan noblewoman. Name variations: Genevra Cavalcanti; Ginevra d'Medici. Married Lorenzo de Medici (1395–1440); children: Pier or Piero Francesco (d. 1467).

Medici, Isabella de (1542–1576)

*Princess of Bracciano. Name variations: Isabella Orsini. Born in 1542; died in July 1576 by her husband's hand; daughter of Cosimo I de Medici (1519–1574), grand duke of Tuscany (r. 1569–1574), and *Eleonora de Medici (1522–1562); married Paolo Giordano Orsini, prince of Bracciano or Brachiano, in 1558.*

In 1558, 16-year-old Isabella de Medici married Paolo Giordano Orsini, prince of Bracciano, the most powerful prince in Rome. It was said that Isabella was highly accomplished, beautiful and kind. In the *Origine e Descendenza de' Medici,* a chronicler writes: "Wit, beauty, and talent made her conspicuous among all the ladies of the day, and she captivated every heart but her husband's. Speaking French, Spanish, and Latin fluently, a perfect musician, singing beautifully, a poetess and *improvisatrice* by nature, Isabella was the soul of all around her, and the fairest star of the Medici." Her fate would bring down the house of Orsini.

After 18 years of marriage, Isabella was residing predominantly in Florence while her husband dallied with the married *Vittoria Accoramboni in Rome. Orsini, corrupted by his enormous power and spurred on by his lover, decided to kill his wife Isabella and Vittoria's husband Francesco Peretti in order to wed Vittoria. Isabella, aware she was in danger, wrote to *Catherine de Medici in France, requesting asylum. Catherine agreed and hastened to make arrangements, but she would be too late. On July 16, 1576, after her husband had unexpectedly arrived in Florence, Isabella accompanied him at his request to their villa of Cerreto Guidi, near Empoli. On the way, Isabella once more

confessed her misgivings, this time to her traveling companion, **Lucrezia Frescobaldi.**

In one historian's version, Orsini had made elaborate preparations for what would follow. A hole had been cut into the ceiling above the bedroom chamber where four men were stationed; a noose had been fed down through the hole and dangled behind a window curtain. That night as Orsini and his wife Isabella retired to the darkened room, he slipped the noose around her neck while kissing her, and, after a violent struggle, she was strangled. Orsini claimed that she had died of apoplexy while "bathing her head," then sent his soldiers to the Villa Negroni in Rome where they killed Francesco Peretti.

Pope Gregory XIII, convinced of foul play, refused to let the widowed Orsini marry the widowed Accoramboni. In defiance, the couple entered into a mock marriage, and for the next four years Orsini and Accoramboni were locked into a struggle with the pope. Then Gregory died and Sixtus V, the uncle of the murdered Francesco Peretti, was elected pope. Accoramboni fled to Padua; Orsini was exiled to Venice. He died there and left his estate to Vittoria. Furious at that turn of events, his nearest relation, Ludovico Orsini, stabbed Vittoria to death. When Ludovico was arrested and put to death, the house of Orsini was ruined and never regained power.

Medici, Joanna de (1546–1578).

See Joanna of Austria.

Medici, Laudomia de (fl. 1460s)

Tuscan noblewoman. Name variations: Laudomia Accaiuoli or Acciaiuoli; Laudomia d'Medici. Born Laudomia Accaiuoli; flourished in the 1460s; married Pier or Piero Francesco d'Medici (d. 1467); children: Lorenzo (1463–1507); Giovanni (1467–1498).

Medici, Laudomia de (fl. 1530s)

*Tuscan noblewoman. Name variations: Laudomia Salviati; Laudomia Strozzi. Flourished in the 1530s; daughter of Pier Francesco de Medici (d. 1525) and *Maria Soderini de Medici; sister of Lorenzino de Medici who assassinated Alessandro de Medici; married Alemanno Salviati (died); married Piero Strozzi.*

The Republic of Florence was abolished in May 1532 and Alessandro de Medici was declared duke of Florence. Alessandro was hated by the Florentines. When he was assassinated on January 5, 1537, by her brother Lorenzino, Laudomia de Medici was innocent but implicated.

Medici, Lucrezia de (1425–1482)

Italian businesswoman. Name variations: Lucrezia Tornabuoni. Born Lucrezia Tornabuoni (of an ancient aristocratic and powerful Florentine family) in 1425; died in 1482 in Florence; married Piero "il Gottoso" de Medici also known as Piero or Pietro de Medici (1416–1469, a preeminent figure in Florence), about 1444; children: Lorenzo de Medici, the Magnificent (1449–1492, unofficial ruler of republican Florence during the Renaissance period, who was a poet, diplomatist, and celebrated patron of the arts); Giuliano (1453–1478); *Bianca de Medici (who married Guglielmo dei Pazzi); *Nannina de Medici (who married Bernardo Rucellai); *Maria de Medici (who married Lionetto de' Rossi).*

Lucrezia de Medici made an important contribution to the emerging prestige of the Medicis. She was born into the wealthy Tornabuoni family and married Piero de Medici when she was about 19. At the time, the Medici of Florence was just establishing itself as a leading Italian dynasty, with great wealth, extensive lands, and close ties to the royal families of Italy; within a century, it would be recognized across Europe as one of its leading political houses. Lucrezia assisted in this development largely through her business acumen, her administrative skills, and her willingness to act as her husband's surrogate in negotiations and financial transactions.

Among other activities, Lucrezia arranged the marriages of her children—a key aspect of creating a stable power base in the Middle Ages. Since the health of Piero de Medici was poor, Lucrezia seems to have been intent on grooming her son Lorenzo the Magnificent to replace his father. Lorenzo's precocious brilliance as an adolescent was manifested in the rapidity with which he learned the ropes of interstate diplomacy and the political management within Florence. After Piero died in 1469, Lucrezia maintained the Medici fortune for Lorenzo, managing their affairs so completely that he was free to occupy himself wherever he wanted.

Lorenzo's formidable mother was as much responsible as his father for setting Lorenzo a good example of how to influence and control events by the cultivation of clients and friends. When she died at age 57, in 1482, Lorenzo wrote that Lucrezia had long been "an instrument who relieved me of many burdens. . . . The sole refuge in my many troubles."

SOURCES:
Anderson, Bonnie S., and Judith P. Zinsser. *A History of Their Own.* Vol. I. NY: Harper & Row, 1988.

SUGGESTED READING:
Brucker, Gene. *Renaissance Florence.* John Wiley, 1969.
Foster, Philip. *A Study of Lorenzo de' Medici's Villa at Poggio a Caiano.* 2 vols. Garland, 1978.
Hale, John. *Florence and the Medici.* Thames & Hudson, 1977.
Hook, Judith. *Lorenzo de' Medici.* Hamish Hamilton, 1984.
Roover, Raymond de. *The Rise and Decline of the Medici Bank (1397–1494).* Harvard University Press, 1963.
Ross, Janet. *Lives of the Early Medici as Shown in Their Correspondence.* Chatto & Windus, 1910.
Rubinstein, Nicolai. *The Government of Florence under the Medici (1434–94).* Clarendon, 1966.

Laura York, M.A. in history,
University of California, Riverside, California

Medici, Lucrezia de (b. around 1480)

Tuscan noblewoman. Name variations: Lucrezia Salviati. Born Lucrezia Giovanni de Medici around 1480; daughter of Lorenzo de Medici (1449–1492), the Magnificent, and *Clarice de Medici (c. 1453–1487); sister of Pope Leo X (1475–1521); married Jacopo also known as Giacomo Salviati; children: Giovanni Salviati, cardinal; *Maria Salviati (1499–1543, who married Giovanni delle Bande Nere); Elena Salviati (who married Jacopo V Appiani).*

The tombs of the two Medici popes, Clement VII (Giulio de Medici) and Leo X (Giovanni de Medici), were completed by Lucrezia de Medici around 1535. The popes were interred in the church of the Santa Maria sopra Minerva.

Medici, Lucrezia de (c. 1544–1561)

Duchess of Ferrara. Born around 1544; died in 1561; daughter of Cosimo I de Medici (1519–1574), grand duke of Tuscany, and *Eleonora de Medici (1522–1562); first wife of Alfonso II (1533–1597), 5th duke of Ferrara and Modena (r. 1559–1597). Alfonso II's second wife was *Margherita Gonzaga (1564–1618).*

In 1561, Lucrezia de Medici, newly married to Alfonso II, the duke of Ferrara, died in Ferrara at age 17. In later years, in light of the propensity for skullduggery at the time, it was rumored that she was poisoned by her husband because of infidelity. The story's origins have now been attributed to enemies of the house of Ferrara.

Medici, Luisa de

Florentine noblewoman. Died before age 12; daughter of Lorenzo de Medici (1449–1492), the Magnificent, and *Clarice de Medici (c. 1453–1487).*

Medici, Maddalena de (d. 1519)

Florentine noblewoman. Name variations: Maddalena Cybo, Cibo, or Cibò. Died at the villa of Careggi in 1519; eldest daughter of Lorenzo de Medici (1449–1492), the Magnificent, and *Clarice de Medici (c. 1453–1487); married Franceschetto or Francesco Cybo (son of Pope Innocent VIII), on January 20, 1488; children: Innocenzo Cibò, cardinal; Lorenzo Cibò (who married Ricciarda Malaspina, princess of Massa); *Caterina Cibò, duchess of Camerino.

Pope Innocent VIII, impressed with the flourishing House of Medici, expressed interest in establishing an alliance with it through one of his sons. Lorenzo the Magnificent offered his eldest daughter Maddalena. When young Francesco Cibò and his retinue arrived from Rome for the marriage, they were feted grandly in separate lodgings from the Medici Palace. But when Cibò was invited to stay with the Medicis, he was affronted by their simple style of living, so unlike the luxuries he was used to in the Papal palace at Rome. Francesco took it as a personal insult until it was explained to him that he was now considered part of the family and that that was how the family lived.

Medici, Maddalena de (1600–1633)

Tuscan noblewoman and nun. Born in 1600; died in 1633; daughter of *Christine of Lorraine (c. 1571–1637) and Ferdinand I de Medici (1549–1609), grand duke of Tuscany (r. 1587–1609); twin sister of Lorenzo de Medici (d. 1648).

At age 20, a few months after her brother Cosimo II's death in 1620, Maddalena de Medici became a nun at the convent of the Crocetta; she died there in 1633, age 33. Her twin brother Lorenzo lived to be 48.

Medici, Madeleine de (1501–1519).

See Madeleine de la Tour d'Auvergne.

Medici, Margaret de.

See Margaret of Parma (1522–1586).
See Margaret of Parma (b. 1612).

Medici, Margherita de.

See Margaret of Parma (1522–1586).
See Margaret of Parma (b. 1612).

Medici, Marguerite Louise de (c. 1645–1721).

See Marguerite Louise of Orleans.

Medici, Maria Cristina de (1610–1632)

Tuscan noblewoman. Born in 1610; died at the villa of Poggio Imperiale at age 22 in August 1632; daughter of *Maria Magdalena of Austria (1589–1631) and Cosimo II de Medici (1590–1620), duke of Tuscany (r. 1609–1620); twin sister of Ferdinand II (1610–1670), grand duke of Tuscany (r. 1620–1670).

Medici, Maria de (fl. late 1400s)

Florentine noblewoman. Name variations: Maria de Rossi. Flourished in late 1400s; daughter of Piero "il Gottoso" de Medici also known as Piero or Pietro de Medici (1416–1469), a preeminent figure in Florence, and *Lucrezia de Medici (1425–1482); sister of Lorenzo de Medici, the Magnificent (1449–1492), unofficial ruler of republican Florence during the Renaissance period; married Lionetto de Rossi.

Medici, Maria de (1499–1543).

See Salviati, Maria.

Medici, Maria de (c. 1573–1642).

See Medici, Marie de.

Medici, Maria Magdalena de (1589–1631).

See Maria Magdalena of Austria.

Medici, Maria Soderini de

Tuscan noblewoman. Name variations: Maria Soderini. Married Pier Francesco de Medici the Younger (d. 1525); children: Lorenzino de Medici (1514–1548, who assassinated Alessandro de Medici in 1537); *Laudomia de Medici (who married Piero Strozzi); Maddalena de Medici (who married Roberto Strozzi); and Giuliano, bishop of Beziers.

Medici, Marie de (c. 1573–1642)

Member of the powerful Florentine family who became a queen of France, hungered for power in the tradition of her blood, and achieved it but only fleetingly, more for lack of wisdom than of spirit. Name variations: (French with the "s" and accent) Marie de Médicis; (Italian without the "s" and accent) Maria de Medici or Marie de' Medici; also Mary de Medici. Pronunciation: MEH-de-chee. Born on April 26, 1573 or 1574 in Florence, Italy; died on July 3, 1642, in poverty and exile, in Cologne, Germany; youngest child of Francis or Francesco I de Medici (1541–1587), grand duke of Tuscany (r. 1574–1587), a scholar and patron of the arts, and Joanna of Austria (1546–1578); married Henri also known as Henry IV the Great (1553–1610), king of France (r. 1589–1610) and Navarre, on October 5, 1600; children: Louis XIII (1601–1643), king of France (r. 1610–1643); Elizabeth Valois (1602–1644, who married Philip IV, king of Spain); Christine of France (1606–1663); Philippe (b. 1607); Gaston d'Orléans (1608–1660), duke of Orléans; Henrietta Maria (1609–1669, who married Charles I, king of England).

Married by proxy to King Henry IV of France and set out from Italy to meet her new husband (1600); became regent to her nine-year-old son, Louis XIII, the day after Henry's assassination (1610); after murder and execution of her court favorites, placed under house arrest at Blois (1617); escaped from Blois and reconciled to the king by Cardinal Richelieu (1619); exiled again, after another confrontation with Cardinal Richelieu, followed by another escape (1630); exiled finally to Cologne, where her remains were held for a year after her death until her debts were paid.

The many dramatic and tragic events in the life of Marie de Medici revolved largely around her relationships to powerful men, including her father and her uncle, the grand dukes of Tuscany Francesco I de Medici and Ferdinand I de Medici; her husband, King Henry IV of France; the wily French minister Cardinal Richelieu; and her son, France's King Louis XIII.

Her childhood in Italy was far from happy. The youngest of four children, she was five years old when her mother *Joanna of Austria died, and she was sent along with her brother and sisters to live at the grandiose Pitti Palace in Florence. Soon after her mother's death, her father, then the grand duke, married his mistress, *Bianca Cappello. According to Marie de Medici's biographer Louis Battifol, Marie was never to forget the humiliation of being forced to take her lessons with Antonio, her father's illegitimate child. In 1583, she was ten when her only brother died, followed the next year by her lively 15-year-old sister **Caterina**; that same year her other sister, *Eleonora de Medici (1567–1611), left to marry the duke of Mantua.

The life of the little princess of Tuscany seemed dogged by physical disasters as well as personal tragedies. Twice the ducal palace was rocked by earthquakes, and lightning struck her bedroom three times. For years, the only bright presence in her life was ◄❧ Leonora Galigaï, a girl three years younger than Marie, with a quick wit and a desire to please, who could make the princess laugh. Lonely survivors in an

Galigaï, Leonora (c. 1570–1617).

See French "Witches."

❧►

unfriendly world, the two became close companions, and out of this innocent friendship formed in difficult times would develop repercussions of catastrophic proportions in later years.

Educated by tutors appointed by her father, Marie de Medici proved to be good at mathematics, and to excel at lapidary, or the evaluation of precious stones, which would prove to be an expensive hobby. She also did well in drawing, engraving, architecture, and sculpture, and acquired a lifelong love of art that would lead her to become an important patron for artists. She was not taught French and seemed uninterested in learning the language even after she moved to France. Raised as she was in guarded isolation, she also had limited knowledge of the social workings of the world.

Marie had reached her teens when her father Grand Duke Francesco died. In the absence of a legitimate male heir, his brother, Cardinal Ferdinand, gave up the religious life to take up the family title in Tuscany. Ferdinand married *Christine of Lorraine, the granddaughter of French queen *Catherine de Medici; at age 16, Marie's new aunt was her senior by two years. The young women became good friends, and the Pitti changed from a stern but luxurious prison into a festive palace, where Marie's uncle now gave her the affection she had never known from her own father.

Ferdinand, meanwhile, became concerned with elevating the Medici name and arranged the best possible marriage for his niece. The effort lasted 13 years. Some negotiations, involving absurd political maneuvering, led nowhere; others were stopped by Marie herself. Ferdinand did not force Marie to marry against her will. Many said that it was the extremely ambitious Leonora Galigaï who made Marie hold out for a king. When Marie was still a small girl, however, a nun had predicted that she would be queen of France, and the childhood companions now waited together for the fulfillment of the prophecy.

When negotiations began between the houses of Medici and Navarre, neither party was blind to the circumstances of the union. For Henry IV, the marriage would be a merger due to necessity, and for Marie, it promised a glorious opportunity. At age 27, she was tall and blonde with her father's broad forehead and direct gaze. From her Austrian mother, she had inherited the Habsburg chin and, some said, a meager intelligence. But her bearing was regal, and she had a radiant complexion and good health—important attributes for Henry IV, as she was untried from the standpoint of giving

Marie
de Medici
(c. 1573–1642)

birth, and his marriage to ***Margaret of Valois** had recently been annulled because of her failure to provide an heir to the throne.

Henry's fertility had been proved many times over with illegitimate births, and the fact that he had recently proposed to two of his mistresses—***Gabrielle d'Estrées** and ❧▶ **Henriette d'Entragues**—was no secret. Had the court of France not been deeply in debt to the Medici family, the marriage to Marie would not even have been considered. As it was, when Henry IV had last borrowed money from the Medicis, 17 wagons had been required to transport the 100,000 crowns from Florence to Paris, with

five companies of cavalry and 200 foot soldiers hired to guard the convoy. While Henry was frantically pleading with one mistress to buy back his written marriage proposal, his councilors were negotiating for an enormous dowry from the Medici.

Ferdinand, whose income equaled almost the entire revenue of France, drew up the final marriage terms. In the contract, signed on April 25, 1600, the grand duke agreed to give France 600,000 crowns, about half of which would come as a cash dowry with the bride, with the rest to be remitted from the king's debt. The wedding took place by proxy in the Duomo of

✦ Entragues, Henriette d' (1579–1633)

Marquise de Verneuil. Name variations: Henriette d'Es-traigues. Born Catherine Henriette de Balzac d'Entragues in 1579; died in 1633; daughter of Charles Balzac d'Entragues and Marie Touchet (who was the mistress of Charles IX); mistress of Henry IV, king of France.

Ambitious and somewhat conniving, Henriette d'Entragues was the mistress of Henry IV, king of France, and succeeded in inducing Henry to promise to marry her after the death of his other mistress *Gabrielle d'Estrées, a promise which led to bitter scenes at court when shortly afterwards Henry married *Marie de Medici. Henriette d'Entragues carried her spite so far as to be deeply compromised in a plot with Marshal Biron against the king in 1606. Though Biron was convicted of treason and conspiracy with Spain, Henriette escaped with only a slight punishment. In 1608, Henry returned her to favor. She seems then to have been involved in the Spanish intrigues which preceded the assassination of the king in 1610.

Florence, since the groom was detained by war. For the first time in her life, Marie de Medici was the center of attention, at festivities that lasted for ten days. One who witnessed the extravagance was the artist Peter Paul Rubens, who worked for Marie's brother-in-law, the duke of Mantua.

*S*he is desirous of honour, and vain-glorious through excess of courage.

—Henry IV

A small fleet debarked, carrying the queen, her jewels, and the dowry to France, and after 23 days of rough sailing landed safely in Marseilles. The Florentines were greeted with pomp, and another reception took place at Lyons, where the queen saw her new husband for the first time. After all the ceremonial build-up, this first encounter must have been a terrible disappointment for the bride. Henry IV was due on December 10, but arrived at Lyons the night before. Because the city gate was closed, he waited in the rain for an hour to be let in. Marie had already retired when he knocked at her door and presented himself, still in wet clothes, and began to cover her with caresses, saying that he hoped to spend the night there, as no bed had been prepared for him. Marie replied to the king that she was his humblest servant, although nothing in her severe upbringing could have prepared her for such informality. The next day, Marie and Henry were married in a second ceremony, and the word that reached the grand duke was that

his niece, instead of showing joy, "did nothing but weep and lament."

A worse incident was in store to deeply wound the new bride soon after her arrival in Paris. At an official function, when Henriette d'Entragues was presented to the queen, Henry IV turned to explain, "Mademoiselle has been my mistress. She will be your most obedient servant." While the queen froze, the mistress bowed, and the king, usually known for his gallantry, suddenly placed a hand on Henriette's head, pushing her to her knees, and forcing her to kiss the hem of the queen's gown. Neither woman ever forgot the incident and less than a year later, when both gave birth to sons within days of each other, their relationship did not improve.

After the shock of introduction to her new life, Marie de Medici experienced a period of contentment. She submitted willingly to the health regimen Henry imposed, which involved a physic and bleeding at regular intervals as a preventive measure. She wrote letters crediting the French doctors with curing a stomach ailment she had endured for years, and declared that she had never felt better. Her first pregnancy was the easiest, and the birth of the dauphin, the future Louis XIII, filled the king with uncontrollable joy. Writers celebrated the queen as a lily among flowers, the public found her beautiful and gracious, and Marie wrote to her uncle that Henry treated her with honor and surrounded her with kindness upon every occasion.

Unaccustomed to consideration from her childhood, however, Marie did not know how to respond to it. Her contemporaries described her as distant, reserved and even cold, and Cardinal Richelieu wrote that she was grave and not very affectionate. With the exception of her third son, Gaston, she seemed indifferent to her children, who did not live with her at the Louvre, although she showed concern when they were sick and asked for reports of their behavior. Henry IV differed from her in that he adored all his children, made them call him Papa, and legitimized the offspring of his mistresses, insisting that five of them be raised with the five royal children. Marie vehemently opposed this coexistence, and young Louis resented the proximity of his half-siblings, playing with them and protecting them but allowing them no familiarities.

Marie was very strict with her oldest son, who proved to be as willful as his mother. On one occasion, when he refused to take medicine, six people were required to administer it. To curb his rebellious outbursts, Marie ordered him to be whipped regularly. Louis fought back, sometimes

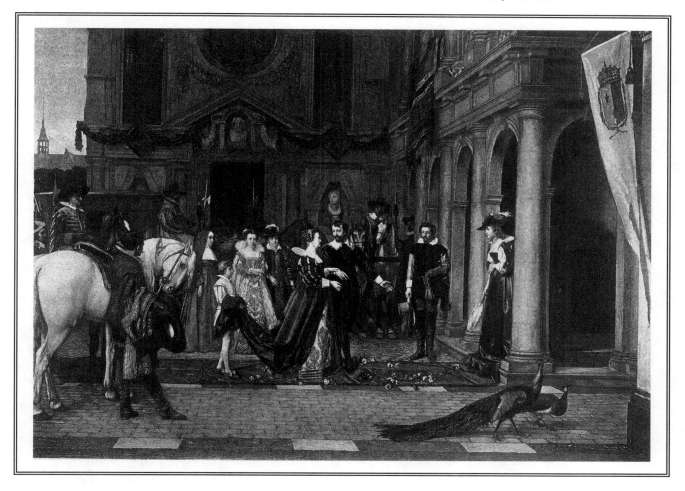

punching his governess, and occasionally became so angered that he would faint. When attendants complained that the floggings threatened the boy's health, the queen relented to the extent of advising that the whip be used more cautiously. Henry warned his wife that there would be trouble ahead, because her son was as opinionated and obstinate as she was. Once, in fact, after the king's death, when the queen had ordered Louis flogged, he entered her room following the beating. As required by court etiquette, the queen rose in his presence, to which young Louis responded, "I would be better pleased with less *obeissance* and less whipping."

Marie's main concern with her three daughters was to provide them with advantageous marriages: *Elizabeth Valois was married to Philip IV of Spain, *Christine of France to Victor Amadeus I, duke of Savoy, and *Henrietta Maria to the ill-fated Charles I of England, who would later be executed by order of Parliament.

At the French court, the queen never felt completely secure, in part because Henry IV's life was constantly threatened. Raised a Protestant Huguenot and a convert to Catholicism, the king believed in religious tolerance and tried to maintain a balance between the two factions, but remained hated by extremists on both sides. Plots against his person were constantly brewing. Because the marriage proposal written to Henriette d'Entragues in Henry's hand had never been retrieved, Marie also feared a threat to the royal succession, and became obsessed with the necessity of a formal coronation. The opportunity came in 1610, when Henry IV was about to engage in a military campaign, requiring that he leave the capital. During his absence, Marie would be designated to act as regent, but prior to his departure she sought to secure her position more firmly through a sanctified ceremony. Henry agreed, but reluctantly, feeling that the event might bring him bad luck.

The coronation took place on May 13, 1610. The following day, Henry IV seemed filled with foreboding, and before leaving the palace he repeatedly kissed the queen goodbye, asking her several times if he should go. He was on his way, and passing through a narrow street, when a religious fanatic who felt that Henry had been too lenient toward the Protestants stepped out and stabbed him.

The news of the king's death was kept secret until his body could be brought back to the Louvre. Marie heard a great noise in the royal chamber, rushed in, and found her husband's body laid out on his bed. Within hours of the tragedy, the Parlement had met to declare her regent of the new king of France, her nine-year-old son Louis XIII. Some said that she had awaited this moment all her life, and that the meters of black crepe she wore enhanced her radiant look. Others described her as genuinely devastated when she addressed the Parlement with the little king beside her.

Marie de Medici, who had always seemed bored when she attended sessions of the Parlement with Henry, now participated willingly. Given genuine responsibility, she proved reasonable at making decisions and continuing Henry's policies, even when they were contrary to her own convictions. At the time of his death, for instance, the war he had undertaken favored the Protestant cause against Catholic interests with which she aligned herself. Nevertheless, she sent a large army to Julich, a Protestant dukedom seized by the Habsburgs, and after a siege of one month, the Austrian imperial garrison capitulated. The French, in league with the Protestant Dutch, English, and German forces, had thus regained territory taken by a Catholic power, thereby antagonizing the pope and Spain—a politically dangerous position for a Catholic queen to be in. It was to appease the Catholic elements at this time that she negotiated a double marriage between her son Louis XIII and *Anne of Austria (1601–1666), and between her daughter Elizabeth Valois and the future Philip IV of Spain. At the very beginning of her regency, the queen whom many had thought to be dull-witted thus accomplished a remarkable coup.

Had she been more insightful, however, she might have recognized that her childhood companion, Leonora Galigaï, who had accompanied her to the French court, and Leonora's husband, Concino Concini, were now vying to become the virtual rulers of France. From the time she set foot on French soil, Leonora Galigaï's main concern had been to elevate her own position. Concini was a Florentine adventurer who had come to France to avoid being expelled from Tuscany, and in their marriage, combining greed, ambition, deviousness and lack of scruples, the couple formed a deadly team. Henry IV had seen the threat well enough to try to banish them, but Marie had stubbornly continued to support them and to lavish money and offices on them.

By 1614, the Concinis had enough influence to be held responsible for depleting the treasury, and several powerful dukes, accusing the queen of squandering money, demanded a session of the Estates General, which had not taken place in 60 years.

The three estates represented at the gathering were the clergy, the nobility, and the commons. The king, now aged 13, attended with his mother. Richelieu was a new delegate from the clergy, and when the queen's power was challenged, he defended her eloquently, thereby saving the regency. Had the queen chosen at this point to distance herself from the Concinis, she might have retained her position. Instead, she outraged the court by allowing Concini to become a marechal de France, a move that would lead to his assassination and the loss of her own power.

The murder was initiated by the king's falconer, Charles d'Albert de Luynes, a courtly and witty man in his 30s. Luynes filled Louis' need for affection and fun, and the two had developed a strong attachment, riding horses together, hunting and training hawks. When Louis XIII ordered the arrest of Concini, a group of conspirators took it upon themselves to kill him instead, and on the morning of April 24, 1617, while Concini was on his way to the Louvre, he was stopped by three bullets fired by men with loaded pistols concealed under their cloaks. Leonora Galigaï was dragged off to the Bastille, and Richelieu passed a frenzied Paris mob as it was hacking the body of Concini to pieces on the Pont Neuf. In a trumped-up trial, Leonora was convicted of witchcraft and executed at the guillotine, while Louis XIII kept his mother confined in the castle of Blois. At age 16, he had, due to his mother, been married for two years to Anne of Austria, whom he disliked.

After two years under house arrest, Marie de Medici and her supporters choreographed a bizarre escape. At midnight, in February, the 46-year-old queen, by then a corpulent mother of six, climbed down a rope ladder carrying only her jewel case. Two men assisted her descent from her bedroom window (one account describes it as 25 feet, another as 120 feet above ground). One man held her around the middle while the other guided her feet, which were bare to assure a better grip. Upon reaching a sloping rampart, she lost her nerve and refused to proceed to a second ladder, and the conspirators had to use ropes and a cloak to assemble a makeshift hammock to lower her the rest of the way.

Through adroit negotiations, Richelieu eventually brought about a reconciliation between mother and son, and Marie returned to Paris undaunted. Instead of playing the role of a subdued and repentant mother, she undertook a monumental project of self-aggrandizement through art. What she had not achieved on a political scale, she now intended to create by ushering in a golden age of baroque extravagance. Throughout her reign, she had patronized the visual arts as well as music, the theater, and architecture. In 1622, she invited Rubens to the French court and embarked on a tremendous project, commissioning 24 huge allegorical paintings to commemorate "the illustrious life and heroic deeds" of her reign. The purpose of the work was to make the queen look sublime, even if history had to be rearranged, and she insisted on having final approval. Because of its propagandistic nature, the work is not considered Rubens' best, but it is fascinating to see how he turned her pathetic escape from Blois into a glorious event. When Louis XIII visited the Luxembourg Palace to see the new works, Rubens became the queen's accomplice in giving her son convoluted explanations of the paintings, so that he had no idea of their real significance.

After the death of his falconer Luynes, Louis began to rely on Richelieu, who was now prime minister. On November 11, 1630, a stormy scene between Marie, Louis, and Richelieu resulted in the king's siding with his minister to exclude the queen from affairs of state. Banished a second time, she escaped, this time on horseback, at age 58, and sought refuge in the Spanish Netherlands.

Alienated from her children and subjects, the spirited exile was not even informed officially of the birth of the future Louis XIV, born to his parents after 23 years of childless marriage. Marie de Medici, princess of Tuscany and queen of France, died in poverty, at age 67, in Cologne, in a house placed at her disposal by Rubens. Ironically, she left her last possession, a pet parrot, to Richelieu, the man whose assassination she had been planning during the last years of her life.

SOURCES:

Battifol, Louis. *Marie de Medicis and the French Court.* 1908. Translated by Mary King. Edited by H.W. Carless Davis. NY: Books for Library Press, 1970.

Hibbert, Christopher. *The House of Medici: Its Rise and Fall.* NY: Morrow Quill Paperbacks, 1980.

Millen, Ronald F., and Robert E. Wolf. *Heroic Deeds and Mystic Figures: A New Reading of Rubens' Life of Maria De' Medici.* NJ: Princeton University Press, 1989.

O'Connell, D.P. *Richelieu.* Cleveland: World, 1968.

Pearson, Hesketh. *Henry of Navarre: The King Who Dared.* NY: Harper and Row, 1963.

Saward, Susan. *The Golden Age of Marie de' Medici.* Ann Arbor, MI: UMI Research Press, 1982.

Tapie, Victor Lucien. *France in the Age of Louis XIII and Richelieu.* Translated and edited by D. McN. Lockie. NY: Praeger, 1975.

SUGGESTED READING:

Hibbert, Christopher. *The Pen and the Sword.* Vol. 6 of the "Milestones of History" series. NY: Newsweek Books, 1974.

Claire Hsu Accomando,
author of *Love and Rutabaga: A Remembrance of the War Years,*
Bonita, California

Medici, Nannina de

Florentine noblewoman. Name variations: Nannina Rucellai. Daughter of Piero de Medici (1416–1469) and *Lucrezia de Medici (1425–1482); sister of Lorenzo de Medici, the Magnificent (1449–1492); married Bernardo Rucellai.

Medici, Philiberta de (c. 1498–1524).

See Philiberta of Savoy.

Medici, Piccarda de

Matriarch of the House of Medici. Name variations: Piccarda Bueri. Buried next to her husband in the "Old Sacristy" in the church of San Lorenzo; married Giovanni de Medici, known as Giovanni di Bicci de Medici (1360–1429 or 1428); children: Cosimo the Elder de Medici (1389–1464), ruler of Florence (r. 1434–1464); Lorenzo de Medici (1395–1440).

Medici, Semiramide de (fl. 1480s)

Tuscan noblewoman. Name variations: Semiramide Appiani or Appiano. Flourished in the 1480s; married Lorenzo the Younger also known as Lorenzo "Popolano" de Medici (1463–1507); children: three sons, including eldest son Pier Francesco "the Younger" de Medici (died 1525, who married *Maria Soderini de Medici); and two daughters (names unknown).

Medici, Violante Beatrice de (d. 1731)

Tuscan noblewoman and governor of Siena. Name variations: Violante of Bavaria; Violante Beatrice of Bavaria; Yolande. Died in 1731; married Ferdinand de Medici (1663–1713, son of Cosimo III, grand duke of Tuscany, and *Marguerite Louise of Orleans), in 1688; no children.

In November 1688, Prince Ferdinand, the son of the grand duke of Tuscany, and Princess Violante Beatrice of Bavaria were married extravagantly. As heir to the House of Medici, Ferdinand was said to be energetic and cultured, one of the more high-minded Medicis. But his weak father bullied him and thwarted his eagerness to take part in public affairs. Eventually, Ferdinand's zeal turned to cynicism, his path turned to debauchery, and he ruined his health by age 40 and died ten years later in 1713. "Unfortunately he did not care for the wife whom his father had chosen for him, the Princess Violante," writes G.F. Young, "though she was in every way worthy of his affection, and deservedly liked by all classes in Florence. She never reproached him for his neglect, and to the last continued to show her affection for him."

Following her husband's death, Violante retired to Siena and was made governor there. When Gian Gastone de Medici became grand duke of Tuscany in 1723, his wife Anne of Saxe-Lauenburg (*Anna Maria de Medici) refused to live there, so he installed his sister-in-law Violante as the social center of life at court. In time, she became "the chief influence, not only in social matters, but also in public affairs; an influence justly deserved, and followed by the best results." For her patronage of the arts and the poor, Pope Benedict XIII bestowed on her the Golden Rose.

When Ferdinand de Medici's coffin was reopened in 1857, it was found to contain the embalmed heart of Violante, which was enclosed in a vase of majolica. An inscription on the vase gave her name, titles, and "amiable qualities," and stated that "this truly royal heart, which in life was full of all virtues, has in accordance with her dying will and testament been placed in this coffin of her husband."

SOURCES:
Young, Col. G.F. *The Medici*. NY: Modern Library, 1930.

Medici, Virginia de (b. 1573?).

See Este, Virginia d'.

Medici, Vittoria de (d. 1694)

Grand duchess of Tuscany. Name variations: Vittoria della Rovere. Born Vittoria della Rovere; died in 1694; daughter of Claudia de Medici (1604–1648) and Federigo Ubaldo also known as Federigo della Rovere, hereditary prince of Urbino; married Ferdinand II de Medici (1610–1670), grand duke of Tuscany (r. 1620–1670), on April 6, 1637; children: Cosimino and Innominata (died young); Cosimo III

*de Medici (1642–1723), grand duke of Tuscany (r. 1670–1723); Francesco Maria de Medici (1660–1711, a cardinal until 1709, who married *Eleonora de Medici [fl. 1690]).*

Vittoria della Rovere, born around 1622, was the last descendant of the noble Rovere family, hereditary rulers of Urbino. She was the only daughter of Duke Federigo della Rovere of Urbino, who died when she was an infant. Her widowed mother *Claudia de Medici brought Vittoria to Florence to stay with their Medici relatives. There, Vittoria, although only a baby, was chosen as the future wife of her young cousin, Grand Duke Ferdinand II of Tuscany. The choice was made by his grandmother *Christine of Lorraine and his mother *Maria Magdalena of Austria (1589–1631), who were serving as joint regents during Ferdinand's minority. Thus Vittoria, who had inherited the duchy of Urbino on her father's death, was raised to be the grand duchess of Tuscany as well. Her character is revealed in the correspondence of the Medici courtiers and in her own letters. All three of her primary influences—her own mother, Christine of Lorraine, and Maria Magdalena—were especially devout Catholics, who instilled in Vittoria a strong sense of religious obligation which at times veered into bigotry. She was proud of her heritage, her family, and her wealth, but showed little interest in practicing or patronizing the arts, sciences, or literature.

Ferdinand and Vittoria were married on April 6, 1637. The couple had three children early in their marriage: Cosimino and Innominata, who both died shortly after birth, and Cosimo, later Cosimo III of Tuscany. Following the birth of Cosimo in 1642, Ferdinand and Vittoria separated. They were too different in personality and interests: Ferdinand seems to have been rather quiet, lacking in the political ambition which characterized his wife. He preferred to spend his time with his scientific and artistic projects, which Vittoria had little use for. His willingness to let the pope claim the duchy of Urbino—which was Vittoria's by right—angered Vittoria and contributed to their separation. Another factor was the irreconcilable differences in their opinions about how to educate their son and heir, Cosimo; Vittoria insisted that he receive a traditional Latin education by priests, while Ferdinand favored a more modern education, including humanist learning and the recent scientific discoveries.

The couple reunited briefly in 1659, and a fourth child, the future cardinal Francesco Maria, was born in 1660. Grand Duchess Vittoria played an important role in her son Cosimo's administration after Ferdinand died in 1670; Cosimo seems to have been content to let Vittoria and her advisors hold the reins of government. Vittoria and Cosimo's wife, Princess *Marguerite Louise of Orleans, developed a mutual antagonism, and Cosimo shared his mother's dislike of the French princess, who eventually left her husband and returned to France. Vittoria continued to play a central role in Cosimo's government until her death about age 72, in 1694.

SOURCES:

Micheletti, Emma. *The Medici of Florence.* Florence: Scala, 1980.

Young, George F. *The Medici.* 2nd ed. NY: E.P. Dutton, 1911.

Laura York, M.A. in history, University of California, Riverside, California

Medicine, Beatrice A. (1923—)

Native-American anthropologist, teacher, and author. Born on the Standing Rock Reservation, Wakpala, South Dakota, on August 1, 1923 (some sources cite 1924); South Dakota State University, B.S.; Michigan State University, M.A.; University of Wisconsin-Madison, Ph.D.; married and divorced; children: one son, Clarence.

Beatrice A. Medicine was born on the Standing Rock Reservation in Wakpala, South Dakota, in 1923. A member of the Lakota (Sioux) Sihasapa tribe, she took up the study of anthropology to better understand her Native American heritage. Medicine received her B.S. in anthropology from South Dakota State University and went on to obtain an M.A. from Michigan State University and a Ph.D. from the University of Wisconsin-Madison. The focus of her studies was the development of Native American family life and the role of women in Native American culture and society, but she also worked to establish a better public understanding of Native American life. Married and divorced, as a single parent Medicine raised her son in accordance with traditional Lakota culture. She taught at many leading centers of Native American studies, including San Francisco State College and the University of Calgary in Alberta, Canada.

In addition to her busy academic career, Medicine promoted the social welfare of Native American communities, advocating public policies to benefit Native Americans and helping to establish leadership development programs as well as urban community centers for Native Americans. In 1977, she was honored as the Sacred Pipe Woman of the revived Lakota Sun Dance. Medicine received the Distinguished Service Award of the American Anthropological Association in 1991.

Beatrice Medicine

Grant Eldridge, freelance writer, Pontiac, Michigan

Medicis.

French variant of Medici.

Medio, Dolores (1914—)

Spanish writer of social-realist fiction. Name variations: Dolores Medio Estrada. Born on December 24, 1914, in Oviedo, Spain; daughter of Ramón Medio-Tuya y Rivero and Maria Teresa Estrada y Pastor.

Dolores Medio was born on December 24, 1914, in Oviedo, Spain, the daughter of Ramón Medio-Tuya y Rivero and Maria Teresa Estrada y Pastor. Her father died when she was a child, leaving the family in poverty. Intellectually precocious, as a 13-year-old Medio taught private lessons to supplement the household income.

Meanwhile, she also began writing short stories and otherwise showed an interest in literature (she wrote her first novel at 12). Medio celebrated Alphonso XIII's abdication and the proclamation of the Second Republic in 1931, but then experienced firsthand the horrors of civil strife. In 1934, radical miners paralyzed Oviedo with a massive strike, which in turn was brutally repressed by the government. Just before the Spanish Civil War began in July 1936, Medio secured a teaching position. Conservatives criticized her classroom innovations and caused her dismissal within a few months. Appalled by the merciless cruelty of both sides during the war, she advocated mutual tolerance despite her sympathies for the middle and lower classes. As well, her fiance died during the war, and persecution of suspected leftists prevented her from securing a teaching position when the conflict ended.

Supporting herself through menial jobs, Medio published "Niña" in 1945, which won a short-story prize. More important, it convinced her to move to Madrid and try to become a full-time writer. From 1945 to 1965, she wrote for *El Domingo*, a newspaper aimed at the lower class. She also wrote novels, short stories, poetry and literary criticism. In 1953, *Nosotros los Rivero* (*We Riveros*) garnered the Nadal Prize, one of Spain's most prestigious literary awards. *Compás de espera* (*Pause*) and *Mañana* (*Tomorrow*) appeared the following year. In 1962, Medio was arrested and jailed for attending a women's demonstration, even though she had not participated in it. In 1966, she published a biography of *Isabella II. Throughout, Medio remained a prolific writer. Her fiction was traditional narrative, which realistically examined the condition of Spain's common people. Some works drew heavily on her own experiences, such as *Diario de una maestra* (*Diary of a School Teacher*, 1961).

SOURCES:
Jones, Margaret E.W. *Dolores Medio*. NY: Twayne, 1974.

Kendall W. Brown,
Professor of History, Brigham Young University, Provo, Utah

Mee, Margaret (1909–1988)

English botanical artist and traveler. Name variations: Margaret Ursula Mee. Born in 1909; died in 1988; attended Camberwell School of Art.

Discovering her life's work in mid-life, Margaret Mee first traveled to the forests of the Amazon at the age of 47, but did not settle in Brazil and take up her career as a botanical artist until ten years later. Mee traveled extensively in the Brazilian Amazonia, collecting new species and making paintings of remarkable technical accuracy and delicate beauty. Her renderings, executed in gouache (a type of watercolor), are the only verification left of some species of the area, which have since become extinct. Mee also became an outspoken crusader against destruction of the Amazonia, which she called "a valley of death." In May 1988, shortly before she died, Mee made her last trip up the Amazon River to locate and paint a night-blooming cactus called the "moonflower" (*Selenicereus wittii*). After tracking down her elusive subject, Mee painted quickly, using only the dim light of a flashlight so as to prevent the flower from fading and closing. Following Mee's death, a trust was established in her name to call attention to the ecological crisis in the area.

SOURCES:
Ben-Ari, Elia T. "Better than a thousand words: botanical artists blend science and aesthetics," in *BioScience*. Vol. 49, no. 8. August 1999, pp. 602–609.

Meg.

Variant of Margaret.

Mehetabel

Biblical woman. The daughter of Matred and the wife of Hadar (or Hadad), one of the kings of Edom.

Mehlig, Anna (1846–1928)

German pianist. Born in Stuttgart, Germany, on July 11, 1846; died in Berlin on July 26, 1928; a pupil of Liszt.

Anna Mehlig was one of many of Franz Liszt's students who studied with the great composer and preserved his style. The art of the great Liszt has been passed from one generation of pianists to the next, and in the musical world, this lineage remains precious. Mehlig's playing was regarded as spirited and energetic. She enjoyed a successful career not only in Europe but in England and America as well. Of her career in America, Liszt said, "Mlle. Mehlig has blossomed so well and borne fruit."

John Haag,
Athens, Georgia

Mehr-un-nisa, Mehrunissa, or Mehrunnissa (1577–1645).

See Nur Jahan.

Mei (d. 1875)

Queen of Cambodia. Reigned from 1835 to 1847; died in 1875; daughter of Ang Chan, king of Cambodia (r. 1797–1835).

On her father Ang Chan's death in 1835, Mei inherited the Cambodian throne, but Cambodia was then controlled by Vietnam and had little power. Mei ruled for 12 years before she was deposed by Ang Duang, son of another former king, Ang Eng. Cambodia was made a French protectorate in 1864.

Mei-Figner, Medea (1859–1952)

Italian soprano, best remembered for her close association with Tchaikovsky. Born Zoraide Amedea in Florence, Italy, in 1859; died on July 8, 1952, in Paris; married Nikolay Figner (a tenor), in 1889 (divorced 1904).

Sang in Italy, Spain, Russia and South America; performed at the St. Petersburg Opera (1887–1912); selected by Tchaikovsky to create Lisa in The Queen of Spades; *remained in Russia and taught after her retirement (1923).*

Although Medea Mei-Figner was Italian, she spent most of her career in Russia after she appeared in St. Petersburg in 1887. She accompanied Nikolay Figner and then married him in 1889. Mei-Figner soon became a member of the Imperial Opera where she created four important Russian roles—Lisa in Tchaikovsky's *The Queen of Spades* and the title role in his *Iolanta,* and Mascha in Napravnik's *Dubrovsky* and Francesca in his *Francesca da Rimini.* For many years, her interpretation of these roles remained preeminent. Mei-Figner and her husband were a tremendous box-office draw, and after their divorce in 1904 they continued to perform together until his retirement in 1907. Mei-Figner made several recordings in the winter of 1901 in St. Petersburg. She recorded again for Pathé in 1903 and for Columbia in 1904, and although she retired in 1923, Mei-Figner was persuaded to record again in 1929. Her close association with Tchaikovsky and her interpretation of Lisa in *The Queen of Spades* make her work especially important. Despite her long sojourn in Russia, Mei-Figner's style was unmistakably Italian. After remaining in Russia for many years, she eventually returned to Paris where she died in 1952.

John Haag,
Athens Georgia

Meigs, Cornelia Lynde (1884–1973)

American writer and educator. Name variations: (pseudonym) Adair Aldon. Born on December 6, 1884, in Rock Island, Illinois; died on September 10, 1973, in Hartford County, Maryland; daughter of Montgomery Meigs and **Grace Lynde Meigs;** *Bryn Mawr College, degree in English, 1908; never married; no children.*

Cornelia Lynde Meigs was a prolific and widely known author of children's literature. Spanning 50 years, her professional career included novels, short stories, biographies, histories, and dramas. The daughter of a civil engineer, Meigs grew up in Rock Island, Illinois, on the Mississippi River. She first attended public school and then entered Bryn Mawr College in Pennsylvania, where she completed a degree in English in 1908.

From 1912 to 1913, she taught at a private school in Davenport, Iowa, where she amused her pupils with original stories. Her inventiveness and ability to capture the imagination of young children led her to write a collection of short stories, published in 1915 as *The Kingdom of the Winding Road.* By the time her first book appeared, Meigs had left her teaching position in Iowa and had returned to her large, close family in Illinois. Her initial publishing success and the support of her family convinced her that she should continue to write for children professionally.

Over the next two decades, Meigs produced 17 more juvenile novels and short story collections, several of which she chose to publish under the pseudonym Adair Aldon. She also wrote many plays for young people, the first of which, *The Steadfast Princess,* won the Drama League prize in 1915. Most of her works received critical praise for their themes of Christian morality and their idealization of family life. They were also enormously popular, as children responded to her realistic young characters and stories of courage and adventure, often in richly detailed historical settings.

In 1932, Meigs accepted a faculty position in English at Bryn Mawr, where she remained until her retirement in 1950. She continued to publish fictional works throughout her tenure at Bryn Mawr, but she expanded her writing interests to include American history and biography as well. A year after moving to Pennsylvania, she published *Invincible Louisa: The Story of the Author of Little Women* (***Louisa May Alcott**), which received the prestigious Newbery Medal in 1934.

After retiring, Meigs divided her time between her homes in Vermont and Maryland. Five more of her juvenile novels were published between 1950 and 1968. In 1953, she edited and contributed to the scholarly *A Critical History of Children's Literature,* a widely acclaimed landmark survey of English juvenile literature from premodern times. Among her other works were a history of Bryn Mawr (1956) and a history of the United Nations (1964). In 1970, she published her final major book, *Jane Addams: Pioneer for Social Justice*, as well as an updated version of *Invincible Louisa*. Cornelia Meigs died at her Hartford County, Maryland, home in September 1973. She was 89.

SOURCES:

Mainiero, Lina, ed. *American Women Writers: A Critical Reference Guide from Colonial Times to the Present*. NY: Ungar, 1994.

Pellowski, Anne. *The World of Children's Literature*. NY: Bowker, 1968.

Laura York, M.A. in history,
University of California, Riverside, California

Meiji empress (1850–1914).

See Haruko.

Meiling Soong (b. 1898).

See Song Meiling.

Meinhof, Ulrike (1934–1972)

German journalist and activist who wrote on social issues but who is mainly remembered as a leader of Germany's notorious Red Army Faction (RAF) or Baader-Meinhof Gang. Name variations: Ulrike Röhl, Rohl, or Roehl. Pronunciation: OOL-re-ka MINE-hawf. Born Ulrike Marie Meinhof on October 7, 1934, in Oldenburg, Germany; died on May 8 or 9, 1976, while imprisoned in Stammheim, Stuttgart, the official cause of death given as suicide; daughter of Walter Meinhof (an art historian) and Ingeborg Meinhof (a teacher); university studies in educational science, psychology and sociology (MA); married Klaus Rainer Röhl, in 1961; children: (twin daughters) Bettina and Regine Röhl (b. 1963).

Awards: student stipend from the Study Foundation of the German People.

Engaged in the anti-bomb movement (1958–59); became journalist for leftist weekly magazine, konkret (1959); was chief editor of konkret (1960–64); published other articles in various media branches focusing on topics concerning fringe groups (to 1969); lectured at the Free University of Berlin (1970); participated in the liberation of Andreas Baader (May 1970); was a fugitive and leader of the Red Army Fraction (RAF) until arrest (1972); was imprisoned and tried for aiding Baader's escape, found guilty, and sentenced to eight years in prison; transferred to Stammheim prison to await the "Baader-Meinhof-Prozesse" (1975); died, allegedly by suicide (May 1976).

Selected publications: Bambule—Fürsorge für wen? (Bambule—Welfare For Whom?, Berlin, Verlag Klaus Wagenbach, 1971); Dokumente einer Rebellion (Hamburg, 1972); Die Würde des Menschen ist antastbar (The Dignity of Man is Infrangible, Berlin, Verlag Klaus Wagenbach, 1980); assorted newspaper and magazine contributions, mainly in konkret.

On June 15, 1972, German police, following evidence found on a recently arrested suspect, tracked down a hideout of reputed terrorists in Hanover, where one woman they arrested, weighing only 90 pounds, was not immediately recognized. X-rays had to be made of her skull and compared with old medical records before the police could confirm that they had captured Germany's most wanted female terrorist, Ulrike Meinhof, even though black-and-white photographs of Meinhof from an earlier time stared out from wanted posters throughout the country. The difference between her appearance when caught and the wanted posters suggested how far she had come in her separation from the ordinary community of German citizens.

Born on October 7, 1934, Ulrike was the younger of two sisters, and the daughter of Walter Meinhof, an art historian, and **Ingeborg Meinhof**. When Ulrike was six and her sister was ten, their father died, leaving their mother with no pension and two children to raise. Ingeborg Meinhof was given a small stipend to acquire training as a teacher, and to ease their desperate economic situation the family took in a lodger, **Renate Reimeck**, who became a friend of the children at first sight, and one of the most important persons in Ulrike's life. In 1949, the year Ingeborg Meinhof died, Reimeck took over the care of the girls.

During Ulrike's early school years, teachers and other adults viewed her as an intelligent and generous-hearted child. According to friends, her high-principled views unconsciously imitated those of Reimeck, who was a professor of educational science in Brunswick and actively engaged in protests against the rearmament of Germany. Ulrike became editor of her school magazine and was a leader among her female classmates, with whom she discussed Franz Kafka, Thomas Mann, Hermann Hesse, and the poetry of Friedrich Hölderlin late into the night.

In 1955, Meinhof started studies in educational science and psychology in the old university town of Marburg. She was awarded a church scholarship and a stipend from the Study Foundation of the German People, the most generous, and one of the most prestigious, scholarships available. Her political interests were considered to have been little more than a general acceptance of leftist views and opposition to "the bomb." More interested in religion, she had joined the Berneuchener Kreis, a Christian brotherhood that revived the liturgy of Luther and practiced spiritual exercises.

In 1956, Meinhof was 22 when she went to work for *konkret,* then a radical leftist political magazine partly funded by the East German Communist Party. Persons working for *konkret* were not allowed to be members of the Social Democrat Party (SPD) or the Socialist German Student's Alliance (SDS). At this point Meinhof's involvement in politics changed, to the degree that one friend has said, "Ulrike forgot herself in politics. There was no distance between herself and politics."

At the end of 1957, Meinhof moved to Münster, where she was the editor of a students' magazine, *Das Argument* (The Argument), and engaged in various campaigns concerning German rearmament, the bomb, and world peace. During one of these events, she became involved in her first authenticated love affair, with Klaus Rainer Röhl, the man she would later marry. In his biographical novel about their relationship, *Die Genossin* (The Female Comrade), Röhl would later describe their initial meeting as "dislike at first sight." Editor at the time of *konkret,* with a reputation as "the Communist womanizer," Röhl, with Meinhof, arranged the first meeting between East German Communists and West German Communists (then forbidden as a party), in East Berlin. He later called this first phase of their affiliation "Ulrike's love-affair with Communism," although in a 1958 article Meinhof wrote about the East German Communist Party as "the freedom-robbing Communists."

In 1960, Meinhof became chief editor of *konkret.* Two articles defending the Berlin Wall led to a burning of copies of the magazine on the campus of the Free University of Berlin and the withdrawal of permission to sell it on campus. In 1961, Meinhof married Röhl, and for a while led a pleasant social and professional life. A lead article she had written, "Hitler in You," a tirade against then minister of defense Franz Josef Strauss, grabbed the attention of the German government. When Strauss sued, Meinhof and *konkret* were represented by Gustav Heinemann, later the attorney general and then president of West Germany, and the magazine and its editor prevailed.

Early in 1963, after Meinhof became pregnant, she retreated from journalism. By the summer, she was suffering from severe headaches and had trouble with her vision before a series of painful examinations forced her to choose between necessary brain surgery and having her baby. Meinhof decided to save the child, and lived with worsening symptoms until she was 7½ months' pregnant, when her twin girls could be delivered by caesarean section. Regine and Bettina were placed in the care of Renate while Meinhof underwent the brain operation.

> [Women] were enfranchised when it was too late to change society with the ballot.
>
> —Ulrike Meinhof

Back at work at *konkret* before the end of 1963, Meinhof found things changed. Following a period of serious economic hazards, Röhl had brought the magazine firmly under his control, by establishing a regular readership as Germany's first "porn with politics" publication. Meinhof resigned her job as chief editor but remained a columnist, and the year ahead proved to be a flourishing period, in which she started to do broadcasting work. She led off with a piece on the trial of a Nazi mass murderer, Karl Wolff, which gained considerable attention, and then a new attack on Franz Josef Strauss in her column for *konkret* led to a second lawsuit. This time Strauss was awarded 600 deutschmarks in damages, but the incident inspired the leading German news magazine, *Der Spiegel,* to refer to Meinhof as "the courageous columnist of *konkret*" and publish a picture that made her face known to the public for the first time. As *konkret* grew into more and more of a commercial enterprise, Meinhof expanded her writing for other papers and radio programs, addressing the problems of foreign workers in Germany and the inequality of women in the job market. The family Röhl became widely known publicly as representatives of leftist chic. Meinhof, political polemicist and champion of the social underdog, was frequently invited to be on television as the token woman on panels covering social problems. Belittling herself as *das Revolutionskasperle* (little revolutionary "punchikin" from Punch and Judy), she wrote in her diary, "life drags on." In 1967, the family moved into a big house in Blankenese, the elegant suburb of Hamburg. Meinhof was alternately shopping for antique furniture and participating in demonstrations against the visit to Germany by the shah of Iran, Reza Pahlavi; in an "Open letter to Farah Diba [*Farah Pahlavi]," Meinhof addressed the shah's wife, calling attention to the social problems, poverty, and torture then rife under his rule.

After a housewarming party in December 1967, Röhl walked out with another woman, the last in a succession of infidelities during his marriage to Meinhof. The next morning, Meinhof moved to Berlin with her daughters, and the divorce is said to have been "very civilized." Berlin, meanwhile, was the center of the German students' revolution then under way: after the Socialists had formed a fusion government with the Christian Democrats, an alliance called the Extra Parliament Opposition (APO) had been formed, uniting all groups to the left of the SPD, and it was responsible for huge German demonstrations against the war in Vietnam. Police force and brutality previously unknown to the young democracy, as well as public hostility towards the demonstrators (reinforced in particular by the tabloid paper *Bild*), were growing. Meinhof supported the actions of the APO, which were sometimes illegal, but was not personally involved in the "street fights." She was prospering financially, and still did work for *konkret*, but she told friends that she did not feel well.

In 1969, an open dispute over undemocratic patterns in the management of *konkret* led to tumultuous infighting between Röhl and the staff. Meinhof stopped contributing to the magazine, and her apartment in Berlin became the meeting place for supporters of APO, SDS members, communards and young women from a nearby welfare home—an environment providing her with close camaraderie. As **Gudrun Ensslin**, Andreas Baader and others formed her new family, a long-time project, a script titled "Bambule" for a teleplay about welfare institutions was finished and filmed. The story describes a welfare home for youths, where the girls are sick of the meaningless labor and lessons, and one girl leads a destructive riot, a "bambule." "Violence produces counterviolence," write Meinhof, "pressure counterpressure. The types of resistance, which evolve in asylums, develop spontaneous and haphazard, unorganized as riots, rebels, hot things, as 'Bambule.' Irene's story is a children's story, a hoax. It ends with police force and the clink." A few weeks after Meinhof was appointed a part-time lecturer at the Free University in Berlin, the airing of "Bambule" would be dropped because of Meinhof's criminal activity.

In April 1968, Andreas Baader and Gudrun Ensslin had been part of a group that set two stores on fire to protest the consumption practices of Western societies while Vietnam was immersed in war. The group had been arrested and tried, but after a year in prison they were out on parole and working in a low-income area on a project for neglected children, where they, and Meinhof, had previously worked. After their appeal was declined, Ensslin and Baader went un-

derground, and, in April 1970, Andreas was arrested again. He was granted a working appointment to read documents with Meinhof in an institute outside prison on May 14, 1970. At the time of the meeting, several persons, including Meinhof, entered the building and led Andreas out through a window. An institute employee was shot but survived, and for Meinhof the escape was to be a leap into life underground. German authorities took out warrants, and photographs of Meinhof now identified her as a leader of the Baader-Meinhof Gang. In June, she, Baader, Ensslin and others left East Berlin on forged passports, with the help of Palestinians, to visit Syria and Jordan, where they joined colleagues in a training camp for Palestinian liberation. In August 1970, Meinhof returned to Germany. With the help of friends who provided cars, apartments, and money acquired through several bank robberies, she and her companions could stay underground. At this time, the group still lacked a theoretical concept and was called the "Baader-Meinhof Group" or "Baader-Meinhof Gang," depending on the speaker's point of view. It was Ulrike who came up with the name "Red Army Faction" (RAF), when she formed the notion of urban guerrillas, who set out to "free" the people, whether they asked for it or not. During this time, Röhl was awarded custody of their daughters, who were in hiding under the care of friends of Meinhof. When he located them, they were tanned and happy, living in Tuscany, Italy.

The hunt for the outlaws intensified after a policeman was killed by the Red Army Faction during a bank robbery, and a U.S. soldier died in a bomb attack on a U.S. base. The public grew increasingly disturbed after another bomb attack, aimed at the judge who had signed most of the search warrants issued against members of the RAF, struck the judge's wife instead, and a bomb planted in the Springer-Verlag building, connected to the newspaper *Bild,* injured the paper's employees. Everyone in Germany was alert to potential terrorists, and the police moved closer. On June 6, 1972, Baader was arrested. When a new RAF pamphlet entitled "To Serve the People" appeared in the streets, its opening line seemed prophetic: "The struggle has just begun." Officials identified the author as Meinhof.

On June 7, 1972, a saleswoman in a boutique spotted firearms in the jacket of a female customer. After informing the police, she hindered the shopper's departure, and the woman taken into custody proved to be Gudrun Ensslin. With evidence found on her, the police traced their way to the apartment of Ulrike Meinhof.

Brought to a prison in Cologne, Meinhof was kept in isolation to prevent any contact with colleagues or possible sympathizers. The cell was totally silent, and visits were restricted to her lawyers; later, she was allowed to correspond with her daughters and wrote, trying to soothe them: "It is very difficult and it is very easy. . . . Don't think that you have to be sad to have a mom in prison. Anyway—it is better to become angry than to become sad."

Meinhof's lawyers fought in vain against her treatment in the penitentiary, while the isolation of the urban guerrilla became a *cause célèbre* across Europe. A French newspaper carried an open letter of protest signed by *Simone de Beauvoir, Jean-Paul Sartre, Michel Foucault, and others. Meanwhile, other RAF comrades went on several hunger strikes against their prison conditions, which were eventually eased.

In 1975, after Meinhof was found guilty of taking part in Baader's liberation, she was moved to a prison in Stuttgart-Stammheim to await trial for other crimes. The proceedings that followed there—known as *Stammheimer Prozess*—evoked the most severe repressions in criminal procedure carried out under Germany's democracy. Meanwhile, deep conflicts had evolved among members of the group held in detention, and only Gudrun Ensslin claimed responsibility for three of the lethal bombings. The others dissociated themselves.

On May 8, 1976, guards have asserted that they heard typing in the cell of Ulrike Meinhof until late in the night. The following morning, she was found dead, hanged by strips of her towel.

SOURCES:

Aust, Stefan. *Der Baader-Meinhof-Komplex.* Hamburg: Hoffmann und Campe Verlag, 1985.

Bakker-Schut, Pieter H. *Stammheim: Der Prozess gegen die Rote Armee Fraktion* (Stammheim: The Red Army Faction on Trial). Kiel: Neuer Malik Verlag, 1986.

Röhl, Klaus Rainer. *Die Genossin* (The Female Comrade). Wien a.o.: Molden, 1975.

Rühmkorf, Peter. *Die Jahre, die Ihr kennt* (The Years You Know). Reinbek b. Hamburg: Rowohlt, 1972.

SUGGESTED READING:

Baader-Meinhof-Gruppe. Berlin: Walter de Gruyter, 1973.

Brückner, Peter. *Ulrike Meinhof und die deutschen Verhältnisse* (Ulrike Meinhof and German Circumstances). Berlin: Wagenbach, 1977.

Sabine Gless,
Strafrechtliches Institut der Universität, Bonn, Germany

Meir, Golda (1898–1978)

Prime minister of Israel from 1969 to 1974, the only woman to hold that position, who was a lifelong worker for the creation and preservation of a secular, social-ist Israel. Name variations: Golda Mabovitch (in Russia); Goldie Mabovitch (in America); Goldie Meyerson or Myerson (after marriage); Golda Meir (from 1956). Pronunciation: May-EAR. Born Goldie Mabovitch on May 3, 1898, in Kiev, Russia; died in Jerusalem on December 8, 1978; daughter of Moshe Yitzhak Mabovitch (a carpenter) and Bluma Mabovitch; attended schools in Milwaukee, Wisconsin, and Denver, Colorado; married Morris Myerson or Meyerson, on December 24, 1917 (separated, 1940); children: Menachem Meyerson also known as Menachem Meir (b. 1924); Sarah Meyerson Rehabi (b. 1926).

Moved from Kiev, Russia, to Milwaukee, Wisconsin (1906); was a Zionist and labor activist and organizer in America, then Palestine; arrived in Tel Aviv (1921); elected to the Woman's Labor Council of Histadruth (trade union for Jewish workers in Palestine), and served as secretary of the Moetzet Hapoalot (Women's Labor Council, 1928); elected a delegate of the Ahdut Haavoda faction to the World Zionist Congress (1929); was chosen secretary of Histadruth's executive committee (1934); served as a Mapai (Israeli Workers Party) delegate to the international congresses (1939); named head of Histadruth's political department (1940); became president of the political bureau of the Jewish Agency (1946); signed the Proclamation declaring the creation of Israel, the new Jewish state (May 14, 1948); appointed Israel's minister to Moscow (1948); elected to the first Knesset (Parliament) as a candidate of the Mapai Party, and appointed Israel's minister of labor and development (1949); served as ambassador to Soviet Union for Israel (1948–49); served as minister of labor (1949–56); served as chair of the Israeli delegation to the U.N. General Assembly (1953–66); served as foreign minister (1956–65); served as secretary general of the Mapai Party (1966–69); served as prime minister of Israel (1969–74).

Golda Meir, prime minister of Israel between 1969 and 1974, was one of a small group of women who rose to positions of supreme national leadership in the late 20th century—*Margaret Thatcher in Britain, *Benazir Bhutto in Pakistan, *Corazon Aquino in the Philippines, and *Indira Gandhi in India are obvious comparisons. She was, as her son wrote, "a woman whose austere bun, deep voice, orthopedic shoes, and capacious handbags were recognized, literally, around the world, a woman like a movie star who was known everywhere by her first name."

She was born in Kiev in 1898, one of seven children, four of whom died in infancy. The family's life was constantly in danger from pogroms—anti-Jewish attacks from the Russian majority, against which the Jews were powerless to resist. When she was five, her father, a carpenter, emigrated to America, hoping to earn enough money there to improve the family's situation. Golda, her mother, and her two sisters, left behind, moved first to Pinsk, but finding conditions equally hard there decided to reunite the family in America rather than Russia and emigrated in 1906. Golda therefore met her father for the first time in three years in Milwaukee, Wisconsin. Like many young émigré Jews, she was soon caught up in the Socialist ferment—Milwaukee had a socialist mayor and congressional representative early in the 20th century.

As a teenager, however, she was in frequent conflict with her parents, who did not want her to finish high school and opposed her early ambition to be a teacher. She reacted by running away, at the age of 14, to stay with her older sister **Sheyna Mabovitch Korngold** in Denver, working in a department store. At Socialist meetings there, she met and fell in love with Morris Meyerson, a sign-painter and aspiring engineer, though she was only 16. A compromise with her parents enabled her to return to Milwaukee to graduate from high school and begin studying for a teaching career at the Normal School.

The Jewish people had been scattered throughout the Western world for centuries. By 1910, there were Jewish communities in all the European countries, a growing population in the United States, in Russia, and in most of the countries of the Middle East and North Africa. Recurrently persecuted, some Jews regarded their suffering as God's punishment for their sins. But in the secular 19th and early 20th centuries, the possibility of a political movement to return to the ancient land of Israel took form, under the leadership of Theodore Herzl and the first Zionists. Goldie Mabovitch joined Poale Zion, a labor-Zionist group whose members pledged themselves to this cause, in 1915. Her effective organizing and vivid street-corner speaking for the group led its leaders to invite her to move to Chicago the next year. She accepted, gave up her teaching plans, worked in the public library during the afternoons, and volunteered for the Zionist cause each evening and night. In 1917, she married Morris Meyerson, despite her knowledge that he was far less enthusiastic about Zionism than she.

Palestine, as it was then known, was part of the decaying Turkish Empire. However, the Turks were on the losing side in the First World War (1914–1918) and their empire was broken up at the Treaty of Versailles. The British, one of the war's victors, took over the government of Palestine with a mandate from the League of Nations. During the war, one British agent, T.E. Lawrence ("Lawrence of Arabia"), had promised the land to Arab leaders in return for their help, whereas the "Balfour Declaration," made at the same time by the British government, had contradicted Lawrence by stating that Britain would work towards the formation of a Jewish homeland-state. Golda and her husband emigrated to Palestine in 1921, at a time when its future was uncertain. Earlier she had struggled to learn English—Yiddish was her first language—now she had to struggle to learn Hebrew, the official language of Zionists returning to Palestine.

In the years between the two world wars (1919–1939), idealistic Zionists like the Meyersons encouraged Jews to emigrate to Israel, to settle there, buy land, and create the foundations of a new nation. After three years of working on a kibbutz at Merhavia, a collective work-farm run on socialist principles in northern Palestine, the couple settled in Tel Aviv, a new settlement on the Mediterranean coast. The move was prompted by Morris' dislike of raising their child, Menachem, on the kibbutz, where he would be in the hands of a child-raising collective. Unlike the ancient cities of Jerusalem and Haifa, Tel Aviv had an all-Jewish population. Golda, after various unsatisfactory jobs, went to work for the Labor movement Histadrut, which was in effect the city's provisional government. She made several trips back to America to spread word of the cause, once staying for two years so that her daughter Sarah might get treatment for a life-threatening kidney disease. Her command of English, her love for the cause, and her skill as a speaker and fund raiser, made her invaluable. It was already clear by 1930 that Golda's passion for politics, and for the ideal of Israel, was greater than Morris' and although the couple remained nominally married until their separation of 1940 they spent increasing periods apart. She had a succession of lovers who shared her ideals, including labor leader David Remez.

In 1934, Meir became a member of the Histadrut leadership and befriended its leader David Ben-Gurion. The British mandate authorities regarded the Zionists with suspicion, fearing that their presence among the Palestinian Arabs would intensify political tensions in the area. Despite the Balfour Declaration, they tried throughout the 1930s and 1940s to restrain immigration, which led most Zionists, including Meir, to re-

gard them as adversaries. On the other hand, some Britons sympathized with the Zionists, notably an unconventional army officer, Orde Wingate, who helped train and lead Jewish resistance fighters against periodic Arab attacks. Moreover the British government's Peel Commission declared, in 1937, that it favored the partition of Palestine into a Jewish homeland and an Arab state. Histadrut leaders were split—Ben-Gurion and Chaim Weitzmann were delighted; Meir countered that the amount of territory offered to Israel by the Peel Commission was far too small. When the Holocaust began, however, she changed her mind, realizing that any homeland, even a weak one, was better than none.

During the late 1930s and the Second World War, Hitler's persecution of German Jews made the moral case for Zionism stronger than ever before. During the war itself, Meir agreed with the principle that Jews should join the British army to fight Nazism, but that they should simultaneously prepare for armed struggle *against* the British when Germany was defeated. A worldwide wave of revulsion against the Holocaust brought more international sympathy to Jews in the mid-1940s than ever before, and the new international arbitration organization, the United Nations, debated the question of how to satisfy all the groups in Palestine when the war ended.

*W*ith her midwestern American accent and flawless English, she won friends easily. The people of the United States could identify with her. Because other Yishuv leaders could not equal her command of the English language. . . . Golda was able to reach the Jewish and non-Jewish communities of America better than anyone else. She became the labor movement's apostle to America, bringing the Yishuv's message of pioneering and heroism to all who would listen.

—**Robert Slater**

With the fighting in Europe finished, Jewish resistance to the British began. Meir's later political antagonist Menachem Begin was among the leaders of Irgun, the anti-British force whose acts of terrorism, such as the bombing of the King David Hotel, increased the pressure on the British to leave. Meir herself joined a hunger strike, trying (like her contemporary, Mohandas Gandhi in India) to use moral pressure against British intransigence, in her case on the continuing sore point of British refusal to admit Jewish refugees. She was appointed provisional head of the Jewish Agency's Political Department when its leaders were imprisoned, and again showed great shrewdness and determination as a negotiator. Britain, its imperial strength dented by the Second World War and now under the leadership of its own Labor Party, finally announced that it would abandon its government of Palestine in May 1948.

In the anxious months between the United Nations decision in favor of a Jewish state, November 1947, and the British departure, Meir again traveled to America in the hope of raising money to help the Yishuv in what she and Ben-Gurion foresaw as the coming war against the Arabs—a war which had already unofficially broken out, making travel between Tel Aviv and Jerusalem hazardous. With her background in the Midwest and her familiarity with the American temperament, she proved phenomenally successful. In her first speech, before the Council of Jewish Federations in Chicago, she declared that the success or failure of the war was in the hands of American Jews, on whose generosity Israel's future depended. She was met with rapturous applause and pledges of over $1 million. By the time she returned to Israel, a month later, she was able to assure Ben-Gurion that an extra $50 million were available to them. On another mission—this one secret—to King Abdallah of Trans-Jordan, she disguised herself as a peasant woman so as not to be recognized, but was unable to convince him not to join in war against Israel.

When Israel officially became an independent state, in accordance with the U.N. Declaration, the British army evacuated Palestine, and the Arab states attacked. Meir expected, and felt she deserved, to be made a Cabinet minister in the new government of Prime Minister Ben-Gurion. In the event, however, she was made ambassador to the Soviet Union, an important post since it was one of the world's two superpowers and had been one of the first nations to recognize Israel diplomatically. Her arrival was delayed when, on another tour of America, she was involved in a taxicab crash in New York and broke her leg. Recovered sufficiently to travel to Moscow in 1948, she soon found her new job vexatious. The dictator Stalin rarely met any diplomats and refused to see her, and she found that information pamphlets her embassy tried to distribute about the new state of Israel were forbidden by the repressive Soviet government.

Recalled to Israel in early 1949, she became minister of labor in Ben-Gurion's Mapai Party government—its only woman member. To Meir, it was a vital post, from which she strove to carry out the principles of her lifelong devotion to Socialism. Creation of adequate housing and full employment were two of the highest priorities of the government, and she played a central role in both—tasks made formidable by the very rapid rate of immigration of Jews from all around the world, averaging more than 1,000 per day in 1949. Again with American financial help, she set up an ambitious public works road-building scheme and an accelerated building program to get refugee-immigrants out of tent encampments and into real housing. One of the policy conflicts within the government was whether to permit continued free immigration of Jews to Israel. In her view, this was a point which must not be compromised—the Holocaust had shown the imperative need, she believed, of a safe haven for Jews from anywhere in the world.

In 1956 during a Cabinet shake-up, Ben-Gurion promoted her to the job of foreign minister, and in accordance with a government regulation she took the occasion to Hebraicize her name, changing it from Meyerson to Meir (which means "illumination"). Although the first war between Israel and the Arabs had ended in a series of truces in 1949, tensions remained very high and Israel went to war against Egypt once more in 1956. Allied with Britain and France, who resented the Egyptian leader Gamel Abdel Nasser's seizure of the Suez Canal, Israel's army advanced successfully and seized the Sinai peninsula. The military success, however, was a diplomatic failure. America's president, Dwight Eisenhower, and secretary of state, John Foster Dulles, insisted that Israel stop its provocative advances and return the over-run territories, in the interest of Middle East peace and stability. It was Meir's humiliating job to accept these terms at the United Nations—she understood perfectly well that Israel's well-being depended on the support of the American government.

The Suez Crisis was the low point of American-Israeli relations, and marked a period of feuding within the Israeli government between three of its strongest and most argumentative personalities, Ben-Gurion, Golda Meir, and Defense Minister Shimon Peres. After Eisenhower's retirement in 1961, Meir set about mending fences in America, and in the ensuing years befriended presidents John F. Kennedy and Lyndon B. Johnson, so that Israel could be assured of whole-hearted American aid if Israel went to war again. (In 1969, just after she had become prime minister, she would make an emotional visit to Milwaukee and to her old school, renamed in her honor.) Meir, now in her mid-60s, discovered that she had cancer of the lymph nodes in 1963. Exhausted by sickness and decades of overwork, she retired from the Foreign Ministry in 1965, soon after Ben-Gurion's decision to create his own splinter political party.

Within a year, however, she was back, trying to heal Mapai, the old party, of which she now took command. Despite her illness (which was kept a closely guarded secret), her moral authority was by now so great that her real power equaled that of Prime Minister Levi Eshkol, a former agricultural economist whom she regarded as unworthy of the job. Mapai put aside its di-

visions in a new war emergency in 1967. In this conflict (unlike the events of 1956), there could be no doubt that Israel was not the aggressor, and that its survival was in jeopardy. The conflict against an Egyptian, Syrian, and Jordanian alliance, soon nicknamed the Six-Day War, witnessed an astonishing victory for Israel's armed forces. They rapidly destroyed enemy air power and, attacking by land, advanced Israel's borders to the banks of the Jordan in the east and the banks of the Suez Canal in the west. These victories gave Israel a greater reputation for power than ever, and increased the possibility that it might find a way to make a lasting settlement with its enemies. It also enhanced the reputation of Moshe Dayan, minister of defense and one of Meir's long-time political opponents. In the wake of the war, and in a mood of national euphoria, she was able to bring together the scattered fragments of the Old Guard and the Ben-Gurionites, to create a new coalition Labor Party.

The sudden death of Prime Minister Eshkol in 1969 led to Meir's final ascent to the premiership: "I could certainly understand the reservations of people who thought that a seventy-year-old grandmother was hardly . . . perfect . . . to head a twenty year old state," she admitted. But as all who knew her recognized, her grandmotherly appearance was offset by her lifetime of political experience, diplomatic skill, and hard-headedness. Her leadership was confirmed later in 1969 when she led her party coalition to victory in national elections. She hoped to achieve a lasting peace but, like her predecessors, believed that it could only be achieved if Israel was militarily strong and vigilant. When the American secretary of state, William Rogers, offered to broker a peace treaty, she cautiously accepted, which led to a split in her fragile government of national unity. Menachem Begin, leader of the right wing Herut Party, refused to consider negotiating over occupied territories and left the Cabinet. Meir, under pressure from Begin on the right but also from a vocal peace faction to her left, also faced the constant threat of Palestinian terrorism. The neighboring countries, Syria, Lebanon, Jordan, and Egypt, were all sympathetic to the Palestinian cause and sheltered anti-Israeli terrorist groups. Even so, the events of her lifetime had borne witness to an astonishing series of successes, both for Israel and for herself personally. As Amos Perlmutter, a shrewd historian of the era, remarks: "The mind set of the Meir government was steeped in success despite enormous adversity. Meir's conspicuous self-righteousness was not without political and realistic foundations. The dream had grown greatly beyond its expected proportions." With the aptness of a Greek tragedy, chastisement was to follow.

On the eve of Yom Kippur, the Day of Atonement, October 1973, the holiest holiday of the year, Egypt and Syria launched another surprise attack on Israel. Israeli intelligence was aware of the possibility of attack, but was wrong about the time, and had become complacent after their armies' smashing victories in 1967. For a few hours, Israel's survival was in grave danger, as army units hastened to the war's two fronts (northeast, against Syria and Iraq, and southwest against Egypt) and reserves were called out of synagogues and straight into action. Egyptian soldiers crossed the Suez Canal, outnumbering the reservists there 70 to 1, and captured the defensive "Bar-Lev Line" while Syrian tanks advanced over the Golan Heights.

Within a week, despite these early reversals, the tide had turned. Golda Meir had continued her lifelong policy of close cooperation with American Jews, and she was on friendly terms with President Richard Nixon who, like a majority in Congress, was pro-Israeli. Five days after the war began, American transport planes began ferrying supplies and munitions into Israel, ensuring Israel's ability to continue the fight to a successful conclusion. The United Nations and U.S. Secretary of State Henry Kissinger intervened to assure a ceasefire and an exchange of prisoners of war. Both sides claimed victory, even though the balance of the military confrontations had gone in favor of Israel, which had sustained 2,500 casualties.

Many Israelis felt angry with Meir, believing that her government had let itself be taken by surprise, with potentially catastrophic effects. Even so, she survived a vote of confidence taken just a month after the war had ended and went on to win the general election of December 1973. She authorized the creation of an independent commission of inquiry, the Agranat Commission, and its report, the following April, recommended that four senior military officers resign or be dismissed. Meir herself, and Minister of Defense Moshe Dayan, the charismatic hero of the Six-Day War, were absolved of blame. Ironically, she and Dayan, who had never been friends or mutual admirers and by now cordially detested each other, both understood the need to stand or fall together, and had to give the appearance of unity. Despite the commission's report, Meir recognized that the strength of the opposition to her continued leadership would mar her effectiveness, and later that month she resigned for the last time, now aged 76. Yitzhak Rabin took her place as premier.

Golda Meir spent her retirement writing her memoirs, which were published in 1975 (and turned into a Broadway play, *Golda*) and remained an influential figure in Israeli politics, able to influence decisions and actions from behind the scenes. She was present for the momentous visit of Egyptian leader Anwar Sadat to Jerusalem in 1977, a prelude to the Camp David Peace Accord which finally normalized relations between Israel and Egypt in 1979. She did not live to see the treaty signed, however, dying from recurrent cancer in 1978. She was mourned by Jews throughout the world and by admiring citizens of other nations for her lifelong dedication to her cause and for her years of effective and powerful leadership.

SOURCES AND SUGGESTED READING:

Martin, Ralph G. *Golda: Golda Meir, the Romantic Years*. NY: Scribner, 1988.

Meir, Golda. *My Life*. NY: Putnam, 1975.

Meir, Menachem. *My Mother, Golda Meir*. NY: Arbor House, 1983.

Perlmutter, Amos. *Israel: The Partitioned State*. NY: Scribner, 1985.

Samuel, Rinna. *A History of Israel*. London: Weidenfeld and Nicolson, 1989.

Slater, Robert. *Golda: The Uncrowned Queen of Israel*. NY: Jonathan David, 1981.

RELATED MEDIA:

"A Woman Called Golda" (four-hour television miniseries), starring *Ingrid Bergman (for which she won an Emmy award), Paramount, 1982.

COLLECTIONS:

Lavon Institute for Labor Research, Tel Aviv.

State Archives of the Prime Minister's Office, Jerusalem.

Patrick Allitt,
Professor of History, Emory University, Atlanta, Georgia

Meireles, Cecília (1901–1964)

Brazilian poet, writer and teacher. Name variations: Cecilia Meireles; Cecília Beneviles Meireles. Born in 1901 in Rio de Janeiro; died on November 9, 1964, in Rio de Janeiro; married Fernando Correia Dias (a painter), in 1921 (died 1935 or 1936); married Heitor Grillo; children: (first marriage) three daughters.

Selected writings: Espectros *(1919);* Nunca Mais . . . e Poema dos Poemas *(1923);* Balada Para El-Rei *(1924);* Viagém *(1939);* Vaga Música *(1942);* Mar Absoluto *(1945);* Retrato Natural *(1949);* Amor em Leonoreta *(1951);* Doze Noturnos de Holanda e o Aeronauta *(1952);* Romanceiro da Inconfidência *(1953);* Pequeno Oratória de Santa Clara *(1955);* Pistóia, Cemitério Militar Brasileiro *(1955);* Canções *(1956);* Giroflê, Giroflá *(1956);* Solombar *(1956);* Romance de Santa Cecília *(1957);* A Rosa *(1957);* Obra Poética *(1958);* Metal Rosicler *(1960);* Poemas Escritos Na Índia *(1961)*; Quadrante 1 e Quadrante 2 *(1962–63)*; Antologia Poética *(1963)*.

Born in Brazil in 1901, Cecília Meireles was orphaned early in life and brought up by her grandmother, a woman of Portuguese descent who had lived in the Azores. Meireles trained to become a teacher but quickly branched out into journalism, contributing to the magazines *Arvore Nova* and *Terra do Sol* from 1919 to 1927, and to the spiritualist periodical *Festa* in 1927. She was active throughout her career not only in teaching and journalism but also in educational reform and library work; as an advocate for the construction of libraries for children, she was instrumental in founding the first children's library in Brazil in 1934. Not long after that her husband, who had been severely depressed, committed suicide, leaving her to raise their three daughters. (She later remarried.) Meireles was a professor at a number of universities, including the University of Texas and the Federal University in Rio de Janeiro. She was considered an expert on Brazilian folklore, and later in life served as a Brazilian cultural attaché.

Partly due to these wide-ranging interests she considered herself somewhat of an outsider in the Brazilian literary scene, but Meireles is nonetheless considered the country's greatest Portuguese-language woman poet. Her first book, *Espectros* (Ghosts), was published in 1919, and displayed a "disciplined formalism" influenced by the Parnassians, French poets who rejected the excesses of Romanticism. She has been praised for her "perfect command of the poetic form," and won a number of important literary prizes; among her most popular works were *Viagém* (Voyage, 1939), which was awarded that year's Poetry Prize from the Brazilian Academy of Letters, and *Mar Absoluto* (Absolute Sea, 1942). *Romanceiro da Inconfidência* (Poet of the Inconfidence), published in 1953, focused on the push for independence led by the Brazilian hero Joaquim José da Silva Xavier. Her later poems are described in *Twentieth-Century Latin American Poetry* as "full of tactile metaphors and verbal sensuality" while "address[ing] a state of vivid internal 'exile,' an ideal transcendental solitude." By the time of her death in 1964 her work had already achieved the renown it maintains.

SOURCES:

Buck, Claire, ed. *The Bloomsbury Guide to Women's Literature.* NY: Prentice Hall General Reference, 1992.

Tapscott, Stephen, ed. *Twentieth-Century Latin American Poetry: A Bilingual Anthology.* Austin, TX: University of Texas Press, 1996.

Grant Eldridge,
freelance writer, Pontiac, Michigan

Meisel-Olday, Hilde (1914–1945).

See Monte, Hilda.

Meisho (1624–1696)

Japanese empress, 109th sovereign of the Empire of Japan according to the traditional count, who came to the throne as a child in 1629 and reigned until 1643. Name variations: *Meishō; Myojo-tenno; Myosho.* Born in 1624 (some sources cite 1623); died in 1696; daughter of Emperor Go-Mizunoo (also seen as Go-Mizuno-o) and Tokugawa Kazuko; had one sister; had three emperor brothers, Go-Komyo (r. 1643–1654, d. 1654), Gosai or Go-Sai (r. 1655–1663, d. 1685), and Reigen (r. 1663–1687, d. 1732); never married.

In 1629, five-year-old Meisho became empress of Japan as a result of her father's abdication. It had been almost a millennium since a woman had been a sovereign ruler of Japan. During the Nara period (710–794 CE), there had been Empress *Kōken-Shōtoku; a zealous Buddhist like her father Emperor Shomu, Kōken-Shōtoku reigned from 749 to 758 and from 764 to 770.

Meisho was born into a troubled and exciting time in her country's history. Although the venerable imperial throne symbolized national unity in Japan, those who sat on it had been virtually powerless for centuries. From the 13th century forward, a shogun (military governor) ruled the island nation through feudal vassals who exchanged their military services for large estates and political rights. Ostensibly, the shogun wielded power only as a temporary stand-in for the emperor, who in theory was to remain the source of all political authority. In reality, however, emperors were no more than figureheads, with shoguns enjoying virtually total power. By 1400, the flaws of this feudal order had revealed themselves, as the conflicting interests of shoguns and their vassals increasingly resulted in protracted and bloody struggles. By the mid-16th century, Japan was torn asunder by internecine conflicts that historians would later call the era of *sengoku*—"the country at war."

By the late 1500s, strong states were emerging in several regions of Japan, with ambitious military leaders in each looking forward to more power as well as to the restoration of peace that would accompany national unification. In 1600, Tokugawa Ieyasu established a military regime known as the Tokugawa *bakufu* ("tent government"), which claimed to be no more than a temporary replacement for the emperor's rule.

But "temporary" rule became very permanent, with Ieyasu and his descendants ruling the *bakufu* as shoguns from 1600 until the end of the Tokugawa Dynasty in 1867. In 1611, while Ieyasu was still alive, Go-Mizunoo became emperor of Japan as the 108th sovereign (*tenno*) in the traditional count (which includes several legendary emperors). In 1620, he was made to marry Tokugawa Kazuko, the daughter of the shogun Tokugawa Hidetada, who had succeeded Ieyasu on the latter's death in 1616. Although Go-Mizunoo's marriage to Kazuko is believed to have been a happy one, he was politically exasperated from repeatedly being dealt with in a peremptory fashion by the shogun and his officials. Consequently, in 1629 Go-Mizunoo made a sudden decision to abdicate the throne in favor of his five-year-old daughter, Meisho.

Meisho was enthroned as empress of Japan in 1630 at Kyoto. At the grand event, lest it be forgotten who actually wielded political power in Japan, the celebrants included Sakai Tadayo and Doi Toshikatsu, chief advisors and councillors (*tairo*) to the current shogun, Iemitsu. The enthronement ceremony took place in the Shishin-den (Purple Dragon Hall). Central to the ceremonial were "announcements" of the reign to the various powerful individuals or groups that were part of the imperial world. Specially commissioned messengers were dispatched, one to the Ise Shrine with a *hohei* (slip of paper) that symbolized the new ruler's report to the Sun Goddess. Others with similar messages were sent to the Kashiwabara Shrine, the tomb of Japan's semi-legendary first emperor Jimmu, and to several other important tomb sites.

By the early 1640s, significant tensions had arisen between the imperial court—where ex-emperor Go-Mizunoo continued to exercise authority behind the scenes—and the shogun. Historians have speculated as to why these stresses appeared, and theories include the possibility that the shogun had always resented the way in which Go-Mizunoo had abdicated in order to wield power unofficially. Despite the fact that Shogun Iemitsu was the Empress Meisho's grandfather (and thus directly linked to the sovereign power in the land), he did not want his authority to be trifled with. Some scholars have detected a conservative anti-feminist undercurrent directed against the Empress Meisho at the Kyoto court.

According to the chronicler Kanzawa Toko, the mechanics of the abdication process were as follows: "The Empress had reigned for thirteen years. Both the civil and military lords thought it time for her to retire. Sakai Tadakatsu and Matsudaira Nobutsuna [Shogun Iemitsu's senior advisors] went to Kyoto to discuss the matter, whereupon the Empress abdicated." Some scholars have argued that the imperial court was able to assert its rights by delaying the abdication, making it appear a free and spontaneous act on the part of the empress. Now a young woman of 20, at the center of the dispute, Meisho did as she was told. She was succeeded on the throne by her brother, Go-Komyo, who died at the age of 21 in 1654. Two more of Meisho's brothers, Gosai and Reigen, would sit on the imperial throne until 1687.

Meisho did not marry while she was on the throne or after her abdication. It has been argued that the reasons for this were political. Had she married, there might well have been serious problems of protocol in the treatment which would have been accorded her spouse and children. According to Japanese law of the time, a man's wife and children belonged to his family unless he had been adopted by the family of his wife. Special usages and traditions, however, applied to the imperial family. These included a prohibition of inheritance through the female line. As a result, any children Meisho might have had would not have belonged to her family but to her husband's. This would have likely caused considerable difficulties because as children of an ex-empress, Meisho's offspring would presumably have been deserving of special treatment. These issues of court etiquette, however, never arose due to her unwed status. Meisho died in her 70s in 1696.

SOURCES:

Elison, George. *Deus Destroyed: The Image of Christianity in Early Modern Japan.* Cambridge, MA: Harvard University Press, 1973.

Hall, John Whitney. "The *bakuhan* system," in John Whitney Hall, ed. *The Cambridge History of Japan*, Volume 4: *Early Modern Japan.* Cambridge, England: Cambridge University Press, 1991, pp. 128–182.

Hanley, Susan B. *Economic and Demographic Change in Pre-Industrial Japan, 1600–1868.* Princeton, NJ: Princeton University Press, 1977.

Iwao, Seiichi, ed. *Biographical Dictionary of Japanese History.* Tokyo and NY: Kodansha International Ltd. & International Society for Educational Information, 1978.

Kasumi Kaikan. Saitama Kenritsu Hakubutsukan. *Jotei Meisho Tenno to Shogun Iemitsu: Matsudaira Nobutsuna to sono jidai.* Tokyo: Kasumi Kaikan, Heisei 9 [1997].

Smith, Robert J. "Divine Kingship in the Formation of the Japanese State, 1868–1945," in John S. Henderson and Patricia J. Netherly, eds., *Configurations of Power: Holistic Anthropology in Theory and Practice.* Ithaca, NY and London: Cornell University Press, 1993, pp. 51–73.

Totman, Conrad. *Japan Before Perry: A Short History.* Berkeley, CA: University of California Press, 1981.

———. *Tokugawa Ieyasu: Shogun.* Torrance, CA: Heian International, 1998.

Webb, Herschel. *The Japanese Imperial Institution in the Tokugawa Period.* NY: Columbia University Press, 1968.

John Haag,
Associate Professor of History,
University of Georgia, Athens, Georgia

Meitner, Lise (1878–1968)

Austrian theoretical physicist, and the first woman in Germany to hold the title professor, who made key contributions to the discovery of nuclear fission. Pronunciation: MITE-ner. Born Lise Meitner in Vienna, Austria, on November 7, 1878; died in Cambridge, England, on October 27, 1968; daughter of Hedwig (Skovran) Meitner and Philip Meitner; attended Academic High School, Vienna, and University of Vienna, 1902–06, awarded Ph.D.; never married; no children.

Awards: Leibnitz Medal of the Berlin Academy of Sciences (1924); Lieber Prize of the Austrian Academy of Sciences (1925); City of Vienna's Prize in Science (1947); Max Planck Medal (1949); Enrico Fermi Award (1966).

Enrolled in Max Planck's lectures, University of Berlin (1907); met Otto Hahn (September 28, 1907) and began collaboration; with Hahn, discovered thorium c (1908); joined Kaiser Wilhelm Institute for Chemistry (1912); became research assistant to Max Planck (1912); was X-ray technician in the Austro-Hungarian Army (1914–18); appointed head of the Department of Physics, Kaiser Wilhelm Institute for Chemistry (1918); with Hahn, discovered protactinium (1918); became a privatdozent, University of Berlin (1919); appointed Professor Extraordinary, University of Berlin (1926); was one of the first to report that positrons were formed by gamma rays (1933); worked with Hahn to confirm Fermi's thesis (1934); fled Nazi Germany (1938); joined the Nobel Institute, Stockholm, Sweden (1938); identified nuclear fission (1939); refused to participate in the Manhattan Project (1942); was a visiting professor, Catholic University, Washington, D.C. (1946); retired from the Nobel Institute (1947); joined the Royal Institute of Technology, Stockholm, Sweden (1947); retired to Cambridge, England (1966); died a few weeks before her 90th birthday (1968).

Selected publications in English: (with O.R. Frisch) "Disintegration of Uranium by Neutrons: A New Type of Nuclear Reaction," in Nature *(1939); "Resonance Energy of the Th Capture Process," in* Physical Review *(1941); "Looking Back," in* Bulletin of Atomic Scientists *(1964).*

On July 16, 1945, at 5:29 AM, the world's first atomic bomb exploded in the New Mexico desert, marking the transition of humanity to the nuclear age. The implications of the blast that was heard around the world are still a matter of considerable conjecture. It can be said with certainty, however, that without the contribution of Lise Meitner, nuclear science would not have come about when it did.

Born in Vienna on November 7, 1878, Lise Meitner was one of seven children of **Hedwig Meitner** and Philip Meitner, a well-known attorney and converted Jew. Though his daughter's interest in physics was apparent from an early age, Philip insisted that she obtain a teaching diploma in order to support herself. After graduation, Lise took the entrance examination and, in 1902, was enrolled at the University of Vienna. By then, her father was willing to subsidize her education.

Fascinated by the work of *Marie Curie, Lise Meitner studied theoretical physics under Ludwig Boltzmann. At the time, not all physicists agreed that the world was comprised of atoms. Fortunately for Meitner, Boltzmann was a firm advocate of the thesis. Notes **Edna Yost**, the debate had a long antecedence:

> The Greek Democritus, who in the fifth century B.C. propounded the theory that all things are composed of invisible particles, all of them in constant motion, and all of them composed of the same matter but different in size, shape and weight, had named these tiny particles atoms because that is the Greek word for "indivisible." Nearly twenty-four centuries elapsed before science had been developed to the stage where men (and women) whose minds were receptive to the atomic theory had scientific equipment and accumulated knowledge to begin to investigate the validity of this theory.

In 1906, when Lise Meitner was awarded a Ph.D. from the University of Vienna, she was only the second woman to receive a doctorate from that institution. Her dissertation dealt with heat conduction in non-homogeneous substances. For a time, she remained in Vienna, undertaking research into radioactivity with Stephan Meyer.

In 1907, Meitner traveled to Berlin, drawn by the prospect of attending Max Planck's lectures on theoretical physics and envisaging only a short stay of one or two years. She also hoped to undertake postgraduate research. As a woman, however, she was barred from entering university laboratories. The Berlin of Meitner's day was a glittering citadel of science, attracting some of the most influential scientific minds of a generation: Max von Laue, Albert Einstein, Gustav Hertz, Max Planck, and Otto Hahn. It was also a city where attitudes towards women were slowly beginning to change.

When Lise Meitner met the gifted organic chemist Otto Hahn at a colloquium at the Institute of Physics on September 28, 1907, she was 29 and had already published two papers on radiation, "On the Absorption of Alpha and Beta Rays" and "On the Dispersion of Alpha Rays." The two scientists seemed an unlikely pair; Hahn was a convivial Rhinelander who enjoyed the outdoors, cigars, and beer, while Meitner was a petite, dark, and pretty Austrian who was morbidly shy. Hahn, an admirer of attractive women, noted: "There was no question of any closer relationship between us outside the laboratory. Lise Meitner had had a strict lady-like upbringing and was very reserved, even shy. . . . And yet we were really close friends." A scientific partnership soon blossomed, enabling Meitner to resume her research. The collaboration lasted for the next 30 years, and proved to be one of the most productive scientific alliances of the 20th century.

Meitner was a victim of the same patterns of prejudice which other women in academia faced. She and Hahn planned to work together at the Chemical Institute in Berlin, but its director, Emil Fischer, did not allow women on the premises. In Meitner's case, a compromise was reached, and she was allowed to work with Hahn provided she did not enter the laboratories where male students were taught. Though Meitner conscientiously kept her part of the bargain, in time Fischer "developed an attitude of fatherly friendship toward Lise Meitner," noted Hahn, and the rules were relaxed.

Meitner and Hahn equipped an old carpentry shop to serve as a laboratory. Here they measured the radioactivity of various substances. While Hahn, the chemist, was interested in the discovery of new compounds, Meitner focused on radiation research. Her inquiry built on the results of work done by Pierre and Marie Curie, Ernest Rutherford, and Niels Bohr. By 1908, Meitner and Hahn had discovered thorium c, and the editor of the *Brockhaus Encyclopedia* asked scientist Meitner to write an entry for the publication. Upon learning that scientist Meitner was a woman, however, he swiftly withdrew the offer.

Soon afterwards, Max Planck (originator of the quantum theory) asked Meitner to become his research assistant. Though few women held such a prestigious position, she served Planck for three years while continuing her work with Hahn. Then, on October 23, 1912, the Kaiser Wilhelm Institute of Chemistry was officially dedicated, and Hahn was invited to join the institute; he asked Meitner to follow him as a guest researcher. Finally, Meitner and Hahn had access to a first-class laboratory. The move was timely, because the old carpentry shop where the pair conducted their early research had become contaminated with radiation. In order to avoid a reoccurrence of this danger, Meitner and Hahn instituted rigorous safety precautions.

World War I disrupted their research. While Hahn served in an army unit specializing in gas warfare, Meitner returned to Austria and became an X-ray technician in a military hospital. As their experiments often took months to come to fruition, they made a virtue of necessity, and whenever their leaves coincided, Meitner and Hahn returned to Berlin and resumed their research.

In 1918, Lise Meitner, who had originally been banned from university laboratories, was asked to organize and head the Department of Physics at the Kaiser Wilhelm Institute. That same year, she and Hahn discovered protactinium. In the history of radioactivity, Lise Meitner was quickly emerging as the best-known female scientist since Marie Curie. The establishment of the Weimar Republic in 1919 opened the doors of academe to women. Shortly thereafter, Meitner became a *privatdozent* (lecturer without pay) at the University of Berlin.

Recognition of her work came in 1924, with the presentation of the Leibnitz Medal of the Berlin Academy of Sciences. A year later, the Lieber Prize of the Austrian Academy of Sciences was awarded. In 1926, Meitner was appointed Professor Extraordinary at the University of Berlin. She continued to focus on the differentiation of beta rays and gamma rays, working with her own independent research team. In 1933, she was one of the first to report that positrons were formed from gamma rays.

By the early 1930s, the science of nuclear physics was making rapid headway. Neutrons were discovered in 1932, positrons the following year, and the existence of artificial radiation was confirmed in 1934. Enrico Fermi, the Italian physicist, was obtaining interesting results by bombarding uranium with neutrons. He found that several radioactive elements were produced, which Fermi described as "elements beyond uranium." Fermi's research hinted that a peaceful use for nuclear energy might lie somewhere in the future. However, as Hahn noted, "among the results are also the atom bomb and the hy-

drogen bomb!" Meitner and Hahn set out to confirm Fermi's results. The young chemist Fritz Strassmann soon joined the team.

Although of Jewish ancestry, Meitner was not initially affected by the rise of National So-

cialism. On April 7, 1933, all non-Aryans were barred from teaching in Germany. Since Meitner was an Austrian citizen, however, the new Nazi legislation did not apply to her. The early "years of the Hitler regime," she said, "were naturally very depressing. But work was a good friend, and I have often thought and said how wonderful it is that by work one may be granted a long respite of forgetfulness from oppressive political conditions." It was not until the German annexation of Austria in 1938 that Meitner lost her position at the Kaiser Wilhelm Institute. The German government deemed her to be "over 50 percent non-Aryan." "Lise Meitner had always kept quiet about her Jewish connection," said her nephew Otto Frisch. "She had never in any way related to the Jewish tradition." Meitner, Hahn, and Strassmann were on the threshold of solving the mystery of nuclear fission when Meitner was forced to flee Berlin. Her loss was deeply felt by Hahn and marked the end of their long collaboration.

Since Meitner attempted to escape Germany without a valid passport, she was terrified:

> I took a train for Holland on the pretext that I wanted to spend a week's vacation. At the Dutch border, I got the scare of my life when a Nazi military patrol of five men going through the coaches picked up my Austrian passport which had expired long ago. I was so frightened, my heart almost stopped beating. I knew that the Nazis had just declared open season on Jews, that the hunt was on. For ten minutes I sat there and waited, ten minutes that seemed like so many hours. Then one of the Nazi officials returned and handed me back the passport without a word. Two minutes later I descended on Dutch territory, where I was met by some of my Holland colleagues.

From Holland, Meitner traveled to Copenhagen where she stayed with Niels Bohr and his wife **Margrethe Bohr**. Although the Danish capital boasted excellent research facilities, as well as well-known scientists, such as Otto Frisch, Meitner chose to move on, and accepted the offer of a position at the Nobel Institute in Stockholm. At 60 years of age, she set out to assemble a small research group and quickly acquired a command of the Swedish language. She also set to work on a number of monographs dealing with the properties of radioactive elements.

A few months after her arrival in Stockholm, Hahn and Strassmann completed their research in Berlin. They discovered that uranium atoms produced barium when bombarded by neutrons. As chemists, however, they were puzzled by these results. Hahn wrote to Meitner on December 19, 1938, informing her of the discovery. In the same month, Otto Frisch visited his Aunt Lise in Sweden. He found her engrossed in the letter from Hahn. Frisch reported:

> We walked up and down in the snow . . . and gradually the idea took shape that this was no chipping nor crackling of the nucleus but rather a process to be explained by Bohr's idea that the nucleus was like a liquid drop; such a drop might elongate and divide itself. But how can one get a nucleus of barium from one of uranium. . . . Could it be that the nucleus got cleaved right across like a chisel? It seemed impossible that a neutron could act like a chisel, and anyhow the idea of a nucleus as a solid object that could be cleaved was all wrong; a nucleus was much more like a liquid drop. Here we stopped and looked at each other.

Over the Christmas holidays, Meitner and Frisch theorized that the positively charged protons within the uranium nucleus repelled each other, and separated into different chemical compounds. In an article co-written with Frisch, "Disintegration of Uranium by Neutrons: A New Type of Nuclear Reaction," Meitner identified the process as "atomic fission," a term first used by her. Employing Einstein's mass energy equivalence theory, she calculated that 200 million electron volts of energy had been created during Hahn's experiment. A few months later, Meitner and Frisch reproduced the experiment and confirmed their hypothesis. The experiment was also reproduced by scientists in Europe and North America.

With the inauguration of the Manhattan Project in the United States, Lise Meitner was invited to participate. She declined the offer on moral grounds, and fervently hoped that the project to build an atomic bomb would fail. "It is an unfortunate accident that this discovery [nuclear fission] came about in time of war," she commented. Except for brief experiments on the asymmetry of fissionable fragments, Meitner never worked on nuclear fission again.

In 1944, Otto Hahn received the Nobel Prize for the discovery of nuclear fission. His results were heavily dependent on the research of Lise Meitner, whom he did not acknowledge and whom the Nobel selection committee ignored. That she had been forced to flee Berlin just before their research bore fruit can account for this exclusion in part. Hahn and Strassman discovered that slow neutrons bombarding uranium produce barium, the first evidence that the uranium atom can be split. This discovery led to the first controlled nuclear reaction and to the first atomic bomb. Without Lise Meitner's expertise, however, their experiment would have been devoid of theoretical meaning. Even today, entries on Hahn in many wide-circulation encyclopedias refer to him as the sole "father" of nuclear fission, and, while those entries may include mention of Strassman, they make no mention of

Lise Meitner or of her critical role in the achievement of nuclear fission.

After World War II, Meitner spent a semester as a visiting professor at the Catholic University in Washington, D.C. Leaving the Nobel Institute in 1947, she undertook research at the Royal Institute of Technology. In the same year, she was awarded the City of Vienna's Prize in Science, and two years later received the Max Planck Medal.

Meitner retired to Cambridge, England, in 1960. Much celebrated in later life, on July 29, 1966, she was honored with the Enrico Fermi Award. The dedication read in part:

> The President of the United States of America . . . awards . . . the Enrico Fermi Award to Lise Meitner for pioneering research in the naturally occurring radioactivities and extensive experimental studies leading to the discovery of fission.

At the turn of the century, women in science were still scorned. As Hahn pointed out:

> Lise Meitner's career is an interesting illustration of the difficulties which confronted a woman interested in an academic career at the beginning of the twentieth century. . . . Of course she could not become a Privatdozent; at that time there were no female professors of any rank in Berlin. But in 1912 Planck took the step of making her an "assistant" at the Institute for Theoretical Physics of the University of Berlin. I think she was one of the first female scientific assistants in all Prussia. . . . After World War One women were admitted to academic careers, and Lise Meitner was able to become Privatdozentin. . . . But to many the concept of a "scientific female" was still somewhat weird.

Despite sexual and racial discrimination, Lise Meitner never failed to contribute to the field which, as a woman, she both pioneered and dominated. Indeed, Albert Einstein, ignoring her Austrian birth, once described her as "the German Madame Curie." Her collaboration with Hahn led to the discovery of new chemical elements, and ultimately to the discovery of nuclear fission. Said Meitner: "I believe all young people think about how they would like their lives to develop, when I did so I always arrived at the conclusion that life need not be easy, provided only that it was not empty. And this wish I have been granted."

SOURCES:

Boorse, Henry A., Lloyd Motz, and Jefferson Hane Weaver. *The Atomic Scientists.* NY: John Wiley and Sons, 1989.

Ermenec, Joseph J., ed. *Atom Bomb Scientist's Memoirs, 1939–1945.* Westport, CT: Meckler, 1989.

Hahn, Otto. *A Scientific Autobiography.* Translated by Willy Ley. NY: Scribner, 1966.

Hermann, Armin. *The New Physics.* Translated by David C. Cassidy. Munich: Inter Nationes: 1979.

Jones, Lorella M. "Intellectual Contributions of Women to Physics," in *Women in Science.* G. Kass-Simon and Patricia Farnes, eds. Bloomington: Indiana University Press, 1990.

Libby, Leona Marshall. *The Uranium People.* NY: Scribner, 1979.

Yost, Edna. *Women of Modern Science.* NY: Dobb, Mead, 1964.

SUGGESTED READING:

Crawford, Deborah. *Lise Meitner: Atomic Pioneer.* NY: Crown, 1969.

Sime, Ruth Lewin. *Lise Meitner: A Life in Physics.* University of California Press, 1996.

Hugh A. Stewart, M.A.,
Guelph, Ontario, Canada

ACKNOWLEDGMENTS

Photographs and illustrations appearing in *Women in World History, Volume 10,* were received from the following sources:

Photo by John Vincent Adams, **p. 739;** © 1991, Hans Namuth Estate. Collection, Center for Creative Photography, The University of Arizona, **p. 423;** Painting by Richard Atkinson, **p. 11;** Painting by Giovanni Bellini, **p. 567;** Compliments of the British Embassy, **p. 285;** Painting by Agnolo Bronzino, **p. 839;** Courtesy of the University of California, San Diego Archives, **p. 669;** Painting by G. Chiari, **p. 523;** Courtesy of Cold Spring Harbor Laboratory/Research Archives, **p. 703;** © Columbia, 1961, **p. 790;** © Columbia Pictures, 1952, **p. 740;** Painting by Correggio, **p. 233;** Photo by Imogen Cunning-

ham, © The Imogen Cunningham Turst, 1978, 1996, **p. 665;** Courtesy of the Royal Danish Ministry of Foreign Affairs, Press Department, Copenhagen, Denmark, **p. 296;** After the painting by E. Debat-Ponsan, **p. 835;** Painting attributed to Corneille de Lyon, **p. 541;** Deutsche Grammophon LP record jacket, **p. 659;** Photo by Ed Estabrook, **p. 136;** Courtesy of the Fisk University Archives, **p. 68;** Photo by Reo Fortune, **p. 809;** Painting by Goya, **p. 331;** Photo by Philippe Halsman, **p. 41;** Harcourt Brace Jovanovich, **p. 695;** Photo by John Hippsley, **p. 769;** Courtesy of Internationaal Informatiecentrum en Archief voor de Vrouwenbeweging, **pp. 197, 199;** Courtesy of the International Swimming Hall of Fame, **pp. 603, 721;** Photo by Lewis-Smith, **p. 720;** Courtesy of the Library of Congress, **pp. 5, 153, 813, 859, 867;** Painting by Filippo Lippi, **p. 563;** © Metro Goldwyn Mayer, **p. 33,** 1940, **p. 49,** 1944, **p. 799,** 1939; Michael Dyer Associates, Ltd., **p. 181;** Painting by Pierre Mignard, **p. 111;** Courtesy of Kristie Miller, **p. 725;** Museum of Modern Art/Film Stills Archive, **p. 419;** Courtesy of the National Archives of Canaca, **p. 379,** C139973, **pp. 59, 709;** Photo by Tyler Dungee, courtesy of the Museum of New Mexico, **p. 489;** Photo by Peter Weil, courtesy of the Newberry Library, **p. 851;** Painting by Allan Ramsay (1749), **p. 26;** Photo by Aaron Rapoport, **p. 118;** Photo by Lilo Raymond, **p. 765;** From the fresco above her tomb at S. Benedetto Polirone, **p. 627;** Photo by Eric Schaal, **p. 773;** Society of Antiquaries, London, **p. 543;** St. Peter's, Rome, **p. 565;** Courtesy of Harriet Thurgren, **p. 495;** Courtesy of the U.S. House of Representatives. **pp. 155, 467, 655, 691, 787;** Painting by Diego Velásquez, **p. 309;** Photo by Bert Six for Warner Bros., **p. 675;** Photo provided by WIBC, **p. 743;** Painting by Florent Willems, **p. 847.**

ISBN 0-7876-4069-7

90000